ACCOUNTING PRINCIPLES

ACCOUNTING PRINCIPLES

5th Edition

JERRY J. WEYGANDT Ph.D., CPA
Arthur Andersen Alumni Professor of Accounting
University of Wisconsin
Madison, Wisconsin

DONALD E. KIESO Ph.D., CPA
KPMG Peat Marwick Emeritus Professor of Accountancy
Northern Illinois University
DeKalb, Illinois

PAUL D. KIMMEL Ph.D., CPA
Associate Professor of Accounting
University of Wisconsin—Milwaukee
Milwaukee, Wisconsin

JOHN WILEY & SONS, INC.
New York • Chichester • Weinheim • Brisbane • Toronto • Singapore

Dedicated to
Walter G. Kell
Scholar–athlete, husband, father, teacher, author, gentleman, and friend

EXECUTIVE EDITOR   Susan Elbe
SENIOR DEVELOPMENT EDITOR   Nancy Perry
ASSOCIATE EDITOR   David B. Kear
SENIOR MARKETING MANAGER   Rebecca Hope
PRODUCTION COORDINATOR   Elm Street Publishing Services, Inc.
DESIGNER   Laura Boucher
PHOTO EDITORS   Alison Bamert, Hilary Newman
PHOTO RESEARCHER   Jennifer Atkins
ILLUSTRATION EDITOR   Anna Melhorn
ART STUDIO   Precision Graphics
COVER PHOTO   © Paul Souders/Tony Stone Images, New York

This book was set in 10.5/12 Palatino by Ruttle, Shaw & Wetherill, Inc. and printed and bound by Von Hoffmann Press. The cover was printed by Phoenix Color Corp.

Recognizing the importance of preserving what has been written, it is a policy of John Wiley & Sons, Inc. to have books of enduring value published in the United States printed on acid-free paper, and we exert our best efforts to that end.

The paper in this book was manufactured by a mill whose forest management programs include sustained yield harvesting of its timberlands. Sustained yield harvesting principles ensure that the number of trees cut each year does not exceed the amount of new growth.

We are grateful for permission to use the following material: The image of *Tony the Tiger*™ throughout the text: *™,® Kellogg Company © 1994 Kellogg Company. All rights reserved, used with permission. Appendix A Specimen Financial Statements of Kellogg Company and Kellogg's 1997 Annual Report: *Kellogg's*® is a registered trademark of Kellogg Company. All rights reserved, used with permission. Appendix B Specimen Financial Statements of General Mills, Inc.: Printed with permission of General Mills, Inc.

Library of Congress Cataloging-in-Publication Data
Weygandt, Jerry J.
    Accounting principles / Jerry J. Weygandt, Donald E. Kieso,
Paul D. Kimmel.—5th ed.
        p.   cm.
    Includes index.
    ISBN 0-471-19096-9 (alk. paper)
    1. Accounting.   I. Kieso, Donald E.   II. Kimmel, Paul D.
III. Title.
HF5635.W524   1998
657—dc21   98-19261
                                                                                                      CIP

ISBN 0-471-19096-9

Printed in the United States of America

10   9   8   7   6   5   4   3   2   1

STUDENT TO STUDENT

Hello!

Congratulations on the beginning of your accounting studies. I'd like to share with you a few ideas I found helpful when I took this course.

Accounting is not only enjoyable but very exciting! As you continue your studies in accounting, you will gain an understanding of why accounting is vital to every business. Accounting gives you a solid background in financial statement analysis. This in turn will help you be a smarter investor. In short, accounting will open up the whole world of commerce and business to you.

Here are some tips I picked up while I used this text. Perhaps you can benefit from them.

- Accounting is a study of concepts and procedures. When studying, be sure you understand the concepts clearly. You might find that sometimes you have to review the text a few times until you fully understand the concepts. Look carefully at the illustrations; they will help you understand the main points of the text. When studying the journal entries, go over every entry until you fully understand it.

- Use the study aids in each chapter to help you understand the key concepts and learn the procedures. The *Feature Story*, list of *Study Objectives*, and *Preview* will help you understand what the chapter is about. Use the *Study Objectives* in the margins and the *Before You Go On* exercises to check whether you have understood and learned the material in each section.

- Use a highlighter. I found it very helpful both in studying and reviewing. Highlight whatever you feel is important.

- After you have done your homework, try some extra problems. Every chapter has two sets of problems on the same material. Try the alternative problems. They will help reinforce what you learned in each chapter.

- If possible, try to get some real-world practice, perhaps by doing some part-time work at an accounting office or just observing an accountant at work. It will bring alive what you study.

After a few short weeks, *you will agree that accounting is exciting and enjoyable!*

Lots of success,

Eli Oelbaum

Eli Oelbaum
Ocean County College

HOW TO USE THE STUDY AIDS IN THIS BOOK

Concepts for Review, listed at the beginning of each chapter from Chapter 2 on, are the accounting concepts you learned in previous chapters that you will need to know in order to understand the topics you are about to learn. Page references are provided if you need to review before reading the chapter.

CONCEPTS FOR REVIEW

Before studying this chapter, you should know or, if necessary, review:

a. The cost principle (Ch. 1, p. 11) and matching principle of accounting. (Ch. 3, p. 94)

b. How to record purchases, sales, and cost of goods sold under a perpetual inventory system. (Ch. 5, pp. 191–199)

c. How to prepare financial statements for a merchandising company. (Ch. 5, pp. 199–201)

FEATURE STORY

Keeping the Books on the Books

If you go to a large college or university, chances are that your bookstore or student union has state-of-the-art computer technology for tracking inventories. In an instant, the clerk at the check-out stand "whooshes" your purchases over a scanning machine that automatically rings up the price and deducts the item from inventory.

Not all schools have such state-of-the-art technology. Some bookstores are even small enough that the person managing it can take a "mom-and-pop corner grocery" approach. One such bookstore is at Erie Community College in Buffalo, New York, which produces annual sales of $500,000 per year. Instead of using "point-of-sale" computer technology, the bookstore uses an old-fashioned cash register. The inventory of textbooks, notebooks, art supplies, and so on is counted every month by Joel Damiani, manager. Because the quantity of inventory is relatively small, Damiani, or his two assistants, can specifically identify each item when sold. A larger bookstore would have too much inventory to use that approach; instead, they would use inventory costing methods that do not specifically match the cost of inventory to the actual sale of goods.

Damiani is candid, too, about some problems at his store. For one thing, the accounting records were in disarray when he took the job. "They told me it was going to be a challenge," he says. "And I like challenges." His challenges have included working with the school's accountant to produce a monthly balance sheet and income statement for the bookstore and making sure he has enough inventory of books and supplies on hand for the start of classes. "Sometimes, students say we're not quick enough."

The Feature Story helps you picture how the chapter topic relates to the real world of accounting and business. You will find references to the story throughout the chapter and in the section called **A Look Back at Our Feature Story** toward the end of the chapter.

The **Navigator** is a learning system designed to guide you through each chapter and help you succeed in learning the material. It consists of (1) a checklist at the beginning of the chapter, which outlines text features and study skills you will need, and (2) a series of check boxes that prompt you to use the learning aids in the chapter and set priorities as you study.

CHAPTER 9

INVENTORIES

THE NAVIGATOR ✓

- ■ Understand *Concepts for Review* ☐
- ■ Read *Feature Story* ☐
- ■ Scan *Study Objectives* ☐
- ■ Read *Preview* ☐
- ■ Read text and answer *Before You Go On*
  p. 370 ☐ p. 376 ☐ p. 385 ☐ p. 390 ☐
- ■ Work *Demonstration Problem* ☐
- ■ Review *Summary of Study Objectives* ☐
- ■ Answer *Self-Study Questions* ☐
- ■ Complete assignments ☐

STUDY OBJECTIVES

After studying this chapter, you should be able to:

1. *Describe the steps in determining inventory quantities.*
2. *Prepare the entries for purchases and sales of inventory under a periodic inventory system.*
3. *Determine cost of goods sold under a periodic inventory system.*
4. *Identify the unique features of the income statement for a merchandising company using a periodic inventory system.*
5. *Explain the basis of accounting for inventories and describe the inventory cost flow methods.*
6. *Explain the financial statement and tax effects of each of the inventory cost flow methods.*
7. *Explain the lower of cost or market basis of accounting for inventories.*
8. *Indicate the effects of inventory errors on the financial statements.*
9. *Compute and interpret the inventory turnover ratio.*

THE NAVIGATOR

Study Objectives at the beginning of each chapter give you a framework for learning the specific concepts and procedures covered in the chapter. You will also see each study objective in the margin where the concept is discussed. Finally, you can review all the study objectives in the **Summary** at the end of the chapter.

365

The **Preview** starts with an introductory paragraph linking the feature story with the major topics of the chapter. It is followed by a graphic outline of major topics and subtopics that will be discussed. This preview gives you a mental framework upon which to arrange the new information you are learning.

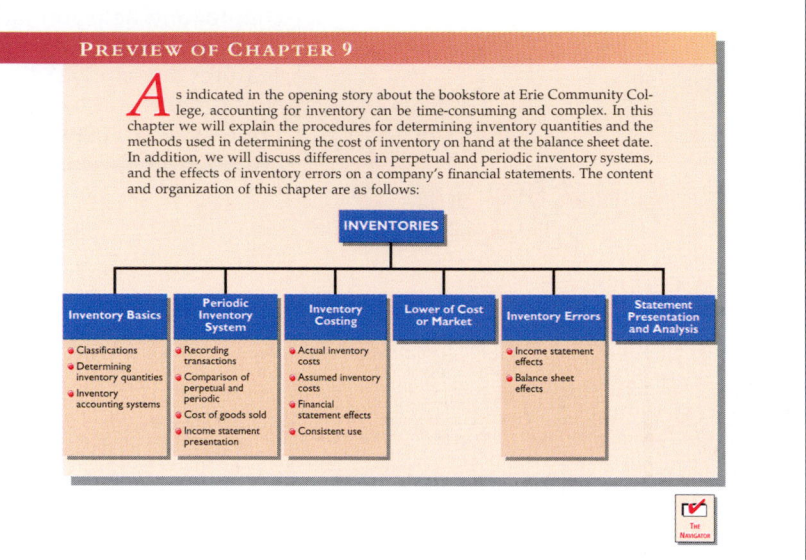

The Accounting Equation has been inserted in the margin next to key journal entries throughout the text. This new feature helps you understand the impact of an accounting transaction on the financial statements.

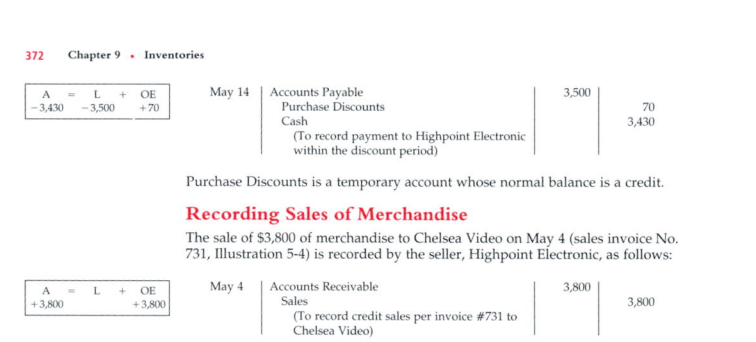

Helpful Hints in the margins help clarify concepts being discussed.

Study Objectives reappear in the margins at the point where the topic is discussed. End-of-chapter assignments are keyed to study objectives.

---

372   Chapter 9 • Inventories

A	=	L	+	OE
−3,430		−3,500		+70

May 14	Accounts Payable	3,500	
	Purchase Discounts		70
	Cash		3,430
	(To record payment to Highpoint Electronic within the discount period)		

Purchase Discounts is a temporary account whose normal balance is a credit.

Recording Sales of Merchandise

The sale of $3,800 of merchandise to Chelsea Video on May 4 (sales invoice No. 731, Illustration 5-4) is recorded by the seller, Highpoint Electronic, as follows:

A	=	L	+	OE
+3,800				+3,800

May 4	Accounts Receivable	3,800	
	Sales		3,800
	(To record credit sales per invoice #731 to Chelsea Video)		

Inventory Basics   367

profit (net sales less cost of goods sold) is closely watched by management, owners, and other interested parties (as explained in Chapter 5).

Classifying Inventory

How a company classifies its inventory depends on whether the firm is a merchandiser or a manufacturer. In a **merchandising enterprise**, inventory consists of many different items. For example, in a grocery store, canned goods, dairy products, meats, and produce are just a few of the inventory items on hand. These items have two common characteristics: (1) they are owned by the company, and (2) they are in a form ready for sale to customers in the ordinary course of business. Thus, only one inventory classification, **merchandise inventory**, is needed to describe the many different items that make up the total inventory.

In a **manufacturing enterprise**, inventories are also owned by the company, but some goods may not yet be ready for sale. As a result, inventory is usually classified into three categories: finished goods, work in process, and raw materials. For example, General Motors classifies automobiles completed and ready for sale as **finished goods**. The automobiles on the assembly line in various stages of production are classified as **work in process**. The steel, glass, upholstery, and other components that are on hand waiting to be used in the production of automobiles are identified as **raw materials**.

The accounting principles and concepts discussed in this chapter apply to inventory classifications of both merchandising and manufacturing companies. In this chapter we will focus on merchandise inventory.

Determining Inventory Quantities

Many businesses take a physical inventory count on the last day of the year. Businesses using the periodic inventory system are required to take an end-of-the-period physical inventory to determine the inventory on hand at the balance sheet date and to compute cost of goods sold. Even businesses using a perpetual inventory system must take a physical inventory at some time during the year.

Determining inventory quantities consists of two steps: (1) taking a physical inventory of goods on hand, and (2) determining the ownership of goods.

HELPFUL HINT
An important inventory management concept is inventory turnover. Inventory that turns means sales and profit; inventory that doesn't turn means costs and losses.

HELPFUL HINT
Regardless of the classification, all inventories are reported under Current Assets on the balance sheet.

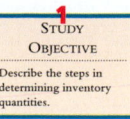

1
STUDY OBJECTIVE

Describe the steps in determining inventory quantities.

Inventory Basics   369

ILLUSTRATION 9-1
Terms of sale

Infographics, a special type of illustration, pictorially link concepts to the real world and provide visual reminders of key concepts.

Significant errors may occur in determining inventory quantities if goods in transit at the statement date are ignored. Assume, for example, that Hargrove Company has 20,000 units of inventory on hand on December 31 and the following goods in transit: (1) **sales** of 1,500 units shipped December 31 FOB destination, and (2) **purchases** of 2,500 units shipped FOB shipping point by the seller on December 31. Hargrove has legal title to both the units sold and the units purchased. Consequently, inventory quantities would be understated by 4,000 units (1,500 + 2,500) if units in transit are ignored.

Technology in Action boxes, identified by a CD icon, show how computers are used by accountants and users of accounting information.

TECHNOLOGY IN ACTION

Many companies have invested large amounts of time and money in automated inventory systems. One of the most sophisticated is Federal Express' Digitally Assisted Dispatch System (DADS). This system uses hand-held "SuperTrackers" to transmit data about the packages and documents to the firm's computer system. Based on bar codes, the system allows the firm to know where any package is at any time to prevent losses and to fulfill the firm's delivery commitments. More recently, FedEx's newly developed software enables customers to track shipments on their own PCs.

Financial statements appear throughout the book. Those from real companies are identified by a logo or related photo. Often, numbers or categories are highlighted in colored type to draw your attention to key information.

Inventory Costing Under a Periodic Inventory System   385

QUAKER OATS COMPANY
Notes to the Financial Statements

ILLUSTRATION 9-22
Disclosure of change in cost flow method

Note 1   Effective July 1, the Company adopted the LIFO cost flow assumption for valuing the majority of U.S. Grocery Products inventories. The Company believes that the use of the LIFO method better matches current costs with current revenues. The effect of this change on the current year was to decrease net income by $16.0 million.

ACCOUNTING IN ACTION
International Insight

U.S. companies typically choose between LIFO and FIFO. Many choose LIFO because it reduces inventory profits and taxes. However, the international community recently considered rules that would ban LIFO entirely and force companies to use FIFO. This proposal was defeated, but the issue will not go away. The issue is sensitive. As John Wulff, controller for Union Carbide noted, "We were in support of the international effort up until the proposal to eliminate LIFO." Wulff says that if Union Carbide had been suddenly forced to switch from LIFO to FIFO, its reported $632 million pretax income would have jumped by $300 million. That would have increased Carbide's income tax bill by as much as $120 million. Given this, do you believe that accounting principles and rules should be the same around the world?

Accounting in Action boxes give you more glimpses into the real world of business. Each type of issue—business, ethics, and international—is identified by its own icon. Don't skip over the photos, figures, and tables.

BEFORE YOU GO ON . . .

Review It

1. How do the cost and matching principles apply to inventoriable costs?
2. How are the three assumed cost flow methods applied in allocating inventoriable costs?
3. What factors should be considered by management in selecting an inventory cost flow method?
4. Which inventory cost flow method produces (a) the highest net income in a period of rising prices, and (b) the lowest income taxes?
5. What amount is reported by Kellogg Company in its 1997 Annual Report as inventories at December 31, 1997? Which inventory cost flow method does Kellogg Company use? The answer to this question is provided on p. 416.

Do It

The accounting records of Shumway Ag Implement show the following data:

Beginning inventory	4,000 units at $3
Purchases	6,000 units at $4
Sales	5,000 units at $12

Determine the cost of goods sold during the period under a periodic inventory system using (a) the FIFO method, (b) the LIFO method, and (c) the average cost method.

Reasoning: Because the units of inventory on hand and available for sale may have been purchased at different prices, a systematic method must be adopted to allocate the costs between the goods sold and the goods on hand (ending inventory).

Solution:
(a) FIFO: (4,000 @ $3) + (1,000 @ $4)] = $12,000 + $4,000 = $16,000.
(b) LIFO: 5,000 @ $4 = $20,000.
(c) Average cost: [(4,000 @ $3) + (6,000 @ $4)] ÷ 10,000 = ($12,000 + $24,000) ÷ 10,000 = $3.60 per unit; 5,000 @ $3.60 = $18,000.

Related exercise material: BE9-6, BE9-7, E9-5, E9-6, E9-7.

Before You Go On *Review It* questions serve as a learning check. If you cannot answer these questions, you should go back and read the section again.

Review It questions marked with the Tony the Tiger™ icon ask you to find information in Kellogg's 1997 Annual Report, which is packaged with this text and excerpted in Appendix A at the end of the text.

Brief *Do It* exercises help you apply what you are learning. They outline the *reasoning* necessary to complete the exercise, and their *solutions* help you see how the problem should be solved. (Keyed to homework exercises.)

The inventory turnover ratio measures the number of times on average the inventory is sold during the period. Its purpose is to measure the liquidity of the inventory. The inventory turnover is computed by dividing cost of goods sold by the average inventory during the period. Unless seasonal factors are significant, average inventory can be computed from the beginning and ending inventory balances. For example, Kellogg Company reported in its 1997 Annual Report a beginning inventory of $424,900,000, and cost of goods sold for the year 1997 of $3,270,100,000; its inventory turnover formula and computation are shown below:

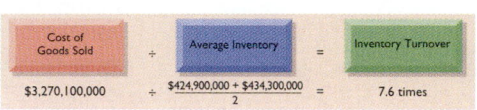

ILLUSTRATION 9-29

Inventory turnover formula and computation for Kellogg Company

Cost of Goods Sold	÷	Average Inventory	=	Inventory Turnover
$3,270,100,000	÷	$\dfrac{\$424,900,000 + \$434,300,000}{2}$	=	7.6 times

A variant of the inventory turnover ratio is the **average days to sell inventory**. For example, the inventory turnover for Kellogg Company of 7.6 times divided into 365 is approximately 48 days. There are typical levels of inventory in every industry. However, companies that are able to keep their inventory at lower levels and higher turnovers and still satisfy customer needs are the most successful.

Key Terms and concepts are printed in blue where they are first explained in the text and are defined again in the end-of-chapter glossary.

One technique for determining the meaning of the information on financial statements is **ratio analysis.** Throughout this text, you will examine key financial ratios using data from Kellogg's financial statements.

Color illustrations visually reinforce important concepts and therefore often contain material that may appear on exams.

---

390   Chapter 9 • Inventories

BEFORE YOU GO ON . . .

Review It

1. Why is it appropriate to report inventories at the lower of cost or market?
2. How do inventory errors affect financial statements?
3. What does the inventory turnover ratio reveal?

A LOOK BACK AT OUR FEATURE STORY

Refer to the opening story concerning the bookstore at Erie Community College, and answer the following questions.
1. Why might a small bookstore use specific identification to determine inventory?
2. If the inventory is overstated at the end of the month, what effect does this error have on the balance sheet and the income statement?

Solution:
1. A small bookstore, as opposed to a large bookstore, might use specific identification because of:
   a. A smaller number of any one book in inventory.
   b. Fewer different books in inventory.
   c. The familiarity of the owner/manager (who handles sales) with the books being sold.
2. An end-of-month, inventory overstatement will result in overstated inventory in the balance sheet along with overstated stockholders' equity, due to overstated net income on the income statement. Cost of goods sold will be understated on the income statement. The next month's income statement will have overstated beginning inventory and understated net income.

The last **Before You Go On** exercise takes you back for a critical look at the chapter-opening feature story.

DEMONSTRATION PROBLEM

Gerald D. Englehart Company has the following inventory, purchases, and sales data for the month of March:

Inventory, March 1	200 units @ $4.00	$ 800
Purchases:		
March 10	500 units @ $4.50	2,250
March 20	400 units @ $4.75	1,900
March 30	300 units @ $5.00	1,500
Sales:		
March 15	500 units	
March 25	400 units	

The physical inventory count on March 31 shows 500 units on hand.

PROBLEM-SOLVING STRATEGIES

1. For FIFO, the latest costs are allocated to inventory.
2. For LIFO, the earliest costs are allocated to inventory.
3. For average costs, use a weighted average for periodic and a moving average for perpetual.
4. Remember, the costs allocated to cost of goods sold can be proved.
5. Total purchases are the same under all three cost flow methods.

Instructions
Under a **periodic inventory system,** determine the cost of inventory on hand at March 31 and the cost of goods sold for March under the (a) first-in, first-out (FIFO) method, (b) last-in, first-out (LIFO) method, and (c) average cost method.

SOLUTION TO DEMONSTRATION PROBLEM

The cost of goods available for sale is $6,450:

Inventory	200 units @ $4.00	$ 800
Purchases:		
March 10	500 units @ $4.50	2,250
March 20	400 units @ $4.75	1,900
March 30	300 units @ $5.00	1,500
Total cost of goods available for sale		$6,450

Demonstration Problems review the chapter material. These problems provide you with *problem-solving strategies* and with *solutions.*

SUMMARY OF STUDY OBJECTIVES

1. *Describe the steps in determining inventory quantities.* The steps in determining inventory quantities are (1) taking a physical inventory of goods on hand and (2) determining the ownership of goods in transit.

2. *Prepare the entries for purchases and sales of inventory under a periodic inventory system.* In recording purchases, entries are required for (a) cash and credit purchases, (b) purchase returns and allowances, (c) purchase discounts, and (d) freight costs. In recording sales, entries are required for (a) cash and credit sales, (b) sales returns and allowances, and (c) sales discounts.

3. *Determine cost of goods sold under a periodic inventory system.* The steps in determining cost of goods sold are (a) recording the purchase of merchandise, (b) determining the cost of goods purchased, and (c) determining the cost of goods on hand at the beginning and end of the accounting period.

4. *Identify the unique features of the income statement for a merchandising company using a periodic inventory system.* The income statement for a merchandising company contains three sections: sales revenue, cost of goods sold, and operating expenses. The cost of goods sold section under a periodic inventory system generally shows more detail by reporting beginning and ending inventory, net purchases, and total goods available for sale.

5. *Explain the basis of accounting for inventories and describe the inventory cost flow methods.* The primary basis of accounting for inventories is cost. Cost includes all expenditures necessary to acquire goods and place them in condition ready for sale. Inventoriable costs include (1) cost of beginning inventory and (2) the cost of goods purchased. The inventory cost flow methods are: specific identification, FIFO, LIFO, and average cost.

6. *Explain the financial statement and tax effects of each of the inventory cost flow methods.* The cost of goods available for sale may be allocated to cost of goods sold and ending inventory by specific identification or by a method based on an assumed cost flow. These methods have different effects on financial statements during periods of changing prices. When prices are rising, the first-in, first-out method (FIFO) results in lower cost of goods sold and higher net income than the average and the last-in, first-out (LIFO) methods. LIFO results in the lowest income taxes (because of lower net income). The reverse is true when prices are falling. In the balance sheet, FIFO results in an ending inventory that is closest to current value, whereas the inventory under LIFO is the farthest from current value.

7. *Explain the lower of cost or market basis of accounting for inventories.* The lower of cost or market basis (LCM) is used when the current replacement cost (market) is less than cost. Under LCM, the loss is recognized in the period in which the price decline occurs. LCM may be applied to individual inventory items, major categories of inventory, or to total inventory.

The **Summary of Study Objectives** relates the study objectives to the key points in the chapter. It gives you another opportunity to review as well as to see how all the key topics within the chapter are related.

---

8. *Indicate the effects of inventory errors on the financial statements.* In the income statement of the current year: (a) an error in beginning inventory will have a reverse effect on net income (overstatement of inventory results in understatement of net income) and (b) an error in ending inventory will have a similar effect on net income (overstatement of inventory results in overstatement of net income). If ending inventory errors are not corrected in the following period, their effect on net income for that period is reversed, and total net income for the two years will be correct. In the balance sheet, ending inventory errors will have the same effect on total assets and total stockholders' equity and no effect on liabilities.

9. *Compute and interpret the inventory turnover ratio.* The inventory turnover ratio is calculated as cost of goods sold divided by average inventory. It can be converted to average days in inventory by dividing 365 days by the inventory turnover ratio. A higher turnover ratio or lower average days in inventory suggests that management is trying to keep inventory levels low relative to its sales level.

GLOSSARY

The **Glossary** defines all the terms and concepts introduced in the chapter. Page references help you find any terms you need to study further.

Average cost method An inventory costing method that assumes that the goods available for sale have the same (average) cost per unit; generally they are homogeneous. (p. 381).

Consigned goods Goods shipped by a consignor, who retains ownership, to another party called the consignee. (p. 369).

Cost of goods available for sale The sum of the beginning merchandise inventory plus the cost of goods purchased. (p. 374).

Cost of goods purchased The sum of net purchases plus freight-in. (p. 374).

Cost of goods sold The total cost of merchandise sold during the period, determined by subtracting ending inventory from the cost of goods available for sale. (p. 374).

Current replacement cost The amount that would be paid at the present time to acquire an identical item. (p. 386).

First-in, first-out method (FIFO) An inventory costing method that assumes that the costs of the earliest goods acquired are the first to be recognized as cost of goods sold. (p. 378).

Inventoriable costs The pool of costs that consists of two elements: (1) the cost of the beginning inventory and (2) the cost of goods purchased during the period. (p. 376).

Inventory turnover ratio A ratio that measures the number of times on average the inventory is sold during the period. It is computed by dividing cost of goods sold by the average inventory during the period. (p. 389).

Last-in, first-out method (LIFO) An inventory costing method that assumes that the costs of the latest units purchased are the first to be allocated to cost of goods sold. (p. 380).

Lower of cost or market basis (LCM) (inventories) A method of valuing inventory that recognizes the decline in the value when the current purchase price (market) is less than cost. (p. 386).

Net purchases Purchases less purchase returns and allowances and purchase discounts. (p. 374).

Periodic inventory system An inventory system in which inventoriable costs are allocated to ending inventory and cost of goods sold at the end of the period. Cost of goods sold is computed at the end of the period by subtracting the ending inventory (costs are assigned to a physical count of items on hand) from the cost of goods available for sale. (p. 370).

Specific identification method An actual physical flow costing method in which items still in inventory are specifically costed to arrive at the total cost of the ending inventory. (p. 377).

APPENDIX 9A ESTIMATING INVENTORIES

10 STUDY OBJECTIVE

Describe the two methods of estimating inventories.

We have assumed throughout the chapter that a company would be able to do a physical count of its inventory. But what if it cannot, as in the example of the lumber inventory destroyed by fire? In that case, we would use an estimate.

Two circumstances explain the reasons for estimating rather than counting inventories. First, management may want monthly or quarterly financial statements but a physical inventory is taken only annually. Second, a casualty such as fire, flood, or earthquake may make it impossible to take a physical inventory. The need for estimating inventories is associated primarily with a periodic inventory system because of the absence of detailed inventory records.

There are two widely used methods of estimating inventories: (1) the gross profit method and (2) the retail inventory method.

End-of-Chapter Appendixes address topics considered optional by some instructors.

400   Chapter 9 • Inventories

*Note: All asterisked Questions, Exercises, and Problems relate to material in the appendixes to the chapter.

SELF-STUDY QUESTIONS

Answers are at the end of the chapter.

(SO 2) 1. When goods are purchased for resale by a company using a periodic inventory system:
   a. purchases on account are debited to Merchandise Inventory.
   b. purchases on account are debited to Purchases.
   c. purchase returns are debited to Purchase Returns and Allowances.
   d. freight costs are debited to Purchases.

(SO 3) 2. In determining cost of goods sold:
   a. purchases discounts are deducted from net purchases.
   b. freight-out is added to net purchases.
   c. purchase returns and allowances are deducted from net purchases.
   d. freight-in is added to net purchases.

8. In periods of rising prices, LIFO will produce:
   a. higher net income than FIFO.
   b. the same net income as FIFO.
   c. lower net income than FIFO.
   d. higher net income than average costing.

9. Factors that affect the selection of an inventory costing method do *not* include:
   a. tax effects.
   b. balance sheet effects.
   c. income statement effects.
   d. perpetual vs. periodic inventory system.

10. The lower of cost or market basis may be applied to:
   a. categories of inventories.
   b. individual items of inventories.
   c. total inventory.
   d. all of the above.

> **Self-Study Questions** are a practice test, keyed to Study Objectives, that gives you an opportunity to check your knowledge of important topics. Answers appear on the last page of the chapter.

QUESTIONS

1. Goods costing $1,700 are purchased on account on July 15 with credit terms of 2/10, n/30. On July 18 a $200 credit memo is received from the supplier for damaged goods. Give the journal entry on July 24 to record payment of the balance due within the discount period.

2. Identify the accounts that are added to or deducted from purchases to determine the cost of goods purchased. For each account, indicate (a) whether it is added or deducted and (b) its normal balance.

3. In the following separate mini cases, using a periodic inventory system, identify the item(s) designated by letter.
   (a) Purchases − X − Y = Net purchases.
   (b) Cost of goods purchased − Net purchases = X.
   (c) Beginning inventory   X = Cost of goods available for sale.
   (d) Cost of goods available for sale − Cost of goods sold = X.

13. "The selection of an inventory cost flow method is a decision made by accountants." Do you agree? Explain. Once a method has been selected, what accounting requirement applies?

14. Which assumed inventory cost flow method:
   (a) usually parallels the actual physical flow of merchandise?
   (b) assumes that goods available for sale during an accounting period are homogeneous?
   (c) assumes that the latest units purchased are the first to be sold?

15. In a period of rising prices, the inventory reported in Jim Groat Company's balance sheet is close to the current cost of the inventory, whereas Greg Hanson Company's inventory is considerably below its current cost. Identify the inventory cost flow method being used by each company. Which company has probably been reporting the higher gross profit?

> **Questions** allow you to explain your understanding of concepts and relationships covered in the chapter.

---

402   Chapter 9 • Inventories

*25. Jana Kingston Company has net sales of $400,000 and cost of goods available for sale of $300,000. If the gross profit rate is 30%, what is the estimated cost of the ending inventory? Show computations.

*26. John Ross Shoe Shop had goods available for sale in 1999 with a retail price of $120,000. The cost of these goods was $84,000. If sales during the period were $90,000, what is the ending inventory at cost using the retail inventory method?

*27. "When perpetual inventory record[s] under the FIFO and LIFO method[s] would be in a periodic invento[ry] agree? Explain.

*28. How does the average method of [transf]er between a perpetual inventory [and periodic] inventory system?

> **Brief Exercises** help you focus on one Study Objective at a time and thus help you build confidence in your basic skills and knowledge. (Keyed to Study Objectives.)

BRIEF EXERCISES

Journalize purchases transactions.
(SO 2)

BE9–1 Prepare the journal entries to record the following transactions on Svenska Company's books using a periodic inventory system.
   (a) On March 2, Svenska Company purchased $900,000 of merchandise from Sing Tao Company, terms 2/10, n/30.
   (b) On March 6, Svenska Company returned $130,000 of the merchandise purchased on March 2 because it was defective.
   (c) On March 12, Svenska Company paid the balance due to Sing Tao Company.

Compute net purchases and cost of goods purchased.
(SO 3)

BE9–2 Assume that Shinhan Company uses a periodic inventory system and has the following account balances: Purchases $440,000, Purchase Returns and Allowances $11,000, Purchase Discounts $8,000, and Freight-in $16,000. Determine (a) net purchases and (b) cost of goods purchased.

EXERCISES

E9–1 Presented below is the following information related to Brazil Co.

1. On April 5, purchased merchandise from Chile Company for $18,000 terms 2/10, net/30, FOB shipping point.
2. On April 6, paid freight costs of $800 on merchandise purchased from Chile.
3. On April 7, purchased equipment on account for $26,000.
4. On April 8, returned damaged merchandise to Chile Company and was granted a $3,000 allowance.
5. On April 15, paid the amount due to Chile Company in full.

Journalize purchases transactions.
(SO 2)

Instructions

(a) Prepare the journal entries to record these transactions on the books of Brazil Co. using a periodic inventory system.
(b) Assume that Brazil Co. paid the balance due to Chile Company on May 4 instead of April 15. Prepare the journal entry to record this payment.

E9–2 The trial balance of Colombia Company at the end of its fiscal year, August 31, 1999, includes the following accounts: Merchandise Inventory $17,200, Purchases $142,400, Sales $190,000, Freight-in $4,000, Sales Returns and Allowances $3,000, Freight-out $1,000, and Purchase Returns and Allowances $2,000. The ending (August 31, 1999) merchandise inventory is $27,000.

Prepare cost of goods sold section.
(SO 3)

Instructions

Prepare a cost of goods sold section for the year ending August 31 (periodic inventory).

E9–3 Presented is information related to Mexico Co. for the month of January 1999.

Prepare an income statement.
(SO 4)

Freight-in	$10,000	Rent expense	19,000
Freight-out	5,000	Salary expense	61,000
Insurance expense	12,000	Sales discounts	8,000
Purchases	200,000	Sales returns and allowances	13,000
Purchase discounts	3,000	Sales	312,000
Purchase returns and allowances	6,000		

Beginning merchandise inventory was $42,000 and ending inventory was $63,000.

> **Exercises,** which are more difficult than Brief Exercises, help you continue to build your confidence. (Keyed to Study Objectives.)

> **Spreadsheet Problems,** identified by [icon], are selected exercises and problems that can be solved using the spreadsheet software *Solving Principles of Accounting Problems Using Lotus 1-2-3 and Excel for Windows.*

406 Chapter 9 · Inventories

Instructions
Calculate the inventory turnover ratio, days in inventory, and gross profit rate (from Chapter 5) for Linda Wasicsko Corporation for 1997, 1998, 1999. Comment on any trends.

Determine merchandise lost using the gross profit method of estimating inventory.
(SO 10)

*E9–12 The inventory of DeBeers Company was destroyed by fire on March 1. From an examination of the accounting records, the following data for the first 2 months of the year are obtained: Sales $51,000, Sales Returns and Allowances $1,000, Purchases $28,200, Freight-in $1,200, and Purchase Returns and Allowances $1,400.

Instructions
Determine the merchandise lost by fire, assuming:

(a) A beginning inventory of $20,000 and a gross profit rate of 30% on net sales.
(b) A beginning inventory of $25,000 and a gross profit rate of 25% on net sales.

Determine ending inventory at cost using retail method.
(SO 10)

*E9–13 Swiss Shoe Store uses the retail inventory method for its two departments: Women's Shoes and Men's Shoes. The following information...

Item		
Beginning inventory at cost		
Cost of goods purchased at cost		
Net sales		
Beginning inventory at retail		
Cost of goods purchased at retail		

Instructions
Compute the estimated cost of the ending inventory... inventory method.

Apply cost flow methods to perpetual records.
(SO 11)

*E9–14 Morocco Appliance uses a perpetual inv... sets, the January 1 inventory was four sets at $60... chase was made: Jan. 10, 6 units at $640 each. T... sales: Jan. 8, 2 units and Jan. 15, 4 units.

Instructions
Compute the ending inventory under (1) FIFO, (2) LIFO, and (3) average cost.

> Two sets of **Problems—Sets A** and **B**—help you pull together and apply several concepts from the chapter. Included in these are problems that help you develop the writing skills that are so important in business. (Keyed to multiple Study Objectives.)

PROBLEMS: SET A

Journalize, post, and prepare trial balance and partial income statement.
(SO 2, 3, 4)

P9–1A Chi Chi Lopez, a former professional golf star, operates Chi Chi's Pro Shop at Bay Golf Course. At the beginning of the current season on April 1, 1999, the ledger of Chi Chi's Pro Shop showed Cash $2,500, Merchandise Inventory $3,500, and Capital $6,000. The following transactions were completed during April.

Apr.	5	Purchased golf bags, clubs, and balls on account from Balata Co. $1,600, FOB shipping point, terms 2/10, n/60.
	7	Paid freight on Balata purchase $80.
	9	Received credit from Balata Co. for merchandise returned $100.
	10	Sold merchandise on account to members $900, terms n/30.
	12	Purchased golf shoes, sweaters, and other accessories on account from Arrow Sportswear $660, terms 1/10, n/30.
	14	Paid Balata Co. in full.
	17	Received credit from Arrow Sportswear for merchandise returned $60.
	20	Made sales on account to members $700, terms n/30.
	21	Paid Arrow Sportswear in full.
	27	Granted credit to members for clothing that did not fit $30.
	30	Made cash sales $600.
	30	Received payments on account from members $1,100.

The chart of accounts for the pro shop includes the following: No. 101 Cash, No. 112 Accounts Receivable, No. 120 Merchandise Inventory, No. 201 Accounts Payable, No. 301 Capital, No. 401 Sales, No. 412 Sales Returns and Allowances, No. 510 Purchases, No. 512 Purchase Returns and Allowances, No. 514 Purchase Discounts, No. 516 Freight-in.

> **General Ledger Problems,** identified by [icon], are selected problems that can be solved using the *General Ledger Software* package.

The **Broadening Your Perspective** section helps you pull together various concepts covered in the chapter and apply them to real-world business decisions.

BROADENING YOUR PERSPECTIVE

FINANCIAL REPORTING AND ANALYSIS

FINANCIAL REPORTING PROBLEM: Kellogg Company

BYP9–1   The notes that accompany a company's financial statements provide informative details that would clutter the amounts and descriptions presented in the statements. Refer to the financial statements of Kellogg Company and the Notes to Consolidated Financial Statements in Appendix A.

Instructions

Answer the following questions. Complete the requirements in millions of dollars, as shown in Kellogg's annual report.

(a) What did Kellogg report for the ...
    Sheet at December 31, 1997? Dec...

A **Financial Reporting Problem** directs you to study various aspects of the financial statements in Kellogg Company's 1997 Annual Report, which is packaged with the text and excerpted in Appendix A at the end of the text.

A **Comparative Analysis Problem** offers the opportunity to compare and contrast the financial reporting of Kellogg with that of a competitor, General Mills, whose financial statements are excerpted in Appendix B.

... does Kellogg use?

(d) What is the cost of sales (cost of goods sold) reported by Kellogg for 1997, 1996, and 1995? Compute the percentage of cost of sales to net sales in 1997.

COMPARATIVE ANALYSIS PROBLEM: Kellogg Company vs. General Mills

BYP9–2   Kellogg's financial statements are presented in Appendix A; General Mills's financial statements are presented in Appendix B.

Instructions

(a) Based on the information contained in these financial statements, compute the following 1997 ratios for each company:
    1. Inventory turnover ratio
    2. Average days to sell inventory
(b) What conclusions concerning the management of the inventory can be drawn from these data?

RESEARCH ASSIGNMENT

BYP9–3   The September 23, 1994, edition of *The Wall Street Journal* includes an article entitled "CompUSA Auctions Notebook Computers Through Bulk Sale."

Instructions

Read the article and answer the following inventory-related questions.

(a) At what amount did CompUSA estimate the retail value of the computers? What was the estimate made by one of the bidders?
(b) What was wrong with the computers?
(c) What were the rules of the auction as specified by CompUSA?
(d) CompUSA had just recorded a $3 million inventory writedown in the preceding quarter. Based on the information in the article, does it appear that additional writedowns were called for?

INTERPRETING FINANCIAL STATEMENTS: Nike and Reebok

BYP9–4   Nike and Reebok compete head-to-head in the sport shoe and sport apparel business. For both companies, inventory is a significant portion of their total assets. The following information was taken from each company's financial statements and notes to those financial statements.

Research Assignments lead you to reports and articles published in various popular business periodicals for further study and analysis of key topics.

NIKE, INC.

Inventory note

Inventories are stated at the lower of cost or market. Cost is determined using the last-in, first-out (LIFO) method for substantially all U.S. inventories. Non-U.S. inventories are valued on a first-in, first-out (FIFO) basis.

Inventories by major classification are as follows (in thousands):

	May 31	
	1997	**1996**
Finished goods	$1,248,401	$ 874,700
Work-in-process	50,245	28,940
Raw materials	39,994	27,511

Other information for Nike:

	May 31	
	1997	**1996**
Inventory	$1,338,640	$ 931,151
Cost of goods sold	5,502,993	3,906,746

Interpreting Financial Statements ask you to read parts of financial statements of actual companies and to interpret that information in light of concepts presented in the chapter.

REAL-WORLD FOCUS: General Motors Corporation

BYP9–5   **General Motors** is the largest producer of automobiles in the world, as well as the world's biggest industrial enterprise. After stumbling in the early 1990s, GM has enacted numerous cost-cutting measures, including downsizing and renegotiating contracts with suppliers. In addition, it has shifted more of its resources to the hot-selling truck market.

The annual report of General Motors Corporation disclosed the following information about its accounting for inventories:

GENERAL MOTORS CORPORATION
Notes to the Financial Statements

Note 5. Inventories
Major Classes of Inventories (in millions)

	December 31	
	1995	**1994**
Productive material, work in process, and supplies	$ 6,570.4	$5,478.3
Finished product, service parts, etc.	4,959.1	4,649.5
Total	$11,529.5	$10,127.8
Memo: Increase in LIFO inventories if valued at FIFO	$ 2,424.4	$2,535.9

Inventories are stated generally at cost, which is not in excess of market. The cost of substantially all U.S. inventories other than the inventories of Saturn Corporation (Saturn) and Hughes is determined by the last-in, first-out (LIFO) method. The cost of non-U.S., Saturn, and Hughes inventories is determined generally by the first-in, first-out (FIFO) or average cost methods.

> The **Real-World Focus** asks you to apply concepts presented in the chapter to specific situations faced by actual companies.

Instructions
(a) What is meant by "Inventories are stated generally at cost, which is not in excess of market"?
(b) The company uses LIFO for most of its inventory. What impact does this have on reported ending inventory if prices are increasing?
(c) General Motors uses different inventory methods for different types of inventory. Why might it do this?

CRITICAL THINKING

GROUP DECISION CASE

BYP9–6   On April 10, 1998, fire damaged the office and warehouse of Gibson Company. Most of the accounting records were destroyed but the following account balances were determined as of March 31, 1998: Merchandise Inventory, January 1, 1998, $80,000; Sales (January 1–March 31, 1998), $150,000; Purchases (January 1–March 31, 1998), $84,000.

The company's fiscal year ends on December 31, and it uses a periodic inventory system.

From an analysis of the April bank statement you discover cancelled checks of $4,200 during the period April 1–10 for cash purchases. Deposits during the same period totaled $18,500 of which 60% were collections on accounts receivable and the balance was cash sales.

Correspondence with the company's principal suppliers revealed $12,400 of purchases on account from April 1 to April 10 of which $1,800 was for merchandise in transit on April 10 that was shipped FOB destination.

Correspondence with the company's principal customers produced acknowledgments of credit sales totaling $28,000 from April 1 to April 10. It was estimated that $4,600 of credit sales will never be acknowledged or recovered from customers.

Gibson Company reached an agreement with the insurance company that its fire-loss claim should be based on the average of the gross profit rates for the preceding 2 years. The financial statements for 1996 and 1997 showed the following data:

	1997	1996
Net sales	$600,000	$480,000
Cost of goods purchased	416,000	356,000
Beginning inventory	60,000	40,000
Ending inventory	80,000	60,000

cost of $19,000 was salvaged from the fire.

vided into groups, answer the following:
e the balances in (1) Sales and (2) Purchases at April 10.
e the average profit rate for the years 1996 and 1997. (*Hint:* Find the gross
e for each year and divide the sum by 2.)
*(c) Determine the inventory loss as a result of the fire, using the gross profit method.

COMMUNICATION ACTIVITY

BYP9–7   You are the controller of Small Toys Inc. Joe Paisley, the president, recently mentioned to you that he found an error in the 1998 financial statements which he believes has corrected itself. He determined, in discussions with the Purchasing Department, that 1998 ending inventory was overstated by $1 million. Joe says that the 1999 ending inventory is correct, thus he assumes that 1999 income is correct. Joe says to you, "What happened has happened—there's no point in worrying about it anymore."

Instructions
You conclude that Joe is incorrect. Write a brief, tactful memo to Joe, clarifying the situation.

ETHICS CASE

BYP9–8   Lonergan Wholesale Corp. uses the LIFO method of inventory costing. In the current year, profit at Lonergan is running unusually high. The corporate tax rate is also high this

> The **Group Decision Case** helps you build decision-making skills by analyzing accounting information in a less structured situation. These cases require evaluation of a manager's decision or lead to a decision among alternative courses of action. As group activities, they prepare you for the business world, where you will be working with many people, by giving you practice in solving problems with colleagues.

> **Communication Activities** ask you to engage in real-world business situations using writing, speaking, or presentation skills.

> Through the **Ethics Cases,** you will reflect on typical ethical dilemmas and decide on an appropriate course of action.

year, but it is scheduled to decline significantly next year. In an effort to lower current year's net income and to take advantage of the changing income tax rate, the president of Lonergan Wholesale instructs the plant accountant to recommend to the purchasing department a large purchase of inventory for delivery 3 days before the end of the year. The price of the inventory to be purchased has doubled during the year and the purchase will represent a major portion of the ending inventory value.

> **Surfing the Net** exercises guide you to Net sites where you can find and analyze information related to the chapter topic.

_____ this transaction on this year's and next year's income statement _____nse? Why?

_____ale had been using the FIFO method of inventory costing, would _____e same directive?

_____ountant order the inventory purchase to lower income? What are the _____ implications of this order?

SURFING THE NET

BYP9–9   A company's annual report usually will identify the inventory method used. Knowing that, you can analyze the effects of the inventory method on the income statement and balance sheet.

Address: http://www.cisco.com

Steps:

1. From Cisco System's homepage, use the **quick search**, type annual report.
2. Choose **Search**.
3. Choose **Cisco System Annual Report**.
4. Choose **Financial Review**.
5. Use the financial statements and relating notes to the financial statements to answer the questions below.

Instructions
Answer the following questions:

(a) At Cisco's fiscal year-end, what was the net i_____

(b) How has this changed from the previous fisca_____

(c) How much of the inventory was finished goo_____

(d) What inventory method do they use?

> **Answers to Self-Study Questions** provide feedback on your understanding of concepts.

Answers to Self-Study Questions

1. b   2. d   3. a   4. a   5. b   6. c   7. d   8. c   9. d   10. d   *11. b
12. b   13. d   *14. d

Answer to Kellogg Review It Question 5, p. 385.
Kellogg Company reported inventories of $434,300,000 at December 31, 1997. Kellogg reports in Note 1—Accounting Policies that it uses the **average cost method** in applying product costs to inventories and cost of goods sold.

> **✓** Remember to go back to the Navigator box on the chapter-opening page and check off your completed work.

> After you complete your homework assignments, it's a good idea to go back to **The Navigator** checklist at the start of the chapter to see if you have used all the study aids of the chapter.

HOW DO YOU LEARN BEST?

Now that you have looked at your Owner's Manual, take time to find out how you learn best. This quiz was designed to help you find out something about your preferred learning method. Research on left brain/right brain differences and also on learning and personality differences suggests that each person has preferred ways to receive and communicate information. After taking the quiz, we will help you pinpoint the study aids in this text that will help you learn the material based on your learning style.

Circle the letter of the answer that best explains your preference. If a single answer does not match your perception, please circle two or more choices. Leave blank any question that does not apply.

1. You are about to give directions to a person. She is staying in a hotel in town and wants to visit your house. She has a rental car. Would you
   V) draw a map on paper?
   R) write down the directions (without a map)?
   A) tell her the directions?
   K) pick her up at the hotel in your car?

2. You are staying in a hotel and have a rental car. You would like to visit friends whose address/location you do not know. Would you like them to
   V) draw you a map on paper?
   R) write down the directions (without a map)?
   A) tell you the directions by phone?
   K) pick you up at the hotel in their car?

3. You have just received a copy of your itinerary for a world trip. This is of interest to a friend. Would you
   A) call her immediately and tell her about it?
   R) send her a copy of the printed itinerary?
   V) show her on a map of the world?

4. You are going to cook a dessert as a special treat for your family. Do you
   K) cook something familiar without need for instructions?
   V) thumb through the cookbook looking for ideas from the pictures?
   R) refer to a specific cookbook where there is a good recipe?
   A) ask for advice from others?

5. A group of tourists has been assigned to you to find out about national parks. Would you
   K) drive them to a national park?
   R) give them a book on national parks?
   V) show them slides and photographs?
   A) give them a talk on national parks?

6. You are about to purchase a new stereo. Other than price, what would most influence your decision?
   A) A friend talking about it.
   K) Listening to it.
   R) Reading the details about it.
   V) Its distinctive, upscale appearance.

7. Recall a time in your life when you learned how to do something like playing a new board game. (Try to avoid choosing a very physical skill, e.g., riding a bike.) How did you learn best? By
   V) visual clues—pictures, diagrams, charts?
   A) listening to somebody explaining it?
   R) written instructions?
   K) doing it?

8. Which of these games do you prefer?
   V) *Pictionary*
   R) *Scrabble*
   K) Charades

9. You are about to learn to use a new program on a computer. Would you
   K) ask a friend to show you?
   R) read the manual that comes with the program?
   A) telephone a friend and ask questions about it?

10. You are not sure whether a word should be spelled "dependent" or "dependant." Do you
    R) look it up in the dictionary?
    V) see the word in your mind and choose the best way it looks?
    A) sound it out in your mind?
    K) write both versions down?

11. Apart from price, what would most influence your decision to buy a particular textbook?
    K) Using a friend's copy.
    R) Skimming parts of it.
    A) A friend talking about it.
    V) It looks OK.

12. A new movie has arrived in town. What would most influence your decision to go or not to go?
    A) Friends talked about it.
    R) You read a review of it.
    V) You saw a preview of it.

13. Do you prefer a lecturer/teacher who likes to use
    R) handouts and/or a textbook?
    V) flow diagrams, charts, slides?
    K) field trips, labs, practical sessions?
    A) discussion, guest speakers?

Results: To determine your learning preference, add up the number of individual Vs, As, Rs, and Ks you have circled. Match the letter you have recorded most frequently to the same letter in the Learning Styles Chart. Next to each letter in the Chart are suggestions that will refer you to different learning aids throughout this text.

LEARNING STYLES CHART

V VISUAL

WHAT TO DO IN CLASS	WHAT TO DO WHEN STUDYING	TEXT FEATURES THAT MAY HELP YOU THE MOST	WHAT TO DO PRIOR TO AND DURING EXAMS
Underline. Use different colors. Use symbols, charts, arrangements on the page.	Use the "In Class" strategies. Reconstruct images in different ways. Redraw pages from memory. Replace words with symbols and initials.	**The Navigator** **Feature Story** **Preview** **Infographics/Illustrations** **Photos** **Accounting in Action** **Accounting Equation Analyses** **Key Terms in blue** **Words in bold** **Questions/Exercises/ Problems** **Financial Reporting Problem** **Comparative Analysis Problem** **Interpreting Financial Statements** **Research Assignments** **Surfing the Net**	Recall the "pictures of the pages." Draw, use diagrams where appropriate. Practice turning visuals back into words.

A AURAL

WHAT TO DO IN CLASS	WHAT TO DO WHEN STUDYING	TEXT FEATURES THAT MAY HELP YOU THE MOST	WHAT TO DO PRIOR TO AND DURING EXAMS
Attend lectures and tutorials. Discuss topics with students. Explain new ideas to other people. Use a tape recorder. Describe overheads, pictures, and visuals to somebody not there. Leave space in your notes for later recall.	You may take poor notes because you prefer to listen. Therefore: Expand your notes. Put summarized notes on tape and listen. Read summarized notes out loud. Explain notes to another "aural" person.	**Infographics/Illustrations** **Accounting in Action** **Review It/Do It** **Summary of Study Objectives** **Glossary** **Demonstration Problem** **Self-Study Questions** **Questions/Exercises/ Problems** **Financial Reporting Problem** **Comparative Analysis Problem** **Real-World Focus** **Group Decision Case** **Communication Activity** **Ethics Case**	Listen to your "voices" and write them down. Speak your answers. Practice writing answers to old exam questions.

Source: Adapted from Neil D. Fleming and Colleen Mills, "Not Another Inventory, Rather a Catalyst for Reflections," *To Improve the Academy*, Volume II (1992), pp. 137-155. Used by permission.

READING/WRITING

WHAT TO DO IN CLASS	WHAT TO DO WHEN STUDYING	TEXT FEATURES THAT MAY HELP YOU THE MOST	WHAT TO DO PRIOR TO AND DURING EXAMS
Use lists, headings. Use dictionaries and definitions. Use handouts and textbooks. Read. Use lecture notes.	Write out words again and again. Reread notes silently. Rewrite ideas into other words. Organize diagrams into statements.	The Navigator Feature Story Study Objectives Preview Review It/Do It Summary of Study Objectives Glossary Self-Study Questions Questions/Exercises/ Problems Writing Problems Financial Reporting Problem Comparative Analysis Problem Real-World Focus Group Decision Case Communication Activity Ethics Case Research Assignment	Practice with multiple-choice questions. Write out lists. Write paragraphs, beginnings and endings.

KINESTHETIC

WHAT TO DO IN CLASS	WHAT TO DO WHEN STUDYING	TEXT FEATURES THAT MAY HELP YOU THE MOST	WHAT TO DO PRIOR TO AND DURING EXAMS
Use all your senses. Go to labs, take field trips. Use trial-and-error methods. Listen to real-life examples. Use hands-on approach.	You may take notes poorly because topics do not seem relevant. Therefore: Put examples in note summaries. Use pictures and photos to illustrate. Talk about notes with another "kinesthetic" person.	The Navigator Feature Story Preview Infographics/Illustrations Review It/Do It Summary of Study Objectives Demonstration Problem Self-Study Questions Questions/Exercises/ Problems Financial Reporting Problem Comparative Analysis Problem Real-World Focus Group Decision Case Communication Activity Research Assignment Surfing the Net	Write practice answers. Role-play the exam situation.

SPECIAL STUDENT SUPPLEMENTS THAT HELP YOU GET THE BEST GRADE YOU CAN

Working Papers, Volume I: Chapters 1–13 and Volume II: Chapters 13–27

These partially completed accounting forms can be used for all end-of-chapter exercises, problems, and cases. They demonstrate how to set up solution formats correctly and are directly tied to textbook assignments.

Student Study Guide, Volume I: Chapters 1–13 and Volume II: Chapters 13–27

The Student Study Guide is a comprehensive review of accounting. In addition to guiding you through chapter content, it provides resources for use during lectures. With additional opportunities to practice your knowledge and skills, this is an excellent resource when preparing for exams.

Self-Study Problems/Solutions Book, Volume I: Chapters 1–13 and Volume II: Chapters 13–27

This tutorial is designed to improve your ability in solving accounting principles homework assignments and exam questions through a wide selection of multiple-choice questions, exercises, and cases. The Self-Study Book also provides additional insights on how to study accounting and tips to alert you to common pitfalls.

PowerNotes, Volume I: Chapters 1–13 and Volume II: Chapters 13–27

This handy note-taking guide includes all the PowerPoint presentations printed out three to a page, with spaces next to them for you to take notes. PowerNotes allow you to focus on the discussions at hand, instead of focusing on copying down slides projected in class.

Financial Accounting Tutor (FAcT)

FAcT is a self-paced CD-ROM tutorial designed to review financial accounting concepts. It uses simple examples that have been carefully crafted to introduce concepts gradually. Throughout, the program emphasizes the logic underlying the accounting process. FAcT uses interactive and graphical tools to enhance the learning process. Intuitive navigation and a powerful search mechanism allow you to easily follow the tutorial from start to finish or skip to the topics you want to complete. The discussions and examples are followed by brief, interactive problems that provide immediate feedback. Built-in tools, such as an on-line financial calculator, help solve the problems.

On-Line Business Survival Guide in Accounting

The journey of 1,000 Web sites begins with one click, and this practical guide gets you on the road. The On-Line Business Survival Guide is a brief, clear introduction to using the World Wide Web as a business research tool. Starting with the basics, this manual covers everything you need to know to become a master sleuth at finding critical information on the Internet. In addition, the guide provides a hands-on guide to using the Wall Street Journal Interactive Edition, as well as a discount offer for a subscription to the Wall Street Journal Interactive on-line.

Business Extra Web Site at http://www.wiley.com/college/businessextra

To complement the On-Line Business Survival Guide in Accounting, the Business Extra Web Site gives you instant access to a wealth of current articles dealing with all aspects of financial accounting. The articles are organized by topic, and discussion questions follow each article. You will find a password inside the On-Line Business Survival Guide that will give you access to the Business Extra Web Site.

The Accounting Principles Web Site at http://www.wiley.com/college/weygandt

As a resource and learning tool, the Accounting Principles Web Site serves as a launching pad to numerous activities, resources, and related sites. Available through the Web site are links to companies discussed in the text, additional cases and problems, and items such as the Checklist of Key Figures and PowerPoint Presentations for download. Sample chapters of the Student Study Guide, Self-Study Book, and PowerNotes are available for download from this site, for you to try out. The site also provides a link to the Wiley Business Extra site, discussed above. Visit the site often for updated and new materials.

Practice Sets

Practice sets expose you to a real-world simulation of maintaining a complete set of accounting records for a business. You'll find that practice sets reinforce the concepts and procedures learned in each chapter of the textbook, and show you how they are brought together to generate the accounting information that is essential in assessing the financial position and operating results of a company. The practice sets available are
- **Campus Cycle Shop**
- **Heritage Home Furniture**
- **University Bookstore, Inc.**

General Ledger Software

The General Ledger Software program allows you to solve selected end-of-chapter text problems using a computerized accounting system. The software also allows you to complete the Campus Cycle Shop, Heritage Home Furniture, and the University Bookstore, Inc., practice sets on a computer.

Solving Accounting Principles Problems Using Lotus 1-2-3 and Solving Accounting Principles Problems Using Excel for Windows

These electronic spreadsheet templates (available in either Lotus or Excel) allow you to complete selected end-of-chapter exercises and problems. The manuals, which include the disks, guide you step-by-step from an introduction to computers and Lotus or Excel, to completing preprogrammed spreadsheets, to designing your own spreadsheets.

MicroStudy, A Computerized Study Guide

A computerized version of the Student Study Guide, MicroStudy is designed to provide more flexible movement through the content of the Study Guide to meet your particular needs. You can select from a number of self-study options, including: chapter summaries, chapter study objectives, and self-test questions. Multiple-choice questions offer you explanations of why the wrong choices are not correct.

ACKNOWLEDGMENTS

During the course of the development of *Accounting Principles*, Fifth Edition, the authors benefited greatly from feedback from numerous instructors and students of accounting principles courses throughout the country, including many users of the Fourth Edition of the text. This feedback (constructive suggestions and innovative ideas) helped focus the revision on the needs of the students. We are indebted to the contributions of the following accounting professionals.

Reviewers and Focus Group Participants for Prior Editions of *Accounting Principles*

Hector Agostini, Middlesex Community College; Linda Alderson, Cabrillo College; Marilyn Allan, Central Michigan University; Walter Allen, North Virginia Community College; Melody Ashenfelter, Southwestern Oklahoma State University; Peter Barton, University of Wisconsin-Whitewater; Abdul Baten, North Virginia Community College; Don Baynham, Eastfield College; Steven Becker, University of Wisconsin-Platteville; Harold Bland, Roosevelt University; Dennis Bolen, Augustana College; Lana Bone, West Valley College; Eugene Braun, North Virginia Community College; Russell Breslaur, Chabot College; William Brooks, Southwestern Oklahoma State University; Virginia Brunell, Diablo Valley College; Jim Bryant, Catonsville Community College; Terry Bullock, College of Dupage; Ashley Burrowes, California State University-Bakersfield; Madeline Carlin, University of Pittsburgh; Janet Cassagio, Nassau Community College; Randy Castello, West Valley College; Barbara Chiapetta, Nassau Community College; John Corradetti, Joliet Junior College; Sharon Cotton, Schoolcraft College; Carolyn Craig, Shepherd College; Mark Dawson, Indiana University of Pennsylvania; Michael Deda, Fairleigh Dickinson University; Irene Douma, Montclair State College; Charles Downing, Massasoit Community College; Roger DuFresne, Northern Essex Community College; Dean Eiteman, Indiana University of Pennsylvania; David Erlich, Queens College; Carl Fisher, Foothills College; Michael Foland, Belleville Area College; Mary Kathryn Gardner, Johnson & Wales University; Angelo Gazzola, University of Wisconsin-Fox Valley; Robert Giacoletti, Eastern Kentucky University; Debra Goorbin, Westchester Community College; Ed Gordon, Triton College; W. Michael Gough, DeAnza College; Don Green, State University of New York-Farmingdale; Gloria Halpern, Montgomery College; Margie Hamilton, Lewis & Clark Community College; Clo Hampton, West Valley College; Ken Hardy, Catonsville Community College; Patricia Harrison, University of New Orleans; John Hartwick, Bucks County Community College; Nabil Hassan, Wright State University; Alene Helling, Stark Technical College; Keith Hendrick, Wallace State College; Sid Hyder, Indiana University of Pennsylvania; Lou Jacoby, Saginaw Valley State University; Joe Kederabek, Baldwin-Wallace College; Janice Kelley, St. Louis Community College; Robert Kirsch, Bowling Green State University; Carol Klinger, Queens College; Jeanette Klosterman, Hutchinson Community College; Roann Kopel, Eastern Illinois University; John Lannen, Salem State College; Doug Larson, Salem State College; Kathy Larson, Middlesex Community College; Larry Larson, Triton College; Marcella Lecky, University of Southwestern Louisiana; Henri LeClerc, Suffolk Community College; Garry Lym, Golden Gate University; Johnnie Mapp, Norfolk State University; Mary Maury, St. John's University; Jean McKenzie, Fergus Falls Community College; Noel McKeon, Florida Community College-Jacksonville; Greg Mostyn, Mission College; Rhonda Mulkonen, University of South Dakota; Deborah Niemer, Oakland Community College-Royal Oak; Betty Nolen, Floyd Junior College; Cletus O'Drobinak, South Suburban College; Lynn Mazzola Paluska, Nassau Community College; Sandra Penn, Wayne State University; Wayne Pfingsten, Belleville Area College; Rose Marie Pilcher, Abilene Christian University; Beverly Piper, Ashland University; Paul Polachek, Loyola University of Chicago; Kay Poston, Arizona State University-West Campus; Charles Reilly, Suffolk Community College; Bill Reynolds, St. Charles Community College; James Rosa, Queensborough Community College; Victoria Rymer, University of Maryland; Stephen Schaefer, Contra Costa College; Barry Smith, DeAnza College; Jerome Spallino, Westmoreland Community College; Carolyn Strikler, Ohlone College; John Sullivan, North Shore Community College; Karen Ulbrich, Parkland College; DuWayne Wacker, University of North Dakota; Janis Waivio, Delta College; Daniel Ward, Southwest Louisiana State University; Michael Watters, New Mexico State University; John Wells, Triton College; Robert Wernagel, College of the Mainland; Kathleen Wessman, Montgomery College; Steven Wong, San Jose City College

Survey Respondents

James Abbott, Broome Community College; Jill Estes Bailey, Abilene Christian University; Peter Barton, University of Wisconsin, Whitewater; Chris Bennett, Taylor University; Mary Bochnak, Hamline University; Michael Brown, Abilene Christian University; M. Patrick Joseph Cahill, R.S.H.M., Marymount University; Joseph D'Adamo, Providence College; S. T. Desai, Cedar Village College; Pamela Druger, Augustana College; Jim Dunigan, University of Wisconsin, Stevens Point; Larry Edwards, Tarrant County South Junior College; Harold Goldde, Marshall University; Mary Greenawalt, The Citadel; Vicki Greshik, Jamestown College; Sue Gunkel, Albuquerque T–VI; John Hartwick, Bucks County Community College; Candie Humphrey, University of Dubuque; Thomas Kam, Hawaii Pacific University; Kenneth Koerber, Bucks County Community College; Teresa Mack, Loras College; Don McDaniel, Clatsop Community College; Jean McKenzie, Fergus Falls Community College; Noel McKeon, Florida Community College; Ben Milchman, Queensborough Community College; Charles Mitchell, Central Carolina Community College; Sally Nelson, Northeast Iowa Community College and University of Dubuque; Jon Nitschke, Montana State University; Daniel Oliveras, Inter American University; William Radig, Marshall University; Reed Reynolds, Sheldon Jackson College; S. C. Schaefer, Contra Costa College; Richard Seek, University of South Alabama; James Segar, Southern College of Seventh-Day Adventists; Robbie Sheffy, Tarrant County South Junior College; Frank Urbancic, University of South Alabama; Du Wayne Wacker, University of North Dakota; Bea Wallace, St. Phillips College; Jack Wiehler, San Joaquin Delta College; Carolyn Woodbury, University of Montana–Missoula

Reviewers and Focus Group Participants for *Accounting Principles*, Fifth Edition

Janet Becker, University of Pittsburgh at Johnstown; Nancy Boyd, Middle Tennessee State University; Lloyd Carroll, Borough of Manhattan Community College; Ed Castelloe, Lincoln Land Community College; Joan Cook, Milwaukee Area Technical College; Cecelia Fewox, Trident Technical College; Jeannie Folk, College of Du Page; Janet Grange, Chicago State University; Thomas Hofmeister, Northwestern Business School; Shirly Kleiner, Johnson County Community College; Robyn Lawrence, University of Scranton; Bruce Leauby, LaSalle University; Paul Lisowski, Edinboro University; Deanne Pannell, Pellissippi State Technical College; Nancy Sheridan, Bucks County Community College; Jerome Spallino, Westmoreland County Community College; Melvin Stinnett, Oklahoma Christian University; Lynda Thompson, Massasoit Community College; Cynthia Tomes, Des Moines Area Community College-Urban Campus; Chris Widmer, Tidewater Community College

Student Reviewers for Prior Editions of *Accounting Principles*—Schools

Appalachian State University; Hofstra University; Nassau Community College; North Carolina A & M University; Ohlone State College; Phoenix College; Providence College, Queensborough Community College; University of Maine-Bangor; University of Texas-San Antonio; Wake Forest Technical College

Student Reviewers for *Accounting Principles*, Fifth Edition

College of Lake County—Professor: Sharon Grove, Student Reviewer: Sheila Anderson, Professor: John Mason, Student Reviewer: Scott Parkerson; Massasoit Community College—Professor: Lynda Thompson, Student Reviewer: Khris Hovagimian; Ocean County Community College—Student Reviewer: Eli Oelbaum; University of Scranton—Professor: Robyn Lawrence, Student Reviewers: Marissa Marsico, Jennifer Medalis; University of Southwestern Louisiana—Professor: Marc Giullian, Student Reviewer: Sloan Richard, Professor: Kathy Hsu, Student Reviewer: Michelle Bryant

Reviewers of Supplements for *Accounting Principles*, Fifth Edition

Jim Benedum, Milwaukee Area Technical College; Joan Cook, Milwaukee Area Technical College; Gaspare DiLorenzo, Gloucester County College; David Erlach, Queens College; Mark Holtzman, Hofstra University; Phil Kishimori, Leeward Community College; Lynn Koshiyama, University of Alaska-Anchorage; Laura Ruff, Milwaukee Area Technical College; Nathan Saltzberg, Milwaukee Area Technical College; Anita Singer, Kings College; Daniel Small, Jay Sargeant Reynolds Community College; David Zaumeyer, Rutgers University

General Ledger Software Advisory Board

Denise Bloom, Upper Iowa University; Kevin Dooley, Kapiolani Community College; Peter Doran, North Shore Community College; Jeannie Folk, College of DuPage; Carolyn Harris, University of Texas-San Antonio; Molly Linksz, Anne Arundel Community College; Shelly Ota, Leeward Community College; Patricia A. Robinson, Johnson & Wales University; Karen Russom, North Harris Community College; Lynda Thompson, Massasoit Community College; Anne Tippitt, Tarrant County Junior College-South Campus.

Special Thanks

Special thanks go to Joey Brenner, University of Wisconsin–Madison; Deanne Pannell, Pellissippi State Technical College; David Ravitch, University of California–Los Angeles; Barbara Trenholm, University of New Brunswick; and a very special thank you for the outstanding editorial efforts of Ann Torbert.

We also sincerely appreciate the work of our supplement authors: Anne Lee Bain, St. Cloud State University; Marianne Bradford, The University of Tennessee; Joan Cook, Milwaukee Area Technical College; Larry Falcetto, Emporia State University; Candace Humphrey, University of Dubuque; Marilyn Hunt, University of Central Florida; Verne Ingram, Red Rocks Community College; Doug Kieso, University of California-Irvine; Greg Lowry, Macon Technical Institute; Gary Lubin, Merck; Sally Nelson, Northeast Iowa Community College; Dick Wasson, Southwestern College.

We also thank those who have assured the accuracy of our supplements: Jack Borke, University of Wisconsin-Platteville; James Benedum, Milwaukee Area Technical College-South; Ed Castelloe, Lincoln Land Community College; Marc Giullian, University of Southwestern Louisiana; Lee Higgins, Southeast Community College; Phil Kishimori, Leeward Community College; Jennifer Laudermilch, Coopers & Lybrand; Scott Peterson, Northern State University; Laura Ruff, Milwaukee Area Technical College-West; Anita Singer, King's College; Teresa Speck, St. Mary's University.

In addition, special recognition goes to Ivan Pagan of the University of Wisconsin-Madison and Jo Koehn of Central Missouri State University for their work in applying Bloom's Taxonomy, to Karen Huffman of Palomar College for her assessment of the text's pedagogy and suggestions on how to increase its helpfulness to students, to Nancy Galli of Palomar College for her work on learning styles and to Wayne Higley of Buena Vista College for his technical proofing.

We also thank the editorial, marketing, production, design, and illustration staff of John Wiley & Sons. The following individuals were particularly helpful: Susan Elbe, Nancy Perry, David Kear, Joe Heider, Kate Yung, Bridget O'Lavin, Evy Fakiris, Rebecca Hope, Susan Nave, Tracy Guyton, Robert Meador, Steve Kazlauskas, Charlotte Hyland, Barbara Russiello, Laura Boucher, Madelyn Lesure, Anna Melhorn, Hilary Newman, Jennifer Atkins, Mary Ann Benson and Alison Bamert. In addition, a note of gratitude to Martha Beyerlein, Barb Lange, Ingrid Mount, and Elizabeth Jahaske of Elm Street Publishing Services and Mike Klinman of Ruttle, Shaw & Wetherill for their help on this project.

Finally, our thanks for the support provided by Will Pesce, President and Chief Executive Officer, and Bonnie Lieberman, Senior Vice-President of the College Division. Suggestions and comments from users—instructors and students alike—will be appreciated.

Jerry J. Weygandt   Donald E. Kieso   Paul D. Kimmel

BRIEF CONTENTS

DETAILED CONTENTS

The Feature Story helps you picture how the chapter topic relates to the real world of accounting and business. You will find references to the story throughout the chapter and in the exercise set toward the end of the chapter.

FEATURE STORY

The Best to You Each Morning

Sometimes it's better to be lucky than good. In 1894 two brothers were working on an experiment to introduce grain into the diet of sanitarium patients. Some of the grain got too wet, but they decided to roll it and toast it anyway. *Voilà*—the Kellogg brothers had just invented flaked cereal. At first they sold it by mail order, but in 1906 William Kellogg, believing he could serve a larger market, started his own company, the Battle Creek Toasted Corn Flake Company.

Today Kellogg produces 12 of the world's top 15 most popular cereals. It sells 40% of the cereal consumed in the world. How did it become so dominant? Kellogg's entrepreneurial vision was grounded in a clever marketing strategy. For example, one early promotion promised a box of cereal to any woman who winked at her grocer. Marketing has been a priority: Think about how many of Kellogg's products, slogans, or advertising jingles are ingrained in your memory such as Tony the Tiger (Frosted Flakes) and Snap! Crackle! and Pop! (Rice Krispies). It is almost impossible to imagine growing up without Rice Krispies bars—those gooey globs of rice are a rite of passage for nearly every American child.

But it takes more than marketing to build a dominant company. Kellogg's success has also come from careful planning. Management must make many decisions: where to locate, whether to buy or rent properties, how to finance current operations and expansion, and what new products to sell. Kellogg's 14,000 employees manufacture its products in 22 countries and distribute them in 160 countries. Managing such a colossal business requires vast amounts of accounting information.

As a business becomes large, its financial needs often exceed the resources of the original owners. When this happens, the company looks for financing from lenders or from additional owners. Kellogg has approximately 27,000 owners, called shareholders. In addition, lenders and creditors have provided it with $3.8 billion. Lenders and investors will not provide financing unless they feel confident about a company's future. In order to obtain additional financing, Kellogg communicates its past performance and its plans for the future to lenders and investors through accounting information.

THE NAVIGATOR

On the World Wide Web
http://www.kelloggs.com

CHAPTER 1

ACCOUNTING IN ACTION

THE NAVIGATOR ✔

- ■ Understand *Concepts for Review* ☐
- ■ Read *Feature Story* ☐
- ■ Scan *Study Objectives* ☐
- ■ Read *Preview* ☐
- ■ Read text and answer *Before You Go On*
  p. 9 ☐ p. 15 ☐ p. 22 ☐ p. 26 ☐
- ■ Work *Demonstration Problem* ☐
- ■ Review *Summary of Study Objectives* ☐
- ■ Answer *Self-Study Questions* ☐
- ■ Complete assignments ☐

The Navigator is a learning system designed to prompt you to use the learning aids in the chapter and set priorities as you study.

STUDY OBJECTIVES

Study Objectives give you a framework for learning the specific concepts covered in the chapter.

After studying this chapter, you should be able to:

1. Explain the meaning of accounting.
2. Identify the users and uses of accounting.
3. Understand why ethics is a fundamental business concept.
4. Explain the meaning of generally accepted accounting principles and the cost principle.
5. Explain the meaning of the monetary unit assumption and the economic entity assumption.
6. State the basic accounting equation and explain the meaning of assets, liabilities, and owner's equity.
7. Analyze the effect of business transactions on the basic accounting equation.
8. Prepare an income statement, owner's equity statement, balance sheet, and statement of cash flows.

THE NAVIGATOR

1

*T*he opening story about the Kellogg Company highlights the need for accurate and sound reporting of financial information. It follows that regardless of one's pursuits or occupation, the need for financial information is inescapable. You cannot earn a living, spend money, buy on credit, make an investment, or pay taxes without receiving, using, or dispensing financial information. Good decision making depends on good information.

The purpose of this chapter is to show you that accounting is the system used to provide useful financial information. The content and organization of the chapter are as follows:

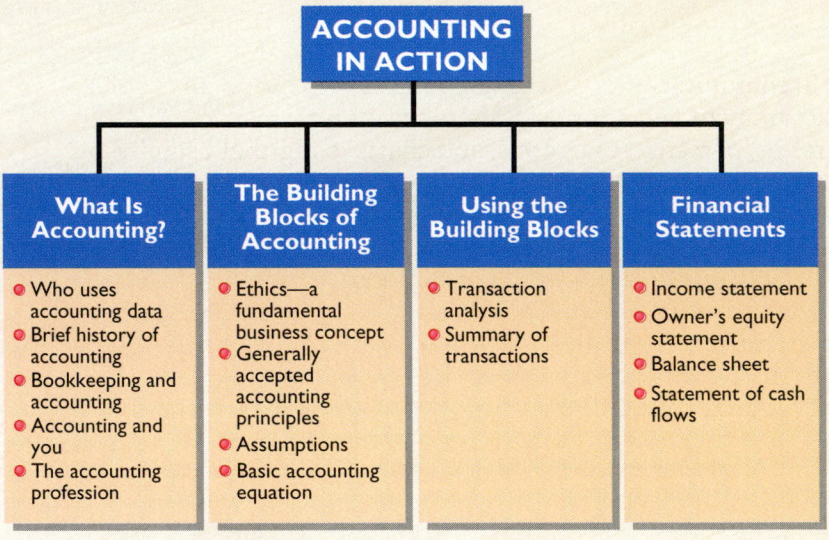

The **Preview** describes and outlines the major topics and subtopics you will see in the chapter.

WHAT IS ACCOUNTING?

1

STUDY
OBJECTIVE

Explain the meaning of accounting.

Essential terms are printed in blue when they first appear, and are defined in the end-of-chapter glossary.

As a financial information system, **accounting** is a process of three activities: **identifying**, **recording**, and **communicating** the economic events of an organization (business or nonbusiness) to interested users of the information. Let's take a closer look at these three activities:

1. The first part of the process—**identifying**—involves selecting those events that are considered **evidence of economic activity relevant to a particular organization**. The sale of goods by Kellogg Company, the rendering of services by American Telephone & Telegraph, the payment of wages by Ford Motor Company, and the collection of ticket and broadcast money and the payment of expenses by major league sports teams are examples of economic events.

2. Once identified and measured in dollars and cents, economic events are **recorded** to provide a permanent history of the financial activities of the organization. Recording consists of keeping a **chronological diary of measured events in an orderly and systematic manner**. In recording, economic events are also classified and summarized.

3. This identifying and recording activity is of little use unless the information is **communicated** to interested users. The information is communicated through the **preparation and distribution of accounting reports**, the most common of which are called **financial statements**. To make the reported financial information meaningful, accountants describe and report the recorded data in a standardized way. Information resulting from similar transactions is accumulated and totaled. Such data are said to be reported **in the aggregate**. For example, all sales transactions of Kellogg Company are accumulated over a certain period of time and reported as one amount in the financial statements of Kellogg Company. By presenting the recorded data in the aggregate, the accounting process simplifies a multitude of transactions and renders a series of activities understandable and meaningful.

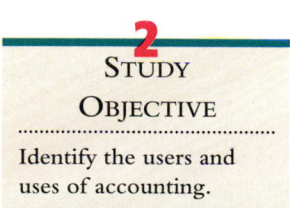

References throughout the chapter tie the accounting concepts you are learning to the story that opened the chapter.

A vital element in communicating economic events is the accountant's ability and responsibility to **analyze** and **interpret** the reported information. Analysis involves the use of ratios, percentages, graphs, and charts to highlight significant financial trends and relationships. Interpretation involves **explaining the uses, meaning, and limitations of reported data**. Appendix A of this textbook illustrates the financial statements and accompanying notes and graphs from Kellogg Company; Appendix B illustrates the financial statements of General Mills. We refer to these statements at various places throughout the text. At this point, they probably strike you as complex and confusing. By the end of this course, you'll be surprised at how much about them you understand.

In summary, the accounting process may be diagrammed as follows:

ILLUSTRATION 1-1

Accounting process

Accounting should consider the needs of the users of financial information. As a consequence, you should know who these users are and something about their needs for information.

Who Uses Accounting Data

Because it communicates financial information about a business enterprise, accounting is often called "the language of business." The information that a specific user of financial information needs depends upon the kinds of decisions that

2
STUDY
OBJECTIVE
....
Identify the users and uses of accounting.

user makes. The differences in the decisions divide the users of financial information into two broad groups: internal users and external users.

Internal Users

ILLUSTRATION 1-2

Questions asked by internal users

Internal users of accounting information are managers who plan, organize, and run a business. These include **marketing managers, production supervisors, finance directors, and company officers.** In running a business, managers must answer many important questions, as shown in Illustration 1-2.

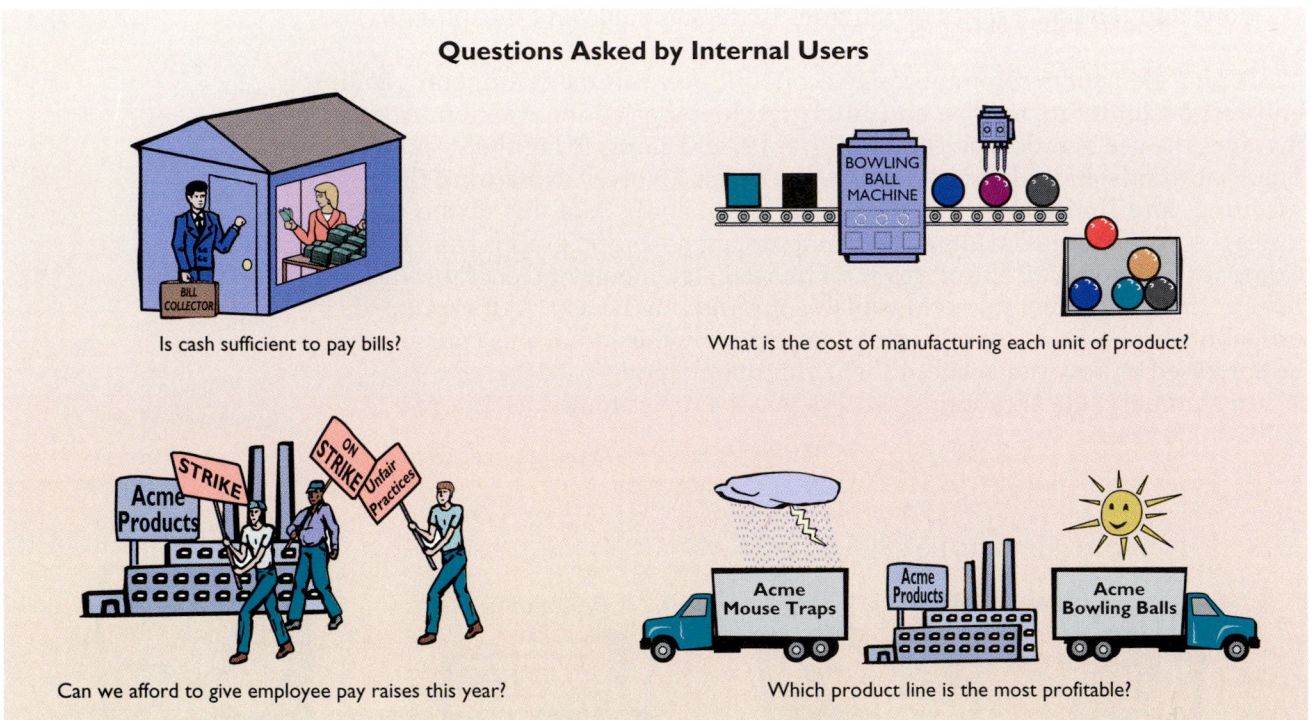

Questions Asked by Internal Users

Is cash sufficient to pay bills?

What is the cost of manufacturing each unit of product?

Can we afford to give employee pay raises this year?

Which product line is the most profitable?

To answer these and other questions, you need detailed information on a timely basis. For internal users, accounting provides internal reports, such as financial comparisons of operating alternatives, projections of income from new sales campaigns, and forecasts of cash needs for the next year. In addition, summarized financial information is presented in the form of financial statements.

External Users

There are several types of **external users** of accounting information. **Investors** (owners) use accounting information to make decisions to buy, hold, or sell stock. **Creditors** such as suppliers and bankers use accounting information to evaluate the risks of granting credit or lending money. Some questions that may be asked by investors and creditors about a company are shown in Illustration 1-3.

The information needs and questions of other external users vary considerably. **Taxing authorities,** such as the Internal Revenue Service, want to know whether the company complies with the tax laws. **Regulatory agencies,** such as the Securities and Exchange Commission or the Federal Trade Commission, want to know whether the company is operating within prescribed rules. **Customers** are interested in whether a company will continue to honor product warranties

HELPFUL HINT

The IRS requires businesses to retain records that can be audited. Also, the Foreign Corrupt Practices Act requires public companies to keep records.

ILLUSTRATION 1-3
Questions asked by external users

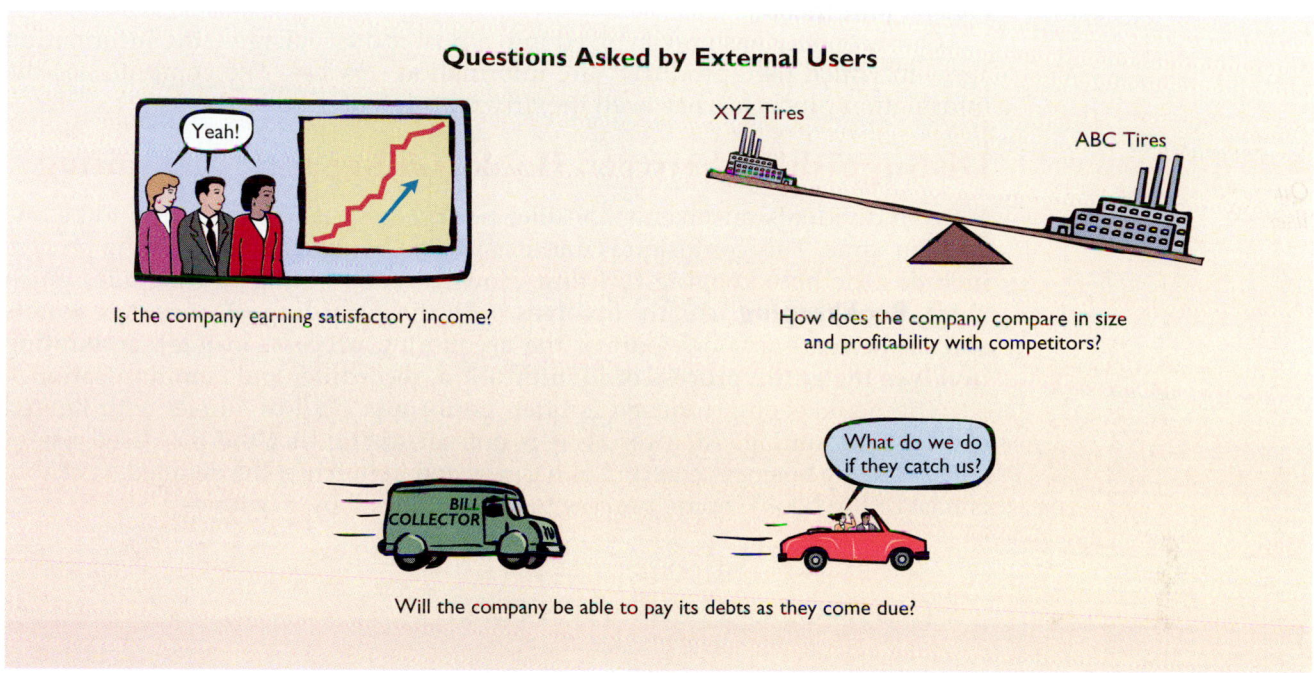

Questions Asked by External Users

Yeah!

Is the company earning satisfactory income?

XYZ Tires

ABC Tires

How does the company compare in size and profitability with competitors?

BILL COLLECTOR

What do we do if they catch us?

Will the company be able to pay its debts as they come due?

and otherwise support its product lines. **Labor unions** want to know whether the owners have the ability to pay increased wages and benefits. **Economic planners** use accounting information to analyze and forecast economic activity.

ACCOUNTING IN ACTION

International Insight

When the chief engineer of Irkutsk Energo, a public utility in Moscow, addressed a gathering of international investors recently, he provided them with all kinds of financial information about the company. The reason: Russians are learning that corporate openness lures much-needed foreign investment. Foreign investors, however, have been reluctant to invest because Russian firms have been secretive (and sometimes deceptive) about their financial affairs. Now, however, things will probably change because firms such as Irkutsk Energo have enjoyed stock price surges after providing candid accounting information. In short, good accounting information may help Russia solve some of its economic problems.

Source: The Wall Street Journal, June 9, 1995, p. A-6.

Accounting in Action examples illustrate important and interesting accounting situations in business.

Brief History of Accounting

The **origins of accounting** are generally attributed to the work of Luca Pacioli, a famous Italian Renaissance mathematician. Pacioli was a close friend and tutor to Leonardo da Vinci and a contemporary of Christopher Columbus. In his text *Summa de Arithmetica, Geometria, Proportione et Proportionalite*, Pacioli described a system to ensure that financial information was recorded efficiently and accurately.

With the advent of the **industrial age** in the nineteenth century and, later, the emergence of large corporations, a separation of the owners from the managers of businesses took place. As a result, the need to report the status of the business enterprise took on increasing importance, to ensure that managers acted in accord with owners' wishes. In addition, transactions between businesses became more complex, making necessary improved approaches for reporting financial information.

Our economy has now evolved into a post-industrial age—**the information age**—in which the "products" are information services. The computer, as the information processor, has been the driver of the information age.

Distinguishing between Bookkeeping and Accounting

Many individuals mistakenly consider bookkeeping and accounting to be one and the same. This confusion is understandable because the accounting process **includes the bookkeeping function**. However, accounting also includes much more. **Bookkeeping usually involves only the recording of economic events** and is therefore just one part of the accounting process. In total, **accounting involves the entire process of identification, recording, and communication.**

The bookkeeping function is often performed by individuals with limited skills in accounting. As a result, it is not surprising that the increased use of computers by business enterprises has resulted in much of the detailed work that is part of the bookkeeping process being performed by machines.

TECHNOLOGY IN ACTION

With the phenomenal growth in computers, more and more record keeping is being performed electronically. Businesses, small as well as large, are finding that through the use of the computer the entire recording process has become more efficient. However, it is important to know the procedures used in a manual system to understand the operations a computer performs.

Technology in Action examples show how computer technology is used in accounting and business.

Accounting and You

One question frequently asked by students of accounting is, "How will the study of accounting help me?" It should help you a great deal, because a working knowledge of accounting is desirable for virtually every field of endeavor. Some illustrations of how accounting is used in other careers include:

General management: Imagine running General Motors, a major hospital, a school, a McDonald's franchise, a bike shop; all general managers need to understand and have access to accounting data in order to make wise business decisions.

Marketing/Advertising: A marketing specialist is someone who develops strategies to help the sales force be successful. But making a sale is meaningless unless it is a profitable sale. Marketing people must be sensitive to costs and benefits, which accounting helps them quantify and understand.

Marketing people are also involved in advertising. What would a flashy field such as advertising have to do with accounting? If you buy a commercial on a radio station, you'll want to know the cost per thousand listeners. You'll deal in ratings numbers and budgets all day. And ad agencies are always under pressure to cut costs, because their clients can be very fickle—particularly if the ad campaign doesn't work.

Finance: Do you want to be a banker, an investment analyst, a stock broker? These fields rely heavily on accounting. Suppose you decide to go into banking. You could become a lending officer, a money manager, a deal-maker, a foreign currency trader, or a retail branch supervisor. Whatever the situation, you will regularly examine and analyze financial statements. In fact, it is difficult to get a good job in a finance function without two or three courses in accounting.

Real estate: Perhaps the most prevalent career in real estate is that of a broker, a person who sells residential or commercial real estate. Because a third party—the bank—is almost always involved in financing a real estate transaction, brokers must understand the numbers involved: Can the buyer of the house afford to make the payments to the bank on a given salary? Does the cash flow from the industrial property justify the purchase price in this market? What are the tax benefits of making the purchase?

Accounting is useful even for occupations you might think completely unrelated. If you become a doctor, a lawyer, a social worker, a teacher, an engineer, an architect, or an entrepreneur—you name it—a working knowledge of accounting is relevant.

The Accounting Profession

What would you do if you joined the accounting profession? You probably would apply your expertise in one of three major fields—public accounting, private accounting, or not-for-profit accounting.

Public Accounting

In **public accounting**, you would offer expert service to the general public in much the same way that a doctor serves patients and a lawyer serves clients. A major portion of public accounting practice is involved with **auditing**. In this area, a certified public accountant (CPA) examines the financial statements of companies and expresses an opinion as to the fairness of presentation. When the presentation is fair, users consider the statements to be **reliable**. For example, Kellogg's investors and creditors would demand audited financial statements before extending it financing.

Taxation is another major area of public accounting. The work performed by tax specialists includes tax advice and planning, preparing tax returns, and representing clients before governmental agencies such as the Internal Revenue Service.

A third area in public accounting is **management consulting**. Management consulting ranges from the installing of basic computerized accounting systems to helping companies determine whether they should use the space shuttle for high-tech research and development projects.

Private Accounting

Instead of working in public accounting, an accountant may be an employee of a business enterprise. In **private (or managerial) accounting**, you would be involved in one of the following activities:

1. **Cost accounting**—determining the cost of producing specific products.
2. **Budgeting**—assisting management in quantifying goals concerning revenues, costs of goods sold, and operating expenses.
3. **General accounting**—recording daily transactions and preparing financial statements and related information.
4. **Accounting information systems**—designing both manual and computerized data processing systems.

5. **Tax accounting**—preparing tax returns and engaging in tax planning for the company.
6. **Internal auditing**—reviewing the company's operations to determine compliance with management policies and evaluating the efficiency of operations.

From the above, you can see that within a specific company, private accountants perform as wide a variety of duties as the public accountant.

Illustration 1-4 presents the general career paths in public and private accounting.

ILLUSTRATION 1-4

Career paths in public and private accounting

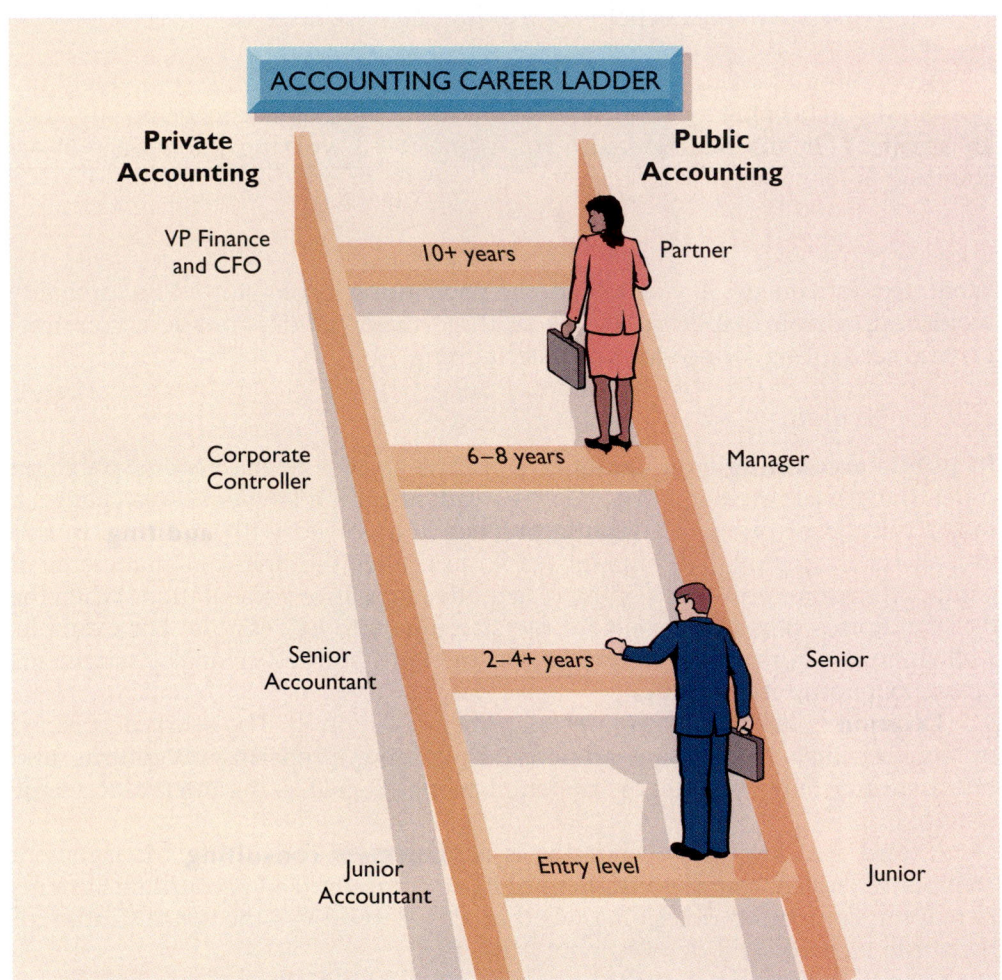

Not-for-Profit Accounting

Like businesses that exist to make a profit, not-for-profit organizations also need sound financial reporting and control. Donors to such organizations as the United Way, the Ford Foundation, and the Red Cross want information about how well the organization has met its objectives and whether continued support is justified. Hospitals, colleges, and universities must make decisions about the allocation of funds. Local, state, and federal governmental units are continually providing financial information to legislators, citizens, employees, and creditors. At the federal level, the largest employers of accountants are the Internal Revenue Service, the General Accounting Office, the Federal Bureau of Investigation, and the Securities and Exchange Commission.

ACCOUNTING IN ACTION

Business Insight

Help Wanted: Forensic CPAs

Tom Taylor's job at the FBI has changed. He used to pack a .357 magnum; now he wields a No. 2 pencil. Taylor, age 37, for two years an FBI agent, is a forensic accountant, somebody who sniffs through company books to ferret out white-collar crime. Demand for this service has surged in the past few years. In one recent year, a recruiter for San Diego's Robert Half International, a headhunting firm, had requests for more than 1,000 such snoops.

Qualification: a CPA with FBI, IRS, or similar government experience. Interestingly, despite its macho image, the FBI has long hired mostly accountants and lawyers as agents.

BEFORE YOU GO ON . . .

Review It

1. What is accounting?
2. Who uses accounting information?
3. What is the difference between bookkeeping and accounting?
4. How can you use your accounting knowledge?

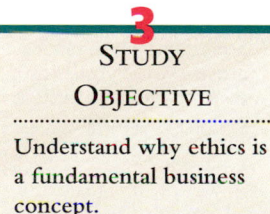

Before You Go On questions at the end of major text sections offer an opportunity to stop and reexamine the key points you have studied.

THE BUILDING BLOCKS OF ACCOUNTING

Every profession develops a body of theory consisting of principles, assumptions, and standards. Accounting is no exception. Just as a doctor follows certain standards in treating a patient's illness, an accountant follows certain standards in reporting financial information. For these standards to work, however, a fundamental business concept is followed—ethical behavior.

Ethics—A Fundamental Business Concept

Wherever you make your career—whether in accounting, marketing, management, finance, government, or elsewhere—your behavior and actions will affect other people and organizations. The standards of conduct by which one's actions are judged as right or wrong, honest or dishonest, fair or not fair, are **ethics**. Imagine trying to carry on a business, perform an audit, or invest money if you could not depend on the individuals you deal with to be honest. If managers, customers, investors, co-workers, and creditors all consistently lied, effective communication and economic activity would be impossible. Information would have no credibility.

Fortunately most individuals in business are ethical. Their actions are both legal and responsible, and they consider the organization's interests in their decision making. However, in some situations public officials, business executives, and respected leaders act unethically. For example, a former chief of the finance committee of the House of Representatives was indicted for possible illegal behavior; Sears was accused of widespread customer overcharging on car repairs; Woolworth Corp. executives were dismissed because they reported false income numbers. As one business leader noted: "We are all embarrassed by the events that make *The Wall Street Journal* read like the *Police Gazette*."

3
STUDY OBJECTIVE
Understand why ethics is a fundamental business concept.

Many companies have developed corporate mission statements. Some of these mission statements include discussion of the company's ethical values. In its statement of company philosophy, for example, Kellogg Company has the following statement regarding integrity and ethics.

ILLUSTRATION 1-5

Corporate ethics statement

KELLOGG COMPANY
Statement of Company Philosophy

Integrity and Ethics
Integrity is the cornerstone of our business practice. We will conduct our affairs in a manner consistent with the highest ethical standards.
   To meet this commitment, we will:

- Engage in fair and honest business practices.
- Show respect for each other, our consumers, customers, suppliers, shareholders and the communities in which we operate.
- Communicate in an honest, factual and accurate manner.

To sensitize you to ethical situations and to give you practice at solving ethical dilemmas, we have included in the book three types of ethics materials: (1) marginal notes that provide helpful hints for developing ethical sensitivity, (2) ethics in accounting boxes that highlight ethics situations and issues, and (3) an ethics case simulating a business situation at the end of the chapter. In the process of analyzing these ethics cases, you should apply the steps outlined in Illustration 1-6.

ILLUSTRATION 1-6

Steps in analyzing ethics cases

Solving an Ethical Dilemma

1. Recognize an ethical situation and the ethical issues involved.

Use your personal ethics to identify ethical situations and issues. Some businesses and professional organizations provide written codes of ethics for guidance in some business situations.

2. Identify and analyze the principal elements in the situation.

Identify the *stakeholders*—persons or groups who may be harmed or benefited. Ask the question: What are the responsibilities and obligations of the parties involved?

3. Identify the alternatives, and weigh the impact of each alternative on various stakeholders.

Select the most ethical alternative, considering all the consequences. Sometimes there will be one right answer. Other situations involve more than one right solution; these situations require an evaluation of each and a selection of the best alternative.

Generally Accepted Accounting Principles

STUDY OBJECTIVE 4

Explain the meaning of generally accepted accounting principles and the cost principle.

The accounting profession has attempted to develop a set of standards that is generally accepted and universally practiced. Its efforts have resulted in a common set of standards called **generally accepted accounting principles (GAAP)**. These standards indicate how to report economic events.

Two organizations are primarily responsible for establishing generally accepted accounting principles. The first is the **Financial Accounting Standards Board (FASB)**, a private organization that establishes broad reporting standards of general applicability as well as specific accounting rules. The second, the **Se-**

curities and Exchange Commission (SEC), is a governmental agency that requires companies filing financial reports with it to follow generally accepted accounting principles. In situations where no principles exist, the SEC often mandates that certain guidelines be used. In general, the FASB and the SEC work hand in hand to assure that timely and useful accounting principles are developed.

One important principle is the cost principle, which states that assets should be recorded at their cost. **Cost is the value exchanged at the time something is acquired.** If you buy a house today, the cost is the amount you pay for it, say $100,000. If you sell the house in two years for $120,000, the sales price is its market value—the value determined by the market for homes at that time. At the time of acquisition, cost and fair market value are the same. In subsequent periods, cost and fair market value may vary, **but the cost amount continues to be used**.

For example, at one time, Greyhound Corporation had 128 bus stations nationwide that cost approximately $200 million. The current market value of the stations is approximately $1 billion. Under the cost principle, the bus stations are recorded and reported at $200 million, not $1 billion. Until the bus stations are actually sold, estimates of market values are considered too subjective.

As the Greyhound example indicates, cost has an important advantage over other valuations: it is reliable. Cost is definite and verifiable. The values exchanged at the time something is acquired generally can be objectively measured. To rely on the information supplied, users must know that the information is based on fact. However, critics argue that cost is often not relevant and that market values provide more useful information. Despite its shortcomings, cost continues to be used in the financial statements because of its reliability.

INTERNATIONAL NOTE

The standard-setting processes in Canada, Mexico, and the United States are quite similar in most respects. All three have relatively open deliberations on new rules, and they support efforts to follow international standards. The use of similar accounting principles within North America has implications for the success of the North American Free Trade Agreement (NAFTA).

ALTERNATIVE TERMINOLOGY

The cost principle is often referred to as the *historical cost principle*.

Assumptions

In developing generally accepted accounting principles, certain basic assumptions are made. These assumptions provide a foundation for the accounting process. Two main assumptions are the **monetary unit assumption** and the **economic entity assumption**.

5
STUDY
OBJECTIVE
....
Explain the meaning of the monetary unit assumption and the economic entity assumption.

Monetary Unit Assumption

The **monetary unit assumption** requires that only transaction data that can be expressed in terms of money be included in the accounting records of the economic entity. Because money is the commonly used medium of exchange, this assumption enables accounting to quantify (measure) the economic event. The monetary unit assumption is vital to applying the cost principle discussed earlier. This assumption prevents such relevant information as the health of the owner, the quality of service, and the morale of employees from being included in the accounting records because they cannot be quantified in terms of money.

An important corollary to the monetary unit assumption is the added assumption that the unit of measure remains sufficiently constant over time. However, the assumption of a stable monetary unit has been challenged because of the significant decline in the purchasing power of the dollar. For example, what used to cost $1.00 in 1960 costs over $4.00 in 1998. In such situations, adding, subtracting, or comparing 1960 dollars with 1998 dollars is highly questionable. The profession has recognized this problem and encourages companies to disclose the effects of changing prices.

Economic Entity Assumption

An economic entity can be any organization or unit in society. It may be a business enterprise (such as General Electric Company), a governmental unit (such as the state of Ohio), a municipality (such as Seattle), a school district (such as St. Louis District 48), or a church (Southern Baptist). The **economic entity assumption** states that economic events can be identified with a particular unit of accountability. This assumption requires that the activities of the entity be kept separate and distinct from (1) the activities of its owner and (2) all other economic entities. To illustrate, if Sally Rider, owner of Sally's Boutique, charges any of her personal living costs as expenses of the Boutique, the economic entity assumption is violated. Similarly, the economic entity assumption assumes that the activities of Kellogg, General Mills, and Quaker Oats can each be segregated into separate economic entities for accounting purposes.

Although the economic entity assumption can be applied to any unit of accountability, we will generally discuss it in relation to a business enterprise, which may be organized as a proprietorship, partnership, or corporation.

ACCOUNTING IN ACTION
Ethics Insight

A violation of the economic entity assumption contributed to the resignation by the chief executive of W.R. Grace and Company. Investors were angered to learn that company funds were used for personal medical care, a Manhattan apartment, and a personal chef for the company's chief. Funds were also used to support a hotel interest owned by the chief executive's son.

HELPFUL HINT
Approximately 70% of United States companies are proprietorships; however, they account for only 6.5% of gross revenues. Corporations, on the other hand, are approximately 19% of all companies, but account for 90% of the revenues.

Proprietorship.   A business owned by one person is generally a **proprietorship**. The owner is often the manager/operator of the business. Small service-type businesses (barber shops, law offices, plumbing companies, and auto repair shops), farms, and small retail stores (antique shops, clothing stores, and book stores) are often sole proprietorships. **Usually only a limited amount of money (capital) is necessary to start in business as a proprietorship, and the owner receives any profits, suffers any losses, and is personally liable for all debts of the business.** Although there is no legal distinction between the business as an economic unit and the owner, the records of the business activities are kept separate from the personal records and activities of the owner. Although sole proprietorships represent the largest number of businesses in the United States, they are typically the smallest in size and volume of business.

Partnership.   A business owned by two or more persons associated as partners is a **partnership**. In most respects a partnership is similar to a sole proprietorship except that more than one owner is involved. When a partnership is created, an agreement (written or oral) should set forth such terms as initial investment of each partner, duties of each partner, division of net income (or net loss), and settlement to be made upon death or withdrawal of a partner. Each partner generally has unlimited personal liability for the debts of the partnership. **Like a proprietorship, for accounting purposes the partnership affairs must be kept separate from the personal activities of the partners.** Partnerships are often used to organize retail and service-type businesses, including professional practices (lawyers, doctors, architects, and certified public accountants).

Corporation.   A business organized as a separate legal entity under state corporation law and having ownership divided into transferable shares of stock is called a corporation. The holders of the shares (stockholders) **enjoy limited liability**; they are not personally liable for the debts of the corporate entity. Stockholders **may transfer all or part of their shares to other investors at any time** (i.e., sell their shares in the securities market). The ease with which ownership can change adds to the attractiveness of investing in a corporation. Because ownership can be transferred without dissolving the corporation, the corporation **enjoys an unlimited life**.

Although the combined number of proprietorships and partnerships in the United States is more than four times the number of corporations, the revenue produced by corporations is nine times greater. Most of the largest enterprises in the United States—for example, Exxon, General Motors, Sears Roebuck, Citicorp, and Kellogg Company—are corporations.

Basic Accounting Equation

Other essential building blocks of accounting are the categories into which economic events are classified. The two basic elements of a business are what it owns and what it owes. **Assets** are the resources owned by a business. For example, Kellogg's competitor, General Mills, has total assets of approximately $3.9 billion. Liabilities and owner's equity are the rights or claims against these resources. Thus, a company such as General Mills that has $3.9 billion of assets also has $3.9 billion of claims against those assets. Claims of creditors are called **liabilities**. Claims of owners are called **owner's equity**. For example, General Mills has liabilities of $3.4 billion and owners' equity of $.5 billion. This equation can be expressed as follows:

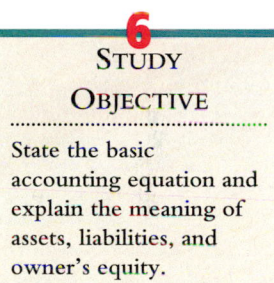

6
STUDY
OBJECTIVE
····················
State the basic accounting equation and explain the meaning of assets, liabilities, and owner's equity.

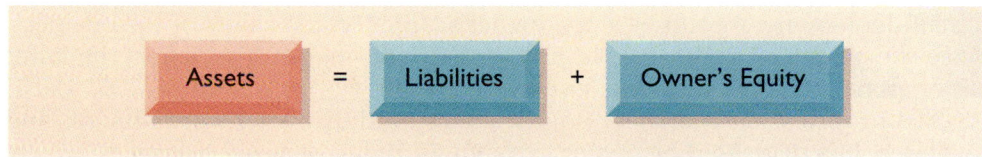

ILLUSTRATION 1-7

The basic accounting equation

This equation is referred to as the basic accounting equation. Assets must equal the sum of liabilities and owner's equity. Because creditors' claims are paid before ownership claims if a business is liquidated, liabilities are shown before owner's equity in the basic accounting equation.

The accounting equation applies to all **economic entities** regardless of size, nature of business, or form of business organization. Thus, it applies to a small proprietorship such as a corner grocery store as well as to a giant corporation such as Kellogg or General Mills. The equation provides the underlying framework for recording and summarizing the economic events of a business enterprise.

Let's look in more detail at the categories in the basic accounting equation.

HELPFUL HINT
In some places we use the term *owner's equity* and in others we use *owners' equity*. *Owner's* refers to one owner—the case with a sole proprietorship, and *owners'* refers to multiple owners—the case with partnerships or corporations.

Assets

As indicated above, assets are resources owned by a business. Thus, they are the things of value used in carrying out such activities as production, consumption, and exchange. The common characteristic possessed by all assets is the capacity to provide future services or benefits to the entities that use them. In a business enterprise, that service potential or future economic benefit eventually results in cash inflows (receipts) to the enterprise.

For example, the enterprise Campus Pizza owns a delivery truck that provides economic benefits because it is used in delivering pizzas. Other assets of Campus Pizza are tables, chairs, jukebox, cash register, oven, mugs and silverware, and, of course, cash.

Liabilities

Liabilities are claims against assets. Put more simply, **liabilities are existing debts and obligations**. For example, businesses of all sizes and degrees of success usually find it necessary to borrow money and to purchase merchandise on credit. Campus Pizza, for instance, purchases cheese, sausage, flour, and beverages on credit from suppliers; these obligations are called **accounts payable**. Additionally, Campus Pizza has a **note payable** to First National Bank for the money borrowed to purchase its delivery truck. Campus Pizza may also have **wages payable** to employees, and **sales and real estate taxes payable** to the local government. Persons or entities to whom Campus Pizza owes money are called **creditors**.

Most claims of creditors attach to **total** enterprise assets rather than to the specific assets provided by the creditor. In the event of nonpayment, creditors may legally force the liquidation of a business. In that case, the law requires that creditor claims be paid before ownership claims.

Owner's Equity

The ownership claim on total assets is known as owner's equity. It is equal to total assets minus total liabilities. Here is why: The assets of a business are supplied or claimed by either creditors or owners. To determine what belongs to owners, we therefore subtract creditors' claims—the liabilities—from assets. The remainder—owner's equity—is the owner's claim on the assets of the business. Since the claims of creditors take precedence over ownership claims, the latter are often referred to as **residual equity**.

In a proprietorship, owner's equity is increased by owner's investments and revenues. It is decreased by owner's drawings and expenses.

Investments by Owner.   Investments by owner are the assets put into the business by the owner. These investments in the business increase owner's equity.

Drawings.   An owner may withdraw cash or other assets during the accounting period for personal use. These withdrawals could be recorded as a direct decrease of owner's equity. However, it is generally considered preferable to use a separate classification referred to as drawings to determine the total withdrawals for the accounting period. **Drawings decrease total owner's equity.**

HELPFUL HINT
The effect of revenues is positive—an increase in owner's equity coupled with an increase in assets or a decrease in liabilities.

Revenues.   Revenues are the **gross increase in owner's equity resulting from business activities entered into for the purpose of earning income.** Generally, revenues result from the sale of merchandise, the performance of services, the rental of property, and the lending of money.

Revenues usually result in an increase in an asset. They may arise from different sources and are identified by various names depending on the nature of the business. Campus Pizza, for instance, has two categories of sales revenues—pizza sales and beverage sales. Other titles for and sources of revenue common to many businesses are: sales, fees, services, commissions, interest, dividends, royalties, and rent.

Expenses. Expenses are **the decreases in owner's equity that result from operating the business.** They are the cost of assets consumed or services used in the process of earning revenue. Expenses represent actual or expected cash outflows (payments). Like revenues, expenses take many forms and are identified by various names depending on the type of asset consumed or service used. For example, Campus Pizza recognizes the following types of expenses: cost of ingredients (meat, flour, cheese, tomato paste, mushrooms, etc.); cost of beverages; wages expense; utility expense (electric, gas, and water expense); telephone expense; delivery expense (gasoline, repairs, licenses, etc.); supplies expense (napkins, detergents, aprons, etc.); rent expense; interest expense; and property tax expense.

In summary, the principal sources (increases) of owner's equity are (1) investments by owners and (2) revenues from business operations. In contrast, reductions in owner's equity are a result of (1) withdrawals of assets by owners and (2) expenses. **Net income** results when revenues exceed expenses; conversely, a **net loss** occurs when expenses exceed revenues.

These relationships are shown in Illustration 1-8.

HELPFUL HINT
The effect of expenses is negative—a decrease in owner's equity coupled with a decrease in assets, or an increase in liabilities.

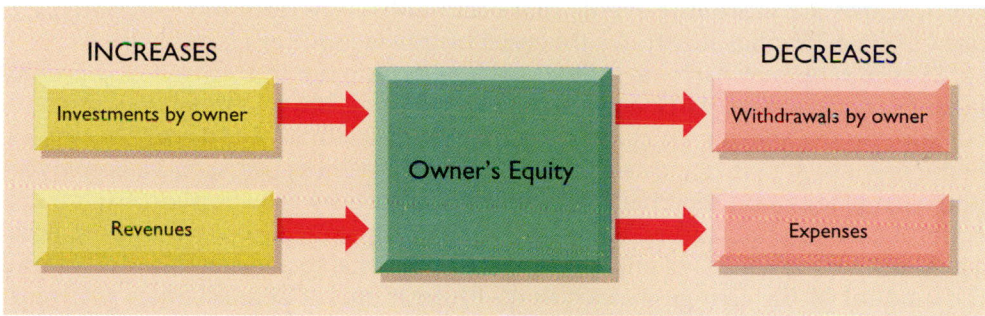

ILLUSTRATION 1-8

Increases and decreases in owner's equity

BEFORE YOU GO ON . . .

Review It

1. Why is ethics considered a fundamental business concept?
2. What are generally accepted accounting principles? Give an example of an accounting principle.
3. Explain the monetary unit and the economic entity assumptions.
4. What is the basic accounting equation? The accounting equation is: Assets = Liabilities + Owner's Equity. Replacing the words in that equation with dollar amounts, what is Kellogg's accounting equation at December 31, 1997? (*Hint:* Owner's equity is equivalent to stockholders' equity. The answer to this question is provided on page 43.)
5. What are assets, liabilities, and owner's equity?

Review It questions marked with this "Tony the Tiger" icon require that you use Kellogg's 1997 Annual Report.

Do It

Classify the following items as investment by owner (I), owner's drawings (D), revenues (R), or expenses (E), and indicate whether these items increase or decrease owner's equity: (1) Rent Expense, (2) Service Revenue, (3) Drawings, and (4) Salaries Expense.

Reasoning: Both investments and revenue increase owner's equity; however, revenue arises from the sale of merchandise, the performance of services, the rental of property, or the lending of money. Investments are resources contributed to the business by the owner. Similarly, expenses and drawings decrease owner's equity; however, expenses arise from consuming assets or services. Drawings are withdrawals of cash or other assets from the business for personal use.

Solution:
(1) Rent Expense is classified as an expense (E); it decreases owner's equity.
(2) Service Revenue is classified as revenue (R); it increases owner's equity.
(3) Drawings is classified as owner's drawings (D); it decreases owner's equity.
(4) Salaries Expense is classified as an expense (E); it decreases owner's equity.

Related exercise material: BE1–1, BE1–2, BE1–3, BE1–4, BE1–5, BE1–6, BE1–7, BE1–9, E1–1, E1–2, E1–3, E1–4, E1–6, and E1–7.

THE
NAVIGATOR

USING THE BUILDING BLOCKS

7
STUDY
OBJECTIVE
....
Analyze the effect of
business transactions on
the basic accounting
equation.

Transactions (often referred to as business transactions) are the economic events of the enterprise that are recorded. Transactions may be identified as external or internal. **External transactions involve economic events between the company and some outside enterprise or party.** For example, for Campus Pizza the purchase of cooking equipment from a supplier, the payment of monthly rent to the landlord, and the sale of pizzas to customers are external transactions. **Internal transactions are economic events that occur entirely within one company.** The use of office supplies illustrates this type of transaction for Campus Pizza.

A company may carry on many activities that do not in themselves represent business transactions. Hiring employees, answering the telephone, talking with customers, and placing an order for merchandise with a supplier are examples. Some of these activities, however, may lead to a business transaction: employees will earn wages, and merchandise will be delivered by the supplier. Each transaction must be analyzed in terms of its effect on the components of the basic accounting equation. This analysis must identify the specific items affected and the amount of the change in each item. Illustration 1-9 demonstrates the transaction identification process.

ILLUSTRATION 1-9

Transaction identification process

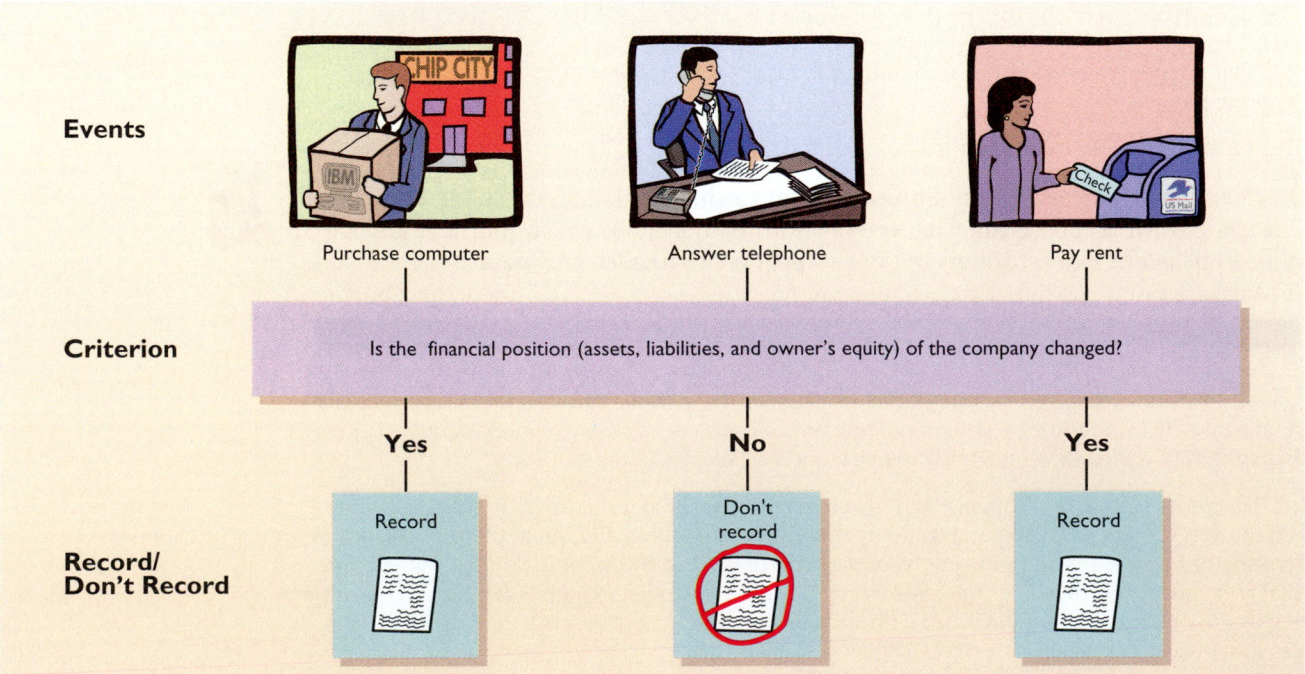

The equality of the basic equation must be preserved. Therefore, each transaction must have a dual effect on the equation. For example, if an individual asset is increased, there must be a corresponding:

1. Decrease in another asset, or
2. Increase in a specific liability, or
3. Increase in owner's equity.

It follows that two or more items could be affected when an asset is increased. For example, as one asset is increased $10,000, another asset could decrease $6,000, and a specific liability could increase $4,000. Note also that any change in an individual liability or ownership claim is subject to similar analysis.

Transaction Analysis

The following examples are business transactions for a new computer programming business during its first month of operations. You will want to study these transactions until you are sure you understand them. They are not difficult but they are important to your success in this course. The ability to analyze transactions in terms of the basic accounting equation is essential for an understanding of accounting.

Transaction (1). Investment by Owner. Ray Neal decides to open a computer programming service. On September 1, 1999, he invests $15,000 cash in the business, which he names Softbyte. This transaction results in an equal increase in assets and owner's equity. In this case, there is an increase in the asset Cash, $15,000, and an equal increase in the owner's equity, R. Neal, Capital, $15,000. The effect of this transaction on the basic equation is:

	Assets	=	Liabilities	+	Owner's Equity
	Cash	=			R. Neal, Capital
(1)	+$15,000	=			+$15,000 Investment

Observe that the equality of the basic equation has been maintained. Note also that the source of the increase in owner's equity is indicated, to make clear that the increase is an investment rather than revenue from operations. Why does this matter? Because investments by the owner do not represent revenues, and they are excluded in determining net income.

Transaction (2). Purchase of Equipment for Cash. Softbyte purchases computer equipment for $7,000 cash. This transaction results in an equal increase and decrease in total assets, though the composition of assets is changed: Cash is decreased $7,000, and the asset Equipment is increased $7,000. Both the specific effect of this transaction and the cumulative effect of the first two transactions are:

		Assets			=	Liabilities	+	Owner's Equity
		Cash	+	Equipment	=			R. Neal, Capital
	Old Bal.	$15,000						$15,000
(2)		−7,000		+$7,000				
	New Bal.	$ 8,000	+	$7,000	=			$15,000
			$15,000					

Observe that total assets are still $15,000 and Neal's equity also remains at $15,000, the amount of his original investment.

Transaction (3). Purchase of Supplies on Credit. Softbyte purchases computer paper and other supplies expected to last several months from Acme Supply Company for $1,600. Acme Company agrees to allow Softbyte to pay this bill in October, a month later. This transaction is often referred to as a purchase on account or a credit purchase. Assets are increased by this transaction because of the expected future benefits of using the paper and supplies, and liabilities are increased by the amount due Acme Company. The asset Supplies is increased $1,600, and the liability Accounts Payable is increased by the same amount. The effect on the equation is:

		Assets			=	Liabilities	+	Owner's Equity
		Cash	+ Supplies	+ Equipment =		Accounts Payable	+	R. Neal, Capital
Old. Bal.		$8,000		$7,000				$15,000
(3)			+$1,600			+$1,600		
New Bal.		$8,000 +	$1,600 +	$7,000	=	$1,600	+	$15,000
			$16,600				$16,600	

Total assets are now $16,600. This total is matched by a $1,600 creditor's claim and a $15,000 ownership claim.

Transaction (4). Services Rendered for Cash. Softbyte receives $1,200 cash from customers for programming services it has provided. This transaction represents the principal revenue-producing activity of Softbyte. Recall that **revenue increases owner's equity**. Both assets and owner's equity are, then, increased by this transaction: In this case, Cash is increased $1,200, and R. Neal, Capital, is increased $1,200. The new balances in the equation are:

		Assets			=	Liabilities	+	Owner's Equity	
	Cash	+	Supplies	+ Equipment =		Accounts Payable	+	R. Neal, Capital	
Old Bal.	$8,000		$1,600	$7,000		$1,600		$15,000	
(4)	+1,200							+1,200	**Service Revenue**
New Bal.	$9,200	+	$1,600	+ $7,000	=	$1,600	+	$16,200	
			$17,800				$17,800		

The two sides of the equation balance at $17,800. Note that owner's equity is increased when revenues are earned. The source of the increase in owner's equity is indicated as service revenue. Service revenue is included in determining Softbyte's net income.

Transaction (5). Purchase of Advertising on Credit. Softbyte receives a bill for $250 from the *Daily News* for advertising the opening of its business but postpones payment of the bill until a later date. This transaction results in an increase in liabilities and a decrease in owner's equity. The specific items involved are Accounts Payable and R. Neal, Capital. The effect on the equation is:

		Assets			=	Liabilities	+	Owner's Equity	
						Accounts		R. Neal,	
	Cash	+ Supplies	+	Equipment	=	Payable	+	Capital	
Old Bal.	$9,200	$1,600		$7,000		$1,600		$16,200	
(5)						+250		−250	Advertising Expense
New Bal.	$9,200	+ $1,600	+	$7,000	=	$1,850	+	$15,950	
		$17,800					$17,800		

The two sides of the equation still balance at $17,800. Observe that owner's equity is decreased when the expense is incurred, and the specific cause of the decrease (advertising expense) is noted. Expenses do not have to be paid in cash at the time they are incurred. When payment is made at a later date, the liability Accounts Payable will be decreased and the asset Cash will be decreased [see Transaction (8)]. The cost of advertising is considered an expense, as opposed to an asset, because the benefits have been used. This expense is included in determining net income.

Transaction (6). Services Rendered for Cash and Credit. Softbyte provides programming services of $3,500 for customers. Cash amounting to $1,500 is received from customers, and the balance of $2,000 is billed to customers on account. This transaction results in an equal increase in assets and owner's equity. Three specific items are affected: Cash is increased $1,500; Accounts Receivable is increased $2,000; and R. Neal, Capital is increased $3,500. The new balances are as follows:

			Assets			=	Liabilities	+	Owner's Equity	
		Accounts					Accounts		R. Neal,	
	Cash	+ Receivable	+	Supplies	+ Equipment	=	Payable	+	Capital	
Old Bal.	$9,200			$1,600	$7,000		$1,850		$15,950	
(6)	+1,500	+2,000							+3,500	Service Revenue
New Bal.	$10,700 +	$2,000	+	$1,600	+ $7,000	=	$1,850	+	$19,450	
		$21,300						$21,300		

Why increase owner's equity by $3,500 when only $1,500 has been collected? Because the inflow of assets resulting from the earning of revenues does not have to be in the form of cash. Remember that owner's equity is increased when revenues are earned, and in Softbyte's case that is when the service is provided. When collections on account are received at a later date, Cash will be increased and Accounts Receivable will be decreased [see Transaction (9)].

Transaction (7). Payment of Expenses. Expenses paid in cash for September are store rent, $600, salaries of employees, $900, and utilities, $200. These payments result in an equal decrease in assets and owner's equity. Cash is decreased $1,700 and R. Neal, Capital is decreased by the same amount. The effect of these payments on the equation is:

	Assets				=	Liabilities	+	Owner's Equity	
	Cash	+ Accounts Receivable	+ Supplies	+ Equipment	=	Accounts Payable	+	R. Neal, Capital	
Old Bal.	$10,700	$2,000	$1,600	$7,000		$1,850		$19,450	
(7)	− 1,700							− 600	Rent Expense
								− 900	Salaries Expense
								− 200	Utilities Expense
New Bal.	$ 9,000 +	$2,000 +	$1,600 +	$7,000	=	$1,850 +		$17,750	
		$19,600					$19,600		

The two sides of the equation now balance at $19,600. Three lines are required in the analysis to indicate the different types of expenses that have been incurred.

Transaction (8).   Payment of Accounts Payable. Softbyte pays its *Daily News* advertising bill of $250 in cash. In analyzing the effect of this transaction, we must recall that the bill has previously been recorded in Transaction (5) as an increase in Accounts Payable and a decrease in owner's equity. Thus, this payment "on account" decreases both assets and liabilities. In this case, the asset Cash and the liability Accounts Payable are decreased by $250. The effect of this transaction on the equation is:

	Assets				=	Liabilities	+	Owner's Equity
	Cash	+ Accounts Receivable	+ Supplies	+ Equipment	=	Accounts Payable	+	R. Neal, Capital
Old Bal.	$9,000	$2,000	$1,600	$7,000		$1,850		$17,750
(8)	− 250					− 250		
New Bal.	$8,750 +	$2,000 +	$1,600 +	$7,000	=	$1,600 +		$17,750
		$19,350					$19,350	

Observe that the payment of a liability related to an expense that has previously been recorded does not affect owner's equity.

Transaction (9).   Receipt of Cash on Account. The sum of $600 in cash is received from customers who have previously been billed for services in Transaction (6). This transaction does not change total assets, but it changes the composition of Softbyte's assets. Cash is increased $600 and Accounts Receivable is decreased $600. The new balances are:

	Assets				=	Liabilities	+	Owner's Equity
	Cash	+ Accounts Receivable	+ Supplies	+ Equipment	=	Accounts Payable	+	R. Neal, Capital
Old Bal.	$8,750	$2,000	$1,600	$7,000		$1,600		$17,750
(9)	+ 600	− 600						
New Bal.	$9,350 +	$1,400 +	$1,600 +	$7,000	=	$1,600 +		$17,750
		$19,350					$19,350	

Note that a collection on account for services previously billed and recorded does not affect owner's equity. Revenue was already recorded in Transaction (6) and should not be recorded again.

Transaction (10).   Withdrawal of Cash by Owner.   Ray Neal withdraws $1,300 in cash from the business for his personal use. This transaction results in an equal decrease in assets and owner's equity. Thus, both Cash and R. Neal, Capital are decreased $1,300, as shown below:

		Assets					=	Liabilities	+	Owner's Equity	
		Cash	+	Accounts Receivable	+ Supplies	+ Equipment	=	Accounts Payable	+	R. Neal, Capital	
	Old Bal.	$9,350		$1,400	$1,600	$7,000		$1,600		$17,750	
(10)		−1,300								−1,300	**Drawings**
	New Bal.	$8,050 +		$1,400	+ $1,600	+ $7,000	=	$1,600	+	$16,450	
					$18,050					$18,050	

Observe that the effect of a cash withdrawal by the owner is the opposite of the effect of an investment by the owner. **Owner's drawings do not represent expenses.** Like owner's investment, they are not included in determining net income.

Summary of Transactions

The transactions of Softbyte are summarized in Illustration 1-10 to show their cumulative effect on the basic accounting equation. The transaction number, the

ILLUSTRATION 1-10

Tabular summary of Softbyte transactions

		Assets				=	Liabilities	+	Owner's Equity	
Transaction	Cash	+ Accounts Receivable	+ Supplies	+ Equipment	=	Accounts Payable	+	R. Neal, Capital	
(1)	+$15,000							+$15,000	**Investment**
(2)	−7,000			+$7,000					
	8,000	+		7,000	=			15,000	
(3)			+$1,600			+$1,600			
	8,000	+	1,600 +	7,000	=	1,600	+	15,000	
(4)	+1,200							+1,200	**Service Revenue**
	9,200	+	1,600 +	7,000	=	1,600	+	16,200	
(5)						+250		−250	**Advertising Expense**
	9,200	+	1,600 +	7,000	=	1,850	+	15,950	
(6)	+1,500	+$2,000						+3,500	**Service Revenue**
	10,700 +	2,000 +	1,600 +	7,000	=	1,850	+	19,450	
(7)	−1,700							−600	**Rent Expense**
								−900	**Salaries Expense**
								−200	**Utilities Expense**
	9,000 +	2,000 +	1,600 +	7,000	=	1,850	+	17,750	
(8)	−250					−250			
	8,750 +	2,000 +	1,600 +	7,000	=	1,600	+	17,750	
(9)	+600	−600							
	9,350 +	1,400 +	1,600 +	7,000	=	1,600	+	17,750	
(10)	−1,300							−1,300	**Drawings**
	$ 8,050 +	$1,400 +	$1,600 +	$7,000	=	$1,600	+	$16,450	
			$18,050					$18,050	

specific effects of the transaction, and the balances after each transaction are indicated. The illustration demonstrates a number of significant facts:

1. Each transaction must be analyzed in terms of its effect on:
   a. the three components of the basic accounting equation.
   b. specific types (kinds) of items within each component.
2. The two sides of the equation must always be equal.
3. The causes of each change in the owner's claim on assets must be indicated in the owner's equity column.

There! You made it through transaction analysis. If you feel a bit shaky on any of the transactions, it would probably be a good idea at this point to get up, take a short break, and come back again for a 10- to 15-minute review of the transactions, to make sure you understand them before you go on to the next section.

BEFORE YOU GO ON . . .

Review It

1. What is an example of an external transaction? What is an example of an internal transaction?
2. If an asset increases, what are the three possible effects on the basic accounting equation?

Do It

A tabular analysis of the transactions made by Roberta Mendez & Co., a certified public accounting firm, for the month of August is shown below. Each increase and decrease in owner's equity is explained.

	Assets			=	Liabilities	+	Owner's Equity	
	Cash	+	Office Equipment	=	Accounts Payable	+	R. Mendez, Capital	
1.	+$25,000						+25,000	Investment
2.			+7,000		+7,000			
3.	+8,000						+8,000	Service Revenue
4.	− 850						− 850	Rent Expense

Describe each transaction that occurred for the month.

Reasoning: The accounting equation must always be in balance. A change in an asset requires a change in another asset, in a liability, or in owner's equity. By analyzing the tabular analysis we can determine each transaction.

Solution:
1. The owner invested an additional $25,000 of cash in the business.
2. The company purchased $7,000 of office equipment on credit.
3. The company received $8,000 of cash in exchange for services performed.
4. The company paid $850 for this month's rent.

Related exercise material: BE1-4, BE1-5, BE1-6, BE1-7, E1-2, E1-3, E1-4, E1-6, and E1-7.

FINANCIAL STATEMENTS

After transactions are identified, recorded, and summarized, four financial statements are prepared from the summarized accounting data:

1. An **income statement** presents the revenues and expenses and resulting net income or net loss of a company for a specific period of time.
2. An **owner's equity statement** summarizes the changes in owner's equity for a specific period of time.
3. A **balance sheet** reports the assets, liabilities, and owner's equity of a business enterprise at a specific date.
4. A **statement of cash flows** summarizes information concerning the cash inflows (receipts) and outflows (payments) for a specific period of time.

Each statement provides management, owners, and other interested parties with relevant financial data. The financial statements of Softbyte and their interrelationships are shown in Illustration 1-11. The statements are interrelated: **(1) Net income of $2,750 shown on the income statement is added to the beginning balance of owner's capital in the owner's equity statement. (2) Owner's capital of $16,450 at the end of the reporting period shown in the owner's equity statement is reported on the balance sheet. (3) Cash of $8,050 on the balance sheet is reported on the statement of cash flows.**

Additionally, every set of financial statements is accompanied by explanatory notes and supporting schedules that are an integral part of the statements. Examples of these notes and schedules are illustrated in later chapters of this textbook.

Be sure to carefully examine the format and content of each statement. The essential features of each are briefly described in the following sections.

8
STUDY
OBJECTIVE

Prepare an income statement, owner's equity statement, balance sheet, and statement of cash flows.

HELPFUL HINT
The income statement, owner's equity statement, and statement of cash flows are all for a *period* of time, whereas the balance sheet is for a *point* in time.

ACCOUNTING IN ACTION

Business Insight

Why do companies choose the particular year-ends that they do? For example, why doesn't every company use December 31 as the accounting year-end? Many companies choose to end their accounting year when inventory or operations are at a low. This is advantageous because compiling accounting information requires much time and effort by managers, so they would rather do it when they aren't as busy operating the business. Also, inventory is easier and less costly to count when it is low. Some companies whose year-ends differ from December 31 are Delta Air Lines, June 30; Walt Disney Productions, September 30; Kmart Corp., January 31; and Dunkin' Donuts, Inc., October 31.

Income Statement

The income statement for Softbyte is prepared from the data appearing in the owner's equity column of Illustration 1-10. The heading of the statement identifies the company, the type of statement, and the time period covered by the statement. Note that the primary focus of the income statement is on reporting the success or profitability of the company's operations over a specified period of time. To indicate that it applies for a period of time, the income statement is dated "For the Month Ended September 30, 1999."

ALTERNATIVE TERMINOLOGY
The income statement is sometimes referred to as the *statement of operations, earnings statement,* or *profit and loss statement.*

ILLUSTRATION 1-11

Financial statements and their interrelationships

HELPFUL HINT

Note that final sums are double-underlined, and negative amounts are presented in parentheses.

HELPFUL HINT

Net income is computed first and is needed to determine the ending balance in owner's equity. The ending balance in owner's equity is needed in preparing the balance sheet. The cash shown on the balance sheet is needed in preparing the statement of cash flows.

SOFTBYTE
Income Statement
For the Month Ended September 30, 1999

Revenues		
Service revenue		$4,700
Expenses		
Salaries expense	$900	
Rent expense	600	
Advertising expense	250	
Utilities expense	200	
Total expenses		1,950
Net income		**$2,750**

SOFTBYTE
Owner's Equity Statement
For the Month Ended September 30, 1999

R. Neal, Capital, September 1		$ –0–
Add: Investments	$15,000	
Net income	2,750	17,750
		17,750
Less: Drawings		1,300
R. Neal, Capital, September 30		**$16,450**

SOFTBYTE
Balance Sheet
September 30, 1999

Assets

Cash	**$ 8,050**
Accounts receivable	1,400
Supplies	1,600
Equipment	7,000
Total assets	$18,050

Liabilities and Owner's Equity

Liabilities	
Accounts payable	$ 1,600
Owner's Equity	
R. Neal, Capital	**16,450**
Total liabilities and owner's equity	$18,050

SOFTBYTE
Statement of Cash Flows
For the Month Ended September 30, 1999

Cash flows from operating activities		
Cash receipts from revenues		$ 3,300
Cash payments for expenses		(1,950)
Net cash provided by operating activities		1,350
Cash flows from investing activities		
Purchase of equipment		(7,000)
Cash flows from financing activities		
Investments by owner	$15,000	
Drawings by owner	(1,300)	13,700
Net increase in cash		8,050
Cash at the beginning of the period		0
Cash at the end of the period		**$ 8,050**

1

2

3

On the income statement, revenues are listed first, followed by expenses. Finally net income (or net loss) is determined. Although practice varies, we have chosen in our illustrations and homework solutions to list expenses in order of magnitude. Alternative formats for the income statement will be considered in later chapters.

Note that investment and withdrawal transactions between the owner and the business are not included in the measurement of net income. For example, the withdrawal by Ray Neal of cash from Softbyte was not regarded as a business expense, as explained earlier.

Owner's Equity Statement

Data for the preparation of the owner's equity statement are obtained from the owner's equity column of the tabular summary (Illustration 1-10) and from the income statement. The heading of this statement identifies the company, the type of statement, and the time period covered by the statement. The time period is the same as that covered by the income statement and therefore is dated "For the Month Ended September 30, 1999." The beginning owner's equity amount is shown on the first line of the statement. Then, the owner's investments, net income, and the owner's drawings are identified in the statement. The information provided by this statement indicates the reasons why owner's equity has increased or decreased during the period.

What if Softbyte reported a net loss in its first month? Let's assume that during the month of September 1999, Softbyte lost $10,000. The presentation in the owner's equity statement of a net loss appears in Illustration 1-12.

ILLUSTRATION 1-12

Presentation of net loss

SOFTBYTE		
Owner's Equity Statement		
For the Month Ended September 30, 1999		
R. Neal, Capital, September 1		$ –0–
Add: Investments		15,000
		15,000
Less: Drawings	$ 1,300	
Net loss	10,000	11,300
R. Neal, Capital, September 30		$3,700

If there are additional investments, they are reported as investments in the owner's equity statement.

Balance Sheet

The balance sheet for Softbyte is prepared from the column headings and the month-end data shown in the last line of the tabular summary (Illustration 1-10). The heading of a balance sheet must identify the company, the statement, and the date. To indicate that the balance sheet is at a specific date, it is dated "September 30, 1999." Observe that the assets are listed at the top, followed by liabilities and owner's equity. Total assets must equal total liabilities and owner's equity. In the Softbyte illustration, only one liability, accounts payable, is reported on the balance sheet. In most cases, there will be more than one liability. When two or more liabilities are involved, a customary way of listing is as follows:

ILLUSTRATION 1-13

Presentation of liabilities

Liabilities	
Notes payable	$10,000
Accounts payable	63,000
Salaries payable	18,000
Total liabilities	$91,000

The balance sheet is like a snapshot of the company's financial condition at a specific moment in time (usually the month-end or year-end).

Statement of Cash Flows

HELPFUL HINT
Investing activities pertain to investments made by the company, not investments made by the owner.

The primary purpose of a statement of cash flows is to provide financial information about the cash receipts and cash payments of an enterprise for a specific period of time. To achieve this purpose and to aid investors, creditors, and others in their analysis of cash, the statement of cash flows reports (1) the cash effects of a company's operations during a period, (2) its investing transactions, (3) its financing transactions, (4) the net increase or decrease in cash during the period, and (5) the cash amount at the end of the period.

Reporting the sources, uses, and net increase or decrease in cash is useful because investors, creditors, and others want to know what is happening to a company's most liquid resource. The statement of cash flows, therefore, provides answers to the following simple but important questions:

1. Where did the cash come from during the period?
2. What was the cash used for during the period?
3. What was the change in the cash balance during the period?

A statement of cash flows for Softbyte is provided in Illustration 1-11.

As shown in the statement, cash increased $8,050 during the year. This increase resulted because net cash flow provided from operating activities increased cash $1,350, cash flow from investing transactions decreased cash $7,000, and cash flow from financing transactions increased cash $13,700. At this time, you need not be concerned with how these amounts are determined. Chapter 18 will examine in detail how the statement is prepared.

BEFORE YOU GO ON . . .

Review It

1. What are the income statement, statement of owner's equity, balance sheet, and statement of cash flows?
2. Indicate how the financial statements are interrelated.

A LOOK BACK AT OUR FEATURE STORY

Refer to the opening story about Kellogg Company, and answer the following questions:

1. If you were interested in investing in Kellogg Company, what would the balance sheet and income statement tell you?
2. Would you request audited financial statements? Explain.
3. Will the financial statements show the market value of the company? Explain.

Solution:

1. The balance sheet reports the assets, liabilities, and owners' equity of the company. The income statement presents the revenues and expenses and resulting net income (or net loss) for a specific period of time. The balance sheet is like a snapshot of the company's financial condition at a point in time. The income statement should give you a good indication of the profitability of the company. Also, the sources of the company's revenues and a picture of its expenses are provided in the income statement.
2. You should request **audited** financial statements—statements that a CPA has examined and expressed an opinion as to the fairness of presentation. You should not make decisions without having audited financial statements.
3. The financial statements will not show the market value of the company. As indicated, one important principle of accounting is the cost principle, which states that assets should be recorded at cost. Cost has an important advantage over other valuations: it is reliable.

A Look Back exercises refer to the chapter opening story. These exercises help you analyze that real-world situation in terms of the accounting topic of the chapter.

DEMONSTRATION PROBLEM

Mary Malone opens her own law office on July 1, 1999. During the first month of operations, the following transactions occurred:

1. Invested $10,000 in cash in the law practice.
2. Paid $800 for July rent on office space.
3. Purchased office equipment on account, $3,000.
4. Rendered legal services to clients for cash, $1,500.
5. Borrowed $700 cash from a bank on a note payable.
6. Rendered legal services to client on account, $2,000.
7. Paid monthly expenses: salaries, $500; utilities, $300; and telephone, $100.

Instructions

(a) Prepare a tabular summary of the transactions.

(b) Prepare the income statement, owner's equity statement, and balance sheet at July 31 for Mary Malone, Attorney at Law.

The **Demonstration Problems** are a final review of the section just completed. The Problem-Solving Strategies in the margin give you tips about how to approach the problem, and the solutions provided demonstrate both the form and content of complete answers.

SOLUTION TO DEMONSTRATION PROBLEM

(a)

Trans-action	Cash	+	Accounts Receivable	+	Equipment	=	Notes Payable	+	Accounts Payable	+	Mary Malone, Capital	
(1)	+$10,000										+$10,000	Investment
(2)	−800										−800	Rent Expense
	9,200					=					9,200	
(3)					+$3,000				+$3,000			
	9,200	+			3,000	=			3,000	+	9,200	
(4)	+1,500										+1,500	Service Revenue
	10,700	+			3,000	=			3,000	+	10,700	
(5)	+700						+$700					
	11,400	+			3,000	=	700	+	3,000	+	10,700	
(6)			+$2,000								+2,000	Service Revenue
	11,400 +		2,000	+	3,000	=	700	+	3,000	+	12,700	
(7)	−900										−500	Salaries Expense
											−300	Utilities Expense
											−100	Telephone Expense
	$10,500 +		$2,000	+	$3,000	=	$700	+	$3,000	+	$11,800	

PROBLEM-SOLVING STRATEGIES

1. Remember that assets must equal liabilities and owner's equity after each transaction.
2. Investments and revenues increase owner's equity.
3. Expenses decrease owner's equity.
4. The income statement shows revenues and expenses for a period of time.
5. The owner's equity statement shows the changes in owner's equity for a period of time.
6. The balance sheet reports assets, liabilities, and owner's equity at a specific date.

(b)
MARY MALONE
Attorney at Law
Income Statement
For the Month Ended July 31, 1999

Revenues		
Service revenue		$3,500
Expenses		
Rent expense	$800	
Salaries expense	500	
Utilities expense	300	
Telephone expense	100	
Total expenses		1,700
Net income		$1,800

MARY MALONE
Attorney at Law
Owner's Equity Statement
For the Month Ended July 31, 1999

Mary Malone, Capital, July 1		$ –0–
Add: Investments	$10,000	
Net income	1,800	11,800
Mary Malone, Capital, July 31		$11,800

MARY MALONE
Attorney at Law
Balance Sheet
July 31, 1999

Assets

Cash	$10,500
Accounts receivable	2,000
Equipment	3,000
Total assets	$15,500

Liabilities and Owner's Equity

Liabilities		
Notes payable		$ 700
Accounts payable		3,000
Total liabilities		3,700
Owner's equity		
Mary Malone, Capital		11,800
Total liabilities and owner's equity		$15,500

This would be a good time to return to the **Student Owner's Manual** at the beginning of the book (or look at it for the first time if you skipped it before) to read about the various types of assignment materials that appear at the end of each chapter. Knowing the purpose of the different assignments will help you appreciate what each contributes to your accounting skills and competencies.

THE NAVIGATOR

SUMMARY OF STUDY OBJECTIVES

1. *Explain the meaning of accounting.* Accounting is the process of identifying, recording, and communicating the economic events of an organization (business or nonbusiness) to interested users of the information.

2. *Identify the users and uses of accounting.* The major users and uses of accounting are: (a) Management uses accounting information in planning, controlling, and evaluating business operations. (b) Investors (owners) judge the wisdom of buying, holding, or selling their financial interests on the basis of accounting data. (c) Creditors (suppliers and bankers) evaluate the risks of granting credit or lending money to particular businesses on the basis of the accounting information obtained about those businesses. Other groups are taxing authorities, regulatory agencies, customers, labor unions, and economic planners.

3. *Understand why ethics is a fundamental business concept.* Ethics are the standards of conduct by which one's actions—both personal and business—are judged as right or wrong. If you cannot depend on the honesty of the individuals you deal with, effective communication and economic activity would be impossible and information would have no credibility.

4. *Explain the meaning of generally accepted accounting principles and the cost principle.* Generally accepted accounting principles are a common set of standards used by accountants. One important principle is the cost principle, which states that assets should be recorded at their cost.

5. *Explain the meaning of the monetary unit assumption and the economic entity assumption.* The monetary unit assumption requires that only transaction data capable of being expressed in terms of money be included in the accounting records of the economic entity. The economic entity assumption states that economic events can be identified with a particular unit of accountability.

6. *State the basic accounting equation and explain the meaning of assets, liabilities, and owner's equity.* The basic accounting equation is:

$$\text{Assets} = \text{Liabilities} + \text{Owner's Equity}$$

Assets are resources owned by a business. Liabilities are creditorship claims on total assets. Owner's equity is the ownership claim on total assets. It is often referred to as residual equity.

7. *Analyze the effect of business transactions on the basic accounting equation.* Each business transaction must have a dual effect on the accounting equation. For example, if an individual asset is increased, there must be a corresponding (1) decrease in another asset, or (2) increase in a specific liability, or (3) increase in owner's equity.

8. *Prepare an income statement, owner's equity statement, balance sheet, and statement of cash flows.* An income statement presents the revenues and expenses of a company for a specified period of time. An owner's equity statement summarizes the changes in owner's equity that have occurred for a specific period of time. A balance sheet reports the assets, liabilities, and owner's equity of a business at a specific date. A statement of cash flows summarizes information concerning the cash inflows (receipts) and outflows (payments) for a specific period of time.

THE NAVIGATOR

GLOSSARY

Accounting   The process of identifying, recording, and communicating the economic events of an organization to interested users of the information. (p. 2).

Assets   Resources owned by a business. (p. 13).

Auditing   The examination of financial statements by a certified public accountant in order to express an opinion as to the fairness of presentation. (p. 7).

Balance sheet   A financial statement that reports the assets, liabilities, and owner's equity at a specific date. (p. 23).

Basic accounting equation   Assets = Liabilities + Owner's equity. (p. 13).

Bookkeeping   A part of accounting that involves only the recording of economic events. (p. 6).

Corporation   A business organized as a separate legal entity under state corporation law having ownership divided into transferable shares of stock. (p. 13).

Cost principle   An accounting principle that states that assets should be recorded at their cost. (p. 11).

Drawings   Withdrawal of cash or other assets from an unincorporated business for the personal use of the owner(s). (p. 14).

Economic entity assumption   An assumption that economic events can be identified with a particular unit of accountability. (p. 12).

Ethics   The standards of conduct by which one's actions are judged as right or wrong, honest or dishonest, fair or not fair. (p. 9).

Expenses   The cost of assets consumed or services used in the process of earning revenue. (p. 15).

Financial Accounting Standards Board (FASB)   A private organization that establishes generally accepted accounting principles. (p. 10).

Generally accepted accounting principles (GAAP)   A common set of standards that indicate how to report economic events. (p. 10).

Income statement   A financial statement that presents the revenues and expenses and resulting net income or net loss of a company for a specific period of time. (p. 23).

Investments by owner   The assets put into the business by the owner. (p. 14).

Liabilities   Creditorship claims on total assets. (p. 14).

Management consulting   An area of public accounting involving financial planning and control and the development of accounting and computer systems. (p. 7).

Monetary unit assumption   An assumption stating that only transaction data that can be expressed in terms of money be included in the accounting records of the economic entity. (p. 11).

Net income The amount by which revenues exceed expenses. (p. 15).

Net loss The amount by which expenses exceed revenues. (p. 15).

Owner's equity The ownership claim on total assets. (p. 14).

Owner's equity statement A financial statement that summarizes the changes in owner's equity for a specific period of time. (p. 23).

Partnership An association of two or more persons to carry on as co-owners of a business for profit. (p. 12).

Private (or managerial) accounting An area of accounting within a company that involves such activities as cost accounting, budgeting, and accounting information systems. (p. 7).

Proprietorship A business owned by one person. (p. 12).

Public accounting An area of accounting in which the accountant offers expert service to the general public. (p. 7).

Revenues The gross increase in owner's equity resulting from business activities entered into for the purpose of earning income. (p. 14).

Securities and Exchange Commission (SEC) A governmental agency that requires companies to file financial reports in accordance with generally accepted accounting principles. (p. 10).

Statement of cash flows A financial statement that provides information about the cash inflows (receipts) and cash outflows (payments) of an entity for a specific period of time. (p. 23).

Taxation An area of public accounting involving tax advice, tax planning, and preparing tax returns. (p. 7).

Transactions The economic events of the enterprise recorded by accountants. (p. 16).

SELF-STUDY QUESTIONS

Answers are on page 43.

(SO 1) 1. Which of the following is *not* a step in the accounting process?
   a. identification.
   b. verification.
   c. recording.
   d. communication.

(SO 2) 2. Which of the following statements about users of accounting information is *incorrect*?
   a. Management is considered an internal user.
   b. Taxing authorities are considered external users.
   c. Present creditors are considered external users.
   d. Regulatory authorities are considered internal users.

(SO 2) 3. Services provided by a public accountant include:
   a. auditing, taxation, and management consulting.
   b. auditing, budgeting, and management consulting.
   c. auditing, budgeting, and cost accounting.
   d. internal auditing, budgeting, and management consulting.

(SO 4) 4. The cost principle states that:
   a. assets should be initially recorded at cost and adjusted when the market value changes.
   b. activities of an entity are to be kept separate and distinct from its owner.
   c. assets should be recorded at their cost.
   d. only transaction data capable of being expressed in terms of money be included in the accounting records.

(SO 5) 5. Which of the following statements about basic assumptions is *incorrect*?
   a. Basic assumptions are the same as accounting principles.
   b. The economic entity assumption states that there should be a particular unit of accountability.
   c. The monetary unit assumption enables accounting to measure economic events.

   d. An important corollary to the monetary unit assumption is the stable monetary unit assumption.

6. Net income will result during a time period when: (SO 6)
   a. assets exceed liabilities.
   b. assets exceed revenues.
   c. expenses exceed revenues.
   d. revenues exceed expenses.

7. Performing services on account will have the following (SO 7) effects on the components of the basic accounting equation:
   a. increase assets and decrease owner's equity.
   b. increase assets and increase owner's equity.
   c. increase assets and increase liabilities.
   d. increase liabilities and increase owner's equity.

8. As of December 31, 1999, Stoneland Company has assets (SO 7) of $3,500 and owner's equity of $2,000. What are the liabilities for Stoneland Company as of December 31, 1999?
   a. $1,500.
   b. $1,000.
   c. $2,500.
   d. $2,000.

9. On the last day of the period, Genesis Company buys a (SO 8) $900 machine on credit. This transaction will affect the:
   a. income statement only.
   b. balance sheet only.
   c. income statement and owner's equity statement only.
   d. income statement, owner's equity statement, and balance sheet.

10. The financial statement that reports assets, liabilities, (SO 8) and owner's equity is the:
   a. income statement.
   b. owner's equity statement.
   c. balance sheet.
   d. statement of cash flow.

THE NAVIGATOR

QUESTIONS

1. "Accounting is ingrained in our society and it is vital to our economic system." Do you agree? Explain.

2. Identify and describe the steps in the accounting process.

3. (a) Who are internal users of accounting data?
   (b) How does accounting provide relevant data to these users?

4. What uses of financial accounting information are made by external users (a) investors and (b) creditors?

5. "Bookkeeping and accounting are the same." Do you agree? Explain.

6. Joe Kirby Travel Agency purchased land for $85,000 cash on December 10, 1999. At December 31, 1999, the land's value has increased to $93,000. What amount should be reported for land on Joe Kirby's balance sheet at December 31, 1999? Explain.

7. What is the monetary unit assumption? What impact does inflation have on the monetary unit assumption?

8. What is the economic entity assumption?

9. What are the three basic forms of business organizations for profit-oriented enterprises?

10. Mary Stone is the owner of a successful printing shop. Recently her business has been increasing, and Mary has been thinking about changing the organization of her business from a proprietorship to a corporation. Discuss some of the advantages Mary would enjoy if she were to incorporate her business.

11. What is the basic accounting equation?

12. (a) Define the terms assets, liabilities, and owner's equity. (b) What items affect owner's equity?

13. Which of the following items are liabilities of Gilt Jewelry Stores?
    (a) Cash.   (f) Equipment.
    (b) Accounts payable.   (g) Salaries payable.
    (c) Drawings.   (h) Service revenue.
    (d) Accounts receivable.   (i) Rent expense.
    (e) Supplies.

14. Can a business enter into a transaction in which only the left side of the basic accounting equation is affected? If so, give an example.

15. Are the following events recorded in the accounting records? Explain your answer in each case.
    (a) The owner of the company dies.
    (b) Supplies are purchased on account.
    (c) An employee is fired.

(d) The owner of the business withdraws cash from the business for personal use.

16. Indicate how the following business transactions affect the basic accounting equation.
    (a) Paid cash for janitorial services.
    (b) Purchased equipment for cash.
    (c) Invested cash in the business.
    (d) Paid an accounts payable in full.

17. Listed below are some items found in the financial statements of Kaustav Sen, M.D. Indicate in which financial statement(s) the following items would appear.
    (a) Service revenue.
    (b) Equipment.
    (c) Advertising expense.
    (d) Accounts receivable.
    (e) Kaustav Sen, Capital.
    (f) Wages payable.

18. In February 1999, John Alcorn invested an additional $10,000 in his business, Alcorn's Pharmacy, which is organized as a proprietorship. Alcorn's accountant, Terry Elliot, recorded this receipt as an increase in cash and revenues. Is this treatment appropriate? Why or why not?

19. A company's net income appears directly on the income statement and the owner's equity statement, and it is included indirectly in the company's balance sheet. Do you agree? Explain.

20. Sotero Enterprises had a capital balance of $168,000 at the beginning of the period. At the end of the accounting period, the capital balance was $198,000.
    (a) Assuming no additional investment or withdrawals during the period, what is the net income for the period?
    (b) Assuming an additional investment of $13,000 but no withdrawals during the period, what is the net income for the period?

21. Summarized operations for the Alberto Rivera Co. for the month of July are as follows:

    Revenues earned: for cash $35,000; on account $70,000.

    Expenses incurred: for cash $26,000; on account $40,000.

    Indicate for Alberto Rivera Co. (a) the total revenues, (b) the total expenses, and (c) net income for the month of July.

BRIEF EXERCISES

Use basic accounting equation.
(SO 6)

BE1–1 Presented below is the basic accounting equation. Determine the missing amounts:

	Assets	=	Liabilities	+	Owner's Equity
(a)	$80,000		$50,000		?
(b)	?		$45,000		$70,000
(c)	$94,000		?		$62,000

Use basic accounting equation.
(SO 6)

BE1–2 Given the accounting equation, answer each of the following questions:

1. The liabilities of Logan Company are $100,000 and the owner's equity is $240,000. What is the amount of Logan Company's total assets?
2. The total assets of Perez Company are $170,000 and its owner's equity is $80,000. What is the amount of its total liabilities?
3. The total assets of Bono Co. are $600,000 and its liabilities are equal to one half of its total assets. What is the amount of Bono Co.'s owner's equity?

Use basic accounting equation.
(SO 6)

BE1–3 At the beginning of the year, Leary Company had total assets of $800,000 and total liabilities of $500,000. Answer the following questions:

1. If total assets increased $150,000 during the year and total liabilities decreased $80,000, what is the amount of owner's equity at the end of the year?
2. During the year, total liabilities increased $100,000 and owner's equity decreased $70,000. What is the amount of total assets at the end of the year?
3. If total assets decreased $90,000 and owner's equity increased $120,000 during the year, what is the amount of total liabilities at the end of the year?

Determine effect of transactions on basic accounting equation.
(SO 7)

BE1–4 Presented below are three business transactions. On a sheet of paper, list the letters a, b, c with columns for assets, liabilities, and owner's equity. For each column, indicate whether the transactions increased (+), decreased (−) or had no effect (NE) on assets, liabilities, and owner's equity:

(a) Purchased supplies on account.
(b) Received cash for providing a service.
(c) Expenses paid in cash.

Determine effect of transactions on basic accounting equation.
(SO 7)

BE1–5 Follow the same format as BE1-4 above. Determine the effect on assets, liabilities, and owner's equity of the following three transactions:

(a) Invested cash in the business.
(b) Withdrawal of cash by owner.
(c) Received cash from a customer who had previously been billed for services provided.

Determine effect of transactions on owner's equity.
(SO 7)

BE1–6 Classify each of the following items as owner's drawing (D), revenue (R), or expense (E).

____ Advertising expense	____ B. Farve, Drawing
____ Commission revenue	____ Rent revenue
____ Insurance expense	____ Utilities expense
____ Salaries expense	

Determine effect of transactions on owner's equity.
(SO 7)

BE1–7 Presented below are three transactions. Mark each transaction as affecting owner's investment (I), owner's drawings (D), revenue (R), expense (E), or not affecting owner's equity (NOE):

____ Received cash for services performed
____ Paid cash to purchase equipment
____ Paid employee salaries

Prepare a balance sheet.
(SO 8)

BE1–8 In alphabetical order below are balance sheet items for Yung Company at December 31, 1999. Kim Yung is the owner of Yung Company. Prepare a balance sheet, following the format of Illustration 1-11.

Accounts payable	$80,000
Accounts receivable	$71,000
Cash	$40,500
Kim Yung, Capital	$31,500

BE1–9 Indicate whether each of the following items is an asset (A), liability (L), or part of owner's equity (OE).

Identify assets, liabilities, and owner's equity.
(SO 6)

_____ Accounts receivable   _____ Office supplies
_____ Salaries payable   _____ Owner's investment
_____ Equipment   _____ Notes payable

BE1–10 Indicate whether the following items would appear on the income statement (IS), balance sheet (BS), or owner's equity statement (OE).

Determine where items appear on financial statements.
(SO 8)

_____ Notes payable   _____ Cash
_____ Advertising expense   _____ Service revenue
_____ S. O'Reiley, Capital

EXERCISES

•••

E1–1 The Otto Cleaners has the following balance sheet items:

Classify accounts as assets, liabilities, and owner's equity.
(SO 6)

Accounts payable   Accounts receivable
Cash   Notes payable
Cleaning equipment   Salaries payable
Cleaning supplies   J. Otto, Capital

Instructions
Classify each item as an asset, liability, or owner's equity.

E1–2 Selected transactions for Lush Lawn Care Company are listed below:

Analyze the effect of transactions.
(SO 6, 7)

1. Made cash investment to start business.
2. Paid monthly rent.
3. Purchased equipment on account.
4. Billed customers for services performed.
5. Withdrew cash for owner's personal use.
6. Received cash from customers billed in (4).
7. Incurred advertising expense on account.
8. Purchased additional equipment for cash.
9. Received cash from customers when service was rendered.

Instructions
List the numbers of the above transactions and describe the effect of each transaction on assets, liabilities, and owner's equity. For example, the first answer is: (1) Increase in assets and increase in owner's equity.

E1–3 Le Wong Computer Timeshare Company entered into the following transactions during May 1999.

Analyze the effect of transactions on assets, liabilities, and owner's equity.
(SO 6, 7)

1. Purchased computer terminals for $19,000 from Digital Equipment on account.
2. Paid $4,000 cash for May rent on storage space.
3. Received $15,000 cash from customers for contracts billed in April.
4. Provided computer services to Barto Construction Company for $3,000 cash.
5. Paid Southern States Power Co. $11,000 cash for energy usage in May.
6. Le Wong invested an additional $32,000 in the business.
7. Paid Digital Equipment for the terminals purchased in (1) above.
8. Incurred advertising expense for May of $1,000 on account.

Instructions
Indicate with the appropriate letter whether each of the transactions above results in:

(a) an increase in assets and a decrease in assets.
(b) an increase in assets and an increase in owner's equity.
(c) an increase in assets and an increase in liabilities.
(d) a decrease in assets and a decrease in owner's equity.
(e) a decrease in assets and a decrease in liabilities.
(f) an increase in liabilities and a decrease in owner's equity.
(g) an increase in owner's equity and a decrease in liabilities.

Analyze transactions and compute net income.
(SO 7)

E1–4   A tabular analysis of the transactions made by Maria Mendoza & Co., a certified public accounting firm, for the month of August is shown below. Each increase and decrease in owner's equity is explained.

	Cash	+ Accounts Receivable	+ Supplies	+ Office Equipment	= Accounts Payable	+ Owner's Equity M. Mendoza, Capital	
1.	+$12,000					+$12,000	Investment
2.	− 2,000			+$5,000	+$3,000		
3.	− 750		+$750				
4.	+2,600	+3,400				+6,000	Service Revenue
5.	−1,500				−1,500		
6.	−2,000					−2,000	Drawings
7.	− 650					− 650	Rent Expense
8.	+ 450	−450					
9.	−2,900					−2,900	Salaries Expense
10.					+ 500	− 500	Utilities Expense

Instructions

(a) ▱▱▱▷ Describe each transaction that occurred for the month.

(b) Determine how much owner's equity increased for the month.

(c) Compute the amount of net income for the month.

Prepare an income statement and owner's equity statement.
(SO 8)

E1–5   The tabular analysis of transactions for Maria Mendoza & Co. is presented in E1–4.

Instructions

Prepare an income statement and an owner's equity statement for August and a balance sheet at August 31, 1999.

Determine net income (or loss).
(SO 7)

E1–6   The Dylan Company had the following assets and liabilities on the dates indicated:

December 31	Total Assets	Total Liabilities
1999	$400,000	$250,000
2000	$460,000	$320,000
2001	$590,000	$400,000

Dylan began business on January 1, 1999, with an investment of $100,000.

Instructions

From an analysis of the change in owner's equity during the year, compute the net income (or loss) for:

(a) 1999, assuming Dylan's drawings were $15,000 for the year.

(b) 2000, assuming Dylan made an additional investment of $50,000 and had no drawings in 2000.

(c) 2001, assuming Dylan made an additional investment of $15,000 and had drawings of $20,000 in 2001.

Analyze financial statements items.
(SO 6, 7)

E1–7   Two items are omitted from each of the following summaries of balance sheet and income statement data for two proprietorships for the year 1999, Anne Wyatt, D.D.S., and Rambo Enterprises.

	Anne Wyatt, D.D.S.	Rambo Enterprises
Beginning of year:		
Total assets	$ 95,000	$125,000
Total liabilities	80,000	(c)
Total owner's equity	(a)	95,000
End of year:		
Total assets	160,000	180,000
Total liabilities	120,000	50,000
Total owner's equity	40,000	130,000
Changes during year in owner's equity:		
Additional investment	(b)	25,000
Drawings	24,000	(d)
Total revenues	215,000	100,000
Total expenses	175,000	85,000

Instructions
Determine the missing amounts.

E1–8 The following information relates to Dyna Seng Co. for the year 1999.

Prepare income statement and owner's equity statement.
(SO 8)

Dyna Seng, Capital, January 1, 1999	$48,000	Advertising expense	1,800
Dyna Seng, Drawing, during 1999	5,000	Rent expense	10,400
Service revenue	55,000	Utilities expense	3,100
Salaries expense	28,000		

Instructions
After analyzing the data, prepare an income statement and an owner's equity statement for the year ending December 31, 1999.

E1–9 Clare Gardner is the bookkeeper for Otago Company. Clare has been trying to get the balance sheet of Otago Company to balance. Otago's balance sheet is as follows:

Correct an incorrectly prepared balance sheet.
(SO 8)

OTAGO COMPANY
Balance Sheet
December 31, 1999

Assets		Liabilities	
Cash	$20,500	Accounts payable	$20,000
Supplies	8,000	Accounts receivable	(10,000)
Equipment	46,000	Otago, Capital	67,500
Otago, Drawing	3,000	Total liabilities and	
Total assets	$77,500	owner's equity	$77,500

Instructions
Prepare a correct balance sheet.

E1–10 Ian King is the sole owner of Bear Park, a public camping ground near the Lake Mead National Recreation Area. Ian has compiled the following financial information as of December 31, 1999.

Compute net income and prepare a balance sheet.
(SO 8)

Revenues during 1999—camping fees	$160,000	Market value of equipment	140,000
Revenues during 1999—general store	40,000	Notes payable	60,000
Accounts payable	11,000	Expenses during 1999	150,000
Cash on hand	20,000	Supplies on hand	2,500
Original cost of equipment	115,500		

Instructions
  (a) Determine Ian King's net income from Bear Park for 1999.
  (b) Prepare a balance sheet for Bear Park as of December 31, 1999.

E1–11 Presented below is financial information related to the 1999 operations of Titanic Cruise Company.

Prepare an income statement.
(SO 8)

Maintenance expense	$ 80,000
Property tax expense (on dock facilities)	10,000
Salaries expense	142,000
Advertising expense	3,500
Ticket revenue	325,000

Instructions
Prepare the 1999 income statement for Titanic Cruise Company.

E1–12 Presented below is information related to the sole proprietorship of Wayne Robinson, attorney.

Prepare an owner's equity statement.
(SO 8)

Legal service revenue—1999	$360,000
Total expenses—1999	205,000
Assets, January 1, 1999	85,000
Liabilities, January 1, 1999	62,000
Assets, December 31, 1999	168,000
Liabilities, December 31, 1999	70,000
Drawings—1999	?

Instructions
Prepare the 1999 owner's equity statement for Wayne Robinson's legal practice.

PROBLEMS: SET A

Analyze transactions and compute net income.
(SO 6, 7)

P1–1A   On April 1, Merle Peper established the Wayne State Travel Agency. The following transactions were completed during the month:

1. Invested $15,000 cash to start the agency.
2. Paid $400 cash for April office rent.
3. Purchased office equipment for $2,500 cash.
4. Incurred $300 of advertising costs in the Chicago Tribune, on account.
5. Paid $600 cash for office supplies.
6. Earned $9,000 for services rendered: Cash of $1,000 is received from customers, and the balance of $8,000 is billed to customers on account.
7. Withdrew $200 cash for personal use.
8. Paid Chicago Tribune amount due in transaction (4).
9. Paid employees' salaries, $2,200.
10. Received $8,000 in cash from customers who have previously been billed in transaction (6).

Instructions
(a) Prepare a tabular analysis of the transactions using the following column headings: Cash, Accounts Receivable, Supplies, Office Equipment, Accounts Payable, and Merle Peper, Capital.
(b) From an analysis of the column, Merle Peper, Capital, compute the net income or net loss for April.

Analyze transactions and prepare income statement and owner's equity statement.
(SO 6, 7, 8)

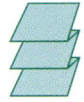

P1–2A   George Kanaan opened a law office, George Kanaan, Attorney at Law, on July 1, 1999. On July 31, the balance sheet showed Cash $4,000, Accounts Receivable $1,500, Supplies $500, Office Equipment $5,000, Accounts Payable $4,200, and George Kanaan, Capital, $6,800. During August the following transactions occurred:

1. Collected $1,400 of accounts receivable.
2. Paid $2,700 cash on accounts payable.
3. Earned revenue of $6,400, of which $3,000 is collected in cash and the balance is due in September.
4. Purchased additional office equipment for $1,000, paying $400 in cash and the balance on account.
5. Paid salaries $2,500, rent for August $900, and advertising expenses $350.
6. Withdrew $550 in cash for personal use.
7. Received $2,000 from Standard Federal Bank—money borrowed on a note payable.
8. Incurred utility expenses for month on account, $250.

Instructions
(a) Prepare a tabular analysis of the August transactions beginning with July 31 balances. The column heading should be as follows: Cash + Accounts Receivable + Supplies + Office Equipment = Notes Payable + Accounts Payable + George Kanaan, Capital.
(b) Prepare an income statement for August, an owner's equity statement for August, and a balance sheet at August 31.

Prepare income statement, owner's equity statement, and balance sheet.
(SO 8)

P1–3A   On June 1, Ann Okah started Secret Cosmetics Co., a company that provides individual skin care treatment to clients, by investing $26,200 cash in the business. Following are the assets and liabilities of the company at June 30 and the revenues and expenses for the month of June.

Cash	$12,000	Notes Payable	$13,000
Accounts Receivable	4,000	Accounts Payable	1,200
Service Revenue	7,500	Supplies Expense	1,200
Cosmetic Supplies	2,400	Gas and Oil Expense	800
Advertising Expense	500	Utilities Expense	300
Equipment	25,000		

Ann made no additional investment in June, but withdrew $1,700 in cash for personal use during the month.

Instructions

(a) Prepare an income statement and owner's equity statement for the month of June and a balance sheet at June 30, 1999.

(b) Prepare an income statement and owner's equity statement for June assuming the following data are not included above: (1) $800 of revenue was earned and billed but not collected at June 30, and (2) $100 of gas and oil expense was incurred but not paid.

P1–4A Jessica Bell started her own consulting firm, Bell Consulting, on May 1, 1999. The following transactions occurred during the month of May:

Analyze transactions and prepare financial statements. (SO 7, 8)

May 1 Bell invested $10,000 cash in the business.
2 Paid $800 for office rent for the month.
3 Purchased $500 of supplies on account.
5 Paid $50 to advertise in the County News.
9 Received $1,000 cash for services provided.
12 Withdrew $700 cash for personal use.
15 Performed $3,000 of services on account.
17 Paid $2,500 for employee salaries.
20 Paid for the supplies purchased on account on May 3.
23 Received a cash payment of $2,000 for services provided on account on May 15.
26 Borrowed $5,000 from the bank on a note payable.
29 Purchased office equipment for $2,400 on account.
30 Paid $150 for utilities.

Instructions

(a) Show the effects of the previous transactions on the accounting equation using the following format:

	Assets				Liabilities		Owner's Equity
Date	Cash +	Accounts Receivable +	Supplies +	Office Equipment =	Notes Payable +	Accounts Payable +	J. Bell, Capital

Include explanations for any changes in the J. Bell, Capital account in your analysis.

(b) Prepare an income statement for the month of May.

(c) Prepare a balance sheet at May 31, 1999.

P1–5A Financial statement information about four different companies is as follows:

Determine financial statement amounts and prepare owner's equity statements. (SO 7, 8)

	Montreal Company	Calgary Company	Edmonton Company	Vancouver Company
January 1, 1999:				
Assets	$ 75,000	$90,000	(g)	$150,000
Liabilities	50,000	(d)	75,000	(j)
Owner's equity	(a)	60,000	55,000	90,000
December 31, 1999:				
Assets	(b)	120,000	180,000	(k)
Liabilities	55,000	62,000	(h)	80,000
Owner's equity	45,000	(e)	110,000	140,000
Owner's equity changes in year:				
Additional investment	(c)	8,000	10,000	15,000
Drawings	10,000	(f)	12,000	10,000
Total revenues	350,000	400,000	(i)	500,000
Total expenses	335,000	385,000	360,000	(l)

Instructions

(a) Determine the missing amounts. (*Hint:* For example, to solve for (a), Assets − Liabilities = Owner's equity = $25,000.)

(b) Prepare the owner's equity statement for Montreal Company.
(c)  Write a memorandum explaining the sequence for preparing financial statements and the interrelationship of the owner's equity statement to the income statement and balance sheet.

PROBLEMS: SET B

Analyze transactions and compute net income.
(SO 6, 7)

P1–1B Kumar's Repair Shop was started on May 1 by U. Kumar. A summary of May transactions is presented below.

1. Invested $15,000 cash to start the repair shop.
2. Purchased equipment for $5,000 cash.
3. Paid $400 cash for May office rent.
4. Paid $500 cash for supplies.
5. Incurred $250 of advertising costs in the Beacon News on account.
6. Received $4,100 in cash from customers for repair service.
7. Withdrew $500 cash for personal use.
8. Paid part-time employee salaries $1,000.
9. Paid utility bills $140.
10. Provided repair service on account to customers, $400.
11. Collected cash of $120 for services billed in transaction (10).

Instructions
(a) Prepare a tabular analysis of the transactions, using the following column headings: Cash, Accounts Receivable, Supplies, Equipment, Accounts Payable, and U. Kumar, Capital. Revenue is called Service Revenue.
(b) From an analysis of the column, U. Kumar, Capital, compute the net income or net loss for May.

Analyze transactions and prepare income statement and owner's equity statement.
(SO 6, 7, 8)

P1–2B Bruce Smith opened a veterinary business in Mankato, Minnesota, on August 1. On August 31, the balance sheet showed Cash $9,000, Accounts Receivable $1,700, Supplies $600, Office Equipment $6,000, Accounts Payable $3,600, and B. Smith, Capital, $13,700. During September the following transactions occurred:

1. Paid $3,100 cash on accounts payable.
2. Collected $1,300 of accounts receivable.
3. Purchased additional office equipment for $2,100, paying $800 in cash and the balance on account.
4. Earned revenue of $5,900, of which $2,500 is paid in cash and the balance is due in October.
5. Withdrew $600 cash for personal use.
6. Paid salaries $700, rent for September $900, and advertising expense $300.
7. Incurred utility expenses for month on account, $170.
8. Received $7,000 from Hilldale Bank—money borrowed on a note payable.

Instructions
(a) Prepare a tabular analysis of the September transactions beginning with August 31 balances. The column headings should be as follows: Cash + Accounts Receivable + Supplies + Office Equipment = Notes Payable + Accounts Payable + B. Smith, Capital.
(b) Prepare an income statement for September, an owner's equity statement for September, and a balance sheet at September 30.

Prepare income statement, owner's equity statement, and balance sheet.
(SO 8)

P1–3B On May 1, Thomas Phillips started Ruston Flying School, a company that provides flying lessons to would-be pilots, by investing $45,000 cash in the business. Following are the assets and liabilities of the company on May 31, 1999, and the revenues and expenses for the month of May.

Cash	$ 6,800	Notes Payable	$30,000
Accounts Receivable	7,200	Rent Expense	1,200
Equipment	64,000	Repair Expense	400
Lesson Revenue	8,600	Fuel Expense	2,200
Advertising Expense	500	Insurance Expense	400
		Accounts Payable	800

Thomas Phillips made no additional investment in May, but he withdrew $1,700 in cash for personal use.

Instructions
(a) Prepare an income statement and owner's equity statement for the month of May and a balance sheet at May 31.
(b) Prepare an income statement and owner's equity statement for May assuming the following data are not included above: (1) $900 of revenue was earned and billed but not collected at May 31, and (2) $3,300 of fuel expense was incurred but not paid.

P1–4B Peter Alex started his own delivery servcice, Alex Deliveries, on June 1, 1999. The following transactions occurred during the month of June:

Analyze transactions and prepare financial statements.
(SO 7, 8)

June 1   Alex invested $15,000 cash in the business.
      2   Purchased a used van for deliveries for $10,000. Alex paid $2,000 cash and signed a note payble for the remaining balance.
      3   Paid $500 for office rent for the month.
      5   Performed $1,000 of services on account.
      9   Withdrew $200 cash for personal use.
      12 Purchased supplies for $150 on account.
      15 Received a cash payment of $750 for services provided on June 5.
      17 Purchased gasoline for $100 on account.
      20 Received a cash payment of $1,500 for services provided.
      23 Made a cash payment of $500 on the note payable.
      26 Paid $250 for utilities.
      29 Paid for the gasoline purchased on account on June 17.
      30 Paid $500 for employee salaries.

Instructions
(a) Show the effects of the previous transactions on the accounting equation using the following format:

		Assets				Liabilities		Owner's Equity
Date	Cash +	Accounts Receivable +	Supplies +	Delivery Van	=	Notes Payable +	Accounts Payable +	P. Alex, Capital

Include explanations for any changes in the P. Alex, Capital account in your analysis.
(b) Prepare an income statement for the month of June.
(c) Prepare a balance sheet at May 31, 1999.

P1–5B Financial statement information about four different companies is as follows:

Determine financial statement amounts and prepare owner's equity statements.
(SO 7, 8)

	Loyola Company	Marshall Company	UNLV Company	UNC Company
January 1, 1999:				
Assets	$ 80,000	$110,000	(g)	$170,000
Liabilities	50,000	(d)	75,000	(j)
Owner's equity	(a)	60,000	50,000	90,000
December 31, 1999:				
Assets	(b)	145,000	200,000	(k)
Liabilities	55,000	65,000	(h)	80,000
Owner's equity	58,000	(e)	130,000	180,000
Owner's equity changes in year:				
Additional investment	(c)	15,000	10,000	15,000
Drawings	25,000	(f)	14,000	20,000
Total revenues	350,000	420,000	(i)	520,000
Total expenses	320,000	385,000	350,000	(l)

Instructions
(a) Determine the missing amounts.
(b) Prepare the owner's equity statement for Marshall Company.
(c) Write a memorandum explaining the sequence for preparing financial statements and the interrelationship of the owner's equity statement to the income statement and balance sheet.

BROADENING YOUR PERSPECTIVE

FINANCIAL REPORTING AND ANALYSIS

FINANCIAL REPORTING PROBLEM: Kellogg Company

BYP1–1   The actual financial statements of Kellogg Company, as presented in the company's 1997 Annual Report, are contained in Appendix A (at the back of the textbook).

Instructions
Refer to Kellogg's financial statements and answer the following questions:

(a) What were Kellogg's total assets at December 31, 1997? At December 31, 1996?
(b) How much cash (and cash equivalents) did Kellogg have on December 31, 1997?
(c) What amount of accounts payable did Kellogg report on December 31, 1997? On December 31, 1996?
(d) What were Kellogg's net sales in 1995? In 1996? In 1997?
(e) What is the amount of the change in Kellogg's net income from 1996 to 1997?

COMPARATIVE ANALYSIS PROBLEM: Kellogg Company vs. General Mills

BYP1–2   Kellogg's financial statements are presented in Appendix A; General Mills's financial statements are presented in Appendix B.

Instructions

(a) Based on the information contained in these financial statements, determine the following for each company;
   (1) Total assets at December 31, 1997, for Kellogg and at May 25, 1997, for General Mills.
   (2) Accounts (notes) receivable, less allowances at December 31, 1997, for Kellogg and at May 25, 1997, for General Mills.
   (3) Net sales for 1997.
   (4) Net income for 1997.
(b) What conclusions concerning the two companies can be drawn from these data?

RESEARCH ASSIGNMENT

BYP1–3   To do financial research, you need to know where to look. This assignment, in two parts, will familiarize you with two important resources.

Part 1:   *The Wall Street Journal* (WSJ), published weekdays by Dow Jones & Company, Inc., is a premier source of business information.

Instructions
Examine a recent copy of the WSJ and answer the following questions:

(a) How many separate sections are included in the WSJ? What are the contents of each?
(b) An index of the companies referenced in each edition is included on page 2 of section B. Select a company from the index and read the associated article. What is the article about? Identify any accounting-related issues discussed in the article.

Part 2:   Most libraries have company annual reports on file or available on microfiche.

Instructions
Examine copies of the financial statements of two companies and answer the following questions:

(a) What were the total assets, total liabilities, and total stockholders' equity at the most recent balance sheet date?
(b) Mathematically demonstrate the basic accounting equation for each company.
(c) What were the total current assets and total current liabilities at the most recent balance sheet date?

41

(d) What were the net sales (or revenue) and net income in the most recent income statement?

INTERPRETING FINANCIAL STATEMENTS: Lincoln Village Properties, Inc.

BYP1–4 Lincoln Village Properites, Inc., is a property management firm in Springfield, Missouri, that provides residential property management such as grounds maintenance, minor repair service, and trash collection for an annual fee. A portion of Lincoln Village's previous year's balance sheet follows:

LINCOLN VILLAGE PROPERTIES, INC.
Balance Sheet (partial)

Assets	
Cash	$ 10,000
Accounts receivable	2,000
Supplies inventory	8,000
Machinery and equipment, net	80,000
Other noncurrent assets	5,000
Total assets	$105,000

During the current year, the following events occurred:
1. $25,000 of machinery, net, was sold for cash.
2. $100,000 was received from cash sales.
3. $115,000 was paid for cash expenses.
4. Customers contracted for $150,000 in services on credit.
5. Lincoln Village Properties collected $148,000 from accounts receivable.

Instructions
Prepare the Assets portion of the current year's balance sheet for Lincoln Village Properties.

REAL-WORLD FOCUS: Air Transportation Holding Company Inc.

BYP1–5 Founded in 1980, **Air Transportation Holding Company** operates contract cargo shipping, specializing in small, overnight deliveries throughout the eastern United States. The company flies approximately 80 routes, as specified in its contracts with Federal Express. It has hangars and maintenance facilities in North Carolina, Michigan, and South Carolina.

The specific assets, liabilities, and subdivisions of owner's equity of any business depend on the type of business being operated. Management of Air Transportation Holding Company explained the year's results of operations as follows:

AIR TRANSPORTATION HOLDING COMPANY
Management Discussion

Operating expenses increased $5,498,000 (29.9%) to $23,904,000 in a recent year compared to the prior year. The increase in operating expenses consisted of the following changes: cost of flight operations increased $2,313,000 (25.7%) as a result of increases in pilot and flight personnel and costs associated with travel and landing fees which were partially offset by decreased aircraft lease and fuel costs; maintenance expense increased $2,850,000 (42.9%) primarily as a result of increases in aircraft parts purchases and mechanic and maintenance personnel costs (due to start-up of satellite maintenance facility and the operation of additional aircraft); the general and administrative expense increase of $470,000 (17.3%) resulted from increases in operational and clerical staffing related to expansion of the aircraft fleet operated.

Instructions

(a) Recall the definition of an asset. Can you identify three specific types of assets owned by Air Transportation Holding Company?

(b) The discussion above is largely about the operating expenses of the company. Identify five expenses of operations that Air Transportation incurs.

(c) When this company renders service by providing air transportation, what account affecting owner's equity is increased?

CRITICAL THINKING

GROUP DECISION CASE

BYP1–6   Patsy and Perry Ross, local golf stars, opened the Long-Shot Driving Range on March 1, 1999, by investing $10,000 of their cash savings in the business. A caddy shack was constructed for cash at a cost of $4,000 and $800 was spent on golf balls and golf clubs. The Rosses leased five acres of land at a cost of $1,000 per month and paid the first month's rent. During the first month, advertising costs totaled $750 of which $150 was unpaid at March 31, and $400 was paid to members of the high school golf team for retrieving golf balls. All revenues from customers were deposited in the company's bank account. On March 15, Patsy and Perry withdrew a total of $800 in cash for personal living expenses. A $100 utility bill was received on March 31 but it was not paid. On March 31, the balance in the company's bank account was $7,550.

Patsy and Perry thought they had a pretty good first month of operations. However, their estimates of profitability ranged from a loss of $2,450 to net income of $2,100.

Instructions

With the class divided into groups, answer the following:

(a) How could the Rosses have concluded that the business operated at a loss of $2,450? Was this a valid basis on which to determine net income?

(b) How could the Rosses have concluded that the business operated at a net income of $2,100? *(Hint:* Prepare a balance sheet at March 31.) Was this a valid basis on which to determine net income?

(c) Without preparing an income statement, determine the actual net income for March.

(d) What was the revenue earned in March?

COMMUNICATION ACTIVITY

BYP1–7   Lynn Bowen is the bookkeeper for Texas Company. Lynn has been trying to get the balance sheet of Texas Company to balance. The company's balance sheet is as follows:

TEXAS COMPANY
Balance Sheet
For the Month Ended December 31, 1999

Assets		Liabilities	
Equipment	$21,500	Thompson, Capital	$21,000
Cash	9,000	Accounts receivable	3,000
Supplies	2,000	Thompson, Drawing	(2,000)
Accounts payable	(6,000)	Notes payable	10,500
	$37,500		$32,500

Instructions

Explain to Lynn Bowen in a memo why the original balance sheet is incorrect, and what should be done to correct it.

ETHICS CASE

BYP1–8   After numerous campus interviews, Steve Pelli, a senior at Great Eastern College, received two office interview invitations from the Baltimore offices of two large firms. Both firms offered to cover his out-of-pocket expenses (travel, hotel, and meal). He scheduled the interviews for both firms on the same day, one in the morning and one in the afternoon. At the conclusion of each interview, he submitted to both firms his total out-of-pocket expenses for the trip to Baltimore, $244: mileage $70 (280 miles at $.25), hotel $120, meals $36, parking and tolls $18, for a total of $244. He believes this approach is appropriate. If he had made two trips, his cost would have been two times $244. He is also certain that neither firm knew he had visited the other on that same trip. Within ten days Steve received two checks in the mail, each in the amount of $244.

Instructions
  (a) Who are the stakeholders (affected parties) in this situation?
  (b) What are the ethical issues in this case?
  (c) What would you do in this situation?

SURFING THE NET

BYP1–9   This exercise will familiarize you with skill requirements, job descriptions, and salaries for accounting careers.

Address: http://www.cob.ohio-state.edu/dept/fin/jobsaccount.htm

Instructions
Go to the site shown above. Answer the following questions:
  (a) What are the three broad areas of accounting?
  (b) List four skills required in these areas.
  (c) How do these areas differ in required skills?
  (d) Explain one of the key job functions in accounting.
  (e) Based on the *Smart Money* survey, what is the salary range for a junior staff accountant with Deloitte & Touche?

Answers to Self-Study Questions
1. b   2. d   3. a   4. c   5. a   6. d   7. b   8. a   9. b   10. c

---

Answer to Kellogg Review It Question 4, p. 15
Kellogg's accounting equation is:

Assets	=	Liabilities	+	Owner's (Stockholders') Equity
$4,877,600,000	=	$3,880,100,000	+	$997,500,000

 ✔ **Remember to go back to the Navigator box on the chapter-opening page and check off your completed work.**

Concepts for Review highlight accounting concepts that you need to understand from earlier chapters before starting the new chapter.

Before studying this chapter, you should know or, if necessary, review:

a. What are assets, liabilities, owner's capital, owner's drawings, revenues, and expenses. (Ch. 1, pp. 13–15)

b. Why assets equal liabilities plus owner's equity. (Ch. 1, pp. 12–13)

c. What transactions are and how they affect the basic accounting equation. (Ch. 1, pp. 16–22)

FEATURE STORY

Her Classroom Is the Real World

Gabriella Torres of San Diego learned how to record transactions on a computer before she took her first accounting course. The reason: by day, she manages the office of Diabetes & Endocrine Associates, a medical practice with an office located near San Diego State University. The doctors' office uses a computer package that makes recording transactions quite easy for Gabriella. She attends night school and hopes to graduate within six years. "The doctors have really been accommodating to my school schedule."

Working during the day allows Gabriella to bring a real-world perspective to the classroom. In turn, studying business subjects at night makes her job easier. She is in charge of paying the bills for the medical practice, making sure the bank statement reconciles with the checkbook, hiring office staff, preparing patient bills, and maintaining accounts receivable. "I really love my job," she says, which is one reason she prefers to work days and go to school at night.

Taking her first accounting course helped Gabriella understand how the journal entries, the accounts, and financial statements fit together. Unlike doing homework assignments, though, the computer package at work catches some of her errors. "It won't let you proceed from one accounting entry to the next unless the entry balances," she says. In fact, there are no "books" at all, just diskettes and printouts.

CHAPTER 2

THE RECORDING PROCESS

THE NAVIGATOR ✔

- ■ Understand *Concepts for Review* ☐
- ■ Read *Feature Story* ☐
- ■ Scan *Study Objectives* ☐
- ■ Read *Preview* ☐
- ■ Read text and answer *Before You Go On*
  p. 51 ☐ p. 54 ☐ p. 64 ☐ p. 69 ☐
- ■ Work *Demonstration Problem* ☐
- ■ Review *Summary of Study Objectives* ☐
- ■ Answer *Self-Study Questions* ☐
- ■ Complete assignments ☐

STUDY OBJECTIVES

After studying this chapter, you should be able to:

1. *Explain what an account is and how it helps in the recording process.*
2. *Define debits and credits and explain how they are used to record business transactions.*
3. *Identify the basic steps in the recording process.*
4. *Explain what a journal is and how it helps in the recording process.*
5. *Explain what a ledger is and how it helps in the recording process.*
6. *Explain what posting is and how it helps in the recording process.*
7. *Prepare a trial balance and explain its purposes.*

THE NAVIGATOR

In Chapter 1, we analyzed business transactions in terms of the accounting equation and presented the cumulative effects of these transactions in tabular form. Imagine a medical practice such as Diabetes & Endocrine Associates using the same tabular format as Softbyte to keep track of every one of its transactions. In a single day, this medical practice engages in hundreds of business transactions. To record each transaction this way would be impractical, expensive, and unnecessary.

As a result, a set of procedures and records are used to make it possible to keep track of and accumulate transaction data more easily. In this chapter we will introduce and illustrate the basic procedures and records that are used. The content and organization of the chapter are as follows:

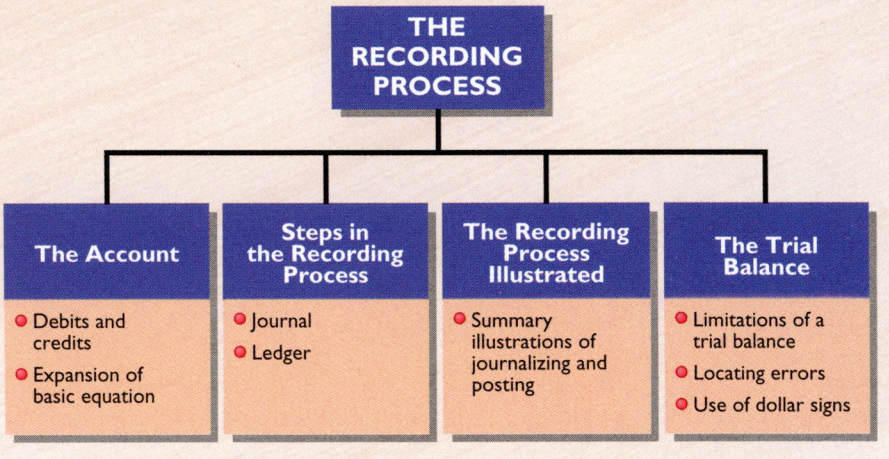

THE NAVIGATOR

1
STUDY
OBJECTIVE

Explain what an account is and how it helps in the recording process.

ILLUSTRATION 2-1

Basic form of account

THE ACCOUNT

An **account** is an individual accounting record of increases and decreases in a specific asset, liability, or owner's equity item. For example, Softbyte (discussed in Chapter 1) would have separate accounts for Cash, Accounts Receivable, Accounts Payable, Service Revenue, Salaries Expense, and so on. In its simplest form, an account consists of three parts: (1) the title of the account, (2) a left or debit side, and (3) a right or credit side. Because the alignment of these parts of an account resembles the letter T, it is referred to as a **T account**. The basic form of an account is shown in Illustration 2-1.

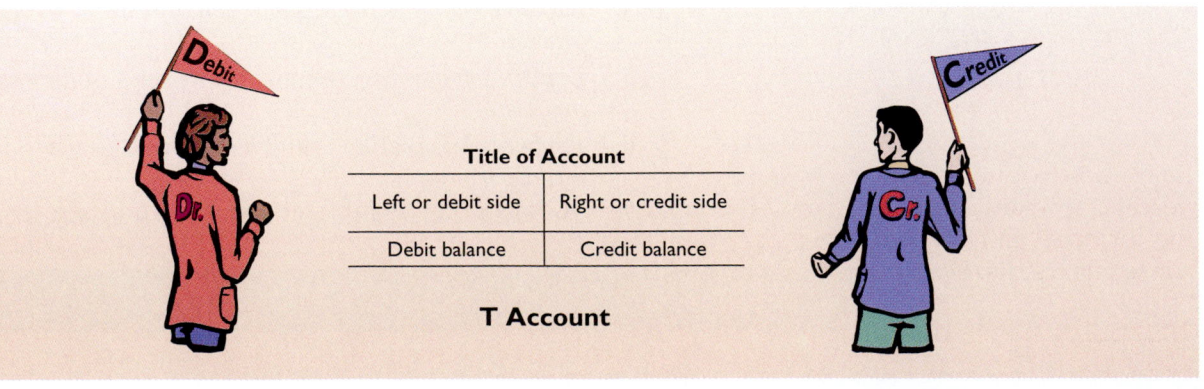

Title of Account	
Left or debit side	Right or credit side
Debit balance	Credit balance

T Account

The T account is a standard shorthand in accounting that helps make clear the effects of transactions on individual accounts. This form of account will be used often throughout this book to explain basic accounting relationships.

TECHNOLOGY IN ACTION

Computerized and manual accounting systems basically parallel one another. Most of the procedures are handled by electronic circuitry in computerized systems. They seem to occur invisibly. Therefore, to fully comprehend how computerized systems operate, it is necessary to illustrate and understand manual approaches for processing accounting data.

Debits and Credits

The terms **debit** and **credit** mean left and right, respectively. They are commonly abbreviated as Dr. for debit and Cr. for credit.[1] These terms do not mean increase or decrease. The terms debit and credit are used repeatedly in the recording process. For example, the act of entering an amount on the left side of an account is called **debiting** the account, and making an entry on the right side is **crediting** the account. When the totals of the two sides are compared, an account will have a **debit balance** if the total of the debit amounts exceeds the credits. Conversely, an account will have a **credit balance** if the credit amounts exceed the debits.

The procedure of having debits on the left and credits on the right is an accounting custom, or rule. We could function just as well if debits and credits were reversed. However, the custom of having debits on the left side of an account and credits on the right side (like the custom of driving on the right-hand side of the road) has been adopted in the United States. **This rule applies to all accounts.**

The procedure of recording debits and credits in an account is shown in Illustration 2-2 for the cash transactions of Softbyte. The data are taken from the cash column of the tabular summary in Illustration 1-10.

STUDY OBJECTIVE 2

Define debits and credits and explain how they are used to record business transactions.

Tabular Summary	Account Form			
Cash	**Cash**			
$15,000	(Debits)	15,000	(Credits)	7,000
−7,000		1,200		1,700
1,200		1,500		250
1,500		600		1,300
−1,700				
−250	Balance	8,050		
600	(Debit)			
−1,300				
$ 8,050				

ILLUSTRATION 2-2

Tabular summary compared to account form

Every positive item in the tabular summary represents a receipt of cash; every negative amount constitutes a payment of cash. Notice that in the account form the increases in cash are recorded as debits, and the decreases in cash are recorded as credits. Having increases on one side and decreases on the other helps

HELPFUL HINT

The word credit has a different meaning in accounting than it has in everyday life. For accounting purposes, think of the terms debit and credit solely as directional signals. Debit—use the left side of the account; credit—use the right side.

---

[1]These abbreviations come from the Latin words *debere* (Dr.) and *credere* (Cr.).

in determining the totals of each side of the account as well as the balance in the account. The account balance, a debit of $8,050, indicates that Softbyte has had $8,050 more increases than decreases in cash. That is, it has $8,050 in its Cash account.

Debit and Credit Procedure

In Chapter 1 you learned the effect of a transaction on the basic accounting equation. Remember that each transaction must affect two or more accounts to keep the basic accounting equation in balance. In other words, for each transaction debits must equal credits in the accounts. The equality of debits and credits provides the basis for the double-entry system of recording transactions (sometimes referred to as double-entry bookkeeping).

Under the universally used **double-entry system**, the dual (two-sided) effect of each transaction is recorded in appropriate accounts. This system provides a logical method for recording transactions. It also offers a means of proving the accuracy of the recorded amounts. If every transaction is recorded with equal debits and credits, then the sum of all the debits to the accounts must equal the sum of all the credits.

The double-entry system for determining the equality of the accounting equation is much more efficient than the plus/minus procedure used in Chapter 1. There, it was necessary after each transaction to compare total assets with total liabilities and owner's equity to determine the equality of the two sides of the accounting equation.

Assets and Liabilities.   In the Softbyte illustration above, increases in cash—an asset—were entered on the left side, and decreases in cash were entered on the right side. We know that both sides of the basic equation (assets = liabilities + owner's equity) must be equal; it then follows that increases and decreases in liabilities will have to be recorded opposite from increases and decreases in assets. Thus, increases in liabilities must be entered on the right or credit side, and decreases in liabilities must be entered on the left or debit side. The effects that debits and credits have on assets and liabilities are summarized as follows:

ILLUSTRATION 2-3

Debit and credit effects— assets and liabilities

Debits	Credits
Increase assets	Decrease assets
Decrease liabilities	Increase liabilities

Debits to a specific asset account should exceed the credits to that account, and credits to a liability account should exceed debits to that account. Thus, asset accounts normally show debit balances, and liability accounts normally show credit balances. The normal balances may be diagrammed as follows:

ILLUSTRATION 2-4

Normal balances—assets and liabilities

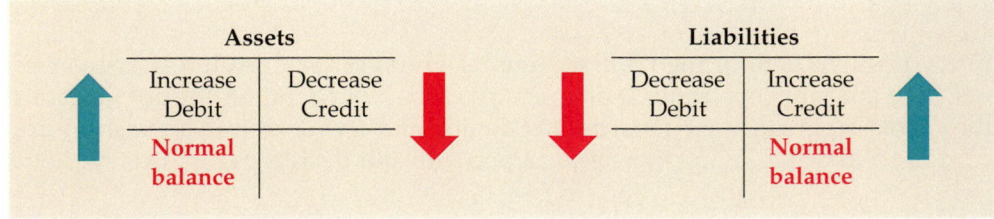

An awareness of the normal balance in an account may help you when you are trying to trace errors. For example, a credit balance in an asset account such as Land or a debit balance in a liability account such as Wages Payable would indicate errors in recording. Occasionally, however, an abnormal balance may be correct. The Cash account, for example, will have a credit balance when a company has overdrawn its bank balance (i.e., written a "bad" check).

Owner's Equity.   As indicated in Chapter 1, owner's equity is increased by owner's investments and revenues. It is decreased by owner's drawings and expenses. In a double-entry system, accounts are kept for each of these types of transactions, as explained below.

Owner's Capital.   Investments by owners are credited to the owner's capital account. The owner's capital account is increased by credits and decreased by debits. For example, when cash is invested in the business, cash is debited and owner's capital is credited. Conversely, owner's capital is debited when the owner's investment in the business is reduced.

The rules of debit and credit for the owner's capital account are stated as follows:

Debits	Credits
Decrease owner's capital	Increase owner's capital

ILLUSTRATION 2-5

Debit and credit effects— owner's capital

The normal balance in this account may be diagrammed as follows:

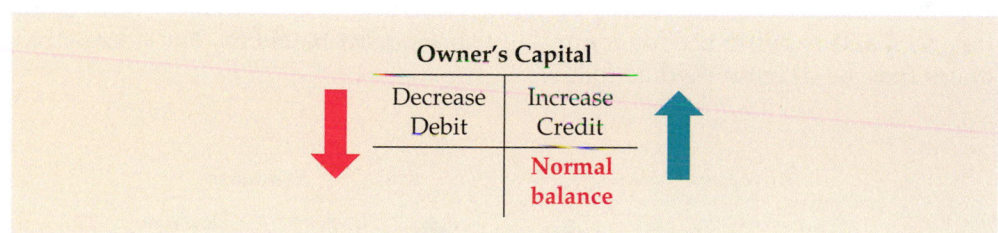

Owner's Capital

Decrease Debit	Increase Credit
	Normal balance

ILLUSTRATION 2-6

Normal balance—owner's capital

Owner's Drawing.   An owner may withdraw cash or other assets for personal use. Withdrawals could be debited directly to owner's capital to indicate a decrease in owner's equity. However, it is preferable to establish a separate account, referred to as the owner's drawing account, in order to determine the total withdrawals for the accounting period. **The drawing account decreases owner's equity. It is not an income statement account like revenues and expenses.** Owner's drawing is increased by debits and decreased by credits. Normally, the drawing account will have a debit balance. The rules of debit and credit for the drawing account are stated as follows:

Debits	Credits
Increase owner's drawing	Decrease owner's drawing

ILLUSTRATION 2-7

Debit and credit effects— owner's drawing

HELPFUL HINT
The normal balance for an account is always the same as the increase side.

The normal balance may be diagrammed as follows:

ILLUSTRATION 2-8

Normal balance—owner's drawing

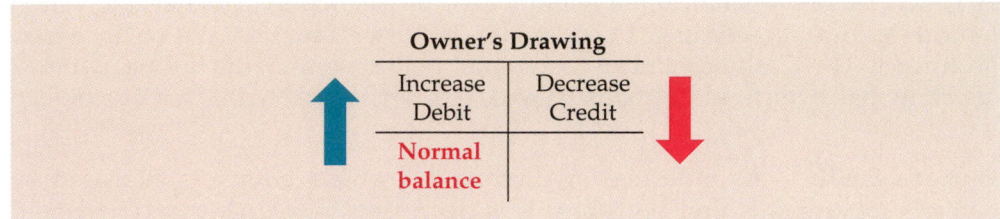

Revenues and Expenses. When revenues are earned, owner's equity is increased. Accordingly, **the effect of debits and credits on revenue accounts is identical to their effect on owner's capital**. Revenue accounts are increased by credits and decreased by debits.

On the other hand, expenses decrease owner's equity. As a result, expenses are recorded by debits. Since expenses are the negative factor in the computation of net income, and revenues are the positive factor, it is logical that the increase and decrease sides of expense accounts should be the reverse of revenue accounts. Thus, expense accounts are increased by debits and decreased by credits. The effect of debits and credits on revenues and expenses may be stated as follows:

> **HELPFUL HINT**
> Because revenues increase owner's equity, a revenue account has the same debit and credit rules as does the owner's capital account. Conversely, expenses have the opposite effect.

ILLUSTRATION 2-9

Debit and credit effects—revenues and expenses

Debits	Credits
Decrease revenues	Increase revenues
Increase expenses	Decrease expenses

Credits to revenue accounts should exceed the debits, and debits to expense accounts should exceed credits. Thus, revenue accounts normally show credit balances and expense accounts normally show debit balances. The normal balances may be diagrammed as follows:

ILLUSTRATION 2-10

Normal balances—revenues and expenses

Revenues		Expenses	
Decrease Debit	Increase Credit	Increase Debit	Decrease Credit
	Normal balance	Normal balance	

ACCOUNTING IN ACTION
Business Insight

The Chicago Cubs baseball team has the following major revenue and expense accounts:

Revenues	Expenses
Admissions (ticket sales)	Players' salaries
Concessions	Administrative salaries
Television and radio	Travel
Advertising	Ballpark maintenance

Expansion of Basic Equation

You have already learned the basic accounting equation. Illustration 2-11 expands this equation to show the accounts that comprise owner's equity. In addition, the debit/credit rules and effects on each type of account are illustrated. Study this diagram carefully. It will help you understand the fundamentals of the double-entry system. Like the basic equation, the expanded basic equation must be in balance (total debits equal total credits).

ILLUSTRATION 2-11

Expanded basic equation and debit/credit rules and effects

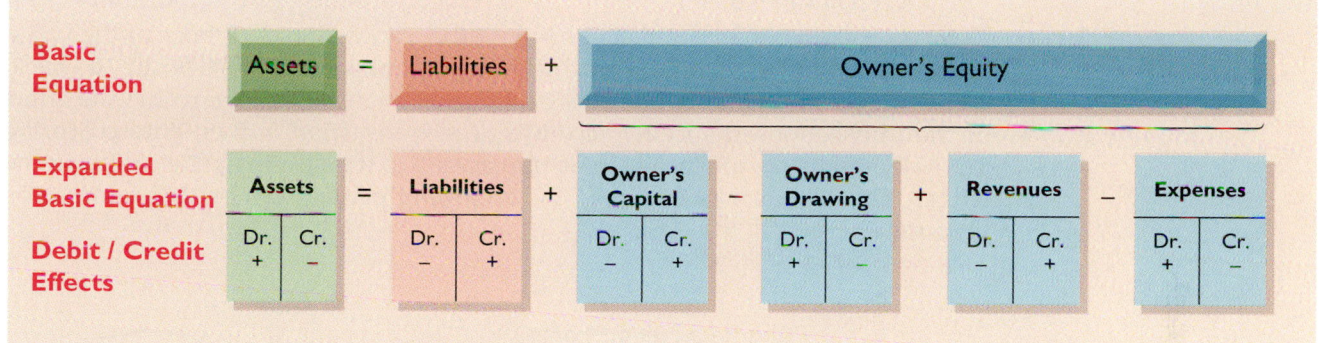

BEFORE YOU GO ON . . .

Review It

1. What do the terms debit and credit mean?
2. What are the debit and credit effects on assets, liabilities, and owner's capital?
3. What are the debit and credit effects on revenues, expenses, and owner's drawing?
4. What are the normal balances for Kellogg Company's cash, accounts payable, and interest expense accounts? The answers to this question are provided on page 88.

Do It

Kate Browne has just rented space in a shopping mall for the purpose of opening and operating a beauty salon, to be called "Hair It Is." Long before opening day and before purchasing equipment, hiring assistants, and remodeling the space, Kate is strongly advised to set up a double-entry set of accounting records in which to record all of her business transactions.

Identify the balance sheet accounts that Kate will likely need to record the transactions necessary to establish and open her business. Also, indicate whether the normal balance of each account is a debit or a credit.

Reasoning: To start her business, Kate will need to have asset accounts for each different type of asset invested in the business. In addition, Kate will need liability accounts for debts incurred by the business. Kate will only need one owner's equity account, owner's capital, when she begins the business. The other owner's equity accounts will only be needed after business has commenced.

Solution: Kate would likely need the following accounts in which to record the transactions necessary to establish and ready her beauty salon for opening day: Cash (debit balance); Equipment (debit balance); Supplies (debit balance); Accounts Payable (credit balance); if she borrows money, Notes Payable (credit balance); K. Browne, Capital (credit balance).

Related exercise material: BE2–1, BE2–2, E2–1, E2–3, and E2–10.

THE
NAVIGATOR

STEPS IN THE RECORDING PROCESS

Although it is possible to enter transaction information directly into the accounts, few businesses do so. In practically every business, the basic steps in the recording process are:

1. Analyze each transaction in terms of its effect on the accounts.
2. Enter the transaction information in a journal (book of original entry).
3. Transfer the journal information to the appropriate accounts in the ledger (book of accounts).

The actual sequence of events begins with the transaction. Evidence of the transaction comes in the form of a **business document**, such as a sales slip, a check, a bill, or a cash register tape. This evidence is analyzed to determine the effect of the transaction on specific accounts. The transaction is then entered in the journal. Finally, the journal entry is transferred to the designated accounts in the ledger. The sequence of events in the recording process can be diagrammed as follows:

The Recording Process

Analyze each transaction   Enter transaction in a journal   Transfer journal information to ledger accounts

ILLUSTRATION 2-12

The recording process

The basic steps in the recording process occur repeatedly in every business enterprise. The analysis of transactions has already been illustrated, and further examples of this step will be given in this and later chapters. The other steps in the recording process are explained in the next sections.

The Journal

Transactions are initially recorded in chronological order in a **journal** before being transferred to the accounts. Thus, the journal is referred to as the book of original entry. For each transaction the journal shows the debit and credit effects on specific accounts. Companies may use various kinds of journals, but every company has the most basic form of journal, a **general journal**. Typically, a general journal has spaces for dates, account titles and explanations, references, and two money columns. Whenever the term journal is used in this textbook without a modifying adjective, it will mean the general journal.

The journal makes several significant contributions to the recording process:

1. It discloses in one place the complete effect of a transaction.
2. It provides a chronological record of transactions.

3. It helps to prevent or locate errors because the debit and credit amounts for each entry can be readily compared.

Journalizing

Entering transaction data in the journal is known as **journalizing**. Separate journal entries are made for each transaction. A complete entry consists of: (1) the date of the transaction, (2) the accounts and amounts to be debited and credited, and (3) a brief explanation of the transaction.

To illustrate the technique of journalizing, the first two transactions of Softbyte are journalized in Illustration 2-13 using the first page (J1) of the general journal. These transactions were: September 1, Ray Neal invested $15,000 cash in the business, and computer equipment was purchased for $7,000 cash.

GENERAL JOURNAL					J1
Date	Account Titles and Explanation	Ref.	Debit	Credit	
1999					
Sept. 1	Cash		15,000		
	R. Neal, Capital			15,000	
	(Owner's investment of cash in business)				
1	Computer Equipment		7,000		
	Cash			7,000	
	(Purchase of equipment for cash)				

ILLUSTRATION 2-13
Technique of journalizing

The standard form and content of journal entries are as follows:

1. The date of the transaction is entered in the Date column. The date recorded should include the year, month, and day of the transaction.
2. The debit account title (that is, the account to be debited) is entered first at the extreme left margin of the column headed "Account Titles and Explanation," and the amount of the debit is recorded in the Debit column.
3. The credit account title (that is, the account to be credited) is indented and entered on the next line in the column headed "Account Titles and Explanation," and the amount of the credit is recorded in the Credit column.
4. A brief explanation of the transaction is given.
5. A space is left between journal entries. The blank space separates individual journal entries and makes the entire journal easier to read.
6. The column entitled Ref. (which stands for reference) is left blank at the time the journal entry is made. The Reference column is used later when the journal entries are transferred to the ledger accounts. At that time, the ledger account number is placed in the Reference column to indicate where the amount in the journal entry was transferred.

It is important to use correct and specific account titles in journalizing. Since most accounts appear later in the financial statements, erroneous account titles lead to incorrect financial statements. Some flexibility exists initially in selecting account titles. The main criterion is that each title must appropriately describe the content of the account. For example, the account title used for the cost of delivery trucks may be Delivery Equipment, Delivery Trucks, or Trucks.

Once a company chooses the specific title to use, all subsequent transactions involving the account should be recorded under that account title.[2]

If an entry involves only two accounts, one debit and one credit, it is considered a **simple entry**. For some transactions, however, it may be necessary to use more than two accounts in journalizing. Imagine, for example, the numerous accounts needed by General Electric to record the acquisition of all the assets and liabilities of RCA in what was one of the largest mergers ever completed. When three or more accounts are required in one journal entry, the entry is referred to as a **compound entry**. To illustrate, assume that on July 1, Butler Company purchases a delivery truck costing $14,000 by paying $8,000 cash and the balance on account (to be paid at a later date). The entry is as follows:

ILLUSTRATION 2-14

Compound journal entry

GENERAL JOURNAL					J1
Date	Account Titles and Explanation		Ref.	Debit	Credit
1999 July 1	Delivery Equipment			14,000	
	Cash				8,000
	Accounts Payable				6,000
	(Purchased truck for cash with balance on account)				

HELPFUL HINT

Assume you find this compound entry:
Wages Expense   700
  Cash   1,200
Advert. Expense 400
(Paid cash for wages and advertising)
Is the entry correct? No. It is incorrect in form because both debits should be listed before the credit. It is incorrect in content because the debit amounts do not equal the credit amount.

In a compound entry, it is important to determine that the total debit and credit amounts are equal. Also, the standard format requires that all debits be listed before the credits are listed.

BEFORE YOU GO ON . . .

Review It

1. What is the correct sequence of the steps in the recording process?
2. What contribution does the journal make to the recording process?
3. What is the standard form and content of a journal entry made in the general journal?

Do It

In establishing her beauty salon, Hair It Is, Kate Browne engaged in the following activities:

1. Opened a bank account in the name of Hair It Is and deposited $20,000 of her own money in this account as her initial investment.
2. Purchased on account (to be paid in 30 days) equipment, for a total cost of $4,800.
3. Interviewed three persons for the position of beautician.

In what form (type of record) should Kate record these three activities? Prepare the entries to record the transactions.

---

[2]In homework problems, when specific account titles are given, they should be used. When account titles are not given, you may select account titles that identify the nature and content of each account. The account titles used in journalizing should not contain explanations such as Cash Paid or Cash Received.

Reasoning: Kate should record the transactions in a journal, which is a chronological record of the transactions. The record should be a complete and accurate representation of the transactions' effects on her business's assets, liabilities, and owner's equity.

Solution: Each transaction that is recorded is entered in the general journal. The three activities would be recorded as follows:

1. Cash   20,000
    K. Browne, Capital   20,000
      (Owner's investment of cash in business)
2. Equipment   4,800
    Accounts Payable   4,800
      (Purchase of equipment on account)
3. No entry because no transaction has occurred.

Related exercise material: BE2–3, BE2–5, BE2–6, E2–2, E2–4, E2–6, E2–7, and E2–8.

THE NAVIGATOR

The Ledger

The entire group of accounts maintained by a company is referred to collectively as the **ledger**. The ledger keeps in one place all the information about changes in specific account balances.

    Companies may use various kinds of ledgers, but every company has a general ledger. A **general ledger** contains all the assets, liabilities, and owner's equity accounts, as shown in Illustration 2-15. A business can use a looseleaf binder or card file for the ledger with each account kept on a separate sheet or card. Whenever the term ledger is used in this textbook without a modifying adjective, it will mean the general ledger.

5
STUDY
OBJECTIVE
·····················
Explain what a ledger is and how it helps in the recording process.

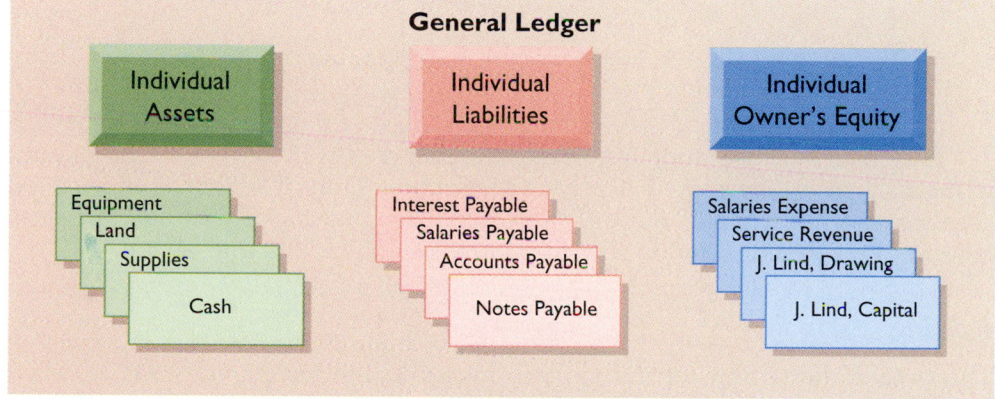

ILLUSTRATION 2-15

The general ledger

    The ledger should be arranged in statement order beginning with the balance sheet accounts. First in order are the asset accounts, followed by liability accounts, owner's capital, owner's drawing, revenues, and expenses. Each account is numbered for easier identification.

    The information in the ledger provides management with the balances in various accounts. For example, the Cash account enables management to determine the amount of cash that is available to meet current obligations. Amounts due from customers and the amounts owed to creditors can be determined by examining the Accounts Receivable and Accounts Payable accounts, respectively.

ACCOUNTING IN ACTION
Business Insight

In his autobiography Sam Walton described the double-entry accounting system he began the Wal-Mart empire with: "We kept a little pigeonhole on the wall for the cash receipts and paperwork of each [Wal-Mart] store. I had a blue binder ledger book for each store. When we added a store, we added a pigeonhole. We did this at least up to twenty stores. Then once a month, the bookkeeper and I would enter the merchandise, enter the sales, enter the cash, and balance it."

Source: Sam Walton, *Made in America* (New York: Doubleday, 1992), p. 53.

Standard Form of Account

The simple T-account form of an account used in an accounting textbook is often very useful for illustration and analysis purposes. However, in practice, the account forms used in ledgers are much more structured. A form widely used in a manual system is shown in Illustration 2-16, using assumed data from a cash account.

ILLUSTRATION 2-16

Three-column form of account

	CASH				No. 10
Date	Explanation	Ref.	Debit	Credit	Balance
1999					
June 1			25,000		25,000
2				8,000	17,000
3			4,200		21,200
9			7,500		28,700
17				11,700	17,000
20				250	16,750
30				7,300	9,450

This form has three money columns—debit, credit, and balance. The balance in the account is determined after each transaction. Thus, this form is often called the **three-column form of account**. Note that the explanation space and reference columns are used to provide special information about the transaction.

Posting

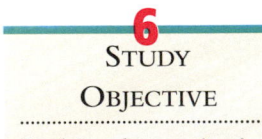

6

STUDY OBJECTIVE

Explain what posting is and how it helps in the recording process.

The procedure of transferring journal entries to the ledger accounts is called **posting**. **This phase of the recording process accumulates the effects of journalized transactions in the individual accounts.**

Posting involves the following steps:

1. In the ledger, enter in the appropriate columns of the account(s) debited the date, journal page, and debit amount shown in the journal.
2. In the reference column of the journal, write the account number to which the debit amount was posted.
3. In the ledger, enter in the appropriate columns of the account(s) credited the date, journal page, and credit amount shown in the journal.
4. In the reference column of the journal, write the account number to which the credit amount was posted.

These four steps are diagrammed in Illustration 2-17 using the first journal entry of Softbyte. The boxed numbers indicate the sequence of the steps.

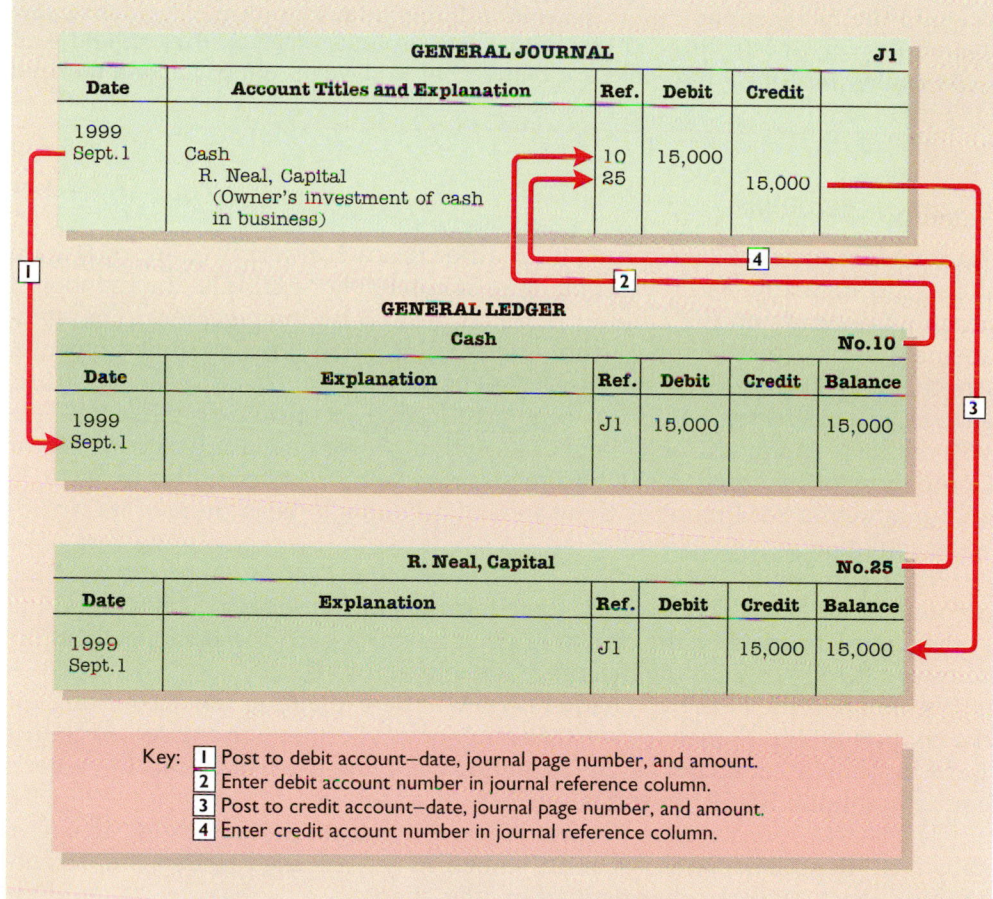

ILLUSTRATION 2-17

Posting a journal entry

Posting should be performed in chronological order. That is, all the debits and credits of one journal entry should be posted before proceeding to the next journal entry. Under the journalizing procedures described in this chapter, postings should be made on a timely basis to ensure that the ledger is up to date.[3]

The reference column **in the journal** serves several purposes. The numbers in this column indicate the entries that have been posted. After the last entry has been posted, the journal reference column should be scanned to see that all postings have been made.

The reference column **of a ledger** account indicates the journal page from which the transaction has been posted. The explanation space of the ledger account is used infrequently because an explanation already appears in the journal. It generally is used only when detailed analysis of account activity is required.

---

[3]In homework problems, it will be permissible to journalize all transactions before posting any of the journal entries.

TECHNOLOGY IN ACTION

Determining what to record is the most critical (and for most businesses the most expensive) point in the accounting process. In computerized systems, after this phase is completed, your input and all further processing just boil down to file merging and report generation. Programmers and management information system types with good accounting backgrounds (such as they should gain from a good principles textbook) are better able to develop effective computerized systems.

Chart of Accounts

The number and type of accounts used differ for each enterprise, depending on the size, complexity, and type of business involved. For example, the number of accounts depends on the amount of detail desired by management. The management of one company may want one account for all types of utility expense. Another may keep separate expense accounts for each type of utility expenditure, such as gas, electricity, and water. Similarly, a single proprietorship like Softbyte will not have many accounts compared with a corporate giant like Ford Motor Company. Softbyte may be able to manage and report its activities in 20 to 30 accounts, while Ford requires thousands of accounts to keep track of its worldwide activities.

Most companies have a **chart of accounts** that lists the accounts and the account numbers which identify their location in the ledger. The numbering system used to identify the accounts usually starts with the balance sheet accounts and follows with the income statement accounts.

In this and the next two chapters, we will be explaining the accounting for the proprietorship Pioneer Advertising Agency (a service enterprise). Accounts 1–19 indicate asset accounts; 20–39 indicate liabilities; 40–49 indicate owner's equity accounts; 50–59, revenues; and 60–69, expenses.

The chart of accounts for Pioneer Advertising Agency (C. R. Byrd, owner) is shown in Illustration 2-18. Accounts shown in red are used in this chapter; accounts shown in black are explained in later chapters.

ILLUSTRATION 2-18

Chart of accounts

Chart of Accounts
Pioneer Advertising Agency

Assets	Owner's Equity
1. Cash	40. C. R. Byrd, Capital
6. Accounts Receivable	41. C. R. Byrd, Drawing
8. Advertising Supplies	49. Income Summary
10. Prepaid Insurance	**Revenues**
15. Office Equipment	
16. Accumulated Depreciation—Office Equipment	50. Service Revenue
Liabilities	**Expenses**
25. Notes Payable	60. Salaries Expense
26. Accounts Payable	61. Advertising Supplies Expense
27. Interest Payable	62. Rent Expense
28. Unearned Revenue	63. Insurance Expense
29. Salaries Payable	64. Interest Expense
	65. Depreciation Expense

You will notice that there are gaps in the numbering system of the chart of accounts for Pioneer Advertising. Gaps are left to permit the insertion of new accounts as needed during the life of the business.

ACCOUNTING IN ACTION
Business Insight

The numbering system used to identify accounts can be quite sophisticated or relatively simple. For example, at Goodyear Tire & Rubber Company an 18-digit system is used. The first three digits identify the division or plant. The second set of three-digit numbers contains the following account classifications:

100–199 Assets	300–399 Revenues
200–299 Liabilities and Owner's Equity	400–599 Expenses

Other digits describe the location of a specific plant, product line, region of the country, and so on. In practice, account numbers are not the same from company to company. Therefore, to reflect the situation you would find in the real world, account numbers in the text and in the homework materials also vary from company to company.

THE RECORDING PROCESS ILLUSTRATED

Illustrations 2-19 through 2-28 show the basic steps in the recording process, using the October transactions of the Pioneer Advertising Agency. Its accounting period is a month. A basic analysis and a debit-credit analysis precede the

(text continues on page 64)

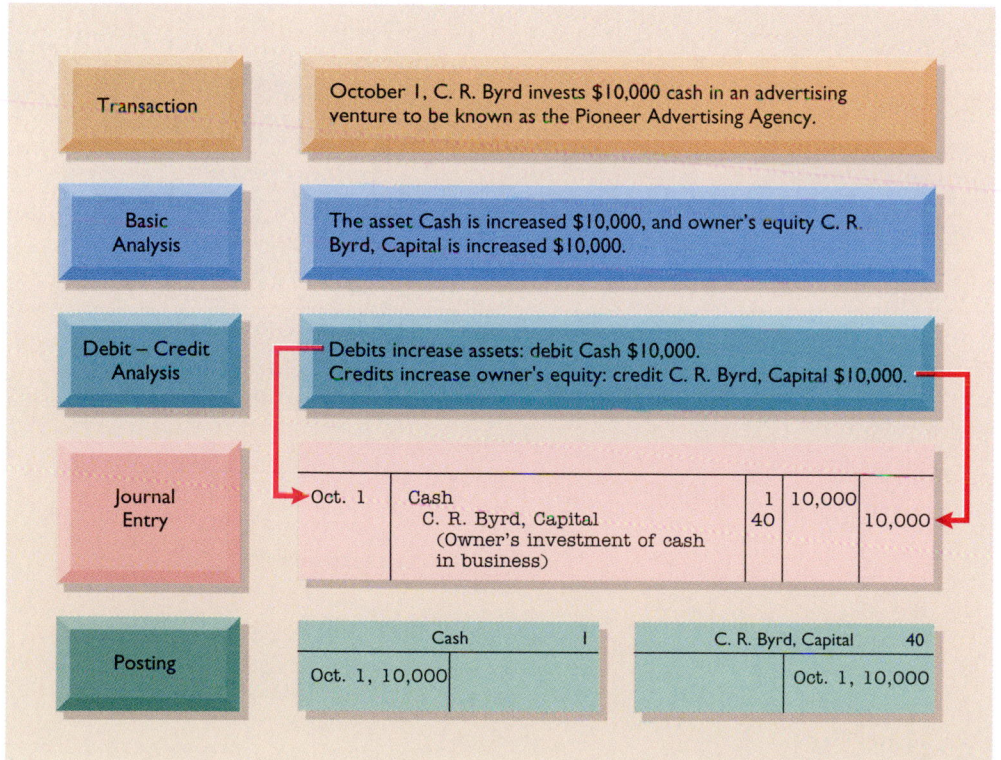

ILLUSTRATION 2-19

Investment of cash by owner

HELPFUL HINT
To correctly record a transaction, you must carefully analyze the event and translate that analysis into debit and credit language.
First: Determine what type of account is involved.
Second: Determine what items increased or decreased and by how much.
Third: Translate the increases and decreases into debits and credits.

ILLUSTRATION 2-20

Purchase of office equipment

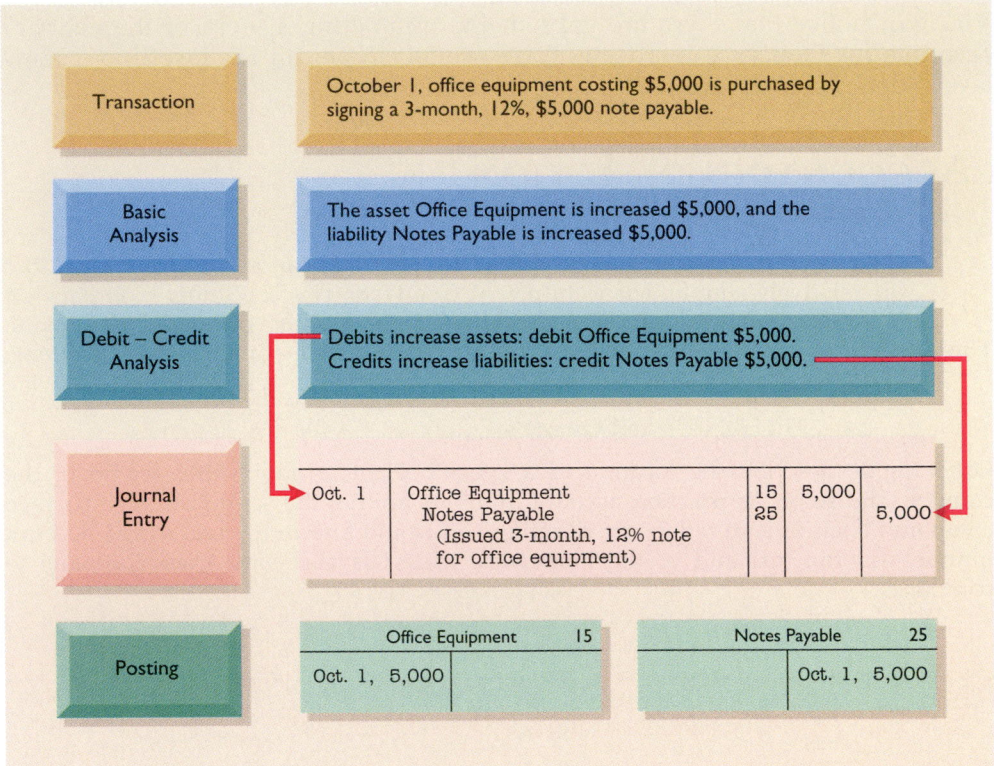

ILLUSTRATION 2-21

Receipt of cash for future service

HELPFUL HINT

When the revenue is earned, the unearned revenue account is debited, and an earned revenue account is credited.

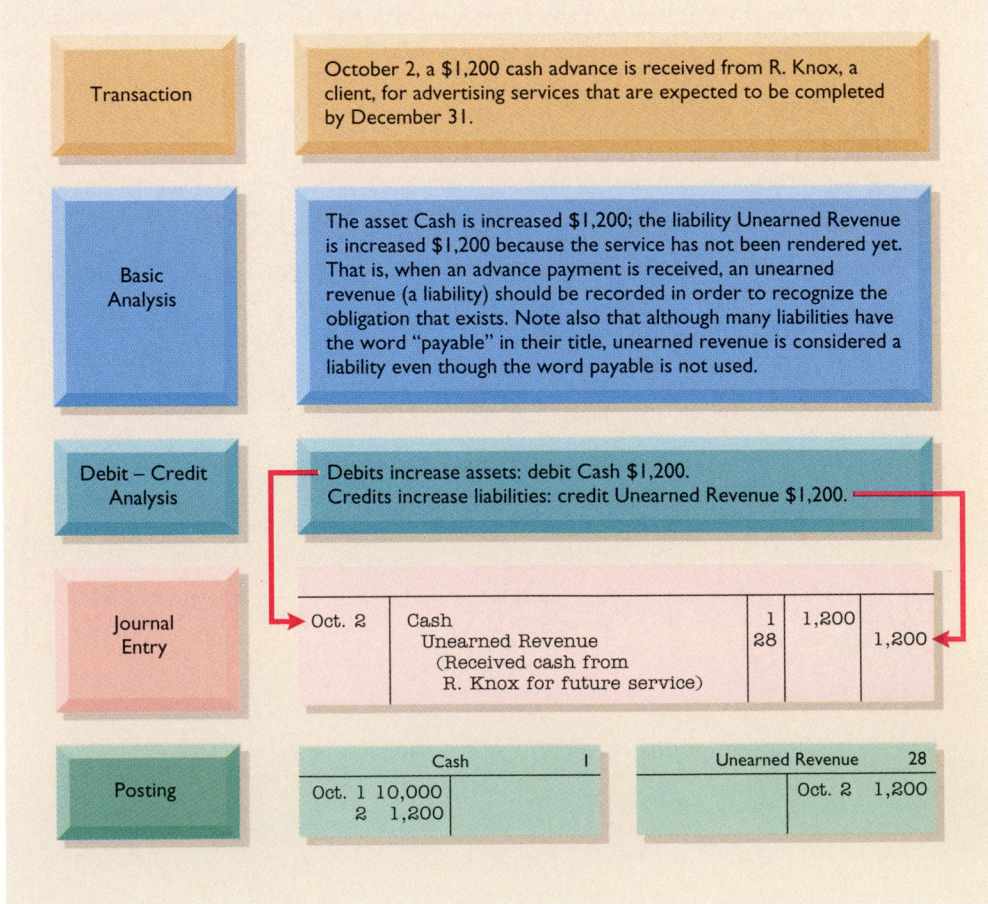

ILLUSTRATION 2-22

Payment of monthly rent

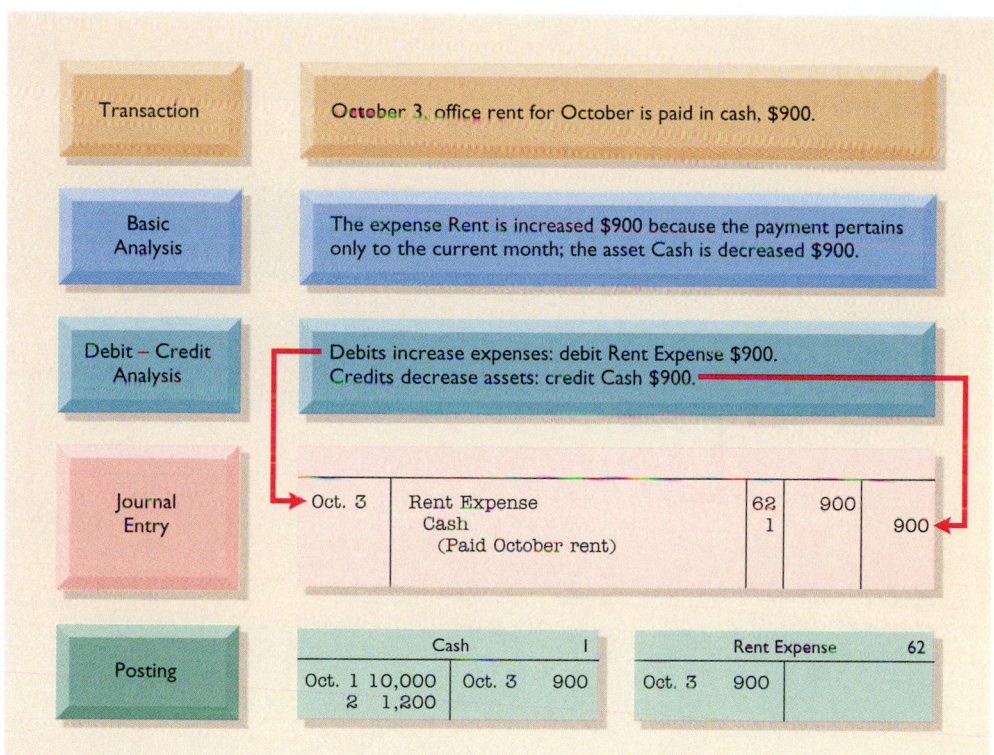

ILLUSTRATION 2-23

Payment for insurance

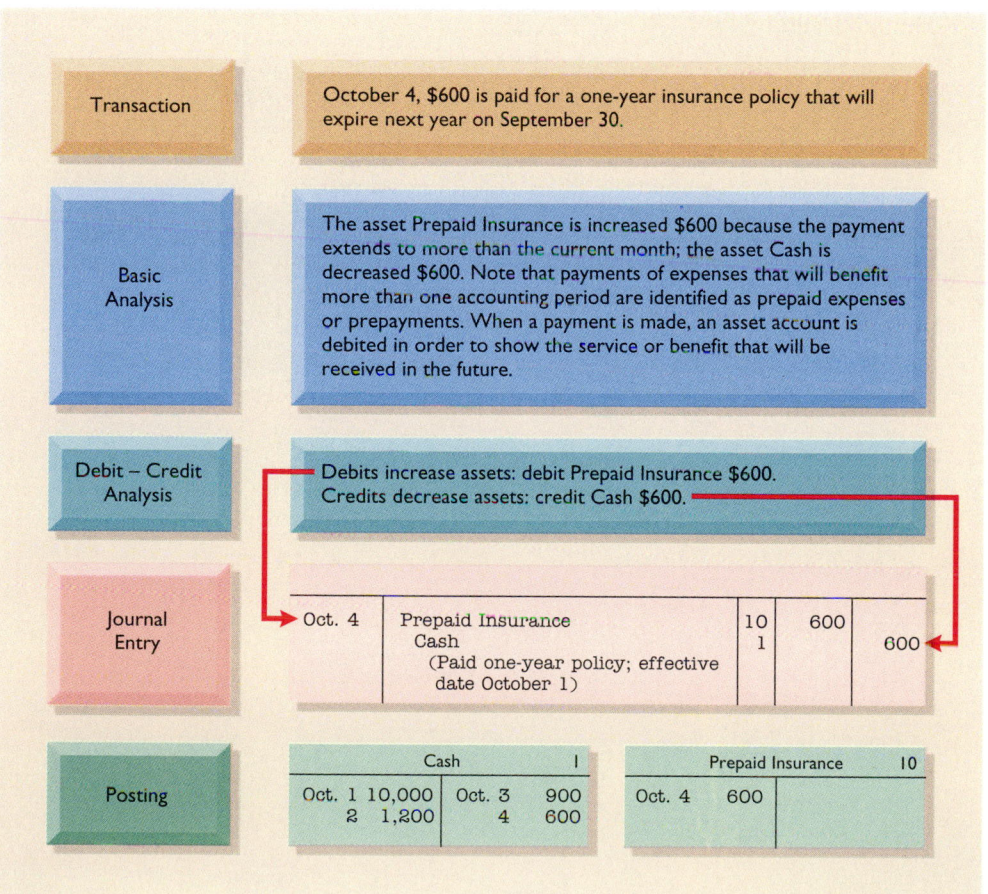

ILLUSTRATION 2-24

Purchase of supplies on credit

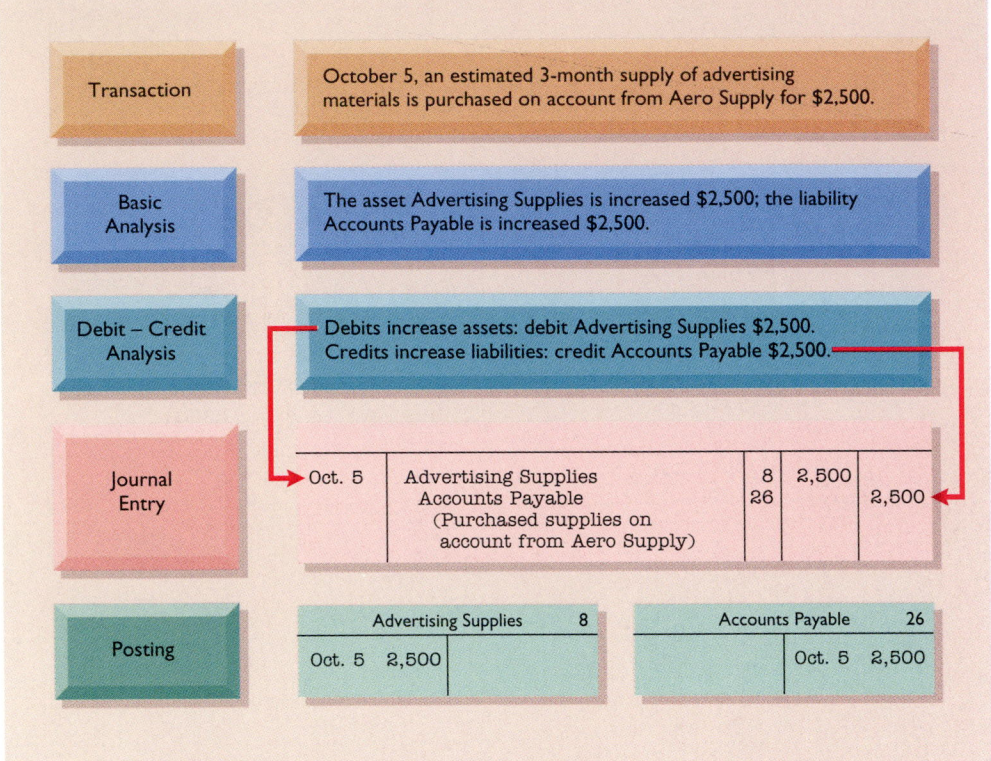

ILLUSTRATION 2-25

Hiring of employees

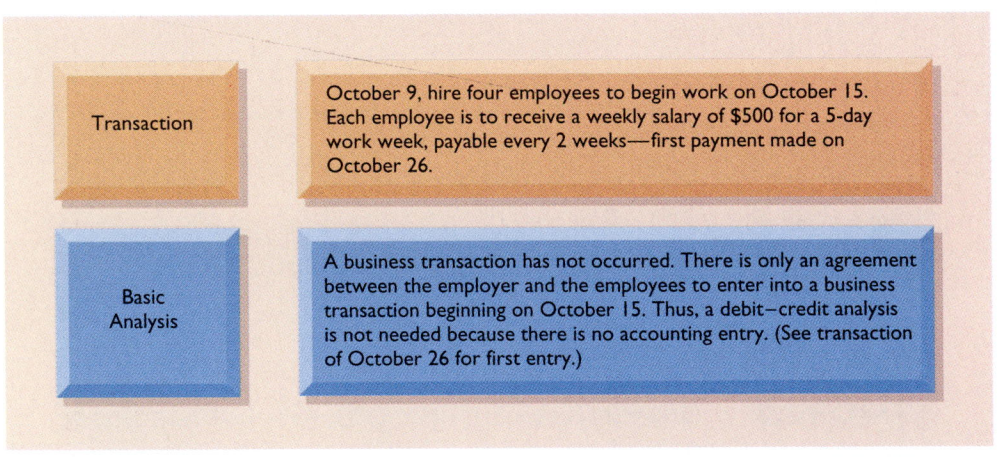

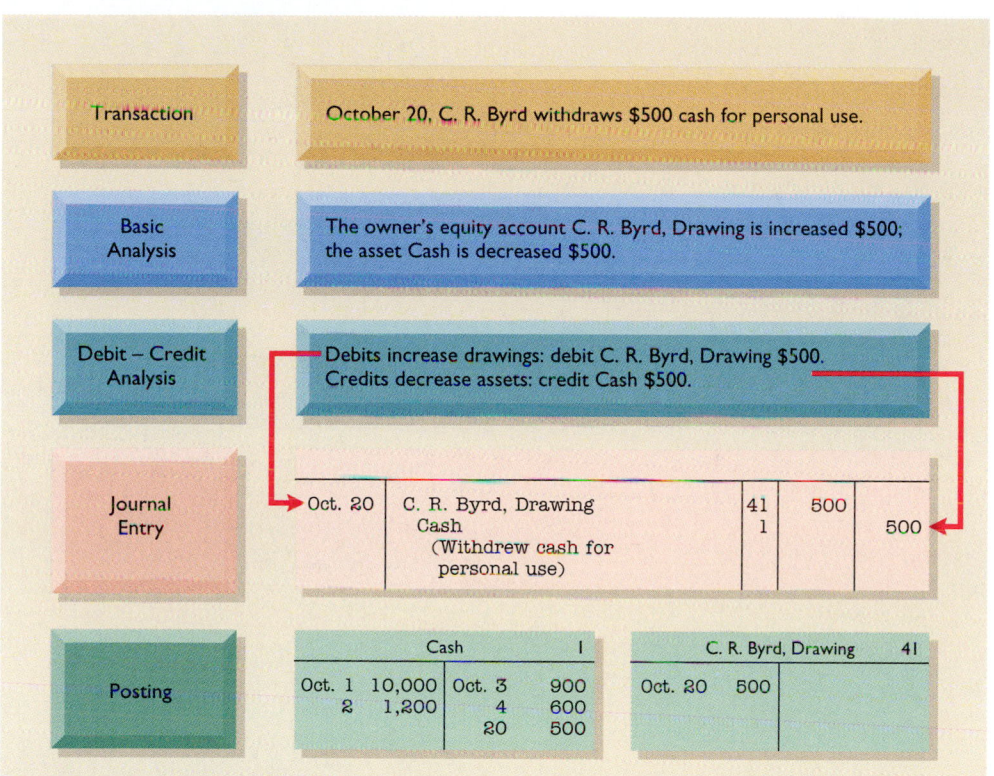

ILLUSTRATION 2-26
Withdrawal of cash by owner

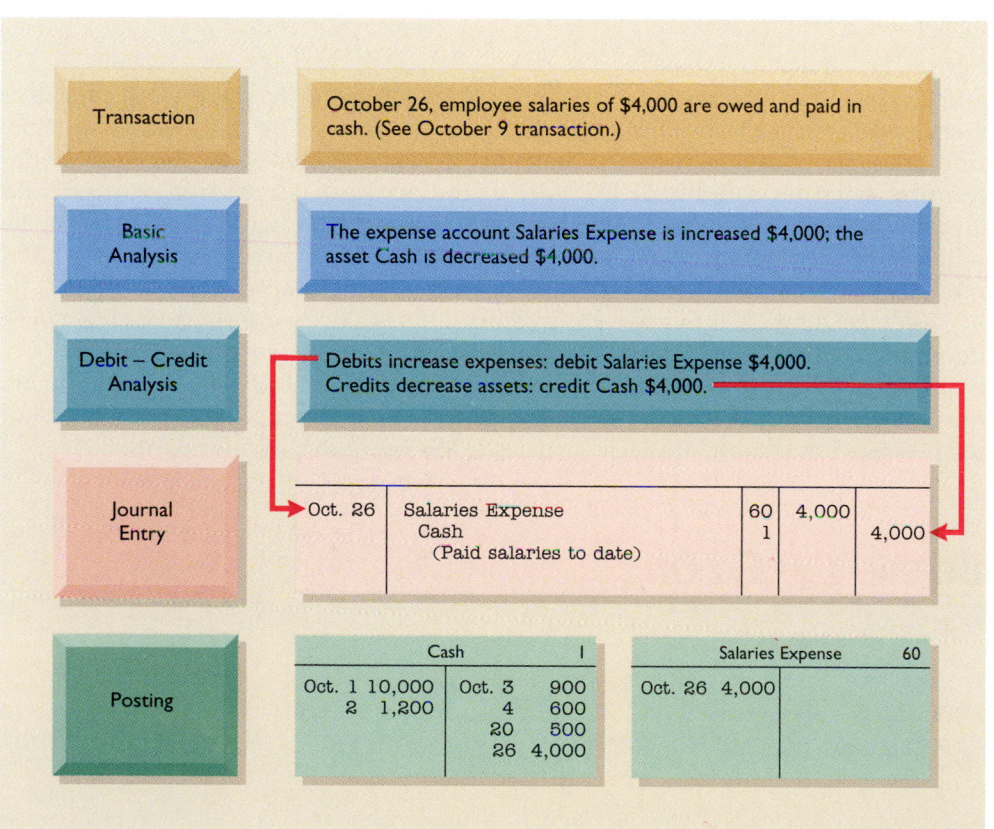

ILLUSTRATION 2-27
Payment of salaries

ILLUSTRATION 2-28

*Receipt of cash for fees
earned*

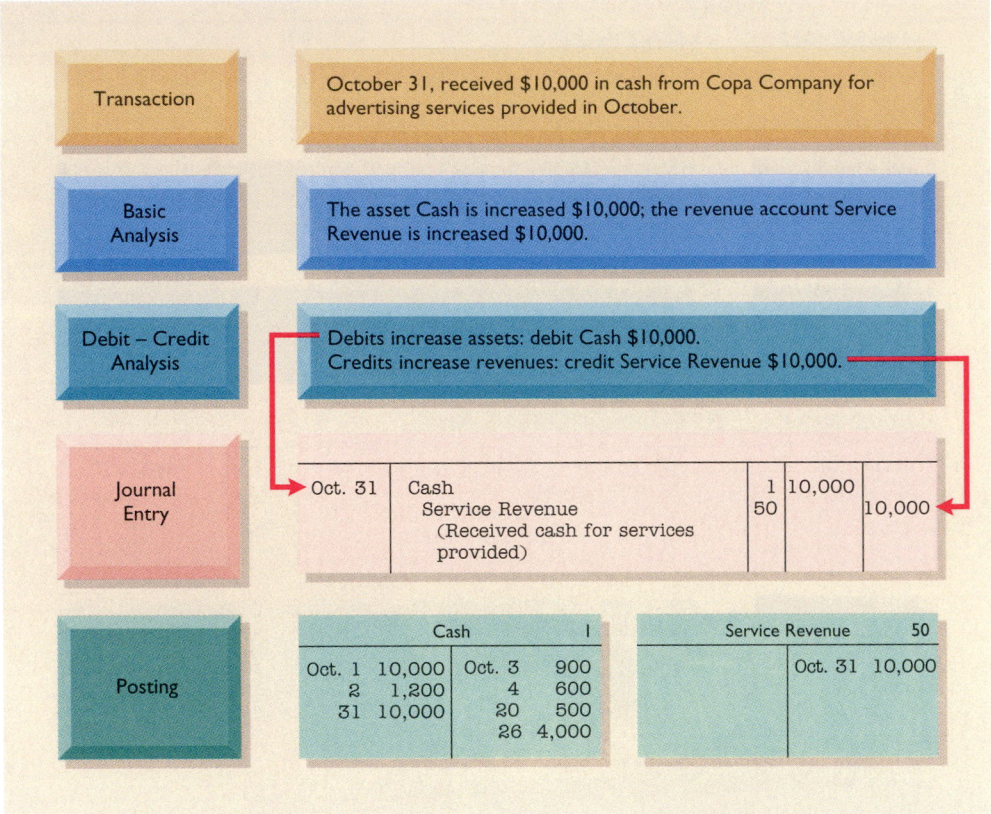

journalizing and posting of each transaction. Go back over the preceding five pages, and study these transaction analyses carefully. **The purpose of transaction analysis is first to identify the type of account involved, and then to determine whether a debit or a credit to the account is required.** You should always perform this type of analysis before preparing a journal entry. Doing so will help you understand the journal entries discussed in this chapter as well as more complex journal entries to be described in later chapters.

Keep in mind that every journal entry affects one or more of the following items: assets, liabilities, owner's capital, owner's drawing, revenues, or expenses. By becoming skilled at transaction analysis, you will be able to recognize quickly the impact of any transaction on these six items. For simplicity, the T-account form is used in the illustrations instead of the standard account form.

BEFORE YOU GO ON . . .

Review It

1. How does journalizing differ from posting?
2. What is the purpose of (a) the ledger and (b) a chart of accounts?

Do It

Kate Browne collected $2,280 in cash for hair styling services, and she paid $400 in wages and $92 for utilities. Kate recorded these transactions in a general journal and posted the entries to the general ledger. Explain the purpose and process of journalizing and posting.

Reasoning: Every business must keep track of its financial activities (receipts, payments, receivables, payables, etc.); journalizing does this. However, just recording every transaction in chronological order does not make the entries useful. To be useful, the entries need to be classified and summarized; posting the entries to specific ledger accounts does this.

Solution: Journalizing records in chronological order every transaction. Journalizing involves dating every transaction, measuring the dollar amount, identifying or labeling each amount with account titles, and recording in a standard format equal debits and credits. Posting involves transferring the journalized debits and credits to specific accounts in the ledger.

Related exercise material: BE2–7, BE2–8, E2–2, E2–5, and E2–8.

THE
NAVIGATOR

Summary Illustration of Journalizing and Posting

The journal for Pioneer Advertising Agency for the month of October is summarized in Illustration 2-29. The ledger is shown in Illustration 2-30, on page 66, with all balances in color.

GENERAL JOURNAL			Page J1	
Date	Account Titles and Explanation	Ref.	Debit	Credit
1999 Oct. 1	Cash	1	10,000	
	C. R. Byrd, Capital	40		10,000
	(Owner's investment of cash in business)			
1	Office Equipment	15	5,000	
	Notes Payable	25		5,000
	(Issued three-month, 12% note for office equipment)			
2	Cash	1	1,200	
	Unearned Revenue	28		1,200
	(Received cash for future services)			
3	Rent Expense	62	900	
	Cash	1		900
	(Paid October rent)			
4	Prepaid Insurance	10	600	
	Cash	1		600
	(Paid one-year policy; effective date, October 1)			
5	Advertising Supplies	8	2,500	
	Accounts Payable	26		2,500
	(Purchased supplies on account from Aero Supply)			
20	C. R. Byrd, Drawing	41	500	
	Cash	1		500
	(Withdrew cash for personal use)			
26	Salaries Expense	60	4,000	
	Cash	1		4,000
	(Paid salaries to date)			
31	Cash	1	10,000	
	Service Revenue	50		10,000
	(Received cash for services provided)			

ILLUSTRATION 2-29
General journal entries

GENERAL LEDGER

	Cash				No. 1
Date	Explanation	Ref.	Debit	Credit	Balance
1999					
Oct. 1		J1	10,000		10,000
2		J1	1,200		11,200
3		J1		900	10,300
4		J1		600	9,700
20		J1		500	9,200
26		J1		4,000	5,200
31		J1	10,000		15,200

	Advertising Supplies				No. 8
Date	Explanation	Ref.	Debit	Credit	Balance
1999					
Oct. 5		J1	2,500		2,500

	Prepaid Insurance				No. 10
Date	Explanation	Ref.	Debit	Credit	Balance
1999					
Oct. 4		J1	600		600

	Office Equipment				No. 15
Date	Explanation	Ref.	Debit	Credit	Balance
1999					
Oct. 1		J1	5,000		5,000

	Notes Payable				No. 25
Date	Explanation	Ref.	Debit	Credit	Balance
1999					
Oct. 1		J1		5,000	5,000

	Accounts Payable				No. 26
Date	Explanation	Ref.	Debit	Credit	Balance
1999					
Oct. 5		J1		2,500	2,500

	Unearned Revenue				No. 28
Date	Explanation	Ref.	Debit	Credit	Balance
1999					
Oct. 2		J1		1,200	1,200

	C. R. Byrd, Capital				No. 40
Date	Explanation	Ref.	Debit	Credit	Balance
1999					
Oct. 1		J1		10,000	10,000

	C. R. Byrd, Drawing				No. 41
Date	Explanation	Ref.	Debit	Credit	Balance
1999					
Oct. 20		J1	500		500

	Service Revenue				No. 50
Date	Explanation	Ref.	Debit	Credit	Balance
1999					
Oct. 31		J1		10,000	10,000

	Salaries Expense				No. 60
Date	Explanation	Ref.	Debit	Credit	Balance
1999					
Oct. 26		J1	4,000		4,000

	Rent Expense				No. 62
Date	Explanation	Ref.	Debit	Credit	Balance
1999					
Oct. 3		J1	900		900

ILLUSTRATION 2-30

General ledger

THE TRIAL BALANCE

A **trial balance** is a list of accounts and their balances at a given time. Customarily, a trial balance is prepared at the end of an accounting period. The accounts are listed in the order in which they appear in the ledger, with debit balances listed in the left column and credit balances in the right column. The totals of the two columns must be in agreement.

The primary purpose of a trial balance is to prove the mathematical equality of debits and credits after posting. Under the double-entry system this equality will occur when the sum of the debit account balances equals the sum of the credit account balances. **A trial balance also uncovers errors in journalizing and posting. In addition, it is useful in the preparation of financial statements,** as will be explained in the next two chapters. The procedures for preparing a trial balance consist of:

1. Listing the account titles and their balances.
2. Totaling the debit and credit columns.
3. Proving the equality of the two columns.

The trial balance prepared from the ledger of Pioneer Advertising Agency is presented below:

ILLUSTRATION 2-31
A trial balance

PIONEER ADVERTISING AGENCY Trial Balance October 31, 1999		
	Debit	Credit
Cash	$15,200	
Advertising Supplies	2,500	
Prepaid Insurance	600	
Office Equipment	5,000	
Notes Payable		$ 5,000
Accounts Payable		2,500
Unearned Revenue		1,200
C. R. Byrd, Capital		10,000
C. R. Byrd, Drawing	500	
Service Revenue		10,000
Salaries Expense	4,000	
Rent Expense	900	
	$28,700	$28,700

Note that the total debits $28,700 equal the total credits $28,700. Account numbers are sometimes shown to the left of the account titles in the trial balance.

A trial balance is a necessary check point before proceeding to other steps in the accounting process. For example, if only the debit portion of a journal entry has been posted, the trial balance would bring this error to light.

Limitations of a Trial Balance

A trial balance does not prove that all transactions have been recorded or that the ledger is correct. Numerous errors may exist even though the trial balance columns agree. For example, the trial balance may balance even when (1) a transaction is not journalized, (2) a correct journal entry is not posted, (3) a journal entry is posted twice, (4) incorrect accounts are used in journalizing or posting, or (5) offsetting errors are made in recording the amount of a transaction. In other words, as long as equal debits and credits are posted, even to the wrong account or in the wrong amount, the total debits will equal the total credits.

Locating Errors

The procedure for preparing a trial balance is relatively simple. However, in manual systems if the trial balance does not balance, locating an error can be

TECHNOLOGY IN ACTION

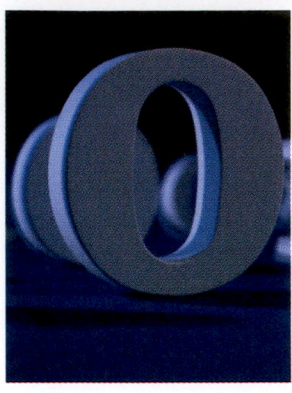

In a computerized system, the trial balance is often only one column (no debit or credit columns), and the accounts have plus and minus signs associated with them. The final balance therefore is zero. Any errors that develop in a computerized system will undoubtedly involve the initial recording rather than some error in the posting or preparation of a trial balance.

time-consuming, tedious, and frustrating. The error(s) generally results from mathematical mistakes, incorrect postings, or simply transcribing the data incorrectly.

What happens if you are faced with a trial balance that does not balance? First determine the amount of the difference between the two columns of the trial balance. After this amount is known, the following steps are often helpful:

1. If the error is $1, $10, $100, or $1,000, re-add the trial balance columns and recompute the account balances.
2. If the error is divisible by two, scan the trial balance to see whether a balance equal to half the error has been entered in the wrong column.
3. If the error is divisible by nine, retrace the account balances on the trial balance to see whether they are incorrectly copied from the ledger. For example, if a balance was $12 and it was listed as $21, a $9 error has been made. Reversing the order of numbers is called a transposition error.
4. If the error is not divisible by two or nine (for example, $365), scan the ledger to see whether an account balance of $365 has been omitted from the trial balance, and scan the journal to see whether a $365 posting has been omitted.

ACCOUNTING IN ACTION
Business Insight

One minute it was flying high, the next minute its very survival was uncertain. That is the story of Informix. It was the best-performing software stock between 1990 and 1995. In early 1997 it seemed well positioned to rival the giants in the industry. But then serious accounting errors and irregularities were detected by the company's auditors. Simply stated, the company had recorded transactions as sales which actually were not sales. Thus its revenues were overstated by as much as $200 million. Problems like this can lead to the ultimate demise of the company. Customers become reluctant to buy from the company because they fear that the company might fail, and consequently won't be available to support the product. Suppliers are reluctant to sell to the company because they fear they won't be paid. Valuable employees begin to leave the company in search of job security. Shareholders are suing the company because of financial losses they sustained when the company's stock price dropped by 35% in a single day after the announcement of the accounting irregularities. The Nasdaq Stock Market threatened to "delist" the company which would mean the company could not trade its shares on that exchange anymore. The company's outside auditor brought in 30 additional staff persons to get to the bottom of the problem. The bottom line is that accounting errors, whether intentional or unintentional, can be very costly.

Use of Dollar Signs

Note that dollar signs do not appear in the journals or ledgers. Dollar signs are usually used only in the trial balance and the financial statements. Generally, a dollar sign is shown only for the first item in the column and for the total of that column. A single line is placed under the column of figures to be added or subtracted; the total amount is double underlined to indicate the final sum.

BEFORE YOU GO ON . . .

Review It

1. What is a trial balance and how is it prepared?
2. What is the primary purpose of a trial balance?
3. What are the limitations of a trial balance?

A LOOK BACK AT OUR FEATURE STORY

Now that you have learned the details of the recording process, think back to the beginning of the chapter to Gabriella Torres and her position as office manager at Diabetes & Endocrine Associates, and answer the following questions:

1. What accounting entries would Gabriella be likely to make to record (a) the rent payment, (b) billing a patient for services provided, and (c) collecting cash from a patient on account.
2. In what way might Gabriella's day-time job as office manager help in her studies as a night student in accounting and business?
3. Prepare a likely list of asset accounts Gabriella has in her general ledger at Diabetes & Endocrine Associates.

Solution:

1. Gabriella would likely make the following entries:
   (a) Rent Expense
             Cash
                 (Paid rent)
   (b) Accounts Receivable
             Service Revenue
                 (Billed a patient for services provided)
   (c) Cash
             Accounts Receivable
                 (Collected cash for amount due)
2. As a result of her office manager's position, Gabriella is able to relate the subject matter as well as much of the assignment material in her business courses to a real-world context. From her job she knows how bills are paid; how to reconcile a bank statement; how employees are hired, managed, evaluated, and paid; how the individual accounts receivable accounts are maintained; how accounting functions are performed on a computer; and much more.
3. A likely list of asset accounts is: Cash, Accounts Receivable, Medical Supplies, Land and Building (if owned), Medical Equipment, Office Furniture and Fixtures, and Prepaid Insurance.

THE
NAVIGATOR

DEMONSTRATION PROBLEM

Bob Sample opened the Campus Laundromat on September 1, 1999. During the first month of operations the following transactions occurred:

Sept. 1 Invested $20,000 cash in the business.

2 Paid $1,000 cash for store rent for the month of September.

3 Purchased washers and dryers for $25,000 paying $10,000 in cash and signing a $15,000 6-month 12% note payable.

4 Paid $1,200 for one-year accident insurance policy.

10 Received bill from the Daily News for advertising the opening of the laundromat, $200.

20 Withdrew $700 cash for personal use.

30 Determined that cash receipts for laundry services for the month were $6,200.

The chart of accounts for the company is the same as in Pioneer Advertising Agency except for the following: No. 15 Laundry Equipment and No. 61 Advertising Expense.

Instructions

(a) Journalize the September transactions. (Use J1 for the journal page number.)

(b) Open ledger accounts and post the September transactions.

(c) Prepare a trial balance at September 30, 1999.

SOLUTION TO DEMONSTRATION PROBLEM

(a) **GENERAL JOURNAL** **J1**

Date	Account Titles and Explanation	Ref.	Debit	Credit
1999				
Sept. 1	Cash	1	20,000	
	Bob Sample, Capital	40		20,000
	(Owner's investment of cash in business)			
2	Rent Expense	62	1,000	
	Cash	1		1,000
	(Paid September rent)			
3	Laundry Equipment	15	25,000	
	Cash	1		10,000
	Notes Payable	25		15,000
	(Purchased laundry equipment for cash and 6-month 12% note payable)			
4	Prepaid Insurance	10	1,200	
	Cash	1		1,200
	(Paid one-year insurance policy)			
10	Advertising Expense	61	200	
	Accounts Payable	26		200
	(Received bill from Daily News for advertising)			
20	Bob Sample, Drawing	41	700	
	Cash	1		700
	(Withdrew cash for personal use)			
30	Cash	1	6,200	
	Service Revenue	50		6,200
	(Received cash for services provided)			

(b)

GENERAL LEDGER

Cash — No. 1

Date	Explanation	Ref.	Debit	Credit	Balance
1999					
Sept. 1		J1	20,000		20,000
2		J1		1,000	19,000
3		J1		10,000	9,000
4		J1		1,200	7,800
20		J1		700	7,100
30		J1	6,200		13,300

Prepaid Insurance — No. 10

Date	Explanation	Ref.	Debit	Credit	Balance
1999					
Sept. 4		J1	1,200		1,200

Laundry Equipment — No. 15

Date	Explanation	Ref.	Debit	Credit	Balance
1999					
Sept. 3		J1	25,000		25,000

Notes Payable — No. 25

Date	Explanation	Ref.	Debit	Credit	Balance
1999					
Sept. 3		J1		15,000	15,000

Accounts Payable — No. 26

Date	Explanation	Ref.	Debit	Credit	Balance
1999					
Sept. 10		J1		200	200

Bob Sample, Capital — No. 40

Date	Explanation	Ref.	Debit	Credit	Balance
1999					
Sept. 1		J1		20,000	20,000

Bob Sample, Drawing — No. 41

Date	Explanation	Ref.	Debit	Credit	Balance
1999					
Sept. 20		J1	700		700

Service Revenue — No. 50

Date	Explanation	Ref.	Debit	Credit	Balance
1999					
Sept. 30		J1		6,200	6,200

Advertising Expense — No. 61

Date	Explanation	Ref.	Debit	Credit	Balance
1999					
Sept. 10		J1	200		200

Rent Expense — No. 62

Date	Explanation	Ref.	Debit	Credit	Balance
1999					
Sept. 2		J1	1,000		1,000

(c)

CAMPUS LAUNDROMAT
Trial Balance
September 30, 1999

	Debit	Credit
Cash	$13,300	
Prepaid Insurance	1,200	
Laundry Equipment	25,000	
Notes Payable		$15,000
Accounts Payable		200
Bob Sample, Capital		20,000
Bob Sample, Drawing	700	
Service Revenue		6,200
Advertising Expense	200	
Rent Expense	1,000	
	$41,400	$41,400

THE NAVIGATOR

SUMMARY OF STUDY OBJECTIVES

1. *Explain what an account is and how it helps in the recording process.* An account is an individual accounting record of increases and decreases in specific asset, liability, and owner's equity items.

2. *Define debits and credits and explain how they are used to record business transactions.* The terms debit and credit are synonymous with left and right. Assets, drawings, and expenses are increased by debits and decreased by credits. Liabilities, owner's capital, and revenues are increased by credits and decreased by debits.

3. *Identify the basic steps in the recording process.* The basic steps in the recording process are: (a) analyze each transaction in terms of its effect on the accounts, (b) enter the transaction information in a journal, (c) transfer the journal information to the appropriate accounts in the ledger.

4. *Explain what a journal is and how it helps in the recording process.* The initial accounting record of a transaction is entered in a journal before the data are entered in the accounts. A journal (a) discloses in one place the complete effect of a transaction, (b) provides a chronological record of transactions, and (c) prevents or locates errors because the debit and credit amounts for each entry can be readily compared.

5. *Explain what a ledger is and how it helps in the recording process.* The entire group of accounts maintained by a company is referred to collectively as a ledger. The ledger keeps in one place all the information about changes in specific account balances.

6. *Explain what posting is and how it helps in the recording process.* Posting is the procedure of transferring journal entries to the ledger accounts. This phase of the recording process accumulates the effects of journalized transactions in the individual accounts.

7. *Prepare a trial balance and explain its purposes.* A trial balance is a list of accounts and their balances at a given time. The primary purpose of the trial balance is to prove the mathematical equality of debits and credits after posting. A trial balance also uncovers errors in journalizing and posting and is useful in preparing financial statements.

THE NAVIGATOR

GLOSSARY

Account An individual accounting record of increases and decreases in specific asset, liability, or owner's equity items. (p. 46).

Chart of accounts A list of accounts and the account numbers which identify their location in the ledger. (p. 58).

Compound entry An entry that involves three or more accounts. (p. 54).

Credit The right side of an account. (p. 47).

Debit The left side of an account. (p. 47).

Double-entry system A system that records the dual effect of each transaction in appropriate accounts. (p. 48).

General journal The most basic form of journal. (p. 52).

General ledger A ledger that contains all asset, liability, and owner's equity accounts. (p. 55).

Journal An accounting record in which transactions are initially recorded in chronological order. (p. 52).

Journalizing The procedure of entering transaction data in the journal. (p. 53).

Ledger The entire group of accounts maintained by a company. (p. 55).

Posting The procedure of transferring journal entries to the ledger accounts. (p. 56).

Simple entry An entry that involves only two accounts. (p. 54).

T account The basic form of an account. (p. 46).

Three-column form of account A form containing money columns for debit, credit, and balance amounts in an account. (p. 56).

Trial balance A list of accounts and their balances at a given time. (p. 66).

SELF-STUDY QUESTIONS

Answers are at the end of the chapter.

(SO 1) 1. Which of the following statements about an account is true?
   a. In its simplest form, an account consists of two parts.
   b. An account is an individual accounting record of increases and decreases in specific asset, liability, and owner's equity items.
   c. There are separate accounts for specific assets and liabilities but only one account for owner's equity items.

   d. The left side of an account is the credit or decrease side.

2. Debits: (SO 2)
   a. increase both assets and liabilities.
   b. decrease both assets and liabilities.
   c. increase assets and decrease liabilities.
   d. decrease assets and increase liabilities.

3. A revenue account: (SO 2)
   a. is increased by debits.
   b. is decreased by credits.

c. has a normal balance of a debit.
d. is increased by credits.

(SO 2)   4. Accounts that normally have debit balances are:
a. assets, expenses, and revenues.
b. assets, expenses, and owner's capital.
c. assets, liabilities, and owner's drawings.
d. assets, owner's drawings, and expenses.

(SO 3)   5. Which of the following is *not* part of the recording process?
a. Analyzing transactions.
b. Preparing a trial balance.
c. Entering transactions in a journal.
d. Posting transactions.

(SO 4)   6. Which of the following statements about a journal is false?
a. It is not a book of original entry.
b. It provides a chronological record of transactions.
c. It helps to locate errors because the debit and credit amounts for each entry can be readily compared.
d. It discloses in one place the complete effect of a transaction.

(SO 5)   7. A ledger:
a. contains only asset and liability accounts.
b. should show accounts in alphabetical order.

c. is a collection of the entire group of accounts maintained by a company.
d. is a book of original entry.

8. Posting: **(SO 6)**
a. normally occurs before journalizing.
b. transfers ledger transaction data to the journal.
c. is an optional step in the recording process.
d. transfers journal entries to ledger accounts.

9. A trial balance: **(SO 7)**
a. is a list of accounts with their balances at a given time.
b. proves the mathematical accuracy of journalized transactions.
c. will not balance if a correct journal entry is posted twice.
d. proves that all transactions have been recorded.

10. A trial balance will not balance if: **(SO 7)**
a. a correct journal entry is posted twice.
b. the purchase of supplies on account is debited to Supplies and credited to Cash.
c. a $100 cash drawing by the owner is debited to Owner's Drawing for $1,000 and credited to Cash for $100.
d. a $450 payment on account is debited to Accounts Payable for $45 and credited to Cash for $45.

THE NAVIGATOR

QUESTIONS

1. Describe a T account.

2. The terms *debit* and *credit* mean increase and decrease, respectively. Do you agree? Explain.

3. Omar Morena, a fellow student, contends that the double-entry system means each transaction must be recorded twice. Is Omar correct? Explain.

4. Kim Nguyen, a beginning accounting student, believes debit balances are favorable and credit balances are unfavorable. Is Kim correct? Discuss.

5. State the rules of debit and credit as applied to (a) asset accounts, (b) liability accounts, and (c) the owner's equity accounts (revenue, expenses, owner's drawing, and owner's capital).

6. What is the normal balance for each of the following accounts? (a) Accounts Receivable. (b) Cash. (c) Owner's Drawing. (d) Accounts Payable. (e) Service Revenue. (f) Salaries Expense. (g) Owner's Capital.

7. Indicate whether each of the following accounts is an asset, a liability, or an owner's equity account and whether it has a normal debit or credit balance: (a) Accounts Receivable, (b) Accounts Payable, (c) Equipment, (d) Owner's Drawing, (e) Supplies.

8. For the following transactions, indicate the account debited and the account credited:
(a) Supplies are purchased on account.
(b) Cash is received on signing a note payable.
(c) Employees are paid salaries in cash.

9. Presented below is a series of accounts. Indicate whether these accounts generally will have (a) debit entries only, (b) credit entries only, (c) both debit and credit entries.
(1) Cash.   (4) Accounts Payable.
(2) Accounts Receivable.   (5) Salaries Expense.
(3) Owner's Drawing.   (6) Service Revenue.

10. What are the basic steps in the recording process?

11. What are the advantages of using a journal in the recording process?

12. (a) When entering a transaction in the journal, should the debit or credit be written first?
(b) Which should be indented, the debit or credit?

13. Describe a compound entry and provide an example of a compound entry.

14. (a) Should business transaction debits and credits be recorded directly in the ledger accounts?
(b) What are the advantages of first recording transactions in the journal and then posting to the ledger?

15. The account number is entered as the last step in posting the amounts from the journal to the ledger. What is the advantage of this step?

16. Journalize the following business transactions.
(a) Dana O'Shea invests $9,000 cash in the business.
(b) Insurance of $800 is paid for the year.
(c) Supplies of $1,500 are purchased on account.
(d) Cash of $7,500 is received for services rendered.

17. (a) What is a ledger?
    (b) What is a chart of accounts and why is it important?
18. What is a trial balance and what are its purposes?
19. Ira Hirsch is confused about how accounting information flows through the accounting system. He believes the flow of information is as follows:
    (a) Debits and credits posted to the ledger.
    (b) Business transaction occurs.
    (c) Information entered in the journal.
    (d) Financial statements are prepared.
    (e) Trial balance is prepared.

Is Ira correct? If not, indicate to Ira the proper flow of the information.

20. Two students are discussing the use of a trial balance. They wonder whether the following errors, each considered separately, would prevent the trial balance from balancing.
    (a) The bookkeeper debited Cash for $600 and credited Wages Expense for $600 for payment of wages.
    (b) Cash collected on account was debited to Cash for $900 and Service Revenue was credited for $90. What would you tell them?

BRIEF EXERCISES

Indicate debit and credit effects and normal balance.
(SO 2)

BE2–1 For each of the following accounts indicate the effects of (a) a debit and (b) a credit on the accounts and (c) the normal balance of the account.

1. Accounts Payable.
2. Advertising Expense.
3. Service Revenue.
4. Accounts Receivable.
5. B. C. Jardine, Capital.
6. B. C. Jardine, Drawing.

Identify accounts to be debited and credited.
(SO 2)

BE2–2 Transactions for the A. D. Ing Company for the month of June are presented below. Identify the accounts to be debited and credited for each transaction.

June 1   A. D. Ing invests $2,000 cash in a small welding business of which he is the sole proprietor.
       2   Purchase of equipment on account for $900.
       3   $500 cash is paid to landlord for June rent.
      12   Bills T. Sargento $300 for welding work done on account.

Journalize transactions.
(SO 4)

BE2–3 Using the data in BE2–2, journalize the transactions. (You may omit explanations.)

Identify and explain steps in recording process.
(SO 3)

BE2–4 ✏️➤ M. Thompson, a fellow student, is unclear about the basic steps in the recording process. Identify and briefly explain the steps in the order in which they occur.

Indicate basic and debit-credit analysis.
(SO 4)

BE2–5 A. Fisher has the following transactions during August of the current year. Indicate (a) the effect on the accounting equation and (b) the debit-credit analysis illustrated on pages 59–64 of the text.

Aug. 1   Opens an office as a financial advisor, investing $6,000 in cash.
       4   Pays insurance in advance for 6 months, $1,800 cash.
      16   Receives $900 from clients for services rendered.
      27   Pays secretary $500 salary.

Journalize transactions.
(SO 4)

BE2–6 Using the data in BE2–5, journalize the transactions. (You may omit explanations.)

Post journal entries to T accounts.
(SO 6)

BE2–7 Selected transactions for the Fernandez Company are presented in journal form below. Post the transactions to T accounts. Make one T account for each item and determine each account's ending balance.

J1

Date	Account Titles and Explanation	Ref.	Debit	Credit
May 5	Accounts Receivable		4,000	
	Service Revenue			4,000
	(Billed for services provided)			
12	Cash		2,400	
	Accounts Receivable			2,400
	(Received cash in payment of account)			
15	Cash		2,000	
	Service Revenue			2,000
	(Received cash for services provided)			

BE2–8 Selected journal entries for the Fernandez Company are presented in BE2–7. Post the transactions using the standard form of account.

Post journal entries to standard form of account.
(SO 6)

BE2–9 From the ledger balances given below, prepare a trial balance for the D. Beirsdorf Company at June 30, 1999. List the accounts in the order shown on page 67 of the text. All account balances are normal.

Prepare a trial balance.
(SO 7)

　　Accounts Payable $5,000, Cash $4,800, D. Beirsdorf, Capital $20,000, D. Beirsdorf, Drawing $1,200, Equipment $17,000, Service Revenue $6,000, Accounts Receivable $3,000, Salaries Expense $4,000, and Rent Expense $1,000.

BE2–10 An inexperienced bookkeeper prepared the following trial balance that does not balance. Prepare a correct trial balance, assuming all account balances are normal.

Prepare a correct trial balance.
(SO 7)

LOPEZ COMPANY
Trial Balance
December 31, 1999

	Debit	Credit
Cash	$16,800	
Prepaid Insurance		$ 3,500
Accounts Payable		3,000
Unearned Revenue	2,200	
P. Lopez, Capital		15,000
P. Lopez, Drawing		4,500
Service Revenue		25,600
Salaries Expense	18,600	
Rent Expense		2,400
	$37,600	$54,000

EXERCISES

E2–1 Selected transactions for L. Visser, an interior decorator, in her first month of business, are as follows:

Identify debits, credits, and normal balances.
(SO 2)

Jan.　2　Invested $8,000 cash in business.
　　　3　Purchased used car for $4,000 cash for use in business.
　　　9　Purchased supplies on account for $500.
　　11　Billed customers $1,800 for services performed.
　　16　Paid $200 cash for advertising start of business.
　　20　Received $700 cash from customers billed on January 11.
　　23　Paid creditor $300 cash on account.
　　28　Withdrew $500 cash for personal use of owner.

Instructions
For each transaction indicate (a) the basic type of account debited and credited (asset, liability, owner's equity); (b) the specific account debited and credited (cash, rent expense, service revenue, etc.); (c) whether the specific account is increased or decreased; and (d) the normal balance of the specific account. Use the following format, in which the January 2 transaction is given as an example:

	Account Debited				Account Credited			
Date	(a) Basic Type	(b) Specific Account	(c) Effect	(d) Normal Balance	(a) Basic Type	(b) Specific Account	(c) Effect	(d) Normal Balance
Jan. 2	Asset	Cash	Increase	Debit	Owner's Equity	L. Visser, Capital	Increase	Credit

E2–2 Data for L. Visser, interior decorator, are presented in E2–1.

Journalize transactions and post using standard account form.
(SO 4)

Instructions
Journalize the transactions using journal page J1. (You may omit explanations.)

Analyze transactions and determine their effect on accounts.
(SO 2)

E2–3 Presented below is information related to Sam Stine Real Estate Agency:

Oct. 1 Sam Stine begins business as a real estate agent with a cash investment of $15,000.
  2 Hires an administrative assistant.
  3 Purchases office furniture for $1,900, on account.
  6 Sells a house and lot for C. Clark; bills Clark $3,200 for realty services provided.
 27 Pays $700 on the balance related to the transaction of October 3.
 30 Pays the administrative assistant $1,050 in salary for October.

Instructions
Prepare the debit-credit analysis for each transaction as illustrated on pages 59–64.

Journalize transactions.
(SO 4)

E2–4 Transaction data for Stine Real Estate Agency are presented in E2–3.

Instructions
Journalize the transactions. Explanations may be omitted.

Post journal entries and prepare a trial balance.
(SO 6, 7)

E2–5 Selected transactions from the journal of J. L. Meche, investment broker, are presented below.

Date	Account Titles and Explanation	Ref.	Debit	Credit
Aug. 1	Cash		2,600	
	J. L. Meche, Capital			2,600
	(Owner's investment of cash in business)			
10	Cash		2,400	
	Service Revenue			2,400
	(Received cash for services provided)			
12	Office Equipment		4,000	
	Cash			1,000
	Notes Payable			3,000
	(Purchased office equipment for cash and notes payable)			
25	Accounts Receivable		1,400	
	Service Revenue			1,400
	(Billed for services provided)			
31	Cash		900	
	Accounts Receivable			900
	(Receipt of cash on account)			

Instructions
(a) Post the transactions to T accounts.
(b) Prepare a trial balance at August 31, 1999.

Journalize transactions from account data and prepare a trial balance.
(SO 4, 7)

E2–6 The T accounts below summarize the ledger of Doty Landscaping Company at the end of the first month of operations:

Cash No. 101

4/1	6,000	4/15	600
4/12	900	4/25	1,500
4/29	400		
4/30	800		

Unearned Revenue No. 205

4/30	800

Accounts Receivable No. 112

4/7	3,200	4/29	400

D. Doty, Capital No. 301

4/1	6,000

Supplies No. 126

4/4	1,800

Service Revenue No. 400

4/7	3,200
4/12	900

Accounts Payable No. 201

4/25	1,500	4/4	1,800

Salaries Expense No. 726

4/15	600

Instructions

(a) Prepare the complete general journal (including explanations) from which the postings to Cash were made.

(b) Prepare a trial balance at April 30, 1999.

E2–7   Presented below is the ledger for McBride Co.

Journalize transactions from account data and prepare a trial balance.
(SO 4, 7)

Cash		No. 101	
10/1	5,000	10/4	400
10/10	650	10/12	1,500
10/10	5,000	10/15	250
10/20	500	10/30	300
10/25	2,000	10/31	500

McBride, Capital		No. 301	
		10/1	5,000
		10/25	2,000

McBride, Drawing		No. 306	
10/30	300		

Accounts Receivable		No. 112	
10/6	800	10/20	500
10/20	940		

Service Revenue		No. 407	
		10/6	800
		10/10	650
		10/20	940

Supplies		No. 126	
10/4	400		

Store Wages Expense		No. 628	
10/31	500		

Furniture		No. 149	
10/3	2,000		

Rent Expense		No. 729	
10/15	250		

Notes Payable		No. 200	
		10/10	5,000

Accounts Payable		No. 201	
10/12	1,500	10/3	2,000

Instructions

(a) Reproduce the journal entries for the transactions that occurred on October 1, 10, and 20 and provide explanations for each.

(b) Determine the October 31 balance for each of the accounts above and prepare a trial balance at October 31, 1999.

E2–8   Selected transactions for the Tracy Lawrence Company during its first month in business are presented below.

Prepare journal entries and post using standard account form.
(SO 4, 6)

Sept. 1   Invested $12,000 cash in the business.

5   Purchased equipment for $10,000 paying $5,000 in cash and the balance on account.

25   Paid $3,000 cash on balance owed for equipment.

30   Withdrew $500 cash for personal use.

Lawrence's chart of accounts shows: Cash, No. 101; Equipment, No. 157; and Accounts Payable, No. 201; Tracy Lawrence, Capital, No. 301; and Tracy Lawrence, Drawing, No. 306.

Instructions

(a) Journalize the transactions on page J1 of the journal.

(b) Post the transactions using the standard account form.

E2–9   The bookkeeper for Gary Allen Equipment Repair made a number of errors in journalizing and posting, as described below:

Analyze errors and their effects on trial balance.
(SO 7)

1. A credit posting of $400 to Accounts Receivable was omitted.

2. A debit posting of $750 for Prepaid Insurance was debited to Insurance Expense.

3. A collection on account of $100 was journalized and posted as a debit to Cash $100 and a credit to Service Revenue $100.

4. A credit posting of $300 to Property Taxes Payable was made twice.
5. A cash purchase of supplies for $250 was journalized and posted as a debit to Supplies $25 and a credit to Cash $25.
6. A debit of $465 to Advertising Expense was posted as $456.

Instructions
For each error, indicate (a) whether the trial balance will balance; if the trial balance will not balance, indicate (b) the amount of the difference, and (c) the trial balance column that will have the larger total. Consider each error separately. Use the following form, in which error (1) is given as an example.

Error	(a) In Balance	(b) Difference	(c) Larger Column
(1)	No	$400	debit

Prepare a trial balance.
(SO 2, 7)

E2–10   The accounts in the ledger of Always Late Delivery Service contain the following balances on July 31, 1999:

Accounts Receivable	$ 7,642	Prepaid Insurance	$ 1,968
Accounts Payable	8,396	Repair Expense	961
Cash	?	Service Revenue	10,610
Delivery Equipment	49,360	J. S. Bach, Drawing	700
Gas and Oil Expense	758	J. S. Bach, Capital	44,636
Insurance Expense	523	Salaries Expense	4,428
Notes Payable	18,450	Salaries Payable	815

Instructions
Prepare a trial balance with the accounts arranged as illustrated in the chapter and fill in the missing amount for Cash.

PROBLEMS: SET A

Journalize a series of transactions.
(SO 2, 4)

P2–1A   The Four Oaks Miniature Golf and Driving Range was opened on March 1 by Joe MacKey. The following selected events and transactions occurred during March:

Mar. 1   Invested $45,000 cash in the business.

3   Purchased Lee's Golf Land for $38,000 cash. The price consists of land, $23,000, building, $9,000, and equipment, $6,000. (Make one compound entry.)

5   Advertised the opening of the driving range and miniature golf course, paying advertising expenses of $1,600.

6   Paid cash $1,480 for a one-year insurance policy.

10   Purchased golf clubs and other equipment for $1,600 from Palmer Company payable in 30 days.

18   Received $800 in cash for golf fees earned.

19   Sold 100 coupon books for $15.00 each. Each book contains 10 coupons that enable the holder to one round of miniature golf or to hit one bucket of golf balls.

25   Withdrew $500 cash for personal use.

30   Paid salaries of $600.

30   Paid Palmer Company in full.

31   Received $500 cash for fees earned.

Joe MacKey uses the following accounts: Cash; Prepaid Insurance; Land; Buildings; Equipment; Accounts Payable; Unearned Revenue; Joe MacKey, Capital; Joe MacKey, Drawing; Golf Revenue; Advertising Expense; and Salaries Expense.

Instructions
Journalize the March transactions.

P2–2A Maria Rojas is a licensed architect. During the first month of the operation of her business, the following events and transactions occurred.

Journalize transactions, post, and prepare a trial balance.
(SO 2, 4, 6, 7)

April 1 Invested $15,000 cash.

   1 Hired a secretary-receptionist at a salary of $300 per week payable monthly.

   2 Paid office rent for the month, $800.

   3 Purchased architectural supplies on account from Halo Company, $1,500.

   10 Completed blueprints on a carport and billed client $900 for services.

   11 Received $500 cash advance from R. Welk for the design of a new home.

   20 Received $1,500 cash for services completed and delivered to P. Donahue.

   30 Paid secretary-receptionist for the month, $1,200.

   30 Paid $600 to Halo Company on account.

Maria uses the following chart of accounts: No. 101 Cash, No. 112 Accounts Receivable, No. 126 Supplies, No. 201 Accounts Payable, No. 205 Unearned Revenue, No. 301 Maria Rojas, Capital, No. 400 Service Revenue, No. 726 Salaries Expense, and No. 729 Rent Expense.

Instructions
   (a) Journalize the transactions.
   (b) Post to the ledger accounts.
   (c) Prepare a trial balance on April 30, 1999.

P2–3A The trial balance of Judy's Laundry on September 30 is shown below:

Journalize transactions, post, and prepare a trial balance.
(SO 2, 4, 6, 7)

JUDY'S LAUNDRY
Trial Balance
September 30, 1999

Account No.		Debit	Credit
101	Cash	$ 8,500	
112	Accounts Receivable	2,200	
126	Supplies	1,700	
157	Equipment	8,000	
201	Accounts Payable		$ 5,000
206	Unearned Laundry Revenue		700
301	Judy Kylie, Capital		14,700
		$20,400	$20,400

The October transactions were as follows:

Oct. 5 Received $800 cash from customers on account.

   10 Billed customers for services performed $5,500.

   15 Paid employee salaries $1,200.

   20 Paid $1,600 to creditors on account.

   29 Withdrew $500 for personal use.

   31 Paid utilities $500.

Instructions
   (a) Enter the opening balances in the ledger accounts as of October 1. Write "Balance" in the explanation space and insert a check mark (√) in the reference column. Provision should be made for the following additional accounts: No. 306 Judy Kylie, Drawing; No. 426 Laundry Revenue; No. 726 Salaries Expense; and No. 732 Utilities Expense.
   (b) Journalize the transactions.
   (c) Post to the ledger accounts.
   (d) Prepare a trial balance on October 31, 1999.

P2–4A The trial balance of Tim Winau Co. shown below does not balance.

TIM WINAU CO.
Trial Balance
June 30, 1999

	Debit	Credit
Cash		$ 2,840
Accounts Receivable	$ 3,231	
Supplies	800	
Equipment	3,000	
Accounts Payable		2,666
Unearned Revenue	1,200	
T. Winau, Capital		9,000
T. Winau, Drawing	800	
Service Revenue		2,380
Salaries Expense	3,400	
Office Expense	910	
	$13,341	$16,886

Each of the listed accounts has a normal balance per the general ledger. An examination of the ledger and journal reveals the following errors.

1. Cash received from a customer on account was debited for $470 and Accounts Receivable was credited for the same amount. The actual collection was for $740.
2. The purchase of a typewriter on account for $340 was recorded as a debit to Supplies for $340 and a credit to Accounts Payable for $340.
3. Services were performed on account for a client for $890. Accounts Receivable was debited for $890 and Service Revenue was credited for $89.
4. A debit posting to Salaries Expense of $600 was omitted.
5. A payment on account for $206 was credited to Cash for $206 and credited to Accounts Payable for $260.
6. The withdrawal of $500 cash for Winau's personal use was debited to Salaries Expense for $500 and credited to Cash for $500.

Instructions
Prepare a correct trial balance. *Hint:* It helps to prepare the correct journal entry for the transaction described and compare it to the mistake made.

P2–5A The Starlite Theater, owned by Lee Baroni, will begin operations in March. The Starlite will be unique in that it will show only triple features of sequential theme movies. As of February 28, the ledger of Starlite showed: No. 101 Cash $16,000; No. 140 Land $42,000; No. 145 Buildings (concession stand, projection room, ticket booth, and screen) $18,000; No. 157 Equipment $16,000; No. 201 Accounts Payable $12,000; and No. 301 L. Baroni, Capital $80,000. During the month of March the following events and transactions occurred:

Mar. 2 Acquired the three *Star Wars* movies (*Star Wars*, *The Empire Strikes Back*, and *The Return of the Jedi*) to be shown for the first 3 weeks of March. The film rental was $9,000; $3,000 was paid in cash and $6,000 will be paid on March 10.

   3 Ordered the first three *Star Trek* movies to be shown the last 10 days of March. It will cost $300 per night.

   9 Received $6,500 cash from admissions.

  10 Paid balance due on *Star Wars* movies rental and $3,000 on February 28 accounts payable.

  11 Starlite Theater contracted with M. Brewer Company to operate the concession stand. Brewer is to pay 15% of gross concession receipts (payable monthly) for the right to operate the concession stand.

  12 Paid advertising expenses $800.

  20 Received $7,200 cash from admissions.

  20 Received the *Star Trek* movies and paid the rental fee of $3,000.

  31 Paid salaries of $3,800.

31   Received statement from M. Brewer showing gross receipts from concessions of
$8,000 and the balance due to Starlite Theater of $1,200 ($8,000 × 15%) for March.
Brewer paid one-half the balance due and will remit the remainder on April 5.

31   Received $12,500 cash from admissions.

In addition to the accounts identified above, the chart of accounts includes: No. 112 Accounts
Receivable, No. 405 Admission Revenue, No. 406 Concession Revenue, No. 610 Advertising
Expense, No. 632 Film Rental Expense, and No. 726 Salaries Expense.

Instructions
   (a) Enter the beginning balances to the ledger. Insert a check mark (√) in the reference
        column of the ledger for the beginning balance.
   (b) Journalize the March transactions.
   (c) Post the March journal entries to the ledger. Assume that all entries are posted from
        page 1 of the journal.
   (d) Prepare a trial balance on March 31, 1999.

PROBLEMS: SET B

P2–1B   The Adventure Park was started on April 1 by Al Rossy. The following selected events
and transactions occurred during April.

Journalize a series of transactions.
(SO 2, 4)

Apr. 1   Rossy invested $50,000 cash in the business.
      4   Purchased land costing $30,000 for cash.
      8   Incurred advertising expense of $1,800 on account.
     11   Paid salaries to employees $1,500.
     12   Hired park manager at a salary of $4,000 per month, effective May 1.
     13   Paid $1,500 cash for a one-year insurance policy.
     17   Withdrew $600 cash for personal use.
     20   Received $5,700 in cash for admission fees.
     25   Sold 100 coupon books for $25 each. Each book contains 10 coupons that entitle
           the holder to one admission to the park.
     30   Received $5,900 in cash admission fees.
     30   Paid $700 on account for advertising incurred on April 8.

Al Rossy uses the following accounts: Cash; Prepaid Insurance; Land; Accounts Payable; Unearned Admissions Revenue; Al Rossy, Capital; Al Rossy, Drawing; Admission Revenue; Advertising Expense; and Salaries Expense.

Instructions
Journalize the April transactions.

P2–2B   Lisa Heins is a licensed CPA. During the first month of operations of her business,
the following events and transactions occurred:

Journalize transactions, post, and prepare a trial balance.
(SO 2, 4, 6, 7)

May 1   Heins invested $32,000 cash.
     2   Hired a secretary-receptionist at a salary of $1,000 per month.
     3   Purchased $1,200 of supplies on account from Read Supply Company.
     7   Paid office rent of $900 cash for the month.
    11   Completed a tax assignment and billed client $1,100 for services rendered.
    12   Received $3,500 advance on a management consulting engagement.
    17   Received cash of $1,200 for services completed for H. Arnold Co.
    31   Paid secretary-receptionist $1,000 salary for the month.
    31   Paid 40% of balance due Read Supply Company.

Lisa uses the following chart of accounts: No. 101 Cash, No. 112 Accounts Receivable, No. 126
Supplies, No. 201 Accounts Payable, No. 205 Unearned Revenue, No. 301 Lisa Heins, Capital,
No. 400 Service Revenue, No. 726 Salaries Expense, and No. 729 Rent Expense.

Instructions
(a) Journalize the transactions.
(b) Post to the ledger accounts.
(c) Prepare a trial balance on May 31, 1999.

Journalize transactions, post,
and prepare a trial balance.
(SO 2, 4, 6, 7)

P2–3B   The trial balance of Steiner Dry Cleaners on June 30 is shown below.

STEINER DRY CLEANERS
Trial Balance
June 30, 1999

Account No.		Debit	Credit
101	Cash	$12,532	
112	Accounts Receivable	10,536	
126	Supplies	4,844	
157	Equipment	25,950	
201	Accounts Payable		$15,878
206	Unearned Revenue		1,730
301	C. Steiner, Capital		36,254
		$53,862	$53,862

The July transactions were as follows:

July 8   Collected $5,936 in cash related to June 30 accounts receivable.
     9   Paid employee salaries $2,100.
    11   Received $4,325 in cash for services rendered.
    14   Paid June 30 creditors $10,750 on account.
    17   Purchased supplies on account $554.
    22   Billed customers for services rendered, $5,700.
    30   Paid employee salaries $3,114, utilities $1,384, and repairs $692, all in cash.
    31   Withdrew $700 cash for personal use of owner.

Instructions
(a) Enter the opening balances in the ledger accounts as of July 1. Write "Balance" in the explanation space and insert a check mark (√) in the reference column. Provision should be made for the following additional accounts: No. 306 C. Steiner, Drawing; No. 428 Dry Cleaning Revenue; No. 622 Repair Expense; No. 726 Salaries Expense; and No. 732 Utilities Expense.
(b) Journalize the transactions.
(c) Post to the ledger accounts.
(d) Prepare a trial balance on July 31, 1999.

Prepare a correct trial balance.
(SO 7)

P2–4B   The trial balance of the Shawnee Company shown below does not balance.

SHAWNEE COMPANY
Trial Balance
May 31, 1999

	Debit	Credit
Cash	$ 5,850	
Accounts Receivable		$ 2,750
Prepaid Insurance	700	
Equipment	8,000	
Accounts Payable		4,500
Property Taxes Payable	560	
M. Flynn, Capital		11,700
Service Revenue	6,690	
Salaries Expense	4,200	
Advertising Expense		1,100
Property Tax Expense	800	
	$26,800	$20,050

Your review of the ledger reveals that each account has a normal balance. You also discover the following errors.

1. The totals of the debit sides of Prepaid Insurance, Accounts Payable, and Property Tax Expense were each understated $100.
2. Transposition errors were made in Accounts Receivable and Service Revenue. Based on postings made, the correct balances were $2,570 and $6,960, respectively.
3. A debit posting to Salaries Expense of $200 was omitted.
4. A $700 cash drawing by the owner was debited to M. Flynn, Capital for $700 and credited to Cash for $700.
5. A $520 purchase of supplies on account was debited to Equipment for $520 and credited to Cash for $520.
6. A cash payment of $250 for advertising was debited to Advertising Expense for $25 and credited to Cash for $25.
7. A collection from a customer for $210 was debited to Cash for $210 and credited to Accounts Payable for $210.

Instructions
Prepare a correct trial balance. (Note: The chart of accounts includes the following: M. A. Flynn, Drawing; Supplies; and Supplies Expense.) *Hint:* It helps to prepare the correct journal entry for the transaction described and compare it to the mistake made.

P2–5B The Grand Theater is owned by Fran Holley. All facilities were completed on March 31. At this time, the ledger showed: No. 101 Cash $6,000; No. 140 Land $10,000; No. 145 Buildings (concession stand, projection room, ticket booth, and screen) $8,000; No. 157 Equipment $6,000; No. 201 Accounts Payable $2,000; No. 275 Mortgage Payable $8,000; and No. 301 Fran Holley, Capital $20,000. During April, the following events and transactions occurred.

Journalize transactions, post, and prepare a trial balance.
(SO 2, 4, 6, 7)

Apr. 2 Paid film rental of $800 on first movie.
  3 Ordered two additional films at $500 each.
  9 Received $1,800 cash from admissions.
  10 Made $2,000 payment on mortgage and $1,000 on accounts payable.
  11 Grand Theater contracted with R. Thoms Company to operate the concession stand. Thoms is to pay 17% of gross concession receipts (payable monthly) for the right to operate the concession stand.
  12 Paid advertising expenses $300.
  20 Received one of the films ordered on April 3 and was billed $500. The film will be shown in April.
  25 Received $5,200 cash from admissions.
  29 Paid salaries $1,600.
  30 Received statement from R. Thoms showing gross concession receipts of $1,000 and the balance due to The Lake Theater of $170 ($1,000 × 17%) for April. Thoms paid one-half of the balance due and will remit the remainder on May 5.
  30 Prepaid $700 rental on special film to be run in May.

In addition to the accounts identified above, the chart of accounts shows: No. 112 Accounts Receivable, No. 136 Prepaid Rentals, No. 405 Admission Revenue, No. 406 Concession Revenue, No. 610 Advertising Expense, No. 632 Film Rental Expense, and No. 726 Salaries Expense.

Instructions
(a) Enter the beginning balances in the ledger as of April 1. Insert a check mark (√) in the reference column of the ledger for the beginning balance.
(b) Journalize the April transactions.
(c) Post the April journal entries to the ledger. Assume that all entries are posted from page 1 of the journal.
(d) Prepare a trial balance on April 30, 1999.

BROADENING YOUR PERSPECTIVE

FINANCIAL REPORTING AND ANALYSIS
••

FINANCIAL REPORTING PROBLEM: Kellogg Company

BYP2–1   The financial statements of Kellogg Company are presented in Appendix A and the notes accompanying the statements contain the following selected accounts, stated in millions of dollars:

Accounts Payable	$ 328.0	Notes Payable	$368.6
Accounts Receivable	587.5	Interest Expense	108.3
Property, net	2,773.3	Inventories	434.3

Instructions

(a) Answer the following questions:
  1. What is the increase and decrease side for each account?
  2. What is the normal balance for each account?
(b) Identify the probable other account in the transaction and the effect on that account when:
  1. Accounts Receivable is decreased.
  2. Accounts Payable is decreased.
  3. Inventories are increased.
(c) Identify the other account(s) that ordinarily would be involved when:
  1. Interest Expense is increased.
  2. Property is increased.

COMPARATIVE ANALYSIS PROBLEM: Kellogg Company vs. General Mills

BYP2–2   Kellogg's financial statements are presented in Appendix A; General Mills's financial statements are presented in Appendix B.

Instructions

(a) Based on the information contained in the financial statements, determine the normal balance of the listed accounts for each company:

Kellogg's	General Mills's
1. Inventories	1. Accounts receivable
2. Property, net	2. Land
3. Accounts payable	3. Depreciation expense
4. Interest expense	4. Sales (revenue)

(b) Identify the other account ordinarily involved when:
  1. Accounts receivable is increased.
  2. Accrued payroll is decreased.
  3. Property is increased.
  4. Interest expense is increased.

RESEARCH ASSIGNMENT

BYP2–3   Several commonly available indexes enable individuals to locate articles previously included in numerous business publications and periodicals. Articles can generally be searched for by company or by subject matter. Four common indexes are *The Wall Street Journal Index*, *Business Abstracts* (formerly the *Business Periodical Index*), *Predicasts F&S Index*, and *ABI/ Inform*. (*Note:* Your library may have hard copy or CD-ROM versions of these indexes.)

Instructions

Use one of these resources to find an article about a New York Stock Exchange company of your choosing. Read the article and answer the following questions.

(a) What is the article about?
(b) What company-specific information is included in the article?
(c) Is the article related to anything you read in Chapter 2 of your accounting textbook?
(d) Identify any accounting-related issues discussed in the article.

INTERPRETING FINANCIAL STATEMENTS: Bob Evans Farms, Inc.

BYP2–4   Bob Evans Farms, Inc. operates 354 restaurants and several food processing plants. The food processing plants primarily process pork into sausage, some of which is used in the restaurants, and some of which is sold to grocery stores. The food processing plants also produce "fast-food"-type frozen sandwiches, which are marketed to grocery stores.

The balance sheet of Bob Evans Farms showed a cash balance of $10 million and trade accounts receivable of $16 million. The notes to the financial statements revealed that there was a line of credit available of $63 million, of which $26 million was then outstanding.

Instructions

(a) Explain why most of the trade accounts receivable would probably not pertain to the restaurant business.
(b) What kind of individuals or companies would you expect to find in the individual accounts receivable accounts?
(c) Why might Bob Evans Farms be keeping the $10 million in cash, instead of using most of it, for example $8 million, to help pay off the line of credit debt?

REAL-WORLD FOCUS: Automated Security Holdings

BYP2–5   **Automated Security Holdings** operates multinationally, with principal markets in the United States and the United Kingdom. The company designs, produces, installs, and maintains security systems to safeguard life and property from a wide range of hazards. The markets for these security products include commercial, industrial, and residential customers.

The following notes to the financial statements identify a few of the accounts found in the general ledger.

AUTOMATED SECURITY HOLDINGS Notes to the Financial Statements		
	November 30,	
	Previous Year	Current Year
	(in thousands)	
Income Tax Payable	$ 3,929	$ 3,919
Accounts Payable	6,499	9,620
Salaries Expense	16,353	9,213
Cash	4,749	2,869
Unearned Revenue	1,211	1,434
Notes Payable	52,000	40,000
Prepaid Insurance	1,333	2,000

Instructions

(a) Identify the accounts of Automated Security Holdings that have debit balances in the trial balance.
(b) What date has Automated Security Holdings adopted for its accounting year-end?
(c) Are the accounts listed above in the order in which they would appear in Automated Security Holdings' general ledger? Explain.

CRITICAL THINKING

· ·

GROUP DECISION CASE

BYP2–6   Greg Daniels operates the Daniels Riding Academy. The academy's primary sources of revenue are riding fees and lesson fees, which are provided on a cash basis. Greg also boards horses for owners, who are billed monthly for boarding fees. In a few cases, boarders pay in advance of expected use. For its revenue transactions, the academy maintains the following accounts: No. 1 Cash, No. 5 Boarding Accounts Receivable, No. 27 Unearned Boarding Revenue, No. 51 Riding Revenue, No. 52 Lesson Revenue, and No. 53 Boarding Revenue.

The academy owns 10 horses, a stable, a riding corral, riding equipment, and office equipment. These assets are accounted for in accounts No. 11 Horses, No. 12 Building, No. 13 Riding Corral, No. 14 Riding Equipment, and No. 15 Office Equipment.

The academy employs stable helpers and an office employee who receive weekly salaries. At the end of each month, the mail usually brings bills for advertising, utilities, and veterinary service. Other expenses include feed for the horses and insurance. For its expenses, the academy maintains the following accounts: No. 6 Hay and Feed Supplies, No. 7 Prepaid Insurance, No. 21 Accounts Payable, No. 60 Salaries Expense, No. 61 Advertising Expense, No. 62 Utilities Expense, No. 63 Veterinary Expense, No. 64 Hay and Feed Expense, and No. 65 Insurance Expense.

Greg Daniels' sole source of income is the academy. Thus, he makes periodic withdrawals of cash for personal living expenses. To record Greg's equity in the business and his drawings, two accounts are maintained: No. 50 Greg Daniels, Capital, and No. 51 Greg Daniels, Drawing.

During the first month of operations an inexperienced bookkeeper was employed. Greg asks you to review the following eight entries of the 50 entries made during the month. In each case, the explanation for the entry is correct.

May 1	Cash		15,000	
	Greg Daniels, Capital			15,000
	(Invested $15,000 cash in business)			
5	Cash		250	
	Riding Revenue			250
	(Received $250 cash for lessons provided)			
7	Cash		500	
	Boarding Revenue			500
	(Received $500 for boarding of horses beginning June 1)			
14	Riding Equipment		80	
	Cash			800
	(Purchased desk and other office equipment for $800 cash)			
15	Salaries Expense		400	
	Cash			400
	(Issued check to Greg Daniels for personal use)			
20	Cash		145	
	Riding Revenue			154
	(Received $154 cash for riding fees)			
30	Veterinary Expense		75	
	Accounts Payable			75
	(Received bill of $75 from veterinarian for services rendered)			
31	Hay and Feed Expense		1,700	
	Cash			1,700
	(Purchased an estimated two months' supply of feed and hay for $1,700 on account)			

Instructions

With the class divided into groups, answer the following:

(a) For each journal entry that is correct, so state. For each journal entry that is incorrect, prepare the entry that should have been made by the bookkeeper.
(b) Which of the incorrect entries would prevent the trial balance from balancing?
(c) What was the correct net income for May, assuming the bookkeeper reported net income of $4,500 after posting all 50 entries?
(d) What was the correct cash balance at May 31, assuming the bookkeeper reported a balance of $12,475 after posting all 50 entries (and the only errors occurred in the items listed above)?

COMMUNICATION ACTIVITY

BYP2–7   Merlynn's Maid Company offers home cleaning service. Two recurring transactions for the company are billing customers for services rendered and paying employee salaries. For example, on March 15 bills totaling $6,000 were sent to customers and $2,000 was paid in salaries to employees.

Instructions

Write a memorandum to your instructor that explains and illustrates the steps in the recording process for each of the March 15 transactions. Use the format illustrated in the text under the heading, "The Recording Process Illustrated" (p. 59).

ETHICS CASE

BYP2–8   Megan Menard is the assistant chief accountant at Staples Company, a manufacturer of computer chips and cellular phones. The company presently has total sales of $20 million. It is the end of the first quarter and Megan is hurriedly trying to prepare a general ledger trial balance so that quarterly financial statements can be prepared and released to management and the regulatory agencies. The total credits on the trial balance exceed the debits by $1,000. In order to meet the 4 p.m. deadline, Megan decides to force the debits and credits into balance by adding the amount of the difference to the Equipment account. She chose Equipment because it is one of the larger account balances: percentage-wise it will be the least misstated. Megan plugs the difference! She believes that the difference is quite small and will not affect anyone's decisions. She wishes that she had another few days to find the error but realizes that the financial statements are already late.

Instructions

(a) Who are the stakeholders in this situation?
(b) What are the ethical issues involved in this case?
(c) What are Megan's alternatives?

SURFING THE NET

BYP2–9   Much information about specific companies is available on the World Wide Web. This information includes basic descriptions of the company's location, activities, industry, financial health, and financial performance.

Address: http://biz.yahoo.com/i (or go to the Wiley home page)

Steps:
1. Choose **Company.**
2. Type in a company name, or use index to find company name.
3. Choose **Profile.** Perform instructions (a)–(c) below.
4. Click on the company's specific industry to identify competitors. Perform instructions (d)–(g) below.

Instructions

Answer the following questions:

(a) What was the company's net income?
(b) What was the company's total sales?
(c) What is the company's industry?
(d) What are the names of four of the company's competitors?
(e) Choose one of these competitors.
(f) What is this competitor's name? What were its sales? What was its net income?
(g) Which of these two companies is larger by size of sales? Which one reported higher net income?

Answers to Self-Study Questions

1. b   2. c   3. d   4. d   5. b   6. a   7. c   8. d   9. a   10. c

---

Answer to Kellogg Review It Question 4, p. 51
Cash—debit; accounts payable—credit; interest expense—debit.

Remember to go back to the Navigator box on the chapter-opening page and check off your completed work.

CONCEPTS FOR REVIEW

Before studying this chapter, you should know, or, if necessary, review:

a. What a double-entry system is. (Ch. 2, p. 48)
b. How to increase or decrease assets, liabilities, and owner's equity using debit and credit procedures. (Ch. 2, pp. 48–50)
c. How to journalize a transaction. (Ch. 2, pp. 53–54)
d. How to post a transaction. (Ch. 2, pp. 56–59)
e. How to prepare a trial balance. (Ch. 2, pp. 66–67)

FEATURE STORY

When Students Leave Campus, This College Adjusts Its Books

Like many colleges, Arizona State University (ASU) uses a June 30 date as the end of its annual accounting period. Rather than using December 31, most colleges use the school year as their primary period of activity. Having an ending date like that seems neat and tidy—and it is in many respects. (If it were not, schools would choose an end-date that made more sense.) But colleges, just like any business organization, have some loose ends that need tying up at the end of the accounting period. For example, at ASU, the second summer session begins around July 5, but registration for the session takes place the prior February. The school collects tuition for the session in one accounting period but will provide the services in the next accounting period. "We have lots of students who are paying tuition in February for a session that begins in July," says Carol Balk, ASU's manager of student tuition payments. In the new accounting year, following completion of the summer session, "We have to account for the revenue collection of five months earlier."

Similarly, ASU has to account for supplies purchased in one accounting year but used the next. Supplies purchased on April 1 for use in the summer session will need to be reported as an expense in the new accounting year.

CHAPTER 3

THE NAVIGATOR ✔

- Understand *Concepts for Review* ☐
- Read *Feature Story* ☐
- Scan *Study Objectives* ☐
- Read *Preview* ☐
- Read text and answer *Before You Go On*
  p. 94 ☐ p. 102 ☐ p. 107 ☐ p. 113 ☐
- Work *Demonstration Problem* ☐
- Review *Summary of Study Objectives* ☐
- Answer *Self-Study Questions* ☐
- Complete assignments ☐

ADJUSTING THE ACCOUNTS

STUDY OBJECTIVES

After studying this chapter, you should be able to:

1. *Explain the time period assumption.*
2. *Distinguish between the revenue recognition principle and the matching principle.*
3. *Explain why adjusting entries are needed.*
4. *Identify the major types of adjusting entries.*
5. *Prepare adjusting entries for prepayments.*
6. *Prepare adjusting entries for accruals.*
7. *Describe the nature and purpose of an adjusted trial balance.*
8. *Explain the accrual basis of accounting.*

*I*n Chapter 2 we examined the basic steps in the recording process through the preparation of the trial balance. Before we will be ready to prepare financial statements from the trial balance, additional steps need to be taken. The timing mismatch between revenues and expenses of Arizona State University illustrates the types of situations that make these additional steps necessary. For example, computer equipment purchased in the prior accounting year is being used to keep student records and accounts in the current year. What portion of the computer cost, if any, should be recognized as an expense of the current period? Before financial statements can be prepared, these and other questions relating to the recognition of revenues and expenses must be answered. With the answers in hand, the relevant account balances can then be adjusted.

The content and organization of the chapter are as follows:

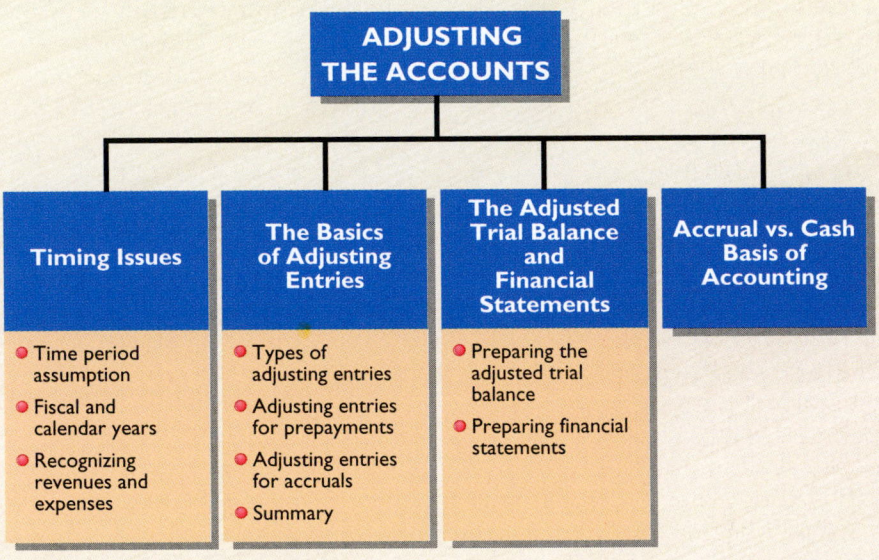

TIMING ISSUES

1

STUDY
OBJECTIVE

Explain the time period
assumption.

No adjustments would be necessary if we waited to prepare financial statements until a company ended its operations. At that point, we could readily determine its final balance sheet and the amount of lifetime income it earned. The following anecdote illustrates one way to compute lifetime income:

A grocery store owner from the old country kept his accounts payable on a spindle, accounts receivable on a note pad, and cash in a cigar box. His daughter, having just passed the CPA exam, chided the father: "I don't understand how you can run your business this way. How do you know what your profits are?"

"Well," the father replied, "when I got off the boat 40 years ago, I had nothing but the pants I was wearing. Today your brother is a doctor, your sister is a college professor, and you are a CPA. Your mother and I have a nice car, a well-furnished house, and a lake home. We have a good business and everything is paid for. So, you add all that together, subtract the pants, and there's your profit."

Selecting an Accounting Time Period

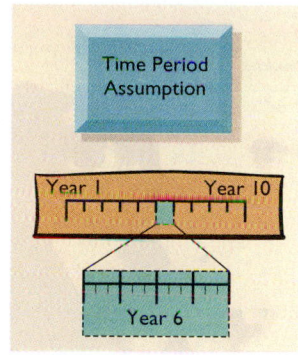

Although the old grocer may be correct in his evaluation, it is impractical to wait so long for the results of operations. All entities, from the corner grocery, to a global company like Kellogg, to your college or university, find it desirable and necessary to report the results of their activities more frequently. For example, management usually wants monthly financial statements, and the Internal Revenue Service requires all businesses to file annual tax returns. As a consequence, **accountants make the assumption that the economic life of a business can be divided into artificial time periods.** This assumption is referred to as the **time period assumption**.

Many business transactions affect more than one of these arbitrary time periods. For example, Farmer Brown's milking machine bought in 1998 and the airplanes purchased by Delta Air Lines 5 years ago are still in use today. Therefore it is necessary to determine the relevance of each business transaction to specific accounting periods. Doing so may involve subjective judgments and estimates. Generally, the shorter the time period (e.g., a month or a quarter of a year), the more difficult it becomes to determine the proper adjustments to be made.

Fiscal and Calendar Years

Both small and large companies prepare financial statements on a periodic basis in order to assess their financial condition and results of operations. **Accounting time periods are generally a month, a quarter, or a year.** Monthly and quarterly time periods are often referred to as **interim periods**. Most large companies are required to prepare both interim (quarterly) and annual financial statements.

An accounting time period that is one year in length is referred to as a **fiscal year**. A fiscal year usually begins with the first day of a month and ends 12 months later on the last day of a month. The accounting period used by most businesses coincides with the **calendar year** (January 1 to December 31). Companies whose fiscal year differs from the calendar year include Delta Air Lines, June 30; Walt Disney Productions, September 30; Kmart Corp., January 31; and Dunkin' Donuts, Inc., October 31. Arizona State University's fiscal year is July 1 through June 30, which is typical of universities and governmental agencies.

Recognizing Revenues and Expenses

Determining the amount of revenues and expenses to be reported in a given accounting period can be difficult. Therefore, accountants have developed two principles as part of generally accepted accounting principles (GAAP) that help in this determination: the revenue recognition principle and the matching principle.

The **revenue recognition principle** dictates that revenue be recognized in the accounting period in which it is earned. **In a service enterprise, revenue is considered to be earned at the time the service is performed.** To illustrate, assume that a dry cleaning business cleans clothing on June 30 but customers do not claim and pay for their clothes until the first week of July. Under the revenue recognition principle, revenue is earned in June when the service is performed and not in July when the cash is received. At June 30, the dry cleaner would report a receivable on its balance sheet and revenue in its income statement for the service performed.

In recognizing expenses, accountants follow the approach of "let the expenses follow the revenues." Thus, expense recognition is tied to revenue recognition. In the preceding example, this principle means that the salary expense

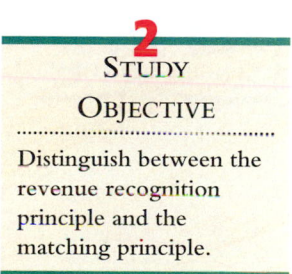

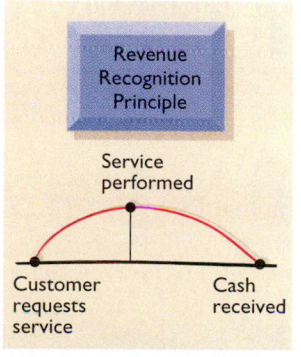

ACCOUNTING IN ACTION
Business Insight

Suppose you are a filmmaker and spend $15 million to produce a film. Over what period should the $15 million be expensed? Yes, it should be expensed over the economic life of the film. But what is its economic life? The filmmaker must estimate how much revenue will be earned from box office sales, video sales, and television—a period that easily can stretch five years or more. If a filmmaker allocates the cost over five years, and the film produces revenue in the sixth year, proper matching has not occurred. Furthermore, in some cases, films flop, and yet the costs are spread out over five years in the hopes that the films will eventually succeed. For example, in the mid-1980s Orion Pictures (now bankrupt) earned $7.3 million in one year, but lost $32 million the next year because it expensed 40 films that were not producing revenue. It was alleged that the company had overstated its income in earlier years because it did not expense these costs earlier. This case demonstrates the difficulty of properly matching expenses to revenues.

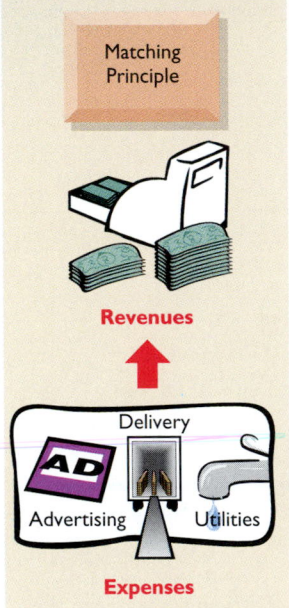

incurred in performing the cleaning service on June 30 should be reported in the income statement for the same period in which the service revenue is recognized. The critical issue in expense recognition is when the expense makes its contribution to revenue. This may or may not be the same period in which the expense is paid. If the salary incurred on June 30 is not paid until July, the dry cleaner would report salaries payable on its June 30 balance sheet. The practice of expense recognition is referred to as the **matching principle** because it dictates that efforts (expenses) be matched with accomplishments (revenues).

Once the assumption is made that the economic life of a business can be divided into artificial time periods, it follows that the revenue recognition and matching principles can be applied. This one assumption and two principles thus provide guidelines as to when revenues and expenses should be reported. These relationships are shown in Illustration 3-1.

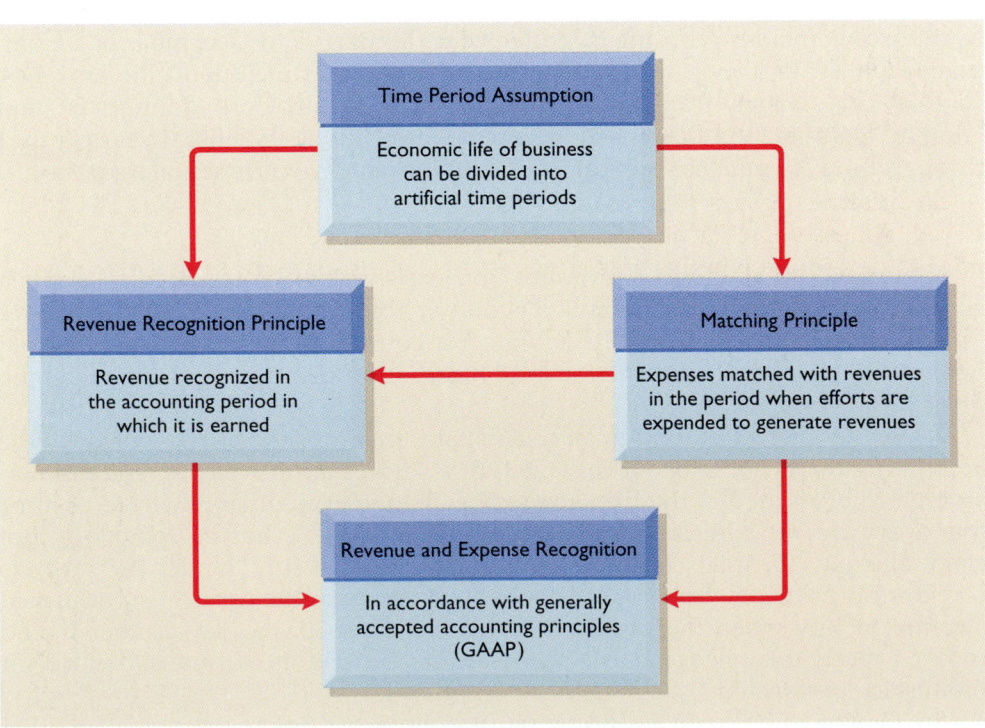

ILLUSTRATION 3-1

GAAP relationships in revenue and expense recognition

BEFORE YOU GO ON . . .

Review It

1. What is the relevance of the time period assumption to accounting?
2. What are the revenue recognition and matching principles?

THE BASICS OF ADJUSTING ENTRIES

In order for revenues to be recorded in the period in which they are earned, and for expenses to be recognized in the period in which they are incurred, adjusting entries are made at the end of the accounting period. In short, **adjusting entries are needed to ensure that the revenue recognition and matching principles are followed.**

The use of adjusting entries makes it possible to report on the balance sheet the appropriate assets, liabilities, and owner's equity at the statement date and to report on the income statement the proper net income (or loss) for the period. However, the trial balance—the first pulling together of the transaction data—may not contain up-to-date and complete data. This is true for the following reasons:

1. Some events are not journalized daily because it is inexpedient to do so. Examples are the consumption of supplies and the earning of wages by employees.
2. Some costs are not journalized during the accounting period because these costs expire with the passage of time rather than as a result of recurring daily transactions. Examples of such costs are building and equipment deterioration and rent and insurance.
3. Some items may be unrecorded. An example is a utility service bill that will not be received until the next accounting period.

Adjusting entries are required every time financial statements are prepared. An essential starting point is an analysis of each account in the trial balance to determine whether it is complete and up-to-date for financial statement purposes. The analysis requires a thorough understanding of the company's operations and the interrelationship of accounts. The preparation of adjusting entries is often an involved process. In accumulating the adjustment data, the company may need to make inventory counts of supplies and repair parts. Also it may be desirable to prepare supporting schedules of insurance policies, rental agreements, and other contractual commitments. Adjustments are often prepared after the balance sheet date. However, the adjusting entries are dated as of the balance sheet date.

Types of Adjusting Entries

Adjusting entries can be classified as either prepayments or accruals. Each of these classes has two subcategories as shown in Illustration 3-2:

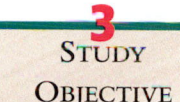

STUDY OBJECTIVE 3

Explain why adjusting entries are needed.

HELPFUL HINT
Adjusting entries are needed to enable financial statements to be in conformity with GAAP.

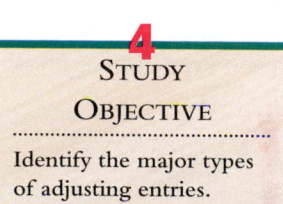

STUDY OBJECTIVE 4

Identify the major types of adjusting entries.

ILLUSTRATION 3-2

Categories of adjusting entries

Prepayments

1. **Prepaid Expenses.** Expenses paid in cash and recorded as assets before they are used or consumed.
2. **Unearned Revenues.** Cash received and recorded as liabilities before revenue is earned.

Accruals

1. **Accrued Revenues.** Revenues earned but not yet received in cash or recorded.
2. **Accrued Expenses.** Expenses incurred but not yet paid in cash or recorded.

Specific examples and explanations of each type of adjustment are given in subsequent sections. Each example is based on the October 31 trial balance of Pioneer Advertising Agency, reproduced in Illustration 3-3 from Chapter 2.

ILLUSTRATION 3-3

Trial balance

PIONEER ADVERTISING AGENCY
Trial Balance
October 31, 1999

	Debit	Credit
Cash	$15,200	
Advertising Supplies	2,500	
Prepaid Insurance	600	
Office Equipment	5,000	
Notes Payable		$ 5,000
Accounts Payable		2,500
Unearned Revenue		1,200
C. R. Byrd, Capital		10,000
C. R. Byrd, Drawing	500	
Service Revenue		10,000
Salaries Expense	4,000	
Rent Expense	900	
	$28,700	$28,700

We assume that Pioneer Advertising uses an accounting period of one month. Thus, monthly adjusting entries will be made. The entries will be dated October 31.

Adjusting Entries for Prepayments

5

STUDY

OBJECTIVE

....

Prepare adjusting entries for prepayments.

HELPFUL HINT

Remember that credits decrease assets and increase revenues. Debits increase expenses and decrease liabilities.

As indicated earlier, prepayments are either prepaid expenses or unearned revenues. Adjusting entries for prepayments are required at the statement date to record the portion of the prepayment that represents the **expense incurred or the revenue earned** in the current accounting period. Assuming an adjustment is needed for both types of prepayments, the asset and liability are overstated and the related expense and revenue are understated. For example, in the trial balance, the balance in the asset, Supplies, shows only supplies purchased. This balance is overstated; the related expense account, Supplies Expense, is understated because the cost of supplies used has not been recognized. Thus the adjusting entry for prepayments will decrease a balance sheet account and increase an income statement account. The effects of adjusting entries for prepayments are graphically depicted in Illustration 3-4.

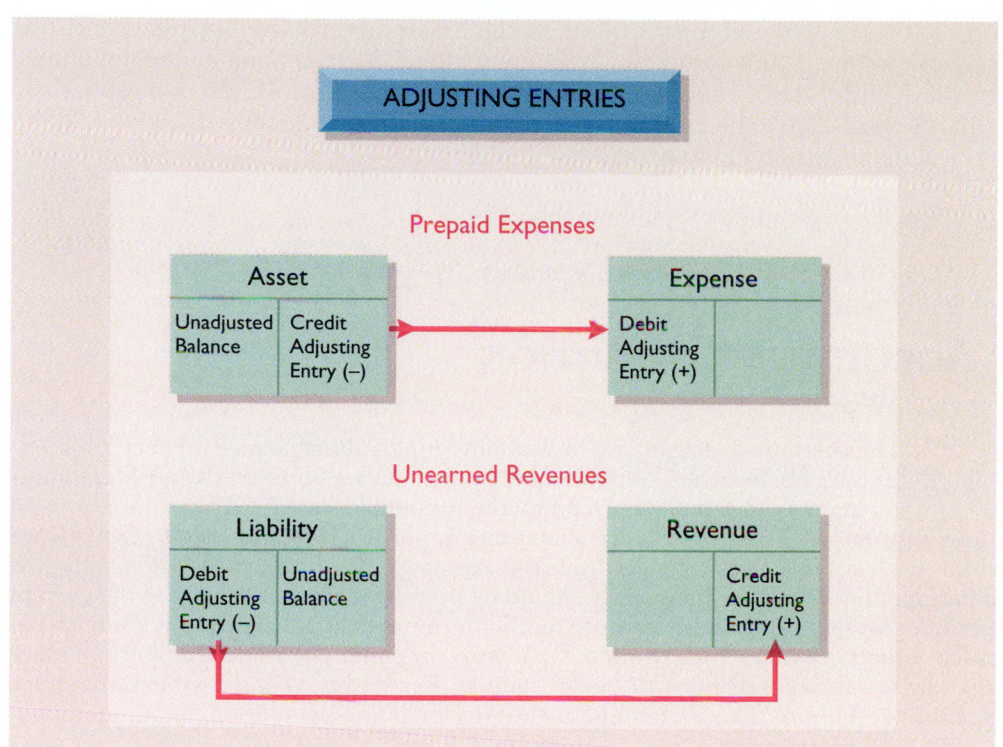

ILLUSTRATION 3-4

Adjusting entries for prepayments

Prepaid Expenses

As stated on page 96, expenses paid in cash and recorded as assets before they are used or consumed are identified as **prepaid expenses**. When a cost is prepaid, an asset account is debited to show the service or benefit that will be received in the future. Prepayments often occur in regard to insurance, supplies, advertising, and rent. In addition, prepayments are made when buildings and equipment are purchased.

Prepaid expenses expire either with the passage of time (e.g., rent and insurance) or through use and consumption (e.g., supplies). The expiration of these costs does not require daily recurring entries, which would be unnecessary and impractical. Accordingly, it is customary to postpone the recognition of such cost expirations until financial statements are prepared. At each statement date, adjusting entries are made to record the expenses that apply to the current accounting period and to show the unexpired costs in the asset accounts.

Prior to adjustment, assets are overstated and expenses are understated. **Thus, the prepaid expense adjusting entry results in a debit to an expense account and a credit to an asset account.**

Supplies. Several different types of supplies are used in a business enterprise. For example, a CPA firm will have **office supplies** such as stationery, envelopes, and accounting paper. In contrast, an advertising firm will have **advertising supplies** such as graph paper, video film, and poster paper. Supplies are generally debited to an asset account when they are acquired. During the course of operations, supplies are depleted or entirely consumed. However, recognition of supplies used is deferred until the adjustment process when a physical inventory (count) of supplies is taken. The difference between the balance in the Supplies (asset) account and the cost of supplies on hand represents the supplies used (expense) for the period.

Pioneer Advertising Agency purchased advertising supplies costing $2,500

Supplies

Oct.5

Supplies purchased; record asset

Oct.31

Supplies used; record supplies expense

In the margins next to key journal entries are **equation analyses** that summarize the effects of the transaction on the three elements of the accounting equation.

Equation Analysis			
A	= L	+	OE
−1,500			−1,500

on October 5. The debit was made to the asset Advertising Supplies, and this account shows a balance of $2,500 in the October 31 trial balance. An inventory count at the close of business on October 31 reveals that $1,000 of supplies are still on hand. Thus, the cost of supplies used is $1,500 ($2,500 − $1,000), and the following adjusting entry is made:

Oct. 31	Advertising Supplies Expense	1,500	
	Advertising Supplies		1,500
	(To record supplies used)		

ACCOUNTING IN ACTION
Business Insight

The costs of advertising on radio, television, and magazines for such products as burgers, bleaches, athletic shoes, and so on are sometimes considered prepayments. As a manager for Procter & Gamble noted, "If we run a long ad campaign for soap and bleach, we sometimes report the costs as prepayments if we think we'll receive sales benefits from the campaign down the road." Presently it is a judgment call whether these costs should be prepayments or expenses in the current period. Developing guidelines consistent with the matching principle is difficult because situations vary widely from company to company. The issue is important since the outlays for advertising can be substantial. Recent big spenders: Sears Roebuck spent $1.28 billion, Nike $978 million, and McDonald's $503 million.

After the adjusting entry is posted, the two supplies accounts in T-account form show:

ILLUSTRATION 3-5

Supplies accounts after adjustment

Advertising Supplies					Advertising Supplies Expense			
10/5	2,500	10/31 **Adj.**	**1,500**		10/31 **Adj.**	**1,500**		
10/31 Bal.	1,000							

Insurance

Oct.4

Insurance purchased; record asset

Insurance Policy			
Oct $50	Nov $50	Dec $50	Jan $50
Feb $50	March $50	April $50	May $50
June $50	July $50	Aug $50	Sept $50
I YEAR $600			

Oct.31

Insurance expired; record insurance expense

The asset account Advertising Supplies now shows a balance of $1,000, which is equal to the cost of supplies on hand at the statement date. In addition, Advertising Supplies Expense shows a balance of $1,500, which equals the cost of supplies used in October. **If the adjusting entry is not made, October expenses will be understated and net income overstated by $1,500. Moreover, both assets and owner's equity will be overstated by $1,500 on the October 31 balance sheet.**

Insurance. Most companies have fire and theft insurance on merchandise and equipment, personal liability insurance for accidents suffered by customers, and automobile insurance on company cars and trucks. The cost of insurance protection is determined by the payment of insurance premiums. The term and coverage are specified in the insurance policy. The minimum term is usually one year, but three- to five-year terms are available and offer lower annual premiums. Insurance premiums normally are charged to the asset account Prepaid Insurance when paid. At the financial statement date it is necessary to debit Insurance Expense and credit Prepaid Insurance for the cost that has expired during the period.

On October 4, Pioneer Advertising Agency paid $600 for a one-year fire insurance policy. The effective date of coverage was October 1. The premium was charged to Prepaid Insurance when it was paid, and this account shows a balance of $600 in the October 31 trial balance. An analysis of the policy reveals that $50 ($600 ÷ 12) of insurance expires each month. Thus, the following adjusting entry is made:

Oct. 31	Insurance Expense	50	
	Prepaid Insurance		50
	(To record insurance expired)		

A	=	L	+	OE
− 50				− 50

After the adjusting entry is posted, the accounts show:

Prepaid Insurance				Insurance Expense		
10/4	600	10/31 **Adj.**	50	10/31 **Adj.**	50	
10/31 Bal.	550					

ILLUSTRATION 3-6

Insurance accounts after adjustment

The asset Prepaid Insurance shows a balance of $550, which represents the unexpired cost applicable to the remaining 11 months of coverage. At the same time, the balance in Insurance Expense is equal to the insurance cost that has expired in October. **If this adjustment is not made, October expenses will be understated by $50 and net income overstated by $50. Moreover, both assets and owner's equity also will be overstated by $50 on the October 31 balance sheet.**

Depreciation.   A business enterprise typically owns a variety of productive facilities such as buildings, equipment, and motor vehicles. These assets provide service for a number of years. The term of service is commonly referred to as the **useful life** of the asset. Because an asset such as a building is expected to provide service for many years, it is recorded as an asset, rather than an expense, in the year it is acquired. As explained in Chapter 1, such assets are recorded at cost, as required by the cost principle.

HELPFUL HINT

Depreciation is an estimate—one of many estimates inherent in accounting.

According to the matching principle, a portion of the cost of a long-lived asset should be reported as an expense during each period of the asset's useful life. **Depreciation** is the process of allocating the cost of an asset to expense over its useful life in a rational and systematic manner.

Need for Depreciation Adjustment.   From an accounting standpoint, the acquisition of productive facilities is viewed essentially as a long-term prepayment for services. The need for making periodic adjusting entries for depreciation is, therefore, the same as described before for other prepaid expenses; that is, to recognize the cost that has expired (expense) during the period and to report the unexpired cost (asset) at the end of the period.

In determining the useful life of a productive facility, the primary causes of depreciation are actual use, deterioration due to the elements, and obsolescence. At the time an asset is acquired, the effects of these factors cannot be known with certainty, so they must be estimated. Thus, you should recognize that depreciation is an estimate rather than a factual measurement of the cost that has expired. A common procedure in computing depreciation expense is to divide the cost of the asset by its useful life. For example, if cost is $10,000 and useful life is expected to be 10 years, annual depreciation is $1,000.[1]

Depreciation

Oct. I

Office equipment purchased; record asset

Office Equipment			
Oct	Nov	Dec	Jan
$40	$40	$40	$40
Feb	March	April	May
$40	$40	$40	$40
June	July	Aug	Sept
$40	$40	$40	$40
Depreciation = $480/year			

Oct.31
    Depreciation recognized; record depreciation expense

---

[1]Additional consideration is given to computing depreciation expense in Chapter 10.

For Pioneer Advertising, depreciation on the office equipment is estimated to be $480 a year, or $40 per month. Accordingly, depreciation for October is recognized by the following adjusting entry:

A	=	L	+	OE
−40				−40

Oct. 31	Depreciation Expense	40	
	Accumulated Depreciation—Office Equipment		40
	(To record monthly depreciation)		

After the adjusting entry is posted, the accounts show:

ILLUSTRATION 3-7

Accounts after adjustment for depreciation

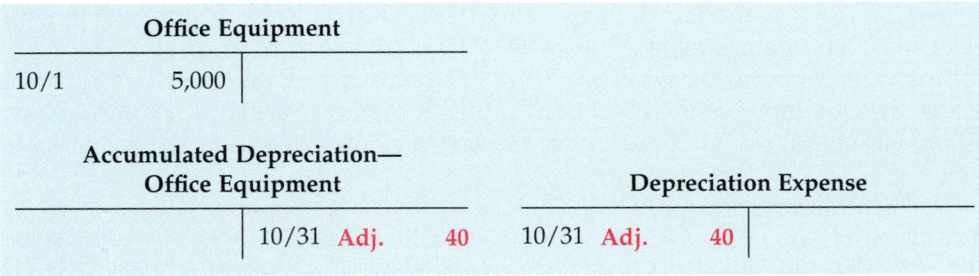

The balance in the accumulated depreciation account will increase $40 each month. Therefore, after journalizing and posting the adjusting entry at November 30, the balance will be $80.

HELPFUL HINT
All contra accounts have increases, decreases, and normal balances opposite to the account to which they relate.

Statement Presentation. Accumulated Depreciation—Office Equipment is a contra asset account. A **contra asset account** is an account that is offset against an asset account on the balance sheet. This means that the accumulated depreciation account is offset against Office Equipment on the balance sheet and that its normal balance is a credit. This account is used instead of crediting Office Equipment in order to permit disclosure of **both the original cost** of the equipment **and the total cost that has expired to date**. In the balance sheet, Accumulated Depreciation—Office Equipment is deducted from the related asset account as follows:

ILLUSTRATION 3-8

Balance sheet presentation of accumulated depreciation

Office equipment		$5,000	
Less: Accumulated depreciation—office equipment		40	**$4,960**

ALTERNATIVE TERMINOLOGY
Book value is sometimes referred to as *carrying value* or *unexpired cost*.

The difference between the cost of any depreciable asset and its related accumulated depreciation is referred to as the **book value** of that asset. In Illustration 3-8, the book value of the equipment at the balance sheet date is $4,960. It is important to realize that the book value and the market value of the asset are generally two different values. The reason the two are different is that depreciation is not a matter of valuation but rather, a means of cost allocation.

Note also that depreciation expense identifies that portion of the asset's cost that has expired in October. As in the case of other prepaid adjustments, the omission of this adjusting entry would cause total assets, total owner's equity, and net income to be overstated and depreciation expense to be understated.

If additional equipment is involved, such as delivery or store equipment, or if the company has buildings, depreciation expense is recorded on each of these items. Related accumulated depreciation accounts also are established. These accumulated depreciation accounts would be described in the ledger as follows:

Accumulated Depreciation—Delivery Equipment; Accumulated Depreciation—Store Equipment; and Accumulated Depreciation—Buildings.

Unearned Revenues

As stated on page 96, cash received and recorded as liabilities before revenue is earned is called **unearned revenues**. Such items as rent, magazine subscriptions, and customer deposits for future service may result in unearned revenues. Airlines such as United, American, and Delta treat receipts from the sale of tickets as unearned revenue until the flight service is provided. Similarly, tuition received prior to the start of a semester, as in the feature story about Arizona State University, is considered to be unearned revenue. Unearned revenues are the opposite of prepaid expenses. Indeed, unearned revenue on the books of one company is likely to be a prepayment on the books of the company that has made the advance payment. For example, if identical accounting periods are assumed, a landlord will have unearned rent revenue when a tenant has prepaid rent.

When the payment is received for services to be provided in a future accounting period, an unearned revenue (a liability) account should be credited to recognize the obligation that exists. Unearned revenues are subsequently earned through rendering service to a customer. During the accounting period it may not be practical to make daily recurring entries as the revenue is earned. In such cases, the recognition of earned revenue is delayed until the adjustment process. Then an adjusting entry is made to record the revenue that has been earned and to show the liability that remains. In the typical case, liabilities are overstated and revenues are understated prior to adjustment. Thus, **the adjusting entry for unearned revenues results in a debit (decrease) to a liability account and a credit (increase) to a revenue account**.

Pioneer Advertising Agency received $1,200 on October 2 from R. Knox for advertising services expected to be completed by December 31. The payment was credited to Unearned Revenue, and this account shows a balance of $1,200 in the October 31 trial balance. When analysis reveals that $400 of those fees has been earned in October, the following adjusting entry is made:

Unearned Revenues

Oct.2 — *Thank you in advance for your work* / *I will finish by Dec. 31* — $1,200

Cash is received in advance; liability is recorded

Oct.31
Service is provided; revenue is recorded

ALTERNATIVE TERMINOLOGY
Unearned revenues is sometimes referred to as *deferred revenues*.

Oct. 31	Unearned Revenue	400	
	Service Revenue		400
	(To record revenue for services provided)		

A	=	L	+	OE
		−400		+400

After the adjusting entry is posted, the accounts show:

Unearned Revenue				Service Revenue		
10/31 Adj. 400	10/2 1,200				10/31 Bal. 10,000	
	10/31 Bal. 800				31 Adj. 400	

ILLUSTRATION 3-9

Revenue accounts after prepayments adjustment

The liability Unearned Revenue now shows a balance of $800, which represents the remaining advertising services expected to be performed in the future. At the same time, Service Revenue shows total revenue earned in October of $10,400. **If this adjustment is not made, revenues and net income will be understated by $400 in the income statement. Moreover, liabilities will be overstated and owner's equity will be understated by $400 on the October 31 balance sheet.**

BEFORE YOU GO ON . . .

Review It

1. What are the four types of adjusting entries?
2. What is the effect on assets, owner's equity, expenses, and net income if a prepaid expense adjusting entry is not made?
3. What is the effect on liabilities, owner's equity, revenues, and net income if an unearned revenue adjusting entry is not made?

4. Using the Selected Financial Data section of Kellogg Company's financial statements what was the amount of depreciation and amortization expense for 1997 and 1996? The answer to this question is provided on page 136.

Do It

The ledger of Hammond, Inc., on March 31, 1999, includes the following selected accounts before adjusting entries are prepared:

	Debit	Credit
Prepaid Insurance	3,600	
Office Supplies	2,800	
Office Equipment	25,000	
Accumulated Depreciation—Office Equipment		5,000
Unearned Revenue		9,200

An analysis of the accounts shows the following:

1. Insurance expires at the rate of $100 per month.
2. Supplies on hand total $800.
3. The office equipment depreciates $200 a month.
4. One-half of the unearned revenue was earned in March.

Prepare the adjusting entries for the month of March.

Reasoning: In order for revenues to be recorded in the period in which they are earned, and for expenses to be recognized in the period in which they are incurred, adjusting entries are made at the end of the accounting period. Adjusting entries for prepayments are required at the statement date to record the portion of the prepayment that represents the expense incurred or the revenue earned in the current accounting period. The failure to adjust for the prepayment leads to overstatement of the asset or liability and a related understatement of the expense or revenue.

Solution:

1. Insurance Expense		100	
Prepaid Insurance			100
(To record insurance expired)			
2. Office Supplies Expense		2,000	
Office Supplies			2,000
(To record supplies used)			
3. Depreciation Expense		200	
Accumulated Depreciation—Office Equipment			200
(To record monthly depreciation)			
4. Unearned Revenue		4,600	
Service Revenue			4,600
(To record revenue for services provided)			

Related exercise material: BE3–3, BE3–4, BE3–5, BE3–6, E3–1, E3–2, E3–3, E3–4, E3–5, E3–6, E3–7, E3–8 and E3–9.

THE NAVIGATOR

Adjusting Entries for Accruals

The second category of adjusting entries is **accruals**. Adjusting entries for accruals are required to record revenues earned and expenses incurred in the current accounting period that have not been recognized through daily entries. If an accrual adjustment is needed, the revenue account (and the related asset account) and/or the expense account (and the related liability account) is understated. Thus, the adjusting entry for accruals will **increase both a balance sheet and an income statement account**. Adjusting entries for accruals are graphically depicted in Illustration 3-10.

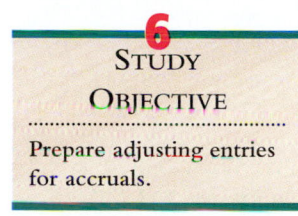

6
STUDY
OBJECTIVE
Prepare adjusting entries for accruals.

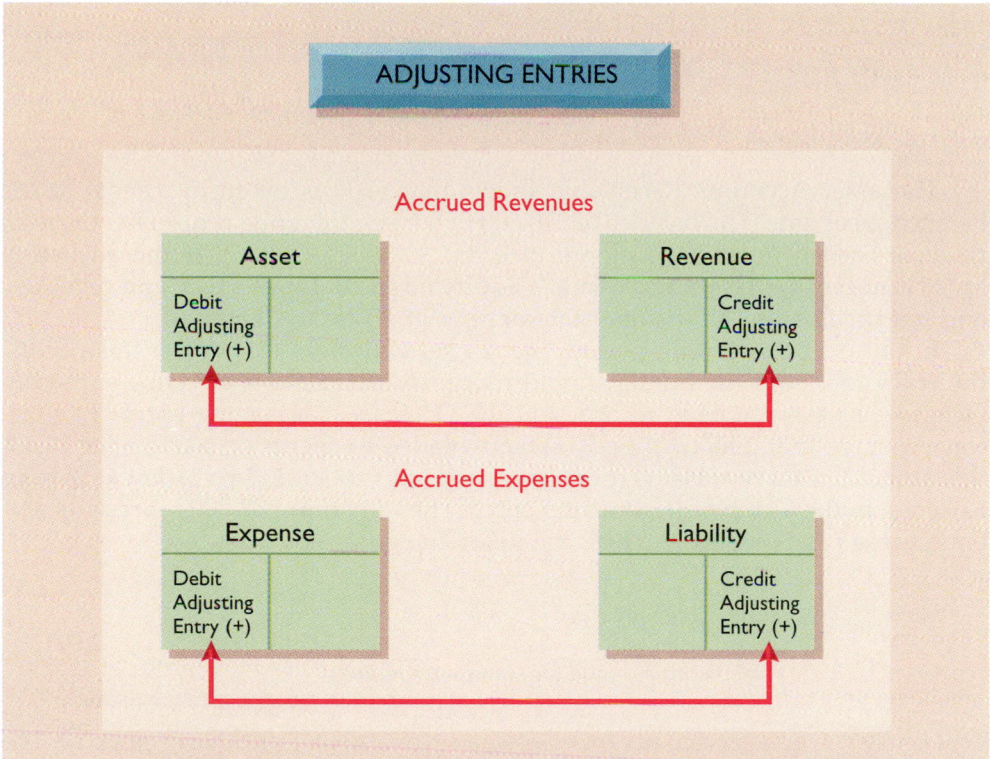

ILLUSTRATION 3-10

Adjusting entries for accruals

Accrued Revenues

As explained on page 96, revenues earned but not yet received in cash or recorded at the statement date are **accrued revenues**. Accrued revenues may accumulate (accrue) with the passing of time, as in the case of interest revenue and rent revenue. Or they may result from services that have been performed but neither billed nor collected, as in the case of commissions and fees. The former are unrecorded because the earning of interest and rent does not involve daily transactions; the latter may be unrecorded because only a portion of the total service has been provided.

An adjusting entry is required to show the receivable that exists at the balance sheet date and to record the revenue that has been earned during the period. Prior to adjustment both assets and revenues are understated. Accordingly, **an adjusting entry for accrued revenues results in a debit (increase) to an asset account and a credit (increase) to a revenue account**.

In October Pioneer Advertising Agency earned $200 for advertising services that were not billed to clients before October 31. Because these services have not been billed, they have not been recorded. Thus, the following adjusting entry is made:

Accrued Revenues

Oct.31

My fee is $200

Revenue and receivable are recorded for unbilled services

Nov.

Cash is received; receivable is reduced

A	=	L	+	OE
+ 200				+ 200

Oct. 31	Accounts Receivable	200	
	Service Revenue		200
	(To record revenue for services provided)		

After the adjusting entry is posted, the accounts show:

ILLUSTRATION 3-11

Receivable and revenue accounts after accrual adjustment

Accounts Receivable		Service Revenue	
10/31 **Adj.** **200**			10/31 10,000
			31 400
			31 **Adj.** **200**
			10/31 Bal. 10,600

ALTERNATIVE TERMINOLOGY

Accrued revenues are also called *accrued receivables*.

The asset Accounts Receivable shows that $200 is owed by clients at the balance sheet date. The balance of $10,600 in Service Revenue represents the total revenue earned during the month ($10,000 + $400 + $200). **If the adjusting entry is not made, assets and owner's equity on the balance sheet, and revenues and net income on the income statement, will all be understated.**

In the next accounting period, the clients will be billed. When this occurs, the entry to record the billing should recognize that $200 of revenue earned in October has already been recorded in the October 31 adjusting entry. To illustrate, assume that bills totaling $3,000 are mailed to clients on November 10. Of this amount, $200 represents revenue earned in October and recorded as Service Revenue in the October 31 adjusting entry. The remaining $2,800 represents revenue earned in November. Thus, the following entry is made:

A	=	L	+	OE
+ 2,800				+ 2,800

Nov. 10	Accounts Receivable	2,800	
	Service Revenue		2,800
	(To record revenue for services provided)		

This entry records service revenue between November 1 and November 10. The subsequent collection of revenue from clients (including the $200 earned in October) will be recorded with a debit to Cash and a credit to Accounts Receivable.

Accrued Expenses

As indicated on page 96, expenses incurred but not yet paid or recorded at the statement date are called **accrued expenses**. Interest, rent, taxes, and salaries can be accrued expenses. Accrued expenses result from the same causes as accrued revenues. In fact, an accrued expense on the books of one company is an accrued revenue to another company. For example, the $200 accrual of fees by Pioneer is an accrued expense to the client that received the service.

ALTERNATIVE TERMINOLOGY

Accrued expenses are also called *accrued liabilities*.

Adjustments for accrued expenses are necessary to record the obligations that exist at the balance sheet date and to recognize the expenses that apply to the current accounting period. Prior to adjustment both liabilities and expenses are understated. Therefore, **the adjusting entry for accrued expenses results in a debit (increase) to an expense account and a credit (increase) to a liability account.**

Accrued Interest. Pioneer Advertising Agency signed a 3-month note payable in the amount of $5,000 on October 1. The note requires interest at an annual rate of 12%. The amount of the interest accumulation is determined by three factors: (1) the face value of the note, (2) the interest rate, which is always expressed as an annual rate, and (3) the length of time the note is outstanding. In this instance, the total interest due on the $5,000 note at its due date 3 months hence is $150 ($5,000 × 12% × 3/12), or $50 for one month. The formula for computing interest and its application to Pioneer Advertising Agency for the month of October[2] are shown in Illustration 3-12.

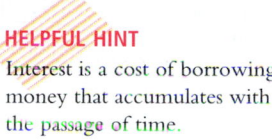

HELPFUL HINT
Interest is a cost of borrowing money that accumulates with the passage of time.

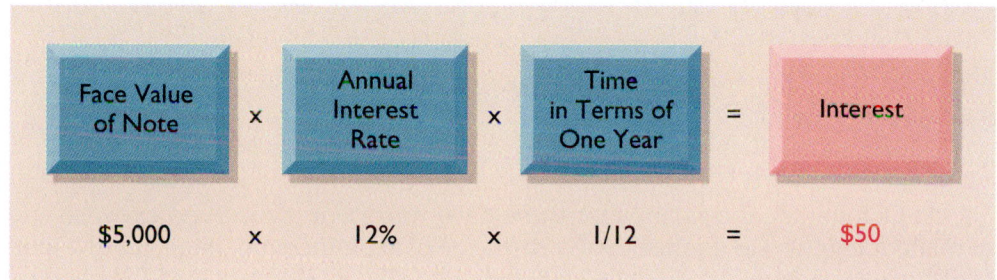

ILLUSTRATION 3-12
Formula for computing interest

Note that the time period is expressed as a fraction of a year. The accrued expense adjusting entry at October 31 is as follows:

Oct. 31	Interest Expense	50	
	Interest Payable		50
	(To record interest on notes payable)		

A	=	L	+	OE
		+50		−50

After this adjusting entry is posted, the accounts show:

Interest Expense			Interest Payable		
10/31 Adj. 50				10/31 Adj. 50	

ILLUSTRATION 3-13
Interest accounts after adjustment

Interest Expense shows the interest charges applicable to the month of October. The amount of interest owed at the statement date is shown in Interest Payable. It will not be paid until the note comes due at the end of three months. The Interest Payable account is used instead of crediting Notes Payable to disclose the two types of obligations (interest and principal) in the accounts and statements. **If this adjusting entry is not made, liabilities and interest expense will be understated, and net income and owner's equity will be overstated.**

Accrued Salaries. Some types of expenses, such as employee salaries and commissions, are paid for after the services have been performed. At Pioneer Advertising, salaries were last paid on October 26; the next payment of salaries will not occur until November 9. As shown in the calendar on page 106, three working days remain in October (October 29–31).

---

[2]The computation of interest will be considered in more depth in later chapters.

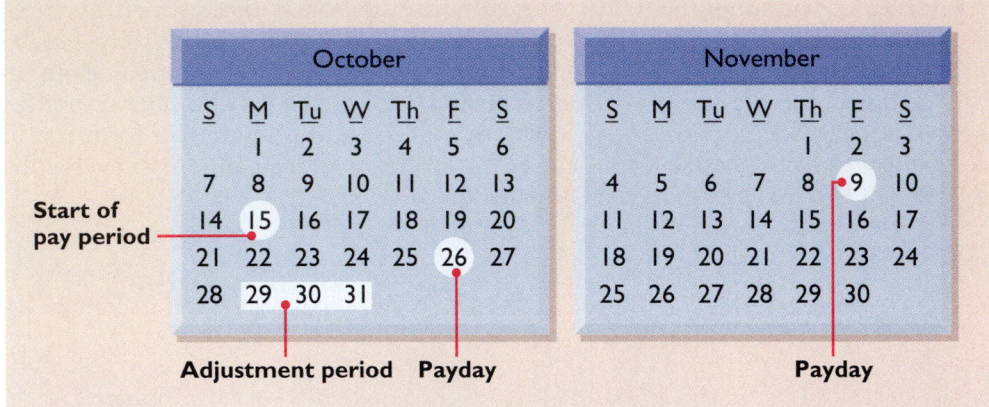

At October 31, the salaries for these days represent an accrued expense and a related liability to Pioneer Advertising. As explained on page 62, the employees receive total salaries of $2,000 for a five-day work week, or $400 per day. Thus, accrued salaries at October 31 are $1,200 ($400 × 3), and the adjusting entry is:

A	=	L	+	OE
		+1,200		−1,200

Oct. 31	Salaries Expense	1,200	
	Salaries Payable		1,200
	(To record accrued salaries)		

After this adjusting entry is posted, the accounts show:

ILLUSTRATION 3-14

Salary accounts after adjustment

Salaries Expense			Salaries Payable	
10/26	4,000			10/31 **Adj.** **1,200**
31 **Adj.** **1,200**				
10/31 Bal. 5,200				

After this adjustment, the balance in Salaries Expense of $5,200 (13 days × $400) is the actual salary expense for October. The balance in Salaries Payable of $1,200 is the amount of the liability for salaries owed as of October 31. **If the $1,200 adjustment for salaries is not recorded, Pioneer's expenses will be understated $1,200, and its liabilities will be understated $1,200.**

At Pioneer Advertising, salaries are payable every two weeks. Consequently, the next payday is November 9, when total salaries of $4,000 will again be paid. The payment consists of $1,200 of salaries payable at October 31 plus $2,800 of salaries expense for November (7 working days as shown in the November calendar × $400). Therefore, the following entry is made on November 9:

A	=	L	+	OE
−4,000		−1,200		−2,800

Nov. 9	Salaries Payable	1,200	
	Salaries Expense	2,800	
	Cash		4,000
	(To record November 9 payroll)		

This entry eliminates the liability for Salaries Payable that was recorded in the October 31 adjusting entry and records the proper amount of Salaries Expense for the period between November 1 and November 9.

TECHNOLOGY IN ACTION

In many computer systems, the adjusting process is handled like any other transaction, with the accountant inputting the adjustment at the time required. The main difference between adjusting entries and regular transactions is that with adjusting entries, one part of the computer system may perform the required calculation for such items as depreciation or interest and then "feed" these figures to the journalizing process.

Such systems are also able to display information before and after changes were made. Management may be interested in such information to highlight the impact that adjustments have on the various accounts and financial statements.

BEFORE YOU GO ON . . .

Review It

1. What is the effect on assets, owner's equity, revenues, and net income if an accrued revenue adjusting entry is not made?
2. What is the effect on liabilities, owner's equity, and interest expense if an accrued expense adjusting entry is not made?

Do It

Calvin and Hobbs are the new owners of Micro Computer Services. At the end of August 1999, their first month of ownership, Calvin and Hobbs are trying to prepare a monthly financial statement. The following information relates to August:

1. At August 31, Calvin and Hobbs owed their employees $800 in salaries that will be paid on September 1.
2. On August 1, Calvin and Hobbs borrowed $30,000 from a local bank on a 15-year mortgage. The annual interest rate is 10%.
3. Service revenue unrecorded in August totaled $1,100.

Prepare the adjusting entries needed at August 31, 1999.

Reasoning: Adjusting entries for accruals are required to record revenues earned and expenses incurred in the current accounting period that have not been recognized through daily entries. An adjusting entry for accruals will increase both a balance sheet and an income statement account.

Solution:

1.	Salaries Expense	800	
	Salaries Payable		800
	(To record accrued salaries)		
2.	Interest Expense	250	
	Interest Payable		250
	(To record interest)		
	($30,000 × 10% × 1/12 = $250)		
3.	Accounts Receivable	1,100	
	Service Revenue		1,100
	(To record revenue for services provided)		

Related exercise material: BE3–7, E3–1, E3–2, E3–3, E3–4, E3–5, E3–6, E3–7, E3–8, and E3–9.

THE
NAVIGATOR

Summary of Basic Relationships

ILLUSTRATION 3-15

Summary of adjusting entries

The four basic types of adjusting entries are summarized in Illustration 3-15. Take some time to study and analyze the adjusting entries shown in the summary. Be sure to note that **each adjusting entry affects one balance sheet account and one income statement account**.

Type of Adjustment	Reason for Adjustment	Accounts before Adjustment	Adjusting Entry
1. Prepaid expenses	(a) Prepaid expenses originally recorded in asset accounts have been used.	Assets overstated Expenses understated	Dr. Expenses Cr. Assets
2. Unearned revenues	(b) Unearned revenues initially recorded in liability accounts have been earned.	Liabilities overstated Revenues understated	Dr. Liabilities Cr. Revenues
3. Accrued revenues	(c) Revenues earned but not yet received in cash or recorded.	Assets understated Revenues understated	Dr. Assets Cr. Revenues
4. Accrued expenses	(d) Expenses incurred but not yet paid in cash or recorded.	Expenses understated Liabilities understated	Dr. Expenses Cr. Liabilities

The journalizing and posting of adjusting entries for Pioneer Advertising Agency on October 31 are shown in Illustrations 3-16 and 3-17. All adjustments are identified in the ledger by the reference J2 because they are journalized on page 2 of the general journal. A center caption entitled Adjusting Entries may be inserted between the last transaction entry and the first adjusting entry to identify these entries. When reviewing the general ledger in Illustration 3-17, note that the adjustments are highlighted in color.

ILLUSTRATION 3-16

General journal showing adjusting entries

HELPFUL HINT

(1) Remember that adjusting entries should not involve debits and credits to cash. (2) Evaluate whether the adjustment makes sense. For example, an adjustment to recognize supplies used should increase supplies expense. (3) Double-check all computations.

	GENERAL JOURNAL			**J2**
Date	**Account Titles and Explanation**	**Ref.**	**Debit**	**Credit**
1999	Adjusting Entries			
Oct. 31	Advertising Supplies Expense	61	1,500	
	Advertising Supplies	8		1,500
	(To record supplies used)			
31	Insurance Expense	63	50	
	Prepaid Insurance	10		50
	(To record insurance expired)			
31	Depreciation Expense	65	40	
	Accumulated Depreciation—Office Equipment	16		40
	(To record monthly depreciation)			
31	Unearned Revenue	28	400	
	Service Revenue	50		400
	(To record revenue for services provided)			
31	Accounts Receivable	6	200	
	Service Revenue	50		200
	(To record revenue for services provided)			
31	Interest Expense	64	50	
	Interest Payable	27		50
	(To record interest on notes payable)			
31	Salaries Expense	60	1,200	
	Salaries Payable	29		1,200
	(To record accrued salaries)			

GENERAL LEDGER

Cash   No. 1

Date	Explanation	Ref.	Debit	Credit	Balance
1999					
Oct. 1		J1	10,000		10,000
2		J1	1,200		11,200
3		J1		900	10,300
4		J1		600	9,700
20		J1		500	9,200
26		J1		4,000	5,200
31		J1	10,000		15,200

Accounts Receivable   No. 6

Date	Explanation	Ref.	Debit	Credit	Balance
1999					
Oct. 31	Adj. entry	J2	200		200

Advertising Supplies   No. 8

Date	Explanation	Ref.	Debit	Credit	Balance
1999					
Oct. 5		J1	2,500		2,500
31	Adj. entry	J2		1,500	1,000

Prepaid Insurance   No. 10

Date	Explanation	Ref.	Debit	Credit	Balance
1999					
Oct. 4		J1	600		600
31	Adj. entry	J2		50	550

Office Equipment   No. 15

Date	Explanation	Ref.	Debit	Credit	Balance
1999					
Oct. 1		J1	5,000		5,000

Accumulated Depreciation—Office Equipment No. 16

Date	Explanation	Ref.	Debit	Credit	Balance
1999					
Oct. 31	Adj. entry	J2		40	40

Notes Payable   No. 25

Date	Explanation	Ref.	Debit	Credit	Balance
1999					
Oct. 1		J1		5,000	5,000

Accounts Payable   No. 26

Date	Explanation	Ref.	Debit	Credit	Balance
1999					
Oct. 5		J1		2,500	2,500

Interest Payable   No. 27

Date	Explanation	Ref.	Debit	Credit	Balance
1999					
Oct. 31	Adj. entry	J2		50	50

Unearned Revenue   No. 28

Date	Explanation	Ref.	Debit	Credit	Balance
1999					
Oct. 2		J1		1,200	
31	Adj. entry	J2	400		800

Salaries Payable   No. 29

Date	Explanation	Ref.	Debit	Credit	Balance
1999					
Oct. 31	Adj. entry	J2		1,200	1,200

C. R. Byrd, Capital   No. 40

Date	Explanation	Ref.	Debit	Credit	Balance
1999					
Oct. 1		J1		10,000	10,000

C. R. Byrd, Drawing   No. 41

Date	Explanation	Ref.	Debit	Credit	Balance
1999					
Oct. 20		J1	500		500

Service Revenue   No. 50

Date	Explanation	Ref.	Debit	Credit	Balance
1999					
Oct. 31		J1		10,000	10,000
31	Adj. entry	J2		400	10,400
31	Adj. entry	J2		200	10,600

Salaries Expense   No. 60

Date	Explanation	Ref.	Debit	Credit	Balance
1999					
Oct. 26		J1	4,000		4,000
31	Adj. entry	J2	1,200		5,200

Advertising Supplies Expense   No. 61

Date	Explanation	Ref.	Debit	Credit	Balance
1999					
Oct. 31	Adj. entry	J2	1,500		1,500

Rent Expense   No. 62

Date	Explanation	Ref.	Debit	Credit	Balance
1999					
Oct. 3		J1	900		900

Insurance Expense   No. 63

Date	Explanation	Ref.	Debit	Credit	Balance
1999					
Oct. 31	Adj. entry	J2	50		50

Interest Expense   No. 64

Date	Explanation	Ref.	Debit	Credit	Balance
1999					
Oct. 31	Adj. entry	J2	50		50

Depreciation Expense   No. 65

Date	Explanation	Ref.	Debit	Credit	Balance
1999					
Oct. 31	Adj. entry	J2	40		40

ILLUSTRATION 3-17

General ledger after adjustment

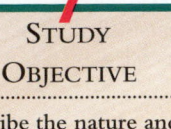

7
STUDY
OBJECTIVE

Describe the nature and
purpose of an adjusted
trial balance.

THE ADJUSTED TRIAL BALANCE AND FINANCIAL STATEMENTS

After all adjusting entries have been journalized and posted, another trial balance is prepared from the ledger accounts. This trial balance is called an **adjusted trial balance**. It shows the balances of all accounts, including those that have been adjusted, at the end of the accounting period. The purpose of an adjusted trial balance is to **prove the equality** of the total debit balances and the total credit balances in the ledger after all adjustments have been made. Because the accounts contain all data that are needed for financial statements, the adjusted trial balance is the primary basis for the preparation of financial statements.

Preparing the Adjusted Trial Balance

The adjusted trial balance for Pioneer Advertising Agency presented in Illustration 3-18 has been prepared from the ledger accounts in Illustration 3-17. To facilitate the comparison of account balances, the trial balance data, labeled "Before Adjustment" (presented earlier in Illustration 3-3), are shown alongside the adjusted data, labeled "After Adjustment." In addition, the amounts affected by the adjusting entries are highlighted in color in the "After Adjustment" columns.

ILLUSTRATION 3-18

Trial balance and adjusted trial balance compared

PIONEER ADVERTISING AGENCY
Trial Balances
October 31, 1999

	Before Adjustment		After Adjustment	
	Dr.	Cr.	Dr.	Cr.
Cash	$15,200		$15,200	
Accounts Receivable			200	
Advertising Supplies	2,500		1,000	
Prepaid Insurance	600		550	
Office Equipment	5,000		5,000	
Accumulated Depreciation— Office Equipment				$ 40
Notes Payable		$ 5,000		5,000
Accounts Payable		2,500		2,500
Interest Payable				50
Unearned Revenue		1,200		800
Salaries Payable				1,200
C. R. Byrd, Capital		10,000		10,000
C. R. Byrd, Drawing	500		500	
Service Revenue		10,000		10,600
Salaries Expense	4,000		5,200	
Advertising Supplies Expense			1,500	
Rent Expense	900		900	
Insurance Expense			50	
Interest Expense			50	
Depreciation Expense			40	
	$28,700	$28,700	$30,190	$30,190

Preparing Financial Statements

Financial statements can be prepared directly from an adjusted trial balance.
The preparation of financial statements from the adjusted trial balance of Pioneer
Advertising Agency and the interrelationship of data are presented in Illustrations 3-19 and 3-20.

As shown in Illustration 3-19 the income statement is prepared from the
revenue and expense accounts; the owner's equity statement is derived from the
owner's capital and drawing accounts and the net income (or net loss) shown in
the income statement. As shown in Illustration 3-20 the balance sheet is then
prepared from the asset and liability accounts and the ending owner's capital
balance as reported in the owner's equity statement.

ILLUSTRATION 3-19

*Preparation of the income
statement and owner's equity
statement from the adjusted
trial balance*

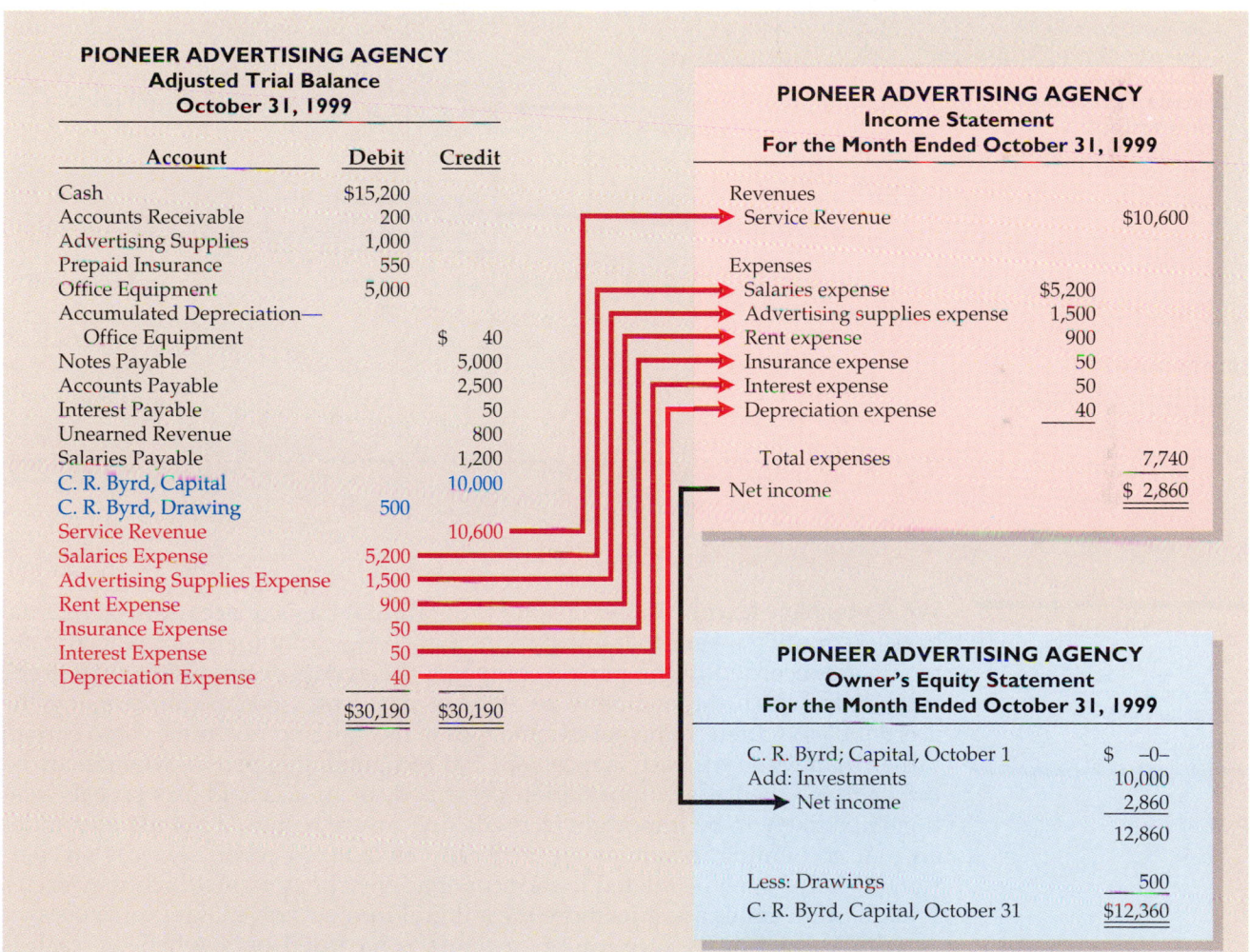

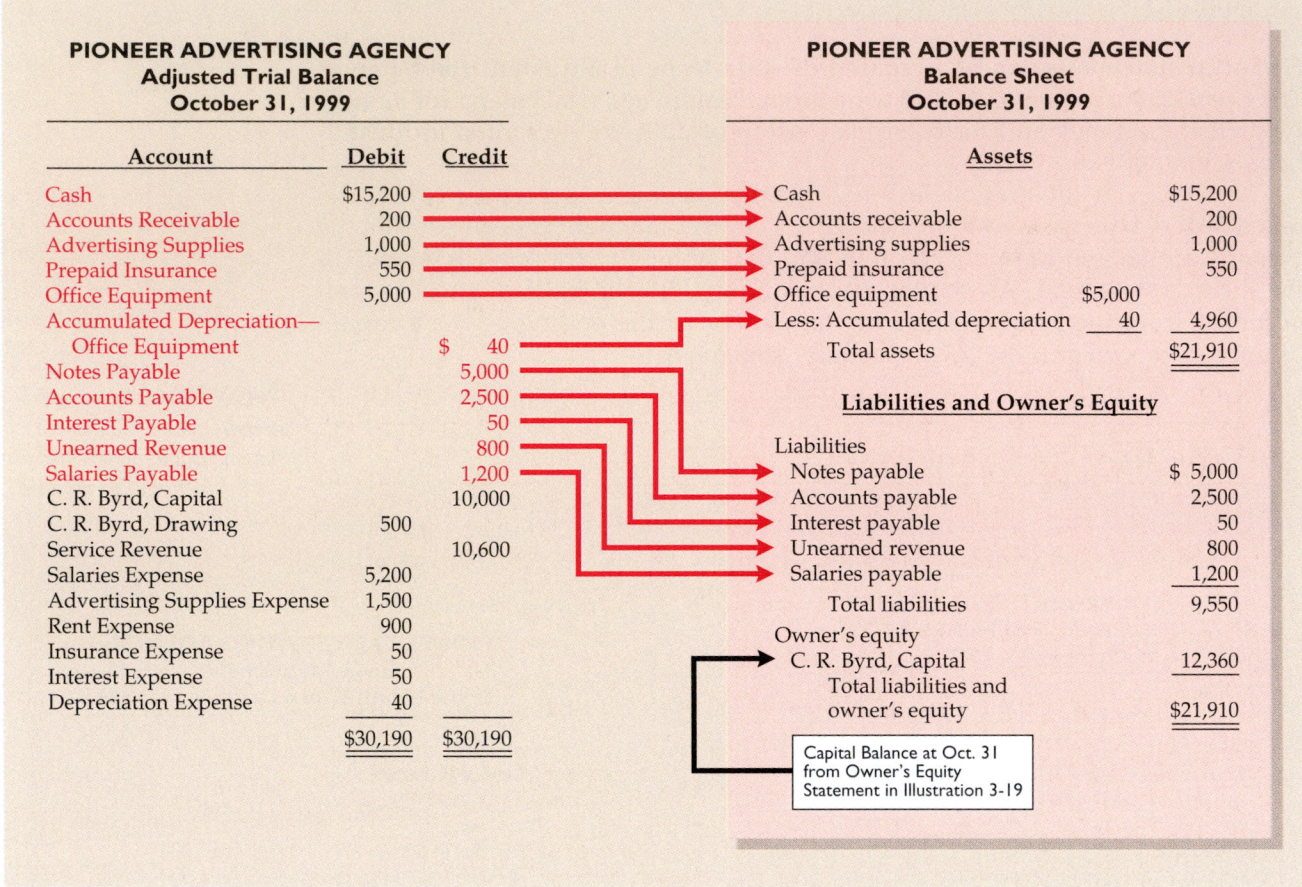

PIONEER ADVERTISING AGENCY Adjusted Trial Balance October 31, 1999			PIONEER ADVERTISING AGENCY Balance Sheet October 31, 1999		
Account	**Debit**	**Credit**	**Assets**		
Cash	$15,200		Cash		$15,200
Accounts Receivable	200		Accounts receivable		200
Advertising Supplies	1,000		Advertising supplies		1,000
Prepaid Insurance	550		Prepaid insurance		550
Office Equipment	5,000		Office equipment	$5,000	
Accumulated Depreciation— Office Equipment		$ 40	Less: Accumulated depreciation	40	4,960
Notes Payable		5,000	Total assets		$21,910
Accounts Payable		2,500			
Interest Payable		50	**Liabilities and Owner's Equity**		
Unearned Revenue		800	Liabilities		
Salaries Payable		1,200	Notes payable		$ 5,000
C. R. Byrd, Capital		10,000	Accounts payable		2,500
C. R. Byrd, Drawing	500		Interest payable		50
Service Revenue		10,600	Unearned revenue		800
Salaries Expense	5,200		Salaries payable		1,200
Advertising Supplies Expense	1,500		Total liabilities		9,550
Rent Expense	900		Owner's equity		
Insurance Expense	50		C. R. Byrd, Capital		12,360
Interest Expense	50		Total liabilities and		
Depreciation Expense	40		owner's equity		$21,910
	$30,190	$30,190			

Capital Balance at Oct. 31 from Owner's Equity Statement in Illustration 3-19

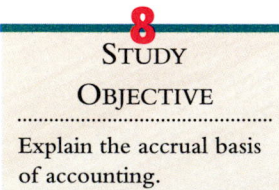

ILLUSTRATION 3-20

Preparation of the balance sheet from the adjusted trial balance

ACCRUAL VS. CASH BASIS OF ACCOUNTING

8
STUDY
OBJECTIVE

Explain the accrual basis of accounting.

What you have learned in this chapter is the **accrual basis of accounting**. Accrual basis accounting means that transactions that change a company's financial statements are recorded **in the periods in which the events occur**, rather than in the periods in which the company receives or pays cash. For example, using the accrual basis to determine net income means recognizing revenues when earned rather than when the cash is received, and recognizing expenses when incurred rather than when paid. Information presented on an accrual basis reveals relationships likely to be important in predicting future results. To illustrate, under accrual accounting, revenues are generally recognized when services are performed so they can be related to the economic environment in which they occur. Trends in revenues are thus more meaningful for decision-making purposes.

Under **cash basis accounting**, revenue is recorded only when the cash is received, and an expense is recorded only when cash is paid. As a result, the cash basis of accounting often leads to misleading financial statements. For example, it fails to record revenue which has been earned but for which the cash has not been received, violating the revenue recognition principle. In addition, expenses are also not matched with earned revenues and therefore the matching principle is not followed. Therefore, **the cash basis of accounting is not in accordance with generally accepted accounting principles.**

INTERNATIONAL NOTE

Although different accounting standards are often used in other major industrialized countries, the accrual basis of accounting is followed by all these countries.

Although most companies use the accrual basis of accounting, some small companies use the cash basis of accounting. The cash basis of accounting is justified by these businesses because they often have few receivables and payables. Accountants are sometimes asked to convert cash basis records to the accrual basis. As you might expect, extensive adjusting entries are required for this task.

BEFORE YOU GO ON . . .

Review It

1. What is the purpose of an adjusted trial balance?
2. How is an adjusted trial balance prepared?
3. What are the differences between the cash and accrual bases of accounting?

A LOOK BACK AT OUR FEATURE STORY

Refer to the opening story about Arizona State University, and answer the following questions.

1. What are the purposes of adjusting entries?
2. Why should Arizona State be concerned about the period in which revenue is recognized?
3. What adjusting entries should be made for tuition revenue and supplies expense at the end of the summer session?
4. What other types of adjusting entries do you believe Arizona State University might make?

Solution:

1. Adjusting entries are necessary to make the financial statements complete and accurate. Adjusting entries are made to record revenues in the period in which they are earned and to recognize expenses in the period in which they are incurred. Therefore, adjustments ensure that the revenue recognition and matching principles are followed.
2. As a not-for-profit institution Arizona State University must operate within its state appropriations and its own budget. It must know what revenues are attributable to each operating/accounting period. Assignment of revenues to the proper operating periods (namely, in the period earned) is necessary in order to make operating/accounting periods (years) comparable.
3. ASU probably used Unearned Tuition Revenue because tuition is generally received before the semester begins. The adjusting entry is debit Unearned Tuition Revenue and credit Tuition Revenue. When supplies were purchased, ASU probably debited Supplies. The adjusting entry is a credit to Supplies and a debit to Supplies Expense.
4. (a) Accrued expenses: rent, salaries, utilities, interest.
   (b) Accrued revenues: unpaid tuition, lab fees, interest earned.
   (c) Prepaid expenses: insurance, depreciation.
   (d) Unearned revenues: tuition, lab fees, theatre tickets, athletic tickets.

THE
NAVIGATOR

DEMONSTRATION PROBLEM

Terry Thomas opens the Green Thumb Lawn Care Company on April 1. At April 30, the trial balance shows the following balances for selected accounts:

Prepaid Insurance	$ 3,600
Equipment	28,000
Notes Payable	20,000
Unearned Revenue	4,200
Service Revenue	1,800

Analysis reveals the following additional data pertaining to these accounts:

1. Prepaid insurance is the cost of a two-year insurance policy, effective April 1.
2. Depreciation on the equipment is $500 per month.
3. The note payable is dated April 1. It is a six-month, 12% note.
4. Seven customers paid for the company's six months' lawn service package of $600 beginning in April. These customers were serviced in April.
5. Lawn services rendered other customers but not billed at April 30 totaled $1,500.

Instructions

Prepare the adjusting entries for the month of April. Show computations.

SOLUTION TO DEMONSTRATION PROBLEM

**PROBLEM-SOLVING
STRATEGIES**

1. Note that adjustments are being made for one month.
2. Make computations carefully.
3. Select account titles carefully.
4. Make sure debits are made first and credits are indented.
5. Check that debits equal credits for each entry.

GENERAL JOURNAL   **J2**

Date	Account Titles and Explanation	Ref.	Debit	Credit
	Adjusting Entries			
Apr. 30	Insurance Expense		150	
	Prepaid Insurance			150
	(To record insurance expired:			
	$3,600 ÷ 24 = $150 per month)			
30	Depreciation Expense		500	
	Accumulated Depreciation—Equipment			500
	(To record monthly depreciation)			
30	Interest Expense		200	
	Interest Payable			200
	(To record interest on notes payable:			
	$20,000 × 12% × 1/12 = $200)			
30	Unearned Revenue		700	
	Service Revenue			700
	(To record service revenue: $600 ÷ 6 = $100;			
	$100 per month × 7 = $700)			
30	Accounts Receivable		1,500	
	Service Revenue			1,500
	(To record revenue for services provided)			

THE
NAVIGATOR

SUMMARY OF STUDY OBJECTIVES

1. Explain the time period assumption. The time period assumption assumes that the economic life of a business can be divided into artificial time periods.

2. Distinguish between the revenue recognition principle and the matching principle. The revenue recognition principle dictates that revenue be recognized in the accounting period in which it is earned. The matching principle dictates that expenses be recognized when they make their contribution to revenues.

3. Explain why adjusting entries are needed. Adjusting entries are made at the end of an accounting period. They ensure that revenues are recorded in the period in which they are earned and that expenses are recognized in the period in which they are incurred.

4. Identify the major types of adjusting entries. The major types of adjusting entries are prepaid expenses, unearned revenues, accrued revenues, and accrued expenses.

5. Prepare adjusting entries for prepayments. Prepayments are either prepaid expenses or unearned revenues. Adjusting entries for prepayments are required at the statement date to record the portion of the prepayment that represents the expense incurred or the revenue earned in the current accounting period.

6. Prepare adjusting entries for accruals. Accruals are either accrued revenues or accrued expenses. Adjusting entries for accruals are required to record revenues earned and expenses incurred in the current accounting period that have not been recognized through daily entries.

7. *Describe the nature and purpose of an adjusted trial balance.* An adjusted trial balance is a trial balance that shows the balances of all accounts, including those that have been adjusted, at the end of an accounting period. The purpose of an adjusted trial balance is to show the effects of all financial events that have occurred during the accounting period.

8. *Explain the accrual basis of accounting.* Accrual basis accounting means that events that change a company's financial statements are recorded in the periods in which the events occur, rather than in the periods in which the company receives or pays cash.

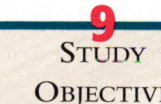

GLOSSARY

Accrual basis of accounting Accounting basis in which transactions that change a company's financial statements are recorded in the periods in which the events occur, rather than in the periods in which the company receives or pays cash. (p. 112).

Accrued expenses Expenses incurred but not yet paid in cash or recorded. (p. 104).

Accrued revenues Revenues earned but not yet received in cash or recorded. (p. 103).

Adjusted trial balance A list of accounts and their balances after all adjustments have been made. (p. 110).

Adjusting entries Entries made at the end of an accounting period to ensure that the revenue recognition and matching principles are followed. (p. 94).

Book value The difference between the cost of a depreciable asset and its related accumulated depreciation. (p. 100).

Calendar year An accounting period that extends from January 1 to December 31. (p. 93).

Cash basis accounting Accounting basis in which revenue is recorded only when cash is received and an expense is recorded only when cash is paid. (p. 112).

Contra asset account An account that is offset against an asset account on the balance sheet. (p. 100).

Depreciation The process of allocating the cost of an asset to expense over its useful life in a rational and systematic manner. (p. 99).

Fiscal year An accounting period that is one year in length. (p. 93).

Interim periods Monthly or quarterly accounting time periods. (p. 93).

Matching principle The principle that efforts (expenses) be matched with accomplishments (revenues). (p. 94).

Prepaid expenses Expenses paid in cash and recorded as assets before they are used or consumed. (p. 97).

Revenue recognition principle The principle that revenue be recognized in the accounting period in which it is earned. (p. 93).

Time period assumption An assumption that the economic life of a business can be divided into artificial time periods. (p. 93).

Unearned revenues Cash received and recorded as liabilities before revenue is earned. (p. 101).

Useful life The length of service of a productive facility. (p. 99).

APPENDIX ALTERNATIVE TREATMENT OF PREPAID EXPENSES AND UNEARNED REVENUES

In our discussion of adjusting entries for prepaid expenses and unearned revenues, we illustrated transactions for which the initial entries were made to balance sheet accounts. That is, in the case of prepaid expenses, the prepayment was debited to an asset account, and in the case of unearned revenue, the cash received was credited to a liability account. Some businesses use an alternative treatment: (1) At the time an expense is prepaid, it is debited to an expense account; (2) at the time of a receipt for future services, it is credited to a revenue account. The circumstances that justify such entries and the different adjusting entries that may be required are described below. The alternative treatment of prepaid expenses and unearned revenues has the same effect on the financial statements as the procedures described in the chapter.

9

STUDY
OBJECTIVE
....
Prepare adjusting entries for the alternative treatment of prepayments.

PREPAID EXPENSES

Prepaid expenses become expired costs either through the passage of time, as in the case of insurance, or through consumption, as in the case of advertising supplies. If, at the time of purchase, the company expects to consume the supplies before the next financial statement date, **it may be more convenient initially to debit (increase) an expense account rather than an asset account**. Assume, for example, that Pioneer Advertising expects that all of the supplies purchased on October 5 will be used before October 31. A debit of $2,500 to Advertising Supplies Expense rather than to the asset account, Advertising Supplies, on October 5 will eliminate the need for an adjusting entry on October 31, if all the supplies are used. At October 31, the Advertising Supplies Expense account will show a balance of $2,500, which is equal to the cost of supplies used between October 5 and October 31.

Assume, however, that the company does not use all the supplies, and an inventory of $1,000 of advertising supplies remains on October 31. What then? Obviously, in such a case an adjusting entry is needed. Prior to adjustment, the expense account, Advertising Supplies Expense, is overstated $1,000, and the asset account, Advertising Supplies, is understated $1,000. Thus the following adjusting entry is made:

A	=	L	+	OE
+1,000				+1,000

Oct. 31	Advertising Supplies	1,000	
	Advertising Supplies Expense		1,000
	(To record supplies inventory)		

After posting the adjusting entry, the accounts show:

ILLUSTRATION 3A-1

Prepaid expenses accounts after adjustment

Advertising Supplies		Advertising Supplies Expense		
10/31 **Adj.** **1,000**		10/5 2,500	10/31 **Adj.** **1,000**
		10/31 **Bal.** **1,500**	

After adjustment, the asset account, Advertising Supplies, shows a balance of $1,000, which is equal to the cost of supplies on hand at October 31. In addition, Advertising Supplies Expense shows a balance of $1,500, which is equal to the cost of supplies used between October 5 and October 31. If the adjusting entry is not made, expenses will be overstated and net income will be understated by $1,000 in the October income statement. Moreover, both assets and owner's equity will be understated by $1,000 on the October 31 balance sheet.

A comparative summary of the entries and accounts for advertising supplies is shown in Illustration 3A-2.

ILLUSTRATION 3A-2

Adjustment approaches— a comparison

Prepayment Initially Debited to Asset Account (per chapter)			Prepayment Initially Debited to Expense Account (per appendix)		
Oct. 5	Advertising Supplies	2,500	Oct. 5	Advertising Supplies	
	Accounts Payable	2,500		Expense	2,500
				Accounts Payable	2,500
Oct. 31	Advertising Supplies		Oct. 31	Advertising Supplies	1,000
	Expense	1,500		Advertising Supplies	
	Advertising Supplies	1,500		Expense	1,000

After posting the entries, the accounts appear as follows:

(per chapter) Advertising Supplies		(per appendix) Advertising Supplies	
10/5 2,500	10/31 Adj. 1,500	10/31 Adj. 1,000	
10/31 Bal. 1,000			
Advertising Supplies Expense		**Advertising Supplies Expense**	
10/31 Adj. 1,500		10/5 2,500	10/31 Adj. 1,000
		10/31 Bal. 1,500	

Note that the account balances under each alternative are the same at October 31; that is, Advertising Supplies $1,000, and Advertising Supplies Expense $1,500.

UNEARNED REVENUES

Unearned revenues become earned either through the passage of time, as in the case of unearned rent, or through rendering the service, as in the case of unearned fees. Like prepaid expenses, a revenue account may be credited when cash is received for future services and a different adjusting entry may be necessary.

To illustrate, assume that when Pioneer Advertising received $1,200 for future services on October 2 the services were expected to be performed before October 31.[3] In such a case, Service Revenue is credited. If revenue is in fact earned before October 31, no adjustment is needed. However, if, at the statement date, $800 of the services have not been performed, an adjusting entry is required. Prior to adjustment, the revenue account, Service Revenue, is overstated $800, and the liability account, Unearned Revenue, is understated $800. Thus, the following adjusting entry is made:

Oct. 31	Service Revenue	800	
	Unearned Revenue		800
	(To record unearned revenue)		

$$A = L + OE$$
$$+800 \quad -800$$

After posting the adjusting entry, the accounts show:

Unearned Revenue		Service Revenue	
	10/31 Adj. 800	10/31 Adj. 800	10/2 1,200
			10/31 Bal. 400

[3]This example focuses only on the alternative treatment of unearned revenues. In the interest of simplicity, the entries to Service Revenue pertaining to the immediate earning of revenue ($10,000) and the adjusting entry for accrued revenue ($200) have been ignored.

The liability account, Unearned Revenue, shows a balance of $800, which is equal to the services that will be rendered in the future. In addition, the balance in Service Revenue equals the services rendered in October. If the adjusting entry is not made, both revenues and net income will be overstated by $800 in the October income statement. Moreover, liabilities will be understated by $800, and owner's equity will be overstated by $800 on the October 31 balance sheet.

A comparative summary of the entries and accounts for service revenue earned and unearned is presented in Illustration 3A-5:

ILLUSTRATION 3A-5

Adjustment approaches— a comparison

	Unearned Revenue Initially Credited to Liability Account (per chapter)			Unearned Revenue Initially Credited to Revenue Account (per appendix)	
Oct. 2	Cash	1,200	Oct. 2	Cash	1,200
	Unearned Revenue	1,200		Service Revenue	1,200
Oct. 31	Unearned Revenue	400	Oct. 31	Service Revenue	800
	Service Revenue	400		Unearned Revenue	800

After posting the entries, the accounts will show:

ILLUSTRATION 3A-6

Comparison of accounts

(per chapter) Unearned Revenue		(per appendix) Unearned Revenue	
10/31 **Adj.** 400	10/2 1,200		10/31 **Adj.** 800
	10/31 Bal. **800**		

(per chapter) Service Revenue		(per appendix) Service Revenue	
	10/31 **Adj.** 400	10/31 **Adj.** 800	10/2 1,200
			10/31 Bal. **400**

Note that the balances in the accounts are the same under the two alternatives: Unearned Revenue $800, and Service Revenue $400.

SUMMARY OF ADDITIONAL ADJUSTMENT RELATIONSHIPS

The use of alternative adjusting entries requires additions to the summary of basic relationships presented earlier in Illustration 3-15. The additions are shown in color in Illustration 3A-7.

Alternative adjusting entries do not apply to accrued revenues and accrued expenses because **no entries occur before these types of adjusting entries are made**. Hence, the summary data shown in Illustration 3-15 for these two types of adjustments remains unchanged.

Type of Adjustment	Reason for Adjustment	Account Balances before Adjustment	Adjusting Entry
1. Prepaid Expenses	(a) Prepaid expenses initially recorded in asset accounts have been used.	Assets overstated Expenses understated	Dr. Expenses Cr. Assets
	(b) Prepaid expenses initially recorded in expense accounts have not been used.	Assets understated Expenses overstated	Dr. Assets Cr. Expenses
2. Unearned Revenues	(a) Unearned revenues initially recorded in liability accounts have been earned.	Liabilities overstated Revenues understated	Dr. Liabilities Cr. Revenues
	(b) Unearned revenues initially recorded in revenue accounts have not been earned.	Liabilities understated Revenues overstated	Dr. Revenues Cr. Liabilities

ILLUSTRATION 3A-7

Summary of basic relationships for prepayments

SUMMARY OF STUDY OBJECTIVE FOR APPENDIX

9. Prepare adjusting entries for the alternative treatment of prepayments. When prepayments are initially recorded in expense and revenue accounts, these accounts are overstated prior to adjustment. The adjusting entries for prepaid expenses are a debit to an asset account and a credit to an expense account. Adjusting entries for unearned revenues are a debit to a revenue account and a credit to a liability account.

*Note: All asterisked Questions, Exercises, and Problems relate to material in the appendix to the chapter.

SELF-STUDY QUESTIONS

Answers are at the end of the chapter.

(SO 1) 1. The time period assumption states that:
   a. revenue should be recognized in the accounting period in which it is earned.
   b. expenses should be matched with revenues.
   c. the economic life of a business can be divided into artificial time periods.
   d. the fiscal year should correspond with the calendar year.

(SO 2) 2. The principle which dictates that efforts (expenses) be matched with accomplishments (revenues) is the:
   a. matching principle.
   b. cost principle.
   c. periodicity principle.
   d. revenue recognition principle.

(SO 3) 3. Adjusting entries are made to ensure that:
   a. expenses are recognized in the period in which they are incurred.
   b. revenues are recorded in the period in which they are earned.
   c. balance sheet and income statement accounts have correct balances at the end of an accounting period.
   d. all of the above.

4. Each of the following is a major type (or category) of (SO 4) adjusting entries *except*:
   a. prepaid expenses.
   b. accrued revenues.
   c. accrued expenses.
   d. earned revenues.

5. The trial balance shows Supplies $1,350 and Supplies (SO 5) Expense $0. If $600 of supplies are on hand at the end of the period, the adjusting entry is:

a. Supplies	600	
Supplies Expense		600
b. Supplies	750	
Supplies Expense		750
c. Supplies Expense	750	
Supplies		750
d. Supplies Expense	600	
Supplies		600

(SO 5) 6. Adjustments for unearned revenues:
   a. decrease liabilities and increase revenues.
   b. have an assets and revenues account relationship.
   c. increase assets and increase revenues.
   d. decrease revenues and decrease assets.

(SO 6) 7. Adjustments for accrued revenues:
   a. have a liabilities and revenues account relationship.
   b. have an assets and revenues account relationship.
   c. decrease assets and revenues.
   d. decrease liabilities and increase revenues.

(SO 6) 8. Kathy Siska earned a salary of $400 for the last week of September. She will be paid on October 1. The adjusting entry for Kathy's employer at September 30 is:
   a. No entry is required

b. Salaries Expense	400	
Salaries Payable		400
c. Salaries Expense	400	
Cash		400
d. Salaries Payable	400	
Cash		400

(SO 7) 9. Which of the following statements is *incorrect* concerning the adjusted trial balance?
   a. An adjusted trial balance proves the equality of the total debit balances and the total credit balances in the ledger after all adjustments are made.
   b. The adjusted trial balance provides the primary basis for the preparation of financial statements.

   c. The adjusted trial balance lists the account balances segregated by assets and liabilities.
   d. The adjusted trial balance is prepared after the adjusting entries have been journalized and posted.

(SO 8) 10. One of the following statements about the accrual basis of accounting is *false*. That statement is:
   a. Events that change a company's financial statements are recorded in the periods in which the events occur.
   b. Revenue is recognized in the period in which it is earned.
   c. This basis is in accord with generally accepted accounting principles.
   d. Revenue is recorded only when cash is received, and expense is recorded only when cash is paid.

(SO 9) *11. The trial balance shows Supplies $0 and Supplies Expense $1,500. If $800 of supplies are on hand at the end of the period, the adjusting entry is:
   a. debit Supplies $800 and credit Supplies Expense $800.
   b. debit Supplies Expense $800 and credit Supplies $800.
   c. debit Supplies $700 and credit Supplies Expense $700.
   d. debit Supplies Expense $700 and credit Supplies $700.

THE NAVIGATOR

QUESTIONS

1. (a) How does the time period assumption affect an accountant's analysis of business transactions?
   (b) Explain the terms *fiscal year*, *calendar year*, and *interim periods*.

2. Identify and state two generally accepted accounting principles that relate to adjusting the accounts.

3. Bon Barone, a lawyer, accepts a legal engagement in March, performs the work in April, and is paid in May. If Barone's law firm prepares monthly financial statements, when should it recognize revenue from this engagement? Why?

4. In completing the engagement in (3) above, Barone incurs $4,500 of expenses in March, which are paid in April. How much expense should be deducted from revenues in the month the revenue is recognized? Why?

5. "Adjusting entries are required by the cost principle of accounting." Do you agree? Explain.

6. Why may a trial balance not contain up-to-date and complete financial information?

7. Distinguish between the two categories of adjusting entries and identify the types of adjustments applicable to each category.

8. What is the debit/credit effect of a prepaid expense adjusting entry?

9. "Depreciation is a process of valuation that results in the reporting of the fair market value of the asset." Do you agree? Explain.

10. Explain the differences between depreciation expense and accumulated depreciation.

11. Shen Company purchased equipment for $15,000. By the current balance sheet date, $7,000 had been depreciated. Indicate the balance sheet presentation of the data.

12. What is the debit/credit effect of an unearned revenue adjusting entry?

13. A company fails to recognize revenue earned but not yet received. Which of the following accounts are involved in the adjusting entry: (a) asset, (b) liability, (c) revenue, or (d) expense? For the accounts selected, indicate whether they would be debited or credited in the entry.

14. A company fails to recognize an expense incurred but not paid. Indicate which of the following accounts is debited and which is credited in the adjusting entry: (a) asset, (b) liability, (c) revenue, or (d) expense.

15. A company makes an accrued revenue adjusting entry for $800 and an accrued expense adjusting entry for $600. How much was net income understated prior to these entries? Explain.

16. On January 9, a company pays $5,000 for salaries of which $2,000 was reported as Salaries Payable on December 31. Give the entry to record the payment.

17. For each of the following items before adjustment, indicate the type of adjusting entry (prepaid expense, unearned revenue, accrued revenue, and accrued expense) that is needed to correct the misstatement. If an item could result in more than one type of adjusting entry, indicate each of the types.
    (a) Assets are understated.
    (b) Liabilities are overstated.
    (c) Liabilities are understated.
    (d) Expenses are understated.
    (e) Assets are overstated.
    (f) Revenue is understated.

18. One-half of the adjusting entry is given below. Indicate the account title for the other half of the entry.
    (a) Salaries Expense is debited.
    (b) Depreciation Expense is debited.
    (c) Interest Payable is credited.
    (d) Supplies is credited.
    (e) Accounts Receivable is debited.
    (f) Unearned Service Revenue is debited.

19. "An adjusting entry may affect more than one balance sheet or income statement account." Do you agree? Why or why not?

20. Why is it possible to prepare financial statements directly from an adjusted trial balance?

21. Why do accrual basis financial statements provide more useful information than cash basis statements?

*22. The Alpha Company debits Supplies Expense for all purchases of supplies and credits Rent Revenue for all advanced rentals. For each type of adjustment, give the adjusting entry.

BRIEF EXERCISES

BE3–1 The ledger of the Hilo Company includes the following accounts. Explain why each account may require adjustment.
a. Prepaid Insurance
b. Depreciation Expense
c. Unearned Revenue
d. Interest Payable

Indicate why adjusting entries are needed.
(SO 3)

BE3–2 The Reno Company accumulates the following adjustment data at December 31. Indicate (a) the type of adjustment (prepaid expense, accrued revenues and so on), and (b) the accounts before adjustment (overstated or understated).

1. Supplies of $600 are on hand.
2. Services provided but unbilled total $900.
3. Interest of $200 has accumulated on a note payable.
4. Rent collected in advance totaling $800 has been earned.

Identify the major types of adjusting entries.
(SO 4)

BE3–3 The Spahn Advertising Company's trial balance at December 31 shows Advertising Supplies $8,700 and Advertising Supplies Expense $0. On December 31, there are $1,500 of supplies on hand. Prepare the adjusting entry at December 31 and, using T accounts, enter the balances in the accounts, post the adjusting entry, and indicate the adjusted balance in each account.

Prepare adjusting entry for supplies.
(SO 5)

BE3–4 At the end of its first year, the trial balance of Tabor Company shows Equipment $25,000 and zero balances in Accumulated Depreciation—Equipment and Depreciation Expense. Depreciation for the year is estimated to be $4,000. Prepare the adjusting entry for depreciation at December 31, post the adjustments to T accounts, and indicate the balance sheet presentation of the equipment at December 31.

Prepare adjusting entries for depreciation.
(SO 5)

BE3–5 On July 1, 1999, Blair Co. pays $18,000 to Hindi Insurance Co. for a three-year insurance contract. Both companies have fiscal years ending December 31. For Blair Co. journalize and post the entry on July 1 and the adjusting entry on December 31.

Prepare adjusting entries for prepaid expense.
(SO 5)

BE3–6 Using the data in BE3–5, journalize and post the entry on July 1 and the adjusting entry on December 31 for Hindi Insurance Co. Hindi uses the accounts Unearned Insurance Revenue and Insurance Revenue.

Prepare adjusting entry for unearned revenue.
(SO 5)

BE3–7 The bookkeeper for DeVoe Company asks you to prepare the following accrued adjusting entries at December 31.

1. Interest on notes payable of $300 is accrued.
2. Services provided but unbilled total $1,400.
3. Salaries earned by employees of $900 have not been recorded.

Use the following account titles: Service Revenue, Accounts Receivable, Interest Expense, Interest Payable, Salaries Expense, and Salaries Payable.

Prepare adjusting entries for accruals.
(SO 6)

BE3–8 The trial balance of Wilson Company includes the following balance sheet accounts. Identify the accounts that require adjustment. For each account that requires adjustment, in-

Analyze accounts in an adjusted trial balance.
(SO 7)

dicate (a) the type of adjusting entry (prepaid expenses, unearned revenues, accrued revenues, and accrued expenses) and (b) the related account in the adjusting entry.

Accounts Receivable	Notes Payable
Prepaid Insurance	Interest Payable
Equipment	Unearned Service Revenue
Accumulated Depreciation—Equipment	

Prepare an income statement from an adjusted trial balance.
(SO 7)

BE3–9   The adjusted trial balance of Klar Company at December 31, 1999, includes the following accounts: S. Klar, Capital $15,600; S. Klar, Drawing $6,000; Service Revenue $38,400; Salaries Expense $13,000; Insurance Expense $2,000; Rent Expense $4,000; Supplies Expense $1,500; and Depreciation Expense $1,000. Prepare an income statement for the year.

Prepare an owner's equity statement from an adjusted trial balance.
(SO 7)

BE3–10   Partial adjusted trial balance data for Klar Company is presented in BE3–9. The balance in S. Klar, Capital is the balance as of January 1. Prepare an owner's equity statement for the year assuming net income is $17,000 for the year.

Prepare adjusting entries under alternative treatment of prepayments.
(SO 9)

*BE3–11**   Phelps Company records all prepayments in income statement accounts. At April 30, the trial balance shows Supplies Expense $2,800, Service Revenue $9,200, and zero balances in related balance sheet accounts. Prepare the adjusting entries at April 30 assuming (a) $1,500 of supplies on hand and (b) $800 of service revenue should be reported as unearned.

EXERCISES

Identify types of adjustments and account relationships.
(SO 4, 5, 6)

E3–1   The McLain Company accumulates the following adjustment data at December 31.

1. Services provided but unbilled total $600.
2. Store supplies of $300 have been used.
3. Utility expenses of $225 are unpaid.
4. Unearned revenue of $260 has been earned.
5. Salaries of $800 are unpaid.
6. Prepaid insurance totaling $350 has expired.

Instructions
For each of the above items indicate:

(a) The type of adjustment (prepaid expense, unearned revenue, accrued revenue, or accrued expense).
(b) The accounts before adjustment (overstatement or understatement).

Prepare adjusting entries from selected account data.
(SO 5, 6, 7)

E3–2   The ledger of Duggan Rental Agency on March 31 of the current year includes the following selected accounts before adjusting entries have been prepared.

	Debit	Credit
Prepaid Insurance	$ 3,600	
Supplies	2,800	
Equipment	25,000	
Accumulated Depreciation—Equipment		$ 8,400
Notes Payable		20,000
Unearned Rent Revenue		9,300
Rent Revenue		60,000
Interest Expense	–0–	
Wage Expense	14,000	

An analysis of the accounts shows the following:

1. The equipment depreciates $250 per month.
2. One-third of the unearned rent was earned during the quarter.
3. Interest of $500 is accrued on the notes payable.
4. Supplies on hand total $850.
5. Insurance expires at the rate of $300 per month.

Instructions
Prepare the adjusting entries at March 31, assuming that adjusting entries are made quarterly. Additional accounts are: Depreciation Expense, Insurance Expense, Interest Payable, and Supplies Expense.

E3–3 Karen Weller, D.D.S., opened a dental practice on January 1, 1999. During the first month of operations the following transactions occurred.

Prepare adjusting entries.
(SO 5, 6, 7)

1. Performed services for patients who had dental plan insurance. At January 31, $750 of such services was earned but not yet billed to the insurance companies.
2. Utility expenses incurred but not paid prior to January 31 totaled $520.
3. Purchased dental equipment on January 1 for $80,000, paying $20,000 in cash and signing a $60,000, three-year-note payable. The equipment depreciates $400 per month. Interest is $500 per month.
4. Purchased a one-year malpractice insurance policy on January 1 for $12,000.
5. Purchased $1,600 of dental supplies. On January 31, determined that $500 of supplies were on hand.

Instructions
Prepare the adjusting entries on January 31. Account titles are: Accumulated Depreciation— Dental Equipment, Depreciation Expense, Service Revenue, Accounts Receivable, Insurance Expense, Interest Expense, Interest Payable, Prepaid Insurance, Supplies, Supplies Expense, Utilities Expense, and Utilities Payable.

E3–4 The trial balance for Pioneer Advertising Agency is shown in Illustration 3-3, p. 96. In lieu of the adjusting entries shown in the text at October 31, assume the following adjustment data:

Prepare adjusting entries.
(SO 5, 6, 7)

1. Advertising supplies on hand at October 31 total $1,400.
2. Expired insurance for the month is $100.
3. Depreciation for the month is $50.
4. Unearned revenue in October totals $600.
5. Services provided but unbilled at October 31 are $300.
6. Interest accrued at October 31 is $70.
7. Accrued salaries at October 31 are $1,500.

Instructions
Prepare the adjusting entries for the items above.

E3–5 The income statement of Ranier Co. for the month of July shows net income of $1,400 based on Service Revenue $5,500, Wages Expense $2,300, Supplies Expense $1,200, and Utilities Expense $600. In reviewing the statement, you discover the following:

Prepare correct income statement.
(SO 2, 5, 6, 7)

1. Insurance expired during July of $300 was omitted.
2. Supplies expense includes $500 of supplies that are still on hand at July 31.
3. Depreciation on equipment of $150 was omitted.
4. Accrued but unpaid wages at July 31 of $300 were not included.
5. Services provided but unrecorded totaled $900.

Instructions
Prepare a correct income statement for July.

E3–6 A partial adjusted trial balance of Piper Company at January 31, 1999, shows the following:

Analyze adjusted data.
(SO 2, 4, 5, 6, 7)

PIPER COMPANY
Adjusted Trial Balance
January 31, 1999

	Debit	Credit
Supplies	$ 700	
Prepaid Insurance	2,400	
Salaries Payable		800
Unearned Revenue		750
Supplies Expense	950	
Insurance Expense	400	
Salaries Expense	1,800	
Service Revenue		2,000

Instructions
Answer the following questions, assuming the year begins January 1:

(a) If the amount in Supplies Expense is the January 31 adjusting entry, and $850 of supplies was purchased in January, what was the balance in Supplies on January 1?

(b) If the amount in Insurance Expense is the January 31 adjusting entry, and the original insurance premium was for one year, what was the total premium and when was the policy purchased?

(c) If $2,500 of salaries was paid in January, what was the balance in Salaries Payable at December 31, 1998?

(d) If $1,600 was received in January for services performed in January, what was the balance in Unearned Revenue at December 31, 1998?

Journalize basic transactions and adjusting entries.
(SO 5, 6, 7)

E3–7 Selected accounts of Felipe Company are shown below:

Supplies Expense

7/31	500	

Supplies

7/1	Bal.	1,100	7/31		500
7/10		200			

Salaries Payable

	7/31	1,200

Accounts Receivable

7/31	500

Unearned Revenue

7/31	900	7/1	Bal.	1,500	
		7/20		700	

Salaries Expense

7/15	1,200
7/31	1,200

Service Revenue

	7/14	3,000
	7/31	900
	7/31	500

Instructions

After analyzing the accounts, journalize (a) the July transactions and (b) the adjusting entries that were made on July 31. (*Hint:* July transactions were for cash.)

Prepare adjusting entries from analysis of trial balances.
(SO 5, 6, 7)

E3–8 The trial balances before and after adjustment for Lund Company at the end of its fiscal year are presented below.

LUND COMPANY
Trial Balance
August 31, 1999

	Before Adjustment Dr.	Before Adjustment Cr.	After Adjustment Dr.	After Adjustment Cr.
Cash	$10,400		$10,400	
Accounts Receivable	8,800		9,400	
Office Supplies	2,300		700	
Prepaid Insurance	4,000		2,500	
Office Equipment	14,000		14,000	
Accumulated Depreciation—Office Equipment		$ 3,600		$ 4,800
Accounts Payable		5,800		5,800
Salaries Payable		–0–		1,100
Unearned Rent Revenue		1,500		700
R. Roni, Capital		15,600		15,600
Service Revenue		34,000		34,600
Rent Revenue		11,000		11,800
Salaries Expense	17,000		18,100	
Office Supplies Expense	–0–		1,600	
Rent Expense	15,000		15,000	
Insurance Expense	–0–		1,500	
Depreciation Expense	–0–		1,200	
	$71,500	$71,500	$74,400	$74,400

Instructions
Prepare the adjusting entries that were made.

E3–9 The adjusted trial balance for the Lund Company is given in E3–8.

*Prepare financial statements
from adjusted trial balance.*
(SO 5, 6, 7)

Instructions
Prepare the income and owner's equity statements for the year and the balance sheet at August 31.

E3–10 On numerous occasions proposals have surfaced to put the federal government on the accrual basis of accounting. This is no small issue because if this basis were used, it would mean that billions in unrecorded liabilities would have to be booked and the federal deficit would increase substantially.

*Distinguish between cash and
accrual basis of accounting.*
(SO 8)

Instructions
(a) What is the difference between accrual basis accounting and cash basis accounting?
(b) Comment on why politicians prefer a cash basis accounting system over an accrual basis system.
(c) Write a letter to your senator explaining why you think the federal government should adopt the accrual basis of accounting.

*E3–11 At the Harmony Company, prepayments are debited to expense when paid and unearned revenues are credited to revenue when received. During January of the current year, the following transactions occurred:

*Journalize transactions and
adjusting entries using
appendix.*
(SO 9)

Jan. 2 Paid $2,400 for fire insurance protection for the year.
   10 Paid $1,700 for supplies.
   15 Received $5,100 for services to be performed in the future.

On January 31, it is determined that $1,500 of the services fees have been earned and that there are $800 of supplies on hand.

Instructions
(a) Journalize and post the January transactions. (Use T accounts.)
(b) Journalize and post the adjusting entries at January 31.
(c) Determine the ending balance in each of the accounts.

PROBLEMS: SET A

P3–1A The trial balance before adjustment of Midwest Tours at the end of its first month of operations is presented below:

*Prepare adjusting entries, post,
and prepare an adjusted trial
balance.*
(SO 5, 6, 7)

MIDWEST TOURS
Trial Balance
June 30, 1999

	Debit	Credit
Cash	$ 3,000	
Prepaid Insurance	7,800	
Office Equipment	1,800	
Buses	140,000	
Notes Payable		$ 62,000
Unearned Tour Revenue		15,000
Alan Kinsley, Capital		70,000
Tour Revenue		15,900
Salaries Expense	8,400	
Advertising Expense	800	
Gas and Oil Expense	1,100	
	$162,900	$162,900

Other data:

1. The insurance policy has a one-year term beginning June 1, 1999.
2. The monthly depreciation is $50 on office equipment and $2,000 on buses.
3. Interest of $700 accrues on the notes payable each month.
4. Deposits of $1,500 each were received for advanced tour reservations from 10 school groups. At June 30, four of these deposits have been earned.
5. Bus drivers are paid a combined total of $400 per day. At June 30, 3 days' salaries are unpaid.
6. A senior citizen's organization that had not made an advance deposit took a Canyon tour on June 30 for $1,200. This group was not billed for the services rendered until July 3.

Instructions

(a) Journalize the adjusting entries at June 30, 1999.
(b) Prepare a ledger using the three-column form of account. Enter the trial balance amounts and post the adjusting entries. (Use J2 as the posting reference.)
(c) Prepare an adjusted trial balance at June 30, 1999.

Prepare adjusting entries, adjusted trial balance, and financial statements.
(SO 5, 6, 7)

P3–2A The Super Motel opened for business on May 1, 1999. Its trial balance before adjustment on May 31 is as follows:

SUPER MOTEL
Trial Balance
May 31, 1999

	Debit	Credit
Cash	$ 2,500	
Prepaid Insurance	1,800	
Supplies	1,900	
Land	15,000	
Lodge	70,000	
Furniture	16,800	
Accounts Payable		$ 4,700
Unearned Rent Revenue		3,600
Mortgage Payable		35,000
Sara Sutton, Capital		60,000
Rent Revenue		9,200
Salaries Expense	3,000	
Utilities Expense	1,000	
Advertising Expense	500	
	$112,500	$112,500

Other data:

1. Insurance expires at the rate of $200 per month.
2. An inventory of supplies shows $1,200 of unused supplies on May 31.
3. Annual depreciation is $3,600 on the lodge and $3,000 on furniture.
4. The mortgage interest rate is 12%. (The mortgage was taken out on May 1.)
5. Unearned rent of $1,500 has been earned.
6. Salaries of $300 are accrued and unpaid at May 31.

Instructions

(a) Journalize the adjusting entries on May 31.
(b) Prepare a ledger using the three-column form of account. Enter the trial balance amounts and post the adjusting entries. (Use J1 as the posting reference.)
(c) Prepare an adjusted trial balance on May 31.
(d) Prepare an income statement and an owner's equity statement for the month of May and a balance sheet at May 31.

Prepare adjusting entries and financial statements.
(SO 5, 6, 7)

P3–3A The Irabu Co. was organized on July 1, 1999. Quarterly financial statements are prepared. The unadjusted and adjusted trial balances as of September 30 are shown below.

IRABU CO.
Trial Balance
September 30, 1999

	Unadjusted Dr.	Unadjusted Cr.	Adjusted Dr.	Adjusted Cr.
Cash	$ 6,700		$ 6,700	
Accounts Receivable	400		1,000	
Prepaid Rent	1,500		900	
Supplies	1,200		1,000	
Equipment	15,000		15,000	
Accumulated Depreciation—Equipment				$ 350
Notes Payable		$ 5,000		5,000
Accounts Payable		1,510		1,510
Salaries Payable				400
Interest Payable				50
Unearned Rent Revenue		900		600
Yosuke Irabu, Capital		14,000		14,000
Yosuke Irabu, Drawing	600		600	
Commission Revenue		14,000		14,600
Rent Revenue		400		700
Salaries Expense	9,000		9,400	
Rent Expense	900		1,500	
Depreciation Expense			350	
Supplies Expense			200	
Utilities Expense	510		510	
Interest Expense			50	
	$35,810	$35,810	$37,210	$37,210

Instructions

(a) Journalize the adjusting entries that were made.

(b) Prepare an income statement and an owner's equity statement for the 3 months ending September 30 and a balance sheet at September 30.

(c) If the note bears interest at 12%, how many months has it been outstanding?

P3–4A A review of the ledger of Davis Company at December 31, 1999, produces the following data pertaining to the preparation of annual adjusting entries:

Prepare adjusting entries.
(SO 5, 6)

1. Prepaid Insurance $12,800. The company has separate insurance policies on its buildings and its motor vehicles. Policy B4564 on the building was purchased on July 1, 1998, for $9,000. The policy has a term of 3 years. Policy A2958 on the vehicles was purchased on January 1, 1999, for $4,800. This policy has a term of 2 years.

2. Unearned Subscription Revenue $49,000. The company began selling magazine subscriptions in 1999 on an annual basis. The selling price of a subscription is $50. A review of subscription contracts reveals the following:

Subscription Date	Number of Subscriptions
October 1	200
November 1	300
December 1	480
	980

3. Notes Payable, $40,000. This balance consists of a note for 6 months at an annual interest rate of 9%, dated September 1.

4. Salaries Payable $0. There are eight salaried employees. Salaries are paid every Friday for the current week. Five employees receive a salary of $600 each per week, and three employees earn $700 each per week. December 31 is a Wednesday. Employees do not work weekends. All employees worked the last 3 days of December.

Instructions

Prepare the adjusting entries at December 31, 1999.

Journalize transactions and follow through accounting cycle to preparation of financial statements.
(SO 5, 6, 7)

P3–5A   On November 1, 1999, the account balances of Delino Equipment Repair were as follows:

No.	Debits		No.	Credits	
101	Cash	$ 2,790	154	Accumulated Depreciation	$ 500
112	Accounts Receivable	2,510	201	Accounts Payable	2,100
126	Supplies	1,000	209	Unearned Service Revenue	400
153	Store Equipment	10,000	212	Salaries Payable	500
			301	P. Delino, Capital	12,800
		$16,300			$16,300

During November the following summary transactions were completed.

Nov. 8   Paid $1,100 for salaries due employees, of which $600 is for November.
      10   Received $1,200 cash from customers on account.
      12   Received $1,400 cash for services performed in November.
      15   Purchased store equipment on account $3,000.
      17   Purchased supplies on account $1,500.
      20   Paid creditors on account $2,500.
      22   Paid November rent $300.
      25   Paid salaries $1,000.
      27   Performed services on account and billed customers for services rendered $900.
      29   Received $550 from customers for future service.

Adjustment data consist of:

1. Supplies on hand $1,600.
2. Accrued salaries payable $500.
3. Depreciation for the month is $120.
4. Unearned service revenue of $300 is earned.

Instructions

(a) Enter the November 1 balances in the ledger accounts.
(b) Journalize the November transactions.
(c) Post to the ledger accounts. Use J1 for posting reference and No. 407 Service Revenue, No. 615 Depreciation Expense, No. 631 Supplies Expense, No. 726 Salaries Expense, and No. 729 Rent Expense.
(d) Prepare a trial balance at November 30.
(e) Journalize and post adjusting entries.
(f) Prepare an adjusted trial balance.
(g) Prepare an income statement and an owner's equity statement for November and a balance sheet at November 30.

Prepare adjusting entries, adjusted trial balance, and financial statements using appendix.
(SO 5, 6, 7, 9)

*P3–6A   Cordero Graphics Company was organized on January 1, 1999, by Jill Batke. At the end of the first 6 months of operations, the trial balance contained the following accounts:

Debits		Credits	
Cash	$ 9,500	Notes Payable	$ 17,000
Accounts Receivable	14,000	Accounts Payable	9,000
Equipment	45,000	Jill Batke, Capital	25,000
Insurance Expense	1,800	Graphic Revenue	52,100
Salaries Expense	30,000	Consulting Revenue	5,000
Supplies Expense	2,700		
Advertising Expense	1,900		
Rent Expense	1,500		
Utilities Expense	1,700		
	$108,100		$108,100

Analysis reveals the following additional data:

1. The $2,700 balance in Supplies Expense represents supplies purchased in January. At June 30, there was $1,500 of supplies on hand.

2. The note payable was issued on February 1. It is a 12%, 6-month note.
3. The balance in Insurance Expense is the premium on a one-year policy, dated March 1, 1999.
4. Consulting fees are credited to revenue when received. At June 30, consulting fees of $1,000 are unearned.
5. Graphic revenue earned but unbilled at June 30 totals $2,000.
6. Depreciation is $2,000 per year.

Instructions
(a) Journalize the adjusting entries at June 30. (Assume adjustments are recorded every 6 months.)
(b) Prepare an adjusted trial balance.
(c) Prepare an income statement and owner's equity statement for the 6 months ended June 30 and a balance sheet at June 30.

PROBLEMS: SET B

P3–1B The Orosco Security Service began operations on January 1, 1999. At the end of the first year of operations, the trial balance before adjustment shows the following:

Prepare adjusting entries, post, and prepare an adjusted trial balance.
(SO 5, 6, 7)

OROSCO SECURITY SERVICE
Trial Balance
December 31, 1999

	Debit	Credit
Cash	$ 12,400	
Accounts Receivable	3,200	
Prepaid Insurance	3,600	
Automobiles	58,000	
Notes Payable		$ 45,000
Unearned Revenue		2,500
C. Orosco, Capital		18,000
Service Revenue		84,000
Salaries Expense	57,000	
Repair Expense	6,000	
Gas and Oil Expense	9,300	
	$149,500	$149,500

Other data:

1. Services provided but unbilled $2,500 at December 31.
2. Insurance coverage began on January 1 under a 2-year policy.
3. Automobile depreciation is $15,000 for the year.
4. Interest of $5,400 accrued on notes payable for the year.
5. $1,000 of the unearned fees has been earned.
6. Drivers' salaries total $500 per day. At December 31, 3 days' salaries are unpaid.
7. Repairs to automobiles of $650 have been incurred, but bills have not been received prior to December 31. (Use Accounts Payable.)

Instructions
(a) Journalize the annual adjusting entries at December 31, 1999.
(b) Prepare a ledger using the three-column account form. Enter the trial balance amounts and post the adjusting entries. (Use J15 as the posting reference.)
(c) Prepare an adjusted trial balance at December 31, 1999.

P3–2B The Spring River Resort opened for business on June 1 with eight air-conditioned units. Its trial balance before adjustment on August 31 is as follows:

Prepare adjusting entries, adjusted trial balance, and financial statements.
(SO 5, 6, 7)

SPRING RIVER RESORT
Trial Balance
August 31, 1999

	Debit	Credit
Cash	$ 19,600	
Prepaid Insurance	5,400	
Supplies	3,300	
Land	25,000	
Cottages	125,000	
Furniture	26,000	
Accounts Payable		$ 6,500
Unearned Rent Revenue		6,800
Mortgage Payable		80,000
P. Villone, Capital		100,000
P. Villone, Drawing	5,000	
Rent Revenue		80,000
Salaries Expense	51,000	
Utilities Expense	9,400	
Repair Expense	3,600	
	$273,300	$273,300

Other data:

1. Insurance expires at the rate of $300 per month.
2. An inventory count on August 31 shows $900 of supplies on hand.
3. Annual depreciation is $4,800 on cottages and $2,400 on furniture.
4. Unearned rent of $5,000 was earned prior to August 31.
5. Salaries of $400 were unpaid at August 31.
6. Rentals of $800 were due from tenants at August 31. (Use Accounts Receivable.)
7. The mortgage interest rate is 12% per year. (The mortgage was taken out on August 1.)

Instructions

(a) Journalize the adjusting entries on August 31 for the 3-month period June 1–August 31.
(b) Prepare a ledger using the three-column form of account. Enter the trial balance amounts and post the adjusting entries. (Use J1 as the posting reference.)
(c) Prepare an adjusted trial balance on August 31.
(d) Prepare an income statement and an owner's equity statement for the 3 months ending August 31 and a balance sheet as of August 31.

Prepare adjusting entries and financial statements.
(SO 5, 6, 7)

P3–3B The Yount Advertising Agency was founded by Thomas Grant in January of 1995. Presented below are both the adjusted and unadjusted trial balances as of December 31, 1999.

YOUNT ADVERTISING AGENCY
Trial Balance
December 31, 1999

	Unadjusted		Adjusted	
	Dr.	Cr.	Dr.	Cr.
Cash	$ 11,000		$ 11,000	
Accounts Receivable	20,000		21,500	
Art Supplies	8,400		5,000	
Prepaid Insurance	3,350		2,500	
Printing Equipment	60,000		60,000	
Accumulated Depreciation		$ 28,000		$ 35,000
Accounts Payable		5,000		5,000
Interest Payable		0		150
Notes Payable		5,000		5,000
Unearned Advertising Revenue		7,000		5,600

	Unadjusted		Adjusted	
	Dr.	Cr.	Dr.	Cr.
Salaries Payable		0		1,300
R. Yount, Capital		25,500		25,500
R. Yount, Drawing	12,000		12,000	
Advertising Revenue		58,600		61,500
Salaries Expense	10,000		11,300	
Insurance Expense			850	
Interest Expense	350		500	
Depreciation Expense			7,000	
Art Supplies Expense			3,400	
Rent Expense	4,000		4,000	
	$129,100	$129,100	$139,050	$139,050

Instructions

(a) Journalize the annual adjusting entries that were made.

(b) Prepare an income statement and a statement of owner's equity for the year ending December 31, 1999, and a balance sheet at December 31.

(c) Answer the following questions:

    (1) If the note has been outstanding 3 months, what is the annual interest rate on that note?

    (2) If the company paid $13,500 in salaries in 1999, what was the balance in Salaries Payable on December 31, 1998?

P3–4B A review of the ledger of Oklahoma Company at December 31, 1999, produces the following data pertaining to the preparation of annual adjusting entries.

Prepare adjusting entries.
(SO 5, 6)

1. Salaries Payable $0. There are eight salaried employees. Salaries are paid every Friday for the current week. Five employees receive a salary of $700 each per week, and three employees earn $500 each per week. December 31 is a Tuesday. Employees do not work weekends. All employees worked the last 2 days of December.

2. Unearned Rent Revenue $369,000. The company began subleasing office space in its new building on November 1. Each tenant is required to make a $5,000 security deposit that is not refundable until occupancy is terminated. At December 31, the company had the following rental contracts that are paid in full for the entire term of the lease.

Date	Term (in months)	Monthly Rent	Number of Leases
Nov. 1	6	$4,000	5
Dec. 1	6	$8,500	4

3. Prepaid Advertising $13,200. This balance consists of payments on two advertising contracts. The contracts provide for monthly advertising in two trade magazines. The terms of the contracts are as follows:

Contract	Date	Amount	Number of Magazine Issues
A650	May 1	$6,000	12
B974	Oct. 1	7,200	24

The first advertisement runs in the month in which the contract is signed.

4. Notes Payable $80,000. This balance consists of a note for one year at an annual interest rate of 12%, dated June 1.

Journalize transactions and follow through accounting cycle to preparation of financial statements.
(SO 5, 6, 7)

Instructions

Prepare the adjusting entries at December 31, 1999. (Show all computations.)

P3–5B On September 1, 1999, the account balances of Silva Equipment Repair were as follows:

No.	Debits		No.	Credits	
101	Cash	$ 4,880	154	Accumulated Depreciation	$ 1,500
112	Accounts Receivable	3,520	201	Accounts Payable	3,400
126	Supplies	1,000	209	Unearned Service Revenue	400
153	Store Equipment	15,000	212	Salaries Payable	500
			301	J. Silva, Capital	18,600
		$24,400			$24,400

During September the following summary transactions were completed.

Sept. 8 Paid $1,100 for salaries due employees, of which $600 is for September.
   10 Received $1,200 cash from customers on account.
   12 Received $3,400 cash for services performed in September.
   15 Purchased store equipment on account $3,000.
   17 Purchased supplies on account $1,500.
   20 Paid creditors $4,500 on account.
   22 Paid September rent $500.
   25 Paid salaries $1,050.
   27 Performed services on account and billed customers for services rendered $700.
   29 Received $650 from customers for future service.

Adjustment data consist of:

1. Supplies on hand $1,800.
2. Accrued salaries payable $400.
3. Depreciation is $200 per month.
4. Unearned service revenue of $350 is earned.

Instructions
(a) Enter the September 1 balances in the ledger accounts.
(b) Journalize the September transactions.
(c) Post to the ledger accounts. Use J1 for posting reference and No. 407 Service Revenue, No. 615 Depreciation Expense, No. 631 Supplies Expense, No. 726 Salaries Expense, and No. 729 Rent Expense.
(d) Prepare a trial balance at September 30.
(e) Journalize and post adjusting entries.
(f) Prepare an adjusted trial balance.
(g) Prepare an income statement and an owner's equity statement for September and a balance sheet at September 30.

BROADENING YOUR PERSPECTIVE

FINANCIAL REPORTING AND ANALYSIS
....

FINANCIAL REPORTING PROBLEM: Kellogg Company

BYP3–1   The financial statements of Kellogg's are presented in Appendix A at the end of this textbook.

Instructions
(a) Using the consolidated financial statements and related information, identify items that may result in adjusting entries for prepayments.
(b) Using the consolidated financial statements and related information, identify items that may result in adjusting entries for accruals.
(c) Using the Selected Financial Data section, what has been the trend since 1990 for depreciation and amortization expense and for advertising expense?

COMPARATIVE ANALYSIS PROBLEM: Kellogg Company vs. General Mills

BYP3–2   Kellogg's financial statements are presented in Appendix A; General Mills's financial statements are presented in Appendix B.

Instructions
Based on information contained in these financial statements, determine the following for each company:

- (a) Net increase (decrease) in property, plant, and equipment from 1996 to 1997.
- (b) Increase (decrease) in selling, general, and administrative expenses from 1996 to 1997.
- (c) Increase (decrease) in accounts payable from 1996 to 1997.
- (d) Increase (decrease) in net income from 1996 to 1997.
- (e) Increase (decrease) in cash and cash equivalents from 1996 to 1997.

RESEARCH ASSIGNMENT

BYP3–3   The Enterprise Standard Industrial Classification (SIC) coding scheme, a published classification of firms into separate industries, is commonly used in practice. SIC codes permit identification of company activities on three levels of detail. Two-digit codes designate a "major group," three-digit codes designate an "industry group," while four-digit codes identify a specific "industry."

Instructions
At your library, find the *Standard Industrial Classification Manual* (published by the U.S. Government's Office of Management and Budget in 1987) to answer the following questions:

- (a) On what basis are SIC codes assigned to companies?
- (b) Identify the major group/industry group/industry represented by the following codes: 12, 271, 3571, 7033, 75, and 872.
- (c) Identify the SIC code for the following industries:
    1. Golfing equipment—manufacturing
    2. Worm farms
    3. Felt tip markers—manufacturing
    4. Household appliance stores, electric, or gas—retail
    5. Advertising agencies
- (d) You are interested in examining several companies in the passenger airline industry. Determine the appropriate two-, three-, and four-digit SIC codes. Use *Wards Business Directory of U.S. Private and Public Companies (Vol. 5)* to compile a list of the five largest parent companies (by total sales) in the industry. Note: If Wards is not available, alternative sources include *Standard & Poor's Register of Corporations, Directors, and Executives, Standard & Poor's Industry Surveys*, and the Dun & Bradstreet *Million Dollar Directory*.

INTERPRETING FINANCIAL STATEMENTS: Smith's Food and Drug Centers, Inc.

BYP3–4   Smith's Food and Drug Centers, Inc. is a supermarket and drug store chain that operates 137 stores in the Intermountain and Southwestern regions of the United States. Smith's competes using a strategy of providing one-stop shopping for customers. This requires large inventories and frequent restocking of inventories. To reduce these costs, Smith's owns and operates its own warehouse and distribution facilities. The Current Liabilities section of the company's balance sheet included the following (dollar amounts are in thousands):

SMITH'S FOOD AND DRUG CO. Balance Sheet (partial)	
Trade accounts payable	$235,843
Accrued sales and other taxes	44,379
Accrued payroll and related benefits	84,083

Instructions

   (a) Why does the company have accrued payroll and related benefits? Does this mean that the company is behind in paying its employees? Explain.

   (b) The company has state-of-the-art scanners at most of its registers. Even at older stores, each cash register computes daily totals for both sales and sales taxes. Why then does the company have accrued sales taxes?

REAL-WORLD FOCUS: Laser Recording Systems Incorporated

BYP3–5 **Laser Recording Systems,** founded in 1981, produces laser disks for use in the home market. Sales since 1985 have increased approximately 15 percent per year. The following is an excerpt from Laser Recording Systems' financial statements (all dollars in thousands):

LASER RECORDING SYSTEMS
Management Discussion

Accrued liabilities increased to $1,642 at January 31, from $138 at the end of the previous fiscal year. Compensation and related accruals increased $195 due primarily to increases in accruals for severance, vacation, commissions, and relocation expenses. Accrued professional services increased by $137 primarily as a result of legal expenses related to several outstanding contractual disputes. Other expense increased $35, of which $18 was for interest payable.

Instructions

   (a) Can you tell from the discussion whether Laser Recording has prepaid its legal expenses and is now making an adjustment to the asset account Prepaid Legal Expenses, or whether the company is handling the legal expense via an accrued expense adjustment?

   (b) Identify each of the adjustments Laser Recording is discussing as one of the four types of possible adjustments discussed in the chapter. How is net income ultimately affected by each of the adjustments?

   (c) What journal entry did Laser Recording make to record the accrued interest?

CRITICAL THINKING

GROUP DECISION CASE

BYP3–6 The Happy Travel Court was organized on April 1, 1998, by Nancy Fox. Nancy is a good manager but a poor accountant. From the trial balance prepared by a part-time bookkeeper, Nancy prepared the following income statement for the quarter that ended March 31, 1999.

HAPPY TRAVEL COURT
Income Statement
For the Quarter Ended March 31, 1999

Revenues		
Travel court rental revenue		$95,000
Operating expenses		
Advertising	$ 5,200	
Wages	29,800	
Utilities	900	
Depreciation	800	
Repairs	4,000	
Total operating expenses		40,700
Net income		$54,300

Nancy knew that something was wrong with the statement because net income had never exceeded $20,000 in any one quarter. Knowing that you are an experienced accountant, she asks you to review the income statement and other data.

You first look at the trial balance. In addition to the account balances reported above in the income statement, the ledger contains the following additional selected balances at March 31, 1999:

Supplies	$ 5,200
Prepaid Insurance	7,200
Notes Payable	12,000

You then make inquiries and discover the following:

1. Travel court rental fees include advanced rentals for summer month occupancy $30,000.
2. There were $1,300 of supplies on hand at March 31.
3. Prepaid insurance resulted from the payment of a one-year policy on January 1, 1999.
4. The mail on April 1, 1999, brought the following bills: advertising for week of March 24, $110; repairs made March 10, $260; and utilities, $180.
5. There are four employees who receive wages totaling $350 per day. At March 31, 2 days' wages have been incurred but not paid.
6. The note payable is a 3-month, 10% note dated January 1, 1999.

Instructions
With the class divided into groups, answer the following:

(a) Prepare a correct income statement for the quarter ended March 31, 1999.
(b) Explain to Nancy the generally accepted accounting principles that she did not recognize in preparing her income statement and their effect on her results.

COMMUNICATION ACTIVITY

BYP3–7   In reviewing the accounts of the Marylee Co. at the end of the year, you discover that adjusting entries have not been made.

Instructions
Write a memorandum to Mary Lee Virgil, the owner of Marylee Co., that explains the following: the nature and purpose of adjusting entries, why adjusting entries are needed, and the types of adjusting entries that may be made.

ETHICS CASE

BYP3–8   Die Hard Company is a pesticide manufacturer. Its sales declined greatly this year due to the passage of legislation outlawing the sale of several of Die Hard's chemical pesticides. During the coming year, Die Hard will have environmentally safe and competitive replacement chemicals to replace these discontinued products. Sales in the next year are expected to greatly exceed any prior year's. The decline in sales and profits appears to be a one-year aberration. But even so, the company president believes that a large dip in current year's profits could cause a significant drop in the market price of Die Hard's stock and make it a takeover target.

To avoid this possibility, the company president urges Becky Freeman, controller, in making this period's year-end adjusting entries to accrue every possible revenue and to defer as many expenses as possible. The president says to Becky, "We need the revenues this year, and next year can easily absorb expenses deferred from this year. We can't let our stock price be hammered down!" Becky didn't get around to recording the adjusting entries until January 17, but she dated the entries December 31 as if they were recorded then. Becky also made every effort to comply with the president's request.

Instructions

(a) Who are the stakeholders in this situation?
(b) What are the ethical considerations of (1) the president's request and (2) Becky's dating the adjusting entries December 31?
(c) Can Becky accrue revenues and defer expenses and still be ethical?

SURFING THE NET

BYP3–9   A wealth of accounting-related information is available via the Internet. For example the Rutgers Accounting Web (http://www.rutgers.edu/accounting/raw.htm) offers access to a great variety of sources.

Instructions
Once in the Rutgers Accounting Web, click on "Accounting Resources" in the left margin, or click on "RAW's Features." (*Note:* Once on this page, you may have to click on the "text only" box to access the available information.)

(a) List the categories of information available through the "Accounting Resources on the Internet" page.
(b) Select any one of these categories and briefly describe the types of information available.

Answers to Self-Study Questions
1. c   2. a   3. d   4. d   5. c   6. a   7. b   8. b   9. c   10. d   11. a

---

Answer to Kellogg Review It Question 4, p. 102
1997 depreciation and amortization expense is \$287.3 million; 1996 depreciation and amortization expense is \$251.5 million.

Remember to go back to the Navigator box on the chapter-opening page and check off your completed work.

Before studying this chapter you should know or, if necessary, review:

a. How to apply the revenue recognition and matching principles. (Ch. 3, pp. 93–94)
b. How to make adjusting entries. (Ch. 3, pp. 94–108)
c. How to prepare an adjusted trial balance. (Ch. 3, p. 110)
d. How to prepare a balance sheet, income statement, and owner's equity statement. (Ch. 3, pp. 110–112)

FEATURE STORY

A Little Knowledge Brings a Lot of Profits

Employee training in financial accounting has paid off for Jack Stack at SRC Corporation in Woodridge, Illinois, which rebuilds engines. President and owner of SRC, he was really concerned when his company lost $61,000 on sales of $16 million. He decided that the "only way to turn things around was to get employees to think like owners." But how to do it? He decided to "teach anyone who moved a broom or operated a grinder everything a bank lender would know. That way they would really understand how each nickel saved could make a difference."

Therefore, SRC spent $300,000 on financial accounting training for its employees. Each week the company stopped its operations for half an hour while its 800 employees broke into small groups to study the latest financial statements. "At first it wasn't easy for everyone to understand the numbers," concedes employee Craig Highbarger, "but we've been over the different figures enough times now, if you hand any one of us a financial statement and leave out a few numbers, we can fill them in." Employees now understand how much it costs to copy a document or turn on a light.

Has it made a difference? Recently SRC earned $6 million on sales of $100 million. As a result of this turnaround, SRC handed out $1.4 million in bonuses to its employees, who are now wealthier in both cash and knowledge.

CHAPTER 4

THE NAVIGATOR ✔

- Understand *Concepts for Review* ☐
- Read *Feature Story* ☐
- Scan *Study Objectives* ☐
- Read *Preview* ☐
- Read text and answer *Before You Go On*
  p. 146 ☐ p. 156 ☐ p. 162 ☐
- Work *Demonstration Problem* ☐
- Review *Summary of Study Objectives* ☐
- Answer *Self-Study Questions* ☐
- Complete assignments ☐

COMPLETION OF THE ACCOUNTING CYCLE

STUDY OBJECTIVES

After studying this chapter, you should be able to:

1. *Prepare a work sheet.*
2. *Explain the process of closing the books.*
3. *Describe the content and purpose of a post-closing trial balance.*
4. *State the required steps in the accounting cycle.*
5. *Explain the approaches to preparing correcting entries.*
6. *Identify the sections of a classified balance sheet.*

THE NAVIGATOR

*A*s was true at SRC Corporation, financial statements can help employees understand what is happening in the business. In Chapter 3, we prepared financial statements directly from the adjusted trial balance. However, with so many details involved in the end-of-period accounting procedures, it is easy to make errors. Locating and correcting errors can cost much time and effort. One way to minimize errors in the records and to simplify the end-of-period procedures is to use a work sheet.

In this chapter we will explain the role of the work sheet in accounting as well as the remaining steps in the accounting cycle, most especially, the closing process, again using Pioneer Advertising Agency as an example. Then we will consider (1) correcting entries and (2) classified balance sheets. The content and organization of the chapter are as follows:

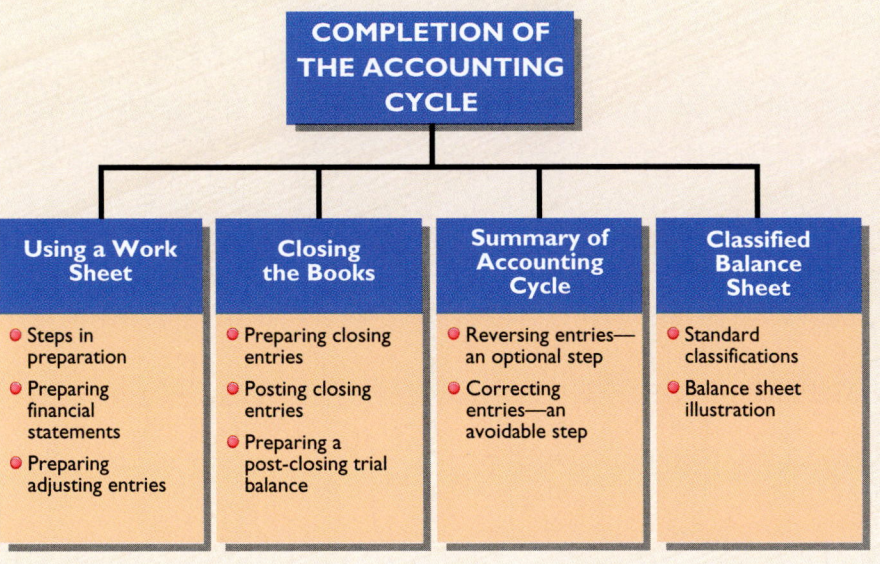

COMPLETION OF THE ACCOUNTING CYCLE

Using a Work Sheet	Closing the Books	Summary of Accounting Cycle	Classified Balance Sheet
• Steps in preparation	• Preparing closing entries	• Reversing entries— an optional step	• Standard classifications
• Preparing financial statements	• Posting closing entries	• Correcting entries—an avoidable step	• Balance sheet illustration
• Preparing adjusting entries	• Preparing a post-closing trial balance		

THE NAVIGATOR

USING A WORK SHEET

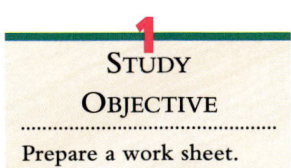

1
STUDY
OBJECTIVE
Prepare a work sheet.

A **work sheet** is a multiple-column form that may be used in the adjustment process and in preparing financial statements. As its name suggests, the work sheet is a working tool or a supplementary device. **A work sheet is not a permanent accounting record;** it is neither a journal nor a part of the general ledger. The work sheet is merely a device used to make it easier to prepare adjusting entries and the financial statements. In small companies with relatively few accounts and adjustments, a work sheet may not be needed. In large companies with numerous accounts and many adjustments, it is almost indispensable.

The basic form of a work sheet and the procedure (5 steps) for preparing a work sheet are shown in Illustration 4-1. Each of the steps in preparing the work sheet must be performed in the prescribed sequence.

ILLUSTRATION 4-1

Form and procedure for a work sheet

Work Sheet

Account Titles	Trial Balance		Adjustments		Adjusted Trial Balance		Income Statement		Balance Sheet	
	Dr.	Cr.	Dr.	Cr.	Dr.	Cr.	Dr.	Cr.	Dr.	Cr.

1 Prepare a trial balance on the work sheet

2 Enter adjustment data

3 Enter adjusted balances

4 Extend adjusted balances to appropriate statement columns

5 Total the statement columns, compute net income (or net loss), and complete work sheet

The use of a work sheet is optional. When a work sheet is used, financial statements are prepared from the work sheet. The adjustments are entered in the work sheet columns and are then journalized and posted after the financial statements have been prepared. Thus, management and other interested parties can receive the financial statements at an earlier date than without a work sheet.

Steps in Preparing a Work Sheet

We will use the October 31 trial balance and adjustment data of Pioneer Advertising in Chapter 3 to illustrate the preparation of a work sheet. Each step of the process is described below and demonstrated in Illustrations 4-2 and 4-3A, B, C, and D following page 143.

Step 1. Prepare a Trial Balance on the Work Sheet. The account title space and trial balance columns are used to prepare a trial balance. The data for the trial balance come directly from the ledger accounts. The trial balance for Pioneer Advertising Agency is entered in the trial balance columns of the work sheet as shown in Illustration 4-2.

Step 2. Enter the Adjustments in the Adjustment Columns. **Turn over the first transparency, Illustration 4-3A.** When a work sheet is used, all adjustments are entered in the adjustment columns. In entering the adjustments, applicable trial balance accounts should be used. If additional accounts are needed, they should be inserted on the lines immediately below the trial balance totals. Each adjustment is indexed and keyed to facilitate the journalizing of the adjusting entry in the general journal. **It is important to recognize that the adjustments are not journalized until after the work sheet is completed and the financial statements have been prepared.**

The adjustments for Pioneer Advertising Agency are the same as the adjustments illustrated on page 108. They are keyed in the adjustment columns of the work sheet as follows:

(a) An additional account, Advertising Supplies Expense, is debited $1,500 for the cost of supplies used, and Advertising Supplies is credited $1,500.

(b) An additional account, Insurance Expense, is debited $50 for the insurance that has expired, and Prepaid Insurance is credited $50.

(c) Two additional accounts are needed. Depreciation Expense is debited $40 for the month's depreciation, and Accumulated Depreciation—Office Equipment is credited $40.

(d) Unearned Revenue is debited $400 for services provided, and Service Revenue is credited $400.

(e) An additional account, Accounts Receivable, is debited $200 for services provided but not billed, and Service Revenue is credited $200.

(f) Two additional accounts are needed. Interest Expense is debited $50 for accrued interest, and Interest Payable is credited $50.

(g) Salaries Expense is debited $1,200 for accrued salaries, and an additional account, Salaries Payable, is credited $1,200.

Note in the illustration that after all the adjustments have been entered, the adjustment columns are totaled and the equality of the column totals is proved.

Step 3.   Enter Adjusted Balances in the Adjusted Trial Balance Columns.   Turn over the second transparency, Illustration 4-3B. The adjusted balance of an account is obtained by combining the amounts entered in the first four columns of the work sheet for each account. For example, the Prepaid Insurance account in the trial balance columns has a $600 debit balance. When this is combined with the $50 credit in the adjustment columns, the result is a $550 debit balance recorded in the adjusted trial balance columns. **For each account on the work sheet, the amount in the adjusted trial balance columns is equal to the account balance that will appear in the ledger after the adjusting entries have been journalized and posted.** The balances in these columns are the same as those in the adjusted trial balance in Illustration 3-18 on page 110.

TECHNOLOGY IN ACTION

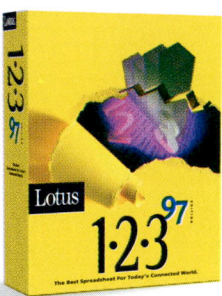

The work sheet can be computerized using an electronic spreadsheet program. The LOTUS 1–2–3 supplement for this textbook is one of the most popular versions of such spreadsheet packages. With a program like LOTUS 1–2–3, you can produce any type of work sheet (accounting or otherwise) that you could produce with paper and pencil on a columnar pad. The tremendous advantage of an electronic work sheet over the paper and pencil version is the ability to change selected data. When data are changed, the computer updates the balance of your computations instantly. More specific applications of electronic spreadsheets will be noted as we proceed.

After the balances of all accounts have been entered in the adjusted trial balance columns, the columns are totaled and their equality is proved. The agreement of the column totals facilitates the completion of the work sheet. If these columns are not in agreement, the statement columns will not balance and the financial statements will be incorrect.

Step 4.   Extend Adjusted Trial Balance Amounts to Appropriate Financial Statement Columns.   Turn over the third transparency, Illustration 4-3C. This step involves the extension of adjusted trial balance amounts to the last four columns of the work sheet. Balance sheet accounts such as Cash and Notes Payable are entered in the balance sheet debit and credit columns, respectively. The balance in accumulated depreciation is extended to the balance sheet credit column. This results because accumulated depreciation is a contra-asset account with a credit balance.

Because the work sheet does not have columns for the owner's equity statement, the balance in owner's capital is extended to the balance sheet credit column. In addition, the balance in owner's drawing is extended to the balance sheet debit column because it is an owner's equity account with a debit balance. The expense and revenue accounts such as Salaries Expense and Service Revenue are entered in the appropriate income statement columns. These extensions are shown in Illustration 4-3C.

Step 5.   Total the Statement Columns, Compute the Net Income (or Net Loss), and Complete the Work Sheet.   Turn over the fourth transparency, Illustration 4-3D. Each of the statement columns must be totaled. The net income or loss for the period is then found by computing the difference between the totals of the two income statement columns. If total credits exceed total debits, net income has resulted. In such a case, as shown in Illustration 4-3D, the words "net income" are inserted in the account title space. The amount then is entered in the income statement debit column and the balance sheet credit column. **The debit amount balances the income statement columns and the credit amount balances the balance sheet columns.** In addition, the credit in the balance sheet column indicates the increase in owner's equity resulting from net income. Conversely, if total debits in the income statement columns exceed total credits, a net loss has occurred. The amount of the net loss is entered in the income statement credit column and the balance sheet debit column.

After the net income or net loss has been entered, new column totals are determined. The totals shown in the debit and credit income statement columns will be identical. The totals shown in the debit and credit balance sheet columns will also be identical. If either the income statement columns or the balance sheet columns are not equal after the net income or net loss has been entered, an error has been made in completing the work sheet. The completed work sheet for Pioneer Advertising Agency is shown in Illustration 4-3D.

Preparing Financial Statements from a Work Sheet

After a work sheet has been completed, the statement columns contain all the data that are required for the preparation of financial statements. The income statement is prepared from the income statement columns, and the balance sheet and owner's equity statement are prepared from the balance sheet columns. The financial statements prepared from the work sheet for Pioneer Advertising Agency are shown in Illustration 4-4. At this point, adjusting entries have not been journalized and posted. Therefore, the ledger does not support all financial statement amounts.

The amount shown for owner's capital on the work sheet is the account balance **before considering drawings and net income (or loss).** When there have been no additional investments of capital by the owner during the period, this amount is the balance at the beginning of the period.

Using a work sheet, financial statements can be prepared before adjusting entries are journalized and posted. **However, the completed work sheet is not a substitute for formal financial statements.** Data in the financial statement columns are not properly arranged for statement purposes. Moreover, as noted above, the financial statement presentation for some accounts differs from their statement columns on the work sheet. **A work sheet is essentially a working tool of the accountant and is not distributed to management and other parties.**

HELPFUL HINT
Every adjusted trial balance amount must be extended to one of the four statement columns. Debit amounts go to debit columns and credit amounts go to credit columns.

HELPFUL HINT
All pairs of columns must balance for a work sheet to be complete.

(Note: Text continues on page 146, following acetate overlays.)

ILLUSTRATION 4-2

Preparing a trial balance

PIONEER ADVERTISING AGENCY
Work Sheet
For the Month Ended October 31, 1999

Account Titles	Trial Balance		Adjustments		Adjusted Trial Balance		Income Statement		Balance Sheet	
	Dr.	Cr.	Dr.	Cr.	Dr.	Cr.	Dr.	Cr.	Dr.	Cr.
Cash	15,200									
Advertising Supplies	2,500									
Prepaid Insurance	600									
Office Equipment	5,000									
Notes Payable		5,000								
Accounts Payable		2,500								
Unearned Revenue		1,200								
C. R. Byrd, Capital		10,000								
C. R. Byrd, Drawing	500									
Service Revenue		10,000								
Salaries Expense	4,000									
Rent Expense	900									
Totals	28,700	28,700								

Include all accounts with balances from ledger.

Trial balance amounts are taken directly from ledger accounts.

ILLUSTRATION 4-4

Financial statements from a work sheet

PIONEER ADVERTISING AGENCY
Income Statement
For the Month Ended October 31, 1999

Revenues		
Service revenue		$10,600
Expenses		
Salaries expense	$5,200	
Advertising supplies expense	1,500	
Rent expense	900	
Insurance expense	50	
Interest expense	50	
Depreciation expense	40	
Total expenses		7,740
Net income		$ 2,860

PIONEER ADVERTISING AGENCY
Owner's Equity Statement
For the Month Ended October 31, 1999

C. R. Byrd, Capital, October 1		$ –0–
Add: Investments	$10,000	
Net income	2,860	12,860
		12,860
Less: Drawings		500
C. R. Byrd, Capital, October 31		$12,360

PIONEER ADVERTISING AGENCY
Balance Sheet
October 31, 1999

Assets

Cash		$15,200
Accounts receivable		200
Advertising supplies		1,000
Prepaid insurance		550
Office equipment	$5,000	
Less: Accumulated depreciation	40	4,960
Total assets		$21,910

Liabilities and Owner's Equity

Liabilities		
Notes payable		$ 5,000
Accounts payable		2,500
Interest payable		50
Unearned revenue		800
Salaries payable		1,200
Total liabilities		9,550
Owner's equity		
C. R. Byrd, Capital		12,360
Total liabilities and owner's equity		$21,910

Preparing Adjusting Entries from a Work Sheet

A work sheet is not a journal, and it cannot be used as a basis for posting to ledger accounts. To adjust the accounts, it is necessary to journalize and post the adjustments to the ledger. **The adjusting entries are prepared from the adjustment columns of the work sheet.** The reference letters in the adjustment columns and the explanation of the adjustments that appear at the bottom of the work sheet help identify entries. However, writing the explanation to the adjustments at the bottom of the work sheet is not required. As indicated previously, the journalizing and posting of adjusting entries **follows** the preparation of financial statements when a work sheet is used. The adjusting entries on October 31 for Pioneer Advertising Agency are the same as those shown in Illustration 3-16 (page 108).

BEFORE YOU GO ON . . .

Review It

1. What are the five steps in preparing a work sheet?
2. How is net income or net loss shown in a work sheet?
3. How does a work sheet relate to preparing financial statements and adjusting entries?

Do It

Melany Newby is preparing a work sheet. Explain to Melany how the following adjusted trial balance accounts should be extended to the financial statement columns of the work sheet: Cash; Accumulated Depreciation; Accounts Payable; R. Kerr, Drawing; Service Revenue; and Salaries Expense.

Reasoning: Asset and liability balances are extended to the balance sheet debit and credit columns, respectively, except for accumulated depreciation which is extended to the balance sheet credit column. The drawing account is extended to the balance sheet debit column. Expenses are extended to the income statement debit column. Revenue accounts are extended to the income statement credit column.

Solution:
Income statement debit column—Salaries Expense
Income statement credit column—Service Revenue
Balance sheet debit column—Cash; R. Kerr, Drawing
Balance sheet credit column—Accumulated Depreciation; Accounts Payable
As indicated in the Technology in Action box on page 142, the work sheet is an ideal application for electronic spreadsheet software like Microsoft Excel and LOTUS 1–2–3.

Related exercise material: BE4–1, BE4–2, BE4–3, E4–1, E4–2, E4–4, and E4–5.

CLOSING THE BOOKS

2
STUDY
OBJECTIVE

Explain the process of closing the books.

In closing the books, it is necessary to distinguish between temporary and permanent accounts. **Temporary** or **nominal accounts** relate only to a given accounting period. They include all income statement accounts and owner's drawing. All temporary accounts are closed. In contrast, **permanent** or **real accounts** relate to one or more future accounting periods. They consist of all balance sheet accounts including owner's capital. Permanent accounts are not closed. Instead, their balances are carried forward into the next accounting period. Illustration 4-5 identifies the accounts in each category.

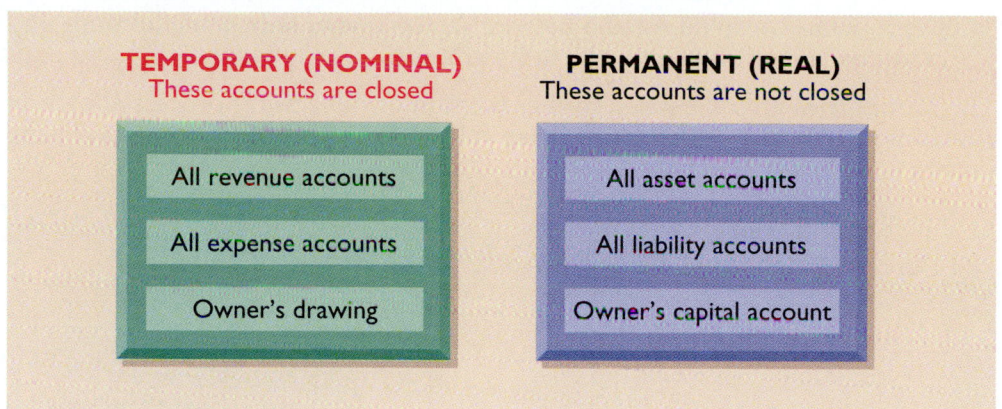

ILLUSTRATION 4-5

Temporary versus permanent accounts

HELPFUL HINT
A contra asset account, such as accumulated depreciation, is a real account also.

Preparing Closing Entries

At the end of the accounting period, the temporary account balances are transferred to the permanent owner's equity account, owner's capital, through the preparation of closing entries.[1] **Closing entries** formally recognize in the ledger the transfer of net income or net loss and owner's drawing to owner's capital as shown in the owner's equity statement. **These entries also produce a zero balance in each temporary account so it can be used to accumulate data in the next accounting period separate from the data of prior periods.** Permanent accounts are not closed.

Journalizing and posting closing entries is a required step in the accounting cycle. (See Illustration 4–12 on page 154.) This step is performed after financial statements have been prepared. In contrast to the steps in the cycle that you have already studied, closing entries are generally journalized and posted **only at the end of a company's annual accounting period**. This practice facilitates the preparation of annual financial statements because all temporary accounts will contain data for the entire year.

In preparing closing entries, each income statement account could be closed directly to owner's capital. However, to do so would result in excessive detail in the permanent owner's capital account. Accordingly, the revenue and expense accounts are closed to another temporary account, **Income Summary**, and only the net income or net loss is transferred from this account to owner's capital.

Closing entries are journalized in the general journal. A center caption entitled Closing Entries may be inserted in the journal between the last adjusting entry and the first closing entry to identify these entries. Then the closing entries are posted to the ledger accounts. Closing entries may be prepared directly from the adjusted balances in the ledger, from the income statement and balance sheet columns of the work sheet, or from the income and owner's equity statements. Separate closing entries could be prepared for each nominal account, but the following four entries accomplish the desired result more efficiently:

1. Debit each revenue account for its balance and credit Income Summary for total revenues.
2. Debit Income Summary for total expenses and credit each expense account for its balance.
3. Debit Income Summary and credit owner's capital for the amount of net income.

---

[1]Closing entries for a partnership and for a corporation are explained in Chapters 13 and 14, respectively.

4. Debit owner's capital for the balance in the owner's drawing account and credit owner's drawing for the same amount.

The four entries are referenced in the diagram of the closing process shown in Illustration 4-6 and in the journal entries in Illustration 4-7. The posting of closing entries is shown in Illustration 4-8.

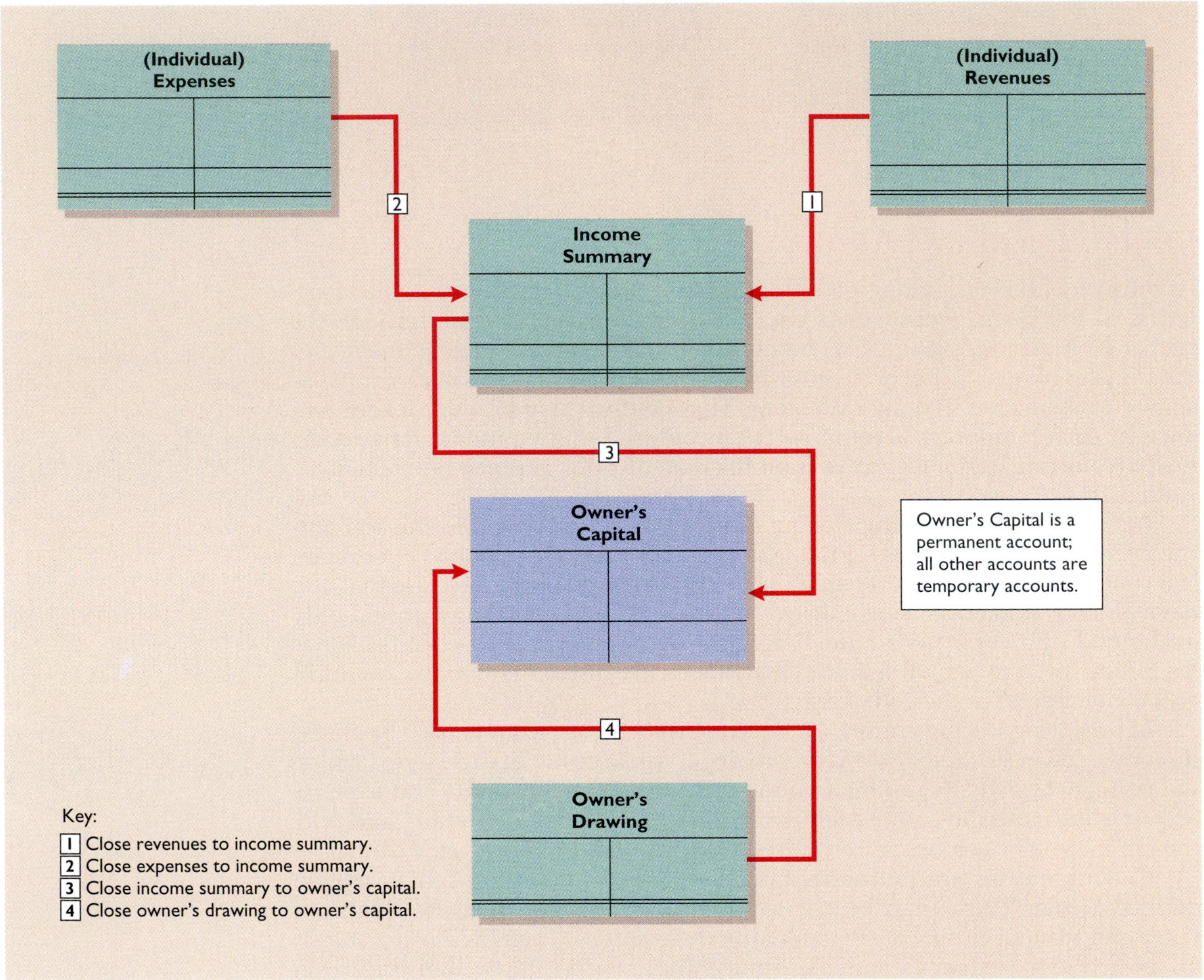

(Individual) Expenses

(Individual) Revenues

Income Summary

Owner's Capital

> Owner's Capital is a permanent account; all other accounts are temporary accounts.

Owner's Drawing

Key:
1. Close revenues to income summary.
2. Close expenses to income summary.
3. Close income summary to owner's capital.
4. Close owner's drawing to owner's capital.

ILLUSTRATION 4-6

Diagram of closing process—proprietorship

If there were a net loss because expenses exceeded revenues, entry 3 in Illustration 4-6 would be reversed: Credit Income Summary and debit Owner's Capital.

ACCOUNTING IN ACTION
Business Insight

Until Sam Walton had opened twenty Wal-Mart stores, he used what he called the "ESP method" of closing the books. ESP was a pretty basic method: If the books didn't balance, Walton calculated the amount by which they were off and entered that amount under the heading ESP—which stood for "Error Some Place." As Walton noted, "It really sped things along when it came time to close those books."

Source: Sam Walton, *Made in America* (New York: Doubleday Publishing Company, 1992), p. 53.

Closing Entries Illustrated

As explained above, closing entries are generally prepared only at the end of a company's annual accounting period. However, to illustrate the journalizing and posting of closing entries, we will assume that Pioneer Advertising Agency closes its books monthly. The closing entries at October 31 are shown in Illustration 4-7.

ILLUSTRATION 4-7
Closing entries journalized

Date		Account Titles and Explanation	Ref.	Debit	Credit
		GENERAL JOURNAL			**J3**
		Closing Entries			
		(1)			
1999					
Oct.	31	Service Revenue	50	10,600	
		Income Summary	49		10,600
		(To close revenue account)			
		(2)			
	31	Income Summary	49	7,740	
		Salaries Expense	60		5,200
		Advertising Supplies Expense	61		1,500
		Rent Expense	62		900
		Insurance Expense	63		50
		Interest Expense	64		50
		Depreciation Expense	65		40
		(To close expense accounts)			
		(3)			
	31	Income Summary	49	2,860	
		C. R. Byrd, Capital	40		2,860
		(To close net income to capital)			
		(4)			
	31	C. R. Byrd, Capital	40	500	
		C. R. Byrd, Drawing	41		500
		(To close drawings to capital)			

HELPFUL HINT
Income Summary is a very descriptive title: total revenues are closed to Income Summary, total expenses are closed to Income Summary, and the balance in the Income Summary is a net income or net loss.

Note that the amounts for Income Summary in entries (1) and (2) are the totals of the income statement credit and debit columns, respectively, in the work sheet.

A couple of cautions in preparing closing entries: (1) Avoid unintentionally doubling the revenue and expense balances rather than zeroing them. (2) Do not close owner's drawing through the Income Summary account. **Owner's drawing is not an expense, and it is not a factor in determining net income.**

Posting Closing Entries

The posting of the closing entries and the ruling of the accounts are shown in Illustration 4-8. Note that all temporary accounts have zero balances after posting the closing entries. In addition, you should realize that the balance in Owner's Capital represents the total equity of the owner at the end of the accounting period. This balance is shown on the balance sheet and is the ending capital reported on the owner's equity statement, as shown in Illustration 4-4 on page 145. **The Income Summary account is used only in closing.** No entries are journalized and posted to this account during the year.

As part of the closing process, the **temporary accounts** (revenues, expenses, and owner's drawing) in T-account form are totaled, balanced, and double ruled as shown in Illustration 4-8. The **permanent accounts** (assets, liabilities, and

HELPFUL HINT
The balance in Income Summary before it is closed must equal the net income or net loss for the period.

ILLUSTRATION 4-8

Posting of closing entries

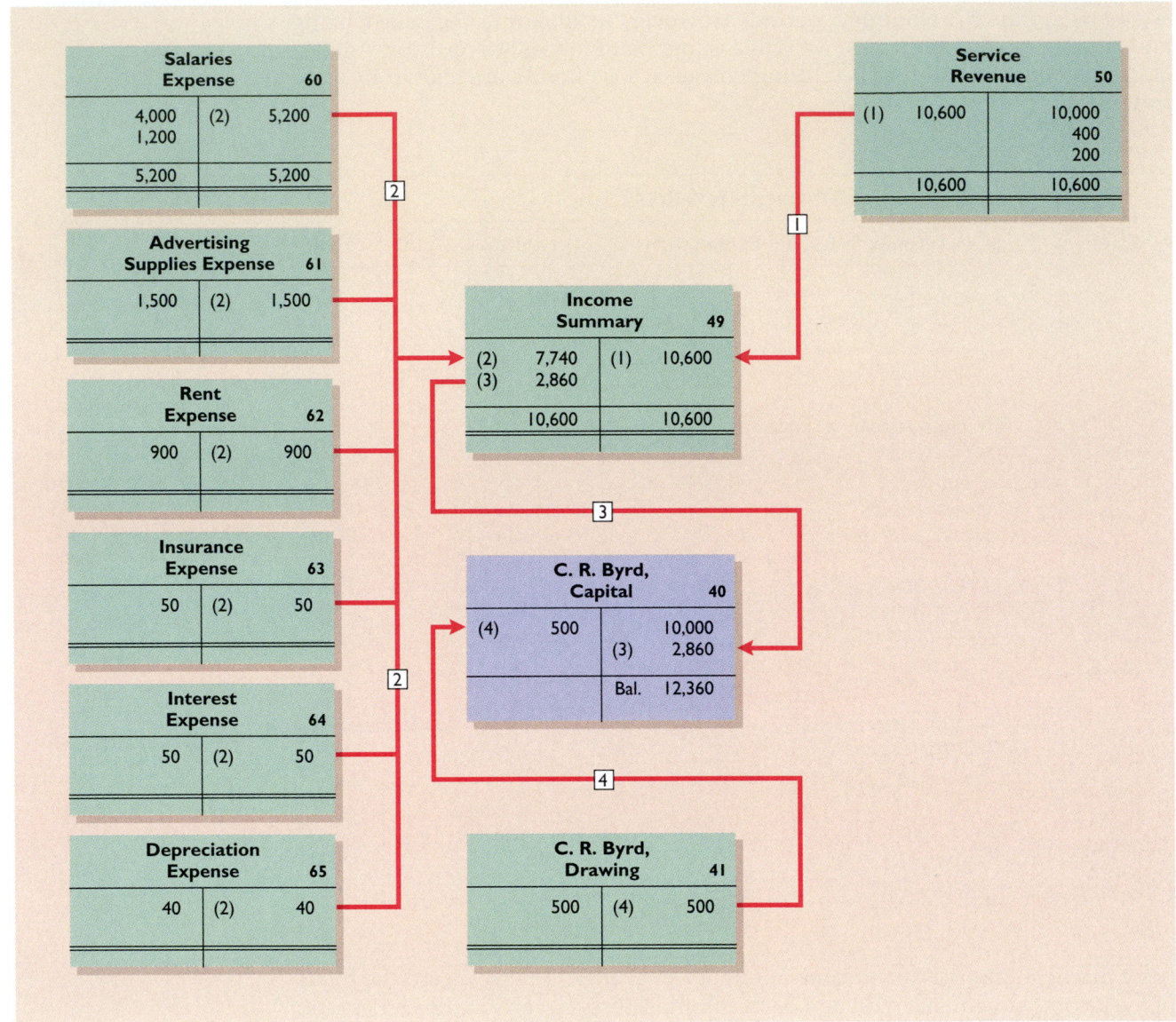

owner's capital) are not closed: A single rule is drawn beneath the current period entries, and the account balance carried forward to the next period is entered below the single rule. (For example, see C. R. Byrd, Capital.)

Preparing a Post-Closing Trial Balance

After all closing entries have been journalized and posted, another trial balance, called a **post-closing trial balance**, is prepared from the ledger. A post-closing trial balance is a list of permanent accounts and their balances after closing entries have been journalized and posted. **The purpose of this trial balance is to prove the equality of the permanent account balances that are carried forward into the next accounting period.** Since all temporary accounts will have zero balances, **the post-closing trial balance will contain only permanent—balance sheet—accounts.**

The procedure for preparing a post-closing trial balance again consists entirely of listing the accounts and their balances. These balances are the same as those reported in the company's balance sheet in Illustration 4-4. The post-closing trial balance for Pioneer Advertising Agency is shown in Illustration 4-9.

PIONEER ADVERTISING AGENCY Post-Closing Trial Balance October 31, 1999		
	Debit	**Credit**
Cash	$15,200	
Accounts Receivable	200	
Advertising Supplies	1,000	
Prepaid Insurance	550	
Office Equipment	5,000	
Accumulated Depreciation—Office Equipment		$ 40
Notes Payable		5,000
Accounts Payable		2,500
Interest Payable		50
Unearned Revenue		800
Salaries Payable		1,200
C. R. Byrd, Capital		12,360
	$21,950	**$21,950**

ILLUSTRATION 4-9

Post-closing trial balance

HELPFUL HINT
Will total debits in a post-closing trial balance equal total assets on the balance sheet? Answer: No. Accumulated depreciation is deducted from assets on the balance sheet but added to the credit balance total in a post–closing trial balance.

The post-closing trial balance is prepared from the permanent accounts in the ledger. The permanent accounts of Pioneer Advertising are shown in the general ledger in Illustration 4-10. Remember that the balance of each permanent account is computed after every posting. Therefore, no additional work on these accounts is needed as part of the closing process. The remaining accounts in the general ledger are temporary accounts (shown in Illustration 4-11 on page 153). After the closing entries are posted, each temporary account has a zero balance. These accounts are double-ruled to finalize the closing process.

A post-closing trial balance provides evidence that the journalizing and posting of closing entries has been properly completed. In addition, it shows that the accounting equation is in balance at the end of the accounting period. However, as in the case of the trial balance, it does not prove that all transactions have been recorded or that the ledger is correct. For example, the post-closing trial balance will balance if a transaction is not journalized and posted or if a transaction is journalized and posted twice.

SUMMARY OF THE ACCOUNTING CYCLE

The steps in the accounting cycle are shown graphically in Illustration 4-12. From the graphic you can see that the cycle begins with the analysis of business transactions and ends with the preparation of a post-closing trial balance. The steps in the cycle are performed in sequence and are repeated in each accounting period.

Steps 1–3 may occur daily during the accounting period, as explained in Chapter 2. Steps 4–7 are performed on a periodic basis, such as monthly, quarterly, or annually. Steps 8 and 9, closing entries, and a post-closing trial balance, are usually prepared only at the end of a company's **annual** accounting period.

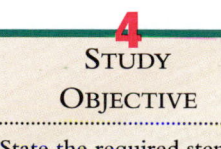

4
STUDY
OBJECTIVE

State the required steps in the accounting cycle.

ILLUSTRATION 4-10

General ledger, permanent accounts

(Permanent Accounts Only)

GENERAL LEDGER

Cash   No. 1

Date	Explanation	Ref.	Debit	Credit	Balance
1999					
Oct. 1		J1	10,000		10,000
2		J1	1,200		11,200
3		J1		900	10,300
4		J1		600	9,700
20		J1		500	9,200
26		J1		4,000	5,200
31		J1	10,000		15,200

Accounts Receivable   No. 6

Date	Explanation	Ref.	Debit	Credit	Balance
1999					
Oct. 31	Adj. entry	J2	200		200

Advertising Supplies   No. 8

Date	Explanation	Ref.	Debit	Credit	Balance
1999					
Oct. 5		J1	2,500		2,500
31	Adj. entry	J2		1,500	1,000

Prepaid Insurance   No. 10

Date	Explanation	Ref.	Debit	Credit	Balance
1999					
Oct. 4		J1	600		600
31	Adj. entry	J2		50	550

Office Equipment   No. 15

Date	Explanation	Ref.	Debit	Credit	Balance
1999					
Oct. 1		J1	5,000		5,000

Accumulated Depreciation—Office Equipment   No. 16

Date	Explanation	Ref.	Debit	Credit	Balance
1999					
Oct. 31	Adj. entry	J2		40	40

Notes Payable   No. 25

Date	Explanation	Ref.	Debit	Credit	Balance
1999					
Oct. 1		J1		5,000	5,000

Accounts Payable   No. 26

Date	Explanation	Ref.	Debit	Credit	Balance
1999					
Oct. 5		J1		2,500	2,500

Interest Payable   No. 27

Date	Explanation	Ref.	Debit	Credit	Balance
1999					
Oct. 31	Adj. entry	J2		50	50

Unearned Revenue   No. 28

Date	Explanation	Ref.	Debit	Credit	Balance
1999					
Oct. 2		J1		1,200	1,200
31	Adj. entry	J2	400		800

Salaries Payable   No. 29

Date	Explanation	Ref.	Debit	Credit	Balance
1999					
Oct. 31	Adj. entry	J2		1,200	1,200

C. R. Byrd, Capital   No. 40

Date	Explanation	Ref.	Debit	Credit	Balance
1999					
Oct. 1		J1		10,000	10,000
31	Closing entry	J3		2,860	12,860
31	Closing entry	J3	500		12,360

Note: The permanent accounts for Pioneer Advertising Agency are shown here; the temporary accounts are shown in Illustration 4-11. Both permanent and temporary accounts are part of the general ledger; they are segregated here to aid in learning.

ILLUSTRATION 4-11

General ledger, temporary accounts

(Temporary Accounts Only)

GENERAL LEDGER

C. R. Byrd, Drawing No. 41

Date	Explanation	Ref.	Debit	Credit	Balance
1999					
Oct. 20		J1	500		500
31	Closing entry	J3		500	–0–

Income Summary No. 49

Date	Explanation	Ref.	Debit	Credit	Balance
1999					
Oct. 31	Closing entry	J3		10,600	10,600
31	Closing entry	J3	7,740		2,860
31	Closing entry	J3	2,860		–0–

Service Revenue No. 50

Date	Explanation	Ref.	Debit	Credit	Balance
1999					
Oct. 31		J1		10,000	10,000
31	Adj. entry	J2		400	10,400
31	Adj. entry	J2		200	10,600
31	Closing entry	J3	10,600		–0–

Salaries Expense No. 60

Date	Explanation	Ref.	Debit	Credit	Balance
1999					
Oct. 26		J1	4,000		4,000
31	Adj. entry	J2	1,200		5,200
31	Closing entry	J3		5,200	–0–

Advertising Supplies Expense No. 61

Date	Explanation	Ref.	Debit	Credit	Balance
1999					
Oct. 31	Adj. entry	J2	1,500		1,500
31	Closing entry	J3		1,500	–0–

Rent Expense No. 62

Date	Explanation	Ref.	Debit	Credit	Balance
1999					
Oct. 3		J1	900		900
31	Closing entry	J3		900	–0–

Insurance Expense No. 63

Date	Explanation	Ref.	Debit	Credit	Balance
1999					
Oct. 31	Adj. entry	J2	50		50
31	Closing entry	J3		50	–0–

Interest Expense No. 64

Date	Explanation	Ref.	Debit	Credit	Balance
1999					
Oct. 31	Adj. entry	J2	50		50
31	Closing entry	J3		50	–0–

Depreciation Expense No. 65

Date	Explanation	Ref.	Debit	Credit	Balance
1999					
Oct. 31	Adj. entry	J2	40		40
31	Closing entry	J3		40	–0–

Note: The temporary accounts for Pioneer Advertising Agency are shown here; the permanent accounts are shown in Illustration 4-10. Both permanent and temporary accounts are part of the general ledger; they are segregated here to aid in learning.

ILLUSTRATION 4-12

Steps in the accounting cycle

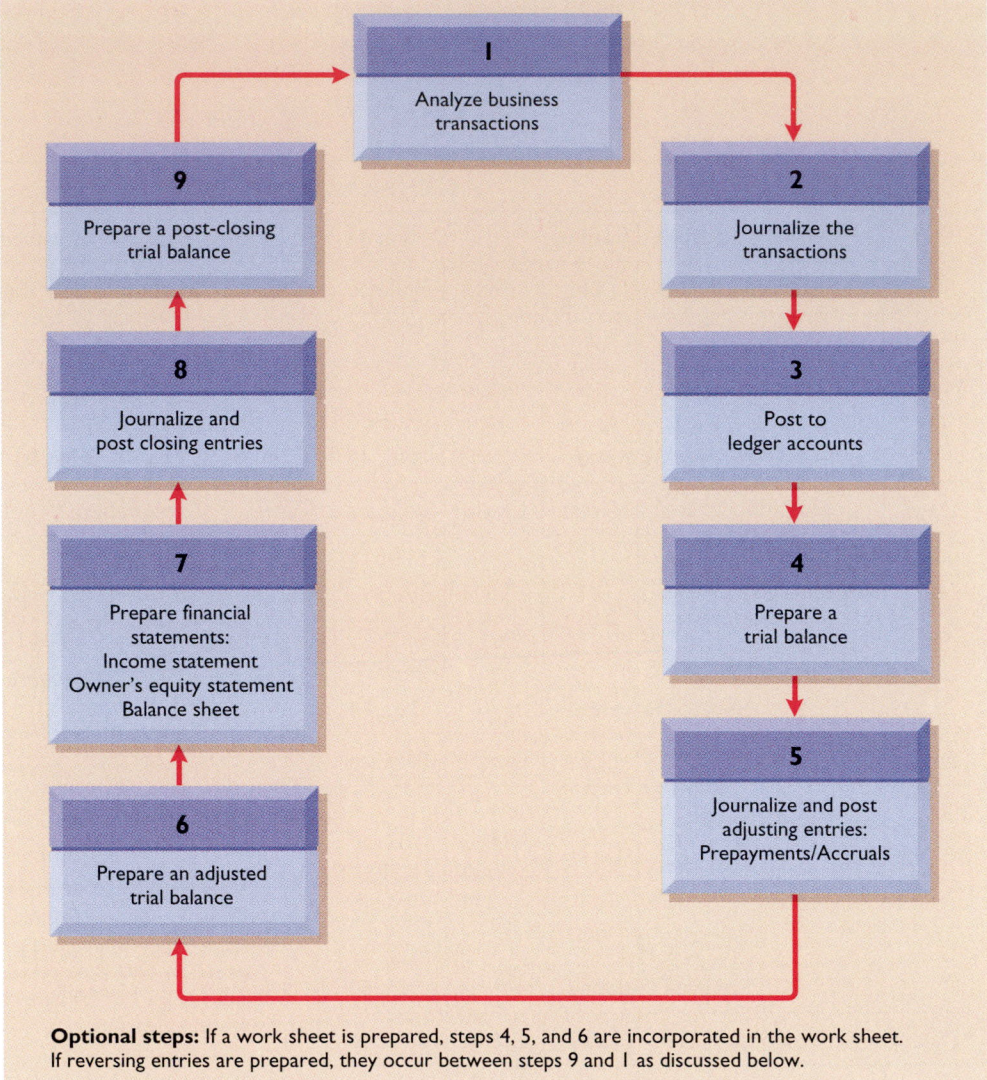

Optional steps: If a work sheet is prepared, steps 4, 5, and 6 are incorporated in the work sheet. If reversing entries are prepared, they occur between steps 9 and 1 as discussed below.

There are also two optional steps in the accounting cycle. As you have seen, a work sheet may be used in preparing adjusting entries and financial statements. In addition, reversing entries may be used as explained in the following section.

Reversing Entries—An Optional Step

Some accountants prefer to reverse certain adjusting entries at the beginning of a new accounting period. A **reversing entry** is made at the beginning of the next accounting period and is the exact opposite of the adjusting entry made in the previous period. **The preparation of reversing entries is an optional bookkeeping procedure that is not a required step in the accounting cycle.** Accordingly, we have chosen to cover this topic in an appendix at the end of the chapter.

Correcting Entries—An Avoidable Step

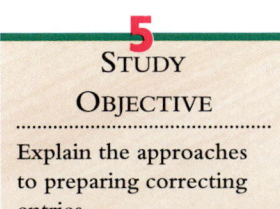

STUDY
OBJECTIVE
....
Explain the approaches
to preparing correcting
entries.

If the accounting records are free of errors, no correcting entries are necessary. Unfortunately, errors may occur in the recording process. Errors should be corrected **as soon as they are discovered** by journalizing and posting **correcting entries**. You should recognize several significant differences between correcting entries and adjusting entries. First, adjusting entries are an integral part of the accounting cycle, whereas correcting entries are unnecessary if the records are free of errors. Second, **adjustments are journalized and posted only at the end of an accounting period; in contrast, correcting entries are made whenever an error is discovered**. Finally, adjusting entries always affect at least one balance sheet account and one income statement account. In contrast, correcting entries may involve any combination of accounts in need of correction. Correcting entries must be posted before closing entries.

To determine the correcting entry, it is useful to compare the incorrect entry with the correct entry. Doing so helps identify the accounts and amounts that should—and should not—be corrected. After comparison, a correcting entry is made to correct the accounts. This approach is illustrated in the following two cases.

Case 1. On May 10, a $50 cash collection on account from a customer is journalized and posted as a debit to Cash $50 and a credit to Service Revenue $50. The error is discovered on May 20, when the customer pays the remaining balance in full.

Incorrect Entry (May 10)			Correct Entry (May 10)		
Cash	50		Cash	50	
Service Revenue		50	Accounts Receivable		50

ILLUSTRATION 4-13

Comparison of entries

A comparison of the incorrect entry with the correct entry reveals that the debit to Cash $50 is correct. However, the $50 credit to Service Revenue should have been credited to Accounts Receivable. As a result, both Service Revenue and Accounts Receivable are overstated in the ledger. The following correcting entry is required:

	Correcting Entry		
May 20	Service Revenue	50	
	Accounts Receivable		50
	(To correct entry of May 10)		

ILLUSTRATION 4-14

Correcting entry

A	=	L	+	OE
−50				−50

Case 2. On May 18, office equipment costing $450 is purchased on account. The transaction is journalized and posted as a debit to Delivery Equipment $45, and a credit to Accounts Payable $45. The error is discovered on June 3, when the monthly statement for May is received from the creditor.

Incorrect Entry (May 18)			Correct Entry (May 18)		
Delivery Equipment	45		Office Equipment	450	
Accounts Payable		45	Accounts Payable		450

ILLUSTRATION 4-15

Comparison of entries

A comparison of the two entries shows that three accounts are incorrect. Delivery Equipment is overstated $45; Office Equipment is understated $450; and Accounts Payable is understated $405. The correcting entry is:

	Correcting Entry		
June 3	Office Equipment	450	
	Delivery Equipment		45
	Accounts Payable		405
	(To correct May 18 entry)		

ILLUSTRATION 4-16

Correcting entry

A	=	L	+	OE
+450				
− 45		+405		

Instead of preparing a correcting entry, **it is possible to reverse the incorrect entry and then prepare the correct entry**. This approach will result in more entries and postings than a correcting entry, but it will accomplish the desired result.

ACCOUNTING IN ACTION
Business Insight

Yale Express, a short-haul trucking firm, turned over much of its cargo to local truckers for delivery completion. Yale collected the entire delivery charge and, when billed by the local trucker, remitted payment for the final phase to the local trucker. Yale used a cutoff period of 20 days into the next accounting period in making its adjusting entries for accrued liabilities. That is, it waited 20 days to receive the local truckers' bills to determine the amount of the unpaid but incurred delivery charges as of the balance sheet date.

On the other hand, Republic Carloading, a nationwide, long-distance freight forwarder, frequently did not receive transportation bills from truckers to whom it passed on cargo until months after the year-end. In making its year-end adjusting entries, Republic waited for months in order to include all of these outstanding transportation bills.

When Yale Express merged with Republic Carloading, Yale's vice president employed the 20-day cutoff procedure for both firms. As a result, millions of dollars of Republic's accrued transportation bills went unrecorded. When the erroneous procedure was detected and correcting entries were made, these and other errors changed a reported profit of $1.14 million into a loss of $1.88 million!

BEFORE YOU GO ON . . .

Review It

1. How do permanent accounts differ from temporary accounts?
2. What four different types of entries are required in closing the books?
3. What is the content and purpose of a post-closing trial balance?
4. What are the required and optional steps in the accounting cycle?

Do It

The work sheet for Hancock Company shows the following in the financial statement columns: R. Hancock, Drawing $15,000, R. Hancock, Capital $42,000, and net income $18,000. Prepare the closing entries at December 31 that affect owner's capital.

Reasoning: Closing entries are made in sequence. The first two entries close revenues and expenses. The remaining two entries close net income and owner's drawing to owner's capital.

Solution:

Dec. 31	Income Summary	18,000	
	R. Hancock, Capital		18,000
	(To close net income to capital)		
31	R. Hancock, Capital	15,000	
	R. Hancock, Drawing		15,000
	(To close drawings to capital)		

THE NAVIGATOR

Related exercise material: BE4–4, BE4–5, BE4–6, E4–3, E4–6, and E4–8.

CLASSIFIED BALANCE SHEET

The financial statements illustrated up to this point were purposely kept simple. We classified items as assets, liabilities, and owner's equity in the balance sheet, and as revenues and expenses in the income statement. **Financial statements, however, become more useful to management, creditors, and potential investors when the elements are classified into significant subgroups.** In the remainder of this chapter we will introduce you to the primary balance sheet classifications. The classified income statement is presented in Chapter 5. The classified financial statements are what Jack Stack, the president of SRC Corporation, gave to his employees to understand what was happening in the business.

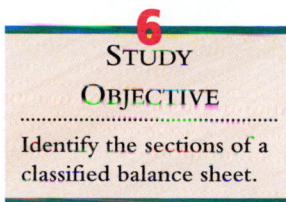

6

STUDY

OBJECTIVE

Identify the sections of a classified balance sheet.

Standard Classifications

A classified balance sheet usually contains these standard classifications:

Assets	Liabilities and Owner's Equity
Current Assets	Current Liabilities
Long-Term Investments	Long-Term Liabilities
Property, Plant, and Equipment	Owner's (Stockholders') Equity
Intangible Assets	

ILLUSTRATION 4-17

Standard balance sheet classifications

These sections help the financial statement user to determine such matters as (1) the availability of assets to meet debts as they come due and (2) the claims of short- and long-term creditors on total assets. A classified balance sheet also makes it easier to compare companies in the same industry, such as GM, Ford, and Chrysler in the automobile industry. Each of the sections is explained below, except for owner's equity, which has already been discussed.

A complete set of specimen financial statements for Kellogg Company is shown in Appendix A at the back of the book.

Current Assets

Current assets are cash and other resources that are reasonably expected to be realized in cash or sold or consumed in the business within one year of the balance sheet date or the company's operating cycle, whichever is longer. For example, accounts receivable are included in current assets because they will be realized in cash through collection within one year. In contrast, a prepayment such as supplies is a current asset because of its expected use or consumption in the business within one year.

The operating cycle of a company is the average time that is required to go from cash to cash in producing revenues. The term "cycle" suggests a circular flow, which in this case, starts and ends with cash. For example, in municipal transit companies, the operating cycle would tend to be very short since services are rendered entirely on a cash basis. On the other hand, the operating cycle in public utility companies is longer: they bill customers for services rendered and the collection period may extend for several months. Most companies have operating cycles of less than one year. More will be said about operating cycles in later chapters.

In a service enterprise, it is customary to recognize four types of current assets: (1) cash, (2) marketable securities such as U.S. government bonds held as a temporary (short-term) investment, (3) receivables (notes receivable, accounts

INTERNATIONAL NOTE

Other countries use a different format for the balance sheet. In Great Britain, for example, property, plant, and equipment are reported first on the balance sheet; assets and liabilities are netted and grouped into net current and net total assets.

receivable, and interest receivable), and (4) prepaid expenses (insurance and supplies). **These items are listed in the order of liquidity**, that is, in the order in which they are expected to be converted into cash. This arrangement is illustrated below in the presentation of UAL, Inc. (United Airlines).

ILLUSTRATION 4-18

Current asset section

UNITED AIRLINES

UAL, INC. (UNITED AIRLINES)
Balance Sheet (partial)
(in thousands)

Current assets	
Cash	$ 52,368
Marketable securities	389,862
Receivables	721,479
Aircraft fuel, spare parts, and supplies	178,840
Prepaid expenses	83,662
Total current assets	$1,426,211

A company's current assets are important in assessing the company's short-term debt-paying ability, as explained later in the chapter.

Long-Term Investments

Like current assets, **long-term investments** are resources that can be realized in cash. However, the conversion into cash is not expected within one year or the operating cycle, whichever is longer. In addition, long-term investments are not intended for use or consumption within the business. This category, often just called "investments," normally includes stocks and bonds of other corporations. Deluxe Corporation reported the following in its balance sheet:

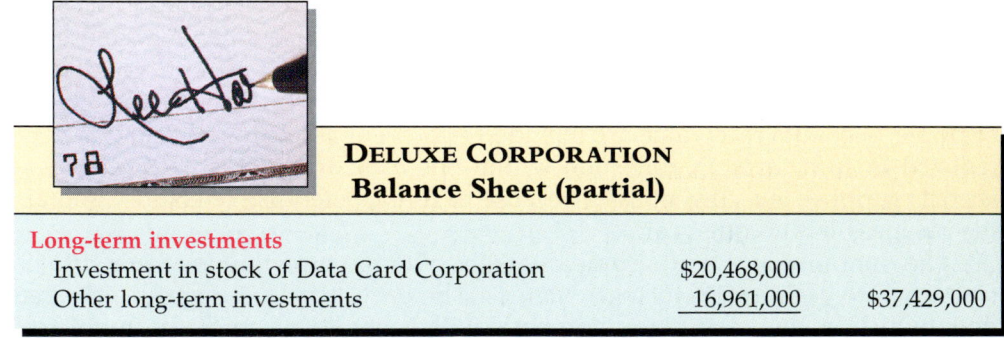

ILLUSTRATION 4-19

Long-term investment section

DELUXE CORPORATION
Balance Sheet (partial)

Long-term investments		
Investment in stock of Data Card Corporation	$20,468,000	
Other long-term investments	16,961,000	$37,429,000

Property, Plant, and Equipment

Property, plant, and equipment are tangible resources of a relatively permanent nature that are used in the business and not intended for sale. This category includes land, buildings, machinery and equipment, delivery equipment, and furniture and fixtures. Assets subject to depreciation should be reported at cost less accumulated depreciation. This practice is illustrated in the following presentation of Delta Air Lines:

ILLUSTRATION 4-20

Property, plant, and equipment section

DELTA AIR LINES, INC.
Balance Sheet (partial)
(in millions)

Property, plant, and equipment			
Flight equipment	$9,619		
Less: Accumulated depreciation	3,510	$6,109	
Ground property and equipment	3,032		
Less: Accumulated depreciation	1,758	1,274	$7,383

Intangible Assets

Intangible assets are noncurrent resources that do not have physical substance. Intangible assets are recorded at cost, and this cost is expensed over the useful life of the intangible asset. Intangible assets include patents, copyrights, and trademarks or trade names that give the holder **exclusive right** of use for a specified period of time. Their value to a company is generally derived from the rights or privileges granted by governmental authority.

In its balance sheet, Brunswick Corporation reported:

ILLUSTRATION 4-21

Intangible assets section

BRUNSWICK

BRUNSWICK CORPORATION
Balance Sheet (partial)

Intangible assets	
Patents, trademarks, and other intangibles	$10,460,000

Current Liabilities

Listed first in the liabilities and owner's equity section of the balance sheet are current liabilities. **Current liabilities** are obligations that are reasonably expected to be paid from existing current assets or through the creation of other current liabilities. As in the case of current assets, the time period for payment is one year or the operating cycle, whichever is longer. Current liabilities include (1) debts related to the operating cycle, such as accounts payable and wages and salaries payable, and (2) other short-term debts, such as bank loans payable, interest payable, taxes payable, and current maturities of long-term obligations (payments to be made within the next year on long-term obligations).

The arrangement of items within the current liabilities section has evolved through custom rather than from a prescribed rule. Notes payable is usually listed first, followed by accounts payable. Other items are then listed in any order. The current liability section adapted from the balance sheet of UAL, Inc. (United Airlines) is as follows:

ILLUSTRATION 4-22

Current liabilities section

Liquidity

Illiquidity

UAL, INC. (UNITED AIRLINES) Balance Sheet (partial) (in thousands)	
Current liabilities	
Notes payable	$ 297,518
Accounts payable	382,967
Current maturities of long-term obligations	81,525
Unearned ticket revenue	432,979
Salaries and wages payable	435,622
Taxes payable	80,390
Other current liabilities	240,652
Total current liabilities	$1,951,653

UNITED AIRLINES

Users of financial statements look closely at the relationship between current assets and current liabilities. This relationship is important in evaluating a company's **liquidity**—its ability to pay obligations that are expected to become due within the next year or operating cycle. When current assets exceed current liabilities at the balance sheet date, the likelihood for paying the liabilities is favorable. When the reverse is true, short-term creditors may not be paid, and the company may ultimately be forced into bankruptcy.

Long-Term Liabilities

Obligations expected to be paid after one year or an operating cycle, whichever is longer, are classified as **long-term liabilities (or long-term debt)**. Liabilities in this category include bonds payable, mortgages payable, long-term notes payable, lease liabilities, and obligations under employee pension plans. Many companies report long-term debt maturing after one year as a single amount in the balance sheet and show the details of the debt in the notes that accompany the financial statements. Others list the various sources of long-term liabilities. In its balance sheet, Consolidated Freightways, Inc. reported:

CONSOLIDATED FREIGHTWAYS

CONSOLIDATED FREIGHTWAYS, INC. Balance Sheet (partial) (in thousands)	
Long-term liabilities	
Bank notes payable	$10,000
Mortgage payable	2,900
Bonds payable	53,422
Other long-term debt	9,597
Total long-term liabilities	$75,919

ILLUSTRATION 4-23

Long-term liabilities section

Owner's Equity

The content of the owner's equity section varies with the form of business organization. In a proprietorship, there is one capital account. In a partnership, there is a capital account for each partner. For a corporation, owners' equity is divided into two accounts—Capital Stock and Retained Earnings. Investments of assets in the business by the stockholders are recorded by debiting an asset account and crediting the Capital Stock account. Income retained for use in the business is recorded in the Retained Earnings account. These two accounts are combined and reported as **stockholders' equity** on the balance sheet. (We'll learn more about these corporation accounts in later chapters.)

In its balance sheet, Dell Computer Corporation reported its owners' (stockholders') equity section in 1997 as follows:

ILLUSTRATION 4-24

Stockholders' equity section

DELL COMPUTER CORPORATION
(in millions)

Stockholders' equity:	
Common stock 173,047,420 shares	$195
Retained earnings	611
Total stockholders' equity	$806

Classified Balance Sheet Illustrated

An unclassified balance sheet of Pioneer Advertising Agency was presented in Illustration 3-20 on page 112. Using the same adjusted trial balance accounts for Pioneer at October 31, 1999, we can prepare the classified balance sheet shown in Illustration 4-25. For illustrative purposes, we have assumed that $1,000 of the notes payable is due currently and $4,000 is long-term.

The balance sheet is most often presented in **report form**, as in Illustration 4-25, with the assets shown above the liabilities and owner's equity. The balance sheet may also be presented in **account form** with the assets section placed on the left and the liabilities and owner's equity sections on the right.

ILLUSTRATION 4-25

Classified balance sheet in report form

PIONEER ADVERTISING AGENCY
Balance Sheet
October 31, 1999

Assets

Current assets		
Cash		$15,200
Accounts receivable		200
Advertising supplies		1,000
Prepaid insurance		550
Total current assets		16,950
Property, plant, and equipment		
Office equipment	$5,000	
Less: Accumulated depreciation	40	4,960
Total assets		$21,910

Liabilities and Owner's Equity

Current liabilities	
Notes payable	$ 1,000
Accounts payable	2,500
Interest payable	50
Unearned revenue	800
Salaries payable	1,200
Total current liabilities	5,550
Long-term liabilities	
Notes payable	4,000
Total liabilities	9,550
Owner's equity	
C. R. Byrd, Capital	12,360
Total liabilities and owner's equity	$21,910

BEFORE YOU GO ON . . .

Review It

1. What are the major sections in a classified balance sheet?
2. Using the Kellogg Company annual report, determine its current liabilities at December 31, 1997, and December 31, 1996. Were current liabilities higher or lower than current assets in these two years? The answers to this question is provided on page 185.
3. What is the difference between the report form and the account form of the classified balance sheet?

A LOOK BACK AT OUR FEATURE STORY

Refer to the opening story about SRC Corporation, and answer the following questions:

1. hat is the lesson of the SRC story and Jack Stack's innovations?
2. How did Craig Highbarger's knowledge of financial statements, especially the income statement, contribute to his effectiveness as an employee?

Solution:

1. If you give employees equity in the company and provide them with the training and the information to understand the financial consequences of their decisions and actions, they will act more responsibly and make a greater contribution to the sales and income of the company. In other words, they begin to think like owners.
2. By understanding the income statement, he now recognizes the impact of revenues and expenses in arriving at net income—as well as how they affect his bonus.

THE NAVIGATOR

DEMONSTRATION PROBLEM

At the end of its first month of operations, the Watson Answering Service has the following unadjusted trial balance:

WATSON ANSWERING SERVICE
August 31, 1999
Trial Balance

	Debit	Credit
Cash	$ 5,400	
Accounts Receivable	2,800	
Prepaid Insurance	2,400	
Supplies	1,300	
Equipment	60,000	
Notes Payable		$40,000
Accounts Payable		2,400
Ray Watson, Capital		30,000
Ray Watson, Drawing	1,000	
Service Revenue		4,900
Salaries Expense	3,200	
Utilities Expense	800	
Advertising Expense	400	
	$77,300	$77,300

Other data consist of the following:

1. Insurance expires at the rate of $200 per month.
2. There are $1,000 of supplies on hand at August 31.
3. Monthly depreciation is $900 on the equipment.
4. Interest of $500 has accrued during August on the notes payable.

PROBLEM-SOLVING STRATEGIES

1. In completing the work sheet, be sure to (a) key the adjustments, (b) extend adjusted balances to the correct statement columns, and (c) enter net income (or net loss) in the proper columns.

2. In preparing a classified balance sheet, know the contents of each of the sections.

3. In journalizing closing entries, remember that there are only four entries and that owner's drawing is closed to owner's capital.

Instructions

(a) Prepare a work sheet.
(b) Prepare a classified balance sheet assuming $35,000 of the notes payable are long-term.
(c) Journalize the closing entries.

SOLUTION TO DEMONSTRATION PROBLEM

(a)

WATSON ANSWERING SERVICE
Work Sheet
For the Month Ended August 31, 1999

Account Titles	Trial Balance Dr.	Trial Balance Cr.	Adjustments Dr.	Adjustments Cr.	Adjusted Trial Balance Dr.	Adjusted Trial Balance Cr.	Income Statement Dr.	Income Statement Cr.	Balance Sheet Dr.	Balance Sheet Cr.
Cash	5,400				5,400				5,400	
Accounts Receivable	2,800				2,800				2,800	
Prepaid Insurance	2,400			(a) 200	2,200				2,200	
Supplies	1,300			(b) 300	1,000				1,000	
Equipment	60,000				60,000				60,000	
Notes Payable		40,000				40,000				40,000
Accounts Payable		2,400				2,400				2,400
Ray Watson, Capital		30,000				30,000				30,000
Ray Watson, Drawing	1,000				1,000				1,000	
Service Revenue		4,900				4,900		4,900		
Salaries Expense	3,200				3,200		3,200			
Utilities Expense	800				800		800			
Advertising Expense	400				400		400			
Totals	77,300	77,300								
Insurance Expense			(a) 200		200		200			
Supplies Expense			(b) 300		300		300			
Depreciation Expense			(c) 900		900		900			
Accumulated Depreciation— Equipment				(c) 900		900				900
Interest Expense			(d) 500		500		500			
Interest Payable				(d) 500		500				500
Totals			1,900	1,900	78,700	78,700	6,300	4,900	72,400	73,800
Net Loss								1,400	1,400	
Totals							6,300	6,300	73,800	73,800

Explanation: (a) Insurance expired, (b) Supplies used, (c) Depreciation expensed, (d) Interest accrued.

(b)

WATSON ANSWERING SERVICE
Balance Sheet
August 31, 1999

Assets

Current assets		
Cash		$ 5,400
Accounts receivable		2,800
Prepaid insurance		2,200
Supplies		1,000
Total current assets		11,400
Property, plant, and equipment		
Equipment	$60,000	
Less: Accumulated depreciation—equipment	900	59,100
Total assets		$70,500

Liabilities and Owner's Equity

Current liabilities		
Notes payable		$ 5,000
Accounts payable		2,400
Interest payable		500
Total current liabilities		7,900
Long-term liabilities		
Notes payable		35,000
Total liabilities		42,900
Owner's equity		
Ray Watson, Capital		27,600*
Total liabilities and owner's equity		$70,500

*Ray Watson, Capital, $30,000 less drawings $1,000 and net loss $1,400.

(c)

Date	Account	Debit	Credit
Aug. 31	Service Revenue	4,900	
	Income Summary		4,900
	(To close revenue account)		
31	Income Summary	6,300	
	Salaries Expense		3,200
	Depreciation Expense		900
	Utilities Expense		800
	Interest Expense		500
	Advertising Expense		400
	Supplies Expense		300
	Insurance Expense		200
	(To close expense accounts)		
31	Ray Watson, Capital	1,400	
	Income Summary		1,400
	(To close net loss to capital)		
31	Ray Watson, Capital	1,000	
	Ray Watson, Drawing		1,000
	(To close drawings to capital)		

THE NAVIGATOR

SUMMARY OF STUDY OBJECTIVES

1. Prepare a work sheet. The steps in preparing a work sheet are: (a) prepare a trial balance on the work sheet, (b) enter the adjustments in the adjustment columns, (c) enter adjusted balances in the adjusted trial balance columns, (d) extend adjusted trial balance amounts to appropriate financial statement columns, and (e) total the statement columns, compute net income (or net loss), and complete the work sheet.

2. Explain the process of closing the books. Closing the books occurs at the end of an accounting period. The process is to journalize and post closing entries and then rule and balance all accounts. In closing the books, separate entries are made to close revenues and expenses to Income Summary, Income Summary to owner's capital, and owner's drawings to owner's capital. Only temporary accounts are closed.

3. Describe the content and purpose of a post-closing trial balance. A post-closing trial balance contains the balances in permanent accounts that are carried forward to the next accounting period. The purpose of this trial balance is to prove the equality of these balances.

4. State the required steps in the accounting cycle. The required steps in the accounting cycle are: (a) analyze business transactions, (b) journalize the transactions, (c) post to ledger accounts, (d) prepare a trial balance, (e) journalize and post adjusting entries, (f) prepare an adjusted trial balance, (g) prepare financial statements, (h) journalize and post closing entries, and (i) prepare a post-closing trial balance.

5. Explain the approaches to preparing correcting entries. One approach for determining the correcting entry is to compare the incorrect entry with the correct entry. After comparison, a correcting entry is made to correct the accounts. An alternative to a correcting entry is to reverse the incorrect entry and then prepare the correct entry.

6. Identify the sections of a classified balance sheet. In a classified balance sheet, assets are classified as current assets; long-term investments; property, plant, and equipment; or intangibles. Liabilities are classified as either current or long-term. There is also an owner's equity section, which varies with the form of business organization.

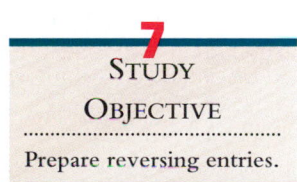

GLOSSARY

Classified balance sheet A balance sheet that contains a number of standard classifications or sections. (p. 157).

Closing entries Entries at the end of an accounting period to transfer the balances of temporary accounts to a permanent owner's equity account, owner's capital. (p. 147).

Correcting entries Entries to correct errors made in recording transactions. (p. 154).

Current assets Cash and other resources that are reasonably expected to be realized in cash or sold or consumed in the business within one year or the operating cycle, whichever is longer. (p. 157).

Current liabilities Obligations reasonably expected to be paid from existing current assets or through the creation of other current liabilities within the next year or operating cycle, whichever is longer. (p. 159).

Income Summary A temporary account used in closing revenue and expense accounts. (p. 147).

Intangible assets Noncurrent resources that do not have physical substance. (p. 159).

Liquidity The ability of a company to pay obligations that are expected to become due within the next year or operating cycle. (p. 160).

Long-term investments Resources not expected to be realized in cash within the next year or operating cycle. (p. 158).

Long-term liabilities (Long-term debt) Obligations expected to be paid after one year. (p. 160).

Operating cycle The average time required to go from cash to cash in producing revenues. (p. 157).

Permanent (real) accounts Balance sheet accounts whose balances are carried forward to the next accounting period. (p. 146).

Post-closing trial balance A list of permanent accounts and their balances after closing entries have been journalized and posted. (p. 150).

Property, plant, and equipment Assets of a relatively permanent nature that are being used in the business and not intended for resale. (p. 158).

Reversing entry An entry at the beginning of the next accounting period that is the exact opposite of the adjusting entry made in the previous period. (p. 154).

Stockholders' equity The ownership claim of shareholders on total assets. It is to a corporation what owner's equity is to a proprietorship. (p. 160).

Temporary (nominal) accounts Revenue, expense, and drawing accounts whose balances are transferred to owner's capital at the end of an accounting period. (p. 146).

Work sheet A multiple-column form that may be used in the adjustment process and in preparing financial statements. (p. 140).

APPENDIX REVERSING ENTRIES

STUDY OBJECTIVE

7

Prepare reversing entries.

After the financial statements are prepared and the books are closed, it is often helpful to reverse some of the adjusting entries before recording the regular transactions of the next period. Such entries are called reversing entries. **A reversing entry is made at the beginning of the next accounting period and is the exact opposite of the adjusting entry made in the previous period.** The recording of reversing entries is an **optional** step in the accounting cycle.

The purpose of reversing entries is to simplify the recording of a subsequent transaction related to an adjusting entry. In Chapter 3, you may recall, the payment of salaries after an adjusting entry resulted in two debits: one to Salaries Payable and the other to Salaries Expense. With reversing entries, the entire subsequent payment can be debited to Salaries Expense. **The use of reversing entries does not change the amounts reported in the financial statements. It does, however, simplify the recording of subsequent transactions.**

ILLUSTRATION OF REVERSING ENTRIES

Reversing entries are most often used to reverse two types of adjusting entries: accrued revenues and accrued expenses. They are seldom made for prepaid expenses and unearned revenues. To illustrate the optional use of reversing entries for accrued expenses, we will use the salaries expense transactions for Pioneer Advertising Agency. The transaction and adjustment data are as follows:

1. October 26 (initial salary entry): $4,000 of salaries earned between October 15 and October 26 are paid.
2. October 31 (adjusting entry): Salaries earned between October 29 and October 31 are $1,200. These will be paid in the November 9 payroll.
3. November 9 (subsequent salary entry): Salaries paid are $4,000. Of this amount, $1,200 applied to accrued wages payable and $2,800 was earned between November 1 and November 9.

ILLUSTRATION 4A-1

*Comparative entries—
not reversing vs. reversing*

The comparative entries with and without reversing entries are shown in Illustration 4A-1.

When Reversing Entries Are Not Used (per chapter)				When Reversing Entries Are Used (per appendix)			
Initial Salary Entry				Initial Salary Entry			
Oct. 26	Salaries Expense	4,000		Oct. 26	Salaries Expense	4,000	
	Cash		4,000		Cash		4,000
Adjusting Entry				Adjusting Entry			
Oct. 31	Salaries Expense	1,200		Oct. 31	Salaries Expense	1,200	
	Salaries Payable		1,200		Salaries Payable		1,200
Closing Entry				Closing Entry			
Oct. 31	Income Summary	5,200		Oct. 31	Income Summary	5,200	
	Salaries Expense		5,200		Salaries Expense		5,200
Reversing Entry				Reversing Entry			
Nov. 1	No reversing entry is made.			Nov. 1	Salaries Payable	1,200	
					Salaries Expense		1,200
Subsequent Salary Entry				Subsequent Salary Entry			
Nov. 9	Salaries Payable	1,200		Nov. 9	Salaries Expense	4,000	
	Salaries Expense	2,800			Cash		4,000
	Cash		4,000				

The comparative entries show that the first three entries are the same whether or not reversing entries are used. The last two entries, however, are different. The November 1 **reversing entry** eliminates the $1,200 balance in Salaries Payable that was created by the October 31 adjusting entry. The reversing entry also creates a $1,200 credit balance in the Salaries Expense account. As you know, it is unusual for an expense account to have a credit balance. The balance is correct in this instance, though, because it anticipates that the entire amount of the first salary payment in the new accounting period will be debited to Salaries Expense. This debit will eliminate the credit balance, and the resulting debit balance in the expense account will equal the salaries expense incurred in the new accounting period ($2,800 in this example).

TECHNOLOGY IN ACTION

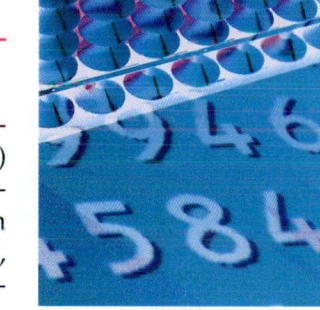

Using reversing entries in a computerized accounting system is more efficient than in a manual system. The reversing entry saves writing a program to locate the amount accrued from the preceding period and making the more complicated entry in the current period. That is, the computer does not have to be programmed to determine whether any accrued items exist.

When reversing entries are made, all cash payments of expenses can be debited to the expense account. This means that on November 9 (and every payday) Salaries Expense can be debited for the amount paid without regard to the existence of any accrued salaries payable. Being able to make the same entry each time simplifies the recording process. Note that when reversing entries are used, the recording of subsequent transactions is simplified because they can be recorded as if the related adjusting entry had never been made.

The posting of the entries with reversing entries is shown in Illustration 4A-2.

Salaries Expense						Salaries Payable				
10/26 Paid	4,000	10/31 Closing	5,200		11/1 Reversing	1,200	10/31 Adjusting	1,200
31 Adjusting	1,200							
	5,200		5,200					
11/9 Paid	4,000	11/1 Reversing	1,200					

ILLUSTRATION 4A-2

Postings with reversing entries

Reversing entries may also be made for accrued revenue adjusting entries. For Pioneer Advertising, the adjusting entry was: Accounts Receivable (Dr.) $200 and Service Revenue (Cr.) $200. Thus, the reversing entry on November 1 is:

Nov. 1	Service Revenue	200	
	Accounts Receivable		200
	(To reverse October 31 adjusting entry)		

A	=	L	+	OE
− 200				− 200

When the accrued fees are collected, Cash is debited and Service Revenue is credited.

SUMMARY OF STUDY OBJECTIVE FOR APPENDIX

7. Prepare reversing entries. Reversing entries are the direct opposite of the adjusting entry made in the preceding period. They are made at the beginning of a new accounting period to simplify the recording of later transactions related to the adjusting entry. In most cases, only accrued adjusting entries are reversed.

*Note: All asterisked Questions, Exercises, and Problems relate to material in the appendix to the chapter.

SELF-STUDY QUESTIONS

Answers are at the end of the chapter.

(SO 1) 1. Which of the following statements is *incorrect* concerning the work sheet?
a. The work sheet is essentially a working tool of the accountant.
b. The work sheet is distributed to management and other interested parties.
c. The work sheet cannot be used as a basis for posting to ledger accounts.
d. Financial statements can be prepared directly from the work sheet before journalizing and posting the adjusting entries.

(SO 1) 2. In a work sheet, net income is entered in the following columns:
a. income statement (Dr) and balance sheet (Dr).
b. income statement (Cr) and balance sheet (Dr).
c. income statement (Dr) and balance sheet (Cr).
d. income statement (Cr) and balance sheet (Cr).

(SO 2) 3. An account that will have a zero balance after closing entries have been journalized and posted is:
a. Service Revenue.
b. Advertising Supplies.
c. Prepaid Insurance.
d. Accumulated Depreciation.

(SO 2) 4. When a net loss has occurred, Income Summary is:
a. debited and owner's capital is credited.
b. credited and owner's capital is debited.
c. debited and owner's drawing is credited.
d. credited and owner's drawing is debited.

(SO 2) 5. The closing process involves separate entries to close (1) expenses, (2) drawings, (3) revenues and (4) income summary. The correct sequencing of the entries is:
a. (4), (3), (2), (1)
b. (1), (2), (3), (4)
c. (3), (1), (4), (2)
d. (3), (2), (1), (4)

(SO 3) 6. Which types of accounts will appear in the post-closing trial balance?
a. Permanent (real) accounts.
b. Temporary (nominal) accounts.
c. Accounts shown in the income statement columns of a work sheet.
d. None of the above.

(SO 4) 7. All of the following are required steps in the accounting cycle *except*:
a. journalizing and posting closing entries.
b. preparing financial statements.
c. journalizing the transactions.
d. preparing a work sheet.

(SO 5) 8. Cash of $100 received at the time the service was rendered was journalized and posted as a debit to Cash $100 and a credit to Accounts Receivable $100. Assuming the incorrect entry is not reversed, the correcting entry is:
a. debit Service Revenue $100 and credit Accounts Receivable $100.
b. debit Accounts Receivable $100 and credit Service Revenue $100.
c. debit Cash $100 and credit Service Revenue $100.
d. debit Accounts Receivable $100 and credit Cash $100.

(SO 6) 9. In a classified balance sheet, assets are usually classified using the following categories:
a. current assets; long-term assets; property, plant, and equipment; and intangible assets.
b. current assets; long-term investments; property, plant, and equipment; and other assets.
c. current assets; long-term investments; tangible assets; and intangible assets.
d. current assets; long-term investments; property, plant, and equipment; and intangible assets.

(SO 6) 10. Current assets are listed:
a. by liquidity.
b. by importance.
c. by longevity.
d. alphabetically.

(SO 7) *11. On December 31, Salerno Company correctly made an adjusting entry to recognize $2,000 of accrued salaries payable. On January 8 of the next year, total salaries of $3,400 were paid. Assuming the correct reversing entry was made on January 1, the entry on January 8 will result in a credit to Cash $3,400, and the following debit(s):
a. Salaries Payable $1,400 and Salaries Expense $2,000.
b. Salaries Payable $2,000 and Salaries Expense $1,400.
c. Salaries Expense $3,400.
d. Salaries Payable $3,400.

THE
NAVIGATOR

QUESTIONS

1. "A work sheet is a permanent accounting record and its use is required in the accounting cycle." Do you agree? Explain.

2. Explain the purpose of the work sheet.

3. What is the relationship, if any, between the amount shown in the adjusted trial balance column for an account and that account's ledger balance?

4. If a company's revenues are $125,000 and its expenses are $113,000, in which financial statement columns of the work sheet will the net income of $12,000 appear? When expenses exceed revenues, in which columns will the difference appear?

5. Why is it necessary to prepare formal financial statements when all of the data are in the statement columns of the work sheet?

6. Identify the account(s) debited and credited in each of the four closing entries, assuming the company has net income for the year.

7. Describe the nature of the Income Summary account and identify the types of summary data that may be posted to this account.

8. What are the content and purpose of a post-closing trial balance?

9. Which of the following accounts would not appear in the post-closing trial balance? Interest Payable; Equipment; Depreciation Expense; Kathy Ho, Drawing; Unearned Revenue; Accumulated Depreciation—Equipment; and Service Revenue.

10. Distinguish between a reversing entry and an adjusting entry. Are reversing entries required?

11. Indicate, in the sequence in which they are made, the three required steps in the accounting cycle that involve journalizing.

12. Identify, in the sequence in which they are prepared, the three trial balances that are often used to report financial information about a company.

13. How do correcting entries differ from adjusting entries?

14. What standard classifications are used in preparing a classified balance sheet?

15. What is meant by the term "operating cycle"?

16. Define current assets. What basis is used for arranging individual items within the current asset section?

17. Distinguish between long-term investments and property, plant, and equipment.

18. How do current liabilities differ from long-term liabilities?

19. (a) What is the term used to describe the owner's equity section of a corporation? (b) Identify the two owner's equity accounts in a corporation and indicate the purpose of each.

20. How does a report form balance sheet differ from an account form balance sheet?

*21. David Biel Company prepares reversing entries. If the adjusting entry for interest payable is reversed, what type of an account balance, if any, will there be in Interest Payable and Interest Expense after the reversing entry is posted?

*22. At December 31, accrued salaries payable totaled $4,500. On January 10, total salaries of $8,000 are paid. (a) Assume that reversing entries are made at January 1. Give the January 10 entry and indicate the Salaries Expense account balance after the entry is posted. (b) Repeat part (a) assuming reversing entries are not made.

BRIEF EXERCISES

BE4–1   The steps in using a work sheet are presented in random order below. List the steps in the proper order.

_____ Prepare a trial balance on the work sheet.
_____ Enter adjusted balances.
_____ Extend adjusted balances to appropriate statement columns.
_____ Total the statement columns, compute net income (loss), and complete the work sheet.
_____ Enter adjustment data.

List the steps in preparing a work sheet.
(SO 1)

BE4–2   The ledger of Warren Company includes the following unadjusted balances: Prepaid Insurance $4,000, Service Revenue $58,000, and Salaries Expense $25,000. Adjusting entries are required for (a) expired insurance $1,600, (b) services provided $900, but unbilled and uncollected, and (c) accrued salaries payable $800. Enter the unadjusted balances and adjustments into a work sheet and complete the work sheet for all accounts. Note: You will need to add the following accounts: Accounts Receivable, Salaries Payable, and Insurance Expense.

Prepare partial work sheet.
(SO 1)

BE4–3   The following selected accounts appear in the adjusted trial balance columns of the work sheet for the Falcetto Company: Accumulated Depreciation; Depreciation Expense;

Identify work sheet columns for selected accounts.
(SO 1)

L. Falcetto, Capital; L. Falcetto, Drawing; Service Revenue; Supplies; and Accounts Payable. Indicate the financial statement column (income statement Dr., balance sheet Cr., etc.) to which each balance should be extended.

Prepare closing entries from ledger balances.
(SO 2)

BE4–4   The ledger of the Perkins Company contains the following balances: R. Perkins, Capital $30,000; R. Perkins, Drawing $2,000; Service Revenue $45,000; Salaries Expense $26,000; and Supplies Expense $4,000. Prepare the closing entries at December 31.

Post closing entries and rule and balance T accounts.
(SO 2)

BE4–5   Using the data in BE4–4, enter the balances in T accounts, post the closing entries, and rule and balance the accounts.

Journalize and post closing entries using the three-column form of account.
(SO 2)

BE4–6   The income statement for Community Golf Club for the month ending July 31 shows Green Fee Revenue $14,000, Salaries Expense $6,200, Maintenance Expense $2,500, and Net Income $7,300. Prepare the entries to close the revenue and expense accounts. Post the entries to the revenue and expense accounts and complete the closing process for these accounts using the three-column form of account.

Identify post-closing trial balance accounts.
(SO 3)

BE4–7   Using the data in BE4–3, identify the accounts that would be included in a post-closing trial balance.

List the required steps in the accounting cycle in sequence.
(SO 4)

BE4–8   The steps in the accounting cycle are listed in random order below. List the steps in proper sequence, assuming no work sheet is prepared.

_____ Prepare a trial balance.
_____ Journalize the transactions.
_____ Journalize and post closing entries.
_____ Prepare financial statements.
_____ Journalize and post adjusting entries.
_____ Post to ledger accounts.
_____ Prepare a post-closing trial balance.
_____ Prepare an adjusted trial balance.
_____ Analyze business transactions.

Prepare correcting entries.
(SO 5)

BE4–9   At Ruhly Company, the following errors were discovered after the transactions had been journalized and posted. Prepare the correcting entries.

1. A collection on account from a customer for $780 was recorded as a debit to Cash $780 and a credit to Service Revenue $780.
2. The purchase of store supplies on account for $1,630 was recorded as a debit to Store Supplies $1,360 and a credit to Accounts Payable $1,360.

Prepare the current asset section of a balance sheet.
(SO 6)

BE4–10   The balance sheet debit column of the work sheet for Rueben Company includes the following accounts: Accounts Receivable $14,500; Prepaid Insurance $3,600; Cash $18,400; Supplies $5,200, and Marketable Securities $8,200. Prepare the current asset section of the balance sheet listing the accounts in proper sequence.

Prepare reversing entries.
(SO 7)

***BE4–11**   At October 31, Julia Company made an accrued expense adjusting entry of $600 for salaries. Prepare the reversing entry on November 1 and indicate the balances in Salaries Payable and Salaries Expense after posting the reversing entry.

EXERCISES

Complete work sheet.
(SO 1)

E4–1   The adjusted trial balance columns of the work sheet for Jose Navarro Company are as follows:

JOSE NAVARRO COMPANY
Work Sheet (partial)
For the Month Ended April 30, 1999

Account Titles	Adjusted Trial Balance		Income Statement		Balance Sheet	
	Dr.	Cr.	Dr.	Cr.	Dr.	Cr.
Cash	17,052					
Accounts Receivable	7,840					

Account Titles	Adjusted Trial Balance		Income Statement		Balance Sheet	
	Dr.	Cr.	Dr.	Cr.	Dr.	Cr.
Prepaid Rent	2,280					
Equipment	23,050					
Accumulated Depreciation		4,921				
Notes Payable		5,700				
Accounts Payable		5,972				
J. Navarro, Capital		33,960				
J. Navarro, Drawing	3,650					
Service Revenue		12,590				
Salaries Expense	7,840					
Rent Expense	760					
Depreciation Expense	671					
Interest Expense	57					
Interest Payable		57				
Totals	63,200	63,200				

Instructions
Complete the work sheet.

E4–2 Work sheet data for the Jose Navarro Company are presented in E4–1. The owner did not make any additional investments in the business in April.

Prepare financial statements from work sheet.
(SO 1, 6)

Instructions
Prepare an income statement, an owner's equity statement, and a classified balance sheet.

E4–3 Work sheet data for the Jose Navarro Company are presented in E4–1.

Journalize and post closing entries and prepare a post-closing trial balance.
(SO 2, 3)

Instructions
(a) Journalize the closing entries at April 30.
(b) Post the closing entries to Income Summary and J. Navarro, Capital. Use T accounts.
(c) Prepare a post-closing trial balance at April 30.

E4–4 The adjustments columns of the work sheet for Goodyear Company are shown below.

Prepare adjusting entries from a work sheet and extend balances to work sheet columns.
(SO 1)

Account Titles	Adjustments	
	Debit	Credit
Accounts Receivable	800	
Prepaid Insurance		400
Accumulated Depreciation		1,000
Salaries Payable		500
Service Revenue		800
Salaries Expense	500	
Insurance Expense	400	
Depreciation Expense	1,000	
	2,700	2,700

Instructions
(a) Prepare the adjusting entries.
(b) Assuming the adjusted trial balance amount for each account is normal, indicate the financial statement column to which each balance should be extended.

Derive adjusting entries from work sheet data.
(SO 1)

E4–5   Selected work sheet data for Marinita Company are presented below.

Account Titles	Trial Balance		Adjusted Trial Balance	
	Dr.	Cr.	Dr.	Cr.
Accounts Receivable	?		34,000	
Prepaid Insurance	24,000		18,000	
Supplies	9,000		?	
Accumulated Depreciation		12,000		?
Salaries Payable		?		6,000
Service Revenue		90,000		95,000
Insurance Expense			?	
Depreciation Expense			10,000	
Supplies Expense			4,000	
Salaries Expense	?		49,000	

Instructions
(a) Fill in the missing amounts.
(b) Prepare the adjusting entries that were made.

Journalize and post closing entries and prepare a post-closing trial balance.
(SO 2, 3)

E4–6   The adjusted trial balance of Rafael Company at the end of its fiscal year is:

RAFAEL COMPANY
Adjusted Trial Balance
July 31, 1999

No.	Account Titles	Debits	Credits
101	Cash	$ 11,940	
112	Accounts Receivable	8,780	
157	Equipment	15,900	
167	Accumulated Depreciation		$ 5,400
201	Accounts Payable		4,220
208	Unearned Rent Revenue		1,800
301	S. Rafael, Capital		45,200
306	S. Rafael, Drawing	14,000	
404	Commission Revenue		65,100
429	Rent Revenue		6,500
711	Depreciation Expense	4,000	
720	Salaries Expense	58,700	
732	Utilities Expense	14,900	
		$128,220	$128,220

Instructions
(a) Prepare the closing entries using page J15.
(b) Post to S. Rafael, Capital and No. 350 Income Summary accounts. (Use the three-column form.)
(c) Prepare a post-closing trial balance at July 31.

E4–7   The adjusted trial balance for Rafael Company is presented in E4–6.

Prepare financial statements.
(SO 6)

Instructions
(a) Prepare an income statement and an owner's equity statement for the year. Rafael did not make any capital investments during the year.
(b) Prepare a classified balance sheet at July 31.

Prepare closing entries and an owner's equity statement.
(SO 2)

E4–8   Selected accounts for Comfort Zone Salon are presented below. All June 30 postings are from closing entries.

Salaries Expense				Service Revenue				L. Pappas, Capital			
6/10	3,200	6/30	8,800	6/30	15,600	6/15	7,200	6/30	2,500	6/1	12,000
6/28	5,600					6/24	8,400			6/30	1,800
										Bal.	11,300

Supplies Expense				Rent Expense				L. Pappas, Drawing			
6/12	800	6/30	1,500	6/1	3,500	6/30	3,500	6/13	1,000	6/30	2,500
6/24	700							6/25	1,500		

Instructions

(a) Prepare the closing entries that were made.
(b) Post the closing entries to Income Summary.

E4–9 The Kumar Company has an inexperienced accountant. During the first 2 weeks on the job, the following errors were made in journalizing transactions. All entries were posted as made.

Prepare correcting entries.
(SO 5)

1. A payment on account to a creditor of $630 was debited to Accounts Payable $360 and credited to Cash $360.
2. The purchase of supplies on account for $600 was debited to Equipment $60 and credited to Accounts Payable $60.
3. A $400 withdrawal of cash for P. Kumar's personal use was debited to Salaries Expense $400 and credited to Cash $400.

Instructions
Prepare the correcting entries.

E4–10 The adjusted trial balance for Bel-Air's Bowling Alley at December 31, 1999, contains the following accounts.

Prepare a classified balance sheet.
(SO 6)

Debits		Credits	
Building	$123,800	T. Henkel, Capital	$110,000
Accounts Receivable	14,520	Accumulated Depreciation—Building	45,600
Prepaid Insurance	4,680	Accounts Payable	13,480
Cash	20,840	Mortgage Payable	93,600
Equipment	62,400	Accumulated Depreciation—Equipment	18,720
Land	61,200	Interest Payable	2,600
Insurance Expense	780	Bowling Revenues	14,180
Depreciation Expense	7,360		$298,180
Interest Expense	2,600		
	$298,180		

Instructions

(a) Prepare a classified balance sheet; assume that $13,600 of the mortgage payable will be paid in 2000.
(b) ▭▭▭▭▷ Comment on the liquidity of the company.

*E4–11 On December 31, the adjusted trial balance of Garrett Employment Agency shows the following selected data:

Prepare closing and reversing entries.
(SO 2, 4, 7)

Accounts Receivable	$4,000	Commission Revenue	$96,000
Interest Expense	7,800	Interest Payable	2,000

Analysis shows that adjusting entries were made to (a) accrue $4,000 of commission revenue and (b) accrue $2,000 interest expense.

Instructions

(a) Prepare the closing entries for the temporary accounts at December 31.
(b) Prepare the reversing entries on January 1.
(c) Post the entries in (a) and (b). Rule and balance the accounts. (Use T accounts.)
(d) Prepare the entries to record (1) the collection of the accrued commissions on January 10 and (2) the payment of all interest due ($2,700) on January 15.
(e) Post the entries in (d) to the temporary accounts.

PROBLEMS: SET A

Prepare a work sheet, financial statements, and adjusting and closing entries.
(SO 1, 2, 3, 6)

P4–1A   The trial balance columns of the work sheet for Spellman Roofing at March 31, 1999, are as follows:

SPELLMAN ROOFING
Work Sheet
For the Month Ended March 31, 1999

Account Titles	Trial Balance Dr.	Trial Balance Cr.
Cash	$ 2,700	
Accounts Receivable	1,600	
Roofing Supplies	1,100	
Equipment	6,000	
Accumulated Depreciation—Equipment		$ 1,200
Accounts Payable		1,100
Unearned Revenue		300
A. Spellman, Capital		7,000
A. Spellman, Drawing	600	
Service Revenue		3,000
Salaries Expense	500	
Miscellaneous Expense	100	
	$12,600	$12,600

Other data:

1. A physical count reveals only $320 of roofing supplies on hand.
2. Depreciation for March is $200.
3. Unearned revenue amounted to $200 after adjustment on March 31.
4. Accrued salaries are $400.

Instructions

(a) Enter the trial balance on a work sheet and complete the work sheet.
(b) Prepare an income statement and owner's equity statement for the month of March and classified balance sheet at March 31. A. Spellman did not make any additional investments in the business in March.
(c) Journalize the adjusting entries from the adjustments columns of the work sheet.
(d) Journalize the closing entries from the financial statement columns of the work sheet.

Complete work sheet and prepare financial statements, closing entries, and post-closing trial balance.
(SO 1, 2, 3, 6)

P4–2A   The adjusted trial balance columns of the work sheet for Perez Company, owned by Jose Perez, are as follows:

PEREZ COMPANY
Work Sheet
For the Year Ended December 31, 1999

Account No.	Account Titles	Adjusted Trial Balance Dr.	Adjusted Trial Balance Cr.
101	Cash	16,600	
112	Accounts Receivable	15,400	
126	Supplies	1,500	
130	Prepaid Insurance	2,800	
151	Office Equipment	34,000	
152	Accumulated Depreciation—Office Equipment		8,000
200	Notes Payable		16,000
201	Accounts Payable		6,000
212	Salaries Payable		3,000
230	Interest Payable		500

Account No.	Account Titles	Adjusted Trial Balance Dr.	Cr.
301	J. Perez, Capital		25,000
306	J. Perez, Drawing	10,000	
400	Service Revenue		88,000
610	Advertising Expense	12,000	
631	Supplies Expense	5,700	
711	Depreciation Expense	4,000	
722	Insurance Expense	5,000	
726	Salaries Expense	39,000	
905	Interest Expense	500	
		146,500	146,500

Instructions

(a) Complete the work sheet by extending the balances to the financial statement columns.

(b) Prepare an income statement, owner's equity statement, and a classified balance sheet. (Note: $10,000 of the notes payable become due in 2000.) J. Perez did not make any additional investments in the business during the year.

(c) Prepare the closing entries. Use J14 for the journal page.

(d) Post the closing entries and rule and balance the accounts. Use the three-column form of account. Income Summary is No. 350.

(e) Prepare a post-closing trial balance.

P4–3A The completed financial statement columns of the work sheet for Strug Company are shown below.

Prepare financial statements, closing entries, and post-closing trial balance.
(SO 1, 2, 3, 6)

STRUG COMPANY
Work Sheet
For the Year Ended December 31, 1999

Account No.	Account Titles	Income Statement Dr.	Cr.	Balance Sheet Dr.	Cr.
101	Cash			13,600	
112	Accounts Receivable			13,500	
130	Prepaid Insurance			3,500	
157	Equipment			26,000	
167	Accumulated Depreciation				5,600
201	Accounts Payable				11,300
212	Salaries Payable				3,000
301	K. Strug, Capital				36,000
306	K. Strug, Drawing			12,000	
400	Service Revenue		56,000		
622	Repair Expense	1,800			
711	Depreciation Expense	2,600			
722	Insurance Expense	2,200			
726	Salaries Expense	35,000			
732	Utilities Expense	1,700			
	Totals	43,300	56,000	68,600	55,900
	Net Income	12,700			12,700
		56,000	56,000	68,600	68,600

Instructions

(a) Prepare an income statement, owner's equity statement, and a classified balance sheet. K. Strug made an additional investment of $6,000 into the business in 1999.

(b) Prepare the closing entries.

(c) Post the closing entries and rule and balance the accounts. Use T accounts. Income Summary is No. 350.

(d) Prepare a post-closing trial balance.

Complete work sheet and prepare classified balance sheet, entries, and post-closing trial balance.
(SO 1, 2, 3, 6)

P4–4A Logan Management Services began business on January 1, 1999, with a capital investment of $120,000. The company manages condominiums for owners (Service Revenue) and rents space in its own office building (Rent Revenue). The trial and adjusted trial balance columns of the work sheet at the end of the first year are as follows:

LOGAN MANAGEMENT SERVICES
Work Sheet
For the Year Ended December 31, 1999

Account Titles	Trial Balance Dr.	Trial Balance Cr.	Adjusted Trial Balance Dr.	Adjusted Trial Balance Cr.
Cash	12,500		12,500	
Accounts Receivable	23,600		23,600	
Prepaid Insurance	3,100		1,600	
Land	56,000		56,000	
Building	106,000		106,000	
Equipment	48,000		48,000	
Accounts Payable		10,400		10,400
Unearned Rent Revenue		4,000		1,800
Mortgage Payable		100,000		100,000
M. Logan, Capital		120,000		120,000
M. Logan, Drawing	20,000		20,000	
Service Revenue		75,600		75,600
Rent Revenue		24,000		26,200
Salaries Expense	32,000		32,000	
Advertising Expense	17,000		17,000	
Utilities Expense	15,800		15,800	
Totals	334,000	334,000		
Insurance Expense			1,500	
Depreciation Expense—Building			2,500	
Accumulated Depreciation—Building				2,500
Depreciation Expense—Equipment			3,900	
Accumulated Depreciation—Equipment				3,900
Interest Expense			10,000	
Interest Payable				10,000
Totals			350,400	350,400

Instructions

(a) Prepare a complete work sheet.

(b) Prepare a classified balance sheet. (Note: $10,000 of the mortgage payable is due for payment next year.)

(c) Journalize the adjusting entries.

(d) Journalize the closing entries.

(e) Prepare a post-closing trial balance.

Complete all steps in accounting cycle.
(SO 1, 2, 3, 4, 6)

P4–5A Jill Marsh opened Jill's Window Washing on July 1, 1999. During July the following transactions were completed.

July 1   Marsh invested $9,000 cash in the business.

1   Purchased used truck for $6,000, paying $3,000 cash and the balance on account.

3   Purchased cleaning supplies for $900 on account.

5   Paid $1,200 cash on one-year insurance policy effective July 1.

12   Billed customers $2,500 for cleaning services.

18   Paid $1,000 cash on amount owed on truck and $500 on amount owed on cleaning supplies.

20   Paid $1,200 cash for employee salaries.
21   Collected $1,400 cash from customers billed on July 12.
25   Billed customers $2,000 for cleaning services.
31   Paid gas and oil for month on truck $200.
31   Withdrew $600 cash for personal use.

The chart of accounts for Jill's Window Washing contains the following accounts: No. 101 Cash, No. 112 Accounts Receivable, No. 128 Cleaning Supplies, No. 130 Prepaid Insurance, No. 157 Equipment, No. 158 Accumulated Depreciation—Equipment, No. 201 Accounts Payable, No. 212 Salaries Payable, No. 301 Jill Marsh, Capital, No. 306 Jill Marsh, Drawing, No. 350 Income Summary, No. 400 Service Revenue, No. 633 Gas & Oil Expense, No. 634 Cleaning Supplies Expense, No. 711 Depreciation Expense, No. 722 Insurance Expense, No. 726 Salaries Expense.

Instructions
(a) Journalize and post the July transactions. Use page J1 for the journal and the three-column form of account.
(b) Prepare a trial balance at July 31 on a work sheet.
(c) Enter the following adjustments on the work sheet and complete the work sheet.
   (1) Services provided but unbilled and uncollected at July 31 were $1,100.
   (2) Depreciation on equipment for the month was $200.
   (3) One-twelfth of the insurance expired.
   (4) An inventory count shows $600 of cleaning supplies on hand at July 31.
   (5) Accrued but unpaid employee salaries were $400.
(d) Prepare the income statement and owner's equity statement for July and a classified balance sheet at July 31.
(e) Journalize and post adjusting entries. Use page J2 for the journal.
(f) Journalize and post closing entries and complete the closing process. Use page J3 for the journal.
(g) Prepare a post-closing trial balance at July 31.

P4–6A   Jenny Denton, CPA, was retained by Everlast TV Repair to prepare financial statements for April 1999. Denton accumulated all the ledger balances per Everlast's records and found the following:

Analyze errors and prepare correcting entries.
(SO 5)

EVERLAST TV REPAIR
Trial Balance
April 30, 1999

	Debit	Credit
Cash	$ 5,100	
Accounts Receivable	3,200	
Supplies	800	
Equipment	10,600	
Accumulated Depreciation		$ 1,350
Accounts Payable		2,100
Salaries Payable		500
Unearned Revenue		890
S. Morris, Capital		13,900
Service Revenue		5,450
Salaries Expense	3,300	
Advertising Expense	400	
Miscellaneous Expense	290	
Depreciation Expense	500	
	$24,190	$24,190

Jenny Denton reviewed the records and found the following errors:

1. Cash received from a customer on account was recorded as $750 instead of $570.
2. A payment of $30 for advertising expense was entered as a debit to Miscellaneous Expense $30 and a credit to Cash $30.

3. The first salary payment this month was for $1,900, which included $500 of salaries payable on March 31. The payment was recorded as a debit to Salaries Expense $1,900 and a credit to Cash $1,900. (No reversing entries were made on April 1.)

4. The purchase, on account, of a typewriter costing $340 was recorded as a debit to Supplies and a credit to Accounts Payable for $340.

5. A cash payment of repair expense on equipment for $86 was recorded as a debit to Equipment $68 and a credit to Cash $68.

Instructions

(a) Prepare an analysis of each error showing (1) the incorrect entry, (2) the correct entry, and (3) the correcting entry. Items 4 and 5 occurred on April 30, 1999.

(b) Prepare a correct trial balance.

PROBLEMS: SET B

....

Prepare work sheet, financial statements, and adjusting and closing entries.

(SO 1, 2, 3, 6)

P4–1B   S. Columbo began operations as a private investigator on January 1, 1999. The trial balance columns of the work sheet for Columbo P.I. at March 31 are as follows:

COLUMBO P.I.
Work Sheet
For the Quarter Ended March 31, 1999

Account Titles	Trial Balance	
	Dr.	Cr.
Cash	$12,400	
Accounts Receivable	5,620	
Supplies	1,050	
Prepaid Insurance	2,400	
Equipment	30,000	
Notes Payable		$10,000
Accounts Payable		12,350
S. Columbo, Capital		20,000
S. Columbo, Drawing	600	
Service Revenue		13,620
Salaries Expense	1,200	
Travel Expense	1,300	
Rent Expense	1,200	
Miscellaneous Expense	200	
	$55,970	$55,970

Other data:

1. Supplies on hand total $750.
2. Depreciation is $400 per quarter.
3. Interest accrued on 6-month note payable, issued January 1, $300.
4. Insurance expires at the rate of $150 per month.
5. Services provided but unbilled at March 31 total $750.

Instructions

(a) Enter the trial balance on a work sheet and complete the work sheet.

(b) Prepare an income statement and owner's equity statement for the quarter and a classified balance sheet at March 31. S. Columbo did not make any additional investments in the business during the quarter ended March 31, 1999.

(c) Journalize the adjusting entries from the adjustments columns of the work sheet.

(d) Journalize the closing entries from the financial statement columns of the work sheet.

P4–2B   The adjusted trial balance columns of the work sheet for Oslo Company is as follows:

Complete work sheet and prepare financial statements, closing entries, and post-closing trial balance.
(SO 1, 2, 3, 6)

OSLO COMPANY
Work Sheet
For the Year Ended December 31, 1999

Account No.	Account Titles	Adjusted Trial Balance Dr.	Cr.
101	Cash	22,800	
112	Accounts Receivable	15,400	
126	Supplies	2,300	
130	Prepaid Insurance	4,800	
151	Office Equipment	44,000	
152	Accumulated Depreciation—Office Equipment		18,000
200	Notes Payable		20,000
201	Accounts Payable		8,000
212	Salaries Payable		3,000
230	Interest Payable		1,000
301	S. Oslo, Capital		36,000
306	S. Oslo, Drawing	12,000	
400	Service Revenue		79,000
610	Advertising Expense	12,000	
631	Supplies Expense	3,700	
711	Depreciation Expense	6,000	
722	Insurance Expense	4,000	
726	Salaries Expense	37,000	
905	Interest Expense	1,000	
		165,000	165,000

Instructions
(a) Complete the work sheet by extending the balances to the financial statement columns.

(b) Prepare an income statement, owner's equity statement, and a classified balance sheet. $10,000 of the notes payable become due in 2000. S. Oslo did not make any additional investments in the business during 1999.

(c) Prepare the closing entries. Use J14 for the journal page.

(d) Post the closing entries and rule and balance the accounts. Use the three-column form of account. Income Summary is No. 350.

(e) Prepare a post-closing trial balance.

P4–3B   The completed financial statement columns of the work sheet for Sierra Company are shown below.

Prepare financial statements, closing entries, and post-closing trial balance.
(SO 1, 2, 3, 6)

SIERRA COMPANY
Work Sheet
For the Year Ended December 31, 1999

Account No.	Account Titles	Income Statement Dr.	Cr.	Balance Sheet Dr.	Cr.
101	Cash			8,200	
112	Accounts Receivable			7,500	
130	Prepaid Insurance			1,800	
157	Equipment			28,000	
167	Accumulated Depreciation				8,600
201	Accounts Payable				12,000
212	Salaries Payable				3,000
301	M. Sierra, Capital				34,000
306	M. Sierra, Drawing			7,200	

Account No.	Account Titles	Income Statement Dr.	Income Statement Cr.	Balance Sheet Dr.	Balance Sheet Cr.
400	Service Revenue		42,000		
622	Repair Expense	3,200			
711	Depreciation Expense	2,800			
722	Insurance Expense	1,200			
726	Salaries Expense	36,000			
732	Utilities Expense	3,700			
	Totals	46,900	42,000	52,700	57,600
	Net Loss		4,900	4,900	
		46,900	46,900	57,600	57,600

Instructions

(a) Prepare an income statement, owner's equity statement, and a classified balance sheet. M. Sierra made an additional investment in the business of $4,000 during 1999.

(b) Prepare the closing entries.

(c) Post the closing entries and rule and balance the accounts. Use T accounts. Income Summary is No. 350.

(d) Prepare a post-closing trial balance.

P4–4B Waterworld Amusement Park has a fiscal year ending on September 30. Selected data from the September 30 work sheet are presented below:

Complete work sheet and prepare classified balance sheet, entries, and post-closing trial balance.
(SO 1, 2, 3, 6)

WATERWORLD AMUSEMENT PARK
Work Sheet
For the Year Ended September 30, 1999

	Trial Balance Dr.	Trial Balance Cr.	Adjusted Trial Balance Dr.	Adjusted Trial Balance Cr.
Cash	37,400		37,400	
Supplies	18,600		1,200	
Prepaid Insurance	31,900		3,900	
Land	80,000		80,000	
Equipment	120,000		120,000	
Accumulated Depreciation		36,200		43,000
Accounts Payable		14,600		14,600
Unearned Admissions Revenue		2,700		1,700
Mortgage Payable		50,000		50,000
N. Y. Berge, Capital		109,700		109,700
N. Y. Berge, Drawing	14,000		14,000	
Admissions Revenue		278,500		279,500
Salaries Expense	109,000		109,000	
Repair Expense	30,500		30,500	
Advertising Expense	9,400		9,400	
Utilities Expense	16,900		16,900	
Property Taxes Expense	18,000		21,000	
Interest Expense	6,000		12,000	
Totals	491,700	491,700		
Insurance Expense			28,000	
Supplies Expense			17,400	
Interest Payable				6,000
Depreciation Expense			6,800	
Property Taxes Payable				3,000
Totals			507,500	507,500

Instructions

(a) Prepare a complete work sheet.

(b) Prepare a classified balance sheet. (Note: $10,000 of the mortgage payable is due for payment in the next fiscal year.)

(c) Journalize the adjusting entries using the work sheet as a basis.

(d) Journalize the closing entries using the work sheet as a basis.

(e) Prepare a post-closing trial balance.

P4–5B   Anna Khan opened Anna's Carpet Cleaners on March 1. During March, the following transactions were completed.

Complete all steps in accounting cycle.
(SO 1, 2, 3, 4, 6)

Mar. 1   Invested $10,000 cash in the business.

1   Purchased used truck for $6,000, paying $4,000 cash and the balance on account.

3   Purchased cleaning supplies for $1,200 on account.

5   Paid $1,800 cash on one-year insurance policy effective March 1.

14   Billed customers $2,800 for cleaning services.

18   Paid $1,500 cash on amount owed on truck and $500 on amount owed on cleaning supplies.

20   Paid $1,500 cash for employee salaries.

21   Collected $1,600 cash from customers billed on July 14.

28   Billed customers $3,500 for cleaning services.

31   Paid gas and oil for month on truck $200.

31   Withdrew $900 cash for personal use.

The chart of accounts for Anna's Carpet Cleaners contains the following accounts: No. 101 Cash, No. 112 Accounts Receivable, No. 128 Cleaning Supplies, No. 130 Prepaid Insurance, No. 157 Equipment, No. 158 Accumulated Depreciation—Equipment, No. 201 Accounts Payable, No. 212 Salaries Payable, No. 301 A. Khan, Capital, No. 306 A. Khan, Drawing, No. 350 Income Summary, No. 400 Service Revenue, No. 633 Gas & Oil Expense, No. 634 Cleaning Supplies Expense, No. 711 Depreciation Expense, No. 722 Insurance Expense, No. 726 Salaries Expense.

Instructions

(a) Journalize and post the March transactions. Use page J1 for the journal and the three-column form of account.

(b) Prepare a trial balance at March 31 on a work sheet.

(c) Enter the following adjustments on the work sheet and complete the work sheet.

   (1) Earned but unbilled revenue at March 31 was $600.

   (2) Depreciation on equipment for the month was $250.

   (3) One-twelfth of the insurance expired.

   (4) An inventory count shows $400 of cleaning supplies on hand at March 31.

   (5) Accrued but unpaid employee salaries were $500.

(d) Prepare the income statement and owner's equity statement for March and a classified balance sheet at March 31.

(e) Journalize and post adjusting entries. Use page J2 for the journal.

(f) Journalize and post closing entries and complete the closing process. Use page J3 for the journal.

(g) Prepare a post-closing trial balance at July 31.

BROADENING YOUR PERSPECTIVE

FINANCIAL REPORTING AND ANALYSIS

FINANCIAL REPORTING PROBLEM: Kellogg Company

BYP4–1   The financial statements of Kellogg Company are presented in Appendix A at the end of this textbook.

Instructions
Answer the following questions using the Consolidated Balance Sheet and the Notes to Consolidated Financial Statements section.

(a) What were Kellogg's total current assets at December 31, 1997, and 1996?
(b) Are assets that Kellogg included under current assets listed in proper order? Explain.
(c) How are Kellogg's assets classified?
(d) What are "cash equivalents"?
(e) What were Kellogg's total current liabilities at December 31, 1997, and 1996?

COMPARATIVE ANALYSIS PROBLEM: Kellogg Company vs. General Mills

BYP4–2   Kellogg's financial statements are presented in Appendix A; General Mills's financial statements are presented in Appendix B.

Instructions

(a) Based on the information contained in these financial statements, determine each of the following for Kellogg at December 31, 1997 and for General Mills at May 25, 1997:
   1. Total current assets.
   2. Net amount of property, plant, and equipment (land, buildings, and equipment).
   3. Total current liabilities.
   4. Total stockholders' (shareholders') equity.
(b) What conclusions concerning the companies' respective financial positions can be drawn from these data?

RESEARCH ASSIGNMENT

BYP4–3   The March 1995 issue of *Management Review* includes an article by Barbara Ettorre, entitled "How Motorola Closes Its Books in Two Days."

Instructions
Read the article and answer the following questions.

(a) How often does Motorola close its books? How long did the process used to take?
(b) What was the major change Motorola initiated to shorten the closing process?
(c) What incentive does Motorola offer to ensure accurate and timely information?
(d) In a given year, how many journal entry lines does Motorola process?
(e) Provide an example of an external force that prevents Motorola from closing faster than a day-and-a-half.
(f) According to Motorola's corporate vice president and controller, how do external financial statement users perceive companies that release information early?

INTERPRETING FINANCIAL STATEMENTS: Case Corporation

BYP4–4   Case Corporation, based in Racine, Wisconsin, manufactures farm tractors, farm equipment, and light- and medium-sized construction equipment. The company's products are distributed through both independent and company-owned distributing companies, which are located throughout the world. Case Corporation's partial income statement is shown on the next page.

CASE

CASE CORPORATION
Income Statement (partial)
(in millions)

Revenues	
Net sales	$ 5,796
Interest income and other	228
	6,024
Costs and expenses	
Cost of goods sold	4,447
Selling, general, and administrative	570
Research, development, and engineering	196
Interest expense	170
Other, net	47
	5,430
Income from operations before taxes	$ 594

The internal audit staff identified the following items that require adjustments:

1. Depreciation on the administrative offices of $13 million needs to be recorded.
2. A physical inventory determined that $1 million in office supplies had been used during the year.
3. $4 million in salaries have been earned but not recorded, and half this amount is for the salaries of the engineering staff; the other half is for the administrative staff.
4. $3 million in annual insurance premiums were prepaid on May 1.
5. $7 million in prepaid rent has expired at year-end.
6. Cost of goods sold of $2 million was recorded in error as interest expense.

Assume that the partial income statement above was prepared before all adjusting entries had been made.

Instructions

(a) Make the adjusting journal entries required. Use standard account titles with prepayments having been recorded as assets.
(b) Which of the entries is not a routine adjusting entry? Explain your answer.
(c) For each of the accounts in these adjusting entries that will be posted to Case's general ledger, tell which item on the income statement will be increased or decreased.
(d) Recast the partial income statement based on the adjusting entries prepared.

REAL-WORLD FOCUS: Bethlehem Corporation

BYP4–5 Located in Easton, Pennsylvania, **Bethlehem Corporation** was established in 1856. Today it offers contract services for industrial products, rebuilding and remanufacturing industrial and military equipment per customer specifications and designs. The company also manufactures and sells a line of equipment used in the chemical, environmental, and food industries.

Bethlehem Corporation had a net loss for the year of $239,251. One reason for the loss is that Bethlehem established an accrual to provide for expenses and costs associated with certain legal proceedings against Bethlehem.

Instructions

(a) Indicate how the net loss would be shown in Bethlehem's work sheet.
(b) Where in the general ledger would you expect to find the two accounts related to the accrual for expenses and costs associated with legal proceedings?
(c) Identify the financial statement columns to which the balances of the two accounts in part (b) would be extended on the work sheet.

CRITICAL THINKING

....

GROUP DECISION CASE

BYP4–6   Cleanfast Janitorial Service was started 2 years ago by Pat Hardy. Because business has been exceptionally good, Pat decided on July 1, 1999, to expand operations by acquiring an additional truck and hiring two more assistants. To finance the expansion, Pat obtained on July 1, 1999, a $25,000, 10% bank loan, payable $10,000 on July 1, 2000, and the balance on July 1, 2001. The terms of the loan require the borrower to have $10,000 more current assets than current liabilities at December 31, 1999. If these terms are not met, the bank loan will be refinanced at 15% interest. At December 31, 1999, the accountant for Cleanfast Janitorial Service Inc. prepared the following balance sheet:

CLEANFAST JANITORIAL SERVICE
Balance Sheet
December 31, 1999

Assets

Current assets		
Cash		$ 6,500
Accounts receivable		9,000
Janitorial supplies		5,200
Prepaid insurance		4,800
Total current assets		25,500
Property, plant, and equipment		
Cleaning equipment (net)	$22,000	
Delivery trucks (net)	34,000	56,000
Total assets		$81,500

Liabilities and Owner's Equity

Current liabilities	
Notes payable	$10,000
Accounts payable	2,500
Total current liabilities	12,500
Long-term liability	
Notes payable	15,000
Total liabilities	27,500
Owner's equity	
Pat Hardy, capital	54,000
Total liabilities and owner's equity	$81,500

Pat presented the balance sheet to the bank's loan office on January 2, 2000, confident that the company had met the terms of the loan. The loan officer was not impressed. She said, "We need financial statements audited by a CPA." A CPA was hired and immediately realized that the balance sheet had been prepared from a trial balance and not from an adjusted trial balance. The adjustment data at the balance sheet date consisted of the following:

1. Earned but unbilled janitorial services were $3,000.
2. Janitorial supplies on hand were $3,500.
3. Prepaid insurance was a 3-year policy dated January 1, 1999.
4. December expenses incurred but unpaid at December 31, $300.
5. Interest on the bank loan was not recorded.
6. The amounts for plant assets were net of accumulated depreciation of $4,000 for cleaning equipment and $5,000 for delivery trucks as of January 1, 1999. Depreciation for 1999 was $2,000 for cleaning equipment and $5,000 for delivery trucks.

Instructions

With the class divided into groups, answer the following:

(a) Prepare a correct balance sheet.

(b) Were the terms of the bank loan met? Explain.

COMMUNICATION ACTIVITY

BYP4–7   The accounting cycle is important in understanding the accounting process.

Instructions

Write a memorandum to your instructor which lists the steps of the accounting cycle in the order in which they should be completed. Complete your memorandum with a paragraph that explains the optional steps in the cycle.

ETHICS CASE

BYP4–8   As the controller of Magnus Perfume Company, you discover a misstatement that overstated net income in the prior year's financial statements. The misleading financial statements appear in the company's annual report which was issued to banks and other creditors less than a month ago. After much thought about the consequences of telling the president, David Rudman, about this misstatement, you gather your courage to inform him. David says, "Hey! What they don't know won't hurt them. But, just so we set the record straight, we'll adjust this year's financial statements for last year's misstatement. We can absorb that misstatement better in this year than in last year anyway! Just don't make such a mistake again."

Instructions

(a) Who are the stakeholders in this situation?

(b) What are the ethical issues in this situation?

(c) What would you do as a controller in this situation?

SURFING THE NET

BYP4–9   Numerous companies have established home pages on the Internet, e.g., Boston Beer Company (http://www.samadams.com), Ford Motor Company (http://www.ford.com), and Kodak (http://www.kodak.com). You may have noticed company Internet addresses in television commercials or magazine advertisements.

Instructions

Examine the home pages of any two companies and answer the following questions.

(a) What type of information is available?

(b) Is any accounting-related information presented?

(c) Would you describe the home page as informative, promotional, or both? Why?

Answers to Self-Study Questions

1. b   2. c   3. a   4. b   5. c   6. a   7. d   8. b   9. d   10. a   11. c

---

Answers to Kellogg Review It Question 2, p. 162

Current liabilities in 1997 were $1,657.3 million and current liabilities in 1996 were $2,199.0 million. In both 1997 and 1996, current liabilities were greater than current assets.

  Remember to go back to the Navigator box on the chapter-opening page and check off your completed work.

CONCEPTS FOR REVIEW

Before studying this chapter, you should know or, if necessary, review:

a. How to prepare a work sheet. (Ch. 4, pp. 141–43)
b. How to close revenue, expense, and drawing accounts. (Ch. 4, pp. 146–50)
c. The steps in the accounting cycle. (Ch. 4, p. 154)

FEATURE STORY

Dropped Courses Produce Bookstore Headaches

Larry Martin is in charge of ordering textbooks for the Washington State University bookstore in Pullman, Washington. The bookstore sells about $4 million in textbooks each year. The average inventory at any point in time is 2,500 titles.

Mr. Martin's big challenge is to order enough books to satisfy demand—but not to order too many. For example, say a course historically has sold 75 books; he'll order 85 to be on the safe side. The reason: if he orders short, he'll have to order additional books by second-day air express—which is expensive and cuts into profits. However, if Martin orders too many, the publisher won't accept for return more than 20% of his original order.

Of course, returns occur all the time, especially when students drop courses during the first week of class. If the returned books are in "new and resalable" condition, the publisher will accept the return of such books and issue Martin a credit memo.

Washington State University starts its fall term before Labor Day. The busy book selling and return period lasts three to four weeks. Therefore, Martin waits until the end of September to take the inventory and determine his returns. That count verifies the accuracy of his computerized perpetual inventory accounting system. At that point, he is ready to order more books.

CHAPTER 5

ACCOUNTING FOR MERCHANDISING OPERATIONS

THE NAVIGATOR ✔

- Understand *Concepts for Review* ☐
- Read *Feature Story* ☐
- Scan *Study Objectives* ☐
- Read *Preview* ☐
- Read text and answer *Before You Go On* p. 196 ☐ p. 201 ☐ p. 207 ☐ p. 210 ☐
- Work *Demonstration Problem* ☐
- Review *Summary of Study Objectives* ☐
- Answer *Self-Study Questions* ☐
- Complete assignments ☐

STUDY OBJECTIVES

After studying this chapter, you should be able to:

1. Identify the differences between a service enterprise and a merchandising company.
2. Explain the entries for purchases under a perpetual inventory system.
3. Explain the entries for sales revenues under a perpetual inventory system.
4. Explain the computation and importance of gross profit.
5. Identify the features of the income statement for a merchandising company.
6. Explain the steps in the accounting cycle for a merchandising company.
7. Distinguish between a multiple-step and a single-step income statement.

THE NAVIGATOR

*A*s indicated in the opening story, Washington State University Bookstore earns a profit by selling goods to customers rather than performing services. Merchandising companies that purchase and sell directly to consumers—such as Kmart, Washington State Bookstore, Safeway, and Toys "R" Us—are called **retailers**. In contrast, merchandising companies that sell to retailers are known as **wholesalers**. For example, retailer Walgreens might buy goods from wholesaler McKesson & Robbins; Office Depot might buy office supplies from wholesaler United Stationers.

The steps in the accounting cycle for a merchandising company are the same as the steps for a service enterprise. However, merchandising companies use additional accounts and entries which are required in recording merchandising transactions. The content and organization of this chapter are as follows:

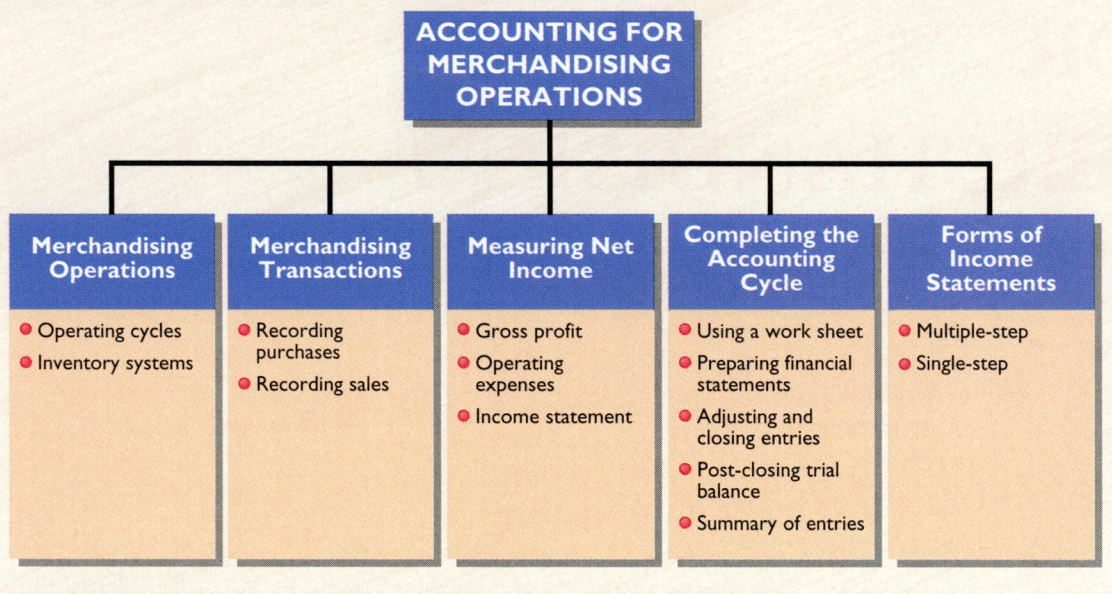

THE NAVIGATOR

MERCHANDISING OPERATIONS

1

STUDY

OBJECTIVE

Identify the differences between a service enterprise and a merchandising company.

Measuring net income for a merchandising company is conceptually the same as for a service enterprise. That is, net income (or loss) results from the matching of expenses with revenues. In a merchandising company, the primary source of revenues is the sale of merchandise, often referred to as **sales revenue** or **sales**. Unlike expenses for a service company, expenses for a merchandising company are divided into two categories: (1) the cost of goods sold and (2) operating expenses.

The **cost of goods sold** is the total cost of merchandise sold during the period. This expense is directly related to the revenue recognized from the sale of the goods. Sales revenue less cost of goods sold is called **gross profit** on sales. For example, when a calculator costing $15 is sold for $25, the gross profit is $10. Merchandising companies report gross profit on sales in the income statement.

After gross profit is calculated, operating expenses are deducted to determine net income (or loss). **Operating expenses** are expenses incurred in the process of earning sales revenue. Examples of operating expenses are sales salaries, advertising expense, and insurance expense. The operating expenses of a merchandising company include many of the expenses found in a service enterprise.

The income measurement process for a merchandiser may be diagrammed as shown in Illustration 5-1. The items in the three blue boxes are peculiar to a merchandising company; they are not used by a service company.

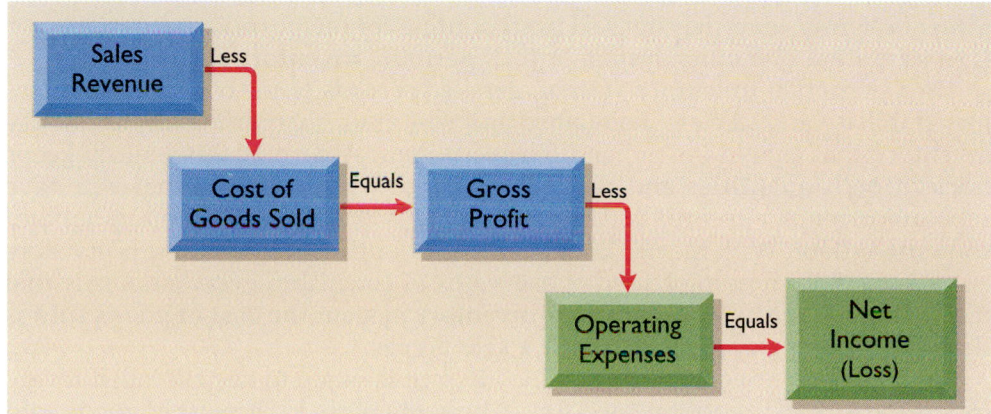

ILLUSTRATION 5-1

Income measurement process for a merchandising company

Operating Cycles

While measuring income for a merchandising company is conceptually the same as for a service company, their operating cycles differ, as shown in Illustration 5-2. The operating cycle of a merchandising company ordinarily is longer than

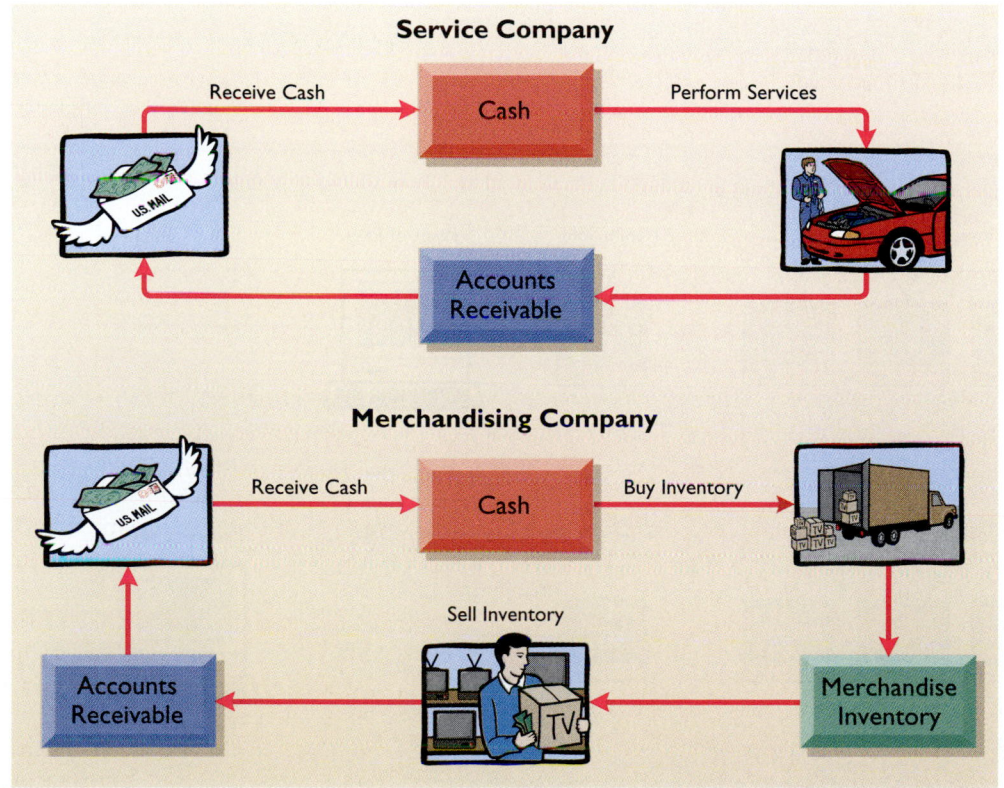

ILLUSTRATION 5-2

Operating cycles for a service company and a merchandising company

that of a service company. The purchase of merchandise inventory and its eventual sale lengthens the cycle. Note that the added asset account for a merchandising company is an **inventory** account (usually entitled Merchandise Inventory). Merchandise inventory is reported as a current asset on the balance sheet.

Inventory Systems

Either of two systems may be used in accounting for merchandising transactions: (1) a **perpetual inventory system** or (2) a **periodic inventory system**.

In a perpetual inventory system, detailed records of the cost of each inventory purchase and sale are maintained and continuously (perpetually) show the inventory that should be on hand for every item. A perpetual inventory keeps track of both **quantities and costs**. For example, a Ford dealership will have separate inventory records for each automobile, truck, and van on its lot and showroom floor. With the use of bar codes and optical scanners, a grocery store can keep a daily running record of every box of cereal and every jar of jelly that it buys and sells. **Under a perpetual inventory system the cost of goods sold is determined and recorded each time a sale occurs.**

In a periodic inventory system, no attempt is made to keep detailed inventory records of the goods on hand throughout the period. **The cost of goods sold is determined only at the end of the accounting period when a physical inventory count is taken to determine the cost of goods on hand.**

To determine the cost of goods sold under a periodic inventory system, it is necessary to (1) record purchases of merchandise, (2) determine the cost of goods purchased, and (3) determine the cost of goods on hand at the beginning and end of the accounting period.

Illustration 5-3 graphically compares the sequence of activities and the timing of the cost of goods sold computation under the two inventory systems.

ILLUSTRATION 5-3

Comparing perpetual to periodic inventory

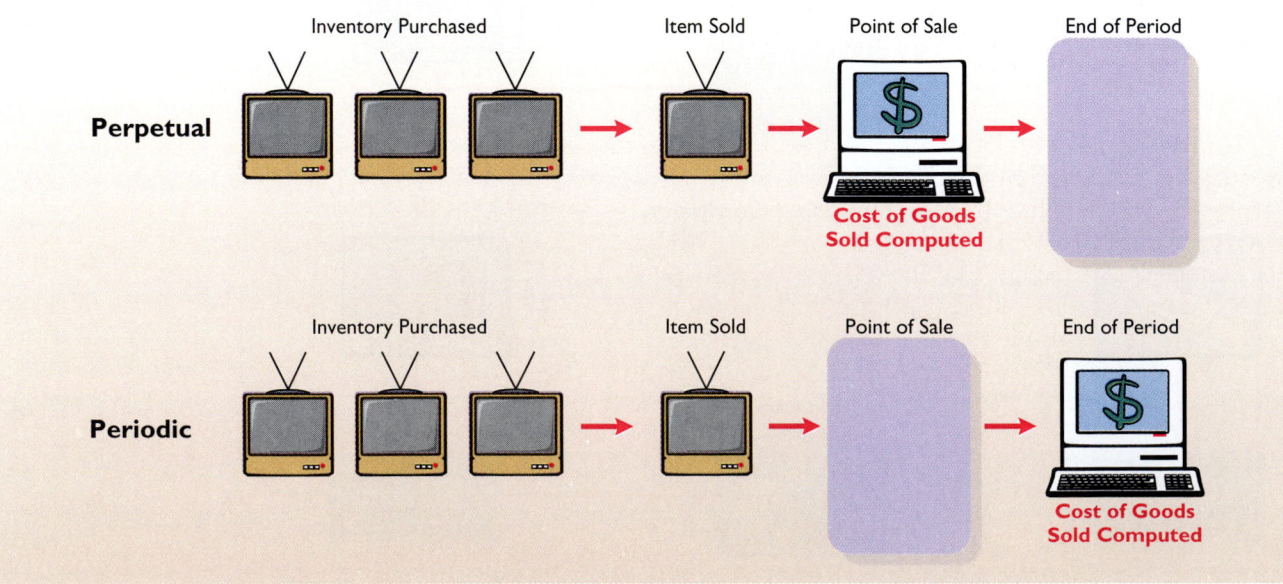

Some businesses employ the periodic system because they can control merchandise and manage day-to-day operations without detailed inventory records. In addition, perpetual systems are in many cases more expensive.

Under a perpetual inventory system, inventory shrinkage and lost or stolen goods are more readily determined. Also, reorder decisions are more accurately made under a perpetual system because exact inventory levels are known constantly. Because the perpetual inventory system is growing in popularity, we illustrate it in this chapter. The periodic system is described in Chapter 9.

MERCHANDISING TRANSACTIONS

Recording merchandising transactions requires the analysis of purchases and sales of merchandise. Related to both purchases and sales are returns and allowances, discounts, and transportation costs.

Recording Purchases

Purchases may be made for cash or on account (credit). Purchases are normally recorded when the goods are received from the supplier. Every purchase should be supported by business documents that provide written evidence of the transaction. Cash purchases should be supported by canceled checks or cash register receipts indicating the items purchased and amounts paid. Credit purchases should be supported by an **invoice**, like the one shown in Illustration 5-4, that indicates the items purchased and the total purchase price. An invoice is a document prepared by the seller that shows the relevant information about a sale. From the seller's perspective this document is a sales invoice, and from the buyer's perspective it is a purchase invoice.

Illustration 5-4 shows a sales invoice prepared by Highpoint Electronic to document a sale to Chelsea Video. Chelsea Video will use this as a purchase invoice to document the purchase from Highpoint. Chelsea will make the following entry to record the purchase of merchandise from Highpoint:

May 4	Merchandise Inventory	3,800	
	Accounts Payable		3,800
	(To record goods purchased on account, terms 2/10, n/30, from Highpoint Electronic)		

A	=	L	+	OE
+3,800		+3,800		

Under the perpetual inventory system, purchases of merchandise for sale are recorded in the Merchandise Inventory account. Thus, Larry Martin, as manager of the Washington State University Bookstore, would **debit Merchandise Inventory for books purchased for resale to students.** However, not all purchases are debited to Merchandise Inventory. Purchases of assets acquired for use and not for resale, such as supplies, equipment, and similar items, should be **debited to specific asset accounts rather than to Merchandise Inventory.** For example, Larry Martin would debit Supplies for the supplies he buys to make shelf signs and labels that identify which books are for which courses.

Purchase Returns and Allowances

A purchaser may be dissatisfied with the merchandise received because the goods are damaged or defective, of inferior quality, or not in accord with the purchaser's specifications. In such cases, the purchaser may return the goods to

ILLUSTRATION 5-4

Invoice

INVOICE NO. 731

HIGHPOINT ELECTRONIC

27 CIRCLE DRIVE
HARDING, MICHIGAN 48281

▼

SOLD TO

Firm Name ___ Chelsea Video

Attention of ___ James Hoover, Purchasing Agent

Address ___ 125 Main Street

Chelsea   Illinois   60915
City   State   Zip

Date 5/4/99	Salesperson Malone	Terms 2/10, n/30	Freight FOB Sh.Pt.		
Catalogue No.	Description		Quantity	Price	Amount
X572Y9820	Printed Circuit Board-prototype		1	2,300	$2,300
A2547Z45	Production Model Circuits		5	300	1,500

IMPORTANT: ALL RETURNS MUST BE MADE WITHIN 10 DAYS   **TOTAL** $3,800

the supplier for credit if the sale was made on credit, or for a cash refund if the purchase was originally for cash. This transaction is known as a **purchase return**. Alternatively, the purchaser may choose to keep the merchandise if the supplier is willing to grant an allowance (deduction) from the purchase price. This transaction is known as a **purchase allowance**.

The purchaser initiates the request for a reduction of the balance due through the issuance of a **debit memorandum**. A debit memorandum is a document issued by a purchaser to inform a supplier that a debit has been made to the supplier's account on the purchaser's books. The original copy of the memorandum is sent to the supplier and one copy is retained by the purchaser. The information contained in a debit memorandum is shown in Illustration 5-5; it relates to the sales invoice shown in Illustration 5-4.

The entry by Chelsea Video for the merchandise returned to Highpoint Electronic on May 8 is:

A	=	L	+	OE
−300		−300		

May 8	Accounts Payable	300	
	Merchandise Inventory		300
	(To record return of inoperable goods		
	received from Highpoint Electronic,		
	DM No. 126)		

ILLUSTRATION 5-5
Debit memorandum

DEBIT-DM126

CHELSEA VIDEO
125 MAIN STREET
CHELSEA, IL 60915

Purchased From:

Firm Name ___Highpoint Electronic___

Attention of ___Susan Malone, Sales Representative___

Address ___27 Circle Drive___

___Harding_____MI_____48281___
City   State   Zip

Date 5/8/99	Salesperson Malone	Invoice No. 731	Invoice Date 5/4/99	Approved Reid

Catalogue No.	Description	Quantity	Price	Amount
A2547Z45	Production Model Circuits (Inoperative)	1	300	$300

Cash Refund ☐   Debit Account ☒   Other ☐

Because Merchandise Inventory was debited when the goods were received, Merchandise Inventory is credited when the goods are returned.

Purchase Discounts

The credit terms of a purchase on account may permit the purchaser to claim a cash discount for the prompt payment of a balance due. The purchaser calls this cash discount a **purchase discount**. This incentive offers advantages to both parties: The purchaser saves money, and the supplier is able to convert the accounts receivable into cash earlier.

The **credit terms** specify the amount and time period for the cash discount. They also indicate the length of time in which the purchaser is expected to pay the full invoice price. In the sales invoice in Illustration 5-4, credit terms are 2/10, n/30, which is read "two-ten, net thirty." This means that a 2% cash discount may be taken on the invoice price (less any returns or allowances) if payment is made within 10 days of the invoice date (the **discount period**); otherwise, the invoice price less any returns or allowances is due 30 days from the invoice date. Alternatively, the discount period may extend to a specified number of days following the month in which the sale occurs. For example, 1/10 EOM (end-of-month) means that a 1% discount is available if the invoice is paid within the first 10 days of the next month.

Purchase Discount

"Get that check in the mail this week so we can save 2%."

Merchandise Inventory	
	XXX

HELPFUL HINT

Assume goods were sold on June 1, terms 1/10, net 30. Question: What is the due date for taking the discount? Answer: June 11. Question: If the terms were 2/10 EOM, what is the due date for taking the discount? Answer: July 10.

When the supplier elects not to offer a cash discount for prompt payment, credit terms will specify only the maximum time period for paying the balance due. For example, the time period may be stated as n/30, n/60, or n/10 EOM.

When an invoice is paid within the discount period, the amount of the discount is credited to Merchandise Inventory. To illustrate, assume Chelsea Video pays the balance due of $3,500 (gross invoice price of $3,800 less purchase returns and allowances of $300) on May 14, the last day of the discount period. The cash discount is $70 ($3,500 × 2%), and the amount of cash paid by Chelsea Video is $3,430 ($3,500 − $70). The entry to record the May 14 payment by Chelsea Video is as follows:

A	=	L	+	OE
−3,430		−3,500		
−70				

May 14	Accounts Payable	3,500	
	Cash		3,430
	Merchandise Inventory		70
	(To record payment within discount period)		

If Chelsea Video had failed to take the discount and full payment is made on June 3, Chelsea would have made the following entry:

A	=	L	+	OE
−3,500		−3,500		

June 3	Accounts Payable	3,500	
	Cash		3,500
	(To record payment with no discount taken)		

ACCOUNTING IN ACTION
Business Insight

In the early 1990s, Sears wielded its retail clout by telling its suppliers that, rather than pay its obligations in the standard 30-day period, it would now pay in 60 days. This practice is often adopted by firms that are experiencing financial distress from a shortage of cash. A Sears spokesperson insisted, however, that Sears did not have cash problems, but, rather, was simply utilizing "vendor-financed inventory methods to improve its return on investment." Supplier trade groups criticized Sears' policy, and pointed out that consumers would be the ultimate victims, because the financing costs would eventually be passed on to them.

HELPFUL HINT

So as not to miss purchase discounts, unpaid invoices should be filed (electronically or manually) by due dates. This procedure helps the purchaser remember the discount date, prevents early payment of bills, and maximizes the time that cash can be used for other purposes.

A buyer usually should take all available discounts. For example, if Chelsea Video takes the discount, it pays $3,430 instead of $3,500, thus saving $70. If it does not take the discount and invests the $3,430 in a bank savings account for 20 days (30 − 10) at 10% interest, it will earn only $19.06 in interest.[1] The savings obtained by taking the discount is computed as follows:

---

[1] If Chelsea Video does not pay at the end of 10 days, it has the use of $3,430 for an additional 20 days at a cost (lost discount) of $70. For the 20-day period, the interest rate on the $3,430 is effectively 2.04% ($70 ÷ $3,430). Interest rates are generally expressed on an annualized basis of 360 days; thus Highpoint Electronic's discount terms are equivalent to 36.72% (360/20 × 2.04%). In view of this high interest rate, it would be better for Chelsea Video to take the discount.

ILLUSTRATION 5-6

Savings obtained by taking purchase discount

Discount of 2% on $3,500	$70.00
Interest received on $3,430	
(for 20 days at 10%)	19.06
Savings by taking the discount	**$50.94**

Freight Costs

The sales agreement should indicate whether the seller or the buyer is to pay the cost of transporting the goods to the buyer's place of business. When a common carrier such as a railroad, trucking company, or airline is used, the transportation company prepares a freight bill (often called a bill of lading) in accordance with the sales agreement. Freight terms are expressed as either **FOB shipping point** or **FOB destination**. The letters FOB mean **free on board**. Thus, FOB shipping point means that goods are placed free on board the carrier by the seller, and the buyer pays the freight costs. Conversely, FOB destination means that the goods are placed free on board to the buyer's place of business, and the seller pays the freight. For example, the sales invoice in Illustration 5-4 on page 192 indicates that freight is FOB shipping point. Thus, the buyer (Chelsea Video) pays the freight charges.

When the purchaser directly incurs the freight costs, the account Merchandise Inventory is debited. For example, if upon delivery of the goods on May 6, Chelsea Video pays Acme Freight Company $150 for freight charges, the entry on Chelsea's books is:

HELPFUL HINT
Freight terms may be stated by location. A Chicago seller may use "FOB Chicago" for FOB shipping point and the buyer's city for FOB destination.

May 6	Merchandise Inventory	150	
	Cash		150
	(To record payment of freight, terms FOB shipping point)		

A	=	L	+	OE
+150				
−150				

In contrast, **freight costs incurred by the seller on outgoing merchandise are an operating expense to the seller**. These costs are debited to Freight-out or Delivery Expense. For example, if the freight terms on invoice no. 731 in Illustration 5-4 had specified FOB destination and Highpoint Electronic paid the $150 freight charges, the entry by Highpoint would be:

HELPFUL HINT
The freight cost under the terms FOB shipping point and paid by Chelsea does not enter into the computation of the discount shown above.

May 4	Freight-out (Delivery Expense)	150	
	Cash		150
	(To record payment of freight on goods sold FOB destination)		

A	=	L	+	OE
−150				−150

When the freight charges are paid by the seller, the seller will usually establish a higher invoice price for the goods, to cover the expense of shipping.

Alternative Accounting for Returns and Allowances, Discounts, and Freight Costs

A business manager may want to keep detailed records of returns and allowances, discounts, and freight costs related to purchases of merchandise. For example, if management wishes to know the amount saved through cash discounts on purchases of merchandise, the amount of discounts taken can be accumulated in a separate Purchase Discounts account. Or, if management wishes to keep track of the purchase returns and allowances due to defective, inferior quality, or damaged goods, a special account, Purchase Returns and Allowances, may be credited to serve as a running record of such transactions. And, Freight-in could be debited for transportation costs on purchased merchandise. In order to report Merchandise Inventory at total cost in the financial statements, these separate accounts may be combined with the amount in Merchandise Inventory as follows:

Merchandise Inventory		$XXXX
Less: Purchase Returns and Allowances	$XXX	
Purchase Discounts	XXX	XXX
Net purchases of merchandise inventory		XXXX
Add: Freight-in		XXX
Total cost of merchandise inventory		$XXXX

BEFORE YOU GO ON . . .

Review It

1. How do the components used in measuring net income in a merchandising company differ from those in a service enterprise?
2. In what ways is a perpetual inventory system different from a periodic inventory system?
3. What entries are made to record purchases of inventory, purchase returns and allowances, purchase discounts, and freight-in under a perpetual inventory system?
4. What is an alternative method of accounting for purchase returns and allowances, discounts, and freight costs?

THE NAVIGATOR

Recording Sales

3
STUDY
OBJECTIVE

Explain the entries for sales revenues under a perpetual inventory system.

Sales revenues, like service revenues, are recorded when earned. This is in accordance with the revenue recognition principle. Typically, sales revenues are earned when the goods are transferred from the seller to the buyer. At this point, the sales transaction is completed and the sales price is established.

Sales may be made on credit or for cash. Every sales transaction should be supported by a **business document** that provides written evidence of the sale. **Cash register tapes** provide evidence of cash sales. A **sales invoice**, like the one shown in Illustration 5-4, provides support for a credit sale. The original copy of the invoice goes to the customer, and a copy is kept by the seller for use in recording the sale. The invoice shows the date of sale, customer name, total sales price, and other relevant information.

For cash sales, the Cash account is debited and the Sales account is credited; and, under the perpetual inventory system, the **cost of the merchandise sold** and the **reduction in merchandise inventory** are also recorded. Therefore, two entries are made for each sale, one at the selling price of the goods and the other at the cost of the goods sold. For example, assume that on May 4 Highpoint Electronic has cash sales of $2,200 from merchandise having a cost of $1,400. The entries to record the day's cash sales are as follows:

A	=	L	+	OE
+2,200				+2,200

May 4	Cash	2,200	
	Sales		2,220
	(To record daily cash sales)		

A	=	L	+	OE
−1,400				−1,400

4	Cost of Goods Sold	1,400	
	Merchandise Inventory		1,400
	(To record cost of merchandise sold for cash)		

For credit sales, Accounts Receivable is debited and Sales is credited; and, Cost of Goods Sold is debited and Merchandise Inventory is credited. In this way, under a perpetual inventory system, the Merchandise Inventory account will show at all times the amount of inventory that should be on hand. To illustrate a credit sales transaction, Highpoint Electronic's sales of $3,800 per invoice No. 731 (Illustration 5-4) of May 4 to Chelsea Video would be recorded as follows (assume the merchandise cost Highpoint $2,400):

ALTERNATIVE TERMINOLOGY

Credit sales are sometimes referred to as *charge sales* or *sales on account*.

May 4	Accounts Receivable	3,800	
	Sales		3,800
	(To record credit sale to Chelsea Video per invoice #731)		
4	Cost of Goods Sold	2,400	
	Merchandise Inventory		2,400
	(To record cost of merchandise sold on invoice #731 to Chelsea Video)		

$$A = L + OE$$
$$+3{,}800 \qquad\qquad +3{,}800$$

$$A = L + OE$$
$$-2{,}400 \qquad\qquad -2{,}400$$

Merchandising companies may use more than one sales account. For example, Highpoint Electronic may decide to keep separate sales accounts for its sales of television sets, videocassette recorders, and microwave ovens. Because sales are the principal source of revenue for a merchandising company, the amount and trend of sales are of critical importance. For example, an increase in sales from the preceding year signifies a growing business and often leads to higher net income. A decrease in sales may suggest an unfavorable trend, and, therefore, lower future earnings.

HELPFUL HINT

The Sales account is credited only for sales of goods held for resale. Sales of assets not held for resale, such as equipment or land, are credited directly to the asset account.

ACCOUNTING IN ACTION
Ethics Insight

Inventory losses can be substantial. Shoplifting is a big crime in the United States, with a cost of more than $18 billion annually, or 5% of retail sales, not including thefts by store employees. Shoplifting losses have led to the demise of many companies. For example, Dayton-Hudson closed its landmark store in downtown Detroit, in part, because of excessive shoplifting losses. Many department stores are trying to reduce shoplifting losses by use of electronic tags on merchandise and by continuous surveillance of customers on closed circuit television.

Sales Returns and Allowances

A purchase return and allowance on the purchaser's books is recorded as a **sales return and allowance** on the books of the seller. To grant the customer a sales return or allowance, the seller normally prepares a **credit memorandum**. This document informs a customer that a credit has been made to the customer's account receivable for a sales return or allowance. The information contained in a credit memorandum is similar to the information found in the debit memorandum in Illustration 5-5 (p. 193). The original copy of the credit memorandum is sent to the customer, and a copy is kept by the seller as evidence of the transaction. Highpoint's entries to record a credit memorandum for returned goods involve (1) a debit to Sales Returns and Allowances and a credit to Accounts Receivable at the $300 selling price, and (2) a debit to Merchandise Inventory (assume a $140 cost) and a credit to Cost of Goods Sold as follows:

ETHICS NOTE

Large retailers of electronics often have generous return policies, allowing returns for any reason within the first 30 days. Unfortunately, unscrupulous customers will "buy" video cameras or large stereos for special events such as weddings, use them, and then return them after the event. The retailer suffers a loss because they must then sell the item as returned merchandise.

A	=	L	+	OE
− 300				− 300

May 8	Sales Returns and Allowances	300	
	Accounts Receivable		300
	(To record return of inoperable goods		
	delivered to Chelsea Video, per credit		
	memorandum)		

A	=	L	+	OE
+ 140				+ 140

8	Merchandise Inventory	140	
	Cost of Goods Sold		140
	(To record cost of goods returned per credit		
	memorandum)		

When a sales allowance for damaged goods is granted on a **credit sale**, no entry to inventory and cost of goods sold is necessary because the supplier receives no returned goods from the customer. As shown in the first entry above, the supplier debits Sales Returns and Allowances and credits Accounts Receivable for the damaged goods allowance.

When goods are returned or an allowance is made on a **cash sale**, the supplier normally provides a cash refund and debits Sales Returns and Allowances and credits Cash. If the supplier **receives returned merchandise** in good condition, a second entry is made debiting Merchandise Inventory and crediting Cost of Goods Sold at cost. If the supplier grants an allowance and the **merchandise is not returned**, no entry affecting inventory and cost of goods sold is necessary by the supplier.

Sales Returns and Allowances is a **contra revenue account** to Sales with a normal debit balance. A contra account is used, instead of debiting Sales, to disclose the amount of sales returns and allowances in the accounts and in the income statement because disclosure of this information is important to management. Excessive returns and allowances suggest inferior merchandise, inefficiencies in filling orders, errors in billing customers, and mistakes in delivery or shipment of the goods. Moreover, a debit directly to Sales would obscure the relative importance of sales returns and allowances as a percentage of sales and could distort comparisons between total sales in different accounting periods.

ACCOUNTING IN ACTION
Business Insight

How high is too high? Returns can become so high that it is questionable whether sales revenue should have been recognized in the first place. An example of high returns is Florafax International Inc., a floral supply company, which was alleged to ship its product without customer authorization on 10 holiday occasions, including 8,562 shipments of its product to customers for Mother's Day and 6,575 for Secretary's Day. The return rate on these shipments went as high as 69% of sales. As one employee noted: "Products went out the front door and came in the back door."

An offshoot of high returns is "channel stuffing." In channel stuffing, the seller "sells" its product by providing substantial inducements to buy. Although this helps the seller's revenue in the short run, the long term can be devastating when the merchandise bought remains on the purchasers' shelves for a long period of time.

Sales Discounts

As mentioned in our discussion of purchase transactions, the seller may offer the customer a cash discount, called by the seller a **sales discount**, for the prompt payment of the balance due. Like a purchase discount, a sales discount is based on the invoice price less returns and allowances, if any. Sales Discounts is debited for the cash discounts that are taken. The entry by Highpoint to record the cash receipt on May 14 from Chelsea Video within the discount period is as follows:

May 14	Cash	3,430	
	Sales Discounts	70	
	Accounts Receivable		3,500
	(To record collection within 2/10, n/30		
	discount period from Chelsea Video)		

A	=	L	+	OE
+3,430				−70
−3,500				

Like Sales Returns and Allowances, Sales Discounts is a **contra revenue account** to Sales. Its normal balance is a debit. This account is used, instead of debiting sales, to accumulate the amount of cash discounts taken by customers. If the discount is not taken, Highpoint Electronic debits Cash for $3,500 and credits Accounts Receivable for $3,500 at the date of the collection.

Statement Presentation of Sales

As contra revenue accounts, sales returns and allowances and sales discounts are deducted from sales in the income statement to arrive at **net sales**. The sales revenues section of the income statement based on assumed data for Highpoint Electronic is as follows:

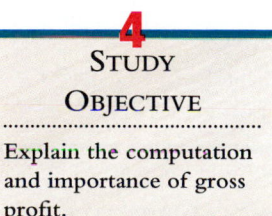

Sales Discount

"That's right, pay within 10 days and you'll get a 2% discount."

Sales Discounts

XXX

Statement presentation of sales revenues section

HIGHPOINT ELECTRONIC
Income Statement (partial)

Sales revenues		
Sales		$480,000
Less: Sales returns and allowances	$12,000	
Sales discounts	8,000	20,000
Net sales		$460,000

This presentation discloses the significant aspects of the company's principal revenue producing activities.

MEASURING NET INCOME

Gross Profit

From Illustration 5-1, you learned that cost of goods sold is deducted from sales revenue to determine **gross profit**. Sales revenue used for this computation is **net sales** (which takes into account sales returns and allowances and sales discounts). On the basis of the sales data presented in Illustration 5-7 (net sales of $460,000) and the cost of goods sold, accumulated under the perpetual inventory system (assume a balance of $316,000), the gross profit for Highpoint Electronic is $144,000, computed as follows:

4
STUDY
OBJECTIVE

Explain the computation and importance of gross profit.

Computation of gross profit

Net sales	$460,000
Cost of goods sold	316,000
Gross profit	**$144,000**

ALTERNATIVE TERMINOLOGY
Gross profit is sometimes referred to as *merchandising profit* or *gross margin*.

A company's gross profit may also be expressed as a percentage by dividing the amount of gross profit by net sales. For Highpoint Electronic the gross profit rate is 31.3% ($144,000 ÷ $460,000). The gross profit rate is generally considered to be more useful than the gross profit amount because it expresses a more meaningful (qualitative) relationship between net sales and gross profit. For example, a gross profit of $1,000,000 may be impressive. But, if it is the result of a gross profit rate of only 7%, it is not so impressive. The gross profit rate tells how many cents of each sales dollar go to gross profit.

Gross profit represents the **merchandising profit** of a company. It is not a measure of the overall profitability of a company, because operating expenses have not been deducted. Nevertheless, the amount and trend of gross profit is closely watched by management and other interested parties. Comparisons of current gross profit with amounts reported in past periods, and comparisons of gross profit rates of competitors and with industry averages provide information about the effectiveness of a company's purchasing function and the soundness of its pricing policies.

ACCOUNTING IN ACTION
Business Insight

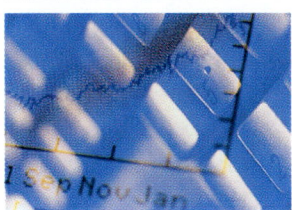

In a recent year, J.C. Penney Company reported a gross profit rate of 31%; Kmart, 24%; and Wal-Mart, 20%. Gross profit is critical. "If you don't have someone monitoring it," says one business consultant, "you are asking for instant death." A decline should trigger a search for the cause. The drop could be due to an increase in cost of goods sold or a decrease in sales revenue, either of which needs prompt attention. The change may be temporary and easily reversed, or it may signal the beginning of a bad trend.

Operating Expenses

Operating expenses are the third component in measuring net income for a merchandising company. As indicated earlier, these expenses are similar in merchandising and service enterprises. At Highpoint Electronic, operating expenses were $114,000. The firm's net income is determined by subtracting operating expenses from gross profit. Thus, net income is $30,000 as shown below:

ILLUSTRATION 5-9

Operating expenses in computing net income

Gross profit	$144,000
Operating expenses	114,000
Net income	$ 30,000

The net income amount is the "bottom line" of a company's income statement.

5
STUDY
OBJECTIVE
··
Identify the features of the income statement for a merchandising company.

Income Statement

The income statement for retailers and wholesalers contains three features not found in the income statement of a service enterprise. These features are: (1) a sales revenue section, (2) a cost of goods sold section, and (3) gross profit. Using assumed data for specific operating expenses, the income statement for Highpoint Electronic, is shown in Illustration 5-10.

ILLUSTRATION 5-10

Income statement for a merchandising company

HIGHPOINT ELECTRONIC
Income Statement
For the Year Ended December 31, 1999

Sales revenues		
Sales		$480,000
Less: Sales returns and allowances	$ 12,000	
Sales discounts	8,000	20,000
Net sales		460,000
Cost of goods sold		316,000
Gross profit		144,000
Operating expenses		
Store salaries expense	45,000	
Rent expense	19,000	
Utilities expense	17,000	
Advertising expense	16,000	
Depreciation expense—store equipment	8,000	
Freight-out	7,000	
Insurance expense	2,000	
Total operating expenses		114,000
Net income		$ 30,000

BEFORE YOU GO ON . . .

Review It

1. What entries are made to record sales, sales returns and allowances, and sales discounts?
2. How are sales and contra revenue accounts reported in the income statement?
3. What is the significance of gross profit?
4. Determine Kellogg Company's gross profit rate for 1997 and 1996. Indicate whether it increased or decreased from 1996 to 1997. The answer to this question is provided on page 229.

COMPLETING THE ACCOUNTING CYCLE

6
STUDY
OBJECTIVE
....
Explain the steps in the accounting cycle for a merchandising company.

Up to this point, we have been primarily concerned with measuring net income in a merchandising company. We have also illustrated the basic entries in recording transactions relating to purchases and sales in a perpetual inventory system. Now it is time to consider the remaining steps in the accounting cycle that were identified in Chapter 4.

Each of the required steps in the cycle applies to a merchandising company. Again, a work sheet is an optional step. To illustrate the steps in the cycle, we will assume that Highpoint Electronic uses a work sheet.

Using a Work Sheet

As indicated in Chapter 4, a work sheet enables financial statements to be prepared before the adjusting entries are journalized and posted. The steps in preparing a work sheet for a merchandising company are the same as they are for

ILLUSTRATION 5-11

Work sheet for merchandising company

a service enterprise (see pp. 141–143). The work sheet for Highpoint Electronic is shown in Illustration 5-11. The unique accounts for a merchandising company, using a perpetual inventory system, are shown in capital letters in red.

	HIGHPOINT ELECTRONIC Work Sheet For the Year Ended December 31, 1999									
	Trial Balance		Adjustments		Adjusted Trial Balance		Income Statement		Balance Sheet	
	Dr.	Cr.	Dr.	Cr.	Dr.	Cr.	Dr.	Cr.	Dr.	Cr.
Cash	9,500				9,500				9,500	
Accounts Receivable	16,100				16,100				16,100	
MERCHANDISE INVENTORY	40,000				40,000				40,000	
Prepaid Insurance	3,800			(a) 2,000	1,800				1,800	
Store Equipment	80,000				80,000				80,000	
Accumulated Depreciation		16,000		(b) 8,000		24,000				24,000
Accounts Payable		20,400				20,400				20,400
R.A. Lamb, Capital		83,000				83,000				83,000
R.A. Lamb, Drawing	15,000				15,000				15,000	
SALES		480,000				480,000		480,000		
SALES RETURNS AND ALLOWANCES	12,000				12,000		12,000			
SALES DISCOUNTS	8,000				8,000		8,000			
COST OF GOODS SOLD	316,000				316,000		316,000			
Freight-out	7,000				7,000		7,000			
Advertising Expense	16,000				16,000		16,000			
Rent Expense	19,000				19,000		19,000			
Store Salaries Expense	40,000		(c) 5,000		45,000		45,000			
Utilities Expense	17,000				17,000		17,000			
Totals	599,400	599,400								
Insurance Expense			(a) 2,000		2,000		2,000			
Depreciation Expense			(b) 8,000		8,000		8,000			
Salaries Payable				(c) 5,000		5,000				5,000
Totals			15,000	15,000	612,400	612,400	450,000	480,000	162,400	132,400
Net Income							30,000			30,000
Totals							480,000	480,000	162,400	162,400

Key: (a) Insurance expired, (b) Depreciation expensed, (c) Salaries accrued.

Trial Balance Columns

Data for the trial balance are obtained from the ledger balances of Highpoint Electronic at December 31. The amount shown for Merchandise Inventory, $40,000, is the year-end inventory amount which results from the application of a perpetual inventory system.

Adjustments Columns

A merchandising company generally has the same types of adjustments as a service company. As you see in the work sheet, adjustments (a), (b), and (c) are for insurance, depreciation, and salaries. These adjustments were also required for Pioneer Advertising Agency, as illustrated in Chapters 3 and 4.

After all adjustment data are entered on the work sheet, the equality of the adjustment column totals is established. The balances in all accounts are then extended to the adjusted trial balance columns.

Adjusted Trial Balance

The adjusted trial balance shows the balance of all accounts after adjustment at the end of the accounting period.

Income Statement Columns

The accounts and balances that affect the income statement are transferred from the adjusted trial balance columns to the income statement columns. For Highpoint Electronic, Sales of $480,000 is shown in the credit column whereas the contra revenue accounts, Sales Returns and Allowances of $12,000 and Sales Discounts of $8,000, are shown in the debit column. Thus, the difference of $460,000 is the net sales shown on the income statement (Illustration 5-10).

Finally, all the credits in the income statement column should be totaled and compared to the total of all the debits in the income statement column. If the credits exceed the debits, then the company has net income. In Highpoint Electronic's case there was net income of $30,000. Conversely if the debits exceed the credits, the company would report a net loss.

Balance Sheet Columns

The major difference between the balance sheets of a service company and a merchandising company is inventory. For Highpoint Electronic, the ending inventory amount of $40,000 is shown in the balance sheet debit column. Note also that the information to prepare the owner's equity statement is also found in these columns. That is, the capital account of R. A. Lamb is $83,000. The drawings for R. A. Lamb are $15,000. Net income results when the total of the debit column exceeds the total of the credit column in the balance sheet columns of the work sheet. Conversely, a net loss results when the total of the credits exceeds the total of the debit balances.

Preparing Financial Statements

As is true in a service enterprise, financial statements for a merchandising company are prepared from the financial statement columns of the work sheet. The income statement for Highpoint Electronic has already been illustrated (see Illustration 5-10).

The owner's equity statement is as follows:

HIGHPOINT ELECTRONIC Owner's Equity Statement For the Year Ended December 31, 1999	
R. A. Lamb, Capital, January 1	$ 83,000
Add: Net income	30,000
	113,000
Less: Drawings	15,000
R. A. Lamb, Capital, December 31	$ 98,000

ILLUSTRATION 5-12

Owner's equity statement

The classified balance sheet, then, is as follows:

ILLUSTRATION 5-13
Classified balance sheet

HIGHPOINT ELECTRONIC
Balance Sheet
December 31, 1999

Assets

Current assets		
Cash		$ 9,500
Accounts receivable		16,100
Merchandise inventory		**40,000**
Prepaid insurance		1,800
Total current assets		67,400
Property, plant, and equipment		
Store equipment	$80,000	
Less: Accumulated depreciation—store equipment	24,000	56,000
Total assets		$123,400

Liabilities and Owner's Equity

Current liabilities		
Accounts payable		$ 20,400
Salaries payable		5,000
Total current liabilities		25,400
Owner's equity		
R.A. Lamb, Capital		98,000
Total liabilities and owner's equity		$123,400

HELPFUL HINT
The $40,000 is the cost of the inventory on hand, not its expected selling price.

HELPFUL HINT
Merchandise inventory is a current asset because it is expected to be sold within one year or the operating cycle, whichever is longer.

In the balance sheet, merchandise inventory is reported as a current asset immediately below accounts receivable. Recall that items are listed under current assets in the order of liquidity. Merchandise inventory is less liquid than accounts receivable because the goods must first be sold and then collection must be made from the customer.

ACCOUNTING IN ACTION

Ethics Insight

Phar Mor was one of the largest and fastest growing retail dry goods and pharmacy chains in the United States until a massive fraud was discovered by the company's auditors, Coopers and Lybrand. Dry goods were Phar Mor's business, but some of its executives had a taste for "raisin cookies." Schemers in Phar Mor's executive suite kept two sets of records, an official ledger that they sometimes manipulated with false entries, and another, nicknamed the "cookies," where they kept track of the false entries, called "raisins." They would refer to their ledger domain as "putting raisins in the cookies."

Based on reports in *The Wall Street Journal*, the assets of the company were overstated by more than $400 million, or about one-third of Phar Mor's gross revenue. Most of this overstatement pertained to fake or overvalued merchandise inventories at various store locations, and was perpetrated by the company's top financial managers.

Adjusting and Closing Entries

Adjusting entries are journalized from the adjustment columns of the work sheet. Because the journalizing and posting of the entries are the same as they are for a service enterprise, they are not illustrated here.

For a merchandising company, like a service enterprise, all accounts that affect the determination of net income are closed to Income Summary. Data for the preparation of closing entries may be obtained from the income statement columns of the work sheet. In journalizing, all debit column amounts are credited, and all credit column amounts are debited, as shown below for Highpoint Electronic. Cost of goods sold is a new account that must be closed to Income Summary.

Dec. 31	Sales	480,000	
	Income Summary		480,000
	(To close income statement accounts with		
	credit balances)		
31	Income Summary	450,000	
	Sales Returns and Allowances		12,000
	Sales Discounts		8,000
	Cost of Goods Sold		316,000
	Store Salaries Expense		45,000
	Rent Expense		19,000
	Freight-out		7,000
	Advertising Expense		16,000
	Utilities Expense		17,000
	Depreciation Expense		8,000
	Insurance Expense		2,000
	(To close income statement accounts with		
	debit balances)		
31	Income Summary	30,000	
	R.A. Lamb, Capital		30,000
	(To close net income to capital)		
31	R.A. Lamb, Capital	15,000	
	R. A. Lamb, Drawing		15,000
	(To close drawings to capital)		

HELPFUL HINT
The easiest way to prepare the first two closing entries is to identify the temporary accounts by their balances and then prepare one entry for the credits and one for the debits.

After the closing entries are posted, all temporary accounts have zero balances. In addition, R.A. Lamb, Capital has a credit balance of $98,000: beginning balance + net income − drawings ($83,000 + $30,000 − $15,000).

Preparing the Post-Closing Trial Balance

After the closing entries are posted, the post-closing trial balance is prepared. The only new account in the post-closing trial balance is Merchandise Inventory. The post-closing trial balance for Highpoint Electronic at December 31, 1999, is shown in Illustration 5-14.

ILLUSTRATION 5-14

Post-closing trial balance

HIGHPOINT ELECTRONIC Post-Closing Trial Balance December 31, 1999		
	Debit	Credit
Cash	$ 9,500	
Accounts receivable	16,100	
Merchandise inventory	40,000	
Prepaid insurance	1,800	
Store equipment	80,000	
Accumulated depreciation		$ 24,000
Accounts payable		20,400
Salaries payable		5,000
R.A. Lamb, Capital		98,000
	$147,400	$147,400

Summary of Merchandising Entries

The entries for the merchandising accounts using a perpetual inventory system are summarized in Illustration 5-15.

ILLUSTRATION 5-15

Daily recurring and closing entries

Transactions	Daily Recurring Entries	Dr.	Cr.
Selling merchandise to customers	Cash or Accounts Receivable	XX	
	Sales		XX
	Cost of Goods Sold	XX	
	Merchandise Inventory		XX
Granting sales returns or allowances to customers	Sales Returns and Allowances	XX	
	Cash or Accounts Receivable		XX
Paying freight costs on sales; FOB destination	Freight-out	XX	
	Cash		XX
Receiving payment from customers within discount period	Cash	XX	
	Sales Discounts	XX	
	Accounts Receivable		XX
Purchasing merchandise for resale	Merchandise Inventory	XX	
	Cash or Accounts Payable		XX
Paying freight costs on merchandise purchased; FOB shipping point	Merchandise Inventory	XX	
	Cash		XX
Receiving purchase returns or allowances from suppliers	Cash or Accounts Payable	XX	
	Merchandise Inventory		XX
Paying suppliers within discount period	Accounts Payable	XX	
	Merchandise Inventory		XX
	Cash		XX

Events	Closing Entries	Dr.	Cr.
Closing accounts with credit balances	Sales	XX	
	Income Summary		XX
Closing accounts with debit balances	Income Summary	XX	
	Sales Returns and Allowances		XX
	Sales Discounts		XX
	Cost of Goods Sold		XX
	Freight-out		XX
	Expenses		XX

BEFORE YOU GO ON . . .

Review It

1. How does a work sheet for a merchandising company differ from a work sheet for a service company? In what ways is the work sheet similar for a merchandising company and a service company?
2. In what columns of the work sheet will (a) merchandise inventory and (b) cost of goods sold be shown?
3. What merchandising account(s) will appear in the post-closing trial balance?

Do It

The trial balance of Revere Clothing Company at December 31 shows Merchandise Inventory $25,000, Sales $162,400, Sales Returns and Allowances $4,800, Sales Discounts $3,600, Cost of Goods Sold $110,000, Rental Revenue $6,000, Freight-out $1,800, Rent Expense $8,800, and Salaries and Wages Expense $22,000. Prepare the closing entries for the above accounts.

Reasoning: The first closing entry for a merchandising company closes temporary accounts with credit balances to Income Summary. The second closing entry closes temporary accounts with debit balances to Income Summary.

Solution: The two closing entries are:

Dec. 31	Sales	162,400	
	Rental Revenue	6,000	
	Income Summary		168,400
	(To close accounts with credit balances)		
Dec. 31	Income Summary	151,000	
	Cost of Goods Sold		110,000
	Sales Returns and Allowances		4,800
	Sales Discounts		3,600
	Freight-out		1,800
	Rent Expense		8,800
	Salaries and Wages Expense		22,000
	(To close accounts with debit balances)		

Related exercise material: BE5–7, E5–5, and E5–6.

THE
NAVIGATOR

FORMS OF INCOME STATEMENTS

Two forms of the income statement are widely used by merchandising companies. These income statements are explained below.

Multiple–Step Income Statement

The **multiple-step income statement** is so named because it shows the numerous steps in determining net income (or net loss). The Highpoint Electronic income statement in Illustration 5-10 is an example. It shows two steps: (1) cost of goods sold was subtracted from net sales, and (2) operating expenses were deducted from gross profit. These steps pertain to the company's principal operating activities. A multiple-step statement provides users with more information about a company's income performance by distinguishing between **operating** and **non-operating activities**. The statement also highlights intermediate components of income and shows subgroupings of expenses.

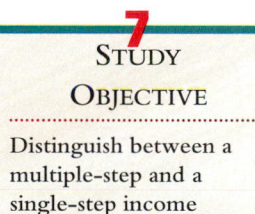

7
STUDY
OBJECTIVE

Distinguish between a multiple-step and a single-step income statement.

Nonoperating Activities

Nonoperating activities consist of (1) revenues and expenses that result from secondary or auxiliary operations and (2) gains and losses that are unrelated to the company's operations. The results of nonoperating activities are shown in two sections: **Other revenues and gains** and **Other expenses and losses**. For a merchandising company, these sections will typically include the following items:

ILLUSTRATION 5-16

Items reported in nonoperating sections

Other Revenues and Gains	Other Expenses and Losses
Interest revenue from notes receivable and marketable securities	Interest expense on notes and loans payable
Dividend revenue from investments in capital stock	Casualty losses from recurring causes such as vandalism and accidents
Rent revenue from subleasing a portion of the store	Loss from the sale or abandonment of property, plant, and equipment
Gain from the sale of property, plant, and equipment	Loss from strikes by employees and suppliers

The nonoperating sections are reported in the income statement immediately after the sections that pertain to the company's primary operating activities. These sections are shown in Illustration 5-17 using assumed data for Highpoint Electronic.

HIGHPOINT ELECTRONIC
Income Statement
For the Year Ended December 31, 1999

Sales revenues			
Sales			$480,000
Less: Sales returns and allowances		$ 12,000	
Sales discounts		8,000	20,000
Net sales			460,000
Cost of goods sold			316,000
Gross profit			144,000
Operating expenses			
Selling expenses			
Store salaries expense	$ 45,000		
Advertising expense	16,000		
Depreciation expense—store equipment	8,000		
Freight-out	7,000		
Total selling expenses		76,000	
Administrative expenses			
Rent expense	19,000		
Utilities expense	17,000		
Insurance expense	2,000		
Total administrative expenses		38,000	
Total operating expenses			114,000
Income from operations			30,000
Other revenues and gains			
Interest revenue	3,000		
Gain on sale of equipment	600	3,600	
Other expenses and losses			
Interest expense	1,800		
Casualty loss from vandalism	200	2,000	1,600
Net income			$ 31,600

When the two nonoperating sections are included, the label **Income from operations** (or Operating income) precedes them. It clearly identifies the results of the company's normal operations. Income from operations is determined by subtracting cost of goods sold and operating expenses from net sales.

Observe that the results of the two nonoperating sections are netted. The difference is added to or subtracted from income from operations to determine net income. Finally, within the nonoperating sections, items are generally reported at the net amount. Thus, if a company received a $2,500 insurance settlement on vandalism losses of $2,700, the loss is reported at $200. It is not uncommon for companies to combine these two nonoperating sections into a single "Other Revenues and Expenses" section.

ACCOUNTING IN ACTION

Business Insight

The distinction between operating and nonoperating activities is crucial to many external users of financial data. The reason is that operating income is viewed as sustainable and therefore long-term, and nonoperating is viewed as nonrecurring and therefore short-term. For example, it was reported that a large cinema chain in North America was selling some of its assets and counting the gains as part of operating income. As a result, operating losses were being offset by these gains. Because of unfavorable press reaction to this practice, the company revised its financial statements. By not counting its nonrecurring items as part of operating income, its first quarter results changed from $24.9 million operating income to a $22.6 million loss. Although the net income figure didn't change, investors were able to see that income was derived from selling assets rather than from selling movie tickets. Thus, with this new information, investors were able to make a more informed decision about the company's earnings.

Subgrouping of Operating Expenses

In larger companies, operating expenses are often subdivided into selling expenses and administrative expenses, as illustrated in the income statement in Illustration 5-17. **Selling expenses** are those associated with making sales. They include sales promotional expenses as well as expenses of completing the sale, such as delivery and shipping expenses. **Administrative expenses** (sometimes called general expenses) relate to general operating activities such as personnel management, accounting, and store security.

When subgroupings are made, some expenses may have to be prorated, e.g., 70% to selling and 30% to administrative expenses. For example, if a store building is used for both selling and general functions, building expenses such as depreciation, utilities, and property taxes will need to be allocated.

Any reasonable classification of expenses that serves to inform those who use the statement is satisfactory. For example, the present tendency in statements prepared for management is to present in considerable detail expense data grouped along lines of responsibility.

Single–Step Income Statement

Another format for income statement presentation is the **single-step income statement**. The statement is so named because only one step, subtracting total expenses from total revenues, is required in determining net income (or net loss).

In a single-step statement, all data are classified under two categories: (1) **Revenues**, which includes both operating revenues and other revenues and gains, or (2) **Expenses**, which includes cost of goods sold, operating expenses, and other expenses and losses. A condensed single-step statement for Highpoint Electronic is illustrated in Illustration 5-18.

ILLUSTRATION 5-18

Single-step income statement

HIGHPOINT ELECTRONIC Income Statement For the Year Ended December 31, 1999		
Revenues		
Net sales		$460,000
Interest revenue		3,000
Gain on sale of equipment		600
Total revenues		463,600
Expenses		
Cost of goods sold	$316,000	
Selling expenses	76,000	
Administrative expenses	38,000	
Interest expense	1,800	
Casualty loss from vandalism	200	
Total expenses		432,000
Net income		$ 31,600

There are two primary reasons for using the single-step form: (1) A company does not realize any type of profit or income until total revenues exceed total expenses, so it makes sense to divide the statement into these two categories. (2) The form is simpler and easier to read than the multiple-step form. For homework problems, the single-step form of income statement should be used only when it is specifically requested.

BEFORE YOU GO ON . . .

Review It

1. What are nonoperating activities and how are they reported in the income statement?
2. How does a single-step income statement differ from a multiple-step income statement?

A LOOK BACK AT OUR FEATURE STORY

Refer to the opening story about the Washington State University bookstore, and answer the following questions:

1. What entry, if any, would the WSU bookstore make when ordering books? When books are received? When returning books? When allowing the students to return books? When purchasing used books from students?
2. How often is it necessary for Larry Martin to take a physical inventory? Why is it necessary to take an inventory? For the inventory taken in September, does Larry need both quantities and costs? Explain.

Solution

1. No entry is made at the time books are ordered. Probably an open purchase order file or memo record is maintained for keeping track of open (unfilled) purchase orders. When books are received, the bookstore would record the purchases at invoice cost as follows:

Merchandise Inventory	XX	
Accounts Payable		XX
(To record goods purchased on account)		

When books are returned to the publisher, the WSU bookstore would prepare a debit memo from which the following entry is made:

Accounts Payable		XX	
Merchandise Inventory			XX
(To record books returned to publisher)			

When the bookstore gives a refund for a returned book (not a used book purchase), the following entry would be made at the book's selling price:

Sales Returns and Allowances		XX	
Cash			XX
(To record payment to customer for returned book)			

And the following entry would be made at the book's cost :

Merchandise Inventory		XX	
Cost of Goods Sold			XX
(To record cost of book returned)			

When used books are bought from students, the bookstore would record the following entry:

Inventory of Used Books		XX	
Cash			XX
(To record purchase of used goods)			

2. Larry Martin waits about 4 weeks after the school term, when the busy book selling and return period ends, to take a physical inventory of books. He does that each school term. In addition Larry takes a physical inventory when the financial statements are prepared at least once a year.

    It is necessary for Larry to take accurate inventory counts in order to ensure the accuracy of the perpetual inventory records. He needs accurate records to make good ordering and return decisions. Accurate ordering coupled with efficient return practices is a must for profitable bookstore operations.

    Larry uses the September inventory balances for ordering books. Thus, only quantities—not costs—are needed by Larry.

THE
NAVIGATOR

DEMONSTRATION PROBLEM

The adjusted trial balance columns of the work sheet for the year ended December 31, 1999, for Dykstra Company are as follows:

Debit		Credit	
Cash	$ 14,500	Accumulated Depreciation	$ 18,000
Accounts Receivable	11,100	Notes Payable	25,000
Merchandise Inventory	29,000	Accounts Payable	10,600
Prepaid Insurance	2,500	Gene Dykstra, Capital	81,000
Store Equipment	95,000	Sales	536,800
Gene Dykstra, Drawing	12,000	Interest Revenue	2,500
Sales Returns and Allowances	6,700		$673,900
Sales Discounts	5,000		
Cost of Goods Sold	363,400		
Freight-out	7,600		
Advertising Expense	12,000		
Store Salaries Expense	56,000		
Utilities Expense	18,000		
Rent Expense	24,000		
Depreciation Expense	9,000		
Insurance Expense	4,500		
Interest Expense	3,600		
	$673,900		

PROBLEM-SOLVING
STRATEGIES

1. Make sure in the adjusted
   trial balance that debits and
   credits are equal before
   transferring amounts to the
   income statement and
   balance sheet columns.

2. Transfer all amounts in the
   adjusted trial balance to
   either the income statement
   or balance sheet columns.

3. The net income or net loss is
   the reconciling item in both
   the income statement and
   the balance sheet columns.

Instructions

(a) Enter the adjusted trial balance data on a work sheet. Complete the work sheet.

(b) Prepare an income statement assuming Dykstra Company does not use subgroupings for operating expenses.

SOLUTION TO DEMONSTRATION PROBLEM

(a)

DYKSTRA COMPANY
Work Sheet
For the Year Ended December 31, 1999

Account Titles	Adjusted Trial Balance		Income Statement		Balance Sheet	
	Dr.	Cr.	Dr.	Cr.	Dr.	Cr.
Cash	14,500				14,500	
Accounts Receivable	11,100				11,100	
Merchandise Inventory	29,000				29,000	
Prepaid Insurance	2,500				2,500	
Store Equipment	95,000				95,000	
Accumulated Depreciation		18,000				18,000
Notes Payable		25,000				25,000
Accounts Payable		10,600				10,600
Gene Dykstra, Capital		81,000				81,000
Gene Dykstra, Drawing	12,000				12,000	
Sales		536,800		536,800		
Sales Returns and Allowances	6,700		6,700			
Sales Discounts	5,000		5,000			
Cost of Goods Sold	363,400		363,400			
Freight-out	7,600		7,600			
Advertising Expense	12,000		12,000			
Store Salaries Expense	56,000		56,000			
Utilities Expense	18,000		18,000			
Rent Expense	24,000		24,000			
Depreciation Expense	9,000		9,000			
Insurance Expense	4,500		4,500			
Interest Expense	3,600		3,600			
Interest Revenue		2,500		2,500		
Totals	673,900	673,900	509,800	539,300	164,100	134,600
Net Income			29,500			29,500
Totals			539,300	539,300	164,100	164,100

PROBLEM-SOLVING
STRATEGIES

1. In preparing the income
   statement, remember that the
   key components are net
   sales, cost of goods sold,
   gross profit, total operating
   expenses, and net income
   (loss). These components are
   reported in the right-hand
   column of the income
   statement.

2. Nonoperating items follow
   income from operations.

(b)

DYKSTRA COMPANY
Income Statement
For the Year Ended December 31, 1999

Sales revenues		
Sales		$536,800
Less: Sales returns and allowances	$ 6,700	
Sales discounts	5,000	11,700
Net sales		525,100
Cost of goods sold		363,400
Gross profit		161,700
Operating expenses		
Store salaries expense	56,000	
Rent expense	24,000	
Utilities expense	18,000	
Advertising expense	12,000	

Account Titles	Adjusted Trial Balance		Income Statement		Balance Sheet	
	Dr.	Cr.	Dr.	Cr.	Dr.	Cr.
Depreciation expense					9,000	
Freight-out					7,600	
Insurance expense					4,500	
Total operating expenses						131,100
Income from operations						30,600
Other revenues and gains						
Interest revenue					2,500	
Other expenses and losses						
Interest expense					3,600	1,100
Net income						$ 29,500

SUMMARY OF STUDY OBJECTIVES

1. Identify the differences between a service enterprise and a merchandising company. Because of the presence of inventory, a merchandising company has sales revenue, cost of goods sold, and gross profit. To account for inventory, a merchandising company must choose between a perpetual inventory system and a periodic inventory system.

2. Explain the entries for purchases under a perpetual inventory system. The Merchandise Inventory account is debited for all purchases of merchandise, for freight-in and other costs, and it is credited for purchase discounts and purchase returns and allowances.

3. Explain the entries for sales revenues under a perpetual inventory system. When inventory is sold, Accounts Receivable (or Cash) is debited and Sales is credited for the **selling price** of the merchandise. At the same time, Cost of Goods Sold is debited and Merchandise Inventory is credited for the **cost** of the inventory items sold.

4. Explain the computation and importance of gross profit. Gross profit is computed by subtracting cost of

goods sold from net sales. Gross profit represents the merchandising profit of a company, and the amount and trend of gross profit is closely watched by management and other interested parties.

5. Identify the features of the income statement for a merchandising company. The income statement for a merchandising company contains three sections: sales revenues, cost of goods sold, and operating expenses.

6. Explain the steps in the accounting cycle for a merchandising company. Each of the required steps in the accounting cycle for a service enterprise applies to a merchandising company. A work sheet is again an optional step.

7. Distinguish between a multiple-step and a single-step income statement. A multiple-step income statement shows numerous steps in determining net income including non-operating sections. In a single-step income statement all data are classified under two categories, revenues or expenses, and net income is determined by one step.

GLOSSARY

Administrative expenses Expenses relating to general operating activities such as personnel management, accounting, and store security. (p. 209).

Contra revenue account An account that is offset against a revenue account on the income statement. (p. 198).

Cost of goods sold The total cost of merchandise sold during the period. (p. 188).

Credit memorandum A document issued by a seller to inform a customer that a credit has been made to the customer's account receivable for a sales return or allowance. (p. 197).

Debit memorandum A document issued by a buyer to inform a seller that a debit has been made to the seller's account because of unsatisfactory merchandise. (p. 192).

FOB destination Freight terms indicating that the goods will be placed free on board at the buyer's place of business, and the seller pays the freight costs. (p. 195).

FOB shipping point Freight terms indicating that goods are placed free on board the carrier by the seller, and the buyer pays the freight costs. (p. 195).

Gross profit The excess of net sales over the cost of goods sold. (p. 188).

Income from operations   Income from a company's principal operating activity determined by subtracting cost of goods sold and operating expenses from net sales. (p. 209).

Invoice   A document that provides support for a credit purchase. (p. 191).

Multiple-step income statement   An income statement that shows numerous steps in determining net income (or net loss). (p. 207).

Net sales   Sales less sales returns and allowances and sales discounts. (p. 199).

Operating expenses   Expenses incurred in the process of earning sales revenues that are deducted from gross profit in the income statement. (p. 188).

Other expenses and losses   A nonoperating section of the income statement that shows expenses from auxiliary operations and losses unrelated to the company's operations. (p. 208).

Other revenues and gains   A nonoperating section of the income statement that shows revenues from auxiliary operations and gains unrelated to the company's operations. (p. 208).

Periodic inventory system   An inventory system in which detailed records are not maintained throughout the accounting period and the cost of goods sold is determined only at the end of an accounting period. (p. 190).

Perpetual inventory system   A detailed inventory system in which the cost of each inventory item is maintained throughout the accounting period and the records continuously show the inventory that should be on hand. (p. 190).

Purchase discount   A cash discount claimed by a buyer for prompt payment of a balance due. (p. 193).

Sales discount   A reduction given by a seller for prompt payment of a credit sale. (p. 198).

Sales invoice   A document that provides support for credit sales. (p. 196).

Sales revenue (sales)   Primary source of revenue in a merchandising company. (p. 188).

Selling expenses   Expenses associated with the making of sales. (p. 209).

Single-step income statement   An income statement that shows only one step in determining net income (or net loss). (p. 209).

Self-Study Questions

Answers are at the end of the chapter.

(SO 1) 1. Gross profit will result if:
a. operating expenses are less than net income.
b. sales revenues are greater than operating expenses.
c. sales revenues are greater than cost of goods sold.
d. operating expenses are greater than cost of goods sold.

(SO 2) 2. Under a perpetual inventory system, when goods are purchased for resale by a company:
a. purchases on account are debited to Merchandise Inventory.
b. purchases on account are debited to Purchases.
c. purchase returns are debited to Purchase Returns and Allowances.
d. freight costs are debited to Freight-out.

(SO 3) 3. The sales accounts that normally have a debit balance are:
a. Sales Discounts.
b. Sales Returns and Allowances.
c. both (a) and (b).
d. neither (a) nor (b).

(SO 3) 4. A credit sale of $750 is made on June 13, terms 2/10, net/30, on which a return of $50 is granted on June 16. The amount received as payment in full on June 23 is:
a. $700.
b. $686.
c. $685.
d. $650.

(SO 3) 5. Which of the following accounts will normally appear in the ledger of a merchandising company that uses a perpetual inventory system?
a. Purchases.
b. Freight-in.
c. Cost of Goods Sold.
d. Purchase Discounts.

(SO 4) 6. If sales revenues are $400,000, cost of goods sold is $310,000, and operating expenses are $60,000, the gross profit is:
a. $30,000.
b. $90,000.
c. $340,000.
d. $400,000.

(SO 5) 7. The multiple-step income statement for a merchandising company shows each of the following features *except*:
a. gross profit.
b. cost of goods sold.
c. a sales revenue section.
d. investing activities section.

(SO 6) 8. In a work sheet, Merchandise Inventory is shown in the following columns:
a. Adjusted trial balance debit and balance sheet debit.
b. Income statement debit and balance sheet debit.
c. Income statement credit and balance sheet debit.
d. Income statement credit and adjusted trial balance debit.

(SO 7)   9. In a single-step income statement:
   a. gross profit is reported.
   b. cost of goods sold is not reported.
   c. sales revenues and other revenues and gains are reported in the revenues section of the income statement.
   d. operating income is separately reported.

10. Which of the following appears on both a single-step (SO 7) and multiple-step income statement?
   a. sales.
   b. gross profit.
   c. income from operations.
   d. cost of goods sold.

QUESTIONS

1. (a) "The steps in the accounting cycle for a merchandising company are different from the accounting cycle for a service enterprise." Do you agree or disagree? (b) Is the measurement of net income in a merchandising company conceptually the same as in a service enterprise? Explain.

2. (a) How do the components of revenues and expenses differ between a merchandising company and a service enterprise? (b) Explain the income measurement process in a merchandising company.

3. How does income measurement differ between a merchandising company and a service company?

4. When is cost of goods sold determined in a perpetual inventory system?

5. Distinguish between FOB shipping point and FOB destination. Identify the freight terms that will result in a debit to Merchandise Inventory by the purchaser and a debit to Freight-out by the seller.

6. Explain the meaning of the credit terms 2/10, n/30.

7. Goods costing $2,000 are purchased on account on July 15 with credit terms of 2/10, n/30. On July 18 a $100 credit memo is received from the supplier for damaged goods. Give the journal entry on July 24 to record payment of the balance due within the discount period using a perpetual inventory system.

8. Patty Loveless believes revenues from credit sales may be earned before they are collected in cash. Do you agree? Explain.

9. (a) What is the primary source document for recording (1) cash sales, (2) credit sales, and (3) sales returns and allowances? (b) Using XXs for amounts, give the journal entry for each of the transactions in part (a).

10. A credit sale is made on July 10 for $800, terms 2/10, n/30. On July 12, $100 of goods are returned for credit. Give the journal entry on July 19 to record the receipt of the balance due within the discount period.

11. Randy Travis Co. has sales revenue of $110,000, cost of goods sold of $70,000, and operating expenses of $20,000. What is its gross profit?

12. Lionel Richie Company reports net sales of $800,000, gross profit of $580,000, and net income of $200,000. What are its operating expenses?

13. Identify the distinguishing features of an income statement for a merchandising company.

14. Indicate the columns of the work sheet in which (a) merchandise inventory, and (b) cost of goods sold will be shown.

15. Why is the normal operating cycle for a merchandising company likely to be longer than for a service company?

16. Prepare the closing entries for the Sales account, assuming a balance of $200,000 and the Cost of Goods Sold account which has a $120,000 balance.

17. What merchandising account(s) will appear in the post-closing trial balance?

18. Identify the sections of a multiple-step income statement that relate to (a) operating activities, and (b) nonoperating activities.

19. Distinguish between the types of functional groupings of operating expenses. What problem is created by these groupings?

20. How does the single-step form of income statement differ from the multiple-step form?

BRIEF EXERCISES

BE5–1 Presented below are the components in Nacho Cano Company's income statement. Determine the missing amounts.

Compute missing amounts in determining net income.
(SO 1)

	Sales	Cost of Goods Sold	Gross Profit	Operating Expenses	Net Income
(a)	$75,000	?	$33,500	?	$10,800
(b)	$108,000	$70,000	?	?	29,500
(c)	?	$71,900	$99,600	$39,500	?

Journalize perpetual inventory entries.
(SO 2, 3)

BE5–2   Chico Company buys merchandise on account from Cesar Company. The selling price of the goods is $800, and the cost of the goods is $600. Both companies use perpetual inventory systems. Journalize the transaction on the books of both companies.

Journalize sales transactions.
(SO 3)

BE5–3   Prepare the journal entries to record the following transactions on Ednita Company's books using a perpetual inventory system.

- (a) On March 2, Ednita Company sold $800,000 of merchandise to Nazario Company, terms 2/10, n/30. The cost of the merchandise sold was $600,000.
- (b) On March 6, Nazario Company returned $120,000 of the merchandise purchased on March 2 because it was defective. The cost of the returned merchandise was $90,000.
- (c) On March 12, Ednita Company received the balance due from Nazario Company.

Journalize purchases transactions.
(SO 2)
Prepare sales revenues section of income statement.
(SO 3)

BE5–4   From the information in BE5–3, prepare the journal entries to record these transactions on Nazario Company's books under a perpetual inventory system.

BE5–5   Matt Damon Company provides the following information for the month ended October 31, 1999: Sales on credit $280,000, Cash sales $100,000, Sales discounts $5,000, Sales returns and allowances $20,000. Prepare the sales revenues section of the income statement based on this information.

Identify work sheet columns for selecting accounts.
(SO 6)

BE5–6   Presented below is the format of the work sheet presented in the chapter.

Trial Balance		Adjustments		Adjusted Trial Balance		Income Statement		Balance Sheet	
Dr.	Cr.	Dr.	Cr.	Dr.	Cr.	Dr.	Cr.	Dr.	Cr.

Indicate where the following items will appear on the work sheet: (a) Cash, (b) Merchandise Inventory, (c) Sales, (d) Cost of goods sold.
Example:
   Cash: Trial balance debit column; Adjusted trial balance debit column; and Balance sheet debit column.

Prepare closing entries for merchandise accounts.
(SO 6)

BE5–7   Cajon Company has the following merchandise account balances: Sales $180,000, Sales Discounts $2,000, Cost of Goods Sold $100,000, and Merchandise Inventory $40,000. Prepare the entries to record the closing of these items to Income Summary.

Contrast presentation in multiple-step and single-step income statements.
(SO 7)
Compute net sales, gross profit, and income from operations.
(SO 3, 4, 7)

BE5–8   ▱▱▱▷ Explain where each of the following items would appear on (1) a multiple-step income statement and on (2) a single-step income statement: (a) gain on sale of equipment, (b) casualty loss from vandalism, and (c) cost of goods sold.

BE5–9   Assume Bayou Company has the following account balances: Sales $500,000, Sales Returns and Allowances $15,000, Cost of Goods Sold $340,000, Selling Expenses $70,000, and Administrative Expenses $40,000. Compute (a) net sales, (b) gross profit, and (c) income from operations.

EXERCISES

Journalize purchases transactions.
(SO 2)

E5–1   Information related to Esplande Co. is presented below.

1. On April 5, purchased merchandise from Dumaine Company for $16,000 terms 2/10, net/30, FOB shipping point.
2. On April 6 paid freight costs of $900 on merchandise purchased from Dumaine.
3. On April 7, purchased equipment on account for $26,000.
4. On April 8, returned damaged merchandise to Dumaine Company and was granted a $3,000 allowance.
5. On April 15 paid the amount due to Dumaine Company in full.

Instructions
- (a) Prepare the journal entries to record these transactions on the books of Esplande Co. under a perpetual inventory system.
- (b) Assume that Esplande Co. paid the balance due to Dumaine Company on May 4 instead of April 15. Prepare the journal entry to record this payment.

E5–2 On September 1, College Office Supply had an inventory of 30 deluxe pocket calculators at a cost of $20 each. The company uses a perpetual inventory system. During September, the following transactions occurred.

Journalize perpetual inventory entries.
(SO 2, 3)

Sept. 6   Purchased 80 calculators at $19 each from Digital Co. for cash.
    9   Paid freight of $80 on calculators purchased from Digital Co.
  10   Returned 2 calculators to Digital Co. for $40 credit because they did not meet specifications.
  12   Sold 26 calculators costing $20 (including freight-in) for $30 each to Campus Book Store, terms, n/30.
  14   Granted credit of $30 to Campus Book Store for the return of one calculator that was not ordered.
  20   Sold 30 calculators costing $20 for $30 each to Varsity Card Shop, terms, n/30.

Instructions
Journalize the September transactions.

E5–3 On June 10, Arcadian Company purchased $6,000 of merchandise from R. Duvall Company FOB shipping point, terms 2/10, n/30. Arcadian pays the freight costs of $300 on June 11. Damaged goods totaling $300 are returned to R. Duvall for credit on June 12. On June 19, Arcadian pays R. Duvall Company in full, less the purchase discount. Both companies use a perpetual inventory system.

Prepare purchase and sale entries and closing entries.
(SO 2, 3)

Instructions
(a) Prepare separate entries for each transaction on the books of Arcadian Company.
(b) Prepare separate entries for each transaction for Duvall Company. The merchandise purchased by Arcadian on June 10 had cost Duvall $3,000.

E5–4 Presented below are transactions related to S. Pippen Company.

Journalize sales transactions.
(SO 3)

1. On December 3, S. Pippen Company sold $480,000 of merchandise to D. Rodman Co., terms 2/10, n/30, FOB shipping point. The cost of the merchandise sold was $320,000.
2. On December 8, D. Rodman Co. was granted an allowance of $20,000 for merchandise purchased on December 3.
3. On December 13, S. Pippen Company received the balance due from D. Rodman Co.

Instructions
(a) Prepare the journal entries to record these transactions on the books of S. Pippen Company using a perpetual inventory system.
(b) Assume that S. Pippen Company received the balance due from D. Rodman Co. on January 2 of the following year instead of December 13. Prepare the journal entry to record the receipt of payment on January 2.

E5–5 The adjusted trial balance of Lopez Company shows the following data pertaining to sales at the end of its fiscal year October 31, 1999: Sales $800,000, Freight-out $12,000, Sales Returns and Allowances $24,000, and Sales Discounts $15,000.

Prepare sales revenues section and closing entries.
(SO 3, 5, 6)

Instructions
(a) Prepare the sales revenues section of the income statement.
(b) Prepare separate closing entries for (1) sales, and (2) the contra accounts to sales.

E5–6 Presented is information related to Gonzales Co. for the month of January 1999.

Prepare closing entries.
(SO 6)

Cost of Goods Sold	208,000	Salary expense	61,000
Freight-out	7,000	Sales discounts	8,000
Insurance expense	12,000	Sales returns and allowances	13,000
Rent expense	20,000	Sales	350,000

Instructions
Prepare the necessary closing entries.

E5–7 Presented below are selected accounts for Alvarez Company as reported in the work sheet at the end of May 1999.

Complete work sheet.
(SO 6)

Accounts	Adjusted Trial Balance		Income Statement		Balance Sheet	
	Dr.	Cr.	Dr.	Cr.	Dr.	Cr.
Cash	9,000					
Merchandise Inventory	80,000					
Sales		450,000				
Sales Returns and Allowances	10,000					
Sales Discounts	5,000					
Cost of Goods Sold	250,000					

Instructions

Complete the work sheet by extending amounts reported in the adjusted trial balance to the appropriate columns in the work sheet. Do not total individual columns.

Prepare multiple-step and single-step income statements.
(SO 7)

E5–8 In its income statement for the year ended December 31, 1999, Acevedo Company reported the following condensed data:

Administrative expenses	$435,000	Selling expenses	$ 690,000
Cost of goods sold	989,000	Loss on sale of equipment	10,000
Interest expense	70,000	Net sales	2,350,000
Interest revenue	45,000		

Instructions

(a) Prepare a multiple-step income statement.
(b) Prepare a single-step income statement.

Prepare correcting entries for sales and purchases.
(SO 2, 3)

E5–9 An inexperienced accountant for Salvador Company made the following errors in recording merchandising transactions:

1. A $150 refund to a customer for faulty merchandise was debited to Sales $150 and credited to Cash $150.
2. A $200 credit purchase of supplies was debited to Merchandise Inventory $200 and credited to Cash $200.
3. An $80 sales discount was debited to Sales.
4. A cash payment of $30 for freight on merchandise purchases was debited to Freight-out $300 and credited to Cash $300.

Instructions

Prepare separate correcting entries for each error, assuming that the incorrect entry is not reversed. (Omit explanations.)

Compute missing amounts.
(SO 3, 4, 5)

E5–10 Presented below is financial information for two different companies:

	Alatorre Company	Eduardo Company
Sales	$90,000	(d)
Sales returns	(a)	$ 5,000
Net sales	81,000	95,000
Cost of goods sold	56,000	(e)
Gross profit	(b)	38,000
Operating expenses	15,000	(f)
Net income	(c)	15,000

Instructions

Determine the missing amounts.

PROBLEMS: SET A

Journalize, post, and prepare partial income statement.
(SO 2, 3, 4, 5)

P5–1A Carlos Hardware Store completed the following merchandising transactions in the month of May. At the beginning of May, the ledger of Carlos showed Cash of $5,000 and J. Carlos, Capital of $5,000.

May   1   Purchased merchandise on account from Depot Wholesale Supply $6,000, terms 2/10, n/30.

2   Sold merchandise on account $4,500, terms 2/10, n/30. The cost of the merchandise sold was $3,000.

5   Received credit from Depot Wholesale Supply for merchandise returned $200.

9   Received collections in full, less discounts, from customers billed on sales of $4,500 on May 2.

10   Paid Depot Wholesale Supply in full, less discount.

11   Purchased supplies for cash $900.

12   Purchased merchandise for cash $2,400.

15   Received refund for poor quality merchandise from supplier on cash purchase $230.

17   Purchased merchandise from Harlow Distributors $1,900, FOB shipping point, terms 2/10, n/30.

19   Paid freight on May 17 purchase $250.

24   Sold merchandise for cash $6,200. The merchandise sold had a cost of $4,340.

25   Purchased merchandise from Horicon Inc. $1,000, FOB destination, terms 2/10, n/30.

27   Paid Harlow Distributors in full, less discount.

29   Made refunds to cash customers for defective merchandise $100. The returned merchandise had a cost of $70.

31   Sold merchandise on account $1,600, terms n/30. The cost of the merchandise sold was $1,120.

Carlos Hardware's chart of accounts includes the following: No. 101 Cash, No. 112 Accounts Receivable, No. 120 Merchandise Inventory, No. 126 Supplies, No. 201 Accounts Payable, No. 301 J. Carlos Capital, No. 401 Sales, No. 412 Sales Returns and Allowances, No. 414 Sales Discounts, No. 505 Cost of Goods Sold.

Instructions
(a) Journalize the transactions using a perpetual inventory system.
(b) Enter the beginning cash and capital balances and post the transactions. (Use J1 for the journal reference.)
(c) Prepare an income statement through gross profit for the month of May 1999.

P5–2A   Presented below are selected transactions for the Anna Mossity Company during September of the current year. Anna Mossity Company uses the perpetual inventory system.

Journalize entries under a perpetual inventory system.
(SO 2,3)

Sept.   2   Purchased delivery equipment on account for $28,000.

4   Purchased merchandise on account from Carol Ling Company at a cost of $50,000, terms FOB shipping point, 2/10, n/30.

5   Paid freight charges of $2,000 on merchandise purchased from Carol Ling Company on September 4.

5   Returned damaged goods costing $7,000 received from Carol Ling Company on September 4.

6   Sold merchandise to Sal A. Mander Company costing $15,000 on account for $21,000, terms 1/10, n/30.

14   Paid Carol Ling balance due related to September 4 transaction.

15   Purchased supplies costing $4,000 for cash.

16   Received balance due from Sal A. Mander Company.

18   Purchased merchandise for cash $6,000.

22   Sold to Wayne E. Weather Company on account for $28,000 inventory costing $20,000, terms 1/10, n/30.

Instructions
Journalize the September transactions.

Complete accounting cycle beginning with a work sheet.
(SO 5, 6, 7)

P5–3A   The trial balance of Monty Zuma Wholesale Company contained the following accounts at December 31, the end of the company's fiscal year:

MONTY ZUMA WHOLESALE COMPANY
Trial Balance
December 31, 1999

	Debit	Credit
Cash	$ 23,400	
Accounts Receivable	37,600	
Merchandise Inventory	90,000	
Land	92,000	
Buildings	197,000	
Accumulated Depreciation—Buildings		$ 54,000
Equipment	83,500	
Accumulated Depreciation—Equipment		42,400
Notes Payable		50,000
Accounts Payable		37,500
M. Zuma, Capital		267,800
M. Zuma, Drawing	10,000	
Sales		902,100
Sales Discounts	4,600	
Cost of Goods Sold	709,900	
Salaries Expense	69,800	
Utilities Expense	19,400	
Repair Expense	5,900	
Gas and Oil Expense	7,200	
Insurance Expense	3,500	
	$1,353,800	$1,353,800

Adjustment data:

1. Depreciation is $10,000 on buildings and $9,000 on equipment. (Both are administrative expenses.)
2. Interest of $7,000 is due and unpaid on notes payable at December 31.

Other data:

1. Salaries are 80% selling and 20% administrative.
2. Utilities expense, repair expense, and insurance expense are 100% administrative.
3. $15,000 of the notes payable are payable next year.
4. Gas and oil expense is a selling expense.

Instructions
(a) Enter the trial balance on a work sheet and complete the work sheet.
(b) Prepare a multiple-step income statement and owner's equity statement for the year, and a classified balance sheet at December 31, 1999.
(c) Journalize the adjusting entries.
(d) Journalize the closing entries.
(e) Prepare a post-closing trial balance.

Prepare financial statements and adjusting and closing entries.
(SO 5, 6, 7)

P5–4A Rowbuck Department Store is located in midtown Metropolis. During the past several years, net income has been declining because of suburban shopping centers. At the end of the company's fiscal year on November 30, 1999, the following accounts appeared in two of its trial balances:

	Unadjusted	Adjusted
Accounts Payable	$ 47,310	$ 47,310
Accounts Receivable	11,770	11,770
Accumulated Depreciation—Delivery Equipment	15,680	19,680
Accumulated Depreciation—Store Equipment	32,300	41,800
Cash	8,000	8,000
N. Rowbuck, Capital	84,200	84,200
Cost of Goods Sold	633,220	633,220

	Unadjusted	Adjusted
Delivery Expense	8,200	8,200
Delivery Equipment	57,000	57,000
Depreciation Expense—Delivery Equipment		4,000
Depreciation Expense—Store Equipment		9,500
N. Rowbuck, Drawing	12,000	12,000
Insurance Expense		9,000
Interest Expense	8,000	8,000
Interest Revenue	5,000	5,000
Merchandise Inventory	36,200	36,200
Notes Payable	46,000	46,000
Prepaid Insurance	13,500	4,500
Property Tax Expense		3,500
Property Taxes Payable		3,500
Rent Expense	19,000	19,000
Salaries Expense	120,000	120,000
Sales	850,000	850,000
Sales Commissions Expense	8,000	14,000
Sales Commissions Payable		6,000
Sales Returns and Allowances	10,000	10,000
Store Equipment	125,000	125,000
Utilities Expense	10,600	10,600

Analysis reveals the following additional data:

1. Salaries expense is 70% selling and 30% administrative.
2. Insurance expense is 50% selling and 50% administrative.
3. Rent expense, utilities expense, and property tax expense are administrative expenses.
4. Notes payable are due in 2002.

Instructions
(a) Prepare a multiple-step income statement, an owner's equity statement, and a classi-fied balance sheet.
(b) Journalize the adjusting entries that were made.
(c) Journalize the closing entries that are necessary.

P5–5A   Chi Chi Garcia, a former professional golf star, operates Chi Chi's Pro Shop at Bay Golf Course. At the beginning of the current season on April 1, the ledger of Chi Chi's Pro Shop showed Cash $2,500, Merchandise Inventory $3,500, and C. C. Garcia, Capital $6,000. The following transactions were completed during April.

Journalize, post, and prepare a trial balance.
(SO 2, 3, 6)

Apr. 5   Purchased golf bags, clubs, and balls on account from Balata Co. $1,600, FOB shipping point, terms 2/10, n/60.
     7   Paid freight on Balata purchase $80.
     9   Received credit from Balata Co. for merchandise returned $100.
    10   Sold merchandise on account to members $900, terms n/30. The merchandise sold had a cost of $630.
    12   Purchased golf shoes, sweaters, and other accessories on account from Titleist Sportswear $660, terms 1/10, n/30.
    14   Paid Balata Co. in full.
    17   Received credit from Titleist Sportswear for merchandise returned $60.
    20   Made sales on account to members $700, terms n/30. The cost of the merchandise sold was $490.
    21   Paid Titleist Sportswear in full.
    27   Granted an allowance to members for clothing that did not fit properly $30.
    30   Received payments on account from members $1,100.

The chart of accounts for the pro shop includes the following: No. 101 Cash, No. 112 Accounts Receivable, No. 120 Merchandise Inventory, No. 201 Accounts Payable, No. 301 C. C. Garcia, Capital, No. 401 Sales, No. 412 Sales Returns and Allowances, No. 505 Cost of Goods Sold.

Instructions

(a) Journalize the April transactions using a perpetual inventory system.
(b) Enter the beginning balances in the ledger accounts and post the April transactions. (Use J1 for the journal reference.)
(c) Prepare a trial balance on April 30, 1999.

PROBLEMS: SET B

Journalize, post, and prepare a partial income statement.
(SO 2, 3, 4, 5)

P5–1B The Maggie Zine Distributing Company completed the following merchandising transactions in the month of April. At the beginning of April, the ledger of Maggie Zine showed Cash of $9,000 and M. Zine, Capital of $9,000.

Apr. 2 Purchased merchandise on account from Ken Tuckee Supply Co. $5,900, terms 2/10, n/30.
   4 Sold merchandise on account $5,000, FOB destination, terms 2/10, n/30. The cost of the merchandise sold was $4,000.
   5 Paid $200 freight on April 4 sale.
   6 Received credit from Ken Tuckee Supply Co. for merchandise returned $300.
  11 Paid Ken Tuckee Supply Co. in full, less discount.
  13 Received collections in full, less discounts, from customers billed on April 4.
  14 Purchased merchandise for cash $4,400.
  16 Received refund from supplier on cash purchase of April 14, $500.
  18 Purchased merchandise from Ida Hoe Distributors $4,200, FOB shipping point, terms 2/10, n/30.
  20 Paid freight on April 18 purchase $100.
  23 Sold merchandise for cash $6,400. The merchandise sold had a cost of $5,120.
  26 Purchased merchandise for cash $2,300.
  27 Paid Ida Hoe Distributors in full, less discount.
  29 Made refunds to cash customers for defective merchandise $90. The returned merchandise had a cost of $70.
  30 Sold merchandise on account $3,700, terms n/30. The cost of the merchandise sold was $3,000.

Maggie Zine Company's chart of accounts includes the following: No. 101 Cash, No. 112 Accounts Receivable, No. 120 Merchandise Inventory, No. 201 Accounts Payable, No. 301 M. Zine, Capital, No. 401 Sales, No. 412 Sales Returns and Allowances, No. 414 Sales Discounts, No. 505 Cost of Goods Sold, and No. 644 Freight-out.

Instructions

(a) Journalize the transactions using a perpetual inventory system.
(b) Enter the beginning cash and capital balances, and post the transactions. (Use J1 for the journal reference.)
(c) Prepare the income statement through gross profit for the month of April 1999.

Journalize transactions under a perpetual inventory system.
(SO 2, 3)

P5–2B Tom E. Hawk Auto Sales uses a perpetual inventory system. On April 1, the new car inventory records show total inventory of $144,000 consisting of the following:

Model	Units	Unit Cost
Custom Sedans	4	$15,000
Convertibles	3	16,000
Recreational Vans	2	18,000

During April, the following purchases and sales were made on account.

April 5 Purchased three custom sedans for $15,000 each.
   7 Sold two custom sedans for $18,200 each.
  13 Purchased two recreational vans for $18,000 each.
  17 Sold one custom sedan for $18,500.

20 Purchased two convertibles for $16,000 each.
22 Returned one convertible purchased on April 20 for $16,000 credit.
24 Sold three recreational vans for $24,000 each.
28 Sold one convertible for $21,000.

Instructions
Journalize the transactions using a perpetual inventory system.

P5–3B The trial balance of Cal A. Fornia Fashion Center contained the following accounts at November 30, the end of the company's fiscal year.

Complete accounting cycle beginning with a work sheet.
(SO 5, 6, 7)

CAL A. FORNIA FASHION CENTER
Trial Balance
November 30, 1999

	Debit	Credit
Cash	$ 26,700	
Accounts Receivable	33,700	
Merchandise Inventory	45,000	
Store Supplies	5,500	
Store Equipment	85,000	
Accumulated Depreciation—Store Equipment		$ 18,000
Delivery Equipment	48,000	
Accumulated Depreciation—Delivery Equipment		6,000
Notes Payable		51,000
Accounts Payable		48,500
C. A. Fornia, Capital		110,000
C. A. Fornia, Drawing	12,000	
Sales		757,200
Sales Returns and Allowances	4,200	
Cost of Goods Sold	497,400	
Salaries Expense	140,000	
Advertising Expense	26,400	
Utilities Expense	14,000	
Repair Expense	12,100	
Delivery Expense	16,700	
Rent Expense	24,000	
	$990,700	$990,700

Adjustment data:

1. Store supplies on hand totaled $3,500.
2. Depreciation is $9,000 on the store equipment and $7,000 on the delivery equipment.
3. Interest of $11,000 is accrued on notes payable at November 30.

Other data:

1. Salaries expense is 70% selling and 30% administrative.
2. Rent expense and utilities expense are 80% selling and 20% administrative.
3. $30,000 of notes payable are due for payment next year.
4. Repair expense is 100% administrative.

Instructions
(a) Enter the trial balance on a work sheet and complete the work sheet.
(b) Prepare a multiple-step income statement and owner's equity statement for the year and a classified balance sheet as of November 30, 1999.
(c) Journalize the adjusting entries.
(d) Journalize the closing entries.
(e) Prepare a post-closing trial balance.

P5–4B The Al Falfa Department Store is located near the Village shopping mall. At the end of the company's fiscal year on December 31, 1999, the following accounts appeared in two of its trial balances.

Prepare financial statements and adjusting and closing entries.
(SO 5, 6, 7)

	Unadjusted	Adjusted
Accounts Payable	$ 79,300	$ 79,300
Accounts Receivable	50,300	50,300
Accumulated Depreciation—Building	42,100	52,500
Accumulated Depreciation—Equipment	29,600	42,900
Building	190,000	190,000
Cash	23,000	23,000
L. Markan, Capital	176,600	176,600
Cost of Goods Sold	412,700	412,700
Depreciation Expense—Building		10,400
Depreciation Expense—Equipment		13,300
L. Markan, Drawing	28,000	28,000
Equipment	110,000	110,000
Insurance Expense		7,200
Interest Expense	3,000	11,000
Interest Payable		8,000
Interest Revenue	4,000	4,000
Merchandise Inventory	75,000	75,000
Mortgage Payable	80,000	80,000
Office Salaries Expense	32,000	32,000
Prepaid Insurance	9,600	2,400
Property Taxes Expense		4,800
Property Taxes Payable		4,800
Sales Salaries Expense	76,000	76,000
Sales	628,000	628,000
Sales Commissions Expense	11,000	14,500
Sales Commissions Payable		3,500
Sales Returns and Allowances	8,000	8,000
Utilities Expense	11,000	11,000

Analysis reveals the following additional data:

1. Insurance expense and utilities expense are 60% selling and 40% administrative.
2. $20,000 of the mortgage payable is due for payment next year.
3. Depreciation on the building and property tax expense are administrative expenses; depreciation on the equipment is a selling expense.

Instructions

(a) Prepare a multiple-step income statement, an owner's equity statement, and a classified balance sheet.
(b) Journalize the adjusting entries that were made.
(c) Journalize the closing entries that are necessary.

Journalize, post, and prepare a trial balance.
(SO 2, 3, 6)

P5–5B   Bobby Jo Evans, a former professional tennis star, operates B.J.'s Tennis Shop at the Jackson Lake Resort. At the beginning of the current season, the ledger of B.J.'s Tennis Shop showed Cash $2,500, Merchandise Inventory $1,700, and B. J. Evans, Capital $4,200. The following transactions were completed during April:

Apr. 4   Purchased racquets and balls from Sampras Co. $640 FOB shipping point, terms 3/10, n/30.
     6   Paid freight on Sampras's purchase $40.
     8   Sold merchandise to members $900, terms n/30. The merchandise sold had a cost of $600.
    10   Received credit of $40 from Sampras Co. for a damaged racquet that was returned.
    11   Purchased tennis shoes from Niki Sports for cash, $300.
    13   Paid Sampras Co. in full.
    14   Purchased tennis shirts and shorts from Martina's Sportswear $700, FOB shipping point, terms 2/10, n/60.
    15   Received cash refund of $50 from Niki Sports for damaged merchandise that was returned.

17 Paid freight on Martina's Sportswear purchase $30.
18 Sold merchandise to members, $800, terms n/30. The cost of the merchandise sold was $530.
20 Received $500 in cash from members in settlement of their accounts.
21 Paid Martina's Sportswear in full.
27 Granted an allowance of $30 to members for tennis clothing that did not fit properly.
30 Received cash payments on account from members, $500.

The chart of accounts for the tennis shop includes the following: No. 101 Cash, No. 112 Accounts Receivable, No. 120 Merchandise Inventory, No. 201 Accounts Payable, No. 301 B. J. Evans, Capital, No. 401 Sales, No. 412 Sales Returns and Allowances, No. 505 Cost of Goods Sold.

Instructions
(a) Journalize the April transactions using a perpetual inventory system.
(b) Enter the beginning balances in the ledger accounts and post the April transactions. (Use J1 for the journal reference.)
(c) Prepare a trial balance on April 30, 1999.

BROADENING YOUR PERSPECTIVE

FINANCIAL REPORTING AND ANALYSIS

FINANCIAL REPORTING PROBLEM: Kellogg Company

BYP5–1 The financial statements of Kellogg Company are presented in Appendix A at the end of this textbook.

Instructions
Answer the following questions using the Consolidated Statement of Earnings.
(a) What was the percentage change in (1) sales and in (2) net income from 1995 to 1996 and from 1996 to 1997?
(b) What was Kellogg's gross profit rate in 1995, 1996, and 1997?
(c) What was Kellogg's percentage of net income to net sales in 1995, 1996, and 1997? Comment on any trend in this percentage.

COMPARATIVE ANALYSIS PROBLEM: Kellogg Company vs. General Mills

BYP5–2 Kellogg's financial statements are presented in Appendix A; General Mills's financial statements are presented in Appendix B.

Instructions
(a) Based on the information contained in these financial statements, determine each of the following for each company:
   (1) Gross profit for 1997.
   (2) Gross profit rate for 1997.
   (3) Operating income for 1997.
   (4) Percent change in operating income from 1996 to 1997.
(b) What conclusions concerning the relative profitability of the two companies can be drawn from these data?

RESEARCH ASSIGNMENT

BYP5–3 The April 1996 issue of the *Journal of Accountancy* includes an article by Dennis R. Beresford, L. Todd Johnson, and Cheri L. Reither, entitled "Is a Second Income Statement Needed?"

Instructions

Read the article and answer the following questions:

   (a) On what basis would the "second income statement" be prepared? Briefly describe this basis.

   (b) Why is there a perceived need for a second income statement?

   (c) Identify three alternatives for reporting the proposed measure of income.

INTERPRETING FINANCIAL STATEMENTS: McDonnell Douglas

BYP5–4   Before being purchased by Boeing Co. in 1997, McDonnell Douglas, based in St. Louis, Missouri, described itself in its Annual Report as the world's largest builder of fighter and military transport aircraft, the third largest commercial aircraft maker, and a leading producer of helicopters, missiles, and satellite launch vehicles. The company's strategy for future growth might have been described as "cautiously aggressive," because it aggressively competed in markets in which it believed that it had a competitive advantage, while it evaluated other markets carefully, and then expanded its product line or divested, depending upon whether it believed that it could remain or become a leading competitor.

   A recent pre-merger McDonnell Douglas income statement is reproduced below. Dollar amounts are in millions.

McDonnell Douglas
Income Statement (partial)

Revenues	$13,176
Costs and expenses:	
Cost of products, services, and rentals	11,026
General and administrative expenses	684
Research and development	297
Interest expense	249
Total costs and expenses	12,256
Earnings before income taxes	920
Income taxes	322
Net earnings	$ 598

Instructions

   (a) What account name appears to represent McDonnell Douglas's cost of goods sold account? Why do you think that company chose the account name that it did? Using that account as cost of goods sold, what is gross profit?

   (b) The income statement shown is in summary form. This means that each account title listed is a summary of several other accounts. For example, the Revenue account includes such things as Commercial Aircraft Revenue, Defense Contract Revenue, and so forth, as well as any offsetting accounts such as Sales Discounts. Indicate in which summary account from the income statement the following merchandising accounts would be located:

     1. Sales returns and allowances.

     2. Freight-in.

     3. Merchandise inventory increases and decreases.

     4. Sales discounts.

   (c) The company was evaluating a divisional plant that would build satellite launch vehicles. The product line consisted of a single vehicle, which was the only one of its kind, but competitors had built vehicles that could launch smaller satellites. The company was confident that it could produce an expanded product line, which would include both larger and smaller vehicles than the one currently made. The two choices being evaluated were: First, spend approximately $17 million in research and development to expand the product line. This cost would be considered an expense immediately. Revenue of about $100 million would be generated each year, beginning two years after development; it would continue at least five years, but possibly more. Second, sell the assets of the existing business to a competitor. This would generate a gain of $315 million next year.

If the choice had been made at the end of this year, how would net income be affected under each alternative? How would gross profit change? Which alternative would you have recommended? Give reasons for your answer.

REAL-WORLD FOCUS: A.L. Laboratories

BYP5–5 **A.L. Laboratories** is headquartered in Ft. Lee, N.J., and also has operations in Scandinavia and Indonesia. The company develops and produces generic pharmaceuticals, specializing in both over-the-counter and prescription creams and ointments, aerosol inhalants, and liquids such as cough syrups. A significant share of its income is also derived from the development and distribution of animal health products such as food additives for poultry. The company was founded in 1975 and today has over 2,700 employees.

Gross profit at A.L. Laboratories declined in both dollars and as a percentage of revenues. The decline was attributed to lower sales volume, customer credits associated with product recalls, inventory disposals, and the impact of higher inventory costs. In addition to the above, the gross profit percentage declined as a result of lower production volumes.

Instructions
(a) What account is affected when A.L. Laboratories has a product recall?
(b) What factors caused gross profit to decline?
(c) What factors could cause this company to have to dispose of inventory?

CRITICAL THINKING

GROUP DECISION CASE

BYP5–6 Three years ago, Kathy Webb and her brother-in-law John Utley opened FedCo Department Store. For the first 2 years, business was good, but the following condensed income results for 1998 were disappointing.

FEDCO DEPARTMENT STORE
Income Statement
For the Year Ended December 31, 1998

Net sales		$700,000
Cost of goods sold		546,000
Gross profit		154,000
Operating expenses		
Selling expenses	$100,000	
Administrative expenses	25,000	125,000
Net income		$ 29,000

Kathy believes the problem lies in the relatively low gross profit rate (gross profit divided by net sales) of 22%. John believes the problem is that operating expenses are too high.

Kathy thinks the gross profit rate can be improved by making both of the following changes: (1) Increase average selling prices by 17%; this increase is expected to lower sales volume so that total sales will increase only 6%. (2) Buy merchandise in larger quantities and take all purchase discounts; these changes are expected to increase the gross profit rate by 3%. Kathy does not anticipate that these changes will have any effect on operating expenses.

John thinks expenses can be cut by making both of the following changes: (1) Cut 1998 sales salaries of $60,000 in half and give sales personnel a commission of 2% of net sales. (2) Reduce store deliveries to one day per week rather than twice a week; this change will reduce 1998 delivery expenses of $30,000 by 40%. John feels that these changes will not have any effect on net sales.

Kathy and John come to you for help in deciding the best way to improve net income.

Instructions

With the class divided into groups, answer the following:

(a) Prepare a condensed income statement for 1999 assuming (1) Kathy's changes are implemented and (2) John's ideas are adopted.

(b) What is your recommendation to Kathy and John?

(c) Prepare a condensed income statement for 1999 assuming both sets of proposed changes are made.

COMMUNICATION ACTIVITY

BYP5–7 The following situation is in chronological order:

1. Dexter decides to buy a surfboard.
2. He calls Surfing USA Co. to inquire about their surfboards.
3. Two days later he requests Surfing USA Co. to make him a surfboard.
4. Three days later, Surfing USA Co. sends him a purchase order to fill out.
5. He sends back the purchase order.
6. Surfing USA Co. receives the completed purchase order.
7. Surfing USA Co. completes the surfboard.
8. Dexter picks up the surfboard.
9. Surfing USA Co. bills Dexter.
10. Surfing USA Co. receives payment from Dexter.

Instructions

In a memo to the president of Surfing USA Co., explain the following:

(a) When should Surfing USA Co. record the sale?

(b) Suppose that with his purchase order, Dexter is required to make a down payment. Would that change your answer?

ETHICS CASE

BYP5–8 Rita Pelzer was just hired as the assistant treasurer of Yorkshire Stores, a specialty chain store company consisting of nine retail stores concentrated in one metropolitan area. Among other things, the payment of all invoices is centralized in one of the departments Rita will manage. Her primary responsibility is to maintain the company's high credit rating by paying all bills when due and to take advantage of all cash discounts. Jamie Caterino, the former assistant treasurer who has been promoted to treasurer, is training Rita in her new duties. He instructs Rita that she is to continue the practice of preparing all checks "net of discount" and dating the checks the last day of the discount period. "But," Jamie continues, "we always hold the checks at least four days beyond the discount period before mailing them. That way we get another four days of interest on our money. Most of our creditors need our business and don't complain. And, if they scream about our missing the discount period, we blame it on the mail room or the post office. We've only lost one discount out of every hundred we take that way. I think everybody does it. By the way, welcome to our team!"

Instructions

(a) What are the ethical considerations in this case?

(b) Who are the stakeholders that are harmed or benefitted in this situation?

(c) Should Rita continue the practice started by Jamie? Does she have any choice?

SURFING THE NET

BYP5–9 No financial decision maker should ever rely solely on the financial information reported in the annual report to make decisions. It is important to keep abreast of financial news. This activity demonstrates how to search for financial news on the Web.

Address: http://biz.yahoo.com

Steps:

1. Choose **Company**.
2. Type in either Kellogg Company or General Mills, Inc.

3. Choose **News**.
4. Select an article that sounds interesting to you.

Instructions

(a) What was the source of the article? (For example, Reuters, Businesswire, Prnews-wire.)

(b) Pretend that you are a personal financial planner and that one of your clients owns stock in the company. Write a brief memo to your client summarizing the article and explaining the implications of the article for their investment.

Answers to Self-Study Questions
1. c   2. a   3. c   4. b   5. c   6. b   7. d   8. a   9. c   10. d

---

Answer to Kellogg Review It Question 4, p. 201
The 1997 gross profit rate is 52.1% ($3,560 ÷ $6,830.1) and the 1996 gross profit rate is 53.2% ($3,553.7 ÷ $6,676.6). The rate therefore decreased by 1.1% from 1996 to 1997. All this information was provided in the Kellogg Company's management discussion and analysis section. It also could be computed from the income statement presented.

 Remember to go back to the Navigator box on the chapter-opening page and check off your completed work.

CONCEPTS FOR REVIEW

Before studying this chapter, you should know or, if necessary, review:

a. How to perform each of the steps in the accounting cycle.
   (Ch. 4, pp. 151–156)

b. How to record transactions for a merchandising company.
   (Ch. 5, pp. 188–199)

c. How to prepare financial statements for a merchandising company.
   (Ch. 5, pp. 200–204)

THE NAVIGATOR

FEATURE STORY

Accidents Happen

How organized are you financially? Take a short quiz.

• Is your wallet jammed full of gas station receipts from places you don't remember ever going?

• Is your wallet such a mess that it is often faster to fish for money in the crack of your car seat than to dig around in your wallet?

• Was Michael Jordan playing high school basketball the last time you balanced your checkbook?

• Have you ever been tempted to burn down your house so you don't have to look for the receipts

and records that you need to fill out your tax returns?

If you think it is hard to keep track of the many transactions that make up *your* life, imagine what it is like for a major corporation like Fidelity Investments, which as the largest mutual fund management firm in the world, manages more than $400 billion of investments. Millions of individuals have the bulk of their life savings invested in mutual funds. If you were one of them, you might be just slightly displeased if, when you called to find out your balance, the representative said, "You know, I kind of remember

someone with a name like yours sending us some money—now what did we do with that?"

To ensure the accuracy of your balance and the security of your funds, Fidelity Investments, like all other companies large and small, relies on a sophisticated accounting information system. That's not to say that Fidelity or anybody else is error-free. In fact, if you've ever really messed up your checkbook register, you may take some comfort from one accountant's mistake at Fidelity Investments. The accountant failed to include a minus sign while doing a calculation, making what was actually a $1.3 billion loss look like a $1.3 billion gain! Fortunately, like most accounting errors, it was detected before any real harm was done.

No one expects that kind of mistake at a firm like Fidelity, which has sophisticated computer systems and top investment managers. In explaining the mistake to shareholders, a spokesperson wrote: "Some people have asked how, in this age of technology, such a mistake could be made. While many of our processes are computerized, accounting systems are complex and dictate that some steps must be handled manually by our managers and accountants, and people can make mistakes."

THE NAVIGATOR

On the World Wide Web
http://www.fidelity.com

CHAPTER 6

ACCOUNTING INFORMATION SYSTEMS

THE NAVIGATOR ✔

- Understand *Concepts for Review* ☐
- Read *Feature Story* ☐
- Scan *Study Objectives* ☐
- Read *Preview* ☐
- Read text and answer *Before You Go On*
  p. 237 ☐ p. 250 ☐ p. 255 ☐
- Work *Demonstration Problem* ☐
- Review *Summary of Study Objectives* ☐
- Answer *Self-Study Questions* ☐
- Complete assignments ☐

STUDY OBJECTIVES

After studying this chapter, you should be able to:

1. *Identify the basic principles of accounting information systems.*
2. *Explain the major phases involved in the development of an accounting system.*
3. *Describe the nature and purpose of a subsidiary ledger.*
4. *Explain how special journals are used in journalizing.*
5. *Indicate how a columnar journal is posted.*
6. *Distinguish between computer hardware and accounting software and the principal methods of data processing.*
7. *Identify the key points in comparing manual and electronic accounting systems.*

THE NAVIGATOR

*A*s you see from the opening story, a reliable information system is a necessity for any company. Whether you use pen, pencil, or computers in maintaining accounting records, certain principles and procedures apply. The purpose of this chapter is to explain and illustrate these features. The content and organization of this chapter are as follows:

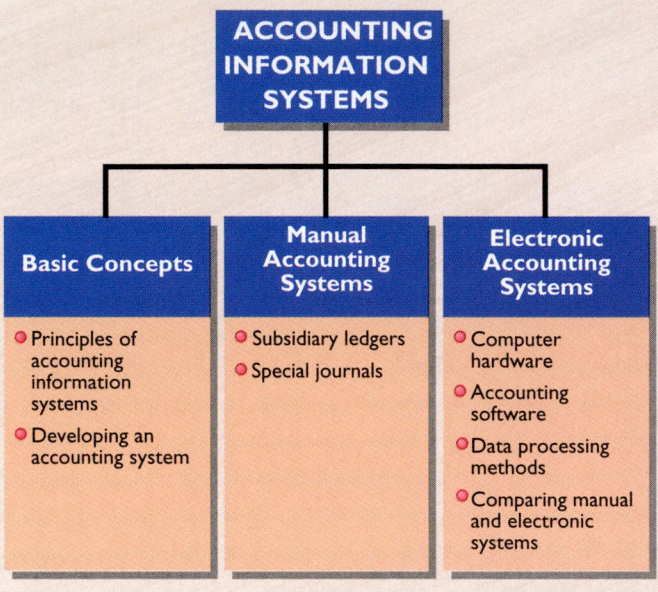

SECTION 1   BASIC CONCEPTS

The system of collecting and processing transaction data and disseminating financial information to interested parties is known as the **accounting information system**. It includes each of the steps in the accounting cycle that you have studied in earlier chapters, the documents that provide evidence of the transactions and events, and the records, trial balances, work sheets, and financial statements that result. An accounting information system may be either manual or electronic.

<table>
<tr><td>1
STUDY
OBJECTIVE

Identify the basic
principles of accounting
information systems.</td></tr>
</table>

PRINCIPLES OF ACCOUNTING INFORMATION SYSTEMS

To have an efficient and effective accounting information system (hereafter referred to simply as the accounting system), certain basic principles must be followed. These principles are: (1) cost awareness, (2) usefulness, and (3) flexibility, as shown in Illustration 6-1.

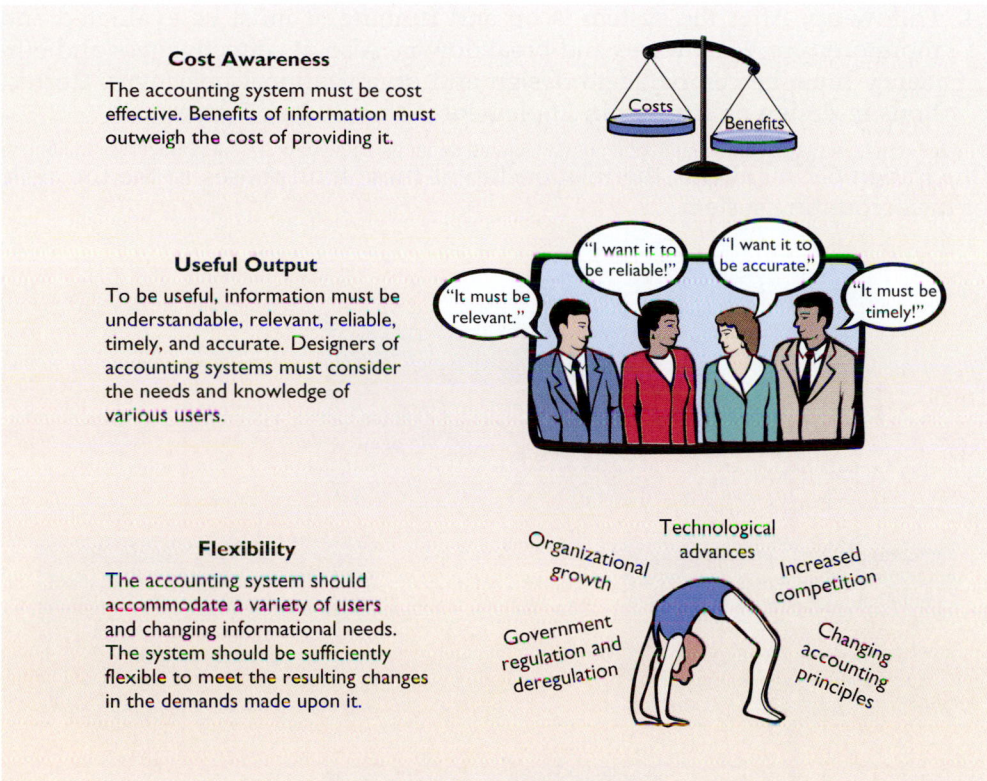

ILLUSTRATION 6-1

Principles of an efficient and effective accounting information system

If the accounting system is cost effective, provides useful output, and has the flexibility to meet future needs, it can provide a valuable service and make a major contribution to both individual and organizational goals.

DEVELOPING AN ACCOUNTING SYSTEM

Good accounting systems do not just happen. They are carefully planned, designed, installed, managed, and refined. Generally, developing an accounting system involves the following four phases:

1. **Analysis.** The starting point of analysis is to determine the information needs of internal and external users. Once this is established, the system analyst proceeds to identify the sources of the information and the records and procedures for collecting and reporting the data. If an existing system is being analyzed, its strengths and weaknesses must be identified.

2. **Design.** For a new system, forms and documents must be designed; methods and procedures selected from alternatives; job descriptions prepared; controls integrated; reports formatted; and equipment selected. Redesigning an existing system may involve only minor changes, a complete overhaul, or replacement of a manual system by a computerized system.

3. **Implementation.** Implementation of either new or revised systems requires that documents, procedures, reports, and processing equipment must be installed and made operational. Personnel must be hired, trained, and closely supervised through a start-up or transition period.

2

STUDY OBJECTIVE

Explain the major phases involved in the development of an accounting system.

4. Follow-up. After the system is up and running, it must be evaluated and monitored for weaknesses and breakdowns. Also, its effectiveness and efficiency must be compared to design and organizational objectives. Corrections in design or changes in implementation may be necessary.

Illustration 6-2 highlights the relationship of these four phases in the life cycle of the accounting system.

ILLUSTRATION 6-2

Phases in the development of an accounting system

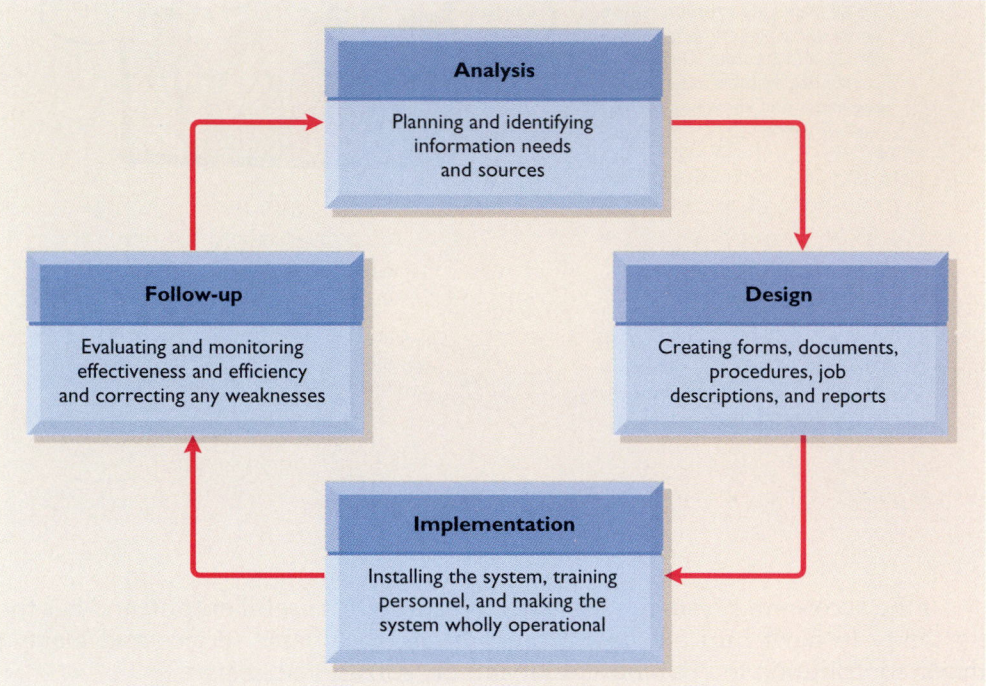

These phases, which represent the life cycle of an accounting system, suggest that few systems remain the same forever. As experience and knowledge are obtained, and as technological and organizational changes occur, the accounting system may also have to grow and change.

The accounting system in the first five chapters is satisfactory in a company where the volume of transactions is extremely low. However, in most companies, it is necessary to add additional ledgers and journals to the accounting system to record transaction data efficiently.

SECTION 2 MANUAL ACCOUNTING SYSTEMS

In a **manual accounting system**, each of the steps in the accounting cycle is performed by hand. For example, each accounting transaction is entered manually in the journal and posted manually to the ledger. To obtain ledger account balances and to prepare a trial balance and financial statements, additional manual computations must be made. In this section, therefore, we discuss how the manual processing system can be more efficiently used to process accounting data.

At this point you might be wondering, "Why cover manual accounting systems if the real world uses computerized systems?" First, small businesses still abound. Most of them begin operations with manual (or even "shoe box") accounting systems and convert to computerized systems as the business grows. Second, to understand what computerized accounting systems do, you need to understand how manual accounting systems work.

SUBSIDIARY LEDGERS

Imagine a business that has several thousand charge (credit) customers and shows the transactions with these customers in only one account—Accounts Receivable—in the general ledger. It would be virtually impossible to determine the balance owed by an individual customer at any specific time. Similarly, the amount payable to one creditor would be difficult to locate quickly from a single Accounts Payable account in the general ledger.

3
STUDY
OBJECTIVE

Describe the nature and purpose of a subsidiary ledger.

To provide such information, companies use subsidiary ledgers to keep track of individual balances. A **subsidiary ledger** is a group of accounts with a common characteristic (for example, all customer accounts—that is, accounts receivable). The subsidiary ledger frees the general ledger from the details of individual balances. A subsidiary ledger is an addition to, and an expansion of, the general ledger.

Two common subsidiary ledgers are:

1. The **accounts receivable** (or **customers'**) **ledger** which accumulates transaction data with individual customers.
2. The **accounts payable** (or **creditors'**) **ledger** which maintains transaction data with individual creditors.

In each of these subsidiary ledgers, individual accounts are usually arranged in alphabetical order.

The detailed data shown in a subsidiary ledger are summarized in a general ledger account. The accounts for the two ledgers above are Accounts Receivable and Accounts Payable, respectively. The general ledger account that summarizes subsidiary ledger data is called a **control account**. **Each general ledger control account balance must equal the composite balance of the individual accounts in the related subsidiary ledger at the end of an accounting period.** An overview of the relationship of subsidiary ledgers to the general ledger is shown in Illustration 6-3, with the general ledger control accounts and subsidiary ledger accounts in green color.

ILLUSTRATION 6-3

Relationship of general ledgers and subsidiary accounts

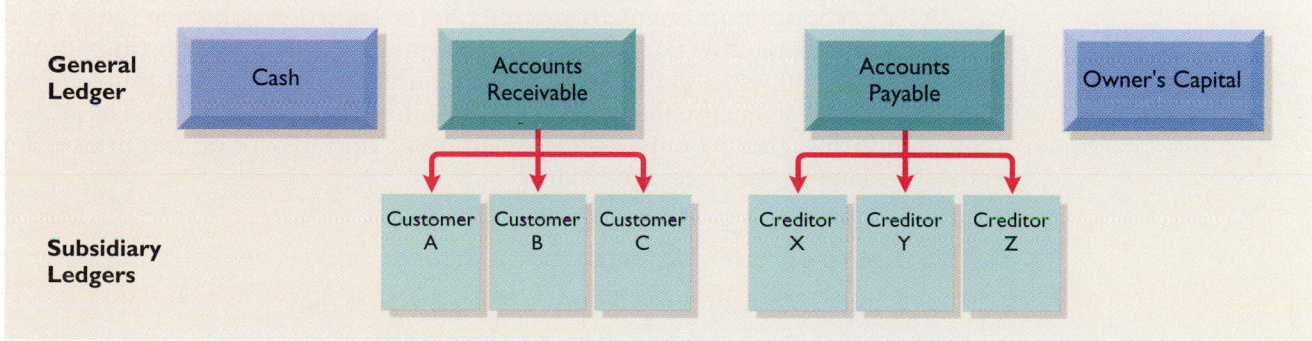

Note that cash and owner's capital in this illustration are not control accounts.

Illustration

An example of a control account and subsidiary ledger for Larson Enterprises is provided in Illustration 6-4. The explanation column in these accounts is not shown in this and subsequent illustrations due to space considerations.

ILLUSTRATION 6-4

Relationship between ledgers

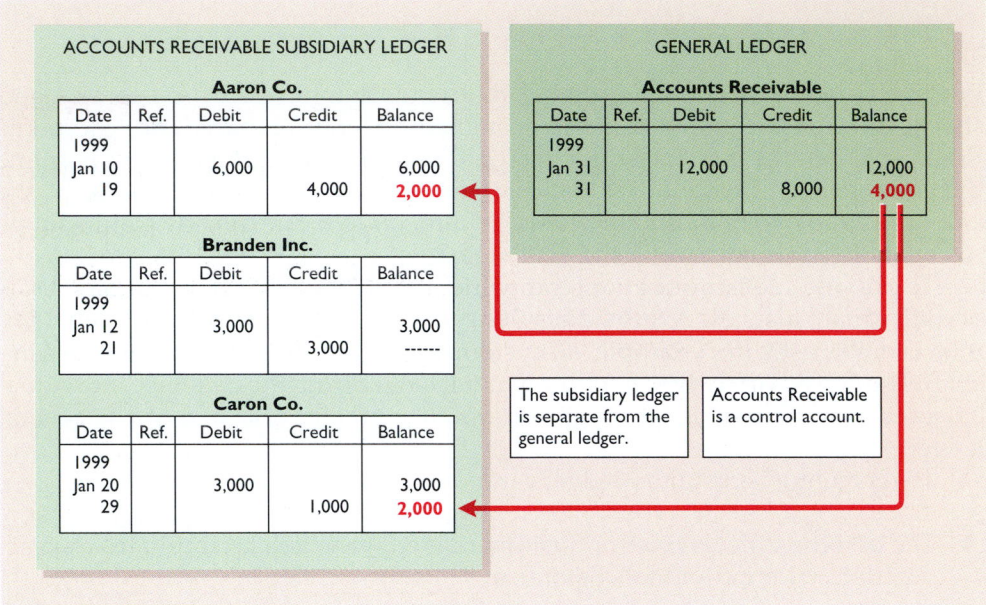

The example is based on the following transactions:

ILLUSTRATION 6-5

Sales and collection transactions

Credit Sales			Collections on Account		
Jan. 10	Aaron Co.	$ 6,000	Jan. 19	Aaron Co.	$ 4,000
12	Branden Inc.	3,000	21	Branden Inc.	3,000
20	Caron Co.	3,000	29	Caron Co.	1,000
		$12,000			$ 8,000

The total debits and credits in Accounts Receivable in the general ledger are reconcilable to the detailed debits and credits in the subsidiary accounts. In addition, the balance of $4,000 in the accounts receivable control account agrees with the total of the balances in the individual accounts (Aaron Co. $2,000 + Branden Inc. $0 + Caron Co. $2,000) in the subsidiary ledger.

As shown, postings are made monthly to the control accounts in the general ledger so that monthly financial statements may be prepared. Postings to the individual accounts in the subsidiary ledger are made daily. The rationale for posting daily is to ensure that current account information can be used as a basis for monitoring credit limits, billing customers, and answering inquiries from customers about their account balances.

Advantages of Subsidiary Ledgers

The advantages of using subsidiary ledgers are that they:

1. **Show transactions affecting one customer or one creditor in a single account**, thus providing necessary up-to-date information on specific account balances.

2. **Free the general ledger of excessive details.** As a result, a trial balance of the general ledger does not contain vast numbers of individual account balances.

3. **Help locate errors in individual accounts** by reducing the number of accounts combined in one ledger and by using controlling accounts.

4. **Make possible a division of labor** in posting by having one employee post to the general ledger and someone else post to the subsidiary ledgers.

TECHNOLOGY IN ACTION

Rather than relying on customer or creditor names in a subsidiary ledger, a computer system expands the account number of the control account in a pre-specified manner. For example, if accounts receivable was numbered 10010, the first account in the accounts receivable subsidiary ledger might be numbered 10010-0001. Most systems allow inquiries about specific accounts in the subsidiary ledger (by account number) or about the control account. With the latter, the system would automatically total all the subsidiary accounts whenever an inquiry to the control account was made.

BEFORE YOU GO ON . . .

Review It

1. What are the basic principles to be followed in designing and developing an efficient and effective accounting information system?
2. What are the major phases in the development of an accounting information system?
3. What is a subsidiary ledger, and what purpose does it serve?

Do It

Presented below is information related to Sims Company for its first month of operations. Identify the balances that appear in the accounts payable subsidiary ledger and the Accounts Payable balance that appears in the general ledger at the end of January.

Credit Purchases			Cash Paid		
Jan 5	Devon Co.	$11,000	Jan 9	Devon Co.	$7,000
Jan 11	Shelby Co.	7,000	Jan 14	Shelby Co.	2,000
Jan 22	Taylor Co.	14,000	Jan 27	Taylor Co.	9,000

Reasoning: Note that only one account appears in the general ledger, but the detail related to this account is shown in the subsidiary ledger.

Solution: Subsidiary ledger balances: Devon Co. $4,000 ($11,000 − $7,000); Shelby Co. $5,000 ($7,000 − $2,000); Taylor Co. $5,000 ($14,000 − $9,000). General ledger Accounts Payable balance $14,000 ($32,000 − $18,000).

Related exercise material: BE6–3, BE6–4, E6–1, E6–2, E6–3, E6–4, E6–5, and E6–9.

THE
NAVIGATOR

SPECIAL JOURNALS

So far you have learned to journalize transactions in a two-column general journal and post these entries individually to the general ledger. This procedure is satisfactory in only the very smallest companies. To expedite journalizing and posting transactions, most companies use special journals **in addition to the general journal**.

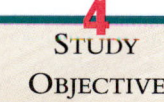

4
STUDY

OBJECTIVE

Explain how special journals are used in journalizing.

A **special journal** is used to record similar types of transactions, such as all sales of merchandise on account, or all cash receipts. The types of special journals used depend largely on the types of transactions that occur frequently in a business enterprise. Most merchandising enterprises use the journals shown in Illustration 6-6 to record transactions daily:

ILLUSTRATION 6-6

Use of special journals and the general journal

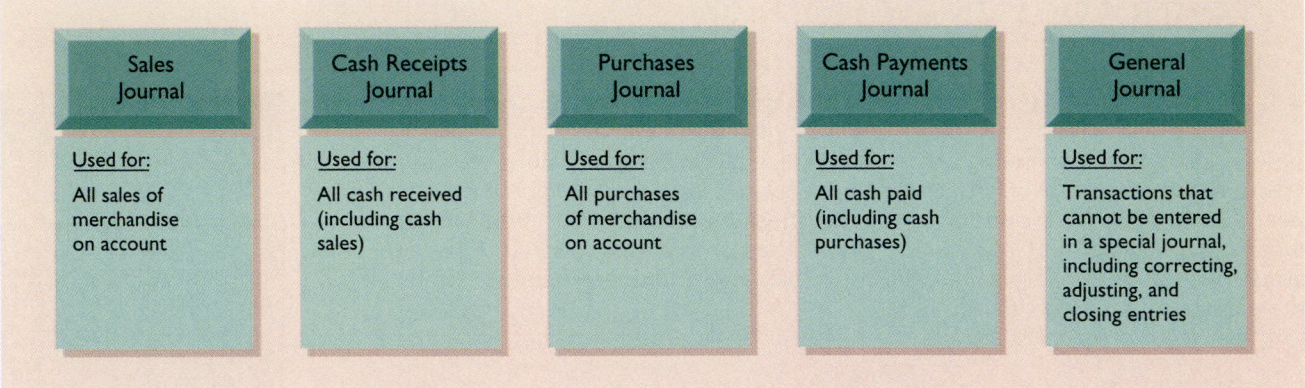

If a transaction cannot be recorded in a special journal, it is recorded in the general journal. For example, if you had special journals only for the four types of transactions listed above, purchase returns and allowances or sales returns and allowances would be recorded in the general journal. Similarly, **correcting, adjusting, and closing entries are recorded in the general journal**. Other types of special journals may be used in some situations. For example, when purchase returns and allowances or sales returns and allowances are frequent, special journals may be used to record these transactions.

Special journals **permit greater division of labor** because several individuals can record entries in different journals at the same time. For example, one employee may be responsible for journalizing all cash receipts, and another for journalizing credit sales. In addition, the use of special journals **reduces the time necessary to complete the posting process**. When special journals are used, monthly postings to some accounts may be substituted for daily postings, as will be illustrated later in the chapter.

Sales Journal

The **sales journal** is used to record sales of merchandise on account. Cash sales of merchandise are entered in the cash receipts journal. Credit sales of assets other than merchandise are entered in the general journal.

Journalizing Credit Sales

Karns Wholesale Supply uses a **perpetual inventory** system. Under a perpetual inventory system, each entry in the sales journal results in one entry **at selling price**—a debit to Accounts Receivable (a control account) and a credit of equal amount to Sales—and another entry **at cost**—a debit to Cost of Goods Sold and a credit of equal amount to Merchandise Inventory (a control account). A sales journal with two amount columns can accommodate a sales transaction recognizing both selling price and cost using only one line. Assuming that Karns Wholesale Supply has the following credit sales transactions (per sales invoices 101–107), its two-column sales journal is shown in Illustration 6-7.

HELPFUL HINT
Postings are also made daily to individual ledger accounts in the inventory subsidiary ledger to maintain a perpetual inventory.

ILLUSTRATION 6-7

Journalizing the sales journal—perpetual inventory system

Karns Wholesale Supply
SALES JOURNAL   S1

Date	Account Debited	Invoice No.	Ref.	Accts. Receivable Dr. Sales Cr.	Cost of Goods Sold Dr. Merchandise Inventory Cr.
1999					
May 3	Abbot Sisters	101		10,600	6,360
7	Babson Co.	102		11,350	7,370
14	Carson Bros.	103		7,800	5,070
19	Deli Co.	104		9,300	6,510
21	Abbot Sisters	105		15,400	10,780
24	Deli Co.	106		21,210	15,900
27	Babson Co.	107		14,570	10,200
				90,230	62,190

The reference (Ref.) column is not used in journalizing. It is used in posting the sales journal, as explained in the next section. Also, note that, unlike the general journal, an explanation is not required for each entry in a special journal. Finally, note that each invoice is prenumbered to ensure that all invoices are journalized.

Posting the Sales Journal

Postings from the sales journal are made **daily to the individual accounts receivable** in the subsidiary ledger and **monthly to the general ledger**, as shown in Illustration 6-8.

A check mark (√) is inserted in the reference posting column to indicate that the daily posting to the customer's account has been made. A check mark (√) is used in this illustration because the subsidiary ledger accounts are not numbered. At the end of the month, the column totals of the sales journal are posted to the general ledger—as a debit of $90,230 to Accounts Receivable (account No. 4), a credit of $90,230 to Sales (account No. 60), a debit of $62,190 to Cost of Goods Sold (account No. 75), and a credit of $62,190 to Merchandise Inventory (account No. 6). The insertion of the respective account numbers below the column total indicates that the postings have been made. In both the general ledger and subsidiary ledger accounts, the reference **S1** indicates that the posting came from page 1 of the sales journal.

Proving the Ledgers

To prove the ledgers it is necessary to determine that (1) the total of the general ledger debit balances equals the total of the general ledger credit balances and (2) the sum of the subsidiary ledger balances equals the balance in the control accounts. The proof of the postings from the sales journal to the general ledger and the accounts receivable subsidiary ledger is shown in Illustration 6-9.

Advantages of the Sales Journal

The use of a special journal to record sales on account has a number of advantages. First, the one-line entry for each sales transaction **saves time**, because it is not necessary to write out the four account titles for each transaction. Second, only totals, rather than individual entries, are posted to the general ledger, thus **saving posting time and reducing the possibilities of errors in posting**. Finally,

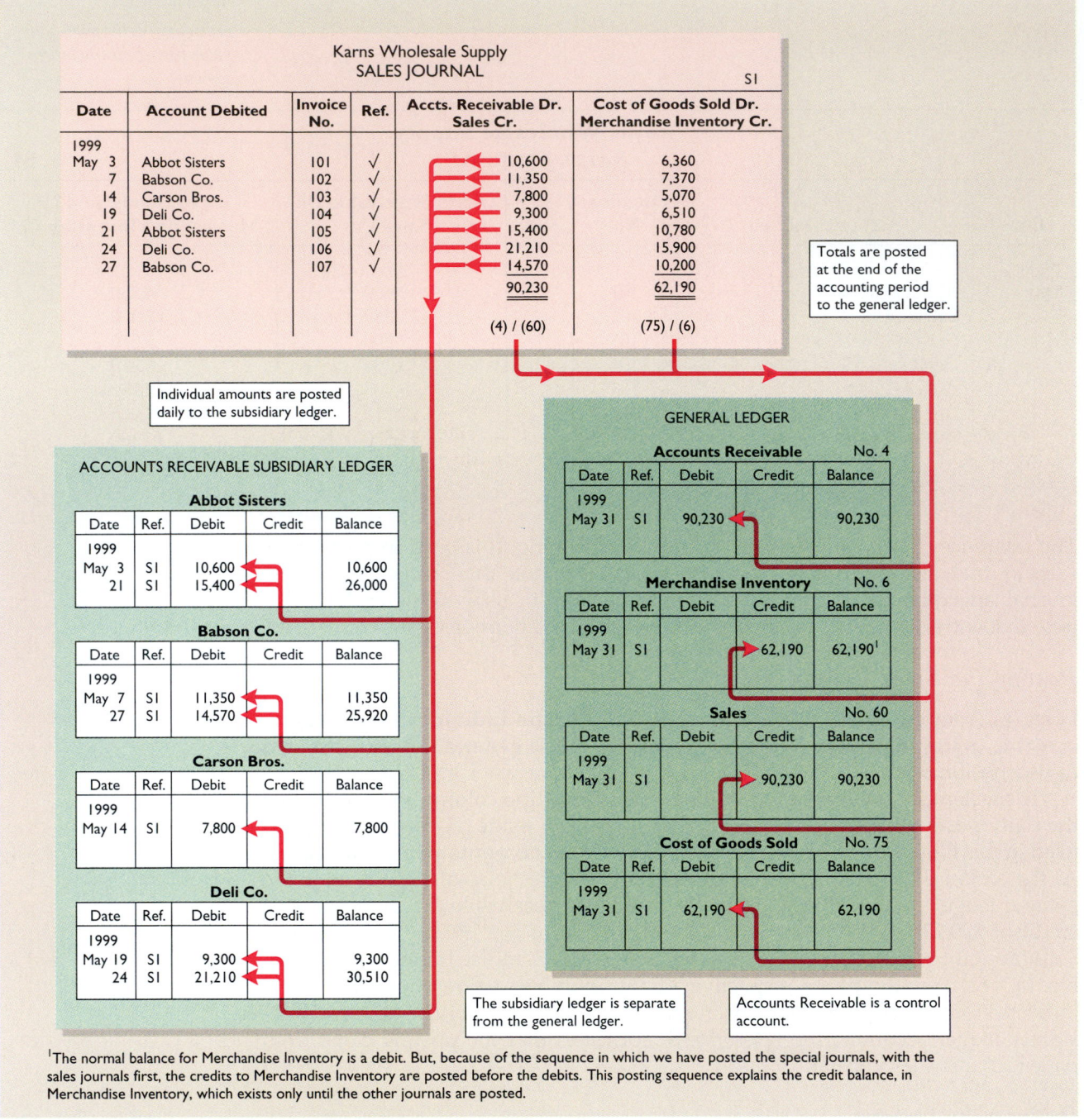

¹The normal balance for Merchandise Inventory is a debit. But, because of the sequence in which we have posted the special journals, with the sales journals first, the credits to Merchandise Inventory are posted before the debits. This posting sequence explains the credit balance, in Merchandise Inventory, which exists only until the other journals are posted.

ILLUSTRATION 6-8

Posting the sales journal

a division of labor results, because one individual can take responsibility for the sales journal.

Cash Receipts Journal

All receipts of cash are recorded in the **cash receipts journal**. The most common types of cash receipts are cash sales of merchandise and collections of accounts receivable. Many other possibilities exist, however, such as receipt of money from bank loans and cash proceeds from disposals of equipment, buildings, or land. A one- or two-column cash receipts journal is not sufficient to accommodate all possible cash receipt transactions. Therefore, a multiple-column cash receipts journal is used.

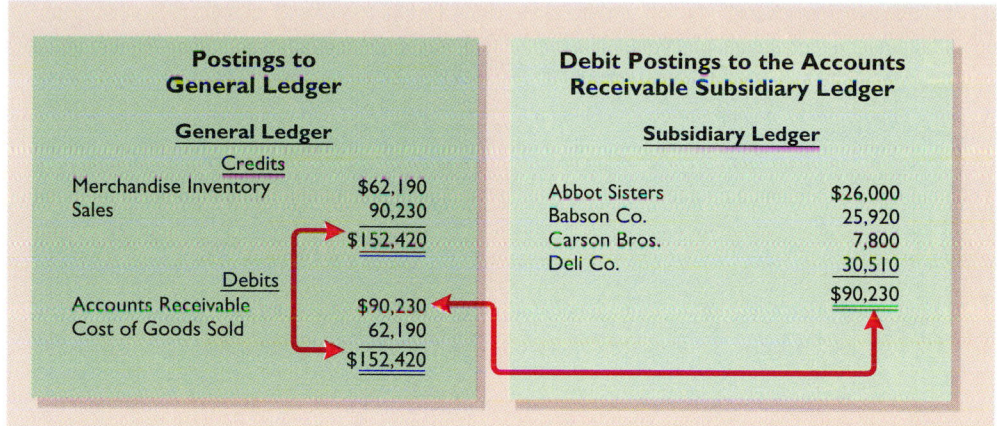

Generally, a cash receipts journal includes debit columns for cash and sales discounts and credit columns for accounts receivable, sales, and "other" accounts. The other accounts category is used when the cash receipt does not involve a cash sale or a collection of accounts receivable. Under a perpetual inventory system, each sales entry is accompanied by another entry that debits Cost of Goods Sold and credits Merchandise Inventory for the cost of the merchandise sold. This entry may be recorded separately. A six-column cash receipts journal that accommodates both entries is shown in Illustration 6-10. When a special journal has more than one account column it is referred to as a **columnar journal**.

Additional credit columns may be used if they significantly reduce postings to a specific account. For example, the cash receipts of a loan company, such as Household International, include thousands of collections from customers. These collections are credited to Loans Receivable and Interest Revenue. A significant saving in posting would result from using separate credit columns for Loans Receivable and Interest Revenue, rather than using the other accounts credit column for these amounts. In contrast, a retailer that has only one interest collection a month would not find it useful to have a separate column for interest revenue.

Journalizing Cash Receipts Transactions

To illustrate the journalizing of cash receipts transactions, we will continue with the transactions of Karns Wholesale Supply during the month of May. Collections from customers relate to the entries recorded in the sales journal in Illustration 6-7. The entries in the cash receipts journal are based on the following cash receipts transactions:

May 1   D. A. Karns makes an investment of $5,000 in the business.
    7   Cash sales of merchandise total $1,900 (cost, $1,240).
  10   A check for $10,388 is received from Abbot Sisters in payment of invoice No. 101 for $10,600 less a 2% discount.
  12   Cash sales of merchandise total $2,600 (cost, $1,690).
  17   A check for $11,123 is received from Babson Co. in payment of invoice No. 102 for $11,350 less a 2% discount.
  22   Cash is received by signing a note for $6,000.
  23   A check for $7,644 is received from Carson Bros. in full for invoice No. 103 for $7,800 less a 2% discount.
  28   A check for $9,114 is received from Deli Co. in full for invoice No. 104 for $9,300 less a 2% discount.

Further information about the columns in the cash receipts journal (see Illustration 6-10) is as follows:

ILLUSTRATION 6-10

Journalizing and posting the cash receipts journal

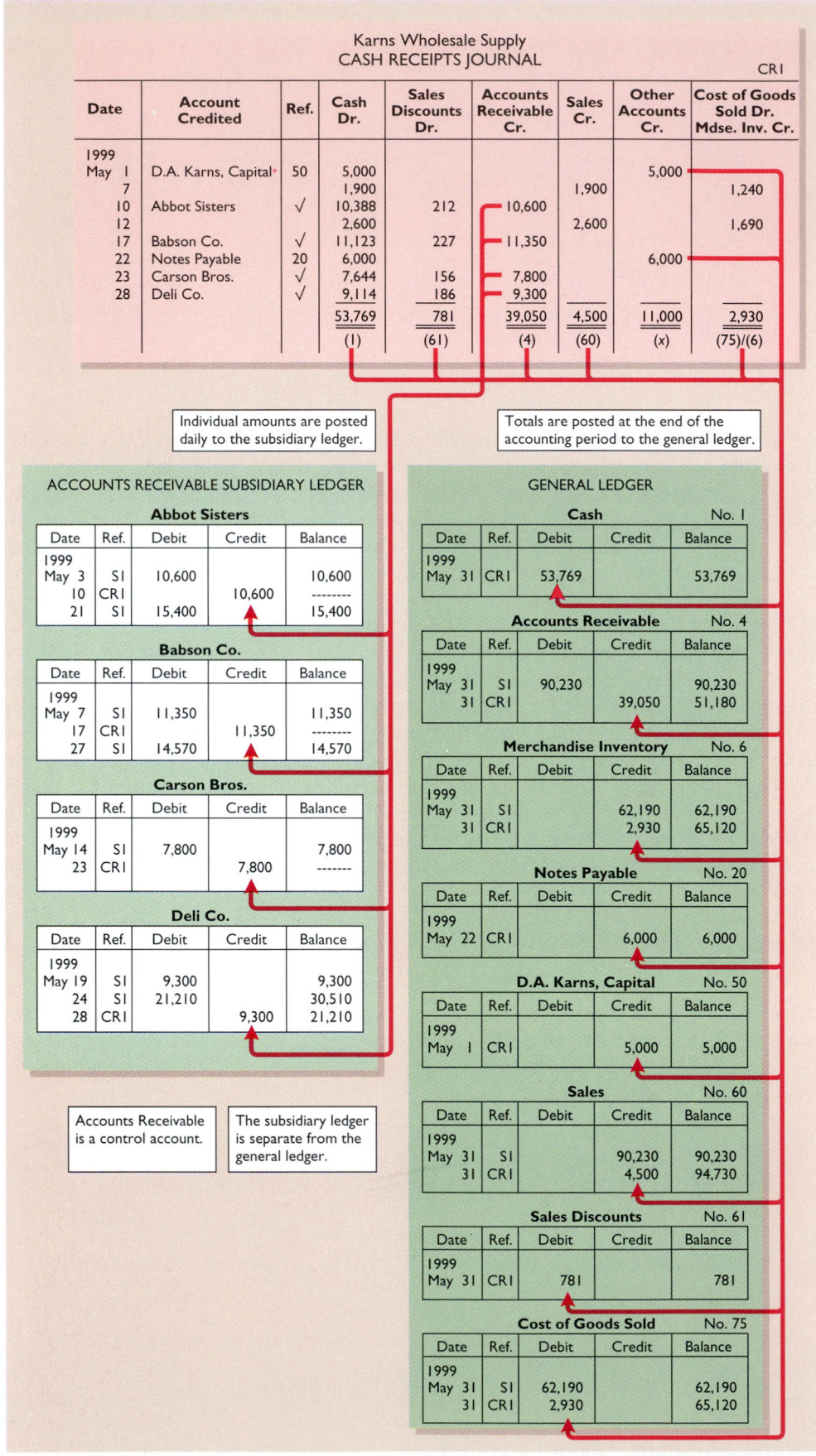

Debit Columns:

1. **Cash.** The amount of cash actually received in each transaction is entered in this column; the column total indicates the total cash receipts for the month.
2. **Sales Discounts.** The Sales Discounts column is included so that it is not necessary to enter sales discount items in the general journal. As a result, the collection of an account receivable within the discount period is expressed on one line in the appropriate columns of the cash receipts journal.

Credit Columns:

3. **Accounts Receivable.** The Accounts Receivable column is used to record cash collections on account. The amount entered in this column is the amount to be credited to the individual customer's account.
4. **Sales.** The Sales column records all cash sales of merchandise. Cash sales of plant assets, for example, are not reported in this column.
5. **Other Accounts.** The Other Accounts column, often referred to as the **sundry accounts column**, is used whenever the credit is other than to Accounts Receivable or Sales. For example, in the first entry, $5,000 is entered as a credit to D. A. Karns, Capital.

Debit and Credit Column:

6. **Cost of Goods Sold and Merchandise Inventory.** This column records debits to Cost of Goods Sold and credits to Merchandise Inventory.

In a columnar journal, as in a single-column journal, generally only one line is needed for each entry. There must be equal debit and credit amounts for each line. When the collection from Abbot Sisters on May 10 is journalized, for example, three amounts are indicated. Note also that the Account Credited column is used to identify both general ledger and subsidiary ledger account titles. The former is illustrated in the May 1 entry for Karns's investment; the latter is illustrated in the May 10 entry for the collection in full from Abbot Sisters.

When the journalizing of a columnar journal has been completed, the amount columns are totaled, and the totals are balanced to prove the equality of debits and credits. The proof of the equality of Karns's cash receipts journal is as follows:

HELPFUL HINT
When is an account title entered in the "Account Credited" column of the cash receipts journal? Answer: A *subsidiary ledger* title is entered there whenever the entry involves a collection of accounts receivable. A *general ledger* account title is entered there whenever the entry involves an account that is not the subject of a special column (and an amount must be entered in the "Other Accounts" column). No account title is entered there if neither of the foregoing applies.

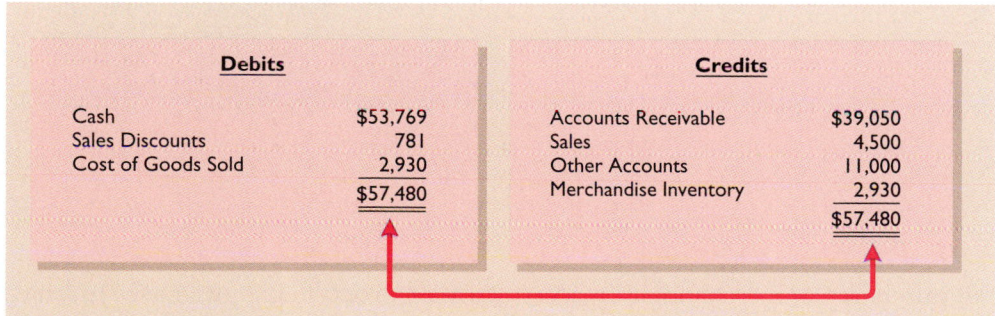

Debits		Credits	
Cash	$53,769	Accounts Receivable	$39,050
Sales Discounts	781	Sales	4,500
Cost of Goods Sold	2,930	Other Accounts	11,000
	$57,480	Merchandise Inventory	2,930
			$57,480

ILLUSTRATION 6-11

Proving the equality of the cash receipts journal

Totaling the columns of a journal and proving the equality of the totals is called **footing** and **cross-footing** a journal.

Posting the Cash Receipts Journal

Posting a columnar journal involves the following procedures.

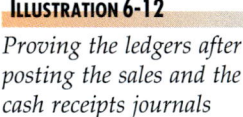

1. All column totals except the total for the Other Accounts column are posted **once at the end of the month** to the account title or titles specified in the column heading, such as Cash or Accounts Receivable. Account numbers are entered below the column totals to show that they have been posted.

2. The total of the Other Accounts column is not posted. Instead, the **individual amounts comprising the total are posted separately** to the general ledger accounts specified in the Accounts Credited column. See, for example, the credit posting to D. A. Karns, Capital. The symbol (X) is inserted below the total to this column to indicate that the amount has not been posted.

3. The individual amounts in a column, posted in total to a control account (Accounts Receivable, in this case), are posted **daily to the subsidiary ledger** account specified in the Account Credited column. See, for example, the credit posting of $10,600 to Abbot Sisters.

Therefore, cash is posted to account No. 1, accounts receivable to account No. 4, merchandise inventory to account No. 6, sales to account No. 60, sales discounts to account No. 61, and cost of goods sold to account No. 75. The symbol **CR** is used in the ledgers to identify postings from the cash receipts journal.

Proving the Ledgers

After the posting of the cash receipts journal is completed, it is necessary to prove the ledgers. As shown in Illustration 6-12, the general ledger totals are in agreement and the sum of the subsidiary ledger balances equals the control account balance.

ILLUSTRATION 6-12

Proving the ledgers after posting the sales and the cash receipts journals

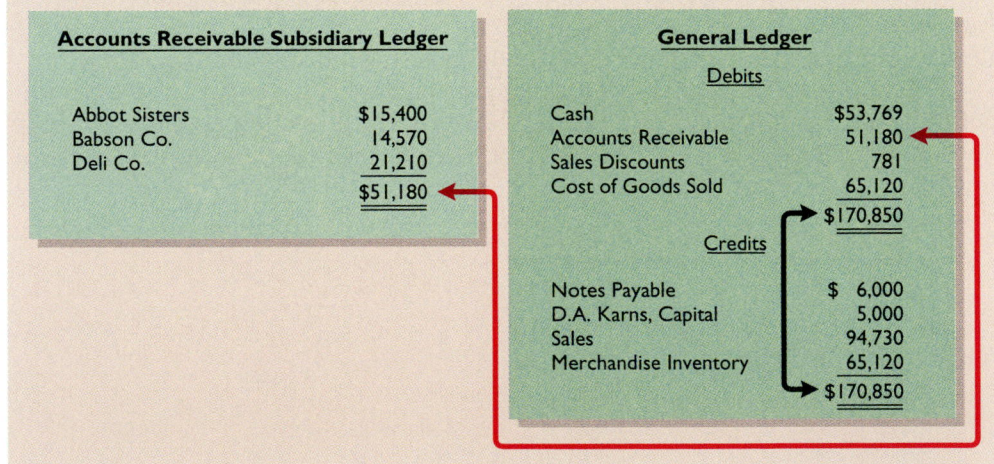

Purchases Journal

All purchases of merchandise on account are recorded in the **purchases journal**. Each entry in this journal results in a debit to Merchandise Inventory and a credit to Accounts Payable. When a one-column purchases journal is used, other types of purchases on account and cash purchases cannot be journalized in it. For example, credit purchases of equipment or supplies must be recorded in the general journal, and all cash purchases are entered in the cash payments journal. As illustrated later, where credit purchases for items other than merchandise are numerous, the purchases journal is often expanded to a multi-column format. The single-column purchases journal for Karns Wholesale Supply is shown in Illustration 6-13.

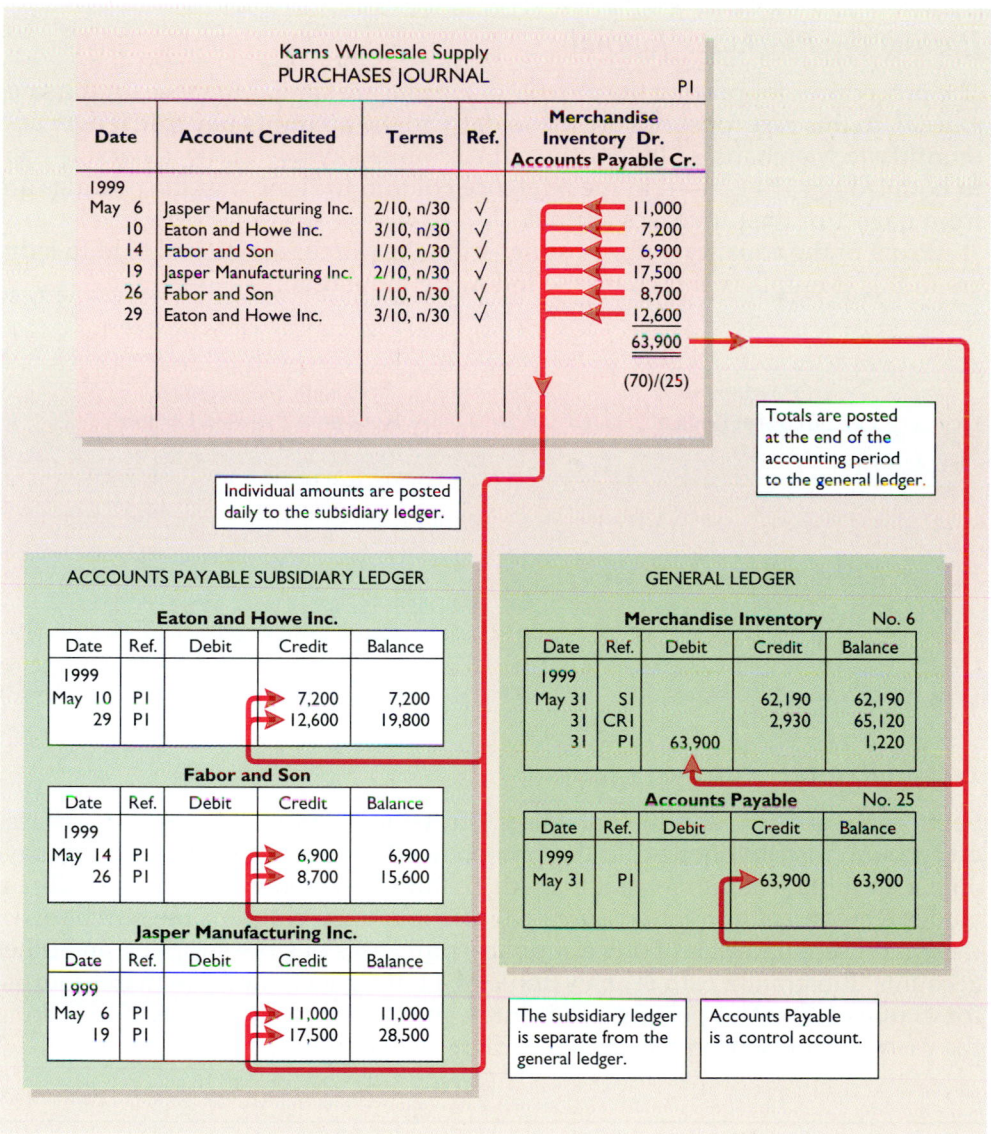

ILLUSTRATION 6-13

Journalizing and posting the purchases journal

Journalizing Credit Purchases of Merchandise

Entries in the purchases journal are made from purchase invoices. The journalizing procedure is similar to the procedures for a single-column sales journal. In contrast to the sales journal, the purchases journal may not have an invoice number column, because invoices received from different suppliers will not be in numerical sequence. To assure that all purchase invoices are recorded, however, some companies consecutively number each invoice upon receipt and then provide for an internal document number column in the purchases journal.

The entries for Karns Wholesale Supply are based on the following assumed purchases on credit transactions:

ILLUSTRATION 6-14

*Credit purchases trans-
actions*

Date	Supplier	Amount	Date	Supplier	Amount
5/6	Jasper Manufacturing Inc.	$11,000	5/19	Jasper Manufacturing Inc.	$17,500
5/10	Eaton and Howe, Inc.	7,200	5/26	Fabor and Son	8,700
5/14	Fabor and Son	6,900	5/29	Eaton and Howe, Inc.	12,600

Posting the Purchases Journal

HELPFUL HINT

Postings to subsidiary ledger accounts are done daily because it is often necessary to know a current balance for the subsidiary accounts.

The procedures for posting the purchases journal are similar to those for the sales journal. In this case, postings are made **daily** to the **accounts payable ledger** and **monthly** to Merchandise Inventory and Accounts Payable in the general ledger. In both ledgers, P1 is used in the reference column to show that the postings are from page 1 of the purchases journal.

Proof of the equality of the postings from the purchases journal to both ledgers in this example is shown by the following tabulation:

ILLUSTRATION 6-15

Proving the equality of the purchases journal

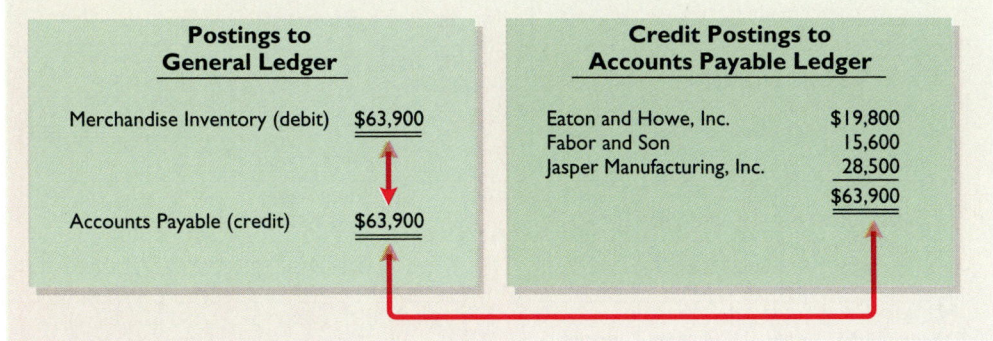

Expanding the Purchases Journal

HELPFUL HINT

A multiple-column purchases journal must be footed and cross-footed to prove the equality of debits and credits.

Some companies expand the purchases journal to include all types of purchases on account. Instead of one column for merchandise inventory and accounts payable, a multiple-column format is used. The multiple-column format usually includes a credit column for accounts payable and debit columns for purchases of merchandise, purchases of office supplies, purchases of store supplies, and other accounts. Illustration 6-16 is an example of a multiple-column purchases journal for Hanover Co. The posting procedures are similar to those used for posting the cash receipts journal illustrated earlier.

ILLUSTRATION 6-16

Columnar purchases journal

Hanover Co.
PURCHASES JOURNAL
P1

Date	Account Credited	Ref.	Accounts Payable Cr.	Merchandise Inventory Dr.	Office Supplies Dr.	Store Supplies Dr.	Other Accounts Dr. Account	Other Accounts Dr. Ref.	Other Accounts Dr. Amount
1999									
June 1	Signe Audio	✓	2,000		2,000				
3	Wright Co.	✓	1,500	1,500					
5	Orange Tree Co.	✓	2,600				Equipment	18	2,600
30	Sue's Business Forms	✓	800			800			
			56,600	43,000	7,500	1,200			4,900

Cash Payments Journal

All disbursements of cash are entered in a **cash payments journal**. Entries in this journal are made from prenumbered checks. Because cash payments may be made for a variety of purposes, the cash payments journal has multiple columns. A four-column journal is shown in Illustration 6-17.

ALTERNATIVE TERMINOLOGY

The cash payments journal is sometimes called the *cash disbursements journal.*

ILLUSTRATION 6-17

Journalizing and posting the cash payments journal

Karns Wholesale Supply
CASH PAYMENTS JOURNAL   CP1

Date	Ck. No.	Account Debited	Ref.	Other Accounts Dr.	Accounts Payable Dr.	Merchandise Inventory Cr.	Cash Cr.
1999							
May 1	101	Prepaid Insurance	10	1,200			1,200
3	102	Mdse. Inventory	6	100			100
8	103	Mdse. Inventory	6	4,400			4,400
10	104	Jasper Manuf. Inc.	✓		11,000	220	10,780
19	105	Eaton & Howe Inc.	✓		7,200	216	6,984
23	106	Fabor and Son	✓		6,900	69	6,831
28	107	Jasper Manuf. Inc.	✓		17,500	350	17,150
30	108	D.A. Karns, Drawing	51	500			500
				6,200	42,600	855	47,945
				(x)	(25)	(6)	(1)

Individual amounts are posted daily to the subsidiary ledger.

Totals are posted at the end of the accounting period to the general ledger.

ACCOUNTS PAYABLE SUBSIDIARY LEDGER

Eaton and Howe Inc.

Date	Ref.	Debit	Credit	Balance
1999				
May 10	P1		7,200	7,200
19	CP1	7,200		-------
29	P1		12,600	12,600

Fabor and Son

Date	Ref.	Debit	Credit	Balance
1999				
May 14	P1		6,900	6,900
23	CP1	6,900		-------
26	P1		8,700	8,700

Jasper Manufacturing Inc.

Date	Ref.	Debit	Credit	Balance
1999				
May 6	P1		11,000	11,000
10	CP1	11,000		-------
19	P1		17,500	17,500
28	CP1	17,500		-------

Accounts Payable is a control account.

The subsidiary ledger is separate from the general ledger.

GENERAL LEDGER

Cash   No. 1

Date	Ref.	Debit	Credit	Balance
1999				
May 31	CR1	53,769		53,769
31	CP1		47,945	5,824

Accounts Payable   No. 25

Date	Ref.	Debit	Credit	Balance
1999				
May 31	P1		63,900	63,900
31	CP1	42,600		21,300

Prepaid Insurance   No. 10

Date	Ref.	Debit	Credit	Balance
1999				
May 1	CP1	1,200		1,200

D.A. Karns, Drawing   No. 51

Date	Ref.	Debit	Credit	Balance
1999				
May 30	CP1	500		500

Merchandise Inventory   No. 6

Date	Ref.	Debit	Credit	Balance
1999				
May 3	CP1	100		100
8	CP1	4,400		4,500
31	S1		62,190	57,690
31	CR1		2,930	60,620
31	P	63,900		3,280
31	CP1		855	2,425

Journalizing Cash Payments Transactions

The procedures for journalizing transactions in this journal are similar to those described earlier for journalizing transactions in the cash receipts journal. For example, each transaction is entered on one line, and for each line there must be equal debit and credit amounts. The entries in the cash payments journal shown in Illustration 6-17 are based on the following transactions for Karns Wholesale Supply:

May 1 Check No. 101 for $1,200 issued for the annual premium on a fire insurance policy.
3 Check No. 102 for $100 issued in payment of freight when terms were FOB shipping point.
8 Check No. 103 for $4,400 issued for the purchase of merchandise.
10 Check No. 104 for $10,780 sent to Jasper Manufacturing Inc. in payment of May 6 invoice for $11,000 less a 2% discount.
19 Check No. 105 for $6,984 mailed to Eaton and Howe, Inc. in payment of May 10 invoice for $7,200 less a 3% discount.
23 Check No. 106 for $6,831 sent to Fabor and Son in payment of May 14 invoice for $6,900 less a 1% discount.
28 Check No. 107 for $17,150 sent to Jasper Manufacturing Inc. in payment of May 19 invoice for $17,500 less a 2% discount.
30 Check No. 108 for $500 issued to D. A. Karns as a cash withdrawal for personal use.

Note that whenever an amount is entered in the Other Accounts column, a specific general ledger account must be identified in the Accounts Debited column. The entries for check Nos. 101, 102, and 103 illustrate this situation. Similarly, a subsidiary account must be identified in the Account Debited column whenever an amount is entered in the Accounts Payable column, as, for example, the entry for check No. 104.

When the journalizing of the cash payments journal has been completed, the amount columns are totaled. The totals are then balanced to prove the equality of debits and credits.

Posting the Cash Payments Journal

The procedures for posting the cash payments journal are similar to those for posting the cash receipts journal. Specifically, the amounts recorded in the Accounts Payable column are posted individually to the subsidiary ledger and in total to the control account. Merchandise Inventory and Cash are posted only in total at the end of the month. When a transaction is recorded in the Other Accounts column, it is posted individually to the appropriate account(s) affected. No totals are posted for this column.

The posting of the cash payments journal is shown in Illustration 6-17. Note that the symbol **CP** is used as the posting reference for this journal. After postings from the journals are completed, the equality of the debit and credit balances in the general ledger should be determined. In addition, the control account balances should agree with the subsidiary ledger total balance. The agreement of these balances is shown in Illustration 6-18.

Effects of Special Journals on General Journal

Special journals for sales, purchases, and cash substantially reduce the number of entries that are made in the general journal. **Only transactions that cannot be entered in a special journal are recorded in the general journal.** For example,

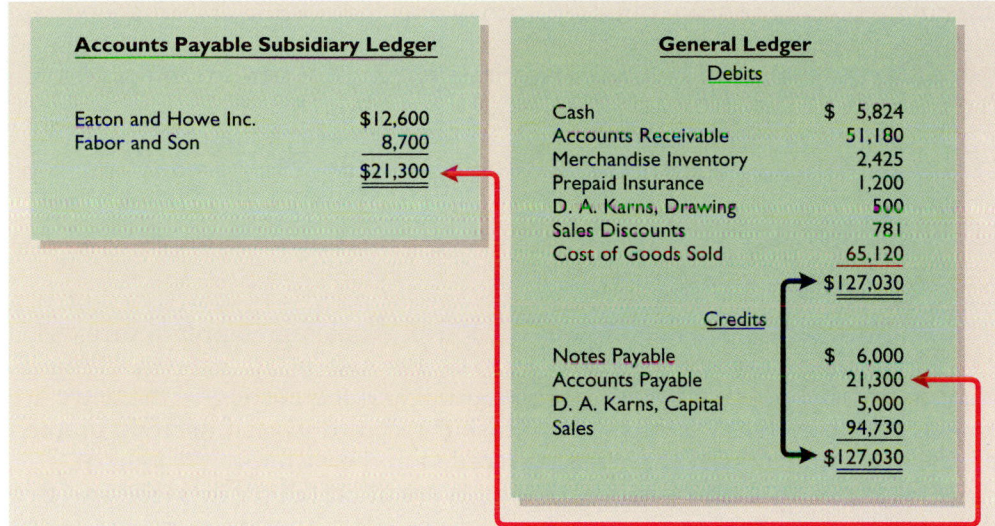

ILLUSTRATION 6-18

Proving the ledgers after postings from the sales, cash receipts, purchases, and cash payments journals

the general journal may be used to record such transactions as granting of credit to a customer for a sales return or allowance, granting of credit from a supplier for purchases returned, acceptance of a note receivable from a customer, and purchase of equipment by issuing a note payable. In addition, correcting, adjusting, and closing entries are made in the general journal.

The general journal has columns for date, account titles and explanation, reference, and debit and credit amounts. When control and subsidiary accounts

ILLUSTRATION 6-19

Journalizing and posting the general journal

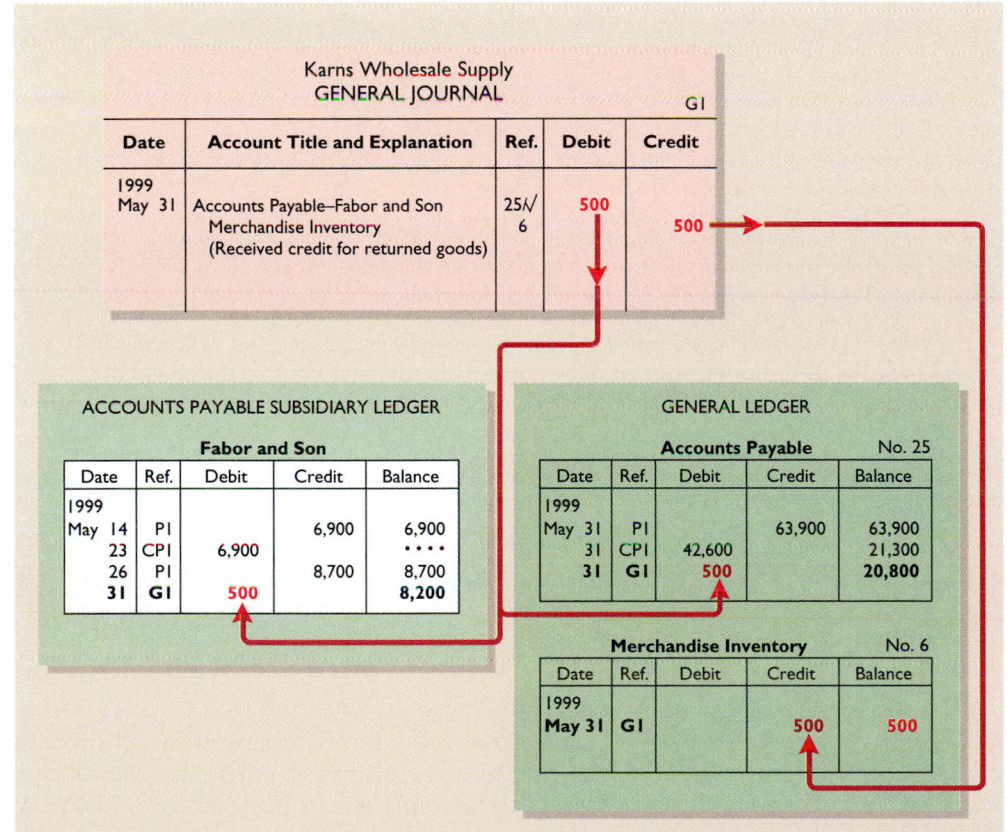

are not involved, the procedures for journalizing and posting of transactions are identical with those described in earlier chapters. However, when control and subsidiary accounts are involved, two modifications of earlier procedures are required:

1. In **journalizing**, both the control and the subsidiary accounts must be identified.
2. In **posting**, there must be a **dual posting**: once to the control account and once to the subsidiary account.

To illustrate, assume that on May 31, Karns Wholesale Supply returns $500 of merchandise for credit to Fabor and Son because of an error in filling its May 26 order. The entry in the general journal and the posting of the entry are shown in Illustration 6-19. Note that if cash is received instead of credit granted on this return, then the transaction is recorded in the cash receipts journal.

Observe in the journal that two accounts are indicated for the debit and two postings are indicated in the reference column. One amount is posted to the control account and the other to the creditor's account in the subsidiary ledger.

BEFORE YOU GO ON . . .

Review It

1. What types of special journals are usually used to record transactions? Why are special journals used?
2. Explain how transactions recorded in the sales journal and the cash receipts journal are posted.
3. Indicate the types of transactions that are recorded in the general journal when special journals are used.

Do It

The Vilas Company has the following selected transactions: (1) purchase of equipment for cash, (2) cash sale, (3) sales returns and allowances, (4) withdrawal of cash for proprietor's personal use, and (5) sale of merchandise on account. Identify the journals in which each transaction should be entered.

Reasoning: It is necessary to know the content of each special journal and the effect of special journals on the general journal. For example, the sales journal contains only sales on account, and the cash payments journal is used for all cash payments.

Solution: (1) Purchase of equipment for cash—cash payments journal. (2) Cash sale—cash receipts journal. (3) Sales return and allowance—general journal. (4) Withdrawal of cash for proprietor's personal use—cash payments journal. (5) Sale of merchandise on account—sales journal.

Related exercise material: BE6–5, BE6–6, E6–1, E6–4, E6–5, E6–6, E6–7, and E6–8.

SECTION 3   ELECTRONIC ACCOUNTING SYSTEMS

An **electronic accounting system** uses computers in processing transaction data and in disseminating accounting information to interested parties. In the following sections, we briefly describe the hardware and accounting software that may be used in such systems, and then we explain and illustrate two common data processing methods.

ACCOUNTING IN ACTION
Business Insight

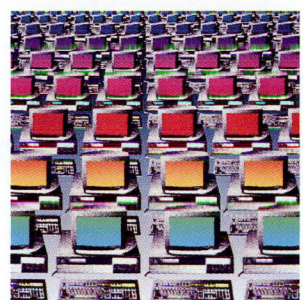

The growth of computers has been phenomenal. The first experimental computers were developed in the 1940s, and primitive computers were used in business in the early 1950s. The first serious business applications for computers were put into use in the mid-1960s. From the time of their invention in the 1940s up to 1980, there were approximately one million computer systems of all kinds. By the middle of the 1990s, it is estimated that *250 million* personal computers (PCs) alone were in use.

COMPUTER HARDWARE

Computers can be divided into three classes, by size: mainframes, minicomputers, and microcomputers. **Mainframes** are large, powerful, very expensive computers that are used by major corporations to process huge volumes of transactions. Mainframes are able to serve many users and perform different processing functions at one time. **Minicomputers** are less powerful and not as expensive as mainframes. They can perform different tasks for several users at a time. The **microcomputer** is commonly referred to as a personal computer (PC). It has speed and power (though generally less than minicomputers), and it is very affordable. In many companies, each employee has his or her own PC.

Computer hardware is the physical equipment associated with a computerized accounting system. The basic hardware configuration consists of the central processing unit (CPU) and peripheral devices. The **central processing unit (CPU)** is composed of three parts:

1. The **control unit**, which directs and coordinates the entire system, including the entry and removal of information from storage.
2. The **internal storage unit**, or computer memory, which stores the program instructions and the data to be processed.
3. The **arithmetic-logic unit**, which performs mathematical computations (addition, subtraction, multiplication, division) and certain logical operations (such as comparisons).

Common types of computer hardware are shown in Illustration 6-20.

6
STUDY
OBJECTIVE
Distinguish between computer hardware and accounting software and the principal methods of data processing.

ILLUSTRATION 6-20

Computer hardware

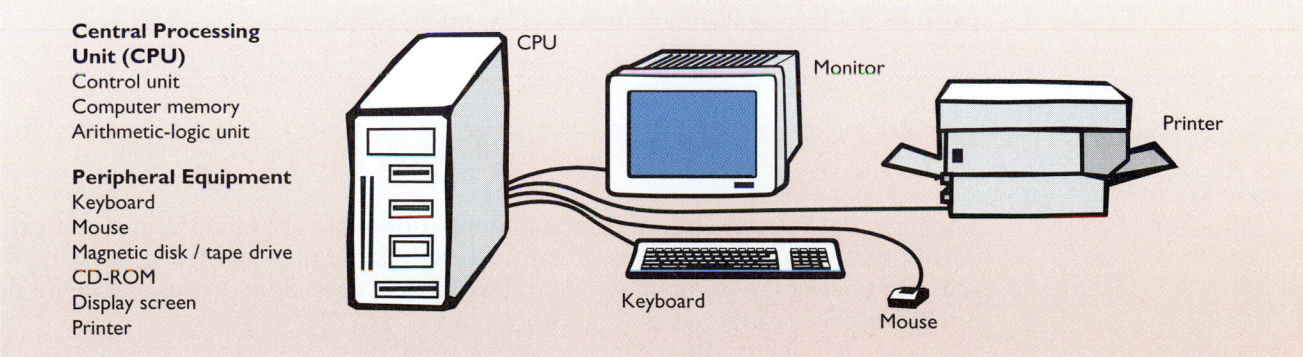

Central Processing Unit (CPU)
Control unit
Computer memory
Arithmetic-logic unit

Peripheral Equipment
Keyboard
Mouse
Magnetic disk / tape drive
CD-ROM
Display screen
Printer

A computer linked with one or more other computers and running with a common software package is called a **network**. A computer network may be as small as two computers in the same dormitory room. In contrast, the Internet is a worldwide network, with a hookup of millions of computers.

ACCOUNTING IN ACTION
Ethics Insight

The Internet is our new frontier—a digital Wild West, with its own forms of lawlessness. By some estimates, roughly $2 billion worth of software was stolen from "the Net" in a recent year. In one year, for example, an international software piracy ring stole 140,000 telephone credit card numbers and sold them to computer hackers who used them to make $140 million worth of long-distance phone calls. As commerce expands on the Internet, such thievery is not likely to stop. Digital socialism rules the Net, not copyright capitalism.

Source: Newsweek, November 14, 1994, pp. 46–47.

ACCOUNTING SOFTWARE

INTERNATIONAL NOTE

It has recently been noted that, in an unusual turning of the tables, some companies in countries such as Brazil that were slow to adopt computer systems early on are often now more advanced than U.S. corporations. The reason: The systems they are buying today are far more sophisticated than many systems that U.S. corporations bought years ago and continue to use.

Accounting software consists of programs that relate to specific parts of the accounting process. For example, there are programs for the general ledger and each subsidiary ledger, and there are programs for performing the steps in the accounting cycle such as journalizing, posting, and preparing a trial balance. In addition, there is software for business functions such as billing customers, preparing the payroll, and budgeting.

Accounting software can be purchased "off the shelf," or it can be custom-made by individual companies and users. For maximum efficiency, related programs are generally used together. For example, a program for paying creditors would be used with programs for journalizing the payments and maintaining both the general ledger and the accounts payable subsidiary ledger. When programs are used together, the company is said to be using **integrated accounting software**.

TECHNOLOGY IN ACTION

For PCs, several leading off-the-shelf accounting software packages are Peachtree's **Complete Accounting**®, Intuit's **Quick Books**®, M-USA's **Pacioli 2000**®, Solomon's **III and IV for Windows**, and DAC Easy's **Accounting and Payroll**®. DAC Easy offers, among other products, accounts receivable, accounts payable, management information, and inventory programs.

DATA PROCESSING METHODS

The term **data processing methods** refers to how data are entered into and processed by a computer. That is, it includes *both* data entry *and* the processing of the data once entered into the system. Two widely used data processing methods are batch processing and on-line processing.

Batch Processing

In **batch processing**, data are accumulated by classes of transactions and are periodically entered into the computer and processed in batches. A batch may include such transaction classes as credit sales, collections on account, or cash payments to creditors.

As shown in Illustration 6-21, transaction data are entered into the computer and coded by batch as they occur. At specified intervals—such as daily or weekly—the coded transactions are sorted (transferred) on computer transaction files that are the equivalent of special journals in a manual system. Next, the transaction files are used to update the master files (the general ledger and subsidiary ledger accounts). This step is similar to posting in a manual system.

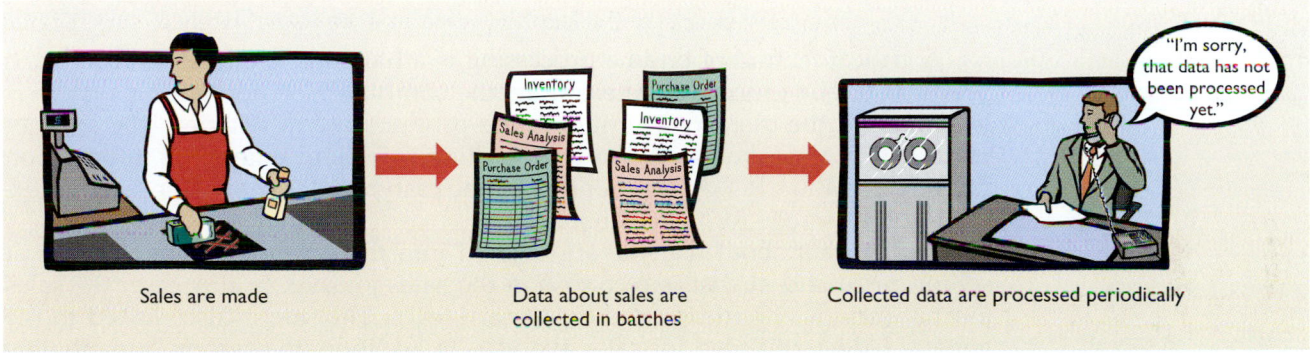

Sales are made   Data about sales are   Collected data are processed periodically
                        collected in batches

ILLUSTRATION 6-21

Batch processing

Batch processing is an efficient method because similar transactions are processed together. The principal disadvantage of batch processing is that files may not always contain up-to-date information. For such files as subsidiary ledgers for accounts receivable and accounts payable, lack of current information could be, at the least, an annoyance.

ACCOUNTING IN ACTION
Business Insight

Under a system called *electronic data interchange (EDI)*, a company's computer can use dial-up communication lines to communicate electronically with other businesses. Recently, EDI was being used in the accounting systems of about 75% of the Fortune 100 companies and 39% of the Fortune 500. For example, computers at over 3,000 suppliers to Chrysler accept purchase orders transmitted by computers from assembly plants, and in turn electronically invoice Chrysler's computers for parts shipped. Wal-Mart, which operates the largest EDI program in the retail industry, processes about 75% of its payments to suppliers using EDI.

On-line Processing

In **on-line processing**, files are updated as data entry takes place. In addition, a transaction log (or tape) is produced that shows a chronological record of all transactions. This processing method is used in airline and hotel reservation systems, among others.

A common accounting application of on-line processing is found in many retail stores, where electronic cash registers are connected directly with the central processing unit of the store's computer. An example of on-line processing in a grocery store is shown in Illustration 6-22.

Data about the sale are scanned
into the cash register/computer.

General and subsidiary ledgers are
updated for sales and inventory.

Reports and other documents
are generated.

ILLUSTRATION 6-22

On-line processing

A critical feature of on-line processing is a **bar code identification** for each product. In our grocery store example, the computerized accounting system is activated by the cashier, who moves the product over a scanner. The scanner reads the product being sold and the selling price and enters the information directly into the CPU. At the same time, the cash register shows the same information on a screen for the customer.[2]

As the data about the sale are entered into the computer, the total sale at selling price and at cost is recorded in the sales journal. In this case, the sales journal includes both cash and credit card sales. The sale is also posted to the general ledger and filed for sales analysis. In addition, the system immediately updates the inventory records. As illustrated, the system can also print out a purchase order when an inventory item reaches a programmed reorder point, and it can generate inventory reports.

TECHNOLOGY IN ACTION

Data processing professionals use the acronym GIGO—garbage-in, garbage-out—to indicate that a computer system is only as good as the data it receives. Data entry is the garbage-in stage of the acronym. Garbage-in is not automated, garbage-out is. The real trick—and the expensive part—of both manual and automated systems (either micros, minis, or mainframes) is to get what we might call DIIO, that is, data-in, information-out.

COMPARING MANUAL AND ELECTRONIC SYSTEMS

7

STUDY

OBJECTIVE

Identify the key points in comparing manual and electronic accounting systems.

Despite the tremendous capabilities of computers, one should not conclude that electronic systems are always better. As with any choice, the costs and benefits of each alternative should be weighed before the choice is made. The following

---

[2]When a product does not have an attached bar code, the cashier must "punch in" the code number and price using the keyboard on the register.

key points should be considered when evaluating and comparing manual and electronic systems.

ILLUSTRATION 6-23
Comparison of manual versus electronic systems

Key Points	Manual Systems	Electronic Systems
Costs	Bookkeepers' salaries. Costs of manual record keeping.	Computer operators' salaries. Costs of computer hardware and software. Usually requires fewer employees than manual systems.
Processing Speed	Fewer delays due to breakdowns or power outages.	Faster.
Errors	People can get fatigued, bored, or can be incompetent, so errors are normal.	Generally more accurate, although errors in data entry or hardware failure may occur.
Report Generation	Reports have to be separately and manually prepared.	Reports can be quickly prepared once data are entered.

BEFORE YOU GO ON . . .

Review It

1. Identify the components of computer hardware.
2. Distinguish between batch and on-line processing.
3. What are the advantages of using a computerized system to record business transactions?

A LOOK BACK AT OUR FEATURE STORY

Refer to the opening story about Fidelity Investments, and answer the following questions:

1. How could a highly sophisticated and computerized firm like Fidelity Investments make an embarrassing $1.3 billion accounting error?
2. What is causing many small businesses to switch to computer bookkeeping systems?
3. Is it likely that in the future some businesses will continue to use manual systems?

Solution:

1. Although Fidelity Investments is highly computerized, some financial information, like the computation of some gains and losses, is generated manually. When people perform such tasks, they occasionally make errors.
2. As discussed in the chapter, more and more small businesses are switching to computerized systems because computers are becoming cheaper, faster, and more reliable, and software is becoming increasingly user-friendly. Furthermore, since a business may have already purchased computers for other parts of its business, it makes sense to employ them for record keeping as well.
3. While the percentage of businesses using manual systems will likely decline, it will probably always make sense for certain businesses to use manual systems. For many start-up businesses, or businesses with few transactions, the advantages of installing a computerized system do not appear to outweigh the costs.

THE NAVIGATOR

DEMONSTRATION PROBLEM

Celine Dion Company uses a six-column cash receipts journal with columns for Cash (Dr.), Sales Discounts (Dr.), Accounts Receivable (Cr.), Sales (Cr.), Other Accounts (Cr.) and Cost of Goods Sold (Dr.) and Merchandise Inventory (Cr.). Cash receipts transactions for the month of July 1999 are as follows:

PROBLEM-SOLVING STRATEGIES

1. All cash receipts are recorded in the cash receipts journal.

2. The "account credited" indicate items posted individually to the subsidiary ledger or general ledger.

3. Cash sales are recorded in the cash receipts journal—not in the sales journal.

4. The total debits must equal the total credits.

July 3 Cash sales total $5,800 (cost, $3,480).

5 A check for $6,370 is received from the Jeltz Company in payment of invoice dated June 26 for $6,500 terms 2/10, n/30.

9 An additional investment of $5,000 in cash is made in the business by Celine Dion, the proprietor.

10 Cash sales total $12,519 (cost, $7,511).

12 A check for $7,275 is received from R. Eliot & Co. in payment of a $7,500 invoice dated July 3, terms 3/10, n/30.

15 A customer advance of $700 cash is received for future sales.

20 Cash sales total $15,472 (cost, $9,283).

22 A check for $5,880 is received from Beck Company in payment of $6,000 invoice dated July 13, terms 2/10, n/30.

29 Cash sales total $17,660 (cost, $10,596).

31 Cash of $200 is received on interest earned for July.

Instructions

(a) Journalize the transactions in the cash receipts journal.

(b) Contrast the posting of the Accounts Receivable and Other Accounts columns.

SOLUTION TO DEMONSTRATION PROBLEM

(a)

Celine Dion Company
CASH RECEIPTS JOURNAL   CR1

Date	Account Credited	Ref.	Cash Dr.	Sales Discounts Dr.	Accounts Receivable Cr.	Sales Cr.	Other Accounts Cr.	Cost of Goods Sold Dr. Mdse. Inv. Cr.
1999								
7/3			5,800			5,800		3,480
5	Jeltz Company		6,370	130	6,500			
9	Celine Dion, Capital		5,000				5,000	
10			12,519			12,519		7,511
12	R. Eliot & Co.		7,275	225	7,500			
15	Unearned Revenues		700				700	
20			15,472			15,472		9,283
22	Beck Company		5,880	120	6,000			
29			17,660			17,660		10,596
31	Interest Revenue		200				200	
			76,876	475	20,000	51,451	5,900	30,870

(b) The Accounts Receivable column is posted as a credit to Accounts Receivable. The individual amounts are credited to the customers' accounts identified in the Account Credited column, which are maintained in the accounts receivable subsidiary ledger.

   The amounts in the Other Accounts Column are only posted individually. They are credited to the account titles identified in the Account Credited column.

SUMMARY OF STUDY OBJECTIVES

1. *Identify the basic principles of accounting information systems.* The basic principles in developing an accounting information system are cost awareness, useful output, and flexibility.

2. *Explain the major phases involved in the development of an accounting system.* The major phases in the development of an accounting system are analysis, design, implementation, and follow-up.

3. *Describe the nature and purpose of a subsidiary ledger.* A subsidiary ledger is a group of accounts with a common characteristic. It facilitates the recording process by freeing the general ledger from details of individual balances.

4. *Explain how special journals are used in journalizing.* A special journal is used to group similar types of transactions. In a special journal, generally only one line is used to record a complete transaction.

5. *Indicate how a columnar journal is posted.* In posting a columnar journal:
(a) all column totals except for the Other Accounts column are posted once at the end of the month to the account title specified in the column heading.

(b) the total of the Other Accounts column is not posted. Instead, the individual amounts comprising the total are posted separately to the general ledger accounts specified in the Account Credited column.

(c) the individual amounts in a column posted in total to a control account are posted daily to the subsidiary ledger accounts specified in the Account Credited column.

6. *Distinguish between computer hardware and accounting software and the principal methods of data processing.* Computer hardware is the physical equipment associated with a computerized accounting system. Accounting software consists of programs that relate to specific parts of the accounting process. The principal methods of data processing are batch processing and on-line processing.

7. *Identify the key points in comparing manual and electronic accounting systems.* The key points in comparing manual and electronic accounting systems are (a) dollar costs, (b) processing speed, (c) processing errors, and (d) report generation.

GLOSSARY

Accounting information system A system that involves collecting and processing transaction data, and disseminating financial information to interested parties. (p. 232).

Accounting software Programs that relate to specific parts of the accounting process. (p. 252).

Accounts payable (creditors') ledger A subsidiary ledger that contains accounts with individual creditors. (p. 235).

Accounts receivable (customers') ledger A subsidiary ledger that contains individual customer accounts. (p. 235).

Batch processing A method in which data are accumulated by classes of transactions and are entered into the computer and processed in batches. (p. 253).

Cash payments journal A special journal used to record all cash paid. (p. 247).

Cash receipts journal A special journal used to record all cash received. (p. 240).

Columnar journal A special journal with more than one column. (p. 241).

Computer hardware The physical equipment associated with an electronic accounting system. (p. 251).

Control account An account in the general ledger that controls a subsidiary ledger. (p. 235).

Electronic accounting system A system that uses computers in processing transaction data and in disseminating accounting information to interested parties. (p. 250).

Manual accounting system A system in which each of the steps in the accounting cycle is performed by hand. (p. 234).

On-line processing A method in which files are updated concurrently with data entry. (p. 253).

Purchases journal A special journal used to record all purchases of merchandise on account. (p. 244).

Sales journal A special journal used to record all sales of merchandise on account. (p. 238).

Special journal A journal that is used to record similar types of transactions such as all credit sales. (p. 238).

Subsidiary ledger A group of accounts with a common characteristic. (p. 235).

SELF-STUDY QUESTIONS

Answers are at the end of the chapter.

(SO 1) 1. The basic principles of an accounting information system include all of the following *except:*
   a. cost awareness.
   b. flexibility.
   c. useful output.
   d. periodicity.

(SO 2) 2. Which of the following is *not* a major phase in the development of an accounting information system?
   a. Design.
   b. Responsiveness.
   c. Implementation.
   d. Follow-up.

(SO 3) 3. Which of the following is *incorrect* concerning subsidiary ledgers?
   a. The purchases ledger is a common subsidiary ledger for creditor accounts.
   b. The accounts receivable ledger is a subsidiary ledger.
   c. A subsidiary ledger is a group of accounts with a common characteristic.
   d. An advantage of the subsidiary ledger is that it permits a division of labor in posting.

(SO 4) 4. A sales journal will be used for:

	Credit Sales	Cash Sales	Sales Discounts
a.	no	yes	yes
b.	yes	no	yes
c.	yes	no	no
d.	yes	yes	no

(SO 5) 5. Which of the following statements is correct?
   a. The sales discount column is included in the cash receipts journal.
   b. The purchases journal records all purchases of merchandise whether for cash or on account.
   c. The cash receipts journal records sales on account.
   d. Merchandise returned by the buyer is recorded by the seller in the purchases journal.

(SO 5) 6. Which of the following is *incorrect* concerning the posting of the cash receipts journal?
   a. The total of the Other Accounts column is not posted.
   b. All column totals except the total for the Other Accounts column are posted once at the end of the month to the account title(s) specified in the column heading.
   c. The total of all columns are posted daily to the accounts specified in the column heading.
   d. The individual amounts in a column posted in total to a control account are posted daily to the subsidiary ledger account specified in the Accounts Credited column.

(SO 5) 7. Postings from the purchases journal to the subsidiary ledger are generally made:
   a. yearly.
   b. monthly.
   c. weekly.
   d. daily.

(SO 4) 8. Which statement is *incorrect* regarding the general journal?
   a. Only transactions that cannot be entered in a special journal are recorded in the general journal.
   b. Dual postings are always required in the general journal.
   c. The general journal may be used to record acceptance of a note receivable for an accounts receivable.
   d. Correcting, adjusting, and closing entries are made in the general journal.

(SO 6) 9. Computer hardware consists of the:
   a. central processing unit.
   b. accounting software.
   c. peripheral equipment.
   d. Both (a) and (c).

(SO 7) 10. Which of the following is *not* a key point in evaluating and comparing manual and electronic systems?
   a. Cost considerations and processing speed.
   b. Processing errors and responsiveness.
   c. Posting general journals and special journals.
   d. Report generation.

THE NAVIGATOR

QUESTIONS

1. (a) What is an accounting information system? (b) "An accounting information system applies only to a manual system." Do you agree? Explain.

2. Certain principles should be followed in the development of an accounting information system. Identify and explain each of the principles.

3. Chandler Company is considering changing its accounting system for its accounts receivable billing procedure. At present, the procedure is performed manually by three clerks. A consultant has recommended that a new computer and related software be purchased for $1,000,000. What basic principle of designing and developing an effective accounting system might be violated by this proposal?

4. There are four phases in the life cycle of an accounting system. Identify and briefly explain each phase.

5. What are the advantages of using subsidiary ledgers?

6. (a) When are postings normally made to (1) the subsidiary accounts and (2) the general ledger control accounts? (b) Describe the relationship between a control account and a subsidiary ledger.

7. Identify and explain the four specific journals discussed in the chapter. List an advantage of using each of these journals rather than using only a general journal.

8. Oliva Company uses special journals. A sale made on account to C. Morton for $435 was recorded in a single-column sales journal. A few days later, Morton returns $70 worth of merchandise for credit. Where should Oliva Company record the sales return? Why?

9. A $500 purchase of merchandise on account from Monico Company was properly recorded in the purchases journal. When posted, however, the amount recorded in the subsidiary ledger was $50. How might this error be discovered?

10. Why would special journals used in different businesses not be identical in format? Can you think of a business that would maintain a cash receipts journal but not include a column for accounts receivable?

11. The cash and the accounts receivable columns in the cash receipts journal were mistakenly overadded by $4,000 at the end of the month. (a) Will the customers' ledger agree with the Accounts Receivable control account? (b) Assuming no other errors, will the trial balance totals be equal?

12. One column total of a special journal is posted at month end to only two general ledger accounts. One of these two accounts is Accounts Receivable. What is the name of this special journal? What is the other general ledger account to which that same month-end total is posted?

13. In what journal would the following transactions be recorded? (Assume that a two-column sales journal and a single-column purchases journal are used.)

(a) Recording of depreciation expense for the year.
(b) Gave credit to a customer for merchandise purchased on credit and returned.
(c) Sales of merchandise for cash.
(d) Sales of merchandise on account.
(e) Collection of cash on account from a customer.
(f) Purchase of office supplies on account.

14. In what journal would the following transactions be recorded? (Assume that a two-column sales journal and a single-column purchases journal are used.)

(a) Cash received from signing a note payable.
(b) Investment of cash by the owner of the business.
(c) Closing of the expense accounts at the end of the year.
(d) Purchase of merchandise on account.
(e) Received credit for merchandise purchased and returned to supplier.
(f) Payment of cash on account due a supplier.

15. What transactions might be included in a multiple-column purchases journal that would not be included in a single-column purchases journal?

16. Give an example of a transaction in the general journal that causes an entry to be posted twice (i.e., to two accounts), one in the general ledger, the other in the subsidiary ledger. Does this affect the debit/credit equality of the general ledger?

17. Give some examples of appropriate general journal transactions for an organization using special journals.

18. (a) Identify and explain the units that comprise the central processing unit (CPU). (b) What types of equipment are considered to be peripheral?

19. (a) What is accounting software? (b) What is integrated computer software?

20. Identify and distinguish between the two widely used methods of data processing in an electronic system.

21. What are the key points to be considered in evaluating and comparing manual and electronic systems?

BRIEF EXERCISES

BE6-1 Indicate whether each of the following statements is true or false.

1. When designing an accounting system, we need to think about the needs and knowledge of both the top management and various other users.
2. When the environment changes as a result of technological advances, increased competition, or government regulation, an accounting system does not have to be sufficiently flexible to meet the changes in order to save money.
3. In developing an accounting system, cost is relevant. The system must be cost effective; that is, the benefits obtained from the information disseminated must outweigh the cost of providing it.

Identify basic principles of accounting information system development.
(SO 1)

BE6-2 The development of an accounting system involves four phases: analysis, design, implementation, and follow-up. Identify the statement that best describes each of these four phases.

1. Determining internal and external information needs, identifying information sources and the needs for controls, and studying alternatives.

Identify major phases in accounting system development.
(SO 2)

2. Evaluation and monitoring of effectiveness and efficiency, and correction of weaknesses, implementation, and design.
3. Creation of forms and documents, selection of procedures, and preparation of job descriptions.
4. Implementing new or revised documents, procedures, reports, and processing equipment; hiring and training personnel through a start-up or transition period.

Identify subsidiary ledger balances.
(SO 3)

BE6–3   Presented below is information related to Bryan Company for its first month of operations. Identify the balances that appear in the accounts receivable subsidiary ledger and the accounts receivable balance that appears in the general ledger at the end of January.

Credit Sales			Cash Collections		
Jan. 7	Ace Co.	$9,000	Jan. 17	Ace Co.	$7,000
15	Bono Co.	$6,000	24	Bono Co.	$5,000
23	Carr Co.	$9,000	29	Carr Co.	$9,000

Identify subsidiary ledger accounts.
(SO 3)

BE6–4   Identify in what ledger (general or subsidiary) each of the following accounts is shown.

1. Rent Expense
2. Accounts Receivable—Olsen
3. Notes Payable
4. Accounts Payable—Kyle

Identify special journals.
(SO 4)

BE6–5   Identify the journal in which each of the following transactions is recorded.

1. Cash sales
2. Owner withdrawal of cash
3. Cash purchase of land
4. Credit sales
5. Purchase of merchandise on account
6. Receipt of cash for services performed

Identify entries to cash receipts journal.
(SO 4)

BE6–6   Indicate whether each of the following debits and credits is included in the cash receipts journal. (Use "Yes" or "No" to answer this question.)

1. Debit to Sales
2. Credit to Merchandise Inventory
3. Credit to Accounts Receivable
4. Debit to Accounts Payable

Indicate postings to cash receipts journal.
(SO 5)

BE6–7   Starr Computer Components Inc. uses a columnar cash receipts journal. Indicate which column(s) is/are posted only in total, only daily, or both in total and daily.

1. Accounts Receivable
2. Sales Discounts
3. Cash
4. Other Accounts

Identify transactions for special journals.
(SO 4)

BE6–8   Coffey Co. uses special journals and a general journal. Identify the journal in which each of the following transactions is recorded.

1. Purchased equipment on account.
2. Purchased merchandise on account.
3. Paid utility expense in cash.
4. Sold merchandise on account.

Identify transactions for special journals.
(SO 4)

BE6–9   Identify the special journal(s) in which the following column headings appear.

1. Sales Discounts Dr.
2. Accounts Receivable Cr.
3. Cash Dr.
4. Sales Cr.
5. Merchandise Inventory Dr.

Prepare a flowchart of the on-line processing method.
(SO 6)

BE6–10   (a) Prepare a flowchart of the on-line processing method in an electronic accounting system. (b) Explain the manual system equivalent of this method of data processing.

EXERCISES

Determine control account balances and explain posting of special journals.
(SO 3, 5)

E6–1   Valdes Company uses both special journals and a general journal as described in this chapter. On June 30, after all monthly postings had been completed, the Accounts Receivable controlling account in the general ledger had a debit balance of $350,000 and the Accounts Payable controlling account had a credit balance of $87,000.

The July transactions recorded in the special journals are summarized below. No entries affecting accounts receivable and accounts payable were recorded in the general journal for July.

Sales journal   Total sales, $161,400
Purchases journal   Total purchases, $54,360
Cash receipts journal   Accounts receivable column total, $135,000
Cash payments journal   Accounts payable column total, $47,500

Instructions
(a) What is the balance of the Accounts Receivable control account after the monthly postings on July 31?
(b) What is the balance of the Accounts Payable control account after the monthly postings on July 31?
(c) To what account(s) is the column total of $161,400 in the sales journal posted?
(d) To what account(s) is the accounts receivable column total of $135,000 in the cash receipts journal posted?

E6–2 Presented below is the subsidiary accounts receivable account of Rico Perez.

Explain postings to subsidiary ledger.
(SO 3)

Date		Ref.	Debit	Credit	Balance
1999					
Sept.	2	S31	61,000		61,000
	9	G4		12,000	49,000
	27	CR8		49,000	—

Instructions
▭▭▭⟹ Write a memo that explains each transaction.

E6–3 On September 1 the balance of the Accounts Receivable controlling account in the general ledger of Cremer Company was $10,960. The customers' subsidiary ledger contained account balances as follows: Alou, $1,440; Farr, $2,640; Keaton, $2,060; Skiles, $4,820. At the end of September the various journals contained the following information:

Post various journals to control and subsidiary accounts.
(SO 3, 5)

Sales journal: Sales to Skiles, $800; to Alou, $1,350; to George, $1,030; to Keaton, $1,100.

Cash receipts journal: Cash received from Keaton, $1,310; from Skiles, $2,300; from George, $410; from Farr, $1,800; from Alou, $1,240.

General journal: An allowance is granted to Skiles, $220.

Instructions
(a) Set up control and subsidiary accounts and enter the beginning balances. Do not construct the journals.
(b) Post the various journals. Post the items as individual items or as totals, whichever would be the appropriate procedure. (No sales discounts given.)
(c) Prepare a list of customers and prove the agreement of the controlling account with the subsidiary ledger at September 30, 1999.

E6–4 Harris Company uses special journals and a general journal. The following transactions occurred during September 1999.

Record transactions in sales and purchases journal.
(SO 3, 4)

Sept. 2 Sold merchandise on account to F. Vina, invoice no. 101, $500, terms n/30. The cost of the merchandise sold was $300.
10 Purchased merchandise on account from F. Kotsch $600, terms 2/10, n/30.
12 Purchased office equipment on account from J. Wells, $6,500.
21 Sold merchandise on account to J. Rich, invoice no. 102 for $800, terms 2/10, n/30. The cost of the merchandise sold was $480.
25 Purchased merchandise on account from M. Watt $900, terms n/30.
27 Sold merchandise to R. Cowan for $700 cash. The cost of the merchandise sold was $420.

Instructions
(a) Draw a sales journal (see Illustration 6-8) and a single-column purchase journal (see Illustration 6-13). (Use page 1 for each journal.)
(b) Record the transaction(s) for September that should be journalized in the sales journal and the purchases journal.

Record transactions in cash receipts and cash payments journal.
(SO 3, 4)

E6–5   Briggs Co. uses special journals and a general journal. The following transactions occurred during May 1999.

May 1   J. Briggs invested $62,000 cash in the business.

2   Sold merchandise to L. Bean for $6,000 cash. The cost of the merchandise sold was $4,200.

3   Purchased merchandise for $9,000 from R. L. Sanchez using check no. 101.

14   Paid salary to F. Sparks $700 by issuing check no. 102.

16   Sold merchandise on account to B. Ready for $900, terms n/30. The cost of the merchandise sold was $630.

22   A check of $9,000 is received from M. Lane in full for invoice 101; no discount given.

Instructions

(a) Draw a multiple-column cash receipts journal (see Illustration 6-10) and a multiple-column cash payments journal (see Illustration 6-17). (Use page 1 for each journal.)

(b) Record the transaction(s) for May that should be journalized in the cash receipts journal and cash payments journal.

Explain journalizing in cash journals.
(SO 4)

E6–6   Abbott Company uses the columnar cash journals illustrated in the textbook. In April, the following selected cash transactions occurred:

1. Made a refund to a customer for the return of damaged goods.
2. Received collection from customer within the 3% discount period.
3. Purchased merchandise for cash.
4. Paid a creditor within the 3% discount period.
5. Received collection from customer after the 3% discount period had expired.
6. Paid freight on merchandise purchased.
7. Paid cash for office equipment.
8. Received cash refund from supplier for merchandise returned.
9. Withdrew cash for personal use of owner.
10. Made cash sales.

Instructions

Indicate (a) the journal, and (b) the columns in the journal that should be used in recording each transaction.

Journalize transactions in general journal and post.
(SO 3, 4)

E6–7   Warner Company has the following selected transactions during March:

Mar. 2   Purchased equipment costing $5,000 from Pena Company on account.

5   Received credit memorandum for $300 from Simon Company for merchandise damaged in shipment to Warner.

7   Issued a credit memorandum for $400 to Farr Company for merchandise the customer returned. The returned merchandise had a cost of $260.

Warner Company uses a one-column purchases journal, a sales journal, the columnar cash journals used in the text, and a general journal.

Instructions

(a) Journalize the transactions in the general journal.

(b) ▭▭▭▷ In a brief memo to the president of Warner Company, explain the postings to the control and subsidiary accounts.

Indicate journalizing in special journals.
(SO 4)

E6–8   Below are some typical transactions incurred by Littlejohn Company.

1. Payment of creditors on account.
2. Return of merchandise sold for credit.
3. Collection on account from customers.
4. Sold land for cash.
5. Sale of merchandise on account.
6. Sale of merchandise for cash.
7. Received credit for merchandise purchased on credit.
8. Sales discount taken on goods sold.
9. Payment of employee wages.
10. Close income summary to owner's capital.
11. Depreciation on building.
12. Purchase of office supplies for cash.
13. Purchase of merchandise on account.

Instructions

For each transaction, indicate whether it would normally be recorded in a cash receipts journal, cash payments journal, sales journal, single-column purchases journal, or general journal.

E6–9 The general ledger of the Torres Company contained the following Accounts Payable control account (in T-account form). Also shown is the related subsidiary ledger.

Explain posting to control account and subsidiary ledger.
(SO 3, 5)

GENERAL LEDGER

Accounts Payable

Feb. 15	General Journal	1,400	Feb. 1	Balance	26,025
28	?	?	5	General Journal	265
			11	General Journal	550
			28	Purchases	13,700
			Feb. 28	Balance	9,640

ACCOUNTS PAYABLE LEDGER

Sealy

Feb. 28 Bal. 4,600	

Wolcott

Feb. 28 Bal. ?	

Gates

Feb. 28 Bal. 2,000	

Instructions
(a) Indicate the missing posting reference and amount in the control account and the missing ending balance in the subsidiary ledger.
(b) Indicate the amounts in the control account that were dual-posted (i.e., posted to the control account and the subsidiary accounts).

E6–10 Selected accounts from the ledgers of Moyer Company at July 31 showed the following:

Prepare purchases and general journals.
(SO 3, 4)

GENERAL LEDGER

Store Equipment   No. 153

Date	Explanation	Ref.	Debit	Credit	Balance
July 1		G1	3,600		3,600

Accounts Payable   No. 201

Date	Explanation	Ref.	Debit	Credit	Balance
July 1		G1		3,600	3,600
15		G1		400	4,000
18		G1	100		3,900
25		G1	200		3,700
31		P1		8,400	12,100

Merchandise Inventory   No. 120

Date	Explanation	Ref.	Debit	Credit	Balance
July 15		G1	400		400
18		G1		100	300
25		G1		200	100
31		P1	8,400		8,500

ACCOUNTS PAYABLE LEDGER

Alcott Equipment Co.

Date	Explanation	Ref.	Debit	Credit	Balance
July 1		G1		3,600	3,600

Delco Co.

Date	Explanation	Ref.	Debit	Credit	Balance
July 14		P1		1,100	1,100
25		G1	200		900

Bradley Co.

Date	Explanation	Ref.	Debit	Credit	Balance
July 3		P1		2,000	2,000
20		P1		700	2,700

Erick Co.

Date	Explanation	Ref.	Debit	Credit	Balance
July 12		P1		500	500
21		P1		600	1,100

Costo Materials

Date	Explanation	Ref.	Debit	Credit	Balance
July 17		P1		1,400	1,400
18		G1	100		1,300
29		P1		2,100	3,400

Gaetti Transit

Date	Explanation	Ref.	Debit	Credit	Balance
July 15		G1		400	400

Instructions

From the data prepare:

(a) the single-column purchases journal for July.

(b) the general journal entries for July.

Determine correct posting amount to control account.
(SO 5)

E6–11   Yan Products uses both special journals and a general journal as described in this chapter. Yan also posts customers' accounts in the accounts receivable subsidiary ledger. The postings for the most recent month are included in the subsidiary T accounts below.

Edmonds

Bal.	340	250
	180	

Roemer

Bal.	150	150
	290	

Schulz

Bal.	–0–	145
	145	

Park

Bal.	120	120
	190	
	170	

Instructions

Determine the correct amount of the end-of-month posting from the sales journal to the Accounts Receivable controlling account.

PROBLEMS: SET A

Journalize transactions in cash receipts journal and post to control account and subsidiary ledger.
(SO 3, 4, 5)

P6–1A   Koslo Company's chart of accounts includes the following selected accounts:

101 Cash	401 Sales
112 Accounts Receivable	414 Sales Discounts
120 Merchandise Inventory	505 Cost of Goods Sold
301 T. Koslo, Capital	

On June 1 the accounts receivable ledger of the Koslo Company showed the following balances: Bell & Son, $2,500; Ellis Co., $1,900; Gant Bros., $1,600; and Mejia Co., $1,000. The June transactions involving the receipt of cash were as follows:

June 1   The owner, T. Koslo, invested additional cash in the business, $9,000.

3   Received check in full from Mejia Co. less 2% cash discount.

6   Received check in full from Ellis Co. less 2% cash discount.

7   Made cash sales of merchandise totaling $6,135. The cost of the merchandise sold was $4,090.

9   Received check in full from Bell & Son less 2% cash discount.

11   Received cash refund from a supplier for damaged merchandise, $200.

15   Made cash sales of merchandise totaling $5,250. The cost of the merchandise sold was $3,500.

20   Received check in full from Gant Bros., $1,600.

Instructions

(a) Journalize the transactions above in a six-column cash receipts journal with columns for Cash Dr.; Sales Discounts Dr.; Accounts Receivable Cr.; Sales Cr.; Other Accounts Cr; and Cost of Goods Sold Dr./Merchandise Inventory Cr. Foot and crossfoot the journal.

(b) Insert the beginning balances in the Accounts Receivable control and subsidiary accounts and post the June transactions to these accounts.

(c) Prove the agreement of the control account and subsidiary account balances.

P6–2A   Cline Company's chart of accounts includes the following selected accounts:

Journalize transactions in cash payments journal and post to the general and subsidiary ledger.

(SO 3, 4, 5)

101 Cash	157 Equipment
120 Merchandise Inventory	201 Accounts Payable
130 Prepaid Insurance	306 B. Cline, Drawing

On November 1 the accounts payable ledger of the Cline Company showed the following balances: S. Haley & Co., $3,750; C. King, $2,350; W. Ortega, $1,000; and Welch Bros., $1,900. The November transactions involving the payment of cash were as follows:

Nov. 1   Purchased merchandise, check no. 11, $900.
  3   Purchased store equipment, check no. 12, $1,650.
  5   Paid Welch Bros. balance due of $1,900, less 1% discount, check no. 13, $1,881.
  11   Purchased merchandise, check no. 14, $2,000.
  15   Paid W. Ortega balance due of $1,000, less 3% discount, check no. 15, $970.
  16   B. Cline, the owner, withdraws $500 cash for own use, check no. 16.
  19   Paid C. King in full for invoice no. 1245, $1,300 less 2% discount, check no. 17, $1,274.
  25   Paid premium due on one year insurance policy, check no. 18, $3,000.
  30   Paid S. Haley & Co. in full for invoice no. 832, $2,250, check no. 19.

Instructions

(a) Journalize the transctions above in a four-column cash payments journal with columns for Other Accounts Dr.; Accounts Payable Dr.; Merchandise Inventory Cr.; and Cash Cr. Foot and crossfoot the journal.

(b) Insert the beginning balances in the Accounts Payable control and subsidiary accounts and post the November transactions to these accounts.

(c) Prove the agreement of the control account and the subsidiary account balances.

P6–3A   The chart of accounts of Pagnozzi Company includes the following selected accounts:

Journalize transactions in multicolumn purchases journal and post to the general and subsidiary ledgers.

(SO 3, 4, 5)

112 Accounts Receivable	401 Sales
120 Merchandise Inventory	412 Sales Returns and Allowances
126 Supplies	505 Cost of Goods Sold
157 Equipment	610 Advertising Expense
201 Accounts Payable	

In May the following selected transactions were completed. All purchases and sales were on account except as indicated. The cost of all merchandise sold was 70% of the sales price.

May 2   Purchased merchandise from Vena Company, $9,000.
  3   Received freight bill from Abel Freight on Vena purchase, $400.
  5   Sales were made to Potts Company, $1,600; Hogan Bros., $2,700; and Nance Company, $1,500.
  8   Purchased merchandise from Gore Company, $8,000 and Deleon Company, $8,700.
  10   Received credit on merchandise returned to Deleon Company, $500.
  15   Purchased supplies from Eaton Supply, $900.
  16   Purchased merchandise from Vena Company, $4,500; and Gore Company, $6,000.
  17   Returned supplies to Eaton Supply, receiving credit, $100. (*Hint:* Credit Supplies.)
  18   Received freight bills on May 16 purchases from Abel Freight, $500.
  20   Returned merchandise to Vena Company receiving credit, $300.
  23   Made sales to Hogan Bros., $2,400; and Nance Company, $2,200.
  25   Received bill for advertising from Beck Advertising, $900.
  26   Granted allowance to Nance Company for merchandise damaged in shipment, $200.
  28   Purchased equipment from Eaton Supply, $250.

Journalize transactions in special journals.

(SO 3, 4, 5)

Instructions

(a) Journalize the transactions above in a purchases journal, a sales journal, and a general journal. The purchases journal should have the following column headings: Date, Accounts Credited (Debited), Ref., Other Accounts Dr., Merchandise Inventory Dr., and Accounts Payable Cr.

(b) Post to both the general and subsidiary ledger accounts. (Assume that all accounts have zero beginning balances.)

(c) Prove the agreement of the control and subsidiary accounts.

P6–4A Selected accounts from the chart of accounts of Santos Company are shown below.

101 Cash	201 Accounts Payable
112 Accounts Receivable	401 Sales
120 Merchandise Inventory	414 Sales Discounts
126 Supplies	505 Cost of Goods Sold
140 Land	610 Advertising Expense
145 Buildings	

The cost of all merchandise sold was 60% of the sales price. During October, Santos Company completed the following transactions:

Oct. 2 Purchased merchandise on account from Ming Company, $17,500.

4 Sold merchandise on account to Pinka Co., $8,000. Invoice no. 204; terms 2/10, n/30.

5 Purchased supplies for cash, $80.

7 Made cash sales for the week totaling $9,160.

9 Paid in full the amount owed the Ming Company less a 2% discount.

10 Purchased merchandise on account from Quayle Corp., $4,200.

12 Received payment from Pinka Co. for invoice no. 204.

13 Issued a debit memorandum to Quayle Corp. and returned $250 worth of damaged goods.

14 Made cash sales for the week totaling $8,180.

16 Sold a parcel of land for $27,000 cash, the land's book value.

17 Sold merchandise on account to C. Baden & Co., $5,350, invoice no. 205, terms 2/10, n/30.

18 Purchased merchandise for cash, $2,125.

21 Made cash sales for the week totaling $8,465.

23 Paid in full the amount owed the Quayle Corp. for the goods kept (no discount).

25 Purchased supplies on account from Flott Co., $260.

25 Sold merchandise on account to Gregg Corp., $5,220, invoice no. 206, terms 2/10, n/30.

25 Received payment from C. Baden & Co. for invoice no. 205.

26 Purchased for cash a small parcel of land and a building on the land to use as a storage facility. The total cost of $35,000 was allocated $21,000 to the land and $14,000 to the building.

27 Purchased merchandise on account from Singer Co., $8,500.

28 Made cash sales for the week totaling $8,540.

30 Purchased merchandise on account from Ming Company, $14,000.

30 Paid advertising bill for the month from the Gazette, $400.

30 Sold merchandise on account to C. Baden & Co., $4,600. Invoice no. 207; terms 2/10, n/30.

Santos Company uses the following journals:

1. Sales journal.

2. Single-column purchases journal.

3. Cash receipts journal with columns for Cash Dr.; Sales Discounts Dr.; Accounts Receivable Cr.; Sales Cr.; Other Accounts Cr.; and Cost of Goods Sold Dr./Merchandise Inventory Cr.

4. Cash payments journal with columns for Other Accounts Dr.; Accounts Payable Dr.; Merchandise Inventory, Cr.; and Cash Cr.

5. General journal.

Instructions

Using the selected accounts provided:

(a) Record, in the appropriate journals, the October transactions.

(b) Foot and crossfoot all special journals.

(c) Show how postings would be made by placing ledger account numbers and check marks as needed in the journals. (Actual posting to ledger accounts is not required.)

P6–5A Presented below are the sales and cash receipts journals for Tino Co. for its first month of operations.

Journalize in purchase and cash payments journals, post, prepare a trial balance, prove control to subsidiary, prepare adjusting entries, and prepare an adjusted trial balance.
(SO 3, 4, 5)

SALES JOURNAL   S1

Date		Account Debited	Ref.	Accounts Receivable Dr. Sales Cr.	Cost of Goods Sold Dr. Merchandise Inventory Cr.
Feb.	3	D. Alco		5,000	3,300
	9	P. Barber		6,500	4,290
	12	D. Casey		8,000	5,280
	26	K. Dennis		6,000	3,960
				25,500	16,830

CASH RECEIPTS JOURNAL   CR1

Date		Account Credited	Ref.	Cash Dr.	Sales Discounts Dr.	Accounts Receivable Cr.	Sales Cr.	Other Accounts Cr.	Cost of Goods Sold Dr. Merchandise Inventory Cr.
Feb.	1	J. Tino, Capital		30,000				30,000	
	2			6,500			6,500		4,290
	13	D. Alco		4,950	50	5,000			
	18	Merchandise Inventory		150				150	
	26	P. Barber		6,500		6,500			
				48,100	50	11,500	6,500	30,150	4,290

In addition, the following transactions have not been journalized for February 1999.

Feb. 2 Purchased merchandise on account from J. Carsen for $3,000, terms 1/10, n/30.

7 Purchased merchandise on account from K. Cooper for $30,000, terms 1/10, n/30.

9 Paid cash of $1,000 for purchase of supplies.

12 Paid $2,970 to J. Carsen in payment for $3,000 invoice, less 1% discount.

15 Purchased equipment for $8,000 cash.

16 Purchased merchandise on account from M. Kim, $2,400, terms 2/10, n/30.

17 Paid $29,700 to K. Cooper in payment of $30,000 invoice, less 1% discount.

20 Withdrew cash of $1,100 from business for personal use.

21 Purchased merchandise on account from G. Azar for $6,500, terms 1/10, n/30.

28 Paid $2,400 to M. Kim in payment of $2,400 invoice.

Instructions

(a) Open the following accounts in the general ledger.

101 Cash	301 J. Tino, Capital
112 Accounts Receivable	306 J. Tino, Drawing
120 Merchandise Inventory	401 Sales
126 Supplies	414 Sales Discounts
157 Equipment	505 Cost of Goods Sold
158 Accumulated Depreciation—Equipment	631 Supplies Expense
201 Accounts Payable	711 Depreciation Expense

(b) Journalize the transactions that have not been journalized in a one-column purchases journal, and the cash payments journal (see Illustration 6-17).

(c) Post to the accounts receivable and accounts payable subsidiary ledgers. Follow the sequence of transactions as shown in the problem.

(d) Post the individual entries and totals to the general ledger.

(e) Prepare a trial balance at February 28, 1999.

(f) Determine that the subsidiary ledgers agree with the control accounts in the general ledger.

(g) The following adjustments at the end of February are necessary.

1. A count of supplies indicates that $300 is still on hand.

2. Depreciation on equipment for February is $200.

Prepare the adjusting entries and then post the adjusting entries to the general ledger.

(h) Prepare an adjusted trial balance.

Journalize in special journals, post, and prepare a trial balance.
(SO 3, 4, 5)

P6–6A   The post-closing trial balance for Gonzalez Co. is as follows:

GONZALES CO.
Post-Closing Trial Balance
December 31, 1999

	Debit	Credit
Cash	$ 39,500	
Accounts Receivable	15,000	
Notes Receivable	45,000	
Merchandise Inventory	23,000	
Equipment	6,450	
Accumulated Depreciation—Equipment		$ 1,500
Accounts Payable		43,000
L. Gonzales, Capital		84,450
	$128,950	$128,950

The subsidiary ledgers contain the following information: (1) accounts receivable—P. Naab $2,500; K. Hoyt $7,500; A. Deitz $5,000; (2) accounts payable—D. Kraft $10,000; W. Henrie $18,000; and J. Fanning $15,000. The cost of all merchandise sold was 65% of the sales price.

The transactions for January 2000 are as follows:

Jan. 3 Sell merchandise to C. Hernandez, $3,000, terms 2/10, n/30.

5 Purchase merchandise from D. Greer, $2,500, terms 2/10, n/30.

7 Receive a check from A. Deitz, $3,500.

11 Pay freight on merchandise purchased, $300.

12 Pay rent of $1,000 for January.

13 Receive payment in full from C. Hernandez.

14 Post all entries to the subsidiary ledgers. Issue a credit memo to acknowledge receipt of damaged merchandise of $700 returned by P. Naab.

15 Send J. Fanning a check for $14,850 in full payment of account, discount, $150.

17 Purchase merchandise from B. Masoni, $1,600, terms 2/10, n/30.

18 Pay sales salaries of $2,800 and office salaries, $1,500.

20 Give W. Henrie a 60-day note for $18,000 in full payment of account payable.

23 Total cash sales amount to $8,600.

24 Post all entries to the subsidiary ledgers. Sell merchandise on account to K. Hoyt, $7,700, terms 1/10, n/30.

27 Send D. Greer a check for $950.

29 Receive payment on a note of $40,000 from L. Danza.

30 Return merchandise of $500 to B. Masoni for credit. Post all journals to the subsidiary ledger.

Instructions

(a) Open general and subsidiary ledger accounts for the following:

101 Cash	157 Equipment
112 Accounts Receivable	158 Accumulated Depreciation—Equipment
115 Notes Receivable	200 Notes Payable
120 Merchandise Inventory	201 Accounts Payable

301 L. Gonzalez, Capital
401 Sales
412 Sales Returns and Allowances
414 Sales Discounts

505 Cost of Goods Sold
726 Sales Salaries Expense
727 Office Salaries Expense
729 Rent Expense

(b) Record the January transactions in a sales journal, a single-column purchases journal, a cash receipts journal (see Illustration 6-10), a cash payments journal (see Illustration 6-17), and a general journal.
(c) Post the appropriate amounts to the general ledger.
(d) Prepare a trial balance at January 31, 2000.
(e) Determine whether the subsidiary ledgers agree with controlling accounts in the general ledger.

PROBLEMS: SET B

P6–1B Morrow Company's chart of accounts includes the following selected accounts:

101 Cash
112 Accounts Receivable
120 Merchandise Inventory
301 T. Morrow, Capital

401 Sales
414 Sales Discounts
505 Cost of Goods Sold

Journalize transactions in cash receipts journal and post to control account and subsidiary ledger.
(SO 3, 4, 5)

On April 1 the accounts receivable ledger of Morrow Company showed the following balances: Horner, $1,550; Kile, $1,200; Nicci Co., $2,900; and Starr, $1,600. The April transactions involving the receipt of cash were as follows:

Apr. 1 The owner, T. Morrow, invested additional cash in the business, $6,000.
4 Received check for payment of account from Starr less 2% cash discount.
5 Received check for $620 in payment of invoice no. 307 from Nicci Co.
8 Made cash sales of merchandise totaling $7,245. The cost of the merchandise sold was $4,347.
10 Received check for $800 in payment of invoice no. 309 from Horner.
11 Received cash refund from a supplier for damaged merchandise, $550.
23 Received check for $1,600 in payment of invoice no. 310 from Nicci Co.
29 Received check for payment of account from Kile.

Instructions
(a) Journalize the transactions above in a six-column cash receipts journal with columns for Cash Dr.; Sales Discounts Dr.; Accounts Receivable Cr.; Sales Cr.; Other Accounts Cr., and Cost of Goods Sold Dr./Merchandise Inventory Cr. Foot and crossfoot the journal.
(b) Insert the beginning balances in the Accounts Receivable control and subsidiary accounts and post the April transactions to these accounts.
(c) Prove the agreement of the control account and subsidiary account balances.

P6–2B Norton Company's chart of accounts includes the following selected accounts:

101 Cash
120 Merchandise Inventory
130 Prepaid Insurance
157 Equipment

201 Accounts Payable
306 R. Norton, Drawing
505 Cost of Goods Sold

Journalize transactions in cash payments journal and post to control account and subsidiary ledger.
(SO 3, 4, 5)

On October 1 the accounts payable ledger of Norton Company showed the following balances: Heston Company, $1,600; Menke & Sons, $2,500; Ogle Co., $1,400; and Paige Company, $3,700. The October transactions involving the payment of cash were as follows:

Oct. 1 Purchased merchandise, check no. 63, $700.
3 Purchased equipment, check no. 64, $800.
5 Paid Heston Company balance due of $1,600, less 2% discount, check no. 65, $1,568.
10 Purchased merchandise, check no. 66, $2,250.
15 Paid Ogle Co. balance due of $1,400, check no. 67.

16 R. Norton, the owner, pays his personal insurance premium of $400, check no. 68.
19 Paid Menke & Sons in full for invoice no. 610, $1,400 less 2% cash discount, check no. 69, $1,372.
29 Paid Paige Company in full for invoice no. 264, $2,500, check no. 70.

Instructions

(a) Journalize the transactions above in a four-column cash payments journal with columns for Other Accounts Dr.; Accounts Payable Dr.; Merchandise Inventory Dr.; and Cash Cr. Foot and crossfoot the journal.
(b) Insert the beginning balances in the Accounts Payable control and subsidiary accounts and post the October transactions to these accounts.
(c) Prove the agreement of the control account and the subsidiary account balances.

Journalize transactions in multi-column purchases journal and post to the general and subsidiary ledgers.
(SO 3, 4, 5)

P6–3B The chart of accounts of Cruz Company includes the following selected accounts:

112 Accounts Receivable	401 Sales
120 Merchandise Inventory	412 Sales Returns and Allowances
126 Supplies	505 Cost of Goods Sold
157 Equipment	610 Advertising Expense
201 Accounts Payable	

In July the following selected transactions were completed. All purchases and sales were on account. The cost of all merchandise sold was 70% of the sales price.

July 1 Purchased merchandise from DeVito Company, $7,000.
2 Received freight bill from Carlin Shipping on DeVito purchase, $400.
3 Made sales to Laird Company, $1,300; and Flood Bros., $1,900.
5 Purchased merchandise from Granger Company, $3,200.
8 Received credit on merchandise returned to Granger Company, $300.
13 Purchased store supplies from Beyer Supply, $720.
15 Purchased merchandise from DeVito Company, $3,600; and Reeble Company, $2,800.
16 Made sales to Marquez Company, $3,450; and Flood Bros., $1,570.
18 Received bill for advertising from Meyer's Advertisements, $600.
21 Sales were made to Laird Company, $310; and Resch Company, $2,200.
22 Granted allowance to Laird Company for merchandise damaged in shipment, $40.
24 Purchased merchandise from Granger Company, $3,000.
26 Purchased equipment from Beyer Supply, $600.
28 Received freight bill from Carlin Shipping on Granger purchase of July 24, $380.
30 Sales were made to Marquez Company, $4,900.

Instructions

(a) Journalize the transactions above in a purchases journal, a sales journal, and a general journal. The purchases journal should have the following column headings: Date, Accounts Credited (Debited), Ref., Other Accounts Dr., Merchandise Inventory Dr., and Accounts Payable Cr.
(b) Post to both the general and subsidiary ledger accounts. (Assume that all accounts have zero beginning balances.)
(c) Prove the agreement of the control and subsidiary accounts.

Journalize transactions in special journals.
(SO 3, 4, 5)

P6–4B Selected accounts from the chart of accounts of Shell Company are shown below.

101 Cash	401 Sales
112 Accounts Receivable	412 Sales Returns and Allowances
120 Merchandise Inventory	414 Sales Discounts
126 Supplies	505 Cost of Goods Sold
157 Equipment	726 Salaries Expense
201 Accounts Payable	

The cost of all merchandise sold was 60% of the sales price. During January, Shell completed the following transactions:

Jan. 3 Purchased merchandise on account from Blue Co., $9,900.
    4 Purchased supplies for cash, $80.
    4 Sold merchandise on account to Grimm, $7,250, invoice no. 371, terms 1/10, n/30.
    5 Issued a debit memorandum to Blue Co. and returned $300 worth of damaged goods.
    6 Made cash sales for the week totaling $3,150.
    8 Purchased merchandise on account from Fritz Co., $4,500.
    9 Sold merchandise on account to Mai Corp., $5,600, invoice no. 372, terms 1/10, n/30.
    11 Purchased merchandise on account from Hatch Co., $3,700.
    13 Paid in full the Blue Co. on account less a 2% discount.
    13 Made cash sales for the week totaling $5,340.
    15 Received payment from Mai Corp. for invoice no. 372.
    15 Paid semi-monthly salaries of $14,300 to employees.
    17 Received payment from Grimm for invoice no. 371.
    17 Sold merchandise on account to Engel Co., $1,200, invoice no. 373, terms 1/10, n/30.
    19 Purchased equipment on account from Jaeger Corp., $5,500.
    20 Cash sales for the week totaled $3,200.
    20 Paid in full the Fritz Co. on account less a 2% discount.
    23 Purchased merchandise on account from Blue Co., $7,800.
    24 Purchased merchandise on account from Rankin Corp., $4,690.
    27 Made cash sales for the week totaling $3,730.
    30 Received payment from Engel Co. for invoice no. 373.
    31 Paid semi-monthly salaries of $13,200 to employees.
    31 Sold merchandise on account to Grimm, $9,330, invoice no. 374, terms 1/10, n/30.

Shell Company uses the following journals:

1. Sales journal.
2. Single-column purchases journal.
3. Cash receipts journal with columns for Cash Dr.; Sales Discounts Dr.; Accounts Receivable Cr.; Sales Cr.; Other Accounts Cr.; and Cost of Goods Sold Dr./Merchandise Inventory Cr.
4. Cash payments journal with columns for Other Accounts Dr.; Accounts Payable Dr.; Merchandise Inventory Cr.; and Cash Cr.
5. General journal.

Instructions
Using the selected accounts provided:

(a) Record, in the appropriate journal noted, the January transactions.
(b) Foot and crossfoot all special journals.
(c) Show how postings would be made by placing ledger account numbers and check-marks as needed in the journals. (Actual posting to ledger accounts is not required.)

P6–5B Presented below are the purchases and cash payments journal for Weber Co. for its first month of operations.

Journalize in sales and cash receipts journals, post, prepare a trial balance, prove control to subsidiary, prepare adjusting entries, and prepare an adjusted trial balance.
(SO 3, 4, 5)

PURCHASES JOURNAL   **P1**

Date		Account Credited	Ref.	Merchandise Inventory Dr. Accounts Payable Cr.
July	4	P. Coley		6,800
	5	S. Farr		7,500
	11	B. Goltra		3,720
	13	C. Hunt		15,300
	20	R. Jenks		8,800
				42,120

CASH PAYMENTS JOURNAL   CP1

Date	Account Debited	Ref.	Other Accounts Dr.	Accounts Payable Dr.	Merchandise Inventory Cr.	Cash Cr.
July 4	Store Supplies		600			600
10	S. Farr			7,500	75	7,425
11	Prepaid Rent		6,000			6,000
15	P. Coley			6,800		6,800
19	Weber, Drawing		2,500			2,500
21	C. Hunt			15,300	153	15,147
			9,100	29,600	228	38,472

In addition, the following transactions have not been journalized for July. The cost of all merchandise sold was 65% of the sales price.

July 1   The founder, M. Weber, invests $80,000 in cash.
     6   Sell merchandise on account to Lantz Co., $5,400 terms 1/10, n/30.
     7   Make cash sales totaling $4,000.
     8   Sell merchandise on account to J. Wenger, $3,600, terms, 1/10, n/30.
    10   Sell merchandise on account to G. Linton, $4,900, terms 1/10, n/30.
    13   Receive payment in full from J. Wenger.
    16   Receive payment in full from G. Linton.
    20   Receive payment in full from Lantz Co.
    21   Sell merchandise on account to A. Kear, $3,000, terms, 1/10, n/30.
    29   Return damaged goods to P. Coley and received cash refund of $450.

Instructions

(a) Open the following accounts in the general ledger.

101 Cash	306 Weber, Drawing
112 Accounts Receivable	401 Sales
120 Merchandise Inventory	412 Sales Returns and Allowances
127 Store Supplies	414 Sales Discounts
131 Prepaid Rent	505 Cost of Goods Sold
201 Accounts Payable	631 Supplies Expense
301 Weber, Capital	729 Rent Expense

(b) Journalize the transactions that have not been journalized in the sales journal, the cash receipts journal (see Illustration 6-10), and the general journal.

(c) Post to the accounts receivable and accounts payable subsidiary ledgers. Follow the sequence of transactions as shown in the problem.

(d) Post the individual entries and totals to the general ledger.

(e) Prepare a trial balance at July 31, 1999.

(f) Determine whether the subsidiary ledgers agree with the controlling accounts in the general ledger.

(g) The following adjustments at the end of July are necessary.
     1. A count of supplies indicates that $140 is still on hand.
     2. Recognize rent expense for July, $500.
     Prepare the necessary entries in the general journal. Post the entries to the general ledger.

(h) Prepare an adjusted trial balance at July 31, 1999.

BROADENING YOUR PERSPECTIVE

FINANCIAL REPORTING AND ANALYSIS
....
FINANCIAL REPORTING PROBLEM—A MINI PRACTICE SET

BYP6–1   (The working papers that accompany this textbook are needed in order to work this mini practice set.)

Stone Co. uses both an accounts receivable and an accounts payable subsidiary ledger. Balances related to both the general ledger and the subsidiary ledger for Stone are indicated in the working papers. Presented below are a series of transactions for Stone Co. for the month of January. Credit sales terms are 2/10, n/30. The cost of all merchandise sold was 60% of the sales price.

Jan. 3   Sell merchandise on credit to B. Sargent $3,200, invoice No. 510, and to J. Eaton $1,800, invoice No. 511.

    5   Purchase merchandise from S. Walden $3,000 and D. Landell $2,200, terms n/30.

    7   Receive checks from S. Lowell, $4,000 and B. Jaggar $2,000 after discount period has lapsed.

    8   Pay freight on merchandise purchased $180.

    9   Send checks to S. Lee for $9,000 less 2% cash discount and D. Nordin for $11,000 less 1% cash discount.

    9   Issue credit memo for $300 to J. Eaton for merchandise returned.

  10   Summary daily cash sales total $15,500.

  11   Sell merchandise on credit to R. Dansig $1,300, invoice No. 512, and to S. Lowell $900, invoice No. 513.

  12   Pay rent of $1,000 for January.

  13   Receive payment in full from B. Sargent and J. Eaton less cash discounts.

  15   Withdraw $800 cash by M. Stone for personal use.

  15   Post all entries to the subsidiary ledgers.

  16   Purchase merchandise from D. Nordin $16,000, terms 1/10, n/30; S. Lee $14,200, terms 2/10, n/30; and S. Walden $1,500, terms n/30.

  17   Pay $400 cash for office supplies.

  18   Return $200 of merchandise to S. Lee and receive credit.

  20   Summary daily cash sales total $17,500.

  21   Issue $15,000 note to R. Mannon in payment of balance due.

  21   Receive payment in full from S. Lowell less cash discount.

  22   Sell merchandise on credit to B. Sargent $1,700, invoice No. 514 and to R. Dansig $800, invoice No. 515.

  22   Post all entries to the subsidiary ledger.

  23   Send checks to D. Nordin and S. Lee in full payment less cash discounts.

  25   Sell merchandise on credit to B. Jaggar $3,500, invoice No. 516 and to J. Eaton $6,100, invoice No. 517.

  27   Purchase merchandise from D. Nordin $14,500, terms 1/10, n/30; D. Landell $1,200, terms n/30; and S. Walden $2,800, terms n/30.

  27   Post all entries to the subsidiary ledger.

  28   Pay $200 cash for office supplies.

  31   Summary daily cash sales total $21,300.

  31   Pay sales salaries $4,300 and office salaries $2,600.

Instructions
  (a) Record the January transactions in a sales journal, a single-column purchases journal, a cash receipts journal as shown on page 242, a cash payments journal as shown on page 247, and a two-column general journal.
  (b) Post the journals to the general ledger.

(c) Prepare a trial balance at January 31, 1999, in the trial balance columns of the work sheet. Complete the work sheet using the following additional information.
   (1) Office supplies at January 31 total $500.
   (2) Insurance coverage expires on October 31, 1999.
   (3) Annual depreciation on the equipment is $1,500.
   (4) Interest of $60 has accrued on the note payable.
(d) Prepare a multiple-step income statement and an owner's equity statement for January and a classified balance sheet at the end of January.
(e) Prepare and post adjusting and closing entries.
(f) Prepare a post-closing trial balance and determine whether the subsidiary ledgers agree with the controlling accounts in the general ledger.

REAL-WORLD FOCUS: Alco Standard Corporation

BYP6–2   **Alco Standard Corporation's** operations are divided into two business groups: Alco Office Products and Unisource. Alco Office Products sells, leases, and rents various electronic office machines; Unisource markets and distributes papers primarily for office use. The company owns or leases facilities in 49 states and 9 foreign countries.

The president of Alco wrote the following in his letter in a recent annual report:

ALCO STANDARD CORPORATION
President's Letter to Stockholders

The creation of Unisource allows us to pursue strategies that are practical only on a unified basis. Our efforts to upgrade information technology, for example, will now be directed to building a common system throughout North America. This unified approach will give us online electronic link suppliers, cutting order entry costs and improving inventory management. As a result, we will be able to improve service to customers with more timely and more accurate order fulfillment, faster inquiry response and enhanced technical support.

Instructions
(a) When a company computerizes customer order entry, what equivalent special journal type must be programmed into such an electronic system?
(b) When a company computerizes inventory management (which involves more timely ordering of new merchandise), what special journal type must be programmed into such an electronic system?

CRITICAL THINKING

GROUP DECISION CASE

BYP6–3   Davis & Ruiz is a wholesaler of small appliances and parts. Davis & Ruiz is operated by two owners, Phil Davis and Tony Ruiz. In addition, the company has one employee, a repair specialist, who is on a fixed salary. Revenues are earned through the sale of appliances to retailers (approximately 75% of total revenues), appliance parts to do-it-yourselfers (10%), and the repair of appliances brought to the store (15%). Appliance sales are made on both a credit and cash basis. Customers are billed on prenumbered sales invoices. Credit terms are always net/30 days. All parts sales and repair work are cash only.

Merchandise is purchased on account from the manufacturers of both the appliances and the parts. Practically all suppliers offer cash discounts for prompt payments, and it is company policy to take all discounts. Most cash payments are made by check. Checks are most frequently issued to suppliers, to trucking companies for freight on merchandise purchases, and to newspapers, radio, and TV stations for advertising. All advertising bills are paid as received. Phil and Tony each make a monthly drawing in cash for personal living expenses. The salaried repairman is paid twice monthly.

Davis & Ruiz currently has a manual accounting system. However, the business is growing and some consideration is being given to an electronic accounting system.

Instructions

With the class divided into groups, answer the following:

  (a) Identify the special journals that Davis & Ruiz should have in its manual system. List the column headings appropriate for each of the special journals.
  (b) What control and subsidiary accounts should be included in Davis & Ruiz's manual system? Why?
  (c) Identify for Phil and Tony the key points they should consider in deciding whether to install an electronic system.

COMMUNICATION ACTIVITY

BYP6–4   Sue Marsh, a classmate, has a part-time bookkeeping job. She is concerned about the inefficiencies in journalizing and posting transactions. Raul Hindi is the owner of the company where Sue works. In response to numerous complaints from Sue and others, Raul hired two additional bookkeepers a month ago. However, the inefficiencies have continued at an even higher rate. The accounting information system for the company has only a general journal and a general ledger. Raul refuses to install an electronic accounting system.

Instructions

Now that Sue is an expert in manual accounting information systems, she decides to send a letter to Raul Hindi explaining (1) why the additional personnel did not help and (2) what changes should be made to improve the efficiency of the accounting department. Write the letter that you think Sue should send.

ETHICS CASE

BYP6–5   Tyler Products Company operates three divisions, each with its own manufacturing plant and marketing/sales force. The corporate headquarters and central accounting office are in Tyler with the plants in Freeport, Rockport, and Bayport, all within 50 miles of Tyler. Corporate management treats each division as an independent profit center and encourages competition among them. They each have similar but different product lines. As a competitive incentive, bonuses are awarded each year to the employees of the fastest growing and most profitable division.

Don Henke is the manager of Tyler's centralized computer accounting operation that keyboards the sales transactions and maintains the accounts receivable for all three divisions. Don came up in the accounting ranks from the Bayport division where his wife, several relatives, and many friends still work.

As sales documents are keyboarded into the computer, the originating division is identified by code. Most sales documents (95%) are coded, but some (5%) are not coded or are coded incorrectly. As the manager, Don has instructed the keyboard operators to assign the Bayport code to all uncoded and incorrectly coded sales documents. This is done he says, ''in order to expedite processing and to keep the computer files current since they are updated daily.'' All receivables and cash collections for all three divisions are handled by Tyler as one subsidiary accounts receivable ledger.

Instructions

  (a) Who are the stakeholders in this situation?
  (b) What are the ethical issues in this case?
  (c) How might the system be improved to prevent this situation?

SURFING THE NET

BYP6–6   Great Plains Dynamics is one of the leading accounting software packages. Information related to this package is found at its web site.

Address: http://www.gps.com/dynamics

Steps:
1. Go to the site shown above.
2. Choose **Product Details** then choose **General Ledger.** Perform instruction (a) below.
3. Choose **Product Details** then choose **Payables Management.** Perform instruction (b) below.
4. Choose **Product Details** then choose **Receivables Management.** Perform instruction (c) below.

Instructions

(a) What are three key features of the general ledger module highlighted by the company?
(b) What are three key features of the payables management module highlighted by the company?
(c) What are three key features of the receivables management module highlighted by the company?

Answers to Self-Study Questions
1. d   2. b   3. a   4. c   5. a   6. c   7. d   8. b   9. d   10. c

Remember to go back to the Navigator box on the chapter-opening page and check off your completed work.

CONCEPTS FOR REVIEW

Before studying this chapter, you should know or, if necessary, review:

a. How cash transactions are journalized in special journals. (Ch. 6, pp. 240–244, 247–248)

b. How postings are made to the cash account from special journals. (Ch. 6, pp. 240–244, 247–248)

c. The phases in developing an accounting system. (Ch. 6, pp. 233–234)

THE NAVIGATOR

FEATURE STORY

No Free Lunch

At Columbia University, thousands of dollars in cash changes hands between students and dining facility cashiers. Making sure that all of the money received by cashiers gets to where it's supposed to go requires various control measures. In accounting, these measures are called internal control.

One control measure used in the cafeteria at Columbia is that the register tape that records the sale and the amount of cash received must reconcile with the amount of cash in the cash drawer at the end of the day. "We see if there are significant overages or shortages at the end of each day for each register," says Susan McLaughlin, director of Columbia's dining facilities. Do cash differences happen very often? "No, because the cashier knows that if there are repeated or significant shortages, disciplinary action will be taken," she says. "There should not be a variance of more than $5, either over or under, at any given time—or else it indicates poor cash handling."

If a student buying a meal at a register sees that a sale isn't rung up or if the student doesn't get a receipt, there is a possibility that the cashier is stealing. "We know that taking the receipt is an annoyance," says Ms. McLaughlin, "but issuing receipts is an absolutely mandatory control for us."

THE NAVIGATOR

CHAPTER 7

INTERNAL CONTROL AND CASH

THE NAVIGATOR ✔

- Understand *Concepts for Review* ☐
- Read *Feature Story* ☐
- Scan *Study Objectives* ☐
- Read *Preview* ☐
- Read text and answer *Before You Go On*
  p. 286 ☐ p. 294 ☐ p. 303 ☐ p. 304 ☐
- Work *Demonstration Problem* ☐
- Review *Summary of Study Objectives* ☐
- Answer *Self-Study Questions* ☐
- Complete assignments ☐

STUDY OBJECTIVES

After studying this chapter, you should be able to:

1. *Define internal control.*
2. *Identify the principles of internal control.*
3. *Explain the applications of internal control principles to cash receipts.*
4. *Describe the applications of internal control principles to cash disbursements.*
5. *Explain the operation of a petty cash fund.*
6. *Indicate the control features of a bank account.*
7. *Prepare a bank reconciliation.*
8. *Explain the reporting of cash.*

THE NAVIGATOR

*A*s the story about the dining facilities at Columbia University indicates, control of cash is important. Similarly, controls are needed to safeguard other types of assets. For example, Columbia University undoubtedly has controls to prevent the theft of food served in the cafeteria and controls to prevent the theft of computer equipment and supplies from its computer laboratories.

In this chapter, we explain the essential features of an internal control system and then describe how those controls apply to cash. The applications include some controls with which you may be already familiar. Toward the end of the chapter, we describe the use of a bank and explain how cash is reported on the balance sheet. The content and organization of Chapter 7 are as follows:

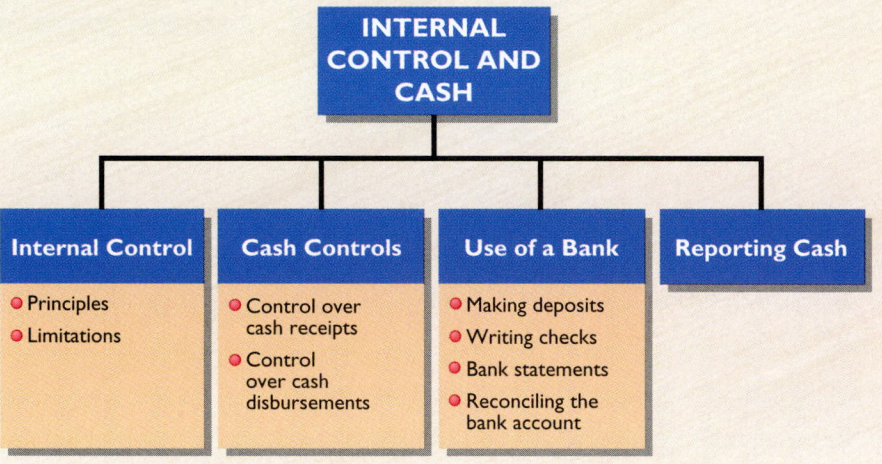

THE NAVIGATOR

INTERNAL CONTROL

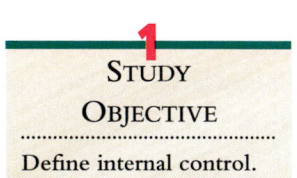

STUDY OBJECTIVE

1

Define internal control.

Could there be dishonest employees in the business that you own or manage? Unfortunately, the answer sometimes is Yes. For example, the financial press recently reported the following:

A bookkeeper in a small company diverted $750,000 of bill payments to a personal bank account over a 3-year period.

A shipping clerk with 28 years of service shipped $125,000 of merchandise to himself.

A computer operator embezzled $21 million from Wells Fargo Bank over a 2-year period.

A church treasurer "borrowed" $150,000 of church funds to finance a friend's business dealings.

These situations emphasize the need for a good system of internal control.

Internal control consists of the plan of organization and all the related methods and measures adopted within a business to:

1. **Safeguard its assets** from employee theft, robbery, and unauthorized use.
2. **Enhance the accuracy and reliability of its accounting records** by reducing the risk of **errors** (unintentional mistakes) and **irregularities** (intentional mistakes and misrepresentations) in the accounting process.

Under the Foreign Corrupt Practices Act of 1977, all major U.S. corporations are required to maintain an adequate system of internal control. Companies that fail to comply are subject to fines, and company officers may be imprisoned. Also, the National Commission on Fraudulent Financial Reporting concluded that all companies whose stock is publicly traded should maintain internal controls that can provide reasonable assurance that fraudulent financial reporting will be prevented or subject to early detection.[1]

> **INTERNATIONAL NOTE**
>
> U.S. companies also adopt model business codes that guide their international operations to provide for a safe and healthy workplace, avoid child and forced labor, abstain from bribes, and follow sound environmental practices.

TECHNOLOGY IN ACTION

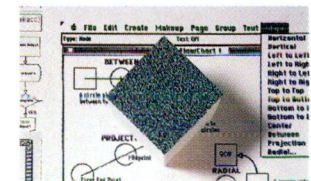

Good internal control must be designed into computerized systems. The starting point is usually flow charts that graphically depict each component of a firm's operations. The assembled flow charts serve as the basis for writing detailed programs. An example of flow charting is given in this chapter. When attempts to automate or improve accounting systems fail, it is often due to the absence of such well-documented procedures.

Principles of Internal Control

To safeguard its assets and enhance the accuracy and reliability of its accounting records, a company follows specific control principles. Of course, internal control measures vary with the size and nature of the business and with management's control philosophy. However, the six principles listed in Illustration 7-1 apply to most enterprises. Each principle is explained in the following sections.

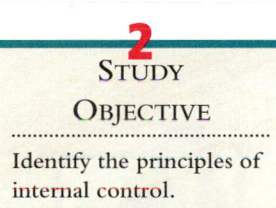

2
STUDY
OBJECTIVE
....
Identify the principles of internal control.

ILLUSTRATION 7-1
Principles of internal control

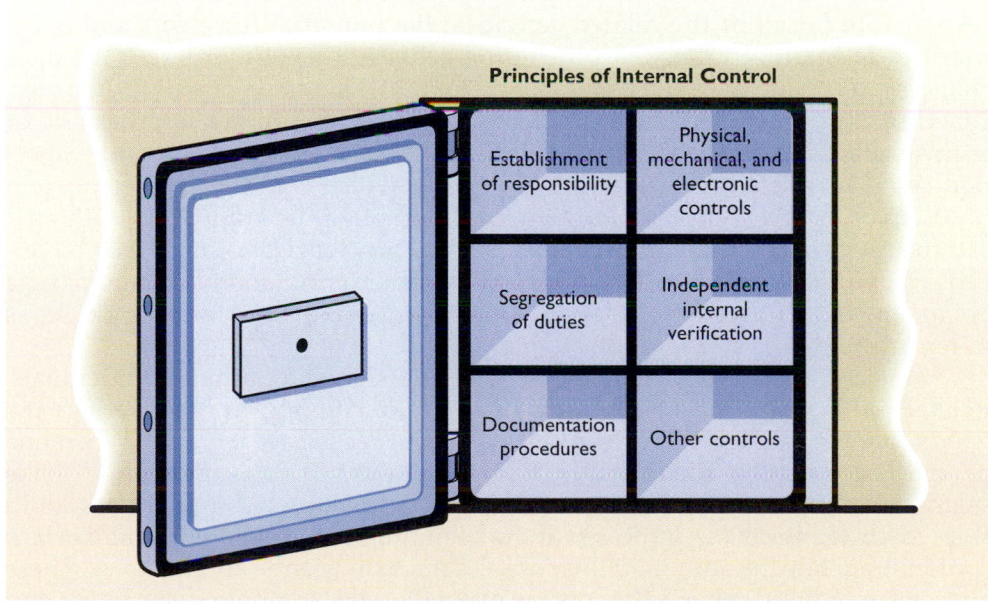

---

[1]Report of the National Commission on Fraudulent Financial Reporting, October 1987, p. 11.

It's your shift now. I'm turning in my cash drawer and heading home.

Transfer of cash drawers

Establishment of Responsibility

An essential characteristic of internal control is the assignment of responsibility to specific individuals. **Control is most effective when only one person is responsible for a given task.** To illustrate, assume that the cash on hand at the end of the day in a Safeway supermarket is $10 short of the cash rung up on the cash register. If only one person has operated the register, responsibility for the shortage can be assessed quickly. However, if two or more individuals have worked the register, it may be impossible to determine who is responsible for the error unless each person is assigned a separate cash drawer and register key. The principle of establishing responsibility was followed by Columbia University's dining services (in the opening story) by assigning a cashier to a cash register and keeping each cashier's cash drawer separate from others.

Establishing responsibility includes the authorization and approval of transactions. For example, the vice president of sales should have the authority to establish policies for making credit sales. The policies ordinarily will require written credit department approval of credit sales.

Segregation of Duties

This principle (also identified as separation of functions or division of work) is indispensable in a system of internal control. There are two common applications of this principle:

1. The responsibility for related activities should be assigned to different individuals.
2. The responsibility for establishing the accountability (keeping the records) for an asset should be separate from the physical custody of that asset.

The rationale for segregation of duties is that the work of one employee should, without a duplication of effort, provide a reliable basis for evaluating the work of another employee.

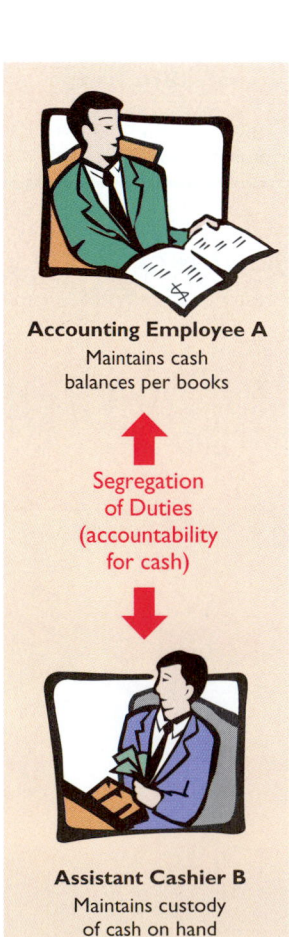

Accounting Employee A
Maintains cash balances per books

Segregation of Duties (accountability for cash)

Assistant Cashier B
Maintains custody of cash on hand

Related Activities.   Related activities that should be assigned to different individuals arise in both the purchasing and selling areas. **When one individual is responsible for all of the related activities, the potential for errors and irregularities is increased.** Related purchasing activities include ordering the merchandise, receiving the goods, and paying (or authorizing payment) for the merchandise. In purchasing, for example, orders could be placed with friends or with suppliers who give kickbacks. Similarly, only a cursory count and inspection could be made upon receiving the goods, which could lead to errors and poor quality merchandise. In addition, payment might be authorized without a careful review of the invoice, or even worse, fictitious invoices might be approved for payment. When the responsibility for ordering, receiving, and paying are assigned to different individuals or departments, the risk of such abuses is minimized.

Similarly, related sales activities should be assigned to different individuals. Related selling activities include making a sale, shipping (or delivering) the goods to the customer, billing the customer, and receiving payment. When one person is responsible for related sales transactions, a salesperson could make sales at unauthorized prices to increase sales commissions; a shipping clerk could ship goods to himself, as indicated at the beginning of the chapter; a billing clerk could understate the amount billed for sales made to friends and relatives. These abuses are reduced when salespersons make the sale, shipping department employees ship the goods on the basis of the sales order, and billing department employees prepare the sales invoice after comparing the sales order with the report of goods shipped.

Accountability for Assets.   If accounting is to provide a valid basis of accountability for an asset, the accountant should have neither physical custody of the asset nor access to it. Moreover, the custodian of the asset should not maintain or have access to the accounting records. **When one employee maintains the record of the asset that should be on hand, and a different employee has physical custody of the asset, the custodian of the asset is not likely to convert the asset to personal use.** The separation of accounting responsibility from the custody of assets is especially important for cash and inventories because these assets are very vulnerable to unauthorized use or misappropriation.

ACCOUNTING IN ACTION
International Insight

Recently Sumitomo Corporation became the fifth Japanese company to announce a huge loss, this time $1.8 billion, due to a single copper trader. Some are blaming Japanese culture because it encourages group harmony over confrontation and thus may contribute to poor internal controls. For example good controls require that both parties to a copper trade send a confirmation slip to management to verify all trades. In Japan the counterparty to the trade often sends the confirmation slip to the trader, who then forwards it to management. Thus, it is possible for the trader to change the confirmation slip. An unethical trader could create fictitious trades to hide losses for an extended period of time or to conceal trades that are larger than allowed limits.

Source: Sheryl Wudunn, "Big New Loss Makes Japan Look Inward," *New York Times*, June 17, 1996, P. D1.

Documentation Procedures

Documents provide evidence that transactions and events have occurred. In the Columbia University cafeteria, the cash register tape was the university's documentation for the sale and the amount of cash received. Similarly, the shipping document indicates that the goods have been shipped, and the sales invoice indicates that the customer has been billed for the goods. By adding signatures (or initials) to the documents, the individual(s) responsible for the transaction or event can be identified. Documentation of transactions should be made when the transaction occurs. Documentation of events, such as those leading to adjusting entries, is generally developed when the adjustments are made.

   Several procedures should be established for documents. First, whenever possible, **documents should be prenumbered and all documents should be accounted for**. Prenumbering helps to prevent a transaction from being recorded more than once, or conversely, to prevent the transactions from not being recorded. Second, documents that are **source documents for accounting entries should be promptly forwarded to the accounting department to help ensure timely recording of the transaction and event**. Thus, this control measure contributes directly to the accuracy and reliability of the accounting records.

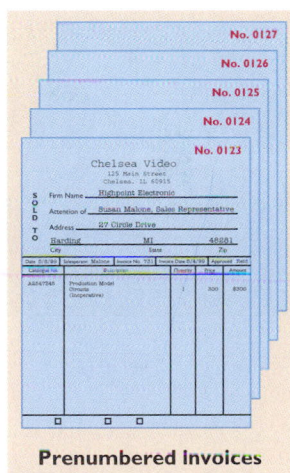

Prenumbered Invoices

HELPFUL HINT
An important corollary to prenumbering is that voided documents be kept until all documents are accounted for.

Physical, Mechanical, and Electronic Controls

Use of physical, mechanical, and electronic controls is essential. Physical controls relate primarily to the safeguarding of assets. Mechanical and electronic controls safeguard assets and enhance the accuracy and reliability of the accounting records. Examples of these controls are shown in Illustration 7-2.

ILLUSTRATION 7-2

Physical, mechanical, and electronic controls

Physical Controls

Safes, vaults, and safety deposit boxes for cash and business papers

Locked warehouses and storage cabinets for inventories and records

Computer facilities with pass key access

Mechanical and Electronic Controls

Alarms to prevent break-ins

Television monitors and garment sensors to deter theft

Time clocks for recording time worked

ACCOUNTING IN ACTION

Business Insight

John Patterson, a young Ohio merchant, couldn't understand why his retail business didn't show a profit. There were lots of customers, but the money just seemed to disappear. Patterson suspected pilferage and sloppy bookkeeping by store clerks. Frustrated, he placed an order with a Dayton, Ohio, company for two rudimentary cash registers. A year later, Patterson's store was in the black.

"What is a good thing for this little store is a good thing for every retail store in the world," he observed. A few months later, in 1884, John Patterson and his brother, Frank, bought the tiny cash register maker for $6,500. The word around Dayton was that the Patterson boys got stung.

In the following 37 years, John Patterson built National Cash Register Co. into a corporate giant. Patterson died in 1922, the year in which NCR sold its two millionth cash register.

Source: The Wall Street Journal, January 28, 1989.

Independent Internal Verification

Most systems of internal control provide for independent internal verification. This principle involves the review, comparison, and reconciliation of data prepared by one or several employees. To obtain maximum benefit from independent internal verification:

1. The verification should be made periodically or on a surprise basis.
2. The verification should be done by an employee who is independent of the personnel responsible for the information.
3. Discrepancies and exceptions should be reported to a management level that can take appropriate corrective action.

Independent internal verification is especially useful in comparing recorded accountability with existing assets. The reconciliation of the cash register tape with the cash in the register in the Columbia University dining facility is an example of this internal control principle. Another common example is the reconciliation by an independent person of the cash balance per books with the cash balance per bank. The relationship between this principle and the segregation of duties principle is shown graphically in Illustration 7-3.

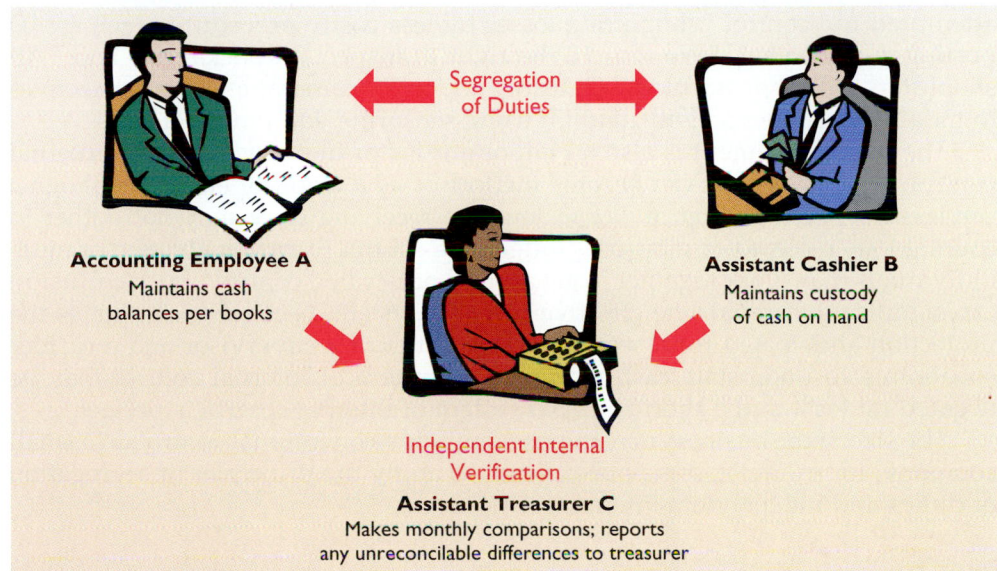

ILLUSTRATION 7-3

Comparison of segregation of duties principle with independent internal verification principle

In large companies, independent internal verification is often assigned to internal auditors. **Internal auditors** are employees of the company who evaluate on a continuous basis the effectiveness of the company's system of internal control. They periodically review the activities of departments and individuals to determine whether prescribed internal controls are being followed and to make recommendations for improvement. The importance of this function is illustrated by the number of internal auditors employed by companies. In a recent year, AT&T had 350 internal auditors, Exxon had 395, and IBM had 142.

Other Controls

Other control measures include the following:

1. **Bonding of employees who handle cash.** Bonding involves obtaining insurance protection against misappropriation of assets by dishonest employees. This measure contributes to the safeguarding of cash in two ways: First, the insurance company carefully screens all individuals before adding them to the policy and may reject risky applicants. Second, bonded employees know that the insurance company will vigorously prosecute all offenders.
2. **Rotating employees' duties and requiring employees to take vacations.** These measures are designed to deter employees from attempting any thefts since they will not be able to permanently conceal their improper actions. Many bank embezzlements, for example, have been discovered when the perpetrator has been on vacation or assigned to a new position.

Limitations of Internal Control

A company's system of internal control is generally designed to provide reasonable assurance that assets are properly safeguarded and that the accounting records are reliable. **The concept of reasonable assurance rests on the premise that the costs of establishing control procedures should not exceed their expected benefit.** To illustrate, consider shoplifting losses in retail stores. Such losses could be completely eliminated by having a security guard stop and search customers as they leave the store. Store managers have concluded, however, that the negative effects of adopting such a procedure cannot be justified. Instead, stores have attempted to "control" shoplifting losses by less costly procedures such as: (1) posting signs saying, "We reserve the right to inspect all packages," and "All shoplifters will be prosecuted," (2) using hidden TV cameras and store detectives to monitor customer activity, and (3) using sensoring equipment at exits.

The **human element** is also an important factor in every system of internal control. A good system can become ineffective as a result of employee fatigue, carelessness, or indifference. For example, a receiving clerk may not bother to count goods received or may just "fudge" the counts. Occasionally, two or more individuals may work together to get around prescribed controls. Such **collusion** can significantly impair the effectiveness of a system, because it eliminates the protection anticipated from segregation of duties. If a supervisor and a cashier collaborate to understate cash receipts, the system of internal control may be negated (at least in the short run). No system of internal control is perfect.

The size of the business may impose limitations on internal control. In a small company, for example, it may be difficult to apply the principles of segregation of duties and independent internal verification.

TECHNOLOGY IN ACTION

Unfortunately, computer-related frauds have become a major concern. The average computer fraud loss is $650,000, compared with an average loss of only $19,000 resulting from other types of white-collar crime.

Computer fraud can be perpetrated almost invisibly and done with electronic speed. Psychologically, stealing with impersonal computer tools can seem far less criminal. Therefore, the moral threshold to commit computer fraud is far lower than fraud involving person-to-person contact.

Preventing and detecting computer fraud represents a major challenge. One of the best ways for a company to minimize the likelihood of computer fraud is to have a good system of internal control that allows the benefits of computerization to be gained without opening the possibility for rampant fraud.

BEFORE YOU GO ON . . .

Review It

1. What are the two primary objectives of internal control?
2. Identify and describe the principles of internal control.
3. What are the limitations of internal control?

Do It

Li Song owns a small retail store. Li wants to establish good internal control procedures but is confused about the difference between segregation of duties and independent internal verification. Explain the differences to Li.

Reasoning: In order to help Li, you need to thoroughly understand each principle. From this knowledge, and a study of Illustration 7-3, it should be possible to explain the differences between the two principles.

Solution: Segregation of duties pertains to the assignment of responsibility so that the work of one employee will permit the evaluation of the work of another employee. Segregation of duties occurs daily in executing and recording transactions. In contrast, independent internal verification involves reviewing, comparing, and reconciling data prepared by one or several employees. Independent internal verification occurs after the fact, as in the case of reconciling cash register totals at the end of the day with cash on hand.

Related exercise material: BE7–1, BE7–2, E7–1, E7–2, and E7–3.

THE NAVIGATOR

CASH CONTROLS

Just as cash is the beginning of a company's operating cycle, it is usually the starting point for a company's system of internal control. Cash is the one asset that is readily convertible into any other type of asset; it is easily concealed and transported; and it is highly desired. Because of these characteristics, **cash is the asset most susceptible to improper diversion and use**. Moreover, because of the large volume of cash transactions, numerous errors may occur in executing and recording cash transactions. To safeguard cash and to assure the accuracy of the accounting records for cash, effective internal control over cash is imperative.

Cash consists of coins, currency (paper money), checks, money orders, and money on hand or on deposit in a bank or similar depository. The general rule is that if the bank will accept it for deposit, it is cash. Items such as postage stamps and postdated checks (checks payable in the future) are not cash. Stamps are a prepaid expense; the postdated checks are accounts receivable. The application of internal control principles to cash receipts and cash disbursements is explained in the following sections.

Internal Control over Cash Receipts

Cash receipts may result from a variety of sources: cash sales; collections on account from customers; the receipt of interest, rents, and dividends; investments by owners; bank loans; and proceeds from the sale of noncurrent assets. The internal control principles explained earlier apply to cash receipts transactions as shown in Illustration 7-4.

As might be expected, companies vary considerably in how they apply these principles. To illustrate internal control over cash receipts, we will examine control measures for a retail store with both over-the-counter and mail receipts.

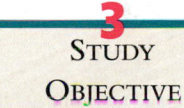
3 STUDY OBJECTIVE

Explain the applications of internal control principles to cash receipts.

Over-the-Counter Receipts

Control of over-the-counter receipts in retail businesses is centered on cash registers that are visible to customers. In supermarkets and variety stores such as Kmart, cash registers are placed in check-out lines near the exit(s). In Sears, Roebuck & Co. and J. C. Penney stores each department has its own cash register. When a cash sale occurs, the sale is "rung up" on a cash register **with the amount clearly visible to the customer**. This measure prevents the cashier from ringing up a lower amount and pocketing the difference. The customer receives an itemized cash register receipt slip and is expected to count the change received. A cash register tape, which is locked into the register until removed by a supervisor or manager, accumulates the daily transactions and totals. When the tape is removed, the supervisor compares the total with the amount of cash in the register. It should show all registered receipts accounted for. The supervisor's findings

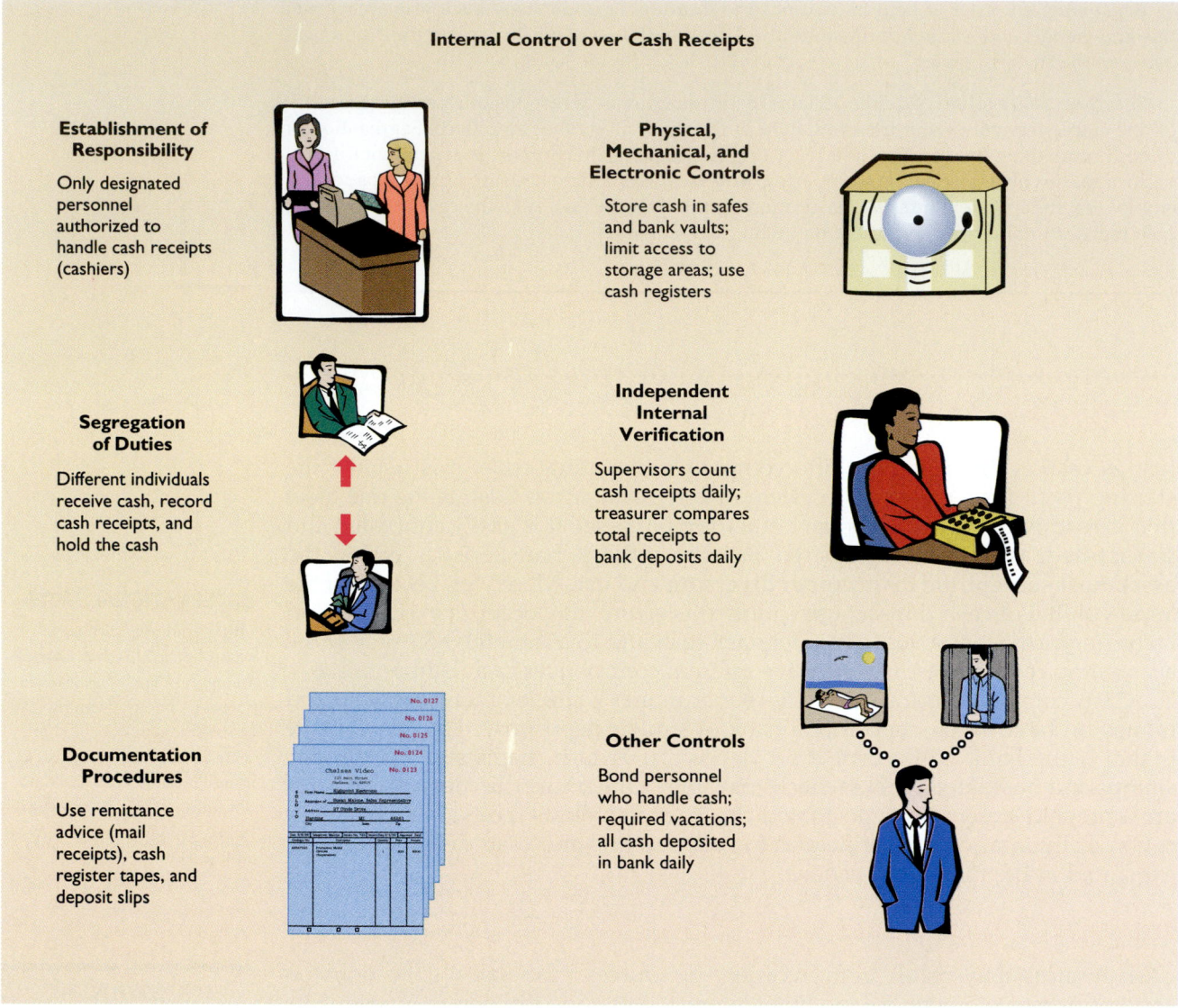

Internal Control over Cash Receipts

Establishment of Responsibility

Only designated personnel authorized to handle cash receipts (cashiers)

Physical, Mechanical, and Electronic Controls

Store cash in safes and bank vaults; limit access to storage areas; use cash registers

Segregation of Duties

Different individuals receive cash, record cash receipts, and hold the cash

Independent Internal Verification

Supervisors count cash receipts daily; treasurer compares total receipts to bank deposits daily

Documentation Procedures

Use remittance advice (mail receipts), cash register tapes, and deposit slips

Other Controls

Bond personnel who handle cash; required vacations; all cash deposited in bank daily

ILLUSTRATION 7-4

Application of internal control principles to cash receipts

are reported on a cash count sheet that is signed by both the cashier and supervisor. The cash count sheet used by Alrite Food Mart is shown in Illustration 7-5.

The count sheets, register tapes, and cash are then given to the head cashier. This individual prepares a daily cash summary showing the total cash received and the amount from each source, such as cash sales and collections on account. The head cashier sends one copy of the summary to the accounting department for entry into the cash receipts journal. The other copy goes to the treasurer's office for subsequent comparison with the daily bank deposit. Next, the head cashier prepares a deposit slip (see Illustration 7-9 on page 296) and makes the bank deposit. The total amount deposited should be equal to the total receipts on the daily cash summary. This will assure that all receipts have been placed in the custody of the bank. In accepting the bank deposit, the bank stamps (authenticates) the duplicate deposit slip and sends it to the company treasurer, who makes the comparison with the daily cash summary. The foregoing measures for cash sales are graphically presented in Illustration 7-6. The activities of the sales department are shown separate from those of the cashier's department to indicate the segregation of duties in handling cash.

ILLUSTRATION 7-5

Cash count sheet

Store No. ___8___   Date   March 8, 1999

1. Opening cash balance $ 50.00
2. Cash sales per tape (attached)   6,956.20
3. Total cash to be accounted for   7,006.20
4. Cash on hand (see list)   6,996.10
5. Cash (short) or over $ (10.10)
6. Ending cash balance $ 50.00
7. Cash for deposit (Line 4 – Line 6) $6,946.10

Cashier *J. Cruse*   Supervisor *M. Braun*

ILLUSTRATION 7-6

Executing over-the-counter cash sales

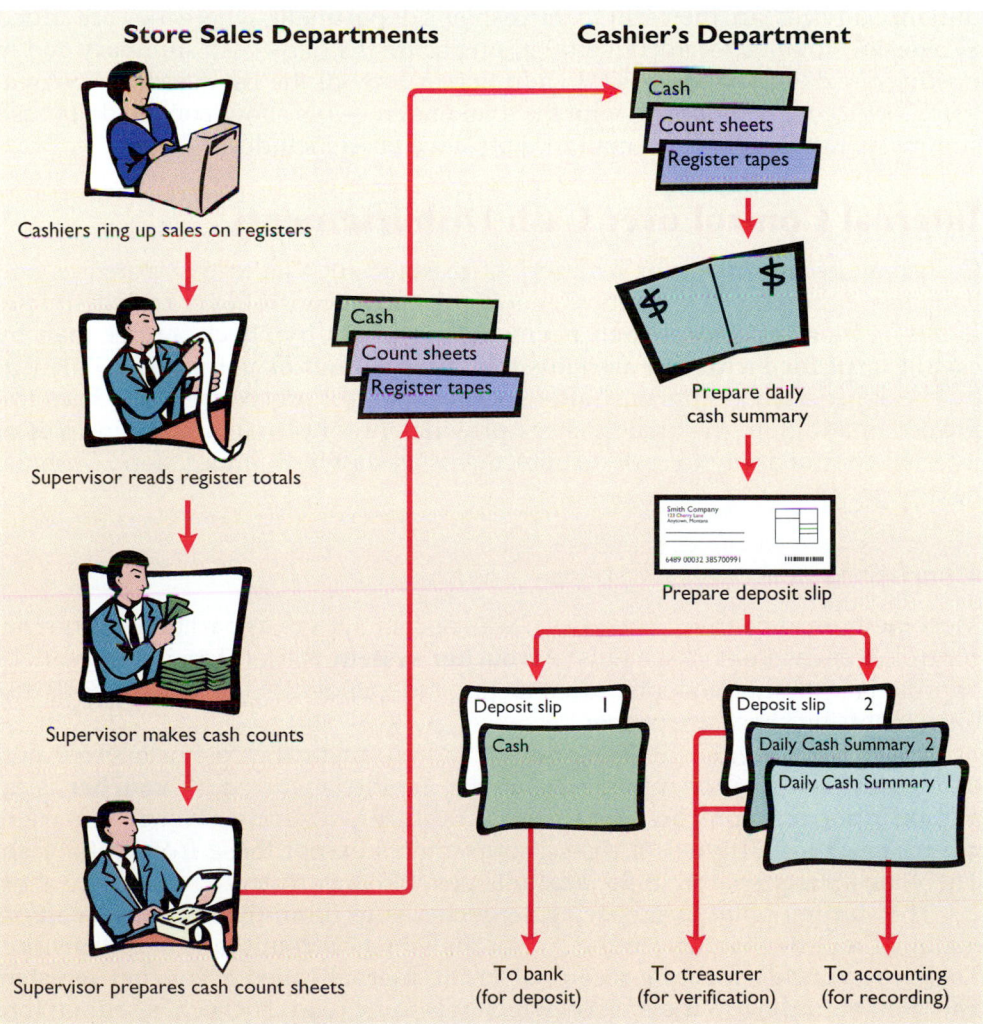

Store Sales Departments

Cashiers ring up sales on registers

Supervisor reads register totals

Supervisor makes cash counts

Supervisor prepares cash count sheets

Cash
Count sheets
Register tapes

Cashier's Department

Cash
Count sheets
Register tapes

Prepare daily cash summary

Smith Company

Prepare deposit slip

Deposit slip   1
Cash

Deposit slip   2
Daily Cash Summary   2
Daily Cash Summary   1

To bank
(for deposit)

To treasurer
(for verification)

To accounting
(for recording)

HELPFUL HINT
Flowcharts enhance the understanding of the flow of documents, the processing steps, and the internal control procedures.

Mail Receipts

Because of your experience as an individual customer, you may be more familiar with over-the-counter receipts than with mail receipts. However, mail receipts resulting from billings and credit sales are by far the most common way cash is received by the greatest variety of businesses. Think, for example, of the number of checks received through the mail daily by a national retailer such as Land's End or L.L. Bean.

All mail receipts should be received in the presence of two mail clerks. These receipts are generally in the form of checks or money orders and frequently are accompanied by a remittance advice stating the purpose of the check. Each check should be promptly endorsed "For Deposit Only" by use of a company stamp. This **restrictive endorsement** reduces the likelihood that the check will be diverted to personal use because banks will not give an individual any cash under this type of endorsement.

A list of the checks received each day should be prepared in duplicate showing the name of the issuer of the check, the purpose of the payment, and the amount of the check. Each mail clerk should sign the list to establish responsibility for the data. The original copy of the list, along with the checks and remittance advices, are then sent to the cashier's department, where they are added to over-the-counter receipts (if any) in preparing the daily cash summary and in making the daily bank deposit. In addition, a copy of the list is sent to the treasurer's office for comparison with the total mail receipts shown on the daily cash summary, to assure that all mail receipts have been included.

Internal Control over Cash Disbursements

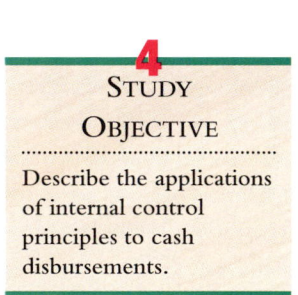

4

STUDY
OBJECTIVE

Describe the applications
of internal control
principles to cash
disbursements.

Cash may be disbursed for a variety of reasons, such as to pay expenses and liabilities, or to purchase assets. **Generally, internal control over cash disbursements is more effective when payments are made by check, rather than by cash, except for incidental amounts that are paid out of petty cash.**[2] Payment by check generally occurs only after specified control procedures have been followed. In addition, the "paid" check provides proof of payment. Principles of internal control apply to cash disbursements as shown in Illustration 7-7 on the next page.

Voucher System

Most medium and large companies use a voucher system as part of their internal control over cash disbursements. A **voucher system** is an extensive network of approvals by authorized individuals acting independently to ensure that all disbursements by check are proper.

The system begins with the authorization to incur the cost or expense and ends with the issuance of a check for the liability incurred. A **voucher** is an authorization form prepared for each expenditure in a voucher system. Vouchers are required for all types of cash disbursements except those from petty cash. The voucher is prepared in the accounts payable department.

The starting point in preparing a voucher is to fill in the appropriate information about the liability on the face of the voucher from the vendor's invoice. Then, the voucher must be recorded (in the journal called a **voucher register**) and filed according to the date on which it is to be paid. A check is sent on that

---

[2]The operation of a petty cash fund is explained on pages 292–94.

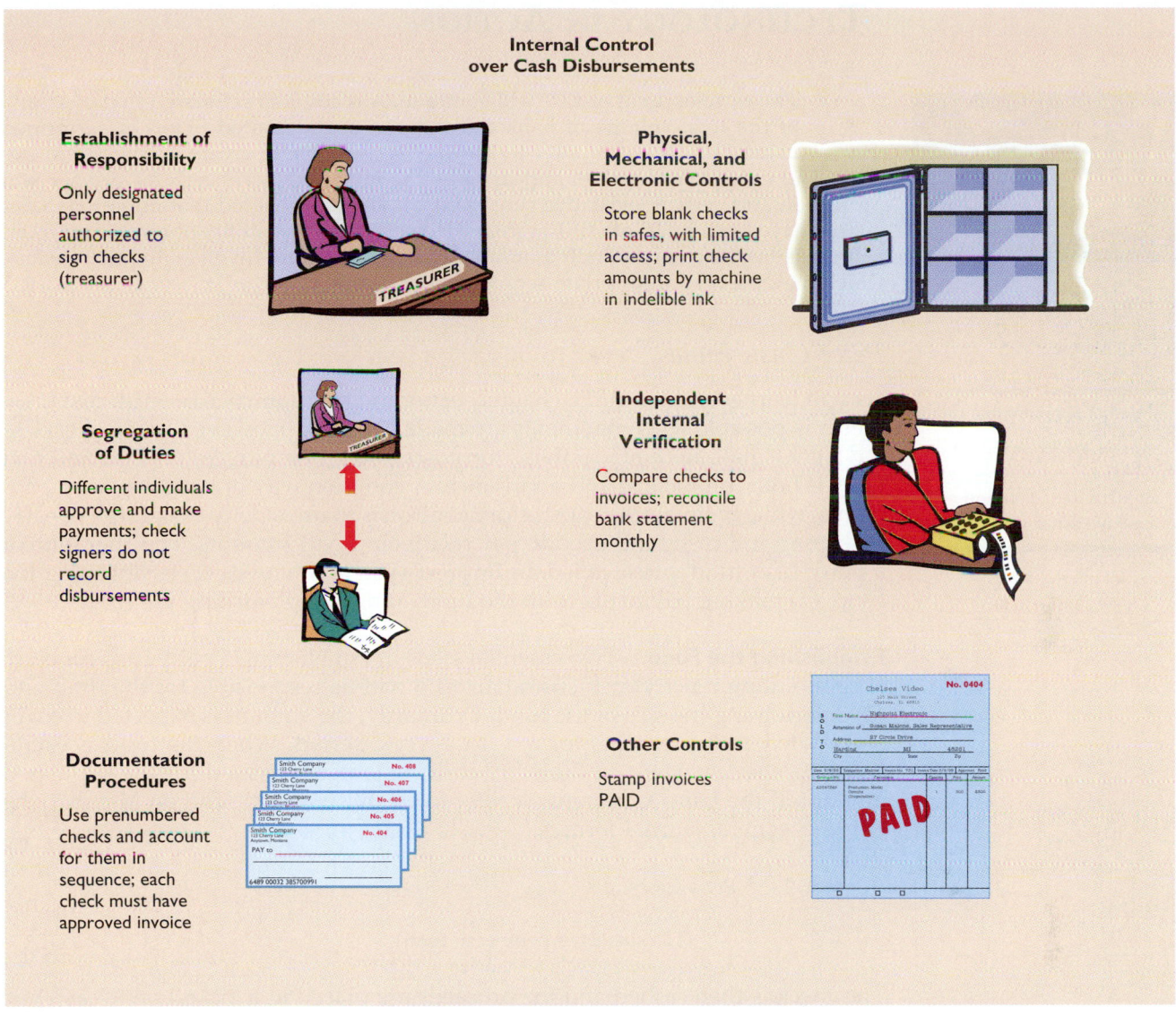

ILLUSTRATION 7-7

Application of internal control principles to cash disbursements

date, the voucher is stamped "paid," and the paid voucher is sent to the accounting department for recording (in a journal called the **check register**).

Electronic Funds Transfer (EFT) System

To account for and control cash is an expensive and time-consuming process. For example, it was estimated recently that the cost to process a check through a bank system ranges from $0.55 to $1.00 and is increasing. It is not surprising, therefore, that new approaches are being developed to transfer funds among parties without the use of paper (deposit tickets, checks, etc.). Such a procedure is called an **electronic funds transfer (EFT)**. EFT is a disbursement system that uses wire, telephone, telegraph, or computer to transfer cash from one location to another. Use of EFT is quite common. For example, the authors receive no formal payroll checks from their universities, which simply send magnetic tapes to the appropriate banks for deposit. Regular payments such as those for house, car, or utilities are frequently made by EFT.

TECHNOLOGY IN ACTION

The development of EFT will continue. Already it is estimated that over 80% of the total volume of bank transactions in the United States is performed using EFT. The computer technology is available to create a "checkless" society. The only major barriers appear to be the individual's concern for privacy and protection and certain legislative constraints. It should be noted that numerous safeguards have been built into EFT systems. However, the possibility of errors and fraud still exists because only a limited number of individuals are involved in the transfers, which may prevent appropriate segregation of duties.

Petty Cash Fund

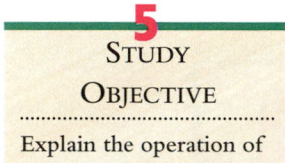

5

STUDY

OBJECTIVE

Explain the operation of
a petty cash fund.

As you learned earlier in the chapter, better internal control over cash disbursements is possible when payments are made by check. However, using checks to pay such small amounts as those for postage due, employee lunches, and taxi fares is both impractical and a nuisance. A common way of handling such payments, while maintaining satisfactory control, is to use a petty cash fund. A **petty cash fund** is a cash fund used to pay relatively small amounts. The operation of a petty cash fund, often called an **imprest system**, involves (1) establishing the fund, (2) making payments from the fund, and (3) replenishing the fund.[3]

Establishing the Fund. Two essential steps in establishing a petty cash fund are (1) appointing a petty cash custodian who will be responsible for the fund and (2) determining the size of the fund. Ordinarily, the amount is expected to cover anticipated disbursements for a 3- to 4-week period. When the fund is established, a check payable to the petty cash custodian is issued for the stipulated amount. If the Laird Company decides to establish a $100 fund on March 1, the entry in general journal form is:

A	=	L	+	OE
+100				
−100				

Mar. 1	Petty Cash	100	
	Cash		100
	(To establish a petty cash fund)		

The check is then cashed and the proceeds are placed in a locked petty cash box or drawer. Most petty cash funds are established on a fixed amount basis. Moreover, no additional entries will be made to the Petty Cash account unless the stipulated amount of the fund is changed. For example, if Laird Company decides on July 1 to increase the size of the fund to $250, it would debit Petty Cash $150 and credit Cash $150.

Making Payments from the Fund. The custodian of the petty cash fund has the authority to make payments from the fund that conform to prescribed management policies. Usually, management limits the size of expenditures that may be made and does not permit use of the fund for certain types of transactions (such as making short-term loans to employees). Each payment from the fund must be documented on a prenumbered petty cash receipt (or petty cash voucher), as shown in Illustration 7-8. Note that the signatures of both the custodian and the individual receiving payment are required on the receipt. If other supporting documents such as a freight bill or invoice are available, they should be attached to the petty cash receipt.

---

[3]The term "imprest" means an advance of money for a designated purpose.

ILLUSTRATION 7-8

Petty cash receipt

| No. 7 | W. A. LAIRD COMPANY | |
| | Petty Cash Receipt | |

Date ___3/6/99___

Paid to ___Acme Express Agency___   Amount ___$18.00___

For ___Collect Express Charges___

CHARGE TO ___Freight-in___

Approved

L. A. Bird Custodian

Received Payment

R. E. Meirs

The receipts are kept in the petty cash box until the fund is replenished. As a result, the sum of the petty cash receipts and money in the fund should equal the established total at all times. This means that surprise counts can be made at any time by an independent person, such as an internal auditor, to determine whether the fund is being maintained intact.

No accounting entry is made to record a payment at the time it is made from petty cash. It is considered to be both inexpedient and unnecessary to do so. Instead, the accounting effects of each payment are recognized when the fund is replenished.

Replenishing the Fund.   When the money in the petty cash fund reaches a minimum level, the fund is replenished. The request for reimbursement is initiated by the petty cash custodian. This individual prepares a schedule (or summary) of the payments that have been made and sends the schedule, supported by petty cash receipts and other documentation, to the treasurer's office. The receipts and supporting documents are examined in the treasurer's office to verify that they were proper payments from the fund. The treasurer then approves the request and a check is prepared to restore the fund to its established amount. At the same time, all supporting documentation is stamped "paid" so that it cannot be submitted again for payment.

To illustrate, assume that on March 15 the petty cash custodian requests a check for $87. The fund contains $13 cash and petty cash receipts for postage $44, freight-out $38, and miscellaneous expenses $5. The entry, in general journal form, to record the check is:

Mar. 15	Postage Expense	44	
	Freight-out	38	
	Miscellaneous Expense	5	
	Cash		87
	(To replenish petty cash fund)		

A	=	L	+	OE
− 87				− 44
				− 38
				− 5

Note that the Petty Cash account is not affected by the reimbursement entry. Replenishment changes the composition of the fund by replacing the petty cash receipts with cash, but it does not change the balance in the fund.

It may be necessary in replenishing a petty cash fund to recognize a cash shortage or overage. This results when the cash plus receipts in the petty cash box do not equal the established amount of the petty cash fund. To illustrate, assume in the example above that the custodian had only $12 in cash in the fund

HELPFUL HINT
Cash over and short situations result from mathematical errors or from failure to keep accurate records.

plus the receipts as listed. The request for reimbursement would, therefore, have been for $88, and the following entry would be made:

A	=	L	+	OE
− 88				− 44
				− 38
				− 5
				− 1

Mar. 15	Postage Expense		44	
	Freight-out		38	
	Miscellaneous Expense		5	
	Cash Over and Short		1	
	Cash			88
	(To replenish petty cash fund)			

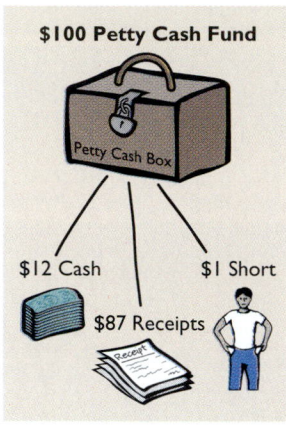

$100 Petty Cash Fund

Petty Cash Box

$12 Cash $1 Short

$87 Receipts

Conversely, if the custodian had $14 in cash, the reimbursement request would have been for $86 and Cash Over and Short would have been credited for $1. A debit balance in Cash Over and Short is reported in the income statement as miscellaneous expense; a credit balance is reported as miscellaneous revenue. Cash Over and Short is closed to Income Summary at the end of the year.

A petty cash fund should be replenished at the end of the accounting period regardless of the cash in the fund. Replenishment at this time is necessary in order to recognize the effects of the petty cash payments on the financial statements.

Internal control over a petty cash fund is strengthened by (1) having a supervisor make surprise counts of the fund to ascertain whether the paid vouchers and fund cash equal the imprest amount and (2) canceling or mutilating the paid vouchers so they cannot be resubmitted for reimbursement.

BEFORE YOU GO ON . . .

Review It

1. How do the principles of internal control apply to cash receipts?
2. How do the principles of internal control apply to cash disbursements?
3. When are entries required in a petty cash system?

Do It

L. R. Cortez is concerned about the control over cash receipts in his fast-food restaurant, Big Cheese. The restaurant has two cash registers. At no time do more than two employees take customer orders and ring up sales. Work shifts for employees range from 4 to 8 hours. Cortez asks your help in installing a good system of internal control over cash receipts.

Reasoning: Cortez needs to understand the principles of internal control, especially the principles of establishing responsibility, the use of electronic controls, and independent internal verification. Using this knowledge, an effective system of control over cash receipts can be designed and implemented.

Solution: Cortez should assign a cash register to each employee at the start of each work shift, with register totals set at zero. Each employee should be instructed to use only the assigned register and to ring up all sales. At the end of each work shift, Cortez or a supervisor/manager should total the register and make a cash count to see whether all cash is accounted for.

Related exercise material: BE7–3 and E7–2.

THE NAVIGATOR

USE OF A BANK

The use of a bank contributes significantly to good internal control over cash. A company can safeguard its cash by using a bank as a depository and clearing house for checks received and checks written. Use of a bank minimizes the amount of currency that must be kept on hand. In addition, the use of a bank facilitates the control of cash because a double record is maintained of all bank transactions—one by the business and the other by the bank. The asset account, Cash, maintained by the depositor is the reciprocal of the bank's liability account for each depositor. It should be possible to **reconcile these accounts** (make them agree) at any time.

Opening a bank checking account is a relatively simple procedure. Typically, the bank makes a credit check on the new customer and the depositor is required to sign a **signature card**. The card should contain the signatures of each person authorized to sign checks on the account. The signature card is used by bank employees to validate signatures on the checks.

As soon as possible after an account is opened, the bank will provide the depositor with a book of serially numbered checks and deposit slips imprinted with the depositor's name and address. Each check and deposit slip is imprinted with both a bank and a depositor identification number in magnetic ink to permit computer processing of the transaction.

Many companies have more than one bank account. For efficiency of operations and better control, national retailers like Wal-Mart Stores and Kmart may have regional bank accounts. Similarly, a company such as Exxon with more than 150,000 employees may have a payroll bank account, as well as one or more general bank accounts. In addition, a company may maintain several bank accounts in order to have more than one source for obtaining short-term loans when needed.

6

STUDY
OBJECTIVE
....
Indicate the control features of a bank account.

Making Bank Deposits

Bank deposits should be made by an authorized employee, such as the head cashier. Each deposit must be documented by a deposit slip (ticket), as shown in Illustration 7-9.

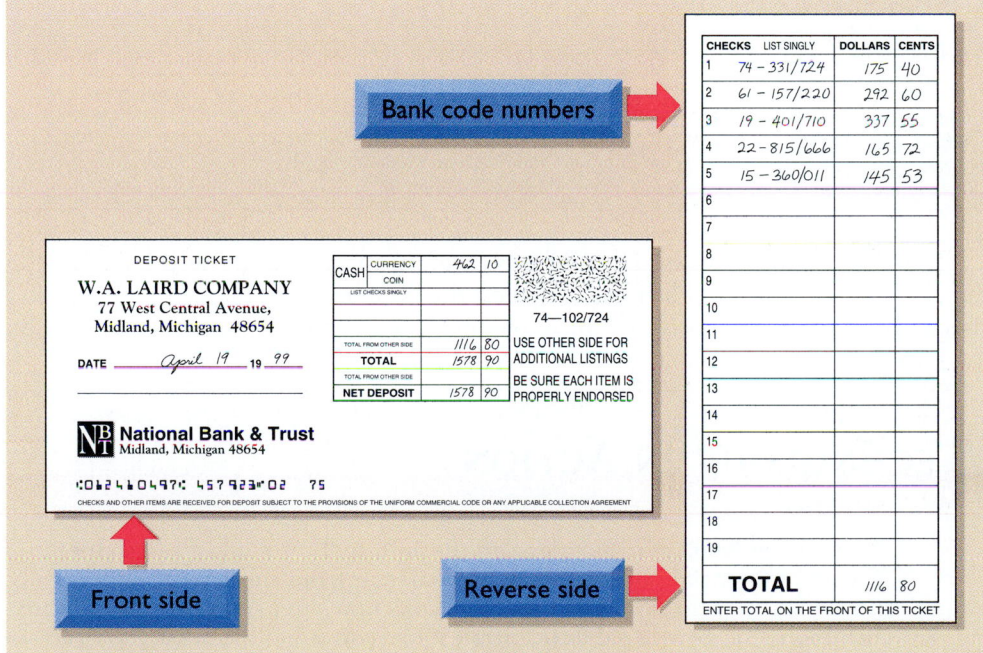

ILLUSTRATION 7-9

Deposit slip

Deposit slips are prepared in duplicate. The original is retained by the bank; the duplicate, machine stamped by the bank to establish its authenticity, is retained by the depositor.

Writing Checks

A **check** is a written order signed by the depositor directing the bank to pay a specified sum of money to a designated recipient. Thus, there are three parties to a check: the **maker** (or drawer) who issues the check, the **bank** (or payer) on which the check is drawn, and the **payee** to whom the check is payable. A check is a negotiable instrument that can be transferred to another party by endorsement. Each check should be accompanied by an explanation of its purposes. In many businesses, this is done by attaching a remittance advice to the check, as shown in Illustration 7-10.

ILLUSTRATION 7-10

Check with remittance advice

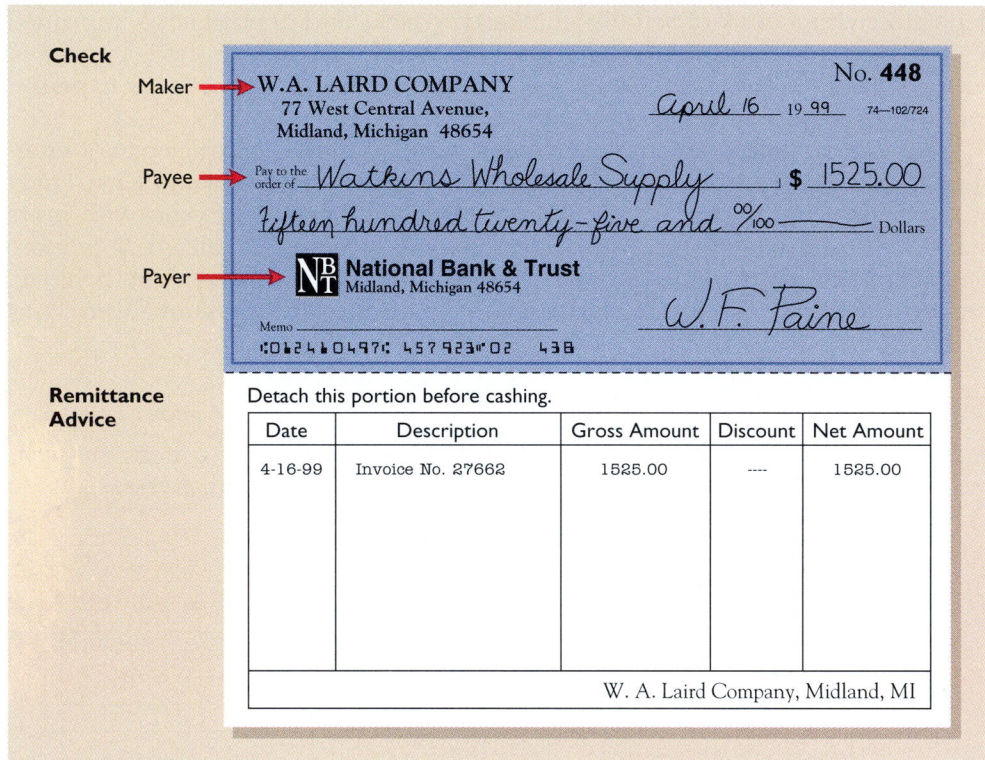

For both individuals and businesses, it is important to know the balance in the checking account at all times. To keep the balance current, each deposit and check should be entered on running balance memorandum forms provided by the bank or on the check stubs contained in the checkbook.

TECHNOLOGY IN ACTION

The first big consumer business on the information highway is shaping up as a set of financial household chores: balancing the checkbook, paying bills, and saving for retirement. Many U.S. banks now offer electronic home banking. For customers, the new capabilities mean more convenient service, more up-to-date information about their finances, and more control over their money. Nearly half-a-million households now do a substantial amount of their money management electronically from home, and this number is expected to increase significantly in the near future.

Bank Statements

Each month, the depositor receives a bank statement from the bank. A **bank statement** shows the depositor's bank transactions and balances. For example, the statement, like the one in Illustration 7-11, shows (1) checks paid and other debits that reduce the balance in the depositor's account, (2) deposits and other credits that increase the balance in the depositor's account, and (3) the account balance after each day's transactions.

HELPFUL HINT
Essentially, the bank statement is a copy of the bank's records sent to the customer for periodic review.

ILLUSTRATION 7-11

Bank statement

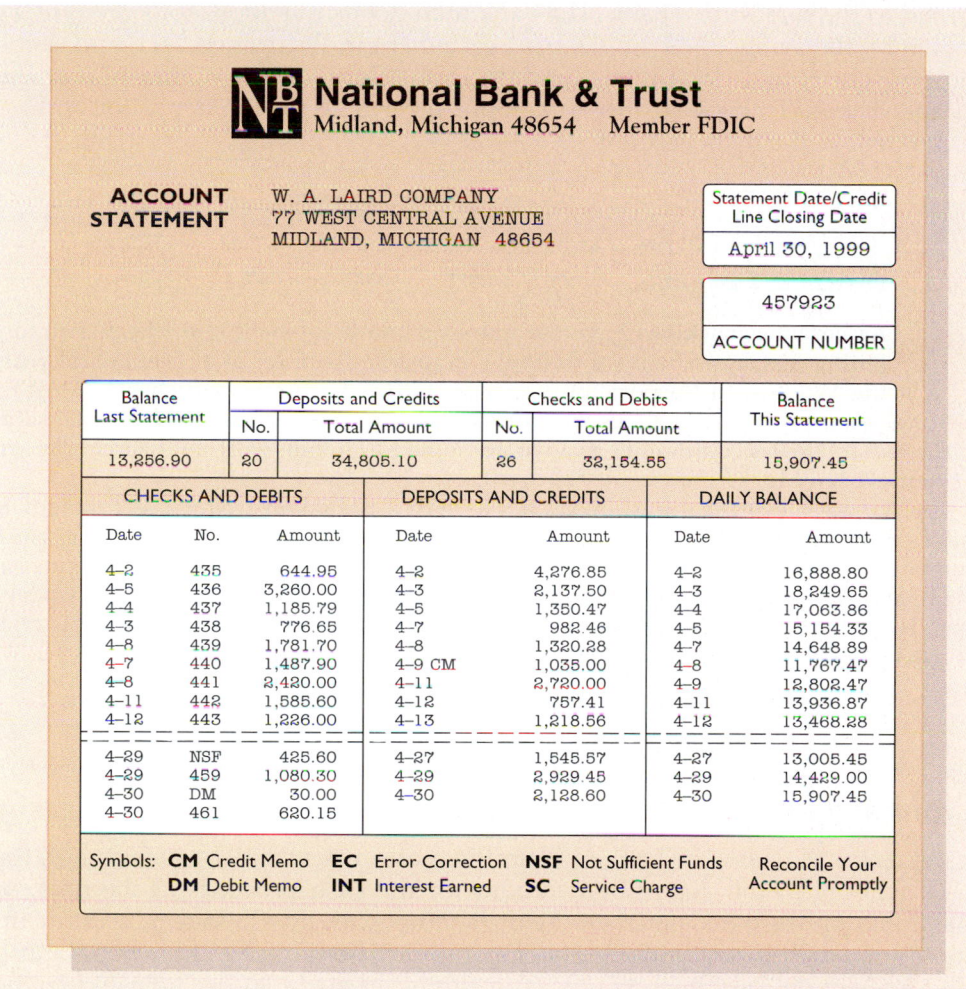

HELPFUL HINT
Every deposit received by the bank is *credited* to the customer's account. The reverse occurs when the bank "pays" a check issued by a company on its checking account balance: Payment reduces the bank's liability and is therefore *debited* to the customer's account with the bank.

Most banks offer depositors the option of receiving "paid" checks with their bank statements. For those who decline, the bank keeps a record of each check on microfilm. Irrespective of the depositor's choice, all "paid" checks are listed in numerical sequence on the bank statement along with the date the check was paid and its amount. Upon paying a check, the bank stamps the check "paid"; a paid check is sometimes referred to as a **canceled** check. In addition, the bank includes with the bank statement memoranda explaining other debits and credits made by the bank to the depositor's account.

Debit Memorandum

Banks charge a monthly fee for the use of their services. Often the fee is charged only when the average monthly balance in a checking account falls below a specified amount. The fee, called a **bank service charge**, is often identified on the bank statement by a code symbol such as SC. A debit memorandum explaining the charge is included with the bank statement. Separate debit memoranda may also be issued for other bank services such as the cost of printing checks, issuing traveler's checks, and wiring funds to other locations. The symbol DM is often used for such charges.

A debit memorandum is used by the bank when a previously deposited customer's check "bounces" because of insufficient funds. In such a case, the check is marked **NSF** (not sufficient funds) by the customer's bank and is returned to the depositor's bank. The bank then debits the depositor's account, as shown by the symbol NSF on the bank statement in Illustration 7-11, and sends the NSF check and debit memorandum to the depositor as notification of the charge. The NSF check creates an account receivable for the depositor and reduces cash in the bank account.

ACCOUNTING IN ACTION
Business Insight

As copying machines have become ever more sophisticated, check counterfeiting has flourished. For example, in just one quarter of a recent fiscal year, the Woolworth Corporation had a $5 million loss from bad checks. Most of the total occurred in the Foot Locker division of the company, a spokesperson said. In the U.S. business community as a whole, some $10 billion worth of bad checks are written every year.

Checkmate Electronic Inc. thinks it has at least a partial answer to this problem. It makes electronic devices that read the magnetic ink used to print account and routing numbers on checks. By identifying the magnetic frequencies as well as the precise shape and size of the numbers, the machine can determine if a check is a fake. Checkmate has a machine small enough to be installed beside cash registers, and it is now in use by such retailers as J.C. Penney, Neiman-Marcus, and Pier 1 Imports.

Source: The Wall Street Journal, March 31, 1994, p. C2; and Business Week, May 23, 1994, p. 9.

Credit Memorandum

A depositor may ask the bank to collect its notes receivable. In such a case, the bank will credit the depositor's account for the cash proceeds of the note, as illustrated on the bank statement by the symbol CM. It will issue a credit memorandum which is sent with the statement to explain the entry. Many banks also offer interest on checking accounts. The interest earned may be indicated on the bank statement by the symbol CM or INT.

Reconciling the Bank Account

7

STUDY

OBJECTIVE

Prepare a bank reconciliation.

Because the bank and the depositor maintain independent records of the depositor's checking account, you might assume that the respective balances will always agree. In fact, the two balances are seldom the same at any given time, and it is necessary to make the balance per books agree with the balance per bank—a process called **reconciling the bank account**. The lack of agreement between the two balances is due to:

1. **Time lags** that prevent one of the parties from recording the transaction in the same period.
2. **Errors** by either party in recording transactions.

Time lags occur frequently. For example, several days may elapse between the time a check is mailed to a payee and the date the check is paid by the bank.

ACCOUNTING IN ACTION
Ethics Insight

Some firms have used time lags to their advantage. For example, E. F. Hutton managers at one time overdrew their accounts by astronomical amounts—on some days the overdrafts totaled $1 billion—creating interest-free loans they could invest. The loans lasted as long as it took for the covering checks to be collected. Although not technically illegal at the time, Hutton's actions were wrong because it did not have bank permission to do so.

Similarly, when the depositor uses the bank's night depository to make its deposits, there will be a difference of at least one day between the time the receipts are recorded by the depositor and the time they are recorded by the bank. A time lag also occurs whenever the bank mails a debit or credit memorandum to the depositor.

The incidence of errors depends on the effectiveness of the internal controls maintained by the depositor and the bank. Bank errors are infrequent. However, either party could inadvertently record a $450 check as $45 or $540. In addition, the bank might mistakenly charge a check drawn by C. D. Berg to the account of C. D. Burg.

TECHNOLOGY IN ACTION

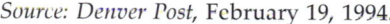

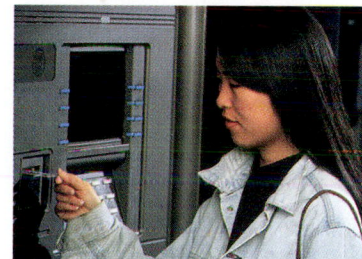

A malfunctioning computer software program doubled all withdrawals and transfers made at Chemical Bank automatic teller machines (ATMs) in New York state for about 12 hours. The printed record of transactions spit out by the ATM was accurate, but the computerized posting of the transactions was automatically doubled. The bank corrected all errors, which in the aggregate may have been $15 million.

Source: Denver Post, February 19, 1994.

Reconciliation Procedure

To obtain maximum benefit from a bank reconciliation, the reconciliation should be prepared by an employee who has no other responsibilities pertaining to cash. When the internal control principle of independent internal verification is not followed in preparing the reconciliation, cash embezzlements may escape unnoticed. For example, a cashier who prepares the reconciliation can embezzle cash and conceal the embezzlement by misstating the reconciliation. Thus, the bank accounts would reconcile and the embezzlement would not be detected.

In reconciling the bank account, it is customary to reconcile the balance per books and balance per bank to their adjusted (correct or true) cash balances. The reconciliation schedule is divided into two sections, as shown in Illustration 7-12. The starting point in preparing the reconciliation is to enter the balance per bank statement and balance per books on the schedule. The following steps should reveal all the reconciling items that cause the difference between the two balances.

HELPFUL HINT

Deposits in transit and outstanding checks are reconciling items because of time lags.

1. Compare the individual deposits on the bank statement with deposits in transit from the preceding bank reconciliation and with the deposits per company records or copies of duplicate deposit slips. Deposits recorded by the depositor that have not been recorded by the bank represent **deposits in transit** and are added to the balance per bank.

2. Compare the paid checks shown on the bank statement or the paid checks returned with the bank statement with (a) checks outstanding from the preceding bank reconciliation and (b) checks issued by the company as recorded in the cash payments journal. Issued checks recorded by the company that have not been paid by the bank represent **outstanding checks** that are deducted from the balance per the bank.

3. Note any **errors** discovered in the foregoing steps and list them in the appropriate section of the reconciliation schedule. For example, if a paid check correctly written by the company for $195 was mistakenly recorded by the company for $159, the error of $36 is deducted from the balance per books. All errors made by the depositor are reconciling items in determining the adjusted cash balance per books. In contrast, all errors made by the bank are reconciling items in determining the adjusted cash balance per the bank.

4. Trace **bank memoranda** to the depositor's records. Any unrecorded memoranda should be listed in the appropriate section of the reconciliation schedule. For example, a $5 debit memorandum for bank service charges is deducted from the balance per books, and $32 of interest earned is added to the balance per books.

ILLUSTRATION 7-12

Bank reconciliation procedures

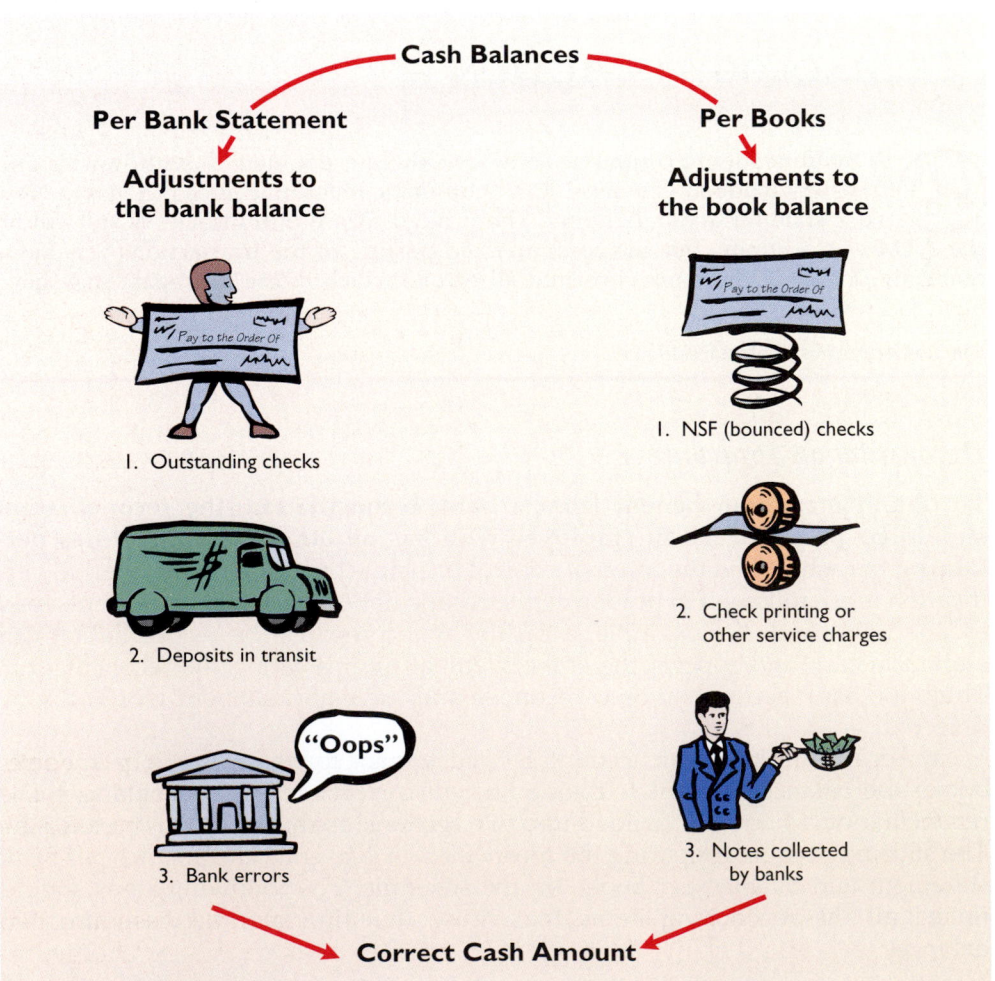

Bank Reconciliation Illustrated

The bank statement for the Laird Company is shown in Illustration 7-11. It shows a balance per bank of $15,907.45 on April 30, 1999. On this date the balance of cash per books is $11,589.45. From the foregoing steps, the following reconciling items are determined.

1. **Deposits in transit:** April 30 deposit (received by bank on May 1). $2,201.40
2. **Outstanding checks:** No. 453 $3,000.00; No. 457 $1,401.30; No. 460 $1,502.70.   5,904.00
3. **Errors:** Check No. 443 was correctly written by Laird for $1,226.00 and was correctly paid by the bank. However, it was recorded for $1,262.00 by Laird Company.   36.00
4. **Bank memoranda:**
   a. Debit—NSF check from J. R. Baron for $425.60   425.60
   b. Debit—Printing company checks charge, $30.00   30.00
   c. Credit—Collection of note receivable for $1,000 plus interest earned $50, less bank collection fee $15.00   1,035.00

HELPFUL HINT
Note in the bank statement that checks No. 459 and 461 have been paid but check No. 460 is not listed. Thus, this check is outstanding. If a complete bank statement were provided, checks No. 453 and 457 would also not be listed. The amounts for these three checks are obtained from the company's cash payments records.

The bank reconciliation is shown in Illustration 7-13.

ILLUSTRATION 7-13

Bank reconciliation

LAIRD COMPANY Bank Reconciliation April 30, 1999		
Cash balance per bank statement		$15,907.45
Add: Deposits in transit		2,201.40
		18,108.85
Less: Outstanding checks		
No. 453	$3,000.00	
No. 457	1,401.30	
No. 460	1,502.70	5,904.00
Adjusted cash balance per bank		**$12,204.85**
Cash balance per books		$11,589.45
Add: Collection of note receivable, $1,000 plus interest earned $50, less collection fee $15	$1,035.00	
Error in recording check No. 443	36.00	1,071.00
		12,660.45
Less: NSF check	425.60	
Bank service charge	30.00	455.60
Adjusted cash balance per books		**$12,204.85**

ALTERNATIVE TERMINOLOGY
The terms *adjusted balance, true cash balance,* and *correct cash balance* may be used interchangeably.

Entries from Bank Reconciliation

Each reconciling item in determining the **adjusted cash balance per books** should be recorded by the depositor. **If these items are not journalized and posted, the Cash account will not show the correct balance.** The entries for the Laird Company on April 30 are as follows:

Collection of Note Receivable.   This entry involves four accounts. Assuming that the interest of $50 has not been accrued and the collection fee is charged to Miscellaneous Expense, the entry is:

HELPFUL HINT
The entries that follow are adjusting entries. In prior chapters, Cash was an account that did not require adjustment because a bank reconciliation had not been explained.

A	=	L	+	OE
+1,035				−15
−1,000				+50

Apr. 30	Cash	1,035.00	
	Miscellaneous Expense	15.00	
	Notes Receivable		1,000.00
	Interest Revenue		50.00
	(To record collection of notes receivable		
	by bank)		

Book Error. An examination of the cash disbursements journal shows that check No. 443 was a payment on account to Andrea Company, a supplier. The correcting entry is:

A	=	L	+	OE
+36		+36		

Apr. 30	Cash	36.00	
	Accounts Payable—Andrea Company		36.00
	(To correct error in recording check		
	No. 443)		

NSF Check. As indicated earlier, an NSF check becomes an accounts receivable to the depositor. The entry is:

A	=	L	+	OE
+425.60				
−425.60				

Apr. 30	Accounts Receivable—J. R. Baron	425.60	
	Cash		425.60
	(To record NSF check)		

Bank Service Charges. Check printing charges (DM) and other bank service charges (SC) are debited to Miscellaneous Expense because they are usually nominal in amount. The entry is:

A	=	L	+	OE
−30				−30

Apr. 30	Miscellaneous Expense	30.00	
	Cash		30.00
	(To record charge for printing company		
	checks)		

The foregoing entries could also be combined into one compound entry. After the entries are posted, the cash account will show the following:

ILLUSTRATION 7-14

Adjusted balance in cash account

Cash				
Apr. 30 Bal.	11,589.45	Apr. 30	425.60
30	1,035.00	30	30.00
30	36.00		
Apr. 30 Bal.	**12,204.85**		

The adjusted cash balance in the ledger should agree with the adjusted cash balance per books in the bank reconciliation in Illustration 7-13.

What entries does the bank make? If any bank errors are discovered in preparing the reconciliation, the bank should be notified so it can make the necessary corrections on its records. The bank does not make any entries for deposits in transit or outstanding checks. Only when these items reach the bank will the bank record these items.

BEFORE YOU GO ON . . .

Review It

1. Why is it necessary to reconcile a bank account?
2. What steps are involved in the reconciliation procedure?
3. What information is included in a bank reconciliation?

Do It

Sally Kist owns Linen Kist Fabrics. Sally asks you to explain how the following reconciling items should be treated in reconciling the bank account at December 31: (1) a debit memorandum for an NSF check, (2) a credit memorandum for a note collected by the bank, (3) outstanding checks, and (4) a deposit in transit.

Reasoning: Sally needs to understand that one cause of a reconciling item is time lags. Items (1) and (2) are reconciling items because Linen Kist Fabrics has not yet recorded the memoranda. Items (3) and (4) are reconciling items because the bank has not recorded the transactions.

Solution: In reconciling the bank account, the reconciling items are treated as follows:

NSF check: Deducted from balance per books.
Collection of note: Added to balance per books.
Outstanding checks: Deducted from balance per bank.
Deposit in transit: Added to balance per bank.

Related exercise material: BE7–6, BE7–7, BE7–8, BE7–9, E7–7, E7–8, E7–9, and E7–10.

THE
NAVIGATOR

REPORTING CASH

Cash on hand, cash in banks, and petty cash are often combined and reported simply as **Cash**. Because it is the most liquid asset owned by a company, cash is listed first in the current asset section of the balance sheet. Some companies use the designation "cash and cash equivalents" in reporting cash as illustrated by the following:

8
STUDY
OBJECTIVE
....
Explain the reporting of cash.

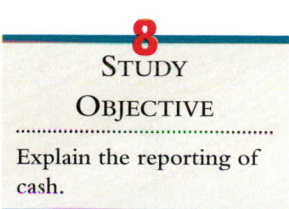

EASTMAN KODAK COMPANY Balance Sheets (partial)		
	1997	1996
Current assets (in millions)		
Cash and cash equivalents	$728	$1,777

ILLUSTRATION 7-15

Presentation of cash and cash equivalents

Cash equivalents are highly liquid investments, with maturities of 3 months or less when purchased, that can be converted into a specific amount of cash. They include money market funds, money market savings certificates, bank certificates of deposit, and U.S. Treasury bills and notes.

A company may have cash that is restricted for a special purpose. Examples include a payroll bank account for paying salaries and wages, and plant expansion fund cash for financing new construction. If the restricted cash is expected to be used within the next year, the amount should be reported as a current asset.

However, when this is not the case, the restricted funds should be reported as a noncurrent asset. Since a payroll bank account will be used as early as the next payday for employees, it is reported as a current asset. In contrast, unless the new construction will begin within the next year, plant expansion fund cash is classified as a noncurrent asset.

In making loans to depositors, it is common for banks to require the borrowers to maintain minimum cash balances. These minimum balances, called **compensating balances**, provide the bank with support for the loans. Compensating balances are a restriction on the use of cash that may affect a company's liquidity. Accordingly, compensating balances should be disclosed in the financial statements.

BEFORE YOU GO ON . . .

Review It

1. What is generally reported as cash on a company's balance sheet?
2. What is meant by cash equivalents and compensating balances?
3. At what amount does Kellogg Company report cash and cash equivalents in its 1997 consolidated balance sheet? The answer to this question is provided on page 322.

A LOOK BACK AT OUR FEATURE STORY

Refer to the opening story about Columbia University, and answer the following questions:

1. Does Susan McLaughlin have a valid basis for establishing responsibility for overages or shortages? Why or why not?
2. What internal control principles are applicable to reconciling cash register tapes and the amount of cash in the cash drawer at the end of the day?
3. What internal control principle is involved in seeing that a student gets a cash register receipt when buying a meal? How does this requirement contribute to good internal control?
4. Do you think the cashiers are, or should be, bonded?

Solution

1. Establishing responsibility for overages or shortages is made only at the end of the day. This will provide a valid basis for evaluation only if one person worked the register for the entire day. If more than one person works the register during the day, the single count will not provide a valid basis for establishing who is responsible for the overage or shortage.
2. Applicable internal control principles are: (a) Segregation of duties—the cashier(s) should not be involved in performing the reconciliation. (b) Documentation procedures—the cash register tape provides the documentation for total receipts for the day. (c) Independent internal verification—a supervisor should perform the reconciliation.
3. The internal control principle of documentation procedures is involved. The control does not reside in the receipt itself. For example, there will not be any subsequent reconciliation of cash register receipts with cash at the end of the day. The control is forcing the cashier to ring up each sale so that a receipt is produced. Each receipt is recorded on the cash register tape. At the end of the day, the tape is used in determining overages or shortages.
4. If the dining facility has nonstudent employees who work as cashiers, they may be bonded. However, if students work part-time as cashiers, it is doubtful that they are bonded. From the employer's standpoint, bonding is protection against major embezzlements. The risk of this occurring with student help is relatively low.

THE NAVIGATOR

DEMONSTRATION PROBLEM

Trillo Company's bank statement for May 1999 shows the following data:

Balance 5/1	$12,650	Balance 5/31	$14,280
Debit memorandum:		Credit memorandum:	
NSF check	$175	Collection of note receivable	$505

The cash balance per books at May 31 is $13,319. Your review of the data reveals the following:

1. The NSF check was from Hup Co., a customer.
2. The note collected by the bank was a $500, three-month, 12% note. The bank charged a $10 collection fee. No interest has been accrued.
3. Outstanding checks at May 31 total $2,410.
4. Deposits in transit at May 31 total $1,752.
5. A Trillo Company check for $352 dated May 10 cleared the bank on May 25. This check, which was a payment on account, was journalized for $325.

Instructions

(a) Prepare a bank reconciliation at May 31.

(b) Journalize the entries required by the reconciliation.

SOLUTION TO DEMONSTRATION PROBLEM

(a)

TRILLO COMPANY
Bank Reconciliation
May 31, 1999

Cash balance per bank statement			$14,280
Add: Deposits in transit			1,752
			16,032
Less: Outstanding checks			2,410
Adjusted cash balance per bank			$13,622
Cash balance per books			$13,319
Add: Collection of note receivable $500, plus $15 interest less			
collection fee $10			505
			13,824
Less: NSF check		$175	
Error in recording check		27	202
Adjusted cash balance per books			$13,622

(b)

May 31	Cash	505	
	Miscellaneous Expense	10	
	Notes Receivable		500
	Interest Revenue		15
	(To record collection of note by bank)		
31	Accounts Receivable—Hup Co.	175	
	Cash		175
	(To record NSF check from Hup Co.)		
31	Accounts Payable	27	
	Cash		27
	(To correct error in recording check)		

PROBLEM-SOLVING STRATEGIES

1. Follow the four steps used in reconciling items (p. 300).
2. Work carefully to minimize mathematical errors in the reconciliation.
3. All entries are based on reconciling items per books.
4. Make sure the cash ledger balance after posting the reconciling entries agrees with the adjusted cash balance per books.

THE
NAVIGATOR

SUMMARY OF STUDY OBJECTIVES

1. Define internal control. Internal control is the plan of organization and related methods and procedures adopted within a business to safeguard its assets and to enhance the accuracy and reliability of its accounting records.

2. Identify the principles of internal control. The principles of internal control are: establishment of responsibility; segregation of duties; documentation procedures; physical, mechanical, and electronic controls; independent internal verification; and other controls.

3. Explain the applications of internal control principles to cash receipts. Internal controls over cash receipts include: (a) designating only personnel such as cashiers to handle cash; (b) assigning the duties of receiving cash, recording cash, and custody of cash to different individuals; (c) obtaining remittance advices for mail receipts, cash register tapes for over-the-counter receipts, and deposit slips for bank deposits; (d) using company safes and bank vaults to store cash with access limited to authorized personnel, and using cash registers in executing over-the-counter receipts; (e) making independent daily counts of register receipts and daily comparisons of total receipts with total deposits; and (f) bonding personnel that handle cash and requiring them to take vacations.

4. Describe the applications of internal control principles to cash disbursements. Internal controls over cash disbursements include: (a) having only specified individuals such as the treasurer authorized to sign checks; (b) assigning the duties of approving items for payment, paying the items, and recording the payment to different individuals; (c) using prenumbered checks and accounting for all checks, with each check supported by an approved invoice; (d) storing blank checks in a safe or vault with access restricted to authorized personnel, and using a checkwriter to imprint amounts on checks; (e) comparing each check with the approved invoice before issuing the check, and making monthly reconciliations of bank and book balances; and (f) after payment, stamping each approved invoice "paid."

5. Explain the operation of a petty cash fund. In operating a petty cash fund, it is necessary to establish the fund, make payments from the fund, and replenish the fund.

6. Indicate the control features of a bank account. A bank account contributes to good internal control by providing physical controls for the storage of cash, minimizing the amount of currency that must be kept on hand, and creating a double record of a depositor's bank transactions.

7. Prepare a bank reconciliation. In reconciling the bank account, it is customary to reconcile the balance per books and balance per bank to their adjusted balances. The steps in determining the reconciling items are to ascertain deposits in transit, outstanding checks, errors by the depositor or the bank, and unrecorded bank memoranda.

8. Explain the reporting of cash. Cash is listed first in the current assets section of the balance sheet. In some cases, cash is reported together with cash equivalents. Cash restricted for a special purpose is reported separately as a current asset or as a noncurrent asset depending on when the cash is expected to be used.

GLOSSARY

Bank service charge A fee charged by a bank for the use of its services. (p. 298).

Bank statement A statement received monthly from the bank that shows the depositor's bank transactions and balances. (p. 297).

Cash Resources that consist of coins, currency, checks, money orders, and money on hand or on deposit in a bank or similar depository. (p. 287).

Cash equivalents Highly liquid investments, with maturities of three months or less when purchased, that can be converted to a specific amount of cash. (p. 303).

Check A written order signed by the depositor directing the bank to pay a specified sum of money to a designated recipient. (p. 295).

Compensating balances Minimum cash balances required by a bank in support of bank loans. (p. 304).

Deposits in transit Deposits recorded by the depositor that have not been recorded by the bank. (p. 300).

Electronic funds transfer (EFT) A disbursement system that uses wire, telephone, telegraph, or computer to transfer cash from one location to another. (p. 291).

Internal auditors Company employees who evaluate on a continuous basis the effectiveness of the company's system of internal control. (p. 285).

Internal control The plan of organization and all the related methods and measures adopted within a business to safeguard its assets and enhance the accuracy and reliability of its accounting records. (p. 280).

NSF check A check that is not paid by a bank because of insufficient funds in a customer's bank account. (p. 298).

Outstanding checks Checks issued and recorded by a company that have not been paid by the bank. (p. 300).

Petty cash fund A cash fund used to pay relatively small amounts. (p. 292).

Voucher An authorization form prepared for each payment by check in a voucher system. (p. 290).

Voucher system An extensive network of approvals by authorized individuals acting independently to ensure that all disbursements by check are proper. (p. 290).

SELF-STUDY QUESTIONS

Answers are at the end of the chapter.

(SO 1)   1. Internal control is used in a business to enhance the accuracy and reliability of its accounting records and to:
   a. safeguard its assets.
   b. prevent fraud.
   c. produce correct financial statements.
   d. deter employee dishonesty.

(SO 2)   2. The principles of internal control do not include:
   a. establishment of responsibility.
   b. documentation procedures.
   c. management responsibility.
   d. independent internal verification.

(SO 2)   3. Physical controls do not include:
   a. safes and vaults to store cash.
   b. independent bank reconciliations.
   c. locked warehouses for inventories.
   d. bank safety deposit boxes for important papers.

(SO 3)   4. Which of the following items in a cash drawer at November 30 is not cash?
   a. Money orders.
   b. Coins and currency.
   c. A customer check dated December 1.
   d. A customer check dated November 28.

(SO 3)   5. Permitting only designated personnel such as cashiers to handle cash receipts is an application of the principle of:
   a. segregation of duties.
   b. establishment of responsibility.
   c. independent check.
   d. other controls.

(SO 4)   6. The use of prenumbered checks in disbursing cash is an application of the principle of:
   a. establishment of responsibility.
   b. segregation of duties.
   c. physical, mechanical, and electronic controls.
   d. documentation procedures.

7. A check is written to replenish a $100 petty cash fund (SO 5) when the fund contains receipts of $94 and $3 in cash. In recording the check,
   a. Cash Over and Short should be debited for $3.
   b. Petty Cash should be debited for $94.
   c. Cash should be credited for $94.
   d. Petty Cash should be credited for $3.

8. The control features of a bank account do not include:
   a. having bank auditors verify the correctness of the (SO 6) bank balance per books.
   b. minimizing the amount of cash that must be kept on hand.
   c. providing a double record of all bank transactions.
   d. safeguarding cash by using a bank as a depository.

9. In a bank reconciliation, deposits in transit are:
   a. deducted from the book balance.   (SO 7)
   b. added to the book balance.
   c. added to the bank balance.
   d. deducted from the bank balance.

10. The reconciling item in a bank reconciliation that will result in an adjusting entry by the depositor is: (SO 7)
   a. outstanding checks.
   b. deposit in transit.
   c. a bank error.
   d. bank service charges.

11. The statement that correctly describes the reporting of cash is: (SO 8)
   a. Cash cannot be combined with cash equivalents.
   b. Restricted cash funds may be combined with Cash.
   c. Cash is listed first in the current asset section.
   d. Restricted cash funds cannot be reported as a current asset.

QUESTIONS

1. "Internal control is concerned only with enhancing the accuracy of the accounting records." Do you agree? Explain.

2. What principles of internal control apply to most business enterprises?

3. In the corner grocery store, all sales clerks make change out of one cash register drawer. Is this a violation of internal control? Why?

4. W. Mozart is reviewing the principle of segregation of duties. What are the two common applications of this principle?

5. How do documentation procedures contribute to good internal control?

6. What internal control objectives are met by physical, mechanical, and electronic controls?

7. (a) Explain the control principle of independent internal verification. (b) What practices are important in applying this principle?

8. The management of Cobo Company asks you, as the company accountant, to explain (a) the concept of reasonable assurance in internal control and (b) the importance of the human factor in internal control.

9. Fauji Fertilizer Co. owns the following assets at the balance sheet date:

Cash in bank-savings account	$ 6,000
Cash on hand	850
Cash refund due from the IRS	1,000
Checking account balance	12,000
Postdated checks	500

What amount should be reported as cash in the balance sheet?

10. What principle(s) of internal control is (are) involved in making daily cash counts of over-the-counter receipts?

11. Metro Department Stores has just installed new electronic cash registers in its stores. How do cash registers improve internal control over cash receipts?

12. In Bangkok Wholesale Company, two mail clerks open all mail receipts. How does this strengthen internal control?

13. "To have maximum effective internal control over cash disbursements, all payments should be made by check." Is this true? Explain.

14. Mardi Gras Company's internal controls over cash disbursements provide for the treasurer to sign checks imprinted by a checkwriter after comparing the check with the approved invoice. Identify the internal control principles that are present in these controls.

15. How do the principles of (a) physical, mechanical, and electronic controls and (b) other controls apply to cash disbursements?

16. (a) What is a voucher system? (b) What principles of internal control apply to a voucher system?

17. What is the essential feature of an electronic funds transfer (EFT) procedure?

18. (a) Identify the three activities that pertain to a petty cash fund, and indicate an internal control principle that is applicable to each activity. (b) When are journal entries required in the operation of a petty cash fund?

19. "The use of a bank contributes significantly to good internal control over cash." Is this true? Why?

20. Lou Reid is confused about the lack of agreement between the cash balance per books and the balance per the bank. Explain the causes for the lack of agreement to Lou, and give an example of each cause.

21. What are the four steps involved in finding differences between the balance per books and balance per banks?

22. Anne Warin asks your help concerning an NSF check. Explain to Anne (a) what an NSF check is, (b) how it is treated in a bank reconciliation, and (c) whether it will require an adjusting entry per bank.

23. (a) "Cash equivalents are the same as cash." Do you agree? Explain. (b) How should restricted cash funds be reported on the balance sheet?

BRIEF EXERCISES

Explain the importance of internal control.
(SO 1)

BE7–1   Sarah McLachlan is the new owner of Galaxy Parking. She has heard about internal control but is not clear about its importance for her business. Explain to Sarah the two purposes of internal control and give her one application of each purpose for Galaxy Parking.

Identify internal control principles.
(SO 2)

BE7–2   The internal control procedures in The Wallflowers Company provide that:
   (a) Employees who have physical custody of assets do not have access to the accounting records.
   (b) Each month the assets on hand are compared to the accounting records by an internal auditor.
   (c) A prenumbered shipping document is prepared for each shipment of goods to customers.

Identify the principles of internal control that are being followed.

Identify the internal control principles applicable to cash receipts.
(SO 3)

BE7–3   Fresno Company has the following internal control procedures over cash receipts. Identify the internal control principle that is applicable to each procedure.
   1. All over-the-counter receipts are registered on cash registers.
   2. All cashiers are bonded.
   3. Daily cash counts are made by cashier department supervisors.
   4. The duties of receiving cash, recording cash, and custody of cash are assigned to different individuals.
   5. Only cashiers may operate cash registers.

Identify the internal control principle applicable to cash disbursements.
(SO 4)

BE7–4   Romez Company has the following internal control procedures over cash disbursements. Identify the internal control principle that is applicable to each procedure.
   1. Company checks are prenumbered.
   2. The bank statement is reconciled monthly by an internal auditor.

3. Blank checks are stored in a safe in the treasurer's office.
4. Only the treasurer or assistant treasurer may sign checks.
5. Check signers are not allowed to record cash disbursement transactions.

BE7–5 On March 20, Grandy's petty cash fund of $100 is replenished when the fund contains $9 in cash and receipts for postage $52, freight-out $26, and travel expense $10. Prepare the journal entry to record the replenishment of the petty cash fund.

Prepare entry to replenish a petty cash fund.
(SO 5)

BE7–6 Olga C. Boad is uncertain about the control features of a bank account. Explain the control benefits of (a) a signature card, (b) a check, and (c) a bank statement.

Identify the control features of a bank account.
(SO 6)

BE7–7 The following reconciling items are applicable to the bank reconciliation for Cindy Crawford Company: (1) outstanding checks, (2) bank debit memorandum for service charge, (3) bank credit memorandum for collecting a note for the depositor, (4) deposit in transit. Indicate how each item should be shown on a bank reconciliation.

Indicate location of reconciling items in a bank reconciliation.
(SO 7)

BE7–8 Using the data in BE7–7, indicate (a) the items that will result in an adjustment to the depositor's records and (b) why the other items do not require adjustment.

Identify reconciling items that require adjusting entries.
(SO 7)

BE7–9 At July 31, Murphy Company has the following bank information: cash balance per bank, $7,920, outstanding checks $762, deposits in transit $1,700, and a bank service charge $20. Determine the adjusted cash balance per bank at July 31.

Prepare partial bank reconciliation.
(SO 7)

BE7–10 At August 31, Rolex Company has a cash balance per books of $9,500 and the following additional data from the bank statement: charge for printing Rolex Company checks $35, interest earned on checking account balance $40, and outstanding checks $800. Determine the adjusted cash balance per books at August 31.

Prepare partial bank reconciliation.
(SO 7)

BE7–11 Dupre Company has the following cash balances: Cash in Bank $15,742, Payroll Bank Account $6,000, and Plant Expansion Fund Cash $25,000. Explain how each balance should be reported on the balance sheet.

Explain the statement presentation of cash balances.
(SO 8)

EXERCISES

E7–1 Fern Galenti is the owner of Galenti's Pizza. Galenti's is operated strictly on a carryout basis. Customers pick up their orders at a counter where a clerk exchanges the pizza for cash. While at the counter, the customer can see other employees making the pizzas and the large ovens in which the pizzas are baked.

Identify the principles of internal control.
(SO 2)

Instructions
Identify the six principles of internal control and give an example of each principle that you might observe when picking up your pizza. (Note: It may not be possible to observe all the principles.)

E7–2 The following control procedures are used in the Seymor Company for over-the-counter cash receipts.

List internal control weaknesses over cash receipts and suggest improvements.
(SO 2, 3)

1. To minimize the risk of robbery, cash in excess of $100 is stored in an unlocked attaché case in the stock room until it is deposited in the bank.
2. All over-the-counter receipts are registered by three clerks who use a cash register with a single cash drawer.
3. The company accountant makes the bank deposit and then records the day's receipts.
4. At the end of each day, the total receipts are counted by the cashier on duty and reconciled to the cash register total.
5. Cashiers are experienced; thus they are not bonded.

Instructions
(a) For each procedure, explain the weakness in internal control and identify the control principle that is violated.
(b) For each weakness, suggest a change in procedure that will result in good internal control.

E7–3 The following control procedures are used in Hilga's Botique Shoppe for cash disbursements.

List internal control weaknesses over cash disbursements and suggest improvements.
(SO 2, 4)

1. The company accountant prepares the bank reconciliation and reports any discrepancies to the owner.

2. The store manager personally approves all payments before signing and issuing checks.
3. Each week, Hilga leaves 100 company checks in an unmarked envelope on a shelf behind the cash register.
4. After payment, bills are "filed" in a paid invoice folder.
5. The company checks are unnumbered.

Instructions

(a) For each procedure, explain the weakness in internal control and identify the internal control principle that is violated.
(b) For each weakness, suggest a change in the procedure that will result in good internal control.

Identify internal control weaknesses for cash disbursements and make recommendations for improvement.
(SO 4)

E7–4   At Vermont Company, checks are not prenumbered because both the purchasing agent and the treasurer are authorized to issue checks. Each signer has access to unissued checks kept in an unlocked file cabinet. The purchasing agent pays all bills pertaining to goods purchased for resale. Prior to payment, the purchasing agent determines that the goods have been received and verifies the mathematical accuracy of the vendor's invoice. After payment, the invoice is filed by vendor, and the purchasing agent records the payment in the cash disbursements journal. The treasurer pays all other bills following approval by authorized employees. After payment, the treasurer stamps all bills PAID, files them by payment date, and records the checks in the cash disbursements journal. Vermont Company maintains one checking account that is reconciled by the treasurer.

Instructions

(a) List the weaknesses in internal control over cash disbursements.
(b) ✏️ Write a memo to your boss indicating your recommendations for improvement.

Prepare journal entries for a petty cash fund.
(SO 5)

E7–5   Acura Company uses an imprest petty cash system. The fund was established on March 1 with a balance of $100. During March the following petty cash receipts were found in the petty cash box:

Date	Receipt No.	For	Amount
3/5	1	Stamp Inventory	$35
7	2	Freight-out	19
9	3	Miscellaneous Expense	12
11	4	Travel Expense	24
14	5	Miscellaneous Expense	5

The fund was replenished on March 15 when the fund contained $2 in cash. On March 20, the amount in the fund was increased to $150.

Instructions
Journalize the entries in March that pertain to the operation of the petty cash fund.

Prepare bank reconciliation and adjusting entries.
(SO 7)

E7–6   Alana Davis is unable to reconcile the bank balance at January 31. Alana's reconciliation is as follows:

Cash balance per bank	$3,660.20
Add: NSF check	430.00
Less: Bank service charge	25.00
Adjusted balance per bank	$4,065.20
Cash balance per books	$3,875.20
Less: Deposits in transit	490.00
Add: Outstanding checks	730.00
Adjusted balance per books	$4,115.20

Instructions
(a) Prepare a correct bank reconciliation.
(b) Journalize the entries required by the reconciliation.

E7-7   On April 30, the bank reconciliation of Bossa Nova Company shows three outstanding checks: No. 254 $650, No. 255 $720, and No. 257 $410. The May bank statement and the May cash payments journal show the following:

Determine outstanding checks.
(SO 7)

Bank Statement			Cash Payments Journal		
Checks Paid			Checks Issued		
Date	Check No.	Amount	Date	Check No.	Amount
5/4	254	650	5/2	258	159
5/2	257	410	5/5	259	275
5/17	258	159	5/10	260	925
5/12	259	275	5/15	261	500
5/20	261	500	5/22	262	750
5/29	263	480	5/24	263	480
5/30	262	750	5/29	264	360

Instructions
Using step 2 in the reconciliation procedure, list the outstanding checks at May 31.

E7-8   The following information pertains to Cody Camera Company.

1. Cash balance per bank, July 31, $7,263.
2. July bank service charge not recorded by the depositor $15.
3. Cash balance per books, July 31, $7,190.
4. Deposits in transit, July 31, $1,700.
5. Bank collected $1,000 note for Cody in July, plus interest $36 less fee $20. The collection has not been recorded by Cody, and no interest has been accrued.
6. Outstanding checks, July 31, $772.

Prepare bank reconciliation and adjusting entries.
(SO 7)

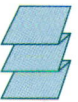

Instructions
(a) Prepare a bank reconciliation at July 31.
(b) Journalize the adjusting entries at July 31 on the books of Cody Company.

E7-9   The information below relates to the Cash account in the ledger of Mawmeg Company.

Prepare bank reconciliation and adjusting entries.
(SO 7)

Balance September 1—$17,150; Cash deposited—$64,000.
Balance September 30—$17,404; Checks written—$63,746.

The September bank statement shows a balance of $16,422 on September 30 and the following memorandum:

Credits		Debits	
Collection of $1,800 note plus interest $30	$1,830	NSF check: J. Hower	$410
Interest earned on checking account	$45	Safety deposit box rent	$30

At September 30, deposits in transit were $4,800 and outstanding checks totaled $2,383.

Instructions
(a) Prepare the bank reconciliation at September 30.
(b) Prepare the adjusting entries at September 30, assuming (1) the NSF check was from a customer on account, and (2) no interest had been accrued on the note.

E7-10   The cash records of Chi Chi Company show the following:

Compute deposits in transit and outstanding checks for two bank reconciliations.
(SO 7)

1. The June 30 bank reconciliation indicated that deposits in transit total $750. During July the general ledger account Cash shows deposits of $15,750, but the bank statement indicates that only $15,600 in deposits were received during the month.
2. The June 30 bank reconciliation also reported outstanding checks of $920. During the month of July, Chi Chi Company books show that $17,200 of checks were issued, yet the bank statement showed that $16,400 of checks cleared the bank in July.
3. In September, deposits per the bank statement totaled $26,700, deposits per books were $25,400, and deposits in transit at September 30 were $2,400.
4. In September, cash disbursements per books were $23,700, checks clearing the bank were $24,000, and outstanding checks at September 30 were $2,100.

There were no bank debit or credit memoranda, and no errors were made by either the bank or Chi Chi Company.

Instructions

Answer the following questions:

(a) In situation (1), what were the deposits in transit at July 31?
(b) In situation (2), what were the outstanding checks at July 31?
(c) In situation (3), what were the deposits in transit at August 31?
(d) In situation (4), what were the outstanding checks at August 31?

PROBLEMS: SET A

Identify internal control weaknesses over cash receipts.
(SO 2, 3)

P7–1A   Burlington Theater is located in the Burlington Mall. A cashier's booth is located near the entrance to the theater. Two cashiers are employed. One works from 1–5 P.M., the other from 5–9 P.M. Each cashier is bonded. The cashiers receive cash from customers and operate a machine that ejects serially numbered tickets. The rolls of tickets are inserted and locked into the machine by the theater manager at the beginning of each cashier's shift.

After purchasing a ticket, the customer takes the ticket to a doorperson stationed at the entrance of the theater lobby some 60 feet from the cashier's booth. The doorperson tears the ticket in half, admits the customer, and returns the ticket stub to the customer. The other half of the ticket is dropped into a locked box by the doorperson.

At the end of each cashier's shift, the theater manager removes the ticket rolls from the machine and makes a cash count. The cash count sheet is initialed by the cashier. At the end of the day, the manager deposits the receipts in total in a bank night deposit vault located in the mall. In addition, the manager sends copies of the deposit slip and the initialed cash count sheets to the theater company treasurer for verification and to the company's accounting department. Receipts from the first shift are stored in a safe located in the manager's office.

Instructions

(a) Identify the internal control principles and their application to the cash receipts transactions of the Burlington Theater.
(b) If the doorperson and cashier decide to collaborate to misappropriate cash, what actions might they take?

Journalize and post petty cash fund transactions.
(SO 5)

P7–2A   ABM Company maintains a petty cash fund for small expenditures. The following transactions occurred over a 2-month period:

July 1   Established petty cash fund by writing a check on Metro Bank for $200.
    15   Replenished the petty cash fund by writing a check for $194.30. On this date the fund consisted of $5.70 in cash and the following petty cash receipts: Freight-out $94.00, postage expense $42.40, entertainment expense $46.60, and miscellaneous expense $10.70.
    31   Replenished the petty cash fund by writing a check for $192.00. At this date, the fund consisted of $8.00 in cash and the following petty cash receipts: Freight-out $82.10, charitable contributions expense $30.00, postage expense $47.80, and miscellaneous expense $32.10.

Aug. 15   Replenished the petty cash fund by writing a check for $188.00. On this date, the fund consisted of $12.00 in cash and the following petty cash receipts: Freight-out $74.40, entertainment expense $43.00, postage expense $33.00, and miscellaneous expense $38.00.
    16   Increased the amount of the petty cash fund to $400 by writing a check for $200.
    31   Replenished petty cash fund by writing a check for $283.00. On this date, the fund consisted of $117 in cash and the following petty cash receipts: Postage expense $145.00, entertainment expense $90.60, and freight-out $45.40.

Instructions

(a) Journalize the petty cash transactions.
(b) Post to the Petty Cash account.
(c) What internal control features exist in a petty cash fund?

P7–3A On July 31, 1999, Long Company had a cash balance per books of $5,815.30. The statement from First State Bank on that date showed a balance of $7,075.80. A comparison of the bank statement with the cash account revealed the following facts:

1. The bank service charge for July was $25.
2. The bank collected a note receivable of $1,200 for Long Company on July 15, plus $48 of interest. The bank made a $10 charge for the collection. Long has not accrued any interest on the note.
3. The July 31 receipts of $1,819.60 were not included in the bank deposits for July. These receipts were deposited by the company in a night deposit vault on July 31.
4. Company check No. 2480 issued to J. Brokaw, a creditor, for $492 that cleared the bank in July was incorrectly entered in the cash payments journal on July 10 for $429.
5. Checks outstanding on July 31 totaled $2,480.10.
6. On July 31, the bank statement showed an NSF charge of $550 for a check received by the company from R. Close, a customer, on account.

Prepare a bank reconciliation and adjusting entries.
(SO 7)

Instructions
(a) Prepare the bank reconciliation as of July 31.
(b) Prepare the necessary adjusting entries at July 31.

P7–4A The bank portion of the bank reconciliation for Zurich Company at October 31, 1999, was as follows:

Prepare a bank reconciliation and adjusting entries from detailed data.
(SO 7)

ZURICH COMPANY
Bank Reconciliation
October 31, 1999

Cash balance per bank		$12,367.90
Add: Deposits in transit		1,530.20
		13,898.10
Less: Outstanding checks		
Check Number	Check Amount	
2451	$1,260.40	
2470	720.10	
2471	844.50	
2472	426.80	
2474	1,050.00	4,301.80
Adjusted cash balance per bank		$ 9,596.30

The adjusted cash balance per bank agreed with the cash balance per books at October 31.
    The November bank statement showed the following checks and deposits:

Bank Statement

	Checks			Deposits	
Date	Number	Amount	Date		Amount
11-1	2470	$ 720.10	11-1		$ 1,530.20
11-2	2471	844.50	11-4		1,211.60
11-5	2474	1,050.00	11-8		990.10
11-4	2475	1,640.70	11-13		2,575.00
11-8	2476	2,830.00	11-18		1,472.70
11-10	2477	600.00	11-21		2,945.00
11-15	2479	1,750.00	11-25		2,567.30
11-18	2480	1,330.00	11-28		1,650.00
11-27	2481	695.40	11-30		1,186.00
11-30	2483	575.50	Total		$16,127.90
11-29	2486	900.00			
	Total	$12,936.20			

The cash records per books for November showed the following:

	Cash Payments Journal						Cash Receipts Journal	
Date	Number	Amount	Date	Number	Amount		Date	Amount
11-1	2475	$1,640.70	11-20	2483	$ 575.50		11-3	$ 1,211.60
11-2	2476	2,830.00	11-22	2484	829.50		11-7	990.10
11-2	2477	600.00	11-23	2485	974.80		11-12	2,575.00
11-4	2478	538.20	11-24	2486	900.00		11-17	1,472.70
11-8	2479	1,570.00	11-29	2487	398.00		11-20	2,954.00
11-10	2480	1,330.00	11-30	2488	800.00		11-24	2,567.30
11-15	2481	695.40	Total		$14,294.10		11-27	1,650.00
11-18	2482	612.00					11-29	1,186.00
							11-30	1,225.00
							Total	$15,831.70

The bank statement contained two bank memoranda:

1. A credit of $1,905.00 for the collection of an $1,800 note for Zurich Company plus interest of $120 and less a collection fee of $15. Zurich Company has not accrued any interest on the note.
2. A debit for the printing of additional company checks, $50.00.

At November 30 the cash balance per books was $11,133.90, and the cash balance per the bank statement was $17,414.60. The bank did not make any errors, but two errors were made by Zurich Company.

Instructions
(a) Using the four steps in the reconciliation procedure described on page 300, prepare a bank reconciliation at November 30.
(b) Prepare the adjusting entries based on the reconciliation. (*Hint:* The correction of any errors pertaining to recording checks should be made to Accounts Payable. The correction of any errors relating to recording cash receipts should be made to Accounts Receivable.)

Prepare a bank reconciliation and adjusting entries.
(SO 7)

P7–5A   Melo Company's bank statement from First National Bank at August 31, 1999, shows the following information:

Balance, August 1	$17,400	Bank credit memorandum:		
August deposits	72,000	Collection of note		
Checks cleared in August	68,660	receivable plus $90		
Balance, August 31	24,850	interest	$4,090	
		Interest earned	45	
		Bank debit memorandum		
		Safety deposit box rent	25	

A summary of the Cash account in the ledger for August shows: Balance, August 1, $16,900; receipts $77,000; disbursements $73,570; and balance, August 31, $20,330. Analysis reveals that the only reconciling items on the July 31 bank reconciliation were a deposit in transit for $4,000 and outstanding checks of $4,500. The deposit in transit was the first deposit recorded by the bank in August. In addition, you determine that there were two errors involving company checks drawn in August: (1) a check for $400 to a creditor on account that cleared the bank in August was journalized and posted for $420, and (2) a salary check to an employee for $275 was recorded by the bank for $285.

Instructions
(a) Prepare a bank reconciliation at August 31.
(b) Journalize the adjusting entries to be made by Melo Company at August 31. Assume the interest on the note has been accrued by the company.

Prepare comprehensive bank reconciliation with theft and internal control deficiencies.
(SO 2, 3, 4, 7)

P7–6A   Giant Company is a very profitable small business. It has not, however, given much consideration to internal control. For example, in an attempt to keep clerical and office expenses to a minimum, the company has combined the jobs of cashier and bookkeeper. As a result, K. Kilgora handles all cash receipts, keeps the accounting records, and prepares the monthly bank reconciliations.

The balance per the bank statement on October 31, 1999, was $18,180. Outstanding checks were: No. 62 for $126.75, No. 183 for $150, No. 284 for $253.25, No. 862 for $190.71, No. 863 for $226.80, and No. 864 for $165.28. Included with the statement was a credit memorandum of $400 indicating the collection of a note receivable for the Giant Company by the bank on October 25. This memorandum has not been recorded by Giant Company.

The company's ledger showed one cash account with a balance of $21,892.72. The balance included undeposited cash on hand. Because of the lack of internal controls, Kilgora took for personal use all of the undeposited receipts in excess of $3,795.51. He then prepared the following bank reconciliation in an effort to conceal his theft of cash.

BANK RECONCILIATION

Cash balance per books, October 31		$21,892.72
Add: Outstanding checks		
No. 862	$190.71	
No. 863	226.80	
No. 864	165.28	482.79
		22,375.51
Less: Undeposited receipts		3,795.51
Unadjusted balance per bank, October 31		18,580.00
Less: Bank credit memorandum		400.00
Cash balance per bank statement, October 31		$18,180.00

Instructions

(a) Prepare a correct bank reconciliation. (*Hint:* Deduct the amount of the theft from the adjusted balance per books.)

(b) Indicate the three ways that Kilgora attempted to conceal the theft and the dollar amount pertaining to each method.

(c) What principles of internal control were violated in this case?

PROBLEMS: SET B

P7–1B   Talley Office Supply Company recently changed its system of internal control over cash disbursements. The system includes the following features.

Instead of being unnumbered and manually prepared, all checks must now be pre-numbered and written by using the new checkwriter purchased by the company. Before a check can be issued, each invoice must have the approval of Lois Bedient, the purchasing agent, and Sara Power, the receiving department supervisor. Checks must be signed by either Amy Rochford, the treasurer, or Joel Reid, the assistant treasurer. Before signing a check, the signer is expected to compare the amounts of the check with the amounts on the invoice.

After signing a check, the signer stamps the invoice PAID and inserts within the stamp, the date, check number, and amount of the check. The "paid" invoice is then sent to the accounting department for recording.

Blank checks are stored in a safe in the treasurer's office. The combination to the safe is known only by the treasurer and assistant treasurer. Each month, the bank statement is reconciled with the bank balance per books by the assistant chief accountant.

Identify internal control principles over cash disbursements.
(SO 2, 4)

Instructions

Identify the internal control principles and their application to cash disbursements of Talley Office Supply Company.

P7–2B   Vickers Company maintains a petty cash fund for small expenditures. The following transactions occurred over a 2-month period:

Journalize and post petty cash fund transactions.
(SO 5)

July 1   Established petty cash fund by writing a check on Metro Bank for $200.

15   Replenished the petty cash fund by writing a check for $195.00. On this date the fund consisted of $5.00 in cash and the following petty cash receipts: Freight-out

$94.00, postage expense $42.40, entertainment expense $46.60, and miscellaneous expense $11.90.

31 Replenished the petty cash fund by writing a check for $192.00. At this date, the fund consisted of $8.00 in cash and the following petty cash receipts: Freight-out $82.10, charitable contributions expense $40.00, postage expense $27.80, and miscellaneous expense $42.10.

Aug. 15 Replenished the petty cash fund by writing a check for $187.00. On this date, the fund consisted of $13.00 in cash and the following petty cash receipts: Freight-out $74.60, entertainment expense $43.00, postage expense $33.00, and miscellaneous expense $37.00.

16 Increased the amount of the petty cash fund to $400 by writing a check for $200.

31 Replenished petty cash fund by writing a check for $283.00. On this date, the fund consisted of $117 in cash and the following petty cash receipts: Postage expense $140.00, travel expense $95.60, and freight-out $46.40.

Instructions
(a) Journalize the petty cash transactions.
(b) Post to the Petty Cash account.
(c) What internal control features exist in a petty cash fund?

Prepare a bank reconciliation and adjusting entries.
(SO 7)

P7–3B   On May 31, 1999, Maris Company had a cash balance per books of $6,781.50. The bank statement from Community Bank on that date showed a balance of $6,804.60. A comparison of the statement with the cash account revealed the following facts:

1. The statement included a debit memo of $40 for the printing of additional company checks.
2. Cash sales of $836.15 on May 12 were deposited in the bank. The cash receipts journal entry and the deposit slip were incorrectly made for $846.15. The bank credited Maris Company for the correct amount.
3. Outstanding checks at May 31 totaled $276.25, and deposits in transit were $936.15.
4. On May 18, the company issued check No. 1181 for $685 to M. Helms, on account. The check, which cleared the bank in May, was incorrectly journalized and posted by Maris Company for $658.
5. A $2,000 note receivable was collected by the bank for Maris Company on May 31 plus $80 interest. The bank charged a collection fee of $20. No interest has been accrued on the note.
6. Included with the cancelled checks was a check issued by Teller Company to P. Jonet for $600 that was incorrectly charged to Maris Company by the bank.
7. On May 31, the bank statement showed an NSF charge of $700 for a check issued by W. Hoad, a customer, to Maris Company on account.

Instructions
(a) Prepare the bank reconciliation at May 31, 1999.
(b) Prepare the necessary adjusting entries for Maris Company at May 31, 1999.

Prepare a bank reconciliation and adjusting entries from detailed data.
(SO 7)

P7–4B   The bank portion of the bank reconciliation for Kona Company at November 30, 1999, was as follows:

KONA COMPANY
Bank Reconciliation
November 30, 1999

Cash balance per bank		$14,367.90
Add: Deposits in transit		2,530.20
		16,898.10
Less: Outstanding checks		

Check Number	Check Amount	
3451	$2,260.40	
3470	720.10	
3471	844.50	
3472	1,426.80	
3474	1,050.00	6,301.80

Adjusted cash balance per bank		$10,596.30

The adjusted cash balance per bank agreed with the cash balance per books at November 30.

The December bank statement showed the following checks and deposits:

		Bank Statement		
	Checks		**Deposits**	
Date	**Number**	**Amount**	**Date**	**Amount**
12-1	3451	$ 2,260.40	12-1	$ 2,530.20
12-2	3471	844.50	12-4	1,211.60
12-7	3472	1,426.80	12-8	2,365.10
12-4	3475	1,640.70	12-16	2,672.70
12-8	3476	1,300.00	12-21	2,945.00
12-10	3477	2,130.00	12-26	2,567.30
12-15	3479	3,080.00	12-29	2,836.00
12-27	3480	600.00	12-30	1,025.00
12-30	3482	475.50	Total	$18,152.90
12-29	3483	1,140.00		
12-31	3485	540.80		
	Total	$15,438.70		

The cash records per books for December showed the following:

	Cash Payments Journal						**Cash Receipts Journal**	
Date	**Number**	**Amount**	**Date**	**Number**	**Amount**		**Date**	**Amount**
12-1	3475	$1,640.70	12-20	3482	$ 475.50		12-3	$ 1,211.60
12-2	3476	1,300.00	12-22	3483	1,140.00		12-7	2,365.10
12-2	3477	2,130.00	12-23	3484	832.00		12-15	2,672.70
12-4	3478	538.20	12-24	3485	450.80		12-20	2,954.00
12-8	3479	3,080.00	12-30	3486	1,389.50		12-25	2,567.30
12-10	3480	600.00	Total		$14,384.10		12-28	2,836.00
12-17	3481	807.40					12-30	1,025.00
							12-31	1,190.40
							Total	$16,822.10

The bank statement contained two memoranda:

1. A credit of $3,145 for the collection of a $3,000 note for Kona Company plus interest of $160 and less a collection fee of $15.00. Kona Company has not accrued any interest on the note.
2. A debit of $547.10 for an NSF check written by D. Lu, a customer. At December 31, the check had not been redeposited in the bank.

At December 31 the cash balance per books was $13,034.30, and the cash balance per the bank statement was $19,680.00. The bank did not make any errors, but two errors were made by Kona Company.

Instructions
(a) Using the four steps in the reconciliation procedure, prepare a bank reconciliation at December 31.
(b) Prepare the adjusting entries based on the reconciliation. (*Hint:* The correction of any errors pertaining to recording checks should be made to Accounts Payable. The correction of any errors relating to recording cash receipts should be made to Accounts Receivable.)

P7–5B Aluminum Company maintains a checking account at the Port City Bank. At July 31, selected data from the ledger balance and the bank statement are as follows:

Prepare a bank reconciliation and adjusting entries.
(SO 7)

	Cash in Bank	
	Per Books	Per Bank
Balance, July 1	$17,600	$19,200
July receipts	82,000	
July credits		80,070
July disbursements	76,900	
July debits		74,740
Balance, July 31	$22,700	$24,530

Analysis of the bank data reveals that the credits consist of $79,000 of July deposits and a credit memorandum of $1,070 for the collection of a $1,000 note plus interest revenue of $70. The July debits per bank consist of checks cleared, $74,700 and a debit memorandum of $40 for printing additional company checks.

You also discover the following errors involving July checks: (1) a check for $230 to a creditor on account that cleared the bank in July was journalized and posted as $320, and (2) a salary check to an employee for $255 was recorded by the bank for $155.

The June 30 bank reconciliation contained only two reconciling items: deposits in transit $5,000 and outstanding checks of $6,600.

Instructions

(a) Prepare a bank reconciliation at July 31.
(b) Journalize the adjusting entries to be made by Aluminum Company at July 31, 1999. Assume that the interest on the note has been accrued.

BROADENING YOUR PERSPECTIVE

FINANCIAL REPORTING AND ANALYSIS

FINANCIAL REPORTING PROBLEM: Kellogg Company

BYP7–1   The financial statements of Kellogg Company are presented in Appendix A at the end of this textbook.

Instructions

(a) What comments, if any, are made about cash in the report of the independent auditors?
(b) What data about cash and cash equivalents are shown in the consolidated balance sheet (statement of financial condition)?
(c) What activities are identified in the consolidated statement of cash flows as being responsible for the changes in cash during 1997?
(d) How are cash equivalents defined under the Notes to Consolidated Financial Statements?

COMPARATIVE ANALYSIS PROBLEM: Kellogg Company vs. General Mills

BYP7–2   Kellogg's financial statements are presented in Appendix A; General Mills's financial statements are presented in Appendix B.

Instructions

(a) Based on the information contained in these financial statements, determine each of the following for each company:
   1. Cash and cash equivalents balance at December 31, 1997, for Kellogg, and May 25, 1997, for General Mills.
   2. Increase (decrease) in cash and cash equivalents from 1996 to 1997.
   3. Cash provided by operating activities during 1997 (from Statement of Cash Flows).
(b) What conclusions concerning the management of cash can be drawn from these data?

RESEARCH ASSIGNMENT

BYP7–3 The "Fortune 500" issue of *Fortune* magazine can serve as a useful reference. This annual issue of *Fortune*, generally appearing in late April or early May, contains a great deal of information regarding the largest U.S. industrial and service companies.

Instructions

Examine the most recent edition and answer the following questions.

  (a) Identify the three largest U.S. corporations in terms of revenues, profits, assets, market value, and employees.
  (b) Identify the largest corporation headquartered (or operating, if needed) in your state (by total revenue). How does this corporation rank in terms of revenues, profits, assets, market value, and number of employees?

INTERPRETING FINANCIAL STATEMENTS: Microsoft, Inc. and Oracle

BYP7–4 Microsoft is the leading developer of software in the world. To continue to be successful Microsoft must generate new products. Generating new products requires significant amounts of cash. Shown below is the current assets section of Microsoft's June 30, 1995, balance sheet and excerpts from a footnote describing the first item listed in the balance sheet, "cash and short-term investments." Below Microsoft is the current asset section of Oracle, another major software developer. (All dollar amounts are in millions.)

MICROSOFT, INC.
Balance Sheets (partial)
As of June 30

	1994	1995
Current assets		
Cash and short-term investments (see Note 1)	$3,614	$4,750
Accounts receivable—net of allowances of $92 and $139	475	581
Inventories	102	88
Other	121	201
Total current assets	$4,312	$5,620
Total current liabilities	$ 913	$1,347

Note 1:	1994	1995
Cash and equivalents	$1,477	$1,962
Short-term investments	2,137	2,788
Cash and short-term investments	$3,614	$4,750

ORACLE
Balance Sheets (partial)
As of May 31

	1994	1995
Current assets		
Cash and cash equivalents	$ 409	$ 480
Short-term cash investments	60	106
Receivables	516	846
Other current assets	95	185
Total current assets	$1,080	$1,617
Current liabilities	$ 682	$1,055

Instructions

(a) What is the definition of a cash equivalent? Give some examples of cash equivalents. How do cash equivalents differ from other types of short-term investments?

(b) Comment on Microsoft's presentation of cash in its balance sheet.

(c) What problems might this presentation of cash pose for a user of Microsoft's financial statements?

(d) Compare the liquidity of Microsoft and Oracle for 1995.

(e) Is it possible to have too many liquid assets?

REAL-WORLD FOCUS: Alternative Distributor Corp.

BYP7–5 **Alternative Distributor Corp.,** a distributor of groceries and related products, is headquartered in Medford, Massachusetts. It was founded in 1980 and today has seven employees, with a total sales of $7 million.

During its audit, the Alternative Distributor Corp. was advised that previously existing internal controls necessary for the company to develop reliable financial statements were inadequate. The audit report stated that the current system of accounting for sales, receivables, and cash receipts constituted a material weakness.

Among other items, the report focused on non-timely deposit of cash receipts, exposing Alternative Distributor to potential loss or misappropriation; excessive past due accounts receivable due to lack of collection efforts; disregard of advantages offered by vendors for prompt payment of invoices; absence of appropriate segregation of duties by personnel consistent with appropriate control objectives; inadequate procedures for applying accounting principles; lack of qualified management personnel; lack of supervision by an outside board of directors; and overall poor record keeping.

Instructions

Identify the principles of internal control violated by Alternative Distributor Corp.

CRITICAL THINKING

GROUP DECISION CASE

BYP7–6 The board of trustees of a local church is concerned about the internal accounting controls pertaining to the offering collections made at weekly services. The trustees ask you to serve on a three-person audit team with the internal auditor of the university and a CPA who has just joined the church.

At a meeting of the audit team and the board of trustees you learn the following:

1. The church's board of trustees has delegated responsibility for the financial management and audit of the financial records to the finance committee. This group prepares the annual budget and approves major disbursements but is not involved in collections or record keeping. No audit has been made in recent years because the same trusted employee has kept church records and served as financial secretary for 15 years. The church does not carry any fidelity insurance.

2. The collection at the weekly service is taken by a team of ushers who volunteer to serve one month. The ushers take the collection plates to a basement office at the rear of the church. They hand their plates to the head usher and return to the church service. After all plates have been turned in, the head usher counts the cash received. The head usher then places the cash in the church safe along with a notation of the amount counted. The head usher volunteers to serve for 3 months.

3. The next morning the financial secretary opens the safe and recounts the collection. The secretary withholds $150–$200 in cash, depending on the cash expenditures expected for the week, and deposits the remainder of the collections in the bank. To facilitate the deposit, church members who contribute by check are asked to make their checks payable to "cash."

4. Each month, the financial secretary reconciles the bank statement and submits a copy of the reconciliation to the board of trustees. The reconciliations have rarely contained any bank errors and have never shown any errors per books.

Instructions

With the class divided into groups, answer the following:

(a) Indicate the weaknesses in internal accounting control over the handling of collections.
(b) List the improvements in internal control procedures that you plan to make at the next meeting of the audit team for (1) the ushers, (2) the head usher, (3) the financial secretary, and (4) the finance committee.
(c) What church policies should be changed to improve internal control?

COMMUNICATION ACTIVITY

BYP7–7 As a new auditor for the CPA firm of Kennedy, Maison, and Davis you have been assigned to review the internal controls over mail cash receipts of Emerik Company. Your review reveals the following: Checks are promptly endorsed "For Deposit Only," but no list of the checks is prepared by the person opening the mail. The mail is opened either by the cashier or by the employee who maintains the accounts receivable records. Mail receipts are deposited in the bank weekly by the cashier.

Instructions

Write a letter to L. S. Croix, owner of the Emerik Company, explaining the weaknesses in internal control and your recommendations for improving the system.

ETHICS CASE

BYP7–8 You are the assistant controller in charge of general ledger accounting at Bad Water Bottling Company. Your company has a large loan from an insurance company. The loan agreement requires that the company's cash account balance be maintained at $200,000 or more as reported monthly. At June 30 the cash balance is $80,000, which you report to Marais Thompson, the financial vice president. Marais excitedly instructs you to keep the cash receipts book open for one additional day for purposes of the June 30 report to the insurance company. Marais says, "If we don't get that cash balance over $200,000, we'll default on our loan agreement. They could close us down, put us all out of our jobs!" Marais continues, "I talked to Grochum Distributors (one of Bad Water's largest customers) this morning and they said they sent us a check for $150,000 yesterday. We should receive it tomorrow. If we include just that one check in our cash balance, we'll be in the clear. It's in the mail!"

Instructions

(a) Who will suffer negative effects if you do not comply with Marais Thompson's instructions? Who will suffer if you do comply?
(b) What are the ethical considerations in this case?
(c) What alternatives do you have?

SURFING THE NET

BYP7–9 All organizations should have systems of internal control. Universities are no exception. This site discusses the basics of internal control in a university setting.

Address: http://www.bc.edu/bc_org/fvp/ia/ic/intro.html

Steps: Go the site shown above.

Instructions

The front page of this site provides links to pages that answer six critical questions. Use these links to answer the following questions:

    (a) In a university setting who has responsibility for evaluating the adequacy of the system of internal control?

    (b) What do reconciliations ensure in the university setting? Who should review the reconciliation?

    (c) What are some examples of physical controls?

    (d) What are two ways to accomplish inventory counts?

Answers to Self-Study Questions

1. a   2. c   3. b   4. c   5. b   6. d   7. a   8. a   9. c   10. d   11. c

---

Answer to Kellogg Review It Question 3, p. 304
Kellogg reports cash and cash equivalents on its balance sheet for 1997 of $173.2 million.

Remember to go back to the Navigator box on the chapter-opening page and check off your completed work.

FEATURE STORY

How Long Should the Check *Be* in the Mail?

Take a look at your campus newspaper. Read the advertisements—the nearby pizza parlor, a local clothing merchant, maybe a review course for the Law School Admission Test. In many cases these advertisers set up accounts with the campus paper and pay their bills 30 days after the ad runs. The paper keeps track of these accounts and bills them on a timely basis.

For more than 70 years, the North Carolina State University newspaper, the *Technician*, has published stories by student writers and run ads by local merchants. "Eighty-five percent of our $400,000 annual operating budget comes from advertising," says Tim Ellington, General Manager—a graduate of NC State. "The rest comes from student fees."

Ellington says that the paper requires prepayment from new advertising accounts. After a trial period, the advertiser will be granted a 30-day payment period. From time to time, however, advertisers don't pay on time. "When it comes to bill paying time, our bill often gets put on the bottom of the pile," says Ellington. "If they are going to anger somebody, they'll anger us before they do a supplier."

The newspaper follows a series of steps in trying to collect late accounts: Once a bill is 30 days past due, the advertiser is sent a letter that says, nicely, "If you haven't sent your payment, please do." At 45 days, the letter isn't as nice: "If we don't receive payment in 30 days, then we could pursue it through small claims court." At 75 days, the newspaper files a small claims suit.

THE
NAVIGATOR

CHAPTER 8

THE NAVIGATOR ✔

- Understand *Concepts for Review* ☐
- Read *Feature Story* ☐
- Scan *Study Objectives* ☐
- Read *Preview* ☐
- Read text and answer *Before You Go On*
  p. 337 ☐   p. 342 ☐   p. 345 ☐
- Work *Demonstration Problem* ☐
- Review *Summary of Study Objectives* ☐
- Answer *Self-Study Questions* ☐
- Complete assignments ☐

ACCOUNTING FOR RECEIVABLES

STUDY OBJECTIVES

After studying this chapter, you should be able to:

1. *Identify the different types of receivables.*
2. *Explain how accounts receivable are recognized in the accounts.*
3. *Distinguish between the methods and bases used to value accounts receivable.*
4. *Describe the entries to record the disposition of accounts receivable.*
5. *Compute the maturity date of, and interest on, notes receivable.*
6. *Explain how notes receivable are recognized in the accounts.*
7. *Describe how notes receivable are valued.*
8. *Describe the entries to record the disposition of notes receivable.*
9. *Explain the statement presentation and analysis of receivables.*

THE NAVIGATOR

*A*s you read this chapter, you will learn what journal entries the *Technician* makes when it sells its ad space, when it collects the cash for those sales, and when it writes off an uncollectible account. The types of entries the *Technician* makes are typical of most businesses, because our economy depends heavily on the use of credit, which takes the form of accounts and notes receivable. The content and organization of this chapter are as follows:

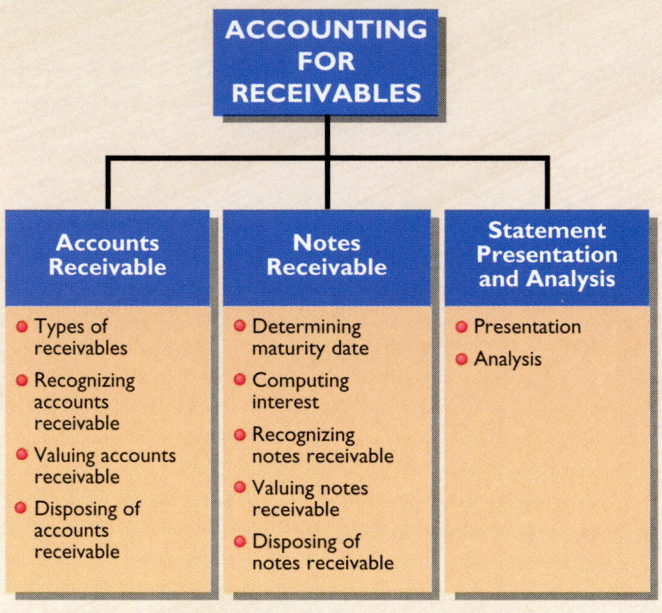

ACCOUNTS RECEIVABLE

Types of Receivables

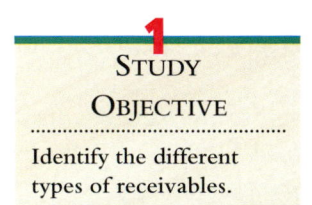

STUDY OBJECTIVE

1

Identify the different types of receivables.

The term "receivables" refers to amounts due from individuals and other companies. Receivables are claims that are expected to be collected in cash. Receivables are frequently classified as (1) accounts, (2) notes, and (3) other.

Accounts receivable are amounts owed by customers on account. They result from the sale of goods and services. These receivables generally are expected to be collected within 30 to 60 days. They are the most significant type of claim held by a company.

Notes receivable represent claims for which formal instruments of credit are issued as evidence of the debt. The credit instrument normally requires the debtor to pay interest and extends for time periods of 60–90 days or longer. Notes and accounts receivable that result from sales transactions are often called **trade receivables**

Other receivables include nontrade receivables such as interest receivable, loans to company officers, advances to employees, and income taxes refundable. These are unusual; therefore, they are generally classified and reported as separate items in the balance sheet.

The three primary accounting problems associated with accounts receivable are:

1. **Recognizing** accounts receivable.
2. **Valuing** accounts receivable.
3. **Disposing of** accounts receivable.

Recognizing Accounts Receivable

Recognizing accounts receivable is relatively straightforward. In Chapter 5 we saw how accounts receivable are affected by the sale of merchandise. To illustrate, assume that Jordache Co. on July 1, 1999, sells merchandise on account to Polo Company for $1,000 terms 2/10, n/30. On July 5, merchandise worth $100 is returned to Jordache Co. On July 11, payment is received from Polo Company for the balance due. The journal entries to record these transactions on the books of Jordache Co. are as follows:

July 1	Accounts Receivable—Polo Company	1,000	
	Sales		1,000
	(To record sales on account)		
July 5	Sales Returns and Allowances	100	
	Accounts Receivable—Polo Company		100
	(To record merchandise returned)		
July 11	Cash ($900 − $18)	882	
	Sales Discounts ($900 × .02)	18	
	Accounts Receivable—Polo Company		900
	(To record collection of accounts receivable)		

The opportunity to receive a cash discount usually occurs when a manufacturer sells to a wholesaler or a wholesaler sells to a retailer. A discount is given in these situations either to encourage prompt payment or for competitive reasons.

On the other hand, retailers rarely grant cash discounts to customers. For example, we would be surprised if you ever received a cash discount in purchasing goods from any well-known retailer, such as Kmart, Sears, Wal-Mart, and so on. In these situations, most sales are either cash or credit card sales. In fact, when you use a retailer's credit card (J. C. Penney or Sears, for example), instead of giving a discount, the retailer charges interest on the balance due if not paid within a specified period (usually 25–30 days).

To illustrate, assume that you charge on your J. C. Penney account an outfit that costs $300. J. C. Penney will make the following entry at the date of sale:

Accounts Receivable	300	
Sales		300
(To record sale of merchandise)		

J. C. Penney will then send you a monthly statement of this transaction and any others that have occurred during the month. If you fail to pay in full within 30 days, J. C. Penney adds an interest (financing) charge to the balance due. Although interest rates vary from state to state and from time to time (depending

2
STUDY
OBJECTIVE
....
Explain how accounts receivable are recognized in the accounts.

| A | = | L | + | OE |
| +1,000 | | | | +1,000 |

| A | = | L | + | OE |
| −100 | | | | −100 |

A	=	L	+	OE
+882				−18
−900				

HELPFUL HINT
These entries are the same as those described in Chapter 5. For simplicity, inventory and cost of goods sold are omitted from this set of journal entries.

| A | = | L | + | OE |
| +300 | | | | +300 |

in part on federal monetary policy), a common rate for retailers is 18% per year or 1.5% per month.

When financing charges are added, the seller recognizes interest revenue. Assuming that you owe $300 at the end of the month, and J. C. Penney charges 1.5% per month on the balance due, the adjusting entry to record interest revenue of $4.50 ($300 × 1.5%) is as follows:

A = L + OE
+4.50   +4.50

Accounts Receivable	4.50	
Interest Revenue		4.50
(To record interest on amount due)		

Interest revenue is often substantial for many retailers.

ACCOUNTING IN ACTION
Business Insight

Interest rates on most credit cards are quite high, averaging approximately 18.8%. As a result, consumers are often looking for companies that charge lower rates. But be careful—some companies offer lower interest rates but have eliminated the standard 25-day grace period before finance charges are incurred. Other companies encourage consumers to get more in debt by advertising that only a $1 minimum payment is due on a $1,000 account balance! They, of course, earn more interest! Chase Manhattan Corp. markets a credit card that allows cardholders to skip a payment twice a year. However, the outstanding balance continues to incur interest. Other credit card companies calculate finance charges initially on two-month, rather than one-month averages, a practice which often translates into higher interest charges. In short, read the fine print.

Valuing Accounts Receivable

3

STUDY

OBJECTIVE

·····························

Distinguish between the methods and bases used to value accounts receivable.

Once receivables are recorded in the accounts, the next question is: How should these receivables be reported on the balance sheet? Determining the amount to report as an asset is important because some receivables will become uncollectible. To ensure that receivables are not overstated on the balance sheet, they are stated at their cash (net) realizable value. **Cash (net) realizable value** is the net amount expected to be received in cash. The cash realizable value excludes amounts that the company estimates it will not be able to collect. Receivables are therefore reduced by estimated uncollectible receivables on the balance sheet.

The income statement also is affected by the amount of uncollectibles. An expense for estimated uncollectibles is recorded to make certain that expenses are not understated and are matched with related sales revenue. This expense is reported as **bad debts expense** on the income statement.

Uncollectible Accounts Receivable

Although each customer must satisfy the credit requirements of the seller before the credit sale is approved, inevitably some accounts receivable become uncollectible. For example, a company may experience a decline in sales because of a downturn in the economy, and as a result, the wholesaler may be unable to collect its accounts receivable from the retailer. Similarly, individuals may be laid off from their jobs or be faced with unexpected hospital bills.

In accounting, credit losses are debited to Bad Debts Expense (or Uncollectible Accounts Expense). Such losses are considered a normal and necessary risk of doing business on a credit basis. In fact, from a management point of view, a reasonable amount of uncollectible accounts is evidence of a sound credit policy.

When bad debts are abnormally low, the company may be losing profitable business by following a credit policy that is too strict. Of course, abnormally high bad debts indicate a credit policy that is too lenient.

Two methods are used in accounting for uncollectible accounts: (1) the allowance method and (2) the direct write-off method. Each of these methods is explained in the following sections.

Allowance Method. The allowance method is required for financial reporting purposes when bad debts are material in amount. Its essential features are:

HELPFUL HINT
In this context, *material* means significant or important.

1. Uncollectible accounts are estimated and the expense for the uncollectible accounts is matched against sales in the same accounting period in which the sales occurred.
2. Estimated uncollectibles are debited to Bad Debts Expense and credited to Allowance for Doubtful Accounts through an adjusting entry at the end of each period.
3. Actual uncollectibles are debited to Allowance for Doubtful Accounts and credited to Accounts Receivable at the time the specific account is written off.

Recording Estimated Uncollectibles. To illustrate the allowance method, assume that Hampson Furniture has credit sales of $1,200,000 in 1998, of which $200,000 remain uncollected at December 31. The credit manager estimates that $12,000 of these sales will prove uncollectible. The adjusting entry to record the estimated uncollectibles is:

Dec. 31	Bad Debts Expense	12,000	
	Allowance for Doubtful Accounts		12,000
	(To record estimate of uncollectible accounts)		

A	=	L	+	OE
−12,000				−12,000

Bad Debts Expense is reported in the income statement as an operating expense (usually as a selling expense). Thus, the estimated uncollectibles are **matched** with sales in 1998 because the expense is recorded in the same year the sales are made.

Allowance for Doubtful Accounts is a contra asset account that shows the claims on customers that are expected to become uncollectible in the future. A contra account is used instead of a direct credit to Accounts Receivable because we do not know which customers will not pay. The credit balance in this account will absorb the specific write-offs when they occur. **Allowance for Doubtful Accounts is not closed at the end of the fiscal year.** It is deducted from Accounts Receivable in the current asset section of the balance sheet as follows:

ALTERNATIVE TERMINOLOGY
Bad debts expense is also called *uncollectible accounts expense.* Allowance for doubtful accounts is also called *allowance for uncollectibles* or *allowance for bad debts.*

ILLUSTRATION 8-1
Presentation of allowance for doubtful accounts

HAMPSON FURNITURE Balance Sheet (partial)		
Current assets		
Cash		$ 14,800
Accounts receivable	$200,000	
Less: Allowance for doubtful accounts	12,000	188,000
Merchandise inventory		310,000
Prepaid expense		25,000
Total current assets		$537,800

The amount of $188,000 represents the expected **cash realizable value** of the accounts receivable at the statement date.

Recording the Write-off of an Uncollectible Account. Companies use various methods of collecting past-due accounts, such as the sequence of letters, calls, and legal action described by Tim Ellington of the NCSU *Technician* in the opening story. When all means of collecting a past-due account have been exhausted and collection appears impossible, the account should be written off. To prevent premature write-offs, each write-off should be formally approved in writing by authorized management personnel.

Assume, for example, that the vice president of finance of Hampson Furniture authorizes the write-off of the $500 balance owed by R. A. Ware on March 1, 1999. The entry to record the write-off is:

A	=	L	+	OE				
+500					Mar. 1	Allowance for Doubtful Accounts	500	
−500						Accounts Receivable—R. A. Ware		500
						(Write-off of R. A. Ware account)		

Bad Debts Expense is not debited when the write-off occurs. **Under the allowance method, every bad debt write-off is debited to the allowance account and not to Bad Debts Expense.** A debit to Bad Debts Expense would be incorrect, because the expense is recognized when the adjusting entry is made for estimated bad debts. After posting, the general ledger accounts will show:

ILLUSTRATION 8-2

General ledger balances after write-off

Accounts Receivable						Allowance for Doubtful Accounts				
1/1/99	Bal.	200,000	3/1/99	500		3/1/99	500	1/1/99	Bal.	12,000
3/1/99	Bal.	199,500						3/1/99		11,500

A write-off affects only balance sheet accounts. The write-off of the account reduces both Accounts Receivable and the Allowance for Doubtful Accounts. Cash realizable value in the balance sheet, therefore, remains the same as illustrated below.

ILLUSTRATION 8-3

Cash realizable value comparison

	Before Write-off	After Write-off
Accounts receivable	$200,000	$199,500
Allowance for doubtful accounts	12,000	11,500
Cash realizable value	**$188,000**	**$188,000**

Recovery of an Uncollectible Account. Occasionally, a company collects from a customer after the account has been written off as uncollectible. Two entries are required to record the recovery of a bad debt: (1) The entry made in writing off the account is reversed to reinstate the customer's account. (2) The collection is journalized in the usual manner. To illustrate, assume that on July 1, R. A. Ware pays the $500 amount that had been written off on March 1. The entries are:

(1)

July 1	Accounts Receivable—R. A. Ware	500		
	Allowance for Doubtful Accounts		500	
	(To reverse write-off of R. A. Ware account)			

A	=	L	+	OE
+ 500				
− 500				

(2)

1	Cash	500		
	Accounts Receivable—R. A. Ware		500	
	(To record collection from R. A. Ware)			

A	=	L	+	OE
+ 500				
− 500				

Note that the recovery of a bad debt, like the write-off of a bad debt, affects only balance sheet accounts. The net effect of the two entries above is a debit to Cash and a credit to Allowance for Doubtful Accounts for $500. Accounts Receivable is debited and the Allowance for Doubtful Accounts is credited for two reasons: First, the company made an error in judgment when it wrote off the account receivable. Second, R. A. Ware did pay, and therefore the Accounts Receivable account in the general ledger and Ware's account in the subsidiary accounts receivable ledger should show this collection for possible future credit purposes.

HELPFUL HINT
Like the write-off, a recovery does not involve the income statement.

Bases Used for Allowance Method.   To simplify the preceding explanation, the amount of the expected uncollectibles was given. However, in "real life" companies must estimate that amount if they use the allowance method. Two bases are used to determine this amount: **(1) percentage of sales**, and **(2) percentage of receivables**. Both bases are generally accepted in accounting. The choice is a management decision. It depends on the relative emphasis that management wishes to give to expenses and revenues on the one hand or to cash realizable value of the accounts receivable on the other. The choice is whether to emphasize income statement or balance sheet relationships. Illustration 8-4 compares the two bases.

ILLUSTRATION 8-4

Comparison of bases of estimating uncollectibles

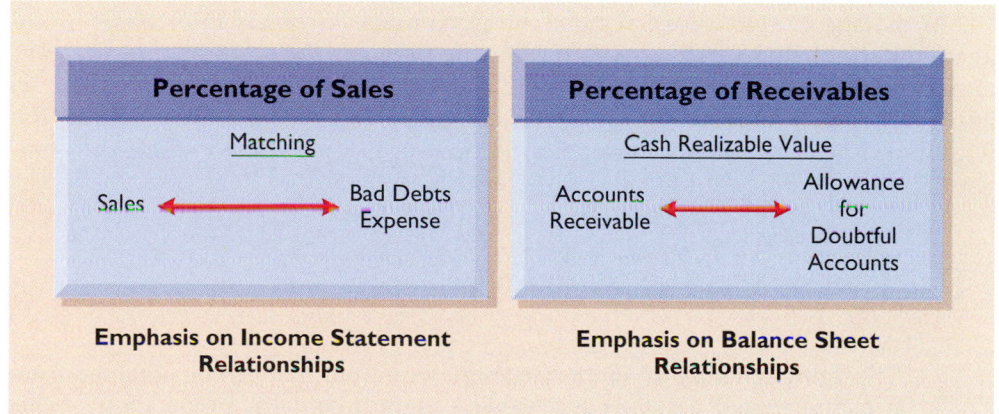

The percentage of sales basis results in a better matching of expenses with revenues—an income statement viewpoint. In contrast, the percentage of receivables basis produces the better estimate of cash realizable value—a balance sheet viewpoint. Under both bases, it is necessary to determine the company's past experience with bad debt losses.

Percentage of Sales.   In the **percentage of sales basis**, management establishes a percentage relationship between the amount of credit sales and expected losses from uncollectible accounts. The percentage is based on past experience and anticipated credit policy.

The percentage is usually applied to either total credit sales or net credit sales of the current year. To illustrate, assume that Gonzalez Company elects to use the percentage of sales basis and concludes that 1% of net credit sales will become uncollectible. If net credit sales for 1999 are $800,000, the estimated bad debts expense is $8,000 (1% × $800,000). The adjusting entry is:

A	=	L	+	OE
−8,000				−8,000

Dec. 31	Bad Debts Expense	8,000	
	Allowance for Doubtful Accounts		8,000
	(To record estimated bad debts for year)		

After the adjusting entry is posted, assuming the allowance account already has a credit balance of $1,723, the accounts of Gonzalez Company will show:

ILLUSTRATION 8-5

Bad debts accounts after posting

Bad Debts Expense		Allowance for Doubtful Accounts	
12/31 Adj. **8,000**			Bal. 1,723
			12/31 Adj. **8,000**
			Bal. 9,723

This basis of estimating uncollectibles emphasizes the matching of expenses with revenues. As a result, Bad Debts Expense will show a direct percentage relationship to the sales base on which it is computed. **When the adjusting entry is made, the existing balance in the Allowance for Doubtful Accounts is disregarded.** The adjusted balance in this account should result in a reasonable approximation of the realizable value of the receivables. If actual write-offs differ significantly from the amount estimated, the percentage for future years should be modified.

Percentage of Receivables.   Under the **percentage of receivables basis**, management establishes a percentage relationship between the amount of receivables and expected losses from uncollectible accounts. A schedule (often called an **aging schedule**) is prepared, in which customer balances are classified by the length of time they have been unpaid. Because of its emphasis on time, the analysis is often called **aging the accounts receivable**.

TECHNOLOGY IN ACTION

The aging schedule is another example of output that can be obtained from a computerized accounts receivable system. Manually, preparation of this schedule is an onerous and time-consuming task. However, the schedule can be done in minutes on computer systems.

After the accounts are aged, the expected bad debt losses are determined by applying percentages based on past experience to the totals of each category. The longer a receivable is past due, the less likely it is to be collected. As a result, the estimated percentage of uncollectible debts increases as the number of days past due increases. An aging schedule for Dart Company is shown in Illustration 8-6. Note the increasing percentages from 2% to 40%.

ILLUSTRATION 8-6
Aging schedule

| Customer | Total | Not Yet Due | Number of Days Past Due | | | |
			1–30	31–60	61–90	Over 90
T. E. Adert	$ 600		$ 300		$ 200	$ 100
R. C. Bortz	300	$ 300				
B. A. Carl	450		200	$ 250		
O. L. Diker	700	500			200	
T. O. Ebbet	600			300		300
Others	36,950	26,200	5,200	2,450	1,600	1,500
	$39,600	$27,000	$5,700	$3,000	$2,000	$1,900
Estimated Percentage Uncollectible		2%	4%	10%	20%	40%
Total Estimated Bad Debts	$ 2,228	$ 540	$ 228	$ 300	$ 400	$ 760

Total uncollectibles for Dart Company ($2,228) represent the amount of existing customer claims expected to become uncollectible in the future. Thus, this amount represents the **required balance** in Allowance for Doubtful Accounts at the balance sheet date. Accordingly, **the amount of the bad debt adjusting entry is the difference between the required balance and the existing balance in the allowance account**. If the trial balance shows Allowance for Doubtful Accounts with a credit balance of $528, an adjusting entry for $1,700 ($2,228 − $528) is necessary, as shown below:

Dec. 31	Bad Debts Expense	1,700	
	Allowance for Doubtful Accounts		1,700
	(To adjust allowance account to total estimated uncollectibles)		

A = L + OE
−1,700   −1,700

After the adjusting entry is posted, the accounts of the Dart Company will show:

Bad Debts Expense	
12/31 Adj. **1,700**	

Allowance for Doubtful Accounts	
	Bal. 528
	12/31 Adj. **1,700**
	Bal. 2,228

ILLUSTRATION 8-7
Bad debt accounts after posting

Occasionally the allowance account will have a **debit balance** prior to adjustment, because write-offs during the year have exceeded previous provisions for bad debts. In such a case **the debit balance is added to the required balance** when the adjusting entry is made. Thus, if there had been a $500 debit balance in the allowance account before adjustment, the adjusting entry would have been for $2,728 ($2,228 + $500) to arrive at a credit balance of $2,228.

The percentage of receivables method will normally result in the better approximation of cash realizable value. This method, however, will not result in the better matching of expenses with revenues if some customers' accounts are more than one year past due. In such a case, bad debts expense for the current period would include amounts applicable to the sales of a prior period.

Direct Write-off Method. Under the direct write-off method, bad debt losses are not estimated and no allowance account is used. When an account is determined to be uncollectible, the loss is charged to Bad Debts Expense. Assume, for example, that Warden Co. writes off M. E. Doran's $200 balance as uncollectible on December 12. The entry is:

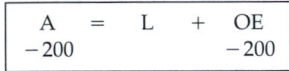

Dec. 12	Bad Debts Expense	200	
	Accounts Receivable—M. E. Doran		200
	(To record write-off of M. E. Doran		
	account)		

A = L + OE
−200   −200

When this method is used, bad debts expense will show only actual losses from uncollectibles. Accounts receivable will be reported at its gross amount.

Under the direct write-off method, bad debts expense is often recorded in a period different from the period in which the revenue was recorded. Thus, no attempt is made to match bad debts expense to sales revenues in the income statement or to show the cash realizable value of the accounts receivable in the balance sheet. **Consequently, unless bad debt losses are insignificant, the direct write-off method is not acceptable for financial reporting purposes.** The direct write-off method is, however, used for tax purposes. The Internal Revenue Service allows a tax deduction for uncollectible accounts only when specific accounts receivable are deemed uncollectible.

Disposing of Accounts Receivable

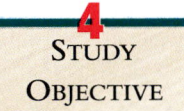

STUDY OBJECTIVE 4

Describe the entries to record the disposition of accounts receivable.

HELPFUL HINT
Two common expressions apply here:
1. Time is money; i.e., waiting for the normal collection process costs money.
2. A bird in the hand is worth two in the bush; i.e., getting the cash now is better than getting it later.

In the normal course of events, accounts receivable are collected in cash and removed from the books. However, as credit sales and receivables have grown in size and significance, the "normal course of events" has changed. In order to accelerate the receipt of cash from receivables, companies frequently sell the receivables to another company for cash, thereby shortening the cash-to-cash operating cycle.

There are several reasons for the sale of receivables. **First, for competitive reasons, sellers** (retailers, wholesalers, and manufacturers) **often must provide financing to purchasers of their goods.** For example, in the sale of durable goods, such as automobiles, trucks, industrial and farm equipment, computers, and appliances, a majority of the sales are on a credit basis. Many major companies in these industries have therefore created companies that accept responsibility for accounts receivable financing. General Motors has General Motors Acceptance Corp. (GMAC), Sears has Sears Roebuck Acceptance Corp. (SRAC), Ford has Ford Motor Credit Corp. (FMCC), and Chrysler has Chrysler Finance Corporation (CFC). These companies are referred to as captive finance companies because they are wholly owned by the company making the product. The purpose of captive financing companies is to encourage the sale of their product by assuring financing to buyers.

Second, receivables may be sold because they may be the only reasonable source of cash. When money is tight, companies may not be able to borrow money in the usual credit markets. If money is available, the cost of borrowing may be prohibitive. A final reason for selling receivables is that **billing and collection are often time consuming and costly.** As a result, it is often easier for a retailer to sell the receivable to another party with expertise in billing and collection matters. Credit card companies such as MasterCard, VISA, American Express, and Diners Club specialize in billing and collecting accounts receivable.

ACCOUNTING IN ACTION
Business Insight

You don't have to go far to find an example of the sale of receivables for competitive reasons. Most local car dealers simply do not have the financial resources to finance the sale of cars, because most loans today are quite large in relationship to the cost of the car. Recently, the percentage of the price financed by the Big Three automobile manufacturers in the United States was 93% of the selling price of the automobile. In addition, the average length of the loan was 53.5 months, compared to 35 months a decade ago. It is no wonder, therefore, that a captive finance subsidiary like General Motors Acceptance Corporation, if it were a bank, would rank among the largest banks in the world in total assets.

Sale of Receivables

A common sale of receivables is a sale to a factor. A **factor** is a finance company or bank that buys receivables from businesses for a fee and then collects the payments directly from the customers. Factoring was traditionally associated with the textiles, apparel, footwear, furniture, and home furnishing industries. It has now spread to many other types of businesses and is a multibillion dollar business. For example, Sears, Roebuck and Co. recently sold $14.8 billion of customer accounts receivable.

Factoring arrangements vary widely, but typically the factor (purchaser of the receivables) charges a commission. It ranges from 1% to 3% of the amount of receivables purchased. To illustrate, assume that Hendredon Furniture factors $600,000 of receivables to Federal Factors, Inc. Federal Factors assesses a service charge of 2% of the amount of receivables sold. The journal entry to record the sale by Hendredon Furniture is as follows:

HELPFUL HINT
The seller can usually earn more than the commission by (1) taking advantage of 2–3% purchase discounts, (2) investing in short-term securities, or (3) reinvesting the money in productive assets.

Cash	588,000	
Service Charge Expense (2% × $600,000)	12,000	
Accounts Receivable		600,000
(To record the sale of accounts receivable)		

A	=	L	+	OE
+ 588,000				− 12,000
− 600,000				

If the company usually sells its receivables, the service charge expense incurred by Hendredon Furniture is recorded as selling expense. If receivables are sold infrequently, this amount may be reported in the Other Expenses and Losses section of the income statement.

ACCOUNTING IN ACTION
Business Insight

"They're the devil in disguise," is how CEO Barry Weinstein described factors. Unable to raise capital from bankers or outside investors, Weinstein turned to factoring receivables. The arrangement was pricey: the factor charged interest of 5% a month, to a maximum of 13% of the total invoice, on any uncollected invoices that were factored. The deal became an endless cycle. Soon Weinstein was factoring all new invoices to get the cash to pay the interest on the older factored invoices.

Source: Inc., July 1994, p. 97.

Credit Card Sales

Approximately 1 billion credit cards were estimated to be in use recently—more than three credit cards for every man, woman, and child in this country. A common type of credit card is a national credit card such as VISA, MasterCard, and American Express. Three parties are involved when national credit cards are used in making retail sales: (1) the credit card issuer, who is independent of the retailer, (2) the retailer, and (3) the customer. A retailer's acceptance of a national credit card is another form of selling (factoring) the receivable.

The major advantages of these national credit cards to the retailer are shown in Illustration 8-8. In exchange for these advantages, the retailer pays the credit card issuer a fee of 2–6% of the invoice price for its services.

ILLUSTRATION 8-8

Advantages of credit cards to the retailer

VISA and MasterCard Sales.   Sales resulting from the use of VISA and MasterCard are considered cash sales by the retailer. These cards are issued by banks. Upon receipt of credit card sales slips from a retailer, the bank immediately adds the amount to the seller's bank balance. These credit card sales slips are therefore recorded in the same manner as checks deposited from a cash sale. Banks generally charge a fee of 2–4% of the credit card sales slips for this service. To illustrate, Anita Ferreri purchases a number of compact discs for her restaurant from Karen Kerr Music Co. for $1,000 using her VISA First Bank Card. The service fee that First Bank charges is 3%. The entry to record this transaction by Karen Kerr Music is as follows:

A	=	L	+	OE
+970				−30
				+1,000

Cash	970	
Service Charge Expense	30	
Sales		1,000
(To record Visa credit card sales)		

ACCOUNTING IN ACTION
Business Insight

Many *are* leaving home without it! Despite long-standing advertisements that urge customers not to leave home without it, more than two million users have cut up their AmEx (American Express) cards and gone in search of better bargains in credit cards. In response, AmEx has staked its future on a new set of twelve different types of credit cards. All offer revolving credit at rates comparable to AmEx's principal rivals, Visa and MasterCard. The U.S. market is saturated with 1 *billion* cards issued by 6,500 companies. Competition is fierce because the pool of potential new customers is shrinking at the same time America's plastic habit is growing. The industry average for bad debt losses on credit cards is 5%.

Source: Time, September 12, 1994, p. 60.

American Express Sales. Sales using American Express cards are reported as credit sales, not cash sales. Conversion into cash does not occur until American Express remits the net amount to the seller. To illustrate, assume that Four Seasons restaurant accepts an American Express card for a $300 bill. The entry for the sale by Four Seasons (assuming a 5% fee) is:

Accounts Receivable—American Express	285	
Service Charge Expense	15	
Sales		300
(To record American Express credit card sales)		

A	=	L	+	OE
+285				−15
				+300

Thus American Express will subsequently pay the restaurant $285 which the restaurant will record as follows:

Cash	285	
Accounts Receivable—American Express		285
(To record redemption of credit card billings)		

A	=	L	+	OE
+285				
−285				

Service Charge Expense is reported as a selling expense in the income statement by the restaurant.

BEFORE YOU GO ON . . .

Review It

1. How are accounts receivable recognized in the accounts?
2. What are the essential features of the allowance method?
3. Explain the difference between the percentage of sales and the percentage of receivables methods.
4. Why do companies sell their receivables?
5. What is the journal entry when a company sells its receivables to a factor?
6. What factors indicate that Kellogg Company has limited its risks related to concentrations of credit? (*Hint:* See "Credit Risk Concentration" paragraph of Note 11 in Kellogg's 1997 Annual Report.) The answer to this question is provided on page 362.

Do It

Peter M. Dell Wholesalers Co. has been expanding faster than it can raise capital and, according to its local banker, the company has reached its debt ceiling. Dell's customers are slow in paying (60–90 days), but its suppliers (creditors) are demanding 30-day payment. Dell has a cash flow problem.

Dell needs to raise $120,000 in cash to safely cover next Friday's employee payroll. Dell's present balance of outstanding receivables totals $750,000. What might Dell do to alleviate this cash crunch? Record the entry that Dell would make when it raises the needed cash.

Reasoning: One source of immediate cash at a competitive cost is the sale of receivables to a factor. Rather than waiting until it can collect receivables, Dell may raise immediate cash by selling its receivables. The last thing Dell (or any employer) wants to do is miss a payroll.

Solution: Assuming that Dell Co. factors $125,000 of its accounts receivable at a 1% service charge, the following entry would be made:

Cash	123,750	
Service Charge Expense	1,250	
Accounts Receivable		125,000
(To record sale of receivables to factor)		

Related exercise material: BE8–9 and E8–5.

THE
NAVIGATOR

NOTES RECEIVABLE

Credit may also be granted in exchange for a formal credit instrument known as a promissory note. A **promissory note** is a written promise to pay a specified amount of money on demand or at a definite time. Promissory notes may be used (1) when individuals and companies lend or borrow money, (2) when the amount of the transaction and the credit period exceed normal limits, and (3) in settlement of accounts receivable.

In a promissory note, the party making the promise to pay is called the **maker**; the party to whom payment is to be made is called the **payee**. The payee may be specifically identified by name or may be designated simply as the bearer of the note. In the note shown in Illustration 8-9, Brent Company is the maker and Wilma Company is the payee. To the Wilma Company, the promissory note is a note receivable; to the Brent Company, the note is a note payable.

Notes receivable give the holder a stronger legal claim to assets than accounts receivable. Like accounts receivable, notes receivable can be readily sold to another party. Promissory notes are negotiable instruments (as are checks), which means that they can be transferred to another party by endorsement.

ILLUSTRATION 8-9

Promissory note

HELPFUL HINT

Who are the two key parties to a note, and what entry does each party make when the note is issued?
Answer:
1. The maker, Brent Company, credits Notes Payable.
2. The payee, Wilma Company, debits Notes Receivable.

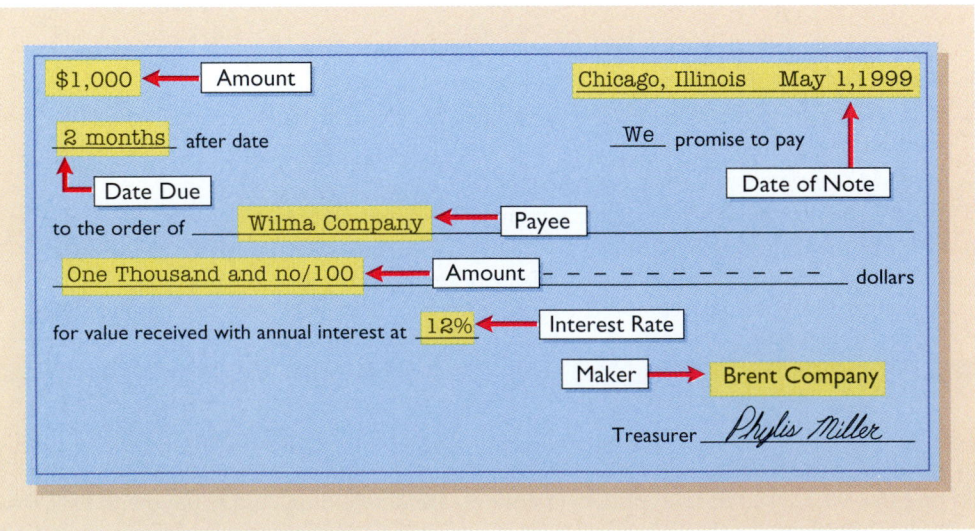

Notes receivable are frequently accepted from customers who need to extend the payment of an outstanding account receivable and are often required from high-risk customers. In some industries (e.g., the pleasure and sport boat industry) all credit sales are supported by notes. The majority of notes, however, originate from lending transactions. The basic issues in accounting for notes receivable are the same as those for accounts receivable.

1. **Recognizing** notes receivable.
2. **Valuing** notes receivable.
3. **Disposing of** notes receivable.

On the following pages, we will look at each of these issues. Before we do, though, we need to consider two issues that did not apply to accounts receivable: the maturity date and the computation of interest.

Determining the Maturity Date

When the life of a note is expressed in terms of months, the due date is found by counting the months from the date of issue. For example, the maturity date of a 3-month note dated May 1 is August 1. A note drawn on the last day of a month matures on the last day of a subsequent month; that is, a July 31 note due in 2 months matures on September 30. When the due date is stated in terms of days, it is necessary to count the exact number of days to determine the maturity date. In counting, **the date the note is issued is omitted but the due date is included**. For example, the maturity date of a 60-day note dated July 17 is September 15, computed as follows:

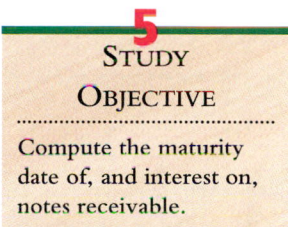

5
STUDY
OBJECTIVE
....
Compute the maturity date of, and interest on, notes receivable.

Term of note		60
July (31 − 17)	14	
August	31	45
Maturity date, September		**15**

ILLUSTRATION 8-10

Computation of maturity date

The due date (maturity date) of a promissory note may be stated in one of three ways, as shown in Illustration 8-11.

ILLUSTRATION 8-11

Maturity date of different notes

"On demand I promise to pay..." — Wilma Co.

On demand

"On July 23, 1999, I promise to pay..." — Wilma Co.

On a stated date

"One year from now I promise to pay..." — Wilma Co. 1999

At the end of a stated period of time

Computing Interest

As indicated in Chapter 3, the basic formula for computing interest on an interest-bearing note is:

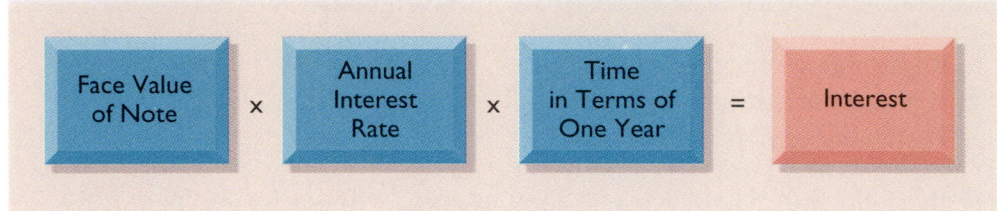

The interest rate specified on the note is an **annual** rate of interest. The time factor in the computation above expresses the fraction of a year that the note is outstanding. When the maturity date is stated in days, the time factor is frequently the number of days divided by 360. When the due date is stated in months, the time factor is the number of months divided by 12. The computation of interest is shown in Illustration 8-13.

Terms of Note	Interest Computation
	Face × Rate × Time = Interest
$ 730, 18%, 120 days	$ 730 × 18% × 120/360 = $ 43.80
$1,000, 15%, 6 months	$1,000 × 15% × 6/12 = $ 75.00
$2,000, 12%, 1 year	$2,000 × 12% × 1/1 = $240.00

There are many different ways to calculate interest. For example, the computation above assumed the total days to be used for the year are 360. Many financial institutions use 365 days to compute interest. It is more profitable, though, to use 360 days because the holder of the note receives more interest than if 365 days are used. For homework problems, assume 360 days.

Recognizing Notes Receivable

To illustrate the basic entry for notes receivable, we will use the $1,000, 2-month, 12% promissory note on page 338. Assuming that the note was written to settle an open account, the entry for the receipt of the note by Wilma Company is:

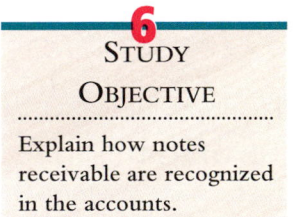

May 1	Notes Receivable	1,000	
	Accounts Receivable—Brent Company		1,000
	(To record acceptance of Brent Company note)		

Observe that the note receivable is recorded at its **face value**, the value shown on the face of the note. No interest revenue is reported when the note is accepted because the revenue recognition principle does not recognize revenue until earned. Interest is earned (accrued) as time passes.

If a note is exchanged for cash, the entry is a debit to Notes Receivable and a credit to Cash in the amount of the loan.

Valuing Notes Receivable

Like accounts receivable, short-term notes receivable are reported at their **cash (net) realizable value**. The notes receivable allowance account is Allowance for

Doubtful Accounts. Valuing short-term notes receivable is the same as valuing accounts receivable. The computations and estimations involved in determining cash realizable value and in recording the proper amount of bad debt expense and related allowance are similar.

Long-term notes receivable, however, pose additional estimation problems. As an example, we need only look at the problems a number of large U.S. banks are having in collecting their receivables. Loans to less-developed countries are particularly worrisome. Developing countries need loans for development but often find repayment difficult. U.S. loans (notes) to less-developed countries at one time totaled approximately $135 billion. In Brazil alone, Citibank at one time had loans equivalent to 80% of its stockholders' equity; Chemical Bank had 77% of its equity lent out in Mexico. Determining the proper allowance is understandably difficult for these types of long-term receivables.

<table>
<tr><td>7</td></tr>
<tr><td>STUDY</td></tr>
<tr><td>OBJECTIVE</td></tr>
<tr><td>Describe how notes receivable are valued.</td></tr>
</table>

ACCOUNTING IN ACTION

International Insight

Varied plans have been proposed to solve the international debt problem. These plans range from encouraging more lending to reducing or forgiving the debt. At one time, this debt burden to banks worldwide exceeded $1.3 trillion. (As an aside, a trillion is a lot of money—enough money to give every man, woman, and child in the world approximately $250 each.) Why were these loans made in the first place? The reasons are numerous, but the three major ones are: (1) to provide stability to these governments and thereby increase trade, (2) the belief that governments would never default on payment, and (3) the desire by banks to increase their income by lending to these countries.

Disposing of Notes Receivable

Notes may be held to their maturity date, at which time the face value plus accrued interest is due. In some situations, the maker of the note defaults and appropriate adjustment must be made. In other situations, similar to accounts receivable, the holder of the note speeds up the conversion to cash by selling the receivables. The entries for honoring and dishonoring notes are illustrated below.

<table>
<tr><td>8</td></tr>
<tr><td>STUDY</td></tr>
<tr><td>OBJECTIVE</td></tr>
<tr><td>Describe the entries to record the disposition of notes receivable.</td></tr>
</table>

Honor of Notes Receivable

A note is **honored** when it is paid in full at its maturity date. For each interest-bearing note, the amount due at maturity is the face value of the note plus interest for the length of time specified on the note.

To illustrate, assume that Betty Co. lends Wayne Higley Inc. $10,000 on June 1, accepting a 4-month, 9% interest note. In this situation, interest is $300 ($10,000 × 9% × 4/12); the amount due, the maturity value, is $10,300. To obtain payment, Betty Co. (the payee) must present the note either to Wayne Higley Inc. (the maker) or to the maker's duly appointed agent, such as a bank. Assuming that Betty Co. presents the note to Wayne Higley Inc. on October 1, the maturity date, the entry by Betty Co. to record the collection is:

Oct. 1	Cash	10,300	
	Notes Receivable		10,000
	Interest Revenue		300
	(To record collection of Higley Inc. note)		

A	=	L	+	OE
+ 10,300				+ 300
− 10,000				

If Betty Co. prepares financial statements as of September 30, it would be necessary to accrue interest. In this case, the adjusting entry by Betty Co. would be for 4 months, or $300, as shown at the top of the next page.

A	=	L	+	OE
+ 300				+ 300

Sept. 30	Interest Receivable	300	
	Interest Revenue		300
	(To accrue 4 months' interest)		

When interest has been accrued, it is necessary to credit Interest Receivable at maturity. The entry by Betty Co. to record the honoring of the Wayne Higley Inc. note on October 1 is:

A	=	L	+	OE
+ 10,300				
− 10,000				
− 300				

Oct. 1	Cash	10,300	
	Notes Receivable		10,000
	Interest Receivable		300
	(To record collection of note at maturity)		

In this case, Interest Receivable is credited because the receivable was established in the adjusting entry.

Dishonor of Notes Receivable

A **dishonored note** is a note that is not paid in full at maturity. A dishonored note receivable is no longer negotiable. However, the payee still has a claim against the maker of the note. Therefore the Notes Receivable account is usually transferred to an Account Receivable.

To illustrate, assume that Wayne Higley Inc. on October 1 indicates that it cannot pay at the present time. The entry to record the dishonor of the note depends on whether eventual collection is expected. If Betty Co. expects eventual collection, the amount due (face value and interest) on the note is debited to Accounts Receivable. Betty Co. would make the following entry at the time the note is dishonored (assuming no previous accrual of interest):

A	=	L	+	OE
+ 10,300				+ 300
− 10,000				

Oct. 1	Accounts Receivable	10,300	
	Notes Receivable		10,000
	Interest Revenue		300
	(To record the dishonor of the note)		

If there is no hope of collection, the face value of the note should be written off by debiting the Allowance for Doubtful Accounts. No interest revenue would be recorded because collection will not occur.

Sale of Notes Receivable

The accounting for the sales of notes receivable is recorded in a manner similar to the sale of accounts receivable. The accounting entries for the sale of notes receivable are left for a more advanced course.

BEFORE YOU GO ON . . .

Review It

1. What is the basic formula for computing interest?
2. At what value are notes receivable reported on the balance sheet?
3. Explain the difference between honoring and dishonoring a note receivable.

Do It

Gambit Stores accepts from Leonard Co. a $3,400, 90-day, 12% note dated May 10 in settlement of Leonard's overdue open account. What is the maturity date of the note? What is the entry made by Gambit at the maturity date, assuming Leonard pays the note and interest in full at that time?

Reasoning: When the due date is stated in terms of days, it is necessary to count the exact number of days to determine the maturity date. In counting, the date the note is issued is omitted, but the due date is included. The entry to record interest at maturity in this solution assumes that no interest is accrued on this note.

Solution: The maturity date is August 8, computed as follows:

Term of note:		90 days
May (31 − 10)	21	
June	30	
July	31	82
Maturity date, August		8

The interest payable at maturity date is $102, computed as follows:

$$\text{Face} \times \text{Rate} \times \text{Time} = \text{Interest}$$
$$\$3,400 \times 12\% \times 90/360 = \$102$$

The entry recorded by Gambit Stores at the maturity date is:

Cash	3,502	
Notes Receivable		3,400
Interest Revenue		102
(To record collection of Leonard note)		

THE NAVIGATOR

Related exercise material: BE8–8, BE8–10, E8–8, and E8–9.

ACCOUNTING IN ACTION
Business Insight

Give the man credit. Like most of us, John Galbreath receives piles of un-solicited, "preapproved" credit card applications in the mail. Galbreath doesn't just toss them out, though. In April he filled out a credit card application on which he stated he was 97 years old and had no income, no telephone, and no Social Security number. In a space inviting him to let the credit card company pay off his other credit card balances, Galbreath said he owed money to the Mafia.

Back came a credit card and a letter welcoming John to the fold with a $1,500 credit limit. Galbreath had requested the card under a false name, John C. Reath, an alias under which he had received two other credit cards—earning exemplary credit. John C. Reath might be a bit "long in the tooth," but it seems he paid his bills on time.

Source: "Forbes Informer," edited by Kate Bohner Lewis, *Forbes*, August 14, 1995, p. 19. Reprinted by permission of FORBES Magazine © Forbes Inc., 1995

STATEMENT PRESENTATION AND ANALYSIS

Presentation

Each of the major types of receivables should be identified in the balance sheet or in the notes to the financial statements. Short-term receivables are reported within the current asset section of the balance sheet below temporary investments. Temporary investments appear before short-term receivables, because these investments are more liquid, or nearer to cash. Both the gross amount of receivables and the allowance for doubtful accounts should be reported. Illus-

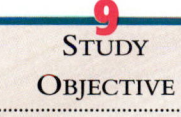

9
STUDY OBJECTIVE

Explain the statement presentation and analysis of receivables.

tration 8-14 shows the current asset presentation of receivables for Kellogg Company, at December 31, 1997.

ILLUSTRATION 8-14

Balance sheet presentation of receivables

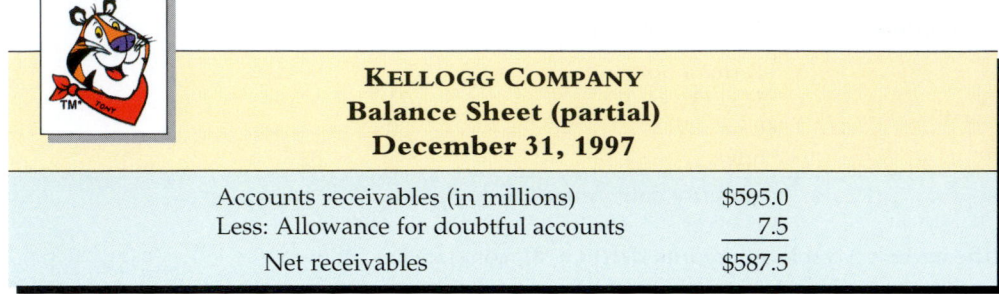

KELLOGG COMPANY **Balance Sheet (partial)** **December 31, 1997**	
Accounts receivables (in millions)	$595.0
Less: Allowance for doubtful accounts	7.5
Net receivables	$587.5

In a multiple-step income statement, Bad Debts Expense and Service Charge Expense are reported as selling expenses in the Operating Expenses section. Interest Revenue is shown under Other Revenues and Gains in the nonoperating section of the income statement.

Analysis

Financial ratios are frequently computed to evaluate the liquidity of a company's accounts receivable. The ratio used to assess the liquidity of the receivables is the **accounts receivables turnover ratio**. This ratio measures the number of times, on average, accounts receivable are collected during the period. The accounts receivable turnover ratio is computed by dividing net credit sales (net sales less cash sales) by the average net accounts receivable during the year. Unless seasonal factors are significant, average net accounts receivable outstanding can be computed from the beginning and ending balance of the net accounts receivable.

For example, in 1997 Kellogg had net sales of $6,830.1 million for the year and a beginning net accounts receivable balance of $592.3 million. Assuming that Kellogg's sales were all on credit, its accounts receivable turnover ratio is computed as follows:

ILLUSTRATION 8-15

Accounts receivable turnover ratio and computation

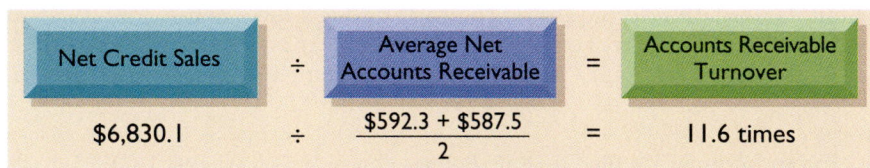

The result indicates an accounts receivable turnover ratio of 11.6 times per year. The higher the turnover ratio the more liquid the company's receivables.

Another variant of the accounts receivable turnover ratio that makes the liquidity even more evident is the conversion of it into an **average collection period** in terms of days. This is done by dividing the turnover ratio into 365 days. For example, Kellogg's turnover of 11.6 times is divided into 365 days, as follows, to obtain approximately 31.5 days:

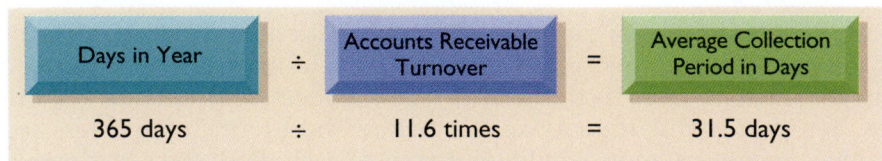

This means that Kellogg's average collection period for accounts receivable is 31.5 days. The average collection period is frequently used to assess the effectiveness of a company's credit and collection policies. The general rule is that the collection period should not greatly exceed the credit term period (i.e., the time allowed for payment).

BEFORE YOU GO ON . . .

Review It

1. Explain where accounts and notes receivable are reported on the balance sheet.
2. Where are bad debts expense, service charge expense, and interest revenue reported on the multiple-step income statement?

A LOOK BACK AT OUR FEATURE STORY

Refer back to the story about the North Carolina State University newspaper at the beginning of the chapter, and answer the following questions:

1. If you had sold advertising space to a tardy paying client, how would you persuade them to pay?
2. At what point would you recommend that the newspaper write off uncollectible receivables?
3. Indicate the accounts to be debited and credited for each of the following transactions of the newspaper: (a) ad space is sold on account; (b) ad space is sold and prepaid; (c) cash is collected on account; (d) the ad is run for the advertiser who prepaid; (e) an uncollectible account is written off.

Solution:

1. The collection process used by the newspaper: a friendly letter at the end of 30 days, a less-than-friendly letter at the end of 45 days, and the filing of a suit in small claims court at the end of 75 days. In addition, a tactful, persuasive telephone call might be added to the attempts to collect.
2. An unpaid receivable should be written off when it is determined that it is uncollectible. Past experience with small unpaid ad bills will usually dictate the appropriate point at which bills are deemed uncollectible. With the limited information given in this case, the write-off would seem proper at the conclusion of an unsuccessful court claim.
3. (a) Debit Accounts Receivable, credit Advertising Revenue.
   (b) Debit Cash, credit Unearned Advertising Revenue.
   (c) Debit Cash, credit Accounts Receivable.
   (d) Debit Unearned Advertising Revenue, credit Advertising Revenue.
   (e) Debit Allowance for Doubtful Accounts, credit Accounts Receivable.

THE
NAVIGATOR

DEMONSTRATION PROBLEM

Presented below are selected transactions related to Falcetto Company.

Mar. 1   Sold $20,000 of merchandise to Potter Company, terms 2/10, n/30.
     11   Received payment in full from Potter Company for balance due.
     12   Accepted Juno Company's $20,000 6-month, 12% note for balance due.
     13   Made Falcetto Company credit card sales for $13,200.
     15   Made American Express credit sales totaling $6,700. A 5% service fee is charged by American Express.
     30   Received payment in full from American Express Company less the 5% service charge.

Apr. 11	Sold accounts receivable of $8,000 to Harcot Factor. Harcot Factor assesses a service charge of 2% of the amount of receivables sold.
13	Received collections of $8,200 on Falcetto Company credit card sales and added finance charges of 1.5% to the remaining balances.
May 10	Wrote off as uncollectible $16,000 of accounts receivable. Falcetto uses the percentage of sales basis to estimate bad debts.
June 30	Credit sales for the first six months total $2,000,000 and the bad debt percentage is 1% of credit sales. At June 30, the balance in the allowance account is $3,500.
July 16	One of the accounts receivable written off in May pays the amount due, $4,000, in full.

Instructions

Prepare the journal entries for the transactions.

SOLUTION TO DEMONSTRATION PROBLEM

Date	Account	Debit	Credit
Mar. 1	Accounts Receivable—Potter	20,000	
	Sales		20,000
	(To record sales on account)		
Mar. 11	Cash	19,600	
	Sales Discounts (2% × $20,000)	400	
	Accounts Receivable—Potter		20,000
	(To record collection of accounts receivable)		
Mar. 12	Notes Receivable	20,000	
	Accounts Receivable—Juno		20,000
	(To record acceptance of Juno Company note)		
Mar. 13	Accounts Receivable	13,200	
	Sales		13,200
	(To record company credit card sales)		
Mar. 15	Accounts Receivable—American Express	6,365	
	Service Charge Expense (5% × $6,700)	335	
	Sales		6,700
	(To record credit card sales)		
Mar. 30	Cash	6,365	
	Accounts Receivable—American Express		6,365
	(To record redemption of credit card billings)		
Apr. 11	Cash	7,840	
	Service Charge Expense (2% × $8,000)	160	
	Accounts Receivable		8,000
	(To record sale of receivables to factor)		
Apr. 13	Cash	8,200	
	Accounts Receivable		8,200
	(To record collection of accounts receivable)		
	Accounts Receivable [($13,200 − $8,200) × 1.5%]	75	
	Interest Revenue		75
	(To record interest on amount due)		

May 10	Allowance for Doubtful Accounts	16,000	
	Accounts Receivable		16,000
	(To record write-off of accounts receivable)		
June 30	Bad Debts Expense ($2,000,000 × 1%)	20,000	
	Allowance for Doubtful Accounts		20,000
	(To record estimate of uncollectible accounts)		
July 16	Accounts Receivable	4,000	
	Allowance for Doubtful Accounts		4,000
	(To reverse write-off of accounts receivable)		
	Cash	4,000	
	Accounts Receivable		4,000
	(To record collection of accounts receivable)		

SUMMARY OF STUDY OBJECTIVES

1. Identify the different types of receivables. Receivables are frequently classified as (1) accounts, (2) notes, and (3) other. Accounts receivable are amounts owed by customers on account. Notes receivable represent claims that are evidenced by formal instruments of credit. Other receivables include nontrade receivables such as interest receivable, loans to company officers, advances to employees, and income taxes refundable.

2. Explain how accounts receivable are recognized in the accounts. Accounts receivable are recorded at invoice price. They are reduced by Sales Returns and Allowances. Cash discounts reduce the amount received on accounts receivable. When interest is charged on a past due receivable, this interest is added to the accounts receivable balance and is recognized as interest revenue.

3. Distinguish between the methods and bases used to value accounts receivable. There are two methods of accounting for uncollectible accounts: (1) the allowance method and (2) the direct write-off method. Either the percentage of sales or the percentage of receivables basis may be used to estimate uncollectible accounts using the allowance method. The percentage of sales basis emphasizes the matching principle. The percentage of receivables basis emphasizes the cash realizable value of the accounts receivable. An aging schedule is frequently used with this basis.

4. Describe the entries to record the disposition of accounts receivable. When an account receivable is collected, Accounts Receivable is credited. When an account receivable is sold, a service charge expense is charged which reduces the amount collected.

5. Compute the maturity date of, and interest on, notes receivable. The maturity date of a note must be computed unless the due date is specified or the note is payable on demand. For a note stated in months, the maturity date is found by counting the months from the date of issue. For a note stated in days, the number of days is counted, omitting the issue date and counting the due date. The formula for computing interest is face value × interest rate × time.

6. Explain how notes receivable are recognized in the accounts. Notes receivable are recorded at face value. In some cases, it is necessary to accrue interest prior to maturity. In this case, Interest Receivable is debited and Interest Revenue is credited.

7. Describe how notes receivable are valued. Like accounts receivable, notes receivable are reported at their cash (net) realizable value. The notes receivable allowance account is the Allowance for Doubtful Accounts. The computation and estimations involved in valuing notes receivables at cash realizable value, and in recording the proper amount of bad debt expense and related allowance are similar to accounts receivable.

8. Describe the entries to record the disposition of notes receivable. Notes can be held to maturity, at which time the face value plus accrued interest is due and the note is removed from the accounts. However, in many cases, similar to accounts receivable, the holder of the note speeds up the conversion by selling the receivable to another party. In some situations, the maker of the note dishonors the note (defaults), and the note is written off.

9. Explain the statement presentation and analysis of receivables. Each major type of receivable should be identified in the balance sheet or in the notes to the financial statements. Short-term receivables are considered current assets. The gross amount of receivables and allowance for doubtful accounts should be reported. Bad debts and service charge expenses are reported in the multiple-step income statement as operating (selling) expenses, and interest revenue is shown as other revenues and gains in the nonoperating section of the statement. Accounts receivables may be evaluated for liquidity by computing a turnover ratio and an average collection period.

GLOSSARY

Accounts receivable turnover ratio A measure of the liquidity of accounts receivable, computed by dividing net credit sales by average net accounts receivable. (p. 344).

Aging of accounts receivable The analysis of customer balances by the length of time they have been unpaid. (p. 332).

Average collection period The average amount of time that a receivable is outstanding, calculated by dividing 365 days by the receivables turnover ratio. (p. 344).

Cash (net) realizable value The net amount expected to be received in cash. (p. 328).

Dishonored note A note that is not paid in full at maturity. (p. 342).

Factor A finance company or bank that buys receivables from businesses for a fee and then collects the payments directly from the customers. (p. 335).

Maker The party in a promissory note who is making the promise to pay. (p. 338).

Payee The party to whom payment of a promissory note is to be made. (p. 338).

Percentage of receivables basis Management establishes a percentage relationship between the amount of receivables and the expected losses from uncollectible accounts. (p. 332).

Percentage of sales basis Management establishes a percentage relationship between the amount of credit sales and expected losses from uncollectible accounts. (p. 331).

Promissory note A written promise to pay a specified amount of money on demand or at a definite time. (p. 338).

Trade receivables Notes and accounts receivable that result from sales transactions. (p. 326).

SELF-STUDY QUESTIONS

Answers are at the end of the chapter.

(SO 2) 1. Remmers Company on June 15 sells merchandise on account to Tucci Co. for $1,000 terms 2/10, n/30. On June 20, Tucci Co. returns merchandise worth $300 to Remmers Company. On June 24, payment is received from Tucci Co. for the balance due. What is the amount of cash received?
   a. $700.
   b. $680.
   c. $686.
   d. None of the above.

(SO 3) 2. Which of the following approaches for bad debts is best described as a balance sheet method?
   a. Percentage of receivables basis.
   b. Direct write-off method.
   c. Percentage of sales basis.
   d. Both a and b.

(SO 3) 3. Net sales for the month are $800,000 and bad debts are expected to be 1.5% of net sales. The company uses the percentage of sales basis. If the Allowance for Doubtful Accounts has a credit balance of $15,000 before adjustment, what is the balance after adjustment?
   a. $15,000.
   b. $27,000.
   c. $23,000.
   d. $31,000.

(SO 3) 4. In 1999, Roland Carlson Company had net credit sales of $750,000. On January 1, 1999, Allowance for Doubtful Accounts had a credit balance of $18,000. During 1999, $30,000 of uncollectible accounts receivable were written off. Past experience indicates that 3% of net credit sales become uncollectible. What should be the adjusted balance of Allowance for Doubtful Accounts at December 31, 1999?
   a. $10,050.
   b. $10,500.
   c. $22,500.
   d. $40,500.

(SO 3) 5. An analysis and aging of the accounts receivable of Machiavelli Company at December 31 reveals the following data:

Accounts Receivable	$800,000
Allowance for Doubtful Accounts per books before adjustment	50,000
Amounts expected to become uncollectible	65,000

The cash realizable value of the accounts receivable at December 31, after adjustment, is:
   a. $685,000.
   b. $750,000.
   c. $800,000.
   d. $735,000.

(SO 6) 6. One of the following statements about promissory notes is incorrect. The *incorrect* statement is:
   a. The party making the promise to pay is called the maker.
   b. The party to whom payment is to be made is called the payee.
   c. A promissory note is not a negotiable instrument.
   d. A promissory note is more liquid than an accounts receivable.

(SO 4) 7. Which of the following statements about VISA credit card sales is *incorrect*?
   a. The credit card issuer makes the credit investigation of the customer.
   b. The retailer is not involved in the collection process.
   c. Two parties are involved.
   d. The retailer receives cash more quickly than it would from individual customers on account.

(SO 4) 8. Morgan Retailers accepted $50,000 of Citibank VISA credit card charges for merchandise sold on July 1. Citibank charges 4% for its credit card use. The entry to record this transaction by Morgan Retailers will include a credit to Sales of $50,000 and a debit(s) to:
   a. Cash $48,000
      and Service Charge Expense $2,000
   b. Accounts Receivable $48,000
      and Service Charge Expense $2,000
   c. Cash $50,000
   d. Accounts Receivable $50,000

(SO 6) 9. Bickner Co. accepts a $1,000, 3-month, 12% promissory note in settlement of an account with Streisand Co. The entry to record this transaction is as follows:

a. Notes Receivable	1,030	
Accounts Receivable		1,030
b. Notes Receivable	1,000	
Accounts Receivable		1,000
c. Notes Receivable	1,000	
Sales		1,000
d. Notes Receivable	1,020	
Accounts Receivable		1,020

10. Schlicht Co. holds Osgrove Inc.'s $10,000, 120-day, 9% **(SO 8)** note. The entry made by Schlicht Co. when the note is collected, assuming no interest has been accrued, is

a. Cash	10,300	
Notes Receivable		10,300
b. Cash	10,000	
Notes Receivable		10,000
c. Accounts Receivable	10,300	
Notes Receivable		10,000
Interest Revenue		300
d. Cash	10,300	
Notes Receivable		10,000
Interest Revenue		300

THE
NAVIGATOR

QUESTIONS

1. What is the difference between an account receivable and a note receivable?

2. What are some common types of receivables other than accounts receivable or notes receivable?

3. Texaco Oil Company issues its own credit cards. Assume that Texaco charges you $40 on an unpaid balance. Prepare the journal entry that Texaco makes to record this revenue.

4. What are the essential features of the allowance method of accounting for bad debts?

5. Dorothy Fleming cannot understand why cash realizable value does not decrease when an uncollectible account is written off under the allowance method. Clarify this point for Dorothy Fleming.

6. Distinguish between the two bases that may be used in estimating uncollectible accounts.

7. Kosinsky Company has a credit balance of $3,500 in Allowance for Doubtful Accounts. The estimated bad debts expense under the percentage of sales basis is $4,100, and the total estimated uncollectibles under the percentage of receivables basis is $5,800. Prepare the adjusting entry under each basis.

8. How are bad debts accounted for under the direct write-off method? What are the disadvantages of this method?

9. Elbe Company accepts both its own credit cards and national credit cards. What are the advantages of accepting both types of cards?

10. An article recently appeared in *The Wall Street Journal* indicating that companies are selling their receivables at a record rate. Why are companies selling their receivables?

11. Southern Textiles decides to sell $800,000 of its accounts receivable to First Central Factors Inc. First Central Factors assesses a service charge of 2% of the amount of receivables sold. Prepare the journal entry that Southern Textiles makes to record this sale.

12. Your roommate is uncertain about the advantages of a promissory note. Compare the advantages of a note receivable with those of an accounts receivable.

13. How may the maturity date of a promissory note be stated?

14. Indicate the maturity date of each of the following promissory notes:

Date of Note	Terms
(a) March 13	one year after date of note
(b) May 4	3 months after date
(c) June 20	30 days after date
(d) July 1	60 days after date

15. Compute the missing amounts for each of the following notes:

	Principal	Annual Interest Rate	Time	Total Interest
(a)	?	9%	120 days	$ 450
(b)	$30,000	10%	3 years	?
(c)	$60,000	?	5 months	$3,000
(d)	$50,000	11%	?	$1,375

16. In determining interest revenue, some financial institutions use 365 days per year whereas others use 360 days. Why might a financial institution use 360 days?

17. Nick Coffin Company dishonors a note at maturity. What actions by Coffin may occur with the dishonoring of the note?

18. Paula Company has accounts receivable and notes receivable. How should the receivables be reported on the balance sheet?

19. If the accounts receivables turnover ratio is 7.15 and average net receivables during the period are $210,000, what is the amount of net credit sales for the period?

BRIEF EXERCISES

•••

Identify different types of receivables.
(SO 1)

BE8–1   Presented below are three receivable transactions. Indicate whether these receivables are reported as accounts receivable, notes receivable, or other receivables on a balance sheet.

1. Sold merchandise on account for $60,000 to a customer.
2. Received a promissory note of $57,000 for services performed.
3. Advanced $10,000 to an employee.

Record basic accounts receivable transactions.
(SO 2)

BE8–2   Record the following transactions on the books of Jose Co.

1. On July 1, Jose Co. sold merchandise on account to Cambridge Inc. for $15,000, terms 2/10, n/30.
2. On July 8, Cambridge Inc. returned merchandise worth $3,800 to Jose Co.
3. On July 11, Cambridge Inc. paid for the merchandise.

Prepare entries for allowance method and classifications.
(SO 3, 9)

BE8–3   During its first year of operations, Alvarado Company had credit sales of $3,000,000, of which $600,000 remained uncollected at year-end. The credit manager estimates that $30,000 of these receivables will become uncollectible. (a) Prepare the journal entry to record the estimated uncollectibles. (b) Prepare the current asset section of the balance sheet for Alvarado Company, assuming that in addition to the receivables it has cash of $90,000, merchandise inventory of $130,000, and prepaid expenses of $13,000.

Prepare entries for write-off and determine cash realizable value.
(SO 3)

BE8–4   At the end of 1999, Delacruz Co. has accounts receivable of $700,000 and an allowance for doubtful accounts of $54,000. On January 24, 2000, it is learned that the company's receivable from Hutley Inc. is not collectible and therefore management authorizes a write-off of $6,000. (a) Prepare the journal entry to record the write-off. (b) What is the cash realizable value of the accounts receivable (1) before the write-off and (2) after the write-off?

Prepare entries for collection of bad debt write-off.
(SO 3)

BE8–5   Assume the same information as BE8–4 and that on March 4, 2000, Delacruz Co. receives payment of $6,000 in full from Hutley Co. Prepare the journal entries to record this transaction.

Prepare entry using percentage of sales method.
(SO 3)

BE8–6   Einhause Co. elects to use the percentage of sales basis in 1999 to record bad debts expense and concludes that 2% of net credit sales will become uncollectible. Sales are $800,000 for 1999, sales returns and allowances are $50,000, and the allowance for doubtful accounts has a credit balance of $12,000. Prepare the adjusting entry to record bad debts expense in 1999.

Prepare entry using percentage of receivables method.
(SO 3)

BE8–7   Grolesky Co. uses the percentage of accounts receivable basis to record bad debt expense, and concludes that 1% of accounts receivable will become uncollectible. Accounts receivable are $400,000 at the end of the year, and the allowance for doubtful accounts has a credit balance of $3,000. (a) Prepare the adjusting journal entry to record bad debt expense for the year. (b) If the allowance for doubtful accounts had a debit balance of $800 instead of credit balance of $3,000, determine the amount to be reported for bad debt expense.

BE8–8 Presented below are three promissory notes. Determine the missing amounts.

Compute maturity date and interest on note. (SO 5)

Date of Note	Terms	Maturity Date	Principal	Annual Interest Rate	Total Interest
(a) April 1	60 days	?	$900,000	9%	?
(b) July 2	30 days	?	90,000	?	$600
(c) March 7	6 months	?	60,000	12%	?

BE8–9 Presented below are the following transactions.

Prepare entries to dispose of accounts receivable. (SO 4)

1. Castle Restaurant accepted a Visa card in payment of a $100 lunch bill. The bank charges a 3% fee. What entry should Castle make?
2. Mayfield Company sold its accounts receivable of $80,000. What entry should Mayfield make, given a service charge of 3% on the amount of receivables sold?

BE8–10 On January 10, 1999, Raja Co. sold merchandise on account to Dewey Yeager for $9,000, n/30. On February 9, Dewey Yeager gave Raja Co. a 10% promissory note in settlement of this account. Prepare the journal entry to record the sale and the settlement of the accounts receivable.

Prepare entry for notes receivable exchanged for account receivable. (SO 6)

BE8–11 The financial statements of Minnesota Mining and Manufacturing Company (3M) report net sales of $9.4 billion. Accounts receivable are $1.6 billion at the beginning of the year and $1.4 billion at the end of the year. Compute 3M's receivable's turnover ratio. Compute 3M's average collection period for accounts receivable in days.

Compute ratios to analyze receivables. (SO 9)

EXERCISES

E8–1 Presented below are two independent situations that occurred during the year.

Journalize entries for recognizing accounts receivable. (SO 2)

1. On January 6, Herzog Co. sells merchandise on account to Watson Inc. for $3,000, terms 2/10, n/30. On January 16, Watson pays the amount due. Prepare the entries on Herzog's books to record the sale and related collection.
2. On January 10, Diane Leto uses her Salizar Co. credit card to purchase merchandise from Salizar Co. for $11,000. On February 10, Leto is billed for the amount due of $11,000. On February 12, Leto pays $6,000 on the balance due. On March 10, Leto is billed for the amount due, including interest at 2% per month on the unpaid balance as of February 12. Prepare the entries on Salizar Co.'s books related to the transactions that occurred on January 10, February 12, and March 10.

E8–2 The ledger of the Kadlec Company at the end of the current year shows Accounts Receivable $90,000, Sales $840,000, and Sales Returns and Allowances $40,000.

Journalize entries to record allowance for doubtful accounts using two different bases. (SO 3)

Instructions

(a) If Allowance for Doubtful Accounts has a credit balance of $800 in the trial balance, journalize the adjusting entry at December 31, assuming bad debts are expected to be (1) 1% of net sales, and (2) 10% of accounts receivable.

(b) If Allowance for Doubtful Accounts has a debit balance of $500 in the trial balance, journalize the adjusting entry at December 31, assuming bad debts are expected to be (1) .75% of net sales and (2) 8% of accounts receivable.

E8–3 Garcia Company has accounts receivable of $92,500 at March 31. An analysis of the accounts shows the following:

Determine bad debts expense and prepare the adjusting entry for bad debts expense. (SO 3)

Month of Sale	Balance, March 31
March	$65,000
February	12,600
December and January	8,500
November and October	6,400
	$92,500

Credit terms are 2/10, n/30. At March 31, there is a $1,600 credit balance in Allowance for Doubtful Accounts prior to adjustment. The company uses the percentage of receivables basis for estimating uncollectible accounts. The company's estimate of bad debts is as follows:

Age of Accounts	Estimated Percentage Uncollectible
1–30 days past due	2.0%
30–60 days past due	5.0%
60–90 days past due	30.0%
Over 90 days	50.0%

Instructions

(a) Determine the total estimated uncollectibles.

(b) Prepare the adjusting entry at March 31 to record bad debts expense.

Journalize percentage of sales basis, write-off, recovery.
(SO 3)

E8–4 On December 31, 1999, Jana Co. estimates that 2% of its net sales of $400,000 will become uncollectible and records this amount as an addition to Allowance for Doubtful Accounts. On May 11, 2000, Jana Co. determined that Bob Knight's account was uncollectible and wrote off $900. On June 12, 2000, Knight paid the amount previously written off.

Instructions

Prepare the journal entries on December 31, 1999, May 11, 2000, and June 12, 2000.

Journalize entries for the sale of accounts receivable.
(SO 4)

E8–5 Presented below are two independent situations:

1. On March 3, Dennis Stoia Appliances sells $800,000 of its receivables to Potter Factors Inc. Potter Factors Inc. assesses a finance charge of 3% of the amount of receivables sold. Prepare the entry on Dennis Stoia Appliances' books to record the sale of the receivables.

2. On May 10, Monee Company sold merchandise for $4,000 and accepted the customer's First Business Bank MasterCard. At the end of the day, the First Business Bank MasterCard receipts were deposited in the company's bank account. First Business Bank charges a 4% service charge for credit card sales. Prepare the entry on Monee Company's books to record the sale of merchandise.

Journalize entries for credit card sales.
(SO 4)

E8–6 Presented below are two independent situations that occurred during the year.

1. On April 2, Elaine Stahl uses her J. C. Penney credit card to purchase merchandise from a J. C. Penney store for $1,300. On May 1, Stahl is billed for the $1,300 amount due. Stahl pays $800 on the balance due on May 3. On June 1, Stahl receives a bill for the amount due, including interest at 1.0% per month on the unpaid balance as of May 3. Prepare the entries on J. C. Penney Co.'s books related to the transactions that occurred on April 2, May 3, and June 1.

2. On July 4, Robyn's Restaurant accepts an American Express card for a $300 dinner bill. American Express charges a 4% service fee. On July 10, American Express pays Robyn $288. Prepare the entries on Robyn's books related to the transactions.

Journalize credit card sales and indicate the statement presentation of financing charges and service charge expense.
(SO 4)

E8–7 Sapaniak Stores accepts both its own and national credit cards. During the year the following selected summary transactions occurred.

Jan. 15 Made Sapaniak credit card sales totaling $15,000. (There were no balances prior to 1y15.)

20 Made American Express credit card sales (service charge fee, 5%) totaling $2,600.

30 Received payment in full from American Express less a 5% service charge.

Feb. 10 Collected $12,000 on Sapaniak credit card sales.

15 Added finance charges of 1.5% to Sapaniak credit card balance.

Instructions

(a) Journalize the transactions for Sapaniak Stores.

(b) Indicate the statement presentation of the financing charges and the credit card service expense for Sapaniak Stores.

Journalize entries for notes receivable transactions.
(SO 5, 6)

E8–8 Marv Tice Supply Co. has the following transactions related to notes receivable during the last 2 months of the year.

Nov. 1 Loaned $18,000 cash to Sheila Skinner on a 1-year, 10% note.
Dec. 11 Sold goods to Lucinda Higdon, Inc., receiving a $3,600, 90-day, 12% note.
     16 Received a $4,000, 6-month, 12% note on account from Deanna Prentice.
     31 Accrued interest revenue on all notes receivable.

Instructions
Journalize the transactions for Marv Tice Supply Co.

E8–9 Record the following transactions for the Plano Molding Co. in the general journal:

Journalize entries for notes receivable.
(SO 5, 6)

1999
May 1 Received a $9,000, 1-year, 10% note on account from John Lewis.
Dec. 31 Accrued interest on the Lewis note.
Dec. 31 Closed the interest revenue account.
2000
May 1 Received principal plus interest on the Lewis note. (No interest has been accrued in 2000.)

E8–10 On May 2, Cynthia Taylor Company lends $6,000 to Nancy Barnes Inc., issuing a 6-month, 10% note. At the maturity date, November 2, Barnes indicates that it cannot pay.

Journalize entries for dishonor of notes receivable.
(SO 5, 8)

Instructions
(a) Prepare the entry to record the dishonor of the note, assuming that Taylor Company expects collection will occur.
(b) Prepare the entry to record the dishonor of the note, assuming that Taylor Company does not expect collection in the future.

PROBLEMS: SET A

P8–1A At December 31, 1999, Mike Muzzillo Imports reported the following information on its balance sheet:

Prepare journal entries related to bad debt expense.
(SO 2, 3)

Accounts receivable	$1,000,000
Less: Allowance for doubtful accounts	60,000

During 2000, the company had the following transactions related to receivables.

1. Sales on account	$2,600,000
2. Sales returns and allowances	40,000
3. Collections of accounts receivable	2,300,000
4. Write-offs of accounts receivable deemed uncollectible	65,000
5. Recovery of bad debts previously written off as uncollectible	25,000

Instructions
(a) Prepare the journal entries to record each of these five transactions. Assume that no cash discounts were taken on the collections of accounts receivable.
(b) Enter the January 1, 1999, balances in Accounts Receivable and Allowance for Doubtful Accounts, post the entries to the two accounts (use T accounts), and determine the balances.
(c) Prepare the journal entry to record bad debts expense for 2000, assuming that an aging of accounts receivable indicates that estimated bad debts are $70,000.
(d) Compute the accounts receivable turnover ratio for the year 2000.

P8–2A Information related to Tisinai Company for 1999 is summarized below:

Compute bad debts amounts.
(SO 3)

Total credit sales	$1,500,000
Accounts receivable at December 31	600,000
Bad debts written off	24,000

Instructions
(a) What amount of bad debts expense will Tisinai Company report if it uses the direct write-off method of accounting for bad debts?

(b) Assume that Tisinai Company decides to estimate its bad debts expense to be 3% of credit sales. What amount of bad debts expense will Tisinai Company record if Allowance for Doubtful Accounts has a credit balance of $3,000?

(c) Assume that Tisinai Company decides to estimate its bad debts expense based on 5% of accounts receivable. What amount of bad debts expense will Tisinai Company record if Allowance for Doubtful Accounts balance has a credit balance of $4,000?

(d) Assume the same facts as in (c), except that there is a $2,000 debit balance in Allowance for Doubtful Accounts. What amount of bad debts expense will Tisinai record?

(e) ▬▬▶ What is the weakness of the direct write-off method of reporting bad debts expense?

Journalize entries to record transactions related to bad debts.

(SO 2, 3)

P8–3A Presented below is an aging schedule for Chris Cain Company.

Customer	Total	Not Yet Due	1–30	31–60	61–90	Over 90
			Number of Days Past Due			
Sandy Freewalt	$ 20,000		$ 9,000	$11,000		
Joni Schnabel	30,000	$ 30,000				
Kay Nelson	50,000	15,000	5,000		$30,000	
Ken Mason	38,000					$38,000
Others	120,000	92,000	15,000	13,000		
	$258,000	$137,000	$29,000	$24,000	$30,000	$38,000
Estimated Percentage Uncollectible			3%	6%	12%	24%	50%
Total Estimated Bad Debts	$ 34,930	$ 4,110	$ 1,740	$ 2,880	$ 7,200	$19,000

At December 31, 1999, the unadjusted balance in Allowance for Doubtful Accounts is a credit of $10,000.

Instructions

(a) Journalize and post the adjusting entry for bad debts at December 31, 1999.

(b) Journalize and post to the allowance account the following events and transactions in the year 2000:
(1) March 1, an $800 customer balance originating in 1999 is judged uncollectible.
(2) May 1, a check for $800 is received from the customer whose account was written off as uncollectible on March 1.

(c) Journalize the adjusting entry for bad debts on December 31, 2000, assuming that the unadjusted balance in Allowance for Doubtful Accounts is a debit of $1,100 and the aging schedule indicates that total estimated bad debts will be $29,100.

Journalize entries to record transactions related to bad debts.

(SO 3)

P8–4A At December 31, 1999, the trial balance of John Gleason Company contained the following amounts before adjustment:

	Debits	Credits
Accounts Receivable	$350,000	
Allowance for Doubtful Accounts		$ 1,500
Sales		875,000

Instructions

(a) Prepare the adjusting entry at December 31, 1999, to record bad debt expense under each of the following independent assumptions:
(1) An aging schedule indicates that $16,750 of accounts receivable will be uncollectible.
(2) It is estimated that 2% of sales will be uncollectible.

(b) Repeat part (a) assuming that instead of a credit balance there is a $1,500 debit balance in the Allowance for Doubtful Accounts.

(c) During the next month, January 2000, a $4,500 account receivable is written off as uncollectible. Prepare the journal entry to record the write-off.

(d) Repeat part (c) assuming that John Gleason Company uses the direct write-off method instead of the allowance method in accounting for uncollectible accounts receivable.

(e) ▓▓▓▷ What are the advantages of using the allowance method in accounting for uncollectible accounts as compared to the direct write-off method?

P8–5A Connie Kolzow Co. closes its books monthly. On June 30, selected ledger account balances are:

Prepare entries for various note receivable transactions.
(SO 2, 4, 5, 8, 9)

Notes Receivable	$20,800
Interest Receivable	$132.80

Notes Receivable include the following:

Date	Maker	Face	Term	Interest
May 21	Don Inc.	$6,000	60 days	12%
May 25	John Co.	4,800	60 days	11%
June 30	Pete Corp.	10,000	6 months	9%

During July, the following transactions were completed.

July 5 Made sales of $6,200 on Connie Kolzow Co. credit cards.

14 Made sales of $700 on VISA credit cards. The credit card service charge is 3%.

16 Added $415 to Connie Kolzow Co. charge customer balances for finance charges on unpaid balances.

20 Received payment in full from Don Inc. on the amount due.

25 Received notice that John Co. note has been dishonored. (Assume that John Co. is expected to pay in the future.)

Instructions

(a) Journalize the July transactions and the July 31 adjusting entry for accrued interest receivable. (Interest is computed using 360 days.)

(b) Enter the balances at July 1 in the receivable accounts and post the entries to all of the receivable accounts.

(c) Show the balance sheet presentation of the receivable accounts at July 31.

P8–6A On January 1, 1999, Judy Elam Company had Accounts Receivable $54,200 and Allowance for Doubtful Accounts $4,700. Judy Elam Company prepares financial statements annually. During the year the following selected transactions occurred.

Prepare entries for various receivables transactions.
(SO 2, 4, 5, 6, 7, 8)

Jan. 5 Sold $6,000 of merchandise to Garth Brooks Company, terms n/30.

Feb. 2 Accepted a $6,000, 4-month, 12% promissory note from Garth Brooks Company for balance due.

12 Sold $7,800 of merchandise to Lynn Easton Company and accepted Easton's $7,800, 2-month, 10% note for the balance due.

26 Sold $4,000 of merchandise to Mathias Co., terms n/10.

Apr. 5 Accepted a $4,000, 3-month, 8% note from Mathias Co. for balance due.

12 Collected Lynne Easton Company note in full.

June 2 Collected Garth Brooks Company note in full.

July 5 Mathias Co. dishonors its note of April 5. It is expected that Mathias will eventually pay the amount owed.

15 Sold $3,000 of merchandise to John Ross Co. and accepted Ross's $3,000, 3-month, 12% note for the amount due.

Oct. 15 John Ross Co. note was dishonored. John Ross Co. is bankrupt, and there is no hope of future settlement.

Instructions
Journalize the transactions.

PROBLEMS: SET B

Prepare journal entries related to bad debts expense.
(SO 2, 3, 4)

P8–1B   At December 31, 1999, Cellular Ten Co. reported the following information on its balance sheet.

Accounts receivable	$960,000
Less: Allowance for doubtful accounts	70,000

During 2000, the company had the following transactions related to receivables.

1. Sales on account	$3,200,000
2. Sales returns and allowances	50,000
3. Collections of accounts receivable	2,800,000
4. Write-offs of accounts receivable deemed uncollectible	90,000
5. Recovery of bad debts previously written off as uncollectible	25,000

Instructions

(a) Prepare the journal entries to record each of these five transactions. Assume that no cash discounts were taken on the collections of accounts receivable.

(b) Enter the January 1, 2000, balances in Accounts Receivable and Allowance for Doubtful Accounts, post the entries to the two accounts (use T accounts), and determine the balances.

(c) Prepare the journal entry to record bad debts expense for 2000, assuming that an aging of accounts receivable indicates that expected bad debts are $100,000.

(d) Compute the accounts receivable turnover ratio for 2000.

Compute bad debts amounts.
(SO 3)

P8–2B   Information related to Sue Hohenberger Company for 1999 is summarized below:

Total credit sales	$2,000,000
Accounts receivable at December 31	800,000
Bad debts written off	36,000

Instructions

(a) What amount of bad debts expense will Hohenberger Company report if it uses the direct write-off method of accounting for bad debts?

(b) Assume that Hohenberger Company decides to estimate its bad debts expense to be 3% of credit sales. What amount of bad debts expense will Hohenberger Company record if it has an Allowance for Doubtful Accounts credit balance of $4,000?

(c) Assume that Hohenberger Company decides to estimate its bad debts expense based on 6% of accounts receivable. What amount of bad debts expense will Hohenberger Company record if it has an Allowance for Doubtful Accounts credit balance of $3,000?

(d) Assume the same facts as in (c), except that there is a $3,000 debit balance in Allowance for Doubtful Accounts. What amount of bad debts expense will Hohenberger record?

(e) What is the weakness of the direct write-off method of reporting bad debts expense?

Journalize entries to record transactions related to bad debts.
(SO 2, 3)

P8–3B   Presented below is an aging schedule for Sandy Hake Company.

Customer	Total	Not Yet Due	Number of Days Past Due			
			1–30	31–60	61–90	Over 90
Ruth Benson	$ 22,000		$10,000	$12,000		
Jean Ripper	40,000	$ 40,000				
Mary Ann Bilek	57,000	16,000	6,000		$35,000	
Sherri Freeland	34,000					$34,000
Others	126,000	96,000	16,000	14,000		
	$279,000	$152,000	$32,000	$26,000	$35,000	$34,000
Estimated Percentage Uncollectible		4%	7%	13%	25%	50%
Total Estimated Bad Debts	$ 37,450	$ 6,080	$ 2,240	$ 3,380	$ 8,750	$17,000

At December 31, 1999, the unadjusted balance in Allowance for Doubtful Accounts is a credit of $12,000.

Instructions

(a) Journalize and post the adjusting entry for bad debts at December 31, 1999.

(b) Journalize and post to the allowance account the following events and transactions in the year 2000:

   (1) March 31, an $800 customer balance originating in 1999 is judged uncollectible.

   (2) May 31, a check for $800 is received from the customer whose account was written off as uncollectible on March 31.

(c) Journalize the adjusting entry for bad debts on December 31, 2000, assuming that the unadjusted balance in Allowance for Doubtful Accounts is a debit of $800 and the aging schedule indicates that total estimated bad debts will be $30,300.

P8–4B   At December 31, 1999, the trial balance of Lexington Company contained the following amounts before adjustment:

Journalize entries to record transactions related to bad debts.
(SO 3)

	Debits	Credits
Accounts Receivable	$400,000	
Allowance for Doubtful Accounts		$ 1,000
Sales		950,000

Instructions

(a) Based on the information given, which method of accounting for bad debts is Lexington Company using—the direct write-off method or the allowance method? How can you tell?

(b) Prepare the adjusting entry at December 31, 1999, for bad debt expense under each of the following independent assumptions:

   (1) An aging schedule indicates that $11,750 of accounts receivable will be uncollectible.

   (2) It is estimated that 1% of sales will be uncollectible.

(c) Repeat part (b) assuming that instead of a credit balance there is a $1,000 debit balance in the Allowance of Doubtful Accounts.

(d) During the next month, January 2000, a $5,000 account receivable is written off as uncollectible. Prepare the journal entry to record the write-off.

(e) Repeat part (d) assuming that Lexington uses the direct write-off method instead of the allowance method in accounting for uncollectible accounts receivable.

(f) ▥▬▶ What type of account is the allowance for doubtful accounts? How does it affect how accounts receivable is reported on the balance sheet at the end of the accounting period?

P8–5B   Cheryl French Company closes its books monthly. On September 30, selected ledger account balances are:

Prepare entries for various note receivable transactions.
(SO 2, 4, 5, 8, 9)

Notes Receivable	$23,200
Interest Receivable	$182.40

Notes Receivable include the following:

Date	Maker	Face	Term	Interest
Aug. 16	Valaitis Co.	$ 8,000	60 days	12%
Aug. 25	Jenelle Co.	5,200	60 days	12%
Sept. 30	Grumieaux Corp.	12,000	6 months	9%

Interest is computed using a 360-day year. During October, the following transactions were completed.

Oct. 7   Made sales of $6,900 on Cheryl French credit cards.

    12   Made sales of $750 on VISA credit cards. The credit card service charge is 4%.

    15   Added $485 to Cheryl French charge customer balance for finance charges on unpaid balances.

    15   Received payment in full from Valaitis Co. on the amount due.

    24   Received notice that Jenelle note has been dishonored. (Assume that Jenelle is expected to pay in future.)

Instructions

(a) Journalize the October transactions and the October 31 adjusting entry for accrued interest receivable.

(b) Enter the balances at October 1 in the receivable accounts and post the entries to all of the receivable accounts.

(c) Show the balance sheet presentation of the receivable accounts at October 31.

Prepare entries for various receivable transactions.
(SO 2, 4, 5, 6, 7, 8)

P8–6B   On January 1, 1999, Paul Gleason Company had Accounts Receivable $146,000, Notes Receivable $15,000, and Allowance for Doubtful Accounts $13,200. The note receivable is from the Linda Johnson Company. It is a 4-month, 12% note dated December 31, 1998. Paul Gleason Company prepares financial statements annually. During the year the following selected transactions occurred.

Jan. 5   Sold $16,000 of merchandise to George Company, terms n/15.
      20   Accepted George Company's $16,000, 3-month, 9% note for balance due.
Feb. 18   Sold $8,000 of merchandise to Swaim Company and accepted Swaim's $8,000, 6-month, 10% note for the amount due.
Apr. 20   Collected George Company note in full.
      30   Received payment in full from Linda Johnson Company on the amount due.
May 25   Accepted Avery Inc.'s $6,000, 3-month, 8% note in settlement of a past-due balance on account.
Aug. 18   Received payment in full from Swaim Company on note due.
      25   The Avery Inc. note was dishonored. Avery Inc. is not bankrupt and future payment is anticipated.
Sept. 1   Sold $10,000 of merchandise to Jose Trevino Company and accepted a $10,000, 6-month, 10% note for the amount due.

Instructions
Journalize the transactions.

BROADENING YOUR PERSPECTIVE

FINANCIAL REPORTING AND ANALYSIS

FINANCIAL REPORTING PROBLEM: SCH Company

BYP8–1   SCH Company sells office equipment and supplies to many organizations in the city and surrounding area on contract terms of 2/10, n/30. In the past, over 75% of the credit customers have taken advantage of the discount by paying within 10 days of the invoice date.

The number of customers taking the full 30 days to pay has increased within the last year. Current indications are that less than 60% of the customers are now taking the discount. Bad debts as a percentage of gross credit sales have risen from the 1.5% provided in past years to about 4% in the current year.

The controller has responded to a request from the Finance Committee for more information on the collections of accounts receivable with the report reproduced below.

SCH COMPANY
Accounts Receivable Collections
May 31, 1999

The fact that some credit accounts will prove uncollectible is normal. Annual bad debt write-offs have been 1.5% of gross credit sales over the past five years. During the last fiscal year, this percentage increased to slightly less than 4%. The current Accounts Receivable balance is $1,400,000. The condition of this balance in terms of age and probability of collection is as follows:

Proportion of Total	Age Categories	Probability of Collection
66%	not yet due	99%
16%	less than 30 days past due	96½%
9%	30 to 60 days past due	95%
5%	61 to 120 days past due	91%
2½%	121 to 180 days past due	75%
1½%	over 180 days past due	30%

The Allowance for Doubtful Accounts had a credit balance of $29,500 on June 1, 1998. SCH has provided for a monthly bad debts expense accrual during the current fiscal year based on the assumption that 4% of gross credit sales will be uncollectible. Total gross credit sales for the 1998–99 fiscal year amounted to $2,800,000. Write-offs of bad accounts during the year totaled $96,000.

Instructions

(a) Prepare an accounts receivable aging schedule for SCH Company using the age categories identified in the controller's report to the Finance Committee showing:
  1. The amount of accounts receivable outstanding for each age category and in total.
  2. The estimated amount that is uncollectible for each category and in total.
(b) Compute the amount of the year-end adjustment necessary to bring Allowance for Doubtful Accounts to the balance indicated by the age analysis. Then prepare the necessary journal entry to adjust the accounting records.
(c) In a recessionary environment with tight credit and high interest rates:
  1. Identify steps SCH Company might consider to improve the accounts receivable situation.
  2. Then evaluate each step identified in terms of the risks and costs involved.

COMPARATIVE ANALYSIS PROBLEM: Kellogg Company vs. General Mills

BYP8–2   Kellogg's financial statements are presented in Appendix A; General Mills's financial statements are presented in Appendix B.

Instructions

(a) Based on the information contained in these financial statements, compute the following 1997 ratios for each company:
  1. Accounts receivable turnover ratio.
  2. Average collection period for receivables.
(b) What conclusions concerning the management of accounts receivable can be drawn from these data?

RESEARCH ASSIGNMENT

BYP8–3   The May 6, 1996, issue of *Forbes* magazine includes an article by Matthew Schifrin and Howard Rudnitsky, entitled "Rx for Receivables."

Instructions

Read the article and answer the following questions:

(a) Why has the pharmacy business moved from a cash-based business to a receivables-based business?
(b) What is the economic motivation for pharmacies to sell their receivables?
(c) What is the economic motivation for the Pharmacy Fund to purchase the receivables?

INTERPRETING FINANCIAL STATEMENTS: Sears Roebuck & Co.

BYP8–4   Sears is one of the world's largest retailers. It is also a huge provider of credit through its Sears credit card. Revenue generated from credit operations was $4.4 billion in 1996. The rate of interest Sears earns on outstanding receivables varies from 10 to 21 percent in the United States to up to 28 percent in Canada. Managing these receivables is critical to the performance of the corporation. One aspect of receivables management is that in some instances, to acquire cash when needed, the company will sell its receivables. At December 31, 1996 Sears had sold $6.33 billion of its receivables.

The following information was available in Sears 1996 financial statements (in millions of dollars).

	1996	1995	1994
Accounts receivable (gross)	$22,371	$20,949	$19,033
Allowance for doubtful accounts	808	843	832
Merchandise sales	33,812	31,035	29,451
Credit revenues	4,424	3,890	3,574
Bad debts expense	1,136	826	698

Instructions

(a) Discuss whether the sale of receivables by Sears represents a significant portion of its receivables. Why might they have sold these receivables? As an investor, what concerns might you have about these sales?

(b) Calculate and discuss the accounts receivable turnover ratio and average collection period for Sears for 1996 and 1995.

(c) Do you think Sears provided credit as a revenue-generating activity, or as a convenience for its customers?

(d) Compute the ratio of Bad Debt Expense to Merchandise sales for 1996 and 1995. Did this ratio improve or get worse? What considerations should Sears make in deciding whether it wants to have liberal or conservative policies?

REAL-WORLD FOCUS: Art World Industries, Inc.

BYP8–5 **Art World Industries, Inc.** was incorporated in 1986 in Delaware, though it is located in Los Angeles. The company employs 25 people to print, publish, and sell limited edition graphics and reproductive prints in the wholesale market.

The operating expenses for the fiscal year for Art World Industries, Inc., include bad debts expense of $6,715.50. The balance sheet shows an allowance for doubtful accounts of $175,477. The allowance was set up against certain Japanese accounts receivable which average over one year in age. The Japanese acknowledge the amount due, but with the slow economy in Japan lack the resources to pay at this time.

Instructions

(a) Which basis for estimating uncollectible accounts does Art World Industries use?

(b) When Art World makes its adjusting entry to record bad debts expense must it consider a previous existing balance in the Allowance for Doubtful Accounts?

(c) Explain the difference between the percentage of sales and percentage of receivables methods. In applying either of these methods, based on Art World's disclosure above, what important factor would you have to consider in arriving at appropriate percentages to apply?

CRITICAL THINKING

GROUP DECISION CASE

BYP8–6 Linda and Gene Shumway own Somonauk Fashions. From its inception Somonauk Fashions has sold merchandise on either a cash or credit basis, but no credit cards have been accepted. During the past several months, the Shumways have begun to question their sales policies. First, they have lost some sales because of refusing to accept credit cards. Second, representatives of two metropolitan banks have been persuasive in convincing them to accept their national credit cards. One bank, City National Bank, has stated that (1) its credit card fee is 4%, and (2) it pays the retailer 96 cents on each $1 of sales within 3 days of receiving the credit card billings.

The Shumways decide that they should determine the cost of carrying their own credit sales. From the accounting records of the past three years they accumulate the following data:

	1999	1998	1997
Net credit sales	$500,000	$600,000	$400,000
Collection agency fees for slow paying customers	2,450	2,500	2,400
Salary of part-time accounts receivable clerk	3,800	3,800	3,800

Credit and collection expenses as a percentage of net credit sales: uncollectible accounts 1.6%, billing and mailing costs 0.5%, and credit investigation fee on new customers 0.15%.

Linda and Gene also determine that the average accounts receivable balance outstanding during the year is 5% of net credit sales. The Shumways estimate that they could earn an average of 10% annually on cash invested in other business opportunities.

Instructions

With the class divided into groups, answer the following:

(a) Prepare a tabulation showing for each year total credit and collection expenses in dollars and as a percentage of net credit sales.

(b) Determine the net credit and collection expense in dollars and as a percentage of sales after considering the revenue not earned from other investment opportunities. (Note: The income lost on the cash held by the bank for 3 days is considered to be immaterial.)

(c) Discuss both the financial and nonfinancial factors that are relevant to the decision.

COMMUNICATION ACTIVITY

BYP8–7 Jackie Henning, a friend of yours who knows little about accounting, asks you to help make sense of a discussion she overheard at work about changes her employer wants to make in accounting for uncollectible accounts. Specifically, she asks you to explain the differences between the percentage of sales, percentage of receivables, and the direct write-off methods for uncollectible accounts.

Instructions

In a letter of one page (or less), explain to Jackie the three methods of accounting for uncollectibles. Be sure to discuss differences among these methods.

ETHICS CASE

BYP8–8 Jacket Co. is a subsidiary of Suit Corp. The controller believes that the yearly allowance for doubtful accounts for Jacket Co. should be 2% of net credit sales. The president of Jacket Co., nervous that the parent company might expect the subsidiary to sustain its 10% growth rate, suggests that the controller increase the allowance for doubtful accounts to 4%. The president thinks that the lower net income, which reflects a 6% growth rate, will be a more sustainable rate for Jacket Co.

Instructions

(a) Who are the stakeholders in this case?

(b) Does the president's request pose an ethical dilemma for the controller?

(c) Should the controller be concerned with Jacket Co.'s growth rate in estimating the allowance? Explain your answer.

SURFING THE NET

BYP8–9 The Security Exchange Act of 1934 requires any firm that is listed on one of the national exchanges to file annual reports (form 10-K), financial statements, and quarterly reports (form 10-Q) with the SEC. This exercise demonstrates how to search and access available SEC filings through the Internet.

Address: http://biz.yahoo.com (May use SEC address instead.)

www.wiley.com/college/weygandt

Steps:
1. Choose **Company.**
2. Type in a company's name, or use index to find a company name.
3. Choose **SEC Filings.**

Instructions
Answer the following questions:
(a) Which SEC filings were available for the company you selected?
(b) In the company's annual report, what was one key point discussed in the "Management's Discussion and Analysis of Results of Operations and Financial Condition"?
(c) What was the net income for the period selected?

———————

Answers to Self-Study Questions
1. c   2. a   3. b   4. b   5. d   6. c   7. c   8. a   9. b   10. d

———————

Answer to Kellogg Review It Question 6, p. 337
Concentrations of credit risk with respect to accounts receivable are limited due to (1) the large number of customers, (2) generally short payment terms, and (3) their dispersion across geographic areas.

 Remember to go back to the Navigator box on the chapter-opening page and check off your completed work.

Before studying this chapter, you should know or, if necessary, review:

a. The cost principle (Ch. 1, p. 11) and matching principle of accounting. (Ch. 3, p. 94)

b. How to record purchases, sales, and cost of goods sold under a perpetual inventory system. (Ch. 5, pp. 191–199)

c. How to prepare financial statements for a merchandising company. (Ch. 5, pp. 199–201)

THE NAVIGATOR

FEATURE STORY

Keeping the Books on the Books

If you go to a large college or university, chances are that your bookstore or student union has state-of-the-art computer technology for tracking inventories. In an instant, the clerk at the check-out stand "whooshes" your purchases over a scanning machine that automatically rings up the price and deducts the item from inventory.

Not all schools have such state-of-the-art technology. Some bookstores are even small enough that the person managing it can take a "mom-and-pop corner grocery" approach. One such bookstore is at Erie Community College in Buffalo, New York, which produces annual sales of $500,000 per year. Instead of using "point-of-sale" computer technology, the bookstore uses an old-fashioned cash register. The inventory of textbooks, notebooks, art supplies, and so on is counted every month by Joel Damiani, manager. Because the quantity of inventory is relatively small, Damiani, or his two assistants, can specifically identify each item when sold. A larger bookstore would have too much inventory to use that approach; instead, they would use inventory costing methods that do not specifically match the cost of inventory to the actual sale of goods.

Damiani is candid, too, about some problems at his store. For one thing, the accounting records were in disarray when he took the job. "They told me it was going to be a challenge," he says. "And I like challenges." His challenges have included working with the school's accountant to produce a monthly balance sheet and income statement for the bookstore and making sure he has enough inventory of books and supplies on hand for the start of classes. "Sometimes, students say we're not quick enough."

THE NAVIGATOR

CHAPTER 9

INVENTORIES

THE NAVIGATOR ✔

- Understand *Concepts for Review*
- Read *Feature Story*
- Scan *Study Objectives*
- Read *Preview*
- Read text and answer *Before You Go On*
  p. 370 ☐ p. 376 ☐ p. 385 ☐ p. 390 ☐
- Work *Demonstration Problem*
- Review *Summary of Study Objectives*
- Answer *Self-Study Questions*
- Complete assignments

STUDY OBJECTIVES

After studying this chapter, you should be able to:

1. *Describe the steps in determining inventory quantities.*
2. *Prepare the entries for purchases and sales of inventory under a periodic inventory system.*
3. *Determine cost of goods sold under a periodic inventory system.*
4. *Identify the unique features of the income statement for a merchandising company using a periodic inventory system.*
5. *Explain the basis of accounting for inventories and describe the inventory cost flow methods.*
6. *Explain the financial statement and tax effects of each of the inventory cost flow methods.*
7. *Explain the lower of cost or market basis of accounting for inventories.*
8. *Indicate the effects of inventory errors on the financial statements.*
9. *Compute and interpret the inventory turnover ratio.*

THE NAVIGATOR

*A*s indicated in the opening story about the bookstore at Erie Community College, accounting for inventory can be time-consuming and complex. In this chapter we will explain the procedures for determining inventory quantities and the methods used in determining the cost of inventory on hand at the balance sheet date. In addition, we will discuss differences in perpetual and periodic inventory systems, and the effects of inventory errors on a company's financial statements. The content and organization of this chapter are as follows:

INVENTORIES

Inventory Basics	Periodic Inventory System	Inventory Costing	Lower of Cost or Market	Inventory Errors	Statement Presentation and Analysis
• Classifications • Determining inventory quantities • Inventory accounting systems	• Recording transactions • Comparison of perpetual and periodic • Cost of goods sold • Income statement presentation	• Actual inventory costs • Assumed inventory costs • Financial statement effects • Consistent use		• Income statement effects • Balance sheet effects	

THE NAVIGATOR

INVENTORY BASICS

In our economy, inventories are an important barometer of business activity. The U.S. Commerce Department, for example, publishes monthly combined inventory data for retailers, wholesalers, and manufacturers. The amount of inventories and the time required to sell the goods on hand are two indicators that are closely watched. During downturns in the economy, there is an initial buildup of inventories, as the length of time needed to sell existing quantities increases. The reverse effects are generally associated with an upturn in business activity. A delicate balance must be maintained between too little inventory and too much. A merchandiser or manufacturer with too little inventory to meet demand will have dissatisfied customers and sales personnel. One with too much inventory will be burdened with unnecessary carrying costs.

Inventories affect both the balance sheet and the income statement. In the **balance sheet** of merchandising companies, inventory is frequently the most significant current asset. Of course, its amount and relative importance can vary, even for enterprises in the same industry. For example, Wal-Mart reported inventory of $14 billion, representing 90% of total current assets, whereas for the same period, J.C. Penney Company reported $3.9 billion of inventory, representing 41% of total current assets. In the **income statement**, inventory is vital in determining the results of operations for a particular period. Moreover, gross profit (net sales less cost of goods sold) is closely watched by management, owners, and other interested parties (as explained in Chapter 5).

Classifying Inventory

How a company classifies its inventory depends on whether the firm is a merchandiser or a manufacturer. In a **merchandising enterprise**, inventory consists of many different items. For example, in a grocery store, canned goods, dairy products, meats, and produce are just a few of the inventory items on hand. These items have two common characteristics: (1) they are owned by the company, and (2) they are in a form ready for sale to customers in the ordinary course of business. Thus, only one inventory classification, **merchandise inventory**, is needed to describe the many different items that make up the total inventory.

In a **manufacturing enterprise**, inventories are also owned by the company, but some goods may not yet be ready for sale. As a result, inventory is usually classified into three categories: finished goods, work in process, and raw materials. For example, General Motors classifies automobiles completed and ready for sale as **finished goods**. The automobiles on the assembly line in various stages of production are classified as **work in process**. The steel, glass, upholstery, and other components that are on hand waiting to be used in the production of automobiles are identified as **raw materials**.

The accounting principles and concepts discussed in this chapter apply to inventory classifications of both merchandising and manufacturing companies. In this chapter we will focus on merchandise inventory.

HELPFUL HINT
Regardless of the classification, all inventories are reported under Current Assets on the balance sheet.

Determining Inventory Quantities

Many businesses take a physical inventory count on the last day of the year. Businesses using the periodic inventory system are required to take an end-of-the-period physical inventory to determine the inventory on hand at the balance sheet date and to compute cost of goods sold. Even businesses using a perpetual inventory system must take a physical inventory at some time during the year.

Determining inventory quantities consists of two steps: (1) taking a physical inventory of goods on hand, and (2) determining the ownership of goods.

1
STUDY
OBJECTIVE
Describe the steps in determining inventory quantities.

Taking a Physical Inventory

Taking a physical inventory involves actually counting, weighing, or measuring each kind of inventory on hand. In many companies, taking an inventory is a formidable task. Retailers, such as Kmart, True Value Hardware, or your favorite music store have thousands of different inventory items. An inventory count is generally more accurate when goods are not being sold or received during the counting. Consequently, companies often "take inventory" when the business is closed or when business is slow. Many retailers, for example, close early on a chosen day in January—after the holiday sales and returns—to count their inventory.

To minimize errors in taking the inventory, a company should adopt the following procedures to adhere to **internal control** principles that safeguard inventory:

1. The counting should be done by employees who do not have custodial responsibility for the inventory. (Segregation of duties)
2. Each counter should establish the authenticity of each inventory item, e.g., each box does contain a 25-inch television set, and each storage tank does contain gasoline. (Establishment of responsibility)

3. There should be a second count by another employee. (Independent internal verification)

4. Prenumbered inventory tags should be used, and all inventory tags should be accounted for. (Documentation procedures)

5. A designated supervisor should ascertain at the conclusion of the count that all inventory items are tagged and that no items have more than one tag. (Independent internal verification)

After the physical inventory is taken, the quantity of each kind of inventory is listed on **inventory summary sheets**. To assure the accuracy of the summary sheets, the listing should be verified by a second employee or supervisor. Subsequently, unit costs will be applied to the quantities in order to determine a total cost of the inventory—which is the topic of later sections.[1]

ACCOUNTING IN ACTION
Business Insight

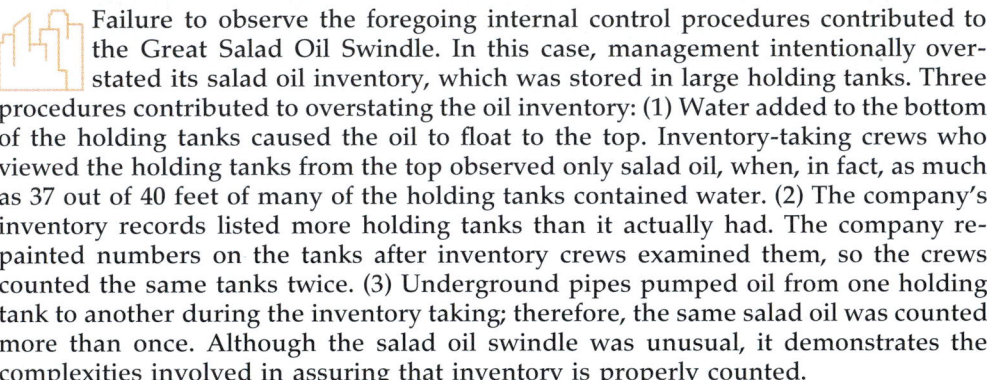

Failure to observe the foregoing internal control procedures contributed to the Great Salad Oil Swindle. In this case, management intentionally overstated its salad oil inventory, which was stored in large holding tanks. Three procedures contributed to overstating the oil inventory: (1) Water added to the bottom of the holding tanks caused the oil to float to the top. Inventory-taking crews who viewed the holding tanks from the top observed only salad oil, when, in fact, as much as 37 out of 40 feet of many of the holding tanks contained water. (2) The company's inventory records listed more holding tanks than it actually had. The company repainted numbers on the tanks after inventory crews examined them, so the crews counted the same tanks twice. (3) Underground pipes pumped oil from one holding tank to another during the inventory taking; therefore, the same salad oil was counted more than once. Although the salad oil swindle was unusual, it demonstrates the complexities involved in assuring that inventory is properly counted.

Determining Ownership of Goods

Before we can begin to calculate the cost of inventory, we need to consider the ownership of goods: specifically, we need to be sure that we have not included in the inventory any goods that do not belong to the company.

Goods in Transit.   Goods are considered to be **in transit** when they are in the hands of a public carrier, such as a railroad, trucking, or airline company at the statement date. Goods in transit should be included in the inventory of the party that has legal title to the goods. Legal title is determined by the terms of sale, as shown in Illustration 9-1 and described below:

1. When the terms are **FOB (free on board) shipping point**, ownership of the goods passes to the buyer when the public carrier accepts the goods from the seller.

2. When the terms are **FOB destination**, legal title to the goods remains with the seller until the goods reach the buyer.

HELPFUL HINT
AMICO Co.'s goods in transit at December 31 consist of sales made (1) FOB destination and (2) FOB shipping point, and purchases made (3) FOB destination and (4) FOB shipping point. Which items should be included in AMICO's inventory at December 31? Answer: Items (1) and (4).

---

[1]To arrive at an estimate of the cost of inventory when a physical inventory cannot be taken (the inventory is destroyed) or when it is inconvenient (during interim periods), estimating methods are applied. These methods (gross profit method and retail inventory method) are discussed in Appendix 9A.

ILLUSTRATION 9-1
Terms of sale

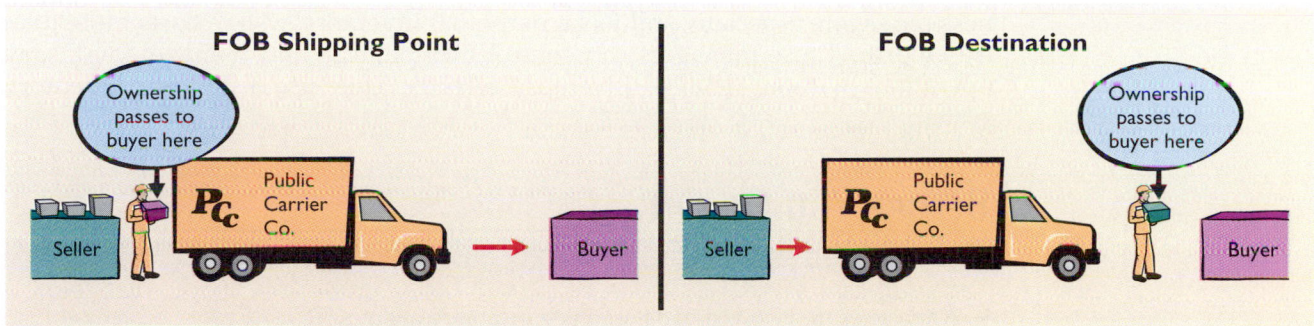

Significant errors may occur in determining inventory quantities if goods in transit at the statement date are ignored. Assume, for example, that Hargrove Company has 20,000 units of inventory on hand on December 31 and the following goods in transit: (1) **sales** of 1,500 units shipped December 31 FOB destination, and (2) **purchases** of 2,500 units shipped FOB shipping point by the seller on December 31. Hargrove has legal title to both the units sold and the units purchased. Consequently, inventory quantities would be understated by 4,000 units (1,500 + 2,500) if units in transit are ignored.

TECHNOLOGY IN ACTION

Many companies have invested large amounts of time and money in automated inventory systems. One of the most sophisticated is Federal Express' Digitally Assisted Dispatch System (DADS). This system uses hand-held "SuperTrackers" to transmit data about the packages and documents to the firm's computer system. Based on bar codes, the system allows the firm to know where any package is at any time to prevent losses and to fulfill the firm's delivery commitments. More recently, FedEx's newly developed software enables customers to track shipments on their own PCs.

Consigned Goods. In some lines of business, it is customary to acquire merchandise on consignment. Under a consignment arrangement, the holder of the goods (called the *consignee*) does not own the goods. Ownership remains with the shipper of the goods (called the *consignor*) until the goods are actually sold to a customer. Because **consigned goods** are not owned by the consignee, they should not be included in the consignee's physical inventory count. Conversely, the consignor should include merchandise held by the consignee as part of its inventory.

Inventory Accounting Systems

One of two basic systems of accounting for inventories may be used: **(1) the perpetual inventory system, or (2) the periodic inventory system.** Chapter 5 of this textbook discussed and illustrated the characteristics of the perpetual inventory system. This chapter discusses and illustrates the periodic inventory system and provides a comparison of it with the perpetual inventory system; Appendix B to this chapter continues coverage of the perpetual inventory system.

Some businesses find it either unnecessary or uneconomical to invest in a computerized perpetual inventory system that maintains up-to-date records of merchandise on hand and cost of goods sold. Many small merchandising business managers especially still feel a perpetual inventory system costs more than it is worth. These managers can control merchandise and manage day-to-day operations without detailed inventory records. They use a periodic inventory system.

BEFORE YOU GO ON . . .

Review It

1. What steps are involved in determining inventory quantities?
2. How is ownership determined for goods in transit at the balance sheet date?
3. Who has title to consigned goods?
4. Name two basic systems of accounting for inventories.

Do It

Hasbeen Company completed its inventory count, arriving at a total value for inventory of $200,000. You have been informed of the information listed below. Discuss how this information affects the reported cost of inventory.

1. Goods held on consignment for Falls Co., costing $15,000, were included in the inventory.
2. Purchased goods of $10,000 which were in transit (terms: FOB shipping point) were not included in the count.
3. Sold inventory with a cost of $12,000 which was in transit (terms: FOB shipping point) was not included in the count.

Reasoning: For goods in transit, ownership is determined by the freight terms. For consigned goods, ownership rests with the consignor until the goods are sold by the consignee.

Solution: The goods held on consignment of $15,000 should be deducted from the inventory count. The goods of $10,000 purchased FOB shipping point should be added to the inventory count. Sold goods of $12,000 which were in transit FOB shipping point should not be included in the ending inventory.

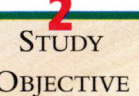

Related exercise material: BE9-4, E9-1, E9-4

PERIODIC INVENTORY SYSTEM

2
STUDY
OBJECTIVE
....
Prepare the entries for
purchases and sales of
inventory under a
periodic inventory
system.

In a **periodic inventory system**, revenues from the sale of merchandise are recorded when sales are made in the same way as in a perpetual system. But, no attempt is made on the date of sale to record the cost of the merchandise sold. Instead, a physical inventory count is taken at the end of the period to determine (1) the cost of the merchandise then on hand and (2) the cost of the goods sold during the period. And, under a periodic system, purchases of merchandise are recorded in a Purchases account rather than a Merchandise Inventory account. Also, under a periodic system, it is customary to record purchase returns and allowances, purchase discounts, and freight-in on purchases in separate accounts so that the accumulated amounts for each are known.

Recording Transactions

To illustrate the recording of merchandise transactions under a periodic inventory system, we will use the purchase/sale transactions between Highpoint Electronic and Chelsea Video discussed in Chapter 5.

Recording Purchases of Merchandise

On the basis of the sales invoice (Illustration 5-4) shown on page 192 and receipt of the merchandise ordered from Highpoint Electronic, Chelsea Video records the $3,800 purchase as follows:

May 4	Purchases	3,800	
	Accounts Payable		3,800
	(To record goods purchased on account,		
	terms 2/10, n/30)		

A	=	L	+	OE
		+3,800		−3,800

Purchases is a temporary account whose normal balance is a debit.

HELPFUL HINT
Be careful not to fall into the trap of debiting purchases of equipment or supplies to Purchases.

Purchase Returns and Allowances

Because $300 of merchandise received from Highpoint Electronic is inoperable, Chelsea Video returns the goods, issues the debit memorandum (Illustration 5-5) shown on page 193, and prepares the following entry to recognize the purchase return:

May 8	Accounts Payable	300	
	Purchase Returns and Allowances		300
	(To record return of inoperable goods		
	purchased from Highpoint Electronic)		

A	=	L	+	OE
		−300		+300

Purchases Returns and Allowances is a temporary account whose normal balance is a credit.

Freight Costs

When the purchaser directly incurs the freight costs, the account Freight-in (or Transportation-in) is debited. For example, if upon delivery of the goods on May 6, Chelsea pays Acme Freight Company $150 for freight charges on its purchase from Highpoint Electronic, the entry on Chelsea's books is:

May 9	Freight-in (Transportation-in)	150	
	Cash		150
	(To record payment of freight, terms FOB		
	shipping point)		

A	=	L	+	OE
−150				−150

Like Purchases, Freight-in is a temporary account whose normal balance is a debit. **Freight-in is part of cost of goods purchased.** The reason is that cost of goods purchased should include any freight charges necessary to bring the goods to the purchaser. Freight costs are not subject to a purchase discount. Purchase discounts apply on the invoice cost of the merchandise.

Purchase Discounts

On May 14 Chelsea Video pays the balance due on account to Highpoint Electronic taking the 2% cash discount allowed by Highpoint for payment within 10 days. The payment and discount are recorded by Chelsea Video as follows:

A	=	L	+	OE
−3,430		−3,500		+70

	May 14	Accounts Payable	3,500	
		Purchase Discounts		70
		Cash		3,430
		(To record payment to Highpoint Electronic within the discount period)		

Purchase Discounts is a temporary account whose normal balance is a credit.

Recording Sales of Merchandise

The sale of $3,800 of merchandise to Chelsea Video on May 4 (sales invoice No. 731, Illustration 5-4) is recorded by the seller, Highpoint Electronic, as follows:

A	=	L	+	OE
+3,800				+3,800

	May 4	Accounts Receivable	3,800	
		Sales		3,800
		(To record credit sales per invoice #731 to Chelsea Video)		

Sales Returns and Allowances

Based on the debit memorandum (Illustration 5-5, page 193) received from Chelsea Video on May 8 for returned goods, Highpoint Electronic records the $300 sales return as follows:

A	=	L	+	OE
−300				−300

	May 8	Sales Returns and Allowances	300	
		Accounts Receivable		300
		(To record return of goods from Chelsea Video)		

Sales Discounts

On May 15, Highpoint Electronic receives payment of $3,430 on account from Chelsea Video. Highpoint honors the 2% cash discount and records the payment of Chelsea's account receivable in full as follows:

A	=	L	+	OE
+3,430				−70
−3,500				

	May 15	Cash	3,430	
		Sales Discounts	70	
		Accounts Receivable		3,500
		(To record collection from Chelsea Video within 2/10, n/30 discount period)		

Comparison of Entries—Perpetual vs. Periodic

The periodic inventory system entries above are shown in Illustration 9-2 on page 373 next to those that were illustrated in Chapter 5 (pages 191–199) under the perpetual inventory system for both Highpoint Electronic and Chelsea Video.

Cost of Goods Sold

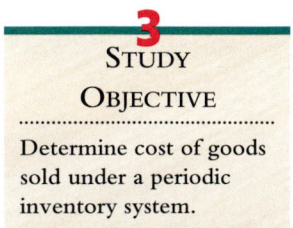

3

STUDY

OBJECTIVE

Determine cost of goods sold under a periodic inventory system.

As noted from the entries in Illustration 9-2, under a periodic inventory system, a running account of the changes in inventory is not recorded as either purchases or sales transactions occur. Neither the daily amount of inventory of merchandise on hand is known nor is the cost of goods sold. To determine the cost of goods sold under a periodic inventory system, it is necessary to (1) record purchases of merchandise (as shown above), (2) determine the cost of goods purchased, and (3) determine the cost of goods on hand at the beginning and end of the accounting period. The cost of goods on hand must be determined by a physical inventory count and application of the cost to the items counted in the inventory.

ENTRIES ON CHELSEA VIDEO'S BOOKS		
Transaction	**Perpetual Inventory System**	**Periodic Inventory System**

May 4 Purchase of merchandise on credit.	Merchandise Inventory 3,800
	  Accounts Payable 3,800
		Purchases 3,800
		  Accounts Payable 3,800

May 8 Purchase returns and allowances.	Accounts Payable 300
	  Merchandise Inventory 300
		Accounts Payable 300
		  Purchase Returns and Allowances 300

May 9 Freight costs on purchases.	Merchandise Inventory 150
	  Cash 150
		Freight-in 150
		  Cash 150

May 14 Payment on account with a discount.	Accounts Payable 3,500
	  Cash 3,430
	  Merchandise Inventory 70
		Accounts Payable 3,500
		  Cash 3,430
		  Purchase Discounts 70

ENTRIES ON HIGHPOINT ELECTRONIC'S BOOKS		
Transaction	**Perpetual Inventory System**	**Periodic Inventory System**

May 4 Sale of merchandise on credit.	Accounts Receivable 3,800
	  Sales 3,800
	Cost of Goods Sold 2,400
	  Merchandise Inventory 2,400
		Accounts Receivable 3,800
		  Sales 3,800
		No entry for cost of goods sold

May 8 Return of merchandise sold.	Sales Returns and Allowances 300
	  Accounts Receivable 300
	Merchandise Inventory 140
	  Cost of Goods Sold 140
		Sales Returns and Allowances 300
		  Accounts Receivable 300
		No entry

May 15 Cash received on account with a discount.	Cash 3,430
	Sales Discounts 70
	  Accounts Receivable 3,500
		Cash 3,430
		Sales Discounts 70
		  Accounts Receivable 3,500

ILLUSTRATION 9-2

Comparison of journal entries under perpetual and periodic inventory systems

Determining Cost of Goods Purchased

We used four accounts to record the purchase of inventory under a periodic inventory system. These accounts are:

Account	Normal Balance
Purchases	Debit
Purchase Returns and Allowances	Credit
Purchase Discounts	Credit
Freight-in	Debit

ILLUSTRATION 9-3

Normal balances: cost of goods purchased accounts

All of these accounts are temporary accounts because they are used to determine the cost of goods sold which is an expense disclosed on the income statement. Therefore, the balances in these accounts must be reduced to zero at the end of each accounting period so that information about cost of goods sold can be accumulated in the next accounting period. The procedure for determining the cost of goods purchased is as follows:

1. The accounts with credit balances (Purchase Returns and Allowances and Purchase Discounts) are subtracted from Purchases to produce **net purchases**.
2. Freight-in is then added to net purchases to produce **cost of goods purchased**.

To illustrate, assume that Highpoint Electronic shows the following balances for the accounts above: Purchases $325,000; Purchase Returns and Allowances $10,400; Purchase Discounts $6,800; and Freight-in $12,200. Net purchases and cost of goods purchased are $307,800 and $320,000, respectively, as computed in Illustration 9-4:

ILLUSTRATION 9-4

Computation of net purchases and cost of goods purchased

Purchases			$325,000
(1) Less: Purchase returns and allowances	$10,400		
Purchase discounts	6,800	17,200	
Net purchases			**307,800**
(2) Add: Freight-in			12,200
Cost of goods purchased			**$320,000**

Determining Cost of Goods on Hand

To **determine the cost of inventory on hand, it is necessary to take a physical inventory**. As explained earlier in this chapter, taking a physical inventory involves:

1. Counting the units on hand for each item of inventory.
2. Applying unit costs to the total units on hand for each item of inventory.
3. Aggregating the costs for each item of inventory to determine the total cost of goods on hand.

A physical inventory should be taken at or near the balance sheet date. To improve the accuracy of the count, many businesses suspend operations while inventory is being taken.

The account Merchandise Inventory is used to record the cost of inventory on hand at the balance sheet date. This amount becomes the beginning inventory for the next accounting period. For Highpoint Electronic, the balance in Merchandise Inventory at December 31, 1998, is $36,000. This amount is also the January 1, 1999, balance in Merchandise Inventory. During 1999, **no entries are made to Merchandise Inventory**. At December 31, 1999, entries are made to eliminate the beginning inventory and to record the ending inventory, which we will assume is $40,000.

Computing Cost of Goods Sold

We have now reached the point where we can compute cost of goods sold. Doing so involves two steps:

1. Add the cost of goods purchased to the cost of goods on hand at the beginning of the period (beginning inventory) to obtain the **cost of goods available for sale**.

ALTERNATIVE TERMINOLOGY

Some use the term *cost of sales* instead of *cost of goods sold.*

2. Subtract the cost of goods on hand at the end of the period (ending inventory) from the cost of goods available for sale to arrive at the **cost of goods sold**.

For Highpoint Electronic the cost of goods available for sale and the cost of goods sold are $356,000 and $316,000, respectively, as shown below.

ILLUSTRATION 9-5

Beginning inventory	$ 36,000
(1) Add: Cost of goods purchased	320,000
Cost of goods available for sale	356,000
(2) Less: Ending inventory	40,000
Cost of goods sold	$316,000

Computation of cost of goods available for sale and cost of goods sold

Gross profit, operating expenses, and net income are computed and reported in a periodic inventory system in the same manner as under a perpetual inventory system as shown in Illustration 9-6. (See also Chapter 5, Illustration 5-17.)

Income Statement Presentation

As under a perpetual inventory system, the income statement for retailers and wholesalers under a periodic inventory system contains three features not found in the income statement of a service enterprise. These features are: (1) a sales

4
STUDY
OBJECTIVE

Identify the unique features of the income statement for a merchandising company using a periodic inventory system.

HIGHPOINT ELECTRONIC
Income Statement
For the Year Ended December 31, 1999

Sales revenues			
Sales			$480,000
Less: Sales returns and allowances		$ 12,000	
Sales discounts		8,000	20,000
Net sales			460,000
Cost of goods sold			
Inventory, January 1		36,000	
Purchases	$325,000		
Less: Purchases returns and allowances	$10,400		
Purchase discounts	6,800	17,200	
Net purchases		307,800	
Add: Freight-in		12,200	
Cost of goods purchased		320,000	
Cost of goods available for sale		356,000	
Inventory, December 31		40,000	
Cost of goods sold			316,000
Gross profit			144,000
Operating expenses			
Store salaries expense		45,000	
Rent expense		19,000	
Utilities expense		17,000	
Advertising expense		16,000	
Depreciation expense—store equipment		8,000	
Freight-out		7,000	
Insurance expense		2,000	
Total operating expenses			114,000
Net income			$ 30,000

HELPFUL HINT
The far right column identifies the major subdivisions of the income statement. The next column identifies the primary items comprising cost of goods sold of $316,000 and operating expenses of $114,000; in addition, contra revenue items of $20,000 are reported. The third column explains cost of goods purchased of $320,000. The fourth column reports contra purchase items of $17,200.

ILLUSTRATION 9-6

Income statement for a merchandising company using a periodic inventory system

ALTERNATIVE TERMINOLOGY

Gross profit is sometimes referred to as *merchandising profit* or *gross margin*.

revenue section, (2) a cost of goods sold section, and (3) gross profit. But, under a periodic inventory system, the cost of goods sold section generally will contain more detail. Using assumed data for specific operating expenses, the income statement for Highpoint Electronic using a periodic inventory system is shown in Illustration 9-6. Whether the periodic or the perpetual inventory system is used, merchandise inventory is reported at the same amount in the current asset section.

BEFORE YOU GO ON . . .

Review It

1. Identify the three steps in determining cost of goods sold.
2. What accounts are used in determining the cost of goods purchased?
3. What is included in cost of goods available for sale?

Do It

Aerosmith Company's accounting records show the following at year-end: Purchase Discounts $3,400; Freight-in $6,100; Sales $240,000; Purchases $162,500; Beginning Inventory $18,000; Ending Inventory $20,000; Sales Discounts $10,000; Purchase Returns $5,200; and Operating Expenses $57,000. Compute the following amounts for Aerosmith Company: net sales, cost of goods purchased, cost of goods sold, gross profit, and net income.

Reasoning: To compute the required amounts, it is important to know the relationships in measuring net income for a merchandising company. For example, it is necessary to know the difference between the following: sales and net sales, goods available for sale and cost of goods sold, and gross profit and net income.

Solution:
Net sales: $240,000 − $10,000 = $230,000.
Cost of goods purchased: $162,500 − $5,200 − $3,400 + $6,100 = $160,000.
Cost of goods sold: $18,000 + $160,000 − $20,000 = $158,000.
Gross profit: $230,000 − $158,000 = $72,000.
Net income: $72,000 − $57,000 = $15,000.

Related exercise material: BE9-2, BE9-3, E9-2, E9-3

INVENTORY COSTING UNDER A PERIODIC INVENTORY SYSTEM

5

STUDY

OBJECTIVE

Explain the basis of accounting for inventories and describe the inventory cost flow methods.

All expenditures necessary to acquire the goods and to make them ready for sale are included as inventoriable costs. **Inventoriable costs** may be regarded as a pool of costs that consists of two elements: (1) the cost of the beginning inventory and (2) the cost of goods purchased during the year. The sum of these two elements equals the cost of goods available for sale. Conceptually, the costs of the purchasing, receiving, and warehousing departments (whose efforts make the goods available for sale) should also be included in inventoriable costs. However, because of the practical difficulties in allocating these costs to inventory, they are generally accounted for as **operating expenses** in the period in which they are incurred.

Inventoriable costs are allocated to ending inventory and to cost of goods sold. Under a periodic inventory system, the allocation is made at the end of the accounting period. First, the costs assignable to the ending inventory are determined. Second, the cost of the ending inventory is subtracted from the cost of goods available for sale to determine the cost of goods sold. Cost of goods sold is then deducted from sales revenues in accordance with the matching principle.

To illustrate, assume that General Suppliers has a cost of goods available for sale of $120,000, based on a beginning inventory of $20,000 and cost of goods purchased of $100,000. The physical inventory indicates that 5,000 units are on hand. The costs applicable to the units are $3.00 per unit. The allocation of the pool of costs is shown in Illustration 9-7. As shown, the $120,000 of goods available for sale are allocated $15,000 to ending inventory and $105,000 to cost of goods sold.

HELPFUL HINT
Under a perpetual inventory system, described in Chapter 5, the allocation is continuously recognized as purchases and sales are made.

ILLUSTRATION 9-7
Allocation (matching) of pool of costs

Pool of Costs

Cost of Goods Available for Sale

Beginning inventory	$ 20,000
Cost of goods purchased	100,000
Cost of goods available for sale	**$120,000**

Step 1			**Step 2**	
Ending Inventory			**Cost of Goods Sold**	
Units	Unit Cost	Total Cost	Cost of goods available for sale	$120,000
			Less: Ending inventory	15,000
5,000	$3.00	**$15,000**	Cost of goods sold	**$105,000**

Using Actual Physical Flow Costing—Specific Identification

Costing of the inventory is complicated because the units on hand for a specific item of inventory may have been purchased at different prices. For example, in a period of rising prices, a company may experience several increases in the cost of identical goods within a given year. Alternatively, unit costs may decline. Under such circumstances, how should the different unit costs in the cost of goods available for sale be allocated between the ending inventory and cost of goods sold?

One answer is to use **specific identification** of the units purchased. This method tracks the **actual physical flow** of the goods. **Each item of inventory is marked, tagged, or coded with its "specific" unit cost.** Items still in inventory at the end of the year are specifically costed to arrive at the total cost of the ending inventory. Assume, for example, that Southland Music Company purchases three 46-inch television sets at costs of $700, $750, and $800, respectively. During the year, two sets are sold at $1,200 each. At December 31, the company determines that the $750 set is still on hand. Accordingly, the ending inventory is $750 and the cost of goods sold is $1,500 ($700 + $800). This is shown graphically in Illustration 9-8.

Specific identification is possible when a company sells a limited variety of high-unit cost items that can be clearly identified from the time of purchase through the time of sale. Examples of such companies are automobile dealerships (cars, trucks, and vans), music stores (pianos and organs), and antique shops (tables and cabinets). Although the bookstore at Erie Community College uses specific identification, it is somewhat unusual to do so for that type of business.

HELPFUL HINT
What gross profit will Southland Music report?
Answer: $900 (Sales $2,400 − CGS $1,500).

ILLUSTRATION 9-8

Specific identification

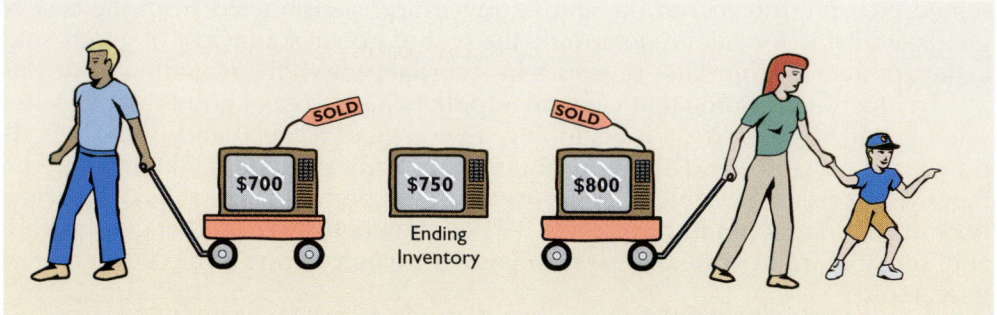

Ordinarily, however, the identity of goods purchased at a specific cost is lost between the date of purchase and the date of sale. For example, drug, grocery, and hardware stores sell thousands of relatively low unit-cost items of inventory. These items are often indistinguishable from one another, making it impossible or impractical to track each item's cost.

When feasible, specific identification seems to be the ideal method of allocating cost of goods available for sale. Under this method, the ending inventory is reported at actual cost and the actual cost of goods sold is matched against sales revenue. This method, however, may enable management to manipulate net income. For example, assume that a music store has three identical Steinway grand pianos that were purchased at different costs. When selling one piano, management could maximize its net income by selecting the piano with the lowest cost to match with revenues. Alternatively, it could minimize net income by selecting the highest-cost piano.

Using Assumed Cost Flow Methods— FIFO, LIFO, and Average Cost

Because specific identification is often impractical, other cost flow methods are allowed. These differ from specific identification in that they assume flows of costs that may be unrelated to the physical flow of goods. For this reason we call them **assumed cost flow methods** or **cost flow assumptions**. They are:

1. First-in, first-out (FIFO).
2. Last-in, first-out (LIFO).
3. Average cost.

INTERNATIONAL NOTE

A survey of accounting standards in 21 major industrial countries found that all three methods were permissible. In Ireland and the U.K., LIFO is permitted only in extreme circumstances.

There is no accounting requirement that the cost flow assumption be consistent with the physical movement of the goods. The selection of the appropriate cost flow assumption (method) is made by management. The management of companies in the same industry may reach different conclusions as to the most appropriate method.

To illustrate these three inventory cost flow methods, we will assume that Bow Valley Electronics uses a **periodic inventory system** and has the information shown in Illustration 9-9 for its Z202 Astro condenser.

First-in, First-out (FIFO)

The **FIFO method** assumes that the **earliest goods** purchased are the first to be sold. FIFO often parallels the actual physical flow of merchandise because it

ILLUSTRATION 9-9

Inventoriable units and costs

BOW VALLEY ELECTRONICS
Z202 Astro Condensers

Date	Explanation	Units	Unit Cost	Total Cost
1/1	Beginning inventory	100	$10	$ 1,000
4/15	Purchase	200	11	2,200
8/24	Purchase	300	12	3,600
11/27	Purchase	400	13	5,200
	Total	1,000		$12,000

During the year, 550 units were sold and 450 units are on hand at December 31.

generally is good business practice to sell the oldest units first. Under the FIFO method, therefore, the **costs** of the earliest goods purchased are the first to be recognized as cost of goods sold. The allocation of the cost of goods available for sale at Bow Valley Electronics under FIFO is shown in Illustrations 9-10 and 9-11.

ILLUSTRATION 9-10

Allocation of costs—FIFO method

Pool of Costs
Cost of Goods Available for Sale

Date	Explanation	Units	Unit Cost	Total Cost
1/1	Beginning inventory	100	$10	$ 1,000
4/15	Purchase	200	11	2,200
8/24	Purchase	300	12	3,600
11/27	Purchase	400	13	5,200
	Total	1,000		$12,000

	Step 1				Step 2	
	Ending Inventory				**Cost of Goods Sold**	

Date	Units	Unit Cost	Total Cost		
11/27	400	$13	$5,200	Cost of goods available for sale	$12,000
8/24	50	12	600	Less: Ending inventory	5,800
Total	450		$5,800	Cost of goods sold	$ 6,200

HELPFUL HINT

Note the sequencing of the allocation: (1) compute ending inventory and (2) determine cost of goods sold.

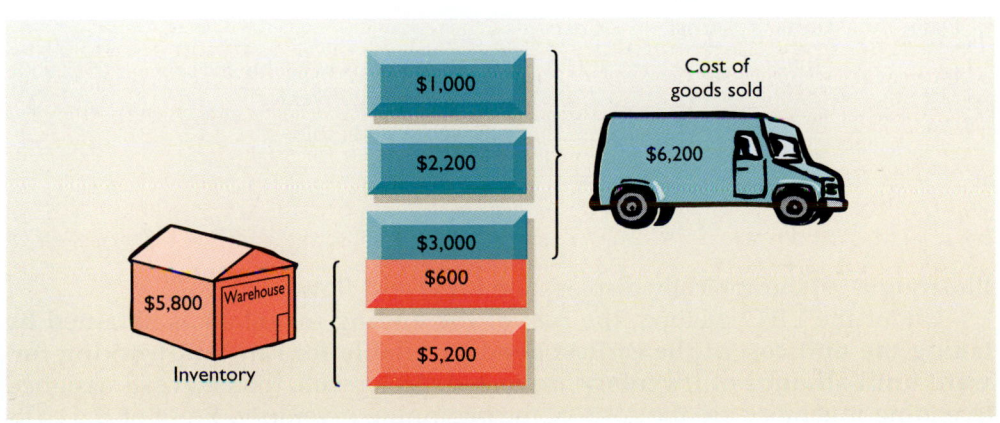

Note that the ending inventory is based on the latest units purchased. That is, **the cost of the ending inventory is obtained by taking the unit cost of the most recent purchase and working backward until all units of inventory have been costed**.

We can verify the accuracy of the cost of goods sold by recognizing that the **first units acquired are the first units sold**. The computations for the 550 units sold are shown in Illustration 9-12.

ILLUSTRATION 9-12

Proof of cost of goods sold

Date	Units		Unit Cost		Total Cost
1/1	100	×	$10	=	$1,000
4/15	200	×	11	=	2,200
8/24	250	×	12	=	3,000
Total	550				$6,200

Last-in, First-out (LIFO)

The **LIFO method** assumes that the **latest goods** purchased are the first to be sold. LIFO seldom coincides with the actual physical flow of inventory. Under the LIFO method, the **costs** of the latest goods purchased are the first to be recognized as cost of goods sold. The allocation of the cost of goods available for sale at Bow Valley Electronics under LIFO is shown in Illustration 9-13.

ILLUSTRATION 9-13

Allocation of costs—LIFO method

Pool of Costs

Cost of Goods Available for Sale

Date	Explanation	Units	Unit Cost	Total Cost
1/1	Beginning inventory	100	$10	$ 1,000
4/15	Purchase	200	11	2,200
8/24	Purchase	300	12	3,600
11/27	Purchase	400	13	5,200
	Total	1,000		$12,000

Step 1				**Step 2**	
Ending Inventory				**Cost of Goods Sold**	

Date	Units	Unit Cost	Total Cost		
1/1	100	$10	$1,000	Cost of goods available for sale	$12,000
4/15	200	11	2,200	Less: Ending inventory	5,000
8/24	150	12	1,800	Cost of goods sold	$ 7,000
Total	450		$5,000		

HELPFUL HINT

The costs allocated to ending inventory ($5,000) plus the costs allocated to CGS ($7,000) must equal CGAS ($12,000).

Illustration 9-14 graphically displays the LIFO cost flow.

Under the LIFO method, **the cost of the ending inventory is obtained by taking the unit cost of the earliest goods available for sale and working forward until all units of inventory are costed**. As a result, the first costs assigned to ending inventory are the costs of the beginning inventory. Proof of the costs allocated to cost of goods sold is shown in Illustration 9-15.

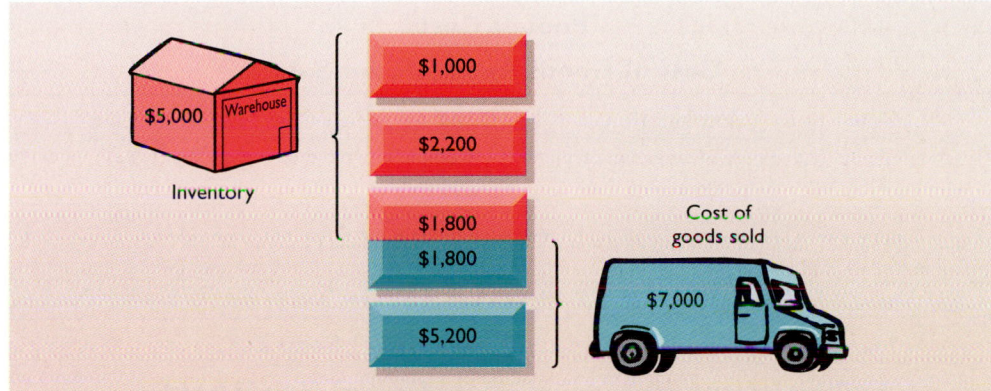

Date	Units		Unit Cost		Total Cost
11/27	400	×	$13	=	$5,200
8/24	150	×	12	=	1,800
Total	550				$7,000

ILLUSTRATION 9-15

Proof of cost of goods sold

Note that the cost of the **last** goods in are the **first** to be assigned to cost of goods sold. Under a periodic inventory system, which we are using here, **all goods purchased during the period are assumed to be available for the first sale, regardless of the date of purchase**.

Average Cost

The **average cost method** assumes that the goods available for sale have the same (average) cost per unit; generally they are homogeneous. Under this method, the allocation of the cost of goods available for sale is made on the basis of the **weighted average unit cost** incurred. The formula and a sample computation of the weighted average unit cost are:

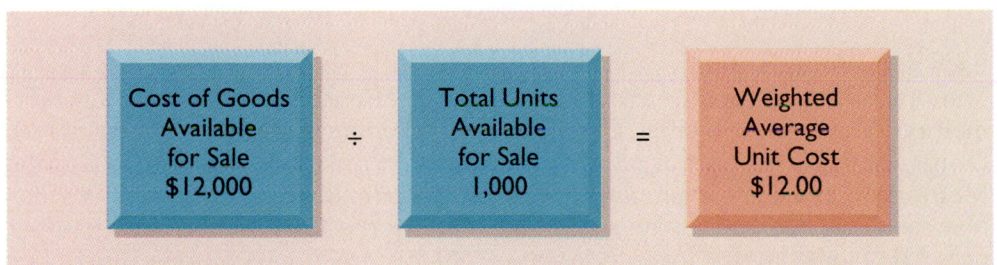

ILLUSTRATION 9-16

Formula for weighted average unit cost

The weighted average unit cost is then applied to the units on hand to determine the cost of the ending inventory. The allocation of the cost of goods available for sale at Bow Valley Electronics using average cost is shown in Illustrations 9-17 and 9-18.

We can verify the cost of goods sold data presented in Illustration 9-17 under this method by multiplying the units sold by the weighted average unit cost ($550 \times \$12 = \$6,600$). Note that this method does not use the average of the unit costs. That average is $11.50 ($10 + $11 + $12 + $13 = $46; $46 \div 4$). The average cost method instead uses the average **weighted** by the quantities purchased at each unit cost.

ILLUSTRATION 9-17

Allocation of costs—average cost method

Pool of Costs
Cost of Goods Available for Sale

Date	Explanation	Units	Unit Cost	Total Cost
1/1	Beginning inventory	100	$10	$ 1,000
4/15	Purchase	200	11	2,200
8/24	Purchase	300	12	3,600
11/27	Purchase	400	13	5,200
	Total	1,000		$12,000

Step 1	Step 2
Ending Inventory	**Cost of Goods Sold**

$12,000 ÷ 1,000 = $12.00
            Unit   Total

Units   Cost   Cost

450 × $12.00 = **$5,400**

Cost of goods available for sale	$12,000
Less: Ending inventory	5,400
Cost of goods sold	$ 6,600

ILLUSTRATION 9-18

Average cost—The average cost of the goods available for sale during the period is the cost used to compute cost of goods sold

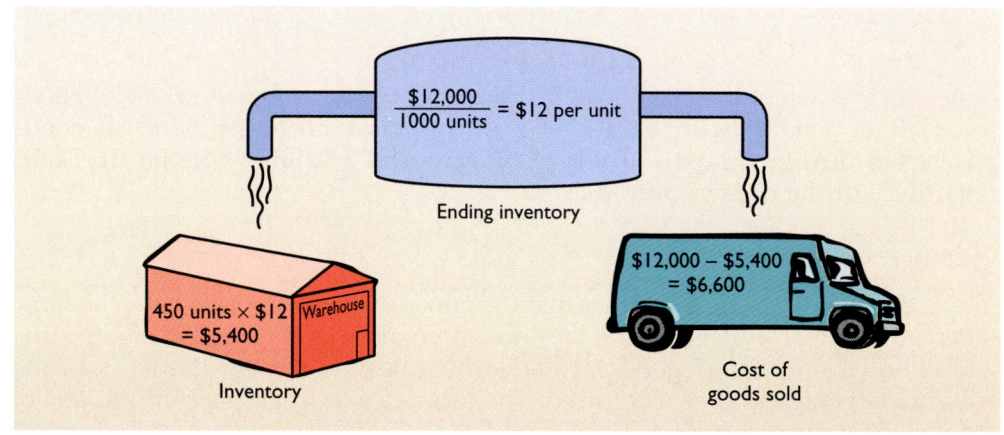

$$\frac{\$12,000}{1000 \text{ units}} = \$12 \text{ per unit}$$

Ending inventory

450 units × $12 Warehouse = $5,400

Inventory

$12,000 − $5,400 = $6,600

Cost of goods sold

6

STUDY

OBJECTIVE

Explain the financial statement and tax effects of each of the inventory cost flow methods.

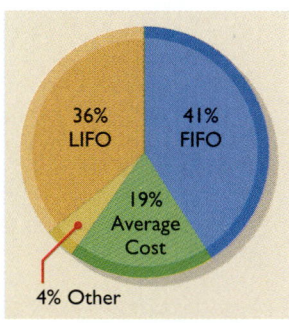

36% LIFO

41% FIFO

19% Average Cost

4% Other

ILLUSTRATION 9-19

Use of cost flow methods in major U.S. companies

Financial Statement Effects of Cost Flow Methods

Each of the three cost flow methods is acceptable. For example, Black and Decker Manufacturing Company and Wendy's International currently use the FIFO method of inventory costing. Campbell Soup Company, Krogers, and Walgreen Drugs use LIFO for part or all of their inventory. Bristol-Myers-Squibb Co. and Motorola, Inc. use the average cost method. A company may also use more than one cost flow method at the same time. Del Monte Corporation, for example, uses LIFO for domestic inventories and FIFO for foreign inventories. Illustration 9-19 shows the use of the three cost flow methods in the 600 largest companies in the U.S. The reasons why companies adopt different inventory cost flow methods are varied, but they usually involve one of the following factors:

1. Income statement effects
2. Balance sheet effects
3. Tax effects

Income Statement Effects

To understand why companies might choose a particular cost flow method, let's examine the effects of the different flow assumptions on the financial statements of Bow Valley Electronics. The condensed income statements in Illustration 9-20 assume that Bow Valley sold its 550 units for $11,500, its operating expenses were $2,000, and its income tax rate is 30%.

BOW VALLEY ELECTRONICS Condensed Income Statements			
	FIFO	**LIFO**	**Average Cost**
Sales	$11,500	$11,500	$11,500
Beginning inventory	1,000	1,000	1,000
Purchases	11,000	11,000	11,000
Cost of goods available for sale	12,000	12,000	12,000
Ending inventory	5,800	5,000	5,400
Cost of goods sold	6,200	7,000	6,600
Gross profit	5,300	4,500	4,900
Operating expenses	2,000	2,000	2,000
Income before income taxes[2]	3,300	2,500	2,900
Income tax expense (30%)	990	750	870
Net income	$ 2,310	$ 1,750	$ 2,030

ILLUSTRATION 9-20

Comparative effects of cost flow methods

Although the cost of goods available for sale ($12,000) is the same under each of the three inventory cost flow methods, both the ending inventories and cost of goods sold are different. This difference is due to the unit costs that are allocated to cost of goods sold and to ending inventory. Each dollar of difference in ending inventory results in a corresponding dollar difference in income before income taxes. For Bow Valley, there is an $800 difference between FIFO and LIFO. In a period of inflation, FIFO produced a higher net income because the lower unit costs of the first units purchased are matched against revenues. In a period of rising prices (as is the case here), FIFO reports the highest net income ($2,310) and LIFO the lowest ($1,750); average cost falls in the middle ($2,030). If prices are falling, the results from the use of FIFO and LIFO are reversed. FIFO will report the lowest net income and LIFO the highest. To management, higher net income is an advantage: it causes external users to view the company more favorably. In addition, if management bonuses are based on net income, FIFO will provide the basis for higher bonuses.

Some argue that the use of LIFO in a period of inflation enables the company to avoid reporting **paper or phantom profit** as economic gain. To illustrate, assume that Kralik Company buys 200 XR492s at $20 per unit on January 10 and 200 more on December 31 at $24 each. During the year, 200 units are sold at $30 each. The results under FIFO and LIFO are shown in Illustration 9-21.

	FIFO		**LIFO**	
Sales (200 × $30)	$6,000		$6,000	
Cost of goods sold	4,000	(200 × $20)	4,800	(200 × $24)
Gross profit	$2,000		$1,200	

ILLUSTRATION 9-21

Income statement effects compared

---

[2]It is assumed that Bow Valley is a corporation, and corporations are required to pay income taxes.

Under LIFO, the company has recovered the current replacement cost ($4,800) of the units sold. Thus, the gross profit in economic terms is real. However, under FIFO, the company has recovered only the January 10 cost ($4,000). To replace the units sold, it must reinvest $800 (200 × $4) of the gross profit. Thus, $800 of the gross profit is said to be phantom or illusory. As a result, reported net income is also overstated in real terms.

Balance Sheet Effects

A major advantage of the FIFO method is that in a period of inflation, the costs allocated to ending inventory will approximate their current cost. For example, for Bow Valley, 400 of the 450 units in the ending inventory are costed at the November 27 unit cost of $13.

Conversely, a major shortcoming of the LIFO method is that in a period of inflation, the costs allocated to ending inventory may be significantly understated in terms of current cost. This is true for Bow Valley, where the cost of the ending inventory includes the $10 unit cost of the beginning inventory. The understatement becomes greater over prolonged periods of inflation if the inventory includes goods purchased in one or more prior accounting periods.

Tax Effects

We have seen that both inventory on the balance sheet and net income on the income statement are higher when FIFO is used in a period of inflation. Yet, many companies have switched to LIFO. The reason is that LIFO results in the lowest income taxes (because of lower net income) during times of rising prices. For example, at Bow Valley Electronics, income taxes are $750 under LIFO, compared to $990 under FIFO. The tax saving of $240 makes more cash available for use in the business.

ACCOUNTING IN ACTION
Business Insight

Most small firms use the FIFO method. But fears of rising inflation often cause many firms to switch to LIFO. For example, Chicago Heights Steel Co. in Illinois boosted cash "by 5% to 10% by lowering income taxes" when it switched to LIFO. Electronic games distributor Atlas Distributing Inc., Chicago, considered a switch "because the costs of our games, made in Japan, are rising 15% a year," says Joseph Serpico, treasurer. When inflation heats up, "the number of companies electing LIFO will rise dramatically," says William Spiro of BDO Seidman, New York.

Using Inventory Cost Flow Methods Consistently

Whatever cost flow method a company chooses, it should be used consistently from one accounting period to another. Consistent application enhances the comparability of financial statements over successive time periods. In contrast, using the FIFO method in one year and the LIFO method in the next year would make it difficult to compare the net incomes of the two years.

Although consistent application is preferred, it does not mean that a company may *never* change its method of inventory costing. When a company adopts a different method, the change and its effects on net income should be disclosed in the financial statements. A typical disclosure is shown in Illustration 9-22, using information from recent financial statements of the Quaker Oats Company.

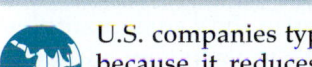

QUAKER OATS COMPANY
Notes to the Financial Statements

ILLUSTRATION 9-22

Disclosure of change in cost flow method

Note 1   Effective July 1, the Company adopted the LIFO cost flow assumption for valuing the majority of U.S. Grocery Products inventories. The Company believes that the use of the LIFO method better matches current costs with current revenues. The effect of this change on the current year was to decrease net income by $16.0 million.

ACCOUNTING IN ACTION
International Insight

U.S. companies typically choose between LIFO and FIFO. Many choose LIFO because it reduces inventory profits and taxes. However, the international community recently considered rules that would ban LIFO entirely and force companies to use FIFO. This proposal was defeated, but the issue will not go away.

The issue is sensitive. As John Wulff, controller for Union Carbide noted, "We were in support of the international effort up until the proposal to eliminate LIFO." Wulff says that if Union Carbide had been suddenly forced to switch from LIFO to FIFO, its reported $632 million pretax income would have jumped by $300 million. That would have increased Carbide's income tax bill by as much as $120 million. Given this, do you believe that accounting principles and rules should be the same around the world?

BEFORE YOU GO ON . . .

Review It

1. How do the cost and matching principles apply to inventoriable costs?
2. How are the three assumed cost flow methods applied in allocating inventoriable costs?
3. What factors should be considered by management in selecting an inventory cost flow method?
4. Which inventory cost flow method produces (a) the highest net income in a period of rising prices, and (b) the lowest income taxes?
5. What amount is reported by Kellogg Company in its 1997 Annual Report as inventories at December 31, 1997? Which inventory cost flow method does Kellogg Company use? The answer to this question is provided on p. 416.

Do It

The accounting records of Shumway Ag Implement show the following data:

Beginning inventory	4,000 units at $3
Purchases	6,000 units at $4
Sales	5,000 units at $12

Determine the cost of goods sold during the period under a periodic inventory system using (a) the FIFO method, (b) the LIFO method, and (c) the average cost method.

Reasoning: Because the units of inventory on hand and available for sale may have been purchased at different prices, a systematic method must be adopted to allocate the costs between the goods sold and the goods on hand (ending inventory).

Solution:

(a) FIFO: (4,000 @ $3) + (1,000 @ $4) = $12,000 + $4,000 = $16,000.

(b) LIFO: 5,000 @ $4 = $20,000.

(c) Average cost: [(4,000 @ $3) + (6,000 @ $4)] ÷ 10,000 = ($12,000 + $24,000) ÷ 10,000 = $3.60 per unit; 5,000 @ $3.60 = $18,000.

Related exercise material: BE9-6, BE9-7, E9-5, E9-6, E9-7.

THE
NAVIGATOR

VALUING INVENTORY AT THE LOWER OF COST OR MARKET (LCM)

7

STUDY
OBJECTIVE

Explain the lower of cost
or market basis
of accounting for
inventories.

When the value of inventory is lower than its cost, the inventory is written down to its market value. This is accomplished by valuing the inventory at the **lower of cost or market (LCM)** in the period in which the price decline occurs. LCM is an example of the accounting concept of conservatism. **Conservatism** means that when choosing among accounting alternatives, the best choice is to select the method that is least likely to overstate assets and net income.

Under the LCM basis, market is defined as **current replacement cost**, not selling price. For a merchandising company, market is the cost of purchasing the same goods at the present time from the usual suppliers in the usual quantities. Current replacement cost is used because a decline in the replacement cost of an item usually leads to a decline in the selling price of the item.

The lower of cost or market basis may be applied to individual items of inventory, major categories of inventory, or total inventory. For example, assume that Len's TV has the following lines of merchandise with costs and market values as indicated. LCM produces the following three results:

ILLUSTRATION 9-23

Alternative lower of cost or market results

	Cost	Market	Lower of Cost or Market by: Individual Items	Major Categories	Total Inventory
Television sets					
Consoles	$ 60,000	$ 55,000	$ 55,000		
Portables	45,000	52,000	45,000		
Total	105,000	107,000		$105,000	
Video equipment					
Recorders	48,000	45,000	45,000		
Movies	15,000	14,000	14,000		
Total	63,000	59,000		59,000	
Total inventory	$168,000	$166,000	$159,000	$164,000	$166,000

The amount entered in the individual items column is the lower of the cost or market amount for **each item**. For the major categories column, the amount is the lower of the total cost or total market for **each category**. Finally, the amount for the total inventory column is the lower of the cost or market for the **entire inventory**. The common practice is to use individual items in determining the LCM valuation. This approach gives the most conservative valuation for balance sheet purposes and also the lowest net income. LCM should be applied consistently from period to period.

LCM is applied to the items in inventory after one of the costing methods (specific identification, FIFO, LIFO, or average cost) has been applied to determine cost.

8

STUDY
OBJECTIVE

Indicate the effects of
inventory errors on the
financial statements.

INVENTORY ERRORS

Unfortunately, errors occasionally occur in taking or costing inventory. In some cases, errors are caused by failure to count or price the inventory correctly. In other cases, errors occur because proper recognition is not given to the transfer of legal title to goods that are in transit. When errors occur, they affect both the income statement and the balance sheet.

Income Statement Effects

Remember that both the beginning and ending inventories are used to determine cost of goods sold in a periodic system. The ending inventory of one period automatically becomes the beginning inventory of the next period. Inventory errors affect the determination of cost of goods sold and net income.

The effects on cost of goods sold can be determined by entering the incorrect data in the following formula and then substituting the correct data.

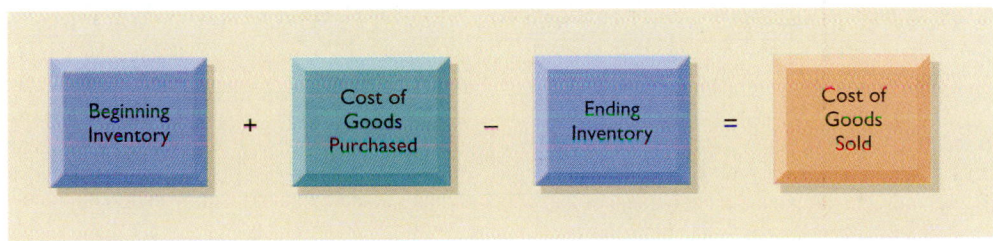

ILLUSTRATION 9-24

Formula for cost of goods sold

ETHICS NOTE

Inventory fraud includes pricing inventory at amounts in excess of their actual value, or claiming to have inventory when no inventory exists. Inventory fraud is usually done to overstate ending inventory, and so understate cost of goods sold and create higher income.

If beginning inventory is understated, cost of goods sold will be understated. On the other hand, an understatement of ending inventory will overstate cost of goods sold. The effects of inventory errors on the current year's income statement are shown in Illustration 9-25.

Inventory Error	Cost of Goods Sold	Net Income
Understate beginning inventory	Understated	Overstated
Overstate beginning inventory	Overstated	Understated
Understate ending inventory	Overstated	Understated
Overstate ending inventory	Understated	Overstated

ILLUSTRATION 9-25

Effects of inventory errors on current year's income statement

An error in ending inventory of the current period will have a **reverse effect on net income of the next accounting period**. This is shown in Illustration 9-26 on the next page. Note that the understatement of ending inventory in 1999 results in an understatement of beginning inventory in 2000 and an overstatement of net income in 2000.

Over the 2 years, total net income is correct because the errors offset one another. Notice that total income using incorrect data is $35,000 ($22,000 + $13,000), which is the same as the total income of $35,000 ($25,000 + $10,000) using correct data. Also note in this example that an error in the beginning inventory does not result in a corresponding error in the ending inventory for that period. The correctness of the ending inventory depends entirely on the accuracy of taking and costing the inventory at the balance sheet date.

Balance Sheet Effects

The effect of ending inventory errors on the balance sheet can be determined by using the basic accounting equation: assets equal liabilities plus owner's

Condensed Income Statement

	1999 Incorrect		1999 Correct		2000 Incorrect		2000 Correct	
Sales		$80,000		$80,000		$90,000		$90,000
Beginning inventory	$20,000		$20,000		$12,000		$15,000	
Cost of goods purchased	40,000		40,000		68,000		68,000	
Cost of goods available for sale	60,000		60,000		80,000		83,000	
Ending inventory	12,000		15,000		23,000		23,000	
Cost of goods sold		48,000		45,000		57,000		60,000
Gross profit		32,000		35,000		33,000		30,000
Operating expenses		10,000		10,000		20,000		20,000
Net income		$22,000		$25,000		$13,000		$10,000

($3,000)
Net income
understated

$3,000
Net income
overstated

Total income for 2 years correct

ILLUSTRATION 9-26

Effects of inventory errors on 2 years' income statements

equity. Errors in the ending inventory have the following effects on these components:

ILLUSTRATION 9-27

Ending inventory error—balance sheet effects

Ending Inventory Error	Assets	Liabilities	Owner's Equity
Overstated	Overstated	None	Overstated
Understated	Understated	None	Understated

The effect of an error in ending inventory on the subsequent period was shown in Illustration 9-26. Recall that if the error is not corrected, total net income for the two periods would be correct. Thus, total owner's equity reported on the balance sheet at the end of 2000 will also be correct.

STATEMENT PRESENTATION AND ANALYSIS

As indicated in an earlier chapter, inventory is classified as a current asset after receivables in the balance sheet, and cost of goods sold is subtracted from sales in a multiple-step income statement. In addition, there should be disclosure of (1) the major inventory classifications, (2) the basis of accounting (cost or lower of cost or market), and (3) the costing method (FIFO, LIFO, or average).

Kellogg Company, for example, in its December 31, 1997, balance sheet reported inventory of $434,300,000 under current assets. The accompanying notes to the financial statements, as shown in Illustration 9-28, disclosed the following information:

KELLOGG COMPANY
Notes to the Financial Statements

Note 1. Accounting Policies

Inventories

Inventories are valued at the lower of cost (principally average) or market.

ILLUSTRATION 9-28

Inventory disclosures by Kellogg Company

As indicated in this brief note, Kellogg Company values its inventories at the lower of cost or market using the average cost method to apply costs to inventory and cost of goods sold.

The amount of inventory carried by a company has significant economic consequences. And, inventory management is a double-edged sword that requires constant attention. On the one hand, management wants to have a great variety and quantity on hand so customers have the greatest selection and inventory items are always in stock. But, such an inventory policy may incur excessive carrying costs (e.g., investment, storage, insurance, taxes, obsolescence, and damage). On the other hand, low inventory levels lead to stockouts, lost sales, and disgruntled customers. Common ratios used in the management and evaluation of inventory levels are inventory turnover and a related measure, average days to sell the inventory.

The **inventory turnover ratio** measures the number of times on average the inventory is sold during the period. Its purpose is to measure the liquidity of the inventory. The inventory turnover is computed by dividing cost of goods sold by the average inventory during the period. Unless seasonal factors are significant, average inventory can be computed from the beginning and ending inventory balances. For example, Kellogg Company reported in its 1997 Annual Report a beginning inventory of $424,900,000, and cost of goods sold for the year 1997 of $3,270,100,000; its inventory turnover formula and computation are shown below:

9
STUDY
OBJECTIVE

Compute and interpret the inventory turnover ratio.

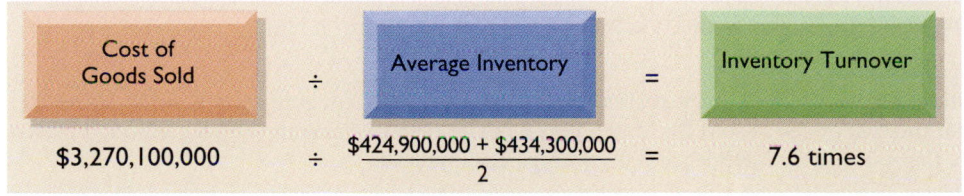

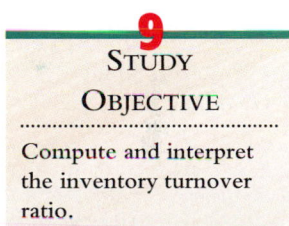

ILLUSTRATION 9-29

Inventory turnover formula and computation for Kellogg Company

A variant of the inventory turnover ratio is the **average days to sell inventory**. For example, the inventory turnover for Kellogg Company of 7.6 times divided into 365 is approximately 48 days. There are typical levels of inventory in every industry. However, companies that are able to keep their inventory at lower levels and higher turnovers and still satisfy customer needs are the most successful.

BEFORE YOU GO ON . . .

Review It

1. Why is it appropriate to report inventories at the lower of cost or market?
2. How do inventory errors affect financial statements?
3. What does the inventory turnover ratio reveal?

A LOOK BACK AT OUR FEATURE STORY

Refer to the opening story concerning the bookstore at Erie Community College, and answer the following questions.
1. Why might a small bookstore use specific identification to determine inventory?
2. If the inventory is overstated at the end of the month, what effect does this error have on the balance sheet and the income statement?

Solution:

1. A small bookstore, as opposed to a large bookstore, might use specific identification because of:
    a. A smaller number of any one book in inventory.
    b. Fewer different books in inventory.
    c. The familiarity of the owner/manager (who handles sales) with the books being sold.
2. An end-of-month, inventory overstatement will result in overstated inventory in the balance sheet along with overstated stockholders' equity, due to overstated net income on the income statement. Cost of goods sold will be understated on the income statement. The next month's income statement will have overstated beginning inventory and understated net income.

THE
NAVIGATOR

DEMONSTRATION PROBLEM

Gerald D. Englehart Company has the following inventory, purchases, and sales data for the month of March:

Inventory, March 1	200 units @ $4.00	$ 800
Purchases:		
March 10	500 units @ $4.50	2,250
March 20	400 units @ $4.75	1,900
March 30	300 units @ $5.00	1,500
Sales:		
March 15	500 units	
March 25	400 units	

The physical inventory count on March 31 shows 500 units on hand.

Instructions

Under a **periodic inventory system**, determine the cost of inventory on hand at March 31 and the cost of goods sold for March under the (a) first-in, first-out (FIFO) method, (b) last-in, first-out (LIFO) method, and (c) average cost method.

SOLUTION TO DEMONSTRATION PROBLEM

The cost of goods available for sale is $6,450:

Inventory	200 units @ $4.00	$ 800
Purchases:		
March 10	500 units @ $4.50	2,250
March 20	400 units @ $4.75	1,900
March 30	300 units @ $5.00	1,500
Total cost of goods available for sale		$6,450

PROBLEM-SOLVING STRATEGIES

1. For FIFO, the latest costs are allocated to inventory.
2. For LIFO, the earliest costs are allocated to inventory.
3. For average costs, use a weighted average for periodic.
4. Remember, the costs allocated to cost of goods sold can be proved.
5. Total purchases are the same under all three cost flow methods.

Under a **periodic inventory system**, the cost of goods sold under each cost flow method is as follows:

FIFO Method

Ending Inventory:

Date	Units	Unit Cost	Total Cost	
March 30	300	$5.00	$1,500	
March 20	200	4.75	950	$2,450

Cost of goods sold: $6,450 − $2,450 = $4,000

LIFO Method

Ending Inventory:

Date	Units	Unit Cost	Total Cost	
March 1	200	$4.00	$ 800	
March 10	300	4.50	1,350	$2,150

Cost of goods sold: $6,450 − $2,150 = $4,300

Weighted Average Cost Method

Weighted average unit cost: $6,450 ÷ 1,400 = $4.607
Ending inventory: 500 × $4.607 = $2,303.50

Cost of goods sold: $6,450 − $2,303.50 = $4,146.50

SUMMARY OF STUDY OBJECTIVES

1. Describe the steps in determining inventory quantities. The steps in determining inventory quantities are (1) taking a physical inventory of goods on hand and (2) determining the ownership of goods in transit.

2. Prepare the entries for purchases and sales of inventory under a periodic inventory system. In recording purchases, entries are required for (a) cash and credit purchases, (b) purchase returns and allowances, (c) purchase discounts, and (d) freight costs. In recording sales, entries are required for (a) cash and credit sales, (b) sales returns and allowances, and (c) sales discounts.

3. Determine cost of goods sold under a periodic inventory system. The steps in determining cost of goods sold are (a) recording the purchase of merchandise, (b) determining the cost of goods purchased, and (c) determining the cost of goods on hand at the beginning and end of the accounting period.

4. Identify the unique features of the income statement for a merchandising company using a periodic inventory system. The income statement for a merchandising company contains three sections: sales revenue, cost of goods sold, and operating expenses. The cost of goods sold section under a periodic inventory system generally shows more detail by reporting beginning and ending inventory, net purchases, and total goods available for sale.

5. Explain the basis of accounting for inventories and describe the inventory cost flow methods. The primary basis of accounting for inventories is cost. Cost includes all expenditures necessary to acquire goods and place them in condition ready for sale. Inventoriable costs include (1) cost of beginning inventory and (2) the cost of goods purchased. The inventory cost flow methods are: specific identification, FIFO, LIFO, and average cost.

6. Explain the financial statement and tax effects of each of the inventory cost flow methods. The cost of goods available for sale may be allocated to cost of goods sold and ending inventory by specific identification or by a method based on an assumed cost flow. These methods have different effects on financial statements during periods of changing prices. When prices are rising, the first-in, first-out method (FIFO) results in lower cost of goods sold and higher net income than the average and the last-in, first-out (LIFO) methods. LIFO results in the lowest income taxes (because of lower net income). The reverse is true when prices are falling. In the balance sheet, FIFO results in an ending inventory that is closest to current value, whereas the inventory under LIFO is the farthest from current value.

7. Explain the lower of cost or market basis of accounting for inventories. The lower of cost or market basis (LCM) is used when the current replacement cost (market) is less than cost. Under LCM, the loss is recognized in the period in which the price decline occurs. LCM may be applied to individual inventory items, major categories of inventory, or to total inventory.

8. *Indicate the effects of inventory errors on the financial statements.* In the income statement of the current year: (a) an error in beginning inventory will have a reverse effect on net income (overstatement of inventory results in understatement of net income) and (b) an error in ending inventory will have a similar effect on net income (overstatement of inventory results in overstatement of net income). If ending inventory errors are not corrected in the following period, their effect on net income for that period is reversed, and total net income for the two years will be correct. In the balance sheet, ending inventory errors will have the same

effect on total assets and total stockholders' equity and no effect on liabilities.

9. *Compute and interpret the inventory turnover ratio.* The inventory turnover ratio is calculated as cost of goods sold divided by average inventory. It can be converted to average days in inventory by dividing 365 days by the inventory turnover ratio. A higher turnover ratio or lower average days in inventory suggests that management is trying to keep inventory levels low relative to its sales level.

GLOSSARY

Average cost method An inventory costing method that assumes that the goods available for sale have the same (average) cost per unit; generally they are homogeneous. (p. 381).

Consigned goods Goods shipped by a consignor, who retains ownership, to another party called the consignee. (p. 369).

Cost of goods available for sale The sum of the beginning merchandise inventory plus the cost of goods purchased. (p. 374).

Cost of goods purchased The sum of net purchases plus freight-in. (p. 374).

Cost of goods sold The total cost of merchandise sold during the period, determined by subtracting ending inventory from the cost of goods available for sale. (p. 374).

Current replacement cost The amount that would be paid at the present time to acquire an identical item. (p. 386).

First-in, first-out method (FIFO) An inventory costing method that assumes that the costs of the earliest goods acquired are the first to be recognized as cost of goods sold. (p. 378).

Inventoriable costs The pool of costs that consists of two elements: (1) the cost of the beginning inventory and (2) the cost of goods purchased during the period. (p. 376).

Inventory turnover ratio A ratio that measures the number of times on average the inventory is sold during the period. It is computed by dividing cost of goods sold by the average inventory during the period. (p. 389).

Last-in, first-out method (LIFO) An inventory costing method that assumes that the costs of the latest units purchased are the first to be allocated to cost of goods sold. (p. 380).

Lower of cost or market basis (LCM) (inventories) A method of valuing inventory that recognizes the decline in the value when the current purchase price (market) is less than cost. (p. 386).

Net purchases Purchases less purchase returns and allowances and purchase discounts. (p. 374).

Periodic inventory system An inventory system in which inventoriable costs are allocated to ending inventory and cost of goods sold at the end of the period. Cost of goods sold is computed at the end of the period by subtracting the ending inventory (costs are assigned to a physical count of items on hand) from the cost of goods available for sale. (p. 370).

Specific identification method An actual physical flow costing method in which items still in inventory are specifically costed to arrive at the total cost of the ending inventory. (p. 377).

APPENDIX 9A ESTIMATING INVENTORIES

10 STUDY OBJECTIVE

Describe the two methods of estimating inventories.

We have assumed throughout the chapter that a company would be able to do a physical count of its inventory. But what if it cannot, as in the example of the lumber inventory destroyed by fire? In that case, we would use an estimate.

Two circumstances explain the reasons for estimating rather than counting inventories. First, management may want monthly or quarterly financial statements but a physical inventory is taken only annually. Second, a casualty such as fire, flood, or earthquake may make it impossible to take a physical inventory. The need for estimating inventories is associated primarily with a periodic inventory system because of the absence of detailed inventory records.

There are two widely used methods of estimating inventories: (1) the gross profit method and (2) the retail inventory method.

GROSS PROFIT METHOD

The **gross profit method** estimates the cost of ending inventory by applying a gross profit rate to net sales. It is used in preparing monthly financial statements under a periodic system when physical inventories are not taken. This method is a relatively simple but effective estimation technique. Accountants, auditors, and managers frequently use the gross profit method to test the reasonableness of the ending inventory amount. This method will detect large errors. To use this method, a company needs to know its net sales, cost of goods available for sale, and gross profit rate. The company then uses the gross profit rate to estimate its gross profit for the accounting period. The formulas for using the gross profit method are given in Illustration 9A-1.

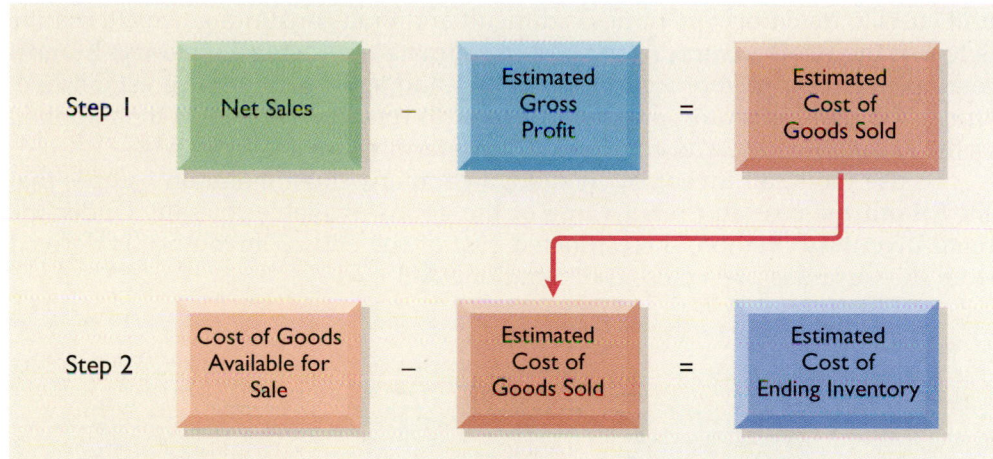

ILLUSTRATION 9A-1

Gross profit method formulas

To illustrate, assume that Williams Company wishes to prepare an income statement for the month of January, when its records show net sales $200,000; beginning inventory $40,000; and cost of goods purchased $120,000. In the preceding year, the company realized a 30% gross profit rate, and it expects to earn the same rate this year. Given these facts and assumptions, the estimated cost of the ending inventory at January 31 under the gross profit method is $20,000, computed as follows:

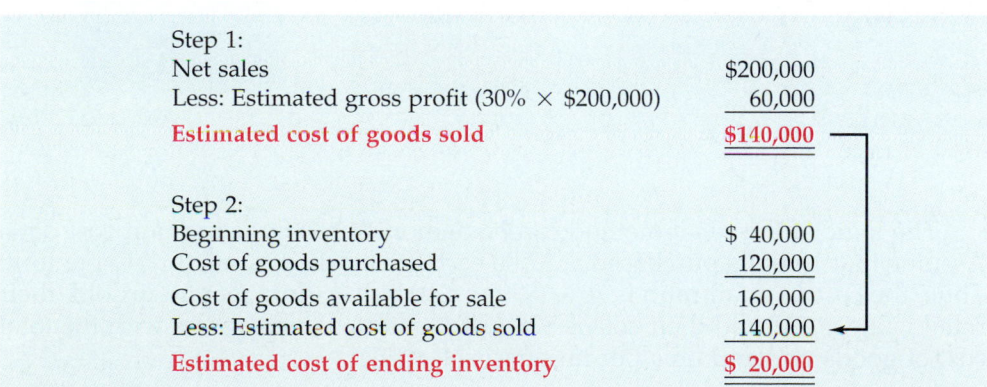

ILLUSTRATION 9A-2

Example of gross profit method

Step 1:		
Net sales		$200,000
Less: Estimated gross profit (30% × $200,000)		60,000
Estimated cost of goods sold		**$140,000**
Step 2:		
Beginning inventory		$ 40,000
Cost of goods purchased		120,000
Cost of goods available for sale		160,000
Less: Estimated cost of goods sold		140,000
Estimated cost of ending inventory		**$ 20,000**

The gross profit method is based on the assumption that the rate of gross profit will remain constant from one year to the next. It may not remain constant, though, because of a change either in merchandising policies or in market conditions. In such cases, the rate of the prior period should be adjusted to reflect current operating conditions. In some cases, a more accurate estimate may be obtained by applying this method on a department or product-line basis.

The gross profit method should not be used in preparing a company's financial statements at the end of the year. These statements should be based on a physical inventory count.

RETAIL INVENTORY METHOD

A retail store such as Kmart, Ace Hardware, or Wal-Mart has thousands of different types of merchandise at low unit costs. In such cases the application of unit costs to inventory quantities is difficult and time-consuming. An alternative is to use the **retail inventory method** to estimate the cost of inventory. In most retail concerns, a relationship between cost and sales price can be established. Under the retail inventory method, the cost to retail percentage is then applied to the ending inventory at retail prices to determine inventory at cost.

To use the retail inventory method, a company must maintain records that show both the cost and retail value of the goods available for sale. Under the retail inventory method, the estimated cost of the ending inventory is derived from the formulas presented in Illustration 9A-3.

ILLUSTRATION 9A-3

Retail inventory method formulas

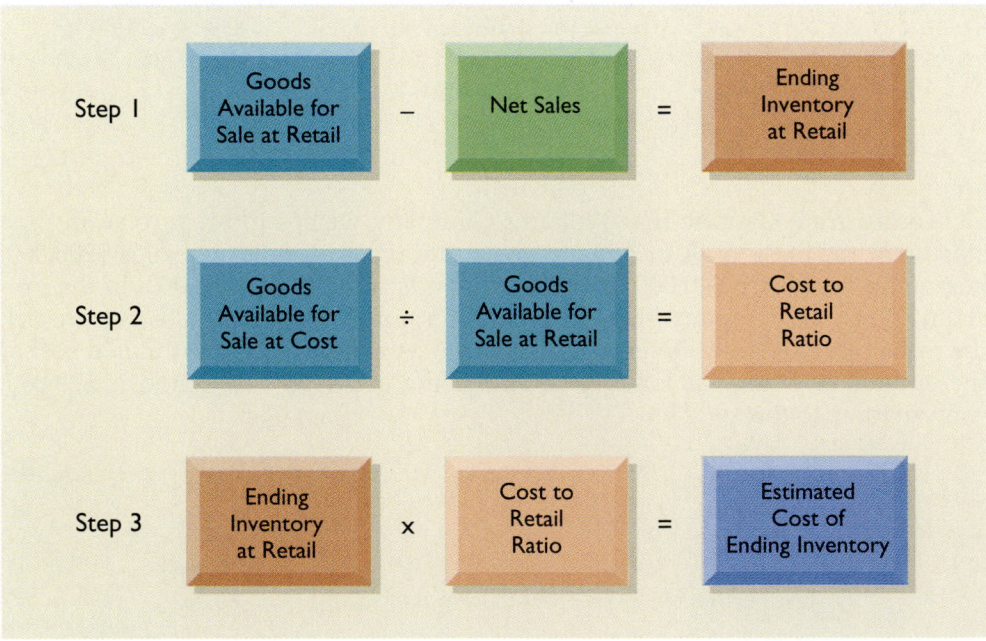

The logic of the retail method can be demonstrated by using unit cost data. Assume that 10 units purchased at $7.00 each are marked to sell for $10 per unit. Thus, the cost to retail ratio is 70% ($70 ÷ $100). If 4 units remain unsold, their retail value is $40 and their cost is $28 ($40 × 70%), which agrees with the total cost of goods on hand on a per unit basis (4 × $7).

The application of the retail method based on the accounting records and supplementary data for Lacy Co. is shown in Illustration 9A-4. Note that it is not necessary to take a physical inventory to determine the estimated cost of goods on hand at any given time.

	At Cost	At Retail
Beginning inventory	$14,000	$ 21,500
Goods purchased	61,000	78,500
Goods available for sale	$75,000	100,000
Net sales		70,000
(1) Ending inventory at retail		$ 30,000

(2) Cost to retail ratio = ($75,000 ÷ $100,000) = 75%
(3) Estimated cost of ending inventory = ($30,000 × 75%) $22,500

ILLUSTRATION 9A-4

Example of retail inventory method

The retail inventory method also facilitates taking a physical inventory at the end of year. With this method, the goods on hand can be valued at the prices marked on the merchandise. The cost to retail ratio is then applied to the goods actually on hand at retail to determine the ending inventory at cost.

The major disadvantage of the retail method is that it is an averaging technique. It may produce an incorrect inventory valuation if the mix of the ending inventory is not representative of the mix in the goods available for sale. Assume, for example, that the cost to retail ratio of 75% in the Lacy Co. consists of equal proportions of inventory items that have cost to retail ratios of 70%, 75%, and 80%, respectively. If the ending inventory contains only items with a 70% ratio, an incorrect inventory cost will result. This problem can be minimized by applying the retail method on a departmental or product-line basis.

HELPFUL HINT
In determining inventory at retail, selling prices on the units are used, and tracing actual unit costs to invoices is unnecessary.

SUMMARY OF STUDY OBJECTIVE FOR APPENDIX 9A

10. Describe the two methods of estimating inventories. The two methods of estimating inventories are the gross profit method and the retail inventory method. Under the gross profit method, a gross profit rate is applied to net sales to determine estimated cost of goods sold. Estimated cost of goods sold is then subtracted from cost of goods available for sale to determine the estimated cost of the ending inventory. Under the retail inventory method, a cost to retail ratio is computed by dividing the cost of goods available for sale by the retail value of the goods available for sale. This ratio is then applied to the ending inventory at retail to determine the estimated cost of the ending inventory.

GLOSSARY FOR APPENDIX 9A

Gross profit method A method for estimating the cost of the ending inventory by applying a gross profit rate to net sales. (p. 393).

Retail inventory method A method used to estimate the cost of the ending inventory by applying a cost to retail ratio to the ending inventory at retail. (p. 394).

APPENDIX 9B   INVENTORY COST FLOW METHODS IN PERPETUAL INVENTORY SYSTEMS

STUDY

OBJECTIVE

Apply the inventory cost flow methods to perpetual inventory records.

Each of the inventory cost flow methods described in the chapter for a periodic inventory system may be used in a perpetual inventory system. To illustrate the application of the three assumed cost flow methods (FIFO, LIFO, and average cost), we will use the data shown below and in this chapter for Bow Valley Electronics' product Z202 Astro Condenser.

ILLUSTRATION 9B-1

Inventoriable units and costs

	BOW VALLEY ELECTRONICS Z202 Astro Condensers				
Date	Explanation	Units	Unit Cost	Total Cost	Balance in Units
1/1	Beginning inventory	100	$10	$1,000	100
4/15	Purchases	200	11	2,200	300
8/24	Purchases	300	12	3,600	600
9/10	Sales	550			50
11/27	Purchases	400	13	5,200	450
				$12,000	

FIRST-IN, FIRST-OUT (FIFO)

Under FIFO, the cost of the earliest goods on hand prior to each sale is charged to cost of goods sold. Therefore, the cost of goods sold on September 10 consists of the units on hand January 1 and the units purchased April 15 and August 24. The inventory on a FIFO method perpetual system is shown in Illustration 9B-2.

ILLUSTRATION 9B-2

Perpetual system—FIFO

Date	Purchases	Sales	Balance
January 1			(100 @ $10) $1,000
April 15	(200 @ $11) $2,200		(100 @ $10) }$3,200 (200 @ $11)
August 24	(300 @ $12) $3,600		(100 @ $10) (200 @ $11) }$6,800 (300 @ $12)
September 10		(100 @ $10) (200 @ $11) (250 @ $12) ——— $6,200	(50 @ $12) $ 600
November 27	(400 @ $13) $5,200		(50 @ $12) }$5,800 (400 @ $13)

The ending inventory in this situation is $5,800 and the cost of goods sold is $6,200 [(100 @ $10) + (200 @ $11) + (250 @ $12)].

The results under FIFO in a perpetual system are the **same as in a periodic system** (see Illustration 9-10 on page 379 where, similarly, the ending inventory is $5,800 and cost of goods sold is $6,200). Regardless of the system, the first costs in are the costs assigned to cost of goods sold.

LAST-IN, FIRST-OUT (LIFO)

Under the LIFO method using a perpetual system, the cost of the most recent purchase prior to sale is allocated to the units sold. Therefore, the cost of the goods sold on September 10 consists of all the units from the August 24 and April 15 purchases and 50 of the units in beginning inventory. The ending inventory on a LIFO method is computed in Illustration 9B-3.

ILLUSTRATION 9B-3

Perpetual system—LIFO

Date	Purchases	Sales	Balance
January 1			(100 @ $10) $1,000
April 15	(200 @ $11) $2,200		(100 @ $10) (200 @ $11) } $3,200
August 24	(300 @ $12) $3,600		(100 @ $10) (200 @ $11) (300 @ $12) } $6,800
September 10		(300 @ $12) (200 @ $11) (50 @ $10) ___ $6,300	(50 @ $10) $ 500
November 27	(400 @ $13) $5,200		(50 @ $10) (400 @ $13) } $5,700

The use of LIFO in a perpetual system will usually produce cost allocations that differ from using LIFO in a periodic system. In a perpetual system, the latest units incurred prior to each sale are allocated to cost of goods sold. In contrast, in a periodic system, the latest units incurred during the period are allocated to cost of goods sold. Thus, when a purchase is made after the last sale, the LIFO periodic system will apply this purchase to the previous sale. See Illustration 9-15 on page 381 where the proof shows the 400 units @ $13 purchased on November 27 applied to the sale of 550 units on September 10.

As shown above under the LIFO perpetual system, the 400 units @ $13 purchased on November 27 are all applied to the ending inventory.

The ending inventory in this LIFO perpetual illustration is $5,700 and cost of goods sold is $6,300 as compared to the LIFO periodic illustration where the ending inventory is $5,000 and cost of goods sold is $7,000.

AVERAGE COST

The average cost method in a perpetual inventory system is called the **moving average method**. Under this method a new average is computed **after each purchase**. The average cost is computed by dividing the cost of goods available for sale by the units on hand. The average cost is then applied to: (1) the units sold, to determine the cost of goods sold, and (2) the remaining units on hand, to determine the ending inventory amount. The application of the average cost method by Bow Valley Electronics is shown in Illustration 9B-4.

ILLUSTRATION 9B-4

Perpetual system—average cost method

Date	Purchases		Sales	Balance	
January 1				(100 @ $10)	$1,000
April 15	(200 @ $11)	$2,200		(300 @ $10.667)	$3,200
August 24	(300 @ $12)	$3,600		(600 @ $11.333)	$6,800
September 10			(550 @ $11.333)	(50 @ $11.333)	$ 567
			($6,233)		
November 27	(400 @ $13)	$5,200		(450 @ $12.816)	$5,767

As indicated above, **a new average is computed each time a purchase is made.** On April 15, after 200 units are purchased for $2,200, a total of 300 units costing $3,200 ($1,000 + $2,200) are on hand. The average unit cost is $10.667 ($3,200 ÷ 300). On August 24, after 300 units are purchased for $3,600, a total of 600 units costing $6,800 ($1,000 + $2,200 + $3,600) are on hand at an average cost per unit of $11.333 ($6,800 ÷ 600). This unit cost of $11.333 is used in costing sales until another purchase is made, when a new unit cost is computed. Accordingly, the unit cost of the 550 units sold on September 10 is $11.333, and the total cost of goods sold is $6,233. On November 27, following the purchase of 400 units for $5,200, there are 450 units on hand costing $5,767 ($567 + $5,200) with a new average cost of $12.816 ($5,767 ÷ 450).

This moving average cost under the perpetual inventory system should be compared to Illustration 9-17 on page 382 showing the weighted average method under a periodic inventory system.

DEMONSTRATION PROBLEM

The Demonstration Problem on page 390 showed cost of goods sold computations under a periodic inventory system. Now let's assume that Gerald D. Englehart Company uses a perpetual inventory system and has the same inventory, purchases, and sales data for the month of March as shown earlier:

Inventory, March 1		200 units @ $4.00	$ 800
Purchases:			
	March 10	500 units @ $4.50	2,250
	March 20	400 units @ $4.75	1,900
	March 30	300 units @ $5.00	1,500
Sales:			
	March 15	500 units	
	March 25	400 units	

The physical inventory count on March 31 shows 500 units on hand.

PROBLEM-SOLVING STRATEGIES

1. For FIFO, the latest costs are allocated to inventory.

2. For LIFO, the earliest costs are allocated to inventory.

3. For average costs, use a weighted average for periodic and a moving average for perpetual.

4. Remember, the costs allocated to cost of goods sold can be proved.

5. Total purchases are the same under all three cost flow methods.

Instructions

Under a **perpetual inventory system**, determine the cost of inventory on hand at March 31 and the cost of goods sold for March under the (a) first-in, first-out (FIFO) method, (b) last-in, first-out (LIFO) method, and (c) average cost method.

SOLUTION TO DEMONSTRATION PROBLEM

The cost of goods available for sale is $6,450:

Inventory		200 units @ $4.00	$ 800
Purchases:			
	March 10	500 units @ $4.50	2,250
	March 20	400 units @ $4.75	1,900
	March 30	300 units @ $5.00	1,500
Total cost of goods available for sale			$6,450

Under a **perpetual inventory system**, the cost of goods sold under each cost flow method is as follows:

FIFO Method

Date	Purchases		Sales		Balance	
March 1					(200 @ $4.00)	$ 800
March 10	(500 @ $4.50)	$2,250			(200 @ $4.00) } (500 @ $4.50) }	$3,050
March 15			(200 @ $4.00) (300 @ $4.50)		(200 @ $4.50)	$ 900
			$2,150			
March 20	(400 @ $4.75)	$1,900			(200 @ $4.50) } (400 @ $4.75) }	$2,800
March 25			(200 @ $4.50) (200 @ $4.75)		(200 @ $4.75)	$ 950
			$1,850			
March 30	(300 @ $5.00)	$1,500			(200 @ $4.75) } (300 @ $5.00) }	$2,450

Ending inventory, $2,450. Cost of goods sold: $6,450 − $2,450 = $4,000

LIFO Method

Date	Purchases		Sales		Balance	
March 1					(200 @ $4.00)	$ 800
March 10	(500 @ $4.50)	$2,250			(200 @ $4.00) } (500 @ $4.50) }	$3,050
March 15			(500 @ $4.50)	$2,250	(200 @ $4.00)	$ 800
March 20	(400 @ $4.75)	$1,900			(200 @ $4.00) } (200 @ $4.75) }	$2,700
March 25			(400 @ $4.75)	$1,900	(200 @ $4.00)	$ 800
March 30	(300 @ $5.00)	$1,500			(200 @ $4.00) } (300 @ $5.00) }	$2,300

Ending inventory, $2,300. Cost of goods sold: $6,450 − $2,300 = $4,150

Moving Average Cost Method

Date	Purchases		Sales		Balance	
March 1					(200 @ $4.00)	$ 800
March 10	(500 @ $4.50)	$2,250			(700 @ $4.357)	$3,050
March 15			(500 @ $4.357)	$2,179	(200 @ $4.357)	$ 871
March 20	(400 @ $4.75)	$1,900			(600 @ $4.618)	$2,771
March 25			(400 @ $4.618)	$1,847	(200 @ $4.618)	$ 924
March 30	(300 @ $5.00)	$1,500			(500 @ $4.848)	$2,424

Ending inventory, $2,424. Cost of goods sold: $6,450 − $2,424 = $4,026

SUMMARY OF STUDY OBJECTIVE FOR APPENDIX 9B

11. *Apply the inventory cost flow methods to perpetual inventory records.* Under FIFO, the cost of the earliest goods on hand prior to each sale is charged to cost of goods sold. Under LIFO, the cost of the most recent purchase prior to sale is charged to cost of goods sold. Under the average cost method, a new average cost is computed after each purchase.

*Note: All asterisked Questions, Exercises, and Problems relate to material in the appendixes to the chapter.

SELF-STUDY QUESTIONS

Answers are at the end of the chapter.

(SO 2) 1. When goods are purchased for resale by a company using a periodic inventory system:
   a. purchases on account are debited to Merchandise Inventory.
   b. purchases on account are debited to Purchases.
   c. purchase returns are debited to Purchase Returns and Allowances.
   d. freight costs are debited to Purchases.

(SO 3) 2. In determining cost of goods sold:
   a. purchases discounts are deducted from net purchases.
   b. freight-out is added to net purchases.
   c. purchase returns and allowances are deducted from net purchases.
   d. freight-in is added to net purchases.

(SO 3) 3. If beginning inventory is $60,000, cost of goods purchased is $380,000, and ending inventory is $50,000, cost of goods sold is:
   a. $390,000.   c. $330,000.
   b. $370,000.   d. $420,000.

(SO 1) 4. Which of the following should *not* be included in the physical inventory of a company?
   a. Goods held on consignment from another company.
   b. Goods shipped on consignment to another company.
   c. Goods in transit from another company shipped FOB shipping point.
   d. None of the above.

(SO 5) 5. Inventoriable costs consist of two elements: beginning inventory and
   a. ending inventory.
   b. cost of goods purchased.
   c. cost of goods sold.
   d. cost of goods available for sale.

(SO 5) 6. Electrolux Company has the following:

	Units	Unit Cost
Inventory, Jan. 1	8,000	$11
Purchase, June 19	13,000	12
Purchase, Nov. 8	5,000	13

   If 9,000 units are on hand at December 31, the cost of the ending inventory under FIFO is:
   a. $99,000.   c. $113,000.
   b. $108,000.   d. $117,000.

(SO 5) 7. Using the data in (6) above, the cost of the ending inventory under LIFO is:
   a. $113,000.   c. $99,000.
   b. $108,000.   d. $100,000.

8. In periods of rising prices, LIFO will produce: (SO 6)
   a. higher net income than FIFO.
   b. the same net income as FIFO.
   c. lower net income than FIFO.
   d. higher net income than average costing.

9. Factors that affect the selection of an inventory costing (SO 6) method do *not* include:
   a. tax effects.
   b. balance sheet effects.
   c. income statement effects.
   d. perpetual vs. periodic inventory system.

10. The lower of cost or market basis may be applied to: (SO 7)
   a. categories of inventories.
   b. individual items of inventories.
   c. total inventory.
   d. all of the above.

*11. Volvo Company has sales of $150,000 and cost of goods (SO 9) available for sale of $135,000. If the gross profit rate is 30%, the estimated cost of the ending inventory under the gross profit method is:
   a. $15,000.
   b. $30,000.
   c. $45,000.
   d. $75,000.

12. Peugeot Company's ending inventory is understated (SO 8) $4,000. The effects of this error on the current year's cost of goods sold and net income, respectively, are:
   a. understated, overstated.
   b. overstated, understated.
   c. overstated, overstated.
   d. understated, understated.

13. Which of these would cause the inventory turnover ratio (SO 9) to increase the most?
   a. Increasing the amount of inventory on hand.
   b. Keeping the amount of inventory on hand constant but increasing sales.
   c. Keeping the amount of inventory on hand constant but decreasing sales.
   d. Decreasing the amount of inventory on hand and increasing sales.

*14. In a perpetual inventory system, (SO 10)
   a. LIFO cost of goods sold will be the same as in a periodic inventory system.
   b. average costs are based entirely on unit cost averages.
   c. a new average is computed under the average cost method after each sale.
   d. FIFO cost of goods sold will be the same as in a periodic inventory system.

THE
NAVIGATOR

QUESTIONS

1. Goods costing $1,700 are purchased on account on July 15 with credit terms of 2/10, n/30. On July 18 a $200 credit memo is received from the supplier for damaged goods. Give the journal entry on July 24 to record payment of the balance due within the discount period.

2. Identify the accounts that are added to or deducted from purchases to determine the cost of goods purchased. For each account, indicate (a) whether it is added or deducted and (b) its normal balance.

3. In the following separate mini cases, using a periodic inventory system, identify the item(s) designated by letter.
   (a) Purchases − X − Y = Net purchases.
   (b) Cost of goods purchased − Net purchases = X.
   (c) Beginning inventory + X = Cost of goods available for sale.
   (d) Cost of goods available for sale − Cost of goods sold = X.

4. "The key to successful business operations is effective inventory management." Do you agree? Explain.

5. An item must possess two characteristics to be classified as inventory by a merchandiser. What are these two characteristics?

6. Your friend Tom Wetzel has been hired to help take the physical inventory in Hitachi Hardware Store. Explain to Tom Wetzel what this job will entail.

7. (a) Janine Company ships merchandise to Laura Company on December 30. The merchandise reaches the buyer on January 6. Indicate the terms of sale that will result in the goods being included in (1) Janine's December 31 inventory, and (2) Laura's December 31 inventory.
   (b) Under what circumstances should Janine Company include consigned goods in its inventory?

8. Mary Ann's Hat Shop received a shipment of hats for which it paid the wholesaler $2,940. The price of the hats was $3,000, but Mary Ann's was given a $60 cash discount and required to pay freight charges of $80. In addition, Mary Ann's paid $130 to cover the travel expenses of an employee who negotiated the purchase of the hats. What amount will Mary Ann record for inventory? Why?

9. What is the primary basis of accounting for inventories? What is the major objective in accounting for inventories? What accounting principles are involved here?

10. Identify the distinguishing features of an income statement for a merchandising company.

11. Roland Carlson believes that the allocation of inventoriable costs should be based on the actual physical flow of the goods. Explain to Roland why this may be both impractical and inappropriate.

12. What is a major advantage and a major disadvantage of the specific identification method of inventory costing?

13. "The selection of an inventory cost flow method is a decision made by accountants." Do you agree? Explain. Once a method has been selected, what accounting requirement applies?

14. Which assumed inventory cost flow method:
    (a) usually parallels the actual physical flow of merchandise?
    (b) assumes that goods available for sale during an accounting period are homogeneous?
    (c) assumes that the latest units purchased are the first to be sold?

15. In a period of rising prices, the inventory reported in Jim Groat Company's balance sheet is close to the current cost of the inventory, whereas Greg Hanson Company's inventory is considerably below its current cost. Identify the inventory cost flow method being used by each company. Which company has probably been reporting the higher gross profit?

16. Char Lewis Company has been using the FIFO cost flow method during a prolonged period of inflation. During the same time period, Char Lewis has been paying out all of its net income as dividends. What adverse effects may result from this policy?

17. Bob Thebeau is studying for the next accounting midterm examination. What should Bob know about (a) departing from the cost basis of accounting for inventories and (b) the meaning of "market" in the lower of cost or market method?

18. John Hohenberger Music Center has 5 CD players on hand at the balance sheet date that cost $400 each. The current replacement cost is $320 per unit. Under the lower of cost or market basis of accounting for inventories, what value should be reported for the CD players on the balance sheet? Why?

19. What methods may be used under the lower of cost or market basis of accounting for inventories? Which method will produce the lowest inventory value?

20. Elaine Stahl Company discovers in 1999 that its ending inventory at December 31, 1998, was $5,000 understated. What effect will this error have on (a) 1998 net income, (b) 1999 net income, and (c) the combined net income for the 2 years?

21. Maureen & Nathan Company's balance sheet shows Inventories $162,800. What additional disclosures should be made?

22. Under what circumstances might the inventory turnover ratio be too high; that is, what possible negative consequences might occur?

*23. When is it necessary to estimate inventories?

*24. Both the gross profit method and the retail inventory method are based on averages. For each method, indicate the average used, how it is determined, and how it is applied.

*25. Jana Kingston Company has net sales of $400,000 and cost of goods available for sale of $300,000. If the gross profit rate is 30%, what is the estimated cost of the ending inventory? Show computations.

*26. John Ross Shoe Shop had goods available for sale in 1999 with a retail price of $120,000. The cost of these goods was $84,000. If sales during the period were $90,000, what is the ending inventory at cost using the retail inventory method?

*27. "When perpetual inventory records are kept, the results under the FIFO and LIFO methods are the same as they would be in a periodic inventory system." Do you agree? Explain.

*28. How does the average method of inventory costing differ between a perpetual inventory system and a periodic inventory system?

BRIEF EXERCISES

Journalize purchases transactions.
(SO 2)

BE9–1 Prepare the journal entries to record the following transactions on Svenska Company's books using a periodic inventory system.

    (a) On March 2, Svenska Company purchased $900,000 of merchandise from Sing Tao Company, terms 2/10, n/30.

    (b) On March 6, Svenska Company returned $130,000 of the merchandise purchased on March 2 because it was defective.

    (c) On March 12, Svenska Company paid the balance due to Sing Tao Company.

Compute net purchases and cost of goods purchased.
(SO 3)

BE9–2 Assume that Shinhan Company uses a periodic inventory system and has the following account balances: Purchases $440,000, Purchase Returns and Allowances $11,000, Purchase Discounts $8,000, and Freight-in $16,000. Determine (a) net purchases and (b) cost of goods purchased.

Compute cost of goods sold and gross profit.
(SO 3)

BE9–3 Assume the same information as in BE9–2, and also that Shinhan Company has beginning inventory of $60,000, ending inventory of $90,000, and net sales of $650,000. Determine the amounts to be reported for cost of goods sold and gross profit.

Identify items to be included in taking a physical inventory.
(SO 1)

BE9–4 Oriental Press Company identifies the following items for possible inclusion in the taking of a physical inventory. Indicate whether each item should be included or excluded from the inventory taking.

    1. Goods shipped on consignment by Oriental Press to another company.

    2. Goods in transit from a supplier shipped FOB destination.

    3. Goods sold but being held for customer pickup.

    4. Goods held on consignment from another company.

Identify the components of inventoriable costs.
(SO 5)

BE9–5 The ledger of Norway Company includes the following items: (1) Freight-in, (2) Purchase Returns and Allowances, (3) Purchases, (4) Sales Discounts, (5) Purchase Discounts. Identify which items are included in inventoriable costs.

Compute ending inventory using FIFO and LIFO.
(SO 5)

BE9–6 In its first month of operations, Finlandia Company made three purchases of merchandise in the following sequence: (1) 300 units at $6, (2) 400 units at $7, and (3) 300 units at $8. Assuming there are 400 units on hand, compute the cost of the ending inventory under the (1) FIFO method and (2) LIFO method. Finlandia uses a periodic inventory system.

Compute the ending inventory using average costs.
(SO 5)

BE9–7 Data for Finlandia Company are presented in BE9–6. Compute the cost of the ending inventory under the average cost method, assuming there are 400 units on hand.

Determine the LCM valuation using inventory categories.
(SO 7)

BE9–8 Germania Appliance Center accumulates the following cost and market data at December 31:

Inventory Categories	Cost Data	Market Data
Cameras	$12,000	$10,200
Camcorders	9,000	9,700
VCRs	14,000	12,800

Compute the lower of cost or market valuation using categories.

Compute inventory turnover ratio and days in inventory.
(SO 9)

BE9–9 At December 31, 1999, the following information was available for Aurora Company: ending inventory $80,000; beginning inventory $60,000; cost of goods sold $210,000; and sales revenue $280,000. Calculate the inventory turnover ratio and days in inventory for Aurora Company.

BE9–10 Italy Company reports net income of $90,000 in 1999. However, ending inventory was understated $7,000. What is the correct net income for 1999? What effect, if any, will this error have on total assets as reported in the balance sheet at December 31, 1999?

Determine correct income statement amounts.
(SO 8)

*BE9–11 At May 31, Poland Company has net sales of $300,000 and cost of goods available for sale of $230,000. Compute the estimated cost of the ending inventory assuming the gross profit rate is 40%.

Apply the gross profit method.
(SO 10)

*BE9–12 On June 30, French Fabrics has the following data pertaining to the retail inventory method: Goods available for sale: at cost $35,000, at retail $50,000; net sales $30,000, and ending inventory at retail $20,000. Compute the estimated cost of the ending inventory using the retail inventory method.

Apply the retail inventory method.
(SO 10)

*BE9–13 Spain Department Store uses a perpetual inventory system. Data for product E2–D2 include the following purchases:

Apply cost flow methods to records.
(SO 11)

Date	Number of Units	Unit Price
May 7	50	$10
July 28	30	15

On June 1 Spain sold 30 units, and on August 27, 33 more units. Prepare the perpetual inventory card for the above transactions using (1) FIFO, (2) LIFO, and (3) average cost.

EXERCISES

E9–1 Presented below is the following information related to Brazil Co.

Journalize purchases transactions.
(SO 2)

1. On April 5, purchased merchandise from Chile Company for $18,000 terms 2/10, net/30, FOB shipping point.
2. On April 6, paid freight costs of $800 on merchandise purchased from Chile.
3. On April 7, purchased equipment on account for $26,000.
4. On April 8, returned damaged merchandise to Chile Company and was granted a $3,000 allowance.
5. On April 15, paid the amount due to Chile Company in full.

Instructions
(a) Prepare the journal entries to record these transactions on the books of Brazil Co. using a periodic inventory system.
(b) Assume that Brazil Co. paid the balance due to Chile Company on May 4 instead of April 15. Prepare the journal entry to record this payment.

E9–2 The trial balance of Colombia Company at the end of its fiscal year, August 31, 1999, includes the following accounts: Merchandise Inventory $17,200, Purchases $142,400, Sales $190,000, Freight-in $4,000, Sales Returns and Allowances $3,000, Freight-out $1,000, and Purchase Returns and Allowances $2,000. The ending (August 31, 1999) merchandise inventory is $27,000.

Prepare cost of goods sold section.
(SO 3)

Instructions
Prepare a cost of goods sold section for the year ending August 31 (periodic inventory).

E9–3 Presented is information related to Mexico Co. for the month of January 1999.

Prepare an income statement.
(SO 4)

Freight-in	$10,000	Rent expense	19,000
Freight-out	5,000	Salary expense	61,000
Insurance expense	12,000	Sales discounts	8,000
Purchases	200,000	Sales returns and allowances	13,000
Purchase discounts	3,000	Sales	312,000
Purchase returns and allowances	6,000		

Beginning merchandise inventory was $42,000 and ending inventory was $63,000.

Instructions

Prepare an income statement using the format presented on page 375. Operating expenses should not be segregated into selling and administrative expenses.

Determine the correct inventory amount.
(SO 1)

E9–4   Yorkville Bank and Trust is considering giving Canada Company a loan. Before doing so, they decide that further discussions with Canada's accountant may be desirable. One area of particular concern is the inventory account, which has a year-end balance of $295,000. Discussions with the accountant reveal the following:

1. Canada sold goods costing $38,000 to Moghul Company FOB shipping point on December 28. The goods are not expected to arrive in India until January 12. The goods were not included in the physical inventory because they were not in the warehouse.
2. The physical count of the inventory did not include goods costing $95,000 that were shipped to Canada FOB destination on December 27, and were still in transit at year-end.
3. Canada received goods costing $25,000 on January 2. The goods were shipped FOB shipping point on December 26 by Cellar Co. The goods were not included in the physical count.
4. Canada sold goods costing $40,000 to Sterling of Mexico FOB destination on December 30. The goods were received in Mexico on January 8. They were not included in Canada's physical inventory.
5. Canada received goods costing $44,000 on January 2 that were shipped FOB destination on December 29. The shipment was a rush order that was supposed to arrive December 31. This purchase was included in the ending inventory of $297,000.

Instructions

Determine the correct inventory amount on December 31.

Compute inventory and cost of goods sold using FIFO and LIFO.
(SO 5)

E9–5   Egypt Co. uses a periodic inventory system. Its records show the following for the month of May, in which 78 units were sold.

		Units	Unit Cost	Total Cost
May 1	Inventory	30	$ 8	$240
15	Purchases	25	10	250
24	Purchases	35	13	455
	Totals	90		$945

Instructions

Compute the ending inventory at May 31 using the FIFO and LIFO methods. Prove the amount allocated to cost of goods sold under each method.

Compute inventory and cost of goods sold using FIFO and LIFO.
(SO 5, 6)

E9–6   In June, Luxemburg Company reports the following for the month of June.

		Units	Unit Cost	Total Cost
June 1	Inventory	200	$5	$1,000
12	Purchases	300	6	1,800
23	Purchases	500	7	3,500
30	Inventory	180		

Instructions

(a) Compute the cost of the ending inventory and the cost of goods sold under (1) FIFO and (2) LIFO.
(b) Which costing method gives the higher ending inventory? Why?
(c) Which method results in the higher cost of goods sold? Why?

Compute inventory and cost of goods sold using average costs.
(SO 5, 6)

E9–7   Inventory data for Luxemburg Company are presented in E9–6.

Instructions

(a) Compute the cost of the ending inventory and the cost of goods sold using the average cost method.
(b) Will the results in (a) be higher or lower than the results under (1) FIFO and (2) LIFO?
(c) Why is the average unit cost not $6?

E9–8 China Camera Shop uses the lower of cost or market basis for its inventory. The following data are available at December 31:

Determine ending inventory under lower of cost or market inventory method.
(SO 7)

Item	Units	Unit Cost	Market
Cameras			
Minolta	5	$170	$160
Canon	7	150	152
Light Meters			
Vivitar	12	125	110
Kodak	10	115	135

Instructions

Determine the amount of the ending inventory by applying the lower of cost or market basis to (a) individual items, (b) inventory categories, and (c) the total inventory.

E9–9 Korea Hardware reported cost of goods sold as follows:

Determine effects of inventory errors.
(SO 8)

	1999	2000
Beginning inventory	$ 20,000	$ 30,000
Cost of goods purchased	150,000	175,000
Cost of goods available for sale	170,000	205,000
Ending inventory	30,000	35,000
Cost of goods sold	$140,000	$170,000

Korea made two errors: (1) 1999 ending inventory was overstated $4,000 and (2) 2000 ending inventory was understated $3,000.

Instructions

Compute the correct cost of goods sold for each year.

E9–10 Zurich Watch Company reported the following income statement data for a 2-year period.

Prepare correct income statements.
(SO 8)

	1999	2000
Sales	$210,000	$250,000
Cost of goods sold		
Beginning inventory	32,000	40,000
Cost of goods purchased	173,000	202,000
Cost of goods available for sale	205,000	242,000
Ending inventory	40,000	52,000
Cost of goods sold	165,000	190,000
Gross profit	$ 45,000	$ 60,000

Zurich uses a periodic inventory system. The inventories at January 1, 1999, and December 31, 2000, are correct. However, the ending inventory at December 31, 1999, was overstated $6,000.

Instructions

(a) Prepare correct income statement data for the 2 years.

(b) What is the cumulative effect of the inventory error on total gross profit for the 2 years?

(c) ▨▨▨▶ Explain in a letter to the president of Zurich Company what has happened—i.e., the nature of the error and its effect on the financial statements.

E9–11 This information is available for Linda Wasisko Corporation for 1997, 1998, and 1999:

Compute inventory turnover ratio, days in inventory, and gross profit rate.
(SO 9, 10)

	1997	1998	1999
Beginning inventory	$ 200,000	$ 300,000	$ 400,000
Ending inventory	300,000	400,000	500,000
Cost of goods sold	900,000	1,120,000	1,250,000
Sales	1,200,000	1,600,000	1,900,000

Determine merchandise lost using the gross profit method of estimating inventory.
(SO 10)

Instructions
Calculate the inventory turnover ratio, days in inventory, and gross profit rate (from Chapter 5) for Linda Wasisko Corporation for 1997, 1998, 1999. Comment on any trends.

*E9–12   The inventory of DeBeers Company was destroyed by fire on March 1. From an examination of the accounting records, the following data for the first 2 months of the year are obtained: Sales $51,000, Sales Returns and Allowances $1,000, Purchases $28,200, Freight-in $1,200, and Purchase Returns and Allowances $1,400.

Instructions
Determine the merchandise lost by fire, assuming:

    (a) A beginning inventory of $20,000 and a gross profit rate of 30% on net sales.
    (b) A beginning inventory of $25,000 and a gross profit rate of 25% on net sales.

Determine ending inventory at cost using retail method.
(SO 10)

*E9–13   Swiss Shoe Store uses the retail inventory method for its two departments: Women's Shoes and Men's Shoes. The following information for each department is obtained:

Item	Women's Department	Men's Department
Beginning inventory at cost	$ 32,000	$ 46,450
Cost of goods purchased at cost	148,000	137,300
Net sales	187,000	195,000
Beginning inventory at retail	45,000	60,000
Cost of goods purchased at retail	182,000	185,000

Instructions
Compute the estimated cost of the ending inventory for each department under the retail inventory method.

Apply cost flow methods to perpetual records.
(SO 11)

*E9–14   Morocco Appliance uses a perpetual inventory system. For its model B47 television sets, the January 1 inventory was four sets at $600 each. During January, the following purchase was made: Jan. 10, 6 units at $640 each. That month, the company had the following sales: Jan. 8, 2 units and Jan. 15, 4 units.

Instructions
Compute the ending inventory under (1) FIFO, (2) LIFO, and (3) average cost.

PROBLEMS: SET A

Journalize, post, and prepare trial balance and partial income statement.
(SO 2, 3, 4)

P9–1A   Chi Chi Lopez, a former professional golf star, operates Chi Chi's Pro Shop at Bay Golf Course. At the beginning of the current season on April 1, 1999, the ledger of Chi Chi's Pro Shop showed Cash $2,500, Merchandise Inventory $3,500, and Capital $6,000. The following transactions were completed during April.

Apr. 5 Purchased golf bags, clubs, and balls on account from Balata Co. $1,600, FOB shipping point, terms 2/10, n/60.
   7 Paid freight on Balata purchase $80.
   9 Received credit from Balata Co. for merchandise returned $100.
  10 Sold merchandise on account to members $900, terms n/30.
  12 Purchased golf shoes, sweaters, and other accessories on account from Arrow Sportswear $660, terms 1/10, n/30.
  14 Paid Balata Co. in full.
  17 Received credit from Arrow Sportswear for merchandise returned $60.
  20 Made sales on account to members $700, terms n/30.
  21 Paid Arrow Sportswear in full.
  27 Granted credit to members for clothing that did not fit $30.
  30 Made cash sales $600.
  30 Received payments on account from members $1,100.

The chart of accounts for the pro shop includes the following: No. 101 Cash, No. 112 Accounts Receivable, No. 120 Merchandise Inventory, No. 201 Accounts Payable, No. 301 Capital, No. 401 Sales, No. 412 Sales Returns and Allowances, No. 510 Purchases, No. 512 Purchase Returns and Allowances, No. 514 Purchase Discounts, No. 516 Freight-in.

Instructions
  (a) Journalize the April transactions using a periodic inventory system.
  (b) Enter the beginning balances in the ledger accounts and post the April transactions. (Use J1 for the journal reference.)
  (c) Prepare a trial balance on April 30, 1999.
  (d) Prepare an income statement through gross profit, assuming merchandise inventory on hand at April 30 is $4,200.

P9–2A Asian Department Store is located in midtown Metropolis. During the past several years, net income has been declining because of suburban shopping centers. At the end of the company's fiscal year on November 30, 1999, the following accounts appeared in its adjusted trial balance:

Prepare an income statement.
(SO 3, 4)

Accounts Payable	$ 35,310
Accounts Receivable	11,770
Accumulated Depreciation—Delivery Equipment	19,680
Accumulated Depreciation—Store Equipment	41,800
Cash	8,000
Delivery Expense	8,200
Delivery Equipment	57,000
Depreciation Expense—Delivery Equipment	4,000
Depreciation Expense—Store Equipment	9,500
Freight-in	5,060
Common Stock	70,000
Retained Earnings	17,200
Dividends	12,000
Insurance Expense	9,000
Merchandise Inventory	34,360
Notes Payable	46,000
Prepaid Insurance	4,500
Property Tax Expense	3,500
Purchases	640,000
Purchase Discounts	7,000
Purchase Returns and Allowances	3,000
Rent Expense	19,000
Salaries Expense	120,000
Sales	860,000
Sales Commissions Expense	12,000
Sales Commissions Payable	8,000
Sales Returns and Allowances	10,000
Store Equipment	125,000
Property Taxes Payable	3,500
Utilities Expense	10,600

Analysis reveals the following additional data:

  1. Salaries expense is 70% selling and 30% administrative.
  2. Insurance expense is 50% selling and 50% administrative.
  3. Merchandise inventory at November 30, 1999, is $36,200.
  4. Rent expense, utilities expense, and property tax expense are administrative expenses.

Instructions
Prepare an income statement for the year ended November 30, 1999.

P9–3A Europe Company had a beginning inventory on January 1 of 100 units of Product WD-44 at a cost of $20 per unit. During the year, the following purchases were made.

Determine cost of goods sold and ending inventory, using FIFO, LIFO, and average cost with analysis.
(SO 5, 6)

Mar. 15	300 units at $24	Sept. 4	300 units at $28
July 20	200 units at 25	Dec. 2	100 units at 30

850 units were sold. Europe Company uses a periodic inventory system.

Instructions
  (a) Determine the cost of goods available for sale.
  (b) Determine (1) the ending inventory, and (2) the cost of goods sold under each of the

assumed cost flow methods (FIFO, LIFO, and average). Prove the accuracy of the cost of goods sold under the FIFO and LIFO methods.

(c) Which cost flow method results in (1) the highest inventory amount for the balance sheet and (2) the highest cost of goods sold for the income statement?

Compute ending inventory, prepare income statements, and answer questions using FIFO and LIFO.

(SO 5, 6)

P9–4A   The management of African Co. asks your help in determining the comparative effects of the FIFO and LIFO inventory cost flow methods. For 1999, the accounting records show the following data:

Inventory, January 1 (10,000 units)	$ 35,000
Cost of 110,000 units purchased	460,000
Selling price of 95,000 units sold	665,000
Operating expenses	120,000

Units purchased consisted of 40,000 units at $4.00 on May 10; 50,000 units at $4.20 on August 15; and 20,000 units at $4.50 on November 20. Income taxes are 28%.

Instructions

(a) Prepare comparative condensed income statements for 1999 under FIFO and LIFO. (Show computations of ending inventory.)

(b) ▭▭▭▭▷ Answer the following questions for management in the form of a business letter:

(1) Which inventory cost flow method produces the most meaningful inventory amount for the balance sheet? Why?

(2) Which inventory cost flow method produces the most meaningful net income? Why?

(3) Which inventory cost flow method is most likely to approximate actual physical flow of the goods? Why?

(4) How much additional cash will be available for management under LIFO than under FIFO? Why?

(5) How much of the gross profit under FIFO is illusionary in comparison with the gross profit under LIFO?

Compute gross profit rate and inventory loss using gross profit method.

(SO 10)

*P9–5A   Australia Company lost all of its inventory in a fire on December 26, 1999. The accounting records showed the following gross profit data for November and December.

	November	December (to 12/26)
Net sales	$400,000	$300,000
Beginning inventory	22,100	29,100
Purchases	314,975	236,000
Purchase returns and allowances	11,800	5,000
Purchase discounts	8,577	6,000
Freight-in	4,402	3,700
Ending inventory	29,100	?

Australia is fully insured for fire losses but must prepare a report for the insurance company.

Instructions

(a) Compute the gross profit rate for November.

(b) Using the gross profit rate for November, determine the estimated cost of the inventory lost in the fire.

Compute ending inventory using retail method.

(SO 10)

*P9–6A   French's Book Store uses the retail inventory method to estimate its monthly ending inventories. The following information is available for two of its departments at October 31, 1999.

	Hardcovers		Paperbacks	
	Cost	Retail	Cost	Retail
Beginning inventory	$ 260,000	$ 400,000	$ 65,000	$ 90,000
Purchases	1,180,000	1,800,000	266,000	380,000
Freight-in	5,000		2,000	
Purchase discounts	15,000		4,000	
Net sales		1,810,000		363,000

At December 31, French's Book Store takes a physical inventory at retail. The actual retail values of the inventories in each department are: Hardcovers $400,000 and Paperbacks $100,000.

Instructions

(a) Determine the estimated cost of the ending inventory for each department at **October 31**, 1999, using the retail inventory method.

(b) Compute the ending inventory at cost for each department at **December 31**, assuming the cost to retail ratios for the year are 65% for hardcovers and 70% for paperbacks.

*P9–7A   Save-Mart Center began operations on July 1. It uses a perpetual inventory system. During July the company had the following purchases and sales:

Determine ending inventory under a perpetual inventory system.
(SO 11)

	Purchases		
Date	Units	Unit Cost	Sales Units
July 1	5	$90	
July 6			3
July 11	4	$99	
July 14			3
July 21	3	$106	
July 27			4

Instructions

(a) Determine the ending inventory under a perpetual inventory system using (1) FIFO, (2) average cost, and (3) LIFO.

(b) Which costing method produces the highest ending inventory valuation?

PROBLEMS: SET B

P9–1B   Billy Jean Evert, a former professional tennis star, operates B.J.'s Tennis Shop at the Jackson Lake Resort. At the beginning of the current season, the ledger of B.J.'s Tennis Shop showed Cash $2,500, Merchandise Inventory $1,700, and Capital $4,200. The following transactions were completed during April:

Journalize, post, and prepare a trial balance and partial income statement.
(SO 2, 3, 4)

Apr. 4   Purchased racquets and balls from Robert Co. $640 FOB shipping point, terms 3/10, n/30.

6   Paid freight on Robert purchase $40.

8   Sold merchandise to members $900, terms n/30.

10   Received credit of $40 from Robert Co. for a damaged racquet that was returned.

11   Purchased tennis shoes from Niki Sports for cash, $300.

13   Paid Robert Co. in full.

14   Purchased tennis shirts and shorts from Martina's Sportswear $700, FOB shipping point, terms 2/10, n/60.

15   Received cash refund of $50 from Niki Sports for damaged merchandise that was returned.

17   Paid freight on Martina's Sportswear purchase $30.

18   Sold merchandise to members, $800, terms n/30.

20   Received $500 in cash from members in settlement of their accounts.

21   Paid Martina's Sportswear in full.

27   Granted credit of $30 to members for tennis clothing that did not fit.

30   Sold merchandise to members $900, terms n/30.

30   Received cash payments on account from members, $500.

The chart of accounts for the tennis shop includes the following: No. 101 Cash, No. 112 Accounts Receivable, No. 120 Merchandise Inventory, No. 201 Accounts Payable, No. 301 Capital, No. 401 Sales, No. 412 Sales Returns and Allowances, No. 510 Purchases, No. 512 Purchase Returns and Allowances, No. 514 Purchase Discounts, No. 516 Freight-in.

Instructions

(a) Journalize the April transactions using a periodic inventory system.
(b) Enter the beginning balances in the ledger accounts and post the April transactions. (Use J1 for the journal reference.)
(c) Prepare a trial balance on April 30, 1999.
(d) Prepare an income statement through gross profit, assuming merchandise inventory on hand at April 30 is $1,800.

Prepare an income statement.
(SO 3, 4)

P9–2B   Austrian Department Store is located near the Village shopping mall. At the end of the company's fiscal year on December 31, 1999, the following accounts appeared in its adjusted trial balance:

Accounts Payable	$ 89,300
Accounts Receivable	50,300
Accumulated Depreciation—Building	52,500
Accumulated Depreciation—Equipment	42,900
Building	190,000
Cash	23,000
Depreciation Expense—Building	10,400
Depreciation Expense—Equipment	13,300
Equipment	110,000
Freight-in	3,600
Insurance Expense	7,200
Merchandise Inventory	40,500
Mortgage Payable	80,000
Office Salaries Expense	32,000
Prepaid Insurance	2,400
Property Taxes Payable	4,300
Purchases	462,000
Purchase Discounts	12,000
Purchase Returns and Allowances	6,400
Sales Salaries Expense	74,000
Sales	618,000
Sales Commissions Expense	14,500
Sales Commissions Payable	4,000
Sales Returns and Allowances	8,000
Capital	177,600
Drawings	28,000
Property Taxes Expense	4,800
Utilities Expense	11,000

Analysis reveals the following additional data:

1. Merchandise inventory on December 31, 1999, is $75,000.
2. Insurance expense and utilities expense are 60% selling and 40% administrative.
3. Depreciation on the building and property tax expense are administrative expenses; depreciation on the equipment is a selling expense.

Instructions

Prepare an income statement for the year ended December 31, 1999.

Determine cost of goods sold and ending inventory, using FIFO, LIFO, and average cost.
(SO 5, 6)

P9–3B   Russia Company had a beginning inventory of 400 units of Product USSR at a cost of $8.00 per unit. During the year, purchases were:

Feb. 20	700 units at $9.00		Aug. 12	300 units at $11.00
May 5	500 units at $10.00		Dec. 8	100 units at $12.00

Russia Company uses a periodic inventory system. Sales totaled 1,550 units.

Instructions

(a) Determine the cost of goods available for sale.
(b) Determine (1) the ending inventory, and (2) the cost of goods sold under each of the assumed cost flow methods (FIFO, LIFO, and average). Prove the accuracy of the cost of goods sold under the FIFO and LIFO methods.
(c) Which cost flow method results in (1) the lowest inventory amount for the balance sheet, and (2) the lowest cost of goods sold for the income statement?

P9–4B   The management of India Co. is reevaluating the appropriateness of using its present inventory cost flow method, which is average cost. They request your help in determining the results of operations for 1999 if either the FIFO method or the LIFO method had been used. For 1999, the accounting records show the following data:

Compute ending inventory, prepare income statements, and answer questions using FIFO and LIFO. (SO 5, 6)

Inventories		Purchases and Sales	
Beginning (15,000 units)	$34,000	Total net sales (225,000 units)	$865,000
Ending (20,000 units)		Total cost of goods purchased (230,000 units)	578,500

Purchases were made quarterly as follows:

Quarter	Units	Unit Cost	Total Cost
1	60,000	$2.30	$138,000
2	50,000	2.50	125,000
3	50,000	2.60	130,000
4	70,000	2.65	185,500
	230,000		$578,500

Operating expenses were $147,000, and the company's income tax rate is 32%.

Instructions
(a) Prepare comparative condensed income statements for 1999 under FIFO and LIFO. (Show computations of ending inventory.)
(b) ▐▐▐▭▭▭▷ Answer the following questions for management:
  (1) Which cost flow method (FIFO or LIFO) produces the more meaningful inventory amount for the balance sheet? Why?
  (2) Which cost flow method (FIFO or LIFO) produces the more meaningful net income? Why?
  (3) Which cost flow method (FIFO or LIFO) is more likely to approximate actual physical flow of the goods? Why?
  (4) How much additional cash will be available for management under LIFO than under FIFO? Why?
  (5) Will gross profit under the average cost method be higher or lower than (a) FIFO and (b) LIFO? (*Note:* It is not necessary to quantify your answer.)

*P9–5B   Tibet Company lost 80% of its inventory in a fire on March 25, 1999. The accounting records showed the following gross profit data for February and March.

Estimate inventory loss using gross profit method. (SO 10)

	February	March (to 3/25)
Net sales	$270,000	$260,000
Net purchases	200,800	191,000
Freight-in	2,900	4,000
Beginning inventory	16,500	20,400
Ending inventory	20,400	?

Tibet Company is fully insured for fire losses but must prepare a report for the insurance company.

Instructions
(a) Compute the gross profit rate for the month of February.
(b) Using the gross profit rate for February, determine both the estimated total inventory and inventory lost in the fire in March.

Compute ending inventory and cost of inventory lost using retail method. (SO 10)

*P9–6B   Japanese Department Store uses the retail inventory method to estimate its monthly ending inventories. The following information is available for two of its departments at August 31, 1999.

	Sporting Goods		Jewelry and Cosmetics	
	Cost	Retail	Cost	Retail
Net sales		$1,020,000		$1,160,000
Purchases	$670,000	1,066,000	$733,000	1,158,000
Purchase returns	(26,000)	(40,000)	(12,000)	(20,000)
Purchase discounts	(15,360)	—	(9,440)	—
Freight-in	6,000	—	8,000	—
Beginning inventory	47,360	74,000	36,440	62,000

At December 31, Japanese Department Store takes a physical inventory at retail. The actual retail values of the inventories in each department are: Sporting Goods $75,000, and Jewelry and Cosmetics $44,000.

Instructions

(a) Determine the estimated cost of the ending inventory for each department on August 31, 1999, using the retail inventory method.

(b) Compute the ending inventory at cost for each department at December 31, assuming the cost-to-retail ratios are 60% for Sporting Goods and 65% for Jewelry and Cosmetics.

Prepare subsidiary ledger records under a perpetual inventory system.
(SO 11)

*P9–7B The Family Home Appliance Mart begins operations on May 1. It uses a perpetual inventory system. During May the company had the following purchases and sales for its Model 25 Sureshot camera.

Date	Purchases		Sales
	Units	Unit Cost	Units
May 1	7	$150	
4			5
8	8	$170	
12			5
15	5	$180	
20			4
25			3

Instructions

(a) Determine the ending inventory under a perpetual inventory system using (1) FIFO, (2) average cost, and (3) LIFO.

(b) Which costing method produces (1) the highest ending inventory valuation and (2) the lowest ending inventory valuation?

BROADENING YOUR PERSPECTIVE

FINANCIAL REPORTING AND ANALYSIS

FINANCIAL REPORTING PROBLEM: Kellogg Company

BYP9–1 The notes that accompany a company's financial statements provide informative details that would clutter the amounts and descriptions presented in the statements. Refer to the financial statements of Kellogg Company and the Notes to Consolidated Financial Statements in Appendix A.

Instructions

Answer the following questions. Complete the requirements in millions of dollars, as shown in Kellogg's annual report.

(a) What did Kellogg report for the amount of inventories in its Consolidated Balance Sheet at December 31, 1997? December 31, 1996?

(b) Compute the dollar amount of change and the percentage change in inventories between 1996 and 1997. Compute inventory as a percentage of current assets for 1997.

(c) How does Kellogg value its inventories? Which inventory cost flow method does Kellogg use?

(d) What is the cost of sales (cost of goods sold) reported by Kellogg for 1997, 1996, and 1995? Compute the percentage of cost of sales to net sales in 1997.

COMPARATIVE ANALYSIS PROBLEM: Kellogg Company vs. General Mills

BYP9–2   Kellogg's financial statements are presented in Appendix A; General Mills's financial statements are presented in Appendix B.

Instructions

(a) Based on the information contained in these financial statements, compute the following 1997 ratios for each company:

  1. Inventory turnover ratio
  2. Average days to sell inventory

(b) What conclusions concerning the management of the inventory can be drawn from these data?

RESEARCH ASSIGNMENT

BYP9–3   The September 23, 1994, edition of *The Wall Street Journal* includes an article entitled "CompUSA Auctions Notebook Computers Through Bulk Sale."

Instructions

Read the article and answer the following inventory-related questions.

(a) At what amount did CompUSA estimate the retail value of the computers? What was the estimate made by one of the bidders?

(b) What was wrong with the computers?

(c) What were the rules of the auction as specified by CompUSA?

(d) CompUSA had just recorded a $3 million inventory writedown in the preceding quarter. Based on the information in the article, does it appear that additional writedowns were called for?

INTERPRETING FINANCIAL STATEMENTS: Nike and Reebok

BYP9–4   Nike and Reebok compete head-to-head in the sport shoe and sport apparel business. For both companies, inventory is a significant portion of their total assets. The following information was taken from each company's financial statements and notes to those financial statements.

NIKE, INC.		

Inventory note

Inventories are stated at the lower of cost or market. Cost is determined using the last-in, first-out (LIFO) method for substantially all U.S. inventories. Non-U.S. inventories are valued on a first-in, first-out (FIFO) basis.

Inventories by major classification are as follows (in thousands):

	May 31	
	1997	**1996**
Finished goods	$1,248,401	$ 874,700
Work-in-process	50,245	28,940
Raw materials	39,994	27,511

Other information for Nike:

	May 31	
	1997	**1996**
Inventory	$1,338,640	$ 931,151
Cost of goods sold	5,502,993	3,906,746

REEBOK INTERNATIONAL, LTD.

Inventory note
Inventory, substantially all finished goods, is recorded at the lower of cost (first-in, first-out method) or market.

Other information for Reebok (in thousands):

	December 31	
	1996	**1995**
Inventory	$ 544,522	$ 635,012
Cost of goods sold	2,144,422	2,114,084

Instructions
Address each of the following questions which deal with how these two companies manage their inventory.

(a) What problems of inventory management face Nike and Reebok in the international sport apparel industry?

(b) What inventory cost flow assumptions does each company use? Why might Nike use a different approach for U.S. operations versus international operations? What are the implications of their respective cost flow assumptions for their financial statements?

(c) Nike provides more detail regarding the nature of its inventory (e.g., raw materials, work-in-process, and finished goods) than does Reebok. How might this additional information be useful in evaluating Nike?

(d) Calculate and interpret the inventory turnover ratio and average days to sell inventory for each company. Comment on how the use of different inventory methods by the two companies impacts your ability to compare their ratios.

REAL-WORLD FOCUS: General Motors Corporation

BYP9–5 **General Motors** is the largest producer of automobiles in the world, as well as the world's biggest industrial enterprise. After stumbling in the early 1990s, GM has enacted numerous cost-cutting measures, including downsizing and renegotiating contracts with suppliers. In addition, it has shifted more of its resources to the hot-selling truck market.

The annual report of General Motors Corporation disclosed the following information about its accounting for inventories:

GENERAL MOTORS CORPORATION
Notes to the Financial Statements

Note 5. Inventories
Major Classes of Inventories (in millions)

	December 31	
	1995	**1994**
Productive material, work in process, and supplies	$ 6,570.4	$5,478.3
Finished product, service parts, etc.	4,959.1	4,649.5
Total	$11,529.5	$10,127.8
Memo: Increase in LIFO inventories if valued at FIFO	$ 2,424.4	$2,535.9

Inventories are stated generally at cost, which is not in excess of market. The cost of substantially all U.S. inventories other than the inventories of Saturn Corporation (Saturn) and Hughes is determined by the last-in, first-out (LIFO) method. The cost of non-U.S., Saturn, and Hughes inventories is determined generally by the first-in, first-out (FIFO) or average cost methods.

Instructions
(a) What is meant by "inventories are stated generally at cost, which is not in excess of market"?
(b) The company uses LIFO for most of its inventory. What impact does this have on reported ending inventory if prices are increasing?
(c) General Motors uses different inventory methods for different types of inventory. Why might it do this?

CRITICAL THINKING
....

GROUP DECISION CASE

BYP9–6   On April 10, 1998, fire damaged the office and warehouse of Gibson Company. Most of the accounting records were destroyed but the following account balances were determined as of March 31, 1998: Merchandise Inventory, January 1, 1998, $80,000; Sales (January 1–March 31, 1998), $150,000; Purchases (January 1–March 31, 1998), $84,000.

The company's fiscal year ends on December 31, and it uses a periodic inventory system.

From an analysis of the April bank statement you discover cancelled checks of $4,200 during the period April 1–10 for cash purchases. Deposits during the same period totaled $18,500 of which 60% were collections on accounts receivable and the balance was cash sales.

Correspondence with the company's principal suppliers revealed $12,400 of purchases on account from April 1 to April 10 of which $1,800 was for merchandise in transit on April 10 that was shipped FOB destination.

Correspondence with the company's principal customers produced acknowledgments of credit sales totaling $28,000 from April 1 to April 10. It was estimated that $4,600 of credit sales will never be acknowledged or recovered from customers.

Gibson Company reached an agreement with the insurance company that its fire-loss claim should be based on the average of the gross profit rates for the preceding 2 years. The financial statements for 1996 and 1997 showed the following data:

	1997	1996
Net sales	$600,000	$480,000
Cost of goods purchased	416,000	356,000
Beginning inventory	60,000	40,000
Ending inventory	80,000	60,000

Inventory with a cost of $19,000 was salvaged from the fire.

Instructions
With the class divided into groups, answer the following:
(a) Determine the balances in (1) Sales and (2) Purchases at April 10.
*(b) Determine the average profit rate for the years 1996 and 1997. (*Hint:* Find the gross profit rate for each year and divide the sum by 2.)
*(c) Determine the inventory loss as a result of the fire, using the gross profit method.

COMMUNICATION ACTIVITY

BYP9–7   You are the controller of Small Toys Inc. Joe Paisley, the president, recently mentioned to you that he found an error in the 1998 financial statements which he believes has corrected itself. He determined, in discussions with the Purchasing Department, that 1998 ending inventory was overstated by $1 million. Joe says that the 1999 ending inventory is correct, thus he assumes that 1999 income is correct. Joe says to you, "What happened has happened—there's no point in worrying about it anymore."

Instructions
You conclude that Joe is incorrect. Write a brief, tactful memo to Joe, clarifying the situation.

ETHICS CASE

BYP9–8   Lonergan Wholesale Corp. uses the LIFO method of inventory costing. In the current year, profit at Lonergan is running unusually high. The corporate tax rate is also high this year, but it is scheduled to decline significantly next year. In an effort to lower current year's net income and to take advantage of the changing income tax rate, the president of Lonergan Wholesale instructs the plant accountant to recommend to the purchasing department a large purchase of inventory for delivery 3 days before the end of the year. The price of the inventory to be purchased has doubled during the year and the purchase will represent a major portion of the ending inventory value.

Instructions
   (a) What is the effect of this transaction on this year's and next year's income statement and income tax expense? Why?
   (b) If Lonergan Wholesale had been using the FIFO method of inventory costing, would the president give the same directive?
   (c) Should the plant accountant order the inventory purchase to lower income? What are the ethical implications of this order?

SURFING THE NET

BYP9–9   A company's annual report usually will identify the inventory method used. Knowing that, you can analyze the effects of the inventory method on the income statement and balance sheet.

Address: http://www.cisco.com

Steps:
   1. From Cisco System's homepage, use the **quick search**, type annual report.
   2. Choose **Search**.
   3. Choose **Cisco System Annual Report**.
   4. Choose **Financial Review**.
   5. Use the financial statements and relating notes to the financial statements to answer the questions below.

Instructions
Answer the following questions:
   (a) At Cisco's fiscal year-end, what was the net inventory on the balance sheet?
   (b) How has this changed from the previous fiscal year-end?
   (c) How much of the inventory was finished goods?
   (d) What inventory method do they use?

Answers to Self-Study Questions
1. b   2. d   3. a   4. a   5. b   6. c   7. d   8. c   9. d   10. d   *11. b
12. b   13. d   *14. d

Answer to Kellogg Review It Question 5, p. 385.
Kellogg Company reported inventories of $434,300,000 at December 31, 1997. Kellogg reports in Note 1—Accounting Policies that it uses the **average cost method** in applying product costs to inventories and cost of goods sold.

Remember to go back to the Navigator box on the chapter-opening page and check off your completed work.

FEATURE STORY

On the Books, Your Classroom May Be Worthless

Take a stroll around your campus. Some of those buildings were built before you were born. How much do you think they cost to build? Are they depreciating? Are they appreciating?

These questions are not merely academic. It costs millions of dollars to construct, maintain, and sometimes demolish these campus buildings. Where does the money come from? Partly your tuition, perhaps tax dollars, perhaps from contributions of wealthy alumni, or from long-term borrowing. How these dollars are allocated can depend upon a reasonable estimate of a building's condition, its remaining life—and of course, how much it would cost to replace (its replacement cost).

At Westbrook College in Portland, Maine, Ms. Betty-Ann Doucette, the school's controller, recently researched the age of certain buildings on campus. The reason: a recent Financial Accounting Standards Board rule mandates that private colleges report fixed assets and depreciate them. Ms. Doucette found that some of the college's buildings go back to the nineteenth century. In order to value each building, she tried to find original construction costs and periodic renovations costs, as well as current replacement costs.

"For example, the building I'm in, Goddard Hall, was built in the early part of this century," says Ms. Doucette. "It's now being depreciated over 40 years, and because it's over eighty years old, I show it as fully depreciated." If it is fully depreciated, does that mean it has a zero value? "On the books it says it does," she says. Of course, that doesn't mean it's worthless. An asset can have a zero value on the books yet have a substantial market value.

CHAPTER 10

THE NAVIGATOR ✔

- Understand *Concepts for Review* ☐
- Read *Feature Story* ☐
- Scan *Study Objectives* ☐
- Read *Preview* ☐
- Read text and answer *Before You Go On*
  p. 425 ☐ p. 437 ☐ p. 440 ☐ p. 447 ☐
- Work *Demonstration Problems* ☐
- Review *Summary of Study Objectives* ☐
- Answer *Self-Study Questions* ☐
- Complete assignments ☐

PLANT ASSETS, NATURAL RESOURCES, AND INTANGIBLE ASSETS

STUDY OBJECTIVES

After studying this chapter, you should be able to:

1. *Describe the application of the cost principle to plant assets.*
2. *Explain the concept of depreciation.*
3. *Compute periodic depreciation using different methods.*
4. *Describe the procedure for revising periodic depreciation.*
5. *Distinguish between revenue and capital expenditures and explain the entries for these expenditures.*
6. *Explain how to account for the disposal of a plant asset through retirement, sale, or exchange.*
7. *Identify the basic accounting issues related to natural resources.*
8. *Contrast the accounting for intangible assets with the accounting for plant assets.*
9. *Indicate how plant assets, natural resources, and intangible assets are reported and analyzed.*

THE NAVIGATOR

A s you can see, the accounting for campus buildings at Westbrook College is complex. In this chapter, we explain the application of the cost principle of accounting to buildings like those at Westbrook, as well as to natural resources and intangible assets such as Westbrook's school logo. We also describe the methods that may be used to allocate an asset's cost over its useful life. In addition, the accounting for expenditures incurred during the useful life of assets is discussed. The content and organization of this chapter are as follows:

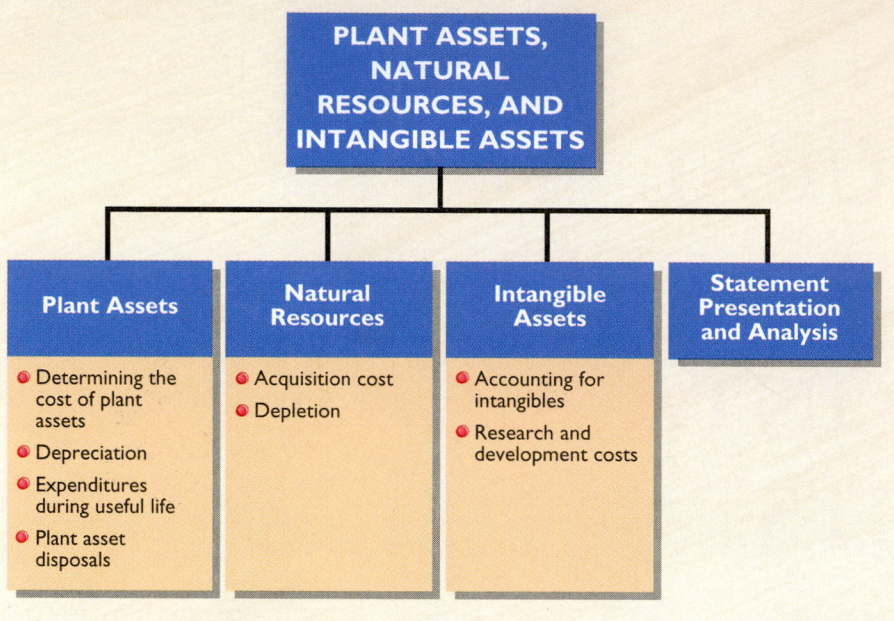

THE NAVIGATOR

SECTION 1 PLANT ASSETS

Plant assets are tangible resources that are used in the operations of the business and are not intended for sale to customers. They are also called **property, plant, and equipment**; **plant and equipment**; or **fixed assets**. These assets are generally long-lived and are expected to provide services to the company for a number of years. Except for land, plant assets decline in service potential over their useful lives.

Many companies have substantial investments in plant assets. In public utility companies, for example, net plant assets (plant assets less accumulated depreciation) often represent more than 70% of total assets. Recently net plant assets were 75% of Citizens Utilities' total assets and 72% of Northern Illinois Gas Company's (NICOR). In other types of companies the percentages of plant assets to total assets were:

McDonald's	86%	Delta Airlines	82%
Marriott Corporation	63%	General Motors Corporation	37%
Caterpillar	26%	Wal-Mart	44%

ILLUSTRATION 10-1

Percentages of plant assets to total assets

In the income statement, the relationship of depreciation expense and maintenance expense to total operating expenses was 10.4% for Consolidated Edison, 9.6% for Delta Airlines, and 6.2% for General Motors.

Plant assets are often subdivided into four classes:

1. **Land**, such as a building site.
2. **Land improvements**, such as driveways, parking lots, fences, and underground sprinkler systems.
3. **Buildings**, such as stores, offices, factories, and warehouses.
4. **Equipment**, such as store check-out counters, cash registers, coolers, office furniture, factory machinery, and delivery equipment.

Like the purchase of a home by an individual, the acquisition of plant assets is an important decision for a business enterprise. It is also important for a business enterprise to (1) keep the asset in good operating condition, (2) replace worn-out or outdated facilities, and (3) expand its productive resources as needed. The decline of rail travel in the United States can be traced in part to the failure of railroad companies to meet the first two conditions. Conversely, the growth of air travel in this country can be attributed in part to the general willingness of airline companies to observe these essential conditions.

DETERMINING THE COST OF PLANT ASSETS

Plant assets are recorded at cost in accordance with the **cost principle** of accounting. Thus the buildings at Westbrook College are recorded at cost. Cost consists of all expenditures necessary to acquire the asset and make it ready for its intended use. For example, the purchase price, freight costs paid by the purchaser, and installation costs are all considered part of the cost of factory machinery.

Cost is measured by the cash paid in a cash transaction or by the cash equivalent price paid when noncash assets are used in payment. **The cash equivalent price is equal to the fair market value of the asset given up or the fair market value of the asset received, whichever is more clearly determinable.** Once cost is established, it becomes the basis of accounting for the plant asset over its useful life. Current market or replacement values are not used after acquisition. The application of the cost principle to each of the major classes of plant assets is explained in the following sections.

1

STUDY

OBJECTIVE

Describe the application of the cost principle to plant assets.

INTERNATIONAL NOTE

The United Kingdom (UK) is more flexible regarding asset valuation. Most companies in the UK make occasional revaluations to fair value when they believe this information is more relevant. Other examples of countries that permit revaluations are Switzerland and the Netherlands.

Land

The cost of land includes (1) the cash purchase price, (2) closing costs such as title and attorney's fees, (3) real estate brokers' commissions, and (4) accrued property taxes and other liens on the land assumed by the purchaser. For example, if the cash price is $50,000 and the purchaser agrees to pay accrued taxes of $5,000, the cost of the land is $55,000.

All necessary costs incurred in making land **ready for its intended use** are debited to the Land account. When vacant land is acquired, these costs include expenditures for clearing, draining, filling, and grading. Sometimes the land has a building on it that must be removed to make the site suitable for construction of a new building. In this case, all demolition and removal costs less any proceeds from salvaged materials are chargeable to the Land account. To illustrate, assume that Hayes Manufacturing Company acquires real estate at a cash cost of $100,000. The property contains an old warehouse that is razed at a net cost of $6,000 ($7,500 in costs less $1,500 proceeds from salvaged materials). Additional expenditures consist of the attorney's fee, $1,000, and the real estate broker's commission, $8,000. Given these factors, the cost of the land is $115,000, computed as follows:

ILLUSTRATION 10-2

Computation of cost of land

Land	
Cash price of property	$100,000
Net removal cost of warehouse	6,000
Attorney's fee	1,000
Real estate broker's commission	8,000
Cost of land	**$115,000**

In recording the acquisition, Land is debited for $115,000 and Cash is credited for $115,000.

Land Improvements

The cost of land improvements includes all expenditures necessary to make the improvements ready for their intended use. For example, the cost of a new company parking lot will include the amount paid for paving, fencing, and lighting. These improvements have limited useful lives and their maintenance and replacement are the responsibility of the company. Thus, these costs are debited to Land Improvements and are depreciated over the useful lives of the improvements.

Buildings

All necessary expenditures relating to the purchase or construction of a building are charged to the Buildings account. When a building is purchased, such costs include the **purchase price, closing costs (attorney's fees, title insurance, etc.), and real estate broker's commission**. Costs to make the building ready for its intended use consist of **expenditures for remodeling rooms and offices and replacing or repairing the roof, floors, electrical wiring, and plumbing**.

When a new building is constructed, such as a new science building by Westbrook College, cost consists of the contract price plus payments made by the owner for architects' fees, building permits, and excavation costs. In addition, interest costs incurred to finance the project are included in the cost of the asset when a significant period of time is required to get the asset ready for use. In these circumstances, interest costs are considered as necessary as materials and labor. The inclusion of interest costs in the cost of a constructed building is **limited to the construction period**. When construction has been completed, subsequent interest payments on funds borrowed to finance the construction are debited to Interest Expense.

Equipment

The cost of equipment consists of the **cash purchase price, sales taxes, freight charges, and insurance during transit paid by the purchaser.** It also includes **expenditures required in assembling, installing, and testing the unit.** However, motor vehicle licenses and accident insurance on company trucks and cars are expensed as incurred, because they represent annual recurring expenditures and do not benefit future periods.

HELPFUL HINT
Two criteria apply in determining cost here: (1) the frequency of the cost—one-time or recurring, and (2) the benefit period—life of asset or one year.

To illustrate, assume that the Lenard Company purchases a delivery truck at a cash price of $22,000. Related expenditures consist of sales taxes $1,320, painting and lettering $500, motor vehicle license $80, and a 3-year accident insurance policy $1,600. The cost of the delivery truck is $23,820, computed as follows:

Delivery Truck	
Cash price	$22,000
Sales taxes	1,320
Painting and lettering	500
Cost of delivery truck	$23,820

ILLUSTRATION 10-3
Computation of cost of delivery truck

The motor vehicle license is expensed when incurred and the insurance policy is a prepaid asset. Thus, the summary entry to record the purchase of the truck and related expenditures is:

Delivery Truck	23,820	
License Expense	80	
Prepaid Insurance	1,600	
Cash		25,500
(To record purchase of delivery truck and related expenditures)		

A	=	L	+	OE
+23,820				−80
+1,600				
−25,500				

For another example, assume the Merten Company purchases factory machinery at a cash price of $50,000. Related expenditures consist of sales taxes $3,000, insurance during shipping $500, and installation and testing $1,000. The cost of the factory machinery is $54,500 computed as follows:

Factory Machinery	
Cash price	$50,000
Sales taxes	3,000
Insurance during shipping	500
Installation and testing	1,000
Cost of factory machinery	$54,500

ILLUSTRATION 10-4
Computation of cost of factory machinery

The summary entry to record the purchase and related expenditures is:

Factory Machinery	54,500	
Cash		54,500
(To record purchase of factory machine)		

A	=	L	+	OE
+54,500				
−54,500				

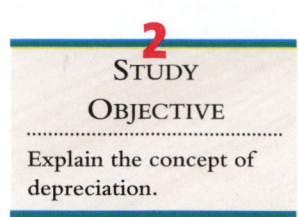

DEPRECIATION

As explained in Chapter 3, **depreciation is the process of allocating to expense the cost of a plant asset over its useful (service) life in a rational and systematic manner.** Cost allocation is designed to provide for the proper matching of expenses with revenues in accordance with the matching principle (see Illustration 10-5).

ILLUSTRATION 10-5

Depreciation as an allocation concept

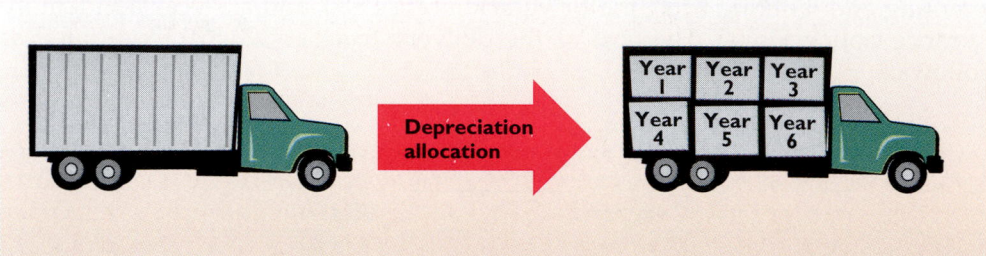

HELPFUL HINT

Remember that depreciation is the process of allocating cost over the useful life of an asset. It is not a measure of value.

HELPFUL HINT

Land does not depreciate because it does not wear out.

Depreciation is a process of cost allocation, not a process of asset valuation. Accountants make no attempt to measure the change in an asset's market value during ownership, because plant assets are not held for resale. Thus, the **book value** (cost less accumulated depreciation) of a plant asset may differ significantly from its market value. This is why Goddard Hall, in the opening story, can have zero book value and still have substantial market value.

Depreciation applies to three classes of plant assets: land improvements, buildings, and equipment. Each of these classes is considered to be a **depreciable asset**, because the usefulness to the company and revenue-producing ability of each class will decline over the asset's useful life. Depreciation does not apply to land because its usefulness and revenue-producing ability generally remain intact as long as the asset is owned. In fact, in many cases, the usefulness of land is greater over time because of the scarcity of good land sites. Thus, **land is not a depreciable asset**.

During a depreciable asset's useful life its revenue-producing ability will decline because of **wear and tear**. A delivery truck that has been driven 100,000 miles will be less useful to a company than one driven only 800 miles. Similarly, trucks and planes exposed to snow and salt will deteriorate faster than equipment that is not exposed to these elements.

A decline in revenue-producing ability may also occur because of **obsolescence**. Obsolescence is the process of becoming out of date before the asset physically wears out. The rerouting of major airlines from Chicago's Midway Airport to Chicago-O'Hare International Airport because Midway's runways were too short for jumbo jets is an example. Likewise, diesel train engines made coal-burning locomotives obsolete, and municipal buses sent streetcars to the scrap heap.

Recognition of depreciation does not result in the accumulation of cash for the replacement of the asset. The balance in Accumulated Depreciation represents the total cost that has been charged to expense; it is not a cash fund.

Factors in Computing Depreciation

Three factors affect the computation of depreciation, as shown in Illustration 10-6.

1. **Cost.** Considerations affecting the cost of a depreciable asset have been explained earlier in this chapter. You will recall that plant assets are recorded at cost, in accordance with the cost principle of accounting.

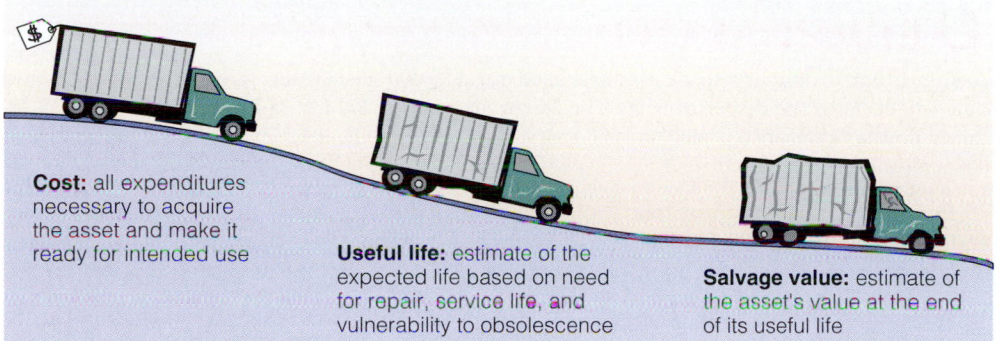

ILLUSTRATION 10-6

Three factors in computing depreciation

HELPFUL HINT
Depreciation expense is reported on the income statement, and accumulated depreciation is reported as a deduction from plant assets on the balance sheet.

2. **Useful life.** Useful life is an estimate of the expected productive life, also called service life, of the asset. Useful life may be expressed in terms of time, units of activity such as machine hours, or in units of output. Like salvage value, useful life is an estimate. In making the estimate, management should consider such factors as the intended use of the asset, its expected repair and maintenance policies, and its vulnerability to obsolescence. The company's past experience with similar assets is often helpful in deciding on expected useful life.

3. **Salvage value.** Salvage value is an estimate of the asset's value at the end of its useful life. The value may be based on the asset's worth as scrap or salvage or on its expected trade-in value. Salvage value is an estimate. In making the estimate, management should consider how it plans to dispose of the asset and its experience with similar assets.

ALTERNATIVE TERMINOLOGY
Another term sometimes used for salvage value is *residual value.*

ACCOUNTING IN ACTION
Business Insight

Not all companies use the same useful life for assets. Compare the useful lives used by the Big Three automakers, for example: At one time General Motors depreciated its machinery over 10 years, compared to Ford's 12 years and Chrysler's 11 years. GM also depreciated its buildings over 28 years while Ford used 30 years and Chrysler used 26 years. General Motors also depreciated its dies and equipment used to manufacture car bodies about twice as fast as Ford and three times as fast as Chrysler. Now GM has changed and aligned itself with its principal competitors by applying more liberal depreciation policies that have increased annual income. Should companies in the same industry be required to use the same useful life for the same type of assets?

BEFORE YOU GO ON . . .
Review It

1. What are plant assets? What are the major classes of plant assets? How is the cost principle applied to accounting for plant assets?
2. What is the relationship, if any, of depreciation to (a) cost allocation, (b) asset valuation, and (c) cash accumulation?
3. Explain the factors that affect the computation of depreciation.
4. Where does Kellogg report the detail about its "Property, net" of $2,773.3 million? What classifications and amounts does Kellogg report in the details of its "Property, net" for 1997? The answer to this question is provided on page 467.

Do It

Assume that a delivery truck is purchased for $15,000 cash, plus sales taxes of $900 and delivery costs to the dealer of $500. The buyer also pays $200 for painting and lettering, $600 for an annual insurance policy, and $80 for a motor vehicle license. Explain how each of these costs would be accounted for.

Reasoning: The cost principle applies to all expenditures made in order to get delivery equipment ready for its intended use. The principle does not apply to operating costs incurred during the useful life of the equipment, such as gas and oil, motor tune-ups, and insurance.

Solution: The first four payments ($15,000, $900, $500, and $200) are considered to be expenditures necessary to make the truck ready for its intended use. Thus, the cost of the truck is $16,600. The payments for insurance and the license are considered to be operating expenses incurred during the useful life of the asset.

Related exercise material: BE10–1, BE10–2, E10–1, and E10–2.

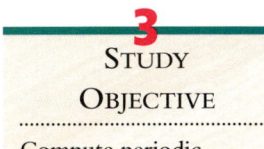

3

STUDY

OBJECTIVE

Compute periodic depreciation using different methods.

Depreciation Methods

Depreciation is generally computed using one of the following methods:

1. Straight-line
2. Units-of-activity
3. Declining-balance

Like the inventory methods discussed in Chapter 9, each method is acceptable under generally accepted accounting principles. Management selects the method or methods it believes to be appropriate in the circumstances. The objective is to select the method that best measures the asset's contribution to revenue over its useful life. Once a method is chosen, it should be applied consistently over the useful life of the asset. Consistency enhances the comparability of financial statements.

To facilitate the comparison of the three depreciation methods, we will base all computations on the following data applicable to a small delivery truck purchased by Barb's Florists on January 1, 1999:

ILLUSTRATION 10-7

Delivery truck data

Cost	$13,000
Expected salvage value	$ 1,000
Estimated useful life in years	5
Estimated useful life in miles	100,000

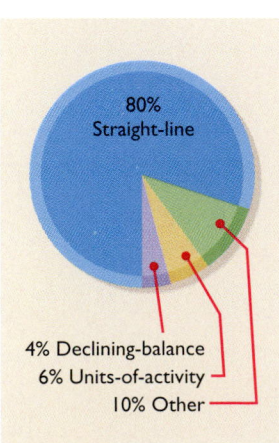

ILLUSTRATION 10-8

Use of depreciation methods

Depreciation affects the balance sheet through accumulated depreciation and the income statement through depreciation expense. Illustration 10-8 shows the use of the different depreciation methods in 600 of the largest companies in the United States.

Straight-Line

Under the **straight-line method**, depreciation is the same for each year of the asset's useful life. It is measured solely by the passage of time. In order to compute depreciation expense, it is necessary to determine depreciable cost. **Depreciable cost** is the cost of the asset less its salvage value. It is the total amount subject to depreciation. Depreciable cost is then divided by the asset's useful life to determine depreciation expense. The formula and computation of depreciation expense in the first year for Barb's Florists are shown in Illustration 10-9.

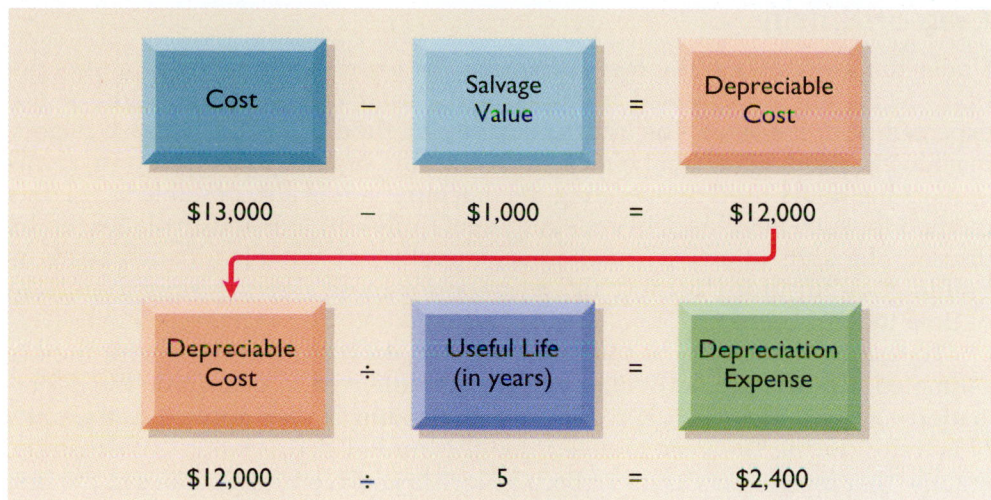

ILLUSTRATION 10-9

Formula for straight-line method

Alternatively, we also can compute an annual rate at which the delivery truck is being depreciated. In this case, the rate is 20% (100% ÷ 5 years). When an annual rate is used under the straight-line method, the percentage rate is applied to the depreciable cost of the asset, as shown in the following **depreciation schedule**:

BARB'S FLORISTS

Year	Computation Depreciable Cost	×	Depreciation Rate	=	Annual Depreciation Expense	End of Year Accumulated Depreciation	Book Value
1999	$12,000		20%		$2,400	$ 2,400	$10,600*
2000	12,000		20		2,400	4,800	8,200
2001	12,000		20		2,400	7,200	5,800
2002	12,000		20		2,400	9,600	3,400
2003	12,000		20		2,400	12,000	1,000

*($13,000 − $2,400).

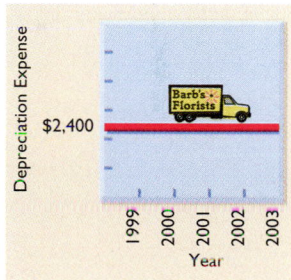

ILLUSTRATION 10-10

Straight-line depreciation schedule

Note that the depreciation expense of $2,400 is the same each year, and that the book value at the end of the useful life is equal to the estimated $1,000 salvage value.

What happens when an asset is purchased **during** the year, rather than on January 1, as in our example? In that case, it is necessary to **prorate the annual depreciation** for the proportion of time used. If Barb's Florists had purchased the delivery truck on April 1, 1999, the depreciation for 1999 would be $1,800 ($12,000 × 20% × 9/12 of a year).

The straight-line method predominates in practice, as shown in Illustration 10-8. For example, such large companies as Campbell Soup, Marriott Corporation, and General Mills use the straight-line method. It is simple to apply, and it matches expenses with revenues appropriately when the use of the asset is reasonably uniform throughout the service life. In the opening story, Westbrook College is probably using the straight-line method of depreciation for its buildings.

ALTERNATIVE TERMINOLOGY
Another term often used is the *units-of-production method.*

HELPFUL HINT
Depreciation stops when the asset's book value equals expected salvage value.

Units-of-Activity

Under the **units-of-activity method**, instead of expressing the life as a time period, useful life is expressed in terms of the total units of production or use expected from the asset. The units-of-activity method is ideally suited to factory machinery: production can be measured in terms of units of output or in terms of machine hours used in operating the machinery. It is also possible to use this method for such items as delivery equipment (miles driven) and airplanes (hours in use). The units-of-activity method is generally not suitable for such assets as buildings or furniture, because depreciation for these assets is more a function of time than of use.

To use this method, the total units of activity for the entire useful life are estimated, the amount is divided into depreciable cost to determine the depreciation cost per unit. The depreciation cost per unit is then applied to the units of activity during the year to determine the annual depreciation. To illustrate, assume that the delivery truck of Barb's Florists is driven 15,000 miles in the first year. The formula and computation of depreciation expense in the first year are:

ILLUSTRATION 10-11

Formula for units-of-activity method

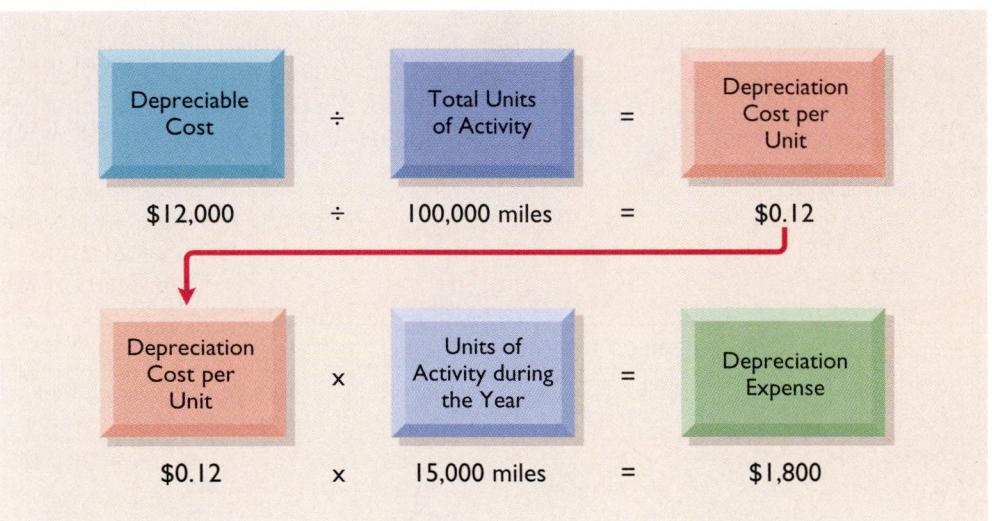

The depreciation schedule, using assumed mileage data, is as follows:

ILLUSTRATION 10-12

Units-of-activity depreciation schedule

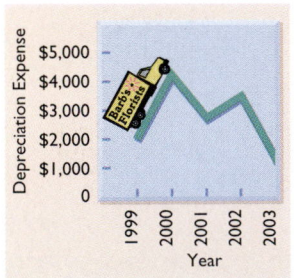

		BARB'S FLORISTS				
		Computation		**Annual**	**End of Year**	
Year	**Units of Activity**	**×** **Depreciation Cost/Unit**	**=**	**Depreciation Expense**	**Accumulated Depreciation**	**Book Value**
1999	15,000	$.12		**$1,800**	$ 1,800	$11,200*
2000	30,000	.12		**3,600**	5,400	7,600
2001	20,000	.12		**2,400**	7,800	5,200
2002	25,000	.12		**3,000**	10,800	2,200
2003	10,000	.12		**1,200**	12,000	1,000

*($13,000 − $1,800).

The units-of-activity method is not nearly as popular as the straight-line method (see Illustration 10-8), primarily because it is often difficult to make a reasonable estimate of total activity. However, this method is used by some very large companies, such as Standard Oil Company of California and Boise Cascade Corporation. When the productivity of the asset varies significantly from one period to another, the units-of-activity method results in the best matching of expenses with revenues. This method is easy to apply when assets are purchased during the year. In such a case, the productivity of the asset for the partial year is used in computing the depreciation.

Declining-Balance

The **declining-balance method** produces a decreasing annual depreciation expense over the useful life of the asset. The method is so named because the computation of periodic depreciation is based on a **declining book value** (cost less accumulated depreciation) of the asset. Annual depreciation expense is computed by multiplying the book value at the beginning of the year by the declining-balance depreciation rate. **The depreciation rate remains constant from year to year, but the book value to which the rate is applied declines each year.**

Book value for the first year is the cost of the asset, because the balance in accumulated depreciation at the beginning of the asset's useful life is zero. In subsequent years, book value is the difference between cost and accumulated depreciation at the beginning of the year. **Unlike the other depreciation methods, salvage value is ignored in determining the amount to which the declining balance rate is applied.** Salvage value, however, does limit the total depreciation that can be taken. Depreciation stops when the asset's book value equals expected salvage value.

A common declining-balance rate is double the straight-line rate. As a result, the method is often referred to as the **double-declining-balance method**. If Barb's Florists uses the double-declining-balance method, the depreciation rate is 40% (2 × the straight-line rate of 20%). The formula and computation of depreciation for the first year on the delivery truck are:

> **HELPFUL HINT**
> Book value is variable and the depreciation rate is constant for this method.

Book Value at Beginning of Year	×	Declining-Balance Rate	=	Depreciation Expense
$13,000	×	40%	=	$5,200

ILLUSTRATION 10-13

Formula for declining-balance method

The depreciation schedule under this method is as follows:

ILLUSTRATION 10-14

Double-declining-balance depreciation schedule

	BARB'S FLORISTS				
	Computation		**Annual**	**End of Year**	
Year	**Book Value Beginning of Year** ×	**Depreciation Rate** =	**Depreciation Expense**	**Accumulated Depreciation**	**Book Value**
1999	$13,000	40%	**$5,200**	$ 5,200	$7,800
2000	7,800	40	**3,120**	8,320	4,680
2001	4,680	40	**1,872**	10,192	2,808
2002	2,808	40	**1,123**	11,315	1,685
2003	1,685	40	**685***	12,000	**1,000**

*Computation of $674 ($1,685 × 40%) is adjusted to $685 in order for book value to equal salvage value.

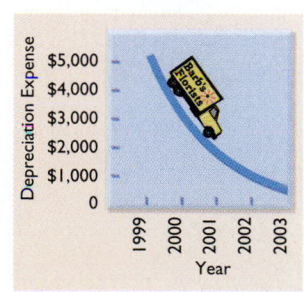

HELPFUL HINT
The method to be used for an asset that is expected to be more productive in the first half of its useful life is the declining-balance method.

You can see that the delivery equipment is 69% depreciated ($8,320 ÷ $12,000) at the end of the second year. Under the straight-line method it would be depreciated 40% ($4,800 ÷ $12,000) at that time. Because the declining-balance method produces higher depreciation expense in the early years than in the later years, it is considered an **accelerated-depreciation method**. The declining-balance method is compatible with the matching principle. The higher depreciation expense in early years is matched with the higher benefits received in these years. Conversely, lower depreciation expense is recognized in later years when the asset's contribution to revenue is less. Also, some assets lose usefulness rapidly because of obsolescence. In these cases, the declining-balance method provides a more appropriate depreciation amount.

When an asset is purchased during the year, it is necessary to prorate the declining-balance depreciation in the first year on a time basis. For example, if Barb's Florists had purchased the delivery equipment on April 1, 1999, depreciation for 1999 would become $3,900 ($13,000 × 40% × 9/12). The book value for computing depreciation in 2000 then becomes $9,100 ($13,000 − $3,900), and the 2000 depreciation is $3,640 ($9,100 × 40%).

ACCOUNTING IN ACTION
Business Insight

Why does Gingiss Formal Wear have 70 depreciation accounts and use the units-of-activity method for its tuxedos? The reason is that Gingiss wants to track wear and tear on each of its 16,000 dinner jackets individually. So each tuxedo has a bar code, like a box of cereal at the supermarket. When a tux is rented, a clerk runs its code across an electronic scanner. At year-end, the computer adds up the total rentals for each of 15 styles, then divides by expected total use to compute the rate. For instance, on one dolphin-gray tux, Gingiss expects a life of 30 rentals. In a recent year the tux was rented 13 times. So depreciation that period was 43% (13 ÷ 30) of the total cost.

Comparison of Methods

A comparison of annual and total depreciation expense under each of the three methods is shown for Barb's Florists in Illustration 10-15.

ILLUSTRATION 10-15

Comparison of depreciation methods

Year	Straight-Line	Units-of-Activity	Declining-Balance
1999	$ 2,400	$ 1,800	$ 5,200
2000	2,400	3,600	3,120
2001	2,400	2,400	1,872
2002	2,400	3,000	1,123
2003	2,400	1,200	685
	$12,000	**$12,000**	**$12,000**

Observe that periodic depreciation varies considerably among the methods, but total depreciation is the same for the 5-year period. Each method is acceptable in accounting, because each recognizes the decline in service potential of the asset in a rational and systematic manner. The depreciation expense pattern under each method is presented graphically in Illustration 10-16.

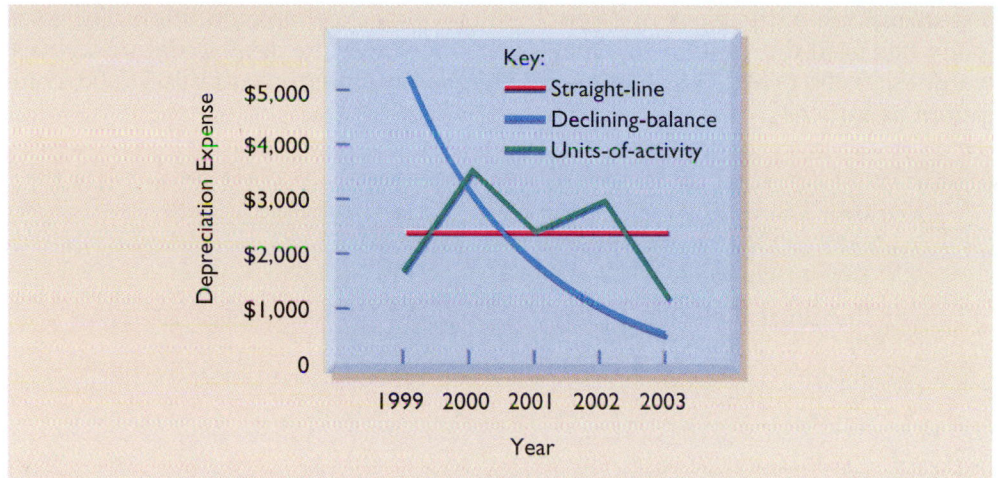

ILLUSTRATION 10-16

Patterns of depreciation

Depreciation and Income Taxes

The Internal Revenue Service (IRS) allows corporate taxpayers to deduct depreciation expense when computing taxable income. However, the IRS does not require the taxpayer to use the same depreciation method on the tax return that is used in preparing financial statements. Consequently, many corporations use straight-line in their financial statements to maximize net income, and at the same time, a special accelerated-depreciation method is generally used on their tax returns to minimize their income taxes. Taxpayers must use on their tax returns either the straight-line method or a special accelerated-depreciation method called **Modified Accelerated Cost Recovery System** (MACRS).

INTERNATIONAL NOTE

In Germany, tax laws have a strong influence on financial accounting. Depreciation expense determined by the tax code must also be used for preparing financial statements.

TECHNOLOGY IN ACTION

Software packages to account for plant assets exist for both large and small computer systems. Even the least sophisticated packages can maintain a control and subsidiary ledger for plant assets and make the necessary depreciation computations and adjusting entries. Many packages also maintain separate depreciation schedules for both financial statement and income tax purposes, with reconciliations made for any differences.

Revising Periodic Depreciation

Depreciation is one example of the estimation procedures that are part of the accounting process. Annual depreciation expense should be reviewed periodically by management. If wear and tear or obsolescence indicate that annual depreciation is inadequate or excessive, a change in the amount should be made.

When a change in an estimate is required, the change is made in **current and future years but not to prior periods**. Thus, (1) there is no correction of previously recorded depreciation expense, and (2) depreciation expense for current and future years is revised. The rationale—continual restatement of prior periods would adversely affect the reader's confidence in financial statements.

To determine the new annual depreciation expense, we compute the asset's depreciable cost at the time of the revision and allocate it to the remaining useful life. To illustrate, assume that Barb's Florists decides on January 1, 2002, to extend

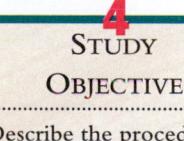

4

STUDY OBJECTIVE

Describe the procedure for revising periodic depreciation.

the useful life of the truck one year because of its excellent condition. The company has used the straight-line method to depreciate the asset to date, and book value is $5,800 ($13,000 − $7,200). The new annual depreciation is $1,600, computed as follows:

ILLUSTRATION 10-17

Revised depreciation computation

Book value, 1/1/02	$5,800
Less: Salvage value	1,000
Depreciable cost	$4,800
Remaining useful life	3 years (2002–2004)
Revised annual depreciation ($4,800 ÷ 3)	**$1,600**

HELPFUL HINT

Use a step-by-step approach: (1) determine new depreciable cost; (2) divide by remaining useful life.

On January 1, 2002, or at any other time, Barb's Florists makes no entry for the change in estimate. On December 31, 2002, during the preparation of adjusting entries, it would record depreciation expense of $1,600. Significant changes in estimates must be described in the financial statements.

EXPENDITURES DURING USEFUL LIFE

5
STUDY OBJECTIVE

Distinguish between revenue and capital expenditures and explain the entries for these expenditures.

During the useful life of a plant asset a company may incur costs for ordinary repairs, additions, and improvements. **Ordinary repairs** are expenditures to maintain the operating efficiency and expected productive life of the unit. They usually are fairly small amounts that occur frequently throughout the asset's service life. Motor tune-ups and oil changes, the painting of buildings, and the replacing of worn-out gears on factory machinery are examples. They are debited to Repair (or Maintenance) Expense as incurred. Because they are immediately charged against revenues as an expense, these costs are often referred to as **revenue expenditures**

Additions and improvements are costs incurred to increase the operating efficiency, productive capacity, or expected useful life of the plant asset. These expenditures are usually material in amount and occur infrequently during the period of ownership. Expenditures for additions and improvements increase the company's investment in productive facilities and are generally debited to the plant asset affected. Accordingly, they are often referred to as **capital expenditures**. Most major U.S. corporations disclose the amount of their annual capital expenditures. In a recent year, both IBM and General Motors reported capital expenditures slightly in excess of $6 billion. The accounting for capital expenditures varies depending on the nature of the expenditure.

PLANT ASSET DISPOSALS

6
STUDY OBJECTIVE

Explain how to account for the disposal of a plant asset through retirement, sale, or exchange.

Plant assets of various types may be disposed of in three ways, as shown in Illustration 10-18. Whatever the method of disposal, at the time of disposal it is necessary to determine the book value of the plant asset. The book value is the difference between the cost of the plant asset and the accumulated depreciation to date. If the disposal occurs at any time during the year, depreciation for the fraction of the year to the date of disposal must be recorded. The book value is then eliminated by debiting Accumulated Depreciation for the total depreciation to the date of disposal and crediting the asset account for the cost of the asset.

In this section we will examine the accounting for each of the three methods of plant asset disposal.

Retirement
Equipment is scrapped or discarded.

Sale
Equipment is sold to another party.

Exchange
Existing equipment is traded for new equipment.

ILLUSTRATION 10-18

Methods of plant asset disposal

Retirement of Plant Assets

To illustrate the accounting for a retirement of plant assets, assume that Hobart Enterprises retires its computer printers, which cost $32,000. The accumulated depreciation on these printers is also $32,000; the equipment, therefore, is fully depreciated (zero book value). The entry to record this retirement is as follows:

Accumulated Depreciation—Printing Equipment	32,000	
Printing Equipment		32,000
(To record retirement of fully depreciated equipment)		

A	=	L	+	OE
+ 32,000				
− 32,000				

What happens if a fully depreciated plant asset is still useful to the company? In this case, the plant asset and the related accumulated depreciation continue to be reported on the balance sheet without further depreciation or adjustment until the asset is retired. Reporting the asset and related accumulated depreciation on the balance sheet informs the reader of the financial statements that the asset is still being used by the company. However, once an asset is fully depreciated, even if it is still being used, no additional depreciation should be taken. In no situation can the accumulated depreciation on the plant asset exceed its cost.

If a plant asset is retired before it is fully depreciated, and no scrap or salvage value is received, a loss on disposal occurs. For example, assume that Sunset Company discards delivery equipment that cost $18,000 and has accumulated depreciation of $14,000 at the date of retirement. The entry is as follows:

HELPFUL HINT
When a plant asset is disposed of, all amounts related to the asset must be removed from the accounts. This includes the original cost in the asset account and the total depreciation to date in the accumulated depreciation account.

Accumulated Depreciation—Delivery Equipment	14,000	
Loss on Disposal	4,000	
Delivery Equipment		18,000
(To record retirement of delivery equipment at a loss)		

A	=	L	+	OE
+ 14,000				− 4,000
− 18,000				

The loss on disposal is reported in the Other Expenses and Losses section of the income statement.

Sale of Plant Assets

In a disposal by sale, the book value of the asset is compared with the proceeds received from the sale. **If the proceeds of the sale exceed the book value of the plant asset, a gain on disposal occurs. If the proceeds of the sale are less than the book value of the plant asset sold, a loss on disposal occurs.**

Only by coincidence will the book value and the fair market value of the asset be the same at the time the asset is sold. Gains and losses on sales of plant assets are, therefore, quite common. As an example, Delta Airlines, Inc. reported a $94,343,000 gain on the sale of five Boeing B-727-200 aircraft and five Lockheed L-1011-1 aircraft.

Gain on Disposal

To illustrate a gain, assume that on July 1, 1999, Wright Company sells office furniture for $16,000 cash. The office furniture originally cost $60,000 and as of January 1, 1999, had accumulated depreciation of $41,000. Depreciation for the first 6 months of 1999 is $8,000. The entry to record depreciation expense and update accumulated depreciation to July 1 is as follows:

A	=	L	+	OE
−8,000				−8,000

July 1	Depreciation Expense		8,000	
	Accumulated Depreciation—Office Furniture			8,000
	(To record depreciation expense for the first			
	six months of 1999)			

After the accumulated depreciation balance is updated, a gain on disposal of $5,000 is computed:

ILLUSTRATION 10-19

Computation of gain on disposal

Cost of office furniture	$60,000
Less: Accumulated depreciation ($41,000 + $8,000)	49,000
Book value at date of disposal	11,000
Proceeds from sale	16,000
Gain on disposal	**$ 5,000**

The entry to record the sale and the gain on disposal is as follows:

A	=	L	+	OE
+16,000				+5,000
+49,000				
−60,000				

July 1	Cash		16,000	
	Accumulated Depreciation—Office Furniture		49,000	
	Office Furniture			60,000
	Gain on Disposal			5,000
	(To record sale of office furniture at a gain)			

The gain on disposal is reported in the Other Revenues and Gains section of the income statement.

Loss on Disposal

Assume that instead of selling the office furniture for $16,000, Wright sells it for $9,000. In this case, a loss of $2,000 is computed:

ILLUSTRATION 10-20

Computation of loss on disposal

Cost of office furniture	$60,000
Less: Accumulated depreciation	49,000
Book value at date of disposal	11,000
Proceeds from sale	9,000
Loss on disposal	**$ 2,000**

The entry to record the sale and the loss on disposal is as follows:

July 1	Cash	9,000		
	Accumulated Depreciation—Office Furniture	49,000		
	Loss on Disposal	2,000		
	Office Furniture		60,000	
	(To record sale of office furniture at a loss)			

A	=	L	+	OE
+9,000				−2,000
+49,000				
−60,000				

The loss on disposal is reported in the Other Expenses and Losses section of the income statement.

Exchange of Plant Assets

Plant assets may also be disposed of through exchange. Exchanges can be for either similar or dissimilar assets. Because exchanges of similar assets are more common, they are discussed here.

    An exchange of similar assets involves assets of the same type. This occurs, for example, when old delivery equipment is exchanged for new delivery equipment or when old office furniture is exchanged for new office furniture. In an exchange of similar assets, the new asset performs the **same function** as the old asset.

    In exchanges of similar plant assets, it is necessary to determine (1) the cost of the asset acquired and (2) the gain or loss on the asset given up. Because a noncash asset is given up in the exchange, cost is equal to the **cash equivalent price** paid. Cost, therefore, is the fair market value of the asset given up plus the cash paid. The gain or loss on disposal is the **difference between the fair market value and the book value of the asset given up**. These determinations and the resulting accounting entries are explained and illustrated below.

Loss Treatment

When a loss occurs on the exchange of similar assets, it is recognized immediately. To illustrate the accounting for a loss, assume that Roland Company exchanged old office equipment for similar new office equipment. The book value of the old office equipment is $26,000 (cost $70,000 less accumulated depreciation $44,000), its fair market value is $10,000, and cash of $81,000 is paid. The cost of the new office equipment, $91,000, is computed as follows:

Fair market value of old office equipment	$10,000
Cash	81,000
Cost of new office equipment	**$91,000**

ILLUSTRATION 10-21

Computation of cost of new office equipment

    Through this exchange, a loss on disposal of $16,000 is incurred. A loss results when the book value is greater than the fair market value of the asset given up. The computation is as follows:

Book value of old office equipment ($70,000 − $44,000)	$26,000
Fair market value of old office equipment	10,000
Loss on disposal	**$16,000**

ILLUSTRATION 10-22

Computation of loss on disposal

In recording an exchange at a loss it is necessary to (1) eliminate the book value of the asset given up, (2) record the cost of the asset acquired, and (3) recognize the loss on disposal. The entry for the Roland Company is as follows:

A	=	L	+	OE
+91,000				−16,000
+44,000				
−70,000				
−81,000				

Office Equipment (new)	91,000	
Accumulated Depreciation—Office Equipment (old)	44,000	
Loss on Disposal	16,000	
Office Equipment (old)		70,000
Cash		81,000
(To record exchange of old office equipment for similar new equipment)		

Gain Treatment

When a gain occurs on the exchange of similar assets, it is not recognized immediately. Instead, the gain is deferred by reducing the cost basis of the new asset. Thus, in determining the cost of the asset acquired, it is necessary to compute the **cost before deferral of the gain** and then the **cost after deferral of the gain**.

To illustrate the accounting for similar assets, assume that Mark's Express Delivery decides to exchange its old delivery equipment plus cash of $3,000 for new delivery equipment. At this time, the book value of the old delivery equipment is $12,000 (cost $40,000 less accumulated depreciation $28,000). In addition, it is determined that the fair market value of the old delivery equipment is $19,000.

The cost of the new asset received (before deferral of the gain) is equal to the **fair market value of the old asset exchanged plus any cash or other consideration given up**. The cost of the new delivery equipment (before deferral of the gain) is $22,000, computed as follows:

HELPFUL HINT

Gains on the exchange of similar assets are not recognized because the earnings process is not considered completed. Losses, however, are recognized, to be conservative.

ILLUSTRATION 10-23

Cost of new equipment (before deferral of gain)

Fair market value of old delivery equipment	$19,000
Cash	3,000
Cost of new delivery equipment (before deferral of gain)	**$22,000**

A gain results when the fair market value is greater than the book value of the asset given up. For Mark's Express, there is a gain of $7,000, computed as follows, on the disposal:

ILLUSTRATION 10-24

Computation of gain on disposal

Fair market value of old delivery equipment	$19,000
Book value of old delivery equipment ($40,000 − $28,000)	12,000
Gain on disposal	**$ 7,000**

The $7,000 gain on disposal is then offset against the $22,000 cost of the new delivery equipment. The result is a $15,000 cost of the new delivery equipment, after deferral of the gain, as shown in Illustration 10-25.

ILLUSTRATION 10-25

Cost of new equipment (after deferral of gain)

Cost of new delivery equipment (before deferral of gain)	$22,000
Less: Gain on disposal	7,000
Cost of new delivery equipment (after deferral of gain)	**$15,000**

The entry to record the exchange is as follows:

Delivery Equipment (new)	15,000	
Accumulated Depreciation—Delivery Equipment (old)	28,000	
Delivery Equipment (old)		40,000
Cash		3,000
(To record exchange of old delivery equipment for		
similar new delivery equipment)		

A	=	L	+	OE
+15,000				
+28,000				
−40,000				
−3,000				

This entry does not eliminate the gain; it just postpones or defers it to future periods. The deferred gain of $7,000 reduces the $22,000 cost to $15,000. As a result, net income in future periods increases because depreciation expense on the newly acquired delivery equipment is less by $7,000.

Summarizing, the rules for accounting for exchanges of similar assets are as follows:

Type of Event	Recognition
Loss	Recognize immediately by debiting Loss on Disposal
Gain	Defer and reduce cost of new asset

ILLUSTRATION 10-26

Accounting rules for plant exchanges

BEFORE YOU GO ON . . .

Review It

1. What are the formulas for computing annual depreciation under each of the depreciation methods?
2. How do the methods differ in terms of their effects on annual depreciation over the useful life of the asset?
3. Are revisions of periodic depreciation made to prior periods? Explain.
4. How does a capital expenditure differ from a revenue expenditure?
5. What is the proper accounting for the retirement and sale of plant assets?
6. What is the proper accounting for the exchange of similar plant assets?

Do It

Overland Trucking has an old truck that cost $30,000, has accumulated depreciation of $16,000, and a fair value of $17,000. It has a choice of either selling the truck for cash of $17,000 or exchanging the old truck and $3,000 cash for a new truck. What is the entry that Overland Trucking would record under each option?

Reasoning: Gains and losses on the sale or exchange of plant assets are determined by the difference between the book value and the fair value of the company's asset. Gains on the exchange of similar assets are deferred.

Solution:
Sale of truck for cash:

Cash	17,000	
Accumulated Depreciation—Truck (old)	16,000	
Truck (old)		30,000
Gain on Disposal [$17,000 − ($30,000 − $16,000)]		3,000
(To record sale of truck at a gain)		

Exchange of old truck and cash for new truck:

Truck (new)*	17,000	
Accumulated Depreciation—Truck (old)	16,000	
Truck (old)		30,000
Cash		3,000
(To record exchange of old truck for similar new truck)		

*($20,000 − $3,000)

If the old truck is exchanged for the new truck, the $3,000 gain is deferred, and the recorded cost of the new truck is reduced by $3,000.

Related exercise material: BE10–8, BE10–9, BE10–10, BE10–11, E10–6, E10–7, E10–8, and E10–9.

SECTION 2 NATURAL RESOURCES

Natural resources consist of standing timber and underground deposits of oil, gas, and minerals. Such resources include the much-publicized offshore oil deposits of major petroleum companies and the oil deposits for which the Alaskan pipeline was built. These long-lived productive assets have two distinguishing characteristics: (1) they are physically extracted in operations (such as mining, cutting, or pumping), and (2) they are replaceable only by an act of nature. Because of these characteristics, natural resources are frequently called **wasting assets.**

HELPFUL HINT
On a balance sheet, natural resources may be described as Timberlands, Mineral Deposits, Oil Reserves, and so on.

ACQUISITION COST

7
STUDY OBJECTIVE

Identify the basic accounting issues related to natural resources.

The acquisition cost of a natural resource is the cash or cash equivalent price necessary to acquire the resource and prepare it for its intended use. For an already discovered resource, such as an existing coal mine, cost is the price paid for the property.

Determining acquisition cost becomes a problem when exploration is involved. For example, some argue that the costs of unsuccessful exploration as well as successful exploration should be capitalized. They believe that, using an oil well as an example, the cost of drilling the dry holes is a cost that is needed to find the commercially profitable wells. As a result, both successful and unsuccessful explorations are capitalized, and the costs are written off to expense over the useful life of the successful wells. This method is often referred to as the **full-cost approach**.

Others disagree, arguing that the costs of only successful projects should be capitalized and unsuccessful projects should be expensed. They maintain that if only one of ten exploratory wells becomes commercially viable, it is inappropriate to assign the costs of the nine unsuccessful wells to the cost of the successful well. This method is referred to as the **successful efforts approach**. At present, both approaches are used in accounting for natural resources. For example, such companies as American Petrofina, DuPont, Callahan Mining, and Copperweld use full costing, whereas Texaco, Mobil, and Gulf use successful efforts.

ACCOUNTING IN ACTION
Business Insight

Should both full cost and successful efforts be permitted in accounting? Views are particularly strong on this subject. As one financial expert, commenting on the full-cost method, noted: "It lets them call a dry hole an asset, and as far as I am concerned, any company that uses full-cost accounting is guilty until proven innocent." On the other hand, companies using the full-cost method argue that "it enables us to undertake risky exploration projects without having sharp swings in reported earnings." Or as one writer noted: "Forcing companies to use successful efforts accounting would retard domestic oil and gas exploration and imperil national security." The debate raises some interesting questions: Does the choice of accounting method actually affect a company's exploration activities? If it does, should accounting be concerned with national security, or should it "tell it like it is"?

DEPLETION

The process of allocating the cost of natural resources to expense in a rational and systematic manner over the resource's useful life is called **depletion**. **The units-of-activity method is generally used to compute depletion, because periodic depletion generally is a function of the units extracted during the year.** Under this method, the total cost of the natural resource minus salvage value, if any, is divided by the number of units estimated to be in the resource. The result is a depletion cost per unit of product. The depletion cost per unit is then multiplied by the number of units extracted and sold, to compute the depletion expense. The formula is as follows:

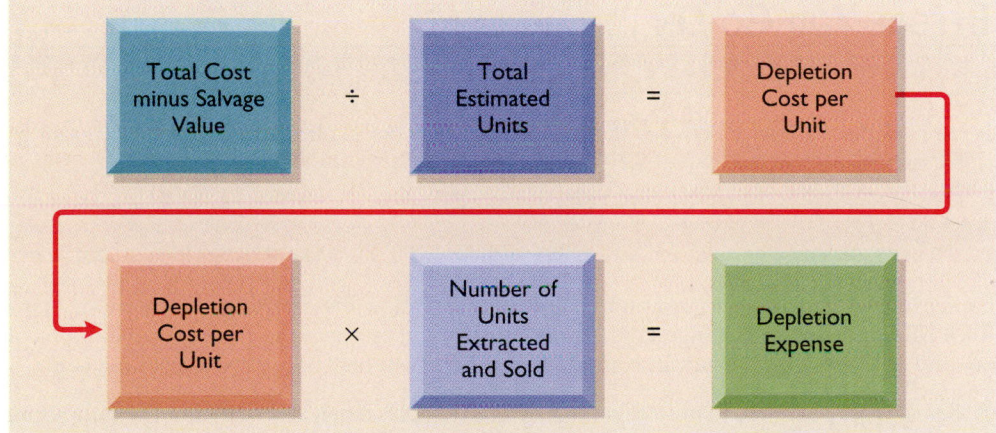

ILLUSTRATION 10-27

Formula to compute depletion expense

HELPFUL HINT
The computation for depletion is similar to the computation for depreciation using the units-of-activity method of depreciation.

To illustrate, assume that the Lane Coal Company invests $5 million in a mine estimated to have 10 million tons of coal and no salvage value. In the first year, 800,000 tons of coal are extracted and sold. Using the formulas above, the computations are as follows:

$$\$5,000,000 \div 10,000,000 = \$.50 \text{ depletion cost per ton}$$

$$\$.50 \times 800,000 = \$400,000 \text{ depletion expense}$$

The entry to record depletion expense for the first year of operation is as follows:

A	= L +	OE	
− 400,000		− 400,000	

Dec. 31	Depletion Expense	400,000	
	Accumulated Depletion		400,000
	(To record depletion expense on coal		
	deposits)		

HELPFUL HINT
Natural resources are generally reported as part of Property, Plant, and Equipment on the balance sheet.

The account Depletion Expense is reported as a part of the cost of producing the product. Accumulated Depletion, a contra asset account similar to accumulated depreciation, is deducted from the cost of the natural resource in the balance sheet as follows:

ILLUSTRATION 10-28

Statement presentation of accumulated depletion

LANE COAL COMPANY		
Balance Sheet (partial)		
Coal mine	$5,000,000	
Less: Accumulated depletion	**400,000**	$4,600,000

However, in many companies an Accumulated Depletion account is not used, and the amount of depletion is credited directly to the natural resource account.

Sometimes, natural resources extracted in one accounting period will not be sold until a later period. In this case, depletion is not expensed until the resource is sold. The amount not sold is reported in the Current Asset section as inventory.

BEFORE YOU GO ON . . .

Review It

1. What is the difference between the full-cost and successful efforts methods in accounting for natural resources?
2. How is depletion expense computed?

Do It

Explain the method used in computing depletion and show the computation, assuming Hard Rock Mining Corporation invests $12 million in a mine estimated to have 10 million tons of ore and a $2 million salvage value. In the first year 40,000 tons of ore are mined and sold.

Reasoning: There are many similarities between depreciation and depletion. In computing depletion expense, the units-of-activity method is generally used.

Solution: Under the units-of-activity method, a depletion cost per unit is determined by dividing total cost minus salvage value by the total estimated units. The computation is as follows:

$$(\$12,000,000 - \$2,000,000) \div 10,000,000 = \$1 \text{ depletion cost per ton}$$

The cost per unit is then multiplied by the number of units extracted and sold to determine depletion expense. Depletion expense for Hard Rock is $40,000 ($1 × 40,000).

THE NAVIGATOR

Related exercise material: BE10–12, BE10–13, and E10–10.

SECTION 3   INTANGIBLE ASSETS

Intangible assets are rights, privileges, and competitive advantages that result from the ownership of long-lived assets that do not possess physical substance. Evidence of intangibles may exist in the form of contracts, licenses, and other documents. Intangibles may arise from:

1. Government grants such as patents, copyrights, franchises, trademarks, and trade names.
2. Acquisition of another business in which the purchase price includes a payment for goodwill.
3. Private monopolistic arrangements arising from contractual agreements, such as franchises and leases.

Some widely known intangibles are the patents of Polaroid, the franchises of McDonald's, the trade name of Col. Sander's Kentucky Fried Chicken, and the trademark 3M of Minnesota Mining and Manufacturing Company.

ACCOUNTING FOR INTANGIBLE ASSETS

STUDY OBJECTIVE

Contrast the accounting for intangible assets with the accounting for plant assets.

In general, accounting for intangible assets parallels the accounting for plant assets. That is, **intangible assets are recorded at cost**, and this cost is expensed **over the useful life of the intangible asset in a rational and systematic manner**. At disposal, the book value of the intangible asset is eliminated, and a gain or loss, if any, is recorded.

There are, however, differences between accounting for intangible assets and accounting for plant assets. First, the term used to describe the allocation of the cost of an intangible asset to expense is **amortization**, rather than depreciation. To record amortization of an intangible, an amortization expense is debited and the specific intangible asset is credited. An alternative is to credit an accumulated amortization account, similar to accumulated depreciation. Most companies, however, choose simply to reduce the cost of the intangible asset.

There is also a difference in determining cost. For plant assets, cost includes both the purchase price of an asset and the costs incurred by a company in designing and constructing the plant asset. In contrast, cost for an intangible asset includes only the purchase price. Costs incurred in developing an intangible asset are expensed as incurred.

A third difference is that **the amortization period of an intangible asset cannot be longer than 40 years**. For example, even if the useful life of an intangible asset is 60 years, it must be written off over 40 years. Conversely, if the useful life is less than 40 years, the useful life is used. This rule ensures that all intangibles, especially those with indeterminable lives, will be written off in a reasonable period of time.

Intangible assets are typically amortized on a straight-line basis. The widespread use of this method adds comparability in accounting for intangible assets.

Patents

A **patent** is an exclusive right issued by the United States Patent Office that enables the recipient to manufacture, sell, or otherwise control an invention for a period of 17 years from the date of the grant. A patent is nonrenewable, but the legal life of a patent may be extended beyond its original term by obtaining new patents for improvements and other changes in the basic design.

The initial cost of a patent is the cash or cash equivalent price paid to acquire the patent. It should be noted that the saying, "A patent is only as good as the money you're prepared to spend defending it," is very true. Most patents are subject to some type of litigation by competitors. A well-known example is the patent infringement suit won by Polaroid against Eastman Kodak in protecting its patent on instant cameras. If the owner incurs legal costs in successfully defending the patent in an infringement suit, such costs are considered necessary to establish the validity of the patent. Thus, **they are added to the Patent account and amortized over the remaining life of the patent**.

The cost of a patent should be amortized over its 17-year legal life or its useful life, whichever is shorter. In determining useful life, obsolescence, inadequacy, and other factors should be considered; these may cause a patent to become economically ineffective before the end of its legal life. To illustrate the computation of patent expense, assume that National Labs purchases a patent at a cost of $60,000. If the useful life of the patent is 8 years, the annual amortization expense is $7,500 ($60,000 ÷ 8). The entry to record the annual amortization is:

A	=	L	+	OE
−7,500				−7,500

Dec. 31	Patent Expense	7,500	
	Patents		7,500
	(To record patent amortization)		

Patent Expense is classified as an **operating expense** in the income statement.

Copyrights

Copyrights are granted by the federal government, giving the owner the exclusive right to reproduce and sell an artistic or published work. Copyrights extend for the life of the creator plus 50 years. The cost of the copyright consists of the **cost of acquiring and defending it**. The cost may be only the $10 fee paid to the U.S. Copyright office, or it may amount to a great deal more if a copyright infringement suit is involved.

The useful life of a copyright generally is significantly shorter than its legal life. Similar to other intangible assets, the maximum write-off is 40 years. However, because of the difficulties of determining the period over which benefits are to be received, copyrights usually are amortized over a relatively short period of time.

ACCOUNTING IN ACTION
International Insight

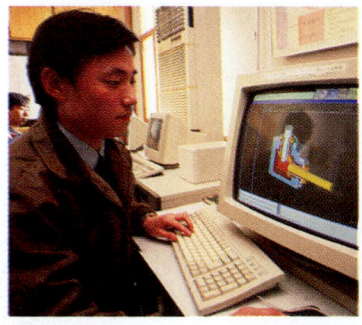

One of the significant new items copyrighted today is computer software. Lotus 1-2-3, Windows 98, and WordPerfect are some examples. These intangible assets—copyrights, in this case—are one of the most valuable assets of these corporations. To illustrate how important copyrights are, consider that in China only $1 million in computer software was sold in two recent years because China had no copyright law to discourage software piracy. Now an agreement has been reached with the Chinese that will provide protection against unlicensed copying of software. As one software maker observed, "If copyrights are protected, the value of the computer-software market in China will skyrocket."

Trademarks and Trade Names

A **trademark** or **trade name** is a word, phrase, jingle, or symbol that distinguishes or identifies a particular enterprise or product. Trade names like Wheaties, Trivial Pursuit, Sunkist, Kleenex, Windows, Coca-Cola, Big Mac, and Cadillac create immediate product identification and generally enhance the sale of the product. The creator or original user may obtain exclusive legal right to the trademark or trade name by registering it with the U.S. Patent Office. Such registration provides 20 years' protection and may be renewed indefinitely as long as the trademark or trade name is in use.

If the trademark or trade name is purchased, the cost is the purchase price. If it is developed by the enterprise itself, the cost includes attorney's fees, registration fees, design costs, successful legal defense costs, and other expenditures directly related to securing it.

As with other intangibles, the cost of trademarks and trade names must be amortized over the shorter of its useful life or 40 years. Because of the uncertainty involved in estimating the useful life, the cost is frequently amortized over a much shorter period.

Franchises and Licenses

When you drive down the street in your Trans-Am purchased from a General Motors dealer, fill up your tank at the corner Standard Oil station, eat lunch at Wendy's, and vacation at a Club Med resort, you are dealing with franchises. A **franchise** is a contractual arrangement under which the franchisor grants the franchisee the right to sell certain products, to render specific services, or to use certain trademarks or trade names, usually within a designated geographical area.

Another type of franchise is that entered into between a governmental body (commonly municipalities) and a business enterprise. This type of franchise permits the enterprise to use public property in performing its services. Examples are the use of city streets for a bus line or taxi service, use of public land for telephone and electric lines, and the use of airwaves for radio or TV broadcasting. Such operating rights are referred to as **licenses**.

Franchises and licenses may be granted for a definite period of time, an indefinite period, or perpetual. **When costs can be identified with the acquisition of the franchise or license, an intangible asset should be recognized.** In the case of a limited life, the cost of a franchise (or license) should be amortized as operating expense over the useful life. If the life is indefinite or perpetual, the cost may be amortized over a reasonable period not to exceed 40 years. Annual payments made under a franchise agreement should be recorded as **operating expenses** in the period in which they are incurred.

ETHICS NOTE

A pharmaceutical company was growing rapidly by buying unwanted drug licensing rights. These licensing rights, reported as intangible assets, represented over 70% of the company's total assets. The company experienced a 50% drop in value when the market realized the rights were being amortized over 40 years. If a more reasonable life had been used to amortize the rights, the company's reported profits would, instead, have been huge losses.

ACCOUNTING IN ACTION
Business Insight

King World's most valuable asset is the right to license television shows such as "Wheel of Fortune," "Jeopardy," "The Oprah Winfrey Show," and "Inside Edition." Almost 90% of its $396.4 million in a recent year came from the fees associated with the rights to license agreements on these intangible assets.

Goodwill

Usually, the largest intangible asset that appears on a company's balance sheet is goodwill. Goodwill is the value of all favorable attributes that relate to a business enterprise. These include exceptional management, desirable location, good customer relations, skilled employees, high-quality products, fair pricing policies, and harmonious relations with labor unions. Some view goodwill as expected earnings in excess of normal earnings. Goodwill is, therefore, unusual: unlike other assets such as investments, plant assets, and other intangibles that can be sold individually in the marketplace, goodwill can be identified only with the business as a whole.

If goodwill can be identified only with the business as a whole, how can it be determined? Certainly, many of the factors above (exceptional management, desirable location, and so on) are present in many business enterprises. However, to determine the amount of goodwill in these types of situations would be too difficult and very subjective. In other words, to recognize goodwill without an exchange transaction would lead to subjective valuations that do not contribute to the reliability of financial statements. **Therefore, goodwill is recorded only when there is an exchange transaction that involves the purchase of an entire business. When an entire business is purchased, goodwill is the excess of cost over the fair market value of the net assets (assets less liabilities) acquired.**

In recording the purchase of a business, the net assets are shown at their fair market values, goodwill is recorded at its cost, and cash is credited for the purchase price. Subsequently, goodwill is written off over its useful life, not to exceed 40 years. The amortization entry generally results in a debit to Goodwill Expense and a credit to Goodwill. Goodwill is reported in the balance sheet under Intangible Assets.

ACCOUNTING IN ACTION
International Insight

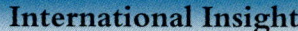

Does the amortization requirement for goodwill create a disadvantage for U.S. companies? British companies, for example, do not have to amortize goodwill against earnings. Rather, they bypass the income statement completely and charge goodwill directly to stockholders' equity. For example, Pillsbury was purchased by Grand Met, a British firm. Many complained that U.S. companies were reluctant to bid for Pillsbury because it would mean that they would have to record a large amount of goodwill, which would substantially depress income in the future. What should be done when accounting practices are different among countries and perhaps give one country a competitive edge?

RESEARCH AND DEVELOPMENT COSTS

Research and development costs are not intangible costs, but because these expenditures may lead to patents and copyrights, they are discussed in this section. Many companies spend considerable sums of money on research and development in an ongoing effort to develop new products or processes. For example, in a recent year IBM spent over $2.5 billion on research and development, an amount greater than the total expenditure budget of some state governments.

Research and development costs present accounting problems: (1) it is sometimes difficult to assign the costs to specific projects, and (2) there are uncertainties in identifying the extent and timing of future benefits. As a result, research and development costs are **usually recorded as an expense when incurred**, whether the research and development is successful or not.

To illustrate, assume that Laser Scanner Company spent $3 million on research and development. These research and development costs resulted in the development of two highly successful patents. The R&D costs, however, cannot be included in the cost of the patent. Rather, they are recorded as an expense when incurred.

Many disagree with this accounting approach. They argue that to expense these costs leads to understated assets and net income. Others, however, argue that capitalizing these costs will lead only to highly speculative assets on the balance sheet. Who is right is difficult to determine. The controversy, however, illustrates how difficult it is to establish proper guidelines for financial reporting.

STATEMENT PRESENTATION AND ANALYSIS

Presentation

Usually plant assets and natural resources are combined under Property, Plant, and Equipment, and intangibles are shown separately under Intangible Assets. Either within the balance sheet or in the notes, there should be disclosure of the balances of the major classes of assets, such as land, buildings, and equipment, and accumulated depreciation by major classes or in total. In addition, the depreciation and amortization methods used should be described and the amount of depreciation and amortization expense for the period disclosed.

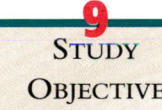

STUDY OBJECTIVE

Indicate how plant assets, natural resources, and intangible assets are reported and analyzed.

The financial statement presentation of property, plant, and equipment by Kellogg Company in its 1997 balance sheet is quite brief, as shown in Illustration 10-29.

KELLOGG COMPANY Balance Sheet (partial) December 31 (in millions)		
	1997	1996
Property, net	$2,773.3	$2,932.9
Other assets	636.6	588.5

ILLUSTRATION 10-29

Kellogg's presentation of property, plant, and equipment, and intangible assets

The notes to Kellogg's financial statements present greater details, namely, that "Other assets" contains goodwill of $194.7 million and other intangibles of $191.2 million.

A more comprehensive presentation of property, plant, and equipment is excerpted from the balance sheet of Owens-Illinois and shown in Illustration 10-30. The notes to the financial statements of Owens-Illinois identify the major classes of property, plant, and equipment. They also indicate that depreciation is by the straight-line method, depletion is by the units-of-activity method, and amortization is by the straight-line method.

ILLUSTRATION 10-30

Statement presentation of property, plant, and equipment and intangible assets

OWENS-ILLINOIS, INC.		
Balance Sheet (partial)		
(in millions of dollars)		
Property, plant, and equipment		
Timberlands, at cost, less accumulated depletion		$ 95.4
Buildings and equipment, at cost	$2,207.1	
Less: Accumulated depreciation	1,229.0	978.1
Total property, plant, and equipment		$1,073.5
Intangibles		
Patents		410.0
Total		$1,483.5

Analysis

Because the original cost ($4,980.6 million), the accumulated depreciation ($2,207.3 million), and the current period's depreciation expense for property, plant, and equipment ($287.3 million), are reported in the notes to Kellogg's 1997 financial statements, it is possible to analyze the lives and ages of these assets (especially for companies, like Kellogg, that use the straight-line method of depreciation). A measure of the **average life** and the **average age** of these assets can be computed using the following formulas and the data above from Kellogg Company:

ILLUSTRATION 10-31

Average life and average age formulas and computations

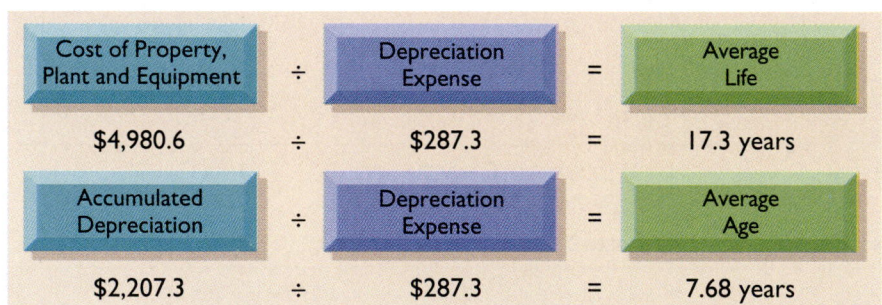

These averages are only rough estimates and possess all the weaknesses of averages. The actual lives of the individual assets that are contained in these averages range from 3 years (tools and office machines) to 35 years (buildings). However, the usefulness of these averages may come from a comparison with averages of other companies in the same industry.

The turnover of assets may be used in analyzing the productivity of a company's assets. That is, the **asset turnover ratio** is computed to measure how efficiently a company uses its assets to generate sales. This ratio is computed by dividing net sales by average total assets for the period, as shown in the formula in Illustration 10-32. (Kellogg's net sales for 1997 are $6,830.1 million, and total ending assets are $4,877.6 million and beginning are $5,050.0 million.)

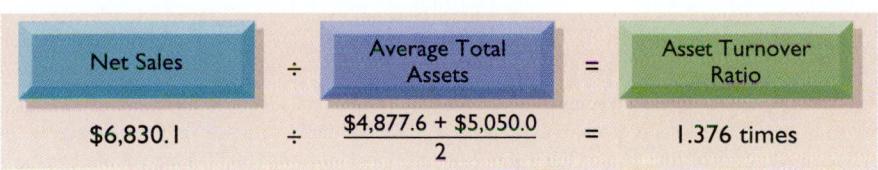

ILLUSTRATION 10-32

Asset turnover formula and computation

This ratio shows the dollars of sales produced for each dollar invested in average total assets. If a company is using its assets efficiently, each dollar of assets will create a high amount of sales. This ratio varies greatly among different industries—from those that are asset intensive (utility) to those that are not (services).

BEFORE YOU GO ON . . .

Review It

1. What are the main differences between accounting for intangible assets and plant assets?
2. Identify the major types of intangibles and the proper accounting for them.
3. Explain the accounting for research and development costs.
4. What ratios may be computed to analyze property, plant, and equipment?

A LOOK BACK AT OUR FEATURE STORY

Refer back to the opening story about Westbrook College, and answer the following questions:

1. Why should Westbrook College depreciate its buildings?
2. How can Westbrook College have a building with a zero book value yet a substantial market value?
3. Give some examples of intangibles other than a trademark that you might find on your college campus.
4. Give some examples of company or product trademarks or trade names. Are trade names and trademarks reported on a company's balance sheet? Explain.

Solution

1. Westbrook College should depreciate its buildings because depreciation is necessary in order to allocate the cost of the buildings to the periods in which they are used.
2. A building can have a zero book value if it has no salvage value and it is fully depreciated—that is, if it has been used for a period longer than its expected life. Because depreciation is used to allocate cost rather than to reflect actual value, it is not at all unlikely that a building could have a low or zero book value, but a positive market value.
3. Examples of other intangibles that might be found on a college campus are franchise of a bookstore chain, license to operate a radio station, patents developed by professors, and a permit to operate a bus service.
4. Typical company or product trade names are:
    Clothes—Gap, Gitano, Dockers, Calvin Klein, Chaus, Guess.
    Perfume—Passion, Ruffles, Chanel No. 5, Diamonds.
    Cars—TransAm, Nova, Prelude, Coupe DeVille, Eclipse.
    Shoes—Nike, Florsheim, L.A. Gear, Adidas.
    Breakfast cereals—Cheerios, Wheaties, Frosted Mini-Wheats, Rice Krispies.

Trade names and trademarks are reported on a balance sheet if there is a cost attached to them. If the trade name or trademark is purchased, the cost is the purchase price. If it is developed by the enterprise, the cost includes attorney's fees, registration fees, design costs, successful legal defense costs, and other expenditures directly related to securing the trade name or trademark.

THE NAVIGATOR

DEMONSTRATION PROBLEM

DuPage Company purchases a factory machine at a cost of $18,000 on January 1, 1999. The machine is expected to have a salvage value of $2,000 at the end of its 4-year useful life.

During its useful life, the machine is expected to be used 160,000 hours. Actual annual hourly use was: Year 1, 40,000; Year 2, 60,000; Year 3, 35,000; and Year 4, 25,000.

Instructions

Prepare depreciation schedules for the following methods: (a) the straight-line, (b) units-of-activity, and (c) declining-balance using double the straight-line rate.

SOLUTION TO DEMONSTRATION PROBLEM

PROBLEM-SOLVING STRATEGIES

1. Under the straight-line method, the depreciation rate is applied to depreciable cost.

2. Under the units-of-activity method, depreciation cost per unit is computed by dividing depreciable cost by total units of activity.

3. Under the declining-balance method, the depreciation rate is applied to **book value** at the beginning of the year.

(a)

Straight-Line Method

Year	Depreciable Cost	×	Depreciation Rate	=	Annual Depreciation Expense	Accumulated Depreciation	Book Value
1999	$16,000		25%		$4,000	$ 4,000	$14,000*
2000	16,000		25%		4,000	8,000	10,000
2001	16,000		25%		4,000	12,000	6,000
2002	16,000		25%		4,000	16,000	2,000

*$18,000 − $4,000.

(b)

Units-of-Activity Method

Year	Units of Activity	×	Depreciation Cost/Unit	=	Annual Depreciation Expense	Accumulated Depreciation	Book Value
1999	40,000		$.10		$4,000	$ 4,000	$14,000
2000	60,000		.10		6,000	10,000	8,000
2001	35,000		.10		3,500	13,500	4,500
2002	25,000		.10		2,500	16,000	2,000

(c)

Declining-Balance Method

Year	Book Value Beginning of Year	×	Depreciation Rate	=	Annual Depreciation Expense	Accumulated Depreciation	Book Value
1999	$18,000		50%		$9,000	$ 9,000	$9,000
2000	9,000		50%		4,500	13,500	4,500
2001	4,500		50%		2,250	15,750	2,250
2002	2,250		50%		250*	16,000	2,000

*Adjusted to $250 because ending book value should not be less than expected salvage value.

THE NAVIGATOR

DEMONSTRATION PROBLEM

On January 1, 1997, the Skyline Limousine Co. purchased a limousine at an acquisition cost of $28,000. The vehicle has been depreciated by the straight-line method using a 4-year service life and a $4,000 salvage value. The company's fiscal year ends on December 31.

Instructions

Prepare the journal entry or entries to record the disposal of the limousine assuming that it was:

(1) Retired and scrapped with no salvage value on January 1, 2001.

(2) Sold for $5,000 on July 1, 2000.

(3) Traded in on a new limousine on January 1, 2000. The fair market value of the old vehicle was $9,000 and $22,000 was paid in cash.

(4) Traded in on a new limousine on January 1, 2000. The fair market value of the old vehicle was $11,000 and $2,000 was paid in cash.

SOLUTION TO DEMONSTRATION PROBLEM

(1)	1/1/01	Accumulated Depreciation—Limousine	24,000	
		Loss on Disposal	4,000	
		Limousine		28,000
		(To record retirement of limousine)		
(2)	7/1/00	Depreciation Expense	3,000	
		Accumulated Depreciation—Limousine		3,000
		(To record depreciation to date of disposal)		
		Cash	5,000	
		Accumulated Depreciation—Limousine	21,000	
		Loss on Disposal	2,000	
		Limousine		28,000
		(To record sale of limousine)		
(3)	1/1/00	Limousine (new)	31,000	
		Accumulated Depreciation—Limousine	18,000	
		Loss on Disposal	1,000	
		Limousine		28,000
		Cash		22,000
		(To record exchange of limousines)		
(4)	1/1/00	Limousine (new)*	12,000	
		Accumulated Depreciation—Limousine (old)	18,000	
		Limousine (old)		28,000
		Cash		2,000
		(To record exchange of limousines)		
		*($11,000 + $2,000 − $1,000)		

PROBLEM-SOLVING STRATEGIES

1. At the time of disposal, determine the book value of the asset.

2. Recognize any gain or loss from disposal of the asset.

3. Remove the book value of the asset from the records by debiting Accumulated Depreciation for the total depreciation to date of disposal and crediting the asset account for the cost of the asset.

THE NAVIGATOR

SUMMARY OF STUDY OBJECTIVES

1. *Describe the application of the cost principle to plant assets.* The cost of plant assets includes all expenditures necessary to acquire the asset and make it ready for its intended use. Cost is measured by the cash or cash equivalent price paid.

2. *Explain the concept of depreciation.* Depreciation is the process of allocating to expense the cost of a plant asset over its useful (service) life in a rational and systematic manner. Depreciation is not a process of valuation, and it is not a process that results in an accumulation of cash. Depreciation is caused by wear and tear and by obsolescence.

3. *Compute periodic depreciation using different methods.* There are three depreciation methods:

Method	Effect on Annual Depreciation	Formula
Straight-line	Constant amount	Depreciable cost ÷ useful life (in years)
Units-of-activity	Varying amount	Depreciation cost per unit × units of activity during the year
Declining-balance	Decreasing amount	Book value at beginning of year × declining-balance rate

4. Describe the procedure for revising periodic depreciation. Revisions of periodic depreciation are made in present and future periods, not retroactively. The new annual depreciation is determined by dividing the depreciable cost at the time of the revision by the remaining useful life.

5. Distinguish between revenue and capital expenditures and explain the entries for these expenditures. Revenue expenditures are incurred to maintain the operating efficiency and expected productive life of the asset. These expenditures are debited to Repair Expense as incurred. Capital expenditures increase the operating efficiency, productive capacity, or expected useful life of the asset. These expenditures are generally debited to the plant asset affected.

6. Explain how to account for the disposal of a plant asset through retirement, sale, or exchange. The accounting for disposal of a plant asset through retirement or sale is as follows:
(a) Eliminate the book value of the plant asset at the date of disposal.
(b) Record cash proceeds, if any.
(c) Account for the difference between the book value and the cash proceeds as a gain or loss on disposal.

In accounting for exchanges of similar assets:
(a) Eliminate the book value of the old asset at the date of the exchange.

(b) Record the acquisition cost of the new asset.
(c) Account for the loss or gain, if any, on the old asset.
  1. If a loss, recognize it immediately.
  2. If a gain, defer and reduce the cost of the new asset.

7. Identify the basic accounting issues related to natural resources. The basic accounting issues related to natural resources are whether exploration costs on unsuccessful explorations should be capitalized or expensed. Under the full-cost approach, both successful and unsuccessful explorations are capitalized and the costs amortized to expense over the useful life of the successful efforts. The other approach is to capitalize only the costs of successful explorations. This is referred to as the successful efforts approach.

8. Contrast the accounting for intangible assets with the accounting for plant assets. The accounting for intangible assets and plant assets is much the same. One difference is that the term used to describe the write-off of an intangible asset is amortization, rather than depreciation. In addition, the amortization of the intangible asset cannot be longer than 40 years. The straight-line method is normally used for amortizing intangible assets.

9. Indicate how plant assets, natural resources, and intangible assets are reported and analyzed. Usually plant assets and natural resources are combined under Property, Plant, and Equipment; intangibles are shown separately under Intangible Assets. Either within the balance sheet or in the notes, the balances of the major classes of assets, such as land, buildings, and equipment, and accumulated depreciation by major classes or in total should be disclosed. Also, the depreciation and amortization methods used should be described, and the amount of depreciation and amortization expense for the period should be disclosed. Assets may be analyzed to measure average life, average age, and asset turnover.

THE
NAVIGATOR

GLOSSARY
••

Accelerated-depreciation method   A depreciation method that produces higher depreciation expense in the early years than in the later years. (p. 430).

Additions and improvements   Costs incurred to increase the operating efficiency, productive capacity, or expected useful life of a plant asset. (p. 432).

Amortization   The allocation of the cost of an intangible asset to expense over its useful life in a systematic and rational manner. (p. 441).

Asset turnover ratio   A measure of how efficiently a company uses its assets to generate sales, calculated as net sales divided by average assets. (p. 446).

Average age of plant assets   A comparative measure of the age of a company's plant assets, calculated as accumulated depreciation divided by depreciation expense. (p. 446).

Average life of plant assets   A comparative measure of a company's plant assets, calculated as cost of plant assets divided by depreciation expense. (p. 446).

Capital expenditures   Expenditures that increase the company's investment in productive facilities. (p. 432).

Cash equivalent price   An amount equal to the fair market value of the asset given up or the fair market value of the asset received, whichever is more clearly determinable. (p. 421).

Copyright   An exclusive right granted by the federal government allowing the owner to reproduce and sell an artistic or published work. (p. 442).

Declining-balance method   A depreciation method that applies a constant rate to the declining book value of the asset and produces a decreasing annual depreciation expense over the useful life of the asset. (p. 429).

Depletion   The process of allocating the cost of a natural resource to expense in a rational and systematic manner over the resources's useful life. (p. 439).

Depreciable cost   The cost of a plant asset less its salvage value. (p. 426).

Franchise (license)   A contractual arrangement under which the franchisor grants the franchisee the right to sell certain products, to render specific services, or to use certain trademarks or trade names, usually within a designated geographical area. (p. 443).

Full-cost approach   Method in which both successful and unsuccessful exploration costs are included in the cost of a natural resource and the costs are written off to expense over the useful life of the successful wells. (p. 438).

Goodwill   The value of all favorable attributes that relate to a business enterprise. (p. 444).

Intangible assets   Rights, privileges, and competitive advantages that result from the ownership of long-lived assets that do not possess physical substance. (p. 441).

Licenses   Operating rights to use public property, granted by a governmental agency to a business enterprise. (p. 443).

Natural resources   Assets that consist of standing timber and underground deposits of oil, gas, and minerals. Also called *wasting assets*. (p. 438).

Ordinary repairs   Expenditures to maintain the operating efficiency and expected productive life of the unit. (p. 432).

Patent   An exclusive right issued by the U.S. Patent Office that enables the recipient to manufacture, sell, or otherwise control an invention for a period of 17 years from the date of the grant. (p. 441).

Plant assets   Tangible resources that are used in the operations of the business and are not intended for sale to customers. (p. 420).

Research and development costs   Expenditures that may lead to patents, copyrights, new processes, and products. (p. 444).

Revenue expenditures   Expenditures that are immediately charged against revenues as an expense. (p. 432).

Straight-line method   A method in which periodic depreciation is the same for each year of the asset's useful life. (p. 426).

Successful efforts approach   Method in which only the costs of successful exploration are included in the cost of a natural resource. (p. 438).

Trademark (trade name)   A word, phrase, jingle, or symbol that distinguishes or identifies a particular enterprise or product. (p. 443).

Units-of-activity method   A depreciation method in which useful life is expressed in terms of the total units of production or use expected from the asset. (p. 428).

SELF-STUDY QUESTIONS

Answers are at the end of the chapter.

(SO 1)   1. Erin Danielle Company purchased equipment and the following costs were incurred:

Cash price	$24,000
Sales taxes	1,200
Insurance during transit	200
Installation and testing	400
Total costs	$25,800

What amount should be recorded as the cost of the equipment?
a. $24,000.
b. $25,200.
c. $25,400.
d. $25,800.

(SO 2)   2. Depreciation is a process of:
a. valuation.
b. cost allocation.
c. cash accumulation.
d. appraisal.

(SO 3)   3. Micah Bartlett Company purchased equipment on January 1, 1998, at a total invoice cost of $400,000. The equipment has an estimated salvage value of $10,000 and an estimated useful life of 5 years. The amount of accumulated depreciation at December 31, 1999, if the straight-line method of depreciation is used, is:
a. $80,000.
b. $160,000.
c. $78,000.
d. $156,000.

(SO 3)   4. Ann Torbert purchased a truck for $11,000 on January 1, 1998. The truck will have an estimated salvage value of $1,000 at the end of 5 years. Using the units-of-activity method, the balance in accumulated depreciation at December 31, 1999, can be computed by the following formula:
a. ($11,000 ÷ Total estimated activity) × Units of activity for 1999.
b. ($10,000 ÷ Total estimated activity) × Units of activity for 1999.
c. ($11,000 ÷ Total estimated activity) × Units of activity for 1998 and 1999.
d. ($10,000 ÷ Total estimated activity) × Units of activity for 1998 and 1999.

(SO 4)   5. When there is a change in estimated depreciation:
a. previous depreciation should be corrected.
b. current and future years' depreciation should be revised.
c. only future years' depreciation should be revised.
d. None of the above.

(SO 5) 6. Additions to plant assets are:
  a. revenue expenditures.
  b. debited to a Repair Expense account.
  c. debited to a Purchases account.
  d. capital expenditures.

(SO 6) 7. Schopenhauer Company exchanged an old machine, with a book value of $39,000 and a fair market value of $35,000, and paid $10,000 cash for a similar new machine. At what amount should the machine acquired in the exchange be recorded on the books of Schopenhauer?
  a. $45,000.
  b. $46,000.
  c. $49,000.
  d. $50,000.

(SO 6) 8. In exchanges of similar assets:
  a. neither gains nor losses are recognized immediately.
  b. gains, but not losses, are recognized immediately.
  c. losses, but not gains, are recognized immediately.
  d. both gains and losses are recognized immediately.

(SO 7) 9. Maggie Sharrer Company expects to extract 20 million tons of coal from a mine that cost $12 million. If no salvage value is expected, and 2 million tons are mined and sold in the first year, the entry to record depletion will include a:

  a. debit to Accumulated Depletion of $2,000,000.
  b. credit to Depletion Expense of $1,200,000.
  c. debit to Depletion Expense of $1,200,000.
  d. credit to Accumulated Depletion of $2,000,000.

10. Martha Beyerlein Company incurred $150,000 of re- (SO 8, 9)
search and development costs in its laboratory to develop a patent granted on January 2, 1999. On July 31, 1999, Beyerlein paid $35,000 for legal fees in a successful defense of the patent. The total amount debited to Patents through July 31, 1999, should be:
  a. $150,000.
  b. $35,000.
  c. $185,000.
  d. some other amount.

11. Indicate which of the following statements is *true*. (SO 9)
  a. Since intangible assets lack physical substance they need be disclosed only in the notes to the financial statements.
  b. Goodwill should be reported as a contra-account in the Stockholder's Equity section.
  c. Totals of major classes of assets can be shown in the balance sheet, with asset details disclosed in the notes to the financial statements.
  d. Intangible assets are typically combined with plant assets and natural resources and then shown in the Property, Plant, and Equipment section.

QUESTIONS

1. Phil Collins is uncertain about the applicability of the cost principle to plant assets. Explain the principle to Phil.

2. How is cost for a plant asset measured in (a) a cash transaction, and (b) a noncash transaction?

3. Winans Company acquires the land and building owned by Corrs Company. What types of costs may be incurred to make the asset ready for its intended use if Winans Company wants to use (a) only the land, and (b) both the land and the building?

4. In a recent newspaper release, the president of Smashing Pumpkins Company asserted that something has to be done about depreciation. The president said, "Depreciation does not come close to accumulating the cash needed to replace the asset at the end of its useful life." What is your response to the president?

5. Michael is studying for the next accounting examination. He asks your help on two questions: (a) What is salvage value? (b) Is salvage value used in determining depreciable cost under each depreciation method? Answer Michael's questions.

6. Contrast the straight-line method and the units-of-activity method as to (a) useful life, and (b) the pattern of periodic depreciation over useful life.

7. Contrast the effects of the three depreciation methods on annual depreciation expense.

8. In the fourth year of an asset's 5-year useful life, the company decides that the asset will have a 6-year service life. How should the revision of depreciation be recorded? Why?

9. Distinguish between revenue expenditures and capital expenditures during useful life.

10. How is a gain or loss on the sale of a plant asset computed?

11. Bimini Corporation owns a machine that is fully depreciated but is still being used. How should Bimini account for this asset and report it in the financial statements?

12. When similar assets are exchanged, how is the gain or loss on disposal computed?

13. Batman Refrigeration Company trades in an old machine on a new model when the fair market value of the old machine is greater than its book value. Should Batman recognize a gain on disposal? If the fair market value of the old machine is less than its book value, should Batmam recognize a loss on disposal?

14. Moon Company experienced a gain on disposal when exchanging similar machines. In accordance with generally accepted accounting principles, the gain was not recognized. How will Moon's future financial statements be affected by not recognizing the gain?

15. What are natural resources, and what are their distinguishing characteristics?

16. Van Amos and Benedict Arnold are arguing about the full-cost approach and the successful efforts approach. Amos says that the full-cost approach will provide a greater reported asset value, while Arnold says that the successful efforts approach would. Who is correct?

17. What are the similarities and differences between the terms depreciation, depletion, and amortization?

18. Mitra Company hires an accounting intern who says that intangible assets should always be amortized over their legal lives. Is the intern correct? Explain.

19. Goodwill has been defined as the value of all favorable attributes that relate to a business enterprise. What types of attributes could result in goodwill?

20. Clint Eastwood, a business major, is working on a case problem for one of his classes. In this case problem, the company needs to raise cash to market a new product it developed. Jack Gleason, an engineering major, takes one look at the company's balance sheet and says, "This company has an awful lot of goodwill. Why don't you recommend that they sell some of it to raise cash?" How should Clint respond to Jack?

21. Under what conditions is goodwill recorded?

22. Often research and development costs provide companies with benefits that last a number of years. (For example, these costs can lead to the development of a patent that will increase the company's income for many years.) However, generally accepted accounting principles require that such costs be recorded as an expense when incurred. Why?

23. McDonald's Corporation reports total average assets of $14.5 billion and net sales of $9.8 billion. What is the company's asset turnover ratio?

24. Morgan Corporation and Fairchild Corporation both operate in the same industry. Morgan uses the straight-line method to account for depreciation, whereas Fairchild uses an accelerated method. Explain what complications might arise in trying to compare the results of these two companies.

25. Lucille Corporation uses straight-line depreciation for financial reporting purposes but an accelerated method for tax purposes. Is it acceptable to use different methods for the two purposes? What is Lucille Corporation's motivation for doing this?

26. You are comparing two companies in the same industry. You have determined that Betty Corp. depreciates its plant assets over a 40-year life, whereas Veronica Corp. depreciates its plant assets over a 20-year life. Discuss the implications this has for comparing the results of the two companies.

27. Pizner Company is doing significant work to revitalize its warehouses. It is not sure whether it should capitalize these costs or expense them. What are the implications for current year net income and future net income of expensing verses capitalizing these costs?

BRIEF EXERCISES

BE10–1 The following expenditures were incurred by JFK Company in purchasing land. Cash price $40,000, accrued taxes $3,000, attorneys' fees $2,500, real estate broker's commission $2,000, and clearing and grading $3,500. What is the cost of the land?

Determine the cost of land.
(SO 1)

BE10–2 Housman Company incurs the following expenditures in purchasing a truck: cash price $20,000, accident insurance $2,000, sales taxes $900, motor vehicle license $100, and painting and lettering $400. What is the cost of the truck?

Determine the cost of a truck.
(SO 1)

BE10–3 Graig Ehlo Company acquires a delivery truck at a cost of $26,000. The truck is expected to have a salvage value of $2,000 at the end of its 4-year useful life. Compute annual depreciation for the first and second years using the straight-line method.

Compute straight-line depreciation.
(SO 3)

BE10–4 Olympic Company purchased land and a building on January 1, 1999. Management's best estimate of the value of the land was $100,000 and of the building $200,000, but management told the accounting department to record the land at $250,000 and the building at $50,000. The building is being depreciated on a straight-line basis over 20 years with no salvage value. Why do you suppose management requested this accounting treatment? Is it ethical?

Compute depreciation and evaluate treatment.
(SO 3)

BE10–5 Depreciation information for Graig Ehlo Company is given in BE10–3. Assuming the declining-balance depreciation rate is double the straight-line rate, compute annual depreciation for the first and second years under the declining-balance method.

Compute declining-balance depreciation.
(SO 3)

BE10–6 Spud Webb Taxi Service uses the units-of-activity method in computing depreciation on its taxicabs. Each cab is expected to be driven 120,000 miles. Taxi No. 10 cost $36,500 and is expected to have a salvage value of $500. Taxi No. 10 is driven 30,000 miles in Year 1 and 20,000 miles in Year 2. Compute the depreciation for each year.

Compute depreciation using the units-of-activity method.
(SO 3)

Compute revised depreciation.
(SO 4)

BE10–7 On January 1, 1999, the Wilkins Company ledger shows Equipment $32,000 and Accumulated Depreciation $9,000. The depreciation resulted from using the straight-line method with a useful life of 10 years and salvage value of $2,000. On this date, the company concludes that the equipment has a remaining useful life of only 4 years with the same salvage value. Compute the revised annual depreciation.

Prepare entries for disposal by retirement.
(SO 6)

BE10–8 Prepare journal entries to record the following:

(a) Arna Company retires its delivery equipment, which cost $41,000. Accumulated depreciation is also $41,000 on this delivery equipment. No salvage value is received.
(b) Assume the same information as (a), except that accumulated depreciation for Arna Company is $38,000, instead of $41,000.

Prepare entries for disposal by sale.
(SO 6)

BE10–9 Garrison Company sells office equipment on September 30, 1999, for $20,000 cash. The office equipment originally cost $72,000 and as of January 1, 1999, had accumulated depreciation of $42,000. Depreciation for the first 9 months of 1999 is $6,250. Prepare the journal entries to (a) update depreciation to September 30, 1999, and (b) record the sale of the equipment.

Prepare entry for disposal by exchange.
(SO 6)

BE10–10 Keillor Company exchanges old delivery equipment for similar new delivery equipment. The book value of the old delivery equipment is $31,000 (cost $61,000 less accumulated depreciation $30,000), its fair market value is $19,000, and cash of $5,000 is paid. Prepare the entry to record the exchange.

Prepare entry for disposal by exchange.
(SO 6)

BE10–11 Assume the same information as BE10–10, except that the fair market value of the old delivery equipment is $42,000. Prepare the entry to record the exchange.

Prepare depletion expense entry and balance sheet presentation for natural resources.
(SO 7)

BE10–12 Adamson Mining Co. purchased for $7 million a mine which is estimated to have 28 million tons of ore and no salvage value. In the first year, 6 million tons of ore are extracted and sold. (a) Prepare the journal entry to record depletion expense for the first year. (b) Show how this mine is reported on the balance sheet at the end of the first year.

Prepare patent expense entry and balance sheet presentation for intangibles.
(SO 8)

BE10–13 Fayne Company purchases a patent for $160,000 on January 2, 1999. Its estimated useful life is 10 years. (a) Prepare the journal entry to record patent expense for the first year. (b) Show how this patent is reported on the balance sheet at the end of the first year.

Classify long-lived assets on balance sheet.
(SO 9)

BE10–14 Information related to plant assets, natural resources and intangibles at the end of 1999 for Riddler Company is as follows: buildings $900,000; accumulated depreciation—buildings $650,000; goodwill $410,000; coal mine $200,000; accumulated depletion—coal mine $108,000. Prepare a partial balance sheet of Riddler Company for these items.

Analyze long-lived assets.
(SO 9)

BE10–15 In its 1996 annual report McDonald's Corporation reported beginning total assets of $15.4 billion; ending total assets of $17.4 billion; property, plant, and equipment (at cost) of $19.1 billion; accumulated depreciation of $4.8 billion; depreciation expense of $673.4 million; and net sales of $10.7 billion. (a) Compute the average life of McDonald's property, plant, and equipment. (b) Compute the average age of McDonald's property, plant, and equipment. (c) Compute McDonald's asset turnover ratio.

EXERCISES

Determine cost of plant acquisitions.
(SO 1)

E10–1 The following expenditures relating to plant assets were made by Salvador Company during the first 2 months of 1999.

1. Paid $5,000 of accrued taxes at time plant site was acquired.
2. Paid $200 insurance to cover possible accident loss on new factory machinery while the machinery was in transit.
3. Paid $850 sales taxes on new delivery truck.
4. Paid $17,500 for parking lots and driveways on new plant site.
5. Paid $250 to have company name and advertising slogan painted on new delivery truck.
6. Paid $8,000 for installation of new factory machinery.
7. Paid $900 for one-year accident insurance policy on new delivery truck.
8. Paid $75 motor vehicle license fee on the new truck.

Instructions

(a)  Explain the application of the cost principle in determining the acquisition cost of plant assets.

(b) List the numbers of the foregoing transactions, and opposite each indicate the account title to which each expenditure should be debited.

E10–2 On March 1, 1999, Neil Young Company acquired real estate, on which it planned to construct a small office building, by paying $90,000 in cash. An old warehouse on the property was razed at a cost of $6,600; the salvaged materials were sold for $1,700. Additional expenditures before construction began included $1,100 attorney's fee for work concerning the land purchase, $4,000 real estate broker's fee, $7,800 architect's fee, and $14,000 to put in driveways and a parking lot.

Determine acquisition costs on land.
(SO 1)

Instructions

(a) Determine the amount to be reported as the cost of the land.

(b) For each cost not used in part (a), indicate the account to be debited.

E10–3 Galactic Bus Lines uses the units-of-activity method in depreciating its buses. One bus was purchased on January 1, 1999, at a cost of $108,000. Over its 4-year useful life, the bus is expected to be driven 100,000 miles. Salvage value is expected to be $8,000.

Compute depreciation under units-of-activity method.
(SO 3)

Instructions

(a) Compute the depreciation cost per unit.

(b) Prepare a depreciation schedule assuming actual mileage was: 1999, 26,000; 2000, 32,000; 2001, 25,000; and 2002, 17,000.

E10–4 Tory Amos Company purchased a new machine on October 1, 1999, at a cost of $96,000. The company estimated that the machine will have a salvage value of $12,000. The machine is expected to be used for 70,000 working hours during its 5-year life.

Determine depreciation for partial periods.
(SO 3)

Instructions

Compute the depreciation expense under the following methods for the year indicated: (a) straight-line for 1999, (b) units-of-activity for 1999, assuming machine usage was 1,700 hours, and (c) declining-balance using double the straight-line rate for 1999 and 2000.

E10–5 Bill Simpson, the new controller of the Bellingham Company, has reviewed the expected useful lives and salvage values of selected depreciable assets at the beginning of 1999. His findings are as follows:

Compute revised annual depreciation.
(SO 3, 4)

Type of Asset	Date Acquired	Cost	Accumulated Depreciation 1/1/99	Useful Life in Years		Salvage Value	
				Old	Proposed	Old	Proposed
Building	1/1/93	$800,000	$114,000	40	50	$40,000	$48,000
Warehouse	1/1/96	100,000	11,400	25	20	5,000	3,600

All assets are depreciated by the straight-line method. Bellingham Company uses a calendar year in preparing annual financial statements. After discussion, management has agreed to accept Bill's proposed changes.

Instructions

(a) Compute the revised annual depreciation on each asset in 1999. (Show computations.)

(b) Prepare the entry (or entries) to record depreciation on the building in 1999.

E10–6 Presented below are selected transactions at Chen Company for 1999.

Journalize entries for disposal of plant assets.
(SO 6)

Jan. 1   Retired a piece of machinery that was purchased on January 1, 1989. The machine cost $62,000 on that date, and had a useful life of 10 years with no salvage value.

June 30   Sold a computer that was purchased on January 1, 1996. The computer cost $35,000, and had a useful life of 7 years with no salvage value. The computer was sold for $25,000.

Dec. 31   Discarded a delivery truck that was purchased on January 1, 1995. The truck cost $27,000 and was depreciated based on a 6-year useful life with a $3,000 salvage value.

Instructions
Journalize all entries required on the above dates, including entries to update depreciation, where applicable, on assets disposed of. Chen Company uses straight-line depreciation. (Assume depreciation is up to date as of December 31, 1998.)

Journalize entries for exchange of similar assets.
(SO 6)

E10–7   Presented below are two independent transactions:

1. White Cloud Co. exchanged trucks (cost $64,000 less $22,000 accumulated depreciation) plus cash of $17,000 for new trucks. The old trucks had a fair market value of $38,000. Prepare the entry to record the exchange of similar assets by White Cloud Co.
2. Nelle Inc. trades its used machine (cost $10,000 less $4,000 accumulated depreciation) for a new machine. In addition to exchanging the old machine (which had a fair market value of $9,000), Nelle also paid cash of $2,000.

Instructions
Prepare the entry to record the exchange of similar assets by Nelle Inc.

Journalize entries for the exchange of similar plant assets.
(SO 6)

E10–8   Wind Company exchanges similar equipment with the Earth Company. Also Sun Company exchanges similar equipment with Moon Company. The following information pertains to these two exchanges:

	Wind Co.	Sun Co.
Equipment (cost)	$28,000	$22,000
Accumulated depreciation	20,000	5,000
Fair market value of equipment	12,000	14,000
Cash paid	2,000	–0–

Instructions
Prepare the journal entries to record the exchange on the books of Wind Company and Sun Company.

Journalize entries for the exchange of similar plant assets.
(SO 6)

E10–9   Peru's Delivery Company and Brazil's Express Delivery exchanged similar delivery trucks on January 1, 1999. Peru's truck cost $20,000, had accumulated depreciation of $13,000, and has a fair market value of $3,000. Brazil's truck cost $10,000, had accumulated depreciation of $8,000, and has a fair market value of $3,000.

Instructions
(a) Journalize the exchange for Peru's Delivery Company.
(b) Journalize the exchange for Brazil's Express Delivery.

Journalize entries for natural resources depletion.
(SO 7)

E10–10   On July 1, 1999, Reggie Inc. invested $360,000 in a mine estimated to have 800,000 tons of ore of uniform grade. During the last 6 months of 1999, 100,000 tons of ore were mined and sold.

Instructions
(a) Prepare the journal entry to record depletion expense.
(b) Assume that the 100,000 tons of ore were mined, but only 80,000 units were sold. How are the costs applicable to the 20,000 unsold units reported?

Prepare adjusting entries for amortization.
(SO 8)

E10–11   The following are selected 1999 transactions of McGillis Corporation.

Jan. 1   Purchased a small company and recorded goodwill of $140,000. The goodwill has a useful life of 55 years.

May 1   Purchased a patent with an estimated useful life of 5 years and a legal life of 17 years for $30,000.

Instructions
Prepare all adjusting entries at December 31 to record amortization required by the events above.

Prepare entries to set up appropriate accounts for different intangibles; amortize intangible assets.
(SO 8)

E10–12   Vail Company, organized in 1999, has the following transactions related to intangible assets.

1/2/99	Purchased patent (7-year life)	$420,000
4/1/99	Goodwill purchased (indefinite life)	360,000
7/1/99	10-year franchise; expiration date 7/1/2009	450,000
9/1/99	Research and development costs	185,000

Instructions

Prepare the necessary entries to record these intangibles. All costs incurred were for cash. Make the entries as of December 31, 1999, recording any necessary amortization and reflecting all balances accurately as of that date.

E10–13 During 1998 Kettle Corporation reported net sales of $2,500,000, net income of $1,500,000, and depreciation expense of $150,000. Its balance sheet reported total assets of $1,400,000, plant assets of $800,000, and accumulated depreciation on plant assets of $300,000.

Calculate average useful life, average age of plant assets, and asset turnover ratio.
(SO 9)

Instructions

Calculate (a) average useful life of plant assets, (b) average age of plant assets, and (c) asset turnover ratio.

PROBLEMS: SET A

P10–1A Superior Company was organized on January 1. During the first year of operations, the following plant asset expenditures and receipts were recorded in random order.

Determine acquisition costs of land and building.
(SO 1)

Debits

1. Cost of real estate purchased as a plant site (land $100,000 and building $25,000)	$125,000
2. Installation cost of fences around property	4,000
3. Cost of demolishing building to make land suitable for construction of new building	13,000
4. Excavation costs for new building	20,000
5. Accrued real estate taxes paid at time of purchase of real estate	2,000
6. Cost of parking lots and driveways	12,000
7. Architect's fees on building plans	10,000
8. Real estate taxes paid for the current year on land	3,000
9. Full payment to building contractor	500,000
	$689,000

Credits

10. Proceeds from salvage of demolished building	$ 2,500

Instructions

Analyze the foregoing transactions using the following tabular arrangement. Insert the number of each transaction in the Item space and insert the amounts in the appropriate columns. For amounts entered in the Other Accounts column also indicate the account title.

Item	Land	Building	Other Accounts

P10–2A In recent years, Erie Company has purchased three machines. Because of heavy turnover in the accounting department, a different accountant was in charge of selecting the depreciation method for each machine, and various methods have been selected. Information concerning the machines is summarized below:

Compute depreciation under different methods.
(SO 3)

Machine	Acquired	Cost	Salvage Value	Useful Life in Years	Depreciation Method
1	1/1/96	$ 96,000	$ 6,000	10	Straight-line
2	1/1/97	80,000	10,000	8	Declining-balance
3	11/1/99	78,000	6,000	6	Units-of-activity

For the declining-balance method, Erie Company uses the double-declining rate. For the units-of-activity method, total machine hours are expected to be 24,000. Actual hours of use in the first 3 years were: 1999, 4,000; 2000, 4,500; and 2001, 5,000.

Instructions

(a) Compute the amount of accumulated depreciation on each machine at December 31, 1999.
(b) If machine 2 was purchased on April 1 instead of January 1, what is the depreciation expense for this machine in (1) 1997 and (2) 1998?

Compute depreciation under different methods.
(SO 3)

P10–3A   On January 1, 1999, Rose Company purchased the following two machines for use in its production process:

Machine A: The cash price of this machine was $30,000. Related expenditures included: sales tax $1,800, shipping costs $175, insurance during shipping $75, installation and testing costs $50, and $90 of oil and lubricants to be used with the machinery during its first year of operation. Rose estimates that the useful life of the machine is 4 years with a $5,000 salvage value remaining at the end of that time period.

Machine B: The recorded cost of this machine was $60,000. Rose estimates that the useful life of the machine is 4 years with a $5,000 salvage value remaining at the end of that time period.

Instructions

(a) Prepare the following for Machine A:
    (1) The journal entry to record its purchase on January 1, 1999.
    (2) The journal entry to record annual depreciation at December 31, 1999 assuming the straight-line method of depreciation is used.
(b) Calculate the amount of depreciation expense that Rose should record for Machine B each year of its useful life assuming:
    (1) Rose uses the straight-line method of depreciation.
    (2) Rose uses the declining-balance method. The rate used is twice the straight-line rate.
    (3) Rose uses the units-of-activity method and estimates that the useful life of the machine is 27,500 units. Actual usage is as follows: 1999, 9,000 units; 2000, 7,500 units; 2001, 6,000 units; 2002, 5,000 units.
(c) Which method used to calculate depreciation on Machine B reports the lowest amount of depreciation expense in year 1 (1999)? The lowest amount in year 4 (2002)? The lowest total amount over the 4-year period?

Journalize a series of equipment transactions related to purchase, sale, retirement, and depreciation.
(SO 6, 9)

P10–4A   At December 31, 1999, Wallace Company reported the following as plant assets:

Land		$ 3,000,000
Buildings	$26,500,000	
Less: Accumulated depreciation—buildings	12,100,000	14,400,000
Equipment	40,000,000	
Less: Accumulated depreciation—equipment	5,000,000	35,000,000
Total plant assets		$52,400,000

During 2000, the following selected cash transactions occurred:

April 1   Purchased land for $2,200,000.
May 1   Sold equipment that cost $600,000 when purchased on January 1, 1996. The equipment was sold for $360,000.
June 1   Sold land purchased on June 1, 1990 for $1,800,000. The land cost $500,000.
July 1   Purchased equipment for $1,400,000.
Dec. 31   Retired equipment that cost $500,000 when purchased on December 31, 1990. No salvage value was received.

Instructions

(a) Journalize the above transactions. Wallace uses straight-line depreciation for buildings and equipment. The buildings are estimated to have a 40-year useful life and no salvage value; the equipment is estimated to have a 10-year useful life and no salvage value. Update depreciation on assets disposed of at the time of sale or retirement.
(b) Record adjusting entries for depreciation for 2000.
(c) Prepare the plant asset section of Wallace's balance sheet at December 31, 2000.

Record disposals.
(SO 6)

P10–5A   Ghani Co. has delivery equipment that cost $50,000 and that has been depreciated $20,000. Record the disposal under the following assumptions:

(a) It was scrapped as having no value.
(b) It was sold for $31,000.
(c) It was sold for $18,000.
(d) It was exchanged for similar delivery equipment. The old delivery equipment has a fair market value of $12,000 and $32,000 was paid.
(e) It was exchanged for similar delivery equipment. The old delivery equipment has a fair market value of $35,000 and $9,000 was paid.

P10–6A   The intangible assets section of El-Gazzar Company at December 31, 1999, is presented below:

Prepare entries to record transactions related to acquisition and amortization of intangibles; prepare the intangible assets section.
(SO 8, 9)

Patent ($60,000 cost less $6,000 amortization)	$54,000
Copyright ($36,000 cost less $14,400 amortization)	21,600
Total	$75,600

The patent was acquired in January 1999 and has a useful life of 10 years. The copyright was acquired in January 1996 and also has a useful life of 10 years. The following cash transactions may have affected intangible assets during 2000:

Jan. 2   Paid $18,000 legal costs to successfully defend the patent against infringement by another company.

Jan.–June   Developed a new product incurring $140,000 in research and development costs. A patent was granted for the product on July 1, and its useful life is equal to its legal life.

Sept. 1   Paid $60,000 to a quarterback to appear in commercials advertising the company's products. The commercials will air in September and October.

Oct. 1   Acquired a copyright for $80,000. The copyright has a useful life of 50 years.

Instructions
(a) Prepare journal entries to record the transactions above.
(b) Prepare journal entries to record the 2000 amortization expense for intangible assets.
(c) Prepare the intangible assets section of the balance sheet at December 31, 2000.
(d) Prepare the note to the financials on El-Gazzar's intangibles as of December 31, 2000.

P10–7A   Due to rapid turnover in the accounting department, a number of transactions involving intangible assets were improperly recorded by Baird Company in 1999.

Prepare entries to correct errors made in recording and amortizing intangible assets.
(SO 8)

1. Baird developed a new manufacturing process, incurring research and development costs of $85,000. The company also purchased a patent for $37,400. In early January, Baird capitalized $122,400 as the cost of the patents. Patent amortization expense of $7,200 was recorded based on a 17-year useful life.
2. On July 1, 1999, Baird purchased a small company and as a result acquired goodwill of $60,000. Baird recorded a half-year's amortization in 1999, based on a 50-year life ($600 amortization).

Instructions
Prepare all journal entries necessary to correct any errors made during 1999. Assume the books have not yet been closed for 1999.

P10–8A   Croix Corporation and Rye Corporation, two corporations of roughly the same size, are both involved in the manufacture of canoes and sea kayaks. Each company depreciates its plant assets using the straight-line approach. An investigation of their financial statements reveals this information:

Calculate and comment on average age, average useful life of plant assets, and asset turnover ratio.
(SO 9)

	Croix Corp.	Rye Corp.
Net income	$ 400,000	$ 600,000
Sales	1,400,000	1,200,000
Total assets	2,000,000	1,500,000
Plant assets	1,500,000	800,000
Accumulated depreciation	300,000	625,000
Depreciation expense	75,000	25,000
Intangible assets (goodwill)	300,000	0
Amortization expense	60,000	0

Instructions
(a) For each company, calculate these values:
   (1) Average age of plant assets.
   (2) Average useful life.
   (3) Asset turnover ratio.
(b) ▭✏▷   Based on your calculations in part (a), comment on the relative effectiveness of the two companies in using their assets to generate sales and produce net income. What factors complicate your ability to compare the two companies?

PROBLEMS: SET B

Determine acquisition costs of land and building.
(SO 1)

P10–1B   Bob Duran Company was organized on January 1. During the first year of operations, the following plant asset expenditures and receipts were recorded in random order.

Debits

1. Cost of real estate purchased as a plant site (land $100,000 and building $45,000)	$145,000
2. Accrued real estate taxes paid at time of purchase of real estate	2,000
3. Cost of demolishing building to make land suitable for construction of new building	12,000
4. Cost of filling and grading the land	4,000
5. Excavation costs for new building	20,000
6. Architect's fees on building plans	10,000
7. Full payment to building contractor	600,000
8. Cost of parking lots and driveways	14,000
9. Real estate taxes paid for the current year on land	5,000
	$812,000

Credits

10. Proceeds for salvage of demolished building	$ 3,500

Instructions
Analyze the foregoing transactions using the following tabular arrangement. Insert the number of each transaction in the Item space and insert the amounts in the appropriate columns. For amounts entered in the Other Accounts column, also indicate the account titles.

Item	Land	Building	Other Accounts

Compute depreciation under different methods.
(SO 3)

P10–2B   In recent years, Lakeshore Transportation purchased three used buses. Because of frequent turnover in the accounting department, a different accountant selected the depreciation method for each bus, and various methods have been selected. Information concerning the buses is summarized below:

Bus	Acquired	Cost	Salvage Value	Useful Life in Years	Depreciation Method
1	1/1/97	$ 86,000	$ 6,000	5	Straight-line
2	1/1/97	140,000	10,000	4	Declining-balance
3	1/1/98	80,000	8,000	5	Units-of-activity

For the declining balance method, Lakeshore Transportation uses the double-declining rate. For the units-of-activity method, total miles are expected to be 120,000. Actual miles of use in the first 3 years were: 1998, 24,000; 1999, 34,000; and 2000, 30,000.

Instructions
(a) Compute the amount of accumulated depreciation on each bus at December 31, 1999.
(b) If Bus No. 2 was purchased on April 1 instead of January 1, what is the depreciation expense for this bus in (1) 1997 and (2) 1998?

P10-3B On January 1, 1999, Axel Company purchased the following two machines for use in its production process:

Compute depreciation under different methods.
(SO 3)

> Machine A: The cash price of this machine was $25,000. Related expenditures included: sales tax $1,500, shipping costs $150, insurance during shipping $80, installation and testing costs $70, and $100 of oil and lubricants to be used with the machinery during its first year of operations. Axel estimates that the useful life of the machine is 5 years with a $5,000 salvage value remaining at the end of that time period. Assume that the straight-line method of depreciation is used.
>
> Machine B: The recorded cost of this machine was $50,000. Axel estimates that the useful life of the machine is 4 years with a $5,000 salvage value remaining at the end of that time period.

Instructions

(a) Prepare the following for Machine A:
   (1) The journal entry to record its purchase on January 1, 1999.
   (2) The journal entry to record annual depreciation at December 31, 1999.
(b) Calculate the amount of depreciation expense that Axel should record for Machine B each year of its useful life assuming:
   (1) Axel uses the straight-line method of depreciation.
   (2) Axel uses the declining-balance method. The rate used is twice the straight-line rate.
   (3) Axel uses the units-of-activity method and estimates that the useful life of the machine is 125,000 units. Actual usage is as follows: 1999, 45,000 units; 2000, 35,000 units; 2001, 25,000 units; 2002, 20,000 units.
(c) Which method used to calculate depreciation on Machine B reports the highest amount of depreciation expense in year 1 (1999)? The highest amount in year 4 (2002)? The highest total amount over the 4-year period?

P10-4B At December 31, 1999, Los Alamos Company reported the following as plant assets:

Journalize a series of equipment transactions related to purchase, sale, retirement, and depreciation.
(SO 6, 9)

Land		$ 4,000,000
Buildings	$28,500,000	
Less: Accumulated depreciation—buildings	12,100,000	16,400,000
Equipment	48,000,000	
Less: Accumulated depreciation—equipment	5,000,000	43,000,000
Total plant assets		$63,400,000

During 2000, the following selected cash transactions occurred:

April 1 Purchased land for $2,630,000.
May 1 Sold equipment that cost $600,000 when purchased on January 1, 1996. The equipment was sold for $350,000.
June 1 Sold land purchased on June 1, 1990, for $1,800,000. The land cost $200,000.
July 1 Purchased equipment for $1,000,000.
Dec. 31 Retired equipment that cost $500,000 when purchased on December 31, 1990. No salvage value was received.

Instructions

(a) Journalize the above transactions. Los Alamos uses straight-line depreciation for buildings and equipment. The buildings are estimated to have a 40-year life and no salvage value; the equipment is estimated to have a 10-year useful life and no salvage value. Update depreciation on assets disposed of at the time of sale or retirement.
(b) Record adjusting entries for depreciation for 2000.
(c) Prepare the plant assets section of Los Alamos's balance sheet at December 31, 2000.

P10-5B Chon Co. has office furniture that cost $80,000 and that has been depreciated $48,000. Record the disposal under the following assumptions:

Record disposals.
(SO 6)

(a) It was scrapped as having no value.
(b) It was sold for $21,000.
(c) It was sold for $61,000.
(d) It was exchanged for similar office furniture. The old office furniture has a fair market value of $46,000 and $8,000 was paid.

(e) It was exchanged for similar office furniture. The old office furniture has a fair market value of $25,000 and $29,000 was paid.

Prepare entries to record transactions related to acquisition and amortization of intangibles; prepare the intangible assets section.
(SO 8, 9)

P10–6B   The intangible assets section of De Paul Company at December 31, 1999, is presented below:

Patent ($70,000 cost less $7,000 amortization)	$63,000
Copyright ($48,000 cost less $19,200 amortization)	28,800
Total	$91,800

The patent was acquired in January 1999 and has a useful life of 10 years. The copyright was acquired in January 1996 and also has a useful life of 10 years. The following cash transactions may have affected intangible assets during 2000:

Jan. 2   Paid $18,000 legal costs to successfully defend the patent against infringement by another company.

Jan.–June   Developed a new product incurring $140,000 in research and development costs. A patent was granted for the product on July 1, and its useful life is equal to its legal life.

Sept. 1   Paid $80,000 to an extremely large defensive lineman to appear in commercials advertising the company's products. The commercials will air in September and October.

Oct. 1   Acquired a copyright for $160,000. The copyright has a useful life of 50 years.

Instructions
(a) Prepare journal entries to record the transactions above.
(b) Prepare journal entries to record the 2000 amortization expense.
(c) Prepare the intangible assets section of the balance sheet at December 31, 2000.

Prepare entries to correct for errors made in recording and amortizing intangible assets.
(SO 8)

P10–7B   Due to rapid turnover in the accounting department, a number of transactions involving intangible assets were improperly recorded by the Coker Company in 1999.

1. Coker developed a new manufacturing process, incurring research and development costs of $153,000. The company also purchased a patent for $39,100. In early January, Coker capitalized $192,100 as the cost of the patents. Patent amortization expense of $11,300 was recorded based on a 17-year useful life.

2. On July 1, 1999, Coker purchased a small company and as a result acquired goodwill of $76,000. Coker recorded a half-year's amortization in 1999, based on a 50-year life ($760 amortization).

Instructions
Prepare all journal entries necessary to correct any errors made during 1999. Assume the books have not yet been closed for 1999.

Calculate and comment on average age, average useful life of plant assets, and asset turnover ratio.
(SO 9)

P10–8B   Reggie Company and Newman Corporation, two corporations of roughly the same size, are both involved in the manufacture of in-line skates. Each company depreciates its plant assets using the straight-line approach. An investigation of their financial statements reveals the information:

	Reggie Co.	Newman Corp.
Net income	$ 800,000	$1,000,000
Sales	1,600,000	1,300,000
Total assets	2,500,000	1,700,000
Plant assets	1,800,000	1,000,000
Accumulated depreciation	500,000	825,000
Depreciation expense	120,000	31,250
Intangible assets (goodwill)	300,000	0
Amortization expense	60,000	0

Instructions
(a) For each company, calculate these values:
(1) Average age of plant assets.
(2) Average useful life.
(3) Asset turnover ratio.

(b) Based on your calculations in part (a), comment on the relative effectiveness of the two companies in using their assets to generate sales and produce net income. What factors complicate your ability to compare the two companies?

BROADENING YOUR PERSPECTIVE

FINANCIAL REPORTING AND ANALYSIS

FINANCIAL REPORTING AND ANALYSIS: Kellogg Company

BYP10–1   The financial statements and the Notes to Consolidated Financial Statements of Kellogg Company are presented in Appendix A.

Instructions

Refer to Kellogg's financial statements and answer the following questions:

- (a) What was the total cost and book value of property, plant, and equipment at December 31, 1997?
- (b) What method or methods of depreciation are used by Kellogg for financial reporting purposes?
- (c) What was the amount of depreciation and amortization expense for each of the three years 1995–1997?
- (d) Using the Statement of Cash Flows, what is the amount of additions to properties in 1997 and 1996?
- (e) Where does Kellogg disclose its intangible assets, and what are the classifications and amounts of its intangibles at December 31, 1997?
- (f) In December 1996, Kellogg acquired Lender's Bagel's business for $466 million in cash. Name the three components and the amounts of the intangible assets included in the acquisition price. What useful life is used to amortize these intangibles?
- (g) What was the amount of research and development expenses Kellogg had in 1997?

COMPARATIVE ANALYSIS PROBLEM: Kellogg Company vs. General Mills

BYP10–2   Kellogg's financial statements are presented in Appendix A; General Mills's financial statements are presented in Appendix B.

Instructions

- (a) The cost of General Mills's plant assets was $2,571.6 and its accumulated depreciation was $1,292.2. Based on the information contained in these financial statements, compute the following 1997 ratios for each company (use "depreciation and amortization expense" amount for both companies):
  1. Average life of plant assets.
  2. Average age of plant assets.
  3. Asset turnover ratio.
- (b) What conclusions concerning the management of assets can be drawn from these data?

RESEARCH ASSIGNMENT

BYP10–3   The December 18, 1995, issue of *Forbes* includes an article by Rita Koselka, entitled "Tall Story."

Instructions

Read the article and answer the following questions:

- (a) What is the biggest expense in running a video rental store?
- (b) Over how long a period does Hollywood Entertainment Corp. depreciate its video tapes? How did the author arrive at this figure?

(c) The author asserts that, once a store is fully stocked, depreciation expense should be approximately equal to the cost of new tapes. Calculate and compare the ratio of depreciation expense to new purchases for Hollywood and Blockbuster.

(d) If Hollywood can open a new store for $400,000 or buy an existing store for $1.2 million, why might investors value Hollywood at an average of $3 million per store?

INTERPRETING FINANCIAL STATEMENTS
Boeing and McDonnell Douglas

BYP10–4   Boeing and McDonnell Douglas were two leaders in the manufacture of aircraft. In 1996 Boeing announced intentions to acquire McDonnell Douglas and create one huge corporation. Its competitors, primarily Airbus of Europe, were very concerned that they would not be able to compete with such a huge rival. In addition, customers are concerned that this will reduce the number of suppliers to a point where Boeing would be able to dictate prices. Provided below are figures taken from the financial statements of Boeing and McDonnell Douglas which allow a comparison of the operations of the two corporations prior to their merger.

(in millions of dollars)	Boeing	McDonnell Douglas
Total revenue	$19,515	$14,322
Net income (loss)	393	(416)
Total assets	22,098	10,466
Land	404	91
Buildings and fixtures	5,791	1,647
Machinery and equipment	7,251	2,161
Total property, plant, and equipment (at cost)	13,744	3,899
Accumulated depreciation	7,288	2,541
Depreciation expense	976	196

Instructions
(a) Which company had older assets?
(b) Which company used a longer average estimated useful life for its assets?
(c) Based on the total asset turnover ratio, which company used its assets more effectively to generate sales?
(d) Besides an increase in size, what other factors might have motivated this merger?

Merck and Johnson & Johnson

BYP10–5   Merck Co., Inc. and Johnson & Johnson are two leading producers of health care products. Each has considerable assets, as well as expending considerable funds each year toward the development of new products. The development of a new health care product is often very expensive, and risky. New products frequently must undergo considerable testing before approval for distribution to the public. For example, it took Johnson & Johnson 4 years and $200 million to develop its 1-DAY ACUVUE contact lenses. Below are some basic data compiled from the financial statements of these two companies.

(all dollars in millions)	Johnson & Johnson	Merck
Total assets	$15,668	$21,857
Total revenue	15,734	14,970
Net income	2,006	2,997
Research and development expense	1,278	1,230
Intangible assets	2,403	7,212

Instructions
(a) What kinds of intangible assets might a health care products company have? Does the composition of these intangibles matter to investors—that is, would it be perceived differently if all of Merck's intangibles were goodwill, than if all of its intangibles were patents?
(b) By employing the asset turnover ratio, determine which company is using its assets more effectively. (*Note*: The previous year's total assets were $19,928 million for Merck and $12,242 million for Johnson & Johnson.)

(c) Suppose the president of Merck has come to you for advice. He has noted that by eliminating research and development expenditures the company could have reported $1.3 billion more in net income in the current year. He is frustrated because much of the research never results in a product, or the products take years to develop. He says shareholders are eager for higher returns, so he is considering eliminating research and development expenditures for at least a couple of years. What would you advise?

(d) The notes to Merck's financial statements indicate that Merck has goodwill of $4.1 billion. Where does recorded goodwill come from? Is it necessarily a good thing to have a lot of goodwill on your books?

REAL-WORLD FOCUS: Clark Equipment Company

BYP10–6   Clark Equipment Company was originally formed in 1902 as a general manufacturing company. During its history it has specialized in the manufacture of drills, gears, towing tractors, lift trucks, and truck transmissions. At the time of the example presented below, Clark operated throughout the U.S. and Europe in the design, manufacture, and sale of skid steer loaders and mini-excavators, golf carts and utility vehicles, axles and transmissions for off-highway vehicles, and asphalt paving equipment. In 1995, Ingersoll-Rand Company acquired Clark and combined its operating units with existing I-R businesses.

The following information relates to the plant assets of Clark Equipment:

CLARK EQUIPMENT COMPANY
Balance Sheet (partial)
(in millions)

	Previous Year	Current Year
Land	$ 7.4	$ 13.2
Land improvements	5.9	8.8
Buildings	77.3	126.0
Machinery and equipment	398.4	451.7
Totals	489.0	599.7
Accumulated depreciation	272.8	315.9
Total plant assets	$216.2	$283.8

Instructions

(a) What type of costs would Clark Equipment capitalize in the land category of plant assets?

(b) Cite several possible types of land improvements that Clark Equipment might have made.

(c) What is the book value of Clark Equipment's plant assets?

CRITICAL THINKING

GROUP DECISION CASE

BYP10–7   Fresno Company and Auburn Company are two proprietorships that are similar in many respects except that Fresno Company uses the straight-line method and Auburn Company uses the declining-balance method at double the straight-line rate. On January 2, 1997, both companies acquired the following depreciable assets.

Asset	Cost	Salvage Value	Useful Life
Building	$320,000	$20,000	40 years
Equipment	110,000	10,000	10 years

Including the appropriate depreciation charges, annual net income for the companies in the years 1997, 1998, and 1999 and total income for the 3 years were as follows:

	1997	1998	1999	Total
Fresno Company	$84,000	$88,400	$90,000	$262,400
Auburn Company	68,000	76,000	85,000	229,000

At December 31, 1999, the balance sheets of the two companies are similar except that Auburn Company has more cash than Fresno Company.

Mary Flaherty is interested in buying one of the companies, and she comes to you for advice.

Instructions

With the class divided into groups, answer the following:

(a) Determine the annual and total depreciation recorded by each company during the 3 years.

(b) Assuming that Auburn Company also uses the straight-line method of depreciation instead of the declining-balance method as in (a), prepare comparative income data for the 3 years.

(c) Which company should Mrs. Flaherty buy? Why?

COMMUNICATION ACTIVITY

BYP10–8   The following was published with the financial statements to American Exploration Company:

AMERICAN EXPLORATION COMPANY
Notes to the Financial Statements

Property, Plant, and Equipment—The Company accounts for its oil and gas exploration and production activities using the successful efforts method of accounting. Under this method, acquisition costs for proved and unproved properties are capitalized when incurred. . . . The costs of drilling exploratory wells are capitalized pending determination of whether each well has discovered proved reserves. If proved reserves are not discovered, such drilling costs are charged to expense. . . . Depletion of the cost of producing oil and gas properties is computed on the units-of-activity method.

Instructions

Write a brief memo to your instructor discussing American Exploration Company's note regarding property, plant, and equipment. Your memo should address what is meant by the "successful efforts method" and "units-of-activity method."

ETHICS CASE

BYP10–9   Finney Container Company is suffering declining sales of its principal product, nonbiodegradeable plastic cartons. The president, Philip Shapeero, instructs his controller, Sharon Fetters, to lengthen asset lives to reduce depreciation expense. A processing line of automated plastic extruding equipment, purchased for $2.7 million in January 1999 was originally estimated to have a useful life of 8 years and a salvage value of $300,000. Depreciation has been recorded for 2 years on that basis. Philip wants the estimated life changed to 12 years total, and the straight-line method continued. Sharon is hesitant to make the change, believing it is unethical to increase net income in this manner. Philip says, "Hey, the life is only an estimate, and I've heard that our competition uses a 12-year life on their production equipment."

Instructions

(a) Who are the stakeholders in this situation?
(b) Is the change in asset life unethical or simply a good business practice by an astute president?
(c) What is the effect of Philip Shapeero's proposed change on income before taxes in the year of change?

SURFING THE NET

BYP10–10 A company's annual report identifies the amount of its plant assets and the depreciation method used.

Address: http://www.reportgallery.com

Steps:

1. From Report Gallery Homepage, choose **Viewing Library.**
2. Select a particular company.
3. Choose **Annual Report.**
4. Follow instructions below.

Instructions
Answer the following questions:

(a) What is the name of the company?
(b) What is the Internet address of the annual report?
(c) At fiscal year-end, what is the net amount of its plant assets?
(d) What is the accumulated depreciation?
(e) Which method of depreciation does the company use?

Answers to Self-Study Questions
1. d   2. b   3. d   4. d   5. b   6. d   7. a   8. c   9. c   10. b   11. c

---

Answer to Kellogg Review It Question 4, p. 425.
Kellogg reports the detail about its "Property, net" in Note 14 "Supplemental financial statement data." The classifications and amounts constituting the detail for "Property, net" are reported by Kellogg as (in millions) land $49; buildings $1,213.8; machinery and equipment $3,434.7; construction in progress $283.1; and accumulated depreciation $2,207.3.

 Remember to go back to the Navigator box on the chapter-opening page and check off your completed work.

CONCEPTS FOR REVIEW

Before studying this chapter, you should know or, if necessary, review:

a. The importance of liquidity in evaluating the financial position of a company. (Ch. 4, p. 160)

b. How to make adjusting entries related to unearned revenue (Ch. 3, pp. 101–102) and accrued expenses. (Ch. 3, pp. 104–107)

c. The principles of internal control. (Ch. 7, p. 281)

FEATURE STORY

No Computer? Your Paycheck May Be Late

When it comes to payroll, colleges are very much like the "real world." There's a payroll supervisor, a few clerks, a giant computer, reams of computer printouts—and, of course, paychecks.

Mrs. Dianna Webb is the payroll supervisor at Casper College in Cas-per, Wyoming, a school with 6,000 students and 550 people on the payroll. "I take out tax deductions, credit union contributions, contributions to tax-sheltered annuities, United Way donations, and even garnishments when an employee has been ordered by a court to pay a debt. Wyoming has no state income tax, so that's one deduction I don't have to worry about."

The payroll staff consists of just Mrs. Webb and the computer. Their job: To process monthly checks for the faculty, administrators, and students and semi-monthly checks for staff. What if she didn't have a computer? "I doubt I'd be able to pay as many people," she laughs.

Just as in any other business, Dianna Webb keeps timecards for all hourly employees. The faculty and administrators—salaried employees—are on the honor system to work the required number of hours, but even their pay has to be authorized.

The computer provides Dianna Webb with many useful reports: The main report shows the payroll in alphabetical order, listing gross pay, tax deductions, other payroll deductions, and net pay. She also gets a report that lists year-to-date totals. "In May, faculty members get paid the balance on their contracts, so I need to know those year-to-date totals."

Student employees provide one extra wrinkle: They don't have Social Security (FICA) taxes withheld during the school year. The reason: Federal regulations consider students who work for the college and are enrolled and attend classes to be exempt from Social Security and Medicare taxes. For work done during the summer months, though, Social Security taxes are withheld.

CHAPTER 11

CURRENT LIABILITIES AND PAYROLL ACCOUNTING

THE NAVIGATOR ✔

- Understand *Concepts for Review* ☐
- Read *Feature Story* ☐
- Scan *Study Objectives* ☐
- Read *Preview* ☐
- Read text and answer *Before You Go On*
  p. 478 ☐ p. 489 ☐ p. 492 ☐ p. 495 ☐
- Work *Demonstration Problems* ☐
- Review *Summary of Study Objectives* ☐
- Answer *Self-Study Questions* ☐
- Complete assignments ☐

STUDY OBJECTIVES

After studying this chapter, you should be able to:

1. *Explain a current liability and identify the major types of current liabilities.*
2. *Describe the accounting for notes payable.*
3. *Explain the accounting for other current liabilities.*
4. *Explain the methods for the financial statement presentation and analysis of current liabilities.*
5. *Describe the accounting and disclosure requirements for contingent liabilities.*
6. *Discuss the objectives of internal control for payroll.*
7. *Compute and record the payroll for a pay period.*
8. *Describe and record employer payroll taxes.*
9. *Identify additional fringe benefits associated with employee compensation.*

THE NAVIGATOR

Whether it be a college like Casper College, a pizza parlor like Pizza Hut, a public accounting firm like Arthur Andersen & Co., or a large multinational company like IBM, all enterprises have liabilities for payroll. In addition, they also have many other types of liabilities. Examples are the purchase of supplies on account, the borrowing of money on a bank loan, and the obligation to pay interest. Liabilities are classified as current or long-term on the balance sheet. We will explain current liabilities in this chapter and long-term liabilities in Chapter 16. The content and organization of this chapter are as follows:

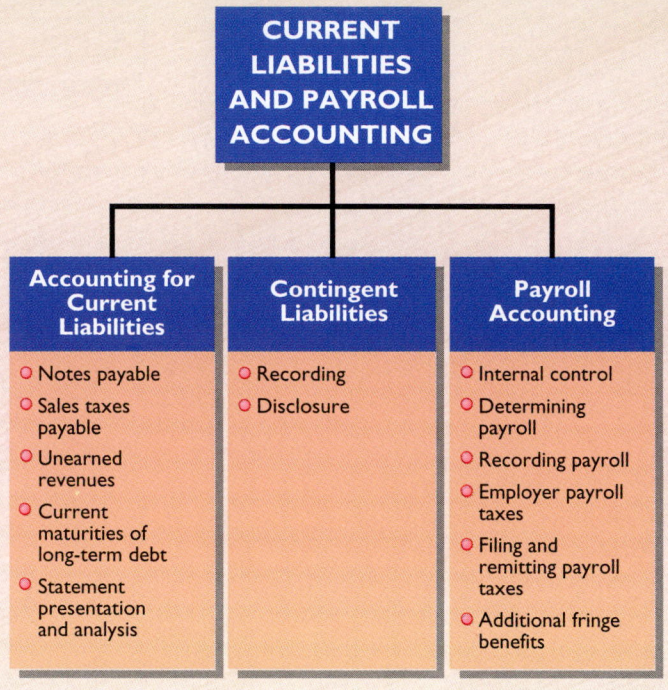

THE
NAVIGATOR

ACCOUNTING FOR CURRENT LIABILITIES

STUDY OBJECTIVE

1

Explain a current liability and identify the major types of current liabilities.

As explained in Chapter 4, a **current liability** is a debt that can reasonably be expected to be paid (1) from existing current assets or through the creation of other current liabilities, and (2) within one year or the operating cycle, whichever is longer. Debts that do not meet both criteria are classified as long-term liabilities. In most companies, current liabilities are paid within one year out of current assets, rather than through the creation of other liabilities.

Companies must carefully monitor the relationship of current liabilities to current assets. This relationship is critical in evaluating a company's liquidity, or short-term debt paying ability. A company that has more current liabilities than current assets is usually the subject of some concern because the company may not be able to meet its current obligations when they become due.

Current liabilities include notes payable, accounts payable, unearned revenues, and accrued liabilities such as taxes, salaries and wages, and interest payable. The entries for accounts payable and adjusting entries for some current liabilities have been explained in previous chapters. Other types of current liabilities that are frequently encountered in practice are discussed in the following sections.

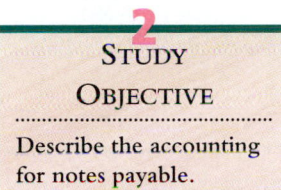

HELPFUL HINT
The current liability section gives creditors a good idea of what obligations are coming due.

Notes Payable

Obligations in the form of written promissory notes are recorded as notes payable. Notes payable are often used instead of accounts payable. Doing so gives the lender written documentation of the obligation in case legal remedies are needed to collect the debt. Notes payable usually require the borrower to pay interest and frequently are issued to meet short-term financing needs.

Notes are issued for varying periods. **Those due for payment within one year of the balance sheet date are usually classified as current liabilities.** Most notes are interest bearing. To illustrate the accounting for notes payable, assume that First National Bank agrees to lend $100,000 on March 1, 1999, if Cole Williams Co. signs a $100,000, 12%, 4-month note. With an interest-bearing promissory note, the amount of assets received upon issuance of the note generally equals the note's face value. Cole Williams Co. therefore will receive $100,000 cash and will make the following journal entry:

2
STUDY
OBJECTIVE
....
Describe the accounting for notes payable.

Mar. 1	Cash	100,000	
	Notes Payable		100,000
	(To record issuance of 12%, 4-month note to		
	First National Bank)		

A	=	L	+ OE
+ 100,000		+ 100,000	

Interest accrues over the life of the note and must be recorded periodically. If Cole Williams Co. prepares financial statements semiannually, an adjusting entry is required to recognize interest expense and interest payable of $4,000 ($100,000 × 12% × 4/12) at June 30. The formula for computing interest and its application to Cole Williams Co. are shown in Illustration 11-1.

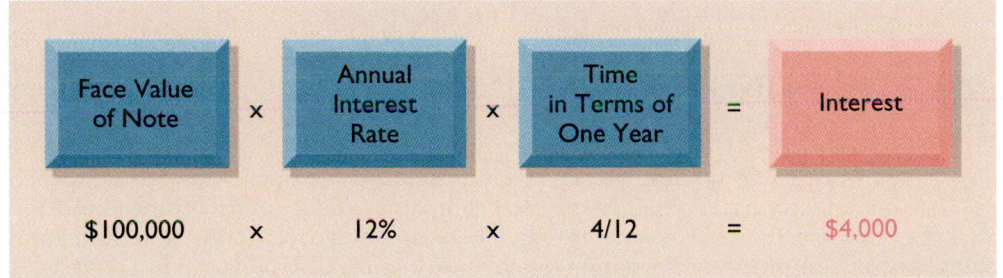

ILLUSTRATION 11-1
Formula for computing interest

The adjusting entry is:

June 30	Interest Expense	4,000	
	Interest Payable		4,000
	(To accrue interest for 4 months on First		
	National Bank note)		

A	=	L	+ OE
		+ 4,000	− 4,000

In the June 30 financial statements, the current liability section of the balance sheet will show notes payable $100,000 and interest payable $4,000. In addition, interest expense of $4,000 will be reported under Other Expenses and Losses in the income statement. If Cole Williams Co. prepared financial statements monthly, the adjusting entry at the end of each month would have been $1,000 ($100,000 × 12% × 1/12).

At maturity (July 1), Cole Williams Co. must pay the face value of the note ($100,000) plus $4,000 interest ($100,000 × 12% × 4/12). The entry to record payment of the note and accrued interest is as follows:

A = L + OE
− 104,000 − 100,000
−   4,000

July 1	Notes Payable	100,000	
	Interest Payable	4,000	
	Cash		104,000
	(To record payment of First National Bank interest-bearing note and accrued interest at maturity)		

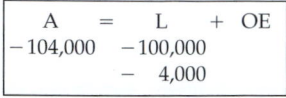

STUDY

OBJECTIVE

Explain the accounting for other current liabilities.

Sales Taxes Payable

As consumers, we are well aware that many of the products we purchase at retail stores are subject to sales taxes. The tax is expressed as a stated percentage of the sales price. The retailer (or selling company) collects the tax from the customer when the sale occurs, and periodically (usually monthly) remits the collections to the state's department of revenue.

Under most state sales tax laws, the amount of the sale and the amount of the sales tax collected must be rung up separately on the cash register. (Gasoline sales are a major exception.) The cash register readings are then used to credit Sales and Sales Taxes Payable. For example, assuming that the March 25 cash register readings for Cooley Grocery show sales of $10,000 and sales taxes of $600 (sales tax rate of 6%), the entry is:

A = L + OE
+ 10,600   + 600   + 10,000

Mar. 25	Cash	10,600	
	Sales		10,000
	Sales Taxes Payable		600
	(To record daily sales and sales taxes)		

When the taxes are remitted to the taxing agency, Sales Taxes Payable is debited and Cash is credited. The company does not report sales taxes as an expense; it simply forwards the amount paid by the customer to the government. Thus, Cooley Grocery serves only as a **collection agent** for the taxing authority.

ACCOUNTING IN ACTION
Business Insight

Sales taxes do not apply exclusively to retail companies. They also apply to manufacturing companies, service companies, and public utilities, and the extent of the taxes is increasing. There are now over 9,000 state and local sales taxes. "Compliance is becoming much more complex as states expand their sales taxes," says an American Telephone and Telegraph (AT&T) tax attorney. They are also becoming more costly. AT&T employs a staff just to file the company's sales tax returns and handle the sales tax audits.

When sales taxes are not rung up separately on the cash register, total receipts are divided by 100% plus the sales tax percentage to determine sales. To illustrate, assume in the above example that Cooley Grocery "rings up" total receipts, which are $10,600. Because the amount received from the sale is equal to the sales price 100% plus 6% of sales, or 1.06 times the sales total, we can compute sales as follows:

$$\$10,600 \div 1.06 = \$10,000$$

Thus, the sales tax amount of $600 is found either by (1) subtracting sales from total receipts ($10,600 − $10,000) or (2) multiplying sales by the sales tax rate ($10,000 × 6%).

Unearned Revenues

A magazine publisher such as Sports Illustrated may receive a customer's check when magazines are ordered, and an airline company, such as American Airlines, often receives cash when it sells tickets for future flights. How do these companies account for unearned revenues that are received before goods are delivered or services are rendered?

1. When the advance is received, Cash is debited, and a current liability account identifying the source of the unearned revenue is credited.
2. When the revenue is earned, the unearned revenue account is debited, and an earned revenue account is credited.

To illustrate, assume that Superior University sells 10,000 season football tickets at $50 each for its five-game home schedule. The entry for the sales of season tickets is:

Aug. 6	Cash	500,000	
	Unearned Football Ticket Revenue		500,000
	(To record sale of 10,000 season tickets)		

| A | = | L | + | OE |
| +500,000 | | +500,000 | | |

As each game is completed, the following entry is made:

Sept. 7	Unearned Football Ticket Revenue	100,000	
	Football Ticket Revenue		100,000
	(To record football ticket revenues earned)		

| A | = | L | + | OE |
| | | −100,000 | | +100,000 |

Unearned Football Ticket Revenue is, therefore, unearned revenue and is reported as a current liability in the balance sheet. As revenue is earned, a transfer from unearned revenue to earned revenue occurs. Unearned revenue is material for some companies: In the airline industry, for example, tickets sold for future flights represent almost 50% of total current liabilities. At United Air Lines, unearned ticket revenue is the largest current liability, recently amounting to over $1 billion.

Illustration 11-2 shows specific unearned and earned revenue accounts used in selected types of businesses.

| Type of Business | Account Title | |
	Unearned Revenue	Earned Revenue
Airline	Unearned Passenger Ticket Revenue	Passenger Revenue
Magazine publisher	Unearned Subscription Revenue	Subscription Revenue
Hotel	Unearned Rental Revenue	Rental Revenue

ILLUSTRATION 11-2

Unearned and earned revenue accounts

Current Maturities of Long-Term Debt

Companies often have a portion of long-term debt that comes due in the current year. For example, assume that Wendy Construction issues a 5-year interest-bearing $25,000 note on January 1, 1999. This note specifies that each January 1, starting January 1, 2000, $5,000 of the note should be paid. When financial statements are prepared on December 31, 1999, $5,000 should be reported as a current liability and $20,000 as a long-term liability. Current maturities of long-term debt are often identified on the balance sheet as **long-term debt due within one year**.

It is not necessary to prepare an adjusting entry to recognize the current maturity of long-term debt. The proper statement classification of each balance sheet account is recognized when the balance sheet is prepared.

Statement Presentation and Analysis

Presentation

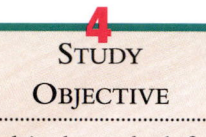

STUDY
OBJECTIVE

Explain the methods for the financial statement presentation and analysis of current liabilities.

As indicated in Chapter 4, current liabilities are the first category under liabilities on the balance sheet. Each of the principal types of current liabilities is listed separately within the category. In addition, the terms of notes payable and other pertinent information concerning the individual items are disclosed in the notes to the financial statements.

Current liabilities are seldom listed in the order of maturity because of the varying maturity dates that may exist for specific obligations such as notes payable. A more common, and entirely satisfactory, method of presenting current liabilities is to list them by **order of magnitude**, with the largest obligations first. Many companies, as a matter of custom, show notes payable and accounts payable first, regardless of amount. The following adapted excerpt from the balance sheet of Kellogg Company illustrates this practice.

ILLUSTRATION 11-3

Balance sheet presentation of current liabilities

HELPFUL HINT

For another example of a current liability section refer to the General Mills balance sheet in Appendix B.

KELLOGG COMPANY
Balance Sheet
December 31, 1997
(in millions)

Assets

Current assets	$1,467.7
Property, plant, and equipment (net)	2,773.3
Identifiable intangible assets and goodwill	636.6
Total assets	$4,877.6

Liabilities and Stockholders' Equity

Current liabilities	
Current maturities of long-term debt	$ 211.2
Notes payable	368.6
Accounts payable	328.0
Other current liabilities	749.5
Total current liabilities	1,657.3
Noncurrent liabilities	2,222.8
Shareholders' equity	997.5
Total liabilities and shareholders' equity	$4,877.6

Analysis

Classifying assets and liabilities into current and noncurrent allows a company's liquidity to be analyzed and evaluated. Liquidity refers to the ability of a company to pay its maturing obligations and meet unexpected needs for cash. The relationship of current assets and current liabilities is critical in analyzing liquidity. This relationship is expressed as a dollar amount called working capital and as a ratio called the current ratio.

The excess of current assets over current liabilities is **working capital**. The formula for the computation of Kellogg's working capital is shown in Illustration 11-4 (dollar amounts in millions).

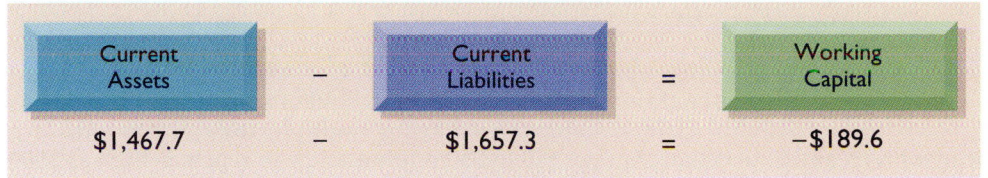

As an absolute dollar amount, working capital is limited in its informational value. For example $1 million of working capital may be far more than needed for a small company but be inadequate for a large corporation. And, $1 million of working capital may be adequate for a company at one time but be inadequate at another time. The **current ratio** permits us to compare the liquidity of different sized companies and of a single company at different times. The current ratio is current assets divided by current liabilities. The formula for this ratio is illustrated below, along with its computation using Kellogg's current asset and current liability data:

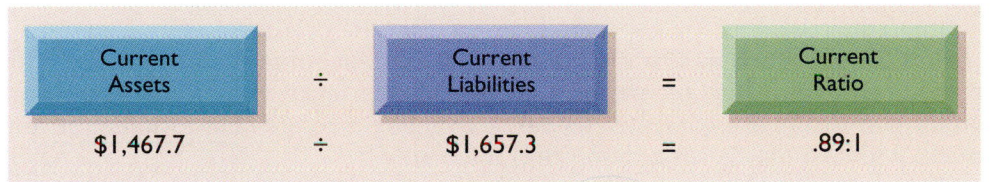

Historically, a ratio of 2:1 was considered to be the standard for a good credit rating. In recent years, however, many healthy companies have maintained ratios well below 2:1. This is exemplified by Kellogg, which is considered a healthy company even though its current ratio is below 1:1.

CONTINGENT LIABILITIES

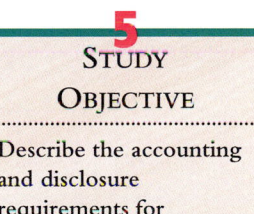

5

STUDY

OBJECTIVE

Describe the accounting and disclosure requirements for contingent liabilities.

With notes payable, interest payable, accounts payable, and sales taxes payable, we know that an obligation exists to make payment. But suppose that your company is currently involved in a dispute with the Internal Revenue Service (IRS) over the amount of its income tax liability. Do you have to report the disputed amount on the balance sheet as a liability? Or suppose your company is the defendant in a lawsuit in which an adverse decision might result in bankruptcy. How should this major contingency be reported? The answers to these questions are difficult, because these liabilities are dependent—contingent—upon some future event. In other words, a **contingent liability** is a potential liability that may become an actual liability in the future.

How, then, should contingent liabilities be reported? Guidelines have been adopted that are helpful in resolving these problems. The guidelines require that:

HELPFUL HINT
Another example of a contingency is toxic waste cleanup costs. Some expect that insurance will cover these costs, but insurance companies are arguing that general liability policies were never meant to cover this type of situation.

1. If the contingency is **probable**—if it is likely to occur—**and** the amount can be **reasonably estimated**, the liability should be recorded in the accounts.

2. If the contingency is only **reasonably possible**—if it could happen—then it need be disclosed only in the notes accompanying the financial statements.

3. If the contingency is **remote**—if it is unlikely to occur—it need not be recorded or disclosed.

ACCOUNTING IN ACTION
Business Insight

Contingent liabilities abound in the real world. Consider the following: Manville Corp. filed bankruptcy when it was hit by billions of dollars in asbestos product liability claims. Companies having multiple toxic waste sites are faced with cleanup costs that average $10 to $30 million and can reach as high as $500 million depending on the type of waste. For life and health insurance companies and their stockholders, the cost of AIDS is like an iceberg—everybody wonders how big it really is and what damage it might do in the future; according to the U.S. Centers for Disease Control treatment costs could be $8 billion to $16 billion. And frequent-flyer programs are so popular that airlines at one time owed participants more than 3 million round-trip domestic tickets. That's enough to fly at least 5.4 billion miles—free for the passengers but at what future cost to the airlines?

Recording a Contingent Liability

INTERNATIONAL NOTE

International accounting standards basically use criteria similar to those in the U.S. in determining how to account for contingencies.

Product warranties are a good example of a contingent liability that should be recorded in the accounts. Warranty contracts result in future costs that may be incurred in replacing defective units or repairing malfunctioning units without charge to the customer for a specified period after the product is sold. Generally, a manufacturer, such as Black & Decker, knows that some warranty costs will be incurred. Moreover, on the basis of prior experience with the product (or similar products), the company usually can make a reasonable estimate of the anticipated cost of servicing (honoring) the contract.

The accounting for warranty costs is based on the matching principle. To comply with this principle, **the estimated cost of honoring product warranty contracts should be recognized as an expense in the period in which the sale occurs**. To illustrate, assume that in 1999 Denson Manufacturing Company sells 10,000 washers and dryers at an average price of $600 each. The selling price includes a one-year warranty on parts. It is expected that 500 units (5%) will be defective and that warranty repair costs will average $80 per unit. In the year of sale, warranty contracts are honored on 300 units at a total cost of $24,000.

At December 31, it is necessary to accrue the estimated warranty costs on the 1999 sales. The computation is as follows:

ILLUSTRATION 11-6

Computation of estimated product warranty liability

Number of units sold	10,000
Estimated rate of defective units	× 5%
Total estimated defective units	500
Average warranty repair cost	× $80
Estimated product warranty liability	**$40,000**

The adjusting entry, therefore, is:

A	=	L	+	OE
		+40,000		−40,000

Dec. 31	Warranty Expense	40,000	
	Estimated Warranty Liability		40,000
	(To accrue estimated warranty costs)		

The entry to record repair costs incurred in 1999 to honor warranty contracts on 1999 sales is shown in summary form below:

Jan. 1– Dec. 31	Estimated Warranty Liability	24,000		
	Repair Parts		24,000	
	(To record honoring of 300 warranty contracts on 1999 sales)			

A	=	L	+	OE
−24,000		−24,000		

Warranty expense of $40,000 is reported under selling expenses in the income statement, and estimated warranty liability of $16,000 ($40,000 − $24,000) is classified as a current liability on the balance sheet.

In the following year, all expenses incurred in honoring warranty contracts on 1999 sales should be debited to Estimated Warranty Liability. To illustrate, assume that 20 defective units are replaced in January 2000, at an average cost of $80 in parts and labor. The summary entry for the month of January is:

Jan. 31	Estimated Warranty Liability	1,600		
	Repair Parts		1,600	
	(To record honoring of 20 warranty contracts on 1997 sales)			

A	=	L	+	OE
−1,600		−1,600		

Disclosure of Contingent Liabilities

When it is probable that a contingent liability will be incurred but the amount cannot be reasonably estimated, or when the contingent liability is only reasonably possible, only disclosure of the contingency is required. Examples of contingencies that may require disclosure are pending or threatened lawsuits and assessment of additional income taxes pending an IRS audit of the tax return.

The disclosure should identify the nature of the item, and if known, the amount of the contingency and the expected outcome of the future event. Disclosure is usually accomplished through a note to the financial statements, as illustrated by the following:

USAIR
Notes to the Financial Statements

Legal Proceedings

The Company and various subsidiaries have been named as defendants in various suits and proceedings which involve, among other things, environmental concerns about noise and air pollution and employment matters. These suits and proceedings are in various stages of litigation, and the status of the law with respect to several of the issues involved is unsettled. For these reasons the outcome of these suits and proceedings is difficult to predict. In the Company's opinion, however, the disposition of these matters is not likely to have a material adverse effect on its financial condition.

ILLUSTRATION 11-7

Disclosure of contingent liability

BEFORE YOU GO ON . . .

Review It

1. What are the two criteria for classifying a debt as a current liability?
2. Identify three liabilities classified as current by Kellogg. The answer to this question is provided on page 512.
3. What entries are made for an interest-bearing note payable?
4. How are sales taxes recorded by a retailer? Identify three unearned revenues.
5. What are the accounting guidelines for contingent liabilities?
6. How may the liquidity of a company be analyzed?

Do It

You and several classmates are studying for the next accounting examination. They ask you to answer the following questions: (1) How is the sales tax amount determined when the cash register total includes sales taxes? (2) When should a contingency be recorded in the accounts?

Reasoning: To answer the first question, you must remove the sales taxes from the total sales. To answer the second question, you need to know the criteria for recording and disclosing contingent liabilities.

Solution:

(1) First, divide the total proceeds by 100% plus the sales tax percentage to find the sales amount; second, subtract the sales amount from the total proceeds to determine the sales taxes.

(2) A contingency should be recorded when it is *probable* that a liability will be incurred *and* the amount can be *reasonably* estimated.

Related exercise material: BE11–3, BE11–4, BE11–5, E11–2, E11–3, E11–4, and E11–5.

THE NAVIGATOR

PAYROLL ACCOUNTING

Payroll and related fringe benefits often constitute a substantial percentage of current liabilities. In addition, employee compensation is often the most significant expense that a company incurs. For example, General Motors recently reported total employees of 516,000 and labor costs of $31.3 billion. Add to labor costs such fringe benefits as health insurance, life insurance, disability insurance, and so on, and you can see why proper accounting and control of payroll are so important.

It should be emphasized that payroll accounting involves more than paying employees' wages. Companies are required by law to maintain payroll records for each employee, file and pay payroll taxes, and comply with numerous state and federal tax laws applicable to employee compensation. Accounting for payroll has become much more complex as a result of these regulations.

The term "payroll" pertains to all salaries and wages paid to employees. Managerial, administrative, and sales personnel are generally paid **salaries**, which are often expressed in terms of a specified amount per month or per year rather than an hourly rate. For example, in the opening story the faculty and administrative personnel at Casper College are paid salaries. In contrast, store clerks, factory employees, and manual laborers are normally paid **wages**, which are based on a rate per hour or on a piecework basis (such as per unit of product). Frequently, the terms "salaries" and "wages" are used interchangeably.

The term "payroll" does not extend to payments made for personal service by professionals such as certified public accountants, attorneys, and architects. Such professionals are independent contractors, and payments to them are called **fees**, rather than salaries or wages. This distinction is important because government regulations relating to the payment and reporting of payroll taxes apply only to employees.

Internal Control

Internal control was introduced in Chapter 7. As applied to payrolls, the objectives of internal control are (1) to safeguard company assets against unauthorized payments of payrolls and (2) to assure the accuracy and reliability of the accounting records pertaining to payrolls.

Unfortunately, irregularities often result if internal control is lax. Overstating hours, using unauthorized pay rates, adding fictitious employees to the payroll, continuing terminated employees on the payroll, and distributing duplicate payroll checks are all methods of stealing from a company. Moreover, inaccurate records will result in incorrect paychecks, financial statements, and payroll tax returns.

6
STUDY
OBJECTIVE
....
Discuss the objectives of internal control for payroll.

TECHNOLOGY IN ACTION

A Senate hearing revealed that the U.S. Army spent $8 million on unauthorized pay, including payments to deserters and "ghost" soldiers. The underlying cause was a computer system so lax that it was possible to create new pay records and destroy old ones without leaving an audit trail.

Payroll activities involve four functions: hiring employees, timekeeping, preparing the payroll, and paying the payroll. For an internal control system to work effectively, these four functions should be assigned to different departments or individuals. To illustrate these functions in more detail, we will examine the case of Academy Company and one of its employees, Michael Jordan.

Hiring Employees

Posting job openings, screening and interviewing applicants, and hiring employees are responsibilities of the personnel department. From a control standpoint, the personnel department provides significant documentation and authorization. When an employee is hired, the personnel department prepares an authorization form like the one used by Academy Company for Michael Jordan shown in Illustration 11-8.

The authorization form is sent to the payroll department, where it is used to place the new employee on the payroll. A chief concern of the personnel department is ensuring the accuracy of this form. The reason is quite simple: one of the most common types of payroll frauds is adding fictitious employees to the payroll.

The personnel department is also responsible for authorizing (1) changes in pay rates during employment and (2) terminations of employment. In each instance, the authorization should be in writing, and a copy of the change in status should be sent to the payroll department. Note in Illustration 11-8 that Jordan received a pay increase of $2 per hour.

Hiring Employees

Personnel department documents and authorizes employment.

ILLUSTRATION 11-8

Personnel authorization form

ACADEMY COMPANY

Employee Name ___Jordan,___ ___Michael___ ___ Starting Date ___9/01/95___
<small>LAST</small> <small>FIRST</small> <small>MI</small>

Classification ___Skilled-Level 10___ Social Security No. ___329-36-9547___

Department ___Shipping___ Division ___Entertainment___

| **NEW HIRE** | Classification ___Clerk___ Salary Grade ___Level 10___ Trans. from Temp. ☐ |
| | Rate $ ___10.00___ per ___hour___ Bonus ___N/A___ Non-exempt ☒ Exempt ☐ |

RATE CHANGE	New Rate $ ___12.00___ Effective Date ___9/1/97___
	Present Rate $ ___10.00___
	Merit ☒ Promotion ☐ Decrease ☐ Other ___
	Previous Increase Date ___None___ Amount $ ___ per ___ Type ___

SEPARATION	Resignation ☐ Discharge ☐ Retirement ☐ Reason ___
	___
	Leave of absence ☐ From ___ to ___ Type ___
	Last Day Worked ___

APPROVALS	*BEW* 9/1/97 *EMW* 9-1-97
	BRANCH OR DEPT. MANAGER DATE DIVISION V.P. DATE
	James E. Speer
	PERSONNEL DEPARTMENT

Timekeeping

Timekeeping

Supervisors monitor hours worked through time cards and time reports.

Another area in which internal control is important is timekeeping. Hourly employees are usually required to record time worked by "punching" a time clock. The time of arrival and departure are automatically recorded by the employee when he or she inserts a time card into the clock. The time card for Michael Jordan is shown in Illustration 11-9.

In large companies, time clock procedures are often monitored by a supervisor or security guard to make sure an employee punches only one card. At the end of the pay period, the employee's supervisor is required to approve the hours shown by signing the time card. When overtime hours are involved, approval by a supervisor is usually mandatory to guard against unauthorized overtime. The approved time card is then sent to the payroll department. For salaried employees, a manually prepared weekly or monthly time report kept by a supervisor may be used to record time worked.

Preparing the Payroll

Preparing the Payroll

Two (or more) employees verify payroll amounts; supervisor approves.

The payroll is prepared in the payroll department on the basis of two sources of input: (1) personnel department authorizations and (2) approved time cards. Because of the numerous calculations involved in determining gross wages and payroll deductions, it is customary for a second payroll department employee, working independently, to verify all amounts, and a payroll department supervisor then approves the payroll. The payroll department is also responsible for preparing (but not signing) payroll checks, maintaining payroll records, and preparing payroll tax returns.

ILLUSTRATION 11-9

Time card

		PAY PERIOD ENDING
No. 17		1/14/99

NAME   Michael Jordan

EXTRA TIME			REGULAR TIME
	1st Day	A.M. IN	8:58
		NOON OUT	12:00
		NOON IN	1:00
		P.M. OUT	5:01
	2nd Day	A.M. IN	9:00
		NOON OUT	11:59
		NOON IN	12:59
		P.M. OUT	5:00
	3rd Day	A.M. IN	8:59
		NOON OUT	12:01
		NOON IN	1:01
		P.M. OUT	5:00
5:00	4th Day	A.M. IN	9:00
9:00		NOON OUT	12:00
		NOON IN	1:00
		P.M. OUT	5:00
	5th Day	A.M. IN	8:57
		NOON OUT	11:58
		NOON IN	1:00
		P.M. OUT	5:01
	6th Day	A.M. IN	8:00
		NOON OUT	1:00
		NOON IN	
		P.M. OUT	
	7th Day	A.M. IN	
		NOON OUT	
		NOON IN	
		P.M. OUT	
TOTAL 4		TOTAL	40

Paying the Payroll

The payroll is paid by the treasurer's department. **Payment by check minimizes the risk of loss from theft, and the endorsed check provides proof of payment.** For good internal control, payroll checks should be prenumbered, and all checks should be accounted for. All checks must be signed by the treasurer (or a designated agent), and their distribution to employees should be controlled by the treasurer's department. Checks may be distributed by the treasurer or paymaster.

If the payroll is paid in currency, it is customary to have a second person count the cash in each pay envelope and for the paymaster to obtain a signed receipt from the employee upon payment. Thus, if alleged discrepancies arise, adequate safeguards have been established to protect each party involved.

Paying the Payroll

Treasurer signs and distributes checks.

Determining the Payroll

Determining the payroll involves computing (1) gross earnings, (2) payroll deductions, and (3) net pay.

Gross Earnings

Gross earnings are the total compensation earned by an employee. There are three major types of gross earnings: wages, salaries, and bonuses.

Total **wages** for an employee are determined by multiplying the hours worked by the hourly rate of pay. In addition to the hourly pay rate, most companies are required by law to pay hourly workers a minimum of one and one-half times the regular hourly rate for overtime work in excess of 8 hours per day

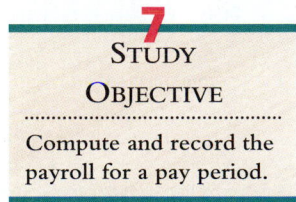

7

STUDY

OBJECTIVE
·····································
Compute and record the payroll for a pay period.

or 40 hours per week. For example, companies involved in interstate commerce are required by the Federal Fair Labor Standards Act to pay one and one-half times the regular wage rate. In addition, many employers pay overtime rates for work done at night, on weekends, and on holidays. The computation of Michael Jordan's gross earnings (total wages) for the 44 hours shown on his time card for the weekly pay period ending January 14 is as follows:

ILLUSTRATION 11-10

Computation of total wages

Type of Pay	Hours	×	Rate	=	Gross Earnings
Regular	40	×	$12.00	=	$480.00
Overtime	4	×	18.00	=	72.00
Total wages					**$552.00**

This computation assumes that Jordan receives one and one-half times his regular hourly rate ($12.00 × 1.5) for his overtime hours. Union contracts often require that overtime rates be as much as twice the regular rates.

The **salary** for an employee is generally based on a monthly or yearly rate rather than on an hourly basis. These rates are then applied ratably to the payroll periods used by the company. Most executive and administrative positions are salaried. The Federal Fair Labor Standards Act does not require overtime pay for such positions. In the Casper College example at the beginning of the chapter, overtime is not given to either faculty or administrative personnel.

Many companies have **bonus** agreements for management personnel and other employees. For example, a recent survey indicated that over 94% of the largest manufacturing companies in the United States provide annual bonuses to their key executives. Bonus arrangements may be based on such factors as increased sales or net income. Bonuses may be paid in cash and/or by granting executives and employees the opportunity to acquire shares of stock in the company at favorable prices (called stock option plans). Bonuses have become very lucrative, as companies attempt to retain the services of key executives—so lucrative, in fact, that they have come under intense public scrutiny.

ETHICS NOTE

Bonuses often reward outstanding individual performance; however, a successful corporation also needs considerable teamwork. A challenge is to motivate individuals while preventing an unethical team member from taking another's idea for his or her own advantage.

ACCOUNTING IN ACTION
Business Insight

In a recent year Amoco Corporation employees received shares of the company's stock equal to 3.5% of their salaries as a result of the company's strong total return to shareholders in the previous year. Amoco's performance plan awards shares to employees when the return to shareholders meets or exceeds the average of seven major oil companies. Amoco's return of 18.8% was the second highest of the group of competitors.

Payroll Deductions

As anyone who has received a paycheck knows, gross earnings are usually very different from the amount actually received. The difference is attributable to **payroll deductions**. Payroll deductions do not result in payroll tax expense to the employer. The employer serves only as a collection agency, and it subsequently transfers the deductions to the government and designated recipients. Payroll deductions may be mandatory or voluntary. The former are required by law and consist of FICA taxes and income taxes. The latter are at the option of the employee. Illustration 11-11 summarizes the types of payroll deductions.

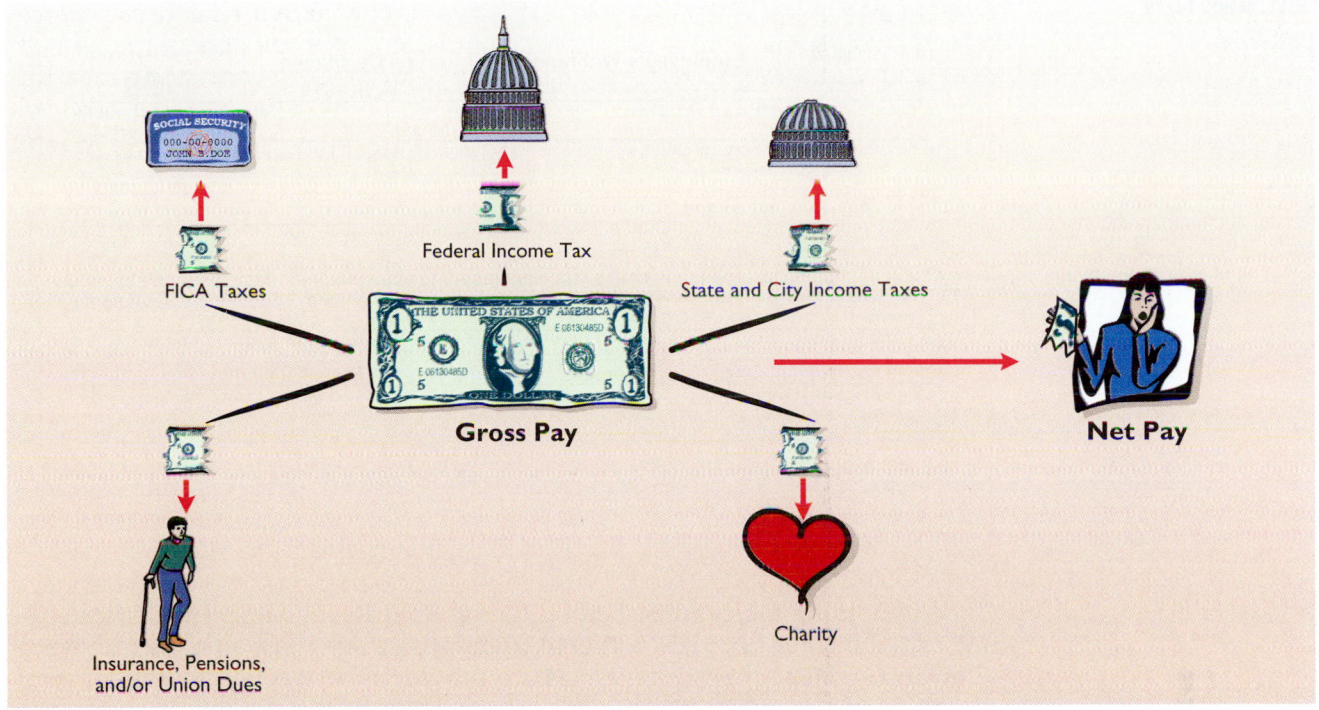

ILLUSTRATION 11-11

Payroll deductions

FICA Taxes. In 1937 Congress enacted the Federal Insurance Contribution Act (FICA). **FICA taxes are designed to provide workers with supplemental retirement, employment disability, and medical benefits.** In 1965, benefits were expanded to include Medicare for individuals over 65 years of age. The benefits are financed by a tax levied on employees' earnings. FICA taxes are commonly referred to as **Social Security taxes**.

The tax rate and the tax base for FICA taxes are set by Congress, and they are changed intermittently. When FICA taxes were first imposed, the rate was 1% on the first $3,000 of gross earnings, or a maximum of $30 per year. The rate and base have changed dramatically since that time! In 1998, that rate was 7.65% (6.2% Social Security and 1.45% Medicare) on the first $68,400 of gross earnings for each employee, or a maximum of $5,232.60.[1] For purpose of illustration in this chapter, we will assume a rate of 8% on the first $65,000 of gross earnings, or a maximum of $5,200. Using the 8% rate, the FICA withholding for Jordan for the weekly pay period ending January 14 is $44.16 ($552 $\times$ 8%).

Income Taxes. Under the United States pay-as-you-go system of federal income taxes, employers are required to withhold income taxes from employees each pay period. The amount to be withheld is determined by three variables: (1) the employee's gross earnings; (2) the number of allowances claimed by the employee for herself or himself, his or her spouse, and other dependents; and (3) the length of the pay period. **To indicate to the Internal Revenue Service the number of allowances claimed, the employee must complete an Employee's Withholding Allowance Certificate (Form W-4).** As shown in Illustration 11-12, Michael Jordan claims two allowances on his W-4.

---

[1]The Medicare provision also includes a tax of 1.45% on gross earnings in excess of $68,400. In the interest of simplification, our end-of-chapter assignment material ignores this 1.45% charge. We assume zero withholdings on gross earnings above $65,000.

ILLUSTRATION 11-12

W-4 form

Form **W-4** Department of the Treasury Internal Revenue Service	**Employee's Withholding Allowance Certificate** ► For Privacy Act and Paperwork Reduction Act Notice, see page 2.	OMB No. 1545-0010 19**98**

1 Type or print your first name and middle initial Michael	Last name Jordan	2 Your social security number 329-36-9547
Home address (number and street or rural route) 2345 Mifflin Ave.	3 ☐ Single ☒ Married ☐ Married, but withhold at higher Single rate. **Note:** *If married, but legally separated, or spouse is a nonresident alien, check the Single box.*	
City or town, State, and ZIP code Hampton, MI 48292	4 If your last name differs from that on your social security card, check here and call 1-800-772-1213 for a new card . . . . . ► ☐	

5 Total number of allowances you are claiming (from line H above or from the worksheet on page 2 if they apply) . . . | 5 | 2
6 Additional amount, if any, you want withheld from each paycheck . . . | 6 | $
7 I claim exemption from withholding for 1998, and I certify that I meet BOTH of the following conditions for exemption:
• Last year I had a right to a refund of ALL Federal income tax withheld because I had NO tax liability AND
• This year I expect a refund of ALL Federal income tax withheld because I expect to have NO tax liability.
If you meet both conditions, enter "Exempt" here . . . . . . ► | 7 |

Under penalties of perjury, I certify that I am entitled to the number of withholding allowances claimed on this certificate or entitled to claim exempt status.

Employee's signature ► *Michael Jordan*   Date ► September 1 , 19 99

8 Employer's name and address (Employer: Complete 8 and 10 only if sending to the IRS)	9 Office code (optional)	10 Employer identification number

Cat. No. 102200

Withholding tables furnished by the Internal Revenue Service indicate the amount of income tax to be withheld from gross wages based on the number of allowances claimed. Separate tables are provided for weekly, biweekly, semi-monthly, and monthly pay periods. The portion of the withholding tax table for Michael Jordan (assuming he earns $552 per week) is shown in Illustration 11-13. As indicated in the table, for a weekly salary of $552 with two allowances, the income tax to be withheld is $49.

ILLUSTRATION 11-13

Withholding tax table

MARRIED Persons — **WEEKLY** Payroll Period
(For Wages Paid in 1998)

If the wages are —		And the number of withholding allowances claimed is —										
At least	But less than	0	1	2	3	4	5	6	7	8	9	10
		The amount of income tax to be withheld is —										
490	500	56	48	40	32	24	17	9	1	0	0	0
500	510	57	49	42	34	26	18	10	3	0	0	0
510	520	59	51	43	35	27	20	12	4	0	0	0
520	530	60	52	45	37	29	21	13	6	0	0	0
530	540	62	54	46	38	30	23	15	7	0	0	0
540	550	63	55	48	40	32	24	16	9	1	0	0
550	560	65	57	**49**	41	33	26	18	10	2	0	0
560	570	66	58	51	43	35	27	19	12	4	0	0
570	580	68	60	52	44	36	29	21	13	5	0	0
580	590	69	61	54	46	38	30	22	15	7	0	0
590	600	71	63	55	47	39	32	24	16	8	1	0
600	610	72	64	57	49	41	33	25	18	10	2	0
610	620	74	66	58	50	42	35	27	19	11	4	0
620	630	75	67	60	52	44	36	28	21	13	5	0
630	640	77	69	61	53	45	38	30	22	14	7	0
640	650	78	70	63	55	47	39	31	24	16	8	0
650	660	80	72	64	56	48	41	33	25	17	10	2
660	670	81	73	66	58	50	42	34	27	19	11	3
670	680	83	75	67	59	51	44	36	28	20	13	5
680	690	84	76	69	61	53	45	37	30	22	14	6

Most states and some cities also require employers to withhold income taxes from the earnings of employees. As a general rule, the amounts to be withheld are determined by applying a percentage specified in the state revenue code to the amount withheld for the federal income tax or to the employee's earnings. For the sake of simplicity, we have assumed that Jordan's wages are subject to state income taxes of 2%, or $11.04 (2% × $552).

There is no limit on the amount of gross earnings subject to income tax withholdings. In fact, the higher the earnings, the higher the amount of taxes withheld.

Other Deductions.   Employees may voluntarily authorize withholdings for charitable, retirement, and other purposes. All voluntary deductions from gross earnings should be authorized in writing by the employee. The authorization(s) may be made individually or as part of a group plan. Deductions for charitable organizations, such as the United Fund, or for financial arrangements, such as U.S. savings bonds and repayment of loans from company credit unions are made individually. In contrast, deductions for union dues, health and life insurance, and pension plans are often made on a group basis. For purpose of illustration, we will assume that Jordan has voluntary deductions of $10 for the United Fund and $5 for union dues.

Net Pay

Net pay is determined by subtracting payroll deductions from gross earnings. For Michael Jordan, net pay for the pay period is $432.80, computed as follows:

ALTERNATIVE TERMINOLOGY

Net pay is also called *take-home pay*.

ILLUSTRATION 11-14

Computation of net pay

Gross earnings		$552.00
Payroll deductions:		
FICA taxes	$44.16	
Federal income taxes	49.00	
State income taxes	11.04	
United Fund	10.00	
Union dues	5.00	119.20
Net pay		**$432.80**

Assuming that Michael Jordan's wages for each week during the year are $552, total wages for the year are $28,704 (52 × $552). Thus, all of Jordan's wages are subject to FICA tax during the year. However, if an employee's wages are $1,350 per week, or $70,200 for the year, only the first $65,000 is subject to FICA taxes. In such case, the maximum FICA withholdings would be $5,200 ($65,000 × 8%).

Recording the Payroll

Recording the payroll involves maintaining payroll department records, recognizing payroll expenses and liabilities, and recording payment of the payroll.

Maintaining Payroll Department Records

To comply with state and federal laws, an employer must keep a cumulative record of each employee's gross earnings, deductions, and net pay during the year. The record that provides this information and other essential data is the **employee earnings record**. Michael Jordan's employee earnings record is shown in Illustration 11-15.

ILLUSTRATION 11-15

Employee earnings record

ACADEMY COMPANY
Employee Earnings Record
For the Year 1999

Name: Michael Jordan   Address: 2345 Mifflin Ave.
Social Security Number: 329-36-9547   Hampton, Michigan 48292
Date of Birth: December 24, 1962   Telephone: 555-238-9051
Date Employed: September 1, 1995   Date Employment Ended:
Sex: Male   Exemptions: 2
Single _____   Married __X__

1999 Period Ending	Total Hours	Regular	Overtime	Total	Cumulative	FICA	Fed. Inc. Tax	State Inc. Tax	United Fund	Union Dues	Total	Net Amount	Check No.
1/7	42	480.00	36.00	516.00	516.00	41.28	43.00	10.32	10.00	5.00	109.60	406.40	974
1/14	44	480.00	72.00	552.00	1,068.00	44.16	49.00	11.04	10.00	5.00	119.20	432.80	1028
1/21	43	480.00	54.00	534.00	1,602.00	42.72	46.00	10.68	10.00	5.00	114.40	419.60	1077
1/28	42	480.00	36.00	516.00	2,118.00	41.28	43.00	10.32	10.00	5.00	109.60	406.40	1133
Jan. Total		1,920.00	198.00	2,118.00		169.44	181.00	42.36	40.00	20.00	452.80	1,665.20	

A separate earnings record is kept for each employee, and it is updated after each pay period. The cumulative payroll data on the earnings record are used by the employer in (1) determining when an employee has earned the maximum earnings subject to FICA taxes, (2) filing state and federal payroll tax returns (as explained later in the chapter), and (3) providing each employee with a statement of gross earnings and tax withholdings for the year, as shown in Illustration 11-19 on page 492. In the opening story about Casper College, Dianna Webb's report that lists the year-to-date totals is the employee earnings record.

In addition to employee earnings records, many companies find it useful to prepare a **payroll register** to accumulate the gross earnings, deductions, and net pay by employee for each pay period. It provides the documentation for preparing a paycheck for each employee. The payroll register is presented in Illustration 11-16, with the data for Michael Jordan shown in the wages section. In this example, Academy Company's total payroll is $17,210, as shown in the gross pay column.

Note that this record is a listing of each employee's payroll data for the pay period. In some companies, a payroll register is a journal or book of original entry, and postings are made directly to ledger accounts from the register. In other companies, the payroll register is a memorandum record that provides the data for a general journal entry and subsequent posting to the ledger accounts. In the Academy Company situation, the latter procedure is followed. The main payroll report provided by the computer at Casper College is the payroll register.

ILLUSTRATION 11-16
Payroll register

ACADEMY COMPANY
Payroll Register
For the Week Ending January 14, 1999

Employee	Total Hours	Regular	Over-time	Gross	FICA	Federal Income Tax	State Income Tax	United Fund	Union Dues	Total	Net Pay	Check No.	Office Salaries Expense	Wages Expense
Office Salaries														
Arnold, Patricia	40	580.00		580.00	46.40	61.00	11.60	15.00		134.00	446.00	998	580.00	
Canton, Matthew	40	590.00		590.00	47.20	63.00	11.80	20.00		142.00	448.00	999	590.00	
Mueller, William	40	530.00		530.00	42.40	54.00	10.60	11.00		118.00	412.0	1000	530.00	
Subtotal		5,200.00		5,200.00	416.00	1,090.00	104.00	120.00		1,730.00	3,470.00		5,200.00	
Wages														
Bennett, Robin	42	480.00	36.00	516.00	41.28	43.00	10.32	18.00	5.00	117.60	398.40	1025		516.00
Jordan, Michael	44	480.00	72.00	552.00	44.16	49.00	11.04	10.00	5.00	119.20	432.80	1028		552.00
Milroy, Lee	43	480.00	54.00	534.00	42.72	46.00	10.68	10.00	5.00	114.40	419.60	1029		534.00
Subtotal		11,000.00	1,010.00	12,010.00	960.80	2,400.00	240.20	301.50	115.00	4,017.50	7,992.50			12,010.00
Total		16,200.00	1,010.00	17,210.00	1,376.80	3,490.00	344.20	421.50	115.00	5,747.50	11,462.50		5,200.00	12,010.00

Recognizing Payroll Expenses and Liabilities

From the payroll register in Illustration 11-16, a journal entry is made to record the payroll. For the week ending January 14 the entry is:

Jan. 14	Office Salaries Expense	5,200.00	
	Wages Expense	12,010.00	
	FICA Taxes Payable		1,376.80
	Federal Income Taxes Payable		3,490.00
	State Income Taxes Payable		344.20
	United Fund Payable		421.50
	Union Dues Payable		115.00
	Salaries and Wages Payable		11,462.50
	(To record payroll for the week ending January 14)		

A = L + OE
+ 1,376.80 − 5,200.00
+ 3,490.00 − 12,010.00
+ 344.20
+ 421.50
+ 115.00
+ 11,462.50

Specific liability accounts are credited for the mandatory and voluntary deductions made during the pay period. In the example, debits to Office Salaries and Wages Expense are used for gross earnings because office workers are on a salary and other employees are paid on an hourly rate. In other cases, there may be additional debits such as Store Salaries and Sales Salaries. The amount credited to Salaries and Wages Payable is the sum of the individual checks the employees will receive.

Recording Payment of the Payroll

Payment by check is made either from the employer's regular bank account or a payroll bank account. Each check is usually accompanied by a detachable **state-**

ment of earnings document that shows the employee's gross earnings, payroll deductions, and net pay. The Academy Company uses its regular bank account for payroll checks. The check and statement of earnings for Michael Jordan are shown in Illustration 11-17.

ILLUSTRATION 11-17

Check and statement of earnings

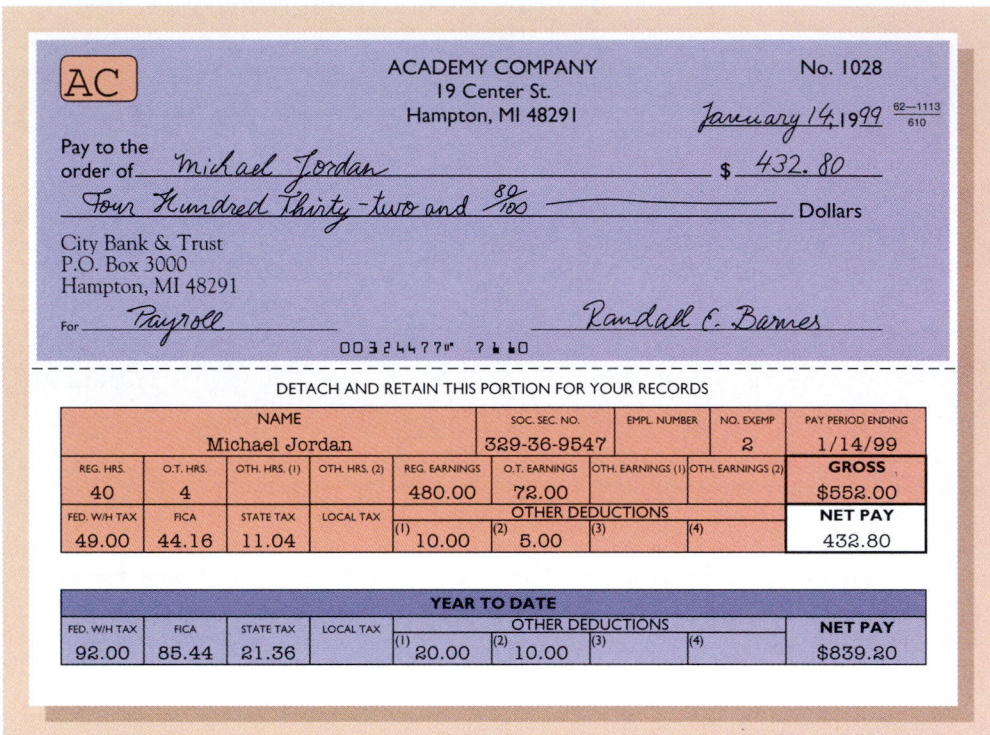

HELPFUL HINT

Do any of the income tax liabilities result in payroll tax expense for the employer? Answer: No, the employer is acting only as a collection agent for the government.

Following payment of the payroll, the check numbers are entered in the payroll register. The entry to record payment of the payroll for Academy Company is as follows:

A	=	L	+ OE
−11,462.50		−11,462.50	

Jan. 14	Salaries and Wages Payable	11,462.50	
	Cash		11,462.50
	(To record payment of payroll)		

When currency is used in payment, one check is prepared for the net pay. The check is then cashed, and the coins and currency are inserted in individual pay envelopes for disbursement to individual employees.

TECHNOLOGY IN ACTION

In addition to supplying the entry to record the payroll, the output for a computerized payroll system would include (1) payroll checks, (2) a payroll check register sorted by check and department, and (3) updated employee earnings records which become the source for monthly, quarterly, and annual reporting of wages to taxing agencies.

Before You Go On . . .

Review It

1. Identify two internal control procedures that are applicable to each payroll function.
2. What are the primary sources of gross earnings?
3. What payroll deductions are (a) mandatory and (b) voluntary?
4. What account titles are used in recording a payroll, assuming only mandatory payroll deductions are involved?

Do It

Your cousin Stan is establishing a house-cleaning business and will have a number of employees working for him. From his prior work experience, he is aware that documentation procedures are an important part of internal control. However, he is confused about the difference between an employee earnings record and a payroll register. He asks you to explain the principal differences, because he wants to be sure that he sets up the proper payroll procedures.

Reasoning: You may need to review the material on payroll department records and study Illustrations 11-15 and 11-16 in order to identify and explain the differences for Stan.

Solution: An employee earnings record is kept for *each* employee. It shows gross earnings, payroll deductions, and net pay for each pay period. It provides cumulative payroll data for that employee. In contrast, a payroll register is a listing of *all* employees' gross earnings, payroll deductions, and net pay for each pay period. It is the documentation for preparing paychecks and for recording the payroll. Of course, Stan will need to keep both documents.

Related exercise material: BE11–7, BE11–8, BE11–9, E11–8, E11–9, E11–10, and E11–11.

THE NAVIGATOR

Employer Payroll Taxes

Payroll tax expense for businesses and educational institutions, like Casper College, results from three taxes **levied on employers** by governmental agencies. These taxes are: FICA, federal unemployment tax, and state unemployment tax. Each of these taxes plus such items as paid vacations and pensions are collectively referred to as "fringe benefits." As indicated earlier, the cost of fringe benefits in many companies is substantial.

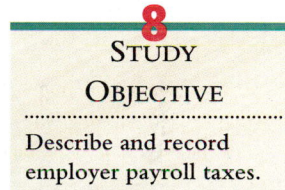

8
STUDY
OBJECTIVE
....
Describe and record employer payroll taxes.

FICA Taxes

We have seen that each employee must pay FICA taxes. The employer must match each employee's FICA contribution. The matching contribution results in **payroll tax expense** to the employer. The employer's tax is subject to the same rate and maximum earnings applicable to the employee. The account, FICA Taxes Payable, is used for both the employee's and the employer's FICA contributions. For the January 14 payroll, Academy Company's FICA tax is $1,376.80 ($17,210.00 × 8%).

Federal Unemployment Taxes

The Federal Unemployment Tax Act (FUTA) is another feature of the federal social security program. **Federal unemployment taxes** provide benefits for a limited period of time to employees who lose their jobs through no fault of their own. Under provisions of the Act, the employer is required to pay a tax of 6.2%

HELPFUL HINT
FICA taxes are paid both by the employer and employee. Federal unemployment taxes and (in most states) the state unemployment taxes are borne entirely by the employer.

on the first $7,000 of gross wages paid to each employee during a calendar year. The law, however, allows the employer a maximum credit of 5.4% on the federal rate for contributions to state unemployment taxes. Because of this provision, state unemployment tax laws generally provide for a 5.4% rate, and the effective federal unemployment tax rate becomes 0.8% (6.2% − 5.4%). This tax is borne **entirely by the employer**; there is no deduction or withholding from employees. The account Federal Unemployment Taxes Payable is used to recognize this liability. The federal unemployment tax for Academy Company for the January 14 payroll is $137.68 ($17,210.00 × 0.8%).

State Unemployment Taxes

All states have unemployment compensation programs under state unemployment tax acts (SUTA). Like federal unemployment taxes, **state unemployment taxes** provide benefits to employees who lose their jobs. These taxes are levied on employers.[2] The basic rate is usually 5.4% on the first $7,000 of wages paid to an employee during the year. The basic rate is adjusted according to the employer's experience rating: Companies with a history of unstable employment may pay more than the basic rate. Companies with a history of stable employment may pay less than 5.4%. Regardless of the rate paid, the credit on the federal unemployment tax is still 5.4%. The account State Unemployment Taxes Payable is used for this liability. The state unemployment tax for Academy Company for the January 14 payroll is $929.34 ($17,210.00 × 5.4%). Illustration 11-18 summarizes the types of employer payroll taxes.

ILLUSTRATION 11-18

Employer payroll taxes

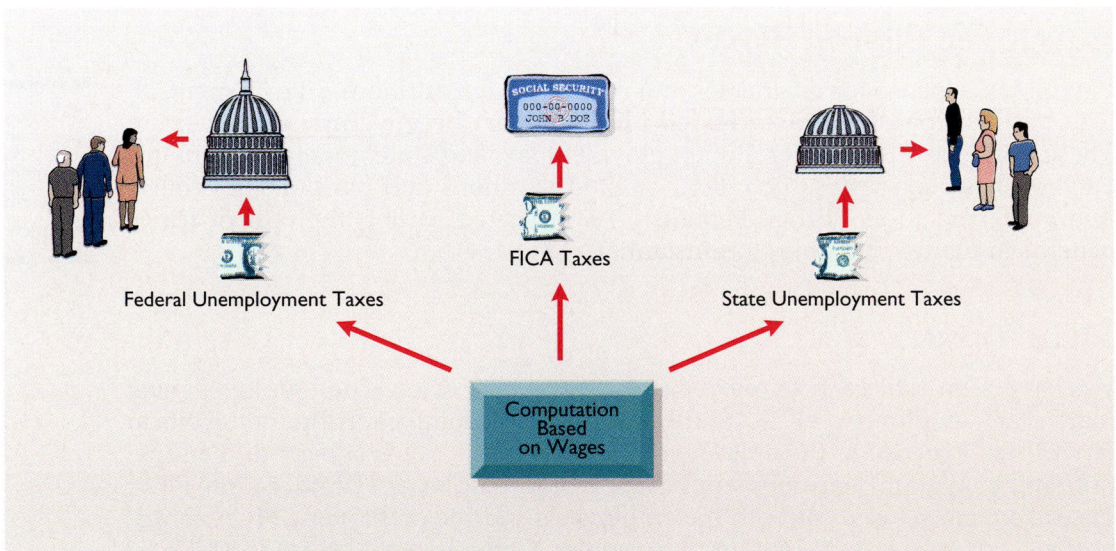

Recording Employer Payroll Taxes

Employer payroll taxes are usually recorded at the same time the payroll is journalized. The entire amount of gross pay ($17,210.00) shown in the payroll register in Illustration 11-16 is subject to each of the three taxes mentioned above. Ac-

---

[2]In a few states, the employee is also required to make a contribution. In this textbook, including the homework, we will assume that the tax is only on the employer.

cordingly, the entry to record the payroll tax expense associated with the January 14 payroll is:

Jan. 14	Payroll Tax Expense	2,443.82	
	FICA Taxes Payable		1,376.80
	Federal Unemployment Taxes Payable		137.68
	State Unemployment Taxes Payable		929.34
	(To record employer's payroll taxes on January 14 payroll)		

A	=	L	+	OE
		+1,376.80		−2,443.82
		+ 137.68		
		+ 929.34		

Separate liability accounts are used instead of a single credit to Payroll Taxes Payable, because these liabilities are payable to different taxing authorities at different dates. The liability accounts are classified as current liabilities since they will be paid within the next year. Payroll Tax Expense is classified on the income statement as an operating expense.

Filing and Remitting Payroll Taxes

Preparation of payroll tax returns is the responsibility of the payroll department; payment of the taxes is made by the treasurer's department. Much of the information for the returns is obtained from employee earnings records.

For purposes of reporting and remitting, FICA taxes and federal income taxes withheld are combined. **The taxes must be reported quarterly**, no later than one month following the close of each quarter. The remitting requirements depend on the amount of taxes withheld and the length of the pay period. Remittances are made through deposits in either a Federal Reserve Bank or an authorized commercial bank.

ACCOUNTING IN ACTION
Business Insight

The owner of a newly restored Victorian hotel, nestled in a small Massachusetts town, skipped payment of withholding taxes for three quarters because of cash flow problems. Before long, he received a call from the IRS. After months of haggling, the hotel owner was told that unless he paid the $70,000 owed, the IRS would be forced to liquidate the hotel, the land, and dozens of antiques in the inn, which had taken him and his wife years to acquire.

As this story indicates, cash-hungry small businesses are often tempted to skip or delay paying withholding taxes. Increasingly, federal and state agencies are cracking down on such cheaters. Penalties for late or nonpayment can be devastating: Fines are levied at the rate of 5% of taxes owed for *each month* a payroll tax isn't filed. And in cases where nothing is paid, penalties of 100% can be applied, with interest added, to the unpaid balance. Under the 100% penalty, the government can padlock the doors, seize assets, and hold the officers or certain other employees personally responsible for the penalties.

What happened to the Massachusetts hotel owner? He's now working on a repayment plan, rather than lose his years of hard work.

Federal unemployment taxes are generally filed and remitted **annually** on or before January 31 of the subsequent year. Earlier payments are required, however, when the tax exceeds a specified amount. State unemployment taxes usually must be filed and paid by the **end of the month following each quarter**. When payroll taxes are paid, payroll liability accounts are debited and cash is credited.

The employer is also required to provide each employee with a **Wage and Tax Statement (Form W-2)** by January 31 following the end of a calendar year.

This statement shows gross earnings, FICA taxes withheld, and income taxes withheld for the year. The required W-2 form for Michael Jordan, using assumed annual data, is shown in Illustration 11-19.

ILLUSTRATION 11-19

W-2 form

Form **W-2 Wage and Tax Statement**

1 Control number		
		OMB No. 1545-0008

2 Employer's name, address and ZIP code	**3** Employer's identification number	**4** Employer's State number
Academy Company 19 Center St. Hampton, MI 48291	36-2167852	

3 Employer's identification number: 36-2167852

5 Stat. employee	Deceased	Legal rep.	942 emp.	Subtotal	Void
☐	☐	☐	☐	☐	☐

6 Allocated tips	**7** Advance EIC payment

8 Employee's social security number	**9** Federal income tax withheld	**10** Wages, tips, other compensation	**11** Social security tax withheld
329-36-9547	$2,248.00	$26,300.00	$2,104.00

12 Employee's name, address, and ZIP code	**13** Social security wages	**14** Social security tips
	$26,300.00	

16

Michael Jordan
2345 Mifflin Ave.
Hampton, MI 48292

17 State income tax	**18** State wages, tips, etc.	**19** Name of State
$526.00		Michigan

20 Local income tax	**21** Local wages, tips, etc.	**22** Name of locality

---

The employer must send a copy of each employee's Wage and Tax Statement to the Social Security Administration. This agency subsequently furnishes the Internal Revenue Service with the income data required.

BEFORE YOU GO ON . . .

Review It

1. What payroll taxes are levied on employers?
2. What accounts are involved in accruing employer payroll taxes?

Do It

In January, the payroll supervisor determines that gross earnings in Halo Company are $70,000. All earnings are subject to 8% FICA taxes, 5.4% state unemployment taxes, and 0.8% federal unemployment taxes. You are asked to record the employer's payroll taxes.

Reasoning: In recording the taxes, you should remember that (1) the total expense can be debited to one account and (2) separate accounts are required for each of the three liabilities.

Solution: The entry to record the employer's payroll taxes is:

Payroll Tax Expense	9,940	
FICA Taxes Payable ($70,000 × 8%)		5,600
Federal Unemployment Taxes Payable ($70,000 × 0.8%)		560
State Unemployment Taxes Payable ($70,000 × 5.4%)		3,780
(To record employer's payroll taxes on January payroll)		

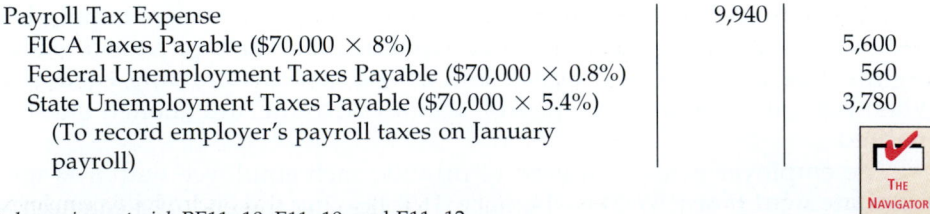

THE NAVIGATOR

Related exercise material: BE11–10, E11–10, and E11–12.

Additional Fringe Benefits

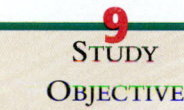

9
STUDY
OBJECTIVE
....
Identify additional fringe
benefits associated with
employee compensation.

In addition to the three payroll tax fringe benefits, employers incur other substantial fringe benefit costs. Two of the most important are paid absences and postretirement benefits.

Paid Absences

Employees often have rights to receive compensation for future absences when certain conditions of employment are met. The compensation may pertain to paid vacations, sick pay benefits, and paid holidays. When the payment of such compensation is **probable** and the amount can be **reasonably estimated**, a liability should be accrued for paid future absences. When the amount cannot be reasonably estimated, the potential liability should be disclosed. Ordinarily, vacation pay is the only paid absence that is accrued; the other types of paid absences are only disclosed.[3]

To illustrate, assume that Academy Company employees are entitled to one day's vacation for each month worked. If thirty employees earn an average of $110 per day in a given month, the accrual for vacation benefits in one month is $3,300. The liability is recognized at the end of the month by the following adjusting entry:

Jan. 31	Vacation Benefits Expense	3,300	
	Vacation Benefits Payable		3,300
	(To accrue vacation benefits expense)		

A	=	L	+	OE
		+3,300		−3,300

This accrual is required by the matching principle. Vacation Benefits Expense is reported as an operating expense in the income statement, and Vacation Benefits Payable is reported as a current liability in the balance sheet. When vacation benefits are paid, Vacation Benefits Payable is debited and Cash is credited. For example if the above benefits for ten employees are paid in July, the entry is:

July 31	Vacation Benefits Payable	1,100	
	Cash		1,100
	(To record payment of vacation benefits)		

A	=	L	+	OE
−1,100		−1,100		

The magnitude of unpaid absences has gained employers' attention. Consider the case of an assistant superintendent of schools who worked for around 20 years and rarely took a vacation or sick day. A month or so before she retired, the school district discovered that she was due nearly $30,000 in accrued benefits. Yet the liability was never accrued.

Postretirement Benefits

Postretirement benefits consist of benefits provided by employers to retired employees for (1) health care and life insurance and (2) pensions. For many years the accounting for postretirement benefits was on a cash basis. However, both types of postretirement benefits are now accounted for on the accrual basis.

Postretirement Health Care and Life Insurance Benefits.   Providing medical and related health care benefits for retirees—at one time an inexpensive and highly effective way of generating employee goodwill—has turned into one of corporate America's most worrisome financial problems. Runaway medical costs, early

---

[3]The typical U.S. company provides an average of 12 days of paid vacations for its employees, at an average cost of 5% of gross earnings.

retirement, and increased longevity are sending the liability for retiree health plans through the roof.

Many companies began offering retiree health care coverage in the form of Medicare supplements in the 1960s. Almost all plans operated on a pay-as-you-go basis—the companies simply paid for the bills as they came in, rather than setting aside funds to meet the cost of future benefits. These plans were accounted for on the cash basis rather than the accrual basis. However, the FASB concluded that shareholders and creditors should know the amount of the employer's obligations. As a result, employers must now use the **accrual basis** in accounting for postretirement health care and life insurance benefits.

ACCOUNTING IN ACTION
Business Insight

The battle over fringe benefits is increasing in intensity as benefits outpace wages and salaries. Growing faster than pay, benefits equaled 38% of wages and salaries in a recent year. While vacations and other forms of paid leave still take the biggest bite of the benefits pie, medical costs are the fastest-growing item.

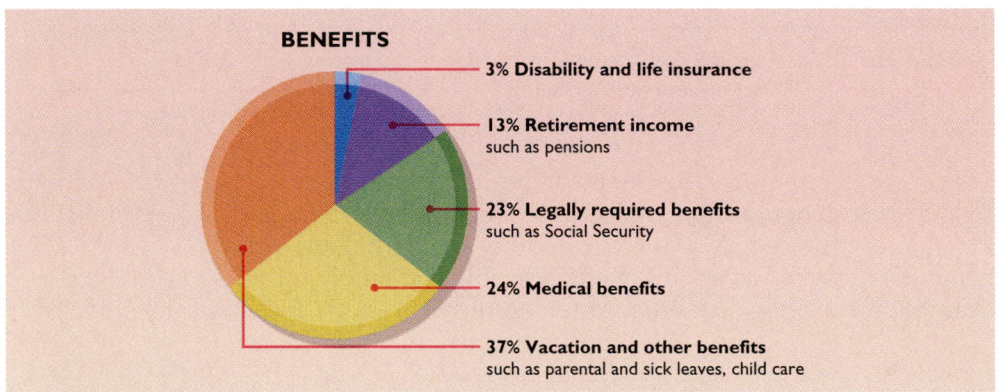

BENEFITS

- 3% Disability and life insurance
- 13% Retirement income such as pensions
- 23% Legally required benefits such as Social Security
- 24% Medical benefits
- 37% Vacation and other benefits such as parental and sick leaves, child care

HELPFUL HINT

With more than $4 trillion in assets overall, both public and private pension funds comprise over one-fifth of the total financial assets in the United States today—and these figures are growing.

ILLUSTRATION 11-20

Parties in a pension plan

Pension Plans.   A **pension plan** is an agreement whereby an employer provides benefits (payments) to employees after they retire. Over 50 million workers currently participate in pension plans in the United States. The need for proper administration of and good accounting for pension plans becomes apparent when one appreciates the size of existing pension funds. Most pension plans are subject to the provisions of ERISA (Employee Retirement Income Security Act), a law enacted to curb abuses in the administration and funding of such plans.

Three parties are generally involved in a pension plan. The **employer** (company) sponsors the pension plan. The **plan administrator** receives the contributions from the employer, invests the pension assets, and makes the benefit payments to the **pension recipients** (retired employees). Illustration 11-20 shows

Employer   **Plan Administrator**   **Pension Recipients**

Contributions   Benefits

Kear Trust Co.

$ $ $ $

Fund Assets:
Investments and Earnings

the three distinct parties involved in a pension plan and indicates the flow of cash among them.

An employer-financed pension is part of the employees' compensation. The provisions of ERISA establish the minimum contribution that a company must make each year toward employee pensions. The company records the pension costs as an expense while the employees are working because that is when the company receives benefits from the employees' services. Generally the pension expense is reported as an operating expense in the company's income statement. Frequently, the amount contributed by the company to the pension plan is different from the amount of the pension expense. A **liability** is recognized when the pension expense to date is **more than** the company's contributions to date; an **asset** is recognized when the pension expense to date is **less than** the company's contributions to date. Further consideration of the accounting for pension plans is left for more advanced courses.

BEFORE YOU GO ON . . .

Review It

1. What accounts are involved in accruing and paying vacation benefits?
2. What basis should be used in accounting for postretirement benefits?

A LOOK BACK AT OUR FEATURE STORY

Refer back to the story about Casper College at the beginning of the chapter, and answer the following questions:

1. In addition to taxes withheld from employees, what employer payroll taxes are remitted by Casper College to governmental agencies?
2. For each of the four payroll functions, give examples of internal control procedures used by Casper College.

Solution:

1. In addition to the amounts withheld for FICA and federal income taxes, Casper College must match the FICA taxes withheld from employees and must pay federal and state unemployment taxes.
2. *Hiring:* Contracts are issued to faculty and administrative personnel, and their pay must be approved.

   Timekeeping: Timecards are used for hourly employees.

   Preparing the payroll: Deductions from gross earnings for each employee are documented. For example, there must be a W-4 form for withholding federal income taxes. The computer prepares useful reports that include maintaining a payroll record for each employee.

   Paying the payroll: Although these procedures are not explicitly stated, the payroll checks generated by the computer would be signed by the school's chief financial officer, and paychecks would be distributed directly to employees.

THE
NAVIGATOR

DEMONSTRATION PROBLEM

Indiana Jones Company had the following selected transactions:

Feb. 1   Signs a $50,000 6-month 9%-interest-bearing note payable to CitiBank receiving $50,000 in cash.

   10   Cash register sales total $43,200 which includes an 8% sales tax.

   28   The payroll for the month consists of Sales Salaries $32,000 and Office Salaries $18,000. All wages are subject to 8% FICA taxes. A total of $8,900 federal income taxes are withheld. The salaries are paid on March 1.

Feb 28 The following adjustment data are developed:
1. Interest expense of $375 has been incurred on the note.
2. Employer payroll taxes include 8% FICA taxes, a 5.4% state unemployment tax, and a 0.8% federal unemployment tax.
3. Some sales were made under warranty. Of the units sold under warranty, 350 are expected to become defective. Repair costs are estimated to be $40 per unit.

Instructions

(a) Journalize the February transactions.
(b) Journalize the adjusting entries at February 28.

PROBLEM-SOLVING STRATEGIES

1. The formula for determining sales is cash register total divided by 100% plus the sales tax percentage.

2. All payroll taxes are based on gross earnings.

3. Warranty costs are expensed in the period in which the sale occurs.

SOLUTION TO DEMONSTRATION PROBLEM

(a) Feb. 1	Cash		50,000	
	Notes Payable			50,000
	(Issued 6-month 9%-interest-bearing note to CitiBank)			
10	Cash		43,200	
	Sales ($43,200 ÷ 1.08)			40,000
	Sales Taxes Payable ($40,000 × 8%)			3,200
	(To record sales and sales taxes payable)			
28	Sales Salaries Expense		32,000	
	Office Salaries Expense		18,000	
	FICA Taxes Payable (8% × $50,000)			4,000
	Federal Income Taxes Payable			8,900
	Salaries Payable			37,100
	(To record February salaries)			
(b) Feb. 28	Interest Expense		375	
	Interest Payable			375
	(To record accrued interest for February)			
28	Payroll Tax Expense		7,100	
	FICA Taxes Payable			4,000
	Federal Unemployment Taxes Payable (0.8% × $50,000)			400
	State Unemployment Taxes Payable (5.4% × $50,000)			2,700
	(To record employer's payroll taxes on February payroll)			
28	Warranty Expense (350 × $40)		14,000	
	Estimated Warranty Liability			14,000
	(To record estimated product warranty liability)			

THE NAVIGATOR

SUMMARY OF STUDY OBJECTIVES

1. *Explain a current liability and identify the major types of current liabilities.* A current liability is a debt that can reasonably be expected to be paid (1) from existing current assets or through the creation of other current liabilities, and (2) within one year or the operating cycle, whichever is longer. The major types of current liabilities are notes payable, accounts payable, sales taxes payable, unearned revenues, and accrued liabilities such as taxes, salaries and wages, and interest payable.

2. *Describe the accounting for notes payable.* When a promissory note is interest-bearing, the amount of assets received upon the issuance of the note is generally equal to the face value of the note, and interest expense is accrued over the life of the note. At maturity, the amount paid is equal to the face value of the note plus accrued interest.

3. *Explain the accounting for other current liabilities.* Sales taxes payable are recorded at the time the related sales occur. The company serves as a collection agent for the taxing authority. Sales taxes are not an expense to the company. Unearned revenues are initially recorded in an unearned revenue account. As the revenue is earned, a transfer from unearned revenue to earned revenue occurs. The current maturities of long-term debt should be reported as a current liability in the balance sheet.

4. *Explain the methods for the financial statement presentation and analysis of current liabilities.* The nature and amount of each current liability should be reported in the balance sheet or in schedules in the notes accompanying the statements. The liquidity of a company may be analyzed by computing working capital and the current ratio.

5. *Describe the accounting and disclosure requirements for contingent liabilities.* If it is probable (likely to occur) that the contingency will happen and the amount is reasonably estimable, the liability should be recorded in the accounts. However, if it is only reasonably possible (it could happen), then it need be disclosed only in the notes to the financial statements. If the possibility that the contingency will happen is remote (unlikely to occur), it need not be recorded or disclosed.

6. *Discuss the objectives of internal control for payroll.* The objectives of internal control for payroll are (1) to safeguard company assets against unauthorized payments of payrolls, and (2) to assure the accuracy and reliability of the accounting records pertaining to payrolls.

7. *Compute and record the payroll for a pay period.* The computation of the payroll involves gross earnings, payroll deductions, and net pay. In recording the payroll, salaries (or wages) expense is debited for gross earnings, individual tax and other liability accounts are credited for payroll deductions, and salaries (wages) payable is credited for net pay. When the payroll is paid, Salaries and Wages Payable is debited, and Cash is credited.

8. *Describe and record employer payroll taxes.* Employer payroll taxes consist of FICA, federal unemployment taxes, and state unemployment taxes. The taxes are usually accrued at the time the payroll is recorded by debiting Payroll Tax Expense and crediting separate liability accounts for each type of tax.

9. *Identify additional fringe benefits associated with employee compensation.* Additional fringe benefits associated with wages are paid absences (paid vacations, sick pay benefits, and paid holidays), and postretirement benefits (health care and life insurance and pensions). Both types of benefits should be accounted for on the accrual basis.

GLOSSARY

Bonus   Compensation to management personnel and other employees, based on factors such as increased sales or the amount of net income. (p. 482)

Contingent liability   A potential liability that may become an actual liability in the future. (p. 475)

Current ratio   A measure of a company's liquidity, computed as current assets divided by current liabilities. (p. 475)

Employee earnings record   A cumulative record of each employee's gross earnings, deductions, and net pay during the year. (p. 486)

Employee's Withholding Allowance Certificate (Form W-4)   An Internal Revenue Service form on which the employee indicates the number of allowances claimed for withholding federal income taxes. (p. 483)

Federal unemployment taxes   Taxes imposed on the employer that provide benefits for a limited time period to employees who lose their jobs through no fault of their own. (p. 489)

FICA taxes   Taxes designed to provide workers with supplemental retirement, employment disability, and medical benefits. (p. 483)

Gross earnings   Total compensation earned by an employee. (p. 481)

Net pay   Gross earnings less payroll deductions. (p. 485)

Payroll deductions   Deductions from gross earnings to determine the amount of a paycheck. (p. 482)

Payroll register   A payroll record that accumulates the gross earnings, deductions, and net pay by employee for each pay period. (p. 486)

Pension plan   An agreement whereby an employer provides benefits to employees after they retire. (p. 494)

Postretirement benefits   Payments by employers to retired employees for health care, life insurance, and pensions. (p. 493)

Salaries   Employee pay that is based on a fixed amount rather than an hourly rate. (p. 478)

Statement of earnings   A document attached to a paycheck that indicates the employee's gross earnings, payroll deductions, and net pay. (p. 488)

State unemployment taxes   Taxes imposed on the employer that provide benefits to employees who lose their jobs. (p. 490)

Wage and Tax Statement (Form W-2)   A form showing gross earnings, FICA taxes withheld, and income taxes withheld which is prepared annually by an employer for each employee. (p. 491)

Wages   Amounts paid to employees based on a rate per hour or on a piece-work basis. (p. 478)

Working capital   A measure of a company's liquidity, computed as the excess of current assets over current liabilities. (p. 475)

SELF-STUDY QUESTIONS

Answers are at the end of the chapter.

(SO 1) 1. The time period for classifying a liability as current is one year or the operating cycle, whichever is:
  a. longer.
  b. shorter.
  c. probable.
  d. possible.

(SO 1) 2. To be classified as a current liability, a debt must be expected to be paid:
  a. out of existing current assets.
  b. by creating other current liabilities.
  c. within two years.
  d. both (a) and (b).

(SO 2) 3. Julie Gilbert Company borrows $88,500 on September 1, 1999, from the Sandwich State Bank by signing an $88,500 12%, one-year note. What is the accrued interest at December 31, 1999?
  a. $2,655.
  b. $3,540.
  c. $4,425.
  d. $10,620.

(SO 3) 4. Reeves Company has total proceeds from sales of $4,515. If the proceeds include sales taxes of 5%, the amount to be credited to Sales is:
  a. $4,000.
  b. $4,300.
  c. $4,289.25.
  d. No correct answer given.

(SO 4) 5. Working capital is calculated as:
  a. current assets minus current liabilities.
  b. total assets minus total liabilities.
  c. long-term liabilities minus current liabilities.
  d. both (b) and (c).

(SO 5) 6. A contingent liability should be recorded in the accounts when:
  a. It is probable the contingency will happen but the amount cannot be reasonably estimated.
  b. It is reasonably possible the contingency will happen and the amount can be reasonably estimated.
  c. It is probable the contingency will happen and the amount can be reasonably estimated.
  d. It is reasonably possible the contingency will happen but the amount cannot be reasonably estimated.

(SO 5) 7. At December 31, Hanes Company prepares an adjusting entry for a product warranty contract. Which of the following accounts is/are included in the entry?
  a. Miscellaneous Expense.
  b. Estimated Warranty Liability.
  c. Repair Parts/Wages Payable.
  d. Both (a) and (b).

(SO 6) 8. The department that should pay the payroll is the:
  a. timekeeping department.
  b. personnel department.
  c. payroll department.
  d. treasurer's department.

(SO 7) 9. J. Barr earns $14 per hour for a 40-hour week and $21 per hour for any overtime work. If Barr works 45 hours in a week, gross earnings are:
  a. $560.
  b. $630.
  c. $650.
  d. $665.

(SO 8) 10. Employer payroll taxes do not include:
  a. federal unemployment taxes.
  b. state unemployment taxes.
  c. federal income taxes.
  d. FICA taxes.

(SO 9) 11. Which of the following is *not* an additional fringe benefit?
  a. Postretirement pensions.
  b. Paid absences.
  c. Paid vacations.
  d. Salaries.

THE NAVIGATOR

QUESTIONS

1. Rubin Ely believes a current liability is a debt that can be expected to be paid in one year. Is Rubin correct? Explain.

2. Mesa Verde Company obtains $25,000 in cash by signing a 9%, 6-month $25,000 note payable to First Bank on July 1. Mesa Verde's fiscal year ends on September 30. What information should be reported for the note payable in the annual financial statements?

3. (a) Your roommate says, "Sales taxes are reported as an expense in the income statement." Do you agree? Explain.

(b) Planet Hollywood has cash proceeds from sales of $10,400. This amount includes $400 of sales taxes. Give the entry to record the proceeds.

4. Colorado State sold 10,000 season football tickets at $80 each for its five-game home schedule. What entries should be made (a) when the tickets were sold and (b) after each game?

5. What is liquidity? What are two measures of liquidity?

6. What is a contingent liability? Give an example of a contingent liability that is usually recorded in the accounts.

7. Under what circumstances is a contingent liability disclosed only in the notes to the financial statements? Under what circumstances is a contingent liability not recorded in the accounts nor disclosed in the notes to the financial statements?

8. You are a newly hired accountant with Goh Company. On your first day, the controller asks you to identify the main internal control objectives related to payroll accounting. How would you respond?

9. What are the four functions associated with payroll activities?

10. What is the difference between gross pay and net pay? Which amount should a company record as wages or salaries expense?

11. Which payroll tax is levied on both employers and employees?

12. Are the federal and state income taxes withheld from employee paychecks a payroll tax expense for the employer? Explain your answer.

13. What do the following acronyms stand for: FICA, FUTA, and SUTA?

14. What information is shown on a W-4 statement? A W-2 statement?

15. Distinguish between the two types of payroll deductions and give examples of each.

16. What are the primary uses of the employee earnings record?

17. (a) Identify the three types of employer payroll taxes. (b) How are tax liability accounts and payroll tax expense classified in the financial statements?

18. Identify three additional types of fringe benefits associated with employees' compensation.

19. Often during job interviews, the candidate asks the potential employer about the firm's paid absences policy. What are paid absences? How are they accounted for?

20. What are two types of postretirement benefits? During what years does the FASB advocate expensing the employer's costs of these postretirement benefits?

21. What basis of accounting for the employer's cost of postretirement health care and life insurance benefits has been used by most companies, and what basis does the FASB now require? Explain the basic difference between these methods in accounting for postretirement benefit costs.

22. Identify the three parties in a pension plan. What role does each party have in the plan?

BRIEF EXERCISES

BE11–1 Toledo Company has the following obligations at December 31: (a) a note payable for $100,000 due in 2 years, (b) a 10-year mortgage payable of $300,000 payable in ten $30,000 annual payments, (c) interest payable of $15,000 on the mortgage, and (d) accounts payable of $60,000. For each obligation, indicate whether it should be classified as a current liability. (Assume an operating cycle of less than one year.)

Identify whether obligations are current liabilities.
(SO 1)

BE11–2 Chi Ho Company borrows $80,000 on July 1 from the bank by signing an $80,000 10%, one-year note payable. Prepare the journal entries to record (a) the proceeds of the note and (b) accrued interest at December 31, assuming adjusting entries are made only at the end of the year.

Prepare entries for an interest-bearing note payable.
(SO 2)

BE11–3 Hobbes Auto Supply does not segregate sales and sales taxes at the time of sale. The register total for March 16 is $8,925. All sales are subject to a 5% sales tax. Compute sales taxes payable and make the entry to record sales taxes payable and sales.

Compute and record sales taxes payable.
(SO 3)

BE11–4 Western Michigan University sells 4,000 season basketball tickets at $60 each for its 12-game home schedule. Give the entry to record (a) the sale of the season tickets and (b) the revenue earned by playing the first home game.

Prepare entries for unearned revenues.
(SO 3)

BE11–5 Motorola's 1995 financial statements contain the following selected data (in millions):

Analyze liquidity.
(SO 4)

Current assets	$10,510
Total assets	22,801
Current liabilities	7,791
Total liabilities	11,753

Compute the following ratios:

(a) Working capital
(b) Current ratio

BE11–6 On December 1, Kearns Company introduces a new product that includes a one-year warranty on parts. In December 1,000 units are sold. Management believes that 5% of the units will be defective and that the average warranty costs will be $60 per unit. Prepare the adjusting entry at December 31 to accrue the estimated warranty cost.

Prepare adjusting entry for warranty costs.
(SO 5)

Identify payroll functions.
(SO 6)

BE11–7 Marmon Company has the following payroll procedures:

1. Supervisor approves overtime work.
2. The personnel department prepares hiring authorization forms for new hires.
3. A second payroll department employee verifies payroll calculations.
4. The treasurer's department pays employees.

Identify the payroll function to which each procedure pertains.

Compute gross earnings and net pay.
(SO 7)

BE11–8 Ellen Monroe's regular hourly wage rate is $14, and she receives an hourly rate of $21 for work in excess of 40 hours. During a January pay period, Ellen works 45 hours. Ellen's federal income tax withholding is $70, and she has no voluntary deductions. Compute Ellen Monroe's gross earnings and net pay for the pay period.

Record a payroll and the payment of wages.
(SO 7)

BE11–9 Data for Ellen Monroe are presented in BE11–8. Prepare the journal entries to record (a) Ellen's pay for the period and (b) the payment of Ellen's wages. Use January 15 for the end of the pay period and the payment date.

Record employer payroll taxes.
(SO 8)

BE11–10 In January, gross earnings in the Poh Company totaled $55,000. All earnings are subject to 8% FICA taxes, 5.4% state unemployment taxes, and 0.8% federal unemployment taxes. Prepare the entry to record January payroll tax expense.

Record estimated vacation benefits.
(SO 9)

BE11–11 At Drexel Company employees are entitled to one day's vacation for each month worked. In January, 50 employees worked the full month. Record the vacation pay liability for January assuming the average daily pay for each employee is $140.

EXERCISES

Prepare entries for interest-bearing notes.
(SO 2)

E11–1 On June 1 Norfolk Company borrows $60,000 from First Bank on a 6-month, $60,000, 12% note.

Instructions
(a) Prepare the entry on June 1.
(b) Prepare the adjusting entry on June 30.
(c) Prepare the entry at maturity (December 1), assuming monthly adjusting entries have been made through November 30.
(d) What was the total financing cost (interest expense)?

Journalize sales and related taxes.
(SO 3)

E11–2 In providing accounting services to small businesses, you encounter the following situations pertaining to cash sales:

1. Jardine Company rings up sales and sales taxes separately on its cash register. On April 10, the register totals are sales $25,000 and sales taxes $2,000.
2. Lim Company does not segregate sales and sales taxes. Its register total for April 15 is $14,840, which includes a 6% sales tax.

Instructions
Prepare the entry to record the sales transactions and related taxes for each client.

Journalize unearned subscription revenue.
(SO 3)

E11–3 Redlands Company publishes a monthly sports magazine, *Fishing Preview*. Subscriptions to the magazine cost $30 per year. During November 1999, Redlands sells 6,000 subscriptions beginning with the December issue. Redlands prepares financial statements quarterly and recognizes subscription revenue earned at the end of the quarter. The company uses the accounts Unearned Subscription Revenue and Subscription Revenue.

Instructions
(a) Prepare the entry in November for the receipt of the subscriptions.
(b) Prepare the adjusting entry at December 31, 1999, to record subscription revenue earned in December of 1999.
(c) Prepare the adjusting entry at March 31, 2000, to record subscription revenue earned in the first quarter of 2000.

Record estimated liability and expense for warranties.
(SO 5)

E11–4 Sangsoo Company sells automatic can openers under a 75-day warranty for defective merchandise. Based on past experience, Sangsoo estimates that 3% of the units sold will become defective during the warranty period. Management estimates that the average cost of replacing or repairing a defective unit is $15. The units sold and units defective that occurred during the last 2 months of 1999 are as follows:

Month	Units Sold	Units Defective Prior to December 31
November	30,000	600
December	32,000	400

Instructions

(a) Determine the estimated warranty liability at December 31 for the units sold in November and December.

(b) Prepare the journal entries to record the estimated liability for warranties and the costs (assume actual costs of $15,000) incurred in honoring 1,000 warranty claims.

(c) Give the entry to record the honoring of 400 warranty contracts in January at an average cost of $15.

E11–5 Lieberman Company has the following liability accounts after posting adjusting entries: Accounts Payable $66,000, Unearned Ticket Revenue $24,000, Estimated Warranty Liability $18,000, Interest Payable $12,000, Mortgage Payable $120,000, Notes Payable $80,000, and Sales Taxes Payable $10,000. Assume the company's operating cycle is less than one year, ticket revenue will be earned within 1 year, warranty costs are expected to be incurred within 1 year, and the notes mature in 3 years.

Prepare the current liability section of the balance sheet.
(SO 1, 2, 3, 4, 5)

Instructions

(a) Prepare the current liability section of the balance sheet, assuming $30,000 of the mortgage is payable next year.

(b) Comment on Lieberman Company's liquidity, assuming total current assets are $300,000.

E11–6 McDonald's 1995 financial statements contained the following selected data (in millions):

Calculate liquidity ratios; discuss impact of unrecorded obligations on liquidity and solvency.
(SO 4)

Current assets	$ 955.8	Interest expense	$ 340.2
Total assets	15,414.6	Income taxes	741.8
Current liabilities	1,794.9	Net income	1,427.3
Total liabilities	7,553.3		
Cash	334.8		
Accounts receivable	377.3		
Notes receivable	36.3		

Instructions

Compute these values:

1. Working capital
2. Current ratio

E11–7 The following financial data were reported by Minnesota Mining and Manufacturing (3M) for 1997 and 1996 ($ in millions):

Calculate current ratios and working capital before and after paying accounts payable.
(SO 4)

MINNESOTA MINING AND MANUFACTURING Balance Sheets (partial)		
	1997	**1996**
Current assets		
Cash and cash equivalents	$ 230	$ 583
Other securities	247	161
Accounts receivable, net	2,434	2,504
Inventories	2,399	2,264
Other current assets	858	974
Total current assets	$6,168	$6,486
Current liabilities	$3,983	$3,606

Instructions

(a) Calculate the current ratio and working capital for 3M for 1997 and 1996.
(b) Suppose that at the end of 1997 3M management used $500 million cash to pay off $500 million of accounts payable. How would its current ratio and working capital have changed?

Compute net pay and record pay for one employee.
(SO 7)

E11–8   Karen Ortega's regular hourly wage rate is $16.00, and she receives a wage of 1½ times the regular hourly rate for work in excess of 40 hours. During a March weekly pay period Karen worked 42 hours. Her gross earnings prior to the current week were $19,000. Karen is married and claims three withholding allowances. Her only voluntary deduction is for group hospitalization insurance at $10.00 per week.

Instructions

(a) Compute the following amounts for Karen's wages for the current week.
   1. Gross earnings.
   2. FICA taxes. (Assume an 8% rate on maximum of $65,000.)
   3. Federal income taxes withheld. (Use the withholding table in the text, page 484.)
   4. State income taxes withheld. (Assume a 2.0% rate.)
   5. Net pay.
(b) Record Karen's pay, assuming she is an office computer operator.

Compute maximum FICA deductions.
(SO 7)

E11–9   Employee earnings records for Kokomo Company reveal the following gross earnings for four employees through the pay period of December 15.

K. Ostman	$63,500	B. Sailors	$64,300
C. Leggett	$64,600	R. Ryan	$65,000

For the pay period ending December 31, each employee's gross earnings is $1,000. The FICA tax rate is 8% on gross earnings of $65,000.

Instructions

Compute the FICA withholdings that should be made for each employee for the December 31 pay period. (Show computations.)

Prepare payroll register and record payroll and payroll tax expense.
(SO 7, 8)

E11–10   Egypt Company has the following data for the weekly payroll ending January 31.

	Hours						Hourly Rate	Federal Income Tax Withholding	Health Insurance
Employee	M	T	W	T	F	S			
S. Rude	8	8	9	8	10	3	$10	$34	$10
N. Siena	8	8	8	8	8	2	12	37	15
V. Ruble	9	10	8	8	9	0	12	58	15

Employees are paid 1½ times the regular hourly rate for all hours worked in excess of 40 hours per week. FICA taxes are 8% on the first $65,000 of gross earnings. Egypt Company is subject to 5.4% state unemployment taxes and 0.8% federal unemployment taxes on the first $7,000 of gross earnings.

Instructions

(a) Prepare the payroll register for the weekly payroll.
(b) Prepare the journal entry to record the payroll and Egypt's payroll tax expense.

Compute missing payroll amounts and record payroll.
(SO 7)

E11–11   Selected data from a February payroll register for Mira Stice Company are presented below with some amounts intentionally omitted.

Gross earnings:			
Regular	$8,900	State income taxes	$ (3)
Overtime	(1)	Union dues	100
Total	(2)	Total deductions	(4)
Deductions:		Net pay	$7,760
FICA taxes	$ 800	Accounts debited:	
Federal income taxes	1,140	Warehouse wages	(5)
		Store wages	$4,000

FICA taxes are 8% and state income taxes are 2% of gross earnings.

Instructions

(a) Fill in the missing amounts.
(b) Journalize the February payroll and the payment of the payroll.

E11–12   According to a payroll register summary of Strickland Company, the amount of employees' gross pay in December was $800,000, of which $60,000 was not subject to FICA tax and $760,000 was not subject to state and federal unemployment taxes.

Determine employer's payroll taxes and record payroll tax expense.
(SO 8)

Instructions
(a) Determine the employer's payroll tax expense for the month, using the following rates: FICA, 8%; state unemployment, 5.4%; federal unemployment, 0.8%.
(b) Prepare the journal entry to record December payroll tax expense.

E11–13   Austin Company has two fringe benefit plans for its employees:

Prepare adjusting entries for fringe benefits.
(SO 9)

1. It grants employees 2 days' vacation for each month worked. Ten employees worked the entire month of March at an average daily wage of $100 per employee.
2. In its pension plan the company recognizes 10% of gross earnings as an expense. Gross earnings in March were $30,000. No contribution has been made to the pension fund.

Instructions
Prepare the adjusting entries at March 31.

PROBLEMS: SET A
••

P11–1A   On January 1, 1999, the ledger of Calcutta Company contains the following liability accounts.

Prepare current liability entries, adjusting entries, and current liability section.
(SO 1, 2, 3, 4, 5)

Accounts Payable	$42,500
Sales Taxes Payable	5,600
Unearned Service Revenue	15,000

During January the following selected transactions occurred:

Jan. 1   Borrowed $15,000 in cash from Midland Bank on a 4-month, 12%, $15,000 note.
   5   Sold merchandise for cash totaling $7,800 which includes 4% sales taxes.
   12   Provided services for customers who had made advance payments of $8,000. (Credit Service Revenue.)
   14   Paid state treasurer's department for sales taxes collected in December 1998 $5,600.
   20   Sold 500 units of a new product on credit at $52 per unit, plus 4% sales tax. This new product is subject to a 1-year warranty.
   25   Sold merchandise for cash totaling $11,440, which includes 4% sales taxes.

Instructions
(a) Journalize the January transactions.
(b) Journalize the adjusting entries at January 31 for (1) the outstanding note payable, and (2) estimated warranty liability, assuming warranty costs are expected to equal 8% of sales of the new product.
(c) Prepare the current liability section of the balance sheet at January 31, 1999. Assume no change in Accounts Payable.

P11–2A   Villanova Drug Store has four employees who are paid on an hourly basis plus time-and-one-half for all hours worked in excess of 40 a week. Payroll data for the week ended February 15, 1999, are presented below:

Prepare payroll register and payroll entries.
(SO 7, 8)

Employees	Hours Worked	Hourly Rate	Federal Income Tax Withholdings	United Fund
O. Stratton	39	$13.00	$?	$ –0–
E. Muse	42	12.00	?	5.00
A. Horton	44	12.00	58	7.50
F. Lupino	46	12.00	33	5.00

Stratton and Muse are married. They claim 2 and 4 withholding allowances, respectively. The following tax rates are applicable: FICA 8%, state income taxes 3%, state unemployment taxes 5.4%, and federal unemployment 0.8%. The first three employees are sales clerks (store wages expense), and the other employee performs administrative duties (office wages expense).

Instructions

(a) Prepare a payroll register for the weekly payroll. (Use the wage-bracket withholding table in the text for federal income tax withholdings.)

(b) Journalize the payroll on February 15, 1999, and the accrual of employer payroll taxes.

(c) Journalize the payment of the payroll on February 16, 1999.

(d) Journalize the deposit in a federal reserve bank on February 28, 1999, of the FICA and federal income taxes payable to the government.

Identify internal control weaknesses and make recommendations for improvement.
(SO 6)

P11–3A   The payroll procedures used by three different companies are described below:

1. In Sanchez Company each employee is required to mark the hours worked on a clock card. At the end of each pay period, the employee must have this clock card approved by the department manager. The approved card is then given to the payroll department by the employee. Subsequently, the treasurer's department pays the employee by check.

2. In Moscove Company clock cards and time clocks are used. At the end of each pay period, the department manager initials the cards, indicates the rates of pay, and sends them to payroll. A payroll register is prepared from the cards by the payroll department. Cash equal to the total net pay in each department is given to the department manager, who pays the employees in cash.

3. In Dominion Company employees are required to record hours worked on clock cards by "punching" a time clock. At the end of each pay period, the clock cards are collected by the department manager. The manager prepares a payroll register in duplicate and forwards the original to payroll. In payroll, the summaries are checked for mathematical accuracy and a payroll supervisor pays each employee by check.

Instructions

(a) 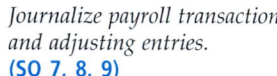 Indicate the weakness(es) in internal control in each company.

(b) For each weakness, describe the control procedure(s) that will provide effective internal control. Use the following format for your answer:

(a) Weaknesses	(b) Recommended Procedures

Journalize payroll transactions and adjusting entries.
(SO 7, 8, 9)

P11–4A   The following payroll liability accounts are included in the ledger of Carlos Costa Company on January 1, 1999:

FICA Taxes Payable	$ 662.20
Federal Income Taxes Payable	954.60
State Income Taxes Payable	102.15
Federal Unemployment Taxes Payable	2,400.00
State Unemployment Taxes Payable	1,954.40
Union Dues Payable	250.00
U.S. Savings Bonds Payable	350.00

In January, the following transactions occurred:

Jan. 10   Sent check for $250.00 to union treasurer for union dues.

12   Deposited check for $1,616.80 in Federal Reserve Bank for FICA taxes and federal income taxes withheld.

15   Purchased U.S. Savings Bonds for employees by writing check for $350.00.

17   Paid state income taxes withheld from employees.

20   Paid federal and state unemployment taxes.

31   Completed monthly payroll register, which shows office salaries $14,600, store wages $27,400, FICA taxes withheld $3,360, federal income taxes payable $1,654, state income taxes payable $360, union dues payable $400, United Fund contributions payable $1,688, and net pay $34,538.

31   Prepared payroll checks for the net pay and distributed checks to employees.

At January 31, the company also makes the following accruals pertaining to employee compensation:

1. Employer payroll taxes: FICA taxes (8%), state unemployment taxes (5.4%), and federal unemployment taxes (0.8%).

2. Vacation pay: 4% of gross earnings.

Instructions

(a) Journalize the January transactions.

(b) Journalize the adjustments pertaining to employee compensation at January 31.

P11–5A   For the year ended December 31, 1999, San Juan Electric Company reports the following summary payroll data:

Prepare entries for payroll and payroll taxes, and prepare W-2 data.
(SO 7, 8, 9)

Gross earnings:	
Administrative salaries	$180,000
Electricians' wages	370,000
Total	$550,000
Deductions:	
FICA taxes	$ 39,600
Federal income taxes withheld	168,000
State income taxes withheld (2.6%)	14,300
United Fund contributions payable	27,500
Hospital insurance premiums	17,200
Total	$266,600

San Juan Company's payroll taxes are: FICA 8%, state unemployment 2.5% (due to a stable employment record), and 0.8% federal unemployment. Gross earnings subject to (1) FICA taxes total $495,000, and (2) unemployment taxes total $400,000.

Instructions

(a) Prepare a summary journal entry at December 31 for the full year's payroll.

(b) Journalize the adjusting entry at December 31 to record the employer's payroll taxes.

(c) The W-2 Wage and Tax Statement requires the following dollar data:

Wages, Tips, Other Compensation	Federal Income Tax Withheld	State Income Tax Withheld	FICA Wages	FICA Tax Withheld

Complete the required data for the following employees:

Employee	Gross Earnings	Federal Income Tax Withheld
R. Cheng	$60,000	$27,500
D. Craig	25,000	10,200

P11–6A   The following are selected transactions of Zimmer Company. Zimmer prepares financial statements *quarterly*.

Journalize and post note transactions and show balance sheet presentation.
(SO 2)

Jan. 2   Purchased merchandise on account from Alicea Company, $18,000, terms 2/10, n/30.

Feb. 1   Issued a 10%, 2-month, $18,000 note to Alicea in payment of account.

Mar. 31   Accrued interest for 2 months on Alicea note.

Apr. 1   Paid face value and interest on Alicea note.

July 1   Purchased equipment from Vincent Equipment paying $11,000 in cash and signing a 10%, 3-month, $24,000 note.

Sept. 30   Accrued interest for 3 months on Vincent note.

Oct. 1   Paid face value and interest on Vincent note.

Dec. 1   Borrowed $10,000 from the Otago Bank by issuing a 3-month, 12%-interest-bearing note with a face value of $10,000.

Dec. 31   Recognized interest expense for 1 month on Otago Bank note.

Instructions

(a) Prepare journal entries for the above transactions and events.

(b) Post to the accounts, Notes Payable, Interest Payable, and Interest Expense.

(c) Show the balance sheet presentation of notes payable at December 31.

(d) What is total interest expense for the year?

PROBLEMS: SET B

Prepare current liability entries, adjusting entries, and current liability section.
(SO 1, 2, 3, 4, 5)

P11–1B   On January 1, 1999, the ledger of El Paso Company contains the following liability accounts:

Accounts Payable	$52,000
Sales Taxes Payable	7,500
Unearned Service Revenue	16,000

During January the following selected transactions occurred:

Jan. 5   Sold merchandise for cash totaling $16,632, which includes 8% sales taxes.

　12   Provided services for customers who had made advance payments of $9,000. (Credit Service Revenue)

　14   Paid state revenue department for sales taxes collected in December 1998 ($7,500).

　20   Sold 500 units of a new product on credit at $50 per unit, plus 8% sales tax. This new product is subject to a 1-year warranty.

　21   Borrowed $18,000 from Midland Bank on a 3-month, 10%, $18,000 note.

　25   Sold merchandise for cash totaling $11,340, which includes 8% sales taxes.

Instructions
(a) Journalize the January transactions.
(b) Journalize the adjusting entries at January 31 for (1) the outstanding notes payable, and (2) estimated warranty liability, assuming warranty costs are expected to equal 8% of sales of the new product. (*Hint*: Use one-third of a month for the Midland Bank note.)
(c) Prepare the current liability section of the balance sheet at January 31, 1999. Assume no change in accounts payable.

Prepare payroll register and payroll entries.
(SO 7, 8)

P11–2B   UCLA Hardware has four employees who are paid on an hourly basis plus time-and-one-half for all hours worked in excess of 40 a week. Payroll data for the week ended March 15, 1999, are presented below:

Employee	Hours Worked	Hourly Rate	Federal Income Tax Withholdings	United Fund
J. Sanders	40	$14.00	$?	$5.00
S. Black	42	13.00	?	5.00
D. Torres	44	13.00	42	8.00
K. Kim	46	13.00	48	5.00

Sanders and Black are married. They claim 0 and 4 withholding allowances, respectively. The following tax rates are applicable: FICA 8%, state income taxes 3%, state unemployment taxes 5.4%, and federal unemployment 0.8%. The first three employees are sales clerks (store wages expense) and the other employee performs administrative duties (office wages expense).

Instructions
(a) Prepare a payroll register for the weekly payroll. (Use the wage-bracket withholding table in the text for federal income tax withholdings.)
(b) Journalize the payroll on March 15, 1999, and the accrual of employer payroll taxes.
(c) Journalize the payment of the payroll on March 16, 1999.
(d) Journalize the deposit in a federal reserve bank on March 31, 1999, of the FICA and federal income taxes payable to the government.

Identify internal control weaknesses and make recommendations for improvement.
(SO 6)

P11–3A   Selected payroll procedures of Merced Sotera Company are described below:

1. Department managers interview applicants and on the basis of the interview either hire or reject the applicants. When an applicant is hired, the applicant fills out a W-4 form (Employer's Withholding Exemption Certificate). One copy of the form is sent to the personnel department and one copy is sent to the payroll department as notice that the individual has been hired. On the copy of the W-4 sent to payroll, the managers manually indicate the hourly pay rate for the new hire.

2. The payroll checks are manually signed by the chief accountant and given to the de-

partment managers for distribution to employees in their department. The managers are responsible for seeing that any absent employees receive their checks.

3. There are two clerks in the payroll department. The payroll is divided alphabetically with one clerk having employees A to L and the other employees M to Z. Each clerk computes the gross earnings, deductions, and net pay for employees in the section and posts the data to the employee earning records.

Instructions

(a) ▰▰▰▰▷ Indicate the weaknesses in internal control.

(b) ▰▰▰▰▷ For each weakness, describe the control procedures that will provide effective internal control. Use the following format for your answer:

(a) Weaknesses	(b) Recommended Procedures

P11–4B   The following payroll liability accounts are included in the ledger of Amora Company on January 1, 1999:

FICA Taxes Payable	$ 760.00
Federal Income Taxes Payable	954.60
State Income Taxes Payable	108.95
Federal Unemployment Taxes Payable	288.95
State Unemployment Taxes Payable	1,954.40
Union Dues Payable	870.00
U.S. Savings Bonds Payable	360.00

Journalize payroll transactions and adjusting entries.
(SO 7, 8, 9)

In January, the following transactions occurred:

Jan. 10   Sent check for $870.00 to union treasurer for union dues.

12   Deposited check for $1,714.60 in Federal Reserve Bank for FICA taxes and federal income taxes withheld.

15   Purchased U.S. Savings Bonds for employees by writing check for $360.00.

17   Paid state income taxes withheld from employees.

20   Paid federal and state unemployment taxes.

31   Completed monthly payroll register, which shows office salaries $14,600, store wages $28,400, FICA taxes withheld $3,440, federal income taxes payable $1,684, state income taxes payable $360, union dues payable $400, United Fund contributions payable $1,888, and net pay $35,228.

31   Prepared payroll checks for the net pay and distributed checks to employees.

At January 31, the company also makes the following accrued adjustments pertaining to employee compensation:

1. Employer payroll taxes: FICA taxes (8%), federal unemployment taxes (0.8%), and state unemployment taxes (5.4%).
2. Vacation pay: 4% of gross earnings.

Instructions

(a) Journalize the January transactions.

(b) Journalize the adjustments pertaining to employee compensation at January 31.

P11–5B   For the year ended December 31, 1999, McMaster Electrical Repair Company reports the following summary payroll data:

Prepare entries for payroll and payroll taxes and prepare W-2 data.
(SO 7, 8, 9)

Gross earnings:	
Administrative salaries	$180,000
Electricians' wages	470,000
Total	$650,000
Deductions:	
FICA taxes	$ 46,000
Federal income taxes withheld	188,000
State income taxes withheld (2.6%)	16,900
United Fund contributions payable	32,500
Hospital insurance premiums	20,300
Total	$303,700

McMaster Company's payroll taxes are: FICA 8%, state unemployment 2.5% (due to a stable employment record), and 0.8% federal unemployment. Gross earnings subject to (1) FICA taxes total $575,000; and (2) unemployment taxes total $450,000.

Instructions
(a) Prepare a summary journal entry at December 31 for the full year's payroll.
(b) Journalize the adjusting entry at December 31 to record the employer's payroll taxes.
(c) The W-2 Wage and Tax Statement requires the following dollar data:

Wages, Tips, Other Compensation	Federal Income Tax Withheld	State Income Tax Withheld	FICA Wages	FICA Tax Withheld

Complete the required data for the following employees:

Employee	Gross Earnings	Federal Income Tax Withheld
J. Walker	$59,000	$28,500
I. Zimmer	28,000	10,800

BROADENING YOUR PERSPECTIVE

FINANCIAL REPORTING AND ANALYSIS

FINANCIAL REPORTING PROBLEM: Kellogg Company

BYP11–1 The financial statements of Kellogg Company and the Notes to Consolidated Financial Statements appear in Appendix A.

Instructions
Refer to Kellogg's financial statements and answer the following questions about current and contingent liabilities and payroll costs:

(a) What were Kellogg's total current liabilities at December 31, 1997? What was the increase/decrease in Kellogg's total current liabilities from the prior year?
(b) How much were the "current maturities of long-term debt" at December 31, 1997?
(c) What were the components of total current liabilities on December 31, 1997 (other than "current maturities of long-term debt" already discussed in b above)?

COMPARATIVE ANALYSIS PROBLEM: Kellogg Company vs. General Mills

BYP11–2   Kellogg's financial statements are presented in Appendix A; General Mills's financial statements are presented in Appendix B.

Instructions
(a) At December 31, 1997, what was Kellogg's largest current liability account? What was its total current liabilities? At May 25, 1997, what was General Mills's largest current liability account? What was its total current liabilities?
(b) Based on information contained in those financial statements, compute the following 1997 values for each company:
  (1) Working capital
  (2) Current ratio
(c) What conclusions concerning the relative liquidity of these companies can be drawn from these data?

RESEARCH ASSIGNMENT

BYP11–3   The December 1995 issue of *Management Accounting* includes a reprint of an article by Glenn Cheney entitled "It's Not Easy Being Green But Top Companies Are Trying."

Instructions

Read the article and answer the following questions.

  (a) What portion of the Fortune 500 companies disclose their position on the environment? What type of information is included in these disclosures?
  (b) How can companies save money by "being green"?
  (c) What is the "take-back" principle"?
  (d) What is the role of public accountants in this area?

INTERPRETING FINANCIAL STATEMENTS: Northland Cranberries

BYP11–4   Despite being a publicly traded company only since 1987, Northland Cranberries of Wisconsin Rapids, Wisconsin, is the world's largest cranberry grower. It has engaged in an aggressive growth strategy, and as a consequence, the company has taken on significant amounts of both short-term and long-term debt. The following information is taken from recent annual reports of the company.

	1995	1994
Current assets	$ 6,745,759	$ 5,598,054
Total assets	107,744,751	83,074,339
Current liabilities	10,168,685	4,484,687
Total liabilities	73,118,204	49,948,787
Stockholders' equity	34,626,547	33,125,552
Net sales	21,783,966	18,051,355
Cost of goods sold	13,057,275	8,751,220
Interest expense	3,654,006	2,393,792
Income tax expense	1,051,000	1,917,000
Net income	1,581,707	2,942,954

Instructions

  (a) Evaluate the company's liquidity by calculating and analyzing working capital and the current ratio.
  (b) The following discussion of the company's liquidity was provided by the company in the Management Discussion and Analysis section of the company's 1995 annual report. Comment on whether you agree with management's statements, and what might be done to remedy the situation.

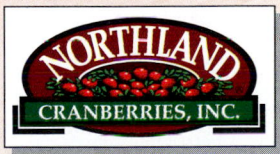

NORTHLAND CRANBERRIES
Management Discussion and Analysis

The lower comparative current ratio at March 31, 1995, was due to $3 million of short-term borrowing then outstanding which was incurred to fund the Company's September 1994 Yellow River Marsh acquisitions. As a result of the extreme seasonality of its business, the Company does not believe that its current ratio or its underlying stated working capital at its March 31, 1995, fiscal year end is a meaningful indication of the Company's liquidity. As of March 31 of each fiscal year, the Company has historically carried no significant amounts of inventories and by such date all of the Company's accounts receivable from its crop sold for processing under the supply agreements have been paid in cash, with the resulting cash received from such payments used to reduce indebtedness. The Company utilizes its revolving bank credit facility, together with cash generated from operations, to fund its working capital requirements throughout its growing season.

REAL-WORLD FOCUS: Capitol American Financial Corporation

BYP11–5 Formed in 1970, **Capitol American Financial Corporation** is licensed throughout most of the United States, Puerto Rico, and the U.S. Virgin Islands. The company's 285 employees develop, underwrite, market, and distribute individual supplemental health and accidental insurance. A primary product line is cancer insurance. Presented below is a note to the financial statements of Capitol American Financial Corporation:

CAPITOL AMERICAN FINANCIAL CORPORATION
Notes to the Financial Statements

The Company is the subject of an employment tax examination by the Internal Revenue Service ("IRS") with respect to the treatment of its agents as independent contractors rather than employees for financial reporting and tax purposes for 1987 and 1988. The IRS has proposed for 1987 and 1988 an increase in the tax liability of the Company in the aggregate amount of approximately $6.1 million, including approximately $1.5 million in penalties, for assessment of Federal Insurance Contributions Act ("FICA") taxes, federal unemployment compensation taxes and federal income taxes on wages not withheld by the Company. Management believes, based in part on the opinion of legal counsel, that the Company's treatment of its agents as independent contractors rather than employees is correct for federal tax purposes and that the Company should prevail. Accordingly, no liability or loss that could result upon adverse resolution of this matter has been recognized in the Company's consolidated financial statements. If the Company does not prevail, it can be expected that the Company would be assessed similar, but generally increasing, amounts for the years 1989 through 1992 (representing a total potential liability to the Company, including penalties, of approximately $28.1 million, for 1987 through 1992), and also for 1993 and future years unless the Company changes certain of its practices regarding the treatment of its agents. In addition, an adverse resolution of this matter could also be expected to have an adverse effect on the Company with respect to certain state and local taxes.

Instructions

(a) How is the company's net income affected by hiring work to be done by independent contractors rather than employees?

(b) If Capitol American Financial Corporation loses the lawsuit, which accounts will have been understated by using the independent contractor arrangement?

(c) What assessment has the Corporation made with respect to the likelihood and estimatability of this contingent liability?

CRITICAL THINKING

GROUP DECISION CASE

BYP11–6 Sauk Processing Company provides word-processing services for clients and students in a university community. The work for clients is fairly steady throughout the year, but the work for students peaks significantly in December and May as a result of term papers, research project reports, and dissertations.

Two years ago, the company attempted to meet the peak demand by hiring part-time help. However, this led to numerous errors and considerable customer dissatisfaction. A year ago, the company hired four experienced employees on a permanent basis instead of using part-time help. This proved to be much better in terms of productivity and customer satisfaction. However, it has caused an increase in annual payroll costs and a significant decline in annual net income.

Recently, Tammy Berg, a sales representative of Harrington Services Inc., has made a proposal to the company. Under the plan, Harrington Services will provide up to four experienced workers at a daily rate of $105 per person for an 8-hour workday. Harrington workers are not available on an hourly basis. Sauk Processing would have to pay only the daily rate for the workers used.

The owner of Sauk Processing, Martha Bell, asks you, as the company's accountant, to prepare a report on the expenses that are pertinent to the decision. If the Harrington plan is adopted, Martha will terminate the employment of two permanent employees who are each earning an average annual salary of $30,000. The remaining permanent employees each earn an annual income of $30,000. Sauk Processing pays 8% FICA taxes, 0.8% Federal Unemployment Taxes, and 5.4% State Unemployment Taxes. The unemployment taxes apply to only the first $7,000 of gross earnings. In addition, Sauk Processing pays $40 per month for each employee for medical and dental insurance.

Martha indicates that if the Harrington Services plan is accepted, her needs for workers will be as follows:

Months	Number	Working Days per Month
January–March	2	20
April–May	3	25
June–October	2	18
November–December	3	23

Instructions

With the class divided into groups, answer the following:
  (a) Prepare a report showing the comparative payroll expense of continuing to employ permanent workers compared to adopting the Harrington Services Inc. plan.
  (b) What other factors should Martha consider before finalizing her decision?

COMMUNICATION ACTIVITY

BYP11–7   Tim Harp, president of the Low Cloud Company, has recently hired a number of additional employees. He recognizes that additional payroll taxes will be due as a result of this hiring, and that the company will serve as the collection agent for other taxes.

Instructions

In a memorandum to Tim Harp, explain each of the taxes, and identify the taxes that result in payroll tax expense to the employer.

ETHICS CASE

BYP11–8   Harry Smith owns and manages Harry's Restaurant, a 24-hour restaurant near the city's medical complex. Harry employs nine full-time employees and sixteen part-time employees. He pays all of the full-time employees by check, the amounts of which are determined by Harry's public accountant, Pam Web. Harry pays all of his part-time employees in currency that he computes and withdraws directly from his cash register. Pam has repeatedly urged Harry to pay all employees by check. But as Harry has told his competitor and friend, Steve Hill, who owns the Greasy Diner, "First of all, my part-time employees prefer the currency over a check, and secondly I don't withhold or pay any taxes or workmen's compensation insurance on those wages because they go totally unrecorded and unnoticed."

Instructions

  (a) Who are the stakeholders in this situation?
  (b) What are the legal and ethical considerations regarding Harry's handling of his payroll?
  (c) Pam Web is aware of Harry's payment of the part-time payroll in currency. What are her ethical responsibilities in this case?
  (d) What internal control principle is violated in this payroll process?

SURFING THE NET

BYP11–9 The Internal Revenue Service provides considerable information over the Internet. The following demonstrates how useful one of its sites is in answering payroll tax questions faced by employers.

Address: http://www.irs.ustreas.gov/prod/forms_pubs/index.html

Steps:
1. Go to the site shown above.
2. Choose **Publications Online.**
3. Choose **Circular E, Employer's Tax Guide.**

Instructions
Answer each of the following questions:

(a) How does the government define "employees"?
(b) What are the special rules for Social Security and Medicare regarding children who are employed by their parents?
(c) How can an employee obtain a Social Security card if he or she doesn't have one?
(d) Must employees report tips received from customers to their employer? If so, what is the process?
(e) Where should the employer deposit Social Security taxes withheld or contributed?

Answers to Self-Study Questions
1. a   2. d   3. b   4. b   5. a   6. c   7. b   8. d   9. d   10. c   11. d

---

Answer to Kellogg Review It Question 2, p. 478
Under the heading of current liabilities Kellogg has listed current maturities of long-term debt, notes payable, and accounts payable.

Remember to go back to the Navigator box on the chapter-opening page and check off your completed work.

Before studying this chapter, you should know or, if necessary, review:

a. The two organizations primarily responsible for setting accounting standards. (Ch. 1, pp. 10–11)

b. The monetary unit assumption, the economic entity assumption, and the time period assumption. (Chs. 1 and 3, pp. 10, 11, 92–93)

c. The cost principle, the revenue recognition principle, and the matching principle. (Chs. 1 and 3, pp. 11, 93–94)

THE NAVIGATOR

FEATURE STORY

Timing Is Everything

A few simple truths:

Truth 1: Net income = Revenues − Expenses

Truth 2: In general, more net income is better than less.

Truth 3: To increase net income you must increase reported revenue or decrease reported expense.

Truth 4: Timing is everything.

So far you have learned some nice orderly rules about how to keep track of corporate transactions. Guess what? It isn't that nice and neat. In fact, it is often difficult to determine in what period some revenues and expenses should be reported. There are rules that give guidance, but occasionally these rules are overlooked, misinterpreted, or even intentionally ignored. Consider the following examples:

• Media Vision Technology Inc., a maker of sound and animation equipment for computers, was accused of operating a "phantom" warehouse to hide inventory for returned products already recorded as sales.

• Policy Management Systems Corp., which makes insurance software, said that it reported some sales before contracts were signed or products delivered.

• Penguin USA, a book publisher, said that it understated expenses in some years because it failed to report expenses for discounts given to customers for paying early.

In each case, accrual accounting concepts were violated. That is, revenues or expenses were not recorded in the proper period, which had a substantial impact on reported income.

Why might management want to report revenues or expenses in the wrong period? One *Wall Street Journal* article states that high-tech firms have intense pressure to report higher earnings every year. If actual performance falls short of expectations, management might be tempted to bend the rules. An accounting expert suggests that investors and auditors should be suspicious of sharp increases in monthly sales at the end of each quarter or big jumps in fourth-quarter sales. Such events don't always mean management is cheating, but they are certainly worth investigating.

Source: Lee Burton, "Tech Concerns Fudge Figures to Buoy Stocks," *The Wall Street Journal*, May 19, 1994, p. B1.

THE NAVIGATOR

CHAPTER 12

ACCOUNTING PRINCIPLES

THE NAVIGATOR

- Understand *Concepts for Review* ☐
- Read *Feature Story* ☐
- Scan *Study Objectives* ☐
- Read *Preview* ☐
- Read text and answer *Before You Go On*
  p. 520 ☐ p. 532 ☐
- Work *Demonstration Problems* ☐
- Review *Summary of Study Objectives* ☐
- Answer *Self-Study Questions* ☐
- Complete assignments ☐

STUDY OBJECTIVES

After studying this chapter, you should be able to:

1. *Explain the meaning of generally accepted accounting principles and identify the key items of the conceptual framework.*
2. *Describe the basic objectives of financial reporting.*
3. *Discuss the qualitative characteristics of accounting information and elements of financial statements.*
4. *Identify the basic assumptions used by accountants.*
5. *Identify the basic principles of accounting.*
6. *Identify the two constraints in accounting.*
7. *Explain the accounting principles used in international operations.*

THE NAVIGATOR

As indicated in the opening story, it is important that general guidelines be available to resolve accounting issues. Without these basic guidelines, each enterprise would have to develop its own set of accounting practices. If this happened, we would have to become familiar with every company's peculiar accounting and reporting rules in order to understand their financial statements. Thus, it would be difficult, if not impossible, to compare the financial statements of different companies.

This chapter explores the basic accounting principles followed in developing specific accounting guidelines. The content and organization of the chapter are as follows:

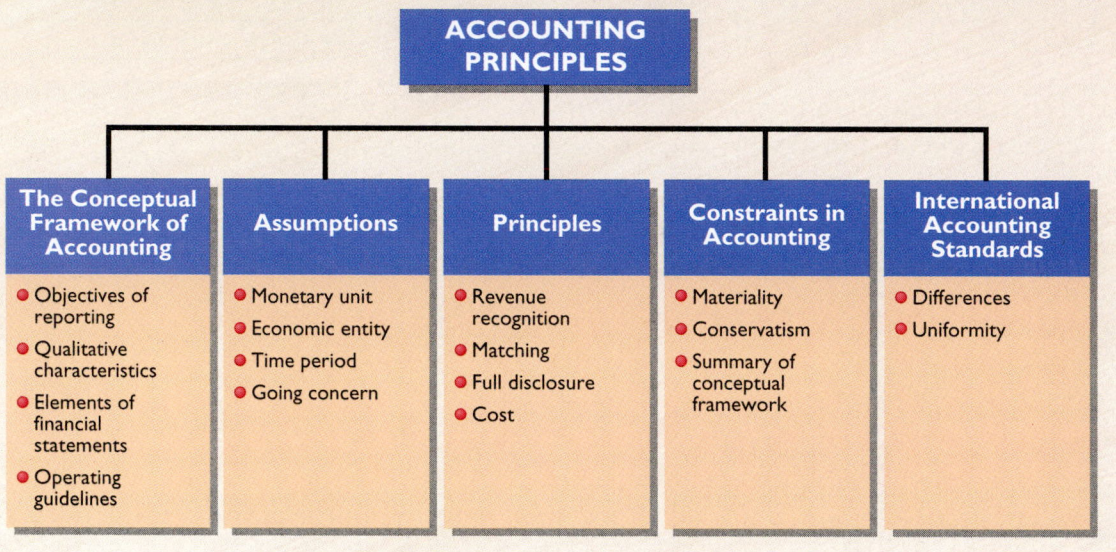

THE CONCEPTUAL FRAMEWORK OF ACCOUNTING

STUDY OBJECTIVE

1

Explain the meaning of generally accepted accounting principles and identify the key items of the conceptual framework.

The accounting profession has established a set of standards and rules that are recognized as a general guide for financial reporting purposes. This recognized set of standards is called **generally accepted accounting principles (GAAP)**. "Generally accepted" means that these principles must have "substantial authoritative support." Such support usually comes from two standard-setting bodies: the Financial Accounting Standards Board (FASB) and the Securities and Exchange Commission (SEC).[1]

Since the early 1970s the business and governmental communities have given the FASB the responsibility for developing accounting principles in this country.

---

[1]The SEC is an agency of the U.S. government that was established in 1933 to administer laws and regulations relating to the exchange of securities and the publication of financial information by U.S. businesses. The agency has the authority to mandate generally accepted accounting principles for companies under its jurisdiction. However, throughout its history, the SEC has been willing to accept the principles set forth by the FASB and similar bodies.

This job is an ongoing process in which accounting principles change to reflect changes in the business environment and in the needs of users of accounting information.

Prior to the establishment of the FASB, accounting principles were developed on a problem-by-problem basis. Thus, rule-making bodies developed and issued accounting rules and methods to solve specific problems. Critics charged that the problem-by-problem approach led to inconsistent rules and practices over time. Unfortunately, no clearly developed conceptual framework of accounting existed for the accounting rule makers to refer to in solving problems.

In response to these criticisms, the FASB developed a **conceptual framework** to serve as the basis for resolving accounting and reporting problems. The FASB spent considerable time and effort on this project. The Board views its conceptual framework as "... a constitution, a coherent system of interrelated objectives and fundamentals."[2]

The FASB's conceptual framework consists of the following four items:

1. Objectives of financial reporting.
2. Qualitative characteristics of accounting information.
3. Elements of financial statements.
4. Operating guidelines (assumptions, principles, and constraints).

We will discuss each of these items on the following pages.

ACCOUNTING IN ACTION
International Insight

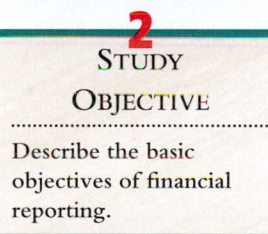

You should recognize that different political and cultural influences affect the accounting that occurs in foreign countries. For example, in Sweden, accounting is considered an instrument to be used to shape fiscal policy. In Europe generally, more emphasis is given to social reporting (more information on employment statistics, health of workers, and so on) because employees and their labor organizations are strong and demand that type of information from management.

Objectives of Financial Reporting

In developing the conceptual framework, the FASB concluded that the first level of study was to determine the objectives of financial reporting. Determining these objectives required answers to such basic questions as: Who uses financial statements? Why? What information do they need? How knowledgeable about business and accounting are the users of financial statements? How should financial information be reported so that it is best understood?

In answering these questions, the FASB concluded that the objectives of financial reporting are to provide information that:

1. Is useful to those making investment and credit decisions.
2. Is helpful in assessing future cash flows.
3. Identifies the economic resources (assets), the claims to those resources (liabilities), and the changes in those resources and claims.

2
STUDY
OBJECTIVE
....
Describe the basic objectives of financial reporting.

---

[2]"Conceptual Framework for Financial Accounting and Reporting: Elements of Financial Statements and Their Measurement," *FASB Discussion Memorandum* (Stamford, Conn.: 1976), p. 1.

The FASB then undertook to describe the characteristics that make accounting information useful.

Qualitative Characteristics of Accounting Information

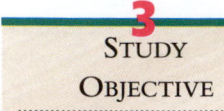

3
STUDY
OBJECTIVE

Discuss the qualitative characteristics of accounting information and elements of financial statements.

How does a company like Microsoft decide on the amount of financial information to disclose? In what format should its financial information be presented? How should assets, liabilities, revenues, and expenses be measured? **The FASB concluded that the overriding criterion by which such accounting choices should be judged is decision usefulness.** The accounting practice selected or the policy adopted should be the one that generates the most useful financial information for making a decision. To be useful, information should possess the following qualitative characteristics: relevance, reliability, comparability, and consistency.

Relevance

Accounting information is **relevant** if it makes a difference in a decision. Relevant information has either predictive or feedback value or both. **Predictive value** helps users forecast future events. For example, when Exxon issues financial statements, the information in the statements is considered relevant because it provides a basis for forecasting (predicting) future earnings. **Feedback value** confirms or corrects prior expectations. When Exxon issues financial statements, in addition to helping predict future events, it confirms or corrects prior expectations about the financial health of the company.

In addition, for accounting information to be relevant it must be **timely**. That is, it must be available to decision makers before it loses its capacity to influence decisions. If Exxon reported its financial information only every 5 years, the information would have limited usefulness for decision-making purposes.

Reliability

Reliability of information means that the information is free of error and bias; it can be depended on. To be reliable, accounting information must be **verifiable**—we must be able to prove that it is free of error and bias. The information must be a **faithful representation** of what it purports to be—it must be factual. If Sears, Roebuck's income statement reports sales of $100 billion when it had sales of $51 billion, then the statement is not a faithful representation. Finally, accounting information must be **neutral**—it cannot be selected, prepared, or presented to favor one set of interested users over another. To ensure reliability, certified public accountants audit financial statements, just as the Internal Revenue Service audits tax returns for the same purpose.

Comparability and Consistency

Accounting information about an enterprise is most useful when it can be compared with accounting information about other enterprises. **Comparability** results when different companies use the same accounting principles. For example, Sears, Roebuck, Montgomery Ward, and J.C. Penney all use the cost principle in reporting plant assets on the balance sheet. Moreover, each company uses the revenue recognition and matching principles in determining its net income.

Conceptually, comparability should also extend to the methods used by companies in complying with an accounting principle. Accounting methods include the FIFO and LIFO methods of inventory costing, and various depreciation methods. At this point, comparability of methods is not required, even for companies in the same industry. Thus, Ford, General Motors, and Chrysler may use different inventory costing and depreciation methods in their financial statements. The

HELPFUL HINT
What makes accounting information relevant? Answer: Relevant accounting information provides feedback, serves as a basis for predictions, and is timely (current).

HELPFUL HINT
What makes accounting information reliable? Answer: Reliable accounting information is free of error and bias, is factual, verifiable, and neutral.

only accounting requirement is that each company **must disclose** the accounting methods used. From the disclosures, the external user can determine whether the financial information is comparable.

Consistency means that a company uses the same accounting principles and methods from year to year. Thus, if a company selects FIFO as the inventory costing method in the first year of operations, it is expected to continue to use FIFO in succeeding years. When financial information has been reported on a consistent basis, the financial statements permit meaningful analysis of trends within a company.

A company can change to a new method of accounting if management can justify that the new method results in more meaningful financial information. In the year in which the change occurs, the change must be disclosed in the notes to the financial statements so that users of the financial statements are aware of the lack of consistency.

ACCOUNTING IN ACTION
Business Insight

There is an old story that professors often tell students about a company looking for an accountant. The company approached the first accountant and asked: "What do you believe our net income will be this year?" The accountant said $4 million dollars. The company asked the second accountant the same question, and the answer was "What would you like it to be?" Guess who got the job? The reason we tell the story here is that, because accounting principles offer flexibility, it is important that a consistent treatment be provided from period to period. Otherwise it would be very difficult to interpret financial statements. Perhaps *no* alternative methods should be permitted in accounting. What do you think?

The qualitative characteristics of accounting information are summarized in Illustration 12-1.

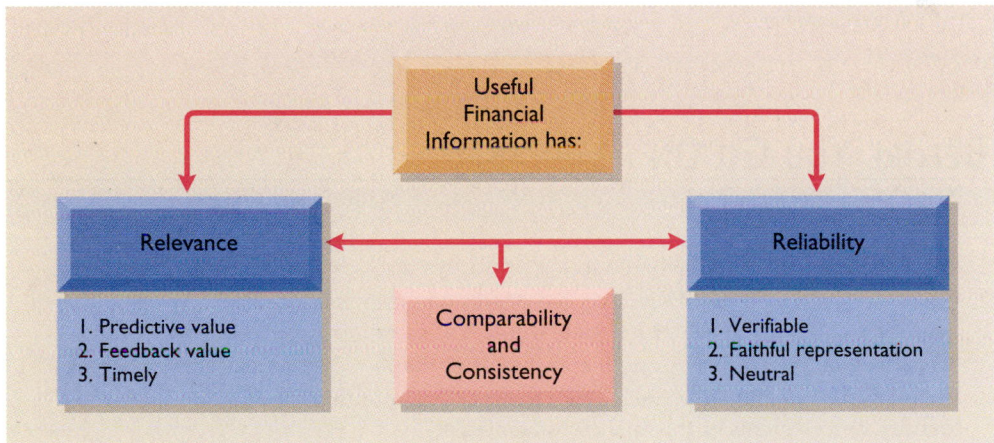

ILLUSTRATION 12-1

Qualitative characteristics of accounting information

Elements of Financial Statements

An important part of an accounting conceptual framework is a set of definitions that describe the basic terms used in accounting. The FASB refers to this set of definitions as the **elements of financial statements**. They include such terms as assets, liabilities, equity, revenues, and expenses.

Because these elements are so important, it is imperative that they be precisely defined and universally understood and applied. Finding the appropriate definition for many of these elements is not easy. For example, how should an asset be defined? Should the value of a company's employees be reported as an asset on a balance sheet? Should the death of the company's president be reported as a loss? A good set of definitions should provide answers to these types of questions. Because you have already encountered most of these definitions in earlier chapters, they are not repeated here.

Operating Guidelines

The objectives of financial statements, the qualitative characteristics of accounting information, and the elements of financial statements are very broad. However, because practicing accountants and standard-setting bodies must solve practical problems, more detailed guidelines are needed. In its conceptual framework, the FASB recognized the need for operating guidelines. We have chosen to classify these guidelines as assumptions, principles, and constraints. These guidelines are well-established and accepted in accounting.

Assumptions provide a foundation for the accounting process. **Principles** are specific rules that indicate how economic events should be reported in the accounting process. **Constraints** on the accounting process allow for a relaxation of the principles under certain circumstances. Illustration 12-2 provides a roadmap of the operating guidelines of accounting. These guidelines are discussed in more detail in the following sections.

ILLUSTRATION 12-2

The operating guidelines of accounting

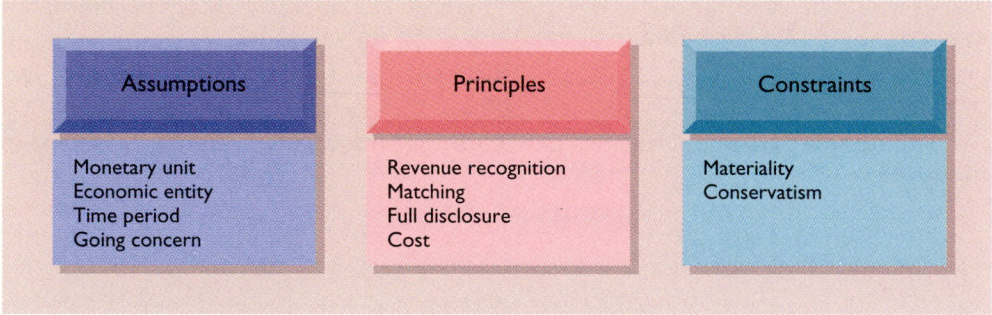

Assumptions	Principles	Constraints
Monetary unit	Revenue recognition	Materiality
Economic entity	Matching	Conservatism
Time period	Full disclosure	
Going concern	Cost	

BEFORE YOU GO ON . . .

Review It

1. What are generally accepted accounting principles?
2. What is stated about generally accepted accounting principles in the Report of Independent Accountants for Kellogg? The answer to this question appears on page 547.
3. What are the basic objectives of financial information?
4. What are the qualitative characteristics that make accounting information useful? Identify two elements of the financial statements.

THE NAVIGATOR

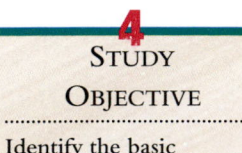

STUDY OBJECTIVE 4

Identify the basic assumptions used by accountants.

ASSUMPTIONS

As noted above, assumptions provide a foundation for the accounting process. You have already studied three of the major assumptions in preceding chapters—the monetary unit, economic entity, and time period assumptions. The fourth is called the going concern assumption.

Monetary Unit Assumption

The **monetary unit assumption** states that only transaction data capable of being expressed in terms of money should be included in the accounting records of the economic entity. For example, the value of a company president is not reported in a company's financial records because it cannot be expressed easily in dollars.

An important corollary to the monetary unit assumption is the added assumption that the unit of measure remains sufficiently constant over time. This point will be discussed in more detail later in this chapter.

Economic Entity Assumption

The **economic entity assumption** states that economic events can be identified with a particular unit of accountability. For example, it is assumed that the activities of IBM can be distinguished from those of other computer companies such as Apple, Compaq, and Hewlett-Packard.

Time Period Assumption

The **time period assumption** states that the economic life of a business can be divided into artificial time periods. Thus, it is assumed that the activities of business enterprises such as General Electric, America Online, Exxon, or any enterprise can be subdivided into months, quarters, or a year for meaningful financial reporting purposes.

Going Concern Assumption

The **going concern assumption** assumes that the enterprise will continue in operation long enough to carry out its existing objectives. Experience indicates that, in spite of numerous business failures, companies have a fairly high continuance rate, and it has proved useful to adopt a going concern assumption for accounting purposes.

The accounting implications of adopting this assumption are critical. If a going concern assumption is not used, then plant assets should be stated at their liquidation value (selling price less cost of disposal)—not at their cost. As a result, depreciation and amortization of these assets would not be needed. Each period these assets would simply be reported at their liquidation value. Also, without this assumption, the current–noncurrent classification of assets and liabilities would have little significance. Labeling anything as fixed or long-term would be difficult to justify.

Acceptance of the going concern assumption gives credibility to the cost principle. If, instead, liquidation were assumed, assets would be better stated at liquidation value than at cost. Only when liquidation appears imminent is the going concern assumption inapplicable.

These basic accounting assumptions are illustrated graphically in Illustration 12-3 on the next page.

INTERNATIONAL NOTE
In an action that sent shock waves through the French business community, the CEO of Alcatel–Alsthom was taken into custody for an apparent violation of the economic entity assumption. Allegedly, the executive improperly used company funds to install an expensive security system in his home.

HELPFUL HINT
(1) Which accounting assumption assumes that an enterprise will remain in business long enough to recover the cost of its assets? (2) Which accounting assumption is justification for the cost principle? Answers: (1) and (2) Going concern assumption.

PRINCIPLES

On the basis of these fundamental assumptions of accounting, the accounting profession has developed principles that dictate how transactions and other economic events should be recorded and reported. In earlier chapters we discussed the cost principle (Chapter 1) and the revenue recognition and matching principles (Chapter 3). We now examine a number of reporting issues related to

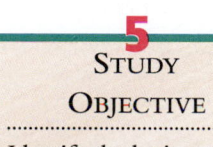

5
STUDY OBJECTIVE
Identify the basic principles of accounting.

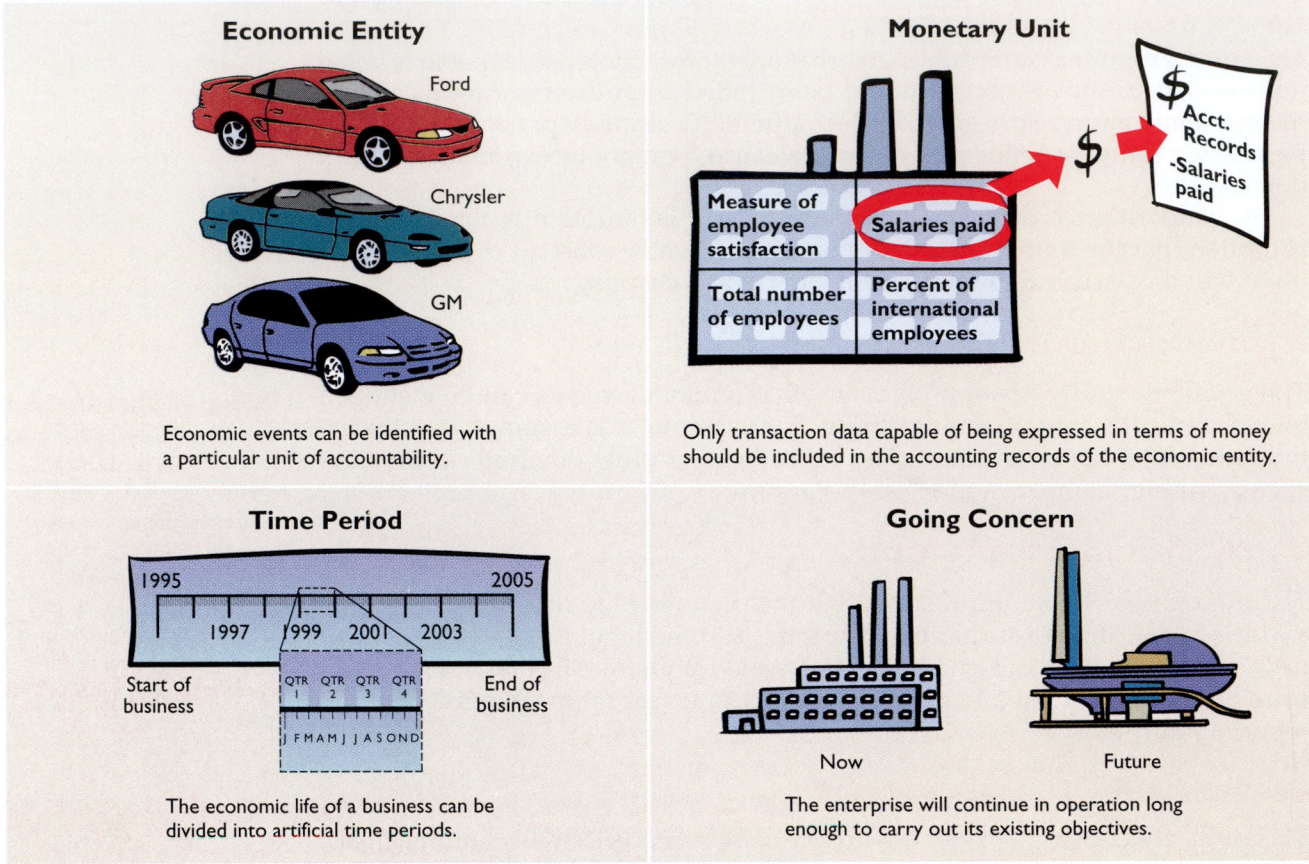

ILLUSTRATION 12-3

Assumptions used in accounting

these principles. In addition, another principle, the full disclosure principle, is discussed.

Revenue Recognition Principle

> **HELPFUL HINT**
> Revenue should be recognized in the accounting period in which it is earned, which may not be the period in which the related cash is received. In a retail establishment the point of sale is often the critical point in the process of earning revenue.

The **revenue recognition principle** dictates that revenue should be recognized in the accounting period in which it is earned. Applying this general principle in practice, however, can be difficult. For example, it was reported that Automatic Inc. was improperly recognizing revenue on goods that had not been shipped to customers. Similarly, many questioned the revenue recognition practices of financial institutions, which until recently recorded a large portion of their fees for granting a loan as revenue immediately rather than spreading those fees over the life of the loan.

When a sale is involved, revenue is recognized at the point of sale. The **sales basis** involves an exchange transaction between the seller and buyer, and the sales price provides an objective measure of the amount of revenue realized. There are, however, two exceptions to the sales basis for revenue recognition that have become generally accepted.

Percentage-of-Completion Method

In long-term construction contracts, recognition of revenue is usually required before the contract is completed. For example, assume that Warrior Construction Co. had a contract to build a dam for the U.S. Department of the Interior for $400 million. Construction is estimated to take 3 years (starting in 1997) at a construction cost of $360 million. If Warrior applies the point-of-sale basis, it will report no revenues and no profit in the first two years. But, in 1999 when completion and sale take place, Warrior will report $400 million in revenues, costs of $360 million, and the entire profit of $40 million. Was Warrior really producing no revenues and earning no profit in 1997 and 1998? Obviously not. The earning process is considered substantially completed at various stages and therefore revenue should be recognized as construction progresses.

In recognizing revenue, Warrior can apply the **percentage-of-completion method**. This method recognizes revenue and income over the life of a long-term project on the basis of reasonable estimates of the project's progress toward completion. Progress toward completion is measured by comparing the costs incurred in a year to the total estimated costs for the entire project. That percentage is multiplied by the total revenue for the project; the result is then recognized as revenue for the period. The formulas for this method are as follows:

HELPFUL HINT
For long-term construction contracts, it is appropriate to use the percentage-of-completion method of revenue recognition because the critical event in the earning process is making progress toward completion. The ultimate sale and selling price are assured by the contract.

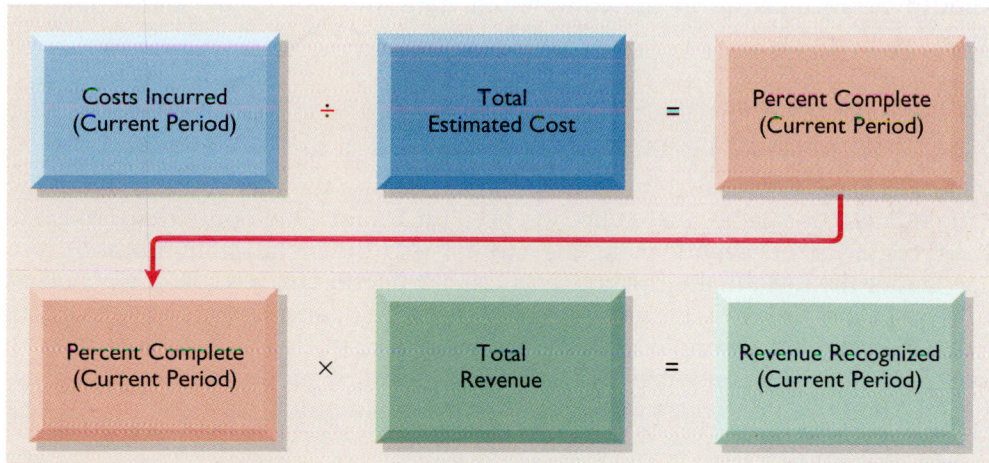

ILLUSTRATION 12-4

Formula to recognize revenue in the percentage-of-completion method

The costs incurred in the current period are then subtracted from the revenue recognized during the current period to arrive at the gross profit.

Let's look at an illustration of the percentage-of-completion method. Assume that Warrior Construction Co. incurs costs of $54 million in 1997, $180 million in 1998, and $126 million in 1999 on the dam project. The portion of the $400 million of revenue recognized in each of the 3 years is shown in Illustration 12-5.

ILLUSTRATION 12-5

Revenue recognized—percentage-of-completion method

Year	Costs Incurred (Current Period)	÷	Total Estimated Cost	=	Percent Complete (Current Period)	×	Total Revenue	=	Revenue Recognized (Current Period)
1997	$ 54,000,000		$360,000,000		15%		$400,000,000		$ 60,000,000
1998	180,000,000		360,000,000		50%		400,000,000		200,000,000
1999	126,000,000		\multicolumn{5}{Balance required to complete the contract}			140,000,000
Totals	$360,000,000								$400,000,000

Note that no estimate is made of the percentage of work completed during the final period. In the final period, all remaining revenue is recognized. In this example, the company's cost estimates have been very accurate; the costs incurred in the third year were 35% of the total estimated cost ($126,000 ÷ $360,000). The gross profit recognized each period is as follows:

ILLUSTRATION 12-6

*Gross profit recognized—
percentage-of-completion
method*

Year	Revenue Recognized (Current Period)	−	Actual Cost Incurred (Current Period)	=	Gross Profit Recognized (Current Period)
1997	$ 60,000,000		$ 54,000,000		$ 6,000,000
1998	200,000,000		180,000,000		20,000,000
1999	140,000,000		126,000,000		14,000,000
Totals	$400,000,000		$360,000,000		$40,000,000

Application of the percentage-of-completion method involves some subjectivity. As a result, there is the possibility of error in determining the amount of revenue recognized and net income reported. Yet to wait until completion would seriously distort each period's financial statements. Naturally, **if it is not possible to obtain dependable estimates of costs and progress, then the revenue should be recognized at the completion date** and not by the percentage-of-completion method.

Installment Method

Another basis for revenue recognition is the receipt of cash. The cash basis is generally used only when it is difficult to determine the revenue amount at the time of a credit sale because collection is so uncertain. One popular approach to the recognition of revenue using the cash basis is the **installment method**.

Under the installment method, each cash collection from a customer consists of (1) a partial recovery of the cost of the goods sold, and (2) partial gross profit from the sale. For example, if the gross profit rate at date of sale is 40%, each subsequent receipt consists of 60% recovery of cost of goods sold and 40% gross profit. The formula to recognize gross profit is as follows:

ILLUSTRATION 12-7

*Gross profit formula—
installment method*

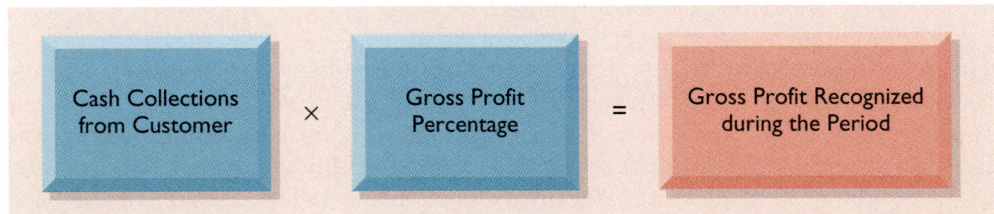

To illustrate, assume that an Iowa farm machinery dealer in the first year of operations had installment sales of $600,000 and a cost of goods sold on installment of $420,000. Total gross profit is, therefore, $180,000 ($600,000 − $420,000), and the gross profit percentage is 30% ($180,000 ÷ $600,000). The collections on the installment sales were as follows: First year, $280,000 (down payment plus monthly payments); second year, $200,000; and, third year, $120,000. The collections of cash and recognition of the gross profit are summarized in Illustration 12-8 (interest charges are ignored in this illustration):

ILLUSTRATION 12-8

*Gross profit recognized—
installment method*

Year	Cash Collected	×	Gross Profit Percentage	=	Gross Profit Recognized
1997	$280,000		30%		$ 84,000
1998	200,000		30%		60,000
1999	120,000		30%		36,000
Total	$600,000				$180,000

Under the installment method of accounting, gross profit is therefore recognized **in the period in which the cash is collected**.

As indicated earlier, use of the installment method is justified when the risk of not collecting an account receivable may be such that the sale is not sufficient evidence for revenue to be recognized.

ACCOUNTING IN ACTION

Business Insight

Datapoint Corp. encouraged its customers to load up with large shipments at the end of the year, allowing Datapoint to report these shipments as revenues, even though payment hadn't been collected. Unfortunately, some of the customers either went broke or quit before paying for the equipment received. As a result, the company had to record substantial bad debts or in some cases reverse previously recorded sales. If Datapoint had used the installment method, this revenue would not have been reported. As a result, revenue recognition practices that are cash-basis oriented, such as the installment method, are becoming more acceptable as it becomes difficult to tell when a sale is a sale.

Matching Principle (Expense Recognition)

Expense recognition is traditionally tied to revenue recognition: "Let the expense follow the revenue." This practice is referred to as the **matching principle**: it dictates that expenses be matched with revenues in the period in which efforts are expended to generate revenues. Expenses are not recognized when cash is paid, or when the work is performed, or when the product is produced; they are recognized when the labor (service) or the product actually makes its contribution to revenue.

The problem is that it is sometimes difficult to determine the accounting period in which the expense contributed to the generation of revenues. Several approaches have therefore been devised for matching expenses and revenues on the income statement.

To understand these approaches, it is necessary to examine the nature of expenses. Costs that will generate revenues only in the current accounting period are expensed immediately. They are reported as operating expenses in the income statement. Examples include such costs as advertising, sales salaries, and repairs. These expenses are often called **expired costs**.

Costs that will generate revenues in future accounting periods are recognized as assets. Examples include merchandise inventory, prepaid expenses, and plant assets. These costs represent **unexpired costs**. Unexpired costs become expenses in two ways:

1. **Cost of goods sold.** Costs carried as merchandise inventory are expensed as cost of goods sold in the period when the sale occurs. Thus, there is a direct matching of expenses with revenues.
2. **Operating expenses.** Unexpired costs become operating expenses through use or consumption (as in the case of store supplies) or through the passage of time (as in the case of prepaid insurance and prepaid rent). The cost of plant assets and other long-lived productive resources is expensed through rational and systematic allocation methods which result in periodic depreciation and amortization. Operating expenses contribute to the revenues of the period but their association with revenues is less direct than for cost of goods sold.

These points about expense recognition are illustrated in Illustration 12-9.

HELPFUL HINT
Costs are the source of expenses. Costs become expenses when they are charged against revenue.

ETHICS NOTE
Many appear to do it, but few like to discuss it: it's earnings management, and it's a clear violation of the revenue recognition and matching principles. Banks sometimes time the sale of investments or the expensing of bad debts to accomplish earnings objectives. Prominent companies, such as GE, have been accused of matching one-time gains with one-time charge-offs so that current period earnings are not so high that they can't be surpassed next period.

ILLUSTRATION 12-9

Expense recognition pattern

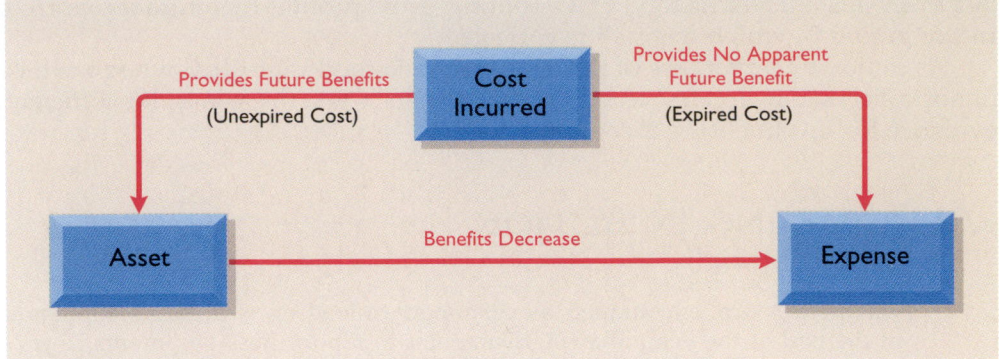

ACCOUNTING IN ACTION
Business Insight

Implementing expense recognition guidelines can be difficult. Consider, for example, Harold's Club (a gambling casino) in Reno, Nevada. How should it report expenses related to the payoff of its progressive slot machines? Progressive slot machines, which generally have no ceiling on their jackpots, are capable of providing a lucky winner with all the money that many losers had previously put in. Payoffs tend to be huge, but infrequent; at Harold's, the progressive slots pay off on average every 4½ months. The basic accounting question is: Can Harold's deduct the millions of dollars sitting in its progressive slot machines from the revenue recognized at the end of the accounting period? One might argue that no, you cannot deduct the money until the "winning handle pull." However, a winning handle pull might not occur for many months or even years. Although admittedly an estimate would have to be used, the better answer is to match these costs with the revenue recognized, assuming that an average 4½ months' payout is well documented. This example demonstrates that the matching principle can be difficult to apply in practice.

Full Disclosure Principle

The **full disclosure principle** requires that circumstances and events that make a difference to financial statement users be disclosed. For example, most accountants would agree that Manville Corporation should have disclosed the 52,000 asbestos liability suits (totaling $2 billion) pending against it so that interested parties were made aware of this contingent loss. Similarly, it is generally agreed that companies should disclose the major provisions of employee pension plans and long-term lease contracts.

Compliance with the full disclosure principle occurs through the data contained in the financial statements and the information in the notes that accompany the statements. The first note in most cases is a **summary of significant accounting policies**. The summary includes, among others, the methods used by the company for inventory costing, depreciation of plant assets, and amortization of intangible assets.

Deciding how much disclosure is enough can be difficult. Accountants could disclose every financial event that occurs and every contingency that exists. However, accounting information must be condensed and combined to make it understandable. Providing additional information entails a cost, and the benefits of providing this information in some cases may be less than the costs. Many companies complain of an accounting standards overload. In addition, they object to requirements that force them to disclose confidential information. Determining where to draw the line on disclosure is not easy.

One thing is certain: financial statements were much simpler years ago, when many companies provided little additional information regarding the financial statements. In 1930, General Electric had no notes to the financial statements; today it has over 10 pages of notes! Why this change? A major reason is that the objectives of financial statements have changed. In the past, information was generally presented on what the business had done. Today the objectives of financial reporting are more future-oriented; accounting is trying to provide information that makes it possible to predict the amount, timing, and uncertainty of future cash flows.

TECHNOLOGY IN ACTION

Some accountants are reconsidering the current means of financial reporting. These accountants propose a data base concept of financial reporting. In such a system, all the information from transactions would be stored in a computerized data base to be accessed by various user groups. The main benefit of such a system is the ability to tailor the information requested to the needs of each user.

What makes it controversial? Discussion currently revolves around access and aggregation issues. Questions such as "Who should be allowed to make inquiries of the system?" "What is the lowest/smallest level of information to be provided?" and "Will such a system necessarily improve on the current means of disclosure?" must be answered before such a system can be implemented on a large scale.

Cost Principle

As you know, the **cost principle** dictates that assets are recorded at their cost. Cost is used because it is both relevant and reliable. Cost is **relevant** because it represents the price paid, the assets sacrificed, or the commitment made at date of acquisition. Cost is **reliable** because it is objectively measurable, factual, and verifiable. It is the result of an exchange transaction. Cost is the basis used in preparing financial statements.

The cost principle, however, has come under much criticism. It is criticized by some as irrelevant. Subsequent to acquisition, the argument goes, cost is not equivalent to market value or current value. For that matter, as the purchasing power of the dollar changes, so also does the meaning associated with the dollar that is used as the basis of measurement. Consider the classic story about the individual who went to sleep and woke up 10 years later. Hurrying to a telephone, he got through to his broker and asked what his formerly modest stock portfolio was worth. He was told that he was a multi-millionaire—his General Motors stock was worth $5 million and his AT&T stock was up to $10 million. Elated, he was about to inquire about his other holdings, when the telephone operator cut in with "Your time is up. Please deposit $100,000 for the next 3 minutes."[3]

This story demonstrates that prices can and do change over a period of time, and that one is not necessarily better off when they do. Although the numbers in the story are extreme, consider some more realistic data that compare prices

---

[3]Adapted from *Barron's*, January 28, 1980, p. 27.

in 1980 with what is expected in 1999, assuming average price increases of 6% and 12% per year.

	1980	1999 6%	1999 12%
Assumed average price increase		**6%**	**12%**
Public college, yearly average cost	$ 3,350.00	$ 10,135.76	$ 28,852.75
Average taxi ride, New York City (before tip)	2.95	8.93	25.40
Slice of pizza	.65	1.97	5.60
First-class postage stamp	.15	.45	1.29
Run-of-the-mill suburban house, New York City	150,000.00	453,840.00	1,291,914.00
McDonald's milk shake	.75	2.27	6.46

Despite the inevitability of changing prices during a period of inflation, the accounting profession still follows the stable monetary unit assumption in preparing a company's primary financial statements. While admitting that some changes in prices do occur, the profession believes the unit of measure—the dollar—has remained sufficiently constant over time to provide meaningful financial information. If presented, the **disclosure of price-level adjusted data is in the form of supplemental information** that accompanies the financial statements.

The basic principles of accounting are summarized in Illustration 12-11.

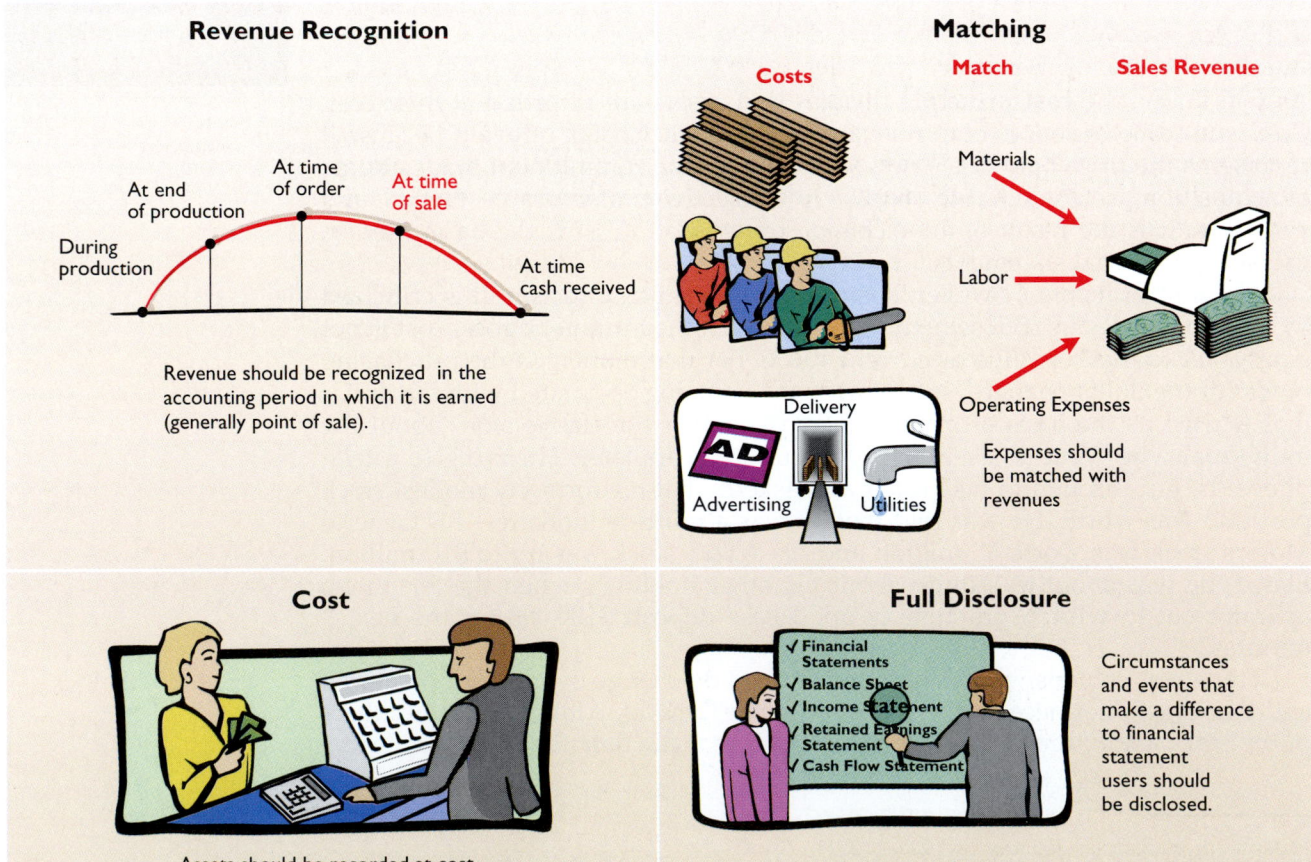

CONSTRAINTS IN ACCOUNTING

Constraints permit a company to modify generally accepted accounting principles without reducing the usefulness of the reported information. The constraints are materiality and conservatism.

Materiality

Materiality relates to an item's impact on a firm's overall financial condition and operations. An item is **material** when it is likely to influence the decision of a reasonably prudent investor or creditor. It is immaterial if its inclusion or omission has no impact on a decision maker. In short, if the item does not make a difference, GAAP does not have to be followed. To determine the materiality of an amount—that is, to determine its financial significance, the accountant usually compares it with such items as total assets, total liabilities, and net income.

To illustrate how the constraint of materiality is applied, assume that Rodriguez Co. purchases a number of low-cost plant assets, such as wastepaper baskets. Although the proper accounting would appear to be to depreciate these wastepaper baskets over their useful life, they are usually expensed immediately. This practice is justified because these costs are considered immaterial. Establishing depreciation schedules for these assets is costly and time-consuming and will not make a material difference on total assets and net income. Other applications of the materiality constraint are the expensing of small tools or the expensing of any plant assets under a certain dollar amount.

Conservatism

Conservatism in accounting means that when in doubt choose the method that will be least likely to overstate assets and income. It does **not** mean **understating** assets or income. Conservatism provides a guide in difficult situations, and the guide is a reasonable one: do not overstate assets and income.

A common application of the conservatism constraint is the use of the lower of cost or market method for inventories. As indicated in Chapter 9, inventories are reported at market value if market value is below cost. This practice results in a higher cost of goods sold and lower net income. In addition, inventory on the balance sheet is stated at a lower amount when market value is below cost. Other examples of conservatism in accounting are the use of the LIFO method for inventory valuation when prices are rising and the use of accelerated depreciation methods for plant assets. Both these methods result in lower asset carrying values and lower net income than alternative methods.

The two constraints are graphically depicted in Illustration 12-12.

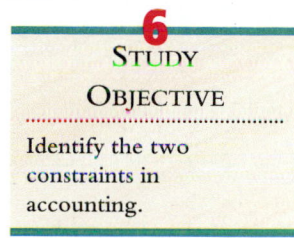

6
STUDY
OBJECTIVE

Identify the two constraints in accounting.

HELPFUL HINT
In other words, if two methods are otherwise equally appropriate, choose the one that will least likely overstate assets and income.

ILLUSTRATION 12-12

Constraints in accounting

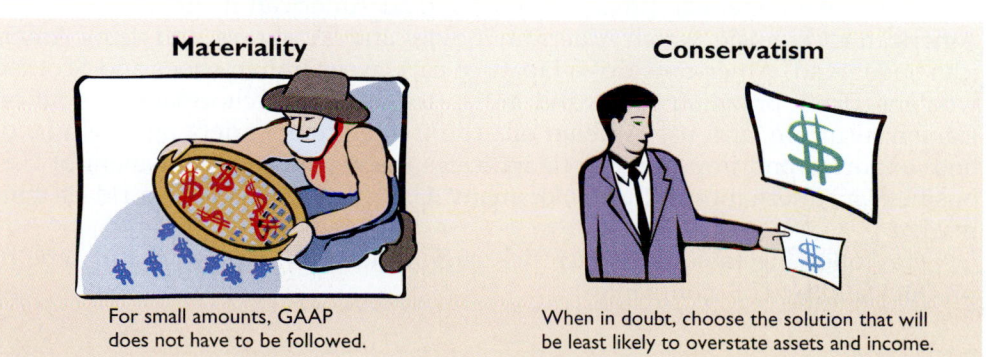

Materiality

For small amounts, GAAP does not have to be followed.

Conservatism

When in doubt, choose the solution that will be least likely to overstate assets and income.

Summary of Conceptual Framework

As we have seen, the conceptual framework for developing sound reporting practices starts with a set of objectives for financial reporting and follows with the development of qualities that make information useful. In addition, elements of financial statements are defined. Operating guidelines in the form of assumptions and principles are then provided. The conceptual framework also recognizes that important constraints exist on the reporting environment. These points are illustrated graphically in Illustration 12-13:

ILLUSTRATION 12-13

Conceptual framework

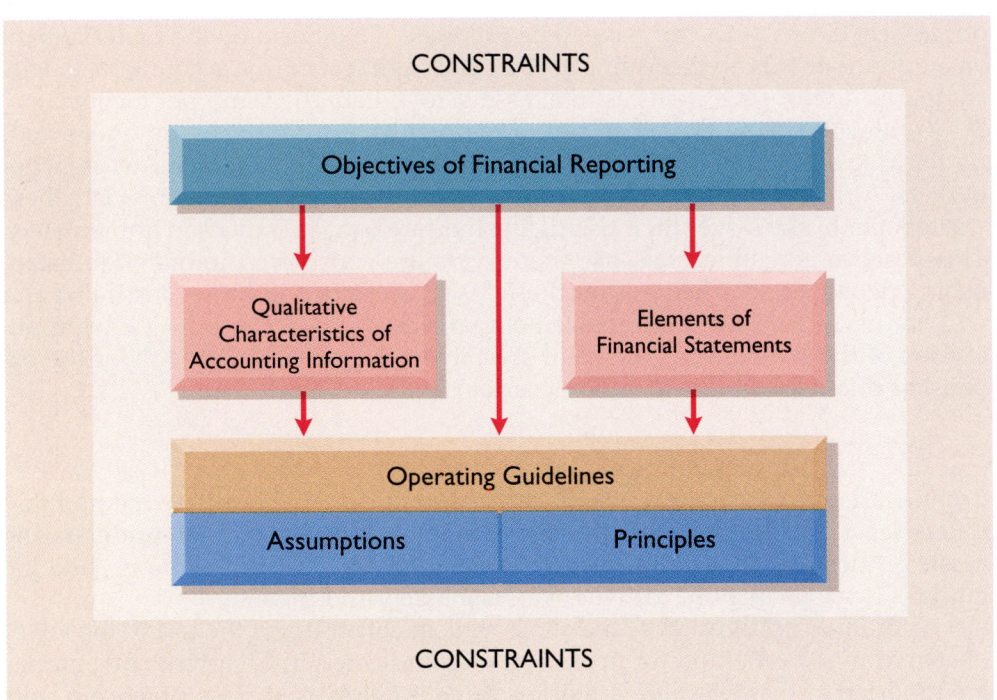

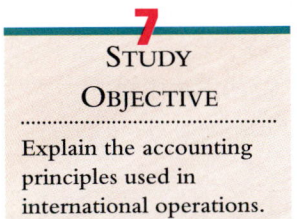

INTERNATIONAL ACCOUNTING STANDARDS

STUDY OBJECTIVE

7

Explain the accounting principles used in international operations.

World markets are becoming increasingly intertwined. Foreigners use American computers, eat American breakfast cereals, read American magazines, listen to American rock music, watch American movies and TV shows, and drink American soda. And, Americans drive Japanese cars, wear Italian shoes and Scottish woolens, drink Brazilian coffee and Indian tea, eat Swiss chocolate bars, sit on Danish furniture, and use Arabian oil. The tremendous variety and volume of both exported and imported goods indicates the extensive involvement of U.S. business in international trade. For many U.S. companies, the world is their market.

The following table illustrates the magnitude of foreign sales and type of product sold by U.S. companies.

Company	Foreign Sales as a % of Total	Product
Reebok	44.3	Sport clothing
Coca-Cola	67.0	Beverages
Disney	23.0	Entertainment
E.I. duPont de Nemours	42.1	Specialty chemicals
General Electric	27.7	Diversified
Ford Motor	32.7	Motor vehicles and parts
Campbell Soup	31.0	Prepared foods
Sears, Roebuck & Co.	8.9	Retail and diversified
Phillip Morris	53.8	Tobacco, beverages, food products
RJR Nabisco	37.0	Tobacco, beverages, food products

ILLUSTRATION 12-14

Foreign sales and type of product

Firms that conduct their operations in more than one country through subsidiaries, divisions, or branches in foreign countries are referred to as **multinational corporations**. The accounting for multinational corporations is complicated because foreign currencies are involved. These international transactions and operations must be translated into U.S. dollars.

Differences in Standards

As the "world economy" is becoming globalized, many investment and credit decisions require the analysis and interpretation of foreign financial statements. Unfortunately, there is a lack of uniformity in accounting standards from country to country. This lack of uniformity is the result of different legal systems, different processes for developing accounting standards, different governmental requirements, and different economic environments.

ACCOUNTING IN ACTION
International Insight

Research and development costs are an example of different international accounting standards. Compare how four countries account for research and development:

Country	Accounting Treatment
United States	Expenditures are expensed.
United Kingdom	Certain expenditures may be capitalized.
Germany	Expenditures are expensed.
Japan	Expenditures may be capitalized and amortized over 5 years.

Thus, a research and development expenditure of $100 million is charged totally to expense in the current period in the United States and Germany. This expense could range from zero to $100 million in the United Kingdom and from $20 million to $100 million in Japan!

Do you believe that accounting principles should be comparable across countries?

Uniformity in Standards

Efforts to obtain uniformity in international accounting practices are taking place. In 1973 the **International Accounting Standards Committee (IASC)** was formed by agreement of accounting organizations in the United States, the United Kingdom, Canada, Australia, France, Germany, Japan, Mexico, and the Netherlands. The purpose of the IASC is to formulate and publish international accounting standards and to promote their acceptance worldwide.

To date, numerous International Accounting Standards have been issued for IASC members to introduce to their respective countries. But, because the IASC has no enforcement powers, these standards are by no means universally applied. They are, however, generally followed by the large multinational companies that are audited by international public accounting firms. Thus, the foundation has been laid for considerable progress toward greater uniformity in international accounting.

BEFORE YOU GO ON . . .

Review It

1. What are the monetary unit assumption, the economic entity assumption, the time period assumption, and the going concern assumption?
2. What are the revenue recognition principle, the matching principle, the full disclosure principle, and the cost principle?
3. What are the materiality constraint and the conservatism constraint?
4. What is the purpose of the International Accounting Standards Committee?

A LOOK BACK AT OUR FEATURE STORY

Refer back to the opening story, and answer the following questions:

1. Policy Management Systems Corp., which produces insurance software, said that it reported some sales before contracts were signed or product delivered. Is the concept of revenue recognition violated in this situation? Explain.
2. In addition, the story noted that Penguin USA failed to report certain expenses for discounts given to customers for paying early. Why might a company overstate revenue or understate expenses in the wrong period?

Solution:

1. The revenue recognition principle dictates that revenue should be recognized in the accounting period in which it is earned. When a sale of product is involved, revenue is generally recognized at the point of sale. Policy Management violated the revenue recognition principle because the sale had not yet occurred.
2. As indicated in the opening story, high-tech firms feel intense pressure to report higher earnings every year. If actual performance falls short of expectations, management might be tempted to bend the rules to prevent its stock price from falling. Although high-tech firms are particularly susceptible to earnings declines, many companies attempt to manage their net income from period to period, as Penguin USA appears to have done.

THE NAVIGATOR

DEMONSTRATION PROBLEM

Carver Construction Company is under contract to build a condominium at a contract price of $2,000,000. The building will take 18 months to complete at an estimated cost of $1,400,000. Construction began in November 1998, and was finished in April 2000. Actual construction costs incurred in each year were: 1998, $140,000; 1999, $910,000; and 2000, $350,000.

Instructions

Compute the gross profit to be recognized in each year.

SOLUTION TO DEMONSTRATION PROBLEM

Year	Costs Incurred (Current Period)	÷ Total Estimated Cost =	Percent Complete (Current Period)	× Total Revenue =	Revenue Recognized (Current Period)
1998	$ 140,000	$1,400,000	10%	$2,000,000	$ 200,000
1999	910,000	1,400,000	65%	2,000,000	1,300,000
2000	350,000	Balance to complete contract			500,000
	$1,400,000				$2,000,000

Year	Revenue Recognized (Current Period)	−	Actual Costs Incurred (Current Period)	=	Gross Profit Recognized (Current Period)
1998	$ 200,000		$ 140,000		$ 60,000
1999	1,300,000		910,000		390,000
2000	500,000		350,000		150,000
	$2,000,000		$1,400,000		$600,000

PROBLEM-SOLVING STRATEGIES

(1) Percent complete is determined by dividing costs incurred by total estimated costs.

(2) Percent complete is multiplied by contract price to find revenue recognized.

(3) Gross profit equals revenue recognized less actual costs incurred.

(4) Percentage-of-completion method recognizes revenue as the construction occurs— it is viewed as a series of sales.

THE NAVIGATOR

DEMONSTRATION PROBLEM

Valdes Inc. uses the installment method in accounting for its sales. During its first year of operations, it had installment sales of $900,000 and a cost of goods sold on installments of $600,000. The collections on installment sales were as follows: Year 1, $330,000; Year 2, $420,000; and Year 3, $150,000.

Instructions

Compute the amount of gross profit to be recognized each year.

SOLUTION TO DEMONSTRATION PROBLEM

Year	Cash Collected	×	Gross Profit Percentage*	=	Gross Profit Recognized
1	$330,000		33⅓%		$110,000
2	420,000		33⅓%		140,000
3	150,000		33⅓%		50,000
	$900,000				$300,000

*$900,000 − $600,000 = $300,000; $300,000 ÷ $900,000 = 33⅓%

PROBLEM-SOLVING STRATEGIES

(1) Installment method used when cash collection is uncertain.

(2) Must always find gross profit percentage.

(3) Gross profit recognized each period results from cash collected times gross profit percentage.

THE NAVIGATOR

SUMMARY OF STUDY OBJECTIVES

1. Explain the meaning of generally accepted accounting principles and identify the key items of the conceptual framework. Generally accepted accounting principles are a set of rules and practices that are recognized as a general guide for financial reporting purposes. Generally accepted means that these principles must have "substantial authoritative support." The key items of the conceptual framework are: (1) objectives of financial reporting; (2) qualitative characteristics of accounting information; (3) elements of financial statements; and (4) operating guidelines (assumptions, principles, and constraints).

2. Describe the basic objectives of financial reporting. The basic objectives of financial reporting are to provide information that is (1) useful to those making investment and credit decisions; (2) helpful in assessing future cash flows; and (3) helpful in identifying economic resources (assets), the claims to those resources (liabilities), and the changes in those resources and claims.

3. Discuss the qualitative characteristics of accounting information and elements of financial statements. To be judged useful, information should possess the following qualitative characteristics: relevance, reliability, comparability, and consistency. The elements of financial statements are a set of definitions that can be used to describe the basic terms used in accounting.

4. *Identify the basic assumptions used by accountants.* The major assumptions are: monetary unit, economic entity, time period, and going concern.

5. *Identify the basic principles of accounting.* The major principles are revenue recognition, matching, full disclosure, and cost.

6. *Identify the two constraints in accounting.* The major constraints are materiality and conservatism.

7. *Explain the accounting principles used in international operations.* There are few recognized worldwide accounting standards. The International Accounting Standards Committee (IASC), of which the United States is a member, is making efforts to obtain conformity in international accounting practices.

GLOSSARY

Comparability Ability to compare accounting information of different companies because they use the same accounting principles. (p. 518).

Conceptual framework A coherent system of interrelated objectives and fundamentals that can lead to consistent standards. (p. 517).

Conservatism The approach of choosing an accounting method when in doubt that will least likely overstate assets and net income. (p. 529).

Consistency Use of the same accounting principles and methods from year to year within a company. (p. 519).

Cost principle Accounting principle that assets should be recorded at their historical cost. (p. 527).

Economic entity assumption Accounting assumption that economic events can be identified with a particular unit of accountability. (p. 521).

Elements of financial statements Definitions of basic terms used in accounting. (p. 519).

Full disclosure principle Accounting principle that circumstances and events that make a difference to financial statement users should be disclosed. (p. 526).

Generally accepted accounting principles (GAAP) A set of rules and practices, having substantial authoritative support, that are recognized as a general guide for financial reporting purposes. (p. 516).

Going concern assumption The assumption that the enterprise will continue in operation long enough to carry out its existing objectives and commitments. (p. 521).

Installment method A method of recognizing revenue using the cash basis; each cash collection consists of a partial recovery of cost of goods sold and partial gross profit from the sale. (p. 524).

International Accounting Standards Committee (IASC) An accounting organization whose purpose is to formulate and publish international accounting standards and to promote their acceptance worldwide. (p. 531).

Matching principle Accounting principle that expenses should be matched with revenues in the period when efforts are expended to generate revenues. (p. 525).

Materiality The constraint of determining if an item is important enough to likely influence the decision of a reasonably prudent investor or creditor. (p. 529).

Monetary unit assumption Accounting assumption that only transaction data capable of being expressed in monetary terms should be included in accounting records. (p. 521).

Percentage-of-completion method Recognizes revenue and income on a construction project on the basis of costs incurred during the period to the total estimated costs for the entire project. (p. 523).

Relevance The quality of information that indicates the information makes a difference in a decision. (p. 518).

Reliability The quality of information that gives assurance that it is free of error and bias. (p. 518).

Revenue recognition principle Accounting principle that revenue should be recognized in the accounting period in which it is earned (generally at the point of sale). (p. 522).

Time period assumption Accounting assumption that the economic life of a business can be divided into artificial time periods. (p. 521).

SELF-STUDY QUESTIONS

Answers are at the end of the chapter.

(SO 1) 1. Generally accepted accounting principles are:
   a. a set of standards and rules that are recognized as a general guide for financial reporting.
   b. usually established by the Internal Revenue Service.
   c. the guidelines used to resolve ethical dilemmas.
   d. fundamental truths that can be derived from the laws of nature.

(SO 2) 2. Which of the following is *not* an objective of financial reporting?
   a. Provide information that is useful in investment and credit decisions.
   b. Provide information about economic resources, claims to those resources, and changes in them.
   c. Provide information that is useful in assessing future cash flows.
   d. Provide information on the liquidation value of a business.

(SO 3) 3. The primary criterion by which accounting information can be judged is:
   a. consistency.
   b. predictive value.
   c. decision-usefulness.
   d. comparability.

(SO 3) 4. Verifiable is an ingredient of:

	Reliability	Relevance
a.	Yes	Yes
b.	No	No
c.	Yes	No
d.	No	Yes

(SO 4, 5, 6) 5. Valuing assets at their liquidation value rather than their cost is *inconsistent* with the:
   a. time period assumption.
   b. matching principle.
   c. going concern assumption.
   d. materiality constraint.

(SO 5) 6. Gonzalez's Construction Company began a long-term construction contract on January 1, 1999. The contract is expected to be completed in 2000 at a total cost of $20,000,000. Gonzalez's revenue for the project is $24,000,000. Gonzalez incurred contract costs of $4,000,000 in 1999. What gross profit should be recognized in 1999?
   a. $800,000.
   b. $1,000,000.
   c. $2,000,000.
   d. $4,000,000.

7. Dunlop Company had installment sales of $1,000,000 in (SO 5) their first year of operations. The cost of goods sold on installment was $650,000, and Dunlop collected a total of $500,000 on the installment sales. Using the installment method, how much gross profit should be recognized in the first year?
   a. $140,000.
   b. $175,000.
   c. $350,000.
   d. $500,000.

8. The full disclosure dictates that: (SO 5)
   a. financial statements should disclose all assets at their cost.
   b. financial statements should disclose only those events that can be measured in dollars.
   c. financial statements should dislose all events and circumstances that would matter to users of financial statements.
   d. financial statements should not be relied on unless an auditor has expressed an unqualified opinion on them.

9. The accounting constraint that means that when in (SO 6) doubt the accountant should choose the method that will be least likely to overstate assets and income is called (the):
   a. matching principle.
   b. materiality.
   c. conservatism.
   d. monetary unit assumption.

10. The organization that issues international accounting (SO 7) standards is the:
   a. Financial Accounting Standards Board.
   b. International Accounting Standards Committee.
   c. International Auditing Standards Committee.
   d. None of the above.

THE NAVIGATOR

QUESTIONS

1. (a) What are generally accepted accounting principles (GAAP)? (b) What bodies provide authoritative support for GAAP?

2. What elements comprise the FASB's conceptual framework?

3. (a) What are the objectives of financial reporting? (b) Identify the qualitative characteristics of accounting information.

4. Doug Evans, the president of Packer Company, is pleased. Packer substantially increased its net income in 1999 while keeping its unit inventory relatively the same. Tom Jones, chief accountant, cautions Evans, however. Jones says that since Packer changed from the LIFO to the FIFO method of inventory valuation, there is a consistency problem and it would be difficult to determine if Packer is better off. Is Jones correct? Why?

5. What is the distinction between comparability and consistency?

6. Why is it necessary for accountants to assume that an economic entity will remain a going concern?

7. When should revenue be recognized? Why has the date of sale been chosen as the point at which to recognize the revenue resulting from the entire producing and selling process?

8. Matson Construction Company has a $210 million contract to build a bridge. Its total estimated cost for the project is $170 million. Costs incurred in the first year of the project were $34 million. Matson appropriately uses the percentage-of-completion method. How much revenue and gross profit should Ryder recognize in the first year of the project?

9. Merchandise with a cost of $80,000 was sold during the year for $100,000. Cash collected for the year amounted to $45,000. How much gross profit should be recognized during the year if the company uses the installment method?

10. Distinguish between expired costs and unexpired costs.

11. (a) Where does the accountant disclose information about an entity's financial position, operations, and cash flows? (b) The full disclosure principle recognizes that the nature and amount of information included in financial reports reflect a series of judgmental trade-offs. What are the objectives of these trade-offs?

12. Sal Troia is the president of Better Books. He has no accounting background. Troia cannot understand why current cost is not used as the basis for accounting measurement and reporting. Explain what basis is used and why.

13. Describe the two constraints inherent in the presentation of accounting information.

14. Your roommate believes that international accounting standards are uniform throughout the world. Is your roommate correct? Explain.

15. What organization establishes international accounting standards?

BRIEF EXERCISES

Identify generally accepted accounting principles.
(SO 1)

BE12–1 Indicate whether each of the following statements is true or false.

1. ____ *"Generally accepted"* means that these principles must have "substantial authoritative support."
2. ____ GAAP is a set of rules and practices established by the accounting profession to serve as a general guide for financial reporting purposes.
3. ____ Substantial authoritative support for GAAP usually comes from two standard-setting bodies: the FASB and the IRS.

Identify items included in conceptual framework.
(SO 1)

BE12–2 Indicate which of the following items is(are) included in the FASB's conceptual framework. (Use "Yes" or "No" to answer this question.)

1. ____ Qualitative characteristics of accounting information.
2. ____ Analysis of financial statement ratios.
3. ____ Objectives of financial reporting.

Identify objectives of financial reporting.
(SO 2)

BE12–3 According to the FASB's conceptual framework, which of the following are objectives of financial reporting? (Use "Yes" or "No" to answer this question.)

1. ____ Provide information that identifies the economic resources (assets), the claims to those resources (liabilities), and the changes in those resources and claims.
2. ____ Provide information that is helpful in assessing past cash flows and stock prices.
3. ____ Provide information that is useful to those making investment and credit decisions.

Identify qualitative characteristics.
(SO 3)

BE12–4 Presented below is a chart of the qualitative characteristics of accounting information. Fill in the blanks from (a) to (e).

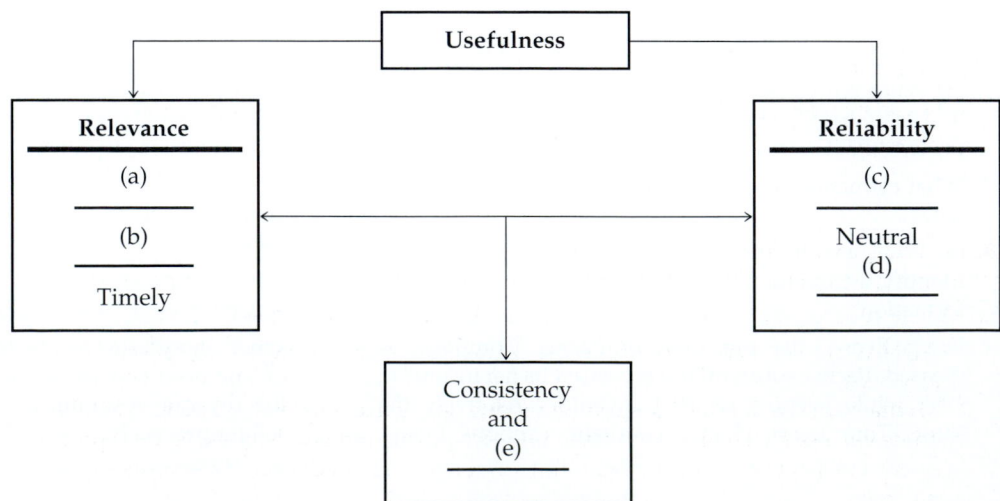

BE12–5   Given the *qualitative characteristics* of accounting established by the FASB's conceptual framework, complete each of the following statements:

1. For information to be _____, it should have predictive or feedback value, and it must be presented on a timely basis.
2. _____ is the quality of information that gives assurance that it is free of error and bias; it can be depended on.
3. _____ means using the same accounting principles and methods from year to year within a company.

BE12–6   Presented below is a set of qualitative characteristics of accounting information.

(a) Predictive value   (c) Verifiable
(b) Neutral   (d) Timely

    Match these qualitative characteristics to the following statements, using letters a through d.

1. _____ Accounting information must be proved to be free of error and bias.
2. _____ Accounting information must be available to decision makers before it loses its capacity to influence their decisions.
3. _____ Accounting information should help users make predictions about the outcome of past, present, and future events.
4. _____ Accounting information cannot be selected, prepared, or presented to favor one set of interested users over another.

BE12–7   Presented below are four concepts discussed in this chapter.

(a) Time period assumption   (c) Full disclosure principle
(b) Cost principle   (d) Conservatism

    Match these concepts to the following accounting practices. Each letter can be used only once.

1. _____ Preparing financial statements on an annual basis.
2. _____ Using the lower of cost or market method for inventory valuation.
3. _____ Recording inventory at its purchase price.
4. _____ Using notes and supplementary schedules in the financial statements.

BE12–8   Won Construction Company is under contract to build a commercial building at a price of $3,600,000. Construction began in January 1998 and was finished in December 2000. Total estimated construction costs are $2,800,000. Actual construction costs incurred in each year were: 1998, $560,000; 1999, $1,820,000; 2000, $420,000. Compute the revenue to be recognized in each year using the *percentage-of-completion* method.

BE12–9   Grasso Co. uses the installment method to determine its net income. During its first year of operations, it had installment sales of $800,000 and a cost of goods sold of $560,000. The collections on installment sales were as follows: Year 1, $360,000; Year 2, $440,000. Determine the gross profit recognized for Year 1 and 2.

BE12–10   Wriston Company uses the following accounting practices:

1. The income statement shows paper clips expense of $10.
2. Revenue on installment sales is recognized at the time of sale.
3. Small tools are recorded as plant assets and depreciated.
4. Inventory is reported at cost when market value is lower.

Indicate the accounting constraint, if any, that has been violated by each practice.

EXERCISES

E12–1   A number of accounting reporting situations are described below.

1. Taylor Company uses the direct write-off method of accounting for uncollectible accounts.
2. Morita Hospital Supply Corporation reports only current assets and current liabilities on its balance sheet. Property, plant, and equipment and bonds payable are reported as current assets and current liabilities, respectively. Liquidation of the company is unlikely.

3. Allen Company is in its fifth year of operation and has yet to issue financial statements. (Do not use full disclosure principle.)
4. Casino Company has inventory on hand that cost $400,000. Casino reports inventory on its balance sheet at its current market value of $425,000. *cost pr. conservatism*
5. Marla Downs, president of the Classic Music Company, bought a computer for her personal use. She paid for the computer by using company funds and debited the "computers" account. *Econ. Ent.*
6. Ruff Company recognizes revenue at the end of the production cycle, but before sale. The price of the product, as well as the amount that can be sold, is not certain. *Rev. Rec.*
7. In preparing its financial statements, Johnson Company omitted information concerning its method of accounting for inventories. *full disclosure*

Instructions

For each of the above, list the assumption, principle, or constraint that has been violated, if any. List only one term for each case.

Identify the assumption, principle, or constraint that has been violated and prepare correct entries.
(SO 4, 5, 6)

E12–2 Presented below are some business transactions that occurred during 1999 for Georgia Co.

(a) Equipment worth $80,000 was acquired at a cost of $64,000 from a company that had water damage in a flood. The following entry was made:

Equipment	80,000	
Cash		64,000
Gain		16,000

(b) Merchandise inventory with a cost of $208,000 is reported at its market value of $260,000. The following entry was made:

Merchandise Inventory	52,000	
Gain		52,000

(c) An account receivable has been deemed to be a bad debt. The following entry was made:

Allowance for Doubtful Accounts	10,000	
Accounts Receivable		10,000

(d) The president of Georgia Co., George Warden, purchased a truck for personal use and charged it to his expense account. The following entry was made:

Travel Expense	18,000	
Cash		18,000

(e) An electric pencil sharpener costing $40 is being depreciated over 5 years. The following entry was made:

Depreciation Expense—Pencil Sharpener	8	
Accumulated Depreciation—Pencil Sharpener		8

Instructions

In each of the situations above, identify the assumption, principle, or constraint that has been violated, if any, and discuss the appropriateness of the journal entries. Give the correct journal entry, if necessary.

Identify accounting assumptions, principles, and constraints to different situations.
(SO 4, 5, 6)

E12–3 Presented below are the assumptions, principles, and constraints discussed in this chapter:

(a) Economic entity assumption
(b) Going concern assumption
(c) Monetary unit assumption
(d) Time period assumption
(e) Cost principle
(f) Matching principle
(g) Full disclosure principle
(h) Revenue recognition principle
(i) Materiality
(j) Conservatism

Instructions

Identify by letter the accounting assumption, principle, or constraint that describes each situation below. Do not use a letter more than once.

1. Requires that the operational guidelines be followed for all significant items.
2. Separates financial information into time periods for reporting purpose.

3. Requires recognition of expenses in the same period as related revenues.
4. Indicates that market value changes subsequent to purchase are not recorded in the accounts.
5. Is the rationale for why plant assets are not reported at liquidation value. (Do not use historical cost principle.)
6. Indicates that personal and business record keeping should be separately maintained.
7. Ensures that all relevant financial information is reported.
8. Assumes that the dollar is the "measuring stick" used to report on financial performance.

E12–4 Consider the following transactions of Brown Group Company for 1999.

Determine the amount of revenue to be recognized.
(SO 5)

1. Leased office space to Patel Supplies for a 1-year period beginning September 1. The rent of $30,000 was paid in advance.
2. Sold a 6-month insurance policy to Oliva Corporation for $8,000 on March 1.
3. A sales order for merchandise costing $9,000 that had a sales price of $12,000 was received on December 28 from Weaver Company. The goods were shipped FOB shipping point on December 31, and Weaver received them on January 3, 2000.
4. Signed a long-term contract to construct a building at a total price of $1,600,000. Total estimated cost of construction is $1,200,000. During 1999, the company incurred $300,000 of costs and collected $330,000 in cash. The percentage-of-completion method is used to recognize revenue.
5. Merchandise inventory on hand at year-end amounted to $160,000. Brown Group expects to sell the inventory in 2000 for $190,000.

Instructions
For each item above, indicate the amount of revenue Brown Group should recognize in calendar year 1999. Explain.

E12–5 Fong Construction Company currently has one long-term construction project. The project has a contract price of $130,000,000 with total estimated costs of $100,000,000. Fong appropriately uses the percentage-of-completion method. After 2 years of construction, the following costs have been accumulated:

Determine gross profit for construction projects.
(SO 5)

Actual cost incurred, Year 1	$30,000,000
Total estimated cost remaining after Year 1	70,000,000
Actual cost incurred, Year 2	50,000,000
Total estimated cost remaining after Year 2	20,000,000

Instructions
Determine the gross profit for each of the first 2 years of the construction contract.

E12–6 Quincy Company sold equipment for $300,000 in 1998. Collections on the sale were as follows: 1998, $70,000; 1999, $190,000; 2000, $40,000. Quincy's cost of goods sold is typically 70% of sales.

Determine gross profit using installment sales and point-of-sale bases.
(SO 5)

Instructions
(a) Determine Quincy's gross profit for 1998, 1999, and 2000, assuming that Quincy recognizes revenue under the installment method.
(b) Determine Quincy's gross profit for 1998, 1999, and 2000, assuming that Quincy recognizes revenue under the point-of-sale basis.

PROBLEMS: SET A

P12–1A Carson and McMann are accountants for Desktop Computers. They are having disagreements concerning the following transactions that occurred during the calendar year 1999.

Analyze transactions to identify accounting principle or assumption violated and prepare correct entries.
(SO 4, 5)

1. Desktop purchased equipment for $35,000 at a going-out-of-business sale. The equipment was worth $45,000. Carson believes that the following entry should be made:

Equipment	45,000	
Cash		35,000
Gain		10,000

2. Land costing $60,000 was appraised at $90,000. Carson suggests the following journal entry:

Land	30,000	
Gain on Appreciation of Land		30,000

3. Depreciation for the year was $18,000. Since net income is expected to be lower this year, Carson suggests deferring depreciation to a year when there is more net income.
4. Desktop bought a custom-made piece of equipment for $18,000. This equipment has a useful life of 6 years. Desktop depreciates equipment using the straight-line method. "Since the equipment is custom-made, it will have no resale value and, therefore, shouldn't be depreciated but instead expensed immediately," argues Carson. "Besides, it provides for lower net income."
5. Carson suggests that equipment should be reported on the balance sheet at its liquidation value, which is $15,000 less than its cost.

McMann disagrees with Carson on each of the above situations.

Instructions

For each transaction, indicate why McMann disagrees. Identify the accounting principle or assumption that Carson would be violating if his suggestions were used. Prepare the correct journal entry for each transaction, if any.

Determine the appropriateness of journal entries in terms of generally accepted accounting principles or assumptions.
(SO 4, 5)

P12–2A   Presented below are a number of business transactions that occurred during the current year for Jose, Inc.

1. Materials were purchased on March 31 for $65,000 and this amount was entered in the Materials account. On December 31, the materials would have cost $85,000, so the following entry was made:

Inventory	20,000	
Gain on Inventories		20,000

2. An order for $30,000 has been received from a customer for products on hand. This order is to be shipped on January 9 next year. The following entry was made:

Accounts Receivable	30,000	
Sales		30,000

3. The president of Jose, Inc. used his expense account to purchase a new Saab 9000 solely for personal use. The following entry was made:

Miscellaneous Expense	34,000	
Cash		34,000

4. Because of a "flood sale," equipment obviously worth $230,000 was acquired at a cost of $150,000. The following entry was made:

Equipment	230,000	
Cash		150,000
Gain on Purchase of Equipment		80,000

5. Because the general level of prices increased during the current year, Jose, Inc. determined that there was a $10,000 understatement of depreciation expense on its equipment and decided to record it in its accounts. The following entry was made:

Depreciation Expense	10,000	
Accumulated Depreciation		10,000

Instructions

 In each of the situations above, discuss the appropriateness of the journal entries in terms of generally accepted accounting principles.

Recognize gross profit using percentage-of-completion.
(SO 5)

P12–3A   Rasheed Construction Company is involved in a long-term construction contract to build an office building at a total estimated cost of $30 million and contract price of $38 million. Additional information follows:

Office Building

	Cash Collections	Actual Costs Incurred
1998	$ 7,000,000	$ 4,500,000
1999	9,000,000	6,000,000
2000	12,500,000	12,000,000
2001	9,500,000	7,500,000

The project is completed in 2001, and all cash to be received from the contract has been received.

Instructions
Prepare a schedule to determine the gross profit in each year for the long-term construction contract using the percentage-of-completion method.

P12–4A Engram Construction sold apartments it had constructed to Fisher Management Company for $2.5 million. Engram's cost to construct the apartments was $1.5 million. Engram appropriately uses the installment method. Additional information follows:

Recognize gross profit using the installment method.
(SO 5)

Cash Collected

1998	$ 800,000
1999	1,200,000
2000	500,000

(a) Determine the gross profit for each year using the installment method.
(b) Repeat (a) assuming the construction costs were $1.6 million.

P12–5A Presented below are the assumptions, principles, and constraints used in this chapter.

Identify accounting assumptions, principles, and constraints.
(SO 4, 5, 6)

(a) Economic entity assumption
(b) Going concern assumption
(c) Monetary unit assumption
(d) Time period assumption
(e) Full disclosure principle
(f) Revenue recognition principle
(g) Matching principle
(h) Cost principle
(i) Materiality
(j) Conservatism

Identify by letter the accounting assumption, principle, or constraint that describes each situation below. Do not use a letter more than once.

1. Market value changes subsequent to purchase are not recorded in the accounts. (Do not use the revenue recognition principle.)
2. Indicates that personal and business record keeping should be separately maintained.
3. Ensures that all relevant financial information is reported.
4. Lower of cost or market is used to value inventories.
5. Repair tools are expensed when purchased. These repair tools have a useful life of more than one accounting period. (Do not use conservatism.)
6. Allocates expenses to revenues in proper period.
7. Assumes that the dollar is the measuring stick used to report financial information.
8. Separates financial information into time periods for reporting purposes.

PROBLEMS: SET B

P12–1B Carlos and Dana are accountants for Arruza Printers. They are having disagreements concerning the following transactions that occurred during the year.

Analyze transactions to identify accounting principle or assumption violated and prepare correct entries.
(SO 4, 5)

1. Arruza purchased equipment at a fire sale for $21,000. The equipment was worth $26,000. Carlos believes that the following entry should be made:

Equipment	26,000	
Cash		21,000
Gain		5,000

2. Carlos suggests that Arruza should carry equipment on the balance sheet at its liquidation value, which is $20,000 less than its cost.

3. Arruza rented office space for 1 year starting October 1, 1999. The total amount of $30,000 was paid in advance. Carlos believes that the following entry should be made on October 1:

| Rent Expense | 30,000 | |
| Cash | | 30,000 |

4. Land costing $41,000 was appraised at $49,000. Carlos suggests the following journal entry:

| Land | 8,000 | |
| Gain on Appreciation of Land | | 8,000 |

5. Arruza bought equipment for $40,000, including installation costs. The equipment has a useful life of 5 years. Arruza depreciates equipment using the straight-line method. "Since the equipment as installed into our system cannot be removed without considerable damage, it will have no resale value, and therefore should not be depreciated but instead expensed immediately," argues Carlos. "Besides, it lowers net income."

6. Depreciation for the year was $26,000. Since net income is expected to be lower this year, Carlos suggests deferring depreciation to a year when there is more net income.

Dana disagrees with Carlos on each of the situations above.

Instructions

For each transaction, indicate why Dana disagrees. Identify the accounting principle or assumption that Carlos would be violating if his suggestions were used. Prepare the correct journal entry for each transaction, if any.

Determine the appropriateness of journal entries in terms of generally accepted accounting principles or assumptions.
(SO 4, 5)

P12–2B Presented below are a number of business transactions that occurred during the current year for Quester, Inc.

1. The president of Quester, Inc., used his expense account to purchase a pre-owned Mercedes-Benz E420 solely for personal use. The following entry was made:

| Miscellaneous Expense | 54,000 | |
| Cash | | 54,000 |

2. Land was purchased on April 30 for $200,000 and this amount was entered in the Land account. On December 31, the land would have cost $230,000, so the following entry was made:

| Land | 30,000 | |
| Gain on Land | | 30,000 |

3. An order for $60,000 has been received from a customer for products on hand. This order is to be shipped on January 9 next year. The following entry was made:

| Accounts Receivable | 60,000 | |
| Sales | | 60,000 |

4. Because of a "flood sale," equipment obviously worth $300,000 was acquired at a cost of $250,000. The following entry was made:

Equipment	300,000	
Cash		250,000
Gain on Purchase of Equipment		50,000

5. Because the general level of prices increased during the current year, Quester, Inc., determined that there was a $40,000 understatement of depreciation expense on its equipment and decided to record it in its accounts. The following entry was made:

| Depreciation Expense | 40,000 | |
| Accumulated Depreciation | | 40,000 |

Instructions

▭▭▭▷ In each of the situations above, discuss the appropriateness of the journal entries in terms of generally accepted accounting principles.

P12–3B Estafan Construction Company is involved in a long-term construction contract. Estafan contracted to build a shopping center with a total estimated cost of $20 million and contract price of $28 million. Additional information follows:

Recognize gross profit using the percentage-of-completion method.
(SO 5)

Shopping Center

	Cash Collections	Actual Costs Incurred
1998	$ 4,500,000	$3,000,000
1999	10,000,000	9,000,000
2000	7,000,000	5,000,000
2001	6,500,000	3,000,000

The project was completed in 2001, and all cash collections related to the contract have been received.

Instructions

Prepare a schedule to determine the gross profit for each year for the long-term construction contract, using the percentage-of-completion method.

P12–4B Donovan Inc. sold condominiums it had constructed to Ashbrook Management Company for $6 million. Donovan's cost to construct the condominiums was $4.2 million. Donovan appropriately uses the installment method. Additional information follows:

Recognize gross profit using the installment method.
(SO 5)

Cash Collected

1998	$ 900,000
1999	3,800,000
2000	1,300,000

Instructions

(a) Prepare a schedule to determine the gross profit for each year using the installment method.
(b) Repeat (a) assuming construction costs were $4.5 million.

P12–5B Presented below are assumptions, principles, and constraints.

Identify accounting assumptions, principles, and constraints.
(SO 4, 5, 6)

(a) Economic entity assumption
(b) Going concern assumption
(c) Monetary unit assumption
(d) Time period assumption
(e) Full disclosure principle
(f) Revenue recognition principle
(g) Matching principle
(h) Cost principle
(i) Materiality
(j) Conservatism

Instructions

Identify by letter the accounting assumption, principle, or constraint that describes each situation below. Do not use a letter more than once.

1. Each entity is kept as a unit distinct from its owner or owners.
2. Reporting must be done at defined intervals.
3. Revenue is recorded at the point of sale.
4. When in doubt, it is better to understate rather than overstate net income.
5. All important information related to inventories is presented in the footnotes or in the financial statements.
6. Assets are not stated at their liquidation value. (Do not use the cost principle.)
7. The death of the president is not recorded in the accounts.
8. Pencil sharpeners are expensed when purchased.
9. An allowance for doubtful accounts is established. (Do not use conservatism.)

BROADENING YOUR PERSPECTIVE

FINANCIAL REPORTING AND ANALYSIS

FINANCIAL REPORTING PROBLEM

BYP12–1   Suzanne Wessels has successfully completed her first accounting course during the spring semester and is now working as a management trainee for First Arizona Bank during the summer. One of her fellow management trainees, Wade Greaton, is taking the same accounting course this summer and has been having a "lot of trouble." On the second examination, for example, Wade became confused about inventory valuation methods and completely missed all the points on a problem involving LIFO and FIFO.

Wade's instructor recently indicated that the third examination will probably have a number of essay questions dealing with accounting principle issues. Wade is quite concerned about the third examination for two reasons. First, he has never taken an accounting examination where essay answers were required. Second, Wade feels he has to do well on this examination to get an acceptable grade in the course.

Wade has therefore asked Suzanne to help him prepare for the next examination. She agrees, and suggests that Wade develop a set of possible questions on the accounting principles material that they might discuss.

Instructions

Answer the following questions that were developed by Wade.

(a) What is a conceptual framework?
(b) Why is there a need for a conceptual framework?
(c) What are the objectives of financial reporting?
(d) If you had to explain generally accepted accounting principles to a nonaccountant, what essential characteristics would you include in your explanation?
(e) What are the qualitative characteristics of accounting? Explain each one.
(f) Identify the basic assumptions used in accounting.
(g) What are two major constraints involved in financial reporting? Explain both of them.

RESEARCH ASSIGNMENT

BYP12–2   During the years 1978–85, the Financial Accounting Standards Board (FASB) issued six *Statements of Financial Accounting Concepts* (SFACs). From the library, obtain copies of SFAC No. 2 (*Qualitative Characteristics of Accounting Information*) and SFAC No. 3 (*Elements of Financial Statements of Business Enterprises*).

Instructions

Use these statements to answer the following questions:

(a) Your textbook indicates that "an item is material when it is likely to influence the decision of a reasonably prudent investor or creditor." SFAC No. 2 identifies a number of examples in which specific quantitative guidelines are provided to accountants and auditors. Identify two of these examples. Do you think that materiality guidelines should be quantified? Why or why not?
(b) SFAC No. 3 discusses the concept of "articulation" between financial statement elements. Briefly summarize the meaning of this term and how it relates to an entity's financial statements.

REAL-WORLD FOCUS: Newcor Incorporated

BYP12–3   **Newcor Inc.** designs, manufactures, and sells specialty-purpose equipment and also manufactures and sells precision-machined parts and molded rubber and plastic products. The company previously had operating facilities in Belgium and Canada, both of which were sold. The company employs 747 employees and has roughly 2,000 shareholders.

The annual report of Newcor Inc. reports the following information in the president's letter to stockholders:

NEWCOR INC.
President's Letter to Stockholders

As indicated in last year's report, we were considering adoption of the percentage-of-completion method of accounting for long-term contracts. During the first quarter this year, we did adopt this method which has the effect of better matching revenues with work performed when compared to the completed-contract method of accounting that had previously been used to report financial results.

Instructions

(a) Which two accounting principles are discussed in Newcor's president's letter?
(b) Explain how the change in method will provide better matching of revenues with work performed.

CRITICAL THINKING

GROUP DECISION CASE

BYP12–4   Margo Industries has two operating divisions—Talley Construction Division and Shumway Securities Division. Both divisions maintain their own accounting system and method of revenue recognition.

Talley Construction Division
During the fiscal year ended November 30, 1999, Talley Construction Division had one construction project in process. A $30,000,000 contract for construction of a civic center was granted on June 19, 1999, and construction began on August 1, 1999. Estimated costs of completion at the contract date were $26,000,000 over a 2-year time period from the date of the contract. On November 30, 1999, construction costs of $8,000,000 had been incurred. The construction costs to complete the remainder of the project were reviewed on November 30, 1999, and were estimated to amount to only $16,000,000 because of an expected decline in raw materials costs. Revenue recognition is based upon a percentage-of-completion method.

Shumway Securities Division
Shumway Securities Division works through manufacturers' agents in various cities. Orders for alarm systems and down payments are forwarded from agents, and the division ships the goods f.o.b. factory directly to customers (usually police departments and security guard companies). Customers are billed directly for the balance due plus actual shipping costs. The firm received orders for $6,000,000 of goods during the fiscal year ended November 30, 1999. Down payments of $600,000 were received and goods with a selling price of $5,000,000 were billed and shipped. Actual freight costs of $100,000 were also billed. Commissions of 10% on product price are paid manufacturing agents after goods are shipped to customers. Such goods are warranted for 90 days after shipment, and warranty returns have been about 1% of sales. Revenue is recognized at the point of sale by this division.

Instructions
With the class divided into groups, answer the following:

(a) There are a variety of methods of revenue recognition. Define and describe each of the following methods of revenue recognition, and indicate whether each is in accordance with generally accepted accounting principles.
  1. Point of sale.
  2. Percentage-of-completion.
  3. Installment contract.
(b) Compute the revenue to be recognized in fiscal year 1999 for both operating divisions of Margo Industries in accordance with generally accepted accounting principles.

COMMUNICATION ACTIVITY

BYP12–5 If you go on to advanced accounting courses, you'll study the differences between accounting in the business world and university accounting. You'll find that there's one major similarity: both depend heavily on the matching principle.

At Long Beach City College, a two-year community college with 30,000 students, most of the revenues come from the state of California and the federal government. As a condition of receiving these grants, "we must match expenses against revenues in the right fiscal year," says the school's accounting manager.

For example, the college receives federal funding under the Job Training Partnership Act. "We receive funding from the federal government, which allows us to offer classes to students for job preparation. The government specifies the grant periods, for instance, from July 1 to June 30. We therefore have to ensure that all transactions for that project are completed within that fiscal year." Another project is the amnesty program, the federal government's legalization of foreign nationals. Expenses to offset the grant money are mostly teaching salaries and instructional materials.

By year-end, the goal is to break even. Excess funds, if any, have to be returned. But program managers do not want a deficit, either, because these projects are accountable to the college administration and any overspending will come from the college's general fund.

Instructions
Write a letter to your instructor covering the following points:

1. Why is the matching principle important in accounting for government grants?
2. Give some examples of grant or special programs to which the matching principle might be applied at your college or university.
3. What are some examples of costs that Long Beach Community College might properly charge to its grant or special programs?

ETHICS CASE

BYP12–6 When the Financial Accounting Standards Board issues new standards, the required implementation date is usually 12 months or more from the date of issuance, with early implementation encouraged. Sarah Lane, accountant at Mintur Corporation, discusses with her financial vice president the need for early implementation of a recently issued standard that would result in a much fairer presentation of the company's financial condition and earnings. When the financial vice president determines that early implementation of the standard will adversely affect reported net income for the year, he strongly discourages Sarah from implementing the standard until it is required.

Instructions
(a) Who are the stakeholders in this situation?
(b) What, if any, are the ethical considerations in this situation?
(c) What does Sarah have to gain by advocating early implementation? Who might be affected by the decision against early implementation?

SURFING THE NET

BYP12–7 The Financial Accounting Standards Board (FASB) is a private organization established to improve accounting standards and financial reporting. The FASB conducts extensive research before issuing a "Statement of Financial Accounting Standards," which represents an authoritative expression of generally accepted accounting principles.

Address: http://www.rutgers.edu/accounting/raw/fasb/home.htm

Steps: Visit the homepage of the FASB

Instructions

Answer the following questions:

(a) What is the mission of the FASB?

(b) Using the table of contents, locate FASB Statement 128. What topic does Statement 128 address? What was the issue date?

———————

Answers to Self-Study Questions

1. a   2. d   3. c   4. c   5. c   6. a   7. b   8. c   9. c   10. b

———————

Answer to Kellogg Review It Question 2, p. 520

The Report of Independent Accountants indicates that the financial statements (balance sheet, income statement, shareholders' equity, and cash flows) are presented fairly, in accordance with generally accepted accounting principles.

Remember to go back to the Navigator box on the chapter-opening page and check off your completed work.

Before studying this chapter, you should know or, if necessary, review:

a. The cost principle of accounting. (Ch. 1, p. 11)
b. The owner's equity statement. (Ch. 1, pp. 23–25)
c. How to make closing entries and prepare the post-closing trial balance. (Ch. 4, pp. 146–151)
d. The steps in the accounting cycle. (Ch. 4, p. 154)
e. The format of classified financial statements. (Ch. 4, pp. 157–161)

THE
NAVIGATOR

FEATURE STORY

From Trials to Top Ten

Razor & Tie Music opened its doors in 1990 when Cliff Chenfield and Craig Balsam gave up the razors, ties, and six-figure salaries they had become accustomed to as New York lawyers to set up a partnership in Cliff's living room. In 1998 the label is at the forefront of marketing contemporary music—the only record company in the country that has achieved success by selling music both on television and in the stores. Razor & Tie's entertaining and ef-

fective TV commercials have yielded unprecedented sales for multi-artist music compilations, while its hot young retail label has been behind some of the most recent original, progressive releases.

Razor & Tie's first TV release, *Those Fabulous '70s* (100,000 copies sold), was followed by *Disco Fever* (over 300,000). These albums generated so much publicity that partners Cliff and Craig were guests on dozens of TV interview shows.

After restoring the respectability of the oft-maligned 1970s, the partners forged into the musical '80s with the same zeal that elicited suc-

cess with their first releases. In July 1993, Razor & Tie released *Totally '80s,* a collection of Top 10 singles from the 1980s that has sold over 450,000 units since its release. Featuring the tag line "The greatest hits from the decade when communism died and music videos were born," *Totally '80s* was the best-selling direct-response album in the country in 1993.

In 1995, Razor & Tie broke into the contemporary music world with *Living In The '90s,* the most successful record in the history of the company. Featuring a number of songs that were still recurrent hits on the radio at the time the package initially aired, *Living In The '90s* was a blockbuster, receiving Gold certification in less than nine months and rewriting the rules on direct-response albums. For the first time, contemporary music was available through an album offered only through direct-response spots.

How has Razor & Tie carved out such a sizable piece of the market? Through the complementary talents of the two partners. Their imagination and savvy, along with exciting new releases planned for the coming years, ensure Razor & Tie such continued growth that the partnership form of organization may be challenged to its limits.

THE
NAVIGATOR

On the World Wide Web
www.razorandtie.com

CHAPTER 13

THE NAVIGATOR ✔

- ■ Understand *Concepts for Review*
- ■ Read *Feature Story*
- ■ Scan *Study Objectives*
- ■ Read *Preview*
- ■ Read text and answer *Before You Go On*
  p. 554 ☐ p. 559 ☐ p. 568 ☐ p. 574 ☐
- ■ Work *Demonstration Problems*
- ■ Review *Summary of Study Objectives*
- ■ Answer *Self-Study Questions*
- ■ Complete assignments

ACCOUNTING FOR PARTNERSHIPS

STUDY OBJECTIVES

After studying this chapter, you should be able to:

1. *Identify the characteristics of the partnership form of business organization.*
2. *Explain the accounting entries for the formation of a partnership.*
3. *Identify the bases for dividing net income or net loss.*
4. *Describe the form and content of partnership financial statements.*
5. *Explain the effects of the entries when a new partner is admitted.*
6. *Describe the effects of the entries when a partner withdraws from the firm.*
7. *Prepare the entries to record the liquidation of a partnership.*

THE NAVIGATOR

*I*t is not surprising that when Cliff Chenfield and Craig Balsam began Razor & Tie, they decided to use the partnership form of organization. Both saw the need for hands-on control of their product and its promotion. In this chapter, we will discuss reasons why the partnership form of organization is often selected and explain the major issues in accounting for partnerships. The content and organization of this chapter are as follows:

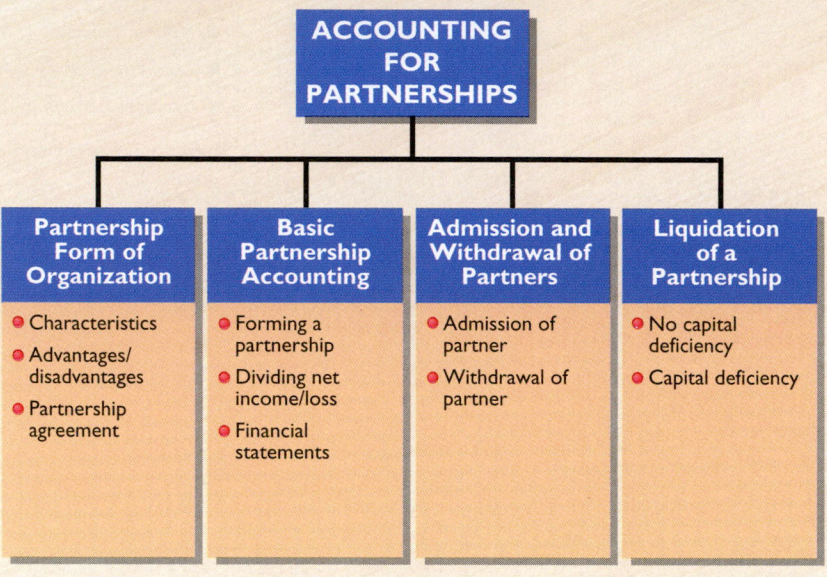

PARTNERSHIP FORM OF ORGANIZATION

The Uniform Partnership Act provides the basic rules for the formation and operation of partnerships in more than 90% of the states. This act defines a **partnership** as "an association of two or more persons to carry on as co-owners of a business for profit." Partnerships are common in retail establishments and in small manufacturing companies. Similarly, if you enter a profession such as accounting, law, or medicine, you may find it desirable to form a partnership with other professionals in your field. Professional partnerships vary in size from a medical partnership of 3 to 5 doctors to 150 to 200 partners in a large law firm and more than 2,000 partners in an international accounting firm.

1
STUDY
OBJECTIVE

Identify the characteristics of the partnership form of business organization.

Characteristics of Partnerships

Partnerships are fairly easy to form. They can be formed by a verbal agreement, although partners who have not taken the next step—to put in writing the rights and obligations of the partners—have found that the characteristics of partnerships can sometimes lead to later difficulties.

The principal characteristics of the partnership form of business organization are shown in Illustration 13-1 and explained in the following sections.

ILLUSTRATION 13-1
Partnership characteristics

Association of Individuals

The voluntary association of two or more individuals in a partnership may be based on as simple an act as a handshake. However, it is preferable to state the agreement in writing. Under the Uniform Partnership Act, a partnership is considered a legal entity for certain purposes. For instance, property (land, buildings, equipment) can be owned in the name of the partnership, and the firm can sue or be sued. **A partnership also represents an accounting entity for financial reporting purposes.** Thus, the purely personal assets, liabilities, and transactions of the partners are excluded from the accounting records of the partnership, just as they are in a proprietorship.

The net income of a partnership is not taxed as a separate entity. However, a partnership is required to file an information tax return showing partnership net income and each partner's share of net income. Each partner's share is taxable at personal tax rates, regardless of the amount of net income withdrawn from the business during the year.

Mutual Agency

Mutual agency means that each partner acts on behalf of the partnership when engaging in partnership business. The act of any partner is binding on all other partners, even when partners act beyond the scope of their authority, so long as the act appears to be appropriate for the partnership. For example, a partner of a grocery store who purchases a delivery truck creates a binding contract in the name of the partnership, even if the partnership agreement denies this authority. On the other hand, if a partner in a law firm purchased a snowmobile for the partnership, such an act would not be binding on the partnership, because it is clearly outside the scope of partnership business.

HELPFUL HINT

Because of mutual agency, an individual should be extremely cautious in selecting partners.

Limited Life

A partnership does not have unlimited life. A partnership may be ended voluntarily at any time through the acceptance of a new partner into the firm or the withdrawal of a partner. A partnership may be ended involuntarily by the death or incapacity of a partner. Thus the life of a partnership is indefinite. **Partnership dissolution** occurs whenever a partner withdraws or a new partner is admitted.

Dissolution of a partnership does not necessarily mean that the business ends. If the continuing partners agree, operations can continue without interruption by forming a new partnership.

Unlimited Liability

Each partner is **personally and individually liable** for all partnership liabilities. Creditors' claims attach first to partnership assets and then to the personal resources of any partner, irrespective of that partner's equity in the partnership. To illustrate, assume that: (1) the Rowe-Sanchez partnership is terminated when the claims of company creditors exceed partnership assets by $30,000, and (2) L. Rowe's personal assets total $40,000 but B. Sanchez has no personal assets. Creditors can collect their total claims from Rowe regardless of Rowe's equity in the firm, even though Sanchez and Rowe may be equal partners. Rowe, in turn, has a legal claim on Sanchez, but this would be worthless under the conditions described.

Some states allow limited partnerships. In a **limited partnership**, one or more partners have unlimited liability and one or more partners have limited liability for the debts of the firm. The former are called **general partners** and the latter are called **limited partners**. The responsibility of limited partners for the debts of the partnership is limited to their investment in the firm. For the privilege of limited liability, the limited partner usually accepts less compensation than a general partner and exercises less influence in the affairs of the firm. This form of organization works well in large partnerships where the partners do not work together closely. In such cases, partners want some protection from liability caused by the acts of partners they may hardly know.

ACCOUNTING IN ACTION
Business Insight

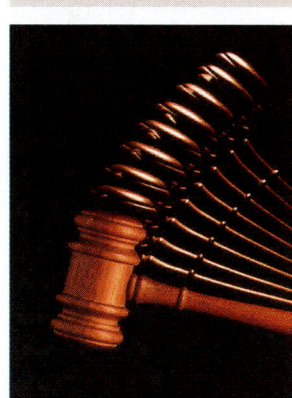

The prestigious New York law firm of Kaye, Scholer, Fierman, Hays, & Handler, accused of withholding damaging information during a federal investigation of its client, Lincoln Savings & Loan, settled out of court for $41 million. The firm's liability insurance covered only $25 million of the total. Thus, its 109 partners had to pay the remaining $16 million out of their own pockets.

In a recent year, court damage awards in malpractice suits against U.S. accountants and attorneys was close to $1 billion.

Co-Ownership of Property

Partnership assets are owned jointly by all the partners. If the partnership is terminated, the assets do not legally revert to the original contributor. Each partner has a claim on total assets equal to the balance in his or her respective capital account. This claim does not attach to specific assets that an individual partner contributed to the firm.

Similarly, if a partner invests a building in the partnership valued at $100,000 and the building is later sold at a gain of $20,000, that partner does not personally receive the entire gain. Partnership net income (or net loss) is also co-owned. **If the partnership contract does not specify to the contrary, all net income or net loss is shared equally by the partners.** As you will see later, however, partners may agree to unequal sharing of net income or net loss.

Advantages and Disadvantages of Partnerships

Why do people choose to form partnerships? One major advantage of doing so is that the **skills and resources of two or more individuals can be combined**. For example, a large public accounting firm such as Ernst & Young must have combined expertise in auditing, taxation, and management consulting, not to mention specialists within each of these areas. In addition, a partnership does not have to contend with the "red tape" that a corporation must face. That is, a partnership is **easily formed and is relatively free from governmental regulations and restrictions**. Decisions can be made quickly on substantive matters affecting the firm, whereas in a corporation, formal meetings with the board of directors are often needed.

On the other hand, partnerships also have some major disadvantages: **mutual agency**, **limited life**, and **unlimited liability**. Unlimited liability is particularly troublesome to many individuals, because they may lose not only their initial investment but also their personal assets, if those assets are needed to pay partnership creditors. As a result, partnerships often find it difficult to obtain large amounts of investment capital. That is one reason why the largest business enterprises in the United States are corporations, not partnerships.

The advantages and disadvantages of the partnership form of business organization are summarized in Illustration 13-2.

Advantages	Disadvantages
Combining skills and resources of two or more individuals	Mutual agency
Ease of formation	Limited life
Freedom from governmental regulations and restrictions	Unlimited liability
Ease of decision making	

ILLUSTRATION 13-2

Advantages and disadvantages of a partnership

ACCOUNTING IN ACTION
Business Insight

With surprising speed, states are creating two new forms of business organizations that are being adopted by many small companies. Known as **limited liability companies (LLCs)** and **limited liability partnerships (LLPs),** they combine the advantages of partnerships and corporations by shielding owners from personal liability while taxing income at the individual level. The LLC structure is an option for many sole proprietorships as well.

The Partnership Agreement

Ideally, the voluntary agreement of two or more individuals to form a partnership should be expressed in writing. This written contract is often referred to as the **partnership agreement** or **articles of co-partnership**. The partnership agreement contains such basic information as the name and principal location of the firm, the purpose of the business, and date of inception. In addition, different relationships that will exist among the partners should be specified, such as the following:

1. Names and capital contributions of partners.
2. Rights and duties of partners.
3. Basis for sharing net income or net loss.
4. Provision for withdrawals of assets.
5. Procedures for submitting disputes to arbitration.
6. Procedures for the withdrawal or addition of a partner.
7. Rights and duties of surviving partners in the event of a partner's death.

The importance of a written contract cannot be overemphasized. The agreement should be drawn with care and should attempt to anticipate all possible situations, contingencies, and disagreements. The help of a lawyer is highly de-

ETHICS NOTE

A well-developed partnership agreement reduces ethical conflict among partners because it specifies in clear and concise language the process by which ethical and legal problems will be resolved. This issue is especially significant when the partnership experiences financial distress.

sirable in preparing the agreement. A poorly drawn contract may create friction among the partners and eventually cause the termination of the partnership.

BEFORE YOU GO ON . . .

Review It

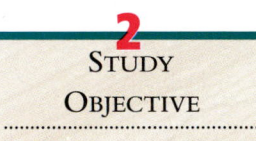

1. What are the distinguishing characteristics of a partnership?
2. What are the principal advantages and disadvantages of a partnership? Why is Kellogg Company not a partnership? The answer to this question is provided on page 586.
3. What are the major items in a partnership agreement?

THE NAVIGATOR

BASIC PARTNERSHIP ACCOUNTING

We now turn our attention to the basic accounting for partnerships. The major accounting issues relate to forming the partnership, dividing net income or net loss, and preparing financial statements.

Forming a Partnership

2

STUDY OBJECTIVE

Explain the accounting entries for the formation of a partnership.

Each partner's initial investment in a partnership should be recorded at the **fair market value of the assets at the date of their transfer to the partnership.** The values assigned must be agreed to by all of the partners.

To illustrate, assume that A. Rolfe and T. Shea combine their proprietorships to start a partnership named U.S. Software. The firm will specialize in developing financial modeling software packages. Rolfe and Shea have the following assets prior to the formation of the partnership:

ILLUSTRATION 13-3

Book and market values of assets invested

	Book Value		Market Value	
	A. Rolfe	**T. Shea**	**A. Rolfe**	**T. Shea**
Cash	$ 8,000	$ 9,000	$ 8,000	$ 9,000
Office equipment	5,000		4,000	
Accumulated depreciation	(2,000)			
Accounts receivable		4,000		4,000
Allowance for doubtful accounts		(700)		(1,000)
	$11,000	$12,300	$12,000	$12,000

The entries to record the investments are:

Investment of A. Rolfe

A = L + OE			
+8,000		+12,000	
+4,000			

Cash	8,000	
Office Equipment	4,000	
A. Rolfe, Capital		12,000
(To record investment of Rolfe)		

Investment of T. Shea

A = L + OE			
+9,000		+12,000	
+4,000			
−1,000			

Cash	9,000	
Accounts Receivable	4,000	
Allowance for Doubtful Accounts		1,000
T. Shea, Capital		12,000
(To record investment of Shea)		

Note that neither the original cost of the equipment ($5,000) nor its book value ($5,000 − $2,000) is recorded by the partnership. The equipment is recorded at its fair market value, $4,000. Since the equipment has not been used by the partnership, there can be no accumulated depreciation. In contrast, the gross claims on customers ($4,000) are carried forward to the partnership, and the allowance for doubtful accounts is adjusted to $1,000 to arrive at a cash (net) realizable value of $3,000. A partnership may start with an Allowance for Doubtful Accounts account, because this balance pertains to existing accounts receivable that are expected to be uncollectible in the future. In addition, this procedure maintains the control and subsidiary relationship between accounts receivable and the accounts receivable subsidiary ledger.

After the partnership has been formed, the accounting for transactions is similar to any other type of business organization. For example, all transactions with outside parties, such as the purchase or sale of merchandise inventory and the payment or receipt of cash, should be recorded in the same manner for a partnership as for a proprietorship.

The steps in the accounting cycle described in Chapter 4 for a proprietorship also apply to a partnership. For example, it is necessary to prepare a trial balance and to journalize and post adjusting entries. In addition, a work sheet may be used. There are minor differences in journalizing and posting closing entries and in preparing financial statements, as explained in the following sections. The differences occur because there is more than one owner in a partnership.

Dividing Net Income or Net Loss

Partnership net income or net loss is shared equally unless the partnership contract specifically indicates otherwise. The same basis of division usually applies to both net income and net loss. As a result, it is customary to refer to the basis as the **income ratio**, the **income and loss ratio**, or the **profit and loss ratio**. Because of its wide acceptance, we will use the term **income ratio** to identify the basis for dividing both net income and net loss. A partner's share of net income or net loss is recognized in the accounts through closing entries.

ALTERNATIVE TERMINOLOGY
The *P&L ratio* terminology is frequently used in business.

Closing Entries

As in the case of a proprietorship, four entries are required in preparing closing entries for a partnership. The entries are:

1. Debit each revenue account for its balance and credit Income Summary for total revenues.
2. Debit Income Summary for total expenses and credit each expense account for its balance.
3. Debit Income Summary for its balance and credit each partner's capital account for his or her share of net income. Conversely, credit Income Summary and debit each partner's capital account for his or her share of net loss.
4. Debit each partner's capital account for the balance in that partner's drawing account, and credit each partner's drawing account for the same amount.

The first two entries are the same as in a proprietorship. The last two entries are different because (1) there are two or more owners' capital and drawing accounts and (2) it is necessary to divide net income (or net loss) among the partners.

To illustrate the last two closing entries, we will assume that the AB Company has net income of $32,000 for 1999. The partners, L. Arbor and D. Barnett, share net income and net loss equally, and drawings for the year were Arbor $8,000 and Barnett $6,000. The last two closing entries are:

ILLUSTRATION 13-4

Closing net income and drawing accounts

Dec. 31	Income Summary	32,000	
	L. Arbor, Capital ($32,000 × 50%)		16,000
	D. Barnett, Capital ($32,000 × 50%)		16,000
	(To transfer net income to owners' capital accounts)		
31	L. Arbor, Capital	8,000	
	D. Barnett, Capital	6,000	
	L. Arbor, Drawing		8,000
	D. Barnett, Drawing		6,000
	(To close drawing accounts to capital accounts)		

Assuming the beginning capital balance is $47,000 for Arbor and $36,000 for Barnett, the capital and drawing accounts will show the following after posting the closing entries:

ILLUSTRATION 13-5

Partners' capital and drawing accounts after closing

L. Arbor, Capital			D. Barnett, Capital		
12/31 Clos. 8,000	1/1 Bal. 47,000		12/31 Clos. 6,000	1/1 Bal. 36,000	
	12/31 Clos. 16,000			12/31 Clos. 16,000	
	12/31 Bal. 55,000			12/31 Bal. 46,000	

L. Arbor, Drawing			D. Barnett, Drawing		
12/31 Bal. 8,000	12/31 Clos. 8,000		12/31 Bal. 6,000	12/31 Clos. 6,000	

As in a proprietorship, the partners' capital accounts are permanent accounts; the partners' drawing accounts are temporary accounts. Normally, the capital accounts will have credit balances and the drawing accounts will have debit balances. Drawing accounts are debited when partners withdraw cash or other assets from the partnership for personal use. For example, the partnership agreement may permit each partner to withdraw cash monthly for personal living expenses.

Income Ratios

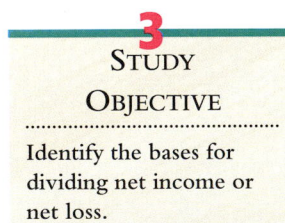

3

STUDY OBJECTIVE

Identify the bases for dividing net income or net loss.

As indicated earlier, the partnership agreement should specify the basis for sharing net income or net loss. The following are typical of the ratios that may be used:

1. A fixed ratio, expressed as a proportion (6:4), a percentage (70% and 30%), or a fraction (2/3 and 1/3).
2. A ratio based either on capital balances at the beginning of the year or on average capital balances during the year.
3. Salaries to partners and the remainder on a fixed ratio.
4. Interest on partners' capitals and the remainder on a fixed ratio.
5. Salaries to partners, interest on partners' capitals, and the remainder on a fixed ratio.

The objective is to reach agreement on a basis that will equitably reflect the differences among partners in terms of their capital investment and service to the partnership.

A fixed ratio is easy to apply, and it may be an equitable basis in some circumstances. Assume, for example, that Hughes and Lane are partners. Each contributes the same amount of capital, but Hughes expects to work full-time in the partnership and Lane expects to work only half-time. Accordingly, the partners agree to a fixed ratio of 2/3 to Hughes and 1/3 to Lane.

A ratio based on capital balances may be appropriate when the funds invested in the partnership are considered the critical factor. Capital balances may also be equitable when a manager is hired to run the business and the partners do not plan to take an active role in daily operations.

The three remaining ratios (3, 4, and 5) give specific recognition to differences that may exist among partners. These ratios provide salary allowances for time worked and interest allowances for capital invested. Then, any remaining net income or net loss is allocated on a fixed ratio. Some caution needs to be exercised in working with these types of income ratios. These ratios pertain exclusively to **the computations that are required in dividing net income or net loss.**

Salaries to partners and interest on partners' capitals are not expenses of the partnership. Therefore, these items do not enter into the matching of expenses with revenues and the determination of net income or net loss. For a partnership, as well as for other entities, salaries expense pertains to the cost of services performed by employees, and interest expense relates to the cost of borrowing money from creditors. Partners in their ownership capacity are not considered either **employees** or **creditors**. Thus, when the income ratio includes a salary allowance for partners, some partnership agreements permit the partner to make monthly withdrawals of cash based on their "salary." In such cases, the withdrawals are debited to the partner's drawing account.

HELPFUL HINT
Use one relationship for all; that is, proportion—3:1 percentage—75% & 25% fraction—¾ & ¼.

ACCOUNTING IN ACTION

Business Insight

Partners in professional firms can and do make substantial incomes. For example, in one large international public accounting firm, the average earnings of all partners in a recent year was over $400,000, and the individual earnings of the five most highly compensated partners was over $1 million. Note, however, that the compensation of partners in most large partnerships differs in both form and substance from the compensation of a corporate executive. Partners are not guaranteed an annual salary. Compensation depends entirely on each year's operating results. Substantial investment is required of each partner. This capital is at risk for the partner's entire career—often 25–30 years—without an established return. Upon leaving, it is repayable without adjustment for inflation or appreciation in value.

Salaries, Interest, and Remainder on a Fixed Ratio

Under this income ratio (item 5 in the list above), the provisions for salaries and interest must be applied **before** the remainder is allocated on the specified fixed ratio. **This is true even if the provisions exceed net income or the partnership has suffered a net loss for the year.** Detailed information concerning the division of net income or net loss should be shown at the bottom of the income statement.

To illustrate this income ratio, assume that Sara King and Ray Lee are co-partners in the Kingslee Company. The partnership agreement provides for (1) salary allowances of $8,400 to King and $6,000 to Lee, (2) interest allowances of 10% on capital balances at the beginning of the year, and (3) the remainder equally. Capital balances on January 1 were King, $28,000, and Lee, $24,000. In 1999, partnership net income is $22,000. The division of net income is as follows:

ILLUSTRATION 13-6

Income statement with division of net income

KINGSLEE COMPANY			
Income Statement			
For the Year Ended December 31, 1999			
Sales			$200,000
Net income			$ 22,000

Division of Net Income			
	Sara King	Ray Lee	Total
Salary allowance	$ 8,400	$6,000	$14,400
Interest allowance			
Sara King ($28,000 × 10%)	2,800		
Ray Lee ($24,000 × 10%)		2,400	
Total interest			5,200
Total salaries and interest	11,200	8,400	19,600
Remaining income, $2,400			
($22,000 − $19,600)			
Sara King ($2,400 × 50%)	1,200		
Ray Lee ($2,400 × 50%)		1,200	
Total remainder			2,400
Total division	**$12,400**	**$9,600**	**$22,000**

The entry to record the division of net income is:

A	=	L	+	OE
				−22,000
				+12,400
				+ 9,600

Dec. 31	Income Summary	22,000	
	Sara King, Capital		12,400
	Ray Lee, Capital		9,600
	(To close net income to partners' capitals)		

To illustrate a situation in which the salary and interest allowances exceed net income, assume that net income in the Kingslee Company is only $18,000. In this case, the salary and interest allowances will create a deficiency of $1,600 ($19,600 − $18,000). Since the computations of the allowances are the same as those in the preceding example, we will begin the division of net income with total salaries and interest as follows:

ILLUSTRATION 13-7

Division of net income—income deficiency

	Sara King	Ray Lee	Total
Total salaries and interest	$11,200	$8,400	$19,600
Remaining deficiency ($1,600)			
($18,000 − $19,600)			
Sara King ($1,600 × 50%)	(800)		
Ray Lee ($1,600 × 50%)		(800)	
Total remainder			(1,600)
Total division	**$10,400**	**$7,600**	**$18,000**

Partnership Financial Statements

The financial statements of a partnership are similar to those of a proprietorship. The differences are related to the fact that a number of owners are involved in a partnership. The income statement for a partnership is identical to the income statement for a proprietorship except for the division of net income, as shown earlier.

The owners' equity statement for a partnership is called the **partners' capital statement**. Its function is to explain the changes in each partner's capital account and in total partnership capital during the year. As in a proprietorship, changes in capital may result from three causes: additional capital investment, drawings, and net income or net loss.

The partners' capital statement for the Kingslee Company shown below is based on the division of $22,000 of net income in Illustration 13-6. The statement includes assumed data for the additional investment and drawings.

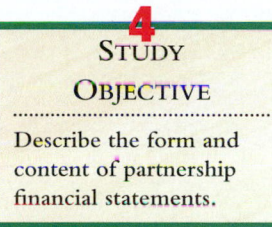

STUDY OBJECTIVE

Describe the form and content of partnership financial statements.

KINGSLEE COMPANY Partners' Capital Statement For the Year Ended December 31, 1999			
	Sara King	Ray Lee	Total
Capital, January 1	$28,000	$24,000	$52,000
Add: Additional investment	2,000		2,000
Net income	12,400	9,600	22,000
	42,400	33,600	76,000
Less: Drawings	7,000	5,000	12,000
Capital, December 31	$35,400	$28,600	$64,000

ILLUSTRATION 13-8
Partners' capital statement

HELPFUL HINT
As in a proprietorship, partners' capital may change due to (1) additional investment, (2) drawings, and (3) net income or loss.

The partners' capital statement is prepared from the income statement and the partners' capital and drawing accounts.

The balance sheet for a partnership is the same as for a proprietorship except in the owner's equity section. In a partnership, the capital balances of each partner are shown in the balance sheet. The owners' equity section for Kingslee Company would show the following:

KINGSLEE COMPANY Balance Sheet (partial) December 31, 1999		
Total liabilities (assumed amount)		$115,000
Owners' equity		
Sara King, Capital	$35,400	
Ray Lee, Capital	28,600	
Total owners' equity		64,000
Total liabilities and owners' equity		$179,000

ILLUSTRATION 13-9
Owners' equity section of a partnership balance sheet

BEFORE YOU GO ON . . .

Review It

1. How should a partner's initial investment of assets be valued?
2. What are the closing entries for a partnership?
3. What income ratios may be used in a partnership?
4. How do partnership financial statements differ from proprietorship financial statements?

Do It

LeMay Company reports net income of $57,000. The partnership agreement provides for salaries of $15,000 to L. Lee and $12,000 to R. May, with the remainder to be shared on a 60:40 basis, respectively. L. Lee asks your help to divide the net income between the partners and to prepare the closing entry.

Reasoning: Salaries to partners and interest on partners' capital are not expenses of the partnership. These items do not enter into the matching of expenses with revenues and the determination of net income or net loss. Therefore, after net income for LeMay is computed, salaries are deducted and then the income ratios are applied to the remainder. The closing entry for net income in a partnership is the same as in a proprietorship except that more than one capital account is credited.

Solution: The division of net income is as follows:

	L. Lee	R. May	Total
Salary allowance	$15,000	$12,000	$27,000
Remaining income ($57,000 − $27,000)			
L. Lee (60% × $30,000)	18,000		
R. May (40% × $30,000)		12,000	
Total remaining income			30,000
Total division of income	$33,000	$24,000	$57,000

The closing entry for net income therefore is:

Income Summary	57,000	
L. Lee, Capital		33,000
R. May, Capital		24,000
(To close net income to partners' capitals)		

Related exercise material: BE13–3, BE13–4, BE13–5, and E13–2.

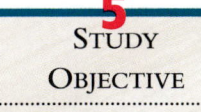

ADMISSION AND WITHDRAWAL OF PARTNERS

We have seen how the basic accounting for a partnership works. We now look at how to account for a common occurrence in partnerships—the addition or withdrawal of a partner.

Admission of a Partner

5
STUDY
OBJECTIVE
·····················
Explain the effects of the entries when a new partner is admitted.

The admission of a new partner results in the **legal dissolution of the existing partnership** and **the beginning of a new partnership**. From an economic standpoint, however, the admission of a new partner (or partners) may be of minor significance in the continuity of the business. For example, in large public accounting or law firms, partners are admitted annually without any change in operating policies established by the continuing partners. **To recognize the economic effects, it is necessary only to open a capital account for each new partner.** The entries described and illustrated below are based on the assumption that the accounting records of the predecessor firm will continue to be used by the new partnership.

A new partner may be admitted either by (1) purchasing the interest of one or more existing partners or (2) investing assets in the partnership, as shown in Illustration 13-10. The former affects only the capital accounts of the partners who are parties to the transaction. The latter increases both net assets (total assets less total liabilities) and total capital of the partnership.

Admission of Partner through:

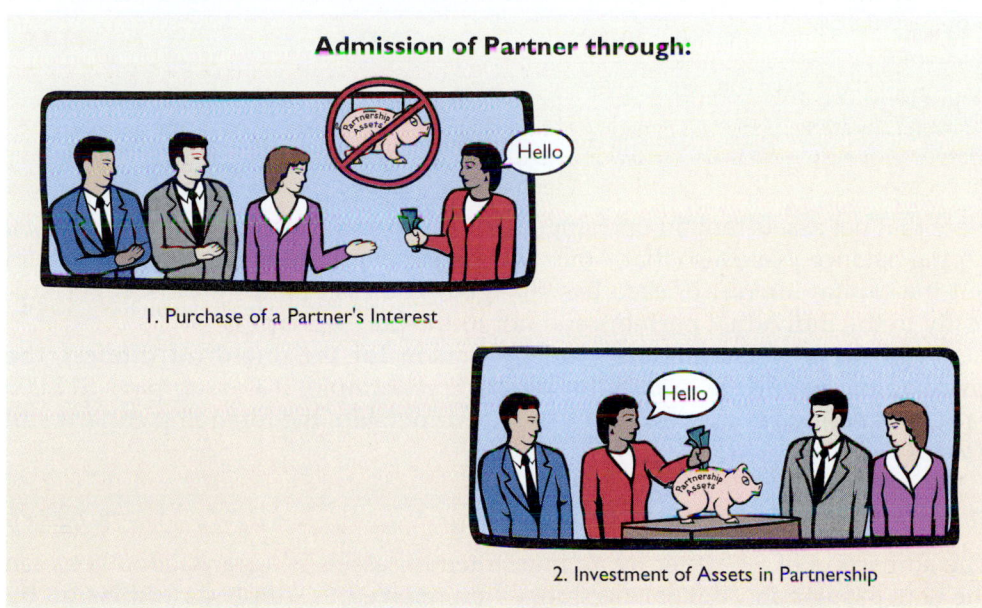

1. Purchase of a Partner's Interest

2. Investment of Assets in Partnership

ILLUSTRATION 13-10

Procedures in adding partners

Purchase of a Partner's Interest

The **admission** of a partner **by purchase of an interest** in the firm is a personal transaction between one or more existing partners and the new partner. Each party acts as an individual separate from the partnership entity. The price paid is negotiated and determined by the individuals involved. It may be equal to or different from the capital equity acquired. The amount of the purchase price passes directly from the new partner to the partners who are giving up part or all of their ownership claims. Any money or other consideration exchanged is the personal property of the participants and **not** the property of the partnership. Upon purchase of an interest, the new partner acquires each selling partner's capital interest and income ratio. A partner does not have to obtain the approval of the other partners to sell his or her interest. However, the Uniform Partnership Act provides that the purchaser does not become a partner until he or she is accepted into the firm by the continuing partners.

Accounting for the purchase of an interest is straightforward. As far as the partnership is concerned, only the realignment of partners' capital is recorded. **Each partner's capital account is debited for the ownership claims that have been relinquished, and the new partner's capital account is credited with the capital equity purchased.** Total assets, total liabilities, and total capital remain unchanged, as do all individual asset and liability accounts.

To illustrate, assume that L. Carson agrees to pay $10,000 each to C. Ames and D. Barker for 33⅓% (one-third) of their interest in the Ames–Barker partnership. At the time of the admission of Carson, each partner has a $30,000 capital balance. Both partners, therefore, give up $10,000 of their capital equity. The entry to record the admission of Carson is:

C. Ames, Capital	10,000	
D. Barker, Capital	10,000	
L. Carson, Capital		20,000
(To record admission of Carson by purchase)		

HELPFUL HINT

In a purchase of an interest, the partnership is **not** a participant in the transaction. For example, no cash is contributed to the partnership.

ILLUSTRATION 13-11

*Ledger balances after pur-
chase of a partner's interest*

The effect of this entry on net assets and partners' capital is shown below:

Net Assets		C. Ames, Capital		D. Barker, Capital		L. Carson, Capital
60,000		**10,000**	30,000	**10,000**	30,000	**20,000**
			Bal. 20,000		Bal. 20,000	

Note that net assets remain unchanged at $60,000 and each partner has a $20,000 capital balance. Note also that Ames and Barker continue as partners in the firm but the capital interest of each has changed. The cash paid by Carson goes directly to the individual partners and not to the partnership.

Regardless of the amount paid by Carson for the one-third interest, the entry above would be exactly the same. For example, if Carson pays $12,000 each to Ames and Barker for 33⅓% of the partnership, the foregoing entry is still made.

Investment of Assets in a Partnership

The admission of a partner by an investment of assets is a transaction between the new partner and the partnership. Often referred to simply as **admission by investment**, the transaction **increases both the net assets and total capital of the partnership**. To illustrate, assume that instead of purchasing an interest, Carson invests $30,000 in cash in the Ames–Barker partnership for a 33⅓% capital interest. In such a case, the entry is:

Cash	30,000	
L. Carson, Capital		30,000
(To record admission of Carson by investment)		

The effects of this transaction on the partnership accounts may be shown as follows:

ILLUSTRATION 13-12

*Ledger balances after invest-
ment of assets*

Net Assets		C. Ames, Capital	D. Barker, Capital	L. Carson, Capital
60,000		30,000	30,000	**30,000**
30,000				
Bal. 90,000				

Note that both net assets and total capital have increased by $30,000.

Remember that Carson's one-third capital interest might not result in a one-third income ratio. Carson's income ratio should be specified in the new partnership agreement, and it may or may not be equal to the one-third capital interest.

The different effects of the purchase of an interest and admission by investment are shown in the comparison of the net assets and capital balances in Illustration 13-13.

Purchase of an Interest		Admission by Investment	
Net Assets	$60,000	Net Assets	$90,000
Capital		Capital	
C. Ames	$20,000	C. Ames	$30,000
D. Barker	20,000	D. Barker	30,000
L. Carson	20,000	L. Carson	30,000
Total capital	$60,000	Total capital	$90,000

ILLUSTRATION 13-13

Comparison of purchase of an interest and admission by investment

When an interest is purchased, the total net assets and total capital of the partnership do not change. However, when a partner is admitted by investment, both the total net assets and the total capital change.

In the case of admission by investment, further complications occur when the new partner's investment differs from the capital equity acquired. When those amounts are not the same, the difference is considered a bonus either to (1) the existing (old) partners or (2) the new partner.

Bonus to Old Partners.   The existing partners may be unwilling to admit a new partner without receiving a bonus for both personal and business reasons. In an established firm, existing partners may insist on a bonus as compensation for the work they have put into the company over the years. Two accounting-related factors underlie the business reason: First, total partners' capital equals the **book value** of the recorded net assets of the partnership. At the time the new partner is admitted, the fair market values of assets such as land and buildings may be higher than their book values. Second, when the partnership has been profitable, goodwill may exist. However, the goodwill will not be recorded or included in total partners' capital. In such cases the new partner is usually willing to pay the bonus to become a partner.

A bonus to old partners results when the new partner's capital credit on the date of admittance is less than his or her investment in the firm. The bonus results in **an increase in the capital balances of the old partners that is allocated to them on the basis of their income ratios before the admission of the new partner.**

To illustrate, assume that the Bart–Cohen partnership owned by Sam Bart and Tom Cohen has total capital of $120,000 when Lea Eden is admitted to the partnership. Lea acquires a 25% ownership (capital) interest by making a cash investment of $80,000 in the partnership. The procedure for determining Eden's capital credit and the bonus to the old partners is as follows:

HELPFUL HINT
(1) The debit to Cash is greater than the new partner's capital credit. (2) Credits to old partners' capitals are needed for equal debits and credits.

1. **Determine the total capital of the new partnership** by adding the new partner's investment to the total capital of the old partnership. In this case the total capital of the new firm is $200,000, computed as follows:

Total capital of existing partnership	$120,000
Investment by new partner, Eden	80,000
Total capital of new partnership	$200,000

2. **Determine the new partner's capital credit** by multiplying the total capital of the new partnership by the new partner's ownership interest. Eden's capital credit is $50,000 ($200,000 × 25%).

3. **Determine the amount of bonus** by subtracting the new partner's capital credit from the new partner's investment. The bonus in this case is $30,000 ($80,000 − $50,000).

4. **Allocate the bonus to the old partners on the basis of their income ratios.** Assuming the ratios are Bart, 60%, and Cohen, 40%, the allocation is: Bart, $18,000 ($30,000 × 60%) and Cohen, $12,000 ($30,000 × 40%).

The entry to record the admission of Eden is:

A	=	L	+	OE
+80,000				+18,000
				+12,000
				+50,000

Cash	80,000	
Sam Bart, Capital		18,000
Tom Cohen, Capital		12,000
Lea Eden, Capital		50,000
(To record admission of Eden and bonus to old		
partners)		

Bonus to New Partner. A bonus to a new partner results when the new partner's capital credit is greater than his or her investment of assets in the firm. This may occur when the new partner possesses resources or special attributes that are desired by the partnership. For example, when bank interest rates are high, the new partner may be able to supply cash that is urgently needed for expansion or to meet maturing debts. Alternatively, the new partner may be a recognized expert or authority in a relevant field. Thus, an engineering firm may be willing to give a world-renowned engineer a bonus to join the firm. Similarly, the partners of a restaurant may offer a bonus to a sports celebrity in order to add the athlete's name to the partnership name. A bonus to a new partner may also result when recorded book values on the partnership books are higher than their market values.

A bonus to a new partner results in a **decrease in the capital balances of the old partners based on their income ratios before the admission of the new partner**. To illustrate, assume that Lea Eden invests $20,000 in cash for a 25% ownership interest in the Bart–Cohen partnership. Using the procedures described in the preceding section, the computations for Eden's capital credit and the bonus are as follows:

ILLUSTRATION 13-14

Computation of capital credit and bonus to new partner

1.	Total capital of Bart–Cohen partnership		$120,000
	Investment by new partner, Eden		20,000
	Total capital of new partnership		$140,000
2.	**Eden's capital credit** (25% × $140,000)		**$ 35,000**
3.	**Bonus to Eden** ($35,000 − $20,000)		**$ 15,000**
4.	Allocation of bonus:		
	Bart ($15,000 × 60%)	$9,000	
	Cohen ($15,000 × 40%)	6,000	$ 15,000

The entry to record the admission of Eden is as follows:

A	=	L	+	OE
+20,000				− 9,000
				− 6,000
				+35,000

Cash	20,000	
Sam Bart, Capital	9,000	
Tom Cohen, Capital	6,000	
Lea Eden, Capital		35,000
(To record Eden's admission and bonus)		

Withdrawal of a Partner

Now let's look at the opposite situation—the withdrawal of a partner. A partner may withdraw from a partnership **voluntarily** by selling his or her equity in the firm or **involuntarily** by reaching mandatory retirement age or by dying. The withdrawal of a partner, like the admission of a partner, legally dissolves the partnership. The legal effects may be recognized in accounting for a withdrawal by dissolving the firm. However, it is customary to record only the economic effects. As indicated earlier, the partnership agreement should specify the terms of withdrawal. The withdrawal of a partner may be accomplished by (1) payment from partners' personal assets or (2) payment from partnership assets, as shown in Illustration 13-15. The former affects only the partners' capital accounts. The latter decreases total net assets and total capital of the partnership.

6
STUDY
OBJECTIVE
....
Describe the effects of the entries when a partner withdraws from the firm.

Withdrawal of Partner through:

1. Payment from Partners' Personal Assets

2. Payment from Partnership Assets

ILLUSTRATION 13-15

Procedures in partnership withdrawal

Payment from Partners' Personal Assets

The withdrawal of a partner when payment is made from partners' personal assets is the direct opposite of admitting a new partner who purchases a partner's interest. Withdrawal by payment from partners' personal assets is a personal transaction between the partners. Payment to the retiring partner is made directly from the remaining partners' personal assets. **Partnership assets are not involved in any way, and total capital does not change.** Thus, the effect on the partnership is limited to a realignment of the partners' capital balances.

To illustrate, assume that Anne Morz, Mary Nead, and Jill Odom have capital balances of $25,000, $15,000, and $10,000, respectively, when Morz and Nead agree to buy out Odom's interest. Each of them agrees to pay Odom $8,000 in exchange for one-half of Odom's total interest of $10,000. The entry to record the withdrawal is:

HELPFUL HINT
If each purchaser acquires one-fourth of Odom's total interest for $8,000 each, the debit becomes $5,000 and the credits $2,500.

Jill Odom, Capital	10,000	
Anne Morz, Capital		5,000
Mary Nead, Capital		5,000
(To record purchase of Odom's interest)		

A	=	L	+	OE
				− 10,000
				+ 5,000
				+ 5,000

ILLUSTRATION 13-16

Ledger balances after payment from partners' personal assets

The effect of this entry on the partnership accounts is shown below:

Net Assets		Anne Morz, Capital		Mary Nead, Capital		Jill Odom, Capital	
50,000			25,000		15,000	10,000	10,000
			5,000		**5,000**		
		Bal.	30,000	Bal.	20,000	Bal.	−0−

Note that net assets and total capital remain the same at $50,000. Note also that the $16,000 paid to Odom is not recorded. Odom's capital is debited only for $10,000, not for the $16,000 that she received. Similarly, both Morz and Nead credit their capital accounts for only $5,000, not the $8,000 they each paid. Morz and Nead will share net income or net loss equally unless they specifically indicate another income ratio in the partnership agreement.

Payment from Partnership Assets

Using partnership assets to pay for a withdrawing partner's interest is the **reverse** of admitting a partner through the investment of assets in the partnership. **Withdrawal by payment from partnership assets** is a transaction that involves the partnership. **Both partnership net assets and total capital are decreased.**

Many partnership agreements provide that the amount paid should be based on the fair market value of the assets at the time of the partner's withdrawal. When this basis is required, some maintain that any differences between recorded asset balances and their fair market values should be (1) recorded by an adjusting entry and (2) allocated to all partners on the basis of their income ratios. This position has serious flaws, however. Recording the revaluations violates the cost principle, which requires that assets be stated at original cost. It also is a departure from the going-concern assumption, which assumes the entity will continue indefinitely. The terms of the partnership contract should not dictate the accounting for the event.

In accounting for a withdrawal by payment from partnership assets:

1. Asset revaluations should not be recorded.
2. Any difference between the amount paid and the withdrawing partner's capital balance should be considered a bonus to the retiring partner or a bonus to the remaining partners.

Bonus to Retiring Partner.   A bonus may be paid to a retiring partner when:

1. The fair market value of partnership assets is more than their book value,
2. There is unrecorded goodwill resulting from the partnership's superior earnings record, or
3. The remaining partners are anxious to remove the partner from the firm.

The bonus is deducted from the remaining partners' capital balances on the basis of their income ratios at the time of the withdrawal.

To illustrate, assume that the following capital balances exist in the RST partnership: Fred Roman $50,000, Dee Sand $30,000, and Betty Terk $20,000. The partners share income in the ratio of 3:2:1, respectively. Terk retires from the partnership and receives a cash payment of $25,000 from the firm. The procedure for determining the bonus to the retiring partner and the allocation of the bonus to the remaining partners is as follows:

1. **Determine the amount of the bonus** by subtracting the retiring partner's capital balance from the cash paid by the partnership. The bonus in this case is $5,000 ($25,000 − $20,000).
2. **Allocate the bonus to the remaining partners on the basis of their income ratios.** The ratios of Roman and Sand are 3:2. Thus, the allocation of the $5,000 bonus is: Roman $3,000 ($5,000 × 3/5) and Sand $2,000 ($5,000 × 2/5).

The entry to record the withdrawal of Terk is:

Betty Terk, Capital	20,000	
Fred Roman, Capital	3,000	
Dee Sand, Capital	2,000	
Cash		25,000
(To record withdrawal of and bonus to Terk)		

The remaining partners, Roman and Sand, will recover the bonus given to Terk as the undervalued assets are sold or used in the partnership.

Bonus to Remaining Partners.   The retiring partner may give a bonus to the remaining partners when:

1. Recorded assets are overvalued,
2. The partnership has a poor earnings record, or
3. The partner is anxious to leave the partnership.

In such cases, the cash paid to the retiring partner will be less than the retiring partner's capital balance. **The bonus is allocated (credited) to the capital accounts of the remaining partners on the basis of their income ratios.**

To illustrate, assume that, instead of the example above, Terk is paid only $16,000 for her $20,000 equity upon withdrawing from the RST partnership. In such case:

1. The bonus to remaining partners is $4,000 ($20,000 − $16,000).
2. The allocation of the $4,000 bonus is: Roman $2,400 ($4,000 × 3/5) and Sand $1,600 ($4,000 × 2/5).

The entry to record the withdrawal is:

Betty Terk, Capital	20,000	
Fred Roman, Capital		2,400
Dee Sand, Capital		1,600
Cash		16,000
(To record withdrawal of Terk and bonus to remaining partners)		

It is important to note that if Sand had withdrawn from the partnership, any bonus would be divided between Roman and Terk on the basis of their income ratio which is 3:1 or 75% and 25%.

Death of a Partner

The death of a partner dissolves the partnership, but provision generally is made for the surviving partners to continue operations. When a partner dies, it usually is necessary to determine the partner's equity at the date of death. This is done by (1) determining the net income or loss for the year to date, (2) closing the books, and (3) preparing financial statements. The partnership agreement may also require an audit of the financial statements by independent auditors and a revaluation of assets by an independent appraisal firm.

The surviving partners may agree either to (1) purchase the deceased partner's equity from their personal assets or (2) use partnership assets to settle with the deceased partner's estate. In both instances, the entries to record the withdrawal of the partner are similar to those presented in previous illustrations.

To facilitate payment from partnership assets, some partnerships obtain life insurance policies on each partner with the partnership as the beneficiary. The proceeds from the insurance policy on the deceased partner are then used to settle with the estate.

BEFORE YOU GO ON . . .

Review It

1. How does the accounting for admission by purchase of an interest differ from admission by investing assets in the partnership?
2. Contrast the accounting effects of the withdrawal of a partner by payment from (a) personal assets and (b) partnership assets.

Do It

Curly, Moe, and Larry have a partnership. Each partner has a $40,000 balance in his capital account. Record journal entries for each of the independent events listed below.

1. Curly, Moe, and Larry agree to admit Stan as a new one-quarter-interest partner. Stan pays $10,000 in cash directly to each partner.
2. Curly, Moe, and Larry agree to admit Stan as a new one-quarter-interest partner. Stan contributes $40,000 into the partnership.
3. Curly and Moe agree to let Larry withdraw from the partnership, and $30,000 of partnership cash is distributed to Larry. Curly and Moe share income and losses equally.
4. Curly and Moe agree to let Larry withdraw from the partnership. Each pays Larry $25,000 out of his personal assets. Curly and Moe share income and losses equally.

Reasoning: You need to understand that admission (withdrawal) by purchase (sale) of an interest is a personal transaction between one or more existing partners and the new (withdrawing) partner. In contrast, admission (withdrawal) by investment (distribution) of partnership assets is a transaction between the new (withdrawing) partner and the partnership.

Solution:

1.

Curly, Capital	10,000	
Moe, Capital	10,000	
Larry, Capital	10,000	
Stan, Capital		30,000
(To record admission of Stan by purchase)		

2.

Cash	40,000	
Stan, Capital		40,000
(To record admission of Stan by investment)		

3.

Larry, Capital	40,000	
Cash		30,000
Curly, Capital		5,000
Moe, Capital		5,000
(To record withdrawal of Larry and bonus to remaining partners)		

4.

Larry, Capital	40,000	
Curly, Capital		20,000
Moe, Capital		20,000
(To record purchase of Larry's interest)		

Related exercise material: BE13–6, BE13–7, BE13–8, BE13–9, E13–4, E13–5, E13–6, and E13–7.

THE NAVIGATOR

LIQUIDATION OF A PARTNERSHIP

The liquidation of a partnership terminates the business. It entails selling the assets of the firm, paying liabilities, and distributing any remaining assets to the partners. Liquidation may result from the sale of the business by mutual agreement of the partners, from the death of a partner, or from bankruptcy. In contrast to the dissolution of a partnership, **partnership liquidation** ends both the legal and economic life of the entity.

From an accounting standpoint, liquidation should be preceded by completing the accounting cycle for the partnership for the final operating period. This includes preparing adjusting entries and financial statements. It also involves preparing closing entries and a post-closing trial balance. Thus, only balance sheet accounts should be open as the liquidation process begins.

The liquidation process may occur at a specific point in time or it may occur over a period of time. In liquidation, the sale of noncash assets for cash is called **realization**, and the difference between book value and the cash proceeds is called the **gain or loss on realization**. To liquidate a partnership, it is necessary to:

1. Sell noncash assets for cash and recognize a gain or loss on realization.
2. Allocate gain/loss on realization to the partners based on their income ratios.
3. Pay partnership liabilities in cash.
4. Distribute remaining cash to partners on the basis of their capital balances.

Each of the steps must be performed in sequence because creditors must be paid **before** partners receive any cash distributions. Each step also must be recorded by an accounting entry.

When a partnership is liquidated, all partners may have credit balances in their capital accounts—a situation termed **no capital deficiency**; or at least one partner's capital account may have a debit balance—a situation termed a **capital deficiency**. To illustrate each of these conditions, assume that the Ace Company is liquidated when its ledger shows the following assets, liabilities, and owners' equity accounts:

7
STUDY
OBJECTIVE

Prepare the entries to record the liquidation of a partnership.

HELPFUL HINT
These steps are indispensable to correct homework and examination results.

Assets		Liabilities and Owners' Equity	
Cash	$ 5,000	Notes payable	$15,000
Accounts receivable	15,000	Accounts payable	16,000
Inventory	18,000	R. Arnet, Capital	15,000
Equipment	35,000	P. Carey, Capital	17,800
Accum. depr.—equipment	(8,000)	W. Eaton, Capital	1,200
	$65,000		$65,000

ILLUSTRATION 13-17
Account balances prior to liquidation

No Capital Deficiency

The partners of Ace Company agree to liquidate the partnership on the following terms: (1) a cash sale of the noncash assets of the partnership to Jackson Enterprises for $75,000, and (2) payment of partnership liabilities by the partnership. The income ratios of the partners are 3:2:1, respectively. The steps in the liquidation process are as follows:

1. The noncash assets (accounts receivable, inventory, and equipment) are sold for $75,000. Since the book value of these assets is $60,000 ($15,000 +

$18,000 + $35,000 − $8,000), a gain of $15,000 is realized on the sale. The entry is:

(1)

A = L + OE
+75,000   +15,000
+ 8,000
− 15,000
− 18,000
− 35,000

Cash	75,000	
Accumulated Depreciation—Equipment	8,000	
Accounts Receivable		15,000
Inventory		18,000
Equipment		35,000
Gain on Realization		15,000
(To record realization of noncash assets)		

2. The gain on realization of $15,000 is allocated to the partners on their income ratios, which are 3:2:1. The entry is:

(2)

A = L + OE
− 15,000
+ 7,500
+ 5,000
+ 2,500

Gain on Realization	15,000	
R. Arnet, Capital ($15,000 × 3/6)		7,500
P. Carey, Capital ($15,000 × 2/6)		5,000
W. Eaton, Capital ($15,000 × 1/6)		2,500
(To allocate gain to partners' capitals)		

3. Partnership liabilities consist of Notes Payable $15,000 and Accounts Payable $16,000. Creditors are paid in full by a cash payment of $31,000. The entry is:

(3)

A = L + OE
− 31,000   − 15,000
− 16,000

Notes Payable	15,000	
Accounts Payable	16,000	
Cash		31,000
(To record payment of partnership liabilities)		

4. The remaining cash is distributed to the partners on the basis of **their capital balances**. After the entries in the first three steps are posted, all partnership accounts, including Gain on Realization, will have zero balances except for four accounts: Cash $49,000; R. Arnet, Capital $22,500; P. Carey, Capital $22,800; and W. Eaton, Capital $3,700, as shown below:

ILLUSTRATION 13-18

Ledger balances before distribution of cash

Cash			R. Arnet, Capital			P. Carey, Capital			W. Eaton, Capital		
Bal. 5,000	(3) 31,000			Bal. 15,000			Bal. 17,800			Bal. 1,200
(1) 75,000				(2) 7,500			(2) 5,000			(2) 2,500
Bal. 49,000				**Bal. 22,500**			**Bal. 22,800**			**Bal. 3,700**

The entry to record the distribution of cash is as follows:

(4)

A = L + OE
− 49,000
− 22,500
− 22,800
− 3,700

R. Arnet, Capital	22,500	
P. Carey, Capital	22,800	
W. Eaton, Capital	3,700	
Cash		49,000
(To record distribution of cash to partners)		

After this entry is posted, all partnership accounts will have zero balances, as shown in Illustration 13-19.

Cash				R. Arnet, Capital				P. Carey, Capital				W. Eaton, Capital			
Bal.	5,000	(3)	31,000	(4)	22,500	Bal.	15,000	(4)	22,800	Bal.	17,800	(4)	3,700	Bal.	1,200
(1)	75,000	(4)	49,000			(2)	7,500			(2)	5,000			(2)	2,500
Bal.	–0–					Bal.	–0–			Bal.	–0–			Bal.	–0–

ILLUSTRATION 13-19
Ledger balances after distribution of cash

A word of caution: **Cash should not be distributed to partners on the basis of their income-sharing ratios.** On this basis, for example, Arnet would receive three-sixths, or $24,500, which would produce an erroneous debit balance of $2,000. The income ratio is a proper basis for allocating net income or loss, **but it is not a proper basis for making the final distribution of cash to the partners.**

HELPFUL HINT
Zero balances after posting is a quick proof of the accuracy of the cash distribution entry.

Schedule of Cash Payments

Some accountants prepare a cash payments schedule to determine the distribution of cash to the partners in the liquidation of a partnership. The **schedule of cash payments**, sometimes called a **safe cash payments schedule**, is organized around the basic accounting equation. The schedule for the Ace Company is shown in Illustration 13-20. The numbers in parentheses refer to the four required steps in the liquidation of a partnership. They also identify the accounting entries that must be made. The cash payments schedule is especially useful when the liquidation process extends over a period of time.

ILLUSTRATION 13-20
Schedule of cash payments, no capital deficiency

ACE COMPANY
Schedule of Cash Payments

Item		Cash	+	Noncash Assets	=	Liabilities	+	R. Arnet Capital	+	P. Carey Capital	+	W. Eaton Capital
Balances before liquidation		5,000	+	60,000	=	31,000	+	15,000	+	17,800	+	1,200
Sales of noncash assets and allocation of gain	(1)&(2)	75,000	+	(60,000)	=			7,500	+	5,000	+	2,500
New balances		80,000	+	–0–	=	31,000	+	22,500	+	22,800	+	3,700
Pay liabilities	(3)	(31,000)			=	(31,000)						
New balances		49,000	+	–0–	=	–0–	+	22,500	+	22,800	+	3,700
Cash distribution to partners	(4)	(49,000)			=			(22,500)	+	(22,800)	+	(3,700)
Final balances		–0–		–0–		–0–		–0–		–0–		–0–

Capital Deficiency

A capital deficiency may be caused by recurring net losses, excessive drawings before liquidation, or by losses from realization suffered during liquidation. To illustrate, assume that Ace Company is on the brink of bankruptcy. The partners decide to liquidate by having a "going-out-of-business" sale in which merchandise is sold at substantial discounts, and the equipment is sold at auction. Cash proceeds from these sales and collections from customers total only $42,000. Accordingly, the loss from liquidation is $18,000 ($60,000 − $42,000). The steps in the liquidation process are as follows:

1. The entry for the realization of noncash assets is:

(1)

Cash	42,000	
Accumulated Depreciation—Equipment	8,000	
Loss on Realization	18,000	
Accounts Receivable		15,000
Inventory		18,000
Equipment		35,000
(To record realization of noncash assets)		

```
A      =  L  +   OE
+42,000        - 18,000
+ 8,000
-15,000
-18,000
-35,000
```

2. The loss on realization is allocated to the partners on the basis of their income ratios. The entry is:

(2)

R. Arnet, Capital ($18,000 × 3/6)	9,000	
P. Carey, Capital ($18,000 × 2/6)	6,000	
W. Eaton, Capital ($18,000 × 1/6)	3,000	
Loss on Realization		18,000
(To allocate loss on realization to partners)		

```
A   =  L  +   OE
           - 9,000
           - 6,000
           - 3,000
           +18,000
```

3. Partnership liabilities are paid. This entry is the same as in the previous example.

(3)

Notes Payable	15,000	
Accounts Payable	16,000	
Cash		31,000
(To record payment of partnership liabilities)		

```
A      =  L    +  OE
-31,000  - 15,000
         - 16,000
```

4. After posting the three entries, two accounts will have debit balances—Cash, $16,000, and W. Eaton, Capital, $1,800—and two accounts will have credit balances—R. Arnet, Capital, $6,000, and P. Carey, Capital, $11,800, as shown below:

ILLUSTRATION 13-21

Ledger balances before distribution of cash

Cash		R. Arnet, Capital		P. Carey, Capital		W. Eaton, Capital	
Bal. 5,000 | (3) 31,000	(2) 9,000 | Bal. 15,000	(2) 6,000 | Bal. 17,800	(2) 3,000 | Bal. 1,200
(1) 42,000			
Bal. 16,000		**Bal. 6,000**	**Bal. 11,800**	**Bal. 1,800**

Eaton has a capital deficiency of $1,800. Eaton, therefore, owes the partnership $1,800, and Arnet and Carey have a legally enforceable claim against Eaton's personal assets. The distribution of cash is still made on the basis of capital balances. However, the amount will vary depending on how the deficiency is settled.

Payment of Deficiency

If the partner with the capital deficiency pays the amount owed the partnership, the deficiency is eliminated. To illustrate, assume that Eaton pays $1,800 to the partnership. The entry is:

(a)

Cash	1,800	
W. Eaton, Capital		1,800
(To record payment of capital deficiency by Eaton)		

```
A      =  L  +  OE
+1,800        +1,800
```

After posting this entry, account balances are as follows:

Cash				R. Arnet, Capital				P. Carey, Capital				W. Eaton, Capital			
Bal.	5,000	(3)	31,000	(2)	9,000	Bal.	15,000	(2)	6,000	Bal.	17,800	(2)	3,000	Bal.	1,200
(1)	42,000													(a)	1,800
(a)	1,800					Bal.	6,000			Bal.	11,800				
Bal.	17,800													Bal.	–0–

ILLUSTRATION 13-22
Ledger balances after paying capital deficiency

The cash balance of $17,800 is now equal to the credit balances in the capital accounts (Arnet $6,000 + Carey $11,800), and cash is distributed on the basis of these balances. The entry is:

R. Arnet, Capital	6,000	
P. Carey, Capital	11,800	
Cash		17,800
(To record distribution of cash to the partners)		

A	=	L	+	OE
−17,800				− 6,000
				−11,800

After this entry is posted, all accounts will have zero balances.

Nonpayment of Deficiency

If a partner with a capital deficiency is unable to pay the amount owed to the partnership, the partners with credit balances must absorb the loss. The loss is allocated on the basis of the income ratios that exist between the partners with credit balances. The income ratios of Arnet and Carey are 3:2 or 3/5 and 2/5, respectively. Thus, the following entry is made to remove Eaton's capital deficiency:

(a)

R. Arnet, Capital ($1,800 × 3/5)	1,080	
P. Carey, Capital ($1,800 × 2/5)	720	
W. Eaton, Capital		1,800
(To record write-off of capital deficiency)		

A	=	L	+	OE
				− 1,080
				− 720
				+1,800

ILLUSTRATION 13-23
Ledger balances after non-payment of capital deficiency

After posting this entry, the cash and capital accounts will have the following balances:

Cash				R. Arnet, Capital				P. Carey, Capital				W. Eaton, Capital			
Bal.	5,000	(3)	31,000	(2)	9,000	Bal.	15,000	(2)	6,000	Bal.	17,800	(2)	3,000	Bal.	1,200
(1)	42,000			(a)	1,080			(a)	720					(a)	1,800
Bal.	16,000					Bal.	4,920			Bal.	11,080			Bal.	–0–

The cash balance of $16,000 now equals the sum of the credit balances in the capital accounts (Arnet $4,920 + Carey $11,080). The entry to record the distribution of cash is:

R. Arnet, Capital	4,920	
P. Carey, Capital	11,080	
Cash		16,000
(To record distribution of cash to partners)		

A	=	L	+	OE
−16,000				− 4,920
				−11,080

After this entry is posted, all accounts will have zero balances.

BEFORE YOU GO ON . . .

Review It

1. Identify the steps in liquidating a partnership.
2. What basis is used in making the final distribution of cash to the partners?

A LOOK BACK AT OUR FEATURE STORY

Refer back to the opening story about Razor & Tie Music, and answer the following questions:

1. Speculate as to why Razor & Tie selected the partnership form of organization for its business.
2. What do you believe are the major items written into the partnership agreement for Razor & Tie?
3. How is net income or loss divided if the partnership is silent regarding the percentage allocation?

Solution:

1. Cliff Chenfield and Craig Balsam may have chosen to form a partnership, rather than a corporation, for a number of reasons. First, the partnership is much quicker and easier to form, with little of the red tape associated with a corporation. Second, the partnership form has distinct tax advantages relative to a corporation. Third, since the two partners knew each other well prior to beginning Razor & Tie, their concerns about the risk of unlimited liabilities that might be incurred due to inappropriate actions by the other partner are reduced.
2. A partnership agreement of Razor & Tie should specify the capital contributed by both partners, and the basis for sharing income and losses and for withdrawing funds from the partnership. In addition, it is good to specify a mechanism for resolving disputes, adding or removing a partner, or what to do in the event of the death of one of the partners. A well-written partnership agreement can significantly reduce conflicts as the firm grows.
3. In this case, income and losses are shared equally.

THE
NAVIGATOR

DEMONSTRATION PROBLEM

On January 1, 1999, the capital balances in Hollingsworth Company are Lois Holly $26,000, and Jim Worth $24,000. In 1999 the company reports net income of $30,000. The income ratio provides for salary allowances of $12,000 for Holly and $10,000 to Worth and the remainder equally. Neither partner had any drawings in 1999.

Assume that the following independent transactions occur on January 1, 2000:

1. Donna Reichenbacher purchases one-half of Holly's capital interest for $25,000.
2. Marsha Mears is admitted with a 25% capital interest by a cash investment of $40,000.
3. Stan Wells is admitted with a 35% capital interest by a cash investment of $40,000.

Instructions

(a) Prepare a schedule showing the distribution of net income in 1999.
(b) Journalize the division of 1999 net income to the partners.
(c) Journalize each of the independent transactions that occurred on January 1, 2000.

SOLUTION TO DEMONSTRATION PROBLEM

(a) Net income $30,000

Division of Net Income

	Lois Holly	Jim Worth	Total
Salary allowance	$12,000	$10,000	$22,000
Remaining income $8,000 ($30,000 − $22,000)			
Lois Holly ($8,000 × 50%)	4,000		
Jim Worth ($8,000 × 50%)		4,000	
Total remainder			8,000
Total division	$16,000	$14,000	$30,000

<table>
<tr><td>(b) 12/31/99</td><td>Income Summary</td><td>30,000</td><td></td></tr>
<tr><td></td><td>   Lois Holly, Capital ($12,000 + $4,000)</td><td></td><td>16,000</td></tr>
<tr><td></td><td>   Jim Worth, Capital ($10,000 + $4,000)</td><td></td><td>14,000</td></tr>
<tr><td></td><td>   (To close net income to partners' capitals)</td><td></td><td></td></tr>
</table>

(1)

<table>
<tr><td>(c) 1/1/00</td><td>Lois Holly, Capital ($26,000 + $16,000) × ½)</td><td>21,000</td><td></td></tr>
<tr><td></td><td>   Donna Reichenbacher, Capital</td><td></td><td>21,000</td></tr>
<tr><td></td><td>   (To record purchase of one-half of Holly's interest)</td><td></td><td></td></tr>
</table>

(2)

<table>
<tr><td>1/1/00</td><td>Cash</td><td>40,000</td><td></td></tr>
<tr><td></td><td>   Lois Holly, Capital</td><td></td><td>5,000</td></tr>
<tr><td></td><td>   Jim Worth, Capital</td><td></td><td>5,000</td></tr>
<tr><td></td><td>   Marsha Mears, Capital</td><td></td><td>30,000</td></tr>
<tr><td></td><td>   (To record admission of Mears and bonus to old partners)</td><td></td><td></td></tr>
</table>

Total capital after investment: $120,000
(Holly, $42,000, Worth $38,000, Mears investment $40,000)

Mears' capital credit (25% × $120,000)		$30,000
Bonus to old partners ($40,000 − $30,000)		$10,000

Allocation of bonus:

Holly ($10,000 × 50%)	$ 5,000	
Worth ($10,000 × 50%)	5,000	$10,000

(3)

<table>
<tr><td>1/1/00</td><td>Cash</td><td>40,000</td><td></td></tr>
<tr><td></td><td>Lois Holly, Capital</td><td>1,000</td><td></td></tr>
<tr><td></td><td>Jim Worth, Capital</td><td>1,000</td><td></td></tr>
<tr><td></td><td>   Stan Wells, Capital</td><td></td><td>42,000</td></tr>
<tr><td></td><td>   (To record Wells's admission and bonus)</td><td></td><td></td></tr>
</table>

Wells's capital credit (35% × $120,000)		$42,000
Bonus to Wells ($42,000 − $40,000)		$ 2,000

Allocation of bonus:

Holly ($2,000 × 50%)	$1,000	
Worth ($2,000 × 50%)	1,000	$ 2,000

PROBLEM-SOLVING STRATEGIES

1. Journalizing the division of net income is a closing entry.
2. The entry for purchase of an interest involves only capital accounts.
3. The entry for admission by investment must have a debit to cash.
4. Allocation of a bonus occurs only in admission by investment.

THE NAVIGATOR

Summary of Study Objectives

1. *Identify the characteristics of the partnership form of business organization.* The principal characteristics of a partnership are: (a) association of individuals, (b) mutual agency, (c) limited life, (d) unlimited liability, and (e) co-ownership of property.

2. *Explain the accounting entries for the formation of a partnership.* When a partnership is formed, each partner's initial investment should be recorded at the fair market value of the assets at the date of their transfer to the partnership.

3. *Identify the bases for dividing net income or net loss.* Net income or net loss is divided on the basis of the income ratio, which may be (a) a fixed ratio, (b) a ratio based on beginning or average capital balances, (c) salaries to partners and the remainder on a fixed ratio, (d) interest on partners' capitals and the remainder on a fixed ratio, and (e) salaries to partners, interest on partners' capitals, and the remainder on a fixed ratio.

4. *Describe the form and content of partnership financial statements.* The financial statements of a partnership are similar to those of a proprietorship. The principal differences are: (a) the division of net income is shown on the income statement, (b) the owners' equity statement is called

a partners' capital statement, and (c) each partner's capital is reported on the balance sheet.

5. *Explain the effects of the entries when a new partner is admitted.* The entry to record the admittance of a new partner by purchase of a partner's interest affects only partners' capital accounts. The entries to record the admittance by investment of assets in the partnership (a) increase both net assets and total capital and (b) may result in recognition of a bonus to either the old partners or the new partner.

6. *Describe the effects of the entries when a partner withdraws from the firm.* The entry to record a withdrawal from the firm when payment is made from partners' personal assets only affects partners' capital accounts. The entry to record a withdrawal when payment is made from partnership assets (a) decreases net assets and total capital and (b) may result in recognizing a bonus either to the retiring partner or the remaining partners.

7. *Prepare the entries to record the liquidation of a partnership.* When a partnership is liquidated, it is necessary to record the (a) sale of noncash assets, (b) allocation of the gain or loss on realization, (c) payment of partnership liabilities, and (d) distribution of cash to the partners.

Glossary

Admission by investment Admission of a partner by investing assets in the partnership, in which both partnership net assets and total capital increase. (p. 562).

Admission by purchase of an interest Admission of a partner in a personal transaction between one or more existing partners and the new partner, which does not change total partnership assets or total capital. (p. 561).

Capital deficiency A debit balance in a partner's capital account after allocation of gain or loss. (p. 569).

General partner A partner who has unlimited liability for the debts of the firm. (p. 552).

Income ratio The basis for dividing both net income and net loss in a partnership. (p. 555).

Limited partner A partner who has limited liability for the debts of the firm. (p. 552).

Limited partnership A partnership in which one or more general partners have unlimited liability and one or more partners have limited liability for the obligations of the firm. (p. 552).

No capital deficiency All partners have credit balances after allocation of gain or loss. (p. 569).

Partners' capital statement The owners' equity statement for a partnership which shows the changes in each partner's

capital balance and in total partnership capital during the year. (p. 559).

Partnership An association of two or more persons to carry on as co-owners of a business for profit. (p. 550).

Partnership agreement A contract expressing the voluntary agreement of two or more individuals in a partnership. (p. 553).

Partnership dissolution A change in partners due to withdrawal or admission which does not necessarily terminate the business. (p. 551).

Partnership liquidation An event that ends both the legal and economic life of a partnership. (p. 569).

Schedule of cash payments A schedule showing the distribution of cash to the partners in the liquidation of a partnership. (p. 571).

Withdrawal by payment from partners' personal assets Withdrawal of a partner in a personal transaction between partners, which does not change total partnership assets or total capital. (p. 565).

Withdrawal by payment from partnership assets Withdrawal of a partner in a transaction involving the partnership which decreases both partnership net assets and total capital. (p. 566).

SELF-STUDY QUESTIONS

Answers are at the end of the chapter.

(SO 1) 1. Which of the following is *not* a characteristic of a partnership?
   a. Taxable entity
   b. Co-ownership of property
   c. Mutual agency
   d. Limited life

(SO 1) 2. The advantages of a partnership do *not* include:
   a. ease of formation.
   b. unlimited liability.
   c. freedom from government regulation.
   d. ease of decision making.

(SO 2) 3. Upon formation of a partnership, each partner's initial investment of assets should be recorded at their:
   a. book values.
   b. cost.
   c. market values.
   d. appraised values.

(SO 3) 4. The XYZ Company reports net income of $60,000. If partners X, Y, and Z have an income ratio of 50%, 30%, and 20%, respectively, Z's share of the net income is:
   a. $30,000.
   b. $12,000.
   c. $18,000.
   d. No correct answer is given.

(SO 3) 5. Using the data in (4) above, what is Y's share of net income if the percentages are applicable after each partner receives a $10,000 salary allowance?
   a. $12,000
   b. $20,000
   c. $19,000
   d. $21,000

(SO 4) 6. Which of the following statements about partnership financial statements is true?
   a. Details of the distribution of net income are shown in the owners' equity statement.
   b. The distribution of net income is shown on the balance sheet.
   c. Only the total of all partner capital balances is shown in the balance sheet.
   d. The owners' equity statement is called the partners' capital statement.

(SO 5) 7. Maria Taxco purchases 50% of Louie Limb capital interest in the K & L partnership for $22,000. If the capital balances of Kim and Louie Limb are $40,000 and $30,000, respectively, Taxco's capital balance following the purchase is:
   a. $22,000.
   b. $35,000.
   c. $20,000.
   d. $15,000.

(SO 5) 8. Capital balances in the DEA partnership are D Capital $60,000, E Capital $50,000, and A Capital $40,000, and income ratios are 5:3:2, respectively. The DEAR partnership is formed by admitting R to the firm with a cash investment of $60,000 for a 25% capital interest. The bonus to be credited to A Capital in admitting R is:
   a. $10,000.
   b. $7,500.
   c. $3,750.
   d. $1,500.

(SO 6) 9. Capital balances in the TERM partnership are T Capital $50,000, E Capital $40,000, R Capital $30,000, and M Capital $20,000, and income ratios are 4:3:2:1, respectively. M withdraws from the firm following payment of $29,000 in cash from the partnership. E's capital balance after recording the withdrawal of M is:
   a. $36,000.
   b. $37,000.
   c. $38,000.
   d. $40,000.

(SO 7) 10. In the liquidation of a partnership it is necessary to (1) distribute cash to the partners, (2) sell noncash assets, (3) allocate any gain or loss on realization to the partners, and (4) pay liabilities. These steps should be performed in the following order:
   a. (2), (3), (4), (1).
   b. (2), (3), (1), (4).
   c. (3), (2), (1), (4).
   d. (3), (2), (4), (1).

THE NAVIGATOR

QUESTIONS

1. The characteristics of a partnership include the following: (a) association of individuals, (b) limited life, and (c) co-ownership of property. Explain each of these terms.

2. Vera Cruz is confused about the partnership characteristics of (a) mutual agency and (b) unlimited liability. Explain these two characteristics for Vera.

3. Swen Varberg and Egor Karlstad are considering a business venture. They ask you to explain the advantages and disadvantages of the partnership form of organization.

4. Ginny Brown and John Fleming form a partnership. Brown contributes land with a book value of $50,000 and a fair market value of $75,000. Brown also contrib-

utes equipment with a book value of $52,000 and a fair market value of $57,000. The partnership assumes a $20,000 mortgage on the land. What should be the balance in Brown's capital account upon formation of the partnership?

5. Roy Orbison, S. Innis, and David Bowie have a partnership called Depeche Mode. A dispute has arisen among the partners because Orbison has invested twice as much in assets as the other two partners and believes net income and net losses should be shared in accordance with the capital ratios. The partnership agreement does not specify the division of profits and losses. How will net income and net loss be divided?

6. Leon Redbone and Elvis Costello are discussing how income and losses should be divided in a partnership they plan to form. What factors should be considered in determining the division of net income or net loss?

7. Doreen Shaffer and Quincy Jones have capital balances of $40,000 and $80,000, respectively, in a partnership. The partnership agreement indicates that net income or net loss should be shared equally. If the net income for the partnership is $24,000, how should the net income be divided?

8. Robben Ford and Gregg Allman share net income and net loss equally. (a) Which account(s) is (are) debited and credited to record the division of net income between the partners? (b) If Robben Ford withdraws $30,000 in cash for personal use in lieu of salary, which account is debited and which is credited?

9. Partners Reba McEntire and B. Zander are provided salary allowances of $30,000 and $25,000, respectively. They divide the remainder of the partnership income in a ratio of 60:40. If partnership net income is $50,000, how much is allocated to McEntire and Zander?

10. Are the financial statements of a partnership similar to those of a proprietorship? Discuss.

11. Patty Loveless decides to pay Mark Waller $50,000 for a one-third interest in the partnership of Waller and Rose. What effect does this transaction have on partnership net assets?

12. Billy Joel decides to invest $25,000 in a partnership for a one-sixth capital interest. How much do the partnership's net assets increase? Does Joel also acquire a one-sixth income ratio through this investment?

13. Pia Zadora purchases Ramos's interest in the Morgan–Ramos partnership for $72,000. Assuming that Ramos has a $63,000 capital balance in the partnership, what journal entry is made by the partnership to record this transaction?

14. Won Jang has a $37,000 capital balance in a partnership. She sells her interest to Carla Cardosa for $45,000 cash. What entry is made by the partnership for this transaction?

15. Natalie Cole retires from the partnership of Suarez, Tanks, and Cole. She receives $89,000 of partnership assets in settlement of her capital balance of $77,000. Assuming that the income-sharing ratios are 5:3:2, respectively, how much of Cole's bonus is debited to Tanks' capital account?

16. Your roommate argues that partnership assets should be revalued in situations like those in question 15. Why is this generally not done?

17. How is a deceased partner's equity determined?

18. How does the liquidation of a partnership differ from the dissolution of a partnership?

19. Phil Collins and Herb Alpert are discussing the liquidation of a partnership. Phil maintains that all cash should be distributed to partners on the basis of their income ratios. Is he correct? Explain.

20. In continuing their discussion, Herb says that even in the case of a capital deficiency, all cash should still be distributed on the basis of capital balances. Is Herb correct? Explain.

21. Mike, Larry, and Joan have income ratios of 5:3:2 and capital balances of $34,000, $31,000, and $28,000, respectively. Noncash assets are sold at a gain. After creditors are paid, $119,000 of cash is available for distribution to the partners. How much cash should be paid to Larry?

22. Before the final distribution of cash, account balances are: Cash $25,000; B. Springsteen, Capital $19,000 (Cr.); M. Moss, Capital $12,000 (Cr.); and T. Zaret, Capital $6,000 (Dr.). Zaret is unable to pay any of the capital deficiency. If the income-sharing ratios are 5:3:2, respectively, how much cash should be paid to M. Moss?

BRIEF EXERCISES

Journalize entries in forming a partnership.
(SO 2)

BE13–1 Elton John and Pablo Cruise decide to organize the ALL-Star partnership. Elton John invests $15,000 cash, and Cruise contributes $10,000 cash and equipment having a book value of $3,500. Prepare the entry to record Cruise's investment in the partnership, assuming the equipment has a fair market value of $6,000.

Prepare portion of opening balance sheet for partnership.
(SO 2)

BE13–2 C. Held and G. Kamp decide to merge their proprietorships into a partnership called HeldKamp Company. The balance sheet of Kamp Co. shows:

Accounts receivable	$15,000	
Less: Allowance for doubtful accounts	1,200	$13,800
Equipment	20,000	
Less: Accumulated depreciation	8,000	12,000

The partners agree that the net realizable value of the receivables is $12,500 and that the fair market value of the equipment is $10,000. Indicate how the four accounts should appear in the opening balance sheet of the partnership.

BE13–3 Fleetwood Mac Co. reports net income of $60,000. The income ratios are: Fleetwood 60% and Mac 40%. Indicate the division of net income to each partner and prepare the entry to distribute the net income.

Journalize the division of net income using fixed income ratios.
(SO 3)

BE13–4 MET Co. reports net income of $60,000. Partner salary allowances are M $20,000, E $5,000, and T $5,000. Indicate the division of net income to each partner, assuming the income ratio is 50:30:20, respectively.

Compute division of net income with a salary allowance and fixed ratios.
(SO 3)

BE13–5 Bill&Til Co. reports net income of $20,000. Interest allowances are Bill $6,000 and Til $5,000; salary allowances are Bill $15,000 and Til $10,000; the remainder is shared equally. Show the distribution of income on the income statement.

Show division of net income when allowances exceed net income.
(SO 3)

BE13–6 In ABC Co. capital balances are: Ali $30,000, Babson $25,000, and Curtis $20,000. The partners share income equally. Daniel is admitted to the firm by purchasing one-half of Curtis's interest for $15,000. Journalize the admission of Daniel to the partnership.

Journalize admission by purchase of an interest.
(SO 5)

BE13–7 In the EZ Co., capital balances are Evelynn $40,000 and Zane $30,000. The partners share income equally. Kerns is admitted to the firm with a 40% interest by an investment of cash of $42,000. Journalize the admission of Kerns.

Journalize admission by investment.
(SO 5)

BE13–8 Capital balances in DEB Co. are Ditka $40,000, Elbert $30,000, and Boyd $28,000. Ditka and Elbert each agree to pay Boyd $12,000 from their personal assets. Ditka and Elbert each receive 50% of Boyd's equity. The partners share income equally. Journalize the withdrawal of Boyd.

Journalize withdrawal paid by personal assets.
(SO 6)

BE13–9 Data pertaining to DEB Co. are presented in BE13–8. Instead of payment from personal assets, assume that Boyd receives $32,000 from partnership assets in withdrawing from the firm. Journalize the withdrawal of Boyd.

Journalize withdrawal paid by partnership assets.
(SO 6)

BE13–10 After liquidating noncash assets and paying creditors, account balances in the ARB Co. are Cash $19,000, A Capital (Cr.) $9,000, R Capital (Cr.) $7,000, and B Capital (Cr.) $3,000. The partners share income equally. Journalize the final distribution of cash to the partners.

Journalize final cash distribution in liquidation.
(SO 7)

EXERCISES

E13–1 Kenny Rogers has owned and operated a proprietorship for several years. On January 1, he decides to terminate this business and become a partner in the firm of Payne and Rogers. Rogers's investment in the partnership consists of $15,000 in cash, and the following assets of the proprietorship: accounts receivable $14,000 less allowance for doubtful accounts of $2,000, and equipment $20,000 less accumulated depreciation of $4,000. It is agreed that the allowance for doubtful accounts should be $4,000 for the partnership, and the fair market value of the equipment is $17,000.

Journalize entry for formation of a partnership.
(SO 2)

Instructions
Journalize Rogers's admission to the firm of Payne and Rogers.

E13–2 B. Manilow and W. How have capital balances on January 1 of $50,000 and $40,000, respectively. The partnership income sharing agreement provides for (1) annual salaries of $14,000 for Manilow and $12,000 for How, (2) interest at 10% on beginning capital balances, and (3) remaining income or loss to be shared 70% by Manilow and 30% by How.

Prepare schedule showing distribution of net income and closing entry.
(SO 3)

Instructions
(a) Prepare a schedule showing the distribution of net income, assuming net income is
    (1) $55,000 and (2) $30,000.
(b) Journalize the allocation of net income in each of the situations above.

E13–3 In Led Zeppelin Co., beginning capital balances on January 1, 1999, are Karen Ackers $20,000 and Chris Cross $18,000. During the year, drawings were Ackers $8,000 and Cross $3,000. Net income was $30,000, and the partners share income equally.

Prepare partners' capital statement and partial balance sheet.
(SO 4)

Instructions

(a) Prepare the partners' capital statement for the year.

(b) Prepare the owners' equity section of the balance sheet at December 31, 1999.

Journalize admission of a new partner by purchase of an interest.

(SO 5)

E13–4   T. Halo, K. Rose, and J. Lamp share income on a 5:3:2 basis. They have capital balances of $30,000, $26,000, and $18,000, respectively, when Tony Bennett is admitted to the partnership.

Instructions

Prepare the journal entry to record the admission of Tony Bennett under each of the following assumptions:

1. Purchase of 50% of Halo's equity for $19,000.
2. Purchase of 50% of Rose's equity for $10,000.
3. Purchase of 33⅓% of Lamp's equity for $9,000.

Journalize admission of a new partner by investment.

(SO 5)

E13–5   Joe Keho and Mike McLain share income on a 6:4 basis. They have capital balances of $90,000 and $70,000, respectively, when Linda Ronstadt is admitted to the partnership.

Instructions

Prepare the journal entry to record the admission of Linda Ronstadt under each of the following assumptions:

1. Investment of $100,000 cash for a 25% ownership interest with bonuses to the existing partners.
2. Investment of $36,000 cash for a 25% ownership interest with a bonus to the new partner.

Journalize withdrawal of a partner with payment from partners' personal assets.

(SO 6)

E13–6   Mary Toshiba, Vera Miles, and Debra Noll have capital balances of $50,000, $30,000, and $22,000, respectively, and their income ratios are 5:3:2. Noll withdraws from the partnership under each of the following independent conditions:

1. Toshiba and Miles agree to purchase Noll's equity by paying $15,000 each from their personal assets. Each purchaser receives 50% of Noll's equity.
2. Miles agrees to purchase all of Noll's equity by paying $22,000 cash from her personal assets.
3. Toshiba agrees to purchase all of Noll's equity by paying $26,000 cash from her personal assets.

Instructions

Journalize the withdrawal of Noll under each of the assumptions above.

Journalize withdrawal of a partner with payment from partnership assets.

(SO 6)

E13–7   Dale Nagel, Keith White, and Todd Rundgren have capital balances of $95,000, $75,000, and $60,000, respectively. They share income or loss on a 5:3:2 basis. White withdraws from the partnership under each of the following conditions:

1. White is paid $82,000 in cash from partnership assets, and a bonus is granted to the retiring partner.
2. White is paid $68,000 in cash from partnership assets, and bonuses are granted to the remaining partners.

Instructions

Journalize the withdrawal of White under each of the assumptions above.

Prepare cash distribution schedule.

(SO 7)

E13–8   The Pips Company at December 31 has cash $20,000, noncash assets $100,000, liabilities $55,000, and the following capital balances: Gladys $45,000 and Knight $20,000. The firm is liquidated, and $120,000 in cash is received for the noncash assets. Gladys and Knight income ratios are 60% and 40%, respectively.

Instructions

Prepare a cash distribution schedule.

Journalize transactions in a liquidation.

(SO 7)

E13–9   Data for The Pips partnership are presented in E13–8.

Instructions

Prepare the entries to record (1) the sale of noncash assets, (2) the allocation of the gain or loss on liquidation to the partners, (3) payment of creditors, and (4) distribution of cash to the partners.

Journalize transactions with a capital deficiency.

(SO 7)

E13–10   Prior to the distribution of cash to the partners, the accounts in the MEL Company are: Cash $30,000, M Capital (Cr.) $18,000, E Capital (Cr.) $15,000, and L Capital (Dr.) $3,000. The income ratios are 5:3:2, respectively.

Instructions

(a) Prepare the entry to record (1) L's payment of $3,000 in cash to the partnership and (2) the distribution of cash to the partners with credit balances.

(b) Prepare the entry to record (1) the absorption of L's capital deficiency by the other partners and (2) the distribution of cash to the partners with credit balances.

PROBLEMS: SET A

P13–1A   The post-closing trial balances of two proprietorships on January 1, 1999, are presented below.

Prepare entries for formation of a partnership and a balance sheet.
(SO 2, 4)

	Roberta Company		Flack Company	
	Dr.	**Cr.**	**Dr.**	**Cr.**
Cash	$ 6,500		$ 8,000	
Accounts receivable	15,000		23,000	
Allowance for doubtful accounts		$ 2,500		$ 4,000
Merchandise inventory	28,000		17,000	
Equipment	52,000		30,000	
Accumulated depreciation—equipment		24,000		13,000
Notes payable		20,000		
Accounts payable		25,000		37,000
Roberta, Capital		30,000		
Flack, Capital				24,000
	$101,500	$101,500	$78,000	$78,000

Roberta and Flack decide to form the Roberta Flack Company with the following agreed upon valuations for noncash assets:

	Roberta Company	Flack Company
Accounts receivable	$15,000	$23,000
Allowance for doubtful accounts	3,500	5,000
Merchandise inventory	32,000	21,000
Equipment	31,000	18,000

All cash will be transferred to the partnership, and the partnership will assume all the liabilities of the two proprietorships. Further, it is agreed that Roberta will invest $15,000 in cash, and Flack will invest $5,000 in cash.

Instructions

(a) Prepare separate journal entries to record the transfer of each proprietorship's assets and liabilities to the partnership.

(b) Journalize the additional cash investment by each partner.

(c) Prepare a balance sheet for the partnership on January 1, 1999.

P13–2A   At the end of its first year of operations on December 31, 1999, the LMC Company's accounts show the following:

Journalize divisions of net income and prepare a partners' capital statement.
(SO 3, 4)

Partner	Drawings	Capital
Lois Lang	$12,000	$30,000
Mary Mio	9,000	20,000
Kim Casey	6,000	10,000

The capital balance represents each partner's initial capital investment. Therefore, net income or net loss for 1999 has not been closed to the partners' capital accounts.

Instructions

(a) Journalize the entry to record the division of net income for 1999 under each of the following independent assumptions:

1. Net income is $32,600, and income is shared 5:3:2.   I/s 16,300

2. Net income is $30,000; Lang and Mio are given salary allowances of $13,000 and $8,000, respectively, and the remainder is shared equally.

30,000 − 13,000 − 8000 = 9,000

3. Net income is $25,200; each partner is allowed interest of 10% on beginning capital balances; Lang is given a $15,000 salary allowance; and the remainder is shared equally.

(b) Prepare a schedule showing the division of net income under assumption (3) above.

(c) Prepare a partner's capital statement for the year under assumption (3) above.

Journalize admission of a partner under different assumptions.
(SO 5)

P13–3A At April 30, partners' capital balances in the ELM Company are: A. Eksjo $49,000, C. Ludvika $24,000, and W. Matt $17,000. The income sharing ratios are 3:2:1, respectively. On May 1, the ELMO Company is formed by admitting N. Ortiz to the firm as a partner.

Instructions

(a) Journalize the admission of Ortiz under each of the following independent assumptions:

1. Ortiz purchases 50% of Matt's ownership interest by paying Matt $9,000 in cash.
2. Ortiz purchases 50% of Ludvika's ownership interest by paying Ludvika $16,000 in cash.
3. Ortiz invests $35,000 cash in the partnership for a 40% ownership interest that includes a bonus to the new partner.
4. Ortiz invests $30,000 in the partnership for a 15% ownership interest and bonuses are given to the old partners.

(b) Matt's capital balance is $18,000 after admitting Ortiz to the partnership by investment. If Matt's ownership interest is 15% of total partnership capital, what was Ortiz's cash investment and the total bonus to the old partners?

Journalize withdrawal of a partner under different assumptions.
(SO 6)

P13–4A On December 31, the capital balances and income ratios in the ART Company are as follows:

Partner	Capital Balance	Income Ratio
E. Arhus	$70,000	60%
P. Ross	30,000	30
L. Tower	20,000	10

Instructions

(a) Journalize the withdrawal of Tower under each of the following independent assumptions:

1. Each of the remaining partners agrees to pay $12,000 in cash from personal funds to purchase Tower's ownership equity. Each receives 50% of Tower's equity.
2. Ross agrees to purchase Tower's ownership interest for $18,000 in cash.
3. From partnership assets, Tower is paid $29,000, which includes a bonus to the retiring partner.
4. Tower is paid $17,000 from partnership assets, and bonuses to the remaining partners are recognized.

(b) If Ross's capital balance after Tower's withdrawal is $33,000, what was the total bonus to the remaining partners and the cash paid by the partnership to Tower?

Prepare entries and schedule of cash payments in liquidation of a partnership.
(SO 7)

P13–5A The partners in Inland Lakes Company decide to liquidate the firm when the balance sheet shows the following:

INLAND LAKES COMPANY
Balance Sheet
April 30, 1999

Assets		Liabilities and Owners' Equity	
Cash	$24,000	Notes payable	$14,000
Accounts receivable	18,000	Accounts payable	24,000
Allowance for doubtful accounts	(1,000)	Wages payable	2,000
Merchandise inventory	30,000	T. E. Huron, Capital	24,000
Equipment	17,000	P. A. Erie, Capital	12,800
Accumulated depreciation—equip.	(8,000)	C. R. Lake, Capital	3,200
Total	$80,000	Total	$80,000

The partners share income and loss 5:3:2. During the process of liquidation, the transactions below were completed in the following sequence:

1. A total of $48,000 was received from converting noncash assets into cash.
2. Liabilities were paid in full.
3. Cash was paid to the partners with credit balances.

Instructions

(a) Prepare a cash distribution schedule.
(b) Prepare the entries to record the transactions.
(c) Post to the cash and capital accounts.

PROBLEMS: SET B

P13–1B The post-closing trial balances of two proprietorships on January 1, 1999, are presented below.

Prepare entries for formation of a partnership and a balance sheet.
(SO 2, 4)

	Elvis Company		Costello Company	
	Dr.	Cr.	Dr.	Cr.
Cash	$ 13,000		$16,000	
Accounts receivable	17,500		26,000	
Allowance for doubtful accounts		$ 3,000		$ 4,400
Merchandise inventory	26,500		18,400	
Equipment	45,000		28,000	
Accumulated depreciation—equipment		24,000		12,000
Notes payable		20,000		15,000
Accounts payable		20,000		31,000
Elvis, Capital		35,000		
Costello, Capital				26,000
	$102,000	$102,000	$88,400	$88,400

Elvis and Costello decide to form the Elvis Costello Company with the following agreed upon valuations for noncash assets:

	Elvis Company	Costello Company
Accounts receivable	$17,500	$26,000
Allowance for doubtful accounts	4,500	4,000
Merchandise inventory	30,000	20,000
Equipment	25,000	18,000

All cash will be transferred to the partnership, and the partnership will assume all the liabilities of the two proprietorships. Further, it is agreed that Elvis will invest $20,000 in cash and Costello will invest $9,000 in cash.

Instructions

(a) Prepare separate journal entries to record the transfer of each proprietorship's assets and liabilities to the partnership.
(b) Journalize the additional cash investment by each partner.
(c) Prepare a balance sheet for the partnership on January 1, 1999.

P13–2B At the end of its first year of operations on December 31, 1999, HRZ Company's accounts show the following:

Journalize divisions of net income and prepare a partners' capital statement.
(SO 3, 4)

Partner	Drawings	Capital
Sue Hidalgo	$23,000	$45,000
Tracey Rugen	14,000	30,000
Eileen Zak	10,000	25,000

The capital balance represents each partner's initial capital investment; therefore, net income or net loss for 1999 has not been closed to the partners' capital accounts.

Instructions

(a) Journalize the entry to record the division of net income for the year 1999 under each of the following independent assumptions:

1. Net income is $28,000, and income is shared 6:3:1.
2. Net income is $34,000; Hidalgo and Rugen are given salary allowances of $18,000 and $10,000, respectively; and the remainder is shared equally.
3. Net income is $22,000; each partner is allowed interest of 10% on beginning capital balances; Hidalgo is given a $15,000 salary allowance; and the remainder is shared equally.

(b) Prepare a schedule showing the division of net income under assumption (3) above.
(c) Prepare a partners' capital statement for the year under assumption (3) above.

Journalize admission of a partner under different assumptions.
(SO 5)

P13–3B   At April 30, partners' capital balances in NSW Company are: A. Nolan $62,000, D. Spoda $36,000, and T. Wuhan $12,000. The income sharing ratios are 5:4:1, respectively. On May 1, the NSWO Company is formed by admitting M. Otton to the firm as a partner.

Instructions

(a) Journalize the admission of Otton under each of the following independent assumptions:
1. Otton purchases 50% of Wuhan's ownership interest by paying Wuhan $16,000 in cash.
2. Otton purchases 33⅓% of Spoda's ownership interest by paying Spoda $15,000 in cash.
3. Otton invests $60,000 for a 30% ownership interest, and bonuses are given to the old partners.
4. Otton invests $40,000 for a 32% ownership interest, which includes a bonus to the new partner.

(b) Spoda's capital balance is $30,000 after admitting Otton to the partnership by investment. If Spoda's ownership interest is 20% of total partnership capital, what was Otton's cash investment and the bonus to the new partner?

Journalize withdrawal of a partner under different assumptions.
(SO 6)

P13–4B   On December 31, the capital balances and income ratios in the BAG Company are as follows:

Partner	Capital Balance	Income Ratio
R. Beano	$60,000	50%
D. Alman	40,000	30%
P. Garth	32,000	20%

Instructions

(a) Journalize the withdrawal of Garth under each of the following assumptions:
1. Each of the continuing partners agrees to pay $17,000 in cash from personal funds to purchase Garth's ownership equity. Each receives 50% of Garth's equity.
2. Alman agrees to purchase Garth's ownership interest for $30,000 cash.
3. Garth is paid $38,000 from partnership assets, which includes a bonus to the retiring partner.
4. Garth is paid $28,000 from partnership assets, and bonuses to the remaining partners are recognized.

(b) If Alman's capital balance after Garth's withdrawal is $43,000, what was the total bonus to the remaining partners and the cash paid by the partnership to Garth?

Prepare entries and schedules of cash payments with a capital deficiency in liquidation of a partnership.
(SO 7)

P13–5B   The partners in the JRS Company decide to liquidate the firm when the balance sheet shows the following:

JRS COMPANY
Balance Sheet
May 31, 1999

Assets		Liabilities and Owners' Equity	
Cash	$ 27,500	Notes payable	$ 13,500
Accounts receivable	24,000	Accounts payable	27,000
Allowance for doubtful accounts	(1,000)	Wages payable	3,800
Merchandise inventory	34,500	M. Jagger, Capital	35,000
Equipment	21,000	K. Richards, Capital	20,000
Accumulated depreciation—equipment	(5,500)	R. Simka, Capital	1,200
Total	$100,500	Total	$100,500

The partners share income and loss 5:3:2. During the process of liquidation, the following transactions were completed in the following sequence:

1. A total of $53,000 was received from converting noncash assets into cash.
2. Liabilities were paid in full.
3. Simka paid his capital deficiency.
4. Cash was paid to the partners with credit balances.

Instructions
(a) Prepare the entries to record the transactions.
(b) Post to the cash and capital accounts.
(c) Assume that Simka is unable to pay the capital deficiency.
  1. Prepare the entry to allocate Simka's debit balance to Jagger and Richards.
  2. Prepare the entry to record the final distribution of cash.

BROADENING YOUR PERSPECTIVE

CRITICAL THINKING

GROUP DECISION CASE

BYP13–1 Dan Staffan and Donna Havasi, two professionals in the finance area, have worked for Advanced Leasing for a number of years. Advanced Leasing is a company that leases high-tech medical equipment to hospitals. Dan and Donna have decided that, with their financial expertise, they might start their own company to provide consulting services to individuals interested in leasing equipment. One form of organization they are considering is a partnership.

If they start a partnership, each individual plans to contribute $15,000 in cash. In addition, Dan has a used IBM microcomputer that originally cost $3,800, which he intends to invest in the partnership. The computer has a present market value of $1,800.

Although both Dan and Donna are financial wizards, they do not know a great deal about how a partnership operates. As a result, they have come to you for advice.

Instructions
With the class divided into groups, answer the following:

(a) What are the major disadvantages of starting a partnership?
(b) What type of document is needed for a partnership and what should this document contain?
(c) Both Dan and Donna plan to work full-time in the new partnership. Therefore they believe that net income or net loss should be shared equally. However, they are wondering how they can provide compensation to Dan Staffan for his additional investment of the microcomputer. What would you tell them?
(d) Dan is not sure how the computer equipment should be reported on his tax return. What would you tell him?
(e) As indicated above, Dan and Donna have worked together for a number of years. Dan's skills complement Donna's and vice versa. If one of them dies, it will be very difficult for the other to maintain the business, not to mention the difficulty of paying the deceased partner's estate for his or her partnership interest. What would you advise them to do?

COMMUNICATION ACTIVITY

BYP13–2 You are an expert in the field of forming partnerships. Doug Stahl and Enid Halsingborg want to establish a partnership to start up "Enid's Pasta Shop," and they are going to meet with you to discuss their plans. Prior to the meeting you will send them a memo discussing the issues they need to consider before their visit.

Instructions
Write a memo in good form to be sent to Doug and Enid.

ETHICS CASE

BYP13–3 Susan and Karen operate a beauty salon as partners who share profits and losses equally. The success of their business has exceeded their expectations and is operating quite profitably. Karen is anxious to maximize profits and schedules appointments from 8 a.m. to 6 p.m. daily, even sacrificing some lunch hours to accommodate regular customers. Susan schedules her appointments from 9 a.m. to 5 p.m. and takes long lunch hours. Susan regularly makes significantly larger withdrawals of cash than Karen does. But, she says, "Karen, you needn't worry, I never make a withdrawal without you knowing about it, so it is properly recorded in my drawing account and charged against my capital at the end of the year." Susan's withdrawals to date are double Karen's.

Instructions

(a) Who are the stakeholders in this situation?
(b) Identify the problems with Susan's actions and discuss the ethical considerations of her actions.
(c) How might the partnership agreement be revised to accommodate the differences in Susan's and Karen's work and withdrawal habits?

SURFING THE NET

BYP13–4 This exercise is an introduction to the Big Six Accounting firms.

Addresses:		
	Arthur Andersen	http://www.arthurandersen.com/
	Coopers & Lybrand	http://www.colybrand.com/
	Deloitte & Touche	http://www.dttus.com/
	Ernst & Young	http://www.ey.com/default.htm
	KPMG Peat Marwick	http://www.us.kpmg.com/
	Price Waterhouse	http://www.pw.com/

Steps:

1. Select a firm that is of interest to you.
2. Go to the firm's homepage.

Instructions

Answer the following questions:

(a) Name two services provided by the firm.
(b) What is the firm's total annual revenue?
(c) How many clients does it service?
(d) How many people are employed by the firm?

Answers to Self-Study Questions

1. a   2. b   3. c   4. b   5. c   6. d   7. d   8. d   9. b   10. a

---

Answer to Kellogg Review It Question 2, p. 554

Mutual agency, limited life, unlimited liability, and co-ownership of property are major characteristics of a partnership. As a company becomes very large, it becomes difficult to remain as a partnership because of these factors. Unlimited liability is particularly troublesome because owners may lose not only their initial investment but also their personal assets, if those assets are needed to pay partnership creditors.

 Remember to go back to the Navigator box on the chapter-opening page and check off your completed work.

CONCEPTS FOR REVIEW

Before studying this chapter, you should know or, if necessary, review:

a. The content of the owner's equity section of a balance sheet. (Ch. 4, pp. 160–161)

b. The content of the owner's equity section of the balance sheet for a proprietorship (Ch. 1, pp. 24–25) and for a partnership. (Ch. 13, p. 559)

c. How to prepare closing entries for a proprietorship (Ch. 4, pp. 146–149) and for a partnership. (Ch. 13, pp. 555–556)

FEATURE STORY

"Have You Driven a Ford Lately?"

A company that has produced such renowned successes as the Model T and the Mustang, and such a dismal failure as the Edsel, would have some interesting tales to tell. Henry Ford was a defiant visionary from the day Ford Motor Company was formed in 1903. His goal from day one was to design a car he could mass-produce and sell at a price that was affordable to the masses. In short order he accomplished this goal, and by 1920 60 percent of all vehicles on American roads were Fords.

Henry Ford was intolerant of anything that stood between himself and success. In the early years Ford issued shares to the public in order to finance the company's exponential growth. In 1916 he decided that, to retain funds to finance expansion, the company would skip a dividend payment to its shareholders. The shareholders sued. Henry Ford's re- action was swift and direct: if the shareholders didn't see things his way, he would get rid of them. In 1919 the Ford family purchased 100 percent of the outstanding shares of Ford, eliminating any outside "interference." It was over 35 years before shares were again issued to the public.

Ford Motor Company has continued to evolve over the years while at the same time it sometimes has appeared to become even more like the company Henry Ford originally dreamed of. Today there are nearly a billion shares of publicly traded Ford stock outstanding, and the President and Chief Executive is not a member of the Ford family. However, the Ford family still retains a significant stake in Ford. In a move Henry Ford might have supported, top management recently decided to centralize decision making—that is, to have more key decisions made by top management, rather than by division managers. And, reminiscent of Henry Ford's most famous car, the company is attempting to make a "global car"—a mass-produced car that can be sold around the world with only minor changes.

On the World Wide Web
http://www.ford.com

CHAPTER 14

THE NAVIGATOR ✔

- Understand *Concepts for Review* ☐
- Read *Feature Story* ☐
- Scan *Study Objectives* ☐
- Read *Preview* ☐
- Read text and answer *Before You Go On*
  p. 596 ☐ p. 600 ☐ p. 603 ☐ p. 607 ☐
  p. 614 ☐
- Work *Demonstration Problems* ☐
- Review *Summary of Study Objectives* ☐
- Answer *Self-Study Questions* ☐
- Complete assignments ☐

CORPORATIONS: ORGANIZATION AND CAPITAL STOCK TRANSACTIONS

STUDY OBJECTIVES

After studying this chapter, you should be able to:

1. *Identify and discuss the major characteristics of a corporation.*
2. *Differentiate between paid-in capital and retained earnings.*
3. *Record the issuance of common stock.*
4. *Explain the accounting for treasury stock.*
5. *Differentiate preferred stock from common stock.*
6. *Prepare a stockholders' equity section.*
7. *Compute book value per share.*

THE NAVIGATOR

Corporations like Ford Motor Company have substantial resources. In fact, the corporation is the dominant form of business organization in the United States in terms of dollar volume of sales, earnings, and employees. All of the 500 largest companies in the United States are corporations. In this chapter we will explain the essential features of a corporation and the accounting for a corporation's capital stock transactions. (In Chapter 15 we will look at other issues related to accounting for corporations.) The content and organization of this chapter are as follows:

CORPORATIONS: Organization and Capital Stock Transactions

The Corporate Form of Organization	Accounting for Common Stock Issues	Accounting for Treasury Stock	Preferred Stock	Statement Presentation and Analysis
• Characteristics • Formation • Stockholder rights • Stock issue considerations • Corporate capital	• Issuing par value stock • Issuing no-par stock • Issuing stock for services or noncash assets	• Purchase of treasury stock • Disposal of treasury stock	• Dividend preferences • Liquidation preference • Convertible preferred • Callable preferred	• Illustrations • Book value

THE
NAVIGATOR

THE CORPORATE FORM OF ORGANIZATION

In 1819, Chief Justice John Marshall defined a corporation as "an artificial being, invisible, intangible, and existing only in contemplation of law." This definition has become the foundation for the prevailing legal interpretation that a **corporation** is an **entity separate and distinct from its owners**.

A corporation is created by law, and its continued existence depends upon the corporate statutes of the state in which it is incorporated. As a legal entity, a corporation has most of the rights and privileges of a person. The major exceptions relate to privileges that can be exercised only by a living person, such as the right to vote or to hold public office. Similarly, a corporation is subject to the same duties and responsibilities as a person, e.g., it must abide by the laws and it must pay taxes.

Corporations may be classified in a variety of ways. Two common bases are by purpose and by ownership. A corporation may be organized for the **purpose** of making a **profit**, or it may be **nonprofit**. Corporations for profit include such well-known companies as McDonald's, General Motors, Kellogg, and Apple

Computer. Nonprofit corporations are organized for charitable, medical, and educational purposes and include the Salvation Army, the American Cancer Society, and the Ford Foundation.

Classification by **ownership** distinguishes between publicly held and privately held corporations. A **publicly held corporation** may have thousands of stockholders, and its stock is regularly traded on a national securities market such as the New York Stock Exchange. Most of the largest U.S. corporations are publicly held. Examples of publicly held corporations are International Business Machines, Caterpillar Inc., and General Electric. In contrast, a **privately held corporation**, often referred to as a closely held corporation, usually has only a few stockholders, and does not offer its stock for sale to the general public. Privately held companies are generally much smaller than publicly held companies.

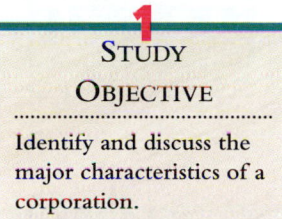

1

STUDY

OBJECTIVE
....
Identify and discuss the major characteristics of a corporation.

Characteristics of a Corporation

A number of characteristics distinguish a corporation from proprietorships and partnerships. The most important of these characteristics are explained below.

Separate Legal Existence

As an entity separate and distinct from its owners, the corporation acts under its own name rather than in the name of its stockholders. A corporation may buy, own, and sell property, borrow money, and enter into legally binding contracts in its own name. It may also sue or be sued, and it pays its own taxes.

In contrast to a partnership, in which the acts of the owners (partners) bind the partnership, the acts of the owners (stockholders) do not bind the corporation unless such owners are duly appointed agents of the corporation. For example, if you owned shares of Ford Motor Company stock, you would not have the right to purchase automobile parts for the company unless you were appointed as an agent of the corporation.

Legal existence separate from owners

Limited Liability of Stockholders

Since a corporation is a separate legal entity, creditors ordinarily have recourse only to corporate assets to satisfy their claims. The liability of stockholders is normally limited to their investment in the corporation, and creditors have no legal claim on the personal assets of the owners unless fraud has occurred. Thus, even in the event of bankruptcy of the corporation, stockholders' losses are generally limited to their capital investment in the corporation.

Limited liability of stockholders

Transferable Ownership Rights

Ownership of a corporation is shown in shares of capital stock, which are transferable units. Stockholders may dispose of part or all of their interest in a corporation simply by selling their stock. In contrast to the transfer of an ownership interest in a partnership, which requires the consent of each owner, the transfer of stock is entirely at the discretion of the stockholder. It does not require the approval of either the corporation or other stockholders. The transfer of ownership rights between stockholders normally has no effect on the operating activities of the corporation or on a corporation's assets, liabilities, and total ownership equity. That is, the enterprise does not participate in the transfer of these ownership rights after it issues the capital stock.

Transferable ownership rights

Ability to Acquire Capital

It generally is relatively easy for a corporation to obtain capital through the issuance of stock. Buying stock in a corporation is often more attractive to an investor than investing in a partnership because a stockholder has limited liability and shares of stock are readily transferable. Moreover, many individuals

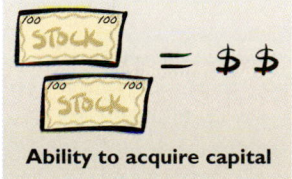

Ability to acquire capital

can become stockholders by investing small amounts of money. In sum, the ability of a successful corporation to obtain capital is virtually unlimited.

Continuous Life

Continuous life

The life of a corporation is stated in its charter; it may be perpetual or it may be limited to a specific number of years. If it is limited, the period of existence can be extended through renewal of the charter. Since a corporation is a separate legal entity, the life of a corporation and its continuance as a going concern are not affected by the withdrawal, death, or incapacity of a stockholder, employee, or officer. As a result, a successful enterprise can have a continuous and perpetual life.

Corporation Management

Although stockholders legally own the corporation, as in Ford Motor Company, they manage the corporation indirectly through a board of directors they elect. The board, in turn, formulates the operating policies for the company and selects officers, such as a president and one or more vice presidents, to execute policy and to perform daily management functions.

A typical organization chart showing the delegation of responsibility is shown in Illustration 14-1. The **president** is the chief executive officer with direct responsibility for managing the business. As the organization chart shows, the president delegates responsibility to other officers. The chief accounting officer is the **controller**. The controller's responsibilities include (1) maintaining the accounting records, (2) maintaining an adequate system of internal control, and (3) preparing financial statements, tax returns, and internal reports. The **treasurer** has custody of the corporation's funds and is responsible for maintaining the company's cash position.

ILLUSTRATION 14-1

Corporation organization chart

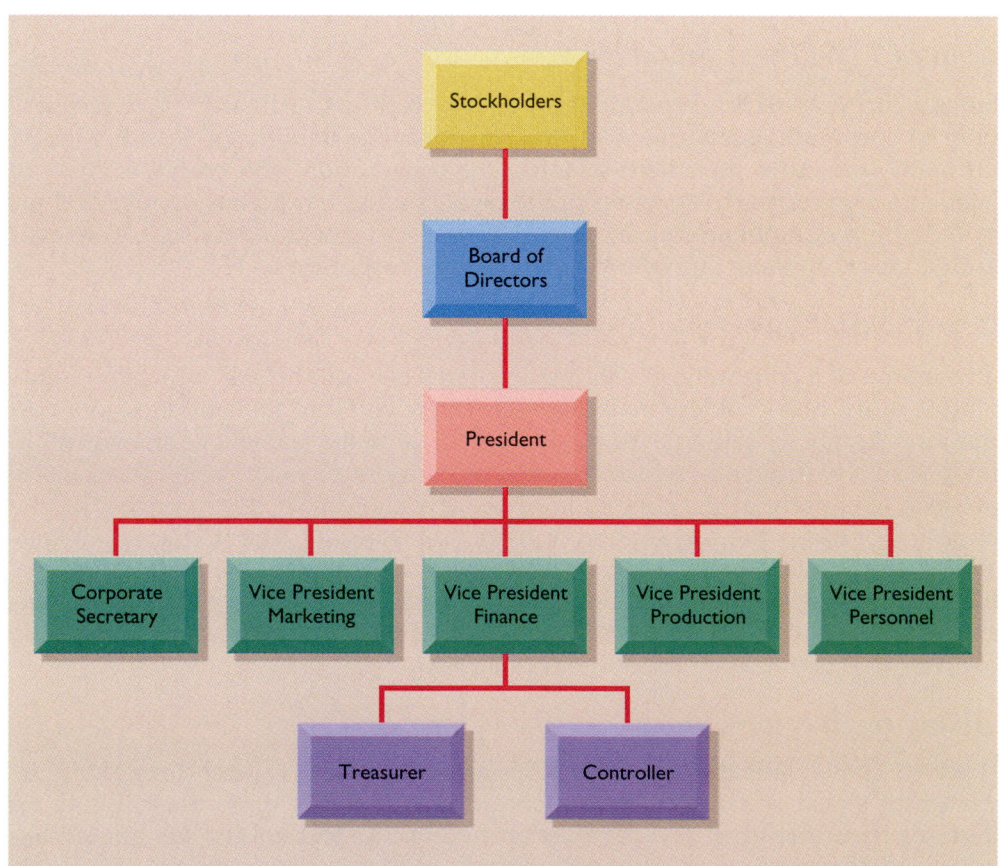

The organizational structure of a corporation enables a company to hire professional managers to run the business. On the other hand, the separation of ownership and management prevents owners from having an active role in managing the company, which some owners like to have.

ACCOUNTING IN ACTION
Business Insight

An interesting question is: Who runs a corporation—the stockholders or the board of directors? This issue has taken on increased importance because stockholders and boards of directors are often on the opposite sides of the fence these days when potential takeovers occur.

A classic example is the unfriendly takeover bid made by Paramount Communication Inc. for Time Inc. Paramount bid up Time's stock price substantially; many stockholders said sell—but Time's board of directors had other plans. They were in the process of trying to make a friendly deal with Warner Communications. Some stockholders said, "Let's vote on what we should do." But Time decided to proceed without a stockholders' vote, even though the board of directors knew the Warner deal would depress Time's stock price. They figured that many stockholders would prefer to accept the Paramount bid. The stockholders sued to overturn the deal with Warner Communications but lost. The judge wrote: "Corporation law does not operate on the theory that directors, in exercising their powers to manage the firm, are obligated to follow the wishes of a majority of stockholders. In fact, the directors, not the stockholders, are charged with the duty to manage the firm."

Government Regulations

A corporation is subject to numerous state and federal regulations. For example, state laws usually prescribe the requirements for issuing stock, the distributions of earnings permitted to stockholders, and the effects of retiring stock, as well as other procedures and restrictions. Similarly, federal securities laws govern the sale of capital stock to the general public. Also, most publicly held corporations are required to make extensive disclosure of their financial affairs to the Securities and Exchange Commission through quarterly and annual reports. In addition, when a corporate stock is listed and traded on organized securities markets, the corporation must comply with the reporting requirements of these exchanges.

Government regulations are designed to protect the owners of the corporation. Unlike the owners of most proprietorships and partnerships, most stockholders do not participate in the day-to-day management of the company.

Goverment regulations

Additional Taxes

Neither proprietorships nor partnerships pay income taxes. The owner's share of these organizations' earnings is reported on his or her personal income tax return. Taxes are then paid by the individual on this amount. Corporations, on the other hand, must pay federal and state income taxes as a separate legal entity. These taxes are substantial: they can amount to as much as 40% of taxable income.

Additional taxes

In addition, stockholders are required to pay taxes on cash dividends, which are pro rata distributions of net income. Thus, many argue that corporate income is **taxed twice (double taxation)**, once at the corporate level, and again at the individual level.

From the foregoing, we can identify the following advantages and disadvantages of a corporation compared to a proprietorship and partnership:

ILLUSTRATION 14-2

Advantages and disadvantages of a corporation

Advantages	Disadvantages
Separate legal existence	Corporation management—separation of
Limited liability of stockholders	ownership and management
Transferable ownership rights	Government regulations
Ability to acquire capital	Additional taxes
Continuous life	
Corporation management—professional	
managers	

Forming a Corporation

The initial step in the formation of a corporation is to file an application with the Secretary of State in the state in which incorporation is desired. The application contains the following types of information: (1) the name, purpose, and duration of the proposed corporation; (2) amounts, kinds, and number of shares of capital stock to be authorized; (3) the address of the corporation's principal office; (4) the names and addresses of the incorporators; and (5) the shares of stock to which each has subscribed.

After the incorporation fee is paid and the application approved, a **charter** is granted. The charter may be an approved copy of the application form or it may be a separate document containing the same basic data. The issuance of the charter, often referred to as the **articles of incorporation**, creates the corporation. Upon receipt of the charter, the corporation develops its by-laws. The **by-laws** establish the internal rules and procedures for conducting the affairs of the corporation and indicate the powers and relationships of the stockholders, directors, and officers of the enterprise.[1]

ACCOUNTING IN ACTION
Business Insight

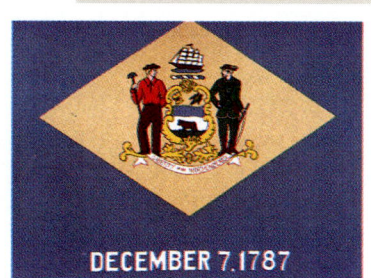

It is not necessary for a corporation to have an office in the state in which it incorporates. In fact, more than 50% of the Fortune 500 corporations are incorporated in Delaware. A primary reason is the Delaware courts' long-standing "business judgment rule." The rule provides that as long as directors exercise "due care" in the interests of stockholders, their actions will not be second-guessed by the courts. The rule has enabled directors to reject hostile takeover offers, even with hefty premiums, or to spurn takeovers simply because they did not want to sell the company. However, new interpretations are emerging. In a recent case, the state court ruled for the company that made a hostile takeover bid. On appeal, the Delaware Supreme Court ruled for the directors but gave the following guideline to the state courts: "Was the board's response reasonable in the light of the threat posed?"

Regardless of the number of states in which a corporation has operating divisions, it is incorporated in only one state. It is to the company's advantage to incorporate in a state whose laws are favorable to the corporate form of business organization. General Motors, for example, is incorporated in Delaware, whereas USX Corp. is a New Jersey corporation. In fact, many corporations choose to incorporate in states with rules favorable to existing management. For example, Gulf Oil changed its state of incorporation to Delaware to thwart possible un-

---

[1]Following approval by two-thirds of the stockholders, the by-laws become binding upon all stockholders, directors, and officers. Legally, a corporation is regulated first by the laws of the state, second by its charter, and third by its by-laws. Care must be exercised to ensure that the provisions of the by-laws are not in conflict with either state laws or the charter.

friendly takeovers. There, certain defensive tactics against takeovers can be approved by the board of directors alone, without a vote by shareholders.

Corporations engaged in interstate commerce must obtain a license from each state in which they do business. The license subjects the corporation's operating activities to the general corporation laws of the state. Costs incurred in the formation of a corporation are called **organization costs**. These costs include fees to underwriters for handling stock and bond issues, legal fees, state incorporation fees, and promotional expenditures involved in the organization of the business.

These organization costs are capitalized by debiting an intangible asset entitled Organization Costs. It may be argued that organization costs have an asset life equal to the life of the corporation. Many companies, however, **amortize these costs** over an arbitrary period of time, up to a maximum of 40 years. Because income tax regulations require the amortization of organization costs over a period of at least five years, some companies prefer to use the same period of amortization for accounting purposes. Determining the amount to be recorded when capital stock is used to pay for organization costs is explained later.

Ownership Rights of Stockholders

When chartered, the corporation may begin selling ownership rights in the form of shares of stock. When a corporation has only one class of stock, it is identified as **common stock**. Each share of common stock gives the stockholder the ownership rights pictured in Illustration 14-3. The ownership rights of a share of stock are stated in the articles of incorporation or in the by-laws.

INTERNATIONAL NOTE

U.S. corporations are identified by *Inc.*, which stands for *incorporated*. In Italy the letters used are *SpA* (Societa per Azioni); in Sweden *AB* (Aktiebolag); in France *SA* (Sociedad Anonima); and in the Netherlands *NV* (Naamloze Vennootschap).

In the United Kingdom public limited corporations are identified by *PLC*, while private corporations are denoted by *LTD*. The parallel designations in Germany are *AG* for public corporations and *GmbH* for private corporations.

Stockholders have the right:

1. To vote in election of board of directors at annual meeting. To vote on actions that require stockholder approval.

2. To share the corporate earnings through receipt of dividends.

3. To keep same percentage ownership when new shares of stock are issued (**preemptive right**[2]).

4. To share in assets upon liquidation, in proportion to their holdings. Called a **residual claim** because owners are paid with assets remaining after all claims have been paid.

ILLUSTRATION 14-3

Ownership rights of stockholders

[2]A number of companies have eliminated the preemptive right, because they believe it makes an unnecessary and cumbersome demand on management. For example, IBM, by stockholder approval, has dropped its preemptive right for stockholders.

ACCOUNTING IN ACTION
International Insight

In Japan, stockholders are considered to be far less important to a corporation than employees, customers, and suppliers. Stockholders are rarely asked to vote on an issue, and the notion of bending corporate policy to favor stockholders borders on the heretical in Japan. This attitude toward stockholders appears to be slowly changing, however, as influential Japanese are advocating listening to investors, raising the extremely low dividends paid by Japanese corporations, and improving disclosure of financial information.

Proof of stock ownership is evidenced by a printed or engraved form known as a **stock certificate**. As shown in Illustration 14-4, the face of the certificate shows the name of the corporation, the stockholder's name, the class and special features of the stock, the number of shares owned, and the signatures of duly authorized corporate officials. Certificates are prenumbered to facilitate their accountability; they may be issued for any quantity of shares.

ILLUSTRATION 14-4

A stock certificate

BEFORE YOU GO ON . . .

Review It

1. What are the advantages and disadvantages of a corporation compared to a proprietorship and a partnership?
2. Identify the principal steps in forming a corporation.
3. What rights are inherent in owning a share of stock in a corporation?

THE NAVIGATOR

Stock Issue Considerations

In considering the issuance (or sale) of stock, a corporation must resolve a number of basic questions: How many shares should be authorized for sale? How should the stock be issued? At what price should the shares be issued? What value should be assigned to the stock? These questions are answered in the following sections.

Authorized Stock

The amount of stock that a corporation is **authorized** to sell is indicated in its charter. The total amount of **authorized stock** at the time of incorporation normally anticipates both initial and subsequent capital needs of a company. As a result, the number of total shares authorized generally exceeds the number of shares initially sold. If all authorized stock is sold, a corporation must obtain consent of the state to amend its charter before it can issue additional shares.

The authorization of capital stock does not result in a formal accounting entry, since the event has no immediate effect on either corporate assets or stockholders' equity. However, disclosure of the number of shares of authorized stock is required in the stockholders' equity section. To determine the number of unissued shares that can be issued without amending the charter, the total shares issued are subtracted from the total authorized. For example, if Advanced Micro was authorized to sell 100,000 shares of common stock and issued 80,000 shares, 20,000 shares would remain unissued.

Issuance of Stock

A corporation has the choice of issuing common stock **directly** to investors or **indirectly** through an investment banking firm (brokerage house) that specializes in bringing securities to the attention of prospective investors. Direct issue is typical in closely held companies, whereas indirect issue is customary for a publicly held corporation.

In an indirect issue, the investment banking firm may agree to **underwrite** the entire stock issue. Under this arrangement, the investment banker buys the stock from the corporation at a stipulated price and resells the shares to investors. The corporation avoids any risk of being unable to sell the shares, and it obtains immediate use of the cash received from the underwriter. The investment banking firm, in turn, assumes the risk of reselling the shares in return for an underwriting fee—the profits expected to be realized from a sales price to the public higher than the price paid to the corporation.[3] For example, Kolff Medical, maker of the Jarvik artificial heart, used an underwriter to help it issue common stock to the public. The underwriter charged a 6.6% underwriting fee on Kolff Medical's approximate $20 million public offering.

How does a corporation set the price for a new issue of stock? Among the factors to be considered are (1) the company's anticipated future earnings, (2) its expected dividend rate per share, (3) its current financial position, (4) the current state of the economy, and (5) the current state of the securities market. The calculation can be complex and is properly the subject of a finance course.

Market Value of Stock

The stock of publicly held companies is traded on organized exchanges at dollar prices per share established by the interaction between buyers and sellers. In general, the prices set by the marketplace tend to follow the trend of a company's earnings and dividends. However, factors beyond a company's control, such as

INTERNATIONAL NOTE

U.S. and U.K. corporations raise most of their capital through millions of outside shareholders and bondholders. In contrast, companies in Germany, France, and Japan acquire financing from large banks or other institutions. Consequently, in the latter environment, shareholders are less important, and external reporting and auditing receive less emphasis.

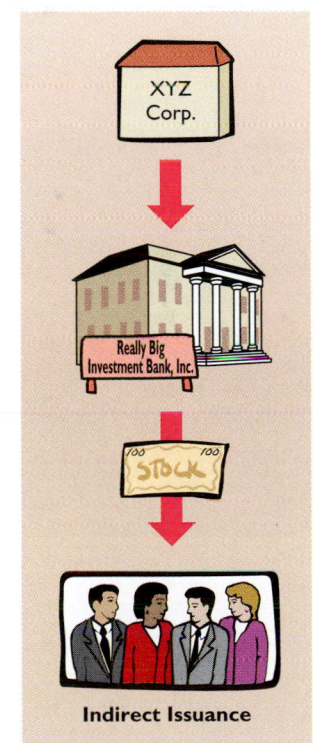

Indirect Issuance

---

[3]Alternatively, the investment banking firm may agree only to enter into a **best efforts** contract with the corporation. In such cases, the banker agrees to sell as many shares as possible at a specified price, and the corporation bears the risk of unsold stock. Under a best efforts arrangement, the banking firm is paid a fee or commission for its services.

the imposition of an oil embargo, changes in interest rates, and the outcome of a presidential election, may cause day-to-day fluctuations in market prices.

The volume of trading on national and international exchanges is heavy. Shares in excess of 600 million are often traded daily on the New York Stock Exchange alone. For each listed security the financial press reports the highs and lows of the stock during the year, the total volume of stock traded for a given day, the high and low price for the day, and the closing market price, with the net change for the day. A recent listing for Kellogg is shown below:

ILLUSTRATION 14-5

Stock market price information

Stock	52 Weeks		Volume	High	Low	Close	Net Change
	High	Low					
Kellogg	50½	34⅞	3303	41¼	40⁹⁄₁₆	41	−⅛

These numbers indicate that Kellogg's high and low market prices for the last 52 weeks have been 50½ and 34⅞; the trading volume was 330,300 shares; the high, low, and closing prices for that date were 41¼, 40⁹⁄₁₆, and 41, respectively; and the net change for the day was a decrease of −⅛, or $.125 per share.

The trading of capital stock on securities exchanges involves the transfer of **already issued shares** from an existing stockholder to another investor. Consequently, these transactions have no impact on a corporation's stockholders' equity section.

TECHNOLOGY IN ACTION

The giant, publicly held corporation could not exist without the organized stock markets, and the stock markets could not exist without massive computerization. Not too many years ago, the NYSE "ticker" would run behind, or trading would even be halted, when sales exceeded 30 million shares or so. Now, with sales sometimes in excess of 600 million shares, the NYSE and its companion exchanges throughout the country operate efficiently with computer technology. Technology has also made possible extended trading hours. An investor in New York, for example, can trade electronically at 3:30 A.M., which is the time in New York when the London Stock Exchange opens. Some predict that 24-hour-trading is not far off.

Par and No-Par Value Stocks

Par value stock is capital stock that has been assigned a value per share in the corporate charter. The par value may be any amount selected by the corporation. Generally, the amount of par value is quite low, because states often levy a tax on the corporation based on par value. For example, International Business Machines has a par of $1.25, Ford Motor Company, $1 par, General Motors Corporation, $1.67, and PepsiCo has 1⅔ cents.

Par value is not indicative of the worth or market value of the stock. As indicated above, IBM has a par value of $1.25, but its recent market price was $120 per share. **The significance of par value is a legal matter.** Par value represents the **legal capital** per share that must be retained in the business for the protection of corporate creditors. That is, it is not available for withdrawal by stockholders. Thus, most states require the corporation to sell its shares at par or above.

No-par value stock is capital stock that has not been assigned a value in the corporate charter. No-par value stock is often issued because some confusion still exists concerning par value and fair market value. If shares have no par value, the questionable treatment of using par value as a basis for fair market value never arises. The major disadvantage of no-par stock is that some states levy a high tax on the shares issued.

No-par value stock is quite common today. For example, Procter & Gamble and North American Van Lines both have no-par stock. In many states the board of directors is permitted to assign a **stated value** to the no-par shares, which becomes the legal capital per share. The stated value of no-par stock may be changed at any time by action of the directors. Stated value, like par value, is not indicative of the market value of the stock. When there is no assigned stated value, the entire proceeds received upon issuance of the stock is considered to be legal capital.

The relationship of par and no-par value to legal capital is shown below.

Stock		Legal Capital per Share
Par value	———————→	Par value
No-par value with stated value	————→	Stated value
No-par value without stated value	——→	Entire proceeds

ILLUSTRATION 14-6

Relationship of par and no-par value stock to legal capital

As will be explained later, a common stock account is credited for the legal capital per share each time stock is issued.

Corporate Capital

Owners' equity is identified as **stockholders' equity, shareholders' equity**, or **corporate capital**. The stockholders' equity section of a corporation's balance sheet consists of: (1) paid-in (contributed) capital, and (2) retained earnings (earned capital). The distinction between paid-in capital and retained earnings is important from both a legal and an economic point of view. Legally, dividends can be declared out of retained earnings in all states, but in many states dividends cannot be declared out of paid-in capital. Economically, management, stockholders, and others look to earnings for the continued existence and growth of the corporation.

2

STUDY OBJECTIVE

···

Differentiate between paid-in capital and retained earnings.

Paid-in Capital

Paid-in capital is the term used to describe the total amount of cash and other assets paid in to the corporation by stockholders in exchange for capital stock. As noted earlier, when a corporation has only one class of stock, it is identified as **common stock**.

Retained Earnings

Retained earnings is net income retained in a corporation. Net income is recorded in Retained Earnings by a closing entry in which Income Summary is debited and Retained Earnings is credited. For example, assuming that net income for Delta Robotics in its first year of operations is $130,000, the closing entry is:

Income Summary	130,000	
Retained Earnings		130,000
(To close income summary and transfer net income to		
retained earnings)		

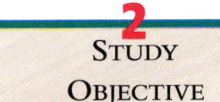

A	=	L	+	SE
				−130,000
				+130,000

If Delta Robotics has a balance of $800,000 in Common Stock at the end of its first year, its stockholders' equity section is as follows:

ILLUSTRATION 14-7

Stockholders' equity section

DELTA ROBOTICS		
Balance Sheet (partial)		
Stockholders' equity		
Paid-in capital		
Common stock	$800,000	
Retained earnings	130,000	
Total stockholders' equity		$930,000

The following illustration compares the owners' equity (stockholders' equity) accounts reported on a balance sheet for a proprietorship, a partnership, and a corporation.

ILLUSTRATION 14-8

Comparison of owners' equity accounts

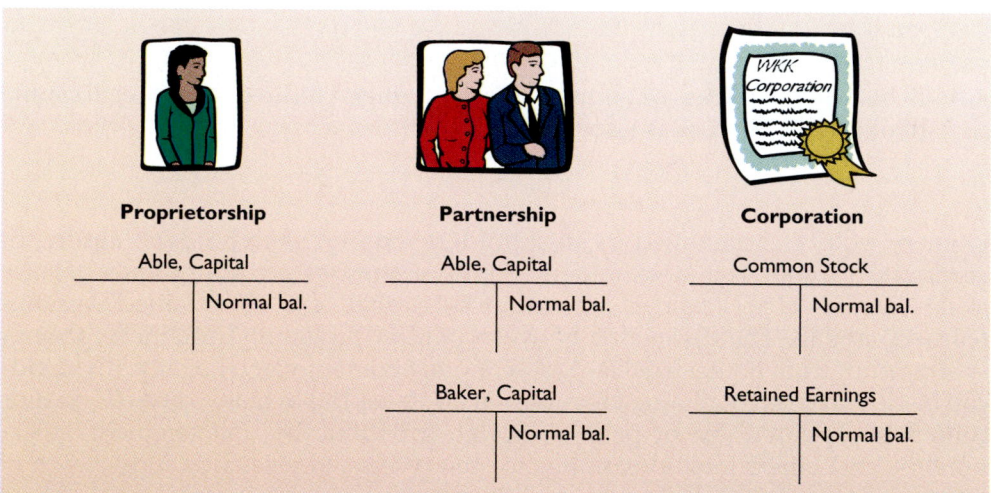

Proprietorship	Partnership	Corporation
Able, Capital	Able, Capital	Common Stock
Normal bal.	Normal bal.	Normal bal.
	Baker, Capital	Retained Earnings
	Normal bal.	Normal bal.

BEFORE YOU GO ON . . .

Review It

1. Of what significance to a corporation is the amount of authorized stock?
2. What alternative approaches may a corporation use in issuing stock?
3. Distinguish between par value and fair market value.

Do It

At the end of its first year of operation, Doral Corporation has $750,000 of common stock and net income of $122,000. Prepare (a) the closing entry for net income and (b) the stockholders' equity section at year-end.

Reasoning: Net income is recorded in Retained Earnings by a closing entry in which Income Summary is debited and Retained Earnings is credited. The stockholders' equity section consists of (1) paid-in capital and (2) retained earnings.

Solution:

(a)	Income Summary	122,000	
	Retained Earnings		122,000
	(To close income summary and transfer net income to retained earnings)		

(b)	Stockholders' equity		
	Paid-in capital		
	Common stock	$750,000	
	Retained earnings	122,000	
	Total stockholders' equity		$872,000

Related exercise material: BE14–2, BE14–8, E14–5, and E14–9.

ACCOUNTING FOR COMMON STOCK ISSUES

3
STUDY
OBJECTIVE
Record the issuance of common stock.

Let's now look at how to account for issues of common stock. The primary objectives in accounting for the issuance of common stock are to (1) identify the specific sources of paid-in capital and (2) maintain the distinction between paid-in capital and retained earnings. As shown below, **the issue of common stock affects only paid-in capital accounts.**

Issuing Par Value Common Stock for Cash

As discussed earlier, par value does not indicate a stock's market value. Therefore, the cash proceeds from issuing par value stock may be equal to, greater than, or less than par value. When the issuance of common stock for cash is recorded, the par value of the shares is credited to Common Stock, and the portion of the proceeds that is above or below par value is recorded in a separate paid-in capital account.

To illustrate, assume that Hydro-Slide, Inc. issues 1,000 shares of $1 par value common stock at par for cash. The entry to record this transaction is:

Cash	1,000	
Common Stock		1,000
(To record issuance of 1,000 shares of $1 par common stock at par)		

A	=	L	+	SE
+1,000				+1,000

If Hydro-Slide, Inc., issues an additional 1,000 shares of the $1 par value common stock for cash at $5 per share, the entry is:

ALTERNATIVE TERMINOLOGY
Paid-in Capital in Excess of Par is also called *Premium on Stock.*

Cash	5,000	
Common Stock		1,000
Paid-in Capital in Excess of Par Value		4,000
(To record issuance of 1,000 shares of common stock in excess of par)		

A	=	L	+	SE
+5,000				+1,000
				+4,000

The total paid-in capital from these two transactions is $6,000, and the legal capital is $2,000. If Hydro-Slide, Inc. has retained earnings of $27,000, the stockholders' equity section is as follows:

ILLUSTRATION 14-9

Stockholders' equity—paid-in capital in excess of par value

HYDRO-SLIDE, INC. Balance Sheet (partial)		
Stockholders' equity		
Paid-in capital		
Common stock	$ 2,000	
Paid-in capital in excess of par value	4,000	
Total paid-in capital	6,000	
Retained earnings	27,000	
Total stockholders' equity	$33,000	

When stock is issued for less than par value, the account Paid-in Capital in Excess of Par Value is debited, if a credit balance exists in this account. If a credit balance does not exist, then the amount less than par is debited to Retained Earnings. This situation occurs only rarely: The sale of common stock below par value is not permitted in most states, because stockholders may be held personally liable for the difference between the price paid upon original sale and par value.

Issuing No-Par Common Stock for Cash

When no-par common stock has a stated value, the entries are similar to those illustrated for par value stock. The stated value represents legal capital and therefore is credited to Common Stock. In addition, when the selling price of no-par stock exceeds stated value, the excess is credited to Paid-in Capital in Excess of Stated Value. For example, assume that instead of $1 par value stock, Hydro-Slide, Inc. has $5 stated value no-par stock and that it issues 5,000 shares at $8 per share for cash. The entry is:

A	=	L	+	SE
+40,000				+25,000
				+15,000

Cash	40,000	
Common Stock		25,000
Paid-in Capital in Excess of Stated Value		15,000
(To record issue of 5,000 shares of $5 stated value no-par stock)		

Paid-in Capital in Excess of Stated Value is reported as part of paid-in capital in the stockholders' equity section.

When no-par stock does not have a stated value, the entire proceeds from the issue become legal capital and are credited to Common Stock. Thus, if Hydro-Slide does not assign a stated value to its no-par stock, the issuance of the 5,000 shares at $8 per share for cash is recorded as follows:

A	=	L	+	SE
+40,000				+40,000

Cash	40,000	
Common Stock		40,000
(To record issue of 5,000 shares of no-par stock)		

The amount of legal capital for Hydro-Slide with a $5 stated value is $25,000; without a stated value, it is $40,000.

Issuing Common Stock for Services or Noncash Assets

Stock may be issued for services (compensation to attorneys, consultants, and others) or for noncash assets (land, buildings, and equipment). In such cases, a question arises as to the cost that should be recognized in the exchange transaction. To comply with the **cost principle** in a noncash transaction, **cost is the cash equivalent price.** Thus, **cost is either the fair market value of the consideration given up or the fair market value of the consideration received,** whichever is more clearly determinable.

To illustrate, assume that the attorneys for The Jordan Company agree to accept 4,000 shares of $1 par value common stock in payment of their bill of $5,000 for services performed in helping the company to incorporate. At the time of the exchange, there is no established market price for the stock. In this case, the market value of the consideration received, $5,000, is more clearly evident. Accordingly, the entry is:

Organization Costs	5,000		
Common Stock		4,000	
Paid-in Capital in Excess of Par Value		1,000	
(To record issuance of 4,000 shares of $1 par value			
stock to attorneys)			

A	=	L	+	SE
+5,000				+4,000
				+1,000

As explained on page 595, organization costs are classified as an intangible asset in the balance sheet.

In contrast, assume that Athletic Research Inc. is a publicly held corporation whose $5 par value stock is actively traded at $8 per share. The company issues 10,000 shares of stock to acquire land recently advertised for sale at $90,000. On the basis of these facts the most clearly evident value is the market price of the consideration given, $80,000. Thus, the transaction is recorded as follows:

Land	80,000		
Common Stock		50,000	
Paid-in Capital in Excess of Par Value		30,000	
(To record issuance of 10,000 shares of $5 par value			
stock for land)			

A	=	L	+	SE
+80,000				+50,000
				+30,000

As illustrated in these examples, **the par value of the stock is never a factor in determining the cost of the assets received.** This is also true of the stated value of no-par stock.

BEFORE YOU GO ON . . .

Review It

1. Explain the accounting for par and no-par common stock issued for cash.
2. Explain the accounting for the issuance of stock for services or noncash assets.
3. What is the par or stated value per share of Kellogg's common stock? How many shares of common stock is Kellogg authorized to issue? How many shares are issued at December 31, 1997? The answers to these questions are provided on page 630.

Do It

Cayman Corporation begins operations on March 1 by issuing 100,000 shares of $10 par value common stock for cash at $12 per share. On March 15, it issues 5,000 shares of common stock to attorneys in settlement of their bill of $50,000 for organization costs. Journalize the issuance of the shares assuming the stock is not publicly traded.

Reasoning: In issuing shares for cash, common stock is credited for par value per share and any additional proceeds are credited to a separate paid-in capital account. When stock is issued for services, the cash equivalent price should be used. In this case, this price is the value of the attorneys' services.

Solution:

Mar. 1	Cash	1,200,000	
	Common Stock		1,000,000
	Paid-in Capital in Excess of Par Value		200,000
	(To record issuance of 100,000 shares at $12 per share)		
Mar. 15	Organization Costs	50,000	
	Common Stock		50,000
	(To record issuance of 5,000 shares for attorneys' fees)		

THE NAVIGATOR

Related exercise material: BE14–3, BE14–4, BE14–5, E14–1, E14–2, E14–3, E14–7, and E14–8.

ACCOUNTING FOR TREASURY STOCK

Treasury stock is a corporation's own stock that has been issued, fully paid for, and reacquired by the corporation but not retired. A corporation may acquire treasury stock for the reasons listed below.

1. Reissue the shares to officers and employees under bonus and stock compensation plans.
2. Increase trading of the company's stock in the securities market in the hopes of enhancing its market value.
3. Have additional shares available for use in the acquisition of other companies.
4. Reduce the number of shares outstanding and thereby increase earnings per share.
5. Rid the company of disgruntled investors, perhaps to avoid a takeover, as illustrated in the Ford Motor Company opening story.

HELPFUL HINT
Treasury stock is so named because the company often holds the shares in its treasury for safekeeping.

Many corporations have treasury stock. For example, one survey of 600 companies in the United States found that 62% have treasury stock.[4] Specifically, Campbell Soup Company recently reported 84 million treasury shares, The Coca-Cola Company 459.5 million, and McDonald's Corporation 135.7 million.

Purchase of Treasury Stock

The cost method is generally used in accounting for treasury stock. This method derives its name from the fact that the Treasury Stock account is maintained at the cost of shares purchased. Under the cost method, **Treasury Stock is debited at the price paid to reacquire the shares, and the same amount is credited to Treasury Stock when the shares are sold.** To illustrate, assume that on January 1, 1999, the stockholders' equity section of Mead, Inc., has 100,000

[4]*Accounting Trends & Techniques 1997* (New York: American Institute of Certified Public Accountants).

ACCOUNTING IN ACTION

Business Insight

Both Nike and Reebok have repurchased many shares in recent years. During 1994 and 1995 Nike repurchased roughly 5 million of its shares—about 10% of those outstanding. Nike's stock price has soared since then. Thus, the stock repurchase worked out well for those investors who kept their shares. With fewer shares outstanding, the surge in Nike's profits dramatically increased the price of the remaining shares.

Reebok, in a bold (and some would say very risky) move in late 1996, brought back nearly a *third* of its shares. This decision was risky because the repurchase of shares dramatically reduced Reebok's available cash. In fact, the company borrowed significant funds to accomplish the repurchase. In a press release, management stated that it was repurchasing the shares because it believed that the stock was severely underpriced. The repurchase of so many shares was meant to signal management's belief in good future earnings. Skeptics, however, suggest that Reebok's management is repurchasing shares to make it less likely that the company will be taken over by a different company (in which case Reebok's top managers would likely lose their jobs). By depleting its cash Reebok is less likely to be acquired because acquiring companies like to purchase companies with large cash reserves so they can pay off debt used in the acquisition.

Reebok stockholders have not profited nearly as much as Nike stockholders did from the repurchase of shares, but that has been due primarily to a decline in Reebok's earnings in 1997.

---

shares of $5 par value common stock outstanding (all issued at par value) and Retained Earnings of $200,000.

The stockholders' equity section before purchase of treasury stock is as follows:

MEAD, INC. Balance Sheet (partial)	
Stockholders' equity	
Paid-in capital	
Common stock, $5 par value, 100,000 shares issued and outstanding	$500,000
Retained earnings	200,000
Total stockholders' equity	$700,000

ILLUSTRATION 14-10

Stockholders' equity with no treasury stock

On February 1, 1999, Mead acquires 4,000 shares of its stock at $8 per share. The entry is:

Feb. 1	Treasury Stock	32,000	
	Cash		32,000
	(To record purchase of 4,000 shares of treasury stock at $8 per share)		

A	=	L	+	SE
−32,000				−32,000

Note that Treasury Stock is debited for the cost of the shares purchased. The original paid-in capital account, Common Stock, is not affected because the number of issued shares does not change. Treasury stock is deducted from total paid-in capital and retained earnings in the stockholders' equity section. Treasury Stock is a contra stockholders' equity account.

HELPFUL HINT
Treasury shares do not have dividend rights or voting rights.

The stockholders' equity section of Mead, Inc., after purchase of treasury stock is as follows:

MEAD, INC. Balance Sheet (partial)	
Stockholders' equity	
Paid-in capital	
Common stock, $5 par value, 100,000 shares issued and 96,000 shares outstanding	$500,000
Retained earnings	200,000
Total paid-in capital and retained earnings	700,000
Less: Treasury stock (4,000 shares)	**32,000**
Total stockholders' equity	$668,000

Thus, the acquisition of treasury stock reduces stockholders' equity.

Both the number of shares issued (100,000) and the number in the treasury (4,000) are disclosed. The difference is the number of shares of stock outstanding (96,000). The term **outstanding stock** means the number of shares of issued stock that are being held by stockholders.

Some maintain that treasury stock should be reported as an asset because it can be sold for cash. Under this reasoning, unissued stock should also be shown as an asset, clearly an erroneous conclusion. Rather than being an asset, treasury stock reduces stockholder claims on corporate assets. This effect is correctly shown by reporting treasury stock as a deduction from total paid-in capital and retained earnings.

Disposal of Treasury Stock

Treasury stock is usually sold or retired. The accounting for its sale is different when treasury stock is sold above cost than when it is sold below cost.

Sale of Treasury Stock above Cost

HELPFUL HINT

Treasury stock transactions are classified as capital stock transactions. As in the case of issuing stock, the income statement is not involved.

If the selling price of the treasury shares is equal to cost, the sale of the shares is recorded by a debit to Cash and a credit to Treasury Stock. When the selling price of the shares is greater than cost, the difference is credited to Paid-in Capital from Treasury Stock. To illustrate, assume that 1,000 shares of treasury stock of Mead, Inc., previously acquired at $8 per share, are sold at $10 per share on July 1. The entry is as follows:

A	=	L	+	SE
+10,000				+8,000
				+2,000

July 1	Cash	10,000	
	Treasury Stock		8,000
	Paid-in Capital from Treasury Stock		2,000
	(To record sale of 1,000 shares of treasury stock above cost)		

The $2,000 credit in the entry is **not** made to Gain on Sale of Treasury Stock for two reasons: (1) Gains on sales occur when assets are sold and treasury stock is not an asset. (2) A corporation does not realize a gain or suffer a loss from stock transactions with its own stockholders. Thus, paid-in capital arising from the sale of treasury stock should not be included in the measurement of net income. Paid-in Capital from Treasury Stock is listed separately on the balance sheet as a part of paid-in capital.

Sale of Treasury Stock below Cost

When treasury stock is sold below its cost, the excess of cost over selling price is usually debited to Paid-in Capital from Treasury Stock. Thus, if Mead, Inc. sells an additional 800 shares of treasury stock on October 1 at $7 per share, the entry is as follows:

Oct. 1	Cash	5,600	
	Paid-in Capital from Treasury Stock	800	
	Treasury Stock		6,400
	(To record sale of 800 shares of treasury		
	stock below cost)		

A	=	L	+	SE
+5,600				− 800
				+6,400

Observe from the two sales entries that (1) Treasury Stock is credited at cost in each entry, (2) Paid-in Capital from Treasury Stock is used for the difference between the cost and resale price of the shares, and (3) the original paid-in capital account, Common Stock, again is not affected. **The sale of treasury stock increases both total assets and total stockholders' equity.**

After posting the foregoing entries, the treasury stock accounts will show the following balances on October 1:

	Treasury Stock				Paid-in Capital from Treasury Stock	
Feb. 1	32,000	July 1	8,000	Oct. 1	800	July 1	2,000
		Oct. 1	6,400				
						Oct. 1 Bal.	1,200
Oct. 1 Bal.	17,600						

ILLUSTRATION 14-12

Treasury stock accounts

When the credit balance in Paid-in Capital from Treasury Stock is eliminated, any additional excess of cost over selling price is debited to Retained Earnings. To illustrate, assume that Mead, Inc., sells its remaining 2,200 shares at $7 per share on December 1. The excess of cost over selling price is $2,200 [2,200 × ($8 − $7)]. In this case, $1,200 of the excess is debited to Paid-in Capital from Treasury Stock, and the remainder is debited to Retained Earnings. The entry is:

Dec. 1	Cash	15,400	
	Paid-in Capital from Treasury Stock	1,200	
	Retained Earnings	1,000	
	Treasury Stock		17,600
	(To record sale of 2,200 shares of treasury		
	stock at $7 per share)		

A	=	L	+	SE
+15,400				− 1,200
				− 1,000
				+17,600

BEFORE YOU GO ON . . .

Review It

1. What is treasury stock, and why do companies acquire it?
2. How is treasury stock recorded?
3. Where is treasury stock reported in the financial statements? Does a company record gains and losses on treasury stock transactions? Explain.
4. How many shares of treasury stock did Kellogg have outstanding at December 31, 1996 and at December 31, 1997? Why the huge difference between 1996 and 1997? The answers to these questions are provided on page 630.

Do It

Santa Anita Inc. purchases 3,000 shares of its $50 par value common stock for $180,000 cash on July 1. The shares are to be held in the treasury until resold. On November 1, the corporation sells 1,000 shares of treasury stock for cash at $70 per share. Journalize the treasury stock transactions.

Reasoning: The purchase of treasury stock is recorded at cost. When treasury stock is sold, the excess of the selling price over cost is credited to Paid-in Capital from Treasury Stock.

Solution:

July 1	Treasury Stock	180,000	
	Cash		180,000
	(To record the purchase of 3,000 shares at $60 per share)		
Nov. 1	Cash	70,000	
	Treasury Stock		60,000
	Paid-in Capital from Treasury Stock		10,000
	(To record the sale of 1,000 shares at $70 per share)		

Related exercise material: BE14–6, E14–2, E14–4, E14–7, and E14–8.

THE
NAVIGATOR

PREFERRED STOCK

To appeal to a larger segment of potential investors, a corporation may issue a class of stock in addition to common stock, called preferred stock. **Preferred stock** has contractual provisions that give it a preference or priority over common stock in certain areas. Typically, preferred stockholders have a priority as to (1) dividends and (2) assets in the event of liquidation. However, they generally do not have voting rights.

Like common stock, preferred stock may be issued for cash or for noncash assets. The entries for these transactions are similar to the entries for common stock. When a corporation has more than one class of stock, each paid-in capital account title should identify the stock to which it relates (e.g., Preferred Stock, Common Stock, Paid-in Capital in Excess of Par Value—Preferred Stock, and Paid-in Capital in Excess of Par Value—Common Stock). Assume that Stine Corporation issues 10,000 shares of $10 par value preferred stock for $12 cash per share. The entry to record the issuance is:

A	= L +	SE
+120,000		+100,000
		+ 20,000

Cash	120,000	
Preferred Stock		100,000
Paid-in Capital in Excess of Par Value—Preferred Stock		20,000
(To record the issuance of 10,000 shares of $10 par value preferred stock)		

Preferred stock may have either a par value or no-par value. For example, Walgreen Drug Co. has $0.50 par value preferred and General Motors has three classes of no-par preferred stock, each with a stated value of $100. In the stockholders' equity section, preferred stock is shown first because of its dividend and liquidation preferences over common stock.

The discussion that follows reflects features associated with the issuance of preferred stock, including dividend preferences, liquidation preferences, convertibility, and callability.

Dividend Preferences

As indicated before, **preferred stockholders have the right to share in the distribution of corporate income before common stockholders.** For example, if the dividend rate on preferred stock is $5 per share, common shareholders will not receive any dividends in the current year until preferred stockholders have received $5 per share. The first claim to dividends does not, however, guarantee dividends. Dividends depend on many factors, such as adequate retained earnings and availability of cash.

The per share dividend amount is stated as a percentage of the par value of preferred stock or as a specified amount. For example, the Crane Company specifies 3¾% dividend on its $100 par value preferred ($100 × 3¾% = $3.75 per share), whereas DuPont has both a $4.50 and a $3.50 series of no-par preferred stock.

I hope there is some money left when it's my turn.

Preferred   Common
stockholders   stockholders

Dividend Preference

Cumulative Dividend

Preferred stock contracts often contain a **cumulative dividend** feature. This right means that preferred stockholders must be paid both current-year dividends and any unpaid prior-year dividends before common stockholders receive dividends. When preferred stock is cumulative, preferred dividends not declared in a given period are called **dividends in arrears**. To illustrate, assume that Scientific-Leasing has 5,000 shares of 7%, $100 par value cumulative preferred stock outstanding. The annual dividend is $35,000 (5,000 × $7 per share). If dividends are 2 years in arrears, preferred stockholders are entitled to receive the following dividends in the current year before any distribution is made to common stockholders:

Dividends in arrears ($35,000 × 2)	$ 70,000
Current-year dividends	35,000
Total preferred dividends	**$105,000**

ILLUSTRATION 14-13

Computation of total dividends to preferred stock

ACCOUNTING IN ACTION
Business Insight

Dividends in arrears can extend for fairly long periods of time. Long Island Lighting Company's directors voted at one time to make up some $390 million in preferred dividends that had been in arrears since 1984 and to resume normal quarterly preferred payments. The announcement resulted from an agreement between the company and New York State to abandon a nuclear power plant in exchange for sizable rate increases over the next 10 years.

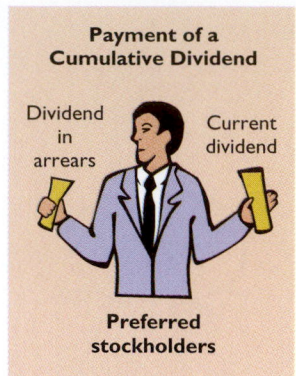

Payment of a Cumulative Dividend

Dividend in arrears

Current dividend

Preferred stockholders

Dividends in arrears are not considered a liability. No obligation exists until a dividend is declared by the board of directors. However, the amount of dividends in arrears should be disclosed in the notes to the financial statements. Doing so enables investors to assess the potential impact of this commitment on the corporation's financial position.

Dividends cannot be paid on common stock while any dividend on preferred stock is in arrears. The cumulative feature is often critical in investor acceptance of a preferred stock issue. When preferred stock is noncumulative, a dividend passed in any year is lost forever. Companies that are unable to meet their dividend obligations are not looked upon favorably by the investment community. As a financial officer noted in discussing one company's failure to pay its cumulative preferred dividend for a period of time, "Not meeting your obligations on something like that is a major black mark on your record." The accounting entries for preferred stock dividends are explained in Chapter 15.

Liquidation Preference

Most preferred stocks have a preference on corporate assets if the corporation fails. This feature provides security for the preferred stockholder. The preference to assets may be for the par value of the shares or for a specified liquidating value. For example, Commonwealth Edison issued preferred stock that entitles the holders to receive $31.80 per share, plus accrued and unpaid dividends, in the event of involuntary liquidation. The liquidation preference is used in litigation pertaining to bankruptcy lawsuits involving the respective claims of creditors and preferred stockholders.

Convertible Preferred Stock

The attractiveness of preferred stock as an investment is enhanced by adding a conversion privilege. **Convertible preferred stock** provides for the exchange of preferred stock into common stock at a specified ratio at the stockholder's option.

Convertible preferred stock is purchased by investors who want the greater security of a preferred stock, but who also desire the added option of conversion if the market value of the common stock increases significantly. To illustrate, assume that Ross Industries issues at par value 1,000 shares of $100 par value convertible preferred stock. One share of preferred is convertible into 10 shares of $5 par value common (current price $9 per share). At this point, it would not be advantageous for the holders of the preferred to convert, because they would exchange preferred stock worth $100,000 (1,000 × $100) for common stock worth $90,000 (10,000 × $9). However, if the price of the common stock were to increase above $10 per share, it usually would be advantageous for the preferred holders to convert.

In recording the conversion, it is customary to transfer the amount paid in on the preferred stock to appropriate common stock accounts. To illustrate, assume that the 1,000 shares of Ross Industries $100 par preferred issued at $105 are converted into 10,000 shares of common stock ($5 par) when the market values per share of the two classes of stock are $101 and $12, respectively. The entry to record the conversion is:

A	=	L	+	SE
				−100,000
				− 5,000
				+ 50,000
				+ 55,000

Preferred Stock	100,000	
Paid-in Capital in Excess of Par Value—Preferred Stock	5,000	
Common Stock		50,000
Paid-in Capital in Excess of Par Value—Common Stock		55,000
(To record conversion of 1,000 shares of preferred stock into 10,000 shares of $5 par value common stock)		

The conversion of preferred stock does not result in either gain or loss to the corporation. If the preferred stock was issued for more than its par value, the paid-in capital in excess of the par value on the preferred stock should be eliminated.

Note that the market values of the shares at the time of the transaction are not considered in recording the transaction. The reason is that the exchange of shares is made directly through the corporation and the corporation has not received any assets equal to fair market value.

Callable Preferred Stock

Many preferred stocks are issued with a call feature. A **callable preferred stock** grants the issuing corporation the right to purchase the stock from stockholders at specified future dates and prices. The call feature offers some flexibility to a corporation by enabling it to eliminate this type of equity security when it is advantageous to do so. The **call (or redemption) price** is frequently slightly above the par or stated value of the shares. When preferred stock is callable, the call price tends to set a ceiling on the market price of the shares. Often shares that are callable are also convertible. Sometimes companies will call their preferred shares to induce investors to convert those preferred shares into common stock.

STATEMENT PRESENTATION AND ANALYSIS

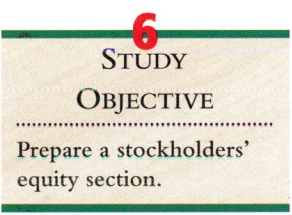

6
STUDY
OBJECTIVE
Prepare a stockholders' equity section.

In the stockholders' equity section of the balance sheet, paid-in capital and retained earnings are reported, and the specific sources of paid-in capital are identified.

Within paid-in capital, two classifications are recognized:

1. **Capital stock**, which consists of preferred and common stock. Preferred stock is shown before common stock because of its preferential rights. Information as to the par value, shares authorized, shares issued, and shares outstanding is reported for each class of stock.

2. **Additional paid-in capital**, which includes the excess of amounts paid in over par or stated value and paid-in capital from treasury stock.

ALTERNATIVE TERMINOLOGY
Paid-in capital is sometimes called *contributed capital*.

Illustrations

The stockholders' equity section of Connally Inc. shown in Illustration 14-14 includes most of the accounts discussed in this chapter. The disclosures pertaining to Connally's common stock indicate that 400,000 shares are issued, 100,000 shares are unissued (500,000 authorized less 400,000 issued), and 390,000 shares are outstanding (400,000 issued less 10,000 shares in treasury).

In published annual reports, subclassifications within the stockholders' equity section are seldom presented. Moreover, the individual sources of additional paid-in capital are often combined and reported as a single amount as shown in Illustration 14-15.

In practice, the term "capital surplus" is sometimes used in place of additional paid-in capital and "earned surplus" in place of retained earnings. The use of the term "surplus" suggests that an excess amount of funds is available. Such is not necessarily the case, which is why **the term surplus should not be employed in accounting**. Unfortunately, a number of financial statements still include these terms.

ILLUSTRATION 14-14

Stockholders' equity section

CONNALLY INC.
Balance Sheet (partial)

Stockholders' equity
  Paid-in capital
    Capital stock

9% preferred stock, $100 par value, callable at $120, cumulative, 10,000 shares authorized, 6,000 shares issued and outstanding		$ 600,000
Common stock, no par, $5 stated value, 500,000 shares authorized, 400,000 shares issued, and 390,000 outstanding		2,000,000
Total capital stock		2,600,000

    Additional paid-in capital

In excess of par value—preferred stock	$ 30,000	
In excess of stated value—common stock	860,000	
From treasury stock	140,000	
Total additional paid-in capital		1,030,000
Total paid-in capital		3,630,000
Retained earnings		1,058,000
Total paid-in capital and retained earnings		4,688,000
Less: Treasury stock—common (10,000 shares) (at cost)		(80,000)
Total stockholders' equity		$4,608,000

ILLUSTRATION 14-15

Published stockholders' equity section

>KR>

KNIGHT-RIDDER INC.
Balance Sheet (partial)
(in millions)

Stockholders' equity	
Preferred stock, $1.00 par value; shares authorized—2,000,000; shares issued—1,754,930	$ 1,755
Common stock, $.02½ par value; shares authorized—250,000,000; shares issued—81,597,631	1,700
Additional paid-in capital	911,572
Retained earnings	636,646
Total stockholders' equity	$1,551,673

Book Value—Another Per Share Amount

7

STUDY OBJECTIVE

Compute book value per share.

You have learned about a number of per share amounts in this chapter. Another per share amount of some importance is **book value per share**. This per share amount represents **the equity a common stockholder has in the net assets of the corporation** from owning one share of stock. Since the net assets of a corporation must be equal to total stockholders' equity, the formula for computing book value per share when a company has only one class of stock outstanding is:

ILLUSTRATION 14-16

Book value per share formula

Thus, if the Marlo Corporation has total stockholders' equity of $1,500,000 (Common Stock $1,000,000 and Retained Earnings $500,000) and 50,000 shares of common stock outstanding, book value per share is $30 ($1,500,000 ÷ 50,000).

When a company has both preferred and common stock, the computation of book value is more complex. Since preferred stockholders have a prior claim on net assets over common stockholders, their equity must be deducted from total stockholders' equity to determine the stockholders' equity that applies to the common stock. The computation of book value per share involves the following steps:

1. Compute the preferred stock equity. This equity is equal to the sum of the call price of preferred stock plus any cumulative dividends in arrears. If the preferred stock does not have a call price, the par value of the stock is used.
2. Determine the common stock equity by subtracting the preferred stock equity from total stockholders' equity.
3. Divide common stock equity by shares of common stock outstanding to determine book value per share.

Illustration

We will use the stockholders' equity section of Connally Inc. shown in Illustration 14-14. Connally's preferred stock is callable at $120 per share and cumulative. Assume that dividends on Connally's preferred stock were in arrears for one year, $54,000 (6,000 × $9). The computation of preferred stock equity is:

Call price (6,000 shares × $120)	$720,000
Dividends in arrears (6,000 shares × $9)	54,000
Preferred stock equity	**$774,000**

ILLUSTRATION 14-17

Computation of preferred stock equity—Step 1

The computation of book value is as follows:

Total stockholders' equity	$4,608,000
Less: Preferred stock equity	774,000
Common stock equity	**$3,834,000**
Shares of common stock outstanding	390,000
Book value per share ($3,834,000 ÷ 390,000)	**$9.83**

ILLUSTRATION 14-18

Computation of book value per share with preferred stock—Steps 2 and 3

The call price of $120 was used instead of the par value of $100. Note also that the paid-in capital in excess of par value of preferred stock, $30,000, **is not assigned to the preferred stock equity**. Preferred stockholders ordinarily do not have a right to amounts paid-in in excess of par value. Accordingly, such amounts are assigned to the common stock equity in computing book value.

Book Value versus Market Value

Book value per share may not equal market value. Book value is based on recorded costs; market value reflects the subjective judgment of thousands of stockholders and prospective investors about a company's potential for future earnings and dividends. Market value per share may exceed book value per share, but that fact does not necessarily mean that the stock is overpriced. The correlation between book value and the annual range of a company's market value per share is often remote, as indicated by the following recent data:

ILLUSTRATION 14-19

Book and market values compared

Company	Book Value (year-end)	Market Range (for year)
Nike, Inc.	$10.63	$47.87–$76.37
Campbell Soup Company	$ 3.10	$32.00–$52.81
Motorola, Inc.	$22.21	$54.00–$90.50
Kellogg Company	$ 2.43	$32.00–$50.38

Book value per share **is** useful in determining the trend of a stockholder's per share equity in a corporation. It is also significant in many contracts and in court cases where the rights of individual parties are based on cost information.

BEFORE YOU GO ON . . .

Review It

1. Identify the classifications within the paid-in capital section and the totals that are stated in the stockholders' equity section of a balance sheet.
2. What is the method for computing book value per share when there is (a) only one class of stock and (b) both preferred and common stock?

A LOOK BACK AT OUR FEATURE STORY

Refer back to the opening story about Ford Motor Company, and answer the following questions.
1. Why did Henry Ford originally choose to form a corporation rather than a sole proprietorship?
2. Why did the Ford Motor Company repurchase all of its shares?
3. What advantages and disadvantages of being organized as a corporation are illustrated by Ford?

Solution:

1. Henry Ford wanted to take full advantage of mass-production. This would require large factories and many employees, which would in turn require considerable funds. The most efficient way to raise these funds was to issue stock.
2. Ford Motor Company initiated a massive treasury stock purchase when Henry Ford's vision was not consistent with the wishes of the shareholders.
3. The history of Ford Motor Company illustrates a number of the strengths and weaknesses of being formed as a corporation. Forming a corporation allowed for more efficient access to funds, and thus more rapid expansion. This was critical because, in the early 1900s, many companies were trying to build cars for the American market. However, by issuing shares, Henry Ford relinquished his control over the firm. This led to a collision in 1916 when the founder believed that it was in the company's best interest to retain funds in the firm rather than to pay dividends. To the extent that outside shareholders are not as well informed as a corporation's managers, the shareholders may force management to do things that hinder the firm's success.

THE
NAVIGATOR

DEMONSTRATION PROBLEM

The Rolman Corporation is authorized to issue 1,000,000 shares of $5 par value common stock. In its first year, the company has the following stock transactions:

Jan. 10   Issued 400,000 shares of stock at $8 per share.

July 1   Issued 100,000 shares of stock for land. The land had an asking price of $900,000. The stock is currently selling on a national exchange at $8.25 per share.

Sept. 1   Purchased 10,000 shares of common stock for the treasury at $9.00 per share.

Dec. 1   Sold 4,000 shares of the treasury stock at $10 per share.

Instructions

(a) Journalize the transactions.
(b) Prepare the stockholders' equity section assuming the company had retained earnings of $200,000 at December 31.

SOLUTION TO DEMONSTRATION PROBLEM

(a) Jan. 10	Cash		3,200,000	
	Common Stock			2,000,000
	Paid-in Capital in Excess of Par Value			1,200,000
	(To record issuance of 400,000 shares of $5 par value stock)			
July 1	Land		825,000	
	Common Stock			500,000
	Paid-in Capital in Excess of Par Value			325,000
	(To record issuance of 100,000 shares of $5 par value stock for land)			
Sept. 1	Treasury Stock		90,000	
	Cash			90,000
	(To record purchase of 10,000 shares of treasury stock at cost)			
Dec. 1	Cash		40,000	
	Treasury Stock			36,000
	Paid-in Capital from Treasury Stock			4,000
	(To record sale of 4,000 shares of treasury stock above cost)			

PROBLEM-SOLVING STRATEGIES

1. When common stock has a par value, Common Stock is always credited for par value.

2. In a noncash transaction, fair market value should be used.

3. The Treasury Stock account is debited and credited at cost.

4. Differences between the cost and selling price of treasury stock are recorded in stockholders' equity accounts, not as gains or losses.

(b)

ROLMAN CORPORATION
Balance Sheet (partial)

Stockholders' equity		
Paid-in capital		
Capital stock		
Common stock, $5 par value, 1,000,000 shares authorized, 500,000 shares issued, 494,000 shares outstanding		$2,500,000
Additional paid-in capital		
In excess of par value	$1,525,000	
From treasury stock	4,000	
Total additional paid-in capital		1,529,000
Total paid-in capital		4,029,000
Retained earnings		200,000
Total paid-in capital and retained earnings		4,229,000
Less: Treasury stock (6,000 shares)		(54,000)
Total stockholders' equity		$4,175,000

THE NAVIGATOR

SUMMARY OF STUDY OBJECTIVES

1. Identify and discuss the major characteristics of a corporation. The major characteristics of a corporation are separate legal existence, limited liability of stockholders, transferable ownership rights, ability to acquire capital, continuous life, corporation management, government regulations, and additional taxes.

2. Differentiate between paid-in capital and retained earnings. Paid-in capital is the total amount paid in on capital stock. It is often referred to as contributed capital. Retained earnings is net income retained in a corporation. It is often referred to as earned capital.

3. Record the issuance of common stock. When the issuance of common stock for cash is recorded, the par value of the shares is credited to Common Stock and the portion of the proceeds that is above or below par value is recorded in a separate paid-in capital account. When no-par common stock has a stated value, the entries are similar to those for par value stock. When no-par does not have a stated value, the entire proceeds from the issue become legal capital and are credited to Common Stock.

4. Explain the accounting for treasury stock. The cost method is generally used in accounting for treasury stock. Under this approach, Treasury Stock is debited at the price paid to reacquire the shares, and the same amount is credited to Treasury Stock when the shares are sold. The difference between the sales price and cost is recorded in stockholders' equity accounts, not in income statement accounts.

5. Differentiate preferred stock from common stock. Preferred stock has contractual provisions that give it priority over common stock in certain areas. Typically, preferred stockholders have a preference as to (1) dividends and (2) assets in the event of liquidation. However, they usually do not have voting rights. In addition, preferred stock may be convertible and/or callable. A convertible preferred stock entitles the holder of the preferred stock to convert those shares to common stock in a specified ratio. The callable feature grants to the issuing corporation the right to purchase the stock from stockholders at specified future dates and prices.

6. Prepare a stockholders' equity section. In the stockholders' equity section, paid-in capital and retained earnings are reported and specific sources of paid-in capital are identified. Within paid-in capital, two classifications are shown: capital stock and additional paid-in capital. If a corporation has treasury stock, the cost of treasury stock is deducted from total paid-in capital and retained earnings to obtain total stockholders' equity.

7. Compute book value per share. Book value per share represents the equity a common stockholder has in the net assets of a corporation from owning one share of stock. When there is only common stock outstanding, the formula for computing book value is: Total Stockholders' Equity ÷ Number of Common Shares Outstanding = Book Value per Share.

THE NAVIGATOR

GLOSSARY

Authorized stock   The amount of stock that a corporation is authorized to sell as indicated in its charter. (p. 597).

Book value per share   The equity a common stockholder has in the net assets of the corporation from owning one share of stock. (p. 612).

By-laws   The internal rules and procedures for conducting the affairs of a corporation. (p. 594).

Callable preferred stock   Preferred stock that grants the issuer the right to purchase the stock from stockholders at specified future dates and prices. (p. 611).

Charter   A document that creates a corporation. (p. 594).

Convertible preferred stock   Preferred stock that provides for the exchange of preferred stock into common stock at a specified ratio at the stockholder's option. (p. 610).

Corporation   A business organized as a legal entity separate and distinct from its owners under state corporation law. (p. 590).

Cumulative dividend   A feature of preferred stock entitling the stockholder to receive current and unpaid prior-year dividends before common stockholders receive any dividends. (p. 609).

Legal capital   The amount per share of stock that must be retained in the business for the protection of corporate creditors. (p. 598).

No-par value stock   Capital stock that has not been assigned a value in the corporate charter. (p. 598).

Organization costs   Costs incurred in the formation of a corporation. (p. 595).

Outstanding stock   Capital stock that has been issued and is being held by stockholders. (p. 606).

Paid-in capital   Total amount of cash and other assets paid in to the corporation by stockholders in exchange for capital stock. (p. 599).

Par value stock   Capital stock that has been assigned a value per share in the corporate charter. (p. 598).

Preferred stock   Capital stock that has contractual preferences over common stock in certain areas. (p. 608).

Privately held corporation   A corporation that has only a few stockholders and whose stock is not available for sale to the general public. (p. 591).

Publicly held corporation   A corporation that may have thousands of stockholders and whose stock is regularly traded on a national securities market. (p. 591).

Retained earnings   Net income retained in the corporation. (p. 599).

Stated value   The amount per share assigned by the board of directors to no-par stock that becomes legal capital per share. (p. 599).

Treasury stock   A corporation's own stock that has been issued, fully paid for, and reacquired by the corporation but not retired. (p. 604).

SELF-STUDY QUESTIONS

Answers are at the end of the chapter.

(SO 1) 1. Which of the following is *not* a major advantage of a corporation?
   a. Separate legal existence.
   b. Continuous life.
   c. Government regulations.
   d. Transferable ownership rights.

(SO 1) 2. A major disadvantage of a corporation is:
   a. limited liability of stockholders.
   b. additional taxes.
   c. transferable ownership rights.
   d. none of the above.

(SO 2) 3. Which of the following statements is *false*?
   a. Ownership of common stock gives the owner a voting right.
   b. The stockholders' equity section begins with paid-in capital.

   c. The authorization of capital stock does not result in a formal accounting entry.
   d. Legal capital per share applies to par value stock but not to no-par value stock.

4. The account, Retained Earnings, is: (SO 2)
   a. a subdivision of paid-in capital.
   b. net income retained in the corporation.
   c. reported as an expense in the income statement.
   d. closed to capital stock.

5. ABC Corporation issues 1,000 shares of $10 par value (SO 3) common stock at $12 per share. In recording the transaction, credits are made to:
   a. Common Stock $10,000 and Paid-in Capital in Excess of Stated Value, $2,000.
   b. Common Stock $12,000.
   c. Common Stock $10,000 and Paid-in Capital in Excess of Par Value $2,000.
   d. Common Stock $10,000 and Retained Earnings $2,000.

(SO 4) 6. XYZ, Inc., sells 100 shares of $5 par value treasury stock at $13 per share. If the cost of acquiring the shares was $10 per share, the entry for the sale should include credits to:

    a. Treasury Stock $1,000 and Paid-in Capital from Treasury Stock $300.

    b. Treasury Stock $500 and Paid-in Capital from Treasury Stock $800.

    c. Treasury Stock $1,000 and Retained Earnings $300.

    d. Treasury Stock $500 and Paid-in Capital in Excess of Par Value $800.

(SO 4) 7. In the stockholders' equity section, the cost of treasury stock is deducted from:

    a. Total paid-in capital and retained earnings.

    b. Retained earnings.

    c. Total stockholders' equity.

    d. Common stock in paid-in capital.

(SO 5) 8. Preferred stock may have priority over common stock *except* in:

    a. dividends.

    b. assets in the event of liquidation.

    c. conversion.

    d. voting.

(SO 6) 9. Which of the following is *not* reported under additional paid-in capital?

    a. Paid-in capital in excess of par value.

    b. Common stock.

    c. Paid-in capital in excess of stated value.

    d. Paid-in capital from treasury stock.

(SO 7) 10. The ledger of JFK, Inc., shows common stock, common treasury stock, and no preferred stock. For this company, the formula for computing book value per share is:

    a. Total paid-in capital and retained earnings divided by the number of shares of common stock issued.

    b. Common stock divided by the number of shares of common stock issued.

    c. Total stockholders' equity divided by the number of shares of common stock outstanding.

    d. Total stockholders' equity divided by the number of shares of common stock issued.

QUESTIONS

1. Vicky Gray, a student, asks your help in understanding the following characteristics of a corporation: (a) separate legal existence, (b) limited liability of stockholders, and (c) transferable ownership rights. Explain these characteristics to Vicky.

2. (a) Your friend Cesar Cedeno cannot understand how the characteristic of corporation management is both an advantage and a disadvantage. Clarify this problem for Cesar.

    (b) Identify and explain two other disadvantages of a corporation.

3. (a) The following terms pertain to the forming of a corporation: (1) charter, (2) by-laws, and (3) organization costs. Explain the terms.

    (b) Jim Henry believes a corporation must be incorporated in the state in which its headquarters office is located. Is Jim correct? Explain.

4. What are the basic ownership rights of common stockholders in the absence of restrictive provisions?

5. (a) What are the two principal components of stockholders' equity?

    (b) What is paid-in capital? Give three examples.

6. How do the financial statements for a corporation differ from the statements for a proprietorship?

7. The corporate charter of Leno Corporation allows the issuance of a maximum of 100,000 shares of common stock. During its first two years of operations, Leno sold 70,000 shares to shareholders and reacquired 7,000 of these shares. After these transactions, how many shares are authorized, issued, and outstanding?

8. Which is the better investment—common stock with a par value of $5 per share or common stock with a par value of $20 per share?

9. What factors help determine the market value of stock?

10. What effect does the issuance of stock at a price above par value have on the issuer's net income? Explain.

11. Why is common stock usually not issued at a price that is less than par value?

12. Land appraised at $80,000 is purchased by issuing 1,000 shares of $20 par value common stock. The market price of the shares at the time of the exchange, based on active trading in the securities market, is $95 per share. Should the land be recorded at $20,000, $80,000, or $95,000? Explain.

13. For what reasons might a company like IBM repurchase some of its stock (treasury stock)?

14. Wilton, Inc., purchases 1,000 shares of its own previously issued $5 par common stock for $12,000. Assuming the shares are held in the treasury, what effect does this transaction have on (a) net income, (b) total assets, (c) total paid-in capital, and (d) total stockholders' equity?

15. The treasury stock purchased in question 14, above, is resold by Wilton Inc., for $14,500. What effect does this transaction have on (a) net income, (b) total assets, (c) total paid-in capital, and (d) total stockholders' equity?

16. (a) What are the principal differences between common stock and preferred stock?
    (b) Preferred stock may be cumulative. Discuss this feature.
    (c) How are dividends in arrears presented in the financial statements?
17. A preferred stockholder exercises her right to convert her convertible preferred stock into common stock. What effect does this have on the corporation's (a) total assets, (b) total liabilities, and (c) total stockholders' equity?
18. What is the formula for computing book value per share when a corporation has only common stock?

19. MCE Inc.'s common stock has a par value of $1, a book value of $29, and a current market value of $15. Explain why these amounts are all different.
20. Indicate how each of the following accounts should be classified in the stockholders' equity section.
    (a) Common stock
    (b) Paid-in capital in excess of par value
    (c) Retained earnings
    (d) Treasury stock
    (e) Paid-in capital from treasury stock
    (f) Paid-in capital in excess of stated value
    (g) Preferred stock

BRIEF EXERCISES

BE14–1 Tammy Barto is studying for her accounting midterm examination. Identify for Tammy the advantages and disadvantages of the corporate form of business organization.

List the advantages and disadvantages of a corporation. (SO 1)

BE14–2 At December 31, Milton Corporation reports net income of $500,000. Prepare the entry to close net income.

Prepare closing entries for a corporation. (SO 2)

BE14–3 On May 10, Alzado Corporation issues 1,000 shares of $10 par value common stock for cash at $15 per share. Journalize the issuance of the stock.

Prepare entries for issuance of par value common stock. (SO 3)

BE14–4 On June 1, Eller Inc. issues 2,000 shares of no-par common stock at a cash price of $6 per share. Journalize the issuance of the shares assuming the stock has a stated value of $1 per share.

Prepare entries for issuance of no-par value common stock. (SO 3)

BE14–5 Stein Inc.'s $10 par value common stock is actively traded at a market value of $15 per share. Stein issues 5,000 shares to purchase land advertised for sale at $80,000. Journalize the issuance of the stock in acquiring the land.

Prepare entries for issuance of stock in a noncash transaction. (SO 3)

BE14–6 On July 1, Ale Corporation purchases 500 shares of its $5 par value common stock for the treasury at a cash price of $8 per share. On September 1, it sells 300 shares of the treasury stock for cash at $10 per share. Journalize the two treasury stock transactions.

Prepare entries for treasury stock transactions. (SO 4)

BE14–7 Omar Inc. issues 5,000 shares of $100 par value preferred stock for cash at $110 per share. Journalize the issuance of the preferred stock.

Prepare entries for issuance of preferred stock. (SO 5)

BE14–8 Brokaw Corporation has the following accounts at December 31: Common Stock, $10 par, 5,000 shares issued, $50,000; Paid-in Capital in Excess of Par Value $10,000; Retained Earnings $39,000; and Treasury Stock—Common, 500 shares, $7,000. Prepare the stockholders' equity section of the balance sheet.

Prepare stockholders' equity section. (SO 6)

BE14–9 The balance sheet for Lott Inc. shows the following: total paid-in capital and retained earnings $860,000, total stockholders' equity $820,000, common stock issued 44,000 shares, and common stock outstanding 40,000 shares. Compute the book value per share.

Compute book value per share. (SO 7)

EXERCISES

E14–1 During its first year of operations, the Levy Corporation had the following transactions pertaining to its common stock.

Journalize issuance of common stock. (SO 3)

Jan. 10   Issued 70,000 shares for cash at $5 per share.
July 1   Issued 30,000 shares for cash at $7 per share.

Instructions
(a) Journalize the transactions, assuming that the common stock has a par value of $5 per share.
(b) Journalize the transactions, assuming that the common stock is no-par with a stated value of $1 per share.

Journalize issuance of common and preferred stock and purchase of treasury stock.
(SO 3, 4, 5)

E14–2 Alomar Co. had the following transactions during the current period:

Mar. 2 Issued 5,000 shares of $1 par value common stock to attorneys in payment of a bill for $25,000 for services rendered in helping the company to incorporate.

June 12 Issued 60,000 shares of $1 par value common stock for cash of $375,000.

July 11 Issued 1,000 shares of $100 par value preferred stock for cash at $108 per share.

Nov. 28 Purchased 2,000 shares of treasury stock for $80,000.

Instructions
Journalize the transactions.

Journalize noncash common stock transactions.
(SO 3)

E14–3 As an auditor for the CPA firm of Barr and Hilo, you encounter the following situations in auditing different clients:

1. The Roth Corporation is a closely held corporation whose stock is not publicly traded. On December 5, the corporation acquired land by issuing 5,000 shares of its $20 par value common stock. The owners' asking price for the land was $120,000, and the fair market value of the land was $115,000.
2. The Weaks Corporation is a publicly held corporation whose common stock is traded on the securities markets. On June 1, it acquired land by issuing 20,000 shares of its $10 par value stock. At the time of the exchange, the land was advertised for sale at $250,000, and the stock was selling at $11 per share.

Instructions
Prepare the journal entries for each of the situations above.

Journalize treasury stock transactions.
(SO 4)

E14–4 On January 1, 1999, the stockholders' equity section of the Mintz Corporation shows: Common stock ($5 par value) $1,500,000; Paid-in capital in excess of par value $1,000,000; and Retained earnings $1,200,000. During the year, the following treasury stock transactions occurred:

Mar. 1 Purchased 50,000 shares for cash at $15 per share.

July 1 Sold 10,000 treasury shares for cash at $16 per share.

Sept. 1 Sold 8,000 treasury shares for cash at $14 per share.

Instructions
(a) Journalize the treasury stock transactions.
(b) Restate the entry for September 1, assuming the treasury shares were sold at $11 per share.

Journalize preferred stock transactions and indicate statement presentation.
(SO 5, 6)

E14–5 Tolan Corporation is authorized to issue both preferred and common stock. The par value of the preferred is $50. During the first year of operations, the company had the following events and transactions pertaining to its preferred stock:

Feb. 1 Issued 30,000 shares for cash at $51 per share.

July 1 Issued 10,000 shares for cash at $57 per share.

Instructions
(a) Journalize the transactions.
(b) Post to the stockholders' equity accounts.
(c) Indicate the statement presentation of the accounts.

Journalize conversion of preferred stock.
(SO 5)

E14–6 Nolte Corporation has 10,000 shares of $100 par value preferred stock outstanding. Each share is convertible into 5 shares of $15 par value common stock. When the market values of the two classes of stock are $110 and $25, respectively, 2,000 shares of preferred stock are converted into common stock.

Instructions
(a) Journalize the conversion of the 2,000 shares.
(b) Repeat (a) assuming that market values at conversion are $105 and $25, respectively.
(c) Repeat (a) assuming each share is convertible into 8 shares of $10 par value common stock.

Prepare correct entries for capital stock transactions.
(SO 3, 4, 5)

E14–7 Fernetti Corporation recently hired a new accountant with extensive experience in accounting for partnerships. Because of the pressure of the new job, the accountant was unable to review what he had learned earlier about corporation accounting. During the first month, the accountant made the following entries for the corporation's capital stock:

May 2	Cash	120,000	
	Capital Stock		120,000
	(Issued 10,000 shares of $5 par value common stock at $12 per share)		
10	Cash	600,000	
	Capital Stock		600,000
	(Issued 10,000 shares of $50 par value preferred stock at $60 per share)		
15	Capital Stock	13,000	
	Cash		13,000
	(Purchased 1,000 shares of common stock for the treasury at $13 per share)		
31	Cash	7,500	
	Capital Stock		2,500
	Gain on Sale of Stock		5,000
	(Sold 500 shares of treasury stock at $15 per share)		

Instructions

On the basis of the explanation for each entry, prepare the entry that should have been made for the capital stock transactions.

E14–8   The stockholders' equity section of Waters Corporation at December 31 is as follows: *Answer questions about stockholders' equity section. (SO 3, 4, 5, 6)*

WATERS CORPORATION
Balance Sheet (partial)

Paid-in capital	
Preferred stock, cumulative, 10,000 shares authorized, 6,000 shares issued and outstanding	$ 600,000
Common stock, no par, 750,000 shares authorized, 600,000 shares issued	1,800,000
Total paid-in capital	2,400,000
Retained earnings	1,158,000
Total paid-in capital and retained earnings	3,558,000
Less: Treasury stock (15,000 common shares)	(64,000)
Total stockholders' equity	$3,494,000

Instructions

▭▭▭▭▭▷   From a review of the stockholders' equity section, as chief accountant, write a memo to the president of the company answering the following questions.

(a) How many shares of common stock are outstanding?
(b) Assuming there is a stated value, what is the stated value of the common stock?
(c) What is the par value of the preferred stock?
(d) If the annual dividend on preferred stock is $36,000, what is the dividend rate on preferred stock?
(e) If dividends of $72,000 were in arrears on preferred stock, what would be the balance reported for Retained Earnings?

E14–9   In a recent year, the stockholders' equity section of the Aluminum Company of America (Alcoa) showed the following (in alphabetical order): Additional (Paid-in) capital $680.5, Common stock $88.3, Preferred stock $66.0, and Retained earnings $3,750.2. All dollar data are in millions.   *Prepare a stockholders' equity section and compute book value. (SO 6, 7)*

The preferred stock has 660,000 shares authorized with a par value of $100 and an annual $3.75 per share cumulative dividend preference. At December 31, all authorized preferred stock is issued and outstanding. There are 300 million shares of $1 par value common stock authorized of which 88.3 million are outstanding at December 31.

Instructions

(a) Prepare the stockholders' equity section, including disclosure of all relevant data.
(b) Compute the book value per share of common stock, assuming there are no preferred dividends in arrears. (Round to two decimals.)

Classify stockholders' equity accounts.
(SO 6)

E14–10 The ledger of Gomez Corporation contains the following accounts: Common Stock, Preferred Stock, Treasury Stock—Common, Paid-in Capital in Excess of Par Value—Preferred Stock, Paid-in Capital in Excess of Stated Value—Common Stock, Paid-in Capital from Treasury Stock, and Retained Earnings.

Instructions
Classify each account using the following tabular alignment:

| | Paid-in Capital | | | |
| | Capital | | Retained | |
Account	Stock	Additional	Earnings	Other

Compute book value per share with preferred stock.
(SO 7)

E14–11 At December 31, Leiter Corporation has total stockholders' equity of $4,000,000. Included in this total are Preferred stock $500,000 and Paid-in capital in excess of par value—Preferred stock $50,000. There are 10,000 shares of $50 par value 10% cumulative preferred stock outstanding. At year-end, 200,000 shares of common stock are outstanding.

Instructions
Compute the book value per share of common stock, under each of the following assumptions:

(a) There are no preferred dividends in arrears, and the preferred stock does not have a call price.
(b) Preferred dividends are one year in arrears, and the preferred stock has a call price of $60 per share.

PROBLEMS: SET A

Journalize stock transactions, post, and prepare paid-in capital section.
(SO 3, 5, 6)

P14–1A Brazil Corporation was organized on January 1, 1999. It is authorized to issue 20,000 shares of 6%, $50 par value preferred stock, and 500,000 shares of no-par common stock with a stated value of $1 per share. The following stock transactions were completed during the first year:

Jan. 10 Issued 100,000 shares of common stock for cash at $3 per share.
Mar. 1 Issued 10,000 shares of preferred stock for cash at $51 per share.
Apr. 1 Issued 25,000 shares of common stock for land. The asking price of the land was $90,000; the company's estimate of fair market value of the land was $85,000.
May 1 Issued 75,000 shares of common stock for cash at $4 per share.
Aug. 1 Issued 10,000 shares of common stock to attorneys in payment of their bill for $50,000 pertaining to services rendered in helping the company organize.
Sept. 1 Issued 5,000 shares of common stock for cash at $6 per share.
Nov. 1 Issued 2,000 shares of preferred stock for cash at $53 per share.

Instructions
(a) Journalize the transactions.
(b) Post to the stockholders' equity accounts. (Use J1 as the posting reference.)
(c) Prepare the paid-in capital section of stockholders' equity at December 31, 1999.

Journalize treasury stock transactions, post, and prepare stockholders' equity section.
(SO 4, 6)

P14–2A Santana Corporation had the following stockholders' equity accounts on January 1, 1999: Common Stock ($1 par) $400,000, Paid-in Capital in Excess of Par Value $500,000, and Retained Earnings $100,000. In 1999, the company had the following treasury stock transactions:

Mar. 1 Purchased 5,000 shares at $7 per share.
June 1 Sold 1,000 shares at $10 per share.
Sept. 1 Sold 2,000 shares at $9 per share.
Dec. 1 Sold 1,000 shares at $6 per share.

Santana Corporation uses the cost method of accounting for treasury stock. In 1999, the company reported net income of $50,000.

Instructions
(a) Journalize the treasury stock transactions, and prepare the closing entry at December 31, 1999, for net income.

(b) Open accounts for (1) Paid-in Capital from Treasury Stock, (2) Treasury Stock, and (3) Retained Earnings. Post to these accounts using J12 as the posting reference.

(c) Prepare the stockholders' equity section for Santana Corporation at December 31, 1999.

P14–3A The stockholders' equity accounts of Chung Corporation on January 1, 1999, were as follows:

Journalize and post transactions, prepare stockholders' equity section, and compute book value.
(SO 2, 3, 4, 5, 6, 7)

Preferred Stock (10%, $100 par noncumulative, 5,000 shares authorized)	$ 300,000
Common Stock ($5 stated value, 300,000 shares authorized)	1,000,000
Paid-in Capital in Excess of Par Value—Preferred Stock	15,000
Paid-in Capital in Excess of Stated Value—Common Stock	400,000
Retained Earnings	488,000
Treasury Stock—Common (5,000 shares)	40,000

During 1999, the corporation had the following transactions and events pertaining to its stockholders' equity:

Feb. 1   Issued 4,000 shares of common stock for $25,000.
Mar. 20   Purchased 1,000 additional shares of common treasury stock at $8 per share.
June 14   Sold 4,000 shares of treasury stock—common for $34,000.
Sept. 3   Issued 2,000 shares of common stock for a patent valued at $13,000.
Dec. 31   Determined that net income for the year was $215,000.

Instructions

(a) Journalize the transactions and the closing entry for net income.

(b) Enter the beginning balances in the accounts and post the journal entries to the stockholders' equity accounts. (Use J1 as the posting reference.)

(c) Prepare a stockholders' equity section at December 31, 1999.

(d) Compute the book value per share of common stock at December 31, 1999, assuming the preferred stock does not have a call price.

P14–4A Jackie Remmers Corporation is authorized to issue 10,000 shares of $100 par value, 10% convertible preferred stock and 200,000 shares of $5 par value common stock. On January 1, 1999, the ledger contained the following stockholders' equity balances:

Journalize and post preferred stock transactions and prepare stockholders' equity section.
(SO 2, 5, 6)

Preferred Stock (4,000 shares)	$400,000
Paid-in Capital in Excess of Par Value—Preferred	40,000
Common Stock (70,000 shares)	350,000
Paid-in Capital in Excess of Par Value—Common	700,000
Retained Earnings	300,000

During 1999, the following transactions occurred:

Feb. 1   Issued 1,000 shares of preferred stock for land having a fair market value of $125,000.

Mar. 1   Issued 1,000 shares of preferred stock for cash at $120 per share.

July 1   Holders of 2,000 shares of preferred stock purchased at $110 per share converted the shares into common stock. Each share of preferred was convertible into 10 shares of common stock. Market values were: preferred stock $122 and common stock $15.

Sept. 1   Issued 400 shares of preferred stock for a patent. The asking price of the patent was $60,000. Market values were: preferred stock $125 and patent, indeterminable.

Dec. 1   Holders of 1,000 shares of preferred stock purchased at $115 per share converted the shares into common stock. Each share of preferred was convertible into 10 shares of common stock. Market values were: preferred stock $125 and common stock $16.

Dec. 31   Net income for the year was $210,000. No dividends were declared.

Prepare stockholders' equity section and compute book value.
(SO 6, 7)

Prepare entries for stock transactions and stockholders' equity section.
(SO 3, 4, 5, 6)

Journalize stock transactions, post, and prepare paid-in capital section.
(SO 3, 5, 6)

Instructions

(a) Journalize the transactions and the closing entry for net income.

(b) Enter the beginning balances in the accounts and post the journal entries to the stock-holders' equity accounts. (Use J2 as the posting reference.)

(c) Prepare a stockholders' equity section at December 31, 1999.

P14–5A   The following stockholders' equity accounts arranged alphabetically are in the ledger of Ireland Corporation at December 31, 1999:

Common Stock ($10 stated value)	$1,500,000
Paid-in Capital from Treasury Stock	6,000
Paid-in Capital in Excess of Stated Value—Common Stock	900,000
Paid-in Capital in Excess of Par Value—Preferred Stock	280,000
Preferred Stock (8%, $100 par, noncumulative)	400,000
Retained Earnings	1,276,000
Treasury Stock—Common (8,000 shares)	88,000

Instructions

(a) Prepare a stockholders' equity section at December 31, 1999.

(b) Compute the book value per share of the common stock, assuming the preferred stock has a call price of $110 per share.

P14–6A   Littell Corporation has been authorized to issue 20,000 shares of $100 par value, 10%, noncumulative preferred stock and 1,000,000 shares of no-par common stock. The cor-poration assigned a $2.50 stated value to the common stock. At December 31, 1999, the ledger contained the following balances pertaining to stockholders' equity:

Preferred Stock	$ 120,000
Paid-in Capital in Excess of Par Value—Preferred	24,000
Common Stock	1,000,000
Paid-in Capital in Excess of Stated Value—Common	2,850,000
Treasury Stock—Common (1,000 shares)	10,000
Paid-in Capital from Treasury Stock	2,000
Retained Earnings	82,000

The preferred stock was issued for land having a fair market value of $144,000. All common stock issued was for cash. In November, 1,500 shares of common stock were purchased for the treasury at a per share cost of $10. In December, 500 shares of treasury stock were sold for $14 per share. No dividends were declared in 1999.

Instructions

(a) Prepare the journal entries for the:

    (1) Issuance of preferred stock for land.

    (2) Issuance of common stock for cash.

    (3) Purchase of common treasury stock for cash.

    (4) Sale of treasury stock for cash.

(b) Prepare the stockholders' equity section at December 31, 1999.

PROBLEMS: SET B

P14–1B   The Wetland Corporation was organized on January 1, 1999. It is authorized to issue 10,000 shares of 8%, $100 par value preferred stock, and 500,000 shares of no-par common stock with a stated value of $2 per share. The following stock transactions were completed during the first year:

Jan. 10   Issued 80,000 shares of common stock for cash at $3 per share.

Mar. 1   Issued 5,000 shares of preferred stock for cash at $104 per share.

Apr. 1   Issued 24,000 shares of common stock for land. The asking price of the land was $90,000; the fair market value of the land was $80,000.

May 1   Issued 80,000 shares of common stock for cash at $4 per share.

Aug. 1   Issued 10,000 shares of common stock to attorneys in payment of their bill of
$50,000 for services rendered in helping the company organize.

Sept. 1   Issued 10,000 shares of common stock for cash at $5 per share.

Nov. 1   Issued 1,000 shares of preferred stock for cash at $108 per share.

Instructions
(a) Journalize the transactions.
(b) Post to the stockholders' equity accounts. (Use J5 as the posting reference.)
(c) Prepare the paid-in capital section of stockholders' equity at December 31, 1999.

P14–2B   Ramos Corporation had the following stockholders' equity accounts on January 1, 1999: Common Stock ($5 par) $500,000, Paid-in Capital in Excess of Par Value $200,000, and Retained Earnings $100,000. In 1999, the company had the following treasury stock transactions: *Journalize treasury stock transactions, post, and prepare stockholders' equity section.* **(SO 4, 6)**

Mar. 1   Purchased 5,000 shares at $8 per share.

June 1   Sold 1,000 shares at $12 per share.

Sept. 1   Sold 2,000 shares at $10 per share.

Dec. 1   Sold 1,000 shares at $7 per share.

Ramos Corporation uses the cost method of accounting for treasury stock. In 1999, the company reported net income of $50,000.

Instructions
(a) Journalize the treasury stock transactions and prepare the closing entry at December 31, 1999, for net income.
(b) Open accounts for (1) Paid-in Capital from Treasury Stock, (2) Treasury Stock, and (3) Retained Earnings. Post to these accounts using J10 as the posting reference.
(c) Prepare the stockholders' equity section for Ramos Corporation at December 31, 1999.

P14–3B   The stockholders' equity accounts of the Capozza Corporation on January 1, 1999, were as follows: *Journalize and post transactions, prepare stockholders' equity section, and compute book value.* **(SO 2, 3, 4, 5, 6, 7)**

Preferred Stock (12%, $50 par cumulative, 10,000 shares authorized)	$ 400,000
Common Stock ($1 stated value, 2,000,000 shares authorized)	1,000,000
Paid-in Capital in Excess of Par Value—Preferred Stock	80,000
Paid-in Capital in Excess of Stated Value—Common Stock	1,400,000
Retained Earnings	1,816,000
Treasury Stock—Common (10,000 shares)	40,000

During 1999, the corporation had the following transactions and events pertaining to its stockholders' equity:

Feb. 1   Issued 20,000 shares of common stock for $100,000.

Apr. 14   Sold 6,000 shares of treasury stock—common for $28,000.

Sept. 3   Issued 5,000 shares of common stock for a patent valued at $25,000.

Nov. 10   Purchased 1,000 shares of common stock for the treasury at a cost of $6,000.

Dec. 31   Determined that net income for the year was $377,000.

The preferred stock has a call price of $55 per share and no dividends were declared during the year.

Instructions
(a) Journalize the transactions and the closing entry for net income.
(b) Enter the beginning balances in the accounts and post the journal entries to the stockholders' equity accounts. (Use J5 for the posting reference.)
(c) Prepare a stockholders' equity section at December 31, 1999, including the disclosure of the preferred dividends in arrears.
(d) Compute the book value per share of common stock at December 31, 1999. (Round to two decimals.)

*Journalize and post preferred
stock transactions and prepare
stockholders' equity section.*
(SO 2, 5, 6)

P14–4B   Shirley Denson Corporation is authorized to issue 10,000 shares of $100 par value, 10% convertible preferred stock and 125,000 shares of $5 par value common stock. On January 1, 1999, the ledger contained the following stockholders' equity balances:

Preferred Stock (5,000 shares)	$500,000
Paid-in Capital in Excess of Par Value—Preferred	50,000
Common Stock (70,000 shares)	350,000
Paid-in Capital in Excess of Par Value—Common	700,000
Retained Earnings	300,000

During 1999, the following transactions occurred:

Feb. 1   Issued 1,000 shares of preferred stock for land having a fair market value of $125,000.

Mar. 1   Issued 1,000 shares of preferred stock for cash at $120 per share.

July 1   Holders of 2,000 shares of preferred stock purchased at $110 per share converted the shares into common stock. Each share of preferred was convertible into 8 shares of common stock. Market values were: preferred stock $122 and common stock $17.

Sept. 1   Issued 400 shares of preferred stock for a patent. The asking price of the patent was $60,000. Market values were: preferred stock $125 and patent indeterminable.

Dec. 1   Holders of 1,000 shares of preferred stock purchased at $120 per share converted the shares into common stock. Each share of preferred was convertible into 8 shares of common stock. Market values were: preferred stock $125 and common stock $16.

Dec. 31   Net income for the year was $260,000. No dividends were declared.

Instructions
   (a) Journalize the transactions and the closing entry for net income.
   (b) Enter the beginning balances in the accounts and post the journal entries to the stockholders' equity accounts. (Use J2 for the posting reference.)
   (c) Prepare a stockholders' equity section at December 31, 1999.

*Prepare stockholders' equity
section and compute book
value.*
(SO 6, 7)

P14–5B   The following stockholders' equity accounts arranged alphabetically are in the ledger of Howitt Corporation at December 31, 1999:

Common Stock ($5 stated value)	$2,500,000
Paid-in Capital from Treasury Stock	10,000
Paid-in Capital in Excess of Stated Value—Common Stock	1,500,000
Paid-in Capital in Excess of Par Value—Preferred Stock	692,000
Preferred Stock (8%, $50 par, noncumulative)	800,000
Retained Earnings	2,448,000
Treasury Stock—Common (10,000 shares)	130,000

Instructions
   (a) Prepare a stockholders' equity section at December 31, 1999.
   (b) Compute the book value per share of the common stock, assuming the preferred stock has a call price of $60 per share.

BROADENING YOUR PERSPECTIVE

FINANCIAL REPORTING AND ANALYSIS
....

FINANCIAL REPORTING PROBLEM: Kellogg Company

BYP14–1   The stockholders' equity section for Kellogg Company is shown in Appendix A. You will also find data relative to this problem on other pages of the appendix.

Instructions
Answer the following questions.

  (a) What is the par or stated value per share of Kellogg's common stock?
  (b) What percentage of Kellogg's authorized common stock was issued at December 31, 1997? (Round to the nearest full percentage.)
  (c) How many shares of common stock were outstanding at December 31, 1997, and at December 31, 1996?
  (d) What was book value per share at December 31, 1997, and at December 31, 1996? (*Note:* The currency translation adjustment is part of stockholders' equity.)
  (e) What was the closing market price per share at December 31, 1997, as reported under Note 12?
  (f) What were the low and high quarterly cash dividends per share during the two-year period 1997 and 1996? What information concerning Kellogg's dividends is reported in the financial highlights section?

COMPARATIVE ANALYSIS PROBLEM: Kellogg Company vs. General Mills

BYP14–2   Kellogg's financial statements are presented in Appendix A; General Mills's financial statements are presented in Appendix B.

Instructions

  (a) Based on the information contained in these financial statements, compute the 1997 book value per share for each company.
  (b) Compare the market value per share for each company to the book value per share at year-end 1997. The market value of General Mills's stock was $64.25 at year-end 1997.
  (c) Why are book value and market value per share different?

RESEARCH ASSIGNMENT

BYP14–3   The September 4, 1995, issue of *Fortune* includes an article by Richard D. Hylton, entitled "Stock Buybacks Are Hot—Here's How You Can Cash In."

Instructions
Read the article and answer the following questions:

  (a) What was the total amount of announced intentions to repurchase shares of stock in 1994? What was this figure during the first six months of 1995?
  (b) The goal of many of these repurchase programs was to increase the price of the remaining outstanding shares. Identify the three factors that will determine the impact of repurchases on share price.
  (c) What did Microsoft do with the shares it repurchased? Why might it use repurchased shares for this purpose rather than issuing new shares?

INTERPRETING FINANCIAL STATEMENTS: Kellogg Company

BYP14–4   In recent years Kellogg Company has taken numerous steps aimed at improving its profitability and earnings per share. Included in these steps was the lay-off of 2,000 employees, roughly 13% of Kellogg's workforce. In addition, in 1995, 1994, and 1993 the company repurchased 5,684,864, 6,194,500, and 9,487,508 of its own shares, and announced plans for significant additional repurchases in the coming year. During 1995, 1994, and 1993 amounts expended for share repurchases were $380 million, $327 million, and $548 million—nearly $1.3 billion over a three-year period. Total amounts expended for new property during this same period was $1.1 billion. Thus the company spent more money repurchasing stock than building the company. Also during this period the company issued $400 million in new debt. Presented below are some basic facts for Kellogg.

(all dollars in millions)	1995	1994
Net sales	$7,003	$6,562
Net income	490	705
Common stock, $.25 par value	78	78
Capital in excess of par value	105	69
Retained earnings	3,963	3,801
Treasury stock, at cost	2,361	1,981
Preferred stock	0	0
Number of shares outstanding (in millions)	217	222

Instructions

(a) What are some of the reasons that management purchases its own stock?
(b) What was the approximate impact on earnings per share of the common stock repurchases during this three-year period? (That is, calculate earnings per share with the share repurchases and without the repurchases for 1995. Use the total repurchases during the three-year period—21,366,872 shares—rounded to 21 million.)

REAL-WORLD FOCUS: Barrister Information Systems Corporation

BYP14–5   **Barrister Information Systems Corp.** develops, assembles, markets, and services computer systems and local area networks for law firms. Headquartered in Buffalo, N.Y., it has offices in 19 U.S. cities. The company has two classes of preferred stock—A and C—in addition to its common stock. The 1,300 shares of Series A preferred stock are nonvoting, have a 12% cumulative dividend, have liquidation preference rights over the Series C preferred stock and the common stock, and are callable by the company at any time for $1,000 per share plus cumulative unpaid dividends. Each share of Series A preferred stock is convertible into 500 shares of common stock. As of March 31, 1993, the cumulative unpaid dividends on the Series A preferred stock totaled $254,000.

Instructions

(a) Should the $254,000 in dividends not paid be reported as a liability on the balance sheet?
(b) If the par value of the Class A preferred stock is $100 per share, what dollar amount in dividends can the shareholders expect annually on the Class A preferred stock?

CRITICAL THINKING

GROUP DECISION CASE

BYP14–6   The stockholders' meeting for McGwire Corporation has been in progress for some time. The chief financial officer for McGwire is presently reviewing the company's financial statements and is explaining the items that comprise the stockholders' equity section of the balance sheet for the current year. The stockholders' equity section of McGwire Corporation at December 31, 1999, is as follows:

McGWIRE CORPORATION
Balance Sheet (partial)
December 31, 1999

Paid-in capital		
Capital stock		
Preferred stock, authorized 1,000,000 shares cumulative, $100 par value, $8 per share, 6,000 shares issued and outstanding		$ 600,000
Common stock, authorized 5,000,000 shares, $1 par value, 3,000,000 shares issued, and 2,700,000 outstanding		3,000,000
Total capital stock		3,600,000
Additional paid-in capital		
In excess of par value-preferred stock	$ 50,000	
In excess of par value-common stock	25,000,000	
Total additional paid-in capital		25,050,000
Total paid-in capital		28,650,000
Retained earnings		900,000
Total paid-in capital and retained earnings		29,550,000
Less: Common treasury stock (300,000 shares)		9,300,000
Total stockholders' equity		$20,250,000

A number of questions regarding the stockholders' equity section of McGwire Corporation's balance sheet have been raised at the meeting.

Instructions

With the class divided into groups, answer the following questions as if you were the chief financial officer for McGwire Corporation.

(a) "What does the cumulative provision related to the preferred stock mean?"

(b) "I thought the common stock was presently selling at $29.75, and yet the company has the stock stated at $1 per share. How can that be?"

(c) "Why is the company buying back its common stock? Furthermore, the treasury stock has a debit balance because it is subtracted from stockholders' equity. Why is treasury stock not reported as an asset if it has a debit balance?"

(d) "Why is it necessary to show additional paid-in capital? Why not just show common stock at the total amount paid in?"

COMMUNICATION ACTIVITY

BYP14–7 Tony Baden, your uncle, is an inventor who has decided to incorporate. Uncle Tony knows that you are an accounting major at U.N.O. In a recent letter to you, he ends with the question, "I'm filling out a state incorporation application; can you tell me the difference in the following terms: (1) authorized stock, (2) issued stock, (3) outstanding stock, (4) preferred stock?"

Instructions

In a brief note, differentiate for Uncle Tony among the four different stock terms. Write the letter to be friendly, yet professional.

ETHICS CASE

BYP14–8 The R & D division of Spencer Chemical Corp. has just developed a chemical for sterilizing the vicious Brazilian "killer bees" which are invading Mexico and the southern states of the United States. The president of Spencer is anxious to get the chemical on the market because Spencer's profits need a boost—his job is in jeopardy because of decreasing sales and profits. Spencer has an opportunity to sell this chemical in Central American countries, where the laws are much more relaxed than in the United States.

The director of Spencer's R & D division strongly recommends further testing in the laboratory for side effects of this chemical on other insects, birds, animals, plants, and even humans. He cautions the president, "We could be sued from all sides if the chemical has tragic side effects that we didn't even test for in the labs." The president answers, "We can't wait an additional year for your lab tests. We can avoid losses from such lawsuits by establishing a separate wholly owned corporation to shield Spencer Corp. from such lawsuits. We can't lose any more than our investment in the new corporation, and we'll invest just the patent covering this chemical. We'll reap the benefits if the chemical works and is safe, and avoid the losses from lawsuits if it's a disaster." The following week Spencer creates a new wholly owned corporation called Zarle Inc., sells the chemical patent to it for $10, and watches the spraying begin.

Instructions

(a) Who are the stakeholders in this situation?
(b) Are the president's motives and actions ethical?
(c) Can Spencer shield itself against losses of Zarle Inc.?

SURFING THE NET

BYP14–9 SEC filings of publicly-traded companies are available to view online.

Address: http://www.yahoo.com/i (or go to the Wiley home page)

Steps:
1. From the Yahoo homepage, choose **Stock Quotes.**
2. Enter stock symbol or use "Symbol Lookup."
3. Choose **Get Quotes.**

Instructions
Answer the following questions:

(a) What company did you select?
(b) What is its stock symbol?
(c) What was the stock's trading range today?
(d) What was the stock's trading range for the year?

Answers to Self-Study Questions
1. c   2. b   3. d   4. b   5. c   6. a   7. a   8. d   9. b   10. c

Answers to Kellogg Review It Question 3, p. 603 and Question 4, p. 607.
3. The par value of Kellogg's common stock is $0.25 per share. Kellogg is authorized to issue 500,000,000 shares of common stock. On December 31, 1997, 414,823,142 shares had been issued.
4. Treasury shares outstanding on December 31, 1996, at Kellogg Company were 101,876,325 and on December 31, 1997, were 4,143,124. The huge decrease was due to the retirement of 105.3 million shares during 1997 as disclosed in the stockholders' equity statement and in Note 1 on Accounting Principles (common stock split).

Remember to go back to the Navigator box on the chapter-opening page and check off your completed work.

Before studying this chapter, you should know or, if necessary, review:

a. Why it is important to distinguish between paid-in capital and retained earnings. (Ch. 14, p. 599)

b. The significance of legal capital in accounting for capital stock transactions. (Ch. 14, p. 598)

c. The form and content of the stockholders' equity section of the balance sheet. (Ch. 14, pp. 611–12)

d. The rights of cumulative preferred stockholders to dividends. (Ch. 14, pp. 609–10)

THE NAVIGATOR

FEATURE STORY

What's Cooking?

What major U.S. corporation got its start 25 years ago with a waffle iron? Hint: It doesn't sell food. Another hint: Swoosh. Another hint: "just do it." That's right, Nike. In 1971 Nike cofounder, Bill Bowerman, put a piece of rubber into a kitchen waffle iron, and the trademark waffle sole was born.

Nike was cofounded by Bowerman and Phil Knight, a member of Bowerman's University of Oregon track team. Each began in the shoe business independently during the early 1960s. Bowerman got his start by making hand-crafted running shoes for his university track team. Knight, after completing graduate school, started a small business importing low-cost, high-quality shoes from Japan. In 1964 the two joined forces, each contributing $500, and formed Blue Ribbon Sports, a partnership. At first they marketed Japanese shoes. It wasn't until 1971 that the company began manufacturing its own line of shoes. With the new shoes came a new corporate name—Nike—the Greek goddess of victory. It is hard to imagine that the com-

pany that now boasts a stable full of world-class athletes as promoters at one time had part-time employees selling shoes out of car trunks at track meets.

By 1980 Nike was sufficiently established that it was able to issue its first stock to the public. In that same year it also created a stock ownership program for its employees, allowing them to share in the company's success. Since then Nike has enjoyed phenomenal growth, with 1997 sales reaching $9.2 billion—fully $2.7 billion over 1996 sales. Its dividend per share to shareholders has increased every year for the last 10 years.

Nike is not alone in its quest for the top of the sport shoe world. Reebok pushes Nike every step of the way. But recently Reebok stumbled. While Reebok shareholders watched their stock price slide, Nike shareholders watched their stock soar. Is the race over? Probably not. The shoe market is fickle, with new styles becoming popular almost daily. Reebok's unwillingness to give up the race was boldly stated in its recent ad campaign: "This is my planet." Whether one of these two giants does eventually take control of the planet remains to be seen. Meanwhile the shareholders sit anxiously in the stands as this Olympic-size drama unfolds.

THE NAVIGATOR

On the World Wide Web
http://www.nike.com
http://www.reebok.com

CHAPTER 15

THE NAVIGATOR ✔

- Understand *Concepts for Review* ☐
- Read *Feature Story* ☐
- Scan *Study Objectives* ☐
- Read *Preview* ☐
- Read text and answer *Before You Go On*
  p. 641 ☐ p. 646 ☐ p. 652 ☐ p. 655 ☐
- Work *Demonstration Problems* ☐
- Review *Summary of Study Objectives* ☐
- Answer *Self-Study Questions* ☐
- Complete assignments ☐

CORPORATIONS: DIVIDENDS, RETAINED EARNINGS, AND INCOME REPORTING

STUDY OBJECTIVES

After studying this chapter, you should be able to:

1. Prepare the entries for cash dividends and stock dividends.
2. Identify the items that are reported in a retained earnings statement.
3. Prepare and analyze a comprehensive stockholders' equity section.
4. Describe the form and content of corporation income statements.
5. Indicate the statement presentation of material items not typical of regular operations.
6. Compute earnings per share.

THE NAVIGATOR

*A*s indicated in the opening story, a corporation like Nike that is profitable often distributes substantial dividends. In addition, it often reinvests a portion of its earnings in the business. This chapter discusses dividends, retained earnings, corporation income statements, and earnings per share. The content and organization of the chapter are as follows:

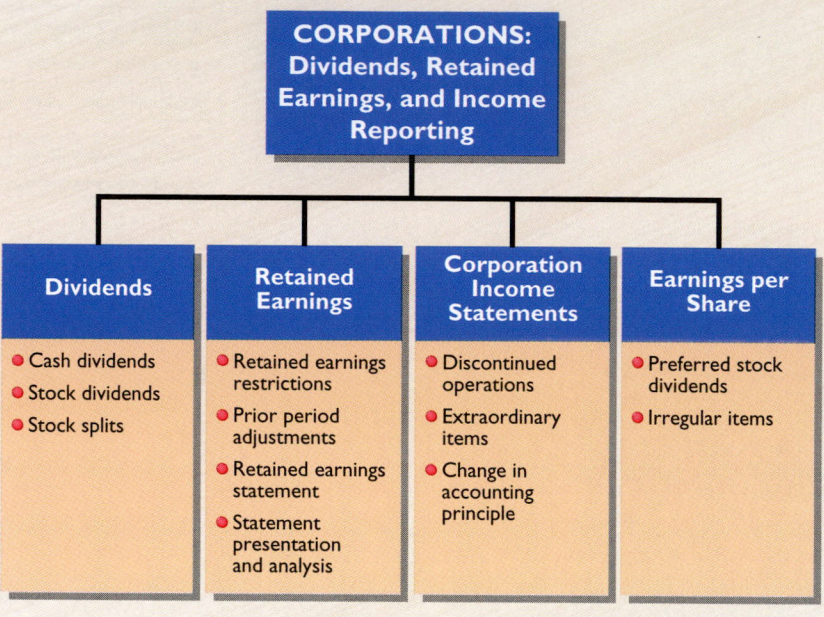

THE NAVIGATOR

DIVIDENDS

A dividend is a distribution by a corporation to its stockholders on a pro rata (proportional) basis. Potential buyers and sellers of a corporation's stock are very interested in a company's dividend policies and practices. Dividends can take four forms: cash, property, scrip (promissory note to pay cash), or (capital) stock. Cash dividends, which predominate in practice, and stock dividends, which are declared with some frequency, will be the focus of discussion in this chapter.

Dividends may be expressed as a percentage of the par or stated value of the stock or as a dollar amount per share. In the financial press, **dividends are generally reported quarterly as a dollar amount per share**. For example, Boeing Company's quarterly dividend rate is 28 cents a share, Ford Motor Company's is 38.5 cents, and Nike's is 9.5 cents.

Cash Dividends

A **cash dividend** is a pro rata distribution of cash to stockholders. For a cash dividend to occur, a corporation must have:

1. **Retained earnings.** The legality of a cash dividend depends on the laws of the state in which the company is incorporated. In general, cash dividends

based on retained earnings are legal, and distributions based on common stock (legal capital) are illegal. Statutory provisions vary considerably with respect to cash dividends based on paid-in capital in excess of par or stated value. Many states permit such dividends. A dividend declared out of paid-in capital is termed a **liquidating dividend**, because the amount originally paid in by stockholders is being reduced or "liquidated."

2. **Adequate cash.** The legality of a dividend does not indicate a company's ability to pay a dividend. For example, a company such as Nike, with a cash balance of $445 million and retained earnings of $2,974 million, could legally declare a dividend of $2,974 million. However, if it attempted to pay the dividend, it would need to raise additional cash through the sale of other assets or through additional financing. It follows that before declaring a cash dividend, the board of directors must carefully consider both current and future demands on the company's cash resources. In some cases, current liabilities may make a cash dividend inappropriate; in other cases, a major plant expansion program may warrant only a relatively small dividend.

3. **Declared dividends.** The board of directors has full authority to determine the amount of income to be distributed in the form of a dividend and the amount to be retained in the business. Dividends do not accrue like interest on a note payable, and they are not a liability until declared.

The amount and timing of a dividend are important issues for management to consider. The payment of a large cash dividend could lead to liquidity problems for the enterprise. Conversely, a small dividend or a missed dividend may cause unhappiness among stockholders who expect to receive a reasonable cash payment from the company on a periodic basis. Many companies declare and pay cash dividends quarterly.

ACCOUNTING IN ACTION
Business Insight

In order to remain in business, companies must honor their interest payments to creditors, bankers, and bondholders. But the payment of dividends to stockholders is another matter. Many companies can survive, even thrive, without such payouts. In fact, managements might consider dividend payments unnecessary, even harmful to the company. Pay your creditors, by all means. But, fork over perfectly good cash to stockholders as dividends? "Why give money to those strangers?" is the response of one company president.

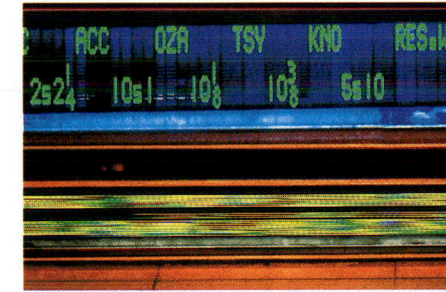

Investors must keep an eye on the company's dividend policy. For most companies, regular boosts in the face of irregular earnings can be a warning signal. So can the refusal of management to lower dividends when earnings fall or capital requirements rise. Companies with high dividends and rising debt may be borrowing money to pay shareholders. For investors who are seeking high returns on their stock investments, low dividends may mean high returns through market appreciation.

Entries for Cash Dividends

Three dates are important in connection with dividends: (1) the declaration date, (2) the record date, and (3) the payment date. Normally, there is a time span of two to four weeks between each date. Accounting entries are required on two of the dates—the declaration date and the payment date.

On the **declaration date**, the board of directors formally declares (authorizes) the cash dividend and announces it to stockholders. The declaration of a cash dividend **commits the corporation to a binding legal obligation** that cannot be rescinded. Thus, an entry is required to recognize the decrease in retained earn-

HELPFUL HINT
What is the effect of the *declaration* of a cash dividend on (1) total stockholders' equity, (2) total liabilities, (3) total assets? Answer: (1) decrease, (2) increase, (3) no effect.

ings and the increase in the liability, Dividends Payable. To illustrate, assume that on December 1, 1999, the directors of Media General declare a 50¢ per share cash dividend on 100,000 shares of $10 par value common stock. The dividend is $50,000 (100,000 × 50¢), and the entry to record the declaration is:

Declaration Date

Dec. 1	Retained Earnings		50,000	
	Dividends Payable			50,000
	(To record declaration of cash dividend)			

A	=	L	+	SE
		+50,000		−50,000

Dividends Payable is a current liability because it will normally be paid within the next several months. Instead of debiting Retained Earnings, the account Dividends may be debited. This account provides additional information in the ledger. For example, a company may have separate dividend accounts for each class of stock. When a dividend account is used, its balance is transferred to Retained Earnings at the end of the year by a closing entry. Consequently, the effect of the declaration is the same: retained earnings is decreased and a current liability is increased. For homework problems, you should use the Retained Earnings account for recording dividend declarations.

The **record date** marks the time when ownership of the outstanding shares is determined for dividend purposes. The stockholders' records maintained by the corporation supply this information. The time interval between the declaration date and the record date enables the corporation to update its stock ownership records. Between the declaration date and record date, the number of shares outstanding should remain the same. Thus, the purpose of the record date is to identify the persons or entities that will receive the dividend, not to determine the amount of the dividend liability. For Media General, the record date is December 22. No entry is required on this date because the corporation's liability recognized on the declaration date is unchanged:

Record Date

Dec. 22				
	No entry necessary			

On the **payment date**, dividend checks are mailed to the stockholders and the payment of the dividend is recorded. Assuming that the payment date is January 20 for Media General, the entry on that date is:

Payment Date

Jan. 20	Dividends Payable		50,000	
	Cash			50,000
	(To record payment of cash dividend)			

A	=	L	+	SE
−50,000		−50,000		

Note that payment of the dividend reduces both current assets and current liabilities but has no effect on stockholders' equity. The cumulative effect of the **declaration and payment** of a cash dividend on a company's financial statements is to **decrease both stockholders' equity and total assets**. Illustration 15-1 summarizes the three important dates associated with dividends.

Allocating Cash Dividends between Preferred and Common Stock

As explained in Chapter 14, preferred stock has priority over common stock in regard to dividends. That is, cash dividends must be paid to preferred stockholders before common stockholders are paid any dividends.

To illustrate, assume that IBR Inc. has 1,000 shares of 8%, $100 par value cumulative preferred stock and 50,000 shares of $10 par value common stock out-

ILLUSTRATION 15-1

Key dividend dates

standing at December 31, 1999. The dividend per share for preferred stock is $8 ($100 par value × 8%), and the required annual dividend for preferred stock is $8,000 (1,000 × $8). At December 31, 1999, the directors declare a $6,000 cash dividend. In this case, the entire dividend amount goes to preferred stockholders because of their dividend preference. The entry to record the declaration of the dividend is:

Dec. 31	Retained Earnings	6,000	
	Dividends Payable		6,000
	(To record $6 per share cash dividend to preferred stockholders)		

A	=	L	+	SE
		+6,000		−6,000

Because of the cumulative feature, dividends of $2 per share are in arrears on preferred stock for 1999. These dividends must be paid to preferred stockholders before any future dividends can be paid to common stockholders. As explained in Chapter 14, dividends in arrears should be disclosed in the financial statements.

At December 31, 2000, IBR declares a $50,000 cash dividend. The allocation of the dividend to the two classes of stock is as follows:

Total dividend		$50,000
Allocated to preferred stock		
Dividends in arrears, 1999 (1,000 × $2)	$2,000	
2000 dividend (1,000 × $8)	8,000	10,000
Remainder allocated to common stock		$40,000

ILLUSTRATION 15-2

Allocating dividends to preferred and common stock

The entry to record the declaration of the dividend is:

Dec. 31	Retained Earnings	50,000	
	Dividends Payable		50,000
	(To record declaration of cash dividends of $10,000 to preferred stock and $40,000 to common stock)		

A	=	L	+	SE
		+50,000		−50,000

If the preferred stock were not cumulative, preferred stockholders would have received only $8,000 in dividends in 2000, and common stockholders would have received $42,000.

Stock Dividends

A **stock dividend** is a pro rata distribution of the corporation's own stock to stockholders. Whereas a cash dividend is paid in cash, a stock dividend is paid in stock. **A stock dividend results in a decrease in retained earnings and an increase in paid-in capital.** Unlike a cash dividend, a stock dividend does not decrease total stockholders' equity or total assets.

To illustrate a stock dividend, assume that you have a 2% ownership interest in Cetus Inc. by virtue of owning 20 of its 1,000 shares of common stock. In a 10% stock dividend, 100 shares (1,000 × 10%) of stock would be issued. You would receive two shares (2% × 100), but your ownership interest would remain at 2% (22 ÷ 1,100). **You now own more shares of stock but your ownership interest has not changed.** Moreover, no cash is disbursed, and no liabilities have been assumed by the corporation. Illustration 15-3 shows the effect of a stock dividend.

ILLUSTRATION 15-3

Effect of stock dividend

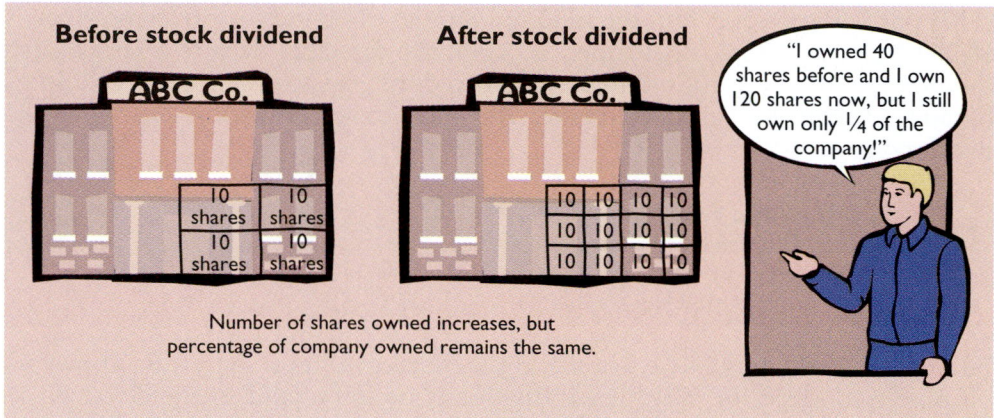

Number of shares owned increases, but percentage of company owned remains the same.

What then are the purposes and benefits of a stock dividend? Corporations issue stock dividends generally for one or more of the following reasons:

1. To satisfy stockholders' dividend expectations without spending cash.
2. To increase the marketability of its stock by increasing the number of shares outstanding and thereby decreasing the market price per share. Decreasing the market price of the stock makes it easier for smaller investors to purchase the shares.
3. To emphasize that a portion of stockholders' equity has been permanently reinvested in the business and therefore is unavailable for cash dividends.

The size of the stock dividend and the value to be assigned to each dividend share are determined by the board of directors when the dividend is declared. The per share amount must be at least equal to the par or stated value in order to meet legal requirements.

The accounting profession distinguishes between a **small stock dividend** (less than 20–25% of the corporation's issued stock) and a **large stock dividend** (greater than 20–25%). It recommends that the directors assign the **fair market value per share** for small stock dividends. The recommendation is based on the assumption that a small stock dividend will have little effect on the market price of the shares previously outstanding. Thus, many stockholders consider small stock dividends to be distributions of earnings equal to the fair market value of the shares distributed. The amount to be assigned for a large stock dividend is not specified by the accounting profession. However, **par or stated value per share** is normally assigned. Small stock dividends predominate in practice. Thus, we will illustrate only the entries for small stock dividends.

Entries for Stock Dividends

To illustrate the accounting for stock dividends, assume that Medland Corporation has a balance of $300,000 in retained earnings and declares a 10% stock dividend on its 50,000 shares of $10 par value common stock. The current fair market value of its stock is $15 per share. The number of shares to be issued is 5,000 (10% × 50,000) and the total amount to be debited to Retained Earnings is $75,000 (5,000 × $15). The entry to record this transaction at the declaration date is as follows:

Retained Earnings	75,000		A	=	L	+	SE
Common Stock Dividends Distributable		50,000					−75,000
Paid-in Capital in Excess of Par Value		25,000					+50,000
(To record declaration of 10% stock dividend)							+25,000

Note that Retained Earnings is debited for the fair market value of the stock issued; Common Stock Dividends Distributable is credited for the par value of the dividend shares (5,000 × $10); and the excess over par (5,000 × $5) is credited to an additional paid-in capital account.

Common Stock Dividends Distributable is a stockholders' equity account; it is not a liability because assets will not be used to pay the dividend. If a balance sheet is prepared before the dividend shares are issued, the distributable account is reported in paid-in capital as an addition to common stock issued, as shown below:

Paid-in capital		
Common stock	$500,000	
Common stock dividends distributable	<u>50,000</u>	$550,000

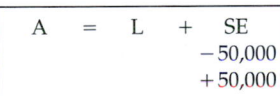

ILLUSTRATION 15-4

Statement presentation of common stock dividends distributable

When the dividend shares are issued, Common Stock Dividends Distributable is debited and Common Stock is credited as follows:

Common Stock Dividends Distributable	50,000		A	=	L	+	SE
Common Stock		50,000					−50,000
(To record issuance of 5,000 shares in a stock dividend)							+50,000

Effects of Stock Dividends

How do stock dividends affect stockholders' equity? They **change the composition of stockholders' equity** because a portion of retained earnings is transferred to paid-in capital. However, **total stockholders' equity remains the same**. Stock dividends also have no effect on the par or stated value per share, but the number of shares outstanding increases and the book value per share decreases. These effects are shown for Medland Corporation in Illustration 15-5.

ILLUSTRATION 15-5

Stock dividend effects

	Before Dividend	After Dividend
Stockholders' equity		
Paid-in capital		
Common stock, $10 par	$500,000	$550,000
Paid-in capital in excess of par value	—	25,000
Total paid-in capital	500,000	575,000
Retained earnings	300,000	225,000
Total stockholders' equity	**$800,000**	**$800,000**
Outstanding shares	**50,000**	**55,000**
Book value per share	**$ 16.00**	**$ 14.55**

In this example, total paid-in capital is increased by $75,000 and retained earnings is decreased by the same amount. Note also that total stockholders' equity remains unchanged at $800,000.

Stock Splits

A **stock split**, like a stock dividend, involves the issuance of additional shares of stock to stockholders according to their percentage ownership. However, **a stock split results in a reduction in the par or stated value per share.** The purpose of a stock split is to increase the marketability of the stock by lowering its market value per share. This, in turn, makes it easier for the corporation to issue additional stock. The effect of a split on market value is generally inversely proportional to the size of the split. For example, after a recent 2-for-1 stock split, the market value of Nike's stock fell from $111 to approximately $55. Within one year it was trading above $100 again.

In a stock split, the number of shares is increased in the same proportion that par or stated value per share is decreased. For example, in a 2-for-1 split, one share of $10 par value stock is exchanged for two shares of $5 par value stock. **A stock split does not have any effect on total paid-in capital, retained earnings, and total stockholders' equity.** However, the number of shares outstanding increases and book value per share decreases. These effects are shown in Illustration 15-6 for Medland Corporation, assuming that it splits its 50,000 shares of common stock on a 2-for-1 basis.

HELPFUL HINT
A stock split changes the par value per share but does not affect any balances in stockholders' equity.

ILLUSTRATION 15-6

Stock split effects

	Before Stock Split	After Stock Split
Stockholders' equity		
Paid-in capital		
Common stock	$500,000	$500,000
Paid-in capital in excess of par value	–0–	–0–
Total paid-in capital	500,000	500,000
Retained earnings	300,000	300,000
Total stockholders' equity	**$800,000**	**$800,000**
Outstanding shares	**50,000**	**100,000**
Book value per share	**$16.00**	**$8.00**

Because a stock split does not affect the balances in any stockholders' equity accounts, **it is not necessary to journalize a stock split**. Significant differences between stock splits and stock dividends are shown in Illustration 15-7:

Item	Stock Split	Stock Dividend
Total paid-in capital	No change	Increase
Total retained earnings	No change	Decrease
Total par value (common stock)	No change	Increase
Par value per share	Decrease	No change

ILLUSTRATION 15-7

Differences between the effects of stock splits and stock dividends

ACCOUNTING IN ACTION
Business Insight

A handful of U.S. companies have no intention of keeping their stock trading in a range accessible to mere mortals. These companies never split their stock, no matter how high their stock price gets. The king of these is investment company Berkshire Hathaway's Class A stock, which goes for a pricey $68,000—per share! The company's Class B stock is a relative bargain at roughly $2,300 per share. Other "premium" stocks are A.D. Makepeace at $9,000 and Mechanics Bank of Richmond, California, at $9,600.

BEFORE YOU GO ON . . .
Review It

1. What entries are made for cash dividends on (a) the declaration date, (b) the record date, and (c) the payment date?
2. Distinguish between a small and large stock dividend and indicate the basis for valuing each kind of dividend.
3. Contrast the effects of a small stock dividend and a 2 for 1 stock split on (a) stockholders' equity, (b) outstanding shares, and (c) book value per share.

Do It

Due to 5 years of record earnings at Sing CD Corporation, the market price of its 500,000 shares of $2 par value common stock tripled from $15 per share to $45. During this period, paid-in capital remained the same at $2,000,000, but retained earnings increased from $1,500,000 to $10,000,000. President Joan Elbert is considering either (1) a 10% stock dividend or (2) a 2-for-1 stock split. She asks you to show the before and after effects of each option on (a) retained earnings and (b) book value per share.

Reasoning: A stock dividend decreases retained earnings and increases paid-in capital, but total stockholders' equity remains the same. Because additional shares of stock are issued in the dividend, book value per share is decreased. A stock split only changes par value per share and the number of shares outstanding. Thus, this event has no effect on the retained earnings balance, and it decreases book value per share.

Solution:

(a) (1) The stock dividend amount is $2,250,000 [(500,000 × 10%) × $45]. The new balance in retained earnings is $7,750,000 ($10,000,000 − $2,250,000).

(2) The retained earnings balance after the stock split is the same as it was before the split: $10,000,000.

(b) The book value effects are as follows:

	Original Balances	After Dividend	After Split
Paid-in capital	$ 2,000,000	$ 4,250,000	$ 2,000,000
Retained earnings	10,000,000	7,750,000	10,000,000
Total stockholders' equity	$12,000,000	$12,000,000	$12,000,000
Shares outstanding	500,000	550,000	1,000,000
Book value per share	$24	$21.82	$12

Related exercise material: BE15–2, BE15–3, E15–3, E15–4, E15–5, E15–6, and E15–7.

THE NAVIGATOR

RETAINED EARNINGS

Retained earnings is net income that is retained in the business. The balance in retained earnings is part of the stockholders' claim on the total assets of the corporation. It does not, however, represent a claim on any specific asset. Nor can the amount of retained earnings be associated with the balance of any asset account. For example, a $100,000 balance in retained earnings does not mean that there should be $100,000 in cash. The reason is that the cash resulting from the excess of revenues over expenses may have been used to purchase buildings, equipment, and other assets. Illustration 15-8 shows the relationship of cash to retained earnings in selected companies.

ILLUSTRATION 15-8

Retained earnings and cash balances

Company	(in millions) Retained Earnings	Cash
Walt Disney Co.	$1,278	$7,933
Sears, Roebuck and Co.	3,330	660
The Home Depot	146	2,173
Netscape	(2)	88

When expenses exceed revenues, a **net loss** results. In contrast to net income, a net loss is debited to Retained Earnings in preparing closing entries. This is done even if a debit balance results in Retained Earnings. **Net losses are not debited to paid-in capital accounts.** To do so would destroy the distinction between paid-in and earned capital. A debit balance in retained earnings is identified as a **deficit** and is reported as a deduction in the stockholders' equity section, as shown below:

ILLUSTRATION 15-9

Stockholders' equity with deficit

Stockholders' equity	
Paid-in capital	
Common stock	$800,000
Retained earnings (deficit)	(50,000)
Total stockholders' equity	$750,000

Retained Earnings Restrictions

The balance in retained earnings is generally available for dividend declarations. Some companies state this fact. For example, in the notes to its financial statements, Martin Lockheed Corporation states:

MARTIN LOCKHEED CORPORATION
Notes to the Financial Statements

At December 31, retained earnings were unrestricted and available for dividend payments.

ILLUSTRATION 15-10

Disclosure of unrestricted retained earnings

In some cases, however, there may be **retained earnings restrictions** that make a portion of the balance currently unavailable for dividends. Restrictions result from one or more of the following causes: legal, contractual, or voluntary.

1. **Legal restrictions.** Many states require a corporation to restrict retained earnings for the cost of treasury stock purchased. The restriction serves to keep intact the corporation's legal capital that is temporarily being held as treasury stock. When the treasury stock is sold, the restriction is lifted.
2. **Contractual restrictions.** Long-term debt contracts may impose a restriction on retained earnings as a condition for the loan. The restriction limits the use of corporate assets for the payment of dividends. Thus, it enhances the likelihood that the corporation will be able to meet required loan payments.
3. **Voluntary restrictions.** The board of directors of a corporation may voluntarily create retained earnings restrictions for specific purposes. For example, the board may authorize a restriction for the purpose of future plant expansion. By reducing the amount of retained earnings available for dividends, more cash may be available for the planned expansion.

Retained earnings restrictions are generally disclosed in the notes to the financial statements. For example, Pratt & Lambert, a leading producer of architectural finishes (paint) has the following note in a recent financial statement:

PRATT & LAMBERT
Notes to the Financial Statements

Note D: Long-term Debt and Retained Earnings Loan agreements contain, among other covenants, a restriction on the payment of dividends, which limits future dividend payments to $20,565,000 plus 75% of future net income.

ILLUSTRATION 15-11

Disclosure of restriction

Prior Period Adjustments

Suppose that after the books have been closed and the financial statements have been issued, a corporation discovers that a material error has been made in reporting net income of a prior year. How should this situation be recorded in the accounts and reported in the financial statements? The correction of an error in previously issued financial statements is known as a **prior period adjustment**. The correction is made directly to Retained Earnings because the effect of the error is now in this account; the net income for the prior period has been recorded in retained earnings through the journalizing and posting of closing entries.

To illustrate, assume that General Microwave discovers in 1999 that it understated depreciation expense in 1998 by $300,000 as a result of computational errors. These errors overstated net income for 1998, and the current balance in retained earnings is also overstated. The entry for the prior period adjustment, assuming all tax effects are ignored, is as follows:

A = L + SE
− 300,000   − 300,000

Retained Earnings	300,000	
Accumulated Depreciation		300,000
(To adjust for understatement of depreciation in a prior period)		

A debit to an income statement account in 1999 would be incorrect because the error pertains to a prior year.

Prior period adjustments are reported in the retained earnings statement.[1] They are added (or deducted) from the beginning retained earnings balance to show the adjusted beginning balance. Assuming General Microwave has a beginning balance of $800,000 in retained earnings, the prior period adjustment is reported as follows:

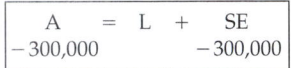

ILLUSTRATION 15-12

Statement presentation of prior period adjustments

GENERAL MICROWAVE **Retained Earnings Statement (partial)**	
Balance, January 1, as reported	$800,000
Correction for overstatement of net income in prior period **(depreciation error)**	**300,000**
Balance, January 1, as adjusted	$500,000

Reporting the correction in the current year's income statement would be incorrect because it applies to a prior year's income statement.

Retained Earnings Statement

The **retained earnings statement** shows the changes in retained earnings during the year. The statement is prepared from the Retained Earnings account. Transactions and events that affect retained earnings are tabulated in account form as shown in Illustration 15-13.

ILLUSTRATION 15-13

Debits and credits to retained earnings

Retained Earnings	
1. Net loss	1. Net income
2. Prior period adjustments for overstatement of net income	2. Prior period adjustments for understatement of net income
3. Cash and stock dividends	
4. Some disposals of treasury stock	

---

[1] A complete retained earnings statement is shown in Illustration 15-14 on the next page.

As indicated, net income increases retained earnings, and a net loss decreases retained earnings. Prior period adjustments may either increase or decrease retained earnings, whereas both cash and stock dividends decrease retained earnings. The circumstances when treasury stock transactions decrease retained earnings are explained in Chapter 14. The retained earnings statement for Graber Inc., based on assumed data, is as follows:

ILLUSTRATION 15-14
Retained earnings statement

GRABER INC. Retained Earnings Statement For the Year Ended December 31, 1999		
Balance, January 1, as reported		$1,050,000
Correction for understatement of net income in prior period (inventory error)		50,000
Balance, January 1, as adjusted		1,100,000
Add: Net income		360,000
		1,460,000
Less: Cash dividends	$100,000	
Stock dividends	200,000	300,000
Balance, December 31		$1,160,000

Statement Presentation and Analysis

Presentation

STUDY OBJECTIVE **3**

Prepare and analyze a comprehensive stockholders' equity section.

The stockholders' equity section of the balance sheet of Graber Inc. is presented in Illustration 15-15. Note that (1) Common Stock Dividends Distributable is shown under capital stock in paid-in capital, and (2) a retained earnings restriction is disclosed in the notes.

ILLUSTRATION 15-15
Comprehensive stockholders' equity section

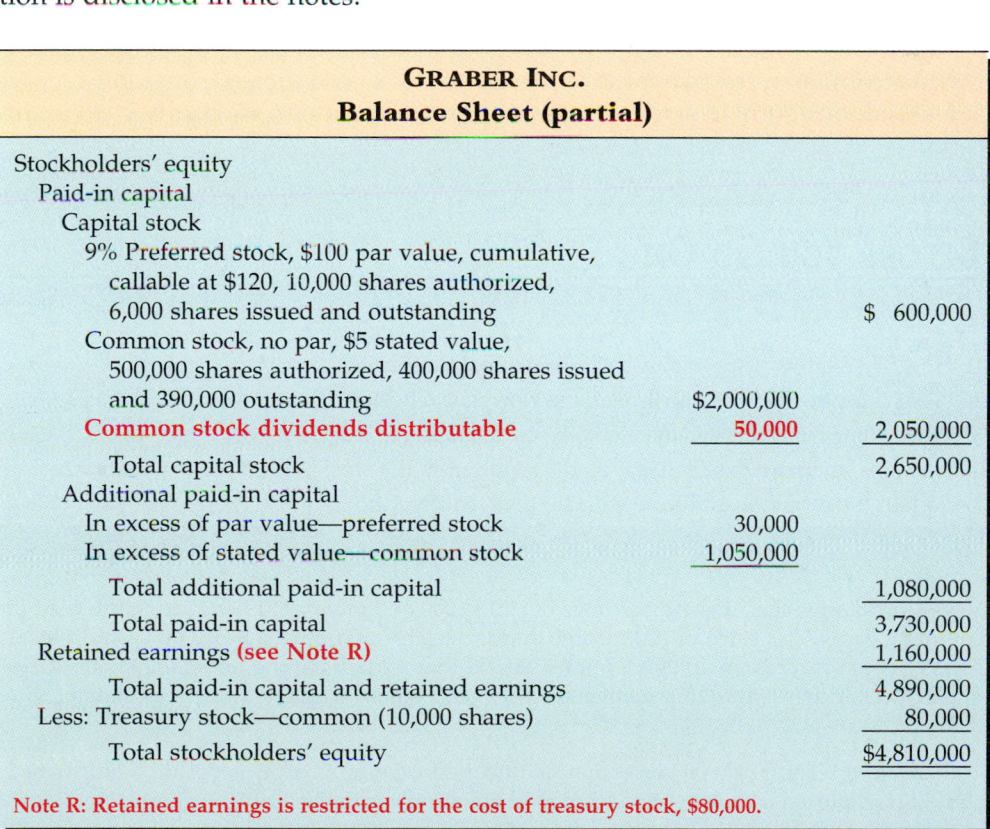

GRABER INC. Balance Sheet (partial)		
Stockholders' equity		
Paid-in capital		
Capital stock		
9% Preferred stock, $100 par value, cumulative, callable at $120, 10,000 shares authorized, 6,000 shares issued and outstanding		$ 600,000
Common stock, no par, $5 stated value, 500,000 shares authorized, 400,000 shares issued and 390,000 outstanding	$2,000,000	
Common stock dividends distributable	50,000	2,050,000
Total capital stock		2,650,000
Additional paid-in capital		
In excess of par value—preferred stock	30,000	
In excess of stated value—common stock	1,050,000	
Total additional paid-in capital		1,080,000
Total paid-in capital		3,730,000
Retained earnings (see Note R)		1,160,000
Total paid-in capital and retained earnings		4,890,000
Less: Treasury stock—common (10,000 shares)		80,000
Total stockholders' equity		$4,810,000

Note R: Retained earnings is restricted for the cost of treasury stock, $80,000.

INTERNATIONAL NOTE

In Switzerland, there are no specific disclosure requirements for stockholders' equity. However, companies typically disclose separate categories of capital on the balance sheet.

Instead of presenting a detailed stockholders' equity section in the balance sheet and a retained earnings statement, many companies prepare a **stockholders' equity statement**. This statement shows the changes in each stockholders' equity account and in total stockholders' equity that have occurred during the year. An example of a stockholders' equity statement is illustrated in the appendix to this chapter and in Kellogg's financial statements in Appendix A.

Analysis

A widely used ratio that measures profitability from the common stockholder's viewpoint is **return on common stockholders' equity**. This ratio shows how many dollars of net income were earned for each dollar invested by the owners. It is computed by dividing net income available to common stockholders (which is Net income − Preferred stock dividends) by average common stockholders' equity. For example, assuming that Kellogg's beginning-of-the-year and end-of-the-year common stockholders' equity were $1,282.4 and $997.5 million respectively, net income was $546.0 million, and no preferred stock was outstanding, the return on common stockholders' equity ratio is shown graphically and computed as follows:

ILLUSTRATION 15-16

Return on common stockholders' equity ratio and computation

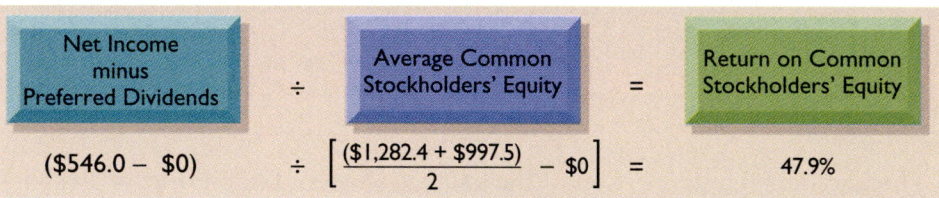

As shown above, if preferred stock is present, **preferred dividend** requirements are deducted from net income to compute income available to common stockholders. Similarly, the par value of preferred stock is deducted from total average stockholders' equity to arrive at the amount of common stock equity used in this ratio.

BEFORE YOU GO ON . . .

Review It

1. How are retained earnings restrictions generally reported?
2. What is a prior period adjustment and how is it reported?
3. What are the principal sources of debits and credits to Retained Earnings?
4. How are stock dividends distributable reported in the stockholders' equity section?
5 Explain the return on common stockholders' equity ratio.

Do It

Vega Corporation has retained earnings of $5,130,000 on January 1, 1999. During the year, the company earns $2,000,000 of net income and it declares and pays a $250,000 cash dividend. In 1999, Vega records an adjustment of $180,000 that pertains to the understatement of 1998 depreciation expense due to a mathematical error. Prepare a retained earnings statement for 1999.

Reasoning: The $180,000 correction of 1998 depreciation is a prior period adjustment. It should be reported as a deduction from the beginning retained earnings balance. Net income is shown as an addition in the statement and dividends are deducted in the statement.

Solution:

VEGA CORPORATION Retained Earnings Statement For the Year Ended December 31, 1999	
Balance, January 1, as reported	$5,130,000
Correction for overstatement of net income in prior period (depreciation error)	180,000
Balance, January 1, as adjusted	4,950,000
Add: Net income	2,000,000
	6,950,000
Less: Cash dividends	250,000
Balance, December 31	$6,700,000

THE NAVIGATOR

Related exercise material: BE15–4 and E15–8.

CORPORATION INCOME STATEMENTS

Income statements for **corporations are the same as the statements for proprietorships or partnerships except for the reporting of income taxes.** For income tax purposes, corporations are considered to be a separate legal entity. As a result, **income taxes (or income tax expense)** are reported in a separate section of the corporation income statement before net income. The condensed income statement for Leads Inc. in Illustration 15-17 shows a typical presentation. Note that income before income taxes is reported before income tax expense.

4
STUDY
OBJECTIVE
Describe the form and content of corporation income statements.

LEADS INC. Income Statement For the Year Ended December 31, 1999	
Sales	$800,000
Cost of goods sold	600,000
Gross profit	200,000
Operating expenses	50,000
Income from operations	150,000
Other revenues and gains	10,000
Other expenses and losses	4,000
Income before income taxes	156,000
Income tax expense	46,800
Net income	$109,200

ILLUSTRATION 15-17
Income statement with income taxes

HELPFUL HINT
Corporations may also use the single-step form of income statement discussed in Chapter 5.

Income tax expense and the related liability for income taxes payable are recorded as part of the adjusting process preceding financial statement preparation. Using the data above for Leads Inc., the adjusting entry for income tax expense at December 31, 1999, would be as follows:

Income Tax Expense	46,800	
Income Taxes Payable		46,800
(To record income taxes for 1999)		

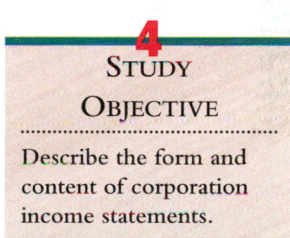

A	=	L	+	SE
		+46,800		−46,800

Another illustration of income taxes is presented in the income statement of Kellogg Company in Appendix A.

ACCOUNTING IN ACTION
Business Insight

Net income and its components reported in the income statement measure a company's performance. The amount and trend of net income (earnings) are, therefore, of vital importance to management, stockholders, and creditors. Net income provides an indication of the amount of dividends that a company may distribute, and it results in an increase in retained earnings.

Reported net income has a major effect on the market price of a company's stock at a given point in time. For example, when IBM announced that its net income would be 7.7% lower, the price of its stock dropped $3.875 per share in one day. Conversely, when Eljer Industries Inc. (a Dallas-based maker of plumbing, heating, and ventilation products) reported a sharp improvement in its earnings, the market price of its stock increased 14% in one day.

The income statements we have studied so far provide considerable insight into a company's income-related activities. In studying such statements, the user may ask: (1) Are the results typical for this company? (2) Are the results a reasonable indicator of the company's future earnings?

To provide answers to these questions, accountants have concluded that additional sections should be added to the income statement to **report material items not typical of regular operations**. These items are reported in the income statement immediately before net income. The nontypical items include (1) discontinued operations, (2) extraordinary items, and (3) changes in accounting principle. All these irregular items are reported net of income taxes. That is, the applicable income tax expense or tax savings is shown for income before income taxes and for each of the listed irregular items. The general concept is "let the tax follow income or loss."

Discontinued Operations

5

STUDY

OBJECTIVE

Indicate the statement presentation of material items not typical of regular operations.

Discontinued operations refers to the disposal of a **significant segment** of a business, such as the cessation of an entire activity or the elimination of a major class of customers. Thus, Kmart's decision to terminate its interest in four business activities, including PACE Membership Warehouse and PayLess Drug Stores Northwest, was reported as discontinued operations. On the other hand, the phasing out of a model such as the GM Chevette or part of a line of business is not considered to be a disposal of a segment.

When the disposal of a significant segment occurs, the income statement should report both income from continuing operations and income (or loss) from discontinued operations. **The income (loss) from discontinued operations consists of the income (loss) from operations and the gain (loss) on disposal of the segment.** To illustrate, assume that during 1999 Acro Energy Inc. has income before income taxes of $800,000. During 1999 the company discontinued and sold its unprofitable chemical division. The loss in 1999 from chemical operations (net of $60,000 taxes) was $140,000, and the loss on disposal of the chemical division (net of $30,000 taxes) was $70,000. Assuming a 30% tax rate on income before income taxes, the income statement presentation is shown on the next page.

ILLUSTRATION 15-18

Statement presentation of discontinued operations

ACRO ENERGY INC.
Income Statement (partial)
For the Year Ended December 31, 1999

Income before income taxes		$800,000
Income tax expense		240,000
Income from continuing operations		560,000
Discontinued operations		
Loss from operations of chemical division, net of		
$60,000 income tax saving	$140,000	
Loss from disposal of chemical division, net of $30,000		
income tax saving	70,000	210,000
Net income		$350,000

HELPFUL HINT
Observe the dual disclosures:
(1) the results of operations of the discontinued division must be eliminated from the results of continuing operations, and (2) the disposal of the operation.

Note that the caption "Income from continuing operations" is used and that a section "Discontinued operations" is added. **Within the new section, both the operating loss and the loss on disposal are reported net of applicable income taxes.** This presentation clearly indicates the separate effects of continuing operations and discontinued operations on net income.

Extraordinary Items

Extraordinary items are events and transactions that meet two conditions: they are (1) **unusual in nature** and (2) **infrequent in occurrence**. To be considered unusual, the item should be abnormal and be only incidentally related to the customary activities of the entity. To be regarded as infrequent, the event or transaction should not be reasonably expected to recur in the foreseeable future. Both criteria must be evaluated in terms of the environment in which the entity operates. Thus, Weyerhaeuser Co. reported the $36 million in damages to its timberland caused by the volcanic eruption of Mount St. Helens as an extraordinary item because the event was both unusual and infrequent. In contrast, Florida Citrus Company does not report frost damage to its citrus crop as an extraordinary item because frost damage is not viewed as infrequent. Illustration 15-19 shows the appropriate classification of extraordinary and ordinary items.

ACCOUNTING IN ACTION
Business Insight

In the recession of the early 1990s, many companies closed some of their plants and reduced the size of their work forces. The costs incurred in these activities, called plant restructuring costs, are reported as other expenses and losses in the income statement. These costs are not considered to be an extraordinary item because plant closings are neither unusual nor infrequent in many industries. Plant restructuring costs often have a significant effect on net income as illustrated by the following:

Union Pacific Corp.	$585 million after-tax charge, of which $492 million applies to the disposal of 7,100 miles of the Union Pacific Railroad.
Borden, Inc.	$71.6 million before-tax charge for business reorganization costs as well as severance, relocation, and other employee-related expenses.

ILLUSTRATION 15-19

Examples of extraordinary and ordinary items

Extraordinary items

1. Effects of major casualties (acts of God), if rare in the area.

2. Expropriation (takeover) of property by a foreign government.

3. Effects of a newly enacted law or regulation, such as a condemnation action.

Ordinary items

1. Effects of major casualties (acts of God), frequent in the area.

2. Write-down of inventories or write-off of receivables.

3. Losses attributable to labor strikes.

4. Gains or losses from sales of property, plant, or equipment.

Extraordinary items are reported net of taxes in a separate section of the income statement immediately below discontinued operations. To illustrate, assume that in 1999 a revolutionary foreign government expropriated property held as an investment by Acro Energy Inc. If the loss is $70,000, before applicable income taxes of $21,000, the income statement presentation will show a deduction of $49,000 as shown in Illustration 15-20.

As illustrated, the caption "Income before extraordinary item" is added immediately before the section for the extraordinary item. This presentation clearly indicates the effect of the extraordinary item on net income. If there are no discontinued operations, the third line of the income statement in Illustration 15-20 would be labeled "Income before extraordinary item."

If a transaction or event meets one (but not both) of the criteria for an extraordinary item, it is reported under either "Other revenues and gains" or "Other expenses and losses" at its gross amount (not net of tax). This is true, for example, of gains (losses) resulting from the sale of property, plant, and equipment, as explained in Chapter 10.

Change in Accounting Principle

For ease of comparison, financial statements are expected to be prepared on a basis **consistent** with that used for the preceding period. That is, where a choice of accounting principles is available, the principle initially chosen should be con-

ILLUSTRATION 15-20

*Statement presentation of
extraordinary items*

ACRO ENERGY INC.
Income Statement (partial)
For the Year Ended December 31, 1999

Income before income taxes		$800,000
Income tax expense		240,000
Income from continuing operations		560,000
Discontinued operations		
Loss from operations of chemical division, net of $60,000 income tax saving	$140,000	
Loss from disposal of chemical division, net of $30,000 income tax saving	70,000	210,000
Income before extraordinary item		350,000
Extraordinary item		
Expropriation of investment, net of $21,000 income tax saving		49,000
Net income		$301,000

sistently applied from period to period. A **change in an accounting principle** occurs when the principle used in the current year is different from the one used in the preceding year. A change is permitted, when (1) management can show that the new principle is preferable to the old principle, and (2) the effects of the change are clearly disclosed in the income statement. Examples of a change in accounting principle include a change in depreciation methods (e.g., declining-balance to straight-line) and a change in inventory costing methods (e.g., FIFO to average cost).

When a change in an accounting principle has occurred,

1. The new principle should be used in reporting the results of operations of the current year.
2. The cumulative effect of the change on all prior year income statements should be disclosed net of applicable taxes in a special section immediately preceding net income.

To illustrate, we will assume that at the beginning of 1999, Acro Energy Inc. changes from the straight-line method of depreciation to the declining-balance method for equipment purchased on January 1, 1996. The cumulative effect on prior year income statements (statements for 1996–1998) is to increase depreciation expense and decrease income before income taxes by $24,000. Assuming a 30% tax rate, the net of tax effect of the change is $16,800 ($24,000 × 70%). The income statement presentation is shown in Illustration 15-21 on page 652.

The income statement for Acro Energy will also show depreciation expense for the current year. The amount is based on the new depreciation method. In this case the caption "Income before extraordinary item and cumulative effect of change in accounting principle" is inserted immediately following the effects of discontinued operations. This presentation clearly indicates the cumulative effect of the change on prior years' income. If a company does not have either discontinued operations or extraordinary items, the label, "Income before cumulative effect of change in accounting principle" is used in place of "Income from continuing operations." A complete income statement showing all material items not typical of regular operations is illustrated in the Demonstration Problem (pp. 655–56).

ETHICS NOTE

Changes in accounting principles should result in financial statements that are more informative for statement users. They should not be used to artificially improve the reported performance and financial position of the corporation.

ILLUSTRATION 15-21

Statement presentation of cumulative effect of change in accounting principle

ACRO ENERGY INC. Income Statement (partial) For the Year Ended December 31, 1999		
Income before income taxes		$800,000
Income tax expense		240,000
Income from continuing operations		560,000
Discontinued operations		
Loss from operations of chemical division, net of $60,000 income tax saving	$140,000	
Loss from disposal of chemical division, net of $30,000 income tax saving	70,000	210,000
Income before extraordinary item and cumulative effect of change in accounting principle		350,000
Extraordinary item		
Expropriation of investment, net of $21,000 income tax saving		49,000
Cumulative effect of change in accounting principle		
Effect on prior years of change in depreciation method, net of $7,200 income tax saving		**16,800**
Net income		$284,200

ACCOUNTING IN ACTION
Business Insight

Sometimes a change in accounting principle is mandated by the Financial Accounting Standards Board. An example is the change in accounting for interperiod income taxes required by Statement of Financial Accounting Standards 109. Such changes can significantly affect net income. For example, in a recent income statement, Consolidated Natural Gas Company reported an increase in income of $17,422,000 under "Cumulative Effect of Accounting Change." An accompanying note explained that the increase in income resulted from a required "change from the deferred method to an asset and liability approach for accounting for and reporting of income taxes."

BEFORE YOU GO ON . . .
Review It

1. What is the unique feature of a corporation income statement?
2. What are the similarities and differences in reporting material items not typical of regular operations?
3. Did Kellogg report any of the three types of irregular items in its 1997 income statement? The answer to this question is provided on p. 673.

Do It

In its proposed 1999 income statement, AIR Corporation reports income before income taxes $400,000, extraordinary loss from fire $100,000, income taxes (30%) $90,000, and net income $210,000. Prepare a correct income statement, beginning with income before income taxes.

Reasoning: The income tax effect of each component is disclosed in the income statement. Thus, the extraordinary loss should be reported net of income taxes.

Solution:

AIR CORPORATION Income Statement (partial)	
Income before income taxes	$400,000
Income tax expense (30%)	120,000
Income before extraordinary item	280,000
Extraordinary loss from fire, net of $30,000 income tax saving	70,000
Net income	$210,000

Related exercise material: BE15–6, BE15–7, BE15–8, E15–12, and E15–13.

EARNINGS PER SHARE

Earnings per share data are frequently reported in the financial press and are widely used by stockholders and potential investors in evaluating the profitability of a company. Investors, especially, attempt to link earnings per share to the market price per share.[2] **Earnings per share (EPS)** indicates the net income earned by each share of outstanding common stock. Thus, **earnings per share is reported only for common stock**. The formula for computing earnings per share is as follows:

6
STUDY
OBJECTIVE
Compute earnings per share.

ILLUSTRATION 15-22

Earnings per share formula

For example, if Modem Inc. has net income of $200,000 and 50,000 shares of common stock outstanding for the year, earnings per share is $4 ($200,000 ÷ 50,000).[3]

Because of the importance of earnings per share (EPS), most companies are required to report it on the face of the income statement. Generally this amount is simply reported below net income on the statement. For Modem Inc. the presentation would be:

---

[2]The ratio of the market price per share to the earnings per share is referred to as the *price-earnings (P/E) ratio*. This ratio is reported in *The Wall Street Journal* and other newspapers for common stocks listed on major stock exchanges.

[3]The calculation of the weighted average of common shares outstanding is discussed in advanced accounting courses.

ILLUSTRATION 15-23

Basic earnings per share disclosure

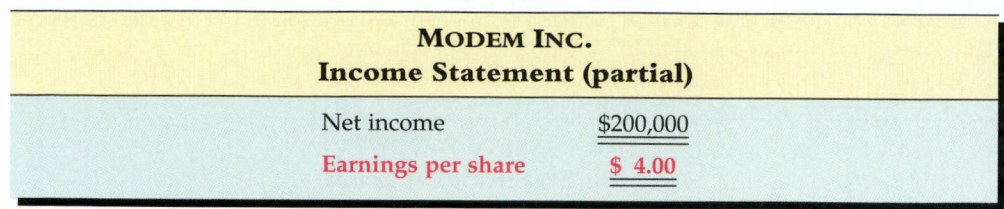

MODEM INC. Income Statement (partial)	
Net income	$200,000
Earnings per share	**$ 4.00**

Preferred Stock Dividends

Earnings per share relates to earnings per share of **common stock**. When a corporation has both preferred and common stock outstanding, the current year's dividend declared on preferred stock is subtracted from net income to arrive at **income available to common stockholders**. The formula for computing EPS in such a case is:

ILLUSTRATION 15-24

Expanded earnings per share formula

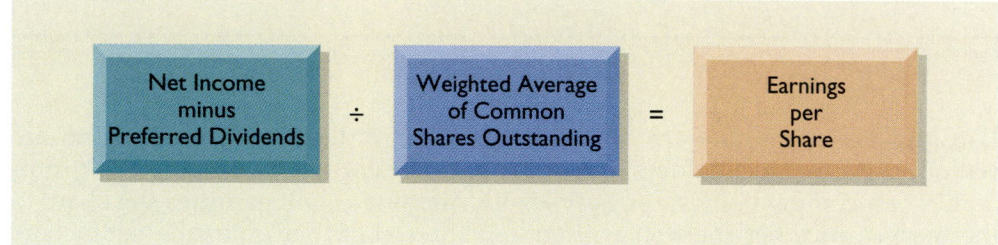

To illustrate, assume that Rally Inc. reports net income of $211,000 on its 102,500 weighted average common shares. During the year it also declares a $6,000 dividend on its preferred stock. Therefore, Rally has $205,000 ($211,000 − $6,000) available for common stock dividends. Earnings per share is $2 ($205,000 ÷ 102,500). If the preferred stock is cumulative, the dividend for the current year is deducted whether or not it is declared.

Irregular Items

When the income statement contains any of the three additional sections that report irregular items described earlier in the chapter, EPS should be disclosed for each component. Assuming that Acro Energy had 100,000 shares of common stock outstanding during the year, the additional EPS disclosures for the income statement shown in Illustration 15-21 would be as shown below.

ILLUSTRATION 15-25

Additional earnings per share disclosures

ACRO ENERGY INC. Income Statement (partial) For the Year Ended December 31, 1999	
Net income	$284,200
Earnings per share	
Income from continuing operations	**$5.60**
Loss from discontinued operations	**(2.10)**
Income before extraordinary item and cumulative effect of change in accounting principle	**3.50**
Extraordinary loss	**(.49)**
Cumulative effect of change in accounting principle	**(.17)**
Net income	**$2.84**

These disclosures enable decision makers to recognize the effects on EPS of income from continuing operations, as distinguished from income or loss from material items not typical of regular operations. **Earnings per share from continuing operations is generally the most useful per share amount**, because it represents the results of continuing and ordinary business activity. Thus, it provides the best basis for predicting future operating results.

BEFORE YOU GO ON . . .

Review It

1. Explain the components of the formula for computing earnings per share when there is only common stock and outstanding shares are unchanged during the year.
2. What effects may preferred stock have on the formula for computing earnings per share?

A LOOK BACK AT OUR FEATURE STORY

To answer the following questions, refer to the opening story.

1. Nike's stock has split numerous times in recent years. What is the likely reason for these splits?
2. Prepare the quarterly journal entry (accounts and amount) recorded by a Nike shareholder when he or she receives a dividend of $1,000 from Nike.
3. Nike has increased its cash dividend per share every year for the past 10 years. What issues must it consider when deciding the level of the divided payment?

Solution:

1. In recent years Nike's stock has experienced a rapid increase in value. To keep the stock in an affordable price range for the average investor, management has split the stock a number of times.
2. The entry to record receipt of a dividend each quarter is:

Cash	1,000	
Dividend Revenue		1,000
(To record quarterly dividend revenue)		

3. Nike should consider the adequacy of its cash, the adequacy of its retained earnings, the level of its future earnings, and its ability to maintain the dividend level in the future.

THE NAVIGATOR

DEMONSTRATION PROBLEM

The events and transactions of the Dever Corporation for the year ending December 31, 1999, resulted in the following data:

Cost of goods sold	$2,600,000
Net sales	4,400,000
Other expenses and losses	9,600
Other revenues and gains	5,600
Selling and administrative expenses	1,100,000
Income from operations of plastics division	70,000
Gain on sale of plastics division	500,000
Loss from tornado disaster (extraordinary loss)	600,000
Cumulative effect of changing from the straight-line depreciation to double-declining-balance (increase in depreciation expense)	300,000

Analysis reveals that:

1. All items are before the applicable income tax rate of 30%.
2. The plastics division was sold on July 1.
3. All operating data for the plastics division have been segregated.
4. There were 100,000 shares of common stock outstanding during the year.

Instructions

Prepare an income statement for the year, including the presentation of earnings per share data.

PROBLEM-SOLVING STRATEGIES

1. Remember that material items not typical of operations are reported in separate sections net of taxes.
2. Income taxes should be associated with the item that affects the taxes.
3. A corporation income statement will have income tax expense when there is income before income tax.
4. All data presented in determining income before income taxes are the same as for unincorporated companies.

SOLUTION TO DEMONSTRATION PROBLEM

DEVER CORPORATION
Income Statement
For the Year Ended December 31, 1999

Net sales		$4,400,000
Cost of goods sold		2,600,000
Gross profit		1,800,000
Selling and administrative expenses		1,100,000
Income from operations		700,000
Other revenues and gains	$ 5,600	
Other expenses and losses	9,600	4,000
Income before income taxes		696,000
Income tax expense ($696,000 × 30%)		208,800
Income from continuing operations		487,200
Discontinued operations		
Income from operations of plastics division, net of		
$21,000 income taxes ($70,000 × 30%)	49,000	
Gain on sale of plastics division, net of $150,000		
income taxes ($500,000 × 30%)	350,000	399,000
Income before extraordinary item and cumulative effect of		
change in accounting principle		886,200
Extraordinary item		
Tornado loss, net of income tax saving $180,000		
($600,000 × 30%)		420,000
Cumulative effect of change in accounting principle		
Effect on prior years of change in depreciation method,		
net of $90,000 income tax saving ($300,000 × 30%)		210,000
Net income		$ 256,200
Earnings per share		
Income from continuing operations		$4.87
Gain from discontinued operations		3.99
Income before extraordinary item and cumulative effect		
of change in accounting principle		8.86
Extraordinary loss		(4.20)
Cumulative effect of change in accounting principle		(2.10)
Net income		$2.56

THE NAVIGATOR

SUMMARY OF STUDY OBJECTIVES

1. Prepare the entries for cash dividends and stock dividends. Entries for both cash and stock dividends are required at the declaration date and the payment date. At the declaration date the entries are: Cash dividend—debit Retained Earnings and credit Dividends Payable; small stock dividend—debit Retained Earnings, credit Paid-in Capital in Excess of Par (or Stated) Value, and credit Common Stock Dividends Distributable. At the payment date, the entries for cash and stock dividends, respectively, are debit Dividends Payable and credit Cash, and debit Common Stock Dividends Distributable and credit Common Stock.

2. Identify the items that are reported in a retained earnings statement. Each of the individual debits and credits to retained earnings should be reported in the retained earnings statement. Additions consist of net income and prior period adjustments to correct understatements of prior years' net income. Deductions consist of net loss, adjustments to correct overstatements of prior years' net income, cash and stock dividends, and some disposals of treasury stock.

3. Prepare and analyze a comprehensive stockholders' equity section. A comprehensive stockholders' equity section includes all stockholders' equity accounts. It consists of two sections: paid-in capital and retained earnings. It should also include notes to the financial statements that explain any restrictions on retained earnings and any dividends in arrears. One measure of profitability is the return on common stockholders' equity. It is calculated by dividing income available to common stockholders by average common stockholders' equity.

4. Describe the form and content of corporation income statements. The form and content of corporation income statements are similar to the statements of proprietorships and partnerships with one exception: Income taxes or income tax expense must be reported in a separate section before net income in the corporation's income statement.

5. Indicate the statement presentation of material items not typical of regular operations. Material items not typical of regular operations are reported net of taxes in sections on the income statement immediately before net income. These items include (a) discontinued operations, (b) extraordinary items, and (c) changes in accounting principle.

6. Compute earnings per share. Earnings per share is computed by dividing net income by the number of common shares outstanding during the period. An additional problem arises when preferred stock dividends exist.

GLOSSARY

Cash dividend A pro rata distribution of cash to stockholders. (p. 634).

Change in accounting principle The use of a principle in the current year that is different from the one used in the preceding year. (p. 650).

Declaration date The date the board of directors formally declares the dividend and announces it to stockholders. (p. 635).

Deficit A debit balance in retained earnings. (p. 642).

Discontinued operations The disposal of a significant segment of a business. (p. 648).

Dividend A distribution by a corporation to its stockholders on a pro rata (proportional) basis. (p. 634).

Earnings per share The net income earned by each share of outstanding common stock. (p. 653).

Extraordinary items Events and transactions that are unusual in nature and infrequent in occurrence. (p. 649).

Liquidating dividend A dividend declared out of paid-in capital. (p. 635).

Payment date The date dividend checks are mailed to stockholders. (p. 636).

Prior period adjustment The correction of an error in previously issued financial statements. (p. 644).

Record date The date when ownership of outstanding shares is determined for dividend purposes. (p. 636).

Retained earnings Net income that is retained in the business. (p. 642).

Retained earnings restrictions Circumstances that make a portion of retained earnings currently unavailable for dividends. (p. 643).

Retained earnings statement A financial statement that shows the changes in retained earnings during the year. (p. 644).

Return on common stockholders' equity A measure of profitability that shows how many dollars of net income were earned for each dollar invested by the owners; computed as net income divided by average common stockholders' equity. (p. 646)

Stock dividend A pro rata distribution of the corporation's own stock to stockholders. (p. 638).

Stockholders' equity statement A statement that shows the changes in each stockholders' equity account and in total stockholders' equity during the year. (p. 646).

Stock split The issuance of additional shares of stock to stockholders according to their percentage ownership, accompanied by a reduction in the par or stated value per share. (p. 640).

APPENDIX STOCKHOLDERS' EQUITY STATEMENT

7

STUDY OBJECTIVE

Describe the use and content of the stockholders' equity statement.

When balance sheets and income statements are presented by a corporation, changes in the separate accounts comprising stockholders' equity should also be disclosed. Disclosure of such changes is necessary to make the financial statements sufficiently informative for users. The disclosures may be made in an additional statement or in the notes to the financial statements.

Many corporations make the disclosures in a stockholders' equity statement. The statement shows the changes in **each** stockholders' equity account and in **total** stockholders' equity during the year. As shown in Illustration 15A-1 the stockholders' equity statement is prepared in columnar form, with columns for each account and for total stockholders' equity. The transactions are then identified and their effects are shown in the appropriate columns.

In practice, additional columns are usually provided to show the number of shares of issued stock and treasury stock. The stockholders' equity statement for Kellogg Company, for a three-year period, is shown in Appendix A. **When this statement is presented, a retained earnings statement is not necessary** because the retained earnings column explains the changes in this account.

ILLUSTRATION 15A-1

Stockholders' equity statement

	Common Stock ($5 Par)	Paid-in Capital in Excess of Par	Retained Earnings	Treasury Stock	Total
HAMPTON CORPORATION Stockholders' Equity Statement For the Year Ended December 31, 1999					
Balance January 1	$300,000	$200,000	$650,000	$(34,000)	$1,116,000
Issued 5,000 shares of common stock at $15	25,000	50,000			75,000
Declared a $40,000 cash dividend			(40,000)		(40,000)
Purchased 2,000 shares for treasury at $16				(32,000)	(32,000)
Net income for year			240,000		240,000
Balance December 31	$325,000	$250,000	$850,000	$(66,000)	$1,359,000

SUMMARY OF STUDY OBJECTIVE FOR APPENDIX

7. *Describe the use and content of the stockholders' equity statement.* Corporations must disclose changes in stockholders' equity accounts and may choose to do so by issuing a separate stockholders' equity statement. This statement, prepared in columnar form, shows changes in each stockholders' equity account and in total stockholders' equity during the accounting period. When this statement is presented, a retained earnings statement is not necessary.

*Note: All asterisked Questions, Exercises, and Problems relate to material in the appendix to the chapter.

SELF-STUDY QUESTIONS

Answers are at the end of the chapter.

(SO 1) 1. Entries for cash dividends are required on the:
    a. declaration date and the payment date.
    b. record date and the payment date.
    c. declaration date, record date, and payment date.
    d. declaration date and the record date.

(SO 1) 2. Which of the following statements about small stock dividends is true?
    a. A debit to Retained Earnings for the par value of the shares issued should be made.
    b. A stock dividend decreases total stockholders' equity.
    c. Market value per share should be assigned to the dividend shares.
    d. A stock dividend ordinarily will have no effect on book value per share of stock.

(SO 2) 3. All *but one* of the following is reported in a retained earnings statement. The exception is:
    a. cash and stock dividends.
    b. net income and net loss.
    c. some disposals of treasury stock below cost.
    d. sales of treasury stock above cost.

(SO 2) 4. A prior period adjustment is:
    a. reported in the income statement as a nontypical item.
    b. a correction of an error that is made directly to retained earnings.
    c. reported directly in the stockholders' equity section.
    d. reported in the retained earnings statement as an adjustment of the ending balance of retained earnings.

(SO 3) 5. In the stockholders' equity section, Stock Dividends Distributable is reported as a(an):
    a. deduction from total paid-in capital and retained earnings.
    b. addition in additional paid-in capital.
    c. deduction from retained earnings.
    d. addition in capital stock.

(SO 4) 6. Corporation income statements may be the same as the income statements for unincorporated companies *except* for:
    a. gross profit.
    b. income tax expense.
    c. operating income.
    d. net sales.

(SO 3) 7. The return on common stockholders' equity is defined as:
    a. Net income divided by total assets.
    b. Cash dividends divided by average common stockholders' equity.
    c. Income available to common stockholders divided by average common stockholders' equity.
    d. None of these is correct.

(SO 5) 8. In reporting discontinued operations, the income statement should show in a special section:
    a. gains and losses on the disposal of the discontinued segment.
    b. gains and losses from operations of the discontinued segment.
    c. Both (a) and (b).
    d. Neither (a) nor (b).

(SO 5) 9. The Rand Corporation has income before taxes of $400,000 and an extraordinary loss of $100,000. If the income tax rate is 25% on all items, the income statement should show income before extraordinary items and extraordinary items, respectively, of:
    a. $325,000 and $100,000.
    b. $325,000 and $75,000.
    c. $300,000 and $100,000.
    d. $300,000 and $75,000.

(SO 6) 10. The income statement for Nadeen, Inc., shows income before income taxes $700,000, income tax expense $210,000, and net income $490,000. If Nadeen has 100,000 shares of common stock outstanding throughout the year, earnings per share is:
    a. $7.00.
    b. $4.90.
    c. $2.10.
    d. no correct answer given.

(SO 7) *11. When a stockholders' equity statement is presented, it is not necessary to prepare a(an):
    a. retained earnings statement.
    b. balance sheet.
    c. income statement.
    d. All of the above must be prepared.

THE NAVIGATOR

QUESTIONS

1. (a) What is a dividend? (b) "Dividends must be paid in cash." Do you agree? Explain.

2. Ruth Hoadley maintains that adequate cash is the only requirement for the declaration of a cash dividend. Is Ruth correct? Explain.

3. (a) Three dates are important in connection with cash dividends. Identify the dates and explain their significance to the corporation and its stockholders.
   (b) Identify the accounting entries that are made for a cash dividend and the date of each entry.

4. Null Inc. declares a $40,000 cash dividend on December 31, 1999. The required annual dividend on preferred stock is $12,000. Determine the allocation of the dividend to preferred and common stockholders assuming the preferred stock is cumulative and dividends are one year in arrears.

5. Contrast the effects of a cash dividend and a stock dividend on a corporation's balance sheet.

6. Laura Fultz asks, "Since stock dividends don't change anything, why declare them?" What is your answer to Laura?

7. Juno Corporation has 20,000 shares of $10 par value common stock outstanding when they announce a 2-for-1 split. Before the split, the stock had a market price of $140 per share. After the split, how many shares of stock will be outstanding, and what will be the approximate market price per share?

8. The board of directors is considering a stock split or a stock dividend. They understand that total stockholders' equity will remain the same under either action. However, they are not sure of the different effects of the two types of actions on other aspects of stockholders' equity. Explain the differences to the directors.

9. What is a prior period adjustment, and how is it reported in the financial statements?

10. ABC Corporation has a retained earnings balance of $210,000 on January 1. During the year, a prior period adjustment of $90,000 is recorded because of the understatement of depreciation in the prior period. Show the retained earnings statement presentation of these data.

11. What is the purpose of a retained earnings restriction? Identify the possible causes of retained earnings restrictions.

12. How are retained earnings restrictions generally reported in the financial statements?

13. Identify the events that result in credits and debits to retained earnings.

14. Ping Liu believes that both the beginning and ending balances in retained earnings are shown in the stockholders' equity section. Is Ping correct? Discuss.

15. Helen Louk, who owns many investments in common stock, says, "I don't care what a company's net income is. The balance sheet tells me everything I need to know!" How do you respond to Helen?

16. What is the unique feature of a corporation income statement? Illustrate this feature, using assumed data.

17. Why is it important to report discontinued operations separately from income from continuing operations?

18. You are considering investing in Alou Transportation, which reports 1999 earnings per share of $6.50 on income before extraordinary items and $4.75 on net income. Which EPS figure would you consider more relevant to your investment decision? Why?

19. Gray Inc. reported 1998 earnings per share of $3.20 and had no extraordinary items. In 1999, EPS on income before extraordinary items was $2.99, and EPS on net income was $3.49. Is this a favorable trend?

20. Indicate which of the following items would be reported as an extraordinary item in Embry Corporation's income statement.
    (a) Loss from damages caused by volcano eruption.
    (b) Loss from sale of temporary investments.
    (c) Loss attributable to a labor strike.
    (d) Loss caused when manufacture of a product was prohibited by the Food and Drug Administration.
    (e) Loss from flood damage. (The nearby Black River floods every two to three years.)
    (f) Write-down of obsolete inventory.
    (g) Expropriation of a factory by a foreign government.

21. When studying for an accounting test, a fellow student says, "Changes in accounting principle are reported in the retained earnings statement." Is your friend correct, or should he study harder?

22. Why must preferred stock dividends be subtracted from net income in computing earnings per share?

*23. What is the purpose of a stockholders' equity statement?

BRIEF EXERCISES

Prepare entries for a cash dividend.
(SO 1)

BE15–1   The Giles Corporation has 20,000 shares of common stock outstanding. It declares a $2 per share cash dividend on November 1 to stockholders of record on December 1. The dividend is paid on December 31. Prepare the entries on the appropriate dates to record the declaration and payment of the cash dividend.

BE15-2   Romano Corporation has 80,000 shares of $10 par value common stock outstanding. It declares a 10% stock dividend on December 1 when the market value per share is $15. The dividend shares are issued on December 31. Prepare the entries for the declaration and payment of the stock dividend.

Prepare entries for a stock dividend.
(SO 1)

BE15-3   The stockholders' equity section of Herrera Corporation consists of common stock ($10 par) $1,000,000 and retained earnings $300,000. A 10% stock dividend (10,000 shares) is declared when the market value per share is $16. Show the before and after effects of the dividend on (a) the components of stockholders' equity, (b) shares outstanding, and (c) book value per share.

Show before and after effects of a stock dividend.
(SO 1)

BE15-4   For the year ending December 31, 1999, Fritz Inc. reports net income $162,000 and dividends $85,000. Prepare the retained earnings statement for the year assuming the balance in retained earnings on January 1, 1999, was $220,000.

Prepare a retained earnings statement.
(SO 2)

BE15-5   Tara Corporation reported net income of $170,000, declared dividends on common stock of $50,000, and had an ending balance in retained earnings of $360,000. Stockholders' equity was $700,000 at the beginning of the year and $800,000 at the end of the year. Compute the return on common stockholders' equity.

Compute return on common stockholders' equity.
(SO 3)

BE15-6   An inexperienced accountant for Ervay Corporation showed the following in the income statement: Income before income taxes and extraordinary item is $300,000, and Extraordinary loss from flood (before taxes) is $70,000. The extraordinary loss and taxable income are both subject to a 30% tax rate. Prepare a correct income statement.

Prepare income statement including extraordinary items.
(SO 5)

BE15-7   On June 30, Ingram Corporation discontinued its operations in Mexico. During the year, the operating loss was $300,000 before taxes. On September 1, Ingram disposed of the Mexico facility at a pretax loss of $160,000. The applicable tax rate is 30%. Show the discontinued operations section of the income statement.

Prepare discontinued operations section of income statement.
(SO 5)

BE15-8   On January 1, 1999, Jimenez Inc., changed from the straight-line method of depreciation to the declining-balance method. The cumulative effect of the change was to increase prior years' depreciation by $60,000 and 1999 depreciation by $8,000. Show the change in accounting principle section of the 1999 income statement, assuming the tax rate is 30%.

Prepare change in accounting principle section of income statement.
(SO 5)

BE15-9   Klumpe Corporation's income statement shows: Income from continuing operations $580,000, Loss from discontinued operations $200,000, Extraordinary loss $90,000, and Cumulative effect of a change in accounting principle that increases net income $30,000. Show the earnings per share data in the income statement, assuming there are 100,000 shares of common stock outstanding at December 31.

Show earnings per share data in income statement.
(SO 6)

BE15-10   Lumley Corporation reports net income of $360,000 and a weighted average of 200,000 shares of common stock outstanding for the year. Compute the earnings per share of common stock.

Compute earnings per share.
(SO 6)

BE15-11   Income and common stock data for Lumley Corporation are presented in BE15-10. Assume also that Lumley has cumulative preferred stock dividends for the current year of $20,000 that were declared and paid. Compute the earnings per share of common stock.

Compute earnings per share with cumulative preferred stock.
(SO 6)

BE15-12   On January 1, 1999, MaGee Corporation had the following stockholders' equity balances: Common Stock $200,000, Paid-in Capital in Excess of Stated Value $300,000, and Retained Earnings $250,000. During 1999, it earned net income of $90,000 and declared a cash dividend of $30,000. Prepare a stockholders' equity statement for the year.

Prepare stockholders' equity statement.
(SO 7)

EXERCISES

E15-1   On January 1, Neill Corporation had 75,000 shares of no-par common stock issued and outstanding. The stock has a stated value of $5 per share. During the year, the following occurred:

Journalize cash dividends and indicate statement presentation.
(SO 1)

Apr. 1   Issued 15,000 additional shares of common stock.
June 15   Declared a cash dividend of $1 per share to stockholders of record on June 30.
July 10   Paid the $1 cash dividend.
Dec. 1   Issued 2,000 additional shares of common stock.
       15   Declared a cash dividend on outstanding shares of $1.50 per share to stockholders of record on December 31.

Instructions

(a) Prepare the entries, if any, on each of the three dividend dates.
(b) How are dividends and dividends payable reported in the financial statements prepared at December 31?

Allocate cash dividends to preferred and common stock.
(SO 1)

E15–2   The Orear Corporation was organized on January 1, 1998. During its first year, the corporation issued 2,000 shares of $50 par value preferred stock and 100,000 shares of $10 par value common stock. At December 31, the company declared the following cash dividends: 1998 $6,000, 1999 $12,000, and 2000 $28,000.

Instructions

(a) Show the allocation of dividends to each class of stock, assuming the preferred stock dividend is 8% and not cumulative.
(b) Show the allocation of dividends to each class of stock assuming the preferred stock dividend is 10% and cumulative.
(c) Journalize the declaration of the cash dividend at December 31, 2000, under part (b).

Journalize stock dividends.
(SO 1)

E15–3   On January 1, 1999, Panek Corporation had $1,000,000 of common stock outstanding that was issued at par and retained earnings of $750,000. The company issued 50,000 shares of common stock at par on July 1 and earned net income of $400,000 for the year.

Instructions

Journalize the declaration of a 10% stock dividend on December 10, 1999, for the following independent assumptions:

1. Par value is $10 and market value is $16.
2. Par value is $5 and market value is $20.

Compare effects of a stock dividend and a stock split.
(SO 1)

E15–4   On October 31, the stockholders' equity section of Rathke Company consists of Common stock $800,000 and Retained earnings $1,000,000. Rathke is considering the following two courses of action: (1) declaring a 10% stock dividend on the 80,000 $10 par value shares outstanding or (2) effecting a 2-for-1 stock split that will reduce par value to $5 per share. The current market price is $14 per share.

Instructions

Prepare a tabular summary of the effects of the alternative actions on the components of stockholders' equity, outstanding shares, and book value per share. Use the following column headings: Before Action, After Stock Dividend, and After Stock Split.

Compute book value per share and indicate account balances after a stock dividend.
(SO 1, 3)

E15–5   On October 1, Savino Corporation's stockholders' equity is as follows:

Common stock $10 par value	$200,000
Paid-in capital in excess of par value	25,000
Retained earnings	75,000
Total stockholders' equity	$300,000

On October 1, Savino declares and distributes a 10% stock dividend when the market value of the stock is $18 per share.

Instructions

(a) Compute the book value per share (1) before the stock dividend and (2) after the stock dividend. (Round to two decimals.)
(b) Indicate the balances in the three stockholders' equity accounts after the stock dividend shares have been distributed.

Indicate the effects on stockholders' equity components.
(SO 1, 2, 3)

E15–6   During 1999, Toso Corporation had the following transactions and events:

1. Declared a cash dividend.
2. Issued par value common stock for cash at par value.
3. Completed a 3-for-1 stock split in which $15 par value stock was changed to $5 par value stock.
4. Declared a stock dividend when the market value was higher than par value.
5. Made a prior period adjustment for overstatement of net income.
6. Issued the shares of common stock required by the stock dividend declaration in no. 4 above.
7. Paid the cash dividend in no. 1 above.
8. Issued par value common stock for cash above par value.

Instructions

Indicate the effect(s) of each of the foregoing items on the subdivisions of stockholders' equity. Present your answer in tabular form with the following columns. Use (I) for increase, (D) for decrease, and (NE) for no effect. Item 1 is given as an example.

	Paid-in Capital		
Item	**Capital Stock**	**Additional**	**Retained Earnings**
1.	NE	NE	D

E15–7 Before preparing financial statements for the current year, the chief accountant for O'Dell Company discovered the following errors in the accounts:

Prepare correcting entries for dividends and a stock split. (SO 1)

1. The declaration and payment of $25,000 cash dividend was recorded as a debit to Interest Expense $25,000 and a credit to Cash $25,000.
2. A 10% stock dividend (1,000 shares) was declared on the $10 par value stock when the market value per share was $14. The only entry made was: Retained Earnings (Dr.) $10,000 and Dividend Payable (Cr.) $10,000. The shares have not been issued.
3. A 4-for-1 stock split involving the issue of 400,000 shares of $5 par value common stock for 100,000 shares of $20 par value common stock was recorded as a debit to Retained Earnings $2,000,000 and a credit to Common Stock $2,000,000.

Instructions

Prepare the correcting entries at December 31.

E15–8 On January 1, 1999, Mayes Corporation had Retained Earnings of $550,000. During the year, Mayes had the following selected transactions:

Prepare a retained earnings statement. (SO 2)

1. Declared cash dividends $120,000.
2. Corrected overstatement of 1998 net income because of depreciation error $20,000.
3. Earned net income $310,000.
4. Declared stock dividends $60,000.

Instructions

Prepare a retained earnings statement for the year.

E15–9 The following accounts appear in the ledger of Osaki Inc. after the books are closed at December 31.

Prepare a stockholders' equity section. (SO 3)

Common Stock, no par, $1 stated value, 400,000 shares authorized; 300,000 shares issued	$ 300,000
Common Stock Dividends Distributable	75,000
Paid-in Capital in Excess of Stated Value—Common Stock	1,200,000
Preferred Stock, $5 par value, 8%, 40,000 shares authorized; 30,000 shares issued	150,000
Retained Earnings	700,000
Treasury Stock (10,000 common shares)	60,000
Paid-in Capital in Excess of Par Value—Preferred Stock	244,000

Instructions

Prepare stockholders' equity section at December 31, assuming retained earnings is restricted for plant expansion in the amount of $100,000.

E15–10 This financial information is available for Mary Jo Corporation:

Calculate ratios to evaluate earnings performance. (SO 3, 6)

	1999	1998
Average common stockholders' equity	$1,200,000	$900,000
Dividends paid to common stockholders	50,000	30,000
Dividends paid to preferred stockholders	10,000	10,000
Net income	200,000	140,000
Market price of common stock	20	15

The weighted average number of shares of common stock outstanding was 80,000 for 1998 and 100,000 for 1999.

Instructions

Calculate earnings per share and return on common stockholders' equity for 1999 and 1998.

Calculate ratios to evaluate earnings performance.
(SO 3, 6)

E15–11 This financial information is available for Fountain City Corporation:

	1999	1998
Average common stockholders' equity	$1,800,000	$1,900,000
Dividends paid to common stockholders	90,000	70,000
Dividends paid to preferred stockholders	10,000	15,000
Net income	230,000	180,000
Market price of common stock	20	25

The weighted number of shares of common stock outstanding was 180,000 for 1998 and 150,000 for 1999.

Instructions
Calculate earnings per share and return on common stockholders' equity for 1999 and 1998.

Prepare a correct income statement.
(SO 4, 5)

E15–12 For its fiscal year ending October 31, 1999, Lorenz Corporation reports the following partial data:

Income before income taxes	$640,000
Income tax expense (30% × $550,000)	165,000
Income before extraordinary items	475,000
Extraordinary loss from fire	90,000
Net income	$385,000

The fire loss is considered an extraordinary item. The income tax rate is 30% on all items.

Instructions
(a) Prepare a correct income statement, beginning with income before income taxes.
(b) 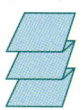 Explain in memo form why the income statement data are misleading.

Prepare income statement.
(SO 4, 5)

E15–13 Kelso Corporation has income from continuing operations of $240,000 for the year ended December 31, 1999. It also has the following items (before considering income taxes): (1) an extraordinary fire loss of $80,000, (2) a gain of $50,000 on the discontinuance of a division, (3) a cumulative change in an accounting principle that resulted in an increase in prior years' depreciation of $30,000, and (4) a correction of an error in last year's financial statements that resulted in a $20,000 understatement of 1998 net income. Assume all items are subject to income taxes at a 30% tax rate.

Instructions
(a) Prepare an income statement, beginning with income from continuing operations.
(b) Indicate the statement presentation of any item not included in (a) above.

Compute earnings per share under different assumptions.
(SO 6)

E15–14 At December 31, 1999, Heimer Corporation has 2,000 shares of $100 par value, 8%, preferred stock outstanding and 100,000 shares of $10 par value common stock issued. Heimer's net income for the year is $500,000.

Instructions
Compute the earnings per share of common stock under the following independent situations. (Round to two decimals.)

1. The dividend to preferred stockholders was declared, and there has been no change in the number of shares of common stock outstanding during the year.
2. The dividend to preferred stockholders was not declared. The preferred stock is cumulative. Heimer held 10,000 shares of common treasury stock throughout the year.

Prepare stockholders' equity statement.
(SO 7)

*E15–15 Jaeger, Inc. has the following stockholders' equity balances at January 1, 1999: Common Stock ($5 par) $600,000, Paid-in Capital in Excess of Par Value $230,000, and Retained Earnings $160,000. In 1999, the following transactions and events occurred:

1. Issued 15,000 additional shares of common stock for $120,000.
2. Declared and paid a cash dividend of $30,000.
3. Net income was $100,000.

Instructions
Prepare a stockholders' equity statement for the year ended December 31, 1999.

PROBLEMS: SET A

. . . .

P15–1A On January 1, 1999, O'Brien Corporation had the following stockholders' equity accounts:

Common Stock ($10 par value, 80,000 shares issued and outstanding)	$800,000
Paid-in Capital in Excess of Par Value	200,000
Retained Earnings	540,000

Prepare dividend entries and stockholders' equity section.
(SO 1, 3)

During the year, the following transactions occurred:

Jan. 15   Declared a $1 cash dividend per share to stockholders of record on January 31, payable February 15.
Feb. 15   Paid the dividend declared in January.
Apr. 15   Declared a 10% stock dividend to stockholders of record on April 30, distributable May 15. On April 15, the market price of the stock was $13 per share.
May 15   Issued the shares for the stock dividend.
July 1   Announced a 2-for-1 stock split. The market price per share prior to the announcement was $15. (The new par value is $5.)
Dec. 1   Declared a $.50 per share cash dividend to stockholders of record on December 15, payable January 10, 2000.
     31   Determined that net income for the year was $250,000.

Instructions
(a) Journalize the transactions and the closing entry for net income.
(b) Enter the beginning balances and post the entries to the stockholders' equity accounts. (*Note:* Open additional stockholders' equity accounts as needed.)
(c) Prepare a stockholders' equity section at December 31.

P15–2A The stockholders' equity accounts of Rodriguez, Inc., at January 1, 1999, are as follows:

Preferred Stock, $100 par, 9%	$400,000
Common Stock, $5 par	900,000
Paid-in Capital in Excess of Par Value—Preferred Stock	100,000
Paid-in Capital in Excess of Par Value—Common Stock	200,000
Retained Earnings	500,000

Journalize and post transactions, and prepare retained earnings statement and stockholders' equity section.
(SO 1, 2, 3)

During 1999, the company had the following transactions and events:

July 1   Declared a $.50 cash dividend on common stock.
Aug. 1   Discovered a $72,000 overstatement of 1998 depreciation. Ignore income taxes.
Sept. 1   Paid the cash dividend declared on July 1.
Dec. 1   Declared a 10% stock dividend on common stock when the market value of the stock was $12 per share.
     15   Declared a 9% cash dividend on preferred stock payable January 31, 2000.
     31   Determined that net income for the year was $350,000.

Instructions
(a) Journalize the transactions and the closing entry for net income.
(b) Enter the beginning balances in the accounts and post to the stockholders' equity accounts. (*Note:* Open additional stockholders' equity accounts as needed.)
(c) Prepare a retained earnings statement for the year.
(d) Prepare a stockholders' equity section at December 31, 1999.

P15–3A The ledger of Quandt Corporation at December 31, 1999, after the books have been closed, contains the following stockholders' equity accounts:

Preferred Stock (10,000 shares issued)	$1,000,000
Common Stock (400,000 shares issued)	2,000,000
Paid-in Capital in Excess of Par Value—Preferred	200,000
Paid-in Capital in Excess of Par Value—Common	1,200,000
Common Stock Dividends Distributable	100,000
Retained Earnings	2,340,000

Prepare retained earnings statement and stockholders' equity section, and compute earnings per share.
(SO 1, 2, 3, 6)

A review of the accounting records reveals the following:

1. No errors have been made in recording 1999 transactions or in preparing the closing entry for net income.
2. Preferred stock is 10% $100 par value, noncumulative, and callable at $125. Since January 1, 1998, 10,000 shares have been outstanding; 20,000 shares are authorized.
3. Common stock is no-par with a stated value of $5 per share; 600,000 shares are authorized.
4. The January 1 balance in Retained Earnings was $2,200,000.
5. On October 1, 100,000 shares of common stock were sold for cash at $8 per share.
6. A cash dividend of $600,000 was declared and properly allocated to preferred and common stock on November 1. No dividends were paid to preferred stockholders in 1998.
7. On December 31, a 5% common stock dividend was declared out of retained earnings on common stock when the market price per share was $7.
8. Net income for the year was $880,000.
9. On December 31, 1999, the directors authorized disclosure of a $100,000 restriction of retained earnings for plant expansion. (Use Note A.)

Instructions
(a) Reproduce the retained earnings account (T-account) for the year.
(b) Prepare a retained earnings statement for the year.
(c) Prepare a stockholders' equity section at December 31.
(d) Compute the earnings per share of common stock using 325,000 as the weighted average shares outstanding for the year.
(e) Compute the allocation of the cash dividend to preferred and common stock.

Prepare income statement with discontinued operations and an extraordinary loss, and compute earnings per share.
(SO 4, 5, 6)

P15–4A   Patel Corporation owns a number of travel agencies and a chain of motels in the Northwest. Its condensed operating results for 1999 show the following:

Operating revenues	$14,580,000
Operating expenses	10,600,000
Income from operations	$ 3,980,000

An additional analysis of the data indicate that the travel agencies are very profitable but the motel chain has been unprofitable. Through September 30, the motels lost $500,000 from operating revenues of $4,200,000 and operating expenses of $4,700,000. On October 1, the motel operation was discontinued and sold at a loss of $1,000,000 before taxes. The motel operating results are included in income from operations, but the loss on disposal is not included in the operating results shown above. During the year, the corporation had other expenses and losses of $80,000, which are not included in the operating results. In November, a condemnation action was taken against the company to obtain property for a new national park. As a result, the corporation suffered an extraordinary loss of $800,000 before taxes which is not included in the operating results. The corporation is in a 30% tax bracket.

Instructions
(a) Prepare a condensed income statement for the year.
(b) Compute all of the earnings per share amounts that should appear on the income statement. Assume weighted average shares of stock equaled 400,000. (Round to two decimals.)

Prepare expanded income statement, and compute earnings per share data.
(SO 4, 5, 6)

P15–5A   The ledger of Mesa Corporation at December 31, 1999, contains the following summary data:

Net sales	$1,500,000	Cost of goods sold	$800,000
Selling expenses	110,000	Administrative expenses	140,000
Other revenues and gains	40,000	Other expenses and losses	30,000

Your analysis reveals the following additional information that is not included in the above data.

1. The entire ceramics division was discontinued on August 31. The loss from operations for this division before income taxes was $150,000. The ceramics division was sold at a gain of $60,000 before income taxes.
2. On July 12, a fire occurred in one plant that resulted in an extraordinary loss of $90,000 before income taxes.

3. During the year, Mesa changed its depreciation method from straight-line to declining balance. The cumulative effect of the change on prior years' net income was a decrease of $30,000 before taxes. (Assume that depreciation under the new method is correctly included in the ledger data.)

4. The income tax rate on all items is 30%.

Instructions

(a) Prepare an income statement for the year ended December 31, 1999, using the format illustrated in the Demonstration Problem (p. 656).

(b) Prepare the earnings per share data that should appear in the income statement, assuming there were 100,000 shares of common stock outstanding throughout the year.

P15–6A   On January 1, 1999, Leiker Inc. had the following stockholders' equity balances:

Prepare stockholders' equity statement.
(SO 7)

Common Stock (500,000 shares issued)	$1,000,000
Paid-in Capital in Excess of Par Value	500,000
Stock Dividends Distributable	100,000
Retained Earnings	600,000

During 1999, the following transactions and events occurred:

1. Issued 50,000 shares of $2 par value common stock as a result of 10% stock dividend declared on December 15, 1998.
2. Issued 40,000 shares of common stock for cash at $5 per share.
3. Purchased 20,000 shares of common stock for the treasury at $6 per share.
4. Declared and paid a cash dividend of $100,000.
5. Sold 5,000 shares of treasury stock for cash at $6 per share.
6. Earned net income of $300,000.

Instructions

Prepare a stockholders' equity statement for the year.

PROBLEMS: SET B

P15–1B   On January 1, 1999, Stengel Corporation had the following stockholders' equity accounts:

Prepare dividend entries and stockholders' equity section.
(SO 1, 3)

Common Stock ($20 par value, 60,000 shares issued and outstanding)	$1,200,000
Paid-in Capital in Excess of Par Value	200,000
Retained Earnings	600,000

During the year, the following transactions occurred:

Feb. 1   Declared a $1 cash dividend per share to stockholders of record on February 15, payable March 1.

Mar. 1   Paid the dividend declared in February.

Apr. 1   Announced a 4-for-1 stock split. Prior to the split, the market price per share was $36.

July 1   Declared a 5% stock dividend to stockholders of record on July 15, distributable July 31. On July 1, the market price of the stock was $13 per share.

     31   Issued the shares for the stock dividend.

Dec. 1   Declared a $.50 per share dividend to stockholders of record on December 15, payable January 5, 2000.

     31   Determined that net income for the year was $350,000.

Instructions

(a) Journalize the transactions and the closing entry for net income.

(b) Enter the beginning balances and post the entries to the stockholders' equity accounts. (*Note:* Open additional stockholders' equity accounts as needed.)

(c) Prepare a stockholders' equity section at December 31.

Journalize and post transactions, and prepare retained earnings statement and stockholders' equity section.
(SO 1, 2, 3)

P15–2B   The stockholders' equity accounts of Fryman Company at January 1, 1999, are as follows:

Preferred Stock, 9%, $50 par	$300,000
Common Stock, $2 par	500,000
Paid-in Capital in Excess of Par Value—Preferred Stock	200,000
Paid-in Capital in Excess of Par Value—Common Stock	300,000
Retained Earnings	600,000

During 1999, the company had the following transactions and events:

July 1 Declared a $.50 cash dividend on common stock.

Aug. 1 Discovered $45,000 understatement of 1998 depreciation. Ignore income taxes.

Sept. 1 Paid the cash dividend declared on July 1.

Dec. 1 Declared 10% stock dividend on common stock when the market value of the stock was $18 per share.

     15 Declared a 9% cash dividend on preferred stock payable January 15, 2000.

     31 Determined that net income for the year was $385,000.

     31 Recognized a $200,000 restriction of retained earnings for plant expansion.

Instructions

(a) Journalize the transactions, events, and closing entries.

(b) Enter the beginning balances in the accounts and post to the stockholders' equity accounts. (*Note:* Open additional stockholders' equity accounts as needed.)

(c) Prepare a retained earnings statement for the year.

(d) Prepare a stockholders' equity section at December 31, 1999.

Prepare retained earnings statement and stockholders' equity section, and compute earnings per share.
(SO 1, 2, 3, 6)

P15–3B   The post-closing trial balance of Javier Corporation at December 31, 1999, contains the following stockholders' equity accounts:

Preferred Stock (15,000 shares issued)	$ 750,000
Common Stock (250,000 shares issued)	2,500,000
Paid-in Capital in Excess of Par Value—Preferred	250,000
Paid-in Capital in Excess of Par Value—Common	500,000
Common Stock Dividends Distributable	200,000
Retained Earnings	803,000

A review of the accounting records reveals the following:

1. No errors have been made in recording 1999 transactions or in preparing the closing entry for net income.

2. Preferred stock is $50 par, 10%, and cumulative. 15,000 shares have been outstanding since January 1, 1998.

3. Authorized stock is 20,000 shares of preferred, 500,000 shares of common with a $10 par value.

4. The January 1 balance in Retained Earnings was $920,000.

5. On July 1, 20,000 shares of common stock were sold for cash at $16 per share.

6. On September 1, the company discovered an understatement error of $60,000 in computing depreciation in 1998. The net of tax effect of $42,000 was properly debited directly to Retained Earnings.

7. A cash dividend of $250,000 was declared and properly allocated to preferred and common stock on October 1. No dividends were paid to preferred stockholders in 1998.

8. On December 31, an 8% common stock dividend was declared out of retained earnings on common stock when the market price per share was $16.

9. Net income for the year was $495,000.

10. On December 31, 1999, the directors authorized disclosure of a $200,000 restriction of retained earnings for plant expansion. (Use Note X.)

Instructions

(a) Reproduce the retained earnings account for the year.

(b) Prepare a retained earnings statement for the year.

(c) Prepare a stockholders' equity section at December 31.

(d) Compute the earnings per share of common stock using 240,000 as the weighted average shares outstanding for the year.

(e) Compute the allocation of the cash dividend to preferred and common stock.

P15–4B Lau Corporation owns a number of cruise ships and a chain of hotels. The hotels, which have not been profitable, were discontinued on September 1, 1999. The 1999 operating results for the company were as follows:

Prepare income statement with discontinued operations and extraordinary loss, and compute earnings per share.
(SO 4, 5, 6)

Operating revenues	$12,600,000
Operating expenses	8,600,000
Operating income	$ 4,000,000

Analysis discloses that these data include the operating results of the hotel chain, which were: operating revenues $3,000,000 and operating expenses $4,000,000. The hotels were sold at a gain of $500,000 before taxes. This gain is not included in the operating results. During the year, Lau suffered an extraordinary fire loss of $800,000 before taxes which is not included in the operating results. In 1999, the company had other revenues and gains of $100,000, which are not included in the operating results. The corporation is in the 30% income tax bracket.

Instructions
(a) Prepare a condensed income statement.
(b) Compute the earnings per share data that should appear in the income statement. Assume weighted average shares of stock equaled 440,000. (Round to two decimals.)

P15–5B The ledger of Yevak Corporation at December 31, 1999, contains the following summary data:

Prepare income statement with nontypical items, and compute earnings per share data.
(SO 4, 5, 6)

Net sales	$1,800,000	Cost of goods sold	$1,000,000
Selling expenses	120,000	Administrative expenses	130,000
Other revenues and gains	20,000	Other expenses and losses	28,000

Your analysis reveals the following additional information that is not included in the above data.

1. The entire puzzles division was discontinued on August 31. The gain from operations for this division before income taxes was $50,000. The puzzles division was sold at a loss of $70,000 before income taxes.
2. On May 15, company property was expropriated for an interstate highway. The settlement resulted in an extraordinary gain of $90,000 before income taxes.
3. During the year, Yevak changed its depreciation method from double-declining balance to straight-line. The cumulative effect of the change on prior years' net income was an increase of $60,000 before taxes. (Assume that depreciation under the new method is correctly included in the ledger data.)
4. The income tax rate on all items is 30%.

Instructions
(a) Prepare an income statement for the year ended December 31, 1999, using the format illustrated in the Demonstration Problem (p. 656).
(b) Prepare the earnings per share data that should appear in the income statement, assuming there were 100,000 shares of common stock outstanding throughout the year.

BROADENING YOUR PERSPECTIVE

FINANCIAL REPORTING AND ANALYSIS
. . . .

FINANCIAL REPORTING PROBLEM: Kellogg Company

BYP15–1 The financial statements of Kellogg Company are presented in Appendix A.

Instructions
Refer to Kellogg's financial statements and answer the following questions:

(a) What was Kellogg's dividend paid per share in 1997? What was the total dividend paid? What percentage of Kellogg's December 31, 1997, retained earnings did this dividend represent? What percentage of reported net income did this dividend represent? What percentage of cash and cash equivalents did this dividend represent?

(b) Kellogg reported nonrecurring charges in its income statement. What was the nature of these nonrecurring charges in 1997? How did these items differ from discontinued operations?

(c) The Selected Financial Data table in the Management Discussion and Analysis section has a footnote describing accounting changes enacted by Kellogg. In what way does adoption of a new standard affect the ability to analyze Kellogg's results over the past 10 years?

COMPARATIVE ANALYSIS PROBLEM: Kellogg Company vs. General Mills

BYP15–2 Kellogg's financial statements are presented in Appendix A; General Mills's financial statements are presented in Appendix B.

Instructions

(a) Compute earnings per share and return on common stockholders' equity for both companies for 1997. Assume Kellogg's weighted average shares were 414,100,000 and General Mills's weighted average shares were 158,200,000. Can these measures be used to compare the profitability of the two companies? Why or why not?

(b) What was the total amount of dividends paid by each company in 1997? What fraction of net income did the dividend represent for each company?

(c) Did either company report one of the three types of irregular items on its income statement? If so, what was the nature of the irregular item?

RESEARCH ASSIGNMENT

BYP15–3 The October 3, 1994, issue of *Barron's* includes an article by Shirley A. Lazo entitled ''Split Decision: One Way to Lift Shares.''

Instructions
Read the article and answer the following questions:

(a) Why might a stock dividend/split have a positive effect on shareholder wealth?

(b) Why might a stock dividend/split have a negative effect on shareholder wealth?

(c) According to the study described in the article, what happens to the stock prices of banks during the month following a stock dividend/split?

(d) What conclusion was drawn from the study?

INTERPRETING FINANCIAL STATEMENTS: BFGoodrich Company

BYP15–4 The BFGoodrich Company is a diversified manufacturer of tires, vinyl products, specialty chemicals, and aerospace products. Selected financial data, in millions of dollars, for a recent two-year period were as follows.

	Current Year	Prior Year
Sales	$2,416.7	$2,023.5
Total operating income	298.0	200.7
Income from continuing operations	209.9	83.6
Income (loss) from discontinued operations (net of taxes)	(16.9)	(4.4)
Extraordinary items (net of taxes)		25.8
Cumulative effect of change in method of accounting for taxes	2.7	
Net income	195.7	105.0
Dividends on preferred stock	8.8	9.8
Dividends on common stock	43.3	37.0
Income retained in the business at end of year	548.9	405.3

The notes to the company's financial statements indicate that the weighted average number of common shares outstanding (in thousands of shares) were 25,179 for the current year and 23,651 for the prior year. In addition, the stockholders' equity section of the balance sheet shows that at December 31 of the current year there were 25,554,627 shares of common stock issued and 352,396 shares of common stock held in the treasury.

Instructions
- (a) Present the earnings per share data for the company for each year.
- (b) Comment on the relative importance of material nontypical items in each year.
- (c) Discuss how you would factor these nontypical items into your prediction of next year's net income for BFGoodrich.
- (d) Prepare a retained earning statement for the current year.
- (e) What was the total dividend per share of common stock for the current year?

REAL-WORLD FOCUS: Diebold, Inc.

BYP15–5   **Diebold, Inc.,** is a world leader in financial self-service transaction systems, security products, and customer service. The company develops, manufactures, sells, and services automated teller machines (ATMs), electronic and physical security systems, and bank facility equipment. It also designs and markets related application software and integrated systems for global financial and commercial markets. Headquartered in Canton, Ohio, Diebold has offices in five countries and manufacturing facilities in the United States and in China.

     The following note related to stockholders' equity was recently reported in Diebold's annual report:

DIEBOLD, INC.
Notes to the Financial Statements

On February 1, 1994, the Board of Directors declared a 3-for-2 stock split, distributed on February 22, 1994, to shareholders of record on February 10, 1994. Accordingly, all numbers of common shares, except authorized shares and treasury shares, and all per share data have been restated to reflect this stock split in addition to the 3-for-2 stock split declared on January 27, 1993, distributed on February 26, 1993, to shareholders of record on February 10, 1993.

     On the basis of amounts declared and paid, the annualized quarterly dividends per share were $0.80 in 1993, $0.75 in 1992, and $0.71 in 1991.

Instructions
- (a) What is the significance of the date of record and the date of distribution?
- (b) Why might Diebold have declared a 3-for-2 stock split?
- (c) What impact does Diebold's stock split have on (1) total stockholders' equity; (2) total par value; (3) outstanding shares, and (4) book value per share?

CRITICAL THINKING

GROUP DECISION CASE

BYP15–6   General Dynamics develops, produces, and supports innovative, reliable, and highly sophisticated military and commercial products. In July of a recent year, the corporation announced that its Quincy Shipbuilding Division (Quincy) will be closed following the completion of the Maritime Prepositioning Ship construction program.

     Prior to discontinuance, the operating results of Quincy were net sales $246.8 million, income from operations before income taxes $28.3 million, and income taxes $12.5 million. The corporation's loss on disposition of Quincy was $5.0 million, net of $4.3 million income tax benefits.

     From its other operating activities, General Dynamics' financial results were net sales $8,163.8 million, cost of goods sold $6,958.8 million, and selling and administrative expenses $537.0 million. In addition, the corporation had interest expense of $17.2 million and interest revenue of $3.6 million. Income taxes were $282.9 million.

General Dynamics had an average of 42.3 million shares of common stock outstanding during the year.

Instructions

With the class divided into groups, answer the following:

(a) Prepare the income statement for the year, assuming that the year ended on December 31, 1999. Show earnings per share data on the income statement. All dollars should be stated in millions, except for per share amounts. (For example, $8 million would be shown as $8.0.)

(b) In the preceding year, Quincy's earnings were $51.6 million before income taxes of $22.8 million. For comparative purposes, General Dynamics reported earnings per share of $0.61 from discontinued operations for Quincy in the preceding year.

  1. What was the average number of common shares outstanding during the preceding year?
  2. If earnings per share from continuing operations was $7.47, what was income from continuing operations during the preceding year? (Round to two decimals.)

COMMUNICATION ACTIVITY

BYP15–7 In the past year, Alameda Corporation declared a 10% stock dividend, and Butte, Inc., announced a 2-for-1 stock split. Your parents own 100 shares of each company's $50 par value common stock. During a recent phone call, your parents ask you, as an accounting student, to explain the difference between the two events.

Instructions

Write a letter to your parents that explains the effects of the two events to them as stockholders and the effects of each event on the financial statements of each corporation.

ETHICS CASE

BYP15–8 Flambeau Corporation has paid 60 consecutive quarterly cash dividends (15 years). The last 6 months, however, have been a cash drain on the company, as profit margins have been greatly narrowed by increasing competition. With a cash balance sufficient to meet only day-to-day operating needs, the president, Vince Ramsey, has decided that a stock dividend instead of a cash dividend should be declared. He tells Flambeau's financial vice president, Janice Rahn, to issue a press release stating that the company is extending its consecutive dividend record with the issuance of a 5% stock dividend. "Write the press release convincing the stockholders that the stock dividend is just as good as a cash dividend," he orders. "Just watch our stock rise when we announce the stock dividend; it must be a good thing if that happens."

Instructions

(a) Who are the stakeholders in this situation?
(b) Is there anything unethical about Ramsey's intentions or actions?
(c) What is the effect of a stock dividend on a corporation's stockholders' equity accounts? Which would you rather receive as a stockholder—a cash dividend or a stock dividend? Why?

SURFING THE NET

BYP15–9 Use the stockholders' equity section of an annual report and identify the major components.

Address: http://www.reportgallery.com

Steps:
  1. From Report Gallery Homepage, choose **Viewing Library.**
  2. Select a particular company.
  3. Choose Annual Report.
  4. Follow instructions below.

Instructions
Answer the following questions:
- (a) What is the company's name?
- (b) What classes of capital stock has the company issued?
- (c) For each class of stock:
    - (1) How many shares are authorized, issued, and/or outstanding?
    - (2) What is the par value?
- (d) What are the company's retained earnings?
- (e) Has the company acquired treasury stock? How many shares?

Answers to Self-Study Questions
1. a   2. c   3. d   4. b   5. d   6. b   7. c   8. c   9. d   10. b   *11. a

---

Answer to Kellogg Review It Question 3, p. 652
In its 1997 income statement Kellogg reported a cumulative effect of accounting change.

 **Remember to go back to the Navigator box on the chapter-opening page and check off your completed work.**

CONCEPTS FOR REVIEW

Before studying this chapter, you should know or, if necessary, review:

a. What is a long-term liability? a current liability? (Ch. 4, pp. 159–160 and Ch. 11, p. 470).

b. How to record adjusting entries for interest expense and payable. (Ch. 3, pp. 104–105).

c. How to record entries for the issuance of notes payable and related interest expense. (Ch. 11, p. 471).

THE
NAVIGATOR

FEATURE STORY

UK Builds with Bonds

Every year, hundreds of colleges around the country build new buildings. Where do most schools get the money for these expensive projects? From long-term bonds, which are obligations in which the issuer of the bond promises to repay the loan amount plus interest on or before a specified date.

The University of Kentucky (UK) has issued "revenue" bonds to build buildings on the 23,000-student Lexington campus, and on 14 community colleges throughout the state. These bonds pledge the school's revenues as collateral to guarantee payment of the bonds. At one time the outstanding debt on the Lexington campus buildings was $137 million. The total debt on the community college buildings equaled $121 million. The bonds generally have maturities ranging from 10 to 20 years.

Additional "guarantees" for bond purchasers are the ratings given the bonds by professional rating agencies. "Our bonds are rated AA− by Standard & Poor's Corp.," says Henry Clay Owen, UK's treasurer. "That's well above investment grade," he says. "We always have a very good market for our bonds. People in Kentucky identify very closely with the university. Even though the bonds are rated AA−, they trade at AAA [the top bond rating] because they're so easy to sell."

One advantage for investors: the bonds' interest revenue is exempt from federal income tax and from state tax for in-state investors. So, an issue offering 6% is the equivalent of 10% to those individuals in the top tax bracket. "I would feel very comfortable buying UK bonds because it's inconceivable to me that there would ever be a default," says Owen.

THE
NAVIGATOR

CHAPTER 16

LONG-TERM LIABILITIES

THE NAVIGATOR ✔

- Understand *Concepts for Review* ☐
- Read *Feature Story* ☐
- Scan *Study Objectives* ☐
- Read *Preview* ☐
- Read text and answer *Before You Go On*
  p. 681 ☐ p. 688 ☐ p. 691 ☐ p. 697 ☐
- Work *Demonstration Problems* ☐
- Review *Summary of Study Objectives* ☐
- Answer *Self-Study Questions* ☐
- Complete assignments ☐

STUDY OBJECTIVES

After studying this chapter, you should be able to:

1. Explain why bonds are issued.
2. Prepare the entries for the issuance of bonds and interest expense.
3. Describe the entries when bonds are redeemed or converted.
4. Indicate the entries required for a bond sinking fund.
5. Describe the accounting for long-term notes payable.
6. Contrast the accounting for operating and capital leases.
7. Identify the methods for the presentation and analysis of long-term liabilities.

THE NAVIGATOR

*A*s you can see from the opening story, the University of Kentucky has chosen to issue long-term bonds to fund its building projects. The UK bonds are classified as long-term liabilities because they are obligations that are expected to be paid after one year. In this chapter we will explain the accounting for the major types of long-term liabilities reported on the balance sheet. These liabilities may be bonds, long-term notes, or lease obligations. The content and organization of the chapter are as follows:

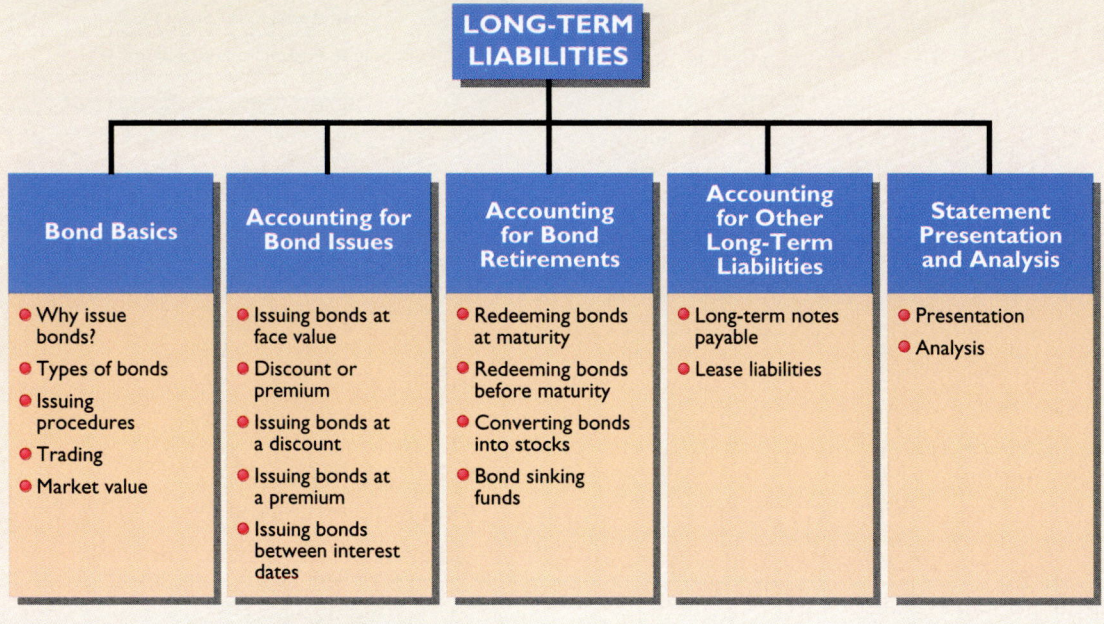

LONG-TERM LIABILITIES

Bond Basics	Accounting for Bond Issues	Accounting for Bond Retirements	Accounting for Other Long-Term Liabilities	Statement Presentation and Analysis
• Why issue bonds? • Types of bonds • Issuing procedures • Trading • Market value	• Issuing bonds at face value • Discount or premium • Issuing bonds at a discount • Issuing bonds at a premium • Issuing bonds between interest dates	• Redeeming bonds at maturity • Redeeming bonds before maturity • Converting bonds into stocks • Bond sinking funds	• Long-term notes payable • Lease liabilities	• Presentation • Analysis

THE NAVIGATOR

BOND BASICS

Bonds are a form of interest bearing notes payable issued by corporations, universities, and governmental agencies. Bonds, like common stock, are sold in small denominations (usually a thousand dollars or multiples of a thousand dollars). As a result, bonds attract many investors.

Why Issue Bonds?

A corporation may use long-term financing other than bonds, such as notes payable and leasing. However, these other forms of financing involve one individual, one company, or a financial institution. Notes payable and leasing are therefore seldom sufficient to furnish the funds needed for plant expansion and major projects like new buildings. To obtain **large amounts of long-term capital**, corporate management usually must decide whether to issue bonds or to use equity financing (common stock).

From the standpoint of the corporation seeking long-term financing, bonds offer the following advantages over common stock:

ILLUSTRATION 16-1

Advantages of bond financing over common stock

Bond Financing	Advantages
(Ballot Box)	1. **Stockholder control is not affected.** Bondholders do not have voting rights, so current owners (stockholders) retain full control of the company.
(Tax Bill)	2. **Tax savings result.** Bond interest is deductible for tax purposes; dividends on stock are not.
($/Stock)	3. **Earnings per share on common stock may be higher.** Although bond interest expense reduces net income, earnings per share on common stock often is higher under bond financing because no additional shares of common stock are issued.

To illustrate the potential effect on earnings per share, assume that Microsystems, Inc., is considering two plans for financing the construction of a new $5 million plant: Plan A involves issuance of 200,000 shares of common stock at the current market price of $25 per share. Plan B involves issuance of $5 million, 12% bonds at face value. Income before interest and taxes on the new plant will be $1.5 million; income taxes are expected to be 30%. Microsystems currently has 100,000 shares of common stock outstanding. The alternative effects on earnings per share are shown in Illustration 16-2.

ILLUSTRATION 16-2

Effects on earnings per share—stocks vs. bonds

	Plan A Issue Stock	Plan B Issue Bonds
Income before interest and taxes	$1,500,000	$1,500,000
Interest (12% × $5,000,000)	—	600,000
Income before income taxes	1,500,000	900,000
Income tax expense (30%)	450,000	270,000
Net income	$1,050,000	$ 630,000
Outstanding shares	300,000	100,000
Earnings per share	$ 3.50	$ 6.30

Note that net income is $420,000 ($1,050,000 − $630,000) less with long-term debt financing (bonds). However, earnings per share is higher because there are 200,000 fewer shares of common stock outstanding.

The major disadvantages resulting from the use of bonds are that interest must be paid on a periodic basis and the principal (face value) of the bonds must be paid at maturity. A company with fluctuating earnings and a relatively weak cash position may experience great difficulty in meeting interest requirements in periods of low earnings.

INTERNATIONAL NOTE

The priority of bondholders' versus stockholders' rights varies across countries. In Japan, Germany, and France stockholders and employees are given priority, with liquidation of the firm to pay creditors seen as a last resort. In Britain creditors' interests are put first—the courts are quick to give control of the firm to creditors.

Types of Bonds

Bonds may have many different features. Some types of bonds commonly issued are described in the following sections:

Secured and Unsecured Bonds

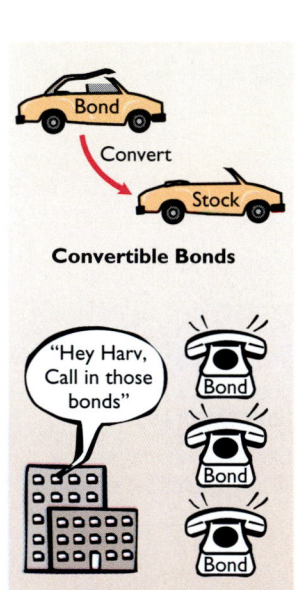

Secured bonds have specific assets of the issuer pledged as collateral for the bonds. A bond secured by real estate, for example, is called a **mortgage bond**. A bond secured by specific assets set aside to retire the bonds is called a **sinking fund bond**. (This type of bond is discussed later in the chapter.) **Unsecured bonds** are issued against the general credit of the borrower. These bonds, called **debenture bonds**, are used extensively by large corporations with good credit ratings. For example, in a recent annual report, DuPont reported over $2 billion of debenture bonds outstanding.

Term and Serial Bonds

Bonds that are due for payment (mature) at a single specified future date are called **term bonds**. In contrast, bonds that mature in installments are called **serial bonds**. For example, Caterpillar Inc. debentures due in 2007 are term bonds, and their debentures due between 1999 and 2007 are serial bonds.

Registered and Bearer Bonds

Bonds issued in the name of the owner are called **registered bonds**; interest payments on registered bonds are made by check to bondholders of record. Bonds not registered are called **bearer (or coupon) bonds**; holders are required to send in coupons to receive interest payments. Coupon bonds may be transferred directly to another party. In contrast, the transfer of registered bonds requires cancellation of the bonds by the corporation and the issuance of new bonds. With minor exceptions, most bonds issued today are registered bonds.

Convertible and Callable Bonds

Bonds that can be converted into common stock at the bondholder's option are called **convertible bonds**. Bonds subject to retirement at a stated dollar amount prior to maturity at the option of the issuer are known as **callable bonds**.

Issuing Procedures

State laws grant corporations the power to issue bonds. Within the corporation, formal approval by both the board of directors and stockholders is usually required before bonds can be issued. **In authorizing the bond issue, the board of directors must stipulate the total number of bonds to be authorized, total face value, and the contractual interest rate**. The total bond authorization often exceeds the number of bonds originally issued. This is done intentionally to help ensure that the corporation will have the flexibility it needs to meet future cash requirements.

The **face value** is the amount of principal due at the maturity date. The **contractual interest rate**, often referred to as the **stated rate**, is the rate used to determine the amount of cash interest the borrower pays and the investor receives. Usually the contractual rate is stated as an annual rate, and interest is generally paid semiannually.

The terms of the bond issue are set forth in a legal document called a **bond indenture**. In addition to the terms, the indenture summarizes the respective rights and privileges of the bondholders and their trustees, as well as the obligations and commitments of the issuing company. The **trustee** (usually a financial institution) keeps records of each bondholder, maintains custody of unissued bonds, and holds conditional title to pledged property.

ACCOUNTING IN ACTION

Business Insight

Although bonds are generally secured by solid, substantial assets like land, buildings, and equipment, exceptions occur. For example Trans World Airlines Inc. (TWA) at one time decided to issue $300 million of high-yielding 5-year bonds. TWA's bonds would be secured by a grab bag of assets, including some durable spare parts, but also a lot of disposable items that TWA had in its warehouses, such as light bulbs and gaskets. Some called the planned TWA bonds "light bulb bonds." As one financial expert noted: "You've got to admit that some security is better than none." However, another noted, "They're digging pretty far down the barrel."

After the bond indenture is prepared, **bond certificates** are printed. The indenture and the certificate are separate documents. As shown in Illustration 16-3, a bond certificate provides information such as the following: name of the issuer, the face value of the bonds, the contractual interest rate, and the maturity date of the bonds. Bonds are generally sold through an investment company that specializes in selling securities. In most cases, the issue is underwritten by the investment company. Under an underwriting arrangement, the company sells the bonds to the investment company, which, in turn, sells the bonds to individual investors.

ILLUSTRATION 16-3

Bond certificate

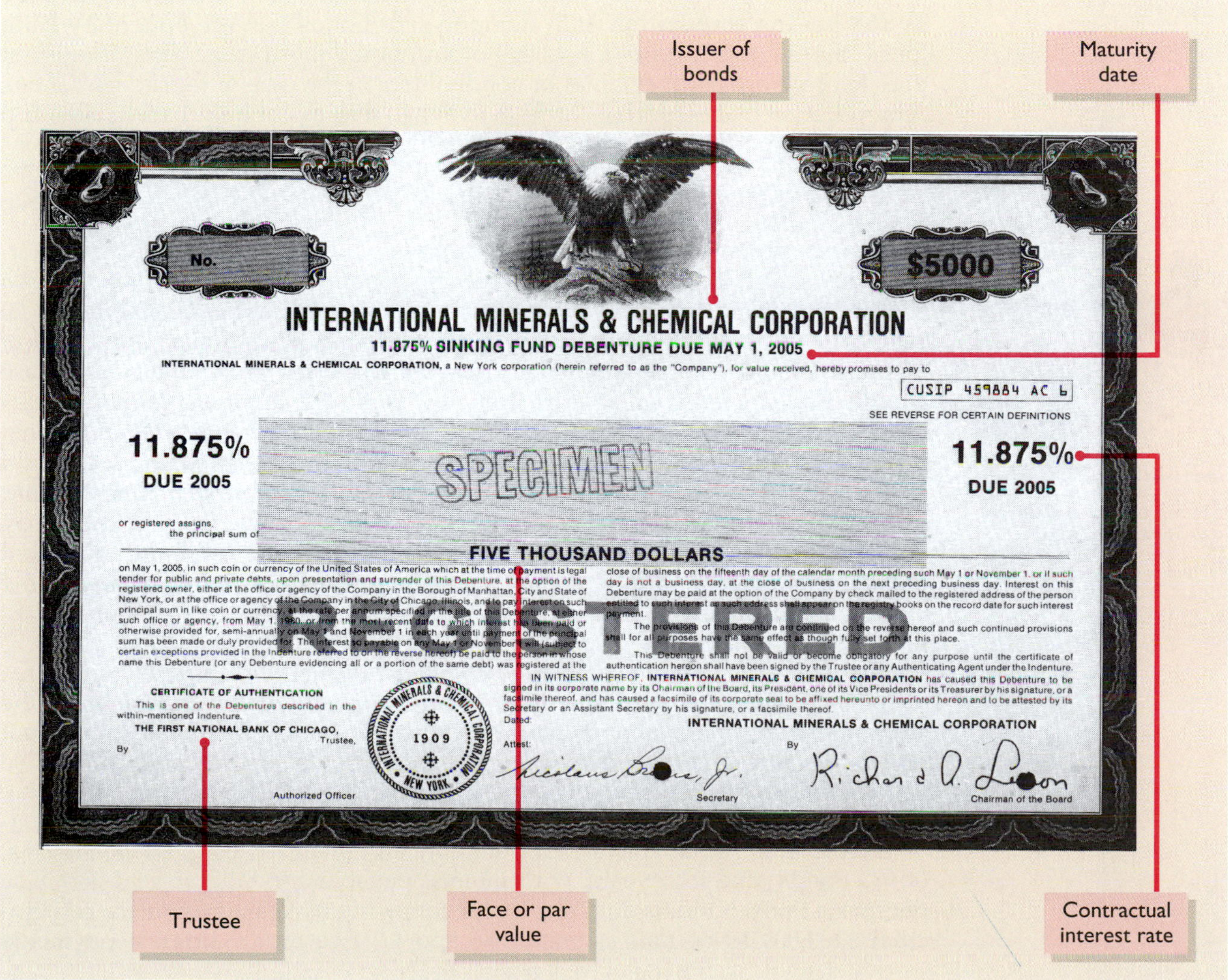

Issuer of bonds

Maturity date

No. $5000

INTERNATIONAL MINERALS & CHEMICAL CORPORATION
11.875% SINKING FUND DEBENTURE DUE MAY 1, 2005
INTERNATIONAL MINERALS & CHEMICAL CORPORATION, a New York corporation (herein referred to as the "Company"), for value received, hereby promises to pay to

CUSIP 459884 AC 6
SEE REVERSE FOR CERTAIN DEFINITIONS

11.875%   SPECIMEN   **11.875%**
DUE 2005   DUE 2005

or registered assigns,
the principal sum of

FIVE THOUSAND DOLLARS

CERTIFICATE OF AUTHENTICATION

This is one of the Debentures described in the within-mentioned Indenture.
THE FIRST NATIONAL BANK OF CHICAGO,
Trustee,
By

1909
NEW YORK

Authorized Officer

INTERNATIONAL MINERALS & CHEMICAL CORPORATION

Attest:

Secretary   Chairman of the Board

Trustee

Face or par value

Contractual interest rate

Bond Trading

Corporate bonds, like capital stock, are traded on national securities markets. Thus, bondholders have the opportunity to convert their holdings into cash at any time by selling the bonds at the current market price.

Bond prices are quoted as a percentage of the face value of the bond, which is usually $1,000. Thus, a $1,000 bond with a quoted price of 97 means that the selling price of the bond is 97% of face value, or $970 in this case. Bond prices and trading activity are published daily in newspapers and the financial press, as illustrated by the following:

ILLUSTRATION 16-4

Market information for bonds

Bonds	Current Yield	Volume	Close	Net Change
Kmart 8⅜ 17	8.4	35	100¼	+⅞

HELPFUL HINT
(1) What is the price of a $1,000 bond trading at 95¼?
(2) What is the price of a $1,000 bond trading at 101⅞?
Answers: (1) $952.50 and (2) $1,018.75.

The information in Illustration 16-4 indicates that Kmart Corporation has outstanding 8⅜%, $1,000 bonds maturing in 2017 and currently yielding an 8.4% return. In addition, 35 bonds were traded on this day; and at the close of trading, the price was 100¼% of face value, or $1,002.50. The net change column indicates the difference between the day's closing price and the previous day's closing price.

Transactions between a bondholder and other investors **are not journalized by the issuing corporation**. If Tom Smith sells bonds that are bought by Faith Jones, the issuing corporation does not journalize the transaction (although it does keep records of the names of bondholders in the case of registered bonds). A corporation makes journal entries only when it issues or buys back bonds, and when bondholders convert bonds into common stock.

Determining the Market Value of Bonds

1999
≠
2019

Same dollars at different times are not equal.

If you were an investor interested in purchasing a bond, how would you determine how much to pay? To be more specific, assume that Coronet, Inc., issues a zero-interest bond (pays no interest) with a face value of $1,000,000 due in 20 years. For this bond, the only cash you receive is a million dollars at the end of 20 years. Would you pay a million dollars for this bond? We hope not, because a million dollars received 20 years from now is not the same as a million dollars received today. The reason you would not pay a million dollars relates to what is called the **time value of money**. If you had a million dollars today, you would invest it and earn interest such that at the end of 20 years, your investment would be worth much more than a million dollars. Thus, if someone is going to pay you a million dollars 20 years from now, you would want to find its equivalent today, or its **present value**. In other words, you would want to determine how much must be invested today at current interest rates to have a million dollars in 20 years.

The market value (present value) of a bond is, therefore, a function of three factors: (1) the dollar amounts to be received, (2) the length of time until the amounts are received, and (3) the market rate of interest. The **market interest rate** is the rate investors demand for loaning funds to the corporation. The process of finding the present value is referred to as **discounting** the future amounts.

To illustrate, assume that Kell Company on January 1, 1999, issues $100,000 of 9% bonds, due in 5 years, with interest payable annually at year-end. The purchaser of the bonds would receive the following two cash payments: (1) **principal** $100,000 to be paid at maturity, and (2) five $9,000 **interest payments**

($100,000 × 9%) over the term of the bonds. The time diagram depicting both cash flows is shown below:

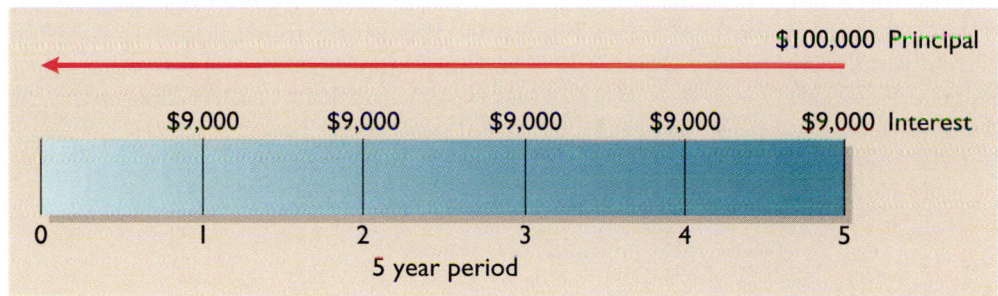

ILLUSTRATION 16-5
Time diagram depicting cash flows

The present values of these amounts are as shown in Illustration 16-6.

Present value of $100,000 received in 5 years	$ 64,993
Present value of $9,000 received annually for 5 years	35,007
Market price of bonds	**$100,000**

ILLUSTRATION 16-6
Computing the market price of bonds

Tables are available to provide the present value numbers to be used, or these values can be determined mathematically.[1] Further discussion of time value of money computations is provided in Appendix C near the end of the book.

BEFORE YOU GO ON . . .

Review It

1. What are the advantages of bond versus stock financing?
2. What are secured versus unsecured bonds, term versus serial bonds, registered versus bearer bonds, and callable versus convertible bonds?
3. Explain the terms face value, contractual interest rate, and bond indenture.
4. Explain why you would prefer to receive $1 million today rather than 5 years from now.

THE
NAVIGATOR

ACCOUNTING FOR BOND ISSUES

Bonds may be issued at face value, below face value (discount), or above face value (premium). They also are sometimes issued between interest dates.

Issuing Bonds at Face Value

To illustrate the accounting for bonds, assume that Devor Corporation issues 1,000, 10-year, 9%, $1,000 bonds dated January 1, 1999, at 100 (100% of face value). The entry to record the sale is:

2
STUDY
OBJECTIVE
....
Prepare the entries for the issuance of bonds and interest expense.

Jan. 1	Cash	1,000,000	
	Bonds Payable		1,000,000
	(To record sale of bonds at face value)		

A	=	L	+	SE
+1,000,000		+1,000,000		

---

[1]For those knowledgeable in the use of present value tables, the computations in this example are:
$100,000 × .64993 = $64,993, and $9,000 × 3.88965 = $35,007 (rounded).

Bonds payable are reported in the long-term liability section of the balance sheet because the maturity date is January 1, 2009 (more than one year away).

Over the term (life) of the bonds, entries are required for bond interest. Interest on bonds payable is computed in the same manner as interest on notes payable, as explained in Chapter 11. Assuming that interest is payable semiannually on January 1 and July 1 on the bonds described above, interest of $45,000 ($1,000,000 × 9% × 6/12) must be paid on July 1, 1999. The entry for the payment, assuming no previous accrual of interest, is:

A	=	L	+	SE
−45,000				−45,000

July 1	Bond Interest Expense	45,000	
	Cash		45,000
	(To record payment of bond interest)		

At December 31, an adjusting entry is required to recognize the $45,000 of interest expense incurred since July 1. The entry is:

A	=	L	+	SE
		+45,000		−45,000

Dec. 31	Bond Interest Expense	45,000	
	Bond Interest Payable		45,000
	(To accrue bond interest)		

Bond interest payable is classified as a current liability, because it is scheduled for payment within the next year. When the interest is paid on January 1, 2000, Bond Interest Payable is debited and Cash is credited for $45,000.

Discount or Premium on Bonds

The previous illustrations assumed that the interest rate paid on bonds, often referred to as the contractual (stated) interest rate and the market (effective) interest rate were the same. The contractual interest rate is the rate applied to the face (par) value to arrive at the interest paid in a year. The market interest rate is the rate investors demand for loaning funds to the corporation. When the contractual interest rate and the market interest rate are the same, bonds sell at face value.

However, market interest rates change daily. They are influenced by the type of bond issued, the state of the economy, current industry conditions, and the company's individual performance. As a result, the contractual and market interest rates often differ and therefore bonds sell below or above face value.

To illustrate, suppose that investors have one of two options: purchase bonds that have a market rate of interest of 10% or purchase bonds that have a contractual rate of interest of 8%. Assuming that the bonds are of equal risk, investors will select the 10% investment. To make the investments equal, investors will demand a rate of interest higher than the contractual interest rate on the 8% bonds. Because investors cannot change the contractual interest rate, they will pay less than the face value for the bonds. By paying less for the bonds, they can obtain the market rate of interest. In these cases, **bonds sell at a discount**.

Conversely, if the market rate of interest is **lower** than the contractual interest rate, investors will have to pay more than face value for the bonds. That is, if the market rate of interest is 8%, but the contractual interest rate is 9%, the issuer will require more funds from the investor. In these cases, **bonds sell at a premium**. These relationships are shown graphically in Illustration 16-7.

Issuance of bonds at an amount different from face value is quite common. By the time a company prints the bond certificates and markets the bonds, it will be a coincidence if the market rate and the contractual rate are the same. Thus, the issuance of bonds at a discount does not mean that the financial strength of the issuer is suspect. Conversely, the sale of bonds at a premium does not indicate that the financial strength of the issuer is exceptional.

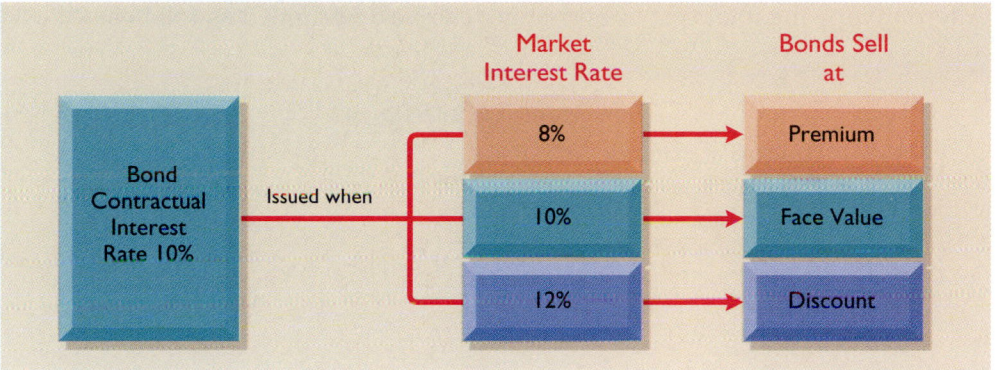

ILLUSTRATION 16-7

Interest rates and bond prices

Issuing Bonds at a Discount

HELPFUL HINT

Discount on Bonds Payable

Increase	Decrease
Debit	Credit
↓	
Normal	
Balance	

To illustrate the issuance of bonds at a discount, assume that on January 1, 1999, Candlestick, Inc., sells $1 million, 5-year, 10% bonds at 98 (98% of face value) with interest payable on July 1 and January 1. The entry to record the issuance is:

Jan. 1	Cash	980,000	
	Discount on Bonds Payable	20,000	
	Bonds Payable		1,000,000
	(To record sale of bonds at a discount)		

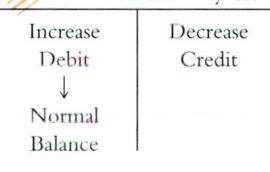

A	=	L	+	SE
+980,000		− 20,000		
		+1,000,000		

Although Discount on Bonds Payable has a debit balance, **it is not an asset**. Rather it is a **contra account**, which is **deducted from bonds payable** on the balance sheet, as illustrated below:

ILLUSTRATION 16-8

Statement presentation of discount on bonds payable

CANDLESTICK, INC.
Balance Sheet (partial)

Long-term liabilities		
Bonds payable	$1,000,000	
Less: Discount on bonds payable	**20,000**	$980,000

The $980,000 represents the **carrying (or book) value** of the bonds. On the date of issue this amount equals the market price of the bonds.

The issuance of bonds below face value causes the total cost of borrowing to differ from the bond interest paid. That is, at maturity the issuing corporation must pay not only the contractual interest rate over the term of the bonds, but also the face value (rather than the issuance price). Therefore, the difference between the issuance price and face value of the bonds—the discount—is an **additional cost of borrowing that should be recorded as bond interest expense over the life of the bonds**. The total cost of borrowing $980,000 for Candlestick, Inc., is $520,000, computed as follows:

HELPFUL HINT

Carrying value (book value) of bonds issued at a discount is determined by subtracting the balance of the discount account from the balance of the Bonds Payable account.

ILLUSTRATION 16-9

Total cost of borrowing— bonds issued at a discount

Bonds Issued at a Discount

Semiannual interest payments	
($1,000,000 × 10% × ½ = $50,000; $50,000 × 10)	$500,000
Add: Bond discount ($1,000,000 − $980,000)	20,000
Total cost of borrowing	**$520,000**

Alternatively, the total cost of borrowing can be determined as follows:

ILLUSTRATION 16-10

Alternative computation of total cost of borrowing— bonds issued at a discount

Bonds Issued at a Discount	
Principal at maturity	$1,000,000
Semiannual interest payments ($50,000 × 10)	500,000
Cash to be paid to bondholders	1,500,000
Cash received from bondholders	980,000
Total cost of borrowing	**$ 520,000**

Amortizing Bond Discount

To comply with the matching principle, it follows that bond discount should be allocated systematically to each accounting period benefiting from the use of the cash proceeds.

One method, the **straight-line method of amortization**, allocates the same amount to interest expense in each interest period.[2] The amount is determined as shown in Illustration 16-11:

ILLUSTRATION 16-11

Formula for straight-line method of bond discount amortization

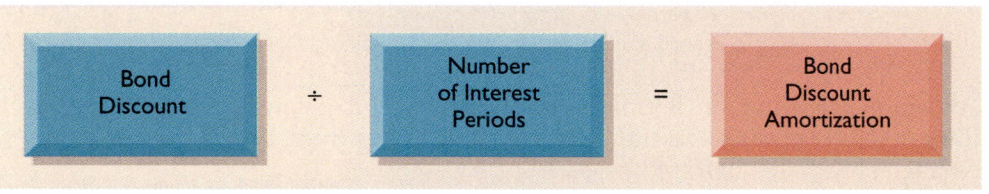

In this example, the bond discount amortization is $2,000 ($20,000 ÷ 10). The entry to record the payment of bond interest and the amortization of bond discount on the first interest date (July 1, 1999) is:

A = L + SE
−50,000 +2,000 −52,000

July 1	Bond Interest Expense	52,000	
	Discount on Bonds Payable		2,000
	Cash		50,000
	(To record payment of bond interest and amortization of bond discount)		

At December 31, the adjusting entry is:

A = L + SE
+ 2,000 −52,000
+50,000

Dec. 31	Bond Interest Expense	52,000	
	Discount on Bonds Payable		2,000
	Bond Interest Payable		50,000
	(To record accrued bond interest and amortization of bond discount)		

ALTERNATIVE TERMINOLOGY
The amount in the Discount on Bonds Payable account is often referred to as *Unamortized Discount on Bonds Payable.*

Over the term of the bonds, the balance in Discount on Bonds Payable will decrease annually by the same amount until it has a zero balance at the maturity date of the bonds. Thus, the carrying value of the bonds at maturity will be equal to the face value of the bonds.

Preparing a bond discount amortization schedule as shown in Illustration 16-12 is useful to determine interest expense, discount amortization and the car-

---

[2]Another method, the effective-interest method, is discussed in the appendix at the end of this chapter.

rying value of the bond. As indicated, the interest expense recorded each period is $52,000. Also note that the carrying value of the bond increases $2,000 each period until it reaches its face value $1,000,000 at the end of period 10.

ILLUSTRATION 16-12

Bond discount amortization schedule

Semiannual Interest Periods	(A) Interest to Be Paid (5% × $1,000,000)	(B) Interest Expense to Be Recorded (A) + (C)	(C) Discount Amortization ($20,000 ÷ 10)	(D) Unamortized Discount (D) − (C)	(E) Bond Carrying Value ($1,000,000 − D)
Issue date				$20,000	$ 980,000
1	$ 50,000	$ 52,000	$ 2,000	18,000	982,000
2	50,000	52,000	2,000	16,000	984,000
3	50,000	52,000	2,000	14,000	986,000
4	50,000	52,000	2,000	12,000	988,000
5	50,000	52,000	2,000	10,000	990,000
6	50,000	52,000	2,000	8,000	992,000
7	50,000	52,000	2,000	6,000	994,000
8	50,000	52,000	2,000	4,000	996,000
9	50,000	52,000	2,000	2,000	998,000
10	50,000	52,000	2,000	–0–	1,000,000
	$500,000	$520,000	$20,000		

Column **(A)** remains constant because the face value of the bonds ($1,000,000) is multiplied by the semiannual contractual interest rate (5%) each period.

Column **(B)** is computed as the interest paid (Column A) plus the discount amortization (Column C).

Column **(C)** indicates the discount amortization each period.

Column **(D)** decreases each period by the same amount until it reaches zero at maturity.

Column **(E)** increases each period by the amount of discount amortization until it equals the face value at maturity.

Issuing Bonds at a Premium

The issuance of bonds at a premium can be illustrated by assuming the Candlestick, Inc., bonds described above are sold at 102 (102% of face value) rather than at 98.

The entry to record the sale is:

Jan. 1	Cash	1,020,000	
	Bonds Payable		1,000,000
	Premium on Bonds Payable		20,000
	(To record sale of bonds at a premium)		

```
A      =    L     +   SE
+1,020,000 +1,000,000
              +    20,000
```

Premium on bonds payable is **added to bonds payable** on the balance sheet, as shown below:

ILLUSTRATION 16-13

Statement presentation of bond premium

CANDLESTICK, INC.
Balance Sheet (partial)

Long-term liabilities		
Bonds payable	$1,000,000	
Add: Premium on bonds payable	20,000	$1,020,000

The sale of bonds above face value causes the total cost of borrowing to be **less than the bond interest paid**, because the borrower is not required to pay the bond premium at the maturity date of the bonds. Thus, the premium is considered to be **a reduction in the cost of borrowing** that should be credited to Bond Interest Expense over the life of the bonds. The total cost of borrowing $1,020,000 for Candlestick, Inc., is $480,000, computed as follows:

ILLUSTRATION 16-14

Total cost of borrowing— bonds issued at a premium

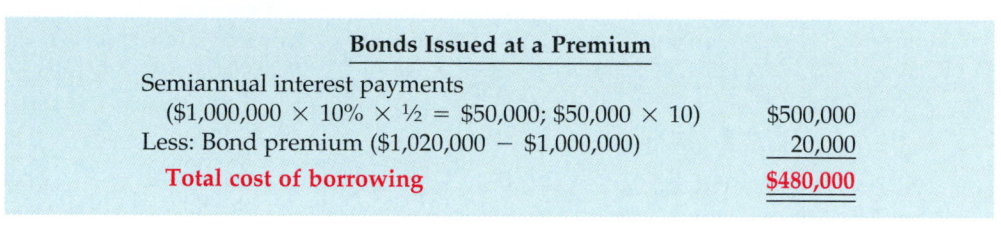

Bonds Issued at a Premium	
Semiannual interest payments ($1,000,000 × 10% × ½ = $50,000; $50,000 × 10)	$500,000
Less: Bond premium ($1,020,000 − $1,000,000)	20,000
Total cost of borrowing	**$480,000**

Alternatively, the cost of borrowing can be computed as follows:

ILLUSTRATION 16-15

Alternative computation of total cost of borrowing— bonds issued at a premium

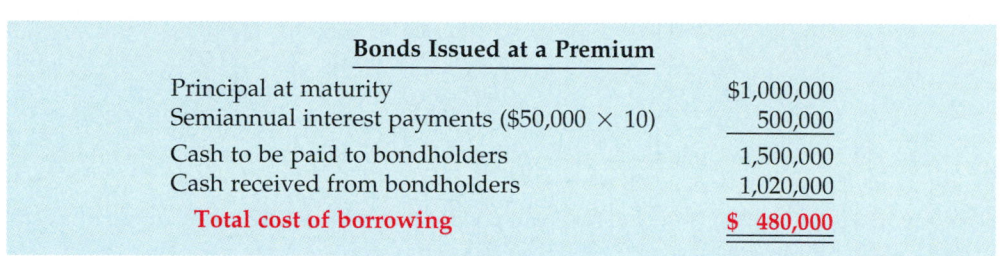

Bonds Issued at a Premium	
Principal at maturity	$1,000,000
Semiannual interest payments ($50,000 × 10)	500,000
Cash to be paid to bondholders	1,500,000
Cash received from bondholders	1,020,000
Total cost of borrowing	**$ 480,000**

Amortizing Bond Premium

The formula for determining bond premium amortization under the straight-line method is presented in Illustration 16-16.

ILLUSTRATION 16-16

Formula for straight-line method of bond premium amortization

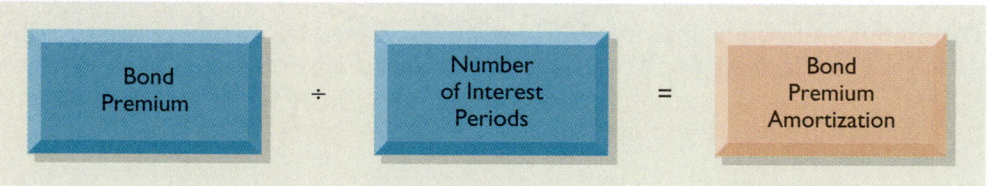

Thus, in our example, the premium amortization for each interest period is $2,000 ($20,000 ÷ 10). The entry to record the first payment of interest on July 1 is:

A	=	L	+	SE
− 50,000		− 2,000		− 48,000

July 1	Bond Interest Expense	48,000	
	Premium on Bonds Payable	2,000	
	Cash		50,000
	(To record payment of bond interest and amortization of bond premium)		

At December 31, the adjusting entry is:

A	=	L	+	SE
		− 2,000		− 48,000
		+ 50,000		

Dec. 31	Bond Interest Expense	48,000	
	Premium on Bonds Payable	2,000	
	Bond Interest Payable		50,000
	(To record accrued bond interest and amortization of bond premium)		

Over the term of the bonds, the balance in Premium on Bonds Payable will decrease annually by the same amount until it has a zero balance at maturity.

Preparing a bond premium amortization schedule as shown in Illustration 16-17 is useful to determine interest expense, premium amortized, and the carrying value of the bond. As indicated, the interest expense recorded each period is $48,000. Also note that the carrying value of the bond decreases $2,000 each period until it reaches its face value $1,000,000 at the end of period 10.

ILLUSTRATION 16-17

Bond premium amortization schedule

Semiannual Interest Periods	(A) Interest to Be Paid (5% × $1,000,000)	(B) Interest Expense to Be Recorded (A) − (C)	(C) Premium Amortization ($20,000 ÷ 10)	(D) Unamortized Premium (D) − (C)	(E) Bond Carrying Value ($1,000,000 + D)
Issue date				$20,000	$1,020,000
1	$ 50,000	$ 48,000	$ 2,000	18,000	1,018,000
2	50,000	48,000	2,000	16,000	1,016,000
3	50,000	48,000	2,000	14,000	1,014,000
4	50,000	48,000	2,000	12,000	1,012,000
5	50,000	48,000	2,000	10,000	1,010,000
6	50,000	48,000	2,000	8,000	1,008,000
7	50,000	48,000	2,000	6,000	1,006,000
8	50,000	48,000	2,000	4,000	1,004,000
9	50,000	48,000	2,000	2,000	1,002,000
10	50,000	48,000	2,000	–0–	1,000,000
	$500,000	$480,000	$20,000		

Column **(A)** remains constant because the face value of the bonds ($1,000,000) is multiplied by the semiannual contractual interest rate (5%) each period.

Column **(B)** is computed as the interest paid (Column A) less the premium amortization (Column C).

Column **(C)** indicates the premium amortization each period.

Column **(D)** decreases each period by the same amount until it reaches zero at maturity.

Column **(E)** decreases each period by the amount of premium amortization until it equals the face value at maturity.

Issuing Bonds between Interest Dates

Bonds are often issued between interest payment dates. **When this occurs, the issuer requires the investor to pay the market price for the bonds plus accrued interest since the last interest date.** At the next interest date, the corporation will return the accrued interest to the investor by paying the full amount of interest due on outstanding bonds.

To illustrate, assume that Deer Corporation sells $1,000,000, 9% bonds at face value plus accrued interest on March 1. Interest is payable semiannually on July 1 and January 1. The accrued interest is $15,000 ($1,000,000 × 9% × 2/12). The total proceeds on the sale of the bonds, therefore, are $1,015,000, and the entry to record the sale is:

Mar. 1	Cash	1,015,000	
	Bonds Payable		1,000,000
	Bond Interest Payable		15,000
	(To record sale of bonds at face value plus accrued interest)		

A	=	L	+	SE
+1,015,000		+1,000,000		
			+	15,000

At the first interest date, it is necessary to eliminate the bond interest payable balance and to recognize interest expense for the 4 months (March 1–June 30) the bonds have been outstanding. Interest expense in this example is, therefore, $30,000 ($1,000,000 $\times$ 9% $\times$ 4/12). The entry on July 1 for the $45,000 interest payment is:

A	=	L	+	SE
$-45,000$		$-15,000$		$-30,000$

July 1	Bond Interest Payable	15,000	
	Bond Interest Expense	30,000	
	Cash		45,000
	(To record payment of bond interest)		

Why does Deer Corporation collect interest at the time of issuance and then return this interest at the time of payment? The rationale: Collection of accrued interest at the issuance date allows the company to pay a full period's interest to all bondholders at the next interest payment date. Deer Corporation does not have to determine the individual amount of interest due each holder based on the time each bond has been outstanding during the interest period.

In other words, if bonds are not sold "with accrued interest," Deer Corporation would have to keep track of the purchaser and the dates that the bonds were purchased. This procedure would be necessary to ensure that each bondholder received the correct amount of interest. By selling the bonds "with accrued interest," Deer does not have to maintain detailed records and cost savings occur.

BEFORE YOU GO ON . . .

Review It

1. What entry is made to record the issuance of bonds payable of $1 million at 100? at 96? at 102?
2. Why do bonds sell at a discount? at a premium? at face value?
3. Explain the accounting for bonds sold between interest dates.

Do It

A bond amortization table shows (a) interest to be paid $50,000, (b) interest expense to be recorded $52,000, and (c) amortization $2,000. Answer the following questions: (1) Were the bonds sold at a premium or a discount? (2) After recording the interest expense, will the bond carrying value increase or decrease?

Reasoning: To answer the questions you need to know the effects that the amortization of bond discount and bond premium have on bond interest expense and on the carrying value of the bonds. Bond discount amortization increases both bond interest expense and the carrying value of the bonds. Bond premium amortization has the reverse effect.

Solution: The bond amortization table indicates that interest expense is $2,000 greater than the interest paid. This difference is equal to the amortization amount. Thus, the bonds were sold at a discount. The interest entry will decrease Discount on Bonds Payable and increase the carrying value of the bonds.

THE NAVIGATOR

Related exercise material: BE16–2, BE16–3, BE16–4, BE16–5, E16–2, E16–3, E16–4, and E16–5.

ACCOUNTING FOR BOND RETIREMENTS

Bonds may be retired either when they are purchased (redeemed) by the issuing corporation or when they are converted into common stock by bondholders. The appropriate entries for these transactions are explained in the following sections.

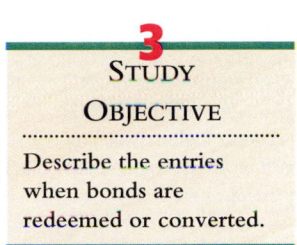

3
STUDY
OBJECTIVE

Describe the entries
when bonds are
redeemed or converted.

Redeeming Bonds at Maturity

Regardless of the issue price of bonds, the book value of the bonds at maturity will equal their face value. This can be seen in Illustrations 16-12 and 16-17 where the carrying value of the bonds at the end of their 10-year life ($1 million) is equal to the face value of the bonds.

Assuming that the interest for the last interest period is paid and recorded separately, the entry to record the redemption of the Candlestick bonds at maturity is:

Bonds Payable		1,000,000	
Cash			1,000,000
(To record redemption of bonds at maturity)			

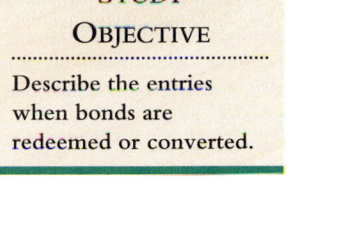

A	=	L	+	SE
−1,000,000		−1,000,000		

Redeeming Bonds before Maturity

Bonds may be redeemed before maturity. A company may decide to retire bonds before maturity to reduce interest cost and remove debt from its balance sheet. A company should retire debt early only if it has sufficient cash resources. When bonds are retired before maturity, it is necessary to: (1) eliminate the carrying value of the bonds at the redemption date, (2) record the cash paid, and (3) recognize the gain or loss on redemption. The carrying value of the bonds is the face value of the bonds less unamortized bond discount or plus unamortized bond premium at the redemption date.

To illustrate, assume at the end of the eighth period Candlestick, Inc. (having sold its bonds at a premium, per Illustration 16-17) retires its bonds at 103 after paying the semiannual interest. The carrying value of the bonds at the redemption date, as shown in the bond premium amortization schedule, is $1,004,000. The entry to record the redemption at the end of the eighth interest period (January 1, 2003) is:

HELPFUL HINT
Question: If a bond is redeemed prior to its maturity date and its carrying value exceeds its redemption price, will the retirement result in a gain or a loss on redemption? Answer: Gain.

Jan. 1	Bonds Payable	1,000,000	
	Premium on Bonds Payable	4,000	
	Loss on Bond Redemption	26,000	
	Cash		1,030,000
	(To record redemption of bonds at 103)		

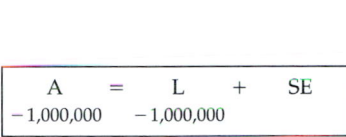

A	=	L	+	SE
−1,030,000		−1,000,000		−26,000
		− 4,000		

Note that the loss of $26,000 is the difference between the cash paid of $1,030,000 and the carrying value of the bonds of $1,004,000. Losses (gains) on bond redemption are reported in the income statement as extraordinary items as required by the accounting profession.

Converting Bonds into Common Stock

Convertible bonds have features that are attractive both to bondholders and to the issuer. The conversion often gives bondholders an opportunity to benefit if the market price of the common stock increases substantially. Furthermore, until conversion, the bondholder receives interest on the bond. For the issuer, the bonds sell at a higher price and pay a lower rate of interest than comparable

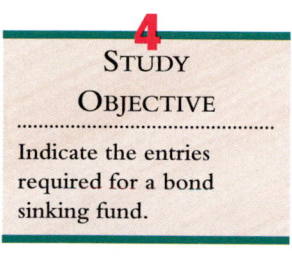

debt securities that do not have a conversion option. Many corporations, such as USAir, USX Corp., and Daimler-Chrysler Corporation, have convertible bonds outstanding.

When bonds are converted into common stocks and the conversion is recorded, the current market prices of the bonds and the stock are ignored. Instead, the **carrying value** of the bonds is transferred to paid-in capital accounts, and **no gain or loss is recognized**. To illustrate, assume that on July 1 Saunders Associates converts $100,000 bonds sold at face value into 2,000 shares of $10 par value common stock. Both the bonds and the common stock have a market value of $130,000. The entry to record the conversion is:

A	=	L	+	SE
		− 100,000		+ 20,000
				+ 80,000

July 1	Bonds Payable	100,000	
	Common Stock		20,000
	Paid-in Capital in Excess of Par Value		80,000
	(To record bond conversion)		

Note that the current market price of the bonds and stock ($130,000) is not considered in making the entry. This method of recording the bond conversion is often referred to as the **carrying (or book) value method**.

Using a Bond Sinking Fund

Many bond issues require the borrower to make periodic cash contributions to a sinking (redemption) fund over the life of the bonds. A **sinking fund** is cash or other assets set aside to retire debt. In other words, it is like a savings account that is used to pay back bondholders. **A sinking fund makes the bonds more attractive to investors, because it enhances the likelihood that the bonds will be redeemed at maturity.** For example, Texaco and Alcoa have sinking funds for their debenture bonds. Such bonds are often referred to as **sinking fund bonds**.

Sinking funds are usually under the control of a trustee, such as a bank or a trust company. The trustee may be permitted to invest the periodic deposits in high-quality income-producing securities. **It is expected that the deposits plus the earnings from the investments will equal the face value of the bonds at maturity.** Shortly before the maturity date, the trustee sells the securities and uses the total cash in the fund to redeem the bonds. Any excess cash in the fund is returned to the bond issuer.

To illustrate, assume that Bountiful Corporation issues $1 million face value, 5-year bonds on January 1. The terms of the bond indenture indicate that Bountiful must make annual deposits with a sinking fund trustee, starting at the end of the first year. The amount of the annual cash contribution is $215,000. The entry to record this contribution by Bountiful Corporation at the end of the first year is as follows:

A	=	L	+	SE
+ 215,000				
− 215,000				

Dec. 31	Bond Sinking Fund	215,000	
	Cash		215,000
	(To record annual contribution)		

At the end of the second year, Bountiful Corporation records actual earnings on the assets in the sinking fund of $16,500. The entry to record this revenue and the required contribution to the fund is as follows:

A	=	L	+	SE
+ 231,500				+ 16,500
− 215,000				

Dec. 31	Bond Sinking Fund	231,500	
	Bond Sinking Fund Revenue		16,500
	Cash		215,000
	(To record sinking fund revenue and annual contribution)		

At the maturity date, sinking fund assets are used to redeem the bonds. The entry to record the redemption, assuming that the sinking fund has $985,000 in cash, is as follows:

Jan. 1	Bonds Payable	1,000,000	
	Bond Sinking Fund		985,000
	Cash		15,000
	(To redeem bonds at maturity)		

A	=	L	+	SE
−985,000		−1,000,000		
− 15,000				

In this case, Bountiful Corporation had to make up for the deficiency by paying an additional $15,000. If the sinking fund had excess cash, it would be returned to Bountiful.

The bond sinking fund is reported as a single amount in the investment section of the balance sheet. Bond sinking fund revenue is classified as other revenues and gains in the income statement.

The bond contract may also require the corporation to establish a restriction on its retained earnings. As explained in Chapter 15, this restriction is reported as a note in the financial statements.

ACCOUNTING IN ACTION
International Insight

Now that you have read about bonds, you may be beginning to realize how significant bond financing can be. A dramatic example of bond financing—which literally changed the course of history—is seen in Britain's struggle for supremacy in the eighteenth and nineteenth centuries. With only a fraction of the population and wealth of France, Britain ultimately humbled its mightier foe through the use of bonds. Because of its effective central bank and a fair system of collecting taxes, Britain developed the capital markets that enabled its government to issue bonds. Britain was able to borrow money at almost half the cost paid by France, and was able to incur more debt as a proportion of the economy than could France. Britain thus could more than match the French navy, raise an army of its own, and lavishly subsidize other armies, eventually destroying Napoleon and his threat to Europe.

Source: "How British Bonds Beat Back Bigger France," *Forbes*, March 13, 1995.

BEFORE YOU GO ON . . .
Review It

1. Explain the accounting for redemption of bonds at maturity, before maturity by payment in cash, and by conversion into common stock.
2. Did Kellogg Company redeem any of its debt during 1997? (*Hint:* To find information related to this question, examine Kellogg Company's statement of cash flows. The answer to this question is provided on page 719.)
3. What is the purpose of the bond sinking fund? Where is a bond sinking fund reported in the financial statements?

Do It

R & B Inc. issued $500,000, 10-year bonds at a premium. Prior to maturity, when the carrying value of the bonds is $508,000, the company retires the bonds at 102. Prepare the entry to record the redemption of the bonds.

Reasoning: In recording the redemption of bonds before maturity, it is necessary to (1) eliminate the carrying value of the bonds, (2) recognize the cash paid, and (3) recognize the gain or loss equal to the difference between (1) and (2).

Solution: There is a loss on redemption because the cash paid, $510,000 ($500,000 × 102), is greater than the carrying value of $508,000. The entry is:

Bonds Payable	500,000	
Premium on Bonds Payable	8,000	
Loss on Bond Redemption	2,000	
Cash		510,000
(To record redemption of bonds at 102)		

Related exercise material: BE16–6, E16–3, E16–4, and E16–6.

THE
NAVIGATOR

ACCOUNTING FOR OTHER LONG-TERM LIABILITIES

Other common types of long-term obligations are notes payable and lease liabilities. The accounting for these liabilities is explained in the following sections.

Long-Term Notes Payable

5

STUDY
OBJECTIVE

Describe the accounting for long-term notes payable.

The use of notes payable in long-term debt financing is quite common. Long-term notes payable are similar to short-term interest-bearing notes payable except that the terms of the notes exceed one year. In periods of unstable interest rates, the interest rate on long-term notes may be tied to changes in the market rate for comparable loans. Examples are the 8.03% adjustable rate notes issued by General Motors and the floating rate notes issued by American Express Company.

A long-term note may be secured by a document called a **mortgage** that pledges title to specific assets as security for a loan. Mortgage notes payable are widely used in the purchase of homes by individuals and in the acquisition of plant assets by many small and some large companies. For example, approximately 18% of McDonald's long-term debt relates to mortgage notes on land, buildings, and improvements. Like other long-term notes payable, the mortgage loan terms may stipulate either a fixed or an adjustable interest rate. Typically, the terms require the borrower to make installment payments over the term of the loan. Each payment consists of (1) interest on the unpaid balance of the loan, and (2) a reduction of loan principal. The interest decreases each period, while the portion applied to the loan principal increases.

Mortgage notes payable are recorded initially at face value, and entries are required subsequently for each installment payment. To illustrate, assume that Porter Technology Inc. issues a $500,000, 12%, 20-year mortgage note on December 31, 1999, to obtain needed financing for the construction of a new research laboratory. The terms provide for semiannual installment payments of $33,231 (not including real estate taxes and insurance). The installment payment schedule for the first 2 years is as follows:

Semiannual Interest Period	(A) Cash Payment	(B) Interest Expense (D) × 6%	(C) Reduction of Principal (A) − (B)	(D) Principal Balance (D) − (C)
Issue date				$500,000
1	$33,231	$30,000	$3,231	496,769
2	33,231	29,806	3,425	493,344
3	33,231	29,601	3,630	489,714
4	33,231	29,383	3,848	485,866

ILLUSTRATION 16-18
Mortgage installment payment schedule

HELPFUL HINT
Electronic spreadsheet programs can create a schedule of installment loan payments. This allows you to put in the data for your own mortgage loan and get an illustration that really hits home.

The entries to record the mortgage loan and first installment payment are as follows:

Dec. 31	Cash	500,000	
	Mortgage Notes Payable		500,000
	(To record mortgage loan)		
June 30	Interest Expense	30,000	
	Mortgage Notes Payable	3,231	
	Cash		33,231
	(To record semiannual payment on		
	mortgage)		

A	=	L	+	SE
+500,000		+500,000		

A	=	L	+	SE
−33,231		−3,231		−30,000

In the balance sheet, the reduction in principal for the next year is reported as a current liability, and the remaining unpaid principal balance is classified as a long-term liability. At December 31, 2000, the total liability is $493,344 of which $7,478 ($3,630 + $3,848) is current, and $485,866 ($493,344 − $7,478) is long-term.

Lease Liabilities

As indicated in Chapter 10, a lease is a contractual arrangement between the lessor (owner of the property) and a lessee (renter of the property) that grants the right to use specific property for a period of time in return for cash payments. Leasing is big business. For example, an estimated $125 billion of capital equipment was leased in a recent year. This represents approximately one-third of equipment financed that year. The two most common types of leases are operating leases and capital leases.

6
STUDY OBJECTIVE
Contrast the accounting for operating and capital leases.

ACCOUNTING IN ACTION

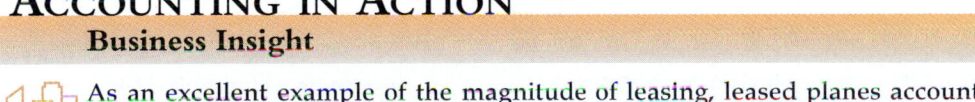

Business Insight

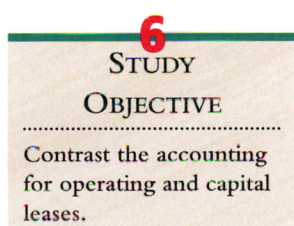

As an excellent example of the magnitude of leasing, leased planes account for nearly 40% of the U.S. fleet of commercial airlines. The reasons for leasing include favorable tax treatment, increased flexibility, and low airline income. As passenger volume is expected to double in the next 20 years, some industry analysts estimate that approximately $400 billion in airplanes will be needed, and it is anticipated that much of the financing will be done through leasing. Leasing is particularly attractive to lessors because airplanes have relatively long lives, a ready secondhand market, and a significant resale value. Or take the commercial truck fleet—over one-third of heavy-duty trucks are presently leased.

Operating Leases

The renting of an apartment and the rental of a car at an airport are examples of **operating leases**. **In an operating lease the intent is temporary use of the property by the lessee with continued ownership of the property by the lessor.** The lease (or rental) payments are recorded as an expense by the lessee and as revenue by the lessor. For example, assuming that a sales representative for Western Inc. leases a car from Hertz Car Rental at the Los Angeles airport and that Hertz charges a total of $275, the entry by the lessee, Western Inc., is:

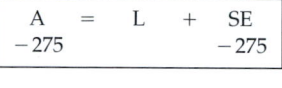

A	=	L	+	SE
− 275				− 275

Car Rental Expense	275	
Cash		275
(To record payment of lease rental charge)		

In addition, the lessee may incur other costs during the lease period. For example, in the case above, the lessee may be required to pay for gas and oil. These costs are also reported as an expense.

Capital Leases

In most lease contracts, a periodic payment is made by the lessee and is recorded as rent expense in the income statement. However, in some cases, the lease contract transfers substantially all the benefits and risks of ownership to the lessee, so that the lease is in effect a purchase of the property. This type of lease is called a **capital lease** because the present value of the cash payments for the lease are capitalized and recorded as an asset. Illustration 16-19 indicates the major difference between an operating and a capital lease.

ILLUSTRATION 16-19

Types of leases

The lessee must record the lease **as an asset**—that is, as a capital lease—if any **one** of the following conditions exists:

1. **The lease transfers ownership of the property to the lessee.** *Rationale:* If during the lease term, the lessee receives ownership of the asset, the leased asset should be reported as an asset on the lessee's books.
2. **The lease contains a bargain purchase option.** *Rationale:* If during the term of the lease, the lessee can purchase the asset at a price substantially below its fair market value, the lessee will obviously exercise this option. Thus, the lease should be reported as a leased asset on the lessee's books.
3. **The lease term is equal to 75% or more of the economic life of the leased property.** *Rationale:* If the lease term is for much of the asset's useful life, the asset should be recorded by the lessee.
4. **The present value of the lease payments equals or exceeds 90% of the fair market value of the leased property.** *Rationale:* If the present value of the lease payments is equal to or almost equal to the fair market value of the asset, the lessee has essentially purchased the asset. As a result, the leased asset should be recorded on the books of the lessee.

To illustrate, assume that Gonzalez Company decides to lease new equipment. The lease period is 4 years; the economic life of the leased equipment is estimated to be 5 years. The present value of the lease payments is $190,000 which is equal to the fair market value of the equipment. There is no transfer of ownership during the lease term nor is there any bargain purchase option.

In this example, Gonzalez has essentially purchased the equipment. Conditions 3 and 4 have been met: First, the lease term is 75% or more of the economic life of the asset, and second, the present value of cash payments is equal to the equipment's fair market value. The entry to record the transaction is as follows:

Leased Asset—Equipment	190,000	
Lease Liability		190,000
(To record leased asset and lease liability)		

A = L + SE
+190,000 +190,000

The leased asset is reported on the balance sheet under plant assets. The lease liability is reported as a liability on the balance sheet. **The portion of the lease liability expected to be paid in the next year is reported as a current liability. The remainder is classified as a long-term liability.**

Most lessees do not like to report leases on their balance sheets. The reason is that the lease liability increases the company's total liabilities. This, in turn, may make it more difficult for the company to obtain needed funds from lenders. As a result, companies attempt to keep leased assets and lease liabilities off the balance sheet by not meeting any one of the four conditions mentioned above. This procedure of keeping liabilities off the balance sheet is often referred to as **off-balance sheet financing.**

STATEMENT PRESENTATION AND ANALYSIS

Presentation

Long-term liabilities are reported in a separate section of the balance sheet immediately following current liabilities, as shown on the next page.

STUDY OBJECTIVE 7

Identify the methods for the presentation and analysis of long-term liabilities.

ILLUSTRATION 16-20

Balance sheet presentation of long-term liabilities

LAX CORPORATION Balance Sheet (partial)		
Long-term liabilities		
Bonds payable 10% due in 2009	$1,000,000	
Less: Discount on bonds payable	80,000	$ 920,000
Mortgage notes payable, 11%, due in 2015 and secured by plant assets		500,000
Lease liability		540,000
Total long-term liabilities		$1,960,000

Alternatively, summary data may be presented in the balance sheet with detailed data (such as interest rates, maturity dates, conversion privileges, and assets pledged as collateral) shown in a supporting schedule. The current maturities of long-term debt should be reported under current liabilities if they are to be paid from current assets.

Analysis

Long-term creditors and stockholders are interested in a company's long-run solvency, particularly its ability to pay interest as it comes due and to repay the face value of the debt at maturity. Debt to total assets and times interest earned are two ratios that provide information about debt-paying ability and long-run solvency.

The **debt to total assets ratio** measures the percentage of the total assets provided by creditors. It is computed, as shown in the formula below, by dividing total debt (both current and long-term liabilities) by total assets. The higher the percentage of debt to total assets, the greater the risk that the company may be unable to meet its maturing obligations.

The **times interest earned ratio** provides an indication of the company's ability to meet interest payments as they come due. It is computed by dividing income before income taxes and interest expense by interest expense.

ILLUSTRATION 16-21

Debt to total assets and times interest earned ratios, with computations

To illustrate these ratios, we will use data from Kellogg Company's annual report which disclosed total liabilities of $3,880.1 million, total assets of $4,877.6 million, interest expense of $108.3 million, income taxes of $340.5 million, and net income of $546.0 million. Kellogg's debt to total assets ratio and times interest earned ratio are shown graphically below, along with their computations.

Total Debt	÷	Total Assets	=	Debt to Total Assets
$3,880.1	÷	$4,877.6	=	79.6%
Income before Income Taxes and Interest Expense	÷	Interest Expense	=	Times Interest Earned
$546.0 + $340.5 + $108.3	÷	$108.3	=	9.2 times

Even though Kellogg Company has a relatively high debt to total assets percentage of 79.6%, its interest coverage of 9.2 times appears very safe.

BEFORE YOU GO ON . . .

Review It

1. Explain the accounting for long-term mortgage notes payable.
2. What is the difference in accounting for an operating lease versus a capital lease? Explain the four conditions used to determine whether the lease contract transfers substantially all the benefits and risks of ownership.
3. What ratios may be computed to analyze a company's long-run solvency?

A LOOK BACK AT OUR FEATURE STORY

Refer to the opening story and answer the following questions:

1. The University of Kentucky's bonds are rated AA– by Standard & Poor's and A1 by Moody's Investor Service. Why is it important to the University of Kentucky that its bonds have a high bond rating?
2. Explain the meaning of the tax-exempt status of the University of Kentucky bonds. What does it mean to say that "a recent issue offering 6% is the equivalent of 10% to those individuals in the top tax bracket"?
3. Why does the state use bonds to finance the buildings rather than taking the funds out of general revenues?

Solution:

1. Having a high (good) bond rating is as important to a university as it is to a business corporation. A high bond rating indicates that the bonds are less risky, and thus more attractive, to purchasers of the bonds. Hence a lower interest rate results, and the cost to the issuer of the bonds is less.
2. Because the University of Kentucky bonds are tax exempt, holders of the bonds do not have to pay federal income tax on the interest received on the bonds. To earn an after-tax return of 6%, a person in the maximum tax bracket would have to receive interest equal to approximately 10% on taxable bonds [10% − (40% × 10%)].
3. Financing the buildings through the issuance of bonds spreads the cost of the buildings over many years and more equitably distributes the costs to a broader base of taxpayers. Future taxpayers pay for the buildings as the buildings are used, rather than the taxpayers of one year absorbing the total cost out of general revenues in the year of construction.

THE
NAVIGATOR

DEMONSTRATION PROBLEM

Snyder Software Inc. has successfully developed a new spreadsheet program. However, to produce and market the program, the company needed $2.0 million of additional financing. On December 31, 1999, Snyder borrowed money as follows:

1. Snyder issued $500,000, 11%, 10-year convertible bonds. The bonds sold at face value and pay semiannual interest on January 1 and July 1. Each $1,000 bond is convertible into 30 shares of Snyder's $20 par value common stock.
2. Snyder issued $1.0 million, 10%, 10-year bonds for $885,301. Interest is payable semiannually on January 1 and July 1. Snyder uses the straight-line method of amortization.
3. Snyder also issued a $500,000, 12%, 15-year mortgage note payable. The terms provide for semiannual installment payments of $36,324 on June 30 and December 31.

Instructions

1. For the convertible bonds, prepare journal entries for:
   (a) the issuance of the bonds on January 1, 2000.

(b) interest expense on July 1 and December 31, 2000.
(c) the payment of interest on January 1, 2001.
(d) the conversion of all bonds into common stock on January 1, 2001, when the market value of the common stock was $67 per share.
2. For the 10-year, 10% bonds:
(a) journalize the issuance of the bonds on January 1, 2000.
(b) prepare a bond discount amortization schedule for the first six interest periods.
(c) prepare the journal entries for interest expense and amortization of bond discount in 2000.
(d) prepare the entry for the redemption of the bonds at 101 on January 1, 2003, after paying the interest due on this date.
3. For the mortgage note payable:
(a) prepare the entry for the issuance of the note on December 31, 1999.
(b) prepare a payment schedule for the first four installment payments.
(c) indicate the current and noncurrent amounts for the mortgage note payable at December 31, 2000.

SOLUTION TO DEMONSTRATION PROBLEM

1. (a) 2000

Jan. 1	Cash	500,000	
	Bonds Payable		500,000
	(To record issue of 11%, 10-year convertible bonds at face value)		

(b) 2000

July 1	Bond Interest Expense	27,500	
	Cash ($500,000 × 0.055)		27,500
	(To record payment of semiannual interest)		
Dec. 31	Bond Interest Expense	27,500	
	Bond Interest Payable		27,500
	(To record accrual of semiannual bond interest)		

(c) 2001

Jan. 1	Bond Interest Payable	27,500	
	Cash		27,500
	(To record payment of accrued interest)		

(d)

Jan. 1	Bonds Payable	500,000	
	Common Stock		300,000*
	Paid-in Capital in Excess of Par Value		200,000
	(To record conversion of bonds into common stock)		
	*($500,000 ÷ $1,000 = 500 bonds; 500 × 30 = 15,000 shares; 15,000 × $20 = $300,000)		

2. (a) 2000

Jan. 1	Cash	885,301	
	Discount on Bonds Payable	114,699	
	Bonds Payable		1,000,000
	(To record issuance of bonds at a discount)		

PROBLEM-SOLVING STRATEGIES

1. Interest is usually paid semiannually. Be careful to use only 6 months' interest in your computations.
2. Upon conversion, the book (carrying) value of the bonds is removed from the liability accounts and recorded as common stock and related paid-in capital.

(b)

Semiannual Interest Period	Interest to Be Paid	Interest Expense to Be Recorded	Discount Amortization	Unamortized Discount	Bond Carrying Value
Issue date				$114,699	$885,301
1	$50,000	$55,735	$5,735	108,964	891,036
2	50,000	55,735	5,735	103,229	896,771
3	50,000	55,735	5,735	97,494	902,506
4	50,000	55,735	5,735	91,759	908,241
5	50,000	55,735	5,735	86,024	913,976
6	50,000	55,735	5,735	80,289	919,711

(c) 2000

July 1	Bond Interest Expense			55,735	
	Discount on Bonds Payable				5,735
	Cash				50,000
	(To record payment of semiannual interest and amortization of bond discount)				
Dec. 31	Bond Interest Expense			55,735	
	Discount on Bonds Payable				5,735
	Bond Interest Payable				50,000
	(To record accrual of semiannual interest and amortization of bond discount)				

(d) 2003

Jan. 1	Bonds Payable			1,000,000	
	Loss on Bond Redemption			90,289*	
	Discount on Bonds Payable				80,289
	Cash				1,010,000
	(To record redemption of bonds at 101)				
	*($1,010,000 − $919,711)				

3. (a) 1999

Dec. 31	Cash			500,000	
	Mortgage Notes Payable				500,000
	(To record issuance of mortgage note payable)				

(b)

Semiannual Interest Period	Cash Payment	Interest Expense	Reduction of Principal	Principal Balance
Issue date				$500,000
1	$36,324	$30,000	$6,324	493,676
2	36,324	29,621	6,703	486,973
3	36,324	29,218	7,106	479,867
4	36,324	28,792	7,532	472,335

(c) Current liability $14,638 ($7,106 + $7,532)
Long-term liability $472,335

PROBLEM-SOLVING STRATEGIES

1. Discount on bonds payable is a contra liability account.

2. Amortization of bond discount increases bond interest expense.

3. Bond interest expense is the same each period when the straight-line method is used.

4. Loss on bond redemption occurs when the cash paid is greater than the bond carrying value.

PROBLEM-SOLVING STRATEGIES

1. Interest expense decreases each period because the principal is decreasing each period.

2. Each payment consists of (1) interest on the unpaid loan balance and (2) a reduction of the loan principal.

THE
NAVIGATOR

SUMMARY OF STUDY OBJECTIVES

1. *Explain why bonds are issued.* Bonds may be sold to many investors, and they offer the following advantages over common stock: (a) stockholder control is not affected, (b) tax savings result, (c) earnings per share of common stock may be higher.

2. *Prepare the entries for the issuance of bonds and interest expense.* When bonds are issued, Cash is debited for the cash proceeds and Bonds Payable is credited for the face value of the bonds. In addition, Bond Interest Payable is credited if there is accrued interest, and the accounts Premium on Bonds Payable or Discount on Bonds Payable are used to show the bond premium or bond discount. Bond discount and bond premium are amortized by the straight-line method.

3. *Describe the entries when bonds are redeemed or converted.* When bonds are redeemed at maturity, Cash is credited and Bonds Payable is debited for the face value of the bonds. When bonds are redeemed before maturity, it is necessary to (a) eliminate the carrying value of the bonds at the redemption date, (b) record the cash paid, and (c) recognize the gain or loss on redemption. When bonds are converted to common stock, the carrying (or book) value of the bonds is transferred to appropriate paid-in capital accounts, and no gain or loss is recognized.

4. *Indicate the entries required for a bond sinking fund.* Entries are required for a bond sinking fund to record (a) periodic contributions, (b) annual revenue, and (c) redemption of the bonds.

5. *Describe the accounting for long-term notes payable.* Each payment consists of (1) interest on the unpaid balance of the loan, and (2) a reduction of loan principal. The interest decreases each period, while the portion applied to the loan principal increases each period.

6. *Contrast the accounting for operating and capital leases.* For an operating lease, lease (or rental) payments are recorded as an expense by the lessee (renter). For a capital lease, the lessee records the asset and related obligation at the present value of the future lease payments.

7. *Identify the methods for the presentation and analysis of long-term liabilities.* The nature and amount of each long-term debt should be reported in the balance sheet or in schedules in the notes accompanying the statements. Stockholders and long-term creditors are interested in a company's long-run solvency, particularly its ability to pay interest as it comes due and to repay the face value of the debt at maturity. Debt to total assets and times interest earned are two ratios that provide information about debt-paying ability and long-run solvency.

THE NAVIGATOR

GLOSSARY

Bearer (coupon) bonds   Bonds not registered. (p. 678).

Bond certificate   A legal document that indicates the name of the issuer, the face value of the bonds, and such other data as the contractual interest rate and maturity date of the bonds. (p. 679).

Bond indenture   A legal document that sets forth the terms of the bond issue. (p. 678).

Bonds   A form of interest bearing notes payable issued by corporations, universities, and governmental entities. (p. 676).

Callable bonds   Bonds that are subject to retirement at a stated dollar amount prior to maturity at the option of the issuer. (p. 678).

Capital lease   A contractual arrangement that transfers substantially all the benefits and risks of ownership to the lessee so that the lease is in effect a purchase of the property. (p. 694).

Convertible bonds   Bonds that permit bondholders to convert them into common stock at their option. (p. 678).

Contractual interest rate   Rate used to determine the amount of interest the borrower pays and the investor receives. (p. 678).

Debenture bonds   Bonds issued against the general credit of the borrower. Also called unsecured bonds. (p. 678).

Debt to total assets ratio   A solvency measure that indicates the percentage of total assets provided by creditors, computed as total debt divided by total assets. (p. 696).

Face value   Amount of principal due at the maturity date of the bond. (p. 678).

Long-term liabilities   Obligations expected to be paid after one year. (p. 676).

Market interest rate   The rate investors demand for loaning funds to the corporation. (p. 680).

Mortgage bond   A bond secured by real estate. (p. 678).

Mortgage note payable   A long-term note secured by a mortgage that pledges title to specific units of property as security for the loan. (p. 692).

Operating lease   A contractual arrangement giving the lessee temporary use of the property with continued ownership of the property by the lessor. (p. 694).

Registered bonds   Bonds issued in the name of the owner. (p. 678).

Secured bonds   Bonds that have specific assets of the issuer pledged as collateral. (p. 678).

Serial bonds   Bonds that mature in installments. (p. 678).

Sinking fund   Cash or other assets set aside to retire debt. (p. 690).

Sinking fund bonds   Bonds secured by specific assets set aside to retire them. (p. 678).

Straight-line method of amortization   A method of amortizing bond discount or bond premium that allocates the same amount to interest expense in each interest period. (p. 684).

Term bonds   Bonds that mature at a single specified future date. (p. 678).

Times interest earned ratio   A solvency measure that indicates a company's ability to meet interest payments, computed by dividing income before income taxes and interest expense by interest expense. (p. 696).

Unsecured bonds   Bonds issued against the general credit of the borrower. Also called debenture bonds. (p. 678).

APPENDIX   EFFECTIVE-INTEREST AMORTIZATION

The straight-line method of amortization that you studied in the chapter has a conceptual deficiency: It does not completely satisfy the matching principle. Under the straight-line method, interest expense as a percentage of the carrying value of the bonds varies each interest period. This can be seen by using data from the first three interest periods of the bond amortization schedule that was shown in Illustration 16-12:

Semiannual Interest Period	Interest Expense to Be Recorded (A)	Bond Carrying Value (B)	Interest Expense as a Percentage of Carrying Value (A) ÷ (B)
1	$52,000	$980,000	5.31%
2	52,000	982,000	5.29%
3	52,000	984,000	5.27%
10	52,000	998,000	5.21%

ILLUSTRATION 16A-1

Interest percentage rates under straight-line method

Note that interest expense as a percentage of carrying value declines in each interest period. However, to completely comply with the matching principle, interest expense as a percentage of carrying value should not change over the life of the bonds. This percentage, referred to as the **effective-interest rate**, is established when the bonds are issued and remains constant in each interest period. The effective-interest method of amortization accomplishes this result.

Under the **effective-interest method**, the amortization of bond discount or bond premium results in periodic interest expense equal to a constant percentage of the carrying value of the bonds. The effective-interest method results in varying amounts of amortization and interest expense per period but a constant percentage rate; the straight-line method results in constant amounts of amortization and interest expense per period but a varying percentage rate.

The following steps are required under the effective-interest method:

1. Compute the **bond interest expense** by multiplying the carrying value of the bonds at the beginning of the interest period by the effective-interest rate.
2. Compute the **bond interest paid** (or accrued) by multiplying the face value of the bonds by the contractual interest rate.
3. Compute the **amortization amount** by determining the difference between the amounts computed in steps (1) and (2).

These steps are graphically depicted in Illustration 16A-2.

8
STUDY OBJECTIVE

Contrast the effects of the straight-line and effective-interest methods of amortizing bond discount and bond premium.

ILLUSTRATION 16A-2

Computation of amortiza-tion—effective-interest method

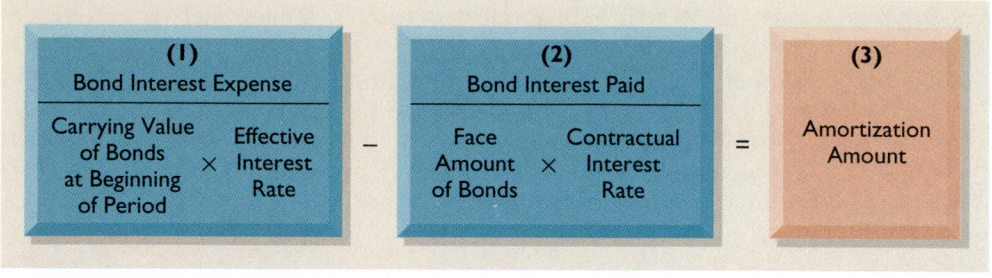

Both the straight-line and effective-interest methods of amortization result in the same total amount of interest expense over the term of the bonds. Furthermore, interest expense each interest period is generally comparable in amount. However, **when the amounts are materially different, the effective-interest method is required under generally accepted accounting principles (GAAP).**

AMORTIZING BOND DISCOUNT

ILLUSTRATION 16A-3

Bond discount amortization schedule

To illustrate the effective-interest method of bond discount amortization, assume that Wrightway Corporation issues $100,000 of 10%, 5-year bonds on January 1,

WRIGHTWAY CORPORATION
Bond Discount Amortization
Effective-Interest Method—Semiannual Interest Payments
10% Bonds Issued at 12%

Semiannual Interest Periods	(A) Interest to Be Paid (5% × $100,000)	(B) Interest Expense to Be Recorded (6% × Preceding Bond Carrying Value)	(C) Discount Amortization (B) − (A)	(D) Unamortized Discount (D) − (C)	(E) Bond Carrying Value ($100,000 − D)
Issue date				$7,361	$ 92,639
1	$ 5,000	$ 5,558 (6% × $92,639)	$ 558	6,803	93,197
2	5,000	5,592 (6% × $93,197)	592	6,211	93,789
3	5,000	5,627 (6% × $93,789)	627	5,584	94,416
4	5,000	5,665 (6% × $94,416)	665	4,919	95,081
5	5,000	5,705 (6% × $95,081)	705	4,214	95,786
6	5,000	5,747 (6% × $95,786)	747	3,467	96,533
7	5,000	5,792 (6% × $96,533)	792	2,675	97,325
8	5,000	5,840 (6% × $97,325)	840	1,835	98,165
9	5,000	5,890 (6% × $98,165)	890	945	99,055
10	5,000	5,945* (6% × $99,055)	945	–0–	100,000
	$50,000	$57,361	$7,361		

Column **(A)** remains constant because the face value of the bonds ($100,000) is multiplied by the semiannual contractual interest rate (5%) each period.

Column **(B)** is computed as the preceding bond carrying value times the semiannual effective-interest rate (6%).

Column **(C)** indicates the discount amortization each period.

Column **(D)** decreases each period until it reaches zero at maturity.

Column **(E)** increases each period until it equals face value at maturity.

*$2 difference due to rounding.

1999, with interest payable each July 1 and January 1. The bonds sell for $92,639 (92.639% of face value), which results in bond discount of $7,361 ($100,000 − $92,639) and an effective-interest rate of 12%. (Note that the $92,639 can be proven as shown in Appendix C at the end of this book.) Preparing a bond discount amortization schedule as shown in Illustration 16A-3 on the previous page facilitates the recording of interest expense and the discount amortization. Note that interest expense as a percentage of carrying value remains constant at 6%.

For the first interest period, the computations of bond interest expense and the bond discount amortization are as follows:

Bond interest expense ($92,639 × 6%)	$5,558
Contractual interest ($100,000 × 5%)	5,000
Bond discount amortization	**$ 558**

ILLUSTRATION 16A-4

Computation of bond discount amortization

As a result, the entry to record the payment of interest and amortization of bond discount by Wrightway Corporation on July 1, 1999, is:

July 1	Bond Interest Expense	5,558	
	Discount on Bonds Payable		558
	Cash		5,000
	(To record payment of bond interest and		
	amortization of bond discount)		

A	=	L	+	SE
−5,000		+558		−5,558

For the second interest period, bond interest expense will be $5,592 ($93,197 × 6%), and the discount amortization will be $592. At December 31, the following adjusting entry is made:

Dec. 31	Bond Interest Expense	5,592	
	Discount on Bonds Payable		592
	Bond Interest Payable		5,000
	(To record accrued interest and		
	amortization of bond discount)		

A	=	L	+	SE
		+ 592		−5,592
		+5,000		

Total bond interest expense for 1999 is $11,150 ($5,558 + $5,592). On January 1, payment of the interest is recorded by a debit to Bond Interest Payable and a credit to Cash.

AMORTIZING BOND PREMIUM

The amortization of bond premium by the effective-interest method is similar to the procedures described for bond discount. As an example, assume that Wrightway Corporation issues $100,000, 10%, 5-year bonds on January 1, 1999, with interest payable on July 1 and January 1. In this case, the bonds sell for $108,111, which results in bond premium of $8,111 and an effective-interest rate of 8%. The bond premium amortization schedule is shown in Illustration 16A-5.

HELPFUL HINT
When a bond sells for $108,111, it is quoted as 108.111% of face value. Note that $108,111 can be proven as shown in Appendix C.

		(B) **Interest Expense**			
		to Be Recorded	**(C)**	**(D)**	**(E)**
Semiannual	**(A)**	**(4% × Preceding Bond**	**Premium**	**Unamortized**	**Bond**
Interest	**Interest to Be Paid**	**Carry Value)**	**Amortization**	**Premium**	**Carrying Value**
Periods	**(5% × $100,000)**		**(A) − (B)**	**(D) − (C)**	**($100,000 + D)**
Issue date				$8,111	$108,111
1	$ 5,000	$ 4,324 (4% × $108,111)	$ 676	7,435	107,435
2	5,000	4,297 (4% × $107,435)	703	6,732	106,732
3	5,000	4,269 (4% × $106,732)	731	6,001	106,001
4	5,000	4,240 (4% × $106,001)	760	5,241	105,241
5	5,000	4,210 (4% × $105,241)	790	4,451	104,451
6	5,000	4,178 (4% × $104,451)	822	3,629	103,629
7	5,000	4,145 (4% × $103,629)	855	2,774	102,774
8	5,000	4,111 (4% × $102,774)	889	1,885	101,885
9	5,000	4,075 (4% × $101,885)	925	960	100,960
10	5,000	4,040* (4% × $100,960)	960	–0–	100,000
	$50,000	$41,889	$8,111		

WRIGHTWAY CORPORATION
Bond Premium Amortization
Effective-Interest Method—Semiannual Interest Payments
10% Bonds Issued at 8%

Column **(A)** remains constant because the face value of the bonds ($100,000) is multiplied by the semiannual contractual interest rate (5%) each period.

Column **(B)** is computed as the carrying value of the bonds times the semiannual effective-interest rate (4%).

Column **(C)** indicates the premium amortization each period.

Column **(D)** decreases each period until it reaches zero at maturity.

Column **(E)** decreases each period until it equals face value at maturity.

*$2 difference due to rounding.

For the first interest period, the computations of bond interest expense and the bond premium amortization are:

Bond interest expense ($108,111 × 4%)	$4,324
Contractual interest ($100,000 × 5%)	5,000
Bond premium amortization	**$ 676**

The entry on the first interest date is:

A	=	L	+	SE
−5,000		−676		−4,324

July 1	Bond Interest Expense	4,324	
	Premium on Bonds Payable	676	
	Cash		5,000
	(To record payment of bond interest and amortization of bond premium)		

For the second interest period, interest expense will be $4,297, and the premium amortization will be $703. Total bond interest expense for 1999 is $8,621 ($4,324 + $4,297).

TECHNOLOGY IN ACTION

The amortization schedule is an excellent example of an accounting computation efficiently and effectively performed by an electronic spreadsheet. Once the selling price, face amount, contractual rate of interest, effective rate of interest, and number of interest periods are determined and entered into the spreadsheet, all of the computations until maturity can be performed by the computer. Note that all data needed for the adjusting entries can be taken directly from the amortization schedule.

DEMONSTRATION PROBLEM

Gardner Corporation issues $1,750,000, 10-year, 12% bonds on January 1, 1999, at $1,820,000 to yield 10%. The bonds pay semiannual interest July 1 and January 1. Gardner uses the effective-interest method of amortization.

Instructions

(a) Prepare the journal entry to record the issuance of the bonds.

(b) Prepare the journal entry to record the payment of interest on July 1, 1999.

SOLUTION TO DEMONSTRATION PROBLEM

(a) 1999

Jan. 1	Cash	1,820,000	
	Bonds Payable		1,750,000
	Premium on Bonds Payable		70,000
	(To record issuance of bonds at a premium)		
1999			
July 1	Bond Interest Expense	91,000*	
	Premium on Bonds Payable	14,000**	
	Cash		105,000
	(To record payment of semiannual interest and amortization of bond premium)		
	*($1,820,000 × 5%)		
	**($105,000 − $91,000)		

PROBLEM-SOLVING STRATEGIES

1. Bond carrying value at beginning of period times effective-interest rate equals interest expense.

2. Credit to cash (or bond interest payable) is computed by multiplying the face value of the bonds by the contractual interest rate.

3. Bond premium or discount amortization is the difference between (1) and (2).

4. Interest expense increases when the effective-interest method is used for bonds issued at a discount. The reason is that a constant percentage is applied to an increasing book value to compute interest expense.

SUMMARY OF STUDY OBJECTIVE FOR APPENDIX

8. Contrast the effects of the straight-line and effective-interest methods of amortizing bond discount and bond premium. The straight-line method of amortization results in a constant amount of amortization and interest expense per period but a varying percentage rate. In contrast, the effective-interest method results in varying amounts of amortization and interest expense per period but a constant percentage rate of interest. The effective-interest method generally results in a better matching of expenses with revenues. When the difference between the straight-line and effective-interest method is material, the use of the effective-interest method is required under GAAP.

GLOSSARY FOR APPENDIX

Effective-interest method of amortization A method of amortizing bond discount or bond premium that results in periodic interest expense equal to a constant percentage of the carrying value of the bonds. (p. 701).

Effective-interest rate Rate established when bonds are issued that remains constant in each interest period. (p. 701).

*Note: All asterisked Questions, Exercises, and Problems relate to material in the appendix to the chapter.

SELF-STUDY QUESTIONS

Answers are at the end of the chapter.

(SO 1) 1. The term used for bonds that are unsecured is:
a. callable bonds.
b. indenture bonds.
c. debenture bonds.
d. bearer bonds.

(SO 2) 2. Karson Inc. issues 10-year bonds with a maturity value of $200,000. If the bonds are issued at a premium, this indicates that:
a. the contractual interest rate exceeds the market interest rate.
b. the market interest rate exceeds the contractual interest rate.
c. the contractual interest rate and the market interest rate are the same.
d. no relationship exists between the two rates.

(SO 2) 3. On January 1, Hurley Corporation issues $500,000, 5-year, 12% bonds at 96 with interest payable on July 1 and January 1. The entry on July 1 to record payment of bond interest and the amortization of bond discount using the straight-line method will include a:
a. debit to Interest Expense, $30,000
b. debit to Interest Expense, $60,000
c. credit to Discount on Bonds Payable, $4,000
d. credit to Discount on Bonds Payable, $2,000

(SO 2) 4. For the bonds issued in question 3, above, what is the carrying value of the bonds at the end of the third interest period?
a. $486,000
b. $488,000
c. $472,000
d. $464,000

(SO 2) 5. When the interest payment dates of a bond are May 1 and November 1, and a bond issue is sold on June 1, the amount of cash received by the issuer will be:
a. decreased by accrued interest from June 1 to November 1.
b. decreased by accrued interest from May 1 to June 1.
c. increased by accrued interest from May 1 to June 1.
d. increased by accrued interest from June 1 to November 1.

(SO 3) 6. Gester Corporation retires its $100,000 face value bonds at 105 on January 1, following the payment of semiannual interest. The carrying value of the bonds at the redemption date is $103,745. The entry to record the redemption will include a:
a. credit of $3,745 to Loss on Bond Redemption.
b. debit of $3,745 to Premium on Bonds Payable.
c. credit of $1,255 to Gain on Bond Redemption.
d. debit of $5,000 to Premium on Bonds Payable.

(SO 3) 7. Colson Inc. converts $600,000 of bonds sold at face value into 10,000 shares of common stock, par value $1. Both the bonds and the stock have a market value of $760,000.

What amount should be credited to Paid-in Capital in Excess of Par as a result of the conversion?
a. $10,000
b. $160,000
c. $600,000
d. $590,000

(SO 4) 8. Sanger Company has a bond sinking fund in the amount of $400,000. Where should this amount be reported on the balance sheet?
a. investments section
b. current asset section
c. current liability section
d. long-term liability section

(SO 5) 9. Andrews Inc. issues a $497,000, 10% 3-year mortgage note on January 1. The note will be paid in three annual installments of $200,000, each payable at the end of the year. What is the amount of interest expense that should be recognized by Andrews Inc. in the second year?
a. $16,567
b. $49,740
c. $34,670
d. $347,600

(SO 6) 10. Lease A does not contain a bargain purchase option, but the lease term is equal to 90 percent of the estimated economic life of the leased property. Lease B does not transfer ownership of the property to the lessee by the end of the lease term, but the lease term is equal to 75 percent of the estimated economic life of the leased property. How should the lessee classify these leases?

	Lease A	Lease B
a.	Operating lease	Capital lease
b.	Operating lease	Operating lease
c.	Capital lease	Operating lease
d.	Capital lease	Capital lease

*11. On January 1, Besalius Inc. issued $1,000,000, 9% bonds (SO 8) for $939,000. The market rate of interest for these bonds is 10%. Interest is payable annually on December 31. Besalius uses the effective interest method of amortizing bond discount. At the end of the first year, Besalius should report unamortized bond discount of:
a. $54,900.
b. $57,100.
c. $51,610.
d. $51,000.

*12. On January 1, Dias Corporation issued $1,000,000, 14%, (SO 8) 5-year bonds with interest payable on July 1 and January 1. The bonds sold for $1,098,540. The market rate of interest for these bonds was 12%. On the first interest date, using the effective-interest method, the debit entry to Bond Interest Expense is for:
a. $60,000.
b. $76,898.
c. $65,912.
d. $131,825.

THE NAVIGATOR

QUESTIONS

1. (a) What are long-term liabilities? Give three examples. (b) What is a bond?

2. (a) As a source of long-term financing, what are the major advantages of bonds over common stock? (b) What are the major disadvantages in using bonds for long-term financing?

3. Contrast the following types of bonds: (a) secured and unsecured, (b) term and serial, (c) registered and bearer, and (d) convertible and callable.

4. The following terms are important in issuing bonds: (a) face value, (b) contractual interest rate, (c) bond indenture, and (d) bond certificate. Explain each of these terms.

5. Describe the two major obligations incurred by a company when bonds are issued.

6. Assume that Shinn Inc. sold bonds with a par value of $100,000 for $104,000. Was the market interest rate equal to, less than, or greater than the bonds' contractual interest rate? Explain.

7. Connie Black and Dan Sells are discussing how the market price of a bond is determined. Connie believes that the market price of a bond is solely a function of the amount of the principal payment at the end of the term of a bond. Is she right? Discuss.

8. If a 10%, 10-year, $800,000 bond is issued at par and interest is paid semiannually, what is the amount of the interest payment at the end of the first semiannual period?

9. If the Bonds Payable account has a balance of $900,000 and the Discount on Bonds Payable account has a balance of $60,000, what is the carrying value of the bonds?

10. Explain the straight-line method of amortizing discount and premium on bonds payable.

11. Darby Corporation issues $300,000 of 8%, 5-year bonds on January 1, 1999, at 104. Assuming that the straight-line method is used to amortize the premium, what is the total amount of interest expense for 1999?

12. Which accounts are debited and which are credited if a bond issue originally sold at a premium is redeemed before maturity at 97 immediately following the payment of interest?

13. Mai Corporation is considering issuing a convertible bond. What is a convertible bond? Discuss the advantages of a convertible bond from the standpoint of (a) the bondholders and (b) the issuing corporation.

14. The financial statements of Landis Inc. disclose that it has a bond sinking fund. What is a bond sinking fund? What is its purpose?

15. Dan Foley, a friend of yours, has recently purchased a home for $125,000, paying $25,000 down and the remainder financed by a 10.5%, 20-year mortgage, payable at $998.38 per month. At the end of the first month, Dan receives a statement from the bank indicating that only $123.38 of principal was paid during the month. At this rate, he calculates that it will take over 67 years to pay off the mortgage. Is he right? Discuss.

16. (a) What is a lease agreement? (b) What are the two most common types of leases? (c) Distinguish between the two types of leases.

17. Seminole Company rents a warehouse on a month-to-month basis for the storage of its excess inventory. The company periodically must rent space when its production greatly exceeds actual sales. What is the nature of this type of lease agreement, and what accounting treatment should be accorded it?

18. Alvarez Company entered into an agreement to lease 12 computers from Estes Electronics Inc. The present value of the lease payments is $186,300. Assuming that this is a capital lease, what entry would Alvarez Company make on the date of the lease agreement?

19. In general, what are the requirements for the financial statement presentation of long-term liabilities?

*20. Janet Hashmi is discussing the advantages of the effective-interest method of bond amortization with her accounting staff. What do you think Janet is saying?

*21. Mobley Corporation issues $500,000 of 9%, 5-year bonds on January 1, 1999, at 104. If Mobley uses the effective-interest method in amortizing the premium, will the annual interest expense increase or decrease over the life of the bonds? Explain.

BRIEF EXERCISES

BE16–1 Mayo Inc. is considering two alternatives to finance its construction of a new $2 million plant:

Compare bond versus stock financing.
(SO 1)

  (a) Issuance of 200,000 shares of common stock at the market price of $10 per share.
  (b) Issuance of $2 million, 8% bonds at par.

Complete the following table and indicate which alternative is preferable.

	Issue Stock	Issue Bond
Income before interest and taxes	$800,000	$800,000
Interest expense from bonds		
Income before income taxes	$	$
Income tax expense (30%)		
Net income	$	$
Outstanding shares		700,000
Earnings per share		

Prepare entries for bonds issued at face value.
(SO 2)

BE16–2   Kaiser Corporation issued 1,000, 8%, 5-year, $1,000 bonds dated January 1, 1999, at 100. (a) Prepare the journal entry to record the sale of these bonds on January 1, 1999. (b) Prepare the journal entry to record the first interest payment on July 1, 1999 (interest payable semiannually), assuming no previous accrual of interest. (c) Prepare the adjusting journal entry on December 31, 1999, to record interest expense.

Prepare entries for bonds issued at a discount.
(SO 2)

BE16–3   Cruyen Company issues $2 million, 10-year, 9% bonds at 97, with interest payable on July 1 and January 1. The straight-line method is used to amortize bond discount. (a) Prepare the journal entry to record the sale of these bonds on January 1, 1999. (b) Prepare the journal entry to record interest expense and bond discount amortization on July 1, 1999, assuming no previous accrual of interest.

Prepare entries for bonds issued at a premium.
(SO 2)

BE16–4   Wiggins Inc. issues $5 million, 5-year, 10% bonds at 102, with interest payable on July 1 and January 1. The straight-line method is used to amortize bond premium. (a) Prepare the journal entry to record the sale of these bonds on January 1, 1999. (b) Prepare the journal entry to record interest expense and bond premium amortization on July 1, 1999, assuming no previous accrual of interest.

Prepare entries for bonds issued between interest dates.
(SO 2)

BE16–5   Quarry Inc. has outstanding $1 million, 10-year, 9% bonds with interest payable on July 1 and January 1. The bonds were dated January 1, 1999, but were issued on May 1, 1999, at face value plus accrued interest. (a) Prepare the journal entry to record the sale of the bonds on May 1, 1999. (b) Prepare the journal entry to record the interest payment on July 1, 1999.

Prepare entry for redemption of bonds.
(SO 3)

BE16–6   The balance sheet for Lopez Company reports the following information on July 1, 1999:

Long-term liabilities		
Bonds payable	$1,000,000	
Less: Discount on bonds payable	60,000	$940,000

Lopez decides to redeem these bonds at 103 after paying semiannual interest. Prepare the journal entry to record the redemption on July 1, 1999.

Prepare entries for bond sinking fund.
(SO 4)

BE16–7   Pasco Company establishes a sinking fund for its $1 million, 5-year bonds. On January 1, 1999, it makes its first annual cash contribution of $180,000. At the end of 1999, the sinking fund had earned $12,000. (a) Prepare the journal entry to record the contribution made into the sinking fund on January 1, 1999. (b) Prepare the journal entry to record the revenue earned in the sinking fund in 1999.

Prepare entries for long-term notes payable.
(SO 5)

BE16–8   O'Neill Inc. issues a $400,000, 10%, 10-year mortgage note on December 31, 1999, to obtain financing for a new building. The terms provide for semiannual installment payments of $32,097. Prepare the entry to record the mortgage loan on December 31, 1999, and the first installment payment.

Contrast accounting for operating and capital lease.
(SO 6)

BE16–9   Prepare the journal entries that the lessee should make to record the following transactions:

1. The lessee makes a lease payment of $70,000 to the lessor in an operating lease transaction.
2. Lloyd Company leases a new building from Chang Construction, Inc. The present value of the lease payments is $600,000. The lease qualifies as a capital lease.

Prepare statement presentation of long-term liabilities.
(SO 7)

BE16–10   Presented below are long-term liability items for Malik Company at December 31, 1999. Prepare the long-term liabilities section of the balance sheet for Malik Company.

Bonds payable, due 2001	$800,000
Lease liability	50,000
Notes payable, due 2003	80,000
Discount on bonds payable	45,000

*BE16–11 Presented below is the partial bond discount amortization schedule for Sauer Corp. Sauer uses the effective-interest method of amortization.

Use effective-interest method of bond amortization.
(SO 8)

Semiannual Interest Periods	Interest to Be Paid	Interest Expense to Be Recorded	Discount Amortization	Unamortized Discount	Bond Carrying Value
Issue date				$62,311	$937,689
1	$45,000	$46,884	$1,884	60,427	939,573
2	45,000	46,979	1,979	58,448	941,552

Instructions

(a) Prepare the journal entry to record the payment of interest and the discount amortization at the end of period 1.
(b) ▉▉▉▶ Explain why interest expense is greater than interest paid.
(c) Explain why interest expense will increase each period.

EXERCISES

E16–1 National Airlines is considering two alternatives for the financing of a purchase of a fleet of airplanes. These two alternatives are:

1. Issue 60,000 shares of common stock at $45 per share. (Cash dividends have not been paid nor is the payment of any contemplated.)
2. Issue 13%, 10-year bonds at par for $2,700,000.

It is estimated that the company will earn $600,000 before interest and taxes as a result of this purchase. The company has an estimated tax rate of 30% and has 90,000 shares of common stock outstanding prior to the new financing.

Compare two alternatives of financing—issuance of common stock vs. issuance of bonds.
(SO 1)

Instructions
Determine the effect on net income and earnings per share for these two methods of financing.

E16–2 On January 1, Madden Company issued $80,000, 10%, 10-year bonds at par. Interest is payable semiannually on July 1 and January 1.

Prepare entries for issuance of bonds and payment and accrual of bond interest.
(SO 2)

Instructions
Present journal entries to record:

(a) The issuance of the bonds.
(b) The payment of interest on July 1, assuming that interest was not accrued on June 30.
(c) The accrual of interest on December 31.

E16–3 Kang Company issued $200,000, 9%, 20-year bonds on January 1, 1999, at 103. Interest is payable semiannually on July 1 and January 1. Kang uses straight-line amortization for bond premium or discount.

Prepare entries to record issuance of bonds, payment of interest, amortization of premium, and redemption at maturity.
(SO 2, 3)

Instructions
Prepare the journal entries to record:

(a) The issuance of the bonds.
(b) The payment of interest and the premium amortization on July 1, 1999, assuming that interest was not accrued on June 30.
(c) The accrual of interest and the premium amortization on December 31, 1999.
(d) The redemption of the bonds at maturity, assuming interest for the last interest period has been paid and recorded.

E16–4 Cortez Company issued $180,000, 11%, 10-year bonds on December 31, 1998, for $170,000. Interest is payable semiannually on June 30 and December 31. Cortez uses the straight-line method to amortize bond premium or discount.

Prepare entries to record issuance of bonds, payment of interest, amortization of discount, and redemption at maturity.
(SO 2, 3)

Instructions
Prepare the journal entries to record:

(a) The issuance of the bonds.
(b) The payment of interest and the discount amortization on June 30, 1999.
(c) The payment of interest and the discount amortization on December 31, 1999.
(d) The redemption of the bonds at maturity, assuming interest for the last interest period has been paid and recorded.

Prepare entries to record issuance of bonds between interest dates, and payment and accrual of interest.
(SO 2)

E16–5 On April 1, Jantz Company issued $80,000, 10%, 10-year bonds dated January 1 at par plus accrued interest. Interest is payable semiannually on July 1 and January 1.

Instructions
Present journal entries to record:

(a) The issuance of the bonds.
(b) The payment of interest on July 1, assuming that interest was not accrued on June 30.
(c) The accrual of interest on December 31.

E16–6 Presented below are three independent situations:

Prepare entries for redemption of bonds and conversion of bonds into common stock.
(SO 3)

1. Noble Corporation retired $130,000 face value, 12% bonds on June 30, 1999, at 102. The carrying value of the bonds at the redemption date was $107,500. The bonds pay semiannual interest and the interest payment due on June 30, 1999, has been made and recorded.
2. Vargas, Inc. retired $150,000 face value, 12.5% bonds on June 30, 1999, at 96. The carrying value of the bonds at the redemption date was $151,000. The bonds pay semiannual interest and the interest payment due on June 30, 1999, has been made and recorded.
3. Lennon Company has $80,000, 8%, 12-year convertible bonds outstanding. These bonds were sold at face value and pay semiannual interest on June 30 and December 31 of each year. The bonds are convertible into 30 shares of Lennon $2 par value common stock for each $1,000 worth of bonds. On December 31, 1999, after the bond interest has been paid, $20,000 face value bonds were converted. The market value of Lennon common stock was $44 per share on December 31, 1999.

Instructions
For each independent situation above, prepare the appropriate journal entry for the redemption or conversion of the bonds.

Prepare entries to record sinking fund deposit, revenue earned on fund assets, and redemption of bonds.
(SO 4)

E16–7 Tabaras Co. decides to establish a sinking fund for its $6,000,000, 20-year bonds that are outstanding. The trustee indicates that an annual contribution of $165,000 should be made at the end of each year. The sinking fund earned $9,700 in the second year. At the maturity date, the sinking fund had a balance of $5,980,000.

Instructions
Prepare the journal entries to record:

(a) The first contribution by Tabaras Co.
(b) The actual earnings in the second year and the second contribution.
(c) The redemption of the bonds at maturity.

Prepare entries to record mortgage note and installment payments.
(SO 5)

E16–8 Neumann Co. receives $120,000 when it issues a $120,000, 10%, mortgage note payable to finance the construction of a building at December 31, 1999. The terms provide for semiannual installment payments of $8,000 on June 30 and December 31.

Instructions
Prepare the journal entries to record the mortgage loan and the first two installment payments.

E16–9 Presented below are two independent situations.

Prepare entries for operating lease and capital lease.
(SO 6)

1. Speedy Car Rental leased a car to Leach Company for one year. Terms of the operating lease agreement call for monthly payments of $500.
2. On January 1, 1999, Knapp Inc. entered into an agreement to lease 20 computers from Guinn Electronics. The terms of the lease agreement require three annual rental payments of $90,000 (including 10% interest) beginning December 31, 1999. The present value of the three rental payments is $223,816. Knapp considers this a capital lease.

Instructions
(a) Prepare the appropriate journal entry to be made by Leach Company for the first lease payment.
(b) Prepare the journal entry to record the lease agreement on the books of Knapp Inc. on January 1, 1999.

Prepare long-term liabilities section.
(SO 7)

E16–10 The adjusted trial balance for Vowell Corporation at the end of the current year contained the following accounts:

Bond Interest Payable	$ 9,000
Lease Liability	59,500
Bonds Payable, due 2007	140,000
Premium on Bonds Payable	32,000
Bond Sinking Fund	241,600

Instructions
(a) Prepare the long-term liabilities section of the balance sheet.
(b) Indicate the proper balance sheet classification for the account(s) listed above that do not belong in the long-term liabilities section.

*E16–11   Pfeifer Corporation issued $390,000, 9%, 10-year bonds on January 1, 1999, for $365,698. This price resulted in an effective interest rate of 10% on the bonds. Interest is payable semiannually on July 1 and January 1. Pfeifer uses the effective-interest method to amortize bond premium or discount.

Prepare entries for issuance of bonds, payment of interest, and amortization of discount using effective-interest method. (SO 8)

Instructions
Prepare the journal entries to record (round to the nearest dollar):

(a) The issuance of the bonds.
(b) The payment of interest and the discount amortization on July 1, 1999, assuming that interest was not accrued on June 30.
(c) The accrual of interest and the discount amortization on December 31, 1999.

*E16–12   Nieto Company issued $360,000, 11%, 10-year bonds on January 1, 1999, for $382,432. This price resulted in an effective interest rate of 10% on the bonds. Interest is payable semiannually on July 1 and January 1. Nieto uses the effective-interest method to amortize bond premium or discount.

Prepare entries for issuance of bonds, payment of interest, and amortization of premium using effective-interest method. (SO 8)

Instructions
Prepare the journal entries (rounded to the nearest dollar) to record:

(a) The issuance of the bonds.
(b) The payment of interest and the premium amortization on July 1, 1999, assuming that interest was not accrued on June 30.
(c) The accrual of interest and the premium amortization on December 31, 1999.

PROBLEMS: SET A

P16–1A   Lorenzo Company sold $4,000,000, 9%, 20-year bonds on January 1, 1999. The bonds were dated January 1, 1999, and pay interest on January 1 and July 1. Lorenzo Company uses the straight-line method to amortize bond premium or discount. The bonds were sold at 98. Assume no interest is accrued on June 30.

Prepare entries to record issuance of bonds, interest accrual, and amortization for 2 years. (SO 2, 7)

Instructions
(a) Prepare the journal entry to record the issuance of the bonds on January 1, 1999.
(b) Prepare a bond discount amortization schedule for the first four interest periods.
(c) Prepare the journal entries for interest and the amortization of the discount in 1999 and 2000.
(d) Show the balance sheet presentation of the bond liability at December 31, 2000.

P16–2A   Cockrill Corporation sold $1,500,000, 8%, 10-year bonds on January 1, 1999. The bonds were dated January 1, 1999, and pay interest on July 1 and January 1. Cockrill Corporation uses the straight-line method to amortize bond premium or discount. Assume no interest is accrued on June 30.

Prepare entries to record issuance of bonds, interest, and amortization of bond premium and discount. (SO 2, 7)

Instructions
(a) Prepare all the necessary journal entries to record the issuance of the bonds and bond interest expense for 1999, assuming that the bonds sold at 103.
(b) Prepare journal entries as in part (a) assuming that the bonds sold at 96.
(c) Show balance sheet presentation for each bond issue at December 31, 1999.

Prepare entries to record interest payments, discount amortization, and redemption of bonds.
(SO 2, 3)

P16–3A   The following is taken from Emig Corp. balance sheet:

EMIG CORPORATION
Balance Sheet (partial)
December 31, 1999

Current liabilities		
Bond interest payable (for 6 months from July 1 to December 31)		$132,000
Long-term liabilities		
Bonds payable, 11%, due January 1, 2010	$2,400,000	
Less: Discount on bonds payable	90,000	$2,310,000

Interest is payable semiannually on January 1 and July 1. The bonds are callable on any semi-annual interest date. Emig uses straight-line amortization for any bond premium or discount. From December 31, 1999, the bonds will be outstanding for an additional 10 years or 120 months.

Instructions
(Round all computations to the nearest dollar.)

(a) Journalize the payment of bond interest on January 1, 2000.
(b) Prepare the entry to amortize bond discount and to pay the interest due on July 1, 2000, assuming that interest was not accrued on June 30.
(c) Assume that on July 1, 2000, after paying interest, Emig Corp. calls bonds having a face value of $800,000. The call price is 102. Record the redemption of the bonds.
(d) Prepare the adjusting entry at December 31, 2000, to amortize bond discount and to accrue interest on the remaining bonds.

Prepare installment payments schedule and journal entries for a mortgage note payable.
(SO 5)

P16–4A   Kinyae Electronics issues a $600,000, 10%, 10-year mortgage note on December 31, 1999, to help finance a plant expansion program. The terms provide for semiannual installment payments, not including real estate taxes and insurance of $48,145. Payments are due June 30 and December 31.

Instructions
(a) Prepare an installment payments schedule for the first 2 years.
(b) Prepare the entries for (1) the mortgage loan and (2) the first two installment payments.
(c) Show how the total mortgage liability should be reported on the balance sheet at December 31, 2000.

Analyze three different lease situations and prepare journal entries.
(SO 6)

P16–5A   Presented below are three different lease transactions in which Foyle Enterprises engaged in 1999. Assume that all lease transactions start on January 1, 1999. In no case does Foyle receive title to the properties leased during or at the end of the lease term.

	Lessor		
	Kasnic Associates	**Dieker Co.**	**Irwin Inc.**
Type of property	Bulldozer	Truck	Furniture
Bargain purchase option	None	None	None
Lease term	4 years	6 years	3 years
Estimated economic life	8 years	7 years	5 years
Yearly rental	$13,000	$ 6,000	$ 4,000
Fair market value of leased asset	$80,000	$29,000	$27,500
Present value of the lease rental payments	$48,000	$25,000	$12,000

Instructions
(a) Identify the leases above as operating or capital leases. Explain.
(b) How should the lease transaction for Dieker Co. be recorded on January 1, 1999?
(c) How should the lease transactions for Irwin Inc. be recorded in 1999?

*P16–6A   On July 1, 1999, Gordon Satellites issued $1,800,000 face value, 9%, 10-year bonds at $1,687,840. This price resulted in an effective-interest rate of 10% on the bonds. Gordon uses the effective-interest method to amortize bond premium or discount. The bonds pay semi-annual interest July 1 and January 1.

Prepare entries to record issuance of bonds, payment of interest, and amortization of bond discount using effective-interest method.
(SO 8)

Instructions
(Round all computations to the nearest dollar.)
(a) Prepare the journal entry to record the issuance of the bonds on July 1, 1999.
(b) Prepare the journal entry to record the accrual of interest and the amortization of the discount on December 31, 1999.
(c) Prepare the journal entry to record the payment of interest and the amortization of the discount on July 1, 2000, assuming that interest was not accrued on June 30.
(d) Prepare the journal entry to record the accrual of interest and the amortization of the discount on December 31, 2000.
(e) Prepare an amortization table through December 31, 2000 (three interest periods) for this bond issue.

*P16–7A   On July 1, 1999, Crose Chemical Company issued $3,000,000 face value, 12%, 10-year bonds at $3,373,868. This price resulted in a 10% effective-interest rate on the bonds. Crose uses the effective-interest method to amortize bond premium or discount. The bonds pay semiannual interest on each July 1 and January 1.

Prepare entries to record issuance of bonds, payment of interest, and amortization of premium using effective-interest method. In addition, answer questions.
(SO 8)

Instructions
(a) Prepare the journal entries to record the following transactions:
   (1) The issuance of the bonds on July 1, 1999.
   (2) The accrual of interest and the amortization of the premium on December 31, 1999.
   (3) The payment of interest and the amortization of the premium on July 1, 2000, assuming no accrual of interest on June 30.
   (4) The accrual of interest and the amortization of the premium on December 31, 2000.
(b) Show the proper balance sheet presentation for the liability for bonds payable on the December 31, 2000, balance sheet.
(c) ▭▬▭▶ Provide the answers to the following questions in letter form.
   (1) What amount of interest expense is reported for 2000?
   (2) Would the bond interest expense reported in 2000 be the same as, greater than, or less than the amount that would be reported if the straight-line method of amortization were used?
   (3) Determine the total cost of borrowing over the life of the bond.
   (4) Would the total bond interest expense be greater than, the same as, or less than the total interest expense if the straight-line method of amortization were used?

PROBLEMS: SET B

P16–1B   Grabowski Electric sold $2,000,000, 10%, 10-year bonds on January 1, 1999. The bonds were dated January 1 and pay interest July 1 and January 1. Grabowski Electric uses the straight-line method to amortize bond premium or discount. The bonds were sold at 104. Assume no interest is accrued on June 30.

Prepare entries to record issuance of bonds, interest accrual, and amortization for 2 years.
(SO 2, 7)

Instructions
(a) Prepare the journal entry to record the issuance of the bonds on January 1, 1999.
(b) Prepare a bond premium amortization schedule for the first four interest periods.
(c) Prepare the journal entries for interest and the amortization of the premium in 1999 and 2000.
(d) Show the balance sheet presentation of the bond liability at December 31, 2000.

P16–2B   O'Meara Company sold $1,500,000, 12%, 10-year bonds on July 1, 1999. The bonds were dated July 1, 1999, and pay interest July 1 and January 1. O'Meara Company uses the straight-line method to amortize bond premium or discount. Assume no interest is accrued on June 30.

Prepare entries to record issuance of bonds, interest, and amortization of bond premium and discount.
(SO 2, 7)

Instructions
  (a) Prepare all the necessary journal entries to record the issuance of the bonds and bond interest expense for 1999, assuming that the bonds sold at 104.
  (b) Prepare journal entries as in part (a) assuming that the bonds sold at 98.
  (c) Show balance sheet presentation for each bond issue at December 31, 1999.

P16–3B The following is taken from the Whitfield Company balance sheet:

Prepare entries to record interest payments, premium amortization, and redemption of bonds.
(SO 2, 3)

WHITFIELD COMPANY
Balance Sheet (partial)
December 31, 1999

Current liabilities		
Bond interest payable (for 6 months		
from July 1 to December 31)		$ 216,000
Long-term liabilities		
Bonds payable, 12% due January 1, 2010	$3,600,000	
Add: Premium on bonds payable	200,000	$3,800,000

Interest is payable semiannually on January 1 and July 1. The bonds are callable on any semi-annual interest date. Whitfield uses straight-line amortization for any bond premium or discount. From December 31, 1999, the bonds will be outstanding for an additional 10 years (120 months).

Instructions
  (a) Journalize the payment of bond interest on January 1, 2000.
  (b) Prepare the entry to amortize bond premium and to pay the interest due on July 1, 2000, assuming no accrual of interest on June 30.
  (c) Assume that on July 1, 2000, after paying interest, Whitfield Company calls bonds having a face value of $1,800,000. The call price is 101. Record the redemption of the bonds.
  (d) Prepare the adjusting entry at December 31, 2000, to amortize bond premium and to accrue interest on the remaining bonds.

Prepare installment schedule and journal entries for a mortgage note payable.
(SO 5)

P16–4B Evans Electronics issues a $400,000, 12%, 10-year mortgage note on December 31, 1998. The proceeds from the note are to be used in financing a new research laboratory. The terms of the note provide for semiannual installment payments, exclusive of real estate taxes and insurance, of $34,874. Payments are due June 30 and December 31.

Instructions
  (a) Prepare an installment payments schedule for the first 2 years.
  (b) Prepare the entries for (1) the loan and (2) the first two installment payments.
  (c) Show how the total mortgage liability should be reported on the balance sheet at December 31, 1999.

Analyze three different lease situations and prepare journal entries.
(SO 6)

P16–5B Presented below are three different lease transactions that occurred for Beck Inc. in 1999. Assume that all lease contracts start on January 1, 1999. In no case does Beck receive title to the properties leased during or at the end of the lease term.

	Lessor		
	Choi Delivery	**Duncan Co.**	**Cagle Auto**
Type of property	Computer	Delivery equipment	Automobile
Yearly rental	$ 8,000	$ 4,200	$ 3,700
Lease term	6 years	4 years	2 years
Estimated economic life	7 years	7 years	5 years
Fair market value of lease asset	$44,000	$19,000	$11,000
Present value of the lease rental payments	$41,000	$13,000	$ 6,400
Bargain purchase option	None	None	None

Instructions

(a) Which of the leases above are operating leases and which are capital leases? Explain.

(b) How should the lease transaction for Duncan Co. be recorded in 1999?

(c) How should the lease transaction for Choi Delivery be recorded on January 1, 1999?

*P16–6B   On July 1, 1999, Keller Corporation issued $2,500,000 face value, 12%, 10-year bonds at $2,811,556. This price resulted in an effective-interest rate of 10% on the bonds. Keller uses the effective-interest method to amortize bond premium or discount. The bonds pay semi-annual interest July 1 and January 1.

Prepare entries to record issuance of bonds, payment of interest, and amortization of bond premium using effective-interest method.
(SO 2)

Instructions

(Round all computations to the nearest dollar.)

(a) Prepare the journal entry to record the issuance of the bonds on July 1, 1999.

(b) Prepare the journal entry to record the accrual of interest and the amortization of the premium on December 31, 1999.

(c) Prepare the journal entry to record the payment of interest and the amortization of the premium on July 1, 2000, assuming no accrual of interest on June 30.

(d) Prepare the journal entry to record the accrual of interest and the amortization of the premium on December 31, 2000.

(e) Prepare an amortization table through December 31, 2000 (three interest periods) for this bond issue.

*P16–7B   On July 1, 1999, Shawnee Company issued $2,000,000 face value, 10%, 10-year bonds at $1,770,592. This price resulted in an effective-interest rate of 12% on the bonds. Shawnee uses the effective-interest method to amortize bond premium or discount. The bonds pay semiannual interest July 1 and January 1.

Prepare entries to record issuance of bonds, payment of interest, and amortization of discount using effective-interest method. In addition, answer questions.
(SO 2, 8)

Instructions

(a) Prepare the journal entries to record the following transactions.

(1) The issuance of the bonds on July 1, 1999.

(2) The accrual of interest and the amortization of the discount on December 31, 1999.

(3) The payment of interest and the amortization of the discount on July 1, 2000, assuming no accrual of interest on June 30.

(4) The accrual of interest and the amortization of the discount on December 31, 2000.

(b) Show the proper balance sheet presentation for the liability for bonds payable on the December 31, 2000, balance sheet.

(c) ▬▬▶ Provide the answers to the following questions in letter form.

(1) What amount of interest expense is reported for 2000?

(2) Would the bond interest expense reported in 2000 be the same as, greater than, or less than the amount that would be reported if the straight-line method of amortization were used?

(3) Determine the total cost of borrowing over the life of the bond.

(4) Would the total bond interest expense be greater than, the same as, or less than the total interest expense that would be reported if the straight-line method of amortization were used?

BROADENING YOUR PERSPECTIVE

FINANCIAL REPORTING AND ANALYSIS
. . . .

FINANCIAL REPORTING PROBLEM: Kellogg Company

BYP16–1   Refer to the financial statements of Kellogg Company and the Notes to Consolidated Financial Statements in Appendix A.

Instructions

Answer the following questions:

(a) What was Kellogg's total long-term debt at December 31, 1997? What was the increase/decrease in Kellogg's total long-term debt (excluding other liabilities) from the prior year?

(b) What were the components of total long-term debt (excluding other liabilities) on December 31, 1997?

(c) What is the amount of leases that are reported as part of long-term debt?

COMPARATIVE ANALYSIS PROBLEM: Kellogg Company vs. General Mills

BYP16–2   Kellogg's financial statements are presented in Appendix A; General Mills's financial statements are presented in Appendix B.

Instructions

(a) Based on the information contained in these financial statements, compute the following 1997 ratios for each company:
(1) Debt to total assets
(2) Times interest earned

(b) What conclusions concerning the companies' long-run solvency can be drawn from these ratios?

RESEARCH ASSIGNMENT

BYP16–3   The November 6, 1995, edition of *The Wall Street Journal* contains an article by Linda Sandler entitled "Kmart Is Pressured Over Obscure Bond 'Puts,' Which Stir Worries Amid Tough Retail Times."

Instructions

Read the article and answer these questions:

(a) What is the total dollar amount of the bond issue in question? Who purchased these bonds?

(b) What right does the "put option" give to bondholders?

(c) What amount is available under Kmart's bank lines? Why can't Kmart borrow under these lines to purchase the bonds? What is the most likely solution to the problem?

(d) Were the terms of the put bonds adquately disclosed?

INTERPRETING FINANCIAL STATEMENTS: Texas Instruments

BYP16–4   Texas Instruments designs and produces devices that use semiconductor technology. You may have one of its calculators on your desk. Because it is in a high-tech industry, the company must constantly invest in new technology, which requires considerable financing. During 1995 Texas Instruments' current liabilities and its long-term liabilities increased by about $1 billion each. Here is additional information (in millions) from Texas Instruments' 1995 annual report:

	1995	1994
Current assets	$ 5,518	$ 4,017
Total assets	9,215	6,980
Current liabilities	3,188	2,199
Total liabilities	5,120	3,950
Stockholders' equity	4,095	3,030
Sales revenue	13,128	10,315
Income taxes	531	351
Interest expense	48	45
Net income	1,088	691

Maturities (in millions) of long-term debt due during the 4 years subsequent to December 31, 1996, are:

1997	$14	1999	$168
1998	18	2000	19

Instructions

Address each of these questions related to the liabilities of Texas Instruments:

    (a) Using both working capital and the current ratio as indicators, evaluate the change in the company's liquidity from 1994 to 1995. Working capital and the current ratio are discussed in Chapter 11.

    (b) Using both the debt to total assets ratio and the times interest earned ratio, evaluate the change in the company's solvency from 1994 to 1995.

    (c) What are the implications of the information provided about the maturities of the company's long-term debt?

REAL-WORLD FOCUS: Apache Corporation

BYP16–5   Apache Corporation is an international, independent energy enterprise engaged in the exploration, development, production, gathering, processing, and marketing of natural gas and crude oil. Its corporate headquarters are located in Houston, Texas, and it has operations in North America, Australia, Egypt, Poland, People's Republic of China, Indonesia, and the Ivory Coast.

    The 1994 annual report of Apache Corporation disclosed the following information in its management discussion section:

APACHE CORPORATION
Management Discussion

In May 1994, Apache issued 9.25% bonds due 2002 in the principal amount of $100 million. The proceeds of $99 million from the offering were used to reduce bank debt, to pay off the 9.5% convertible debentures due 1996, and for general corporate purposes. In December 1994, the company privately placed 3.93% convertible notes due 1997 in the principal amount of $75 million. The notes are not redeemable before maturity and are convertible into Apache common stock at the option of the holders at any time prior to maturity, at a conversion price of $27 per share. Proceeds from the sale of the notes were used for the repayment of bank debt.

Instructions

    (a) Identify the face amount, contractual interest rate, and selling price of the newly issued bonds due in 2002. Explain whether the bonds sold at a premium or a discount.

    (b) For what purposes has Apache Corporation been incurring more debt?

CRITICAL THINKING

GROUP DECISION CASE

BYP16–6 On January 1, 1998, Marsh Corporation issued $1,200,000 of 5-year, 8% bonds at 96; the bonds pay interest semiannually on July 1 and January 1. By January 1, 2000, the market rate of interest for bonds of risk similar to those of Marsh Corporation had risen. As a result the market value of these bonds was $1,000,000 on January 1, 2000—below their carrying value. Tom Marsh, president of the company, suggests repurchasing all of these bonds in the open market at the $1,000,000 price. To do so the company will have to issue $1,000,000 (face value) of new 10-year, 12% bonds at par. The president asks you, as controller, "What is the feasibility of my proposed repurchase plan?"

Instructions

With the class divided into groups, answer the following:

    (a) What is the carrying value of the outstanding Marsh Corporation 5-year bonds on January 1, 2000? (Assume straight-line amortization.)

(b) Prepare the journal entry to retire the 5-year bonds on January 1, 2000. Prepare the journal entry to issue the new 10-year bonds.
(c) Prepare a short memo to the president in response to his request for advice. List the economic factors that you believe should be considered for his repurchase proposal.

COMMUNICATION ACTIVITY

BYP16–7   Dane Ely, president of the Briley Corporation, is considering the issuance of bonds to finance an expansion of his business. He has asked you to (1) discuss the advantages of bonds over common stock financing, (2) indicate the type of bonds he might issue, and (3) explain the issuing procedures used in bond transactions.

Instructions
Write a memorandum to the president, answering his request.

ETHICS CASE

BYP16–8   Ron Gant is the president, founder, and majority owner of Newman Medical Corporation, an emerging medical technology products company. Newman is in dire need of additional capital to keep operating and to bring several promising products to final development, testing, and production. Ron, as owner of 51% of the outstanding stock, manages the company's operations. He places heavy emphasis on research and development and on long-term growth. The other principal stockholder is Judy Costello who, as a nonemployee investor, owns 40% of the stock. Judy would like to deemphasize the R&D functions and emphasize the marketing function, to maximize short-run sales and profits from existing products. She believes this strategy would raise the market price of Newman's stock.

All of Ron's personal capital and borrowing power is tied up in his 51% stock ownership. He knows that any offering of additional shares of stock will dilute his controlling interest because he won't be able to participate in such an issuance. But, Judy has money and would likely buy enough shares to gain control of Newman. She then would dictate the company's future direction, even if it meant replacing Ron as president and CEO.

The company already has considerable debt. Raising additional debt will be costly, will adversely affect Newman's credit rating, and will increase the company's reported losses due to the growth in interest expense. Judy and the other minority stockholders express opposition to the assumption of additional debt, fearing the company will be pushed to the brink of bankruptcy. Wanting to maintain his control and to preserve the direction of "his" company, Ron is doing everything to avoid a stock issuance and is contemplating a large issuance of bonds, even if it means the bonds are issued with a high effective-interest rate.

Instructions

(a) Who are the stakeholders in this situation?
(b) What are the ethical issues in this case?
(c) What would you do if you were Ron?

SURFING THE NET

BYP16–9   Bond or debt securities pay a stated rate of interest. This rate of interest is dependent on the risk associated with the investment. Moody's Investment Service provides ratings for companies that issue debt securities.

Address: http://www.moodys.com/index.shtml

Steps: From Moody's homepage choose **SiteMap.**

Instructions

Answer the following questions:

(a) What year did Moody's introduce the first bond rating?

(b) List three basic principles Moody's uses in rating bonds.

(c) What is the definition of Moody's Aaa rating on long-term taxable debt?

Answers to Self-Study Questions

1. c   2. a   3. d   4. a   5. c   6. b   7. d   8. a   9. c   10. d   *11. b

*12. c

Answer to Kellogg Review It Question 2, p. 691

An examination of Kellogg Company's statement of cash flows indicates the following reductions of debt: reductions of notes payable, with maturities less than or equal to 90 days ($374.7 million); reductions of notes payable, with maturities greater than 90 days ($14.1 million), and reductions of long-term debt ($507.9 million).

Remember to go back to the Navigator box on the chapter-opening page and check off your completed work.

CONCEPTS FOR REVIEW

Before studying this chapter, you should know or, if necessary, review:

a. How to record the issuance of bonds. (Ch. 16, pp. 681–688)

b. How to compute and record interest. (Ch. 3, pp. 104–5, Ch. 8, p. 340, and Ch. 16, pp. 684–88)

c. How to record amortization of bond discount and bond premium using the straight-line method. (Ch. 16, pp. 684–87)

d. Where temporary and long-term investments are classified on a balance sheet. (Ch. 4, pp. 157–58)

THE NAVIGATOR

FEATURE STORY

Is There Anything Else We Can Buy?

In a rapidly changing world you must change rapidly or suffer the consequences. In business, to change means to invest. A case in point is found in the entertainment industry. Technology is bringing about new innovations so quickly that it is nearly impossible to guess which technologies will last and which will soon fade away. For example, consider the publishing industry. Will paper newspapers and magazines be replaced by online news via the World Wide Web? If you are a publisher, you have to make your best guess about what the future holds and invest accordingly.

Time Warner Corporation lives at the center of this arena. It is not an environment for the timid, and Time Warner's philosophy is anything but timid. It might be characterized as "If we can't beat you, we will buy you." Its mantra is "invest, invest, invest." An abbreviated list of Time Warner's holdings gives an idea of its reach. Magazines: *People, Time, Life, Sports Illustrated, Fortune.*

Book publishers: Time-Life Books, Book-of-the-Month Club, Little, Brown & Co. Music: Warner Bros., Reprise, Atlantic, Rhino. Television and movies: Warner Bros. ("ER" and "Friends"), HBO, and movies like *Batman Forever.* And, in 1996 Time Warner merged with Turner Broadcasting, so it now owns TNT, CNN, and Turner's library of thousands of classic movies. Even before the Turner merger, Time Warner owned more information and entertainment copyrights and brands than any other company in the world.

So what has Time Warner's aggressive acquisition spree meant for the bottom line? It has left Time Warner with huge debt and massive interest costs. In addition, some of the acquisitions have not come cheap, resulting in large amounts of reported goodwill and goodwill amortization. As a consequence, since the merger of Time and Warner in 1988, the combined corporation has reported net losses in all but two years through 1997, and many analysts expect losses for some time longer. With so much investing by Time Warner and so little profit to show for it, one is reminded of one more of its companies, Looney Tunes cartoons—"That's all, folks."

THE NAVIGATOR

On the World Wide Web
http://www.timewarner.com

CHAPTER 17

INVESTMENTS

THE NAVIGATOR ✔

- Understand *Concepts for Review* ☐
- Read *Feature Story* ☐
- Scan *Study Objectives* ☐
- Read *Preview* ☐
- Read text and answer *Before You Go On*
  p. 725 ☐ p. 730 ☐ p. 736 ☐
- Work *Demonstration Problems* ☐
- Review *Summary of Study Objectives* ☐
- Answer *Self-Study Questions* ☐
- Complete assignments ☐

STUDY OBJECTIVES

After studying this chapter, you should be able to:

1. *Identify the reasons corporations invest in stocks and debt securities.*
2. *Explain the accounting for debt investments.*
3. *Explain the accounting for stock investments.*
4. *Describe the purpose and usefulness of consolidated financial statements.*
5. *Indicate how debt and stock investments are valued and reported on the financial statements.*
6. *Distinguish between temporary and long-term investments.*

THE NAVIGATOR

Time Warner's management believes in a policy of aggressive growth through investing in the stock of existing companies. In addition to purchasing stock, companies also purchase other securities such as debt securities issued by corporations or by governments. Investments can be purchased for a short or long period of time, as a passive investment, or with the intent to control another company. As you will see later in the chapter, the way in which a company accounts for its investments is determined by a number of factors.

The content and organization of this chapter are as follows:

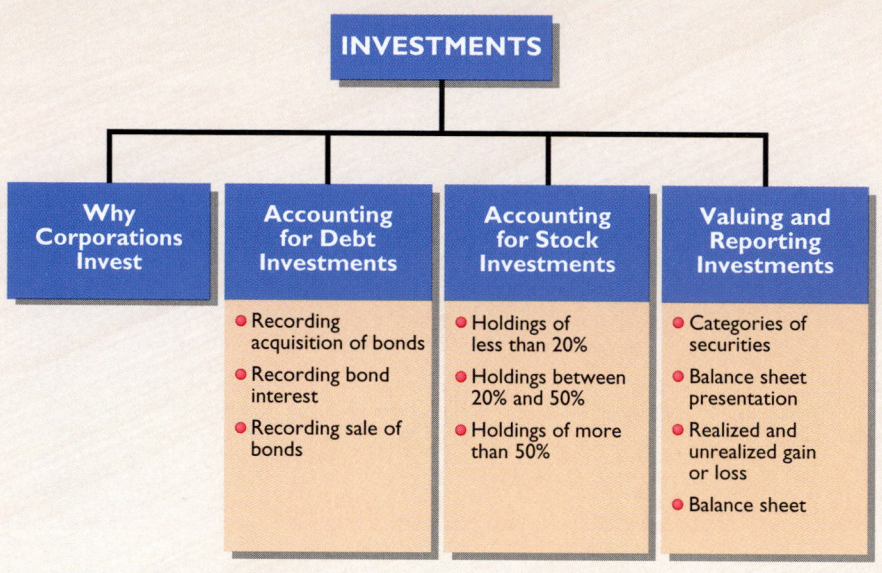

THE NAVIGATOR

WHY CORPORATIONS INVEST

STUDY OBJECTIVE

1

Identify the reasons corporations invest in stocks and debt securities.

Corporations purchase investments in debt or equity securities generally for one of three reasons. First, a corporation may **have excess cash** that it does not need for the immediate purchase of operating assets. For example, many companies experience seasonal fluctuations in sales. A Cape Cod marina has more sales in the spring and summer than in the fall and winter, whereas the reverse is true for an Aspen ski shop. Thus, at the end of an operating cycle, many companies may have cash on hand that is temporarily idle pending the start of another operating cycle. Until the cash is needed, these companies may invest the excess funds to earn, through interest and dividends, a greater return than they would get by just holding the funds in the bank. The role played by such temporary investments in the operating cycle is depicted in Illustration 17-1.

A second reason some companies purchase investments is that they generate a **significant portion of their earnings from investment income.** Although banks make most of their earnings by lending money, they also generate earnings by investing in debt and equity securities. Banks purchase investment securities because loan demand varies both seasonally and with changes in the economic climate. Thus, when loan demand is low, a bank must find other uses for its cash. Investing in securities also allows banks to diversify some of their risk. Bank

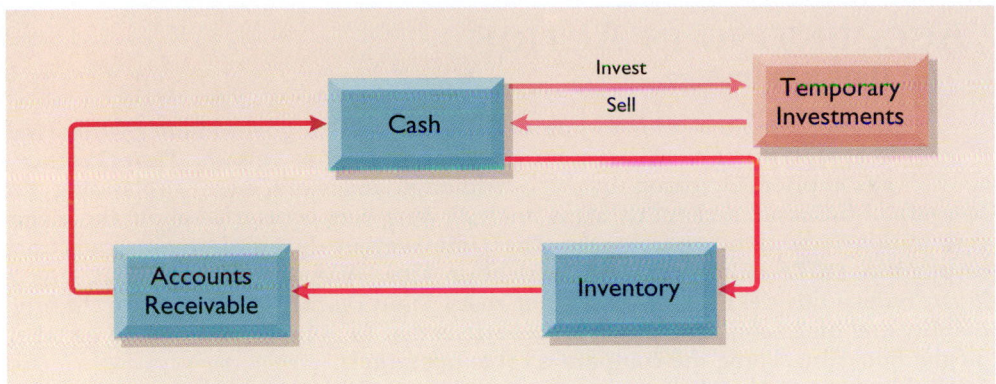

ILLUSTRATION 17-1

Temporary investments and the operating cycle

regulators severely limit the ability of banks to invest in common stock; therefore, most investments held by banks are debt securities.

Pension funds and mutual funds are corporations that also regularly invest to generate earnings. However, they do so for **speculative reasons**; that is, they are speculating that the investment will increase in value and thus result in positive returns. Therefore, they invest primarily in the common stock of other corporations. These investments are passive in nature; the pension fund or mutual fund does not usually take an active role in controlling the affairs of the companies in which they invest.

A third reason why companies invest is for **strategic reasons**. A company may purchase a noncontrolling interest in another firm in a related industry in which it wishes to establish a presence. For example, Time Warner initially purchased an interest of less than 20% in Turner Broadcasting to have a stake in Turner's expanding business opportunities. Similarly, Canadian giant Seagram purchased a significant interest in Time Warner. (Thus, not even a huge corporation like Time Warner is at the top of the corporate "food chain.") Alternatively, a company can exercise some influence over one of its customers or suppliers by purchasing a significant, but not controlling, interest in that company.

In summary, businesses invest in other companies for the reasons shown in Ilustration 17-2.

Reason	**Typical Investment**
To house excess cash until needed	Low-risk, high-liquidity, short-term securities such as government-issued securities
To generate earnings *I need 1,000 Treasury bills by tonight* BANK	Debt securities (banks and other financial institutions); and stock securities (mutual funds and pension funds)
To meet strategic goals	Stocks of companies in a related industry or in an unrelated industry that the company wishes to enter

ILLUSTRATION 17-2

Why corporations invest

In the 2 months prior to approval by the federal government of the Time Warner/Turner deal, as approval appeared more certain, Time Warner's stock price increased by 30%. Although investors were applauding the strength of the combined entity, many analysts were very concerned about the mega-corporation's ability to control costs. The Time Warner deal and other acquisitions resulted in a $17.5 billion mountain of debt on Time Warner's balance sheet. Unless it can reduce this debt and control other costs, Time Warner will not return to profitability any time soon. One possible scenario is that $8 billion in debt could be taken off the books by selling the company's cable operations.

Observers were also interested to see how the two corporate cultures would merge. Ted Turner had been openly critical of Time Warner's management for running a loose ship, with far too much being spent on unnecessary extravagances such as corporate jets. Time Warner executives privately responded that if Mr. Turner was really concerned, he might consider taking a cut in his salary of $10 millon a year.

ACCOUNTING FOR DEBT INVESTMENTS

2
STUDY
OBJECTIVE

Explain the accounting for debt investments.

Debt investments are investments in government and corporation bonds. In accounting for debt investments, entries are required to record (1) the acquisition, (2) the interest revenue, and (3) the sale.

Recording Acquisition of Bonds

At acquisition, the cost principle applies. Cost includes all expenditures necessary to acquire these investments, such as the price paid plus brokerage fees (commissions), if any. Assume, for example, that Kuhl Corporation acquires 50 Doan Inc. 12%, 10-year, $1,000 bonds on January 1, 1999, for $54,000, including brokerage fees of $1,000. The entry to record the investment is:

A	=	L	+	SE
+54,000				
−54,000				

Jan. 1	Debt Investments	54,000	
	Cash		54,000
	(To record purchase of 50 Doan Inc. bonds)		

Recording Bond Interest

The bonds pay interest of $3,000 semiannually on July 1 and January 1 ($50,000 × 12% × ½). The entry for the receipt of interest on July 1 is:

A	=	L	+	SE
+3,000				+3,000

July 1	Cash	3,000	
	Interest Revenue		3,000
	(To record receipt of interest on Doan Inc. bonds)		

If Kuhl Corporation's fiscal year ends on December 31, it is necessary to accrue the interest of $3,000 earned since July 1. The adjusting entry is:

A	=	L	+	SE
+3,000				+3,000

Dec. 31	Interest Receivable	3,000	
	Interest Revenue		3,000
	(To accrue interest on Doan Inc. bonds)		

Interest Receivable is reported as a current asset in the balance sheet; Interest Revenue is reported under Other Revenues and Gains in the income statement. When the interest is received on January 1, the entry is:

Jan. 1	Cash	3,000	
	Interest Receivable		3,000
	(To record receipt of accrued interest)		

A	=	L	+	SE
+3,000				
−3,000				

A credit to Interest Revenue at this time is incorrect because the interest revenue was earned and accrued in the preceding accounting period.

Recording Sale of Bonds

When the bonds are sold, it is necessary to credit the investment account for the cost of the bonds. Any difference between the net proceeds (sales price less brokerage fees) from sale and the cost of the bonds is recorded as a gain or loss. Assume, for example, that Kuhl Corporation receives net proceeds of $58,000 on the sale of the Doan Inc. bonds on January 1, 2000, after receiving the interest due. Since the securities cost $54,000, a gain of $4,000 has been realized. The entry to record the sale is:

Jan. 1	Cash	58,000	
	Debt Investments		54,000
	Gain on Sale of Debt Investments		4,000
	(To record sale of Doan Inc. bonds)		

A	=	L	+	SE
+58,000				
−54,000				+4,000

The gain on sale of debt investments is reported under Other Revenues and Gains in the income statement.

The accounting for temporary debt investments and for long-term debt investments is similar. The major exception is when bonds are purchased at a premium or discount. For temporary investments, the bond premium or discount is not amortized to interest revenue because the bonds are held for a short period of time and a misstatement of interest revenue for such a period is not considered material. For long-term investments, however, any bond premium or discount is amortized to interest revenue over the remaining term of the bonds. Like the issuer of the bonds, the investor uses either the straight-line or the effective-interest method of amortization. The effective-interest method is required under generally accepted accounting principles when the annual amounts of the two amortization methods are materially different.

BEFORE YOU GO ON . . .

Review It

1. Why might a company purchase debt or equity investments?
2. What entries are required in accounting for debt investments?
3. How does the accounting for a temporary debt investment differ from that for a long-term debt investment?

Do It

The Waldo Corporation had the following transactions pertaining to debt investments:

Jan. 1   Purchased 30 10%, $1,000 Hillary Co. bonds for $30,000 plus brokerage fees of $900. Interest is payable semiannually on July 1 and January 1.
July 1 Received semiannual interest on Hillary Co. bonds.
July 1 Sold 15 Hillary Co. bonds for $15,000 less $400 brokerage fees.

(a) Journalize the transactions, and (b) prepare the adjusting entry for the accrual of interest on December 31.

Reasoning: Bond investments are recorded at cost. Interest is recorded when received and/or accrued. When bonds are sold, the investment account is credited for the cost of the bonds. Any difference between the cost and the net proceeds is recorded as a gain or loss.

Solution:

(a)	Jan. 1	Debt Investments	30,900	
		Cash		30,900
		(To record purchase of 30 Hillary Co. bonds)		
	July 1	Cash	1,500	
		Interest Revenue ($30,000 × .10 × 6/12)		1,500
		(To record receipt of interest on Hillary Co. bonds)		
	July 1	Cash	14,600	
		Loss on Sale of Debt Investments	850	
		Debt Investments ($30,900 ÷ 15/30)		15,450
		(To record sale of 15 Hillary Co. bonds)		
(b)	Dec. 31	Interest Receivable	750	
		Interest Revenue ($15,000 × .10 × 6/12)		750
		(To accrue interest on Hillary Co. bonds)		

Related exercise material: BE17–1 and E17–1.

THE
NAVIGATOR

ACCOUNTING FOR STOCK INVESTMENTS

STUDY OBJECTIVE 3

Explain the accounting for stock investments.

Stock investments are investments in the capital stock of corporations. When a company holds stock (and/or debt) of several different corporations, the group of securities is identified as an **investment portfolio**. The accounting for investments in common stock is based on the extent of the investor's influence over the operating and financial affairs of the issuing corporation (commonly called the **investee**) as shown in Illustration 17-3. In some cases, depending on the degree of investor influence, net income of the investee is considered to be income to the investor.

The presumed influence may be negated by extenuating circumstances. For example, a company that acquires a 25% interest in another company in a "hostile" takeover may not have any significant influence over the investee.[1] In other words, companies are required to use judgment instead of blindly following the guidelines. On the following pages we will explain and illustrate the application of each guideline.

INTERNATIONAL NOTE

A recent study demonstrated the peril of investing overseas. For the same company under different reporting systems, income was $84,600, $260,600, $240,600, and $10,402 in the United States, the United Kingdom, Australia, and West Germany, respectively.

---

[1]Among the factors that should be considered in determining an investor's influence are whether (1) the investor has representation on the investee's board of directors, (2) the investor participates in the investee's policy-making process, (3) there are material transactions between the investor and investee, and (4) the common stock held by other stockholders is concentrated or dispersed.

ILLUSTRATION 17-3

Accounting guidelines for stock investments

Investor's Ownership Interest in Investee's Common Stock	Presumed Influence on Investee	Accounting Guidelines
Less than 20%	Insignificant	Cost method
Between 20% and 50%	Significant	Equity method
More than 50%	Controlling	Consolidated financial statements

Holdings of Less Than 20%

In accounting for stock investments of less than 20%, the cost method is used. Under the **cost method**, the investment is recorded at cost and revenue is recognized only when cash dividends are received.

Recording Acquisition of Stock Investments

At acquisition, the cost principle applies. Cost includes all expenditures necessary to acquire these investments, such as the price paid plus brokerage fees (commissions), if any. Assume, for example, that on July 1, 1999, Sanchez Corporation acquires 1,000 shares (10% ownership) of Beal Corporation common stock at $40 per share plus brokerage fees of $500. The entry for the purchase is:

July 1	Stock Investments	40,500	
	Cash		40,500
	(To record purchase of 1,000 shares of Beal Corporation common stock)		

A	=	L	+	SE
+40,500				
−40,500				

Recording Dividends

During the time the stock is held, entries are required for any cash dividends received. Thus, if a $2.00 per share dividend is received by Sanchez Corporation on December 31, the entry is:

Dec. 31	Cash (1,000 × $2)	2,000	
	Dividend Revenue		2,000
	(To record receipt of a cash dividend)		

A	=	L	+	SE
+2,000				+2,000

Dividend Revenue is reported under Other Revenues and Gains in the income statement. Unlike interest on notes and bonds, dividends do not accrue. Therefore, adjusting entries are not made to accrue dividends.

Recording Sale of Stock

When stock is sold, the difference between the net proceeds (sales price less brokerage fees) from the sale and the cost of the stock is recognized as a gain or a loss. Assume, for instance, that Sanchez Corporation receives net proceeds of $39,500 on the sale of its Beal stock on February 10, 2000. Because the stock cost $40,500, a loss of $1,000 has been incurred. The entry to record the sale is:

A	=	L	+	SE
+39,500				−1,000
−40,500				

Feb. 10	Cash	39,500	
	Loss on Sale of Stock Investments	1,000	
	Stock Investments		40,500
	(To record sale of Beal common stock)		

HELPFUL HINT
The entries for investments in common stock also apply to investments in preferred stock.

The loss account is reported under Other Expenses and Losses in the income statement, whereas a gain on sale is shown under Other Revenues and Gains.

Holdings between 20% and 50%

When an investor company owns only a small portion of the shares of stock of another company (the investee), the investor cannot exercise control over the company. When an investor owns between 20% and 50% of the common stock of a corporation, however, it is generally presumed that the investor has significant influence over the financial and operating activities of the investee. The investor probably has a representative on the investee's board of directors. With a representative on the board, the investor begins to exercise some control over the investee—and the investee company in some sense really becomes part of the investor company.

For example, even prior to purchasing all of Turner Broadcasting, Time Warner owned 20% of Turner. Because it exercised significant control over major decisions made by Turner, Time Warner used an approach called the equity method. Under the **equity method,** the investor records its share of the net income of the investee in the year when it is earned. To delay recognizing the investor's share of net income until a cash dividend is declared ignores the fact that the investor and investee are, in some sense, one company, so the investor is better off by the investee's earned income.

HELPFUL HINT
Revenue is recognized under the equity method on the accrual basis—i.e., when it is earned by the investee.

Under the equity method, the investment in common stock is initially recorded at cost, and the investment account is **adjusted annually** to show the investor's equity in the investee. Each year, the investor (1) increases (debits) the investment account and increases (credits) revenue for its share of the investee's net income[2] and (2) decreases (credits) the investment account for the amount of divideds received. The investment account is reduced for dividends received because the net assets of the investee are decreased when a dividend is paid.

Recording Acquisition of Stock Investments

Assume that Milar Corporation acquires 30% of the common stock of Beck Company for $120,000 on January 1, 1999. The entry to record this transaction is:

A	=	L	+	SE
+120,000				
−120,000				

Jan. 1	Stock Investments	120,000	
	Cash		120,000
	(To record purchase of Beck common stock)		

Recording Revenue and Dividends

For 1999, Beck reports net income of $100,000 and declares and pays a $40,000 cash dividend. Milar is required to record (1) its share of Beck's income, $30,000 (30% × $100,000) and (2) the reduction in the investment account for the dividends received, $12,000 ($40,000 × 30%). The entries are:

(1)

A	=	L	+	SE
+30,000				+30,000

Dec. 31	Stock Investments	30,000	
	Revenue from Investment in Beck Company		30,000
	(To record 30% equity in Beck's 1999 net income)		

[2]Conversely, the investor increases (debits) a loss account and decreases (credits) the investment account for its share of the investee's net loss.

(2)

Dec. 31	Cash		12,000	
	Stock Investments			12,000
	(To record dividends received)			

A	=	L	+	SE
+12,000				
−12,000				

After posting the transactions for the year, the investment and revenue accounts will show the following:

ILLUSTRATION 17-4

Investment and revenue accounts after posting

Stock Investments				Revenue from Investment in Beck Company		
Jan. 1	120,000	Dec. 31	12,000		Dec. 31	30,000
Dec. 31	30,000					
Dec. 31 Bal.	138,000					

During the year, the investment account has increased by $18,000. This $18,000 is Milar's 30% equity in the $60,000 increase in Beck's retained earnings ($100,000 − $40,000). In addition, Milar will report $30,000 of revenue from its investment, which is 30% of Beck's net income of $100,000. Note that the difference between reported income under the cost method and reported revenue under the equity method can be significant. For example, Milar would report only $12,000 of dividend revenue (30% × $40,000) if the cost method were used.

Holdings of More Than 50%

A company that owns more than 50% of the common stock of another entity is known as the **parent company**. The entity whose stock is owned by the parent company is called the **subsidiary (affiliated) company**. Because of its stock ownership, the parent company has a **controlling interest** in the subsidiary company.

When a company owns more than 50% of the common stock of another company, **consolidated financial statements** are usually prepared. Consolidated financial statements present the assets and liabilities controlled by the parent company and the aggregate profitability of the subsidiary companies. They are prepared **in addition to** the financial statements for each of the individual parent and subsidiary companies. As noted earlier, prior to acquiring all of Turner Broadcasting, Time Warner accounted for its investment in Turner using the equity method. Time Warner's net investment in Turner was reported in a single line item—Other Investments. After the merger, Time Warner instead consolidated Turner's results with its own. Under this approach, the individual assets and liabilities of Turner are included with those of Time Warner; its plant and equipment are added to Time Warner's plant and equipment, its receivables are added to Time Warner's receivables, and so on.

Consolidated statements are especially useful to the stockholders, board of directors, and management of the parent company. Moreover, consolidated statements inform creditors, prospective investors, and regulatory agencies as to the magnitude and scope of operations of the companies under common control. For example, regulators and the courts undoubtedly used the consolidated statements of AT&T to determine whether a breakup of AT&T was in the public interest. Listed at the top of page 730 are three companies that prepare consolidated statements and some of the companies they have owned. Note that one, Disney, is Time Warner's arch rival.

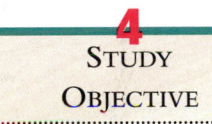

STUDY OBJECTIVE

4

Describe the purpose and usefulness of consolidated financial statements.

HELPFUL HINT

If parent (A) has three wholly owned subsidiaries (B, C, & D), there are four separate legal entities, but only one economic entity from the viewpoint of the shareholders of the parent company.

Beatrice Foods	American Brands, Inc.	The Walt Disney Company
Tropicana Frozen Juices	American Tobacco Company	Capital Cities/ABC, Inc.
Switzer Candy Company	Master Lock Company	Disneyland, Disney World
Samsonite Corporation	Pinkerton's Security Service	Mighty Ducks
Dannon Yogurt Company	Titleist Golf Company	Anaheim Angels
		ESPN

ACCOUNTING IN ACTION
Business Insight

Time Warner, Inc., owns 100% of the common stock of Home Box Office (HBO) Corporation. The common stockholders of Time Warner elect the board of directors of the company, who, in turn, select the officers and managers of the company. The board of directors controls the property owned by the corporation, which includes the common stock of HBO. Thus, they are in a position to elect the board of directors of HBO and, in effect, control its operations. These relationships are graphically illustrated here:

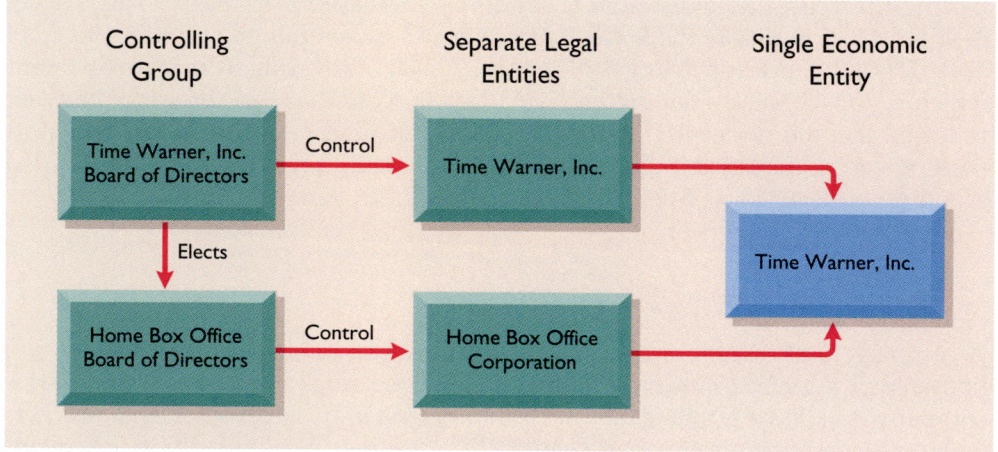

BEFORE YOU GO ON . . .

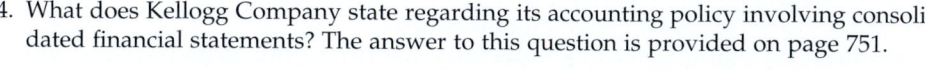
Review It

1. What are the accounting entries for investments in stock for which ownership is less than 20%?
2. What entries are made under the equity method when (a) the investor receives a cash dividend from the investee and (b) the investee reports net income for the year?
3. What is the purpose of consolidated financial statements?
4. What does Kellogg Company state regarding its accounting policy involving consolidated financial statements? The answer to this question is provided on page 751.

Do It

Presented below are two independent situations:

1. Rho Jean Inc. acquired 5% of the 400,000 shares of common stock of Stillwater Corp. at a total cost of $6 per share on May 18, 1999. On August 30, Stillwater declared and paid a $75,000 dividend. On December 31, Stillwater reported net income of $244,000 for the year.

2. Debbie, Inc., obtained significant influence over North Sails by buying 40% of North Sails' 60,000 outstanding shares of common stock at a cost of $12 per share on January 1, 1999. On April 15, North Sails declared and paid a cash dividend of $45,000. On December 31, North Sails reported a net income of $120,000 for the year.

Prepare all necessary journal entries for 1999 for (1) Rho Jean Inc. and (2) Debbie, Inc.

Reasoning: When an investor owns less than 20% of the common stock of another corporation, it is presumed that the investor has relatively little influence over the investee. As a result, net income earned by the investee is not considered a proper basis for recognizing income from the investment by the investor. For investments of 20%–50%, significant influence is presumed and therefore the investor's share of the net income of the investee should be recorded.

Solution:

(1)	May 18	Stock Investments (20,000 × $6)	120,000	
		Cash		120,000
		(To record purchase of 20,000 shares of Stillwater Co. stock)		
	Aug. 30	Cash	3,750	
		Dividend Revenue ($75,000 × 5%)		3,750
		(To record receipt of cash dividend)		
(2)	Jan. 1	Stock Investments (60,000 × 40% × $12)	288,000	
		Cash		288,000
		(To record purchase of 24,000 shares of North Sails' stock)		
	Apr. 15	Cash	18,000	
		Stock Investments ($45,000 × 40%)		18,000
		(To record receipt of cash dividend)		
	Dec. 31	Stock Investments ($120,000 × 40%)	48,000	
		Revenue from Investment in North Sails		48,000
		(To record 40% equity in North Sails' net income)		

Related exercise material: BE17–2, BE17–3, E17–1, E17–2, E17–3, E17–4, and E17–5.

THE
NAVIGATOR

VALUING AND REPORTING INVESTMENTS

The value of debt and stock investments may fluctuate greatly during the time they are held. For example, in one 12-month period, the stock of Digital Equipment Corporation hit a high of 76½ and a low of 28⅜. In light of such price fluctuations, how should investments be valued at the balance sheet date? Valuation could be at cost, at fair value (market value), or at the lower of cost or market value. Many people argue that fair value offers the best approach because it represents the expected cash realizable value of securities. **Fair value** is the amount for which a security could be sold in a normal market. Others counter that, unless a security is going to be sold soon, the fair value is not relevant because the price of the security will likely change again.

5

STUDY
OBJECTIVE
....

Indicate how debt and stock investments are valued and reported on the financial statements.

Categories of Securities

For purposes of valuation and reporting at a financial statement date, debt and stock investments are classified into three categories of securities:

1. **Trading securities** are securities bought and held primarily for sale in the near term to generate income on short-term price differences.
2. **Available-for-sale securities** are securities that may be sold in the future.
3. **Held-to-maturity securities** are debt securities that the investor has the intent and ability to hold to maturity.

The valuation guidelines for these securities are shown in Illustration 17-5. These guidelines apply to all debt securities and all stock investments where the holdings are less than 20%.

ILLUSTRATION 17-5

Valuation guidelines

Trading Securities

Trading securities are held with the intention of selling them in a short period of time (generally less than a month). Trading means frequent buying and selling. As indicated in Illustration 17-5, trading securities are reported at fair value, and changes from cost are reported as part of net income. The changes are reported as **unrealized gains or losses** because the securities have not been sold. The unrealized gain or loss is the difference between the **total cost** of the securities in the category and their **total fair value**.

As an example, Illustration 17-6 shows the cost and fair values for investments classified as trading securities for Pace Corporation on December 31, 1999. Pace Corporation has an unrealized gain of $7,000 because total fair value ($147,000) is $7,000 greater than total cost ($140,000).

ILLUSTRATION 17-6

Valuation of trading securities

Trading Securities, December 31, 1999			
Investments	Cost	Fair Value	Unrealized Gain (Loss)
Yorkville Company bonds	$ 50,000	$ 48,000	$(2,000)
Kodak Company stock	90,000	99,000	9,000
Total	$140,000	$147,000	$ 7,000

---

[3]This category is provided for completeness. The accounting and valuation issues related to held-to-maturity securities are discussed in more advanced accounting courses.

The fact that trading securities are a short-term investment increases the likelihood that they will be sold at fair value (the company may not be able to time their sale) and the likelihood that there will be an unrealized gain or loss. Fair value and unrealized gain or loss are recorded through an adjusting entry at the time financial statements are prepared. In the entry, a valuation allowance account, Market Adjustment—Trading, is used to record the difference between the total cost and the total fair value of the securities. The adjusting entry for Pace Corporation is:

Dec. 31	Market Adjustment—Trading	7,000	
	Unrealized Gain—Income		7,000
	(To record unrealized gain on trading securities)		

HELPFUL HINT
An unrealized gain or loss is reported in the income statement because of the likelihood that the securities will be sold at fair value since they are a short-term investment.

A	=	L	+	SE
+7,000				+7,000

The use of a Market Adjustment–Trading account enables the company to maintain a record of the investment cost. Actual cost is needed to determine the gain or loss realized when the securities are sold. The Market Adjustment–Trading balance is added to the cost of the investments to arrive at a fair value for the trading securities.

The fair value of the securities is the amount reported on the balance sheet. The unrealized gain is reported on the income statement in the Other Revenues and Gains section. The term income is used in the account title to indicate that the gain affects net income. When the total cost of the trading securities is greater than total fair value, an unrealized loss has occurred. In such a case, the adjusting entry is a debit to Unrealized Loss—Income and a credit to Market Adjustment—Trading. The unrealized loss is reported under Other Expenses and Losses in the income statement.

The market adjustment account is carried forward into future accounting periods. No entries are made to this account during the period. At the end of each reporting period, the balance in the account is adjusted to the difference between cost and fair value. The Unrealized Gain or Loss–Income account is closed at the end of the reporting period.

Available-for-Sale Securities

As indicated earlier, available-for-sale securities are held with the intent of selling them sometime in the future. If the intent is to sell the securities within the next year or operating cycle, the securities are classified as current assets in the balance sheet. Otherwise, they are classified as long-term assets in the investments section of the balance sheet.

Available-for-sale securities are also reported at fair value. The procedure for determining fair value and the unrealized gain or loss for these securities is the same as for trading securities. To illustrate, assume that Elbert Corporation has two securities that are classified as available-for-sale. Illustration 17-7 provides information on cost, fair value, and the amount of the unrealized gain or loss. For Elbert Corporation, there is an unrealized loss of $9,537 because total cost ($293,537) is $9,537 more than total fair value ($284,000).

ETHICS NOTE
Some managers appear to hold their available-for-sale securities that have experienced losses, while selling those that have gains, thus increasing income. Do you think this is ethical?

Available-for-Sale Securities, December 31, 1999

Investments	Cost	Fair Value	Unrealized Gain (Loss)
Campbell Soup Corporation 8% bonds	$ 93,537	$103,600	$ 10,063
Hersey Corporation stock	200,000	180,400	(19,600)
Total	$293,537	$284,000	$ (9,537)

ILLUSTRATION 17-7
Valuation of available-for-sale securities

Both the adjusting entry and the reporting of the unrealized gain or loss from available-for-sale securities differ from those illustrated for trading securities. The differences result because these securities are not going to be sold in the near term. Thus, prior to actual sale there is a much greater likelihood of changes in fair value that may reverse either unrealized gains or losses. Accordingly, an unrealized gain or loss is not reported in the income statement. Instead, it is reported as a **separate component of stockholders' equity.** In the adjusting entry, the market adjustment account is identified with available-for-sale securities, and the unrealized gain or loss account is identified with stockholders' equity. The adjusting entry for Elbert Corporation to record the unrealized loss of $9,537 is as follows:

A	=	L	+	SE
−9,537				−9,537

Dec. 31	Unrealized Loss—Equity	9,537	
	Market Adjustment—Available-for-Sale		9,537
	(To record unrealized loss on available-for-sale securities)		

If total fair value exceeds total cost, the adjusting entry would have a debit to the market adjustment account and a credit to an unrealized gain account.

For available-for-sale securities, the unrealized gain or loss account is carried forward to future periods. At each future balance sheet date, it is adjusted with the market adjustment account to show the difference between cost and fair value at that time.

Balance Sheet Presentation

For balance sheet presentation, investments are classified as either temporary or long-term.

Temporary Investments

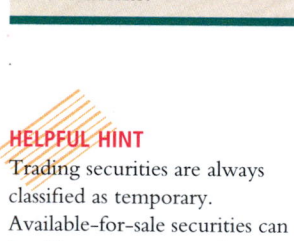

6

STUDY
OBJECTIVE

Distinguish between temporary and long-term investments.

Temporary investments are securities held by a company that are (1) **readily marketable** and (2) **intended to be converted into cash** within the next year or operating cycle, whichever is longer. Investments that do not meet **both criteria** are classified as **long-term investments.** In a recent survey of 600 large U.S. companies, over 400 reported temporary investments.

Readily Marketable.   **An investment is readily marketable when it can be sold easily whenever the need for cash arises.** Short-term paper[4] meets this criterion because it can be sold readily to other investors. Stocks and bonds traded on organized securities markets, such as the New York Stock Exchange, are readily marketable because they can be bought and sold daily. In contrast, there may be only a limited market for the securities issued by small corporations and no market for the securities of a privately held company.

HELPFUL HINT
Trading securities are always classified as temporary. Available-for-sale securities can be either temporary or long-term.

Intent to Convert.   **Intent to convert means that management intends to sell the investment within the next year or operating cycle, whichever is longer.** Generally, this criterion is satisfied when the investment is considered a resource that will be used whenever the need for cash arises. For example, a ski resort may invest idle cash during the summer months with the intent to sell the securities to buy supplies and equipment shortly before the next winter season.

---

[4]Short-term paper includes (1) certificates of deposits (CDs) issued by banks, (2) money market certificates issued by banks and savings and loan associations, (3) Treasury bills issued by the U.S. government, and (4) commercial paper issued by corporations with good credit ratings.

This investment is considered temporary even if lack of snow cancels the next ski season and eliminates the need to convert the securities into cash as intended.

Because of their high liquidity, temporary investments are listed immediately below Cash in the current asset section of the balance sheet. Temporary investments are reported at fair value. For example, Pace Corporation would report its trading securities as shown in Illustration 17-8.

PACE CORPORATION Balance Sheet (partial)	
Current assets	
Cash	$ 21,000
Temporary investments, at fair value	147,000

ILLUSTRATION 17-8
Presentation of temporary investments

Long-Term Investments

Long-term investments are generally reported in a separate section of the balance sheet immediately below Current assets, as shown later in Illustration 17-11. Long-term investments in available-for-sale securities are reported at fair value, and investments in common stock accounted for under the equity method are reported at equity.

Presentation of Realized and Unrealized Gain or Loss

Gains and losses on investments, whether realized or unrealized, must be presented in the financial statements. In the income statement, gains and losses, as well as interest and dividend revenue, are reported in the nonoperating section under the categories listed in Illustration 17-9.

Other Revenue and Gains	Other Expenses and Losses
Interest Revenue	Loss on Sales of Investments
Dividend Revenue	Unrealized Loss—Income
Gain on Sale of Investments	
Unrealized Gain—Income	

ILLUSTRATION 17-9
Nonoperating items related to investments

As indicated earlier, an unrealized gain or loss on available-for-sale securities is reported as a separate component of stockholders' equity. To illustrate, assume that Dawson Inc. has common stock of $3,000,000, retained earnings of $1,500,000, and an unrealized loss on available-for-sale securities of $100,000. The statement presentation of the unrealized loss is shown in Illustration 17-10.

DAWSON INC. Balance Sheet (partial)	
Stockholders' equity	
Common stock	$3,000,000
Retained earnings	1,500,000
Total paid-in capital and retained earnings	4,500,000
Less: Unrealized loss on available-for-sale securities	(100,000)
Total stockholders' equity	$4,400,000

ILLUSTRATION 17-10
Unrealized loss in stockholders' equity section

Note that the presentation of the loss is similar to the presentation of the cost of treasury stock in the stockholders' equity section. An unrealized gain is added in this section. Reporting the unrealized gain or loss in the stockholders' equity section serves two important purposes: (1) It reduces the volatility of net income due to fluctuations in fair value, and (2) it informs the financial statement user of the gain or loss that would occur if the securities were sold at fair value.

A new accounting standard requires that items such as this, which affect stockholders' equity but are not included in the calculation of net income, must be reported as part of a more inclusive measure called *comprehensive income.* Comprehensive income is discussed in more advanced courses.

Balance Sheet

Many sections of classified balance sheets have been presented in this and preceding chapters. The comprehensive balance sheet in Illustration 17-11 on page 737 includes such topics from previous chapters as the issuance of par value common stock, organization costs, restrictions of retained earnings, issuance of long-term bonds, and bond sinking funds. From this chapter, the statement includes (highlighted in red) temporary and long-term investments. The investments in temporary securities are considered trading securities; the long-term investments in stock of less than 20% owned companies are considered available-for-sale securities. Illustration 17-11 also includes a long-term investment reported at equity and descriptive notations within the statement, such as the basis for valuing merchandise and two notes to the statement.

BEFORE YOU GO ON . . .

Review It

1. What is the proper valuation and reporting of trading and available-for-sale securities on a balance sheet?
2. Explain how the unrealized gain or loss for both trading and available-for-sale securities is reported.
3. Explain where temporary and long-term investments are reported on a balance sheet.

A LOOK BACK AT OUR FEATURE STORY

Refer back to the opening story about Time Warner Corporation, and answer the following questions:

1. For what reason(s) is Time Warner investing in equity securities?
2. Would you expect Time Warner to prepare consolidated financial statements for the many companies it owns? Explain your answer.
3. What has Time Warner's aggressive acquisition spree meant for its bottom line?

Solution:
1. Time Warner is investing for strategic reasons. As indicated in the feature story, the company's attitude is "If we can't beat you, we will buy you." Time Warner is diversifying because it is not sure what industry or set of industries will be successful in the future. As a result, Time Warner now owns more information and entertainment copyrights and brands than any other company in the world.
2. When a company owns more than 50% of the common stock of another company, consolidated financial statements are usually prepared. Because Time Warner owns over 50% of the companies mentioned in the opening story, Time Warner would consolidate these subsidiary companies with its own.
3. To date, Time Warner's acquisition spree has left it with huge debt and massive interest costs. In addition, some of the acquisitions have not come cheap, resulting in large amounts of reported goodwill and goodwill amortization. As a result, Time Warner has reported net losses in all but two years from 1989 through 1997.

THE NAVIGATOR

ILLUSTRATION 17-11

Comprehensive balance sheet

PACE CORPORATION
Balance Sheet
December 31, 1999

Assets

Current assets

Cash			$ 21,000
Temporary investments, at fair value			147,000
Accounts receivable		$ 84,000	
Less: Allowance for doubtful accounts		4,000	80,000
Merchandise inventory, at FIFO cost			43,000
Prepaid insurance			23,000
Total current assets			314,000

Investments

Bond sinking fund			100,000
Investments in stock of less than 20% owned companies, at fair value			50,000
Investment in stock of 20–50% owned company, at equity			150,000
Total investments			300,000

Property, plant, and equipment

Land			200,000
Buildings	$800,000		
Less: Accumulated depreciation	200,000	600,000	
Equipment	180,000		
Less: Accumulated depreciation	54,000	126,000	
Total property, plant, and equipment			926,000

Intangible assets

Goodwill (Note 1)			100,000
Organization costs			70,000
Total intangible assets			170,000
Total assets			$1,710,000

Liabilities and Stockholders' Equity

Current liabilities

Accounts payable		$185,000
Bond interest payable		10,000
Federal income taxes payable		60,000
Total current liabilities		255,000

Long-term liabilities

Bonds payable, 10%, due 2010	$ 300,000	
Less: Discount on bonds	10,000	
Total long-term liabilities		290,000
Total liabilities		545,000

Stockholders' equity

Paid-in capital

Common stock, $10 par value, 200,000 shares authorized, 80,000 shares issued and outstanding	800,000	
Paid-in capital in excess of par value	100,000	
Total paid-in capital	900,000	
Retained earnings (Note 2)	255,000	
Total paid-in capital and retained earnings	1,155,000	
Add: Unrealized gain on available-for-sale securities	10,000	
Total stockholders' equity		1,165,000
Total liabilities and stockholders' equity		$1,710,000

Note 1. Goodwill is amortized by the straight-line method over 40 years.

Note 2. Retained earnings of $100,000 is restricted for plant expansion.

DEMONSTRATION PROBLEM

In its first year of operations, the DeMarco Company had the following selected transactions in stock investments which are considered trading securities:

June 1 Purchased for cash 600 shares of Sanburg common stock at $24 per share plus $300 brokerage fees.

July 1 Purchased for cash 800 shares of Cey common stock at $33 per share plus $600 brokerage fees.

Sept. 1 Received a $1 per share cash dividend from Cey Corporation.

Nov. 1 Sold 200 shares of Sanburg common stock for cash at $27 per share less $150 brokerage fees.

Dec. 15 Received a $.50 per share cash dividend on Sanburg common stock.

At December 31, the fair values per share were: Sanburg $25 and Cey $30.

Instructions

(a) Journalize the transactions.
(b) Prepare the adjusting entry at December 31 to report the securities at fair value.

**PROBLEM-SOLVING
STRATEGIES**

1. Cost includes the price paid plus brokerage fees.

2. Gain or loss on sales is determined by the difference between net selling price and the cost of the securities.

3. The adjustment to fair value is based on the total difference between cost and fair value of the securities.

SOLUTION TO DEMONSTRATION PROBLEM

(a) June	1	Stock Investments	14,700	
		Cash		14,700
		(To record purchase of 600 shares of Sanburg common stock)		
July	1	Stock Investments	27,000	
		Cash		27,000
		(To record purchase of 800 shares of Cey common stock)		
Sept.	1	Cash	800	
		Dividend Revenue		800
		(To record receipt of $1 per share cash dividend from Cey Corporation)		
Nov.	1	Cash	5,250	
		Stock Investments		4,900
		Gain on Sale of Stock Investments		350
		(To record sale of 200 shares of Sanburg common stock)		
Dec.	15	Cash	200	
		Dividend Revenue		200
		(To record receipt of $.50 per share dividend from Sanburg Corporation)		
(b) Dec.	31	Unrealized Loss—Income	2,800	
		Market Adjustment—Trading		2,800
		(To record unrealized loss on trading securities)		

Investment	Cost	Fair Value	Unrealized Gain (Loss)
Sanburg common stock	$ 9,800	$10,000	$ 200
Cey common stock	27,000	24,000	(3,000)
Totals	$36,800	$34,000	$(2,800)

THE
NAVIGATOR

SUMMARY OF STUDY OBJECTIVES

1. *Identify the reasons corporations invest in stocks and debt securities.* Corporations invest for three primary reasons: (a) They have excess cash; (b) they view investments as a significant revenue source; or (c) they have strategic goals such as gaining control of a competitor or moving into a new line of business.

2. *Explain the accounting for debt investments.* Entries for investments in debt securities are required when the bonds are purchased, interest is received or accrued, and the bonds are sold. The accounting for long-term investments in bonds is the same as for temporary investments in bonds, except that bond premium and bond discount must be amortized.

3. *Explain the accounting for stock investments.* Entries for investments in common stock are required when the stock is purchased, dividends are received, and stock is sold. When ownership is less than 20%, the cost method is used. When ownership is between 20% and 50%, the equity method should be used. When ownership is more than 50%, consolidated financial statements should be prepared.

4. *Describe the purpose and usefulness of consolidated financial statements.* When a company owns more than 50% of the common stock of another company, consolidated financial statements are usually prepared. These statements are especially useful to the stockholders, board of directors, and management of the parent company.

5. *Indicate how debt and stock investments are valued and reported on the financial statements.* Investments in debt and stock securities are classified as trading, available-for-sale, or held-to-maturity securities for valuation and reporting purposes. Trading securities are reported in current assets at fair value with changes from cost reported in net income. Available-for-sale securities are also reported at fair value with the changes from cost reported in stockholders' equity. Available-for-sale securities are classified as temporary or long-term depending on their expected realization.

6. *Distinguish between temporary and long-term investments.* Temporary investments are securities, held by a company, that are readily marketable and intended to be converted to cash within the next year or operating cycle, whichever is longer. Investments that do not meet both criteria are classified as long-term investments.

THE
NAVIGATOR

GLOSSARY

Available-for-sale securities   Securities that may be sold in the future. (p. 732)

Consolidated financial statements   Financial statements that present the assets and liabilities controlled by the parent company and the aggregate profitability of the affiliated companies. (p. 729)

Controlling interest   Ownership of more than 50% of the common stock of another entity. (p. 729)

Cost method   An accounting method in which the investment in common stock is recorded at cost and revenue is recognized only when cash dividends are received. (p. 727)

Debt investments   Investments in government and corporation bonds. (p. 724)

Equity method   An accounting method in which the investment in common stock is initially recorded at cost, and the investment account is then adjusted annually to show the investor's equity in the investee. (p. 728)

Fair value   Amount for which a security could be sold in a normal market. (p. 731)

Held-to-maturity securities   Debt securities which the investor has the intent and ability to hold to their maturity date. (p. 732)

Investment portfolio   A group of stocks in different corporations held for investment purposes. (p. 726)

Long-term investments   Investments that are not readily marketable or that management does not intend to convert into cash within the next year or operating cycle, whichever is longer. (p. 734)

Parent company   A company that owns more than 50% of the common stock of another entity. (p. 729)

Stock investments   Investments in the capital stock of corporations. (p. 726)

Subsidiary (affiliated) company   A company in which more than 50% of its stock is owned by another company. (p. 729)

Temporary investments   Investments that are readily marketable and intended to be converted into cash within the next year or operating cycle, whichever is longer. (p. 734)

Trading securities   Securities bought and held primarily for sale in the near term to generate income on short-term price differences. (p. 732)

SELF-STUDY QUESTIONS

Answers are at the end of the chapter.

(SO 2) 1. Debt investments are initially recorded at:
   a. cost.
   b. cost plus accrued interest.
   c. fair value.
   d. None of the above.

(SO 2) 2. Hanes Company sells debt investments costing $26,000 for $28,000 plus accrued interest that has been recorded. In journalizing the sale, credits are:
   a. Debt Investments and Loss on Sale of Debt Investments.
   b. Debt Investments, Gain on Sale of Debt Investments, and Bond Interest Receivable.
   c. Stock Investments and Bond Interest Receivable.
   d. No correct answer given.

(SO 3) 3. Pryor Company receives net proceeds of $42,000 on the sale of stock investments that cost $39,500. This transaction will result in reporting in the income statement a:
   a. loss of $2,500 under Other Expenses and Losses.
   b. loss of $2,500 under Operating Expenses.
   c. gain of $2,500 under Other Revenues and Gains.
   d. gain of $2,500 under Operating Revenues.

(SO 3) 4. The equity method of accounting for long-term investments in stock should be used when the investor has significant influence over an investee and owns:
   a. between 20% and 50% of the investee's common stock.
   b. 20% or more of the investee's common stock.
   c. more than 50% of the investee's common stock.
   d. less than 20% of the investee's common stock.

(SO 4) 5. Which of the following statements is *not true*? Consolidated financial statements are useful to:
   a. determine the profitability of specific subsidiaries.
   b. determine the aggregate profitability of enterprises under common control.
   c. determine the breadth of a parent company's operations.
   d. determine the full extent of aggregate obligations of enterprises under common control.

(SO 5) 6. At the end of the first year of operations, the total cost of the trading securities portfolio is $120,000, and total fair value is $115,000. The financial statements should show:
   a. a reduction of an asset of $5,000 and a realized loss of $5,000.
   b. a reduction of an asset of $5,000 and an unrealized loss of $5,000 in the stockholders' equity section.
   c. a reduction of an asset of $5,000 in the current asset section and an unrealized loss in Other Expenses and Losses of $5,000.
   d. a reduction of an asset of $5,000 in the current asset section and a realized loss of $5,000 in Other Expenses and Losses.

(SO 5) 7. In the balance sheet, Unrealized Loss—Equity is reported as a:
   a. contra asset account.
   b. contra stockholders' equity account.
   c. loss in the income statement.
   d. loss in the retained earnings statement.

(SO 6) 8. Temporary debt investments must be readily marketable and be expected to be sold within:
   a. 3 months from the date of purchase.
   b. the next year or operating cycle, whichever is shorter.
   c. the next year or operating cycle, whichever is longer.
   d. the operating cycle.

QUESTIONS

1. What are the reasons that corporations invest in securities?

2. (a) What is the cost of an investment in bonds?
   (b) When is interest on bonds recorded?

3. Sara Stine is confused about losses and gains on the sale of debt investments. Explain to Sara (a) how the gain or loss is computed, and (b) the statement presentation of the gains and losses.

4. Cline Company sells Hope's bonds costing $40,000 for $45,000, including $2,000 of accrued interest. In recording the sale, Cline books a $5,000 gain. Is this correct? Explain.

5. What is the cost of an investment in stock?

6. To acquire May Corporation stock, B. Mallon pays $60,000 in cash plus $1,500 broker's fees. What entry should be made for this investment, assuming the stock is readily marketable?

7. (a) When should a long-term investment in common stock be accounted for by the equity method? (b) When is revenue recognized under this method?

8. Marx Corporation uses the equity method to account for its ownership of 25% of the common stock of Welch Packing. During 1999 Welch reported a net income of $80,000 and declares and pays cash dividends of $10,000. What recognition should Marx Corporation give to these events?

9. What constitutes "significant influence" when an investor's financial interest is below the 50% level?

10. Distinguish between the cost and equity methods of accounting for investments in stocks.

11. What are consolidated financial statements?

12. What are the valuation guidelines for investments at a balance sheet date?

13. Kim Carley is the controller of Roarke, Inc. At December 31, the company's investments in trading securities cost $74,000 and have a fair value of $68,000. Indicate how Kim would report these data in the financial statements prepared on December 31.

14. Using the data in question 13, how would Kim report the data if the investment were long-term and the securities were classified as available-for-sale?

15. Colby Company's investments in available-for-sale securities at December 31 show total cost of $192,000 and total fair value of $205,000. Prepare the adjusting entry.

16. Using the data in question 15, prepare the adjusting entry assuming the securities are classified as trading securities.

17. What is the proper statement presentation of the account Unrealized Loss—Equity?

18. What purposes are served by reporting Unrealized Gains (Losses)—Equity in the stockholders' equity section?

19. Kiley Wholesale Supply owns stock in Sharp Corporation, which it intends to hold indefinitely because of some negative tax consequences if sold. Should the investment in Sharp be classified as a temporary investment? Why?

BRIEF EXERCISES

BE17–1 DeShields Corporation purchased debt investments for $41,500 on January 1, 1999. On July 1, 1999, DeShields received cash interest of $2,490. Journalize the purchase and the receipt of interest. Assume that no interest has been accrued.

Journalize entries for debt investments.
(SO 2)

BE17–2 On August 1, Lolich Company buys 1,000 shares of Stead common stock for $36,000 cash plus brokerage fees of $600. On December 1, the stock investments are sold for $38,000 in cash. Journalize the purchase and sale of the common stock.

Journalize entries for stock investments.
(SO 3)

BE17–3 Arkin Company owns 30% of Hines Company. For the current year Hines reports net income of $180,000 and declares and pays a $50,000 cash dividend. Record Arkin's equity in Hines's net income and the receipt of dividends from Hines.

Record transactions under the equity method of accounting.
(SO 3)

BE17–4 Cost and fair value data for the trading securities of Mingo Company at December 31, 1999, are $64,000 and $59,000, respectively. Prepare the adjusting entry to record the securities at fair value.

Prepare adjusting entry using fair value.
(SO 5)

BE17–5 For the data presented in BE17–4, show the financial statement presentation of the trading securities and related accounts.

Indicate statement presentation using fair value.
(SO 5, 6)

BE17–6 Dexter Corporation holds available-for-sale stock securities costing $72,000 as a long-term investment. At December 31, 1999, the fair value of the securities is $68,000. Prepare the adjusting entry to record the securities at fair value.

Prepare adjusting entry using fair value.
(SO 5)

BE17–7 For the data presented in BE17–6, show the financial statement presentation of the available-for-sale securities and related accounts. Assume the available-for-sale securities are noncurrent.

Indicate statement presentation using fair value.
(SO 5, 6)

BE17–8 Thesh Corporation has the following long-term investments: common stock of Kubek Co. (10% ownership) held as available-for-sale securities, cost $108,000, fair value $110,000; common stock of Ely Inc. (30% ownership), cost $210,000, equity $250,000; and a bond sinking fund of $150,000. Prepare the investments section of the balance sheet.

Prepare investment section of balance sheet.
(SO 5, 6)

EXERCISES

E17–1 Greer Corporation had the following transactions pertaining to debt investments:

Jan. 1 Purchased 90 10%, $1,000 Ford Co. bonds for $90,000 cash plus brokerage fees of $900. Interest is payable semiannually on July 1 and January 1.

July 1 Received semiannual interest on Ford Co. bonds.

July 1 Sold 30 Ford Co. bonds for $32,000 less $400 brokerage fees.

Journalize debt investment transactions and accrue interest.
(SO 2)

Instructions
(a) Journalize the transactions.
(b) Prepare the adjusting entry for the accrual of interest at December 31.

Journalize stock investment transactions.
(SO 3)

E17–2 Jacobs Company had the following transactions pertaining to stock investments:

Feb. 1 Purchased 800 shares of Aber common stock (2%) for $9,000 cash plus brokerage fees of $200.

July 1 Received cash dividends of $1 per share on Aber common stock.

Sept. 1 Sold 300 shares of Aber common stock for $4,000 less brokerage fees of $100.

Dec. 1 Received cash dividends of $1 per share on Aber common stock.

Instructions
(a) Journalize the transactions.
(b) Explain how dividend revenue and the gain (loss) on sale should be reported in the income statement.

Journalize transactions for investments in stocks.
(SO 3)

E17–3 Crosby Inc. had the following transactions pertaining to investments in common stock:

Jan. 1 Purchased 1,000 shares of Hannah Corporation common stock (5%) for $70,000 cash plus $2,100 broker's commission.

July 1 Received a cash dividend of $9 per share.

Dec. 1 Sold 500 shares of Hannah Corporation common stock for $37,000 cash less $800 broker's commission.

Dec. 31 Received a cash dividend of $9 per share.

Instructions
Journalize the transactions.

Journalize and post transactions and contrast cost and equity method results.
(SO 3)

E17–4 On January 1 Howell Corporation purchased a 30% equity in Louise Corporation for $150,000. At December 31 Louise declared and paid a $60,000 cash dividend and reported net income of $200,000.

Instructions
(a) Journalize the transactions.
(b) Determine the amount to be reported as an investment in Louise stock at December 31.

Journalize entries under cost and equity methods.
(SO 3)

E17–5 Presented below are two independent situations:

1. Ritter Cosmetics acquired 10% of the 200,000 shares of common stock of Mai Fashion at a total cost of $13 per share on March 18, 1999. On June 30, Mai declared and paid a $75,000 dividend. On December 31, Mai reported net income of $122,000 for the year. At December 31, the market price of Mai Fashion was $15 per share. The stock is classified as available-for-sale.

2. Somer, Inc., obtained significant influence over Ortiz Corporation by buying 40% of Ortiz's 30,000 outstanding shares of common stock at a total cost of $9 per share on January 1, 1999. On June 15, Ortiz declared and paid a cash dividend of $35,000. On December 31, Ortiz reported a net income of $80,000 for the year.

Instructions
Prepare all the necessary journal entries for 1999 for (a) Ritter Cosmetics and (b) Somer, Inc.

Prepare adjusting entry to record fair value and indicate statement presentation.
(SO 5, 6)

E17–6 At December 31, 1999, the trading securities for Yanik, Inc., are as follows:

Security	Cost	Fair Value
A	$17,500	$16,000
B	12,500	14,000
C	23,000	21,000
	$53,000	$51,000

Instructions
(a) Prepare the adjusting entry at December 31, 1999, to report the securities at fair value.
(b) Show the balance sheet and income statement presentation at December 31, 1999, after adjustment to fair value.

Prepare adjusting entry to record fair value and indicate statement presentation.
(SO 5, 6)

E17–7 Data for investments in stock classified as trading securities are presented in E17–6. Assume instead that the investments are classified as available-for-sale securities with the same cost and fair value data. The securities are considered to be a long-term investment.

Instructions
  (a) Prepare the adjusting entry at December 31, 1999, to report the securities at fair value.
  (b) Show the statement presentation at December 31, 1999, after adjustment to fair value.
  (c) ▭▬▬▶ M. Wise, a member of the board of directors, does not understand the reporting of the unrealized gains or losses. Write a letter to Mr. Wise explaining the reporting and the purposes that it serves.

E17–8 Quayle Company has the following data at December 31, 1999:

Securities	Cost	Fair Value
Trading	$120,000	$128,000
Available-for-sale	100,000	94,000

Prepare adjusting entries for fair value and indicate statement presentation for two classes of securities.
(SO 5, 6)

The available-for-sale securities are held as a long-term investment.

Instructions
  (a) Prepare the adjusting entries to report each class of securities at fair value.
  (b) Indicate the statement presentation of each class of securities and the related unrealized gain (loss) accounts.

PROBLEMS: SET A

P17–1A The following transactions related to long-term bonds occurred for Wolfe Corporation:

Journalize transactions and show financial statement presentation.
(SO 2, 5, 6)

1999
 Jan. 1   Purchased $50,000 Lake Corporation 10% bonds for $50,000.
 July 1   Received interest on Lake bonds.
 Dec. 31 Accrued interest on Lake bonds.

2000
 Jan. 1   Received interest on Lake bonds.
 Jan. 1   Sold $25,000 Lake bonds for $26,500.
 July 1   Received interest on Lake bonds.

Instructions
  (a) Journalize the transactions.
  (b) Assume that the fair value of the bonds at December 31, 1999, was $55,000. These bonds are classified as available-for-sale securities. Prepare the adjusting entry to record these bonds at fair value.
  (c) Show the balance sheet presentation of the bonds and interest receivable at December 31, 1999, and indicate where any unrealized gain or loss is reported in the financial statements.

P17–2A In January 1999, the management of Mann Company concludes that it has sufficient cash to purchase some temporary investments in debt and stock securities. During the year, the following transactions occurred:

Journalize investment transactions, prepare adjusting entry, and show statement presentation.
(SO 2, 3, 5, 6)

 Feb. 1   Purchased 800 shares of SRI common stock for $32,000 plus brokerage fees of $800.
 Mar. 1   Purchased 500 shares of FGH common stock for $15,000 plus brokerage fees of $300.
 Apr. 1   Purchased 60 $1,000, 12% XYZ bonds for $60,000 plus $1,200 brokerage fees. Interest is payable semiannually on April 1 and October 1.
 July 1   Received a cash dividend of $.60 per share on the SRI common stock.
 Aug. 1   Sold 200 shares of SRI common stock at $42 per share less brokerage fees of $350.
 Sept. 1 Received a $1 per share cash dividend on the FGH common stock.
 Oct. 1   Received the semiannual interest on the XYZ bonds.
 Oct. 1   Sold the XYZ bonds for $63,000 less $1,000 brokerage fees.

At December 31, the fair value of the SRI and FGH common stocks were $39 and $30 per share, respectively.

Instructions

    (a) Journalize the transactions and post to the accounts Debt Investments and Stock Investments. (Use the T-account form.)

    (b) Prepare the adjusting entry at December 31, 1999, to report the investments at fair value. All securities are considered to be trading securities.

    (c) Show the balance sheet presentation of investment securities at December 31, 1999.

    (d) Identify the income statement accounts and give the statement classification of each account.

Journalize transactions and adjusting entry for stock investments.
(SO 3, 5, 6)

P17–3A On December 31, 1999, Kern Associates owned the following securities that are held as long-term investments:

Common Stock	Shares	Cost
A Co.	1,000	$50,000
B Co.	6,000	36,000
C Co.	1,200	24,000

On this date, the total fair value of the securities was equal to its cost. The securities are not held for influence or control over the investees. In 2000, the following transactions occurred:

July 1 Received $1 per share semiannual cash dividend on B Co. common stock.

Aug. 1 Received $.50 per share cash dividend on A Co. common stock.

Sept. 1 Sold 500 shares of B Co. common stock for cash at $7 per share less brokerage fees of $100.

Oct. 1 Sold 400 shares of A Co. common stock for cash at $56 per share less brokerage fees of $600.

Nov. 1 Received $1 per share cash dividend on C Co. common stock.

Dec. 15 Received $.50 per share cash dividend on A Co. common stock.

    31 Received $1 per share semiannual cash dividend on B Co. common stock.

At December 31, the fair values per share of the common stocks were: A Co. $47, B Co. $6, and C Co. $19.

Instructions

    (a) Journalize the 2000 transactions and post to the account Stock Investments. (Use the T-account form.)

    (b) Prepare the adjusting entry at December 31, 2000, to show the securities at fair value. The stock should be classified as available-for-sale securities.

    (c) Show the balance sheet presentation of the investments at December 31, 2000. At this date, Kern Associates has common stock $2,000,000 and retained earnings $1,200,000.

Prepare entries at cost and at equity and prepare memorandum.
(SO 3)

P17–4A Jantz Concrete acquired 20% of the outstanding common stock of Hawes, Inc., on January 1, 1999, by paying $1,200,000 for 50,000 shares. Hawes declared and paid a $0.60 per share cash dividend on June 30 and again on December 31, 1999. Hawes reported net income of $800,000 for the year.

Instructions

    (a) Prepare the journal entries for Jantz Concrete for 1999 assuming Jantz cannot exercise significant influence over Hawes. (Use the cost method.)

    (b) Prepare the journal entries for Jantz Concrete for 1999, assuming Jantz can exercise significant influence over Hawes. (Use the equity method.)

    (c) ▯▭▭▶ The board of directors of Jantz Concrete is confused about the differences between the cost and equity methods. Prepare a memorandum for the board that (1) explains each method and (2) shows, in tabular form, the account balances under each method at December 31, 1999.

Journalize stock transactions and show statement presentation.
(SO 3, 5, 6)

P17–5A The following are in Hyatt Company's portfolio of long-term available-for-sale securities at December 31, 1999:

	Cost
500 shares of Aglar Corporation common stock	$26,000
700 shares of BAL Corporation common stock	42,000
400 shares of Hicks Corporation preferred stock	16,800

On December 31, the total cost of the portfolio equaled total fair value. Hyatt had the following transactions related to the securities during 2000:

Jan. 7 Sold 500 shares of Aglar Corporation common stock at $56 per share less brokerage fees of $700.

Jan. 10 Purchased 200 shares, $70 par value common stock of Miley Corporation at $78 per share, plus brokerage fees of $240.

26 Received a cash dividend of $1.15 per share on BAL Corporation common stock.

Feb. 2 Received cash dividends of $.40 per share on Hicks Corporation preferred stock.

10 Sold all 400 shares of Hicks Corporation preferred stock at $30.00 per share less brokerage fees of $180.

July 1 Received a cash dividend of $1.00 per share on BAL Corporation common stock.

Sept. 1 Purchased an additional 400 shares of the $70 par value common stock of Miley Corporation at $82 per share, plus brokerage fees of $400.

Dec. 15 Received a cash dividend of $1.50 per share on Miley Corporation common stock.

At December 31, 2000, the fair values of the securities were:

BAL Corporation common stock	$64 per share
Miley Corporation common stock	$72 per share

Hyatt uses separate account titles for each investment, such as Investment in BAL Corporation Common Stock.

Instructions
(a) Prepare journal entries to record the transactions.
(b) Post to the investment accounts. (Use T accounts.)
(c) Prepare the adjusting entry at December 31, 2000, to report the porfolio at fair value.
(d) Show the balance sheet presentation at December 31, 2000.

P17–6A The following data, presented in alphabetical order, are taken from the records of Lehman Corporation.

Prepare a balance sheet.
(SO 5, 6)

Accounts payable	$ 220,000
Accounts receivable	90,000
Accumulated depreciation—building	180,000
Accumulated depreciation—equipment	52,000
Allowance for doubtful accounts	6,000
Bonds payable (10%, due 2012)	400,000
Bond sinking fund	360,000
Buildings	900,000
Cash	92,000
Common stock ($5 par value; 500,000 shares authorized,	
300,000 shares issued)	1,500,000
Discount on bonds payable	20,000
Dividends payable	50,000
Equipment	275,000
Goodwill	200,000
Income taxes payable	120,000
Investment in Houston Inc, stock (30% ownership), at equity	240,000
Land	500,000
Temporary stock investment, at fair value	185,000
Merchandise inventory	170,000
Notes payable (due 2000)	70,000
Organization costs	50,000
Paid-in capital in excess of par value	200,000
Prepaid insurance	16,000
Retained earnings	300,000

Instructions
Prepare a balance sheet at December 31, 1999.

PROBLEMS: SET B

....

Journalize transactions and show financial statement presentation.
(SO 2, 5, 6)

P17–1B   The following transactions related to long-term bonds occurred for Gomez Corporation:

1999

Jan. 1   Purchased $100,000 Horton Corporation 9% bonds for $100,000.
July 1   Received interest on Horton bonds.
Dec. 31   Accrued interest on Horton bonds.

2000

Jan. 1   Received interest on Horton bonds.
Jan. 1   Sold $25,000 Horton bonds for $28,500.
July 1   Received interest on Horton bonds.

Instructions

(a) Journalize the transactions.
(b) Assume that the fair value of the bonds at December 31, 1999, was $96,000. These bonds are classified as available-for-sale securities. Prepare the adjusting entry to record these bonds at fair value.
(c) Show the balance sheet presentation of the bonds and interest receivable at December 31, 1999, and indicate where any unrealized gain or loss is reported in the financial statements.

Journalize investment transactions, prepare adjusting entry, and show statement presentation.
(SO 2, 3, 5, 6)

P17–2B   In January 1999, the management of the Norris Company concludes that it has sufficient cash to permit some temporary investments in debt and stock securities. During the year, the following transactions occurred:

Feb. 1   Purchased 600 shares of CBA common stock for $31,800 plus brokerage fees of $600.
Mar. 1   Purchased 800 shares of GHI common stock for $20,000 plus brokerage fees of $400.
Apr. 1   Purchased 50 $1,000, 12% UVW bonds for $50,000 plus $1,000 brokerage fees. Interest is payable semiannually on April 1 and October 1.
July 1   Received a cash dividend of $.60 per share on the CBA common stock.
Aug. 1   Sold 200 shares of CBA common stock at $58 per share less brokerage fees of $200.
Sept. 1   Received a $1 per share cash dividend on the GHI common stock.
Oct. 1   Received the semiannual interest on the UVW bonds.
Oct. 1   Sold the UVW bonds for $51,000 less $1,000 brokerage fees.

At December 31, the fair value of the CBA and GHI common stocks were $55 and $23 per share, respectively.

Instructions

(a) Journalize the transactions and post to the accounts Debt Investments and Stock Investments. (Use the T-account form.)
(b) Prepare the adjusting entry at December 31, 1999, to report the investment securities at fair value. All securities are considered to be trading securities.
(c) Show the balance sheet presentation of investment securities at December 31, 1999.
(d) Identify the income statement accounts and give the statement classification of each account.

Journalize transactions and adjusting entry for stock investments.
(SO 3, 5, 6)

P17–3B   On December 31, 1999, Milner Associates owned the following securities that are held as a long-term investment. The securities are not held for influence or control of the investee.

Common Stock	Shares	Cost
X Co.	2,000	$90,000
Y Co.	5,000	45,000
Z Co.	1,500	30,000

On this date, the total fair value of the securities was equal to its cost. In 2000, the following transactions occurred.

July 1   Received $1 per share semiannual cash dividend on Y Co. common stock.
     8   Received 4,000 shares of X Co. common stock in a 3 for 1 stock split.

Aug. 1 Received $.50 per share cash dividend on X Co. common stock.

Sept. 1 Sold 700 shares of Y Co. common stock for cash at $8 per share less brokerage fees of $200.

Oct. 1 Sold 600 shares of X Co. common stock for cash at $17 per share less brokerage fees of $500.

Nov. 1 Received $1 per share cash dividend on Z Co. common stock.

Dec. 15 Received $.50 per share cash dividend on X Co. common stock.

     31 Received $1 per share semiannual cash dividend on Y Co. common stock.

At December 31, the fair values per share of the common stocks were: X Co. $16, Y Co. $8, and Z Co. $18.

Instructions

(a) Journalize the 2000 transactions and post to the account Stock Investments. (Use the T-account form.)

(b) Prepare the adjusting entry at December 31, 2000, to show the securities at fair value. The stock should be classified as available-for-sale securities.

(c) Show the balance sheet presentation of the investments at December 31, 2000. At this date, Milner Associates has common stock $1,500,000 and retained earnings $1,000,000.

P17–4B Nayler Services acquired 30% of the outstanding common stock of Quinn Company on January 1, 1999, by paying $800,000 for the 40,000 shares. Quinn declared and paid $0.40 per share cash dividends on March 15, June 15, September 15, and December 15, 1999. Quinn reported net income of $360,000 for the year.

Prepare entries under the cost and equity methods and tabulate differences.
(SO 3)

Instructions

(a) Prepare the journal entries for Nayler Services for 1999 assuming Nayler cannot exercise significant influence over Quinn. (Use the cost method.)

(b) Prepare the journal entries for Nayler Services for 1999, assuming Nayler can exercise significant influence over Quinn. (Use the equity method.)

(c) In tabular form, indicate the investment and income statement account balances at December 31, 1999, under each method of accounting.

P17–5B The following data, presented in alphabetical order, are taken from the records of Scheer Corporation:

Prepare a balance sheet.
(SO 5, 6)

Accounts payable	$ 270,000
Accounts receivable	140,000
Accumulated depreciation—building	180,000
Accumulated depreciation—equipment	52,000
Allowance for doubtful accounts	6,000
Bonds payable (10%, due 2010)	500,000
Bond sinking fund	150,000
Buildings	950,000
Cash	92,000
Common stock ($10 par value; 500,000 shares authorized, 150,000 shares issued)	1,500,000
Dividends payable	80,000
Equipment	275,000
Goodwill	200,000
Income taxes payable	120,000
Investment in Dodge common stock (10% ownership), at cost	278,000
Investment in Huston common stock (30% ownership), at equity	230,000
Land	500,000
Market adjustment—available-for-sale securities (Dr)	8,000
Merchandise inventory	170,000
Notes payable (due 2000)	70,000
Organization costs	50,000
Paid-in capital in excess of par value	200,000
Premium on bonds payable	40,000
Prepaid insurance	16,000
Retained earnings	213,000
Temporary stock investment, at fair value	180,000
Unrealized gain—available-for-sale securities	8,000

The investment in Dodge common stock is considered to be a long-term available-for-sale security.

Instructions
Prepare a balance sheet at December 31, 1999.

BROADENING YOUR PERSPECTIVE

FINANCIAL REPORTING AND ANALYSIS

FINANCIAL REPORTING PROBLEM: Kellogg Company

BYP17–1   The annual report of Kellogg Company is presented in Appendix A.

Instructions
Answer the following questions:

(a) What information about investments is reported in the consolidated balance sheet?
(b) Based on the information in Note 1 accompanying the financial statements, what is the nature of Kellogg's short-term investments?
(c) How much was spent in acquisition of new businesses in 1997 compared with 1996?

COMPARATIVE ANALYSIS PROBLEM: Kellogg Company vs. General Mills

BYP17–2   Kellogg's financial statements are presented in Appendix A; General Mills's financial statements are presented in Appendix B.

Instructions

(a) Based on the information contained in these financial statements, determine each of the following for each company:
 (1) Cash used in (by) investing (investment) activities during 1997 (from the Statement of Cash Flows).
 (2) Cash used for acquisitions and investments in businesses during 1997.
(b) Based on the information contained in the notes to the financial statements, explain the major acquisitions made by these two companies in the last two years.

RESEARCH ASSIGNMENT

BYP17–3   The July 6, 1995, edition of *The Wall Street Journal* includes an article by Jim Carlton and David P. Hamilton, entitled "Packard Bell Sells 20% Stake to NEC for $170 Million; Deal Gives Japanese Firm Unprecedented Access to the U.S. PC Market."

Instructions
Read the article and answer the following questions:

(a) Why did Packard Bell sell shares to NEC?
(b) Identify a similar transaction between two other computer companies.
(c) Under U.S. GAAP, how would NEC account for its investment in Packard Bell?
(d) Packard Bell was considering a sale of common shares to the general public. Why didn't it select this option?

INTERPRETING FINANCIAL STATEMENTS: Xerox Corporation

BYP17–4   Xerox Corporation has a 50% investment interest in a joint venture with the Japanese corporation Fuji, called Fuji Xerox. Xerox accounts for this investment using the equity method. The following additional information regarding this investment was taken from Xerox's 1995 annual report:

Investment in Fuji Xerox per balance sheet	$ 1,223
Xerox's equity in Fuji Xerox net income	88
Xerox total assets	25,969
Xerox total liabilities	21,328
Fuji Xerox total assets	6,603
Fuji Xerox total liabilities	4,153

Instructions

(a) What alternative approaches are available for accounting for long-term investments in stock? Discuss whether Xerox is correct in using the equity method to account for this investment.

(b) Under the equity method, how does Xerox reports its investment in Fuji Xerox? If Xerox owned a majority of Fuji Xerox, it then would have to consolidate Fuji Xerox instead of using the equity method. Discuss how this would change Xerox's financial statements. That is, in what way and by how much would assets and liabilities change?

(c) The use of 50% joint ventures is becoming a fairly common practice. Why might companies like Xerox prefer to participate in a joint venture rather than own a majority share?

REAL-WORLD FOCUS: SPS Technologies, Inc.

BYP17–5 **SPS Technologies, Inc.,** was formed in 1903 as Standard Pressed Steel. Today the company is engaged in the design, manufacture, and marketing of high-strength mechanical fasteners, superalloys, and magnetic materials for the aerospace, automotive, and off-highway equipment industries. The company owns plants in the United States, United Kingdom, Ireland, Australia, and Spain, and has minority interests in facilities in Brazil and India.

The following note to the financial statements appears in a recent SPS annual report:

SPS TECHNOLOGIES
Notes to the Financial Statements

Investments: The Company's investments in affiliates consist of a 16.75% interest in Precision Fasteners Ltd., Bombay, India; a 46.49% interest in Metalac S.A. Industria e Comercio, Sao Paulo, Brazil; a 51.0% interest in Pacific Products Limited, Guernsey, Channel Islands, United Kingdom; and a 51.0% interest in National-Arnold Magnetics Company, Adelanto, California, United States. Dividends received from these companies were $42,000, $44,000, and $66,000 in 1993, 1992 and 1991, respectively.

Instructions

(a) Does the investment in these companies represent short- or long-term investments? Are these investments in stocks or in bonds of these companies?

(b) The ownership percentages in these companies vary. Based upon the information given, which accounting method would appear appropriate for each company? What other information would you like to know before deciding how to account for each investment?

(c) What is the most likely method used to account for dividends received from Precision Fasteners? From National-Arnolds Magnetics Company?

CRITICAL THINKING

GROUP DECISION CASE

BYP17–6 At the beginning of the question and answer portion of the annual stockholders' meeting of Powell Corporation, stockholder Cindy Olson asks, "Why did management sell the holdings in BMA Company at a loss when this company has been very profitable during the period its stock was held by Powell?"

Since president Tony Perez has just concluded his speech on the recent success and bright future of Powell, he is taken aback by this question and responds, "I remember we paid $1,100,000 for that stock some years ago, and I am sure we sold that stock at a much higher price. You must be mistaken."

Olson retorts, "Well, right here in footnote number 7 to the annual report it shows that 240,000 shares, a 25% interest in BMA, were sold on the last day of the year. Also, it states that BMA earned $550,000 this year and paid out $150,000 in cash dividends. Further, a summary statement indicates that in past years, while Powell held BMA stock, BMA earned

$1,240,000 and paid out $440,000 in dividends. Finally, the income statement for this year shows a loss on the sale of BMA stock of $180,000. So, I doubt that I am mistaken.''

Red-faced, president Perez turns to you.

Instructions

With the class divided into groups, answer the following:

(a) What dollar amount did Powell receive upon the sale of the BMA stock?
(b) Explain why both stockholder Olson and president Perez are correct.

COMMUNICATION ACTIVITY

BYP17–7   Ramariz Corporation has purchased two securities for its portfolio. The first is a stock investment in Thome Corporation, one of its suppliers. Ramariz purchased 10% of Thome with the intention of holding it for a number of years, but has no intention of purchasing more shares. The second investment was a purchase of debt securities. Ramariz purchased the debt securities because its analysts believe that changes in market interest rates will cause these securities to increase in value in a short period of time. Ramariz intends to sell the securities as soon as they have increased in value.

Instructions

Write a memo to Crus Carey, the chief financial officer, explaining how to account for each of these investments, and what the implications for reported income are from this accounting treatment.

ETHICS CASE

BYP17–8   Kimble Financial Services Company holds a large portfolio of debt and stock securities as an investment. The total fair value of the portfolio at December 31, 1999, is greater than total cost, with some securities having increased in value and others having decreased. Ann Osborn, the financial vice president, and Sue Ling, the controller, are in the process of classifying for the first time the securities in the portfolio.

Osborn suggests classifying the securities that have increased in value as trading securities in order to increase net income for the year. She also wants to classify the securities that have decreased in value as long-term available-for-sale securities so that the decreases in value will not affect 1999 net income.

Ling disagrees. She recommends classifying the securities that have decreased in value as trading securities and those that have increased in value as long-term available-for-sale securities. Ling argues that the company is having a good earnings year and that recognizing the losses now will help to smooth income for this year. Moreover, for future years, when the company may not be as profitable, the company will have built-in gains.

Instructions

(a) Will classifying the securities as Osborn and Ling suggest actually affect earnings as each says it will?
(b) Is there anything unethical in what Osborn and Ling propose? Who are the stakeholders affected by their proposals?
(c) Assume that Osborn and Ling properly classify the portfolio. Assume, at year-end, that Osborn proposes to sell the securities that will increase 1999 net income, and that Ling proposes to sell the securities that will decrease 1999 net income. Is this unethical?

SURFING THE NET

BYP17–9   Bonds, similar to stocks, can be purchased by investors in an initial public offering or through a secondary market. Secondary markets can be reached via the Internet and provide users with investment information. Bonds Online is one site that provides a bond-specific glossary of terms.

Address: http://www.bondsonline.com

Steps:

1. From the Bonds Online homepage, choose **Bond Professor.**
2. Choose **Glossary.**

Instructions

Using the glossary, find the definition of:

    (a) discount rate.
    (b) capital market.
    (c) rating.

BYP17–10   Most publicly traded companies are analyzed by numerous analysts. These analysts often don't agree about a company's future prospects. In this exercise you will find analysts' ratings about companies and make comparisons over time and across companies in the same industry. You will also see to what extent the analysts experienced "earnings surprises." Earnings surprises can cause changes in stock prices.

Address: http://biz.yahoo.com/i (or go to the Wiley home page)

Steps:

1. Choose a company.
2. Use the index to find the company's name.
3. Choose **Research.**

Instructions

Answer the following questions:

    (a) How many brokers rated the company?
    (b) What percentage rated it a strong buy?
    (c) What was the average rating for the week?
    (d) Did the average rating improve or decline relative to last week?
    (e) How do the brokers rank this company among all the companies in its industry?
    (f) What was the amount of the earnings surprise during the last quarter (that is, to what extent were analysts' expectations of earnings incorrect)?
    (g) Are earnings expected to increase or decrease this quarter compared to last?

Answers to Self-Study Questions

1. a   2. b   3. c   4. a   5. a   6. c   7. b   8. c

Answer to Kellogg Review It Question 4, page 730

In Note 1, the following statement is made regarding the consolidation policy of Kellogg Company: "The consolidated financial statements include the accounts of Kellogg Company and its majority-owned subsidiaries. Intercompany balances and transactions are eliminated. Certain amounts in the prior year financial statements have been reclassified to conform to the current year presentation."

Remember to go back to the Navigator box on the chapter-opening page and check off your completed work.

Before studying this chapter, you should know or, if necessary, review:

a. The difference between the accrual basis and the cash basis of accounting. (Ch. 3, pp. 112–113)

b. The major items included in a corporation's balance sheet. (Ch. 17, p. 737)

c. The major items included in a corporation's income statement. (Ch. 15, p. 652)

THE NAVIGATOR

FEATURE STORY

"Cash Is Cash, and Everything Else Is Accounting"

For Gerald Biby, vice president and chief financial officer of Kilian Community College in Sioux Falls, South Dakota, the statement of cash flows was the difference between being

able to refinance a mortgage and being turned down by six local banks. "We recently wanted to refinance a $125,000 mortgage on a piece of property that we own," he says. "It was the statement of cash flows that finally showed our lender that we had the cash flow to service the debt."

As he explains, the traditional financial statement for a not-for-

profit, educational institution shows revenues and all expenditures, even the capital expenditures. According to this format, which the banks focused on initially, Kilian Community College was just breaking even. "In the business world, if we had spent $250,000 on a computer system, then we would have put that on a depreciation schedule. But in the non-profit arena, it's typical that the entire $250,000 is written off as an expense against the general fund." The statement of cash flows showed the bankers that one of the uses of funds was really the purchase of computer equipment that had several years of life.

The college's statement of cash flows has over 30 classifications including tuition, fees, bookstore revenues, and so on. The school has 250 students, charges $70 a credit hour (12 hours is a full-time schedule), and has five terms each year.

The bankers granted the refinancing when they saw that the college's sources of funds exceeded the loan repayments, including principal and interest, by a ratio of 3-to-1. Not only did the school get the loan, but it did so at a favorable rate. "We were able to cut the mortgage rate to prime plus 1% from prime plus 3%."

THE NAVIGATOR

CHAPTER 18

THE STATEMENT
OF CASH FLOWS

THE NAVIGATOR

- Understand *Concepts for Review*
- Read *Feature Story*
- Scan *Study Objectives*
- Read *Preview*
- Read text and answer *Before You Go On*
  p. 761 ☐ p. 771 ☐ p. 784 ☐ p. 789 ☐
- Work *Demonstration Problems*
- Review *Summary of Study Objectives*
- Answer *Self-Study Questions*
- Complete assignments

STUDY OBJECTIVES

After studying this chapter, you should be able to:

1. *Indicate the primary purpose of the statement of cash flows.*
2. *Distinguish among operating, investing, and financing activities.*
3. *Prepare a statement of cash flows using the indirect method.*
4. *Prepare a statement of cash flows using the direct method.*
5. *Analyze the statement of cash flows.*

THE
NAVIGATOR

*A*s the story about Kilian Community College indicates, the balance sheet, income statement, and retained earnings statement do not always show the whole picture of the financial condition of a company or institution. In fact, looking at the three traditional financial statements of some well-known companies, a thoughtful investor might have questions like the following: How did Eastman Kodak finance cash dividends of $649 million in a year in which it earned only $17 million? How could Delta Airlines purchase new planes costing $900 million in a year in which it reported a net loss of $86 million? How did Kohlberg Kravis Roberts finance its record-shattering $25 billion purchase of RJR Nabisco? Answers to these and similar questions can be found in this chapter, which presents the **statement of cash flows**. The content and organization of this chapter are as follows:

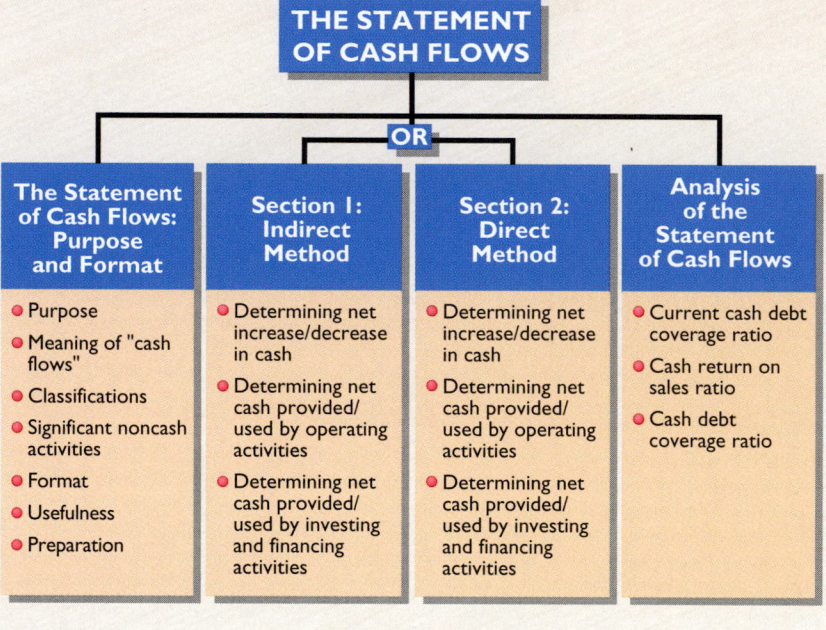

THE STATEMENT OF CASH FLOWS: PURPOSE AND FORMAT

The three basic financial statements we've studied so far present only limited and fragmentary information about a company's cash flows (cash receipts and cash payments). For example, comparative balance sheets show the increase in property, plant, and equipment during the year, but they do not show how the additions were financed or paid for. The income statement shows net income, but it does not indicate the amount of cash generated by operating activities. Similarly, the retained earnings statement shows cash dividends declared but not the cash dividends paid during the year. None of these statements presents a detailed summary of the net change in cash as a result of operating, investing, and financing activities during the period.

ACCOUNTING IN ACTION

Business Insight

Libby-Owens-Ford (LOF) Company's mission statement in its annual report emphasizes the importance of cash flow as follows: "LOF stresses the importance of cash flow measurement and performance. Individual companies must analyze the cash flow effects of running their business. Where cash comes from and what cash is used for must be simply and clearly set forth."

Purpose of the Statement of Cash Flows

The primary purpose of the statement of cash flows is to provide information about the cash receipts and cash payments of an entity during a period. A secondary objective is to provide information about the operating, investing, and financing activities of the entity during the period.[1] The **statement of cash flows** reports the cash receipts, cash payments, and net change in cash resulting from the operating, investing, and financing activities of an enterprise during a period in a format that reconciles the beginning and ending cash balances.

Reporting the causes of changes in cash is considered useful because investors, creditors, and other interested parties want to know what is happening to a company's most liquid resource—its cash. As the opening story about Kilian Community College demonstrates, a statement of cash flows helps us understand what is happening. It provides answers to the following simple, but important, questions about the enterprise:

1. Where did the cash come from during the period?
2. What was the cash used for during the period?
3. What was the change in the cash balance during the period?

1

STUDY OBJECTIVE

Indicate the primary purpose of the statement of cash flows.

Meaning of "Cash Flows"

The statement of cash flows is generally prepared using "**cash and cash equivalents**" as its basis. Cash equivalents are short-term, highly liquid investments that are both:

1. Readily convertible to known amounts of cash, and
2. So near their maturity that their market value is relatively insensitive to changes in interest rates.

Generally, only investments with original maturities of three months or less qualify under this definition. Examples of cash equivalents are Treasury bills, commercial paper (short-term corporate notes), and money market funds. All typically are purchased with cash that is in excess of immediate needs. Note that since cash and cash equivalents are viewed as the same, transfers between cash and cash equivalents are not treated as cash receipts and cash payments—i.e., they are not reported in the statement of cash flows. The term "cash" when used in this chapter includes cash and cash equivalents.

Classification of Cash Flows

The statement of cash flows classifies cash receipts and cash payments by operating, investing, and financing activities. Transactions and other events char-

2

STUDY OBJECTIVE

Distinguish among operating, investing, and financing activities.

---

[1]"Statement of Cash Flows," *Statement of Financial Accounting Standards No. 95* (Stamford, Conn.: FASB, 1987).

acteristic of each kind of activity are described in the list below and pictured in Illustration 18-1:

1. **Operating activities** include the cash effects of transactions that create revenues and expenses and thus enter into the determination of net income.
2. **Investing activities** include (a) acquiring and disposing of investments and productive long-lived assets, and (b) lending money and collecting the loans.
3. **Financing activities** include (a) obtaining cash from issuing debt and repaying the amounts borrowed, and (b) obtaining cash from stockholders and providing them with a return on their investment.

ILLUSTRATION 18-1

Business activities shown on the statement of cash flows

| Operating activities | Investing activities | Financing activities |

The category of operating activities is the most important because it shows the cash provided by company operations. This source of cash is generally considered to be the best measure of a company's ability to generate sufficient cash to continue as a going concern.

Illustration 18-2 on page 757 lists typical cash receipts and cash payments within each of the three classifications. Study the list carefully. It will prove very useful in solving homework exercises and problems.

As you can see, some cash flows relating to investing or financing activities are classified as operating activities. For example, **receipts of investment revenue (interest and dividends) and payments of interest to lenders are classified as operating activities because these items are reported in the income statement.**

Note that, generally, (1) operating activities involve income determination (income statement) items, (2) investing activities involve cash flows resulting from changes in investments and long-term asset items, and (3) financing activities involve cash flows resulting from changes in long-term liability and stockholders' equity items.

Significant Noncash Activities

Not all of a company's significant activities involve cash. Examples of significant noncash activities are:

1. Issuance of common stock to purchase assets.
2. Conversion of bonds into common stock.
3. Issuance of debt to purchase assets.
4. Exchanges of plant assets.

Significant financing and investing activities that do not affect cash are not reported in the body of the statement of cash flows. However, these activities

ILLUSTRATION 18-2
Typical receipts and payments classified by activity

Types of Cash Inflows and Outflows

Operating activities
Cash inflows:
From sale of goods or services.
From returns on loans (interest received) and on equity securities (dividends received).
Cash outflows:
To suppliers for inventory.
To employees for services.
To government for taxes.
To lenders for interest.
To others for expenses.

Investing activities
Cash inflows:
From sale of property, plant, and equipment.
From sale of debt or equity securities of other entities.
From collection of principal on loans to other entities.
Cash outflows:
To purchase property, plant, and equipment.
To purchase debt or equity securities of other entities.
To make loans to other entities.

Financing activities
Cash inflows:
From sale of equity securities (company's own stock).
From issuance of debt (bonds and notes).
Cash outflows:
To stockholders as dividends.
To redeem long-term debt or reacquire capital stock.

HELPFUL HINT
Operating activities generally relate to changes in current assets and current liabilities. Investing activities generally relate to changes in noncurrent assets. Financing activities relate to changes in noncurrent liabilities and stockholders' equity accounts.

HELPFUL HINT
Do not include noncash investing and financing activities in the body of the statement of cash flows. Report this information in a separate schedule at the bottom of the statement.

are reported in either a separate schedule at the bottom of the statement of cash flows or in a separate note or supplementary schedule to the financial statements.

The reporting of these activities in a separate note or supplementary schedule satisfies the **full disclosure principle** because it identifies significant noncash investing and financing activities of the enterprise. In solving homework assignments you should present significant noncash investing and financing activities in a separate schedule at the bottom of the statement of cash flows. (See lower section of Illustration 18-3, on page 758, for an example.)

ACCOUNTING IN ACTION
Business Insight

Differences between net income and net cash provided by operating activities are illustrated by the following results from recent annual reports for the same fiscal year (all data are in millions of dollars):

Company	Net Income	Net Cash from Operations
Kmart Corporation	$ 296	$ 76
Wal-Mart Stores, Inc.	2,681	2,906
Gap Inc.	452	845
J.C. Penney Company, Inc.	1,057	738
Sears Roebuck & Co.	1,454	1,930
The May Department Stores Company	782	999

Note the wide disparity among the companies that engaged in similar types of retail merchandising.

Format of the Statement of Cash Flows

The three activities discussed previously—operating, investing, and financing—plus the significant noncash investing and financing activities constitute the general format of the statement of cash flows. A widely used form of the statement of cash flows is shown in Illustration 18-3.

ILLUSTRATION 18-3

Format of statement of cash flows

COMPANY NAME Statement of Cash Flows Period Covered		
Cash flows from operating activities		
(List of individual items)	XX	
Net cash provided (used) by operating activities		XXX
Cash flows from investing activities		
(List of individual inflows and outflows)	XX	
Net cash provided (used) by investing activities		XXX
Cash flows from financing activities		
(List of individual inflows and outflows)	XX	
Net cash provided (used) by financing activities		XXX
Net increase (decrease) in cash		XXX
Cash at beginning of period		XXX
Cash at end of period		XXX
Noncash investing and financing activities		
(List of individual noncash transactions)		XXX

As illustrated, the cash flows from operating activities section always appears first, followed by the investing activities and the financing activities sections. Also, **the individual inflows and outflows from investing and financing activities are reported separately**. Thus, cash outflow for the purchase of property, plant, and equipment is reported separately from the cash inflow from the sale of property, plant, and equipment. Similarly, the cash inflow from the issuance of debt securities is reported separately from the cash outflow for the retirement of debt. If a company did not report the inflows and outflows separately, it would obscure the investing and financing activities of the enterprise and thus make it more difficult to assess future cash flows.

The reported operating, investing, and financing activities result in either net cash **provided or used** by each activity. The net cash provided or used by each activity is totaled to show the net increase (decrease) in cash for the period. The net increase (decrease) in cash for the period is then added to or subtracted from the beginning-of-the-period cash balance to obtain the end-of-the-period cash balance. Finally, any significant noncash investing and financing activities are reported in a separate schedule at the bottom of the statement.

Usefulness of the Statement of Cash Flows

The information in a statement of cash flows should help investors, creditors, and others assess various aspects of the firm's financial position:

1. **The entity's ability to generate future cash flows.** By examining relationships between such items as sales and net cash provided by operating activities, or cash provided by operations and increases or decreases in cash, investors and others can make predictions of the amounts, timing, and uncertainty of future cash flows better than from accrual basis data.

ETHICS NOTE

Many investors believe that "Cash is cash and everything else is accounting"—that is, cash flow is less susceptible to management manipulation and fraud than traditional accounting measures such as net income. Though we would discourage reliance on cash flows to the exclusion of accrual accounting, comparing cash from operations to net income can reveal important information about the "quality" of reported net income—that is, the extent to which net income provides a good measure of actual performance.

2. **The entity's ability to pay dividends and meet obligations.** Simply put, if a company does not have adequate cash, employees cannot be paid, debts settled, or dividends paid. Employees, creditors, stockholders, and customers should be particularly interested in this statement, because it alone shows the flows of cash in a business.

3. **The reasons for the difference between net income and net cash provided (used) by operating activities.** Net income is important, because it provides information on the success or failure of a business enterprise. However, some are critical of accrual basis net income because it requires many estimates; as a result, the reliability of the number is often challenged. Such is not the case with cash. Thus, many readers of the financial statement want to know the reasons for the difference between net income and net cash provided by operating activities. Then they can assess for themselves the reliability of the income number.

4. **The cash investing and financing transactions during the period.** By examining a company's investing activities and its financing transactions, a financial statement reader can better understand why assets and liabilities increased or decreased during the period. In summary, the information in the statement of cash flows is useful in answering the following questions:

> How did cash increase when there was a net loss for the period?
> How were the proceeds of the bond issue used?
> How was the expansion in the plant and equipment financed?
> Why were dividends not increased?
> How was the retirement of debt accomplished?
> How much money was borrowed during the year?
> Is cash flow greater or less than net income?

HELPFUL HINT
Income from operations and cash flow from operating activities are different. Income from operations is based on accrual accounting; cash flow from operating activities is prepared on a cash basis.

ACCOUNTING IN ACTION
Business Insight

Cash flow is also sometimes used to determine the price of a company. Page Net, a company in the telephone beeper business, had an initial public offering (IPO) in which $590 million of stock was sold. In December 1993 the stock had a market value of $1.5 billion. Yet Page Net reported losses in every quarter since it went public. However, its cash flow the year before the IPO was $39 million, $57 million in the IPO year, $75 million in 1992, and approximately $99 million in 1993. As one expert noted, "It is a classic example of a company valued by cash flow."

Preparing the Statement of Cash Flows

The statement of cash flows is prepared differently from the three other basic financial statements. First, it is not prepared from an adjusted trial balance. Because the statement requires detailed information concerning the changes in account balances that occurred between two periods of time, an adjusted trial balance will not provide the necessary data for the statement. Second, the statement of cash flows deals with cash receipts and payments. As a result, **the accrual concept is not used in the preparation of a statement of cash flows**.

The information to prepare this statement usually comes from three sources:

Comparative balance sheet. Information in this statement indicates the amount of the changes in assets, liabilities, and stockholders' equities from the beginning to the end of the period.

Current income statement. Information in this statement helps the reader determine the amount of cash provided by or used by operations during the period.

Additional information. Additional information includes transaction data that are needed to determine how cash was provided or used during the period.

ILLUSTRATION 18-4

Three major steps in preparing the statement of cash flows

Preparing the statement of cash flows from these data sources involves three major steps, explained in Illustration 18-4.

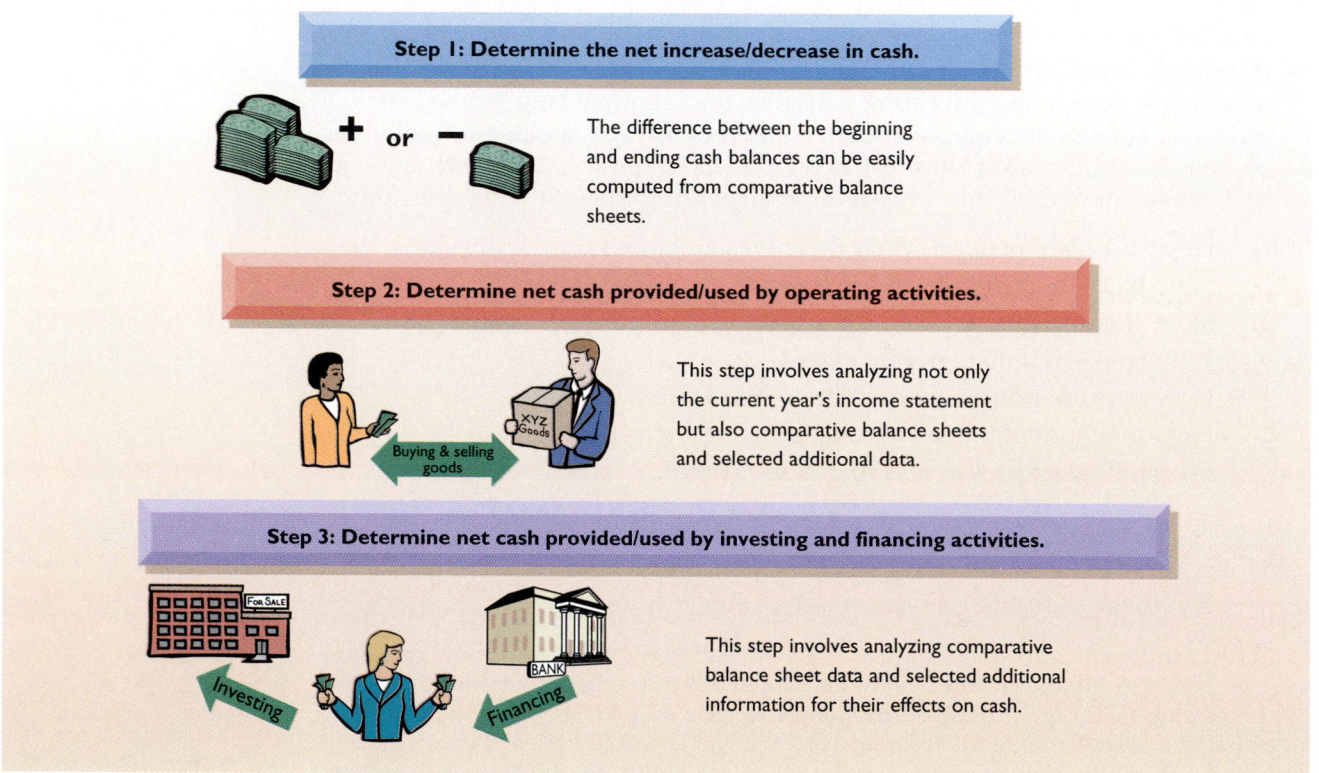

Step 1: Determine the net increase/decrease in cash.

The difference between the beginning and ending cash balances can be easily computed from comparative balance sheets.

Step 2: Determine net cash provided/used by operating activities.

This step involves analyzing not only the current year's income statement but also comparative balance sheets and selected additional data.

Buying & selling goods

Step 3: Determine net cash provided/used by investing and financing activities.

This step involves analyzing comparative balance sheet data and selected additional information for their effects on cash.

Investing   Financing

Indirect and Direct Methods

In order to perform step 2, the operating activities section of the statement of cash flows **must be converted from an accrual basis to a cash basis**. This conversion may be done by either of two methods: (1) the indirect method or (2) the direct method. **Both methods arrive at the same total amount** for "Net cash provided by operating activities," but they differ in disclosing the items that comprise the total amount.

The indirect method is used extensively in practice, as shown in the nearby chart.[2] Companies (98%) favor the indirect method for two reasons: (1) it is easier to prepare, and (2) it focuses on the differences between net income and net cash flow from operating activities.

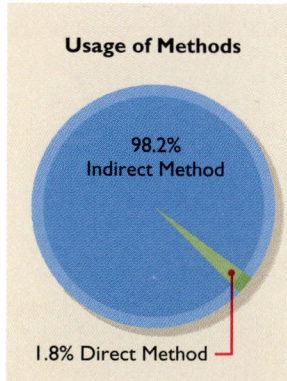

Usage of Methods

98.2% Indirect Method

1.8% Direct Method

---

[2]*Accounting Trends and Techniques* survey of 600 companies indicated that 589 use the indirect method and 11 use the direct method.

Others, however, favor the direct method. The direct method shows operating cash receipts and payments. Thus, it is more consistent with the objective of a statement of cash flows. The FASB has expressed a preference for the direct method, but allows the use of either method. However, when the direct method is used, the net cash flow from operating activities as computed using the indirect method must also be reported in a separate schedule.

INTERNATIONAL NOTE

International accounting requirements are quite similar in most respects with regard to the cash flow statement. Some interesting exceptions: In Japan, operating and investing activities are combined; in Australia, the direct method is mandatory; in Spain, the indirect method is mandatory. Also, in a number of European and Scandinavian countries a cash flow statement is not required at all, although in practice most publicly traded firms provide one.

BEFORE YOU GO ON . . .

Review It

1. What is the primary purpose of a statement of cash flows?
2. What are the major classifications of cash flows on the statement of cash flows?
3. What are the three major steps in the preparation of a statement of cash flows?
4. Why is the statement of cash flows useful? What key information does it convey?

Do It

During its first week of existence, Plano Molding Company had the following transactions:

1. Issued 100,000 shares of $5 par value common stock for $800,000 cash.
2. Borrowed $200,000 from Sandwich State Bank, signing a 5-year note bearing 8% interest.
3. Purchased two semi-trailer trucks for $170,000 cash.
4. Paid employees $12,000 for salaries and wages.
5. Collected $20,000 cash for services rendered.

Classify by type of cash flow activity each of these transactions.

Reasoning: All cash flows are classified into three types of activities for purposes of reporting cash inflows and outflows: operating activities, investing activities, and financing activities. Operating activities include the cash effects of transactions that create revenues and expenses and thus enter into the determination of net income. Investing activities include (a) acquiring and disposing of investments and productive long-lived assets, and (b) lending money and collecting the loans. Financing activities include (a) obtaining cash from issuing debt and repaying the amounts borrowed, and (b) obtaining cash from stockholders and providing them with a return on their investment.

Solution:
1. Financing activity.
2. Financing activity.
3. Investing activity.
4. Operating activity.
5. Operating activity.

Related exercise material: BE18–3, BE18–5, E18–1, and E18–6.

THE
NAVIGATOR

On the following pages, in two separate sections, we describe the use of the two methods. Section 1 illustrates the indirect method, and Section 2 illustrates the direct method. These sections are independent of each other; *only one or the other* need be covered in order to understand and prepare the statement of cash flows. When you have finished the section assigned by your instructor, turn to the next topic, on page 786—"Analysis of the Statement of Cash Flows."

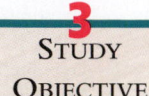

SECTION 1   STATEMENT OF CASH FLOWS— INDIRECT METHOD

3

STUDY OBJECTIVE

Prepare a statement of cash flows using the indirect method.

To explain and illustrate the indirect method, we will use the transactions of the Computer Services Company for two years—1999 and 2000. Annual statements of cash flows will be prepared. Basic transactions will be used in the first year with additional transactions added in the second year.

FIRST YEAR OF OPERATIONS—1999

Computer Services Company started on January 1, 1999, when it issued 50,000 shares of $1.00 par value common stock for $50,000 cash. The company rented its office space and furniture and performed consulting services throughout the first year. The comparative balance sheets at the beginning and end of 1999, showing increases or decreases, appear in Illustration 18-5.

ILLUSTRATION 18-5

Comparative balance sheet, 1999, with increases and decreases

HELPFUL HINT

Note that although each of the balance sheet items of Computer Services increased, their individual effects are not the same. Some of these increases are cash inflows, and some are cash outflows.

COMPUTER SERVICES COMPANY
Comparative Balance Sheet

Assets	Dec. 31, 1999	Jan. 1, 1999	Change Increase/Decrease
Cash	$34,000	$ –0–	$34,000 Increase
Accounts receivable	30,000	–0–	30,000 Increase
Equipment	10,000	–0–	10,000 Increase
Total	$74,000	$ –0–	
Liabilities and Stockholders' Equity			
Accounts payable	$ 4,000	$ –0–	$ 4,000 Increase
Common stock	50,000	–0–	50,000 Increase
Retained earnings	20,000	–0–	20,000 Increase
Total	$74,000	$ –0–	

The income statement and additional information for Computer Services Company are shown in Illustration 18-6.

ILLUSTRATION 18-6

Income statement and additional information, 1999

COMPUTER SERVICES COMPANY
Income Statement
For the Year Ended December 31, 1999

Revenues	$85,000
Operating expenses	40,000
Income before income taxes	45,000
Income tax expense	10,000
Net income	$35,000

Additional information:
(a) A dividend of $15,000 was declared and paid during the year.
(b) The equipment was purchased at the end of 1999. No depreciation was taken in 1999.

Determining the Net Increase/Decrease in Cash (Step 1)

To prepare a statement of cash flows, the first step is **determining the net increase or decrease in cash**. This is a simple computation. For example, Computer Services Company had no cash on hand at the beginning of 1999, but had $34,000 on hand at the end of 1999. Thus, the change in cash for 1999 was an increase of $34,000.

Determining Net Cash Provided/Used by Operating Activities (Step 2)

To determine net cash provided by operating activities under the indirect method, **net income is adjusted for items that did not affect cash**. A useful starting point in determining net cash provided by operating activities is to understand **why** net income must be converted. Under generally accepted accounting principles, most companies use the accrual basis of accounting. As you have learned, this basis requires that revenue be recorded when earned and that expenses be recorded when incurred. Earned revenues may include credit sales that have not been collected in cash and expenses incurred that may not have been paid in cash. Thus, under the accrual basis of accounting, net income does not indicate the net cash provided by operating activities. Therefore, under the indirect method, net income must be adjusted to convert certain items to the cash basis.

The **indirect method** (or reconciliation method) starts with net income and converts it to net cash provided by operating activities. In other words, **the indirect method adjusts net income for items that affected reported net income but did not affect cash**, as shown in Illustration 18-7. That is, noncash charges in the income statement are added back to net income and noncash credits are deducted to compute net cash provided by operating activities. A useful starting point in identifying the adjustments to net income is the current asset and current liability accounts other than cash. Those accounts—receivables, payables, prepayments, and inventories—should be analyzed for their effects on cash.

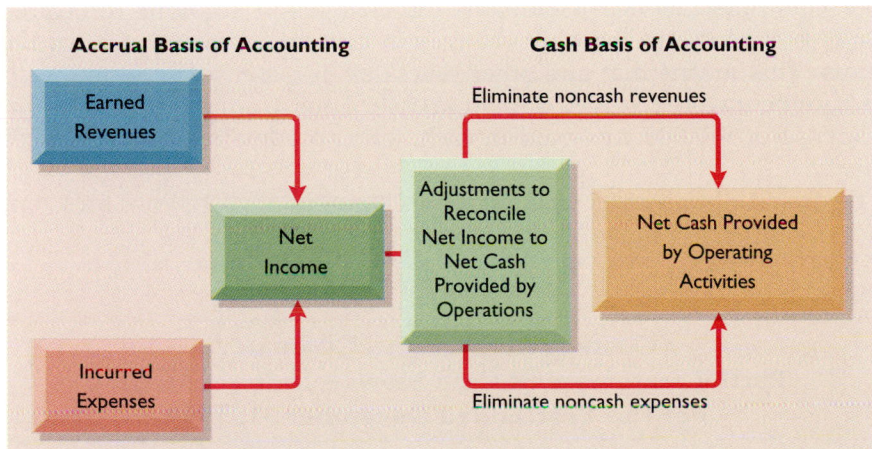

ILLUSTRATION 18-7

Net income versus net cash provided by operating activities

Increase in Accounts Receivable. When accounts receivable increase during the year, revenues on an accrual basis are higher than revenues on a cash basis. In other words, operations of the period led to increased revenues, **but not all of these revenues resulted in an increase in cash**; some of the increase in revenues resulted in an increase in accounts receivable.

Illustration 18-8 shows that Computer Services Company had $85,000 in revenues, but it collected only $55,000 in cash. Therefore, to convert net income to net cash provided by operating activities, the increase of $30,000 in accounts receivable must be deducted from net income.

ILLUSTRATION 18-8

Analysis of accounts receivable

Accounts Receivable				
1/1/99	Balance	–0–	Receipts from customers	55,000
	Revenues	**85,000**		
12/31/99	Balance	30,000		

Increase in Accounts Payable. In the first year, operating expenses incurred on account were credited to Accounts Payable. When accounts payable increase during the year, operating expenses on an accrual basis are higher than they are on a cash basis. For Computer Services, operating expenses reported in the income statement were $40,000. However, since Accounts Payable increased $4,000, only $36,000 ($40,000 − $4,000) of the expenses were paid in cash. To adjust net income to net cash provided by operating activities, the increase of $4,000 in accounts payable must be added to net income.

A T-account analysis also indicates that payments to creditors are less than operating expenses.

ILLUSTRATION 18-9

Analysis of accounts payable

Accounts Payable				
Payments to creditors	**36,000**	1/1/99	Balances	–0–
			Operating expenses	**40,000**
		12/31/99	Balance	4,000

For Computer Services Company, the changes in accounts receivable and accounts payable were the only changes in current asset and current liability accounts. This means that any other revenues or expenses reported in the income statement were received or paid in cash. Thus, Computer Services' income tax expense of $10,000 was paid in cash, and no adjustment of net income is necessary.

The operating activities section of the statement of cash flows for Computer Services Company is shown in Illustration 18-10.

ILLUSTRATION 18-10

Presentation of net cash provided by operating activities, 1999—indirect method

COMPUTER SERVICES COMPANY		
Partial Statement of Cash Flows—Indirect Method		
For the Year Ended December 31, 1999		
Cash flows from operating activities		
Net income		$35,000
Adjustments to reconcile net income to net cash provided by operating activities:		
Increase in accounts receivable	$(30,000)	
Increase in accounts payable	4,000	(26,000)
Net cash provided by operating activities		**$ 9,000**

Determining Net Cash Provided/Used by Investing and Financing Activities (Step 3)

The third and final step in preparing the statement of cash flows begins with a study of the balance sheet to determine changes in noncurrent accounts. The changes in each noncurrent account are then analyzed using selected transaction data to determine the effect, if any, the changes had on cash.

In Computer Services Company, the three noncurrent accounts are Equipment, Common Stock, and Retained Earnings, and all three have increased during the year. What caused these increases? No transaction data are given for the increases in Equipment of $10,000 and Common Stock of $50,000. In solving your homework, you can conclude that **any unexplained differences in noncurrent accounts involve cash**. Thus, the increase in equipment is assumed to be a purchase of equipment for $10,000 cash. This purchase is reported as a cash outflow in the investing activities section. The increase in common stock is assumed to result from the issuance of common stock for $50,000 cash. It is reported as an inflow of cash in the financing activities section of the statement of cash flows.

The reasons for the net increase of $20,000 in the Retained Earnings account are determined by analysis. First, net income increased retained earnings by $35,000. Second, the additional information provided below the income statement in Illustration 18-6 indicates that a cash dividend of $15,000 was declared and paid. The $35,000 increase due to net income is reported in the operating activities section. The cash dividend paid is reported in the financing activities section.

This analysis can also be made directly from the Retained Earnings account in the ledger of Computer Services Company as shown in Illustration 18-11:

Retained Earnings			
12/31/99 Cash dividend	15,000	1/1/99 Balance	–0–
		12/31/99 Net income	35,000
		12/31/99 Balance	20,000

ILLUSTRATION 18-11

Analysis of retained earnings

The $20,000 increase in Retained Earnings in 1999 is a **net** change. When a net change in a noncurrent balance sheet account has occurred during the year, it generally is necessary to report the causes of the net change separately in the statement of cash flows.

Statement of Cash Flows—1999

Having completed the three steps above, we can prepare the statement of cash flows. The statement starts with the operating activities section, followed by the investing activities section, and then the financing activities section. The 1999 statement of cash flows for Computer Services is shown in Illustration 18-12.

Computer Services' statement of cash flows for 1999 shows that operating activities **provided** $9,000 cash; investing activities **used** $10,000 cash; and financing activities **provided** $35,000 cash. The increase in cash of $34,000 reported in the statement of cash flows agrees with the increase of $34,000 shown as the change in the cash account in the comparative balance sheet.

ILLUSTRATION 18-12

*Statement of cash flows,
1999—indirect method*

COMPUTER SERVICES COMPANY
Statement of Cash Flows—Indirect Method
For the Year Ended December 31, 1999

Cash flows from operating activities		
Net income		$35,000
Adjustments to reconcile net income to net cash provided by operating activities:		
Increase in accounts receivable	$(30,000)	
Increase in accounts payable	4,000	(26,000)
Net cash provided by operating activities		9,000
Cash flows from investing activities		
Purchase of equipment	(10,000)	
Net cash used by investing activities		(10,000)
Cash flows from financing activities		
Issuance of common stock	50,000	
Payment of cash dividends	(15,000)	
Net cash provided by financing activities		35,000
Net increase in cash		34,000
Cash at beginning of period		–0–
Cash at end of period		$34,000

SECOND YEAR OF OPERATIONS—2000

Presented in Illustrations 18-13 and 18-14 is information related to the second year of operations for Computer Services Company.

ILLUSTRATION 18-13

*Comparative balance sheet,
2000, with increases and
decreases*

COMPUTER SERVICES COMPANY
Comparative Balance Sheet
December 31

Assets	2000	1999	Change Increase/Decrease
Cash	$ 56,000	$34,000	$ 22,000 Increase
Accounts receivable	20,000	30,000	10,000 Decrease
Prepaid expenses	4,000	–0–	4,000 Increase
Land	130,000	–0–	130,000 Increase
Building	160,000	–0–	160,000 Increase
Accumulated depreciation—building	(11,000)	–0–	11,000 Increase
Equipment	27,000	10,000	17,000 Increase
Accumulated depreciation—equipment	(3,000)	–0–	3,000 Increase
Total	$383,000	$74,000	
Liabilities and Stockholders' Equity			
Accounts payable	$ 59,000	$ 4,000	$ 55,000 Increase
Bonds payable	130,000	–0–	130,000 Increase
Common stock	50,000	50,000	–0–
Retained earnings	144,000	20,000	124,000 Increase
Total	$383,000	$74,000	

COMPUTER SERVICES COMPANY		
Income Statement		
For the Year Ended December 31, 2000		
Revenues		$507,000
Operating expenses (excluding depreciation)	$261,000	
Depreciation expense	15,000	
Loss on sale of equipment	3,000	279,000
Income from operations		228,000
Income tax expense		89,000
Net income		$139,000

Additional information:

(a) In 2000, the company declared and paid a $15,000 cash dividend.

(b) The company obtained land through the issuance of $130,000 of long-term bonds.

(c) A building costing $160,000 was purchased for cash; equipment costing $25,000 was also purchased for cash.

(d) During 2000, the company sold equipment with a book value of $7,000 (cost $8,000, less accumulated depreciation $1,000) for $4,000 cash.

ILLUSTRATION 18-14

Income statement and additional information, 2000

Determining the Net Increase/Decrease in Cash (Step 1)

To prepare a statement of cash flows from this information, the first step is to **determine the net increase or decrease in cash**. As indicated from the information presented, cash increased $22,000 ($56,000 − $34,000).

Determining Net Cash Provided/Used by Operating Activities (Step 2)

As in step 2 in 1999, net income on an accrual basis must be adjusted to arrive at net cash provided/used by operating activities. Explanations for the adjustments to net income for Computer Services in 2000 are as follows:

Decrease in Accounts Receivable.   Accounts receivable decreases during the period because cash receipts are higher than revenues reported on an accrual basis. To adjust net income to net cash provided by operating activities, the decrease of $10,000 in accounts receivable must be added to net income.

Increase in Prepaid Expenses.   Prepaid expenses increase during a period because cash paid for expenses is higher than expenses reported on an accrual basis. Cash payments have been made in the current period, but expenses (as charges to the income statement) have been deferred to future periods. To adjust net income to net cash provided by operating activities, the increase of $4,000 in prepaid expenses must be deducted from net income. An increase in prepaid expenses results in a decrease in cash during the period.

Increase in Accounts Payable.   Like the increase in 1999, the 2000 increase of $55,000 in accounts payable must be added to net income to convert to net cash provided by operating activities.

Depreciation Expense.   During 2000, Computer Services Company reported depreciation expense of $15,000. Of this amount, $11,000 related to the building and $4,000 to the equipment. These two amounts were determined by analyzing the accumulated depreciation accounts.

HELPFUL HINT
Decrease in accounts receivable indicates that cash collections were greater than sales. **Increase in accounts receivable** indicates that sales were greater than cash collections. **Increase in prepaid expenses** indicates that the amount paid for the prepayments exceeded the amount that was recorded as an expense. **Decrease in prepaid expenses** indicates that the amount recorded as an expense exceeded the amount of cash paid for the prepayments. **Increase in accounts payable** indicates that expenses incurred exceed the cash paid for expenses that period.

Increase in Accumulated Depreciation—Building.   As shown in Illustration 18-13, accumulated depreciation increased $11,000. This change represents the depreciation expense on the building for the year. **Because depreciation expense is a noncash charge, it is added back to net income** in order to arrive at net cash provided by operating activities.

Increase in Accumulated Depreciation—Equipment.   The increase in the Accumulated Depreciation—Equipment account was $3,000. This amount does not represent depreciation expense for the year because the additional information indicates that this account was decreased (debited $1,000) as a result of the sale of some equipment. Thus depreciation expense for 2000 was $4,000 ($3,000 + $1,000). This amount is added to net income to determine net cash provided by operating activities. The T-account below provides information about the changes that occurred in this account in 2000.

ILLUSTRATION 18-15

Analysis of accumulated depreciation—equipment

Accumulated Depreciation—Equipment			
Accumulated depreciation on equipment sold	1,000	1/1/00 Balance	–0–
		Depreciation expense	4,000
		12/31/00 Balance	3,000

Depreciation expense on the building of $11,000 plus depreciation expense on the equipment of $4,000 equals the depreciation expense of $15,000 reported on the income statement.

Other charges to expense that do not require the use of cash, such as the amortization of intangible assets and depletion expense, are treated in the same manner as depreciation. Depreciation and similar noncash charges are frequently listed in the statement of cash flows as the first adjustments to net income.

Loss on Sale of Equipment.   On the income statement, Computer Services Company reported a $3,000 loss on the sale of equipment (book value $7,000, less cash proceeds $4,000). The loss reduced net income but **did not reduce cash**. Thus the loss is **added to net income** in determining net cash provided by operating activities.[3]

As a result of the previous adjustments, net cash provided by operating activities is $218,000 as computed in Illustration 18-16.

Determining Net Cash Provided/Used by Investing and Financing Activities (Step 3)

After finding net cash provided by operating activities, the next step involves analyzing the remaining changes in balance sheet accounts to determine net cash provided (used) by investing and financing activities.

---

[3]If a gain on sale occurs, a different situation results. To allow a gain to flow through to net cash provided by operating activities would be double-counting the gain—once in net income and again in the investing activities section as part of the cash proceeds from sale. As a result, a gain is deducted from net income in reporting net cash provided by operating activities.

ILLUSTRATION 18-16
Presentation of net cash provided by operating activities, 2000—indirect method

COMPUTER SERVICES COMPANY
Partial Statement of Cash Flows—Indirect Method
For the Year Ended December 31, 2000

Cash flows from operating activities		
Net income		$139,000
Adjustments to reconcile net income to net cash provided		
by operating activities:		
Depreciation expense	$15,000	
Loss on sale of equipment	3,000	
Decrease in accounts receivable	10,000	
Increase in prepaid expenses	(4,000)	
Increase in accounts payable	55,000	79,000
Net cash provided by operating activities		$218,000

Increase in Land.   As indicated from the change in the Land account, land of $130,000 was purchased through the issuance of long-term bonds. Although the issuance of bonds payable for land has no effect on cash, it is a significant noncash investing and financing activity that merits disclosure. As indicated earlier, these activities are disclosed in a separate schedule at the bottom of the statement of cash flows.

Increase in Building.   As indicated in the additional data, an office building was acquired using cash of $160,000. This transaction is a cash outflow reported in the investing section.

Increase in Equipment.   The Equipment account increased $17,000. Based on the additional information, this was a net increase that resulted from two transactions: (1) a purchase of equipment of $25,000 and (2) the sale for $4,000 of equipment costing $8,000. These transactions are classified as investing activities, and each transaction should be reported separately. Thus the purchase of equipment should be reported as an outflow of cash for $25,000 and the sale should be reported as an inflow of cash for $4,000. The T-account below shows the reasons for the change in this account during the year.

ILLUSTRATION 18-17
Analysis of equipment

Equipment

1/1/00 Balance	10,000	Cost of equipment sold	8,000
Purchase of equipment	25,000		
12/31/00 Balance	27,000		

The following entry shows the details of the equipment sale transactions:

Cash	4,000	
Accumulated Depreciation	1,000	
Loss on Sale of Equipment	3,000	
Equipment		8,000

A	=	L	+	OE
+4,000				−3,000
+1,000				
−8,000				

Increase in Bonds Payable.   The Bonds Payable account increased $130,000. As shown in the additional information, land was acquired from the issuance of these bonds. As indicated earlier, this noncash transaction is reported in a separate schedule at the bottom of the statement.

Increase in Retained Earnings.   Retained earnings increased $124,000 during the year. This increase can be explained by two factors: (1) net income of $139,000 increased retained earnings, and (2) dividends of $15,000 decreased retained earnings. Net income is adjusted to net cash provided by operating activities in the operating activities section. Payment of the dividends is a **cash outflow that is reported as a financing activity**.

Statement of Cash Flows—2000

Combining the previous items, we obtain a statement of cash flows for 2000 for Computer Services Company as presented in Illustration 18-18.

COMPUTER SERVICES COMPANY
Statement of Cash Flows—Indirect Method
For the Year Ended December 31, 2000

Cash flows from operating activities		
Net income		$139,000
Adjustments to reconcile net income to net cash		
provided by operating activities:		
Depreciation expense	$ 15,000	
Loss on sale of equipment	3,000	
Decrease in accounts receivable	10,000	
Increase in prepaid expenses	(4,000)	
Increase in accounts payable	55,000	79,000
Net cash provided by operating activities		218,000
Cash flows from investing activities		
Purchase of building	$(160,000)	
Purchase of equipment	(25,000)	
Sale of equipment	4,000	
Net cash used by investing activities		(181,000)
Cash flows from financing activities		
Payment of cash dividends	(15,000)	
Net cash used by financing activities		(15,000)
Net increase in cash		22,000
Cash at beginning of period		34,000
Cash at end of period		$ 56,000
Noncash investing and financing activities		
Issuance of bonds payable to purchase land		$130,000

Summary of Conversion to Net Cash Provided by Operating Activities—Indirect Method

As shown in the previous illustrations, the statement of cash flows prepared by the indirect method starts with net income and adds (or deducts) items not affecting cash to arrive at net cash provided by operating activities. The additions and deductions consist of (1) changes in specific current assets and current liabilities and (2) noncash charges reported in the income statement. A summary of the adjustments for current assets and current liabilities is provided in Illustration 18-19.

Current Assets and Current Liabilities	Adjustments to Convert Net Income to Net Cash Provided by Operating Activities	
	Add to Net Income	Deduct from Net Income
Accounts receivable	Decrease	Increase
Inventory	Decrease	Increase
Prepaid expenses	Decrease	Increase
Accounts payable	Increase	Decrease
Accrued expenses payable	Increase	Decrease

ILLUSTRATION 18-19

Adjustments for current assets and current liabilities

HELPFUL HINT
1. Increase in a current asset is deducted from net income.
2. Decrease in a current asset is added to net income.
3. Increase in a current liability is added to net income.
4. Decrease in a current liability is deducted from net income.

Adjustments for the noncash charges reported in the income statement are made as shown in Illustration 18-20.

Noncash Charges	Adjustments to Convert Net Income to Net Cash Provided by Operating Activities
Depreciation expense	Add
Patent amortization expense	Add
Depletion expense	Add
Loss on sale of asset	Add

ILLUSTRATION 18-20

Adjustments for noncash charges

BEFORE YOU GO ON . . .

Review It

1. What is the format of the operating activities section of the statement of cash flows using the indirect method?
2. Where is depreciation expense shown on a statement of cash flows using the indirect method?
3. Where are significant noncash investing and financing activities shown in a statement of cash flows? Give some examples.
4. Which method of computing net cash provided by operating activities does Kellogg use? What single item provided the largest amount of cash inflow for Kellogg in 1997? The answers to these questions are provided on page 816.

Do It

Presented below is information related to Reynolds Company. Use it to prepare a statement of cash flows using the indirect method.

REYNOLDS COMPANY
Comparative Balance Sheet
December 31

Assets	2000	1999	Change Increase/Decrease
Cash	$ 54,000	$ 37,000	$ 17,000 Increase
Accounts receivable	68,000	26,000	42,000 Increase
Inventories	54,000	–0–	54,000 Increase
Prepaid expenses	4,000	6,000	2,000 Decrease
Land	45,000	70,000	25,000 Decrease
Buildings	200,000	200,000	–0–
Accumulated depreciation—buildings	(21,000)	(11,000)	10,000 Increase
Equipment	193,000	68,000	125,000 Increase
Accumulated depreciation—equipment	(28,000)	(10,000)	18,000 Increase
Totals	$569,000	$386,000	
Liabilities and Stockholders' Equity			
Accounts payable	$ 23,000	$ 40,000	$ 17,000 Decrease
Accrued expenses payable	10,000	–0–	10,000 Increase
Bonds payable	110,000	150,000	40,000 Decrease
Common stock ($1 par)	220,000	60,000	160,000 Increase
Retained earnings	206,000	136,000	70,000 Increase
Totals	$569,000	$386,000	

REYNOLDS COMPANY
Income Statement
For the Year Ended December 31, 2000

Revenues		$890,000
Cost of goods sold	$465,000	
Operating expenses	221,000	
Interest expense	12,000	
Loss on sale of equipment	2,000	700,000
Income from operations		190,000
Income tax expense		65,000
Net income		$125,000

Additional information:
(a) Operating expenses include depreciation expense of $33,000 and charges from prepaid expenses of $2,000.
(b) Land was sold at its book value for cash.
(c) Cash dividends of $55,000 were declared and paid in 2000.
(d) Interest expense of $12,000 was paid in cash.
(e) Equipment with a cost of $166,000 was purchased for cash. Equipment with a cost of $41,000 and a book value of $36,000 was sold for $34,000 cash.
(f) Bonds of $10,000 were redeemed at their book value for cash; bonds of $30,000 were converted into common stock.
(g) Common stock ($1 par) of $130,000 was issued for cash.
(h) Accounts payable pertain to merchandise suppliers.

HELPFUL HINT
You may wish to insert the beginning and ending cash balances and the increase/decrease in cash necessitated by these balances immediately into the statement of cash flows. The net increase/decrease is the target amount. The net cash flows from the three classes of activities must equal the target amount.

Reasoning: As you have learned, the balance sheet and the income statement are prepared from an adjusted trial balance of the general ledger. The statement of cash flows is prepared from an analysis of the content and changes in the balance sheet and the income statement.

Solution:

REYNOLDS COMPANY
Statement of Cash Flows—Indirect Method
For the Year Ended December 31, 2000

Cash flows from operating activities		
Net income		$125,000
Adjustments to reconcile net income to net cash provided by operating activities:		
Depreciation expense	$ 33,000	
Increase in accounts receivable	(42,000)	
Increase in inventories	(54,000)	
Decrease in prepaid expenses	2,000	
Decrease in accounts payable	(17,000)	
Increase in accrued expenses payable	10,000	
Loss on sale of equipment	2,000	(66,000)
Net cash provided by operating activities		59,000
Cash flows from investing activities		
Sale of land	25,000	
Sale of equipment	34,000	
Purchase of equipment	(166,000)	
Net cash used by investing activities		(107,000)
Cash flows from financing activities		
Redemption of bonds	(10,000)	
Sale of common stock	130,000	
Payment of dividends	(55,000)	
Net cash provided by financing activities		65,000
Net increase in cash		17,000
Cash at beginning of period		37,000
Cash at end of period		$ 54,000
Noncash investing and financing activities		
Conversion of bonds into common stock		$ 30,000

Related exercise material: BE18–1, BE18–2, BE18–4, E18–2, E18–3, E18–4, and E18–5.

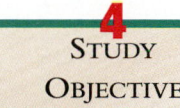

THE NAVIGATOR

Note: This concludes Section 1 on preparation of the statement of cash flows using the indirect method. Unless your instructor assigns Section 2, you should turn to the concluding section of the chapter, "Analysis of the Statement of Cash Flows," on page 786.

SECTION 2   STATEMENT OF CASH FLOWS— DIRECT METHOD

To explain and illustrate the direct method, we will use the transactions of Juarez Company for two years, 1999 and 2000. Annual statements of cash flow will be prepared. Basic transactions will be used in the first year with additional transactions added in the second year.

4
STUDY OBJECTIVE

Prepare a statement of cash flows using the direct method.

FIRST YEAR OF OPERATIONS—1999

Juarez Company began business on January 1, 1999, when it issued 300,000 shares of $1 par value common stock for $300,000 cash. The company rented office and sales space along with equipment. The comparative balance sheet at the beginning and end of 1999 and the changes in each account are shown in Illustration 18-21. The income statement and additional information for Juarez Company are shown in Illustration 18-22.

ILLUSTRATION 18-21

Comparative balance sheet, 1999, with increases and decreases

JUAREZ COMPANY
Comparative Balance Sheet

Assets	Dec. 31, 1999	Jan. 1, 1999	Change Increase/Decrease
Cash	$159,000	$–0–	$159,000 Increase
Accounts receivable	15,000	–0–	15,000 Increase
Inventory	160,000	–0–	160,000 Increase
Prepaid expenses	8,000	–0–	8,000 Increase
Land	80,000	–0–	80,000 Increase
Total	$422,000	$–0–	
Liabilities and Stockholders' Equity			
Accounts payable	$ 60,000	$–0–	$ 60,000 Increase
Accrued expenses payable	20,000	–0–	20,000 Increase
Common stock	300,000	–0–	300,000 Increase
Retained earnings	42,000	–0–	42,000 Increase
Total	$422,000	$–0–	

ILLUSTRATION 18-22

Income statement and additional information, 1999

JUAREZ COMPANY
Income Statement
For the Year Ended December 31, 1999

Revenues	$780,000
Cost of goods sold	450,000
Gross profit	330,000
Operating expenses	170,000
Income before income taxes	160,000
Income tax expense	48,000
Net income	$112,000

Additional information:
(a) Dividends of $70,000 were declared and paid in cash.
(b) The accounts payable increase resulted from the purchase of merchandise.

The three steps cited on page 760 for preparing the statement of cash flows are used in the direct method.

Determining the Net Increase/Decrease in Cash (Step 1)

The comparative balance sheet for Juarez Company shows a zero cash balance at January 1, 1999, and a cash balance of $159,000 at December 31, 1999. Thus, the change in cash for 1999 was a net increase of $159,000.

Determining Net Cash Provided/Used by Operating Activities (Step 2)

Under the direct method, net cash provided by operating activities is computed by **adjusting each item in the income statement** from the accrual basis to the cash basis. To simplify and condense the operating activities section, **only major classes of operating cash receipts and cash payments are reported**. The difference between these major classes of cash receipts and cash payments is the net cash provided by operating activities as shown in Illustration 18-23.

ILLUSTRATION 18-23

Major classes of cash receipts and payments

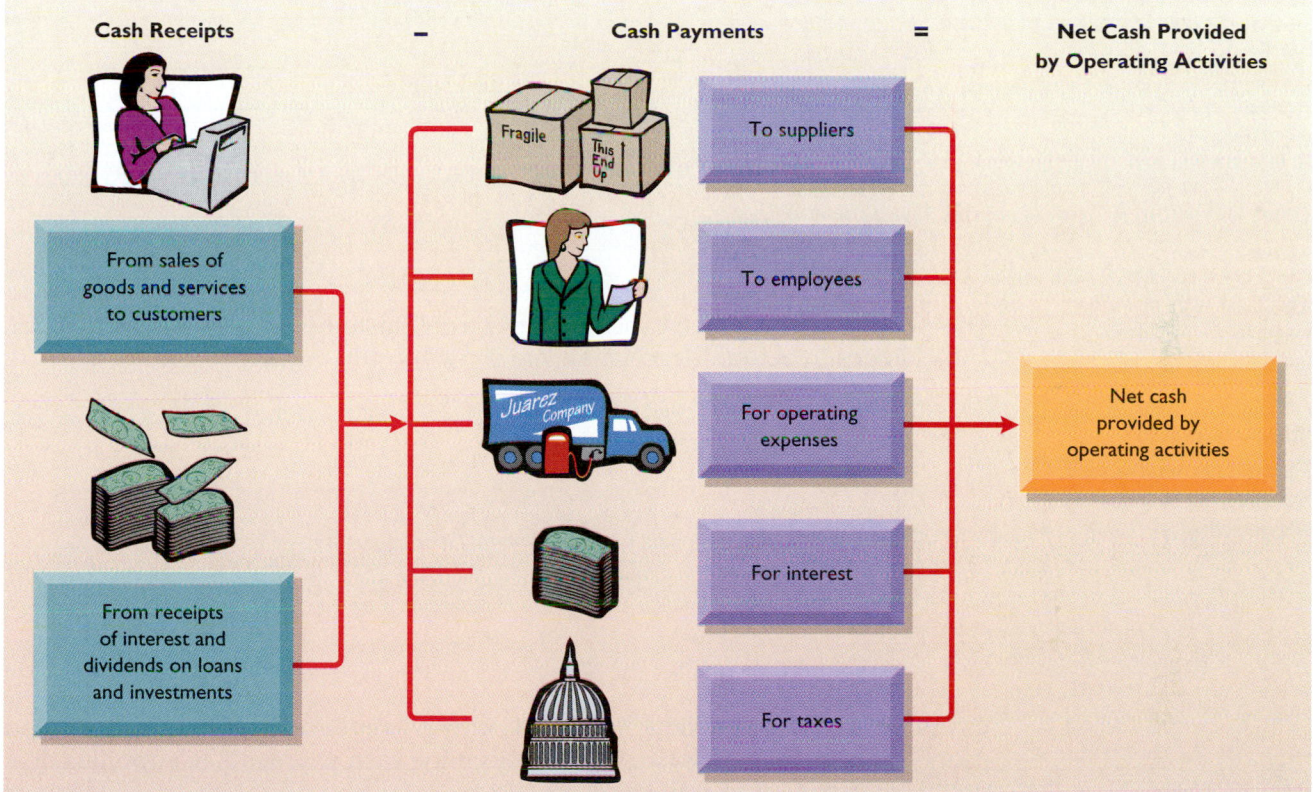

An efficient way to apply the direct method is to analyze the revenues and expenses reported in the income statement in the order in which they are listed. Cash receipts and cash payments related to these revenues and expenses are then determined. The direct method adjustments for Juarez Company in 1999 to determine net cash provided by operating activities are presented in the following sections.

Cash Receipts from Customers.   The income statement for Juarez Company reported revenues from customers of $780,000. To determine cash receipts from customers, it is necessary to consider the change in accounts receivable during the year. When accounts receivable increase during the year, revenues on an accrual basis are higher than cash receipts from customers. In other words, operations led to increased revenues, but not all of these revenues resulted in cash receipts. To determine the amount of cash receipts, the increase in accounts receivable is deducted from sales revenues. Conversely, a decrease in accounts receivable is added to sales revenues, because cash receipts from customers then exceed sales revenues.

For Juarez Company, accounts receivable increased $15,000. Thus, cash receipts from customers were $765,000, computed as follows:

ILLUSTRATION 18-24

Computation of cash receipts from customers

Revenues from sales	$780,000
Deduct: Increase in accounts receivable	15,000
Cash receipts from customers	**$765,000**

Cash receipts from customers may also be determined from an analysis of the Accounts Receivable account as shown in Illustration 18-25.

ILLUSTRATION 18-25

Analysis of accounts receivable

Accounts Receivable				
1/1/99	Balance	–0–	**Receipts from customers**	**765,000**
	Revenues from sales	780,000		
12/31/99	Balance	15,000		

HELPFUL HINT
The T-account shows that revenue less increase in receivables equals cash receipts.

The relationships between cash receipts from customers, revenues from sales, and changes in accounts receivable are shown in Illustration 18-26.

ILLUSTRATION 18-26

Formula to compute cash receipts from customers— direct method

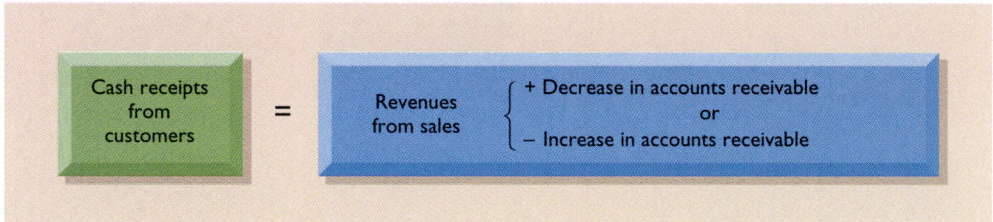

Cash Payments to Suppliers. Juarez Company reported cost of goods sold on its income statement of $450,000. To determine cash payments to suppliers, it is first necessary to find purchases for the year. To find purchases, cost of goods sold is adjusted for the change in inventory. When inventory increases during the year, it means that purchases this year exceed cost of goods sold. As a result, the increase in inventory is added to cost of goods sold to arrive at purchases.

In 1999, Juarez Company's inventory increased $160,000. Purchases, therefore, are computed as follows:

ILLUSTRATION 18-27

Computation of purchases

Cost of goods sold	$450,000
Add: Increase in inventory	160,000
Purchases	**$610,000**

After purchases are computed, cash payments to suppliers are determined by adjusting purchases for the change in accounts payable. When accounts payable increase during the year, purchases on an accrual basis are higher than they are on a cash basis. As a result, an increase in accounts payable is deducted from purchases to arrive at cash payments to suppliers. Conversely, a decrease in accounts payable is added to purchases because cash payments to suppliers exceed purchases. Cash payments to suppliers were $550,000, computed as follows:

Purchases	$610,000	
Deduct: Increase in accounts payable	60,000	
Cash payments to suppliers	**$550,000**	

ILLUSTRATION 18-28

Computation of cash payments to suppliers

Cash payments to suppliers may also be determined from an analysis of the Accounts Payable account as shown in Illustration 18-29.

Accounts Payable

Payments to suppliers	550,000	1/1/99 Balance	–0–	
		Purchases	610,000	
		12/31/99 Balance	60,000	

ILLUSTRATION 18-29

Analysis of accounts payable

> **HELPFUL HINT**
> The T-account shows that purchases less increase in accounts payable equals payments to suppliers.

The relationship between cash payments to suppliers, cost of goods sold, changes in inventory, and changes in accounts payable is shown in the following formula:

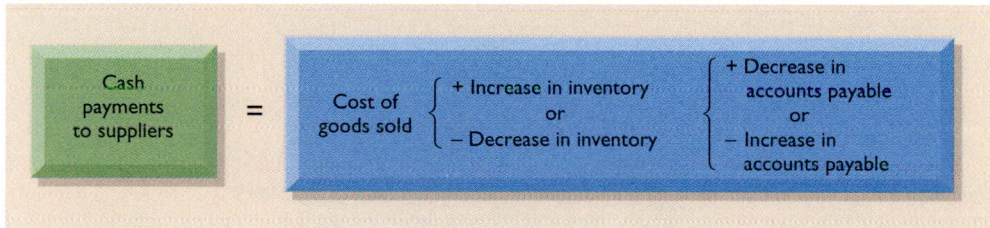

Cash Payments for Operating Expenses. Operating expenses of $170,000 were reported on Juarez's income statement. To determine the cash paid for operating expenses, this amount must be adjusted for any changes in prepaid expenses and accrued expenses payable. For example, when prepaid expenses increased $8,000 during the year, cash paid for operating expenses was $8,000 higher than operating expenses reported on the income statement. To convert operating expenses to cash payments for operating expenses, the increase of $8,000 must be added to operating expenses. Conversely, if prepaid expenses decrease during the year, the decrease must be deducted from operating expenses.

Operating expenses must also be adjusted for changes in accrued expenses payable. When accrued expenses payable increase during the year, operating expenses on an accrual basis are higher than they are in a cash basis. As a result, an increase in accrued expenses payable is deducted from operating expenses to arrive at cash payments for operating expenses. Conversely, a decrease in accrued expenses payable is added to operating expenses because cash payments exceed operating expenses.

Juarez Company's cash payments for operating expenses were $158,000, computed as follows:

> **HELPFUL HINT**
> **Decrease in accounts receivable** indicates that cash collections were greater than sales. **Increase in accounts receivable** indicates that sales were greater than cash collections. **Increase in prepaid expenses** indicates that the amount paid for the prepayments exceeded the amount that was recorded as an expense. **Decrease in prepaid expenses** indicates that the amount recorded as an expense exceeded the amount of cash paid for the prepayments. **Increase in accounts payable** indicates that expenses incurred exceed the cash paid for expenses that period.

Operating expenses	$170,000	
Add: Increase in prepaid expenses	8,000	
Deduct: Increase in accrued expenses payable	(20,000)	
Cash payments for operating expenses	**$158,000**	

ILLUSTRATION 18-31

Computation of cash payments for operating expenses

The relationships among cash payments for operating expenses, changes in prepaid expenses, and changes in accrued expenses payable are shown in the following formula:

ILLUSTRATION 18-32

Formula to compute cash payments for operating expenses—direct method

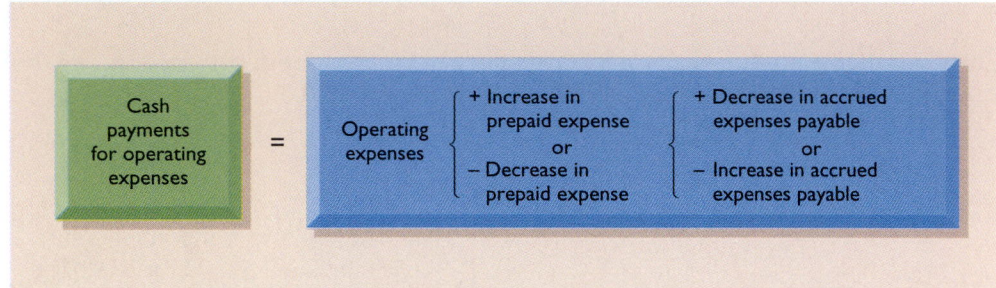

Cash Payments for Income Taxes.   The income statement for Juarez shows income tax expense of $48,000. This amount equals the cash paid because the comparative balance sheet indicated no income taxes payable at either the beginning or end of the year.

All of the revenues and expenses in the 1999 income statement have now been adjusted to a cash basis. The operating activities section of the statement of cash flows is as follows:

ILLUSTRATION 18-33

Operating activities section—direct method

JUAREZ COMPANY
Partial Statement of Cash Flows—Direct Method
For the Year Ended December 31, 1999

Cash flows from operating activities		
Cash receipts from customers		$765,000
Cash payments:		
To suppliers	$550,000	
For operating expenses	158,000	
For income taxes	48,000	756,000
Net cash provided by operating activities		**$ 9,000**

HELPFUL HINT

This is the same procedure used under the indirect method; the investing and financing activities are measured and reported the same under both methods.

Determining Net Cash Provided/Used by Investing and Financing Activities (Step 3)

Preparing the investing and financing activities sections of the statement of cash flows begins with a determination of the changes in noncurrent accounts reported in the comparative balance sheet. The change in each account is then analyzed using the additional information to determine the effect, if any, the change had on cash.

Increase in Land.   No additional information is given for the increase in land. In such case, you should assume that the increase affected cash. You should also make the same assumption in solving homework problems when the cause of a change in a noncurrent account is not explained. The purchase of land is an investing activity. Thus, an outflow of cash of $80,000 for the purchase of land should be reported in the investing activities section.

Increase in Common Stock.   As indicated earlier, 300,000 shares of $1 par value stock were sold for $300,000 cash. The issuance of common stock is a financing activity. Thus, a cash inflow of $300,000 from the issuance of common stock is reported in the financing activities section.

Increase in Retained Earnings.   For the Retained Earnings account, the reasons for the net increase of $42,000 are determined by analysis. First, net income increased retained earnings by $112,000. Second, the additional information section indicates that a cash dividend of $70,000 was declared and paid. The adjustment of revenues and expenses to arrive at net cash provided by operations was done in step 2 above. The cash dividend paid is reported as an outflow of cash in the financing activities section.

This analysis can also be made directly from the Retained Earnings account in the ledger of Juarez Company as shown in Illustration 18-34.

HELPFUL HINT
It is the **payment** of dividends, not the declaration, that appears on the cash flow statement.

ILLUSTRATION 18-34
Analysis of retained earnings

Retained Earnings				
12/31/99	Cash dividend	70,000	1/1/99 Balance	–0–
			12/31/99 Net income	112,000
			12/31/99 Balance	42,000

The $42,000 increase in Retained Earnings in 1999 is a net change. When a net change in a noncurrent balance sheet account has occurred during the year, it generally is necessary to report the individual items that cause the net change.

Statement of Cash Flows—1999

The statement of cash flows can now be prepared. The operating activities section is reported first, followed by the investing and financing activities sections. The statement of cash flows for Juarez Company for 1999 is shown in Illustration 18-35.

ILLUSTRATION 18-35
Statement of cash flows, 1999—direct method

JUAREZ COMPANY
Statement of Cash Flows—Direct Method
For the Year Ended December 31, 1999

Cash flows from operating activities		
Cash receipts from customers		$765,000
Cash payments:		
To suppliers	$550,000	
For operating expenses	158,000	
For income taxes	48,000	756,000
Net cash provided by operating activities		9,000
Cash flows from investing activities		
Purchase of land	(80,000)	
Net cash used by investing activities		(80,000)
Cash flows from financing activities		
Issuance of common stock	300,000	
Payment of cash dividend	(70,000)	
Net cash provided by financing activities		230,000
Net increase in cash		159,000
Cash at beginning of period		–0–
Cash at end of period		$159,000

HELPFUL HINT
Note that in the investing and financing activities sections, positive numbers indicate cash inflows (receipts) and negative numbers indicate cash outflows (payments).

The statement of cash flows shows that operating activities provided $9,000 of the net increase in cash of $159,000. Financing activities **provided** $230,000 of cash, and investing activities **used** $80,000 of cash. The net increase in cash for the year of $159,000 agrees with the increase in cash of $159,000 reported in the comparative balance sheet.

SECOND YEAR OF OPERATIONS—2000

Illustrations 18-36 and 18-37 present the comparative balance sheet, the income statement, and additional information pertaining to the second year of operations for Juarez Company.

ILLUSTRATION 18-36

Comparative balance sheet, 2000, with increases and decreases

JUAREZ COMPANY
Comparative Balance Sheet
December 31

Assets	2000	1999	Change Increase/Decrease
Cash	$191,000	$159,000	$ 32,000 Increase
Accounts receivable	12,000	15,000	3,000 Decrease
Inventory	130,000	160,000	30,000 Decrease
Prepaid expenses	6,000	8,000	2,000 Decrease
Land	180,000	80,000	100,000 Increase
Equipment	160,000	–0–	160,000 Increase
Accumulated depreciation—equipment	(16,000)	–0–	16,000 Increase
Total	$663,000	$422,000	
Liabilities and Stockholders' Equity			
Accounts payable	$ 52,000	$ 60,000	$ 8,000 Decrease
Accrued expenses payable	15,000	20,000	5,000 Decrease
Income taxes payable	12,000	–0–	12,000 Increase
Bonds payable	90,000	–0–	90,000 Increase
Common stock	400,000	300,000	100,000 Increase
Retained earnings	94,000	42,000	52,000 Increase
Total	$663,000	$422,000	

ILLUSTRATION 18-37

Income statement and additional information, 2000

JUAREZ COMPANY
Income Statement
For the Year Ended December 31, 2000

Revenues		$975,000
Cost of goods sold	$660,000	
Operating expenses (excluding depreciation)	176,000	
Depreciation expense	18,000	
Loss on sale of store equipment	1,000	855,000
Income before income taxes		120,000
Income tax expense		36,000
Net income		$ 84,000

Additional information:
(a) In 2000, the company declared and paid a $32,000 cash dividend.
(b) Bonds were issued at face value for $90,000 in cash.
(c) Equipment costing $180,000 was purchased for cash.
(d) Equipment costing $20,000 was sold for $17,000 cash when the book value of the equipment was $18,000.
(e) Common stock of $100,000 was issued to acquire land.

Determining the Net Increase/Decrease in Cash (Step 1)

The comparative balance sheet shows a beginning cash balance of $159,000 and an ending cash balance of $191,000. Thus, there was a net increase in cash in 2000 of $32,000.

Determining Net Cash Provided/Used by Operating Activities (Step 2)

Cash Receipts from Customers. Revenues from sales were $975,000. Since accounts receivable decreased $3,000, cash receipts from customers were greater than sales revenues. Cash receipts from customers were $978,000, computed as follows:

Revenues from sales	$975,000
Add: Decrease in accounts receivable	3,000
Cash receipts from customers	**$978,000**

ILLUSTRATION 18-38

Computation of cash receipts from customers

Cash Payments to Suppliers. The conversion of cost of goods sold to purchases and purchases to cash payments to suppliers is similar to the computations made in 1999. For 2000, purchases are computed using cost of goods sold of $660,000 from the income statement and the decrease in inventory of $30,000 from the comparative balance sheet. Purchases are then adjusted by the decrease in accounts payable of $8,000. Cash payments to suppliers were $638,000, computed as follows:

Cost of goods sold	$660,000
Deduct: Decrease in inventory	30,000
Purchases	630,000
Add: Decrease in accounts payable	8,000
Cash payments to suppliers	**$638,000**

ILLUSTRATION 18-39

Computation of cash payments to suppliers

Cash Payments for Operating Expenses. Operating expenses (exclusive of depreciation expense) for 2000 were reported at $176,000. This amount is then adjusted for changes in prepaid expenses and accrued expenses payable to arrive at cash payments for operating expenses.

As indicated from the comparative balance sheet, prepaid expenses decreased $2,000 during the year. This means that $2,000 was allocated to operating expenses (thereby increasing operating expenses), but cash payments did not increase by that $2,000. To arrive at cash payments for operating expenses, the decrease in prepaid expenses is deducted from operating expenses.

Accrued operating expenses decreased $5,000 during the period. As a result, cash payments were higher by $5,000 than the amount reported for operating expenses. The decrease in accrued expenses payable is added to operating expenses. Cash payments for operating expenses were $179,000, computed as follows:

ILLUSTRATION 18-40

Computation of cash payments for operating expenses

Operating expenses, exclusive of depreciation	$176,000
Deduct: Decrease in prepaid expenses	(2,000)
Add: Decrease in accrued expenses payable	5,000
Cash payments for operating expenses	**$179,000**

Depreciation Expense and Loss on Sale of Equipment.   Operating expenses are shown exclusive of depreciation. Depreciation expense in 2000 was $18,000. Depreciation expense is not shown on a statement of cash flows because it is a noncash charge. If the amount for operating expenses includes depreciation expense, operating expenses must be reduced by the amount of depreciation to determine cash payments for operating expenses.

The loss on sale of equipment of $1,000 is also a noncash charge. The loss on sale of equipment reduces net income, but it does not reduce cash. Thus, the loss on sale of equipment is not reported on a statement of cash flows.

Other charges to expense that do not require the use of cash, such as the amortization of intangible assets and depletion expense, are treated in the same manner as depreciation.

Cash Payments for Income Taxes.   Income tax expense reported on the income statement was $36,000. Income taxes payable, however, increased $12,000 which means that $12,000 of the income taxes have not been paid. As a result, income taxes paid were less than income taxes reported on the income statement. Cash payments for income taxes were, therefore, $24,000 as shown below.

ILLUSTRATION 18-41

Computation of cash payments for income taxes

Income tax expense	$36,000
Deduct: Increase in income taxes payable	12,000
Cash payments for income taxes	**$24,000**

The relationships of cash payments for income taxes, income tax expense, and changes in income taxes payable are shown in the following formula:

ILLUSTRATION 18-42

Formula to compute cash payments for income taxes—direct method

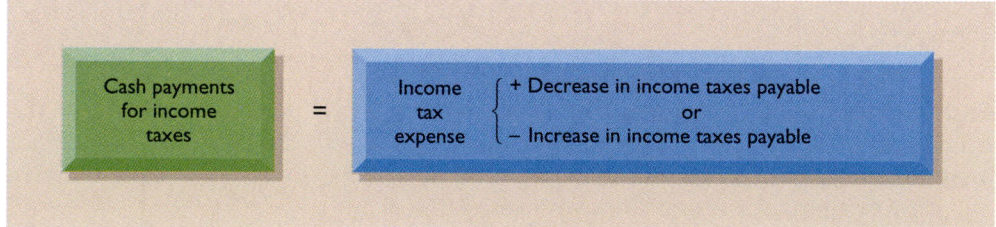

Determining Net Cash Provided/Used by Investing and Financing Activities (Step 3)

Increase in Land.   Land increased $100,000. The additional information section indicates that common stock was issued to purchase the land. Although the issuance of common stock for land has no effect on cash, it is a **significant non-cash investing and financing transaction**. This transaction requires disclosure in a separate schedule at the bottom of the statement of cash flows.

Increase in Equipment. The comparative balance sheet shows that equipment increased $160,000 in 2000. The additional information in Illustration 18-37 indicates that the increase resulted from two investing transactions: (1) equipment costing $180,000 was purchased for cash, and (2) equipment costing $20,000 was sold for $17,000 cash when its book value was $18,000. The relevant data for the statement of cash flows is the cash paid for the purchase and the cash proceeds from the sale. For Juarez Company, the investing activities section will show: Purchase of equipment $180,000, as an outflow of cash; and sale of equipment $17,000, as an inflow of cash. The two amounts **should not be netted** because one is an outflow of cash and the other is an inflow of cash; **both flows should be shown**.

The analysis of the changes in equipment should include the related Accumulated Depreciation account. These two accounts for Juarez Company are shown in Illustration 18-43.

ILLUSTRATION 18-43

Analysis of equipment and related accumulated depreciation

Equipment				
1/1/00	Balance	–0–	Cost of equipment sold	20,000
	Cash purchase	180,000		
12/31/00	Balance	160,000		

Accumulated Depreciation—Equipment				
Sale of equipment	2,000	1/1/00	Balance	–0–
			Depreciation expense	18,000
		12/31/00	Balance	16,000

Increase in Bonds Payable. Bonds Payable increased $90,000. The additional information in Illustration 18-37 indicates that bonds with a face value of $90,000 were issued for $90,000 cash. The issuance of bonds is a financing activity. For Juarez Company, there is an inflow of cash of $90,000 from the issuance of bonds.

Increase in Common Stock. The Common Stock account increased $100,000. As indicated from the additional information, land was acquired from the issuance of common stock. This transaction is a **significant noncash investing and financing transaction** that should be reported in a separate schedule at the bottom of the statement.

Increase in Retained Earnings. The net increase in Retained Earnings of $52,000 resulted from net income of $84,000 and the declaration and payment of a cash dividend of $32,000. **Net income is not reported in the statement of cash flows**

under the direct method. Cash dividends paid of $32,000 are reported in the financing activities section as an outflow of cash.

Statement of Cash Flows—2000

The statement of cash flows for Juarez Company is shown in Illustration 18-44.

JUAREZ COMPANY Statement of Cash Flows—Direct Method For the Year Ended December 31, 2000		
Cash flows from operating activities		
Cash receipts from customers		$978,000
Cash payments:		
To suppliers	$638,000	
For operating expenses	179,000	
For income taxes	24,000	841,000
Net cash provided by operating activities		137,000
Cash flows from investing activities		
Purchase of equipment	(180,000)	
Sale of equipment	17,000	
Net cash used by investing activities		(163,000)
Cash flows from financing activities		
Issuance of bonds payable	90,000	
Payment of cash dividends	(32,000)	
Net cash provided by financing activities		58,000
Net increase in cash		32,000
Cash at beginning of period		159,000
Cash at end of period		$191,000
Noncash investing and financing activities		
Issuance of common stock to purchase land		$100,000

BEFORE YOU GO ON . . .

Review It

1. What is the format of the operating activities section of the statement of cash flows using the direct method?
2. Where is depreciation expense shown on a statement of cash flows using the direct method?
3. Where are significant noncash investing and financing activities shown on a statement of cash flows? Give some examples.

Do It

Presented below is information related to Reynolds Company. Use it to prepare a statement of cash flows using the direct method.

REYNOLDS COMPANY
Comparative Balance Sheet
December 31

Assets	2000	1999	Change Increase/Decrease
Cash	$ 54,000	$ 37,000	$ 17,000 Increase
Accounts receivable	68,000	26,000	42,000 Increase
Inventories	54,000	–0–	54,000 Increase
Prepaid expenses	4,000	6,000	2,000 Decrease
Land	45,000	70,000	25,000 Decrease
Buildings	200,000	200,000	–0–
Accumulated depreciation—buildings	(21,000)	(11,000)	10,000 Increase
Equipment	193,000	68,000	125,000 Increase
Accumulated depreciation—equipment	(28,000)	(10,000)	18,000 Increase
Totals	$569,000	$386,000	
Liabilities and Stockholders' Equity			
Accounts payable	$ 23,000	$ 40,000	$ 17,000 Decrease
Accrued expenses payable	10,000	–0–	10,000 Increase
Bonds payable	110,000	150,000	40,000 Decrease
Common stock ($1 par)	220,000	60,000	160,000 Increase
Retained earnings	206,000	136,000	70,000 Increase
Totals	$569,000	$386,000	

REYNOLDS COMPANY
Income Statement
For the Year Ended December 31, 2000

Revenues		$890,000
Cost of goods sold	$465,000	
Operating expenses	221,000	
Interest expense	12,000	
Loss on sale of equipment	2,000	700,000
Income from operations		190,000
Income tax expense		65,000
Net income		$125,000

Additional information:

(a) Operating expenses include depreciation expense of $33,000 and charges from prepaid expenses of $2,000.

(b) Land was sold at its book value for cash.

(c) Cash dividends of $55,000 were declared and paid in 2000.

(d) Interest expense of $12,000 was paid in cash.

(e) Equipment with a cost of $166,000 was purchased for cash. Equipment with a cost of $41,000 and a book value of $36,000 was sold for $34,000 cash.

(f) Bonds of $10,000 were redeemed at their book value for cash; bonds of $30,000 were converted into common stock.

(g) Common stock ($1 par) of $130,000 was issued for cash.

(h) Accounts payable pertain to merchandise suppliers.

Reasoning: The indirect and the direct methods differ primarily in their presentation of the cash flows from the operating activities. The direct method reports cash receipts less cash payments to arrive at net cash provided by operating activities.

Solution:

REYNOLDS COMPANY
Statement of Cash Flows
For the Year Ended December 31, 2000

Cash flows from operating activities		
Cash receipts from customers		$848,000[a]
Cash payments:		
To suppliers	$536,000[b]	
For operating expenses	176,000[c]	
For interest expense	12,000	
For income taxes	65,000	789,000
Net cash provided by operating activities		59,000
Cash flows from investing activities		
Sale of land	25,000	
Sale of equipment	34,000	
Purchase of equipment	(166,000)	
Net cash used by investing activities		(107,000)
Cash flows from financing activities		
Redemption of bonds	(10,000)	
Sale of common stock	130,000	
Payment of dividends	(55,000)	
Net cash provided by financing activities		65,000
Net increase in cash		17,000
Cash at beginning of period		37,000
Cash at end of period		$ 54,000
Noncash investing and financing activities		
Conversion of bonds into common stock		$ 30,000

Computations:

[a]$848,000 = $890,000 − $42,000
[b]$536,000 = $465,000 + $54,000 + $17,000
[c]$176,000 = $221,000 − $33,000 − $2,000 − $10,000
Technically, an additional schedule reconciling net income to net cash provided by operating activities should be presented as part of the statement of cash flows when using the direct method.

Related exercise material: BE18–6, BE18–7, BE18–8, E18–7, E18–8, E18–9, and E18–10.

THE NAVIGATOR

Note: This concludes Section 2 on preparation of the statement of cash flows using the direct method. You should now turn to the next—and concluding—section of the chapter, "Analysis of the Statement of Cash Flows."

5
STUDY
OBJECTIVE

Analyze the statement of cash flows.

ANALYSIS OF THE STATEMENT OF CASH FLOWS

The statement of cash flows provides information about a company's financial health that is not evident from analysis of the balance sheet or the income statement. Bankers, creditors, and other users of the statement of cash flows are as concerned with cash flow from operations as they are with net income because they are interested in a company's ability to pay its bills. Does accrual accounting conceal cash flow problems? What can be learned about a company and its management from the statement of cash flows?

In the following discussion of cash flow analysis, we use financial information from the fiscal 1997 annual report of Gap Inc. (manufacturer and retailer of Gap, Banana Republic, and Old Navy brands). Gap Inc. reported the following relevant information:

Gap Inc.
Gap
Banana Republic
Old Navy

Gap Inc.

($ in millions)	Fiscal 1997	Fiscal 1996
Current liabilities	$ 992	$ 775
Total liabilities	1,754	973
Net sales	6,508	5,284
Net cash provided by operating activities	845	835

ILLUSTRATION 18-45
Gap Inc. data used in cash flow analysis

As with the balance sheet and the income statement, ratio analysis of the statement of cash flows can evaluate Gap Inc.'s liquidity, profitability, and solvency. Three cash flow ratios that contribute to these evaluations are (a) the current cash debt coverage ratio, (b) the cash return on sales ratio, and (c) the cash debt coverage ratio. Each of these ratios uses net cash provided by operating activities as the numerator.

Current Cash Debt Coverage Ratio

A disadvantage of the current ratio is that it employs year-end balances of current asset and current liability accounts. These year-end balances may not be representative of what the company's current position was during most of the year. A ratio that partially corrects for this problem is the ratio of net cash provided by operating activities to average current liabilities, referred to as the **current cash debt coverage ratio**. Because it uses net cash provided by operating activities during the period, rather than a balance at a point in time, it may provide a better representation of **liquidity**. Using Gap Inc.'s financial data, the current cash debt coverage ratio is computed as follows:

HELPFUL HINT
Recall that the current ratio is current assets divided by current liabilities.

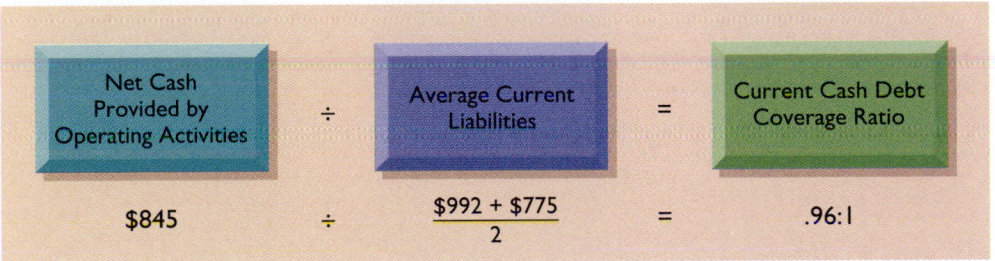

ILLUSTRATION 18-46
Current cash debt coverage ratio

This ratio indicates that for every dollar of debt due during the year, $0.96 of cash was generated from operations to pay that debt.

Cash Return on Sales Ratio

One measure of profitability using accrual accounting is the profit margin ratio. This ratio is defined as net income divided by net sales and measures net income generated by each dollar of sales. The cash-based ratio that is the counterpart of the profit margin ratio is the cash return on sales ratio (sometimes referred to as "cash flow margin"), computed by dividing net cash provided by operating activities by net sales. For Gap Inc, this ratio is computed as follows:

ILLUSTRATION 18-47

Cash return on sales ratio

Although differences are expected between cash and accrual accounting, significant differences should be investigated. When Gap Inc.'s "cash flow margin"—its cash return on sales—of 13% is compared with its profit margin of 5.3%, it appears that Gap Inc. is very efficient at turning sales into cash—since its cash flow margin is more than double its profit margin (accrual basis).

Cash Debt Coverage Ratio

In Chapter 16 we introduced the debt to total assets ratio as one measure of long-term **solvency**. The cash basis measure of solvency is the cash debt coverage ratio—the ratio of net cash provided by operating activities to average total liabilities. This ratio demonstrates a company's ability to repay its liabilities from net cash provided by operating activities, without having to liquidate the assets employed in its operations. Gap Inc.'s cash debt coverage ratio is computed as follows:

ILLUSTRATION 18-48

Cash debt coverage ratio

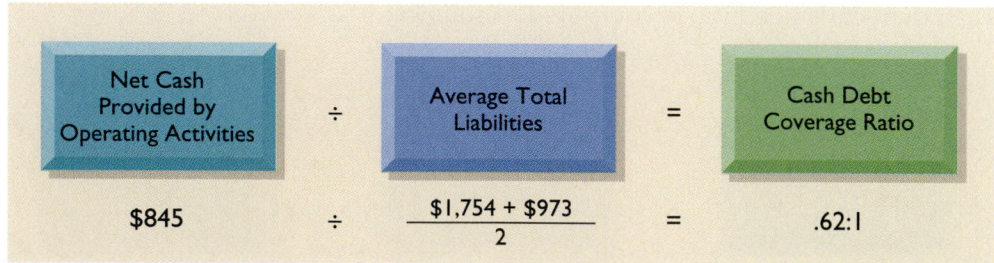

The three cash-based ratios illustrated above show that Gap Inc. is efficiently generating cash, and its cash flow coverage ratios are in line with industry averages. These ratios indicate that the company is liquid, profitable, and solvent.

BEFORE YOU GO ON . . .

Review It

1. Why might an analyst want to supplement accrual-based ratios with cash-based ratios?
2. What cash-basis ratios may be prepared to evaluate liquidity, profitability, and solvency?

A LOOK BACK AT OUR FEATURE STORY

Refer to the opening story of Gerald Biby's attempt to refinance Kilian Community College's mortgage, and answer the following questions:

1. How was the purchase of the $250,000 computer system presented on the "traditional educational institution financial statement" so that it negatively affected Biby's ability to refinance the mortgage?
2. How was the purchase of the $250,000 computer system presented on the statement of cash flows? How did the preparation of the statement of cash flows aid Biby in securing the refinancing of the mortgage?

Solution:

1. A traditional financial statement for a not-for-profit, educational institution reports receipts as revenues and expenses all expenditures, even capital expenditures such as the $250,000 computer system. That is, the traditional financial statement reported the entire $250,000 as an expense in one year, making it look like the college was just breaking even.
2. When the computer purchase was classified as an investing activity, the statement of cash flows showed the bankers that one of the uses of funds was really the purchase of computer equipment that had several years of life. In addition, the bankers noted from the statement of cash flows "that the college's sources of funds exceeded the loan repayments, including principal and interest, by a ratio of 3-to-1."

THE
NAVIGATOR

DEMONSTRATION PROBLEM

The income statement for the year ended December 31, 1999, for John Kosinski Manufacturing Company contains the following condensed information:

JOHN KOSINSKI MANUFACTURING COMPANY
Income Statement

Revenues		$6,583,000
Operating expenses (excluding depreciation)	$4,920,000	
Depreciation expense	880,000	5,800,000
Income before income taxes		783,000
Income tax expense		353,000
Net income		$ 430,000

Included in operating expenses is a $24,000 loss resulting from the sale of machinery for $270,000 cash. Machinery was purchased at a cost of $750,000. The following balances are reported on Kosinski's comparative balance sheet at December 31:

JOHN KOSINSKI MANUFACTURING COMPANY
Balance Sheet (partial)

	1999	1998
Cash	$672,000	$130,000
Accounts receivable	775,000	610,000
Inventories	834,000	867,000
Accounts payable	521,000	501,000

Income tax expense of $353,000 represents the amount paid in 1999. Dividends declared and paid in 1999 totaled $200,000.

Instructions

(a) Prepare the statement of cash flows using the indirect method.

OR

(b) Prepare the statement of cash flows using the direct method.

SOLUTION TO DEMONSTRATION PROBLEM

PROBLEM-SOLVING STRATEGY

This demonstration problem illustrates both the direct and indirect methods using the same basic data. Note the similarities and the differences between the two methods. Both methods report the same information in the investing and financing activities sections. The cash flow from operating activities section reports different information, but the amount—net cash provided by operating activities—is the same for both methods.

(a)

JOHN KOSINSKI MANUFACTURING COMPANY
Statement of Cash Flows—Indirect Method
For the Year Ended December 31, 1999

Cash flows from operating activities		
Net income		$ 430,000
Adjustments to reconcile net income to net cash		
provided by operating activities:		
Depreciation expense	$880,000	
Loss on sale of machinery	24,000	
Increase in accounts receivable	(165,000)	
Decrease in inventories	33,000	
Increase in accounts payable	20,000	792,000
Net cash provided by operating activities		1,222,000
Cash flows from investing activities		
Sale of machinery	270,000	
Purchase of machinery	(750,000)	
Net cash used by investing activities		(480,000)
Cash flows from financing activities		
Payment of cash dividends		(200,000)
Net increase in cash		542,000
Cash at beginning of period		130,000
Cash at end of period		$672,000

(b)

JOHN KOSINSKI MANUFACTURING COMPANY
Statement of Cash Flows—Direct Method
For the Year Ended December 31, 1999

Cash flows from operating activities		
Cash collections from customers		$6,418,000 *
Cash payments:		
For operating expenses	$4,843,000 **	
For income taxes	353,000	5,196,000
Net cash provided by operating activities		1,222,000
Cash flows from investing activities		
Sale of machinery	$270,000	
Purchase of machinery	(750,000)	
Net cash used by investing activities		(480,000)
Cash flows from financing activities		
Payment of cash dividends		(200,000)
Net increase in cash		542,000
Cash at beginning of period		130,000
Cash at end of period		$ 672,000

Direct Method Computations:

* Computation of cash collections from customers:	
Revenues per the income statement	$6,583,000
Less increase in accounts receivable	165,000
Cash collections from customers	$6,418,000

**	Computation of cash payments for operating expenses:	
	Operating expenses per the income statement	$4,920,000
	Deduct loss from sale of machinery	(24,000)
	Deduct decrease in inventories	(33,000)
	Deduct increase in accounts payable	(20,000)
	Cash payments for operating expenses	$4,843,000

SUMMARY OF STUDY OBJECTIVES

1. Indicate the primary purpose of the statement of cash flows. The primary purpose of the statement of cash flows is to provide information about the cash receipts and cash payments of an entity during a period. A secondary objective is to provide information about the operating, investing, and financing activities of the entity during the period.

2. Distinguish among operating, investing, and financing activities. Operating activities include the cash effects of transactions that enter into the determination of net income. Investing activities involve cash flows resulting from changes in investments and long-term asset items. Financing activities involve cash flows resulting from changes in long-term liability and stockholders' equity items.

3. Prepare a statement of cash flows using the indirect method. The preparation of a statement of cash flows involves three major steps: (1) determine the net increase or decrease in cash; (2) determine net cash provided (used) by operating activities; and (3) determine net cash flows provided (used) by investing and financing activities. Under the indirect method, accrual basis net income is adjusted to net cash provided by operating activities.

4. Prepare a statement of cash flows using the direct method. The preparation of the statement of cash flows involves three major steps: (1) determine the net increase or decrease in cash; (2) determine net cash provided (used) by operating activities; and (3) determine net cash flows provided (used) by investing and financing activities. The direct method reports cash receipts less cash payments to arrive at net cash provided by operating activities.

5. Analyze the statement of cash flows. Ratio analysis of the statement of cash flows can evaluate liquidity, profitability, and solvency by computing (a) the current cash debt coverage ratio, (b) the cash return on sales ratio, and (c) the cash debt coverage ratio.

GLOSSARY

Cash debt coverage ratio A cash-basis measure of solvency, computed as net cash provided by operating activities divided by average total liabilities. (p. 788)

Cash return on sales ratio A cash-basis measure of profitability, computed as net cash provided by operating activities divided by net sales. Also called *cash flow margin*. (p.788)

Current cash debt coverage ratio A cash-basis measure of liquidity, computed as net cash provided by operating activities divided by average current liabilities. (p.787)

Direct method A method of determining the "net cash provided by operating activities" by adjusting each item in the income statement from the accrual basis to the cash basis. (p. 775)

Financing activities Cash flow activities that include (a) obtaining cash from issuing debt and repaying the amounts borrowed and (b) obtaining cash from stockholders and providing them with a return on their investment. (p. 756)

Indirect method A method of preparing a statement of cash flows in which net income is adjusted for items that did not affect cash, to determine net cash provided by operating activities. (p. 763)

Investing activities Cash flow activities that include (a) acquiring and disposing of investments and productive long-lived assets and (b) lending money and collecting on those loans. (p. 756)

Operating activities Cash flow activities that include the cash effects of transactions that create revenues and expenses and thus enter into the determination of net income. (p. 756)

Statement of cash flows A basic financial statement that provides information about the cash receipts and cash payments of an entity during a period, classified as operating, investing, and financing activities, in a format that reconciles the beginning and ending cash balances. (p. 755)

APPENDIX   USING A WORK SHEET TO PREPARE THE STATEMENT OF CASH FLOWS—INDIRECT METHOD

6

STUDY OBJECTIVE

Explain the guidelines and procedural steps in using a work sheet to prepare the statement of cash flows.

When numerous adjustments of net income are necessary, **a work sheet is often used to assemble and classify the data that will appear on the statement of cash flows**. The work sheet is merely a device that aids in the preparation of the statement; its use is optional. The skeleton format of the work sheet for preparation of the statement of cash flows is shown in Illustration 18A-1.

XYZ COMPANY
Work Sheet
Statement of Cash Flows
For the Year Ended . . .

Balance Sheet Accounts	End of Last Year Balances	Reconciling Items Debits	Reconciling Items Credits	End of Current Year Balances
Debit balance accounts	XX	XX	XX	XX
	XX	XX	XX	XX
Totals	XXX			XXX
Credit balance accounts	XX	XX	XX	XX
	XX	XX	XX	XX
Totals	XXX			XXX
Statement of Cash Flows Effects				
Operating activities				
Net income		XX		
Adjustments to net income		XX	XX	
Investing activities				
Receipts and payments		XX	XX	
Financing activities				
Receipts and payments		XX	XX	
Totals		XXX	XXX	
Increase (decrease) in cash		(XX)	XX	
Totals		XXX	XXX	

ILLUSTRATION 18A-1

Format of work sheet

The following guidelines are important in using a work sheet:

1. In the balance sheet accounts section, **accounts with debit balances are listed separately from those with credit balances**. This means, for example, that Accumulated Depreciation is listed under credit balances and not as a contra account under debit balances. The beginning and ending balances of each account are entered in the appropriate columns. The transactions that caused the change in the account balance during the year are entered as reconciling items in the two middle columns. After all reconciling items have been entered, each line pertaining to a balance sheet account should "foot across." That is, the beginning balance plus or minus the reconciling item(s) must equal the ending balance. When this agreement exists for all balance sheet accounts, all changes in account balances have been reconciled.

2. The bottom portion of the work sheet consists of the operating, investing, and financing activities sections. Accordingly, it provides the information necessary to prepare the formal statement of cash flows. **Inflows of cash are entered as debits in the reconciling columns, and outflows of cash are entered as credits in the reconciling columns.** Thus, in this section, the sale of equipment for cash at book value is entered as a debit under investing activities. Similarly, the purchase of land for cash is entered as a credit under investing activities.

3. **The reconciling items shown in the work sheet are not entered in any journal or posted to any account.** They do not represent either adjustments or corrections of the balance sheet accounts. They are used only to facilitate the preparation of the statement of cash flows.

PREPARING THE WORK SHEET

As in the case of work sheets illustrated in earlier chapters, the preparation of a work sheet involves a series of prescribed steps. The steps in this case are:

1. Enter in the balance sheet accounts section the balance sheet accounts and their beginning and ending balances.
2. Enter in the reconciling columns of the work sheet the data that explain the changes in the balance sheet accounts other than cash and their effects on the statement of cash flows.
3. Enter on the cash line and at the bottom of the work sheet the increase or decrease in cash. This entry should enable the totals of the reconciling columns to be in agreement.

To illustrate the preparation of a work sheet, we will use the 2000 data for Computer Services Company. Your familiarity with these data should help you understand the use of a work sheet. For ease of reference, the comparative balance sheets, income statement, and selected data for 2000 are presented in Illustrations 18A-2 and 18A-3.

ILLUSTRATION 18A-2

Comparative balance sheet, 2000, with increases and decreases

COMPUTER SERVICES COMPANY Comparative Balance Sheet December 31			
Assets	**2000**	**1999**	**Change Increase/Decrease**
Cash	$ 56,000	$34,000	$ 22,000 Increase
Accounts receivable	20,000	30,000	10,000 Decrease
Prepaid expenses	4,000	–0–	4,000 Increase
Land	130,000	–0–	130,000 Increase
Building	160,000	–0–	160,000 Increase
Accumulated depreciation—building	(11,000)	–0–	11,000 Increase
Equipment	27,000	10,000	17,000 Increase
Accumulated depreciation—equipment	(3,000)	–0–	3,000 Increase
Totals	$383,000	$74,000	
Liabilities and Stockholders' Equity			
Accounts payable	$ 59,000	$ 4,000	55,000 Increase
Bonds payable	130,000	–0–	130,000 Increase
Common stock	50,000	50,000	–0–
Retained earnings	144,000	20,000	124,000 Increase
Totals	$383,000	$74,000	

ILLUSTRATION 18A-3

Income statement and additional information, 2000

COMPUTER SERVICES COMPANY
Income Statement
For the Year Ended December 31, 2000

Revenues		$507,000
Operating expenses (excluding depreciation)	$261,000	
Depreciation expense	15,000	
Loss on sale of equipment	3,000	279,000
Income from operations		228,000
Income tax expense		89,000
Net income		$139,000

Additional information:
(a) In 2000, the company declared and paid a $15,000 cash dividend.
(b) The company obtained land through the issuance of $130,000 of long-term bonds.
(c) A building costing $160,000 was purchased for cash; equipment costing $25,000 was also purchased for cash.
(d) During 2000, the company sold equipment with a book value of $7,000 (cost $8,000, less accumulated depreciation $1,000) for $4,000 cash.

Determining the Reconciling Items

Several approaches may be used to determine the reconciling items. For example, the changes affecting net cash provided by operating activities could be completed first and then the effects of financing and investing transactions could be determined. Alternatively, the balance sheet accounts can be analyzed in the order in which they are listed on the work sheet. We will follow this latter approach for Computer Services, except for cash. As indicated above, **cash is handled last**.

Accounts Receivable.   The decrease of $10,000 in accounts receivable means that cash collections from revenues are higher than the revenues reported in the income statement. To convert net income to net cash provided by operating activities, the decrease of $10,000 is added to net income. The entry in the reconciling columns of the work sheet is:

(a)	Operating—Decrease in Accounts Receivable	10,000	
	Accounts Receivable		10,000

Prepaid Expenses.   An increase of $4,000 in prepaid expenses means that expenses deducted in determining net income are less than expenses that were paid in cash. Thus, the increase of $4,000 must be deducted from net income in determining net cash provided by operating activities. The work sheet entry is:

(b)	Prepaid Expenses	4,000	
	Operating—Increase in Prepaid Expenses		4,000

HELPFUL HINT
These amounts are asterisked in the work sheet to indicate that they result from a significant noncash transaction.

Land.   The increase in land of $130,000 resulted from a purchase through the issuance of long-term bonds. This transaction should be reported as a significant noncash investing and financing activity. The work sheet entry is:

(c)	Land	130,000	
	Bonds Payable		130,000

Building.   The cash purchase of a building for $160,000 is an investing activity cash outflow. The entry in the reconciling columns of the work sheet is:

| (d) | Building | 160,000 | |
| | Investing—Purchase of Building | | 160,000 |

Equipment. The increase in equipment of $17,000 resulted from a cash purchase of $25,000 and the sale of equipment costing $8,000. The book value of the equipment was $7,000, the cash proceeds were $4,000, and a loss of $3,000 was recorded. The work sheet entries are:

| (e) | Equipment | 25,000 | |
| | Investing—Purchase of Equipment | | 25,000 |

(f)	Investing—Sale of Equipment	4,000	
	Operating—Loss on Sale of Equipment	3,000	
	Accumulated Depreciation—Equipment	1,000	
	Equipment		8,000

Accounts Payable. The increase of $55,000 in accounts payable must be added to net income to obtain net cash provided by operating activities. The following work sheet entry is made:

| (g) | Operating—Increase in Accounts Payable | 55,000 | |
| | Accounts Payable | | 55,000 |

Bonds Payable. The increase of $130,000 in this account resulted from the issuance of bonds for land. This is a significant noncash investing and financing activity. Work sheet entry (c) above is the only entry necessary.

Accumulated Depreciation—Building, and Accumulated Depreciation—Equipment. The increases in these accounts of $11,000 and $4,000, respectively, resulted from depreciation expense. Depreciation expense is a **noncash charge that must be added to net income** in determining net cash provided by operating activities. The work sheet entries are:

| (h) | Operating—Depreciation Expense—Building | 11,000 | |
| | Accumulated Depreciation—Building | | 11,000 |

| (i) | Operating—Depreciation Expense—Equipment | 4,000 | |
| | Accumulated Depreciation—Equipment | | 4,000 |

Retained Earnings. The $124,000 increase in retained earnings resulted from net income of $139,000 and the declaration of a $15,000 cash dividend that was paid in 2000. Net income is included in net cash provided by operating activities, and the dividends are a financing activity cash outflow. The entries in the reconciling columns of the work sheet are:

| (j) | Operating—Net Income | 139,000 | |
| | Retained Earnings | | 139,000 |

| (k) | Retained Earnings | 15,000 | |
| | Financing—Payment of Dividends | | 15,000 |

Disposition of Change in Cash. The firm's cash increased $22,000 in 2000. The final entry on the work sheet, therefore, is:

| (l) | Cash | 22,000 | |
| | Increase in cash | | 22,000 |

As shown in the work sheet, the increase in cash is entered in the reconciling credit column as a **balancing** amount. This entry should complete the reconciliation of the changes in the balance sheet accounts. In addition, it should permit the totals of the reconciling columns to be in agreement. When all changes have been explained and the reconciling columns are in agreement, the reconciling columns are ruled to complete the work sheet. The completed work sheet for Computer Services Company is shown in Illustration 18A-4.

ILLUSTRATION 18A-4

Completed work sheet—indirect method

COMPUTER SERVICES COMPANY
Work Sheet
Statement of Cash Flows
For the Year Ended December 31, 2000

Balance Sheet Accounts	Balance 12/31/99	Reconciling Items Debit	Reconciling Items Credit	Balance 12/31/00
Debits				
Cash	34,000	(l) 22,000		56,000
Accounts receivable	30,000		(a) 10,000	20,000
Prepaid expenses	–0–	(b) 4,000		4,000
Land	–0–	(c) 130,000*		130,000
Building	–0–	(d) 160,000		160,000
Equipment	10,000	(e) 25,000	(f) 8,000	27,000
Total	74,000			397,000
Credits				
Accounts payable	4,000		(g) 55,000	59,000
Bonds payable	–0–		(c) 130,000*	130,000
Accumulated depreciation—building	–0–		(h) 11,000	11,000
Accumulated depreciation—equipment	–0–	(f) 1,000	(i) 4,000	3,000
Common stock	50,000			50,000
Retained earnings	20,000	(k) 15,000	(j) 139,000	144,000
Total	74,000			397,000
Statement of Cash Flows Effects				
Operating activities				
Net income		(j) 139,000		
Decrease in accounts receivable		(a) 10,000		
Increase in prepaid expenses			(b) 4,000	
Increase in accounts payable		(g) 55,000		
Depreciation expense—building		(h) 11,000		
Depreciation expense—equipment		(i) 4,000		
Loss on sale of equipment		(f) 3,000		
Investing activities				
Purchase of building			(d) 160,000	
Purchase of equipment			(e) 25,000	
Sale of equipment		(f) 4,000		
Financing activities				
Payment of dividends			(k) 15,000	
Totals		583,000	561,000	
Increase in cash			(l) 22,000	
Totals		583,000	583,000	

*Significant noncash investing and financing activity.

PREPARING THE STATEMENT

The statement of cash flows is prepared primarily from the data that appear in the work sheet under Statement of Cash Flows Effects. The reconciling columns should also be scanned for any asterisked items that designate significant non-cash activities. The formal statement was shown in Illustration 18-18.

SUMMARY OF STUDY OBJECTIVE FOR APPENDIX

6. Explain the guidelines and procedural steps in using a work sheet to prepare the statement of cash flows. When there are numerous adjustments, a work sheet can be a helpful tool in preparing the statement of cash flows. Key guidelines for using a work sheet are: (1) list accounts with debit balances separately from those with credit balances; (2) in the reconciling columns in the bottom portion of the work sheet, show cash inflows as debits and cash outflows as

credits; (3) do not enter reconciling items in any journal or account but use them only to help prepare the statement of cash flows.

The steps in preparing the work sheet are: (1) enter beginning and ending balances of balance sheet accounts; (2) enter debits and credits in reconciling columns; (3) enter the increase or decrease in cash in two places as a balancing amount.

*Note: All asterisked Questions, Exercises, and Problems relate to material in the appendix to the chapter.

SELF-STUDY QUESTIONS

Answers are at the end of the chapter.

(SO 1)   1. Which of the following is *incorrect* about the statement of cash flows?
   a. It is a fourth basic financial statement.
   b. It provides information about cash receipts and cash payments of an entity during a period.
   c. It reconciles the ending cash account balance to the balance per the bank statement.
   d. It provides information about the operating, investing, and financing activities of the business.

(SO 2)   2. The statement of cash flows classifies cash receipts and cash payments by the following activities:
   a. operating and nonoperating.
   b. investing, financing, and operating.
   c. financing, operating, and nonoperating.
   d. investing, financing, and nonoperating.

(SO 2)   3. An example of a cash flow from an operating activity is:
   a. payment of cash to lenders for interest.
   b. receipt of cash from the sale of capital stock.
   c. payment of cash dividends to the company's stockholders.
   d. none of the above.

(SO 2)   4. An example of a cash flow from an investing activity is:
   a. receipt of cash from the issuance of bonds payable.
   b. payment of cash to repurchase outstanding capital stock.
   c. receipt of cash from the sale of equipment.
   d. payment of cash to suppliers for inventory.

5. Cash dividends paid to stockholders are classified on the statement of cash flows as: (SO 2)
   a. operating activities.
   b. investing activities.
   c. a combination of the above.
   d. financing activities.

6. An example of a cash flow from a financing activity is: (SO 2)
   a. receipt of cash from sale of land.
   b. issuance of debt for cash.
   c. purchase of equipment for cash.
   d. none of the above.

7. Which of the following about the statement of cash (SO 2) flows is *incorrect*?
   a. The direct method may be used to report cash provided by operations.
   b. The statement shows the cash provided (used) for three categories of activity.
   c. The operating section is the last section of the statement.
   d. The indirect method may be used to report cash provided by operations.

Questions 8 and 9 apply only to the indirect method.

8. Net income is $132,000, accounts payable increased (SO 3) $10,000 during the year, inventory decreased $6,000 during the year, and accounts receivable increased $12,000 during the year. Under the indirect method, net cash provided by operations is:

a. $102,000.
b. $112,000.
c. $124,000.
d. $136,000.

(SO 3) 9. Noncash charges that are added back to net income in determining cash provided by operations under the indirect method do *not* include:
  a. depreciation expense.
  b. an increase in inventory.
  c. amortization expense.
  d. loss on sale of equipment.

Questions 10 and 11 apply only to the direct method.

(SO 4) 10. The beginning balance in accounts receivable is $44,000, and the ending balance is $42,000. Sales during the period are $129,000. Cash receipts from customers are:
  a. $127,000.
  b. $129,000.
  c. $131,000.
  d. $141,000.

11. Which of the following items is reported on a cash flow (SO 4) statement prepared by the direct method?
  a. Loss on sale of building.
  b. Increase in accounts receivable.
  c. Depreciation expense.
  d. Cash payments to suppliers.

12. The statement of cash flows should *not* be used to eval- (SO 3) uate an entity's ability to:
  a. earn net income.
  b. generate future cash flows.
  c. pay dividends.
  d. meet obligations.

*13. In a work sheet for the statement of cash flows, a de- (SO 5) crease in accounts receivable is entered in the reconciling columns as a credit to Accounts Receivable and a debit in the:
  a. investing activities section.
  b. operating activities section.
  c. financing activities section.
  d. none of the above.

QUESTIONS

1. (a) What is the statement of cash flows? (b) Alice Weiseman maintains that the statement of cash flows is an optional financial statement. Do you agree? Explain.

2. What questions about cash are answered by the statement of cash flows?

3. What are "cash equivalents"? How do cash equivalents affect the statement of cash flows?

4. Distinguish among the three types of activities reported in the statement of cash flows.

5. What are the major sources (inflows) of cash in a statement of cash flows? What are the major uses (outflows) of cash?

6. Why is it important to disclose certain noncash transactions? How should they be disclosed?

7. Wilma Flintstone and Barny Rublestone were discussing the presentation format of the statement of cash flows of Stone Candy Co. At the bottom of Stone Candy's statement of cash flows was a separate section entitled "Noncash investing and financing activities." Give three examples of significant noncash transactions that would be reported in this section.

8. Why is it necessary to use comparative balance sheets, a current income statement, and certain transaction data in preparing a statement of cash flows?

9. Contrast the advantages and disadvantages of the direct and indirect methods. Are both methods acceptable? Which method is preferred by the FASB? Which method is more popular?

10. When the total cash inflows exceed the total cash outflows in the statement of cash flows, how and where is this excess identified?

11. Describe the indirect method for determining net cash provided by operating activities.

12. Why is it necessary to convert accrual based net income to cash basis income when preparing a statement of cash flows?

13. The president of Styx Company is puzzled. During the last year, the company experienced a net loss of $800,000, yet its cash increased $300,000 during the same period of time. Explain to the president how this situation could occur.

14. Identify five items that are adjustments to reconcile net income to net cash provided by operating activities under the indirect method.

15. Why and how is depreciation expense reported in a statement prepared using the indirect method?

16. Why is the statement of cash flows useful?

17. During 1999, James Brown Company converted $1,600,000 of its total $2,000,000 of bonds payable into common stock. Indicate how the transaction would be reported on a statement of cash flows, if at all.

18. Describe the direct method for determining net cash provided by operating activities.

19. Give the formulas under the direct method for computing (a) cash receipts from customers and (b) cash payments to suppliers.

20. Sharon Stone Inc. reported sales of $2 million for 1999. Accounts receivable decreased $100,000 and accounts payable increased $325,000. Compute cash receipts from customers, assuming that the receivable and payable transactions related to operations.

21. Why is depreciation expense not reported in the direct-method cash flow from operating activities section?

22. Give an example of one accrual-based ratio and one cash-based ratio to measure these characteristics of a company: (a) liquidity, (b) solvency, and (c) profitability.

*23. Why is it advantageous to use a work sheet when preparing a statement of cash flows? Is a work sheet required to prepare a statement of cash flows?

BRIEF EXERCISES

BE18–1 DiCaprio Co., reported net income of $2.5 million in 1999. Depreciation for the year was $280,000, accounts receivable decreased $350,000, and accounts payable decreased $310,000. Compute net cash provided by operating activities using the indirect approach.

Compute cash provided by operating activities—indirect method.
(SO 3)

BE18–2 The net income for Kate Winslet Co. for 1999 was $280,000. For 1999, depreciation on plant assets was $60,000, and the company incurred a loss on sale of plant assets of $10,000. Compute net cash provided by operating activities under the indirect method.

Compute cash provided by operating activities—indirect method.
(SO 3)

BE18–3 Each of the following items must be considered in preparing a statement of cash flows for Matt Damon Co. for the year ended December 31, 1999. For each item, state how it should be shown in the statement of cash flows for 1999.

(a) Issued bonds for $200,000 cash.
(b) Purchased equipment for $180,000 cash.
(c) Sold land costing $20,000 for $20,000 cash.
(d) Declared and paid a $50,000 cash dividend.

Indicate statement presentation of selected transactions.
(SO 2)

BE18–4 The comparative balance sheet for the Amistad Company shows the following changes in noncash current asset accounts: accounts receivable decrease $95,000, prepaid expenses increase $12,000, and inventories increase $30,000. Compute net cash provided by operating activities using the indirect method assuming that net income is $220,000.

Compute net cash provided by operating activities using indirect method.
(SO 3)

BE18–5 Classify the following items as an operating, investing, or financing activity. Assume all items involve cash unless there is information to the contrary.

(a) Purchase of equipment.
(b) Sale of building.
(c) Redemption of bonds.
(d) Depreciation.
(e) Payment of dividends.
(f) Issuance of capital stock.

Classify items by activities.
(SO 2)

BE18–6 Julie Christie Co. has accounts receivable of $14,000 at January 1, 1999, and $24,000 at December 31, 1999. Sales revenues were $490,000 for the year 1999. What is the amount of cash receipts from customers in 1999?

Compute receipts from customers using direct method.
(SO 4)

BE18–7 Joe Pesci Company reported income taxes of $90,000 on its 1999 income statement and income taxes payable of $12,000 at December 31, 1998, and $9,000 at December 31, 1999. What amount of cash payments was made for income taxes during 1999?

Compute cash payments for income taxes using direct method.
(SO 4)

BE18–8 Titanic Company reports operating expenses of $100,000 excluding depreciation expense of $15,000 for 1999. During the year prepaid expenses decreased $6,600 and accrued expenses payable increased $4,400. Compute the cash payments for operating expenses in 1999.

Compute cash payments for operating expenses using direct method.
(SO 4)

BE18–9 The T-accounts for Equipment and the related Accumulated Depreciation for Kim Bassinger Company at the end of 1999 are as follows:

Determine cash received in sale of equipment.
(SO 3, 4)

Equipment			
Beg. bal.	80,000	Disposals	22,000
Acquisitions	41,600		
End. bal.	99,600		

Accumulated Depreciation			
Disposals	5,500	Beg. bal.	44,500
		Depr.	12,000
		End. bal.	51,000

In addition, Kim Bassinger Company's income statement reported a loss on the sale of equipment of $6,900. What amount was reported on the statement of cash flows as "cash flow from sale of equipment"?

Identify financing activity transactions.
(SO 2)

BE18–10 The following T-account is a summary of the cash account of Robin Williams Company.

Cash (Summary Form)

Balance, 1/1/99	8,000		
Receipts from customers	364,000	Payments for goods	200,000
Dividends on stock investments	6,000	Payments for operating expenses	140,000
Proceeds from sale of equipment	36,000	Interest paid	10,000
Proceeds from issuance of bonds		Taxes paid	8,000
payable	100,000	Dividends paid	45,000
Balance, 12/31/99	111,000		

For Robin Williams Company what amount of net cash provided (used) by financing activities should be reported in the statement of cash flows?

Calculate cash-based ratios.
(SO 5)

BE18–11 Alice Weiseman Company reported cash from operations of $300,000, net sales $1,500,000, average current liabilities of $150,000 and average total liabilities of $225,000. Calculate these ratios:
(a) Current cash debt coverage ratio.
(b) Cash debt coverage ratio.
(c) Cash return on sales ratio.

Indicate entries in work sheet.
(SO 6)

*BE18–12 Using the data in BE18–8, indicate how the changes in prepaid expenses and accrued expenses payable should be entered in the reconciling columns of a work sheet. Assume that beginning balances were: prepaid expenses, $18,600 and accrued expenses payable, $8,200.

EXERCISES

Classify transactions by type of activity.
(SO 2)

E18–1 Depeche Mode Corporation had the following transactions during 1999:

1. Issued $50,000 par value common stock for cash.
2. Collected $16,000 of accounts receivable.
3. Declared and paid a cash dividend of $25,000.
4. Sold a long-term investment with a cost of $15,000 for $15,000 cash.
5. Issued $200,000 par value common stock upon conversion of bonds having a face value of $200,000.
6. Paid $18,000 on accounts payable.
7. Purchased a machine for $30,000, giving a long-term note in exchange.

Instructions
Analyze the transactions above and indicate whether each transaction resulted in a cash flow from (a) operating activities, (b) investing activities, (c) financing activities, or (d) noncash investing and financing activities.

Prepare the operating activities section—indirect method.
(SO 3)

E18–2 Burt Reynolds Company reported net income of $195,000 for 1999. Reynolds also reported depreciation expense of $45,000, and a loss of $5,000 on the sale of equipment. The comparative balance sheet shows an increase in accounts receivable of $15,000 for the year, an $8,000 increase in accounts payable, and a decrease in prepaid expenses $4,000.

Instructions
Prepare the operating activities section of the statement of cash flows for 1999. Use the indirect method.

E18–3   The current sections of Greg Kinnear Co. balance sheets at December 31, 1998 and 1999, are presented below.

Prepare the operating activities section—indirect method.
(SO 3)

GREG KINNEAR CO.
Balance Sheet (partial)
December 31

	1999	1998	
Current assets			
Cash	$105,000	$ 99,000	*Increase 6,000*
Accounts receivable	110,000	89,000	*increase 21000*
Inventory	171,000	186,000	*decrease 15000*
Prepaid expenses	27,000	32,000	*decrease 5000*
Total current assets	$413,000	$406,000	
Current liabilities			
Accrued expenses payable	$ 15,000	$ 5,000	*increase 10000*
Accounts payable	$ 85,000	$ 92,000	*decrease 7000*
Total current liabilities	$100,000	$ 97,000	

Kinnear's net income for 1999 was $153,000. Depreciation expense was $24,000.

Instructions
Prepare the net cash provided by operating activities section of Kinnear's statement of cash flows for the year ended December 31, 1999, using the indirect method.

E18–4   Presented below are three accounts that appear in the general ledger of Anthony Hopkins Co. during 1999:

Prepare a partial statement of cash flows—indirect method.
(SO 3)

Equipment

Date		Debit	Credit	Balance
Jan. 1	Balance			160,000
July 31	Purchase of equipment	70,000		230,000
Sept. 2	Cost of equipment constructed	53,000		283,000
Nov. 10	Cost of equipment sold		45,000	238,000

Accumulated Depreciation—Equipment

Date		Debit	Credit	Balance
Jan. 1	Balance			71,000
Nov. 10	Accumulated depreciation on equipment sold	30,000		41,000
Dec. 31	Depreciation for year		24,000	65,000

Retained Earnings

Date		Debit	Credit	Balance
Jan. 1	Balance			105,000
Aug. 23	Dividends (cash)	14,000		91,000
Dec. 31	Net income		67,000	158,000

Instructions
From the postings in the accounts above, indicate how the information is reported on a statement of cash flows by preparing a partial statement of cash flows using the indirect method. The loss on sale of equipment was $6,000.

E18–5   A comparative balance sheet for Rupert Everett Company is presented below.

Prepare a statement of cash flows—indirect method.
(SO 3, 5)

RUPERT EVERETT COMPANY
Balance Sheet
December 31

Assets	1999	1998
Cash	$ 63,000	$ 22,000
Accounts receivable	85,000	76,000
Inventories	180,000	189,000
Land	75,000	100,000
Equipment	260,000	200,000
Accumulated depreciation	(66,000)	(42,000)
Total	$597,000	$545,000

Liabilities and Stockholders' Equity	1999	1998
Accounts payable	$ 34,000	$ 47,000
Bonds payable	150,000	200,000
Common stock ($1 par)	214,000	164,000
Retained earnings	199,000	134,000
Total	$597,000	$545,000

Additional information:

1. Net income for 1999 was $105,000.
2. Cash dividends of $40,000 were declared and paid.
3. Bonds payable amounting to $50,000 were redeemed for cash $50,000.
4. Common stock was issued for $50,000 cash.
5. Depreciation expense was $24,000.
6. Sales for the year were $978,000.

Instructions

(a) Prepare a statement of cash flows for 1999 using the indirect method.
(b) Compute the following cash-basis ratios:
    (1) Current cash debt coverage ratio.
    (2) Cash return on sales ratio.
    (3) Cash debt coverage ratio.

Classify transactions by type of activity.
(SO 2)

E18–6 An analysis of comparative balance sheets, the current year's income statement, and the general ledger accounts of Kevin Spacey Corp. uncovered the following items. Assume all items involve cash unless there is information to the contrary.

(a) Issuance of capital stock.
(b) Amortization of patent.
(c) Issuance of bonds for land.
(d) Payment of interest on notes payable.
(e) Conversion of bonds into common stock.
(f) Sale of land at a loss.
(g) Receipt of dividends on investment in stock.
(h) Purchase of land.
(i) Payment of dividends.
(j) Sale of building at book value.
(k) Exchange of land for patent.
(l) Depreciation.
(m) Redemption of bonds.
(n) Receipt of interest on notes receivable.

Instructions
Indicate how the above items should be classified in the statement of cash flows using the following four major classifications: operating activity (indirect method), investing activity, financing activity, and significant noncash investing and financing activity.

Compute cash provided by operating activities—direct method.
(SO 4)

E18–7 Judi Dench Company has just completed its first year of operations on December 31, 1999. Its initial income statement showed that Judi Dench had revenues of $157,000 and operating expenses of $88,000. Accounts receivable and accounts payable at year-end were $42,000 and $33,000, respectively. Assume that accounts payable related to operating expenses. Ignore income taxes.

Instructions
Compute net cash provided by operating activities using the direct method.

E18-8 The income statement for Helen Hunt Company shows cost of goods sold $355,000 and operating expenses (exclusive of depreciation) $250,000. The comparative balance sheet for the year shows that inventory increased $6,000, prepaid expenses decreased $6,000, accounts payable (merchandise suppliers) decreased $8,000, and accrued expenses payable increased $8,000.

Compute cash payments— direct method. (SO 4)

Instructions
Using the direct method, compute (a) cash payments to suppliers and (b) cash payments for operating expenses.

E18-9 The 1999 accounting records of Helena Bonham Co. reveal the following transactions and events.

Compute cash flow from operating activities— direct method. (SO 2, 4)

Payment of interest	$ 6,000	Collection of accounts receivable	$180,000
Cash sales	48,000	Payment of salaries and wages	68,000
Receipt of dividend revenue	14,000	Depreciation expense	18,000
Payment of income taxes	15,000	Proceeds from sale of aircraft	812,000
Net income	38,000	Purchase of equipment for cash	22,000
Payment of accounts payable for		Loss on sale of aircraft	3,000
merchandise	90,000	Payment of dividends	14,000
Payment for land	74,000	Payment of operating expenses	20,000

Instructions
Prepare the cash flows from operating activities section using the direct method. (Not all of the above items will be used.)

E18-10 The following information is taken from the 1999 general ledger of Robert Duvall Company:

Calculate cash flows—direct method. (SO 4)

Rent	Rent expense	$ 33,000
	Prepaid rent, January 1	5,900
	Prepaid rent, December 31	3,000
Salaries	Salaries expense	$ 54,000
	Salaries payable, January 1	5,000
	Salaries payable, December 31	8,000
Sales	Revenue from sales	$180,000
	Accounts receivable, January 1	12,000
	Accounts receivable, December 31	9,000

Instructions
In each of above cases, compute the amount that should be reported in the operating activities section of the statement of cash flows applying the direct method.

E18-11 Presented here is information for two companies in the same industry: Morgan Corporation and Cole Corporation.

Compare two companies by using cash-based ratios. (SO 5)

	Morgan Corporation	Cole Corporation
Cash provided by operations	$200,000	$200,000
Average current liabilities	50,000	100,000
Average total libilities	200,000	250,000
Net income	200,000	200,000
Sales	400,000	800,000

Instructions
Using the cash-based ratios presented in this chapter, compare the (a) liquidity, (b) solvency, and (c) profitability of the two companies.

*E18-12 Information for Rupert Everett Company is presented in E18-5.

Prepare a work sheet. (SO 6)

Instructions
Use the data in E18-5 to prepare a work sheet for a statement of cash flows for 1999. Enter the reconciling items directly on the work sheet, identifying the entries alphabetically.

PROBLEMS: SET A

Prepare the operating activities section—indirect method.
(SO 3)

P18–1A   The income statement of Oprah Winfrey Company is shown below:

OPRAH WINFREY COMPANY
Income Statement
For the Year Ended November 30, 1999

Sales		$6,900,000
Cost of goods sold		
Beginning inventory	$2,000,000	
Purchases	4,300,000	
Goods available for sale	6,300,000	
Ending inventory	1,600,000	
Cost of goods sold		4,700,000
Gross profit		2,200,000
Operating expenses		
Selling expenses	450,000	
Administrative expenses	700,000	1,150,000
Net income		$1,050,000

Additional information:

1. Accounts receivable decreased $290,000 during the year.
2. Prepaid expenses increased $150,000 during the year.
3. Accounts payable to suppliers of merchandise decreased $300,000 during the year.
4. Accrued expenses payable decreased $100,000 during the year.
5. Administrative expenses include depreciation expense of $90,000.

Instructions
Prepare the operating activities section of the statement of cash flows for the year ended November 30, 1999, for Oprah Winfrey Company using the indirect method.

Prepare the operating activities section—direct method.
(SO 4)

P18–2A   Data for the Oprah Winfrey Company are presented in P18–1A.

Instructions
Prepare the operating activities section of the statement of cash flows using the direct method.

Prepare the operating activities section—direct method.
(SO 4)

P18–3A   Pierce Brosnan Company's income statement for the year ended December 31, 1999, contained the following condensed information:

Revenue from fees		$900,000
Operating expenses (excluding depreciation)	$624,000	
Depreciation expense	60,000	
Loss on sale of equipment	26,000	710,000
Income before income taxes		190,000
Income tax expense		40,000
Net income		$150,000

Brosnan's balance sheet contained the following comparative data at December 31:

	1999	1998
Accounts receivable	$47,000	$55,000
Accounts payable	41,000	33,000
Income taxes payable	4,000	9,000

(Accounts payable pertains to operating expenses.)

Prepare the operating activities section—indirect method.
(SO 3)

Instructions
Prepare the operating activities section of the statement of cash flows using the direct method.

P18–4A   Data for Pierce Brosnan Company are presented in P18–3A.

Instructions
Prepare the operating activities section of the statement of cash flows for Pierce Brosnan Company using the indirect method.

P18–5A   The financial statements of Joan E. Robinson Company appear below:

Prepare a statement of cash flows—indirect method.
(SO 3, 5)

JOAN E. ROBINSON COMPANY
Comparative Balance Sheet
December 31

Assets	1999	1998	
Cash	$ 29,000	$ 13,000	↑ 16,000
Accounts receivable	28,000	14,000	↑ 14,000
Merchandise inventory	25,000	35,000	↓ 10,000
Property, plant, and equipment	60,000	78,000	↓ 18,000
Accumulated depreciation	(20,000)	(24,000)	↑ 4,000
Total	$122,000	$116,000	

Liabilities and Stockholders' Equity			
Accounts payable	$ 29,000	$ 23,000	↑ 6,000
Income taxes payable	5,000	8,000	↓ 3,000
Bonds payable	27,000	33,000	↓ 6,000
Common stock	18,000	14,000	↓ 4,000
Retained earnings	43,000	38,000	↑ 5,000
Total	$122,000	$116,000	

JOAN E. ROBINSON COMPANY
Income Statement
For the Year Ended December 31, 1999

Sales		$220,000
Cost of goods sold		180,000
Gross profit		40,000
Selling expenses	$14,000	
Administrative expenses	10,000	24,000
Income from operations		16,000
Interest expense		2,000
Income before income taxes		14,000
Income tax expense		4,000
Net income		$ 10,000

The following additional data were provided:

1. Dividends declared and paid were $5,000.
2. During the year equipment was sold for $8,500 cash. This equipment cost $18,000 originally and had a book value of $8,500 at the time of sale.
3. All depreciation expense is in the selling expense category.
4. All sales and purchases are on account.

Instructions

(a) Prepare a statement of cash flows using the indirect method.
(b) Compute the following cash-basis ratios:
  (1) Current cash debt coverage ratio.
  (2) Cash return on sales ratio.
  (3) Cash debt coverage ratio.

P18–6A   Data for the Joan E. Robinson Company are presented in P18–5A. Further analysis reveals the following:

1. Accounts payable pertain to merchandise suppliers.
2. All operating expenses except for depreciation were paid in cash.

Prepare a statement of cash flows—direct method.
(SO 4, 5)

Instructions

(a) Prepare a statement of cash flows for Joan E. Robinson Company using the direct method.

(b) Compute the following cash-basis ratios:
 (1) Current cash debt coverage ratio.
 (2) Cash return on sales ratio.
 (3) Cash debt coverage ratio.

Prepare a statement of cash flows—indirect method.
(SO 3)

P18–7A The financial statements of Charlie Brown Company appear below:

CHARLIE BROWN COMPANY
Balance Sheet
December 31

Assets	1999	1998
Cash	$ 25,000	$ 11,000
Accounts receivable	22,000	33,000
Merchandise inventory	20,000	29,000
Prepaid expenses	15,000	13,000
Land	40,000	40,000
Property, plant, and equipment	210,000	225,000
Less: Accumulated depreciation	(55,000)	(67,500)
Total	$277,000	$283,500

Liabilities and Stockholders' Equity		
Accounts payable	$ 11,000	$ 18,500
Accrued expenses payable	9,500	7,500
Interest payable	1,000	1,500
Income taxes payable	3,000	2,000
Bonds payable	50,000	80,000
Common stock	125,000	105,000
Retained earnings	77,500	69,000
Total	$277,000	$283,500

CHARLIE BROWN COMPANY
Income Statement
For the Year Ended December 31, 1999

Revenues		
Sales	$600,000	
Gain on sale of plant assets	2,500	$602,500
Less: Expenses		
Cost of goods sold	$500,000	
Operating expenses (excluding depreciation)	60,000	
Depreciation expense	7,500	
Interest expense	5,000	
Income tax expense	9,000	581,500
Net income		$ 21,000

Additional information:

1. Plant assets were sold at a sales price of $37,500.
2. Additional equipment was purchased at a cost of $40,000.
3. Dividends of $12,500 were paid.
4. All sales and purchases were on account.
5. Bonds were redeemed at face value.
6. Additional shares of stock were issued for cash.

Instructions

Prepare a statement of cash flows for Charlie Brown Company for the year ended December 31, 1999, using the indirect method.

P18–8A Data for Charlie Brown Company is presented in P18–7A. Further analysis reveals the following:

Prepare a statement of cash flows—direct method.
(SO 4)

1. Accounts payable relates to merchandise creditors.
2. All operating expenses, except depreciation expense, were paid in cash.

Instructions

Prepare a statement of cash flows for Charlie Brown Company for the year ended December 31, 1999, using the direct method.

P18–9A Presented below is the comparative balance sheet for Karin Weigle Company as of December 31:

Prepare a statement of cash flows—indirect method.
(SO 3, 5)

KARIN WEIGLE COMPANY
Comparative Balance Sheet
December 31

Assets	1999	1998
Cash	$ 41,000	$ 45,000
Accounts receivable	47,500	52,000
Inventory	151,450	142,000
Prepaid expenses	16,780	21,000
Land	100,000	130,000
Equipment	228,000	155,000
Accumulated depreciation—equipment	(45,000)	(35,000)
Building	200,000	200,000
Accumulated depreciation—building	(60,000)	(40,000)
	$679,730	$670,000
Liabilities and Stockholders' Equity		
Accounts payable	$ 43,730	$ 40,000
Bonds payable	250,000	300,000
Common stock, $1 par	200,000	150,000
Retained earnings	186,000	180,000
	$679,730	$670,000

Additional information:

1. Operating expenses include depreciation expense of $42,000.
2. Land was sold for cash at book value.
3. Cash dividends of $32,000 were paid.
4. Net income for 1999 was $38,000.
5. Equipment was purchased for $95,000 cash. In addition, equipment costing $22,000 with a book value of $10,000 was sold for $8,100 cash.
6. Bonds were converted at face value by issuing 50,000 shares of $1 par value common stock.
7. Net sales for 1999 totaled $420,000.

Instructions

(a) Prepare a statement of cash flows for the year ended December 31, 1999, using the indirect method.
(b) Compute the following cash-basis ratios for 1999:
   (1) Current cash debt coverage ratio.
   (2) Cash return on sales ratio.
   (3) Cash debt coverage ratio.

Prepare a work sheet.
(SO 6)

*P18–10A Data for Charlie Brown Company are presented in P18–7A.

Instructions
Prepare a work sheet for a statement of cash flows for 1999. Enter the reconciling entries directly on the work sheet, identifying the entries alphabetically.

PROBLEMS: SET B

Prepare the operating activities section—indirect method.
(SO 3)

P18–1B   The income statement of Emma Thompson Company is shown below:

EMMA THOMPSON COMPANY
Income Statement
For the Year Ended December 31, 1999

Sales		$7,100,000
Cost of goods sold		
Beginning inventory	$1,700,000	
Purchases	5,430,000	
Goods available for sale	7,130,000	
Ending inventory	1,920,000	
Cost of goods sold		5,210,000
Gross profit		1,890,000
Operating expenses		
Selling expenses	380,000	
Administrative expense	525,000	
Depreciation expense	75,000	
Amortization expense	30,000	1,010,000
Net income		$ 880,000

Additional information:

1. Accounts receivable increased $510,000 during the year.
2. Prepaid expenses increased $170,000 during the year.
3. Accounts payable to merchandise suppliers increased $50,000 during the year.
4. Accrued expenses payable decreased $180,000 during the year.

Instructions
Prepare the operating activities section of the statement of cash flows for the year ended December 31, 1999, for Emma Thompson Company using the indirect method.

Prepare the operating activities section—direct method.
(SO 4)

P18–2B   Data for the Emma Thompson Company are presented in P18–1B.

Instructions
Prepare the operating activities section of the statement of cash flows using the direct method.

Prepare the operating activities section—direct method.
(SO 4)

P18–3B   The income statement of Kanapilei International Co. for the year ended December 31, 1999, reported the following condensed information:

Revenue from fees	$470,000
Operating expenses	280,000
Income from operations	190,000
Income tax expense	47,000
Net income	$143,000

Kanapilei's balance sheet contained the following comparative data at December 31:

	1999	1998
Accounts receivable	$50,000	$40,000
Accounts payable	30,000	41,000
Income taxes payable	6,000	4,000

Kanapilei has no depreciable assets. (Accounts payable pertains to operating expenses.)

Instructions
Prepare the operating activities section of the statement of cash flows using the direct method.

P18–4B Data for Kanapilei International Co. are presented in P18–3B.

Instructions
Prepare the operating activities section of the statement of cash flows using the indirect method.

Prepare the operating activities section—indirect method.
(SO 3)

P18–5B The financial statements of Adam Sandler Company appear below:

Prepare a statement of cash flows—indirect method.
(SO 3, 5)

ADAM SANDLER COMPANY
Comparative Balance Sheet
December 31

Assets		1999		1998
Cash		$ 26,000		$ 13,000
Accounts receivable		18,000		14,000
Merchandise inventory		38,000		35,000
Property, plant, and equipment	$70,000		$78,000	
Less accumulated depreciation	(30,000)	40,000	(24,000)	54,000
Total		$122,000		$116,000

Liabilities and Stockholders' Equity		1999		1998
Accounts payable		$ 29,000		$ 33,000
Income taxes payable		15,000		20,000
Bonds payable		20,000		10,000
Common stock		25,000		25,000
Retained earnings		33,000		28,000
Total		$122,000		$116,000

ADAM SANDLER COMPANY
Income Statement
For the Year Ended December 31, 1999

Sales		$240,000
Cost of goods sold		180,000
Gross profit		60,000
Selling expenses	$24,000	
Administrative expenses	10,000	34,000
Income from operations		26,000
Interest expense		2,000
Income before income taxes		24,000
Income tax expense		7,000
Net income		$ 17,000

The following additional data were provided:

1. Dividends of $12,000 were declared and paid.
2. During the year equipment was sold for $10,000 cash. This equipment cost $15,000 originally and had a book value of $10,000 at the time of sale.
3. All depreciation expense, $11,000, is in the selling expense category.
4. All sales and purchases are on account.
5. Additional equipment was purchased for $7,000 cash.

Instructions
(a) Prepare a statement of cash flows using the indirect method.
(b) Compute the following cash-basis ratios:
   (1) Current cash debt coverage ratio.
   (2) Cash return on sales ratio.
   (3) Cash debt coverage ratio.

Prepare a statement of cash flows—direct method.
(SO 4, 5)

P18–6B Data for the Adam Sandler Company are presented in P18–5B. Further analysis reveals the following:

1. Accounts payable pertains to merchandise creditors.
2. All operating expenses except for depreciation are paid in cash.

Instructions

(a) Prepare a statement of cash flows using the direct method.
(b) Compute the following cash-basis ratios:
    (1) Current cash debt coverage ratio.
    (2) Cash return on sales ratio.
    (3) Cash debt coverage ratio.

Prepare a statement of cash flows—indirect method.
(SO 3)

P18–7B Condensed financial data of Dan Aykroyd Company appear below:

DAN AYKROYD COMPANY
Comparative Balance Sheet
December 31

Assets	1999	1998
Cash	$ 96,700	$ 47,250
Accounts receivable	86,800	57,000
Inventories	121,900	102,650
Investments	84,500	87,000
Plant assets	250,000	205,000
Accumulated depreciation	(49,500)	(40,000)
	$590,400	$458,900

Liabilities and Stockholders' Equity	1999	1998
Accounts payable	$ 52,700	$ 48,280
Accrued expenses payable	12,100	18,830
Bonds payable	100,000	70,000
Common stock	250,000	200,000
Retained earnings	175,600	121,790
	$590,400	$458,900

DAN AYKROYD COMPANY
Income Statement Data
For the Year Ended December 31, 1999

Sales		$297,500
Gain on sale of plant assets		8,750
		306,250
Less:		
Cost of goods sold	$99,460	
Operating expenses (excluding depreciation expense)	14,670	
Depreciation expense	49,700	
Income taxes	7,270	
Interest expense	2,940	174,040
Net income		$132,210

Additional information:

1. New plant assets costing $92,000 were purchased for cash during the year.
2. Investments were sold at cost.
3. Plant assets costing $47,000 were sold for $15,550, resulting in a gain of $8,750.
4. A cash dividend of $78,400 was declared and paid during the year.

Instructions
Prepare a statement of cash flows using the indirect method.

P18–8B   Data for Dan Aykroyd Company are presented in P18–7B. Further analysis reveals that accounts payable pertains to merchandise creditors.

Prepare a statement of cash flows—direct method.
(SO 4)

Instructions
Prepare a statement of cash flows for Dan Aykroyd Company using the direct method.

P18–9B   Presented below is the comparative balance sheet for Andy Garcia Company at December 31:

Prepare a statement of cash flows—indirect method.
(SO 3, 5)

ANDY GARCIA COMPANY
Comparative Balance Sheet
December 31

Assets	1999	1998
Cash	$ 40,000	$ 57,000
Accounts receivable	77,000	64,000
Inventory	132,000	140,000
Prepaid expenses	12,140	16,540
Land	125,000	150,000
Equipment	200,000	175,000
Accumulated depreciation—equipment	(60,000)	(42,000)
Building	250,000	250,000
Accumulated depreciation—building	(75,000)	(50,000)
	$701,140	$760,540
Liabilities and Stockholders' Equity		
Accounts payable	$ 33,000	$ 45,000
Bonds payable	235,000	265,000
Common stock, $1 par	280,000	250,000
Retained earnings	153,140	200,540
	$701,140	$760,540

Additional information:

1. Operating expenses include depreciation expense of $70,000 and charges from prepaid expenses of $4,400.
2. Land was sold for cash at cost.
3. Cash dividends of $74,290 were paid.
4. Net income for 1999 was $26,890.
5. Equipment was purchased for $65,000 cash. In addition, equipment costing $40,000 with a book value of $13,000 was sold for $14,000 cash.
6. Bonds were converted at face value by issuing 30,000 shares of $1 par value common stock.
7. Net sales in 1999 were $367,000.

Instructions

(a) Prepare a statement of cash flows for 1999 using the indirect method.
(b) Compute the following cash-basis ratios for 1999:
    (1) Current cash debt coverage ratio.
    (2) Cash return on sales ratio.
    (3) Cash debt coverage ratio.

*P18–10B   Data for Dan Aykroyd Company are presented in P18–7B.

Prepare a work sheet
(SO 6)

Instructions
Prepare a work sheet for a statement of cash flows. Enter the reconciling items directly in the work sheet columns, identifying the debit and credit amounts alphabetically.

BROADENING YOUR PERSPECTIVE

FINANCIAL REPORTING AND ANALYSIS

FINANCIAL REPORTING PROBLEM: Kellogg Company

BYP18–1   Refer to the financial statements of Kellogg Company, presented in Appendix A and answer the following questions:

(a) What was the amount of net cash provided by operating activities for the year 1997? For the year 1996?

(b) What was the amount of increase or decrease in cash and cash equivalents for the year 1997? For the year 1996?

(c) Which method of computing net cash provided by operating activities does Kellogg use?

(d) From your analysis of the 1997 statement of cash flows, did the change in accounts receivable require or provide cash? Did the change in inventories require or provide cash? Did the change in accounts payable require or provide cash?

(e) What was the net outflow or inflow of cash from investing activities for 1997?

(f) What was the amount of interest paid in 1997? What was the amount of income taxes paid in 1997?

COMPARATIVE ANALYSIS PROBLEM: Kellogg Company vs. General Mills

BYP18–2   Kellogg's financial statements are presented in Appendix A; General Mills's financial statements are presented in Appendix B.

Instructions

(a) Based on the information contained in these financial statements, compute the following 1997 ratios for each company:
(1) Current cash debt coverage ratio
(2) Cash return on sales ratio
(3) Cash debt coverage ratio

(b) What conclusions concerning the management of cash can be drawn from these data?

RESEARCH ASSIGNMENT

BYP18–3   The March 25, 1996, issue of *Barron's* includes an article by Harry B. Ernst and Jeffrey D. Fotta, entitled "Weary Bull."

Instructions

Read the article and answer the following questions:

(a) The article describes a cash flow-based model used by investors. Identify the model and briefly describe its purpose.

(b) How does the model classify a firm's cash flows?

(c) Identify one way in which the cash flow classifications described in the article differ from those under GAAP.

(d) How can the model be used to predict stock prices?

INTERPRETING FINANCIAL STATEMENTS: Vermont Teddy Bear Co.

BYP18–4   Founded in the early 1980s, the Vermont Teddy Bear Co. designs and manufactures American-made teddy bears and markets them primarily as gifts called Bear-Grams or Teddy Bear-Grams. Bear-Grams are personalized teddy bears delivered directly to the recipient for special occasions such as birthdays and anniversaries. The Shelburne, Vermont, company's primary markets are New York, Boston, and Chicago. Sales have jumped dramatically in recent years, exceeding 50% increases in several consecutive years prior to 1994. Such dramatic growth has significant implications for cash flows. Provided below are the company's cash flow statements for 1993 and 1994.

VERMONT TEDDY BEAR CO. Comparative Statement of Cash Flows For the Years Ended December 31	1994	1993
Cash flows from operating activities		
Net income	$ 17,523	$ 838,955
Adjustments to reconcile net income to net cash provided by operating activities		
Deferred income taxes	(69,524)	(146,590)
Depreciation and amortization	316,416	181,348
Changes in assets and liabilities		
Accounts receivable, trade	(38,267)	(25,947)
Inventories	(1,599,014)	(1,289,293)
Prepaid and other current assets	(444,794)	(113,205)
Deposit and other assets	(24,240)	(83,044)
Accounts payable	2,017,059	(284,567)
Accrued expenses	61,321	170,755
Accrued interest payable, debentures	—	(58,219)
Other	—	(8,960)
Income taxes payable	—	117,810
Net cash provided by (used for) operating activities	236,480	(700,957)
Net cash used for investing activities	(2,102,892)	(4,422,953)
Net cash (used for) provided by financing activities	(315,353)	9,685,435
Net change in cash and cash equivalents	$(2,181,765)	$ 4,561,525

Other information:

	1994	1993
Current liabilities	$ 4,055,465	$ 1,995,600
Total liabilities	4,620,085	2,184,386
Net sales	20,560,566	17,025,856

Instructions

(a) Note that net income in 1994 was only $17,523 compared to 1993 income of $838,955, but cash flow from operations was $236,480 in 1994 and a negative $700,957 in 1993. Explain the causes of this apparent paradox.

(b) Evaluate Vermont Teddy Bear's liquidity, solvency, and profitability for 1994 using cash-based ratios.

REAL-WORLD FOCUS: Praxair Incorporated

BYP18–5   Praxair was founded in 1907 as Linde-Air Products Company and was a pioneer in separating oxygen from air. It was purchased and run as a division of Union Carbide. In 1992 Praxair became an independent public company. Today, the company is one of the top three largest suppliers of industrial gases worldwide. Praxair has operations in all regions of the world, with half of its sales occurring outside of the United States.

The following management discussion was included in a recent annual report:

PRAXAIR INCORPORATED
Management Discussion and Analysis

Liquidity, Capital Resources and Other Financial Data: This year, Praxair changed its presentation of the Statement of Cash Flows to the direct method to report major classes of cash receipts and payments from operations. Praxair believes the direct method more clearly presents its operating cash flows. Prior years' cash flow information has been reclassified to conform to the current year presentation.

Instructions

(a) What method has Praxair changed from?
(b) What will the newly prepared cash flow statement show that the former one did not?
(c) Will the cash flows from investing and financing appear any differently under the new method of preparation than they did under the old method?

CRITICAL THINKING

GROUP DECISION CASE

BYP18–6   Greg Rhoda and Debra Sondgeroth are examining the following statement of cash flows for K.K. Bean Trading Company for the year ended January 31, 1998.

K.K. BEAN TRADING COMPANY
Statement of Cash Flows
For the Year Ended January 31, 1998

Sources of cash	
From sales of merchandise	$370,000
From sale of capital stock	420,000
From sale of investment (purchased below)	80,000
From depreciation	55,000
From issuance of note for truck	20,000
From interest on investments	6,000
Total sources of cash	951,000
Uses of cash	
For purchase of fixtures and equipment	340,000
For merchandise purchased for resale (all sold)	258,000
For operating expenses (including depreciation)	160,000
For purchase of investment	75,000
For purchase of truck by issuance of note	20,000
For purchase of treasury stock	10,000
For interest on note payable	3,000
Total uses of cash	866,000
Net increase in cash	$ 85,000

Greg claims that K.K. Bean's statement of cash flows is an excellent portrayal of a superb first year with cash increasing $85,000. Debra replies that it was not a superb first year—but rather, that the year was an operating failure, that the statement was incorrectly presented, and that $85,000 is not the actual increase in cash. The cash balance at the beginning of the year was $140,000.

Instructions

With the class divided into groups, answer the following:

  (a) With whom do you agree, Greg or Debra? Explain your position.
  (b) Using the data provided, prepare a statement of cash flows in proper form using the indirect method. The only noncash items in the income statement are depreciation and the gain from the sale of the investment.

COMMUNICATION ACTIVITY

BYP18–7   Arnold Byte, the owner-president of Computer Services Company, is unfamiliar with the statement of cash flows which you, as his accountant, prepared. He asks for further explanation.

Instructions

Write him a brief memo explaining the form and content of the statement of cash flows as shown in Illustration 18-18 on page 770.

ETHICS CASE

BYP18–8   Puebla Corporation is a medium-sized wholesaler of automotive parts. It has 10 stockholders, who have been paid a total of $1 million in cash dividends for 8 consecutive years. The policy of the Board of Directors requires that in order for this dividend to be declared, net cash provided by operating activities as reported in Puebla's current year's statement of cash flows must be in excess of $1 million. President and CEO Phil Monat's job is secure so long as he produces annual operating cash flows to support the usual dividend.

At the end of the current year, controller Rick Rodgers presents president Monat with some disappointing news—the net cash provided by operating activities is calculated by the indirect method to be only $970,000. The president says to Rick, "We must get that amount above $1 million. Isn't there some way to increase operating cash flow by another $30,000?" Rick answers, "These figures were prepared by my assistant. I'll go back to my office and see what I can do." The president replies, "I know you won't let me down, Rick."

Upon close scrutiny of the statement of cash flows, Rick concludes that he can get the operating cash flows above $1 million by reclassifying a $60,000, 2-year note payable listed in the financing activities section as "Proceeds from bank loan—$60,000." He will report the note instead as "Increase in payables—$60,000" and treat it as an adjustment of net income in the operating activities section. He returns to the president saying, "You can tell the Board to declare their usual dividend. Our net cash flow provided by operating activities is $1,030,000." "Good man, Rick! I knew I could count on you," exults the president.

Instructions

  (a) Who are the stakeholders in this situation?
  (b) Was there anything unethical about the president's actions? Was there anything unethical about the controller's actions?
  (c) Are the Board members or anyone else likely to discover the misclassification?

SURFING THE NET

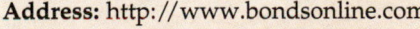

BYP18–9   Bonds, similar to stocks, can be purchased by investors in an initial public offering or through a secondary market. Secondary markets can be reached via the Internet and provide users with investment information. Bonds Online is one site that provides a bond-specific glossary of terms.

Address: http://www.bondsonline.com

Steps:
1. From the Bonds Online homepage, choose **Bond Professor.**
2. Choose **Glossary.**

Instructions
Using the glossary, find the definition of:

    (a) discount rate.
    (b) capital market.
    (c) rating.

Answers to Self-Study Questions
1. c   2. b   3. a   4. c   5. d   6. b   7. c   8. d   9. b   10. c   11. d
12. a   13. b

Answer to Kellogg Review It Question 4, p. 771
4. Kellogg uses the indirect method of computing net cash provided by operating activities. The largest single item of cash flow for Kellogg in 1997 is "Issuance of long-term debt, $1 billion."

Remember to go back to the Navigator box on the chapter-opening page and check off your completed work.

CONCEPTS FOR REVIEW

Before studying this chapter, you should know or, if necessary, review:

a. The contents and classification of a corporate balance sheet. (Ch. 4, pp. 157–162)

b. The contents and classification of a corporate income statement. (Ch. 5, pp. 200–202, 207–210)

c. Who are the various users of financial statement information. (Ch. 1, pp. 3–5)

d. How to compute earnings per share (EPS). (Ch. 15, p. 653–55)

e. How the liquidity of a company is determined. (Ch. 4, p. 160)

FEATURE STORY

Just Fooling Around?

The information superhighway added a new lane recently when two brothers, Tom and David Gardner, created an online investor service called the Motley Fool. The name comes from Shakespeare's *As You Like It*. The fool in Shakespeare's plays was the only one who could speak unpleasant truths to kings and queens without being killed. Tom and David view themselves as 20th-century "fools," revealing the "truths" of Wall Street to the small investor, who they feel has been taken advantage of by Wall Street insiders. They provide a bulletin board service where America Online subscribers can exchange information and insights about companies that may be of interest to investors.

One company, Iomega, has captured the interest of Motley Fool subscribers more than all others. Iomega makes a new kind of computer disk drive called a Zip drive. In less than one year, Iomega's stock price soared by a multiple of 16; that is, a $1,000 investment was suddenly worth $16,000! Many people suggest that this tremendous run-up in price (one of the highest increases experienced by any U.S. company during that period) was caused by the attention the stock received on the Motley Fool bulletin board. Supporters of the Motley Fool say that this is an example of how the Internet can be used by small investors to make the kind of returns that the "big guys" make. Participants share any information they can find about the company and its product: Are Zip drive users happy with the product? How quickly are Zip drives moving off store shelves? How full is the employee parking lot at Iomega on Sundays?

Critics, however, contend that the bulletin board is merely a high-tech rumor mill that has built a speculative house of cards. One potentially troubling aspect of the bulletin board is that participants on the board don't have to give their identities. Consequently, there is little to stop people from putting misinformation on the board to influence the price in the direction they desire.

As information services such as Motley Fool proliferate, gathering information will become easier, and evaluating it will become the harder task.

On the World Wide Web:
http://fool.yahoo.com
http://www.iomega.com

CHAPTER 19

FINANCIAL STATEMENT ANALYSIS

THE NAVIGATOR ✔

- Understand *Concepts for Review* ☐
- Read *Feature Story* ☐
- Scan *Study Objectives* ☐
- Read *Preview* ☐
- Read text and answer *Before You Go On*
  p. 827 ☐ p. 844 ☐ p. 845 ☐
- Work *Demonstration Problems* ☐
- Review *Summary of Study Objectives* ☐
- Answer *Self-Study Questions* ☐
- Complete assignments ☐

STUDY OBJECTIVES

After studying this chapter, you should be able to:

1. *Discuss the need for comparative analysis.*
2. *Identify the tools of financial statement analysis.*
3. *Explain and apply horizontal analysis.*
4. *Describe and apply vertical analysis.*
5. *Identify and compute ratios and describe their purpose and use in analyzing a firm's liquidity, profitability, and solvency.*
6. *Recognize the limitations of financial statement analysis.*

THE NAVIGATOR

*I*f you are thinking of purchasing Iomega Corporation stock, or the stock of any company, how can you determine the worth of the stock? How can you determine the company's financial soundness or its profitability? How does Iomega compare financially with other companies in the high-tech industry of computer disk-drive manufacturers? To answer these types of questions, it is helpful for you to understand how to analyze financial statement information.

Financial statement analysis, the topic of this chapter, enhances the usefulness of published financial statements in making decisions about a company. The content and organization of this chapter are shown below.

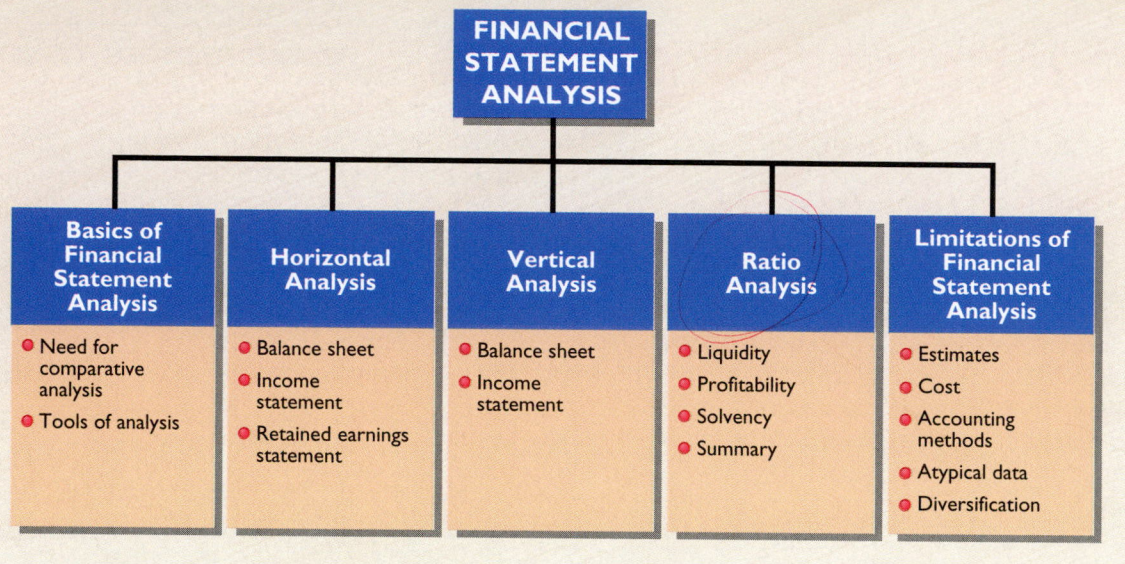

THE
NAVIGATOR

BASICS OF FINANCIAL STATEMENT ANALYSIS

Analyzing financial statements involves evaluating three characteristics of a company: its liquidity, its profitability, and its solvency. For example, a **short-term creditor**, such as a bank, is primarily interested in the ability of the borrower to pay obligations when they come due. The liquidity of the borrower in such a case is extremely important in evaluating the safety of a loan. A **long-term creditor**, such as a bondholder, however, looks to indicators such as profitability and solvency that indicate the firm's ability to survive over a long period of time. Long-term creditors consider such measures as the amount of debt in the company's capital structure and the ability to meet interest payments. Similarly, **stockholders** are interested in the profitability and solvency of the enterprise when they assess the likelihood of dividends and the growth potential of the stock.

Need for Comparative Analysis

Every item reported in a financial statement has significance. For example, when Iomega Corporation reports cash of $108 million on its balance sheet, we know the company had that amount of cash on the balance sheet date. However, we do not know whether the amount represents an increase over prior years or whether the amount is adequate in relation to the company's need for cash. To obtain this information, it is necessary to compare the amount of cash with other financial statement data.

Comparisons can be made on a number of different bases—three are illustrated in this chapter:

1. **Intracompany basis.** This basis compares an item or financial relationship **within a company** in the current year with the same item or relationship in one or more prior years. For example, a comparison of Iomega's cash balance at the end of the current year with last year's balance will show the amount of the increase or decrease. Likewise, Iomega can compare the percentage of cash to current assets at the end of the current year with the percentage in one or more prior years. Intracompany comparisons are useful in detecting changes in financial relationships and significant trends.
2. **Industry averages.** This basis compares an item or financial relationship of a company with **industry averages** (or **norms**) published by financial ratings organizations such as Dun & Bradstreet, Moody's, and Standard & Poor's. For example, Iomega's net income can be compared with the average net income of all companies in the computer hard-drive and storage solutions industry. Comparisons with industry averages provide information as to a company's relative performance within the industry.
3. **Intercompany basis.** This basis compares an item or financial relationship of one company with the same item or relationship in **one or more competing companies**. The comparisons are made on the basis of the published financial statements of the individual companies. For example, Iomega's total sales for the year can be compared with the total sales of its major competitors such as IBM and Nomai. Intercompany comparisons are useful in determining a company's competitive position.

Tools of Financial Statement Analysis

Various tools are used to evaluate the significance of financial statement data. Three commonly used tools are these:

Horizontal analysis is a technique for evaluating a series of financial statement data over a period of time.

Vertical analysis is a technique for evaluating financial statement data that expresses each item in a financial statement in terms of a percent of a base amount.

Ratio analysis expresses the relationship among selected items of financial statement data.

Horizontal analysis is used primarily in intracompany comparisons. Two features in published financial statements facilitate this type of comparison: First, each of the basic financial statements is presented on a comparative basis for a minimum of two years. Second, a summary of selected financial data is presented for a series of 5 to 10 years or more. Vertical analysis is used in both intra- and intercompany comparisons. Ratio analysis is used in all three types of compar-

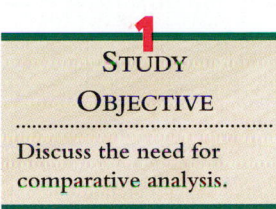

1
STUDY OBJECTIVE
Discuss the need for comparative analysis.

Intracompany

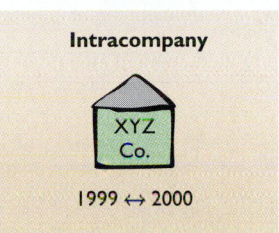

Industry averages

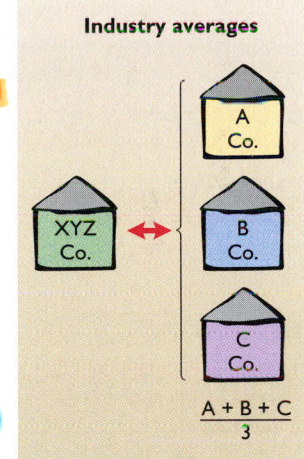

Intercompany

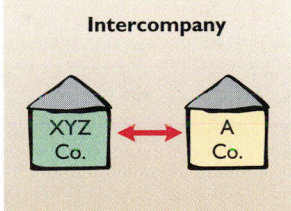

2
STUDY OBJECTIVE
Identify the tools of financial statement analysis.

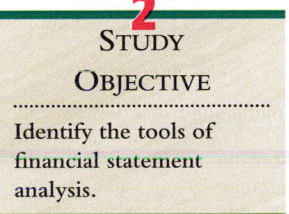

isons. In the following sections, we will explain and illustrate each of the three types of analysis.

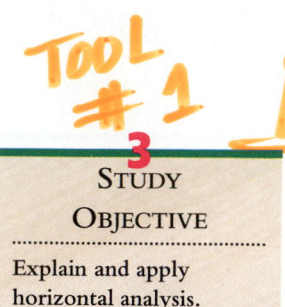

HORIZONTAL ANALYSIS

Horizontal analysis, also called trend analysis, is a technique for evaluating a series of financial statement data over a period of time. Its purpose is to determine the increase or decrease that has taken place, expressed as either an amount or a percentage. For example, the recent net sales figures of Sears, Roebuck and Co. are as follows (yes, that's $41 **billion** 296 million in 1997):

ILLUSTRATION 19-1

Sears, Roebuck's net sales

SEARS, ROEBUCK AND CO. Net Sales (in millions)				
1997	1996	1995	1994	1993
$41,296	$38,064	$34,835	$33,110	$30,518

If we assume that 1993 is the base year, we can measure all percentage increases or decreases from this base period amount as follows:

ILLUSTRATION 19-2

Formula for horizontal analysis of changes since base period

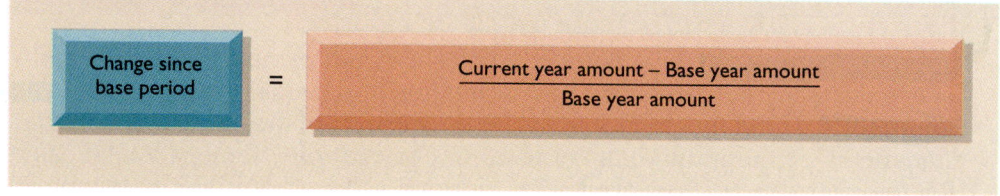

$$\text{Change since base period} = \frac{\text{Current year amount} - \text{Base year amount}}{\text{Base year amount}}$$

For example, we can determine that net sales for Sears, Roebuck increased approximately 8.5% [($33,110 − $30,518) ÷ $30,518] from 1993 to 1994. Similarly, we can determine that net sales increased over 35.3% [($41,296 − $30,518) ÷ $30,518] from 1993 to 1997.

Alternatively, we can express current year sales as a percentage of the base period by dividing the current year amount by the base year amount, as shown below:

ILLUSTRATION 19-3

Formula for horizontal analysis of current year in relation to base year

$$\text{Current results in relation to base period} = \frac{\text{Current year amount}}{\text{Base year amount}}$$

Illustration 19-4 presents this analysis for Sears for a 5-year period using 1993 as the base period.

SEARS, ROEBUCK AND CO. Net Sales (in millions) in relation to base period 1993				
1997	**1996**	**1995**	**1994**	**1993**
$41,296	$38,064	$34,835	$33,110	$30,518
135%	125%	114%	108%	100%

ILLUSTRATION 19-4

Horizontal analysis of Sears, Roebuck's net sales in relation to base period

Balance Sheet

To further illustrate horizontal analysis, we will use the financial statements of Quality Department Store Inc., a downtown full-line department store in a southeastern city of 55,000 population. Its 2-year condensed balance sheets for 1997 and 1996 showing dollar and percentage changes are presented in Illustration 19-5.

ILLUSTRATION 19-5

Horizontal analysis of a balance sheet

QUALITY DEPARTMENT STORE INC. Condensed Balance Sheet December 31				
			Increase or (Decrease) during 1997	
	1997	**1996**	**Amount**	**Percent**
Assets				
Current assets	$1,020,000	$ 945,000	$ 75,000	7.9%
Plant assets (net)	800,000	632,500	167,500	26.5%
Intangible assets	15,000	17,500	(2,500)	(14.3%)
Total assets	$1,835,000	$1,595,000	$240,000	15.0%
Liabilities				
Current liabilities	$ 344,500	$ 303,000	$ 41,500	13.7%
Long-term liabilities	487,500	497,000	(9,500)	(1.9%)
Total liabilities	832,000	800,000	32,000	4.0%
Stockholders' Equity				
Common stock, $1 par	275,400	270,000	5,400	2.0%
Retained earnings	727,600	525,000	202,600	38.6%
Total stockholders' equity	1,003,000	795,000	208,000	26.2%
Total liabilities and stockholders' equity	$1,835,000	$1,595,000	$240,000	15.0%

HELPFUL HINT

It is difficult to comprehend the significance of a change when only the dollar amount of change is examined. When the change is expressed in percentage form, it is easier to grasp the true magnitude of the change.

The comparative balance sheet in Illustration 19-5 shows that a number of significant changes have occurred in Quality Department Store's financial structure from 1996 to 1997. In the asset section, plant assets (net) increased $167,500, or 26.5%. In the liabilities section, current liabilities increased $41,500, or 13.7%. In the stockholders' equity section, we find that retained earnings increased $202,600, or 38.6%. This suggests that the company expanded its asset base during 1997 and financed this expansion primarily by retaining income in the business rather than assuming additional long-term debt.

Income Statement

Presented in Illustration 19-6 is a 2-year comparative income statement of Quality Department Store Inc. for the years 1997 and 1996, in a condensed format.

ILLUSTRATION 19-6

Horizontal analysis of an income statement

QUALITY DEPARTMENT STORE INC. Condensed Income Statement For the Years Ended December 31				
			Increase or (Decrease) during 1997	
	1997	1996	Amount	Percent
Sales	$2,195,000	$1,960,000	$235,000	12.0%
Sales returns and allowances	98,000	123,000	(25,000)	(20.3%)
Net sales	2,097,000	1,837,000	260,000	14.2%
Cost of goods sold	1,281,000	1,140,000	141,000	12.4%
Gross profit	816,000	697,000	119,000	17.1%
Selling expenses	253,000	211,500	41,500	19.6%
Administrative expenses	104,000	108,500	(4,500)	(4.1%)
Total operating expenses	357,000	320,000	37,000	11.6%
Income from operations	459,000	377,000	82,000	21.8%
Other revenues and gains				
Interest and dividends	9,000	11,000	(2,000)	(18.2%)
Other expenses and losses				
Interest expense	36,000	40,500	(4,500)	(11.1%)
Income before income taxes	432,000	347,500	84,500	24.3%
Income tax expense	168,200	139,000	29,200	21.0%
Net income	$ 263,800	$ 208,500	$ 55,300	26.5%

HELPFUL HINT

Note that while the amount column is additive (the total is $55,300), the percentage column is not additive (26.5% is not the total). A separate percentage has been calculated for each item.

Horizontal analysis of the income statements shows the following changes:

1. Net sales increased $260,000, or 14.2% ($260,000 ÷ $1,837,000).
2. Cost of goods sold increased $141,000, or 12.4% ($141,000 ÷ $1,140,000).
3. Total operating expenses increased $37,000, or 11.6% ($37,000 ÷ $320,000).

Overall, gross profit and net income were up substantially. Gross profit, for example, increased 17.1% and net income 26.5%. It appears, therefore, that Quality's profit trend is favorable.

Retained Earnings Statement

Quality Department Store's comparative retained earnings statement for the years 1997 and 1996 is presented in Illustration 19-7. Analyzed horizontally, net income increased $55,300, or 26.5%, whereas dividends on the common stock increased only $1,200, or 2%. Ending retained earnings, as shown in the horizontal analysis of the balance sheet, increased 38.6%. As indicated earlier, Quality Department Store Inc. retained a significant portion of its net income to finance expenditures for additional plant facilities.

QUALITY DEPARTMENT STORE INC. Retained Earnings Statement For the Years Ended December 31				
			Increase or (Decrease) during 1997	
	1997	**1996**	**Amount**	**Percent**
Retained earnings, Jan. 1	$525,000	$376,500	$148,500	39.4%
Add: Net income	263,800	208,500	55,300	26.5%
	788,800	585,000	203,800	
Deduct: Dividends	61,200	60,000	1,200	2.0%
Retained earnings, Dec. 31	$727,600	$525,000	$202,600	38.6%

ILLUSTRATION 19-7

*Horizontal analysis of a
retained earnings statement*

The measurement of changes from period to period in terms of percentages is relatively straightforward and is quite useful. However, complications can result in making the computations. For example, if an item has no value in a base year or preceding year and a value in the next year, no percentage change can be computed. Similarly, if a negative amount appears in the base or preceding period and a positive amount exists the following year, or vice versa, no percentage change can be computed.

VERTICAL ANALYSIS

Tool #2

Vertical analysis, sometimes referred to as **common size analysis**, is a technique for evaluating financial statement data that expresses each item within a financial statement in terms of a percent of a base amount. For example, on a balance sheet we might say that current assets are 22% of total assets (total assets being the base amount). Or on an income statement, we might say that selling expenses are 16% of net sales (net sales being the base amount).

4
STUDY
OBJECTIVE

Describe and apply
vertical analysis.

Balance Sheet

Presented in Illustration 19-8 on page 826 is the comparative balance sheet of Quality Department Store Inc. for 1997 and 1996, analyzed vertically. The base for the asset items is **total assets**, and the base for the liability and stockholders' equity items is **total liabilities and stockholders' equity**.

In addition to showing the relative size of each category on the balance sheet, vertical analysis may show the **percentage change** in the individual asset, liability, and stockholders' equity items. In this case, even though current assets increased $75,000 from 1996 to 1997, they decreased from 59.2% to 55.6% of total assets. Plant assets (net) have increased from 39.7% to 43.6% of total assets, and retained earnings have increased from 32.9% to 39.7% of total liabilities and stockholders' equity. These results reinforce the earlier observations that Quality is choosing to finance its growth through retention of earnings rather than through the issuance of additional debt.

Income Statement

Vertical analysis of the comparative income statements of Quality, shown in Illustration 19-9, reveals that cost of goods sold as a percentage of net sales de-

ILLUSTRATION 19-8

*Vertical analysis of a balance
sheet*

QUALITY DEPARTMENT STORE INC.
Condensed Balance Sheet
December 31

	1997		1996	
	Amount	Percent	Amount	Percent
Assets				
Current assets	$1,020,000	55.6%	$ 945,000	59.2%
Plant assets (net)	800,000	43.6%	632,500	39.7%
Intangible assets	15,000	.8%	17,500	1.1%
Total assets	$1,835,000	100.0%	$1,595,000	100.0%
Liabilities				
Current liabilities	$ 344,500	18.8%	$ 303,000	19.0%
Long-term liabilities	487,500	26.5%	497,000	31.2%
Total liabilities	832,000	45.3%	800,000	50.2%
Stockholders' Equity				
Common stock, $1 par	275,400	15.0%	270,000	16.9%
Retained earnings	727,600	39.7%	525,000	32.9%
Total stockholders' equity	1,003,000	54.7%	795,000	49.8%
Total liabilities and stockholders' equity	$1,835,000	100.0%	$1,595,000	100.0%

HELPFUL HINT

The formula for calculating these balance sheet percentages is:

$$\frac{\text{Each item on B/S}}{\text{Total assets}} = \%$$

clined 1% (62.1% vs. 61.1%) and total operating expenses declined 0.4% (17.4% vs. 17.0%). As a result, it is not surprising to see net income as a percent of net sales increase from 11.4% to 12.6%. As indicated from the horizontal analysis, Quality appears to be a profitable enterprise that is becoming even more successful.

ILLUSTRATION 19-9

*Vertical analysis of an
income statement*

QUALITY DEPARTMENT STORE INC.
Condensed Income Statement
For the Years Ended December 31

	1997		1996	
	Amount	Percent	Amount	Percent
Sales	$2,195,000	104.7%	$1,960,000	106.7%
Sales returns and allowances	98,000	4.7%	123,000	6.7%
Net sales	2,097,000	100.0%	1,837,000	100.0%
Cost of goods sold	1,281,000	61.1%	1,140,000	62.1%
Gross profit	816,000	38.9%	697,000	37.9%
Selling expenses	253,000	12.0%	211,500	11.5%
Administrative expenses	104,000	5.0%	108,500	5.9%
Total operating expenses	357,000	17.0%	320,000	17.4%
Income from operations	459,000	21.9%	377,000	20.5%
Other revenues and gains				
Interest and dividends	9,000	0.4%	11,000	0.6%
Other expenses and losses				
Interest expense	36,000	1.7%	40,500	2.2%
Income before income taxes	432,000	20.6%	347,500	18.9%
Income tax expense	168,200	8.0%	139,000	7.5%
Net income	$ 263,800	12.6%	$ 208,500	11.4%

HELPFUL HINT

The formula for calculating these income statement percentages is:

$$\frac{\text{Each item on I/S}}{\text{Net sales}} = \%$$

An associated benefit of vertical analysis is that it enables you to compare companies of different sizes. For example, Quality's main competitor is a Sears store in a nearby town. Using vertical analysis, the condensed income statements of the small local retail enterprise, Quality Department Store Inc., can be more meaningfully compared with the 1997 income statement of the giant international retailer, Sears, Roebuck and Co., as shown in Illustration 19-10.

ILLUSTRATION 19-10

Intercompany income statement comparison

Condensed Income Statements (in thousands)				
	Quality Department Store Inc.		Sears, Roebuck and Co.[1]	
	Dollars	**Percent**	**Dollars**	**Percent**
Net sales	$2,097	100.0%	$41,296,000	100.0%
Cost of goods sold	1,281	61.1%	26,769,000	64.8%
Gross profit	816	38.9%	14,527,000	35.2%
Selling and administrative expenses	357	17.0%	10,649,000	25.8%
Income from operations	459	21.9%	3,878,000	9.4%
Other expenses and revenues (including income taxes)	195	9.3%	2,690,000	6.5%
Net income	$ 264	12.6%	$ 1,188,000	2.9%

Although Sears' net sales are 19,693 times greater than the net sales of relatively tiny Quality Department Store, vertical analysis eliminates this difference in size. The percentages show that Quality's and Sears' gross profit rates were somewhat comparable at 38.9% and 35.2%, although the percentages related to income from operations were significantly different at 21.9% and 9.4%. This disparity can be attributed to Quality's selling and administrative expense percentage (17%) which is much lower than Sears' (25.8%). Although Sears earned net income more than 4,500 times larger than Quality's, Sears' net income as a **percent of each sales dollar** (2.9%) is only 23% of Quality's (12.6%).

BEFORE YOU GO ON . . .

Review It

1. What are the different tools that might be used to compare financial information?
2. What is horizontal analysis?
3. What is vertical analysis?
4. Identify the specific sections in Kellogg's 1997 Annual Report where horizontal and vertical analysis of financial data is presented. The answer to this question is provided on page 866.

Do It

Summary financial information for Rosepatch Company is as follows:

	December 31, 1999	December 31, 1998
Current assets	$234,000	$180,000
Plant assets (net)	756,000	420,000
Total assets	$990,000	$600,000

---

[1]Sears, Roebuck and Co., *1997 Annual Report* (Hoffman Estates, Illinois).

Compute the amount and percentage changes in 1999 using horizontal analysis, assuming 1998 is the base year.

Reasoning: Since 1998 is the base year, the percentage change is found by dividing the amount of the increase by the 1998 amount.

Solution:

	Increase in 1999	
	Amount	**Percent**
Current assets	$ 54,000	30% [($234,000 − $180,000) ÷ $180,000]
Plant assets (net)	336,000	80% [($756,000 − $420,000) ÷ $420,000]
Total assets	$390,000	65% [($990,000 − $600,000) ÷ $600,000]

Related exercise material: BE19–1, BE19–3, BE19–4, BE19–6, E19–1, E19–3, and E19–4.

Tool #3

5
STUDY
OBJECTIVE
....
Identify and compute ratios and describe their purpose and use in analyzing a firm's liquidity, profitability, and solvency.

HELPFUL HINT

Each of these is illustrated in the following sections.

RATIO ANALYSIS

Ratio analysis expresses the relationship among selected items of financial statement data. A **ratio** expresses the mathematical relationship between one quantity and another. The relationship is expressed in terms of either a percentage, a rate, or a simple proportion. To illustrate, recently Nike, Inc., had current assets of $3,830 million and current liabilities of $1,867 million. The relationship is determined by dividing current assets by current liabilities. The alternative means of expression are:

Percentage: Current assets are 205% of current liabilities.
Rate: Current assets are 2.05 times greater than current liabilities.
Proportion: The relationship of current assets to liabilities is 2.05:1.

TECHNOLOGY IN ACTION

Many general ledger accounting programs include the generation of financial ratios as routine output. All the ratio computations presented in this chapter can be done with electronic spreadsheets as well. There are also many programs written specifically for financial statement analysis. These packages are written for both general purpose use and use in specific industries. For example, financial institutions routinely use over 60 ratios geared specifically to the banking industry.

For analysis of the primary financial statements, ratios can be classified as pictured in Illustration 19-11.

Ratios can provide clues to underlying conditions that may not be apparent from inspection of the individual components of a particular ratio. However, a single ratio by itself is not very meaningful. Accordingly, in the following discussion we will use:

1. **Intracompany comparisons** covering 2 years for the Quality Department Store.

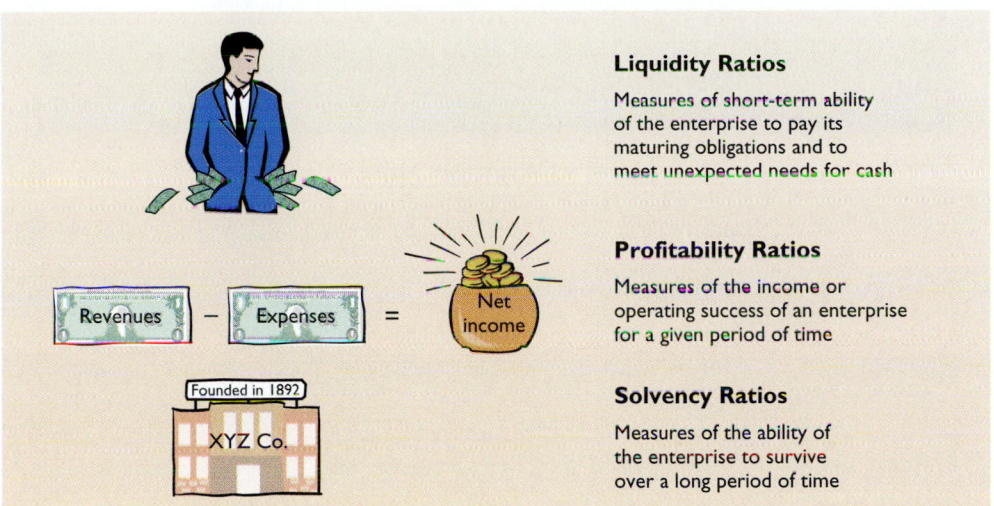

ILLUSTRATION 19-11
Financial ratio classifications

Liquidity Ratios

Measures of short-term ability of the enterprise to pay its maturing obligations and to meet unexpected needs for cash

Profitability Ratios

Measures of the income or operating success of an enterprise for a given period of time

Solvency Ratios

Measures of the ability of the enterprise to survive over a long period of time

2. **Industry average comparisons** based on Dun & Bradstreet's median ratios for department stores and Robert Morris Associates' median ratios for department stores.
3. **Intercompany comparisons** based on Sears, Roebuck and Co. as Quality Department Store's principal competitor.

Liquidity Ratios

Liquidity ratios measure the short-term ability of the enterprise to pay its maturing obligations and to meet unexpected needs for cash. Short-term creditors such as bankers and suppliers are particularly interested in assessing **liquidity**. The ratios that can be used to determine the enterprise's short-term debt-paying ability are the current ratio, the acid-test ratio, the current cash debt coverage ratio, receivables turnover, and inventory turnover.

1. Current Ratio

The current ratio is a widely used measure for evaluating a company's liquidity and short-term debt-paying ability. The ratio is computed by dividing current assets by current liabilities. It is sometimes referred to as the **working capital ratio** because **working capital** is the excess of current assets over current liabilities. The current ratio is a more dependable indicator of liquidity than working capital. Two companies with the same amount of working capital may have significantly different current ratios. The 1997 and 1996 current ratios for Quality Department Store and comparative data are shown in Illustration 19-12 on page 830.

What does the ratio actually mean? The 1997 ratio of 2.96:1 means that for every dollar of current liabilities, Quality has $2.96 of current assets. Quality's current ratio has decreased in the current year. However, compared to the industry average of 3.2:1, and Sears' 1.94:1 current ratio, Quality appears to be reasonably liquid.

The current ratio is only one measure of liquidity. It does not take into account the composition of the current assets. For example, a satisfactory current ratio does not disclose the fact that a portion of the current assets may be tied up in slow-moving inventory. A dollar of cash is more readily available to pay the bills than is a dollar of slow-moving inventory.

$$\text{current ratio} = \frac{\text{current assets}}{\text{current liability}}$$

ILLUSTRATION 19-12

Current ratio

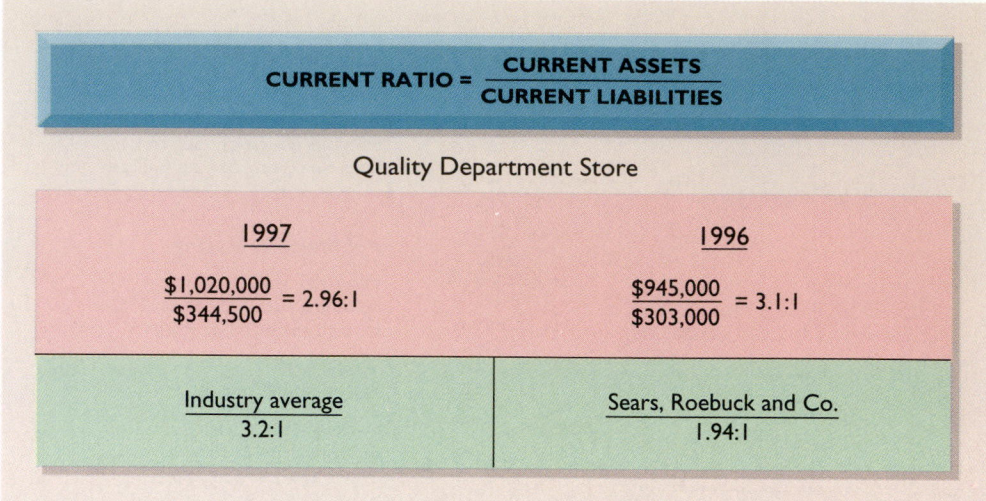

$$\text{CURRENT RATIO} = \frac{\text{CURRENT ASSETS}}{\text{CURRENT LIABILITIES}}$$

Quality Department Store

1997	1996
$\frac{\$1,020,000}{\$344,500} = 2.96:1$	$\frac{\$945,000}{\$303,000} = 3.1:1$
Industry average 3.2:1	Sears, Roebuck and Co. 1.94:1

2. Acid-Test Ratio

ALTERNATIVE TERMINOLOGY
The acid-test ratio is also called the *quick ratio.*

The **acid-test ratio** is a measure of a company's immediate short-term liquidity, computed by dividing the sum of cash, marketable securities, and net receivables by current liabilities. Thus, it is an important complement to the current ratio. For example, assume that the current assets of Quality Department Store for 1997 and 1996 consist of the following items:

ILLUSTRATION 19-13

Current assets of Quality Department Store

QUALITY DEPARTMENT STORE INC. Balance Sheet (partial)		
	1997	1996
Current assets		
Cash	$ 100,000	$155,000
Marketable securities	20,000	70,000
Receivables (net)	230,000	180,000
Inventory	620,000	500,000
Prepaid expenses	50,000	40,000
Total current assets	$1,020,000	$945,000

ACCOUNTING IN ACTION
Business Insight

The apparent simplicity of the current ratio can have real-world limitations because an addition of equal amounts to both the numerator and the denominator causes the ratio to decrease. Assume, for example, that a company has $2,000,000 of current assets and $1,000,000 of current liabilities; its current ratio is 2:1. If it purchases $1,000,000 of inventory on account, it will have $3,000,000 of current assets and $2,000,000 of current liabilities; its current ratio will decrease to 1.5:1. If, instead, the company pays off $500,000 of its current liabilities, it will have $1,500,000 of current assets and $500,000 of current liabilities, and its current ratio will increase to 3:1. Thus, any trend analysis should be done with care, since the ratio is susceptible to quick changes and is easily influenced by management.

Cash, marketable securities (short-term), and receivables (net) are highly liquid compared to inventory and prepaid expenses. The inventory may not be readily saleable and the prepaid expenses may not be transferable to others.

Thus, the acid-test ratio measures **immediate** liquidity. The 1997 and 1996 acid-test ratios for Quality Department Store and comparative data are as follows:

ILLUSTRATION 19-14

Acid-test ratio

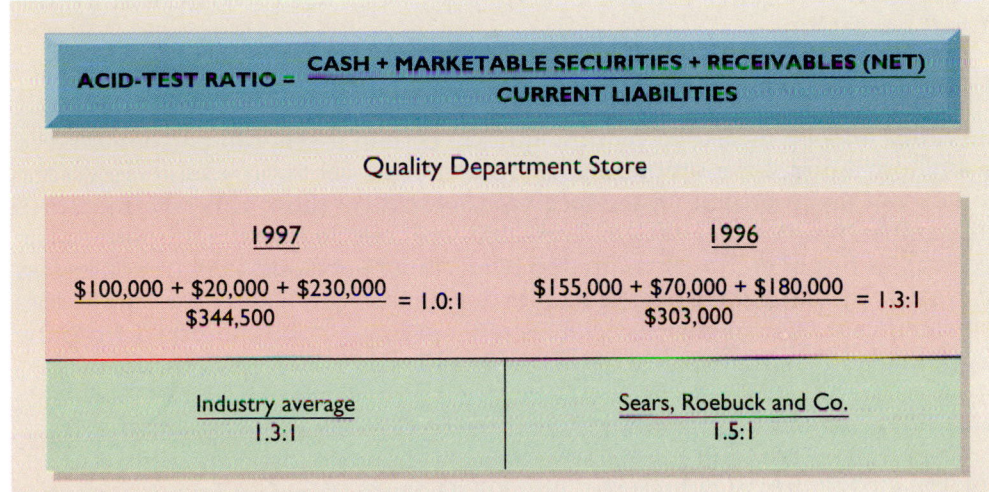

Is an acid-test ratio of 1.0:1 adequate? The ratio has declined in 1997. However, when compared with the industry median of 1.3:1 and Sears' of 1.5:1, Quality's acid-test ratio seems adequate.

3. Current Cash Debt Coverage Ratio

A disadvantage of the current and acid-test ratios is that they use year-end balances of current asset and current liability accounts. These year-end balances may not be representative of what the company's current position was during most of the year. A ratio that partially corrects for this problem is the ratio of net cash provided by operating activities to average current liabilities, referred to as the current cash debt coverage ratio. Because it uses net cash provided by operating activities rather than a balance at a point in time, it may provide a better representation of liquidity.

To illustrate the computation of this ratio, assume that Quality Department Store's statement of cash flows shows net cash flows provided by operating activities of $404,000 in 1997 and $340,000 in 1996 and that current liabilities at January 1, 1996, are $290,000. The current cash debt coverage ratio for Quality Department Store and comparative data are as follows:

ILLUSTRATION 19-15

Current cash debt coverage ratio

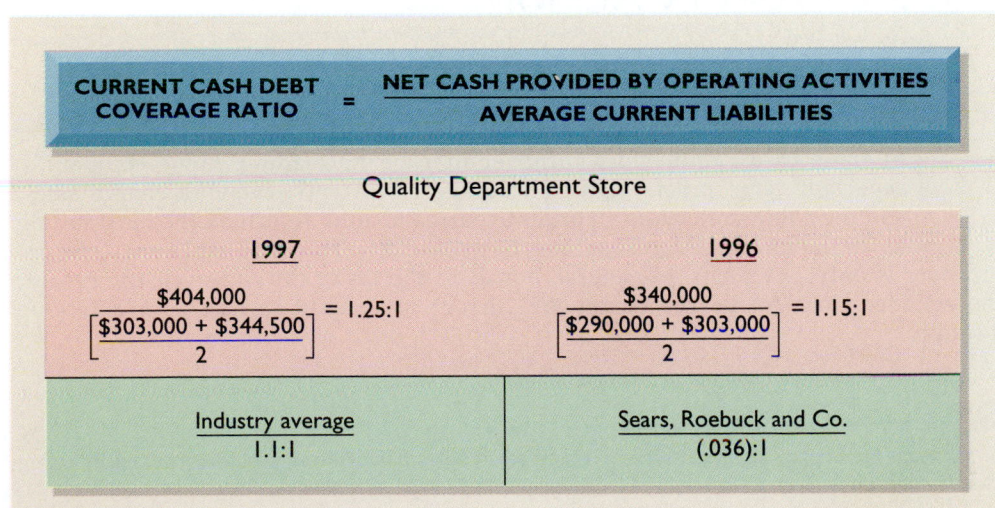

The ratio has increased in 1997. Is the coverage adequate? Probably so. Quality's operating cash flow coverage of average current liabilities is slightly greater than the industry average. Sears' current cash debt coverage ratio in 1997 was (.036):1. It was negative because operating activities **used** (as opposed to provided) net cash.

4. Receivables Turnover

Liquidity may be measured by how quickly certain assets can be converted to cash. How liquid, for example, are the receivables? The ratio used to assess the liquidity of the receivables is the **receivables turnover ratio**. This ratio measures the number of times, on average, receivables are collected during the period. The receivables turnover ratio is computed by dividing net credit sales (net sales less cash sales) by the average net receivables during the year. Unless seasonal factors are significant, average net receivables outstanding can be computed from the beginning and ending balance of the net receivables.[2]

Assuming that all sales are credit sales and the balance of accounts receivable (net) at the beginning of 1996 is $200,000, the receivables turnover ratio for Quality Department Store and comparative data are shown in Illustration 19-16. Quality's receivables turnover improved in 1997. The turnover of 10.2 times compares quite favorably with Sears' 2.11 times and the department store industry's average of 7.0 times.

ILLUSTRATION 19-16

Receivables turnover

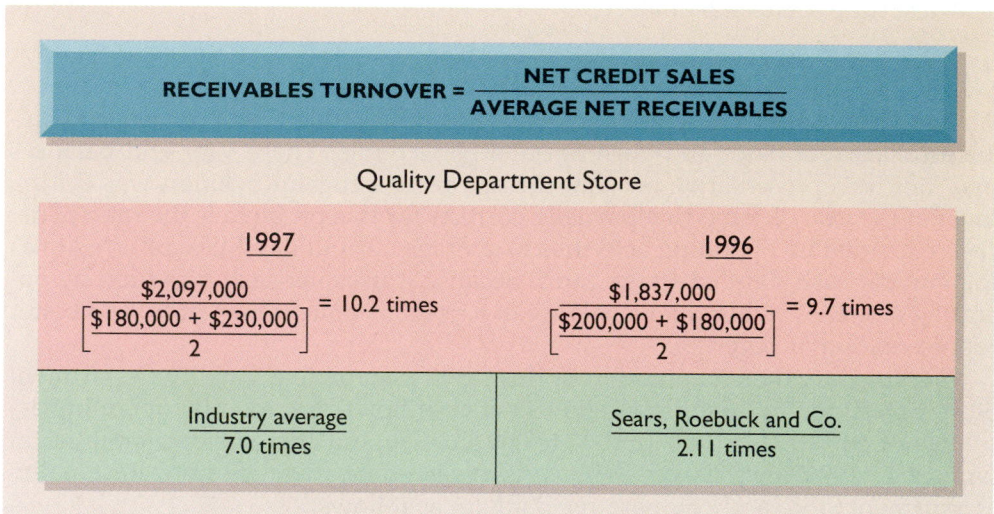

$$\text{RECEIVABLES TURNOVER} = \frac{\text{NET CREDIT SALES}}{\text{AVERAGE NET RECEIVABLES}}$$

Quality Department Store

1997	1996
$\dfrac{\$2,097,000}{\left[\dfrac{\$180,000 + \$230,000}{2}\right]}$ = 10.2 times	$\dfrac{\$1,837,000}{\left[\dfrac{\$200,000 + \$180,000}{2}\right]}$ = 9.7 times
Industry average 7.0 times	Sears, Roebuck and Co. 2.11 times

ACCOUNTING IN ACTION
Business Insight

In some cases, receivables turnover may be misleading. Some companies, especially large retail chains, encourage credit and revolving charge sales, and they slow collections in order to earn a healthy return on the outstanding receivables in the form of interest at rates of 18% to 22%. This may explain why Sears' turnover is only 2.11 times. In general, however, the faster the turnover, the greater the reliance that can be placed on the current and acid-test ratios for assessing liquidity.

---

[2] If seasonal factors are significant, the average receivables balance might be determined by using monthly amounts.

A popular variant of the receivables turnover ratio is to convert it into an **average collection period** in terms of days. This is done by dividing the receivables turnover ratio into 365 days. For example, the receivables turnover in 1997 of 10.2 times is divided into 365 days to obtain approximately 35.8 days. This means that the average collection period for receivables is 36 days, or approximately every 5 weeks. The average collection period is frequently used to assess the effectiveness of a company's credit and collection policies. The general rule is that the collection period should not greatly exceed the credit term period (i.e., the time allowed for payment).

5. Inventory Turnover

The **inventory turnover ratio** measures the number of times on average the inventory is sold during the period. Its purpose is to measure the liquidity of the inventory. The inventory turnover is computed by dividing cost of goods sold by the average inventory during the period. Unless seasonal factors are significant, average inventory can be computed from the beginning and ending inventory balances. Assuming that the inventory balance for Quality Department Store at the beginning of 1996 was $450,000, its inventory turnover and comparative data are as shown in Illustration 19-17. Quality's inventory turnover declined slightly in 1997. The turnover ratio of 2.3 times is relatively low compared with the industry average of 3.4 and Sears' 5.5. Generally, the faster the inventory turnover, the less cash that is tied up in inventory and the less the chance of inventory obsolescence.

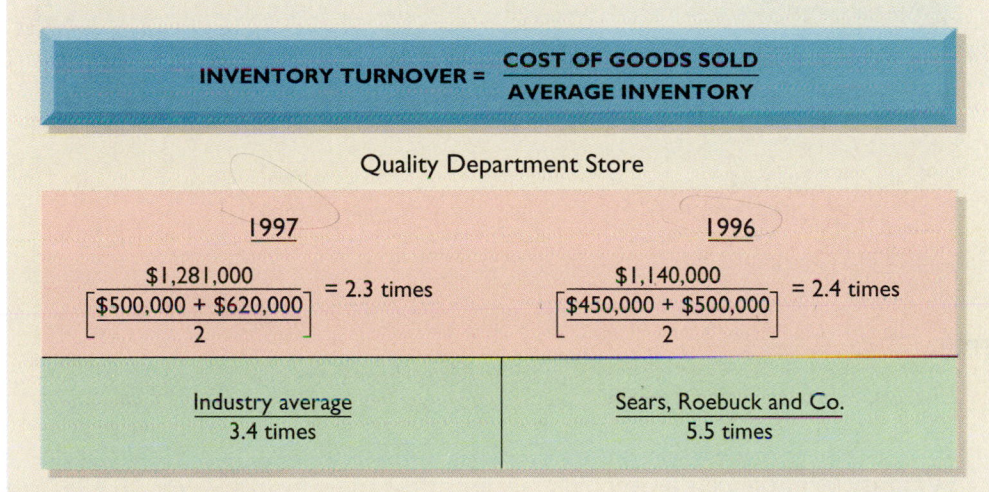

ILLUSTRATION 19-17

Inventory turnover

A variant of the inventory turnover ratio is the **average days to sell the inventory**. For example, the inventory turnover in 1997 of 2.3 times divided into 365 is approximately 159 days. An average selling time of 159 days is also relatively high compared with the industry average of 107 days (365 ÷ 3.4) and Sears' 66 days (365 ÷ 5.5).

Profitability Ratios

Profitability ratios measure the income or operating success of an enterprise for a given period of time. Income, or the lack of it, affects the company's ability to obtain debt and equity financing, the company's liquidity position, and the com-

ACCOUNTING IN ACTION
Business Insight

Inventory turnover ratios vary considerably among industries. For example, grocery store chains have a turnover of 10 times and an average selling period of 37 days. In contrast, jewelry stores have an average turnover of 1.3 times and an average selling period of 281 days. Within a company there may be significant differences in inventory turnover among different types of products. Thus, in a grocery store the turnover of perishable items such as produce, meats, and dairy products will be faster than the turnover of soaps and detergents.

pany's ability to grow. As a consequence, creditors and investors alike are interested in evaluating earning power (profitability). Profitability is frequently used as the ultimate test of management's operating effectiveness.

6. Profit Margin

ALTERNATIVE TERMINOLOGY

The profit margin ratio is also called the *rate of return on sales.*

The **profit margin ratio** is a measure of the percentage of each dollar of sales that results in net income. It is computed by dividing net income by net sales for the period. Quality Department Store's profit margin ratios and comparative data are shown in Illustration 19-18.

ILLUSTRATION 19-18

Profit margin ratio

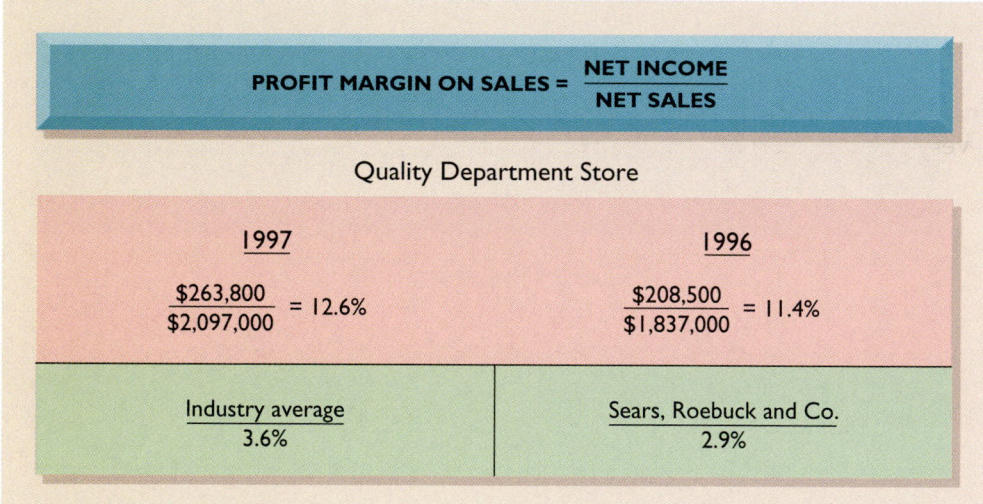

$$\text{PROFIT MARGIN ON SALES} = \frac{\text{NET INCOME}}{\text{NET SALES}}$$

Quality Department Store

1997	1996
$\dfrac{\$263,800}{\$2,097,000} = 12.6\%$	$\dfrac{\$208,500}{\$1,837,000} = 11.4\%$
Industry average 3.6%	Sears, Roebuck and Co. 2.9%

Quality experienced an increase in its profit margin from 1996 to 1997. Its profit margin is unusually high in comparison with the industry average of 3.6% and Sears' 2.9%.

High-volume (high inventory turnover) enterprises such as grocery stores (Safeway or Kroger) and discount stores (Kmart or Wal-Mart) generally experience low profit margins, whereas low-volume enterprises such as jewelry stores (Tiffany & Co.) or airplane manufacturers (Boeing Aircraft) have high profit margins.

7. Cash Return on Sales Ratio

The profit margin ratio discussed above is an accrual-based ratio using net income as the numerator. The cash-basis counterpart to that ratio is the **cash return on sales ratio** which uses net cash provided by operating activities as the numerator and net sales as the denominator. The difference between these two ratios should be explainable as differences between accrual accounting and cash-basis accounting, i.e., differences in the timing of revenue and expense recognition. Using net cash provided by operating activities of $404,000 in 1997 and $340,000 in 1996, Quality Department Store's cash return on sales ratios are computed as follows:

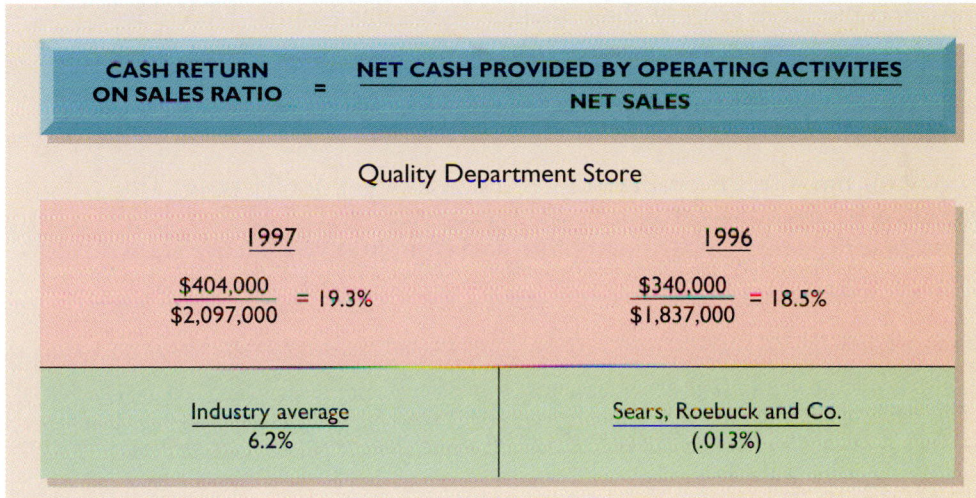

ILLUSTRATION 19-19

Cash return on sales ratio

Quality's cash return on sales is considerably higher than its profit margin on sales. The difference of 6.7% (19.3% − 12.6%) in 1997 is due to excess noncash charges over noncash credits to the income statement. Quality appears to have a very healthy cash return on sales.

8. Asset Turnover

The **asset turnover ratio** measures how efficiently a company uses its assets to generate sales. It is determined by dividing net sales by average assets for the period. The resulting number shows the dollars of sales produced by each dollar invested in assets. Unless seasonal factors are significant, average total assets can be computed from the beginning and ending balance of total assets. Assuming that the total assets at the beginning of 1996 were $1,446,000, the 1997 and 1996 asset turnover ratios for Quality Department Store and comparative data are as follows:

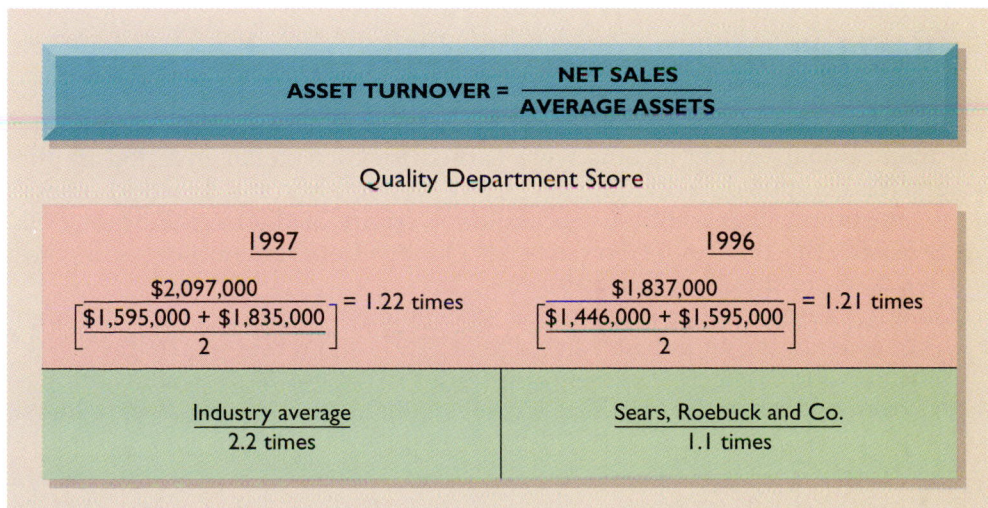

ILLUSTRATION 19-20

Asset turnover

The asset turnover ratio shows that Quality generated sales of $1.22 in 1997 for each dollar it had invested in assets. The ratio changed little from 1996 to 1997. Quality's asset turnover ratio is below the industry average of 2.2 times and above Sears' ratio of 1.1 times.

Asset turnover ratios vary considerably among industries. For example, a large utility company like Consolidated Edison (New York) has a ratio of 0.49 times, and the large grocery chain Kroger Stores has a ratio of 4.3 times.

9. Return on Assets Ratio

An overall measure of profitability is the **return on assets ratio**. This ratio is computed by dividing net income by average assets. The 1997 and 1996 return on assets for Quality Department Store and comparative data are shown below.

ILLUSTRATION 19-21

Return on assets

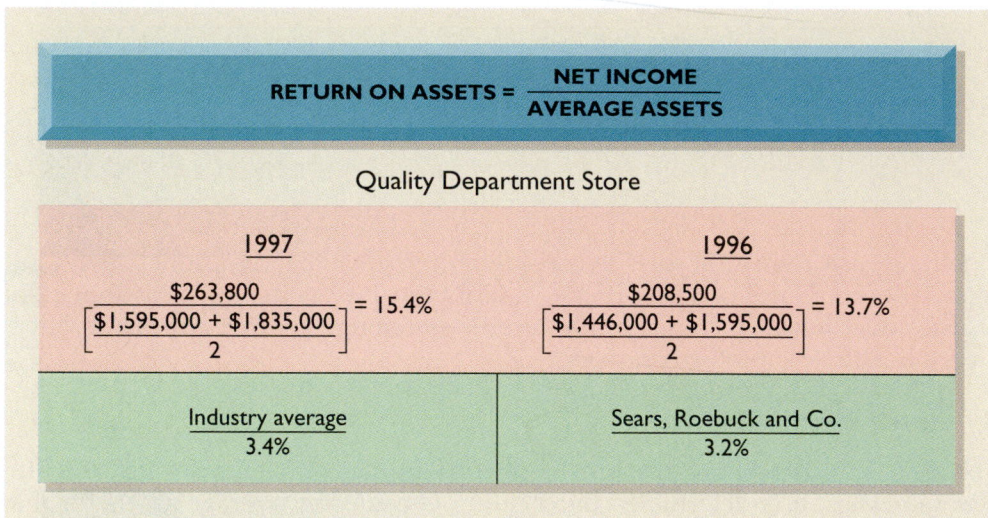

$$\text{RETURN ON ASSETS} = \frac{\text{NET INCOME}}{\text{AVERAGE ASSETS}}$$

Quality Department Store

1997	1996
$\dfrac{\$263,800}{\left[\dfrac{\$1,595,000 + \$1,835,000}{2}\right]} = 15.4\%$	$\dfrac{\$208,500}{\left[\dfrac{\$1,446,000 + \$1,595,000}{2}\right]} = 13.7\%$
Industry average 3.4%	Sears, Roebuck and Co. 3.2%

Quality's return on assets improved from 1996 to 1997. Its return of 15.4% is very high, compared with the department store industry average of 3.4% and Sears' 3.2%.

10. Return on Common Stockholders' Equity

Another widely used ratio that measures profitability from the common stockholder's viewpoint is **return on common stockholders' equity**. This ratio shows how many dollars of net income were earned for each dollar invested by the owners. It is computed by dividing net income by average common stockholders' equity. Assuming that common stockholders' equity at the beginning of 1996 was $667,000, the 1997 and 1996 ratios for Quality Department Store and comparative data are shown in Illustration 19-22.

Quality's rate of return on common stockholders' equity is unusually high at 29.3%, considering an industry average of 12.9% and a rate of 22% for Sears.

When preferred stock is present, **preferred dividend** requirements are deducted from net income to compute income available to common stockholders.

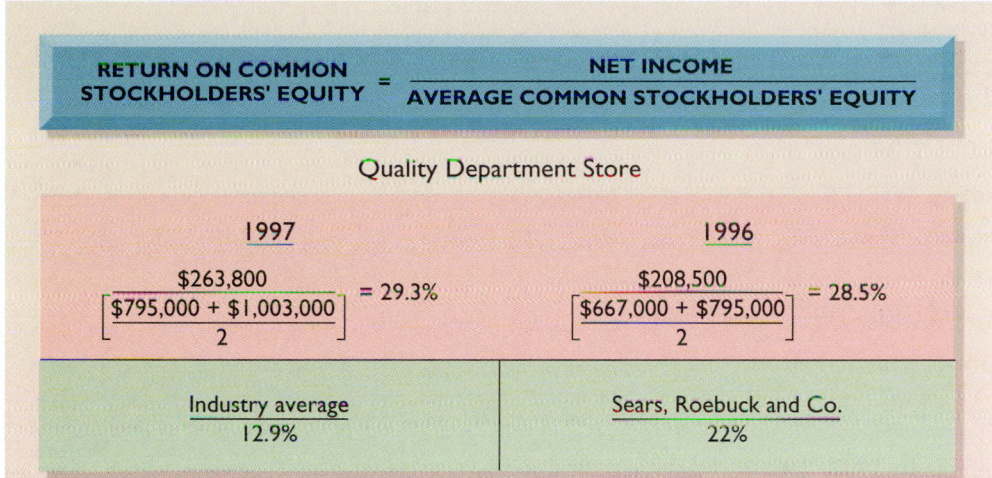

ILLUSTRATION 19-22
Return on common stockholders' equity

Similarly, the par value of preferred stock (or call price, if applicable) must be deducted from total stockholders' equity to arrive at the amount of common stock equity used in this ratio. The ratio then appears as follows:

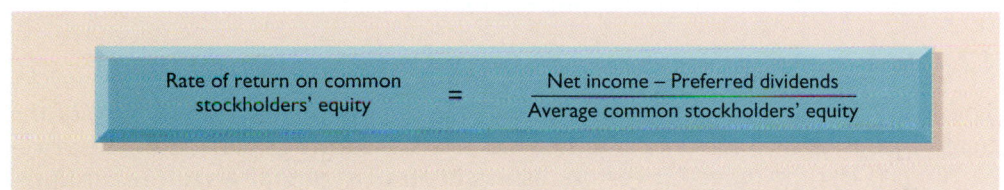

ILLUSTRATION 19-23
Return on common stockholders' equity with preferred stock

Note that Quality's rate of return on stockholders' equity (29.3%) is substantially higher than its rate of return on assets (15.38%). The reason is that Quality has made effective use of leverage or **trading on the equity** at a gain. Trading on the equity at a gain means that the company has borrowed money through the issuance of bonds or notes at a lower rate of interest than it is able to earn by using the borrowed money. Leverage is using money supplied by nonowners to increase the return to the owners. A comparison of the rate of return on total assets with the rate of interest paid for borrowed money indicates the profitability of trading on the equity. Quality Department Store earns more on its borrowed funds than it has to pay in the form of interest. Thus the return to stockholders exceeds the return on the assets, benefiting from the positive leveraging.

ALTERNATIVE TERMINOLOGY
Trading on the equity is also called *leveraging*.

11. Earnings per Share (EPS)

Earnings per share of stock is a measure of the net income earned on each share of common stock. It is computed by dividing net income by the number of weighted average common shares outstanding during the year. Reducing net income earned to a per share basis provides a useful perspective for determining profitability. Assuming that there is no change in the number of outstanding shares during 1996 and that the 1997 increase occurred midyear, the net income per share for Quality Department Store for 1997 and 1996 is computed as shown in Illustration 19-24 on page 838.

Note that no industry or Sears data are presented. Such comparisons are not meaningful because of the wide variations in the number of shares of outstanding stock among companies. Quality's earnings per share increased 20 cents per

ILLUSTRATION 19-24

Earnings per share

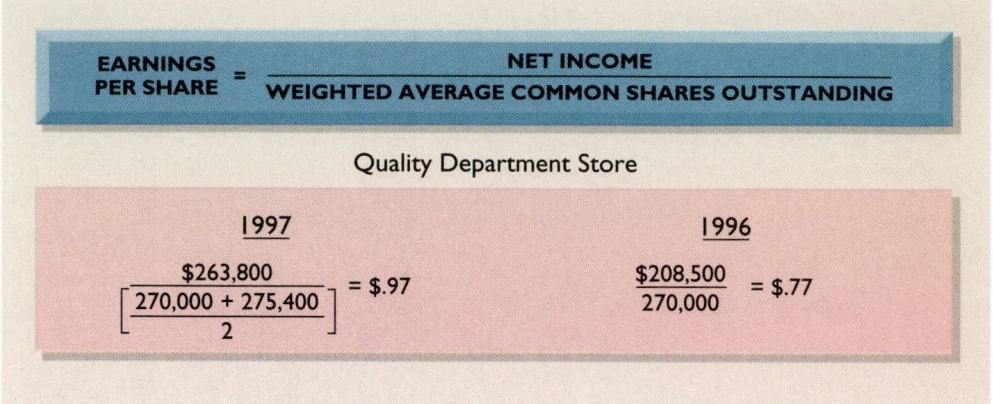

share in 1997. This represents a 26% increase over the 1996 earnings per share of 77 cents.

When the term "net income per share" or "earnings per share" is used, it refers to the amount of net income applicable to each share of **common stock**. Therefore, in computing net income per share, if there are preferred dividends declared for the period, they must be deducted from net income to arrive at income available to the common stockholders.

12. Price-Earnings Ratio

The price-earnings ratio is an oft-quoted statistic that measures the ratio of the market price of each share of common stock to the earnings per share. The price-earnings (PE) ratio reflects investors' assessments of a company's future earnings. It is computed by dividing the market price per share of the stock by earnings per share. Assuming that the market price of Quality Department Store Inc. stock is $8 in 1996 and $12 in 1997, the price-earnings ratio is computed as follows:

ILLUSTRATION 19-25

Price-earnings ratio

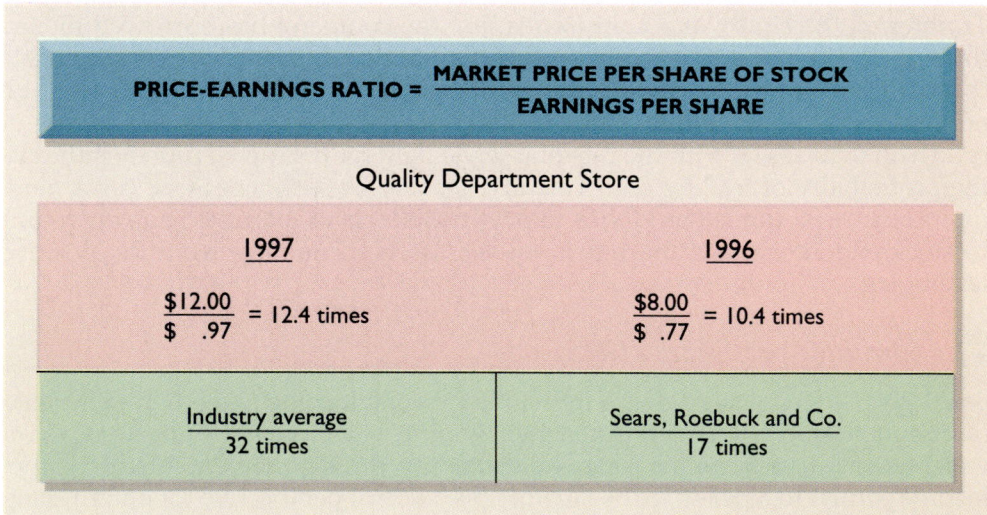

In 1997 each share of Quality's stock sold for 12.4 times the amount that was earned on each share. Quality's price-earnings ratio is significantly lower than the industry average of 32 times, and it is less than the ratio of 17 times for Sears. The average price-earnings ratio for the stocks that constitute the Dow-Jones industrial average on the New York Stock Exchange in March 1998 was an unusually high 21 times.

ACCOUNTING IN ACTION
Business Insight

For the stock of some companies, investors are willing to pay over 20 times the current per-share earnings because they feel the future growth in earnings will provide an adequate return on the investment. Examples of companies with price-earnings ratios over 20 are America Online (101), Microsoft (54), Coca-Cola (41), and Gillette Co. (40). Examples of companies with low price-earnings ratios are Ford Motor (9), General Motors (8), and Northwest Airlines (7).

13. Payout Ratio

The **payout ratio** measures the percentage of earnings distributed in the form of cash dividends. It is computed by dividing cash dividends by net income. Companies that have high growth rates are characterized by low payout ratios because they reinvest most of their net income into the business. The 1997 and 1996 payout ratios for Quality Department Store are computed as follows:

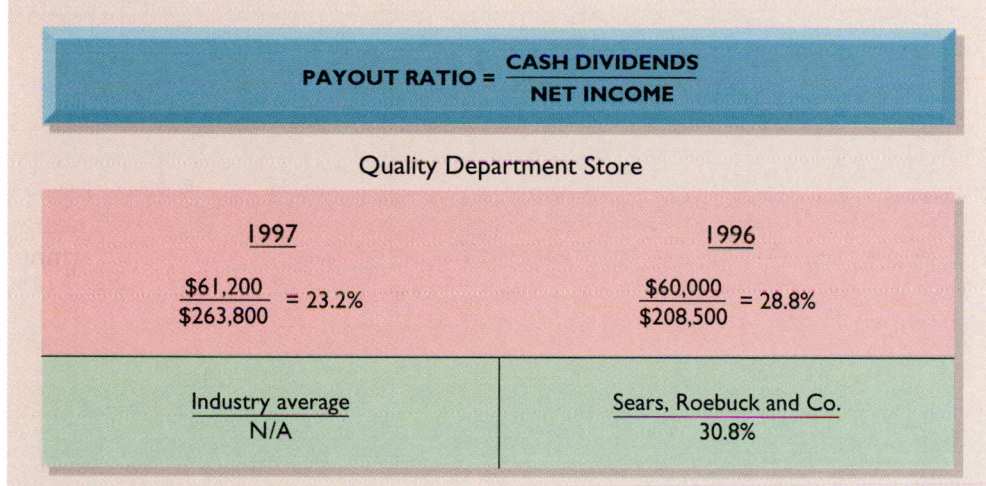

$$\text{PAYOUT RATIO} = \frac{\text{CASH DIVIDENDS}}{\text{NET INCOME}}$$

Quality Department Store

1997	1996
$\frac{\$61,200}{\$263,800} = 23.2\%$	$\frac{\$60,000}{\$208,500} = 28.8\%$
Industry average N/A	Sears, Roebuck and Co. 30.8%

ILLUSTRATION 19-26

Payout ratio

Quality's payout ratio is lower than Sears' payout ratio of 30.8%. As indicated earlier, the company has apparently decided to fund its purchase of plant assets through retention of earnings.

ACCOUNTING IN ACTION
Business Insight

Many companies with stable earnings have high payout ratios. For example, Baltimore Gas and Electric has had an 84% payout ratio over the last 5 years, and Omega Healthcare's dividends exceeded net income over the same period. Conversely, companies that are expanding rapidly, such as Toys 'R' Us, Microsoft, and Telecommunications Inc. (TCI) have never paid a cash dividend.

Solvency Ratios

Solvency ratios measure the ability of the enterprise to survive over a long period of time. Long-term creditors and stockholders are interested in a company's long-run solvency, particularly its ability to pay interest as it comes due and to repay the face value of the debt at maturity. Debt to total assets, times interest earned, and cash debt coverage are three ratios that provide information about debt-paying ability.

14. *Debt to Total Assets Ratio*

HELPFUL HINT

A variation of this ratio is the **equity to debt ratio**. It is computed by dividing total stockholders' equity by total liabilities. The higher this ratio, the more protection creditors have in a period of financial distress.

The **debt to total assets ratio** measures the percentage of the total assets provided by creditors (this ratio indicates the degree of leveraging). It is computed by dividing total debt (both current and long-term liabilities) by total assets. This ratio provides some indication of the company's ability to withstand losses without impairing the interests of creditors. The higher the percentage of debt to total assets, the greater the risk that the company may be unable to meet its maturing obligations. The 1997 and 1996 ratios for Quality Department Store and comparative data are as follows:

ILLUSTRATION 19-27

Debt to total assets

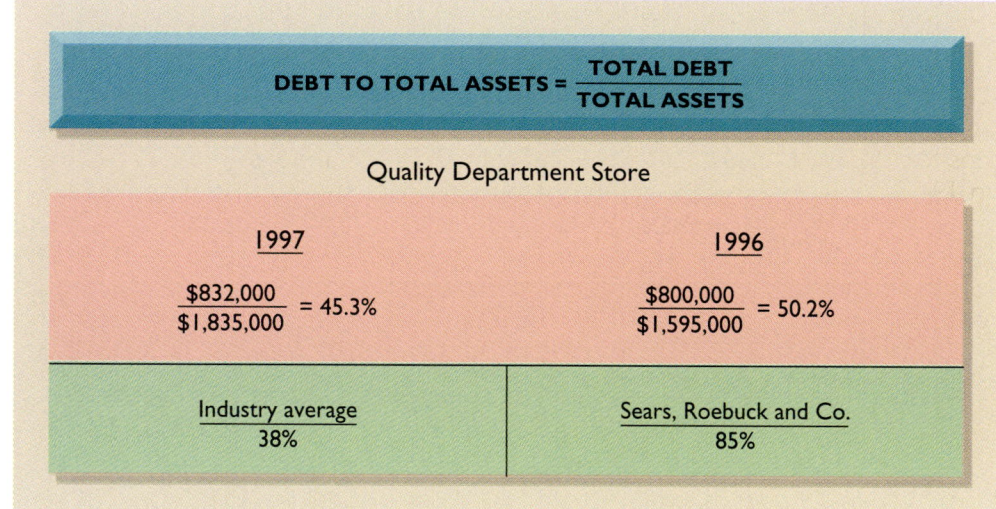

A ratio of 45.3% means that creditors have provided 45.3% of Quality Department Store's total assets. Quality's 45.3% is above the industry average of 38%, but it is considerably below the incredibly high 85% ratio of Sears. The lower the ratio, the more equity "buffer" there is available to the creditors if the company becomes insolvent. Thus, from the creditors' point of view, a low ratio of debt to total assets is usually desirable.

The adequacy of this ratio is often judged in the light of the company's earnings. Generally, companies with relatively stable earnings, such as public utilities, have higher debt to total assets ratios than cyclical companies with widely fluctuating earnings, such as many high-tech companies. (See *Accounting in Action* for examples of debt to total assets ratios for selected companies.)

ACCOUNTING IN ACTION

Business Insight

Examples of debt to total assets ratios for selected companies are:

	Total Debt to Total Assets as a Percent
Advanced Micro Devices	19%
Ford Motor Company	42%
Merck	9%
Caterpillar	37%
Bob Evans Farms	0%
Revlon	56%

Another means used in practice to measure this same leverage phenomenon is the debt to equity ratio. It shows the relative use of borrowed funds (total liabilities) as compared to resources invested by the owners. Because this ratio may be computed in several ways, care should be taken when making comparisons. Debt may be defined to include only the noncurrent portion of the liabilities, and intangible assets may be excluded from owners' equity (resulting in tangible net worth).

15. Times Interest Earned Ratio

The **times interest earned ratio** provides an indication of the company's ability to meet interest payments as they come due. It is computed by dividing income before interest expense and income taxes by interest expense. The 1997 and 1996 ratios for Quality Department Store and comparative data are shown in Illustration 19-28. Note that the times interest earned ratio uses income before income taxes and interest expense, because this amount represents the amount available to cover interest. For Quality Department Store the 1997 amount of $468,000 is computed by taking the income before income taxes of $432,000 and adding back the $36,000 of interest expense. The interest expense of Quality is well covered at 13 times relative to the industry average of 2.7 times and Sears' 2.49 times.

ALTERNATIVE TERMINOLOGY

The times interest earned ratio is also called the *interest coverage ratio*.

ILLUSTRATION 19-28

Times interest earned

$$\text{TIMES INTEREST EARNED} = \frac{\text{INCOME BEFORE INCOME TAXES AND INTEREST EXPENSE}}{\text{INTEREST EXPENSE}}$$

Quality Department Store

1997	1996
$\dfrac{\$468,000}{\$36,000} = 13$ times	$\dfrac{\$388,000}{\$40,500} = 9.6$ times
Industry average 2.7 times	Sears, Roebuck and Co. 2.49 times

Technology in Action

In terms of the types of financial information that are available and the ratios used by various industries, you should be aware that what can be practically covered in this textbook gives you only the "Titanic approach." That is, you are seeing only the tip of the iceberg compared to the vast data bases and different types of ratio analysis that are available on computers. The availability of information is not a problem. The real trick is to be discriminating enough to perform relevant analysis and to select pertinent comparative data.

16. *Cash Debt Coverage Ratio*

The ratio of net cash provided by operating activities to average total liabilities, referred to as the cash debt coverage ratio, is a cash-basis measure of **solvency**. This ratio demonstrates a company's ability to repay its liabilities from cash generated from operating activities, without having to liquidate the assets employed in its operations. Using Quality's net cash provided by operating activities of $404,000 in 1997 and $340,000 in 1996 and assuming total liabilities of $740,000 on January 1, 1996, the cash debt coverage ratios are computed as follows:

ILLUSTRATION 19-29

Cash debt coverage ratio

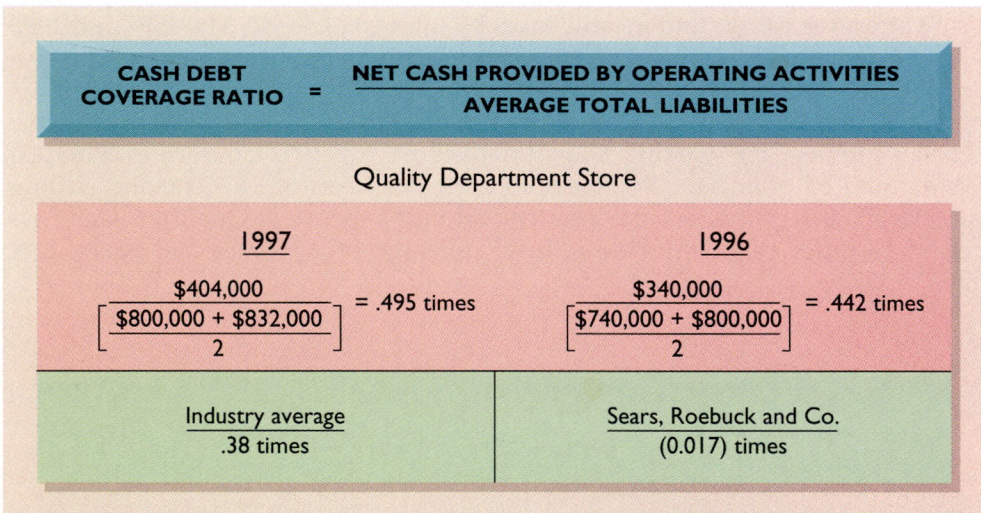

Based on net cash generated from operations in 1997, it would take Quality approximately 2 years to generate enough cash to pay off all its liabilities (assuming all of the net cash generated were used for that purpose only). Its ratio is also superior to that of the retail industry and Sears. (Sears' ratio is negative because its operating activities **used** net cash during 1997.)

Summary of Ratios

A summary of the ratios discussed in the chapter is presented in Illustration 19-30. The summary includes the formula and purpose or use of each ratio.

ILLUSTRATION 19-30

Summary of liquidity, profit-ability, and solvency ratios

Ratio	Formula	Purpose or Use
Liquidity Ratios		
1. Current ratio	$\dfrac{\text{Current assets}}{\text{Current liabilities}}$	Measures short-term debt-paying ability.
2. Acid-test or quick ratio	$\dfrac{\text{Cash + marketable securities + receivables (net)}}{\text{Current liabilities}}$	Measures immediate short-term liquidity.
3. Current cash debt coverage ratio	$\dfrac{\text{Net cash provided by operating activities}}{\text{Average current liabilities}}$	Measures short-term debt-paying ability (cash basis).
4. Receivables turnover	$\dfrac{\text{Net credit sales}}{\text{Average net receivables}}$	Measures liquidity of receivables.
5. Inventory turnover	$\dfrac{\text{Cost of goods sold}}{\text{Average inventory}}$	Measures liquidity of inventory.
Profitability Ratios		
6. Profit margin	$\dfrac{\text{Net income}}{\text{Net sales}}$	Measures net income generated by each dollar of sales.
7. Cash return on sales ratio	$\dfrac{\text{Net cash provided by operating activities}}{\text{Net sales}}$	Measures the net cash flow generated by each dollar of sales.
8. Asset turnover	$\dfrac{\text{Net sales}}{\text{Average assets}}$	Measures how efficiently assets are used to generate sales.
9. Return on assets	$\dfrac{\text{Net income}}{\text{Average assets}}$	Measures overall profitability of assets.
10. Return on common stockholders' equity	$\dfrac{\text{Net income}}{\text{Average common stockholders' equity}}$	Measures profitability of owners' investment.
11. Earnings per share	$\dfrac{\text{Net income}}{\text{Weighted average common shares outstanding}}$	Measures net income earned on each share of common stock.
12. Price-earnings ratio	$\dfrac{\text{Market price per share of stock}}{\text{Earnings per share}}$	Measures the ratio of the market price per share to earnings per share.
13. Payout ratio	$\dfrac{\text{Cash dividends}}{\text{Net income}}$	Measures percentage of earnings distributed in the form of cash dividends.
Solvency Ratios		
14. Debt to total assets	$\dfrac{\text{Total debt}}{\text{Total assets}}$	Measures the percentage of total assets provided by creditors.
15. Times interest earned	$\dfrac{\text{Income before income taxes and interest expense}}{\text{Interest expense}}$	Measures ability to meet interest payments as they come due.
16. Cash debt coverage ratio	$\dfrac{\text{Net cash provided by operating activities}}{\text{Average total liabilities}}$	Measures the long-term debt-paying ability (cash basis).

BEFORE YOU GO ON . . .

Review It

1. What are liquidity ratios? Explain the current ratio, acid-test ratio, current cash debt coverage ratio, receivables turnover ratio, and inventory turnover ratio.
2. What are profitability ratios? Explain the profit margin ratio, cash return on sales ratio, asset turnover ratio, return on assets ratio, return on common stockholders' equity ratio, earnings per share, price-earnings ratio, and payout ratio.
3. What are solvency ratios? Explain the debt to total assets ratio, times interest earned ratio, and cash debt coverage ratio.

Do It

Selected financial data for Drummond Company at December 31, 1999, are as follows: cash $60,000; receivables (net) $80,000; inventory $70,000; current liabilities $140,000. Compute the current and acid-test ratios.

Reasoning: The formula for the current ratio is: current assets ÷ current liabilities. The formula for the acid-test ratio is: cash + marketable securities + receivables (net) ÷ current liabilities.

Solution: The current ratio is 1.5:1 ($210,000 ÷ $140,000). The acid-test ratio is 1:1 ($140,000 ÷ $140,000).

Related exercise material: BE19–7, BE19–8, BE19–9, BE19–10, BE19–11, E19–5, E19–6, and E19–7.

THE NAVIGATOR

LIMITATIONS OF FINANCIAL STATEMENT ANALYSIS

6
STUDY
OBJECTIVE

Recognize the limitations of financial statement analysis.

Significant business decisions are frequently made using one or more of the three analytical tools illustrated in this chapter. However, you should be aware of some of the limitations of these tools and of the financial statements on which they are based.

Estimates

Financial statements contain numerous estimates. Estimates, for example, are used in determining the allowance for uncollectible receivables, periodic depreciation, the costs of warranties, and contingent losses. To the extent that these estimates are inaccurate, the financial ratios and percentages are inaccurate.

Cost

Traditional financial statements are based on cost and are not adjusted for price-level changes. Comparisons of unadjusted financial data from different periods may be rendered invalid by significant inflation or deflation. For example, a 5-year comparison of Sears' revenues might show a growth of 36%. But this growth trend would be misleading if the general price-level had increased significantly during the same 5-year period.

Alternative Accounting Methods

Variations among companies in the application of generally accepted accounting principles may hamper comparability. For example, one company may use the

FIFO method of inventory costing, whereas another company in the same industry may use LIFO. If inventory is a significant asset to both companies, it is unlikely that their current ratios are comparable. For example, if General Motors Corporation had used FIFO instead of LIFO in valuing its inventories, its inventories would have been 26% higher, significantly affecting the current ratio (and other ratios as well). In addition to differences in inventory costing methods, differences also exist in reporting such items as depreciation, depletion, and amortization. Although these differences in accounting methods might be detectable from reading the notes to the financial statements, adjusting the financial data to compensate for the different methods is difficult, if not impossible in some cases.

Atypical Data

Fiscal year-end data may not be typical of the financial condition during the year. Firms frequently establish a fiscal year-end that coincides with the low point in operating activity or in inventory levels. Therefore, certain account balances (cash, receivables, payables, and inventories) may not be representative of the balances in the accounts during the year.

Diversification of Firms

Diversification in American industry also limits the usefulness of financial analysis. Many firms today are so diversified that they cannot be classified by a single industry—they are true conglomerates. Others appear to be comparable but are not.

INTERNATIONAL NOTE

In many industries competition is global: To evaluate a firm's standing, an investor or analyst must make comparisons to firms from other countries. However, given the many differences in accounting practices, these comparisons can be both difficult and misleading.

ETHICS NOTE

When investigating diversified firms, investors are often most interested to learn about the results of particular divisions. Firms are required to disclose the results of distinct lines of business separately if they are a material part of operations. Unfortunately, shifting revenues and expenses across divisions to achieve desired results reduces the usefulness of this information for financial statement analysis.

BEFORE YOU GO ON . . .

Review It

1. What are some limitations of financial statement analysis?
2. Give examples of alternative accounting methods that hamper comparability.
3. In what way does diversification limit the usefulness of financial statement analysis?

A LOOK BACK AT OUR FEATURE STORY

Refer to the opening story and answer the following questions:

1. How is the Motley Fool bulletin board like the fool in Shakespeare's plays?
2. What makes the Motley Fool bulletin board attractive to Internet subscribers?
3. What are the dangers of using the Motley Fool bulletin board for investment purposes?

Solution:

1. The fool in Shakespeare's play was the only one who could speak unpleasant truths to kings and queens without being killed. The creators of the Motley Fool bulletin board view themselves as twentieth-century "fools," revealing the "truths" of Wall Street to the small investor, who the Gardner brothers believe has been taken advantage of by Wall Street insiders. That is, both Shakespeare's fools and the Motley Fool are irreverent attacks on the establishment.
2. The Motley Fool provides a bulletin board service where America Online subscribers can exchange information and insights about companies of interest to investors and potential investors. The information sources are endless (grassroots, insiders, anyone), worldwide, and nearly costless.

3. Critics contend that the bulletin board is nothing more than a high-tech rumor mill that tends to build a speculative house of cards. Participants on the board don't have to give their identities. Consequently, there is little to stop people from putting misinformation on the board to influence stock prices in the direction they want. Much of the information is soft and stands in sharp contrast to the data and ratios provided by analysis of financial statements as illustrated in this chapter.

DEMONSTRATION PROBLEM

The condensed financial statements of The Estée Lauder Companies, Inc., for the years ended June 30, 1997 and 1996, are presented below:

THE ESTÉE LAUDER COMPANIES, INC.
Balance Sheet
June 30

| | (in millions) | |
Assets	1997	1996
Current assets		
Cash and cash equivalents	$ 255.6	$ 254.8
Accounts receivable (net)	471.7	434.0
Inventories	440.6	452.8
Prepaid expenses and other current assets	143.2	148.8
Total current assets	1,311.1	1,290.4
Property, plant, and equipment (net)	265.0	229.3
Investments	25.9	24.7
Intangibles and other assets	271.1	235.0
Total assets	$1,873.1	$1,779.4
Liabilities and Stockholders' Equity		
Current liabilities	$759.5	$822.9
Long-term liabilities	565.9	562.3
Stockholders' equity—common	547.7	394.2
Total liabilities and stockholders' equity	$1,873.1	$1,779.4

THE ESTÉE LAUDER COMPANIES, INC.
Income Statement
For the Year Ended June 30

| | (in millions) | |
	1997	1996
Revenues	$3,381.6	$3,194.5
Costs and expenses		
Cost of goods sold	765.1	731.0
Selling and administrative expenses	2,224.6	2,116.0
Interest expense and royalties	52.4	92.0
Total costs and expenses	3,042.1	2,939.0
Income before income taxes	339.5	255.5
Income tax expense	165.3	152.6
Net income	$ 174.2	$ 102.9

Instructions

Compute the following ratios for 1997 and 1996.

  (a) Current ratio.

  (b) Inventory turnover (Inventory 6/30/95, $437.4).

  (c) Profit margin ratio.

  (d) Return on assets (Assets 6/30/95, $1,701.4).

  (e) Return on common stockholders' equity (Equity 6/30/95, $335.1).

  (f) Debt to total assets.

  (g) Times interest earned.

SOLUTION TO DEMONSTRATION PROBLEM

		1997	1996
(a)	Current ratio:		
	$1,311.1 ÷ $759.5 =	1.7:1	
	$1,290.4 ÷ $822.9 =		1.6:1
(b)	Inventory turnover:		
	$765.1 ÷ [($440.6 + $452.8) ÷ 2] =	1.7 times	
	$731.0 ÷ [($452.8 + $437.4) ÷ 2] =		1.6 times
(c)	Profit margin:		
	$174.2 ÷ $3,381.6 =	5.2%	
	$102.9 ÷ $3,194.5 =		3.2%
(d)	Return on assets:		
	$174.2 ÷ [($1,873.1 + $1,779.4) ÷ 2] =	9.5%	
	$102.9 ÷ [($1,779.4 + $1,701.4) ÷ 2] =		5.9%
(e)	Return on common stockholders' equity:		
	$174.2 ÷ [($547.7 + $394.2) ÷ 2] =	37%	
	$102.9 ÷ [($394.2 + $335.1) ÷ 2] =		28%
(f)	Debt to total assets:		
	$1,325.4 ÷ $1,873.1 =	70.8%	
	$1,385.2 ÷ $1,779.4 =		77.8%
(g)	Times interest earned:		
	($174.2 + $165.3 + $52.4) ÷ $52.4 =	7.5 times	
	($102.9 + $152.6 + $92.0) ÷ $92.0 =		3.8 times

PROBLEM-SOLVING STRATEGIES

1. Remember that the current ratio includes all current assets; acid-test ratio uses only cash, marketable securities, and net receivables.

2. Use average balances for turnover ratios like inventory, receivables, and assets.

3. Return on assets is greater or smaller than return on common stockholders' equity depending on cost of debt.

THE
NAVIGATOR

SUMMARY OF STUDY OBJECTIVES

1. *Discuss the need for comparative analysis.* There are three bases of comparison: (1) Intracompany, which compares an item or financial relationship with other data within a company. (2) Industry, which compares company data with industry averages. (3) Intercompany, which compares an item or financial relationship of a company with data of one or more competing companies.

2. *Identify the tools of financial statement analysis.* Financial statements may be analyzed horizontally, vertically, and with ratios.

3. *Explain and apply horizontal (trend) analysis.* Horizontal analysis is a technique for evaluating a series of data over a period of time to determine the increase or decrease that has taken place, expressed as either an amount or a percentage.

4. *Describe and apply vertical analysis.* Vertical analysis is a technique that expresses each item within a financial statement in terms of a percentage of a relevant total or a base amount.

5. *Identify and compute ratios and describe their purpose and use in analyzing a firm's liquidity, profitability, and solvency.* The formula and purpose of each ratio is presented in Illustration 19-30.

6. *Recognize the limitations of financial statement analysis.* The usefulness of analytical tools is limited by the use of estimates, the cost basis, the application of alternative accounting methods, atypical data at year-end, and the diversification of firms.

GLOSSARY

Acid-test ratio   A measure of a company's immediate short-term liquidity, computed by dividing the sum of cash, marketable securities, and (net) receivables by current liabilities. (p. 830).

Asset turnover ratio   A measure of how efficiently a company uses its assets to generate sales, computed by dividing net sales by average assets. (p. 835).

Cash debt coverage ratio   A cash-basis measure of long-term debt-paying ability, computed as net cash provided by operating activities divided by average total liabilities. (p.842).

Cash return on sales ratio   A measure of the cash generated by each dollar of sales, computed as net cash provided by operating activities divided by net sales. (p.834).

Current cash debt coverage ratio   A cash-basis measure of short-term debt-paying ability, computed as net cash provided by operating activities divided by average current liabilities. (p.831).

Current ratio   A measure used to evaluate a company's liquidity and short-term debt-paying ability, computed by dividing current assets by current liabilities. (p. 829).

Debt to total assets ratio   Measures the percentage of total assets provided by creditors, computed by dividing total debt by total assets. (p. 840).

Earnings per share   The net income earned by each share of common stock, computed by dividing net income by the weighted average common shares outstanding. (p. 837).

Horizontal analysis   A technique for evaluating a series of financial statement data over a period of time to determine the increase (decrease) that has taken place, expressed as either an amount or a percentage. (p. 822).

Inventory turnover ratio   A measure of the liquidity of inventory, computed by dividing cost of goods sold by average inventory. (p. 833).

Liquidity ratios   Measures of the short-term ability of the enterprise to pay its maturing obligations and to meet unexpected needs for cash. (p. 829).

Payout ratio   Measures the percentage of earnings distributed in the form of cash dividends, computed by dividing cash dividends by net income. (p. 839).

Price-earnings ratio   Measures the ratio of the market price of each share of common stock to the earnings per share, computed by dividing the market price of the stock by earnings per share. (p. 838).

Profitability ratios   Measures of the income or operating success of an enterprise for a given period of time. (p. 833).

Profit margin ratio   Measures the percentage of each dollar of sales that results in net income, computed by dividing net income by net sales. (p. 834).

Ratio   An expression of the mathematical relationship between one quantity and another. The relationship may be expressed either as a percentage, a rate, or a simple proportion. (p. 828).

Ratio analysis   A technique for evaluating financial statements that expresses the relationship among selected financial statement data. (p. 828).

Receivables turnover ratio   A measure of the liquidity of receivables, computed by dividing net credit sales by average net receivables. (p. 832).

Return on assets ratio   An overall measure of profitability, computed by dividing net income by average assets. (p. 836).

Return on common stockholders' equity   Measures the dollars of net income earned for each dollar invested by the owners, computed by dividing net income by average common stockholders' equity. (p. 836).

Solvency ratios   Measures of the ability of the enterprise to survive over a long period of time. (p. 840).

Times interest earned ratio   Measures a company's ability to meet interest payments as they come due, computed by dividing income before interest expense and income taxes by interest expense. (p. 841).

Trading on the equity (leverage)   Borrowing money at a lower rate of interest than can be earned by using the borrowed money. (p. 837).

Vertical analysis   A technique for evaluating financial statement data that expresses each item within a financial statement in terms of a percent of a base amount. (p. 825).

SELF-STUDY QUESTIONS

Answers are at the end of the chapter.

(SO 1) 1. Comparisons of data within a company are an example of the following comparative basis:
   a. Industry averages.
   b. Intracompany.
   c. Intercompany.
   d. Both (b) and (c).

2. In horizontal analysis, each item is expressed as a percentage of the: (SO 2)
   a. net income amount.
   b. stockholders' equity amount.
   c. total assets amount.
   d. base year amount.

(SO 4) 3. In vertical analysis, the base amount for depreciation expense is generally:
   a. net sales.
   b. depreciation expense in a previous year.
   c. gross profit.
   d. fixed assets.

(SO 4) 4. The following schedule is a display of what type of analysis?

	Amount	Percent
Current assets	$200,000	25%
Property, plant, and equipment	600,000	75%
Total assets	$800,000	

   a. Horizontal analysis.
   b. Differential analysis.
   c. Vertical analysis.
   d. Ratio analysis.

(SO 3) 5. Leland Corporation reported net sales of $300,000, $330,000, and $360,000 in the years 1997, 1998, and 1999, respectively. If 1997 is the base year, what is the trend percentage for 1999?
   a. 77%.
   b. 108%.
   c. 120%.
   d. 130%.

(SO 5) 6. Which of the following measures is an evaluation of a firm's ability to pay current liabilities?
   a. Acid-test ratio.
   b. Current ratio.
   c. Both (a) and (b).
   d. None of the above.

(SO 5) 7. A measure useful in evaluating the efficiency in managing inventories is:
   a. inventory turnover ratio.
   b. average days to sell inventory.
   c. Both (a) and (b).
   d. None of the above.

(SO 5) 8. Which of the following is *not* a liquidity ratio?
   a. Current ratio.
   b. Asset turnover.
   c. Inventory turnover.
   d. Receivables turnover.

(SO 5) 9. Plano Corporation reported net income $24,000, net sales $400,000, and average assets $600,000 for 1999. The 1999 profit margin was:
   a. 6%.
   b. 12%.
   c. 40%.
   d. 200%.

(SO 6) 10. Which of the following is generally *not* considered to be a limitation of financial analysis?
   a. Use of estimates.
   b. Use of ratio analysis.
   c. Use of cost.
   d. Use of alternative accounting methods.

THE NAVIGATOR

QUESTIONS

1. (a) Tara Goff believes that the analysis of financial statements is directed at two characteristics of a company: liquidity and profitability. Is Tara correct? Explain.
   (b) Are short-term creditors, long-term creditors, and stockholders interested primarily in the same characteristics of a company? Explain.

2. (a) Distinguish among the following bases of comparison: (1) intracompany, (2) industry averages, and (3) intercompany.
   (b) Give the principal value of using each of the three bases of comparison.

3. Two popular methods of financial statement analysis are horizontal analysis and vertical analysis. Explain the difference between these two methods.

4. (a) If Roy Company had net income of $480,000 in 1999 and it experienced a 24.5% increase in net income for 2000, what is its net income for 2000?
   (b) If six cents of every dollar of Roy's revenue is net income in 1999, what is the dollar amount of 1999 revenue?

5. What is a ratio? What are the different ways of expressing the relationship of two amounts? What information does a ratio provide?

6. Name the major ratios useful in assessing (a) liquidity and (b) solvency.

7. Bob Thebeau is puzzled. His company had a profit margin of 10% in 1999. He feels that this is an indication that the company is doing well. Loren Foelske, his accountant, says that more information is needed to determine the firm's financial well-being. Who is correct? Why?

8. What do the following classes of ratios measure? (a) Liquidity ratios. (b) Profitability ratios. (c) Solvency ratios.

9. What is the difference between the current ratio and the acid-test ratio?

10. Payne Company, a retail store, has a receivables turnover ratio of 4.5 times. The industry average is 12.5 times. Does Payne have a collection problem with its receivables?

11. Which ratios should be used to help answer the following questions?
    (a) How efficient is a company in using its assets to produce sales?
    (b) How near to sale is the inventory on hand?
    (c) How many dollars of net income were earned for each dollar invested by the owners?
    (d) How able is a company to meet interest charges as they fall due?

12. The price-earnings ratio of General Motors (automobile builder) was 9, and the price-earnings ratio of Microsoft (computer software) was 49. Which company did the stock market favor? Explain.

13. What is the formula for computing the payout ratio? Would you expect this ratio to be high or low for a growth company?

14. Holding all other factors constant, indicate whether each of the following changes generally signals good or bad news about a company:
    (a) Increase in profit margin.
    (b) Decrease in inventory turnover.
    (c) Increase in the current ratio.
    (d) Decrease in earnings per share.
    (e) Increase in price-earnings ratio.
    (f) Increase in debt to total assets ratio.
    (g) Decrease in times interest earned.
    (h) Increase in book value per share.

15. The return on total assets for Matson Corporation is 7.6%. During the same year Matson's return on common stockholders' equity is 12.8%. What is the explanation for the difference in the two rates?

16. Which two ratios do you think should be of greatest interest to:
    (a) A pension fund considering the purchase of 20-year bonds?
    (b) A bank contemplating a short-term loan?
    (c) A common stockholder?

17. (a) What is meant by trading on the equity?
    (b) How would you determine the profitability of trading on the equity?

18. Kiser Inc. has net income of $210,000, weighted average shares of common stock outstanding of 50,000, and preferred dividends for the period of $40,000. What is Kiser's earnings per share of common stock? Jim Akins, the president of Kiser Inc., believes the computed EPS of the company is high. Comment.

19. Identify and briefly explain five limitations of financial analysis.

20. Explain how the choice of one of the following accounting methods over the other raises or lowers a company's net income during a period of continuing inflation:
    (a) Use of FIFO instead of LIFO for inventory costing.
    (b) Use of a 6-year life for machinery instead of a 9-year life.
    (c) Use of straight-line depreciation instead of accelerated declining-balance depreciation.

21. What three ratios are partially dependent on cash-basis data, that is, data from the statement of cash flows?

BRIEF EXERCISES*

Prepare horizontal analysis.
(SO 3)

BE19–1 Using the following data from the comparative balance sheet of Jackie Remmers Company, illustrate horizontal analysis:

	December 31, 2000	December 31, 1999
Accounts receivable	$ 500,000	$ 400,000
Inventory	$ 840,000	$ 600,000
Total assets	$3,220,000	$2,800,000

Prepare vertical analysis.
(SO 4)

BE19–2 Using the same data presented above in BE19–1 for Jackie Remmers Company, illustrate vertical analysis.

Calculate percentage of change.
(SO 3)

BE19–3 Net income was $500,000 in 1998, $400,000 in 1999, and $504,000 in 2000. What is the percentage of change from (1) 1998 to 1999 and (2) 1999 to 2000? Is the change an increase or a decrease?

Calculate net income.
(SO 3)

BE19–4 If Hal Adelman Company had net income of $662,500 in 2000 and it experienced a 25% increase in net income over 1999, what was its 1999 net income?

Calculate change in net income.
(SO 4)

BE19–5 Vertical analysis (common size) percentages for Domingo Company's sales, cost of goods sold, and expenses are shown below:

Vertical Analysis	2000	1999	1998
Sales	100.0	100.0	100.0
Cost of goods sold	59.5	61.4	64.5
Expenses	25.0	26.6	28.5

*Follow the rounding procedures used in the chapter.

Did Domingo's net income as a percent of sales increase, decrease, or remain unchanged over the 3-year period presented above? Provide numerical support for your answer.

BE19–6 Horizontal analysis (trend analysis) percentages for Foltz Company's sales, cost of goods sold, and expenses are shown below:

Calculate change in net income.
(SO 3)

Horizontal Analysis	2000	1999	1998
Sales	96.2	106.8	100.0
Cost of goods sold	102.0	97.0	100.0
Expenses	110.6	95.4	100.0

Did Foltz's net income increase, decrease, or remain unchanged over the 3-year period presented above?

BE19–7 Selected condensed data taken from a recent balance sheet of Jensen Farms are as follows:

Calculate liquidity ratios.
(SO 5)

JENSEN FARMS
Balance Sheet (partial)

Cash	$ 8,241,000
Marketable securities	1,947,000
Accounts receivable	12,545,000
Inventories	14,814,000
Other current assets	5,371,000
Total current assets	$42,918,000
Total current liabilities	$45,844,000

What are the (1) working capital, (2) current, and (3) acid-test ratios?

BE19–8 Hawkins Corporation has net income of $12 million and net revenue of $100 million in 1999. Its assets were $12 million at the beginning of the year and $18 million at the end of the year. What are (a) the Hawkins' asset turnover ratio and (b) profit margin ratio? (Round to two decimals.)

Calculate profitability ratios.
(SO 5)

BE19–9 The following data are taken from the financial statements of Geitz Company:

Evaluate collection of accounts receivable.
(SO 5)

	2000	1999
Accounts receivable (net), end of year	$ 560,000	$ 540,000
Net sales on account	4,400,000	3,100,000
Terms for all sales are 1/10, n/60.		

Compute for each year (1) the receivables turnover and (2) the average collection period. What conclusions about the management of accounts receivable can be drawn from these data? At the end of 1998, accounts receivable (net) was $490,000.

BE19–10 The following data were taken from the income statements of Lester Fredrick Company:

Evaluate management of inventory.
(SO 5)

	2000	1999
Sales	$6,420,000	$6,240,000
Beginning inventory	980,000	860,000
Purchases	4,440,000	4,661,000
Ending inventory	1,020,000	980,000

Compute for each year (1) the inventory turnover ratio and (2) the average days to sell the inventory. What conclusions concerning the management of the inventory can be drawn from these data?

BE19–11 McCarty Company has owners' equity of $400,000 and net income of $60,000. It has a payout ratio of 20% and a rate of return on assets of 16%. How much did McCarty pay in cash dividends, and what were its average assets?

Calculate profitability ratios.
(SO 5)

BE19–12 Selected data taken from the 1999 financial statements of Shirley Denson Manufacturing Company are as follows:

Calculate cash-basis liquidity, profitability, and solvency ratios. (SO 5)

Net sales for 1999	$6,860,000
Current liabilities, January 1, 1999	180,000
Current liabilities, December 31, 1999	240,000
Net cash provided by operating activities	760,000
Total liabilities, January 1, 1999	1,500,000
Total liabilities, December 31, 1999	1,300,000

Compute the following ratios at December 31, 1999: (a) the current cash debt coverage ratio, (b) the cash return on sales ratio, and (c) the cash debt coverage ratio.

EXERCISES*

• •

Prepare horizontal analysis.
(SO 3)

E19-1 Financial information for Lister Inc. is presented below:

	December 31, 2000	December 31, 1999
Current assets	$125,000	$100,000
Plant assets (net)	400,000	330,000
Current liabilities	91,000	70,000
Long-term liabilities	144,000	95,000
Common stock, $1 par	155,000	115,000
Retained earnings	135,000	150,000

Instructions
Prepare a schedule showing a horizontal analysis for 2000 using 1999 as the base year.

Prepare vertical analysis.
(SO 4)

E19-2 Operating data for Khan Corporation are presented below:

	2000	1999
Sales	$800,000	$600,000
Cost of goods sold	464,000	378,000
Selling expenses	120,000	72,000
Administrative expenses	80,000	54,000
Income tax expense	38,400	25,200
Net income	97,600	70,800

Instructions
Prepare a schedule showing a vertical analysis for 2000 and 1999.

Prepare horizontal and vertical analyses.
(SO 3, 4)

E19-3 The comparative balance sheets of Barkley Corporation are presented below:

BARKLEY CORPORATION
Comparative Balance Sheets
December 31

	2000	1999
Assets		
Current assets	$ 76,000	$ 80,000
Property, plant, & equipment (net)	99,000	90,000
Intangibles	25,000	40,000
Total assets	$200,000	$210,000
Liabilities & stockholders' equity		
Current liabilities	$ 45,800	$ 48,000
Long-term liabilities	138,000	150,000
Stockholders' equity	16,200	12,000
Total liabilities & stockholders' equity	$200,000	$210,000

*Follow the rounding procedures used in the chapter.

Instructions

(a) Prepare a horizontal analysis of the balance sheet data for Barkley Corporation using 1999 as a base. (Show the amount of increase or decrease as well.)

(b) Prepare a vertical analysis of the balance sheet data for Barkley Corporation in columnar form for 2000.

E19–4   The comparative income statements of LaGalle Corporation are shown below:

Prepare horizontal and vertical analyses.
(SO 3, 4)

LAGALLE CORPORATION
Comparative Income Statements
For the Years Ended December 31

	2000	1999
Net sales	$550,000	$500,000
Cost of goods sold	440,000	420,000
Gross profit	110,000	80,000
Operating expenses	57,200	44,000
Net income	$ 52,800	$ 36,000

Instructions

(a) Prepare a horizontal analysis of the income statement data for LaGalle Corporation using 1999 as a base. (Show the amounts of increase or decrease.)

(b) Prepare a vertical analysis of the income statement data for LaGalle Corporation in columnar form for both years.

E19–5   Nordstrom, Inc., operates department stores in numerous states. Selected financial statement data in millions of dollars for a recent year are as follows:

Compute liquidity ratios and compare results.
(SO 5)

NORDSTROM, INC.
Balance Sheet (partial)

	End-of-Year	Beginning-of-Year
Cash and cash equivalents	$ 33	$ 91
Receivables (net)	676	586
Merchandise Inventory	628	586
Prepaid expenses	61	52
Total current assets	$1,398	$1,315
Total current liabilities	$690	$627

For the year, net sales were $3,894 and cost of goods sold was $2,600. Net cash provided by operating activities was $800.

Instructions

(a) Compute the five liquidity ratios at the end of the current year.

(b) Using the data in the chapter, compare Nordstrom's liquidity with (1) Sears, Roebuck and (2) the industry averages for department stores.

E19–6   Fargo Incorporated had the following transactions occur involving current assets and current liabilities during February 1999:

Perform current and acid-test ratio analysis.
(SO 5)

Feb.   3   Accounts receivable of $15,000 are collected.
     7   Equipment is purchased for $25,000 cash.
   11   Paid $3,000 for a 3-year insurance policy.
   14   Accounts payable of $14,000 are paid.
   18   Cash dividends are declared, $6,000.

Additional information:

1. As of February 1, 1999, current assets were $120,000 and current liabilities were $50,000.

2. As of February 1, 1999, current assets included $15,000 of inventory and $5,000 of prepaid expenses.

Instructions

(a) Compute the current ratio as of the beginning of the month and after each transaction.

(b) Compute the acid-test ratio as of the beginning of the month and after each transaction.

Compute selected ratios.
(SO 5)

E19–7 Georgette Company has the following comparative balance sheet data:

GEORGETTE COMPANY
Balance Sheet
December 31

	1999	1998
Cash	$ 20,000	$ 30,000
Receivables (net)	65,000	60,000
Inventories	60,000	50,000
Plant assets (net)	200,000	180,000
	$345,000	$320,000
Accounts payable	$ 50,000	$ 60,000
Mortgage payable (15%)	100,000	100,000
Common stock, $10 par	140,000	120,000
Retained earnings	55,000	40,000
	$345,000	$320,000

Additional information for 1999:

1. Net income was $25,000.
2. Sales on account were $420,000. Sales returns and allowances amounted to $20,000.
3. Cost of goods sold was $198,000.
4. Net cash provided by operating activities was $44,000.

Instructions
Compute the following ratios at December 31, 1999:

(a) Current.   (e) Cash return on sales.
(b) Acid-test.   (f) Cash debt coverage.
(c) Receivables turnover.   (g) Current cash debt coverage.
(d) Inventory turnover.

Compute selected ratios.
(SO 5)

E19–8 Selected comparative statement data for Meng Products Company are presented below. All balance sheet data are as of December 31.

	2000	1999
Net sales	$800,000	$720,000
Cost of goods sold	480,000	40,000
Interest expense	7,000	5,000
Net income	64,000	42,000
Accounts receivable	120,000	100,000
Inventory	85,000	75,000
Total assets	600,000	500,000
Total common stockholders' equity	450,000	310,000

Instructions
Compute the following ratios for 2000:

(a) Profit margin.
(b) Asset turnover.
(c) Return on assets.
(d) Return on common stockholders' equity.

E19–9 The income statement for Cheryl Countryman, Inc., appears below.

Compute selected ratios.
(SO 5)

CHERYL COUNTRYMAN, INC.
Income Statement
For the Year Ended December 31, 1999

Sales	$400,000
Cost of goods sold	230,000
Gross profit	170,000
Expenses (including $20,000 interest and $24,000 income taxes)	100,000
Net income	$ 70,000

Additional information:

1. Common stock outstanding January 1, 1999, was 35,000 shares.
2. The market price of Cheryl Countryman, Inc., stock was $15 in 1999.
3. Cash dividends of $21,000 were paid, $5,000 of which were to preferred stockholders.
4. Net cash provided by operating activities $98,000.

Instructions
Compute the following ratios for 1999.

(a) Earnings per share.   (d) Times interest earned.
(b) Price-earnings.   (e) Cash return on sales.
(c) Payout.

E19–10 Perez Corporation experienced a fire on December 31, 2000, in which its financial records were partially destroyed. It has been able to salvage some of the records and has ascertained the following balances:

Compute amounts from ratios.
(SO 5)

	December 31, 2000	December 31, 1999
Cash	$ 30,000	$ 10,000
Receivables (net)	72,500	126,000
Inventory	200,000	180,000
Accounts payable	50,000	90,000
Notes payable	30,000	60,000
Common stock, $100 par	400,000	400,000
Retained earnings	115,000	101,000

Additional information:

1. The inventory turnover is 3.8 times.
2. The return on common stockholders' equity is 22%. The company had no additional paid-in capital.
3. The receivables turnover is 8.4 times.
4. The return on assets is 20%.
5. Total assets at December 31, 1999, were $605,000.

Instructions
Compute the following for Perez Corporation:

(a) Cost of goods sold for 2000.
(b) Net sales for 2000.
(c) Net income for 2000.
(d) Total assets at December 31, 2000.

PROBLEMS*

P19–1 Comparative statement data for Eller Company and Foley Company, two competitors, appear below. All balance sheet data are as of December 31, 2000, and December 31, 1999.

Prepare vertical analysis and comment on profitability.
(SO 4, 5)

*Follow the rounding procedures used in the chapter.

	Eller Company		Foley Company	
	2000	1999	2000	1999
Net sales	$1,549,035		$339,038	
Cost of goods sold	1,080,490		238,006	
Operating expenses	302,275		79,000	
Interest expense	6,800		1,252	
Income tax expense	51,030		6,650	
Current assets	325,975	$312,410	83,336	$ 79,467
Plant assets (net)	521,310	500,000	139,728	125,812
Current liabilities	66,325	75,815	35,348	30,281
Long-term liabilities	108,500	90,000	29,620	25,000
Common stock, $10 par	500,000	500,000	120,000	120,000
Retained earnings	172,460	146,595	38,096	29,998

Instructions

(a) Prepare a vertical analysis of the 2000 income statement data for Eller Company and Foley Company in columnar form.

(b) ▇▇▇▶ Comment on the relative profitability of the companies by computing the return on assets and the return on common stockholders' equity ratios for both companies.

Compute ratios from balance sheet and income statement. (SO 5)

P19–2 The comparative statements of Dorothy Fleming Company are presented below:

DOROTHY FLEMING COMPANY
Income Statement
For the Year Ended December 31

	1999	1998
Net sales	$1,818,500	$1,750,500
Cost of goods sold	1,005,500	996,000
Gross profit	813,000	754,500
Selling and administrative expense	506,000	479,000
Income from operations	307,000	275,500
Other expenses and losses		
Interest expense	18,000	19,000
Income before income taxes	289,000	256,500
Income tax expense	86,700	77,000
Net income	$ 202,300	$ 179,500

DOROTHY FLEMING COMPANY
Balance Sheet
December 31

Assets	1999	1998
Current assets		
Cash	$ 60,100	$ 64,200
Marketable securities	54,000	50,000
Accounts receivable (net)	107,800	102,800
Inventory	123,000	115,500
Total current assets	344,900	332,500
Plant assets (net)	625,300	520,300
Total assets	$970,200	$852,800

Liabilities and Stockholders' Equity	1999	1998
Current liabilities		
Accounts payable	$150,000	$145,400
Income taxes payable	43,500	42,000
Total current liabilities	193,500	187,400
Bonds payable	210,000	200,000
Total liabilities	403,500	387,400
Stockholders' equity		
Common stock ($5 par)	280,000	300,000
Retained earnings	286,700	165,400
Total stockholders' equity	566,700	465,400
Total liabilities and stockholders' equity	$970,200	$852,800

On April 1, 1999, 4,000 shares were repurchased and canceled. All sales were on account. Net cash provided by operating activities for 1999 was $280,000.

Instructions
Compute the following ratios for 1999:

(a) Earnings per share.
(b) Return on common stockholders' equity.
(c) Return on assets.
(d) Current.
(e) Acid-test.
(f) Receivables turnover.
(g) Inventory turnover.

(h) Times interest earned.
(i) Asset turnover.
(j) Debt to total assets.
(k) Current cash debt coverage.
(l) Cash return on sales.
(m) Cash debt coverage.

P19–3 Condensed balance sheet and income statement data for Roland Carlson Corporation appear below:

Perform ratio analysis.
(SO 5)

ROLAND CARLSON CORPORATION
Balance Sheet
December 31

	2000	1999	1998
Cash	$ 25,000	$ 20,000	$ 18,000
Receivables (net)	50,000	45,000	48,000
Other current assets	90,000	85,000	64,000
Investments	75,000	70,000	45,000
Plant and equipment (net)	400,000	370,000	358,000
	$640,000	$590,000	$533,000
Current liabilities	$ 75,000	$ 80,000	$ 70,000
Long-term debt	80,000	85,000	50,000
Common stock, $10 par	340,000	300,000	300,000
Retained earnings	145,000	125,000	113,000
	$640,000	$590,000	$533,000

ROLAND CARLSON CORPORATION
Income Statement
For the Years Ended December 31

	2000	1999
Sales	$740,000	$700,000
Less: Sales returns and allowances	40,000	50,000
Net sales	700,000	650,000
Cost of goods sold	420,000	400,000
Gross profit	280,000	250,000
Operating expenses (including income taxes)	230,000	215,000
Net income	$ 50,000	$ 35,000

Additional information:

1. The market price of Carlson's common stock was $4.00, $5.00, and $7.95 for 1998, 1999, and 2000, respectively.
2. All dividends were paid in cash.
3. On July 1, 2000, 4,000 shares of common stock were issued.

Instructions

(a) Compute the following ratios for 1999 and 2000:
   (1) Profit margin.
   (2) Asset turnover.
   (3) Earnings per share.
   (4) Price-earnings.
   (5) Payout.
   (6) Debt to total assets.

(b) ▭▭▭▭▶ Based on the ratios calculated, discuss briefly the improvement or lack thereof in financial position and operating results from 1999 to 2000 of Roland Carlson Corporation.

Compute ratios, commenting on overall liquidity and profitability.
(SO 5)

P19–4 Financial information for Callaway Company is presented below:

CALLAWAY COMPANY
Balance Sheet
December 31

Assets	2000	1999
Cash	$ 60,000	$ 55,000
Short-term investments	45,000	40,000
Receivables (net)	94,000	90,000
Inventories	130,000	125,000
Prepaid expenses	25,000	23,000
Land	140,000	140,000
Building and equipment (net)	190,000	175,000
	$684,000	$648,000

Liabilities and Stockholders' Equity		
Notes payable	$100,000	$100,000
Accounts payable	45,000	42,000
Accrued liabilities	40,000	40,000
Bonds payable, due 2003	150,000	150,000
Common stock, $10 par	200,000	200,000
Retained earnings	149,000	116,000
	$684,000	$648,000

CALLAWAY COMPANY
Income Statement
For the Years Ended December 31

	2000	1999
Sales	$850,000	$790,000
Cost of goods sold	610,000	570,000
Gross profit	240,000	220,000
Operating expenses	194,000	180,000
Net income	$ 46,000	$ 40,000

Additional information:

1. Inventory at the beginning of 1999 was $115,000.
2. Receivables at the beginning of 1999 were $88,000.
3. Total assets at the beginning of 1999 were $630,000.
4. No common stock transactions occurred during 1999 or 2000.
5. All sales were on account.

Instructions

(a) Indicate, by using ratios, the change in liquidity and profitability of Callaway Company from 1999 to 2000. (Note: Not all profitability ratios can be computed.)

(b) Given below are three independent situations and a ratio that may be affected. For each situation, compute the affected ratio (1) as of December 31, 2000, and (2) as of December 31, 2001, after giving effect to the situation. Net income for 2001 was $45,000. Total assets on December 31, 2001, were $700,000.

Situation	Ratio
1. 18,000 shares of common stock were sold at par on July 1, 2001.	Return on common stockholders' equity
2. All of the notes payable were paid in 2001.	Debt to total assets
3. Market price of common stock was $9 and $12.80 on December 31, 2000, and 2001, respectively.	Price-earnings ratio

P19-5   Selected financial data of two intense competitors in a recent year are presented below in millions of dollars.

Compute selected ratios and compare liquidity, profitability, and solvency for two companies.
(SO 5)

	Kmart Corporation	Wal-Mart Stores, Inc.
Income Statement Data for Year		
Net sales	$34,025	$82,494
Cost of goods sold	25,992	65,586
Selling and administrative expenses	7,701	12,858
Interest expense	494	706
Other income (net)	572	918
Income taxes	114	1,581
Net income	$ 296	$ 2,681
Balance Sheet Data (End-of-Year)		
Current assets	$ 9,187	$15,338
Property, plant, and equipment (net)	7,842	17,481
Total assets	$17,029	$32,819
Current liabilities	$ 5,626	$ 9,973
Long-term debt	5,371	10,120
Total stockholders' equity	6,032	12,726
Total liabilities and stockholders' equity	$17,029	$32,819
Beginning-of-Year Balances		
Total assets	$17,504	$26,441
Total stockholders' equity	6,093	10,753
Other Data		
Average net receivables	$ 1,570	$ 695
Average inventory	7,317	12,539
Net cash provided by operating activities	351	3,106

Instructions

(a) For each company, compute the following ratios:

(1) Current
(2) Receivables turnover
(3) Inventory turnover
(4) Profit margin
(5) Asset turnover
(6) Return on assets

(7) Return on common stockholders' equity
(8) Debt to total assets
(9) Times interest earned
(10) Current cash debt coverage
(11) Cash return on sales
(12) Cash debt coverage

(b) Compare the liquidity, profitability, and solvency of the two companies.

Compute numerous ratios.
(SO 5)

P19–6   The comparative statements of Swanson Company are presented below:

SWANSON COMPANY
Income Statement
For Year Ended December 31

	2000	1999
Net sales (all on account)	$650,000	$520,000
Expenses		
Cost of goods sold	415,000	354,000
Selling and administrative	150,800	114,800
Interest expense	7,200	6,000
Income tax expense	18,000	14,000
Total expenses	591,000	488,800
Net income	$ 59,000	$ 31,200

SWANSON COMPANY
Balance Sheet
December 31

Assets	2000	1999
Current assets		
Cash	$ 41,000	$ 18,000
Marketable securities	18,000	15,000
Accounts receivable (net)	92,000	74,000
Inventory	84,000	70,000
Total current assets	235,000	177,000
Plant assets (net)	403,000	383,000
Total assets	$638,000	$560,000
Liabilities and Stockholders' Equity		
Current liabilities		
Accounts payable	$112,000	$110,000
Income taxes payable	23,000	20,000
Total current liabilities	135,000	130,000
Long-term liabilities		
Bonds payable	130,000	80,000
Total liabilities	265,000	210,000
Stockholders' equity		
Common stock ($5 par)	150,000	150,000
Retained earnings	223,000	200,000
Total stockholders' equity	373,000	350,000
Total liabilities and stockholders' equity	$638,000	$560,000

Additional data:
The common stock recently sold at $19.50 per share.

Instructions
Compute the following ratios for 2000:

(a) Current.
(b) Acid-test.
(c) Receivables turnover.
(d) Inventory turnover.
(e) Profit margin.
(f) Asset turnover.
(g) Return on assets.

(h) Return on common stockholders' equity.
(i) Earnings per share.
(j) Price-earnings.
(k) Payout.
(l) Debt to total assets.
(m) Times interest earned.

P19–7 Presented below is an incomplete income statement and an incomplete comparative balance sheet of Vickers Corporation:

Compute missing information given a set of ratios.
(SO 5)

VICKERS CORPORATION
Income Statement
For the Year Ended December 31, 2000

Sales	$12,000,000
Cost of goods sold	?
Gross profit	?
Operating expenses	2,665,000
Income from operations	?
Other expenses and losses	
Interest expense	?
Income before income taxes	?
Income tax expense	580,000
Net income	$?

VICKERS CORPORATION
Balance Sheet
December 31

Assets	2000	1999
Current assets		
Cash	$ 440,000	$ 375,000
Accounts receivable (net)	?	950,000
Inventory	?	1,720,000
Total current assets	?	3,045,000
Plant assets (net)	4,550,000	3,955,000
Total assets	$?	$7,000,000
Liabilities and Stockholders' Equity		
Current liabilities	$?	$ 825,000
Long-term notes payable	?	2,800,000
Total liabilities	?	3,625,000
Common stock, $1 par	3,000,000	3,000,000
Retained earnings	400,000	375,000
Total stockholders' equity	3,400,000	3,375,000
Total liabilities and stockholders' equity	$?	$7,000,000

Additional information:

1. The receivables turnover for 2000 is 10 times.
2. All sales are on account.
3. The profit margin for 2000 is 15%.
4. Return on assets is 25% for 2000.
5. The current ratio on December 31, 2000, is 3:1.
6. The inventory turnover for 2000 is 5 times.

Instructions

Compute the missing information given the ratios above. Show computations. (Note: Start with one ratio and derive as much information as possible from it before trying another ratio. List all missing amounts under the ratio used to find the information.)

BROADENING YOUR PERSPECTIVE

FINANCIAL REPORTING AND ANALYSIS

FINANCIAL REPORTING PROBLEM: Kellogg Company

BYP19–1   Your parents are considering investing in Kellogg Company, Inc., common stock. They ask you, as an accounting expert, to make an analysis of the company for them. Fortunately, excerpts from a current annual report of Kellogg are presented in Appendix A of this textbook. Note that all amounts omit 000,000's (i.e., all dollar amounts are in millions).

Instructions
(Follow the approach in the chapter for rounding numbers.)

(a) Make a 5-year trend analysis, using 1993 as the base year, of (1) net sales and (2) operating profit. Comment on the significance of the trend results.
(b) Compute for 1997 and 1996 the (1) profit margin, (2) asset turnover, (3) return on assets, and (4) return on common stockholders' equity. How would you evaluate Kellogg's profitability? Total assets at December 31, 1995, were $4,414.6, and total stockholders' equity at December 31, 1995, was $1,590.9.
(c) Compute for 1997 and 1996 the (1) debt to total assets and (2) times interest earned ratio. How would you evaluate Kellogg's long-term solvency?
(d) What information outside the annual report may also be useful to your parents in making a decision about Kellogg Company?

COMPARATIVE ANALYSIS PROBLEM: Kellogg Company vs. General Mills

BYP19–2   Kellogg's financial statements are presented in Appendix A; General Mills's financial statements are presented in Appendix B.

Instructions
(a) Based on the information contained in these financial statements, determine each of the following for each company:
  1. The percentage increase (decrease) in (i) net sales and (ii) net income from 1996 to 1997.
  2. The percentage increase in (i) total assets and (ii) total stockholders' (shareholders') equity from 1996 to 1997.
  3. The earnings per share and price-earnings ratio for 1997. General Mills's common stock had a market price of $64.25 at the end of 1997.
(b) What conclusions concerning the two companies can be drawn from these data?

RESEARCH ASSIGNMENT

BYP19–3   The chapter stresses the importance of comparing an individual firm's financial ratios to industry norms. Robert Morris Associates (RMA), a national association of bank loan and credit officers, publishes industry-specific financial data in its *Annual Statement Studies.* This publication includes common-size financial statements and various ratios classified by four-digit SIC code. (Note: An alternative source is Dun & Bradstreet's *Industry Norms and Key Business Ratios.*)

Obtain the 1997 edition of *Annual Statement Studies* (covering fiscal years ended 4/1/96 through 3/31/97) and the 1997 (or 1998) Annual Report of Wal-Mart Stores, Inc.

Instructions
(a) Prepare a 1997 common-size (vertical analysis) balance sheet and income statement for Wal-Mart.
(b) Calculate those 1997 ratios for Wal-Mart which are covered by RMA. (Note: The specific ratio definitions used by RMA are described in the beginning of the book. Use ending values for balance sheet items.)

(c) What is Wal-Mart's SIC code? Use your answers from parts (a) and (b) to compare Wal-Mart to the appropriate current industry data. How does Wal-Mart compare to its competitors? (Note: RMA sorts current-year data by firm assets and sales, while five years of historical data are presented on an aggregate basis.)

(d) How many sets of financial statements did RMA use in compiling the current industry data sorted by sales?

INTERPRETING FINANCIAL STATEMENTS: Manitowoc Company and Caterpillar Corp.

BYP19–4 The Manitowoc Company and Caterpillar Corporation are both producers and sellers of large fixed assets. Caterpillar is substantially larger than Manitowoc. Financial information taken from each company's financial statements is provided below.

Financial highlights	Caterpillar (in millions)		Manitowoc (in thousands)	
	1995	1994	1995	1994
Cash and short-term investments	$ 638	$ 419	$ 16,635	$ 16,163
Accounts receivable	4,285	4,290	51,011	29,500
Inventory	1,921	1,835	52,928	36,793
Other current assets	803	865	14,571	14,082
Current assets	7,647	7,409	135,145	96,538
Total assets	16,830	16,250	324,915	159,465
Current liabilities	6,049	5,498	110,923	54,064
Total liabilities	13,442	13,339	243,254	84,408
Total stockholders' equity	3,388	2,911	81,661	75,057
Sales	15,451		313,149	
Cost of goods sold	12,000		237,679	
Interest expense	191		1,865	
Income tax expense	501		8,551	
Net income	1,136		14,569	
Cash provided from operations	2,190		16,367	

Instructions

(a) Calculate the following liquidity ratios and provide a discussion of the relative liquidity of the two companies.
   1. Current ratio
   2. Quick or acid-test ratio
   3. Current cash debt coverage
   4. Accounts receivable turnover
   5. Inventory turnover

(b) Calculate the following profitability ratios and provide a discussion of the relative profitability of the two companies.
   1. Asset turnover
   2. Profit margin on sales
   3. Return on assets
   4. Return on common equity

(c) Calculate the following solvency ratios and provide a discussion of the relative solvency of the two companies.
   1. Debt to assets
   2. Times interest earned

REAL-WORLD FOCUS: The Coca-Cola Company and PepsiCo, Inc.

BYP19–5 The Coca-Cola Company and PepsiCo, Inc., provides refreshments to every corner of the world. Both believe that great potential still exists—to satisfy the thirst of the world's population. Selected data from the consolidated financial statements for The Coca-Cola Company and for PepsiCo, Inc., are presented below. (All dollars are in millions.)

	Coca-Cola	PepsiCo
Total current assets (including cash, accounts receivable, and marketable securities totaling $3,056 and $3,539, respectively)	$ 5,205	$ 5,546
Total current liabilities	6,177	5,230
Net sales	16,172	30,421
Cost of goods sold	6,167	14,886
Net income	2,554	1,606
Average receivables for the year	1,384	2,229
Average inventories for the year	1,048	1,011
Average total assets	12,947	25,112
Average common stockholders' equity	4,910	7,085
Net cash provided by operating activities	3,115	3,742
Average current liabilities	6,763	5,250
Total assets	13,873	25,432
Total liabilities	8,638	18,119
Income before income taxes	3,728	2,432
Interest expense	199	682

Instructions

(a) Compute the following liquidity ratios for Coca-Cola and for PepsiCo.:
  (1) Current
  (2) Acid-test
  (3) Current cash debt coverage
  (4) Receivables turnover
  (5) Inventory turnover
(b) Comment on the relative liquidity of the two competitors.
(c) Compute the following profitability ratios for the two companies:
  (1) Profit margin
  (2) Cash return on sales
  (3) Asset turnover
  (4) Return on assets
  (5) Return on common stockholders' equity
(d) Comment on the relative profitability of the two competitors.

CRITICAL THINKING

GROUP DECISION CASE

BYP19–6   As the CPA for L. Gonzalez Manufacturing Inc., you have been requested to develop some key ratios from the comparative financial statements. This information is to be used to convince creditors that L. Gonzalez Manufacturing Inc. is solvent and to support the use of going-concern valuation procedures in the financial statements.

The data requested and the computations developed from the financial statements follow:

	2000	1999
Current ratio	3.1 times	2.1 times
Acid-test ratio	.8 times	1.4 times
Asset turnover	2.8 times	2.2 times
Sales to stockholders' equity	2.3 times	2.7 times
Net income	Up 32%	Down 8%
Earnings per share	$3.30	$2.50
Book value per share	Up 8%	Up 11%

Instructions

With the class divided into groups, answer the following:

(a) L. Gonzalez Manufacturing Inc. asks you to prepare a list of brief comments stating how each of these items supports the solvency and going-concern potential of the business. The company wishes to use these comments to support its presentation of data to its creditors. You are to prepare the comments as requested, giving the implications and the limitations of each item separately, and then the collective inference that may be drawn from them about L. Gonzales's solvency and going-concern potential.

(b) What warnings should you offer these creditors about the limitations of ratio analysis for the purpose stated here?

COMMUNICATION ACTIVITY

BYP19–7   Ken Powell is the Chief Executive Officer of Midwest Electronics. Powell is an expert engineer but a novice in accounting. Powell asks you, as an accounting major, to explain (1) the bases for comparison in analyzing Midwest's financial statements and (2) the limitations, if any, in financial statement analysis.

Instructions

Write a letter to Powell that explains the bases for comparison and the limitations of financial statement analysis.

ETHICS CASE

BYP19–8   Ron Staub, president of Staub Industries, wishes to issue a press release to bolster his company's image and maybe even its stock price, which has been gradually falling. As controller, you have been asked to provide a list of twenty financial ratios along with some other operating statistics relative to Staub Industries' first quarter financials and operations.

Two days after you provide the ratios and data requested, you are asked by Manny Alomar, the public relations director of Staub, to prove the accuracy of the financial and operating data contained in the press release written by the president and edited by Manny. In the news release, the president highlights the sales increase of 25% over last year's first quarter and the positive change in the current ratio from 1.5:1 last year to 3:1 this year. He also emphasizes that production was up 50% over the prior year's first quarter. You note that the release contains only positive or improved ratios and none of the negative or deteriorated ratios. For instance, no mention is made that the debt to total assets ratio has increased from 35% to 55%, that inventories are up 89%, and that while the current ratio improved, the acid-test ratio fell from 1:1 to .5:1. Nor is there any mention that the reported profit for the quarter would have been a loss had not the estimated lives of Staub's plant and machinery been increased by 30%. Manny emphasized, ''The Pres wants this release by early this afternoon.''

Instructions

(a) Who are the stakeholders in this situation?
(b) Is there anything unethical in president Staub's actions?
(c) Should you as controller remain silent? Does Manny have any responsibility?

SURFING THE NET

BYP19–9   The Management Discussion and Analysis (MD&A) section of an annual report addresses corporate performance for the year, and sometimes uses financial ratios to support its claims.

Addresses: http://www.ibm.com/financialguide
http://www.yahoo.com

Steps:
1. From IBM's Financial Guide, choose **Guides Contents.**
2. Choose **Anatomy of an Annual Report.**
3. Follow instruction (a).
4. From Yahoo Homepage, choose **Stock Quotes.**
5. Enter **GE.**
6. Choose **Get Quotes.**
7. Choose **SEC filing** (this will take you to Yahoo-Edgar Online).
8. Choose the most recent annual report.
9. Follow instructions (b)-(e).

Instructions

(a) Using IBM's Financial Guide, describe the contents of the Management Discussion and Analysis.
(b) In the overview section, GE's management discusses the company's performance. What were the net corporate earnings in the most recent year?
(c) Compare current year earnings with the previous year's earnings.
(d) What were management's reasons for the change in net earnings?

Answers to Self-Study Questions

1. b   2. d   3. a   4. c   5. c   6. c   7. c   8. b   9. a   10. b

---

Answer to Kellogg Review It Question 4, p. 827.

4. Kellogg presents horizontal analyses in its "Financial Highlights" section, its Management's Discussion and Analysis section, and its Note 13 on Operating Segments. Vertical analysis is used in schedules presented in the Management's Discussion and Analysis section.

Remember to go back to the Navigator box on the chapter-opening page and check off your completed work.

Before studying this chapter, you should know or, if necessary, review:

a. The cost principle. (Ch. 1, p. 11)

b. Ethics in accounting. (Ch. 1, p. 9)

c. The computation of cost of goods sold. (Ch. 9, p. 374–375)

d. The adjusting and closing process used in a merchandising firm. (Ch. 5, pp. 205–206)

e. The use of a work sheet in the preparation of financial statements. (Ch. 4, pp. 140–45 and Ch. 5, pp. 201–204)

FEATURE STORY

Spokesman Says, "Cut the Scrap"

You've heard of the Big Three automakers—that's shorthand for General Motors, Ford, and Chrysler, the three big domestic car companies. Well, there's also the Big Three U.S. bicycle makers—Huffy, Murray, and Roadmaster. Like their automotive counterparts, the bike makers have a big challenge: produce domestically a bicycle at a reasonable sticker price when there's a lot of foreign competition.

Murray (short for Murray Ohio Manufacturing Co.) has found a way to keep costs and prices down—and to make a profit. The company manufactures 15,000 bicycles per day at its plant in southern Tennessee. Instead of marketing the bikes to independent bicycle stores, they sell their products to mass merchants such as Sears.

A bicycle's direct materials include steel, tires, spokes, hubs, and brakes. "We take steel and turn it into tubing which, in turn, becomes the bike frame," says Tom Appleton, product manager. "You do have some planned scrap," he says, because you might want to stamp a round sprocket out of a square piece of steel. "By taking a round part out of a square piece, you've automatically got around 25% scrap," he says, "which we sell to scrap dealers at 5 percent of its original cost. Then, there's unplanned scrap which occurs when one of the workers—to put it bluntly—makes a mistake. We also sell this scrap, but we lose the labor cost."

The direct labor time to make a Murray bike is only about 30 minutes. That's one good reason why an American manufacturer can do well against global competition. "The key is to manage your costs better than the next guy," says Appleton. The most expensive Murray bicycle retails for around $250 and they sold approximately 3 million units to the U.S. market in a recent year.

On the World Wide Web
http://www.huffy.com

CHAPTER 20

MANAGERIAL ACCOUNTING

THE NAVIGATOR ✔

- ■ Understand *Concepts for Review* ☐
- ■ Read *Feature Story* ☐
- ■ Scan *Study Objectives* ☐
- ■ Read *Preview* ☐
- ■ Read text and answer *Before You Go On*
  p. 873 ☐ p. 876 ☐ p. 884 ☐
- ■ Work *Demonstration Problems* ☐
- ■ Review *Summary of Study Objectives* ☐
- ■ Answer *Self-Study Questions* ☐
- ■ Complete assignments ☐

STUDY OBJECTIVES

After studying this chapter, you should be able to:

1. *Explain the distinguishing features of managerial accounting.*
2. *Identify the three broad functions of management.*
3. *Define the three classes of manufacturing costs.*
4. *Distinguish between product and period costs.*
5. *Explain the difference between a merchandising and a manufacturing income statement.*
6. *Indicate how cost of goods manufactured is determined.*
7. *Explain the difference between a merchandising and a manufacturing balance sheet.*

THE NAVIGATOR

Beginning with this chapter, we turn our attention to issues illustrated in the opening story about Murray Ohio Manufacturing Co., such as the costs of materials and labor and the relationship between costs and profits. To this point in the text, we have described the form and content of **financial statements** for **external users** such as stockholders and creditors. These statements represent the principal end-product of financial accounting. The remaining chapters of this textbook focus primarily on the preparation of **reports** for **internal users**, such as the managers and officers of a company. These reports are an integral part of managerial accounting. The content and organization of this chapter are as follows:

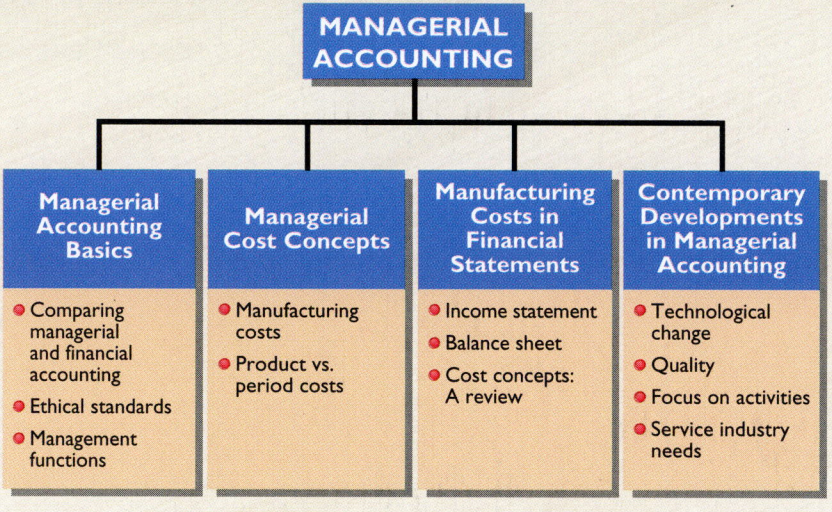

THE
NAVIGATOR

MANAGERIAL ACCOUNTING BASICS

Managerial accounting, also called management accounting, is a field of accounting that provides economic and financial information for managers and other internal users. The activities that are part of managerial accounting (and the chapters in which they are discussed) are as follows:

1. Explaining manufacturing and nonmanufacturing costs and how they are reported in the financial statements (Chapter 20).
2. Computing the cost of rendering a service or manufacturing a product (Chapters 21 and 22).
3. Determining the behavior of costs and expenses as activity levels change and analyzing cost–volume–profit relationships within a company (Chapter 23).
4. Assisting management in profit planning and formalizing the plans in the form of budgets (Chapter 24).
5. Providing a basis for controlling costs and expenses by comparing actual results with planned objectives and standard costs (Chapters 25 and 26).
6. Accumulating and presenting relevant data for management decision making (Chapter 27).

Managerial accounting applies to all types of businesses—service, merchandising, and manufacturing—and to all forms of business organizations—proprietorships, partnerships, and corporations. Moreover, managerial accounting is needed in not-for-profit entities as well as in profit-oriented enterprises.

Comparing Managerial and Financial Accounting

There are both similarities and differences between managerial and financial accounting. An important similarity is that each field of accounting deals with the economic events of an enterprise. Thus, their interests overlap. For example, determining the unit cost of manufacturing a product is part of managerial accounting. In contrast, reporting the total cost of goods manufactured and sold is part of financial accounting. In addition, both managerial and financial accounting require that the results of an entity's economic events be quantified and be communicated to interested parties. The diverse needs for economic data among parties interested in an enterprise are responsible for many of the differences between the two fields of accounting.

The principal differences between financial accounting and managerial accounting are summarized in Illustration 20-1.

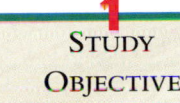

1
STUDY
OBJECTIVE
....
Explain the distinguishing features of managerial accounting.

ILLUSTRATION 20-1

Differences between financial and managerial accounting

	Financial Accounting		**Managerial Accounting**
Primary Users of Reports	• External users, who are stockholders, creditors, and regulatory agencies.		• Internal users, who are officers, department heads, managers, and supervisors in the company.
Types and Frequency of Reports	• Classified financial statements. • Issued quarterly and annually.		• Internal reports. • Issued as frequently as the need arises.
Purpose of Reports	• To provide general-purpose information for all users.		• To provide special-purpose information for a particular user for a specific decision.
Content of Reports	• Pertains to entity as a whole and is highly aggregated (condensed). • Limited to double-entry accounting system and cost data. • Reporting standard is generally accepted accounting principles.		• Pertains to subunits of the entity and may be very detailed. • May extend beyond double-entry accounting system to any type of relevant data. • Reporting standard is relevance to the decision to be made.
Verification Process	• Annual independent audit by certified public accountant.		• No independent audits.

Ethical Standards for Managerial Accountants

We have emphasized throughout the textbook the importance of ethics in business and in accounting. Managerial accountants recognize that they have an ethical obligation to their companies and the public. To provide guidance for managerial accountants in the performance of their duties, the Institute of Management Accountants (IMA) has developed a code of ethical standards, entitled *Standards of Ethical Conduct for Management Accountants*. This code divides the managerial accountants' responsibilities into four areas: (1) competence, (2) confidentiality, (3) integrity, and (4) objectivity. The code states that management accountants should not commit acts in violation of these standards, nor should they condone such acts by others within their organizations. You may wish to review the code to understand the importance of ethics in companies today.

HELPFUL HINT
The IMA code of ethical standards is provided in Appendix E.

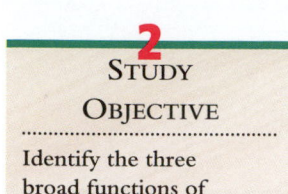

2

STUDY

OBJECTIVE

....

Identify the three
broad functions of
management.

Management Functions

The management of an organization performs three broad functions. They are:

1. Planning.
2. Organizing and directing.
3. Controlling.

In performing these functions, management must make decisions that have a significant impact on the organization.

Planning requires management to look ahead and to establish objectives. These objectives are often as diverse as maximizing short-term profits and market share, maintaining a commitment to environmental protection, and contributing to social programs. Today, a key objective of management appears to be to add **value** to the business under its control. Value is usually measured by the trading price of the company's stock and by the potential selling price of the company.

Organizing and directing involves coordinating a company's diverse activities and human resources to produce a smooth-running operation. This function relates to the implementation of planned objectives. For example, in companies such as Campbell Soup Company, IBM, General Motors, and Oscar Mayer, purchasing, manufacturing, warehousing, and selling must be coordinated. Similarly, it is necessary to select executives, appoint managers and supervisors, and hire and train employees. Most companies prepare **organization charts** to show the interrelationship of activities and the delegation of authority and responsibility within the company.

ACCOUNTING IN ACTION
Business Insight

Business researchers have identified different organization types, or "corporate cultures." The ways in which the management function of organizing and directing are carried out differ from one organization type to another. Researcher Jeffrey Sonnenfeld has labeled four types of corporate culture:

1. Academies—For the steady climber who must thoroughly master each new job and make one company his or her career home. A classic academy is IBM because as one expert noted: "You don't move ahead until you perform where you are."
2. Clubs—For the individual who strives to fit in. What counts isn't individual achievement, but sincerity, commitment, and doing things for the good of the group. An example is United Parcel Service where one executive noted: "When decisions have to be made we get everyone's opinion, and the company feels like a family to a lot of us."
3. Baseball teams—For those who like to consider themselves free agents. In these situations, companies seek out talent of all ages and experience and reward them by what they produce. They don't care how committed you'll be tomorrow—they want cutting-edge results today. Examples are accounting firms like Arthur Andersen and consulting firms like First Boston Corp.
4. Fortresses—For those who like crisis situations. Many fortresses are companies concerned with survival. Fortresses may be academies, clubs, or baseball teams that have failed in the market place and are struggling to reverse their fortunes. Other fortresses are in a perpetual boom-and-bust cycle, such as natural resources companies.

Companies do change over time. Apple Computer started out as a baseball team but is now becoming an academy. And with deregulation, banks—once clubs—are fast evolving into baseball teams.

Source: Adapted from an article by Carol Hymowitz, "Which Corporate Culture Fits You?" *The Wall Street Journal,* July 17, 1989.

The third management function, **controlling**, is the process of keeping the firm's activities on track. In controlling operations, management determines whether planned goals are being met and what changes are necessary when there are deviations from targeted objectives.

How do managers achieve control? In small organizations, a manager might use personal observation. A smart manager in a small operation should know the right questions to ask and how to evaluate the answers. But such a system in a large organization would be chaotic. Imagine the president of Ford Motor Company attempting to determine whether planned objectives are being met without some record of what has happened and what is expected to occur. Thus, a formal system of evaluation that includes such items as budgets, responsibility centers, and performance evaluation reports is typically used in large businesses.

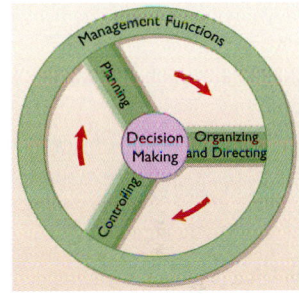

As shown by the graphic in the margin, the three functions of management may be depicted as the spokes of a wheel that move around the axle or hub of decision making. Decision making is not a separate management function. Rather, it is the outcome of the exercise of good judgment in planning, organizing and directing, and controlling.

You are now ready to study specific applications of managerial accounting. As you study the managerial chapters, you will encounter many new terms, concepts, and reports. At the same time, you will find some new uses and interpretations of a number of familiar financial accounting terms.

BEFORE YOU GO ON . . .

Review It

1. Compare financial accounting and managerial accounting, identifying the principal differences.
2. Give three examples of the expanding role of managerial accounting.
3. Identify and discuss the three broad functions of management.

THE
NAVIGATOR

MANAGERIAL COST CONCEPTS

To perform the three management functions effectively, management needs information. One very important type of information is related to costs. For example, questions such as the following need answering:

1. What costs are involved in making a product?
2. If production volume is decreased, will costs decrease?
3. What impact will automation have on total costs?
4. How can costs best be controlled in the organization?

To answer these questions, management needs reliable and relevant cost information. We now explain and illustrate the costs that management uses.

Manufacturing Costs

Manufacturing consists of activities and processes that convert raw materials into finished goods. Contrast this type of operation with merchandising, which sells merchandise in the form in which it is purchased. Manufacturing costs are typically classified as shown in Illustration 20-2.

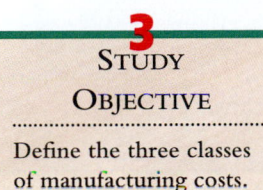

3
STUDY
OBJECTIVE
....
Define the three classes
of manufacturing costs.

ILLUSTRATION 20-2
*Classifications of manufac-
turing costs*

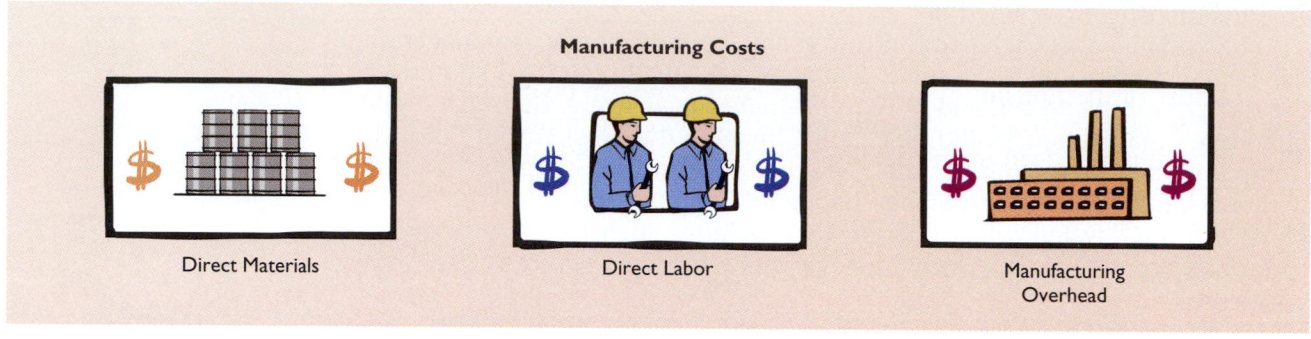

Manufacturing Costs

Direct Materials   Direct Labor   Manufacturing Overhead

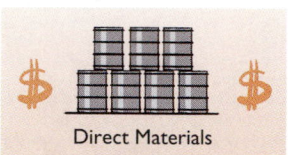

Direct Materials

Direct Labor

Direct Materials

To obtain the materials that will be converted into the finished product, the manufacturer purchases raw materials. **Raw materials** represent the basic materials and parts that are to be used in the manufacturing process. For example, steel, plastics, and tires are raw materials in making automobiles.

Raw materials that can be physically and conveniently associated with the finished product during the manufacturing process are called **direct materials**. Examples include flour in the baking of bread, syrup in the bottling of soft drinks, and steel in the making of automobiles. In the opening story, direct materials for the bicycles included steel, tires, spokes, hubs, and brakes.

Conversely, some raw materials cannot be easily associated with the finished product; these are considered indirect materials. **Indirect materials** (1) do not physically become part of the finished product, such as lubricants, rosin, and polishing compounds used in the manufacturing process, or (2) cannot be traced because their physical association with the finished product is too small in terms of cost, such as cotter pins, lock washers, and the like. Indirect materials are accounted for as part of **manufacturing overhead**.

Direct Labor

The work of factory employees that can be physically and conveniently associated with converting raw materials into finished goods is considered **direct labor**. In the story about Murray Ohio Manufacturing, it took 30 minutes of direct labor to make a bicycle. Bottlers in a soft drink plant, bakers in a bakery, and typesetters in a print shop are examples of employees whose activities are usually classified as direct labor. In contrast, the wages of maintenance people, timekeepers, and supervisors are usually identified as **indirect labor** because their efforts have no physical association with the finished product, or it is impractical

ACCOUNTING IN ACTION
Business Insight

The trend toward more automated and computerized factories will change the way managers and employees interact. For one thing, managers will have fewer direct labor employees to supervise because fewer will be needed on the line. Instead of standing in one spot all day, employees and managers will become more mobile, monitoring the computers that handle the production, and involving themselves in a variety of jobs.

Jobs will be more varied. As machines do more of the repetitive work, employees and managers will need to be more problem-solvers than "cogs in a machine." They will need to be more analytical, to receive more technical training, and to be more highly educated. As a result, they also will be more highly paid.

to trace the costs to the goods produced. Like indirect materials, indirect labor is classified as **manufacturing overhead**.

Manufacturing Overhead

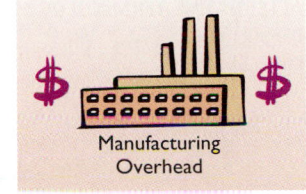
Manufacturing Overhead

Manufacturing overhead consists of costs that are indirectly associated with the manufacture of the finished product. These costs may also be defined as manufacturing costs that cannot be classified as either direct materials or direct labor. Manufacturing overhead includes indirect materials, indirect labor, depreciation on factory buildings and machinery, and insurance, taxes, and maintenance on factory facilities.

The magnitude of the three different product costs in terms of the total product cost is provided in the following chart, which covers seven industries:[1]

ILLUSTRATION 20-3

Product cost components by industry

	PRODUCT COST BY INDUSTRY		
	Percentage of Total Manufacturing Cost		
Industry	**Direct Materials**	**Direct Labor**	**Manufacturing Overhead**
Aerospace	51.7%	19.3%	29.0%
Computers	69.9	7.5	22.5
Electronics	48.6	15.1	36.3
Industrial and farm equipment	46.0	12.8	41.2
Metal products	52.0	15.7	32.3
Motor vehicles and parts	63.8	7.8	28.4
Scientific and photographic equipment	52.3	11.3	36.5
Average for seven industries	54.4%	12.9%	32.6%

ALTERNATIVE TERMINOLOGY

Terms such as *factory overhead, indirect manufacturing costs,* and *burden* are sometimes used instead of manufacturing overhead.

Note that the direct labor component is the smallest. This component of product cost is dropping substantially because of automation. In some companies, direct labor has become as little as 5% of the total cost.

ACCOUNTING IN ACTION
Business Insight

In valuing inventories, accountants include three types of costs: materials, overhead, and labor. Allocating materials and labor costs to specific products is fairly straightforward. But accountants have big trouble dealing with overhead, a black hole that swallows up everything from the equipment used to fashion a product to the security guard who watches over the plant at night. How much of the purchasing agent's salary is attributable to the semiconductor chip, how much to the personal computer on his or her desk, how much to the hundred other products made in the same plant? What about the grease that keeps the machines humming, or the computers that make sure paychecks come out on time? Boiled down to its simplest form, the question becomes: Which products cause which costs?

Product versus Period Costs

Each of the manufacturing cost elements (direct materials, direct labor, and manufacturing overhead) are product costs. As the term suggests, **product costs** are costs that are a necessary and integral part of producing the finished product. These costs do not become expenses under the matching principle until the finished goods inventory is sold. The expense is cost of goods sold. Direct materials

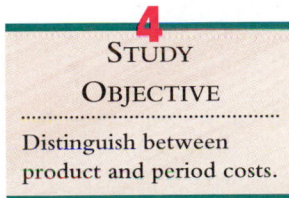
STUDY OBJECTIVE
....
Distinguish between product and period costs.

---

[1]James A. Hendricks, "Applying Cost Accounting to Factory Automation," *Management Accounting,* December 1988, p. 26.

and direct labor are often referred to as **prime costs** because of their direct association with the manufacturing of the finished product. In addition, because direct labor and manufacturing overhead are incurred in converting raw materials into finished goods, these two cost elements are often referred to as **conversion costs**.

Period costs are costs that are identified with a specific time period rather than with a salable product. These costs relate to nonmanufacturing costs and therefore are not inventoriable costs. Period costs include selling and administrative expenses that are deducted from revenues in the period in which they are incurred.

The foregoing relationships and cost terms are summarized in Illustration 20-4. Our main concern in this chapter is with product costs.

ILLUSTRATION 20-4

Product versus period costs

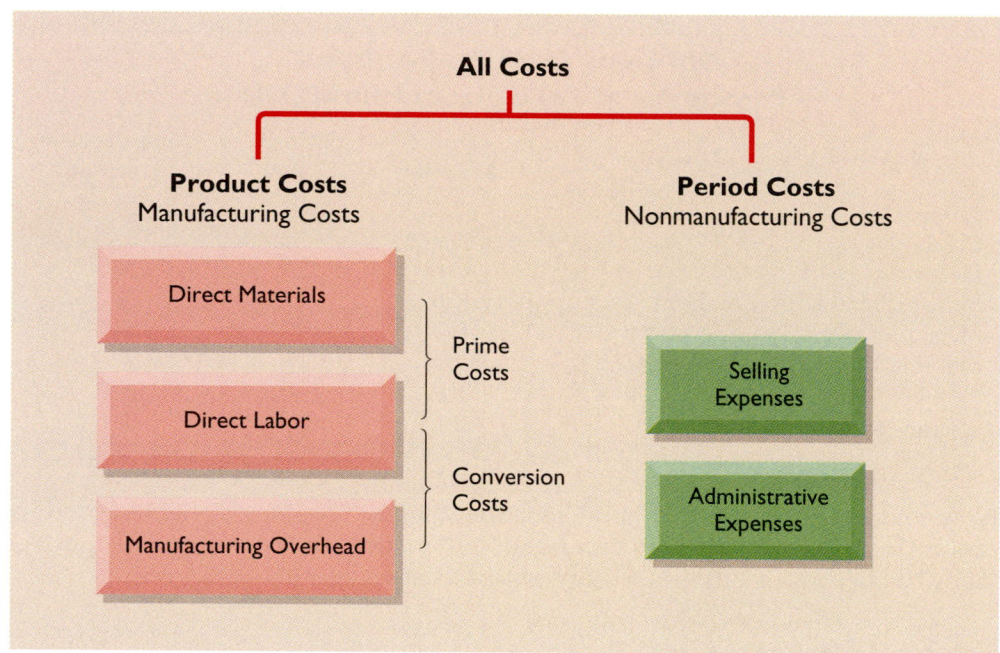

BEFORE YOU GO ON . . .

Review It

1. What are the major cost classifications involved in manufacturing a product?
2. What are product and period costs and their relationship to the manufacturing process?

Do It

In making bicycles, a company has the following costs: tires, salaries of employees who put tires on the wheels, factory building depreciation, wheel nuts, spokes, salary of factory foreman, handle bars, and salaries of factory maintenance employees. Classify each cost as direct materials, direct labor, or manufacturing overhead.

Reasoning: Direct materials are raw materials that can be physically and conveniently associated with the finished product. Direct labor is the work of factory employees that can be physically and conveniently associated with the finished product. Manufacturing overhead are costs that are indirectly associated with the finished product.

Solution: Tires, spokes, and handle bars are direct materials. Salaries of employees who put tires on the wheels are direct labor. All of the other costs are manufacturing overhead.

Related exercise material: BE20–4, BE20–6, BE20–11, E20–1, and E20–2.

MANUFACTURING COSTS IN FINANCIAL STATEMENTS

The financial statements of a manufacturing company are very similar to those of a merchandising company. The principal differences pertain to the cost of goods sold section of the income statement and the current assets section of the balance sheet.

Income Statement

Under a periodic inventory system, the income statements of a merchandising company and a manufacturing company differ in the cost of goods sold section. For a merchandising company, cost of goods sold is computed by adding the beginning merchandise inventory and the **cost of goods purchased** and subtracting the ending merchandise inventory. For a manufacturing company, cost of goods sold is computed by adding the beginning finished goods inventory and **cost of goods manufactured** and subtracting the ending finished goods inventory. The different components are shown graphically below:

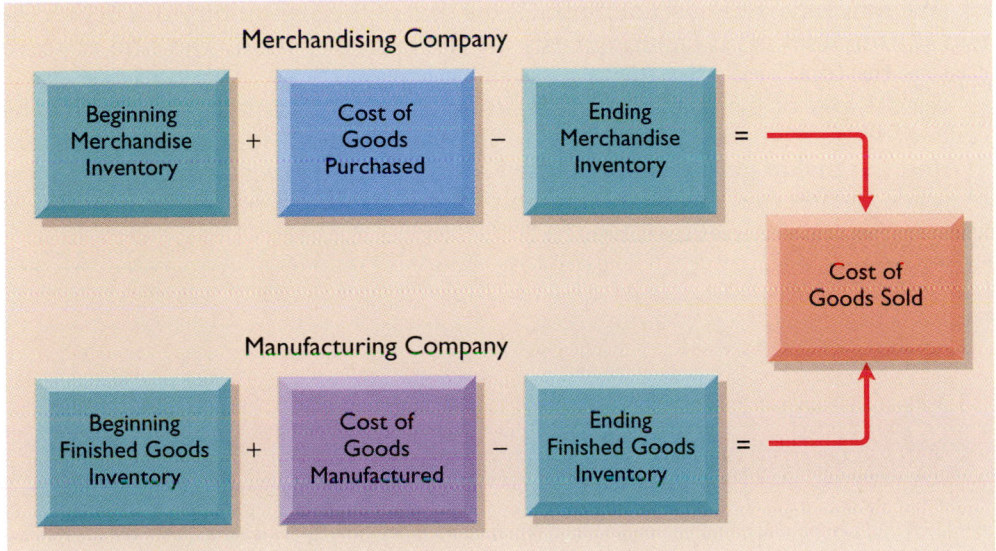

ILLUSTRATION 20-5

Cost of goods sold components

HELPFUL HINT

Note that a periodic inventory system is used here.

The cost of goods sold sections for merchandising and manufacturing enterprises presented below illustrate the different presentations:

ILLUSTRATION 20-6

Cost of goods sold sections of merchandising and manufacturing income statements

MERCHANDISE COMPANY Income Statement (partial) For the Year Ended December 31, 1999		MANUFACTURING COMPANY Income Statement (partial) For the Year Ended December 31, 1999	
Cost of goods sold		Cost of goods sold	
Merchandise inventory, January 1	$ 70,000	Finished goods inventory, January 1	$ 90,000
Cost of goods purchased	650,000	Cost of goods manufactured	
		(see Illustration 20-8)	370,000
Cost of goods available for sale	720,000	Cost of goods available for sale	460,000
Merchandise inventory, December 31	400,000	Finished goods inventory, December 31	80,000
Cost of goods sold	$320,000	Cost of goods sold	$380,000

The other sections of an income statement are similar for both a merchandising and a manufacturing company.

A number of accounts are involved in determining the cost of goods manufactured. To eliminate excessive detail in the income statement, it is customary to show in the income statement only the total cost of goods manufactured and to present the details in a Cost of Goods Manufactured Schedule. The form and content of this schedule are shown in Illustration 20-8 (page 879).

Determining the Cost of Goods Manufactured

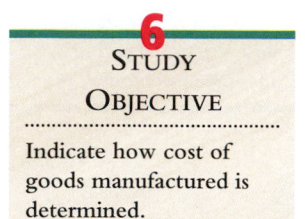

STUDY OBJECTIVE 6

Indicate how cost of goods manufactured is determined.

An example may be helpful in showing how the cost of goods manufactured for a period is determined. Assume that Ford Motor Company has a number of automobiles in various stages of production on January 1. In total, these partially completed units are called **beginning work in process inventory**. The costs assigned to beginning work in process inventory are based on the **manufacturing costs incurred in the prior period**. In the current year, Ford Motor continues the production of automobiles. The manufacturing costs incurred in the current year are used first to complete the work in process on January 1 and then to start the production of other vehicles. The sum of the direct materials costs, direct labor costs, and manufacturing overhead incurred in the current year is the total manufacturing costs.

HELPFUL HINT

Does the amount of "total manufacturing costs for the current year" include the amount of "beginning work in process inventory?"
Answer: No.

We now have two cost amounts: (1) the cost of the beginning work in process and (2) the total manufacturing costs for the current period. The sum of these costs is the total cost of work in process for the year.

At the end of the year, some vehicles may be only partially completed. The costs of these units become the cost of the **ending work in process inventory**. To find the cost of goods manufactured, we subtract this cost from the total cost of work in process. The determination of the cost of goods manufactured is shown graphically in Illustration 20-7.

ILLUSTRATION 20-7

Cost of goods manufactured formula

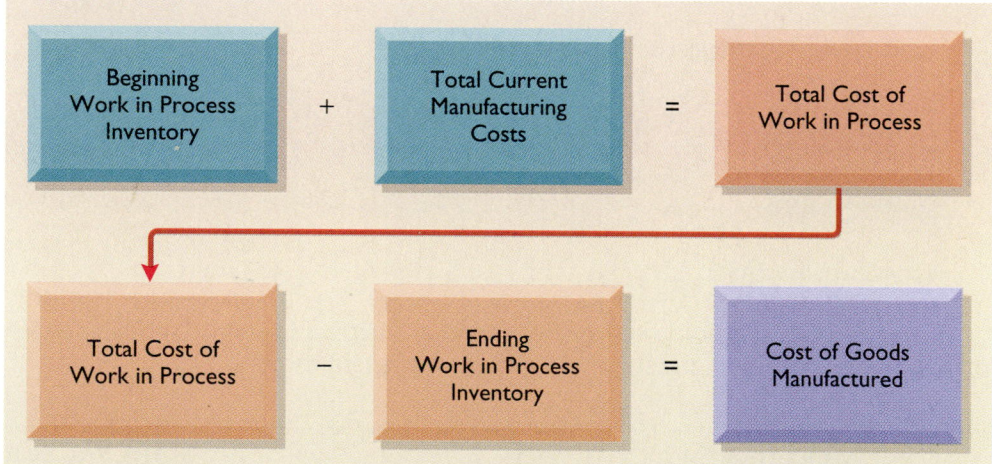

Cost of Goods Manufactured Schedule

An internal financial schedule called the **cost of goods manufactured schedule** shows each of the cost elements explained in Illustration 20-7. The schedule for Olsen Manufacturing Company using assumed data is shown in Illustration 20-8. Note that detailed data are presented for direct materials and manufacturing overhead.

A review of Illustration 20-7 along with an examination of the cost of goods manufactured schedule, Illustration 20-8, should help you distinguish between "total manufacturing costs" and "cost of goods manufactured." The difference is the effect of the change in work in process during the period.

ILLUSTRATION 20-8

Cost of goods manufactured schedule

OLSEN MANUFACTURING COMPANY Cost of Goods Manufactured Schedule For the Year Ended December 31, 1999			
Work in process, January 1			$ 18,400
Direct materials			
Raw materials inventory, January 1	$ 16,700		
Raw materials purchases	152,500		
Total raw materials available for use	169,200		
Less: Raw materials inventory, December 31	22,800		
Direct materials used		$146,400	
Direct labor		175,600	
Manufacturing overhead			
Indirect labor	14,300		
Factory repairs	12,600		
Factory utilities	10,100		
Factory depreciation	9,440		
Factory insurance	8,360		
Total manufacturing overhead		54,800	
Total manufacturing costs			376,800
Total cost of work in process			395,200
Less: Work in process, December 31			25,200
Cost of goods manufactured			$370,000

267 200

Balance Sheet

Unlike the balance sheet for a merchandising company, which shows just one category of inventory, the balance sheet for a manufacturing company may have three inventory accounts. They are:

Finished Goods Inventory, which shows the cost of completed goods on hand.

Work in Process Inventory, which shows the cost applicable to units that have been started into production but are only partially completed.

Raw Materials Inventory, which shows the cost of raw materials on hand.

Finished Goods Inventory is to a manufacturing enterprise what Merchandise Inventory is to a merchandising firm because it represents the goods that are available for sale.

The current assets sections presented in Illustration 20-9 contrast the presentation of inventories of a merchandising company with those of a manufacturing company. Manufacturing inventories are generally listed in the order of their liquidity—their expected realization in cash. Thus, finished goods inventory is listed first. The remainder of the balance sheet is similar for the two types of companies.

Each step in the accounting cycle for a merchandising company is applicable to a manufacturing company. For example, prior to preparing financial statements, adjusting entries are required. The adjusting entries are essentially the same as those of a merchandising company.

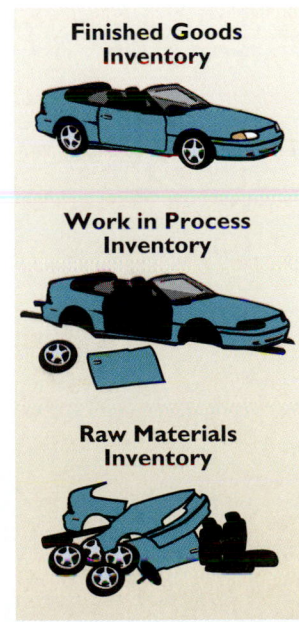

Finished Goods Inventory

Work in Process Inventory

Raw Materials Inventory

ILLUSTRATION 20-9

Current assets sections of merchandising and manufacturing balance sheets

MERCHANDISING COMPANY Balance Sheet December 31, 1999			MANUFACTURING COMPANY Balance Sheet December 31, 1999		
Current assets			Current assets		
Cash		$100,000	Cash		$180,000
Receivables (net)		210,000	Receivables (net)		210,000
Merchandise inventory		400,000	Inventories:		
Prepaid expenses		22,000	Finished goods	$80,000	
Total current assets		$732,000	Work in process	25,200	
			Raw materials	22,800	128,000
			Prepaid expenses		18,000
			Total current assets		$536,000

The closing entries for a manufacturing company are also similar to those of a merchandising company. The use of a work sheet in the accounting cycle and the journalizing of closing entries for a manufacturing company are illustrated in the appendix at the end of this chapter.

Cost Concepts—A Review

You have learned a number of cost concepts in this chapter. Because many of these concepts are new, we believe an extended example will be helpful in illustrating how these various cost concepts are used. To illustrate, assume that Northridge Company manufactures and sells pre-hung metal doors. Recently, it has decided to start selling pre-hung wood doors as well. An old warehouse that the company presently owns will be used to manufacture the new product. To manufacture and sell these pre-hung wood doors, Northridge identifies the following costs:

1. The material cost (wood) for each door is $10.
2. Labor costs involved in constructing a wood door are $8 per door.
3. Depreciation on the new equipment used to make the wood door using the straight-line method is $25,000 per year.
4. Property taxes on the old warehouse used to make the wood doors are $6,000 per year.
5. Advertising costs for the pre-hung wood doors total $2,500 per month or $30,000 per year.
6. Sales commissions related to pre-hung wood doors sold are $4 per door.
7. Maintenance salaries for the old warehouse are $28,000.
8. Salary of plant manager in charge of pre-hung wood doors is $70,000.
9. Cost of shipping pre-hung wood doors is $12 per door sold.

These manufacturing and selling costs can be assigned to the various categories shown in Illustration 20-10.

ILLUSTRATION 20-10

Assignment of costs to cost categories

| | Product Costs | | | | | |
Cost Item	Direct Materials	Direct Labor	Manufacturing Overhead	Period Costs	Prime Costs	Conversion Costs
1. Material cost ($10) per door	X				X	
2. Labor costs ($8) per door		X			X	X
3. Depreciation on new equipment ($25,000 per year)			X			X
4. Property taxes ($6,000 per year)			X			X
5. Advertising costs ($30,000 per year)				X		
6. Sales commissions ($4 per door)				X		
7. Maintenance salaries ($28,000 per year)			X			X
8. Salary of plant manager ($70,000)			X			X
9. Cost of shipping pre-hung doors ($12 per door)				X		

Remember that total manufacturing costs are the sum of the product costs—direct materials, direct labor, and manufacturing overhead costs. For example, assume that Northridge Company produces 10,000 pre-hung wood doors the first year. The total manufacturing costs are:

ILLUSTRATION 20-11

Computation of total manufacturing cost

Cost Number and Item	Manufacturing Cost
1. Material cost ($10 × 10,000)	$100,000
2. Labor cost ($8 × 10,000)	80,000
3. Depreciation on new equipment	25,000
4. Property taxes	6,000
7. Maintenance salaries	28,000
8. Salary of plant manager	70,000
Total manufacturing costs	**$309,000**

If total manufacturing costs are $309,000, then the manufacturing cost per unit (cost to produce one pre-hung wood door) is $30.90 ($309,000 ÷ 10,000 units).

The cost concepts above will be used extensively in subsequent chapters. Study Illustration 20-10 carefully. If you do not understand any of these classifications, go back and reread the appropriate section in this chapter.

CONTEMPORARY DEVELOPMENTS IN MANAGERIAL ACCOUNTING

Since the early 1970s, the competitive environment for U.S. businesses has changed significantly. Within the United States, for example, the airline, financial services, and telecommunication industries have been deregulated. Globally, competition from such countries as Japan and Germany has intensified, particularly in the automotive and electronics industries. Consequently, contemporary business managers demand from managerial accountants different and better information than they needed just a few years ago. Such factors as those discussed below contribute to the expanding role of managerial accounting as we look toward the next century.

Technological Change

Through **computer-integrated manufacturing (CIM),** many companies can now manufacture products that are untouched by human hands. An example is the use of robotic equipment in the steel and automobile industries. Automation significantly reduces the importance of direct labor costs in some cases, because the worker simply monitors the manufacturing process by watching instrument panels.

Also, the widespread use of computers has greatly reduced the cost of accumulating, storing, and reporting managerial accounting information. Computers now make it possible to do more detailed costing of products, processes, and services than is possible under manual processing.

Technology in Action

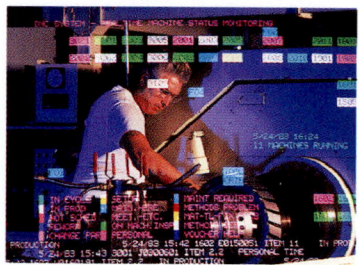

The use of computers is as important in managerial accounting as in financial accounting. As one expert on manufacturing recently noted "I am convinced that the manufacturers that survive will be those with an unbelievable amount of automation and computerization. The winners will have true computer-integrated manufacturing (CIM). In such a scenario, computers will do everything. They will design the parts, tell you if they can be built, set up the machines on the line, inspect the products, and pop them out on the loading dock with a computerized bill of lading."

Quality

Many companies have installed a **total quality control (TQC) system** to reduce defects in finished products. This system requires timely data on defective products, rework costs, and the cost of honoring warranty contracts. As a result, more emphasis is now put on **nonfinancial measures** such as customer satisfaction, number of service calls, and time to generate reports. Attention to these measures, which employees can control, leads to increased profitability.

In addition, many companies have significantly lowered inventory levels and costs using **just-in-time inventory methods (JIT).** Under a just-in-time method, goods are manufactured or purchased just in time for use, which lowers costs of holding and storing inventory. More will be said about this factor in Chapter 22.

Focus on Activities

In order to obtain more accurate product costs, many companies are accounting for overhead costs by the activities used in making the product. Activities include purchasing materials, handling raw materials, and production order scheduling. This development, called **activity-based costing (ABC),** is further explained in Chapter 22.

Service Industry Needs

Service industries and companies include the following:

ILLUSTRATION 20-12

Service industries and companies

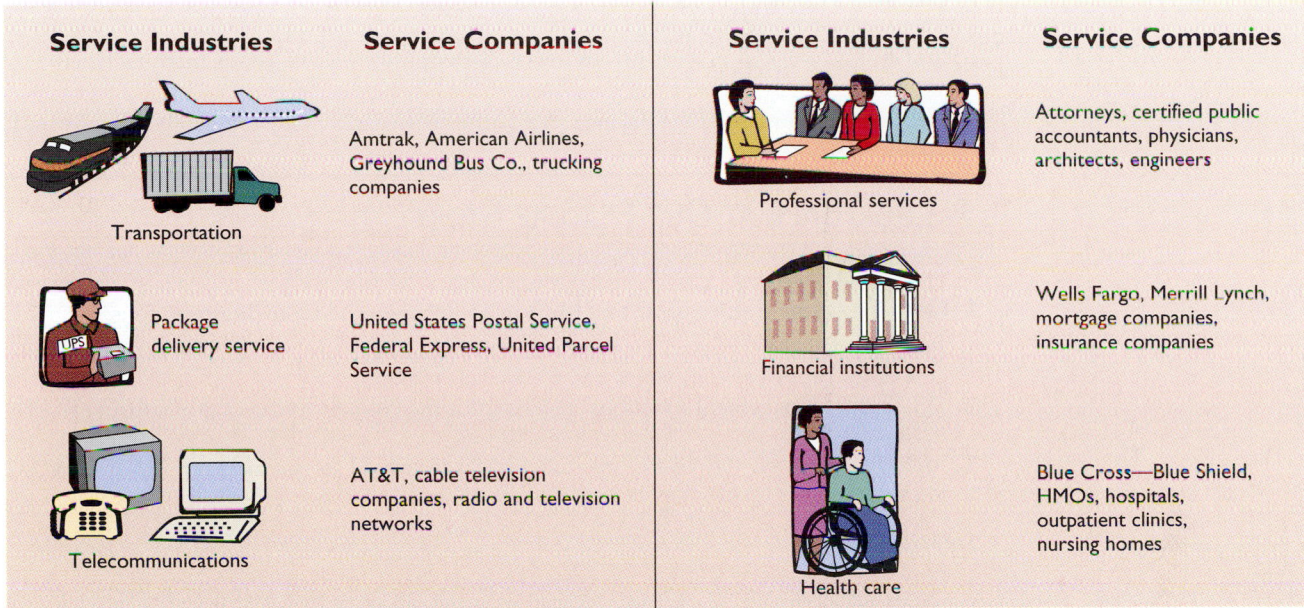

Service Industries	Service Companies
Transportation	Amtrak, American Airlines, Greyhound Bus Co., trucking companies
Package delivery service	United States Postal Service, Federal Express, United Parcel Service
Telecommunications	AT&T, cable television companies, radio and television networks

Service Industries	Service Companies
Professional services	Attorneys, certified public accountants, physicians, architects, engineers
Financial institutions	Wells Fargo, Merrill Lynch, mortgage companies, insurance companies
Health care	Blue Cross—Blue Shield, HMOs, hospitals, outpatient clinics, nursing homes

In some respects, the challenges for managerial accounting are greater in services enterprises than in manufacturing companies. How does a professional firm measure the efficiency and productivity of its professional staff? How does a brokerage firm measure the cost of serving individual customers? What measures can be used to evaluate the quality of services in a hospital or a bank?

Managers of service enterprises look to managerial accounting to answer these questions. In some companies, it may be necessary for the managerial accountant to develop new systems for measuring the cost of serving individual customers and new operating controls to improve the quality and efficiency of specific services.

ACCOUNTING IN ACTION
Business Insight

At South Central Bell (Telephone), management accountants have shed their scorekeeping image. A corporate reorganization plan challenged the accountants to "show their stuff." The accountants took on the roles of interpreter, advisor, and partner. To do so, the management accountants had to understand what the numbers mean, relate the numbers to business activity, and recommend alternative courses of action. In addition, they evaluate alternatives and make decisions to maximize business efficiency.

Final Comment

Not long ago, the managerial accountant was primarily engaged in cost accounting—collecting and reporting manufacturing cost to management. Today, the managerial accountant's responsibilities extend to cost management—providing managers with data on the efficient use of company resources in both manufacturing and service industries.

BEFORE YOU GO ON . . .

Review It

1. How does the content of an income statement differ between a merchandising company and a manufacturing company?
2. How are the work in process inventories reported in the cost of goods manufactured schedule?
3. How does the content of the balance sheet differ between a merchandising company and a manufacturing company?

A LOOK BACK AT OUR FEATURE STORY

Refer to the opening story regarding Murray and answer the following questions:

1. What are the similarities in the production processes, general product cost accounts, and cost flows of the car companies and the bicycle makers?
2. Relate the management functions discussed in the chapter to the manufacturing of bicycles.
3. Identify some of the likely manufacturing overhead costs incurred by a bicycle manufacturer.

Solution:

1. Both car companies and bicycle makers are engaged in a manufacturing process that involves designing, producing, assembling, finishing, and marketing a multi-piece, multi-model product line. Both use general product cost accounts such as direct materials, direct labor, and overhead cost accounts, along with raw material, work in process, and finished goods inventory accounts. The cost flows would also be similar through these accounts.
2. Manufacturing bicycles involves **planning**, that is, establishing production and marketing objectives; **organizing** assets and employees into a production work force; implementing planned objectives by coordinating purchasing, manufacturing, warehousing, and selling functions; and **directing** and **controlling** activities and operations through supervision, training, evaluation, reporting, and analysis.
3. A bicycle manufacturer would likely incur overhead costs such as indirect materials (abrasives, lubricants, etc.); indirect labor (supervisors, maintenance, etc.); depreciation of factory buildings and machinery; and factory insurance, taxes, and utilities.

THE
NAVIGATOR

DEMONSTRATION PROBLEM 1

Superior Manufacturing Company has the following cost and expense data for the year ending December 31, 1999.

Raw materials, 1/1/99	$ 30,000	Insurance, factory	$ 14,000
Raw materials, 12/31/99	20,000	Property taxes, factory building	6,000
Raw materials purchased	205,000	Sales (net)	1,500,000
Indirect materials	15,000	Delivery expenses	100,000
Work in process, 1/1/99	80,000	Sales commissions	150,000
Work in process, 12/31/99	50,000	Indirect labor	90,000
Finished goods, 1/1/99	110,000	Factory machinery rent	40,000
Finished goods, 12/31/99	120,000	Factory utilities	65,000
Direct labor	350,000	Depreciation, factory building	24,000
Factory manager's salary	35,000	Administrative expenses	300,000

Instructions

(a) Prepare a cost of goods manufactured schedule for Superior Company for 1999.

(b) Prepare an income statement for Superior Company for 1999.

(c) Assume that Superior Company's ledgers show the balances of the following current asset accounts: Cash, $17,000, Accounts Receivable (net), $120,000, Prepaid Expenses, $13,000, and Short-term Investments, $26,000. Prepare the current assets section of the balance sheet for Superior Company as of December 31, 1999.

SOLUTION TO DEMONSTRATION PROBLEM

(a)
SUPERIOR MANUFACTURING COMPANY
Cost of Goods Manufactured Schedule
For the Year Ended December 31, 1999

Work in process, 1/1			$ 80,000
Direct materials			
Raw materials inventory, 1/1	$ 30,000		
Raw materials purchased	205,000		
Total raw materials available for use	235,000		
Less: Raw materials inventory, 12/31	20,000		
Direct materials used		$215,000	
Direct labor		350,000	
Manufacturing overhead			
Indirect labor	90,000		
Factory utilities	65,000		
Factory machinery rent	40,000		
Factory manager's salary	35,000		
Depreciation on building	24,000		
Indirect materials	15,000		
Factory insurance	14,000		
Property taxes	6,000		
Total manufacturing overhead		289,000	
Total manufacturing costs			854,000
Total cost of work in process			934,000
Less: Work in process, 12/31			50,000
Cost of goods manufactured			$884,000

(b)
SUPERIOR MANUFACTURING COMPANY
Income Statement
For the Year Ended December 31, 1999

Sales (net)		$1,500,000
Cost of goods sold		
Finished goods inventory, January 1	$110,000	
Cost of goods manufactured	884,000	
Cost of goods available for sale	994,000	
Less: Finished goods inventory, December 31	120,000	
Cost of goods sold		874,000
Gross profit		626,000
Operating expenses		
Administrative expenses	300,000	
Sales commissions	150,000	
Delivery expenses	100,000	
Total operating expenses		550,000
Net income		$ 76,000

PROBLEM-SOLVING STRATEGIES

1. Beginning work in process is the first item in the cost of goods manufactured schedule.

2. Total manufacturing costs are the sum of direct materials used, direct labor, and total manufacturing overhead.

3. Total cost of work in process is the sum of beginning work in process and total manufacturing costs.

4. Cost of goods manufactured is the total cost of work in process less ending work in process.

5. The cost of goods sold section of the income statement shows beginning and ending finished goods inventory and cost of goods manufactured.

6. In the balance sheet, manufacturing inventories are listed in the order of their expected realization in cash, with finished goods first.

(c)

SUPERIOR MANUFACTURING COMPANY
Balance Sheet (partial)
December 31, 1999

Current assets		
Cash		$ 17,000
Short-term investments		26,000
Accounts receivable (net)		120,000
Inventories:		
Finished goods	$120,000	
Work in process	50,000	
Raw materials	20,000	190,000
Prepaid expenses		13,000
Total current assets		$366,000

THE
NAVIGATOR

DEMONSTRATION PROBLEM 2

Giant Company specializes in manufacturing different models of racing bicycles. A new model, the Jaguar, has been well accepted. As a result, the company has established a separate manufacturing facility to produce these bicycles. The company produces 1,000 bicycles per month. Giant's monthly manufacturing cost and other expenses data related to these bicycles are as follows:

1. Rent on manufacturing equipment (lease cost) $2,000/month
2. Insurance on manufacturing building $750/month
3. Raw materials (frames, tires, etc.) $80/bicycle
4. Utility costs for manufacturing facility $1,000/month
5. Supplies for general office $800/month
6. Wages for assembly line workers in manufacturing facility $30/bicycle
7. Depreciation on office equipment $650/month
8. Miscellaneous materials (lubricants, solders, etc.) $1.20/bicycle
9. Property taxes on manufacturing building $2,400/year
10. Manufacturing supervisor's salary $3,000/month
11. Advertising for bicycles $30,000/year
12. Sales commissions $10/bicycle
13. Depreciation on manufacturing building $1,500/month

Instructions

(a) Prepare an answer sheet with the following column headings:

	Product Costs					
Cost Item	Direct Materials	Direct Labor	Manufacturing Overhead	Period Costs	Prime Costs	Conversion Costs

Enter each cost item on your answer sheet, placing an "X" mark under the appropriate headings.

(b) Compute total manufacturing costs for the month.

SOLUTION TO DEMONSTRATION PROBLEM

(a)

Cost Item	Product Costs			Period Costs	Prime Costs	Conversion Costs
	Direct Materials	Direct Labor	Manufacturing Overhead			
1. Rent on equipment ($2,000/month)			X			X
2. Insurance on manufacturing building ($750/month)			X			X
3. Raw materials ($80/bicycle)	X				X	
4. Manufacturing utilities ($1,000/month)			X			X
5. Office supplies ($800/month)				X		
6. Wages for workers ($30/bicycle)		X			X	X
7. Depreciation on office equipment ($650/month)				X		
8. Miscellaneous materials ($1.20/bicycle)			X			X
9. Property taxes on building ($2,400/year)			X			X
10. Manufacturing supervisor's salary ($3,000/month)			X			X
11. Advertising cost ($30,000/year)				X		
12. Sales commissions ($10/bicycle)				X		
13. Depreciation on manufacturing building ($1,500/month)			X			X

PROBLEM-SOLVING STRATEGIES

1. Remember the definitions of: Prime costs = direct materials + direct labor. Conversion costs = Direct labor + manufacturing overhead costs incurred in converting raw materials into finished goods.

2. Make sure you are doing the computations for the appropriate period: month, year, unit, etc.

3. Period costs are not manufacturing costs and, therefore, are not inventoriable.

4. Product costs are manufacturing costs and are inventoriable.

(b)

Cost Item	Manufacturing Cost
Rent on equipment	$ 2,000
Insurance	750
Raw materials ($80 × 1,000)	80,000
Manufacturing utilities	1,000
Labor ($30 × 1,000)	30,000
Miscellaneous materials ($1.20 × 1,000)	1,200
Property taxes ($2,400 ÷ 12)	200
Manufacturing supervisor's salary	3,000
Depreciation on building	1,500
Total manufacturing costs	$119,650

THE NAVIGATOR

1. *Explain the distinguishing features of managerial accounting.* The distinguishing features of managerial accounting are:

Primary users of reports—internal users, who are officers, department heads, managers, and supervisors in the company.

Type and frequency of reports—internal reports that are issued as frequently as the need arises.

Purpose of reports—to provide special-purpose information for a particular user for a specific decision.

Content of reports—pertains to subunits of the entity and may be very detailed; may extend beyond double-entry accounting system; the reporting standard is relevance to the decision being made.

Verification of reports—no independent audits.

2. *Identify the three broad functions of management.* The three functions are planning, organizing and directing, and controlling. Planning requires management to look ahead and to establish objectives. Organizing and directing involves coordinating the diverse activities and human resources of a company to produce a smooth-running operation. Controlling is the process of keeping the activities on track.

3. *Define the three classes of manufacturing costs.* Manufacturing costs are typically classified as either (1) direct materials, (2) direct labor, or (3) manufacturing overhead. Raw materials that can be physically and conveniently associated with the finished product during the manufacturing process are called direct materials. The work of factory employees that can be physically and conveniently associated with converting raw materials into finished goods is considered di-

rect labor. Manufacturing overhead consists of costs that are indirectly associated with the manufacture of the finished product.

4. *Distinguish between product and period costs.* Product costs are costs that are a necessary and integral part of producing the finished product. Product costs are also called inventoriable costs. These costs do not become expenses under the matching principle until the inventory to which they attach is sold. Period costs are costs that are identified with a specific time period rather than with a salable product. These costs relate to nonmanufacturing costs and therefore are not inventoriable costs.

5. *Explain the difference between a merchandising and a manufacturing income statement.* The difference between a merchandising and a manufacturing income statement is in the cost of goods sold section. A manufacturing cost of goods sold section shows beginning and ending finished goods inventories and the cost of goods manufactured.

6. *Indicate how cost of goods manufactured is determined.* The cost of the beginning work in process is added to the total manufacturing costs for the current year to arrive at the total cost of work in process for the year. The ending work in process is then subtracted from the total cost of work in process to arrive at the cost of goods manufactured.

7. *Explain the difference between a merchandising and a manufacturing balance sheet.* The difference between a manufacturing and a merchandising balance sheet is in the current asset section. In the current asset section of a manufacturing company's balance sheet, three inventory accounts are presented: finished goods inventory, work in process inventory, and raw materials inventory.

GLOSSARY

Conversion costs Direct labor and manufacturing overhead costs incurred in converting raw materials into finished goods. (p. 876).

Cost of goods manufactured Total cost of work in process less the cost of the ending work in process inventory. (p. 878).

Direct labor The work of factory employees that can be physically and conveniently associated with converting raw materials into finished goods. (p. 874).

Direct materials Raw materials that can be physically and conveniently associated with manufacturing the finished product. (p. 874).

Indirect labor Work of factory employees that has no physical association with the finished product, or it is impractical to trace the costs to the goods produced. (p. 874).

Indirect materials Raw materials that do not physically become part of the finished product or cannot be traced because their physical association with the finished product is too small. (p. 874).

Managerial accounting A field of accounting that provides economic and financial information for managers and other internal users. (p. 870).

Manufacturing overhead Manufacturing costs that are indirectly associated with the manufacture of the finished product. (p. 875).

Period costs Costs that are identified with a specific time period and charged to expense as incurred. (p. 876).

Prime costs Direct materials and direct labor. (p. 876).

Product costs Costs that are a necessary and integral part of producing the finished product. (p. 875).

Total cost of work in process Cost of the beginning work in process plus total manufacturing costs for the current period. (p. 878).

Total manufacturing costs The sum of direct materials, direct labor, and manufacturing overhead incurred in the current period. (p. 878).

APPENDIX   ACCOUNTING CYCLE FOR A MANUFACTURING COMPANY

The accounting cycle for a manufacturing company is the same as for a merchandising company when a periodic inventory system is used. Except for the additional manufacturing inventories and manufacturing cost accounts, the journalizing and posting of transactions is the same. Similarly, the preparation of a trial balance and the journalizing and posting of adjusting entries are the same. Some changes, however, occur in the use of a work sheet and in preparing closing entries.

    To illustrate the changes in the work sheet, we will use the cost of goods manufactured schedule for Olsen Manufacturing presented in Illustration 20-8 of the chapter and other assumed data. For convenience, the cost of goods manufactured schedule is reproduced below:

8
STUDY
OBJECTIVE
....
Prepare a work sheet and closing entries for a manufacturing company.

ILLUSTRATION 20A-1

Cost of goods manufactured schedule

OLSEN MANUFACTURING COMPANY Cost of Goods Manufactured Schedule For the Year Ended December 31, 1999		
Work in process, January 1		$ 18,400
Direct materials		
Raw materials inventory, January 1	$ 16,700	
Raw materials purchases	152,500	
Total raw materials available for use	169,200	
Less: Raw materials inventory, December 31	22,800	
Direct materials used		$146,400
Direct labor		175,600
Manufacturing overhead		
Indirect labor	14,300	
Factory repairs	12,600	
Factory utilities	10,100	
Factory depreciation	9,440	
Factory insurance	8,360	
Total manufacturing overhead		54,800
Total manufacturing costs		376,800
Total cost of work in process		395,200
Less: Work in process, December 31		25,200
Cost of goods manufactured		$370,000

WORK SHEET

When a work sheet is used in preparing financial statements, two additional columns are needed for the cost of goods manufactured schedule. As illustrated in the work sheet in Illustration 20A-2, debit and credit columns for this schedule have been inserted before the income statement columns.

    In the cost of goods manufactured columns, the beginning inventories of raw materials and work in process are entered as debits. In addition, all the manufacturing costs are entered as debits. The reason is that each of these amounts increases cost of goods manufactured. Ending inventories for raw materials and

ILLUSTRATION 20A-2

Partial work sheet

OLSEN MANUFACTURING COMPANY
Work Sheet (partial)
For the Year Ended December 31, 1999

	Adjusted Trial Balance		Cost of Goods Manufactured		Income Statement		Balance Sheet	
	Dr.	Cr.	Dr.	Cr.	Dr.	Cr.	Dr.	Cr.
Cash	42,500						42,500	
Accounts Receivable (Net)	71,900						71,900	
Finished Goods Inv.	24,600				24,600	19,500	19,500	
Work in Process Inv.	18,400		18,400	25,200			25,200	
Raw Materials Inv.	16,700		16,700	22,800			22,800	
Plant Assets	724,000						724,000	
Accumulated Depr.		278,400						278,400
Notes Payable		100,000						100,000
Accounts Payable		40,000						40,000
Income Taxes Payable		5,000						5,000
Common Stock		200,000						200,000
Retained Earnings		205,100						205,100
Sales		680,000				680,000		
Raw Materials Purchases	152,500		152,500					
Direct Labor	175,600		175,600					
Indirect Labor	14,300		14,300					
Factory Repairs	12,600		12,600					
Factory Utilities	10,100		10,100					
Factory Depreciation	9,440		9,440					
Factory Insurance	8,360		8,360					
Selling Expenses	114,900				114,900			
Administrative Exp.	92,600				92,600			
Income Tax Exp.	20,000				20,000			
Totals	1,508,500	1,508,500	418,000	48,000				
Cost of Goods Manufactured				370,000	370,000			
Totals			418,000	418,000	622,100	699,500	905,900	828,500
Net Income					77,400			77,400
Totals					699,500	699,500	905,900	905,900

work in process are entered as credits in the cost of goods manufactured columns because they have the opposite effect—they decrease cost of goods manufactured. The balancing amount for these columns is the cost of goods manufactured. Note that the amount, $370,000, agrees with the amount reported for cost of goods manufactured in Illustration 20A-1. This amount is also entered in the income statement debit column.

The income statement and balance sheet columns for a manufacturing company are basically the same as for a merchandising company. For example, the treatment of the finished goods inventories is identical with the treatment of merchandise inventory. That is, the beginning inventory is entered in the debit column, and the ending finished goods inventory is entered in the income statement credit column and the balance sheet debit column.

As in the case of a merchandising company, financial statements can be prepared from the statement columns of the work sheet. In addition, the cost of goods manufactured schedule can also be prepared directly from the work sheet.

CLOSING ENTRIES

The closing entries for a manufacturing company are different than for a merchandising company. **A Manufacturing Summary account is used to close all accounts that appear in the cost of goods manufactured schedule.** The balance of the Manufacturing Summary account is the Cost of Goods Manufactured for the period. Manufacturing Summary is then closed to Income Summary. The closing entries can be prepared from the work sheet. As illustrated below, the closing entries for the manufacturing accounts are prepared first. The closing entries for Olsen Manufacturing are as follows:

Dec. 31	Work in Process Inventory (Dec. 31)	25,200	
	Raw Materials Inventory (Dec. 31)	22,800	
	Manufacturing Summary		**48,000**
	(To record ending raw materials and work		
	in process inventories)		
31	**Manufacturing Summary**	**418,000**	
	Work in Process Inventory (Jan. 1)		18,400
	Raw Materials Inventory (Jan. 1)		16,700
	Raw Materials Purchases		152,500
	Direct Labor		175,600
	Indirect Labor		14,300
	Factory Repairs		12,600
	Factory Utilities		10,100
	Factory Depreciation		9,440
	Factory Insurance		8,360
	(To close beginning raw materials and		
	work in process inventories and		
	manufacturing cost accounts)		
31	Finished Goods Inventory (Dec. 31)	19,500	
	Sales	680,000	
	Income Summary		699,500
	(To record ending finished goods inventory		
	and close sales account)		
31	Income Summary	622,100	
	Finished Goods Inventory (Jan. 1)		24,600
	Manufacturing Summary		**370,000**
	Selling Expenses		114,900
	Administrative Expenses		92,600
	Income Tax Expense		20,000
	(To close beginning finished goods		
	inventory, manufacturing summary, and		
	expense accounts)		
31	Income Summary	77,400	
	Retained Earnings		77,400
	(To close net income to retained earnings)		

After posting, the summary accounts will show the following:

ILLUSTRATION 20A-3

Summary accounts for a manufacturing company, after posting

Manufacturing Summary				
Dec. 31	Close	418,000	Dec. 31 Close	48,000
			31 Close	370,000

Income Summary				
Dec. 31	Close	622,100	Dec. 31 Close	699,500
31	Close	77,400		

These data precisely track the closing entries. It also would be possible to post each account balance to the Manufacturing Summary account.

SUMMARY OF STUDY OBJECTIVE FOR APPENDIX

8. *Prepare a work sheet and closing entries for a manufacturing company.* Two additional columns are needed in the work sheet for the cost of goods manufactured. In these columns, the beginning inventories of raw materials and work in process are entered as debits and the ending inventories are entered as credits; all manufacturing costs are entered as debits. To close all of the accounts that appear in the cost of goods manufactured schedule, a Manufacturing Summary account is used.

*Note: All asterisked Questions, Exercises, and Problems relate to material in the appendix to the chapter.

SELF-STUDY QUESTIONS

Answers are at the end of the chapter.

(SO 1) 1. Managerial accounting:
   a. is governed by generally accepted accounting principles.
   b. places emphasis on special-purpose information.
   c. pertains to the entity as a whole and is highly aggregated.
   d. is limited to cost data.

(SO 1) 2. Which of the following is *not* one of the categories in *Standards of Ethical Conduct for Management Accountants*?
   a. Confidentiality.   c. Integrity.
   b. Competence.   d. Independence.

(SO 2) 3. The management of an organization performs three broad functions. They are:
   a. planning, organizing and directing, and selling.
   b. planning, organizing and directing, and controlling.
   c. planning, manufacturing, and controlling.
   d. organizing and directing, manufacturing, and controlling.

4. Direct materials are a: (SO 3)

	Conversion Cost	Manufacturing Cost	Prime Cost
a.	Yes	Yes	No
b.	No	Yes	Yes
c.	Yes	Yes	Yes
d.	No	No	No

5. Indirect labor is a: (SO 4)
   a. nonmanufacturing cost.
   b. prime cost.
   c. product cost.
   d. period cost.

6. Which of the following costs would be included in manufacturing overhead of a computer manufacturer?   (SO 3)
   a. The cost of the 3½-inch disk drives.
   b. The wages earned by computer assemblers.
   c. The cost of the memory chips.
   d. Depreciation on testing equipment.

(SO 3) 7. Which of the following is *not* an element of manufacturing overhead?
   a. Sales manager's salary.
   b. Plant manager's salary.
   c. Factory repairman's wages.
   d. Product inspector's salary.

(SO 5) 8. For the year, Redder Company has cost of goods manufactured of $600,000, beginning finished goods inventory of $200,000, and ending finished goods inventory of $250,000. The cost of goods sold is:
   a. $450,000.   c. $550,000.
   b. $500,000.   d. $600,000.

9. A cost of goods manufactured schedule shows begin- (SO 6) ning and ending inventories for:
   a. raw materials and work in process only.
   b. work in process only.
   c. raw materials only.
   d. raw materials, work in process, and finished goods.

10. In a manufacturing company balance sheet, three inven- (SO 7) tories may be reported: (1) raw materials, (2) work in process, and (3) finished goods. Indicate in what sequence these inventories generally appear on a balance sheet.
   a. (1), (2), (3)   c. (3), (1), (2)
   b. (2), (3), (1)   d. (3), (2), (1)

QUESTIONS

1. (a) "Managerial accounting is a field of accounting that provides economic information for all interested parties." Do you agree? Explain.
   (b) Pat Gonzalez believes that managerial accounting serves only manufacturing firms. Is Pat correct? Explain.

2. Distinguish between managerial and financial accounting as to (a) primary users of reports, (b) types and frequency of reports, and (c) purpose of reports.

3. How does the content of reports and the verification of reports differ between managerial and financial accounting?

4. (a) Identify the four categories of ethical standards for management accountants.
   (b) Is the responsibility of the management accountant limited to only his or her own acts? Explain.

5. Karen Pedigo is studying for the next accounting midterm examination. Summarize for Karen what she should know about management functions.

6. "Decision making is management's most important function." Do you agree? Why or why not?

7. Sue McCabe is studying for her next accounting examination. Explain to Sue what she should know about the differences between the income statements for a manufacturing company and a merchandising company.

8. Bob Segar is unclear as to the difference between the balance sheets of a merchandising company and a manufacturing company. Explain the difference to Bob.

9. How are manufacturing costs classified?

10. Gene Decker claims that the distinction between direct and indirect materials is based entirely on physical association with the product. Is Gene correct? Why?

11. Andrea Leite is confused about the differences between a product cost and a period cost. Explain the differences to Andrea.

12. Amy Haas asks your help with the terms (a) prime costs and (b) conversion costs. Distinguish between the terms.

13. In Modine Molding Company, direct materials are $12,000, direct labor is $15,000, and manufacturing overhead is $9,000. What is the amount of (a) prime costs and (b) conversion costs?

14. Identify the differences in the cost of goods sold section of an income statement between a merchandising company and a manufacturing company.

15. The determination of the cost of goods manufactured involves the following factors: (A) beginning work in process inventory, (B) total manufacturing costs, and (C) ending work in process inventory. Identify the meaning of x in the following formulas:
   (a) $A + B = x$
   (b) $A + B - C = x$

16. Sajjad Manufacturing has beginning raw materials inventory $24,000, ending raw materials inventory $18,000, and raw materials purchases $180,000. What is the cost of direct materials used?

17. Griggs Manufacturing Inc. has beginning work in process $27,200, direct materials used $240,000, direct labor $200,000, total manufacturing overhead $120,000, and ending work in process $32,000. What are total manufacturing costs?

18. Using the data in Q17, what are (a) the total cost of work in process and (b) the cost of goods manufactured?

19. In what order should manufacturing inventories be listed in a balance sheet?

*20. How, if at all, does the accounting cycle differ between a manufacturing company and a merchandising company?

*21. What typical account balances are carried into the cost of goods manufactured columns of the manufacturing work sheet?

*22. Prepare the closing entries for (a) ending work in process and raw materials inventories and (b) manufacturing summary. Use XXXs for amounts.

BRIEF EXERCISES

....

Distinguish between managerial and financial accounting.
(SO 1)

BE20–1 Complete the following comparison table between managerial and financial accounting.

	Financial Accounting	Managerial Accounting
Primary users		
Type of reports		
Frequency of reports		
Purpose of reports		
Reporting standards		
Verification		

Identify ethical standards.
(SO 1)

BE20–2 The Institute of Management Accountants has promulgated ethical standards for managerial accountants. Identify the four specific standards.

Identify the three management functions.
(SO 2)

BE20–3 Listed below are three functions of the management of an organization:

(a) Planning   (b) Organizing and directing   (c) Controlling

Identify each of the following statements that best describes each of the above functions.

1. ____ require(s) management to look ahead and to establish objectives. A key objective of management appears to be to add value to the business.
2. ____ involve(s) coordinating the diverse activities and human resources of a company to produce a smooth-running operation. This function relates to the implementation of planned objectives.
3. ____ is the process of keeping the activities on track. Management must determine whether goals are being met and what changes are necessary when there are deviations.

Classify manufacturing costs.
(SO 3)

BE20–4 Determine whether each of the following costs should be classified as direct materials (DM), direct labor (DL), or manufacturing overhead (MO):

1. ____ Frames and tires used in manufacturing bicycles.
2. ____ Wages paid to production workers.
3. ____ Insurance on factory equipment and machinery.
4. ____ Depreciation on factory equipment.

Identify product and period costs.
(SO 4)

BE20–5 Identify whether each of the following costs should be classified as product costs or period costs:

1. ____ Manufacturing overhead.
2. ____ Selling expenses.
3. ____ Administrative expenses.
4. ____ Advertising expenses.
5. ____ Direct labor.
6. ____ Direct material.

Classify manufacturing costs.
(SO 3)

BE20–6 Indicate whether each of the following costs of an automobile manufacturer would be classified as direct materials, direct labor, or manufacturing overhead:

1. ____ Windshield.
2. ____ Engine.
3. ____ Wages of assembly line worker.
4. ____ Depreciation of factory machinery.
5. ____ Factory machinery lubricants.
6. ____ Tires.
7. ____ Steering wheel.
8. ____ Salary of painting supervisor.

Compute total manufacturing costs and total cost of work in process.
(SO 6)

BE20–7 Chinn Manufacturing Company has the following data: direct labor $250,000, direct materials used $180,000, total manufacturing overhead $208,000, and beginning work in process $25,000. Compute (a) total manufacturing costs and (b) total cost of work in process.

Prepare current assets section.
(SO 7)

BE20–8 In alphabetical order below are current asset items for Judd Company's balance sheet at December 31, 1999. Prepare the current asset section (including a complete heading).

Accounts receivable	$200,000
Cash	62,000
Finished goods	75,000
Prepaid expenses	38,000
Raw materials	68,000
Work in process	91,000

BE20–9 Presented below are incomplete 1999 manufacturing cost data for Kelser Corporation. Determine the missing amounts.

Determine missing amounts in computing total manufacturing costs. (SO 6)

	Direct Material Used	Direct Labor Used	Factory Overhead	Total Manufacturing Costs
1.	$49,000	$61,000	$ 50,000	?
2.	?	$88,000	$120,000	$296,000
3.	$55,000	?	$ 95,000	$300,000

BE20–10 Use the same data from BE20–9 above. Compute the cost of goods manufactured for Kelser Corporation in 1999.

Determine missing amounts in computing cost of goods manufactured. (SO 6)

	Total Manufacturing Costs	Work in Process (1/1)	Work in Process (12/31)	Cost of Goods Manufactured
1.	?	$120,000	$86,000	?
2.	$296,000	?	$98,000	$318,000
3.	$300,000	$470,000	?	$715,000

BE20–11 Presented below are Sabino Company's monthly manufacturing cost data related to its personal computer product:

Classify manufacturing costs. (SO 3, 4)

(a) Utilities for manufacturing equipment $116,000
(b) Raw material (CPU, chips, etc.) $ 85,000
(c) Depreciation on manufacturing building $880,000
(d) Wages for production workers $191,000

Enter each cost item on the following table, placing an "X" under the appropriate headings.

	Direct Material	Direct Labor	Factory Overhead	Prime Costs	Conversion Costs
(a)					
(b)					
(c)					
(d)					

Product Costs (heading over Direct Material, Direct Labor, Factory Overhead)

*BE20–12 A work sheet is used in preparing financial statements for Lawney Manufacturing Company. The following accounts are included in the adjusted trial balance: Finished Goods Inventory $28,000, Work in Process Inventory $21,600, Raw Materials Purchases $175,000, and Direct Labor $140,000. Indicate the work sheet column(s) to which each account should be extended.

Identify work sheet columns for selected accounts. (SO 8)

EXERCISES

E20–1 Presented below is a list of costs and expenses usually incurred by Mauer Corporation, a manufacturer of furniture, in its factory:

Classify costs into three classes of manufacturing costs. (SO 3)

1. Salaries for assembly line inspectors.
2. Insurance on factory machines.
3. Property taxes on the factory building.
4. Factory repairs.
5. Upholstery used in manufacturing furniture.
6. Wages paid to assembly line workers.
7. Factory machinery depreciation.
8. Glue, nails, paint, and other small parts used in production.
9. Factory supervisors' salaries.
10. Wood used in manufacturing furniture.

Instructions
Classify the above items into the following categories: (a) direct materials, (b) direct labor, and (c) manufacturing overhead.

Determine the total amount of various types of costs.
(SO 3, 4)

E20–2   Nevitt Company reports the following costs and expenses in May:

Factory utilities	$ 8,500	Direct labor	$69,100
Depreciation on factory equipment	12,650	Sales salaries	49,400
Depreciation on delivery trucks	3,500	Property taxes on factory building	2,500
Indirect factory labor	48,900	Repairs to office equipment	1,300
Indirect materials	96,200	Factory repairs	2,000
Direct materials used	137,600	Advertising	18,000
Factory manager's salary	8,000	Office supplies used	3,000

Instructions
From the information, determine the total amount of:

(a) Prime costs.
(b) Manufacturing overhead.
(c) Conversion costs.
(d) Product costs.
(e) Period costs.

Indicate in which schedule or financial statement(s) different cost items will appear.
(SO 5, 6, 7)

E20–3   Piazza Manufacturing Company produces blankets. From its accounting records it prepares the following schedule and financial statements on a yearly basis:

(a) Cost of goods manufactured schedule
(b) Income statement
(c) Balance sheet

The following items are found in its ledger and accompanying data:

1. Direct labor
2. Raw materials inventory, 1/1
3. Work in process inventory, 12/31
4. Finished goods inventory, 1/1
5. Indirect labor
6. Depreciation on factory machinery
7. Work in process, 1/1
8. Finished goods inventory, 12/31

9. Factory maintenance salaries
10. Cost of goods manufactured
11. Depreciation on delivery equipment
12. Cost of goods available for sale
13. Direct materials used
14. Heat and electricity for factory
15. Repairs to roof of factory building
16. Cost of raw materials purchases

Instructions
List the items (1)–(16). For each item, indicate by using the appropriate letter or letters, the schedule and/or financial statement(s) in which the item will appear.

Determine the missing amount of different cost items.
(SO 6)

E20–4   Manufacturing cost data for Rathke Company are presented below:

	Case A	Case B	Case C
Direct materials used	(a)	$70,000	$130,000
Direct labor	$ 60,000	86,000	(g)
Manufacturing overhead	42,500	81,600	102,000
Total manufacturing costs	180,650	(d)	260,000
Work in process 1/1/00	(b)	16,500	(h)
Total cost of work in process	221,500	(e)	327,000
Work in process 12/31/00	(c)	9,000	70,000
Cost of goods manufactured	185,275	(f)	(i)

Determine the missing amount of different cost items and prepare a condensed cost of goods manufactured schedule.
(SO 5, 6)

Instructions
Indicate the missing amount for each letter.

E20–5   Incomplete manufacturing cost data for Cepada Company for 2000 are presented as follows:

	Direct Materials Used	Direct Labor Used	Manufacturing Overhead	Total Manufacturing Costs	Work in Process 1/1	Work in Process 12/31	Cost of Goods Manufactured
(1)	$120,000	$140,000	$ 77,000	(a)	$30,000	(b)	$360,000
(2)	(c)	200,000	130,000	$440,000	(d)	$40,000	470,000
(3)	80,000	100,000	(e)	260,000	60,000	80,000	(f)
(4)	70,000	(g)	75,000	290,000	45,000	(h)	270,000

Instructions

(a) Indicate the missing amount for each letter.

(b) Prepare a condensed cost of goods manufactured schedule for situation (1) for the year ended December 31, 2000.

E20–6 Tressler Corporation has the following cost records for June 2000:

Prepare a cost of goods manufactured schedule and a partial income statement.
(SO 5, 6)

Indirect factory labor	$ 4,500	Factory utilities	$ 400
Direct materials used	20,000	Depreciation, factory equipment	1,700
Work in process, 6/1/00	3,000	Direct labor	25,000
Work in process, 6/30/00	3,500	Maintenance, factory equipment	1,300
Finished goods, 6/1/00	5,000	Indirect materials	2,200
Finished goods, 6/30/00	6,000	Factory manager's salary	3,000

Instructions

(a) Prepare a cost of goods manufactured schedule for June 2000.

(b) Prepare an income statement through gross profit for June 2000 assuming net sales are $98,100.

E20–7 An analysis of the accounts of Salazar Manufacturing reveals the following manufacturing cost data for the month ended June 30, 2000:

Prepare a cost of goods manufactured schedule and present the ending inventories of the balance sheet.
(SO 5, 6, 7)

Inventories:	Beginning	Ending
Raw materials	$9,000	$10,000
Work in process	5,000	8,000
Finished goods	8,000	6,000

Costs incurred:

Raw materials purchases $64,000, direct labor $50,000, manufacturing overhead $19,200. The specific overhead costs were: indirect labor $5,500, factory insurance $4,000, machinery depreciation $4,000, machinery repairs $1,800, factory utilities $2,400, miscellaneous factory costs $1,500.

Instructions

(a) Prepare the cost of goods manufactured schedule for the month ended June 30, 2000.

(b) Show the presentation of the ending inventories on the June 30, 2000, balance sheet.

E20–8 The cost of goods manufactured schedule shows each of the cost elements. Complete the following schedule for Lanier Manufacturing Company:

Determine missing amounts in cost of goods manufactured schedule.
(SO 5, 6)

LANIER MANUFACTURING COMPANY
Cost of Goods Manufactured Schedule
For the Year Ended December 31, 2000

Work in process (1/1)		$200,000
Direct materials		
Raw materials inventory (1/1)	$?	
Add: Raw material purchases	158,000	
Less: Raw material inventory (12/31)	6,500	
Direct materials used		$190,000
Direct labor		?
Manufacturing overhead		
Indirect labor	$ 18,000	
Factory depreciation	36,000	
Factory utilities	68,000	
Total overhead		122,000
Total manufacturing costs		?
Total cost of work in process		$?
Less: Work in process (12/31)		87,000
Cost of goods manufactured		$560,000

E20–9 Fiero Motor Company manufactures automobiles. During September 2000 the company purchased 5,000 head lamps at a cost of $8 per lamp. Fiero withdrew 4,650 lamps from the warehouse during the month. Fifty of these lamps were used to replace the head lamps in autos used by traveling sales staff. The remaining 4,600 lamps were put in autos manufactured during the month.

Determine the amount of cost to appear in various accounts and indicate in which financial statements these accounts would appear.
(SO 5, 6, 7)

Of the autos put into production during September 2000, 90% were completed and transferred to the company's storage lot. Eighty percent of the cars completed during the month were sold by September 30.

Instructions

(a) Determine the cost of head lamps that would appear in each of the following accounts at September 30, 2000: Raw Materials, Work in Process, Finished Goods, Cost of Goods Sold, and Selling Expenses.

(b) ▐▬▬▬▶ Write a short memorandum to the chief accountant, indicating whether and where each of the accounts in (a) would appear on the income statement or on the balance sheet at September 30, 2000.

Classify various costs into different cost categories.
(SO 3, 4)

E20–10 Caudell Company is a manufacturer of personal computers. Various costs and expenses associated with its operations are as follows:

1. Property taxes on the factory building.
2. Production superintendents' salaries.
3. Memory boards and chips used in assembling computers.
4. Depreciation on the factory equipment.
5. Salaries for assembly line quality control inspectors.
6. Sales commissions paid to sell personal computers.
7. Electrical wiring in assembling computers.
8. Wages of workers assembling personal computers.
9. Soldering materials used on factory assembly lines.
10. Salaries for the night security guards for the factory building.

The company intends to classify these costs and expenses into the following categories: (a) direct materials, (b) direct labor, (c) manufacturing overhead, and (d) period costs.

Instructions
List the items (1)–(10). For each item, indicate the cost category to which the item belongs.

Prepare a partial work sheet for a manufacturing firm.
(SO 8)

*****E20–11** Data for Salazar Manufacturing are presented in Exercise 20-7.

Instructions
Prepare a partial work sheet for Salazar Manufacturing.

PROBLEMS: SET A

Classify manufacturing costs into different categories and compute the unit cost.
(SO 3, 4)

P20–1A Glazier Company specializes in manufacturing motorcycles. The model is well accepted by consumers, and the company has a large number of orders to keep the factory production at 1,000 motorcycles per month. Glazier's monthly manufacturing cost and other expense data are as follows:

Maintenance costs on factory building	$ 300
Factory manager's salary	5,000
Advertising for motorcycles	10,000
Sales commissions	5,000
Depreciation on factory building	700
Rent on factory equipment	5,000
Insurance on factory building	3,000
Raw materials (frames, tires, etc.)	20,000
Utility costs for factory	800
Supplies for general office	200
Wages for assembly line workers	35,000
Depreciation on office equipment	500
Miscellaneous materials (lubricants, solders, etc.)	700

Instructions

(a) Prepare an answer sheet with the following column headings:

	Product Costs					
Cost Item	Direct Materials	Direct Labor	Manufacturing Overhead	Period Costs	Prime Costs	Conversion Costs

Enter each cost item on your answer sheet, placing the dollar amount under the appropriate headings. Total the dollar amounts in each of the columns.

(b) Compute the cost to produce one motorcycle.

P20–2A Hewitt Company, a manufacturer of tennis rackets, started its production in November 1999. For the preceding 5 years Hewitt had been a retailer of sports equipment. After a thorough survey of tennis racket markets, Hewitt Company decided to turn its retail store into a tennis racket factory.

Classify manufacturing costs into different categories and compute the unit cost.
(SO 3, 4)

Raw materials cost for a tennis racket will total $20 per racket. Workers on the production lines are on average paid $12 per hour. A racket usually takes two hours to complete. In addition, the rent on the equipment used to produce rackets amounts to $1,000 per month. Indirect materials cost $3 per racket. A supervisor was hired to oversee production; her monthly salary will be $2,000.

Janitorial costs were $1,200 monthly. Advertising costs for the rackets will be $6,000 per month. The factory building depreciation expense is $8,400 per year. Property taxes on the factory building will be $3,600 per year.

Instructions
(a) Prepare an answer sheet with the following column headings:

	Product Costs					
Cost Item	Direct Materials	Direct Labor	Manufacturing Overhead	Period Costs	Prime Costs	Conversion Costs

Assuming that Hewitt manufactures, on average, 2,000 tennis rackets per month, enter each cost item on your answer sheet, placing the dollar amount per month under the appropriate headings. Total the dollar amounts in each of the columns.

(b) Compute the cost to produce one racket.

P20–3A Incomplete manufacturing costs, expenses, and selling data for two different cases are as follows:

Indicate the missing amount of different cost items; prepare a condensed cost of goods manufactured schedule, an income statement, and a partial balance sheet.
(SO 5, 6, 7)

	Case	
	1	2
Direct Materials Used	$ 9,000	(g)
Direct Labor	3,000	4,000
Manufacturing Overhead	4,000	5,000
Total Manufacturing Costs	(a)	20,000
Beginning Work in Process Inventory	1,000	(h)
Ending Work in Process Inventory	(b)	2,000
Sales	21,500	(i)
Sales Discounts	1,500	1,200
Cost of Goods Manufactured	13,500	21,000
Beginning Finished Goods Inventory	(c)	3,500
Goods Available for Sale	18,000	(j)
Cost of Goods Sold	(d)	(k)
Ending Finished Goods Inventory	1,000	2,500
Gross Profit	(e)	6,000
Operating Expenses	2,700	(l)
Net Income	(f)	2,200

Instructions
(a) Indicate the missing amount for each letter.
(b) Prepare a condensed cost of goods manufactured schedule for Case 1.
(c) Prepare an income statement and the current assets section of the balance sheet for Case 1, assuming that in Case 1 the other items in the current assets section are as follows: Cash, $3,000, Receivables (net), $10,000, Raw Materials, $700, and Prepaid Expenses, $200.

Prepare a cost of goods manufactured schedule, a partial income statement, and a partial balance sheet.
(SO 5, 6, 7)

P20–4A The following data were taken from the records of Buckley Manufacturing Company for the year ended December 31, 2000.

Raw Materials		Factory Insurance	$ 5,400
Inventory 1/1/00	$ 43,500	Factory Machinery	
Raw Materials		Depreciation	7,700
Inventory 12/31/00	44,200	Freight-in on Raw Materials	
Finished Goods		Purchased	3,900
Inventory 1/1/00	85,000	Factory Utilities	15,900
Finished Goods		Office Utilities Expense	8,600
Inventory 12/31/00	77,800	Sales	475,000
Work in Process		Sales Discounts	3,200
Inventory 1/1/00	10,200	Plant Manager's Salary	30,000
Work in Process		Factory Property Taxes	6,100
Inventory 12/31/00	6,500	Factory Repairs	800
Direct Labor	145,100	Raw Materials Purchases	64,600
Indirect Labor	19,100	Cash	28,000
Accounts Receivable	27,000		

Instructions

(a) Prepare a cost of goods manufactured schedule.

(b) Prepare an income statement through gross profit.

(c) Prepare the current assets section of the balance sheet at December 31.

*Prepare a cost of goods manufactured schedule and a correct income statement.
(SO 5, 6)*

P20–5A   Hawkinson Company is a manufacturer of toys. Its controller, Al Duryea, resigned in August 2000. An inexperienced assistant accountant has prepared the following income statement for the month of August 2000.

HAWKINSON COMPANY
Income Statement
For the Month Ended August 31, 2000

Sales (net)		$670,000
Less: Operating expenses		
Raw materials purchased	$200,000	
Direct labor cost	150,000	
Advertising expense	80,000	
Selling and administrative salaries	70,000	
Rent on factory facilities	60,000	
Depreciation on sales equipment	55,000	
Depreciation on factory equipment	40,000	
Indirect labor cost	20,000	
Factory utilities	10,000	
Factory insurance	5,000	690,000
Net loss		$ (20,000)

Prior to August 2000 the company had been profitable every month. The company's president is concerned about the accuracy of the income statement above. As a friend of the president, you have been asked to review the income statement and make necessary corrections. After examining other manufacturing cost data, you have acquired additional information as follows:

1. Inventory balances at the beginning and end of August were:

	August 1	August 31
Raw materials	$18,000	$33,000
Work in process	25,000	21,000
Finished goods	40,000	62,000

2. Only 70% of the utilities expense and 80% of the insurance expense apply to factory operations; the remaining amounts should be charged to selling and administrative activities.

Instructions

(a) Prepare a cost goods manufactured schedule for August 2000.

(b) Prepare a correct income statement for August 2000.

*P20–6A   Everheart Manufacturing Company uses a simple manufacturing accounting system. At the end of its fiscal year on August 31, 2000, the adjusted trial balance contains the following accounts.

Complete a work sheet; prepare a cost of goods manufactured schedule, an income statement, and a balance sheet; journalize and post the closing entries.
(SO 8)

Debits			Credits		
Cash	$	16,700	Accumulated Depreciation	$	353,000
Accounts Receivable (net)		62,900	Notes Payable		45,000
Finished Goods Inventory		56,000	Accounts Payable		38,200
Work in Process Inventory		27,800	Income Taxes Payable		9,000
Raw Materials Inventory		37,200	Common Stock		352,000
Plant Assets		890,000	Retained Earnings		205,300
Raw Materials Purchases		236,500	Sales		996,000
Direct Labor		280,900			
Indirect Labor		27,400			
Factory Repairs		17,200			
Factory Depreciation		19,000			
Factory Manager's Salary		40,000			
Factory Insurance		11,000			
Factory Property Taxes		12,900			
Factory Utilities		13,300			
Selling Expenses		98,500			
Administrative Expenses		115,200			
Income Tax Expense		36,000			
		$1,998,500			$1,998,500

Physical inventory accounts on August 31, 2000, show the following inventory amounts: Finished Goods $54,600, Work in Process $23,400, and Raw Material $46,500.

Instructions
(a) Enter the adjusted trial balance data on a work sheet in financial statement order and complete the work sheet.
(b) Prepare a cost of goods manufactured schedule for the year.
(c) Prepare an income statement for the year and a balance sheet at August 31, 2000.
(d) Journalize the closing entries.
(e) Post the closing entries to Manufacturing Summary and to Income Summary.

PROBLEMS: SET B

P20–1B   Marek Company specializes in manufacturing a unique model of bicycle helmet. The model is well accepted by consumers, and the company has a large number of orders to keep the factory production at 10,000 helmets per month (80% of its full capacity). Marek's monthly manufacturing cost and other expense data are as follows.

Classify manufacturing costs into different categories and compute the unit cost.
(SO 3, 4)

Rent on factory equipment	$ 6,000
Insurance on factory building	1,500
Raw materials (plastics, polystyrene, etc.)	70,000
Utility costs for factory	900
Supplies for general office	300
Wages for assembly line workers	46,000
Depreciation on office equipment	800
Miscellaneous materials (lubricants, solders, etc.)	1,100
Factory manager's salary	5,700
Property taxes on factory building	400
Advertising for helmets	11,000
Sales commissions	7,000
Depreciation on factory building	1,500

Instructions

(a) Prepare an answer sheet with the following column headings:

	Product Costs					
Cost Item	Direct Materials	Direct Labor	Manufacturing Overhead	Period Costs	Prime Costs	Conversion Costs

Enter each cost item on your answer sheet, placing the dollar amount under the appropriate headings. Total the dollar amounts in each of the columns.

(b) Compute the cost to produce one helmet.

Classify manufacturing costs into different categories and compute the unit cost.
(SO 3, 4)

P20–2B Vargas Company, a manufacturer of stereo systems, started its production in October 1999. For the preceding 3 years Vargas had been a retailer of stereo systems. After a thorough survey of stereo system markets, Vargas Company decided to turn its retail store into a stereo equipment factory.

Raw materials cost for a stereo system will total $70 per unit. Workers on the production lines are on average paid $10 per hour. A stereo system usually takes five hours to complete. In addition, the rent on the equipment used to assemble stereo systems amounts to $1,200 per month. Indirect materials cost $5 per system. A supervisor was hired to oversee production; her monthly salary will be $2,400.

Janitorial costs were $1,300 monthly. Advertising costs for the stereo system will be $8,500 per month. The factory building depreciation expense is $7,200 per year. Property taxes on the factory building will be $6,000 per year.

Instructions

(a) Prepare an answer sheet with the following column headings:

	Product Costs					
Cost Item	Direct Materials	Direct Labor	Manufacturing Overhead	Period Costs	Prime Costs	Conversion Costs

Assuming that Vargas manufactures, on average, 1,200 stereo systems per month, enter each cost item on your answer sheet, placing the dollar amount per month under the appropriate headings. Total the dollar amounts in each of the columns.

(b) Compute the cost to produce one stereo system.

Indicate the missing amount of different cost items; prepare a condensed cost of goods manufactured schedule, an income statement, and a partial balance sheet.
(SO 5, 6, 7)

P20–3B Incomplete manufacturing costs, expenses, and selling data for two different cases are as follows.

	Case	
	1	2
Direct Materials Used	$ 8,000	(g)
Direct Labor	6,000	8,000
Manufacturing Overhead	5,000	4,000
Total Manufacturing Costs	(a)	21,000
Beginning Work in Process Inventory	1,000	(h)
Ending Work in Process Inventory	(b)	3,000
Sales	24,500	(i)
Sales Discounts	2,500	1,400
Cost of Goods Manufactured	16,500	22,000
Beginning Finished Goods Inventory	(c)	3,500
Goods Available for Sale	18,000	(j)
Cost of Goods Sold	(d)	(k)
Ending Finished Goods Inventory	3,000	2,500
Gross Profit	(e)	7,000
Operating Expenses	2,500	(l)
Net Income	(f)	2,800

Instructions

(a) Indicate the missing amount for each letter.

(b) Prepare a condensed cost of goods manufactured schedule for Case 1.

(c) Prepare an income statement and the current assets section of the balance sheet for Case 1, assuming that in Case 1 the other items in the current assets section are as follows: Cash, $4,000, Receivables (net), $15,000, Raw Materials, $600, and Prepaid Expenses, $400.

P20–4B The following data were taken from the records of Scheve Manufacturing Company for the fiscal year ended June 30, 2000.

Prepare a cost of goods manufactured schedule, a partial income statement, and a partial balance sheet.
(SO 5, 6, 7)

Raw Materials		Factory Insurance	$ 4,600
Inventory 7/1/99	$ 46,500	Factory Machinery	
Raw Materials		Depreciation	15,000
Inventory 6/30/00	39,600	Freight-in on Raw Materials	
Finished Goods		Purchased	8,600
Inventory 7/1/99	96,000	Factory Utilities	24,600
Finished Goods		Office Utilities Expense	8,650
Inventory 6/30/00	95,900	Sales	547,000
Work in Process		Sales Discounts	3,300
Inventory 7/1/99	21,000	Plant Manager's Salary	29,000
Work in Process		Factory Property Taxes	9,600
Inventory 6/30/00	18,700	Factory Repairs	1,400
Direct Labor	147,250	Raw Materials Purchases	89,800
Indirect Labor	24,460	Cash	32,000
Accounts Receivable	27,000		

Instructions

(a) Prepare a cost of goods manufactured schedule.
(b) Prepare an income statement through gross profit.
(c) Prepare the current asset section of the balance sheet at June 30, 2000.

P20–5B Noonan Company is a manufacturer of computers. Its controller, Jason Petry, re-signed in October 2000. An inexperienced assistant accountant has prepared the following income statement for the month of October 2000.

Prepare a cost of goods manufactured schedule and a correct income statement.
(SO 5, 6)

NOONAN COMPANY
Income Statement
For the Month Ended October 31, 2000

Sales (net)		$780,000
Less: Operating expenses		
Raw materials purchased	$260,000	
Direct labor cost	190,000	
Advertising expense	90,000	
Selling and administrative salaries	75,000	
Rent on factory facilities	60,000	
Depreciation on sales equipment	45,000	
Depreciation on factory equipment	30,000	
Indirect labor cost	25,000	
Factory utilities	12,000	
Factory insurance	8,000	795,000
Net loss		$ (15,000)

Prior to October 2000 the company had been profitable every month. The company's president is concerned about the accuracy of the income statement above. As a friend of the president, you have been asked to review the income statement and make necessary correc-tions. After examining other manufacturing cost data, you have acquired additional infor-mation as follows:

1. Inventory balances at the beginning and end of October were:

	October 1	October 31
Raw materials	$15,000	$31,000
Work in process	16,000	14,000
Finished goods	30,000	48,000

2. Only 80% of the utilities expense and 70% of the insurance expense apply to factory operations; the remaining amounts should be charged to selling and administrative activities.

Instructions
(a) Prepare a schedule of cost of goods manufactured for October 2000.
(b) Prepare a correct income statement for October 2000.

BROADENING YOUR PERSPECTIVE

GROUP DECISION CASE

BYP20–1 Deskins Manufacturing Company specializes in producing fashion outfits. On July 31, 1999, a tornado touched down at its factory and general office. The inventories in the warehouse and the factory were totally damaged due to heavy rain and moisture. The general office nearby was completely destroyed. Next morning, through a careful search over the disaster site, however, Ed Loder, the company's controller, and Susan Manning, the cost accountant, were able to recover a small part of manufacturing cost data for the current month.

"What a horrible experience," sighed Ed. "And the worst part is that we may not have enough records to use in filing an insurance claim."

"It was terrible," replied Susan. "However, I managed to recover some of the manufacturing cost data that I was working on yesterday afternoon. The data indicate that our direct labor cost in July totaled $250,000 and that we had purchased $345,000 of raw materials. In addition, I recall that the raw materials used for July was $350,000. But I'm not sure this information will help; the rest of our records are blown away."

"Well, not exactly," said Ed. "I was working on the year-to-date income statement when the tornado warning was announced. My recollection is that our sales in July were $1,250,000 and our gross profit ratio has been 40% of sales. Also, I can remember that our cost of goods available for sale was $790,000 for July."

"Maybe we can work something out from this information!" exclaimed Susan. "My experience tells me that our manufacturing overhead is usually 60% of direct labor."

"Hey, look what I just found," cried Susan. "It's a copy of this June's balance sheet, and it shows that our inventories as of June 30 are Finished goods, $36,000, Work in process, $22,000, and Raw materials, $19,000."

"Super," yelled Ed. "Let's go work something out."

In order to file an insurance claim Deskins Company must determine the amount of its inventories as of July 31, 1999, the date of the tornado touchdown.

Instructions
With the class divided into groups, determine the amount of cost in the Raw Materials, Work in Process, and Finished Goods inventory accounts as of the date of the tornado touchdown.

MANAGERIAL ANALYSIS

BYP20–2 Tennis, Anyone? is a fairly large manufacturing company located in the southern United States. The company manufactures tennis rackets, tennis balls, tennis clothing, and tennis shoes, all bearing the company's distinctive logo, a large green question mark on a white flocked tennis ball. The company's sales have been increasing over the past 10 years. The tennis racket division has recently implemented several advanced manufacturing techniques. Robot arms hold the tennis rackets in place while glue dries, machine vision systems check for defects, and the engineering and design team use computerized drafting and testing of new products. The following managers work in the tennis racket division:

Wayne Gryer, Sales Manager (supervises all sales representatives)
Tommye Stevens, technical specialist (supervises computer programmers)
Martie Lefever, cost accounting manager (supervises cost accountants)
Jack Marler, production supervisor (supervises all manufacturing employees)
Tina Roy, engineer (supervises all new product design teams)

Instructions

With the class divided into groups, answer the following questions:

(a) What are the primary information needs of each manager?
(b) Which, if any, financial accounting report(s) is each likely to use?
(c) Name one special-purpose management accounting report that could be designed for each manager. Include the name of the report, the information it contains, and how frequently it should be issued.

REAL-WORLD FOCUS:
Anchor Glass Container Corporation

BYP20–3 **Anchor Glass Container Corporation,** the third largest manufacturer of glass containers in the U.S., supplies beverage and food producers and consumer products manufacturers nationwide. Based in Tampa, Florida, Anchor employs 4,500 at ten U.S. locations. Parent company Consumers Packaging Inc. (*Toronto Stock Exchange:* CGC) is a leading international designer and manufacturer of glass containers.

The following management discussion appeared in a recent annual report of Anchor Glass:

ANCHOR GLASS CORPORATION
Management Discussion

Cost of Products Sold   Cost of products sold as a percentage of net sales was 89.3% in the current year compared to 87.6% in the prior year. The increase in cost of products sold as a percentage of net sales principally reflected the impact of operational problems during the second quarter of the current year at a major furnace at one of the Company's plants, higher downtime, and costs and expenses associated with an increased number of scheduled capital improvement projects, increases in labor, and certain other manufacturing costs (with no corresponding selling price increases in the current year). Reduced fixed costs from the closing of the Streator, Illinois, plant in June of the current year and productivity and efficiency gains partially offset these cost increases.

Instructions

What factors affect the costs of products sold at Anchor Glass Container Corporation?

COMMUNICATION ACTIVITY

BYP20–4   Refer to Problem 20-5A and add the following requirement:

Prepare a letter to the president of the company, Marie Klinger, describing the changes you made. Explain clearly why net income is different after the changes. Keep the following points in mind as you compose your letter:

1. This is a letter to the president of a company, who is your friend. The style should be generally formal, but you may relax some requirements; for example, you may call the president by her first name.

2. Executives are very busy. Your letter should tell the president your main results first (for example, the amount of net income).
3. You should include brief explanations so that the president can understand the changes you made in the calculations.

RESEARCH ASSIGNMENT

BYP20–5 The December 1995 issue of *Management Accounting* includes an article by William L. Ferrara entitled ''Cost/Management Accounting: The 21st Century Paradigm.'' The article contains a historical perspective on management accounting as well as a prediction of the future.

Instructions
Read the article and answer the following questions:
 (a) What are the four eras into which management accounting is divided? (Identify the dates of each era. These are labeled paradigm A, B, C, and D in the article.)
 (b) What is the costing/pricing formula shown in Table 1 for paradigm (model) D, the fourth era?
 (c) What are the three ''provocative new issues'' created by the future model of management accounting (paradigm D)?

ETHICS CASE

BYP20–6 Carlos Morales, controller for Tredway Industries, was reviewing production cost reports for the year. One amount in these reports continued to bother him—advertising. During the year, the company had instituted an expensive advertising campaign to sell some of its slower moving products. It was still too early to tell whether the advertising campaign was successful. There had been much internal debate as how to report advertising costs. The Vice President of Finance argued that advertising costs should be reported as a cost of production, just like direct materials and direct labor. He therefore recommended that this cost be identified as manufacturing overhead and reported as part of inventory costs until sold. Others disagreed. Morales believed that this cost should be reported as an expense of the current period based on the conservatism principle. Others argued that it should be reported as Prepaid Advertising and reported as a current asset.

The president finally had to decide the issue. He argued that these costs should be reported as inventory. His arguments were practical ones. He noted that the company was experiencing financial difficulty and expensing this amount in the current period might jeopardize a planned bond offering. Also by reporting the advertising costs as inventory rather than as prepaid advertising, less attention would be directed to it by the financial community.

Instructions
 (a) Who are the stakeholders in this situation?
 (b) What are the ethical issues involved in this situation?
 (c) What would you do if you were Carlos Morales?

SURFING THE NET

BYP20–7 Dofasco Inc., located in Hamilton, Ontario, is one of Canada's largest integrated steelmakers. The home page of Dofasco Inc., includes information about the company, its markets, people, technology, and the environment, in addition to a wealth of financial information.

Address: https://www.dofasco.ca/

Instructions
At Dofasco's home page, choose the current **Annual Report** and locate the answers to the following questions:

(a) What does Dofasco produce? How much of this product did it produce in the current year?

(b) Explain the term "a shipped yield." What is Dofasco's current shipped yield? What are the factors influencing its increase or decrease?

(c) Did revenue per ton increase or decrease in the current year? Did cost per ton increase or decrease? What are the factors influencing these changes?

(d) How much was Dofasco's cost of sales in the current year? Its inventory? What inventory valuation method does Dofasco use?

Answers to Self-Study Questions
1. b   2. d   3. b   4. b   5. c   6. d   7. a   8. c   9. a   10. d

Remember to go back to the Navigator box on the chapter-opening page and check off your completed work.

Before studying this chapter, you should know or, if necessary, review:

a. How a perpetual inventory system works. (Ch. 5, pp. 189–199)
b. The three classifications of manufacturing costs. (Ch. 20, pp. 873–74)
c. The difference between product and period costs. (Ch. 20, pp. 875–76)
d. The form and content of a cost of goods manufactured schedule. (Ch. 20, pp. 878–79)

THE NAVIGATOR

FEATURE STORY

"We'd Like It in Red"

Western States Fire Apparatus, Inc., of Cornelius, Oregon, is one of the few American companies that makes fire trucks. The company builds about 25 trucks per year. Founded in 1941, the company is run by the children and grandchildren of the original founder.

"We buy the chassis, which is the cab and the frame," says Susan Scott, the company's bookkeeper. "In our computer, we set up an account into which all of the direct material that is purchased for that particular job is charged." Other direct materials include the fire pump—which can cost $10,000—the lights, the siren, ladders, and hoses.

As for direct labor, the production workers fill out job sheets that tell what jobs they worked on. Usually, the company is building four trucks at any one time. On payday, the controller allocates the payroll to the appropriate job record.

Indirect materials, such as nuts and bolts, wiring, lubricants, and abrasives are allocated to each job in proportion to direct material dollars. Other costs, such as insurance and supervisors' salaries, are allocated based on direct labor hours. "We need to allocate overhead in order to know what kind of price we have to charge when we submit our bids," she says.

Western gets orders through a "blind-bidding" process; that is, Western submits its bid without knowing the bid prices made by its competitors. "If we bid too low, we won't make a profit. If we bid too high, we don't get the job."

Regardless of the final price for the truck, the quality had better be first-rate. "The fire departments let you know if they don't like what you did, and you usually end up fixing it."

THE NAVIGATOR

CHAPTER 21

JOB ORDER COST ACCOUNTING

THE NAVIGATOR ✔

- ■ Understand *Concepts for Review*
- ■ Read *Feature Story*
- ■ Scan *Study Objectives*
- ■ Read *Preview*
- ■ Read text and answer *Before You Go On*
  p. 912 ☐ p. 922 ☐ p. 927 ☐
- ■ Work *Demonstration Problems*
- ■ Review *Summary of Study Objectives*
- ■ Answer *Self-Study Questions*
- ■ Complete assignments

STUDY OBJECTIVES

After studying this chapter, you should be able to:

1. *Explain the characteristics and purposes of cost accounting.*
2. *Describe the flow of costs in a job order cost accounting system.*
3. *Explain the nature and importance of a job cost sheet.*
4. *Indicate how the predetermined overhead rate is determined and used.*
5. *Prepare entries for jobs completed and sold.*
6. *Distinguish between under- and overapplied manufacturing overhead.*

THE NAVIGATOR

aving read the story about Western States Fire Apparatus, Inc., you should now be familiar with the manufacturing costs used in making a fire truck. This chapter illustrates how these manufacturing costs would be assigned to specific jobs, such as the manufacture of individual fire trucks. We begin the discussion in this chapter with an overview of the flow of costs in a job order cost accounting system. We then use a case study to explain and illustrate the documents, entries, and accounts in this type of cost accounting system. The content and organization of this chapter are as follows:

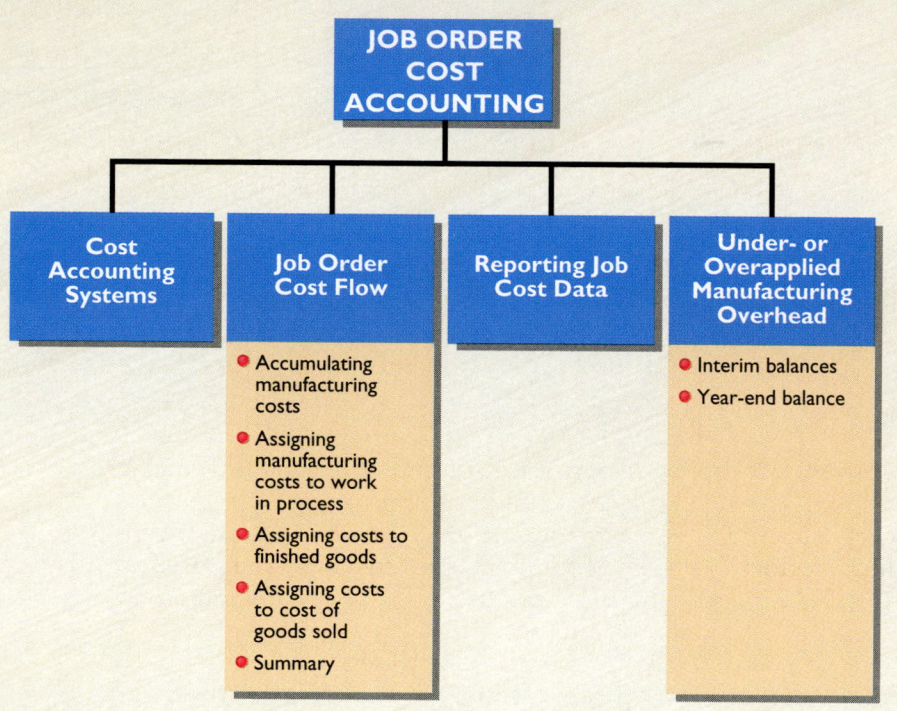

THE
NAVIGATOR

COST ACCOUNTING SYSTEMS

1

STUDY

OBJECTIVE

Explain the
characteristics and
purposes of cost
accounting.

Cost accounting involves the measuring, recording, and reporting of product costs. From the data accumulated, both the total cost and the unit cost of each product is determined.

A cost accounting system consists of manufacturing cost accounts that are fully integrated into the general ledger of a company. **An important feature of a cost accounting system is the use of a perpetual inventory system that provides information immediately on the cost of a product.** There are two basic types of cost accounting systems: (1) a job order cost system and (2) a process cost system. Although cost accounting systems differ widely from company to company, most are based on one of these two traditional product costing systems.

Under a job order cost system, costs are assigned to each **job**, such as the manufacture of a high-speed drilling machine, or to each **batch** of goods, such as 500 wedding invitations. Jobs or batches may be completed to fill a specific customer order or to replenish inventory. An important feature of job order costing is that each job (or batch) has its own distinguishing characteristics. For example, each house is custom built, each motion picture is unique, and each printing job is different. **The objective is to compute the cost per job.** At each point in the manufacturing process, the job and its associated costs can be identified. A job order cost system measures costs for each completed job, rather than for set time periods. The recording of costs in a job order cost system is shown in Illustration 21-1.

ILLUSTRATION 21-1

Job order cost system

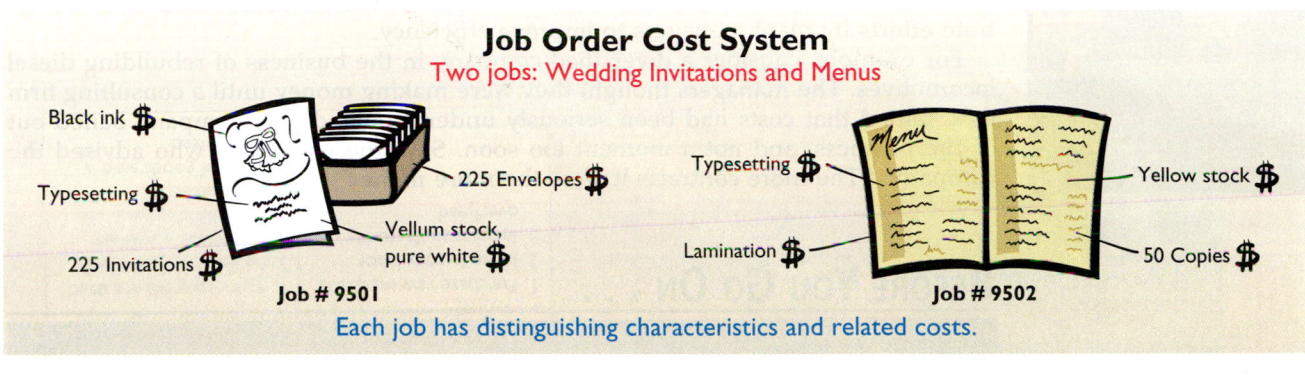

Job Order Cost System
Two jobs: Wedding Invitations and Menus

Black ink $
Typesetting $
225 Invitations $
225 Envelopes $
Vellum stock, pure white $
Job # 9501

Typesetting $
Lamination $
Yellow stock $
50 Copies $
Job # 9502

Each job has distinguishing characteristics and related costs.

A process cost system is used when a series of connected manufacturing processes or departments produce a large volume of uniform or relatively homogeneous products. Production is continuous to ensure that adequate inventories of the finished product(s) are on hand. A process cost system is used in the manufacture of cereal, the refining of petroleum, and the production of automobiles. Process costing accounts for and accumulates product-related costs for a period of time (such as a week or a month) as opposed to assigning costs to specific products or job orders. In process costing, the costs are assigned to or accumulated by departments or processes for a set period of time. The recording of costs in a process cost system is shown in Illustration 21-2. The process cost system will be discussed further in Chapter 22.

ILLUSTRATION 21-2

Process cost system

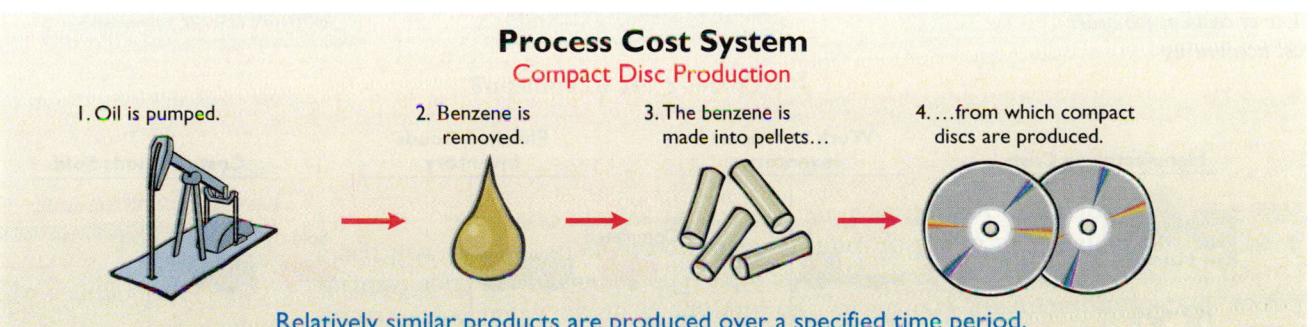

Process Cost System
Compact Disc Production

1. Oil is pumped.
2. Benzene is removed.
3. The benzene is made into pellets...
4. ...from which compact discs are produced.

Relatively similar products are produced over a specified time period.

A company may use both types of cost systems. For example, General Motors uses process cost accounting for its standard model cars, such as Saturns and Corvettes, and job order cost accounting for a custom-made limousine for the President of the United States. The objective of both systems is to provide product unit cost information for product pricing, cost control, inventory valuation, and

ILLUSTRATION 21-6

Job cost sheet

Job Cost Sheet

Job No. _____   Quantity _____

Item _____   Date Requested _____

For _____   Date Completed _____

Date	Direct Materials	Direct Labor	Manufacturing Overhead

Cost of completed job
  Direct materials $ _____
  Direct labor   _____
  Manufacturing overhead   _____
Total cost $ _____
Unit cost (total dollars ÷ quantity) $ _____

ETHICS NOTE

The misallocation of costs in a job order system can be a serious legal and ethical problem. For example, the Department of Defense sued General Dynamics Corporation at one time for over-allocating production costs that were not related to the underlying contract for U.S. Navy nuclear submarines.

in Process Inventory must be accompanied by a corresponding posting to one or more job cost sheets.

Raw Materials Costs

Raw materials costs are assigned when the materials are issued by the storeroom. To achieve effective internal control over the issuance of materials, the storekeeper should obtain a written authorization each time materials are released to production. The authorization for issuing raw materials is made on a prenumbered **materials requisition slip** signed by an authorized employee such as a department supervisor. Materials may be used directly on a job, or they may be considered to be indirect materials. As shown in Illustration 21-7, the requi-

ILLUSTRATION 21-7

Materials requisition slip

HELPFUL HINT

The internal control principle of documentation includes prenumbering to enhance subsequent accountability.

Wallace Manufacturing Company
Materials Requisition Slip

Deliver to: _____ Assembly Department _____   Req. No. __R247__

Charge to: __ Work in Process—Job No. 101 __   Date: __1/6/99__

Quantity	Description	Stock No.	Cost per Unit	Total
200	Handles	AA2746	$5.00	$1,000

Requested by _Bruce Howart_   Received by _Herb Crowley_

Approved by _Kap Shin_   Costed by _Heather Remmers_

sition should indicate the quantity and type of materials withdrawn and the account to be charged. The account is Work in Process Inventory for direct materials and Manufacturing Overhead for indirect materials.

The requisition is prepared in duplicate. A copy is retained in the storeroom as evidence of the materials released; the original is sent to accounting, where the cost per unit and total cost of the materials used are determined. Any of the inventory costing methods (FIFO, LIFO, or average cost) may be used in costing the requisitions; the method selected by management should be followed consistently. After the requisition slips have been costed, they are posted daily to the materials inventory records. In addition, **requisitions for direct materials are posted daily to the individual job cost sheets.**

Periodically, the requisitions are sorted, totaled, and journalized. For example, if $24,000 of direct materials and $6,000 of indirect materials are used in Wallace Manufacturing in January, the entry is:

(4)

Jan. 31	Work in Process Inventory	24,000	
	Manufacturing Overhead	6,000	
	Raw Materials Inventory		30,000
	(To assign materials to jobs and overhead)		

The requisition slips show total direct materials costs of $12,000 for Job No. 101, $7,000 for Job No. 102, and $5,000 for Job No. 103. The posting of requisition slip R247 and other assumed postings to the job cost sheets for materials are shown in Illustration 21-8. After all postings have been completed, the sum of the totals of the direct materials columns of the job cost sheets should equal the direct materials debited to Work in Process Inventory.

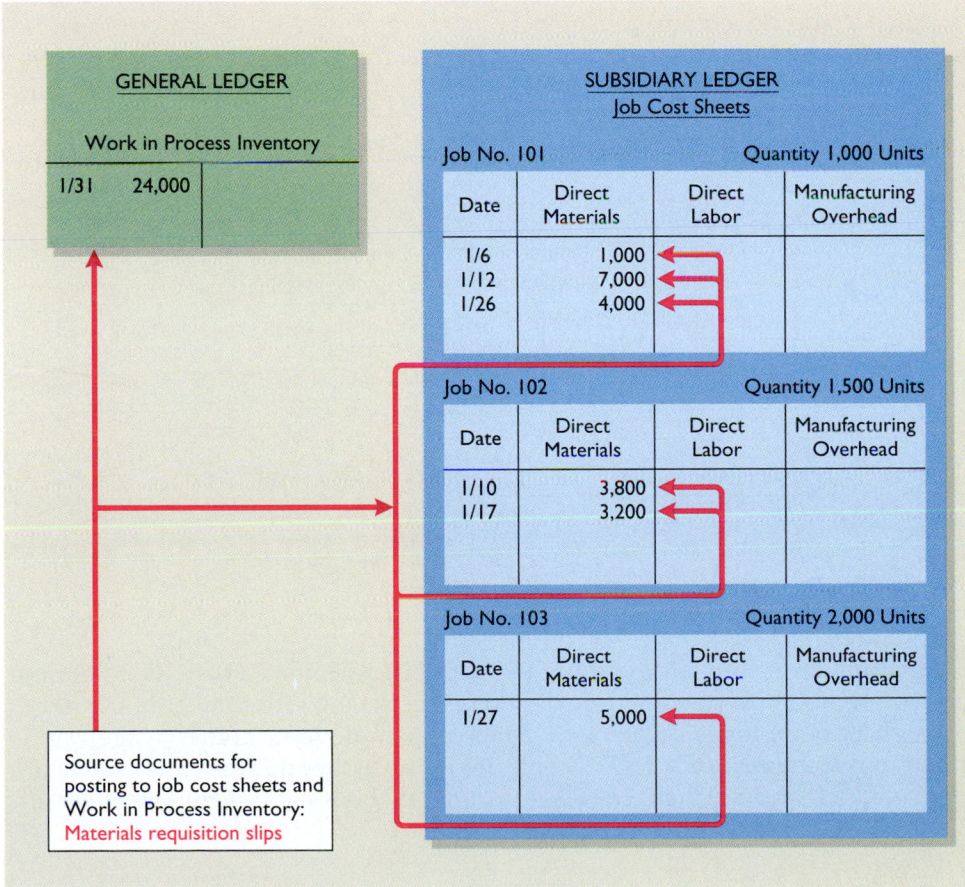

The materials inventory record for Part No. AA2746, after posting requisition slip R247 and an assumed requisition slip for 760 handles costing $3,800 on January 10 for Job 102, is shown in Illustration 21-9.

ILLUSTRATION 21-9

Materials inventory card following issuances

Item: Handles							Part No: AA2746		
	Receipts			Issues			Balance		
Date	Units	Cost	Total	Units	Cost	Total	Units	Cost	Total
1/4	2,000	$5	$10,000				2,000	$5	$10,000
1/6				200	$5	$1,000	1,800	$5	9,000
1/10				760	$5	3,800	1,040	$5	5,200

Factory Labor Costs

Factory labor costs are assigned to jobs on the basis of time tickets prepared when the work is performed. The **time ticket** should indicate the employee, the hours worked, the account and job to be charged, and the total labor cost. The account Work in Process Inventory is debited for direct labor, and Manufacturing Overhead is debited for indirect labor. When direct labor is involved, the job number must be indicated as shown in Illustration 21-10. In some companies, different colored time tickets are used for direct and indirect labor. All time tickets should be approved by the employee's supervisor.

ILLUSTRATION 21-10

Time ticket

Wallace Manufacturing Company
Time Ticket

Date: 1/6/99

Employee _____ John Nash _____   Employee No. ____ 124
Charge to: _____ Work in Process _____   Job No. ____ 101

Time			Hourly Rate	Total Cost
Start	Stop	Total Hours		
0800	1200	4	10.00	40.00

Approved by *Bob Kadler*   Costed by *M Cher*

The time tickets are later sent to the payroll department where the total time reported for an employee for a pay period is reconciled with total hours worked, shown on the employee's time card. Then the employee's hourly wage rate is applied and the total labor cost is computed. Subsequently, the time tickets are sorted, totaled, and journalized. For example, if the total factory labor cost incurred of $32,000 consists of $28,000 of direct labor and $4,000 of indirect labor, the entry is:

	(5)		
Jan. 31	Work in Process Inventory	28,000	
	Manufacturing Overhead	4,000	
	Factory Labor		32,000
	(To assign labor to jobs and overhead)		

As a result of this entry, Factory Labor is left with a zero balance, and gross earnings are assigned to the appropriate manufacturing accounts.

We will assume that the labor costs chargeable to the three jobs are $15,000, $9,000, and $4,000. The Work in Process Inventory and job cost sheets after posting are shown in Illustration 21-11. As in the case of direct materials, the postings to the direct labor columns of the job cost sheets should equal the posting of direct labor to Work in Process Inventory.

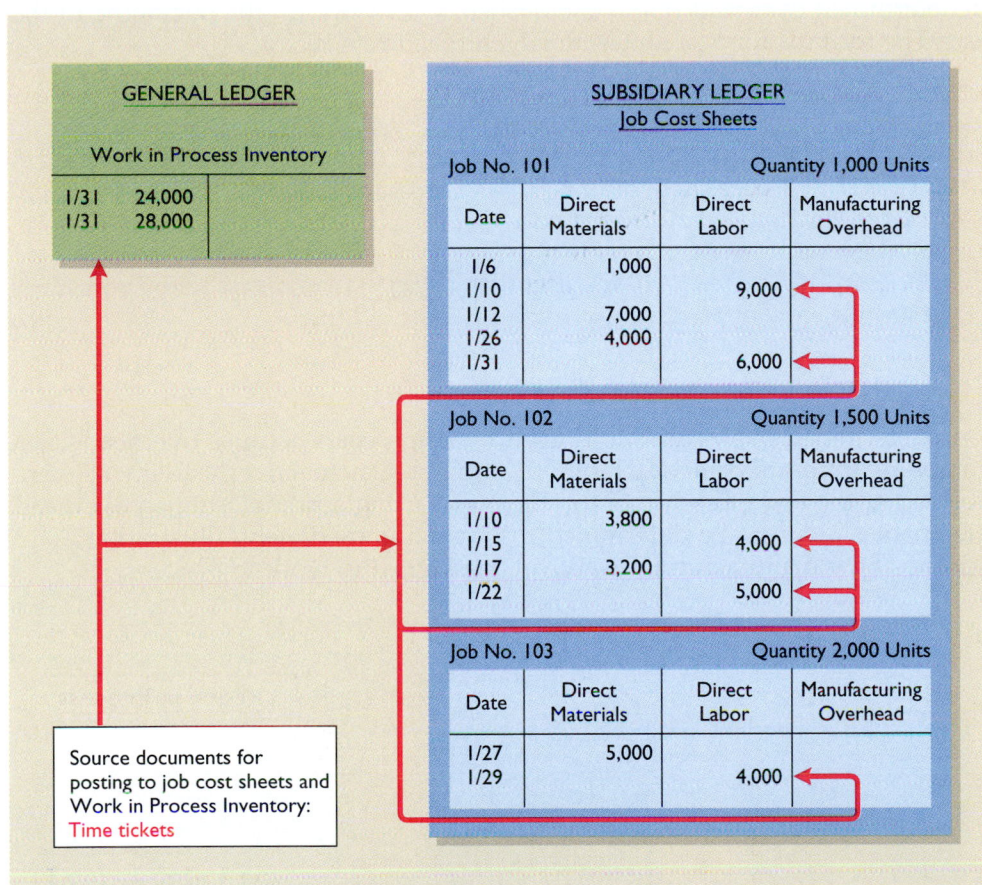

ILLUSTRATION 21-11

Job cost sheets—direct labor

HELPFUL HINT

Prove the $28,000 by totaling the charges by jobs:

101	$15,000
102	9,000
103	4,000
	$28,000

Manufacturing Overhead Costs

Unlike direct materials and direct labor that apply to specific jobs, manufacturing overhead relates to production operations as a whole. Consequently, these costs cannot be assigned to specific jobs on the basis of actual costs incurred. Instead, **manufacturing overhead is assigned to work in process and to specific jobs on an estimated basis through the use of a predetermined overhead rate.**

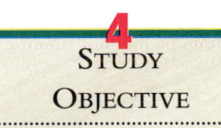

STUDY OBJECTIVE

Indicate how the predetermined overhead rate is determined and used.

TECHNOLOGY IN ACTION

A job cost computer program provides summaries of material and labor expenses by job. The program enables the company to accumulate costs by jobs, provide data to accounts receivable for billings, assign overhead costs, and provide up-to-date management reports. The paperwork and reports generated by such systems are basically the same as shown for Wallace Manufacturing Company. The major difference between manual and computerized systems is the time involved in converting data into information and in getting feedback (reports) to management.

The **predetermined overhead rate** is based on the relationship between estimated annual overhead costs and expected annual operating activity, expressed in terms of a common **activity base**. The common activity base may be stated in terms of direct labor costs, direct labor hours, machine hours, or any other measure that will provide an equitable basis for applying overhead costs to jobs. The predetermined overhead rate is established at (or prior to) the beginning of the year. The formula for a predetermined overhead rate is:

ILLUSTRATION 21-12

Formula for predetermined overhead rate

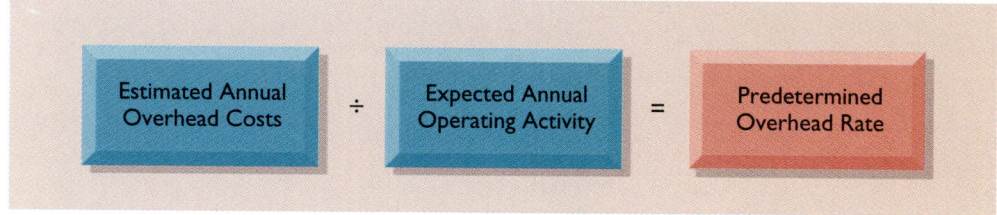

HELPFUL HINT

In contrast to overhead, actual costs for direct materials and direct labor are used to assign costs to Work in Process because the time delay to get cost information is short.

A predetermined overhead rate is used to assign costs because overhead costs are not incurred uniformly each month, and not all actual overhead invoices are received at the end of each month. Therefore, using a predetermined overhead rate enables a cost to be determined for the job immediately. Illustration 21-13 indicates how manufacturing overhead is assigned to work in process.

ILLUSTRATION 21-13

Using predetermined overhead rates

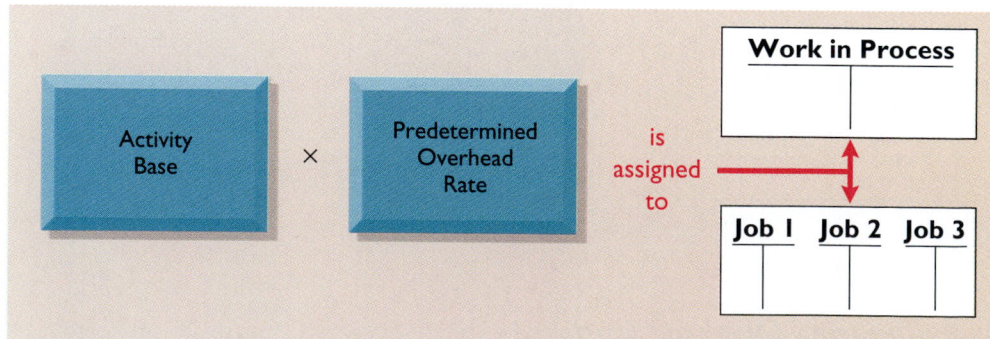

At Wallace Manufacturing, direct labor cost is the activity base. Assuming that annual overhead costs are expected to be $280,000 and that $350,000 of direct labor costs are anticipated, the overhead rate is 80%, computed as follows:

$$\$280,000 \div \$350,000 = 80\%$$

This means that for every dollar of direct labor, 80 cents of manufacturing overhead will be assigned to a job. The use of a predetermined overhead rate enables the company to determine the approximate total cost of each job **when the job is completed**.

Historically, direct labor costs or direct labor hours have often been used as the activity base because of the relatively high correlation between direct labor and manufacturing overhead. In recent years, however, **there has been a significant trend toward use of machine hours as the activity base because of increased reliance on automation in manufacturing operations.**

A company may use more than one activity base. For example, if a job order is manufactured in more than one factory department, each department may have its own overhead rate. In the opening story about fire trucks, two bases were used in assigning overhead to jobs: direct material dollars for indirect materials, and direct labor hours for such costs as insurance and supervisors' salaries.

For Wallace Manufacturing, manufacturing overhead is assigned to work in process and **charged to jobs when direct labor costs are assigned**. Overhead applied for January is $22,400 ($28,000 × 80%), and the application is recorded through the following entry.

	(6)		
Jan. 31	Work in Process Inventory	22,400	
	Manufacturing Overhead		22,400
	(To assign overhead to jobs)		

After posting, the Work in Process Inventory account and the job cost sheets will appear as shown in Illustration 21-14.

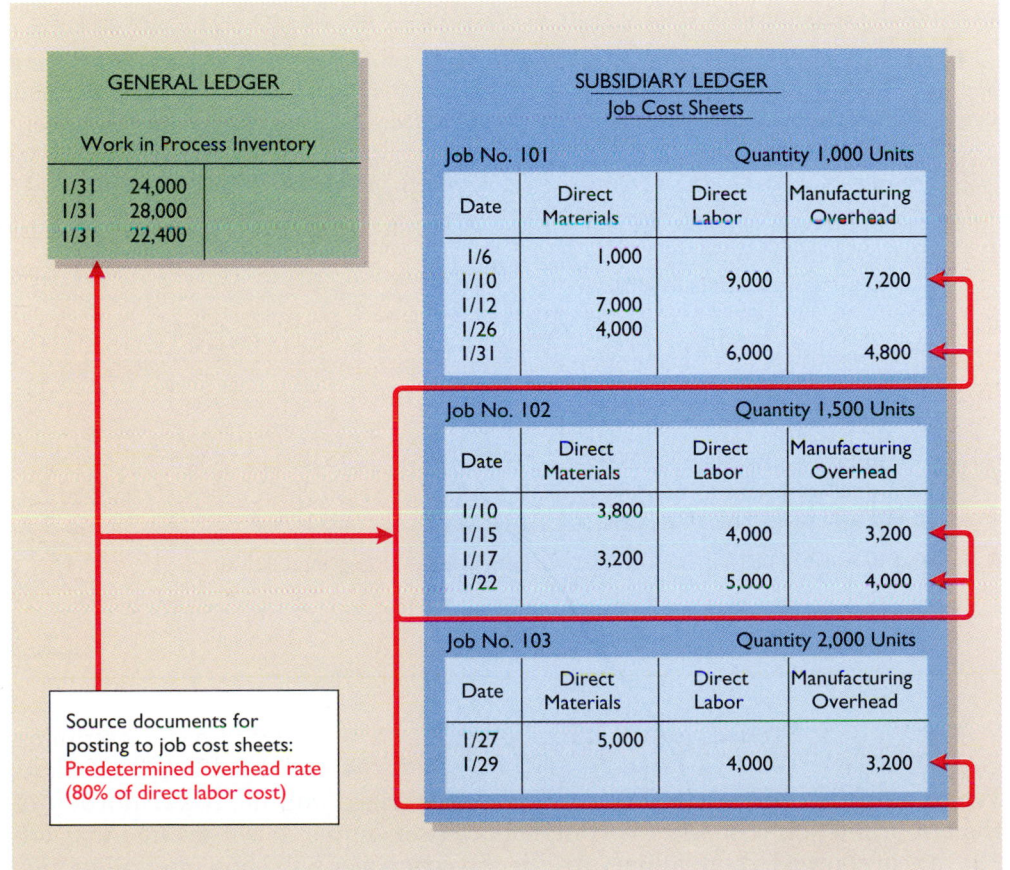

ILLUSTRATION 21-14

Job cost sheets—manufacturing overhead applied

Note that the debit of $22,400 of Work in Process Inventory equals the sum of the overhead assigned to jobs: Job 101 $12,000 + Job 102 $7,200 + Job 103 $3,200.

At the end of each month, **the balance in Work in Process Inventory should equal the sum of the costs shown on the job cost sheets of unfinished jobs**. Assuming that all jobs are unfinished, proof of the agreement of the control and subsidiary accounts in Wallace Manufacturing is shown below.

ILLUSTRATION 21-15

Proof of job cost sheets to work in process inventory

Work in Process Inventory		Job Cost Sheets	
Jan. 31	24,000	No. 101	$39,000
31	28,000	102	23,200
31	22,400	103	12,200
	74,400		**$74,400**

BEFORE YOU GO ON . . .

Review It

1. What source documents are used in assigning manufacturing costs to Work in Process Inventory?
2. What is a job cost sheet, and what is its primary purpose?
3. What is the formula for computing a predetermined overhead rate?

Do It

Danielle Company is working on two job orders. The job cost sheets show the following: direct materials—Job 120 $6,000, Job 121 $3,600; direct labor—Job 120 $4,000, Job 121 $2,000; and manufacturing overhead—Job 120 $5,000, Job 121 $2,500. Prepare the three summary entries to record the assignment of costs to Work in Process from the data on the job cost sheets.

Reasoning: Each cost charged to a job must be accompanied by a debit to the control account, Work in Process Inventory. The credits in the summary entries are the accounts debited when the manufacturing costs were accumulated.

Solution: The three summary entries are:

Work in Process Inventory ($6,000 + $3,600)	9,600	
Raw Materials Inventory		9,600
(To assign materials to jobs)		
Work in Process Inventory ($4,000 + $2,000)	6,000	
Factory Labor		6,000
(To assign labor to jobs)		
Work in Process Inventory ($5,000 + $2,500)	7,500	
Manufacturing Overhead		7,500
(To assign overhead to jobs)		

Related exercise material: BE21–3, BE21–4, BE21–7, E21–2, E21–3, E21–7, and E21–8.

THE NAVIGATOR

5
STUDY OBJECTIVE
....
Prepare entries for jobs completed and sold.

Assigning Costs to Finished Goods

When a job is completed, the costs are summarized and the lower portion of the applicable job cost sheet is completed. For example, if we assume that Job No. 101 is completed on January 31, the job cost sheet will show the following:

ILLUSTRATION 21-16
Completed job cost sheet

Job Cost Sheet

Job No. _____ 101 _____ Quantity _____ 1,000 _____
Item _____ Magnetic Sensors _____ Date Requested _____ February 5 _____
For _____ Tanner Company _____ Date Completed _____ January 31 _____

Date	Direct Materials	Direct Labor	Manufacturing Overhead
1/6	$ 1,000		
1/10		$ 9,000	$ 7,200
1/12	7,000		
1/26	4,000		
1/31		6,000	4,800
	$12,000	$15,000	$12,000

Cost of completed job

Direct materials	$ 12,000
Direct labor	15,000
Manufacturing overhead	12,000
Total cost	$ 39,000
Unit cost ($39,000 ÷ 1,000)	$ 39.00

When a job is finished, an entry is made to transfer its total cost to finished goods inventory. The entry for Wallace Manufacturing is:

		(7)		
Jan. 31	Finished Goods Inventory		39,000	
	Work in Process Inventory			39,000
	(To record completion of Job No. 101)			

Finished Goods Inventory is a control account that controls individual finished goods records in a finished goods subsidiary ledger. Postings to the receipts columns are made directly from completed job cost sheets. The finished goods inventory record for Job No. 101 is shown below in Illustration 21-17.

ILLUSTRATION 21-17
Finished goods record

Item: Magnetic Sensors   Job No: 101

	Receipts			Issues			Balance		
Date	Units	Cost	Total	Units	Cost	Total	Units	Cost	Total
1/31	1,000	$39	$39,000				1,000	$39	$39,000
2/2				1000	$39	$39,000			–0–

Assigning Costs to Cost of Goods Sold

Recognition of the cost of goods sold is made when each sale occurs. To illustrate the entries when a completed job is sold, we will assume that on January 31 Wallace Manufacturing sells, on account, Job 101, costing $39,000, for $50,000.

The entries are:

		(8)		
Jan. 31	Accounts Receivable		50,000	
	Sales			50,000
	(To record sale of Job No. 101)			
31	Cost of Goods Sold		39,000	
	Finished Goods Inventory			39,000
	(To record cost of Job No. 101)			

ILLUSTRATION 21-18

Job order cost system—flow of costs and documents

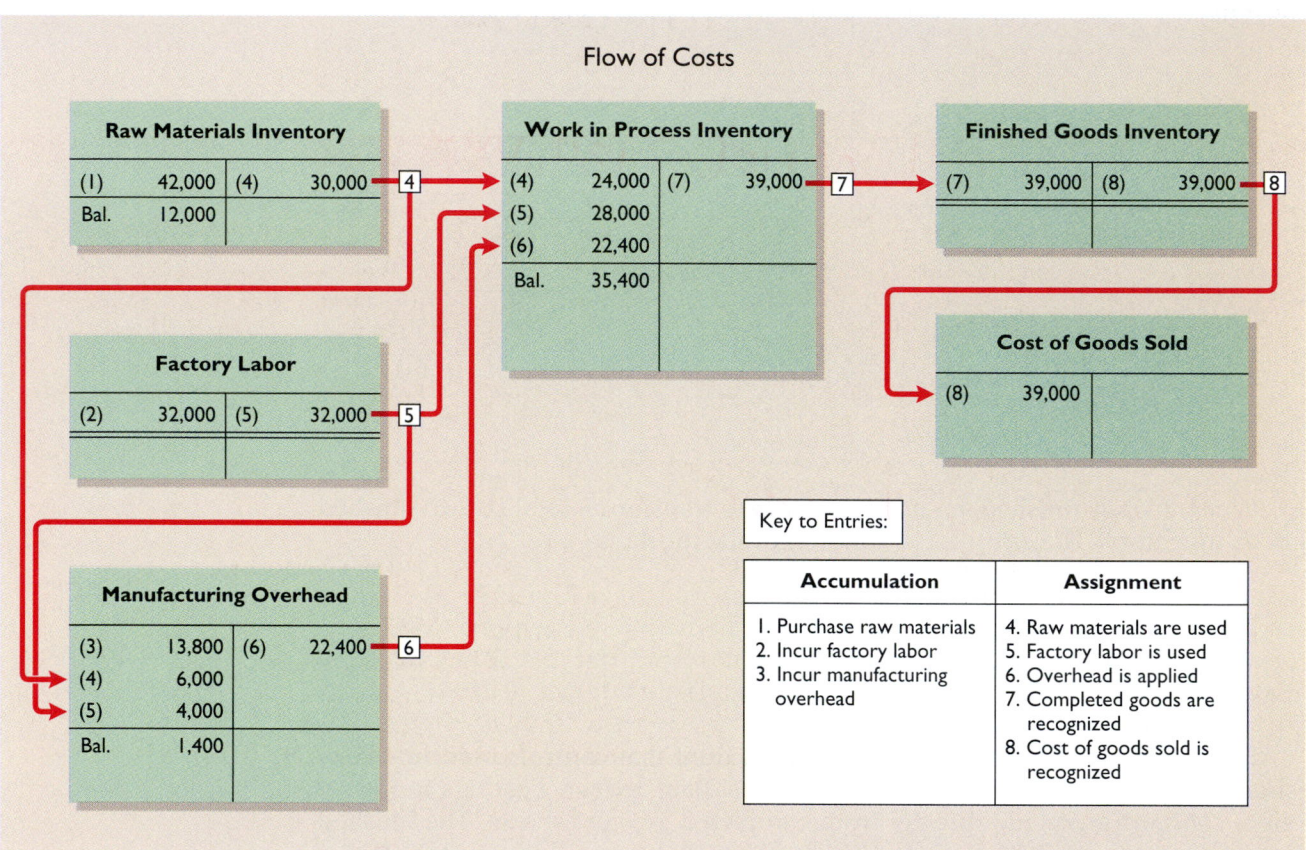

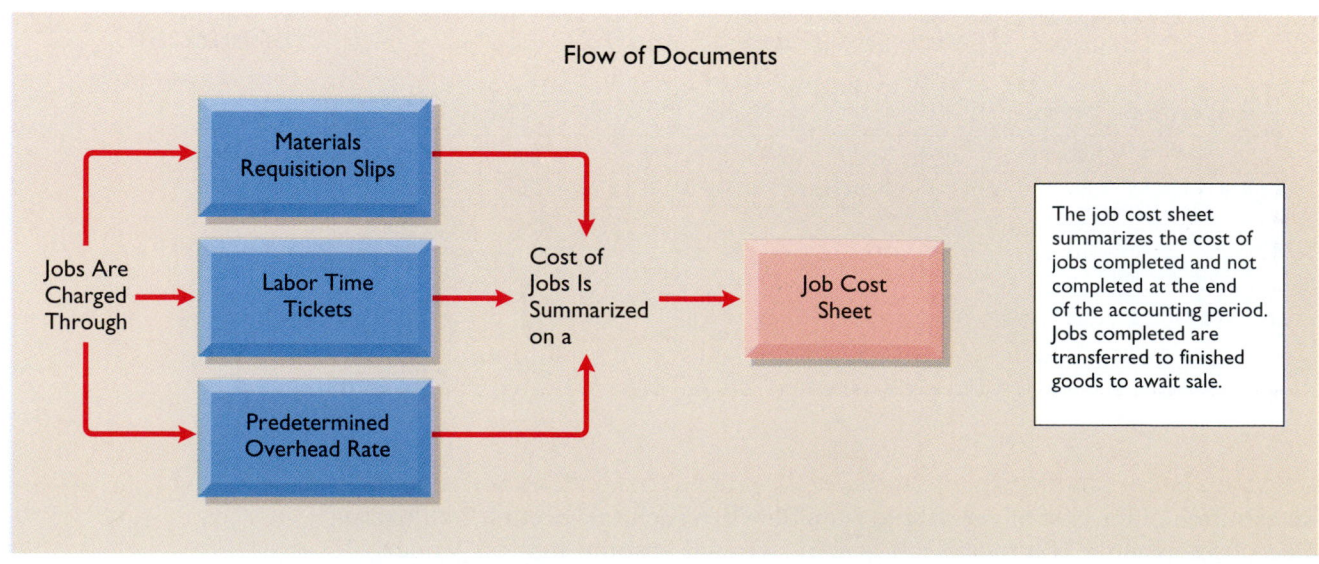

The units sold, the cost per unit, and the total cost of goods sold for each job sold are recorded in the issues section of the finished goods record as shown in Illustration 21-17.

Summary of Job Order Cost Flows

A completed flow chart for a job order cost accounting system is shown in Illustration 21-18 on page 924. All postings are keyed to entries 1–8 in Wallace Manufacturing Company's accounts presented in the cost flow graphic in Illustration 21-4. The graphic also provides a summary of the inventory control accounts, subsidiary ledgers, and source documents for assigning costs to jobs.

TECHNOLOGY IN ACTION

With the increased sophistication of microcomputers, small manufacturers can now use micros to perform (1) computer-aided manufacturing (CAM), (2) computer-aided testing (CAT), (3) computer-aided design (CAD), (4) electronic data interchange (EDI), and (5) materials requirement planning (MRP). For a small investment, manufacturers can now use software with capabilities only dreamed about a few years ago.

REPORTING JOB COST DATA

At the end of a period, financial statements are prepared that present aggregate data on all jobs manufactured and sold. The cost of goods manufactured schedule in job order costing is the same as in Chapter 20 with one exception: **Manufacturing overhead applied, rather than actual overhead costs, is added to direct materials and direct labor in determining total manufacturing costs.** The schedule is prepared directly from the Work in Process Inventory account. A condensed schedule for Wallace Manufacturing Company for January is as follows:

HELPFUL HINT
Monthly financial statements are usually prepared for management use only.

ILLUSTRATION 21-19

Cost of goods manufactured schedule

WALLACE MANUFACTURING COMPANY Cost of Goods Manufactured Schedule For the Month Ended January 31, 1999		
Work in process, January 1		$ –0–
Direct materials used	$24,000	
Direct labor	28,000	
Manufacturing overhead applied	22,400	
Total manufacturing costs		74,400
Total cost of work in process		74,400
Less: Work in process, January 31		35,400
Cost of goods manufactured		$39,000

Note that the cost of goods manufactured ($39,000) agrees with the amount transferred from Work in Process Inventory to Finished Goods Inventory in journal entry No. 7 in Illustration 21-18.

The income statement and balance sheet are the same as those illustrated in Chapter 20. For example, the partial income statement for Wallace Manufacturing Company for the month of January is as follows:

ILLUSTRATION 21-20

Partial income statement

WALLACE MANUFACTURING COMPANY		
Income Statement (partial)		
For the Month Ending January 31, 1999		
Sales		$50,000
Less: Cost of goods sold		
Finished goods inventory, January 1	$ –0–	
Cost of goods manufactured (See Illustration 21-19)	39,000	
Cost of goods available for sale	39,000	
Finished goods inventory, January 31	–0–	
Cost of goods sold		39,000
Gross profit		$11,000

6

STUDY OBJECTIVE

Distinguish between under- and overapplied manufacturing overhead.

ILLUSTRATION 21-21

Under- and overapplied overhead

UNDER- OR OVERAPPLIED MANUFACTURING OVERHEAD

When Manufacturing Overhead has a **debit balance**, overhead is said to be underapplied. Underapplied overhead means that the overhead assigned to work in process is less than the overhead incurred. Conversely, when manufacturing overhead has a **credit balance**, overhead is overapplied. Overapplied overhead means that the overhead assigned to work in process is greater than the overhead incurred. These concepts are shown in Illustration 21-21:

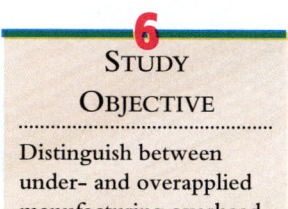

Manufacturing Overhead	
Actual (Costs incurred)	Applied (Costs assigned)

If actual is *greater* than applied, manufacturing overhead is underapplied.

If actual is *less* than applied, manufacturing overhead is overapplied.

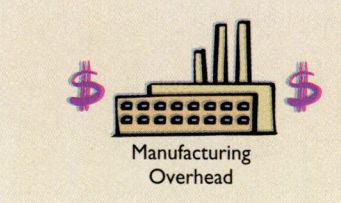

HELPFUL HINT

True or false: Underapplied overhead is reported as a current liability in an interim balance sheet. Answer: False; it is reported as a current asset.

Interim Balances

The existence of under- or overapplied overhead at the end of a month is expected and usually does not require corrective action by management. It is anticipated that monthly differences between actual and applied overhead will be offsetting over the course of the year.

When monthly financial statements are prepared, under- or overapplied overhead is reported on the balance sheet. Underapplied overhead is shown as a prepaid expense in the current asset section. Overapplied overhead is reported as unearned revenue in the current liability section.

Year-End Balance

At the end of the year, all manufacturing overhead transactions are complete; thus, there is no further opportunity for offsetting events to occur. Accordingly, any balance in Manufacturing Overhead is eliminated by an adjusting entry. Usually, under- or overapplied overhead is considered to be an **adjustment to cost of goods sold**. Thus, **underapplied overhead is debited to Cost of Goods Sold, and overapplied overhead is credited to Cost of Goods Sold**. To illustrate, assume that Wallace Manufacturing has a $2,500 credit balance in Manufacturing Overhead at December 31. The adjusting entry for the overapplied overhead is:

Dec. 31	Manufacturing Overhead	2,500	
	Cost of Goods Sold		2,500
	(To transfer overapplied overhead to cost of goods sold)		

After this entry is posted, Manufacturing Overhead will have a zero balance. In preparing an income statement for the year, the amount reported for cost of goods sold will be the account balance after the adjustment for either under- or overapplied overhead.

ACCOUNTING IN ACTION
Business Insight

Overhead also applies in nonmanufacturing companies. The State of Michigan found that auto dealers were charging documentary and service fees ranging from $18 to $445 per automobile and inspection fees from $88 to $360. These fees often were charged auto buyers after a base price had been negotiated. The Attorney General of the State of Michigan ruled that auto dealers cannot charge customers additional fees for routine overhead costs. The attorney general said: "Overhead is part of the sales price of a motor vehicle. Processing paper work, dealer incurred costs, and inspection fees to qualify cars for extended warranty plans are ordinary overhead expenses."

    Conceptually, it can be argued that under- or overapplied overhead at the end of the year should be allocated among ending work in process, finished goods, and cost of goods sold. However, most management accountants do not believe allocation is worth the cost and effort. The bulk of the under- or overapplied amount will be allocated to cost of goods sold anyway, because most of the jobs will be sold during the year.

BEFORE YOU GO ON . . .

Review It

1. When are entries made to record the completion and sale of a job?
2. What costs are included in total manufacturing costs in the cost of goods manufactured schedule?
3. How is under- or overapplied manufacturing overhead reported in monthly financial statements?

A LOOK BACK AT OUR FEATURE STORY

Refer to the opening story, and answer the following questions.

1. Would you expect Western States to use a job order or a process cost system? Why?
2. Is the flow of costs consistent with the cost flow used in the text? Explain.
3. On what basis does Western States allocate its overhead?
4. Why is the allocation of costs important to Western States Fire Apparatus?

Solution:

1. Western States uses job cost sheets; thus, the company uses a job order cost system. The use of a job order, rather than process cost, system by Western States makes sense because each job is custom built to fill a specific customer order, and each has its own distinguishing characteristics.
2. Western States follows the approach used in the text: it accumulates material, labor, and overhead costs and then assigns these costs to specific jobs and work in process.
3. Western States' overhead includes indirect materials (such as nuts and bolts, wiring, lubricants, and abrasives), which are allocated to each job in proportion to direct material costs. Its overhead also includes other costs such as insurance and supervisors' salaries, which are assigned based on direct labor hours.
4. Western States engages in blind-bidding to win contracts. In order to avoid over- or underbidding, the firm must have precise knowledge about costs.

DEMONSTRATION PROBLEM

During February, Cardella Manufacturing works on two jobs: Numbers A16 and B17. Summary data concerning these jobs are as follows:

Manufacturing Costs Incurred:

Purchased $54,000 of raw materials on account.
Factory labor $76,000 plus $4,000 employer payroll taxes.
Manufacturing overhead exclusive of indirect materials and indirect labor $59,800.

Assignment of Costs:

Direct materials:	Job A16 $27,000, Job B17 $21,000
Indirect materials:	$3,000
Direct labor:	Job A16 $52,000, Job B17 $26,000
Indirect labor:	$2,000

Manufacturing overhead rate 80% of direct labor costs.

Job A16 was completed and sold on account for $150,000. Job B17 was only partially completed.

Instructions

(a) Journalize the February transactions in the sequence followed in the chapter.

(b) What was the amount of under- or overapplied manufacturing overhead?

PROBLEM-SOLVING STRATEGIES

1. In accumulating costs, three accounts are debited: Raw Materials Inventory, Factory Labor, and Manufacturing Overhead.

2. When Work in Process Inventory is debited, one of the three accounts in strategy (1), above, must be credited.

3. Finished Goods Inventory is debited for the cost of completed jobs, and Cost of Goods Sold is debited for the cost of jobs sold.

4. Overhead is underapplied when Manufacturing Overhead has a debit balance.

SOLUTION TO DEMONSTRATION PROBLEM

(a)

1.

Feb. 28	Raw Materials Inventory	54,000	
	Accounts Payable		54,000
	(Purchase of raw materials on account)		

2.

28	Factory Labor	80,000	
	Factory Wages Payable		76,000
	Employer Payroll Taxes Payable		4,000
	(To record factory labor costs)		

3.

28	Manufacturing Overhead	59,800	
	Accounts Payable, Accumulated Depreciation, and Prepaid Insurance		59,800
	(To record overhead costs)		

4.

28	Work in Process Inventory	48,000	
	Manufacturing Overhead	3,000	
	Raw Materials Inventory		51,000
	(To assign raw materials to production)		

5.

28	Work in Process Inventory	78,000	
	Manufacturing Overhead	2,000	
	Factory Labor		80,000
	(To assign factory labor to production)		

6.

28	Work in Process Inventory	62,400	
	Manufacturing Overhead		62,400
	(To assign overhead to jobs—80% × $78,000)		

7.

28	Finished Goods Inventory	120,600	
	Work in Process Inventory		120,600
	(To record completion of Job A16: direct		
	materials, $27,000, direct labor $52,000 and		
	manufacturing overhead $41,600)		

8.

28	Accounts Receivable	150,000	
	Cost of Goods Sold	120,600	
	Sales		150,000
	Finished Goods Inventory		120,600
	(To record sale of Job A16)		

(b) Manufacturing Overhead has a debit balance of $2,400 as shown below:

Manufacturing Overhead

(3)	59,800	(6)	62,400
(4)	3,000		
(5)	2,000		
Bal.	2,400		

Thus, manufacturing overhead is underapplied for the month.

THE NAVIGATOR

SUMMARY OF STUDY OBJECTIVES

1. *Explain the characteristics and purposes of cost accounting.* Cost accounting involves the procedures for measuring, recording, and reporting product costs. From the data accumulated, the total cost and the unit cost of each product is determined.

2. *Describe the flow of costs in a job order cost accounting system.* In job order cost accounting, manufacturing costs are first accumulated in three accounts: Raw Materials Inventory, Factory Labor, and Manufacturing Overhead. The accumulated costs are then assigned to Work in Process Inventory and eventually to Finished Goods Inventory and Cost of Goods Sold.

3. *Explain the nature and importance of a job cost sheet.* A job cost sheet is a form used to record the costs chargeable to a specific job and to determine the total and unit cost of the completed job. Job cost sheets constitute the subsidiary ledger for the Work in Process Inventory control account.

4. *Indicate how the predetermined overhead rate is determined and used.* The predetermined overhead rate is based on the relationship between estimated annual overhead costs and expected annual operating capacity expressed in terms of a common activity base, such as direct labor cost. The rate is used in assigning overhead costs to work in process and to specific jobs.

5. *Prepare entries for jobs completed and sold.* When jobs are completed, the cost is debited to Finished Goods Inventory and credited to Work in Process Inventory. When a job is sold the entries are: (a) Debit Cash or Accounts Receivable and credit Sales for the selling price and (b) Debit Cost of Goods Sold and credit Finished Goods Inventory for the cost of the goods.

6. *Distinguish between under- and overapplied manufacturing overhead.* Underapplied manufacturing overhead means that the overhead assigned to work in process is less than the overhead incurred. Conversely, overapplied overhead means that the overhead assigned to work in process is greater than the overhead incurred.

THE NAVIGATOR

GLOSSARY

Cost accounting   An area of accounting that involves the measuring, recording, and reporting of product costs. (p. 910).

Cost accounting system   Manufacturing cost accounts that are fully integrated into the general ledger of a company. (p. 910).

Job cost sheet   A form used to record the costs chargeable to a job and to determine the total and unit cost of the completed job. (p. 915).

Job order cost system   A cost accounting system in which costs are assigned to each job or batch. (p. 910).

Materials requisition slip   A document authorizing the issuance of raw materials from the storeroom to production. (p. 916).

Overapplied overhead   A situation in which overhead assigned to work in process is greater than the overhead incurred. (p. 926).

Predetermined overhead rate   A rate based on the relationship between estimated annual overhead costs and expected annual operating activity, expressed in terms of a common activity base. (p. 920).

Process cost system   A system of accounting used by companies that manufacture relatively homogeneous products through a series of continuous processes or operations. (p. 911).

Time ticket   A document that indicates the employee, the hours worked, the account and job to be charged, and the total labor cost. (p. 918).

Underapplied overhead   A situation in which overhead assigned to work in process is less than the overhead incurred. (p. 926).

SELF-STUDY QUESTIONS

Answers are at the end of the chapter.

(SO 1) 1. Cost accounting involves the measuring, recording, and reporting of:
  a. product costs.
  b. future costs.
  c. manufacturing processes.
  d. managerial accounting decisions.

(SO 2) 2. In accumulating raw materials costs, the cost of raw materials purchased in a perpetual system is debited to:
  a. Raw Material Purchases.
  b. Raw Materials Inventory.
  c. Purchases.
  d. Work in Process.

(SO 2) 3. When incurred, factory labor costs are debited to:
  a. Work in Process.
  b. Factory Wages Expense.
  c. Factory Labor.
  d. Factory Wages Payable.

(SO 3) 4. The source documents for assigning costs to job cost sheets are:
  a. invoices, time tickets, and the predetermined overhead rate.
  b. materials requisition slips, time tickets, and the actual overhead costs.

  c. materials requisition slips, payroll register, and the predetermined overhead rate.
  d. materials requisition slips, time tickets, and the predetermined overhead rate.

(SO 3) 5. In recording the issuance of raw materials in a job order cost system, it would be *incorrect* to:
  a. debit Work in Process Inventory.
  b. debit Finished Goods Inventory.
  c. debit Manufacturing Overhead.
  d. credit Raw Materials Inventory.

(SO 3) 6. The entry when direct factory labor is assigned to jobs is a debit to:
  a. Work in Process Inventory and a credit to Factory Labor.
  b. Manufacturing Overhead and a credit to Factory Labor.
  c. Factory Labor and a credit to Manufacturing Overhead.
  d. Factory Labor and a credit to Work in Process Inventory.

(SO 4) 7. The formula for computing the predetermined manufacturing overhead rate is estimated annual overhead costs divided by an expected annual operating activity, expressed as:

a. direct labor cost.   c. machine hours.

b. direct labor hours.   (d.) any of the above.

(SO 4) 8. In the Cleo Company, the predetermined overhead rate is 80% of direct labor cost. During the month, $210,000 of factory labor costs are incurred, of which $180,000 is direct labor and $30,000 is indirect labor. Actual overhead incurred was $200,000. The amount of overhead debited to Work in Process Inventory should be:

a. $120,000.   c. $168,000.

b. $144,000.   (d.) $160,000.

(SO 5) 9. In BAC Company, Job No. 26 is completed at a cost of $4,500 and later sold for $7,000 cash. A correct entry is:

a. Debit Finished Goods Inventory $7,000 and credit Work in Process Inventory $7,000.

b. Debit Cost of Goods Sold $7,000 and credit Finished Goods Inventory $7,000.

c. Debit Finished Goods Inventory $4,500 and credit Work in Process Inventory $4,500.

(d.) Debit Accounts Receivable $7,000 and credit Sales $7,000.

10. In preparing monthly financial statements, overapplied (SO 6) overhead is reported in the balance sheet as a(an):

a. prepaid expense.

(b.) unearned revenue.

c. noncurrent asset.

d. noncurrent liability.

QUESTIONS

1. Kenna Quayle is studying for an accounting midterm examination. What should Kenna know about how management may use job cost data?

2. (a) Nels Hoadley is not sure about the differences between cost accounting and a cost accounting system. Explain the difference to Nels. (b) What is an important feature of a cost accounting system?

3. (a) Distinguish between the two types of cost accounting systems. (b) May a company use both types of cost accounting systems?

4. What type of industry is likely to use a job order cost system? Give some examples.

5. What type of industry is likely to use a process cost system? Give some examples.

6. Your roommate asks your help in understanding the major steps in the flow of costs in a job order cost system. Identify the steps for your roommate.

7. There are three inventory control accounts in a job order system. Identify the control accounts and their subsidiary ledgers.

8. What source documents are used in accumulating direct labor costs?

9. Entries to manufacturing overhead normally are only made daily. Do you agree? Explain.

10. Elaine Gould is confused about the source documents used in assigning materials and labor costs. Identify the documents and give the entry for each document.

11. What is the purpose of a job cost sheet?

12. Indicate the source documents that are used in charging costs to specific jobs.

13. Differentiate between a "materials inventory record" and a "materials requisition slip" as used in a job order cost system.

14. Phil Agler believes actual manufacturing overhead should be charged to jobs. Do you agree? Why or why not?

15. What relationships are involved in computing a predetermined overhead rate?

16. How can the agreement of Work in Process Inventory and job cost sheets be verified?

17. Judy Jansen believes that the cost of goods manufactured schedule in job order cost accounting is the same as in manufacturing accounting. Is Judy correct? Explain.

18. Ron Patten is confused about under- and overapplied manufacturing overhead. Define the terms for Ron and indicate the balance in the manufacturing overhead account applicable to each term.

19. Under- or overapplied overhead is reported in the income statement when monthly financial statements are prepared. Do you agree? If not, indicate the proper presentation.

20. At the end of the year, under- or overapplied overhead is closed to Income Summary. Is this correct? If not, indicate the customary treatment of this account.

BRIEF EXERCISES

BE21–1   Redeker Tool & Die begins operations on January 1. Because all work is done to customer specifications, the company decides to use a job cost accounting system. Prepare a flow chart of a typical job order system with arrows showing the flow of costs. Identify the eight transactions.

Prepare a flowchart of a job order cost accounting system, and identify transactions.
(SO 2)

Prepare entries in accumulating manufacturing costs.
(SO 2)

BE21–2 During the first month of operations, Redeker Tool & Die accumulated the following manufacturing costs: raw materials $8,000 on account, factory labor $4,000 of which $3,600 relates to factory wages payable and $400 relates to payroll taxes payable, and utilities payable $2,000. Prepare separate journal entries for each type of manufacturing cost.

Prepare entry for the assignment of raw materials costs.
(SO 2)

BE21–3 In January, Redeker Tool & Die requisitions raw materials for production as follows: Job 1 $1,000, Job 2 $1,200, Job 3 $1,600, and general factory use $600. Prepare a summary journal entry to record raw materials used.

Prepare entry for the assignment of factory labor costs.
(SO 2)

BE21–4 Factory labor data for Redeker Tool & Die is given in BE21–2. During January, time tickets show that the factory labor of $4,000 was used as follows: Job 1 $1,200, Job 2 $1,300, Job 3 $1,000, and general factory use $500. Prepare a summary journal entry to record factory labor used.

Prepare job cost sheets.
(SO 3)

BE21–5 Data pertaining to job cost sheets for Redeker Tool & Die are given in BE21–3 and BE21–4. Prepare the job cost sheets for each of the three jobs. (Note: You may omit the column for Manufacturing Overhead.)

Compute predetermined overhead rates.
(SO 4)

BE21–6 Oliva Company estimates that annual manufacturing overhead costs will be $300,000. Estimated annual operating activity bases are: direct labor cost $500,000, direct labor hours 50,000, and machine hours 100,000. Compute the predetermined overhead rate for each activity base.

Assign manufacturing overhead to production.
(SO 4)

BE21–7 During the first quarter, Oliva Company incurs the following direct labor costs: January $40,000, February $30,000, and March $50,000. For each month, prepare the entry to assign overhead to production using a predetermined rate of 60% of direct labor cost.

Prepare entries for completion and sale of completed jobs.
(SO 5)

BE21–8 In March, Glendo Company completes Jobs 10 and 11 costing $28,000 and $32,000, respectively. On March 31, Job 10 is sold to the customer for $35,000 in cash. Journalize the entries for the completion of the two jobs and the sale of Job 10.

Indicate statement classification of under- or overapplied overhead.
(SO 6)

BE21–9 On September 30, balances in Manufacturing Overhead are: Oliva Company—Debit $1,500, Glendo Company—Credit $3,000. Indicate how each company should report its balance at September 30, assuming each company prepares annual financial statements on December 31.

Prepare adjusting entries for under- and overapplied overhead.
(SO 6)

BE21–10 At December 31, balances in Manufacturing Overhead are: Oliva Company—Debit $1,000, Glendo Company—Credit $1,200. Prepare the adjusting entry for each company at December 31, assuming the adjustment is made to cost of goods sold.

EXERCISES

Prepare entries for factory labor.
(SO 2)

E21–1 The gross earnings of the factory workers for Gaetti Company during the month of January are $90,000. The employer's payroll taxes for the factory payroll are $9,000 and the fringe benefits to be paid by the employer on this payroll are $4,000. Of the total accumulated cost of factory labor, 90% is related to direct labor and 10% is attributable to indirect labor.

Instructions
  (a) Prepare the entry to record the factory labor costs for the month of January.
  (b) Prepare the entry to assign factory labor to production.

Prepare journal entries for manufacturing costs.
(SO 2, 3, 4, 5)

E21–2 Lorenzo Manufacturing uses a job order cost accounting system. On May 1, the company has a balance in Work in Process Inventory of $3,200 and two jobs in process: Job No. 429 $2,000, and Job No. 430 $1,200. During May, a summary of source documents reveals the following:

Job Number	Materials Requisition Slips	Labor Time Tickets
429	$2,500	$ 2,400
430	2,000	3,000
431	4,400	7,600
General use	800	1,200
	$9,700	$14,200

Lorenzo Manufacturing applies manufacturing overhead to jobs at an overhead rate of 70% of direct labor cost. Job No. 429 is completed during the month.

Instructions

(a) Prepare summary journal entries to record the requisition slips, time tickets, the assignment of manufacturing overhead to jobs, and the completion of Job No. 429.

(b) Post the entries to Work in Process Inventory and prove the agreement of the control account with the job cost sheets.

E21–3   A job order cost sheet for Free Company is shown below.

Analyze a job cost sheet and prepare entries for manufacturing costs.
(SO 2, 3, 4, 5)

Job No. 92			For 2,000 Units
Date	Direct Materials	Direct Labor	Manufacturing Overhead
Beg. bal. Jan. 1	5,000	6,000	4,200
8	6,000		
12		8,000	6,000
25	2,000		
27		4,000	3,000
	13,000	18,000	13,200

Cost of completed job:
Direct materials	$13,000
Direct labor	18,000
Manufacturing overhead	13,200
Total cost	$44,200
Unit cost ($44,200 ÷ 2,000)	$22.10

Instructions

(a) On the basis of the foregoing data answer the following questions:

(1) What was the balance in Work in Process Inventory on January 1 if this was the only unfinished job?

(2) If manufacturing overhead is applied on the basis of direct labor cost, what overhead rate was used in each year?

(b) Prepare summary entries at January 31 to record the current year's transactions pertaining to Job No. 92.

E21–4   Manufacturing cost data for Kosko Company, which uses a job order cost system, are presented below:

Analyze costs of manufacturing and determine missing amounts.
(SO 2, 5)

	Case A	Case B	Case C
Direct materials	(a)	$83,000	$ 65,000
Direct labor used	$ 50,000	90,000	(h)
Manufacturing overhead applied	42,500	(d)	(i)
Total manufacturing costs	190,650	(e)	287,000
Work in process 1/1/99	(b)	15,500	18,000
Total cost of work in process	201,500	(f)	(j)
Work in process 12/31/99	(c)	11,800	(k)
Cost of goods manufactured	192,300	(g)	262,000

Instructions

Indicate the missing amount for each letter. Assume that in all cases manufacturing overhead is applied on the basis of direct labor cost and the rate is the same.

E21–5   Gomez Company applies manufacturing overhead to jobs on the basis of machine hours used. Overhead costs are expected to total $275,000 for the year, and machine usage is estimated at 125,000 hours.

In January, $26,000 of overhead costs are incurred and 10,000 machine hours are used. For the remainder of the year, $274,000 of overhead costs are incurred and 120,000 machine hours are worked.

Compute the manufacturing overhead rate and under- or overapplied overhead.
(SO 4, 6)

Instructions

(a) Compute the manufacturing overhead rate for the year.

(b) What is the amount of under- or overapplied overhead at January 31? How should this amount be reported in the financial statements prepared on January 31?

(c) What is the amount of under- or overapplied overhead at December 31?

(d) Assuming the under- or overapplied overhead for the year is not allocated to inventory accounts, prepare the adjusting entry to assign the amount to cost of goods sold.

Analyze job cost sheet and prepare entry for completed job.
(SO 2, 3, 4, 5)

E21–6   A job cost sheet of Duc Mai Company is given below:

Job Cost Sheet			
JOB NO. 469		Quantity	2,000
ITEM White Lion Cages		Date Requested	7/2
FOR Tesla Company		Date Completed	7/31

Date	Direct Materials	Direct Labor	Manufacturing Overhead
7/10	825		
12	900		
15		440	550
22		380	475
24	1,600		
27	1,500		
31		540	675

Cost of completed job: 1360   1700
  Direct materials
  Direct labor
  Manufacturing overhead
Total cost   7986
Unit cost   3.95

Instructions

(a)   Answer the following questions:

(1) What are the source documents for direct materials, direct labor, and manufacturing overhead costs assigned to this job?

(2) What is the predetermined manufacturing overhead rate? 1.25%

(3) What is the total cost and unit cost of the completed job?

(b) Prepare the entry to record the completion of the job.

Prepare entries for manufacturing costs.
(SO 2, 4, 5)

E21–7   Kiefer Corporation incurred the following transactions.

1. Purchased raw materials on account, $48,900.

2. Raw Materials of $36,000 were requisitioned to the factory. An analysis of the materials requisition slips indicated that $8,800 was classified as indirect materials.

3. Factory labor costs incurred were $64,900 of which $59,000 pertained to factory wages payable and $5,900 pertained to employer payroll taxes payable.

4. Time tickets indicated that $60,000 was direct labor and $4,900 was indirect labor.

5. Overhead costs incurred on account were $80,500.

6. Manufacturing overhead was applied at the rate of 150% of direct labor cost.

7. Goods costing $88,000 were completed and transferred to finished goods.

8. Finished goods costing $68,000 to manufacture were sold on account for $103,000.

Instructions

Journalize the transactions. (Omit explanations.)

Prepare entries for manufacturing costs.
(SO 2, 3, 4, 5)

E21–8   Ikerd Printing Corp. uses a job order cost system. The following data summarize the operations related to the first quarter's production:

1. Materials purchased on account $172,000 and factory wages incurred, $87,300.

2. Materials requisitioned and factory labor used by job:

Job Number	Materials	Factory Labor
A20	$ 32,240	$18,000
A21	40,920	26,000
A22	36,100	15,000
A23	39,270	25,000
General factory use	4,470	3,300
	$153,000	$87,300

3. Manufacturing overhead costs incurred on account, $39,500.
4. Depreciation on machinery and equipment, $14,550.
5. Manufacturing overhead rate is 75% of direct labor cost.
6. Jobs completed during the quarter: A20, A21, and A23.

Instructions
Prepare entries to record the operations summarized above. (Prepare a schedule showing the individual cost elements and total cost for each job in item 6.)

E21–9   At May 31, the accounts of Ginavan Manufacturing Company show the following:

Prepare a cost of goods manufactured schedule and partial financial statements. (SO 2, 5)

1. May 1 inventories—finished goods $12,600, work in process $14,700, and raw materials $8,200.
2. May 31 inventories—finished goods $10,500, work in process $16,900, and raw materials, $7,100.
3. Debit postings to work in process were: direct materials $62,400, direct labor $32,000, and manufacturing overhead applied $64,000.
4. Sales totaled $200,000.

Instructions
(a) Prepare a condensed cost of goods manufactured schedule.
(b) Prepare an income statement for May through gross profit.
(c) Indicate the balance sheet presentation of the manufacturing inventories at May 31, 1999.

E21–10   Krumme Company begins operations on April 1. Information from job cost sheets shows the following:

Compute work in process and finished goods from job cost sheets. (SO 3, 5)

Job Number	Manufacturing Costs Assigned		
	April	May	June
10	$5,200	$4,400	
11	4,100	3,900	$3,000
12	1,200		
13		4,700	4,500
14		3,900	3,600

Job 12 was completed in April. Job 10 was completed in May, and Jobs 11 and 13 were completed in June. Each job was sold for 50% above its cost in the month following completion.

Instructions
Answer the following questions:

1. What is the balance in Work in Process Inventory at the end of each month?
2. What is the balance in Finished Goods Inventory at the end of each month?
3. What is the gross profit for May, June, and July?

PROBLEMS: SET A

P21–1A   Good Manufacturing uses a job order cost system and applies overhead to production on the basis of direct labor hours. On January 1, 1999, Job No. 25 was the only job in process. The costs incurred prior to January 1 on this job were as follows: direct materials,

Prepare entries in a job cost system and job costs sheets (SO 2, 3, 4, 5, 6)

$10,000; direct labor, $6,000; and manufacturing overhead, $10,500. In addition, Job No. 23 had been completed at a cost of $45,000 and was part of finished goods inventory, and there was a $5,000 balance in the Raw Materials inventory account.

During the month of January, Good Manufacturing began production on Jobs 26 and 27, and completed Jobs 25 and 26. Jobs 23 and 25 were also sold on account during the month for $52,000 and $58,000 respectively. The following additional events occurred during the month:

1. Purchased additional raw materials of $45,000 on account.
2. Incurred factory labor costs of $31,500. Of this amount $6,500 related to employer payroll taxes.
3. Incurred manufacturing overhead costs as follows; indirect materials, $10,000; indirect labor, $7,500; depreciation expense, $10,000; and various other manufacturing overhead costs on account, $15,000.
4. Assigned direct materials and direct labor to jobs as follows:

Job No.	Direct Materials	Direct Labor
25	$ 5,000	$ 3,000
26	20,000	12,000
27	15,000	9,000

5. The company uses direct labor hours as the activity base to assign overhead. Direct labor hours incurred on each job were as follows: Job No. 25, 200; Job No. 26, 800; and Job No. 27, 600.

Instructions

(a) Calculate the predetermined overhead rate for the year 1999, assuming Good Manufacturing estimates total manufacturing overhead costs of $500,000, direct labor costs of $300,000, and direct labor hours of 20,000 for the year.
(b) Open job cost sheets for Jobs 25, 26, and 27. Enter the January 1 balances on the job cost sheet for Job No. 25.
(c) Prepare the journal entries to record the purchase of raw materials, the factory labor costs incurred, and the manufacturing overhead costs incurred during the month of January.
(d) Prepare the journal entries to record the assignment of direct materials, direct labor, and manufacturing overhead costs to production. In assigning manufacturing overhead costs, use the overhead rate calculated in (a). Post all costs to the job cost sheets as necessary.
(e) Total the job cost sheets for any job(s) completed during the month. Prepare the journal entry (or entries) to record the completion of any job(s) during the month.
(f) Prepare the journal entry (or entries) to record the sale of any job(s) during the month.
(g) What is the balance in the Work-In-Process Inventory account at the end of the month? What does this balance consist of?
(h) What is the amount of over- or underapplied overhead for the month? How would this be reported on the financial statements for the month of January?

Prepare entries in a job cost system and partial income statement.
(SO 2, 3, 4, 5, 6)

P21–2A For the year ended December 31, 1999, the job cost sheets of Asticio Company contained the following data.

Job Number	Explanation	Direct Materials	Direct Labor	Manufacturing Overhead	Total Costs
7650	Balance 1/1	$18,000	$20,000	$25,000	$ 63,000
	Current year's costs	22,000	30,000	37,500	89,500
7651	Balance 1/1	12,000	18,000	22,500	52,500
	Current year's costs	28,000	40,000	50,000	118,000
7652	Current year's costs	40,000	60,000	75,000	175,000

Other data:

1. Raw materials inventory totaled $20,000 on January 1. During the year, $100,000 of raw materials were purchased on account.
2. Finished goods on January 1 consisted of Job No. 7648 for $98,000 and Job No. 7649 for $62,000.

3. Job No. 7650 and Job No. 7651 were completed during the year.
4. Job Nos. 7648, 7649, and 7650 were sold on account for $390,000.
5. Manufacturing overhead incurred on account totaled $120,000.
6. Other manufacturing overhead consisted of indirect materials $12,000, indirect labor $18,000, and depreciation on factory machinery $6,000.

Instructions
(a) Prove the agreement of Work in Process Inventory with job cost sheets pertaining to unfinished work.
(b) Prepare the adjusting entry for manufacturing overhead, assuming the balance is allocated entirely to cost of goods sold.
(c) Determine the gross profit to be reported for 1999.

P21–3A Joe Witten is a contractor specializing in custom-built jacuzzis. On May 1, 1999, his ledger contains the following data:

Prepare entries in a job cost system and cost of goods manufactured schedule.
(SO 2, 3, 4, 5)

Raw Materials Inventory	$30,000
Work in Process Inventory	12,200
Manufacturing Overhead	2,500 (dr.)

The Manufacturing Overhead account has debit totals of $12,500 and credit totals of $10,000. Subsidiary data for Work in Process Inventory on May 1 include:

Job Cost Sheets

Job by Customer	Direct Materials	Direct Labor	Manufacturing Overhead
Jovi	$2,500	$2,000	$1,400
Roth	2,000	1,200	840
Nicks	900	800	560
	$5,400	$4,000	$2,800

A summary of materials requisition slips and time tickets for the month of May reveals the following:

Job by Customer	Materials Requisition Slips	Time Tickets
Jovi	$ 500	$ 400
Roth	600	1,000
Nicks	2,300	1,300
Jett	2,400	3,300
	5,800	6,000
General use	1,500	2,600
	$7,300	$8,600

During May, the following costs were incurred: (a) raw materials purchased on account, $5,000, (b) labor paid, $8,200, (c) manufacturing overhead paid $1,400. Overhead was charged to jobs on the basis of direct labor cost at the same rate as in the previous month.

The jacuzzis for customers Jovi, Roth, and Nicks were completed during May. Each jacuzzi was sold for $12,500 cash.

Instructions
(a) Prepare journal entries for the May transactions.
(b) Post the entries to Work in Process Inventory.
(c) Reconcile the balance in Work in Process Inventory with the costs of unfinished jobs.
(d) Prepare a cost of goods manufactured schedule for May.

Compute predetermined overhead rates, apply overhead, and indicate statement presentation of under- or overapplied overhead.
(SO 4, 6)

P21–4A Navarro Manufacturing uses a job order cost system in each of its three manufacturing departments. Manufacturing overhead is applied to jobs on the basis of direct labor cost in Department A, direct labor hours in Department B, and machine hours in Department C.

In establishing the predetermined overhead rates for 1999 the following estimates were made for the year:

	Department		
	A	B	C
Manufacturing overhead	$900,000	$760,000	$780,000
Direct labor cost	$600,000	$100,000	$600,000
Direct labor hours	50,000	40,000	50,000
Machine hours	100,000	120,000	150,000

During January, the job cost sheets showed the following costs and production data:

	Department		
	A	B	C
Direct materials used	$92,000	$86,000	$64,000
Direct labor cost	$48,000	$35,000	$50,400
Manufacturing overhead incurred	$76,000	$67,000	$64,500
Direct labor hours	4,000	3,500	4,200
Machine hours	8,000	10,500	12,600

Instructions

(a) Compute the predetermined overhead rate for each department.
(b) Compute the total manufacturing cost assigned to jobs in January in each department.
(c) Compute the under- or overapplied overhead for each department at January 31.
(d) Indicate the statement presentation of the under- or overapplied overhead at January 31.
(e) If the amount in (d) was the same at December 31, how would it be reported in the year-end financial statements?

Analyze manufacturing cost accounts and determine missing amounts.
(SO 2, 3, 4, 5, 6)

P21–5A Wagaman Company's fiscal year ends on June 30. The following accounts are found in its job order cost accounting system for the first month of the new fiscal year.

Raw Materials Inventory

July 1	Beginning balance	19,000	July 31	Requisitions	(a)
31	Purchases	88,400			
July 31	Ending balance	(b)			

Work in Process Inventory

July 1	Beginning balance	(c)	July 31	Jobs completed	(f)
31	Direct materials	75,000			
31	Direct labor	(d)			
31	Overhead	(e)			
July 31	Ending balance	(g)			

Finished Goods Inventory

July 1	Beginning balance	(h)	July 31	Cost of goods sold	(j)
31	Completed jobs	(i)			
July 31	Ending balance	(k)			

Factory Labor

July 31	Factory wages	(l)	July 31	Wages assigned	(m)

Manufacturing Overhead

July 31	Indirect materials	8,900	July 31	Overhead applied	91,000
31	Indirect labor	16,000			
31	Other overhead	(n)			

Other data:

1. On July 1, two jobs were in process: Job No. 4085 and Job No. 4086 with costs of $17,000 and $8,200, respectively.
2. During July, Job Nos. 4087, 4088, and 4089 were started. On July 31, only Job No. 4089 was unfinished. This job had charges for direct materials $2,000, direct labor $1,500 plus manufacturing overhead.
3. On July 1, Job No. 4084, costing $135,000, was in the finished goods warehouse. On July 31, Job No. 4088, costing $143,000, was in finished goods.
4. Manufacturing overhead was applied at the rate of 130% of direct labor cost. Overhead was $4,000 underapplied in July.

Instructions

List the letters (a) through (n) and indicate the amount pertaining to each letter. Show computations.

PROBLEMS: SET B

P21–1B Great Manufacturing uses a job order cost system and applies overhead to production on the basis of direct labor costs. On January 1, 1999, Job No. 50 was the only job in process. The costs incurred prior to January 1 on this job were as follows: direct materials, $20,000; direct labor, $12,000; and manufacturing overhead, $21,000. In addition as of January 1, Job No. 49 had been completed at a cost of $90,000 and was part of finished goods inventory, and there was a $15,000 balance in the Raw Materials inventory account.

Prepare entries in a job cost system and job cost sheets.
(SO 2, 3, 4, 5)

During the month of January, Great Manufacturing began production on Jobs 51 and 52, and completed Jobs 50 and 51. Jobs 49 and 50 were also sold on account during the month for $89,000 and $115,000 respectively. The following additional events occurred during the month:

1. Purchased additional raw materials of $90,000 on account.
2. Incurred factory labor costs of $63,000. Of this amount $13,000 related to employer payroll taxes.
3. Incurred manufacturing overhead costs as follows: indirect materials, $14,000; indirect labor, $15,000; depreciation expense, $18,000; and various other manufacturing overhead costs on account, $23,000.
4. Assigned direct materials and direct labor to jobs as follows:

Job No.	Direct Materials	Direct Labor
50	$10,000	$ 6,000
51	39,000	24,000
52	30,000	18,000

5. The company uses direct labor hours as the activity base to assign overhead. Direct labor hours incurred on each job were as follows: Job No. 50, 400; Job No. 51, 1,600; and Job No. 52, 1,200.

Instructions

(a) Calculate the predetermined overhead rate for the year 1999, assuming Great Manufacturing estimates total manufacturing overhead costs of $1,050,000, direct labor costs of $700,000 and direct labor hours of 20,000 for the year.
(b) Open job cost sheets for Jobs 50, 51, and 52. Enter the January 1 balances on the job cost sheet for Job No. 50.
(c) Prepare the journal entries to record the purchase of raw materials, the factory labor costs incurred, and the manufacturing overhead costs incurred during the month of January.
(d) Prepare the journal entries to record the assignment of direct materials, direct labor, and manufacturing overhead costs to production. In assigning manufacturing overhead costs, use the overhead rate calculated in (a). Post all costs to the job cost sheets as necessary.

(e) Total the job cost sheets for any job(s) completed during the month. Prepare the journal entry (or entries) to record the completion of any job(s) during the month.

(f) Prepare the journal entry (or entries) to record the sale of any job(s) during the month.

(g) What is the balance in the Finished Goods Inventory account at the end of the month? What does this balance consist of?

(h) What is the amount of over- or underapplied overhead for the month? How would this be reported on the financial statements for the month of January?

Prepare entries in a job cost system and partial income statement.
(SO 2, 3, 4, 5, 6)

P21–2B For the year ended December 31, 1999, the job cost sheets of Brazil Company contained the following data.

Job Number	Explanation	Direct Materials	Direct Labor	Manufacturing Overhead	Total Costs
7640	Balance 1/1	$25,000	$24,000	$28,800	$ 77,800
	Current year's costs	34,000	36,000	43,200	113,200
7641	Balance 1/1	11,000	18,000	21,600	50,600
	Current year's costs	40,000	48,000	57,600	145,600
7642	Current year's costs	48,000	55,000	66,000	169,000

Other data:

1. Raw materials inventory totaled $15,000 on January 1. During the year, $140,000 of raw materials were purchased on account.
2. Finished goods on January 1 consisted of Job No. 7638 for $87,000 and Job No. 7639 for $92,000.
3. Job No. 7640 and Job No. 7641 were completed during the year.
4. Job Nos. 7638, 7639, and 7641 were sold on account for $530,000.
5. Manufacturing overhead incurred on account totaled $135,000.
6. Other manufacturing overhead consisted of indirect materials $14,000, indirect labor $20,000, and depreciation on factory machinery $8,000.

Instructions

(a) Prove the agreement of Work in Process Inventory with job cost sheets pertaining to unfinished work.

(b) Prepare the adjusting entry for manufacturing overhead, assuming the balance is allocated entirely to Cost of Goods Sold.

(c) Determine the gross profit to be reported for 1999.

Prepare entries in a job cost system and cost of goods manufactured schedule.
(SO 2, 3, 4, 5)

P21–3B Ehrlich Inc. is a construction company specializing in custom patios. The patios are constructed of concrete, brick, fiberglass, and lumber, depending upon customer preference. On June 1, 1999, the general ledger for Ehrlich Inc. contains the following data:

Raw Material Inventory	$4,200	Manufacturing Overhead Applied	$27,200
Work in Process Inventory	$5,540	Manufacturing Overhead Incurred	$26,375

Subsidiary data for Work in Process Inventory on June 1 are as follows:

Job Cost Sheets

	Customer Job		
Cost Element	Dion	Cole	Kix
Direct materials	$ 600	$ 800	$ 900
Direct labor	320	540	580
Manufacturing overhead	400	675	725
	$1,320	$2,015	$2,205

A summary of materials requisition slips and time tickets for June shows the following:

Customer Job	Materials Requisition Slips	Time Tickets
Dion	$ 800	$ 450
Lock	2,000	800
Cole	500	360
Kix	1,300	800
Dion	300	250
	4,900	2,660
General use	1,500	1,200
	$6,400	$3,860

During June, raw materials purchased on account were $3,900 and all wages were paid. Additional overhead costs consisted of depreciation on equipment $700 and miscellaneous costs of $400 incurred on account. Overhead was charged to jobs at the same rate that was used in May. The patios for customers Dion, Cole, and Kix were completed during June and sold for a total of $18,900. Each customer paid in full.

Instructions
(a) Journalize the June transactions.
(b) Post the entries to Work in Process Inventory.
(c) Reconcile the balance in Work in Process Inventory with the costs of unfinished jobs.
(d) Prepare a cost of goods manufactured schedule for June.

P21–4B Salinas Manufacturing Company uses a job order cost system in each of its three manufacturing departments. Manufacturing overhead is applied to jobs on the basis of direct labor cost in Department X, direct labor hours in Department Y, and machine hours in Department Z.

Compute predetermined overhead rate, apply overhead, and indicate statement presentation of under- or overapplied overhead.
(SO 4, 6)

In establishing the predetermined overhead rates for 2000 the following estimates were made for the year:

	Department		
	X	Y	Z
Manufacturing overhead	$1,170,000	$1,500,000	$960,000
Direct labor cost	$1,500,000	$1,250,000	$450,000
Direct labor hours	100,000	125,000	40,000
Machine hours	400,000	500,000	120,000

During January, the job cost sheets showed the following costs and production data:

	Department		
	X	Y	Z
Direct materials used	$140,000	$126,000	$78,000
Direct labor costs	$120,000	$110,000	$37,500
Manufacturing overhead incurred	$98,000	$129,000	$80,000
Direct labor hours	8,000	11,000	3,500
Machine hours	34,000	45,000	10,400

Instructions
(a) Compute the predetermined overhead rate for each department.
(b) Compute the total manufacturing costs assigned to jobs in January in each department.
(c) Compute the under- or overapplied overhead for each department at January 31.
(d) Indicate the statement presentation of the under- or overapplied overhead at January 31.
(e) If the amount in (d) was the same at December 31, how would it be reported in the year-end financial statements?

Analyze manufacturing accounts and determine missing amounts.
(SO 2, 3, 4, 5, 6)

P21–5B   Laguna Corporation's fiscal year ends on November 30. The following accounts are found in its job order cost accounting system for the first month of the new fiscal year.

Raw Materials Inventory

Dec. 1	Beginning balance	(a)	Dec. 31	Requisitions	14,850
31	Purchases	17,225			
Dec. 31	Ending balance	7,975			

Work in Process Inventory

Dec. 1	Beginning balance	(b)	Dec. 31	Jobs completed	(f)
31	Direct materials	(c)			
31	Direct labor	8,100			
31	Overhead	(d)			
Dec. 31	Ending balance	(e)			

Finished Goods Inventory

Dec. 1	Beginning balance	(g)	Dec. 31	Cost of goods sold	(i)
31	Completed jobs	(h)			
Dec. 31	Ending balance	(j)			

Factory Labor

Dec. 31	Factory wages	10,600	Dec. 31	Wages assigned	(k)

Manufacturing Overhead

Dec. 31	Indirect materials	1,900	Dec. 31	Overhead applied	(m)
31	Indirect labor	(l)			
31	Other overhead	1,445			

Other data:

1. On December 1, two jobs were in process: Job No. 154 and Job No. 155. These jobs had combined direct materials costs of $9,750 and direct labor costs of $12,000. Overhead was applied at a rate that was 75% of direct labor cost.
2. During December, Job Nos. 156, 157, and 158, were started. On December 31, Job No. 158 was unfinished. This job had charges for direct materials $3,800, direct labor $4,400 plus manufacturing overhead. All jobs, except for Job No. 158, were completed in December.
3. On December 1, Job No. 153 was in the finished goods warehouse. It had a total cost of $5,000. On December 31, Job No. 157 was the only job finished that was not sold. It had a cost of $4,000.
4. Manufacturing overhead was $230 overapplied in December.

Instructions

List the letters (a) through (m) and indicate the amount pertaining to each letter.

BROADENING YOUR PERSPECTIVE

GROUP DECISION CASE
••

BYP21–1 Costello Products Company uses a job order cost system. For a number of months there has been an ongoing rift between the sales department and the production department concerning a special-order product, TC-1. TC-1 is a seasonal product that is manufactured in batches of 1,000 units. TC-1 is sold at cost plus a markup of 40% of cost.

The sales department is unhappy because fluctuating unit production costs significantly affect selling prices. Sales personnel complain that this has caused excessive customer complaints and the loss of considerable orders for TC-1.

The production department maintains that each job order must be fully costed on the basis of the costs incurred during the period in which the goods are produced. Production personnel maintain that the only real solution to the problem is for the sales department to increase sales in the slack periods.

Linda Gurney, president of the company, asks you as the company accountant to collect quarterly data for the past year on TC-1. From the cost accounting system, you accumulate the following production quantity and cost data:

| | | Quarter | | |
Costs	1	2	3	4
Direct materials	$100,000	$220,000	$ 80,000	$200,000
Direct labor	60,000	132,000	48,000	120,000
Manufacturing overhead	105,000	123,000	97,000	125,000
Total	$265,000	$475,000	$225,000	$445,000
Production in batches	5	11	4	10
Unit cost (per batch)	$ 53,000	$ 43,182	$ 56,250	$ 44,500

Instructions
With the class divided into groups, answer the following questions:

(a) What manufacturing cost element is responsible for the fluctuating unit costs? Why?
(b) What is your recommended solution to the problem of fluctuating unit cost?
(c) Restate the quarterly data on the basis of your recommended solution.

MANAGERIAL ANALYSIS
••

BYP21–2 In the course of routine checking of all journal entries prior to preparing month-end reports, Li Chin discovered several strange entries. She recalled that the president's son Jeff had come in to "help out" during an especially busy time and that he had recorded some journal entries. She was relieved that there were only a few of his entries, and even more relieved that he had included rather lengthy explanations. The entries Jeff made were:

Work in Process	20,000	
Cash		20,000

(This is for materials put into process. I don't find the record that we paid for these, so I'm crediting Cash, because I know we'll have to pay for them sooner or later.)

Manufacturing Overhead	12,000	
Cash		12,000

(This is for bonuses paid to salespeople. I know they're part of overhead, and I can't find an account called "Non-factory Overhead" or "Other Overhead" so I'm putting it in Manufacturing Overhead. I have the check stubs, so I know we paid these.)

Wages Expense	120,000	
Cash		120,000

(This is for the factory workers' wages. I have a note that payroll taxes are $8,000. I still think that's part of wages expense, and that we'll have to pay it all in cash sooner or later, so I credited Cash for the wages and the taxes.)

Work in Process	3,000	
Raw Materials Inventory		3,000

(This is for the glue used in the factory. I know we used this to make the products, even though we didn't use very much on any one of the products. I got it out of inventory, so I credited an inventory account.)

Instructions

Using the information above, answer the following questions:

(a) How should Jeff have recorded each of the four events?
(b) If the entry was not corrected, which financial statements (income statement or balance sheet) would be affected? What balances would be overstated or understated?

REAL-WORLD FOCUS: PARLEX COMPANY

BYP21–3   Founded in 1970, **Parlex Corporation** is a world leader in the design and manufacture of flexible interconnect products. Parlex produces custom flexible circuits and laminated cables utilizing proprietary processes and patented technologies which are designed to satisfy the unique requirements of a wide range of customers. Its facilities are located in Methuen, Mass., Salem, N.H., Shanghai, China, and Empalmè, Mexico. Parlex provides its products and engineering services to a variety of markets including automotive, computer, telecommunciations, industrial controls, medical, consumer, and military-aerospace. Parlex's common stock trades on the Nasdaq stock market under the symbol PRLX.

The following information was provided in the company's annual report:

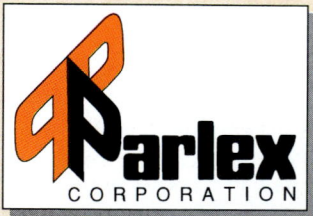

PARLEX COMPANY
Notes to the Financial Statements

The Company's products are manufactured on a job order basis to customers' specifications. Customers submit requests for quotations on each job, and the Company prepares bids based on its own cost estimates. The Company attempts to reflect the impact of changing costs when establishing prices. However, during the past several years, the market conditions for flexible circuits and the resulting price sensitivity haven't always allowed this to transpire. Although still not satisfactory, the Company was able to reduce the cost of products sold as a percentage of sales to 85% this year versus 87% that was experienced in the two immediately preceding years. Management continues to focus on improving operational efficiency and further reducing costs.

Instructions

(a) Parlex management discusses the job order cost system employed by their company. What are several advantages of using the job order approach to costing?

(b) Contrast the products produced in a job order environment, like Parlex, to those produced when process cost systems are used.

COMMUNICATION ACTIVITY

BYP21–4   You are the management accountant for Modine Manufacturing. Your company does custom carpentry work and uses a job order cost accounting system. Modine sends detailed job cost sheets to its customers, along with an invoice. The job cost sheets show the date materials were used, the dollar cost of materials, and the hours and cost of labor. A predetermined overhead application rate is used, and the total overhead applied is also listed.

Cindy Ross is a customer who recently had custom cabinets installed. Along with her check in payment for the work done, she included a letter. She thanked the company for including the detailed cost information but questioned why overhead was estimated. She stated that she would be interested in knowing exactly what costs were included in overhead, and she thought that other customers would, too.

Instructions

Prepare a letter to Ms. Ross (address: 123 Cedar Lane, Altoona, Kansas 66651) and tell her why you did not send her information on exact costs of overhead included in her job. Respond to her suggestion that you provide this information.

RESEARCH ASSIGNMENT

BYP21–5   The February 1994 issue of *Ohio CPA Journal* includes an article by Eun-Sup Shim and Joseph M. Larkin, entitled "A Survey of Current Managerial Accounting Practices: Where Do We Stand?"

Instructions

Read the article and answer the following questions:

(a) What percent of manufacturers surveyed used job order costing?

(b) What was the smallest cost component of the three factors of production? What portion of total manufacturing costs does it represent?

(c) What percent of manufacturers surveyed operate in a single product environment— that is, what percent produce only one product?

(d) What two managerial decisions were considered most affected by overhead allocation?

ETHICS CASE

BYP21–6   Roblez Printing provides printing services to many different corporate clients. Although Roblez bids most jobs, some jobs, particularly new ones, are often negotiated on a cost plus basis. Cost plus means that the buyer is willing to pay the actual cost plus a return (profit) on these costs to Roblez.

Kristi Peat, controller for Roblez, has recently returned from a meeting where Roblez's president stated that he wanted her to find a way to charge most costs to any project that was on a cost plus basis. The president noted that the company needed more profits to meet its stated goals this period. By charging more costs to the cost plus projects and therefore less cost to the jobs that were bid, the company should be able to increase its profits for the current year.

Kristi knew why the president wanted to take this action. Rumors were that he was looking for a new position and if the company reported strong profits the president's opportunities would be enhanced. Kristi also recognized that she could probably increase the cost of certain jobs by changing the basis used to allocate manufacturing overhead.

Instructions

   (a) Who are the stakeholders in this situation?
   (b) What are the ethical issues in this situation?
   (c) What would you do if you were Kristi Peat?

SURFING THE NET

BYP21–7   The Institute of Management Accountants sponsors a certification for management accountants, allowing them to obtain the title of Certified Management Accountant.

Address: http://www.rutgers.edu/Accounting/raw/ima/certletter.htm

Steps:
1. Go to the site shown above.
2. Under the heading "About the Certification Programs," choose **Objectives**.

Instructions
Answer the following questions:

   (a) What are the objectives of the certification program?
   (b) What is the "experience requirement"?
   (c) How many hours of continuing education are required, and what types of courses qualify?

Answers to Self-Study Questions
1. a   2. b   3. c   4. d   5. b   6. a   7. d   8. b   9. c   10. b

Remember to go back to the Navigator box on the chapter-opening page and check off your completed work.

Before studying this chapter, you should know or, if necessary, review:

a. The three manufacturing cost elements. (Ch. 20, pp. 873–874)

b. How manufacturing costs are accumulated in the accounts. (Ch. 21, pp. 913–915)

c. How manufacturing costs are assigned to work in process, finished goods, and cost of goods sold. (Ch. 21, pp. 915–924)

d. The flow of costs and supporting documents in a job order cost accounting system. (Ch. 21, pp. 924–925)

FEATURE STORY

Ben & Jerry's Tracks Its Mix-Ups

One of the fastest growing companies in the nation is Ben & Jerry's Homemade, Inc., based in Waterbury, Vermont. The ice cream company that started out of a garage in 1978 is now a public company with sales exceeding $174 million.

Making ice cream is a process— a movement of product from a mixing department to a prepping department to a pint department. The mixing department is where the ice cream is created. The prep area is where extras such as cherries and walnuts are added to make plain ice cream into "Cherry Garcia." And the pint department is where the ice cream is actually put into containers.

As the product is processed from one department to the next, the appropriate materials, labor, and overhead are added to it.

"The incoming ingredients from the shipping and receiving departments are stored in certain locations, either in a freezer or dry warehouse," says Beecher Eurich, staff accountant. "As ingredients get added, so do the costs associated with them." How much ice cream is actually produced? Running the plant around the clock, 24,000 pints are produced per 8-hour shift, or 72,000 pints per day.

Using the FIFO method, Eurich can tell you how much a certain batch of ice cream costs to make— its materials, labor, and overhead in each of the production departments. She generates reports for the production department heads, but makes sure not to overdo it. "You can get bogged down in numbers," says Eurich. "If you're generating a report that no one can use, then that's a waste of time." More likely, though, Ben & Jerry's production people want to know how efficient they are. Why? Many own stock in the company.

On the World Wide Web:
http://www.benjerry.com

CHAPTER 22

THE NAVIGATOR ✔

- ■ Understand *Concepts for Review* ☐
- ■ Read *Feature Story* ☐
- ■ Scan *Study Objectives* ☐
- ■ Read *Preview* ☐
- ■ Read text and answer *Before You Go On*
  p. 956 ☐ p. 968 ☐ p. 971 ☐
- ■ Work *Demonstration Problems* ☐
- ■ Review *Summary of Study Objectives* ☐
- ■ Answer *Self-Study Questions* ☐
- ■ Complete assignments ☐

PROCESS COST ACCOUNTING

STUDY OBJECTIVES

After studying this chapter, you should be able to:

1. *Explain the flow of costs in process cost accounting.*
2. *State the end-of-period procedures in process cost accounting.*
3. *Compute the physical units of production.*
4. *Compute equivalent units of production.*
5. *Indicate how unit costs are computed.*
6. *Explain the method and objective of assigning costs to units of output.*
7. *Prepare a production cost report.*
8. *Apply end-of-period procedures to a second process.*
9. *Explain just-in-time (JIT) processing.*
10. *Explain activity-based costing (ABC).*

THE NAVIGATOR

*T*he cost accounting system used by companies such as Ben & Jerry's is called process cost accounting. In contrast to job order cost accounting, which focuses on the individual job, process cost accounting focuses on the processes involved in producing homogeneous products. The primary objective of this chapter is to explain and illustrate process cost accounting. At the end of the chapter, two contemporary developments, just-in-time (JIT) processing and activity-based costing (ABC) are considered. The content and organization of this chapter are as follows:

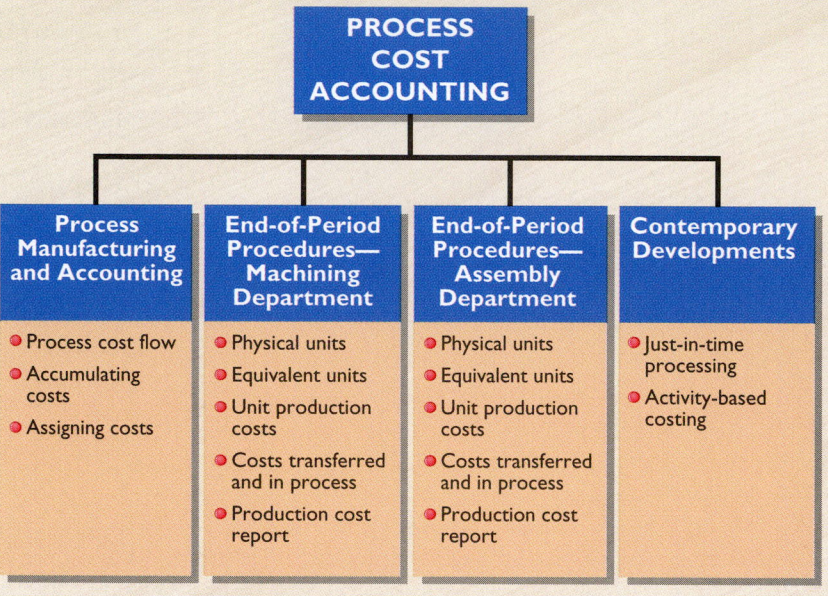

PROCESS MANUFACTURING AND ACCOUNTING

Continuous process manufacturing, sometimes referred to as mass production operations, occurs in producing such items as steel by USX Corp., cereals by Kellogg's, petroleum products by Exxon, and paint by Sherwin-Williams. One characteristic of this type of manufacturing is that **once the production begins, it continues until the finished product emerges**. For example, in a beverage company such as Coca-Cola, the process begins with the blending of the beverage. Next, the beverage is dispensed into bottles that are moved into position by automated machinery. The bottles are then capped, packaged, and forwarded to the finished goods warehouse.

A second characteristic of continuous process manufacturing is that **when the finished product emerges, all units will have been processed in the same manner with precisely the same amount of materials, labor, and overhead**. Each finished unit, such as a bottle of Coke, will therefore be indistinguishable one from another.

A process cost accounting system is used for continuous process manufacturing. In process cost accounting, as in a job order system, it is necessary to record both the accumulation and assignment of manufacturing costs. A distinc-

ACCOUNTING IN ACTION

Business Insight

The new General Motors Corporation assembly plants are missing a key element of traditional mass production: the assembly line. Instead, the company utilizes hundreds of automated, unmanned carriers to carry a car as it goes through the assembly process. With the carriers, each car follows a prescribed path, receiving instructions from computers through wires buried in the plant floor. Cars with extensive options are moved out of the main path until the options are installed.

ILLUSTRATION 22-1

Manufacturing processes and work in process accounts

tive feature of process cost accounting, however, is that **individual work in process accounts are maintained for each production department or manufacturing process**. For example, in a beverage company there would be a work in process account for each of the manufacturing processes, as illustrated below:

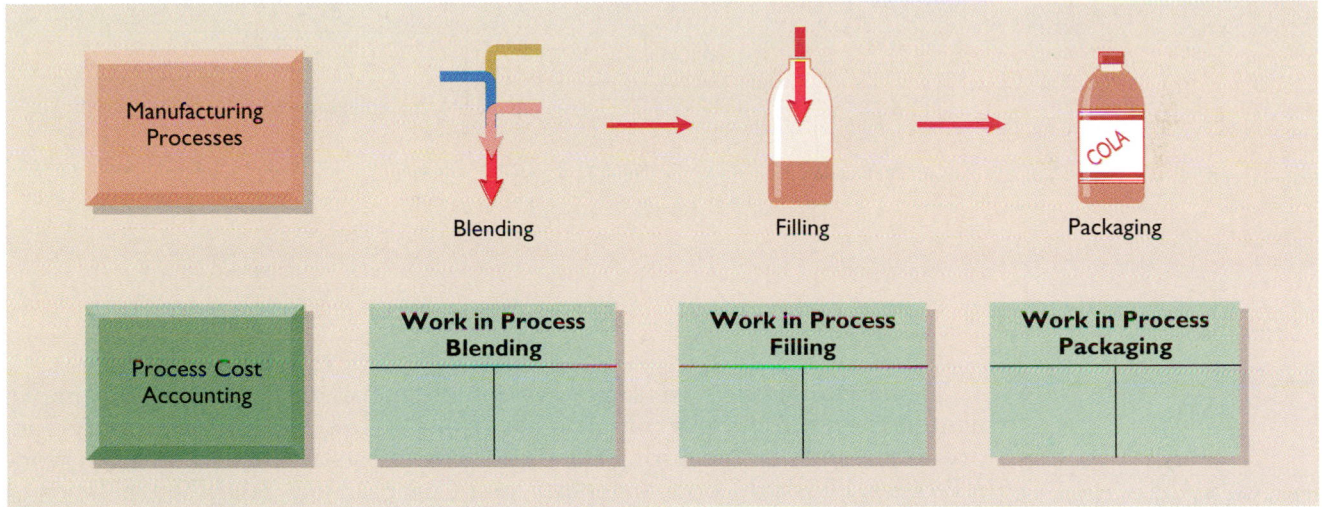

A second feature of process costing is that **costs charged to work in process are summarized in production cost reports rather than in job cost sheets**. There are also significant differences between process and job order cost accounting in determining total manufacturing costs and unit costs. In process cost accounting, **total costs are determined at the end of a period of time**, such as a month, rather than when a job is finished. **Unit costs are computed by dividing total manufacturing costs for the period by the units produced during the period.**

The major differences between job order cost accounting and process cost accounting are summarized in Illustration 22-2.

Feature	Job Order Cost Accounting	Process Cost Accounting
1. Work in process accounts	One for each job	One for each process
2. Summary of manufacturing costs	Job cost sheets	Production cost reports
3. Determination of total manufacturing costs	Each job	Each period
4. Unit cost computation	Cost of each job ÷ Units produced for the job	Total manufacturing costs ÷ Units produced during the period

ILLUSTRATION 22-2

Differences between job order and process cost accounting

Process Cost Flow

Illustration 22-3 shows one possible flow of costs in a process cost system. Note that separate work in process accounts are provided for each producing department.

ILLUSTRATION 22-3

Flow of costs in process cost system

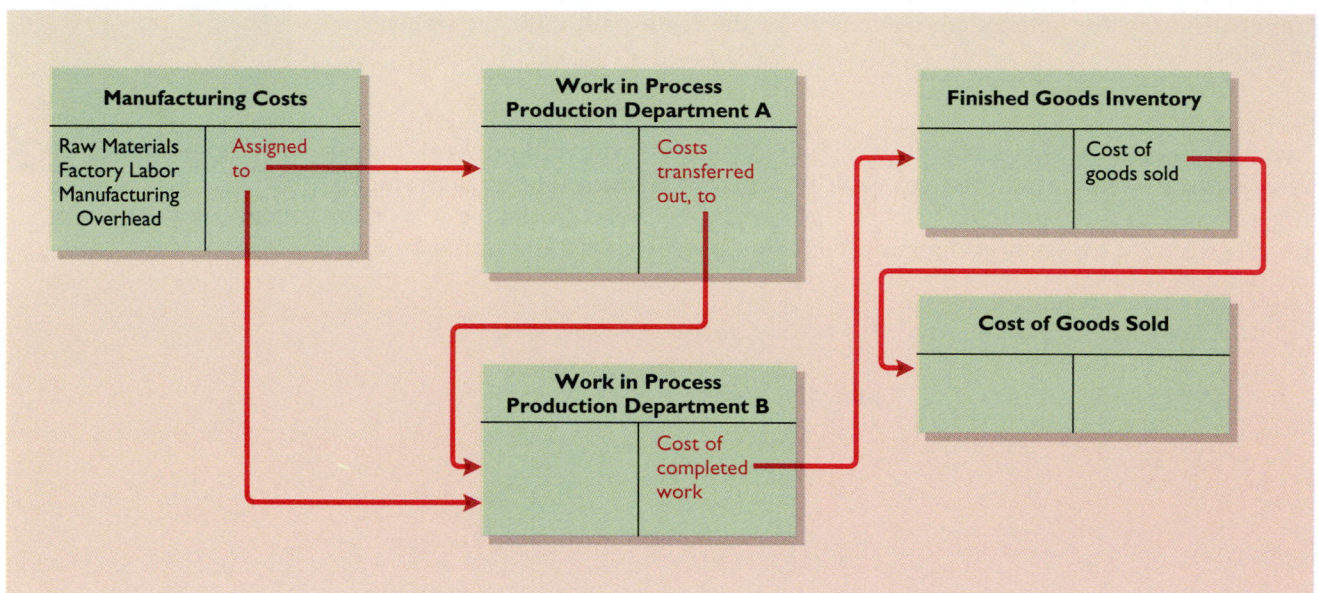

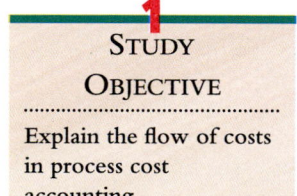

STUDY OBJECTIVE 1

Explain the flow of costs in process cost accounting.

The flow of costs is the same as in job order cost accounting. For example, manufacturing costs are accumulated by debits to Raw Materials Inventory, Factory Labor, and Manufacturing Overhead. These costs are then assigned to Work in Process, Finished Goods Inventory, and Cost of Goods Sold. The methods of assigning costs, however, differ significantly. These differences are explained and illustrated later in the chapter. Illustration 22-4 provides a more detailed analysis of the flow of costs in a process cost system.

The entries pertaining to the accumulation and assignment of costs are explained in the following pages, using the June transactions of Tyler Manufacturing Company. The entries are keyed to the numbers in Illustration 22-4. Tyler Company manufactures automatic can openers that are sold to retail outlets. Manufacturing consists of two processes: machining and assembly. In the Machining Department, the raw materials are shaped, honed, and drilled. In the Assembly Department, the parts are assembled and packaged. On June 1, the ledger includes the following balances:

| Raw Materials Inventory | $24,000 | Work in Process—Machining | $ –0– |
| Finished Goods Inventory | 6,000 | Work in Process—Assembly | 3,600 |

Accumulation of Manufacturing Costs

Each of the three manufacturing cost elements presented in Chapter 20—direct materials, direct labor, and overhead—occurs in a process cost system. **The accumulation of the costs of materials and labor is the same in process costing as in job order costing.** All raw materials are debited to Raw Materials Inventory

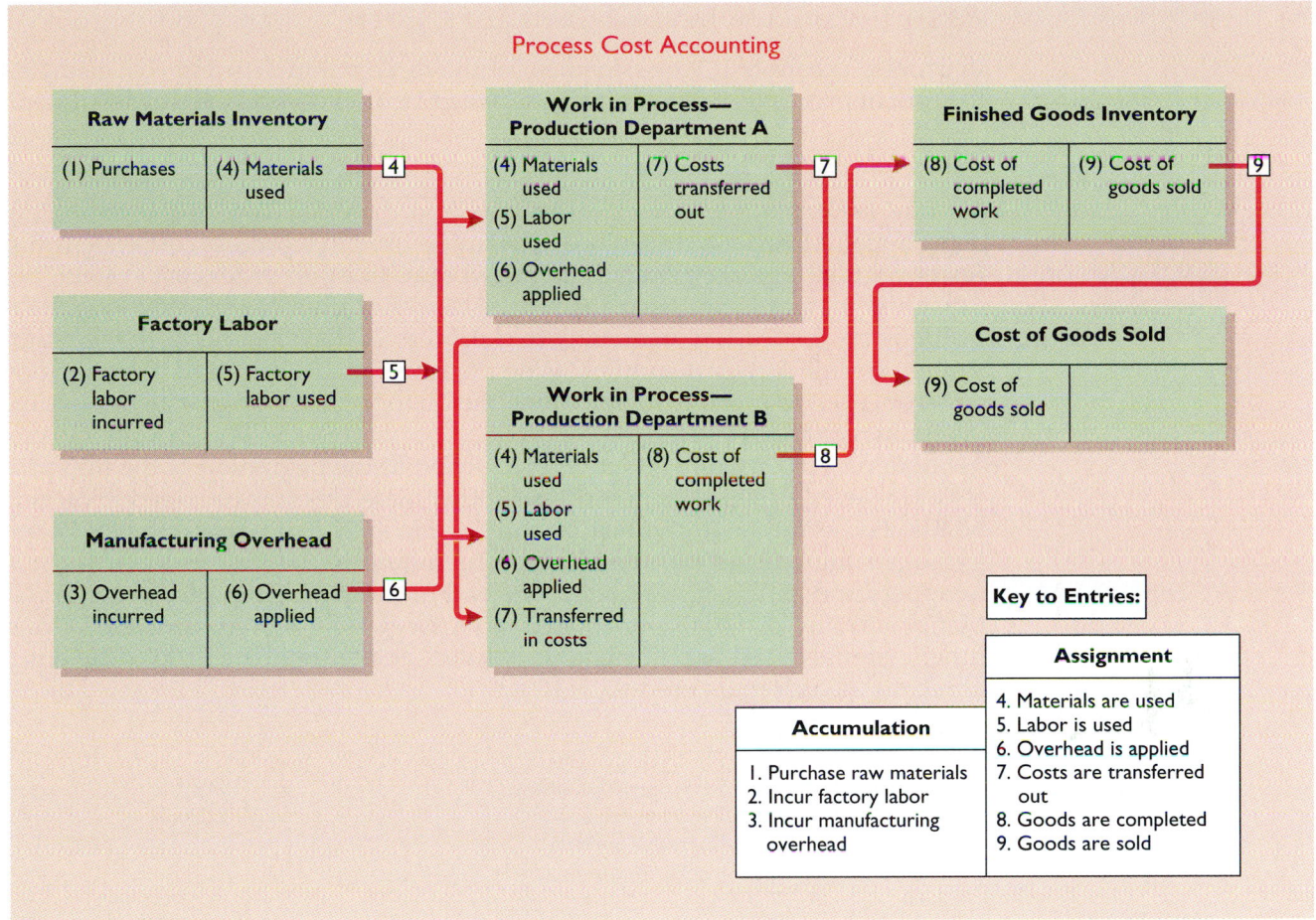

ILLUSTRATION 22-4

Detailed flow of costs in process cost accounting

when the materials are purchased. Similarly, all factory labor is debited to Factory Labor when the labor costs are incurred. In the month of June, Tyler Manufacturing purchases $17,000 of raw materials and incurs $20,400 of factory labor. The summary entries for these costs are as follows:

		(1)		
June 30	Raw Materials Inventory		17,000	
	Accounts Payable			17,000
	(To record purchases of raw materials on account)			

		(2)		
June 30	Factory Labor		20,400	
	Wages Payable			20,400
	(To record factory labor costs)			

The accumulation of manufacturing overhead costs may also be the same as in job order costing. That is, overhead costs are debited to Manufacturing Overhead as they are incurred. During June, overhead costs were $41,800 in Tyler Manufacturing. The summary entry to record these costs is:

		(3)		
June 30	Manufacturing Overhead		41,800	
	Cash (Accounts Payable, etc.)			41,800
	(To record overhead incurred)			

Assignment of Manufacturing Costs

In process accounting the assignment of the three manufacturing cost elements to work in process is different from the assignment of costs in a job order system.

Materials Costs

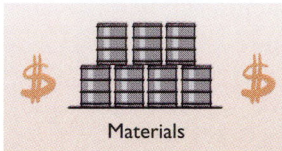

Materials

All raw materials issued for production are a materials cost to the producing department. Materials requisition slips may be used in a process cost system, but **fewer requisitions are generally required than in a job order cost system, because the materials are used for processes rather than for specific jobs**. Requisitions are issued less frequently in a process cost system because the requisitions are for larger quantities. When a raw material is used by only one department, it is possible to determine the quantity used by making a physical inventory count.

Materials are usually added to production at the beginning of the first process. However, in subsequent processes, other materials may be added at various points. For example, in the manufacture of Hershey candy bars, the chocolate and other ingredients are added at the beginning of the first process, and the wrappers and cartons are added at the end of the packaging process. At Tyler Manufacturing, materials are entered at the beginning of each process. During June, materials used are: Machining, $15,000, and Assembly, $4,000. The entry to record the materials used is:

	(4)		
June 30	Work in Process—Machining	15,000	
	Work in Process—Assembly	4,000	
	Raw Materials Inventory		19,000
	(To record materials used)		

In our ice cream story at the beginning of the chapter, materials are added in three departments: milk and flavoring in the mixing department; extras such as cherries and walnuts in the prepping department; and cardboard containers in the pinting (packaging) department.

Factory Labor Costs

Factory Labor

In process costing, as in job order costing, time tickets may be used in determining the cost of labor assignable to the production departments. Since labor costs are assigned to a process rather than a job, the labor cost chargeable to a process can be obtained from the payroll register or departmental payroll summaries.

All labor costs incurred within a producing department are a cost of processing the raw materials. Thus, labor costs for the Machining Department will include the wages of employees who shape, hone, and drill the raw materials. During June, the labor costs in Tyler Manufacturing are: Machining $14,000 and Assembly $6,400. The entry to assign these costs is:

	(5)		
June 30	Work in Process—Machining	14,000	
	Work in Process—Assembly	6,400	
	Factory Labor		20,400
	(To assign factory labor to production)		

Manufacturing Overhead Costs

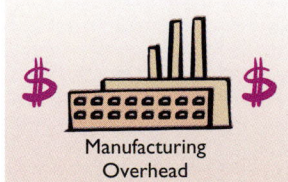

Manufacturing Overhead

The objective in assigning overhead in process cost accounting is to allocate the overhead costs to the production departments on an objective and equitable basis. That basis is the activity that "drives" or causes the costs. For most compa-

ACCOUNTING IN ACTION
Business Insight

In one of Caterpillar's automated cost centers, work is fed into the cost center, processed by robotic machines, and transferred to the next cost center without human intervention. One person tends all of the machines and spends more time maintaining machines than operating them. In such cases, overhead rates based on direct labor hours may be misleading. Surprisingly, some companies continue to assign manufacturing overhead on the basis of direct labor despite the fact that there is no cause-and-effect relationship between labor and overhead.

nies, today, the primary driver of overhead costs in continuous manufacturing operations is **machine time used**, not direct labor. Thus, **machine hours are widely used** in allocating manufacturing overhead costs.

To illustrate the assignment of overhead costs, we will assume in Tyler Manufacturing that overhead is charged to production departments at the rate of $10 per machine hour. In June, machine hours were 2,280 in the Machining Department and 1,820 in the Assembly Department. Thus, the entry to allocate overhead to the two processes is:

		(6)		
June 30		Work in Process—Machining	22,800	
		Work in Process—Assembly	18,200	
		Manufacturing Overhead		41,000
		(To assign overhead to processes)		

After the foregoing entries are posted, the work in process accounts of Tyler Manufacturing Company show the data indicated in Illustration 22-5. The ques-

ILLUSTRATION 22-5

Work in process accounts

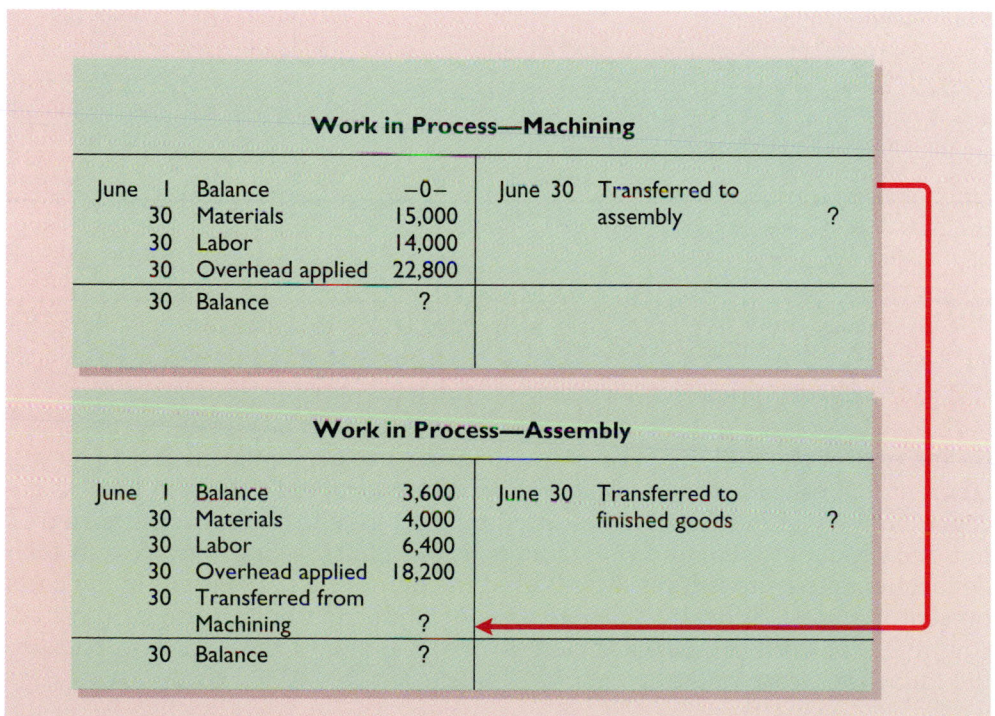

Work in Process—Machining

June	1	Balance	–0–	June 30	Transferred to assembly	?
	30	Materials	15,000			
	30	Labor	14,000			
	30	Overhead applied	22,800			
	30	Balance	?			

Work in Process—Assembly

June	1	Balance	3,600	June 30	Transferred to finished goods	?
	30	Materials	4,000			
	30	Labor	6,400			
	30	Overhead applied	18,200			
	30	Transferred from Machining	?			
	30	Balance	?			

HELPFUL HINT
When should overhead be applied on the basis of machine hours? Answer: When machine hours "drive" overhead costs; i.e., when there is a cause-and-effect relationship between machine hours and overhead.

tion marks indicate the amounts that are yet to be determined. The answers to the question marks are obtained through special end-of-period procedures explained in the following sections.

Before You Go On . . .

Review It

1. What type of manufacturing companies might use a process cost accounting system?
2. What are the principal differences between job order cost accounting and process cost accounting?

Do It

Ruth Company manufactures ZEBO through two processes: Blending and Bottling. In June, raw materials used were Blending $18,000 and Bottling $4,000; factory labor costs were Blending $12,000 and Bottling $5,000. Journalize the assignment of these costs to the two processes.

Reasoning: In process cost accounting, separate work in process accounts are kept for each process. Raw materials are accumulated in the account titled Raw Materials Inventory. Factory labor is accumulated in the account titled Factory Labor. These accounts are credited when the costs are assigned to production.

   Solution: The entries are:

Work in Process—Blending	18,000	
Work in Process—Bottling	4,000	
Raw Materials Inventory		22,000
(To record materials used)		
Work in Process—Blending	12,000	
Work in Process—Bottling	5,000	
Factory Labor		17,000
(To assign factory labor to production)		

Related exercise material: BE22–1, BE22–2, BE22–3, and E22–10.

THE
NAVIGATOR

END-OF-PERIOD PROCEDURES— MACHINING DEPARTMENT

2

STUDY

OBJECTIVE

State the end-of-period procedures in process cost accounting.

By the end of the period, Tyler Manufacturing has accumulated the materials, labor, and overhead costs in each production department's work in process account. Now Tyler must assign these accumulated costs to (1) the units transferred out of each department and (2) the units in the ending work in process in each department. The procedures (steps) used in computing and assigning the costs present the most difficult challenge to your understanding of process cost accounting. For each process, it is necessary at the end of the period to perform the following procedures:

1. Compute the physical units.
2. Compute equivalent units of production.

3. Compute unit costs of production.
4. Assign costs to the units transferred and in process.
5. Prepare the production cost report.

We will explain these procedures in detail. First, we will make all of the required computations for the Machining Department of Tyler Manufacturing. Then we will explain the computations for the Assembly Department.

Computing Physical Units

Physical units are the actual units to be accounted for during a period irrespective of any work performed. To keep track of these units, it is necessary to add the units started (or transferred) into production during the period to the units in process at the beginning of the period. This amount is referred to as the **total units to be accounted for**.

These units then are accounted for by the output of the period, which consists of units transferred out during the period and any units in process at the end of the period. This amount is referred to as the **total units accounted for**. Illustration 22-6 shows the flow of physical units for Tyler Manufacturing for the month of June for both the Machining and Assembly Departments.

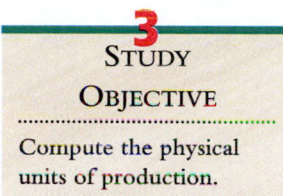

STUDY OBJECTIVE

Compute the physical units of production.

ILLUSTRATION 22-6

Production data in units

Tyler Manufacturing Company

	Machining Department	Assembly Department	
Work in process, June 1	–0–	500	(40% complete)
Started (transferred) into production	10,000	8,000	
Total units to be accounted for	10,000	8,500	
Transferred out	8,000	8,100 *	
Work in process, June 30	2,000 (60% complete)	400 (75% complete)	
Total units accounted for	10,000	8,500	
*Transferred to finished goods			

The records indicate that 10,000 units must be accounted for in the Machining Department. Of this sum, 8,000 units were transferred to the Assembly Department and 2,000 units are still in process. A similar record is made in the Assembly Department, where the units to be accounted for include the units transferred in from the Machining Department.

The percentages pertaining to the units in work in process in Illustration 22-6 refer to the percentage of completion of the units. The percentages are not relevant in accounting for physical units, but they are needed in the other end-of-period procedures.

Computing Equivalent Units of Production

Once the physical flow of the units is established, it is necessary to measure each department's productivity in terms of **equivalent units of production**. Equiva-

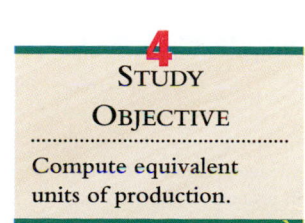

STUDY OBJECTIVE

Compute equivalent units of production.

lent units of production are the work done during the period on the physical units of output, expressed in terms of fully completed units. For example, if a department's output consists entirely of 4,000 units of work in process that are 60% complete, equivalent units of production are 2,400 (4,000 × 60%).

ACCOUNTING IN ACTION
Business Insight

An example of equivalent units close to home: Your university probably expresses enrollment statistics in terms of equivalent full-time students, in addition to keeping tabs of the total number of students. For example, a student taking 9 hours of course work when 15 hours is considered full-time would be counted as a 60% equivalent full-time student. Two half-time students would be counted as one equivalent full-time student. This information is of particular use when the school is projecting tuition income and planning departmental staffing needs.

Equivalent units of production are determined by applying the percentage of work done to the physical units of output. Equivalent units are the sum of the work performed to:

1. Finish the units of beginning work in process inventory.
2. Complete the units started into production during the period.
3. Start, but only partially complete, the units in ending work in process inventory.

Normally, in continuous processing, some units will always be in process at both the beginning and end of the period.

Equivalent Units for Materials

HELPFUL HINT
Materials are not always added at the beginning of the process. For example, materials are sometimes added uniformly during the process.

At Tyler Manufacturing, materials are entered at the beginning of each process, and conversion costs (labor and overhead) are incurred uniformly during the process. Thus, two computations of equivalent units are required: one for materials and the other for conversion costs. From the production data given in Illustration 22-6, we know that the 2,000 units in ending work in process are 60% complete. **This percentage pertains only to conversion costs.** The percentage of completion for materials is not stated, because in this case it is 100%. The computation of equivalent units for materials is as follows:

ILLUSTRATION 22-7

Computation of equivalent units—materials

	Machining Department		
Production Data	Physical Units	Materials Added This Period	Equivalent Units
Work in process, June 1	–0–	–0–	–0–
Started and finished	8,000	100%	8,000
Work in process, June 30	2,000	100%	2,000
Total	10,000		10,000

HELPFUL HINT
If 30,000 units are started into production and 5,000 units are in process at the end of the period, how many units were started and finished? Answer: 25,000 (30,000 − 5,000)

In the Machining Department, the equivalent units for materials (10,000) equal the physical units to be accounted for (10,000).

The term **units started and finished** may be confusing. **It means the number of units that were both started and completed during the period.** As a consequence, the units in work in process at the beginning and at the end of the period are not included in "units started and finished." The easiest way to compute the units started and finished is to determine the units of completed work transferred out of the department and subtract the units in work in process at the beginning of the period. The computation for the Machining Department is as follows:

Units transferred out	8,000
Less: Units of work in process, June 1	–0–
Units started and finished	**8,000**

ILLUSTRATION 22-8

Computation of units started and finished

Note that the units in ending work in process are ignored in determining the units started and finished.

Equivalent Units for Conversion Costs

The computation of equivalent units for conversion costs is basically the same as for material costs, as illustrated below:

Machining Department			
Production Data	Physical Units	Work Added This Period	Equivalent Units
Work in process, June 1	–0–	–0–	–0–
Started and finished	8,000	100%	**8,000**
Work in process, June 30	2,000	60%	**1,200**
Total	10,000		**9,200**

ILLUSTRATION 22-9

Computation of equivalent units—conversion costs

Alternatively, the graphic in Illustration 22-10 may be used in computing the equivalent units of conversion costs:

Machining Department				
Production Data	Physical Units	Work Added This Period	%	Equivalent Units
Work in process, June 1	–0–		–0–	–0–
Started and finished	8,000		100	**8,000**
Work in process, June 30	2,000		60	**1,200**
Total	10,000			**9,200**
		0% 20 40 60 80 100%		

ILLUSTRATION 22-10

Equivalent units for conversion costs—graphic illustration

Note in this case, that equivalent units (9,200), do not equal the physical units to be accounted for (10,000).

Computing Unit Production Costs

Armed with knowledge of the equivalent units of production, we can now compute the unit production costs. **Unit production costs** are costs expressed in terms of equivalent units of production. When equivalent units of production are different for materials and conversion costs, three unit costs are computed: (1) materials, (2) conversion, and (3) total manufacturing.

As shown in Illustration 22-5, costs in June for the Machining Department are materials $15,000 and conversion costs $36,800 (labor $14,000 plus overhead $22,800). The formulas and computations of the unit costs are as follows:

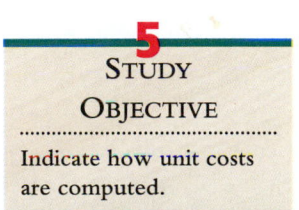

5
STUDY
OBJECTIVE
....
Indicate how unit costs are computed.

ILLUSTRATION 22-11

*Unit cost formulas and
computations—Machining
Department*

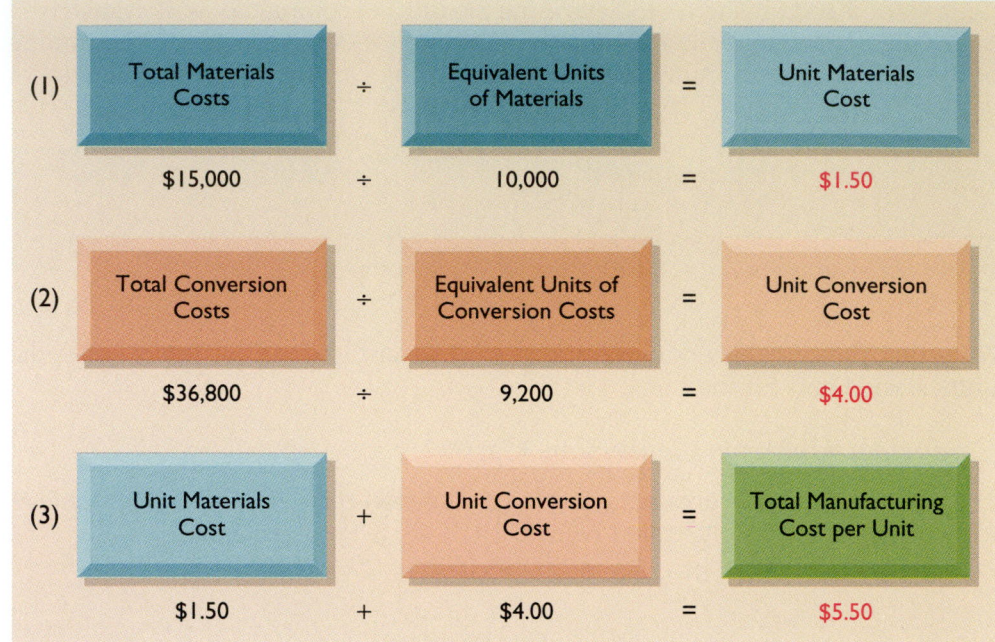

When equivalent units of production are the same for materials and conversion costs, it is necessary to compute only the total manufacturing cost per unit. The computation is total manufacturing cost divided by equivalent units of production.

6

STUDY

OBJECTIVE

....

Explain the method and
objective of assigning
costs to units of output.

Assigning Costs to Units Transferred and in Process

Our next task is to determine the total cost of the units transferred out in June and the total cost of the units in ending work in process at June 30. To obtain these amounts, unit costs are assigned to the equivalent units of production for the period. The computations for the Machining Department are shown in Illustration 22-12. Note that total manufacturing cost per unit, $5.50, is used in costing the units started and finished. In contrast, the unit cost of materials and the unit cost of conversion are needed in costing the units in process. As indicated in the schedule, **the total costs charged to the department must equal the total costs accounted for**.

ILLUSTRATION 22-12

*Assignment of costs—
Machining Department*

Machining Department

Costs Charged to Department		Assignment of Costs	Equivalent Units	Unit Cost		Costs Accounted For
		Transferred out				
Materials	$15,000	Work in process, June 1				$ –0–
Conversion costs	36,800	Started and finished	8,000	$5.50		44,000
	$51,800	Work in process, June 30				44,000
		Materials	2,000	$1.50	3,000	
		Conversion costs	1,200	$4.00	4,800	7,800
						$51,800

When the costs have been assigned, an entry is needed to record the cost of goods transferred out of the department. In this case, the transfer is to the Assembly Department, and the following entry is made:

	(7)			
June 30	Work in Process—Assembly		44,000	
	Work in Process—Machining			44,000
	(To record transfer of 8,000 units to the Assembly Department)			

Preparing the Production Cost Report

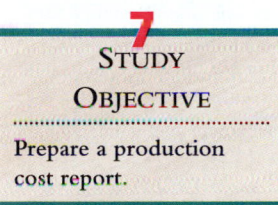

7 STUDY OBJECTIVE

Prepare a production cost report.

The final end-of-period procedure is the preparation of a **production cost report**, as shown in Illustration 22-13. This is an internal report for management that shows **production quantity and cost data** for a production department. In the opening story, the staff accountant prepares the production cost report for each department in Ben & Jerry's.

ILLUSTRATION 22-13

Production cost report— Machining Department

TYLER MANUFACTURING COMPANY
Machining Department
Production Cost Report
For the Month Ended June 30, 1999

		Equivalent Units	
	Physical Units	Materials	Conversion Costs
	Step 1		Step 2
QUANTITIES			
Units charged to department			
In process, June 1	–0–		
Started into production	10,000		
Total units charged	10,000		
Units accounted for			
Transferred out			
In process, June 1	–0–	–0–	–0–
Started and finished	8,000	8,000	8,000
Total	8,000	8,000	8,000
In process, June 30	2,000	2,000	1,200 (2,000 × 60%)
Total units accounted for	10,000	10,000	9,200

COSTS

		Materials	Conversion Costs	Total
Unit costs Step 3				
Costs in June	(a)	$15,000	$36,800	$51,800
Equivalent units	(b)	10,000	9,200	
Unit costs (a) ÷ (b)		$1.50	$4.00	$5.50

Costs charged to department		
In process, June 1		$ –0–
Costs in June		51,800
Total costs charged		$51,800

Costs accounted for Step 4			
Transferred out			
In process, June 1			$ –0–
Started and finished (8,000 × $5.50)			44,000	$44,000
In process, June 30			
Materials (2,000 × $1.50)		3,000	
Conversion costs (1,200 × $4.00)		4,800	7,800
Total costs accounted for			$51,800

The production cost report has the following sections: (1) Units charged to department, (2) Units accounted for, (3) Unit costs, (4) Costs charged to department, and (5) Costs accounted for. The production cost report for the Machining Department of Tyler Manufacturing was shown in Illustration 22-13. All of the end-of-period procedures (steps 1 thru 4) are identified in the report. As shown, the **total physical units accounted for must equal the total units charged to the department**. Similarly, **the total costs accounted for must equal the total costs charged to the department**.

Production cost reports provide a basis for evaluating the productivity of a department. In addition, the cost data can be used to assess whether unit costs and total costs are reasonable. When the quantity and cost data are compared with predetermined goals, top management can also ascertain whether current performance is meeting planned objectives.

END-OF-PERIOD PROCEDURES— ASSEMBLY DEPARTMENT

Computing Physical Units

8 STUDY OBJECTIVE

Apply end-of-period procedures to a second process.

The physical units to be accounted for in the Assembly Department are determined in the same manner as in the Machining Department. From the Tyler Manufacturing production data presented earlier, the physical units for the Assembly Department are shown in Illustration 22-14.

ILLUSTRATION 22-14

Production data in physical units

Assembly Department	Units
Work in process, June 1 (40% complete)	500
Transferred in	8,000
Total units to be accounted for	8,500
Transferred out	8,100
Work in process, June 30 (75% complete)	400
Units accounted for	8,500

In this case the units transferred out (8,100) plus the units in ending work in process (400) equal the total units to be accounted for (8,500).

Computing Equivalent Units of Production

The equivalent units of production for the Assembly Department are computed in the same way as for the Machining Department. However, the presence of a beginning work in process adds a new dimension to process cost accounting.

When there are units in process at the beginning of the period, it is necessary to **identify the cost flow assumption** to be used. We will use the first-in, first-out (FIFO) costing method in this text and in homework problems. As indicated in the opening story, this is the method used by Ben & Jerry's in costing batches of ice cream. Other methods are discussed in cost accounting courses.

Under the **FIFO costing method**, the computation of equivalent units of production (as well as the computation of unit production costs and the assignment of costs to units transferred out and in process) is done on a first-in, first-out basis. The FIFO cost flow assumption usually corresponds to the actual physical flow of the goods because beginning work in process is normally completed before new work is started. This assumption affects the determination of equivalent units as follows:

1. The first units finished during the current period are the units in beginning work in process. Thus, units started and finished during the current period are the units transferred out minus the units in beginning work in process. For the Assembly Department, units started and finished in June are 7,600 (8,100 − 500).
2. Only the work required to finish the units of beginning work in process is included in the equivalent units of production for the current period.

Equivalent Units for Materials

Since materials are entered at the beginning of the process, no additional materials costs are required to complete the beginning work in process. In addition, 100% of the materials costs has been incurred on the ending work in process. Thus, the computation of equivalent units for materials is as follows:

	Assembly Department		
Production Data	Physical Units	Materials Added This Period	Equivalent Units
Work in process, June 1	500	–0–	–0–
Started and finished	7,600	100%	7,600
Work in process, June 30	400	100%	400
Total	8,500		8,000

ILLUSTRATION 22-15

Computation of equivalent units—materials

Equivalent units can also be determined graphically as was shown in Illustration 22-10.

Equivalent Units for Conversion Costs

The 500 units of beginning work in process were 40% complete in terms of conversion costs. Thus, 300 equivalent units (60% × 500 units) of conversion costs were required to complete the beginning inventory. In addition, the 400 units of ending work in process were 75% complete in terms of conversion costs. Thus the equivalent units for conversion costs is 8,200, computed as follows:

	Assembly Department		
Production Data	Physical Units	Work Added This Period	Equivalent Units
Work in process, June 1	500	60%	300
Started and finished	7,600	100%	7,600
Work in process, June 30	400	75%	300
Total	8,500		8,200

ILLUSTRATION 22-16

Computation of equivalent units—conversion costs

Computing Unit Costs of Production

The production costs chargeable to the Assembly Department in June consist of the following debits to work in process.

ILLUSTRATION 22-17

Costs charged to Assembly Department

Work in Process—Assembly Department		
June 1 Balance	3,600	
30 Materials	4,000	
30 Labor	6,400	
30 Overhead	18,200	
30 Transferred from Machining Dept.	44,000	
Total	**76,200**	

Our objective is to determine the unit costs of production for the month of June. **Under the FIFO method, this determination is based entirely on the production costs incurred on work done during the month.** Thus, the costs in the beginning work in process are not relevant, because they were incurred on work done in the preceding month.

HELPFUL HINT

In a second department, total materials costs equals the sum of (1) materials added in the department plus (2) costs transferred in.

The June costs for the Assembly Department include the same types of costs as in the Machining Department with one exception: the costs tranferred in from the Machining Department. **Transferred-in costs are recognized as materials cost to the receiving department.** At Tyler Manufacturing, these costs are a cost to the Assembly Department. Therefore, total materials costs are $48,000 (materials added by the Assembly Department $4,000 + the transferred-in costs $44,000). Conversion costs total $24,600 (labor $6,400 + overhead $18,200). The computations of unit costs in the Assembly Department are as follows:

ILLUSTRATION 22-18

Unit cost formulas and computations—Assembly Department

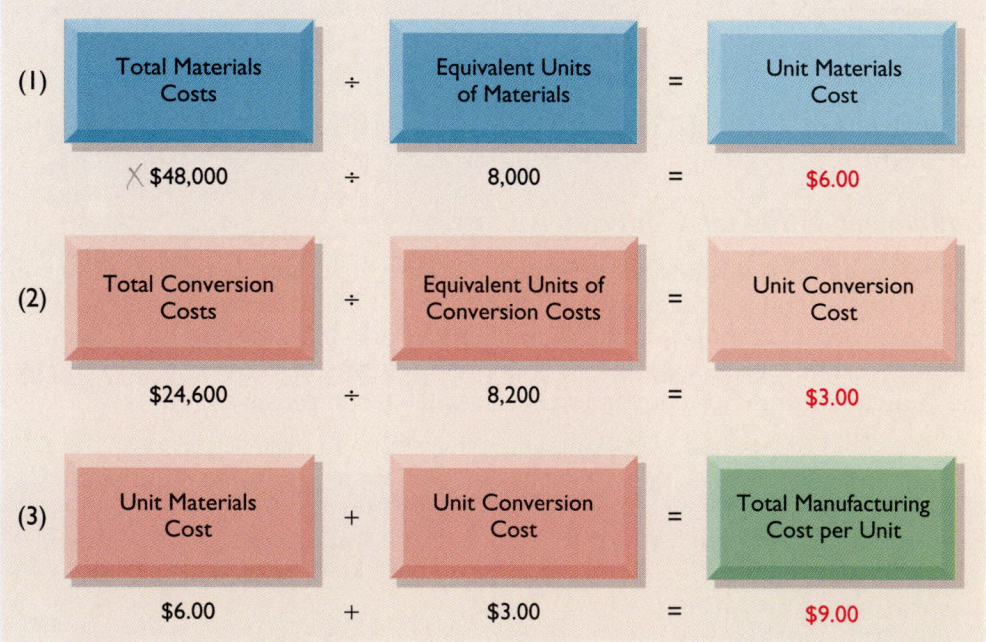

As shown, the unit costs are $6.00 for materials, $3.00 for conversion costs, and $9.00 for total manufacturing costs.

Assigning Costs to Units Transferred and in Process

Under the FIFO method, the first goods to be completed during the period are the units in beginning work in process. Thus, the cost of the beginning work

ACCOUNTING IN ACTION
Business Insight

Chrysler Corp.'s low product development costs made it the lowest-cost automotive producer in the world, according to the *Harbour Report* published by Harbour & Associates Inc., a Troy, Michigan, consulting firm. The finding was based on the total cost of both product development and vehicle assembly. Among the Big Three auto makers, Ford leads in efficiency of assembly operations. The comparative costs of assembling a vehicle in a recent year were Ford $1,563, Chrysler $1,872, and GM $2,358.

in process is always assigned to the goods transferred to finished goods (or to the next department). The FIFO method also means that ending work in process will be assigned only production costs that are incurred in the current period. The assignment of the manufacturing costs in the Assembly Department is shown in Illustration 22-19.

ILLUSTRATION 22-19

Assignment of costs— Assembly Department

Costs Charged to Department	Assignment of Costs	Equivalent Units	Unit Cost		Costs Accounted For
(See Ilustration 22-17 for computation.)	Transferred out				
	Work in process, June 1			$3,600	
$76,200	Conversion costs	300	$3.00	900	$ 4,500
	Started and finished	7,600	$9.00		68,400
	Ending work in process				72,900
	Materials	400	$6.00	2,400	
	Conversion costs	300	$3.00	900	3,300
					$76,200

Again, you can see that the costs assigned ($72,900 + $3,300) equal the costs to be assigned ($76,200). In this case, the total costs assigned to units transferred out can be obtained by multiplying the units (8,100) by the unit cost of the goods started and finished ($9.00). This procedure is valid only if there has been no change in unit costs between the preceding and current months. In solving homework problems, the step-by-step approach should be followed.

The units completed in the Assembly Department are transferred to the finished goods warehouse. The entry for this transfer is:

		(8)		
June 30	Finished Goods Inventory		72,900	
	Work in Process—Assembly			72,900
	(To record transfer of 8,100 units to finished goods)			

Preparing the Production Cost Report

The procedure for preparing a production report is the same for every department. The report for the Assembly Department is shown in Illustration 22-20. As in the report for the Machining Department, **the total physical units accounted for must equal the units charged to the department.** Similarly, the **total costs accounted for must equal the total costs charged to the department.**

ETHICS NOTE

Because production cost reports are used as the basis for evaluating department productivity and efficiency, the units, costs, and computations reported therein should be independently accumulated and analyzed to prevent misstatements by department managers.

TYLER MANUFACTURING COMPANY
Assembly Department
Production Cost Report
For the Month Ended June 30, 1999

		Equivalent Units		
	Physical Units	Materials	Conversion Costs	
QUANTITIES	Step 1		Step 2	
Units charged to department				
In process, June 1	500			
Transferred in	8,000			
Total units charged	8,500			
Units accounted for				
Transferred out				
In process, June 1	500	–0–	300	(500 × 60%)
Started and finished	7,600	7,600	7,600	
Total	8,100	7,600	7,900	
In process, June 30	400	400	300	(400 × 75%)
Total units accounted for	8,500	8,000	8,200	

COSTS				
			Conversion	
Unit costs Step 3		Materials	Costs	Total
Costs in June	(a)	$48,000	$24,600	$72,600
Equivalent units	(b)	8,000	8,200	
Unit costs (a) ÷ (b)		$6.00	$3.00	$9.00
Costs charged to department				
In process, June 1				$ 3,600
Costs in June				72,600
Total costs charged				$76,200
Costs accounted for Step 4				
Transferred out				
In process, June 1		$ 3,600		
Conversion costs (300 × $3.00)		900	$ 4,500	
Started and finished (7,600 × $9.00)			68,400	$72,900
In process, June 30				
Materials (400 × $6.00)			2,400	
Conversion costs (300 × $3.00)			900	3,300
Total costs accounted for				$76,200

ILLUSTRATION 22-20

Production cost report—
Assembly Department

Process Cost Flow Summary

The flow of costs in process cost accounting was graphically presented in Illustrations 22-3 and 22-4 earlier in this chapter (pages 952 and 953). The ledger accounts after posting the nine June transactions of Tyler Manufacturing Company and the flow of documents are shown in Illustration 22-21.

Each posting is based on journal entries illustrated earlier except for the posting pertaining to the cost of goods sold. Data for this entry are obtained from finished goods perpetual inventory records. Assuming 6,000 of the can openers

ILLUSTRATION 22-21

*Process cost accounts and
document flow*

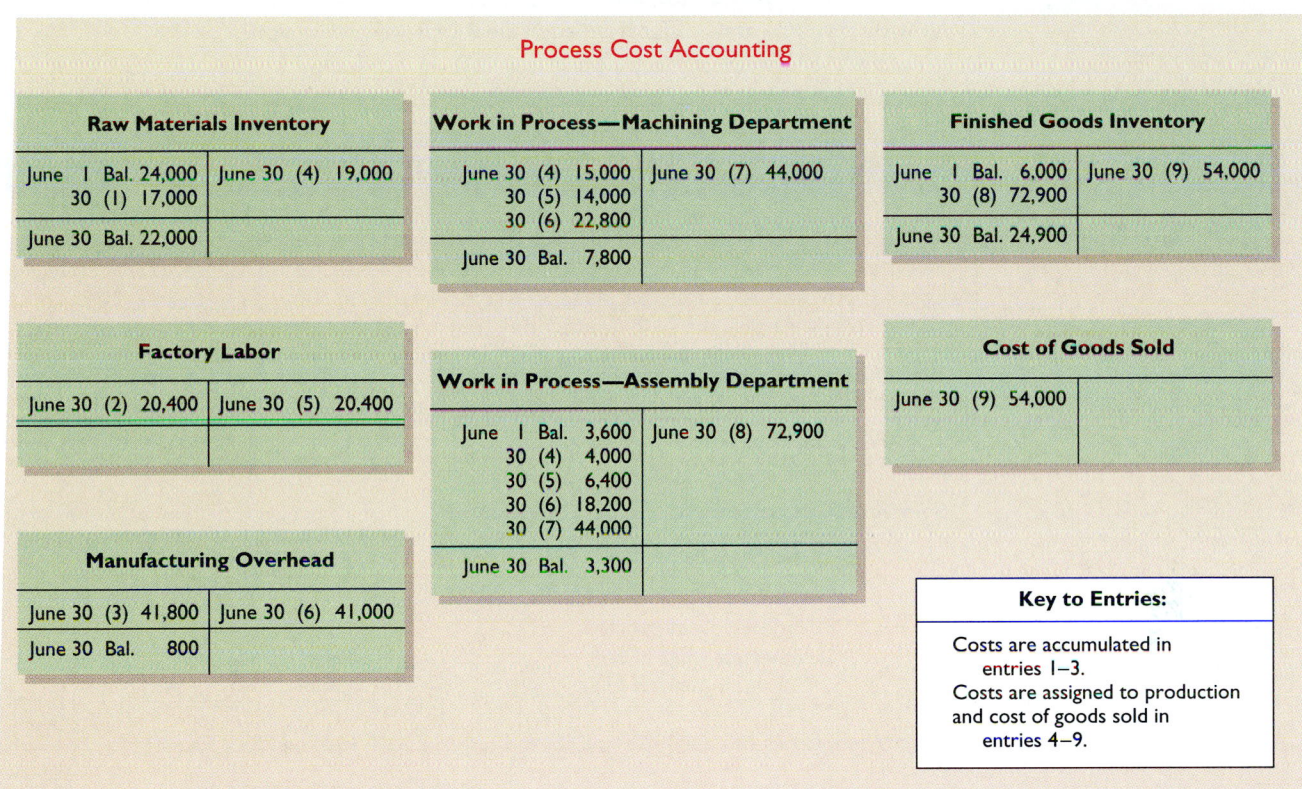

Process Cost Accounting

Raw Materials Inventory

June 1 Bal. 24,000	June 30 (4) 19,000
30 (1) 17,000	
June 30 Bal. 22,000	

Work in Process—Machining Department

June 30 (4) 15,000	June 30 (7) 44,000
30 (5) 14,000	
30 (6) 22,800	
June 30 Bal. 7,800	

Finished Goods Inventory

June 1 Bal. 6,000	June 30 (9) 54,000
30 (8) 72,900	
June 30 Bal. 24,900	

Factory Labor

June 30 (2) 20,400	June 30 (5) 20,400

Work in Process—Assembly Department

June 1 Bal. 3,600	June 30 (8) 72,900
30 (4) 4,000	
30 (5) 6,400	
30 (6) 18,200	
30 (7) 44,000	
June 30 Bal. 3,300	

Cost of Goods Sold

June 30 (9) 54,000	

Manufacturing Overhead

June 30 (3) 41,800	June 30 (6) 41,000
June 30 Bal. 800	

Key to Entries:

Costs are accumulated in
entries 1–3.
Costs are assigned to production
and cost of goods sold in
entries 4–9.

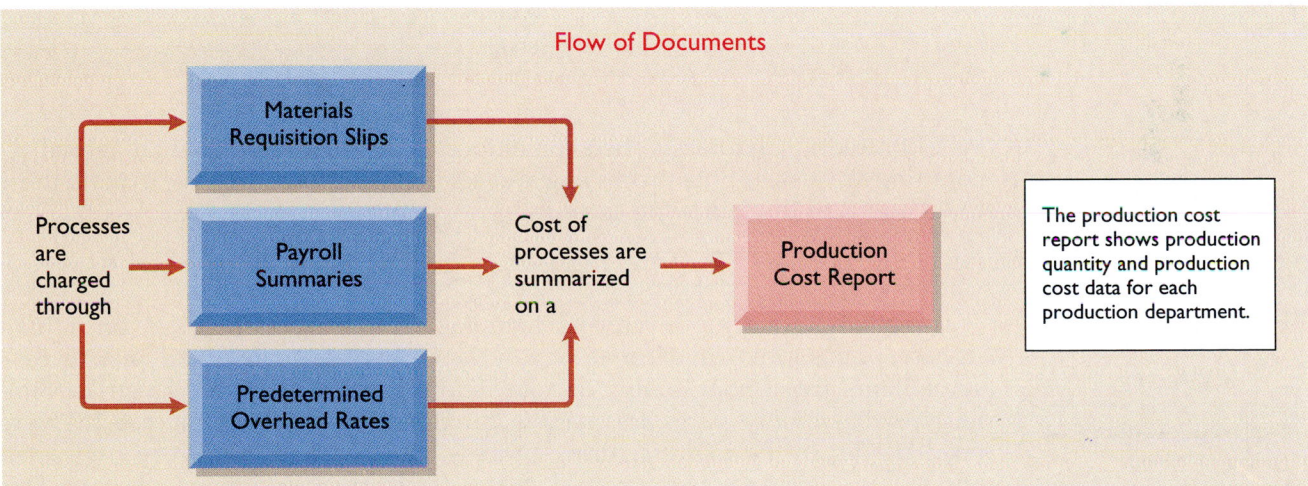

Flow of Documents

Processes are charged through → Materials Requisition Slips / Payroll Summaries / Predetermined Overhead Rates → Cost of processes are summarized on a → Production Cost Report

The production cost report shows production quantity and production cost data for each production department.

costing $9.00 each are sold in June, the entry to record the cost of goods sold is as follows:

	(9)		
June 30	Cost of Goods Sold	54,000	
	Finished Goods Inventory		54,000
	(To record cost of 6,000 units sold)		

In addition, an entry would be made to record the sale of the units for $119,700 (6,000 × the selling price of $19.95).

BEFORE YOU GO ON . . .

Review It

1. How do physical units differ from equivalent units of production?
2. What are the formulas for computing unit costs of production?
3. How are costs assigned to units transferred out and in process?
4. What are the five sections of a production cost report?

Do It

In March, Rodayo Manufacturing had the following unit production costs: materials $6 and conversion costs $9. On March 1, it had zero work in process. During March, 12,000 units were transferred out, and 800 units that were 25% completed as to conversion costs were in ending work in process. Assign the costs to the units transferred and in process.

Reasoning: The units transferred are the 12,000 units started and finished. These units should be assigned the total manufacturing cost of $15 per unit. The assignment of costs to units in process consists of the materials cost and conversion cost based on equivalent units of production.

Solution: The assignment of costs is as follows:

Transferred out:		
Started and finished (12,000 × $15)		$180,000
Ending work in process:		
Materials (800 × $6)	$4,800	
Conversion costs (200 × $9)	1,800	$ 6,600

THE NAVIGATOR

Related exercise material: BE22–4, BE22–5, BE22–6, BE22–7, E22–1, E22–2, E22–3, E22–4, and E22–8.

CONTEMPORARY DEVELOPMENTS

As indicated in Chapter 20, two contemporary developments in managerial accounting are just-in-time processing and activity-based costing. We explain these innovations in the following sections.

Just-in-Time Processing

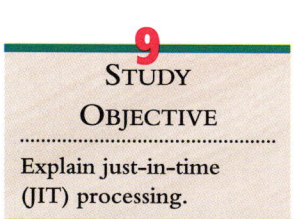

9

STUDY OBJECTIVE

Explain just-in-time (JIT) processing.

Traditionally, continuous process manufacturing has been based on a **just-in-case** philosophy: Inventories of raw materials are maintained **just in case** some items are of poor quality or a key supplier is shut down by a strike. Similarly, subassembly parts are manufactured and stored **just in case** they are needed later in the manufacturing process, and finished goods are completed and stored **just in case** unexpected and rush customer orders are received. This philosophy often results in a **"push approach"** in which raw materials and subassembly parts are pushed through each process. Traditional processing often results in the buildup of extensive manufacturing inventories.

Primarily in response to foreign competition, many U.S. firms have switched to **just-in-time (JIT) processing**. JIT manufacturing is dedicated to producing the right products (or parts) at the right time as they are needed. Under JIT processing, raw materials are received **just in time** for use in production, subassembly parts are completed **just in time** for use in finished goods, and finished goods are completed **just in time** to be sold. Illustration 22-22 shows the sequence of activities in just-in-time processing.

ILLUSTRATION 22-22

Just-in-time processing

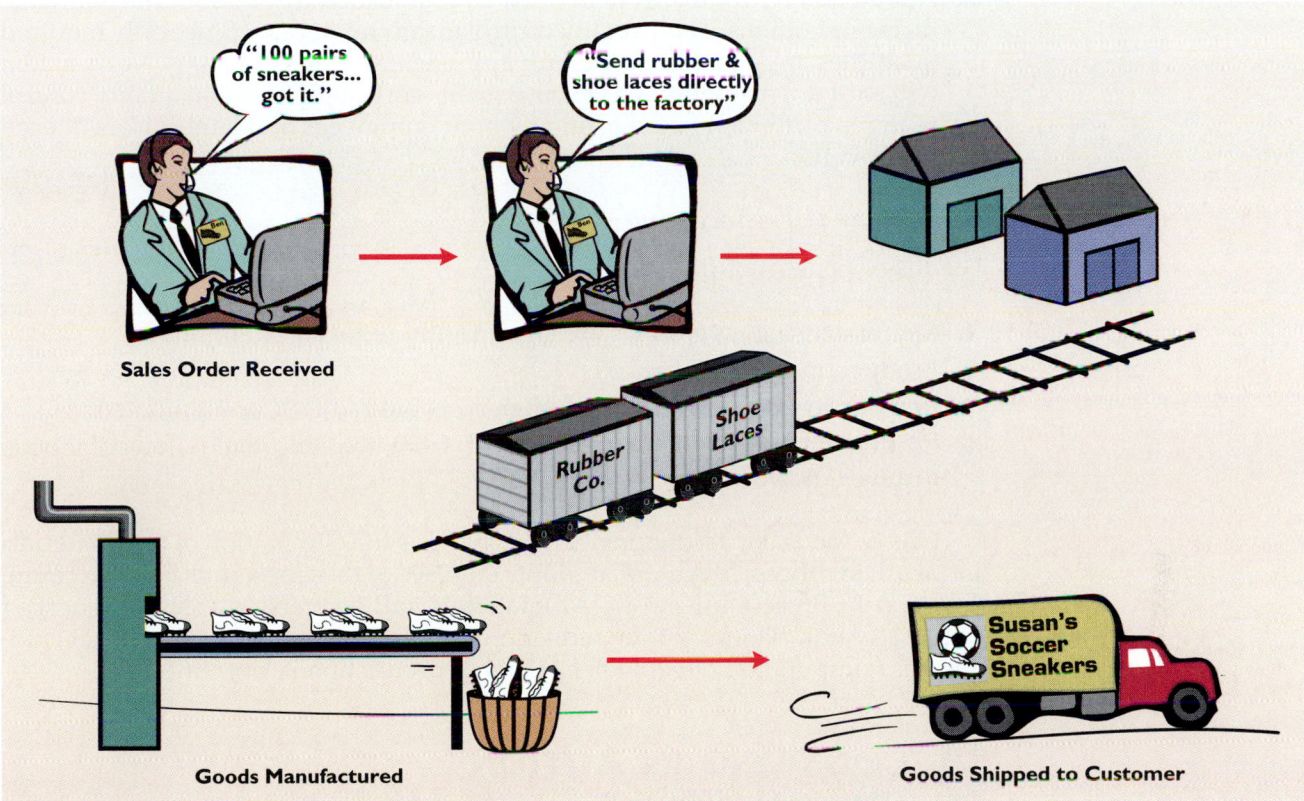

A primary objective of JIT is to eliminate all manufacturing inventories. Inventories are considered to have an adverse effect on net income because they tie up funds and storage space that could be made available for more productive purposes. JIT strives to eliminate inventories by using a **"pull approach"** in manufacturing. This approach begins at the final process (cell or work station) where a signal is sent via a computer to the next preceding work station indicating the exact materials (parts and subassemblies) needed for a time period, such as four hours or an eight-hour shift, to complete the production of a specified product. The preceding process, in turn, sends its signal to other processes so that there is a smooth continuous flow in the manufacturing process and no buildup of inventories at any point.

Elements of JIT Processing

There are three important elements in JIT processing:

1. A company must have dependable suppliers who are willing to deliver on short notice exact quantities of raw materials according to precise quality specifications (even including multiple deliveries within the same day). Suppliers must also be willing to deliver the raw materials at specified work stations rather than at a central receiving department. This type of purchasing requires constant and direct communication with suppliers, which is facilitated by an on-line computer linkage between the company and its suppliers.

2. A multiskilled workforce must be developed. Under JIT, machines are often strategically grouped around work cells or centers and much of the work is

automated. As a result, one worker may have the responsibility to operate and maintain several different types of machines.

3. A total quality control system must be established throughout the manufacturing operations. Total quality control means **no defects**. Since only required quantities are signaled by the **pull approach**, any defects at any work station will shut down operations at subsequent work stations. Total quality control requires continuous monitoring by both employees and supervisors at each work station.

Benefits of JIT Processing

The major benefits of JIT processing are:

1. Manufacturing inventories are significantly reduced or eliminated.
2. Product quality is enhanced.
3. Rework costs and inventory storage costs are reduced or eliminated.
4. Production cost savings are realized from the improved flow of goods through the processes.

One of the major accounting benefits of JIT is the elimination of raw materials and work in process inventory accounts. In place of these accounts is one account, Raw and In-Process Inventory. All materials and conversion costs are charged to this account. Because of the reduction (or elimination) of in-process inventories, the computation of equivalent units of production is simplified.

ACCOUNTING IN ACTION
Business Insight

JIT first hit the USA in the early 1980s when it was adopted by automobile companies to meet foreign competition. It is now being successfully used in many companies, including General Electric, Caterpillar, and Harley-Davidson. The effects in most cases have been dramatic. For example, after using JIT for two years, a major division of Hewlett-Packard found that work in process inventories (in dollars) were down 82%, scrap/rework costs were down 30%, space utilization was down 40%, and labor efficiency improved 50%. As indicated, JIT not only reduces inventory but also enables a manufacturer to produce a better product faster and with less waste.

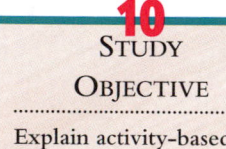

STUDY OBJECTIVE

Explain activity-based costing (ABC).

Activity-Based Costing

Activity-based costing (ABC) is a development in product costing that has received much attention in recent years. **Activity-based costing** focuses on the activities performed in producing a product. An ABC system is similar to conventional costing systems in accounting for direct materials and direct labor but differs in regard to manufacturing overhead.

In a conventional cost system, a **single unit-level** basis of allocation is used to allocate overhead costs to products. As explained in this text, the basis may be direct labor or machine hours used to manufacture the product. The assumption in this approach is that as volume of units produced increases, so does the cost of overhead. However, in some cases, the overhead cost is unrelated to the number of units produced.

In ABC, the cost of a product is equal to the sum of the costs of all activities performed to manufacture it. ABC recognizes that to have accurate and meaningful cost data, more than one basis of allocating activity costs to products is needed. In selecting the basis, ABC seeks to identify the **cost drivers** that measure the activities performed on the product. Examples of activities and possible cost drivers are as follows:

Activity	Cost Driver
Ordering raw materials	Ordering hours; number of orders
Receiving raw materials	Receiving hours; number of shipments
Materials handling	Number of requisitions; weight of materials; handling hours
Production scheduling	Number of orders
Machine setups	Setup hours; number of setups
Machining (fabricating, assembling, etc.)	Machine hours
Quality control inspections	Number of inspections
Factory supervision	Number of employees

ILLUSTRATION 22-23

Activities and cost drivers in ABC

Two important assumptions must be met in order to obtain accurate product costs under ABC:

1. All overhead costs related to the activity must be driven by the cost driver used to assign costs to products.
2. All overhead costs related to the activity should respond proportionally to changes in the activity level of the cost driver.

For example, if there is little or no correlation between changes in the cost driver and consumption of the overhead cost, inaccurate product costs are inevitable. A case example in the use of ABC is explained and illustrated in the appendix at the end of this chapter.

Activity-based costing may be used with either a job order or a process cost accounting system. The primary benefit of ABC is more accurate and meaningful product costing. Also, improved cost data about an activity can lead to reduced costs for the activity. In sum, ABC makes managers realize that it is activities and not products that determine the profitability of a company.

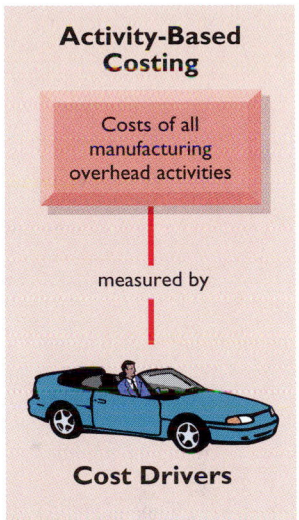

Activity-Based Costing

Costs of all manufacturing overhead activities

measured by

Cost Drivers

ACCOUNTING IN ACTION
International Insight

Contrary to popular opinion, ABC was not a Japanese invention. ABC was developed in France in the 1950s, but most Japanese corporations have used a form of ABC since that time. In Japan, ABC is called "target costing." Exhaustive market research is done on a new product to determine a price the market will accept. This becomes the target cost that designers, engineers, and production managers must meet. The use of target costing has resulted in products that are priced properly and profitably and that promptly win market share.

BEFORE YOU GO ON . . .
Review It

1. What are the principal accounting effects of just-in-time (JIT) processing?
2. What are the primary differences between activity-based costing (ABC) and traditional costing?

A LOOK BACK AT OUR FEATURE STORY

Refer to the opening story and answer the following questions.

1. How many processes are used by Ben & Jerry's to make ice cream? Identify the processes.
2. Why does Ben & Jerry's use a process costing system rather than a job order system?
3. How does the production report satisfy the needs of the department heads?

Solution:

1. The three processes used by Ben & Jerry's to make ice cream are (1) mixing, (2) prepping, and (3) pinting.
2. Ben & Jerry's uses a process costing system because making ice cream is continuous process manufacturing; it is mass production of many homogeneous units. Making ice cream fits the manufacturing characteristics of (1) "once the production begins, it continues until the finished product emerges," and (2) "when the finished product emerges, all units will have been processed in the same manner with precisely the same amount of materials, labor, and overhead." Each finished pint of ice cream is indistinguishable one from another.
3. The production report provides current cost data that can be compared with previous cost data and with budget expectations so that efficiency can be evaluated. The production report shows how much was processed (manufactured) and at what cost. These data are needed by department heads to manage and control production.

THE NAVIGATOR

DEMONSTRATION PROBLEM

Karlene Industries produces plastic ice cube trays in two processes: heating and stamping. All materials are added at the beginning of the Heating Department.

On November 1, 1,000 trays that were 70% complete were in process in the Heating Department. During November 12,000 trays were started into production. On November 30, 2,000 trays that were 60% complete were in process.

The following cost information for the Heating Department was also available:

Work in process, November 1	$1,000	Labor	$2,300
Materials	3,000	Overhead	4,600

Instructions

(a) Prepare a production cost report for the Heating Department for the month of November 1999.

(b) Journalize the transfer of costs to the Stamping Department.

SOLUTION TO DEMONSTRATION PROBLEM

(a)

KARLENE INDUSTRIES
Heating Department
Production Cost Report
For the Month Ended November 30, 1999

	Physical Units (Step 1)	Equivalent Units	
		Materials	Conversion Costs (Step 2)
QUANTITIES			
Units charged to department			
In process, November 1	1,000		
Started into production	12,000		
Total units charged	13,000		

PROBLEM-SOLVING STRATEGIES

1. Remember that total units accounted for must equal total units charged.
2. Similarly, total costs accounted for must equal total costs charged.
3. Equivalent units used for unit costs must equal equivalent units shown under total units accounted for.
4. The total costs charged must equal the debit total in work in process.

		Equivalent Units	
QUANTITIES	**Physical Units (Step 1)**	**Materials**	**Conversion Costs**
		(Step 2)	

QUANTITIES	Physical Units (Step 1)	Materials	Conversion Costs	
Units accounted for				
Transferred out				
In process, November 1	1,000	–0–	300	(1,000 × 30%)
Started and finished	10,000	10,000	10,000	
Total	11,000	10,000	10,300	
In process, November 30	2,000	2,000	1,200	(2,000 × 60%)
Total units accounted for	13,000	12,000	11,500	

COSTS

Unit costs **(Step 3)**		**Materials**	**Conversion Costs**	**Total**
Costs in November	(a)	$ 3,000	$ 6,900 *	$ 9,900
Equivalent units	(b)	12,000	11,500	
Unit costs (a) ÷ (b)		$.25	$.60	$.85

Costs charged to department				
In process, November 1				$ 1,000
Costs in November				9,900
Total costs charged				$10,900

Costs accounted for **(Step 4)**	**Materials**	**Conversion Costs**	**Total**
Transferred out			
In process, November 1	$ 1,000		
Conversion costs (300 × $.60)	180	$ 1,180	
Started and finished (10,000 × $.85)		8,500	$ 9,680
In process, November 30			
Materials (2,000 × $.25)		500	
Conversion costs (1,200 × $.60)		720	1,220
Total costs accounted for			$10,900

* Labor $2,300 plus overhead of $4,600.

(b) Nov. 30	Work in Process—Stamping	9,680	
	Work in Process—Heating		9,680
	(To record transfer of 11,000 units to Stamping Department)		

THE NAVIGATOR

SUMMARY OF STUDY OBJECTIVES

1. Explain the flow of costs in process cost accounting. The cost flow in process cost accounting is basically the same as in job order cost accounting. The accumulation of manufacturing costs (materials, labor, and overhead) is the same in process cost accounting as in job order costing. In process costing, costs are assigned to more than one work in process account, and the method of assigning costs is different.

2. State the end-of-period procedures in process cost accounting. End-of-period procedures are used to:
(a) Compute the physical units.
(b) Compute equivalent units of production.
(c) Compute unit costs of production.
(d) Assign costs to units transferred and in process.
(e) Prepare the production cost report.

3. *Compute the physical units of production.* Keeping track of the physical units of product consists of adding the units started into production during the period to the units in process at the beginning of the period to determine the total units to be accounted for. These units then are accounted for by the output of the period, which consists of units transferred out during the period and any units in process at the end of the period.

4. *Compute equivalent units of production.* Equivalent units of production are the sum of the work performed to (a) finish the units of beginning work in process inventory, if any; (b) complete the units started into production during the period; and (c) start, but only partially complete, the units in ending work in process inventory.

5. *Indicate how unit costs are computed.* There are two steps in determining unit costs: (a) determine the equivalent units of production, and (b) divide the appropriate costs by the equivalent units. Unit costs are computed for total manufacturing costs and generally it is also necessary to compute unit costs separately for materials and conversion costs.

6. *Explain the method and objective of assigning costs to units of output.* Costs are assigned to work done by applying unit costs to the equivalent units of work done. The objective of assigning costs is to determine the costs to be assigned to units transferred out and the units in ending work in process.

7. *Prepare a production cost report.* The production cost report contains both quantity and cost data for a production department. There are five sections in the report: (a) Units charged to department, (b) Units accounted for, (c) Unit costs, (d) Costs charged to department, and (e) Costs accounted for.

8. *Apply end-of-period procedures to a second process.* For a second process, (a) work done to complete beginning inventory is added in computing equivalent units, (b) costs transferred in are a materials cost, and (c) costs are assigned to beginning work in process in determining the cost of units transferred out.

9. *Explain just-in-time (JIT) processing.* JIT is a manufacturing technique that is dedicated to producing the right products at the right time as needed. One of the principal accounting effects is that a Raw and In-Process Inventory account replaces both the raw materials and work in process inventory accounts.

10. *Explain activity-based costing (ABC).* ABC is a method of product costing that focuses on the activities performed to produce products. It then assigns the cost of the activities to products by using cost drivers that measure the activities performed. The primary objective of ABC is accurate and meaningful product costs.

GLOSSARY

Activity-based costing A cost accounting system that focuses on the activities performed in manufacturing a specific product. (p. 970).

Equivalent units of production The work done during the period on the physical units of output expressed in terms of fully completed units. (p. 957).

Just-in-time processing A processing system dedicated to producing the right products (or parts) as they are needed. (p. 968).

Physical units Actual units to be accounted for during a period irrespective of any work performed. (p. 957).

Production cost report An internal report for management that shows both production quantity and cost data for a production department. (p. 961).

Process cost accounting A system of accounting used by companies that manufacture relatively homogeneous prod-

ucts through a series of continuous processes or operations. (p. 950).

Total units accounted for The sum of the units transferred out during the period plus the units in process at the end of the period. (p. 957).

Total units to be accounted for The sum of the units started (or transferred) into production during the period plus the units in process at the beginning of the period. (p. 957).

Transferred-in costs Costs transferred in from a department that are considered to be a materials cost to the receiving department. (p. 964).

Unit production costs Costs expressed in terms of equivalent units of production. (p. 959).

Units started and finished Units both started and completed during the period. (p. 958).

APPENDIX CASE EXAMPLE OF TRADITIONAL COSTING VERSUS ACTIVITY-BASED COSTING

PRODUCTION AND COST DATA

In this appendix we'll look at a case example of activity-based costing and compare that approach to traditional costing. Assume that Atlas Company produces two products, Product X and Product Y. Product X is a high-volume item totaling 25,000 units annually, and Product Y is a low-volume item totaling only 5,000 units per year. Both products require one hour of direct labor for completion. Therefore, total direct labor hours are 30,000 (25,000 + 5,000). Expected annual manufacturing overhead costs are $900,000. Thus, the overhead rate is $30 ($900,000 ÷ 30,000) per direct labor hour.

The direct materials cost per unit is $40 for Product X and $30 for Product Y. The direct labor cost is $12 per unit for each product.

11
STUDY OBJECTIVE
....
Apply activity-based costing to specific company data.

Unit Costs Under Traditional Costing

The unit cost for each product under traditional costing is shown below.

	Product	
Manufacturing Costs	**X**	**Y**
Direct materials	$40	30
Direct labor	12	12
Overhead	30	30
Total unit cost	$82	$72

ILLUSTRATION 22A-1

Unit costs—traditional costing

Determining Overhead Rates Under ABC

Analysis reveals that Atlas Company's expected annual overhead costs of $900,000 relate to three activities—machine setups, machining, and inspections. The cost driver and overhead rate for each activity are shown in Illustration 22A-2.

ILLUSTRATION 22A-2

Computing overhead rates—ABC

Activity	Cost Driver	Total Expected Overhead Cost	Total Expected Use of Driver	Overhead Rate
Machine setups	Number of setups	$300,000	1,500	$200
Machining	Machine hours	500,000	50,000	10
Inspections	Number of inspections	100,000	2,000	50

Assigning Overhead Costs to Products Under ABC

In assigning costs, it is necessary to know the expected number of cost drivers for each product. Because of its low volume, Product Y requires more setups and inspections than Product X. The expected number of cost drivers for each product is as follows:

ILLUSTRATION 22A-3

Expected number of cost drivers

Cost Driver	Product X	Product Y	Total Usage
Number of machine setups	500	1,000	1,500
Machine hours	30,000	20,000	50,000
Number of inspections	500	1,500	2,000

Using these data, the assignment of the expected annual overhead cost to each product is as follows:

ILLUSTRATION 22A-4

Assignment of overhead costs to products

Activity	Product X Number	Product X Cost	Product Y Number	Product Y Cost	Total Cost
Machine setups ($200)	500	$100,000	1,000	$200,000	$300,000
Machining ($10)	30,000	300,000	20,000	200,000	500,000
Inspections ($50)	500	25,000	1,500	75,000	100,000
Total assigned costs (a)		$425,000		$475,000	$900,000
Units produced (b)		25,000		5,000	
Overhead cost per unit (a) ÷ (b)		$17		$95	

These data show that under ABC, overhead costs are shifted from the high-volume product (Product X) to the low-volume product (Product Y). This shift results in more accurate costing for two reasons:

1. Low-volume products often require more special handling, such as more machine setups and inspections, than high-volume products. This is true for Atlas Company, for example. Thus, the low-volume product frequently is responsible for more overhead costs per unit than a high-volume product.

2. The overhead costs incurred by the low-volume product often are disproportionate to a traditional allocation base such as direct labor hours. Therefore, direct labor hours is usually a poor cost driver for assigning overhead costs to low-volume products. When overhead is properly assigned in ABC, it will usually increase the unit cost of low-volume products.

TECHNOLOGY IN ACTION

Many software packages designed especially for ABC costing are available for a personal computer or network. EASYABC developed by ABC Technologies includes three modules: overhead, activity, and cost object. The overhead module contains the overhead costs that are to be allocated to activities. In the activity module a user identifies the activities that are consumed by products. In the final module, the user defines the cost object such as a product, a customer, a product line, or any combination of the three. EASYABC also generates reports.

COMPARING UNIT COSTS

A comparison of unit manufacturing costs under traditional costing and ABC shows the following significant differences:

Manufacturing Costs	Traditional Costing Product		ABC Product	
	X	**Y**	**X**	**Y**
Direct materials	$40	$30	$40	$ 30
Direct labor	12	12	12	12
Overhead	30	30	17	95
Total	$82	$72	$69	$137

The comparison shows that unit costs under traditional costing have been significantly distorted. The cost of Product X has been overstated $13 per unit ($82 − $69), and the cost of Product Y has been understated $65 per unit ($137 − $72). The differences are attributable entirely to how manufacturing overhead is assigned. A likely consequence of the differences is that Atlas Company has been overpricing Product X and possibly losing market share to competitors. In addition, it has been sacrificing profitability by underpricing Product Y.

As illustrated in the above case, ABC involves the following steps:

1. Identify the major activities that pertain to the manufacture of specific products.
2. Accumulate manufacturing overhead costs by activities.
3. Identify the cost driver(s) that accurately measure(s) each activity's contribution to the finished product.
4. Assign manufacturing overhead costs for each activity to products using the cost driver(s).

BENEFITS AND LIMITATIONS OF ACTIVITY-BASED COSTING

We have already seen that a primary benefit of ABC is more accurate product costing. In addition, ABC offers the following other benefits:

1. **Control over overhead costs** is enhanced. Many overhead costs are incurred directly by activities. Thus, managers become more aware of their responsibility to control the activities that generate the costs.
2. **Better management decisions** can be made. More accurate product costing should contribute to setting selling prices that will achieve desired product profitability levels. In addition, the cost data should be helpful in deciding whether to discontinue or expand a product line or in deciding whether to make or buy a product component.

The principal disadvantages or limitations of ABC generally focus on two factors. First, **the expense of obtaining the cost data** required by the system is relatively high. ABC requires data that are not normally generated within a company such as the number of setups, inspections, orders placed, and orders received. In addition, numerous computations are involved in assigning overhead costs to individual products.

ACCOUNTING IN ACTION
Business Insight

ABC enabled Digital Communications Associates, a computer hardware and software manufacturer, to discover why profit margins slipped from 18.6% to 8% over a 3-year period. Digital boiled down 600 production activities to 136. ABC helped Digital and its 1,300 employees to bring costs under control.

Second, **ABC does not eliminate arbitrary assignments** of overhead. For example, plant-wide overhead costs such as depreciation, insurance, and property taxes on the factory building should be allocated to the activity centers in determining the cost of a product. These allocations may be more difficult to do accurately than in a traditional cost system because of the increased number of activity centers. As a result, accuracy of product costs could be adversely affected.

SUMMARY OF STUDY OBJECTIVE FOR APPENDIX

11. *Apply activity-based costing to specific company data.* In applying ABC, it is necessary to compute the overhead rate for each activity by dividing total expected overhead by the total expected usage of the cost driver. The overhead cost for each activity is then assigned to products on the basis of each product's use of the cost driver.

*****Note:** All asterisked Questions, Exercises, and Problems relate to material contained in the appendix to the chapter.

SELF-STUDY QUESTIONS

Answers are at the end of the chapter.

(SO 1) 1. Which of the following items is *not* a characteristic of continuous process manufacturing?
   a. Once production begins, it continues until the finished product emerges.
   b. The products produced are heterogeneous in nature.
   c. The focus is on continually producing homogeneous products.
   d. When the finished product emerges, all units have precisely the same amount of materials, labor, and overhead.

(SO 2) 2. End-of-period procedures in process cost accounting do *not* include:
   a. computing physical units of production.
   b. computing equivalent units of production.
   c. assigning costs to units transferred and in process.
   d. preparing a job cost sheet.

(SO 3) 3. In the RYZ Company, there are zero units in beginning work in process, 7,000 units started into production, and 500 units in ending work in process 20% completed. The physical units to be accounted for are:
   a. 7,000.
   b. 7,360.
   c. 7,600.
   d. 7,340.

(SO 4) 4. The Mora Company has 2,000 units in beginning work in process, 20% complete as to conversion costs, 25,000 units started and finished, and 3,000 units in ending work in process, 30% complete as to conversion costs. Equivalent units for materials and conversion costs are, respectively:
   a. 28,000 and 26,600.
   b. 28,000 and 27,500.
   c. 27,000 and 26,200.
   d. 27,000 and 29,600.

(SO 5) 5. KLM Company has no beginning work in process; 9,000 units are started and finished and 3,000 units in ending work in process are one-third finished. If total materials cost is $60,000, the unit materials cost is:
   a. $5.00.
   b. $6.00.
   c. $6.67 (rounded).
   d. No correct answer given.

(SO 6) 6. Toney Company has unit costs of $10 for materials and $30 for conversion costs. If there are 2,500 units in ending work in process, 40% complete as to conversion costs, the total cost assignable to the ending work in process inventory is:
   a. $45,000.
   b. $55,000.
   c. $75,000.
   d. $100,000.

(SO 7)   7. A production cost report:
   a. is an external report.
   b. shows costs charged to department and costs accounted for.
   c. shows equivalent units of production but not physical units.
   d. contains four sections.

(SO 8)   8. In determining unit costs in a second department:
   a. costs in beginning inventory are added to costs incurred during the period.
   b. only costs incurred on units transferred in are used.
   c. only costs incurred during the period are used.
   d. No correct answer is given.

(SO 9)   9. Just-in-time processing (JIT):
   a. strives to eliminate inventories.
   b. uses a pull approach in manufacturing.
   c. Neither of the above.
   d. Both (a) and (b).

10. Activity-based costing (ABC):   (SO 10)
   a. can be used only in a process cost system.
   b. focuses on units of production.
   c. focuses on activities performed to produce a product.
   d. uses only a single basis of allocation.

*11. The overhead rate for Machine Setups is $100 per setup. (SO 11) Products A and B have 80 and 60 setups, respectively. The overhead assigned to each product is:
   a. Product A $8,000, Product B $8,000.
   b. Product A $8,000, Product B $6,000.
   c. Product A $6,000, Product B $6,000.
   d. Product A $6,000, Product B $8,000.

QUESTIONS

1. Contrast the primary focus of job order cost accounting and of process cost accounting.

2. Your roommate is confused about the features of process cost accounting. Identify and explain the four distinctive features for your roommate.

3. Yang Woo believes there are no significant differences in the flow of costs between job order cost accounting and process cost accounting. Is Yang correct? Explain.

4. (a) What source documents are used in assigning (1) materials and (2) labor to production?
   (b) What criterion and basis are commonly used in allocating overhead to processes?

5. In Renfro Company, overhead is assigned to production departments at the rate of $15 per machining hour. In July, machine hours were 3,000 in the Machining Department and 2,400 in the Assembly Department. Prepare the entry to assign overhead to production.

6. Penny Griffen is uncertain about the end-of-period procedures in process cost accounting. State the procedures that are required in the sequence in which they are performed.

7. Karl Lange is confused about computing physical units. Explain to Karl how physical units to be accounted for and physical units accounted for are determined.

8. What is meant by the term "equivalent units of production"?

9. How are equivalent units computed?

10. Irvine Company had zero units of beginning work in process. During the period, 8,000 units were completed, and there were 500 units of ending work in process. What were the units started into production?

11. Tabaras Co. has zero units of beginning work in process. During the period 10,000 units were completed, and there were 500 units of ending work in process one-fifth complete. What were the equivalent units of production

for (a) materials and (b) conversion costs? Materials are added at the beginning of the process.

12. Sielert Co. started and finished 2,000 units for the period. Its beginning inventory is 600 units one-fourth complete and its ending inventory is 400 units one-fifth complete. How many units were transferred out this period?

13. Osgood Company transfers out 12,000 units and has 2,000 units of ending work in process that are 25% complete. Materials are entered at the beginning of the process and there is no beginning work in process. Assuming unit materials costs of $3 and unit conversion costs of $9, what are the costs to be assigned to units (a) transferred out and (b) in ending work in process?

14. (a) Lori Lang believes the production cost report is an external report for stockholders. Is Lori correct? Explain.
   (b) Identify the sections in a production cost report.

15. What purposes are served by a production cost report?

16. When units are transferred from one department to another, how should the receiving department handle the costs transferred in?

17. In Mercer Company, there are 800 units of ending work in process that are 100% complete as to materials and 25% complete as to conversion costs. If the unit cost of materials is $4 and the costs assigned to the 800 units is $6,600, what is the per-unit conversion cost?

18. (a) Describe the philosophy and approach of just-in-time processing.
   (b) Identify the major elements of JIT processing.

19. (a) What are the principal differences between activity-based costing (ABC) and traditional product costing?
   (b) What assumptions must be met for ABC costing to be useful?

20. Hoy Co. identifies the following activities that pertain to manufacturing overhead: Materials Handling, Machine Setups, Factory Machine Maintenance, Factory Supervision, and Quality Control. For each activity identify an appropriate cost driver.

*21. (a) Identify the steps that pertain to activity-based costing.
(b) What are the advantages of ABC costing?

BRIEF EXERCISES

Journalize entries for accumulating costs.
(SO 1)

BE22–1 Petty Manufacturing purchases $40,000 of raw materials on account, and it incurs $30,000 of factory labor costs. Journalize the two transactions on March 31 assuming the labor costs are not paid until April.

Journalize the assignment of materials and labor costs.
(SO 1)

BE22–2 Data for Petty Manufacturing are given in BE22–1. Supporting records show that (a) the Assembly Department used $14,000 of raw materials and $18,000 of the factory labor, and (b) the Finishing Department used the remainder. Journalize the assignment of the costs to the processing departments on March 31.

Journalize the assignment of overhead costs.
(SO 1)

BE22–3 Factory labor data for Petty Manufacturing are given in BE22–2. Manufacturing overhead is assigned to departments on the basis of 200% of labor costs. Journalize the assignment of overhead to the Assembly and Finishing Departments.

Compute physical units of production.
(SO 3)

BE22–4 Sorvino Manufacturing Company has the following production data for selected months:

Month	Beginning Work in Process	Units Started and Finished	Ending Work in Process Units	% Complete
January	–0–	30,000	10,000	40%
March	–0–	50,000	4,000	75
July	–0–	40,000	6,000	25

Compute the physical units for each month.

Compute equivalent units of production.
(SO 4)

BE22–5 Using the data in BE22–4, compute equivalent units of production for materials and conversion costs, assuming materials are entered at the beginning of the process.

Compute unit costs of production.
(SO 5)

BE22–6 In Unger Company, total material costs are $48,000, and total conversion costs are $60,000. Equivalent units of production are materials 12,000 and conversion costs 10,000. Compute the unit costs for materials, conversion costs, and total manufacturing costs.

Assign costs to units transferred out and in process.
(SO 6)

BE22–7 Motta Company has the following production data for April: units started and finished 40,000, and ending work in process 5,000 units that are 100% complete for materials and 40% complete for conversion costs. If unit materials cost is $8 and unit conversion cost is $12, determine the costs to be assigned to the units transferred out and the units in ending work in process. The total costs to be assigned are $864,000.

Prepare a partial production cost report.
(SO 7)

BE22–8 Using the data in BE22–7, prepare the cost section of the production cost report for Motta Company.

Compute unit costs in a second processing department.
(SO 8)

BE22–9 Production costs chargeable to the Finishing Department in June in Berger Company are materials $8,000, labor $20,000, overhead $18,000, and transferred in costs $72,000. Equivalent units of production are materials 20,000 and conversion costs 19,000. Compute the unit costs for materials and conversion costs.

Assign costs in a second processing department.
(SO 8)

BE22–10 Data for Berger Company are given in BE22–9. Production records indicate that 18,000 units were started and finished, and 2,000 units in ending work in process were 50% completed. Show the assignment of costs to the units transferred out and in process.

Compute overhead rates for activities.
(SO 11)

*BE22–11 Dooley Company identifies three activities in its manufacturing process: machine setups, machining, and inspections. Estimated annual overhead cost for each activity is $180,000, $300,000, and $70,000, respectively. The cost driver for each activity and the expected annual usage are: number of setups 1,000, machine hours 25,000, and number of inspections 1,400. Compute the overhead rate for each activity.

EXERCISES

E22–1 In Estes Company, materials are entered at the beginning of each process. Work in process inventories, with the percentage of work done on conversion costs, and production data for its Sterilizing Department in selected months during 1999 are as follows:

Compute physical units and equivalent units of production.
(SO 3, 4)

	Beginning Work in Process		Units Started	Ending Work in Process	
Month	Units	Conversion Cost %	and Finished	Units	Conversion Cost %
January	–0–	—	7,000	1,000	60
March	–0–	—	10,000	3,000	30
May	–0–	—	16,000	2,500	80
July	–0–	—	9,000	1,500	40

Instructions

(a) Compute the physical units for January and May.

(b) Compute the equivalent units of production for (1) materials and (2) conversion costs for each month.

E22–2 The Cutting Department of Cruz Manufacturing has the following production and cost data for July:

Determine equivalent units, unit costs, and assignment of costs.
(SO 4, 5, 6)

Production	Costs	
1. Started and finished 9,000 units.	Beginning work in process	$ –0–
2. Started 1,000 units that are 40%	Materials	45,000
completed at July 31.	Labor	14,000
	Manufacturing overhead	18,900

Materials are entered at the beginning of the process. Conversion costs are incurred uniformly during the process.

Instructions

(a) Determine the equivalent units of production for (1) materials and (2) conversion costs.

(b) Compute unit costs and show the assignment of manufacturing costs to units transferred out and in work in process.

E22–3 The Sanding Department of Lore Furniture Company has the following production and manufacturing cost data for March 1999:

Prepare a production cost report.
(SO 3, 4, 5, 6, 7)

Production: 12,000 units started and finished; 4,000 units started that are 100% completed as to materials and 25% completed as to conversion costs.

Manufacturing costs: Materials $32,000; labor $30,000; overhead $35,000.

Instructions

Prepare a production cost report.

E22–4 The Smelting Department of Agler Manufacturing Company has the following production and cost data for November:

Compute equivalent units, unit costs, and costs assigned.
(SO 4, 5, 6)

Production: Beginning work in process 2,000 units that are 100% complete as to materials and 20% complete as to conversion costs; units started and finished 9,000 units; and ending work in process 1,000 units that are 100% complete as to materials and 40% complete as to conversion costs.

Manufacturing costs: Work in process, November 1, $15,200; materials added $60,000; labor and overhead $121,000.

Instructions

(a) Compute the equivalent units of production for (1) materials and (2) conversion costs for the month of November.

(b) Compute the unit costs for the month.

(c) Determine the costs to be assigned to the units transferred out and in process.

Explain the production cost report.
(SO 7)

E22–5 Jerry Lundy has recently been promoted to production manager, and so he has just started to receive various managerial reports. One of the reports he has received is the production cost report that you prepared. It showed that his department had 1,000 equivalent units in ending inventory. His department has had a history of not keeping enough inventory on hand to meet demand. He has come to you, very angry, and wants to know why you credited him with only 1,000 units when he knows he had at least twice that many on hand.

Instructions

Explain to him why his production cost report showed only 1,000 equivalent units in ending inventory. Write an informal memo. Be kind and explain very clearly why he is mistaken.

Answer questions on costs and production.
(SO 3, 4, 5, 6)

E22–6 The ledger of Grogan Company has the following work in process account:

Work in Process—Painting

5/1	Balance	3,680	5/31	Transferred out	?
5/31	Materials	6,600			
5/31	Labor	2,500			
5/31	Overhead	1,400			
5/31	Balance	?			

Production records show that there were 800 units in the beginning inventory, 30% complete, 1,100 units started, and 1,300 units transferred out. The units in ending inventory were 40% complete. Materials are entered at the beginning of the painting process.

Instructions

Answer the following questions:

(a) How many units are in process at May 31?
(b) What is the unit materials cost for May?
(c) What is the unit conversion cost for May?
(d) What is the total cost of units started in April and completed in May?
(e) What is the total cost of units started and finished in May?
(f) What is the cost of the May 31 inventory?

Journalize transactions for two processes.
(SO 8)

E22–7 Hendrix Manufacturing Company has two production departments: Cutting and Assembly. July 1 inventories are Raw Materials $4,200, Work in Process—Cutting $2,900, Work in Process—Assembly $10,600, and Finished Goods $31,000. During July, the following transactions occurred:

1. Purchased $35,600 of raw materials on account.
2. Incurred $56,000 of factory labor. (Credit Wages Payable.)
3. Incurred $70,000 of manufacturing overhead; $42,000 was paid and the remainder is unpaid.
4. Requisitioned materials for Cutting $15,700 and Assembly $8,900.
5. Used factory labor for Cutting $29,000 and Assembly $27,000.
6. Applied overhead at the rate of $20 per machine hour. Machine hours were Cutting 1,740 and Assembly 1,620.
7. Transferred goods costing $67,700 from the Cutting Department to the Assembly Department.
8. Transferred goods costing $134,900 from Assembly to Finished Goods.
9. Sold goods costing $130,000 for $200,000 on account.

Instructions

Journalize the transactions. (Omit explanations.)

Compute equivalent units, unit costs, and costs assigned in a second process.
(SO 8)

E22–8 The Polishing Department of Longbine Manufacturing Company has the following production and manufacturing cost data for September. Materials are entered at the beginning of the process.

Production: Beginning inventory 2,600 units that are 100% complete as to materials and 30% complete as to conversion costs; units started that came from a prior department 12,000; ending inventory of 3,000 units 10% complete as to conversion costs.

Manufacturing costs: Beginning inventory costs of $63,180; costs transferred into Polishing during the month, $120,000; materials costs added in Polishing during the month,

$48,000; labor and overhead applied in Polishing during the month, $100,080 and $278,000, respectively.

Instructions

(a) Compute the equivalent units of production for materials and conversion costs for the month of September.

(b) Compute the unit costs for materials and conversion costs for the month.

(c) Determine the costs to be assigned to the units transferred out and in process.

E22–9 The Welding Department of Nagano Manufacturing Company has the following production and manufacturing cost data for February 1999. All materials are added at the beginning of the process.

Prepare a production cost report for a second process.
(SO 8)

Manufacturing Costs		Production Data	
Beginning work in process	$ 32,175	Beginning work in process	15,000 units
Costs transferred in	135,000		1/10 complete
Materials	45,000	Units transferred out	49,000
Labor	35,100	Units transferred in	60,000
Overhead	70,300	Ending work in process	26,000
			1/5 complete

Instructions

Prepare a production cost report for the Welding Department for the month of February.

E22–10 Niemann Company manufactures pizza sauce through two production departments: Cooking and Canning. In each process, materials and conversion costs are incurred evenly throughout the process. For the month of April, the work in process accounts show the following debits:

Journalize transactions and answer questions for two processes.
(SO 1, 6, 8)

	Cooking	Canning
Beginning work in process	$ –0–	$ 4,000
Materials	19,000	6,000
Labor	8,500	5,000
Overhead	29,500	21,800
Costs transferred in		50,000

Instructions

(a) Journalize the April transactions.

(b) If 110,000 units were started into production in Cooking and 100,000 units were transferred to Canning, what is the cost per unit of the goods transferred out?

(c) What is the total materials cost for the Canning Department in April?

*E22–11 Amend Instrument Inc. manufactures two products: missile range instruments and space pressure gauges. During January, 50 range instruments and 300 pressure gauges were produced, and overhead costs of $81,000 were incurred. An analysis of overhead costs reveals the following activities:

Compute overhead rates and assign overhead using ABC.
(SO 11)

Activity	Cost Driver	Total Cost
1. Materials handling	Number of requisitions	$30,000
2. Machine setups	Number of setups	27,000
3. Quality inspections	Number of inspections	24,000

The cost driver volume for each product was as follows:

Cost Driver	Instruments	Gauges	Total
Number of requisitions	400	600	1,000
Number of setups	150	300	450
Number of inspections	200	400	600

Instructions

(a) Determine the overhead rate for each activity.

(b) Assign the manufacturing overhead costs for January to the two products using activity-based costing.

(c) [pencil icon] Write a memorandum to the president of Amend Instrument, explaining the benefits of activity-based costing.

PROBLEMS: SET A

Complete end-of-period procedures for first process.
(SO 3, 4, 5, 6, 7)

P22–1A Buehler Corporation manufactures water skis through two processes: Molding and Packaging. In the Molding Department fiber glass is heated and shaped into the form of a ski. In the Packaging Department, the skis are placed in cartons and sent to the finished goods warehouse. Materials are entered at the beginning of both processes. Labor and manufacturing overhead are incurred uniformly throughout each process. Production and cost data for the Molding Department for January 1999 are presented below.

Production Data	January
Beginning work in process units	–0–
Units started into production	42,500
Ending work in process units	2,500
Percent complete—ending inventory	40%

Cost Data	
Materials	$510,000
Labor	96,000
Overhead	150,000
Total	$756,000

Instructions
(a) Compute the physical units of production.
(b) Determine the equivalent units of production for materials and conversion costs.
(c) Compute the unit costs of production.
(d) Determine the costs to be assigned to the units transferred out and in process.
(e) Prepare a production cost report for the Molding Department for the month of January.

Complete end-of-period procedures for first process.
(SO 3, 4, 5, 6, 7)

P22–2A Clemente Corporation manufactures in separate processes refrigerators and freezers for homes. In each process, materials are entered at the beginning and conversion costs are incurred uniformly. Production and cost data for the first process in making two products in two different manufacturing plants are as follows:

	Stamping Department	
	Plant A	**Plant B**
Production Data—June	**R12 Refrigerators**	**F24 Freezers**
Work in process units, June 1	–0–	–0–
Units started into production	21,000	20,000
Work in process units, June 30	4,000	2,500
Work in process percent complete	75	60
Cost Data—June		
Work in process, June 1	$ –0–	$ –0–
Materials	840,000	720,000
Labor	220,000	221,000
Overhead	420,000	292,000
Total	$1,480,000	$1,233,000

conversion cost

Instructions
(a) For each plant:
    (1) Compute the physical units of production.
    (2) Compute equivalent units of production for materials and for conversion costs.
    (3) Determine the unit costs of production.
    (4) Show the assignment of costs to units transferred out and in process.
(b) Prepare the production cost report for Plant A for June 1999.

Journalize and post transactions and show assignment of costs.
(SO 1, 3, 4, 5, 6)

P22–3A Pickard Company manufactures a nutrient, Everlife, through two manufacturing processes: Blending and Packaging. All materials are entered at the beginning of each process.

On August 1, 1999, inventories consisted of Raw Materials $5,000, Work in Process—Blending $0, Work in Process—Packaging $3,945, and Finished Goods $7,500. The beginning inventory for Packaging consisted of 500 units, two-fifths complete as to conversion costs. During August, 9,000 units were star _____ ___ ___ ___ in Blending and the following transactions were completed:

1. Purchased $25,000 _____
2. Issued raw materia_____ _____ _____690.
3. Incurred labor cost _____
4. Used factory labor _____
5. Incurred $36,500 _____
6. Applied manufac_____ _____ _____ _____lachine hours were Blending 90____
7. Transferred 8,200 _____ _____ _____ _____Unfinished units in Blending _____
8. Transferred 8,60_____ _____ _____ _____74,490. Unfinished units in th_____ _____ _____ _____rsion costs.
9. Sold goods costi_____

Instructions

(a) Journalize the _____
(b) Post the entrie_____
(c) Compute the _____ _____ _____n Blending.

P22–4A Cheng Company has sev____ p_____ _____ _____ged to the Assembly Department for October 1999 totaled $1,347,500 as follows.

Work in process inventory, October 1	$ 67,500	Overhead	$121,000
Materials added	166,000	Costs transferred in	913,000
Labor	80,000		

Assign costs and prepare production cost report with transferred-in costs.
(SO 8)

Production records show that 25,000 units were in beginning work in process 40% complete, 415,000 units were transferred in, and 35,000 units were in ending work in process 20% complete. Materials are entered at the beginning of each process.

Instructions

(a) Determine the equivalent units of production and the unit costs for the Assembly Department.
(b) Determine the assignment of costs to goods transferred out and in process.
(c) Prepare a production cost report for the Assembly Department.

P22–5A Jessica Company manufactures bicycles and tricycles. For both products, materials are added at the beginning of the production process, and conversion costs are incurred uniformly. Production and cost data for the month of May are as follows:

Determine equivalent units and unit costs and assign costs for processes with transferred-in costs.
(SO 8)

Production Data—Bicycles	Units	Percent Complete
Work in process units, May 1	200	80%
Units started into production	1,000	
Work in process units, May 31	300	30%

Cost Data—Bicycles	
Work in process, May 1	$19,280
Direct materials	50,000
Direct labor	18,140
Manufacturing overhead	30,000

Production Data—Tricycles	Units	Percent Complete
Work in process units, May 1	100	75%
Units started into production	800	
Work in process units, May 31	60	25%

Cost Data—Tricycles	
Work in process, May 1	$ 6,125
Direct materials	38,000
Direct labor	15,100
Manufacturing overhead	20,000

Instructions

(a) Calculate the following for both the bicycles and the tricycles:
  (1) The equivalent units of production for materials and conversion.
  (2) The unit costs of production for materials and conversion costs.
  (3) The assignment of costs to units transferred out and in process at the end of the accounting period.
(b) Prepare a production cost report for the month of May for the bicycles only.

Answer questions relating to percentage of completion, unit costs, and costs assigned.
(SO 4, 5, 6, 8)

P22–6A   Dwyer Furniture Company manufactures living room furniture through two departments: Framing and Upholstering. Materials are entered at the beginning of each process. For May, the following cost data are obtained from the two work in process accounts.

	Framing	Upholstering
Work in process, May 1	$–0–	$?
Materials	420,000	?
Conversion costs	210,000	330,000
Costs transferred in	–0–	550,000
Costs transferred out	550,000	?
Work in process, May 31	80,000	?

Instructions

Answer the following questions:

(a) If 3,000 sofas were started into production on May 1 and 2,500 sofas were transferred to Upholstering, what was the unit cost of materials for May in the Framing Department?
(b) Using the data in (a) above, what was the per unit conversion cost of the sofas transferred to Upholstering?
(c) Continuing the assumptions in (a) above, what is the percentage of completion of the units in process at May 31 in the Framing Department?
(d) If the materials cost per unit in Upholstering is $370, what was the cost of materials added in Upholstering in May?
(e) If the conversion cost per unit in Upholstering is $150, what are the equivalent units of conversion costs for May?
(f) Assuming there is no beginning work in process in Upholstering, what is the cost of the work in process at May 31 if 800 units are 25% completed?
(g) Assuming the per unit conversion costs for Upholstering in (d) and (e), what is the percentage of completion of 1,000 units of ending work in process inventory if the total costs assigned are $415,000?
(h) If unit costs were the same in April as in May, what is the cost of the May 1 work in process inventory in Upholstering if there are 1,000 units 60% complete?

PROBLEMS: SET B

Complete end-of-period procedures for first process.
(SO 3, 4, 5, 6, 7)

P22–1B   Fortner Company manufactures bowling balls through two processes: Molding and Packaging. In the Molding Department, the urethane, rubber, plastics, and other materials are molded into bowling balls. In the Packaging Department, the balls are placed in cartons and sent to the finished goods warehouse. All materials are entered at the beginning of each process. Labor and manufacturing overhead are incurred uniformly throughout each process. Production and cost data for the Molding Department during June 1999 are presented below.

Production Data	June
Beginning work in process units	–0–
Units started into production	22,000
Ending work in process units	2,000
Percent complete—ending inventory	45%

Cost Data	
Materials	$264,000
Labor	92,200
Overhead	116,800
Total	$473,000

Instructions
 (a) Prepare a schedule showing physical units of production.
 (b) Determine the equivalent units of production for materials and conversion costs.
 (c) Compute the unit costs of production.
 (d) Determine the costs to be assigned to the units transferred and in process for June.
 (e) Prepare a production cost report for the Molding Department for the month of June only.

P22–2B Enright Industries Inc. manufactures in separate processes furniture for homes. In each process, materials are entered at the beginning, and conversion costs are incurred uniformly. Production and cost data for the first process in making two products in two different manufacturing plants are as follows:

Complete end-of-period procedures for first process.
(SO 3, 4, 5, 6, 7)

	Cutting Department	
	Plant 1	Plant 2
Production Data—July	T12-Tables	C10-Chairs
Work in process units, July 1	–0–	–0–
Units started into production	20,000	18,000
Work in process units, July 31	1,000	500
Work in process percent complete	60	80

Cost Data—July		
Work in process, July 1	$ –0–	$ –0–
Materials	360,000	270,000
Labor	180,000	110,200
Overhead	94,400	86,700
Total	$634,400	$466,900

Instructions
 (a) For each plant:
   (1) Compute the physical units of production.
   (2) Compute equivalent units of production for materials and for conversion costs.
   (3) Determine the unit costs of production.
   (4) Show the assignment of costs to units transferred out and in process.
 (b) Prepare the production cost report for Plant 1 for July 1999.

P22–3B Vargas Company manufactures its product, Vitadrink, through two manufacturing processes: Mixing and Packaging. All materials are entered at the beginning of each process. On October 1, 2000, inventories consisted of Raw Materials $26,000, Work in Process—Mixing $0, Work in Process—Packaging $250,000, and Finished Goods $89,000. The beginning inventory for Packaging consisted of 10,000 units that were 50% complete as to conversion costs. During October, 50,000 units were started into production in the Mixing Department and the following transactions were completed:

Journalize and post transactions and show assignment of costs.
(SO 1, 3, 4, 5, 6)

 1. Purchased $300,000 of raw materials on account.
 2. Issued raw materials for production: Mixing $210,000 and Packaging $45,000.

3. Incurred labor costs of $238,900.
4. Used factory labor: Mixing $182,500 and Packaging $56,400.
5. Incurred $820,000 of manufacturing overhead on account.
6. Applied indirect manufacturing overhead on the basis of $25 per machine hour. Machine hours were 26,000 in Mixing and 6,600 in Packaging.
7. Transferred 45,000 units from Mixing to Packaging at a cost of $999,000. Unfinished units in Mixing are 25% complete as to conversion costs.
8. Transferred 53,000 units from Packaging to Finished Goods at a cost of $1,455,000. Units unfinished in the Packaging Department are 60% complete as to conversion costs.
9. Sold goods costing $1,460,000 for $2,100,000 on account.

Instructions
(a) Journalize the October transactions.
(b) Post the entries to the work in process accounts.
(c) Compute the costs assigned to units transferred out and in process in Mixing.

Assign costs and prepare production cost report with transferred in costs.
(SO 8)

P22–4B   Falcone Company has several processing departments. Costs charged to the Assembly Department for November 2000 totaled $2,064,100 as follows:

Inventory, November 1	$ 75,300	Overhead	$ 330,880
Materials added	160,000	Costs transferred in	1,312,000
Labor	185,920		

Production records show that 30,000 units were in beginning work in process 30% complete, 640,000 units were transferred in, and 25,000 units were in ending work in process 40% complete. Materials are entered at the beginning of each process.

Instructions
(a) Determine the equivalent units of production and the units costs for the Assembly Department.
(b) Determine the assignment of costs to goods transferred out and in process.
(c) Prepare a production cost report for the Assembly Department.

Determine equivalent units and unit costs and assign costs for processes with transferred in costs.
(SO 8)

P22–5B   Nicholas Company manufactures basketballs and soccer balls. For both products, materials are added at the beginning of the production process and conversion costs are incurred uniformly. Production and cost data for the month of July are as follows:

Production Data—Basketballs	Units	Percent Complete
Work in process units, July 1	500	60%
Units started into production	1,600	
Work in process units, July 31	600	40%

Cost Data—Basketballs	
Work in process, July 1	$1,125
Direct materials	1,600
Direct labor	1,160
Manufacturing overhead	1,000

Production Data—Soccer Balls	Units	Percent Complete
Work in process units, July 1	200	80%
Units started into production	2,000	
Work in process units, July 31	150	70%

Cost Data—Soccer Balls	
Work in process, July 1	$ 450
Direct materials	2,500
Direct labor	1,000
Manufacturing overhead	995

Instructions

(a) Calculate the following for both the basketballs and the soccer balls:
  (1) The equivalent units of production for materials and conversion.
  (2) The unit costs of production for materials and conversion costs.
  (3) The assignment of costs to units transferred out and in process at the end of the accounting period.
(b) Prepare a production cost report for the month of July for the basketballs only.

P22–6B Novacek Electronics manufactures two large-screen television models: the Royale which sells for $1,500, and a new model, the Majestic, which sells for $1,200. The production cost per unit for each model in 1999 was as follows:

Assign overhead to products using ABC.
(SO 11)

	Royale	Majestic
Direct materials	$ 700	$420
Direct labor ($20 per hour)	100	80
Manufacturing overhead ($40 per DLH)	200	160
Total per unit cost	$1,000	$660

In 1999, Novacek manufactured 30,000 units of the Royale and 10,000 units of the Majestic. The overhead rate of $40 per direct labor hour was determined by dividing total expected manufacturing overhead of $7,600,000 by the total direct labor hours (190,000) for the two models.

The gross profit on the models was: Royale $500 ($1,500 − $1,000) and Majestic $540 ($1,200 − $660). Because of this difference, management is considering phasing out the Royale model and increasing the production of the Majestic model.

Before finalizing its decision, management asks the controller of Novacek to prepare an analysis using activity-based costing. The controller accumulates the following information about overhead for the year ended December 31, 1999:

Activity	Cost Driver	Total Cost	Cost Driver Volume	Overhead Rate
Purchase orders	Number of orders	$1,200,000	30,000	$40
Machine setups	Number of setups	900,000	15,000	60
Machining	Machine hours	4,800,000	160,000	30
Quality control	Number of inspections	700,000	35,000	20

The cost driver volume for each product was:

Cost Driver	Royale	Majestic	Total
Purchase orders	10,000	20,000	30,000
Machine setups	5,000	10,000	15,000
Machine hours	100,000	60,000	160,000
Inspections	10,000	25,000	35,000

Instructions

(a) Assign the total 1999 manufacturing overhead costs to the two products using activity-based costing (ABC).
(b) What was the cost per unit and gross profit of each model using ABC costing?
(c) Are management's future plans for the two models sound?

BROADENING YOUR PERSPECTIVE

GROUP DECISION CASE

BYP22–1 Mendoza Company manufactures suntan lotion, called Surtan, in 11-ounce plastic bottles. Surtan is sold in a competitive market. As a result, management is very cost-conscious. Surtan is manufactured through two processes: mixing and filling. Materials are entered at the beginning of each process and labor and manufacturing overhead occur uniformly throughout each process. Unit costs are based on the cost per gallon of Surtan using FIFO costing.

On June 30, 1999, Sue Noller, the chief accountant for the past 20 years, opted to take early retirement. Her replacement, Jeff Mura, had extensive accounting experience with motels in the area but only limited contact with manufacturing accounting.

During July, Jeff correctly accumulated the following production quantity and cost data for the Mixing Department.

Production quantities: Work in process, July 1, 8,000 gallons 75% complete; started into production 100,000 gallons; work in process, July 31, 5,000 gallons 20% complete.

Production costs: Beginning work in process $88,000; incurred in July: materials $600,000, conversion costs $784,000.

Jeff then prepared a production cost report on the basis of physical units involved. His report showed a production cost of $15.49 per gallon of Surtan. The management of Mendoza was shocked at the high unit cost. The president comes to you, as Sue's top assistant, to review Jeff's report and prepare a correct report if necessary.

Instructions
With the class divided into groups, answer the following questions:

(a) Show how Jeff arrived at the unit cost of $15.49 per gallon of Surtan.
(b) What error(s) did Jeff make in preparing his production cost report?
(c) Prepare a correct production cost report for July.

MANAGERIAL ANALYSIS

BYP22–2 Logan Company manufactures bird houses in four departments. The first department is Sawing. It is responsible for cutting the pieces of lumber to be used to manufacture the houses. The second department is Construction. In the Construction Department the houses are nailed together; no other materials are added in the Construction Department. The third department is Painting. In the Painting Department, each house receives a primer and then two coats of weather-resistant paint. The fourth and last department is Finishing. Workers in the Finishing Department add trim and pack the bird houses for shipment. Data for March follow:

Started by Sawing:	10,000 units
Transferred to Construction	11,000
Transferred to Painting	12,000
Transferred to Finishing	10,000
Transferred to Finished Goods warehouse	11,000

Each department had 2,000 bird houses on hand at the beginning of the month, which were 25% complete as to conversion costs. Each department's ending inventory was 50% complete as to conversion costs.

Instructions
Compute the physical units for each department, or for only one of the departments, as your instructor directs.

REAL-WORLD FOCUS: General Microwave Corp.
• •

BYP22-3   **General Microwave Corp.** is engaged primarily in the design, development, manufacture, and marketing of microwave, electronic, and fiber optic test equipment, components, and subsystems. A substantial portion of the company's microwave product is sold to manufacturers and users of microwave systems and equipment for applications in the defense electronics industry.

General Microwave Corp. reports the following information in one of the notes to its financial statements:

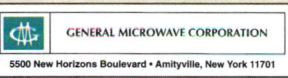

GENERAL MICROWAVE CORPORATION
Notes to the Financial Statement
Work in process inventory reflects all accumulated production costs, which are comprised of direct production costs and overhead, reduced by amounts attributable to units delivered. Work in process inventory is reduced to its estimated net realizable value by a charge to cost of sales in the period [in which] excess costs are identified. Raw materials and finished goods inventories are reflected at the lower of cost or market, computed on the first-in, first-out (FIFO) method.

Instructions
(a) What types of manufacturing costs are accumulated in the work in process inventory account?
(b) What types of information must General Microwave have to be able to compute equivalent units of production?
(c) How does General Microwave assign costs to the units transferred out of work in process that are completed?

COMMUNICATION ACTIVITY
• •

BYP22-4   Clara Pipken was a good friend of yours in high school and is from your home town. While you chose to major in accounting when you both went away to college, she majored in marketing and management. You have recently been promoted to accounting manager for the Snack Foods Division of Romero Enterprises, and your friend was promoted to regional sales manager for the same division of Romero. Clara recently telephoned you. She explained that she was familiar with job cost sheets, which had been used by the Special Projects division where she had formerly worked. She was, however, very uncomfortable with the production cost reports prepared by your division. She faxed you a list of her particular questions. These included the following:

1. Since Romero occasionally prepares snack foods for special orders in the Snack Foods Division, why don't we track costs of the orders separately?
2. What is an equivalent unit?
3. Why am I getting four production cost reports? Isn't there only one Work in Process account?

Instructions
Prepare a memorandum to Clara. Answer her questions, and include any additional information you think would be helpful. You may write informally, but be careful to use proper grammar and punctuation.

RESEARCH ASSIGNMENT
• •

BYP22-5   The August 1994 issue of *Management Accounting* includes an article by Daniel P. Keegan and Robert T. Eiler entitled "Let's Reengineer Cost Accounting."

Instructions

Read the article and answer the following questions:

(a) What percentage of service companies have experimented with activity-based costing?

(b) What do the authors cite as the positive aspects of activity-based costing? What example do they cite?

(c) What do the authors cite as the chief problem with activity-based costing? What do they propose as the solution to this problem?

(d) In reengineering a cost system, what do the authors suggest that most companies should do with their labor reporting systems? Why do they suggest this?

ETHICS CASE

BYP22–6   J. R. Snider Company manufactures a high-tech component that passes through two production processing departments, Molding and Assembly. Department managers are partially compensated on the basis of units of products completed and transferred out relative to units of product put into production. This was intended as encouragement to be efficient and to minimize waste.

Bill Fortuno is the department head in the Molding Department, and Steve Drummond is his quality control inspector. During the month of June, Bill had three new employees who were not yet technically skilled. As a result, many of the units produced in June had minor molding defects. In order to maintain the department's normal high rate of completion, Bill told Steve to pass through inspection and on to the Assembly Department all units that had defects nondetectable to the human eye. "Company and industry tolerances on this product are too high anyway," says Bill. "Less than 2% of the units we produce are subjected in the market to the stress tolerance we've designed into them. The odds of those 2% being any of this month's units are even less. Anyway, we're saving the company money."

Instructions

(a) Who are the potential stakeholders involved in this situation?

(b) What alternatives does Steve have in this situation? What might the company do to prevent this from occurring?

SURFING THE NET

BYP22–7   Search the Internet and find the Web sites of two manufacturers that you think are likely to use process costing. Are there any specifics included in their Web sites that confirm the use of process costing for each of these companies?

Answers to Self-Study Questions

1. b   2. d   3. a   4. b   5. a   6. b   7. b   8. c   9. d   10. c   *11. b

Remember to go back to the Navigator box on the chapter-opening page and check off your completed work.

CONCEPTS FOR REVIEW

Before studying this chapter, you should know or, if necessary, review:

a. The three manufacturing cost elements. (Ch. 20, pp. 873–75)

b. The difference between product and period costs. (Ch. 20, pp. 875–76)

c. The income statement for a manufacturing company. (Ch. 20, pp. 877–79)

THE NAVIGATOR

FEATURE STORY

Growing by Leaps and Leotards

When the last of her three children went off to kindergarten, Amy began looking for a part-time job. At this same time, her daughter asked to take dance classes. The nearest dance studio was over 20 miles away, and Amy didn't know how she would balance a new job and driving her daughter to dance classes. Suddenly it hit her—she knew a little bit about dance and she had a physical education degree, so why not start her own dance studio?

With a piece of paper and pencil Amy sketched out a business plan: A

local church would rent its basement for $6 per hour. Because the basement was small she was limited in the number of students she could teach, but at least the rent was low. Insurance for a small studio was $50 per month. Initially she would teach classes only for young kids since that was all she felt qualified to do. She thought she could charge $2.50 per each one-hour class. There was room in the basement for 8 students per class. She wasn't going to get rich—but at least it would be fun, and she didn't have much at risk.

Early in the first year Amy realized that the demand for dance classes far exceeded her capacity. She began to consider renting an empty

retail space. With the bigger space she could serve as many as 15 students per class, but her rent would also increase significantly. Also, rather than paying rent by the hour, she would have to pay $600 per month, and she would have to pay this even during the summer months when demand for dance classes was low. In addition she would have to pay utilities—roughly $70 per month.

However, with a bigger space she could offer classes for teens and adults. Teens and adults would pay a higher fee—$5 per hour—though the number of students per class would have to be smaller, probably only 8 per class. She would hire a part-time instructor to teach advanced classes, and a good instructor demands at least $18 per hour. With a bigger operation her insurance costs would increase to $100 per month. Amy also realized she could increase her income by selling dance supplies such as shoes, towels, and leotards. In addition, she would hire a part-time administrator at $100 per month to keep records.

Amy laid out a new business plan based on these estimates. If she failed, she stood to lose real money. Convinced she could make a go of it, she made the big plunge.

Within ten years of starting her business in a church basement Amy had over 800 students, 7 instructors, two administrators, and a facility with three separate studios.
THE NAVIGATOR

CHAPTER 23

COST-VOLUME-PROFIT RELATIONSHIPS

THE NAVIGATOR ✔

- ■ Understand *Concepts for Review* □
- ■ Read *Feature Story* □
- ■ Scan *Study Objectives* □
- ■ Read *Preview* □
- ■ Read text and answer *Before You Go On*
  p. 1002 □ p. 1009 □ p. 1014 □ p. 1018 □
- ■ Work *Demonstration Problems* □
- ■ Review *Summary of Study Objectives* □
- ■ Answer *Self-Study Questions* □
- ■ Complete assignments □

STUDY OBJECTIVES

After studying this chapter, you should be able to:

1. *Distinguish between variable and fixed costs.*
2. *Explain the meaning and importance of the relevant range.*
3. *Explain the concept of mixed costs.*
4. *State the five components of cost-volume-profit analysis.*
5. *Indicate the meaning of contribution margin and the ways it may be expressed.*
6. *Identify the three ways that the break-even point may be determined.*
7. *Define margin of safety and give the formulas for computing it.*
8. *Give the formulas for determining sales required to earn target net income.*
9. *Describe the essential features of a cost-volume-profit income statement.*
10. *Explain the difference between absorption costing and variable costing.*

THE NAVIGATOR

*A*s the opening story indicates, to manage any size business you must understand how costs respond to changes in sales volume and the effect of the
interaction of costs and revenues on profits. A prerequisite to understanding cost-
volume-profit (CVP) relationships is knowledge of the behavior of costs. In this chapter, we first explain the considerations involved in cost behavior analysis. Then we
discuss and illustrate CVP analysis and variable costing. The content and organization
of the chapter are as follows:

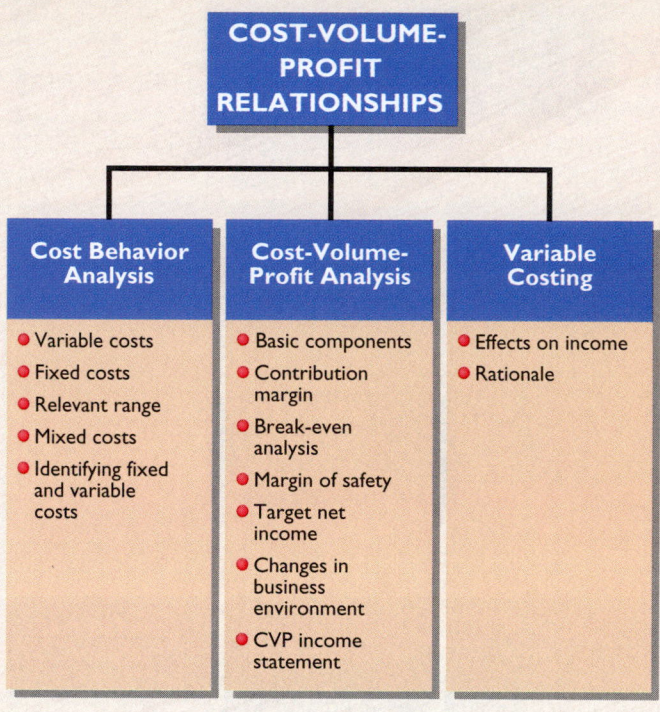

THE
NAVIGATOR

COST BEHAVIOR ANALYSIS

Cost behavior analysis is the study of how specific costs respond to changes in
the level of activity within a company. As you might expect, some costs change
and others remain the same. A knowledge of cost behavior helps management
plan business operations and decide between alternative courses of action. Cost
behavior analysis applies to all types of entities as the story about Amy's Dance
Studio indicates.

 The starting point in cost behavior analysis is measuring the key activities in
the company's business. Activity levels may be expressed in terms of sales dollars (in a retail company), miles driven (in a trucking company), room occupancy
(in a hotel), or dance classes taught (by a dance studio). Many companies use
more than one measurement base. A manufacturing company, for example, may
use direct labor hours or units of output for manufacturing costs and sales revenue or units sold for selling expenses.

 For an activity level to be useful in cost behavior analysis, there should be
correlation between changes in the level or volume of activity and changes in

costs. The activity level selected is referred to as the activity (or volume) index. The **activity index** identifies the activity that causes changes in the behavior of costs. Once an appropriate activity index is selected, it is possible to classify the behavior of costs in response to changes in activity levels into three categories: variable, fixed, or mixed.

Variable Costs

Variable costs are costs that vary **in total** directly and proportionately with changes in the activity level. If the level increases 10%, total variable costs will increase 10%. If the level of activity decreases by 25%, variable costs will be reduced 25%. Examples of variable costs include direct materials and direct labor in a manufacturing company; cost of goods sold, sales commissions, and freight-out in a merchandising company; and gasoline in airline and trucking companies. A variable cost may also be defined as a cost that **remains the same** *per unit* **at every level of activity**.

To illustrate the behavior of a variable cost, assume that Damon Company manufactures radios that contain a $10 digital clock. The activity index is the number of radios produced. As each radio is manufactured, the total cost of the clocks increases by $10. As shown in part (a) of Illustration 23-1, total cost of the clocks will be $20,000 if 2,000 radios are produced, and $100,000 when 10,000 radios are produced. The digital clocks can also be used to show that a variable cost remains the same per unit as the level of activity changes. As shown in part (b) of Illustration 23-1, the unit cost of $10 for the clocks is the same whether 2,000 or 10,000 radios are produced.

STUDY OBJECTIVE

Distinguish between variable and fixed costs.

ILLUSTRATION 23-1

Behavior of total and unit variable costs

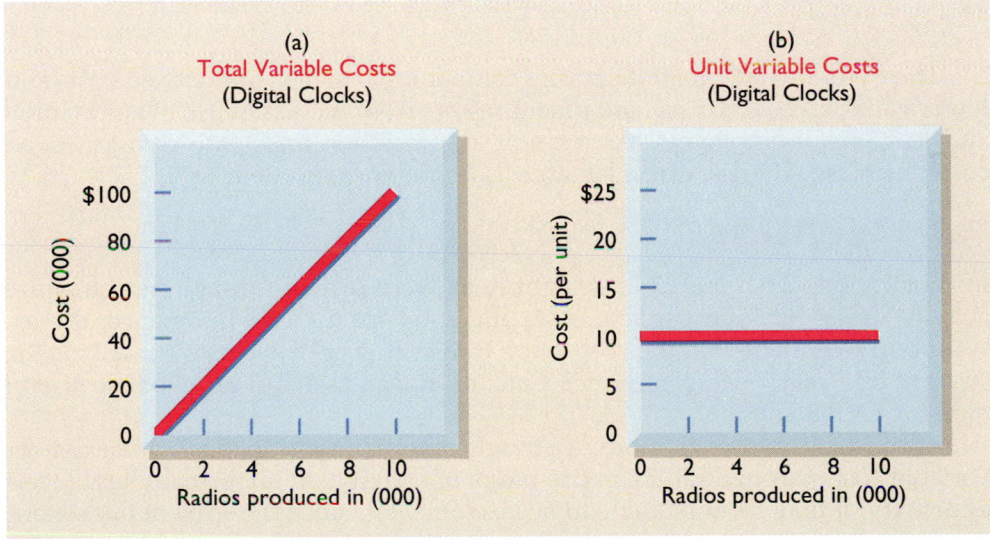

HELPFUL HINT

True or false: Variable cost per unit changes directly and proportionately with changes in activity. Answer: False; per unit cost remains constant at all levels of activity.

Companies that rely heavily on labor to manufacture a product or to render a service are likely to have many variable costs. In contrast, companies that use a high proportion of machinery and equipment in producing revenue, such as public utilities, may have few variable costs.

Fixed Costs

Fixed costs are costs that **remain the same in total** regardless of changes in the activity level. Examples include property taxes, insurance, rent, supervisory salaries, and depreciation on buildings and equipment. Because fixed costs remain constant in total as activity changes, it follows that **fixed costs per unit vary inversely with activity. As volume increases, unit cost declines and vice versa.**

To illustrate the behavior of fixed costs, assume that Damon Company leases all of its productive facilities at a cost of $10,000 per month. Total fixed costs of the facilities will remain constant at every level of activity, as shown in part (a) of Illustration 23-2. However, on a per unit basis, the cost of rent will decline as activity increases, as shown in part (b) of Illustration 23-2. At 2,000 units, the unit cost is $5 ($10,000 ÷ 2,000); when 10,000 radios are produced, the unit cost is only $1 ($10,000 ÷ 10,000).

ILLUSTRATION 23-2

Behavior of total and unit fixed costs

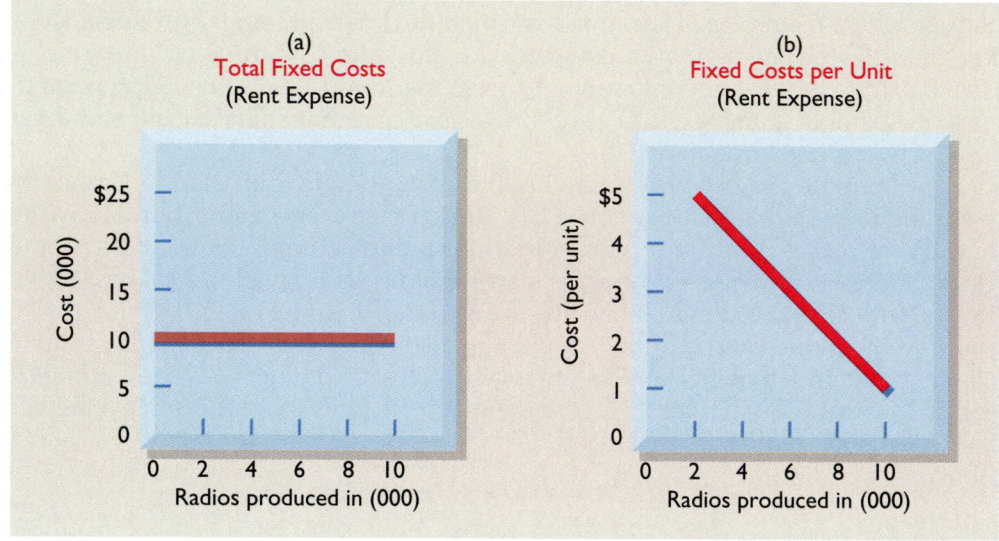

The trend in many manufacturing companies is to have more fixed costs and fewer variable costs. This development results from increased use of automation and less use of employees. As a result, depreciation and lease charges (fixed costs) increase whereas direct labor costs (variable costs) decrease.

Relevant Range

2
STUDY
OBJECTIVE

Explain the meaning and importance of the relevant range.

In Illustrations 23-1 and 23-2, straight lines were drawn throughout the entire activity index for total variable costs and total fixed costs. In essence, the assumption was made that the costs were **linear**. It is now necessary to ask: Is the straight-line relationship realistic? Can the linear assumption produce useful data for CVP analysis?

In most business situations, a straight-line relationship **does not exist** for variable costs throughout the entire range of activity. At abnormally low levels of activity, it may be impossible to be cost efficient, since the scale of operations may not allow the company to obtain quantity discounts in the purchase of raw materials or use specialization of labor. In contrast, at abnormally high levels of activity, labor costs may increase sharply because of overtime pay, and materials costs may jump significantly because of excess spoilage caused by worker fatigue. Consequently, in the real world, the relationship between the behavior of a variable cost and changes in the activity level is often **curvilinear**, as shown in part (a) of Illustration 23-3.

Total fixed costs also do not have a straight-line relationship over the entire range of activity. While some fixed costs will not change, it is possible for management to change other fixed costs. For example, in the feature story the dance studio's rent was originally variable, then became fixed at a certain level, then increased to a new fixed amount when the size of the studio increased beyond

HELPFUL HINT

Fixed costs that may be changeable include research, such as new product development, and management training programs.

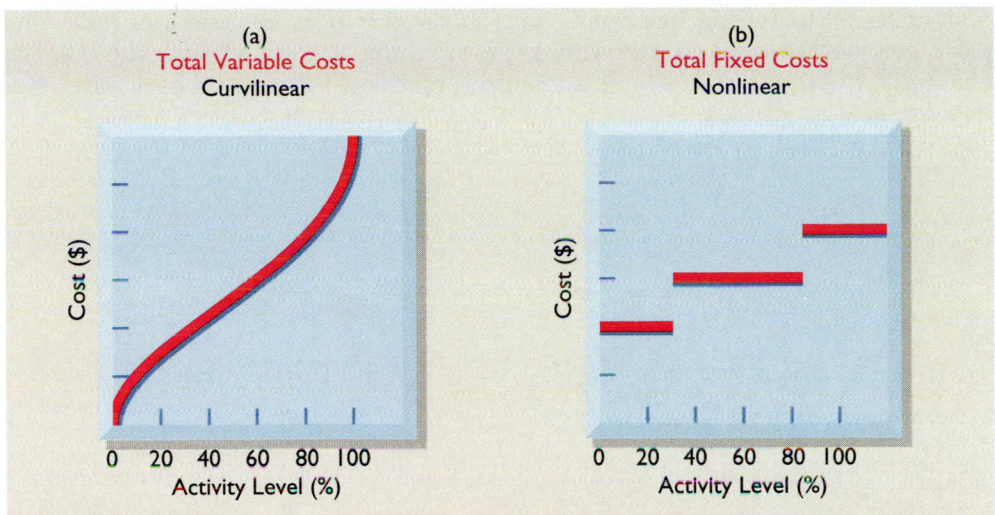

ILLUSTRATION 23-3
Nonlinear behavior of variable and fixed costs

a certain point. The behavior of total fixed costs through all levels of activity is shown in part (b) of Illustration 23-3.

For most companies, operating at almost zero or at 100% capacity is the exception rather than the rule. Instead, companies often operate over a somewhat narrower range, such as 40–80% of capacity. The range over which a company expects to operate during a year is called the **relevant range** of the activity index. Within this range, as shown in both diagrams in Illustration 23-4, a straight-line relationship generally exists for both variable and fixed costs.

ALTERNATIVE TERMINOLOGY

The relevant range is also called the *normal* or *practical range*.

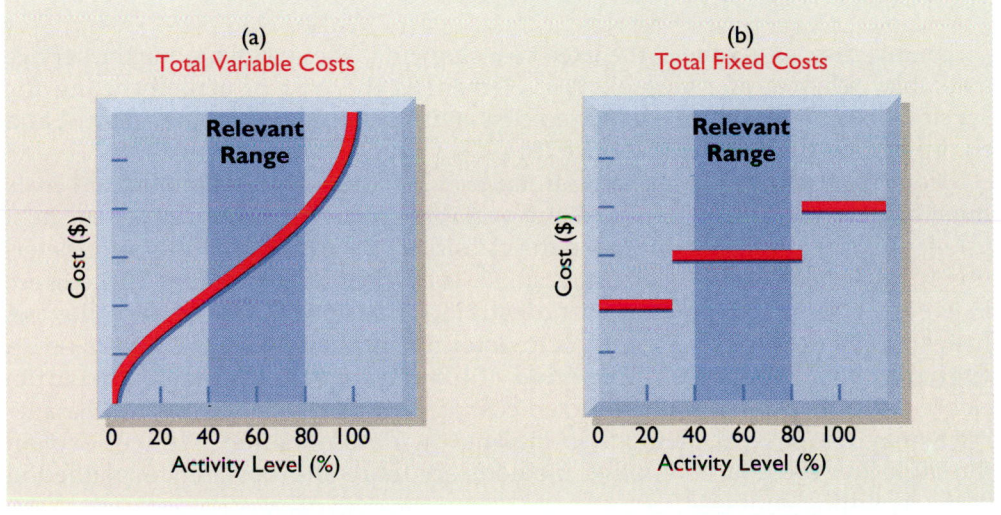

ILLUSTRATION 23-4
Linear behavior within relevant range

As you can see, although the straight-line relationship may not be completely realistic, the linear assumption produces useful data for CVP analysis as long as the level of activity remains within the relevant range.

Mixed Costs

Mixed costs contain both a variable cost element and a fixed cost element. Sometimes called **semivariable costs, mixed costs change in total but not proportionately with changes in the activity level**. The rental of a U-Haul truck is a good example of a mixed cost. To illustrate, assume that local rental terms for a

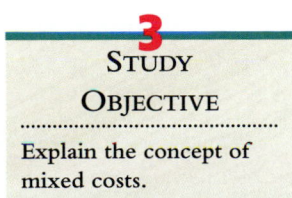

3
STUDY
OBJECTIVE
·····························
Explain the concept of mixed costs.

17-foot truck, including insurance, are $50 per day plus 50 cents per mile. The per diem charge is a fixed cost with respect to miles driven, whereas the mileage charge is a variable cost. The graphic presentation of the rental cost for a one-day rental is as follows:

ILLUSTRATION 23-5

Behavior of a mixed cost

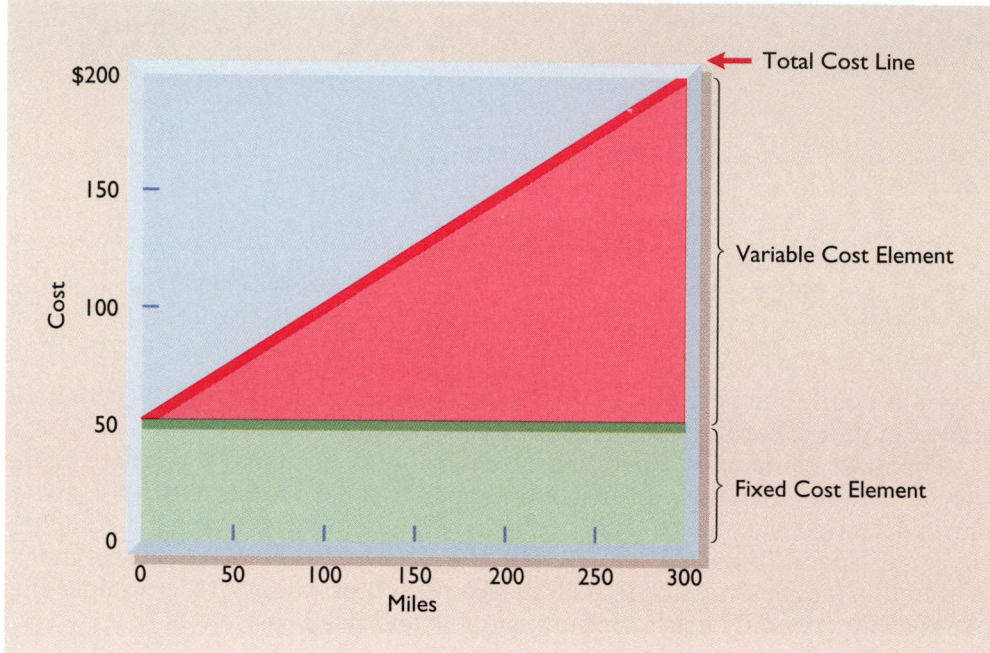

In this case, as in others, the fixed cost element is the cost of having the service available, whereas the variable cost element is the cost of actually using the service. Another example of a mixed cost is utility costs (electric, telephone, and so on), where there is a flat service fee plus a usage charge.

For purposes of CVP analysis, an underlying assumption is that **mixed costs must be classified into their fixed and variable elements**. Accordingly, we must ask: How does management make the classification? One possibility is to determine the variable and fixed components each time a mixed cost is incurred. However, because of time and cost constraints, this approach is rarely followed. Instead, the customary approach is to determine variable and fixed costs on an **aggregate basis at the end of a period of time**, using the company's past experience with the behavior of the mixed cost at various levels of activity. Management may use several methods in making the determination. We will explain the **high-low method** here; other methods are more appropriately explained in cost accounting courses.[1]

High-Low Method

The **high-low method** is a mathematical method that uses the total costs incurred at the high and low levels of activity. The difference in costs between the high and low levels represents variable costs, since only the variable cost element can change as activity levels change. The steps in computing fixed and variable costs under this method are as follows:

---

[1]Other methods include the scatter diagram method and least squares regression analysis.

1. **Determine variable cost per unit from the following formula:**

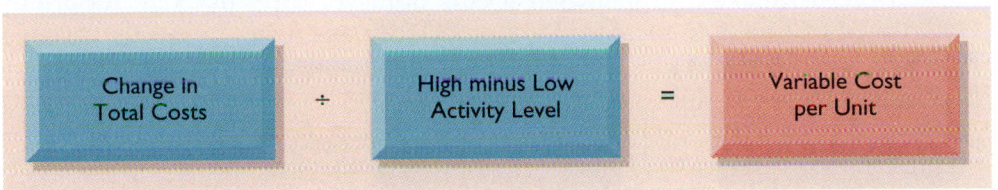

ILLUSTRATION 23-6

Formula for variable cost per unit using high-low method

To illustrate, assume that Metro Transit Company has the following maintenance costs and mileage data for its fleet of buses over a 4-month period:

ILLUSTRATION 23-7

Assumed maintenance costs and mileage data

Month	Miles Driven	Total Cost	Month	Miles Driven	Total Cost
January	20,000	$30,000	March	35,000	$49,000
February	40,000	48,000	April	50,000	63,000

The high and low levels of activity are 50,000 miles in April and 20,000 miles in January. The maintenance costs at these two levels are $63,000 and $30,000, respectively. The difference in maintenance costs is $33,000 ($63,000 − $30,000) and the difference in miles is 30,000 (50,000 − 20,000). Therefore, for Metro Transit, variable cost per unit is $1.10, computed as follows:

$$\$33,000 \div 30,000 = \$1.10$$

2. **Determine the fixed cost by subtracting the total variable cost at either the high or the low activity level from the total cost at that activity level.**

For Metro Transit, the computations are shown in Illustration 23-8:

ILLUSTRATION 23-8

High-low method computation of fixed costs

	Activity Level	
	High	**Low**
Total cost	$63,000	$30,000
Less: Variable costs		
50,000 × $1.10	55,000	
20,000 × $1.10		22,000
Total fixed costs	$ 8,000	$ 8,000

Maintenance costs are therefore $8,000 per month plus $1.10 per mile. For example, at 45,000 miles, estimated maintenance costs would be $49,500 variable (45,000 × $1.10) and $8,000 fixed. The high-low method generally produces a reasonable estimate for analysis. However, it does not produce a precise measurement of the fixed and variable elements in a mixed cost because other activity levels are ignored in the computation.

Importance of Identifying Variable and Fixed Costs

Why is it important to segregate costs into variable and fixed elements? The answer may become apparent if we look at the following five business decisions:

1. If American Airlines is to make a profit when it reduces all domestic fares by 50%, what reduction in costs or increase in passengers will be required? **Answer:** To make a profit when it cuts domestic fares by 50%, American Airlines will have to increase the number of passengers or cut its variable costs for those flights. Its fixed costs will not change.

2. What increase in sales revenue will be needed to maintain current profit levels if Ford Motor Company meets the United Auto Workers' demands for higher wages? **Answer:** Higher wages to UAW members at Ford Motor Company will increase the variable costs of manufacturing automobiles. To maintain present profit levels, Ford will have to cut other variable costs or increase the price of its automobiles.

3. What level of sales will General Motors need to cover its costs exactly for the Saturn automobile in the next model year? **Answer:** To cover its costs exactly on the Saturn automobile for the next model year, General Motors must determine the sales volume at which sales revenue will equal total costs, both fixed and variable.

4. What will be the effect on the cost of producing one ton of steel at USX Corp. if its program to modernize plant facilities reduces the work force by 50%? **Answer:** The modernizing of plant facilities at USX Corp. changes the proportion of fixed and variable costs of producing one ton of steel. Fixed costs increase because of higher depreciation charges whereas variable costs decrease due to the reduction in the number of steelworkers.

5. What happens if Kellogg Company increases its advertising expenses? **Answer:** Sales volume must be increased to cover three items: (1) the increase in advertising, (2) the variable cost of the increased sales volume, and (3) the desired additional net income.

BEFORE YOU GO ON . . .

Review It

1. What are the effects on (a) a variable cost and (b) a fixed cost due to a change in activity?
2. What is the relevant range and the behavior of costs within this range?
3. What are the steps in applying the high-low method to mixed costs?

Do It

Helena Company reports the following total costs at two levels of production:

	10,000 units	20,000 units
Direct materials	$20,000	$40,000
Maintenance	8,000	10,000
Depreciation	4,000	4,000

Classify each cost as either variable, fixed, or mixed.

Reasoning: A variable cost varies in total directly and proportionately with each change. A fixed cost remains the same in total with each change. A mixed cost changes in total but not proportionately with each change.

Solution: Direct materials is a variable cost. Maintenance is a mixed cost. Depreciation is a fixed cost.

Related exercise material: BE23–1, E23–1, and E23–2.

COST-VOLUME-PROFIT ANALYSIS

Cost-volume-profit (CVP) analysis is the study of the effects of changes in costs and volume on a company's profits. CVP analysis is important in profit planning. It also is a critical factor in such management decisions as setting selling prices, determining the best product mix, and making maximum use of production facilities.

4
STUDY
OBJECTIVE
····························
State the five components of cost–volume-profit analysis.

Basic Components

CVP analysis involves a consideration of the interrelationships among the components shown in Illustration 23-9.

ILLUSTRATION 23-9

Components of CVP analysis

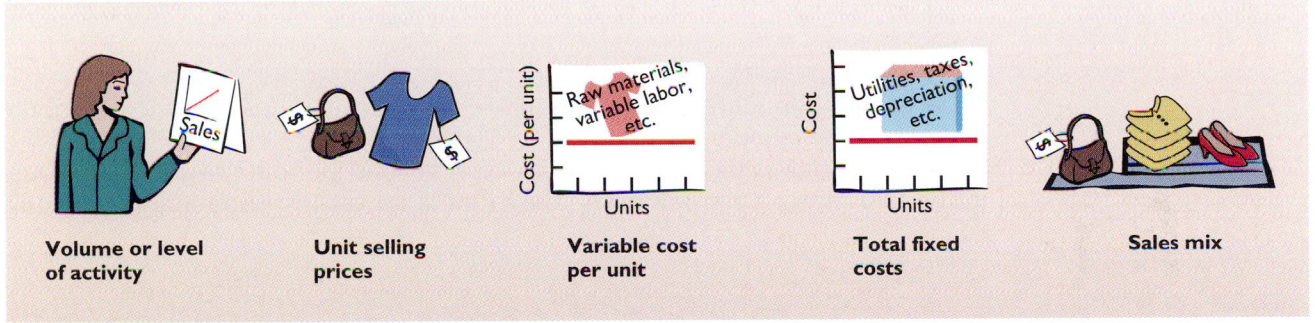

| Volume or level of activity | Unit selling prices | Variable cost per unit | Total fixed costs | Sales mix |

The following assumptions underlie each CVP application:

1. The behavior of both costs and revenues is linear throughout the relevant range of the activity index.
2. All costs can be classified as either variable or fixed with reasonable accuracy.
3. Changes in activity are the only factors that affect costs.
4. All units produced are sold.
5. When more than one type of product is sold, total sales will be in a constant sales mix. Sales mix complicates CVP analysis because different products will have different cost relationships. In this text we assume a single product. Technical issues of addressing sales mix problems are dealt with in advanced accounting courses.

When these five assumptions are not valid, the results of CVP analysis may be inaccurate.

In the applications of CVP analysis that follow, we will assume that the term "cost" includes **all** costs and expenses pertaining to production and sale of the product. That is, **cost includes manufacturing costs plus selling and administrative expenses**. We will use Vargo Video Company as an example. Relevant data for the videocassette recorders (VCRs) made by this company are as follows:

Unit selling price	$500
Unit variable costs	$300
Total monthly fixed costs	$200,000

ILLUSTRATION 23-10

Assumed selling price and cost data for Vargo Video

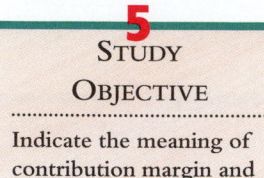

5
STUDY
OBJECTIVE

Indicate the meaning of contribution margin and the ways it may be expressed.

Contribution Margin

One of the key relationships in CVP analysis is **contribution margin (CM)**. **Contribution margin is the amount of revenue remaining after deducting variable costs.** For example, if we assume that Vargo Video sells 1,000 VCRs in one month, sales are $500,000 (1,000 × $500) and variable costs are $300,000 (1,000 × $300). Thus, contribution margin is $200,000 computed as follows:

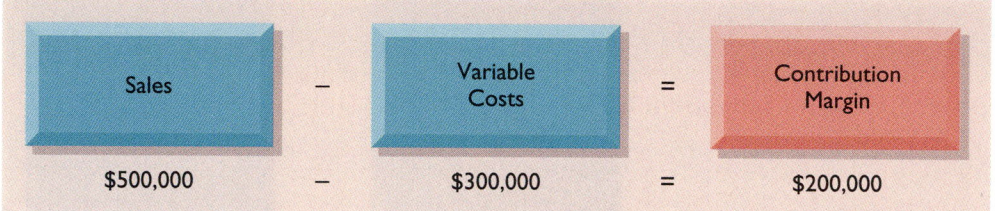

ILLUSTRATION 23-11

Formula for and computation of contribution margin

This contribution margin is then available to cover fixed costs and to contribute income for the company.

Views differ as to the best way to express contribution margin (CM). Some individuals favor a per unit basis. The formula for **contribution margin per unit** is:

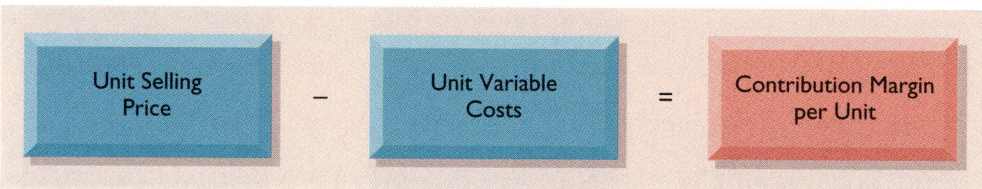

ILLUSTRATION 23-12

Formula for contribution margin per unit

At Vargo Video, the contribution margin per unit is $200, computed as follows:

$$\$500 - \$300 = \$200$$

Contribution margin per unit indicates that for every VCR sold, Vargo will have $200 to cover fixed costs and contribute to income. Since fixed costs are $200,000, Vargo Video must sell 1,000 VCRs ($200,000 ÷ $200) before there is any income. Above that sales volume, every sale will contribute $200 to income. Thus, if 1,500 units are sold, income will be $100,000 (500 × $200).

Others prefer to use a **contribution margin ratio**. The formula for this ratio is:

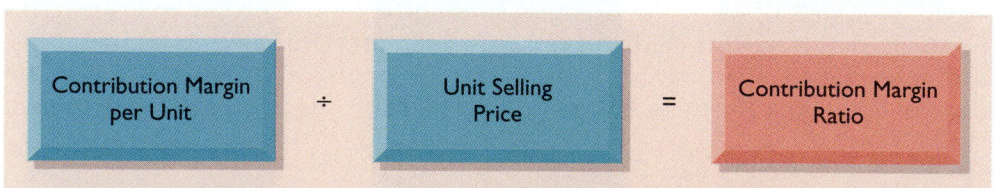

ILLUSTRATION 23-13

Formula for contribution margin ratio

HELPFUL HINT

The same ratio results from dividing total CM by total sales; i.e., $200,000 ÷ $500,000 = 40%.

At Vargo Video, the ratio is 40%, as shown below.

$$\$200 \div \$500 = 40\%$$

The CM ratio of 40% means that 40 cents of each sales dollar ($1 × 40%) is available to apply to fixed costs and to contribute to income. This expression of contribution margin is very helpful in determining the effect of changes in sales on income. To illustrate, if the management of Vargo Video wants to know the effect of a $50,000 increase in sales, they simply multiply $50,000 by the CM ratio (40%) to determine that income will increase $20,000.

Break–Even Analysis

A second key relationship in CVP analysis is the level of activity at which total revenues equal total costs, both fixed and variable. This level of activity is called the **break-even point**. At this volume of sales, the company will realize no income and suffer no loss. Since no income is involved when the break-even point is the objective, the analysis is often referred to simply as **break-even analysis**. Knowledge of the break-even point is useful to management in deciding whether to introduce new product lines, change sales prices on established products, or enter new market areas.

The break-even point can be:

1. Computed from a mathematical equation.
2. Computed by using contribution margin.
3. Derived from a cost-volume-profit (CVP) graph.

The break-even point can be expressed **either in sales dollars or sales units**.

6
STUDY OBJECTIVE

....

Identify the three ways that the break-even point may be determined.

ACCOUNTING IN ACTION

Business Insight

It pays to know how break-even is defined. For example, *Forrest Gump*, a highly successful film, provided little to the movie producers initially because of the definitions used for profits. As one producer noted, "The studios do not cheat and they do not lie—they just have very creative accounting methods. A studio, for example, has at least four ways to define 'break-even' and 24 different types of 'gross,' and they're all legitimate." Perhaps the Hollywood bookkeeper is right when he observed, "Most of the creative work in this business is done in the accounting department."

ILLUSTRATION 23-14

Break-even equation

Mathematical Equation

In its simplest form, the equation for break-even sales is:

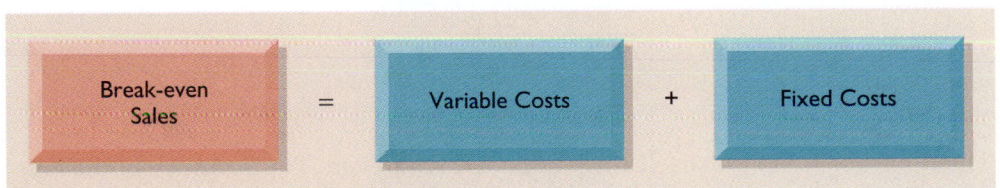

| Break-even Sales | = | Variable Costs | + | Fixed Costs |

The break-even point **in dollars** is found by expressing **variable costs as a percentage of unit selling price.** For Vargo Video, the percentage is 60% ($300 ÷ $500). The computation to determine sales dollars at the break-even point is:

ILLUSTRATION 23-15

Computation of break-even point in dollars

$$X = .60X + \$200,000$$
$$.40X = \$200,000$$
$$X = \textbf{\$500,000}$$

where:

X = sales dollars at the break-even point
$.60$ = variable costs as a percentage of unit selling price
$\$200,000$ = total fixed costs

Sales, therefore, must be $500,000 for Vargo Video to break even.

ACCOUNTING IN ACTION
Business Insight

As the accompanying chart shows, the level of break-even sales of the Big Three automakers moved lower in recent years. This meant increased profits for Detroit.

Source: Fortune, December 12, 1994, p. 32.

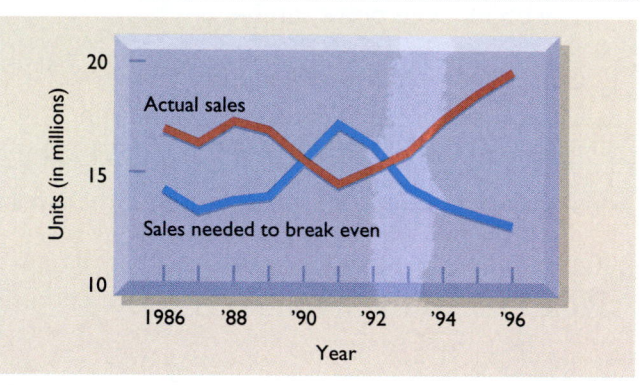

The break-even point **in units** can be computed directly from the mathematical equation by **using unit selling prices** and **unit variable costs**. The computation is:

ILLUSTRATION 23-16

Computation of break-even point in units

$$\$500X = \$300X + \$200,000$$
$$\$200X = \$200,000$$
$$X = \textbf{1,000 units}$$

where:

X = sales volume
$\$500$ = unit selling price
$\$300$ = variable cost per unit
$\$200,000$ = total fixed costs

Thus, Vargo Video must sell 1,000 units to break even. The accuracy of the computations can be proved as follows:

ILLUSTRATION 23-17

Break-even proof

Sales (1,000 × $500)		$500,000
Total costs:		
Variable (1,000 × $300)	$300,000	
Fixed	200,000	500,000
Net income		**$ –0–**

Contribution Margin Technique

Because we know that contribution margin equals total revenues less variable costs, it follows that at the break-even point, **contribution margin must equal total fixed costs**. On the basis of this relationship, the break-even point can be computed by using either the contribution margin per unit or the contribution margin ratio.

When the contribution margin per unit is used, the formula to compute break-even point in units is as follows:

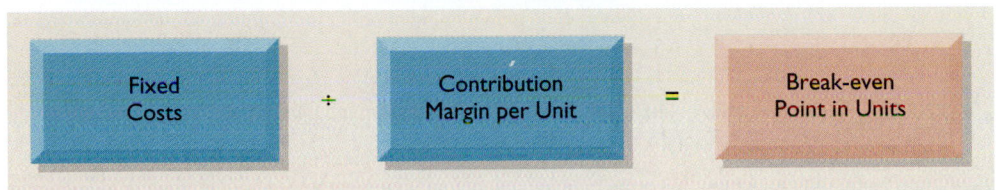

ILLUSTRATION 23-18

Formula for break-even point in units using contribution margin

For Vargo Video, the contribution margin per unit is $200, as explained above. Thus, the computation is:

$$\$200{,}000 \div \$200 = 1{,}000 \text{ units}$$

When the contribution margin ratio is used, the formula to compute break-even point in dollars is:

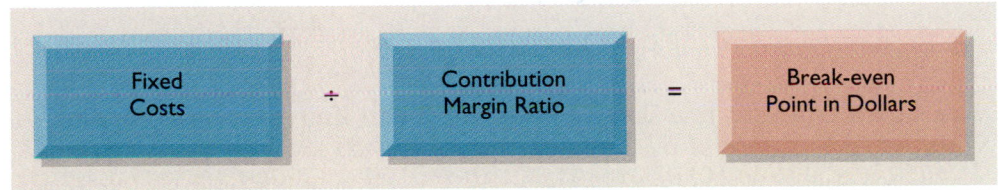

ILLUSTRATION 23-19

Formula for break-even point in dollars using contribution margin ratio

We know that the contribution margin ratio for Vargo Video is 40%. Thus, the computation is:

$$\$200{,}000 \div 40\% = \$500{,}000$$

Graphic Presentation

An effective way to derive the break-even point is to prepare a break-even graph. Because this graph also shows costs, volume, and profits, it is referred to as the **cost-volume-profit (CVP) graph**.

In the graph in Illustration 23-20, sales volume is recorded along the horizontal axis. This axis should extend to the maximum level of expected sales. Both total revenues (sales) and total costs (fixed plus variable) are recorded on the vertical axis.

The construction of the graph, using the data for Vargo Video, is as follows:

1. Plot the total revenue line starting at the zero activity level. For every VCR sold, total revenue increases by $500. For example, at 200 units, sales are $100,000, and at the upper level of activity (1,800 units), sales are $900,000. Note that the revenue line is assumed to be linear throughout the full range of activity.
2. Plot the total fixed cost by a horizontal line. For the VCRs, this line is plotted at $200,000, and it is the same at every level of activity.

ILLUSTRATION 23-20

CVP graph

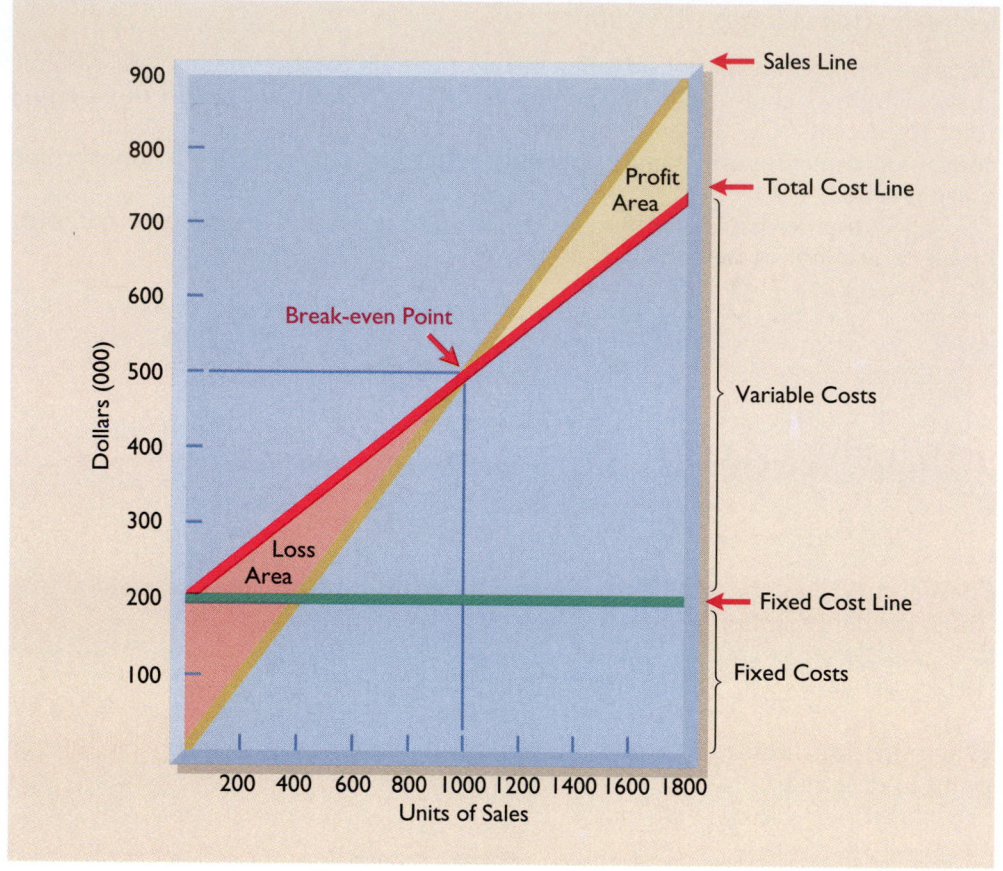

3. Plot the total cost line starting at the fixed cost line at zero activity and increasing the amount by the variable cost at each level of activity. For each VCR, variable costs are $300. Thus, at 200 units, total variable cost is $60,000 and the total cost is $260,000; at 1,800 units total variable cost is $540,000, and total cost is $740,000. On the graph, the amount of the variable cost can be derived from the difference between the total cost and fixed cost lines at each level of activity.

4. Determine the break-even point from the intersection of the total cost line and the total revenue line. The break-even point in dollars is found by drawing a horizontal line from the break-even point to the vertical axis. The break-even point in units is obtained by drawing a vertical line from the break-even point to the horizontal axis. For the VCRs, the break-even point is $500,000 of sales, or 1,000 units. At this sales level, Vargo Video will cover costs but make no profit.

In addition to identifying the break-even point, the CVP graph shows both the net income and net loss areas. Thus, the amount of income or loss at each level of sales can be derived from the total sales and total cost lines.

A CVP graph is especially useful in management meetings because the effects of a change in any element in the CVP analysis can be promptly portrayed. For example, a 10% increase in selling price will change the location of the total revenue line. Likewise, the effects on total costs of wage increases to both office employees and factory workers can be quickly observed.

TECHNOLOGY IN ACTION

Computer graphics are a valuable companion to an increasing number of computer software packages. Graphs can be instantly changed to provide visual "what if" analysis. This can all be done in color for either video or hard copy output.

Current technology allows for stunning graphs in a variety of different formats (pie charts, bar, stacked bar, two-dimensional, three-dimensional, etc.). In the appropriate situation, a graph can literally be worth a thousand words. However, just because graphs can be quickly generated does not mean they can convey all the needed information for a management decision.

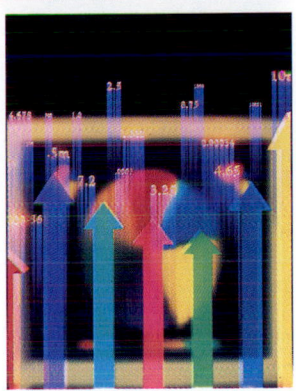

BEFORE YOU GO ON . . .

Review It

1. What are the assumptions that underlie each CVP application?
2. What is contribution margin and how may it be expressed?
3. How can the break-even point be determined?

Do It

Lombardi Company has a unit selling price of $400, variable costs per unit of $240, and fixed costs of $160,000. Compute the break-even point in units using (a) a mathematical equation and (b) contribution margin per unit.

Reasoning: The mathematical equation is Break-even Sales = Variable Costs + Fixed Costs. Using contribution margin per unit, the formula is Fixed Costs ÷ Contribution Margin per Unit = Break-even Point in Units.

Solution: (a) The equation is $400X = $240X + $160,000. Thus, the break-even point in units is 1,000 ($160,000 ÷ $160X). (b) Contribution margin per unit is $160 ($400 − $240). The formula is $160,000 ÷ $160, and the break-even point in units is 1,000.

Related exercise material: BE23–5, BE23–6, E23–3, E23–4, E23–5, E23–6, and E23–7.

Margin of Safety

The margin of safety is another relationship that may be calculated in CVP analysis. **Margin of safety** is the difference between actual or expected sales and sales at the break-even point. This relationship measures the "breathing room" or "cushion" that management has in order to break even if actual or expected sales fail to materialize. The margin of safety may be expressed in dollars or as a ratio.

The formula for stating the **margin of safety in dollars** is:

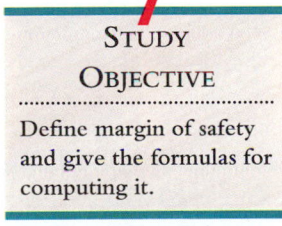
STUDY OBJECTIVE 7

Define margin of safety and give the formulas for computing it.

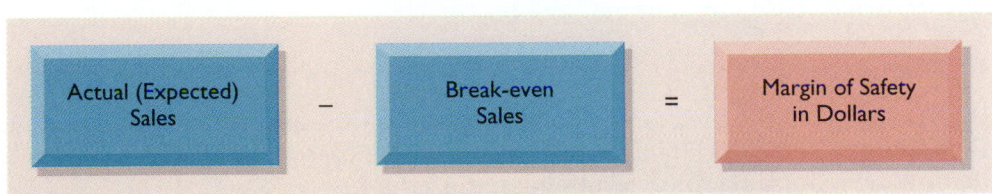

ILLUSTRATION 23-21
Formula for margin of safety in dollars

Assuming that actual (expected) sales for Vargo Video are $750,000, the computation is:

$$\$750{,}000 - \$500{,}000 = \$250{,}000$$

In contrast, the formula and computation for determining the **margin of safety ratio** are:

ILLUSTRATION 23-22

Formula for margin of safety ratio

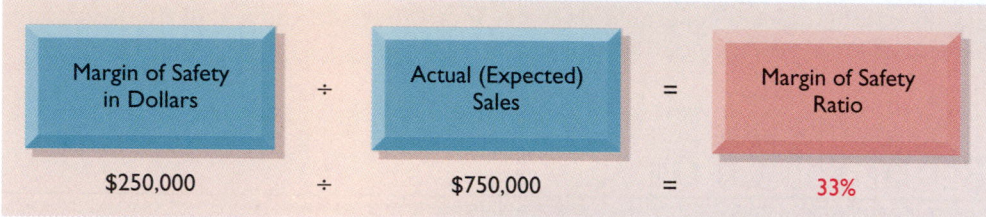

Margin of Safety in Dollars	÷	Actual (Expected) Sales	=	Margin of Safety Ratio
$250,000	÷	$750,000	=	33%

ACCOUNTING IN ACTION
Business Insight

Computation of break-even and margin of safety is important for various types of business. Consider how the promoter for the Rolling Stones' tour used the break-even point and margin of safety. For example, one outdoor show should bring 70,000 individuals for a gross of $2.45 million. The promoter guarantees $1.2 million to the Rolling Stones. In addition, 20% of gross or approximately $500,000 goes to the stadium in which the performance is staged. Add another $400,000 for other expenses such as ticket takers, parking attendants, advertising, and so on. This leaves $350,000 per show to the promoter, if it sells out. At 75%, the promoter breaks about even, and at 50%, the promoter loses hundreds of thousands of dollars. However, the promoter also shares in sales of T-shirts and memorabilia for which the promoter will net over $7 million during the tour. If the Rolling Stones' tour is a success, the promoter could make $35 million!

The higher the dollars or the percentage, the greater the margin of safety. The adequacy of the margin of safety should be evaluated by management in terms of such factors as the vulnerability of the product to competitive pressures and to downturns in the economy.

Target Net Income

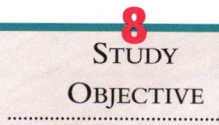

Management usually sets an income objective for individual product lines. This objective called **target net income** is extremely useful to management because it indicates the sales necessary to achieve a specified level of income. The amount of sales necessary to achieve target net income can be determined from each of the approaches used in determining break-even sales.

Mathematical Equation

We know that at the break-even point no profit or loss results for the company. By adding a factor for target net income to the break-even equation, we obtain the following formula for determining required sales:

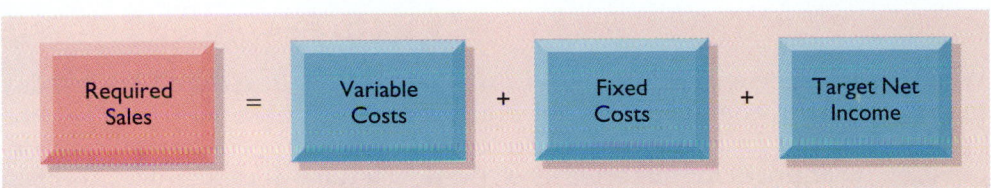

ILLUSTRATION 23-23

Formula for required sales to meet target net income

Required sales may be expressed in **either sales dollars or sales units**. Assuming that target net income is $120,000 for Vargo Video, the computation of required sales in dollars is as follows:

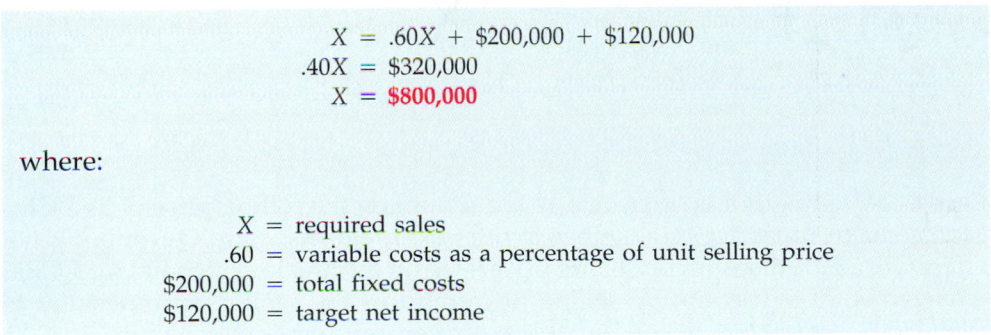

ILLUSTRATION 23-24

Computation of required sales

$$X = .60X + \$200,000 + \$120,000$$
$$.40X = \$320,000$$
$$X = \mathbf{\$800,000}$$

where:

$$X = \text{required sales}$$
$$.60 = \text{variable costs as a percentage of unit selling price}$$
$$\$200,000 = \text{total fixed costs}$$
$$\$120,000 = \text{target net income}$$

HELPFUL HINT
Alternatively, the required sales units can be computed directly by using unit prices in the equation: $500X = $300X + $200,000 + $120,000; $200X = $320,000 or 1,600 units.

The sales volume in units at the targeted income level is found by dividing the sales dollars by the unit selling price ($800,000 ÷ $500) = 1,600 units.

Contribution Margin Technique

As in the case of break-even sales, the sales required to meet a target net income can be computed in either dollars or units. The formula using the contribution margin ratio is as follows:

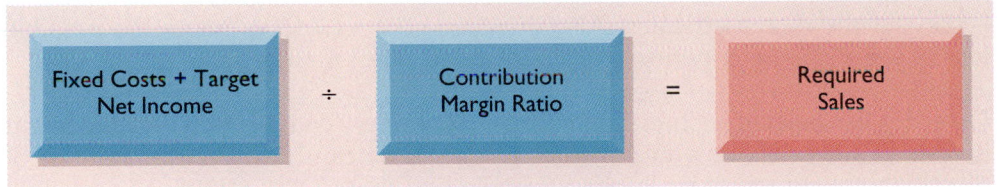

ILLUSTRATION 23-25

Formula for required sales in dollars using contribution margin ratio

The computation for Vargo Video is as follows:

$$\$320,000 \div 40\% = \$800,000$$

Graphic Presentation

The CVP graph presented in Illustration 23-20 can also be used to derive the sales required to meet target net income. In the profit area of the graph, the distance between the sales line and the total cost line at any point equals net income. Required sales are found by analyzing the differences between the two lines until the desired net income is found.

CVP and Changes in the Business Environment

When the IBM personal computer (PC) was introduced, it sold for $2,500; today the same type of computer sells for much less. When high oil prices fell, the break-even point for airline and trucking companies dropped dramatically. Because of lower prices for imported steel, the demand for domestic steel dropped significantly. The point should be clear: Business conditions change rapidly and management must respond intelligently to these changes. CVP analysis can help.

To illustrate how CVP analysis can be used in responding to change, we will use the following independent situations that might occur at Vargo Video. Each case is based on the original VCR sales and cost data, which were:

ILLUSTRATION 23-26

Original VCR sales and cost data

Unit selling price	$500
Unit variable cost	$300
Total fixed costs	$200,000
Break-even sales	$500,000 or 1,000 units

Case I. A competitor is offering a 10% discount on the selling price of its VCRs. Management must decide whether to offer a similar discount. **Question:** What effect will a 10% discount on selling price have on the break-even point for VCRs? **Answer:** A 10% discount on selling price reduces the selling price per unit to $450 [$500 − ($500 × 10%)]. Variable costs per unit remain unchanged at $300. Thus, the contribution margin per unit is $150. Assuming no change in fixed costs, break-even sales are 1,333 units, computed as follows:

ILLUSTRATION 23-27

Computation of break-even sales in units

Fixed Costs	÷	Contribution Margin per Unit	=	Break-even Sales
$200,000	÷	$150	=	1,333 units (rounded)

For Vargo Video, this change would require monthly sales to increase by 333 units or 33⅓% in order to break even. In reaching a conclusion about offering a 10% discount to customers, management must determine the likelihood of achieving the increased sales. Also, management should estimate the possible loss of sales if the competitor's discount price is not matched.

Case II. To meet the continuing threat of foreign competition, management invests in new robotic equipment that will significantly lower the amount of direct labor required to make the VCRs. It is estimated that total fixed costs will increase 30% and that variable cost per unit will decrease 30%. **Question:** What effect will the new equipment have on the sales volume required to break even? **Answer:** Total fixed costs become $260,000 [$200,000 + (30% × $200,000)], and variable cost per unit is now $210 [$300 − (30% × $300)]. The new break-even point is approximately 900 units, computed as follows:

ILLUSTRATION 23-28

Computation of break-even sales in units

Fixed Costs	÷	Contribution Margin per Unit	=	Break-even Sales
$260,000	÷	($500 − $210)	=	900 units (rounded)

These changes appear to be advantageous for Vargo Video because the break-even point is reduced by 10%, or 100 units.

Case III. The principal supplier of raw materials has just announced a price increase. It is estimated that the higher cost will increase the variable cost of VCRs by $25 per unit. Management would like to hold the line on the selling price of VCRs. It plans a cost-cutting program that will save $17,500 in fixed costs per month. Vargo is currently realizing monthly net income of $80,000 on sales of 1,400 VCRs. **Question:** What increase in sales will be needed to maintain the same level of net income? **Answer:** The variable cost per unit increases to $325 ($300 + $25), and fixed costs are reduced to $182,500 ($200,000 − $17,500). Because of the change in variable cost, the variable cost becomes 65% of sales ($325 ÷ $500). Using the equation for target net income, we find that required sales are $750,000, computed as follows:

ILLUSTRATION 23-29

Computation of required sales

Required Sales = Variable Costs + Fixed Costs + Target Net Income

$$X = .65X + \$182,500 + \$80,000$$
$$.35X = \$262,500$$
$$X = \mathbf{\$750,000}$$

To achieve the required sales, 1,500 VCRs will have to be sold ($750,000 ÷ $500), an increase of 100 units. If this does not seem to be a reasonable expectation, management will either have to effect further reductions in costs or accept less net income if the selling price remains unchanged.

CVP Income Statement

As you have learned, cost behavior and contribution margin are key factors in CVP analysis. Because management makes its decisions on these factors, it often wants the results of these decisions reported in a similar format. This has led to the development for **internal use only** of a **CVP** or **contribution margin format** for the income statement. The **CVP income statement** classifies costs and expenses as variable or fixed and specifically reports contribution margin in the body of the statement. This is in contrast to the income statement traditionally prepared for external use, in which no disclosure is made of the behavior of costs and expenses. In the traditional statement, costs and expenses are classified only by function, such as cost of goods sold, selling expenses, and administrative expenses.

To illustrate the CVP income statement, we will assume that Vargo Video reaches its target net income of $120,000 (see page 1011). From an analysis of the transactions, the following information is obtained on the $680,000 of costs that were incurred in June:

9

STUDY
OBJECTIVE
....
Describe the essential features of a cost–volume–profit income statement.

ILLUSTRATION 23-30

Assumed cost and expense data

	Variable	Fixed	Total
Cost of goods sold	$400,000	$120,000	$520,000
Selling expenses	60,000	40,000	100,000
Administrative expenses	20,000	40,000	60,000
	$480,000	$200,000	$680,000

The CVP income statement and the conventional income statement based on these data are shown side-by-side for comparative purposes in Illustration 23-31.

VARGO VIDEO COMPANY **Income Statements** **For the Month Ended June 30, 1999**				
Traditional Format			**CVP Format**	
Sales		$800,000	Sales		$800,000
Cost of goods sold		520,000	Variable expenses		
Gross profit		280,000	Cost of goods sold	$400,000	
Operating expenses			Selling expenses	60,000	
Selling expenses	$100,000		Administrative expenses	20,000	
Administrative expenses	60,000		Total variable expenses		480,000
Total operating expenses		160,000	**CONTRIBUTION MARGIN**		**320,000**
Net income		**$120,000**	Fixed expenses		
			Cost of goods sold	120,000	
			Selling expenses	40,000	
			Administrative expenses	40,000	
			Total fixed expenses		200,000
			Net income		**$120,000**

ILLUSTRATION 23-31

*Traditional versus CVP
income statement*

Note that net income is the same ($120,000) in both of the statements. The major difference is the format for the expenses. As illustrated, the CVP statement classifies costs and expenses as either variable or fixed. Another difference is that the traditional statement shows gross profit, whereas the CVP statement shows contribution margin. Study the CVP form carefully. It will be used in remaining chapters, and it is often used in business in internal reporting to management.

BEFORE YOU GO ON . . .

Review It

1. What is the formula for computing the margin of safety (a) in dollars and (b) as a ratio?
2. How does a CVP income statement differ from a traditional income statement?

Do It

At Kimoto Company, variable costs are 65% of sales, fixed costs are $245,000, and target net income is $70,000. Compute the required sales in dollars using the mathematical equation approach.

    Reasoning: The mathematical equation is Required Sales = Variable Costs + Fixed Costs + Target Net Income.

    Solution: Required sales are $900,000; the computation is: $X = (.65X + \$245,000 + \$70,000)$.

Related exercise material: BE23–7, BE23–8, E23–4, and E23–6.

10
STUDY
OBJECTIVE
....
Explain the difference
between absorption
costing and variable
costing.

VARIABLE COSTING

In the earlier managerial chapters, both variable and fixed manufacturing costs have been classified as product costs. In job order costing, for example, a job is assigned the costs of direct materials, direct labor, and both variable and fixed manufacturing overhead. This costing approach is referred to as full or **absorption costing**, because all manufacturing costs are charged to, or absorbed by, the product. An alternative approach is to use variable costing. Under **variable costing** only direct materials, direct labor, and variable manufacturing overhead costs are considered product costs; fixed manufacturing overhead costs are recognized as period costs (expenses) when incurred. The difference between absorption costing and variable costing is graphically shown as follows:

ILLUSTRATION 23-32

Difference between absorption costing and variable costing

Selling and administrative expenses are period costs under both absorption and variable costing.

To illustrate the computation of unit production cost under absorption and variable costing, assume that Premium Products Corporation manufactures a polyurethane sealant called Fix-it for car windshields. Relevant data for Fix-it in January 1999, the first month of production, are as follows:

Selling price: $20 per unit.

Units: Produced 30,000; sold 20,000; beginning inventory zero.

Variable unit costs: Manufacturing $9 (direct materials $5, direct labor $3, and variable overhead $1), and selling and administrative expenses $2.

Fixed costs: Manufacturing overhead $120,000 and selling and administrative expenses $15,000.

The per unit production cost under each costing approach is:

Type of Cost	Absorption Costing	Variable Costing
Direct materials	$ 5	$5
Direct labor	3	3
Variable manufacturing overhead	1	1
Fixed manufacturing overhead		
($120,000 ÷ 30,000 units produced)	4	0
Total unit cost	**$13**	**$9**

ILLUSTRATION 23-33

Computation of per unit production cost

The difference in total unit cost of $4 ($13 − $9) occurs because fixed manufacturing costs are a product cost under absorption costing and a period cost under variable costing. Based on these data, each unit sold and each unit remaining in inventory is costed at $13 under absorption costing and at $9 under variable costing.

Effects on Income

The income statements under the two costing approaches are shown in Illustrations 23-34 and 23-35. The conventional income statement format is used with absorption costing, and the cost-volume-profit format is used with variable costing. Computations are inserted parenthetically in the statements to facilitate your understanding of the amounts.

PREMIUM PRODUCTS COMPANY **Income Statement** **For the Month Ended January 31, 1999** **(Absorption Costing)**		
Sales (20,000 units × $20)		$400,000
Cost of goods sold		
Inventory, January 1	$ –0–	
Cost of goods manufactured (30,000 units × $13)	390,000	
Cost of goods available for sale	390,000	
Inventory, January 31 (10,000 units × $13)	**130,000**	
Cost of goods sold (20,000 units × $13)		260,000
Gross profit		140,000
Selling and administrative expenses		
(Variable 20,000 units × $2 + fixed $15,000)		55,000
Income from operations		**$ 85,000**

Income from operations under absorption costing shown in Illustration 23-34 is $40,000 higher than under variable costing ($85,000 − $45,000) shown in Illustration 23-35.

As highlighted in the two income statements, there is a $40,000 difference in the ending inventories ($130,000 under absorption costing and $90,000 under variable costing). Under absorption costing, $40,000 of the fixed overhead costs (10,000 units × $4) have been deferred to a future period as a product cost. In contrast, under variable costing the entire fixed manufacturing costs are expensed when incurred.

PREMIUM PRODUCTS COMPANY **Income Statement** **For the Month Ended January 31, 1999** **(Variable Costing)**		
Sales (20,000 units × $20)		$400,000
Variable expenses		
Variable cost of goods sold		
Inventory, January 1	$ –0–	
Variable manufacturing costs (30,000 units × $9)	270,000	
Cost of goods available for sale	270,000	
Inventory, January 31 (10,000 units × $9)	**90,000**	
Variable cost of goods sold	180,000	
Variable selling and administrative expenses		
(20,000 units × $2)	40,000	
Total variable expenses		220,000
Contribution margin		180,000
Fixed expenses		
Manufacturing overhead	120,000	
Selling and administrative expenses	15,000	
Total fixed expenses		135,000
Income from operations		**$ 45,000**

As shown, when units produced exceed units sold, income under absorption costing is higher than under variable costing. Conversely, when units produced are less than units sold, income under absorption costing is lower than under variable costing. The reason is that the cost of the **ending inventory will be higher under absorption costing** than under variable costing. For example, if 30,000 units of Fix-it are sold in January and only 20,000 units are produced, income from operations will be $40,000 less under absorption costing than under variable costing because of the $40,000 difference ($130,000 vs. $90,000) in the ending inventories.

When units produced and sold are the same, income from operations will be equal under the two costing approaches. Since there is no increase in ending inventory, fixed overhead costs of the current period are not deferred to future periods through the ending inventory. The foregoing effects of the two costing approaches on income from operations may be summarized as follows:

ILLUSTRATION 23-36

Summary of income effects

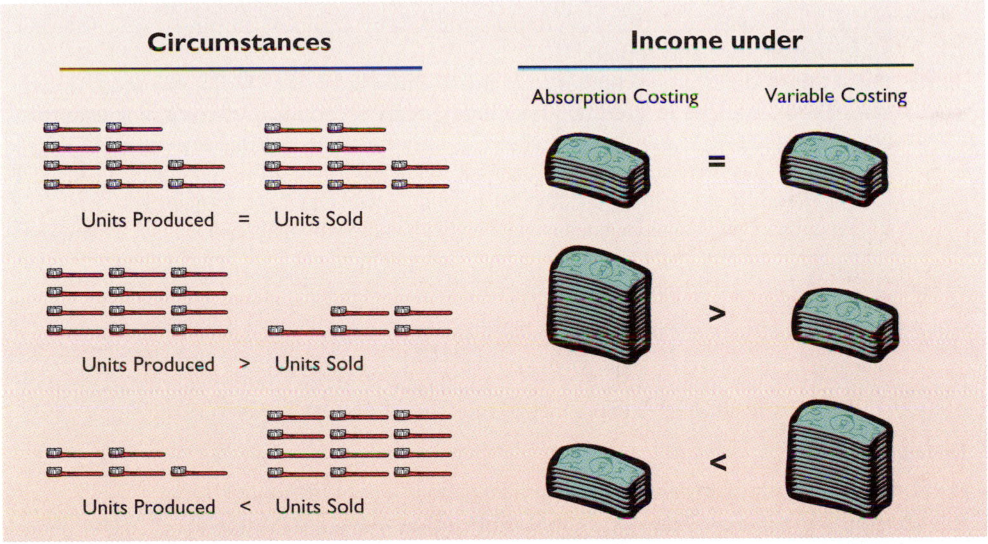

Rationale for Variable Costing

The rationale for variable costing centers on the purpose of fixed manufacturing costs which is **to have productive facilities available for use**. Conceptually, these costs are incurred whether a company operates at zero or at 100% of capacity. Thus, proponents of variable costing argue that these costs should be expensed in the period in which they are incurred.

Supporters of absorption costing defend the assignment of fixed manufacturing overhead costs to inventory on the basis that these costs are as much a cost of getting a product (such as Fix-it) ready for sale as direct materials or direct labor. Accordingly, these costs should not be matched with revenues until the product is sold.

The use of variable costing in product costing is acceptable **only for internal use by management**. It cannot be used in determining product costs in financial statements prepared in accordance with generally accepted accounting principles because it understates inventory costs. To comply with the matching principle, a company must use absorption costing for its work in process and finished goods inventories. Similarly, absorption costing must be used for income tax purposes.

BEFORE YOU GO ON . . .

Review It

1. What is variable costing?
2. What is the rationale for variable costing?

A LOOK BACK AT OUR FEATURE STORY

Refer to the opening story and answer the following questions:

(a) What are some variable costs that Amy's Dance Studio might incur?
(b) What are some fixed costs that Amy's Dance Studio might incur?
(c) Why is it important to segregate costs into variable and fixed costs when analyzing profitability?

Solution:

(a) Some variable costs are instructors' wages, dance towels, dance shoes, and leotards.
(b) Some fixed costs are insurance, depreciation, rent, utilities, administrative salaries, and maintenance and repairs.
(c) For Amy to determine whether to increase the size of her studio, she must understand how changes in volume affect changes in revenues and costs. For example, when advertising expense is increased, it may increase volume and revenue, or it may increase revenue but not generate any additional profit. By segregating costs into variable and fixed, Amy can determine what dollar impact a change in sales revenue will have on overall profit.

DEMONSTRATION PROBLEM

Mabo Company makes calculators that sell for $20 each. For the coming year, management expects fixed costs to total $220,000 and variable costs to be $9.00 per unit.

Instructions

(a) Compute break-even sales in dollars using the mathematical equation.
(b) Compute break-even sales using the contribution margin (CM) ratio.
(c) Compute the margin of safety percentage assuming actual sales are $500,000.
(d) Compute the sales required to earn net income of $165,000.

PROBLEM-SOLVING STRATEGIES

1. Know the formulas.
2. Recognize that variable costs change with sales volume; fixed costs do not.
3. Avoid computational errors.
4. Prove your answers.

SOLUTION TO DEMONSTRATION PROBLEM

(a) Break-even sales = Variable costs + Fixed costs
$$X = .45X + \$220,000$$
$$.55X = \$220,000$$
$$X = \$400,000$$

(b) Contribution margin per unit = Unit selling price − Unit variable costs
$$\$11 = \$20 - \$9$$
Contribution margin ratio = Contribution margin per unit ÷ Unit selling price
$$55\% = \$11 \div \$20$$
Break-even sales = Fixed cost ÷ Contribution margin ratio
$$X = \$220,000 \div 55\%$$
$$X = \$400,000$$

(c) Margin of safety = $\dfrac{\text{Actual sales} - \text{Break-even sales}}{\text{Actual sales}}$

$$= \frac{\$500,000 - \$400,000}{\$500,000}$$

$$= 20\%$$

(d) Required sales = Variable costs + Fixed costs + Net income
$$X = .45X + \$220,000 + \$165,000$$
$$.55X = \$385,000$$
$$X = \$700,000$$

SUMMARY OF STUDY OBJECTIVES

1. *Distinguish between variable and fixed costs.* Variable costs are costs that vary in total directly and proportionately with changes in the activity index. Fixed costs are costs that remain the same in total regardless of changes in the activity index.

2. *Explain the meaning and importance of the relevant range.* The relevant range is the range of activity in which a company expects to operate during a year. It is important in CVP analysis because the behavior of costs is linear throughout the relevant range.

3. *Explain the concept of mixed costs.* Mixed costs increase in total but not proportionately with changes in the activity level. For purposes of CVP analysis, mixed costs must be classified into their fixed and variable elements. One method that management may use is the high-low method.

4. *State the five components of cost-volume-profit analysis.* The five components of CVP analysis are (a) volume or level of activity, (b) unit selling prices, (c) variable cost per unit, (d) total fixed costs, and (e) sales mix.

5. *Indicate the meaning of contribution margin and the ways it may be expressed.* Contribution margin is the amount of revenue remaining after deducting variable costs. It can be expressed as a per unit amount or as a ratio.

6. *Identify the three ways that the break-even point may be determined.* The break-even point can be (a) computed from a mathematical equation, (b) computed by using a contribution margin technique, and (c) derived from a CVP graph.

7. *Define margin of safety and give the formulas for computing it.* Margin of safety is the difference between actual or expected sales and sales at the break-even point. The formulas for margin of safety are Actual (Expected) Sales − Break-even Sales = Margin of Safety in Dollars; Margin of Safety in Dollars ÷ Actual (Expected) Sales = Margin of Safety Ratio.

8. *Give the formulas for determining sales required to earn target net income.* One formula is: Required Sales = Variable Costs + Fixed Costs + Target Net Income. Another formula is: Fixed Costs + Target Net Income ÷ Contribution Margin Ratio = Required Sales.

9. *Describe the essential features of a cost-volume-profit income statement.* The CVP income statement classifies costs and expenses as variable or fixed and reports contribution margin in the body of the statement.

10. *Explain the difference between absorption costing and variable costing.* Under absorption costing, fixed manufacturing costs are product costs; under variable costing, fixed manufacturing costs are period costs.

GLOSSARY

Absorption costing   A costing approach in which all manufacturing costs are charged to the product. (p. 1015).

Activity index   The activity that causes changes in the behavior of costs. (p. 997).

Break-even point   The level of activity at which total revenues equal total costs. (p. 1005).

Contribution margin (CM)   The amount of revenue remaining after deducting variable costs. (p. 1004).

Cost behavior analysis   The study of how specific costs respond to changes in the level of activity within a company. (p. 996).

Cost-volume-profit (CVP) analysis   The study of the effects of changes in costs and volume on a company's profits. (p. 1003).

Cost-volume-profit (CVP) graph   A graph showing the relationship between costs, volume, and profits. (p. 1007).

Cost-volume-profit (CVP) income statement   A statement for internal use that classifies costs and expenses as fixed or variable and reports contribution margin in the body of the statement. (p. 1013).

Fixed costs   Costs that remain the same in total regardless of changes in the activity level. (p. 997).

High-low method   A mathematical method that uses the total costs incurred at the high and low levels of activity. (p. 1000).

Margin of safety   The difference between actual or expected sales and sales at the break-even point. (p. 1009).

Mixed costs   Costs that contain both a variable and a fixed cost element and change in total but not proportionately with changes in the activity level. (p. 999).

Relevant range   The range of the activity index over which the company expects to operate during the year. (p. 999).

Target net income   The income objective for individual product lines. (p. 1010).

Variable costing   A costing approach in which only variable manufacturing costs are product costs and fixed manufacturing costs are period costs (expenses). (p. 1015).

Variable costs   Costs that vary in total directly and proportionately with changes in the activity level. (p. 997).

SELF-STUDY QUESTIONS

Answers are at the end of the chapter.

(SO 1) 1. Variable costs are costs that:
  a. vary in total directly and proportionately with changes in the activity level.
  b. remain the same per unit at every activity level.
  c. None of the above.
  d. Both (a) and (b) above.

(SO 2) 2. The relevant range is:
  a. the range of activity in which variable costs will be curvilinear.
  b. the range of activity in which fixed costs will be curvilinear.
  c. the range over which the company expects to operate during a year.
  d. usually from zero to 100% of operating capacity.

(SO 3) 3. Mixed costs consist of a:
  a. variable cost element and a fixed cost element.
  b. fixed cost element and a controllable cost element.
  c. relevant cost element and a controllable cost element.
  d. variable cost element and a relevant cost element.

(SO 4) 4. One of the following is *not* involved in CVP analysis. That factor is:
  a. sales mix.
  b. unit selling prices.
  c. fixed costs per unit.
  d. volume or level of activity.

(SO 5) 5. Contribution margin:
  a. is revenue remaining after deducting variable costs.
  b. may be expressed as contribution margin per unit.
  c. is selling price less cost of goods sold.
  d. Both (a) and (b) above.

(SO 6) 6. Gossen Company is planning to sell 200,000 pliers for $4.00 per unit. The contribution margin ratio is 25%. If

Gossen will break even at this level of sales, what are the fixed costs?
  a. $100,000.
  b. $160,000.
  c. $200,000.
  d. $300,000.

(SO 7) 7. Marshall Company had actual sales of $600,000 when break-even sales were $420,000. What is the margin of safety ratio?
  a. 25%.
  b. 30%.
  c. 33⅓%.
  d. 45%.

(SO 8) 8. The mathematical equation for computing required sales to obtain target net income is: Required sales =
  a. Variable costs + Target net income.
  b. Variable costs + Fixed costs + Target net income.
  c. Fixed costs + Target net income.
  d. No correct answer is given.

(SO 9) 9. Cournot Company sells 100,000 wrenches for $12.00 a unit. Fixed costs are $300,000 and net income is $200,000. What should be reported as variable expenses in the CVP income statement?
  a. $700,000.
  b. $900,000.
  c. $500,000.
  d. $1,000,000.

(SO 10) 10. Under variable costing, fixed manufacturing costs are classified as:
  a. period costs.
  b. product costs.
  c. both (a) and (b).
  d. neither (a) nor (b).

QUESTIONS

1. (a) What is cost behavior analysis?
   (b) Why is cost behavior analysis important to management?

2. (a) Jenny Beason asks your help in understanding the term "activity index." Explain the meaning and importance of this term for Jenny.
   (b) State the two ways that variable costs may be defined.

3. Contrast the effects of changes in the activity level on total and on unit fixed costs.

4. R.E. Chang claims that the relevant range concept is important only for variable costs.
   (a) Explain the relevant range concept.
   (b) Do you agree with R.E.'s claim? Explain.

5. "The relevant range is indispensable in cost behavior analysis." Is this true? Why?

6. Bart Detar is confused. He does not understand why rent on his apartment is a fixed cost and rent on a Hertz rental truck is a mixed cost. Explain the difference to Bart.

7. How should mixed costs be classified in CVP analysis? What approach is used to effect the appropriate classification?

8. At the high and low levels of activity during the month, direct labor hours are 90,000 and 40,000, respectively, and the related costs are $150,000 and $100,000. What are the fixed and variable costs at any level of activity?

9. "Cost-volume-profit (CVP) analysis is based entirely on unit costs." Do you agree? Explain.

10. Patty Dye defines contribution margin as the amount of profit available to cover operating expenses. Is there any truth in this definition? Discuss.

11. In Eusey Company, the Speedo pocket calculator sells for $40, and variable costs per unit are estimated to be $22. What is the contribution margin per unit and the contribution margin ratio?

12. "Break-even analysis is of limited use to management because a company cannot survive by just breaking even." Do you agree? Explain.

13. Total fixed costs are $18,000 for Froelich Inc.; it has a contribution margin per unit of $15, and a contribution margin ratio of 20%. Compute the break-even sales in dollars.

14. Linda Gibbons asks your help in constructing a CVP graph. Explain to Linda how (a) the break-even point is plotted and (b) the level of activity and dollar sales at the break-even point are determined.

15. Define the term "margin of safety." If Hancock Company expects to sell 1,250 units of its product at $12 per unit, and break-even sales for the product are $12,000, what is the margin of safety ratio?

16. Inwood Company's break-even sales are $600,000. Assuming fixed costs are $210,000, what sales dollars are needed to achieve a target net income of $56,000?

17. What are the similarities and differences between a CVP income statement and a traditional income statement?

18. The traditional income statement for Reeves Company shows sales $900,000, cost of goods sold $500,000, and operating expenses $200,000. Assuming all costs and expenses are 70% variable and 30% fixed, prepare a CVP income statement through contribution margin.

19. Distinguish between absorption costing and variable costing.

20. (a) What is the major rationale for the use of variable costing? (b) Discuss why variable costing may not be used for financial reporting purposes.

BRIEF EXERCISES

BE23–1 Monthly production costs in Kasnic Company for two levels of production are as follows:

Cost	2,000 units	4,000 units
Indirect labor	$10,000	$20,000
Supervisory salaries	5,000	5,000
Maintenance	3,000	3,600

Indicate which costs are variable, fixed, and mixed, and give the reason for each answer.

Classify costs as variable, fixed, or mixed.
(SO 1, 3)

BE23–2 In Manhart Company, the relevant range of production is 40–80% of capacity. At 40% of capacity, a variable cost is $2,000 and a fixed cost is $4,000. Diagram the behavior of each cost within the relevant range assuming the behavior is linear.

Diagram the behavior of costs within the relevant range.
(SO 2)

BE23–3 In Leyva Company, a mixed cost is $40,000 plus $8 per direct labor hour. Diagram the behavior of the cost using increments of 1,000 hours up to 5,000 hours on the horizontal axis and increments of $20,000 up to $80,000 on the vertical axis.

Diagram the behavior of a mixed cost.
(SO 3)

BE23–4 Neufeld Company accumulates the following data concerning a mixed cost, using miles as the activity level.

	Miles Driven	Total Cost		Miles Driven	Total Cost
January	8,000	$14,100	March	8,500	$14,800
February	7,500	13,400	April	8,200	14,400

Compute the variable and fixed cost elements using the high-low method.

Determine variable and fixed cost elements using the high-low method.
(SO 3)

BE23–5 Determine the missing amounts.

	Unit Selling Price	Unit Variable Costs	Contribution Margin per Unit	Contribution Margin Ratio
1.	$250	$180	(a)	(b)
2.	$500	(c)	$140	(d)
3.	(e)	(f)	$360	40%

Determine missing amounts for contribution margin.
(SO 5)

BE23–6 Cajun Company has a unit selling price of $400, variable costs per unit of $280, and fixed costs of $120,000. Compute the break-even point using (a) a mathematical equation and (b) contribution margin per unit.

Compute the break-even point.
(SO 6)

Compute the margin of safety and the margin of safety ratio.
(SO 7)
Compute sales for target net income.
(SO 8)
Prepare CVP income statement.
(SO 9)

BE23–7 In Petry Company actual sales are $1,200,000 and break-even sales are $840,000. Compute (a) the margin of safety in dollars and (b) the margin of safety ratio.

BE23–8 In Riddell Company, variable costs are 75% of sales, fixed costs are $160,000, and management's net income goal is $60,000. Compute the required sales needed to achieve management's target net income of $60,000. (Use the mathematical equation approach.)

BE23–9 Zimmerman Manufacturing Inc. has sales of $1,900,000 for the first quarter of 1999. In making the sales, the company incurred the following costs and expenses:

	Variable	Fixed
Cost of goods sold	$760,000	$540,000
Selling expenses	95,000	60,000
Administrative expenses	79,000	66,000

Prepare a CVP income statement for the quarter ended March 31, 1999.

Compute net income under absorption and variable costing.
(SO 10)

BE23–10 ▱▱▱▷ Sayler Company's fixed overhead costs are $5 per unit, and its variable overhead costs are $8 per unit. In the first month of operations, 50,000 units are produced, and 45,000 units are sold. Write a short memorandum to the chief financial officer of Sayler Company explaining which costing approach will produce the higher income and what the difference will be.

EXERCISES

Define and classify variable, fixed, and mixed costs.
(SO 1, 3)

E23–1 Massey Company manufactures a single product. Annual production costs incurred in the manufacturing process are shown below for two levels of production:

	Costs Incurred			
Production in Units	**5,000**		**10,000**	
Production Costs	**Total Cost**	**Cost/ Unit**	**Total Cost**	**Cost/ Unit**
Direct materials	$8,250	$1.65	$16,500	$1.65
Direct labor	9,500	1.90	19,000	1.90
Utilities	1,400	.28	2,300	.23
Rent	4,000	.80	4,000	.40
Maintenance	800	.16	1,100	.11
Supervisory salaries	1,000	.20	1,000	.10

Instructions
(a) Define the terms variable costs, fixed costs, and mixed costs.
(b) Classify each cost above as either variable, fixed, or mixed.

Determine fixed and variable costs using the high-low method and prepare graph.
(SO 1, 3)

E23–2 The controller of Jimenez Industries has collected the following monthly expense data for use in analyzing the cost behavior of maintenance costs:

Month	Total Maintenance Costs	Total Machine Hours
January	$ 2,900	3,000
February	3,000	4,000
March	3,600	6,000
April	4,500	7,900
May	3,200	5,000
June	4,650	8,000

Instructions
(a) Determine the fixed and variable cost components using the high-low method.
(b) Prepare a graph showing the behavior of maintenance costs and identify the fixed and variable cost elements. Use 2,000 unit increments and $1,000 cost increments.

E23–3   In the month of June, Jan's Beauty Salon gave 2,400 haircuts, shampoos, and permanents at an average price of $30. During the month, fixed costs were $18,000 and variable costs were 60% of sales.

Compute contribution margin, break-even point, and margin of safety.
(SO 5, 6, 7)

Instructions

(a) Determine the contribution margin in dollars, per unit, and as a ratio.

(b) Using the contribution margin technique, compute the break-even point in dollars and in units.

(c) Compute the margin of safety in dollars and as a ratio.

E23–4   Unruh Company estimates that variable costs will be 50% of sales and fixed costs will total $700,000. The selling price of the product is $4.

Prepare a CVP graph and compute break-even point and margin of safety.
(SO 6, 7)

Instructions

(a) Prepare a CVP graph, assuming maximum sales of $3,200,000. (Note: Use $400,000 increments for sales and costs and 100,000 increments for units.)

(b) Compute the break-even point in (1) units and (2) dollars.

(c) Compute the margin of safety in (1) dollars and (2) as a ratio, assuming actual sales are $2 million.

E23–5   In 1999, Wiggins Company had a break-even point of $350,000 based on a selling price of $7 per unit and fixed costs of $105,000. In 2000, the selling price and the variable cost per unit did not change, but the break-even point increased to $455,000.

Compute variable cost per unit, contribution margin ratio, and increase in fixed costs.
(SO 5)

Instructions

(a) Compute the variable cost per unit and the contribution margin ratio for 1999.

(b) Compute the increase in fixed costs for 2000.

E23–6   Vowell Company had $90,000 of net income in 1999 when the selling price per unit was $150, the variable costs per unit were $90, and the fixed costs were $630,000. Management expects per unit data and total fixed costs to remain the same in 2000. The president of Vowell Company is under pressure from stockholders to increase net income by $60,000 in 2000.

Compute various components to derive target net income under different assumptions.
(SO 6, 8)

Instructions

(a) Compute the number of units sold in 1999.

(b) Compute the number of units that would have to be sold in 2000 to reach the stockholders' desired profit level.

(c) Assume that Vowell Company sells the same number of units in 2000 as it did in 1999. What would the selling price have to be in order to reach the stockholders' desired profit level?

E23–7   Angell Company reports the following operating results for the month of August: Sales $300,000 (units 5,000); variable costs $210,000; and fixed costs $80,000. Management is considering the following independent courses of action to increase net income.

Compute net income under different alternatives.
(SO 8)

1. Increase selling price by 15% with no change in total variable costs.

2. Reduce variable costs to 60% of sales.

3. Reduce fixed costs by $20,000.

Instructions

Compute the net income to be earned under each alternative. Which course of action will produce the highest net income?

E23–8   Healy Company had sales in 1999 of $1,500,000 on 60,000 units. Variable costs totaled $720,000, and fixed costs totaled $500,000.

Prepare a CVP income statement before and after changes in business environment.
(SO 9)

A new raw material is available that will decrease the variable costs per unit by 20% (or $2.40). However, to process the new raw material, fixed operating costs will increase by $50,000. Management feels that one-half of the decline in the variable costs per unit should be passed on to the company's customers in the form of a sales price reduction. The marketing department expects that this sales price reduction will result in a 10% increase in the number of units sold.

Instructions

Prepare a CVP income statement for 1999, assuming the changes are made as described.

E23–9   DeLong Equipment Company manufactures and distributes industrial air compressors. The following costs are available for the year ended December 31, 1999. The company has no beginning inventory. In 1999, 1,500 units were produced, but only 1,200 units were sold. The unit selling price was $4,500. Costs and expenses were:

Compute total product cost and prepare an income statement using variable costing.
(SO 10)

Variable costs per unit	
Direct materials	$ 600
Direct labor	1,500
Variable manufacturing overhead	300
Variable selling and administrative expenses	70
Annual fixed costs and expenses	
Manufacturing overhead	$1,200,000
Selling and administrative expenses	100,000

Instructions

(a) Compute the manufacturing cost of one unit of product using variable costing.
(b) Prepare a 1999 income statement for DeLong Company using variable costing.

PROBLEMS: SET A

Determine variable and fixed costs, compute break-even point, prepare a CVP graph, and determine net income.
(SO 1, 3, 5, 6)

P23–1A The College Barber Shop employs four barbers. One barber, who also serves as the manager, is paid a salary of $1,600 per month. The other barbers are paid $1,200 per month. In addition, each barber is paid a commission of $4 per haircut. Other monthly costs are: store rent $800 plus 60 cents per haircut, depreciation on equipment $500, barber supplies 40 cents per haircut, utilities $300, and advertising $200. The price of a haircut is $10.

Instructions

(a) Determine the variable cost per haircut and the total monthly fixed costs.
(b) Compute the break-even point in units and dollars.
(c) Prepare a CVP graph, assuming a maximum of 1,800 haircuts in a month. Use increments of 300 haircuts on the horizontal axis and $3,000 increments on the vertical axis.
(d) Determine the net income, assuming 1,600 haircuts are given in a month.

Prepare a CVP income statement, compute break-even point, contribution margin ratio, margin of safety ratio, and sales for target net income.
(SO 5, 6, 7, 8, 9)

P23–2A Corbin Company bottles and distributes LOKAL, a fruit drink. The beverage is sold for 50 cents per 16-oz. bottle to retailers, who charge customers 70 cents per bottle. At full (100%) plant capacity, management estimates the following revenues and costs.

Net sales	$2,000,000	Selling expenses—variable	$ 90,000
Direct materials	360,000	Selling expenses—fixed	150,000
Direct labor	450,000	Administrative expenses—	
Manufacturing overhead—		variable	30,000
variable	270,000	Administrative expenses—	
Manufacturing overhead—		fixed	70,000
fixed	380,000		

Instructions

(a) Prepare a CVP income statement for the year 1999 based on management's estimates.
(b) Compute the break-even point in (1) units and (2) dollars.
(c) Compute the contribution margin ratio and the margin of safety ratio.
(d) Determine the sales required to earn net income of $220,000.

Compute break-even point under alternative courses of action.
(SO 5, 6)

P23–3A Griffey Manufacturing had a bad year in 1999. For the first time in its history it operated at a loss. The company's income statement showed the following results from selling 60,000 units of product: Net sales $1,500,000; total costs and expenses $1,890,000; and net loss $390,000. Costs and expenses consisted of the following:

	Total	Variable	Fixed
Cost of goods sold	$1,350,000	$930,000	$420,000
Selling expenses	420,000	75,000	345,000
Administrative expenses	120,000	45,000	75,000
	$1,890,000	$1,050,000	$840,000

Management is considering the following independent alternatives for 2000:

1. Increase unit selling price 40% with no change in costs, expenses, and sales volume.
2. Change the compensation of salespersons from fixed annual salaries totaling $200,000 to total salaries of $50,000 plus a 6% commission on net sales.

3. Purchase new high-tech factory machinery that will change the proportion between variable and fixed cost of goods sold to 50:50.

Instructions

(a) Compute the break-even point in dollars for the year 1999.
(b) Compute the break-even point in dollars under each of the alternative courses of action. Which course of action do you recommend?

P23–4A Cindy Henning is the advertising manager for Thrifty Shoe Store. She is currently working on a major promotional campaign. Her ideas include the installation of a new lighting system and increased display space that will add $37,000 in fixed costs to the $210,000 currently spent. In addition, Cindy is proposing that a 6⅔% price decrease (from $30.00 to $28.00) will produce an increase in sales volume from 16,000 to 21,000 units. Variable costs will remain at $15.00 per pair of shoes. Management is impressed with Cindy's ideas but concerned about the effects that these changes will have on the break-even point and the margin of safety.

Compute break-even point and margin of safety ratio and prepare a CVP income statement before and after changes in business environment.
(SO 6, 7, 9)

Instructions

(a) Compute the current break-even point in units, and compare it to the break-even point in units if Cindy's ideas are used.
(b) Compute the margin of safety ratio for current operations and after Cindy's changes are introduced. (Round to nearest full percent.)
(c) Prepare a CVP income statement for current operations and after Cindy's changes are introduced. Would you make the changes suggested?

P23–5A Karmik Metal Company produces the steel wire that goes into the production of paper clips. In 1999, the first year of operations, Karmik produced 40,000 miles of wire and sold 30,000 miles. In 2000, the production and sales results were exactly reversed. In each year, selling price per mile was $80, variable manufacturing costs were 20% of the sales price, variable selling expenses were $8.00 per mile sold, fixed manufacturing costs were $1,200,000, and fixed administrative expenses were $200,000.

Prepare income statements under absorption and variable costing.
(SO 10)

Instructions

(a) Prepare comparative income statements for each year using variable costing.
(b) Prepare comparative income statements for each year using absorption costing.
(c) Reconcile the differences each year in income from operations under the two costing approaches.
(d) Comment on the effects of production and sales on net income under the two costing approaches.

PROBLEMS: SET B

P23–1B Joe Wong owns the Peace Barber Shop. He employs five barbers and pays each a base rate of $1,000 per month. One of the barbers serves as the manager and receives an extra $400 per month. In addition to the base rate, each barber also receives a commission of $3.50 per haircut.

Determine variable and fixed costs, compute break-even point, prepare a CVP graph, and determine net income.
(SO 1, 3, 5, 6)

Other costs are as follows:

Advertising	$200 per month
Rent	$800 per month
Barber supplies	$.30 per haircut
Utilities	$175 per month plus $.20 per haircut
Magazines	$25 per month

Joe currently charges $10 per haircut.

Instructions

(a) Determine the variable cost per haircut and the total monthly fixed costs.
(b) Compute the break-even point in units and dollars.
(c) Prepare a CVP graph, assuming a maximum of 1,800 haircuts in a month. Use increments of 300 haircuts on the horizontal axis and $3,000 on the vertical axis.
(d) Determine net income, assuming 1,500 haircuts are given in a month.

Prepare a CVP income statement, compute break-even point, contribution margin ratio, margin of safety ratio, and sales for target net income.
(SO 5, 6, 7, 8, 9)

P23–2B Newsom Company bottles and distributes NOKAL, a diet soft drink. The beverage is sold for 40 cents per 16-oz. bottle to retailers, who charge customers 60 cents per bottle. At full (100%) plant capacity, management estimates the following revenues and costs.

Net sales	$1,800,000	Selling expenses—variable	$80,000
Direct materials	400,000	Selling expenses—fixed	65,000
Direct labor	460,000	Administrative expenses—	
Manufacturing overhead—		variable	20,000
variable	300,000	Administrative expenses—	
Manufacturing overhead—		fixed	52,000
fixed	243,000		

Instructions

(a) Prepare a CVP income statement for the year 1999 based on management's estimates.
(b) Compute the break-even point in (1) units and (2) dollars.
(c) Compute the contribution margin ratio and the margin of safety ratio. (Round to full percents.)
(d) Determine the sales required to earn net income of $150,000.

Compute break-even point under alternative courses of action.
(SO 5, 6)

P23–3B Masoni Manufacturing's sales slumped badly in 1999. For the first time in its history, it operated at a loss. The company's income statement showed the following results from selling 600,000 units of product: Net sales $2,400,000; total costs and expenses $2,490,000; and net loss $90,000. Costs and expenses consisted of the following:

	Total	Variable	Fixed
Cost of goods sold	$1,980,000	$1,320,000	$ 660,000
Selling expenses	310,000	72,000	238,000
Administrative expenses	200,000	48,000	152,000
	$2,490,000	$1,440,000	$1,050,000

Management is considering the following independent alternatives for 2000:

1. Increase unit selling price 20% with no change in costs, expenses, and sales volume.
2. Change the compensation of salespersons from fixed annual salaries totaling $210,000 to total salaries of $70,000 plus a 5% commission on net sales.
3. Purchase new automated equipment that will change the proportion between variable and fixed cost of goods sold to 60% variable and 40% fixed.

Instructions

(a) Compute the break-even point in dollars for the year 1999.
(b) Compute the break-even point in dollars under each of the alternative courses of action. (Round to full percents.) Which course of action do you recommend?

Compute break-even point and margin of safety ratio and prepare a CVP income statement before and after changes in business environment.
(SO 6, 7, 9)

P23–4B Kathy Short is the advertising manager for Value Shoe Store. She is currently working on a major promotional campaign. Her ideas include the installation of a new lighting system and increased display space that will add $48,000 in fixed costs to the $240,000 currently spent. In addition, Kathy is proposing that a 5% price decrease ($40.00 to $38.00) will produce a 20% increase in sales volume (20,000 to 24,000). Variable costs will remain at $20.00 per pair of shoes. Management is impressed with Kathy's ideas but concerned about the effects that these changes will have on the break-even point and the margin of safety.

Instructions

(a) Compute the current break-even point in units, and compare it to the break-even point in units if Kathy's ideas are used.
(b) Compute the margin of safety ratio for current operations and after Kathy's changes are introduced. (Round to nearest full percent.)
(c) Prepare a CVP income statement for current operations and after Kathy's changes are introduced. Would you make the changes suggested?

Prepare income statements under absorption and variable costing.
(SO 10)

P23–5B ADC produces plastic that is used for injection molding applications such as gears for small motors. In 1999, the first year of operations, ADC produced 4,000 tons of plastic and sold 3,000 tons. In 2000, the production and sales results were exactly reversed. In each year, selling price per ton was $2,500, variable manufacturing costs were 15% of the sales price of units produced, variable selling expenses were 10% of the selling price of units sold, fixed manufacturing costs were $3,000,000, and fixed administrative expenses were $600,000.

Instructions

(a) Prepare comparative income statements for each year using variable costing.
(b) Prepare comparative income statements for each year using absorption costing.

(c) Reconcile the differences each year in income from operations under the two costing approaches.
(d) Comment on the effects of production and sales on net income under the two costing approaches.

BROADENING YOUR PERSPECTIVE

GROUP DECISION CASE

BYP23–1 Cedeno Company has decided to introduce a new product. The new product can be manufactured by either a capital-intensive method or a labor-intensive method. The manufacturing method will not affect the quality of the product. The estimated manufacturing costs by the two methods are as follows:

	Capital-Intensive	Labor-Intensive
Raw materials	$5 per unit	$5.50 per unit
Direct labor	$6 per unit	$7.20 per unit
Variable overhead	$3 per unit	$4.80 per unit
Fixed manufacturing costs	$2,300,000	$1,285,000

Cedeno's market research department has recommended an introductory unit sales price of $30. The incremental selling expenses are estimated to be $500,000 annually plus $2 for each unit sold, regardless of manufacturing method.

Instructions
With the class divided into groups, answer the following:

(a) Calculate the estimated break-even point in annual unit sales of the new product if Cedeno Company uses the:
   (1) capital-intensive manufacturing method.
   (2) labor-intensive manufacturing method.
(b) Determine the annual unit sales volume at which Cedeno Company would be indifferent between the two manufacturing methods.
(c) Explain the circumstances under which Cedeno should employ each of the two manufacturing methods.

(CMA adapted)

MANAGERIAL ANALYSIS

BYP23–2 The condensed income statement for the Rivera and Santos partnership for 1999 is as follows:

RIVERA AND SANTOS COMPANY
Income Statement
For the Year Ended December 31, 1999

Sales (200,000 units)		$1,200,000
Cost of goods sold		800,000
Gross profit		400,000
Operating expenses		
Selling	320,000	
Administrative	160,000	480,000
Net loss		($80,000)

A cost behavior analysis indicates that 75% of the cost of goods sold are variable; 50% of the selling expenses are variable; and 25% of the administrative expenses are variable.

Instructions
(Round to nearest unit, dollar, and percentage, where necessary. Use the CVP income statement format in computing profits.)

(a) Compute the break-even point in total sales dollars and in units for 1999.

(b) Rivera has proposed a plan to get the partnership "out of the red" and improve its profitability. She feels that the quality of the product could be substantially improved by spending $0.55 more per unit on better raw materials. The selling price per unit could be increased to only $6.50 because of competitive pressures. Rivera estimates that sales volume will increase by 30%. What effect will Rivera's plan have on the profits and the break-even point in dollars of the partnership?

(c) Santos was a marketing major in college. He believes that sales volume can be increased only by intensive advertising and promotional campaigns. He therefore proposed the following plan as an alternative to Rivera's: (1) increase variable selling expenses to $0.85 per unit, (2) lower the selling price per unit by $0.20, and (3) increase fixed selling expenses by $20,000. Santos quoted an old marketing research report that said that sales volume would increase by 50% if these changes were made. What effect will Santos's plan have on the profits and the break-even point in dollars of the partnership?

(d) Which plan should be accepted? Explain your answer.

REAL-WORLD FOCUS: The Coca-Cola Company
....

BYP23–3 The **Coca-Cola Company** hardly needs an introduction. A line taken from the cover of its 1996 annual report says it all: If you measured time in servings of Coca-Cola, "a billon Coca-Cola's ago was yesterday morning." On average, every U.S. citizen drinks 363 eight-ounce servings of Coca-Cola products each year. Coca-Cola's primary line of business is the making and selling of syrup to bottlers. These bottlers then sell the finished bottles and cans of Coca-Cola to the consumer.

In the 1996 annual report of Coca-Cola, the following information was provided:

> ### THE COCA-COLA COMPANY
> ### Management Discussion
>
> Our gross margin declined to 61 percent in 1995 from 62 percent in 1994, primarily due to costs for materials such as sweeteners and packaging.
>
> The increases (in selling expenses) in 1996 and 1995 were primarily due to higher marketing expenditures in support of our Company's volume growth.
>
> We measure our sales volume in two ways: (1) gallon shipments of concentrates and syrups and (2) unit cases of finished product (bottles and cans of Coke sold by bottlers).

Instructions
Answer the following questions:

(a) Are sweeteners and packaging a variable cost or a fixed cost? What is the impact on the contribution margin of an increase in the per unit cost of sweeteners or packaging? What are the implications for profitability?

(b) In your opinion, are marketing expenditures a fixed cost, variable cost, or mixed cost to The Coca-Cola Company? Give justification for your answer.

(c) Which of the two measures cited for measuring volume represents the activity index as defined in this chapter? Why might Coca-Cola use two different measures?

COMMUNICATION ACTIVITY

BYP23–4   In CVP analysis there are many formulas. Your roommate asks your help on the following questions:

   (a) How can the mathematical equation for break-even sales show both sales dollars and sales units?
   (b) How do the formulas differ, if at all, for contribution margin per unit and contribution margin ratio?
   (c) How can contribution margin be used to determine break-even sales in dollars and in units?

Instructions
Write a memorandum to your roommate stating the relevant formulas and the answers to each of the foregoing questions.

RESEARCH ASSIGNMENT

BYP23–5   The February 1998 issue of *Management Accounting* includes an article by Bonnie Stivers, Teresa Covin, Nancy Green Hall, and Steven Smalt entitled "How Nonfinancial Performance Measures Are Used."

Instructions
Read the article and answer the following questions:

   (a) The article is based on a study and survey. What is the objective of this study? Describe the specific nature of the survey that was conducted.
   (b) What were the five categories of nonfinancial performance measures identified and surveyed in this study?
   (c) What factors were identified, as a result of the survey, to be the most important nonfinancial measures?
   (d) What are the "three red flags" (conclusions) that the study results highlight?

ETHICS CASE

BYP23–6   Donny Blake is an accountant for Swenson Company. Early this year Donny made a highly favorable projection of sales and profits over the next 3 years for its hot-selling computer PLEX. As a result of the projections Donny presented to senior management, they decided to expand production in this area. This decision led to dislocations of some plant personnel who were reassigned to one of the company's newer plants in another state. However, no one was fired, and in fact the company expanded its work force slightly.

   Unfortunately Donny rechecked his computations on the projections a few months later and found that he had made an error that would have reduced his projections substantially. Luckily, sales of PLEX have exceeded projections so far, and management is satisfied with its decision. Donny, however, is not sure what to do. Should he confess his honest mistake and jeopardize his possible promotion? He suspects that no one will catch the error because sales of PLEX have exceeded his projections, and it appears that profits will materialize close to his projections.

Instructions
   (a) Who are the stakeholders in this situation?
   (b) Identify the ethical issues involved in this situation.
   (c) What are the possible alternative actions for Donny? What would you do in Donny's position?

SURFING THE NET

....

BYP23–7 Ganong Bros. Ltd., located in St. Stephen, New Brunswick, is Canada's independent candy company. Its products are distributed worldwide. In 1885, Ganong invented the popular "chicken bone," a cinnamon flavored, pink, hard candy jacket over a chocolate center. The home page of Ganong, listed below, includes information about the company and its products.

Address: http://www.gulliver.nb.ca/pcsolve/ganong/index.htm

Instructions
Choose the **Ganong Times,** and answer the following:

   (a) Describe the steps in making "chicken bones."
   (b) Identify at least two variable and two fixed costs that are likely to affect the production of "chicken bones."

————————

Answers to Self-Study Questions
1. d   2. c   3. a   4. c   5. d   6. c   7. b   8. b   9. a   10. a

Remember to go back to the Navigator box on the chapter-opening page and check off your completed work.

Before studying this chapter, you should know or, if necessary, review:

a. The meaning of the management function of planning. (Ch. 20, p. 872)

b. The difference between variable costs and fixed costs. (Ch. 23, pp. 997–998)

FEATURE STORY

Big Red's Biennial Budget

Every university has a budget. Usually, there's a capital budget for big projects such as new buildings, and there's an operating budget for the day-to-day expenditures.

At the University of Nebraska, the operating budget request takes up four volumes totaling nearly 900 pages. Because the university is funded by the state of Nebraska, the budget must be submitted to the state legislature for approval. That means the university has to pay lobbyists to plead its case with legislators. The budget is due September 15th of every other year. The lawmakers consider it during their sessions, which begin in January.

As you might expect, increases in expenses are resisted because money is tight. "Roughly 70% of our budget goes toward salaries," says Paula Boroff, budget officer at the Omaha campus. "A university is a very labor-intensive institution," she observes. The total budget for a recent fiscal year is about $95 million, reflecting a 1% cut in state funds from the prior year.

One budget item of interest to students is the "remission" category. That's where scholarships are funded. "This year, the budget for honor students and needy students is nearly $2 million—$1,994,488 to be exact," says Boroff, who recently received her MBA from the University of Nebraska graduate school. "Of our 16,000 students, we had 8,274 on some kind of aid," she says.

CHAPTER 24

BUDGETARY PLANNING

THE NAVIGATOR ✓

- ■ Understand *Concepts for Review* ☐
- ■ Read *Feature Story* ☐
- ■ Scan *Study Objectives* ☐
- ■ Read *Preview* ☐
- ■ Read text and answer *Before You Go On* p. 1039 ☐ p. 1049 ☐ p. 1052 ☐
- ■ Work *Demonstration Problems* ☐
- ■ Review *Summary of Study Objectives* ☐
- ■ Answer *Self-Study Questions* ☐
- ■ Complete assignments ☐

STUDY OBJECTIVES

After studying this chapter, you should be able to:

1. *Indicate the benefits of budgeting.*
2. *State the essentials of effective budgeting.*
3. *Identify the budgets that comprise the master budget.*
4. *Describe the sources for preparing the budgeted income statement.*
5. *Explain the principal sections of a cash budget.*
6. *Indicate the applicability of budgeting in nonmanufacturing companies.*

THE NAVIGATOR

A s the story about the University of Nebraska indicates, budgeting is an integral part of our society. As students, you budget your study time and your money. Families budget income and expenses, and governmental agencies budget revenues and expenditures. Business enterprises use budgets in planning and controlling their operations.

Our primary focus in this chapter is budgeting—specifically, how budgeting is used as a *planning tool* by management. Through budgeting, it should be possible for management to maintain enough cash to pay creditors, to have sufficient raw materials to meet production requirements, and to have adequate finished goods to meet expected sales. The content and organization of this chapter are as follows:

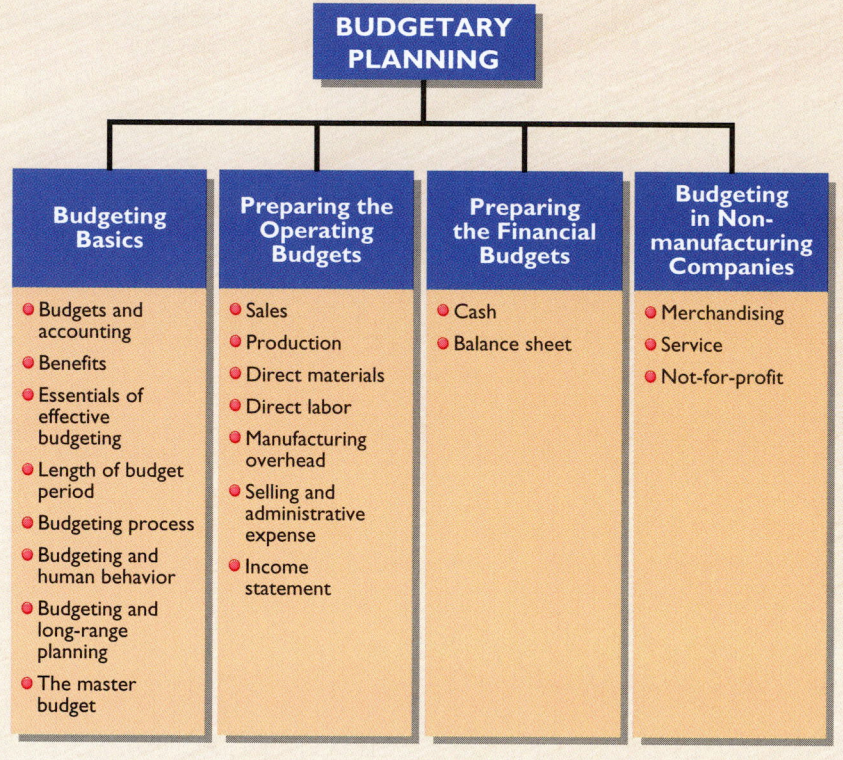

BUDGETARY PLANNING

Budgeting Basics	Preparing the Operating Budgets	Preparing the Financial Budgets	Budgeting in Non-manufacturing Companies
• Budgets and accounting • Benefits • Essentials of effective budgeting • Length of budget period • Budgeting process • Budgeting and human behavior • Budgeting and long-range planning • The master budget	• Sales • Production • Direct materials • Direct labor • Manufacturing overhead • Selling and administrative expense • Income statement	• Cash • Balance sheet	• Merchandising • Service • Not-for-profit

THE NAVIGATOR

BUDGETING BASICS

One of management's major responsibilities is planning. As explained in Chapter 20, **planning** is the process of establishing enterprise objectives. A successful organization establishes both long-term and short-term plans that set forth the objectives of the company and the proposed means of accomplishing them.

A **budget** is a formal written summary (or statement) of management's plans for a specified future time period, expressed in financial terms. It normally represents the primary means of communicating agreed-upon objectives throughout the business organization. Once adopted, a budget becomes an important basis for evaluating performance. Thus, it promotes efficiency and serves as a deterrent to waste and inefficiency. We consider the role of budgeting as a **control device** in Chapter 25.

Budgeting and Accounting

Accounting information makes major contributions to the budgeting process. From the accounting records, historical data on revenues, costs, and expenses can be obtained. These data may be helpful in formulating future budget goals.

Normally, accounting has the responsibility for expressing management's budgeting goals in financial terms. In this role, it becomes the translator of management's plans, and it provides the means of communicating the budget to all areas of responsibility. Accounting also prepares periodic budget reports that provide the basis for measuring performance and comparing actual results with planned objectives. The budget itself, and the administration of the budget, however, are entirely management responsibilities.

TECHNOLOGY IN ACTION

In large firms, the computer is an essential tool in the budgeting process. Entire computer programs are designed to aid in budget preparation. These systems can also be integrated into the general ledger and provide a complete reporting package for monitoring budgeted vs. actual results. Packages with similar features are available for microcomputers so even small companies can adopt the budgeting practices found in major companies.

A powerful feature of many spreadsheet packages is the ability to merge and consolidate budget data as they flow up the organizational chain of command.

The Benefits of Budgeting

The primary benefits of budgeting are:

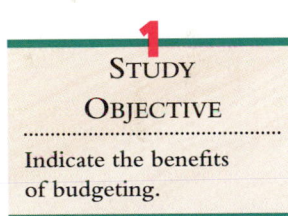

STUDY OBJECTIVE

Indicate the benefits of budgeting.

1. It requires all levels of management to **plan ahead** and to formalize their future goals on a recurring basis.
2. It provides **definite objectives** for evaluating performance at each level of responsibility.
3. It creates an **early warning system** for potential problems. With early warning, management has time to solve the problem before things get out of hand. For example, the cash budget may reveal the need for outside financing several months before an actual cash shortage occurs.
4. It facilitates the **coordination of activities** within the business by correlating the goals of each segment with overall company objectives. Thus, production and sales promotion can be integrated with expected sales.
5. It results in greater **management awareness** of the entity's overall operations and the impact of external factors, such as economic trends, on the company's operations.
6. It contributes to **positive behavior patterns** throughout the organization by motivating personnel to meet planned objectives.

A budget is an aid to management; it is not a substitute for management. A budget cannot operate or enforce itself. The benefits of budgeting will be realized only when budgets are carefully prepared and properly administered by management.

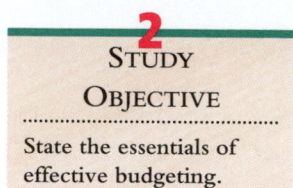

Essentials of Effective Budgeting

Effective budgeting depends on a **sound organizational structure** in which authority and responsibility over all phases of operations are clearly defined. Budgets based on **research and analysis** should result in realistic goals that will contribute to the growth and profitability of a company. And, the effectiveness of a budget program is directly related to its **acceptance by all levels of management**.

Once the buget has been adopted, it should be an important basis for evaluating performance. Variations between actual and expected results should be systematically and periodically reviewed to determine their cause(s). However, care should be exercised to see that individuals are not held responsible for variations that are beyond their control.

Length of the Budget Period

As indicated in the opening story about the University of Nebraska budget, the budget period is not necessarily one year in length. **A budget may be prepared for any period of time.** Such factors as the type of budget, the nature of the organization, the need for periodic appraisal, and prevailing business conditions will influence the length of the budget period. For example, cash may be budgeted monthly, whereas a plant expansion program budget may cover a 10-year period.

The budget period should be long enough to provide an attainable goal under normal business conditions. Ideally, the time period should minimize the impact of seasonal and cyclical business fluctuations. On the other hand, the budget period should not be so long that reliable estimates are impossible.

The **most common budget period is one year**. The annual budget, in turn, is often supplemented by monthly and quarterly budgets. Many companies today use **continuous 12-month budgets** by dropping the month just ended and adding a future month. One advantage of continuous budgeting is that it keeps management planning a full year ahead.

The Budgeting Process

The development of the budget for the coming year generally starts several months before the end of the current year. The budgeting process usually begins with the collection of data from each of the organizational units of the company. Past performance is often the starting point in budgeting, from which future budget goals are formulated.

The budget is developed within the framework of a sales forecast that shows potential sales for the industry and the company's expected share of such sales. Sales forecasting involves a consideration of such factors as (1) general economic conditions, (2) industry trends, (3) market research studies, (4) anticipated advertising and promotion, (5) previous market share, (6) changes in prices, and (7) technological developments. The input of sales personnel and top management are essential in preparing the sales forecast.

In many companies, responsibility for coordinating the preparation of the budget is assigned to a budget committee. The committee, often headed by a budget director, ordinarily includes the president, treasurer, chief accountant (controller), and management personnel from each of the major areas of the company, such as sales, production, and research. The budget committee serves as a review board where managers and supervisors can defend their budget goals and requests. After differences are reviewed, modified if necessary, and reconciled, the budget is prepared by the budget committee, put in its final form, approved, and distributed.

TECHNOLOGY IN ACTION

Because a forecast involves many uncertainties, various approaches are taken in an effort to increase the reliability of the forecast. These include a variety of sophisticated statistical and mathematical techniques. Today, many companies use **financial planning models** to forecast sales. A model can express the effects of both internal and external factors on sales.

Budgeting and Human Behavior

A budget can have a significant effect on human behavior. On the one hand, a budget may have a strong positive influence that inspires a manager to higher levels of performance. On the other hand, a budget may discourage additional effort and have a negative impact on the morale of a manager. Why do these diverse effects occur? The answer is found in the manner in which the budget is developed and administered.

In **developing the budget**, each level of management should be invited and encouraged to participate. The overall objective is to reach agreement on a budget that the manager considers to be fair and achievable. When this objective is met, the budget will have a positive effect on the manager. In contrast, if the manager views the budget as being unfair and unrealistic, he or she may become discouraged and uncommitted to the budget goals. The risk of having unrealistic budgets is generally greater when the budget is developed from top management down to lower management than vice versa. Illustration 24-1 graphically displays the flow of budget data from bottom to top in an organization.

ILLUSTRATION 24-1

Flow of budget data from lower levels of management to top

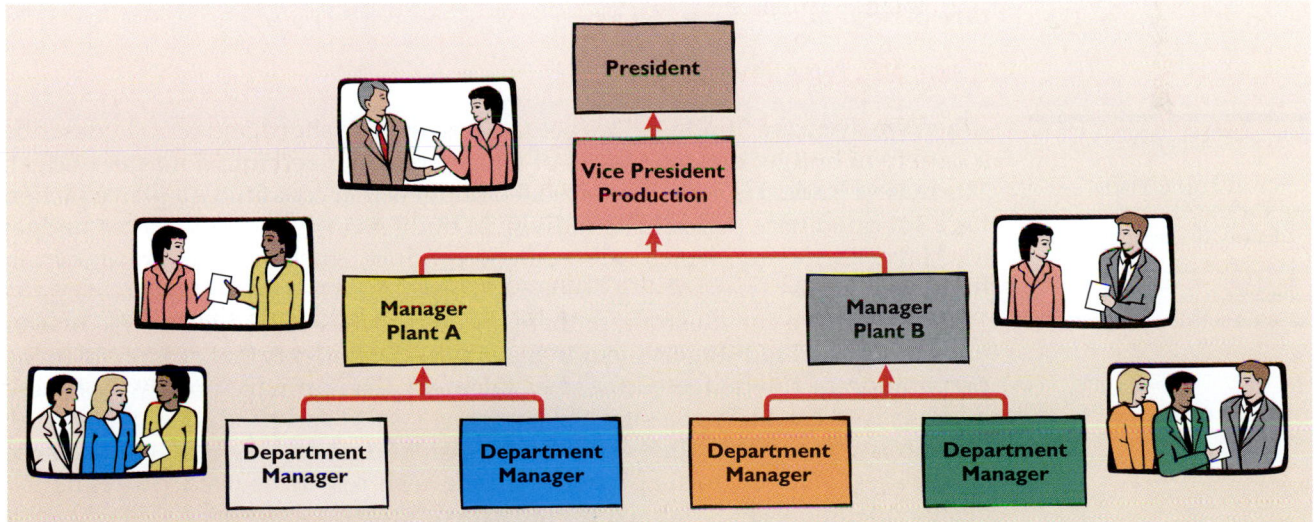

Administering the budget relates to the manner in which the budget is used by top management. As explained earlier, the budget should have the complete support of top management. In addition, the budget should be an important basis for evaluating performance. The effect of an evaluation on a manager will be positive when top management tempers criticism with advice and assistance. In contrast, the response of a manager is likely to be negative when the budget is used exclusively to assess blame. Top management should also be sensitive to the behavioral implications of its actions. An understanding and flexible attitude has a positive influence on human behavior. Conversely, a rigid and inflexible attitude has a negative effect on the manager who is being evaluated.

A budget may be used improperly as a pressure device to force improved performance. Alternatively, it can be used as a positive aid in achieving projected goals. In sum, a budget can become a friend or a foe to the manager.

Budgeting and Long-Range Planning

In business, you may hear management talk about the need for long-range planning. Budgeting and long-range planning are not the same. One important difference is the **time period involved**. The maximum length of a budget is usually one year, and budgets are often prepared for shorter periods of time, such as a month or a quarter. In contrast, long-range planning usually encompasses a period of at least five years.

A second significant difference is **in emphasis**. Budgeting is concerned with the achievement of specific short-term goals, such as meeting annual profit objectives. Long-range planning, on the other hand, is a formalized process of selecting strategies to achieve long-term goals and developing policies and plans to implement the strategies. In long-range planning, management also considers anticipated trends in the economic and political environment and policies the company should follow to cope with them.

The final difference between budgeting and long-range planning pertains to the **amount of detail presented**. Budgets, as you have seen earlier in this chapter, can be very detailed. The detail is needed to provide a basis for control. Long-range plans contain considerably less detail, because the data are intended more for a review of progress toward long-term goals than for an evaluation of specific results to be achieved. The primary objective of long-range planning is to develop the best strategy to maximize the company's performance over an extended future period.

The Master Budget

When we discuss a "budget," we actually are using a shorthand term to describe a variety of budget documents, all of which are combined into a master budget. The master budget is a set of interrelated budgets that constitutes a plan of action for a specified time period. The individual budgets included in a master budget for Hayes Company, which sells a single product, Kitchen-mate, are shown in Illustration 24-2.

As shown in the illustration, there are two classes of budgets in the master budget. Operating budgets include the individual budgets that culminate in the preparation of the budgeted income statement. The primary objective of these budgets is to establish goals for the company's sales and production personnel. In contrast, financial budgets include the cash budget and the budgeted balance sheet. These budgets focus primarily on the cash resources needed to fund expected operations and planned capital expenditures.

The master budget is prepared in the sequence shown in Illustration 24-2. The operating budgets are developed first beginning with the sales budget. After these budgets have been determined, the financial budgets are prepared. We will explain and illustrate each budget shown in Illustration 24-2 except the capital expenditure budget. This budget is discussed under the topic, Capital Budgeting, in Chapter 27.

ILLUSTRATION 24-2

Components of the master budget

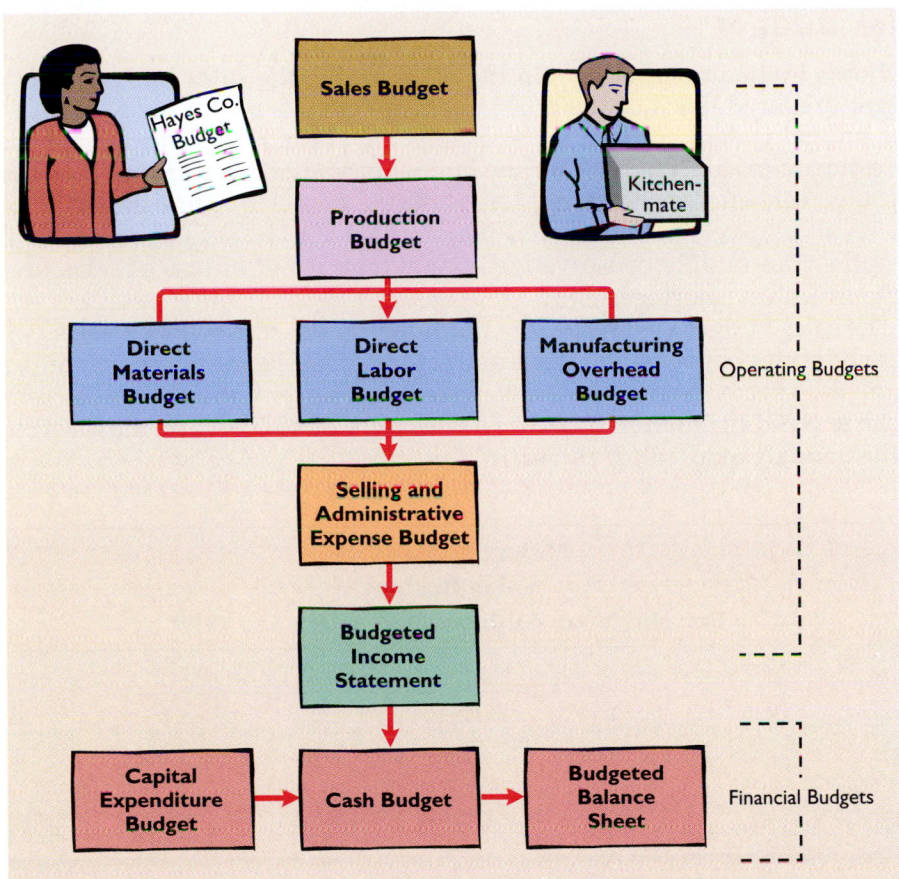

BEFORE YOU GO ON . . .

Review It

1. What are the benefits of budgeting?
2. What are the factors essential to effective budgeting?
3. How does the budget process work?
4. How does budgeting differ from long-range planning?
5. What is a master budget?

THE NAVIGATOR

PREPARING THE OPERATING BUDGETS

A case study of Hayes Company will be used in preparing the operating budgets. Hayes Company manufactures and sells a single product, Kitchen-mate. The budgets will be prepared by quarters for the year ending December 31, 1999. Hayes Company begins its annual budgeting process on September 1, 1998, and it completes the budget for 1999 by December 1, 1998.

Sales Budget

As shown in the master budget in Illustration 24-2, **the sales budget is the first budget prepared**. Each of the other budgets depends on the sales budget. The sales budget is derived from the sales forecast, and it represents management's best estimate of sales revenue for the budget period. An inaccurate sales budget may adversely affect net income. For example, an overly optimistic sales budget may result in excessive inventories that may have to be sold at reduced prices. In contrast, an unduly conservative budget may result in loss of sales revenue due to inventory shortages.

The sales budget is prepared by multiplying the expected unit sales volume for each product by its anticipated unit selling price. For Hayes Company, sales volume is expected to be 3,000 units in the first quarter with 500-unit increments in each succeeding quarter. Based on a sales price of $60 per unit, the sales budget for the year, by quarters, is shown in Illustration 24-3.

ILLUSTRATION 24-3

Sales budget

HAYES COMPANY					
Sales Budget					
For the Year Ending December 31, 1999					
	Quarter				
	1	**2**	**3**	**4**	**Year**
Expected unit sales	3,000	3,500	4,000	4,500	15,000
Unit selling price	× $60	× $60	× $60	× $60	× $60
Total sales	$180,000	$210,000	$240,000	$270,000	$900,000

The anticipated sales revenue may be classified as cash or credit sales and by geographical regions, territories, or salespersons.

Production Budget

The **production budget** shows the units that must be produced to meet anticipated sales. Production requirements are determined from the following formula:[1]

ILLUSTRATION 24-4

Production requirements formula

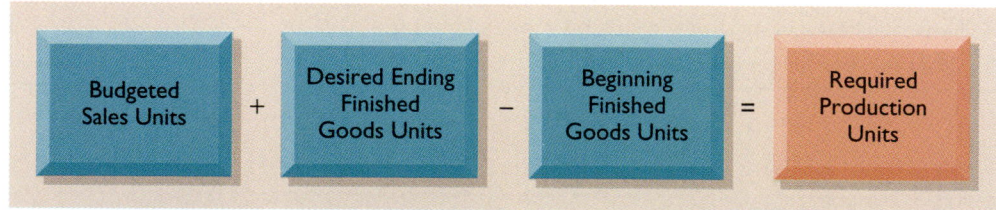

A realistic estimate of ending inventory is essential in scheduling production requirements. Excessive inventories in one quarter may lead to cutbacks in production and layoffs of employees in a subsequent quarter. Conversely, inadequate inventories may result either in added costs for overtime work or in lost sales in a later period. On the basis of past experience, Hayes Company believes it can meet future sales requirements by maintaining an ending inventory equal to 20% of the next quarter's budgeted sales volume. For example, the

---

[1]This formula ignores any work in process inventories, which are assumed to be nonexistent in Hayes Company.

ending finished goods inventory for the first quarter is 700 units (20% × anticipated second-quarter sales of 3,500 units). The production budget is shown in Illustration 24-5.

ILLUSTRATION 24-5

Production budget

HAYES COMPANY Production Budget For the Year Ending December 31, 1999					
	Quarter				
	1	2	3	4	Year
Expected unit sales (Illustration 24-3)	3,000	3,500	4,000	4,500	
Add: Desired ending finished goods units[a]	700	800	900	1,000[b]	
Total required units	3,700	4,300	4,900	5,500	
Less: Beginning finished goods units	600[c]	700	800	900	
Required production units	3,100	3,600	4,100	4,600	15,400

[a]20% of next quarter's sales
[b]Expected 2000 first-quarter sales, 5,000 units × 20%
[c]20% of estimated first-quarter 1999 sales units

The production budget, in turn, provides the basis for determining the budgeted costs for each manufacturing cost element, as explained in the following pages.

ACCOUNTING IN ACTION
Business Insight

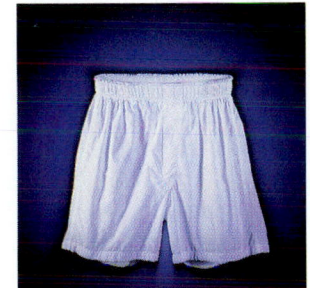

Wrong move, wrong time, poor planning. Recently, Fruit of the Loom Inc. saw underwear and apparel sales slowing. It cut back production sharply. Too sharply, in fact: almost overnight, demand soared. Caught with its shorts down, the company hired back thousands of workers and frantically increased production. The mistimed production cuts contributed to a 43% fall in first-quarter profits. For the year, Fruit stood to lose $200 million in sales, and analysts expected an 11% drop in profits for the year.

Source: Business Week, June 6, 1994, p. 38.

Direct Materials Budget

The **direct materials budget** contains both the quantity and cost of direct materials to be purchased. The quantities of direct materials are derived from the following formula:

ILLUSTRATION 24-6

Formula for direct materials quantities

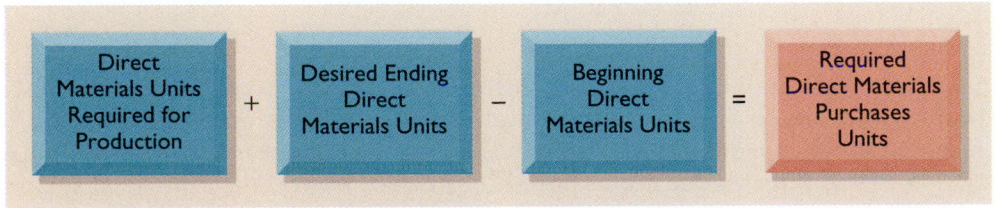

The budgeted cost of direct materials to be purchased is then computed by multiplying the required units of direct materials by the anticipated cost per unit.

TECHNOLOGY IN ACTION

The successful manufacturers of the twenty-first century will be fully computerized. A crucial step on the way is material requirements planning (MRP) systems. Early MRP systems accepted a sales forecast and computed how much materials, inventory, people, and machinery a company needed to manufacture the product. Current MRP systems link the company's manufacturing resource planning with its financial management, creating a powerful system of control over the entire business planning and operating process. With MRP, management can make decisions on facts rather than on "hunches" and "instinct."

The desired ending inventory is again a critical component in the budgeting process. For example, inadequate inventories could result in temporary shutdowns of production. Because of its close proximity to suppliers, Hayes Company has found that an ending inventory of raw materials equal to 10% of the next quarter's production is sufficient. The manufacture of each Kitchen-mate requires 2 pounds of raw materials and the expected cost per pound is $4. The direct materials budget is shown in Illustration 24-7.

ILLUSTRATION 24-7

Direct materials budget

HAYES COMPANY
Direct Materials Budget
For the Year Ending December 31, 1999

	Quarter				
	1	2	3	4	Year
Units to be produced (Illustration 24-5)	3,100	3,600	4,100	4,600	
Direct materials per unit	× 2	× 2	× 2	× 2	
Total pounds needed for production	6,200	7,200	8,200	9,200	
Add: Desired ending direct materials (pounds)[a]	720	820	920	1,020[b]	
Total materials required	6,920	8,020	9,120	10,220	
Less: Beginning direct materials (pounds)	620[c]	720	820	920	
Direct materials purchases	6,300	7,300	8,300	9,300	
Cost per pound	× $4	× $4	× $4	× $4	
Total cost of direct materials purchases	**$25,200**	**$29,200**	**$33,200**	**$37,200**	**$124,800**

[a]10% of next quarter's production
[b]Estimated 2000 first-quarter pounds needed for production, 10,200 × 10%
[c]10% of estimated first-quarter pounds needed for production

Direct Labor Budget

Like the direct materials budget, the **direct labor budget** contains the quantity (hours) and cost of direct labor necessary to meet production requirements. Direct labor hours are determined from the production budget. At Hayes Company, two hours of direct labor are required to produce each unit of finished goods, and the anticipated hourly wage rate is $10. These data are shown in Illustration 24-8. The direct labor budget is critical in maintaining a labor force that can meet the expected levels of production.

ILLUSTRATION 24-8

Direct labor budget

HAYES COMPANY **Direct Labor Budget** **For the Year Ending December 31, 1999**					
	Quarter				
	1	2	3	4	Year
Units to be produced (Illustration 24-5)	3,100	3,600	4,100	4,600	
Direct labor time (hours) per unit	× 2	× 2	× 2	× 2	
Total required direct labor hours	6,200	7,200	8,200	9,200	
Direct labor cost per hour	× $10	× $10	× $10	× $10	
Total direct labor cost	**$62,000**	**$72,000**	**$82,000**	**$92,000**	**$308,000**

Manufacturing Overhead Budget

The manufacturing overhead budget shows the expected manufacturing overhead costs for the budget period. As shown in Illustration 24-9, **this budget distinguishes between variable and fixed overhead costs**. From previous experience, Hayes Company expects variable costs to fluctuate with production volume on the basis of the following rates per direct labor hour: indirect materials $1.00, indirect labor $1.40, utilities $0.40, and maintenance $0.20. Thus, for 6,200 direct labor hours, budgeted indirect materials are $6,200 (6,200 × $1), and budgeted indirect labor is $8,680 (6,200 × $1.40). Hayes Company also recognizes that some maintenance is fixed. The amounts reported for fixed costs are assumed.

At Hayes Company, overhead is applied to production on the basis of direct labor hours. Thus, as shown in Illustration 24-9, the annual rate is $8 per hour ($246,400 ÷ 30,800).

ILLUSTRATION 24-9

Manufacturing overhead budget

HAYES COMPANY **Manufacturing Overhead Budget** **For the Year Ending December 31, 1999**					
	Quarter				
	1	2	3	4	Year
Variable costs					
Indirect materials	$ 6,200	$ 7,200	$ 8,200	$ 9,200	$ 30,800
Indirect labor	8,680	10,080	11,480	12,880	43,120
Utilities	2,480	2,880	3,280	3,680	12,320
Maintenance	1,240	1,440	1,640	1,840	6,160
Total variable	18,600	21,600	24,600	27,600	92,400
Fixed costs					
Supervisory salaries	20,000	20,000	20,000	20,000	80,000
Depreciation	3,800	3,800	3,800	3,800	15,200
Property taxes and insurance	9,000	9,000	9,000	9,000	36,000
Maintenance	5,700	5,700	5,700	5,700	22,800
Total fixed	38,500	38,500	38,500	38,500	154,000
Total manufacturing overhead	**$57,100**	**$60,100**	**$63,100**	**$66,100**	**$246,400**
Direct labor hours	**6,200**	**7,200**	**8,200**	**9,200**	**30,800**
Manufacturing overhead rate per direct labor hour ($246,400 ÷ 30,800)					**$8.00**

Selling and Administrative Expense Budget

Hayes Company combines its operating expenses into one budget, the **selling and administrative expense budget**. This budget is a projection of anticipated selling and administrative expenses for the budget period. In this budget, as in the preceding budget, expenses are classified as either variable or fixed. In this case, the variable expense rates per unit of sales are sales commissions $3.00, and freight-out $1.00. Variable expenses per quarter are based on the unit sales projected in the sales budget (Illustration 24-3). For example, sales in the first quarter are expected to be 3,000 units. Thus, Sales Commissions Expense is $9,000 (3,000 × $3), and Freight-out is $3,000 (3,000 × $1). Fixed expenses are based on assumed data. The selling and administrative expense budget is shown in Illustration 24-10.

ILLUSTRATION 24-10

Selling and administrative expense budget

HAYES COMPANY					
Selling and Administrative Expense Budget					
For the Year Ending December 31, 1999					
	Quarter				
	1	**2**	**3**	**4**	**Year**
Variable expenses					
Sales commissions	$ 9,000	$10,500	$12,000	$13,500	$ 45,000
Freight-out	3,000	3,500	4,000	4,500	15,000
Total variable	12,000	14,000	16,000	18,000	60,000
Fixed expenses					
Advertising	5,000	5,000	5,000	5,000	20,000
Sales salaries	15,000	15,000	15,000	15,000	60,000
Office salaries	7,500	7,500	7,500	7,500	30,000
Depreciation	1,000	1,000	1,000	1,000	4,000
Property taxes and insurance	1,500	1,500	1,500	1,500	6,000
Total fixed	30,000	30,000	30,000	30,000	120,000
Total selling and administrative expenses	**$42,000**	**$44,000**	**$46,000**	**$48,000**	**$180,000**

Budgeted Income Statement

4
STUDY OBJECTIVE

Describe the sources for preparing the budgeted income statement.

The **budgeted income statement** is the important end-product in preparing operating budgets. This budget indicates the expected profitability of operations for the budget period. Once established, the budgeted income statement provides the basis for evaluating company performance. As you would expect, this budget is prepared from the previous budgets. For example, to find the cost of goods sold, it is first necessary to determine the total unit cost of producing one Kitchen-mate as follows:

ILLUSTRATION 24-11

Computation of total unit cost

	Cost of One Kitchen-mate			
Cost Element	**Illustration**	**Quantity**	**Unit Cost**	**Total**
Direct materials	24-7	2 pounds	$ 4.00	$ 8.00
Direct labor	24-8	2 hours	$10.00	20.00
Manufacturing overhead	24-9	2 hours	$ 8.00	16.00
Total unit cost				**$44.00**

Cost of goods sold can then be determined by multiplying the units sold by the unit cost. For Hayes Company, budgeted cost of goods sold is $660,000 (15,000 × $44). All data for the statement are obtained from the individual operating budgets except the following: (1) interest expense is expected to be $100 and (2) income taxes are estimated to be $12,000. The budgeted income statement is shown in Illustration 24-12.

ILLUSTRATION 24-12

Budgeted income statement

HAYES COMPANY Budgeted Income Statement For the Year Ending December 31, 1999	
Sales (Illustration 24-3)	$900,000
Cost of goods sold (15,000 × $44)	660,000
Gross profit	240,000
Selling and administrative expenses (Illustration 24-10)	180,000
Income from operations	60,000
Interest expense	100
Income before income taxes	59,900
Income tax expense	12,000
Net income	$ 47,900

PREPARING THE FINANCIAL BUDGETS

As shown in Illustration 24-2, the financial budgets consist of the capital expenditure budget, the cash budget, and the budgeted balance sheet. The capital expenditure budget is discussed in Chapter 27; the other budgets are explained in the following sections.

Cash Budget

The **cash budget** shows anticipated cash flows. Because cash is so vital in a company, this budget is considered to be the most important output in preparing financial budgets. The cash budget contains three sections (cash receipts, cash disbursements, and financing) and the beginning and ending cash balances as shown in Illustration 24-13.

5

STUDY OBJECTIVE

Explain the principal sections of a cash budget.

ILLUSTRATION 24-13

Basic form of a cash budget

ANY COMPANY Cash Budget	
Beginning cash balance	$X,XXX
Add: Cash receipts (Itemized)	X,XXX
Total available cash	X,XXX
Less: Cash disbursements (Itemized)	X,XXX
Excess (deficiency) of available cash over cash disbursements	X,XXX
Financing	X,XXX
Ending cash balance	$X,XXX

The **cash receipts section** includes expected receipts from the company's principal source(s) of revenue such as cash sales and collections from customers on credit sales. This section also shows anticipated receipts of interest and dividends, and proceeds from planned sales of investments, plant assets, and the company's capital stock.

The **cash disbursements section** shows expected payments for direct materials, direct labor, manufacturing overhead, and selling and administrative expenses. This section also includes projected payments for income taxes, dividends, investments, and plant assets.

The **financing section** shows expected borrowings and the repayment of the borrowed funds plus interest. This section is needed when there is a cash deficiency or when the cash balance is below management's minimum required balance.

Data in the cash budget must be prepared in sequence because the ending cash balance of one period becomes the beginning cash balance for the next period. Data for preparing the cash budget are obtained from other budgets and from information provided by management. In practice, cash budgets are often prepared for the year on a monthly basis.

HELPFUL HINT

Why is the cash budget prepared after the other budgets are prepared? Answer: Because the information generated by the other budgets dictates the need for and the inflows and outflows of cash.

ACCOUNTING IN ACTION
Business Insight

Douglas Roberson, president of Atlantic Network, woke up one morning to find that his company was out of cash. At that point, Roberson realized that managing cash flow is different from simply accumulating sales. He says: "If you don't do serious projections about how much cash you will need to handle sales—and how long it will take to collect on invoices—you can end up out of business no matter how fast you are growing." In fact, Roberson says, fast growth exacerbates cash flow problems because the company can be spending cash on supplies and payroll at an accelerated pace while waiting 45 days or longer to collect receivables.

To minimize detail, we will assume that Hayes Company prepares an annual cash budget by quarters. The cash budget for Hayes Company is based on the following assumptions:

1. The January 1, 1999, cash balance is expected to be $38,000.
2. Sales (Illustration 24-3)—60% are collected in the quarter sold and 40% are collected in the following quarter. Accounts receivable of $60,000 at December 31, 1998, are expected to be collected in full in the first quarter of 1999.
3. Marketable securities are expected to be sold for $2,000 cash in the first quarter.
4. Direct materials (Illustration 24-7)—50% are paid in the quarter purchased and 50% are paid in the following quarter. Accounts payable of $10,600 at December 31, 1998, are expected to be paid in full in the first quarter of 1999.
5. Direct labor (Illustration 24-8)—100% is paid in the quarter incurred.
6. Manufacturing overhead (Illustration 24-9) and selling and administrative expenses (Illustration 24-10). All items except depreciation are paid in the quarter incurred.
7. Management plans to purchase a new truck in the second quarter for $10,000 cash.
8. The company makes equal quarterly payments of its estimated annual income taxes.

9. Loans are repaid in the first subsequent quarter in which there is sufficient cash.

Preparing schedules for collections from customers (assumption No. 2, above) and cash payments for direct materials (assumption No. 4, above) is useful in preparing the cash budget. The schedules are shown in Illustrations 24-14 and 24-15.

Schedule of Expected Collections from Customers

	Quarter			
	1	**2**	**3**	**4**
Accounts receivable, 12/31/98	$ 60,000			
First quarter ($180,000)	108,000	$ 72,000		
Second quarter ($210,000)		126,000	$ 84,000	
Third quarter ($240,000)			144,000	$ 96,000
Fourth quarter ($270,000)				162,000
Total collections	$168,000	$198,000	$228,000	$258,000

ILLUSTRATION 24-14

Collections from customers

Schedule of Expected Payments for Direct Materials

	Quarter			
	1	**2**	**3**	**4**
Accounts payable, 12/31/98	$10,600			
First quarter ($25,200)	12,600	$12,600		
Second quarter ($29,200)		14,600	$14,600	
Third quarter ($33,200)			16,600	$16,600
Fourth quarter ($37,200)				18,600
Total payments	$23,200	$27,200	$31,200	$35,200

ILLUSTRATION 24-15

Payments for direct materials

The cash budget for the Hayes Company is shown in Illustration 24-16. The budget indicates that $3,000 of financing will be needed in the second quarter to maintain a minimum cash balance of $15,000. Since there is an excess of available cash over disbursements of $22,500 at the end of the third quarter, the borrowing is repaid in this quarter plus $100 interest.

A cash budget contributes to more effective cash management. For example, it can show when additional financing will be necessary well before the actual need arises. Conversely, it can indicate when excess cash will be available for investments or other purposes.

Budgeted Balance Sheet

The **budgeted balance sheet** is a projection of financial position at the end of the budget period. This budget is developed from the budgeted balance sheet for the preceding year and the budgets for the current year. Pertinent data from the budgeted balance sheet at December 31, 1998, are as follows:

Building and equipment	$182,000	Common stock	$225,000
Accumulated depreciation	$ 28,800	Retained earnings	$ 46,480

ILLUSTRATION 24-16

Cash budget

HAYES COMPANY
Cash Budget
For the Year Ending December 31, 1999

	Assumption	Quarter 1	Quarter 2	Quarter 3	Quarter 4
Beginning cash balance	1	$ 38,000	$ 25,500	$ 15,000	$ 19,400
Add: Receipts					
Collections from customers	2	168,000	198,000	228,000	258,000
Sale of securities	3	2,000	0	0	0
Total receipts		170,000	198,000	228,000	258,000
Total available cash		208,000	223,500	243,000	277,400
Less: Disbursements					
Direct materials	4	23,200	27,200	31,200	35,200
Direct labor	5	62,000	72,000	82,000	92,000
Manufacturing overhead	6	53,300[1]	56,300	59,300	62,300
Selling and administrative expenses	6	41,000[2]	43,000	45,000	47,000
Purchase of truck	7	0	10,000	0	0
Income tax expense	8	3,000	3,000	3,000	3,000
Total disbursements		182,500	211,500	220,500	239,500
Excess (deficiency) of available cash over disbursements		25,500	12,000	22,500	37,900
Financing					
Borrowings		0	3,000	0	0
Repayments—plus $100 interest	9	0	0	3,100	0
Ending cash balance		$ 25,500	$ 15,000	$ 19,400	$ 37,900

[1]$57,100 − $3,800 depreciation
[2]$42,000 − $1,000 depreciation

The budgeted balance sheet at December 31, 1999, is shown below.

ILLUSTRATION 24-17

Budgeted balance sheet

HAYES COMPANY
Budgeted Balance Sheet
December 31, 1999

Assets

Cash		$ 37,900
Accounts receivable		108,000
Finished goods inventory		44,000
Raw materials inventory		4,080
Buildings and equipment	$192,000	
Less: Accumulated depreciation	48,000	144,000
Total assets		$337,980

Liabilities and Stockholders' Equity

Accounts payable	$ 18,600
Common stock	225,000
Retained earnings	94,380
Total liabilities and stockholders' equity	$337,980

The computations and sources of the amounts are explained below.

Cash—Ending cash balance $37,900, shown in the cash budget (Illustration 24-16).

Accounts receivable—40% of fourth-quarter sales $270,000, shown in the schedule of expected collections from customers (Illustration 24-14).

Finished goods inventory—Desired ending inventory 1,000 units, shown in production budget (Illustration 24-5) times the total unit cost, $44 (shown in Illustration 24-11).

Raw materials inventory—Desired ending inventory 1,020 pounds, times the cost per pound, $4 shown in the direct materials budget (Illustration 24-7).

Buildings and equipment—December 31, 1998, balance $182,000, plus purchase of truck for $10,000.

Accumulated depreciation—December 31, 1998, balance $28,800, plus $15,200 depreciation shown in manufacturing overhead budget (Illustration 24-9) and $4,000 depreciation shown in selling and administrative expense budget (Illustration 24-10).

Accounts payable—50% of fourth-quarter purchases $37,200, shown in schedule of expected payments for direct materials (Illustration 24-15).

Common stock—Unchanged from the beginning of the year.

Retained earnings—December 31, 1998, balance $46,480, plus net income, $47,900, shown in budgeted income statement (Illustration 24-12).

TECHNOLOGY IN ACTION

After the budgeting data are entered into the computer, the various budgets (sales, cash, etc.) can be prepared, as well as the budgeted financial statements. Management can also manipulate the budgets in "what if" (sensitivity) analyses based on different hypothetical assumptions. For example, suppose that sales were budgeted to be 10 percent higher in the coming quarter. What impact would the change have on the rest of the budgeting process and the financing needs of the business? The computer can quickly "play out" the impact of the various assumptions on the budgets. Armed with these analyses, management can make more informed decisions about the impact of various projects and anticipate future problems and business opportunities. Budgeting is one of the top uses of electronic spreadsheets. Template versions of every one of the Hayes Company budgets shown in this chapter could easily be prepared.

BEFORE YOU GO ON . . .

Review It

1. How may the individual budgets in the master budget be classified?
2. What is the sequence for preparing the budgets that comprise the operating budgets?
3. What are the three principal sections of the cash budget?
4. Obviously, Kellogg does not present its detailed budgets in its 1997 Annual Report, but, in the "1998 Outlook" in its Management Discussion and Analysis section, what general expectations and what specific hard-data expectations does Kellogg provide about 1998 operations? The answer to this question is provided on page 1069.

Do It

In Martian Company, management wants to maintain a minimum monthly cash balance of $15,000. At the beginning of March, the cash balance is $16,500, expected cash receipts for March are $210,000, and cash disbursements are expected to be $220,000. How much cash, if any, must be borrowed to maintain the desired minimum monthly balance?

Reasoning: The best way to answer this question is to insert the dollar data into the basic form of the cash budget.

Solution:

MARTIAN COMPANY
Cash Budget
For the Month Ending March 31, 1999

Beginning cash balance	$ 16,500
Add: Cash receipts for March	210,000
Total available cash	226,500
Less: Cash disbursements for March	220,000
Excess of available cash over cash disbursements	6,500
Financing	8,500
Ending cash balance	$ 15,000

To maintain the desired minimum cash balance of $15,000, $8,500 of cash must be borrowed.

Related exercise material: BE24–9 and E24–9.

BUDGETING IN NONMANUFACTURING COMPANIES

6
STUDY
OBJECTIVE
....
Indicate the applicability of budgeting in nonmanufacturing companies.

Budgeting is not limited to manufacturing companies. Budgets may also be used in profit planning by merchandising companies, service enterprises, and not-for-profit organizations.

Merchandising Companies

As in manufacturing operations, the sales budget is both the starting point and the key factor in the development of the master budget for a merchandising company. The major differences between the master budgets of a merchandising company and a manufacturing company are that a merchandiser **(1) uses a merchandise purchases budget instead of a production budget and (2) does not use the manufacturing budgets (direct materials, direct labor, and manufacturing overhead).** The merchandise purchases budget shows the estimated cost of goods to be purchased to meet expected sales. The formula for determining budgeted merchandise purchases is:

ILLUSTRATION 24-18

Merchandise purchases formula

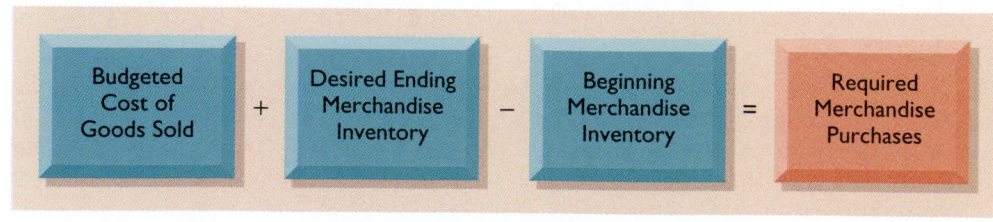

To illustrate, assume that the budget committee of Lima Company is preparing the merchandise purchases budget for July. It estimates that budgeted sales will be $300,000 in July and $320,000 in August. Cost of goods sold is expected to be 70% of sales, and the company's desired ending inventory is 30% of the following month's cost of goods sold. Required merchandise purchases for July are $214,200, computed as follows:

Budgeted cost of goods sold (budgeted sales for July, $300,000 × 70%)	$210,000
Desired ending merchandise inventory (budgeted cost of goods sold for August, $320,000 × 70% × 30%)	67,200
Total	277,200
Less: Beginning merchandise inventory (budgeted sales for July, $300,000 × 70% × 30%)	63,000
Required merchandise purchases for July	**$214,200**

ILLUSTRATION 24-19

Computation of required merchandise purchases

When the merchandising company is departmentalized, separate budgets are prepared for each department. For example, a grocery store may start by preparing sales budgets and purchases budgets for each of its major departments, such as meats, dairy, and produce. These budgets are then combined into a master budget for the store. When a retailer has branch stores, separate master budgets are prepared for each store. Then these budgets are incorporated into master budgets for the company as a whole.

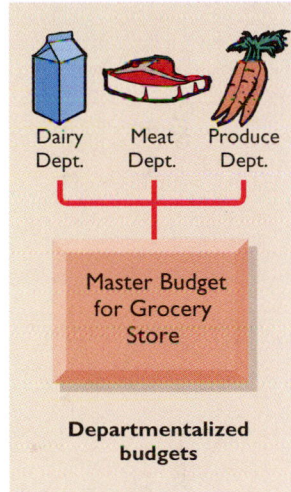

Dairy Dept.   Meat Dept.   Produce Dept.

Master Budget for Grocery Store

Departmentalized budgets

Service Enterprises

In service enterprises, such as a public accounting firm, a law office, or a medical practice, the critical factor in budgeting is **coordinating professional staff needs with anticipated services**. If a firm is overstaffed, (1) labor costs will be disproportionately high, (2) profits will be lower because of the additional salaries, and (3) staff turnover may increase because of lack of challenging work. In contrast, if an enterprise is understaffed, revenue may be lost because existing and prospective client needs for service cannot be met, and professional staff may seek other positions because of excessive work loads.

Budget data for service revenue may be obtained from expected output or expected input. When output is used, it is necessary to determine the expected billings of clients for services rendered. In a public accounting firm, for example, output would be the sum of its billings in auditing, tax, and consulting services. When service revenue is derived from input data, each professional staff member is required to project his or her billable time. Billing rates are then applied to billable time to produce expected service revenue.

ACCOUNTING IN ACTION

Business Insight

Lucy Carter, managing partner of a small CPA firm in Nashville, uses formal budgets as the principal tool for keeping cash flow on an even keel throughout the year. The firm budgets annually for both revenues and expenses on a month-by-month basis. For example, the revenue budget is derived from chargeable-hour goals set by the staff, with a threshold of 1,800 hours for each staff member and 1,700 hours for each manager. Each month the budget is compared with the financial statements, and adjustments are made if necessary.

Not-for-Profit Organizations

Budgeting is just as important for not-for-profit organizations as for profit-oriented enterprises. The budget process, however, is significantly different. In most cases not-for-profit entities budget **on the basis of cash flows (expenditures and receipts), rather than on a revenue and expense basis.** Further, the starting point in the process is usually expenditures, not receipts. For the not-for-profit entity, management's task generally is to find the receipts needed to support the planned expenditures. This was the case for the University of Nebraska in the opening story. The activity index is also likely to be significantly different. For example, in a not-for-profit entity, such as a university, budgeted faculty positions may be based on full-time equivalent students or credit hours expected to be taught in a department.

For some governmental units, the budget must be approved by voters. In other cases, such as state governments and the federal government, legislative approval is required. After the budget is adopted, it must be strictly followed, and overspending is often illegal. In governmental budgets, authorizations tend to be on a line-by-line basis. That is, the budget for a municipality may have a specified authorization for police and fire protection, garbage collection, street paving, and so on. The line item authorization of governmental budgets significantly limits the amount of discretion management can exercise. The city manager often cannot use savings in one line item, such as street paving, to cover increased spending in another line item, such as snow removal.

BEFORE YOU GO ON . . .

Review It

1. What is the formula for computing required merchandise purchases?
2. How does budgeting in service and not-for-profit organizations differ from budgeting in manufacturing and merchandising companies?

A LOOK BACK AT OUR FEATURE STORY

Refer to the opening story and answer the following questions.

1. How does the length of the budget period for the University of Nebraska compare with the guidelines given for businesses in the chapter?
2. What is the difference between a capital budget and an operating budget?
3. Who do you believe comprises the budget committee at your college or university?

Solution:

1. The University of Nebraska must submit its budget to the state legislature on September 15 *every other year*. Thus, the length of the budget period is 2 years. For businesses, the length of the budget period is normally one year, and for some items, such as cash, monthly budgets may be prepared.
2. A capital budget is for big projects, such as buildings, which span more than a year. An operating budget is established to plan for day-to-day expenditures.
3. The budget committee at many universities consists of key officers and the deans of the various colleges. Key officers would be the president, vice president for academic affairs (sometimes called the provost), and the vice president of finance.

DEMONSTRATION PROBLEM

The Soroco Company is preparing its master budgets for 1999. Relevant data pertaining to its sales and production budgets are as follows:

Sales: Sales for the year are expected to total 1,200,000 units. Quarterly sales are 20%, 25%, 30%, and 25%, respectively. The sales price is expected to be $50 per unit for the first three quarters and $55 per unit beginning in the fourth quarter. Sales in the first quarter of 2000 are expected to be 10% higher than the budgeted sales volume for the first quarter of 1999.

Production: Management desires to maintain ending finished goods inventories at 25% of the next quarter's budgeted sales volume.

Instructions

Prepare the sales budget and production budget by quarters for 1999.

SOLUTION TO DEMONSTRATION PROBLEM

SOROCO COMPANY
Sales Budget
For the Year Ending December 31, 1999

| | \multicolumn{5}{c}{Quarter} | | | | |
	1	2	3	4	Year
Expected unit sales	240,000	300,000	360,000	300,000	1,200,000
Unit selling price	× $50	× $50	× $50	× $55	—
	$12,000,000	$15,000,000	$18,000,000	$16,500,000	$61,500,000

SOROCO COMPANY
Production Budget
For the Year Ending December 31, 1999

| | \multicolumn{4}{c}{Quarter} | | | | |
	1	2	3	4	Year
Expected unit sales	240,000	300,000	360,000	300,000	
Add: Desired ending finished goods units	75,000	90,000	75,000	66,000[1]	
Total required units	315,000	390,000	435,000	366,000	
Less: Beginning finished goods units	60,000[2]	75,000	90,000	75,000	
Units to be produced	255,000	315,000	345,000	291,000	1,206,000

[1]Estimated first-quarter 2000 sales volume 240,000 + (240,000 × 10%) = 264,000; 264,000 × 25%.
[2]25% of estimated first-quarter 1999 sales units.

PROBLEM-SOLVING STRATEGIES

1. For the sales budget, know the form and content.
2. The sales budget is the first budget prepared.
3. Each of the other budgets is dependent on the sales budget.
4. The production budget shows the units that must be produced to meet anticipated sales.
5. The production budget provides the bases for determining the budgeted cost for each manufacturing cost element.
6. Know how to compute the beginning and ending finished goods units.

THE NAVIGATOR

SUMMARY OF STUDY OBJECTIVES

1. *Identify the benefits of budgeting.* The primary advantages of budgeting are that it (a) requires management to plan ahead, (b) provides definite objectives for evaluating performance, (c) creates an early warning system for potential problems, (d) facilitates coordination of activities, (e) results in greater management awareness, and (f) contributes to positive behavior patterns.

2. *State the essentials of effective budgeting.* The essentials of effective budgeting are (a) sound organizational structure, (b) research and analysis, and (c) acceptance by all levels of management.

3. *Identify the budgets that comprise the master budget.* The master budget consists of the following budgets:

(a) sales, (b) production, (c) direct materials, (d) direct labor, (e) manufacturing overhead, (f) selling and administrative expense, (g) budgeted income statement, (h) capital expenditure budget, (i) cash budget, and (j) budgeted balance sheet.

4. *Describe the sources for preparing the budgeted income statement.* The budgeted income statement is prepared from (a) the sales budget, (b) the budgets for direct materials, direct labor, and manufacturing overhead, and (c) the selling and administrative expense budget.

5. *Explain the principal sections of a cash budget.* The cash budget has three sections (receipts, disbursements, and financing) and the beginning and ending cash balances.

6. *Indicate the applicability of budgeting in nonmanufacturing companies.* Budgeting may be used in merchandising companies for development of a master budget. In service enterprises budgeting is a critical factor in coordinating staff needs with anticipated services. In not-for-profit organizations, the starting point in budgeting is usually expenditures, not receipts.

GLOSSARY

Budget A formal written summary of management's plans for a specified future time period, expressed in financial terms. (p. 1034).

Budget committee A group responsible for coordinating the preparation of the budget. (p. 1036).

Budgeted balance sheet A projection of financial position at the end of the budget period. (p. 1047).

Budgeted income statement An estimate of the expected profitability of operations for the budget period. (p. 1044).

Cash budget A projection of anticipated cash flows. (p. 1045).

Direct labor budget A projection of the quantity and cost of direct labor to be incurred to meet production requirements. (p. 1042).

Direct materials budget An estimate of the quantity and cost of direct materials to be purchased. (p. 1041).

Financial budgets Individual budgets that indicate the cash resources needed for expected operations and planned capital expenditures. (p. 1038).

Long-range planning A formalized process of selecting strategies to achieve long-term goals and developing policies and plans to implement the strategies. (p. 1038).

Manufacturing overhead budget An estimate of expected manufacturing overhead costs for the budget period. (p. 1043).

Master budget A set of interrelated budgets that constitutes a plan of action for a specific time period. (p. 1038).

Merchandise purchases budget The estimated cost of goods to be purchased in a merchandising company to meet expected sales. (p. 1050).

Operating budgets Individual budgets that culminate in a budgeted income statement. (p. 1038).

Production budget A projection of the units that must be produced to meet anticipated sales. (p. 1040).

Sales budget An estimate of expected sales for the budget period. (p. 1040).

Sales forecast The projection of potential sales for the industry and the company's expected share of such sales. (p. 1036).

Selling and administrative expense budget A projection of anticipated selling and administrative expenses for the budget period. (p. 1044).

SELF-STUDY QUESTIONS

Answers are at the end of the chapter.

(SO 1) 1. The benefits of budgeting include *all but one* of the following:
   a. Management can plan ahead.
   b. An early warning system is provided for potential problems.
   c. It enables disciplinary action to be taken at every level of responsibility.
   d. The coordination of activities is facilitated.

(SO 2) 2. The essentials of effective budgeting do *not* include:
   a. top down budgeting.
   b. management acceptance.
   c. research and analysis.
   d. sound organizational structure.

3. Compared to budgeting, long-range planning generally (SO 2) has the:
   a. same amount of detail.
   b. longer time period.
   c. same emphasis.
   d. same time period.

4. A sales budget is: (SO 3)
   a. derived from the production budget.
   b. management's best estimate of sales revenue for the year.
   c. not the starting point for the master budget.
   d. prepared only for credit sales.

(SO 3) 5. The formula for the production budget is budgeted sales in units plus:
a. desired ending merchandise inventory less beginning merchandise inventory.
b. beginning finished goods units less desired ending finished goods units.
c. desired ending direct materials units less beginning direct materials units.
d. desired ending finished goods units less beginning finished goods units.

(SO 3) 6. Direct materials inventories are kept in pounds in Byrd Company, and the total pounds of direct materials needed for production is 9,500. If the beginning inventory is 1,000 pounds and the desired ending inventory is 2,200 pounds, the total pounds to be purchased is:
a. 9,400.
b. 9,500.
c. 9,700.
d. 10,700.

(SO 3) 7. The formula for computing the direct labor cost budget is to multiply the direct labor cost per hour by the:
a. total required direct labor hours.
b. physical units to be produced.
c. equivalent units to be produced.
d. no correct answer is given.

8. Each of the following budgets is used in preparing the (SO 4) budgeted income statement *except* the:
a. sales budget.
b. selling and administrative budget.
c. capital expenditure budget.
d. direct labor budget.

9. Expected direct materials purchases in Read Company (SO 5) are $70,000 in the first quarter and $90,000 in the second quarter. Forty percent of the purchases are paid in cash as incurred, and the balance is paid in the following quarter. The budgeted cash payments for purchases in the second quarter are:
a. $96,000.
b. $90,000.
c. $78,000.
d. $72,000.

10. The budget for a merchandising company differs from (SO 6) a budget for a manufacturing company because:
a. a merchandise purchases budget replaces the production budget.
b. the manufacturing budgets are not applicable.
c. None of the above.
d. Both (a) and (b) above.

THE NAVIGATOR

QUESTIONS

1. (a) What is a budget?
   (b) How does a budget contribute to good management?

2. Alemeda and Delino are discussing the benefits of budgeting. They ask you to identify the primary advantages of budgeting. Comply with their request.

3. Ramon Martinez asks your help in understanding the essentials of effective budgeting. Identify the essentials for Ramon.

4. (a) "Accounting plays a relatively unimportant role in budgeting." Do you agree? Explain.
   (b) What responsibilities does management have in budgeting?

5. What criteria are helpful in determining the length of the budget period? What is the most common budget period?

6. Kathy Fernetti maintains that the only difference between budgeting and long-range planning is time. Do you agree? Why or why not?

7. Distinguish between a master budget and a sales forecast.

8. What budget is the starting point in preparing the master budget? What may result if this budget is inaccurate?

9. "The production budget shows both unit production data and unit cost data." Is this true? Explain.

10. Klaus Company has 6,000 beginning finished goods units. Budgeted sales units are 150,000. If management

desires 10,000 ending finished goods units, what are the required units of production?

11. In preparing the direct materials budget for Matsakis Company, management concludes that required purchases are 48,000 units. If 46,000 direct materials units are required in production and there are 4,000 units of beginning direct materials, what is the desired units of ending direct materials?

12. The production budget of Piper Company calls for 80,000 units to be produced. If it takes 30 minutes to make one unit and the direct labor rate is $14 per hour, what is the total budgeted direct labor cost?

13. Schultz Company's manufacturing overhead budget shows total variable costs of $186,000 and total fixed costs of $174,000. Total production in units is expected to be 160,000. It takes 15 minutes to make one unit, and the direct labor rate is $15 per hour. Express the manufacturing overhead rate as (a) a percentage of direct labor cost and (b) an amount per direct labor hour.

14. Tabor Company's variable selling and administrative expenses are 10% of net sales and fixed expenses are $60,000 per quarter. The sales budget shows expected sales of $200,000 and $250,000 in the first and second quarters, respectively. What are the total budgeted selling and administrative expenses for each quarter?

15. For Franco Company, the budgeted cost for one unit of product is direct materials $10, direct labor $20, and manufacturing overhead 75% of direct labor cost. If

25,000 units are expected to be sold at $77 each, what is the budgeted gross profit?

16. Indicate the supporting schedules used in preparing a budgeted income statement through gross profit for a manufacturing company.

17. Identify the three sections of a cash budget. What balances are also shown in this budget?

18. Garcia Company has credit sales of $400,000 in January. Past experience suggests that 40% is collected in the month of sale, 50% in the month following the sale, and 4% in the second month following the sale. Compute the cash collections from January sales in January, February, and March.

19. What is the formula for determining required merchandise purchases in a merchandising company?

20. How may expected revenues in a service enterprise be computed?

BRIEF EXERCISES

••

Prepare a diagram of a master budget.
(SO 3)

BE24–1 O'Connor Manufacturing Company uses the following budgets: Balance Sheet, Capital Expenditure, Cash, Direct Labor, Direct Materials, Income Statement, Manufacturing Overhead, Production, Sales, and Selling and Administrative. Prepare a diagram of the interrelationships of the budgets in the master budget. Indicate whether each budget is an operating or a financial budget.

Prepare a sales budget.
(SO 3)

BE24–2 Delgado Company estimates that unit sales will be 10,000 in quarter 1; 12,000 in quarter 2; 14,000 in quarter 3; and 15,000 in quarter 4. Using a sales price of $60 per unit, prepare the sales budget, by quarters, for the year ending December 31, 1999.

Prepare a production budget for 2 quarters.
(SO 3)

BE24–3 Sales budget data for Delgado Company are given in BE24–2. Management desires to have an ending finished goods inventory equal to 25% of the next quarter's expected unit sales. Prepare a production budget, by quarters, for the first 6 months of 1999.

Prepare a direct materials budget for one month.
(SO 3)

BE24–4 Fosdick Company has 1,200 pounds of raw materials in its December 31, 1999, ending inventory. Required production for January and February are 4,000 and 5,000 units, respectively. Three pounds of raw materials are needed for each unit, and the estimated cost per pound is $6. Management desires an ending inventory equal to 10% of next month's materials requirements. Prepare the direct materials budget for January.

Prepare a direct labor budget for 2 quarters.
(SO 3)

BE24–5 For Haught Company, units to be produced are 5,000 in quarter 1 and 6,000 in quarter 2. It takes 1.5 hours to make a finished unit, and the expected hourly wage rate is $12 per hour. Prepare a direct labor budget, by quarters, for the 6 months ending June 30, 1999.

Prepare a manufacturing overhead budget.
(SO 3)

BE24–6 For McNulty, Inc., variable manufacturing overhead costs are expected to be $30,000 in the first quarter of 1999 with $4,000 increments in each of the remaining three quarters. Fixed overhead costs are estimated to be $35,000 in each quarter. Prepare the manufacturing overhead budget, by quarters, for the year.

Prepare a selling and administrative expense budget.
(SO 3)

BE24–7 Newlin Company classifies its selling and administrative expense budget into variable and fixed components. Variable expenses are expected to be $21,000 in the first quarter, and $3,000 increments are expected in the remaining quarters of 1999. Fixed expenses are expected to be $40,000 in each quarter. Prepare the selling and administrative expense budget, by quarters, for 1999.

Prepare a budgeted income statement for the year.
(SO 4)

BE24–8 Markowitz Company has completed all of its operating budgets. The sales budget for the year shows 50,000 units and total sales of $2,000,000. The total unit cost of making one unit of sales is $30. Selling and administrative expenses are expected to be $300,000, and income taxes are estimated to be $50,000. Prepare a budgeted income statement for the year ending December 31, 1999.

Prepare data for a cash budget.
(SO 5)

BE24–9 Liang Industries expects credit sales for January, February, and March to be $200,000, $275,000, and $310,000, respectively. It is expected that 60% of the sales will be collected in the month of sale, and 40% will be collected in the following month. Compute cash collections from customers for each month.

Determine required merchandise purchases for one month.
(SO 6)

BE24–10 GRS Wholesalers is preparing its merchandise purchases budget. Budgeted sales are $400,000 for April and $450,000 for May. Cost of goods sold is expected to be 70% of sales, and the company's desired ending inventory is 20% of the following month's cost of goods sold. Compute the required purchases for April.

EXERCISES

· ·

E24–1   Kohler Electronics Inc. produces and sells two models of pocket calculators, XQ-103 and XQ-104. The calculators sell for $10 and $15, respectively. Because of the intense competition Kohler faces, management budgets sales semiannually. Its projections for the first 2 quarters of 1999 are as follows:

Prepare a sales budget for 2 quarters.
(SO 3)

| Product | Unit Sales | |
	Quarter 1	Quarter 2
XQ-103	30,000	27,000
XQ-104	12,000	13,000

No changes in selling prices are anticipated.

Instructions
Prepare a sales budget for the two quarters ending June 30, 1999. List the products and show for each quarter and for the 6 months, units, selling price, and total sales by product and in total.

E24–2   Ghosh Company produces and sells two types of automobile batteries, the heavy-duty HD-240 and the long-life LL-250. The 1999 sales budget for the two products is as follows:

Prepare quarterly production budgets.
(SO 3)

Quarter	HD-240	LL-250
1	5,000	10,000
2	7,000	18,000
3	8,000	20,000
4	10,000	35,000

The January 1, 1999, inventory of HD-240 and LL-250 units is 4,000 and 8,000, respectively. Management desires an ending inventory each quarter equal to 70% of the next quarter's sales. Sales in the first quarter of 2000 are expected to be 40% higher than sales in the same quarter in 1999.

Instructions
Prepare separate quarterly production budgets for each product by quarters for 1999.

E24–3   Herrara Industries has adopted the following production budget for the first 4 months of 2000.

Prepare a direct materials purchases budget.
(SO 3)

Month	Units	Month	Units
January	10,000	March	6,000
February	8,000	April	4,000

Each unit requires 6 pounds of raw materials costing $1.50 per pound. On December 31, 1999, the ending raw materials inventory was 36,000 pounds. Management wants to have a raw materials inventory at the end of the month equal to 60% of next month's production requirements.

Instructions
Prepare a direct materials purchases budget by months for the first quarter.

E24–4   The Kasper Company budget committee has reached agreement on the following data for the 6 months ending June 30, 2000:

Prepare production and direct materials budgets by quarters for 6 months.
(SO 3)

Sales units (by quarters):	(1) 5,000, (2) 8,000
Ending raw materials inventory:	50% of the next quarter's production requirements
Ending finished goods inventory:	25% of the next quarter's expected sales units

The ending raw materials and finished goods inventories at December 31, 1999, follow the same percentage relationships to production and sales that occur in 2000. Three pounds of raw materials are required to make each unit of finished goods. Raw materials purchased are expected to cost $4 per pound. Sales of 7,000 units and required production of 7,250 units are expected in the third quarter of 2000.

Instructions
(a) Prepare a production budget by quarters for the 6 months.
(b) Prepare a direct materials budget by quarters for the 6 months.

Prepare a direct labor budget.
(SO 3)

E24–5   Manies, Inc., is preparing its direct labor budget for 1999 from the following production budget based on a calendar year:

Quarter	Units	Quarter	Units
1	20,000	3	35,000
2	25,000	4	30,000

Each unit requires 1.6 hours of direct labor.

Instructions
Prepare a direct labor cost budget for 1999. Wage rates are expected to be $14 for the first 2 quarters and $15 for quarters 3 and 4.

Prepare a manufacturing overhead budget for the year.
(SO 3)

E24–6   Napier Company is preparing its manufacturing overhead budget for 1999. Relevant data consist of the following:

Units to be produced (by quarters):   10,000; 12,000; 14,000; 16,000.

Direct labor: Time is 1.5 hours per unit.

Variable overhead costs per direct labor hour: Indirect materials $0.70; indirect labor $1.20; and maintenance $0.30.

Fixed overhead costs per quarter: Supervisory salaries $30,000; depreciation $8,000; and maintenance $6,000.

Instructions
Prepare the manufacturing overhead budget for the year, showing quarterly data.

Prepare a selling and administrative expense budget for 2 quarters.
(SO 3)

E24–7   Ortega Company combines its operating expenses for budget purposes in a selling and administrative expense budget. For the first 6 months of 1999, the following data are developed:

1. Sales: 12,000 units quarter 1; 15,000 units quarter 2.
2. Variable costs per dollar of sales: Sales commissions 5%; delivery expense 2%; and advertising 3%.
3. Fixed costs per quarter: Sales salaries $10,000; office salaries $6,000; depreciation $4,200; insurance $1,500; utilities $800, and repairs expense $600.
4. Unit selling price: $20.

Instructions
Prepare a selling and administrative expense budget by quarters for the first 6 months of 1999.

Prepare a budgeted income statement for the year.
(SO 3, 4)

E24–8   Renfro Company has accumulated the following budget data for the year 1999:

1. Sales: 25,000 units; unit selling price $80.
2. Cost of one unit of finished goods: Direct materials 2 pounds at $5 per pound; direct labor 3 hours at $12 per hour; and manufacturing overhead $6 per direct labor hour.
3. Inventories (raw materials only):   Beginning, 10,000 pounds; ending, 15,000 pounds.
4. Raw materials cost: $5 per pound.
5. Selling and administrative expenses: $150,000.
6. Income taxes: 30% of income before income taxes.

Instructions
Prepare a budgeted income statement for 1999. Show the computation of cost of goods sold.

Prepare a cash budget for 2 months.
(SO 5)

E24–9   Peres Company expects to have a cash balance of $46,000 on January 1, 1999. Relevant monthly budget data for the first 2 months of 1999 are as follows:

Collections from customers: January $70,000; February $150,000.

Payments to suppliers: January $40,000; February $75,000.

Direct labor: January $30,000; February $40,000. Wages are paid in the month they are incurred.

Manufacturing overhead: January $21,000; February $30,000. These costs include depreciation of $1,000 per month. All other overhead costs are paid as incurred.

Selling and administrative expenses: January $15,000; February $20,000. These costs are exclusive of depreciation. They are paid as incurred.

Sales of marketable securities in January are expected to realize $10,000 in cash. Peres Company has a line of credit at a local bank that enables it to borrow up to $25,000. The company wants to maintain a minimum monthly cash balance of $20,000.

Instructions
Prepare a cash budget for January and February.

E24–10   In May 1999, the budget committee of Union Street Stores assembles the following data in preparation of budgeted merchandise purchases for the month of June.

Prepare a purchases budget and budgeted income statement for a merchandising company.
(SO 6)

1. Expected sales: June $500,000, July $600,000.
2. Cost of goods sold is expected to be 60% of sales.
3. Desired ending merchandise inventory is 30% of the following (next) month's cost of goods sold.
4. The beginning inventory at June 1 will be the desired amount.

Instructions
(a) Compute the budgeted merchandise purchases for June.
(b) Prepare the budgeted income statement for June through gross profit on sales.

PROBLEMS: SET A

P24–1A   Bluestem Farm Supply Company manufactures and sells a fertilizer called Basic II. The following data are developed for preparing budgets for Basic II for the first 2 quarters of 1999:

Prepare a budgeted income statement and supporting budgets.
(SO 3, 4)

1. Sales: Quarter 1, 40,000 bags; quarter 2, 60,000 bags. Selling price is $60 per bag.
2. Direct materials: Each bag of Basic II requires 6 pounds of Crup at a cost of $3 per pound and 10 pounds of Dert at $1.50 per pound.
3. Desired inventory levels:

Type of Inventory	January 1	April 1	July 1
Basic II (bags)	10,000	15,000	20,000
Crup (pounds)	9,000	12,000	15,000
Dert (pounds)	15,000	20,000	25,000

4. Direct labor: Direct labor time is 15 minutes per bag at an hourly rate of $10 per hour.
5. Selling and administrative expenses are expected to be 10% of sales plus $150,000 per quarter.
6. Income taxes are expected to be 30% of income from operations.

Your assistant has prepared two budgets: the manufacturing overhead budget that shows expected costs to be 100% of direct labor cost, and the direct materials budget for Dert which shows the cost of Dert to be $682,500 in quarter 1 and $982,500 in quarter 2.

Instructions
Prepare the budgeted income statement for the first 6 months of 1999 and all required supporting budgets by quarters. (*Note:* Use variable and fixed in the selling and administrative expense budget.)

P24–2A   Reneau Inc. is preparing its annual budgets for the year ending December 31, 1999. Accounting assistants furnish the following data:

Prepare sales, production, direct materials, direct labor, and income statement budgets.
(SO 3, 4)

	Product LN 35	Product LN 40
Sales budget:		
Anticipated volume in units	400,000	180,000
Unit selling price	$20.00	$30.00
Production budget:		
Desired ending finished goods units	30,000	25,000
Beginning finished goods units	20,000	15,000

	Product LN 35	Product LN 40
Direct materials budget:		
Direct materials per unit (pounds)	2	3
Desired ending direct materials pounds	50,000	20,000
Beginning direct materials pounds	40,000	10,000
Cost per pound	$2.00	$3.00
Direct labor budget:		
Direct labor time per unit	.5	.75
Direct labor rate per hour	$8.00	$8.00
Budgeted income statement:		
Total unit cost	$10.00	$20.00

An accounting assistant has prepared the detailed manufacturing overhead budget and the selling and administrative expense budget. The latter shows selling expenses of $460,000 for product LN 35 and $440,000 for product LN 40, and administrative expenses of $420,000 for product LN 35 and $380,000 for product LN 40. Income taxes are expected to be 30%.

Instructions
Prepare the following budgets for the year. Show data for each product. Quarterly budgets should not be prepared.

(a) Sales
(b) Production
(c) Direct materials
(d) Direct labor
(e) Income statement (*Note:* Income taxes are not allocated to the products.)

Prepare sales and production budgets and compute cost per unit under two plans.
(SO 3, 4)

P24–3A Prothe Industries had sales in 1999 of $5,250,000 (875,000 units) and gross profit of $1,587,500. Management is considering two alternative budget plans to increase its gross profit in 2000.

Plan A would increase the selling price per unit from $6.00 to $6.60. Sales volume would decrease by 10% from its 1999 level. Plan B would decrease the selling price per unit by 5%. The marketing department expects that the sales volume would increase by 100,000 units.

At the end of 1999, Prothe has 75,000 units on hand. If Plan A is accepted, the 2000 ending inventory should be equal to 87,500 units. If Plan B is accepted, the ending inventory should be equal to 100,000 units. Each unit produced will cost $2.00 in direct materials, $1.00 in direct labor, and $.50 in variable overhead. The fixed overhead for 2000 should be $1,000,000.

Instructions
(a) Prepare a sales budget for 2000 under (1) Plan A and (2) Plan B.
(b) Prepare a production budget for 2000 under (1) Plan A and (2) Plan B.
(c) Compute the cost per unit under (1) Plan A and (2) Plan B. Explain why the cost per unit is different for each of the two plans. (Round to two decimals.)
(d) Which plan should be accepted? (*Hint:* Compute the gross profit under each plan.)

Prepare cash budget for 2 months.
(SO 5)

P24–4A Sielert Company prepares monthly cash budgets. Relevant data from operating budgets for 2000 are:

	January	February
Sales	$350,000	$400,000
Direct materials purchases	95,000	110,000
Direct labor	80,000	95,000
Manufacturing overhead	60,000	75,000
Selling and administrative expenses	75,000	85,000

All sales are on account. Collections are expected to be 50% in the month of sale, 30% in the first month following the sale, and 20% in the second month following the sale. Forty percent (40%) of direct material purchases are paid in cash in the month of purchase, and the balance due is paid in the month following the purchase. All other items above are paid in the month incurred. Depreciation has been excluded from manufacturing overhead and selling and administrative expenses.

Other data:

(1) Credit sales: November 1999, $200,000; December 1999, $280,000.
(2) Purchases of direct materials: December 1999, $90,000.

(3) Other receipts: January—Collection of December 31, 1999, interest receivable $3,000;
February—Proceeds from sale of securities $5,000.

(4) Other disbursements: February—payment of $20,000 for land.

The company's cash balance on January 1, 2000, is expected to be $60,000. The company wants to maintain a minimum cash balance of $50,000.

Instructions
(a) Prepare schedules for (1) expected collections from customers and (2) expected payments for direct materials purchases.
(b) Prepare a cash budget for January and February in columnar form.

P24–5A The budget committee of Taberes Company collects the following data for its Westwood Store in preparing budgeted income statements for July and August 1999.

Prepare purchases and income statement budgets for a merchandising company.
(SO 6)

1. Expected sales: July $400,000, August $450,000, September $500,000.
2. Cost of goods sold is expected to be 70% of sales.
3. Company policy is to maintain ending merchandise inventory at 25% of the following month's cost of goods sold.
4. Operating expenses are estimated to be:

Sales salaries	$20,000 per month
Advertising	4% of monthly sales
Delivery expense	2% of monthly sales
Sales commissions	3% of monthly sales
Rent expense	$3,000 per month
Depreciation	$700 per month
Utilities	$500 per month
Insurance	$300 per month

5. Income taxes are estimated to be 30% of income from operations.

Instructions
(a) Prepare the merchandise purchases budget for each month in columnar form.
(b) Prepare budgeted income statements for each month in columnar form. Show the details of cost of goods sold in the statements.

P24–6A Viola Industries' balance sheet at December 31, 1999, is presented below.

Prepare budgeted income statement and balance sheet.
(SO 3, 4)

VIOLA INDUSTRIES
Balance Sheet
December 31, 1999

Assets

Current assets		
Cash		$ 7,500
Accounts receivable		82,500
Finished goods inventory (2,000 units)		30,000
Total current assets		120,000
Property, plant, and equipment		
Equipment	$40,000	
Less: Accumulated depreciation	10,000	30,000
Total assets		$150,000

Liabilities and Stockholders' Equity

Liabilities		
Notes payable		$ 25,000
Accounts payable		45,000
Total liabilities		70,000
Stockholders' equity		
Common stock	$50,000	
Retained earnings	30,000	
Total stockholders' equity		80,000
Total liabilities and stockholders' equity		$150,000

Additional information accumulated for the budgeting process:
Budgeted data for the year 2000 include the following:

	4th Qtr. of 2000	Year 2000 Total
Sales budget (8,000 units at $35)	$80,000	$280,000
Direct materials used	17,000	67,200
Direct labor	8,500	33,600
Manufacturing overhead applied	10,000	42,000
Selling and administrative expenses	18,000	76,000

To meet sales requirements and to have 2,400 units of finished goods on hand at December 31, 2000, the production budget shows 8,400 required units of output. The total unit cost of production is expected to be $17. Viola Industries uses the first-in, first-out (FIFO) inventory costing method. Selling and administrative expenses include $4,000 for depreciation on equipment. Interest expense is expected to be $3,500 for the year. Income taxes are expected to be 30% of income before income taxes.

All sales and purchases are on account. It is expected that 60% of quarterly sales are collected in cash within the quarter and the remainder is collected in the following quarter. Direct materials purchased from suppliers are paid 50% in the quarter incurred and the remainder in the following quarter. Purchases in the fourth quarter were the same as the materials used. In 2000, the company expects to purchase additional equipment costing $24,000. It expects to pay $8,000 on notes payable plus all interest due and payable to December 31 (included in interest expense $3,500 above). Accounts payable at December 31, 2000, includes amounts due suppliers (see above) plus other accounts payable of $7,500. In 2000, the company expects to declare and pay a $2,000 cash dividend. Unpaid income taxes at December 31 will be $5,000. The company's cash budget shows an expected cash balance of $41,150 at December 31, 2000.

Instructions
Prepare a budgeted income statement for 2000 and a budgeted balance sheet at December 31, 2000. In preparing the income statement, you will need to compute cost of goods manufactured (materials + labor + overhead) and finished goods inventory (December 31, 2000).

PROBLEMS: SET B

Prepare budgeted income statement and supporting budgets.
(SO 3, 4)

P24–1B Hindi Farm Supply Company manufactures and sells a pesticide called Snare. The following data are developed for preparing budgets for Snare for the first 2 quarters of 2000.

1. Sales: Quarter 1, 32,000 bags: quarter 2, 48,000 bags. Selling price is $60 per bag.
2. Direct materials: Each bag of Snare requires 6 pounds of Gumm at a cost of $3 per pound and 8 pounds of Tarr at $1.50 per pound.
3. Desired inventory levels:

Type of Inventory	January 1	April 1	July 1
Snare (bags)	8,000	12,000	18,000
Gumm (pounds)	9,000	10,000	13,000
Tarr (pounds)	14,000	20,000	25,000

4. Direct labor: Direct labor time is 20 minutes per bag at an hourly rate of $12 per hour.
5. Selling and administrative expenses are expected to be 8% of sales plus $175,000 per quarter.
6. Income taxes are expected to be 30% of income from operations.

Your assistant has prepared two budgets: the manufacturing overhead budget that shows expected costs to be 150% of direct labor cost, and the direct materials budget for Tarr which shows the cost of Tarr to be $441,000 in quarter 1 and $655,500 in quarter 2.

Instructions
Prepare the budgeted income statement for the first 6 months and all required supporting budgets by quarters. (*Note:* Use variable and fixed in the selling and administrative expense budget.)

P24–2B Kaminski Inc. is preparing its annual budgets for the year ending December 31, 2000. Accounting assistants furnish the following data:

Prepare sales, production, direct materials, direct labor, and income statement budgets.
(SO 3, 4)

	Product JB 50	Product JB 60
Sales budget:		
Anticipated volume in units	450,000	160,000
Unit selling price	$20.00	$25.00
Production budget:		
Desired ending finished goods units	25,000	15,000
Beginning finished goods units	30,000	10,000
Direct materials budget:		
Direct materials per unit (pounds)	2	3
Desired ending direct materials pounds	30,000	15,000
Beginning direct materials pounds	40,000	10,000
Cost per pound	$3.00	$4.00
Direct labor budget		
Direct labor time per unit	.4	.6
Direct labor rate per hour	$10.00	$10.00
Budgeted income statement:		
Total unit cost	$12.00	$20.00

An accounting assistant has prepared the detailed manufacturing overhead budget and the selling and administrative expense budget. The latter shows selling expenses of $660,000 for product JB 50 and $360,000 for product JB 60 and administrative expenses of $420,000 for product JB 50 and $340,000 for product JB 60. Income taxes are expected to be 30%.

Instructions
Prepare the following budgets for the year. Show data for each product. Quarterly budgets should not be prepared.

(a) Sales
(b) Production
(c) Direct materials
(d) Direct labor
(e) Income statement (*Note:* Income taxes are not allocated to the products.)

P24–3B Latham Industries had sales in 1999 of $6,000,000, and gross profit of $1,500,000. Management is considering two alternative budget plans to increase its gross profit in 2000.

Plan A would increase the selling price per unit from $8.00 to $8.40. Sales volume would decrease by 5% from its 1999 level. Plan B would decrease the selling price per unit by $0.50. The marketing department expects that the sales volume would increase by 150,000 units.

At the end of 1999, Latham has 30,000 units of inventory on hand. If Plan A is accepted, the 2000 ending inventory should be equal to 4% of the 2000 sales. If Plan B is accepted, the ending inventory should be equal to 40,000 units. Each unit produced will cost $1.50 in direct labor, $2.00 in direct materials, and $.90 in variable overhead. The fixed overhead for 2000 should be $1,800,000.

Prepare sales and production budgets and compute cost per unit under two plans.
(SO 3, 4)

Instructions
(a) Prepare a sales budget for 2000 under each plan.
(b) Prepare a production budget for 2000 under each plan.
(c) Compute the production cost per unit under each plan. Why is the cost per unit different for each of the two plans? (Round to two decimals.)
(d) Which plan should be accepted? (*Hint:* Compute the gross profit under each plan.)

Prepare cash budget for 2 months.
(SO 5)

P24–4B   Gagney Company prepares monthly cash budgets. Relevant data from operating budgets for 2000 are:

	January	February
Sales	$360,000	$400,000
Direct materials purchases	125,000	130,000
Direct labor	80,000	95,000
Manufacturing overhead	70,000	75,000
Selling and administrative expenses	79,000	86,000

All sales are on account. Collections are expected to be 50% in the month of sale, 40% in the first month following the sale, and 10% in the second month following the sale. Fifty percent (50%) of direct material purchases are paid in cash in the month of purchase, and the balance due is paid in the month following the purchase. All other items above are paid in the month incurred except for selling and administrative expenses that include $1,000 of depreciation per month.

   Other data:

(1) Credit sales: November 1999, $260,000; December 1999, $300,000.
(2) Purchases of direct materials: December 1999, $100,000.
(3) Other receipts: January—Collection of December 31, 1999, notes receivable $15,000;
                      February—Proceeds from sale of securities $6,000.
(4) Other disbursements: February—Withdrawal of $5,000 cash for personal use of owner, T. Kempen.

   The company's cash balance on January 1, 2000, is expected to be $55,000. The company wants to maintain a minimum cash balance of $50,000.

Instructions
(a) Prepare schedules for (1) expected collections from customers and (2) expected payments for direct materials purchases.
(b) Prepare a cash budget for January and February in columnar form.

Prepare purchases and income statement budgets for a merchandising company.
(SO 6)

P24–5B   The budget committee of Hernandez Company collects the following data for its San Miguel Store in preparing budgeted income statements for May and June 2000.

1. Sales for May are expected to be $600,000. Sales in June and July are expected to be 10% higher than the preceding month.
2. Cost of goods sold is expected to be 75% of sales.
3. Company policy is to maintain ending merchandise inventory at 30% of the following month's cost of goods sold.
4. Operating expenses are estimated to be:

Sales salaries	$25,000 per month
Advertising	5% of monthly sales
Delivery expense	3% of monthly sales
Sales commissions	4% of monthly sales
Rent expense	$5,000 per month
Depreciation	$800 per month
Utilities	$600 per month
Insurance	$500 per month

5. Income taxes are estimated to be 30% of income from operations.

Instructions
(a) Prepare the merchandise purchases budget for each month in columnar form.
(b) Prepare budgeted income statements for each month in columnar form. Show the details of cost of goods sold in the statements.

BROADENING YOUR PERSPECTIVE

GROUP DECISION CASE

. . . .

BYP24–1   Henigen Corporation operates on a calendar-year basis. It begins the annual budgeting process in late August when the president establishes targets for the total dollar sales and net income before taxes for the next year.

The sales target is given to the marketing department where the marketing manager formulates a sales budget by product line in both units and dollars. From this budget, sales quotas by product line in units and dollars are established for each of the corporation's sales districts. The marketing manager also estimates the cost of the marketing activities required to support the target sales volume and prepares a tentative marketing expense budget.

The executive vice president uses the sales and profit targets, the sales budget by product line, and the tentative marketing expense budget to determine the dollar amounts that can be devoted to manufacturing and corporate office expense. The executive vice president prepares the budget for corporate expenses, and then forwards to the production department the product-line sales budget in units and the total dollar amount that can be devoted to manufacturing.

The production manager meets with the factory managers to develop a manufacturing plan that will produce the required units when needed within the cost constraints set by the executive vice president. The budgeting process usually comes to a halt at this point because the production department does not consider the financial resources allocated to be adequate.

When this standstill occurs, the vice president of finance, the executive vice president, the marketing manager, and the production manager meet together to determine the final budgets for each of the areas. This normally results in a modest increase in the total amount available for manufacturing costs while the marketing expense and corporate office expense budgets are cut. The total sales and net income figures proposed by the president are seldom changed. Although the participants are seldom pleased with the compromise, these budgets are final. Each executive then develops a new detailed budget for the operations in his or her area.

None of the areas has achieved its budget in recent years. Sales often run below the target. When budgeted sales are not achieved, each area is expected to cut costs so that the president's profit target can still be met. However, the profit target is seldom met because costs are not cut enough. In fact, costs often run above the original budget in all functional areas (marketing, production, and corporate office). The president is disturbed that Henigen has not been able to meet the sales and profit targets. He hired a consultant with considerable experience with companies in Henigen's industry. The consultant reviewed the budgets for the past four years. He concluded that the product-line sales budgets were reasonable and that the cost and expense budgets were adequate for the budgeted sales and production levels.

Instructions

With the class divided into groups, answer the following:

  (a) Discuss how the budgeting process employed by Henigen Corporation contributes to the failure to achieve the president's sales and profit targets.

  (b) Suggest how Henigen Corporation's budgeting process could be revised to correct the problems.

  (c) Should the functional areas be expected to cut their costs when sales volume falls below budget? Explain your answer.   (CMA adapted.)

MANAGERIAL ANALYSIS

. . . .

BYP24–2   Thebeau & Carlson Inc. manufactures ergonomic devices for computer users. Some of their more popular products include glare screens (for computer monitors), keyboard stands with wrist rests, and carousels that allow easy access to floppy disks. Over the past 5 years, they experienced rapid growth, with sales of all products increasing 20% to 50% each year.

Last year, some of the primary manufacturers of computers began introducing new products with some of the ergonomic designs, such as glare screens and wrist rests, already built in. As a result, sales of Thebeau & Carlson's accessory devices have declined somewhat. The company believes that the disk carousels will probably continue to show growth, but that the other products will probably continue to decline. When the next year's budget was prepared, increases were built in to research and development so that replacement products could be developed or the company could expand into some other product line. Some product lines being considered are general-purpose ergonomic devices including back supports, foot rests, and sloped writing pads.

The most recent results have shown that sales decreased more than was expected for the glare screens. As a result, the company may have a shortage of funds. Top management has therefore asked that all expenses be reduced 10% to compensate for these reduced sales. Summary budget information is as follows:

Raw materials	$240,000
Direct labor	110,000
Insurance	50,000
Depreciation	90,000
Machine repairs	30,000
Sales salaries	50,000
Office salaries	80,000
Factory salaries (indirect labor)	50,000
Total	$700,000

Instructions

Using the information above, answer the following questions:

(a) What are the implications of reducing each of the costs? For example, if the company reduces raw materials costs, it may have to do so by purchasing lower quality materials. This may affect sales in the long term.

(b) Based on your analysis in (a), what do you think is the best way to obtain the $70,000 in cost savings requested? Be specific. Are there any costs that cannot or should not be reduced? Why?

REAL-WORLD FOCUS:
Network Computing Devices Inc.

BYP24–3 **Network Computing Devices Inc.** was founded in 1988 in Mountain View, Calif. The company, which has 375 employees, develops software products such as X-terminals, Z-mail, PC X-ware, and related hardware products. Presented below is a discussion by management in its annual report.

NETWORK COMPUTING DEVICES, INC.
Management Discussion

The Company's operating results have varied significantly, particularly on a quarterly basis, as a result of a number of factors, including general economic conditions affecting industry demand for computer products, the timing and market acceptance of new product introductions by the Company and its competitors, the timing of significant orders from large customers, periodic changes in product pricing and discounting due to competitive factors, and the availability of key components, such as video monitors and electronic subassemblies, some of which require substantial order lead times. The Company's operating results may fluctuate in the future as a result of these and other factors, including the Company's success in developing and introducing new products, its product and customer mix, and the level of competition which it experiences. The Company operates with a small backlog. Sales and operating results, therefore, generally depend on the volume and timing of orders received, which are difficult to forecast. The Company has experienced slowness in orders from some customers during the first quarter of each calendar year due to budgeting cycles common in the computer industry. In addition, sales in Europe typically are adversely affected in the third calendar quarter as many European customers reduce their business activities during the month of August.

Due to the Company's rapid growth rate and the effect of new product introductions on quarterly revenues, these seasonal trends have not materially impacted the Company's results of operations to date. However, as the Company's product lines mature and its rate of revenue growth declines, these seasonal factors may become more evident. Additionally, the Company's international sales are denominated in U.S. dollars, and an increase or decrease in the value of the U.S. dollar relative to foreign currencies could make the Company's products less or more competitive in those markets.

Instructions

(a) Identify the factors that affect the budgeting process at Network Computing Devices Inc.

(b) Explain the additional budgeting concerns created by the international operations of the Company.

COMMUNICATION ACTIVITY

BYP24–4 In order to better serve their rural patients, Drs. Jim and Jeff Howell (brothers) began giving safety seminars. Especially popular were their "emergency-preparedness" talks given to farmers. Many people asked whether the "kit" of materials the doctors recommended for common farm emergencies was commercially available.

After checking with several suppliers, the doctors realized that no other company offered the supplies they recommended in their seminars, packaged in the way they described. Their wives, Marie and Pam, agreed to make a test package by ordering supplies from various medical supply companies and assembling them into a "kit" that could be sold at the seminars. When these kits proved a runaway success, the sisters-in-law decided to market them. At the advice of their accountant, they organized this venture as a separate company, called Life Protection Products (LPP), with Marie Howell as CEO and Pam Howell as Secretary-Treasurer.

LPP soon started receiving requests for the kits from all over the country, as word spread about their availability. Even without advertising, LPP was able to sell its full inventory every month. However, the company was becoming financially strained. Marie and Pam had about $100,000 in savings, and invested about half that amount initially. They believed that this venture would allow them to make money. However, at the present time, only about $30,000 of the cash remains, and the company is constantly short of cash.

Marie Howell has come to you for advice. She does not understand why the company is having cash flow problems. She and Pam have not even been withdrawing salaries. However, they have rented a local building and have hired two more full-time workers to help them cope with the increasing demand. They do not think they could handle the demand without this additional help.

Marie is also worried that the cash problems mean that the company may not be able to support itself. She has prepared the cash budget shown below. All seminar customers pay for their products in full at the time of purchase. In addition, several large companies have ordered the kits for use by employees who work in remote sites. They have requested credit terms and have been allowed to pay in the month following the sale. These large purchasers amount to about 25% of the sales at the present time. LPP purchases the materials for the kits about 2 months ahead of time. Marie and Pam are considering slowing the growth of the company by simply purchasing less materials, which will mean selling fewer kits.

The workers are paid in cash weekly. Marie and Pam need about $15,000 cash on hand at the beginning of the month to pay for purchases of raw materials. Right now they have been using cash from their savings, but as noted, only $30,000 is left.

The cash budget that Marie Howell has given you is as follows:

LIFE PROTECTION PRODUCTS
Cash Budget
For the Quarter Ending June 30, 2000

	April	May	June
Cash balance, beginning	$15,000	$15,000	$15,000
Cash received			
From prior month sales	5,000	7,500	12,500
From current sales	15,000	22,500	37,500
Total cash on hand	35,000	45,000	65,000
Cash payments			
To employees	3,000	3,000	3,000
For products	25,000	35,000	45,000
Miscellaneous expenses	5,000	6,000	7,000
Postage	1,000	1,000	1,000
Total cash payments	34,000	45,000	56,000
Cash balance	$ 1,000	$ 0	$ 9,000
Borrow from savings	$14,000	$15,000	$ 1,000
Borrow from bank?	$ 0	$ 0	$ 7,000

Instructions

Write a response to Marie Howell. Explain why LPP is short of cash. Will this company be able to support itself? Explain your answer. Make any recommendations you deem appropriate.

RESEARCH ASSIGNMENT

BYP24–5 The January 1997 issue of *Management Accounting* contains an article by Robert West and Amy Snyder entitled "How to Set Up a Budgeting and Planning System." The article is a description of Penn Fuel Gas, Inc.'s experience of initiating its first annual and long-range operating budget process.

Instructions

Read the article and answer the following questions:

(a) What were the "three primary tasks" first faced by the new budget director in developing the new budget process?

(b) After solving the initial challenges of developing and installing a new budget process, what were four ongoing challenges faced by the new budget director?

(c) What benefits has Penn Fuel Gas, Inc., derived from its budgeting process?

ETHICS CASE

BYP24–6 You are an accountant in the budgetary, projections, and special projects department of Vek-Tek Corp., a large manufacturing company. The president, Warren Bleeker, asks you on very short notice to prepare some sales and income projections covering the next 2 years of the company's much heralded new product lines. He wants these projections for a series of speeches he is making while on a 2-week trip to eight East Coast brokerage firms. The president hopes to bolster Vek-Tek's stock sales and price.

You work 23 hours in 2 days to compile the projections, hand deliver them to the president, and are swiftly but graciously thanked as he departs. A week later you find time to go over some of your computations and discover a miscalculation that makes the projections grossly overstated. You quickly inquire about the president's itinerary and learn that he has made half of his speeches and has half yet to make. You are in a quandary as to what to do.

Instructions
   (a) What are the consequences of telling the president of your gross miscalculations?
   (b) What are the consequences of *not* telling the president of your gross miscalculations?
   (c) What are the ethical considerations to you and the president in this situation?

SURFING THE NET

BYP24–7   In its annual report Mark's Work Wearhouse Ltd. publishes a forecast for the up-coming year and a ''post-mortem'' on how well it met the prior year's forecast. The company also publishes senior management performance targets and corporate goals. Because of this, and other extensive disclosures, Mark's Work Wearhouse Ltd. received the gold prize in the merchandising category of the Canadian Institute of Chartered Accountants/Financial Post Annual Report Awards program.

Address: http://www.cica.ca/new/index.htm.

Steps:

   1. Go to the Canadian Institute of Chartered Accountants web site, at the above address.
   2. Choose the **Annual Report Awards** button. Explore each of the 1996 and 1997 Annual Report Awards. Choose **Merchandising** in each category. Highlight **Mark's Work Wearhouse Ltd.**

Instructions

   (a) Explain, with particular emphasis on budgetary disclosures, what Mark's Work Wearhouse includes in its annual report that persuades the judges that it repeatedly deserves the gold prize.
   (b) Relate Mark's Work Wearhouse's budget disclosures to the budget process outlined in Chapter 24. What has Mark's done right, in terms of the ideal budget process?

Answers to Self-Study Questions
1. c   2. a   3. b   4. b   5. d   6. d   7. a   8. c   9. c   10. d

---

Answer to Kellogg Review It Question 4, page 1049

Kellogg offers the following general expectation: ''continued cereal volume growth, strong results from product innovation, and the global introduction of other convenience foods will deliver sales and earnings growth for the full year 1998.'' Kellogg's hard-data expectations ''for 1998 include a gross profit margin of 53–54%, an SGA (selling, general, and administrative expense) of 35–36%, an effective income tax rate of 36–37%, capital spending of approximately $400 million, common stock repurchase activity of $390 million, and an increase in interest expense of 10%.''

Remember to go back to the Navigator box on the chapter-opening page and check off your completed work.

CONCEPTS FOR REVIEW

Before studying this chapter, you should know or, if necessary, review:

a. The meaning and scope of the management function of controlling. (Ch. 20, p. 873)

b. The cost elements that produce a total cost per unit of finished goods. (Ch. 20, pp. 873–76)

c. How variable costs differ from fixed costs. (Ch. 23, pp. 997–1000)

THE NAVIGATOR

FEATURE STORY

"If Money Is Low, We'll Take the Bus"

Virtually every department on a college campus develops a budget and then compares that budget to the amount actually spent. As the school term progresses, the person in charge of the budget can see how well the department is doing compared to expectations.

One of the most expensive departments on campus is the athletic department. That fact usually rankles the academic department heads. They argue that a university exists first and foremost to educate. But the money for sports is often justified because the sports teams—particu-larly at big schools—generate large incomes from television contracts that can then be used for a variety of educational purposes.

At the University of Nevada, Las Vegas, each athletic team has its own budget and its own financial statements. This financial information "shows what the teams have spent for the month and for the year to date, and how the actual expenditures compare to the budget," says Merv Gupton, athletic accounting manager. The biggest budget items: scholarships for student athletes, payroll, and travel costs.

UNLV sports teams include football, basketball, tennis, baseball, softball, soccer, track, cross country, golf, and swimming. Travel costs are usually the most uncontrollable item in the budget. What if you get two-thirds through the season and run out of money? "One sports team might be able to help out another," says Gupton. Or more likely, "if a coach is running low on money, the team won't fly—it'll take the bus."

THE NAVIGATOR

CHAPTER 25

THE NAVIGATOR ✔

- Understand *Concepts for Review* ☐
- Read *Feature Story* ☐
- Scan *Study Objectives* ☐
- Read *Preview* ☐
- Read text and answer *Before You Go On*
  p. 1082 ☐ p. 1090 ☐ p. 1095 ☐
- Work *Demonstration Problems* ☐
- Review *Summary of Study Objectives* ☐
- Answer *Self-Study Questions* ☐
- Complete assignments ☐

BUDGETARY CONTROL AND RESPONSIBILITY ACCOUNTING

STUDY OBJECTIVES

After studying this chapter, you should be able to:

1. *Describe the concept of budgetary control.*
2. *Evaluate the usefulness of static budget reports.*
3. *Explain the development of flexible budgets and the usefulness of flexible budget reports.*
4. *Describe the concept of responsibility accounting.*
5. *Indicate the features of responsibility reports for cost centers.*
6. *Identify the content of responsibility reports for profit centers.*
7. *Explain the basis and formula used in evaluating performance in investment centers.*

THE NAVIGATOR

The opening story indicates not only that budgets are necessary for an athletic department, but also that they can be used to control the department's activities. For example, if you were the athletic director at UNLV, you might require periodic updates from each coach, showing actual and budgeted expenses.

In contrast to Chapter 24, we now consider how budgets are used by management to control operations. This chapter focuses on two aspects of management control: (1) budgetary control and (2) responsibility accounting. The content and organization of this chapter are as follows:

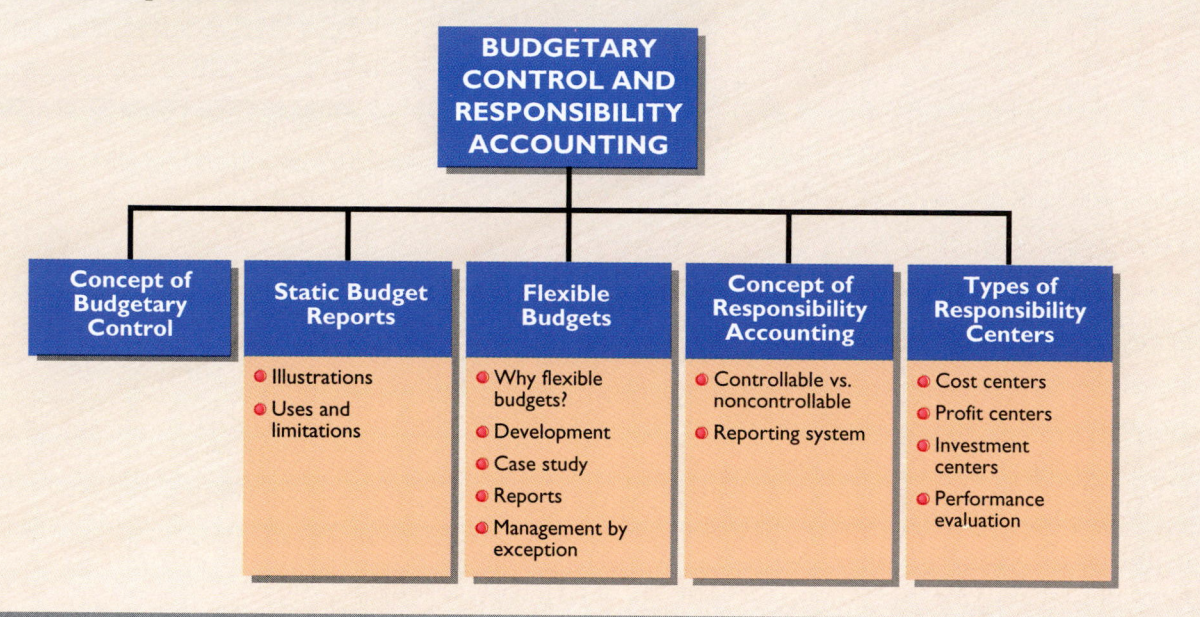

THE NAVIGATOR

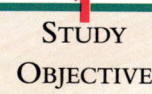

CONCEPT OF BUDGETARY CONTROL

As stated at the beginning of the managerial accounting chapters, one of management's major functions is controlling the operations of the company. Control was defined as the steps taken by management to see that planned objectives are met. We now ask: How do budgets assist management in controlling operations?

The use of budgets in controlling operations is known as **budgetary control**. The centerpiece of budgetary control is the use of **budget reports** that compare actual results with planned objectives. The preparation and use of budget reports is based on the belief that planned objectives lose much of their potential value without some monitoring of progress along the way. Just as your professors give midterm examinations to evaluate your progress, so top management requires periodic reports on the progress that department managers are making toward planned annual objectives.

Budget reports provide the feedback needed by management to see whether actual operations are on course. The feedback for a crucial objective, such as having enough cash on hand to pay bills, may be made daily. For other objectives, such as meeting budgeted annual sales and operating expenses, monthly budget reports may suffice. Because of the flexibility of managerial accounting, budget reports can be prepared as frequently as needed. On the basis of the budget reports, management first analyzes any differences between actual and planned results to determine their causes. From this analysis, management may take corrective action, or it may decide to modify future plans.

Budgetary control involves the following:

ILLUSTRATION 25-1

Budgetary control

Budgetary control works best when a company has a formalized reporting system. The system should (1) identify the name of the budget report, such as the sales budget or the manufacturing overhead budget; (2) state the frequency of the report, such as weekly or monthly; (3) specify the purpose of the report; and (4) indicate the primary recipient(s) of the report. The following schedule illustrates a partial budgetary control system for a manufacturing company. Note the emphasis on control in the reports and the frequency of the reports. For example, there is a daily report on scrap and a weekly report on labor.

ILLUSTRATION 25-2

Budgetary control reporting system

Name of Report	Frequency	Purpose	Primary Recipient(s)
Sales	Weekly	Determine whether sales goals are being met	Top management and sales manager
Labor	Weekly	Control direct and indirect labor costs	Vice president of production and production department managers
Scrap	Daily	Determine efficient use of materials	Production manager
Departmental overhead costs	Monthly	Control overhead costs	Department manager
Selling expenses	Monthly	Control selling expenses	Sales manager
Income statement	Monthly and quarterly	Determine whether income objectives are being met	Top management

STATIC BUDGET REPORTS

You learned in Chapter 24 that the master budget formalizes management's planned objectives for the coming year. When used in budgetary control, each budget included in the master budget is considered to be a static budget. A static budget is a projection of budget data at one level of activity. In such a budget, data for different levels of activity are ignored. As a result, actual results are always compared with budget data at the activity level used in developing the master budget.

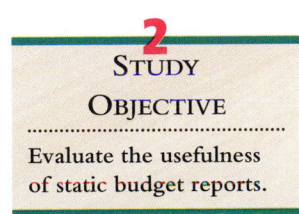

2
STUDY
OBJECTIVE
....
Evaluate the usefulness of static budget reports.

Illustrations

To illustrate the role of a static budget in budgetary control, we will use selected budget data prepared for Hayes Company in Chapter 24. Budget and actual sales data for the Kitchen-mate product in the first and second quarters of 1999 are as follows:

ILLUSTRATION 25-3

Budget and actual sales data

Sales	First Quarter	Second Quarter	Total
Budgeted	$180,000	$210,000	$390,000
Actual	179,000	199,500	378,500
Difference	$ 1,000	$ 10,500	$ 11,500

The sales budget report for Hayes Company's first quarter is shown below.

ILLUSTRATION 25-4

Sales budget report—first quarter

ALTERNATIVE TERMINOLOGY
The difference between budget and actual is sometimes called a *budget variance.*

HAYES COMPANY
Sales Budget Report
For the Quarter Ended March 31, 1999

Product Line	Budget	Actual	Difference Favorable F Unfavorable U
Kitchen-mate[a]	$180,000	$179,000	$1,000 U

[a]In practice, each product line would be included in the report.

The report shows that sales are $1,000 under budget—an unfavorable result. This difference is less than 1% of budgeted sales ($1,000 ÷ $180,000 = .0056). Top management's analysis of unfavorable differences is often influenced by the materiality (significance) of the difference. Since the difference of $1,000 is immaterial in this case, we will assume that the management of Hayes Company does not investigate the difference and takes no specific action.

The budget report for the second quarter presented in Illustration 25-5 contains one new feature: cumulative year-to-date information. This report indicates that sales for the second quarter were $10,500 below budget, which is 5% of budgeted sales ($10,500 ÷ $210,000). Top management may conclude that the difference between budgeted and actual sales in the second quarter merits investigation.

ILLUSTRATION 25-5

Sales budget report—second quarter

HAYES COMPANY
Sales Budget Report
For the Quarter Ended June 30, 1999

Product Line	Second Quarter			Year-to-Date		
	Budget	Actual	Difference Favorable F Unfavorable U	Budget	Actual	Difference Favorable F Unfavorable U
Kitchen-mate	$210,000	$199,500	$10,500 U	$390,000	$378,500	$11,500 U

Management's analysis should start by asking the sales manager the cause(s) of the shortfall. The need for corrective action should be considered. For example, management may decide to spur sales by offering sales incentives to customers or by increasing the advertising of Kitchen-mates. On the other hand, if management concludes that a downturn in the economy is responsible for the lower sales, it may decide to modify planned sales and profit goals for the remainder of the year.

Uses and Limitations

From the examples above, you can see that a master sales budget is useful in evaluating the performance of a sales manager. It is now necessary to ask: How appropriate is the master budget for evaluating a manager's performance in controlling costs? Recall that in a static budget, budget data are not modified or adjusted, regardless of changes in activity during the year. It follows, then, that a static budget is appropriate in evaluating a manager's effectiveness in controlling costs when:

1. The actual level of activity closely approximates the master budget activity level, and/or
2. The behavior of the costs in response to changes in activity is fixed.

A static budget report is, therefore, appropriate for fixed manufacturing costs and fixed selling and administrative expenses. However, as you will see shortly, static budget reports may not be a proper basis for evaluating a manager's performance in controlling variable costs.

Static budgets are best for fixed costs and expenses

FLEXIBLE BUDGETS

In contrast to a static budget, which is based on one level of activity, a **flexible budget** projects budget data for various levels of activity. In essence, **the flexible budget is a series of static budgets at different levels of activity**. The flexible budget recognizes that the budgetary process has greater usefulness if it is adaptable to changed operating conditions.

Flexible budgets can be prepared for each of the types of budgets included in the master budget. For example, Marriott Hotels can budget revenues and net income on the basis of 60%, 80%, and 100% of room occupancy. Similarly, American Van Lines can budget its operating expenses on the basis of various levels of truck miles driven. Likewise, the bottling department of Coca-Cola can budget manufacturing costs on the basis of 70%, 80%, and 100% of direct labor costs or machine hours. In the following pages, we will illustrate a flexible budget for manufacturing overhead.

3
STUDY
OBJECTIVE
Explain the development of flexible budgets and the usefulness of flexible budget reports.

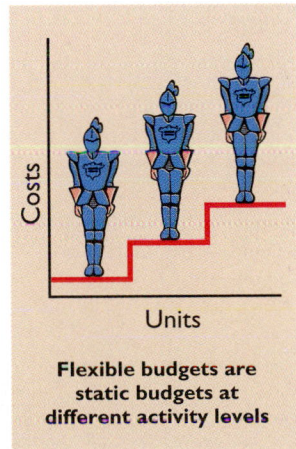

Flexible budgets are static budgets at different activity levels

Why Flexible Budgets?

Assume that you are the manager in charge of manufacturing overhead in the Forging Department of Barton Steel. In preparing the manufacturing overhead budget for 1999, you prepare the following static budget based on a production volume of 10,000 units of steel ingots:

BARTON STEEL **Manufacturing Overhead Budget (Static)** **Forging Department** **For the Year Ended December 31, 1999**	
Budgeted production in units (steel ingots)	10,000
Budgeted costs	
Indirect materials	$ 250,000
Indirect labor	260,000
Utilities	190,000
Depreciation	280,000
Property taxes	70,000
Supervision	50,000
	$1,100,000

Fortunately for the company, the demand for steel ingots has increased, and 12,000 units are produced during the year, rather than 10,000. You are elated because increased sales means increased profitability, which should mean a large raise for you and the employees in your department. Unfortunately, a comparison of the actual costs incurred with the budgeted costs for the year in the Forging Department has put you on the spot. The budget report is shown below.

BARTON STEEL **Manufacturing Overhead Budget Report (Static)** **Forging Department** **For the Year Ended December 31, 1999**			
	Budget	**Actual**	**Difference** **Favorable F** **Unfavorable U**
Production in units	10,000	12,000	
Costs			
Indirect materials	$ 250,000	$ 295,000	$ 45,000 U
Indirect labor	260,000	312,000	52,000 U
Utilities	190,000	225,000	35,000 U
Depreciation	280,000	280,000	–0–
Property taxes	70,000	70,000	–0–
Supervision	50,000	50,000	–0–
	$1,100,000	$1,232,000	$132,000 U

Note that this comparison is based on budget data based on the original activity level (10,000 steel ingots). The comparison indicates that the Forging Department is significantly **over budget** for three of the six overhead costs. Moreover, there is a total unfavorable difference of $132,000, which is 12% over budget ($132,000 ÷ $1,100,000). Your supervisor is very unhappy! Instead of sharing in the company's success, you may find yourself looking for another job. What would you do in this situation?

When you calm down and carefully examine the manufacturing overhead budget, you identify the problem: The budget data are not relevant! At the time the budget was developed, the company anticipated that only 10,000 units of steel ingots would be produced, **not** 12,000 ingots. As a result, the comparison of actual variable costs with budgeted costs is meaningless. The reason is that as production increases, the budget allowances for variable costs should increase both directly and proportionately. The variable costs in this example are indirect materials, indirect labor, and utilities.

An analysis of the budget data for these costs at 10,000 units produces the following per unit results:

Item	Total Cost	Per Unit
Indirect materials	$250,000	$25
Indirect labor	260,000	26
Utilities	190,000	19
	$700,000	$70

ILLUSTRATION 25-8

Variable costs per unit

The budgeted variable costs at 12,000 units, therefore, are as follows:

Item	Computation	Total
Indirect materials	$25 × 12,000	$300,000
Indirect labor	26 × 12,000	312,000
Utilities	19 × 12,000	228,000
		$840,000

ILLUSTRATION 25-9

Budgeted variable costs (12,000 units)

Because fixed costs do not change in total as activity changes, the budgeted amounts for these costs remain the same. The budget report based on the flexible budget for 12,000 units of production is shown in Illustration 25-10. (Compare this to Illustration 25-7.)

ILLUSTRATION 25-10

Flexible overhead budget report

BARTON STEEL
Manufacturing Overhead Budget Report (Flexible)
Forging Department
For the Year Ended December 31, 1999

	Budget	Actual	Difference Favorable F Unfavorable U
Production in units	12,000	12,000	
Variable costs			
Indirect materials	$ 300,000	$ 295,000	$5,000 F
Indirect labor	312,000	312,000	–0–
Utilities	228,000	225,000	3,000 F
Total variable	840,000	832,000	8,000 F
Fixed costs			
Depreciation	280,000	280,000	–0–
Property taxes	70,000	70,000	–0–
Supervision	50,000	50,000	–0–
Total fixed	400,000	400,000	–0–
Total costs	$1,240,000	$1,232,000	$8,000 F

This report indicates that the Forging Department is below budget—a favorable difference. Instead of worrying about being fired, you may be in line for a raise or a promotion after all! As indicated from the foregoing analysis, the only appropriate comparison is between actual costs at 12,000 units of production and budgeted costs at 12,000 units of production. Flexible budget reports provide this comparison.

Developing the Flexible Budget

The flexible budget uses the master budget as its basis. To develop the flexible budget, management should take the following steps:

1. Identify the activity index and the relevant range of activity.
2. Identify the variable costs and determine the budgeted variable cost per unit of activity for each cost.
3. Identify the fixed costs and determine the budgeted amount for each cost.
4. Prepare the budget for selected increments of activity within the relevant range.

The activity index chosen should be one that significantly influences the costs that are being budgeted. For manufacturing overhead costs, for example, the activity index is usually the same as the index used in developing the predetermined overhead rate—that is, direct labor hours or machine hours. For selling and administrative expenses, the activity index usually is sales or net sales.

The choice of selected increments of activity is largely a matter of judgment. For example, if the relevant range is 8,000 to 12,000 direct labor hours, increments of 1,000 hours may be selected. The flexible budget is then prepared in columnar form for each increment within the relevant range.

Flexible Budget—A Case Study

To illustrate the preparation of the flexible budget, we will use Fox Manufacturing Company. The management of Fox Manufacturing wants to use the **flexible budget for monthly comparisons** of actual and budgeted manufacturing overhead costs of the Finishing Department. The master budget for the year ending December 31, 1999, shows expected annual operating capacity of 120,000 direct labor hours and the following overhead costs:

ILLUSTRATION 25-11

Master budget data

Variable Costs		Fixed Costs	
Indirect materials	$180,000	Depreciation	$180,000
Indirect labor	240,000	Supervision	120,000
Utilities	60,000	Property taxes	60,000
Total	$480,000	Total	$360,000

The application of the four steps is as follows:

Step 1. Identify the activity index and the relevant range of activity. The activity index is direct labor hours. Management concludes that the relevant range is 8,000–12,000 direct labor hours per month.

Step 2. Identify the variable costs and determine the budgeted variable cost per unit of activity for each cost. There are three variable costs. The variable cost per unit is found by dividing each total budgeted cost by the direct labor hours used in preparing the master budget (120,000 hours). For Fox Manufacturing, the computations are:

ILLUSTRATION 25-12

Computation of variable costs per direct labor hour

Variable Cost	Computation	Variable Cost per Direct Labor Hour
Indirect materials	$180,000 ÷ 120,000	$1.50
Indirect labor	240,000 ÷ 120,000	2.00
Utilities	60,000 ÷ 120,000	.50
Total		$4.00

Step 3. Identify the fixed costs and determine the budgeted amount for each cost. There are three fixed costs. Since Fox Manufacturing desires **monthly budget data**, the budgeted amount is found by dividing each annual budgeted cost by 12. For Fox Manufacturing, the monthly budgeted fixed costs are: Depreciation $15,000, Supervision $10,000, and Property taxes $5,000.

Step 4. Prepare the budget for selected increments of activity within the relevant range. Management decides that the budget be prepared in increments of 1,000 direct labor hours.

The flexible budget is shown in Illustration 25-13.

ILLUSTRATION 25-13

Flexible monthly overhead budget

FOX MANUFACTURING COMPANY
Flexible Monthly Manufacturing Overhead Budget
Finishing Department
For the Year 1999

Activity level					
Direct labor hours	8,000	9,000	10,000	11,000	12,000
Variable costs					
Indirect materials	$12,000	$13,500	$15,000	$16,500	$18,000
Indirect labor	16,000	18,000	20,000	22,000	24,000
Utilities	4,000	4,500	5,000	5,500	6,000
Total variable	32,000	36,000	40,000	44,000	48,000
Fixed costs					
Depreciation	15,000	15,000	15,000	15,000	15,000
Supervision	10,000	10,000	10,000	10,000	10,000
Property taxes	5,000	5,000	5,000	5,000	5,000
Total fixed	30,000	30,000	30,000	30,000	30,000
Total costs	$62,000	$66,000	$70,000	$74,000	$78,000

From the budget, the following formula may be used to determine total budgeted costs at any level of activity:

ILLUSTRATION 25-14

Formula for total budgeted costs

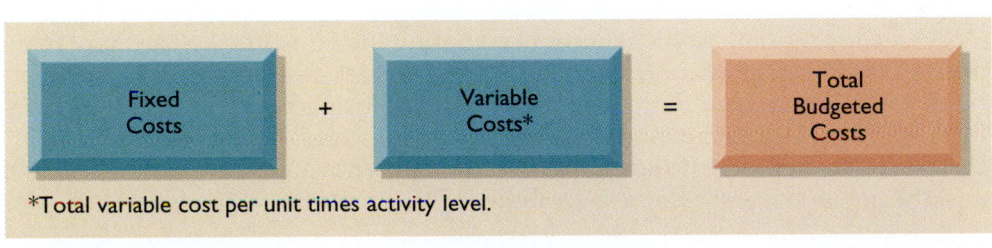

Fixed Costs + Variable Costs* = Total Budgeted Costs

*Total variable cost per unit times activity level.

For Fox Manufacturing, fixed costs are $30,000, and total variable cost per unit is $4.00. Thus, at 9,000 direct labor hours, total budgeted costs are $66,000 [fixed costs, $30,000 + ($4.00 × 9,000)]. Similarly, at 8,622 direct labor hours, total budgeted costs are $64,488 [$30,000 + ($4.00 × 8,622)].

Total budgeted costs can also be shown graphically, as in Illustration 25-15. In the graph, the activity index is shown on the horizontal axis and costs are indicated on the vertical axis. The graph highlights two of the 1,000 increments (10,000 and 12,000). As shown in Illustration 25-15, total budgeted costs are $70,000 [$30,000 + ($4.00 × 10,000)] and $78,000 [$30,000 + ($4.00 × 12,000)], respectively.

ILLUSTRATION 25-15

Graphic flexible budget data highlighting 10,000 and 12,000 activity levels

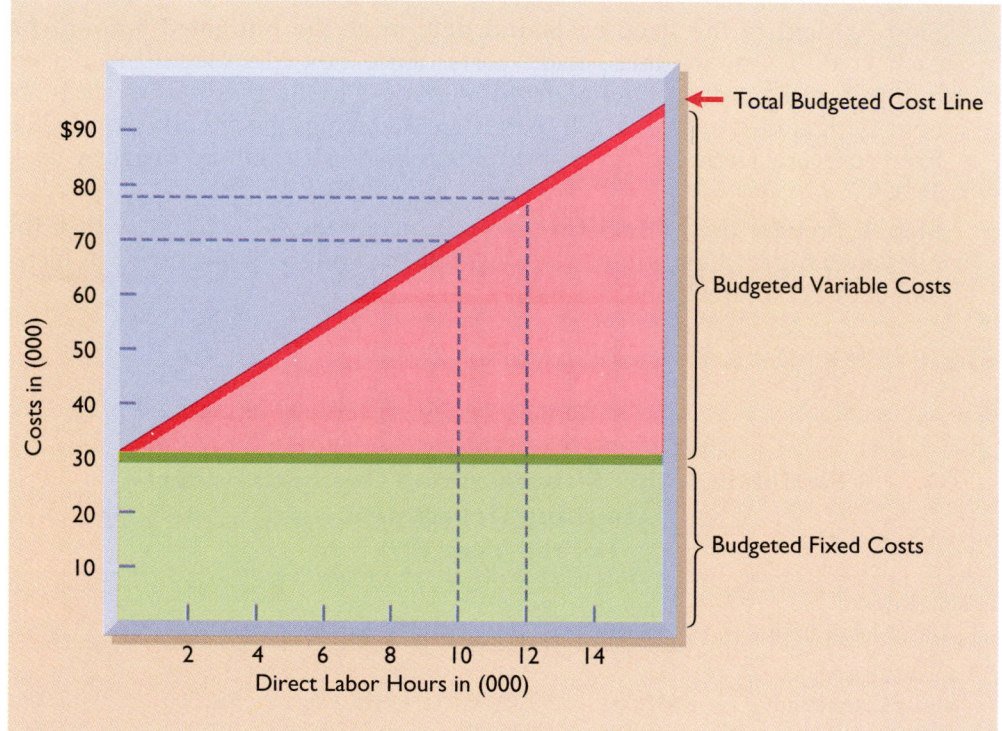

Flexible Budget Reports

Flexible budget reports represent another type of internal report produced by managerial accounting. The flexible budget report consists of two sections: (1) production data such as direct labor hours and (2) cost data for variable and fixed costs. Consequently, the report provides a basis for evaluating a manager's performance in two areas: production control and cost control. Flexible budgets are widely used in production and service departments.

A budget report for the Finishing Department of Fox Company for the month of January is shown in Illustration 25-16. In this month, 8,800 direct labor hours were expected but 9,000 hours were worked. The budget data are based on the flexible budget for 9,000 hours in Illustration 25-13. The actual cost data are assumed.

How appropriate is this report in evaluating the Finishing Department manager's performance in controlling costs? The report clearly provides a reliable basis for this purpose. Both actual and budget costs are based on the activity level worked during January. Since variable costs generally are incurred directly by the department, the difference between the budget allowance for those hours and the actual costs are the responsibility of the department manager.

ILLUSTRATION 25-16

Flexible overhead budget report

FOX MANUFACTURING COMPANY
Manufacturing Overhead Budget Report (Flexible)
Finishing Department
For the Month Ended January 31, 1999

Direct labor hours (DLH)				Difference
Expected	8,800	**Budget at**	**Actual Costs**	**Favorable F**
Actual	9,000	**9,000 DLH**	**9,000 DLH**	**Unfavorable U**
Variable costs				
Indirect materials		$13,500	$14,000	$ 500 U
Indirect labor		18,000	17,000	1,000 F
Utilities		4,500	4,600	100 U
Total variable		36,000	35,600	400 F
Fixed costs				
Depreciation		15,000	15,000	–0–
Supervision		10,000	10,000	–0–
Property taxes		5,000	5,000	–0–
Total fixed		30,000	30,000	–0–
Total costs		$66,000	$65,600	$ 400 F

From the standpoint of production control, the report shows a 200-hour difference between actual direct labor hours and expected hours. This difference is favorable if actual production orders required 9,000 direct labor hours. The difference is unfavorable if actual production orders required only 8,800 direct labor hours. In either case, the budget for purposes of cost control is based on 9,000 direct labor hours.

In subsequent months, other flexible budget reports will be prepared. For each month, the budget data are based on the actual activity level attained. In February that level may be 11,000 direct labor hours, in July, 10,000, and so on.

Management by Exception

Management by exception means that top management's review of a budget report is directed either entirely or primarily to differences between actual results and planned objectives. This approach enables top management to focus on problem areas that need attention. Management by exception does not mean that top management will investigate every difference. For this approach to be effective, there must be some guidelines for identifying an exception. The usual criteria are materiality and controllability of the item.

Materiality

Without quantitative guidelines, management would have to investigate every budget difference regardless of the amount. Materiality is usually expressed as a percentage difference from budget. For example, management may set the percentage difference at 5% for important items and 10% for other items. This means that all differences either over or under budget by the specified percentage will be investigated. Costs over budget warrant investigation to determine why they were not controlled. In contrast, costs under budget merit investigation to determine whether costs critical to the profitability of the division are being curtailed. For example, if maintenance costs are budgeted at $80,000 and only $40,000 is spent, major unexpected breakdowns in productive facilities may occur in the future.

Alternatively, a company may specify a single percentage difference from budget for all items and supplement this guideline with a minimum dollar limit. For example, the exception criteria may be stated at 5% of budget or more than $10,000.

Controllability of the Item

Exception guidelines are more restrictive for controllable items than for items that are not controllable by the manager being evaluated. In fact, there may be no guidelines for noncontrollable items. For example, a large unfavorable difference between actual and budgeted property tax expense may not be flagged by management for investigation because the only possible causes are an unexpected increase in the tax rate or in the assessed value of the property. An investigation into the difference will be useless because the manager cannot control either cause.

BEFORE YOU GO ON . . .

Review It

1. What is the meaning of budgetary control?
2. When is a static budget appropriate for evaluating a manager's effectiveness in controlling costs?
3. What is a flexible budget?
4. How is a flexible budget developed?
5. What are the criteria used in management by exception?

Do It

Your roommate asks your help in understanding how total budgeted costs are computed at any level of activity. Compute total budgeted costs at 30,000 direct labor hours, assuming that in the flexible budget graph, the fixed cost line and the total budgeted cost line intersect the vertical axis at $36,000 and that the total budget cost line is $186,000 at an activity level of 50,000 direct labor hours.

Reasoning: The formula for the computation is: Fixed Costs + Variable Costs (Total Variable Costs per Unit × Activity Level) = Total Budgeted Costs.

Solution: Using the graph, fixed costs are $36,000 and variable costs are $3 per direct labor hour [($186,000 − $36,000) ÷ 50,000]. Thus, at 30,000 direct labor hours total budgeted costs are $126,000 [$36,000 + ($3 × 30,000)].

Related exercise material: BE25–3, BE25–4, BE25–5, E25–1, E25–2, E25–3, E25–4, E25–5, E25–6, and E25–7.

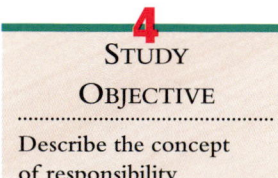

THE CONCEPT OF RESPONSIBILITY ACCOUNTING

Like budgeting, responsibility accounting is an important part of management accounting. **Responsibility accounting** involves accumulating and reporting costs (and revenues, where relevant) on the basis of the individual manager who has the authority to make the day-to-day decisions about the items. Under responsibility accounting, the evaluation of a manager's performance is based on matters directly under that manager's control. Responsibility accounting can be used at every level of management in which the following conditions exist:

1. Costs and revenues can be directly associated with the specific level of management responsibility.
2. The costs and revenues are controllable at the level of responsibility with which they are associated.
3. Budget data can be developed for evaluating the manager's effectiveness in controlling the costs and revenues.

The levels of responsibility for controlling costs are depicted in Illustration 25-17.

ILLUSTRATION 25-17
Responsibility for controllable costs at varying levels of management

Responsibility accounting personalizes the managerial accounting system. Under responsibility accounting, any individual who has control and is accountable for a specified set of activities can be recognized as a responsibility center. Thus, responsibility accounting may extend from the lowest level of control to the top strata of management. Once responsibility has been established, the effectiveness of the individual's performance is first measured and reported for the specified activity, and it is then reported upward throughout the organization.

Responsibility accounting is especially valuable in a decentralized company. **Decentralization** means that the control of operations is delegated by top management to many individuals (managers) throughout the organization. The term **segment** is sometimes used to identify an area of responsibility in decentralized operations. Under responsibility accounting, reports are prepared periodically such as monthly, quarterly, and annually, to provide a basis for evaluating the performance of each manager.

Responsibility accounting is an essential part of any effective system of budgetary control. The reporting of costs and revenues under responsibility accounting differs from budgeting in two respects:

1. A distinction is made between controllable and noncontrollable items.
2. Performance reports either emphasize or include only items controllable by the individual manager.

HELPFUL HINT
All companies use responsibility accounting. Without some form of responsibility accounting, there would be chaos in discharging management's control function.

Responsibility accounting applies to both profit and not-for-profit entities. The former seek to maximize net income, whereas the latter wish to minimize the cost of providing the service.

ACCOUNTING IN ACTION
Business Insight

Since devising the budgeting system, JKL, Inc., a large New York advertising agency, has become aware of which specific customer accounts are unprofitable and the reasons why. Since the budgeting and control system has been instituted, the agency has dropped several unprofitable accounts that otherwise would have gone unnoticed. Account managers and supervisors now feel responsible for the profitability of their accounts. They carefully monitor actual hours spent on each account to make sure the account is being managed and run as efficiently as possible. For example, an account manager noticed a large amount of supervisory creative time was being spent on an account. Further investigation showed that the supervisors, rather than the creative department, were doing the actual creative work. The account manager pointed this out, and a junior creative team was appointed to the account, saving a great deal of money.

Controllable versus Noncontrollable Revenues and Costs

All costs and revenues are controllable at some level of responsibility within a company. This truth underscores the adage by the chief executive officer of any organization that "the buck stops here." Under responsibility accounting, the critical issue is **whether the cost or revenue is controllable at the level of responsibility with which it is associated**.

A cost is considered to be controllable at a given level of managerial responsibility if that manager has the power to incur it within a given period of time. From this criterion, it follows that

1. All costs are controllable by top management because of the broad range of its authority.
2. Fewer costs are controllable as one moves down to each lower level of managerial responsibility because of the manager's decreasing authority.

In general, **costs incurred directly by a level of responsibility are controllable at that level**. In contrast, costs incurred indirectly and allocated to a responsibility level are considered to be noncontrollable at that level.

Responsibility Reporting System

A responsibility reporting system involves the preparation of a report for each level of responsibility shown in the company's organization chart. To illustrate a responsibility reporting system, we will use the partial organization chart and production departments of the Francis Company in Illustration 25-18.

The responsibility reporting system begins with the lowest level of responsibility for controlling costs and moves upward to each higher level, as detailed in Illustration 25-19. A brief description of the four reports is as follows:

1. **Report D** is typical of reports that go to managers at the lowest level of responsibility shown in the organization chart—department managers. In this report, additional detail may be presented for manufacturing overhead. Similar reports are prepared for the managers of the Enameling and Assembly Departments.

HELPFUL HINT
Are there more or fewer controllable costs as you move to higher levels of management? Answer: More.

HELPFUL HINT
The longer the time span, the more likely that the cost becomes controllable.

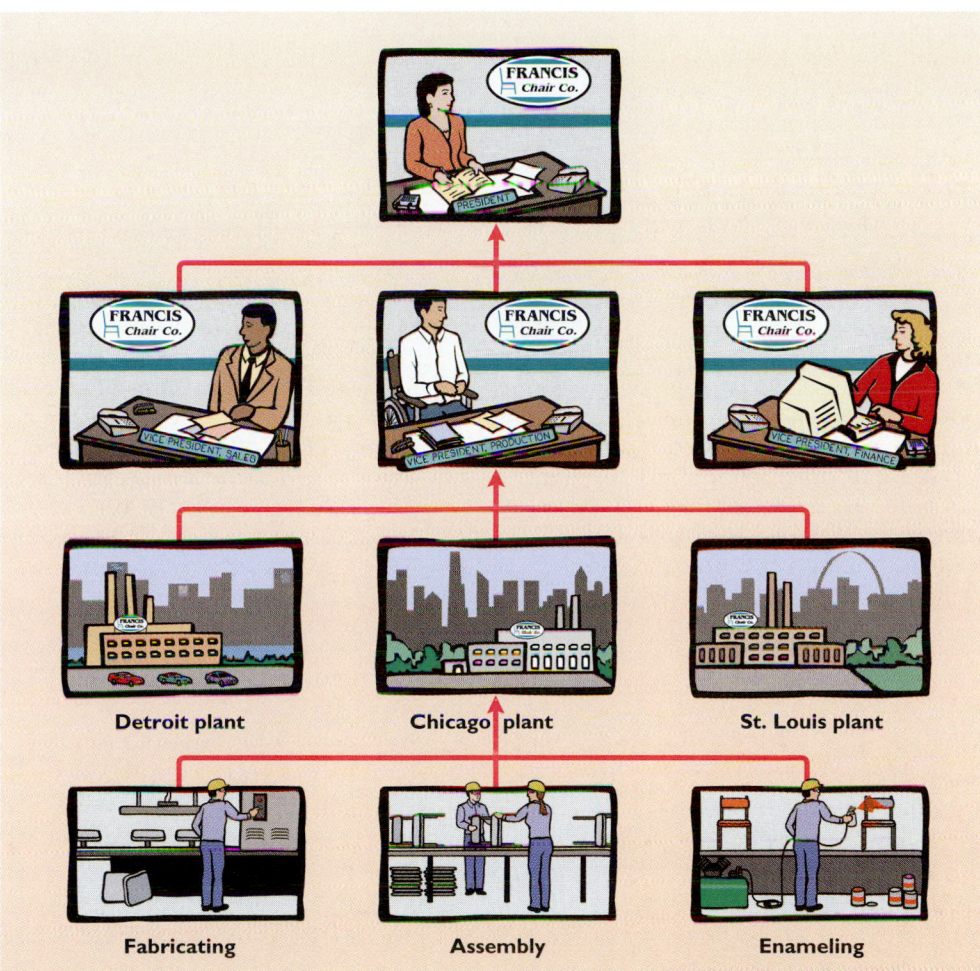

Report A
President sees summary data of vice presidents.

Report B
Vice president sees summary of controllable costs in his/her functional area.

Report C
Plant manager sees summary of controllable costs for each department in plant.

Report D
Department manager sees controllable costs of his/her department.

2. **Report C** is an example of reports that are sent to plant managers. This report shows the costs of the Chicago plant that are controllable at the second level of responsibility. In addition, Report C shows summary data for each department that is controlled by the plant manager. Similar reports are prepared for the Detroit and St. Louis plant managers.

3. **Report B** illustrates the reports at the third level of responsibility. It shows the controllable costs of the vice president of production and summary data on the three assembly plants for which this officer is responsible.

4. **Report A** is typical of the reports that go to the top level of responsibility—the president. This report shows the controllable costs and expenses of this office and summary data on the vice presidents that are accountable to the president.

A responsibility reporting system permits management by exception at each level of responsibility within the organization. In addition to the information shown in Illustration 25-19, each higher level of responsibility can obtain the detailed report for each lower level of responsibility. For example, the vice president of production in the Francis Company may request the Chicago plant manager's report because this plant is $5,300 over budget.

This type of reporting system also permits comparative evaluations. In Illustration 25-19, the Chicago plant manager can easily rank the department man-

ILLUSTRATION 25-19

Responsibility reporting system

REPORT A

To President		Month:	January
Controllable Costs:	Budget	Actual	Fav/Unfav
President	$ 150,000	$ 151,500	$ 1,500 U
Vice Presidents:			
Sales	185,000	187,000	2,000 U
Production	1,179,000	1,186,300	7,300 U
Finance	100,000	101,000	1,000 U
Total	$1,614,000	$1,625,800	$11,800 U

REPORT B

To Vice President Production		Month:	January
Controllable Costs:	Budget	Actual	Fav/Unfav
V P Production	$ 125,000	$ 126,000	$ 1,000 U
Assembly Plants:			
Detroit	420,000	418,000	2,000 F
Chicago	304,000	309,300	5,300 U
St. Louis	330,000	333,000	3,000 U
Total	$1,179,000	$1,186,300	$ 7,300 U

REPORT C

To Plant Manager-Chicago		Month:	January
Controllable Costs:	Budget	Actual	Fav/Unfav
Chicago Plant	$110,000	$113,000	$ 3,000 U
Departments:			
Fabricating	84,000	85,300	1,300 U
Enameling	62,000	64,000	2,000 U
Assembly	48,000	47,000	1,000 F
Total	$304,000	$309,300	$ 5,300 U

REPORT D

To Fabricating Department Manager		Month:	January
Controllable Costs:	Budget	Actual	Fav/Unfav
Direct Materials	$ 20,000	$ 20,500	$ 500 U
Direct Labor	40,000	41,000	1,000 U
Overhead	24,000	23,800	200 F
Total	$ 84,000	$ 85,300	$ 1,300 U

agers' effectiveness in controlling manufacturing costs. Comparative rankings provide further incentive for a manager to control costs. For example, the Detroit plant manager will want to continue to be No. 1 in the report to the vice president of production, and the Chicago plant manager will not want to remain No. 3 in future reporting periods.

TECHNOLOGY IN ACTION

Computerized accounting systems can play a major role in increasing the timeliness of performance reports. The computer's speed in processing and reorganizing information has enabled management to receive feedback reports of exceptions much sooner after the exceptions have occurred than would have been possible with a manual system. Efficiency is increased because management's attention is directed to significant deviations requiring corrective action before these deviations get too far "out of hand."

Management has also come to rely on personal computers to increase the timeliness of information receipt. When connected to the main computer system, a manager can "download" financial information and perform additional calculations and manipulations on the information for a decision at hand in a fraction of the time needed to request such information from the EDP Department. Though more timely, accuracy must not be sacrificed, and all calculations should be tested for correctness before being used for decision making.

TYPES OF RESPONSIBILITY CENTERS

There are three basic types of responsibility centers: cost centers, profit centers, and investment centers. These centers indicate the degree of responsibility the manager has for the performance of the center.

A **cost center** incurs costs (and expenses) but does not directly generate revenues. Managers of cost centers have the authority to incur costs. They are evaluated on their ability to control costs. Cost centers are usually either production departments or service departments. The former participate directly in making the product whereas the latter provide only support services. In a Ford Motor Company automobile plant, the welding, painting, and assembling departments are production departments, and the maintenance, cafeteria, and personnel departments are service departments. All of these departments are cost centers.

A **profit center** incurs costs (and expenses) but also generates revenues. Managers of profit centers are judged on the profitability of their centers. Examples of profit centers include the individual departments of a retail store, such as clothing, furniture, and automotive products, and branch offices of banks.

Like a profit center, an **investment center** incurs costs (and expenses) and generates revenues. In addition, an investment center has control over the investment funds available for use. Managers of investment centers are evaluated on the profitability of the center and on the rate of return earned on the funds invested. Investment centers are often associated with subsidiary companies. For example, Kellogg produces several product lines including ready-to-eat cereals, toaster pastries, frozen waffles, cereal bars, and bagels; General Mills's product lines include cereals, helper dinner mixes, fruit snacks, popcorn, and yogurt. In each of these instances, the manager of the investment center (product line or segment) is able to control or significantly influence investment decisions pertaining to such matters as plant expansion and entry into new market areas. These three types of responsibility centers are depicted in Illustration 25-20.

The evaluation of a manager's performance in each type of responsibility center is explained in the remainder of this chapter.

HELPFUL HINT
(1) Is the jewelry department of Marshall Field's department store a profit center or a cost center? (2) Is the props department of a movie studio a profit center or a cost center? Answers: (1) Profit center. (2) Cost center.

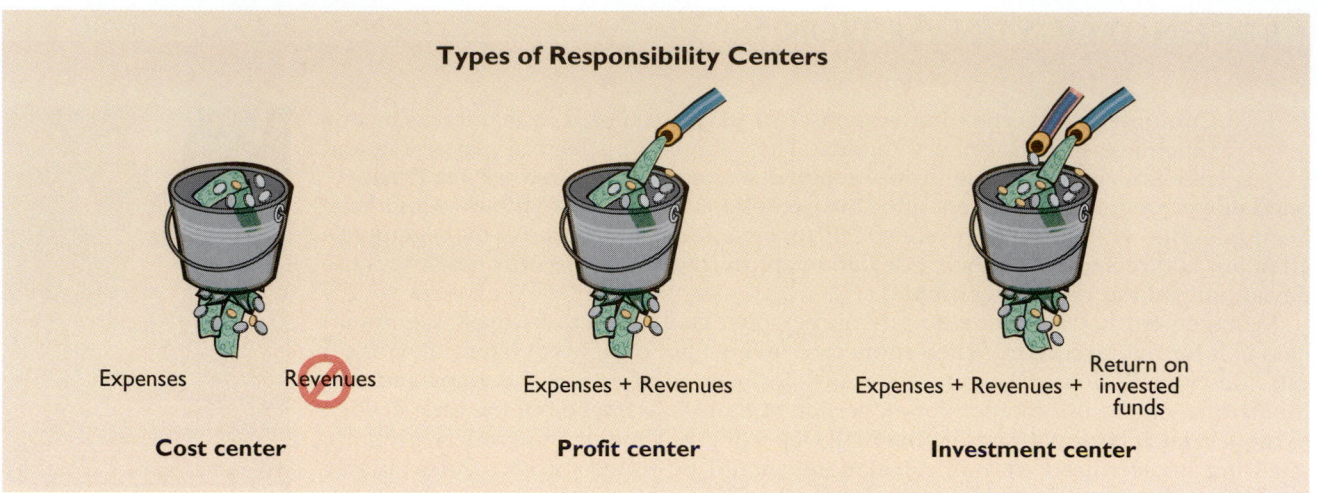

Types of Responsibility Centers

Expenses | Revenues

Cost center

Expenses + Revenues

Profit center

Expenses + Revenues + Return on invested funds

Investment center

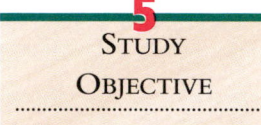

ILLUSTRATION 25-20

Types of responsibility centers

5

STUDY
OBJECTIVE

Indicate the features of responsibility reports for cost centers.

Responsibility Accounting for Cost Centers

The evaluation of a manager's performance for cost centers is based on the manager's ability to meet budgeted goals for controllable costs. **Responsibility reports for cost centers compare actual controllable costs with flexible budget data.**

A responsibility report is illustrated in Illustration 25-21. The report is adapted from the budget report for Fox Manufacturing Company in Illustration 25-16 on page 1081. It assumes that the Finishing Department manager is able to control all manufacturing overhead costs except depreciation, property taxes, and his own monthly supervisory salary of $6,000. The remaining $4,000 of supervision costs are assumed to apply to other supervisory personnel within the Finishing Department, whose salaries are controllable by the manager.

ILLUSTRATION 25-21

Responsibility report for a cost center

FOX MANUFACTURING COMPANY
Finishing Department
Responsibility Report
For the Month Ended January 31, 1999

Controllable Cost	Budget	Actual	Difference Favorable F Unfavorable U
Indirect materials	$13,500	$14,000	$ 500 U
Indirect labor	18,000	17,000	1,000 F
Utilities	4,500	4,600	100 U
Supervision	4,000	4,000	–0–
	$40,000	$39,600	$ 400 F

Only controllable costs are included in the report, and no distinction is made between variable and fixed costs. As in budget reports, the responsibility report continues the concept of management by exception. In this case, top management may request an explanation of the $1,000 favorable difference in indirect labor and/or the $500 unfavorable difference in indirect materials.

Responsibility Accounting for Profit Centers

To evaluate the performance of a manager of a profit center properly, detailed information is needed about both controllable revenues and controllable costs. The operating revenues earned by a profit center, such as sales, are controllable by the manager. All variable costs (and expenses) incurred by the center are also controllable by the manager because they vary with sales. However, to determine the controllability of fixed costs, it is necessary to distinguish between direct and indirect fixed costs.

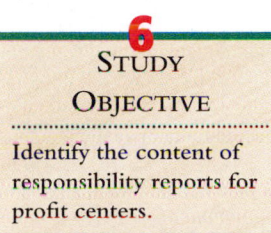

6
STUDY
OBJECTIVE
....
Identify the content of responsibility reports for profit centers.

Direct and Indirect Fixed Costs

A profit center may have both direct and indirect fixed costs. **Direct fixed costs** are costs that relate specifically to one center and are incurred for the sole benefit of that center. Examples of such costs include the salaries established by the profit center manager for supervisory personnel and the cost of maintaining a time-keeping department for the center's employees. Since these fixed costs can be traced directly to a center, they are also called **traceable costs**. **Most direct fixed costs are controllable by the profit center manager.**

In contrast, **indirect fixed costs** pertain to a company's overall operating activities and they are incurred for the benefit of more than one profit center. Indirect fixed costs are allocated to profit centers on some type of equitable basis. For example, property taxes on a building occupied by more than one center may be allocated on the basis of square feet of floor space used by each center. Alternatively, the costs of a company's personnel department may be allocated to profit centers on the basis of the number of employees in each center. Because these fixed costs apply to more than one center, they are also called **common costs. Most indirect fixed costs are not controllable by the profit center manager.**

Responsibility Report

The responsibility report for a profit center shows budgeted and actual **controllable revenues and costs**. The report is prepared using the cost-volume-profit income statement explained in Chapter 23. In the report:

1. Controllable fixed costs are deducted from contribution margin.
2. The excess of contribution margin over controllable fixed costs is identified as **controllable margin**.
3. Noncontrollable fixed costs are not reported.

The responsibility report for the manager of the Marine Division, a profit center of Mantle Manufacturing Company, is shown in Illustration 25-22. For the year, the Marine Division also had $60,000 of indirect fixed costs that were not controllable by the profit center manager.

Controllable margin is considered to be the best measure of the manager's performance **in controlling revenues and costs**. This report shows that the manager's performance was below budgeted expectations by approximately 10% ($36,000 ÷ $360,000). Top management would likely investigate the causes of this unfavorable result. Note that the report does not show the Marine Division's

ILLUSTRATION 25-22

*Responsibility report for
profit center*

HELPFUL HINT
Recognize that we are
emphasizing financial measures
of performance. More effort is
now being made to stress
nonfinancial performance
measures such as product
quality, labor productivity,
market growth, material's yield,
manufacturing flexibility, and
technological capability.

ETHICS NOTE

Responsibility reports are
helpful tools for evaluating the
performance of management.
Too much emphasis on profits
or investments, however, can
be harmful because it ignores
other important performance
issues such as quality and social
responsibility.

MANTLE MANUFACTURING COMPANY
Marine Division
Responsibility Report
For the Year Ended December 31, 1999

	Budget	Actual	Difference Favorable F Unfavorable U
Sales	$1,200,000	$1,150,000	$50,000 U
Variable costs			
Cost of goods sold	500,000	490,000	10,000 F
Selling and administrative	160,000	156,000	4,000 F
Total	660,000	646,000	14,000 F
Contribution margin	540,000	504,000	36,000 U
Controllable fixed costs			
Cost of goods sold	100,000	100,000	–0–
Selling and administrative	80,000	80,000	–0–
Total	180,000	180,000	–0–
Controllable margin	$ 360,000	$ 324,000	$36,000 U

noncontrollable fixed costs of $60,000. These costs would be included in a report on the profitability of the profit center.

Responsibility reports for profit centers may also be prepared monthly. In addition, they may include cumulative year-to-date results.

BEFORE YOU GO ON . . .

Review It

1. What conditions are essential for responsibility accounting?
2. What is involved in a responsibility reporting system?
3. What is the primary objective of a responsibility report for a cost center?
4. How does contribution margin differ from controllable margin in a responsibility report for a profit center?

Do It

Midwest Division, which operates as a profit center, reports the following actual results for the year: Sales $1,700,000, variable costs $800,000, controllable fixed costs $400,000, noncontrollable fixed costs $200,000. Annual budgeted amounts were $1,500,000, $700,000, $400,000, and $200,000 respectively. Prepare a responsibility report for the Midwest Division for December 31, 1999.

Reasoning: In the responsibility report, variable costs are deducted from sales to show contribution margin. Controllable fixed costs are then deducted to show controllable margin. Noncontrollable fixed costs are not reported.

Solution:

MIDWEST DIVISION
Responsibility Report
For the Year Ended December 31, 1999

	Budget	Actual	Difference Favorable F Unfavorable U
Sales	$1,500,000	$1,700,000	$200,000 F
Variable costs	700,000	800,000	100,000 U
Contribution margin	800,000	900,000	100,000 F
Controllable fixed costs	400,000	400,000	–0–
Controllable margin	$ 400,000	$ 500,000	$100,000 F

Related exercise material: BE25–7 and E25–9.

THE
NAVIGATOR

Responsibility Accounting for Investment Centers

As explained earlier, an important characteristic of an investment center is that the manager can control or significantly influence the investment funds available for use. Thus, the primary basis for evaluating the performance of a manager of an investment center is **return on investment (ROI)**. The return on investment is considered to be superior to any other performance measurement because it shows the **effectiveness of the manager in utilizing the assets at the manager's disposal**.

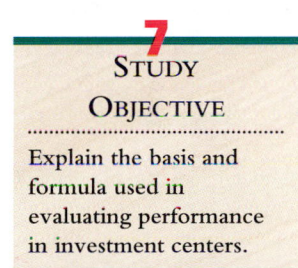

7
STUDY
OBJECTIVE
....
Explain the basis and formula used in evaluating performance in investment centers.

Return on Investment (ROI)

The formula for computing ROI for an investment center, together with assumed illustrative data, is shown in Illustration 25-23. Both factors in the formula are controllable by the investment center manager. Operating assets consist of current assets and plant assets used in operations by the center and controlled by the manager. Nonoperating assets such as idle plant assets and land held for future use are excluded. Average operating assets are usually based on the cost or book value of the assets at the beginning and end of the year.

ILLUSTRATION 25-23
ROI formula

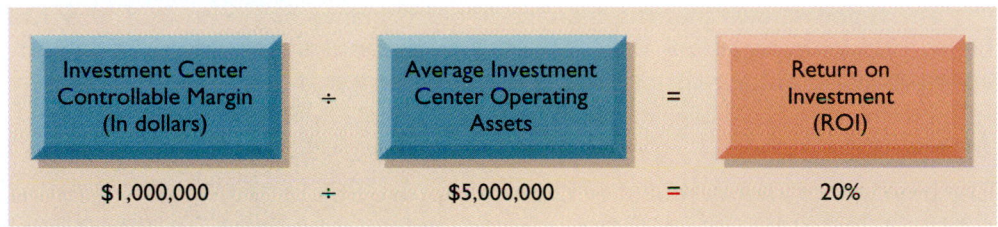

Responsibility Report

The scope of the investment center manager's responsibility significantly affects the content of the performance report. Since an investment center is an independent entity for operating purposes, **all fixed costs are controllable by the investment center manager**. For example, the manager is responsible for depreciation on investment center assets. Accordingly, more fixed costs are identified as controllable in the performance report for an investment center manager than in a performance report for a profit center manager. In addition, the report shows budgeted and actual ROI below controllable margin.

To illustrate the responsibility report, we will now assume that the Marine Division of Mantle Manufacturing Company is an investment center with budgeted and actual average operating assets of $2,000,000. In addition, we will assume that the manager can control the $60,000 of fixed costs that were not controllable when the division was a profit center. The responsibility report is shown in Illustration 25-24.

ILLUSTRATION 25-24

Responsibility report for investment center

MANTLE MANUFACTURING COMPANY
Marine Division
Responsibility Report
For the Year Ended December 31, 1999

	Budget	Actual	Difference Favorable F Unfavorable U
Sales	$1,200,000	$1,150,000	$50,000 U
Variable costs			
Cost of goods sold	500,000	490,000	10,000 F
Selling and administrative	160,000	156,000	4,000 F
Total	660,000	646,000	14,000 F
Contribution margin	540,000	504,000	36,000 U
Controllable fixed costs			
Cost of goods sold	100,000	100,000	–0–
Selling and administrative	80,000	80,000	–0–
Other fixed costs	60,000	60,000	–0–
Total	240,000	240,000	–0–
Controllable margin	$ 300,000	$ 264,000	$36,000 U
Return on investment	15%	13.2%	1.8% U
	(a)	(b)	(c)

(a) $\dfrac{\$300,000}{\$2,000,000}$ (b) $\dfrac{\$264,000}{\$2,000,000}$ (c) $\dfrac{\$36,000}{\$2,000,000}$

The report shows that the manager's performance based on ROI was 12% below budget expectations (1.8% ÷ 15%). Top management would likely want an explanation of the reasons for this unfavorable result.

Improving ROI

The manager of an investment center can improve ROI in two ways: (1) increase controllable margin and/or (2) reduce average operating assets. To illustrate, we will use the following assumed data for the Marine Division of Mantle Manufacturing:

ILLUSTRATION 25-25

Assumed data for Marine Division

Sales	$2,000,000
Variable cost	1,100,000
Contribution margin (45%)	900,000
Controllable fixed costs	300,000
Controllable margin (a)	$ 600,000
Average operating assets (b)	$5,000,000
Return on investment (a) ÷ (b)	12%

Increasing Controllable Margin.   Controllable margin can be increased by increasing sales or by reducing variable and controllable fixed costs as follows:

1. **Increase sales 10%.** Sales will increase $200,000 ($2,000,000 × .10). Assuming no change in the contribution margin percentage of 45%, contribution margin will increase $90,000 ($200,000 × .45). Controllable margin will increase by the same amount because controllable fixed costs will not change. Thus, controllable margin becomes $690,000 ($600,000 + $90,000), and the new ROI is 13.8%, computed as follows:

$$\text{ROI} = \frac{\text{Controllable margin}}{\text{Average operating assets}} = \frac{\$690,000}{\$5,000,000} = 13.8\%$$

ILLUSTRATION 25-26

ROI computation—increase in sales

An increase in sales benefits both the investment center and the company if it results in new business. It would not benefit the company if the increase was achieved at the expense of other investment centers.

2. **Decrease variable and fixed costs 10%.** Total costs will decrease $140,000 [($1,100,000 + $300,000) × .10]. This reduction will result in a corresponding increase in controllable margin. Thus, this margin becomes $740,000 ($600,000 + $140,000), and the new ROI is 14.8%, computed as follows:

$$\text{ROI} = \frac{\text{Controllable margin}}{\text{Average operating assets}} = \frac{\$740,000}{\$5,000,000} = 14.8\%$$

ILLUSTRATION 25-27

ROI computation—decrease in costs

This course of action is clearly beneficial when waste and inefficiencies are eliminated. However, a reduction in vital costs such as required maintenance and inspections are not likely to be acceptable to top management.

Reducing Average Operating Assets.   Assume that average operating assets are reduced 10% or $500,000 ($5,000,000 × .10). Average operating assets become $4,500,000 ($5,000,000 − $500,000). Since controllable margin remains unchanged at $600,000, the new ROI is 13.3%, computed as follows:

$$\text{ROI} = \frac{\text{Controllable margin}}{\text{Average operating assets}} = \frac{\$600,000}{\$4,500,000} = 13.3\%$$

ILLUSTRATION 25-28

ROI computation—decrease in operating assets

Reductions in operating assets may or may not be prudent. It is beneficial to eliminate overinvestment in inventories and to dispose of excessive plant assets. However, it is unwise to reduce inventories below expected needs or to dispose of essential plant assets.

Judgmental Factors in ROI

The return on investment approach includes two judgmental factors:

1. **Valuation of operating assets.** Operating assets may be valued at acquisition cost, book value, appraised value, or market value. The first two bases are readily available from the accounting records.
2. **Margin (income) measure.** This measure may be controllable margin, income from operations, or net income.

Each of the alternative values for operating assets can provide a reliable basis for evaluating a manager's performance as long as it is consistently applied between reporting periods. However, the use of income measures other than controllable margin will not result in a valid basis for evaluating the performance of an investment center manager because they will include some noncontrollable revenues and costs.

Principles of Performance Evaluation

Performance evaluation is at the center of responsibility accounting. **Performance evaluation** is a management function that compares actual results with budget goals. It is based on internal reports prepared by the managerial accountant. Performance evaluation involves both behavioral and reporting principles.

Behavioral Principles

The human factor is critical in evaluating performance. Behavioral principles include the following:

1. **Managers of responsibility centers should have direct input into the process of establishing budget goals of their area of responsibility.** Without such input, managers may view the goals as unrealistic or arbitrarily set by top management. Such views adversely affect the managers' motivation to meet the targeted objectives.
2. **The evaluation of performance should be based entirely on matters that are controllable by the manager being evaluated.** Criticism of a manager on matters outside his or her control reduces the effectiveness of the evaluation process. Moreover, it leads to negative reactions by a manager and to doubts about the fairness of the company's evaluation policies.
3. **Top management should support the evaluation process.** As explained earlier, the evaluation process begins at the lowest level of responsibility and extends upward to the highest level of management. Managers quickly lose faith in the process when top management ignores, overrules, or bypasses established procedures for evaluating a manager's performance.
4. **The evaluation process must allow managers to respond to their evaluations.** Evaluation is not a one-way street. Managers should have the opportunity to defend their performance. Evaluation without feedback is both impersonal and ineffective.
5. **The evaluation should identify both good and poor performance.** Praise for good performance is a powerful motivating factor for a manager. This is especially true when a manager's compensation includes rewards for meeting budget goals.

Reporting Principles

Performance evaluation under responsibility accounting also involves reporting principles. These principles pertain primarily to the internal reports that provide the basis for evaluating performance. Performance reports should:

1. Contain only data that are controllable by the manager of the responsibility center.
2. Provide accurate and reliable budget data to measure performance.
3. Highlight significant differences between actual results and budget goals.
4. Be tailor-made for the intended evaluation.
5. Be prepared at reasonable intervals.

BEFORE YOU GO ON . . .

Review It

1. What is the formula for computing return on investment (ROI)?
2. Identify three actions a manager may take to improve ROI.
3. What responsibility centers (investment type) might Kellogg be utilizing in determining ROI? The answer to this question is provided on page 1113.

A LOOK BACK AT OUR FEATURE STORY

Refer to the opening story about the athletic department of UNLV, and answer the following questions.

1. Would you expect a static or a flexible budget to be used in comparing actual and budgeted expenditures for each team?
2. Which of the biggest budget items are variable and which are fixed?
3. What is the relationship, if any, of the budgets used at UNLV and the allocation of cash to each team?

Solution:

1. At the time of preparing the budget, if a sports team has a fixed schedule of games (meets) along with a fixed number of players and coaches, a static budget might be sufficient. That is, if the predetermined activity level is static or fixed, the budget may be static. However, if the activity level (games/meets along with the roster size, number of scholarships, and coaches) is flexible and not predeterminable, a flexible budget tied to the activity driver is necessary in order to evaluate budget compliance at different activity levels.
2. The biggest variable expense is travel cost, which varies with distance, the number in the traveling party, and number of trips. Once the coaches, trainers, and managers are hired, payroll is a fixed cost for the season. Scholarships, once the number of in-state and out-of-state scholarships has been granted, is also a fixed cost for the season.
3. Once approved, the budget becomes the basis for the appropriation of funds and the allocation of cash to each team. Cash is allocated to each team in accordance with the approved budget. The budget sets the limits and the categories of expenditures.

DEMONSTRATION PROBLEM

Glenda Company uses a flexible budget for manufacturing overhead based on direct labor hours. For 1999 the master overhead budget for the Packaging Department at normal capacity of 300,000 direct labor hours was as follows:

Variable Costs		Fixed Costs	
Indirect labor	$360,000	Supervision	$ 60,000
Supplies and lubricants	150,000	Depreciation	24,000
Maintenance	210,000	Property taxes	18,000
Utilities	120,000	Insurance	12,000
	$840,000		$114,000

During July, 24,000 direct labor hours were worked when 25,000 hours were expected to be worked. The company incurred the following variable costs in July: Indirect labor $30,200, supplies and lubricants $11,600, maintenance $17,500, and utilities $9,200. Actual fixed overhead costs were the same as monthly budgeted fixed costs.

Instructions

Prepare a flexible budget report for the Packaging Department for July.

PROBLEM-SOLVING
STRATEGIES
1. Use budget data for actual
   direct labor hours worked.
2. Classify each cost as variable
   or fixed.
3. Determine the difference
   between budgeted and actual
   costs.
4. Identify the difference as
   favorable or unfavorable.
5. Determine the difference in
   total variable costs, total
   fixed costs, and total costs.

SOLUTION TO DEMONSTRATION PROBLEM

GLENDA COMPANY
Manufacturing Overhead Budget Report (Flexible)
Packaging Department
For the Month Ended July 31, 1999

Direct labor hours (DLH) Expected 25,000 Actual 24,000	Budget 24,000 DLH	Actual Costs 24,000 DLH	Difference Favorable F Unfavorable U
Variable costs			
Indirect labor	$28,800	$30,200	$1,400 U
Supplies and lubricants	12,000	11,600	400 F
Maintenance	16,800	17,500	700 U
Utilities	9,600	9,200	400 F
Total variable	67,200	68,500	1,300 U
Fixed costs			
Supervision	5,000	5,000	–0–
Depreciation	2,000	2,000	–0–
Property taxes	1,500	1,500	–0–
Insurance	1,000	1,000	–0–
Total fixed	9,500	9,500	–0–
Total costs	$76,700	$78,000	$1,300 U

THE NAVIGATOR

SUMMARY OF STUDY OBJECTIVES

1. Describe the concept of budgetary control. Budgetary control consists of (a) preparing periodic budget reports that compare actual results with planned objectives, (b) analyzing the differences to determine their causes, (c) taking appropriate corrective action, and (d) modifying future plans, if necessary.

2. Evaluate the usefulness of static budget reports. Static budget reports are useful in evaluating the progress toward meeting planned sales and profit goals. They are also appropriate in assessing a manager's effectiveness in controlling fixed costs and expenses when (a) actual activity closely approximates the master budget activity level and/or (b) the behavior of the costs in response to changes in activity is fixed.

3. Explain the development of flexible budgets and the usefulness of flexible budget reports. To develop the flexible budget it is necessary to:
(a) Identify the activity index and the relevant range of activity.
(b) Identify the variable costs and determine the budgeted variable cost per unit of activity for each cost.
(c) Identify the fixed costs and determine the budgeted amount for each cost.
(d) Prepare the budget for selected increments of activity within the relevant range.

Flexible budget reports permit an evaluation of a manager's performance in controlling production and costs.

4. Describe the concept of responsibility accounting. Responsibility accounting involves the accumulation and reporting of revenues and costs on the basis of the individual manager who has the authority to make the day-to-day decisions about the items. Under responsibility accounting, the evaluation of a manager's performance is based on the matters directly under the manager's control. In responsibility accounting, it is necessary to distinguish between controllable and noncontrollable fixed costs and to identify three types of responsibility centers: cost, profit, and investment.

5. Indicate the features of responsibility reports for cost centers. Responsibility reports for cost centers compare actual costs with flexible budget data. The reports show only controllable costs and no distinction is made between variable and fixed costs.

6. Identify the content of responsibility reports for profit centers. Responsibility reports show contribution margin, controllable fixed costs, and controllable margin for each profit center.

7. Explain the basis and formula used in evaluating performance in investment centers. The primary basis for evaluating performance in investment centers is return on investment (ROI). The formula for computing ROI for investment centers is: Controllable Margin (in dollars) ÷ Average Operating Assets.

THE NAVIGATOR

GLOSSARY

Budgetary control The use of budgets to control operations. (p. 1072).

Controllable costs Costs that a manager has the authority to incur within a given period of time. (p. 1084).

Controllable margin Contribution margin less controllable fixed costs. (p. 1089).

Cost center A responsibility center that incurs costs but does not directly generate revenues. (p. 1087).

Decentralization Control of operations is delegated by top management to many managers throughout the organization. (p. 1083).

Direct fixed costs Costs that relate specifically to a responsibility center and are incurred for the sole benefit of the center. (p. 1089).

Flexible budget A projection of budget data for various levels of activity. (p. 1075).

Indirect fixed costs Costs that are incurred for the benefit of more than one profit center. (p. 1089).

Investment center A responsibility center that incurs costs, generates revenues, and has control over the investment funds available for use. (p. 1087).

Management by exception The review of budget reports by top management directed entirely or primarily to differ-

ences between actual results and planned objectives. (p. 1081).

Noncontrollable costs Costs incurred indirectly and allocated to a responsibility center that are not controllable at that level. (p. 1084).

Profit center A responsibility center that incurs costs and also generates revenues. (p. 1087).

Responsibility accounting A part of management accounting that involves accumulating and reporting revenues and costs on the basis of the individual manager who has the authority to make the day-to-day decisions about the items. (p. 1082).

Responsibility reporting system The preparation of reports for each level of responsibility shown in the company's organization chart. (p. 1084).

Return on investment (ROI) A measure of management's effectiveness in utilizing assets at its disposal in an investment center. (p. 1091).

Segment An area of responsibility in decentralized operations. (p. 1083).

Static budget A projection of budget data at one level of activity. (p. 1073).

SELF-STUDY QUESTIONS

Answers are at the end of the chapter.

(SO 1) 1. Budgetary control involves all but one of the following:
   a. modifying future plans.
   b. analyzing differences.
   c. using static budgets.
   d. determining differences between actual and planned results.

(SO 2) 2. A static budget is useful in controlling costs when cost behavior is:
   a. mixed.
   b. fixed.
   c. variable.
   d. linear.

(SO 3) 3. At zero direct labor hours in a flexible budget graph, the total budgeted cost line intersects the vertical axis at $30,000. At 10,000 direct labor hours, the line drawn from the total budgeted cost line intersects the vertical axis at $90,000. Fixed and variable costs may be expressed as:
   a. $30,000 fixed plus $6 per direct labor hour variable.
   b. $30,000 fixed plus $9 per direct labor hour variable.
   c. $60,000 fixed plus $3 per direct labor hour variable.
   d. $60,000 fixed plus $6 per direct labor hour variable.

(SO 3) 4. At 9,000 direct labor hours, the flexible budget for indirect materials is $27,000. If $28,000 of indirect materi-

als costs are incurred at 9,200 direct labor hours, the flexible budget report should show the following difference for indirect materials:
   a. $1,000 unfavorable.
   b. $1,000 favorable.
   c. $400 favorable.
   d. $400 unfavorable.

5. Under responsibility accounting, the evaluation of a (SO 4) manager's performance is based on matters that the manager:
   a. directly controls.
   b. directly and indirectly controls.
   c. indirectly controls.
   d. has shared responsibility with another manager.

6. Responsibility centers include: (SO 4)
   a. cost centers.
   b. profit centers.
   c. investment centers.
   d. all of the above.

7. Responsibility reports for cost centers: (SO 5)
   a. distinguish between fixed and variable costs.
   b. use static budget data.
   c. include both controllable and noncontrollable costs.
   d. include only controllable costs.

(SO 6) 8. In a responsibility report for a profit center, controllable fixed costs are deducted from contribution margin to show:
  a. profit center margin.
  b. controllable margin.
  c. net income.
  d. income from operations.

(SO 7) 9. In the formula for return on investment (ROI), the factors for controllable margin and operating assets are, respectively:
  a. controllable margin percentage and total operating assets.
  b. controllable margin dollars and average operating assets.
  c. controllable margin dollars and total assets.
  d. controllable margin percentage and average operating assets.

10. A manager of an investment center can improve ROI (SO 7) by:
  a. increasing average operating assets.
  b. reducing sales.
  c. increasing variable costs.
  d. reducing variable and/or controllable fixed costs.

QUESTIONS

1. (a) What is budgetary control?
   (b) Tony Crespino is describing budgetary control. What steps should be included in Tony's description?

2. The following purposes are part of a budgetary reporting system: (a) determine efficient use of materials, (b) control overhead costs, and (c) determine whether income objectives are being met. For each purpose, indicate the name of the report, the frequency of the report, and the primary recipient(s) of the report.

3. How may a budget report for the second quarter differ from a budget report for the first quarter?

4. Don Cox questions the usefulness of a master sales budget in evaluating sales performance. Is there justification for Don's concern? Explain.

5. Under what circumstances may a static budget be an appropriate basis for evaluating a manager's effectiveness in controlling costs?

6. "A flexible budget is really a series of static budgets." Is this true? Why?

7. The static manufacturing overhead budget based on 40,000 direct labor hours shows budgeted indirect labor costs of $56,000. During March, the department incurs $66,000 of indirect labor while working 45,000 direct labor hours. Is this a favorable or unfavorable performance? Why?

8. A static overhead budget based on 40,000 direct labor hours shows Factory Insurance $6,500 as a fixed cost. At the 50,000 direct labor hours worked in March, factory insurance costs were $6,200. Is this a favorable or unfavorable performance? Why?

9. Kate Coulter is confused about how a flexible budget is prepared. Identify the steps for Kate.

10. Alou Company has prepared a graph of flexible budget data. At zero direct labor hours, the total budgeted cost line intersects the vertical axis at $25,000. At 10,000 direct labor hours, the line drawn from the total budgeted cost line intersects the vertical axis at $85,000. How may the fixed and variable costs be expressed?

11. The flexible budget formula is fixed costs $40,000 plus variable costs of $2 per direct labor hour. What is the total budgeted cost at (a) 9,000 hours and (b) 12,345 hours?

12. What is management by exception? What criteria may be used in identifying exceptions?

13. What is responsibility accounting? Explain the purpose of responsibility accounting.

14. Ann Wilkins is studying for an accounting examination. Describe for Ann what conditions are necessary for responsibility accounting to be used effectively.

15. Distinguish between controllable and noncontrollable costs.

16. How do responsibility reports differ from budget reports?

17. What is the relationship, if any, between a responsibility reporting system and a company's organization chart?

18. Distinguish among the three types of responsibility centers.

19. (a) What costs are included in a performance report for a cost center? (b) In the report, are variable and fixed costs identified?

20. How do direct fixed costs differ from indirect fixed costs? Are both types of fixed costs controllable?

21. Lori Quan is confused about controllable margin reported in an income statement for a profit center. How is this margin computed, and what is its primary purpose?

22. What is the primary basis for evaluating the performance of the manager of an investment center? Indicate the formula for this basis.

23. Explain the ways that ROI can be improved.

24. Indicate two behavioral principles that pertain to (a) the manager being evaluated and (b) top management.

BRIEF EXERCISES

BE25–1   For the quarter ended March 31, 1999, Elsie Company accumulates the following sales data for its product, Garden-Tools: $315,000 budget; $300,000 actual. Prepare a static budget report for the quarter.

Prepare static budget report.
(SO 2)

BE25–2   Data for Elsie Company are given in BE25–1. In the second quarter, budgeted sales were $380,000, and actual sales were $390,000. Prepare a static budget report for the second quarter and for the year to date.

Prepare static budget report for two quarters.
(SO 2)

BE25–3   In Finney Company, direct labor is $20 per hour, and the company expects to operate at 10,000 direct labor hours each month. In January 1999, direct labor totaling $207,000 is incurred in working 10,800 hours. Prepare a static budget report and a flexible budget report. Evaluate the usefulness of each report.

Show usefulness of flexible budgets in evaluating performance.
(SO 3)

BE25–4   Kandt Company expects to produce 1,200,000 units of Product XX in 1999. Monthly production is expected to range from 80,000 to 120,000 units. Budgeted variable manufacturing costs per unit are: direct materials $5, direct labor $6, and overhead $3. Prepare a flexible manufacturing budget for the relevant range value using 20,000 unit increments.

Prepare a flexible budget for variable costs.
(SO 3)

BE25–5   Data for Kandt Company are given in BE25–4. In March 1999, the company incurs the following costs in producing 100,000 units: direct materials $520,000, direct labor $590,000, and variable overhead $305,000. Prepare a flexible budget report for March. Were costs controlled?

Prepare flexible budget report.
(SO 3)

BE25–6   In the Assembly Department of Jurgens Company, budgeted and actual manufacturing overhead costs for the month of April 1999 were as follows:

Prepare a responsibility report for a cost center.
(SO 5)

	Budget	Actual
Indirect materials	$15,000	$14,500
Indirect labor	20,000	20,800
Utilities	10,000	10,600
Supervision	5,000	5,000

All costs are controllable by the department manager. Prepare a responsibility report for April for the cost center.

BE25–7   Lehman Manufacturing Company accumulates the following summary data for the year ending December 31, 1999, for its Aqua Division which it operates as a profit center: Sales—$2,000,000 budget, $2,080,000 actual; variable costs—$1,000,000 budget, $1,050,000 actual; and controllable fixed costs—$300,000 budget, $310,000 actual. Prepare a responsibility report for the Aqua Division.

Prepare a responsibility report for a profit center.
(SO 6)

BE25–8   For the year ending December 31, 1999, Ming Chow Company accumulates the following data for the Plastics Division which it operates as an investment center: contribution margin—$700,000 budget, $715,000 actual; controllable fixed costs—$300,000 budget, $295,000 actual. Average operating assets for the year were $2,000,000. Prepare a responsibility report for the Plastics Division beginning with contribution margin.

Prepare a responsibility report for an investment center.
(SO 7)

BE25–9   For its three investment centers, Huskey Company accumulates the following data:

Compute return on investment using the ROI formula.
(SO 7)

	I	II	III
Sales	$2,000,000	$3,000,000	$ 4,000,000
Controllable margin	1,500,000	2,400,000	3,200,000
Average operating assets	6,000,000	8,000,000	10,000,000

Compute the return on investment (ROI) for each center.

BE25–10   Data for the investment centers for Huskey Company are given in BE25–9. The centers expect the following changes in the next year: (I) increase sales 10%; (II) decrease costs $200,000; (III) decrease average operating assets $400,000. Compute the expected return on investment (ROI) for each center. Assume center I has a contribution margin percentage of 80%.

Compute return on investment under changed conditions.
(SO 7)

EXERCISES

Prepare flexible manufacturing overhead budget.
(SO 3)

E25–1 Paola Company uses a flexible budget for manufacturing overhead based on direct labor hours. Variable manufacturing overhead costs per direct labor hour are as follows:

Indirect labor	$1.00
Indirect materials	.50
Utilities	.30

Fixed overhead costs per month are: Supervision $3,000, Depreciation $1,500, and Property Taxes $800. The company believes it will normally operate in a range of 7,000–10,000 direct labor hours per month.

Instructions
Prepare a monthly flexible manufacturing overhead budget for 1999 for the expected range of activity, using increments of 1,000 direct labor hours.

Prepare flexible budget reports for manufacturing overhead costs and comment on findings.
(SO 3)

E25–2 Using the information in E25–1, assume that in July 1999, Paola Company incurs the following manufacturing overhead costs:

Variable Costs		Fixed Costs	
Indirect labor	$8,700	Supervision	$3,000
Indirect materials	4,300	Depreciation	1,500
Utilities	2,500	Property taxes	800

Instructions
(a) Prepare a flexible budget performance report, assuming that the company worked 9,000 direct labor hours during the month. The company expected to work 9,000 direct labor hours.
(b) Prepare a flexible budget performance report, assuming that the company worked 8,500 direct labor hours during the month. The company expected to work 8,500 direct labor hours.
(c) ▆▐▤▥▻ Comment on your findings.

Prepare flexible selling expense budget.
(SO 3)

E25–3 Mallory Company uses flexible budgets to control its selling expenses. Monthly sales are expected to range from $170,000 to $200,000. Variable costs and their percentage relationship to sales are: Sales Commissions (5%), Advertising (4%), Traveling (3%), and Delivery (2%). Fixed selling expenses will consist of Sales Salaries $30,000, Depreciation on Delivery Equipment $5,000, and Insurance on Delivery Equipment $1,000.

Instructions
Prepare a monthly flexible budget for each $10,000 increment of sales within the relevant range for the year ending December 31, 1999.

Prepare flexible budget reports for selling expenses.
(SO 3)

E25–4 The actual selling expenses incurred in March 1999 by Mallory Company are as follows:

Variable Expenses		Fixed Expenses	
Sales commissions	$9,200	Sales salaries	$30,000
Advertising	7,000	Depreciation	5,000
Travel	5,100	Insurance	1,000
Delivery	3,500		

Instructions
(a) Prepare a flexible budget performance report for March using the budget data in E25–3, assuming that March sales were $170,000. Expected and actual sales are the same.
(b) Prepare a flexible budget performance report, assuming that March sales were $180,000. Expected sales and actual sales are the same.
(c) Comment on the importance of using flexible budgets in evaluating the performance of the sales manager.

Prepare flexible budget and responsibility report for manufacturing overhead.
(SO 3, 5)

E25–5 Jabarra Company's manufacturing overhead budget for the first quarter of 1999 contained the following data:

Variable Costs		Fixed Costs	
Indirect materials	$12,000	Supervisory salaries	$30,000
Indirect labor	10,000	Depreciation	7,000
Utilities	8,000	Property taxes and insurance	8,000
Maintenance	5,000	Maintenance	5,000

Actual variable costs were: indirect materials $14,200, indirect labor $9,600, utilities $8,700, and maintenance $4,200. Actual fixed costs equaled budgeted costs except for property taxes and insurance, which were $8,100.

All costs are considered controllable by the production department manager except for depreciation, property taxes, and insurance.

Instructions

(a) Prepare a flexible overhead budget report for the first quarter.

(b) Prepare a responsibility report for the first quarter.

E25–6 As sales manager, Todd Keyser was given the following static budget report for selling expenses in the Clothing Department of O'Keefe Company for the month of October.

Prepare flexible budget report and answer question.
(SO 2, 3)

O'KEEFE COMPANY
Clothing Department
Budget Report
For the Month Ended October 31, 1999

	Budget	Actual	Difference Favorable F Unfavorable U
Sales in units	8,000	10,000	2,000 F
Variable costs			
Sales commissions	$ 2,000	$ 2,200	$ 200 U
Advertising expense	800	850	50 U
Travel expense	4,400	4,900	500 U
Free samples given out	1,000	1,300	300 U
Total variable	8,200	9,250	1,050 U
Fixed costs			
Rent	1,500	1,500	–0–
Sales salaries	1,200	1,200	–0–
Office salaries	800	800	–0–
Depreciation—autos (sales staff)	500	500	–0–
Total fixed	4,000	4,000	–0–
Total costs	$11,800	$13,250	$1,050 U

As a result of this budget report, Todd was called into the president's office and congratulated on his fine sales performance. He was reprimanded, however, for allowing his costs to get out of control. Todd knew something was wrong with the performance report that he had been given. However, he was not sure what to do, and comes to you for advice.

Instructions

(a) Prepare a budget report based on flexible budget data to help Todd.

(b) Should Todd have been reprimanded? Explain.

E25–7 Gonzalez Company has two production departments, Fabricating and Assembling. At a department managers' meeting, the controller uses flexible budget graphs to explain total budgeted costs. Separate graphs based on direct labor hours are used for each department. The graphs show the following:

State total budgeted cost formulas and prepare flexible budget graph.
(SO 3)

1. At zero direct labor hours, the total budgeted cost line and the fixed cost line intersect the vertical axis at $50,000 in the Fabricating Department and $48,000 in the Assembling Department.

2. At normal capacity of 50,000 direct labor hours, the line drawn from the total budgeted cost line intersects the vertical axis at $160,000 in the Fabricating Department, and $108,000 in the Assembling Department.

Instructions

(a) State the total budgeted cost formula for each department.

(b) Compute the total budgeted cost for each department, assuming actual direct labor hours worked were 53,000 and 47,000, in the Fabricating and Assembling Departments, respectively.

(c) Prepare the flexible budget graph for the Fabricating Department, assuming the maximum direct labor hours in the relevant range is 100,000. Use increments of 10,000 direct labor hours on the horizontal axis and increments of $50,000 on the vertical axis.

Prepare reports in a responsibility reporting system.
(SO 4)

E25–8 Abotteen Company's organization chart includes the president; the vice president of production; three assembly plants—Dallas, Atlanta, and Tucson; and two departments within each plant—Machining and Finishing. Budget and actual manufacturing cost data for July 1999 are as follows:

Finishing Department—Dallas: Direct materials $42,000 actual, $46,000 budget; direct labor $83,000 actual, $82,000 budget; manufacturing overhead $51,000 actual, $49,200 budget.

Machining Department—Dallas: Total manufacturing costs $218,000 actual, $214,000 budget.

Atlanta Plant: Total manufacturing costs $426,000 actual, $421,000 budget.

Tucson Plant: Total manufacturing costs $494,000 actual, $499,000 budget.

The Dallas plant manager's office costs were $95,000 actual and $92,000 budget. The vice president of production's office costs were $132,000 actual and $130,000 budget. Office costs are not allocated to departments and plants.

Instructions

Prepare the reports in a responsibility system for (a) the Finishing Department—Dallas, (b) the plant manager—Dallas, and (c) the vice president of production. Use the format on page 1086.

Compute missing amounts in responsibility reports for three profit centers and prepare a report.
(SO 6)

E25–9 Pavlik Manufacturing Inc. has three divisions which are operated as profit centers. Operating data for the divisions listed alphabetically are as follows:

Operating Data	Women's Shoes	Men's Shoes	Children's Shoes
Contribution margin	$250,000	(3)	$160,000
Controllable fixed costs	100,000	(4)	(5)
Controllable margin	(1)	$ 90,000	96,000
Sales	600,000	450,000	(6)
Variable costs	(2)	310,000	250,000

Instructions

(a) Compute the missing amounts. Show computations.

(b) Prepare a responsibility report for the Women's Shoe Division assuming (1) the data are for the month ended June 30, 1999, and (2) all data equal budget except variable costs which are $10,000 over budget.

Compute ROI for current year and for possible future changes.
(SO 7)

E25–10 The Mastercraft Division of Nunez Company reported the following data for the current year:

Sales	$3,000,000
Variable costs	1,800,000
Controllable fixed costs	600,000
Average operating assets	5,000,000

Top management is unhappy with the investment center's return on investment (ROI). It asks the manager of the Mastercraft Division to submit plans to improve ROI in the next year. The manager believes it is feasible to consider the following independent courses of action.

1. Increase sales by $320,000 with no change in the contribution margin percentage.
2. Reduce variable costs by $100,000.
3. Reduce average operating assets by 5%.

Instructions

(a) Compute the return on investment (ROI) for the current year.

(b) Using the ROI formula, compute the ROI under each of the proposed courses of action. (Round to one decimal.)

PROBLEMS: SET A

P25–1A Rossi Company estimates that 240,000 direct labor hours will be worked during 1999 in the Assembly Department. On this basis, the following budgeted manufacturing overhead data are computed:

Prepare flexible budget and budget report for manufacturing overhead.
(SO 3)

Variable Overhead Costs		Fixed Overhead Costs	
Indirect labor	$ 72,000	Supervision	$ 72,000
Indirect materials	48,000	Depreciation	30,000
Repairs	24,000	Insurance	9,600
Utilities	14,400	Rent	7,200
Lubricants	9,600	Property taxes	6,000
	$168,000		$124,800

It is estimated that direct labor hours worked each month will range from 18,000 to 24,000 hours.

During January, 20,000 direct labor hours were worked and the following overhead costs were incurred.

Variable Overhead Costs		Fixed Overhead Costs	
Indirect labor	$ 6,200	Supervision	$ 6,000
Indirect materials	3,600	Depreciation	2,500
Repairs	1,600	Insurance	800
Utilities	900	Rent	700
Lubricants	830	Property taxes	500
	$13,130		$10,500

Instructions

(a) Prepare a monthly flexible manufacturing overhead budget for each increment of 2,000 direct labor hours over the relevant range for the year ending December 31, 1999.

(b) Prepare a manufacturing overhead budget report for January, assuming 20,500 direct labor hours were expected.

(c) Comment on management's efficiency in controlling manufacturing overhead costs in January.

P25–2A Tariq Manufacturing Company produces one product, Kebo. Because of wide fluctuations in demand for Kebo, the Assembly Department experiences significant variations in monthly production levels.

Prepare flexible budget, budget report, and graph for manufacturing overhead.
(SO 3)

The master manufacturing overhead budget **for the year,** based on 300,000 direct labor hours, and the actual overhead costs incurred in July in which 27,500 labor hours were worked, and 27,500 hours were expected to be worked, are as follows:

Overhead Costs	Master Budget (annual)	Actual in July
Variable		
Indirect labor	$ 360,000	$32,000
Indirect materials	210,000	17,000
Utilities	90,000	8,100
Maintenance	60,000	5,400
Fixed		
Supervision	180,000	15,000
Depreciation	120,000	10,000
Insurance and taxes	60,000	5,000
Total	$1,080,000	$92,500

Instructions

(a) Prepare a monthly flexible overhead budget for the year ending December 31, 1999, assuming monthly production levels range from 22,500 to 30,000 direct labor hours. Use increments of 2,500 direct labor hours.

(b) Prepare a budget performance report for the month of July 1999 comparing actual results with budget data based on the flexible budget.

(c) ▭▭▭▶ Were costs effectively controlled? Explain.

(d) State the formula for computing the total monthly budgeted costs in Tariq Company.

(e) Prepare the flexible budget graph showing total budgeted costs at 25,000 and 27,500 direct labor hours. Use increments of 5,000 on the horizontal axis and increments of $10,000 on the vertical axis.

State total budgeted cost formula and prepare flexible budget reports for two time periods.
(SO 2, 3)

P25–3A Uphoff Company uses budgets in controlling costs. The May 1999 budget report for the company's Packaging Department is as follows:

UPHOFF COMPANY
Budget Report
Packaging Department
For the Month Ended May 31, 1999

Manufacturing Costs	Budget	Actual	Difference Favorable F Unfavorable U
Variable costs			
Direct materials	$ 30,000	$ 32,000	$2,000 U
Direct labor	40,000	43,000	3,000 U
Indirect materials	15,000	15,200	200 U
Indirect labor	12,500	13,000	500 U
Utilities	7,500	7,100	400 F
Maintenance	5,000	5,200	200 U
Total variable	110,000	115,500	5,500 U
Fixed costs			
Rent	9,000	9,000	–0–
Supervision	8,000	8,000	–0–
Depreciation	5,000	5,000	–0–
Total fixed	22,000	22,000	–0–
Total costs	$132,000	$137,500	$5,500 U

The budget amounts in the report were on the master budget for the year, which assumed that 600,000 units would be produced. (*Hint:* The budget amounts above are one-twelfth of the master budget for the year.)

The company president was displeased with the department manager's performance. The department manager, who thought he had done a good job, could not understand the unfavorable results. In May, 55,000 units were produced.

Instructions

(a) State the total budgeted cost formula.

(b) Prepare a budget report for May using flexible budget data. Why does this report provide a better basis for evaluating performance than the report based on static budget data? Assume 57,000 units were expected to be produced in the Packaging Department.

(c) In June, 40,000 units were produced when 39,000 were expected. Prepare the budget report using flexible budget data, assuming (1) each variable cost was 20% less in June than its actual cost in May, and (2) fixed costs were the same in the month of June as in May.

Prepare responsibility report for a profit center.
(SO 6)

P25–4A McCluskey Manufacturing Inc. operates the Home Appliance Division as a profit center. Operating data for this division for the year ended December 31, 1999, are as follows:

	Budget	Difference from Budget
Sales	$2,400,000	$100,000 U
Cost of goods sold		
Variable	1,200,000	60,000 U
Controllable fixed	200,000	10,000 F

	Budget	Difference from Budget
Selling and administrative		
Variable	240,000	10,000 F
Controllable fixed	60,000	6,000 U
Noncontrollable fixed costs	50,000	2,000 U

In addition, McCluskey Manufacturing incurs $150,000 of indirect fixed costs that were budgeted at $155,000. Twenty percent (20%) of these costs are allocated to the Home Appliance Division. None of these costs are controllable by the division manager.

Instructions
(a) Prepare a responsibility report for the Home Appliance Division (a profit center) for the year.
(b) ▇▇▇▇▷ Comment on the manager's performance in controlling revenues and costs.
(c) Identify any costs excluded from the responsibility report and explain why they were excluded.

P25–5A Ninemire Manufacturing Company manufactures a variety of garden and lawn equipment. The company operates through three divisions. Each division is an investment center. Operating data for the Lawnmower Division for the year ended December 31, 1999, and relevant budget data are as follows:

Prepare responsibility report for an investment center and compute ROI.
(SO 7)

	Actual	Comparison with Budget
Sales	$2,800,000	$200,000 unfavorable
Variable cost of goods sold	1,400,000	150,000 unfavorable
Variable selling and administrative expenses	300,000	50,000 favorable
Controllable fixed cost of goods sold	270,000	On target
Controllable fixed selling and administrative expenses	130,000	On target

Average operating assets for the year for the Lawnmower Division were $5,000,000 which was also the budgeted amount.

Instructions
(a) Prepare a responsibility report (in thousands of dollars) for the Lawnmower Division.
(b) Evaluate the manager's performance. Which items will likely be investigated by top management?
(c) Compute the expected ROI in 2000 for the Lawnmower Division, assuming the following changes:
   1. Variable cost of goods sold is decreased by 15%.
   2. Average operating assets are decreased by 20%.
   3. Sales are increased by $500,000 and this increase is expected to increase contribution margin by $200,000.

P25–6A Ohse Company uses a responsibility reporting system. It has divisions in Denver, Seattle, and San Diego. Each division has three production departments: Cutting, Shaping, and Finishing. The responsibility for each department rests with a manager who reports to the division production manager. Each division manager reports to the vice president of production. There are also vice presidents for marketing and finance. All vice presidents report to the president.

Prepare reports for cost centers under responsibility accounting and comment on performance of managers.
(SO 4)

In January 1999, controllable actual and budget manufacturing overhead cost data for the departments and divisions were as follows:

Manufacturing Overhead	Actual	Budget
Individual costs—Cutting Department—Seattle		
Indirect labor	$ 73,000	$ 70,000
Indirect materials	46,700	46,000
Maintenance	20,500	18,000
Utilities	20,100	17,000
Supervision	20,000	20,000
	$ 180,300	$ 171,000

Manufacturing Overhead	Actual	Budget
Total costs		
Shaping Department—Seattle	$ 158,000	$ 148,000
Finishing Department—Seattle	210,000	208,000
Denver division	676,000	673,000
San Diego division	722,000	715,000
	$1,766,000	$1,744,000

Additional overhead costs were incurred as follows: Seattle division production manager—actual costs $52,500, budget $51,000; vice president of production—actual costs $65,000, budget $64,000; president—actual costs $76,400, budget $74,200. These expenses are not allocated.

The vice presidents who report to the president, other than the vice president of production, had the following expenses:

Vice president	Actual	Budget
Marketing	$133,600	$130,000
Finance	107,000	105,000

Instructions

(a) Prepare the following responsibility reports:
    (1) Manufacturing overhead—Cutting Department manager—Seattle division.
    (2) Manufacturing overhead—Seattle division manager.
    (3) Manufacturing overhead—vice president of production.
    (4) Manufacturing overhead and expenses—president. Use the format on page 1086.
(b) Comment on the comparative performances of
    (1) Department managers in the Seattle division.
    (2) Division managers.
    (3) Vice presidents.

PROBLEMS: SET B

Prepare flexible budget and budget report for manufacturing overhead.
(SO 3)

P25–1B Petrova Company estimates that 360,000 direct labor hours will be worked during the coming year, 1999, in the Packaging Department. On this basis, the following budgeted manufacturing overhead cost data are computed for the year:

Fixed Overhead Costs		Variable Overhead Costs	
Supervision	$ 90,000	Indirect labor	$144,000
Depreciation	54,000	Indirect materials	90,000
Insurance	27,000	Repairs	54,000
Rent	36,000	Utilities	72,000
Property taxes	18,000	Lubricants	18,000
	$225,000		$378,000

It is estimated that direct labor hours worked each month will range from 27,000 to 36,000 hours.

During October, 27,000 direct labor hours were worked and the following overhead costs were incurred:

Fixed overhead costs: Supervision $7,500, Depreciation $4,500, Insurance $2,225, Rent $3,000, and Property taxes $1,500.

Variable overhead costs: Indirect labor $11,760, Indirect materials, $6,400, Repairs $4,000, Utilities $5,900, and Lubricants $1,640.

Instructions

(a) Prepare a monthly flexible manufacturing overhead budget for each increment of 3,000 direct labor hours over the relevant range for the year ending December 31, 1999.

(b) Prepare a flexible budget report for October, when 27,500 direct labor hours were expected.

(c) Comment on management's efficiency in controlling manufacturing overhead costs in October.

P25–2B Matheny Company manufactures tablecloths. Sales have grown rapidly over the past 2 years. As a result, the president has installed a budgetary control system for 1999. The following data were used in developing the master manufacturing overhead budget for the Ironing Department, which is based on an activity index of direct labor hours.

Prepare flexible budget, budget report, and graph for manufacturing overhead.
(SO 3)

Variable Costs	Rate per Direct Labor Hour	Annual Fixed Costs	
Indirect labor	$.40	Supervision	$30,000
Indirect materials	.50	Depreciation	18,000
Factory utilities	.30	Insurance	12,000
Factory repairs	.20	Rent	24,000

The master overhead budget was prepared on the expectation that 480,000 direct labor hours will be worked during the year. In June, 42,000 direct labor hours were worked and 42,000 were expected. At that level of activity, actual costs were as follows:

Variable—per direct labor hour: Indirect labor $.42, Indirect materials $.50, Factory utilities $.32, and Factory repairs $.21.

Fixed: same as budgeted.

Instructions
(a) Prepare a monthly flexible manufacturing overhead budget for the year ending December 31, 1999, assuming production levels range from 35,000 to 50,000 direct labor hours. Use increments of 5,000 direct labor hours.
(b) Prepare a budget performance report for June comparing actual results with budget data based on the flexible budget.
(c) Were costs effectively controlled? Explain.
(d) State the formula for computing the total budgeted costs for Matheny Company.
(e) Prepare the flexible budget graph, showing total budgeted costs at 35,000 and 45,000 direct labor hours. Use increments of 5,000 direct labor hours on the horizontal axis and increments of $10,000 on the vertical axis.

P25–3B Fernandez Company uses budgets in controlling costs. The August 1999 budget report for the company's Assembling Department is as follows:

State total budgeted cost formula and prepare flexible budget reports for two time periods.
(SO 2, 3)

FERNANDEZ COMPANY
Budget Report
Assembling Department
For the Month Ended August 31, 1999

Manufacturing Costs	Budget	Actual	Difference Favorable F Unfavorable U
Variable costs			
Direct materials	$ 48,000	$ 47,000	$1,000 F
Direct labor	72,000	68,000	4,000 F
Indirect materials	24,000	24,200	200 U
Indirect labor	18,000	17,500	500 F
Utilities	15,000	14,900	100 F
Maintenance	9,000	9,200	200 U
Total variable	186,000	180,800	5,200 F
Fixed costs			
Rent	10,000	10,000	–0–
Supervision	15,000	15,000	–0–
Depreciation	7,000	7,000	–0–
Total fixed	32,000	32,000	–0–
Total costs	$218,000	$212,800	$5,200 F

The budget data in the report are based on the master budget for the year, which assumed that 720,000 units would be produced. The Assembling Department manager is pleased with the report and expects a raise, or at least praise for a job well done. The company president, however, is unhappy with the results for August, because only 58,000 units were produced. (*Hint:* The budget amounts above are one-twelfth of the master budget.)

Instructions

(a) State the total budgeted cost formula.

(b) Prepare a budget report for August using flexible budget data. Why does this report provide a better basis for evaluating performance than the report based on static budget data? Assume 62,000 units were expected to be produced.

(c) In September, 64,000 units were produced when 65,000 were expected. Prepare the budget report using flexible budget data, assuming (1) each variable cost was 10% higher than its actual cost in August, and (2) fixed costs were the same in September as in August.

Prepare responsibility report for a profit center.
(SO 6)

P25–4B Kohler Manufacturing Inc. operates the Patio Furniture Division as a profit center. Operating data for this division for the year ended December 31, 1999, are as follows:

	Budget	Difference from Budget
Sales	$2,500,000	$50,000 F
Cost of goods sold		
Variable	1,300,000	40,000 F
Controllable fixed	200,000	5,000 U
Selling and administrative		
Variable	220,000	5,000 U
Controllable fixed	50,000	2,000 U
Noncontrollable fixed costs	70,000	4,000 U

In addition, Kohler Manufacturing incurs $180,000 of indirect fixed costs that were budgeted at $175,000. Twenty percent (20%) of these costs are allocated to the Patio Furniture Division.

Instructions

(a) Prepare a responsibility report for the Patio Furniture Division for the year.

(b) Comment on the manager's performance in controlling revenues and costs.

(c) Identify any costs excluded from the responsibility report and explain why they were excluded.

Prepare responsibility report for an investment center and compute ROI.
(SO 7)

P25–5B Ingalls Manufacturing Company manufactures a variety of tools and industrial equipment. The company operates through three divisions. Each division is an investment center. Operating data for the Home Division for the year ended December 31, 1999, and relevant budget data are as follows:

	Actual	Comparison with Budget
Sales	$1,500,000	$100,000 favorable
Variable cost of goods sold	700,000	100,000 unfavorable
Variable selling and administrative expenses	125,000	25,000 unfavorable
Controllable fixed cost of goods sold	170,000	On target
Controllable fixed selling and administrative expenses	100,000	On target

Average operating assets for the year for the Home Division were $2,500,000 which was also the budgeted amount.

Instructions

(a) Prepare a responsibility report (in thousands of dollars) for the Home Division.

(b) Evaluate the manager's performance. Which items will likely be investigated by top management?

(c) Compute the expected ROI in 2000 for the Home Division, assuming the following changes:

1. Variable cost of goods sold is decreased by 6%.
2. Average operating assets are decreased by 10%.
3. Sales are increased by $200,000, and this increase is expected to increase contribution margin by $90,000.

BROADENING YOUR PERSPECTIVE

GROUP DECISION CASE

BYP25–1   Green Pastures is a 400-acre farm on the outskirts of the Kentucky Bluegrass, specializing in the boarding of broodmares and their foals. A recent economic downturn in the thoroughbred industry has led to a decline in breeding activities, and it has made the boarding business extremely competitive. To meet the competition, Green Pastures planned in 1999 to entertain clients, advertise more extensively, and absorb expenses formerly paid by clients such as veterinary and blacksmith fees.

The budget report for 1999 is presented below. As shown, the static income statement budget for the year is based on an expected 21,900 boarding days at $25 per mare. The variable expenses per mare per day were budgeted: Feed $5, Veterinary fees $3, Blacksmith fees $0.30, and Supplies $0.40. All other budgeted expenses were either semifixed or fixed.

During the year, management decided not to replace a worker who quit in March, but it did issue a new advertising brochure and did more entertaining of clients.[1]

GREEN PASTURES
Static Budget Income Statement
Year Ended December 31, 1999

	Actual	Master Budget	Difference
Number of mares	52	60	8*
Number of boarding days	18,980	21,900	2,920*
Sales	$379,600	$547,500	$167,900*
Less variable expenses:			
Feed	104,390	109,500	5,110
Veterinary fees	58,838	65,700	6,862
Blacksmith fees	6,074	6,570	496
Supplies	7,402	8,760	1,358
Total variable expenses	176,704	190,530	13,826
Contribution margin	202,896	356,970	154,074*
Less fixed expenses:			
Depreciation	40,000	40,000	–0–
Insurance	11,000	11,000	–0–
Utilities	12,000	14,000	2,000
Repairs and maintenance	10,000	11,000	1,000
Labor	88,000	96,000	8,000
Advertisement	12,000	8,000	4,000*
Entertainment	7,000	5,000	2,000*
Total fixed expense	180,000	185,000	5,000
Net income	$ 22,896	$171,970	$149,074*

*Unfavorable.

Instructions
With the class divided into groups, answer the following:

(a) Based on the static budget report,
  (1) What was the primary cause(s) of the loss in net income?
  (2) Did management do a good, average, or poor job of controlling expenses?
  (3) Were management's decisions to stay competitive sound?

[1]Data for this case are based on Hans Sprohge and John Talbott, "New Applications for Variance Analysis," *Journal of Accountancy* (AICPA, New York), April 1989, pp. 137–41.

(b) Prepare a flexible budget report for the year.

(c) Based on the flexible budget report, answer the three questions in part (a) above.

(d) What course of action do you recommend for the management of Green Pastures?

MANAGERIAL ANALYSIS

BYP25–2 Lakenvelder Dutch manufactures expensive watch cases sold as souvenirs. Three of its sales departments are: Retail Sales, Wholesale Sales, and Outlet Sales. The Retail Sales Department is a profit center. The Wholesale Sales Department, however, is a cost center, because its managers merely take orders from customers who purchase through the company's wholesale catalog. The Outlet Sales Department is an investment center, because each manager is given full responsibility for an outlet store location. The manager can hire and discharge employees, purchase, maintain, and sell equipment, and in general is fairly independent of company control.

Rena Worthington is a manager in the Retail Sales Department; Winston Hillhouse manages the Wholesale Sales Department; Oscar Hadley manages the Golden Gate Club outlet store in San Francisco. The following are the budget responsibility reports for each of the three departments:

Budget

	Retail Sales	Wholesale Sales	Outlet Sales
Sales	$ 750,000	$ 400,000	$200,000
Variable costs			
Cost of goods sold	150,000	100,000	25,000
Advertising	100,000	30,000	5,000
Sales salaries	75,000	15,000	3,000
Printing	10,000	20,000	5,000
Travel	20,000	30,000	2,000
Fixed costs			
Rent	50,000	30,000	10,000
Insurance	5,000	2,000	1,000
Depreciation	75,000	100,000	40,000
Investment in assets	$1,000,000	$1,200,000	$800,000

Actual Results

	Retail Sales	Wholesale Sales	Outlet Sales
Sales	$ 750,000	$ 400,000	$200,000
Variable costs			
Cost of goods sold	195,000	120,000	26,250
Advertising	100,000	30,000	5,000
Sales salaries	75,000	15,000	3,000
Printing	10,000	20,000	5,000
Travel	15,000	20,000	1,500
Fixed costs			
Rent	40,000	50,000	12,000
Insurance	5,000	2,000	1,000
Depreciation	80,000	90,000	60,000
Investment in assets	$1,000,000	$1,200,000	$800,000

Instructions

(a) Determine which of the items should be included in the responsibility report for each of the three managers.

(b) Compare the budgeted measures with the actual results. Decide which results should be called to the attention of each manager.

REAL-WORLD FOCUS:
Computer Associates International, Inc.

BYP25–3   **Computer Associates International** was incorporated in 1974. Today it designs, develops, markets, and supports standardized computer software products for use with mainframe, midrange, and desktop computers. The company has 6,900 employees who work in its 55 offices in the U.S. or its 62 offices throughout the world including Europe, Asia, Russia, Israel, South America, and New Zealand.

Presented below is information from the company's annual report:

COMPUTER ASSOCIATES INTERNATIONAL
Management Discussion

The Company has experienced a pattern of business whereby revenue for its third and fourth fiscal quarters reflects an increase over first- and second-quarter revenue. The Company attributes this increase to clients' increased spending at the end of their calendar year budgetary periods and the culmination of its annual sales plan. Since the Company's costs do not increase proportionately with the third- and fourth-quarters' increase in revenue, the higher revenue in these quarters results in greater profit margins and income. Fourth-quarter profitability is traditionally affected by significant new hirings, training, and education expenditures for the succeeding year.

Instructions
(a) Why don't the company's costs increase proportionately as the revenues increase in the third and fourth quarters?
(b) What type of budgeting seems appropriate for Computer Associate's situation?

COMMUNICATION ACTIVITY

BYP25–4   The manufacturing overhead budget for Reebles Company contains the following items:

Variable expenses	
Indirect materials	$25,000
Indirect labor	12,000
Maintenance expenses	10,000
Manufacturing supplies	6,000
Total variable	$53,000
Fixed expenses	
Supervision	$17,000
Inspection costs	1,000
Insurance expenses	2,000
Depreciation	15,000
Total fixed	$35,000

The budget was based on an estimated 2,000 units being produced. During the past month, 1,500 units were produced, and the following costs incurred:

Variable expenses		
Indirect materials	$25,200	
Indirect labor	13,500	
Maintenance expenses	8,200	
Manufacturing supplies	5,100	
Total variable		$52,000
Fixed expenses		
Supervision	$19,300	
Inspection costs	1,200	
Insurance expenses	2,200	
Depreciation	14,700	
Total fixed		$37,400

Instructions
(a) Determine which items would be controllable by Ed Lopat, the production manager.
(b) How much should have been spent during the month for the manufacture of the 1,500 units?
(c) Prepare a flexible manufacturing overhead budget report for Mr. Lopat.
(d) Prepare a responsibility report. Include only the costs that would have been controllable by Mr. Lopat. In an attached memo, describe clearly for Mr. Lopat the areas in which his performance needs to be improved.

RESEARCH ASSIGNMENT

BYP25–5   The January 1998 issue of *Management Accounting* contains an article by Guy Haddleton entitled "10 Rules for Selecting Budget Management Software."

Instructions
Read the article and answer the following questions:
(a) In December 1996, International Data Corp. identified a new category of business management software—budget management. What is the meaning of budget management? Why is budget management complicated for any mid- to large-scale organization?
(b) As the foundation for the budget management system, why is the spreadsheet solution failing?
(c) The author of the article classifies his 10 rules into four categories that identify the demands of a budget management system, the demands that the spreadsheet solution fails to satisfy. What are these four categories of demands?
(d) What are the 10 requirements for a budget management system?

ETHICS CASE

BYP25–6   National Products Corporation participates in a highly competitive industry. In order to meet this competition and achieve profit goals, the company has chosen the decentralized form of organization. Each manager of a decentralized investment center is measured on the basis of profit contribution, market penetration, and return on investment. Failure to meet the objectives established by corporate management for these measures has not been acceptable and usually has resulted in demotion or dismissal of an investment center manager.

An anonymous survey of managers in the company revealed that the managers feel the pressure to compromise their personal ethical standards to achieve the corporate objectives. For example, at certain plant locations there was pressure to reduce quality control to a level which could not assure that all unsafe products would be rejected. Also, sales personnel were encouraged to use questionable sales tactics to obtain orders, including gifts and other incentives to purchasing agents.

The chief executive officer is disturbed by the survey findings. In his opinion such behavior cannot be condoned by the company. He concludes that the company should do something about this problem.

Instructions
(a) Who are the stakeholders (the affected parties) in this situation?
(b) Identify the ethical implications, conflicts, or dilemmas in the above described situation.
(c) What might the company do to reduce the pressures on managers and decrease the ethical conflicts?

(CMA adapted)

SURFING THE NET

BYP25–7 Genelle and Doug have recorded the story of their wedding planning. They are on a strict budget and need help in preparing what they call "a somewhat flexible budget."

Address: http://www.wednet.com/inspire/wedstory/story1.htm

Steps:
1. Go to Genelle and Doug's Web site and read about their trials and tribulations in planning a wedding.
2. Review the **Planning and Budgeting** section in "Part 1" of their story. They mention that this is a "somewhat flexible budget" for 250 guests, totalling $7,150. They would like to reduce their total costs to $7,000, if at all possible.

Instructions
Recast Genelle and Doug's budget into a truly flexible budget so that they can see the effects on their total costs of reducing the number of invited guests to 225 or 200.

Answers to Self-Study Questions
1. c   2. b   3. a   4. d   5. a   6. d   7. d   8. b   9. b   10. d

Answer to Kellogg Review It Question 3, p. 1095
3. Kellogg does not say in its annual report that it uses investment centers but does characterize its business by the following product lines: ready-to-eat cereals, toaster pastries, frozen waffles, cereal bars, and bagels.

Remember to go back to the Navigator box on the chapter-opening page and check off your completed work.

FEATURE STORY

Highlighting Performance Efficiency

There's a very good chance that the highlighter you're holding in your hand was made by Sanford, a maker of markers and other writing instruments. Sanford, headquartered in Illinois, annually sells hundreds of millions of dollars' worth of ACCENT highlighters, fine-point pens, Sharpie markers for overhead projectors, and other writing instruments.

Since Sanford makes literally billions of writing utensils per year, the company must keep tight control over manufacturing costs. As a result, a very important part of Sanford's manufacturing process is the determination of how much direct materials, labor, and overhead should cost. These costs are then compared to actual costs to assess performance efficiency. Raw materials for Sanford's markers include a barrel, plug, cap, ink reservoir, and a nib (tip). These parts are assembled by machine to produce thousands of units per hour. A major component of manufacturing overhead, then, includes machine maintenance—some fixed, some variable.

There's still a labor component, though: the machine operator, who makes or breaks productivity. "We try to control labor efficiency the best we can," says Tom Beyer, Sanford's vice president–controller. "But excessive labor time is often due to malfunctioning equipment—which is difficult to control."

In contrast, labor rates are more predictable because the hourly workers are covered by a union contract. The story is the same with the fringe benefits and some supervisory salaries. Even volume levels are fairly predictable—demand for the product is high—so that fixed overhead is efficiently absorbed. Raw material standard costs are based on the previous year's actual prices plus any anticipated inflation. Lately, though, inflation has been so low that the company is considering any price increase in raw material to be unfavorable.

THE NAVIGATOR

On the World Wide Web
http://www.sanfordcorp.com

CHAPTER 26

PERFORMANCE EVALUATION THROUGH STANDARD COSTS

THE NAVIGATOR ✔

- ■ Understand *Concepts for Review* ☐
- ■ Read *Feature Story* ☐
- ■ Scan *Study Objectives* ☐
- ■ Read *Preview* ☐
- ■ Read text and answer *Before You Go On*
  p. 1122 ☐ p. 1133 ☐ p. 1138 ☐
- ■ Work *Demonstration Problems* ☐
- ■ Review *Summary of Study Objectives* ☐
- ■ Answer *Self-Study Questions* ☐
- ■ Complete assignments ☐

STUDY OBJECTIVES

After studying this chapter, you should be able to:

1. *Distinguish between a standard and a budget.*
2. *Identify the advantages of standard costs.*
3. *Describe how standards are set.*
4. *Indicate the formulas for determining direct materials and direct labor variances.*
5. *State the formulas for determining manufacturing overhead variances.*
6. *Discuss the reporting of variances.*
7. *Enumerate the features of a standard cost accounting system.*

*I*n this chapter we continue the study of controlling costs by considering additional measures that permit the evaluation of performance. The content and organization of this chapter are as follows:

PERFORMANCE EVALUATION THROUGH STANDARD COSTS

Need for Standards
- Standards vs. budgets
- Why standard costs?

Setting Standards
- Ideal vs. normal
- Case study

Variances from Standards
- Analyzing
- Reporting

Standard Cost Accounting System
- Journal entries
- Ledger accounts
- Statement presentation

THE NAVIGATOR

THE NEED FOR STANDARDS

Standards are a fact of life. You met the admission standards for the college or university you are attending. The automobile that you drive had to meet certain governmental emissions standards. The hamburgers and salads you eat in a restaurant have to meet certain health and nutritional standards before they can be sold. The reason for standards in these cases is very simple: They help to ensure that the overall quality of the product produced is high. Without standards, quality control is lost.

Standards are also common in business. Those imposed by government agencies are often called **regulations**. They include the Fair Labor Standards Act, the Equal Employment Opportunity Act, and a multitude of environmental standards. Standards established internally by a company may extend to personnel matters, such as employee absenteeism and ethical codes of conduct, quality control standards for products, and standard costs for goods and services. In managerial accounting, standard costs are predetermined unit costs, which are used as measures of performance.

Although we will focus on manufacturing operations in the remainder of this chapter, you should also recognize that standard costs are also applicable to many other types of businesses. For example, a fast-food restaurant such as McDonald's knows not only the price it should pay for pickles, beef, buns, and other ingredients, but also how much time it should take an employee to flip hamburgers. If too much is paid for pickles or too much time is taken to prepare Big Macs, the deviations are noticed and corrective action is taken. Moreover, standard costs may be used in not-for-profit enterprises such as universities, charitable organizations, and governmental agencies.

Distinguishing between Standards and Budgets

In concept, **standards** and **budgets** are essentially the same. Both are predetermined costs and both contribute significantly to management planning and control. There is a difference, however, in the way the terms are expressed. A standard is a **unit** amount, whereas a budget is a **total** amount. Thus, it is customary to state that the standard cost of direct labor for a unit of product is $10. However, if 5,000 units of the product are produced, the $50,000 of direct labor is the budgeted labor cost. In this context, a standard is the budgeted cost per unit of product. A standard is, therefore, concerned with each individual cost component that makes up the entire budget.

There are important accounting differences between budgets and standards. Except in the application of manufacturing overhead to jobs and processes, budget data are not journalized in cost accounting systems. In contrast, as will be illustrated later in the chapter, standard costs may be incorporated into cost accounting systems. It is also possible for a company to report its inventories at standard cost in its financial statements, but it is not possible to report inventories at budgeted costs.

Why Standard Costs?

Standard costs offer a number of advantages to an organization, as shown in Illustration 26-1. These advantages will be realized only when standard costs are carefully established and prudently used. Using standards solely as a means of finding fault or placing blame can have a negative effect on managers and em-

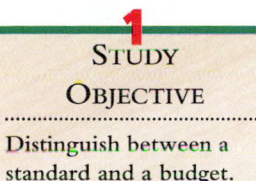

STUDY OBJECTIVE

Distinguish between a standard and a budget.

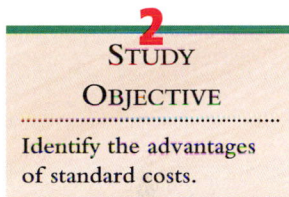

STUDY OBJECTIVE

Identify the advantages of standard costs.

ILLUSTRATION 26-1

Advantages of standard costs

Advantages of standard costs

Facilitate management planning

Promote greater economy by making employees more "cost-conscious"

Useful in setting selling prices

Contribute to management control by providing basis for evaluation of cost control

Useful in highlighting variances in management by exception

Simplify costing of inventories and reduce clerical costs

ployees. In an effort to minimize this effect, many companies offer wage incentives to those who meet their standards.

SETTING STANDARD COSTS— A DIFFICULT TASK

3

STUDY

OBJECTIVE

Describe how standards are set.

The setting of standard costs to produce a unit of product is a difficult task. It requires input from all persons who have responsibility for costs and quantities. To determine the standard cost of direct materials, management may have to consult the purchasing agents, product managers, quality control engineers, and production supervisors. In setting the cost standard for direct labor, pay rate data are obtained from the payroll department, and the labor time requirements may be determined by industrial engineers. The managerial accountant provides input into the standards-setting process by accumulating historical cost data and by knowing how costs respond to changes in activity levels. The decision as to what the standard cost should be is, of course, a management responsibility.

To be effective in controlling costs, standard costs need to be current at all times. Thus, standards should be under continuous review and should be changed whenever it is determined that the existing standard is not a good measure of performance. Circumstances that may warrant revision of a standard include changed wage rates resulting from a new union contract, a change in product specifications, or the implementation of a new manufacturing method.

TECHNOLOGY IN ACTION

Computerized standard cost systems represent one of the most complex accounting systems to develop and maintain. The standard cost system must be fully integrated into the general ledger, allow for the creation and timely maintenance of the data base of standard usage and costs for every product, and perform various variance computations. Such systems must also produce variance reports by product, department, or employee. With the increased use of automation and robotics, the computerized standard cost system may even be tied directly into these systems to gather variance information.

Ideal versus Normal Standards

Standards may be set at one of two levels: ideal or normal. **Ideal standards** represent optimum levels of performance under perfect operating conditions. In contrast, **normal standards** represent efficient levels of performance that are attainable under expected operating conditions.

Some managers believe ideal standards will stimulate the conscientious worker to ever-increasing improvement. However, most managers believe that because these standards are so difficult, if not impossible, to meet, they discourage self-improvement and lower the morale of the entire workforce. Very few companies use ideal standards.

Most companies that use standards set them at a normal level. Properly set, normal standards should be **rigorous but attainable**. Normal standards allow for rest periods, machine breakdowns, and other "normal" contingencies in the production process. It will be assumed in the remainder of this chapter that standard costs are set at a normal level.

ETHICS NOTE

When standards are set too high, employees sometimes feel pressure to consider unethical practices to meet these standards.

A Case Study

To establish the standard cost of producing a product, it is necessary to establish standards for each manufacturing cost element—direct materials, direct labor, and manufacturing overhead. The standard for each element is derived from a consideration of the standard price to be paid and the standard quantity to be used. To illustrate, in the remainder of this section we will look at a case study of how standard costs are set. In this extended example, we will assume that Xonic, Inc., wishes to use standard costs to measure performance in filling an order for 1,000 gallons of Weed-O, a liquid weed killer.

Direct Materials

The **direct materials price standard** is the cost per unit of direct materials that should be incurred. This standard should be based on the purchasing department's best estimate of the **cost of raw materials**. This is frequently based on an analysis of current purchase prices. The price standard should also include an amount for related costs such as receiving, storing, and handling. The materials price standard per pound of material for Xonic's weed killer is:

Item	Price
Purchase price, net of discounts	$2.70
Freight	.20
Receiving and handling	.10
Standard direct materials price per pound	**$3.00**

ILLUSTRATION 26-2

Setting direct materials price standard

The **direct materials quantity standard** is the quantity of direct materials that should be used per unit of finished goods. This standard is expressed as a physical measure, such as pounds, barrels, or board feet. In setting the standard, management should consider both the quality and quantity of materials required to manufacture the product. The standard should include allowances for unavoidable waste and normal spoilage. To illustrate, the standard quantity per unit for Xonic, Inc., is as follows:

Item	Quantity (Pounds)
Required materials	3.5
Allowance for waste	.4
Allowance for spoilage	.1
Standard direct materials quantity per unit	**4.0**

ILLUSTRATION 26-3

Setting direct materials quantity standard

The standard direct materials cost per unit is the standard direct materials price times the standard direct materials quantity. For Xonic, Inc., the standard direct material costs per gallon of Weed-O is $12.00 ($3.00 × 4.0 pounds).

Direct Labor

The **direct labor price standard** is the rate per hour that should be incurred for direct labor. This standard is based on current wage rates adjusted for anticipated changes, such as cost of living adjustments (COLAs) included in many union contracts. In addition, the price standard generally includes employer payroll

ALTERNATIVE TERMINOLOGY

The direct labor price standard is also called the *direct labor rate standard*.

taxes and fringe benefits, such as paid holidays and vacations. For Xonic, Inc., the direct labor price standard is as follows:

ILLUSTRATION 26-4

Setting direct labor price standard

Item	Price
Hourly wage rate	$ 7.50
COLA	.25
Payroll taxes	.75
Fringe benefits	1.50
Standard direct labor rate per hour	**$10.00**

ALTERNATIVE TERMINOLOGY

The direct labor quantity standard is also called the *direct labor efficiency standard.*

The **direct labor quantity standard** is the time that should be required to make one unit of the product. This standard is especially critical in labor-intensive (as opposed to capital-intensive) companies. Allowances should be made in this standard for rest periods, cleanup, machine setup, and machine downtime. For Xonic, Inc., the direct labor quantity standard is as follows:

ILLUSTRATION 26-5

Setting direct labor quantity standard

Item	Quantity (Hours)
Actual production time	1.5
Rest periods and cleanup	.2
Setup and downtime	.3
Standard direct labor hours per unit	**2.0**

The standard direct labor cost per unit is the standard direct labor rate times the standard direct labor hours. For Xonic, Inc., the standard direct labor cost per gallon of Weed-O is $20 ($10.00 × 2.0 hours).

Manufacturing Overhead

Calculating the overhead rate

Overhead ÷ Labor hours

For manufacturing overhead, a **standard predetermined overhead rate** is used in setting the standard. This overhead rate is determined by dividing budgeted overhead costs by an expected standard activity index. For example, the index may be standard direct labor hours or standard machine hours. Xonic, Inc., uses standard direct labor hours as the activity index. The company expects to produce 13,200 gallons of Weed-O during the year at normal capacity. Since it takes two direct labor hours for each gallon, total standard direct labor hours are 26,400 (13,200 × 2). At this level of activity, overhead costs are expected to be $132,000, of which $79,200 are variable and $52,800 are fixed. The standard predetermined overhead rates, therefore, are computed as shown in Illustration 26-6:

ILLUSTRATION 26-6

Computing predetermined overhead rates

Budgeted Overhead Costs	Amount	÷	Standard Direct Labor Hours	=	Overhead Rate per Direct Labor Hour
Variable	$ 79,200		26,400		**$3.00**
Fixed	52,800		26,400		**2.00**
Total	$132,000		26,400		**$5.00**

The standard manufacturing overhead rate per unit is the predetermined overhead rate times the activity index quantity standard. For Xonic, Inc., which uses direct labor hours as its activity index, the standard manufacturing overhead rate per gallon of Weed-O is $10 ($5 × 2 hours).

Total Standard Cost per Unit

Now that the standard quantity and price have been established per unit of product, the total standard cost can be determined. The total standard cost per unit is the sum of the standard costs of direct materials, direct labor, and manufacturing overhead. For Xonic, Inc., the total standard cost per gallon of Weed-O is $42, as shown on the following standard cost card:

ILLUSTRATION 26-7

Standard cost per gallon of Weed-O

Product: Weed-O		Unit Measure: Gallon		
Manufacturing Cost Elements	Standard Quantity	×	Standard Price	= Standard Cost
Direct materials	4 pounds		$ 3.00	$12.00
Direct labor	2 hours		$10.00	$20.00
Manufacturing overhead	2 hours		$ 5.00	$10.00
				$42.00

A standard cost card is prepared for each product. This card provides the basis for determining variances from standards.

ACCOUNTING IN ACTION
Business Insight

Setting standards can be difficult. Consider Susan's Chili Factory, which manufactures and sells chili. The cost of manufacturing Susan's chili consists of the costs of raw materials, labor to convert the basic ingredients to chili, and overhead. We will use material cost as an example. Three standards need to be developed: (1) What should be the formula (mix) of ingredients for one gallon of chili? (2) What should be the normal wastage (or shrinkage) for the individual ingredients? (3) What should be the standard cost for the individual ingredients that go into the chili?

Susan's Chili Factory also illustrates how standard costs can be used by management in controlling costs. Suppose that summer droughts have reduced crop yields and, as a result, prices have doubled for beans, onions, and peppers. In such a case, actual costs will be significantly higher than standard costs, which will cause management to evaluate the situation. Such an evaluation might lead to an increase in the price charged for a gallon of chili, reexamination of the product mix to see if other types of ingredients can be used, or curtailment of production until ingredients can be purchased at or near standard costs. Similarly, assume that poor maintenance procedures caused the onion-dicing blades to become dull. As a result, usage of onions to make a gallon of chili tripled. Because this deviation is quickly highlighted through standard costs, corrective action can be promptly taken.

Source: Adapted from David R. Beran, "Cost Reduction Through Control Reporting," Management Accounting, April 1982, pp. 29–33.

BEFORE YOU GO ON . . .

Review It

1. How do standards differ from budgets?
2. What are the advantages of standard costs to an organization?
3. Distinguish between normal standards and ideal standards. Which standard is more widely used? Why?

Do It

The management of Arapahoe Company has decided to use standard costs. Management asks you to explain the components used in setting the standard cost per unit for direct materials, direct labor, and manufacturing overhead.

Reasoning: Each standard has two components: price and quantity.

Solution: The standard direct materials cost per unit is the standard direct materials price times the standard direct materials quantity. The standard direct labor cost per unit is the standard direct labor rate times the standard direct labor hours. The standard manufacturing overhead rate per unit is the standard predetermined overhead rate times the activity index quantity standard.

Related exercise material: BE26–2, BE26–3, and E26–1.

VARIANCES FROM STANDARDS

ALTERNATIVE TERMINOLOGY

In business, the term *variance* is also used to indicate differences between total budgeted and total actual costs.

One of the major management uses of standard costs is to identify variances from standards. **Variances** are the differences between total actual costs and total standard costs. To illustrate, we will assume that in producing 1,000 gallons of Weed-O in the month of June, Xonic, Inc., incurred the following costs:

ILLUSTRATION 26-8

Actual production costs

Direct materials	$13,020
Direct labor	20,580
Variable overhead	6,500
Fixed overhead	4,400
Total actual costs	$44,500

Total standard costs are determined by multiplying the units produced by the standard cost per unit. The total standard cost of Weed-O is $42,000 (1,000 gallons × $42). Thus, the total variance is $2,500, as shown below:

ILLUSTRATION 26-9

Computation of total variance

Actual costs	$44,500
Standard costs	42,000
Total variance	**$ 2,500**

Note that the variance is expressed in total dollars and not on a per unit basis.

When actual costs exceed standard costs, the variance is **unfavorable**. Thus, the $2,500 variance is unfavorable. An unfavorable variance has a negative con-

notation. It suggests that too much was paid for one or more of the manufacturing cost elements or that the elements were used inefficiently.

If actual costs are less than standard costs, the variance is **favorable**. A favorable variance has a positive inference. It suggests efficiencies in incurring manufacturing costs and in using direct materials, direct labor, and manufacturing overhead. However, be careful: A favorable variance could be obtained by using inferior materials. In printing wedding invitations, for example, a favorable variance could result from using an inferior grade of paper. Similarly, a favorable variance might be achieved in installing tires on an automobile assembly line by tightening only half of the lug bolts. The point should be obvious: A variance is not favorable if quality control standards have been sacrificed.

Analyzing Variances

To interpret properly the significance of a variance, you must analyze it to determine the underlying factors. Analyzing variances begins with a determination of the cost elements that comprise the variance. **For each manufacturing cost element, a total dollar variance is computed. Then this variance is analyzed into a price variance and a quantity variance.** The relationships are shown graphically as follows:

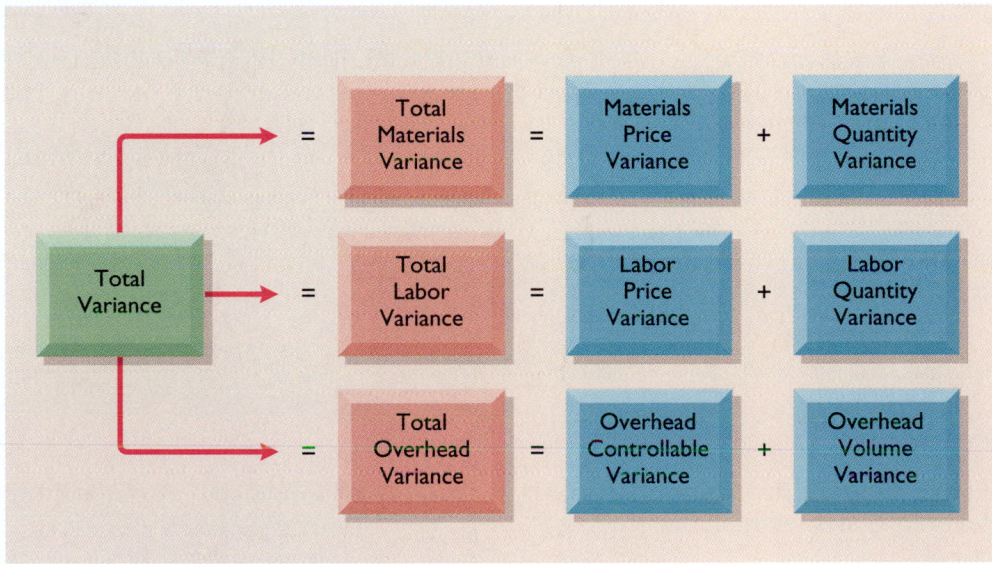

ILLUSTRATION 26-10

Relationships of variances

Each of the variances is explained below.

Direct Materials Variances

In completing the order for 1,000 gallons of Weed-O, Xonic used 4,200 pounds of direct materials purchased at a cost of $3.10 per unit. The **total materials variance** is computed from the following formula:

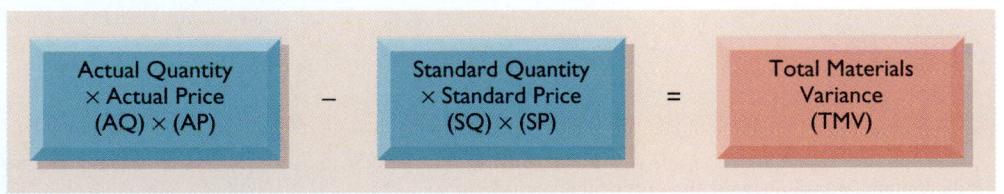

4

STUDY
OBJECTIVE

Indicate the formulas for determining direct materials and direct labor variances.

ILLUSTRATION 26-11

Formula for total materials variance

For Xonic, Inc., the total materials variance is $1,020 ($13,020 − $12,000) unfavorable as shown below:

$$(4,200 \times \$3.10) - (4,000 \times \$3.00) = \$1,020 \text{ U}$$

Next, the total variance is analyzed to determine the amount attributable to costs and to quantity (use). The **materials price variance** is computed from the formula shown in Illustration 26-12.[1]

ILLUSTRATION 26-12

Formula for materials price variance

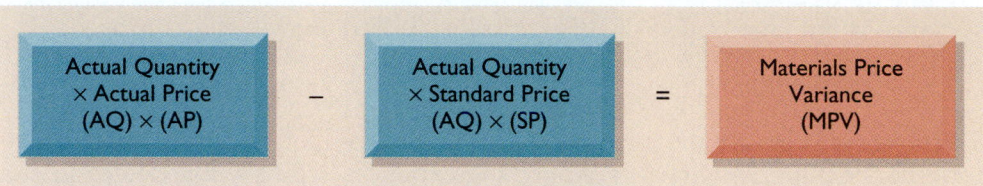

For Xonic, Inc., the materials price variance is $420 ($13,020 − $12,600) unfavorable as shown below:

$$(4,200 \times \$3.10) - (4,200 \times \$3.00) = \$420 \text{ U}$$

HELPFUL HINT

The alternative formula is:

$$\boxed{\text{AQ}} \times \boxed{\text{AP} - \text{SP}} = \boxed{\text{MPV}}$$

The price variance can also be computed by multiplying the actual quantity purchased by the difference between the actual and standard price per unit. The computation in this case is $4,200 \times (\$3.10 - \$3.00) = \$420$ U.

The **materials quantity variance** is determined from the following formula:

ILLUSTRATION 26-13

Formula for materials quantity variance

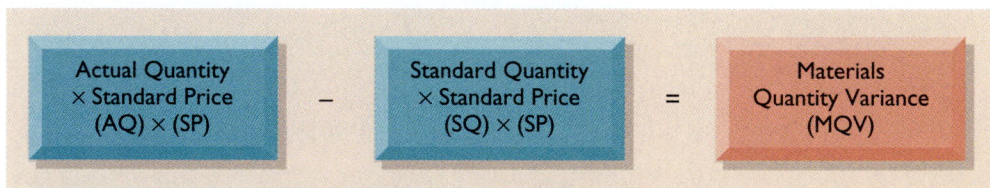

For Xonic, Inc., the materials quantity variance is $600 ($12,600 − $12,000) unfavorable, as shown below:

$$(4,200 \times \$3.00) - (4,000 \times \$3.00) = \$600 \text{ U}$$

HELPFUL HINT

The alternative formula is:

$$\boxed{\text{SP}} \times \boxed{\text{AQ} - \text{SQ}} = \boxed{\text{MQV}}$$

This variance can also be computed by applying the standard price to the difference between actual and standard quantities used. The computation in this example is $3.00 \times (4,200 - 4,000) = \$600$ U.

The total materials variance of $1,020(U), therefore, consists of the following:

ILLUSTRATION 26-14

Summary of materials variance

Materials price variance	$ 420 U
Materials quantity variance	600 U
Total materials variance	**$1,020 U**

---

[1]We will assume that all materials purchased during the period are used in production and that no units remain in inventory at the end of the period.

A matrix is sometimes used to determine and analyze a variance. **When the matrix is used, the formulas for each cost element are computed first and then the variances.** The completed matrix for the direct materials variance for Xonic, Inc. is shown in Illustration 26-15. The matrix provides a convenient structure for determining each variance.

ILLUSTRATION 26-15

Matrix for direct materials variance

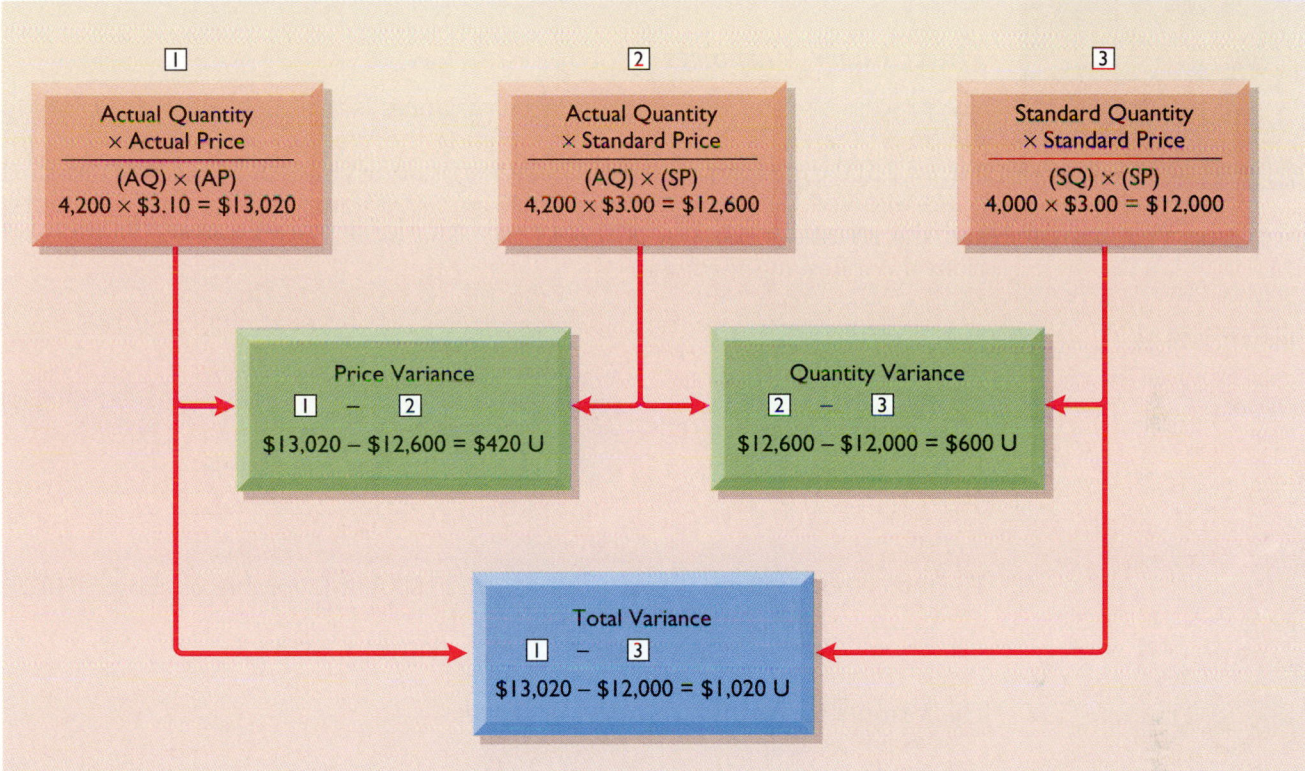

Causes of Materials Variances. What are the causes of a variance? The causes may relate to both internal and external factors. **The investigation of a materials price variance usually begins in the purchasing department.** Many factors affect the price paid for raw materials. These include the delivery method used, availability of quantity and cash discounts, and the quality of the materials requested. To the extent that these factors have been considered in setting the price standard, the purchasing department should be responsible for any variances. However, a variance may be beyond the control of the purchasing department. In a period of inflation, prices may rise faster than expected. Moreover, actions by groups over which the company has no control, such as the OPEC nations' oil price increases, may cause an unfavorable variance. There are also times when a production department may be responsible for the price variance. This may occur when a rush order forces the company to pay a higher price for the materials.

The starting point for determining the cause(s) of an unfavorable **materials quantity variance** is in the **production department**. If the variances are due to inexperienced workers, faulty machinery, or carelessness, the production department would be responsible. However, if the materials obtained by the purchasing department were of inferior quality, then the purchasing department should be responsible.

ACCOUNTING IN ACTION
Business Insight

If purchase price variances are used as a basis for measuring performance, purchasing departments often will continually search for the lowest cost item. However, this situation can become counterproductive if it leads to late deliveries of the goods or the purchase of inferior quality goods.

Direct Labor Variances

The process of determining direct labor variances is the same as for determining the direct materials variances. In completing the Weed-O order, Xonic, Inc., incurred 2,100 direct labor hours at an average hourly rate of $9.80. The standard hours allowed for the units produced were 2,000 hours (1,000 units × 2 hours) and the standard rate was $10 per hour. The **total labor variance** is obtained from the following formula:

ILLUSTRATION 26-16

Formula for total labor variance

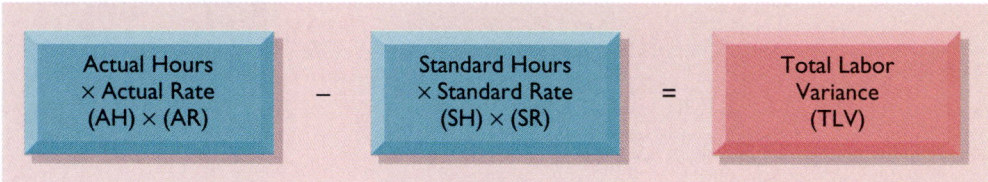

The total labor variance is $580 ($20,580 − $20,000) unfavorable, as shown below:

$$(2,100 \times \$9.80) - (2,000 \times \$10.00) = \$580 \text{ U}$$

The formula for the **labor price variance** is:

ILLUSTRATION 26-17

Formula for labor price variance

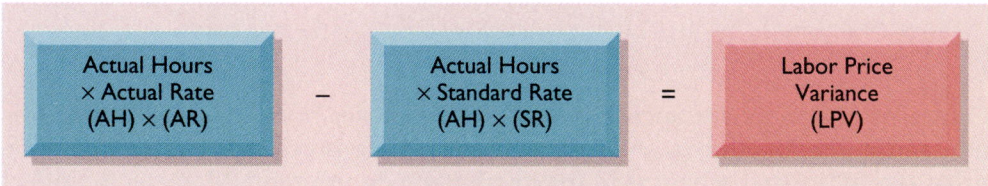

For Xonic, Inc., the labor price variance is $420 ($20,580 − $21,000) favorable as shown below.

$$(2,100 \times \$9.80) - (2,100 \times \$10.00) = \$420 \text{ F}$$

HELPFUL HINT

The alternative formula is:

This variance can also be computed by multiplying actual hours worked by the difference between the actual pay rate and the standard pay rate. The computation in this example is 2,100 × ($10.00 − $9.80) = $420 F.

The **labor quantity variance** is derived from the following formula:

ILLUSTRATION 26-18

Formula for labor quantity variance

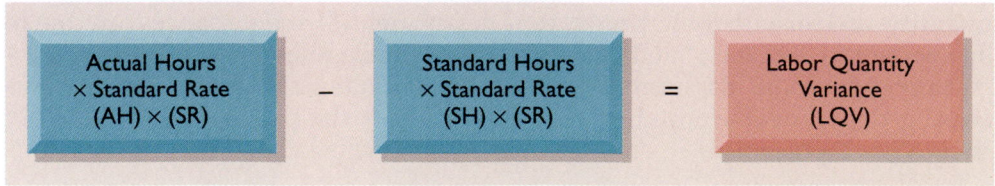

For Xonic, Inc., the labor quantity variance is $1,000 ($21,000 − $20,000) un-favorable:

$$(2,100 \times \$10.00) - (2,000 \times \$10.00) = \$1,000 \text{ U}$$

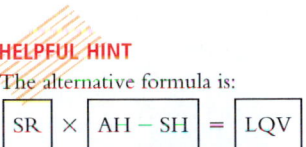

HELPFUL HINT
The alternative formula is:

$$\boxed{SR} \times \boxed{AH - SH} = \boxed{LQV}$$

The same result can be obtained by multiplying the standard rate by the difference between actual hours worked and standard hours allowed. In this case the computation is $10.00 × (2,100 − 2,000) = $1,000 U.

The total direct labor variance of $580 U, therefore, consists of:

ILLUSTRATION 26-19

Summary of labor variances

Labor price variance	$ 420 F
Labor quantity variance	1,000 U
Total direct labor variance	**$ 580 U**

ILLUSTRATION 26-20

Matrix for direct labor variances

These results can also be obtained from the matrix in Illustration 26-20.

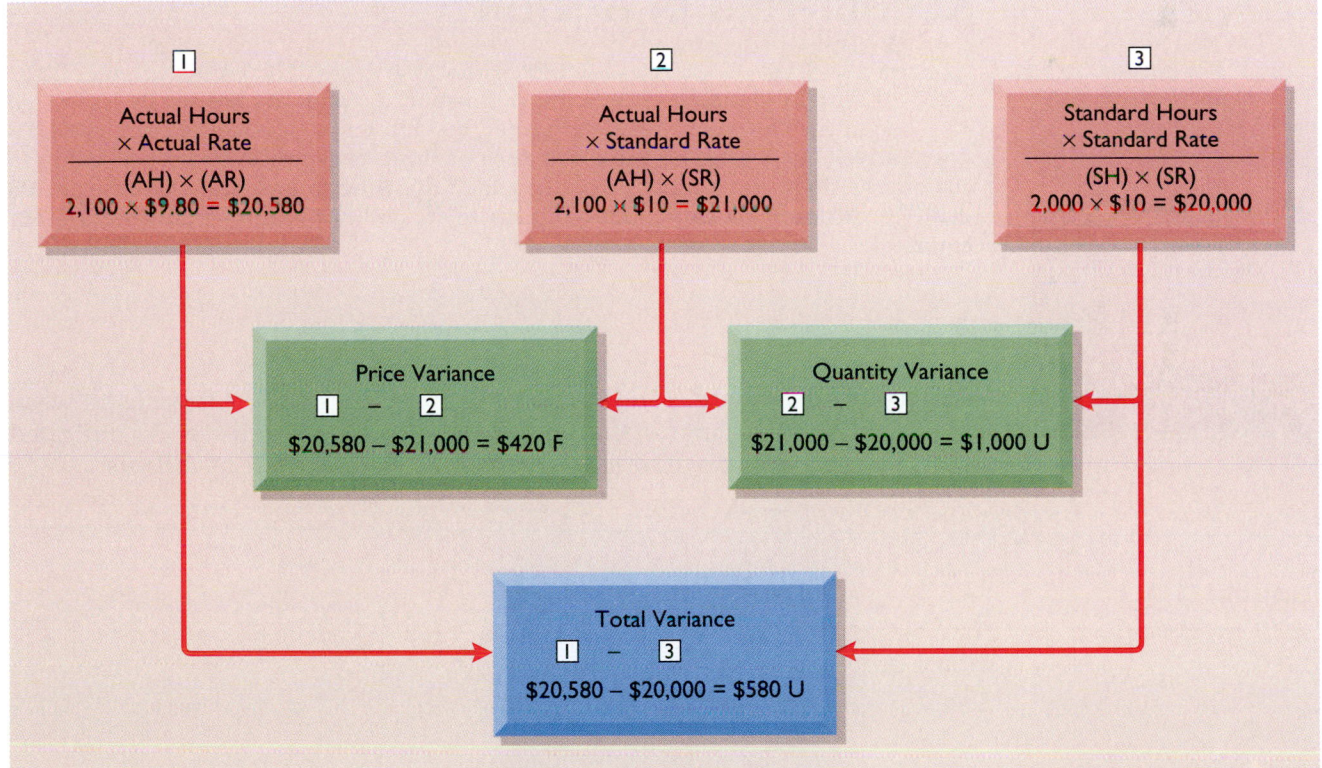

Causes of Labor Variances. **Labor price variances** usually result from two factors: (1) paying workers **higher wages than expected**, and **(2) misallocation of workers**. In companies where pay rates are determined by union contracts, labor price variances should be infrequent. When workers are not unionized, there is a much higher likelihood of such variances. The responsibility for these variances rests with the manager who authorized the wage increase. Misallocation of the workforce refers to using skilled workers in place of unskilled workers and vice versa. The use of an inexperienced worker instead of an experienced one will result in a favorable price variance because of the lower pay rate of the unskilled

"What caused labor price variances?"

Personnel decisions

worker. An unfavorable price variance would result if the skilled worker were substituted for the inexperienced employee. The production department generally is responsible for labor price variances resulting from misallocation of the workforce.

Labor quantity variances relate to the **efficiency of workers**. An investigation of the causes of a quantity variance generally focuses on the production department. The causes of an unfavorable variance may be poor training, worker fatigue, faulty machinery, or carelessness. These causes are the responsibility of the **production department**. However, if the excess time is due to inferior materials, the responsibility falls outside the production department.

5
STUDY
OBJECTIVE
....
State the formulas for determining manufacturing overhead variances.

Manufacturing Overhead Variances

The computation of the manufacturing overhead variances is conceptually the same as the computation of the materials and labor variances. However, the task is more challenging for manufacturing overhead because both variable and fixed overhead costs must be considered.

ACCOUNTING IN ACTION
Business Insight

At United Parcel Service (UPS) performance standards are set by industrial engineers for many tasks performed by UPS employees. For example, a UPS driver is expected to walk at a pace of three feet per second when going to a customer's door and knock rather than take the time to look for a doorbell. UPS executives attribute the company's success to its ability to manage and hold labor accountable.

Total Overhead Variance.   The total overhead variance is the difference between actual overhead costs and overhead costs applied to work done. As indicated earlier, manufacturing overhead costs incurred were $10,900, as follows:

ILLUSTRATION 26-21

Actual overhead costs

Variable overhead	$ 6,500
Fixed overhead	4,400
Total actual overhead	$10,900

With standard costs, manufacturing overhead costs are applied to work in process on the basis of the **standard hours allowed** for the work done. Standard hours allowed are the hours that should have been worked for the units produced. For the Weed-O order, the standard hours allowed are 2,000 and the predetermined overhead rate is $5 per direct labor hour. Thus, overhead applied is $10,000 (2,000 × $5). Note that actual hours of direct labor (2,100) are not used in applying manufacturing overhead.

The formula for the total overhead variance is:

ILLUSTRATION 26-22

Formula for total overhead variance

Thus, for Xonic, Inc., the total overhead variance is $900 unfavorable as shown below:

$$\$10,900 - \$10,000 = \$900 \text{ U}$$

The overhead variance is generally analyzed through a price variance and a quantity variance. The name usually given to the price variance is the **overhead controllable variance**, whereas the quantity variance is referred to as the **overhead volume variance**.

Overhead Controllable Variance. The overhead controllable variance shows whether overhead costs were effectively controlled. To compute this variance, actual overhead costs incurred are compared with budgeted costs for the **standard hours allowed**. The budgeted costs are determined from the flexible manufacturing overhead budget. The budget for Xonic, Inc., is as follows:

ALTERNATIVE TERMINOLOGY
The overhead controllable variance is also called the *budget* or *spending variance.*

ILLUSTRATION 26-23

Flexible budget using standard direct labor hours

XONIC, INC. Flexible Manufacturing Overhead Budget				
Activity Index				
Standard direct labor hours	1,800	2,000	2,200	2,400
Costs				
Variable costs				
Indirect materials	$1,800	$ 2,000	$ 2,200	$ 2,400
Indirect labor	2,700	3,000	3,300	3,600
Utilities	900	1,000	1,100	1,200
Total variable	5,400	6,000	6,600	7,200
Fixed costs				
Supervision	3,000	3,000	3,000	3,000
Depreciation	1,400	1,400	1,400	1,400
Total fixed	4,400	4,400	4,400	4,400
Total costs	$9,800	$10,400	$11,000	$11,600

As shown, the budgeted costs for 2,000 standard hours are $10,400 ($6,000 variable and $4,400 fixed).[2]

---

[2]The flexible budget formula is: fixed costs $4,400 plus variable costs $3 per hour. Thus, total budgeted costs are $4,400 + ($3 × 2,000), or $10,400.

The formula for the overhead controllable variance is:

ILLUSTRATION 26-24

Formula for overhead controllable variance

* Based on standard hours allowed.

The overhead controllable variance for Xonic, Inc., is $500 unfavorable as shown below:

$$\$10,900 - \$10,400 = \$500 \text{ U}$$

Most controllable variances are associated with variable costs which are controllable costs. Fixed costs are usually known at the time the budget is prepared. In Xonic, Inc., the variance is accounted for by comparing the actual variable overhead costs ($6,500) with the budgeted variable costs ($6,000).

If management desires, actual and budgeted overhead for each manufacturing overhead cost that contributes to the controllable variance can be compared. In addition, cost and quantity variances can be developed for each overhead cost, such as indirect materials and indirect labor.

Overhead Volume Variance.   The **overhead volume variance** indicates whether plant facilities were efficiently used during the period. The formula for computing the volume variance is as follows:

ILLUSTRATION 26-25

Formula for overhead volume variance

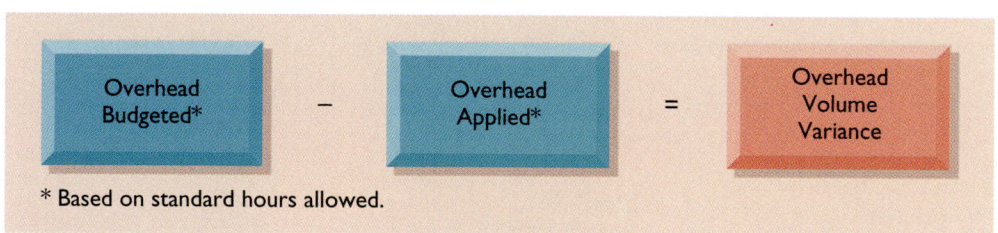

* Based on standard hours allowed.

Both the factors in this formula have been explained above. The overhead budgeted is the same as the amount used in computing the controllable variance or $10,400 in our example. Overhead applied of $10,000 is the amount used in determining the total overhead variance. For Xonic Inc., the overhead volume variance is $400 unfavorable as shown below:

$$\$10,400 - \$10,000 = \$400 \text{ U}$$

Further insight into the volume variance can be obtained from a detailed analysis of the two factors. As shown in the flexible manufacturing overhead budget, the budgeted overhead of $10,400 consists of $6,000 variable and $4,400 fixed. As indicated in determining the predetermined overhead rate in Illustration 26-6 (p. 1120), the rate of $5 consists of $3 variable and $2 fixed. The detailed analysis, therefore, is:

ILLUSTRATION 26-26

Detailed analysis of overhead volume variance

Overhead budgeted		
Variable costs	$6,000	
Fixed costs	4,400	$10,400
Overhead applied		
Variable costs (2,000 × $3)	6,000	
Fixed costs (2,000 × $2)	4,000	10,000
Overhead volume variance—unfavorable		$ 400

A careful examination of this analysis indicates that **the overhead volume variance relates solely to fixed costs** (fixed costs budgeted $4,400 − fixed costs applied $4,000). Thus, **the volume variance measures the amount that fixed overhead costs are under- or overapplied**.

We have already established that total fixed costs remain the same at every level of activity within the relevant range. Since a predetermined overhead rate based on normal capacity is used in applying overhead, **it follows that if the standard hours allowed are less than the standard hours at normal capacity, fixed overhead costs will be underapplied**. In contrast, **if production exceeds normal capacity, fixed overhead costs will be overapplied**.

An alternative formula for computing the overhead volume variance is shown in Illustration 26-27.

ILLUSTRATION 26-27

Alternative formula for overhead volume variance

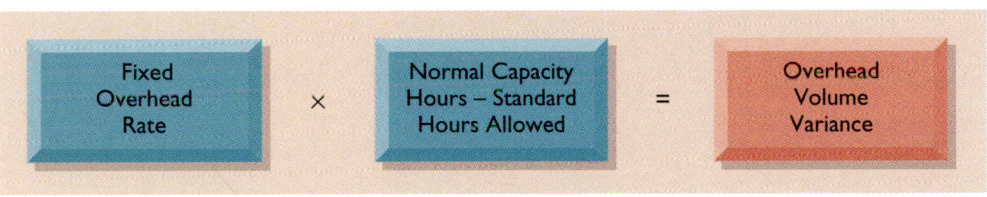

In Xonic, Inc., normal capacity is 26,400 hours for the year or 2,200 hours for a month (26,400 ÷ 12), and the fixed overhead rate is $2 per hour. Thus, the volume variance is $400 unfavorable as shown below:

$$\$2 \times (2,200 - 2,000) = \$400 \text{ U}$$

The total overhead variance of $900 unfavorable for Xonic, Inc., therefore, consists of the following:

ILLUSTRATION 26-28

Summary of overhead variance

Overhead controllable variance	$500 U
Overhead volume variance	400 U
Total overhead variance	**$900 U**

The results can also be obtained from the matrix in Illustration 26-29 shown on the next page.

In computing the overhead variances, it is important to remember the following:

1. Standard hours allowed are used in each of the variances.
2. Budgeted costs for the controllable variance are derived from the flexible budget.

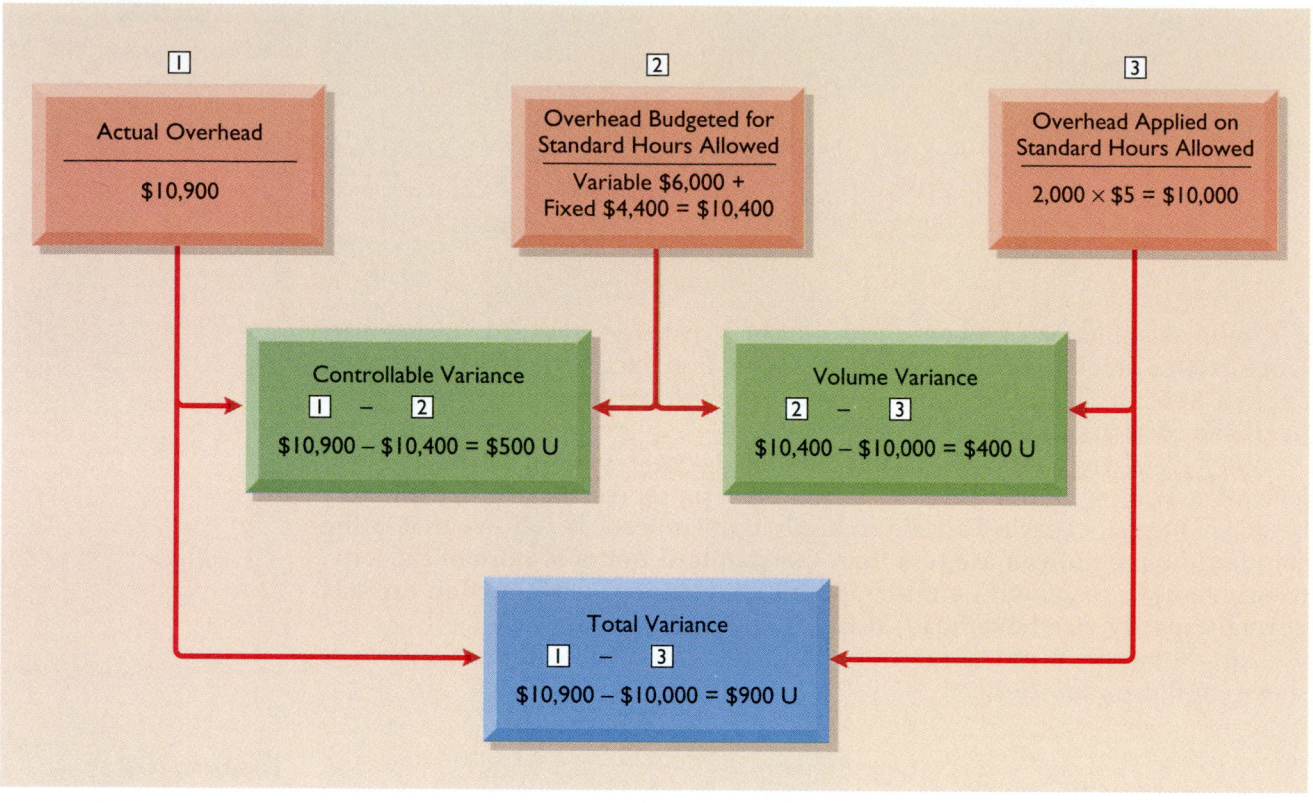

ILLUSTRATION 26-29

Matrix for manufacturing overhead variance

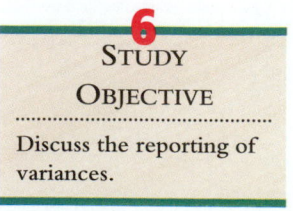

Controllable Variance — Production Dept.

Overhead Volume Variance — Production or Sales Dept.

3. The controllable variance generally pertains to variable costs.
4. The volume variance pertains solely to fixed costs.

Causes of Manufacturing Overhead Variances. Since the **controllable variance** relates to variable manufacturing costs, the responsibility for the variance rests with the **production department**. The cause of an unfavorable variance may be (1) **higher than expected use** of indirect materials, indirect labor, and factory supplies or (2) **increases in indirect manufacturing costs**, such as fuel and maintenance costs.

The **overhead volume variance** is the responsibility of the **production department** if the cause is inefficient use of direct labor or machine breakdowns. However, when the cause is a **lack of sales orders**, the responsibility rests **outside** the production department.

Reporting Variances

All variances should be reported to appropriate levels of management as soon as possible. The sooner management is informed, the sooner problems can be evaluated and corrective actions taken if necessary.

The form, content, and frequency of variance reports vary considerably among companies. One approach is to prepare a weekly report for each department that has primary responsibility for cost control. Under this approach, materials price variances are reported to the purchasing department, and all other variances are reported to the production department that did the work. The

6
STUDY OBJECTIVE

Discuss the reporting of variances.

following report for Xonic, Inc., with the materials for the Weed-O order listed first, illustrates this approach:

Type of Materials	Quantity Purchased	Actual Price	Standard Price	Price Variance	Explanation
X 100	4,200 lbs.	$3.10	$3.00	$420 U	Rush order
X 142	1,200 units	2.75	2.80	60 F	Quantity discount
A 85	600 doz.	5.20	5.10	60 U	Regular supplier on strike
Total price variance				**$420 U**	

XONIC, INC.
Variance Report—Purchasing Department
For Week Ended June 8, 1999

ILLUSTRATION 26-30
Materials price variance report

The explanation column is completed after consultation with the purchasing department manager.

Variance reports facilitate the principle of "management by exception" explained in Chapter 25. For example, the vice president of purchasing can use the report illustrated above to evaluate the effectiveness of the purchasing department manager. Similarly, the vice president of production can use production department variance reports to determine how well each production manager is controlling costs. In using variance reports, top management normally looks for **significant variances**. The significance of a variance may be judged on the basis of some quantitative measure, such as more than 10% of the standard or more than $1,000.

BEFORE YOU GO ON . . .

Review It

1. What are the formulas for computing the total, price, and quantity variances for direct materials?
2. What are the formulas for computing the total, price, and quantity variances for direct labor?
3. What are the formulas for computing the total, controllable, and volume variances for manufacturing overhead?

Do It

The standard cost of Product XX includes two units of direct materials at $8.00 per unit. During July, 22,000 units of direct materials are purchased at $7.50 and used to produce 10,000 units. Compute the total, price, and quantity variances for materials.

Reasoning: It is necessary to know the formulas for computing each of the materials variances. The formulas are:

Total materials variance = (actual quantity × actual price) − (standard quantity × standard price)

Materials price variance = (actual quantity × actual price) − (actual quantity × standard price)

Materials quantity variance = (actual quantity × standard price) − (standard quantity × standard price)

Solution: Substituting amounts into the formulas, the variances are:

$$\text{Total materials variance} = (22{,}000 \times \$7.50) - (20{,}000 \times \$8.00) = \$5{,}000 \text{ unfavorable.}$$

$$\text{Materials price variance} = (22{,}000 \times \$7.50) - (22{,}000 \times \$8.00) = \$11{,}000 \text{ favorable.}$$

$$\text{Materials quantity variance} = (22{,}000 \times \$8.00) - (20{,}000 \times \$8.00) = \$16{,}000 \text{ unfavorable.}$$

Related exercise material: BE26–4, BE26–5, BE26–6, BE26–7, BE26–8, E26–2, E26–3, E26–4, E26–6, E26–7, E26–8, E26–9, and E26–12.

THE NAVIGATOR

STANDARD COST ACCOUNTING SYSTEM

7

STUDY

OBJECTIVE

Enumerate the features of a standard cost accounting system.

A standard cost accounting system is a double-entry system of accounting in which standard costs are used in making entries and variances are formally recognized in the accounts. A standard cost system may be used with either job order or process costing. At this point, we will explain and illustrate a **standard cost, job order cost accounting system**. The system includes two important assumptions: (1) variances from standards are recognized at the earliest opportunity, and (2) the Work in Process account is maintained exclusively on the basis of standard costs. In practice, there are many variations among standard cost systems. However, the system described here should facilitate your transition to a specific company's system.

Journal Entries

The transactions of Xonic, Inc., will be used to illustrate the journal entries. Note as you study the entries that the major difference between the entries here and those for the job order cost accounting system in Chapter 21 is the **variance accounts**.

1. Purchase raw materials on account for $13,020 when the standard cost is $12,600.

Raw Materials Inventory	12,600	
Materials Price Variance	420	
Accounts Payable		13,020
(To record purchase of materials)		

The inventory account is debited for actual quantities at standard cost. This enables the perpetual materials records to show actual quantities. The price variance, which is unfavorable, is debited to Materials Price Variance.

2. Incur direct labor costs of $20,580 when the standard labor cost is $21,000.

Factory Labor	21,000	
Labor Price Variance		420
Wages Payable		20,580
(To record direct labor costs)		

Like the raw materials inventory account, Factory Labor is debited for actual hours worked at the standard hourly rate of pay. In this case, the labor variance is favorable. Thus, Labor Price Variance is credited.

3. Incur actual manufacturing overhead costs of $10,900.

Manufacturing Overhead	10,900	
Accounts Payable/Cash/Acc. Depreciation		10,900
(To record overhead incurred)		

The controllable overhead variance is not recorded at this time. It depends on standard hours applied to work in process, which is not known at the time overhead is incurred.

4. Issue raw materials for production at a cost of $12,600 when the standard cost is $12,000.

Work in Process Inventory	12,000	
Materials Quantity Variance	600	
Raw Materials Inventory		12,600
(To record issuance of raw materials)		

Work in Process Inventory is debited for standard materials quantities used at standard prices. The variance account is debited because the variance is unfavorable. Raw Materials Inventory is credited for actual quantities at standard prices.

5. Assign factory labor to production at a cost of $21,000 when standard cost is $20,000.

Work in Process Inventory	20,000	
Labor Quantity Variance	1,000	
Factory Labor		21,000
(To assign factory labor to jobs)		

Work in Process Inventory is debited for standard labor hours at standard rates, and the unfavorable variance is debited to Labor Quantity Variance. The credit to Factory Labor produces a zero balance in this account.

6. Applying manufacturing overhead to production, $10,000.

Work in Process Inventory	10,000	
Manufacturing Overhead		10,000
(To assign overhead to jobs)		

Work in Process Inventory is debited for standard hours allowed multiplied by the standard overhead rate.

7. Transfer completed work to finished goods, $42,000.

Finished Goods Inventory	42,000	
Work in Process Inventory		42,000
(To record transfer of completed work to		
finished goods)		

In this example, both inventory accounts are at standard cost.

8. The 1,000 gallons of Weed-O are sold for $60,000.

Accounts Receivable	60,000	
Cost of Goods Sold	42,000	
Sales		60,000
Finished Goods Inventory		42,000
(To record sale of finished goods and the cost of goods sold)		

Cost of Goods Sold is debited at standard cost. Gross profit, in turn, is the difference between sales and the standard cost of goods sold.

9. Recognize unfavorable overhead variances: controllable, $500; volume, $400.

Overhead Controllable Variance	500	
Overhead Volume Variance	400	
Manufacturing Overhead		900
(To recognize overhead variances)		

Prior to this entry, a debit balance of $900 existed in Manufacturing Overhead. The above entry therefore produces a zero balance in the Manufacturing Overhead account. The information needed for this entry is often not available until the end of the accounting period.

Ledger Accounts

The cost accounts for Xonic, Inc., after posting the entries, are shown in Illustration 26-31 on the next page. Note that six variance accounts are included in the ledger. The remaining accounts are the same as those illustrated for a job order cost system in Chapter 21 in which only actual costs were used.

Statement Presentation of Variances

In income statements **prepared for management** under a standard cost accounting system, **cost of goods sold is stated at standard cost and the variances are separately disclosed**, as shown in Illustration 26-32 on the next page. The statement shown is based entirely on the production and sale of Weed-O and assumes selling and administrative costs of $3,000. Observe that each variance is shown, as well as the total net variance. In this example, variations from standard costs reduced net income by $2,500.

In financial statements prepared for stockholders and other external users, standard costs may be used. The costing of inventories at standard costs is in accordance with generally accepted accounting principles when there are no significant differences between actual costs and standard costs. Hewlett-Packard and Westinghouse Electric, for example, report their inventories at standard costs. However, if there are significant differences between actual and standard costs, inventories and cost of goods sold must be reported at actual costs.

It is also possible to show the variances in an income statement prepared in the contribution margin format. To do so, it is necessary to analyze the overhead variances into variable and fixed components. This type of analysis is explained in cost accounting textbooks.

ILLUSTRATION 26-31

Cost accounts with variances

Raw Materials Inventory			
(1)	12,600	(4)	12,600

Materials Price Variance			
(1)	420		

Work in Process Inventory			
(4)	12,000	(7)	42,000
(5)	20,000		
(6)	10,000		

Factory Labor			
(2)	21,000	(5)	21,000

Materials Quantity Variance			
(4)	600		

Finished Goods Inventory			
(7)	42,000	(8)	42,000

Manufacturing Overhead			
(3)	10,900	(6)	10,000
		(9)	900

Labor Price Variance			
		(2)	420

Cost of Goods Sold			
(8)	42,000		

Labor Quantity Variance		
(5)	1,000	

Overhead Controllable Variance		
(9)	500	

Overhead Volume Variance		
(9)	400	

HELPFUL HINT
All debit balances in variance accounts indicate unfavorable variances; all credit balances indicate favorable variances.

ILLUSTRATION 26-32

Variances in income statement for management

XONIC, INC.
Income Statement
For the Month Ended June 30, 1999

Sales		$60,000
Cost of goods sold (at standard)		42,000
Gross profit (at standard)		18,000
Variances		
Materials price	$ 420	
Materials quantity	600	
Labor price	(420)	
Labor quantity	1,000	
Overhead controllable	500	
Overhead volume	400	
Total variance unfavorable		2,500
Gross profit (actual)		15,500
Selling and administrative expenses		3,000
Net income		$12,500

BEFORE YOU GO ON . . .

Review It

1. Does a debit balance in a variance account indicate favorable or unfavorable performance?
2. What entry is made to recognize overhead variances in the accounts?
3. How are standard costs and variances reported in income statements prepared for management?

A LOOK BACK AT OUR FEATURE STORY

Refer to the data in the opening story and answer the following questions.

1. Should standard unit costs be based on normal or ideal manufacturing activity?
2. What factor is critical in controlling costs? How might Sanford improve its control over this factor?
3. For internal reporting to top management, should Sanford report actual costs, standard costs, or both? Why?
4. In financial statements for stockholders, should Sanford report actual costs, standard costs, or both? Why?

Solution:

1. Normal standards are more widely used because they represent an efficient level of performance that is attainable under expected operating conditions. Most managers believe that because ideal standards are so difficult to meet, they discourage self-improvement and lower morale.
2. The critical factor in controlling costs is the efficiency of the machine operator. However, excess labor time is often due to malfunctioning equipment. Management admits that this factor is difficult to control. However, the following steps may reduce or eliminate malfunctions: (1) increase maintenance on the equipment and (2) purchase new equipment.
3. Both standard costs and actual costs should be reported to top management. In addition, differences between the two costs should be reported. Then, by scanning the differences, management can quickly identify those that are significant. This approach follows the principle of "management by exception." When a significant variance is identified, management can investigate the cause and take corrective action.
4. For financial statements, actual costs should be used. Standard costs are permissible but only if standard costs are not significantly different from actual costs. GAAP requires the use of actual costs if standard costs are not current and comparable to actual costs.

THE
NAVIGATOR

DEMONSTRATION PROBLEM

Manlow Company makes a cologne called Allure. The standard cost for one bottle of Allure is as follows:

Manufacturing Cost Elements	Standard		
	Quantity ×	Price =	Cost
Direct materials	6 oz.	× $ .90 =	$ 5.40
Direct labor	0.5 hrs.	× $12.00 =	6.00
Manufacturing overhead	0.5 hrs.	× $ 4.80 =	2.40
			$13.80

During the month, the following transactions occurred in manufacturing 10,000 bottles of Allure.

1. 58,000 ounces of materials were purchased at $1.00 per ounce.
2. All the materials purchased were used to produce the 10,000 bottles of Allure.
3. 4,900 direct labor hours were worked at a total labor cost of $56,350.
4. Variable manufacturing overhead incurred was $15,000 and fixed overhead incurred was $10,400.

The manufacturing overhead rate of $4.80 is based on a normal capacity of 5,200 direct labor hours. The total budget at this capacity is $10,400 fixed and $14,560 variable.

Instructions

Compute the total variance and the variances for each of the manufacturing cost elements.

SOLUTION TO DEMONSTRATION PROBLEM

Total Variance

Actual costs incurred:	
Direct materials	$ 58,000
Direct labor	56,350
Manufacturing overhead	25,400
	139,750
Standard cost (10,000 × $13.80)	138,000
Total variance	$ 1,750 (U)

Direct Materials Variances

Total	=	$58,000 (58,000 × $1.00)	−	$54,000 (60,000 × $.90)	=	$4,000 U
Price	=	$58,000 (58,000 × $1.00)	−	$52,200 (58,000 × $.90)	=	$5,800 U
Quantity	=	$52,200 (58,000 × $.90)	−	$54,000 (60,000 × $.90)	=	$1,800 F

Direct Labor Variances

Total	=	$56,350 (4,900 × $11.50)	−	$60,000 (5,000 × $12.00)	=	$3,650 F
Price	=	$56,350 (4,900 × $11.50)	−	$58,800 (4,900 × $12.00)	=	$2,450 F
Quantity	=	$58,800 (4,900 × $12.00)	−	$60,000 (5,000 × $12.00)	=	$1,200 F

Overhead Variances

Total	=	$25,400 ($15,000 + $10,400)	−	$24,000 (5,000 × $4.80)	=	$1,400 U
Controllable	=	$25,400 ($15,000 + $10,400)	−	$24,400 ($14,000 + $10,400)	=	$1,000 U
Volume	=	$24,400 ($14,000 + $10,400)	−	$24,000 (5,000 × $4.80)	=	$ 400 U

PROBLEM-SOLVING STRATEGIES

1. Check to make sure the total variance and the sum of the individual variances are equal.
2. Find the price variance first, then the quantity variance.
3. Budgeted overhead costs are based on flexible budget data.
4. Overhead applied is based on standard hours allowed.
5. Actual hours worked is not relevant in computing overhead variances.
6. The overhead volume variance relates solely to fixed costs.

THE NAVIGATOR

SUMMARY OF STUDY OBJECTIVES

1. Distinguish between a standard and a budget. Both standards and budgets are predetermined costs. The primary difference is that a standard is a unit amount, whereas a budget is a total amount. A standard may be regarded as the budgeted cost per unit of product.

2. Identify the advantages of standard costs. Standard costs offer a number of advantages to an organization. They (a) facilitate management planning, (b) promote greater economy and efficiency, (c) are useful in setting selling prices, (d) contribute to management control, (e) permit

"management by exception," and (f) simplify the costing of inventories and reduce clerical costs.

3. Describe how standards are set. The direct materials price standard should be based on the delivered cost of raw materials plus an allowance for receiving and handling. The direct materials quantity standard should establish the required quantity plus an allowance for waste and spoilage.

The direct labor price standard should be based on current wage rates and anticipated adjustments such as COLAs. In addition, it generally includes payroll taxes and fringe benefits. Direct labor quantity standards should be based on required production time plus an allowance for rest periods, cleanup, machine setup, and machine downtime.

For manufacturing overhead, a standard predetermined overhead rate is used based on an expected standard activity index such as standard direct labor hours or standard direct labor cost.

4. Indicate the formulas for determining direct materials and direct labor variances. The formulas for the direct materials variances are:

$$\begin{pmatrix} \text{Actual quantity} \\ \times \text{ Actual price} \end{pmatrix} - \begin{pmatrix} \text{Standard quantity} \\ \times \text{ Standard price} \end{pmatrix} = \begin{matrix} \text{Total} \\ \text{materials} \\ \text{variance} \end{matrix}$$

$$\begin{pmatrix} \text{Actual quantity} \\ \times \text{ Actual price} \end{pmatrix} - \begin{pmatrix} \text{Actual quantity} \\ \times \text{ Standard price} \end{pmatrix} = \begin{matrix} \text{Materials} \\ \text{price} \\ \text{variance} \end{matrix}$$

$$\begin{pmatrix} \text{Actual quantity} \\ \times \text{ Standard price} \end{pmatrix} - \begin{pmatrix} \text{Standard quantity} \\ \times \text{ Standard price} \end{pmatrix} = \begin{matrix} \text{Materials} \\ \text{quantity} \\ \text{variance} \end{matrix}$$

The formulas for the direct labor variances are:

$$\begin{pmatrix} \text{Actual hours} \\ \times \text{ Actual rate} \end{pmatrix} - \begin{pmatrix} \text{Standard hours} \\ \times \text{ Standard rate} \end{pmatrix} = \begin{matrix} \text{Total} \\ \text{labor} \\ \text{variance} \end{matrix}$$

$$\begin{pmatrix} \text{Actual hours} \\ \times \text{ Actual rate} \end{pmatrix} - \begin{pmatrix} \text{Actual hours} \\ \times \text{ Standard rate} \end{pmatrix} = \begin{matrix} \text{Labor} \\ \text{price} \\ \text{variance} \end{matrix}$$

$$\begin{pmatrix} \text{Actual hours} \\ \times \text{ Standard rate} \end{pmatrix} - \begin{pmatrix} \text{Standard hours} \\ \times \text{ Standard rate} \end{pmatrix} = \begin{matrix} \text{Labor} \\ \text{quantity} \\ \text{variance} \end{matrix}$$

5. State the formulas for determining manufacturing overhead variances. The formulas for the manufacturing overhead variances are:

$$\begin{matrix} \text{Actual} \\ \text{overhead} \end{matrix} - \begin{matrix} \text{Overhead} \\ \text{applied} \end{matrix} = \begin{matrix} \text{Total overhead} \\ \text{variance} \end{matrix}$$

$$\begin{matrix} \text{Actual} \\ \text{overhead} \end{matrix} - \begin{matrix} \text{Overhead} \\ \text{budgeted} \end{matrix} = \begin{matrix} \text{Overhead control-} \\ \text{lable variance} \end{matrix}$$

$$\begin{matrix} \text{Overhead} \\ \text{budgeted} \end{matrix} - \begin{matrix} \text{Overhead} \\ \text{applied} \end{matrix} = \begin{matrix} \text{Overhead volume} \\ \text{variance} \end{matrix}$$

6. Discuss the reporting of variances. Variances are reported to management in variance reports. The reports facilitate management by exception because significant differences can be highlighted.

7. Enumerate the features of a standard cost accounting system. In a standard cost accounting system, standard costs are journalized and posted and separate variance accounts are maintained in the ledger. When differences between actual costs and standard costs do not differ significantly, inventories may be reported at standard costs.

THE NAVIGATOR

GLOSSARY

• •

Direct labor price standard   The rate per hour that should be incurred for direct labor. (p. 1119).

Direct labor quantity standard   The time that should be required to make one unit of product. (p. 1120).

Direct materials price standard   The cost per unit of direct materials that should be incurred. (p. 1119).

Direct materials quantity standard   The quantity of direct materials that should be used per unit of finished goods. (p. 1119).

Ideal standards   Standards based on the optimum level of performance under perfect operating conditions. (p. 1118).

Labor price variance   The difference between the actual hours times the actual rate and the actual hours times the standard rate. (p. 1126).

Labor quantity variance   The difference between actual hours times the standard rate and standard hours times the standard rate. (p. 1126).

Materials price variance   The difference between the actual quantity times the actual price and the actual quantity times the standard price. (p. 1124).

Materials quantity variance   The difference between the actual quantity times the standard price and the standard quantity times the standard price. (p. 1124).

Normal standards   Standards based on an efficient level of performance that are attainable under expected operating conditions. (p. 1118).

Overhead controllable variance   The difference between actual overhead incurred and overhead budgeted for the standard hours allowed. (p. 1129).

Overhead volume variance   The difference between overhead budgeted for the standard hours allowed and the overhead applied. (p. 1130).

Standard cost accounting system   A double-entry system of accounting in which standard costs are used in making entries and variances are recognized in the accounts. (p. 1134).

Standard costs   Predetermined unit costs which are used as measures of performance. (p. 1116).

Standard hours allowed   The hours that should have been worked for the units produced. (p. 1128).

Standard predetermined overhead rate   An overhead rate determined by dividing budgeted overhead costs by an expected standard activity index. (p. 1120).

Total labor variance   The difference between actual hours times the actual rate and standard hours times the standard rate for labor. (p. 1126).

Total materials variance   The difference between the actual quantity times the actual price and the standard quantity times the standard price of materials. (p. 1123).

Total overhead variance   The difference between actual overhead costs and overhead costs applied to work done. (p. 1128).

Variances   The difference between total actual costs and total standard costs. (p. 1122).

SELF-STUDY QUESTIONS

Answers are at the end of the chapter.

(SO 1) 1. Standards differ from budgets in that:
   a. budgets may be used in valuing inventories but not standards.
   b. budgets may be journalized and posted but not standards.
   c. budgets are a total amount and standards are a unit amount.
   d. only budgets contribute to management planning and control.

(SO 2) 2. The advantages of standard costs include all of the following *except*:
   a. management by exception may be used.
   b. management planning is facilitated.
   c. they may simplify the costing of inventories.
   d. management must use a static budget.

(SO 3) 3. The setting of standards is:
   a. a managerial accountant decision.
   b. a management decision.
   c. a worker decision.
   d. preferably set at the ideal level of performance.

(SO 4) 4. Each of the following formulas is correct except:
   a. Labor price variance = (actual hours × actual rate) − (actual hours × standard rate).
   b. Overhead controllable variance = actual overhead − overhead budgeted.
   c. Materials price variance = (actual quantity × actual cost) − (standard quantity × standard cost).
   d. Overhead volume variance = overhead budgeted − overhead applied.

(SO 4) 5. In producing product AA, 6,300 pounds of direct materials were used at a cost of $1.10 per pound when the standard was 6,000 pounds at $1 per pound. The direct materials quantity variance is:
   a. $330 unfavorable.
   b. $300 unfavorable.
   c. $600 unfavorable.
   d. $630 unfavorable.

6. In producing product ZZ, 14,800 direct labor hours were (SO 4) used at a rate of $8.20 per hour when the standard was 15,000 hours at $8.00 per hour. Based on these data, the direct labor:
   a. quantity variance is $1,600 favorable.
   b. quantity variance is $1,600 unfavorable.
   c. price variance is $2,960 favorable.
   d. price variance is $3,000 unfavorable.

7. Which of the following is *correct* about overhead vari- (SO 5) ances?
   a. The controllable variance generally pertains to fixed overhead costs.
   b. The volume variance pertains solely to variable overhead costs.
   c. Standard hours actually worked are used in each variance.
   d. Budgeted overhead costs are based on the flexible overhead budget.

8. The formula for computing the total overhead variance (SO 5) is:
   a. actual overhead less overhead applied.
   b. overhead budgeted less overhead applied.
   c. actual overhead less overhead budgeted.
   d. no correct answer given.

9. Which of the following is *incorrect* about variance re- (SO 6) ports?
   a. They facilitate "management by exception."
   b. They should only be sent to the top level of management.
   c. They should be prepared as soon as possible.
   d. They may vary in form, content, and frequency among companies.

10. Which of the following is *incorrect* about a standard cost (SO 7) accounting system?
   a. It is applicable to job order costing.
   b. It is applicable to process costing.
   c. It is a single-entry system.
   d. It keeps separate accounts for each variance.

THE NAVIGATOR

QUESTIONS

1. (a) "Standard costs are the expected total cost of completing a job." Is this correct? Explain.
   (b) "A standard imposed by a governmental agency is known as a regulation." Do you agree? Explain.

2. (a) Explain the similarities and differences between standards and budgets.
   (b) Contrast the accounting for standards and budgets.

3. Standard costs facilitate management planning. What are the other advantages of standard costs?

4. Contrast the roles of the management accountant and management in setting standard costs.

5. Distinguish between an ideal standard and a normal standard.

6. What factors should be considered in setting (a) the materials price standard and (b) the materials quantity standard?

7. "The objective in setting the direct labor quantity standard is to determine the aggregate time required to make one unit of product." Do you agree? What allowances should be made in setting this standard?

8. How is the predetermined overhead rate determined when standard costs are used?

9. What is the difference between a favorable cost variance and an unfavorable cost variance?

10. In each of the following formulas, supply the words that should be inserted for each number in parentheses.
    (a) (Actual quantity × (1)) − (standard quantity × (2)) = Total materials variance
    (b) ((3) × actual price) − (actual quantity × (4)) = Materials price variance
    (c) (Actual quantity × (5)) − ((6) × standard price) = Materials quantity variance

11. In the direct labor variance matrix, there are three factors: (1) actual hours × actual rate, (2) actual hours × standard rate, and (3) standard hours × standard rate. Using the numbers, indicate the formulas for each of the direct labor variances.

12. Keene Company's standard predetermined overhead rate is $6.00 per direct labor hour. For the month of June, 26,000 actual hours were worked and 27,500 standard hours were allowed. Normal capacity hours were 28,000. How much overhead was applied?

13. If the $6.00 per hour overhead rate in question 12 consists of $4.00 variable, and actual overhead costs were $163,000, what is the overhead controllable variance for June? Is the variance favorable or unfavorable?

14. Using the data in questions 12 and 13, what is the overhead volume variance for June? Is the variance favorable or unfavorable?

15. What is the purpose of computing the overhead volume variance? What is the basic formula for this variance?

16. Ellen Landis does not understand why the overhead volume variance indicates that fixed overhead costs are under- or overapplied. Clarify this matter for Ellen.

17. Stan LaRue is attempting to outline the important points about overhead variances on a class examination. List four points that Stan should include in his outline.

18. How often should variances be reported to management? What principle may be used with variance reports?

19. What circumstances may cause the purchasing department to be responsible for both an unfavorable materials price variance and an unfavorable materials quantity variance?

20. (a) Explain the basic features of a standard cost accounting system. (b) What type of balance will exist in the variance account when (1) the materials price variance is unfavorable and (2) the labor quantity variance is favorable?

21. (a) How are variances reported in income statements prepared for management? (b) May standard costs be used in preparing financial statements for stockholders? Explain.

BRIEF EXERCISES

Distinguish between a standard and a budget.
(SO 1)

BE26–1   Valdez Company uses both standards and budgets. For the year, estimated production of Product X is 400,000 units. Total estimated cost for materials and labor are $1,200,000 and $1,600,000. Compute the estimates for (a) a standard cost and (b) a budgeted cost.

Set direct materials standard.
(SO 3)

BE26–2   Hideo Company accumulates the following data concerning raw materials in making one gallon of finished product: (1) Price—net purchase price $3.40, freight-in $0.20 and receiving and handling $0.10; (2) quantity—required materials 2.6 pounds, allowance for waste and spoilage 0.4 pounds. Compute the (a) standard direct materials price per gallon; (b) standard direct materials quantity per gallon and (c) total standard material cost per gallon.

Set direct labor standard.
(SO 3)

BE26–3   Labor data for making one gallon of finished product in Hideo Company are as follows: (1) Price—hourly wage rate $10.00, payroll taxes $0.80, and fringe benefits $1.20; (2) Quantity—actual production time 1.4 hours, rest periods and clean up 0.25 hours, and setup and downtime 0.15 hours. Compute the (a) standard direct labor rate per hour, (b) standard direct labor hours per gallon, and (c) the standard labor cost per gallon.

BE26–4 Sprague Company's standard materials cost per unit of output is $10 (2 pounds × $5.00). During July, the company purchases and uses 3,300 pounds of materials costing $16,830 in making 1,500 units of finished product. Compute the total, price, and quantity materials variances.

Compute direct materials variances.
(SO 4)

BE26–5 Talbot Company's standard labor cost per unit of output is $20 (2 hours × $10.00 per hour). During August, the company incurs 1,850 hours of direct labor at an hourly cost of $9.60 per hour in making 1,000 units of finished product. Compute the total, price, and quantity labor variances.

Compute direct labor variances.
(SO 4)

BE26–6 In October, Russo Company reports 21,000 actual direct labor hours and it incurs $101,000 of manufacturing overhead costs. Standard hours allowed for the work done is 20,000 hours and the predetermined overhead rate is $5.00 per direct labor hour. Compute the total manufacturing overhead variance.

Compute total manufacturing overhead variance.
(SO 5)

BE26–7 Some overhead data for Russo Company are given in BE26–6. In addition, the flexible manufacturing overhead budget shows that budgeted costs are $4.00 variable per direct labor hour and $24,000 fixed. Compute the manufacturing overhead controllable variance.

Compute the manufacturing overhead controllable variance.
(SO 5)

BE26–8 Using the data in BE26–6 and BE26–7, compute the manufacturing overhead volume variance.

Compute overhead volume variance.
(SO 5)

BE26–9 Journalize the following transactions for McBee Manufacturing:

Journalize materials variances.
(SO 7)

1. Purchased 6,000 units of raw materials on account for $12,300 when the standard cost was $12,000.
2. Issued 6,000 units of raw materials for production when the standard units were 5,800.

BE26–10 Journalize the following transactions for Worrel Manufacturing:

Journalize labor variances.
(SO 7)

1. Incurred direct labor costs of $24,300 for 3,000 hours when the standard labor cost was $24,000.
2. Assigned 3,000 direct labor hours costing $24,300 to production when standard hours were 3,100.

EXERCISES

E26–1 Raul Montanez manufactures and sells homemade wine, and he wants to develop a standard cost per gallon. The following are required for production of a 50-gallon batch:

Compute standard materials costs.
(SO 3)

3,000 ounces of grape concentrate at $0.04 per ounce

55 pounds of granulated sugar at $0.30 per pound

60 lemons at $0.65 each

50 yeast tablets at $0.25 each

50 nutrient tablets at $0.20 each

2,500 ounces of water at $0.004 per ounce

Raul estimates that 4% of the grape concentrate is wasted, 12% of the sugar is lost, and 20% of the lemons cannot be used.

Instructions

Compute the standard cost of the ingredients for one gallon of wine. (Carry computations to three decimal places.)

E26–2 The standard cost of Product B manufactured by Nang Company includes three units of direct materials at $5.00 per unit. During June, 30,000 units of direct materials are purchased at a cost of $4.70 per unit, and 27,600 units of direct materials are used to produce 9,000 units of Product B.

Compute materials price and quantity variances.
(SO 4)

Instructions

(a) Compute the materials price and quantity variances.

(b) Repeat (a), assuming the purchase price is $5.20 and the quantity used is 26,600 units.

Compute labor price and quantity variances.
(SO 4)

E26–3 Pagnozzi Company's standard labor cost of producing one unit of Product DD is 4 hours at the rate of $12.00 per hour. During August, 40,800 hours of labor are incurred at a cost of $12.20 per hour to produce 10,000 units of Product DD.

Instructions
(a) Compute the labor price and quantity variances.
(b) Repeat (a), assuming the standard is 4.2 hours of direct labor at $12.40 per hour.

Compute materials and labor variances.
(SO 4)

E26–4 Kopecky Inc., which produces a single product, has prepared the following standard cost sheet for one unit of the product.

Direct materials (8 pounds at $2.50 per pound)	$20.00
Direct labor (3 hours at $12.00 per hour)	$36.00

During the month of April, the company manufactures 245 units and incurs the following actual costs:

Direct materials (1,900 pounds)	$4,940
Direct labor (700 hours)	$8,120

Instructions
Compute the total, price, and quantity variances for materials and labor.

Journalize entries for materials and labor variances.
(SO 7)

E26–5 Data for Kopecky Inc. are given in E26–4.

Instructions
Journalize the entries to record the materials and labor variances.

Compute the materials and labor variances and list reasons for unfavorable variances.
(SO 4, 6)

E26–6 The following direct materials and direct labor data pertain to the operations of Batista Manufacturing Company for the month of August.

Costs		Quantities	
Actual labor rate	$13.00 per hour	Actual hours incurred and used	4,250 hours
Actual materials price	$128.00 per ton	Actual quantity of materials purchased and used	1,225 tons
Standard labor rate	$12.00 per hour	Standard hours used	4,300 hours
Standard materials price	$130.00 per ton	Standard quantity of materials used	1,200 tons

Instructions
(a) Compute the total, price, and quantity variances for materials and labor.
(b) ▨▨▨▷ Provide two possible explanations for each of the unfavorable variances calculated above and suggest where responsibility for the unfavorable result might be placed.

Compute manufacturing overhead variances and interpret findings.
(SO 5)

E26–7 The following information was taken from the annual manufacturing overhead cost budget of Guardino Company:

Variable manufacturing overhead costs	$33,000
Fixed manufacturing overhead costs	$20,625
Normal production level in hours	16,500
Normal production level in units	4,125

During the year, 4,000 units were produced, 16,100 hours were worked, and the actual manufacturing overhead was $55,000. Actual fixed manufacturing overhead costs equaled budgeted fixed manufacturing overhead costs. Overhead is applied on the basis of direct labor hours.

Instructions
(a) Compute the total, fixed, and variable predetermined manufacturing overhead rates.
(b) Compute the total, controllable, and volume overhead variances.
(c) ▨▨▨▷ Briefly interpret the overhead controllable and volume variances computed in (b).

Compute overhead variances and journalize transactions and adjusting entry.
(SO 5, 7)

E26–8 Manufacturing overhead data for the production of Product H by DeDonder Company are as follows:

Overhead incurred for 51,000 actual direct labor hours worked	$213,000
Overhead rate (variable $3.00; fixed $1.00) at normal capacity of 54,000	
direct labor hours	$ 4.00
Standard hours allowed for work done	52,000

Instructions

(a) Compute the total, controllable, and volume overhead variances.

(b) Journalize the incurrence of the overhead costs and the application of overhead to the job, assuming a standard cost accounting system is used.

(c) Prepare the adjusting entry for the overhead variances.

E26–9 During March 1999, Tovar Tool & Die Company worked on four jobs. A review of direct labor costs reveals the following summary data:

Prepare a variance report for direct labor.
(SO 4, 6)

Job	Actual		Standard		Total
Number	Hours	Costs	Hours	Costs	Variance
A257	220	$ 4,400	225	$4,500	$ 100 F
A258	450	10,350	420	8,400	1,950 U
A259	300	6,150	300	6,000	150 U
A260	115	2,070	110	2,200	130 F
Total variance					$1,870 U

Analysis reveals that Job A257 was a repeat job. Job A258 was a rush order that required overtime work at premium rates of pay. Job A259 required a more experienced replacement worker on one shift. Work on Job A260 was done for one day by a new trainee when a regular worker was absent.

Instructions

Prepare a report for the plant supervisor on direct labor cost variances for March. The report should have columns for (1) Job No., (2) Actual Hours, (3) Standard Hours, (4) Labor Quantity Variance, (5) Actual Rate, (6) Standard Rate, (7) Labor Price Variance, and (8) Explanations.

E26–10 Aladen Company uses a standard cost accounting system. During January, the company reported the following manufacturing variances:

Prepare income statement for management.
(SO 7)

Material price variance	$2,250 debit	Labor quantity variance	$ 725 debit
Material quantity variance	700 credit	Overhead controllable	200 credit
Labor price variance	525 debit	Overhead volume	1,000 debit

In addition, 6,000 units of product were sold at $8.00 per unit. Each unit sold had a standard cost of $6.00. Selling and administrative expenses were $7,000 for the month.

Instructions

Prepare an income statement for management for the month ending January 31, 1999.

E26–11 Frizell Company installed a standard cost system on January 1. Selected transactions for the month of January are as follows:

Journalize entries in a standard cost accounting system.
(SO 7)

1. Purchased 18,000 units of raw materials on account at a cost of $4.30 per unit. Standard cost was $4.00 per unit.
2. Issued 18,000 units of raw materials for jobs that required 17,500 standard units of raw materials.
3. Incurred 15,200 actual hours of direct labor at an actual rate of $4.90 per hour. The standard rate is $5.00 per hour. (Credit Wages Payable)
4. Performed 15,200 hours of direct labor on jobs when standard hours were 15,300.
5. Applied overhead to jobs at the rate of 100% of direct labor cost for standard hours allowed.

Instructions

Journalize the January transactions.

E26–12 Lacruz Company uses a standard cost accounting system. Some of the ledger accounts have been destroyed in a fire. The controller asks your help in reconstructing some missing entries and balances.

Answer questions concerning missing entries and balances.
(SO 4, 5, 7)

Instructions

Answer the following questions:

(a) Materials Price Variance shows a $2,000 favorable balance, and Accounts Payable shows $126,000 of raw materials purchases. What was the amount debited to Raw Materials Inventory for raw materials purchased?

(b) Materials Quantity Variance shows a $3,000 unfavorable balance, and Raw Materials Inventory shows a zero balance. What was the amount debited to Work in Process Inventory for direct materials used?

(c) Labor Price Variance shows a $1,500 unfavorable balance, and Factory Labor shows a debit of $153,000 for wages incurred. What was the amount credited to Wages Payable?

(d) Factory Labor shows a credit of $153,000 for direct labor used, and Labor Quantity Variance shows a $900 unfavorable balance. What was the amount debited to Work in Process for direct labor used?

(e) Overhead applied to Work in Process totaled $165,000. If the total overhead variance was $1,200 unfavorable, what was the amount of overhead costs debited to Manufacturing Overhead?

(f) Overhead Controllable Variance shows a debit balance of $1,500. What was the amount and type of balance (debit or credit) in Overhead Volume Variance?

PROBLEMS: SET A

Compute variances, and prepare income statement.
(SO 4, 5, 7)

P26–1A   Roniger Manufacturing Company uses a standard cost accounting system. In July 1999, it accumulates the following data relative to jobs started and finished:

Cost and Production Data	Actual	Standard
Raw materials		
Units purchased	17,700	
Units used	17,700	18,000
Unit cost	$3.40	$3.00
Direct labor		
Hours worked	2,950	3,000
Hourly rate	$11.80	$12.00
Manufacturing overhead		
Incurred	$87,500	
Applied		$90,000

Manufacturing overhead was applied on the basis of direct labor hours. Normal capacity for the month was 2,800 direct labor hours. At normal capacity, budgeted overhead costs were: variable $56,000 and fixed $28,000.

Jobs finished during the month were sold for $240,000; selling and administrative expenses were $25,000.

Instructions

(a) Compute all of the variances for direct materials, direct labor, and manufacturing overhead.

(b) Prepare an income statement for management. Ignore income taxes.

Compute variances.
(SO 4, 5, 7)

P26–2A   Moreno Corporation manufactures a single product. The standard cost per unit of product is as follows:

Direct materials—2 pounds of plastic at $5.00 per pound	$10.00
Direct labor—2 hours at $12.00 per hour	24.00
Variable manufacturing overhead	12.00
Fixed manufacturing overhead	6.00
Total standard cost per unit	$52.00

The master manufacturing overhead budget for the year based on normal productive capacity of 180,000 direct labor hours (90,000 units) shows total variable costs of $1,080,000 and total fixed costs of $540,000. Overhead is applied on the basis of direct labor hours. Actual costs for November in producing 7,600 units were as follows:

Direct materials (15,000 pounds)	$ 73,500
Direct labor (14,900 hours)	181,780
Variable overhead	88,990
Fixed overhead	44,000
Total manufacturing costs	$388,270

The purchasing department normally buys the quantities of raw materials that are expected to be used in production each month. Raw materials inventories, therefore, can be ignored.

Instructions
Compute all of the materials, labor, and overhead variances.

P26–3A Harbaugh Clothiers manufactures women's business suits. The company uses a standard cost accounting system. In March 1999, 12,000 suits were made. The following standard and actual cost data applied to the month of March when normal capacity was 15,000 direct labor hours.

Compute variances, journalize entries, and identify significant variances.
(SO 4, 5, 6, 7)

Cost Element	Standard (per unit)	Actual
Direct materials	5 yards at $7.00 per yard	$423,400 for 58,000 yards ($7.30 per yard)
Direct labor	1.0 hours at $12.00 per hour	$128,800 for 11,500 hours ($11.20 per hour)
Overhead	1.0 hours at $9.00 per hour (fixed $6.00; variable $3.00)	$90,000 fixed overhead $42,000 variable overhead

Overhead is applied on the basis of direct labor hours. At normal capacity, budgeted fixed overhead costs were $90,000 and budgeted variable overhead costs were $45,000.

Instructions
(a) Compute the total, price, and quantity variances for (1) materials and (2) labor, and compute the total, controllable, and volume variances for manufacturing overhead.
(b) Journalize the entries to record the variances assuming (1) all purchases of materials were on account and (2) Wages Payable was credited for factory labor incurred.
(c) ▣▣▣▶ Which of the materials and labor variances should be investigated if management considers a variance of more than 6% from standard to be significant?

P26–4A Soriano Manufacturing Company uses standard costs with its job order cost accounting system. In January, an order (Job 84) was received for 4,000 units of Product D. The standard cost of 1 unit of Product D is as follows:

Journalize and post standard cost entries and prepare income statement.
(SO 4, 5, 7)

Direct materials—1.5 pounds at $4.00 per pound	$ 6.00
Direct labor—1 hour at $9.00 per hour	9.00
Overhead—1 hour (variable $6.00; fixed $10.00)	16.00
Standard cost per unit	$31.00

Overhead is applied on the basis of direct labor hours. Normal capacity for the month of January was 4,500 direct labor hours. During January, the following transactions applicable to Job No. 84 occurred.

1. Purchased 6,200 pounds of raw materials on account at $3.60 per pound.
2. Requisitioned 6,200 pounds of raw materials for production.
3. Incurred 3,800 hours of direct labor at $9.20 hour.
4. Worked 3,800 hours of direct labor on Job No. 84.
5. Incurred $67,650 of manufacturing overhead on account.
6. Applied overhead to Job No. 84 on the basis of direct labor hours.
7. Transferred Job No. 84 to finished goods.
8. Billed customer for Job No. 84 at a selling price of $250,000.
9. Incurred selling and administrative expenses on account $61,000.

Instructions
(a) Journalize the transactions.
(b) Post to the job order cost accounts.

(c) Prepare the entry to recognize the overhead variances.
(d) Prepare the income statement for management for January 1999.

Answer questions about variances.
(SO 4, 5, 7)

P26–5A   Inwood Manufacturing Company uses a standard cost accounting system. In 1999, 36,000 units were produced. Each unit took several pounds of direct materials and 1⅓ standard hours of direct labor at a standard hourly rate of $12.00. Normal capacity was 42,000 direct labor hours. During the year, 140,000 pounds of raw materials were purchased at $0.94 per pound. All pounds purchased were used during the year.

Instructions
Answer the following questions:

(a) If the materials price variance was $5,600 unfavorable, what was the standard materials price per pound?
(b) If the materials quantity variance was $3,600 favorable, what was the standard materials quantity per unit?
(c) What were the standard hours allowed for the units produced?
(d) If the labor quantity variance was $9,600 unfavorable, what were the actual direct labor hours worked?
(e) If the labor price variance was $7,320 favorable, what was the actual rate per hour?
(f) If total budgeted manufacturing overhead was $315,000 at normal capacity, what was the predetermined overhead rate?
(g) What was the standard cost per unit of product?
(h) How much overhead was applied to production during the year?
(i) If the fixed overhead rate was $2.50, what was the overhead volume variance?
(j) If the overhead controllable variance was $3,000 favorable, what were the total variable overhead costs incurred?
(k) Using selected answers above, what were the total costs assigned to work in process?

Problems: Set B

* *

Compute variances and prepare income statement.
(SO 4, 5, 7)

P26–1B   Mattivi Manufacturing Corporation accumulates the following data relative to jobs started and finished during the month of June 1999:

Costs and Production Data	Actual	Standard
Raw materials purchases, 10,300 units	$22,660	$20,000
Raw materials units used	10,300	10,000
Direct labor payroll	$120,450	$120,000
Direct labor hours worked	14,600	15,000
Manufacturing overhead incurred	$178,500	
Manufacturing overhead applied		$180,000
Machine hours expected to be used at normal capacity		42,500
Budgeted fixed overhead for June		$42,500
Variable overhead rate per hour		$3.00

Overhead is applied on the basis of standard machine hours. Three hours of machine time are required for each direct labor hour. The jobs were sold for $400,000; selling and administrative expenses were $40,000.

Instructions
(a) Compute all of the variances for direct materials, direct labor, and manufacturing overhead.
(b) Prepare an income statement for management. Ignore income taxes.

Compute variances.
(SO 4, 5, 7)

P26–2B   Fuqua Corporation manufactures a single product. The standard cost per unit of product is shown below:

Direct materials—1 pound plastic at $7.00 per pound	$ 7.00
Direct labor—1.5 hours at $12.00 per hour	18.00
Variable manufacturing overhead	11.25
Fixed manufacturing overhead	3.75
Total standard cost per unit	$40.00

The predetermined manufacturing overhead rate is $10 per direct labor hour ($15.00 ÷ 1.5). This rate was computed from a master manufacturing overhead budget based on normal production of 90,000 direct labor hours (60,000 units) for the year. The master budget showed total variable costs of $675,000 and total fixed costs of $225,000. Actual costs for October in producing 4,900 units were as follows:

Direct materials (5,100 pounds)	$ 37,230
Direct labor (7,000 hours)	87,500
Variable overhead	56,170
Fixed overhead	18,750
Total manufacturing costs	$199,650

The purchasing department normally buys the quantities of raw materials that are expected to be used in production each month. Raw materials inventories, therefore, can be ignored.

Instructions
Compute all of the materials, labor, and overhead variances.

P26–3B Drago Clothiers is a small company that manufactures tall men's suits. The company has used a standard cost accounting system. In May 2000, 11,250 suits were produced.

Compute variances, journalize entries, and identify significant variances.
(SO 4, 5, 6, 7)

The following standard and actual cost data applied to the month of May when normal capacity was 14,000 direct labor hours.

Cost Element	Standard (per unit)	Actual
Direct materials	8 yards at $4.50 per yard	$366,000 for 91,500 yards ($4.00 per yard)
Direct labor	1.2 hours at $13.00 per hour	$203,000 for 14,500 hours ($14.00 per hour)
Overhead	1.2 hours at $6.00 per hour (fixed $3.50; variable $2.50)	$49,000 fixed overhead $36,000 variable overhead

Overhead is applied on the basis of direct labor hours. At normal capacity, budgeted fixed overhead costs were $49,000 and budgeted variable overhead was $35,000.

Instructions
(a) Compute the total, price, and quantity variances for (1) materials and (2) labor, and the total, controllable, and volume variances for manufacturing overhead.
(b) Journalize the entries to record the variances assuming (1) all purchases of materials were on account and (2) Wages Payable was credited for factory labor incurred.
(c) ▮▮▮▭▷ Which of the materials and labor variances should be investigated if management considers a variance of more than 7% from standard to be significant?

P26–4B Grassie Corporation uses standard costs with its job order cost accounting system. In January, an order (Job No. 12) for 2,000 units of Product B was received. The standard cost of 1 unit of Product B is as follows:

Journalize and post standard cost entries and prepare income statement.
(SO 4, 5, 7)

Direct materials	3 pounds at $1.00 per pound	$ 3.00
Direct labor	1 hour at $8.00 per hour	8.00
Overhead	2 hours (variable $4.00 per machine hour; fixed $2.00 per machine hour)	12.00
Standard cost per unit		$23.00

Normal capacity for the month was 4,200 machine hours. During January, the following transactions applicable to Job No. 12 occurred:

1. Purchased 6,150 pounds of raw materials on account at $1.10 per pound.
2. Requisitioned 6,150 pounds of raw materials for Job No. 12.
3. Incurred 2,100 hours of direct labor at a rate of $7.80 per hour.
4. Worked 2,100 hours of direct labor on Job No. 12.
5. Incurred manufacturing overhead on account $24,200.
6. Applied overhead to Job No. 12 on basis of standard machine hours used.
7. Completed Job No. 12.
8. Billed customer for Job No. 12 at a selling price of $70,000.
9. Incurred selling and administrative expenses on account $2,000.

Instructions

    (a) Journalize the transactions.

    (b) Post to the job order cost accounts.

    (c) Prepare the entry to recognize the overhead variances.

    (d) Prepare the January 2000 income statement for management.

Answer questions about variances.
(SO 4, 5, 7)

P26–5B Diego Manufacturing Company uses a standard cost accounting system. In 1999, 32,000 units were produced. Each unit took several pounds of direct materials and 1½ standard hours of direct labor at a standard hourly rate of $12.00. Normal capacity was 50,000 direct labor hours. During the year, 133,000 pounds of raw materials were purchased at $0.96 per pound. All pounds purchased were used during the year.

Instructions

Answer the following questions:

    (a) If the materials price variance was $2,660 favorable, what was the standard materials price per pound?

    (b) If the materials quantity variance was $4,900 unfavorable, what was the standard materials quantity per unit?

    (c) What were the standard hours allowed for the units produced?

    (d) If the labor quantity variance was $7,200 unfavorable, what were the actual direct labor hours worked?

    (e) If the labor price variance was $9,720 favorable, what was the actual rate per hour?

    (f) If total budgeted manufacturing overhead was $350,000 at normal capacity, what was the predetermined overhead rate?

    (g) What was the standard cost per unit of product?

    (h) How much overhead was applied to production during the year?

    (i) If the fixed overhead rate was $2.00, what was the overhead volume variance?

    (j) If the overhead controllable variance is $3,000 unfavorable, what were the total variable overhead costs incurred?

    (k) Using one or more answers above, what were the total costs assigned to work in process?

BROADENING YOUR PERSPECTIVE

GROUP DECISION CASE

BYP26–1 Admar Professionals, a management consulting firm, specializes in strategic planning for financial institutions. Tim Adler and Joan Marley, partners in the firm, are assembling a new strategic planning model for use by clients. The model is designed for use on most microcomputers and replaces a rather lengthy manual model currently marketed by the firm. To market the new model Tim and Joan will need to provide clients with an estimate of the number of labor hours and computer time needed to operate the model. The model is currently being test marketed at five small financial institutions. These financial institutions are listed below, along with the number of combined computer/labor hours used by each institution to run the model one time.

Financial Institutions	Computer/Labor Hours Required
Midland National	25
First State	45
Financial Federal	40
Pacific America	30
Lakeview National	30
Total	170
Average	34

Any company that purchases the new model will need to purchase user manuals to access and operate the system. Also required are specialized computer forms that are sold only by Admar Professionals. User manuals will be sold to clients in cases of 20, at a cost of $400 per case. One manual must be used each time the model is run because each manual includes a nonreusable computer accessed password for operating the system. The specialized computer forms are sold in packages of 250, at a cost of $75 per package. One application of the model requires the use of 50 forms. This sum includes two forms that are generally wasted in each application due to printer alignment errors. The overall cost of the strategic planning model to user clients is $12,000. Most clients will use the model four times annually.

Admar Professionals must provide its clients with estimates of ongoing costs incurred in operating the new strategic planning model. They would like to provide this information in the form of standard costs.

Instructions

With the class divided into groups, answer the following:

(a) What factors should be considered in setting a standard for computer/labor hours?
(b) What alternatives for setting a standard for computer/labor hours might be used?
(c) What standard for computer/labor hours would you select? Justify your answer.
(d) Determine the standard material cost associated with the user manuals and computer forms for each application of the strategic planning model.

MANAGERIAL ANALYSIS
••

BYP26–2 Jake Ryan and Associates is a medium-sized company located near a large metropolitan area in the Midwest. The company manufactures cabinets of mahogany, oak, and other fine woods for use in expensive homes, restaurants, and hotels. Although some of the work is custom, many of the cabinets are a standard size. One such model is called Luxury Base Frame. Standard production is 1,000 units. Each unit has a direct labor hour standard of 5 hours. Overhead is applied to production based on standard direct labor hours. During the most recent month, only 900 units were produced; 4,500 direct labor hours were allowed for standard production, but only 4,000 hours were used. Standard and actual overhead costs were as follows:

	Standard (1,000 units)	Actual (900 units)
Indirect materials	$ 12,000	$ 12,300
Indirect labor	43,000	51,000
(Fixed) Manufacturing supervisors salaries	22,000	22,000
(Fixed) Manufacturing office employees salaries	13,000	11,500
(Fixed) Engineering costs	27,000	25,000
Computer costs	10,000	10,000
Electricity	2,500	2,500
(Fixed) Manufacturing building depreciation	8,000	8,000
(Fixed) Machinery depreciation	3,000	3,000
(Fixed) Trucks and forklift depreciation	1,500	1,500
Small tools	700	1,400
(Fixed) Insurance	500	500
(Fixed) Property taxes	300	300
Total	$143,500	$149,000

Instructions

(a) Determine the overhead application rate.
(b) Determine how much overhead was applied to production.
(c) Calculate the controllable overhead variance and the overhead volume variance.
(d) Decide which overhead variances should be investigated.
(e) Discuss causes of the overhead variances. What can management do to improve its performance next month?

REAL-WORLD FOCUS: Glassmaster Company

BYP26–3 **Glassmaster Co.** was incorporated in 1946 as Koolvent Metal Awning Company. Its current name was adopted in 1982 to reflect the more general nature of its products. The company is organized as two divisions and one subsidiary. One division focuses on the manufacture of filaments such as fishing line and sewing thread; the other division manufactures antennas and specialty fiberglass products. Its subsidiary manufactures flexible steel wire controls and molded control panels.

The annual report of Glassmaster provides the following information:

**GLASSMASTER COMPANY
Management Discussion**

Gross profit margins for the year improved to 20.9% of sales compared to last year's 18.5%. All operations reported improved margins due in large part to improved operating efficiencies as a result of cost reduction measures implemented during the second and third quarters of the fiscal year and increased manufacturing throughout due to higher unit volume sales. Contributing to the improved margins was a favorable materials price variance due to competitive pricing by suppliers as a result of soft demand for petrochemical-based products. This favorable variance is temporary and will begin to reverse itself as stronger worldwide demand for commodity products improves in tandem with the economy. Partially offsetting these positive effects on profit margins were competitive pressures on sales prices of certain product lines. The company responded with pricing strategies designed to maintain and/or increase market share.

Instructions
  (a) Is it apparent from the information whether Glassmaster utilizes standard costs?
  (b) Do you think the price variance experienced should lead to changes in standard costs for the next fiscal year?

COMMUNICATION ACTIVITY

BYP26–4   The setting of standards is critical to the effective use of standards in evaluating performance.

Instructions
Explain in a memorandum to your instructor (a) the comparative advantages and disadvantages of ideal versus normal standards, and (b) the factors that should be included in setting the price and quantity standards for direct materials, direct labor, and manufacturing overhead.

RESEARCH ASSIGNMENT

BYP26–5   The December 1996 issue of *Accounting Horizons* contains an article by Carol B. Cheatham and Leo R. Cheatham entitled ''Redesigning Cost Systems: Is Standard Costing Obsolete?''

Instructions
Read the article and answer the following questions:
  (a) For what percent of U.S. manufacturing firms are standard cost systems still the cost system of choice?
  (b) What are the major criticisms of standard cost systems?
  (c) How does a standard cost system relate to activity-based costing (ABC)? And, how might activity-based costing (ABC) be used to enhance a company's costing system when standard costing is the primary system?
  (d) What do the authors conclude from their study of standard cost systems?

ETHICS CASE

BYP26–6   In Corolla Manufacturing Company production workers in the Painting Department are paid on the basis of productivity. The labor time standard for a unit of production is established through periodic time studies conducted by the Manpower Management Department. In a time study, the actual time required to complete a specific task by a worker is observed. Allowances are then made for preparation time, rest periods, and clean up time. Jeff Jorden is one of several veterans in the Painting Department.

Jeff is informed by Manpower Management that he will be used in the time study for the painting of a new product. The findings will be the basis for establishing the labor time standard for the next 6 months. During the test, Jeff deliberately slows his normal work pace in an effort to obtain a labor time standard that will be easy to meet. Because it is a new product, the Manpower Management representative who conducted the test is unaware that Jeff did not give the test his best effort.

Instructions
- (a) Who was benefited and who was harmed by Jeff's actions?
- (b) Was Jeff ethical in the way he performed the time study test?
- (c) What measure(s) might the company take to obtain valid data for setting the labor time standard?

SURFING THE NET

BYP26–7   Computer manufacturer Hewlett-Packard's Web site provides information about Hewlett-Packard's 25,000 electronic products and services, its worldwide operations, and its financial picture.

Address: http://www.hp.com/

Steps:
1. Choose **HP Financials.**
2. Choose the current **Annual Report.**
3. Review the Summary of Significant Accounting Policies in the Notes to the Financial Statements.

Instructions
- (a) At what cost does Hewlett-Packard report its inventories?
- (b) What inventory costing method does standard cost approximate for Hewlett-Packard?
- (c) Has the lower-of-cost-or-market rule been applied to the Hewlett-Packard inventories?
- (d) Why do you suppose that Hewlett-Packard accounts for and reports its inventories at standard cost?

Answers to Self-Study Questions
1. c   2. d   3. b   4. c   5. b   6. a   7. d   8. a   9. b   10. c

Remember to go back to the Navigator box on the chapter-opening page and check off your completed work.

CONCEPTS FOR REVIEW

Before studying this chapter, you should know or, if necessary, review:

a. The difference between variable and fixed costs. (Ch. 23, pp. 997–1000)
b. The meaning of the term contribution margin. (Ch. 23, pp. 1004)
c. How to use present value tables. (Appendix C)

THE NAVIGATOR

FEATURE STORY

What's in a Word?

What's the difference between gross and net? About $20 million if you're Tom Hanks, the actor who played Forrest Gump, or novelist Winston Groom, the creator of the character. Although the movie grossed over $661 million in box office sales, Paramount Pictures says *Forrest Gump* lost millions.

How does Paramount show a loss when it appears to have a real winner? It starts by charging a distribution fee—of nearly a third of the movie's ticket sales—that goes to the

studio as almost pure profit. Distribution *expenses*—for everything from making and shipping copies of the film to opening-night parties in posh places—are also added. The costs of actually making the movie have to be accounted for as well, including such costs as office staff, valets and personal trainers for the stars, and even take-out meals from fast-food restaurants. Finally, 50% of each movie's revenues go to theater owners.

For *Forrest Gump*, the distribution fees, expenses, and advertising costs totaled $135 million. The costs

of making the movie, including $20 million each to the star and the director, were $112 million. Studio overhead, computed as about 15% of the cost of making the film, was another $14.5 million. And let's not forget $6 million in interest the studio calculates it *would have earned* if it had put the money it cost to make the movie into the bank—or as some have called it, "interest on money never borrowed."

Thus, accountants for Paramount have managed to make *Forrest Gump* look like a financial loser. Why do that? Because the author and the screenwriter had contracts that provided a fixed percentage of the movie's net profits—repeat, *net profits*. Hanks, knowledgeable to Hollywood's ways, specified that he wanted his contract to be a percentage of *gross profits*—that is, profit before the chicanery.

The author and screenwriter are taking this issue to the courts, where it could be tied up for years. Before the accounting issues were resolved in this and other pending lawsuits, though, a committee on accounting procedures of the American Institute of Certified Public Accountants in February 1998 approved new rules that will remove some of the creativity from Hollywood accounting.

THE NAVIGATOR

On the World Wide Web
http://www.paramount.com

CHAPTER 27

INCREMENTAL ANALYSIS AND CAPITAL BUDGETING

THE NAVIGATOR ✓

- ■ Understand *Concepts for Review* ☐
- ■ Read *Feature Story* ☐
- ■ Scan *Study Objectives* ☐
- ■ Read *Preview* ☐
- ■ Read text and answer *Before You Go On* p. 1164 ☐
- ■ Work *Demonstration Problem 1* ☐
- ■ Read text and answer *Before You Go On* p. 1174 ☐
- ■ Work *Demonstration Problem 2* ☐
- ■ Review *Summary of Study Objectives* ☐
- ■ Answer *Self-Study Questions* ☐
- ■ Complete assignments ☐

STUDY OBJECTIVES

After studying this chapter, you should be able to:

1. *Identify the steps in management's decision-making process.*
2. *Describe the concept of incremental analysis.*
3. *Identify the relevant costs in accepting an order at a special price.*
4. *Indicate the relevant costs in a make-or-buy decision.*
5. *Give the decision rule in deciding whether to sell or process materials further.*
6. *Identify the factors to be considered in retaining or replacing equipment.*
7. *Explain the factors that are relevant in deciding whether to eliminate an unprofitable segment.*
8. *Determine which products to make and sell when a company has limited resources.*
9. *Contrast the annual rate of return and cash payback techniques in capital budgeting.*
10. *Distinguish between the net present value and internal rate of return methods.*

*A*n important purpose of management accounting is to provide management with relevant information for decision making. Examples of these decisions might include:

1. Paramount Picture's decision to produce *Forrest Gump* rather than some other movie.
2. Boeing's strategic decisions to spend $5 billion to build a plane for the 21st century—the B-777—and to cancel development of a larger version of the B-747.
3. Intel Corporation's decision to bring out the Pentium Pro processor, a power-house chip that runs at initial speeds of up to 200 MHz, demands 32-bit soft-ware, and drives network servers.

This chapter begins with an explanation of management's decision-making pro-cess. It then considers the topics of incremental analysis and capital budgeting. The content and organization of this chapter are as follows:

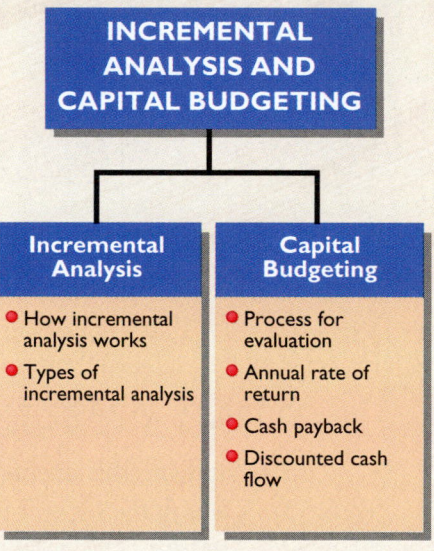

THE
NAVIGATOR

SECTION 1 INCREMENTAL ANALYSIS

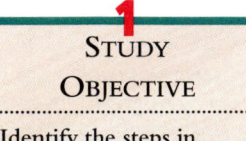

STUDY OBJECTIVE

1

Identify the steps in management's decision-making process.

Making decisions is an important part of management. Management's decision-making process does not always follow a set pattern, because decisions vary significantly in their scope, urgency, and importance. It is possible, however, to identify some steps that are frequently involved in the process. These steps are graphically shown in Illustration 27-1.

Accounting's contribution to the decision-making process occurs primarily in Steps 2 and 4. In Step 2, for each possible course of action, relevant revenue and cost data are provided to show the expected overall effect on net income. In Step 4, internal reports are prepared that review the actual impact of the decision.

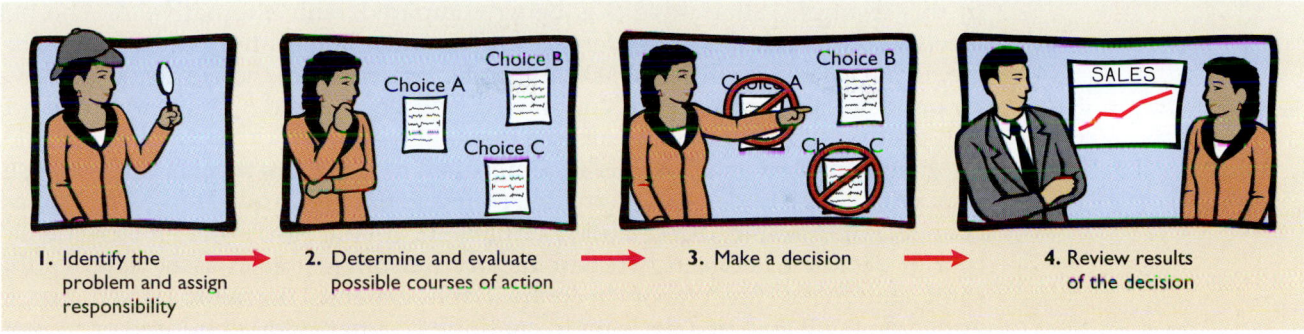

1. Identify the problem and assign responsibility → 2. Determine and evaluate possible courses of action → 3. Make a decision → 4. Review results of the decision

ILLUSTRATION 27-1

Management's decision-making process

In making business decisions, management ordinarily considers both financial and nonfinancial information. **Financial** information is related to revenues and costs and their effect on the company's overall profitability. **Nonfinancial** information relates to such factors as the effect of the decision on employee turnover, the environment, or the overall image of the company in the community. Although the nonfinancial information can be as important as, and in some cases more important than, the financial information, we will limit our discussion primarily to financial information that is relevant to the decision.

Decisions involve a choice among alternative courses of action. Suppose that you were deciding whether to purchase or lease an IBM PC for use in doing your accounting homework. The financial data relate to the cost of leasing versus the cost of purchasing. For example, leasing would involve periodic lease payments; purchasing would require payment of the purchase price. In other words, the financial data relevant to the decision are the data that would vary in the future among the possible alternatives. The process used to identify the financial data that change under alternative courses of action is called **incremental analysis**. In some cases, you will find that when you use incremental analysis, both costs and revenues will change. In other cases, only costs or revenues will vary.

Just as your decision to buy or lease a PC will affect your future, similar decisions—on a larger scale—will affect a company's future. It follows, therefore, that incremental analysis includes the probable effects of those decisions on future earnings. Such data inevitably involve estimates and uncertainty. Gathering data for incremental analyses may involve market analysts, engineers, and accountants. In quantifying the data, the accountant is expected to exercise professional judgment to produce the most reliable information available at the time the decision must be made.

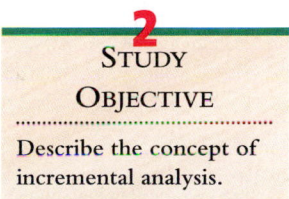

STUDY OBJECTIVE

Describe the concept of incremental analysis.

ALTERNATIVE TERMINOLOGY
Incremental analysis is also called *differential analysis* because the analysis focuses on differences.

HOW INCREMENTAL ANALYSIS WORKS

The basic approach in incremental analysis is illustrated in the following example:

	Alternative A	Alternative B	Net Income Increase (Decrease)
Revenues	$125,000	$110,000	$(15,000)
Costs	100,000	80,000	20,000
Net income	$ 25,000	$ 30,000	$ 5,000

ILLUSTRATION 27-2

Basic approach in incremental analysis

In this example, alternative B is being compared with alternative A. The net income column shows the differences between the alternatives. In this case, incremental revenue will be $15,000 less under alternative B than under alternative A, but a $20,000 incremental cost saving will be realized.[1] Thus, alternative B will produce $5,000 more net income than alternative A.

In incremental analysis, it is also important to recognize that (1) variable costs may not change under the alternative courses of action, and (2) fixed costs may change. For example, direct labor, normally a variable cost, is not an incremental cost in deciding between two new factory machines if each asset requires the same amount of direct labor. In contrast, rent expense, normally a fixed cost, is an incremental cost in a decision to continue occupancy of a building or to purchase or lease a new building.

TYPES OF INCREMENTAL ANALYSIS

A number of different types of decisions involve incremental analysis. The more common types of decisions are whether to:

1. Accept an order at a special price.
2. Make or buy.
3. Sell or process further.
4. Retain or replace equipment.
5. Eliminate an unprofitable business segment.
6. Allocate limited resources.

We will consider each of these types of analysis in the following pages.

Accept an Order at a Special Price

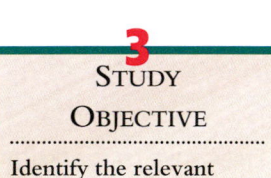

STUDY OBJECTIVE 3

Identify the relevant costs in accepting an order at a special price.

HELPFUL HINT

This is a good example of different costs for different purposes. In the long-run all costs are relevant, but for this decision only costs that change are relevant.

Sometimes, a company may have an opportunity to obtain additional business if it is willing to make a major price concession to a specific customer. To illustrate, assume that Sunbelt Company produces 100,000 automatic blenders per month, which is 80% of plant capacity. Variable manufacturing costs are $8 per unit, and fixed manufacturing costs are $400,000, or $4 per unit. The blenders are normally sold directly to retailers at $20 each. Sunbelt has an offer from Mexico Co. (a foreign wholesaler) to purchase an additional 2,000 blenders at $11 per unit. Acceptance of the offer would not affect normal sales of the product, and the additional units can be manufactured without increasing plant capacity. What should management do?

If management makes its decision on the basis of the total cost per unit of $12 ($8 + $4), the order would be rejected, because costs ($12) would exceed revenues ($11) by $1 per unit. However, since the units can be produced within existing plant capacity, the special order **will not increase fixed costs**. The relevant data for the decision, therefore, are the variable manufacturing costs per unit of $8 and the expected revenue of $11 per unit. Thus, as shown in Illustration 27-3, Sunbelt will increase its net income by $6,000 by accepting this special order.

Two points should be emphasized: First, it is assumed that sales of the product in other markets would not be affected by this special order. If other sales were affected, then Sunbelt would have to consider the lost sales in making the

---

[1]Although income taxes are sometimes important in incremental analysis, they are ignored in the chapter for simplicity's sake.

	Reject Order	Accept Order	Net Income Increase (Decrease)
Revenues	$-0-	$22,000	$22,000
Costs	-0-	16,000	(16,000)
Net income	$-0-	$ 6,000	$ 6,000

ILLUSTRATION 27-3
Incremental analysis— accepting an order at a special price

decision. Second, if Sunbelt is operating at full capacity, it is likely that the special order would be rejected. Under such circumstances, the company would have to expand plant capacity, and, the special order would have to absorb these additional fixed manufacturing costs, as well as the variable manufacturing costs.

Make or Buy

When a manufacturer assembles component parts in producing a finished product, management must decide whether to make or buy the components. For example, General Motors Corporation may either make or buy the batteries, tires, and radios used in its cars. Similarly, Zenith Corporation may make or buy the electronic circuitry, cabinets, and speakers for its television sets. The decision to make or buy components should be made on the basis of incremental analysis.

To illustrate the analysis, assume that Baron Company incurs the following annual costs in producing 25,000 ignition switches for motor scooters:

4
STUDY OBJECTIVE

Indicate the relevant costs in a make-or-buy decision.

Direct materials	$ 50,000
Direct labor	75,000
Variable manufacturing overhead	40,000
Fixed manufacturing overhead	60,000
Total manufacturing costs	$225,000
Total cost per unit ($225,000 ÷ 25,000)	$9.00

ILLUSTRATION 27-4
Annual product cost data

Alternatively, Baron Company may purchase the ignition switches from Ignition, Inc., at a price of $8 per unit. The question again is, "What should management do?"

On the one hand, it appears that management should purchase the ignition switches for $8, rather than make them at a cost of $9. However, a review of operations indicates that if the ignition switches are purchased from Ignition, Inc., all of Baron's variable costs but only $10,000 of its fixed manufacturing costs will be eliminated. Thus, $50,000 of the fixed manufacturing costs will remain if the ignition switches are purchased. The relevant costs for incremental analysis, therefore, are as follows:

	Make	Buy	Net Income Increase (Decrease)
Direct materials	$ 50,000	$ -0-	$ 50,000
Direct labor	75,000	-0-	75,000
Variable manufacturing costs	40,000	-0-	40,000
Fixed manufacturing costs	60,000	50,000	10,000
Purchase price (25,000 × $8)	-0-	200,000	(200,000)
Total annual cost	$225,000	$250,000	$ (25,000)

ILLUSTRATION 27-5
Incremental analysis—make or buy

This analysis indicates that Baron Company will incur $25,000 of additional cost by buying the ignition switches. Therefore, Baron should continue to make the ignition switches, even though the total manufacturing cost is $1 higher than the purchase price. The reason is that if the company purchases the ignition switches, it will still have fixed costs of $50,000 to absorb.

The foregoing analysis is complete only if it is assumed that the productive capacity used to make the ignition switches cannot be converted to another purpose. If there is an opportunity to use this productive capacity in some other manner, then this opportunity cost must be considered. **Opportunity cost** is the potential benefit that may be obtained by following an alternative course of action. To illustrate, assume that through buying the switches, Baron Company can use the released productive capacity to generate additional income of $28,000. This lost income is an additional cost of continuing to make the switches in the make-or-buy decision. This opportunity cost therefore is added to the "Make" column, for comparison. As shown, it is now advantageous to buy the ignition switches.

ILLUSTRATION 27-6

Incremental analysis—make or buy, with opportunity cost

	Make	Buy	Net Income Increase (Decrease)
Total annual cost	$225,000	$250,000	$(25,000)
Opportunity cost	28,000	–0–	28,000
Total cost	$253,000	$250,000	$ 3,000

The qualitative factors in this decision include the possible loss of jobs for employees who produce the ignition switches. In addition, management must assess how long the supplier will be able to satisfy the company's quality control standards at the quoted price per unit.

ACCOUNTING IN ACTION
Business Insight

As an example of opportunity cost, one construction company with a heavy load of debt had several pieces of very expensive equipment that had been fully depreciated. The company's books told management that this equipment wasn't tying up any capital. Supposedly it didn't cost the company anything to keep that equipment, except for maintenance expenses. But the equipment could have been sold for a good price. Therefore that zero book value was misleading. The equipment was actually taking up a substantial amount of expensive capital and contributing to the company's weak financial position.

Sell or Process Further

Many manufacturers have the option of selling products at a given point in the production cycle or continuing to process with the expectation of selling them at a higher price. For example, a bicycle manufacturer such as Schwinn could sell its 10-speed bicycles to retailers either unassembled or assembled, and a furniture manufacturer such as Ethan Allen could sell its dining room sets to furniture stores either unfinished or finished. The sell-or-process further decision should be made on the basis of incremental analysis. The basic decision rule is: **Process further as long as the incremental revenue from such processing exceeds the incremental processing costs.**

Assume, for example, that Woodmasters Inc. makes tables. The cost to manufacture an unfinished table is $35, computed as follows:

Direct material	$15
Direct labor	10
Variable manufacturing overhead	6
Fixed manufacturing overhead	4
Manufacturing cost per unit	**$35**

The selling price per unfinished unit is $50. Woodmasters currently has unused productive capacity that is expected to continue indefinitely. Management concludes that some of this capacity may be used to finish the tables and sell them at $60 per unit. For a finished table, it is anticipated that direct materials and direct labor costs will increase $2 and $4, respectively. In addition, variable manufacturing overhead costs will increase by $2.40 (60% of direct labor). No increase is anticipated in fixed manufacturing overhead. The incremental analysis on a per unit basis is as follows:

	Sell	Process Further	Net Income Increase (Decrease)
Sales per unit	$50.00	$60.00	**$10.00**
Cost per unit			
Direct materials	15.00	17.00	**(2.00)**
Direct labor	10.00	14.00	**(4.00)**
Variable manufacturing overhead	6.00	8.40	**(2.40)**
Fixed manufacturing overhead	4.00	4.00	**–0–**
Total	$35.00	$43.40	**$ (8.40)**
Net income per unit	$15.00	$16.60	**$ 1.60**

HELPFUL HINT
Current net income is known. Net income from processing further is an estimate. In making its decision, management could add a "risk" factor for the estimate.

As indicated from the analysis, it would be advantageous for Woodmaster to process the tables further. In this case, the incremental revenue of $10.00 from the additional processing is $1.60 higher than the incremental processing costs of $8.40.

Retain or Replace Equipment

Management often has to decide whether to continue using an asset or replace it. To illustrate, assume that Jeffcoat Company has a factory machine with a book value of $40,000 and a remaining useful life of four years. A new machine is available that costs $120,000 and is expected to have zero salvage value at the end of its 4-year useful life. If the new machine is acquired, variable manufacturing costs are expected to decrease from $160,000 to $125,000 annually and the old unit will be scrapped. The incremental analysis for the 4-year period is as follows:

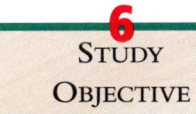

6
STUDY
OBJECTIVE
....
Identify the factors to be considered in retaining or replacing equipment.

ILLUSTRATION 27-9

Incremental analysis—retain or replace equipment

	Retain Equipment	Replace Equipment	Net Income Increase (Decrease)
Variable manufacturing costs	$640,000[a]	$500,000[b]	$140,000
New machine cost		120,000	(120,000)
Total	$640,000	$620,000	$ 20,000

[a](4 years × $160,000)
[b](4 years × $125,000)

In this case, it would be to the company's advantage to replace the equipment. The lower variable manufacturing costs due to replacement more than offset the cost of the new equipment.

One other point should be mentioned regarding Jeffcoat's decision: **The book value of the old machine does not affect the decision.** Book value is a sunk cost, which is a cost that cannot be changed by any present or future decision. Sunk costs, therefore, **are not relevant in incremental analysis**. In this example, if the asset is retained, book value will be depreciated over its remaining useful life. On the other hand, if the new unit is acquired, book value will be recognized as a loss of the current period. Thus, the effect of book value on current and future earnings is the same regardless of the replacement decision. **Any trade-in allowance or cash disposal value of the existing asset, however, is relevant** to the decision, because this value will not be realized if the asset is continued in use.

Eliminate an Unprofitable Segment

Management sometimes needs to decide whether to eliminate an unprofitable business segment. Again, the key is to focus on the data that change under the alternative courses of action. To illustrate, assume that Martina Company manufactures tennis racquets in three models: Pro, Master, and Champ. Pro and Master are profitable lines, whereas Champ (highlighted in color in the table below) operates at a loss. Condensed income statement data are:

ILLUSTRATION 27-10

Segment income data

HELPFUL HINT

A decision to discontinue a segment based solely on the bottom line—net loss—is inappropriate.

	Pro	Master	Champ	Total
Sales	$800,000	$300,000	$100,000	$1,200,000
Variable expenses	520,000	210,000	90,000	820,000
Contribution margin	280,000	90,000	10,000	380,000
Fixed expenses	80,000	50,000	30,000	160,000
Net income	$200,000	$ 40,000	$ (20,000)	$ 220,000

It might be expected that total net income will increase by $20,000 to $240,000 if the unprofitable line of racquets is eliminated. However, **it is possible for net income to decrease if the Champ line is discontinued**. The reason is that the fixed expenses allocated to the Champ racquets will have to be absorbed by the other products. To illustrate, assume that the $30,000 of fixed costs applicable to the unprofitable segment are allocated ⅔ and ⅓ to the Pro and Master product lines, respectively. Fixed expenses will increase to $100,000 ($80,000 + $20,000) in the Pro line and to $60,000 ($50,000 + $10,000) in the Master line. The revised income statement is:

ILLUSTRATION 27-11

Income data after eliminating unprofitable product line

	Pro	Master	Total
Sales	$800,000	$300,000	$1,100,000
Variable expenses	520,000	210,000	730,000
Contribution margin	280,000	90,000	370,000
Fixed expenses	100,000	60,000	160,000
Net income	$180,000	$ 30,000	$ 210,000

Total net income has decreased $10,000 ($220,000 − $210,000). This result is also obtained in the following incremental analysis of the Champ racquets:

ILLUSTRATION 27-12

Incremental analysis— eliminating an unprofitable segment

	Continue	Eliminate	Net Income Increase (Decrease)
Sales	$100,000	$ –0–	$(100,000)
Variable expenses	90,000	–0–	90,000
Contribution margin	10,000	–0–	(10,000)
Fixed expenses	30,000	30,000	–0–
Net income	$ (20,000)	$(30,000)	$ (10,000)

The loss in net income is attributable to the contribution margin ($10,000) that will not be realized if the segment is discontinued.

In deciding on the future status of an unprofitable segment, management should consider the effect of elimination on related product lines. It may be possible for continuing product lines to obtain some or all of the sales lost by the discontinued product line. In some businesses, services or products may be linked—for example, free checking accounts at a bank, or coffee at a donut shop. In addition, management should consider the effect of eliminating the product line on employees who may have to be discharged or retrained.

Allocate Limited Resources

Everyone's resources are limited. For a company, the limited resource may be floor space in a retail department store, or raw materials, direct labor hours, or machine capacity in a manufacturing company. When a company has limited resources, management must decide which products to make and sell in order to maximize net income.

To illustrate, assume that Collins Company manufactures deluxe and standard pen and pencil sets. The limiting resource is machine capacity, which is 3,600 hours per month. Relevant data consist of the following:

8
STUDY OBJECTIVE
....
Determine which products to make and sell when a company has limited resources.

ILLUSTRATION 27-13

Contribution margin and machine hours

	Deluxe Sets	Standard Sets
Contribution margin per unit	$8	$6
Machine hours required	4	2

The deluxe sets may appear to be more profitable since they have a higher contribution margin ($8) than the standard sets ($6). However, note that the standard sets take fewer machine hours to produce than the deluxe sets. Therefore, it is necessary to find the **contribution margin per unit of limited resource,** in this case, contribution margin per machine hour. This is obtained by dividing the contribution margin per unit of each product by the number of units of the limited resource required for each product. The computation shows that the standard sets have a higher contribution margin per unit of limited resource.

ILLUSTRATION 27-14

Contribution margin per unit of limited resource

	Deluxe Sets	Standard Sets
Contribution margin per unit (a)	$8	$6
Machine hours required (b)	4	2
Contribution margin per unit of limited resource (a) ÷ (b)	**$2**	**$3**

If Collins Company is able to increase machine capacity from 3,600 hours to 4,200 hours, the additional 600 hours could be used to produce either the standard or deluxe pen and pencil sets. The total contribution margin under each alternative is found by multiplying the machine hours by the contribution margin per unit of limited resource as shown below.

ILLUSTRATION 27-15

Incremental analysis—computation of total contribution margin

	Produce Deluxe Sets	Produce Standard Sets
Machine hours (a)	600	600
Contribution margin per unit of limited resource (b)	$2	$3
Contribution margin (a) × (b)	$1,200	$1,800

From this analysis, we can see that to maximize net income, all of the increased capacity should be used to make and sell the standard sets.

BEFORE YOU GO ON . . .

Review It

1. Give three examples of how incremental analysis might be used.
2. What is the decision rule in deciding to sell or process products further?
3. How may the elimination of an unprofitable segment decrease the overall net income of a company?
4. What is the critical factor in allocating limited resources?

Do It

Cobb Company incurs a cost of $28 per unit, of which $18 is variable, to make a product that normally sells for $42. A foreign wholesaler offers to buy 5,000 units at $25 each. Cobb will incur shipping costs of $1 per unit. Compute the net income (loss) Cobb will realize by accepting the special order, assuming Cobb has excess operating capacity.

Reasoning: The decision in this case involves incremental analysis. Thus, Cobb must identify the revenues and costs that change by accepting the special order.

Solution:

	Reject	Accept	Net Income Increase (Decrease)
Revenues	$-0-	$125,000	$125,000
Costs	-0-	95,000*	(95,000)
Net income	$-0-	$ 30,000	$ 30,000

*(5,000 × $18) + (5,000 × $1)

Related exercise material: BE27-2, BE27-3, and E27-1.

THE NAVIGATOR

DEMONSTRATION PROBLEM 1

Juanita Company must decide whether to make or buy some of its components. The costs of producing 50,000 electrical cords for its floor lamps are as follows:

Direct materials	$60,000	Variable overhead	$12,000
Direct labor	30,000	Fixed overhead	8,000

Instead of making the electrical cords at an average cost per unit of $2.20 ($110,000 ÷ 50,000), the company has an opportunity to buy the cords at $2.30 per unit. If the cords are purchased all variable costs and one-half of the fixed costs will be eliminated.

Instructions

(a) Prepare an incremental analysis showing whether the company should make or buy the electrical cords.

(b) Will your answer be different if the released productive capacity will generate additional income of $25,000?

SOLUTION TO DEMONSTRATION PROBLEM

(a)

	Make	Buy	Net Income Increase (Decrease)
Direct materials	$ 60,000	$ -0-	$ 60,000
Direct labor	30,000	-0-	30,000
Variable manufacturing costs	12,000	-0-	12,000
Fixed manufacturing costs	8,000	4,000	4,000
Purchase price	-0-	115,000	(115,000)
Total cost	$110,000	$119,000	$ (9,000)

This analysis indicates that Juanita Company will incur $9,000 of additional costs if it buys the electrical cords.

(b)

	Make	Buy	Net Income Increase (Decrease)
Total cost	$110,000	$119,000	$ (9,000)
Opportunity cost	25,000		25,000
Total cost	$135,000	$119,000	$ 16,000

Yes, the answer is different because the analysis shows that net income will be increased by $16,000 if the electrical cords are purchased.

PROBLEM-SOLVING STRATEGIES

1. Look for the costs that change.

2. Ignore the costs that do not change.

3. Use the format in the chapter for your answer.

4. Recognize that opportunity cost can make a difference.

THE NAVIGATOR

SECTION 2   CAPITAL BUDGETING

Individuals make capital expenditures when they buy a new home, car, or television set. Similarly, businesses make capital expenditures when they modernize plant facilities or expand operations. Examples include the new engine plant recently built in Detroit by Chrysler Corporation and the new baseball stadium built in Denver by the Colorado Rockies team.

The amounts spent by companies on capital expenditures each year are substantial. For example, in a recent year, U.S. businesses spent approximately $375 billion on capital expenditures. More specifically, in 1996, Intel Corporation spent $4.1 billion, Burlington Northern Santa Fe Corp. spent $2.2 billion, and Caterpillar spent $771 million. In business enterprises, as for individuals, the amount of possible capital expenditures usually exceeds the funds available for such expenditures. Thus, the resources available must be allocated (or budgeted) among the competing alternatives. The process of making capital expenditure decisions in business is known as **capital budgeting**. Capital budgeting involves choosing among various capital projects to find the one(s) that will maximize a company's return on investment.

PROCESS FOR EVALUATION

Many companies follow a carefully prescribed process in capital budgeting. At least once a year, proposals for projects are requested from each department and plant and from authorized personnel. The proposals are screened by a capital budgeting committee, which submits its findings to the officers of the company. The officers, in turn, select the projects they believe to be most worthy of funding and submit them to the board of directors. Ultimately, the directors approve the capital expenditure budget for the year. The involvement of top management and the board of directors in the process demonstrates the importance of capital budgeting decisions. These decisions often have a significant impact on a company's future profitability. Indeed, poor capital budgeting decisions have led to the bankruptcy of some companies. Accounting data are indispensable in assessing the probable effects of capital expenditures.

To provide management with relevant data for capital budgeting decisions, you should be familiar with the quantitative techniques that may be used. The three most common techniques are: (1) annual rate of return, (2) cash payback, and (3) discounted cash flow. To illustrate the three quantitative techniques, assume that Tappan Company is considering an investment of $130,000 in new equipment. The new equipment is expected to last 10 years and have zero salvage value at the end of its useful life. The straight-line method of depreciation is used for accounting purposes. The expected annual revenues and costs of the new product that will be produced from the investment are:

INTERNATIONAL NOTE

The World Bank estimates that Asian, Latin American, and other developing nations will be spending over $200 billion annually on infrastructure in the years just ahead. U.S. manufacturers of equipment used to build the infrastructure will benefit greatly.

ILLUSTRATION 27-16

Estimated annual net income from capital expenditure

Sales		$200,000
Less: Costs and expenses		
Manufacturing costs (exclusive of depreciation)	$145,000	
Depreciation expense ($130,000 ÷ 10)	13,000	
Selling and administrative expenses	22,000	180,000
Income before income taxes		20,000
Income tax expense		7,000
Net income		$ 13,000

ANNUAL RATE OF RETURN

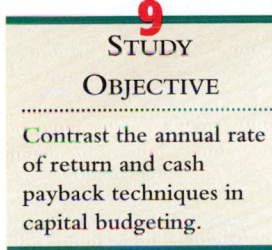

9
STUDY
OBJECTIVE
....
Contrast the annual rate
of return and cash
payback techniques in
capital budgeting.

The **annual rate of return technique** is based directly on accounting data. It indicates **the profitability of a capital expenditure** by dividing expected annual net income by the average investment. The formula for computing annual rate of return is shown in Illustration 27-17.

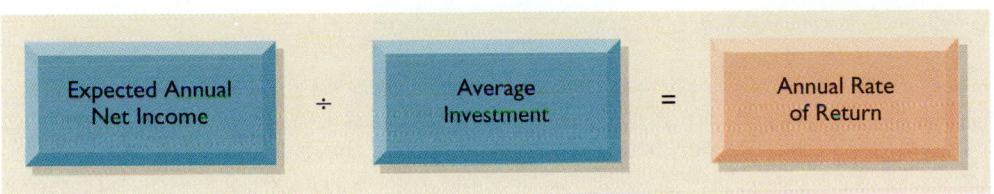

ILLUSTRATION 27-17

Annual rate of return formula

Expected annual net income is obtained from the projected income statement. Tappan Company's expected annual net income is $13,000. Average investment is derived from the following formula:

$$\text{Average investment} = \frac{\text{Original investment} + \text{Investment at end of useful life}}{2}$$

ILLUSTRATION 27-18

Formula for computing average investment

The investment at the end of useful life is equal to the asset's salvage value, if any. For Tappan Company, average investment is $65,000 [($130,000 + $0) ÷ 2]. The expected annual rate of return for Tappan Company's investment in new equipment is therefore 20%, computed as follows:

$$\$13,000 \div \$65,000 = 20\%$$

The annual rate of return is then compared with the management's required minimum rate of return for investments of similar risk. The minimum rate of return (also called the **hurdle rate** or **cutoff rate**) is generally based on the company's **cost of capital**. The **cost of capital** is the rate of return that management expects to pay on all borrowed and equity funds. It does not relate to the cost of funding a specific project. The decision rule is: **A project is acceptable if its rate of return is greater than management's minimum rate of return; it is unacceptable when the reverse is true.** When the rate of return technique is used in deciding among several acceptable projects, **the higher the rate of return for a given risk, the more attractive the investment.**

The principal advantages of this technique of analysis are the simplicity of its calculation and management's familiarity with the accounting terms used in the computation. A major limitation of the annual rate of return approach is that it does not consider the time value of money. For example, no consideration is given as to whether cash inflows from the investment will occur early or late in the life of the investment. As explained in Appendix C, recognition of the time value of money can make a significant difference between the future value and the discounted present value of an investment.

HELPFUL HINT
A capital budgeting decision based on only one technique may be misleading. It is often wise to analyze the situation from a number of different perspectives.

CASH PAYBACK

The **cash payback technique** identifies the time period required to recover the cost of the capital investment from the annual cash inflow produced by the investment. The formula for computing the cash payback period is:

ILLUSTRATION 27-19

Cash payback formula

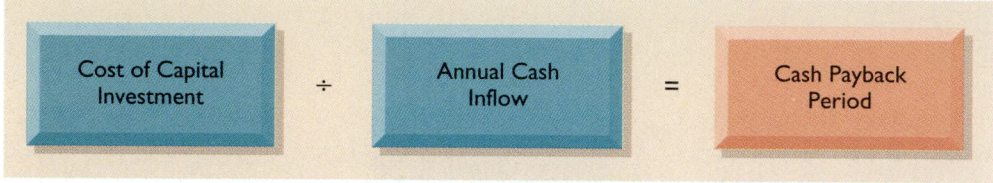

Annual cash inflow, also known as net cash inflow, is approximated by taking net income and adding back depreciation expense. Depreciation expense is added back because depreciation on the capital expenditure does not involve an annual outflow of cash. Accordingly, the depreciation deducted in determining net income must be added back to determine annual cash inflows. In the Tappan Company example, annual cash inflow is $26,000, as shown below.

ILLUSTRATION 27-20

Computation of annual cash inflow

Net income	$13,000
Add: Depreciation expense	13,000
Annual cash inflow	**$26,000**

The cash payback period in this example is therefore 5 years, computed as follows:

$$\$130,000 \div \$26,000 = 5 \text{ years}$$

The evaluation of the payback period is often related to the expected useful life of the asset. For example, assume that at Tappan Company a project is unacceptable if the payback period is longer than 60% of the asset's expected useful life. The five-year payback period in this case is 50% of the project's expected useful life. Thus, the project is acceptable. It follows that when the payback technique is used to decide among acceptable alternative projects, **the shorter the payback period, the more attractive the investment**. The reason is that: (1) the earlier the investment is recovered, the sooner the cash funds can be used for other purposes, and (2) the risk of loss from obsolescence and changed economic conditions is less in a shorter payback period.

The cash payback technique may be useful as an initial screening tool. It also may be the most critical factor in the capital budgeting decision for a company that desires a fast turnaround of its investment because of a weak cash position. Like the annual rate of return technique, the cash payback technique is relatively easy to compute and understand. However, it should not ordinarily be the only basis for the capital budgeting decision because it ignores the expected profitability of the project. To illustrate, assume that Projects A and B have the same payback period, but Project A's useful life is double the useful life of Project B. Project A's earning power, therefore, is twice as long as Project B's. A further disadvantage of this technique is that it ignores the time value of money.

DISCOUNTED CASH FLOW

The **discounted cash flow technique** is generally recognized as the most informative and best conceptual approach to making capital budgeting decisions. This technique considers both the estimated total cash inflows from the investment and the time value of money. As indicated previously, consideration of the time value of money is critical because of the long-term impact of the capital budgeting decision. The expected total cash inflow consists of the sum of the annual cash inflows plus the estimated liquidation proceeds when the asset is sold for salvage at the end of its useful life. Because liquidation proceeds are generally immaterial, they are ignored in subsequent discussions. Two methods are used with the discounted cash flow technique: (1) net present value and (2) internal rate of return. Before we discuss the methods, we recommend that you examine Appendix C if you need a review of present value concepts.

10
STUDY
OBJECTIVE

Distinguish between the net present value and internal rate of return methods.

Net Present Value Method

Under the **net present value method**, cash inflows are discounted to their present value and then compared with the capital outlay required by the investment. The difference between these two amounts is referred to as **net present value**. The interest rate to be used in discounting the future cash inflows is the required minimum rate of return. **A proposal is acceptable when net present value is zero or positive**, because this means the rate of return on the investment equals or exceeds the required rate of return. When net present value is negative, the project is unacceptable. Illustration 27-21 shows the net present value decision criteria.

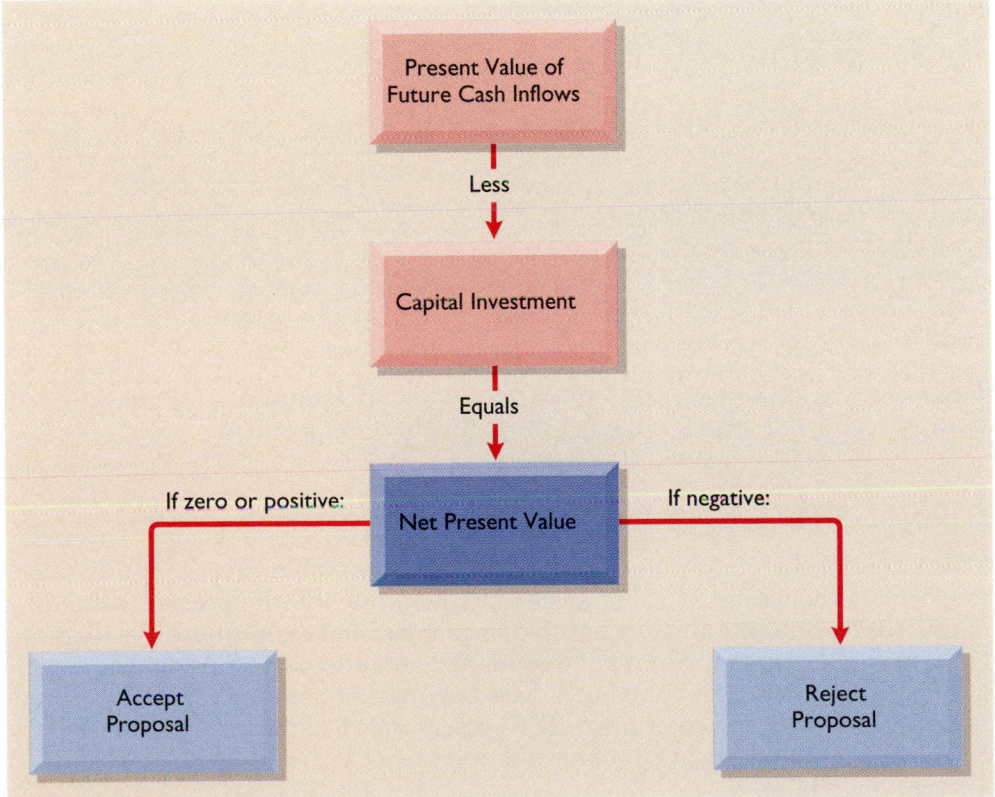

ILLUSTRATION 27-21

Net present value decision criteria

When making a selection among acceptable proposals, **the higher the positive net present value, the more attractive the investment**. The application of this method to two cases is described in the next two sections. In each case, we will assume that the investment has no salvage value at the end of its useful life.

Equal Annual Cash Flows

Tappan Company's annual cash inflows are $26,000. If we assume this amount **is uniform over the asset's useful life**, the present value of the annual cash inflows can be computed by using the present value of an annuity of 1 for 10 periods (in Table 2, Appendix C). The computations at rates of return of 12% and 15%, respectively, are:

ILLUSTRATION 27-22

Present value of annual cash inflows

	Present Values at Different Discount Rates	
	12%	**15%**
Discount factor for 10 periods	5.65022	5.01877
Present value of cash inflows:		
$26,000 × 5.65022	**$146,906**	
$26,000 × 5.01877		**$130,488**

Therefore, the analysis of the proposal by the net present value method is as follows:

ILLUSTRATION 27-23

Computations of net present value

	12%	**15%**
Present value of future cash inflows	$146,906	$130,488
Capital investment	130,000	130,000
Positive (negative) net present value	**$ 16,906**	**$ 488**

The proposed capital expenditure is acceptable at a required rate of return of both 12% and 15% because the net present values are positive.

Unequal Annual Cash Inflows

When annual cash inflows are unequal, it is not possible to use annuity tables to calculate their present value. Instead, tables showing the **present value of a single future amount must be applied to each annual cash inflow**. To illustrate, assume in the Tappan Company that management expects the same aggregate annual cash inflow ($260,000) but a declining market demand for the new product over the life of the equipment. The present value of the annual cash flows is calculated as follows using Table 1 in Appendix C:

ILLUSTRATION 27-24

Computing present value of unequal annual cash inflows

Year	Assumed Annual Cash Inflows	Discount Factor 12%	Discount Factor 15%	Present Value 12%	Present Value 15%
	(1)	(2)	(3)	(1) × (2)	(1) × (3)
1	$ 36,000	.89286	.86957	$ 32,143	$ 31,305
2	32,000	.79719	.75614	25,510	24,196
3	29,000	.71178	.65752	20,642	19,068
4	27,000	.63552	.57175	17,159	15,437
5	26,000	.56743	.49718	14,753	12,927
6	24,000	.50663	.43233	12,159	10,376
7	23,000	.45235	.37594	10,404	8,647
8	22,000	.40388	.32690	8,885	7,192
9	21,000	.36061	.28426	7,573	5,969
10	20,000	.32197	.24719	6,439	4,944
	$260,000			**$155,667**	**$140,061**

Therefore, the analysis of the proposal by the net present value method is as follows:

ILLUSTRATION 27-25

Analysis of proposal using net present value method

	12%	15%
Present value of future cash inflows	$155,667	$140,061
Capital investment	130,000	130,000
Positive (negative) net present value	$ 25,667	$ 10,061

In this example, the present values of the cash inflows are greater than the $130,000 capital investment. Thus, the project is acceptable at both a 12% and 15% required rate of return. The difference between the present values using the 12% rate under equal cash inflows ($146,906) and unequal cash inflows ($155,667) is due to the pattern of the inflows.

Internal Rate of Return Method

The **internal rate of return method** differs from the net present value method in that it results in finding the **interest yield of the potential investment**. The **internal rate of return** is the rate that will cause the present value of the proposed capital expenditure to equal the present value of the expected annual cash inflows. The determination of the internal rate of return involves two steps.

   Step 1. Compute the internal rate of return factor. The formula for this factor is:

ILLUSTRATION 27-26

Formula for internal rate of return factor

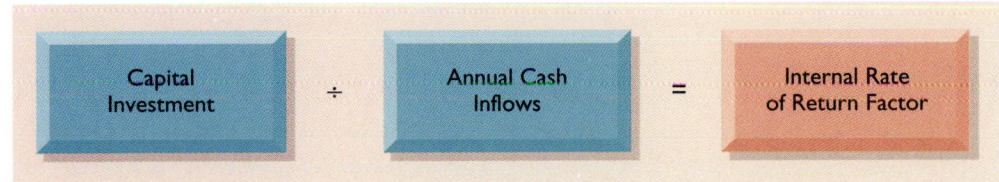

The computation for the Tappan Company, assuming equal annual cash inflows is:

$$\$130,000 \div \$26,000 = 5.0^2$$

Step 2. Use the factor and the present value of an annuity of 1 table to find the internal rate of return. Table 2 of Appendix C is used in this step. The internal rate of return is found by locating the discount factor in the table that is closest to the internal rate of return factor for the time period covered by the annual cash flows.

In Tappan Company, the annual cash inflows are expected to continue for 10 years. Thus, it is necessary to read across the period 10 row in Table 2 to find the discount factor. Row 10 is reproduced below for your convenience.

TABLE 2
PRESENT VALUE OF AN ANNUITY OF 1

(n) Periods	5%	6%	8%	9%	10%	11%	12%	15%
10	7.72173	7.36009	6.71008	6.41766	6.14457	5.88923	5.65022	5.01877

In this case, the closest discount factor to 5.0 is 5.01877 which represents an interest rate of approximately 15%. The approximate rate can be determined by interpolation, but since we are using estimated annual cash flows such precision is seldom required.

When the internal rate of return has been determined, it is compared to management's required minimum rate of return. The decision rule, therefore, is: **Accept the project when the internal rate of return is equal to or greater than the required rate of return, and reject the project when the internal rate of return is less than the required rate.** These relationships are shown graphically in Illustration 27-27. Assuming the minimum required rate of return is 10% for

ILLUSTRATION 27-27

Internal rate of return decision criteria

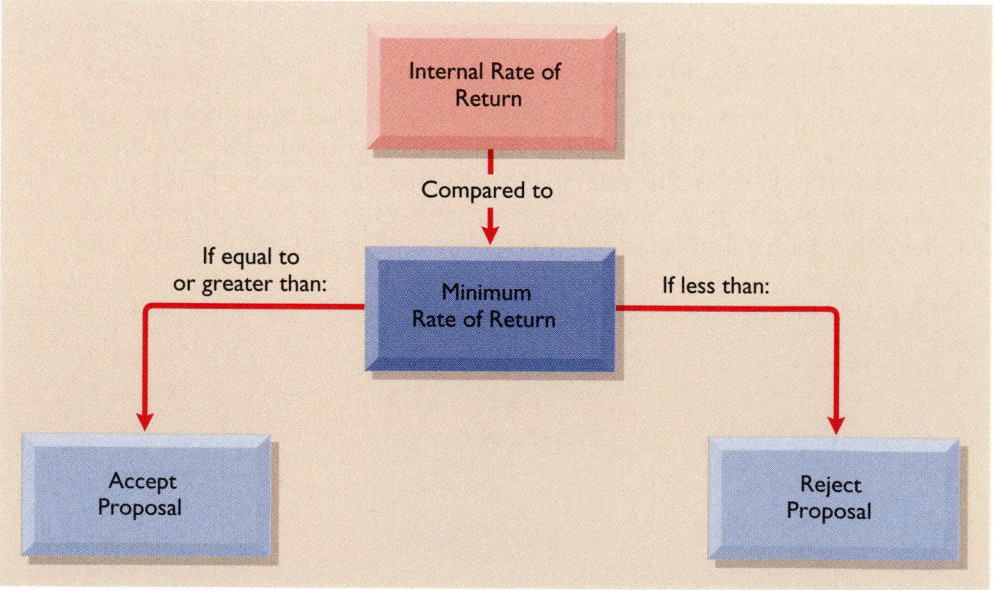

---

[2]When annual cash inflows are equal, the internal rate of return factor is the same as the cash payback period.

Tappan Company, the project is acceptable because the 15% internal rate of return is greater than the required rate.

The internal rate of return method is widely used in practice. Most managers find the internal rate of return easy to interpret.

ACCOUNTING IN ACTION
Business Insight

Which capital budgeting methods are used the most? One survey asked financial officers which method they used in considering expenditures for factory automation. Internal rate of return and cash payback were the most popular methods. Subjective evaluation—though not, strictly speaking, a capital budgeting method—also turned out to be popular with finance professionals.

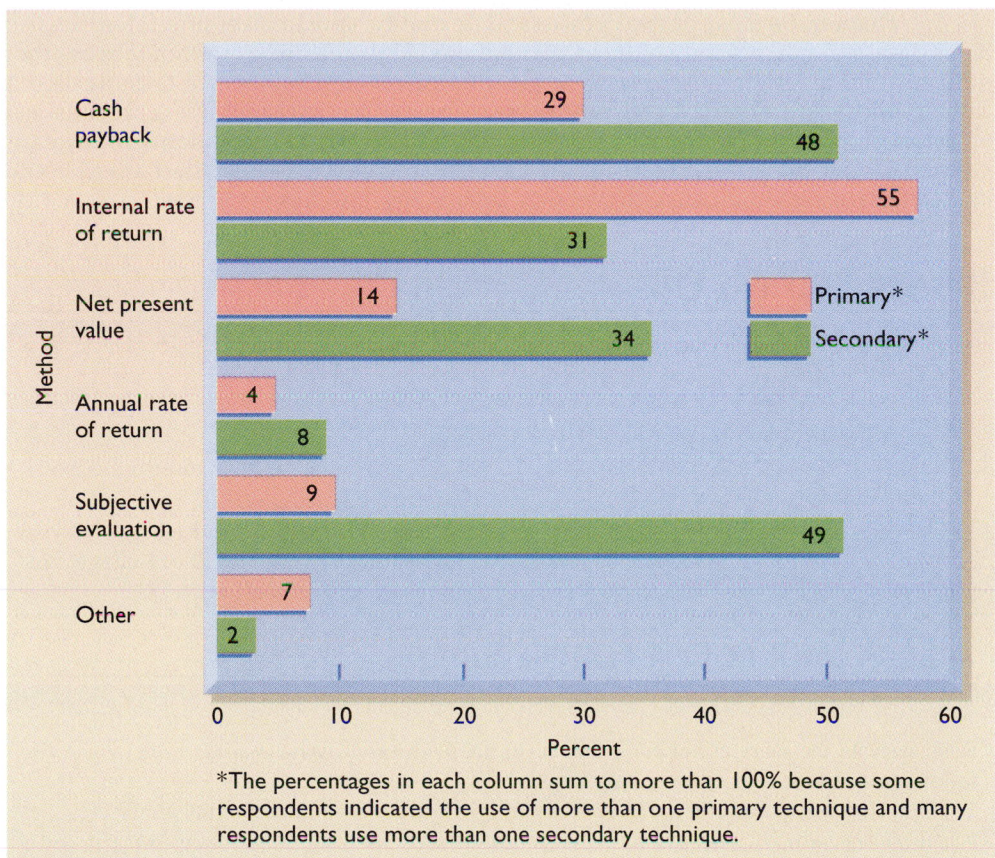

*The percentages in each column sum to more than 100% because some respondents indicated the use of more than one primary technique and many respondents use more than one secondary technique.

Source: James A. Hendricks, "Applying Cost Accounting to Factory Automation," *Management Accounting.*

Comparison of Discounted Cash Flow Methods

A comparative summary of the two discounted cash flow methods—net present value and internal rate of return—is presented in Illustration 27-28. When properly used, either method will provide management with relevant quantitative data for making capital budgeting decisions.

ILLUSTRATION 27-28

Comparison of discounted cash flow methods

Item	Net Present Value	Internal Rate of Return
1. Objective	Compute net present value.	Compute internal rate of return.
2. Decision rule	If net present value is zero or positive, accept the proposal; if net present value is negative, reject the proposal.	If internal rate of return is equal to or greater than the minimum required rate of return, accept the proposal; if internal rate of return is less than the minimum rate, reject the proposal.

TECHNOLOGY IN ACTION

There are software packages available for each of the decision situations described in the incremental analysis and capital budgeting sections of this chapter. Because of their power and flexibility, spreadsheet programs can also be designed to perform any of these calculations. Thus, businesses often face another decision: Should they purchase packages dedicated only to specific tasks (called a canned approach) or will a general-purpose application package, like a spreadsheet or database program, be better? Management often turns to accountants to help answer such questions. As discussed in Chapter 6, the costs of each alternative should be carefully weighed against the benefits before any purchase is made.

BEFORE YOU GO ON . . .

Review It

1. What is the formula for and the decision rule in using the annual rate of return method?
2. What is the formula for the cash payback method?
3. When is a proposal acceptable under (a) the net present value method and (b) the internal rate of return method?
4. What does Kellogg report as its return on average assets for 1997? (See Kellogg's 10-year summary of selected financial data.) Since 1987, what has been the trend in Kellogg's return on average assets? The answer to this question is provided on page 1189.

A LOOK BACK AT OUR FEATURE STORY

Refer back to the story about *Forrest Gump* at the beginning of the chapter, and answer the following questions:
1. What decisions faced by a movie studio might benefit from incremental analysis?
2. Comment on the usefulness of the accounting methods used by Paramount Pictures for incremental analysis.

Solution:

1. Studio decisions that might benefit from incremental analysis would be: (a) the choice of which two movies to produce (allocation of limited resources); (b) whether to upgrade audio and video equipment (retain or replace); and (c) the sale of distribution rights to a movie (sell or process further).
2. It appears that Paramount Pictures is allocating its costs in a manner that would minimize the payments made on contingent contracts, such as those of the screenwriter and author. If these same accounting methods were employed in deciding whether to produce a movie, some very profitable opportunities might be forgone.

THE NAVIGATOR

DEMONSTRATION PROBLEM 2

Sierra Company is considering a long-term capital investment project called ZIP. ZIP will require an investment of $120,000, and it will have a useful life of 4 years. Annual net income is expected to be: Year 1, $12,000; Year 2, $10,000; Year 3, $8,000; and Year 4, $6,000. Depreciation is computed by the straight-line method with no salvage value. The company's cost of capital is 12%.

Instructions

(Round all computations to two decimal places.)

(a) Compute the annual rate of return for the project.
(b) Compute the cash payback period for the project. (Round to two decimals.)
(c) Compute the net present value for the project. (Round to nearest dollar.)
(d) Should the project be accepted? Why?

SOLUTION TO DEMONSTRATION PROBLEM

(a) $9,000 ($36,000 ÷ 4) ÷ $60,000 ($120,000 ÷ 2) = 15%

(b) $120,000 ÷ $39,000 ($9,000 + $30,000) = 3.08 years

(c)

Year	Discount Factor	Cash Inflow	Present Value
1	.89286	$42,000	$ 37,500
2	.79719	40,000	31,888
3	.71178	38,000	27,048
4	.63552	36,000	22,879
			119,315
Capital investment			120,000
Negative net present value			$ (685)

(d) The annual rate of return of 15% is good. However, the cash payback period is 77% of the project's useful life, and net present value is negative. The recommendation is to reject the project.

PROBLEM-SOLVING STRATEGIES

1. The formula for annual rate of return is expected annual net income divided by average investment.

2. The formula for the cash payback method is cost of the investment divided by annual cash inflows.

3. Annual cash inflow equals annual net income plus annual depreciation expense.

4. Be careful to use the correct discount factor in using the net present value method.

THE NAVIGATOR

SUMMARY OF STUDY OBJECTIVES

1. Identify the steps in management's decision-making process. Management's decision-making process consists of (a) identifying the problem or opportunity, (b) assigning responsibility for the decision, (c) determining possible courses of action, (d) developing data relevant to each course of action, (e) making the decision, and (f) reviewing the results of the decision.

2. Describe the concept of incremental analysis. Incremental analysis is the process that is used to identify financial data that change under alternative courses of action. These data are relevant to the decision because they will vary in the future among the possible alternatives.

3. Identify the relevant costs in accepting an order at a special price. The relevant information in accepting an order at a special price is the difference between the variable manufacturing costs to produce the special order and expected revenues.

4. Indicate the relevant costs in a make-or-buy decision. In a make-or-buy decision, the relevant costs are (a) the vari-

able manufacturing costs that will be saved, (b) the purchase price, and (c) opportunity costs.

5. Give the decision rule in deciding whether to sell or process materials further. The decision rule in deciding whether to sell or process materials further is: process further as long as the incremental revenue from processing exceeds the incremental processing costs.

6. Identify the factors to be considered in retaining or replacing equipment. The factors to be considered in determining whether equipment should be retained or replaced are the effects on variable costs and the cost of the new equipment. In addition, any disposal value of the existing asset must be considered.

7. Explain the factors that are relevant in deciding whether to eliminate an unprofitable segment. In deciding whether to eliminate an unprofitable segment, it is necessary to determine the contribution margin, if any, produced by the segment and the disposition of the segment's fixed expenses.

8. Determine which products to make and sell when a company has limited resources. When a company has limited resources, it is necessary to find the contribution margin per unit of limited resource. This amount is then multiplied by the units of limited resource to determine which product maximizes net income.

9. Contrast the annual rate of return and cash payback techniques in capital budgeting. The annual rate of return is obtained by dividing expected annual net income by the average investment. The higher the rate of return, the more attractive the investment. The cash payback technique identifies the time period to recover the cost of the investment. The formula is: Cost of capital expenditure divided by estimated annual cash inflow equals cash payback period. The shorter the payback period, the more attractive the investment.

10. Distinguish between the net present value and internal rate of return methods. Under the net present value method, the present value of future cash inflows is compared with the capital investment to determine net present value. The decision rule is: Accept the project if net present value is zero or positive; reject the investment if net present value is negative.

Under the internal rate of return method, the objective is to find the true interest yield of the potential investment. The decision rule is: Accept the project when the internal rate of return is equal to or greater than the required rate of return; reject the project when the internal rate of return is less than the required rate.

GLOSSARY

Annual rate of return technique The determination of the profitability of a capital expenditure by dividing expected annual net income by the average investment. (p. 1167).

Capital budgeting The process of making capital expenditure decisions in business. (p. 1166).

Cash payback technique A capital budgeting technique that identifies the time period required to recover the cost of a capital investment from the annual cash inflow produced by the investment. (p. 1168).

Cost of capital The rate of return that management expects to pay on all borrowed and equity funds. (p. 1167).

Discounted cash flow technique A capital budgeting technique that considers both the estimated total cash inflows from the investment and the time value of money. (p. 1169).

Incremental analysis The process of identifying the financial data that change under alternative courses of action. (p. 1157).

Internal rate of return method A method used in capital budgeting that results in finding the interest yield of the potential investment. (p. 1171).

Net present value method A method used in capital budgeting in which cash inflows are discounted to their present value and then compared to the capital outlay required by the investment. (p. 1169).

Opportunity cost The potential benefit that may be obtained from following an alternative course of action. (p. 1160).

Sunk cost A cost that cannot be changed by any present or future decision. (p. 1162).

SELF-STUDY QUESTIONS

Answers are at the end of the chapter.

(SO 1) 1. Three of the steps in management's decision process are (1) review results of decision, (2) develop data relevant to each course of action, and (3) make the decision. The steps are prepared in the following order:
a. (1), (2), (3).
b. (3), (2), (1).
c. (2), (1), (3).
d. (2), (3), (1).

(SO 2) 2. Incremental analysis is the process of identifying the financial data that:
a. do not change under alternative courses of action.
b. change under alternative courses of action.
c. are mixed under alternative courses of action.
d. No correct answer is given.

3. It costs a company $14 of variable costs and $6 of fixed (SO 3) costs to produce product A that sells for $30. A foreign buyer offers to purchase 3,000 units at $18 each. If the special offer is accepted and produced with unused capacity, net income will:
a. decrease $6,000.
b. increase $6,000.
c. increase $12,000.
d. increase $9,000.

4. In a make-or-buy decision, relevant costs are: (SO 4)
a. manufacturing costs that will be saved.
b. the purchase price of the units.
c. opportunity costs.
d. all of the above.

(SO 5) 5. The decision rule in a sell-or-process-further decision is: process further as long as the incremental revenue from process exceeds:
   a. incremental processing costs.
   b. variable processing costs.
   c. fixed processing costs.
   d. No correct answer is given.

(SO 6) 6. In a decision to retain or replace equipment, the book value of the old equipment is a (an):
   a. opportunity cost.
   b. sunk cost.
   c. incremental cost.
   d. marginal cost.

(SO 7) 7. If an unprofitable segment is eliminated:
   a. net income will always increase.
   b. variable expenses of the eliminated segment will have to be absorbed by other segments.
   c. fixed expenses allocated to the eliminated segment will have to be absorbed by other segments.
   d. net income will always decrease.

(SO 8) 8. If the contribution margin per unit is $15 and it takes 3.0 machine hours to produce the unit, the contribution margin per unit of limited resource is:
   a. $25.
   b. $5.
   c. $4.
   d. No correct answer is given.

(SO 9) 9. Which of the following is *incorrect* about the annual rate of return technique?
   a. The calculation is simple.
   b. The accounting terms used are familiar to management.
   c. The timing of the cash inflows is not considered.
   d. The time value of money is considered.

(SO 10) 10. A positive net present value means that the:
   a. project's rate of return is less than the cutoff rate.
   b. project's rate of return exceeds the required rate of return.
   c. project's rate of return equals the required rate of return.
   d. project is unacceptable.

QUESTIONS

1. What steps are frequently involved in management's decision-making process?

2. Your roommate, John Ross, contends that accounting contributes to most of the steps in management's decision-making process. Is your roommate correct? Explain.

3. "Incremental analysis involves the accumulation of information concerning a single course of action." Do you agree? Why?

4. Ron Schoffer asks your help concerning the relevance of variable and fixed costs in incremental analysis. Help Ron with his problem.

5. What data are relevant in deciding whether to accept an order at a special price?

6. Roland Carlson Company has an opportunity to buy parts at $7 each that currently cost $10 to make. What manufacturing costs are relevant to this make-or-buy decision?

7. Define the term "opportunity cost." How may this cost be relevant in a make or buy decision?

8. What is the decision rule in deciding whether to sell a product or process it further?

9. Your roommate, John Lewis, is confused about sunk costs. Explain to your roommate the meaning of sunk costs and their relevance to a decision to retain or replace equipment.

10. Anita Ferraro Inc. has one product line that is unprofitable. What circumstances may cause overall company net income to be lower if the unprofitable product line is eliminated?

11. How is the contribution margin per unit of limited resources computed?

12. Describe the process a company may use in screening and approving the capital expenditure budget.

13. Your classmate, Jana Kingston, is confused about the factors that are included in the annual rate of return technique. What is the formula for this technique?

14. Ernie Lobb is trying to understand the term "cost of capital." Define the term and indicate its relevance to the decision rule under the annual rate of return technique.

15. Pete Henning claims the formula for the cash payback technique is the same as the formula for the annual rate of return technique. Is Pete correct? What is the formula for the cash payback technique?

16. What are the advantages and disadvantages of the cash payback technique?

17. Two types of present value tables may be used with the discounted cash flow technique. Identify the tables and the circumstance(s) when each table should be used.

18. What is the decision rule under the net present value method?

19. Identify the steps required in using the internal rate of return method.

20. Cheryl Munns Company uses the internal rate of return method. What is the decision rule for this method?

BRIEF EXERCISES

Identify the steps in management's decision-making process.
(SO 1)

BE27–1 The steps in management's decision-making process are listed in random order below. Indicate the order in which the steps should be executed.

____ Make decision   ____ Review results of decision

____ Identify the opportunity or problem   ____ Determine possible courses of action

____ Assign responsibility for decision   ____ Develop data relevant to each course of action

Determine incremental changes.
(SO 2)

BE27–2 Jeong Company is considering two alternatives. Alternative A will have sales of $150,000 and costs of $100,000. Alternative B will have sales of $180,000 and costs of $125,000. Compare Alternative A to Alternative B showing incremental revenues, costs, and net income.

Determine whether to accept a special order.
(SO 3)

BE27–3 In Essex Company it costs $30 per unit ($20 variable and $10 fixed) to make a product that normally sells for $45. A foreign wholesaler offers to buy 4,000 units at $25 each. Essex will incur special shipping costs of $1 per unit. Assuming that Essex has excess operating capacity, indicate the net income (loss) Essex would realize by accepting the special order.

Determine whether to make or buy a part.
(SO 4)

BE27–4 Wirtz Manufacturing incurs unit costs of $8 ($5 variable and $3 fixed) in making a sub-assembly part for its finished product. A supplier offers to make 10,000 of the assembly part at $5.50 per unit. If the offer is accepted, Wirtz will save all variable costs but no fixed costs. Prepare an analysis showing the total cost saving, if any, Wirtz will realize by buying the part.

Determine whether to sell or process further.
(SO 5)

BE27–5 Trujillo Inc. makes unfinished bookcases that it sells for $60. Production costs are $30 variable and $10 fixed. Because it has unused capacity, Trujillo is considering finishing the bookcases and selling them for $70. Variable finishing costs are expected to be $8 per unit with no increase in fixed costs. Prepare an analysis on a per unit basis showing whether Trujillo should sell unfinished or finished bookcases.

Determine whether to retain or replace equipment.
(SO 6)

BE27–6 Roark Company has a factory machine with a book value of $90,000 and a remaining useful life of 4 years. A new machine is available at a cost of $200,000. This machine will have a 4-year useful life with no salvage value. The new machine will lower annual variable manufacturing costs from $600,000 to $420,000. Prepare an analysis showing whether the old machine should be retained or replaced.

Determine whether to eliminate an unprofitable segment.
(SO 7)

BE27–7 Parmely, Inc., manufactures golf clubs in three models. For the year, the Eagle line has a net loss of $20,000 from sales $200,000, variable expenses $180,000, and fixed expenses $40,000. If the Eagle line is eliminated, $28,000 of fixed costs will remain. Prepare an analysis showing whether the Eagle line should be eliminated.

Show allocation of limited resources.
(SO 8)

BE27–8 In Cruz Company, data concerning two products are: Contribution margin per unit—Product A $10, Product B $12; machine hours required for one unit—Product A 2, Product B 3. Compute the contribution margin per unit of limited resource for each product.

Compute the cash payback period for a capital investment.
(SO 9)

BE27–9 Mouser Company is considering purchasing new equipment for $400,000. It is expected that the equipment will produce annual net income of $10,000 over its 10-year useful life. Annual depreciation will be $40,000. Compute the payback period.

Compute net present value of an investment.
(SO 10)

BE27–10 Weng Company accumulates the following data concerning a proposed capital investment: cash cost $225,000, annual cash inflow $40,000, present value of cash inflows for 10 years 5.65 (rounded). Determine the net present value, and indicate whether the investment should be made.

EXERCISES

Make incremental analysis for special order.
(SO 3)

E27–1 Giraldi Company manufactures toasters. For the first 8 months of 2000, the company reported the following operating results while operating at 75% of plant capacity:

Sales (400,000 units)	$4,000,000
Cost of goods sold	2,400,000
Gross profit	1,600,000
Operating expenses	900,000
Net income	$ 700,000

Cost of goods sold was 70% variable and 30% fixed; operating expenses were 60% variable and 40% fixed.

In September, Giraldi Company receives a special order for 15,000 toasters at $6.00 each from Alazar Company of Mexico City. Acceptance of the order would result in $3,000 of shipping costs but no increase in fixed operating expenses.

Instructions

(a) Prepare an incremental analysis for the special order.

(b) ▰▰▰▷ Should Giraldi Company accept the special order? Why or why not?

E27–2 Cinelli Inc. has been manufacturing its own shades for its table lamps. The company is currently operating at 100% of capacity, and variable manufacturing overhead is charged to production at the rate of 50% of direct labor cost. The direct materials and direct labor cost per unit to make the lamp shades are $4.00 and $6.00, respectively. Normal production is 30,000 table lamps per year.

Make incremental analysis for make-or-buy decision.
(SO 4)

A supplier offers to make the lamp shades at a price of $13.50 per unit. If Cinelli Inc. accepts the supplier's offer, all variable manufacturing costs will be eliminated, but the $40,000 of fixed manufacturing overhead currently being charged to the lamp shades will have to be absorbed by other products.

Instructions

(a) Prepare the incremental analysis for the decision to make or buy the lamp shades.

(b) ▰▰▰▷ Should Cinelli Inc. buy the lamp shades?

(c) ▰▰▰▷ Would your answer be different in (b) if the productive capacity released by not making the lamp shades could be used to produce income of $35,000?

E27–3 Debbie Sondgeroth recently opened her own basketweaving studio. She sells finished baskets in addition to the raw materials needed by customers to weave baskets of their own. Debbie has put together a variety of raw material kits, each including materials at various stages of completion. Unfortunately, owing to space limitations, Debbie is unable to carry all varieties of kits originally assembled and must choose between two basic packages.

Make incremental analysis for further processing of materials.
(SO 5)

The basic introductory kit includes undyed, uncut reeds (with dye included) for weaving one basket. This basic package costs Debbie $12 and sells for $27. The second kit, called Stage 2, includes cut reeds that have already been dyed. With this kit the customer need only soak the reeds and weave the basket. Debbie is able to produce the second kit by using the basic materials included in the first kit and adding one hour of her own time, which she values at $16 per hour. Because she is more efficient at cutting and dying reeds than her average customer, Debbie is able to make two kits of the dyed reeds, in one hour, from one kit of undyed reeds. The kit of dyed and cut reeds sells for $32.

Instructions

Determine whether Debbie's basketweaving shop should carry the basic introductory kit with undyed and uncut reeds or the Stage 2 kit with reeds already dyed and cut. Prepare an incremental analysis to support your answer.

E27–4 Yan Enterprises uses a word processing computer to handle its sales invoices. Lately, business has been so good that it takes an extra 3 hours per night, plus every third Saturday, to keep up with the volume of sales invoices. Management is considering updating its computer with a faster model that would eliminate all of the overtime processing.

Make incremental analysis for retaining or replacing equipment.
(SO 6)

	Current Machine	New Machine
Original purchase cost	$15,000	$24,000
Accumulated depreciation	6,000	—
Estimated operating costs	21,000	16,000
Useful life	5 years	5 years

If sold now, the current machine would have a salvage value of $3,000. If operated for the remainder of its useful life, the current machine would have zero salvage value. The new machine is expected to have zero salvage value after five years.

Instructions

Should the current machine be replaced? (Ignore the time value of money.)

E27–5 Lisa Hollern, a recent graduate of Rolling's accounting program, evaluated the operating performance of Winser Company's six divisions. Lisa made the following presentation to Winser's Board of Directors and suggested the Hudson Division be eliminated. "If the Hudson Division is eliminated," she said, "our total profits would increase by $16,870."

Make incremental analysis concerning elimination of division.
(SO 7)

	The Other Five Divisions	Hudson Division	Total
Sales	$1,664,200	$ 98,200	$1,762,400
Cost of goods sold	978,520	76,470	1,054,990
Gross profit	685,680	21,730	707,410
Operating expenses	527,940	38,600	566,540
Net income	$ 157,740	$(16,870)	$ 140,870

In the Hudson Division, cost of goods sold is $60,000 variable and $16,470 fixed, and operating expenses are $12,000 variable and $24,600 fixed. None of the Hudson Division's fixed costs will be eliminated if the division is discontinued.

Instructions

Is Lisa right about eliminating the Hudson Division? Prepare a schedule to support your answer.

Compute contribution margin and determine the product to be manufactured.
(SO 8)

E27–6 Lazarus Company manufactures and sells three products. Relevant per unit data concerning each product are given below:

	Product		
	A	**B**	**C**
Selling price	$8	$12	$14
Variable costs and expenses	$4	$ 9	$12
Machine hours to produce	2	1	2

Instructions

(a) Compute the contribution margin per unit of the limited resource (machine hour) for each product.

(b) Assuming 1,500 additional machine hours are available, which product should be manufactured?

(c) Prepare an analysis showing the total contribution margin if the additional hours are (1) divided equally among the products, and (2) allocated entirely to the product identified in (b) above.

Compute cash payback period and annual rate of return.
(SO 9)

E27–7 Wamser Service Center just purchased an automobile hoist for $13,000. The hoist has a 5-year life and an estimated salvage value of $940. Installation costs and freight charges were $2,900 and $740, respectively. Wamser uses straight-line depreciation.

The new hoist will be used to replace mufflers and tires on automobiles. Wamser estimates that the new hoist will enable his mechanics to replace four extra mufflers per week. Each muffler sells for $65 installed. The cost of a muffler is $35 and the labor cost to install a muffler is $10.

Instructions

(a) Compute the payback period for the new hoist.

(b) Compute the annual rate of return for the new hoist. (Round to one decimal.)

Compute cash payback period and net present value.
(SO 9, 10)

E27–8 Jimmy Smits Manufacturing Company is considering three new projects, each requiring an equipment investment of $22,000. Each project will last for 3 years and produce the following cash inflows:

Year	AA	BB	CC
1	$ 7,500	$ 9,500	$13,000
2	9,000	9,500	9,000
3	15,000	9,500	11,000
Total	$31,500	$28,500	$33,000

The equipment's salvage value is zero, and Smits uses straight-line depreciation. Smits will not accept any project with a payback period over 2 years. Smits's minimum required rate of return is 15%.

Instructions

(a) Compute each project's payback period, indicating the most desirable project and the least desirable project using this method. (Round to two decimals.)

(b) Compute the net present value of each project. Does your evaluation change? (Round to nearest dollar.)

E27–9 Silva Company is considering a capital investment of $150,000 in additional productive facilities. The new machinery is expected to have a useful life of 5 years with no salvage value. Depreciation is by the straight-line method. During the life of the investment, annual net income and cash inflows are expected to be $18,000 and $48,000 respectively. Silva has a 15% cost of capital rate which is the minimum acceptable rate of return on the investment.

Compute annual rate of return, cash payback period, and net present value.
(SO 9, 10)

Instructions
(Round to two decimals.)

(a) Compute (1) the annual rate of return and (2) the cash payback period on the proposed capital expenditure.
(b) Using the discounted cash flow technique, compute the net present value.

E27–10 Novak Company is considering three capital expenditure projects. Relevant data for the projects are as follows:

Determine internal rate of return.
(SO 10)

Project	Investment	Annual Income	Life of Project
22A	$240,000	$15,000	6 years
23A	270,000	26,400	9 years
24A	288,000	22,000	8 years

Annual income is constant over the life of the project. Each project is expected to have zero salvage value at the end of the project. Novak Company uses the straight-line method of depreciation.

Instructions
(a) Determine the internal rate of return for each project. Round the internal rate of return factor to three decimals.
(b) If Novak Company's minimum required rate of return is 12%, which projects are acceptable?

PROBLEMS: SET A

P27–1A All Sports Inc. manufactures basketballs for the National Basketball Association (NBA). For the first 6 months of 2000, the company reported the following operating results while operating at 90% of plant capacity.

Make incremental analysis for special order and identify nonfinancial factors in decision.
(SO 3)

	Amount	Per Unit
Sales	$4,500,000	$50.00
Cost of goods sold	3,600,000	40.00
Selling and administrative expenses	360,000	4.00
Net income	$ 540,000	$ 6.00

Fixed costs for the period were: cost of goods sold $900,000, and selling and administrative expenses $180,000.

In July, normally a slack manufacturing month, All Sports receives a special order for 10,000 basketballs at $34 each from the Italian Basketball Association (IBA). Acceptance of the order would increase variable selling and administrative expenses $.35 per unit because of shipping costs but would not increase fixed costs and expenses.

Instructions
(a) Prepare an incremental analysis for the special order.
(b) Should All Sports Inc. accept the special order?
(c) What is the minimum selling price on the special order to produce net income of $2.50 per ball?
(d) ▣▭▭▷ What nonfinancial factors should management consider in making its decision?

*Make incremental analysis
related to make or buy;
consider opportunity cost, and
identify nonfinancial factors.*
(SO 4)

P27–2A The management of Francona Manufacturing Company is trying to decide whether to continue manufacturing a part or to buy it from an outside supplier. The part, called WISCO, is a component of the company's finished product.

The following information was collected from the accounting records and production data for the year ending December 31, 2000:

1. 7,000 units of WISCO were produced in the Machining Department.
2. Variable manufacturing costs applicable to the production of each WISCO unit were: direct materials $4.75, direct labor $4.60, indirect labor $0.45, utilities $0.35.
3. Fixed manufacturing costs applicable to the production of WISCO were:

Cost Item	Direct	Allocated
Depreciation	$1,600	$ 900
Property taxes	400	200
Insurance	900	600
	$2,900	$1,700

All variable manufacturing and direct fixed costs will be eliminated if WISCO is purchased. Allocated costs will have to be absorbed by other production departments.

4. The lowest quotation for 7,000 WISCO units from a supplier is $75,000.
5. If WISCO units are purchased, freight and inspection costs would be $0.30 per unit, and receiving costs totaling $750 per year would be incurred by the Machining Department.

Instructions
(a) Prepare an incremental analysis for WISCO. Your analysis should have columns for (1) Make WISCO, (2) Buy WISCO, and (3) Net Income Increase/Decrease.
(b) Based on your analysis, what decision should management make?
(c) Would the decision be different if Francona Company has the opportunity to produce $4,000 of net income with the facilities currently being used to manufacture WISCO? Show computations.
(d) ▨▨▨▷ What nonfinancial factors should management consider in making its decision?

*Compute contribution margin
and prepare incremental
analysis concerning
elimination of divisions.*
(SO 7)

P27–3A Bailor Manufacturing Company has four operating divisions. During the first quarter of 2000, the company reported aggregate income from operations of $145,000 and the following divisional results:

	\multicolumn{4}{c}{Division}			
	I	**II**	**III**	**IV**
Sales	$490,000	$410,000	$300,000	$190,000
Cost of goods sold	300,000	250,000	280,000	180,000
Selling and administrative expenses	60,000	80,000	35,000	60,000
Income (loss) from operations	$130,000	$ 80,000	$ (15,000)	$ (50,000)

Analysis reveals the following percentages of variable costs in each division.

	I	II	III	IV
Cost of goods sold	70%	80%	75%	90%
Selling and administrative expenses	40	50	60	70

Discontinuance of any division would save 50% of the fixed costs and expenses for that division.

Top management is very concerned about the unprofitable divisions (III and IV). Consensus is that one or both of the divisions should be discontinued.

Instructions
(a) Compute the contribution margin for Divisions III and IV.
(b) Prepare an incremental analysis concerning the possible discontinuance of (1) Division III and (2) Division IV. What course of action do you recommend for each division?
(c) Prepare a columnar condensed income statement for Bailor Manufacturing, assuming

Division IV is eliminated. Use the CVP format. Division IV's unavoidable fixed costs are allocated equally to the continuing divisions.

(d) Reconcile the total income from operations ($145,000) with the total income from operations without Division IV.

P27–4A The Vera and Tucker partnership is considering three long-term capital investment proposals. Each investment has a useful life of 5 years. Relevant data on each project are as follows:

Compute rate of return, cash payback, and net present value.
(SO 9, 10)

	Project Tic	Project Tac	Project Toe
Capital investment	$150,000	$160,000	$200,000
Annual net income:			
Year 1	13,000	18,000	27,000
2	13,000	17,000	22,000
3	13,000	16,000	21,000
4	13,000	12,000	18,000
5	13,000	9,000	12,000
Total	$ 65,000	$ 72,000	$100,000

Depreciation is computed by the straight-line method with no salvage value. The company's cost of capital is 15%.

Instructions

(a) Compute the annual rate of return for each project. (Round to two decimals.)
(b) Compute the cash payback period for each project. (Round to two decimals.)
(c) Compute the net present value for each project. (Round to nearest dollar.)
(d) Rank the projects on each of the foregoing bases. Which project do you recommend?

P27–5A Jill Kobe is an accounting major at a midwestern state university located approximately 60 miles from a major city. Many of the students attending the university are from the metropolitan area and visit their homes regularly on the weekends. Jill, an entrepreneur at heart, realizes that few good commuting alternatives are available for students doing weekend travel. She believes that a weekend commuting service could be organized and run profitably from several suburban and downtown shopping mall locations. Jill has gathered the following investment information:

Compute annual rate of return, cash payback, and net present value.
(SO 9, 10)

1. Six used vans would cost a total of $69,000 to purchase and would have a 3-year useful life with negligible salvage value. Jill plans to use straight-line depreciation.
2. Ten drivers would have to be employed at a total payroll expense of $48,000.
3. Other annual out of pocket expenses associated with running the commuter service would include Gasoline $12,000, Maintenance $2,800, Repairs $3,500, Insurance $3,200, Advertising $1,500.
4. Jill has visited several financial institutions to discuss funding for her new venture. The best interest rate she has been able to negotiate is 12%. Use this rate for cost of capital.
5. Jill expects each van to make nine round trips weekly and carry an average of five students each trip. The service is expected to operate 30 weeks each year, and each student will be charged $12.00 for a round-trip ticket.

Instructions

(a) Determine the annual (1) net income, and (2) cash inflow for the commuter service.
(b) Compute (1) the annual rate of return, and (2) the cash payback period. (Round to two decimals.)
(c) Compute the net present value of the commuter service. (Round to the nearest dollar.)
(d) ▱▱▱▱➤ What should Jill conclude from these computations?

PROBLEMS: SET B

Make incremental analysis for special order and identify nonfinancial factors in decisions.
(SO 3)

P27–1B Escobar Company is currently producing 15,000 units per month, which is 75% of its production capacity. Variable manufacturing costs are currently $11.00 per unit, and fixed manufacturing costs are $48,000 per month. Escobar pays a 9% sales commission to its sales people, has $30,000 in fixed administrative expenses per month, and is averaging $300,000 in sales per month.

A special order received from a foreign company would enable Escobar Company to operate at 100% capacity. The foreign company offered to pay 75% of Escobar's current selling price per unit. If the order is accepted, Escobar will have to spend an extra $2.00 per unit to package the product for overseas shipping. Also, Escobar Company would need to lease a new stamping machine to imprint the foreign company's logo on the product, at a monthly cost of $2,500. The special order would require a sales commission of $3,000.

Instructions
(a) Compute the number of units involved in the special order and the foreign company's offered price per unit.
(b) What is the manufacturing cost of producing one unit of Escobar's product for regular customers?
(c) Prepare an incremental analysis of the special order. Should management accept the order?
(d) What is the lowest price that Escobar could accept for the special order to earn net income of $1.20 per unit?
(e) ▭▭▭▷ What nonfinancial factors should management consider in making its decision?

Make incremental analysis related to make or buy, consider opportunity cost, and identify nonfinancial factors.
(SO 4)

P27–2B   The management of Mareno Manufacturing Company has asked for your assistance in deciding whether to continue manufacturing a part or to buy it from an outside supplier. The part, called Tropica, is a component of Mareno's finished product.

An analysis of the accounting records and the production data revealed the following information for the year ending December 31, 1999:

1. The Machinery Department produced 36,000 units of Tropica.
2. Each Tropica unit requires 10 minutes to produce. Three people in the Machinery Department work full time (2,000 hours per year) producing Tropica. Each person is paid $10.00 per hour.
3. The cost of materials per Tropica unit is $2.00.
4. Manufacturing costs directly applicable to the production of Tropica are: indirect labor, $5,500; utilities, $1,300; depreciation, $1,600; property taxes and insurance, $1,000. All of the costs will be eliminated if Tropica is purchased.
5. The lowest price for a Tropica from an outside supplier is $3.50 per unit. Freight charges will be $0.30 per unit, and a part-time receiving clerk at $8,500 per year will be required.
6. If Tropica is purchased, the excess space will be used to store Mareno's finished product. Currently, Mareno rents storage space at approximately $0.60 per unit stored per year. Approximately 4,500 units per year are stored in the rented space.

Instructions
(a) Prepare an incremental analysis for the make or buy decision. Should Mareno make or buy the part? Why?
(b) Prepare an incremental analysis, assuming the released facilities can be used to produce $10,000 of net income in addition to the savings on the rental of storage space. What decision should now be made?
(c) ▭▭▭▷ What nonfinancial factors should be considered in the decision?

Compute contribution margin and prepare incremental analysis concerning elimination of divisions.
(SO 7)

P27–3B   Modine Manufacturing Company has four operating divisions. During the first quarter of 1999, the company reported total income from operations of $61,000 and the following results for the divisions:

	Division			
	Denver	**Helena**	**Portland**	**Seattle**
Sales	$440,000	$730,000	$920,000	$520,000
Cost of goods sold	380,000	480,000	576,000	420,000
Selling and administrative expenses	120,000	207,000	246,000	120,000
Income (loss) from operations	$ (60,000)	$ 43,000	$ 98,000	$ (20,000)

Analysis reveals the following percentages of variable costs in each division.

	Denver	Helena	Portland	Seattle
Cost of goods sold	95%	80%	90%	90%
Selling and administrative expenses	80	60	70	60

Discontinuance of any division would save 60% of the fixed costs and expenses for that division.

Top management is deeply concerned about the unprofitable divisions (Denver and Seattle). The consensus is that one or both of the divisions should be eliminated.

Instructions
   (a) Compute the contribution margin for the two unprofitable divisions.
   (b) Prepare an incremental analysis concerning the possible elimination of (1) the Denver Division and (2) the Seattle Division. What course of action do you recommend for each division?
   (c) Prepare a columnar condensed income statement using the CVP format for Modine Manufacturing Company, assuming (1) the Denver Division is eliminated, and (2) the unavoidable fixed costs and expenses of the Denver Division are allocated 30% to Helena, 50% to Portland, and 20% to Seattle.
   (d) Compare the total income from operations with the Denver Division ($61,000) to total income from operations without this division.

P27–4B The partnership of Malle and Stine is considering three long-term capital investment proposals. Relevant data on each project are as follows:

Compute rate of return, cash payback, and net present value.
(SO 9, 10)

	Project		
	Brown	Red	Yellow
Capital investment	$180,000	$220,000	$250,000
Annual net income:			
Year 1	25,000	20,000	31,000
2	16,000	20,000	24,000
3	13,000	20,000	23,000
4	10,000	20,000	22,000
5	8,000	20,000	20,000
Total	$72,000	$100,000	$120,000

Salvage value is expected to be zero at the end of each project. Depreciation is computed by the straight-line method. The company's minimum rate of return is the company's cost of capital which is 12%.

Instructions
   (a) Compute the average annual rate of return for each project. (Round to two decimals.)
   (b) Compute the cash payback period for each project. (Round to two decimals.)
   (c) Compute the net present value for each project. (Round to nearest dollar.)
   (d) Rank the projects on each of the foregoing bases. What project do you recommend?

P27–5B Tammy Yewell is managing director of the Village Day Care Center. Village is currently set up as a full-time child care facility for children between the ages of 12 months and 6 years. Tammy is trying to determine whether the center should expand its facilities to incorporate a newborn care room for infants between the ages of 6 weeks and 12 months. The necessary space already exists. An investment of $25,000 would be needed, however, to purchase cribs, high chairs, etc. The equipment purchased for the room would have a 5-year useful life with zero salvage value.

Compute annual rate of return, cash payback, and net present value.
(SO 9, 10)

The newborn nursery would be staffed to handle 12 infants on a full-time basis. The parents of each infant would be charged $150 weekly, and the facility would operate 52 weeks of the year. Staffing the nursery would require two full-time specialists and five part-time assistants at an annual cost of $74,000. Food, diapers, and other miscellaneous supplies are expected to total $12,500 annually.

Instructions
   (a) Determine (1) annual net income and (2) cash inflow for the new nursery.
   (b) Compute (1) the annual rate of return and (2) the cash payback period for the new nursery. (Round to two decimals.)

(c) Assuming that Village can borrow the money needed for expansion at 12%, compute the net present value of the new room. (Round to the nearest dollar.)

(d) ◼▰▰▰▷   What should Tammy conclude from these computations?

BROADENING YOUR PERSPECTIVE

GROUP DECISION CASE

BYP27–1   Sanchez Company is considering the purchase of a new machine. The invoice price of the machine is $115,000, freight charges are estimated to be $4,000, and installation costs are expected to be $6,000. Salvage value of the new equipment is expected to be zero after a useful life of 4 years. Existing equipment could be retained and used for an additional 4 years if the new machine is not purchased. At that time, the salvage value of the equipment would be zero. If the new machine is purchased now, the existing machine would have to be scrapped. Sanchez's accountant, Diane Gallup, has accumulated the following data regarding annual sales and expenses with and without the new machine:

1. Without the new machine, Sanchez can sell 11,000 units of product annually at a per unit selling price of $100. If the new unit is purchased, the number of units produced and sold would increase by 20%, and the selling price would remain the same.
2. The new machine is faster than the old machine, and it is more efficient in its usage of materials. With the old machine the gross profit rate will be 27.5% of sales, whereas the rate will be 29% of sales with the new machine.
3. Annual selling expenses are $180,000 with the current equipment. Because the new equipment would produce a greater number of units to be sold, annual selling expenses are expected to increase by 10% if it is purchased.
4. Annual administrative expenses are expected to be $100,000 with the old machine, and $113,000 with the new machine.
5. The current book value of the existing machine is $36,000. Sanchez uses straight-line depreciation.
6. Sanchez's management wants a minimum rate of return of 15% on its investment and a payback period of no more than 3 years.

Instructions
With the class divided into groups, answer the following (ignore income tax effects):

(a) Prepare an incremental analysis for the 4 years showing whether Sanchez should keep the existing machine or buy the new machine.
(b) Calculate the annual rate of return for the new machine. (Round to two decimals.)
(c) Compute the payback period for the new machine. (Round to two decimals.)
(d) Compute the net present value of the new machine. (Round to the nearest dollar.)
(e) On the basis of the foregoing data, would you recommend that Sanchez buy the machine? Why?

MANAGERIAL ANALYSIS

BYP27–2   Electro-More manufactures private-label small electronic products, such as alarm clocks, calculators, kitchen timers, stopwatches, and automatic pencil sharpeners. Some of the products are sold as sets, and others are sold individually. Products are studied as to their sales potential, and then cost estimates are made. The Engineering Department develops production plans, and then production begins. The company has generally had very successful product introduction. Only two products introduced by the company have been discontinued.

One of the products currently sold is a multi-alarm alarm clock. The clock has four alarms that can be programmed to sound at various times and for varying lengths of time. The company has experienced a great deal of difficulty in making the circuit boards for the clocks. The production process has never operated smoothly. The product is unprofitable at the present time, primarily because of warranty repairs and product recalls. Two models of the clocks were recalled, for example, because they sometimes caused an electric shock when the alarms were being shut off. The Engineering Department is attempting to revise the manufacturing process, but the revision will take another 6 months at least.

The clocks were very popular when they were introduced, and since they are private-label, the company has not suffered much from the recalls. Presently, the company has a very large order for several items from Kmart Stores. The order includes 5,000 of the multi-alarm clocks. When the company suggested that Kmart purchase the clocks from another manufacturer, Kmart threatened to rescind the entire order unless the clocks were included.

The company has therefore investigated the possibility of having another company make the clocks for them. The clocks were bid for the Kmart order based on an estimated $5 cost to manufacture:

Circuit board, 1 each @ $1.50	$1.50
Plastic case, 1 each @ $0.50	0.50
Alarms, 4 @ $0.10 each	0.10
Labor, 15 minutes @ $10/hour	2.50
Overhead, $1.60 per labor hour	0.40

Electro-More could purchase clocks to fill the Kmart order for $10 from Silver Star, a Korean manufacturer with a very good quality record. Silver Star has offered to reduce the price to $7.50 after Electro-More has been a customer for 6 months, placing an order of at least 1,000 units per month. If Electro-More becomes a "preferred customer" by purchasing 15,000 units per year, the price would be reduced still further to $4.50.

Alpha Products, a local manufacturer, has also offered to make clocks for Electro-More. They have offered to sell 5,000 clocks for $3 each. However, Alpha Products has been in business for only 6 months. They have experienced significant turnover in their labor force, and the local press has reported that the owners may face tax evasion charges soon. The owner of Alpha Products is an electronic engineer, however, and the quality of the clocks is likely to be good.

If Electro-More decides to purchase the clocks from either Silver Star or Alpha, all the costs to manufacture could be avoided, except a total of $5,000 in overhead costs for machine depreciation. The machinery is fairly new, and has no alternate use.

Instructions

(a) What is the difference in profit under each of the alternatives if the clocks are to be sold for $12.50 each to Kmart?

(b) What are the most important nonfinancial factors that Electro-More should consider when making this decision?

(c) What do you think Electro-More should do in regard to the Kmart order? What should it do in regard to continuing to manufacture the multi-alarm alarm clocks? Be prepared to defend your answer.

Real-World Focus: Beverly Hills Fan Company

BYP27–3 Founded in 1983, the **Beverly Hills Fan Company** is located in Woodland Hills, California. With 23 employees and sales of less than $10 million, the company is relatively small. Management feels that there is potential for growth in the upscale market for ceiling fans and lighting. They are particularly optimistic about growth in Mexican and Canadian markets.

Presented below is information from the president's letter in the company's annual report:

BEVERLY HILLS FAN COMPANY
President's Letter

An aggressive product development program was initiated during the past year resulting in new ceiling fan models planned for introduction in 1993. Award winning industrial designer Ron Rezek created several new fan models for the Beverly Hills Fan and L.A. Fan lines, including a new Showroom Collection, designed specifically for the architectural and designer markets. Each of these models has received critical acclaim, and order commitments for 1993 have been outstanding. Additionally, our Custom Color and special order fans continued to enjoy increasing popularity and sales gains as more and more customers desire fans that match their specific interior decors. Currently, Beverly Hills Fan Company offers a product line of over 100 models of contemporary, traditional, and transitional ceiling fans.

Instructions
  (a) What points did the company management need to consider before deciding to offer the special-order fans to customers?
  (b) How would incremental analysis be employed to assist in this decision?

COMMUNICATION ACTIVITY

BYP27–4   Refer back to Exercise 27–7 to address the following:

Instructions
Prepare a memo to Mary Ann Griffin, your supervisor. Show your calculations from E27–7, (a) and (b). In one or two paragraphs, discuss important nonfinancial considerations. Make any assumptions you believe to be necessary. Make a recommendation, based on your analysis.

RESEARCH ASSIGNMENT

BYP27–5   The April 21, 1997, issue of *Forbes* includes an article by Toni Mack entitled, "The Tiger Is on the Prowl."

Instructions
Read the article and answer the following questions:
  (a) What have been the relative capital spending practices of Royal Dutch Shell versus Mobil Corp. versus Exxon?
  (b) What has been "the religion" (business objective) of Exxon's headquarters since 1983?
  (c) What was Exxon's capital budget in 1994 and 1995? What is Exxon's capital budget expected to swell to in 2 or 3 years?
  (d) Did Exxon's capital spending strategy pay off during the past 15 years?

ETHICS CASE

BYP27–6   Bristle Brush Company operates in a state where corporate taxes and workmen's compensation insurance rates have recently doubled. Bristle's president has just assigned you the task of preparing an economic analysis and making a recommendation relative to moving the company's entire operation to Missouri. The president is slightly in favor of such a move because Missouri is his boyhood home and he also owns a fishing lodge there.

You have just completed building your dream house, moved in, and sodded the lawn. Your children are all doing well in school and sports and, along with your spouse, want no part of a move to Missouri. If the company does move, so will you because the town is a one-industry community and you and your spouse will have to move to have employment. Moving when everyone else does will cause you to take a big loss on the sale of your house. The same hardships will be suffered by your coworkers, and the town will be devastated.

In compiling the costs of moving versus not moving, you have latitude in the assumptions you make, the estimates you compute, and the discount rates and time periods you project. You are in a position to influence the decision singlehandedly.

Instructions
- (a) Who are the stakeholders in this situation?
- (b) What are the ethical issues in this situation?
- (c) What would you do in this situation?

SURFING THE NET

BYP27-7 Campbell Soup Company is an international provider of soup products. Management is very interested in continuing to grow the company in its core business, while "spinning off" those businesses that are not part of its core operation.

Address: http://www.campbellsoups.com

Steps:
1. Go to the home page of Campbell Soup Company at the address shown above.
2. Choose the current annual report.

Instructions
Review the financial statements and management's discussion and analysis, and answer the following questions:

- (a) What was the total amount of capital expenditures in the current year, and how does this amount compare with the previous year? If next year's projected expenditures are presented, provide this amount also.
- (b) What interest rate did the company pay new borrowings in the current year?
- (c) Assume that this year's capital expenditures are expected to increase cash flows by $54 million. What is the expected internal rate of return (IRR) for these capital expenditures? (Assume a 10-year period for the cash flows.)

Answers to Self-Study Questions
1. d   2. b   3. c   4. d   5. a   6. b   7. c   8. b   9. d   10. b

---

Answer to Kellogg Review It Question 4, p. 1174
Kellogg's return on average assets for 1997 was 11%. Kellogg's return on average assets was 17% in 1987, and it was 14% or above in 6 of the 10 years since then; but, it has been 11% for the 3 most recent years.

Remember to go back to the Navigator box on the chapter-opening page and check off your completed work.

APPENDIXES A – E

APPENDIX A

SPECIMEN FINANCIAL STATEMENTS:
Kellogg Company

THE ANNUAL REPORT

Once each year a corporation communicates to its stockholders and other interested parties by issuing a complete set of audited financial statements. The **annual report**, as this communication is called, summarizes the financial results of its operations for the year and its plans for the future. Many such annual reports have become attractive, multicolored, glossy public relations ad pieces containing pictures of corporate officers and directors as well as photos and descriptions of new products and new buildings. Yet the basic function of every annual report is to report **financial information**, almost all of which is a product of the corporation's accounting system.

The content and organization of corporate annual reports have become fairly standardized. Excluding the public relations part of the report (pictures and products), the following items are the traditional financial portions of the annual report:

> Financial Highlights
> Letter to the Stockholders
> Auditor's Report
> Management Discussion and Analysis
> Financial Statements and Accompanying Notes
> Five- or Ten-Year Summary

In this appendix we illustrate current financial reporting with a comprehensive set of corporate financial statements that are prepared in accordance with generally accepted accounting principles and audited by an international independent certified public accounting firm. We are grateful for permission to use the actual financial statements and other accompanying financial information from the annual report of a large, publicly held company, Kellogg Company.

FINANCIAL HIGHLIGHTS

The financial highlights section is usually presented inside the front cover or on the first two pages of the annual report. This section generally reports the total or per share amounts for five to ten financial items for the current year and one or more previous years. Financial items from the income statement and the balance sheet that typically are presented are sales, income from continuing operations, net income, net income per share, dividends per common share, and the amount of capital expenditures. The financial highlights section from Kellogg's Annual Report is shown below:

FINANCIAL HIGHLIGHTS

(millions, except per share data)	1997	Change	1996	Change	1995	Change
Net sales	$6,830.1	+2%	$6,676.6	-5%	$7,003.7	+7%
Operating profit, excluding non-recurring charges (a)	1,193.2	+9%	1,095.0	-13%	1,259.3	+8%
Earnings, excluding non-recurring charges and other unusual items (a) and before cumulative effect of accounting change (b)	704.5	+8%	651.1	-14%	761.6	+8%
Earnings per share (basic and diluted), excluding non-recurring charges and other unusual items (a) and before cumulative effect of accounting change (b) (c)	1.70	+11%	1.53	-12%	1.74	+10%
Operating profit	1,009.1	+5%	958.9	+14%	837.5	-28%
Net earnings	546.0	+3%	531.0	+8%	490.3	-30%
Net earnings per share (basic and diluted) (c)	1.32	+6%	1.25	+12%	1.12	-29%
Net cash provided by operating activities	879.8	+24%	711.5	-32%	1,041.0	+8%
Capital expenditures	312.4	+2%	307.3	-3%	315.7	-11%
Average shares outstanding (c)	414.1		424.9		438.3	
Dividends per share (c)	$ .87	+7%	$ .81	+8%	$ .75	+7%
Year-end stock price (c)	$ 49^{5}/$_{8}$	+51%	$ 32^{13}/$_{16}$	-15%	$ 38^{5}/$_{8}$	+33%

(a) Refer to Management's Discussion and Analysis on pages A9-A14 and Notes 3 and 4 within the Notes to Consolidated Financial Statements for further explanation of non-recurring charges and other unusual items for years 1995 - 1997.

(b) Refer to Management's Discussion and Analysis on pages A9-A14 and Note 1 within the Notes to Consolidated Financial Statements for further explanation of cumulative effect of accounting change in 1997.

(c) Restated for two-for-one stock split effective August 22, 1997.

As shown above, Kellogg chose also to present the percent change from last year to the current year for each of the reported items.

LETTER TO THE STOCKHOLDERS

Nearly every annual report contains a letter to the stockholders from the Chairman of the Board or the President (or both). This letter typically discusses the company's accomplishments during the past year and highlights significant

Arnold G. Langbo

Kellogg Company recorded solid growth in 1997, as we prepared to assume an even stronger leadership position among the global food companies of the 21st century.

Your Company's earnings per share increased 11 percent in 1997, excluding unusual items. Global volume was up 11 percent, helped by the strong performance of new products and the impact of our new Lender's Bagels business. Excluding Lender's, global volume was up 5 percent.

Kellogg Company stock split two-for-one, and our stock price advanced by 51 percent. The Kellogg dividend rose for the 41st straight year, with a split-adjusted increase of 6 cents per share to $.87.

We also continued our program of purchasing Kellogg shares. These purchases totaled $426 million in 1997, and the Board of Directors has authorized $389 million in additional purchases during 1998.

Building on a heritage of leadership and excellence, we are shaping Kellogg Company into a value-focused global growth company of the future. To reach that goal, we must:

- **Gain a clear competitive advantage** in certain critical aspects of our business; and
- **Build from strength**, taking full advantage of the equity assets that make Kellogg unique among the world's food companies.

I am pleased to report substantial progress in meeting these two requirements.

Gaining a Competitive Advantage

Kellogg Company's foundation for leadership in the 21st century will be clear competitive superiority in *innovation*, *cost structure*, and *global capabilities*.

Innovation. Leadership in innovation is leadership in ideas. One imperative of this leadership is knowing and understanding the vast diversity of consumers around the world and organizing Kellogg Company's resources to respond with high-value products.

To enhance our leadership in global food innovation, the W.K. Kellogg Institute for Food and Nutrition Research (WKKI) in Battle Creek, Michigan, began operations during 1997. At this world-class facility, we have brought together Kellogg research and development people from 23 nations. At the WKKI, we are strengthening our product development effort and building our capability to generate products for launch in multiple markets. This new system allows us to allocate resources to the highest-value ideas and take them to market rapidly around the world.

The success of three of our newest products – *Kellogg's® Honey Crunch Corn Flakes™* and *Kellogg's Cocoa Frosted Flakes™* cereals and *Kellogg's® Rice Krispies Treats™* squares – demonstrates the value of innovative product development. We also are optimistic about our

events such as mergers and acquisitions, new products, operating achievements, business philosophy, changes in officers or directors, financing commitments, expansion plans, and future prospects. The letter to the stockholders signed by Arnold G. Langbo, Chairman of the Board and Chief Executive Officer of Kellogg, is shown on pages A4 to A7.

most-recent cereal launch, *Kellogg's®* *Razzle Dazzle Rice Krispies.™* Kellogg Company's consumer-focused thinking, backed by the WKKI's unmatched R&D facilities, is continuing to fill our new product pipeline for 1998 and beyond.

The European initiative reduced the number of plants from seven to four, while actually enhancing our ability to serve the pan-European marketplace.

As we continue to improve our supply chain, we expect additional savings and an increasingly advantaged cost structure.

decisions that create value for shareholders.

The Enterprise Business Applications (EBA) initiative, centerpiece of our business transformation, is currently under way for our supply chain, financial, and performance management processes.

SHAREHOLDERS

Our quest to sustain our leadership in innovation extends to all aspects of our business. Examples are the mutually beneficial global relationships we are developing with major retailers and, in the U.S., our new *"Cereal. Eat it for Life."™* television and print advertisements. Leading-edge efforts such as these will deliver value to consumers and to Kellogg shareholders. **Cost structure.** A relentless commitment to be the low-cost producer of cereal and convenience foods enables us to offer *Kellogg's®* products at a competitive value advantage in diverse markets around the world.

To further strengthen our cost positioning, we are realigning what we call our global supply chain. This supply chain extends from the grain in the field through the purchasing, manufacturing, and distribution processes to the ultimate consumer.

Over the past two years, we have aggressively streamlined major parts of our supply chain. In 1996, we completed significant manufacturing efficiency initiatives in the U.S. and Australia. Then, in 1997, we restructured our European cereal manufacturing and distribution network.

Global capabilities. Leadership in the 21st century requires that we build greater global capabilities to fully leverage our worldwide resources and knowledge. Advances in information technology are enabling us to manage our business processes, people, and technology very differently to better serve our customers and consumers.

We are transforming the Company by engineering our major processes worldwide for improved effectiveness and efficiency. These processes, and the responsibilities of Kellogg people, will transcend today's functional and country boundaries. There will be greater collaboration and sharing of intellectual capital. Our people will have worldwide access to critical information to accelerate fact-based

Building from Strength Our initiatives to assure long-term superiority in innovation, cost structure, and global capabilities have made this a time of dynamic change at Kellogg Company.

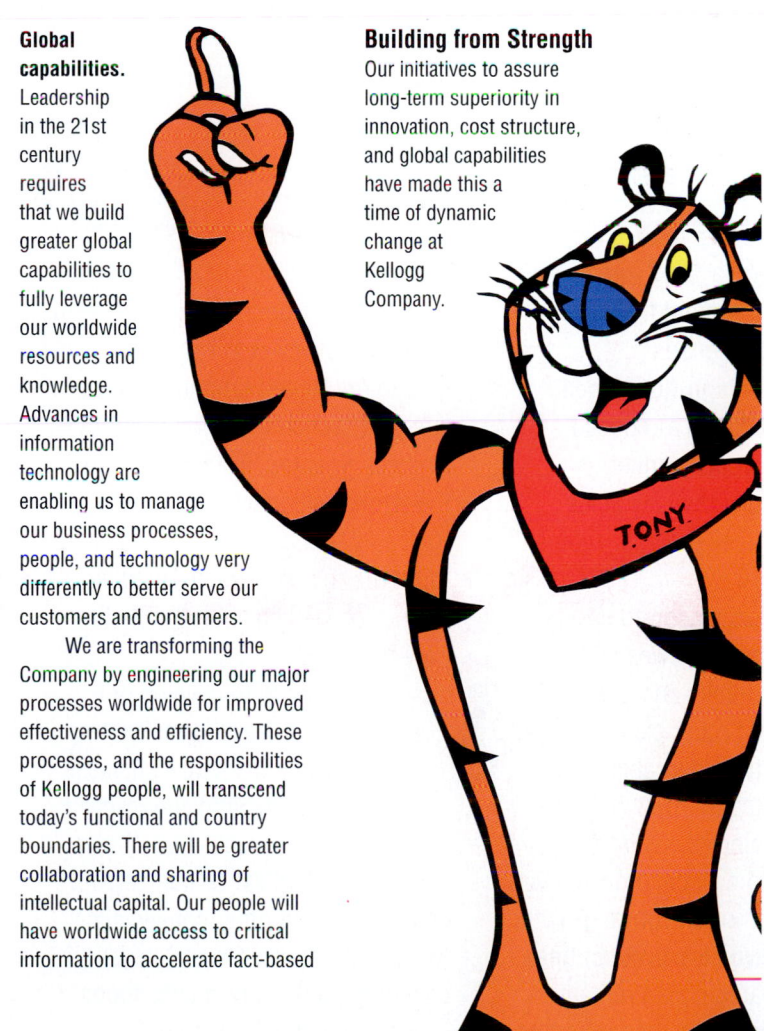

Our accomplishments from these initiatives are of great strategic importance.

Just as significant, however, is how your Company is using its unique strengths to deliver solid growth today and set the stage for consistent growth and superior returns to shareholders in the 21st century.

Building on a commitment to nutrition. This Company was founded on a belief in the dietary goodness of grain-based food. We continue to be driven by that same belief. An ever-growing base of scientific evidence provides a solid foundation for the Company's efforts to communicate the value of wheat-bran fiber, folic acid, and other attributes of our products in a healthy diet.

As we prepare to begin a new millennium, a 1997 meeting of scientists from around the world reached this consensus:

- A diet rich in high-fiber cereal is associated with a reduced risk of colo-rectal cancer.
- There is suggestive evidence that cereal fiber protects against breast cancer.
- There is good reason to examine the relationship between cereal fiber intake and the prevention of other cancers.

With further favorable reports expected in 1998, the health positioning of *Kellogg's*® products could well become an even stronger factor in our future growth.

Building our two core product lines. Our global strategic plan remains centered on Kellogg Company's two immensely valuable core businesses: ready-to-eat cereal and grain-based convenience foods. We acted decisively in 1997 to further develop both.

To foster the continued growth of our cereal business, we opened an efficient new plant in Thailand, streamlined our European cereal infrastructure, and purchased cereal businesses in Ecuador and Brazil. We also adjusted our development strategies in emerging Asian markets to better respond to local taste preferences.

Our global roll-out of convenience foods accelerated with the highly successful introduction of *Kellogg's*® *Nutri-Grain*® cereal bars in the United Kingdom, the late-year launch of *Kellogg's*® *Rice Krispies Squares*™ in the U.K., and the strong national introductions of *Kellogg's*® *Rice Bubbles Treats*™ and four other cereal bars in Australia. Further convenience food launches are planned for 1998.

Continuing to develop our convenience foods infrastructure, we invested in a bagel business in the United Kingdom and reached agreement to purchase Day Dawn, a producer of wheat biscuit cereal, cereal bars, and other convenience foods in Australia. We also began construction of convenience foods capacity in Latin America and

carefully integrated the Lender's Bagels business, purchased in December 1996, into our U.S. operations.

Building by understanding and responding to consumers. Building on strength also means delivering products where and when consumers want them.

One of our biggest ongoing initiatives in 1997 was the expanded delivery of *Kellogg's*® products through new, non-traditional channels such as vending machines and kiosks, as well as convenience,

Kellogg's Corn Flakes® cereal, a family favorite around the world, is one of Kellogg Company's many growth equities. It is popular in diverse markets and in our growing single-serve business. The potential of the *Kellogg's Corn Flakes*® equity has been broadened by *Kellogg's*® *Honey Crunch Corn Flakes*™ cereal, which has achieved exceptionally strong results in the United States since its introduction in 1996. International marketing of *Honey Crunch Corn Flakes*™ begins in 1998.

Dig 'Em™ the frog, and *Snap!*® *Crackle!*® and *Pop!*®; and the *Kellogg's*® name itself, associated worldwide with great taste, nutrition, quality, and value.

The pages that follow describe how we are taking increasing advantage of this equity base to enhance the growth and development of our business.

People: Our Most Important Advantage

As we grow globally, we continue to recognize, as did our founder W.K. Kellogg, that people represent Kellogg Company's greatest competitive advantage. Our global team turned in another strong performance during 1997 and is totally focused on delivering superior value to consumers and to Kellogg shareholders in the future. The wide-ranging talents and perspectives of our people are of great value to Kellogg Company, and we are strongly committed to diversity in our workforce.

Special recognition is due several members of the Kellogg family. Dolores D. Wharton and

club, and general merchandise stores. Our introduction of *Nutri-Grain*® cereal bars in the U.K. marked the first presence of *Kellogg's*® products in nearly 30,000 additional food outlets, primarily convenience stores.

Building on a strong equity base. Perhaps the most important way Kellogg Company builds on strength is through our exceptionally powerful equity base. No other food company can match the Kellogg combination of internationally recognized brands such as *Kellogg's Frosted Flakes*,® *Rice Krispies*,® *Pop-Tarts*® and *Special K*®; widely known and loved characters such as *Tony the Tiger*,® *Toucan Sam*,® *Corny*™ the rooster,

Timothy P. Smucker left our Board of Directors in 1997 after 21 and 7 years, respectively, of dedicated service. We extend sincere thanks and best wishes to both Dolores and Tim.

Joining the Board during 1997 were Dr. Benjamin S. Carson, a world-renowned neurosurgeon, and Carleton (Carly) S. Fiorina, group president of Lucent Technologies' Global Service Provider Business.

Promotions among Kellogg Company officers during 1997 included William A. Camstra to vice chairman; Alan F. Harris to executive vice president and president – Kellogg Latin America; John R. Hinton to executive vice president – administration and chief financial officer; and Donna J. Banks to senior vice president – research and development.

Our fine team of Kellogg people is executing growth strategies that we believe are right for Kellogg Company and right for the future. We look forward with excitement to the challenges and global growth opportunities of 1998, 1999, and the new century.

Arnold G. Langbo
Chairman of the Board
Chief Executive Officer

AUDITOR'S REPORT

All publicly held corporations, as well as many other enterprises and organizations (both profit and not-for-profit, large and small) engage the services of independent certified public accountants for the purpose of obtaining an objective, expert report on their financial statements. Based on a comprehensive examination of the company's accounting system and records, and of the financial statements, the outside CPA issues the auditor's report.

The standard auditor's report consists of three pieces of information, expressed in separate sentences or paragraphs: (1) a responsibilities statement, (2) a scope statement, and (3) the opinion. In the **responsibilities statement**, the auditor identifies who and what was audited and indicates the responsibilities of management and the auditor relative to the financial statements. In the **scope statement**, the auditor states that the audit was conducted in accordance with generally accepted auditing standards and discusses the nature and limitations of the audit. In the **opinion statement**, (which is first in Kellogg's auditor's report), the auditor expresses an informed opinion as to (1) the fairness of the financial statements and (2) their conformity with generally accepted accounting principles. The **Report of Price Waterhouse Independent Auditors** appearing in Kellogg's Annual Report is shown below:

REPORT OF INDEPENDENT ACCOUNTANTS

Price Waterhouse LLP

To the Shareholders and Board of Directors of Kellogg Company

In our opinion, the accompanying consolidated balance sheet and the related consolidated statements of earnings, of shareholders' equity and of cash flows present fairly, in all material respects, the financial position of Kellogg Company and its subsidiaries at December 31, 1997 and 1996, and the results of their operations and their cash flows for each of the three years in the period ended December 31, 1997, in conformity with generally accepted accounting principles. These financial statements are the responsibility of the Company's management; our responsibility is to express an opinion on these financial statements based on our audits. We conducted our audits of these statements in accordance with generally accepted auditing standards which require that we plan and perform the audit to obtain reasonable assurance about whether the financial statements are free of material misstatement. An audit includes examining, on a test basis, evidence supporting the amounts and disclosures in the financial statements, assessing the accounting principles used and significant estimates made by management, and evaluating the overall financial statement presentation. We believe that our audits provide a reasonable basis for the opinion expressed above.

As discussed in Note 1 to the financial statements, the Company changed its method of accounting for business process reengineering costs effective October 1, 1997.

Price Waterhouse LLP

Battle Creek, Michigan
January 30, 1998

The auditor's report above contains an additional paragraph wherein Price Waterhouse reports that Kellogg changed its method of accounting for business process reengineering costs as discussed in notes to the financial statements.

The auditor's report issued on Kellogg's financial statements is **unqualified** or "clean"; that is, it contains no qualifications or exceptions. In other words, the auditor conformed completely with generally accepted auditing standards in performing the audit, and the financial statements conformed in all material respects with generally accepted accounting principles.

When the financial statements do not conform with generally accepted accounting principles, the auditor must issue a **qualified** opinion and describe the exception. If the lack of conformity with GAAP is sufficiently material, the auditor is compelled to issue an **adverse** or negative opinion. An adverse opinion means that the financial statements do not present fairly the company's financial condition and/or the results of the company's operations at the dates and for the periods reported.

In circumstances where the auditor is unable to perform all the auditing procedures necessary to reach a conclusion as to the fairness of the financial statements, a **disclaimer** must be issued. In these rare instances, the auditor must report the reason for failure to reach a conclusion on the fairness of the financial statements.

Companies strive to obtain an unqualified auditor's report. Hence, only infrequently are you likely to encounter anything other than this type of opinion on the financial statements.

MANAGEMENT DISCUSSION AND ANALYSIS

The **management discussion and analysis (MD&A)** section covers three financial aspects of a company: its results of operations, its ability to pay near-term obligations, and its ability to fund operations and expansion. Management must highlight favorable or unfavorable trends and identify significant events and uncertainties that affect these three factors. This discussion obviously involves a number of subjective estimates and opinions. The MD&A section of Kelloggs' annual report is presented on the following pages.

Management's Discussion and Analysis

Results of operations

Overview

Kellogg Company operates in a single industry – manufacturing and marketing grain-based convenience food products, including ready-to-eat cereal, toaster pastries, frozen waffles, cereal bars, and bagels, throughout the world. The Company leads the global ready-to-eat cereal category, with an estimated 39% annualized share of worldwide volume. Additionally, the Company is the North American market leader in the toaster pastry, cereal/granola bar, frozen waffle, and pre-packaged bagel categories.

During 1997, the Company returned to growth in earnings per share (excluding unusual items, discussed below), as management continued with its global strategy of brand-differentiated pricing, investment in new product research, brand-building marketing activities, and cost structure reduction initiatives. Results for 1997

were significantly improved over 1996, a year in which earnings were negatively impacted by competitive conditions in the Company's major markets.

For the full year of 1997, Kellogg Company reported net earnings and earnings per share of $546.0 million and $1.32, respectively, compared to 1996 net earnings of $531.0 million and net earnings per share of $1.25. Net earnings and earnings per share for 1995 were $490.3 million and $1.12, respectively. (All per share amounts reflect the 2-for-1 stock split effective August 22, 1997. All earnings per share presented represent both basic and diluted earnings per share.)

During the current and prior years, the Company reported nonrecurring charges and other unusual items that have been excluded from all applicable amounts presented below for purposes of comparison between years. Additionally, results for 1997 are presented before the cumulative effect of a change in the method of accounting for business process reengineering costs. Refer to the separate section below on non-recurring charges and other unusual items for further information.

1997 compared to 1996

Excluding non-recurring charges and other unusual items, the Company reported 1997 earnings per share of $1.70, an 11% increase over the prior-year results of $1.53. The year-over-year increase in earnings per share of $.17 resulted from $.12 of business growth, $.03 of common stock repurchases, and $.04 of favorable tax rate movements, partially offset by $.02 of unfavorable foreign currency movements. The business growth was principally attributable to cereal volume growth in the Company's U.S. and Latin American markets, continued double-digit growth in other convenience foods volume, and reductions in manufacturing and marketing costs. Foreign currency movements negatively impacted earnings by 2% in Europe, 3% in other non-U.S. areas, and 1% on a consolidated basis. The negative impact on 1997 earnings per share due to results of the Lender's Bagels business, acquired in December 1996, was approximately $.05.

The Company achieved the following volume growth during 1997:

	Change
Global cereal	+3.4%
U.S. cereal	+3.9%
Global total	+11.3%
Global total excluding Lender's (a)	+5.0%

(a) Lender's Bagels business acquired in December 1996.

Within the U.S. market, the Company recovered cereal volume declines of the prior year, and slightly exceeded 1995 results. Growth in most other non-U.S. cereal markets offset softness in the Company's United Kingdom, Canada, and Australia volume. The Company's Latin American region achieved record annual volume results. Other convenience foods volume continued to increase at a double-digit rate, even after excluding sales from the Lender's Bagels business.

On an annualized basis, regional volume share of the ready-to-eat cereal category remained strong during the year, at approximately 34% in North America, 44% in Europe, 43% in Asia-Pacific, and 60% in Latin America.

Consolidated net sales increased 2% for 1997. The favorable impact of strong volumes was partially offset by unfavorable pricing and product mix movements, and a negative foreign currency impact of 2%. Excluding the Lender's business, consolidated net sales were even with the prior year. On a geographic basis, net sales versus the prior year were:

Net sales by geographic area – 1997 vs. 1996 % change

	U.S.	Europe	All other	Consolidated
Business	+5%	+2%	+6%	+4%
Foreign currency impact	—	-5%	-4%	-2%
Total change	**+5%**	**-3%**	**+2%**	**+2%**

Margin performance for 1997 was:

	1997	1996	Change
Gross margin	52.1%	53.2%	-1.1%
SGA%(a)	-34.6%	-36.8%	+2.2%
Operating margin	17.5%	16.4%	+1.1%

(a) Selling, general, and administrative expense as a percentage of net sales.

Gross margin performance for 1997 benefited from volume increases and year-over-year operational cost savings. However, these favorable factors were outweighed by the negative impact of prior-year pricing actions. The improvement in SGA% primarily reflects reduced promotional spending in the U.S. market, in line with the Company's integrated pricing strategy.

Operating profit results on a geographic basis were:

Operating profit by geographic area – 1997 vs. 1996

(millions)	U.S.	Europe	All other	Consolidated
1997 operating profit as reported	$706.8	$158.9	$143.4	$1,009.1
Non-recurring charges	35.2	119.1	29.8	184.1
1997 operating profit excluding non-recurring charges	**$742.0**	**$278.0**	**$173.2**	**$1,193.2**
1996 operating profit as reported	$611.2	$204.4	$143.3	$958.9
Non-recurring charges	24.1	76.5	35.5	136.1
1996 operating profit excluding non-recurring charges	**$635.3**	**$280.9**	**$178.8**	**$1,095.0**
% change – 1997 vs. 1996 excluding non-recurring charges:				
Business	+17%	+3%	+1%	+11%
Foreign currency impact	—	-4%	-4%	-2%
Total change	**+17%**	**-1%**	**-3%**	**+9%**

Gross interest expense, prior to amounts capitalized, increased 70% versus the prior year to $117.9 million. The higher interest expense resulted from increased debt levels to fund the Lender's Bagels business acquisition and the Company's common stock repurchase program.

Excluding the impact of non-recurring charges and other unusual items, the effective income tax rate was 35.3%, 1.5 percentage points lower than the prior-year rate. The lower effective tax rate is primarily due to enactment of a 2% statutory rate reduction in the United Kingdom, effective April 1, 1997, as well as favorable adjustments in other jurisdictions. The effective income tax rate based on reported earnings (before cumulative effect of accounting change) was 37.6% in 1997 and 38.2% in 1996. For both 1997 and 1996, the higher reported rate (as compared to the rate excluding the impact of unusual items) primarily relates to certain non-recurring charges for which no tax benefit was provided, based on management's assessment of the likelihood of recovering such benefit in future years.

1996 compared to 1995

The Company's 1996 results were negatively impacted by competitive conditions in the U.S. ready-to-eat cereal market, in which significant price reductions were undertaken by all major competitors during the year. In an effort to improve the brand value proposition to the consumer, the Company implemented several pricing actions in 1996, most notably reductions announced June 10, 1996, averaging 19% on brands comprising approximately two-thirds of its U.S. cereal business. Following an integrated strategy, the Company combined its price reductions with reduced marketing expenditures, while competitors continued heavy deep-discount promotional spending during most of the year. As a result, the Company reported a 12% decline in 1996 earnings per share (excluding non-recurring charges and other unusual items) to $1.53, versus $1.74 in 1995. The $.21 decrease was comprised of $.22 in business decline and $.03 in unfavorable foreign currency movements, mitigated by $.03 of common stock repurchases, and $.01 from a lower effective tax rate. Foreign currency movements negatively impacted earnings by 3% in Europe, 4% in other non-U.S. areas, and 1% on a consolidated basis.

The Company experienced the following volume results during 1996:

	Change
Global cereal	-.7%
U.S. cereal	-3.6%
Global total	+1.2%

Total volume growth was led by strength in the Company's Asia-Pacific and Latin American ready-to-eat cereal shipments and low double-digit growth in other convenience foods volume. These volume gains offset softness in the Company's U.S. and United Kingdom ready-to-eat cereal markets.

Net sales were down 5%, primarily reflecting the price reductions, ready-to-eat cereal volume loss, and unfavorable product mix and foreign currency movements. On a geographic basis, net sales versus the prior year were:

Net sales by geographic area – 1996 vs. 1995 % change				
	U.S.	Europe	All other	Consolidated
Business	-7%	-1%	+8%	-4%
Foreign currency impact	—	-3%	-3%	-1%
Total change	-7%	-4%	+5%	-5%

Margin performance for 1996 was:

	1996	1995	Change
Gross margin	53.2%	54.6%	-1.4%
SGA%	-36.8%	-36.6%	-.2%
Operating margin	16.4%	18.0%	-1.6%

The decline in gross profit margin reflected the price reductions, partially offset by the effect of operational cost savings. The SGA% was maintained at nearly a constant level versus the prior year despite the relatively high level of spending related to the Company's 90th Anniversary promotional programs, implementation costs associated with pricing actions, and competitive conditions in the U.S. cereal market.

Operating profit results on a geographic basis were:

Operating profit by geographic area – 1996 vs. 1995				
(millions)	U.S.	Europe	All other	Consolidated
1996 operating profit excluding non-recurring charges	**$635.3**	**$280.9**	**$178.8**	**$1,095.0**
1995 operating profit as reported	$ 443.1	$ 293.6	$ 100.8	$ 837.5
Non-recurring charges	325.0	38.4	58.4	421.8
1995 operating profit excluding non-recurring charges	**$768.1**	**$332.0**	**$159.2**	**$1,259.3**
% change – 1996 vs. 1995 excluding non-recurring charges:				
Business	-17%	-11%	+16%	-11%
Foreign currency impact	—	-4%	-4%	-2%
Total change	**-17%**	**-15%**	**+12%**	**-13%**

Gross interest expense prior to amounts capitalized was $69.4 million, compared to $69.8 million in 1995. Despite an increase in debt during the year, total interest expense was maintained at prior-year levels due to the favorable effect of lower rates on short-term borrowings.

Other expense for 1996 included a charge of $35.0 million for a contribution to the Kellogg's Corporate Citizenship Fund, a private trust established for charitable donations. Excluding this unusual item, other income, net, decreased $19.5 million to $1.6 million, primarily due to foreign currency losses in Latin American markets and lower interest income during 1996.

Excluding the impact of non-recurring charges and other unusual items, the effective income tax rate was 36.8%, .7 percentage points lower than the prior-year rate, primarily due to favorable audit settlements in foreign jurisdictions and country mix.

Liquidity and capital resources

The Company's financial condition remained strong throughout 1997. A strong cash flow, combined with a program of issuing commercial paper and maintaining worldwide credit facilities, provides adequate liquidity to meet the Company's operational needs.

Net cash provided by operating activities during 1997 was $879.8 million, compared to $711.5 million in 1996, with the increase due principally to higher earnings, lower benefit plan contributions, and favorable working capital movements. The ratio of current assets to current liabilities was .9 at December 31, 1997, compared to .7 at December 31, 1996.

Net cash used in investing activities was $329.3 million, principally comprised of $312.4 million in property additions. Net cash used in investing activities decreased significantly from the prior year, in which the Company paid $466 million to purchase the Lender's Bagels business.

Net cash used in financing activities was $607.3 million, primarily related to common stock repurchases of $426.0 million and dividend payments of $360.1 million, partially offset by a net increase in total debt of $108.1 million. The Company's total 1997 per share dividend payment was $.87, a 7.4% increase over the prior-year payment of $.81.

On August 1, 1997, the Company's Board of Directors approved a 2-for-1 stock split to shareholders of record at the close of business August 8, 1997, effective August 22, 1997, and also authorized retirement of 105.3 million common shares (pre-split) held in treasury. All per share and shares outstanding data have been restated retroactively to reflect the stock split.

Under existing plans authorized by the Company's Board of Directors, management spent $426.0 million during 1997 to repurchase 10.9 million shares (on a post-split basis) of the Company's common stock at an average price of $39 per share. The open repurchase authorization, which extends through December 31, 1998, was $389.1 million at year-end 1997.

Notes payable consist principally of commercial paper borrowings in the United States. Associated with these borrowings, during September 1997, the Company purchased a $225 million notional, four-year fixed interest rate cap. Under the terms of the cap, if the Federal Reserve AA composite rate on 30-day commercial paper increases to 6.33%, the Company will pay this fixed rate on $225 million of its commercial paper borrowings. If the rate increases to 7.83% or above, the cap will expire. As of year-end 1997, the rate was 5.65%.

To reduce short-term borrowings, on February 4, 1998, the Company issued $400 million of three-year 5.75% fixed rate U.S. Dollar Notes. Accordingly, an equivalent amount of commercial paper borrowings was classified as long-term debt in the December 31, 1997, balance sheet. These Notes were issued under an existing "shelf registration" with the Securities and Exchange Commission, and provide an option to holders to extend the obligation for an additional four years at a predetermined interest rate of 5.63% plus the Company's then-current credit spread. Concurrent with this issuance, the Company entered into a $400 million notional, three-year fixed-to-floating

interest rate swap, indexed to the Federal Reserve AA composite rate on 30-day commercial paper.

As of December 31, 1997, current maturities of long-term debt primarily consisted of $200 million of five-year notes due October 1998. Management currently intends to replace these notes with new long-term debt issuances as of the maturity date and, as of year-end 1997, had entered into $25 million notional amount of interest rate hedges to effectively fix the U.S. Treasury rate on which an equivalent amount of future issuances would be priced. Subject to market conditions, management intends to gradually increase the notional amount of interest rate hedges to $200 million, prior to the maturity date of the notes.

On January 29, 1997, the Company issued $500 million of seven-year 6.625% fixed rate Euro Dollar Notes. This debt was issued primarily to fund the purchase of the Lender's Bagels business, acquired in December 1996. In conjunction with this issuance, the Company settled $500 million notional amount of interest rate forward swap agreements, which effectively fixed the interest rate on the debt at 6.354%. Associated with this debt, during September 1997, the Company entered into a $225 million notional, 4 ½-year fixed-to-floating interest rate swap, indexed to the three-month London Interbank Offered Rate (LIBOR). Under the terms of the swap, if three-month LIBOR decreases to 4.71% or below, the swap will expire. At year-end 1997, three-month LIBOR was 5.81%.

To replace other long-term debt maturing during the year, the Company issued $500 million of four-year 6.125% Euro Dollar Notes on August 5, 1997. In conjunction with this issuance, the Company settled $400 million notional amount of interest rate forward swap agreements that effectively fixed the interest rate on the debt at 6.4%. Associated with this debt, during September 1997, the Company entered into a $200 million notional, four-year fixed-to-floating interest rate swap, indexed to three-month LIBOR.

The ratio of total debt to market capitalization at December 31, 1997, was 10%, down from 14% at December 31, 1996, principally due to an increase in the market price of the Company's stock since that date.

Non-recurring charges and other unusual items

From 1995 to the present, management has commenced major productivity and operational streamlining initiatives in an effort to optimize the Company's cost structure and move toward a global business model. The incremental costs of these programs have been reported throughout 1995-1997 as non-recurring charges.

In addition to the non-recurring charges reported during 1995-1997 for streamlining initiatives, the Company incurred charges for other unusual items. Furthermore, net earnings for 1997 included a cumulative effect of accounting change related to business process reengineering costs. In summary, the following charges were excluded from reported results for purposes of comparison within the "Results of operations" section above:

Non-recurring charges & other unusual items

Impact on (millions, except per share data):	Operating profit	Earnings before income taxes and cumulative effect of accounting change	Net earnings	Net earnings per share
1997:				
Streamlining initiatives	$161.1	$161.1		
Impairment losses	23.0	23.0		
Total non-recurring charges	**$184.1**	**$184.1**	**$140.5**	**$.34**
Cumulative effect of accounting change	—	—	**$ 18.0**	**$.04**
1996:				
Streamlining initiatives	$121.1	$121.1		
Litigation provision	15.0	15.0		
Private trust contribution (a)	—	35.0		
Total	**$136.1**	**$171.1**	**$120.1**	**$.28**
1995:				
Streamlining initiatives	$348.0	$348.0		
Impairment losses	73.8	73.8		
Total	**$421.8**	**$421.8**	**$271.3**	**$.62**

(a) Recorded in other income (expense), net.

The 1997 charges for streamlining initiatives relate principally to management's plan to optimize the Company's pan-European operations, as well as ongoing productivity programs in the United States and Australia. A major component of the pan-European initiatives was the late 1997 closing of manufacturing plants and separation of employees in Riga, Latvia; Svendborg, Denmark; and Verola, Italy.

Approximately 50% of the total 1997 streamlining charges consist of manufacturing asset write-downs, with the balance comprised of current and anticipated cash outlays for employee separation benefits, equipment removal, production redeployment, associated management consulting, and similar costs. Related primarily to the pan-European initiatives, streamlining programs begun in 1997 will result in employee headcount reductions of approximately 600 and are expected to deliver annual pre-tax savings of approximately $60 million when fully implemented. Total cash outlays for streamlining initiatives were approximately $85 million during 1997 and are expected to be approximately $50 million in 1998. Refer to Note 3 within Notes to Consolidated Financial Statements for additional information.

The streamlining programs commenced since 1995, including the aforementioned pan-European initiatives, are expected to result in the elimination of approximately 3,000 employee positions by the end of 1998, with approximately 90% of this reduction already achieved. These programs are expected to deliver average annual pre-tax sav-

ings in excess of $200 million by the year 2000, with approximately 75% of that amount being realized currently. These savings are not necessarily indicative of current and future incremental earnings due to management's commitment to invest in competitive business strategies, new markets, and growth opportunities.

Also included in the 1997 charges are $23.0 million of asset impairment losses, which result from evaluation of the Company's ability to recover components of its investments, based on management's ongoing strategic assessment of local conditions, in the emerging markets of Asia-Pacific.

In addition to the non-recurring charges reported during 1995 and 1996 for streamlining initiatives, the Company incurred charges for the following unusual items:

• During 1996, the Company included in non-recurring charges a provision of $15.0 million for the potential settlement of certain litigation.

• During 1996, the Company included in other expense a charge of $35.0 million for a contribution to the Kellogg's Corporate Citizenship Fund, which is expected to satisfy the charitable-giving plans of this private trust through the year 2000.

• During 1995, the Company included in non-recurring charges $73.8 million of asset impairment losses that resulted from the evaluation of the Company's ability to recover asset costs given changes in local market conditions, sourcing of products, and other strategic factors in its North American and Asia-Pacific operations.

The foregoing discussion of streamlining initiatives contains forward-looking statements regarding headcount reductions, cash requirements, and realizable savings. Actual amounts may vary depending on the final determination of important factors, such as identification of specific employees to be separated from predetermined pools, actual amounts of asset removal and relocation costs, dates of asset disposal and costs to maintain assets up to the date of disposal, proceeds from asset disposals, final negotiation of third party contract buy-outs, and other items.

On November 20, 1997, the Emerging Issues Task Force (EITF) of the Financial Accounting Standards Board reached a consensus in Issue 97-13 that the costs of business process reengineering activities are to be expensed as incurred. This consensus also applies to business process reengineering activities that are part of an information technology project. Beginning in 1996, the Company has undertaken an Enterprise Business Applications (EBA) initiative that combines design and installation of business processes and software packages to achieve global best practices. Under the EBA initiative, the Company had capitalized certain external costs associated with business process reengineering activities as part of the software asset. EITF Issue 97-13 prescribes that previously capitalized business process reengineering costs should be expensed and reported as a cumulative effect of a change in accounting principle. Accordingly, for the fourth quarter of 1997, the Company reported a charge of $18.0 million (net of tax benefit of $7.7 million) or $.04 per share for write-off of business process reengineering costs. Such costs were expensed as incurred during the fourth quarter of 1997, and were insignificant.

1998 outlook

Management is not aware of any adverse trends that would materially affect the Company's strong financial position. Should suitable investment opportunities or working capital needs arise that would require additional financing, management believes that the Company's strong credit rating, balance sheet, and earnings history provide a base for obtaining additional financial resources at competitive rates and terms. Based on the expectation of continued cereal volume growth, and strong results from product innovation and the global introduction of other convenience foods, management believes the Company is well-positioned to deliver sales and earnings growth for the full year 1998. The Company will continue to identify and pursue streamlining and productivity initiatives to optimize its cost structure.

Additional expectations for 1998 include a gross profit margin of 53-54%, an SGA% of 35-36%, an effective income tax rate of 36-37%, capital spending of approximately $400 million, common stock repurchase activity of $390 million, and an increase in interest expense of 10%.

To address the millennium date change issue (the inability of certain computer software, hardware, and other equipment with embedded computer chips to properly process two-digit year-date codes after 1999), the Company formed a global task force to perform a risk assessment, and develop and execute action plans, as necessary. The global risk assessment is substantially complete. Remediation and testing activities for critical business operations are under way, with completion scheduled by year-end 1998. Remediation and testing of non-critical business operations will continue, as necessary, throughout 1999. Management currently believes that the total cost of becoming Year 2000 compliant will not be significant to the Company's financial results, partly due to other significant systems initiatives currently under way. While the Company believes all necessary work will be completed, there can be no guarantee that all systems will be in compliance by the year 2000 or that the systems of other companies and government agencies on which the Company relies will be converted in a timely manner. Such failure to complete the necessary work by the year 2000 could result in material financial risk.

The foregoing projections of volume growth, profitability, capital spending, and common stock repurchase activity are forward-looking statements that involve risks and uncertainties. Actual results may differ materially due to the impact of competitive conditions, marketing spending, and/or incremental pricing actions on actual volumes and product mix; the levels of spending on system initiatives, properties, business opportunities, continued streamlining initiatives, and other general and administrative costs; raw material price and labor cost fluctuations; foreign currency exchange rate fluctuations; changes in statutory tax law; interest rates available on short-term financing; the impact of stock market conditions on common stock repurchase activity; and other items.

FINANCIAL STATEMENTS AND ACCOMPANYING NOTES

The standard set of financial statements consists of: (1) a comparative income statement (statement of earnings) for 3 years, (2) a comparative balance sheet for 2 years, (3) a comparative statement of cash flows for 3 years, (4) a statement of retained earnings (or stockholders' equity) for 3 years, and (5) a set of accompanying notes that are considered an integral part of the financial statements. The auditor's report, unless stated otherwise, covers the financial statements and the accompanying notes. The financial statements and accompanying notes plus some supplementary data for Kellogg Company appear on the following pages.

Kellogg Company and Subsidiaries

CONSOLIDATED STATEMENT OF EARNINGS

Year ended December 31,

(millions, except per share data)	1997	1996	1995
Net sales	**$6,830.1**	$6,676.6	$7,003.7
Cost of goods sold	3,270.1	3,122.9	3,177.7
Selling and administrative expense	2,366.8	2,458.7	2,566.7
Non-recurring charges	184.1	136.1	421.8
Operating profit	**1,009.1**	958.9	837.5
Interest expense	108.3	65.6	62.6
Other income (expense), net	3.7	(33.4)	21.1
Earnings before income taxes and cumulative effect of accounting change	**904.5**	859.9	796.0
Income taxes	340.5	328.9	305.7
Earnings before cumulative effect of accounting change	**564.0**	531.0	490.3
Cumulative effect of accounting change (net of tax)	(18.0)	—	—
Net earnings	**$ 546.0**	$ 531.0	$ 490.3
Per share amounts (basic and diluted):			
Earnings before cumulative effect of accounting change	**$ 1.36**	$ 1.25	$ 1.12
Cumulative effect of accounting change	(0.04)	—	—
Net earnings per share	**$ 1.32**	$ 1.25	$ 1.12

Refer to Notes to Consolidated Financial Statements.

Kellogg Company and Subsidiaries

CONSOLIDATED STATEMENT OF SHAREHOLDERS' EQUITY

(millions, except per share data)	Common stock shares	Common stock amount	Capital in excess of par value	Retained earnings	Treasury stock shares	Treasury stock amount	Currency translation adjustment	Total shareholders' equity
Balance, January 1, 1995	310.4	$ 77.6	$ 68.6	$ 3,801.2	88.7	($ 1,980.6)	($ 159.3)	$ 1,807.5
Stock options exercised	.7	.2	36.6					36.8
Common stock repurchases					5.7	(374.7)		(374.7)
Net earnings				490.3				490.3
Dividends				(328.5)				(328.5)
Currency translation adjustments							(34.6)	(34.6)
Other					—	(5.9)		(5.9)
Balance, December 31, 1995	**311.1**	**77.8**	**105.2**	**3,963.0**	**94.4**	**(2,361.2)**	**(193.9)**	**1,590.9**
Stock options exercised	.4	.1	18.7					18.8
Common stock repurchases					7.4	(535.7)		(535.7)
Net earnings				531.0				531.0
Dividends				(343.7)				(343.7)
Currency translation adjustments							27.6	27.6
Other					.1	(6.5)		(6.5)
Balance, December 31, 1996	**311.5**	**77.9**	**123.9**	**4,150.3**	**101.9**	**(2,903.4)**	**(166.3)**	**1,282.4**
Stock options exercised (pre-split)	.6	.1	31.9		(.1)	2.1		34.1
Common stock repurchases (pre-split)					3.9	(290.9)		(290.9)
Other (pre-split)					.1	(6.0)		(6.0)
Retirement of treasury stock	(105.3)	(26.3)	(55.8)	(3,095.8)	(105.3)	3,177.9		—
Two-for-one stock split	206.8	51.7	(51.7)		.5	—		—
Stock options exercised (post-split)	1.2	.3	44.3		(.1)	2.1		46.7
Common stock repurchases (post-split)					3.1	(135.1)		(135.1)
Net earnings				546.0				546.0
Dividends				(360.1)				(360.1)
Currency translation adjustments							(115.6)	(115.6)
Other (post-split)					.1	(4.0)		(4.0)
Balance, December 31, 1997	**414.8**	**$103.7**	**$ 92.6**	**$1,240.4**	**4.1**	**($ 157.3)**	**($281.9)**	**$ 997.5**

Refer to Notes to Consolidated Financial Statements.

Kellogg Company and Subsidiaries

CONSOLIDATED BALANCE SHEET

At December 31,

(millions, except share data)	1997	1996
Current assets		
Cash and cash equivalents	$ 173.2	$ 243.8
Accounts receivable, less allowances of $7.5 and $6.6	587.5	592.3
Inventories	434.3	424.9
Other current assets	272.7	267.6
Total current assets	1,467.7	1,528.6
Property, net	2,773.3	2,932.9
Other assets	636.6	588.5
Total assets	$4,877.6	$5,050.0
Current liabilities		
Current maturities of long-term debt	$ 211.2	$ 501.2
Notes payable	368.6	652.6
Accounts payable	328.0	335.2
Other current liabilities	749.5	710.0
Total current liabilities	1,657.3	2,199.0
Long-term debt	1,415.4	726.7
Other liabilities	807.4	841.9
Shareholders' equity		
Common stock, $.25 par value, 500,000,000 shares authorized Issued: 414,823,142 shares in 1997 and 311,524,437 in 1996	103.7	77.9
Capital in excess of par value	92.6	123.9
Retained earnings	1,240.4	4,150.3
Treasury stock, at cost: 4,143,124 shares in 1997 and 101,876,325 in 1996	(157.3)	(2,903.4)
Currency translation adjustment	(281.9)	(166.3)
Total shareholders' equity	997.5	1,282.4
Total liabilities and shareholders' equity	$4,877.6	$5,050.0

Refer to Notes to Consolidated Financial Statements.

Kellogg Company and Subsidiaries

CONSOLIDATED STATEMENT OF CASH FLOWS

Year ended December 31,

(millions)	1997	1996	1995
Operating activities			
Net earnings	$ 546.0	$ 531.0	$ 490.3
Items in net earnings not requiring (providing) cash:			
Depreciation and amortization	287.3	251.5	258.8
Deferred income taxes	38.5	58.0	(78.7)
Non-recurring charges, net of cash paid	133.8	90.6	385.3
Other	9.5	14.5	9.1
Pension and other postretirement benefit contributions	(114.5)	(156.8)	(74.5)
Changes in operating assets and liabilities	(20.8)	(77.3)	50.7
Net cash provided by operating activities	879.8	711.5	1,041.0
Investing activities			
Additions to properties	(312.4)	(307.3)	(315.7)
Acquisitions of businesses	(25.4)	(505.2)	—
Property disposals	5.9	11.6	6.3
Other	2.6	14.1	.5
Net cash used in investing activities	(329.3)	(786.8)	(308.9)
Financing activities			
Net issuances (reductions) of notes payable, with maturities less than or equal to 90 days	(374.7)	906.6	(86.8)
Issuances of notes payable, with maturities greater than 90 days	4.8	137.0	—
Reductions of notes payable, with maturities greater than 90 days	(14.1)	(79.0)	—
Issuances of long-term debt	1,000.0	—	—
Reductions of long-term debt	(507.9)	(3.4)	(.4)
Net issuances of common stock	70.7	12.2	31.2
Common stock repurchases	(426.0)	(535.7)	(374.7)
Cash dividends	(360.1)	(343.7)	(328.5)
Net cash provided by (used in) financing activities	(607.3)	94.0	(759.2)
Effect of exchange rate changes on cash	(13.8)	3.2	(17.3)
Increase (decrease) in cash and cash equivalents	(70.6)	21.9	(44.4)
Cash and cash equivalents at beginning of year	243.8	221.9	266.3
Cash and cash equivalents at end of year	$ 173.2	$ 243.8	$ 221.9

Refer to Notes to Consolidated Financial Statements.

Notes to Consolidated Financial Statements
Kellogg Company and Subsidiaries

Note 1 Accounting policies
Consolidation
The consolidated financial statements include the accounts of Kellogg Company and its majority-owned subsidiaries. Intercompany balances and transactions are eliminated.

Certain amounts in the prior year financial statements have been reclassified to conform to the current year presentation.

Cash and cash equivalents
Highly liquid temporary investments with original maturities of less than three months are considered to be cash equivalents. The carrying amount approximates fair value.

Inventories
Inventories are valued at the lower of cost (principally average) or market.

Property
Fixed assets are recorded at cost and depreciated over estimated useful lives using straight-line methods for financial reporting and accelerated methods for tax reporting. Cost includes an amount of interest associated with significant capital projects.

Advertising
The costs of advertising are generally expensed as incurred.

Stock compensation
The Company follows Accounting Principles Board Opinion (APB) #25, "Accounting for Stock Issued to Employees," in accounting for its employee stock options and other stock-based compensation. Under APB #25, because the exercise price of the Company's employee stock options equals the market price of the underlying stock on the date of the grant, no compensation expense is recognized. As permitted, the Company has elected to adopt the disclosure provisions only of Statement of Financial Accounting Standards (SFAS) #123, "Accounting for Stock-Based Compensation." (Refer to Note 7 for further information.)

Net earnings per share
Basic net earnings per share is determined by dividing net earnings by the weighted average number of common shares outstanding during the period. Weighted average shares outstanding, in millions, were 414.1, 424.9, and 438.3 for the years 1997, 1996, and 1995, respectively. Diluted net earnings per share is similarly determined except that the denominator is increased to include the number of additional common shares that would have been outstanding if all dilutive potential common shares had been issued. Dilutive potential common shares are principally comprised of employee stock options issued by the Company and had an insignificant impact on the computation of diluted net earnings per share during the periods presented.

Change in accounting principle
On November 20, 1997, the Emerging Issues Task Force (EITF) of the Financial Accounting Standards Board reached a consensus in EITF 97-13 that the costs of business process reengineering activities are to be expensed as incurred. This consensus also applies to business process reengineering activities that are part of an information technology project. Beginning in 1996, the Company has undertaken an Enterprise Business Applications (EBA) initiative that combines design and installation of business processes and software packages to achieve global best practices. Under the EBA initiative, the Company had capitalized certain external costs associated with business process reengineering activities as part of the software asset. EITF Issue 97-13 prescribes that previously capitalized business process reengineering costs should be expensed and reported as a cumulative effect of a change in accounting principle. Accordingly, for the fourth quarter of 1997, the Company reported a charge of $18.0 million (net of tax benefit of $7.7 million) or $.04 per share for write-off of business process reengineering costs. Such costs were expensed as incurred during the fourth quarter of 1997, and were insignificant.

Common stock split
On August 1, 1997, the Company's Board of Directors approved a 2-for-1 stock split to shareholders of record at the close of business August 8, 1997, effective August 22, 1997, and also authorized retirement of 105.3 million common shares (pre-split) held in treasury. All per share and shares outstanding data in the Consolidated Statement of Earnings and Notes to Consolidated Financial Statements have been retroactively restated to reflect the stock split.

Use of estimates
The preparation of financial statements in conformity with generally accepted accounting principles requires management to make estimates and assumptions that affect the reported amounts of assets and liabilities and disclosure of contingent assets and liabilities at the date of the financial statements and the reported amounts of revenues and expenses during the reporting period. Actual results could differ from those estimates.

Note 2 Acquisition
On December 16, 1996, the Company purchased certain assets and liabilities of the Lender's Bagels business from Kraft Foods, Inc. for $466 million in cash, including related acquisition costs. The acquisition was accounted for as a purchase. The assets and liabilities of the acquired business are included in the consolidated balance sheet as of December 31, 1996. The results of Lender's operations from the date of the acquisition to December 31, 1996, were not significant. The acquisition was initially financed through commercial paper borrowings that were replaced with long-term debt in January 1997.

The components of intangible assets included in the allocation of purchase price, along with the related straight-line amortization periods, were:

	Amount (millions)	Amortization period (yrs.)
Trademarks and tradenames	$150.0	40
Non-compete covenants	20.0	5
Goodwill	179.0	40
Total	$349.0	

The unaudited pro forma combined historical results, as if the Lender's Bagels business had been acquired at the beginning of fiscal 1996 and 1995, respectively, are estimated to be:

(millions, except per share data)	1996	1995
Net sales	$6,873.1	$7,219.4
Net earnings	$ 524.3	$ 489.3
Net earnings per share	$ 1.23	$ 1.12

The pro forma results include amortization of the intangibles presented above and interest expense on debt presumed issued to finance the purchase. The pro forma results are not necessarily indicative of what actually would have occurred if the acquisition had been completed as of the beginning of each of the fiscal periods presented, nor are they necessarily indicative of future consolidated results.

Note 3 Non-recurring charges
Operating profit for 1997 includes non-recurring charges of $184.1 million ($140.5 million after tax or $.34 per share), comprised of $161.1 million for streamlining initiatives and $23.0 million for asset impairment losses.

Operating profit for 1996 includes non-recurring charges of $136.1 million ($97.8 million after tax or $.23 per share), comprised of $121.1 million for streamlining initiatives and $15.0 million for potential settlement of certain litigation.

Operating profit for 1995 includes non-recurring charges of $421.8 million ($271.3 million after tax or $.62 per share), comprised of $348.0 million for streamlining initiatives and $73.8 million for asset impairment losses.

Streamlining initiatives
From 1995 to the present, management has commenced major productivity and operational streamlining initiatives in an effort to optimize the Company's cost structure and move toward a global business model. The incremental costs of these programs have been reported throughout 1995-1997 as non-recurring charges.

The 1997 charges for streamlining initiatives relate principally to management's plan to optimize the Company's pan-European operations, as well as ongoing productivity programs in the United States and Australia. A major component of the pan-European initiatives was the late-1997 closing of plants and separation of employees in Riga, Latvia; Svendborg, Denmark; and Verola, Italy. Approximately 50% of the total 1997 streamlining charges consist of manufacturing asset write-downs, with the balance comprised of current and anticipated cash outlays for employee separation benefits, equipment removal, production redeployment, associated management consulting, and similar costs. Principally related to the pan-European initiatives, streamlining programs commenced in 1997 will result in employee headcount reductions of approximately 600. Total cash outlays during 1997 for streamlining initiatives were approximately $85 million.

The 1996 and 1995 charges for streamlining initiatives result from management's actions to consolidate and reorganize operations in the United States, Europe, and other international locations. Cash outlays for streamlining initiatives were approximately $120 million in 1996 and $40 million in 1995. The streamlining programs commenced since 1995, including the aforementioned pan-European initiatives, are expected to result in the elimination of approximately 3,000 employee positions by the end of 1998, with approximately 90% of this headcount reduction already achieved.

The components of the streamlining charges, as well as reserve balances remaining at December 31, 1997, 1996, and 1995, were:

(millions)	Employee retirement & severance benefits (a)	Asset write-offs	Asset removal	Other costs	Total
1995 streamlining charges	$183.6	$106.5	$39.5	$18.4	$348.0
Amounts utilized during 1995	(126.1)	(106.5)	(3.0)	(18.4)	(254.0)
Remaining reserve at December 31, 1995	57.5	—	36.5	—	94.0
1996 streamlining charges (b)	31.4	37.5	13.5	38.7	121.1
Amounts utilized during 1996	(65.0)	(37.5)	(19.6)	(38.7)	(160.8)
Remaining reserve at December 31, 1996	23.9	—	30.4	—	54.3
1997 streamlining charges	22.4	78.1	19.3	41.3	161.1
Amounts utilized during 1997	(22.7)	(78.1)	(21.4)	(41.3)	(163.5)
Remaining reserve at December 31, 1997	$ 23.6	$—	$28.3	$—	$ 51.9

(a) Includes approximately $100 and $5 of pension and postretirement health care curtailment losses and special termination benefits recognized in 1995 and 1996, respectively. (Refer to Notes 8 and 9.)

(b) Includes $23 of reversals of prior-year reserves due to lower than expected employee severance payments and asset removal costs, and other favorable factors.

Other

In addition to the non-recurring charges reported for streamlining initiatives, the Company incurred charges for the following unusual items:

- During 1997, asset impairment losses of $23.0 million, which resulted from evaluation of the Company's ability to recover components of its investments, based on management's ongoing strategic assessment of local conditions, in the emerging markets of Asia-Pacific.

- During 1996, a provision of $15.0 million for the potential settlement of certain litigation.

- During 1995, asset impairment losses of $73.8 million which resulted from the evaluation of the Company's ability to recover asset costs given changes in local market conditions, sourcing of products, and other strategic factors in its North American and Asia-Pacific operations.

Note 4 Other income and expense

Other income and expense includes non-operating items such as interest income, foreign exchange gains and losses, and charitable donations.

Other expense for 1996 includes a charge of $35.0 million ($22.3 million after tax or $.05 per share) for a contribution to the Kellogg's Corporate Citizenship Fund, a private trust established for charitable donations. This contribution is expected to satisfy the charitable-giving plans of this trust through the year 2000.

Note 5 Leases

Operating leases are generally for equipment and warehouse space. Rent expense on all operating leases was $38.6 million in 1997, $37.9 million in 1996, and $32.0 million in 1995. At December 31, 1997, future minimum annual rental commitments under non-cancelable operating leases totaled $68 million consisting of (in millions): 1998-$17; 1999-$12; 2000-$9; 2001-$8; 2002-$7; 2003 and beyond-$15.

Note 6 Debt

Notes payable consist principally of commercial paper borrowings in the United States at the highest credit rating available and, to a lesser extent, bank loans of foreign subsidiaries at competitive market rates. U.S. borrowings at December 31, 1997 (including $400 million classified in long-term debt, as discussed in (f) below), were $744.2 million with an effective interest rate of 5.7%. U.S. borrowings at December 31, 1996 (including $500 million classified in long-term debt, as discussed in (f) below), were $1.12 billion with an effective interest rate of 5.4%. Associated with these borrowings, during September 1997, the Company purchased a $225 million notional, four-year fixed interest rate cap. Under the terms of the cap, if the Federal Reserve AA composite rate on 30-day commercial paper increases to 6.33%, the Company will pay this fixed rate on $225 million of its commercial paper borrowings. If the rate increases to 7.83% or above, the cap will expire. As of year-end 1997, the rate was 5.65%. At December 31, 1997, the Company had $775.1 million of short-term lines of credit, of which $749.4 million were unused and available for borrowing on an unsecured basis.

Long-term debt at year-end consisted of:

(millions)	1997	1996
(a) Seven-Year Notes due 2004	$ 500.0	$ —
(b) Four-Year Notes due 2001	500.0	—
(c) Five-Year Notes due 1998	200.0	200.0
(d) Three-Year Notes due 1997	—	200.0
(e) Five-Year Notes due 1997	—	299.9
(f) Commercial paper	400.0	500.0
Other	26.6	28.0
	1,626.6	1,227.9
Less current maturities	(211.2)	(501.2)
Balance, December 31	$1,415.4	$ 726.7

(a) In January 1997, the Company issued $500 of seven-year 6.625% fixed rate Euro Dollar Notes. In conjunction with this issuance, the Company settled $500 notional amount of interest rate forward swap agreements, which effectively fixed the interest rate on the debt at 6.354%. Associated with this debt, during September 1997, the Company entered into a $225 notional, 4½-year fixed-to-floating interest rate swap, indexed to the three-month London Interbank Offered Rate (LIBOR). Under the terms of the swap, if three-month LIBOR decreases to 4.71% or below, the swap will expire. At year-end 1997, three-month LIBOR was 5.81%.

(b) In August 1997, the Company issued $500 of four-year 6.125% Euro Dollar Notes. In conjunction with this issuance, the Company settled $400 notional amount of interest rate forward swap agreements which effectively fixed the interest rate on the debt at 6.4%. Associated with this debt, during September 1997, the Company entered into a $200 notional, four-year fixed-to-floating interest rate swap, indexed to three-month LIBOR.

(c) In October 1993, the Company issued $200 of five-year 6.25% Euro Canadian Dollar Notes which were swapped into 4.629% fixed rate U.S. Dollar obligations for the duration of the five-year term.

(d) In September 1994, the Company issued $200 of three-year debt consisting of both 8.125% Euro Canadian Dollar Secured Notes and 5.25% Swiss Franc Secured Notes. These Notes were swapped into U.S. Dollar obligations, with a variable rate indexed to the Federal Reserve AA composite rate on 30-day commercial paper, for the duration of the three-year term.

(e) In July 1992, the Company issued $300 of five-year 5.9% U.S. Dollar obligations.

(f) At December 31, 1997, $400 of the Company's commercial paper was classified as long-term, based on the Company's intent and ability to refinance as evidenced by an issuance of $400 of three-year 5.75% fixed rate U.S. Dollar Notes on February 4, 1998. These Notes were issued under an existing "shelf registration" with the Securities and Exchange Commission, and provide an option to holders to extend the obligation for an additional four years at a predetermined interest rate of 5.63% plus the Company's then-current credit spread. Concurrent with this issuance, the Company entered into a $400 notional, three-year fixed-to-floating interest rate swap, indexed to the Federal Reserve AA composite rate on 30-day commercial paper.

At December 31, 1996, $500 of the Company's commercial paper was classified as long-term, based on the Company's intent and ability to refinance as evidenced by the issuance described in (a) above.

The $200 million of five-year notes will mature during the fourth quarter of 1998 and are classified in current maturities as of December 31, 1997. Management currently intends to replace these borrowings with new long-term debt issuances as of the maturity date and, as of year-end 1997, had entered into $25 million notional amount of interest rate forward swap agreements to pay fixed and receive variable interest, effectively fixing the U.S. Treasury rate on which an equivalent amount of future issuances would be priced.

Scheduled principal repayments on long-term debt are (in millions): 1998-$211; 1999-$2; 2000-$1; 2001-$901; 2002-$5; 2003 and beyond-$507.

Interest paid was $85 million for 1997 and approximated interest expense for 1996 and 1995. Interest expense capitalized as part of the construction cost of fixed assets was (in millions): 1997- $9.6; 1996-$3.8; 1995-$7.2.

Note 7 Stock options

The Key Employee Long-Term Incentive Plan provides for benefits to be awarded to executive-level employees in the form of stock options, performance shares, performance units, incentive stock options, restricted stock grants, and other stock-based awards. Options granted under this plan generally vest over two years and, prior to September 1997, vested at the date of grant. The Bonus Replacement Stock Option Plan allows certain key executives to receive stock options that generally vest immediately in lieu of part or all of their respective bonus. Options granted under this plan are issued from the Key Employee Long-Term Incentive Plan. The Kellogg Employee Stock Ownership Plan is designed to offer stock and other incentive awards based on Company performance to employees who are not eligible to participate in the Key Employee Long-Term Incentive Plan or the Bonus Replacement Stock Option Plan. Options awarded under the Kellogg Employee Stock Ownership Plan are subject to graded vesting over a five-year period. Under these plans (the "stock option plans"), options are granted with exercise prices equal to the fair market value of the Company's common stock at the time of grant, exercisable for a 10-year period following the date of grant, subject to vesting rules.

The Key Employee Long-Term Incentive Plan contains an accelerated ownership feature ("AOF"). An AOF option is granted when Company stock is surrendered to pay the exercise price of a stock option. The holder of the option is granted an AOF option for the number of shares surrendered. For all AOF options, the original expiration date is not changed, but the options vest immediately.

As permitted by SFAS #123 "Accounting for Stock-Based Compensation," the Company has elected to account for the stock option plans under APB #25 "Accounting for Stock Issued to Employees." Accordingly, no compensation cost has been recognized for these plans.

For purposes of pro forma disclosures, the estimated fair value of the options is amortized to expense over the options' vesting period. Had compensation cost for the stock option plans been determined based on the fair value at the grant date consistent with SFAS #123, the Company's net earnings and earnings per share for employee stock options granted after December 31, 1994, are estimated as follows:

(millions, except per share data)	1997	1996	1995
Net earnings			
As reported	$546.0	$531.0	$490.3
Pro forma	$520.8	$514.1	$476.4
Net earnings per share (basic and diluted)			
As reported	$ 1.32	$ 1.25	$ 1.12
Pro forma	$ 1.26	$ 1.21	$ 1.09

The fair value of each option grant was estimated at the date of grant using a Black-Scholes option pricing model with the following weighted average assumptions:

	1997	1996	1995
Risk-free interest rate	6.31%	6.16%	6.89%
Dividend yield	1.97%	2.30%	2.30%
Volatility	19.83%	19.16%	21.45%
Average expected term (years)	3.52	3.34	3.02
Fair value of options granted	$7.48	$6.32	$5.47

Under the Key Employee Long-Term Incentive Plan, options for 13.2 million and 15.5 million shares were available for grant at December 31, 1997 and 1996, respectively. Under the Kellogg Employee Stock Ownership Plan, options for 6.9 million and 8.3 million shares were available for grant at December 31, 1997 and 1996, respectively. Transactions under these plans were:

(millions, except per share data)	1997	1996	1995
Under option, January 1	11.2	8.4	7.6
Granted	6.0	5.2	4.8
Exercised	(4.5)	(2.1)	(3.8)
Cancelled	(.3)	(.3)	(.2)
Under option, December 31	12.4	11.2	8.4
Exercisable, December 31	8.1	7.6	6.1
Shares available, December 31, for options that may be granted	20.1	23.8	27.4
	Average prices per share		
Under option, January 1	$33	$30	$28
Granted	36	38	31
Exercised	33	30	28
Cancelled	34	30	27
Under option, December 31	$35	$33	$30
Exercisable, December 31	$36	$35	$31

Employee stock options outstanding and exercisable under these plans as of December 31, 1997, were:

(millions, except per share data) Range of exercise prices	Outstanding			Exercisable	
	Number of options	Weighted average exercise price	Weighted average remaining contractual life (yrs.)	Number of options	Weighted average exercise price
$15 – 34	6.4	$31	8.0	3.4	$31
35 – 39	4.7	38	8.3	3.4	38
40 – 44	.7	44	9.8	.7	44
45 – 50	.6	48	9.7	.6	48
	12.4			8.1	

Note 8 Pension benefits

The Company has a number of U.S. and foreign pension plans to provide retirement benefits for its employees. Benefits for salaried employees are generally based on salary and years of service, while union employee benefits are generally a negotiated amount for each year of service. Plan funding strategies are influenced by tax regulations. Plan assets consist primarily of equity securities with smaller holdings of bonds, real estate, and other investments. Investment in Company common stock represented 4.2% and 6.8% of consolidated plan assets at December 31, 1997, and 1996, respectively.

The components of pension expense were:

(millions)	1997	1996	1995
Service cost	$ 29.9	$ 27.6	$ 27.4
Interest cost	79.6	72.8	66.0
Actual return on plan assets	(210.4)	(102.8)	(163.3)
Net amortization and deferral	118.0	19.7	100.3
Curtailment loss and special termination benefits expense	—	4.0	77.7
Pension expense – Company plans	17.1	21.3	108.1
Pension expense – multiemployer plans	1.9	2.0	1.8
Total pension expense	$ 19.0	$ 23.3	$109.9

The worldwide weighted average actuarial assumptions were:

	1997	1996	1995
Discount rate	7.6%	7.9%	7.5%
Long-term rate of compensation increase	4.9%	5.2%	5.1%
Long-term rate of return on plan assets	10.5%	10.5%	9.6%

Reconciliation of funded status of the plans at year-end was:

	Underfunded		Overfunded	
(millions)	1997	1996	1997	1996
Accumulated benefit obligation:				
Nonvested	$ 6.6	$ 6.0	$ 60.0	$ 46.9
Vested	62.5	41.5	926.3	845.2
Total	69.1	47.5	986.3	892.1
Projected salary increases	18.0	17.4	60.0	79.3
Projected benefit obligation	87.1	64.9	1,046.3	971.4
Plan assets at fair value	15.4	—	1,193.6	1,048.7
Assets (less) greater than projected benefit obligation	(71.7)	(64.9)	147.3	77.3
Unrecognized net (gain) loss	14.4	15.0	(7.0)	28.8
Unrecognized transition amount	2.6	(2.8)	1.8	.6
Unrecognized prior service cost	3.9	3.4	43.3	49.3
Minimum liability adjustment	(10.7)	(5.7)	—	—
Prepaid (accrued) pension	($61.5)	($55.0)	$ 185.4	$ 156.0

Curtailment losses and special termination benefits expense recognized in 1996 and 1995 relate to operational workforce reduction initiatives undertaken during these years and are recorded as a component of non-recurring charges. (Refer to Note 3 for further information.)

The amount of intangible assets related to underfunded pension plans was $10.7 million and $5.7 million at year-end 1997 and 1996, respectively. All gains and losses, other than curtailment losses, are recognized over the average remaining service period of active employees.

Certain of the Company's subsidiaries sponsor 401(k) or similar savings plans for active employees. Expense related to these plans was (in millions): 1997-$16; 1996-$17; 1995-$18.

Note 9 Nonpension postretirement benefits

Certain of the Company's North American subsidiaries provide health care and other benefits to substantially all retired employees, their covered dependents, and beneficiaries. Generally, employees are eligible for these benefits when one of the following service/age requirements is met: 30 years and any age; 20 years and age 55; 5 years and age 62.

Components of postretirement benefit expense were:

(millions)	1997	1996	1995
Service cost	$ 9.6	$11.2	$11.8
Interest cost	37.2	40.2	41.5
Actual return on plan assets	(23.0)	—	—
Net amortization and deferral	2.9	.3	(.6)
Curtailment loss	—	1.0	26.3
Postretirement benefit expense	$26.7	$52.7	$79.0
Discount rate used for accumulated benefit obligation	7.25%	7.75%	7.25%

The assumed health care cost trend rate was 7.0% for 1997, decreasing gradually to 4.5% by the year 2003 and remaining at that level thereafter. These trend rates reflect the Company's prior experience and management's expectation that future rates will decline. Increasing the assumed health care cost trend rates by 1 percentage point in each year would increase the accumulated postretirement benefit obligation as of December 31, 1997, by $63.5 million and postretirement benefit expense for 1997 by $6.8 million. All gains and losses, other than curtailment losses, are recognized over the average remaining service period of active plan partici-

pants. Curtailment losses recognized in 1996 and 1995 relate to operational workforce reduction initiatives undertaken during these years and were recorded as a component of non-recurring charges. (Refer to Note 3 for further information.) Since December 1996, the Company has contributed to a voluntary employee benefit association (VEBA) trust for funding of its nonpension postretirement benefit obligations. Plan assets consist primarily of equity securities with smaller holdings of bonds.

The accrued postretirement benefit cost included in the balance sheet at year-end was:

(millions)	1997	1996
Accumulated benefit obligation:		
Retirees	$347.4	$305.9
Active plan participants	175.9	188.2
	523.3	494.1
Plan assets at fair value	(150.7)	(81.0)
Accumulated benefit obligation greater than assets	372.6	413.1
Unrecognized experience gain	86.5	95.1
Unrecognized prior service adjustments	8.1	8.6
Accrued postretirement benefit cost	$467.2	$516.8

Note 10 Income taxes

Earnings before income taxes and cumulative effect of accounting change, and the provision for U.S. federal, state, and foreign taxes on these earnings, were:

(millions)	1997	1996	1995
Earnings before income taxes and cumulative effect of accounting change:			
United States	$576.4	$516.7	$430.9
Foreign	328.1	343.2	365.1
	$904.5	$859.9	$796.0
Income taxes:			
Currently payable:			
Federal	$129.4	$130.6	$205.2
State	29.6	21.9	34.7
Foreign	143.0	118.4	144.5
	302.0	270.9	384.4
Deferred:			
Federal	50.2	45.7	(81.0)
State	4.0	11.4	(10.7)
Foreign	(15.7)	.9	13.0
	38.5	58.0	(78.7)
Total income taxes	$340.5	$328.9	$305.7

The difference between the U.S. federal statutory tax rate and the Company's effective rate was:

	1997	1996	1995
U.S. statutory rate	35.0%	35.0%	35.0%
Foreign rates varying from 35%	.1	.7	.2
State income taxes, net of federal benefit	2.4	2.5	2.0
Net change in valuation allowance	1.6	(.1)	1.9
Statutory rate changes, deferred tax impact	(.5)	—	.4
Other	(1.0)	.1	(1.1)
Effective income tax rate	37.6%	38.2%	38.4%

The 1997 increase in valuation allowance on deferred tax assets and corresponding impact on the effective income tax rate, as presented above, primarily result from management's assessment of the Company's ability to utilize certain operating loss and tax credit carryforwards. Total tax benefits of carryforwards at year-end 1997 were $30.4 million and principally expire after the year 2002.

The 1995 increase in valuation allowance on deferred tax assets and corresponding impact on the effective income tax rate, as presented above, primarily relate to asset impairment losses recorded as non-recurring charges (refer to Note 3) for which no tax benefit was provided, based on management's assessment of the likelihood of recovering such benefit in future years.

The deferred tax assets and liabilities included in the balance sheet at year-end were:

(millions)	Deferred tax assets 1997	1996	Deferred tax liabilities 1997	1996
Current:				
Promotion and advertising	**$ 65.0**	$ 78.4	**$ 10.5**	$ 6.7
Wages and payroll taxes	**13.8**	13.8	**—**	—
Health and postretirement benefits	**15.7**	17.2	**2.4**	6.3
State taxes	**8.1**	8.6	**—**	—
Operating loss and credit carryforwards	**2.1**	.1	**—**	—
Other	**24.2**	23.4	**12.3**	23.3
	128.9	141.5	**25.2**	36.3
Less valuation allowance	**(4.1)**	(2.5)	**—**	—
	124.8	139.0	**25.2**	36.3
Noncurrent:				
Depreciation and asset disposals	**18.8**	25.6	**326.0**	337.0
Health and postretirement benefits	**163.5**	179.6	**56.2**	43.0
Capitalized interest	**3.5**	3.3	**32.3**	31.5
State taxes	**—**	.9	**2.6**	—
Operating loss and credit carryforwards	**28.3**	1.4	**—**	—
Other	**26.6**	26.3	**5.8**	.7
	240.7	237.1	**422.9**	412.2
Less valuation allowance	**(41.8)**	(29.1)	**—**	—
	198.9	208.0	**422.9**	412.2
Total deferred taxes	**$323.7**	$347.0	**$448.1**	$448.5

At December 31, 1997, foreign subsidiary earnings of $1.3 billion were considered permanently invested in those businesses. Accordingly, U.S. income taxes have not been provided on these earnings. Foreign withholding taxes of approximately $64 million would be payable upon remittance of these earnings. Subject to certain limitations, the withholding taxes would then be available for use as credits against the U.S. tax liability.

Cash paid for income taxes was (in millions): 1997-$332; 1996-$281; 1995-$404.

Note 11   Financial instruments and credit risk concentration

The fair values of the Company's financial instruments are based on carrying value in the case of short-term items, quoted market prices for derivatives and investments, and, in the case of long-term debt, incremental borrowing rates currently available on loans with similar terms and maturities. The carrying amounts of the Company's cash, cash equivalents, receivables, notes payable, and long-term debt approximate fair value.

The Company is exposed to certain market risks which exist as a part of its ongoing business operations and uses derivative financial and commodity instruments, where appropriate, to manage these risks. In general, instruments used as hedges must be effective at reducing the risk associated with the exposure being hedged and must be designated as a hedge at the inception of the contract. Deferred gains or losses related to any instrument 1) designated but ineffective as a hedge of existing assets, liabilities, or firm commitments, or 2) designated as a hedge of an anticipated transaction which is no longer likely to occur, are recognized immediately in the statement of earnings.

For all derivative financial and commodity instruments held by the Company, changes in fair values of these instruments and the resultant impact on the Company's cash flows and/or earnings would generally be offset by changes in values of underlying exposures. The impact on the Company's results and financial position of holding derivative financial and commodity instruments was insignificant during the periods presented.

Foreign exchange risk

The Company is exposed to fluctuations in foreign currency cash flows primarily related to third party purchases, intercompany product shipments, and intercompany loans. The Company is also exposed to fluctuations in the value of foreign currency investments in subsidiaries and cash flows related to repatriation of these investments. Additionally, the Company is exposed to volatility in the translation of foreign currency earnings to U.S. Dollars.

The Company assesses foreign currency risk based on transactional cash flows and enters into forward contracts of generally less than twelve months duration to reduce fluctuations in net long or short currency positions. Foreign currency contracts are marked-to-market with net amounts due to or from counterparties recorded in accounts receivable or payable. For contracts hedging firm commitments, mark-to-market gains and losses are deferred and recognized as adjustments to the basis of the transaction. For contracts hedging subsidiary investments, mark-to-market gains and losses are recorded in the currency translation adjustment component of shareholders' equity. For all other contracts, mark-to-market gains and losses are recognized currently in other income or expense.

The notional amounts of open forward contracts were $143.2 million and $80.0 million at December 31, 1997, and 1996, respectively. Refer to Supplemental Financial Information on page 33 for further information regarding these contracts.

Interest rate risk

The Company is exposed to interest rate volatility with regard to future issuances of fixed rate debt and existing issuances of variable rate debt. The Company uses interest rate caps, and currency and interest rate swaps, including forward swaps, to reduce interest rate volatility and funding costs associated with certain debt issues, and to achieve a desired proportion of variable versus fixed rate debt, based on current and projected market conditions.

Interest rate forward swaps are marked-to-market with net amounts due to or from counterparties recorded in interest receivable or payable. Mark-to-market gains and losses are deferred and recognized over the life of the debt issue as a component of interest expense. For other caps and swaps entered into concurrently with the debt issue, the interest or currency differential to be paid or received on the instrument is recognized in the statement of earnings as incurred, as a component of interest expense. If a position were to be terminated prior to maturity, the gain or loss realized upon termination would be deferred and amortized to interest expense over the remaining term of the underlying debt issue or would be recognized immediately if the underlying debt issue was settled prior to maturity.

The notional amounts of currency and interest rate swaps were $875.0 million and $1.05 billion at December 31, 1997, and 1996, respectively. Refer to Note 6 and Supplemental Financial Information on page 33 for further information regarding these swaps.

Price risk

The Company is exposed to price fluctuations primarily as a result of anticipated purchases of raw and packaging materials. The Company uses the combination of long cash positions with vendors, and exchange-traded futures and option contracts to reduce price fluctuations in a desired percentage of forecasted purchases over a duration of generally less than one year. Commodity contracts are marked-to-market with net amounts due to or from brokers recorded in accounts receivable or payable. Mark-to-market gains and losses are deferred and recognized as adjustments to the basis of the underlying material purchases.

Credit risk concentration

The Company is exposed to credit loss in the event of nonperformance by counterparties on derivative financial and commodity contracts. This credit loss is limited to the cost of replacing these contracts at current market rates. Management believes that the probability of such loss is remote.

Financial instruments which potentially subject the Company to concentrations of credit risk are primarily cash, cash equivalents, and accounts receivable. The Company places its investments in highly rated financial institutions and investment grade short-term debt instruments, and limits the amount of credit exposure to any one entity. Concentrations of credit risk with respect to accounts receivable are limited due to the large number of customers, generally short payment terms, and their dispersion across geographic areas.

Note 12 Quarterly financial data (unaudited)

(millions, except per share data)	Net sales 1997	Net sales 1996	Gross profit 1997	Gross profit 1996
First	**$1,688.9**	$1,785.9	**$ 860.9**	$ 995.5
Second	**1,719.7**	1,651.4	**908.9**	876.2
Third	**1,803.8**	1,681.6	**944.4**	865.6
Fourth	**1,617.7**	1,557.7	**845.8**	816.4
	$6,830.1	$6,676.6	**$3,560.0**	$3,553.7

	Earnings before cumulative effect of accounting change (a) 1997	1996	Earnings per share before cumulative effect of accounting change (a)(b) 1997	1996
First	**$160.6**	$206.1	**$.38**	$.48
Second	**163.6**	78.1	**.39**	.18
Third	**207.2**	159.5	**.50**	.38
Fourth	**32.6**	87.3	**.08**	.21
	$564.0	$531.0		

	Net earnings (a) 1997	1996	Net earnings per share (a)(b) 1997	1996
First	**$160.6**	$206.1	**$.38**	$.48
Second	**163.6**	78.1	**.39**	.18
Third	**207.2**	159.5	**.50**	.38
Fourth	**14.6**	87.3	**.04**	.21
	$546.0	$531.0		

(a) The quarterly results of 1997 and 1996 include the following non-recurring charges, other unusual items, and cumulative effect of accounting change. (Refer to Notes 1, 3, and 4 for further information.)

	Earnings 1997	1996	Earnings per share 1997	1996
Non-recurring charges and other unusual items:				
First	$ —	($ 6.1)	$ —	($.01)
Second	**(8.0)**	(16.9)	**(.02)**	(.04)
Third	**(6.6)**	(21.3)	**(.02)**	(.05)
Fourth	**(125.9)**	(75.8)	**(.31)**	(.18)
Earnings before cumulative effect of accounting change	**(140.5)**	(120.1)		
Cumulative effect of accounting change - Fourth	**(18.0)**	—	**(.04)**	—
Net earnings	**($158.5)**	($120.1)		

(b) Earnings per share presented represent both basic and diluted earnings per share.

The principal market for trading Kellogg shares is the New York Stock Exchange (NYSE). The shares are also traded on the Boston, Chicago, Cincinnati, Pacific, and Philadelphia Stock Exchanges. At year-end 1997, the closing price (on the NYSE) was $49 5/8 and there were 25,305 shareholders of record.

Dividends paid and the quarterly price ranges on the NYSE during the last two years were:

1997 – Quarter	Dividend	Stock Price High	Low
Fourth	**$.225**	$50.38	$40.00
Third	.225	50.38	42.00
Second	.210	43.44	32.00
First	.210	36.38	32.06
	$.870		
1996 – Quarter			
Fourth	$.210	$34.56	$31.00
Third	.210	38.69	32.81
Second	.195	37.88	33.69
First	.195	40.31	36.25
	$.810		

Note 13 Operating segments

The Company operates in a single industry – manufacturing and marketing grain-based convenience food products including ready-to-eat cereal, toaster pastries, frozen waffles, cereal bars, and bagels throughout the world. The following table describes operations by geographic area. Geographic operating profit includes allocated corporate overhead expenses. Corporate assets are comprised principally of cash and cash equivalents held for general corporate purposes.

(millions)	1997	% change	1996	% change	1995	% change
Net sales						
United States	**$3,961.8**	**+5**	$3,779.5	−7	$4,080.3	+6
% of total	**58%**		57%		58%	
Europe	**1,702.0**	**−3**	1,749.6	−4	1,829.1	+9
% of total	**25%**		26%		26%	
Other areas	**1,166.3**	**+2**	1,147.5	+5	1,094.3	+5
% of total	**17%**		17%		16%	
Consolidated	**$6,830.1**	**+2**	$6,676.6	−5	$7,003.7	+7
Operating profit (a)						
United States	**$ 706.8**	**+16**	$ 611.2	+38	$ 443.1	−37
% of total	**70%**		64%		53%	
Europe	**158.9**	**−22**	204.4	−30	293.6	+2
% of total	**16%**		21%		35%	
Other areas	**143.4**	**—**	143.3	+42	100.8	−39
% of total	**14%**		15%		12%	
Consolidated	**$1,009.1**	**+5**	$ 958.9	+14	$ 837.5	−28
Identifiable assets						
United States	**$2,819.9**	**+1**	$2,785.9	+27	$2,194.8	−1
% of total	**58%**		55%		50%	
Europe	**1,160.2**	**−8**	1,258.2	−1	1,269.4	−1
% of total	**24%**		25%		29%	
Other areas	**882.3**	**−9**	973.3	+5	929.7	−1
% of total	**18%**		19%		21%	
Corporate assets	**15.2**	**−53**	32.6	+57	20.7	+9
% of total	**—**		1%		—	
Consolidated	**$4,877.6**	**−3**	$5,050.0	+14	$4,414.6	−1

(a) Operating profit includes the following non-recurring charges, by geographic area. (Refer to Note 3 for further information.)

	1997	1996	1995
United States	**($ 35.2)**	($ 24.1)	($325.0)
Europe	**(119.1)**	(76.5)	(38.4)
All other	**(29.8)**	(35.5)	(58.4)
Consolidated	**($184.1)**	($136.1)	($421.8)

Note 14 Supplemental financial statement data

(millions)

Consolidated Statement of Earnings	1997	1996	1995
Research and development expense	$106.1	$ 84.3	$ 72.2
Advertising expense	$780.4	$778.9	$891.5

Consolidated Statement of Cash Flows	1997	1996	1995
Accounts receivable	$ 5.1	$ 10.9	($ 25.6)
Inventories	(8.1)	(35.4)	19.6
Other current assets	(11.0)	(.5)	(33.7)
Accounts payable	(8.7)	(41.0)	36.3
Other current liabilities	1.9	(11.3)	54.1
Changes in operating assets and liabilities	**($ 20.8)**	($ 77.3)	$ 50.7

Consolidated Balance Sheet	1997	1996
Raw materials and supplies	$ 135.0	$ 135.2
Finished goods and materials in process	299.3	289.7
Inventories	**$ 434.3**	$ 424.9
Deferred income taxes	$ 113.4	$ 117.9
Prepaid advertising and promotion	95.2	83.4
Other	64.1	66.3
Other current assets	**$ 272.7**	$ 267.6
Land	$ 49.0	$ 52.4
Buildings	1,213.8	1,226.1
Machinery and equipment	3,434.7	3,464.1
Construction in progress	283.1	277.5
Accumulated depreciation	(2,207.3)	(2,087.2)
Property, net	**$2,773.3**	$2,932.9
Goodwill	$ 194.3	$ 193.7
Other intangibles	191.2	186.6
Other	251.1	208.2
Other assets	**$ 636.6**	$ 588.5
Accrued income taxes	$ 30.5	$ 50.5
Accrued salaries and wages	99.7	84.6
Accrued advertising and promotion	308.8	336.8
Other	310.5	238.1
Other current liabilities	**$ 749.5**	$ 710.0
Nonpension postretirement benefits	$ 444.1	$ 494.2
Deferred income taxes	237.7	226.3
Other	125.6	121.4
Other liabilities	**$ 807.4**	$ 841.9

Supplemental Financial Information

Quantitative & qualitative disclosures related to market risk sensitive instruments

The Company is exposed to certain market risks which exist as a part of its ongoing business operations and uses derivative financial and commodity instruments, where appropriate, to manage these risks. The Company, as a matter of policy, does not engage in trading or speculative transactions. Refer to Note 11 within Notes to Consolidated Financial Statements for further information on accounting policies related to derivative financial and commodity instruments.

Foreign exchange risk

The Company is exposed to fluctuations in foreign currency cash flows related to third party purchases, intercompany product shipments, and intercompany loans. The Company is also exposed to fluctuations in the value of foreign currency investments in subsidiaries and cash flows related to repatriation of these investments. Additionally, the Company is exposed to volatility in the translation of foreign currency earnings to U.S. Dollars. Primary exposures include the U.S. Dollar versus functional currencies of the Company's major markets, i.e. British Pound, German Deutchmark, French Franc, Australian Dollar, Canadian Dollar, and Mexican Peso, and in the case of inter-subsidiary transactions, the British Pound versus other European currencies. The Company assesses foreign currency risk based on transactional cash flows and enters into forward contracts of generally less than twelve months duration to reduce fluctuations in net long or short currency positions.

The tables below summarize forward contracts held at year-end 1997. All contracts are valued in U.S. Dollars using year-end 1997 exchange rates, are hedges of anticipated transactions (unless indicated otherwise), and mature in 1998.

Contracts to sell foreign currency

Currency sold	Currency received	Notional value (millions)	Exchange rate (fc/1US$)	Fair value (millions)
Belgian Franc	British Pound	$ 11.7	35.19	$ .5
Swiss Franc	German Deutchmark	3.9	1.46	—
French Franc	German Deutchmark	4.3	6.08	—
French Franc	Danish Kroner	.6	6.06	—
Danish Kroner	British Pound	5.4	6.67	.1
Belgian Franc	French Franc	1.0	36.87	—
French Franc	British Pound	48.0	5.70	2.3
Irish Punt	British Pound	27.4	.66	1.7
Spanish Peseta	British Pound	1.3	134.72	.2
Swedish Kroner	Danish Kroner	16.0	7.89	.1
	Total	$119.6		$4.9

Contracts to purchase foreign currency

Currency purchased	Currency exchanged	Notional value (millions)	Exchange rate (fc/1US$)	Fair value (millions)
Swiss Franc (a)	British Pound	$ 4.7	1.42	($.1)
German Deutchmark (a)	British Pound	.3	1.72	—
German Deutchmark	British Pound	18.6	1.71	(.8)
	Total	$23.6		($.9)

(a) Designated as hedge of firm committment.

Interest rate risk

The Company is exposed to interest rate volatility with regard to future issuances of fixed rate debt and existing issuances of variable rate debt. Primary exposures include movements in U.S. Treasury rates, London Interbank Offered rates (LIBOR), and commercial paper rates. The Company uses interest rate caps, and currency and interest rate swaps, including forward swaps, to reduce interest rate volatility and funding costs associated with certain debt issues, and to achieve a desired proportion of variable versus fixed rate debt, based on current and projected market conditions.

The tables below provide information on the Company's significant debt issues and related hedging instruments at year-end 1997. For foreign currency-denominated debt, the information is presented in U.S. Dollar equivalents. Variable interest rates are based on effective rates or implied forward rates as of year-end 1997. Refer to Note 6 within the Notes to Consolidated Financial Statements for further information.

Significant debt issues

Debt characteristics	Principal by year of maturity (millions)			Fair value (millions)
	1998	2001	2004	
Euro Canadian Dollar	$200.0			$186.6
fixed rate	6.25%			
Euro Dollar		$500.0		$502.6
fixed rate		6.125%		
effective rate (a)		6.400%		
Euro Dollar			$500.0	$515.3
fixed rate			6.625%	
effective rate (a)			6.354%	
U.S. commercial paper (b)	$744.2			$744.2
weighted av. variable	5.74%			

(a) Effective fixed interest rate paid, as a result of settlement of forward interest rate swap at date of debt issuance.

(b) $400 million of commercial paper classified in long-term debt as of year-end 1997. Refer to Note 6 within Notes to Consolidated Financial Statements for further information.

Interest & currency swaps & caps

Instrument characteristics		Year of maturity (millions)			Fair value (millions)
		1998	2001	2002	
Mixed swap – currency/interest – pay/receive fixed – hedge of existing debt issue	Notional amt.	$200.0			($10.8)
	Pay	US$/4.629%			
	Receive	C$/6.250%			
Interest rate swap – pay variable/receive fixed – hedge of existing debt issue	Notional amt.		$200.0		1.3
	Pay		5.96%		
	Receive		6.40%		
Interest rate swap – pay variable/receive fixed – hedge of existing debt issue (a)	Notional amt.			$225.0	1.2
	Pay			5.600%	
	Receive			6.354%	
Interest rate forward swap – pay fixed/receive variable – hedge of future debt issue	Notional amt.	$25.0			(.1)
	Pay	5.8125%			
	Receive	5.7730%			
Interest rate cap – pay fixed if 30-day C.P. rate rises to strike rate – hedge of U.S. commercial paper (b)	Notional amt.			$225.0	(.4)
	Strike			6.33%	
	Reference			5.65%	

(a) Under the terms of this swap, if three-month LIBOR falls to 4.71% or below, the swap will expire. At year-end 1997, three-month LIBOR was 5.81%.

(b) Under the terms of this cap, if the Federal Reserve AA composite rate on 30-day commercial paper increases to 7.83% or above, the cap will expire. At year-end 1997 the rate was 5.65%.

Price risk

The Company is exposed to price fluctuations primarily as a result of anticipated purchases of raw and packaging materials. Primary exposures include corn, wheat, soybean oil, sugar, and other ingredients for the Company's grain-based convenience food products. The Company uses the combination of long cash positions with vendors, and exchange-traded futures and option contracts to reduce price fluctuations in a desired percentage of forecasted purchases over a duration of generally less than one year. The fair values of commodity contracts held at year-end 1997 were insignificant, and potential near-term changes in commodity prices are not expected to have a significant impact on the Company's future earnings or cash flows.

For all derivative financial instruments presented in the tables above, changes in fair values of these instruments and the resultant impact on the Company's cash flows and/or earnings would generally be offset by changes in values of underlying transactions and positions. Therefore, it should be noted that the exclusion of certain of the underlying exposures from the tables above may be a limitation in assessing the net market risk of the Company.

FIVE- OR TEN-YEAR SUMMARY

Usually presented in close proximity to the audited financial statements is a 5- or 10-year summary of selected financial data. From such a summary, one can determine trends and growth patterns over a fairly long period of time. Kellogg

Value-Focused Global Growth

Kellogg Company has a governing objective of creating shareholder value by maximizing economic profit.* Applying value-based management principles, with economic profit as a key measure, to our exceptionally strong brand equities will be our foundation for future growth. Management strongly believes stock price appreciation is linked to growth in economic profit. To align our people behind this objective, Kellogg managers have incentive components of their compensation linked directly to value creation. Also, employees are strongly encouraged to become shareholders.

Market Value Added
(billions)

Compound Annual Growth Rate 14%

$6 $20
$1 $1
1987   1997

☐ Market Value of Equity   ☐ Book Value of Equity

This value-focused formula has clearly delivered historic wealth creation for Kellogg shareholders. Over the past ten years, your Company's equity market value has increased from $6 billion to $20 billion. In this same time period, equity book value has remained unchanged at $1 billion, mainly due to our aggressive share repurchase program. As a result, market value added, which measures the wealth created for shareholders, has increased at a compound annual growth rate of 14%. In 1997, you received a 54% total return on your investment (stock appreciation plus reinvested dividends).

Management remains committed to finding new and innovative ways to leverage our global resources in pursuit of value-focused global growth and long-term shareholder value.

*Defined as net operating profit after tax (excluding non-recurring charges), less a financing charge for capital utilization.

SELECTED FINANCIAL DATA

(millions, except per share data and number of employees)

	Net sales	% Growth	(a) Operating profit	% Growth
10-year compound growth rate	6%		4%	
1997	**$6,830.1**	**2%**	**$1,009.1**	**5%**
1996	6,676.6	(5)	958.9	14
1995	7,003.7	7	837.5	(28)
1994	6,562.0	4	1,162.6	16
1993	6,295.4	2	1,004.6	(5)
1992	6,190.6	7	1,062.8	3
1991	5,786.6	12	1,027.9	16
1990	5,181.4	11	886.0	21
1989	4,651.7	7	732.5	(8)
1988	4,348.8	15	794.1	15
1987	3,793.0	14	691.2	7

	Total assets	Return on average assets	Shareholders' equity	Return on average equity
1997	**$4,877.6**	**11%**	**$ 997.5**	**49%**
1996	5,050.0	11	1,282.4	37
1995	4,414.6	11	1,590.9	29
1994	4,467.3	16	1,807.5	40
1993	4,237.1	16	1,713.4	37
1992	4,015.0	11	1,945.2	21
1991	3,925.8	16	2,159.8	30
1990	3,749.4	14	1,901.8	28
1989	3,390.4	14	1,634.4	30
1988	3,297.9	16	1,483.2	36
1987	2,680.9	17	1,211.4	38

(a) Operating profit for 1997 includes non-recurring charges of $184.1 ($140.5 after tax or $.34 per share). Operating profit for 1996 includes non-recurring charges of $136.1 ($97.8 after tax or $.23 per share). Earnings before accounting change for 1996 include a charge of $35.0 ($22.3 after tax or $.05 per share) for a contribution to the Kellogg's Corporate Citizenship Fund. Operating profit for 1995 includes non-recurring charges of $421.8 ($271.3 after tax or $.62 per share). Operating profit for 1993 includes non-recurring charges of $64.3 ($41.1 after tax or $.09 per share). Refer to Management's Discussion and Analysis on pages 18–22 and Notes 3 and 4 within Notes to Consolidated Financial Statements for further explanation of non-recurring charges and other unusual items for years 1995–1997.

presents selected financial data that includes operating data, financial position data, and selected statistics and ratios. In addition, it provides a discussion of its value-based management principles.

(a)(b) Earnings before accounting change	% Growth	Average shares outstanding(c)	Per Common Share Data (c)		(d) Price/ earnings ratio	Stock price range	Net cash provided by operating activities	Net cash provided by/ (used in) financing activities	Common stock repurchases
			(a)(b) Earnings before accounting change	Cash dividends					
4%			5%	11%					
$564.0	6%	414.1	$1.36	$.87	36	$32-50	$ 879.8	$(607.3)	$426.0
531.0	8	424.9	1.25	.81	26	31-40	711.5	94.0	535.7
490.3	(30)	438.3	1.12	.75	34	26-40	1,041.0	(759.2)	374.7
705.4	4	448.6	1.57	.70	18	24-30	966.8	(559.5)	327.3
680.7	—	463.0	1.47	.66	19	23-34	800.2	(464.2)	548.1
682.8	13	477.7	1.43	.60	23	27-37	741.9	(422.6)	224.1
606.0	21	482.4	1.26	.54	26	17-33	934.4	(537.7)	83.6
502.8	19	483.2	1.04	.48	18	14-19	819.2	(490.9)	86.9
422.1	(12)	488.4	.87	.43	20	14-20	533.5	(143.2)	78.6
480.4	21	492.8	.98	.38	16	12-17	492.3	52.1	33.6
395.9	24	494.8	.80	.32	16	9-17	523.5	(130.5)	22.6

Property, net	Capital expenditures	Depreciation and amortization	Long-term debt	(e) Debt to market capitalization	Pretax interest coverage (times)	Current ratio	Advertising expense	R&D expense	Number of employees
$2,773.3	$312.4	$287.3	$1,415.4	10%	9	.9	$780.4	$106.1	14,339
2,932.9	307.3	251.5	726.7	14	13	.7	778.9	84.3	14,511
2,784.8	315.7	258.8	717.8	5	12	1.1	891.5	72.2	14,487
2,892.8	354.3	256.1	719.2	8	23	1.2	856.9	71.7	15,657
2,768.4	449.7	265.2	521.6	7	27	1.0	772.4	59.2	16,151
2,662.7	473.6	231.5	314.9	3	33	1.2	782.3	56.7	16,551
2,646.5	333.5	222.8	15.2	3	17	.9	708.3	34.7	17,017
2,595.4	320.5	200.2	295.6	7	10	.9	648.5	38.3	17,239
2,406.3	508.7	167.6	371.4	10	10	.9	611.4	42.9	17,268
2,131.9	538.1	139.7	272.1	9	14	.9	560.9	42.0	17,461
1,738.8	478.4	113.1	290.4	7	14	.9	486.9	40.0	17,762

(b) Earnings before accounting change for 1997 exclude the effect of a charge of $18.0 after tax ($.04 per share) to write off business process reengineering costs in accordance with guidance issued by the Emerging Issues Task Force of the FASB. Earnings before accounting change for 1992 and 1989 exclude the effect of adopting the following Statements of Financial Accounting Standards (SFAS): in 1992, a charge of $251.6 ($.53 per share) net of $144.6 of income tax benefit for the transition effect of SFAS #106, "Employers' Accounting for Postretirement Benefits Other Than Pensions," and, in 1989, a gain of $48.1 ($.10 per share) for SFAS #96 "Accounting for Income Taxes."

(c) All share data retroactively restated to reflect 2-for-1 stock splits in 1997 and 1991. All earnings per share presented represent both basic and diluted earnings per share.

(d) The price/earnings ratio was calculated based on year-end stock price divided by earnings before the accounting changes referred to in note (b). These earnings include the non-recurring charges and other unusual items referred to in note (a). Excluding the impact of these unusual items, the price/earnings ratio in 1997, 1996, 1995, and 1993 would have been 29, 21, 22, and 19, respectively.

(e) Debt to market capitalization was calculated based on year-end total debt balance divided by market capitalization. Market capitalization was calculated based on year-end stock price multiplied by the number of shares outstanding at year-end.

SPECIMEN FINANCIAL STATEMENTS:
General Mills, Inc.

Continuing Operations

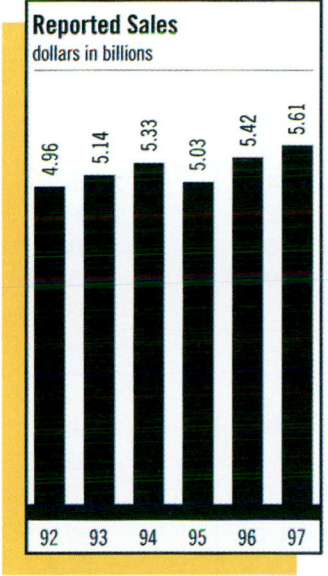

Reported Sales
dollars in billions

92	93	94	95	96	97
4.96	5.14	5.33	5.03	5.42	5.61

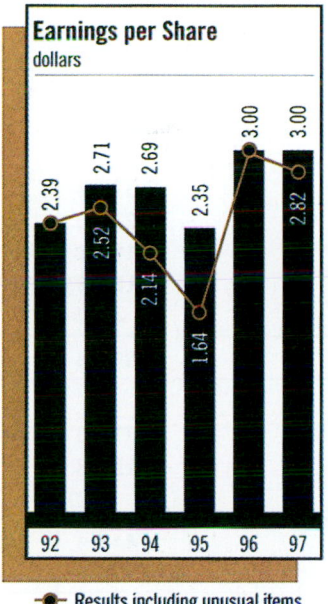

Earnings per Share
dollars

92	93	94	95	96	97
2.39	2.71	2.69	2.35	3.00	3.00
2.52	2.14	1.64			2.82

— Results including unusual items

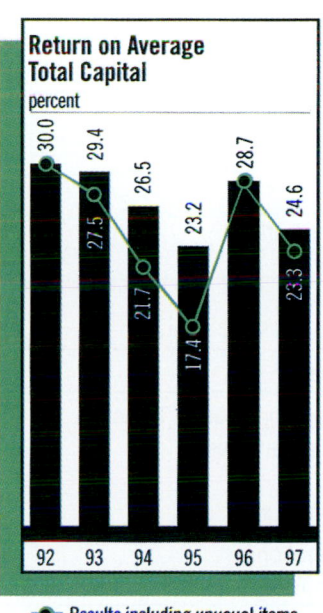

Return on Average Total Capital
percent

92	93	94	95	96	97
30.0	29.4	26.5	23.2	28.7	24.6
27.5	21.7	17.4			23.3

— Results including unusual items

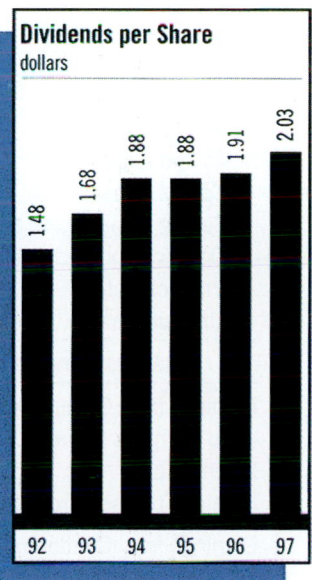

Dividends per Share
dollars

92	93	94	95	96	97
1.48	1.68	1.88	1.88	1.91	2.03

Financial Highlights

Dollars In Millions, Except per Share Data; Fiscal Year Ended	May 25, 1997	May 26, 1996	May 28, 1995
Continuing Operations			
Sales	**$5,609.3**	$5,416.0	$5,026.7
Earnings after Taxes	**445.4**	476.4	259.7
Earnings per Share	**2.82**	3.00	1.64
Return on Average Total Capital	**23.3%**	28.7%	17.4%
Results After Discontinued Operations			
Discontinued Operations after Taxes	**$ –**	$ –	$ 107.7
Net Earnings	**445.4**	476.4	367.4
Net Earnings per Share	**2.82**	3.00	2.33
Average Shares Outstanding	**158.2**	158.9	158.0
Dividends per Share	**$ 2.03**	$ 1.91	$ 1.88

Consolidated Statements of Earnings

In Millions, Except per Share Data, Fiscal Year Ended	May 25, 1997	May 26, 1996	May 28, 1995
Continuing Operations:			
Sales	**$5,609.3**	$5,416.0	$5,026.7
Costs and Expenses:			
Cost of sales	**2,328.4**	2,241.0	2,123.0
Selling, general and administrative	**2,239.2**	2,128.3	2,008.3
Depreciation and amortization	**182.8**	186.7	191.4
Interest, net	**100.5**	101.4	101.2
Unusual items	**48.4**	–	183.2
Total Costs and Expenses	**4,899.3**	4,657.4	4,607.1
Earnings from Continuing Operations before Taxes and Earnings (Losses) of Joint Ventures	**710.0**	758.6	419.6
Income Taxes	**258.3**	279.4	153.3
Earnings (Losses) from Joint Ventures	**(6.3)**	(2.8)	(6.6)
Earnings from Continuing Operations	**445.4**	476.4	259.7
Discontinued Operations after Taxes	**–**	–	107.7
Net Earnings	**$ 445.4**	$ 476.4	$ 367.4
Earnings per Share:			
Continuing operations	**$ 2.82**	$ 3.00	$ 1.64
Discontinued operations	**–**	–	.69
Net Earnings per Share	**$ 2.82**	$ 3.00	$ 2.33
Average Number of Common Shares	**158.2**	158.9	158.0

Consolidated Balance Sheets

In Millions	May 25, 1997	May 26, 1996
Assets		
Current Assets:		
Cash and cash equivalents	$ 12.8	$ 20.6
Receivables, less allowance for doubtful accounts of $4.1 in both 1997 and 1996	419.1	337.8
Inventories	364.4	395.5
Prepaid expenses and other current assets	107.3	132.6
Deferred income taxes	107.7	108.6
Total Current Assets	1,011.3	995.1
Land, Buildings and Equipment, at cost	1,279.4	1,312.4
Other Assets	1,611.7	987.2
Total Assets	$3,902.4	$3,294.7
Liabilities and Equity		
Current Liabilities:		
Accounts payable	$ 599.7	$ 590.7
Current portion of long-term debt	139.0	75.4
Notes payable	204.3	141.6
Accrued taxes	97.0	124.3
Accrued payroll	129.4	124.7
Other current liabilities	123.1	135.2
Total Current Liabilities	1,292.5	1,191.9
Long-term Debt	1,530.4	1,220.9
Deferred Income Taxes	272.1	250.0
Deferred Income Taxes – Tax Leases	143.7	157.5
Other Liabilities	169.1	166.7
Total Liabilities	3,407.8	2,987.0
Stockholders' Equity:		
Cumulative preference stock, none issued	–	–
Common stock, 204.2 shares issued	578.0	384.3
Retained earnings	1,535.4	1,408.6
Less common stock in treasury, at cost, shares of 44.3 in 1997 and 45.2 in 1996	(1,501.9)	(1,367.4)
Unearned compensation and other	(58.0)	(61.2)
Cumulative foreign currency adjustment	(58.9)	(56.6)
Total Stockholders' Equity	494.6	307.7
Total Liabilities and Equity	$3,902.4	$3,294.7

Consolidated Statements of Cash Flows

In Millions, Fiscal Year Ended	May 25, 1997	May 26, 1996	May 28, 1995
Cash Flows – Operating Activities:			
Earnings from continuing operations	$ 445.4	$ 476.4	$ 259.7
Adjustments to reconcile earnings to cash flow:			
Depreciation and amortization	182.8	186.7	191.4
Deferred income taxes	20.9	42.4	59.0
Change in current assets and liabilities, net of effects			
from business acquired	(86.4)	(25.9)	(227.8)
Unusual expenses	48.4	–	183.2
Other, net	(17.0)	(3.2)	(8.1)
Cash provided by continuing operations	594.1	676.4	457.4
Cash provided (used) by discontinued operations	(6.8)	(16.6)	210.1
Net Cash Provided by Operating Activities	587.3	659.8	667.5
Cash Flows – Investment Activities:			
Purchases of land, buildings and equipment	(162.5)	(128.8)	(156.5)
Investments in businesses, intangibles and affiliates, net of dividends	(42.0)	(40.0)	(48.8)
Purchases of marketable securities	(8.0)	(21.6)	(21.7)
Proceeds from sale of marketable securities	47.7	22.5	49.1
Proceeds from disposal of land, buildings and equipment	2.6	6.2	1.2
Proceeds from disposition of businesses	6.5	–	188.3
Other, net	(29.9)	(11.3)	(27.5)
Discontinued operations investment activities, net (primarily new restaurants)	–	–	(357.5)
Net Cash Used by Investment Activities	(185.6)	(173.0)	(373.4)
Cash Flows – Financing Activities:			
Increase (decrease) in notes payable	312.7	(42.4)	(330.4)
Issuance of long-term debt	76.2	42.3	135.0
Payment of long-term debt	(167.0)	(164.7)	(117.2)
Common stock issued	60.5	38.0	24.3
Purchases of common stock for treasury	(361.8)	(35.6)	(57.7)
Dividends paid	(320.7)	(303.6)	(297.2)
Other, net	(9.4)	(13.2)	(13.6)
Pre spin-off borrowings by Darden (Note Three)	–	–	347.9
Net Cash Used by Financing Activities	(409.5)	(479.2)	(308.9)
Increase (Decrease) in Cash and Cash Equivalents	(7.8)	7.6	(14.8)
Cash and Cash Equivalents – Beginning of Year	20.6	13.0	27.8
Cash and Cash Equivalents – End of Year	$ 12.8	$ 20.6	$ 13.0
Cash Flow from Changes in Current Assets and Liabilities:			
Receivables	$ (80.0)	$ (59.5)	$ (11.9)
Inventories	45.0	(23.7)	(52.7)
Prepaid expenses and other current assets	2.5	(6.3)	(11.9)
Accounts payable	(27.8)	93.2	(18.1)
Other current liabilities	(26.1)	(29.6)	(133.2)
Change in Current Assets and Liabilities	$ (86.4)	$ (25.9)	$(227.8)

Consolidated Statement of Stockholders' Equity

In Millions, Except per Share Data	$.10 Par Value Common Stock (One Billion Shares Authorized)				Retained Earnings	Unearned Compensation and Other	Cumulative Foreign Currency Adjustment	Total
	Issued		Treasury					
	Shares	Amount	Shares	Amount				
Balance at May 29, 1994	204.2	$251.0	(45.7)	$(1,334.4)	$2,457.9	$(160.2)	$(63.1)	$1,151.2
Unrealized gain, net of income taxes of $14.0, on available-for-sale securities at May 30, 1994						22.0		22.0
Net earnings					367.4			367.4
Cash dividends declared ($1.88 per share), net of income taxes of $3.1					(294.1)			(294.1)
Stock option, profit sharing and ESOP plans	–	10.0	.4	17.2				27.2
Shares purchased via puts, or on open market			(1.0)	(57.7)				(57.7)
Put option premium/settlements, net	–	(3.5)	–	2.8				(.7)
Transfer of put options	–	122.0						122.0
Unearned compensation related to restricted stock awards						(5.6)		(5.6)
Earned compensation and other						11.0		11.0
Change in unrealized gain, net of income taxes of $3.7, on available-for-sale securities						5.8		5.8
Amount charged to gain on sale of foreign operations							3.6	3.6
Translation adjustments, net of income tax benefit of $.2							7.6	7.6
Transfer of equity components to Darden prior to spin-off						69.1	10.1	79.2
Distribution of equity to stockholders from spin-off of Restaurant operations					(1,297.9)			(1,297.9)
Balance at May 28, 1995	204.2	379.5	(46.3)	(1,372.1)	1,233.3	(57.9)	(41.8)	141.0
Net earnings					476.4			476.4
Cash dividends declared ($1.91 per share), net of income taxes of $2.5					(301.1)			(301.1)
Stock option, profit sharing and ESOP plans	–	4.6	1.7	40.3				44.9
Shares purchased on open market			(.6)	(35.6)				(35.6)
Put option premium/settlements, net	–	.2						.2
Unearned compensation related to restricted stock awards						(6.5)		(6.5)
Earned compensation and other						7.1		7.1
Change in unrealized gain, net of income taxes of $2.0, on available-for-sale securities						(3.1)		(3.1)
Minimum pension liability adjustment						(.8)		(.8)
Translation adjustments, net of income tax benefit of $.2							(14.8)	(14.8)
Balance at May 26, 1996	204.2	384.3	(45.2)	(1,367.4)	1,408.6	(61.2)	(56.6)	307.7
Net earnings					445.4			445.4
Cash dividends declared ($2.03 per share), net of income taxes of $2.1					(318.6)			(318.6)
Shares issued in acquisition	–	181.4	5.4	173.0				354.4
Stock option, profit sharing and ESOP plans	–	9.3	1.7	57.4				66.7
Shares purchased via puts, or on open market			(6.2)	(368.0)				(368.0)
Put and call option premium/settlements, net	–	3.0	–	3.1				6.1
Unearned compensation related to restricted stock awards						(7.9)		(7.9)
Earned compensation and other						13.1		13.1
Change in unrealized gain, net of income taxes of $.1, on available-for-sale securities						(.1)		(.1)
Minimum pension liability adjustment						(1.9)		(1.9)
Amount removed on disposition of foreign operation							6.1	6.1
Translation adjustments							(8.4)	(8.4)
Balance at May 25, 1997	204.2	$578.0	(44.3)	$(1,501.9)	$1,535.4	$ (58.0)	$(58.9)	$ 494.6

APPENDIX C

PRESENT VALUE CONCEPTS

Business enterprises borrow and invest large sums of money. Both of these types of transactions involve the use of **present value computations**. A present value computation is based on the concept of the **time value of money**. For example, would you rather be given $1,000 today or be given $1,000 a year from today? If you get the $1,000 today and invest it to earn 10% per year, the $1,000 will accumulate to $1,100 ($1,000 plus the $100 interest) one year from today. The $1,000 received today is the present value amount that is equivalent to $1,100 one year from now. The present value, therefore, is based on three variables: (1) the dollar amount to be received (the future amount), (2) the length of time until the amount is received (the number of periods), and (3) the interest rate (the discount rate). The process of determining the present value is referred to as **discounting the future amount**. The relationship of these fundamental variables is depicted in the following time diagram:

ILLUSTRATION C-1

Time diagram

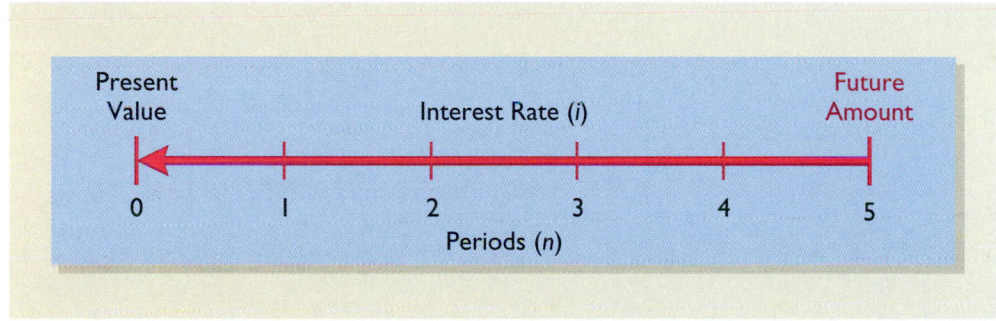

To better understand the variables involved in present value analysis, we encourage you to use time diagrams such as the one in Illustration C-1.

In this textbook, present value computations are used in measuring several items. For example, in Chapter 16, to determine the market price of a bond, the present value of the principal and interest payments is computed. In addition, the determination of the amount to be reported for notes payable and lease liability involves present value computations. And, in Chapter 27, the discounted cash flow technique and the net present value method are used to make capital budget decisions.

PRESENT VALUE OF A SINGLE FUTURE AMOUNT

To illustrate present value concepts, assume that you are willing to invest a sum of money that will yield $1,000 at the end of one year. In other words, what amount would you need to invest today to have $1,000 one year from now? If you want a 10% rate of return, the investment or present value is $909.09 ($1,000 ÷ 1.10). The computation of this amount is shown in Illustration C-2.

ILLUSTRATION C-2

*Present value computation—
$1,000 discounted at 10%
for 1 year*

Present value × (1 + interest rate) = Future amount
Present value × (1 + 10%)   = $1,000
Present value   = $1,000 ÷ 1.10
Present value   = $909.09

The future amount ($1,000), the discount rate (10%), and the number of periods (1) are known. The variables in this situation can be depicted in the following time diagram:

ILLUSTRATION C-3

*Finding present value if dis-
counted for one period*

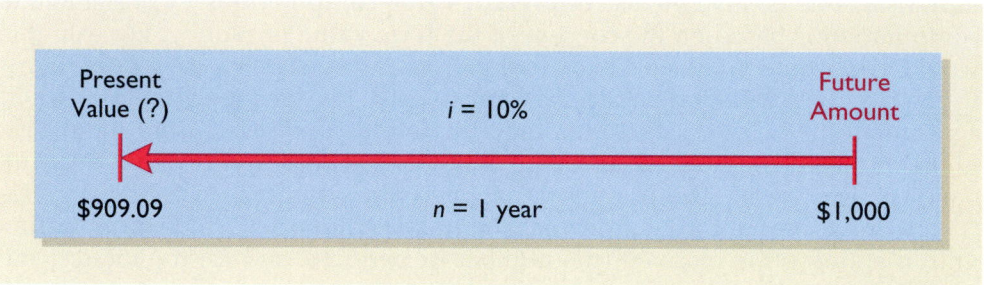

If the single future amount of $1,000 is to be received **in 2 years** and discounted at 10%, its present value is $826.45 [($1,000 ÷ 1.10) ÷ 1.10], depicted as follows:

ILLUSTRATION C-4

*Finding present value if dis-
counted for two periods*

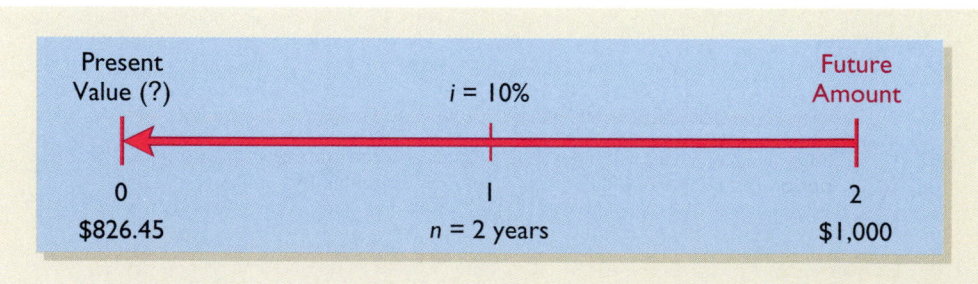

The present value of 1 may also be determined through tables that show the present value of 1 for n periods. In Table C-1 on page C3, n is the number of discounting periods involved. The percentages are the periodic interest rates or discount rates, and the 5-digit decimal numbers in the respective columns are the factors for the present value of 1.

When Table C-1 is used, the future amount is multiplied by the present value factor specified at the intersection of the number of periods and the discount rate. For example, the present value factor for 1 period at a discount rate of 10% is .90909, which equals the $909.09 ($1,000 × .90909) computed in Illustration C-2.

TABLE C-1
Present Value of 1

(n) Periods	4%	5%	6%	8%	9%	10%	11 %	12%	15%
1	.96154	.95238	.94340	.92593	.91743	.90909	.90090	.89286	.86957
2	.92456	.90703	.89000	.85734	.84168	.82645	.81162	.79719	.75614
3	.88900	.86384	.83962	.79383	.77218	.75132	.73119	.71178	.65752
4	.85480	.82270	.79209	.73503	.70843	.68301	.65873	.63552	.57175
5	.82193	.78353	.74726	.68058	.64993	.62092	.59345	.56743	.49718
6	.79031	.74622	.70496	.63017	.59627	.56447	.53464	.50663	.43233
7	.75992	.71068	.66506	.58349	.54703	.51316	.48166	.45235	.37594
8	.73069	.67684	.62741	.54027	.50187	.46651	.43393	.40388	.32690
9	.70259	.64461	.59190	.50025	.46043	.42410	.39092	.36061	.28426
10	.67556	.61391	.55839	.46319	.42241	.38554	.35218	.32197	.24719
11	.64958	.58468	.52679	.42888	.38753	.35049	.31728	.28748	.21494
12	.62460	.55684	.49697	.39711	.35554	.31863	.28584	.25668	.18691
13	.60057	.53032	.46884	.36770	.32618	.28966	.25751	.22917	.16253
14	.57748	.50507	.44230	.34046	.29925	.26333	.23199	.20462	.14133
15	.55526	.48102	.41727	.31524	.27454	.23939	.20900	.18270	.12289
16	.53391	.45811	.39365	.29189	.25187	.21763	.18829	.16312	.10687
17	.51337	.43630	.37136	.27027	.23107	.19785	.16963	.14564	.09293
18	.49363	.41552	.35034	.25025	.21199	.17986	.15282	.13004	.08081
19	.47464	.39573	.33051	.23171	.19449	.16351	.13768	.11611	.07027
20	.45639	.37689	.31180	.21455	.17843	.14864	.12403	.10367	.06110

For 2 periods at a discount rate of 10%, the present value factor is .82645, which equals the $826.45 ($1,000 × .82645) computed previously.

Note that **a higher discount rate produces a smaller present value**. For example, using a 15% discount rate, the present value of $1,000 due one year from now is $869.57 versus $909.09 at 10%. It should also be recognized that **the further removed from the present the future amount is, the smaller the present value**. For example, using the same discount rate of 10%, the present value of $1,000 due **in five years** is $620.92 versus the present value of $1,000 due in **one** year, which is $909.09.

The following two demonstration problems (Illustrations C-5 and C-6) illustrate how to use Table C-1.

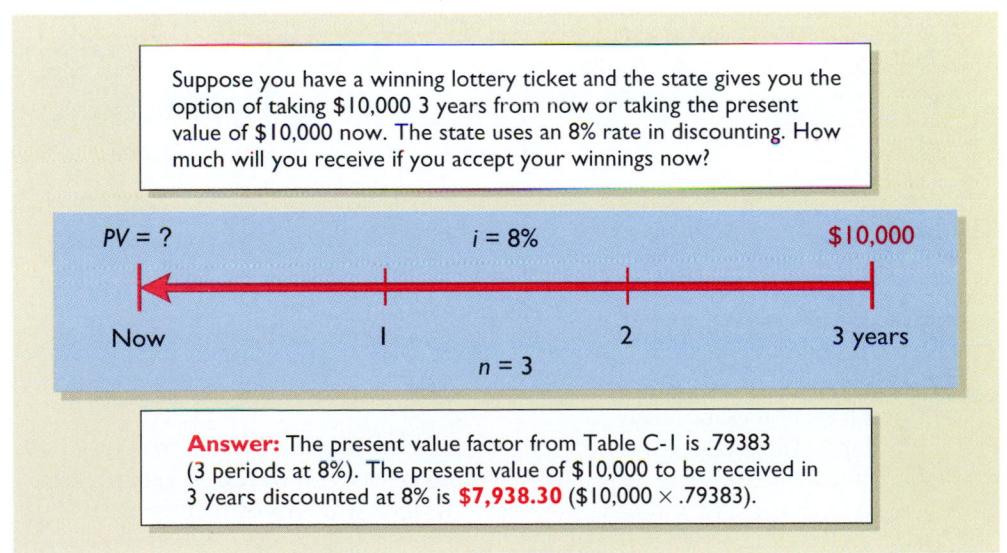

ILLUSTRATION C-5

Demonstration Problem—
Using Table C-1 for PV of 1

Suppose you have a winning lottery ticket and the state gives you the option of taking $10,000 3 years from now or taking the present value of $10,000 now. The state uses an 8% rate in discounting. How much will you receive if you accept your winnings now?

PV = ? $i = 8\%$ $10,000

Now   1   2   3 years

$n = 3$

Answer: The present value factor from Table C-1 is .79383 (3 periods at 8%). The present value of $10,000 to be received in 3 years discounted at 8% is **$7,938.30** ($10,000 × .79383).

ILLUSTRATION C-6

*Demonstration Problem—
Using Table C-1 for PV of 1*

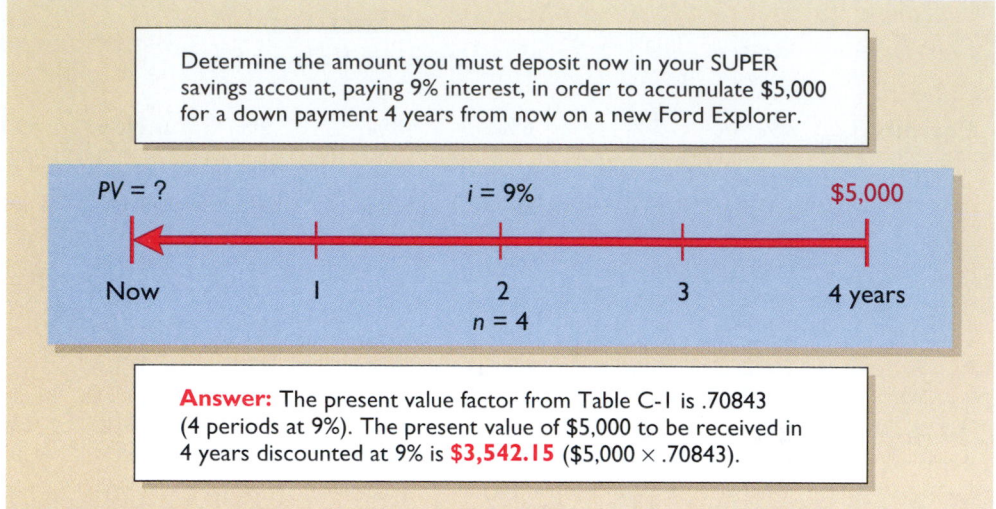

Determine the amount you must deposit now in your SUPER savings account, paying 9% interest, in order to accumulate $5,000 for a down payment 4 years from now on a new Ford Explorer.

Answer: The present value factor from Table C-1 is .70843 (4 periods at 9%). The present value of $5,000 to be received in 4 years discounted at 9% is **$3,542.15** ($5,000 × .70843).

PRESENT VALUE OF A SERIES OF FUTURE AMOUNTS (ANNUITIES)

The preceding discussion involved the discounting of only a single future amount. Businesses and individuals frequently engage in transactions in which a series of equal dollar amounts are to be received or paid periodically. Examples of a series of periodic receipts or payments are loan agreements, installment sales, mortgage notes, lease (rental) contracts, and pension obligations. These series of periodic receipts or payments are called **annuities**. In computing the present value of an annuity, it is necessary to know the (1) discount rate, (2) the number of discount periods, and (3) the amount of the periodic receipts or payments. To illustrate the computation of the present value of an annuity, assume that you will receive $1,000 cash annually for 3 years and the discount rate is 10%. This situation is depicted in the following time diagram:

ILLUSTRATION C-7

Time diagram for a 3-year annuity

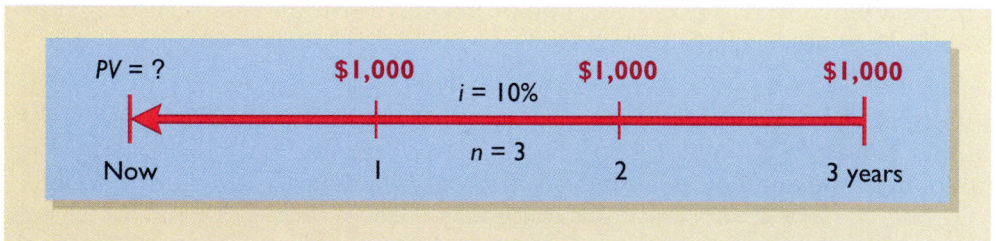

The present value in this situation may be computed as follows:

ILLUSTRATION C-8

Present value of a series of future amounts computation

Future Amount	×	Present Value of 1 Factor at 10%	=	Present Value
$1,000 (One year away)		.90909		$ 909.09
1,000 (Two years away)		.82645		826.45
1,000 (Three years away)		.75132		751.32
		2.48686		**$2,486.86**

This method of calculation is required when the periodic cash flows are not uniform in each period. However, when the future receipts are the same in each period, there are two other ways to compute present value. First, the annual cash flow can be multiplied by the sum of the three present value factors. In the example above, $1,000 × 2.48686 equals $2,486.86. Second, annuity tables may be used. As illustrated in Table C-2 below, these tables show the present value of 1 to be received periodically for a given number of periods.

TABLE C-2
Present Value of an Annuity of 1

(n) Periods	4%	5%	6%	8%	9%	10%	11 %	12%	15%
1	.96154	.95238	.94340	.92593	.91743	.90909	.90090	.89286	.86957
2	1.88609	1.85941	1.83339	1.78326	1.75911	1.73554	1.71252	1.69005	1.62571
3	2.77509	2.72325	2.67301	2.57710	2.53130	2.48685	2.44371	2.40183	2.28323
4	3.62990	3.54595	3.46511	3.31213	3.23972	3.16986	3.10245	3.03735	2.85498
5	4.45182	4.32948	4.21236	3.99271	3.88965	3.79079	3.69590	3.60478	3.35216
6	5.24214	5.07569	4.91732	4.62288	4.48592	4.35526	4.23054	4.11141	3.78448
7	6.00205	5.78637	5.58238	5.20637	5.03295	4.86842	4.71220	4.56376	4.16042
8	6.73274	6.46321	6.20979	5.74664	5.53482	5.33493	5.14612	4.96764	4.48732
9	7.43533	7.10782	6.80169	6.24689	5.99525	5.75902	5.53705	5.32825	4.77158
10	8.11090	7.72173	7.36009	6.71008	6.41766	6.14457	5.88923	5.65022	5.01877
11	8.76048	8.30641	7.88687	7.13896	6.80519	6.49506	6.20652	5.93770	5.23371
12	9.38507	8.86325	8.38384	7.53608	7.16073	6.81369	6.49236	6.19437	5.42062
13	9.98565	9.39357	8.85268	7.90378	7.48690	7.10336	6.74987	6.42355	5.58315
14	10.56312	9.89864	9.29498	8.24424	7.78615	7.36669	6.98187	6.62817	5.72448
15	11.11839	10.37966	9.71225	8.55948	8.06069	7.60608	7.19087	6.81086	5.84737
16	11.65230	10.83777	10.10590	8.85137	8.31256	7.82371	7.37916	6.97399	5.95424
17	12.16567	11.27407	10.47726	9.12164	8.54363	8.02155	7.54879	7.11963	6.04716
18	12.65930	11.68959	10.82760	9.37189	8.75563	8.20141	7.70162	7.24967	6.12797
19	13.13394	12.08532	11.15812	9.60360	8.95012	8.36492	7.83929	7.36578	6.19823
20	13.59033	12.46221	11.46992	9.81815	9.12855	8.51356	7.96333	7.46944	6.25933

From Table C-2 it can be seen that the present value factor of an annuity of 1 for three periods at 10% is 2.48685.[1] This present value factor is the total of the three individual present value factors as shown in Illustration C-8. Applying this amount to the annual cash flow of $1,000 produces a present value of $2,486.85.

The following demonstration problem (Illustration C-9) illustrates how to use Table C-2.

---

[1]The difference of .00001 between 2.48686 amd 2.48685 is due to rounding.

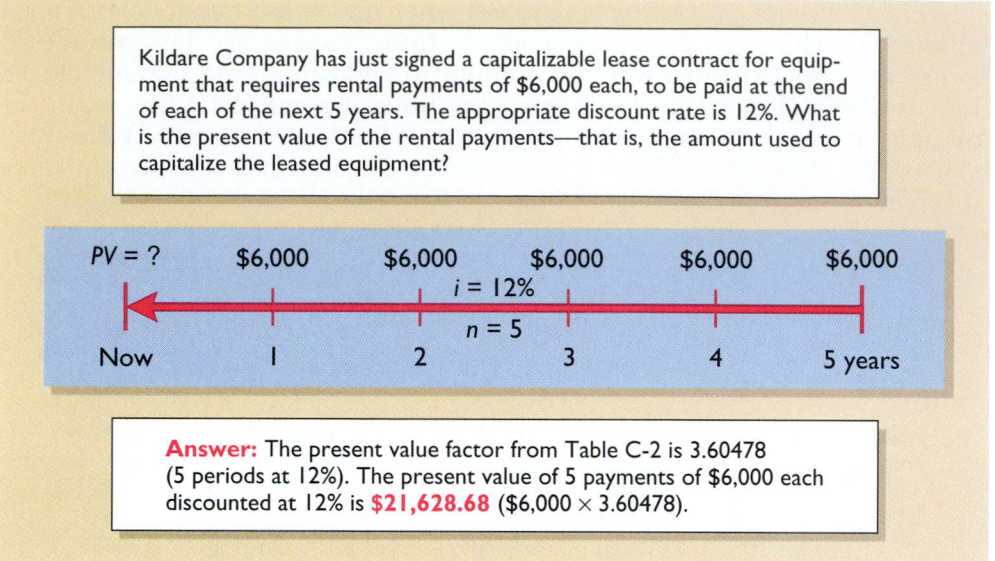

Kildare Company has just signed a capitalizable lease contract for equipment that requires rental payments of $6,000 each, to be paid at the end of each of the next 5 years. The appropriate discount rate is 12%. What is the present value of the rental payments—that is, the amount used to capitalize the leased equipment?

Answer: The present value factor from Table C-2 is 3.60478 (5 periods at 12%). The present value of 5 payments of $6,000 each discounted at 12% is **$21,628.68** ($6,000 × 3.60478).

TIME PERIODS AND DISCOUNTING

In the preceding calculations, the discounting has been done on an annual basis using an annual interest rate. Discounting may also be done over shorter periods of time such as monthly, quarterly, or semiannually. When the time frame is less than one year, it is necessary to convert the annual interest rate to the applicable time frame. Assume, for example, that the investor in Illustration C-8 received $500 **semiannually** for 3 years instead of $1,000 annually. In this case, the number of periods becomes 6 (3 × 2), the discount rate is 5% (10% ÷ 2), the present value factor from Table C-2 is 5.07569, and the present value of the future cash flows is $2,537.85 (5.07569 × $500). This amount is slightly higher than the $2,486.86 computed in Illustration C-8 because interest is computed twice during the same year; therefore interest is earned on the first half year's interest.

COMPUTING THE PRESENT VALUE OF A BOND

The present value (or market price) of a bond is a function of three variables: (1) the payment amounts, (2) the length of time until the amounts are paid, and (3) the discount rate.

The first variable (dollars to be paid) is made up of two elements: (1) a series of interest payments (an annuity) and (2) the principal amount (a single sum). To compute the present value of the bond, both the interest payments and the principal amount must be discounted—two different computations. The time diagrams for a bond due in 5 years are shown in Illustration C-10.

When the investor's discount rate is equal to the bond's contractual interest rate, the present value of the bonds will equal the face value of the bonds. To

ILLUSTRATION C-10

Time diagram for the present value of a bond

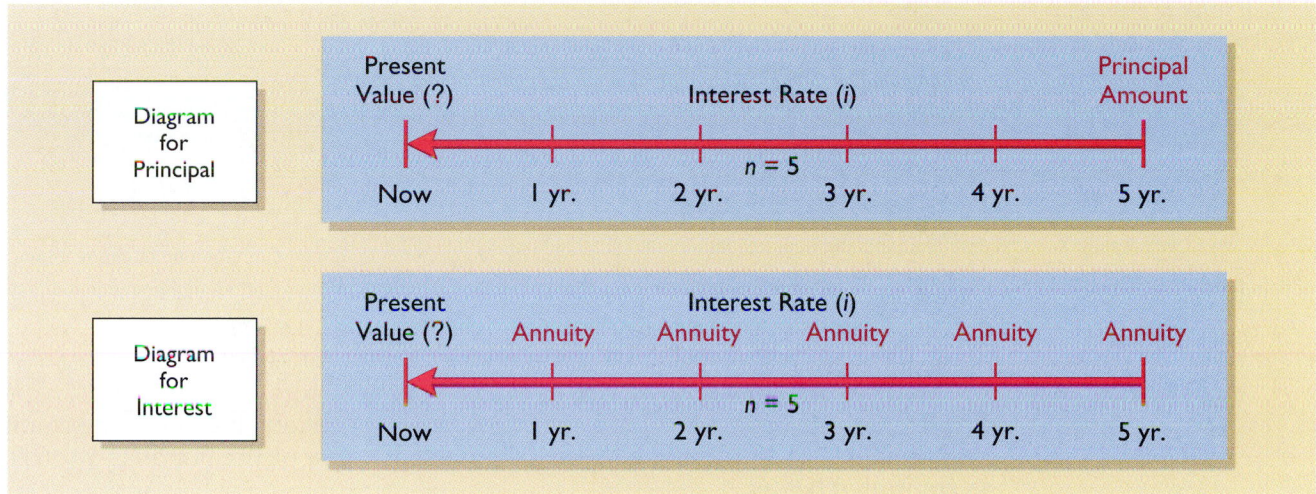

illustrate, assume a bond issue of 10%, 5-year bonds with a face value of $100,000 with interest payable **semiannually** on January 1 and July 1. If the discount rate is the same as the contractual rate, the bonds will sell at face value. In this case, the investor will receive (1) $100,000 at maturity and (2) a series of ten $5,000 interest payments [($100,000 × 10%) ÷ 2] over the term of the bonds. The length of time is expressed in terms of interest periods, in this case, 10, and the discount rate per interest period, 5%. The following time diagram (Illustration C-11) depicts the variables involved in this discounting situation:

ILLUSTRATION C-11

Time diagram for the present value of a 10%, 5-year bond paying interest semiannually

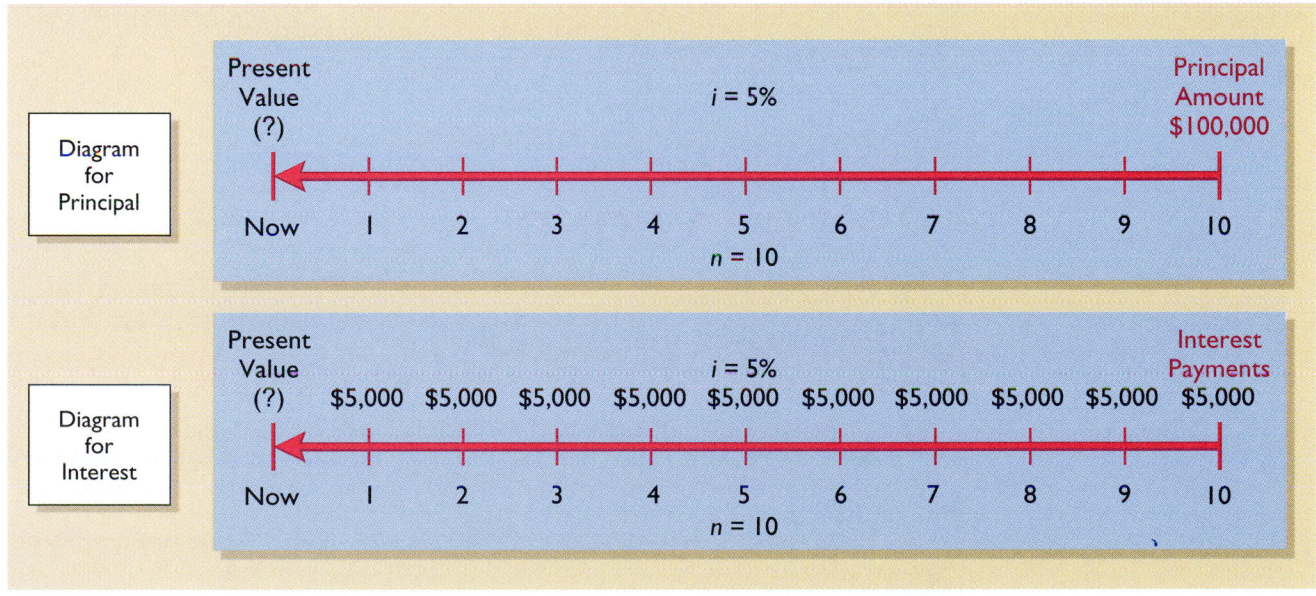

The computation of the present value of these bonds is shown below.

ILLUSTRATION C-12

Present value of principal and interest (face value)

10% Contractual Rate—10% Discount Rate	
Present value of principal to be received at maturity	
$100,000 × PV of 1 due in 10 periods at 5%	
$100,000 × .61391 (Table C-1)	$ 61,391
Present value of interest to be received periodically over the term of the bonds	
$5,000 × PV of 1 due periodically for 10 periods at 5%	
$5,000 × 7.72173 (Table C-2)	38,609*
Present value of bonds	**$100,000**

*(Rounded).

Now assume that the investor's required rate of return is 12%, not 10%. The future amounts are again $100,000 and $5,000, respectively, but now a discount rate of 6% (12% ÷ 2) must be used. The present value of the bonds is $92,639, as computed below:

ILLUSTRATION C-13

Present value of principal and interest (discount)

10% Contractual Rate—12% Discount Rate	
Present value of principal to be received at maturity	
$100,000 × .55839 (Table C-1)	$55,839
Present value of interest to be received periodically over the term of the bonds	
$5,000 × 7.36009 (Table C-2)	36,800
Present value of bonds	**$92,639**

Conversely, if the discount rate is 8% and the contractual rate is 10%, the present value of the bonds is $108,111, computed as follows:

ILLUSTRATION C-14

Present value of principal and interest (premium)

10% Contractual Rate—8% Discount Rate	
Present value of principal to be received at maturity	
$100,000 × .67556 (Table C-1)	$ 67,556
Present value of interest to be received periodically over the term of the bonds	
$5,000 × 8.11090 (Table C-2)	40,555
Present value of bonds	**$108,111**

TECHNOLOGY IN ACTION

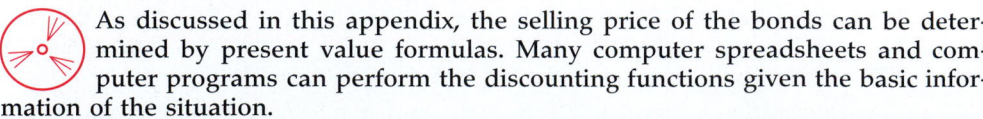

As discussed in this appendix, the selling price of the bonds can be determined by present value formulas. Many computer spreadsheets and computer programs can perform the discounting functions given the basic information of the situation.

The above discussion relied on present value tables in solving present value problems. Electronic hand-held calculators may also be used to compute present values without the use of these tables. Some calculators, especially the "business" or "financial" type calculators, have present value (PV) functions that allow you to calculate present values by merely punching in the proper amount, discount rate, periods, and pressing the PV key.

BRIEF EXERCISES
(Use Tables to Solve Exercises)

BEC–1 For each of the following cases, indicate (a) to what interest rate columns and (b) to what number of periods you would refer in looking up the discount rate.

Using present value tables.

1. In Table C-1 (present value of 1):

	Annual Rate	Number of Years Involved	Discounts Per Year
a.	12%	6	Annually
b.	10%	15	Annually
c.	8%	8	Semiannually

2. In Table C-2 (present value of an annuity of 1):

	Annual Rate	Number of Years Involved	Number of Payments Involved	Frequency of Payments
a.	12%	20	20	Annually
b.	10%	5	5	Annually
c.	8%	4	8	Semiannually

BEC–2 (a) What is the present value of $10,000 due 8 periods from now, discounted at 8%? (b) What is the present value of $10,000 to be received at the end of each of 6 periods, discounted at 9%?

Determining present values.

BEC–3 Smolinski Company is considering an investment that will return a lump sum of $500,000 5 years from now. What amount should Smolinski Company pay for this investment in order to earn a 15% return?

Compute the present value of a single-sum investment.

BEC–4 Pizzeria Company earns 11% on an investment that will return $875,000 8 years from now. What is the amount Pizzeria should invest now in order to earn this rate of return?

Compute the present value of a single-sum investment.

BEC–5 Shake-A-Soda Company sold a 5-year, noninterest-bearing $27,000 note receivable to Valley Inc. Valley wishes to earn 12% over the remaining 4 years of the note. How much cash will Shake-A-Soda receive upon sale of the note?

Compute the present value of a single-sum noninterest-bearing note.

BEC–6 Roberto Company issues a 3-year, zero-interest-bearing $66,000 note. The interest rate used to discount the zero-interest-bearing note is 8%. What are the cash proceeds that Roberto Company should receive?

Compute the present value of a single-sum noninterest-bearing note.

BEC–7 Kilarny Company is considering investing in an annuity contract that will return $20,000 annually at the end of each year for 15 years. What amount should Kilarny Company pay for this investment if it earns a 6% return?

Compute the present value of an annuity investment.

BEC–8 Zarita Enterprises earns 11% on an investment that pays back $110,000 at the end of each of the next 4 years. What is the amount Zarita Enterprises invested to earn the 11% rate of return?

Compute the present value of an annuity investment.

BEC–9 Hernandez Railroad Co. is about to issue $100,000 of 10-year bonds paying a 12% interest rate, with interest payable semiannually. The discount rate for such securities is 10%. How much can Hernandez expect to receive for the sale of these bonds?

Compute the present value of bonds.

BEC–10 Assume the same information as BEC–9 except that the discount rate is 12% instead of 10%. In this case, how much can Hernandez expect to receive from the sale of these bonds?

Compute the present value of bonds.

BEC–11 Caledonian Taco Company receives a $50,000, 6-year note bearing interest of 11% (paid annually) from a customer at a time when the discount rate is 12%. What is the present value of the note received by Caledonian?

Compute the present value of a note.

Compute the present value of bonds.

BEC–12   Galway Bay Enterprises issued 10%, 8-year, $2,000,000 par value bonds that pay interest semiannually on October 1 and April 1. The bonds are dated April 1, 1999, and are issued on that date. The discount rate of interest for such bonds on April 1, 1999, is 12%. What cash proceeds did Galway Bay receive from issuance of the bonds?

Compute the value of a machine for purposes of making a purchase decision.

BEC–13   Barney Googal owns a garage and is contemplating purchasing a tire retreading machine for $16,280. After estimating costs and revenues, Barney projects a net cash flow from the retreading machine of $2,790 annually for 8 years. Barney hopes to earn a return of 11% on such investments. What is the present value of the retreading operation? Should Barney Googal purchase the retreading machine?

Compute the present value of a note.

BEC–14   Hung-Chao Yu Company issues a 10%, 6-year mortgage note on January 1, 1999, to obtain financing for new equipment. Land is used as collateral for the note. The terms provide for semiannual installment payments of $112,825. What were the cash proceeds received from the issuance of the note?

Compute the maximum price to pay for a machine.

BEC–15   Ramos Company is considering purchasing equipment. The equipment will produce the following cash flows: Year 1, $30,000; Year 2, $40,000; Year 3, $50,000. Ramos requires a minimum rate of return of 15%. What is the maximum price Ramos should pay for this equipment?

Compute the interest rate on a single sum.

BEC–16   If Kerry Rodriquez invests $1,827 now, she will receive $10,000 at the end of 15 years. What annual rate of interest will Kerry earn on her investment? (Hint: Use Table C-1.)

Compute the number of periods of a single sum.

BEC–17   Maloney Cork has been offered the opportunity of investing $24,719 now. The investment will earn 15% per year and at the end of that time will return Maloney $100,000. How many years must Maloney wait to receive $100,000? (Hint: Use Table C-1.)

Compute the interest rate on an annuity.

BEC–18   Annie Dublin purchased an investment for $11,469.92. From this investment, she will receive $1,000 annually for the next 20 years, starting one year from now. What rate of interest will Annie's investment be earning for her? (Hint: Use Table C-2.)

Compute the number of periods of an annuity.

BEC–19   Andy Sanchez invests $8,851.37 now for a series of $1,000 annual returns, beginning one year from now. Andy will earn a return of 8% on the initial investment. How many annual payments of $1,000 will Andy receive? (Hint: Use Table C-2.)

COMPLETING THE ACCOUNTING CYCLE UNDER THE PERIODIC INVENTORY SYSTEM

In Chapter 5, the **perpetual inventory method** was explained and illustrated. That presentation, using a merchandising firm, demonstrated the use of a work sheet and closing entries. Our presentation of the **periodic inventory method** in Chapter 9 did not include these steps. The purpose of this appendix is to explain these two steps.

Under a periodic inventory system the ending inventory and the cost of goods sold are determined at the end of the period. And, once determined, the ending inventory replaces the beginning inventory in the general ledger. There are two ways to record the newly determined ending inventory: (1) as part of the closing process, or (2) as part of the adjusting process. We demonstrate both ways, using a work sheet.

SECTION **I** CLOSING ENTRY METHOD FOR MERCHANDISE INVENTORY

USING A WORK SHEET

As indicated in Chapters 4 and 5, a work sheet enables financial statements to be prepared before the adjusting entries are journalized and posted. The work sheet for Highpoint Electronic, shown in Illustration D-1, contains all the income statement data explained in Chapter 9 plus other noninventory data from Chapter 5. The unique accounts for a merchandising company using a periodic inventory system are shown in capital letters in red.

Trial Balance Columns

Data for the trial balance are obtained from the ledger balances of Highpoint Electronic at December 31. The amount shown for Merchandise Inventory, $36,000, is the beginning inventory.

HIGHPOINT ELECTRONIC
Work Sheet
For the Year Ended December 31, 1999

	Trial Balance		Adjustments		Adjusted Trial Balance		Income Statement		Balance Sheet	
	Dr.	Cr.	Dr.	Cr.	Dr.	Cr.	Dr.	Cr.	Dr.	Cr.
Cash	9,500				9,500				9,500	
Accounts Receivable	16,100				16,100				16,100	
MERCHANDISE INVENTORY	36,000				36,000		36,000	40,000	40,000	
Prepaid Insurance	3,800			(a) 2,000	1,800				1,800	
Store Equipment	80,000				80,000				80,000	
Accumulated Depreciation		16,000		(b) 8,000		24,000				24,000
Accounts Payable		20,400				20,400				20,400
R. A. Lamb, Capital		83,000				83,000				83,000
R. A. Lamb, Drawing	15,000				15,000				15,000	
SALES		480,000				480,000		480,000		
SALES RETURNS AND ALLOWANCES	12,000				12,000		12,000			
SALES DISCOUNTS	8,000				8,000		8,000			
PURCHASES	325,000				325,000		325,000			
PURCHASE RETURNS AND ALLOWANCES		10,400				10,400		10,400		
PURCHASE DISCOUNTS		6,800				6,800		6,800		
FREIGHT-IN	12,200				12,200		12,200			
Freight-out	7,000				7,000		7,000			
Advertising Expense	16,000				16,000		16,000			
Rent Expense	19,000				19,000		19,000			
Store Salaries Expense	40,000		(c) 5,000		45,000		45,000			
Utilities Expense	17,000				17,000		17,000			
Totals	616,600	616,600								
Insurance Expense			(a) 2,000		2,000		2,000			
Depreciation Expense			(b) 8,000		8,000		8,000			
Salaries Payable				(c) 5,000		5,000				5,000
Totals			15,000	15,000	629,600	629,600	507,200	537,200	162,400	132,400
Net Income							30,000			30,000
Totals							537,200	537,200	162,400	162,400

Key: (a) Insurance expired, (b) Depreciation expensed, (c) Salaries accrued.

ILLUSTRATION D-1

Work sheet for merchandising company using a periodic inventory system

Adjustments Columns

After all adjustment data are entered on the work sheet, the equality of the adjustment column totals is established. The balances in all accounts are then extended to the adjusted trial balance columns.[1]

---

[1]Conceptually, it can be argued that the change between the beginning and ending inventory balances should be shown on the work sheet as an adjustment. The adjusting entry approach is explained and illustrated in Section II of this appendix.

Adjusted Trial Balance

The adjusted trial balance shows the balance of all accounts after adjustment at the end of the accounting period. **Note that beginning inventory was not adjusted.** Therefore, it is extended to the adjusted trial balance in the amount of $36,000.

Income Statement Columns

The accounts and balances that affect the income statement are transferred from the adjusted trial balance columns to the income statement columns. For Highpoint Electronic, Sales of $480,000 is shown in the credit column whereas the contra revenue accounts, Sales Returns and Allowances of $12,000 and Sales Discounts of $8,000, are shown in the debit column. Thus, the difference of $460,000 is the net sales shown on the income statement. Similarly, Purchases of $325,000 and Freight-in of $12,200 are extended to the debit column. The contra purchase accounts, Purchase Returns and Allowances of $10,400 and Purchase Discounts of $6,800, are extended to the credit columns.

The work sheet procedures for the account Merchandise Inventory merit specific comment. The procedures are:

1. The beginning balance, $36,000, is extended from the adjusted trial balance column to the **income statement debit column**. From there it can be used (added) in reporting cost of goods available for sale in the income statement.
2. The ending inventory, $40,000, is added to the work sheet by an **income statement credit and a balance sheet debit**. The credit makes it possible to deduct ending inventory from the cost of goods available for sale in the income statement to determine cost of goods sold. The debit means the ending inventory can be reported as an asset on the balance sheet.

These two procedures are specifically illustrated below:

	Income Statement		Balance Sheet	
	Dr.	Cr.	Dr.	Cr.
Merchandise Inventory	(1) 36,000	40,000 ◄——(2)——► 40,000		

ILLUSTRATION D-2
Work sheet procedures for inventories—periodic inventory system

The computation for cost of goods sold, taken from the income statement columns in Illustration D-1, is as follows:

Debit Column		Credit Column	
Beginning inventory	$ 36,000	Ending inventory	$40,000
Purchases	325,000	Purchase returns and allowances	10,400
Freight-in	12,200	Purchase discounts	6,800
Total debits	373,200	Total credits	$57,200
Less: Total credits	57,200		
Cost of goods sold	$316,000		

ILLUSTRATION D-3
Computation of cost of goods sold from work sheet columns

HELPFUL HINT
In a periodic system, cost of goods sold is a computation—it is not a separate account with a balance.

Balance Sheet Columns

For Highpoint Electronic, the ending inventory amount of $40,000 is shown in the balance sheet debit column (see Illustration D-2).

PREPARING FINANCIAL STATEMENTS

Financial statements for a merchandising company are prepared from the financial statement columns of the work sheet. The income statement for Highpoint Electronic has already been illustrated (see Illustration 9-6, page 375). The owner's equity statement (see Illustration 5-12, page 203) and the balance sheet (see Illustration 5-13, page 204) appear as already reported in Chapter 5.

Closing Entries

All accounts (including beginning and ending inventory under a periodic inventory system) that affect the determination of net income are closed to Income Summary. Data for the preparation of closing entries may be obtained from the income statement columns of the work sheet. In journalizing, all debit column amounts are credited, and all credit column amounts are debited.

The closing of merchandise inventory is included with other closing entries, as shown below for Highpoint Electronic.

Dec. 31	Merchandise Inventory (Dec. 31)	40,000	
	Sales	480,000	
	Purchase Returns and Allowances	10,400	
	Purchase Discounts	6,800	
	Income Summary		537,200
	(To record ending inventory and close accounts with credit balances)		

HELPFUL HINT
Except for merchandise inventory, the easiest way to prepare the first two closing entries is to identify the temporary accounts by their balances and then prepare one entry for the credits and one for the debits.

31	Income Summary	507,200	
	Merchandise Inventory (Jan. 1)		36,000
	Sales Returns and Allowances		12,000
	Sales Discounts		8,000
	Purchases		325,000
	Freight-in		12,200
	Store Salaries Expense		45,000
	Rent Expense		19,000
	Freight-out		7,000
	Advertising Expense		16,000
	Utilities Expense		17,000
	Depreciation Expense		8,000
	Insurance Expense		2,000
	(To close beginning inventory and other income statement accounts with debit balances)		
31	Income Summary	30,000	
	R. A. Lamb, Capital		30,000
	(To transfer net income to capital)		
31	R. A. Lamb, Capital	15,000	
	R. A. Lamb, Drawing		15,000
	(To close drawings to capital)		

SECTION II   ADJUSTING ENTRY METHOD FOR MERCHANDISE INVENTORY

As previously stated, the change between the beginning and ending inventory balances may be made through adjusting entries rather than through closing entries. Some favor this method because they believe that changes in merchandise inventory should receive the same accounting treatment as changes in the cost of supplies on hand between two points in time. The adjusting entry method is just as acceptable as the closing entry method, and it accomplishes the same objective.

The adjusting entry method affects several steps in the accounting cycle, beginning with the use of a work sheet. Again, these effects are explained and illustrated using Highpoint Electronic as an example.

USING A WORK SHEET

In Illustration D-4, you will see a work sheet similar to the work sheet presented in Section I (Illustration D-1). The major difference in these two work sheets relates to merchandise inventory. In Illustration D-4, the accounting for merchandise inventory uses the adjusting entry method. In Illustration D-1, the closing entry method was used. The unique accounts for the adjusting entry method are shown in capital letters in red.

Trial Balance Columns

The trial balance columns are self-explanatory. The inventory before adjustment is the beginning inventory.

TECHNOLOGY IN ACTION

The adjusting entry method is used in most computerized systems since the programming logic involved is more straightforward. That is, in a computerized system, the command to close the books will close all the temporary accounts to Income Summary. However, if the inventory has not been adjusted, it will not be up-to-date and therefore a misstatement can occur. Some accountants favor the adjusting entry method in manual systems as well.

Adjustments Columns

In the adjustments columns of Illustration D-4, you will see two adjusting entries related to inventory. The objective of preparing adjusting entries for merchandise inventory is to adjust the asset balance to the cost of goods on hand at the balance sheet date. To accomplish this objective for merchandise inventory, two adjusting entries are made: (1) the beginning inventory amount is removed from merchandise inventory, and (2) the ending inventory amount is recorded in merchandise inventory. The adjusting entries, using the inventory data for Highpoint Electronic, are shown below the worksheet on page D6.

HIGHPOINT ELECTRONIC
Work Sheet
For the Year Ended December 31, 1999

	Trial Balance Dr.	Trial Balance Cr.	Adjustments Dr.	Adjustments Cr.	Adjusted Trial Balance Dr.	Adjusted Trial Balance Cr.	Income Statement Dr.	Income Statement Cr.	Balance Sheet Dr.	Balance Sheet Cr.
Cash	9,500				9,500				9,500	
Accounts Receivable	16,100				16,100				16,100	
MERCHANDISE INVENTORY	36,000		(e) 40,000	(d) 36,000	40,000				40,000	
Prepaid Insurance	3,800			(a) 2,000	1,800				1,800	
Store Equipment	80,000				80,000				80,000	
Accumulated Depreciation		16,000		(b) 8,000		24,000				24,000
Accounts Payable		20,400				20,400				20,400
R. A. Lamb, Capital		83,000				83,000				83,000
R. A. Lamb, Drawing	15,000				15,000				15,000	
SALES		480,000				480,000		480,000		
SALES RETURNS AND ALLOWANCES	12,000				12,000		12,000			
SALES DISCOUNTS	8,000				8,000		8,000			
PURCHASES	325,000				325,000		325,000			
PURCHASE RETURNS AND ALLOWANCES		10,400				10,400		10,400		
PURCHASE DISCOUNTS		6,800				6,800		6,800		
FREIGHT-IN	12,200				12,200		12,200			
Freight-out	7,000				7,000		7,000			
Advertising Expense	16,000				16,000		16,000			
Rent Expense	19,000				19,000		19,000			
Store Salaries Expense	40,000		(c) 5,000		45,000		45,000			
Utilities Expense	17,000				17,000		17,000			
Totals	616,600	616,600								
Insurance Expense			(a) 2,000		2,000		2,000			
Depreciation Expense			(b) 8,000		8,000		8,000			
Salaries Payable				(c) 5,000		5,000				5,000
INCOME SUMMARY			(d) 36,000	(e) 40,000	36,000	40,000	36,000	40,000		
Totals			91,000	91,000	669,600	669,600	507,200	537,200	162,400	132,400
Net Income							30,000			30,000
Totals							537,200	537,200	162,400	162,400

Key: (a) Insurance expired, (b) Depreciation expensed, (c) Salaries accrued, (d) Beginning merchandise inventory, (e) Ending merchandise inventory.

ILLUSTRATION D-4

Work sheet—adjusting inventory method

Dec. 31	Income Summary	36,000	
	Merchandise Inventory		36,000
	(To remove beginning inventory)		
31	Merchandise Inventory	40,000	
	Income Summary		40,000
	(To record ending inventory)		

These entries are identified as adjustments (d) and (e), respectively, in the work sheet.

After posting, the accounts will show:

Merchandise Inventory	Income Summary
Jan. 1 Bal. 36,000 Dec.31 Adj. 36,000	Dec.31 Adj. 36,000 Dec.31 Adj. 40,000
Dec.31 Adj. 40,000	
Dec.31 Bal. 40,000	

Adjusted Trial Balance Columns

In Illustration D-4, the merchandise inventory amount is extended to the adjusted trial balance debit column. **This amount is the ending inventory for the period.** Both amounts reported in Income Summary are transferred to the adjusted trial balance columns to ensure that these two amounts are reported in the income statement columns. Therefore the net amount, in this case, $4,000 ($40,000 − $36,000), is not reported.

Financial Statement Columns

Complete financial statements are prepared directly from the income statement and balance sheet columns of the work sheet. The use of the financial statement columns should be familiar to you. One difficult subject is the treatment of merchandise inventory and income summary adjustments. A partial work sheet showing just these two items is presented below:

	Trial Balance Dr.	Trial Balance Cr.	Adjustments Dr.	Adjustments Cr.	Adjusted Trial Balance Dr.	Adjusted Trial Balance Cr.	Income Statement Dr.	Income Statement Cr.	Balance Sheet Dr.	Balance Sheet Cr.
Merchandise Inventory	36,000		(e) 40,000	(d) 36,000	40,000				40,000	
Income Summary			(d) 36,000	(e) 40,000	36,000	40,000	36,000	40,000		

In the merchandise inventory line, the $40,000 in the balance sheet debit column is the ending inventory. In the income summary line, the debit in the income statement column indicates the cost of the beginning inventory, and the credit in the income statement column shows the cost of the ending inventory. Complete financial statements are then prepared directly from the income statement and balance sheet columns of the work sheet.

JOURNALIZING AND POSTING CLOSING ENTRIES

When the adjusting entry method is followed, merchandise inventory is not part of the closing process. As a result, entries to close the books are as follows:

Dec. 31	Sales	480,000	
	Purchase Returns and Allowances	10,400	
	Purchase Discounts	6,800	
	Income Summary		497,200
	(To close income statement accounts with credit balances)		

Dec. 31	Income Summary	471,200	
	Sales Returns and Allowances		12,000
	Sales Discounts		8,000
	Purchases		325,000
	Freight-in		12,200
	Store Salaries Expense		45,000
	Rent Expense		19,000
	Freight-out		7,000
	Advertising Expense		16,000
	Utilities Expense		17,000
	Depreciation Expense		8,000
	Insurance Expense		2,000
	(To close income statement accounts with debit balances)		

These entries produce a credit balance in the Income Summary account of $30,000. This amount equals the net income reported for Highpoint Electronic using the closing method. The postings to Income Summary are as follows:

ILLUSTRATION D-7

Postings to Income Summary

	Income Summary			
Dec. 31 **Adj.**	**36,000**	Dec. 31 **Adj.**	**40,000**	
31 Close	471,200	31 Close	497,200	
31 to Cap.	30,000			
	537,200		537,200	

Both the closing entry method and the adjusting entry method result in the same accounts and amounts reported in the financial statements. It is a matter of personal preference which method is used.

QUESTIONS

1. Assuming the closing entry method is used, indicate the columns of the work sheet in which (a) the beginning merchandise inventory, and (b) the ending merchandise inventory will be shown.

2. Prepare the closing entries for the merchandise inventory account, assuming the closing entry method is used with a beginning inventory of $48,000 and an ending inventory of $58,000.

3. What merchandising account(s) will appear in the post-closing trial balance (assume the closing entry method is used)?

4. Assuming the adjusting entry method is used, indicate the columns of the work sheet in which (a) the beginning merchandise inventory, and (b) the ending merchandise inventory will be shown.

5. Prepare the adjusting entry for the merchandise inventory account, assuming the adjusting entry method is used with a beginning inventory of $48,000 and an ending inventory of $58,000.

6. What merchandising account(s) will appear in the post-closing trial balance (assume the adjusting entry method is used)?

BRIEF EXERCISES

Identify work sheet columns for selected accounts.

BED–1   Presented below is the format of the work sheet presented in the chapter.

Trial Balance		Adjustments		Adjusted Trial Balance		Income Statement		Balance Sheet	
Dr.	Cr.	Dr.	Cr.	Dr.	Cr.	Dr.	Cr.	Dr.	Cr.

Assuming the closing entry method is used, indicate where the following items will appear on the work sheet: (a) cash, (b) beginning inventory, (c) purchases, (d) ending inventory. *Example:*

   Cash: Trial balance debit column; Adjusted trial balance debit column; and Balance sheet debit column.

BED–2   Pema Company has the following merchandise account balances: Sales $180,000, Sales Discounts $2,000, Purchases $120,000, Purchase Returns and Allowances $30,000. In addition, it has a beginning inventory of $50,000 and an ending inventory of $30,000. Assuming the closing entry method is used, prepare the entries to record the closing of these items to Income Summary.

Prepare closing entries for merchandise accounts.

BED–3   Using the information from BED–1, indicate how these four items are presented on the work sheet if the adjusting entry method is used.

Adjusting entry method.

EXERCISES

ED–1   The adjusted trial balance of Cecilie Company shows the following data pertaining to sales at the end of its fiscal year October 31, 1999: Sales $900,000, Freight-out $12,000, Sales Returns and Allowances $24,000, Sales Discounts $2,000, beginning inventory $155,000, and ending inventory $176,000. The closing entry method is used.

Prepare sales revenues section and closing entries, using the closing entry method.

Instructions

   (a) Prepare the sales revenues section of the income statement.
   (b) Prepare the closing entries for Cecilie Company.

ED–2   On June 10, L. Pele Company purchased $5,000 of merchandise from R. Duvall Company FOB shipping point, terms 2/10, n/30. L. Pele pays the freight costs of $300 on June 11. Damaged goods totaling $300 are returned to R. Duvall for credit on June 12. On June 19, L. Pele pays R. Duvall Company in full, less the purchase discount. Pele had a beginning inventory of $25,000, sales of $40,000, and ending inventory of $10,000.

Prepare purchase entries and closing entries, using the closing entry method.

Instructions

   (a) Prepare separate entries for each purchase related transaction on the books of L. Pele Company.
   (b) Using the closing entry method, prepare separate closing entries on June 30 for the temporary accounts with (1) debit balances, and (2) credit balances.

ED–3   The trial balance of G. Garbo Company at the end of its fiscal year, August 31, 1999, includes the following accounts: Merchandise Inventory $17,200, Purchases $142,400, Sales $190,000, Freight-in $4,000, Sales Returns and Allowances $3,000, Freight-out $1,000, and Purchase Returns and Allowances $2,000. The ending merchandise inventory is $26,000. Garbo uses the closing entry method for inventory.

Prepare cost of goods sold section and closing entries, using the closing entry method.

Instructions

   (a) Prepare a cost of goods sold section for the year ending August 31.
   (b) Prepare the closing entries for all accounts.
   (c) Post the closing entries to Merchandise Inventory.

ED–4   Use the information provided in ED-3 to complete the following instructions; assume Garbo uses the adjusting entry method for inventory.

Prepare cost of goods sold section and adjusting and closing entries, using the adjusting entry method.

Instructions

   (a) Prepare a cost of goods sold section for the year ending August 31.
   (b) Prepare the adjusting entries for inventory.
   (c) Prepare the closing entries for all accounts.

ED–5   Presented on page D10 are selected accounts for B. Milia Company as reported in the work sheet at the end of May 1999. Ending merchandise inventory is $72,000.

Complete work sheet and identify accounts for post-closing trial balance, using the closing entry method.

Accounts	Adjusted Trial Balance		Income Statement		Balance Sheet	
	Dr.	Cr.	Dr.	Cr.	Dr.	Cr.
Cash	9,000					
Merchandise Inventory	80,000					
Purchases	240,000					
Purchase Returns and Allowances		30,000				
Sales		450,000				
Sales Returns and Allowances	10,000					
Sales Discounts	5,000					
Rent Expense	42,000					

Instructions

(a) Complete the work sheet by extending amounts reported in the adjusted trial balance to the appropriate columns in the work sheet. The closing entry method is used to account for merchandise inventory. Do not total individual columns.

(b) Identify the merchandising account(s) that are in the post-closing trial balance.

PROBLEMS

. . . .

Complete accounting cycle beginning with a work sheet, using the closing entry method.

PD-1 The trial balance of Mesa Wholesale Company contained the following accounts at December 31, the end of the company's fiscal year. Mesa uses the closing entry method for inventory.

MESA WHOLESALE COMPANY
Trial Balance
December 31, 1999

	Debit	Credit
Cash	$ 33,400	
Accounts Receivable	37,600	
Merchandise Inventory	62,400	
Land	92,000	
Buildings	197,000	
Accumulated Depreciation—Buildings		$ 54,000
Equipment	83,500	
Accumulated Depreciation—Equipment		42,400
Notes Payable		50,000
Accounts Payable		37,500
G. Mesa, Capital		267,800
G. Mesa, Drawing	10,000	
Sales		886,100
Sales Discounts	4,600	
Purchases	725,100	
Purchase Discounts		16,000
Freight-in	12,400	
Salaries Expense	69,800	
Utilities Expense	9,400	
Repair Expense	5,900	
Gas and Oil Expense	7,200	
Insurance Expense	3,500	
	$1,353,800	$1,353,800

Adjustment data:

1. Depreciation is $10,000 on buildings and $9,000 on equipment. (Both are administrative expenses.)
2. Interest of $7,000 is due and unpaid on notes payable at December 31.

Other data:

1. Merchandise inventory on hand at December 31, 1999, is $90,000.
2. Salaries are 80% selling and 20% administrative.
3. Utilities expense, repair expense, and insurance expense are 100% administrative.
4. $15,000 of the notes payable are payable next year.
5. Gas and oil expense is a selling expense.

Instructions

(a) Enter the trial balance on a work sheet and complete the work sheet.
(b) Prepare a multiple-step income statement and owner's equity statement for the year, and a classified balance sheet at December 31, 1999.
(c) Journalize the adjusting entries.
(d) Journalize the closing entries.
(e) Prepare a post-closing trial balance.

PD–2 The trial balance of Ivanna Fashion Center contained the following accounts at November 30, the end of the company's fiscal year. Ivanna uses the closing entry method for inventory.

Complete accounting cycle beginning with a work sheet, using the closing entry method.

IVANNA FASHION CENTER Trial Balance November 30, 1999		
	Debit	Credit
Cash	$ 16,700	
Accounts Receivable	33,700	
Merchandise Inventory	38,000	
Store Supplies	5,500	
Store Equipment	85,000	
Accumulated Depreciation—Store Equipment		$ 18,000
Delivery Equipment	48,000	
Accumulated Depreciation—Delivery Equipment		6,000
Notes Payable		51,000
Accounts Payable		48,500
L. Ivanna, Capital		110,000
L. Ivanna, Drawing	12,000	
Sales		746,600
Sales Returns and Allowances	4,200	
Purchases	503,600	
Purchase Returns and Allowances		6,900
Purchase Discounts		3,700
Freight-in	10,800	
Salaries Expense	140,000	
Advertising Expense	26,400	
Utilities Expense	14,000	
Repair Expense	12,100	
Delivery Expense	16,700	
Rent Expense	24,000	
	$990,700	$990,700

Adjustment data:

1. Store supplies on hand totaled $3,500.
2. Depreciation is $9,000 on the store equipment and $7,000 on the delivery equipment.
3. Interest of $11,000 is accrued on notes payable at November 30.

Other data:

1. Merchandise inventory on hand at November 30, 1999 is $45,000.
2. Salaries expense is 70% selling and 30% administrative.
3. Rent expense and utilities expense are 80% selling and 20% administrative.
4. $30,000 of notes payable are due for payment next year.
5. Repair expense is 100% administrative.

Instructions

(a) Enter the trial balance on a work sheet and complete the work sheet.
(b) Prepare a multiple-step income statement and owner's equity statement for the year and a classified balance sheet as of November 30, 1999.
(c) Journalize the adjusting entries.
(d) Journalize the closing entries.
(e) Prepare a post-closing trial balance.

Complete a work sheet using the adjusting entry method, prepare adjusting and closing entries and post to some accounts.

PD–3 The trial balance of World Enterprises for the year ending December 31, 1999, is shown below. World Enterprises uses the adjusting entry method for inventory.

WORLD ENTERPRISES
Trial Balance
December 31, 1999

	Debit	Credit
Cash	$ 14,000	
Accounts Receivable	27,600	
Merchandise Inventory	27,500	
Prepaid Insurance	1,800	
Store Equipment	42,000	
Accumulated Depreciation—Store Equipment		$ 9,000
Accounts Payable		31,200
R. Roger, Capital		50,300
Sales		238,500
Sales Returns and Allowances	4,600	
Sales Discounts	3,900	
Purchases	172,000	
Freight-in	5,000	
Purchase Returns and Allowances		1,200
Purchase Discounts		2,000
Salaries Expense	27,700	
Utilities Expense	6,100	
	$332,200	$332,200

Other data:

1. Merchandise inventory on hand at December 31, $38,600.
2. Insurance expired $800.
3. Depreciation expense, $3,000.
4. The company uses the adjusting entry method for merchandise inventory.

Instructions

(a) Enter the trial balance on a work sheet and complete the work sheet using the adjusting entry method.
(b) Journalize the adjusting entries.
(c) Prepare the closing entries.
(d) Post the entries in (b) and (c) to Merchandise Inventory and Income Summary.

APPENDIX E

STANDARDS OF ETHICAL CONDUCT FOR MANAGEMENT ACCOUNTANTS

Management accountants have an obligation to the organizations they serve, their profession, the public, and themselves to maintain the highest standards of ethical conduct. In recognition of this obligation, the Institute of Management Accountants, formerly the National Association of Accountants, has published and promoted the following standards of ethical conduct for management accountants. Adherence to these standards is integral to achieving the *Objectives of Management Accounting*.[1] Management accountants shall not commit acts contrary to these standards nor shall they condone the commission of such acts by others within their organizations.

COMPETENCE

Management accountants have a responsibility to:
- Maintain an appropriate level of professional competence by ongoing development of their knowledge and skills.
- Perform their professional duties in accordance with relevant laws, regulations, and technical standards.
- Prepare complete and clear reports and recommendations after appropriate analyses of relevant and reliable information.

CONFIDENTIALITY

Management accountants have a responsibility to:
- Refrain from disclosing confidential information acquired in the course of their work except when authorized, unless legally obligated to do so.

---

[1] Institute of Management Accountants, formerly National Association of Accountants, *Statements on Management Accounting: Objectives of Management Accounting*, Statement No. 1B, June 17, 1982.

- Inform subordinates as appropriate regarding the confidentiality of information acquired in the course of their work and monitor their activities to assure the maintenance of that confidentiality.
- Refrain from using or appearing to use confidential information acquired in the course of their work for unethical or illegal advantage either personally or through third parties.

INTEGRITY

Management accountants have a responsibility to:
- Avoid actual or apparent conflicts of interest and advise all appropriate parties of any potential conflict.
- Refrain from engaging in any activity that would prejudice their ability to carry out their duties ethically.
- Refuse any gift, favor, or hospitality that would influence or would appear to influence their actions.
- Refrain from either actively or passively subverting the attainment of the organization's legitimate and ethical objectives.
- Recognize and communicate professional limitations or other constraints that would preclude responsible judgment or successful performance of an activity.
- Communicate unfavorable as well as favorable information and professional judgments or opinions.
- Refrain from engaging in or supporting any activity that would discredit the profession.

OBJECTIVITY

Management accountants have a responsibility to:
- Communicate information fairly and objectively.
- Disclose fully all relevant information that could reasonably be expected to influence an intended user's understanding of the reports, comments, and recommendations presented.

PHOTO CREDITS

Chapter 1
Page 1: Chris Everard/Tony Stone Images/New York, Inc. Page 5: Murray Alcosser/The Image Bank. Page 6: Ivan Chermayeff/Nonstock, Inc. Page 9: Ann Sates/SABA. Page 12: Laurence Dutton/Tony Stone Images/New York, Inc. Page 23: Will Crocker/The Image Bank.

Chapter 2
Page 44: James Cotier/Tony Stone Images/New York, Inc. Page 47: Matthew Borkoski/Index Stock. Page 50: Jonathan Daniel/Allsport. Page 56: Mike Stewart/Sygma. Page 58: Stephen Marks/The Image Bank. Page 59: Arthur Meyerson/The Image Bank. Page 68 (top): Frank Wing/Stock, Boston/PNI. Page 68 (bottom): Nick Koudis/The Stock Market.

Chapter 3
Page 90: Craig Aurness/West Light. Page 94: Courtesy Jerry Ohlinger. Page 98: Romily Lockyer/The Image Bank. Page 111: Peter Poulides/Tony Stone Images/New York, Inc.

Chapter 4
Page 138: Bartee Stock Imagery. Page 142: ©1998 Lotus Corporation. Used with permission of Lotus Development Corporation. Lotus® and 1-2-3® are registered trademarks of Lotus Development Corporation. Page 148: Courtesy Wal-Mart Stores. Page 156: Miguel S. Salmeron/FPG International. Page 158 (top): Courtesy United Airlines. Page 158 (bottom): Leland Bobbe/Tony Stone Images/New York, Inc. Page 159 (top): John Fiordalisi/SUPERSTOCK. Page 159 (bottom): Courtesy Brunswick Corporation. Page 160 (top): Courtesy United Airlines. Page 160 (bottom): Courtesy Consolidated Freightways. Page 161: Michel Tcherevkoff/The Image Bank. Page 167: Lonnie Duka/Tony Stone Images/New York, Inc. Page 183: Courtesy Case Corporation.

Chapter 5
Page 186: Simon Battensby/Tony Stone Images/New York, Inc. Page 194: G. Covian/The Image Bank. Page 197: Richard Hutchings/Photo Researchers. Page 198: Lorentz Gullachsen/Tony Stone Images/New York, Inc. Page 200: Mark Harmel/Tony Stone Images/New York, Inc. Page 204: Murray Alcosser/The Image Bank. Page 209: Comstock, Inc. Page 226: Courtesy McDonnell Douglas.

Chapter 6
Page 230: ©SUPERSTOCK. Page 237: Earl Glass/Stock, Boston/PNI. Page 251: Frank Levy/The Stock Market. Page 252: Mitchell Funk/The Image Bank. Page 253: Gary Kaemmer/The Image Bank. Page 254: Garry Gay/The Image Bank.

Chapter 7
Page 278: G. & V. Chapman/The Image Bank. Page 281: Gary Buss/FPG International. Page 283: Mike Blank/Tony Stone Images/New York, Inc. Page 284: R. Michael Stuckey/Comstock, Inc. Page 286: Michael Murphy/The Image Bank. Page 292: Telegraph Colour Library/FPG International. Page 295: David Leach/Tony Stone Images/New York, Inc. Page 298: Jon Riley/Tony Stone Images/New York, Inc. Page 299 (top): J.W. Burkey/Tony Stone Images/New York, Inc. Page 299 (bottom): Comstock, Inc. Page 303: Courtesy Eastman Kodak Company. Page 319 (top): Courtesy Microsoft. Page 319 (bottom): Courtesy Oracle Corporation.

Chapter 8
Page 324: Doug Armand/Tony Stone Images/New York, Inc. Page 328: David Gould/The Image Bank. Page 332: Zefa/Stock Imagery. Page 335 (top): Zigy Kaluzny/Tony Stone Images/New York, Inc. Page 335 (bottom): Brian Smale Photography. Page 337: A Berliner/Gamma Liaison. Page 341: John Lund/Tony Stone Images/New York, Inc. Page 343: Laurence Dutton/Tony Stone Images/New York, Inc.

Chapter 9
Page 364: Bob Handelman/Tony Stone Images/New York, Inc. Page 368: Luigi Giordano/The Stock Market. Page 369: Tom Tracey/FPG International. Page 384: Tommy Ewasko/The Image Bank. Page 385 (top): Courtesy The Quaker Oats Company. Page 385 (bottom): Bob Krist/Tony Stone Images/New York, Inc. Page 413: Courtesy Nike Corporation. Page 414 (top): Courtesy Reebok International, Ltd. Page 414 (bottom): Courtesy General Motors Corporation.

Chapter 10
Page 418: Bob Krist/Tony Stone Images/New York, Inc. Page 425: International Stock Photo. Page 430: Michael Krasowitz/FPG International. Page 431: Thierry Dosogne/The Image Bank. Page 439: N. Cotton/International Stock Photo. Page 442: Forrest Anderson/Gamma Liaison. Page 443: ©Schnepf/Gamma Liaison. Page 444: Courtesy Grand Met. Page 465: Courtesy Clark Equipment Company.

Chapter 11
Page 468: Ralph Mercer/Gamma Liaison. Page 473: Laurence Dutton/Tony Stone Images/New York, Inc. Page 476: Peter Gridley/FPG International. Page 477: The Image Bank. Page 479: Steve Bronstein/The Image Bank. Page 482: Adam Woolfitt/Woodfin Camp & Associates. Page 487: ©1994 Turner & Devries/The Image Bank. Page 491: Randy O'Rourke/The Stock Market. Page 501: Courtesy 3M. Page 509: Courtesy Northland Cranberries.

PC-2 Photo Credits

Chapter 12
Page 514: Walter Geiersperger/Index Stock. Page 517: Donald Struthers/Tony Stone Images/New York, Inc. Page 519: Comstock, Inc. Page 525: Henry Sims/The Image Bank. Page 526: Comstock, Inc. Page 527: Andy Zito/The Image Bank. Page 531: Olney Vasan/Tony Stone Images/New York, Inc. Page 545: Courtesy Newcor, Inc.

Chapter 13
Page 548: Andy Washnik. Page 552: Jim Scruggs/Gamma Liaison. Page 553: Walter Bibikow/The Image Bank. Page 557: Robert Cattan/Index Stock.

Chapter 14
Page 588: Rick Graves/Tony Stone Images/New York, Inc. Page 593: Jaques Chenet/Woodfin Camp & Associates. Page 594: Courtesy Delaware State Travel Service. Page 596: Paul Van Riel/Black Star. Page 598: Dave Wilhelm/The Stock Market. Page 605: Courtesy Reebok International, Ltd. Page 609: Will Crocker/The Image Bank. Page 612: Courtesy Knight-Ridder.

Chapter 15
Page 632: Mike Powell/Tony Stone Images/New York, Inc. Page 635: Sandra Baker/Tony Stone Images/New York, Inc. Page 641: John Labbe/The Image Bank. Page 643 (top): Courtesy Lockheed Martin. Page 643 (bottom): Ken Whitmore/Tony Stone Images/New York, Inc. Page 648: Robert Kristofik/The Image Bank. Page 649: Rob Nelson/Black Star. Page 652: Mitchell Funk/The Image Bank. Page 671: Courtesy DIEBOLD, Inc.

Chapter 16
Page 674: Mark Burnside/Tony Stone Images/New York, Inc. Page 679: Steven Wilkes/The Image Bank. Page 691: Archiv/Photo Researchers. Page 693: Mitchell Funk/The Image Bank. Page 705: Ken Whitmore/Tony Stone Images/New York, Inc. Page 717: Courtesy Apache Corporation.

Chapter 17
Page 720: Sven Annstein/Photofest. Page 724: Steve Allen/Gamma Liaison. Page 749: Courtesy SPS Technologies.

Chapter 18
Page 752: John Lund/Tony Stone Images/New York, Inc. Page 755: R. Rathe/FPG International. Page 757: Jonathan Elderfield/Gamma Liaison. Page 759: Garry Gay/The Image Bank. Page 787: Courtesy Gap, Inc. Page 813: Courtesy The Vermont Teddy Bear Company. Page 814: Courtesy Praxair, Inc.

Chapter 19
Page 818: Jeanne Strongin. Page 828: D. Sarraute/The Image Bank. Page 830: Nora Good/Masterfile. Page 832: Christopher Morris/Black Star. Page 834: Phil Banko/Tony Stone Images/New York, Inc. Page 839 (top): Michael Skott/The Image Bank. Page 839 (bottom): Eric Sander/Gamma Liaison. Page 841: Vladimir Pcholkin/FPG International. Page 842: Tom Stewart/The Stock Market. Page 846: Jan Cobb/The Image Bank.

Chapter 20
Page 868: David Epperson/Tony Stone Images/New York, Inc. Page 872: Jorgen Vogt/The Image Bank. Page 874: Brownie Harris/The Stock Market. Page 875: Steve Dunwell/The Image Bank. Page 882: Will McIntyre/Photo Researchers. Page 883: Eric Kamp/Index Stock. Page 905: Courtesy Anchor Glass Container Corp.

Chapter 21
Page 908: Kathi Lamm/Tony Stone Images/New York, Inc. Page 912: David Plowden/Photo Researchers. Page 915: Courtesy Federal Express Corp. Used by permission. Page 920: Andy Zito/The Image Bank. Page 925: Robert Tinney/The Stock Market. Page 927: Bob Daemmrich/The Image Works. Page 944: Courtesy Parlex Corporation.

Chapter 22
Page 948: Pete McArthur/Tony Stone Images/New York, Inc. Page 951: Andrew Sacks/Tony Stone Images/New York, Inc. Page 955: Rick Altman/The Stock Market. Page 958: Loren Santow/Tony Stone Images/New York, Inc. Page 965: Stephen Simpson/FPG International. Page 970: Nick Vedros, Vedros & Associates/Tony Stone Images/New York, Inc. Page 971: Will Crocker/The Image Bank. Page 976: Courtesy ABC Technologies, Inc. Page 978: M & C Werner/Comstock, Inc. Page 991: Courtesy General Microwave Corporation.

Chapter 23
Page 994: Simon Norfolk/Tony Stone Images/New York, Inc. Page 1005: Reza Estakhrian/Tony Stone Images/New York, Inc. Page 1009: Cyberimage/Tony Stone Images/New York, Inc. Page 1010: ©Yael/Retna.

Chapter 24
Page 1032: Courtesy University of Nebraska. Page 1035: Gary Conner/Index Stock. Page 1037: Tony Stone Images/New York, Inc. Page 1041: Peter Zeray/Photonica. Page 1042: Peter Vadnai/The Stock Market. Page 1046: Larry Gilpin/Tony Stone Images/New York, Inc. Page 1049: Rosanne Olson/Tony Stone Images/New York, Inc. Page 1051: David Blum/Pixel Studios/The Stock Market. Page 1067: Courtesy Network Computing Devices, Inc.

Chapter 25
Page 1070: Comstock, Inc. Page 1084: Comstock, Inc. Page 1087: David Chambers/Tony Stone Images/New York, Inc. Page 1111: Courtesy Computer Associates.

Chapter 26
Page 1114: Dick Luria/FPG International. Page 1118: ©SUPERSTOCK. Page 1121: Naideau/The Stock Market. Page 1126: Michel Tchervkoff/The Image Bank. Page 1128: Courtesy United Parcel Service. Page 1152: Courtesy Glassmaster Company.

Chapter 27
Page 1154: Photofest. Page 1160: Chris Jones/The Stock Market. Page 1174: Ken Ross/Gamma Liaison.

INDEX

COMPANY INDEX